Current Law

YEAR BOOK
2002

VOLUME TWO

THOMSON

SWEET & MAXWELL

AUSTRALIA
LBC Information Services
Sydney

CANADA & USA
Carswell
Toronto

NEW ZEALAND
Brooker's
Auckland

SINGAPORE and MALAYSIA
Sweet & Maxwell Asia
Singapore and Kuala Lumpur

Current Law

YEAR
BOOK 2002

Being a Comprehensive Statement of the Law of 2002

SWEET & MAXWELL EDITORIAL TEAM

James Aidoo-Baidoe	Stephanie Armytage	Raffia Arshad
Shahnaila Aziz	Catherine Berry	Chris Blagg
Caroline Bury	Catherine Collins	Daniel Collins
Lisa Fergusson	Emma Fielden	Heidi Fletcher
Jonathan Hilton	Jonathan Langtry-Langton	
Jonathan Lonergan	Mairead O'Grady	Colette Rybicki
Martin Syrett	Nina Taylor	Natasha Wadsworth
Patricia Williams	Hilary Wyles	Jennifer Young

PUBLISHING CO-ORDINATOR
Philip Dye

SWEET & MAXWELL PRODUCTION TEAM
Elizabeth Risdon   Roger Greenwood

Editors

English and Commonwealth Law
MICHAEL BLACK, LL.B., *Solicitor*
PATRICK CLARKE, *Barrister*
CRAIG DUNFORD, *Barrister*
SHAUN FERRIS, B.A., *Barrister*
STEPHEN GARNER, *LL.B., Barrister*
Dr. ALASTAIR HUDSON, LL.B., LL.M., *Barrister*
CHARLES H JOSEPH, B.A., *Barrister, FCI Arb*
EILEEN O'GRADY, LL.B. (Hons), *Barrister*
PETER OSBORNE, PhD, *Solicitor (Ireland and N Ireland)*
JESSICA PENROSE, LL.B., *Solicitor*
WILLIAM VANDYCK, B.A., *Barrister*
GORDON WIGNALL, M.A., *Barrister*

Scotland
MALCOLM THOMSON, Q.C., LL.B.

Damages Awards
DAVID KEMP, Q.C., B.A., *Barrister*   PETER MANTLE, *Barrister*

The Mode of Citation
of the Current Law Year Book is
[2002] C.L.Y. 1282
The 2002 Year Book is published in two volumes.

Published in 2003 by
Sweet & Maxwell Limited of
100 Avenue Road, Swiss Cottage, London NW3 3PF
Typeset by Sweet & Maxwell Limited,
Mytholmroyd, Hebden Bridge
Printed in England by William Clowes Ltd

A CIP catalogue record for this book is available
from the British Library

ISBN: 2002 Yearbook: 0421 844 701
2002 Yearbook with Case and Legislation Citators: 0421 844 507

No forests were destroyed to make this product;
farmed timber was used and then replanted.

PREFACE

The 2002 Current Law Year Book supersedes the issues of *Current Law Monthly Digest* for 2002 and covers the law from January 1 to December 31 of that year.

Jurisdiction

The text of the 2002 Current Law Year Book is divided into three sections respectively: UK, England and Wales and EU, Northern Ireland and Scotland. The European material comprises: cases appearing before the Court of First Instance and European Court of Justice which are published in the reports series and newspapers, and a selection of books.

Cases

The 2002 Current Law Year Book includes digests of 3,077 cases published in over 90 reports series, journals, *The Times* and *Independent* newspapers, transcripts and ex relatione contributions from barristers and solicitors. A number of reports edited by David Kemp Q.C. concerning damages awards in personal injury cases in England and Wales appears under the subject heading DAMAGES and is collated in tabular form together with Scottish personal injuries cases at the beginning of Vol. 1.

The editor thanks those barristers and solicitors who have submitted case reports, many of which demonstrate developments in county court litigation. Whilst all reasonable care is taken in the preparation of the digests it is not possible to guarantee the accuracy of each digest, particularly those cases ex relatione which are not taken from an authorised judgment.

An alphabetical Table of Cases digested in the 2002 Year Book appears at the beginning of Volume 1. The Current Law Case Citator 2002 forms part of the permanent bound volume series for the years 1947-76, 1977-1997, 1998-2001, 2002.

Legislation

All public and private Acts of Parliament published in 2002 are abstracted and indexed. All Statutory Instruments, Scottish Statutory Instruments and Statutory Rules of Northern Ireland are abstracted. Cumulative tables of Statutory Instruments, arranged alphabetically, numerically and by subject are published in Vol. 1. Cumulative tables of Statutory Rules of Northern Ireland arranged alphabeticially, numerically and by subject are also published in Vol. 1.

The Current Law Legislation Citators for 2001 and 2002 appear as a separate bound volume and form part of the series of permanent bound volumes for the years 1989-1995, 1996-1999 and 2000-2001, 2002.

Books

The full title, reference and author of books of interest to the legal profession published in 2001/2002 are arranged by subject heading. A separate list, arranged by author is included in Volume 2.

Index

The subject-matter index is closely associated with a Legal Taxonomy from Sweet & Maxwell. The 30-year Index from 1947-76 may be found in the 1976 *Current Law Year Book*. The Scottish Index for the years 1972-86 may be found in the Scottish 1986 *Year Book*. Scottish material prior to 1972 can be found in the *Scottish Current Law Year Book Master Volumes*, published in 1956, 1961, 1966 and 1971.

August 2003

CONTENTS

VOLUME 1

THE LAW OF 2002 DIGESTED UNDER TITLES:
Note: Italicised entries refer to Scotland only.

Accountancy, §1
Administration of Justice, §2, 4822, *5209*
Administrative Law, §45, 4836, *5239*
Agency, §62, *5249*
Agriculture, §70, 4839, *5251*
Animals, §189, 4868, *5294*
Arbitration, §207, *5302*
Armed Forces, §222

Arts and Culture, §231
Aviation, §234, 4873, *5305*

Banking and Finance, §246, 4874, *5306*

Charities, §265
Civil Evidence, §270, 4875, *5310*
Civil Procedure, §279, 4876, *5313*
Commercial Law, §511, 4877,

CONTENTS

CURRENT LAW

YEAR BOOK 2002

UK, ENGLAND & WALES & EU

(continued)

INTERNATIONAL TRADE

2967. **Animal products–bone in beef–despatch to domestic market**

BOVINES AND BOVINE PRODUCTS (TRADE) (AMENDMENT) (ENGLAND) REGULATIONS 2002, SI 2002 2357; made under the European Communities Act 1972 s.2. In force: October 7, 2002; £2.00.

These Regulations amend the Bovines and Bovine Products (Trade) Regulations 1999 (SI 1999 1103) which gives effect to Commission Decision 98/692 ([1998] OJ L328/28) amending Commission Decision 98/256 to provide for the export from the UK of deboned beef and beef products under the strict conditions of the Date-based Export Scheme; and Commission Decision 98/564 ([1998] OJ L273/37) amending Council Decision 98/256 as regards certain emergency measures to protect against bovine spongiform encephalopathy. The amendments give effect to Commission Decision 2002/670 ([2002] OJ L228/22) amending Council Decision 98/256 concerning emergency measures to protect against bovine spongiform encephalopathy to enable the despatch from England of bovine embryos and bone in veal carcases from calves between six and nine months exported under the Date Based Export Scheme. The Regulations also prohibit offering to despatch or consign goods which may not be despatched or consigned whether on the internet or otherwise and provide for the payment of expenses reasonably incurred in connection with storage by the owner of the consignment and in some circumstances the payment of compensation to the owner for any depreciation in value of the consignment.

2968. **Animal products–bone in beef–despatch to domestic market–Wales**

BOVINES AND BOVINE PRODUCTS (TRADE) (AMENDMENT) (WALES) REGULATIONS 2002, SI 2002 1174; made under the European Communities Act 1972 s.2. In force: July 1, 2002; £1.75.

These Regulations amend the Bovines and Bovine Products (Trade) Regulations 1999 (SI 1999 1103) which give effect to Commission Decision 98/692 ([1992]

OJ L328/28) and Commission Decision 98/564 ([1998] OJ L273/37) which amended Council Decision 98/256 ([1998] OJ L113/32). The effect of these amendments is to permit the despatch of bone-in beef from premises approved under the Date Based Export Scheme to the domestic market.

2969. Animal products—bone in beef—despatch to domestic market—Wales

BOVINES AND BOVINE PRODUCTS (TRADE) (AMENDMENT) (WALES) (NO.2) REGULATIONS 2002, SI 2002 2325; made under the European Communities Act 1972 s.2. In force: September 11, 2002; £3.00.

These Regulations amend the Bovines and Bovine Products (Trade) Regulations 1999 (SI 1999 1103) which gives effect to Commission Decision 98/692 ([1998] OJ L328/28) amending Decision 98/256/EC as regards certain emergency measures to protect against bovine spongiform encephalopathy under the strict conditions of the Date-based Export Scheme; and Commission Decision 98/564 ([1998] OJ L273/37) amending Council Decision 98/256 as regards certain emergency measures to protect against bovine spongiform encephalopathy. The amendments give effect to Commission Decision 2002/670 ([2002] OJ L228/22) amending Council Decision 98/256 concerning emergency measures to protect against bovine spongiform encephalopathy to enable the despatch from Wales of bovine embryos and bone in veal carcases from calves between six and nine months exported under the Date Based Export Scheme. The Regulations also prohibit offering to despatch or consign goods which may not be despatched or consigned whether on the internet or otherwise and provide for the payment of expenses reasonably incurred in connection with storage by the owner of the consignment and in some circumstances the payment of compensation to the owner for any depreciation in value of the consignment.

2970. Animal products—import and export controls

ANIMALS AND ANIMAL PRODUCTS (IMPORT AND EXPORT) (ENGLAND AND WALES) (AMENDMENT) (ENGLAND) (NO.2) REGULATIONS 2002, SI 2002 956; made under the European Communities Act 1972 s.2. In force: April 4, 2002 at 8 pm; £1.50.

These Regulations amend the Animals and Animal Products (Import and Export) (England and Wales) Regulations 2000 (SI 2000 1673) in relation to England to give effect to Commission Decision 2002/242 ([2002] OJ L82/18) amending for the ninth time Decision 2001/327 ([2001] OJ L115/12) concerning restrictions to the movement of animals of susceptible species with regard to foot and mouth disease.

2971. Animal products—import and export controls—Wales

ANIMALS AND ANIMAL PRODUCTS (IMPORT AND EXPORT) (ENGLAND AND WALES) (AMENDMENT) (WALES) (NO.2) REGULATIONS 2002, SI 2002 1039; made under the European Communities Act 1972 s.2. In force: April 10, 2002 at 12 pm; £1.75.

These Regulations amend the Animals and Animal Products (Import and Export) (England and Wales) Regulations 2000 (SI 2000 1673) in relation to Wales to give effect to Commission Decision 2002/242 ([2002] OJ L82/18) amending for the ninth time Decision 2001/327 ([2001] OJ L115/12) concerning restrictions to the movement of animals of susceptible species with regard to foot and mouth disease.

2972. Animal products—imports—licences—Commission Regulation

Commission Regulation 285/2003 on the issue of import licences for sheepmeat and goatmeat products under GATT-WTO non-country-specific tariff quotas for the first quarter of 2003. [2003] OJ L42/28.

2973. Animal products—origin marking—third country imports

PRODUCTS OF ANIMAL ORIGIN (THIRD COUNTRY IMPORTS) (ENGLAND) REGULATIONS 2002, SI 2002 1227; made under the European Communities Act 1972 s.2. In force: May 22, 2002; £7.50.

These Regulations amend the Imported Food Regulations 1984 (SI 1984 1918), the Dairy Products (Hygiene) Regulations 1995 (SI 1995 1086), the Products of Animal Origin (Import and Export) Regulations 1996 (SI 1996 3124), the Fresh Meat (Import Conditions) Regulations 1996 (SI 1996 3125), the Imported Food Regulations 1997 (SI 1997 2537) and the Miscellaneous Products of Animal Origin (Import Conditions) Regulations 1999 (SI 1999 157). They implement Council Directive 97/78 ([1997] OJ L24/9) laying down the principles governing the organisation of veterinary checks on products entering the Community from third countries which applies to products of animal origin. The Regulations establish the inspection system which will apply to the generality of products, lay down special provisions which apply to particular categories of product and deal with the calculation and payment of charges for the veterinary checks.

2974. Animal products—origin marking—third country imports

PRODUCTS OF ANIMAL ORIGIN (THIRD COUNTRY IMPORTS) (ENGLAND) (AMENDMENT) (NO.2) REGULATIONS 2002, SI 2002 2570; made under the European Communities Act 1972 s.2. In force: October 11, 2002; £1.50.

These Regulations amend the Products of Animal Origin (Third Country Imports) (England) Regulations 2002 (SI 2002 1227) to give effect in England to Commission Decision 2002/768 ([2002] OJ L260/31) amending Decision 2002/69 concerning certain protective measures with regard to the products of animal origin imported from China; Commission Decision 2002/770 ([2002] OJ L265/16) amending Commission Decision 2001/699 and repealing Commission Decision 2002/250 to revoke the protective measures with regard to the fishery and aquaculture products imported from Vietnam; and Commission Decision 2002/771 ([2002] OJ L265/18) repealing Decision 2002/62 concerning protective measures with regard to the fishery and aquaculture products imported from Pakistan.

2975. Animal products—origin marking—third country imports

PRODUCTS OF ANIMAL ORIGIN (THIRD COUNTRY IMPORTS) (ENGLAND) (AMENDMENT) (NO.4) REGULATIONS 2002, SI 2002 3206; made under the European Communities Act 1972 s.2. In force: January 1, 2003; £3.50.

These Regulations revoke the Products of Animal Origin (Third Country Imports) (England) (Amendment) Regulations 2002 (SI 2002 2151), the Products of Animal Origin (Third Country Imports) (England) (Amendment) (No.2) Regulations 2002 (SI 2002 2570) and the Products of Animal Origin (Third Country Imports) (England) (Amendment) (No.3) Regulations 2002 (SI 2002 2639) and amend the Products of Animal Origin (Third Country Imports) (England) Regulations 2002 (SI 2002 1227) to implement Commission Decision 2002/995 ([2002] OJ L353/1) laying down interim safeguard measures with regard to imports of products of animal origin for personal consumption.

2976. Animal products—origin marking—third country imports—China

PRODUCTS OF ANIMAL ORIGIN (THIRD COUNTRY IMPORTS) (ENGLAND) (AMENDMENT) REGULATIONS 2002, SI 2002 2151; made under the European Communities Act 1972 s.2. In force: August 20, 2002; £1.50.

These Regulations, which revoke the Food and Animal Feedingstuffs (Products of Animal Origin from China) (Emergency Control) (England) Regulations 2002 (SI 2002 1614), amend the Products of Animal Origin (Third Country Imports) (England) Regulations 2002 (SI 2002 1227) by updating the reference to Commission Decision 2002/69 ([2002] OJ L30/50) concerning certain protective measures with regard to the products of animal origin imported from

China by including references to Commission Decision 2002/441 ([2002] OJ L161/16) amending Decision 2002/69 concerning certain protective measures with regard to the products of animal origin imported from China; and Commission Decision 2002/573 amending Decision 2002/69 concerning certain protective measures with regard to the products of animal origin imported from China.

2977. Animal products–origin marking–third country imports–Wales

PRODUCTS OF ANIMAL ORIGIN (THIRD COUNTRY IMPORTS) (WALES) REGULATIONS 2002, SI 2002 1387; made under the European Communities Act 1972 s.2. In force: May 22, 2002; £7.50.

These Regulations amend the Dairy Products (Hygiene) Regulations 1995 (SI 1995 1086), the Fresh Meat (Import Conditions) Regulations 1996 (SI 1996 3125) and the Imported Food Regulations 1997 (SI 1997 2537). They also revoke the Importation of Animal Products and Poultry Products Order 1980 (SI 1980 14), the Imported Food Regulations 1984 (SI 1984 1918), the Products of Animal Origin (Import and Export) Regulations 1996 (SI 1996 3124), the Fresh Meat (Import Conditions) Regulations 1996 (SI 1996 3125) and the Miscellaneous Products of Animal Origin (Import Conditions) Regulations 1999 (SI 1999 157). They implement Council Directive 97/78 ([1998] OJ L24/9) laying down the principles governing the organisation of veterinary checks on products entering the Community from third countries which applies to products of animal origin. The Regulations establish the inspection system which will apply to the generality of products, lay down special provisions which apply to particular categories of product and deal with the calculation and payment of charges for the veterinary checks.

2978. Animal products–origin marking–third country imports–Wales

PRODUCTS OF ANIMAL ORIGIN (THIRD COUNTRY IMPORTS) (WALES) (AMENDMENT) REGULATIONS 2002, SI 2002 3011 (W.283); made under the European Communities Act 1972 s.2. In force: December 7, 2002; £1.75.

These Regulations amend the Products of Animal Origin (Third Country Imports) (Wales) Regulations 2002 (SI 2002 1387) in order to give effect to Commission Decision 2002/794 ([2002] OJ L 276/66) concerning certain protective measures with regard to poultry meat, poultry meat products and poultry meat preparations intended for human consumption and imported from Brazil.

2979. Animal products–origin marking–third country imports–Wales

PRODUCTS OF ANIMAL ORIGIN (THIRD COUNTRY IMPORTS) (WALES) (AMENDMENT) (NO.2) REGULATIONS 2002, SI 2002 3230 (W.307); made under the European Communities Act 1972 s.2. In force: January 1, 2003; £3.50.

These Regulations, which amend the Products of Animal Origin (Third Country Imports) (Wales) Regulations 2002 (SI 2002 1387 (W.136)), implement Commission Decision of December 9, 2002 which lays down interim safeguard measures with regard to imports of products of animal origin for personal consumption (not yet published in the Official Journal). They also remove the power of the Secretary of State for Health to appoint independent persons to hear appeals against charges levied by the Food Standards Agency and makes this a function of the National Assembly for Wales.

2980. Customs duty–origin of goods–petroleum products

ORIGIN OF GOODS (PETROLEUM PRODUCTS) (REVOCATION) REGULATIONS 2002, SI 2002 2266; made under the Customs and Excise Management Act 1979 s.120. In force: October 1, 2002; £1.50.

These Regulations revoke the Origin of Goods (Petroleum Products) Regulations 1988 (SI 1988 1) which laid down the conditions under which certain petroleum products specified were to be treated as originating in a particular country for the purposes of preferential rates of, or exemption from, customs duties charged in accordance with the European Communities Act 1972 s.5(1)(2). The Regulations also revoke the Origin of Goods (Petroleum Products) (Amendment) Regulations 1992 (SI 1992 3289) which reflected the changes given effect by Council Regulation 3576/92 ([1992] OJ L374/1) on the definition of the concept of "originating products" applicable to certain mineral products and to certain products of the chemical or allied industries, within the framework of preferential tariff arrangements granted by the Community to third countries; and by Commission Regulation 3660/92 ([1992] OJ L370/11) amending Commission Regulation 693/88, Commission Regulation 809/88 and Commission Regulation 343/92 on the definition of the concept of originating products and methods of administrative cooperation with regard to imports into the Community of products originating in developing countries, in the Occupied Territories and in the Republics of Bosnia-Herzegovina, Croatia and Slovenia and the former Yugoslav Republic of Macedonia. Council Decision 2001/822 ([2001] OJ L314/1) on the association of the overseas countries and territories with the European Community now provides Community origin rules for petroleum products from the overseas countries and territories.

2981. EFTA—free movement of goods—state monopoly on retail sale of domestically produced beer—discriminatory effect on sale of imported pre packaged alcoholic beverages

The EFTA Surveillance Authority applied for a declaration that Norway had failed to comply with the Agreement on a European Economic Area 1992 Art.11 and Art.16. Norwegian law provided that beer of between 2.5 and 4.75 per cent alcohol could be sold by duly licensed grocery stores, although other drinks with the same level of alcohol could only be sold by the state retail monopoly. Norway contended that these provisions formed the foundation of its comprehensive strategy aimed at the protection of public health and were necessary in particular to protect young people from the harmful effects of alcopops.

Held, granting the declaration, that (1) there was no established definition of "alcopops" which was a common trade term for pre packaged beverages aimed at young people and consisting of beer, wine or spirits, combined with a mixer. Based on the classification of their alcohol content, beer and spirit based alcopops fell within the ambit of the Agreement Arts.11 and 16, whereas wine based alcopops fell only within the scope of Art.16; (2) Norway was entitled to maintain a strict regime in relation to alcohol sales, provided that in so doing, it did not contravene the rules of the Agreement in relation to the free movement of goods; (3) EEA states could legitimately pursue policies aimed at fighting alcohol abuse, including operating a state retail alcohol monopoly, provided that such a monopoly did not place trade in goods from other EEA states at a disadvantage when compared to domestically produced goods; (4) since beer of between 2.5 and 4.75 per cent alcohol was domestically produced and sold outside the state monopoly, while other pre packaged beverages of the same alcohol content were mostly imported from other EEA states and could only be sold through the state monopoly, Norwegian law discriminated against products from other EEA states and so contravened Art.16; (5) the relevant Norwegian law could not be justified on the grounds of public health, since Art.13 did not provide for derogations from Art.16, and (6) the more restrictive measures on licences to serve pre packaged beverages with an alcohol content between 2.5 and 4.75 per cent, most of which were imported from other EEA states, amounted to a quantitative restriction within the meaning of Art.11. Since those measures could not be justified on the grounds of public health under Art.13, Norway had failed to comply with Art.11.

EFTA SURVEILLANCE AUTHORITY v. NORWAY (E9/00) [2002] 2 C.M.L.R.17, Vilhjalmsson (President), EFTA.

2982. Embargoes–arms trade–refusal to pay outstanding amount after adoption of Council Regulation 2340/90

[EC Treaty Art.215; European Convention on Human Rights 1950; Council Regulation 2340/90 preventing trade by the Community as regards Iraq and Kuwait; Security Council Resolution 661 (United Nations).]

E, a company incorporated under Greek law, made and sold arms and ammunition on an international basis. In 1987, E had contracts with Iraq to supply ammunition worth over $83 million with 90 per cent of that cost due for payment two years after shipment. Before full payment, however, the United Nations declared, by Security Council Resolution 661, that Iraq's invasion of Kuwait should be punished by an embargo on trade with both countries. Accordingly, the European Union adopted Council Regulation 2340/90. The Central Bank of Iraq then refused to pay E the remaining 90 per cent of the price owing plus the agreed interest, a total of over $75 million. E took action against the Bank in the Court of First Instance, Athens and also negotiated the possibility of being paid either in crude oil or through Iraqi assets frozen in the United States, *Dorsch Consult Ingenieurgesellschaft mbH v. Council of the European Union (T184/95)* [1998] E.C.R. II-667, which was appealed as *Dorsch Consult Ingenieurgesellschaft mbH v. Council of the European Union (C237/98 P)* [2000] E.C.R. I-4549, [2002] 5 C.L.M. 212, was an application for compensation analogous to E's case and was heard, and dismissed, after E had sought action before the CFI claiming non contractual liability by the Council and the Commission. Proceedings in the instant case were suspended pending that judgment but E then insisted that its case proceed. Its claim against the Council and the Commission for damages resulting from the adoption of the Regulation totalled $75,451,500, with interest. E claimed breach of (1) the right to property under the European Convention on Human Rights 1950; (2) the principle of non discrimination; (3) EC Treaty Art.133, and (4) the principle of proportionality. Alternatively, it claimed breach of the legitimate expectations of economic operators.

Held, dismissing the application, that to succeed under EC Treaty Art.215, the application would have to prove the unlawfulness of the conduct alleged against the Community institutions, actual damage and the existence of a causal link between that conduct and the damage complained of. As a direct causal link was not proved, and as all three points stood together, the action had to fail. Moreover, the plea of breach of the principle of non discrimination also failed and the application was therefore dismissed in its entirety.

ELLINIKI VIOMICHANIA OPLON AE (EVO) v. COUNCIL OF THE EUROPEAN UNION (T220/96) [2002] 2 C.M.L.R. 32, Mengozzi (President), CFI.

2983. Embargoes–beef–breach of legitimate expectation–review of Directive in context of WTO rules

[EC Treaty Art.288; Council Directive 88/146 on imports into the Community of beef and veal from non-Member States containing substances having a hormonal action and of any substances having a thyrostatic action.]

E, a major shareholder in a meat trading company, brought an action for damages under the EC Treaty Art.288 claiming that the prohibition in Council Directive 88/146 on imports into the Community of beef and veal from non Member States containing substances which had a hormonal action, breached the principle of the protection of legitimate expectations and the World Trade Organisation, WTO, Agreement on the application of Sanitary and Phytosanitary Measures, "SPS Agreement".

Held, refusing the application, that (1) E could not have had a legitimate expectation in respect of the embargo being lifted since E was incorporated after the Directive came into force. Furthermore, traders could not have a legitimate expectation that an existing situation capable of being altered by Community institutions in the exercise of their discretionary power would be maintained, *Edeka Zentrale AG v. Germany (C245/81)* [1982] E.C.R. 2745, [1983] C.L.Y. 1379 applied. In an area such as the Common Agricultural Policy, because of its potential effects on public health, any legislative amendments depended on unpredictable developments in scientific knowledge and complex assessments to be made by the legislature, and (2) the Community judicature was only entitled to review the legality of a Community measure in the light of the WTO rules where the Community intended to implement a particular obligation assumed in the context of the WTO, or where the Community measure referred expressly to the precise provisions of the WTO agreements. Since Directive 88/146 preceded the SPS agreement by several years E could not therefore rely on an infringement of that agreement, *EEC Seed Crushers' and Oil Processors' Federation (FEDIOL) v. Commission of the European Communities (C70/87)* [1989] E.C.R. 1781, [1991] C.L.Y. 3918 and *Nakajima All Precision Co Ltd v. Council of the European Communities (C69/89)* [1991] E.C.R. I-2069 applied.

ETABLISSEMENTS BIRET & CIE SA v. COUNCIL OF THE EUROPEAN UNION (T210/00) [2002] 2 C.M.L.R. 31, Vesterdorf (President), CFI.

2984. Export Control 2002 (28)

This Act makes provision enabling controls to be imposed on the exportation of goods, the transfer of technology, the provision of technical assistance overseas and activities connected with trade in controlled goods.

This Act received Royal Assent on July 24, 2002.

2985. Export controls–dual use goods

DUAL-USE ITEMS (EXPORT CONTROL) (AMENDMENT) REGULATIONS 2002, SI 2002 50; made under the European Communities Act 1972 s.2. In force: February 5, 2002; £1.50.

These Regulations amend the Dual-Use Items (Export Control) Regulations 2000 (SI 2000 3620) by extending the definition of "the Regulation" to include Council Regulation 2432/2001 ([2001] OJ L338/1) amending and updating Regulation 1334/2000 setting up a Community regime for the control of exports of dual-use items and technology and removing the general prohibition on exportation to any destination except Member States of Materials and Technology covered by 1C950 and 1E950 respectively.

2986. Export controls–dual use goods–Americium

DUAL-USE ITEMS (EXPORT CONTROL) (AMENDMENT) (NO.2) REGULATIONS 2002, SI 2002 2033; made under the European Communities Act 1972 s.2. In force: August 21, 2002; £1.50.

These Regulations, which amend the Dual-Use Items (Export Control) Regulations 2000 (SI 2000 2620) made in implementation of and pursuant to Council Regulation 1334/2000 ([2000] OJ L159/1) on the control of exports of dual-use item and technology, add "Americium" to the list of prohibited materials, chemicals, micro-organisms and toxins. They also add a new Council Regulation to the list of Regulations applicable to export control.

2987. Export controls–sanctions–Zimbabwe–restrictive measures

OVERSEAS TERRITORIES (ZIMBABWE) (RESTRICTED MEASURES) ORDER 2002, SI 2002 1077; made under the Saint Helena Act 1833 s.112; the British Settlements Act 1887; and the British Settlements Act 1945. In force: April 19, 2002; £3.00.

This Order, which applies to each of the specified British overseas territories, imposes restrictive measures in respect of Zimbabwe and those who bear a wide responsibility for the serious violations of human rights and of the freedom of opinion, of association and of peaceful assembly in that country. These measures include the prohibition of the delivery or supply of arms and related matriel and equipment that might be used for internal repression to Zimbabwe, and the prohibition of making available funds, financial assets or economic resources to persons specified and the freezing of their funds, financial assets or economic resources.

2988. Export controls–weapons–Yugoslavia

EXPORT OF GOODS (CONTROL) (AMENDMENT) ORDER 2002, SI 2002 2059; made under the Import, Export and Customs Powers (Defence) Act 1939 s.1. In force: August 28, 2002; £2.00.

The Export of Goods (Control) (Amendment) Order 2002 makes a number of changes to the Export of Goods (Control) Order 1994 by deleting the national controls on four wheel drive civil vehicles to the Federal Republic of Yugoslavia; deleting the definitions of additives, military explosives and pyrotechnics; broadens the definition of explosives and pyrotechnics by widening what can constitute these materials; extends the scope of the principal Order to cover "special forces" parachuting equipment; replaces the current explosives Military List with the Schedule to this Order and removes countries from Sch.3 which are no longer subject to arms embargoes

2989. Export controls–weapons–Yugoslavia

EXPORT OF GOODS (FEDERAL REPUBLIC OF YUGOSLAVIA) (CONTROL) (REVOCATION) ORDER 2002, SI 2002 315; made under the Import, Export and Customs Powers (Defence) Act 1939 s.1. In force: March 7, 2002; £1.50.

This Order revokes the Export of Goods (Federal Republic of Yugoslavia) (Control) Order 1998 (SI 1998 1530) which prohibited the exportation of any goods specified in Council Regulation 926/98 ([1998] OJ L130/1) to any destination in the Federal Republic of Yugoslavia.

2990. Export licences–procedure–duties of importing authority when presented with export permit

[Convention on International Trade in Endangered Species of Wild Fauna and Flora 1976 Art.V (2) (a); Convention on International Trade in Endangered Species of Wild Fauna and Flora 1976 Appendix III; Council Regulation 338/97 on the protection of species of wild fauna and flora by regulating trade therein Annex C.]

G, an environmental group, sought judicial review of a decision to allow an importation of mahogany from Brazil. The exploitation of mahogany in Brazil was prohibited by the Brazilian constitution unless it had been authorised by the Brazilian Institute of Environment and Renewable Resources. In 2001 the Institute issued decrees suspending the transportation, processing and commercialisation of mahogany after becoming concerned that widespread illegal logging was taking place. Without notice applications were made to the Brazilian court by timber companies seeking orders requiring the Institute to issue export permits for mahogany. Pressurised by a court order granting the applications, the Institute issued export permits. The issue before the court was whether, where an apparently valid export permit was presented to the competent authorities of a Member State to support the importation into that state of flora or fauna covered by the Convention on International Trade in Endangered Species of Wild Fauna and Flora 1976 Appendix III or Council Regulation 338/97 Annex C, the authorities were obliged to accept the permit and allow the importation even though they knew that the management authority which had issued the permit in the exporting state had not, for the purposes of Art.V (2) (a) of the Convention, been satisfied that the specimen in question had not been obtained in contravention of the laws of that state for the protection of fauna and flora.

Held, refusing the application (Laws, L.J. dissenting), that unless and until an authentic export permit was unilaterally revoked or cancelled by the authority which had issued it or was set aside by consent or by a court order, the importing authority was entitled to treat it as a valid and subsisting permit. The importing authority's sole concern was to check that the permit complied with the provisions for documentary evidence in the Convention and it was not bound to investigate the correctness or validity of the decision of the management authority of the exporting state that the conditions for the grant of the export permit had been satisfied. Such a conclusion created commercial certainty, the need for which was as great in cases where a permit had been issued incorrectly or unwillingly as it was in cases where the permit had been issued correctly and willingly. The decision to allow the importation in the instant case had therefore been lawful.

R. (ON THE APPLICATION OF GREENPEACE LTD) v. SECRETARY OF STATE FOR THE ENVIRONMENT, FOOD AND RURAL AFFAIRS, [2002] EWCA Civ 1036, [2002] 1 W.L.R. 3304, Laws, L.J., CA.

2991. Gem industry–imports–Sierra Leone–Council Regulation

Council Regulation 2290/2002 of December 19, 2002 concerning the importation into the Community of rough diamonds from Sierra Leone. [2002] OJ L348/56.

2992. Government aid–African Development Fund–additional subscriptions

AFRICAN DEVELOPMENT FUND (ADDITIONAL SUBSCRIPTIONS) ORDER 2002, SI 2002 2404; made under the International Development Act 2002 s.11. In force: September 16, 2002; £1.50.

This Order approves the making of a payment on behalf of the Government of the UK of a sum not exceeding £40,000,000 as a further contribution to the African Development Fund in accordance with the arrangements made with the Fund pursuant to Resolution F//BG/2002/03 adopted by the Board of Governors of the Fund on May 28, 2002. This payment is by way of an additional contribution to the Fund pending conclusion of negotiations on the next routine replenishment (the Ninth Replenishment), and will score as a contribution to the Ninth Replenishment of the Fund. The Order approves the redemption of non-interest-bearing and non-negotiable notes issued by the Secretary of State in payment of the further contribution.

2993. Import controls–import licences–retrospective application

[Council Regulation 338/97 on the protection of species of wild fauna and flora by regulating trade therein Art.4(2); Commission Regulation 939/97 laying down detailed rules concerning the implementation of Council Regulation 338/97 Art.8(3); European Convention on Human Rights 1950 Art.1.]

W sought judicial review of decisions of the Secretary of State refusing to grant a retrospective permit for the import of Russian caviar. W had taken delivery of an amount of caviar which was found to exceed the export and import permits granted in respect of the consignment. W reported the discrepancy to the Secretary of State who advised that W apply for a retrospective import licence. Meanwhile customs officials had seized the excess quantity of caviar valued at over $40,000. The Russian authorities refused to issue an export permit for the excess caviar and therefore the Secretary of State took the view that the conditions laid down in Council Regulation 338/97 Art.4(2) and Commission Regulation 939/97 Art.8(3) for the issue of a retrospective import licence had not been satisfied and refused W's application.

Held, refusing the application, that (1) the Secretary of State had no general discretion to issue a retrospective import licence in an appropriate case under Art.8(3) of Regulation 939/97. Art.8(3) provided for the possibility of a limited derogation and had to be strictly construed. The derogation related only to the requirements as to time limits and did not permit a derogation from the fundamental and mandatory requirement contained in Art.4 of Regulation 338/97 that an export permit must be obtained in respect of a consignment. In the present case that mandatory requirement had not been met and therefore the Secretary of State had no power to issue a retrospective import permit, and (2) the refusal to issue a retrospective import permit did not violate W's right to property under European Convention on Human Rights 1950 Art.1. The Secretary of State's decision complied with and enforced the relevant EC provisions since without an export licence there was no discretion to grant an import licence.

R. (ON THE APPLICATION OF WG WHITE LTD) v. SECRETARY OF STATE FOR THE ENVIRONMENT,TRANSPORT AND THE REGIONS, [2001] EWHC Admin 1151, [2002] 2 C.M.L.R. 19, Forbes, J., QBD (Admin Ct).

2994. **Import licences–declarations–innocent falsehoods–fairness of exclusion of application–proportionality**

[Council Regulation 520/94 laying down rules for establishing a procedure for administering quantitative quotas Art.4; Commission Regulation 738/94 relating to the establishment of a procedure for administering quantitative quotas Art.3(2)(g).]

C sought to challenge a refusal by the Secretary of State to grant an import licence relating to certain goods originating from China. The Secretary of State refused the licence on the basis that C's application contained a false declaration. The application had contained a statement that C was established as a company within the European Community as required by Council Regulation 520/94 Art.4 together with a declaration, pursuant to Commission Regulation 738/94 Art.3(2)(g), that the information contained within the application was accurate as at the date signed. However, C was not established at the date of the declaration but was established by the closing date for submitting applications. It was argued that (1) Art.3(2)(g) of Regulation 738/94 should be construed purposively such that the relevant day for determining the accuracy of the application was the closing date for submitting applications and not the date of the declaration; (2) the requirement that the application was valid at the date of declaration was disproportionate to the aims of Regulation 520/94, and (3) the exclusion of C's application was disproportionate, the false statement being a technical error.

Held, refusing the application for judicial review, that (1) on a correct interpretation of the Regulations, the licensing authorities were entitled to assume that an application was accurate as at the date the declaration was signed; (2) the aim of the Regulations was to ensure uniform administrative procedures and it was proportionate to require that information contained within an application was accurate as at the date the declaration was signed, and (3) in the instant case, the false declaration was not a mere technical error but was a failure to satisfy a vital procedural requirement. The Secretary of State had been entitled to exclude C's application notwithstanding the fact that the error had been made in good faith, *R. v. Intervention Board for Agricultural Produce, ex p. ED&F Man (Sugar) Ltd (C181/84)* [1986] 2 All E.R. 115, [1986] C.L.Y. 1303 considered.

R. (ON THE APPLICATION OF CASTILLE LTD) v. SECRETARY OF STATE FOR TRADE AND INDUSTRY, [2002] EWHC 16, [2002] Eu. L.R. 209, Elias, J., QBD (Admin Ct).

2995. **Imports–bananas–Commission Regulation**

Commission Regulation 323/2003 of February 20, 2003 amending Regulation 896/2001 as regards the list of national authorities competent to apply the arrangements for importing bananas into the UK. [2003] OJ L47/12.

2996. **Imports–fruit–origin mark on packaging of citrus fruit–affixing mark–appropriate country**

[Council Directive 77/93 on protective measures against the introduction into the Community of organisms harmful to plants or plant products and against their spread within the Community Annex IV Part A Item 16.1.]

In a dispute relating to the importation of citrus fruits from the northern part of Cyprus into the United Kingdom, A sought leave to raise a further issue, namely whether the special requirements of Council Directive 77/93 Annex IV Part A Item

16.1, as amended, requiring the packaging of citrus fruits to bear an appropriate mark of origin, could be fulfilled in a place other than in the place of origin.

Held, referring questions to the ECJ, that it was appropriate, given the absence of agreement on the proper interpretation of Item 16.1, to make a reference to the ECJ. Accordingly, the following questions concerning the interpretation of the Directive, as amended, would be referred: (1) whether the appropriate origin mark had to be affixed in the country of origin or whether it could be affixed in a third country, and (2) whether the official statement that the particular citrus fruits originated from a country recognised to be free from harmful organisms had to be made by an official in the country of origin.

R. v. MINISTRY OF AGRICULTURE, FISHERIES AND FOOD, *ex p.* SP ANASTASIOU (PISSOURI) LTD (NO.4), [2001] UKHL 71, [2002] Eu. L.R. 55, Lord Slynn of Hadley, HL.

2997. Imports–third country imports–hemp

HEMP (THIRD COUNTRY IMPORTS) REGULATIONS 2002, SI 2002 787; made under the European Communities Act 1972 s.2. In force: May 1, 2002; £2.00.

These Regulations, which introduce provisions concerning the UK of true hemp, hemp seed for sowing and hemp seeds other than for sowing from countries other than Member States of the European Community, implement Commission Regulation 245/2001 ([2001] OJ L150/17) concerning imported hemp. The Regulations require that hemp from third countries be imported under a licence, and, in the case of hemp seeds other than for sowing, under an authorisation, issued by the Secretary of State for Environment, Food and Rural Affairs in respect of imports into England, the National Assembly for Wales in respect of imports into Wales, the Scottish Ministers in respect of imports into Scotland, and the Department of Agriculture and Rural Development in respect of imports into Northern Ireland. They establish procedures for the application for, and the grant and variation of, import licences as well as specifying the scope of those licences, and introduce similar procedures for authorisations. In addition, they introduce requirements in relation to the tetrahydrocannabinol content of the variety of true hemp or hemp seeds for sowing imported and the content of attestations provided by importers or subsequent users on the use made of hemp seeds other than for sowing. The Regulations also introduce information and record keeping requirements and establish provisions on enforcement.

2998. Imports–third country imports–hemp–suspension of licences

HEMP (THIRD COUNTRY IMPORTS) (AMENDMENT) REGULATIONS 2002, SI 2002 1924; made under the European Communities Act 1972 s.2. In force: September 1, 2002; £1.50.

These Regulations amend the Hemp (Third Country Imports) Regulations 2002 (SI 2002 787) by extending the scope of the written representations procedures to include the suspension of licences or authorisations for the import into the UK of hemp from third countries.

2999. Sale of goods–prohibition–Yugoslavia–revocation

FEDERAL REPUBLIC OF YUGOSLAVIA (SUPPLY AND SALE OF EQUIPMENT) (PENALTIES AND LICENCES) (REVOCATION) REGULATIONS 2002, SI 2002 316; made under the European Communities Act 1972 s.2. In force: March 7, 2002; £1.50.

These Regulations revoke the Federal Republic of Yugoslavia (Supply and Sale of Equipment) (Penalties and Licences) Regulations 1998 (SI 1998 1531) and the Federal Republic of Yugoslavia (Supply and Sale of Equipment) (Penalties and Licences) (Amendment) Regulations 1999 (SI 1999 1775) which made provision for national enforcement measures and penalties for the infringement of Council Regulation 926/98 ([1998] OJ L139/1) which prohibited the sale or supply to the Federal Republic of Yugoslavia of specified equipment which may be used for internal repression or terrorism.

3000. Sale of goods—prohibition—Zimbabwe

ZIMBABWE (SALE, SUPPLY, EXPORT AND SHIPMENT OF EQUIPMENT) (PENALTIES AND LICENCES) REGULATIONS 2002, SI 2002 868; made under the European Communities Act 1972 s.2. In force: March 31, 2002; £1.75.

These Regulations provide that breaches of certain provisions of Council Regulation 310/2002 ([2002] OJ L50/4) concerning certain restrictive measures in respect of Zimbabwe are to be criminal offences. They prohibit the provision of technical training or, assistance related to the provision, manufacture, maintenance or use of arms and related material of all types including weapons and ammunition, military vehicles and equipment, paramilitary equipment and spare parts for the aforementioned; prohibit the sale and supply to Zimbabwe of, specified equipment, which might be used for internal repression or terrorism; and prohibit participation in activities the object of which is to promote the transactions or activities specified. In addition, they provide for the licensing of exports, sales or supplies in accordance with the Regulations and provide for enforcement and penalties for breach of the Regulation.

3001. Single market—beef and veal—premium schemes—Commission Regulation

Commission Regulation 2381/2002 of December 30, 2002 amending Regulation 2342/199 laying down detailed rules for the application of Council Regulation 1254/199 on the common organisation of the market in beef and veal as regards premium schemes. [2002] OJ L358/119.

3002. Books

Andenas, Mads; Roth, Wulf-Henning—Services and Free Movement in EU Law. Hardback: £60.00. ISBN 0-19-829938-9. Oxford University Press.

Benitah, Marc—Law of Subsidies Under the GATT/WTO System. Hardback: £69.00. ISBN 90-411-9827-X. Kluwer Law International.

Bunter, Michael A.G.—Promotion and Licensing of Petroleum Prospective Acreage. International Energy and Resources Law and Policy, 16. Hardback: £83.00. ISBN 90-411-1712-1. Kluwer Law International.

Desta, Melaku Geboye—Law of International Trade in Agricultural Products. Hardback: £99.00. ISBN 90-411-9865-2. Kluwer Law International.

Dillon, Sara—International Trade and Economic Law and the European Union. Paperback: £25.00. ISBN 1-84113-113-X. Hart Publishing.

Dispute Settlement Reports 1999. World Trade Organization Dispute Settlement Reports. Paperback: £30.00. ISBN 0-521-00565-5. Cambridge University Press.

Dispute Settlement Reports 1999: Volume 1. World Trade Organization Dispute Settlement Reports. Paperback: £30.00. ISBN 0-521-00562-0. Cambridge University Press.

Dispute Settlement Reports 1999: Volume I. World Trade Organization Dispute Settlement Reports. Hardback: £75.00. ISBN 0-521-80320-9. Cambridge University Press.

Dispute Settlement Reports 1999: Volume II. World Trade Organization Dispute Settlement Reports. Hardback: £75.00. ISBN 0-521-80321-7. Paperback: £30.00. ISBN 0-521-00564-7. Cambridge University Press.

Dispute Settlement Reports 1999: Volume III. World Trade Organization Dispute Settlement Reports. Hardback: £75.00. ISBN 0-521-80322-5. Cambridge University Press.

Frase, Dick; Parry, Helen—Exchanges and Alternative Trading Systems-Law and Regulation. Hardback: £150.00. ISBN 0-421-73930-4. Sweet & Maxwell.

Kelsey, Jane—International Economic Regulation. The Library of Essays in International Law. Hardback: £110.00. ISBN 0-7546-2225-8. Dartmouth.

Letterman, G. Gregory—Basics of International Sales of Goods. The Basics of International Law. Paperback: £76.99. ISBN 1-57105-255-0. Transnational Publishers, Inc.

Sellman, Pamela—Law of International Trade. Revision Workbook. Paperback: £9.95. ISBN 1-85836-465-5. Old Bailey Press.

Sellman, Pamela; Evans, Judith–Law of International Trade. Old Bailey Press Leading Cases. Paperback: £11.95. ISBN 1-85836-364-0. Old Bailey Press.

Snyder, Francis–Regional and Global Regulation of International Trade. Hardback: £35.00. ISBN 1-84113-218-7. Hart Publishing.

Todd, Paul–Cases and Materials on International Trade Law. Paperback: £40.00. ISBN 0-421-82710-6. Sweet & Maxwell.

Van Houtte, Hans–Law of International Trade. 2nd Ed. Hardback: £140.00. ISBN 0-421-76480-5. Sweet & Maxwell. Paperback: £40.00. ISBN 0-421-76490-2. Sweet & Maxwell International Student Editions.

World Trade Organization–WTO Agreements on CD-ROM Issue 1-The Legal Texts (English, French and Spanish) and Schedules: Services (English Only). World Trade Organization Schedules. CD-ROM: £406.35. ISBN 0-521-79645-8. Cambridge University Press.

Zanettin, Bruno–Cooperation Between Antitrust Agencies At the International Level. Hardback: £50.00. ISBN 1-84113-351-5. Hart Publishing.

JURISPRUDENCE

3003. Books

Alberstein, Michal–Pragmatism and Law-From Philosophy to Dispute Resolution. Law, Justice and Power. Hardback: £55.00. ISBN 0-7546-2208-8. Dartmouth.

Alexander, Larry; Sherwin, Emily–Rule of Rules-Morality, Rules, and the Dilemmas of Law. Hardback: £34.95. ISBN 0-8223-2736-8. Duke University Press.

Allan, James Plunkett–Sympathy and Antipathy. Hardback: £50.00. ISBN 0-7546-2289-4. Dartmouth.

Atria, Fernando–On Law and Legal Reasoning. Hardback: £35.00. ISBN 1-84113-275-6. Hart Publishing.

Austin, John; Campbell, Robert–Lectures on Jurisprudence: 2 Volumes (1879 Ed.). Hardback: £175.00. ISBN 1-85506-962-8. Thoemmes Press.

Banakar, Reza; Travers, Max–Introduction to Law and Social Theory. Hardback: £40.00. ISBN 1-84113-208-X. Paperback: £20.00. ISBN 1-84113-209-8. Hart Publishing.

Barendt, Eric M.–Privacy. International Library of Essays in Law and Legal Theory (Second Series). Hardback: £100.00. ISBN 0-7546-2071-9. Dartmouth.

Bass, Gary Jonathan–Stay the Hand of Vengeance. Princeton Studies in International History and Politics. Paperback: £13.95. ISBN 0-691-09278-8. Princeton University Press.

Bauman, Richard W.–Ideology and Community in the First Wave of Critical Legal Studies. Paperback: £18.00. ISBN 0-8020-8341-2. University of Toronto Press Inc.

Berk-Seligson, Susan–Bilingual Courtroom. Paperback: £14.50. ISBN 0-226-04378-9. University of Chicago Press.

Blackstone, William–Commentaries on the Laws of England-A Facsimile of the First Edition of 1765-1769. Hardback: £123.00. ISBN 0-226-05547-7. University of Chicago Press.

Bottomley, Anne–Feminist Perspectives on the Foundational Subjects of Law. Feminist Perspectives. Paperback: £32.95. ISBN 1-85941-590-3. Cavendish Publishing Ltd.

Byrne, John; Glover, Leigh; Martinez, Celia–Environmental Justice: International Discourses in Political Economy, Energy and Environmental Policy, Volume 2. Energy and Environmental Policy Series, Vol 8. Paperback: £22.95. ISBN 0-7658-0751-3. Transaction Publishers.

Campbell, Tom D.; Stone, Adrienne–Law and Democracy. International Library Essays in Law and Legal Theory. Hardback: £100.00. ISBN 0-7546-2214-2. Dartmouth.

Cane, Peter–Responsibility in Law and Morality. Hardback: £25.00. ISBN 1-841-13321-3. Hart Publishing.

Cartledge, Paul; Millett, Paul; Todd, Stephen–Nomos-Essays in Athenian Law, Politics and Society. Paperback: £18.95. ISBN 0-521-52209-9. Cambridge University Press.

Cohn, Marjorie; Dow, David–Cameras in the Courtroom. Paperback: £14.95. ISBN 0-7425-2023-4. Rowman & Littlefield Publishers.

Coleman, Jules L.–Markets, Morals, and the Law. Paperback: £25.00. ISBN 0-19-925360-9. Oxford University Press.

Coleman, Jules L.–Risks and Wrongs. Paperback: £25.00. ISBN 0-19-925361-7. Oxford University Press.

Cotterrell, Roger–Politics of Jurisprudence. 2nd Ed. Paperback: £22.95. ISBN 0-406-93055-4. Butterworths Law.

Dan-Cohen, Meir–Harmful Thoughts-Essays on Law, Self, and Morality. Hardback: £45.00. ISBN 0-691-09006-8. Paperback: £13.95. ISBN 0-691-09007-6. Princeton University Press.

Dnes, Antony; Rowthorn, Robert–Law and Economics of Marriage and Divorce. Hardback: £45.00. ISBN 0-521-80933-9. Cambridge University Press.

Doherty, Michael–Jurisprudence, 2nd Edition. Sourcebook. Paperback: £11.95. ISBN 1-85836-456-6. Old Bailey Press.

Doherty, Michael–Jurisprudence. Revision Workbook. Paperback: £9.95. ISBN 1-85836-427-2. Old Bailey Press.

Duxbury, Neil–Random Justice: on Lotteries and Legal Decision Making. Paperback: £19.99. ISBN 0-19-925353-6. Oxford University Press.

Dworkin, Ronald–Sovereign Virtue. Paperback: £13.95. ISBN 0-674-00810-3. Harvard University Press.

Edgeworth, Brendan–Law, Modernity, Postmodernity: Legal Change in Advanced Societies. Hardback: £45.00. ISBN 1-84014-009-7. Dartmouth.

Eskridge Jr., William N.–Equality Practice-Civil Unions and the Future of Gay Rights. Hardback: £50.00. ISBN 0-415-93072-3. Paperback: £11.99. ISBN 0-415-93073-1. Routledge, an imprint of Taylor & Francis Books Ltd.

Felson, Richard B.–Violence and Gender Reexamined. Law and Public Policy: Psychology and the Social Sciences. Hardback: £33.95. ISBN 1-55798-895-1. American Psychological Association.

Freeman, Michael–Current Legal Problems: Vol 54. 2001. Current Legal Problems. Hardback: £65.00. ISBN 0-19-924780-3. Oxford University Press.

Freeman, Michael–Lloyd's Introduction to Jurisprudence. 7th Ed. Paperback: £17.95. ISBN 0-421-75330-7. Sweet & Maxwell International Student Editions. Paperback: £36.00. ISBN 0-421-69020-8. Sweet & Maxwell.

Garnett, George; Hudson, John–Law and Government in Medieval England and Normandy. Paperback: £25.95. ISBN 0-521-52009-6. Cambridge University Press.

Gibbons, John–Forensic Linguistics. Language in Society. Hardback: £55.00. ISBN 0-631-21246-9. Paperback: £16.99. ISBN 0-631-21247-7. Blackwell Publishers.

Gillroy, John Martin–Justice and Nature-Kantian Philosophy, Environmental Policy, and the Law. American Governance and Public Policy. Paperback: £26.00. ISBN 0-87840-796-0. Georgetown University Press.

Goldsworthy, Jeffrey; Campbell, Tom–Legal Interpretation in Democratic States. Applied Legal Philosophy. Hardback: £55.00. ISBN 0-7546-2215-0. Dartmouth.

Grana, Sheryl J.; Ollenburger Jane C.; Nicholas, Mark–Social Context of Law. 2nd Ed. Paperback: £24.99. ISBN 0-13-041374-7. Prentice Hall.

Halpin, Andrew–Reasoning with Law. Hardback: £25.00. ISBN 1-84113-070-2. Paperback: £20.00. ISBN 1-84113-244-6. Hart Publishing.

Harris, J.W.–Property and Justice. Paperback: £18.99. ISBN 0-19-925140-1. Oxford University Press.

Hartogh, Govert A. den–Mutual Expectations-A Conventionalist Theory of Law. Law and Philosophy Library. Hardback: £61.00. ISBN 90-411-1796-2. Kluwer Law International.

Haslanger, Sally; Witt, Charlotte–View from Home. Feminist Theory and Politics. Hardback: £46.99. ISBN 0-8133-6616-X. Westview Press.

Hayden, Patrick—John Rawls-Towards a Just World Order. Political Philosophy Now. Hardback: £30.00. ISBN 0-7083-1729-4. Paperback: £14.99. ISBN 0-7083-1728-6. University of Wales Press.

Hinterseer, Kris—Criminal Finance-The Political Economy of Money Laundering in a Comparative Legal Context. Studies in Comparative Corporate and Financial Law. Hardback: £100.00. ISBN 90-411-9864-4. Kluwer Law International.

Hoecke, Mark Van—Law As Communication. European Academy of Legal Theory Series. Hardback: £35.00. ISBN 1-84113-341-8. Hart Publishing.

Honore, Tony—Ulpian: Pioneer of Human Rights. 2nd Ed. Hardback: £55.00. ISBN 0-19-924424-3. Oxford University Press.

Hopkins, John—Devolution in Context-Regional, Federal and Devolved Government in the EU. Paperback: £48.40. ISBN 1-85941-637-3. Cavendish Publishing Ltd.

Hunter, Ian; Saunders, David; Hunter, Ian; Saunders, David—Natural Law and Civil Sovereignty-Moral Right and State Authority in Early Modern Political Thought. Hardback: £45.00. ISBN 0-333-96459-4. Palgrave Macmillan.

Hutchinson, Dennis J.; Strauss, David A.; Stone, Geoffrey R.—Supreme Court Review: 2001. Hardback: £34.50. ISBN 0-226-36250-7. University of Chicago Press.

James, Susan; Palmer, Stephanie—Visible Women-Essays on Feminist Legal Theory and Political Philosophy. Hardback: £25.00. ISBN 1-84113-195-4. Hart Publishing.=j

Johnston, David; Zimmermann, Reinhard—Comparative Law of Unjust Enrichment. Hardback: £80.00. ISBN 0-521-80820-0. Cambridge University Press.

Jurisprudence. 3rd Ed. Law Cards Series. Paperback: £6.95. ISBN 1-85941-518-0. Cavendish Publishing Ltd.

Kaplow, Louis; Shavell, Steven—Fairness Versus Welfare. Hardback: £30.95. ISBN 0-674-00622-4. Harvard University Press.

Kapp, Marshall B.—Lessons in Law and Aging. Hardback: £38.95. ISBN 0-8261-1411-3. Springer Publishing Company.

Kerson, Toba Schwaber—Boundary Spanning-An Ecological Reinterpretation of Social Work Practice in Health and Mental Health Systems. Hardback: £39.50. ISBN 0-231-11036-7. Columbia University Press.

Kolm, Serge-Christophe—Modern Theories of Justice. Paperback: £26.50. ISBN 0-262-61180-5. The MIT Press.

Langlois, Anthony J.—Politics of Justice and Human Rights-Southeast Asia and Universalist Theory. Cambridge Asia-Pacific Studies. Hardback: £45.00. ISBN 0-521-80785-9. Cambridge University Press.

Macdonald, Roderick A.—Lessons of Everyday Law. Hardback: £49.90. ISBN 0-88911-913-9. Paperback: £18.90. ISBN 0-88911-915-5. McGill-Queen's University Press.

Marsh, James L.—Unjust Legality. New Critical Theory. Hardback. ISBN 0-7425-1260-6. Rowman & Littlefield Publishers.

Martin, Jacqueline—AQA Law for AS. Paperback: £14.99. ISBN 0-340-84741-7. Hodder & Stoughton Educational.

McConnell, Michael W.; Cochran Jr, Robert F.; Carmella, Angela C.—Christian Perspectives on Legal Thought. Hardback: £35.00. ISBN 0-300-08749-7. Paperback: £18.95. ISBN 0-300-08750-0. Yale University Press.

Menuge, Noel James—Medieval English Wardship in Romance and Law. Hardback: £40.00. ISBN 0-85991-632-4. D.S. Brewer.

Montagu—Legal Practice Companion 2002-2003. Paperback: £29.99. ISBN 0-19-925540-7. Oxford University Press.

Moore, Randy—Evolution in the Courtroom. Hardback: £55.95. ISBN 1-57607-420-X. ABC CLIO (Reference Books).

Naffine, Ngaire—Gender and Justice. International Library of Essays in Law and Legal Theory: Second Series. Hardback: £110.00. ISBN 0-7546-2087-5. Dartmouth.

Naffine, Ngaire; Owens, Rosemary J.; Williams, John—Intention in Law and Philosophy. Applied Legal Philosophy. Hardback: £50.00. ISBN 0-7546-2171-5. Dartmouth.

Neumann, Michael – Rule of Law-Politicizing Ethics. Ashgate New Critical Thinking in Philosophy. Hardback: £40.00. ISBN 0-7546-0525-6. Ashgate Publishing Limited.

Ogloff, James R.P. – Taking Psychology and Law Into the Twenty-first Century. Perspectives in Law & Psychology. Hardback: £55.00. ISBN 0-306-46760-7. Kluwer Academic / Plenum Publishers.

Omar, Paul J. – Procedures to Enforce Foreign Judgments. Association of European Lawyers. Hardback: £40.00. ISBN 0-7546-2010-7. Dartmouth.

Peach, Lucinda – Legislating Morality. Hardback: £32.50. ISBN 0-19-514371-X. Oxford University Press Inc, USA.

Perry, Michael J. – We the People: The Fourteenth Amendment and the Supreme Court. Paperback: £15.99. ISBN 0-19-515125-9. Oxford University Press Inc, USA.

Platts-Mills, John – Muck, Silk and Socialism. Hardback: £28.00. ISBN 0-9539949-0-2. Paper Publishing, London.

Posner, Eric A. – Law and Social Norms. Paperback: £12.95. ISBN 0-674-00814-6. Harvard University Press.

Posner, Richard – Problematics of Moral and Legal Theory. Paperback: £13.95. ISBN 0-674-00799-9. Harvard University Press.

Post, Robert; Appiah, Anthony; Butler, Judith; et al-Prejudicial Appearances-The Logic of American Antidiscrimination Law. Hardback: £41.95. ISBN 0-8223-2702-3. Duke University Press.

Postema, Gerald J. – Philosophy and the Law of Torts. Cambridge Studies in Philosophy and Law. Hardback: £40.00. ISBN 0-521-62282-4. Cambridge University Press.

Priban, Jiri – Dissidents of Law-On the 1989 Revolutions, Legitimations, Fictions of Legality and Contemporary Version of the Social Contract. Law, Justice and Power. Paperback: £50.00. ISBN 0-7546-2284-3. Dartmouth.

Reay, Rosamund – Evidence. 1999-2000 Suggested Solutions. Paperback: £6.95. ISBN 1-85836-444-2. Old Bailey Press.

Rescher, Nicholas – Fairness: Theory and Practice of Distributive Justice. Hardback: £29.50. ISBN 0-7658-0110-8. Transaction Publishers.

Roberts, J. Timmons – Chronicles from the Environmental Justice Frontline. Hardback: £40.00. ISBN 0-521-66062-9. Paperback: £14.95. ISBN 0-521-66900-6. Cambridge University Press.

Robison, Wade L. – Legal Essays of Michael Bayles. Law and Philosophy Library. Hardback: £60.00. ISBN 90-411-1835-7. Kluwer Law International.=j

Rollins, Joe – Ironic Jurisprudence. Hardback: £22.99. ISBN 0-312-24006-6. Palgrave Macmillan.

Santos, Boaventura De Sousa – Toward a New Common Sense. 2nd Ed. Paperback: £34.95. ISBN 0-406-94997-2. Butterworths Law.

Schneider, Elizabeth M. – Battered Women and Feminist Lawmaking. Paperback: £12.95. ISBN 0-300-09411-6. Yale University Press.

Shute, Stephen; Simester, Andrew – Criminal Law Theory-Doctrines of the General Part. Oxford Monographs on Criminal Law and Justice. Hardback: £45.00. ISBN 0-19-924349-2. Oxford University Press.

Shytov, Alexander Nikolaevich – Conscience and Love in Making Judicial Decisions. Law and Philosophy Library, 54. Hardback: £56.00. ISBN 1-4020-0168-1. Kluwer Academic Publishers.

Sosa, Ernest – Philosophical Issues: Vol 11. Philosophy of Law and Social Philosophy. Philosophical Issues, 11, 2002. Paperback: £19.99. ISBN 0-631-23029-7. Blackwell Publishers.

Stetson, Dorothy McBride – Abortion Politics, Women's Movements, and the Democratic State-A Comparative Study of State Feminism. Gender and Politics. Hardback: £45.00. ISBN 0-19-924265-8. Oxford University Press.=j

Tate, C. Neal – Comparative Judicial Systems. Hardback: £117.00. ISBN 1-56802-684-6. CQ Press.

Teitel, Ruti G. – Transitional Justice. Paperback: £15.99. ISBN 0-19-515126-7. Oxford University Press Inc, USA.

Tonry, Michael – Crime and Justice: 29. Hardback: £38.00. ISBN 0-226-80861-0. Newberry Library.

Tuori, Kaarlo–Critical Legal Positivism. Applied Legal Philosophy. Hardback: £60.00. ISBN 0-7546-2272-X. Dartmouth.

Tur, Richard–Different Concept of Law. Paperback: £22.00. ISBN 1-85941-641-1. Cavendish Publishing Ltd.

Twining, William L.–Great Juristic Bazaar-Juristic Texts and Lawyers' Stories. Collected Essays in Law. Hardback: £60.00. ISBN 0-7546-2211-8. Dartmouth.

Twining, William; Hampsher-Monk, Iain–Evidence and Inference in History and Law-Interdisciplinary Dialogues. Hardback: £75.50. ISBN 0-8101-1893-9. Paperback: £24.95. ISBN 0-8101-1756-8. Northwestern University Press.

Valdes, Francisco; Culp, Jerome McCristal; Harris, Angela P.–Crossroads, Directions, and a New Critical Race Theory. Hardback: £66.95. ISBN 1-56639-929-7. Paperback: £24.95. ISBN 1-56639-930-0. Temple University Press.

Van Pelt, Robert–Case for Auschwitz-Evidence from the Irving Trial. Hardback: £34.50. ISBN 0-253-34016-0. Indiana University Press.

Verheij, B.; Lodder, A.R.; Loui, R.P.; Muntjewerff, A.–Legal Knowledge and Information Systems. Frontiers in Artificial Intelligence and Applications, Vol 70. Hardback: £48.00. ISBN 1-58603-201-1. IOS Press.

Viscusi, W. Kip–Regulation Through Litigation. Hardback: £41.00. ISBN 0-8157-0610-3. Paperback: £18.50. ISBN 0-8157-0609-X. The Brookings Institution.

Walzer, Lee–Gay Rights on Trial. Hardback: £29.95. ISBN 1-57607-254-1. ABC CLIO (Reference Books).

Wickham, Gary; Pavlich, George–Rethinking Law Society and Governance-Foucault's Bequest. Onati International Series in Law and Society. Hardback: £45.00. ISBN 1-84113-293-4. Paperback: £20.00. ISBN 1-84113-294-2. Hart Publishing.

Williams, Melanie–Empty Justice: One Hundred Years of Law, Literature and Philosophy. Feminist Perspectives. Paperback: £40.00. ISBN 1-85941-614-4. Cavendish Publishing Ltd.

Winston, Kenneth–Fuller's Principles of Social Order. Paperback: £25.00. ISBN 1-84113-234-9. Hart Publishing.

Winter, Steven L.–Clearing in the Forest-Law, Life, and Mind. Hardback: £24.00. ISBN 0-226-90221-8. University of Chicago Press.

Wintgens, Luc–Legisprudence. Hardback: £50.00. ISBN 1-84113-342-6. Hardback: £50.00. ISBN 1-84113-342-6. Hart Publishing.

LANDLORD AND TENANT

3004. Agricultural holdings–equitable relief–protected tenancy defeated by proprietary estoppel

[Agricultural Holdings Act 1986 s.2, s.25.]

B, a property development company, sought declarations that it was entitled to occupy certain land and proceed with its development of it without interference from C and that any tenancy of that land which C might hold was unenforceable against it. B had purchased 38 acres of agricultural land from another developer. It had emerged, however, that C claimed a tenancy of the land and that such tenancy, if it existed, would be protected under the provisions of the Agricultural Holdings Act 1986. C had brought proceedings in the county court for, inter alia, an injunction but the judge had found that C had disentitled himself through his conduct from receiving equitable relief. In the instant proceedings, B maintained that C's conduct had, pursuant to the doctrine of proprietary estoppel, resulted in an equity in its favour. C argued that the statutory protection established under s.2 and s.25 of the Act could not be defeated by an alleged proprietary estoppel.

Held, granting the declarations, that there was nothing within the Act to prevent B from placing reliance on the doctrine of proprietary estoppel, be that by positively claiming the right to use the land during what would otherwise be the remainder of the tenancy, or negatively by denying C damages in relation to such use. Given that an existing agricultural tenant could surrender his tenancy, that surrender having immediate effect, by conduct contrary to the continued subsistence of the tenancy, it was appropriate that a landlord should, in appropriate circumstances, be able to invoke the doctrine of proprietary estoppel against that tenant in order to prevent him from attempting to assert his tenancy or some incident of it; a tenant's ability to end a tenancy through consensual surrender had to include the ability, through acts falling short of a surrender, to create an equity in the landlord's favour. It followed that the tenancy was unenforceable against B, *Keen v. Holland* [1984] 1 W.L.R. 251, [1984] C.L.Y. 34 distinguished. *Keen v. Holland* had been limited to the issue of estoppel by convention and had decided nothing in relation to the applicability of the doctrine of proprietary estoppel.

JS BLOOR (MEASHAM) LTD v. CALCOTT (NO.2) [2002] 1 E.G.L.R.1, Hart, J., Ch D.

3005. Agricultural holdings—notice to quit—breaches of covenant—validity of notices

T, an agricultural tenant, appealed against a judge's decision to dismiss his application challenging an arbitrator's award in favour of LCC, his landlord, on the basis of three successive notices to quit, following three previous notices to remedy breaches of covenant. The arbitrator had held that although the first two notices to quit were invalid, the third was valid and effective since T had been given 12 months in which to remedy the breach which was reasonable. T submitted that (1) the arbitrator had erred by failing to account for the expansion of the business since the first notice was served and the time needed for relocation, and (2) the judge was wrong to impeach the arbitrator's finding that LCC's conduct in relation to the first notice amounted to a representation that it would not insist on the strict operation of the notice with the effect that the period specified in the notice was suspended and the notice was impugned. T contended that the failure to respond to enquiries regarding future proceedings estopped LCC from serving the subsequent notices as it had indicated a willingness to review its position.

Held, dismissing the appeal, that (1) there was no error of law in the arbitrator's award concerning the notice period contained in the third notice, and there was no evidence to show that the expansion of the business, which had been taken into account at the hearing, would have made it more difficult to relocate, and (2) LCC's representation had not been so clear and unequivocal as to found a claim in promissory estoppel, *Hughes v. Metropolitan Railway Co* (1876-77) L.R. 2 App. Cas. 439 applied, and accordingly the judge's decision to impeach the arbitrator's finding was correct.

TAYLOR v. LANCASHIRE CC [2001] EWCA Civ 174, Dyson, L.J., CA.

3006. Agricultural holdings—rent reviews—variation of tenancy to include small amount of additional land—jurisdiction of arbitrator to determine landlord's application for rent review

[Agricultural Holdings Act 1986 s.12, Sch.2 para.4(1), Sch.2 para.6.]

The Secretary of State in his capacity as the owner of 256 acres of farmland and the buildings thereon, appealed against a finding that an arbitrator had no jurisdiction to determine the rent payable under an annual tenancy which had been originally granted to the tenant, T, in 1987. On September 21, 1998, T served a notice under the Agricultural Holdings Act 1986 s.12 seeking a review of the rent with effect from September 29, 1999. Meanwhile, T had written to the Secretary of State offering to include a small parcel of adjoining land into the tenancy agreement in return for a small increase in the rent. T accepted the proposal and went into occupation of the additional land, but the agreement was only formalised on February 28, 2000. T then contended that the effect of the 2000 agreement was to preclude the Secretary of State from continuing with the rent review, because Sch.2 para.4(1) of the 1986 Act rendered ineffective any demand for arbitration that sought a review from a date not less than three years from the date on which any previous increase in the rent took effect. The Secretary of State contended that he was entitled to benefit from exceptions to Sch.2

para.4(1) given in Sch.2 para.6, as the 2000 agreement made provision for (1) "adjustment of the boundaries of the holding", or (2) "any other variation of the terms of the tenancy".

Held, allowing the appeal, that (1) the agreement allowing for the inclusion of the additional land did not fall within the natural meaning of the words "adjustment of the boundaries of the holding". An agreement did not make provision for the adjustment of boundaries to a holding merely because it happened to have that consequence, *Mann v. Gardner* (1991) 61 P & C.R. 1, [1991] C.L.Y. 116 followed, however (2) upon a proper consideration of the statutory context, it was clear that the natural meaning of the words "any other variation of the terms of the tenancy" included the extension of the tenancy to include a small amount of additional land. Accordingly, Sch.2 para.4(1) was not engaged in circumstances where the increase in rent was attributable to the variation in the terms of the tenancy.

SECRETARY OF STATE FOR DEFENCE v. SPENCER, [2002] EWHC 2116, [2003] 1 W.L.R. 75, Neuberger, J., Ch D.

3007. Agricultural holdings—units of production—net annual income

AGRICULTURAL HOLDINGS (UNITS OF PRODUCTION) (ENGLAND) ORDER 2002, SI 2002 1925; made under the Agricultural Holdings Act 1986 Sch.6 para.4. In force: September 12, 2002; £2.00.

This Order, which revokes the Agricultural Holdings (Units of Production) (England) Order 2001 (SI 2001 2751), prescribes units of production for the assessment of the productive capacity of agricultural land situated in England and sets out the amount which is to be regarded as the net annual income from each such unit for the year September 12, 2002 to September 11, 2003.

3008. Assured shorthold tenancies—notices—effect of defects in pre tenancy notice

[Housing Act 1988 s.20(2).]

H, who had occupied a flat under a four year assured shorthold tenancy, appealed against a finding that the pre tenancy notice which had been served on her by her landlord, R, pursuant to the Housing Act 1988 s.20(2) was valid. H argued that the notice was defective in that it stated that the tenancy commenced on the date on which the term of years created by the tenancy began rather than on the date when the tenancy agreement had been executed.

Held, dismissing the appeal, that the sole question was whether, despite any errors or omissions, the notice was substantially to the same effect as a correct notice in serving the statutory purpose of informing the prospective tenant of the special nature of an assured shorthold tenancy, *Mannai Investment Co Ltd v. Eagle Star Life Assurance Co Ltd* [1997] A.C. 749, [1997] C.L.Y. 3256 and *Manel v. Memon* (2001) 33 H.L.R. 24, [2000] C.L.Y. 3875 applied. In the instant case, although R's notice had failed to specify the correct commencement date of the tenancy, it had been substantially to the same effect as a correct notice and was therefore valid.

RAVENSEFT PROPERTIES LTD v. HALL; KASSEER v. FREEMAN; WHITE v. CHUBB; *sub nom.* RAVENSCROFT PROPERTIES LTD v. HALL, [2001] EWCA Civ 2034, [2002] H.L.R. 33, Mummery, L.J., CA.

3009. Assured shorthold tenancies—notices—notice to quit by tenant—rent in lieu of notice

[Protection from Eviction Act 1977 s.5(1); Housing Act 1996 s.5.]

In January 1998 L granted an assured shorthold tenancy to C for six months at a rent of £390 per calendar month, payable in advance at two monthly intervals. The tenancy agreement contained a clause requiring C to give one calendar month's notice of termination. The tenancy continued after the end of the six months, and in September 1998 C left the property, depositing the keys through L's letterbox. L's applications to the court to recover rent arrears and funds to repair damage caused by C were successful, although her associated claim for four weeks' rent in lieu of notice was refused. L appealed.

Held, allowing the appeal, that at the end of the term certain the tenancy took effect as a periodic assured tenancy under the Housing Act 1996 s.5, the periods being calendar months. Although the notice clause in the tenancy agreement no longer applied after the expiration of the term certain, C was required by the Protection from Eviction Act 1977 s.5(1) to give at least four weeks notice to quit. The act of putting the keys through L's letterbox amounted to an offer by C to terminate the tenancy, which L by implication accepted as four weeks' notice commencing on that day. L was therefore entitled to recover rent equivalent to that four week notice period.

LAINE v. CADWALLADER (2001) 33 H.L.R. 36, Kennedy, L.J., CA.

3010. Assured shorthold tenancies–notices–service of pre tenancy notice on tenant's agent

[Housing Act 1988 s.20.]

N, the tenant of a residential property, appealed against a finding (Times, August 1, 2001) that the tenancy which he had entered into with Y, the landlord, was an assured shorthold tenancy rather than an assured tenancy. Y's notice, served pursuant to the Housing Act 1988 s.20, stating that the tenancy was to be an assured shorthold tenancy had been served on N's agent rather than on N himself. N argued that it was not permissible to serve such a notice on the tenant's agent.

Held, dismissing the appeal, that a notice under s.20 of the 1988 Act could be served on the tenant's authorised agent, *Galinski v. McHugh* (1989) 21 H.L.R. 47, [1989] C.L.Y. 2162 applied.

YENULA PROPERTIES LTD v. NAIDU; *sub nom.* NAIDU v. YENULA PROPERTIES LTD, [2002] EWCA Civ 719, [2003] H.L.R. 18, Robert Walker, L.J., CA.

3011. Assured shorthold tenancies–possession orders–automatic continuation of tenancy–definition of term of lease

[Housing Act 1988 s.45(1).]

E, the lessee of a property owned by G, appealed against an order allowing the appeal of G against the decision not to grant G an order for possession. The issue to be resolved was whether E's tenancy was an assured shorthold tenancy for the purposes of the Housing Act 1988. E submitted that the lease was in effect a single tenancy for a one year term thereafter determinable on one month's notice, and that it formed a periodic tenancy in part and was therefore not a fixed term tenancy within s.45(1) of the Act.

Held, dismissing the appeal, that the tenancy was not a periodic tenancy because the automatic continuation at the end of the term was not for the same one year period. Consequently, the tenancy did not fall within the exclusion to s.45(1) of the Act and was therefore an assured shorthold tenancy, G being entitled to possession.

GOODMAN v. EVELY, [2001] EWCA Civ 104, [2002] H.L.R. 53, Sir Robert Andrew Morritt V.C., CA.

3012. Assured tenancies–agricultural occupancies

ASSURED TENANCIES AND AGRICULTURAL OCCUPANCIES (FORMS) (AMENDMENT) (ENGLAND) REGULATIONS 2002, SI 2002 337; made under the Housing Act 1988 s.13, s.45. In force: Reg.4: June 20, 2002; remainder: February 20, 2002; £2.00.

These Regulations, which amend the Assured Tenancies and Agricultural Occupancies (Forms) Regulations 1997 (SI 1997 194), prescribe a new form to be used by landlords in proposing a new rent for an assured tenancy or an assured agricultural occupancy under the Housing Act 1988 s.13.

3013. Assured tenancies–landlords powers and duties–possession sought to effect works–work falling outside scope of Landlord and Tenant Act 1954 s.11

[Landlord and Tenant Act 1954 s.11, s.30(1)(f); Housing Act 1988 s.16, Sch.2.]

S claimed possession of a property from his assured tenant, A, relying upon ground 6 of the Housing Act 1988 Sch.2. S produced a specification setting out a complex programme of works to be carried out to the premises. Whilst it was common ground that part of the programme included works which S was required to carry out in any event pursuant to his duty under the Landlord and Tenant Act 1954 s.11, A contended that, by virtue of s.16 of the 1988 Act, S already had a right to enter the premises to carry out works. Therefore, A argued, S was only entitled to claim possession in respect of work that was outside the scope of s.11 of the 1954 Act in the same way that a landlord seeking possession of property from a business tenant under s.30(1)(f) of the 1954 Act could seek possession, *Heath v. Drown* [1973] A.C. 498, [1972] C.L.Y. 1983 and *Cerex Jewels v. Peachey Property Corp* (1986) 52 P. & C.R. 127, [1987] C.L.Y. 2112 cited. S submitted that (1) cases decided under the 1954 Act were not authoritative in respect of claims under the 1988 Act, and (2) in the context of ground D in Sch.2 of the 1988 Act, the landlord was only required to show that he required physical possession of the premises to be entitled to an order for legal possession of the same.

Held, granting judgment in favour of A, that (1) cases decided under s.30(1)(f) of the 1954 Act were authority for matters to be decided under the 1988 Act, *Heath* and *Cerex* applied, and (2) to succeed under ground 6, S was required to satisfy the court that the proposed works not only fell outside of the scope of s.11 of the 1954 Act but also were of such a nature that legal, rather than physical, possession of the property was necessary in order for them to be carried out.

SUGARWHITE v. AFRIDI, January 11, 2002, Judge Collins, CC (Central London). [*Ex rel.* James Browne, Barrister, 96 Gray's Inn Road, London].

3014. Assured tenancies–notices–notice proposing statutory tenancy not addressed to tenant–rent assessment committee setting rent above maximum for assured tenancy

[Landlord and Tenant Act 1954 Part I.]

M, the tenant, appealed against the dismissal of his application for judicial review of a rent assessment committee decision. The landlord, C, had granted a headlease of a flat to D in 1962. D granted an underlease to B. The headlease and the underlease were later assigned to F. M went into occupation in 1990. The headlease expired in September 1995 and, in April 1995, C sent a notice to B under the Landlord and Tenant Act 1954 Part I, proposing a statutory tenancy. M then acquired the underlease from F and a notice was served on M by C in June 1999. This terminated his previous tenancy and proposed an assured tenancy at an annual rent of £46,800. No agreement was reached on the rent and so the matter was referred to the rent assessment committee, which set the rent at £32,496 per annum. It was also held that M was an assured tenant. M asserted that he was a statutory tenant as the April 1995 notice had been properly served. Alternatively, if he was an assured tenant, that the committee could not set a rent in excess of £25,000.

Held, dismissing the appeal, that the April 1995 notice was addressed to B, not M, and B was not the tenant at that time. The notice was therefore invalid. However, both the 1999 notice and the determination of the rent committee were valid. Setting a figure in excess of £25,000 meant that M was no longer an assured tenant.

R. (ON THE APPLICATION OF MORRIS) v. LONDON RENT ASSESSMENT COMMITTEE; *sub nom.* MORRIS v. LONDON RENT ASSESSMENT COMMITTEE, [2002] EWCA Civ 276, [2002] H.L.R. 48, Mummery, L.J., CA.

3015. Assured tenancies–security of tenure–premises vacated–effect of subtenancy

[Housing Act 1988.]

F appealed against a decision that her assured tenancy of a house had come to an end after she had vacated the house and her letting agent had sub-let it for a period of 12 months.

Held, dismissing the appeal, that it was possible for a tenant who had sub-let assured premises to retain his entitlement to an assured tenancy by showing that he had a genuine intention to return to the premises and use them as his permanent residence. The decisions of the Court of Appeal in relation to this issue appeared to be irreconcilable. It was therefore appropriate to apply the underlying reasoning of *Ujima Housing Association v. Ansah* (1998) 30 H.L.R. 831, [1997] C.L.Y. 3251, which was the only case decided under the Housing Act 1988, *Crawley BC v. Sawyer* (1988) 20 H.L.R. 98, [1988] C.L.Y. 2078 and *Hussey v. Camden LBC* (1995) 27 H.L.R. 5, [1996] C.L.Y. 3835 considered, and *Ujima* applied. It could not be said that, having regard to the facts, the judge had erred in finding that F had not established a genuine intention to return to the house.

FANNING v. WALTHAM FOREST COMMUNITY BASED HOUSING ASSOCIATION; *sub nom.* WALTHAM FOREST COMMUNITY BASED HOUSING ASSOCIATION v. FANNING [2001] L. & T.R. 41, Rougier, J., QBD.

3016. Assured tenancies–security of tenure–transitional provisions–protected tenancies

[Rent Act 1977 s.20; Housing Act 1988 s.34, s.36.]

R appealed against a possession order granted in respect of premises which he occupied as a tenant and against a judgment in respect of rent arrears. R submitted that, at the relevant time, he had been a protected tenant under the Rent Act 1977 with the result that the possession order and money judgment should be set aside.

Held, dismissing the appeal, that under the provisions of the 1977 Act, R had never been a protected tenant but that R's tenancy had, by virtue of s.20, acquired status as a restricted contract. Following a consensual variation of R's rent in 1990, R must be regarded, pursuant to the Housing Act 1988 s.36, as having entered into a new tenancy which had the effect of removing any protection afforded under the restricted contract. Since the new tenancy had begun after the date of commencement of the 1988 Act, s.34 prevented R from gaining a status, never previously attained, as a protected tenant. Upon correct interpretation, s.36(2) of the 1988 Act having prevented a new restricted contract from arising also had the effect of treating the subsequent contract as being "entered into" for the purposes of s.34(1) of the 1988 Act with the result that the new contract was prevented from conferring protection previously afforded by the Rent Acts. Accordingly, R had, at the material time, been an assured tenant within the meaning of the 1988 Act.

ROWE v. MATTHEWS (2001) 33 H.L.R. 81, McCombe, J., QBD.

3017. Business tenancies–access–balance of convenience–estoppel or positive right over landlord's property–adequacy of damages

R, a tenant, operated a nightclub from basement premises and sought an interlocutory injunction preventing C, the landlord, from interfering with its enjoyment of access to this property. The premises were subject to a 25 year lease granted to R by C's predecessor in title and were accessed through a separate ground floor property, unit four. R previously enjoyed the use of unit four under a 10 year lease and a series of fixed term tenancies all of which had expired. Unusually the basement lease contained no express right of access other than in an emergency but obliged C to apply for and use reasonable endeavours to obtain all necessary consents to achieve access to the basement through specific points. If C failed to secure this access R was entitled to determine the basement lease upon expiration of the unit four lease. It was submitted that the problems faced given lack of access to the basement were due to C's failure to discharge its obligations under the lease and so R had an arguable right to continue to use unit four as access. Alternatively it was contended that, in the light of negotiations which had taken place, an estoppel had arisen entitling R to access the basement.

Held, granting an interlocutory injunction, that R had an arguable case and the balance of convenience favoured an injunction so that it could continue to enjoy access through unit four. Under the terms of the lease it was difficult to see how there was any right to use unit four after the expiry of the lease relating to it; moreover, any action brought in respect of C's failure to comply with its contractual obligations would lie in damages not in asserting a positive right over the landlord's property. However, there was an argument that one could imply a positive right to use an alternative route over C's property analogous to the principles of rights of way. Although this reasoning was regarded as adventurous an arguable estoppel was also found relating to R having desisted from enforcing his right that C should seek to provide access during negotiations regarding redevelopment of the site. The difficulty in quantifying lost trade and goodwill made damages inadequate and it was also tentatively suggested that the balance of convenience included a consideration of the adequacy of an award of damages.

ROCK GARDEN LTD v. COVENT GARDEN MARKET LP, [2002] EWHC 1666, *The Times*, October 3, 2002, Neuberger, J., Ch D.

3018.   Business tenancies–access–renewal of tenancy–property treated as landlocked for purposes of fixing rent

[Landlord and Tenant Act 1954 s.34.]

R appealed against a preliminary finding that, in fixing the rent payable for a new tenancy granted to J, the property was to be treated as landlocked. The judge fixed the rent, incorporating a 40 per cent discount, to take account of access difficulties. R submitted that the judge should have disregarded the access difficulties when assessing the rent in accordance with the Landlord and Tenant Act 1954 s.34, arguing that s.34 required that there be the assumption of an open market and a willing lessor, which in turn implied that there was a willing lessee.

Held, dismissing the appeal, that the lack of access to the property could not be disregarded for the purposes of s.34 and was therefore capable of providing a further deduction in rent. The judge had been correct to find that, notwithstanding that the property was landlocked, there was an open market for the property and as such an open market rent should be ascertained, *Jefferies v. O'Neill* (1983) 46 P. & C.R. 376, [1984] C.L.Y. 1955 and *British Airways Plc v. Heathrow Airport* [1992] 1 E.G.L.R. 141, [1992] C.L.Y. 2730 considered.

J MURPHY & SONS LTD v. RAILTRACK PLC; *sub nom.* MURPHY & SONS LTD v. RAILTRACK PLC, [2002] EWCA Civ 679, [2003] 1 P. & C.R. 7, Peter Gibson, L.J., CA.

3019.   Business tenancies–assignment–authorised guarantee agreements– requirement of reasonableness

[Landlord and Tenant (Covenants) Act 1995 s.16(3)(b).]

W, tenants of shop premises, brought proceedings against CGU, the freehold owner and landlord, concerning the wording of an alienation clause in the proposed new tenancy agreement following the expiry of the original lease. The alienation clause in the new lease purported to require W to enter into an authorised guarantee agreement, AGA, guaranteeing the keeping of covenants by its assignees, in return for CGU's consent to the assignment. W contended that, by virtue of the Landlord and Tenant (Covenants) Act 1995 s.16(3)(b), the clause should include wording to the effect that it would only be required to enter into an AGA "where reasonable". CGU argued that (1) the requirement should be automatic as the lease would otherwise be more favourable to W than the previous lease, and (2) a requirement for reasonableness could lead to uncertainty.

Held, allowing the application, that the purpose of the Act had been to substantially alter a landlord's rights to impose terms on a tenant's assignment of a lease and that he could not, therefore, lawfully require an AGA where one was not provided for either in the lease or by order of the court. In order to show that a landlord's requirement for an AGA was unreasonable, a tenant would have to show that no reasonable landlord could require it in the circumstances.

WALLIS FASHION GROUP LTD v. CGU LIFE ASSURANCE LTD; *sub nom.* WALLIS FASHION GROUP LTD v. GENERAL ACCIDENT LIFE ASSURANCE LTD (2001) 81 P. & C.R. 28, Neuberger, J., Ch D.

3020. Business tenancies–contract terms–no commencement date in lease

The court was asked to determine certain issues relating to the respective rights and obligations of the local authority and W, a developer, under an agreement entered into for the redevelopment of a city centre site. Under Clause 4.13 of the agreement, subject to certain conditions precedent being fulfilled, a decision notice had to be issued by the local authority and a lease granted to W for 999 years on the terms of a draft lease annexed to the agreement. The draft lease did not, however, contain a commencement date. The local authority argued, inter alia, that such an omission rendered the lease void for uncertainty.

Held, giving judgment for W, that as a matter of construction and having regard to authority, the lease, if and when granted, would be for a term of 999 years from the date upon which it was executed. Alternatively, if such a conclusion was wrong, the term would be 999 years from the date upon which the local authority served its decision notice, *Marshall v. Berridge* (1881-82) L.R. 19 Ch. D. 233 and *Harvey v. Pratt* [1965] 1 W.L.R. 1025, [1965] C.L.Y. 2183 distinguished. If, contrary to those conclusions, the lease was void, an equity had arisen in favour of W and the parties were bound by Clause 4.13. W had spent significant amounts of time and money reasonably believing that the agreement was enforceable. It would not be unfair or oppressive for the local authority to be required to grant W a 999 year lease on the terms of the draft lease, *Dodsworth v. Dodsworth* (1973) 228 E.G. 1115, [1974] C.L.Y. 3144 considered.

LIVERPOOL CITY COUNCIL v. WALTON GROUP PLC [2002] 1 E.G.L.R. 149, Neuberger, J., Ch D.

3021. Business tenancies–forfeiture–wrongful termination–recognition of borrowing costs of small businesses

See DAMAGES: Jaura v. Ahmed. §925

3022. Business tenancies–grant–demolition and reconstruction works–terms granting access and facilities to carry out works

[Landlord and Tenant Act 1954 s.30(1)(f), s.31A(1)(a).]

P, a tenant, appealed against a decision upholding the opposition of its landlord to the grant of a new lease. The tenancy in question had been of what was commonly called an "eggshell tenancy"; only the internal "skin" of that part of the building P occupied being included in the demise, all load bearing structures being specifically excluded. L intended to carry out works on the building including removal of the material enclosing the demised premises such that what had been P's shop would become part of a larger open space. L argued that the intended works amounted to demolition and reconstruction and that those works could not reasonably be carried out with his obtaining possession of the holding. P contended that the judge at first instance had erred in concluding (1) that L had satisfied the requirements of the Landlord and Tenant Act 1954 s.30(1)(f), and/or (2) that P had not been entitled to rely upon s.31A of the Act.

Held, dismissing the appeal, that for the purpose of s.30(1)(f) and s.31A(1)(a) "obtaining possession of the holding" meant the tenant being deprived of his legal right to possession rather than the landlord obtaining mere physical possession, *Heath v. Drown* [1973] A.C. 498, [1972] C.L.Y. 1983 applied. A tenant could rely on s31A(1)(a) to defeat his landlord's reliance on s30(1)(f) if he could show that the intended works could be reasonably carried out by inclusion in the new tenancy of terms granting the landlord access and other facilities for the purpose of those works being carried out. In the instant case, the granting of such access and facilities would not avail P as the works in question would result in P being unable to use the premises demised by the new tenancy for the purpose of its business without it reinstating those parts of the premises it had agreed to L removing. Thus, the intended works could not reasonably be carried out without granting L legal possession of the premises demised to P.

PUMPERNINKS OF PICCADILLY LTD v. LAND SECURITIES PLC; *sub nom.* PUMPERNINKS OF PICCADILLY LTD v. LAND SECURITIES LTD, [2002] EWCA Civ 621, [2002] Ch. 332, Charles, J., CA.

3023. Business tenancies—implied terms—rent review clause—appointment of surveyor—tenant able to make time of the essence for landlord's application

B, the tenant, appealed against an order allowing S's appeal from a master's refusal to grant S summary judgment on B's claim. B had sought a declaration that the proper construction of the lease allowed it to make time of the essence for the appointment of an independent surveyor for a rent review. The lease provided for rent reviews every seven years with the rent to be agreed by the next quarter day before the rent review date. In the absence of agreement, the rent was to be determined by a surveyor to be appointed on S's application to the Royal Institution of Chartered Surveyors. B and S failed to agree on the rent and B required S to apply for the appointment of a surveyor within 28 days, contending that time was of the essence. S did not apply within that time period, so B sought the declaration.

Held, allowing the appeal, that a term would be implied into the lease that the application was to be made within a reasonable time of the relevant quarter day. B could therefore make time of the essence and had done so in its letter to S requesting the application to be made.

BARCLAYS BANK PLC v. SAVILE ESTATES LTD; *sub nom.* BARCLAYS BANK PLC v. SAVILLE ESTATES LTD, [2002] EWCA Civ 589, [2002] L. & T.R. 28, Aldous, L.J., CA.

3024. Business tenancies—licensed premises—options—surrender of equitable tenancy in return for 20 year full repairing lease—availability of damages for breach of contract

P was the licensee of a public house with a five year tenancy and an option to renew for a further five years. P exercised the option at the end of the first term. By then T, the landlord, was only granting 20 year terms under a full repairing lease. After negotiations, P entered into an agreement for a 20 year term and agreed to surrender his earlier tenancy. P subsequently claimed damages for breach of contract arising from the failure to grant a second term following the exercise of the option. P succeeded at first instance and was awarded £20,930 damages on the basis that, although the equitable tenancy had been surrendered, the fact that the agreement was no longer enforceable did not prevent P from claiming damages for breach of the agreement. T appealed.

Held, allowing the appeal, that the breach of contract found at first instance consisted of the failure to grant P a second five year term. After exercising the option, P had an equitable tenancy that allowed him to occupy for the remainder of the term. The surrender ended his right of renewal and meant that T was not obliged to let P occupy on the previous terms. No compensation was available for the loss of that right as it had been compromised by the surrender. Although a claim for breach could survive the surrender, P was actually claiming for performance of the agreement and this had not survived the surrender.

PLUMMER v. TIBSCO LTD, [2002] EWCA Civ 102, [2002] 1 E.G.L.R. 29, Aldous, L.J., CA.

3025. Business tenancies—local authorities—permitted use as retail—change of use to food outlet

[Local Government Act 1972 s.123(2).]

M applied for judicial review of the local authority's decision not to allow M to change the use of premises leased by him from the local authority. The lease allowed the premises to be used only as a retail delicatessen, in accordance with local planning policy. Over the years, M began selling food to be eaten on the premises and applied for planning permission for a change of use. This was granted on appeal, but the local authority refused to permit the change of use under the lease. M contended that that decision was in breach of (1) the Local Government Act 1972 s.123(2) as it prevented the local authority from obtaining the best possible consideration for the lease; (2) the local authority's fiduciary duty and therefore irrational, and (3) a legitimate expectation that the local authority would make the decision without recourse to local planning policy.

Held, dismissing the application, that the decision should not be quashed because (1) given that at the time of granting the lease planning policy restricted the use of the premises to retail, it could not be said that the local authority was reducing its chances of getting the best possible consideration for the lease by restricting the use in line with planning policy; (2) irrationality and breach of fiduciary duty were in the circumstances of this case one and the same. The local authority had been in the best position to judge local planning need and its decision was not so surprising as to be irrational, and (3) the local authority had made it clear throughout that it objected to a change of use and therefore there had been nothing in its dealings with M which could be said to have given rise to a legitimate expectation.

R. (ON THE APPLICATION OF MOLINARO) v. KENSINGTON AND CHELSEA RLBC, [2001] EWHC Admin 896, [2002] B.L.G.R. 336, Elias, J., QBD (Admin Ct).

3026. Business tenancies—notice to quit—delayed payment of rent—post dated cheques—validity of notice

L, a tenant of premises leased from C, had exercised an option and served a valid notice to determine the lease. However, C sought a declaration that the lease had not been determined effectively, contending that (1) L was in material breach of a repair covenant, and (2) L had also breached a covenant to pay all outstanding rent by the determination date.

Held, granting a declaration in favour of the defendant, that (1) L had made a genuine attempt to comply with the repair covenant. Both the interior and exterior of the premises had been left in good order by L and L had carried out certain repairs to the property. Any remaining breaches of the covenant to repair could not be viewed as material, especially in the light of C's attempt to take advantage of L's alleged non compliance, and (2) L had, however, made a deliberate attempt to delay payment of the rent insofar as it had initially disregarded the invoice and by post-dating the cheque it sent to C. This amounted to a material breach of covenant since the exercise of an option was a privilege that necessitated the strict observance of any conditions and therefore the lease had not been validly determined, *Finch v. Underwood* (1875-76) L. R. 2 Ch. D. 310 applied.

COMMERCIAL UNION LIFE ASSURANCE CO LTD v. LABEL INK LTD [2001] L. & T.R. 29, Judge Rich Q.C., Ch D.

3027. Business tenancies–rent–persistent late payment–landlord's assent– landlord estopped from refusing new tenancy

[Landlord and Tenant Act 1954 Part II, s.30(1)(a), s.30(1)(b).]

H appealed against the refusal of his application pursuant to the Landlord and Tenant Act 1954 Part II for the grant of a new business tenancy. The application had been opposed by A, the landlord of the relevant premises, on the grounds set out in s.30(1)(a) and s.30(1)(b) of the Act, namely that H had failed to comply with his repair obligations and had persistently delayed in paying rent. It had been the normal practice for H to pay rent to the previous landlords of the premises slightly late, a practice that had continued after A had become the landlord. After A had become the new landlord, a letter containing a demand for the rent for two previous quarters had been sent wrongly to H. The county court judge had considered the letter as indicative of H's attitude in persistently delaying payment of the rent. H argued that the judge had erred in failing to give sufficient consideration to the fact that it had been the normal practice for rent to be paid late and that no complaint, request or demand had been made by the landlords that he pay the rent more timeously.

Held, allowing the appeal, that the judge had erred, in particular by mistakenly regarding the wrongful demand letter as notice to H that late payment of rent would no longer be tolerated. Given that H had habitually paid his rent slightly late and that his landlords had assented to his doing so, an estoppel had arisen such that A could only rely on H's persistent late payment if notice had been given to him that strict compliance with the lease covenant was required. Such notice had not been given. It was apparent that the prior history of rent payments did not indicate a "persistent" failure for the purposes of s.30(1)(b) of the Act and that, in the circumstances, it was appropriate to grant H a new business tenancy.

HAZEL v. AKHTAR, [2001] EWCA Civ 1883, [2002] 2 P. & C.R. 17, Sir Anthony Evans, CA.

3028. Business tenancies–repair covenants–interpretation of clause

On a trial of preliminary issues, the wording of a landlord's repair covenant in a lease of business premises between HB, the landlord, and H, the tenant, fell to be interpreted. The clause required HB to keep the structure and exterior in good order but also contained words in round brackets, which read "other than those parts comprised in the property". At first instance an alternative interpretation put forward by H to the effect that it was liable for the parts defined by the words in brackets was accepted. HB appealed and H cross appealed, on the basis that the words should have been omitted as they made no sense in relation to the actual premises concerned.

Held, dismissing the appeal and allowing the cross appeal, that the words in brackets made no literal sense because they came from a repairing covenant used in a lease over a part of a building and had wrongly been used in a lease for the entire building. The covenant was therefore to be interpreted as meaning that HB was responsible for repairing the roof, foundations and external structure, *East v. Pantiles (Plant Hire)* [1982] 2 E.G.L.R. 111, [1982] C.L.Y. 1803 and *Investors Compensation Scheme Ltd v. West Bromwich Building Society (No.1)* [1998] 1 W.L.R. 896, [1997] C.L.Y. 2537 applied.

HOLDING & BARNES PLC v. HILL HOUSE HAMMOND LTD (PRELIMINARY ISSUE), [2001] EWCA Civ 1334, [2002] 2 P. & C.R. 11, Clarke, L.J., CA.

3029. Business tenancies–tenancies at will–implied intentions of parties

[Landlord and Tenant Act 1954 Part II; Companies Act 1985 s.652.]

M, the landlord, appealed against a finding that W, as underlessee of shop premises, had been granted a quarterly periodic tenancy which was protected by the Landlord and Tenant Act 1954 Part II. The headlease was vested in a company R which granted an underlease for a term of seven years to a company F which was owned by W, in partnership with others. Rent at the premises was paid on partnership cheques in response to demands addressed to F, however, W, not F, traded at and from the shop premises. Subsequently F was struck off the register pursuant to the Companies Act 1985 s.652. An associate company of M acquired the freehold reversion in the premises and prior to the expiry of the underlease R served notices to terminate the tenancy under s.25 of the 1954 Act on the non existent F. There followed a meeting between R and W in which W informed R that F had ceased to exist but that W wanted a new seven year underlease on the same covenants and terms as before. No documents were signed but it was agreed that the legal formalities would be concluded at a later date. W stayed in occupation and R continued to send quarterly rent demands to F, which were paid. M contended that following expiry of the underlease in 1996, R had allowed W into possession as a tenant at will pending the outcome of the negotiations which followed their meeting.

Held, dismissing the appeal, that the inference sensibly and reasonably drawn from what had been expressly agreed and all the surrounding circumstances, was that W had a periodic quarterly tenancy, *Javad v. Aqil* [1991] 1 W.L.R. 1007, [1991] C.L.Y. 2218 applied.

WALJI v. MOUNT COOK LAND LTD [2002] 1 P. & C.R. 13, Charles, J., CA.

3030. Business tenancies—termination—notice followed by counter notice and application for new tenancy—effect of tenant vacating before term date

[Landlord and Tenant Act 1954 s.25(1), s.64(1).]

SCC, which had occupied premises under a business tenancy, appealed against an order requiring it to pay rent to S, the landlord, in respect of a period beyond the term of the lease. S had served a notice on SCC under the Landlord and Tenant Act 1954 s.25(1), whereupon SCC had served a counter notice and applied to the court for a new tenancy. After taking those steps, however, and before the term of the lease had expired, SCC had decided to vacate the premises.

Held, allowing the appeal, that where after receiving a s.25(1) notice, serving a counter notice and applying to the court for a new tenancy, a business tenant vacated the premises before the term date, s.64(1) of the Act, which concerned the interim continuation of tenancies pending a determination by the court, did not operate to continue the tenancy beyond the term date, *Esselte AB v. Pearl Assurance Plc* [1997] 1 W.L.R. 891, [1996] C.L.Y. 3705 applied. A tenant who decided to vacate premises after serving a counter notice and applying to the court for a new tenancy should inform his landlord of his decision so that his application to the court could be dismissed, failing which he might be estopped from denying that he continued to occupy the premises at the term date and be liable for rent in respect of a period beyond the term date.

SURREY CC v. SINGLE HORSE PROPERTIES LTD; *sub nom.* SINGLE HORSE PROPERTIES LTD v. SURREY CC, [2002] EWCA Civ 367, [2002] 1 W.L.R. 2106, Arden, L.J., CA.

3031. Business tenancies—termination—notice returned to sender after despatch by recorded delivery—validity of notice where service by post required

[Law of Property Act 1925 s.196(3); Landlord and Tenant Act 1927 s.23(1); Landlord and Tenant Act 1954 s.25.]

B, a business tenant, appealed against the dismissal of his action against former landlord, F. The retail premises leased by B had sustained damage as a result of a terrorist bombing. F subsequently erected a secure hoarding around the premises following the service by the local authority of a dangerous building notice and ultimately exercised its power under a clause in the lease to determine the tenancy, serving a notice under the Landlord and Tenant Act 1954 s.25. F sent the notices by recorded delivery to B at three separate addresses but all were returned by the Post Office. F also affixed copies of the notices to the outside of B's business premises. At first instance, B contended that he had not had actual knowledge of any of the notices and that F had been aware that he had not been permitted to enter the business premises. The court had found that B's action had no real prospect of success as F had effected valid service of the notices both pursuant to the terms of the lease and by affixing the notice to the business premises, notwithstanding that they had not come to B's knowledge. On appeal, B argued, inter alia, that (1) the contractual clause should be construed so that the notice was required to be sent and delivered in order to effect valid service; (2) it was not possible to effect valid service by post under the Landlord and Tenant Act 1927 s.23(1) if the letter was not actually delivered, and (3) the copy of the notice affixed to the leased premises did not amount to valid service in the circumstances.

Held, dismissing the appeal, that (1) although it might be fairer as between the parties to construe the phrase "sent by post" in the lease as meaning "sent and delivered", such a construction could not be extracted from the language of the contract; (2) s.23(1) of the 1927 Act contained no express provision excluding letters which were returned undelivered, *Railtrack Plc v. Gojra* [1998] 1 E.G.L.R. 63, [1998] C.L.Y. 3600 and *Commercial Union Life Assurance Co Ltd v. Moustafa* [1999] L. & T.R. 489, [1999] C.L.Y. 3667 applied, and (3) (Carnwath L.J. and Schiemann L.J. expressing no concluded view) F had in the circumstances achieved good service by affixing a copy of the notice to the outside of the cordoned off premises both under the terms of the lease and under the Law of Property Act 1925 s.196(3), *Kinch v. Bullard* [1999] 1 W.L.R. 423, [1998] C.L.Y. 4347 followed.

BLUNDEN v. FROGMORE INVESTMENTS LTD, [2002] EWCA Civ 573, [2002] L. & T.R. 31, Robert Walker, L.J., CA.

3032. Commonhold and Leasehold Reform Act 2002 (c.15)–Commencement No.1, Savings and Transitional Provisions Order–England

COMMONHOLD AND LEASEHOLD REFORM ACT 2002 (COMMENCEMENT NO.1, SAVINGS AND TRANSITIONAL PROVISIONS) (ENGLAND) ORDER 2002, SI 2002 1912; made under the Commonhold and Leasehold Reform Act 2002 s.181. Commencement details: bringing into force various provisions of the 2002 Act on July 26, 2002; £2.00.

This Order brings into force various provisions of the Commonhold and Leasehold Reform Act 2002 in relation to collective enfranchisement by tenants of flats; acquisition of new leases by tenants of flats; enfranchisement and lease extension by tenants of houses; applications to a leasehold valuation tribunal for the appointment of a manager to a block of flats; and the grounds for applying to vary a lease.

3033. Covenants–landlords powers and duties–liability for defective works–operation of notice releasing landlord from obligations–personal covenants

[Landlord and Tenant (Covenants) Act 1995 s.8.]

C, the landlord, appealed against a decision ([2002] Ch. 12) that a notice served by it pursuant to the Landlord and Tenant (Covenants) Act 1995 s.8 did not release it from liability for defects in works carried out to the demised premises. By the agreement for lease, B had undertaken to carry out specified works to the premises. C had transferred the reversionary interest and served the notice pursuant to s.8 applying to be released from "the landlord's obligations under the tenancy". B did not serve a counternotice and, after physical damage to the building became apparent, claimed that C was in breach of its covenant. C contended that service of the s.8 notice had operated to release it from such liability. B cross appealed against the judge's interpretation of the contractual extent of C's liability.

Held, dismissing the appeal and allowing the cross appeal, that the covenant was personal to C and was therefore not a "landlord covenant" for the purposes of the Act. The fact that the covenant "touched and concerned" the land did not preclude it from also being a personal covenant. Consequently service of the notice had not released C from its liability for the building defects. Further, the terms of the agreement provided that C was liable for making good defects which appeared prior to the expiry of the six year defect period but which did not cause physical damage until afterwards.

BHP PETROLEUM GREAT BRITAIN LTD v. CHESTERFIELD PROPERTIES LTD; *sub nom.* CHESTERFIELD PROPERTIES LTD v. BHP PETROLEUM GREAT BRITAIN LTD; BHP GREAT BRITAIN PETROLEUM LTD v. CHESTERFIELD

PROPERTIES LTD, [2001] EWCA Civ 1797, [2002] Ch. 194, Jonathan Parker, L.J., CA.

3034. Derogation from grant–implied terms–landlord restricted from competing with tenant

O, who ran the gift shop at the London Aquarium, brought an action against its landlord, S, who proposed to erect two kiosks on a walkway and sell items usually found in gift shops. O contended that S was prevented from building the kiosks by either an express covenant in the lease, or by the fact that it was not entitled to derogate from its grant. Clause 4 in the lease specified that S could not permit another gift shop to be run "in the building", and it fell to the court to determine whether the walkway fell within that definition.

Held, giving judgment for O in part, that the walkway was in fact a roof for part of the building. However, it did not form part of the building but was a separate public footpath, and therefore the erecting of kiosks on the site would not constitute being "in the building". The doctrine of non derogation from grant applied, and the court had to consider what was reasonably in the minds of O and S at the time the lease was entered into. The lease had been granted in order for O to run the aquarium gift shop and with this an exclusivity had been granted to O to sell aquarium related products. Therefore, there was an implied term in the lease restricting any other gift shop from selling aquarium related goods, *Johnston & Sons Ltd v. Holland* [1988] 1 E.G.L.R. 264, [1988] C.L.Y. 478 applied.

OCEANIC VILLAGE LTD v. SHIRAYAMA SHOKUSAN CO LTD; *sub nom.* OCEANIC VILLAGE LTD v. SHIRAYMA SHOKUSSAN CO LTD [2001] L. & T.R. 35, Nicholas Warren Q.C., Ch D.

3035. Enfranchisement–leaseholds–notices

LEASEHOLD REFORM (NOTICES) (AMENDMENT) (ENGLAND) REGULATIONS 2002, SI 2002 1715; made under the Landlord and Tenant Act 1954 s.66. In force: July 26, 2002; £2.50.

These Regulations, which amend the Leasehold Reform (Notices) Regulations 1997 (SI 1997 640), provide new forms of notices to be used by tenants applying for enfranchisement and extension of long leaseholds under the Leasehold Reform Act 1967.

3036. Enfranchisement–leaseholds–notices–Wales

LEASEHOLD REFORM (NOTICES) (AMENDMENT) (WALES) REGULATIONS 2002, SI 2002 3187 (W.303); made under the Landlord and Tenant Act 1954 s.66. In force: January 1, 2003; £3.00.

These Regulations, which amend the Leasehold Reform (Notices) Regulations 1997 (SI 1997 640), provide new forms of notices to be used by tenants applying for enfranchisement and extension of long leaseholds under the Leasehold Reform Act 1967.

3037. Introductory tenancies–notices–possession proceedings–requirement to serve second notice following review

[Housing Act 1996 s.128, s.129(1).]

S, an introductory tenant, appealed against a ruling on a preliminary issue in favour of her landlord, the local housing authority, C. S had fallen into arrears with her rent and C issued a notice pursuant to the Housing Act 1996 s.128 indicating its intention to instigate possession proceedings. S sought a review of that decision in accordance with s.129(1) of the Act. The review board upheld the authority's decision. C advised S they would not seek possession so long as she repaid the arrears at £3 per week. The arrears increased and proceedings were duly commenced. S contended that s.128 had not been complied with because the authority, in seeking possession, had relied on her failure to adhere to the post review agreement rather than the arrears specified in the pre review notice. S maintained that in consequence a further notice should have been served.

Held, dismissing the appeal, that a housing authority which had served notice of proceedings on an introductory tenant and conducted a review was not obliged to serve a second notice or conduct a further review before commencing possession proceedings, even where several months had elapsed between the review and the issue of proceedings and the authority wished to rely on events which had occurred during that period. There was no substantial difference between the ground on which possession had been obtained and that given in the notice. The tenant had failed to pay rent regularly, and a substantial amount of the original arrears had remained outstanding.

CARDIFF CITY COUNCIL v. STONE, [2002] EWCA Civ 298, *The Times,* February 19, 2002, Arden, L.J., CA.

3038. **Landlords powers and duties—breach of covenant—capacity in which claim brought by manager appointed under Housing Act 1996 s.85—no entitlement for tenant to claim set off for breach of covenants**

[Landlord and Tenant Act 1987 s.24(1); Housing Act 1996 s.85.]

B, a tenant, appealed against a decision ([2002] 2 E.G.L.R. 35) made in favour of M, who had been appointed as a manager under the Landlord and Tenant Act 1987 s.24(1), as amended by the Housing Act 1996 s.85, that B was not entitled to set off against M's claim in respect of repair costs. B's tenancy was derived from an underlease, which provided for payment of a proportion of the "annual cost or anticipated cost in connection with the building". B's flat suffered disrepair as a result of the underlessor's breach of covenant, as a consequence of which M was appointed as manager. M brought claims against B for a proportion of the repair costs and service charge, and B sought to set off those costs against the duties of repair which B alleged were owed by M in his capacity as manager, contending that these duties were equivalent to those owed by the underlessor in respect of the landlord's covenants.

Held, dismissing the appeal, that the central issue was the capacity in which M made his claims. The purpose of Part II of the 1987 Act was to make provision for the appointment of a manager who would carry out duties required by the court. Accordingly, M's functions were those of a court appointed official rather than those of the landlord, and were not confined to carrying out the terms of the lease or the landlord's obligations under it. M's claims were made in his capacity as manager, notwithstanding the fact that his duties and liabilities as set out in the order appointing him were defined by reference to the lease. It followed that M's right to the sums claimed arose from his appointment rather than from the lease and there was no mutuality between his claim and that of B. The remedy of set off was therefore not available.

MAUNDER TAYLOR v. BLAQUIERE; *sub nom.* TAYLOR v. BLAQUIERE; MAUNDER TAYLOR v. BLAQUIRE, [2002] EWCA Civ 1633, [2003] 1 W.L.R. 379, Aldous, L.J., CA.

3039. **Landlords powers and duties—harassment—extent of justices' obligation to give reasons for conviction—procedural unfairness**

[Protection from Eviction Act 1977 s.1 (3A), s.1 (3B); Human Rights Act 1998.]

M applied for judicial review of the justices' decision convicting him of harassment under the Protection from Eviction Act 1977 s.1 (3A). M had bought a building and sought to convert the ground floor of it into a pub. H occupied the first floor of the building and complained that M's acts in converting the ground floor interfered with her occupation of the premises and were calculated to cause her to give up her occupation. On M's request, the justices gave further reasons for their decision, stating that M was entitled to make such a request under the Human Rights Act 1998. M brought his application on the basis of (1) procedural unfairness, contending that the justices had failed to give adequate reasons for their decision, and (2) a contention that the justices had misdirected themselves as to the ingredients of the offence. M argued that the justices had approached the matter too broadly and their consideration should have been confined to the matters specified in the information.

Held, dismissing the application for judicial review, that (1) the justices were not obliged to give detailed reasons for their decision, *McKerry v. Teesdale and Wear Valley Justices* (2000) 164 J.P. 355, [2000] C.L.Y. 1306 applied, and in the instant case the justices' initial reasons showed that they had appreciated that M's state of mind was the relevant issue and had properly considered the ingredients of the offence. In a criminal case, the extent of the justices' duty was to inform the defendant why he had been found guilty, *R. v. Westminster City Council, ex p. Ermakov* [1996] 2 All E.R. 302, [1996] C.L.Y. 2568 applied, and (2) s.1 (3B) of the 1977 Act required that the information be directed at a course of conduct which produced an effect upon the victim. In the instant case, the justices decided that the acts alleged cumulatively had an effect upon H which interfered with her peace or comfort; therefore they had followed the correct approach.

R. (ON THE APPLICATION OF McGOWAN) v. BRENT JUSTICES, [2001] EWHC Admin 814, (2002) 166 J.P. 29, Tuckey, L.J., QBD (Admin Ct).

3040. Landlords powers and duties—repair covenants—assignment of freehold— liability of new landlord for pre-assignment repairs

P, long leaseholders of a flat within premises owned by W, claimed damages against W for disrepair. W's predecessor, S, had failed to maintain the roof of the flat and rainwater had penetrated the premises damaging furnishings and making it generally damp. In consequence, P had withheld service charges which fell due both before and after the assignment of freehold to W. P brought proceedings against S and W for specific performance of W's covenant to repair and for damages for disrepair. S went into voluntary liquidation and P claimed to be entitled to claim damages against W for disrepair predating the assignment or in the alternative to set off those damages against W's claims for arrears of service charges.

Held, determining the preliminary issue in favour of P, that W had taken the assignment of the reversion expectant on P's leasehold interest subject to any breaches by S of the covenants for quiet enjoyment and repair prior to the assignment. Accordingly, P were entitled not only to set off damages in respect of such breaches against any claim by W for service charges but could also claim against W for damages in respect of the breaches, whether by action or counterclaim. It could not be right that a successor landlord could be free to pursue claims against a tenant for breach of both pre and post assignment obligations, whether of the tenant or the tenant's predecessor, whilst avoiding even an equitable set off in respect of pre-assignment breaches of obligations by a predecessor landlord, *Duncliffe v. Caerfelin Properties* [1989] 27 E.G. 89, [1989] C.L.Y. 2118 and *Kemra (Management) Ltd v. Lewis* (Unreported, July 7, 1999), [1999] C.L.Y. 3729 not followed, *Lotteryking Ltd v. Amec Properties Ltd* [1995] 2 E.G.L.R. 13, *Business Computers Ltd v. Anglo-African Leasing Ltd* [1977] 1 W.L.R. 578, [1977] C.L.Y. 385 and *Reeves v. Pope* [1914] 2 K.B. 284 referred to.

PANTON v. ST. MARY'S ESTATES LTD, Judge Kennedy Q.C., CC (Brighton). [*Ex rel.* Christopher Wilson, Barrister, 9 Gough Square, London].

3041. Landlords powers and duties—repair covenants—obligation to keep installations for the supply of water, gas and electricity in "proper working order"

[Landlord and Tenant Act 1985 s.11 (1) (b).]

OE, the landlord, appealed against a decision that it had breached its obligation under the Landlord and Tenant Act 1985 s.11 (1) (b) to keep pipes carrying water in "proper working order". Following refurbishment of OE's property, the pipework had been replaced with pipework of a smaller bore. The pipes had worked successfully for a number of years until a fall in the water pressure which had been outside OE's control. OE could have installed a pump to make the smaller pipes carry the water but had not done so. The judge had found that the obligation to keep the pipes in proper working order was an obligation "to ensure that the pipes were physically or mechanically capable of supplying water". He had concluded that OE could have met such an obligation but had not done so. The issue before the court was whether a breach of the obligation imposed by s.11 (1) (b) could occur where an installation was in mechanical working order but, because of something for which the landlord was not responsible, it failed to perform its function.

Held, allowing the appeal, that installations for the supply of water, gas and electricity would be in "proper working order" at the commencement of a tenancy if they had been designed and constructed so as to be capable of performing their functions. It was apparent that the characteristics of the supply of water, gas and electricity were capable of varying, either intentionally or unintentionally. An installation would be in proper working order if it continued to function under such conditions as it was reasonable to anticipate would prevail. The landlord's obligations were likely to be dependent on the degree to which variations in supply could reasonably be anticipated and provided for. The question of whether a landlord was obliged to make modifications following such variations would depend on the circumstances. A landlord would be required to make any necessary modifications where a deliberate change in supply, such as a change in the voltage of electrical supply, had occurred. However, where the change was unforeseen and likely to be short in duration, modification of the relevant installations might be disproportionate.

O'CONNOR v. OLD ETONIAN HOUSING ASSOCIATION LTD; *sub nom.* O'CONNOR v. OLD ETON HOUSING ASSOCIATION; O'CONNOR v. OLD ETONIANS HOUSING ASSOCIATION LTD, [2002] EWCA Civ 150, [2002] Ch. 295, Lord Phillips of Worth Matravers, M.R., CA.

3042. Leaseholds–enfranchisement–assignment–impact of assignment of statutory right to enfranchise prior to assignment of tenancy

[Leasehold Reform Act 1967 s.5(2).]

S applied for summary judgment in her claim for specific performance of C's statutory obligation to sell and transfer to S the freehold in a property for the sum of £2.395 million following service by S of the requisite notice to enfranchise pursuant to the Leasehold Reform Act 1967. S had already entered into a contract for the subsale of the property to E for the sum of £4.5 million and executed an assignment to E of her right to acquire the freehold. The trustees of the property contended that the assignment extinguished S's right to purchase under the 1967 Act, thus relieving them of their obligation to transfer the property to either S or E.

Held, granting the application, that pursuant to s.5(2) of the Act, the statutory right of enfranchisement was assignable with, but not separately from, the tenancy itself. Whilst an assignment of the tenancy itself without the statutory right would be effective to extinguish the statutory right, an assignment of the statutory right without the tenancy was of no legal effect, *Linden Gardens Trust Ltd v. Lenesta Sludge Disposals Ltd* [1994] 1 A.C. 85, [1993] C.L.Y. 303 applied. Accordingly the purported assignment in the instant case was of no legal effect and the lease and statutory right of enfranchisement remained vested in S.

SOUTH v. CHAMBERLAYNE [2002] L. & T.R. 26, Lightman, J., Ch D.

3043. Leaseholds–enfranchisement–lease providing for early termination by tenant–tenant's rights

[Leasehold Reform Act 1967 s.3(1).]

S appealed against a finding that she did not enjoy a long tenancy under the Leasehold Reform Act 1967 s.3(1) entitling her to acquire the freehold. In 1960 S's parents granted her and her husband a lease of a house for a term of 90 years. The lease provided that at any time after the death of the last to die of the two persons comprising the tenant, the lease could be determined by giving one month's notice. The husband died in 1996 and in 1998 S claimed the right to enfranchise under the Leasehold Reform Act 1967. G, the landlord, disputed the right, contending that the lease was not a long tenancy within the meaning of the Act.

Held, dismissing the appeal, that a tenancy was not a long tenancy within the meaning of s.3(1) because the notice was capable of being given at any time after the death of the surviving tenant. The reference points were the terms of the lease and not the terms of the notice.

SKINNS v. GREENWOOD, [2002] EWCA Civ 424, [2002] H.L.R. 50, Kennedy, L.J., CA.

3044. Leaseholds–enfranchisement–vesting orders–terms of conveyance not agreed

[Leasehold Reform, Housing and Urban Development Act 1993 s.13, s.24.]

P appealed against an order allowing an appeal against a vesting order in his favour made pursuant to the Leasehold Reform, Housing and Urban Development Act 1993 s.24 in respect of the flat he occupied. P was the nominee purchaser pursuant to a collective enfranchisement notice which the tenants of the property had served on their landlord, U, under s.13 of the Act, stating their intention to buy the freehold. The leasehold valuation tribunal determined the price but no other terms of the conveyance, which were still not agreed when P applied for, and obtained, the vesting order. On appeal, the judge held that the court had no jurisdiction to make a vesting order until the leasehold valuation tribunal had determined an outstanding issue as to whether the conveyance should contain an indemnity clause in the terms sought by U. P submitted that the the tribunal's earlier determination was final, that it had no power to alter its decisions nor could it determine issues sequentially.

Held, dismissing the appeal, that under s.24(3)(b) of the 1993 Act, before a court could make a vesting order, an agreement between the parties, or determination by the leasehold valuation tribunal, had to be reached on all the terms of the acquisition. Therefore, the court had no jurisdiction to make the vesting order, given that there were outstanding issues to be determined by the tribunal. A tribunal was not prohibited from determining matters sequentially.

PENMAN v. UPAVON ENTERPRISES LTD, [2001] EWCA Civ 956, [2002] L. & T.R. 10, Arden, L.J., CA.

3045. Leases–assignment–landlord's consent–guidance on interpretation of third edition of Standard Conditions of Sale

A appealed against a decision ([2001] 10 E.G.C.S. 155) dismissing its application for a declaration that it had validly rescinded a contract to purchase a commercial leasehold interest from L. The contract had incorporated the 3rd edition of the Standard Conditions of Sale which stipulated, by standard conditions 8.3.1 and 8.3.2(a), that where consent to assign was required from a landlord the seller was to apply for that consent and to use all reasonable efforts to secure it. Under standard condition 8.3.4, either party could rescind the contract if consent had not been given three working days prior to the completion date or where consent had been given subject to a condition to which the buyer was reasonably entitled to object. Clause 4.18.3 of the lease required the landlord's prior written consent to assign. A contended that it should be entitled to rescind as L had failed to obtain the landlord's written consent prior to the completion date in accordance with cl. 4.18.3. The issues on appeal were whether (1) the landlord's consent was required to be in writing; (2) that consent should be unequivocal, and (3) standard condition 8.3.4 was to be interpreted so as to give either party a right to rescind only after the inception of three working days before contractual completion.

Held, dismissing the appeal (Ward L.J. dissenting) that (1) in employing the words "if a consent to assign...is required to complete the contract", standard condition 8.3.1 plainly referred to the requirement of prior written consent as found in cl. 4.18.3 of the lease; (2) standard condition 8.3.1 did not confine prior written consent to an unconditional consent or consent by deed or other formal document. Conditional assent was plainly within the contemplation of standard conditions 8.3.2.(b) and 8.3.4.(b). Thus, a clear expression of a willingness to consent was not rendered uncertain by the inclusion of conditions or by the fact that the landlord's solicitor had headed relevant correspondence "Subject to licence", *Mount Eden Land Ltd v. Prudential Assurance Co Ltd* (1997) 74 P. & C.R. 377, [1997] C.L.Y. 3269 followed, and (3) the purpose of the timing imposed by standard condition 8.3.4 was to create a readily identifiable contractual time limit within which the landlord's consent would be secured and accordingly no extension would be permitted.

AUBERGINE ENTERPRISES LTD v. LAKEWOOD INTERNATIONAL LTD, [2002] EWCA Civ 177, [2002] 1 W.L.R. 2149, Auld, L.J., CA.

3046. Leases–change of use–consent withheld by landlord–reasonableness of refusal

L, which leased nightclub premises from A, challenged the decision of A to refuse consent for the subletting of the premises for use as a gym and health club. A had refused to consent to the proposed subletting or to a change of use in the belief that to do so would result in a diminution of the value of the reversion. A clause in the lease provided that the landlord's consent to any subletting or change of use would not be unreasonably withheld and L maintained that A had unreasonably withheld his consent. A argued that the burden of proof was upon L to establish that the refusal was unreasonable and that L could not discharge that burden having regard to the expert evidence he had obtained by way of a valuation of the reversion.

Held, giving judgment for L, that the burden of proof was upon L, as lessee, and the refusal of consent had been unreasonable. The refusal had essentially been concerned with the issue of change of use rather than the issue of subletting and the valuation obtained by A had been so unreliable as to make reliance upon its conclusions unreasonable. The valuer had approached his task in the belief that health and fitness clubs were a passing fad. It had not been reasonable to adopt such an approach in the absence of any evidence as to the state of the health and fitness market sector. Such evidence, had it been obtained, would have revealed a market with significant growth potential such as to justify a conclusion that the proposed change of use would marginally enhance, rather than diminish, the value of the reversion.

LUMINAR LEISURE LTD v. APOSTOLE [2001] 3 E.G.L.R. 23, Alan Wilkie Q.C., Ch D.

3047. Leases–contract terms–options to renew–notice periods

B appealed against a possession order for premises which it had leased from H. The lease, which expired on May 6, 2000, had contained a clause granting B an option to renew the lease by six months' notice given "at any time after the 6th day of May 1999". B did not send notice until less than six months before the expiry of the term. The judge in the court below held that the six month period had to have elapsed before the date of expiry of the lease and that the notice was therefore invalid. H contended that considerations of business efficacy favoured its interpretation of the clause.

Held, allowing the appeal, that there was nothing in the wording of the clause to support the judge's finding. The argument of business convenience was weak and did not take precedence over the natural express meaning of the words themselves.

HART INVESTMENTS LTD v. BURTON HOTEL LTD; *sub nom.* HART INVESTMENTS PLC v. BURTON HOTEL LTD [2002] L. & T.R. 6, Patten, J., Ch D.

3048. Leases–covenants–attempt to circumvent underletting covenant

H appealed against an order that the terms of an underlease did not meet the terms on underletting contained in a proviso to the headlease ([2002] 1 P. & C.R. 1). The proviso required that any underlease should not be granted at a rent of less than the full market rent reasonably obtainable. H's prospective subtenant, L, was not prepared to pay the rent currently payable by H under the headlease and furthermore was not prepared to undertake H's repairing obligations. Accordingly, H and L entered into two separate agreements, an underlease which H believed satisfied the conditions of the headlease, and a collateral agreement expressed to be personal to H and L. Under the collateral agreement H indemnified L for the difference between the rent actually payable by L and the amount payable by L to H under the underlease and also against the cost of complying with the repairing obligations. On receiving copies of the draft agreements from H, A, the landlord under the headlease, commenced proceedings to restrain H and L from completing the proposed transactions. A also withheld its consent to the proposed underlease.

Held, dismissing the appeal, that it was not disputed that had the underlease contained the terms as to rent and repairs contained in the collateral deed, it would not have complied with the headlease. H had not managed to avoid the requirements of the headlease by means of the collateral deed. The underlease and the collateral deed had to be read together as if the relevant provisions had been included in the underlease. The original parties to the headlease could not have intended that the proviso as to underletting would not have to be met in a case where undertakings in relation to the rent and the repairing obligations inconsistent with the requirements of the proviso were only enforceable as between the original parties to the underlease. It was therefore unnecessary to consider whether A had unreasonably withheld its consent.

ALLIED DUNBAR ASSURANCE PLC v. HOMEBASE LTD; *sub nom.* HOMEBASE LTD v. ALLIED DUNBAR ASSURANCE PLC, [2002] EWCA Civ 666, [2003] 1 P. & C.R. 6, Chadwick, L.J., CA.

3049. Leases—forfeiture—denial of title—repudiatory breach

[Law of Property Act 1925 s.146.]

A appealed against the refusal of his claim for the forfeiture of a lease. The action had been grounded on, inter alia, a denial of title by F, the tenant. The court had held that a right to forfeit by reason of denial of title was subject to the requirements of the Law of Property Act 1925 s.146, with which A had failed to comply. A contended that a denial of title involved a repudiation of the landlord and tenant relationship, which repudiation had been accepted by A, and that repudiation fell outside the scope of s.146.

Held, dismissing the appeal, that denial of title conferred a right to forfeiture by implication of law, as distinct from an operation of law, and was subject to the requirements of s.146, *WG Clarke (Properties) Ltd v. Dupre Properties Ltd* [1992] Ch. 297, [1992] C.L.Y. 2681 applied. In any event, the conduct of F, which took the form of a submission to the court for a determination of the issue as to title, was not such as to amount to a repudiation of the lease nor was A's conduct such as to amount to an acceptance of repudiation.

ABIDOGUN v. FROLAN HEALTH CARE LTD, [2001] EWCA Civ 1821, [2002] L. & T.R. 16, Arden, L.J., CA.

3050. Leases—forfeiture—subtenancies—underletting without consent— availability of relief

[Law of Property Act 1925 s.146 (4).]

D, the sub lessees under a lease between M, the tenant, and MC, the landlord, sought relief from forfeiture claiming that a purported sale agreement of M's lease to them was a sham. The head lease contained a prohibition on underletting or assignment without MC's consent. Contrary to that provision, M effected a sub lease to D at a weekly rent of £2,000. MC learned of the sub lease and was eager to have D as tenants in place of M. Negotiations to that effect began between the parties. M failed to maintain his rental payments and MC exercised a right of peaceable reentry as part of its negotiating strategy with D and a purported sale of M's lease to D was effected while negotiations for a new lease continued. A new lease, on terms favourable to MC, was negotiated between the parties at an annual rent of £65,000. Subsequently, MC sought to impose a rent of £150,000 on D as tenants. D refused and MC claimed forfeiture of the lease and the eviction of D.

Held, granting the application, that the sale of the lease had been a sham and D had really been sub lessees under a weekly tenancy from M. MC's consent to the sub-letting had not been sought, neither had D established that MC's agents had waived the right to forfeiture. The jurisdiction to grant relief from forfeiture under the Law of Property Act 1925 s.146(4) would be used only sparingly particularly where the landlord had tenants which it had never sanctioned foisted on it. However, in the instant case, MC had been eager to have D as tenants and furthermore, had sought to impose a large increase in their rent. Consequently, D would suffer hardship if their rights were terminated, whereas MC would suffer none.

DUARTE v. MOUNT COOK LAND LTD [2002] L. & T.R. 21, John Crowley Q.C., QBD.

3051. Leases—service charges—inclusion of notional cost of caretaker's flat

S appealed against a decision that it was not entitled to recover from its tenant, G, by way of service charge, the notional costs of a caretaker's flat. G's lease contained a clause requiring G to pay a proportion of "all monies expended by [S] in... providing the services and management" required by the lease, which included the provision of a "resident housekeeper". S paid a wage to the caretaker and did not charge rent, but levied the wage and the notional rent that could have been charged as service charges on G. The judge in the court below held that there was nothing in the lease justifying inclusion of the notional rent in the service charge. On appeal S argued that the notional rent on the caretaker's flat was included in the term "all monies expended" and was therefore properly part of the service charge.

Held, dismissing the appeal, that inclusion of such a sum in the service charge could only be procured by an unequivocal and clear clause in the lease, so that tenants would be fully aware of what was required of them under the lease. No such clause existed in the instant case.

GILJE v. CHARLGROVE SECURITIES LTD; *sub nom.* GILJE v. CHARLEGROVE SECURITIES LTD, [2001] EWCA Civ 1777, [2002] L. & T.R. 33, Laws, L.J., CA.

3052. Licences—car parks—no exclusive possession

N appealed against the dismissal of its application for a declaration that an agreement made by it with T was a tenancy not a licence. The agreement was expressed to be a licence and permitted N to "manage and administer" a car park, in which T would be allowed 40 spaces at no charge. T sought to end the agreement but N contended that T's notice was invalid as N was a tenant not a licensee. The judge in the court below held that the substance of the agreement amounted to a licence as N did not have exclusive possession. On appeal, N argued that the right to run the car park business on the premises amounted to exclusive possession and that T had a right of reentry for maintenance purposes.

Held, dismissing the appeal, that the judge's decision had been correct. Although the label the parties chose to put on the agreement was not conclusive, it did carry weight. The overall thrust of the agreement was one of imposing obligations on N rather than granting rights, and did not point towards a grant of exclusive possession. N was obliged to make it possible for T to resurface the car park by providing whatever assistance was required, but T's presence would only be temporary and would only happen in exceptional circumstances and this did not therefore amount to a right of reentry.

NATIONAL CAR PARKS LTD v. TRINITY DEVELOPMENT CO (BANBURY) LTD; *sub nom.* R. (ON THE APPLICATION OF NATIONAL CAR PARKS LTD) v. TRINITY DEVELOPMENT CO (BANBURY) LTD, [2001] EWCA Civ 1686, [2002] 2 P. & C.R. 18, Arden, L.J., CA.

3053. Possession orders—consent orders—jurisdiction of court to enforce order—failure to establish compliance with Housing Act 1988

[Housing Act 1988.]

G appealed against a consent order granting her landlord, B, possession of a room in respect of which she had had an assured tenancy. B had sought possession on the ground that there were arrears of rent. G had counterclaimed, seeking damages for breach of covenant. G had contended that as the damages sought exceeded the arrears no rent had been lawfully due. At the hearing the parties had reached a compromise under which G had agreed to vacate the room in return for B paying her a lump sum.

Held, allowing the appeal, that the court had had no jurisdiction to endorse the private agreement reached by the parties regarding possession in circumstances where the judge had failed to establish that the requirements of the Housing Act 1988 had been met, particularly where the tenant did not accept the allegation of rent arrears.

BAYGREEN PROPERTIES LTD v. GIL; *sub nom.* GIL v. BAYGREEN PROPERTIES LTD, [2002] EWCA Civ 1340, [2003] H.L.R. 12, Clarke, L.J., CA.

3054. Possession orders—drug offences—tenant convicted—reasonableness of possession proceedings

[Housing Act 1985 Sch.2.]

H, a secure tenant, was convicted of offences of cultivating cannabis at the property and unlawful abstraction of electricity. He received a community service order and a fine. The landlord then proceeded to commence possession proceedings under the Housing Act 1985 Sch.2 ground 1 and ground 2 on the basis that H had been convicted of an arrestable offence. There had been no other complaints in relation to H's behaviour. H defended the claim on the basis that it was not reasonable to make an order for posession, contending that he had grown the cannabis for his personal use to alleviate recurring back pain.

Held, dismissing the possession proceedings, that in the exercise of the judge's discretion it was not reasonable to make an order for possession. There had been no serious breach of the tenancy agreement, *Bristol City Council v. Mousah* (1998) 30 H.L.R. 32, [1998] C.L.Y. 3044 distinguished, and no other complaints about H in the duration of the tenancy. There was no evidence that other residents had been upset by H living at the premises and H had not grown any cannabis since his arrest.

LIVERPOOL HOUSING ACTION TRUST v. HANKIN, July 26, 2002, District Judge Dignan, CC (Liverpool). [*Ex rel.* Nazmun Ismail, Barrister, Central Chambers, 89 Princess Street, Manchester].

3055. Possession orders—introductory tenancies—approach to be taken by court

[Housing Act 1996 Part V; Human Rights Act 1998.]

The local authority appealed against a decision setting aside a possession order granted in its favour and adjourning the possession proceedings to enable the tenant, W, to make an application for judicial review. W had been granted an introductory tenancy of a property for a trial period of 12 months under the Housing Act 1996 Part V. The local authority had sought possession of the property on the grounds of W's failure to take up occupation of the property and that there were arrears of rent. The order for possession had been set aside on the basis that the local authority's decision may have been unlawful and in breach of W's Convention rights.

Held, allowing the appeal, that in possession proceedings relating to introductory tenancies the court had a duty to consider the procedure which had been followed, bearing in mind the statutory procedure under the 1996 Act and the tenant's rights under the Human Rights Act 1998, *R. (on the application of McLellan) v. Bracknell Forest BC* [2001] EWCA Civ 1510, [2002] 2 W.L.R. 1448, [2001] C.L.Y. 4170 applied. Where a tenant alleged, as in the instant case, that the procedure adopted by the local authority had been flawed, the court, having raised the issue, should give the parties the opportunity to consider it. However, in the instant case, where there had been no realistic prospect of W sustaining his excuse for the non payment of rent and where the local authority had correctly asserted in its notice of proceedings that W had failed to take up occupation, the judge had erred in adjourning the proceedings. Accordingly, the order for possession was restored.

MERTON LBC v. WILLIAMS, [2002] EWCA Civ 980, [2003] H.L.R. 20, Mance, L.J., CA.

3056. Possession orders–secure tenancies–payment of arrears–revival of tenancy

[Housing Act 1985 s.82(2), s.85(2), s.85(2)(b), s.85(4).]

M, who occupied property which had formerly been rented to her and her husband, but which had since been made subject to a possession order following arrears of rent, appealed against a decision that her payment of the arrears had not automatically revived the tenancy, and the striking out of disrepair proceedings against her landlord, B. B had obtained the possession order 11 years previously but it was suspended under the Housing Act 1985 s.85(2) on the condition that the arrears were paid. M had complied with the conditions but no application to revive the tenancy had been made, and M had continued to occupy the property as a tolerated trespasser. M contended that (1) the tenancy had been automatically revived upon payment of the arrears, and (2) the judge had erred by exercising his discretion to strike out the disrepair claim on the ground that it was beyond the limitation period, notwithstanding that an application to revive the tenancy would be likely to succeed.

Held, dismissing the appeal, that (1) the tenancy had not been automatically revived by the discharge of the arrears. Where, as in the instant case, the tenancy had been brought to an end under s.82(2), there had to be a further order under s.85(2), varying the conditions in the original order or postponing the date of possession. Furthermore, s.85(4) of the Act did not empower the court to discharge or rescind the order, and (2) it had been a proper exercise of the court's discretion to strike out the disrepair proceedings. In the instant case it was unlikely that an order to postpone the date of possession under s.85(2)(b) would be made due to difficulties arising from the joint obligations of M's husband, who was no longer living at the property. It would also have been unjust to deprive B of a limitation defence by reviving the secure tenancy with the effect of retrospectively validating proceedings which could not otherwise have been commenced.

MARSHALL v. BRADFORD MDC, [2001] EWCA Civ 594, [2002] H.L.R. 22, Chadwick, L.J., CA.

3057. Possession orders–secure tenancies–termination–breach of occupancy condition–assessment of intention

H appealed against the dismissal of its application for possession of premises for breach of the tenant's occupancy condition by JC, who was the grandmother of DC and a secure tenant. DC and her husband had moved into the house after JC had suffered a stroke and DC had been caring for JC until she was admitted to a nursing home for respite care. DC and her husband remained in the house but during her stay JC obtained a permanent place at the home and signed a note indicating that she did not intend to return home. H contended that (1) the judge below had failed to determine whether JC was occupying the premises as her only or principal home as at the correct date, namely upon expiration of the notice to quit, and (2) that there was no reason to believe that JC had changed her mind in the two month interval between signing the note and expiration of the notice to quit.

Held, dismissing the appeal, that (1) while it had been correct to assess JC's intention at the date that the notice to quit took effect, *Hussey v. Camden LBC* (1995) 27 H.L.R. 5, [1996] C.L.Y. 3835 applied, it was also appropriate to take into account relevant evidence both before and after that date, and (2) when assessing intention with regard to occupancy the court was required to determine the enduring intention of the tenant, and while JC may have changed her mind on various occasions, the judge had been entitled to conclude, particularly having regard to her poor state of health and associated depression, that nevertheless her enduring intention had been to return to her home, *Crawley BC v. Sawyer* (1988) 20 H.L.R. 98, [1988] C.L.Y. 2078 applied.

HAMMERSMITH AND FULHAM LBC v. CLARKE (2001) 33 H.L.R. 77, Keene, L.J., CA.

3058. **Public sector tenancies–landlords powers and duties–contracting out waste disposal function–requirement for adequate supervision**

S appealed against a damages award of £13,500 in favour of L in respect of breaches of a tenancy agreement. L had been granted a secure tenancy by S of a flat which was adjacent to a large bin into which ran a rubbish chute. The chute was inadequate to deal with the volume of rubbish produced by the surrounding flats on the estate and L complained to S about the noise, smells and maggot infestation caused by tenants using the chute and leaving the excess rubbish beside the bin. L contended that S had breached its covenant to "take reasonable steps to keep the estate and common parts clean and tidy" contained within her tenancy agreement and that it had also breached the implied covenant of quiet enjoyment. S maintained that (1) in contracting out the waste disposal function it had fulfilled its obligations by instructing the contractors to clean the common parts, and (2) it had taken reasonable steps to prevent the tenants from using the rubbish chute inappropriately by giving them written notice reminding them of the permitted use of the chute and bin.

Held, dismissing the appeal, that (1) the obligation to take reasonable steps could not be satisfied by contracting out the waste disposal function unless there was an adequate system in place for monitoring the performance of that function. Furthermore, because of L's complaints, S had been put on notice of the fact that the contractors were not performing their function adequately. Accordingly, the failure to adequately supervise the contractors amounted to a breach of the covenant. When considering whether S's actions constituted reasonable steps it was relevant that S provided low cost housing and that the steps taken must be appropriate to such housing. However, the basic standards of cleanliness could not be compromised and there was no implicit proviso that the landlord should have the resources available to fund the steps otherwise considered reasonable. (2) Notifying the tenants about appropriate use of the waste facilities was not in itself sufficient to fulfil the obligation especially since there was a distinct possibility that a high proportion of tenants would ignore such a notice. On the issue of breach of the implied covenant of quiet enjoyment the judge concluded that there had been no breach, *Southwark LBC v. Mills* [2001] 1 A.C. 1, [1999] C.L.Y. 3672 followed.

SOUTHWARK LBC v. LONG; *sub nom.* LONG v. SOUTHWARK LBC, [2002] EWCA Civ 403, [2002] H.L.R. 56, Arden, L.J., CA.

3059. **Public sector tenancies–right to family life–property unfit for human habitation–obligation to remedy design faults**

[Defective Premises Act 1972 s.4; Landlord and Tenant Act 1985 s.8; Human Rights Act 1998 s.6; European Convention on Human Rights 1950 Art.8.]

R appealed against a decision that the local authority was not obliged to remedy design faults in their rented accommodation. The faults had led to condensation and mould growth, aggravating R's asthma. R had brought a claim for damages for personal injury under the Defective Premises Act 1972 s.4. R submitted that the Human Rights Act 1998 s.6 imposed a duty on the local authority landlord to comply with the European Convention on Human Rights 1950 Art.8.

Held, dismissing the appeal, that (1) there was no evidence to show that there had been a breach of s.6 of the 1998 Act in conjunction with Art.8 of the Convention, despite the fact that the property was unfit for human habitation or in a state prejudicial to health; (2) there was no statutory basis for the assertion that landlords were obliged to ensure that housing was to be fit for human habitation, *Quick v. Taff Ely BC* [1986] Q.B. 809, [1985] C.L.Y. 1610 considered, and there was no conflict between the Landlord and Tenant Act

1985 s.8 and the Convention; (3) there was no requirement that a term be implied at common law into the tenancy agreement to ensure that the property was fit for habitation, since s.8 of the 1985 Act clearly contemplated that there may be such premises which were let for occupation, and (4) the obligation to repair only arose where there was a need for repair, thus if a defect causing injury which was the subject of a claim under s.4 of the 1972 Act did not arise from lack of repair, it did not constitute a "relevant defect" for the purposes of the section and no deemed obligation arose.

RATCLIFFE v. SANDWELL MBC; LEE v. LEEDS CITY COUNCIL, [2002] EWCA Civ 6, [2002] 1 W.L.R. 1488, Chadwick, L.J., CA.

3060. Public sector tenancies—termination—notice to quit former matrimonial home given by husband—right of wife to remain—proportionality

[Human Rights Act 1998 Sch.1 Part I Art.8(1), Art.8(2), Art.14.]

K, a local housing authority, sought possession of premises that had been O's former matrimonial home. K's predecessor had granted a weekly tenancy to the husband alone in 1970. Ultimately, the husband gave notice to quit in 2001 and moved into sheltered accommodation provided by K. The husband had informed K that his marriage had broken down and that he had been living alone when, in fact, the wife had been residing with him at the premises with one of her grandchildren. The wife resisted the making of a possession order, contending that (1) the tenancy had not been validly determined; (2) the grant of the tenancy to the husband alone amounted to an act of discrimination contrary to the Human Rights Act 1998 Sch.1 Part 1 Art.14; (3) the premises were her home within the meaning of Art.8(1) of the 1998 Act, and (4) she was entitled to relief pursuant to Art.8(2) of the Act.

Held, granting an order for possession, that (1) the notice was not bad for ambiguity as the intentions of K and the husband had been clear; (2) Art.14 was not engaged. It was common practice in 1970 to grant tenancies to the husband alone but had K refused to grant a joint tenancy after the coming into force of the 1998 Act such a refusal would have clearly engaged that provision; (3) it was clear on the facts that the wife had lived at the premises as her home within the meaning of *Qazi v. Harrow LBC* [2001] EWCA Civ 1834, [2002] U.K.H.R.R. 316, [2002] 6 C.L. 455. Her status had initially been that of a qua licensee and, although she became a trespasser when the husband's tenancy determined, she had sufficient and continuous links with the property and Art.8(2) was therefore engaged, however (4) K had not behaved unreasonably or with impropriety as it had been unaware of the wife's presence at the premises. Accordingly, K's decision was not amenable to judicial review; rather the wife's right to relief was to be determined summarily, *Poplar Housing & Regeneration Community Association Ltd v. Donoghue* [2001] EWCA Civ 595, [2002] Q.B. 48, [2001] C.L.Y. 4145 followed. On the facts of the instant case, the grant of a possession order was not disproportionate as K sought fair and orderly management of its housing stock. If the wife remained in occupation, she would remain in five bedroomed accommodation that was clearly surplus to her needs, *Sheffield City Council v. Smart* [2002] EWCA Civ 4, [2002] H.L.R. 34, [2002] 3 C.L. 333 followed.

KENSINGTON AND CHELSEA RLBC v. O'SULLIVAN, February 27, 2002, Judge Green, CC (Central London). [*Ex rel.* Richard Nall-Cain, Barrister, St Albans Chambers, 11 London Road, St Albans].

3061. Rent—fair rent—assessment—hypothetical regulated tenancy market—deduction for void periods

[Rent Acts (Maximum Fair Rent) Order 1999 (SI 1999 6).]

S, a landlord, appealed against a decision of a rent assessment committee determining a fair rent for a regulated tenancy. The committee applied a cap to the fair rent figure pursuant to the Rent Acts (Maximum Fair Rent) Order 1999 and then deducted one twelfth from that figure to take account of the costs associated with "void" periods where the property might be vacant between lets. The justification for that deduction was based on the assumption that in respect of assured shorthold tenancies, S built into their market rents an element in respect of such periods but in the hypothetical market for regulated tenancies, such "void" periods did not exist. S contended that (1) the committee had not been entitled to apply the cap under the Order either as a matter of law, because the Order should apply to the existing rent rather than the registered rent, or as a matter of fairness, as it had failed to disclose the basis for its capping calculations, and (2) the committee had not been permitted to make a deduction for "voids".

Held, allowing the appeal, that (1) the purpose of registration was to protect tenants and the fact that the tenant had been paying a higher rent than that registered was irrelevant to the application of the Order. Furthermore, the figures used for the capping calculation were all in the public domain and when dealing with an apparently competent and experienced landlord there was no requirement to supply the calculations, and (2) in the absence of any evidence that S had taken account of voids when fixing the rent for tenants of its assured shorthold tenancies, the committee had not been entitled to assume that S had built into its agreed market rents an element in respect of such periods. Furthermore, the committee had erred in assuming an absence of voids in the hypothetical market for regulated tenancies, since a landlord in such a market would face voids and therefore, letting costs, to a similar extent as for assured tenancies, *Queensway Housing Association Ltd v. Chiltern, Thames and Eastern Rent Assessment Committee* (1999) 31 H.L.R. 945, [1999] C.L.Y. 3721 not followed.

SPATH HOLME LTD v. NORTH WESTERN RENT ASSESSMENT COMMITTEE, [2001] EWHC Admin 541, [2003] H.L.R. 13, Collins, J., QBD (Admin Ct).

3062. Rent reviews−service of process−assumption of available recipient for deemed service

[Law of Property Act 1925 s.196.]

W, a landlord, appealed a decision that although B, a tenant, had not served a counter notice in time in relation to a rent review W could not rely on that failure because it had not taken reasonable steps to accept delivery. F, the Part 20 defendant, was a surveyor who had served the counter notice on behalf of B by recorded delivery. The lease expressly incorporated the provisions as to notices contained in the Law of Property Act 1925 s.196. F contended that the counter notice was deemed served prior to the date of its actual receipt, pursuant to s.196(4).

Held, dismissing the appeal, that the counter notice had been served in time for the purpose of the rent review provisions in the lease. For the purposes of s.196(4) the actual date of delivery was irrelevant as the inclusion of a deeming provision in the subsection introduced a presumed date of delivery which was determined by the court on the basis of the ordinary operation of the postal service, *Holwell Securities Ltd v. Hughes* [1973] 1 W.L.R. 757 applied. The purpose of the subsection in referring to a hypothetical delivery was to introduce certainty. The subsection required an assumption to be made that a recipient was available on the presumed date of delivery.

WX INVESTMENTS LTD v. BEGG; *sub nom.* WX INVESTMENTS LTD v. BEG, [2002] EWHC 925, [2002] 1 W.L.R. 2849, Patten, J., Ch D.

3063. Rent reviews−time limits−interpretation of rent review clause

F, the landlord of premises of which R was the tenant, applied to the court to determine the meaning of the rent review provisions in the lease. The lease provided for the service by F of a notice to "be given at any time not more than twelve months before the expiration of each or any of the following years of the said terms that is to say every fifth year thereof but not at any other time". The lease term commenced on May 7,1995. The last rent review had been on May 7,1990. F served notice on April 25, 2001. R contended that the notice was invalid, as it had not been served within 12 months of a "fifth year". F argued that so long as the notice was served no more than 12 months before the expiration of the fifth year, there was no end date for the giving of a notice.

Held, ruling in favour of R, that the relevant clause in the lease meant that the review notice might be given at any time during each of the fifth years but not more than 12 months before the expiration of those years. The phrase "but not at any other time" made time of the essence of the clause.

FIRST PROPERTY GROWTH PARTNERSHIP LP v. ROYAL & SUN ALLIANCE PROPERTY SERVICES LTD, [2002] EWHC 305, [2002] 2 E.G.L.R.11, Rimer, J., Ch D.

3064. Rent reviews—time limits—interpretation of rent review clause

I applied for declaratory relief in respect of the rent review provisions of its lease. I held a lease of business premises from D with rent reviews in April 1980 and every seventh anniversary thereafter. A schedule to the lease provided that where D sought a review they should serve a trigger notice before the rent review date. The schedule provided that if the parties had not agreed a rent at least two months prior to the rent review date, the rent was to be determined by a surveyor, to be agreed at least one month before the review date, and, in default of agreement on a surveyor, by the President of the Royal Institution of Chartered Surveyors. The schedule also provided that if the parties had not agreed the rent at least two months before the review date and D had neglected to make an application to the President, then the trigger notice would be void. In May 2001 D served a notice purporting to implement the rent review and, following an application by D, the President appointed a surveyor in August 2001.

Held, refusing the application, that it was inappropriate and unnecessary to imply a time limit into the schedule. Unless the tenant served a notice making time of the essence, time was not of the essence of the clauses governing the service of the notice and the application to the President. The use of the word "neglect" in the clause governing D's application to the President indicated that D was under a duty to get on with any such application within a reasonable period of time, but D had complied with that obligation. Accordingly, D was entitled to a review of the rent and the appointment of the surveyor was valid.

ICELAND FOODS PLC v. DANGOOR, [2002] EWHC 107, [2002] 2 E.G.L.R. 5, Neuberger, J., Ch D.

3065. Rent reviews—underleases—interpretation of "the said term"

The habendum of a sublease provided that the tenant hold "from the date hereof for the residue of a term of 125 years from December 21, 1960". The sublease was granted on March 30, 1962. The lessor was entitled to give notice of rent review during certain specified periods "of the said term". The arbitrator held that the said term commenced on December 21, 1960. The landlord appealed.

Held, allowing the appeal, that "the said term" meant the period from the date of the grant of the sublease. The rent review clause was intended to run from the date for the first payment of rent.

BISICHI MINING LTD v. BASS HOLDINGS LTD, [2002] EWHC 375, [2002] L. & T.R. 30, Jacob, J., Ch D.

3066. Repair covenants—secure tenancies—damp affecting property—no evidence due to damage to property

[Landlord and Tenant Act 1985 s.11.]

S owned a maisonette which was occupied by M under a secure tenancy. M complained that the premises were damp and sought damages for breach of the implied repairing covenant in the Landlord and Tenant Act 1985 s.11. At trial, issues arose as to whether (1) S had a duty to warn M not to dry clothes in a heated cupboard. She had done so and this had caused condensation to spread throughout the property; (2) the damp was due to a breach of the repairing covenant, and (3) a leak from a washing machine pipe which had caused water to come through M's ceiling was due to a breach of covenant. M succeeded at first instance and was awarded damages of £7,850. S appealed.

Held, allowing the appeal, that (1) S had no duty to advise M not to use the cupboard to dry clothes and no such duty arose under the implied repairing covenant. M's pleading did not allege that the damp was caused by actual damage to the property or entered from the outside, *Quick v. Taff Ely BC* [1986] Q.B. 809, [1985] C.L.Y. 1610 considered. In the absence of such allegations, the existence of damp was insufficient to found a claim, and (3) there was no evidence that the leak which affected the ceiling was due to a breach of covenant or that S had been responsible for it.

SOUTHWARK LBC v. McINTOSH [2002] 1 E.G.L.R. 25, Lightman, J., Ch D.

3067. Repair covenants–secure tenancies–possession given up without execution of possession order–retrospective reinstatement of tenancies

[Housing Act 1985 s.85(2).]

D appealed against the dismissal of her application to reinstate her tenancy. L, a local authority landlord, appealed against an order postponing the date for possession of M's tenancy. The common question raised by these appeals was whether the court had power under the Housing Act 1985 s.85(2) to postpone the date of possession of a dwelling house let under a secure tenancy by a local authority landlord in circumstances where there was an existing order for possession and the tenant had given up possession without the need for execution of a warrant of possession. In each case, the tenants sought postponement of possession under the existing orders to the dates on which possession had been given up, in order to enable them to bring claims against their landlords alleging breach of repairing obligations in respect of the whole of the period during which they had remained in possession.

Held, dismissing D's appeal and allowing L's appeal, that the court could not exercise its discretionary powers under s.85(2) to retrospectively reinstate tenancies which had been given up by secure tenants without the need for execution of a suspended possession order. The extended powers under s.85(2) were enacted to enable the courts to maintain a former tenant in possession. Those powers would no longer be needed once possession had been given up. In the instant cases, as the tenants had failed to make any application for reinstatement prior to giving up possession, they could not claim compensation under the repairing covenants in respect of the period between the determination of their tenancies and their giving up possession.

DUNN v. BRADFORD MDC; MARSTON v. LEEDS CITY COUNCIL, [2002] EWCA Civ 1137, [2003] H.L.R. 15, Chadwick, L.J., CA.

3068. Residential tenancies–forms

LONG RESIDENTIAL TENANCIES (PRINCIPAL FORMS) (AMENDMENT) (ENGLAND) REGULATIONS 2002, SI 2002 2227; made under the Local Government and Housing Act 1989 Sch.10 para.4. In force: September 30, 2002; £1.75.

These Regulations amend two forms set out in the Long Residential Tenancies (Principal Forms) Regulations 1997 (SI 1997 3008) which are prescribed for the purposes of the Local Government and Housing Act 1989 Sch.10.

3069. Residential tenancies–termination–right to a home–sufficient and continuous links

[Human Rights Act 1998 Sch.1 Part I Art.8.]

Q appealed against the possession order made against him following the refusal by H of his application for tenancy. The application had been unsuccessful on the grounds that as a single person, Q was not entitled to family accommodation. Q argued that by seeking possession of the property, in which Q had formerly lived with his wife and child, H was in breach of the Human Rights Act 1998 Sch.1 Part I Art.8. The judge had found that Q's rights were not engaged as he ceased to have an interest in the home following the decision of his wife and joint tenant to leave and to determine the tenancy. On appeal, Q argued that case law showed that it was not necessary to prove a legal or equitable interest in the land in order to establish that the property was a home, which had an autonomous meaning under the Act, and that a matrimonial home continued to be a home after a joint tenancy had ended.

Held, allowing the appeal, that the test established in *Buckley v. United Kingdom* (1997) 23 E.H.R.R. 101, [1996] C.L.Y. 4838 applied. "Home" within the meaning of the Act was autonomous and it was inappropriate to introduce references to concepts such as landlord and tenant within the term. Q did have a right to a home at the time that the possession proceedings were served on him and therefore the case was remitted to the lower court to determine whether the interference with Q's rights was justified under Art.8(2) of the Act, *Gillow v. United Kingdom (A/109)* (1989) 11 E.H.R.R. 335, [1986] C.L.Y. 1654 considered, *Chapman v. United Kingdom (27238/95)* (2001) 33 E.H.R.R. 18, [2001] C.L.Y. 4744 distinguished.

QAZI v. HARROW LBC; *sub nom.* HARROW LBC v. QUAZI; HARROW LBC v. QAZI, [2001] EWCA Civ 1834, [2002] U.K.H.R.R. 316, Arden, L.J., CA.

3070. Restrictive covenants–breach–car parking–interpretation of restrictive covenant

A lessor, M, appealed against the grant of a declaration permitting the lessee, S, to park cars on a part of the demised premises. A 999 year lease had been granted on a property occupying a position on the corner of two streets in central London. The basement areas had originally been open, but had subsequently been completely covered with pavement lights at the same level as the pavement itself. Occupiers of the property had, for many years, parked cars on those pavement lights. Clause II(9) of the lease concluded with the statement "no goods shall at any time be or remain placed outside the said premises which are of any nature which the lessor shall have forbidden to be or to remain so placed". M relied on clause II(9) in seeking to prevent S from continuing to park cars in the relevant area. In response, S contended that (1) motor cars were not "goods"; (2) a parked car could not be said to have been "placed" outside the said premises, and (3) the words "outside the said premises" meant outside the boundaries of the demised premises.

Held, dismissing the appeal, that (1) the plain and ordinary meaning of the word "goods" included motor cars; (2) it was not inappropriate to say that a parked car had been "placed" outside the premises, and (3) clause II(9) was pervaded by inconsistency. Accordingly, the court was driven to construe the clause against the grantor and thus "outside the said premises" was taken to mean outside the premises the subject of the demise.

SPRING HOUSE (FREEHOLD) LTD v. MOUNT COOK LAND LTD; *sub nom.* MOUNT COOK LAND LTD v. SPRING HOUSE (FREEHOLD) LTD, [2001] EWCA Civ 1833, [2002] 2 All E.R. 822, Ward, L.J., CA.

3071. Restrictive covenants–breach–covenant requiring residential use of property–use as private study–business use not established

C, the landlord of L, the assignee of a 20 year lease of a mews property in London, commenced proceedings for forfeiture on the basis of an alleged breach of covenant. The lease contained a covenant that the lessee "will not use or permit or suffer to be used the demised premises or any part thereof otherwise than as a single private dwelling house in one family residential occupation only" nor "for any business whatsoever". The lease also contained a forfeiture clause. L was an 83 year old lady with an active social life and extensive involvement in a number of charities. L gave evidence that, she used the property only in the daytime on Tuesday, Wednesday and Thursday when, in the company of a private secretary, she carried out various administrative tasks relating to her charity work and social and private life, and entertained friends for lunch or tea. She never spent evenings or nights at the property, residing in a flat over a mile away. The main room was furnished as an office with two desks and ancillary office paraphernalia. There was a small bedroom with a fold down bed on which L occasionally slept in the afternoons, and a galley style kitchen with a microwave oven.

Held, dismissing the claim, that to describe L's activities at the premises as "business" would be "to fall into the pond of absurdity", *Abernethie v. Kleiman Ltd* [1970] 1 QB 10, [1969] C.L.Y. 2035 applied. The covenant required that such use as was made of the premises was of a residential nature, not that its use served to make it a complete home, *Kavanagh v. Lyroudias* [1985] 1 All E.R. 560, [1985] C.L.Y. 1907 and *Wimbush v. Cibulia* [1949] 2 K.B. 564 distinguished. L was under no obligation to use the premises at all and the fact that she did so effectively as a private study did not amount to a breach of covenant.

CHURCH COMMISSIONERS v. LEIGH, March 7, 2002, Judge Colin Smith Q.C., CC (Central London). [*Ex rel.* Andrew Butler, Barrister, Tanfield Chambers, Francis Taylor Building, Temple, London].

3072. Restrictive covenants–rental agreements–meaning of "to rent"

C appealed against a decision that a rental agreement for a mountain chalet which restricted L, who had hired the chalet from C, from directly or indirectly renting chalets named in the agreement for a period of 18 months did not prohibit L from entering into a rental agreement for one of the named chalets within the 18 month period where occupation would not take place until after the expiry of such period. C contended that L had breached the agreement by entering into a rental agreement for one of the chalets.

Held, allowing the appeal, that the agreement did prohibit L from entering into rental agreements within the 18 month period even though occupation would not take place until after the expiration of that period. The verb "to rent" could be interpreted so as to include the making of an agreement for the future occupation of premises, and that interpretation more closely reflected the intention of the parties when entering the agreement.

CARTER v. LOTUS LEISURE GROUP LTD, [2001] EWCA Civ 1205, [2002] 2 P. & C.R. 2, Mummery, L.J., CA.

3073. Restrictive covenants–restraint of trade–pharmacy business–loss of goodwill

[National Health Service (Pharmaceutical Services) Regulations 1992 (SI 1992 662) Reg.4.]

Y appealed against a decision that a restraint of trade clause in a lease of pharmacy premises was valid. The lease had been granted to Y by a partnership of doctors, E, whose practice formed part of the same premises leased to Y. The lease provided that upon its expiration, the lessee would use his best endeavours to procure the transfer of his licence to operate a pharmacy in order to facilitate the continued use of the premises as a pharmacy. The court at first instance held that the restraint of trade arising as a result of the clause was reasonable from the point of view of both the parties and the public interest. Y contended that if the clause was valid then, upon the expiration of the lease, the goodwill that he had established would be appropriated by E without any compensation. Y further maintained that E was not obliged to provide a pharmacy upon the expiration of the lease and that accordingly E did not have a sufficient interest to protect.

Held, dismissing the appeal, that whilst E was not obliged to provide a pharmacy, it had a clear interest in doing so both from a financial viewpoint and from the viewpoint of patient welfare. Accordingly, E undoubtedly had a sufficient interest to protect and the clause as formulated was reasonably necessary to protect that interest. If Y was unable to negotiate a renewal of the lease upon satisfactory terms then he retained the option of assignment to be negotiated on terms which acknowledged the goodwill built up in the business, a course of action to which E could not unreasonably withhold consent. Whilst the clause hindered Y in any attempt at a minor relocation of his business, such hindrance was not a product of E's unreasonable attitude but rather a by product of the limitations imposed by the National Health Service (Pharmaceutical Services) Regulations 1992 Reg.4. It was however observed that it would not be appropriate to view either the lease or clause in the instant case as a precedent to be followed in future cases.

YOUNG v. EVANS-JONES, [2001] EWCA Civ 732, [2002] 1 P. & C.R.14, Robert Walker, L.J., CA.

3074. **Right to buy–green belt–restrictions on alienation of green belt land by local authorities–compulsory sale of green belt land**

[Green Belt (London and Home Counties) Act 1938 s.5; Housing Act 1985 Part V, s.118.]

The Secretary of State appealed against a decision ([2001] EWCA Civ 499, [2002] H.L.R. 30) overturning a ruling that his consent was necessary for the sale of a flat owned by a local authority. O was the secure tenant of the flat and had attempted to exercise her right to buy under the Housing Act 1985 Part V. The local authority contended that as the flat was situated on green belt land it was necessary that the procedures prescribed by the Green Belt (London and Home Counties) Act 1938 s.5, including the need to obtain consent from the Secretary of State, be complied with. The issue that arose was whether the restrictions under s.5 of the 1938 Act could operate to deprive a secure tenant of the right to buy under Part V of the 1985 Act.

Held, dismissing the appeal, that the requirement in the Green Belt (London and Home Counties) Act 1938 s.5 for ministerial consent to sale by local authorities of green belt land did not apply to a council tenant's right to buy under the provisions of the Housing Act 1985 Part V. It was reasonable to infer that Parliament had omitted any reference to the 1938 Act in Part V of the 1985 Act because it took the view that the environmental objectives of the earlier Act were not undermined by an involuntary disposal of housing accommodation by a local authority. The omission of any reference to the 1938 Act in s.118 of the 1985 Act and the absence of any mention of a requirement for obtaining ministerial consent in Part V of the 1985 Act justified such an interpretation.

R. (ON THE APPLICATION OF O'BYRNE) v. SECRETARY OF STATE FOR THE ENVIRONMENT, TRANSPORT AND THE REGIONS; *sub nom.* O'BYRNE v. SECRETARY OF STATE FOR THE ENVIRONMENT, TRANSPORT AND THE REGIONS; R. v. SECRETARY OF STATE FOR THE ENVIRONMENT, TRANSPORT AND THE REGIONS, *ex p.* O'BYRNE, [2002] UKHL 45, [2002] 1 W.L.R. 3250, Lord Scott of Foscote, HL.

3075. **Security of tenure–eviction–excluded tenancies–temporary sleeping arrangements of landlord–determination of principal home of landlord**

[Protection from Eviction Act 1977 s.3A(2)(a).]

M, a landlord, appealed against a decision that S was not an excluded tenant under the Protection from Eviction Act 1977 s.3A(2)(a). M had granted tenancy of a room to S in April 1998 at "no.70", which M had temporarily moved into following his divorce. Between April and September 1998, M used two rooms at no.70 as living and bedroom accommodation. M however spent much of his time at an adjacent house, "no.72", with his children until they left to get married in 1998. In August 1998 M gave S notice to quit and evicted her in September 1998. Under the 1977 Act, it fell to be decided whether M had used no.70 as his only or principal home. The judge at first instance concluded that on the facts, M's main residence was no.72 as his occupancy of no.70 had been a temporary arrangement. M submitted that the judge was wrong in his decision contending that he had occupied a bedroom and a living room at the property in question. S however submitted that a place where a person slept was irrelevant in determining the principal residence of M.

Held, allowing the appeal, that a place where a person slept was of the utmost importance and that for the purposes of s.3A(2)(a) M had been using the property in question as "his only and principal home" at the beginning and termination of the tenancy because he had a bedroom and slept there. The tenancy was therefore an excluded tenancy.

SUMEGHOVA v. McMAHON; *sub nom*. SUMEGHOVO v. McMAHON, [2002] EWCA Civ 1581, [2003] H.L.R. 26, Longmore, L.J., CA.

3076. Service charges–costs–legal costs irrecoverable under service charge provisions

V, the lessee of a flat held on a long lease, appealed against a ruling that, inter alia, the lessor, S, was entitled to charge her as part of her service charge contributions the balance of costs incurred but not reimbursed in respect of current and past proceedings for the recovery of service charges and ground rent. The lease entitled S to recover as part of the service charge the "cost of all other services which the lessor may at its absolute discretion provide or install in the said buildings for the comfort and convenience of the lessees" (clause A) and the "reasonable and proper fees of the lessor's auditors and the reasonable and proper fees of the lessor's managing agents for the collection of the rents of the flats in the said buildings and for the general management thereof" (clause B).

Held, allowing the appeal in part, that giving clause A its ordinary and natural meaning, it permitted S to charge for other services that it provided or installed in the building; it concerned physical facilities, not legal advice. Furthermore, the ordinary natural meaning of clause B was to provide for the recovery of the reasonable and proper fees of S's auditors as one category and, as the other, the reasonable and proper fees of S's managing agents, both for their collection of rents in the buildings and for their general management of the buildings. Neither clause enabled S to recover legal costs as part of the service charge.

ST MARY'S MANSIONS LTD v. LIMEGATE INVESTMENT CO LTD, [2002] EWCA Civ 1491, [2003] H.L.R. 24, Ward, L.J., CA.

3077. Service charges–management companies–reasonableness–scope of Landlord and Tenant Act 1985

[Landlord and Tenant Act 1985 s.18, s.19, s.30.]

M, the tenant of a residential property, appealed against a decision that charges incurred by the landlord's management company were not "relevant costs" within the meaning of the Landlord and Tenant Act 1985 s.18(2) thus denying M the opportunity to apply to a leasehold valuation tribunal for a determination as to whether the relevant charges had been reasonably incurred.

Held, allowing the appeal, that having regard to the definitions of "service charge", "relevant costs" and "landlord" set out in s.18(1), s.18(2) and s.30 of the Act respectively, it had been intended that a person who had a right under a lease to enforce a charge for services, repairs and maintenance which varied according to the costs incurred by that person in providing those services under the lease was a "landlord" for the purposes of the Act insofar as it related to service charges. Accordingly, service charges capable of being enforced by a management company which varied according to the costs actually incurred by the management company fell within the scope of the provisions as to reasonableness set out in s.19 of the Act. There was no reason why a management company should not fall within the definition of a landlord in the context of service charges, *Berrycroft Management Co Ltd v. Sinclair Gardens Investments (Kensington) Ltd* (1997) 29 H.L.R. 444, [1997] C.L.Y. 3331 considered.

CINNAMON LTD v. MORGAN, [2001] EWCA Civ 1616, [2002] 2 P. & C.R. 10, Chadwick, L.J., CA.

3078. Service charges—repairs—landlord seeking contribution from tenants—failure to carry out consultation required by Landlord and Tenant Act 1985 s.20

[Landlord and Tenant Act 1985 s.18, s.20.]

H, the freehold owner of a building divided into commercial and residential properties, sought a contribution of £17,665 for repairs from C, tenant under the headleases of the lifts, lift shaft, hallways and flats, and B, tenant of the same parts under a sublease. Both headlease and sublease allowed for the recovery of expenses by way of service charge. C and B contended that they were not liable to contribute as H had not carried out the consultation required by the Landlord and Tenant Act 1985 s.20, which applied as flats were included in their demised holding. H asserted that s.20 did not apply because C and B held other parts of the property apart from the flats. The matter was determined on a trial of preliminary issues.

Held, determining the preliminary issue in favour of the defendants, that s.20 applied. H could not recover the sum sought from C and B. Under s.18, service charges were payable by the "tenant of a dwelling" and there was no further requirement for the tenant to be in actual occupation. Neither was there a restriction that prevented C or B from being a "tenant" for the purposes of the Act by virtue of their additional tenancies of other parts of the building where these were separately identified in the headlease and sublease.

HERON MAPLE HOUSE LTD v. CENTRAL ESTATES LTD [2002] 1 E.G.L.R. 35, Judge Roger Cooke, CC (Central London).

3079. Statutory tenancies—succession—lawfulness of statutory provision excluding survivors of same sex relationships

[Rent Act 1977 Sch.1 para.2, Sch.1 para.3; Human Rights Act 1998 Sch. Part I Art.8, Art.14.]

M, who had shared a property with W, his homosexual partner and the tenant of the property, appealed against a finding that, upon W's death, he had become an assured tenant of the property under the Rent Act 1977 Sch.1 para.3 rather than a statutory tenant under Sch.1 para.2. He alleged that to grant a statutory tenancy to the survivor of a heterosexual relationship when the survivor of a homosexual relationship was entitled only to the less beneficial assured tenancy amounted to discrimination on the ground of sexual orientation. The issues before the court were whether the facts of the case fell within the ambit of one or more of the substantive provisions of the Human Rights Act 1998 Sch. Part I and whether the different treatment of survivors of heterosexual relationships and survivors of homosexual relationships had an objective and reasonable justification. G, the landlord, argued, inter alia, that the court should defer to Parliament, which had been entitled to legislate as it had done.

Held, allowing the appeal, that Art.14 would be engaged even where there was "the most tenuous link with another provision in the Convention", *Petrovic v. Austria (20458/92)* (2001) 33 E.H.R.R. 14, [1998] C.L.Y. 3155 considered. The positive obligation on the part of the state to promote the values that Art.8 protected was wide enough to bring legislation that affected the home within the ambit of Art.8, *Marckx v. Belgium (A/31)* (1979-80) 2 E.H.R.R. 330 applied and *Michalak v. Wandsworth LBC* [2002] EWCA Civ 271, [2002] H.L.R. 39 followed. The facts of M's case did therefore fall within the ambit of Art.8 as that Article was understood for the purposes of Art.14. Moreover, discrimination by reason of sexual orientation fell within Art.14, *Salgueiro da Silva Mouta v. Portugal (33290/96)* [2001] 1 F.C.R. 653, [2001] C.L.Y. 2587 considered. The principle of deference to the will of Parliament could not assist G. Once discrimination had been established, it was for the discriminator to show an objective and reasonable justification for that discrimination, *Michalak* applied. Furthermore, issues of discrimination had a high constitutional importance, and in such cases deference had only a minor role, *R. v. DPP, ex p. Kebilene* [2000] 2 A.C. 326, [1999] C.L.Y. 1045 applied. Once it was accepted that the court was not bound by what Parliament had decided, it was a case of considering whether the steps taken by Parliament in implementing its policy were reasonable, proportionate and logically explicable. That could not be done. As to the interests of landlords and flexibility in the housing market, Parliament had already extended full Rent Act protection to survivors of heterosexual unmarried partnerships, a class that appeared to much more numerous than a class made up of same sex partnerships. As to the protection of the family, it was quite unclear how heterosexual family life, which included unmarried partnerships, was promoted by handicapping people who were constitutionally unable or strongly unwilling to enter into family relationships so defined. In addition, the more the court was told that a person holding an assured tenancy was very little, if at all, worse off than a statutory tenant, the less it seemed that any effective social policy could be achieved through the grant of an assured rather than a statutory tenancy. In the circumstances, it was clear that Sch.1 para.2 of the 1977 Act infringed Art.14. That breach could be remedied by construing the words "as his or her wife or husband" in Sch.1 para.2 as if they meant "as if they were his or her wife or husband".

GHAIDAN v. GODIN-MENDOZA; *sub nom.* GHAIDAN v. MENDOZA; GODIN-MENDOZA v. GHAIDAN; MENDOZA v. GHAIDAN, [2002] EWCA Civ 1533, [2003] 2 W.L.R. 478, Buxton, L.J., CA.

3080. Tenants–access orders–access for alterations to be carried out–refusal of consent–court orders empowering landlord–statutory requirements

[Rent Act 1977 s.98(1)(a), s.116)2), s.116(3).]

BA appealed against an order that he give his landlord, MA, access to his room for works to be carried out for the provision of alternative accommodation. BA occupied a ground floor room in MA's house and had shared use of the kitchen and bathroom. MA had sought a possession order but this had been refused and instead a declaration was made that MA's proposals to convert BA's room into a self contained unit would provide BA with "suitable alternative accommodation" pursuant to the Rent Act 1977 s.98(1)(a). The following year the judge had granted the order for access to BA's room.

Held, allowing the appeal, that the order requiring BA to give his landlord access to the room he rented in order for works to be carried out was unlawful as it failed to meet the conditions specified in s.116(3) of the 1977 Act. In cases where a tenant was unwilling to allow his landlord access, the court could, if satisfied that the condition in s.116(3) had been met, that is that the proposed works had been specified in an application for a statutory grant, make an order under s.116(3) giving the landlord power to carry out the works. In the instant case, MA's proposed works had not been the subject of a grant application. The judge had failed to exercise the power under s.116(2) and had not addressed the issue of interim accommodation for BA. In the absence of any consensual arrangement between MA and BA, there was no basis on which the judge could require BA to give his landlord access to his room for the works to be carried out.

AKRAM v. ADAM, [2002] EWCA Civ 1679, [2003] H.L.R. 28, Chadwick, L.J., CA.

3081. Books

Agreement for the Creation of an Assured Shorthold Tenancy. Paperback: £9.50. RICS Books.

Barnes, Michael–Hill and Redmans Guide to Rent Review. Paperback: £60.00. ISBN 0-406-93756-7. Butterworths Law.

Brennan, Gabriel–Landlord and Tenant Law. Paperback: £34.99. ISBN 0-19-925555-5. Oxford University Press.

Dowding, Nicholas–Landlord and Tenant Reports 2001. Hardback: £265.00. ISBN 0-421-75630-6. Sweet & Maxwell.

Fraser, Marge–Michigan Real Estate. Paperback: £26.99. ISBN 0-324-14374-5. South Western College Publishing.

Furber John; Karas, Jonathan; Evans Jonathan; Scott, Tiffany–Furber: Commonhold and Leasehold Reform Act 2002. Butterworth's New Law Guides. Paperback: £35.00. ISBN 0-406-94557-8. Butterworths Law.

Garner–Practical Approach to Landlord and Tenant Law. Paperback: £24.95. ISBN 0-19-925452-4. Oxford University Press.

Irvin, Carol; Irvin, James–Ohio Real Estate Law. 7th Ed. Paperback: £37.99. ISBN 0-324-14383-4. South Western College Publishing.

Jourdan, Stephen–Jourdan: Adverse Possession. Hardback: £55.00. ISBN 0-406-98251-1. Butterworths Law.

Luba, J.; Madge, N.; McConnell, D.–Defending Possession Proceedings. 5th Ed. Paperback: £42.00. ISBN 1-903307-06-6. The Legal Action Group.

Smith, P.F.–Evans and Smith: the Law of Landlord and Tenant. 6th Ed. Paperback: £23.95. ISBN 0-406-94679-5. Butterworths Law.

Social Housing Law-A Practical Guide. Hardback: £65.00. ISBN 0-406-90314-X. Butterworths Law.

Sweet, Robert–Commercial Leases: Tenants' Amendments. 4th Ed. Paperback: £65.00. ISBN 0-421-77210-7. Sweet & Maxwell.

Wilde, Peter; Butt, Paul–"Which?" Guide to Renting and Letting. Revised Ed. Which? Consumer Guides. Paperback (C format): £11.99. ISBN 0-85202-894-6. Which? Books.

LEGAL ADVICE AND FUNDING

3082. Barristers–fees–travelling expenses–case conference with client on remand

[Legal Aid in Criminal and Care Proceedings (Costs) Regulations 1989 (SI 1989 343) Reg.19, Reg.24.]

Held, that the assessment of counsel's fees and travelling expenses for attending a conference with a client held on remand under the Legal Aid in Criminal and Care Proceedings (Costs) Regulations 1989 Reg.19 was to be carried out without being subject to the provisions of Reg.24.

R. v. CARLYLE (COSTS) [2002] 1 Costs L.R. 192, Costs Judge Rogers, Supreme Court Costs Office.

3083. Barristers–fees–travelling expenses–meeting with defendant at scene of crime

[Legal Aid in Criminal and Care Proceedings (Costs) Regulations 1989 (SI 1989 343) Reg.19.]

B, a barrister, appealed against an assessment in which the costs of time spent travelling to view the scene of the crime with the client were not allowed.

Held, allowing the appeal, that the Legal Aid in Criminal and Care Proceedings (Costs) Regulations 1989 Reg.19 applied. It was reasonable for B to view the scene and the meeting with S could not have been properly conducted in chambers. B could therefore claim both his travelling time and expenses.

R. v. SINGH (HARDEV) (COSTS) [2002] 1 Costs L.R. 196, Costs Judge Pollard, Supreme Court Costs Office.

3084. Civil procedure–legal aid–costs

CIVIL LEGAL AID (GENERAL) (AMENDMENT) REGULATIONS 2002, SI 2002 711; made under the Legal Aid Act 1988 s.34, s.43. In force: April 8, 2002; £1.50.

These Regulations amend the Civil Legal Aid (General) Regulations 1989 (SI 1989 339) in order to provide for the imposition of an embargo against any further work being carried out under a legal aid certificate once notice has been served that it may be discharged or revoked. They also clarify the position regarding amendments of certificates and apply to transitional cases to which the 1989

Regulations continue to apply by virtue of the provisions in the Access to Justice Act 1999 (Commencement No.3 Transitional Provisions and Savings) Order 2000 (SI 2000 774).

3085. Civil procedure-legal aid-costs

CIVIL LEGAL AID (GENERAL) (AMENDMENT NO.2) REGULATIONS 2002, SI 2002 3033; made under the Legal Aid Act 1988 s.16, s.34, s.43. In force: December 31, 2002; £1.75.

These Regulations make amendments to the Civil Legal Aid (General) Regulations 1989 (SI 1989 339). They apply to transitional cases to which the principal Regulations continue to apply by virtue of the provisions in the Access to Justice Act 1999 (Commencement No. 3, Transitional Provisions and Savings) Order 2000 (SI 2000 774).

3086. Community Legal Service-assessment of financial resources

COMMUNITY LEGAL SERVICE (FINANCIAL) (AMENDMENT) REGULATIONS 2002, SI 2002 709; made under the Access to Justice Act 1999 s.7, s.10. In force: April 8, 2002; £1.50.

These Regulations amend the Community Legal Service (Financial) Regulations 2000 (SI 2000 516) so as to increase the income limits for the purposes of determining eligibility for services provided by the Legal Services Commission as part of the Community Legal Service. This is in line with the relevant uprating of social security benefits.

3087. Community Legal Service-assessment of financial resources

COMMUNITY LEGAL SERVICE (FINANCIAL) (AMENDMENT NO.2) REGULATIONS 2002, SI 2002 1766; made under the Access to Justice Act 1999 s.7. In force: August 5, 2002; £1.50.

These Regulations, which amend the provisions relating to the gross income cap in the Community Legal Service (Financial) Regulations 2000 (SI 2000 516), increase the gross income limit beyond which an individual is not eligible for services funded by the Legal Services Commission as part of the Community Legal Service. They also provide for deductions of benefits to be made in assessing gross income. In addition they provide for the limit to be increased for individuals who have more than four dependant children.

3088. Criminal Defence Service-recovery of costs

CRIMINAL DEFENCE SERVICE (RECOVERY OF DEFENCE COSTS ORDERS) (AMENDMENT) REGULATIONS 2002, SI 2002 713; made under the Access to Justice Act 1999 s.17. In force: April 8, 2002; £1.50.

These Regulations amend the Criminal Defence Service (Recovery of Defence Costs Orders) Regulations 2001 (SI 2001 856) so as to increase the level of income a funded defendant must have before his income is taken into account for the purpose of calculating his financial resources.

3089. Family proceedings-remuneration

LEGAL AID IN FAMILY PROCEEDINGS (REMUNERATION) (AMENDMENT) REGULATIONS 2002, SI 2002 710; made under the Legal Aid Act 1988 s.34, s.43. In force: April 8, 2002; £1.50.

These Regulations amend the Legal Aid in Family Proceedings (Remuneration) Regulations 1991 (SI 1991 2038) so as to add the Law Society Family Law Panel Advanced to those panels whose members receive an uplift in relation to the sums payable for work carried out by them.

3090. Legal aid—costs—appropriate circumstances for award of indemnity costs in favour of legally aided litigants

See CIVIL PROCEDURE: Brawley v. Marczynski (No.2). §350

3091. Legal aid—costs—claim for enhanced rates—failure to claim when bill first submitted

[Legal Aid in Criminal and Care Proceedings (Costs) Regulations 1989 (SI 1989 343) Reg.14(2).]

R made a claim for the payment of enhanced legal aid rates on a redetermination, having failed to do so when the bill of costs was first submitted.

Held, refusing the application, that such a claim was precluded by the Legal Aid in Criminal and Care Proceedings (Costs) Regulations 1989 Reg.14(2) which provided that only matters first considered by the determining officer could form the basis for a redetermination. As R had failed to claim enhanced rates when the bill was first submitted, such a course was not open to them on a redetermination, *Ali v. Lord Chancellor's Department* [2002] 2 Costs L.R. 258 applied.

R. v. WALPOLE (JOHN) (COSTS) [2002] 1 Costs L.R. 199, Costs Judge Rogers, Supreme Court Costs Office.

3092. Legal aid—criminal appeals—legal representation

See CRIMINAL PROCEDURE: R. v. Oates (Emma Louise). §847

3093. Legal aid—discharge—validity of embargo on certificate prior to discharge decision—procedural fairness

[Legal Aid Act 1988 s.4(1); Civil Legal Aid (General) Regulations 1989 (SI 1989 339) Reg.67.]

The Legal Services Commission, L, appealed against a decision ([2001] EWHC Admin 580) that it had not had the power to place an embargo on a legal aid certificate issued to M. M had obtained legal aid to pursue his claim for damages for personal injuries. His counsel had advised him to consider seriously any offer over £9,000. He was offered £10,000 but refused to accept it, whereupon his solicitors, B, reported him to L pursuant to the Civil Legal Aid (General) Regulations 1989 Reg.67. L had placed an embargo on further work under the certificate, and consequently M was obliged to represent himself. He had, however, accepted an offer at the court door of £15,000 plus costs. M had subsequently brought proceedings contending that the imposition of the embargo on the day before the trial was unlawful. The judge had found that there was no power in law to place such an embargo on a full legal aid certificate pending its possible discharge, and that even if there was such a power, it had not been used fairly. The judge had concluded that the presence of such a power in relation to emergency certificates and its absence in relation to full certificates excluded the use of any residual power under the Legal Aid Act 1988 s.4(1). L contended that if the judge's decision was correct it would have no power to prevent a solicitor incurring fruitless expense in the interim between notice of possible withdrawal and eventual revocation or discharge.

Held, dismissing the appeal (Simon Brown, L.J. dissenting in part), that the duty under the 1989 Regulations to report unreasonable conduct lay with the solicitors. If, as it appeared was the case, neither the solicitor's report to L or L's notice to the legally aided person, suspended his representation, it was the duty of the solicitor to decide that expenditure which could properly be incurred in the interim. L could remind the solicitor that although the certificate remained in place, any expenditure had to be strictly necessary. Furthermore, if L had been within its powers in imposing the embargo, it had not gone about it fairly.

R. (ON THE APPLICATION OF MACHI) v. LEGAL SERVICES COMMISSION, [2001] EWCA Civ 2010, [2002] 1 W.L.R. 983, Sedley, L.J., CA.

3094. Legal representation–committals–right to seek public funding–court's approach to adjournment application

[Human Rights Act 1998 Sch.1 Part I Art.6.]

M appealed against a refusal to grant a further adjournment of committal proceedings on the application of B for alleged breaches of worldwide search and seizure orders. The adjournment had been sought to enable M to apply for publicly funded legal representation. Although M had previously submitted two unsuccessful applications for funding, the matter remained under consideration by the Legal Services Commission. Since several adjournments had already been granted, B had offered to fund legal representation of M's own choosing so as to enable the committal proceedings to be heard, but M refused the offer.

Held, allowing the appeal, that committal applications were criminal proceedings for the purposes of the Human Rights Act 1998. Thus, in order to protect the right to fair trial under Sch.1 Part I Art.6 of the Act, M should have been given an effective opportunity to apply for public funding for legal representation. That opportunity had to outweigh all other considerations such as the inconvenience to other parties and the use of court resources. The court had to have regard to the accused's view as to his representation. Although the right to free legal assistance was not absolute, unjustified interference with a defendant's application for public funding ran contrary to the notion of a fair trial, *Croissant v. Germany (A/237B)* (1993) 16 E.H.R.R. 135, [1993] C.L.Y. 2136 considered.

BERRY TRADE LTD v. MOUSSAVI (NO.1), [2002] EWCA Civ 477, [2002] 1 W.L.R. 1910, Arden, L.J., CA.

3095. Books

Directory of Local Authorities: 2002. Paperback: £38.50. ISBN 0-421-77220-4. Sweet & Maxwell.

Directory of Local Authorities: 2002 (CD-ROM). CD-ROM: £80.00. ISBN 0-421-77230-1. Sweet & Maxwell.

Directory of Local Authorities: 2002 (special Bundle Offer). Paperback: CD-ROM: £99.00. ISBN 0-421-77240-9. Sweet & Maxwell.

Exall, Gordon–APIL Guide to Fatal Injury Claims. Paperback: £30.00. ISBN 0-85308-757-1. Jordans.

Martin, Jacqueline; Gibbins, Mary–Complete A-Z Law Handbook. 2nd Ed. Complete A-Z. Paperback: £9.99. ISBN 0-340-84716-6. Hodder & Stoughton Educational.

Morris, Gordon–Shaw's Directory of Courts in the United Kingdom: 2002/03. Paperback: £39.50. ISBN 0-7219-1409-8. Shaw & Sons.

O'Floinn, Benedict; Gannon, The Hon Mr Justice Sean–Practice and Procedure in the Superior Courts. Hardback: £91.54. ISBN 1-85475-263-4. Butterworths Law (Ireland).

Pegg, Samantha–Good Web Guide to Legal Advice Online. Paperback: £9.99. ISBN 1-903282-41-1. Paperback: £9.99. ISBN 1-903282-41-1. The Good Web Guide.

Simons, Alan; Harmer, Caroline–Practical Guide to the Small Claims Court. Paperback: £22.95. ISBN 0-754-51760-8. Butterworths Law.

LEGAL METHODOLOGY

3096. Precedent–Court of Appeal authority–effect of unargued point

[Law of Property Act 1925 s.193(4).]

BM, which owned roughly 144 acres of common land, sought a declaration as to whether B and others who resided in houses constructed around the edges of that land had vehicular rights of access across the land. BM relied on the Law of Property Act 1925 s.193(4), which made it an offence for a person to drive a vehicle across such land without lawful authority, and on the decision of the Court of Appeal in

Hanning v. Top Deck Travel Group Ltd (1994) 68 P. & C.R. 14, [1995] C.L.Y. 1858, in which it was held that an easement by prescription could not be acquired by conduct which amounted to a crime. The defendants argued that they had acquired easements under the doctrine of lost modern grant and that the decision in *Hanning* should not be followed since they were relying on an argument which had not been put before the Court of Appeal when it had decided that case.

Held, giving judgment for BM, that the decision in *Hanning* was binding and should be followed. The defendants had not therefore acquired an easement by prescription. A High Court judge should not hold that a Court of Appeal decision had been arrived at per incuriam on the basis that he was presented with an argument which had not been put to the Court of Appeal. That was all the more so where, as in *Hanning*, the House of Lords had refused an application for permission to appeal. A court might regard an earlier decision as per incuriam if the court which made it had failed to take into account a relevant statutory provision or a yet earlier decision by which it would have been bound. Other situations might arise in which a decision would be found to have been given per incuriam; such situations would, however, be very rare, *Young v. Bristol Aeroplane Co Ltd* [1944] K.B. 718 considered.

BAKEWELL MANAGEMENT LTD v. BRANDWOOD, [2002] EWHC 472, *The Times*, April 19, 2002, Park, J., Ch D.

3097. Books

Barker, D.L.–Law. 11th Ed. Made Simple Series. Paperback: £14.99. ISBN 0-7506-5405-8. Butterworth-Heinemann.

Bennion, Francis A.R.–Bennion: Statutory Interpretation. 4th Ed. Hardback: £275.00. ISBN 0-406-94305-2. Butterworths Law.

DCG: Law: 2002/2003. Paperback: £5.50. ISBN 1-86017-937-1. Hobsons plc.

Garner, Bryan A.–Elements of Legal Style. 2nd Ed. Hardback: £21.99. ISBN 0-19-514162-8. Oxford University Press Inc, USA.

Greenberg, Daniel; Milbrook, Alexandra–Stroud's Judicial Dictionary of Words and Phrases: 2nd Supplement to the 6th Edition. Paperback: £55.00. ISBN 0-421-82880-3. Sweet & Maxwell.

Halsbury's Statutes Citator 2002. Paperback: £103.00. ISBN 0-406-94620-5. Butterworths Law.

Is It in Force? 2002. Paperback: £45.00. ISBN 0-406-94710-4. Butterworths Law.

Keenan, Denis–English Law Update: Bulletin No 1: September 2001. Paperback. ISBN 0-582-47306-3. Longman.

Lasok, Paul; Paines, Nicholas–Common Market Law Reports 2001: Vol 1. Hardback: £250.00. ISBN 0-421-79320-1. Sweet & Maxwell.

Lasok, Paul; Paines, Nicholas–Common Market Law Reports 2001: Vol 2. Hardback: £250.00. ISBN 0-421-79340-6. Sweet & Maxwell.

Lasok, Paul; Paines, Nicholas–Common Market Law Reports 2001: Vol 3. Hardback: £250.00. ISBN 0-421-79360-0. Sweet & Maxwell.

Law Update 2002. Paperback: £9.95. ISBN 1-85836-435-3. Old Bailey Press.

Lewis, Robyn–Geiriadur Newydd Y Gyfraith/The New Legal Dictionary. Hardback: £75.00. ISBN 1-84323-101-8. Gomer Press.

Martin, Elizabeth A.–Dictionary of Law. 5th Ed. Oxford Paperback Reference. Paperback: £9.99. ISBN 0-19-860399-1. Oxford University Press.

McEldowney, J.F.–Public Law. Paperback: £27.95. ISBN 0-421-78070-3. Sweet & Maxwell.

McLeod, Ian–Legal Method. 4th Ed. Palgrave Law Masters. Paperback: £14.99. ISBN 0-333-97025-X. Palgrave Macmillan.

Ramage, Roderick W.–Kelly's Draftsman. Hardback: CD-ROM: £178.00. ISBN 0-406-94834-8. Butterworths Law.

Sherwin, Richard K.–When Law Goes Pop. Paperback: £12.00. ISBN 0-226-75292-5. University of Chicago Press.

Smith, A.T.H.–Learning the Law. 12th Ed. Paperback: £9.95. ISBN 0-421-74420-0. Sweet & Maxwell.

Steiner, Eva—French Legal Method. Paperback: £24.99. ISBN 1-84174-185-X. Oxford University Press.

Urbina, Sebastian—Legal Method and the Rule of Law. Law and Philosophy Library, 59. Hardback: £56.00. ISBN 90-411-1870-5. Kluwer Law International.

Wittman, Donald—An Economic Analysis of the Law. Hardback: £60.00. ISBN 0-631-23157-9. Paperback: £21.99. ISBN 0-631-23158-7. Blackwell Publishers.

Yalof, David Alistair—Pursuit of Justices-Presidential Politics and the Selection of Supreme Court Nominees. Paperback: £11.50. ISBN 0-226-94546-4. University of Chicago Press.

LEGAL PROFESSION

3098. Bar Council—fees—anti competitive activity—approval of draft tariff— exercise of State legislative powers—admissibility

See COMPETITION LAW: Criminal Proceedings against Arduino (C35/99). §573

3099. Barristers—advocacy—conduct of defence—effect of counsel's illness during trial

See CRIMINAL PROCEDURE: R. v. Hall (Terry). §886

3100. Barristers—bias—counsel's knowledge of appellant's wife—applicability of code of conduct

S appealed against an order ([2002] EWHC 269) dismissing his appeal against the refusal of his application for a retrial of bankruptcy proceedings brought by G. During the hearing of the bankruptcy petition it had become apparent that M, who was acting counsel for G, had known S's wife approximately 10 years previously. It was argued that during the course of this acquaintance M might have formed conscious or unconscious impressions of S's family which could have affected his views on the dispute regarding S's domicile of choice. S submitted that this situation amounted to "professional embarrassment" under the Code of Conduct for the Bar of England and Wales para.603 (7th ed. 2000) and that accordingly M should have refused to accept instructions. Alternatively it was argued that, in accordance with the test for determining impartiality in a tribunal, the current circumstances would lead a fair minded observer to deduce a risk of bias.

Held, dismissing the appeal, that no objection could be raised to M's representation of G. A party to proceedings could not rely on the Bar Code of Conduct when objecting to an advocate as the content and enforcement of the code were not a matter for the court. Moreover, given the difference in the roles of an advocate and a judge, the test for determining the impartiality of a tribunal did not apply to counsel, *Director General of Fair Trading v. Proprietary Association of Great Britain* [2001] 1 W.L.R. 700, [2001] C.L.Y. 14 distinguished. There remained an inherent power to prevent abuse of the judicial process and an advocate, as an officer of the court, had to ensure that any procedural irregularity was brought to the court's attention. It was well established that an advocate who held confidential information was liable to be restrained from acting for another party but, beyond such circumstances, the court should only interfere in exceptional cases where there was a real risk that the advocate's participation would lead to the court's order being set aside on appeal.

SKJEVESLAND v. GEVERAN TRADING CO LTD (NO.2); *sub nom.* GEVERAN TRADING CO LTD v. SKJEVESLAND (NO.2), [2002] EWCA Civ 1567, [2003] 1 W.L.R. 912, Arden, L.J., CA.

3101. Barristers—Queens Counsel—appointments—fees

APPOINTMENT OF QUEEN'S COUNSEL FEES ORDER 2002, SI 2002 2037; made under the Access to Justice Act 1999 s.45. In force: August 27, 2002; £1.50.

This Order, which revokes the Appointment of Queen's Counsel Fees Order 1999 (SI 1999 2138), increases the fee payable by a person who wishes to apply to the Lord Chancellor to be recommended for appointment as Queen's Counsel in England and Wales to £720.

3102. Foreign lawyers—right to peaceful enjoyment of possessions—law preventing claiming of costs awarded by court

See HUMAN RIGHTS: Ambruosi v. Italy (31227/96). §2507

3103. Law society—intervention—right to peaceful enjoyment of possessions—manner of intervention

[Solicitors Act 1974 Sch.1 Part II para.6, Part II para.9; Human Rights Act 1998 Sch.1 Part II Art.1.]

H, a solicitor, appealed against a summary judgment ordered in favour of L, the Law Society, and the refusal of H's application to have a notice of intervention set aside. L had made an emergency decision to intervene in H's practice and had exercised powers pursuant to the Solicitors Act 1974 Sch.1 Part II para.6 and para.9 to vest practice monies in L and to require H to deliver practice documents to L's agent. The intervention had followed allegations which had raised a reasonable suspicion of dishonesty in relation to H's operation of the Client Account and his involvement with moneylenders which had led him to make a potentially fraudulent misuse of the Solicitors Compensation Fund. H contended that the intervention had infringed his right to peaceful enjoyment of his possessions, pursuant to the Human Rights Act 1998 Sch.1 Part II Art.1. H contended that the statutory power of intervention was not justified in any circumstances because intervention was disproportionate as it destroyed solicitors' practices, goodwill, and the recoverability of work in progress and left a solicitor without recourse. H submitted that there were alternative procedures which were more balanced and reasonable.

Held, allowing the appeal, that it could not be concluded on the evidence that there was no realistic prospect of H establishing an infringement of his human rights. A full analysis of H's practice, assets and liabilities was required to determine whether his rights had been infringed. In balancing an individual's rights against the rights of the public and the State interest in the maintenance of solicitors' conduct to the highest professional standards of integrity, the power of intervention was a necessary power and was not of itself contrary to the Human Rights Act 1998. However, interventions usually destroyed practices. The use of the power could infringe human rights and was a question of fact and degree in each case. Even where an intervention was justified, it was appropriate to consider what manner of intervention was necessary. In the instant case the additional use of receivership ought to have been considered.

HOLDER v. LAW SOCIETY, [2002] EWHC 1559, *The Times*, September 9, 2002, Peter Smith, J., Ch D.

3104. Law Society—intervention powers—recovery of outstanding fees

[Solicitors Act 1974 Sch.1 Part II, Part II para.6(1).]

D, a solicitor in whose practice the Law Society had intervened, applied for the determination of various issues relating to the provisions of the Solicitors Act 1974 Sch.1 Part II. The Society had intervened on the ground of suspected knowing and dishonest involvement in bank instruments fraud and money laundering. D sought the determination of six questions, including (1) whether the Law Society's resolution to exercise its intervention powers under the Act in relation to his practice vested in the Society monies paid or payable for professional services after the date of the resolution; (2) whether para.6(1) of Sch.1 Part II of the Act vested in the Society the right to receive or recover practice monies and, or alternatively, professional fees paid or payable after the date of the resolution; (3) whether para.6(1) imposed an obligation on the Society to recover practice monies and, or alternatively, professional fees payable after the date of the resolution, and (4) in the absence of a duty to recover outstanding fees, the entitlement of the solicitor.

Held, determining the issues, that (1) para.6(1) of Sch.1 Part II of the Act applied to monies held at the date of the resolution and for the full subsequent period while the resolution remained in force; (2) the right to recover sums due to the solicitor from former clients remained vested in the solicitor alone; the Society did not have the right to recover sums due. The solicitor alone could bring proceedings to recover a debt. However, any debt recovered would automatically vest in the Society; (3) as there was no right to recover outstanding fees, the Society was not under a duty to seek to recover such fees, and (4) the solicitor was not entitled to unsupervised access to confiscated files in order to assist in the recovery of fees. The Society's policy of supervised access reflected a fair and reasonable balance in accordance with the Society's public law duties. Where fees had been recovered, the solicitor had no right to payment of disbursements in the absence of an agreement with the Society.

DOOLEY v. LAW SOCIETY *The Times*, January 16, 2002, Lightman, J., Ch D.

3105. Legal representation–prisoners–Italian avvocato denied access to client prisoner–right to fair trial

See HUMAN RIGHTS: R. (on the application of Van Hoogstraten) v. Governor of Belmarsh Prison. §2448

3106. Practising certificates–solicitors–fees

ACCESS TO JUSTICE ACT 1999 (SOLICITORS' PRACTISING CERTIFICATES) ORDER 2002, SI 2002 3235; made under the Access to Justice Act 1999 s.47. In force: December 19, 2002; £1.50.

This Order amends the Solicitors Act 1974, which sets out the purposes for which the Law Society may apply fees received from the issue of practising certificates, to allow the Law Society to apply the fees for the purposes of the regulation, accreditation, education and training of solicitors and those wishing to become solicitors and for the other purposes set out in this Order.

3107. Solicitors–accounts–disciplinary proceedings–statutory demands–alleged negligence on part of investigating accountant–counterclaims

[Solicitors Act 1974.]

M, a solicitor, appealed against the dismissal of his application to set aside a statutory demand served on him by the Law Society for the costs of its investigations. M had been investigated by an accountant appointed by the Law Society under the Solicitors' Accounts Rules 1991 para.27 to inspect his books of accounts. The accountant had concluded that, although M had not been dishonest, there was a shortage in the client account. The compliance and supervision committee of the Office for the Supervision of Solicitors had subsequently intervened in M's practice and the practice's money was vested with the Law Society on trust, and M's practising certificate was suspended. M did not exercise his right to challenge the intervention within the time limits. A hearing of the Solicitors' Disciplinary Tribunal later found that M had allowed his accounts to fall into disarray and had used clients' funds for the wrong purposes. M was suspended and ordered to pay the costs of the investigation. M applied to have the statutory demand set aside, contending that he had a triable counterclaim for damages because the investigation had been carried out negligently, and that, had it been carried out competently, there would have been no intervention in his practice and he would have continued to receive a profit.

Held, dismissing the appeal, that M's rights of appeal in relation to the conduct of the investigation into his accounts prior to the Law Society's intervention, were confined to the High Court under the Solicitors Act 1974. The investigation by the accountant was part of the disciplinary process laid down by the 1974 Act, and a private law action could not intrude into the public field of solicitors' disciplinary processes. M could not identify any loss arising from the alleged negligence of the investigation, save for that which resulted from the intervention itself, and he could not claim those losses given that the allegations had been established. There was a distinction between those actions brought against a body undertaking a public duty where there was no statutory remedy for an aggrieved party, and situations such as the instant case, where Parliament had given a specific remedy to aggrieved persons.

MILLER v. LAW SOCIETY, [2002] EWHC 1453, [2002] 4 All E.R. 312, Geoffrey Vos Q.C., Ch D.

3108. Solicitors—conflict of interest—previous role in proceedings—disclosure of confidential material

B sought an interlocutory injunction to restrain D, a firm of solicitors, from continuing to act for the defendants in a Chancery action in which he was the claimant. B was one of the two originators of the Eden Project, an exhibition centre opened in celebration of the millennium, but he had been dismissed from the project and in the Chancery action sought monies due. B argued that D had previously acted for him personally, and that there was therefore a risk that confidential information would be imparted to the defendants. D accepted that it had formerly acted for B but disputed B's view of the nature of the retainer, arguing that their advice had only related to the establishment of the trust. D contended that B's delay in applying for injunctive relief was a bar to his claim.

Held, granting the injunction, that there was an arguable case that confidential information existed which was at risk of being disclosed, *Bolkiah v. KPMG* [1999] 2 A.C. 222, [1999] C.L.Y. 1 applied. Damages would not be an adequate remedy. Any delay in bringing the case was explicable when the chronology was examined.

BALL v. DRUCES & ATTLEE (A FIRM) [2002] P.N.L.R. 23, Burton, J., QBD.

3109. Solicitors—costs—assessment—entitlement to taxation of costs of Law Society's agent in intervention

[Solicitors Act 1974 s.70(1), s.71, Sch.1 Part II para.13.]

The Law Society appealed against a decision that P, a solicitor in whose practice it had intervened, was entitled under the Solicitors Act 1974 s.71 to a detailed assessment of bills submitted by the solicitor who had been appointed to act as the Society's agent in the intervention. The Law Society had sought payment of the relevant bills from P under Sch.1 Part II para.13 of the Act.

Held, dismissing the appeal, that the bills submitted by the Law Society's agent were "solicitor's bills" within the meaning of s.70(1) of the Act. The work carried out by the agent was business connected with the profession of a solicitor. What was more, he had been employed because he was a solicitor and would not have been appointed had he not been a solicitor. In addition, s.71 recognised that the person chargeable with the bill might not ultimately be liable to pay the costs sought; the aim of s.71 was to confer on a person with a secondary liability for those costs a right equivalent to that enjoyed by the person who was primarily liable, and that right was not overriden or excluded by Sch.1 Part II para.13.

PINE v. LAW SOCIETY (NO.2), [2002] EWCA Civ 175, [2002] 1 W.L.R. 2189, Sir Andrew Morritt V.C., CA.

3110. Solicitors—fees—adequacy of information provided to client in bill

[Solicitors Act 1974 s.69.]

G appealed against the refusal of his application to strike out proceedings commenced by his former solicitors, R, in respect of unpaid fees. G was a solicitor who had retained R in connection with a partnership dispute. When G failed to pay the sum of £127,935 which was owed to R by way of professional fees, R initiated proceedings which G defended on the basis that he had a claim for professional negligence by way of set off. Prior to trial, G applied to strike out the proceedings on the basis that no reasonable cause of action had been disclosed. G contended that R was not entitled to sue on the basis of the bills submitted since they did not contain sufficient information as required by the Solicitors Act 1974 s.69.

Held, dismissing the appeal, that the interests of justice required the court to strike the appropriate balance between the right of an individual client to challenge the contents of a bill by way of taxation and the right of a solicitor to obtain monies owed to him without being defeated by an opportunistic and technical challenge. In order to satisfy the requirements of s.69(2) and establish that the bill was not a bill "bona fide complying with the Act", it was necessary for a client to establish (1) that there was insufficient narrative in the bill such as to identify what he was being charged for, and (2) that he did not have sufficient other information in his possession from other documents or from what he had been told in order reasonably to take advice as to whether to seek taxation. On the facts of the instant case it was clear that the bill identified the relevant matter and the period over which the work had been carried out and accordingly the requirements of the Act were satisfied, *Cook v. Gillard* (1852) 1 El. & Bl. 26 and *Eversheds v. Osman* [2000] 1 Costs L.R. 54, [2000] C.L.Y. 4027 applied and *Haigh v. Ousey* (1857) 7 El. & Bl. 578, *Solicitor (Taxation of Costs), Re* [1955] 2 Q.B. 252, [1955] C.L.Y. 2625, *A Solicitor, Re* (Unreported, October 10, 1994), *Ring Sights Holding Co Ltd v. Graham* (Unreported, October 8, 2001) and *Pender, Re* (1847) 10 Beav. 390 considered.

RALPH HUME GARRY (A FIRM) v. GWILLIM, [2002] EWCA Civ 1500, [2003] 1 W.L.R. 510, Ward, L.J., CA.

3111. **Solicitors–legal professional privilege–breach of confidence–solicitor previously acting for defendants' group of companies**

Y owned a Guernsey registered company, G, which in turn owned a UK company, U. In 1998, U went into administrative receivership and the receivers sold U's assets, including patents and know how, to N who sold them on to ST. ST and N subsequently made claims against U and Y relating to the ownership of the patents and know how and included a claim for breach of confidence against B, a firm of solicitors that had acted for Y, G and U. ST and N objected to B accepting instructions from Y on the ground that there was a conflict of interest. The court gave guidance so that B could consider its position.

Held, giving judgment, that (1) ST and N could claim legal professional privilege against Y and G on the basis of the title to property which passed under the asset sale agreement; (2) a duty of confidence could be imposed after information was communicated as long as the material concerned had not been published and the obligation was drawn to the attention of the person to whom it had been confided, and (3) any information that was not privileged was liable to be treated as confidential and could not be used.

SURFACE TECHNOLOGY PLC v. YOUNG [2002] F.S.R. 25, Pumfrey, J., Ch D.

3112. **Solicitors–retainers–solicitor continuing to act for company following death of majority shareholder–authority to act surviving death**

Held, allowing the appeal, that solicitors, H, had been retained to conduct litigation by R, the sole director and majority shareholder of a client company, under a retainer that was not subject to any limitation. The facts showed that R wanted the matter to go to trial and H's authority to act in the proceedings survived R's death, even though there was no one who could give instructions on behalf of the company.

DONSLAND LTD v. VAN HOOGSTRATEN; *sub nom.* HEALYS v. VAN HOOGSTRATEN, [2002] EWCA Civ 253, [2002] P.N.L.R. 26, Tuckey, L.J., CA.

3113. **Solicitors–Solicitors** **Indemnity** **Fund–conveyancing** **transaction–dishonesty**

M, a mortgage lender, brought a claim against N, a solicitor, for damages in respect of loss suffered by M upon a sale of a property as mortgagee in possession. N brought a Part 20 claim against the Solicitors Indemnity Fund, SIF, who denied liability on the ground that N's conduct as the solicitor acting on the purchase of the property had been fraudulent, such conduct being excluded from indemnity cover by the Solicitors Indemnity Fund Rules 1993 r.14 (f). Inter alia, SIF alleged that N had (1) altered the date for exchange of contracts on the report on title; (2) failed to seek an interview with and written instructions from the purchaser; (3) known of the existence of tenancies in the property when the purchase was apparently being conducted on the basis of vacant possession, and (4) failed to advise M of a sub sale arrangement without exchange of contracts revealing a price differential of some £165,000, leading to the conclusion that N had wilfully shut her eyes to the obvious or wilfully and recklessly failed to make enquiries which an honest and reasonable solicitor would have made because she did not want to know what the answer might be.

Held, giving judgment for N on the Part 20 claim, that N had not been dishonest in failing to make further enquiries about the transaction or in failing to appreciate that it might have been a dishonest transaction. N's secretary had informed M that the report on title had been completed incorrectly in specifying that contracts had been exchanged on a particular date. Although N had been aware of the price differential between what the vendor had paid and what her client, the purchaser, had agreed to pay for the property, she would have been satisfied, had she addressed her mind to it, that this was explained by the fact that the sale to the vendor was subject to tenancies whereas the sale to her client was with vacant possession. Account had to be taken of the state of knowledge within the solicitors' profession at the time of the transaction; the Law Society's "Green Card" warning on mortgage fraud had not been issued in 1990 when the transaction had been completed. Having regard to N's limited experience of conveyancing and applying an objective test and standard, her conduct had not been dishonest.

MORTGAGE EXPRESS LTD v. S NEWMAN & CO (NO.3) [2001] Lloyd's Rep. P.N. 669, Etherton, J., Ch D.

3114. **Solicitors–undertakings–change** **of** **circumstances–enforcement** **of** **undertaking**

S applied for summary enforcement of a solicitor's undertaking given by H relating to the apportionment of the proceeds of a property sale. M and her husband held a beneficial interest in their matrimonial home. The trustees decided to sell the property and, as the couple had been undergoing marital difficulties, they instructed separate firms of solicitors to act for them in relation to the sale. In the course of correspondence, the husband's solicitors, H, undertook to pay £275,000 from the proceeds to a third party bank so as to discharge a second mortgage on the property. H agreed that, should the bank demand a higher settlement figure, the excess would be charged against the husband's half share of the final net proceeds. In the event, the second mortgage was only redeemed after the payment of a sum far in excess of the original estimate and consequently, S was deprived of the whole of the share of the balance she had expected to receive upon completion. H maintained that (1) they had rid themselves of liability in respect of the undertaking as they had informed S of the change in circumstances at the earliest opportunity, and (2) the relief claimed was inappropriate in the circumstances.

Held, granting the application for summary enforcement, that (1) there was no general principle under which a solicitor could rid himself of liability for an undertaking by notifying the recipient of a change of circumstances, *Citadel Management Inc v. Equal Ltd* [1999] 1 F.L.R. 21 considered. In any event, in the instant case the court was not satisfied that the circumstances outlined in the notification letter could be classified as a change of circumstances or that the communication had been made at the earliest possible opportunity, and (2) as it was for H to satisfy themselves that they could safely give the undertaking that had been sought and as there was no "real scope for genuine misunderstanding" in the interpretation of the correspondence, it was appropriate for the court to exercise its residual discretion to grant compensation, *Udall (t/a Udall Sheet Metal & Co) v. Capri Lighting Ltd* [1988] Q.B. 907, [1987] C.L.Y. 3562 applied.

HOLE & PUGSLEY v. SUMPTION [2002] Lloyd's Rep. P.N. 419, Hart, J., Ch D.

3115. Solicitors Disciplinary Tribunal–appeals–appropriate respondent to appeal against Tribunal's finding of no case to answer

[Solicitors Act 1974 s.49(2); Civil Procedure Rules 1998 (SI 1998 3132) Sch.1 RSC Ord.106 r.12, r.13, r.15, Part 52.]

L appealed against a finding of the Solicitors Disciplinary Tribunal that the solicitor, M, who had been the subject of L's complaint had no case to answer. The court was required to determine whether the proper respondent to an appeal under Solicitors Act 1974 s.49(2) was the Tribunal, the Law Society or the solicitor complained about.

Held, dismissing the appeal, that upon consideration of s.49(2) of the 1974 Act, the Civil Procedure Rules 1998 Sch.1 RSC Ord.106 r.12, r.13 and r.15 and Part 52 PD 52 para.17.5 of the Rules the proper parties to such an appeal were the appellant and the solicitor complained about. There was a further requirement that the Tribunal and the Law Society should be notified.

LUCAS v. MILLMAN, [2002] EWHC 2470, [2003] 1 W.L.R. 271, Kennedy, L.J., QBD (Admin Ct).

3116. Solicitors Disciplinary Tribunal–costs–apportionment–culpability of partner

S appealed against a decision of the Solicitors Disciplinary Tribunal that he pay 80 per cent of the costs incurred by the Law Society in bringing charges against him. S had pleaded guilty to the charges of unreasonable delay in the conduct of professional business, failing to to keep proper accounts, and drawing money out of client accounts for his own use and the use of other clients. S submitted that, because of the culpability of his former partner, he should not have been ordered to pay such a large proportion of the costs, notwithstanding the fact that the partner had not been brought before the tribunal.

Held, dismissing the appeal, that where, as in the case of S, one partner in a firm was subject to disciplinary proceedings but another partner might also have been at fault, the tribunal was entitled to make the single partner charged pay all the costs of the proceedings.

SINGH (JUSVINDER) v. LAW SOCIETY, [2001] EWHC Admin 1106, *The Times*, January 21, 2002, Kennedy, L.J., QBD (Admin Ct).

3117. Solicitors disciplinary tribunal–right to fair trial–absence of legal representation

[Human Rights Act 1998 Sch.1 Part I Art.6.]

P, a solicitor, appealed against a decision (Daily Telegraph, December 5, 2000) that the absence of legal representation at a hearing before the Solicitors' Disciplinary Tribunal had not deprived him of a fair hearing contrary to the Human Rights Act 1998 Sch.1 Part I Art.6. P, whose practising certificate had been suspended prior to the disciplinary proceedings, had not been present or represented before the tribunal. In a letter faxed to the tribunal prior to the hearing he had explained that he could not afford the expenses involved in travelling to London. The High Court, in finding that the absence of legal representation had not rendered the proceedings unfair, had observed that the tribunal hearing had not been complex and that since P had not shown any difficulty in understanding the issues he could have represented himself. P submitted that the nature of the allegations before the tribunal had been such that the absence of legal representation had resulted in obvious unfairness.

Held, dismissing the appeal, that having regard to the nature of the allegations and to the fact that the procedure had not been complex, the tribunal hearing had not been rendered unfair due to the absence of legal representation. For the purposes of Art.6(1), proceedings would be unfair only in such exceptional circumstances as where the absence of representation made the assertion of a civil claim practically impossible or where there would be obvious unfairness if a party was not represented, *Airey v. Ireland (No.1) (A/32)* (1979-80) 2 E.H.R.R. 305 applied. Whilst in certain circumstances the fact that a party was unrepresented at a hearing would constitute a breach of Art.6, it would depend on the facts of each case. In the instant case, the procedure was not complex and P could have represented himself. Further, the seriousness of the consequences for P did not give rise to any unfairness.

PINE v. LAW SOCIETY (NO.1); *sub nom.* SOLICITOR (CO/1385/2000), *Re*, [2001] EWCA Civ 1574, [2002] U.K.H.R.R. 81, Sir Andrew Morritt V.C., CA.

3118. **Books**

Abrahamson, Debbie–Bar Manual: Professional Conduct 2002/2003. Blackstone Bar Manual. Paperback: £21.99. ISBN 0-19-925505-9. Oxford University Press.

Alschuler, Albert W.–Law Without Values-The Life, Work, and Legacy of Justice Holmes. Paperback: £11.50. ISBN 0-226-01521-1. University of Chicago Press.

Anderson, Ellen Mary–Judging Bertha Wilson-Law As Large As Life. Osgoode Society for Canadian Legal History. Hardback: £32.00. ISBN 0-8020-3648-1. University of Toronto Press Inc.

Blake, Susan–Bar Manual: Remedies 2002/2003. Blackstone Bar Manual. Paperback: £21.99. ISBN 0-19-925506-7. Oxford University Press.

Blakemore, Timothy; Greene, Brendan–Law for Legal Executives: Part One Year One. 6th Ed. Paperback: £21.99. ISBN 0-19-925526-1. Oxford University Press.

Bobb-Semple, Colin; Inns of Court School of Law–Bar Manual: Criminal Litigation and Sentencing 2002/2003. Blackstone Bar Manual. Paperback: £21.99. ISBN 0-19-925499-0. Oxford University Press.

Brockman, Joan–Gender in the Legal Profession-Fitting or Breaking the Mould. Paperback: £25.50. ISBN 0-7748-0835-7. University of British Columbia Press.

Cain, George H.–Law Partnership Revisited. Hardback: £46.95. ISBN 1-59031-032-2. American Bar Association.

Camp, Peter–Solicitors and Financial Services-A Compliance Handbook. 3rd Ed. Paperback: £69.95. ISBN 1-85328-805-5. Law Society Publications.

Carman, Dominic–No Ordinary Man. Paperback: £7.99. ISBN 0-340-82099-3. Coronet.

Chapman, Michael D.–Waterlow's Solicitors' & Barristers' Directory: 2002. Hardback: £61.95. ISBN 1-85783-982-X. Waterlow Professional Publishing.

Cheyne, Ann–Legal Secretary's Guide. Paperback: £25.99. ISBN 0-19-925422-2. Oxford University Press.

Congressional Quarterly's Judicial Staff Directory: December 2001/Winter. 19th Ed. Paperback: £167.00. ISBN 0-87289-193-3. CQ Press.

Dershowitz, Alan–Letters to a Young Lawyer. The Art of Mentoring Series. Hardback: £15.99. ISBN 0-465-01631-6. Basic Books.

Duncan, Nigel–Bar Manual: Case Preparation 2002/2003. Blackstone Bar Manual. Paperback: £21.99. ISBN 0-19-925497-4. Oxford University Press.

Echaore-McDavid, Susan–Career Opportunities in Law and the Legal Industry. Career Opportunities Series. Hardback: £38.50. ISBN 0-8160-4552-6. Paperback: £14.95. ISBN 0-8160-4553-4. Facts on File Inc.

Edwards, R.–Introduction to Paralegal Studies and the Law. Paperback: £38.00. ISBN 0-7668-3589-8. Delmar.

Emmet, David–Bar Manual: Drafting 2002/2003. Blackstone Bar Manual. Paperback: £21.99. ISBN 0-19-925501-6. Oxford University Press.

Fleming, Macklin–Lawyers, Money, and Success-The Consequences of Dollar Obsession. Paperback: £20.95. ISBN 1-56720-595-X. Quorum Books.

Gray, Barry; Jackson, Robin—Advocacy and Learning Difficulties. Paperback: £24.95. ISBN 1-85302-942-4. Jessica Kingsley Publishers.

Griffiths-Baker, Janine—Serving Two Masters. Onati International Series in Law and Society. Hardback: £30.00. ISBN 1-84113-229-2. Hart Publishing.

Harris, Phil—Harris: An Introduction to Law. 6th Ed. Law in Context. Paperback: £15.95. ISBN 0-406-94672-8. Butterworths Law.

Hobsons Guide to Careers in Law: 2003. Hobsons Casebooks. Paperback: £9.99. ISBN 1-86017-946-0. Hobsons plc.

Hughesdon, John; Russell, Neville—Butterworths Solicitors Accounts and Financial Management. Looseleaf/ring bound: £90.00. ISBN 0-406-05370-7. Butterworths Tolley.

Kay, D.—Bar Manual: Solicitors Accounts/practice Guide 2002/2003. 6th Ed. Blackstone Bar Manual. Paperback: £22.99. ISBN 0-19-925508-3. Oxford University Press.

Kerr, Michael—As Far As I Remember. Hardback: £22.50. ISBN 1-901362-87-6. Hart Publishing.

Koch, Hugh—Interface Between Medical Expert and Lawyer. Spiral/comb bound: £165.00. ISBN 1-84311-028-8. LLP Professional Publishing.

Law Society's Directory of Solicitors and Barristers 2002-2003. 11th Ed. Hardback: £94.95. ISBN 1-85328-811-X. Law Society Publications.

MacDowell, Laurel Sefton—Renegade Lawyer. Osgoode Society for Canadian Legal History. Hardback: £42.00. ISBN 0-8020-3513-2. University of Toronto Press Inc.

McPeake, Robert—Bar Manual: Advocacy 2002/2003. Blackstone Bar Manual. Paperback: £21.99. ISBN 0-19-925496-6. Oxford University Press.

Medical Records for Lawyers. Paperback: £42.00. ISBN 1-85811-259-1. EMIS Professional Publishing.

Morrish, Peter; McLean, Ian; Selwood, David—Crown Court Index: 2002. Hardback: £75.00. ISBN 0-421-76820-7. Sweet & Maxwell.

Murray, Len—Pleader-An Autobiography. Hardback: £15.99. ISBN 1-84018-642-9. Mainstream Publishing.

Postgraduate Guide: Business, Economics and Law: Vol 1. 2003. Paperback: £6.50. ISBN 1-86017-955-X. Hobsons plc.

Pound, R.W.—History of Stikeman Elliott. Hardback: £37.90. ISBN 0-7735-2411-8. McGill-Queen's University Press.

Rowley, Graham; Stevenson, Janet; Greene, Brendan; Blakemore, Timothy—Law for Legal Executives: Part One Year Two. 6th Ed. Paperback: £21.99. ISBN 0-19-925527-X. Oxford University Press.

Ruiter, Dick W.P.—Legal Institutions. Law and Philosophy Library, 55. Hardback: £56.00. ISBN 1-4020-0186-X. Kluwer Academic Publishers.

Sinclair, William—Drafting. Hardback: £19.95. ISBN 0-414-01284-4. W. Green & Son.

Smith, Rosemary S.—Bar Manual: Conference Skills 2002/2003. Blackstone Bar Manual. Paperback: £21.99. ISBN 0-19-925500-8. Oxford University Press.

Solicitors' Professional Handbook 2002. A Parliament House Book. Paperback: £24.00. ISBN 0-414-01499-5. W. Green & Son.

Taylor, Margot—Bar Manual: Negotiation 2002/2003. Blackstone Bar Manual. Paperback: £21.99. ISBN 0-19-925503-2. Oxford University Press.

The Lawyer's Remembrancer 2003. Paperback: £36.00. ISBN 0-406-95927-7. Butterworths Law.

Underwood, Kerry—No Win, No Fee, No Worries! (New Ed.). Paperback: £38.00. ISBN 1-858-11216-8. EMIS Professional Publishing.

Webb, Julian—LPC Lawyer Skills 2002/2003. 9th Ed. Blackstone Bar Manual. Paperback: £22.99. ISBN 0-19-925509-1. Oxford University Press.

Wolfgarten, Alison—Bar Manual: Opinion Writing 2002/2003. Blackstone Bar Manual. Paperback: £21.99. ISBN 0-19-925504-0. Oxford University Press.

LEGAL SYSTEMS

3119. Books

Anderson, David; Demetriou, Marie—References to the European Court. 2nd Ed. Litigation Library. Hardback: £160.00. ISBN 0-421-75350-1. Sweet & Maxwell.

Bahaa Ali El-Dean—Privatisation and the Creation of a Market Based Legal System. Social, Economic and Political Studies of the Middle East and Asia, 82. Hardback. ISBN 90-04-12580-9. Brill.

Bailey, Stephen; Gunn, Michael—Smith, Bailey and Gunn on the Modern English Legal System. Paperback: £14.95. ISBN 0-421-75080-4. Sweet & Maxwell International Student Editions.

Bailey, Stephen; Gunn, Michael—Smith, Bailey and Gunn on the Modern English Legal System. 4th Ed. Paperback: £30.00. ISBN 0-421-74130-9. Sweet & Maxwell.

Basedow, Jurgen—European Private Law/Droit Prive Europeen/Europaisches Privatrecht/Diritto Privato Europeo-Sources/quellen/fonti, III. Hardback: £164.00. ISBN 90-411-1329-0. Kluwer Law International.

Berg, Alan—Common Law in Practice: Understanding Common Problems. ISBN 1-84311-001-6. LLP Professional Publishing.

Binder, Sarah—Stalemate-Causes and Consequences of Legislative Gridlock. Hardback: £29.25. ISBN 0-8157-0910-2. Paperback: £12.50. ISBN 0-8157-0911-0. The Brookings Institution.

Birks, Peter—English Private Law-Main Volumes and First Cumulative Supplement (Updated Ed). Oxford English Law. Hardback: £175.00. ISBN 0-19-925576-8. Oxford University Press.

Birks, Peter—English Private Law: First Cumulative Supplement. English Private Law Series. Paperback: £30.00. ISBN 0-19-924754-4. Oxford University Press.

Breen, P.J.—Round Hall's Consolidated Superior Court Rules. Hardback. ISBN 1-85800-303-2. Round Hall Ltd.

Burton, Michael—Civil Appeals. Looseleaf release (unbound): £250.00. ISBN 1-858-11284-2. Spiral/comb bound: £275.00. ISBN 1-858-11284-2. EMIS Professional Publishing.

Collin, P.H.—Pocket German Law Dictionary-English-German/German-English. Paperback: £6.95. ISBN 1-903856-26-4. Peter Collin Publishing.

Collin, P.H.—Pocket Spanish Law Dictionary. Paperback: £6.95. ISBN 1-903856-25-6. Peter Collin Publishing.

Congressional Quarterly's Congressional Staff Directory: March 2002/Spring. 63rd Ed. Paperback: £167.00. ISBN 0-87289-194-1. CQ Press.

Cossman, Brenda; Fudge, Judy—Privatization, Law, and the Challenge of Feminism. Hardback: £48.00. ISBN 0-8020-3699-6. Paperback: £22.50. ISBN 0-8020-8509-1. University of Toronto Press Inc.

Cotterill, Janet—Language in the Legal Process. Hardback: £50.00. ISBN 0-333-96902-2. Macmillan.

Darbyshire, Penny—Eddey and Darbyshire on the English Legal System. 7th Ed. Paperback: £14.95. ISBN 0-421-75070-7. Sweet & Maxwell.

Elliott, Catherine; Quinn, Frances—AS Law. Paperback: £19.99. ISBN 0-582-47319-5. Longman.

Elliott, Catherine; Quinn, Francis—English Legal System. 4th Ed. Paperback: £19.99. ISBN 0-582-47313-6. Longman.

English Legal System. 3rd Ed. LawCards Series. Paperback: £6.00. ISBN 1-85941-711-6. Cavendish Publishing Ltd.

Foskett, David—Law and Practice of Compromise. 5th Ed. Litigation Library. Hardback: £145.00. ISBN 0-421-76600-X. Sweet & Maxwell.

Foster, Charles—Tripping and Slipping Cases-a Practitioner's Guide. 3rd Ed. Personal Injury Library. Paperback: £55.00. ISBN 0-421-77850-4. Sweet & Maxwell.

Foster, Nigel; Sule, Satish—German Legal System and Laws. 3rd Ed. Paperback: £29.99. ISBN 0-19-925483-4. Oxford University Press.

Greenhill, John–Work of a Magistrate. 6th Ed. Paperback: £13.95. ISBN 0-7219-0563-3. Shaw & Sons.

Grove, Trevor–Magistrate's Tale. Hardback: £14.99. ISBN 0-7475-6055-2. Bloomsbury.

Guttenplan, D.D.–Holocaust on Trial: History, Justice and the David Irving Libel Case. Paperback (B format): £9.99. ISBN 1-86207-486-0. Granta Books.

Ingman, Terence–English Legal Progress. 9th Ed. Paperback: £19.99. ISBN 0-19-925495-8. Oxford University Press.

Jaconelli, Joseph–Open Justice: Critique of the Public Trial. Hardback: £50.00. ISBN 0-19-825258-7. Oxford University Press.

Komesar, Neil–Law's Limits. Hardback: £45.00. ISBN 0-521-80629-1. Cambridge University Press.

Komesar, Neil–Law's Limits: The Role of Courts, the Rule of Law, and the Supply and Demand of Rights. Hardback: £45.00. ISBN 0-521-80629-1. Cambridge University Press.

Koo, John–English Legal System. 2nd Ed. 150 Leading Cases. Paperback: £11.95. ISBN 1-85836-451-5. Old Bailey Press.

Krishnan, Vickneswaren–English Legal System. 2nd Ed. Revision Workbook. Paperback: £9.95. ISBN 1-85836-426-4. Old Bailey Press.

Kritzer, Herbert M.–Legal Systems of the World-A Political, Social, and Cultural Encyclopedia. Hardback: £265.50. ISBN 1-57607-231-2. ABC CLIO (Reference Books).

Lush, Master Denzil–Heywood and Massey: Court of Protection Practice. 13th Ed. Looseleaf/ring bound: £195.00. ISBN 0-421-82680-0. Sweet & Maxwell.

Mundy, Martha–Law and Anthropology. International Library of Essays in Law and Legal Theory: Second Series. Hardback: £115.00. ISBN 0-7546-2082-4. Dartmouth.

Murphy–Counting Nine Analyzing the Supreme Court. Paperback: £33.99. ISBN 0-205-29008-6. Allyn & Bacon.

Naffine, Ngaire–Gender and Justice. International Library of Essays in Law and Legal Theory: Second Series. Hardback: £110.00. ISBN 0-7546-2087-5. Dartmouth.

Osin, Paul–Point of Law: PACE Explained. The Point of Law. Paperback: £25.00. ISBN 0-11-702836-3. The Stationery Office Books.

Phillips, Alfred–Lawyer's Language-The Distinctiveness of Legal Language. Hardback: £50.00. ISBN 0-7007-1688-2. RoutledgeCurzon.

Powers, Stephen P.; Rothman, Stanley–The Least Dangerous Branch? Hardback: £58.50. ISBN 0-275-97536-3. Praeger Publishers.

Riesenfeld, Stefan A.; Pakter, Walter J.–Casebook on Comparative Law. Hardback: £68.99. ISBN 1-57105-220-8. Transnational Publishers, Inc.

Rose, William–Pleading Without Tears-A Guide to Legal Drafting Under the Civil Procedure Rules. 6th Ed. Paperback: £19.95. ISBN 0-19-925438-9. Oxford University Press.

Sarat, A.; Ewick, P.–Studies in Law, Politics and Society: Vol 26. Studies in Law, Politics and Society, Vol 26. Hardback. ISBN 0-7623-0894-X. JAI Press.

Short, Martin–Secrets of the Jury Room. Paperback. ISBN 0-00-638776-4. HarperCollins.

Stevens, Robert–English Judges-Their Role in the Changing Constitution. Hardback: £22.50. ISBN 1-84113-226-8. Hart Publishing.

Tate, C. Neal–Comparative Judicial Systems. Hardback: £117.00. ISBN 1-56802-684-6. CQ Press.

Van Caenegem, R.C.–Unity and Diversity: European Law in the Past and the Future. Paperback: £14.95. ISBN 0-521-80938-X. Paperback: £14.95. ISBN 0-521-00648-1. Cambridge University Press.

Watkins, Michael; Gordon, Winston–Sentence of the Court. Revised 3rd Ed. Paperback: £17.00. ISBN 1-904380-01-8. Waterside Press.

Watson, Brian–Litigation Liabilities. Hardback: £105.00. ISBN 1-902558-52-9. Palladian Law Publishing Ltd.

Wheeler, John–English Legal System. Frameworks Series. Paperback: £21.99. ISBN 0-582-42405-4. Longman.

Woolf, Lord–Zamir and Woolf: The Declaratory Judgement. 3rd Ed. Litigation
Library. Hardback: £130.00. ISBN 0-421-71710-6. Sweet & Maxwell.
Youngs, Raymond–Sourcebook on German Law. 2nd Ed. SOURCEBOOK SERIES.
Paperback: £35.95. ISBN 1-85941-678-0. Cavendish Publishing Ltd.

LICENSING

3120. Alcohol–licensed premises–permitted hours–Golden Jubilee

REGULATORY REFORM (GOLDEN JUBILEE LICENSING) ORDER 2002, SI
2002 1062; made under the Regulatory Reform Act 2001 s.1. In force: March
29, 2002; £1.75.

This Order reforms the law relating to licensing hours which has the effect of
imposing burdens on people carrying out certain activities with a view to
reducing those burdens on the occasion of Her Majesty's Golden Jubilee. It does
so by amending provisions in the Regulatory Reform (Special Occasions
Licensing) Order 2001 (SI 2001 3937) to allow the sale of intoxicating liquor in
licensed premises other than off-licences, in registered clubs and in licensed
canteens in the period between what would otherwise be the end of the
permitted hours on June 3, 2002 and 1.00 am on June 4, 2002.

3121. Alcohol–licensed premises–special hours licences

REGULATORY REFORM (SPECIAL OCCASIONS LICENSING) ORDER 2002, SI
2002 3205; made under the Regulatory Reform Act 2001 s.1. In force: December
21, 2002; £1.75.

This Order, which amends the London Government Act 1963, the Local
Government (Miscellaneous Provisions) Act 1982 and the Regulatory Reform
(Special Occasions Licensing) Order 2001 (SI 2001 3937), reforms the law
relating to licensing hours which has the effect of imposing burdens on people
carrying out certain activities with a view to reducing those burdens in respect of
New Year's Eve. It allows allow the sale of intoxicating liquor in licensed premises
(other than off-licences), in registered clubs and in licensed canteens in the period
between what would otherwise be the end of the permitted hours on New Year's
Eve and the beginning of permitted hours on the following day. Provision is also
made for reforming the law relating to the licensing of public entertainments, in
particular the licensing of public music and dancing, with a view to reducing the
burdens it imposes on people carrying out certain activities where they take place
at New Year's Eve. It also allows premises in respect of which there are Special
Occasions licensing hours, and in respect of which there is an entertainment
licence in force, to be kept open on New Year's Eve and during the Special
Occasions licensing hours for any purposes authorised by the entertainment
licence beyond the time authorised by the licence itself.

3122. Betting offices–refreshments–removal of restrictions

BETTING, GAMING AND LOTTERIES ACT 1963 (SCHEDULE 4)
(AMENDMENT) ORDER 2002, SI 2002 1930; made under the Betting, Gaming
and Lotteries Act 1963 s.10. In force: August 19, 2002; £1.50.

This Order amends the Betting, Gaming and Lotteries Act 1963 Sch.4 to remove
the restrictions on the form of refreshments, other than alcohol, which may be sold
in a licensed betting office in Great Britain.

3123. Gambling–bingo–charges

GAMING CLUBS (CHARGES) (AMENDMENT) REGULATIONS 2002, SI 2002
1902; made under the Gaming Act 1968 s.14. In force: August 12, 2002; £1.50.

These Regulations, which amend the Gaming Clubs (Hours and Charges)
Regulations 1984 (SI 1984 248) and the Gaming Clubs (Hours and Charges)

(Scotland) Regulations 1984 (SI 1984 470), increase the maximum admission charge to a bingo club from £10 to £20, and increase the maximum participation charge in a game of bingo from £5 to £10.

3124. Gambling–bingo–fees

GAMING (BINGO) ACT (FEES) (AMENDMENT) ORDER 2002, SI 2002 640; made under the Gaming (Bingo) Act 1985 Sch.1 para.5. In force: April 1, 2002; £1.50.

This Order, which revokes the Gaming (Bingo) Act (Fees) (Amendment) Order 2001 (SI 2001 727), amends the Gaming (Bingo) Act (Fees) Order 1986 (SI 1986 833) so as to increase the fee payable to the Gaming Board for Great Britain for the issue of a certificate issued by the Board to an organiser of games of multiple bingo from £150,168 to £167,000. It also increases the fee payable to the Gaming Board for Great Britain for the continuing in force, for a period of three years, of such a certificate from £144,576 to £160,000.

3125. Gambling–bingo–increase of number of games

GAMING CLUBS (MULTIPLE BINGO) (AMENDMENT) REGULATIONS 2002, SI 2002 1901; made under the Gaming (Bingo) Act 1985 s.3. In force: August 12, 2002; £1.50.

These Regulations amend the Gaming Clubs (Multiple Bingo) Regulations 1986 (SI 1986 834) to increase from three to five the number of games of multiple bingo that may be played on any licensed bingo club premises in any period of 24 hours.

3126. Gambling–bingo–increase of prize limit

GAMING (BINGO) ACT (VARIATION OF MONETARY LIMIT) ORDER 2002, SI 2002 1909; made under the Gaming (Bingo) Act 1985 s.2. In force: August 12, 2002; £1.50.

This Order, which revokes the Gaming (Bingo) Act (Variation of Monetary Limit) Order 1998 (SI 1998 2153), provides that the maximum amount to be paid as a prize in respect of a game of multiple bingo shall be £2,000,000 and replaces the limit of £500,000 specified for the purposes of the Gaming (Bingo) Act 1985.

3127. Gambling–bingo and other gaming–deregulation

DEREGULATION (BINGO AND OTHER GAMING) ORDER 2002, SI 2002 460; made under the Deregulation and Contracting Out Act 1994 s.1. In force: March 29, 2002; £1.75.

This Order amends the Gaming Act 1968 by removing the requirement for bingo operators to notify the licensing authority of changes to their charges 14 days in advance. It also makes amendments to allow a licensing authority to direct that jackpot gaming machines may be available on bingo club premises together with "amusements with prizes" gaming machines. In addition, the Order amends the Gaming (Bingo) Act 1985 to allow organisers of "multiple bingo" to offer more than one prize in each of the three possible categories of prize.

3128. Gambling–casino premises–live music and entertainment–removal of restrictions

GAMING CLUBS (LICENSING) (AMENDMENT) REGULATIONS 2002, SI 2002 1910; made under the Gaming Act 1968 s.22, s.51. In force: August 12, 2002; £1.50.

These Regulations amend the Gaming Clubs (Licensing) Regulations 1969 (SI 1969 1110) to remove the requirement that licensing authorities must impose a restriction on casino premises, prohibiting the premises from being used for dancing, or live music or entertainment.

3129. Gambling–gaming clubs–bankers games

GAMING CLUBS (BANKERS' GAMES) (AMENDMENT) REGULATIONS 2002, SI 2002 1130; made under the Gaming Act 1968 s.13, s.15, s.51. In force: May 13, 2002; £2.00.

The Gaming Act 1968 prohibits the playing of bankers' games and games of unequal chance on premises licensed under that Act. However, it also authorises the making of regulations to provide that this prohibition shall not have effect in relation to games specified in the Regulations, if so played as to comply with the Regulations. These Regulations amend the Gaming Clubs (Bankers' Games) Regulations 1994 (SI 1994 2899) to introduce The Big Six, Sic Bo and Three Card Poker as new games, to allow the option of offering fewer wagers in Roulette, to allow two further wagers in Dice, to allow the banker to draw on a "soft" 17 in Blackjack and to allow an optional side bet in Casino Stud Poker.

3130. Gambling–gaming clubs–bankers games

GAMING CLUBS (BANKERS' GAMES) (AMENDMENT) (NO.2) REGULATIONS 2002, SI 2002 1407; made under the Gaming Act 1968 s.13, s.51. In force: June 17, 2002; £1.50.

These Regulations amend the Gaming Clubs (Bankers' Games) Regulations 1994 (SI 1994 2899) to correct a defect introduced by Gaming Clubs (Bankers' Games) (Amendment) Regulations 2002 (SI 2002 1130). It is now provided that in Three Card Poker where a player's hand is out-ranked or equalled by a banker's hand which does not contain a Queen or better, the player's Ante wager will win and his Play wager will be returned to him.

3131. Gambling–licences and certificates–fees

GAMING ACT (VARIATION OF FEES) (ENGLAND AND WALES AND SCOTLAND) ORDER 2002, SI 2002 642; made under the Gaming Act 1968 s.48, s.51. In force: April 1, 2002; £1.75.

This Order, which amends the Gaming Act (Variation of Fees) Order 2000 (SI 2000 1212) and the Gaming Act (Variation of Fees) (England and Wales and Scotland) Order 2001 (SI 2001 726), amends the fees to be charged in England and Wales under the Gaming Act 1968 for specified matters.

3132. Gambling–prizes–variation of monetary limits

GAMING ACT (VARIATION OF MONETARY LIMITS) ORDER 2002, SI 2002 1904; made under the Gaming Act 1968 s.20, s.21, s.51. In force: August 12, 2002; £1.75.

This Order, which amends the Gaming Act 1968, the Gaming Act (Variation of Monetary Limits) Order 2000 (SI 2000 1213) and the Gaming Act (Variation of Monetary Limits) Order 2001 (SI 2001 757), increases the maximum added weekly prize money for bingo games played in any one club to £20,000; increases the aggregate weekly prize in linked bingo games played in any club to £500,000; and increases the total take, and total prizes, in prize bingo games, as played in bingo clubs to £500.

3133. Gambling–prizes–variation of monetary limits

LOTTERIES (VARIATION OF MONETARY LIMITS) ORDER 2002, SI 2002 1410; made under the Lotteries and Amusements Act 1976 s.18, s.24. In force: June 17, 2002; £1.50.

This Order amends the Lotteries and Amusements Act 1976, the Lotteries (Variation of Monetary Limits) (Scotland) Order 1989 (SI 1989 1214) and the Lotteries (Variation of Monetary Limits) Order 1989 (SI 1989 1218) which apply to societies' lotteries and local lotteries. The maximum price of a ticket or chance in such a lottery is increased from £1 to £2, the maximum value of tickets or chances which may be sold in one such lottery is increased from £1,000,000 to £2,000,000 and the maximum value of tickets or chances sold in all such lotteries held in any one year and promoted on behalf of the same society or by the same local authority is increased from £5,000,000 to £10,000,000.

3134. Gambling–renewal of licences–fees

GAMING ACT (VARIATION OF FEES) (ENGLAND AND WALES) ORDER 2002, SI 2002 637; made under the Gaming Act 1968 s.48, s.51. In force: April 1, 2002; £1.75.

This Order, which amends the Gaming Act (Variation of Fees) Order 2000 (SI 2000 1212) and the Gaming Act (Variation of Fees) (England and Wales) Order 2001 (SI 2001 725), amends the fees to be charged in England and Wales under the Gaming Act 1968 for specified matters.

3135. Licensed premises–companies–suitability–failure to disclose identity of shareholders

[Licensing Act 1964.]

The Chief Constable appealed against a decision ([2001] 1 W.L.R. 2239) upholding a declaration that the Crown Court had erred in law in dismissing the appeal of R, an unlimited company, against the refusal of the licensing justices to grant an application by K, an employee of R, for a licence to sell intoxicating liquor. The licensing justices and the Crown Court had concluded that since R's shareholders had refused to disclose their identity, the possibility existed that they were involved in some nefarious activity, with the result that it could not be said that K was a fit and proper person to hold a licence.

Held, dismissing the appeal, that the crucial issue was whether the applicant for a licence was, was not or might not be a fit and proper person. The focus, as was made clear by the Licensing Act 1964, was on the particular applicant's suitability to run the public house in question. In deciding that issue, the licensing justices and the Crown Court had to form a judgment based on the evidence before them. The findings of fact in the instant case showed that K was, both personally and professionally, a fit and proper person. He was answerable to his area manager and to his managing director, who had also been found to be fit and proper persons. Those findings precluded any inference that K was no more than a stooge for others or that he would be pressurised into acting unlawfully or improperly. While R's shareholders' refusal to disclose their identity raised speculation as to their motives, such speculation was relevant only if and to the extent that it cast doubt on K's ability to carry out his duties as a licensee.

R. (ON THE APPLICATION OF RBNB) v. WARRINGTON CROWN COURT; *sub nom.* R. v. WARRINGTON CROWN COURT, *ex p.* RBNB, [2002] UKHL 24, [2002] 1 W.L.R. 1954, Lord Bingham of Cornhill, HL.

3136. Licensed premises–exemptions–special order of exemption for extended hours–World Cup 2002

[Licensing Act 1964 s.74(4).]

G, a licensee, appealed against the decision of the justices dismissing his application under the Licensing Act 1964 s.74(4) for a special order of exemption for extended hours in relation to the World Cup 2002. The justices had concluded that they were bound by the decisions of *R. v. Leicester Justices, ex p. Watchorn* Times, June 9, 1978, [1978] C.L.Y. 1742 and *R. v. Commissioner of Police of the Metropolis, ex p. Maynard* Times, June 1, 1982, [1982] C.L.Y. 1696. The issue before the court was whether the World Cup amounted to a special occasion for the purposes of s.74(4).

Held, allowing the appeal, that the World Cup 2002 did constitute a special occasion. The decisions of *Watchorn* and *Maynard* reflected the time at which they had been made; the way in which people now watched sporting events at public houses had altered significantly. Customers attended a public house showing a sporting event to take part and collectively enjoy that event. However, it was important to distinguish between public houses which provided facilities, such as large screen televisions, to enable matches to be watched collectively as a shared experience and those merely providing a small television, perhaps at the corner of the bar. It followed that the justices had erred in not exercising their discretion and allowing G's application, *R. v. Berwyn Justices, ex p. Edwards* [1980] 1 W.L.R. 1045, [1980] C.L.Y. 1554 applied and *Watchorn* and *Maynard* distinguished. It was observed that, in the light of the instant decision, where an application for a special order of exemption had recently been refused, a fresh application should be made rather than an appeal.

GOUGH v. AVON AND SOMERSET POLICE LICENSING BUREAU; *sub nom.* GOUGH v. AVON JUSTICES; GOUGH v. BRISTOL LICENSING JUSTICES, [2002] EWHC 658, (2003) 2 J.P. 79, Lord Woolf, L.C.J., QBD.

3137. Licensed premises–public entertainments–karaoke machines–requirement for licence–meaning of "recorded sounds"

[London Government Act 1963 Sch.12 para.10(1)(b)(i); Licensing Act 1964 s.182.]

T appealed against the dismissal of his appeal against his conviction for allowing premises to be used for entertainment purposes without the provision of a licence in breach of the London Government Act 1963 Sch.12 para.10(1)(b)(i). The entertainment consisted of a karaoke session using a machine which generated accompaniment by sending MIDI instructions to a synthesiser. T had maintained that he was entitled to take advantage of the statutory exception contained within the Licensing Act 1964 s.182. However the exception did not apply to entertainment provided by a combination of live performance and recorded sound. The Crown Court held that use of the equipment consisted of "recorded sound" and that accordingly operating the machine amounted to the "reproduction of recorded sound" for the purposes of s.182 such as to preclude the application of the statutory exception. On appeal the court had to determine whether the Crown Court had been correct in its conclusion that operation of the equipment in question amounted to the "reproduction of recorded sound".

Held, dismissing the appeal, that the musicians who had prepared the instructions for the MIDI had done so by listening to an audio recording of the relevant songs that they wished to reproduce. They had then inputted the necessary instructions onto a CD Rom in order that the synthesiser could reproduce the relevant sounds. The musical sounds had accordingly been recorded in the instructions and were in consequence "recorded sounds" within the meaning of s.182.

TOYE v. SOUTHWARK LBC, [2002] EWHC 292, (2002) 166 J.P. 389, Forbes, J., QBD (Admin Ct).

3138. Licensed premises–restaurants–deregulation

DEREGULATION (RESTAURANT LICENSING HOURS) ORDER 2002, SI 2002 493; made under the Deregulation and Contracting Out Act 1994 s.1. In force: April 2, 2002; £1.50.

This Order amends the Licensing Act 1964 by removing the requirement for the licensee of a restaurant which serves alcohol with meals until midnight on weekdays and 11.30pm on Sundays to obtain a supper hour certificate.

3139. Licensed premises–tied estates–supply of beer–revocation

SUPPLY OF BEER (TIED ESTATE) (REVOCATION) ORDER 2002, SI 2002 3204; made under the Fair Trading Act 1973 s.56, s.90, s.124, Sch.8 para.1, Sch.8 para.2, Sch.8 para.14. In force: January 17, 2003; £1.50.

This Order revokes the Supply of Beer (Tied Estate) Order 1989 (SI 1989 2390) and the Supply of Beer (Tied Estate) (Amendment) Order 1997 (SI 1997 1740).

3140. Lotteries–Gaming Board fees

LOTTERIES (GAMING BOARD FEES) ORDER 2002, SI 2002 639; made under the Lotteries and Amusements Act 1976 s.18, s.24, Sch.1A para.6, Sch.2 para.7. In force: April 1, 2002; £1.75.

This Order, which revokes the Lotteries (Gaming Board Fees) Order 2001 (SI 2001 728), provides for the fees payable to the Gaming Board for Great Britain by societies under the Lotteries and Amusements Act 1976 Sch.1A; by local authorities under Sch.2 to that Act; and by lottery managers for certification under Sch.2A to that Act.

3141. National lottery–licence fees–prescribed sum

NATIONAL LOTTERY (LICENCE FEES) (AMENDMENT) ORDER 2002, SI 2002 3124; made under the National Lottery etc. Act 1993 s.7, s.60. In force: January 13, 2003; £1.50.

This Order amends the National Lottery (Licence Fees) Order 2001 (SI 2001 2506) which prescribes the fees payable on all licences granted under the National Lottery etc. Act 1993. The Order prescribes the sums payable by the licensee to the National Lottery Commission by way of fees on the grant of a licence under the Act, which authorises the promotion by the licensee of an unrestricted number of lotteries which fall within a description specified in the licence.

3142. Books

Douglas, Andrew–National Lottery: Its Regulation Process, Problems and Personalities. Hardback: £40.00. ISBN 0-485-11572-7. Continuum International Publishing Group-Athlone Press.

Phillips, Jeremy–Phillips: Licensing Law Guide. 3rd Ed. Paperback: £45.00. ISBN 0-406-95226-4. Butterworths Law.

Robinson, Duncan; Butterfield, Roger; Chambers, David–Entertainments Licensing Law and Practice. Law in Practice. Paperback: £9.95. ISBN 1-85836-436-1. Old Bailey Press.

LOCAL GOVERNMENT

3143. Benefits–contracting out–income related benefits–local authorities

CONTRACTING OUT (FUNCTIONS OF LOCAL AUTHORITIES: INCOME-RELATED BENEFITS) ORDER 2002, SI 2002 1888; made under the Deregulation and Contracting Out Act 1994 s.69, s.70, s.77. In force: July 25, 2002; £1.75.

This Order provides that, with specified exceptions, functions of a local authority exercisable under the Social Security and Benefits Act 1992, the Social Security Administration Act 1992, Social Security Act 1998 and the Child Support, Pensions and Social Security Act 2000 and Regulations and Orders made thereunder, in relation to community charge benefits, council tax benefit and housing benefit, may be exercised by such persons as the authority may authorise to do so.

3144. Best value–local authorities powers and duties–analyses and improvement plans–Wales

LOCAL GOVERNMENT (WHOLE AUTHORITY ANALYSES AND IMPROVEMENT PLANS) (WALES) ORDER 2002, SI 2002 886; made under the Local Government Act 1999 s.5, s.6, s.7, s.29. In force: April 1, 2002; £1.75.

The Local Government Act 1999 imposes duties on local and other authorities to conduct best value reviews of their functions and to prepare a best value performance plan for each financial year. This Order, which revokes the Local Government (Best Value) (Reviews and Performance Plans) (Wales) Order 2000 (SI 2000 1271), specifies the review period, the date before which an authority's plan for a financial year must be published and the date by which copies of an auditor's report are to be sent.

3145. **Best value–local authorities powers and duties–performance indicators–Wales**

LOCAL GOVERNMENT (BEST VALUE PERFORMANCE INDICATORS) (WALES) ORDER 2002, SI 2002 757; made under the Local Government Act 1999 s.4, s.29. In force: April 1, 2002; £4.00.

This Order, which revokes the Local Government (Best Value Performance Indicators) (Wales) Order 2001 (SI 2001 1337), prescribes for Wales performance indicators by reference to which the performance of county councils, county borough councils and National Park authorities, in exercising their functions, will be measured from April 1, 2002.

3146. **Best value–local authorities powers and duties–performance indicators and standards**

LOCAL GOVERNMENT (BEST VALUE) PERFORMANCE INDICATORS AND PERFORMANCE STANDARDS ORDER 2002, SI 2002 523; made under the Local Government Act 1999 s.4, s.28. In force: April 1, 2002; £4.00.

The Local Government Act 1999 imposes requirements on local authorities and other authorities relating to economy, efficiency and effectiveness in exercise of their functions and confers a power on the Secretary of State to specify by Order best value performance indicators and standards. This Order, which revokes the Local Government (Best Value) Performance Indicators and Performance Standards Order 2001 (SI 2001 724), specifies performance indicators by reference to which a best value authority's performance in exercising functions can be measured and the standards in respect of particular functions and particular best value authorities.

3147. **Best value–non commercial matters–contract workers–Wales**

LOCAL GOVERNMENT BEST VALUE (EXCLUSION OF NON-COMMERCIAL CONSIDERATIONS) (WALES) ORDER 2002, SI 2002 678; made under the Local Government Act 1999 s.19, s.29. In force: March 31, 2002; £1.75.

The Local Government Act 1988 contains a list of non-commercial matters by reference to which a public authority may not exercise the functions specified, which include functions in relation to proposed public supply or works contracts with the authority. This Order provides for the specified matters and of the 1988 Act to cease to be non-commercial matters for the purposes of that section. The matters concerned relate to the terms and conditions of employment etc. of the contractor's workforce and the conduct of contractors or their workers in industrial disputes.

3148. **Best value–performance plans and reviews**

LOCAL GOVERNMENT (BEST VALUE) PERFORMANCE PLANS AND REVIEWS AMENDMENT AND SPECIFIED DATES ORDER 2002, SI 2002 305; made under the Local Government Act 1999 s.5, s.6, s.7. In force: March 8, 2002; £1.50.

This Order, which amends the Local Government (Best Value) Performance Plans and Reviews Order 1999 (SI 1999 3251), specifies the matters which best value authorities must include in their performance plans. It also specifies matters that should be included in their performance reviews and the time period in which all of their reviews should be carried out.

3149. Capital finance–rate of discount

LOCAL AUTHORITIES (CAPITAL FINANCE) (RATE OF DISCOUNT FOR 2002/03) (ENGLAND) REGULATIONS 2002, SI 2002 110; made under the Local Government and Housing Act 1989 s.49. In force: April 1, 2002; £1.50.

The Local Government and Housing Act 1989 makes provision for the capital finance of local authorities and sets out a formula for determining the value of the consideration falling to be given by a local authority under a credit arrangement in any financial year after the one in which the arrangement comes into being. The percentage rate of discount prescribed for the financial year is one of the factors referred to in the formula. These Regulations prescribe, for the financial year beginning on April 1, 2002, 7.2 per cent which is 0.3 per cent less than the rate of discount prescribed for 2001/2002.

3150. Capital finance–rate of discount–Wales

LOCAL AUTHORITIES (CAPITAL FINANCE) (RATE OF DISCOUNT FOR 2002/2003) (WALES) REGULATIONS 2002, SI 2002 785; made under the Local Government and Housing Act 1989 s.49. In force: April 1, 2002; £1.75.

The Local Government and Housing Act 1989 makes provision for the capital finance of local authorities and sets out a formula for determining the value of the consideration falling to be given by an authority under a credit arrangement in any financial year after the year in which the arrangement comes into being. The percentage rate of discount prescribed for a financial year is one of the elements which make up the formula. These Regulations prescribe a percentage rate of 6.7 per cent which is 0.3 per cent less than the rate of discount prescribed for 2001/2002.

3151. Civil Defence (Grant) Act 2002 (c.5)

This Act replaces Civil Defence Act 1948 s.3 in so far as it applies to authorities in England or Wales.

This Act received Royal Assent on February 26, 2002.

3152. Community charge–computers–evidence of liability to pay–admissibility

See CIVIL EVIDENCE: Sutton v. Islington LBC. §272

3153. Contracting out–local education authorities

CONTRACTING OUT (LOCAL EDUCATION AUTHORITY FUNCTIONS) (ENGLAND) ORDER 2002, SI 2002 928; made under the Deregulation and Contracting Out Act 1994 s.70, s.77. In force: April 1, 2002; £2.00.

This Order enables a local education authority in England to authorise another person, or that person's employees, to exercise certain functions of local education authorities on behalf of that authority.

3154. Council tax–assessment–first floor flat located above Indian restaurant– failure to consider detrimental effect

C appealed against the dismissal by the valuation tribunal of his appeal against the listing officer's decision to list his first floor flat, which was situated directly above an Indian restaurant, in band F, along with all the other first floor flats.

Held, allowing the appeal and remitting the matter for reconsideration, that the flats should have been treated separately and the tribunal had erred, due largely to the way in which the case had been presented, by not considering the detrimental effect that the restaurant would have on the value of C's property.

CSELKO v. CAMDEN LISTING OFFICER [2001] R.V.R. 280, Collins, J., QBD.

3155. Council tax—exemptions—vacant property formerly in multiple occupation subject to repairs notice

[Housing Act1985 s.189, s.352; Council Tax (Exempt Dwellings) Order1992 (SI 1992 558) Art.3 Class G.]

W owned a property which was rented out and in multiple occupation. He had received a repairs notice from the local authority under the Housing Act1985 s.189 and a notice under s.352, which stipulated the works necessary to make the property fit for multiple occupation. As a result he had allowed the property to become vacant. Although the local authority had withdrawn the notices, W had been warned that another notice would be served if he rented the property out again. He had received demands for the payment of council tax in respect of the property which he did not pay, claiming that the property was exempt under the Council Tax (Exempt Dwellings) Order 1992 Art.3 Class G. W appealed against a valuation tribunal decision dismissing his appeal against the local authority's decision that a council tax Class G exemption did not apply.

Held, dismissing the appeal, that the Class G exemption only included dwellings whose occupation was prohibited by law. On the facts of the instant case, W's property was unoccupied because he had decided not to let it so that he could avoid carrying out the repairs specified in the notices.

WATSON v. RHONDDA CYNON TAFF CBC, [2001] EWHC Admin 913, [2002] R.V.R. 132, Gibbs, J., QBD (Admin Ct).

3156. Council tax—houses—self contained flat within house

[Local Government Finance Act 1992; Council Tax (Chargeable Dwellings) Order 1992 (SI 1992 549).]

M appealed against the decisions of a valuation tribunal that both a flat situated within a house and the house itself amounted to "self contained" units for the purposes of the Council Tax (Chargeable Dwellings) Order 1992 with the result that each was a "chargeable dwelling" within the meaning of the Local Government Finance Act 1992. The flat, which consisted of two bedrooms, a kitchen and a bathroom, could only be accessed by passing through the hall, stairs and landing of the house. In relation to the flat, the tribunal had concluded that the fact that access could only be gained through the house was not sufficient to prevent it from being self contained. In relation to the house, the tribunal had found that the right of passage through the house of the person residing in the flat, whilst inconvenient, did not prevent the house from being a self contained unit in its own right. M claimed that the valuation list should contain only one entry relating to the flat and house as one self contained unit.

Held, dismissing the appeal, that the fact that the flat could only be reached through the house did not preclude it from being a separate "self contained unit" for the purposes of the Order. Similarly, the fact that the occupier of the flat had been granted a licence to pass through the house did not preclude it from being a separate dwelling for the purposes of the Order.

McCOLL v. LISTING OFFICER, [2001] EWHC Admin 712, [2001] R.A. 342, Sir Christopher Bellamy, Q.C., QBD (Admin Ct).

3157. Council tax—property bands—appeals—time limits

[Council Tax (Alteration of Lists and Appeals) Regulations 1993 (SI 1993 290) Reg.5.]

S complained that his flat had been rated in band B, contended that it have been listed in band A. The valuation list came into force on April 1, 1993 and S acquired the property in May 1993 but he did not make his proposal for a change to the valuation list until September 1, 1996. The listing officer refused S's application and he appealed to the valuation tribunal. The tribunal dismissed his appeal and S appealed. The six month time limit for proposing alterations to the list under the Council Tax (Alteration of Lists and Appeals) Regulations 1993 Reg.5(4) and Reg.5(5) was not raised before the tribunal but was relied on by W at the appeal.

Held, dismissing the appeal, that S's application was long out of time and neither the tribunal nor the court had jurisdiction to hear the appeal. The mere fact that the tribunal had heard the application did not serve to confer jurisdiction or give rise to an estoppel on which S could rely, *Upper Agbrigg Assessment Committee v. Bents Brewery Co* [1945] K.B. 196 considered.

SCRIVNER v. WOJCIK [2001] R.V.R. 248, Turner, J., QBD.

3158. Council tax–property bands–error in determining reduction in value–lack of evidence

[Rules of the Supreme Court Ord.55 r.7.]

T sought an alteration in the valuation list, asserting that her flat should not have been placed in band C but in some lower band. It was in fact in band C because she had earlier successfully sought a reduction from band D, in which the property had originally been placed. In her current application she relied upon environmental pollution caused by construction works in the vicinity. The listing officer refused her application and she appealed to the valuation tribunal. Her appeal was dismissed on the basis that the pollution she now sought to rely on had been known at the date of the earlier application. She appealed to the High Court.

Held, dismissing the appeal, that in terms of the pollution, the question was not whether the pollution was known about, but whether the alleged reduction in the value of the property was known about, at the material time. It followed that the tribunal had asked itself the wrong question and had erred in law. However, T had not adduced any evidence as to the value of her property either before the tribunal or the court. Accordingly, even if the tribunal had asked itself the right question it would have dismissed the appeal as there was no evidential basis for any alteration in the list. In the circumstances, therefore, the appeal would be dismissed, notwithstanding the Tribunal's error of law, as no wrong or miscarriage had occurred, as required by the Rules of the Supreme Court Ord.55 r.7.

TILLY v. TOWER HAMLETS LBC LISTING OFFICER; *sub nom.* TILLY v. VALUATION OFFICER [2001] R.V.R. 250, Jowitt, J., QBD.

3159. Council tax–residence–no alternative permanent residence

W owned a property which was tenanted to N and T. Following investigations which tended to show that W resided at the property with his tenants, the local authority determined that W was the resident owner and therefore liable for payment of the council tax. W appealed to the Valuation Tribunal arguing that his work as a joiner and comedian took him all over the country where he stayed in bed and breakfast accommodation. During other times he stayed with his mother or friends. The local authority produced statements from N and T and from neighbours to the effect that W was resident at the property. The Tribunal found that, given no alternative permanent residence, W was indeed the resident owner. W appealed to the court arguing that he was not resident anywhere due to the nature of his occupation.

Held, dismissing the appeal, that no error in law had been made by the Tribunal in their determination that the property was W's sole or main place of residence even though the evidence relied on by the Tribunal was the minimum level of evidence capable of supporting such a finding.

R. (ON THE APPLICATION OF WRIGHT) v. LIVERPOOL CITY COUNCIL, [2002] EWHC 626, [2002] R.A. 73, George Bartlett Q.C., QBD (Admin Ct).

3160. Council tax–residence–sole or main residence

[Local Government Finance Act 1992 s.6(5).]

N applied for judicial review of the decision of a valuation tribunal that he was liable to pay council tax on a chargeable dwelling owned by him but which was not occupied for a period of five months while he was in the USA. N claimed that during this period the property was unfurnished and was not his "sole or main residence" within the meaning of the Local Government Finance Act 1992 s.6(5) and that therefore he was not liable for council tax on the property.

Held, refusing the application for judicial review, that the evidence supported the tribunal's conclusion that the property was N's sole or main residence. It was where he usually lived, he was only away temporarily and, when compared with any other property, for instance the one he lived in while abroad, it was his sole or main residence. Whether the premises were furnished or not was irrelevant to this issue.

R. (ON THE APPLICATION OF NAVABI) v. CHESTER LE STREET DC, [2001] EWHC Admin 796, [2002] R.V.R. 10, Elias, J., QBD (Admin Ct).

3161. **Councillors–breach of statutory duty–former councillor guilty of wilful misconduct–nature of remedy available to local authority**

[Audit Commission Act 1998 s.18.]

W sought summary judgment in its claim against a former councillor, P, for breach of trust. W maintained that as a result of P's wilful misconduct the authority had incurred losses of approximately £26 million. W contended that P was liable for the sum plus interest calculated to run from 14 days after the auditor's certificate had been issued since her liability arose not only pursuant to statute but also as a trustee of local authority assets. P maintained that (1) a remedy by way of a claim for breach of trust and the statutory remedy arising as a result of the issue of an auditor's certificate were alternative and not cumulative with the consequence that W was required to elect which remedy it was to pursue, and (2) it was appropriate to grant a stay of execution pending her application to the European Court of Human Rights.

Held, granting the application for summary judgment, that (1) when enacting the relevant legislation enabling a local authority to pursue a claim based upon an auditor's certificate, Parliament had left intact the existing equitable jurisdiction whereby a corporate authority could sue its own members for abuse of power, *Attorney General v. Wilson* (1840) 1 Cr. & Ph. 1 and *Tang Man Sit (Deceased) v. Capacious Investments Ltd* [1996] A.C. 514, [1996] C.L.Y. 3789 considered. However the remedy available to a claimant seeking to pursue a claim for breach of the duty owed to it was not the same as the remedy sought when pursuing a claim under the Audit Commission Act 1998 s.18. In an ordinary case the pursuit of the equitable cause of action would result in an order for an inquiry as to the extent of the loss suffered. Accordingly unless such a claimant wished to obtain an order for an inquiry into the losses suffered, it had to restrict itself to the statutory remedy, and (2) there was no basis for the imposition of a stay pending P's application to the European Court since the European Court of Human Rights was not an appellate court in the English jurisdiction, *Locabail (UK) Ltd v. Waldorf Investment Corp (No.4)* [2000] H.R.L.R. 623, [2000] C.L.Y. 3236 applied.

WESTMINSTER CITY COUNCIL v. PORTER (NO. 1), [2002] EWHC 1589, [2003] 2 W.L.R. 420, Hart, J., Ch D.

3162. **Local authorities–access to meetings and documents–period of notice**

LOCAL AUTHORITIES (ACCESS TO MEETINGS AND DOCUMENTS) (PERIOD OF NOTICE) (ENGLAND) ORDER 2002, SI 2002 715; made under the Local Government Act 1972 s.100K. In force: October 1, 2002; £1.50.

This Order amends the Local Government Act 1972 in relation to provisions about access to meetings and documents relating to those meetings of principal councils in England and Wales, their committees and sub-committees. In particular, public notice of a meeting must normally be given at least three clear days before the meeting is held. The agenda and certain other documents must be open to inspection at least three clear days before the meeting. An item of business may not normally be considered at a meeting unless a copy of the agenda including the item has been available for public inspection for three clear days before the meeting. This Order extends each of these periods of three clear days to five clear days as respects principal councils in England, their committees and sub-committees.

3163. Local authorities–allowances–Wales

LOCAL AUTHORITIES (ALLOWANCES FOR MEMBERS OF COUNTY AND COUNTY BOROUGH COUNCILS AND NATIONAL PARK AUTHORITIES) (WALES) REGULATIONS 2002, SI 2002 1895; made under the Local Government and Housing Act 1989 s.18. In force: August 9, 2002; £3.00.

These Regulations, which amend the Local Authorities (Members' Allowances) Regulations 1991 (SI 1991 351), require county and county borough councils and National Park Authorities in Wales to make a scheme for the payment of allowances in respect of the current year and subsequent years.

3164. Local authorities–boundaries–Blaenau Gwent and Caerphilly–Wales

BLAENAU GWENT AND CAERPHILLY (TREDEGAR AND RHYMNEY) ORDER 2002, SI 2002 651; made under the Local Government Act 1972 s.58. In force: April 6, 2002; £2.00.

This Order gives effect to proposals by the Local Government Boundary Commission for Wales. The effect of those proposals will see an area of the community of Rhymney in Caerphilly in the area of Tafarnau-bach become part of the community of Tredegar in Blaenau Gwent.

3165. Local authorities–boundaries–Cardiff and Vale of Glamorgan–Wales

CARDIFF AND VALE OF GLAMORGAN (MICHAELSTON AND GRANGETOWN) ORDER 2002, SI 2002 3273 (W.311); made under the Local Government Act 1972 s.58. In force: in accordance with Art.1 (2); £3.00.

This Order gives effect to the proposals made by the Local Government Boundary Commission for Wales, so that the specified area will be transferred from the community of Michaelston in the County Borough of The Vale of Glamorgan to the community of Grangetown in the City and County of Cardiff.

3166. Local authorities–boundaries–Carmarthenshire and Pembrokeshire–Wales

CARMARTHENSHIRE AND PEMBROKESHIRE (CLYNDERWEN, CILYMAENLLWYD AND HENLLANFALLTEG) ORDER 2002, SI 2002 3270 (W.308); made under the Local Government Act 1972 s.58. In force: in accordance with Art.1 (2); £6.00.

This Order, which gives effect with modifications to proposals by the Local Government Boundary Commission for Wales, provides the community of Clynderwen will be transferred from Carmarthenshire and become part of Pembrokeshire; the area which is part of the community of Cilymaenllwyd in Carmarthenshire will become part of the community of Clynderwen in Pembrokeshire; the area which is part of the community of Clynderwen will become part of the community of Cilymaenllwyd in Carmarthenshire; the area which is part of the community of Henllanfallteg in Carmarthenshire will become part of the community of Clynderwen in Pembrokeshire; and the area which is part of the community of Clynderwen in Carmarthenshire in the vicinity of Pen-deri Farm and which does not include any dwellings will become part of the community of Henllanfallteg in Pembrokeshire so that the boundary in that area will follow the centre of the Afon Daulan.

3167. Local authorities–boundaries–Ceredigion and Pembrokeshire–Wales

CEREDIGION AND PEMBROKESHIRE (ST DOGMAELS) ORDER 2002, SI 2002 3272 (W.310); made under the Local Government Act 1972 s.58. In force: in accordance with Art.1 (2); £4.00.

This Order gives effect to proposals by the Local Government Boundary Commission for Wales so that the specified area of the community of St. Dogmaels in the County of Ceredigion will be transferred from the County of Ceredigion to the County of Pembrokeshire.

3168. Local authorities-boundaries-Neath Port Talbot and Swansea-Wales

NEATH PORT TALBOT AND SWANSEA (TREBANOS AND CLYDACH) ORDER 2002, SI 2002 652; made under the Local Government Act 1972 s.58. In force: April 6, 2002; £2.00.

This Order made in accordance with the Local Government Act 1972 s.58(2) gives effect to proposals by the Local Government Boundary Commission for Wales. The effect of those proposals will see an area of the community of Pontardawe in Neath Port Talbot become part of the community of Clydach in Swansea.

3169. Local authorities-boundaries-Newport-Wales

NEWPORT (CAERLEON AND MALPAS) ORDER 2002, SI 2002 3271 (W.309); made under the Local Government Act 1972 s.58. In force: in accordance with Art.1 (2); £3.00.

This Order gives effect to proposals made by the Local Government Boundary Commission for Wales so the specified area will be transferred from the community of Caerleon to the community of Malpas.

3170. Local authorities-boundaries-Rhondda Cynon Taff and Vale of Glamorgan-Wales

RHONDDA CYNON TAFF AND VALE OF GLAMORGAN (LLANHARRY, PONT-Y-CLUN, PENLLYN, WELSH ST DONATS AND PENDOYLAN) ORDER 2002, SI 2002 654; made under the Local Government Act 1972 s.58. In force: April 6, 2002; £2.00.

This Order gives effect to proposals by the Local Government Boundary Commission for Wales, the effect of which is that an area of the community of Llanharry in Rhondda Cynon Taff in the vicinity of two properties known as "Brynderwen" and "Two Hoots" becomes part of the community of Penllyn in the Vale of Glamorgan.

3171. Local authorities-companies-credit cover-Wales

LOCAL AUTHORITIES (COMPANIES) (AMENDMENT) (WALES) ORDER 2002, SI 2002 2118; made under the Local Government and Housing Act 1989 s.39. In force: September 1, 2002; £2.00.

The Local Authorities (Companies) Order 1995 (SI 1995 849) Art.14 requires an authority to have available an amount of credit cover for the liabilities of companies treated as companies regulated by the authority. This Order makes amendments to that Order so as to provide an additional mechanism by which an authority can provide that credit cover.

3172. Local authorities-companies-Greater London Authority

LOCAL AUTHORITIES (COMPANIES) (AMENDMENT) (ENGLAND) ORDER 2002, SI 2002 2298; made under the Local Government and Housing Act 1989 s.39. In force: September 30, 2002; £1.75.

This Order amends the Local Authorities (Companies) Order 1995 (SI 1995 849) so that it applies to the Greater London Authority and functional bodies in a similar way as it applies to other authorities.

3173. Local authorities-conduct-model codes of practice

LOCAL GOVERNMENT ACT 2000 (MODEL CODE OF CONDUCT) (AMENDMENT) ORDER 2002, SI 2002 1719; made under the Local Government Act 2000 s.50, s.105. In force: July 27, 2002; £1.50.

This Order amends the Local Authorities (Model Code of Conduct) (England) Order 2001 (SI 2001 3575), the Parish Councils (Model Code of Conduct) Order 2001 (SI 2001 3576), the National Park and Broads Authorities (Model Code of Conduct) (England) Order 2001 (SI 2001 3577) and the Police Authorities (Model

Code of Conduct) Order 2001 (SI 2001 3578). The amendments disapply the specified enactments to authorities where a code of conduct in the schedules to those orders has been adopted or applied to it.

3174. Local authorities–conduct of referendums

LOCAL AUTHORITIES (CONDUCT OF REFERENDUMS) (ENGLAND) (AMENDMENT) REGULATIONS 2002, SI 2002 521; made under the Local Government Act 2000 s.45, s.105. In force: March 8, 2002; £1.75.

These Regulations amend the Local Authorities (Conduct of Referendums) (England) Regulations 2001 (SI 2001 1298). Referendums under those Regulations relate to the question whether a county, district or London borough council should adopt executive arrangements that include a mayor and cabinet executive, a mayor and council manager executive or a leader and cabinet executive. The Regulations enable voting at a referendum to be taken together with an election of a description to be conducted wholly by post where the election is also to be conducted wholly by post. They also apply the Representation of the People Act 2000 s.10 to referendums and enable the Secretary of State to approve pilot schemes submitted by county, district or London borough councils for the conduct of referendums.

3175. Local authorities–council meetings–access and disclosure

LOCAL AUTHORITIES (EXECUTIVE ARRANGEMENTS) (ACCESS TO INFORMATION) (ENGLAND) AMENDMENT REGULATIONS 2002, SI 2002 716; made under the Local Government Act 2000 s.22, s.105. In force: Reg.1-13: April 15, 2002 : Reg.14: October 1, 2002; £1.75.

These Regulations apply to county councils, district councils and London borough councils in England which are operating executive arrangements under the Local Government Act 2002 and amend the Local Authorities (Executive Arrangements) (Access to Information) Regulations 2000 (SI 2000 3272) which made provision relating to public access to meetings of local authority executives and their committees. The Regulations make amendments to provide that papers, agendas and documents relating to meeting of local authority executives and their committees have to be available to the public at least five days instead of three clear days before the date of the meeting or, in the case of a decision being taken by an individual member, the date that the decision is taken.

3176. Local authorities–council meetings–modification of enactments

LOCAL AUTHORITIES (EXECUTIVE ARRANGEMENTS) (MODIFICATION OF ENACTMENTS) (ENGLAND) ORDER 2002, SI 2002 1057; made under the Local Government Act 2000 s.47, s.105. In force: May 6, 2002; £2.00.

This Order amends the Fund Reorganisation Act1903, so as to exclude a member of an executive of a London borough from appointment to the membership of the constitution of the Royal Patriotic Fund Corporation, the Naval and Military War Pensions, &c, Act1915 so that a mayor of a London borough who is a member of the constitution of the Royal Patriotic Fund Corporation by virtue of the Patriotic Fund Reorganisation Act1903, cannot appoint a member of an executive to be a member in his place, the Local Government Act1972 to make provision for a principal council which is operating executive arrangements involving an elected mayor, to fix the date of the annual meeting in a year of an election for the return of the elected mayor, which is not a year of ordinary elections of councillors to the council and the Administration of Justice Act 1973 so that where a London borough council is operating executive arrangements involving an elected mayor, the chairman of the council, not the elected mayor, is to undertake certain acts prescribed in the Justices of the Peace Act 1997. The Order also makes amendments to the Local Government Act 1974 so that where an authority are operating executive arrangements which involve an elected mayor, the Local Commissioner's report into an investigation is sent to the chairman of the authority, to the the the Representation of the People Act 1983 so that where a London borough council is operating executive arrangements which involve an elected mayor, the chairman of the council, not the elected mayor, is to be the returning officer for a parliamentary election and the Parliamentary Writs Order 1983 (SI 1983 605). In addition, the Order amends the Local Government Act 1985 so that it is extended to include appointments made by the elected mayor of an authority, the Returning Officers (Parliamentary Constituencies) (England) Order 1995 (SI 1995 2061), the Defamation Act 1996 and the Local Authorities (Executive and Alternative Arrangements) (Modification of Enactments and Other Provisions) (England) Order 2001 (SI 2001 2237).

3177. Local authorities–council meetings–modification of enactments–Wales

LOCAL AUTHORITIES (EXECUTIVE ARRANGEMENTS) (MODIFICATION OF ENACTMENTS AND FURTHER PROVISIONS) (WALES) ORDER 2002, SI 2002 803; made under the Local Government Act 2000 s.47, s.105, s.106. In force: April 1, 2002; £2.00.

These Regulations, which amend the Local Government Act 1972, the Local Government and Housing Act 1989 and the Local Government Act 2000, prevent local authorities from making arrangements for the discharge of functions by another local authority to the extent that the function in question is the responsibility of the executive of that other local authority. They provide that the arrangements for the discharge of a local authority's functions, by either another local authority or a joint committee, existing at the time when any of the participating local authorities begin to operate executive arrangements, shall cease to the extent that the function in question becomes the responsibility of the executive of any of those authorities; enable local authorities to appoint advisory committees to advise the executive of the local authority and any committee or individual member of that executive; and introduces a requirement for local authorities who are or will be operating executive arrangements to make standing orders in respect of local authority contracts and specify the provisions to be included in the standing orders, including the procedure to be followed in the making of such contracts.

3178. Local authorities–executive arrangements–discharge of functions–Wales

LOCAL AUTHORITIES (EXECUTIVE ARRANGEMENTS) (DISCHARGE OF FUNCTIONS) (AMENDMENT) (WALES) REGULATIONS 2002, SI 2002 2941 (W.282); made under the Local Government Act 2000 s.18, s.19, s.20, s.105, s.106. In force: December 20, 2002; £1.75.

These Regulations amend the Local Authorities (Executive Arrangements) (Discharge of Functions) (Wales) Regulations 2002 (SI 2002 802) which made provision enabling a local authority in Wales operating executive arrangements to make arrangements for the discharge of its executive functions by area committees, the executive of another local authority or jointly with one or more other local authorities by way of joint committee. The 2002 Regulations provide that only a member of the executive can be appointed to a joint committee which exercises executive functions. These Regulations make amendments to ensure that local authority executives are permitted to appoint either members of the local authority who are not executive members or officers of the authority to serve on joint committees on their behalf.

3179. Local authorities–executive arrangements–discharge of functions–Wales

LOCAL AUTHORITIES (EXECUTIVE ARRANGEMENTS) (DISCHARGE OF FUNCTIONS) (WALES) REGULATIONS 2002, SI 2002 802; made under the Local Government Act 2000 s.18, s.19, s.20, s.105, s.106. In force: April 1, 2002; £2.50.

The Local Government Act 2000 Part II provides for local authorities to make arrangements for the creation and operation of an executive of the authority under which certain functions of the authority are the responsibility of the executive. The National Assembly for Wales may by regulations make provision which enables an executive of a local authority in Wales, or a committee or a specified member of such an executive, to make arrangements for the discharge by an area committee of the authority or by another local authority of any functions which, under executive arrangements, are the responsibility of the authority. The National Assembly for Wales may by regulations make provision which enables a local authority in Wales to make arrangements for the discharge by that authority and one or more other local authorities jointly of any functions which, under the executive arrangements, are the responsibility of the executive of the authority. These Regulations, which revoke the Local Authorities (Executive Arrangements) (Discharge of Functions) (Wales) Regulations 2001 (SI 2001 2287), specify the persons who have the power to make such arrangements in the case of a mayor and cabinet executive, a leader and cabinet executive and a mayor and council manager executive respectively and provide for the making of arrangements for the discharge of functions which are the responsibility of the executive of a local authority in Wales by an area committee of that authority. They provide for the making of arrangements for the discharge of functions which are the responsibility of the executive of a local authority in Wales by another local authority and also for the making, in specified circumstances, of arrangements for the discharge of functions which are not the responsibility of the executive of a local authority in Wales by the executive of another local authority.

3180. Local authorities–executive arrangements–functions and responsibilities–Wales

LOCAL AUTHORITIES EXECUTIVE ARRANGEMENTS (FUNCTIONS AND RESPONSIBILITIES) (AMENDMENT) (WALES) REGULATIONS 2002, SI 2002 783; made under the Local Government Act 2000 s.13, s.105, s.106. In force: April 1, 2002; £1.75.

The Local Government Act 2000 Part II provides for the discharge of a local authority's functions by an executive of the authority unless those functions are specified as functions that are not the responsibility of the authority's executive. These Regulations amend the Local Authorities Executive Arrangements (Functions and Responsibilities) (Wales) Regulations 2001 (SI 2001 2291) which specified functions that are not to be the responsibility of an authority's executive or are to be the responsibility of such an executive only to a limited extent or only in specified circumstances. The Regulations clarify that determination of terms and conditions are not to be the responsibility of the executive of a local authority and insert a reference to the Criminal Justice and Police Act 2001 s.13 so that the power to make an Order identifying a place as a designated public place for the purposes of police powers is one that must not be exercised by the executive of a local authority.

3181. Local authorities–executive arrangements–modification of enactments

LOCAL AUTHORITIES (EXECUTIVE AND ALTERNATIVE ARRANGEMENTS) (MODIFICATION OF ENACTMENTS AND OTHER PROVISIONS) (WALES) ORDER 2002, SI 2002 808; made under the Local Government Act 2000 s.47, s.105, s.106. In force: April 1, 2002; £6.00.

This Order amends the Local Government Act 1972, the Local Government Act 1974, the Local Government (Miscellaneous Provisions) Act 1976, the Adoption Agencies Regulations 1983 (SI 1983 1964), the Transport Act 1985, the Weights and Measures Act 1985, the Local Government Act 1986, the Airports Act 1986, the Pilotage Act 1987, the Local Government Finance Act 1988, the Local Government Act 1988, the Local Government and Housing Act 1989, the Water Industry Act 1991, the Definition of Independent Visitors (Children) Regulations 1991 (SI 1991 892), the Children (Secure Accommodation) Regulations 1991 (SI 1991 1505), the Local Government Finance Act 1992, the Council Tax (Administration and Enforcement) Regulations 1992 (SI 1992 613), the Deregulation and Contracting out Act 1994, the Education (Special Educational Needs) (Approval of Independent Schools) Regulations 1994 (SI 1994 651), the Employment Rights Act 1996, the Defamation Act 1996, the Education Act 1996, theJusticesof the PeaceAct1997, theTeaching and Higher Education Act1998 and the Powers of the Criminal Courts (Sentencing) Act 2000. This Order makes modifications to the specified primary and secondary legislation in consequence of, or for giving full effect to provisions of the Local Government Act 2000 Part II.

3182. Local authorities–executive arrangements–powers and duties–Wales

LOCAL AUTHORITIES (EXECUTIVE ARRANGEMENTS) (DECISIONS, DOCUMENTS AND MEETINGS) (WALES) (AMENDMENT) REGULATIONS 2002, SI 2002 1385; made under the Local Government Act 2000 s.22, s.105, s.106. In force: May 17, 2002; £1.75.

The National Assembly for Wales made the Local Authorities (Executive Arrangements) (Decisions, Documents and Meetings) (Wales) Regulations 2001 (SI 2001 2290) to regulate various matters in respect of the business conducted by local authorities operating executive arrangements. These Regulations are made using the same powers to make an addition to those earlier Regulations. They make provision for the chairperson of a meeting of the executive, or a committee of the executive, of a local authority to make additions to the agenda for the meeting where that person is of the view that the additional matter should be considered, by reason of special circumstance, as a matter of urgency.

3183. Local authorities–proposals–executive or alternative arrangements–Wales

LOCAL AUTHORITIES (OPERATION OF DIFFERENT EXECUTIVE OR ALTERNATIVE ARRANGEMENTS) (WALES) REGULATIONS 2002, SI 2002 2880 (W.276); made under the Local Government Act 2000 s.30, s.33, s.105, s.106. In force: November 25, 2002; £2.00.

The Local Government Act 2000 provides for local authorities to draw up proposals for the operation of executive arrangements or, in the case of certain authorities, for the operation of alternative arrangements. These Regulations enable a local authority, which is operating executive or alternative arrangements, to draw up proposals to change those arrangements.

3184. Local authorities–supply of goods and services–designation of public bodies

LOCAL AUTHORITIES (GOODS AND SERVICES) (PUBLIC BODIES) (ENGLAND) (NO.3) ORDER 2002, SI 2002 2624; made under the Local Authorities (Goods and Services) Act1970 s.1. In force: November14, 2002; £1.50.

This Order designates Active Life Ltd as a public body enabling Canterbury City Council to provide goods and services to the designated public body by way of an agreement for any purposes prescribed by the Local Authorities (Goods and Services) Act 1970 s.1. It also imposes restrictions on the agreements that can be made by the body designated.

3185. Local authorities powers and duties–abuse of power–exercise of statutory power for improper purpose

[Local Government FinanceAct1982 s.20; Human Rights Act1998 Sch.1 Part I Art.6.]

M, the council auditor, appealed against a decision of the Court of Appeal ([2000] 2 W.L.R. 1420) allowing the appeals of P and W, the former leader and deputy leader respectively of Westminster City Council, against a decision ((1998) 30 H.L.R. 997) upholding the issue of a certificate by M pursuant to the Local Government Finance Act 1982 s.20 following a finding of wilful misconduct. M had found that P and W had formulated and implemented a policy whereby council homes would be sold in marginal wards for the purpose of increasing the number of voters in those wards likely to vote for the Conservative Party, that P and W had known that the policy was unlawful, and that the policy had caused financial loss to the council. P and W contended that (1) they had acted in accordance with legal advice and accordingly were not guilty of wilful misconduct; (2) the existence of an improper motive did not render the decision of the housing committee to implement the policy unlawful, since the committee had reached its decision independently and by applying lawful housing objectives, and (3) they had been denied a fair trial since M was not an independent and impartial tribunal for the purposes of the Human Rights Act 1998 Sch.1 Part I Art.6. Further, that in view of a statement M had made at a press conference, there was an inference of apparent bias and that there had been an unreasonable delay of eight years between the first objection and the judgment of the Divisional Court.

Held, allowing the appeal and upholding the certificate, that powers conferred on local authority councillors had to be used for the purposes for which they were conferred and use for unauthorised purposes amounted to misconduct. Where such misconduct was knowing or reckless, it constituted wilful misconduct and if it resulted in loss the councillors concerned could be liable to compensate the council for such loss pursuant to s.20 of the 1982 Act. Whilst it was inevitable that councillors would act in a manner which they hoped would strengthen their position with the electorate, P and W had used their powers purely to promote electoral advantage which was an abuse of their powers. In relation to the contentions of P and W: (1) reliance on legal advice was not a defence to a finding of wilful misconduct; (2) the majority of members of the housing committee had had insufficient knowledge of the rationale behind the housing policy to enable them to make an informed judgment with the consequence that the causal link between the conduct of P and W and its consequences had not been broken, and (3) given the existence, by virtue of s.20(3), of a power of the court to hold a complete rehearing, the various functions of the auditor as investigator, prosecutor and judge did not constitute a breach of Art.6(1). The test to be applied for determining the existence of apparent bias was whether a fair minded and informed observer would conclude that there was a real possibility of bias. Applying such test, P's claim was unsubstantiated and, in view of the nature of the investigation, the delay was not unreasonable.

PORTER v. MAGILL; WEEKS v. MAGILL; HARTLEY v. MAGILL; ENGLAND v. MAGILL; PHILLIPS v. MAGILL; *sub nom.* MAGILL v. PORTER; MAGILL v. WEEKS, [2001] UKHL 67, [2002] 2 A.C. 357, Lord Bingham of Cornhill, HL.

3186. Local authorities powers and duties–alternative arrangements–Wales

LOCAL AUTHORITIES (ALTERNATIVE ARRANGEMENTS) (AMENDMENT) (WALES) REGULATIONS 2002, SI 2002 810; made under the Local Government Act 2000 s.31, s.32, s.106. In force: April 1, 2002; £2.00.

The Local Government Act 2000 Part II provides for the National Assembly for Wales to specify which local authorities may operate "alternative arrangements" and what form those arrangements should take. These Regulations amend the Local Authorities (Alternative Arrangements) (Wales) Regulations 2001 (SI 2001 2284) to make minor changes to the required form of the alternative arrangements and to determine how a council may discharge its function in relation to certain additional specified powers. They provide that the Board of a local authority must act as its social services committee unless a sub-committee of the Board is designated for that purpose; permits the creation of a sub-committee of the Board to undertake the social services committee role if the local authority so chooses, the creation of an employment appeals committee and up to four other committees; and prohibit the chairperson or vice-chairperson of a local authority from being a member of the Board.

3187. Local authorities powers and duties–contracting out–waste disposal function–requirements for adequate supervision

See LANDLORD AND TENANT: Southwark LBC v. Long. §3058

3188. **Local authorities powers and duties–data protection–lapse of registration for data use–recklessness**

[Data Protection Act 1984 s.5, s.5(2).]

The Information Commissioner appealed against the dismissal of seven charges laid against the local authority alleging the use of data held on a computer for an unauthorised purpose contrary to the Data Protection Act 1984 s.5. In spite of the issue of reminder letters, the local authority failed to renew its registration to use or hold data for certain specified purposes. The Commissioner charged the local authority with breaching s.5(2) by recklessly continuing to "use" the data subsequent to the lapse of the registration. The council maintained that the Commissioner was required to prove that the council officer who used the data for the unlawful purpose knew or should have known that the registration had expired.

Held, allowing the appeal, that, as a body corporate, the local authority could be a person for the purposes of s.5 and could, therefore, act knowingly or recklessly. Thus, in failing to comply with the duty to implement a system to ensure compliance with the 1984 Act, the local authority would or should have known that the continued use of the data contravened s.5. There was no need to prove that the individual officer who accessed and used the data had acted recklessly. For the purposes of s.5, the knowledge and actions of the "directing minds" of a corporate body were to be taken together with actions of those to whom administrative functions were delegated.

INFORMATION COMMISSIONER v. ISLINGTON LBC, [2002] EWHC 1036, [2003] B.L.G.R. 38, Hallett, J., QBD.

3189. **Local authorities powers and duties–duty of care–staffing requirements at residential case homes–economic loss**

See NEGLIGENCE: Douce v. Staffordshire CC. §3316

3190. **Local authorities powers and duties–fly posting–political posters placed on highway without lawful authority–entitlement to claim cost of removal**

See AGENCY: Hackney LBC v. Arrowsmith. §63

3191. **Local authorities powers and duties–housing benefit–criteria relevant to restriction of benefit**

See SOCIAL SECURITY: R. (on the application of Laali) v. Westminster Housing Benefit Review Board. §4194

3192. **Local authorities powers and duties–maladministration–right to respect for private and family life–failure of local authority to provide suitably adapted accommodation for disabled tenant–measure of damages**

[National Assistance Act 1948 s.21 (1) (a); Human Rights Act 1998 s.8, Sch.1 Part I Art.3, Sch.1 Part 1 Art.8.]

B claimed damages under the Human Rights Act 1998 s.8 against E in respect of its failure to provide her with appropriate accommodation. B was severely disabled, had limited mobility and suffered from incontinence and diabetes. B and her family lived in a property provided by E. Assessments of B's needs, carried out by E's social services department, indicated that the property was unsuitable as, inter alia, B could not use her electronic wheelchair or access the first floor. The occupational therapist instructed by B's solicitor had concluded that the property was not adaptable and the care plan stated that B needed assistance to move to suitably adapted accommodation. Whilst E accepted that it was under a duty to make arrangements for the provision of suitably adapted accommodation under the National Assistance Act 1948 s.21 (1) (a), it failed to comply with that duty or to act on social services' recommendation until judicial review proceedings had been commenced. B contended that leaving her in such unsuitable accommodation for a period of more than 20 months amounted to a breach of her rights under Sch.1 Part I Art.3 and Art.8 of the 1998 Act.

Held, assessing total damages in the sum of £10,000, that (1) there had been no breach of B's Art.3 rights. Although the conditions in which she had been forced to live could be described as degrading, the minimum threshold level of severity had not been crossed, *A v. United Kingdom* [1998] 2 F.L.R. 959, [1998] C.L.Y. 3065 applied. The fact that E had not intended to humiliate or debase B was an important consideration; (2) B's Art.8 rights had been breached. Following the initial assessments, E had been under an obligation to take positive steps to enable B and her family to lead as normal a family life as possible. The failure to act showed a singular lack of respect for B's private and family life; (3) if a public body took appropriate steps once a problem had been drawn to its attention, it might be that nothing further was required. However, in the instant case, an award of damages was just and necessary, and (4) there was no justification for the assertion that, generally, awards under s.8(3) of the 1998 Act should not be comparable to tortious awards. However, in the instant case there was no comparable tort. Minor psychiatric injuries were not truly comparable with the humiliating conditions endured by B and her husband over a period of 20 months. To make a minimal award would diminish respect for the policy underlying the 1998 Act that all public authorities should observe Convention rights. The local government ombudsman's recommended awards in cases where there had been a failure to provide care facilities for the disabled provided the best available comparison because the instant case was, in essence, one of maladministration. Therefore the level of award fell within the range £5,000 to £10,000. Given, that B's problems were compounded by E's conduct an award of £10,000 was appropriate, apportioned £8,000 to B and £2,000 to her husband.

R. (ON THE APPLICATION OF BERNARD) v. ENFIELD LBC, [2002] EWHC 2282, [2003] H.R.L.R. 4, Sullivan, J., QBD (Admin Ct).

3193. Local authorities powers and duties–repairs–responsibility of tenant to report disrepair

See NEGLIGENCE: Jeffers v. West Lancashire DC. §3278

3194. Local authorities powers and duties–road signs–marking of hazards

See NEGLIGENCE: Calderdale MBC v. Gorringe. §3315

3195. Local authorities powers and duties–sale of land–obligation to obtain highest price–commercial value of consideration

[Local Government Act 1972 s.123(2).]

L applied for judicial review of the decision of HLBC, the local authority, to sell a property within its control to the London Development Agency, LDA, despite the fact that L had offered a higher price for it. The local authority in reaching its decision had had regard to the job creation prospects of LDA's offer. The issue before the court related to whether for the purposes of the Local Government Act 1972 s.123(2), which provided that land could not be disposed of "for a consideration less than the best that can reasonably be obtained" without the consent of the Secretary of State, a local authority could treat as part of the relevant consideration the perceived job prospects created. HLBC maintained that it was not required to gain the consent of the Secretary of State.

Held, granting the application, that the provisions of s.123(2) of the Act did not allow a local authority to treat any part of the value attributable to job creation as part of the purchase "consideration" and accordingly, HLBC was in breach of its obligation to obtain the highest possible price for the property. The elements of consideration had to have a commercial or monetary value to the council, *R. v. Pembrokeshire CC, ex p. Coker* [1999] 4 All E.R. 1007, [2000] C.L.Y. 4111 applied. In effect, the element of consideration attributed to job creation was a disguised grant to the LDA for what was perceived as a socially desirable project. Where an element of grant or discount existed, the Secretary of State's consent to the transaction was required.

R. (ON THE APPLICATION OF LEMON LAND LTD) v. HACKNEY LBC, [2001] EWHC Admin 336, (2001) 3 L.G.L.R. 42, Lightman, J., QBD (Admin Ct).

3196. **Local authorities powers and duties–wrongful interference with goods– mistaken removal of property by refuse collectors–responsibility for identifying waste**

H brought an action against the local authority for damages alleging the wrongful removal of items. H had left newly laundered clothes in plastic bags in an outhouse which also housed the dustbin. Refuse collectors removed the bags as items of refuse.

Held, dismissing the action, that the local authority had not breached its duty to H. The refuse collectors had not been negligent in treating bags as rubbish and should not have regard to the placement of rubbish bags provided they were in the vicinity of the dustbin. It would impose too high a burden on the collectors to expect them to decide whether it was rubbish or not and members of the public should make it clear if they did not want items to be removed.

HADWIN v. LEEDS CITY COUNCIL, August 15, 2001, Deputy District Judge Saffman, CC (Leeds). [*Ex rel.* Department of Legal Services, Leeds City Council, Civic Hall, Leeds].

3197. **Local authority inquiries–duty of care–supply of information from statutory list**

See NEGLIGENCE: Gooden v. Northamptonshire CC. §3317

3198. **Local Government Act 2000 (c.22)–Commencement No.3 Order–Wales**

LOCAL GOVERNMENT ACT 2000 (COMMENCEMENT NO.3) (WALES) ORDER 2002, SI 2002 1359; made under the Local Government Act 2000 s.108. Commencement details: bringing into force various provisions of the 2000 Act on June 30, 2002; £2.00.

This Order brings into force the Local Government Act 2000 s.93 which enables grants to be made to local authorities in Wales for welfare services.

3199. **Local Government Act 2000 (c.22)–Commencement No.8 Order**

LOCAL GOVERNMENT ACT 2000 (COMMENCEMENT NO.8) ORDER 2002, SI 2002 1718; made under the Local Government Act 2000 s.105, s.108. Commencement details: bringing into force various provisions of the 2000 Act on July 27, 2002; £1.75.

This Order brings into force further provisions of the Local Government Act 2000 relating to the repeal of surcharge.

3200. **Local government finance–allocation of grants–council tax calculations**

GREATER LONDON AUTHORITY (ALLOCATION OF GRANTS FOR PRECEPT CALCULATIONS) REGULATIONS 2002, SI 2002 267; made under the Greater London Authority Act 1999 s.88, s.89. In force: February 13, 2002; £1.50.

The Greater London Authority Act 1999 sets out how the Greater London Authority is to calculate the amounts of its council tax for the City of London and the remainder of Greater London. Separate calculations are necessary for these two parts of Greater London because the Metropolitan Police Authority is not responsible for the provision of police services in the City of London. These Regulations prescribe the amounts of redistributed non-domestic rates and specified grants, which the Secretary of State considers relate to the police and non-police expenditure of the Greater London Authority and functional bodies, which the Greater London Authority must take into account when carrying out the calculations of the amounts of council tax for the two parts of Greater London.

3201. Local government finance–billing authorities–calculations

LOCAL AUTHORITIES (ALTERATION OF REQUISITE CALCULATIONS) (ENGLAND) REGULATIONS 2002, SI 2002 155; made under the Local Government Finance Act 1992 s.32, s.33, s.43, s.44, s.113; and the Greater London Authority Act 1999 s.86, s.88, s.89, s.420. In force: February 1, 2002; £1.75.

The Local Government Finance Act 1992 sets out how a billing authority and a major precepting authority other than the Greater London Authority are to calculate their budget requirements for a financial year and how to calculate the basic amount of their council tax. These Regulations amend the definition of "police grant" for the financial year beginning on April 1, 2002 within the Local Government Finance Act 1992 and the Greater London Authority Act 1999.

3202. Local government finance–budget requirements–amendment to calculations–Wales

LOCAL AUTHORITIES (ALTERATION OF REQUISITE CALCULATIONS) (WALES) REGULATIONS 2002, SI 2002 328; made under the Local Government Finance Act 1992 s.32, s.33. In force: February 28, 2002; £1.75.

The Local Government Finance Act 1992 sets out how a billing authority is to calculate its budget requirement and the basic amount of its council tax for a financial year. These Regulations amend the definition of "relevant special grant" in the 1992 Act for the financial year beginning on April 1, 2002 in relation to Wales only.

3203. Local government finance–capital finance–investments

LOCAL AUTHORITIES (CAPITAL FINANCE AND APPROVED INVESTMENTS) (AMENDMENT) (ENGLAND) REGULATIONS 2002, SI 2002 451; made under the Local Government and Housing Act 1989 s.58, s.66, s.190. In force: April 1, 2002; £1.75.

The Local Authorities (Capital Finance) (Approved Investments) Regulations 1990 (SI 1990 426) contain a list of investments approved by the Secretary of State for the purposes of Part IV of the Local Government and Housing Act 1989. These Regulations amend the 1990 Regulations by adding investments in money market funds and deposits with the Treasury to the list of approved investments. They also make consequential amendments to the Local Authorities (Capital Finance) Regulations 1997 (SI 1997 319).

3204. Local government finance–capital finance–investments–Wales

LOCAL AUTHORITIES (CAPITAL FINANCE AND APPROVED INVESTMENTS) (AMENDMENT) (WALES) REGULATIONS 2002, SI 2002 885; made under the Local Government and Housing Act 1989 s.58, s.66. In force: April 1, 2002; £1.75.

These Regulations amend the Local Authorities (Capital Finance) (Approved Investments) Regulations 1990 (SI 1990 426) by adding investments in money market funds and deposits with the Treasury to the list of approved investments. They also make consequential amendments to the Local Authorities (Capital Finance) Regulations 1997 (SI 1997 319).

3205. Local government finance–capital finance–investments and contracts–Wales

LOCAL AUTHORITIES (CAPITAL FINANCE) (APPROVED INVESTMENTS) (AMENDMENT) (NO.2) (WALES) REGULATIONS 2002, SI 2002 1884; made under the Local Government and Housing Act 1989 s.66. In force: September 1, 2002; £1.75.

These Regulations amend the Local Authorities (Capital Finance) (Approved Investments) Regulations 1990 (SI 1990 426) by extending the list of approved investments include securities issued by a body mentioned in Part I of the Schedule to the 1990 Regulations which have been admitted to the official list maintained by the competent authorities in other Member States of the European Economic Area.

3206. Local government finance—capital finance—private finance transactions—disposal of property

LOCAL AUTHORITIES (CAPITAL FINANCE) (AMENDMENT) (ENGLAND) REGULATIONS 2002, SI 2002 2299; made under the Local Government and Housing Act 1989 s.61, s.190, Sch.3 para.11, Sch.3 para.15. In force: September 30, 2002; £1.50.

These Regulations amend the Local Authorities (Capital Finance) Regulations 1997 (SI 1997 319) which extend the description of private finance transactions under or in connection with which a local authority can dispose of property without having to set aside an amount in respect of the non-monetary consideration received for the disposal under the transaction; make provision in respect of a local authority's credit ceiling, which is one of the components of the aggregate credit limit; and make provision for determining a local authority's minimum revenue provision. They make amendments so that specified provisions apply in a similar way to the Greater London Authority and functional bodies (as provided for in the Greater London Authority Act 1999) as they do to other authorities.

3207. Local government finance—public expenditure—limits

LOCAL AUTHORITIES (DISCRETIONARY EXPENDITURE LIMITS) (ENGLAND) ORDER 2002, SI 2002 2878; made under the Local Government Act 1972 s.137. In force: March 31, 2003; £1.50.

The Local Government Act 1972 s.137 enables parish councils in England to incur expenditure for certain purposes not otherwise authorised. This expenditure must not exceed the amount produced by multiplying a specified sum by the relevant population of the authority's area. In the case of a parish council in England, the specified sum is £3.50 or other such sum as by Order be specified. This Order increases to £5.00 the sum specified.

3208. Maladministration—Local Government Ombudsman—failure to issue exemption notice in respect of access road

[Highways Act 1980 s.219(4).]

H, P and L applied for judicial review of the Local Government Ombudsman's decision to make no order or recommendation in spite of her finding that there had been serious maladministration on the part of the local authority following its failure to issue an exemption notice pursuant to the Highways Act 1980 s.219(4) in respect of an access road to new houses which they had acquired. The Ombudsman, who concluded that there had been no injustice as a result of the maladministration, supported the applicants' contention that her decision should be quashed but submitted that the court should make no further order and that she should be permitted to reconsider the matter without fetter.

Held, granting the application for judicial review in part, that it had not been open to the Ombudsman on the evidence before her to conclude that no injustice had been caused to the applicants. If the local authority had acted reasonably H, P and L would undoubtedly have adopted a different course and would not have incurred the costs of improving the standard of the access road to their houses following the liquidation of the property developer's business; therefore, the Ombudsman's decision that there had been no injustice was quashed. However, it was not appropriate for the court to make a direction as to the conclusion that the Ombudsman should reach when the matter came before her for reconsideration.

R. (ON THE APPLICATION OF HUGHES) v. LOCAL GOVERNMENT OMBUDSMAN; *sub nom.* R. (ON THE APPLICATION OF HUGHES) v. LOCAL ADMINISTRATION COMMISSIONER, [2001] EWHC Admin 349, (2001) 3 L.G.L.R. 50, Burton, J., QBD (Admin Ct).

3209. Maladministration–Local Government Ombudsman–refusal to investigate planning complaint

T sought judicial review of a decision of L, that a local authority, C, was not guilty of maladministration and therefore did not warrant further investigation. T had built a property and anticipated that any property built next to their home would be just over six metres from the edge of their house in accordance with an existing planning permission. Subsequently a housing society started to build houses, without formal planning permission, at a distance of only four metres from T's property. T submitted that (1) the alteration of the distance between the properties and the resulting narrowness of the spacing between the houses should have been brought to the attention of the planning committee; (2) following a meeting between T, the principal planning officer and the chairman of the planning committee at which T had raised his objections, the matter should have been put back before the planning committee, and (3) L's interview notes should have been disclosed.

Held, granting the application, that (1) the proposed alteration did not constitute a material consideration which should have been brought to the committee's attention; (2) the reasons put forward for L's failure to investigate the matter were flawed given that it was arguable that the principal planning officer's failure to put the matter back before the planning committee when objections had been raised by T, amounted to maladministration, and (3) the refusal by L to disclose interview notes had been unfair given that there had to be good reasons for such a refusal and in the instant case there had been nothing to justify the decision, *R. v. Chelsea College of Art and Design, ex p. Nash (Application for Judicial Review)* [2000] Ed. C.R. 571, [2000] C.L.Y. 1787 applied.

R. (ON THE APPLICATION OF TURPIN) v. COMMISSIONER FOR LOCAL ADMINISTRATION, [2001] EWHC Admin 503, [2003] B.L.G.R. 133, Collins, J., QBD (Admin Ct).

3210. Non domestic rates–rural rate relief–maximum rateable values–Wales

NON-DOMESTIC RATING (RURAL RATE RELIEF) (WALES) ORDER 2002, SI 2002 331; made under the Local Government Finance Act 1988 s.43, s.47. In force: April 1, 2002; £2.00.

Each county and county borough council in Wales is required by the Local Government Finance Act 1988 to compile and maintain for each chargeable financial year a list which identifies settlements which are wholly or partly within the authority's area, appear to the authority to have had a population of not more than 3,000 on December 31 immediately preceding the beginning of the chargeable financial year in question and are in that financial year wholly or partly within an area designated by order as a rural area for the purposes of the section. This Order amends the Non-Domestic Rating (Rural Settlements) (Wales) Order 1998 (SI 1998 2963), which designates rural areas in Wales, and prescribes £9,000 in the case of a public house or a petrol filling station and £6,000 in any other case as the maximum chargeable amount of non-domestic rate for a chargeable day.

3211. Public authorities–standards committees–dispensations

RELEVANT AUTHORITIES (STANDARDS COMMITTEE) (DISPENSATIONS) REGULATIONS 2002, SI 2002 339; made under the Local Government Act 2000 s.53, s.81, s.105. In force: March 18, 2002; £1.75.

These Regulations prescribe the circumstances in which a standards committee may grant dispensations to members and co-opted members of relevant authorities in England, and police authorities in Wales. If a member or co-opted member acts in accordance with the grant of a dispensation, any participation in business prohibited by the mandatory provisions of a model code of conduct issued under the Local Government Act 2000 s.50 is not a failure to comply with the authority's code of conduct. The Regulations set out the circumstances in which standards committees may grant dispensations, specify that dispensations may only be granted if half the members entitled or required to participate in the business of the authority would not otherwise be able to, or the authority would not able to comply with political balance principles, specify that the member must submit a written request for a dispensation and that the standards committee must conclude that having regard to these matters and all the other circumstances of the case, it is appropriate to grant the dispensation. They also provide that a dispensation cannot be granted in respect of business conducted after four years and specify that the circumstances in which dispensations can be granted do not extend to allowing a member of an overview and scrutiny committee to participate in the scrutiny of the decision of another committee in which he was involved or to allowing an individual to exercise executive functions where he is prohibited by the mandatory provisions from doing so.

3212. Street trading–tenancies–trading from permanent structure–power to grant tenancy over highway

[Local Government Act 1972 s.111; London Local Authorities Act 1990 Part III.]

S, who traded from a permanent structure in the street, appealed against the decision of the deputy judge ([2002] E.H.L.R. 3) that she was engaged in "street trading" for the purposes of the London Local Authorities Act 1990 Part III and was therefore subject to the regulatory scheme within the Act and the judge's dismissal of her counterclaim that she was entitled to the grant of a 25 year lease, or, in the alternative, a licence from the date on which the structure had been erected. S traded from a purpose built kiosk which had been built on foundations and was connected to the mains supplies of the usual services. The kiosk had been erected at considerable expense with the consent of the local authority and to designs of which it had approved. The judge had found that a "general reassurance" had been given by the local authority that while a street trading licence rather than a lease was on offer, if S conducted herself properly the licence would be renewed for at least 20 years. As to the question of whether S was engaged in "street trading", the judge had concluded that while S remained in the kiosk, her customers remained in the street at all times with the result that the actual "selling" of goods took place on the customer's side, namely the street. In relation to whether S was entitled to a lease, the judge found that no right to hold a tenancy had arisen since Part III of the 1990 Act did not encompass the "question of the nature of any right that [might] have been granted by the [local authority] in respect of occupation of the land itself". She had rejected the contention that the local authority's ancillary powers provided under the Local Government Act 1972 s.111 enabled it to create a tenancy over a highway.

Held, allowing the appeal in part, that the judge had erred in her conclusion that S was engaged in "street trading" and therefore subject to the regulatory scheme within Part III of the 1990 Act. The street trading legislation was not intended to apply to trading from within a permanent structure erected in a street; it could not have been the case that Parliament had intended that the issue of whether an offence of street trading had taken place rested on a detailed analysis of the moment at which the contract for sale had been made, *Newman v. Lipman* [1951] 1 K.B. 333 considered. The judge had, however, been correct in her conclusion that no right to hold a tenancy had been created. The grant of a tenancy over the surface of a highway could not be seen as being calculated to facilitate, or as conducive or incidental to, the discharge of a local authority's functions as highway authority and therefore did not fall within the subsidiary powers provided under s.111 of the 1972 Act. Even if a tenancy could be granted, no tenancy had arisen since S had entered into occupation of the site on the basis that no tenancy was on offer.

TOWER HAMLETS LBC v. SHERWOOD, [2002] EWCA Civ 229, [2002] E.H.L.R. 13, Chadwick, L.J., CA.

3213. Supply of services–designation of public bodies

LOCAL AUTHORITIES (GOODS AND SERVICES) (PUBLIC BODIES) (ENGLAND) ORDER 2002, SI 2002 522; made under the Local Authorities (Goods and Services) Act 1970 s.1. In force: April 1, 2002; £1.50.

This Order designates bodies of the description specified under the Local Authorities (Goods and Services) Act 1970 s.1 (5) to allow a local authority to provide certain goods and services to the designated public body which, in this case is a housing management organisation.

3214. Supply of services–designation of public bodies

LOCAL AUTHORITIES (GOODS AND SERVICES) (PUBLIC BODIES) (ENGLAND) (NO.2) ORDER 2002, SI 2002 2244; made under the Local Authorities (Goods and Services) Act 1970 s.1. In force: September 30, 2002; £1.50.

This Order designates Kirklees Active Leisure as a public body enabling Kirklees Metropolitan Borough Council to provide goods and services to the designated body by way of an agreement for any purposes prescribed by the Local Authorities (Goods and Services) Act 1970 s.1. It also imposes restrictions on the agreements that can be made by the body designated.

3215. Supply of services–designation of public bodies–Wales

LOCAL AUTHORITIES (GOODS AND SERVICES) (PUBLIC BODIES) (WALES) ORDER 2002, SI 2002 1729; made under the Local Authorities (Goods and Services) Act 1970 s.1. In force: July 19, 2002; £1.75.

This Order designates the National Assembly for Wales, the Care Council for Wales and the National Council for Education and Training for Wales as public bodies for the purposes of the Local Authorities (Goods and Services) Act 1970.

3216. Books

Drabble, Richard; Maurici, James–Local Authorities and Human Rights. Blackstone's Human Rights Act Series. Paperback: £25.00. ISBN 1-84174-135-3. Blackstone Press.

Greene, Abner S.–Understanding the 2000 Election: A Guide to the Legal Battles That Decided the Presidency. Hardback: £20.00. ISBN 0-8147-3148-1. New York University Press.

Henriques, Jack; Winter, Richard–Henriques and Winter on Local Authority Prosecutions. Paperback: £45.00. ISBN 1-85941-697-7. Cavendish Publishing Ltd.

McDonald, Laughlin–Voting Rights Odyssey. Hardback: £37.50. ISBN 0-521-81232-1. Paperback: £13.95. ISBN 0-521-01179-5. Cambridge University Press.

Randall, Helen–Local Government Contracts and Procurement. Hardback: £115.00. ISBN 0-406-94897-6. Hardback: £115.00. ISBN 0-406-94897-6. Butterworths Law.

MEDIA AND ENTERTAINMENT

3217. Digital television–satellite television–conditional fee operators–Spanish registration requirements–free movement of goods–freedom to provide services

[EC Treaty Art.30 (now, after amendment, Art.28 EC), Art.59 (now, after amendment, Art.49 EC); Parliament and Council Directive 95/47 on the use of standards for transmission of television signals.]

The Spanish Supreme Court referred questions to the ECJ on the interpretation of the EC Treaty Art.30 (now, after amendment, Art.28 EC) and EC Treaty Art.59

(now, after amendment, Art.49 EC), read in conjunction with Council Directive 95/47. C, a provider of conditional access services for digital satellite television broadcasting, supplied special decoding equipment in Spain. National provisions transposing Directive 95/47 made the marketing of digital and satellite television equipment subject to a compulsory registration scheme which required conditional access operators to obtain prior administrative certification that compliance with technical specifications had been achieved. The ECJ was asked to rule on whether the registration scheme unlawfully restricted the free movement of goods and the freedom to provide services as guaranteed by Art.30 and Art.59 respectively.

Held, giving a preliminary ruling, that the Spanish provisions restricted the free movement of goods and the freedom to provide services. However, where the legislation pursued the legitimate public interest of protecting and informing consumers, such a restriction could be justified insofar as the Member State complied with the principle of proportionality. In determining whether a national provision was compliant with that principle, it was necessary to take the following considerations into account: (1) a prior administrative authorisation scheme had to be based on objective, non discriminatory criteria which were known in advance, in such a way as to circumscribe the national authorities' discretion; (2) a measure could not be regarded as necessary if it duplicated controls already carried out in the context of other procedures, either in the same State or in another Member State; (3) a prior authorisation procedure would only be necessary where subsequent controls would be too late to be genuinely effective, and (4) any procedure which, on account of its duration and disproportionate costs, deterred operators from pursuing a business plan could not be justified.

CANAL SATELITE DIGITAL SL v. ADMINISTRACION GENERAL DEL ESTADO (C390/99) [2003] 1 C.M.L.R. 27, GC Rodriguez Iglesias (President), ECJ.

3218. Film industry–cinemas–safety on premises

CINEMATOGRAPH (SAFETY) (AMENDMENT) REGULATIONS 2002, SI 2002 1903; made under the Cinemas Act 1985 s.4. In force: August 12, 2002; £1.50.

These Regulations amend the Cinematograph (Safety) Regulations 1955 (SI 1955 1129) to lower the age from 21 to 18 of a licensee or a person nominated by the licensee to be responsible for the premises at all times when the public are on the premises; a person is responsible for ensuring that electrical installations and equipment in the projection room are kept in good order; and a person in charge of and present in the projection room whenever inflammable film is being projected.

3219. Newspapers–confidential   information–celebrities–confidentiality attaching to sexual relations–freedom of expression

[Human Rights Act 1998 s.12(3), Sch.1 Part I Art.8, Sch.1 Part I Art.10.]

T, a television presenter, sought an injunction restraining the "Sunday People", a newspaper published by M, from publishing certain photographs and an article stating that he had visited a Mayfair brothel and had engaged in sexual activity with three prostitutes. T had been out drinking with friends. They had entered an establishment, which T claimed not to have realised was a brothel, but had later left. T had, however, subsequently returned to the establishment and the alleged sexual activity had taken place. T maintained that he had been in a private place with friends and that publication of the material would constitute a breach of confidentiality and a breach of his right to privacy as provided under the Human Rights Act 1998 Sch.1 Part I Art.8 and reflected in the Press Complaints Commission Code. In particular, T argued that sexual relations should be regarded as confidential and that confidentiality could arise from certain circumstances and did not require an agreement, either express or implied, to such effect.

Held, granting the injunction in part, that (1) for the purposes of s.12(3) of the Act, the party seeking an injunction had to show that it was more probable than not that he would succeed in obtaining an injunction at trial; (2) where there was an evidential conflict, there was no obligation to assume that what the party seeking the injunction said was true. Any factual disputes, and their nature, formed part of the consideration as to the prospects of injunctive relief being granted; (3) confidentiality did not attach to all acts of physical intimacy regardless of circumstances. It was necessary to consider the degree of intimacy but not in isolation from the relationship within which the physical intimacy had occurred. The impact of any disclosure on others, such as the children of a relationship, could be relevant to the existence of confidentiality. A "one night stand" or a brief relationship were at the outer limits of relationships which required the protection of the law; a transitory engagement in a brothel was even further from such a limit, *A v. B Plc* [2001] 1 W.L.R. 2341, [2001] C.L.Y. 4415 considered, and (4) T had visited an establishment which was obviously a brothel. A brothel did not constitute a private place for the purposes of the Code. The relationship between a prostitute in a brothel and the customer was not confidential in nature and the fact that sexual activity had taken place did not, of itself, create a relationship of confidentiality. T had previously courted publicity about various aspects of his private life and had not made complaint on previous occasions when articles had been published discussing his sexual relations. Furthermore, given that T was a presenter of television programmes aimed at younger viewers, there was an element of public interest in some of the material being published. Having regard to both Art.8 and Art.10, the freedom of expression of the "Sunday People" and the prostitute would, at trial, be given greater weight than the intrusion into T's privacy. It was, however, appropriate to restrain publication of the photographs; there was no public interest in their publication, no consent had been given to their being taken and there was no similar material that had been placed in the public domain.

THEAKSTON v. MGN LTD, [2002] EWHC 137, [2002] E.M.L.R. 22, Ouseley, J., QBD.

3220. **Newspapers—confidential information—freedom of expression—celebrities—transient sexual relationships—guidelines for assessment of injunction applications**

[Human Rights Act 1998.]

B, a Sunday newspaper, appealed against a decision ([2001] 1 W.L.R. 2341) refusing to set aside an injunction granted in favour of A, a married professional footballer, preventing the disclosure or publication of details of his sexual relationships with two women, C and D. The fact that A had been involved in adulterous relationships with C and D was not disputed. However, A maintained that publication would amount to breach of confidentiality, prejudice his marriage and thus, indirectly harm his children.

Held, allowing the appeal, that since the coming into force of the Human Rights Act 1998, the courts had witnessed a sharp increase in applications for injunctions which sought to prevent the publication of newspaper articles which contained information which was alleged to be confidential. As such applications had been characterised by the citation of large numbers of authorities, it was necessary to issue guidelines in order to assist the judiciary in dealing with such applications in a more proportionate manner by shifting attention away from technical aspects of law in favour of a focus on balancing facts. Thus, it was appropriate to consider, inter alia, that any interference with the freedom of the press had to be justified irrespective of whether publication of information was in the public interest, that the protection of any duty of confidence was dependent upon the relationship between the parties at the time of the actual or threatened breach, and that the courts should not act as arbiters of taste in assessing the balance between the respective interests. In the instant case, the judge below had erred in (1) finding that A had a right to privacy which could only be overridden where publication was in the public interest; (2) offering the same protection in respect of transient relationships as would have applied had the parties been married; (3) failing to consider C and D's right to freedom of expression and thus, how their desire to disclose affected A's right to protection; (4) assuming that preventing publication was in the interests of A's wife and family, and (5) rejecting the argument that publication of the article could have been in the public interest as although A had not courted publicity, he held a position of responsibility which inevitably attracted the interest of the public and the media.

A v. B PLC; *sub nom.* A v. B (A FIRM); B & C v. A, [2002] EWCA Civ 337, [2003] Q.B. 195, Lord Woolf of Barnes, L.C.J., CA.

3221. Newspapers−confidential information−medical records−disclosure− identity of source−scope of court's jurisdiction

[Contempt of Court Act 1981 s.10; Human Rights Act 1998 Sch.1 Part I Art.10.]

M, a newspaper publishing group, appealed against a decision ([2001] 1 W.L.R. 515) which affirmed a disclosure order made in favour of A, the body responsible for the management of a high security mental hospital. M had published an article which included verbatim extracts from the medical records of a well known mental patient. The order required M to make and serve a witness statement explaining how they had come into possession of the records and to identify any employee of A and the name of any person or persons involved in their acquisition. M contended that (1) the information relating to the patient was not confidential in the sense that it was neither secret nor not in the public domain, and consequently disclosure could not be ordered as the publication of extracts from the records did not amount to a tortious wrong, and (2) the *Norwich Pharmacal* jurisdiction to order disclosure did not extend to cases where a claimant had neither brought nor intended to bring proceedings.

Held, dismissing the appeal, that (1) there was no requirement that the person against whom proceedings had been brought should have committed a civil or criminal wrong. It was sufficient that the source was a wrongdoer and that M, in publishing the information acquired, had become involved in that wrongdoing. The need for involvement was a threshold requirement which enabled the court to then consider whether it was appropriate to make the order sought. The fact that the patient in the instant case had put similar information into the public domain did not destroy A's independent interest in retaining the confidentiality of its medical records, and (2) an order for disclosure could be made even where the information was not required for the purposes of a bringing an action against an informant, *British Steel Corp v. Granada Television Ltd* [1981] A.C. 1096, [1980] C.L.Y. 2132 followed and *Interbrew SA v. Financial Times Ltd* [2002] EWCA Civ 274, [2002] E.M.L.R. 24, [2002] 4 C.L. 52 considered. However, the protection which the Human Rights Act 1998 Sch.1 Part I Art.10 and the Contempt of Court Act 1981 s.10 provided for freedom of expression required the court to stringently scrutinise any request for relief and to ensure that there was a sufficiently strong positive case in favour of disclosure. In the light of Art.10(2), the exercise of the jurisdiction was only to be permitted where there was a pressing social need. Moreover, any restriction on the right to free expression was to be proportionate to the legitimate aim being pursued. As the disclosure of medical records increased the difficulties and dangers facing staff and patients at the hospital and in light of the need to prevent future wrongdoing, it was essential in the instant case that the source be identified. Accordingly, the order was necessary, proportionate and justified.

ASHWORTH HOSPITAL AUTHORITY v. MGN LTD; *sub nom.* ASHWORTH SECURITY HOSPITAL v. MGN LTD, [2002] UKHL 29, [2002] 1 W.L.R. 2033, Lord Woolf of Barnes, L.C.J., HL.

3222. Newspapers−freedom of expression−report on celebrity's drug addiction− public interest disclosure−data protection

See DEFAMATION: Campbell v. Mirror Group Newspapers Ltd. §951

3223. Press Complaints Commission−judicial review−threshold for interference

[Human Rights Act 1998.]

F, a well-known media figure, sought permission to apply for judicial review of the decision of the Press Complaints Commission that the publication of certain photographs of her whilst on holiday had not infringed her privacy in breach of the Commission's Code of Practice. The photographs had been taken with the use of a long-lens camera. The Commission had determined that F had not had a "reasonable expectation of privacy" whilst on a beach that had been accessible to the public.

Held, refusing permission to apply for judicial review, that given that the membership and expertise of the Commission placed it in a better position than the courts to resolve the issue of the appropriate balance between an individual's right to privacy and the right of newspapers to publish, it was necessary to show that it was clearly desirable for the court to interfere with one of its decisions. The Commission had a broad discretion and the deference given to its decisions by the courts was unaffected by the coming into force of the Human Rights Act 1998, *R. v. Broadcasting Standards Commission, ex p. BBC* [2000] 3 W.L.R. 1327, [2000] C.L.Y. 4163 applied. In the instant case, F had not shown that it was clearly desirable to interfere with the Commission's decision. The Commission had had before it sufficient material to entitle it to reach the determination that it had reached. Furthermore, F had brought her application outside the three month time limit and, in the absence of justification for such delay, her application was time barred.

R. (ON THE APPLICATION OF FORD) v. PRESS COMPLAINTS COMMISSION, [2001] EWHC Admin 683, [2002] E.M.L.R. 5, Silber, J., QBD (Admin Ct).

3224. **Publications–anonymity–effect of investigative journalism on presumption of innocence–relationship between privacy and confidentiality–remedies**

[Human Rights Act 1998 Sch.1 Part I Art.3, Art.8; Criminal Appeal (Reference of Points of Law) Rules 1973 (SI 1973 1114) r.6; Civil Procedure Rules 1998 (SI 1998 3132) Part 3 r.3(4).]

H, a publishing company, applied under the Civil Procedure Rules 1998 Part 3 r.3.4 to strike out proceedings instigated against it by B. B, who had been acquitted of rape despite compelling evidence of his guilt, had alleged breach of his right to privacy and violation of his fundamental rights enshrined in the Human Rights Act 1998 Sch.1 Part I Art.3 and Art.8 following H's breach of an anonymity order made under the Criminal Appeal (Reference of Points of Law) Rules 1973 r.6. B submitted that an article published by H, in which he had been named, had undermined the presumption of innocence and had caused him to suffer distress, anxiety and a reasonable apprehension of violence, because he feared that readers of the article might feel inclined to inflict a punishment upon him which they perceived the criminal justice system had "failed to deliver". He further submitted that he was entitled to damages to compensate him for H's breach of the presumption of innocence.

Held, granting the application, that (1) there was no bar to exposing an acquitted defendant to further enquiry, for example through investigative journalism, with a view to determining whether he was the true culprit and a restriction upon the right to do so would severely damage the right to freedom of expression, *Minelli v. Switzerland (A/62)* (1983) 5 E.H.R.R. 554 and *Nolkenbockhoff v. Germany (A/123-C)* (1991) 13 E.H.R.R. 360 distinguished; (2) the purpose of the 1973 Rules was to protect the presumption of innocence, to protect a person's privacy and to avoid undermining an acquittal in circumstances where there was an aspect of the law which required clarification after the conclusion of the trial. There was no statutory penalty for breach and the only effective sanction was to be found in the ordinary law of contempt, which was designed, not for the protection of the individual, but for the protection of administration of justice, and (3) the anonymity order had not received sufficient publicity to make it effective. However, it was impossible to reach a finding that the matter was in the public domain to such an extent as to extinguish any supposed confidentiality, *Attorney General v. Guardian Newspapers Ltd (No.2)* [1990] 1 A.C. 109, [1989] C.L.Y. 3103 and *R. v. Broadcasting Complaints Commission, ex p. Granada Television Ltd* [1995] E.M.L.R. 163, [1995] C.L.Y. 7 considered. On the evidence there was no information which would have led H to recognise or acknowledge an obligation of confidence, since there was nothing inherently confidential about the fact that B had been charged with, and acquitted of, rape, nor would the information which B was seeking to withhold normally be considered to be of a personal or private nature. Consequently, B's reliance upon Art.8 was flawed because the court's approach to the right to privacy was inextricably linked with the development of the law of confidence. To sanction B's argument would militate against open justice and require anonymity throughout the trial.

B v. H BAUER PUBLISHING LTD [2002] E.M.L.R. 8, Eady, J., QBD.

3225. Publishing—breach of contract—implied terms—requirement for consistency with express terms

T claimed damages for breach of contract from W, contending that W broke an agreement to provide T with the serialisation rights to the memoirs of a famous politician, and that T was entitled to the extra cost of purchasing the serialisation rights it eventually bought from D. T submitted that under the agreement, W had the publishing rights to the memoirs and sub sold the serialisation rights to T, before relinquishing its power of disposal of the rights; therefore W should pay damages for its failure to meet the agreement. It was further submitted that (1) there was an implied term in the agreement that W would not act in relation to the publishing agreement in such a way as to put the serialisation agreement beyond its or T's reach, and (2) there was also an implied term that W had the power to dispose of the first serialisation rights to T and would continue to have the right.

Held, giving judgment for W, that the court had to be wary of implying terms in instances where a carefully written agreement had been drafted. Furthermore, an implied term could not go further than what was required to give business efficacy to the contract and could not be inconsistent with the effect of the express terms, *Philips Electronique Grand Public SA v. British Sky Broadcasting Ltd* [1995] E.M.L.R. 472, [1997] C.L.Y. 4845 applied. Therefore (1) the implied term sought did not conform with the express terms of the agreement, which defined the serial rights and specified that the book might never materialise because W had the right to end the publishing agreement at any time, and (2) the term could not be implied into the agreement as it would have placed an excessive burden on W.

TIMES NEWSPAPER LTD v. GEORGE WEIDENFELD & NICOLSON LTD; *sub nom.* TIMES NEWSPAPERS LTD v. GEORGE WEIDENFELD & NICOLSON LTD [2002] F.S.R. 29, Bell, J., QBD.

3226. Television—political parties—party election broadcasts—refusal to transmit on grounds of taste and decency

P, a registered political party, appealed against the decision of the judge ([2001] EWHC Admin 607) refusing it permission to apply for judicial review of the decision of the BBC and other terrestrial broadcasters not to transmit a party election broadcast in Wales. P opposed abortion, euthanasia, destructive embryo research and human cloning. In the 2001 General Election P had put up enough candidates in Wales to entitle it to screen a single party election broadcast. A video had been submitted to the BBC depicting the products of suction abortion and describing various abortion techniques. The BBC and other terrestrial broadcasters had refused to show the broadcast because, in their view, having regard to the guidelines of taste and decency it constituted a breach of their obligations. A broadcast was eventually approved and transmitted which contained no visual images. By consent, the court approached the hearing as a substantive appeal against the disposal of judicial review at first instance. The issue for determination was whether the considerations of taste and offensiveness were sufficient to warrant what was effectively an act of censorship, banning P's proposed broadcast.

Held, allowing the appeal, that the judge had erred in approaching the issue on *Wednesbury* grounds. At the time of an election the right to freedom of speech was imperative; the State should, in principle, possess little discretion to interfere with it, *Bowman v. United Kingdom* (1998) 26 E.H.R.R. 1, [1998]

C.L.Y. 3086 applied. The court owed a special responsibility to the public to preserve the freedom of political debate, especially during a general election. The nature of a party election broadcast was such that the court would give only limited deference to the broadcaster's views. There was a constitutional duty to protect political speech. The proposed broadcast contained disturbing images but was not gratuitous, untrue or sensational. To campaign against abortion was a legitimate political aim and the images in the broadcast were an important element of P's message. The BBC and other terrestrial broadcasters had been wrong to approach the issue merely as a question of taste and decency; insufficient weight had been given to the pressing need for free political expression.

R. (ON THE APPLICATION OF PROLIFE ALLIANCE) v. BBC; *sub nom.* PROLIFE ALLIANCE v. BBC, [2002] EWCA Civ 297, [2002] 3 W.L.R. 1080, Laws, L.J., CA.

3227. Books

Arnold, Richard—Entertainment and Media Law Reports: 2001. Hardback: £430.00. ISBN 0-421-75670-5. Sweet & Maxwell.

Crone, Tom; Alberstat, Philip; Cassels, Tom—Law and the Media. 4th Ed. Paperback: £19.99. ISBN 0-240-51629-X. Focal Press.

Fenwick and Phillipson: Media Freedom and the Human Rights Act. Paperback. ISBN 0-406-94289-7. Butterworths Law.

Gilboa, Eytan—Media and Conflict-Framing Issues, Making Policy, Shaping Opinions. Hardback: £28.50. ISBN 1-57105-270-4. Paperback: £28.50. ISBN 1-57105-276-3. Transnational Publishers, Inc.

Goldstein, Norm; Goldstein, Norma—Associated Press Stylebook and Briefing on Media Law. Paperback: £12.99. ISBN 0-7382-0740-3. Perseus Books.

Harcourt, Amanda; Parker, Nigel—Music Business. Paperback: £52.00. ISBN 1-902558-42-1. Palladian Law Publishing Ltd.

Jones, Hugh; Benson, Chris—Publishing Law. 2nd Ed. Hardback: £65.00. ISBN 0-415-26153-8. Paperback: £24.99. ISBN 0-415-26154-6. Routledge, an imprint of Taylor & Francis Books Ltd.

Lutzker, Arnold P.—Content Rights for Creative Professionals. Paperback: CD-ROM: £27.50. ISBN 0-240-80484-8. Paperback: CD-ROM: £27.50. ISBN 0-240-80484-8. Focal Press.

Lynn, Michael—Media Law in Ireland. Hardback. ISBN 1-85475-209-X. Butterworths Law (Ireland).

Martino, Tony; Miskin, Claire—Entertainment Law Review 2001. Hardback: £435.00. ISBN 0-421-77320-0. Sweet & Maxwell.

Miller, Phillip—Media Law for Producers. Paperback: £27.50. ISBN 0-240-80478-3. Focal Press.

Miller, Phillip—Media Law for Producers. 4th Ed. Paperback: £27.50. ISBN 0-240-80478-3. Focal Press.

Morgan, Owen—International Protection of Performers Rights. Hardback: £35.00. ISBN 1-84113-285-3. Hart Publishing.

Parker, Nigel—Music Business. Paperback: £52.00. ISBN 1-902558-42-1. Palladian Law Publishing Ltd.

Robertson, Geoffrey; Nicol, Andrew—Media Law. 4th Ed. Paperback (C format): £30.00. ISBN 0-14-024769-6. Penguin Books.

Russomanno, Joseph—Speaking Our Minds-Conversations with the People Behind Landmark First Amendment Cases. Hardback: £51.50. ISBN 0-8058-3767-1. Paperback: £25.50. ISBN 0-8058-3768-X. Lawrence Erlbaum Associates, Inc.

Tugendhat, Michael; Christie, Iain—Law of Privacy and the Media. Hardback: £145.00. ISBN 0-19-925430-3. Oxford University Press.

MENTAL HEALTH

3228. Hospital orders–jurisdiction–power to quash Crown Court order–test for inappropriateness of trial

[Supreme Court Act 1981 s.29(3); Mental Health Act 1983 s.51(5).]

K, a schizophrenic, applied for judicial review of a decision of the Crown Court to make a hospital order with a restriction order pursuant to the Mental Health Act 1983 s.51(5). K had pleaded not guilty to two charges of indecent assault of young girls. An order was made under s.51(5) at the behest of K's counsel, on the basis of medical evidence which indicated that K would be liable to behave in a disruptive manner during a trial. The Crown Court contended that the court had no jurisdiction to quash its order, since it related to a trial on indictment within the meaning of the Supreme Court Act 1981 s.29(3).

Held, granting the application (Pill L.J. dissenting in part), that it was not clear whether the power to make an order under s.51(5) of the Act was an exercise of the Crown Court's jurisdiction in matters relating to trial on indictment within the meaning of s.29(3) with the result that the High Court did not have the power to quash such an order. The High Court did, however, have the power to quash an order if the Crown Court had made a jurisdictional error of the type which took the case outside the scope of the Crown Court's jurisdiction in matters relating to trial on indictment, *R. v. Maidstone Crown Court, ex p. Harrow LBC* [2000] Q.B. 719, [1999] C.L.Y. 99 considered. The judge had erred in failing to scrutinise the word "inappropriate" for the purposes of s.51(5); the section had to be construed restrictively and was not to be used as a convenient means of avoiding a potentially inconvenient and embarrassing trial. A "high degree of disablement or relative disorder" had to be present. A broader view of the word "inappropriate" was permissible where a defendant had already been convicted, but to pass sentence without first convicting the defendant was a step which could only be taken in exceptional circumstances.

R. (ON THE APPLICATION OF KENNEALLY) v. SNARESBROOK CROWN COURT; R. (ON THE APPLICATION OF KENNEALLY) v. RAMPTON HOSPITAL AUTHORITY, [2001] EWHC Admin 968, [2002] Q.B. 1169, Pill, L.J., QBD (Admin Ct).

3229. Learning difficulties–guardianship–confidential information–disclosure sought by mother

[Mental Health Act 1983 s.29; Human Rights Act 1998 Sch.1 Part I Art.6, Art.8.]

S, the mother of C who had learning and behavioural difficulties, appealed against the dismissal of her application for judicial review of the decision by the local social services to refuse her permission to see C's social services files and other material upon which guardianship decisions had been made. As C grew older there was a professional view that it would be better if he were cared for in a residential environment, away from home where S had been caring for him. The local social services authority invited S to agree to guardianship or face an application under the Mental Health Act 1983 to replace her as nearest relative. S agreed and there followed a number of renewals of guardianship. S sought access to C's files, particularly the material upon which the decisions to continue the guardianship had been made but her requests were refused.

Held, allowing the appeal, that at common law and under the Human Rights Act 1998 Sch.1 Part I Art.6 and Art.8 it was necessary to strike a balance between maintaining confidentiality of information and permitting or requiring that information to be disclosed in certain cases. The information sought by S was of a type covered by the common law obligation of confidence but that did not generally confer a privilege against disclosure in legal proceedings. Normally the court would require all relevant material to be before it for the proper administration of justice and in cases where the material concerned a child or patient, the child or patient had an interest in ensuring that all relevant material was before the court. S had an obvious interest in seeing the material so that she could respond properly to the social services' requests for guardianship. S and C's right to a family life under Art.8 was engaged but S's right under Art.6 to be involved in the decision making concerning C outweighed C's rights under Art.8. This was particularly so where there was no suggestion that C objected to disclosure or where there was any risk of harm to C as a result of such disclosure.

R. (ON THE APPLICATION OF S) v. PLYMOUTH CITY COUNCIL, [2002] EWCA Civ 388, [2002] 1 W.L.R 2583, Hale, L.J., CA.

3230. Mental health review tribunals–discharge–stay of decision to discharge pending judicial review challenge–lawfulness of decision to resection claimant

[Mental Health Act 1983 s.3, s.13.]

H appealed against a decision ([2001] EWHC Admin 901) and contended that (1) the court could not lawfully grant a stay of the Mental Health Review Tribunal's decision to discharge H, pending the outcome of AHA's application for judicial review of that decision, once the time stipulated for discharge had been reached; (2) AHA's decision to readmit and detain H under the Mental Health Act 1983 s.3 and s.13 in the interim period was unlawful; (3) the tribunal's decision to discharge was not *Wednesbury* unreasonable, and (4) the tribunal had given adequate reasons for its decision.

Held, allowing the appeal in part, that (1) the court had jurisdiction to grant a stay of a tribunal decision that was subject to a judicial review challenge, even where that decision had already been fully implemented, provided that (a) there was a strong case that the decision was unlawful; (b) there was cogent evidence of risk and dangerousness, and (c) the validity of the tribunal's decision was to be determined with the greatest possible speed; (2) the judge had erred in finding that the decision to readmit H was lawful. AHA were not entitled to overrule a discharge order except where they were conscientiously able to suppose that, had the tribunal been aware of fresh circumstances, it would have reached a different conclusion and not ordered the discharge. Although AHA had been advised and believed that the tribunal's decision was unlawful, no new circumstances had arisen which justified AHA's decision to resection H and thus, AHA had acted unlawfully, *R. (on the application of von Brandenburg) v. East London and the City Mental Health NHS Trust* [2001] EWCA Civ 239, [2002] Q.B. 235, [2001] C.L.Y. 4429 followed; (3) the tribunal had acted unreasonably in failing to consider the availability of suitable after care and accommodation when deciding to order H's immediate discharge. Where a tribunal had doubts as to whether such services would be available on discharge, it should adjourn so as to obtain the necessary information, and (4) the tribunal had failed to meet the obligation to give adequate reasons for its rejection of the powerful expert evidence against discharge.

R. (ON THE APPLICATION OF H) v. ASHWORTH HOSPITAL AUTHORITY; R. (ON THE APPLICATION OF ASHWORTH HOSPITAL AUTHORITY) v. MENTAL HEALTH REVIEW TRIBUNAL FOR WEST MIDLANDS AND NORTH WEST REGION, [2002] EWCA Civ 923, [2003] 1 W.L.R. 127, Dyson, L.J., CA.

3231. Mental health review tribunals–judgments and orders–provision of information to non party

[Administration of Justice Act 1960 s.12; Mental Health Act 1983 s.78 (2); Mental Health Review Tribunal Rules 1983 (SI 1983 942) r.21 (5).]

T, the former partner of a mental patient, G, applied for judicial review of the decision of the Mental Health Review Tribunal not to provide her with certain information relating to its decision whereby it had ordered a deferred conditional discharge. T believed that G posed a threat to her life. The Tribunal had previously refused her interim application to be made a party to any hearing concerning G. In a letter explaining its reasons for not providing her with information about the conditions imposed on G and the reason for the deferral, the Tribunal had stated that the combined effect of the Administration of Justice Act 1960 s.12 and the Mental Health Review Tribunal Rules 1983 r.21(5) was that the requested information could only be given to a party to the Tribunal hearing. T argued that r.21(5) of the Rules, properly construed, provided the Tribunal with a discretion to decide whether or not to make public the information that she sought.

Held, granting the application, that a Tribunal did have a discretion under r.21(5) of the Rules to decide whether or not to provide T with the information that she sought. The blanket approach expressed by the Tribunal in its letter to T had been unlawful. The Tribunal had erred in placing reliance on the decision of *Pickering v. Liverpool Daily Post and Echo* [1991] 2 A.C. 370, [1991] C.L.Y. 2456 as establishing that it did not have the power to provide the information sought; the decision in *Pickering* did not establish that the Tribunal could never direct the publication of the conditions imposed on a patient's discharge, *Pickering* considered. It was necessary, when considering the Rules, to have regard to the statute from which they were derived, namely the Mental Health Act 1983. Rule 21 was probably derived from s.78(2)(e) of the Act. However, that section could not be read in isolation from s.78(2)(j). Against that background, it was apparent that the ambit of r.21(5) of the Rules was sufficiently wide to enable the Tribunal to make public at least some of the information that T was seeking. Given T's genuine fear, the provision of some information about the Tribunal's decision would provide her with considerable peace of mind.

R. (ON THE APPLICATION OF T) v. MENTAL HEALTH REVIEW TRIBUNAL; *sub nom*. T v. MENTAL HEALTH REVIEW TRIBUNAL, [2002] EWHC 247, [2002] Lloyd's Rep. Med. 354, Scott Baker, J., QBD (Admin Ct).

3232. Mental hospitals—medical treatment—decision of hospital managers—susceptibility to judicial review

[Mental Health Act 1983 s.3; Registered Homes Act 1984 Part II; Nursing Homes and Mental Nursing Homes Regulations 1984 (SI 1984 1578) Reg.12(1); Civil Procedure Rules 1998 (SI 1998 3132) Part 54 r.54.1.]

In proceedings brought by A, a woman with a severe personality disorder, seeking judicial review of the decision of the managers of a private psychiatric hospital to alter the nature of care provided in one of its wards, the preliminary issue arose as to whether the decision had been made "in relation to the exercise of a public function" within the meaning of the Civil Procedure Rules 1998 Part 54 r.54.1 and was therefore susceptible to judicial review. The hospital had been registered as a mental nursing home under the provisions of the Registered Homes Act 1984 Part II and admitted patients under the Mental Health Act 1983 s.3. A, whose placement at the hospital was funded by her local health authority, maintained that the ward had been intended to be a single unit dedicated to working therapeutically with female patients with a primary diagnosis of personality disorder. According to A, the decision of the managers to change the focus of the ward meant that it would cater for women with a primary diagnosis of mental illness. The provision of care for such persons differed from that provided to those with a primary diagnosis of personality disorder.

Held, determining the preliminary issue in favour of A, that the decision of the managers was an act of a public nature and therefore susceptible to judicial review. While decisions relating to treatment were clinical in nature, decisions relating to the facilities provided and whether the hospital had adequate staff with the appropriate training were another matter; since the hospital was registered under the 1984 Act, such a decision was subject to the statutory duty imposed under the Nursing Homes and Mental Nursing Homes Regulations 1984 Reg.12(1) to provide adequate professional staff and treatment facilities. Furthermore, there was a public interest in the care and treatment provided by the hospital given that as a result of any deficiencies, a patient detained pursuant to the 1983 Act might have their detention prolonged or their recovery might be hindered. Accordingly, the managers of the hospital were a "functional" public authority, *Poplar Housing & Regeneration Community Association Ltd v. Donoghue* [2001] EWCA Civ 595, [2002] Q.B. 48, [2001] C.L.Y. 4415 and *R.*

(on the application of Heather) v. Leonard Cheshire Foundation [2001] EWHC Admin 429, [2001] A.C.D. 75 considered.
R. (ON THE APPLICATION OF A) v. PARTNERSHIPS IN CARE LTD, [2002] EWHC 529, [2002] 1 W.L.R. 2610, Keith, J., QBD (Admin Ct).

3233. Mental patients–capacity–late term abortion–best interests of patient

[Abortion Act 1967 s.1 (1) (1) (a); Mental Health Act 1983 s.3.]
S was a 34 year old schizophrenic of Indian origin, detained in a psychiatric hospital under the Mental Health Act 1983 s.3. She was 24 weeks pregnant, the limit for a termination under the Abortion Act 1967 s.1 (1) (1) (a), and applied for declarations that (1) she did not have the capacity to decide on an abortion, and (2) an abortion was in her best interests. Expert evidence showed that the procedure used for a late termination would be as stressful as a normal birth followed by removal of the child for adoption. Further, that the child would be of mixed race, giving rise to attendant adoption difficulties.
Held, refusing the applications, that none of the expert evidence favoured a termination or viewed that course of action as being in S's best interests. The other circumstances of the case, including the procedure necessary for a 24 week termination, showed that an abortion would not be in S's best interests either. The issue of the termination of pregnancies in psychiatric patients required that hospitals had protocols in place to deal with such cases well before the 24 week statutory limit and that such patients obtained independent legal advice.
SS (MEDICAL TREATMENT: LATE TERMINATION), *Re*; *sub nom*. SS (AN ADULT: MEDICAL TREATMENT), *Re* [2002] 1 F.L.R. 445, Wall, J., Fam Div.

3234. Mental patients–consent–certification of administration of medical treatment to competent, non consenting adult patient–duty to give reasons

[Mental Health Act 1983 s.58.]
W, a competent patient detained under the Mental Health Act 1983, sought judicial review of the decision of F, a Second Opinion Appointed Doctor (SOAD) under the 1983 Act, that anti psychotic medication should be administered to W without his consent. F had carried out an assessment of W so as to facilitate the renewal of certification for medical treatment without consent under s.58 of the 1983 Act. W sought, inter alia, a declaration that fairness demanded that F should have provided him with adequate written reasons when certifying under s.58.
Held, granting the application, that where a decision to administer medical treatment sanctioned the violation of the autonomy of a competent, non consenting adult patient the common law implied a duty to give reasons as of right, *R. (on the application of Wilkinson) v. Broadmoor Hospital* [2001] EWCA Civ 1545, [2002] 1 W.L.R. 419, [2001] C.L.Y. 4431, *R. v. Civil Service Appeal Board, ex p. Cunningham* [1991] 4 All E.R. 310, [1991] C.L.Y. 18, *R. v. Secretary of State for the Home Department, ex p. Doody* [1994] 1 A.C. 531, [1993] C.L.Y. 1213 and *R. v. Higher Education Funding Council, ex p. Institute of Dental Surgery* [1994] 1 W.L.R. 242, [1995] C.L.Y. 162 considered. However, an exemption from that general duty would arise where disclosure would be likely to cause serious harm to the physical or mental health of the patient or any other person
R. (ON THE APPLICATION OF WOODER) v. FEGGETTER, [2002] EWCA Civ 554, [2003] Q.B. 219, Brooke, L.J., CA.

3235. Mental patients–discharge–failure to adduce evidence at original hearing– referral to fresh tribunal–lawfulness of referral

[Mental Health Act 1983 s.70, s.71 (1), s.73.]
The Secretary of State appealed against a ruling that there was no justification for the referral of the case of a restricted patient, C, back to a fresh tribunal. C had previously applied to a Mental Health Review Tribunal for discharge pursuant to the Mental Health Act 1983 s.70. The Tribunal concluded that C should be

conditionally discharged subject to conditions which included, inter alia, access to, rather than supervision by, a psychiatrist. The community social worker who had prepared a statement of needs recommending that any conditions should include supervision by a psychiatrist, subsequently discovered that her report had not been made available to the Tribunal. In view of this omission the Secretary of State referred the case back to a fresh tribunal pursuant to s.71 (1).

Held, dismissing the appeal, that a decision directing conditional discharge was provisional and a Tribunal was accordingly entitled to reconsider its decision pursuant to s.73 if, prior to directing a conditional discharge, there was a change of circumstances or additional material was made available, *R. (on the application of H) v. Secretary of State for the Home Department* [2002] EWCA Civ 646, Times, May 24, 2002 applied and *R. v. Oxford Regional Mental Health Tribunal, ex p. Secretary of State for the Home Department* [1988] A.C. 120, [1987] C.L.Y. 2425 overruled.

R. (ON THE APPLICATION OF C) v. SECRETARY OF STATE FOR THE HOME DEPARTMENT, [2002] EWCA Civ 647, *The Times*, May 24, 2002, Lord Phillips of Worth Matravers, M.R., CA.

3236. Mental patients–infectious disease control–no condoms policy–no "real and immediate threat to life"

[Human Rights Act 1998 Sch.1 Part I Art.2, Art.8.]

H, a homosexual mental patient with hepatitis C, applied for judicial review of the policy of A, a special hospital, not to issue condoms to patients. The policy was part of A's "Patients' Relationships Policy" which had been adopted in October 2000. Although A operated a no-sex policy, H maintained that he was sexually active and that a patient care team had approved the use of condoms by him. H submitted, inter alia, that the policy of not issuing condoms was in breach of the right to life and the right to private life under the Human Rights Act 1998 Sch.1 Part I Art.2 and Art.8 respectively.

Held, refusing the application, that H was effectively arguing that A was, by virtue of its no-condoms policy, failing to protect others from harm from him. It was necessary to show, for the purposes of Art.2, that the policy was one that involved "a real and immediate threat to life" and that A was not doing everything that could be reasonably expected to obviate that threat, *Osman v. United Kingdom* [1999] 1 F.L.R. 193, [1998] C.L.Y. 3102 and *Keenan v. United Kingdom (27229/95)* 10 B.H.R.C. 319, [2001] C.L.Y. 3572 applied. The relevant type of sexual activity was that of anal penetrative intercourse. Whilst it was impossible to say that there was no risk of such intercourse, on the available evidence it was apparent that it was unlikely to occur. M's assertions that he was sexually active were doubtful and the evidence of A was to be preferred. The likelihood of a patient becoming infected with hepatitis B or C due to sexual activity was extremely low. It followed that the policy did not present "a real and immediate threat to life" for the purposes of Art.2. Furthermore, it could not be said that A had acted unreasonably in adopting the policy. Applying the same "real and immediate threat" test for the purposes of Art.8, H's claim failed for the same reasons.

R. (ON THE APPLICATION OF H) v. ASHWORTH HOSPITAL AUTHORITY, [2001] EWHC Admin 872, [2002] 1 F.C.R. 206, Sir Christopher Bellamy, Q.C., QBD (Admin Ct).

3237. Mental patients–local authorities powers and duties–entitlement to charge for after care services

[Mental Health Act 1983 s.3, s.117.]

M, together with various other local authorities, appealed against a ruling ([2001] Q.B. 370) that it was not entitled to charge former mental patients for after care services provided pursuant to the Mental Health Act 1983 s.117. All the cases before the court were concerned with persons suffering from mental illness who had been admitted to hospital pursuant to s.3 of the 1983 Act and then subsequently discharged and placed in residential accommodation pursuant to s.117(2). M submitted that whilst there was a duty under s.117 to provide after care services, there was no actual power to do so.

Held, dismissing the appeal, that s.117 was free standing. If there had been any intention on the part of Parliament that after care services would be provided under other statutory provisions, then s.117(2) would have been expected to specify such provisions. In the absence of any such clearly worded "gateway" provision, it was clear that s.117(2) was incapable of being read as imposing a duty to provide services under other unspecified legislation. The natural and obvious interpretation of s.117(2) was that the duty carried with it a concomitant power to carry out the duty.

R. (ON THE APPLICATION OF STENNETT) v. MANCHESTER CITY COUNCIL; R. (ON THE APPLICATION OF ARMSTRONG) v. REDCAR AND CLEVELAND BC; R. (ON THE APPLICATION OF COBHAM) v. HARROW LBC; *sub nom.* R. v. RICHMOND LBC, *ex p.* WATSON; R. v. MANCHESTER CITY COUNCIL, *ex p.* STENNETT; R. v. HARROW LBC, *ex p.* COBHAM; R. v. REDCAR AND CLEVELAND BC, *ex p.* ARMSTRONG, [2002] UKHL 34, [2002] 2 A.C. 1127, Lord Steyn, HL.

3238. Mental patients rights–right to liberty and security–criteria for renewal of detention

[Mental Health Act 1983 s.3, s.20; Human Rights Act 1998 Sch.1 Part I Art.5.]

A schizophrenic, R, who had been living at home pursuant to a treatment plan, challenged a decision by hospital managers to renew their authority to detain her under the Mental Health Act 1983 s.3 on the basis that she constituted a danger to herself and others without her medication. R had a history of past readmissions to hospital resulting from her refusal to take her medication voluntarily. R contended that the decision had been unlawful since the renewal conditions specified in s.20 had not been fulfilled, or, in the alternative, that renewed detention breached her right to liberty under the Human Rights Act 1998 Sch.1 Part I Art.5. R maintained that the power to detain or renew could only be used where the condition of a patient required treatment in hospital.

Held, refusing the application, that the applicable test was whether treatment in hospital formed a substantial part of the treatment regime and not whether the treatment plan envisaged that the patient would be treated as an in patient. The managers in question had not erred in considering the renewal process as opposed to the criteria governing an initial admission. On the facts of the instant case treatment in hospital constituted a significant part of the treatment plan for R and accordingly the criteria for renewal had been satisfied. Art.5 was not engaged since under the existing law the only way in which medication could be administered on a compulsory basis was by detaining a patient or renewing the patient's liability to detention.

R. (ON THE APPLICATION OF DR) v. MERSEY CARE NHS TRUST; *sub nom.* R. (ON THE APPLICATION OF R) v. MERSEY CARE NHS TRUST *The Times*, October 11, 2002, Wilson, J., QBD (Admin Ct).

3239. Mental patients rights–right to liberty and security–discharge– reconsideration by tribunal of deferred decision

[Mental Health Act 1983 s.73; Human Rights Act 1998 Sch.1 Part I Art.5.]

IH, a restricted patient, appealed against the refusal ([2001] EWHC Admin 1037, Independent, January 14, 2002 (C.S.)) of his application for judicial review of his continued detention. A Mental Health Review Tribunal had directed that IH be discharged subject to certain arrangements being made, including that he be supervised by a psychiatrist. No psychiatrist had been found and IH had accordingly remained in detention. IH had sought a declaration that the Mental Health Act 1983 s.73 was incompatible with the right to liberty and security provided by the Human Rights Act 1998 Sch.1 Part I Art.5 as a Tribunal did not have the power to guarantee that any conditions attached to a direction of conditional discharge would be implemented within a reasonable time. The judge had found that s.73 of the 1983 Act could be interpreted in a way that was compatible with Art.5 if, after a deferred conditional discharge had been directed, theTribunal monitored attempts made to comply with the conditions and amended the discharge order in the light of any problems encountered. Although not expressly stated by the judge, such a conclusion was incompatible with the decision of the House of Lords in *R. v. Oxford Regional Mental Health Tribunal, ex p. Secretary of State for the Home Department* [1988] A.C. 120, [1987] C.L.Y. 2425.

Held, dismissing the appeal, that where, despite its best endeavours, a local authority was unable to provide the necessary services to fulfil the conditions set by a Tribunal when ordering the conditional discharge of a patient, it was appropriate for the Tribunal to reconsider its decision and, where necessary, to make appropriate modifications to the conditions imposed. There was a potential conflict between the decision of the House of Lords in *R. v. Oxford Regional Mental Health Tribunal* and Art.5(4). If, however, a Tribunal no longer proceeded on the basis that it could not reconsider a conditional discharge on specified conditions where there was a change in circumstances, the scheme would be compatible with Art.5(1), *R. v. Oxford Regional Mental Health Tribunal, Johnson v. United Kingdom* (1999) 27 E.H.R.R. 296, [1998] C.L.Y. 3898, *Winterwerp v. Netherlands (A/33)* (1979-80) 2 E.H.R.R. 387, [1981] C.L.Y. 1089 and *R. (on the application of K) v. Camden and Islington HA* [2001] EWCA Civ 240, [2002] Q.B. 198, [2001] C.L.Y. 4430 considered.

R. (ON THE APPLICATION OF H) v. SECRETARY OF STATE FOR THE HOME DEPARTMENT; *sub nom.* R. (ON THE APPLICATION OF IH) v. NOTTINGHAMSHIRE HEALTHCARE NHS TRUST; R. (ON THE APPLICATION OF IH) v. SECRETARY OF STATE FOR THE HOME DEPARTMENT, [2002] EWCA Civ 646, [2003] Q.B. 320, Lord Phillips of Worth Matravers, M.R., CA.

3240. Mental patients rights—right to liberty and security—seclusion of patient in non secure hospital

[Mental Health Act 1983; Human Rights Act 1998 Sch.1 Part I Art.3, Art.5.]

S, a mental patient, applied for judicial review in relation to his seclusion in a non secure hospital for a period of twelve days. Following his admission, S had been violent and had repeatedly absconded, and had been secluded as he was potentially dangerous. S had previous convictions for sexual offences. S had been secluded in a non secure hospital because of the unavailability of a bed in a secure unit. S contended that his seclusion was unlawful under domestic law and that it infringed his rights under the Human Rights Act 1998 Sch.1 Part I Art.3 and Art.5, particularly with regard to the length of his seclusion. S further submitted that, in respect of his convictions, the hospital had not been entitled to consider additional information relating to the offences which went further than the court's findings.

Held, refusing the application for judicial review, that (1) under the Mental Health Act 1983 a power to seclude a patient where necessary, could be implied, although a significant degree of anxious scrutiny was required at common law which should achieve a similar result to the application of the necessity and proportionality tests in ECHR cases. The review of seclusion and decisions as to the conditions of seclusion were decisions as to medical treatment within the Act, *R. (on the application of Colonel M) v. Ashworth Hospital Authority (now Mersey Care NHS Trust)* [2002] EWHC 1521 applied, (2) although the use of seclusion had to be minimised, where there was genuinely no sensible alternative to its use Art.3 was not necessarily infringed even if the seclusion was not short term and was not an emergency measure. In the present case the seclusion did not reach the necessary levels of seriousness to constitute a breach, (3) seclusion was not detention but rather it affected the conditions of detention, and for the purposes of Art.5 it was the detention that deprived a mental patient of his liberty, *R. v. Deputy Governor of Parkhurst Prison, ex p. Hague* [1992] 1 A.C. 58, [1992] C.L.Y. 3651 applied, (4) the underlying cause for the duration of the seclusion in the instant case was the lack of a secure bed, but this did not make the decision to seclude unlawful for, as a general rule, the problem of resources was not one for the courts, and

(5) in the determination of treatment and assessment of risk, a responsible medical officer had to take into account all of the apparently reliable information that he was provided with.

S v. AIREDALE NHS TRUST, [2002] EWHC 1780, [2003] Lloyd's Rep. Med. 21, Stanley Burnton, J., QBD (Admin Ct).

3241. Mental patients rights—right to respect for private and family life—cross dressing—detention

[Human Rights Act 1998 Sch.1 Part I Art.8(1).]

E, a mentally ill male patient with a preference for dressing in women's clothing and who was detained in hospital, applied for judicial review of the hospital's decision to limit his access to female garments and to specify that those available to him could only be worn privately in his own room. E had been detained following commission of criminal offences. E contended that the restrictions imposed upon him constituted an interference with his right to a private life under the Human Rights Act 1998 Sch.1 Part I Art.8(1).

Held, refusing the application, that there was a pressing and self evident need for the hospital to be able to control what its patients wore and that was to be implied into the power to detain a mentally ill offender. The decision to impose the restriction was a rational one and the restriction itself was necessary for the purposes of both detention and treatment.

R. (ON THE APPLICATION OF E) v. ASHWORTH HOSPITAL AUTHORITY, [2001] EWHC Admin 1089, *The Times*, January 17, 2002, Richards, J., QBD (Admin Ct).

3242. Mental patients rights—right to respect for private and family life—residential care—transfer from care home

[Human Rights Act 1998 Sch.1 Part I Art.8.]

C and three others, all of whom suffered from mental disorders, sought judicial review of the decision of B to transfer them from a care home on the ground that it was to be refurbished for use as a rehabilitation unit for other patients. C argued that (1) B had promised that he could remain at the home for the rest of his life; (2) B had breached an obligation to consult with him about proposals for the future of the home; (3) when making a decision on the future of the home, B had not properly assessed his needs, and (4) B's decision to move him from the home amounted to a breach of his rights under the Human Rights Act 1998 Sch.1 Part I Art.8.

Held, refusing the applications, that (1) the evidence revealed that no promise of a "home for life" had been made; the home had been intended only as an interim placement; (2) given that C had not been promised a home for life and that his placement had only been on an interim basis, B had not been under a duty to consult with him about his move. That conclusion was not altered by the fact that C had occupied the home for over three years; (3) it could not be said that C's needs had not been properly assessed. He had received careful assessments and the doctor responsible for his care had concluded that a move from the home would be beneficial for him, and (4) a health authority responsible for the long term care of mental patients and their placement in suitable accommodation had to act compatibly with Art.8 of the 1998 Act. B had to strike a fair balance between the interference with C's Convention rights in connection with the home and the requirements of other patients for whom it was responsible and to involve C in the process of making its decision so that it was sensitive to his needs. It was a necessary consequence of the engagement of Art.8(1) that C's rights were inextricably linked with the primary obligation to supply medical care from which the provision of a home arose. In the instant case, B had acted honestly and reasonably and had not breached Art.8. The court observed that it was regrettable that court proceedings were not avoided in the instant case, *R. (on the application of Cowl) v. Plymouth City*

Council [2001] EWCA Civ 1935, [2002] 1 W.L.R. 803, [2002] 2 C.L. 183 considered.

R. (ON THE APPLICATION OF C) v. BRENT, KENSINGTON AND CHELSEA, AND WESTMINSTER MENTAL HEALTH NHS TRUST, [2002] EWHC 181, [2002] Lloyd's Rep. Med. 321, Newman, J., QBD (Admin Ct).

3243. **Restricted patients–leave–deferred conditional discharge–consent of Secretary of State**

[Mental Health Act 1983 s.17, s.41 (3) (c) (i), s.42, s.73(7); Human Rights Act 1998 s.3(1), s.6, Sch.1 Part I Art.5(1), Sch.1 Part I Art.5(4).]

A, a restricted patient, applied for judicial review of the Secretary of State's refusal of consent to his leave of absence from hospital under the Mental Health Act 1983 s.17. A conditional discharge had been granted to A by the Mental Health Review Tribunal, but this had been deferred under s.73(7) of the 1983 Act until appropriate accommodation had been found. A sought declarations that (1) the Secretary of State's refusal of consent was unlawful for the purposes of the Human Rights Act 1998 s.6, and (2) the 1983 Act was incompatible with his rights under Sch.1 Part I Art.5(1) and Art.5(4) of the 1998 Act. A also sought review of the Secretary of State's policy of limiting the grant of consent to s.17 leave to cases where there were exceptional circumstances. The Secretary of State submitted that his approach to giving consent under s.17 was flexible and no such policy existed.

Held, granting the application for judicial review, that the Secretary of State's practice or policy of using s.42 of the 1983 Act in preference to s.17 when considering the grant of leave in such circumstances was wrong. It was clear that such a preference existed and there appeared to be evidence of a policy to that effect. The normal method should have been to use s.17 in relation to restricted patients who had been granted deferred conditional discharge. The Secretary of State was obliged to respond with reasonable promptness to a tribunal's recommendations unless there were sound reasons to the contrary or new circumstances arose. It was possible to operate the provisions of s.17 and s.41 (3) (c) (i) of the 1983 Act without causing unreasonable delay and it was not necessary to use s.3(1) of the 1998 Act to read the provisions of s.41 (3) (c) (i) of the 1983 Act in a way that rendered them compatible with Convention rights. In the instant case, the Secretary of State's refusal of leave and his policy in relation to leave of this nature for restricted patients had caused an unreasonable delay of about six weeks, resulting in a violation of A's rights under Art.5(1) and Art.5(4).

R. (ON THE APPLICATION OF A) v. SECRETARY OF STATE FOR THE HOME DEPARTMENT; *sub nom.* R. (ON THE APPLICATION OF RA) v. SECRETARY OF STATE FOR THE HOME DEPARTMENT, [2002] EWHC 1618, [2003] 1 W.L.R. 330, Crane, J., QBD (Admin Ct).

3244. **Books**

Roesch, Ronald; Corrado, Raymond; Dempster, Rebecca–Psychology in the Courts: International Advances in Knowledge. Hardback: £38.00. ISBN 90-5823-123-2. Harwood Academic (Medical, Reference and Social Sciences).

Slovenko, Ralph–Law in Psychiatry. Hardback. ISBN 0-415-93364-1. Brunner-Routledge.

Slovenko, Ralph–Psychiatry in Law / Law in Psychiatry. 2 Volume Set. Hardback: £99.95. ISBN 0-415-93365-X. Brunner-Routledge.

NEGLIGENCE

3245. Causation–consent orders–fatal mesothelioma–full liability consent order prior to death

G, the widow of a former employee of V, appealed against a decision that the issue of causation in respect of her late husband's fatal mesothelioma was still open notwithstanding that V had entered into a consent order on a full liability basis whilst G's husband was still alive. Before the mesothelioma had been diagnosed, G's husband had claimed against V for his suffering from pleural plaques caused by his exposure to asbestos whilst employed by V. Under a consent order V had agreed to an immediate award of £4,000 on a full liability basis on the assumption that G's husband would not thereafter develop mesothelioma. On his death, G sought to rely on the consent order to establish entitlement to damages on a full liability basis. Relying on *Fairchild v. Glenhaven Funeral Services Ltd (t/a GH Dovener & Son)* [2001] EWCA Civ 1881, [2002] 1 W.L.R. 1052, [2002] 1 C.L. 278 V contended that G had to establish which employer was responsible for the fatal exposure since G's husband had in fact been employed by different legal entities. V conceded that the mesothelioma had been caused by exposure to asbestos.

Held, allowing the appeal, that although when formulating a consent order the parties were entitled to leave issues of causation open, in the present case that had not been done and V had agreed to an award on a full liability basis, *Fairchild* considered. Accordingly, V was precluded from contesting liability since on a true construction of the consent order V had accepted that if G's husband suffered from any of the conditions referred to in the order and established that such conditions were caused by exposure to asbestos, then he would receive damages on a full liability basis.

GREEN v. VICKERS DEFENCE SYSTEMS, [2002] EWCA Civ 904, *The Times*, July 1, 2002, Collins, J., CA.

3246. Causation–duty of care–motorcycle event organisers–causative effect of mixed ability groupings

C, a quadriplegic, appealed against the dismissal of his claim in negligence against R. C had broken his neck in a motorcycling accident which had taken place at an event organised by R. C contended that R had failed to ensure that the groups of riders, which had been categorised according to their ability, were kept separate with the result that C had been hindered by slow riders on the race track, a factor which had been causative of the accident.

Held, allowing the appeal, that R's duty of care had extended to preventing faster riders from being obstructed by slower riders, the solution to which was to stop the separate groups from being on the race track at the same time. The judge in the first instance had failed to draw a correct conclusion on the causative effect of mixing different groups of riders on the race track and whilst C was guilty of contributory negligence to a certain extent, R's breach of duty had been the principal causative factor.

CRAVEN v. RICHES, [2001] EWCA Civ 375, [2002] P.I.Q.R. P23, Sedley, L.J., CA.

3247. Clinical negligence–causation–doctors–failure to diagnose lymphoma–diminution in life expectancy

G appealed against the dismissal of his claim against S, his former general practitioner, for negligence in failing to diagnose his tumour. G had developed a non Hodgkin's lymphoma in the form of a lump under his left arm. In 1994 S had diagnosed the lump as a lipoma, a benign collection of fatty tissue, and consequently failed to refer him to a specialist. The following year, G had moved house and had consulted a new general practitioner who referred him to hospital. The examining surgeon suspected lymphoma and this was confirmed. The judge at first instance found that S's failure to refer G to a specialist in 1994 delayed his treatment by about nine months. The judge concluded however that there would have been no material change in the tumour during this time and that any escalation occurred in the following autumn. It was found that the delay in treatment had reduced G's chances of survival by 25 percent, however G's claim for damages was dismissed on the ground that G had failed to establish on the balance of probabilities that S's negligence had had a material outcome on the disease. Basing his decision on the decision reached in *Hotson v. East Berkshire HA* [1987] A.C. 750, [1987] C.L.Y. 2604, the judge at first instance had held that, on the evidence, for a person suffering from the same type of lymphoma as G, the prospects of a cure were less than 50 percent, so that it was more probable than not that G would have been in the same position even had the treatment commenced earlier. G submitted that the judge's assessment of the medical evidence was wrong and that on the balance of probabilities, had he received treatment earlier, he would have required only one course of chemotherapy and would have been cured. He further contended that even if the judge was correct in his assessment of the evidence, he failed to appreciate that the exercise he was carrying out in relation to G's statistical chances of survival was not one of causation but one of quantification, or alternatively, that following the decision in *Fairchild v. Glenhaven Funeral Services Ltd (t/a GH Dovener & Son)* [2002] UKHL 22, [2002] 3 W.L.R. 89, [2002] 7 C.L. 300 the court could revisit the issue of whether or not a loss of chance in respect of a diminution in a risk of an adverse outcome as a result of medical advice or intervention should be recognised as damage giving rise to a claim in negligence.

Held, dismissing the appeal (Lord Justice Latham dissenting), that G had sought to argue that his loss was a diminution in his life expectancy. G could have only succeeded in this claim if he could show that on the balance of probability S's negligence had caused it. This he failed to do. G could not show that he was not already going to suffer such loss notwithstanding any negligence on the part of S, *Hotson* applied. *Fairchild* differed from the instant case in that it concerned employers and indisputable and already sustained injury or illness and in which the defendants were 100 percent liable for the illnesses or injury. The approach taken in *Fairchild* applied only to the most narrowly defined circumstances and there was nothing to suggest a generally more relaxed approach to the issue of causation, *Fairchild* considered. In his dissenting judgment, Latham LJ, argued that there were stark differences between *Hotson* and the instant case. In *Hotson* the claim had proceeded on the basis that the necrosis either would or would not have resulted despite timeous intervention. The lymphoma in the instant case however was susceptible to treatment, the issue was to what extent the chances of treating successfully had been reduced. Latham LJ contended that *Hotson* was not authority for the proposition that the loss of a chance was not capable of forming the basis for an award of damages in medical negligence cases.

GREGG v. SCOTT, [2002] EWCA Civ 1471, *The Times*, November 4, 2002, Latham, L.J., CA.

3248. Clinical negligence–causation–patient with uncontrolled blood pressure–risk of second stroke–failure to adjust medication after dangerously high readings obtained

L suffered a mild stroke at the age of 36 and was found to be suffering from chronic hypertension. He was seen by P, a consultant clinical pharmacologist employed by H, four times over a four week period, then seen again after a break of two months and a further appointment was booked. After the fifth appointment, but three weeks before the next, L's blood pressure was measured continuously over two days and found to be dangerously high, as subsequently agreed by all the expert witnesses. P did not bring the next appointment forward, however, and when he saw L he only made a slight change to his medication. On the following day, L suffered a stroke that was much more serious than the first and which left him severely disabled and unable to speak. L sued H, alleging negligence in failing to monitor his blood pressure between the last two appointments; failure to analyse the blood pressure readings prior to the last appointment and a failure to prescribe proper treatment.

Held, giving judgment for L on liability, that (1) in assessing whether P had been negligent, regard had to be paid to the risk that L would suffer another stroke, the consequences if he did and the ways in which the likelihood could be reduced; (2) P's expert had failed to give proper weight to the uncontrolled state of L's blood pressure or that P had been concerned as to whether L was taking the prescribed medication properly and the fact that he was a young married man with a family, and (3) the facts showed that the risk of the second stroke would have been reduced by over 50 per cent if L's medication had been changed soon after the readings were taken.

LOWE v. HAVERING HOSPITALS NHS TRUST (2001) 62 B.M.L.R. 69, Judge Peter Crawford Q.C., QBD.

3249. Clinical negligence–causation–severe brain damage–sufficiency of evidence

G, who suffered from severe permanent brain damage, appealed against a finding ((2001) 57 B.M.L.R. 148) that her injury had not been caused by the negligence of S following brain surgery 16 years earlier. The trial judge found that G's brain damage was the result of systemic hypoxia or hypertension which should not have been permitted but held that G's condition could not be attributed to improper management by anaesthetist, R, during the post operative recovery period. S maintained that G's injury resulted from status epilepticus. G contended that the finding that R had exercised an appropriate standard of care and skill was against the weight of the evidence.

Held, dismissing the appeal, that the judge's decision could not be impugned. He had been entitled to conclude, on the balance of probabilities, that G's brain damage was the result of systemic hypoxia or hypertension. However, the expert witnesses had been unable to state with any degree of certainty whether a failure to treat the hypoxia had caused permanent brain damage or if G's condition had been otherwise caused. Therefore, G's claim that her injury would not have occurred but for S's negligence had not been proved to the required standard.

GRAY v. SOUTHAMPTON AND SOUTH WEST HAMPSHIRE HA, [2001] EWCA Civ 855, (2002) 67 B.M.L.R. 1, May, L.J., CA.

3250. Clinical negligence–causation–wrongful evaluation of cervical smear test– refusal to undergo further smear tests–contributory negligence

P brought a claim for damages in respect of a cervical smear which was wrongly evaluated in 1988 as being negative, when the correct result was that it was abnormal and showing a pre cancerous condition. In 1997, P was referred to a gynaecologist after suffering heavy bleeding and cervical carcinoma was discovered. The Trust defended the claim, contending that if P had responded to urgings on some seven occasions by her GP to have further smear tests between 1991 and 1997, her condition would have come to light earlier and appropriate treatment could have been given. The Trust submitted that (1) P's refusal to undergo screening had broken the chain of causation; (2) the Trust's duty in respect of the 1988 smear only extended until 1991 when the first repeat test ought to have taken place in accordance with their screening programme, and (3) P was contributorily negligent. P's evidence was that she had failed to have the smear tests because she found the procedure painful and embarrassing, although she acknowledged that she understood the potential risk involved in not having the tests.

Held, finding that P had been contributorily negligent, that (1) P's conduct in failing to undergo subsequent smear tests was not so unreasonable as to break the chain of causation because she had been misled by the inaccurate results of the 1988 test, in relation to which the Trust had been negligent; (2) the Trust's duty was not limited to the time when a repeat test ought to have been conducted as P had never participated in a screening programme, nor agreed to do so. The effects of the Trust's negligence in respect of the 1988 test would have been the same if there had been no screening programme at all, since the purpose of the test was merely diagnostic and not to serve as an entry into a screening programme, and (3) P had failed to take many opportunities to have further tests, the purpose of which she understood. Although her reasons for such failure were real, she had undergone a number of intimate examinations in connection with a miscarriage and subsequent pregnancy and birth of a baby, and as such it was not unreasonable to expect that the level of embarrassment she experienced would have lessened. Her repeated failure to undergo the tests despite warnings from her GP was blameworthy and the proper apportionment was to hold her responsible as to two thirds.

PIDGEON v. DONCASTER HA; *sub nom.* PIDGEON v. DONCASTER ROYAL INFIRMARY & MONTAGU HOSPITAL NHS TRUST [2002] Lloyd's Rep. Med. 130, Judge Bullimore, CC (Sheffield).

3251. **Clinical negligence–consultation–adequacy of pre-surgical advice to patient**

In April 1996, C underwent surgery for a revision decompression of his spine at L4/5. A consultant orthopaedic surgeon, U, carried out the procedure. Four days later C suffered loss of spinal fluid from the operation wound and was re-admitted to hospital. Arrangements were subsequently made for a repair of the meningomyelocele. In May 1996, U and a consultant neurosurgeon carried out a posterior exploration of C's lower lumbar spine. The dura was inspected and there was no obvious leak. A muscle patch was applied to the dura and C was later discharged home. C suffered constant and debilitating pain and an inability to return to work after the procedures and claimed that he was not given proper advice before the decompression procedure. Had he received proper advice, he would not have consented to that procedure.

Held, granting judgment in favour of C, that in the circumstances C's recollection of the pre-operative discussion was to be preferred. Both C and his wife's version were the same, they were convincing witnesses and they had had the benefit of consulting solicitors no later than a year after the operation and so events were fresh in their minds. U's evidence had changed and he had been in a difficult position, as he had not had to try to recall events until four years after the operation. On the evidence, C had not been advised of alternative procedures nor had he been warned of the possible risks consequent upon undergoing revision surgery, in fact U had conveyed reassurance that it would be fine and C had not been told that the surgery was urgent. The advice given did not satisfy the minimum standards of professional competence. There should have been a clear warning of the higher incidence of problems arising from revision surgery and other options should have been discussed. U admitted he had not explained to C that any course of action was available other than surgery. In the instant circumstances, had C received the appropriate advice he would not have agreed to undergo the operation. The judge found that there was a causal and temporal connection between the surgery and the symptoms, which were different and worse very soon after the surgery. The two operations had occurred within a short period on a site previously operated upon and had caused damage resulting in C's condition. The symptoms were much worse than they would have been without the surgery.

CHINCHEN v. UNIVERSITY HOSPITAL OF WALES HEALTHCARE NHS TRUST, November 8, 2001, Deputy High Court Judge Graham Jones, QBD. [*Ex rel.* Howard Shaw, Barrister, 29 Bedford Row Chambers, 29 Bedford Row, London].

3252. **Clinical negligence–expert evidence–judge;s failure to find facts–retrial**

The Trust appealed against a decision (Unreported, June 29, 2000) giving judgment for G who claimed that emergency surgery had been performed negligently. G, who suffered from a complex medical condition, was admitted to hospital with a suspected hernia. The central issue for the judge at first instance was the positioning of the abdominal incision by the surgeon. On appeal, the Trust contended that the judge had misinterpreted the expert evidence, had failed to consider whether one expert view withstood logical analysis and, in the alternative, had reached a perverse conclusion.

Held, allowing the appeal, that in an action for medical negligence a failure by the judge to make a reasoned rebuttal of any of the expert evidence adduced by the parties meant that the finding as to liability was fatally flawed. In the instant case, the judge had expressed her findings as conclusions, without dealing with the subsidiary issues raised by counsel or attempting any rebuttal of any expert view. Further, she had failed to define the issues, marshall the evidence or give reasons, *Eckersley v. Binnie* 18 Con. L.R. 1 applied. Accordingly, the judgment was set aside and a retrial was ordered.

GLICKSMAN v. REDBRIDGE HEALTHCARE NHS TRUST; *sub nom.* GLICKSMAN v. REDBRIDGE NHS TRUST, [2001] EWCA Civ 1097, (2002) 63 B.M.L.R. 109, Henry, L.J., CA.

3253. Clinical negligence–medical treatment–divers–treatment of decompression illness

H, a deep sea diver, sought damages against N and the local police force, for their alleged negligence in the treatment of the decompression illness he suffered following a dive. After attempting recompression himself, he alerted the coast guard and was airlifted to a hospital a short distance away from the dive site. However, because its decompression chamber was closed, he was taken to the police diving school chamber which was used as an alternative in such circumstances. H submitted that the N and police had both been negligent in their arrangements. He alleged that the delay in him receiving treatment caused by the diversion to the hospital, compounded by the fact that when he arrived at the police diving school, the chamber was not ready, meant that his recovery was impeded. Furthermore, he contended that when he finally received treatment, a doctor was negligent in not catheterising him and failing to rehydrate him intravenously. N and the police alleged that H was contributorily negligent by re-entering the water to attempt recompression and by failing to contact the coast guard earlier.

Held, giving judgment for the defendants, that given their undertaking to provide the compression facility in the event of the hospital's chamber being unavailable, the police owed a duty of care in their provision of the chamber. However, given that the function of the police was not medical care, the standard of care required was not that of a hospital. They did not have adequate information before the call from the hospital to justify alerting their team earlier. Accordingly, H's claim against the police had to fail. N owed H a duty of care, but this duty was qualified by the resources it had available. It was not negligent in ordering that H attend the hospital, given that if he was diagnosed as not suffering from decompression he could have received treatment there. The doctor's decisions were supported by expert witnesses, and when judged against those expected of a reasonably competent casualty doctor, he could not be said to have been negligent. Furthermore, there was no evidence that a shorter delay in H entering the compression chamber would have resulted in a better recovery.

HARDAKER v. NEWCASTLE HA [2001] Lloyd's Rep. Med. 512, Stanley Burnton, J., QBD.

3254. Clinical negligence–warnings–doctors–failure to give warning as to risk of post operative paralysis

A, a neurosurgeon who had carried out a back operation on C, appealed against the decision (Unreported, December 21, 2000) that although he had not performed the operation negligently, he had been negligent in not warning C of the slight risk of paralysis, which she in fact had suffered after the operation.

Held, dismissing the appeal, that even where surgery had been carried out successfully, a doctor remained liable in negligence if when seeking a patient's consent to the operation he had not provided a warning of the slight risk of post operative paralysis and that paralysis had been suffered by the patient. Accordingly, while in the instant case the operation had been completed successfully, A remained liable because he had failed to warn C prior to the operation of the risk of post operative paralysis. The rule that doctors were required to give patients appropriate information surrounding operations was to enable patients to choose whether or not to have the operation for which they were required to give their consent. Liability for failing to give adequate warning lay in negligence not trespass, but a patient still had the right to choose what could be done to her body. It followed that a doctor should take reasonable care to ensure that the information relevant to that choice was given. The judge had been correct to follow the decision of the majority in *Chappel v. Hart* [1999] Lloyd's Rep. Med. 223, [1999] C.L.Y. 3987.

CHESTER v. AFSHAR, [2002] EWCA Civ 724, [2003] Q.B. 356, Sir Denis Henry, CA.

3255. Clinical negligence–wrongful birth–intervening events–development of meningitis following birth–entitlement to damages for economic loss

S appealed against a ruling ([2001] Lloyd's Rep. Med. 39, [2001] C.L.Y. 4462) that G was entitled to recover damages representing the additional costs of rearing her disabled daughter, M. S had admitted to a negligent failure to diagnose or test for pregnancy at a consultation with G as a result of which G had been deprived of an opportunity to terminate the pregnancy. M was born premature and approximately four weeks later developed salmonella meningitis complicated by bilateral front brain abscesses, as a result of which she became severely handicapped. S contended that M was a healthy child at birth and that a subsequent infection could not found a claim for damages.

Held, dismissing the appeal, that M could not properly be described as a "healthy child" at birth since the bacterium responsible for the meningitis had already been present on her skin. All the ingredients for the condition to develop had been present and there had been no novus actus interveniens. Since the birth of a premature child who developed salmonella meningitis as a result of her exposure to a bacterium during the normal birth process was a foreseeable consequence of S's admitted negligence, G was entitled to recover damages for economic loss, *P v. St James and Seacroft University Hospital NHS Trust* [2001] EWCA Civ 530, [2001] 3 W.L.R. 376, [2001] C.L.Y. 1509 applied.

GROOM v. SELBY, [2001] EWCA Civ 1522, [2002] P.I.Q.R. P18, Brooke, L.J., CA.

3256. Contributory negligence–breach of statutory duty–highway maintenance– tripping incident resulting from gap in steps

[Highways Act 1980 s.41.]

W brought a claim against the local authority for damages for personal injuries following an incident in which he put his foot in a gap between two paving stones on a flight of steps outside his home and fell, sustaining injuries to his shoulder. W's claim was for breach of statutory duty under the Highways Act 1980 s.41, alleging that the local authority had failed to maintain the steps and had allowed one paving slab to become loose and move sideways, leaving a gap approximately two inches deep, three to four inches wide and 10 inches long. W's witness evidence was that the gap had been present for nine to 14 months. The local authority's evidence was that the area had been inspected two months before the accident and no problem had been perceived.

Held, finding in favour of W, that the gap had been present for at least eight to nine months prior to the accident and constituted a danger. On the facts, the local authority inspector must have failed to notice the gap when the inspection was carried out. However, W was found to be contributorily negligent as to one third, *Brown v. Edinburgh City Council* 1999 S.L.T. (Sh Ct) 43, [1999] C.L.Y. 6366 considered. W had been aware of the gap in the step outside his house for all the time it had been present and had taken steps to avoid it repeatedly as he passed up and down the steps approximately five times each week. He had never reported it to the local authority and had fallen while talking to friends; therefore W had failed to take appropriate care to avoid a danger of which he was well aware.

WALKER v. NEWHAM LBC, May 10, 2002, Judge Ryland, CC (Central London). [*Ex rel.* Guy Opperman, Barrister, 3 Paper Buildings, Temple, London].

3257. Contributory negligence–causation–damage to water main during construction work–subsequent burst causing flood damage–duty of water company to provide accurate mapping

[Metropolis Water Act 1852 s.17; Civil Liability (Contribution) Act 1978 s.1 (1); Water Act 1989 s.165; Water Industry Act 1991 s.209(1).]

T brought an action against D for a contribution under the Civil Liability (Contribution) Act 1978. T had paid out over £700,000 to property owners under the strict liability provisions of the Water Industry Act 1991 s.209(1) in respect of damage caused by a burst water main. The damage to the water main had occurred during cable laying work that was being carried out by D. D accepted that it owed a duty of care to those affected by the burst water main to prevent damage to their property but claimed that T had been negligent in failing to respond promptly to the problem of the damaged main and in failing to provide adequate information as to the location of the main. T submitted, inter alia, that the Metropolis Water Act 1852 s.17 had been impliedly repealed following the coming into force of the Water Act 1989 s.165 and that therefore it did not owe any private law duty to D.

Held, giving judgment for D, that s.17 of the 1852 Act was still in force. The duty under that section was to maintain accurate maps of mains and pipes and to allow interested parties to inspect and take copies of those maps; the duty was not to take care to protect from damage the property of occupiers of premises covered by maps by supplying accurate information to those whose activities might cause damage if inaccurate information was given. The immediate cause of the damage to the main was D's use of a JCB to break through concrete found under the road surface. Expert evidence showed that although D had properly referred to plans and used detection equipment prior to excavating, it had been negligent in using a JCB when it did not know what lay beneath the concrete. However, the loss suffered by the property owners was not directly caused by the initial damage to the main resulting from D's negligence; rather the loss was caused by the escape of water following the burst of the main which occurred over three hours after the initial damage. T's staff had failed to make a sensible assessment of the situation on the basis of available information as to the location and depth of the main. T had followed mechanistically its rigid procedure for shutting down smaller mains first when it should have been obvious that it was the larger main that needed to be shut down. The burst would not have occurred if the larger main had been shut down immediately. Furthermore, T had not updated its plans following a similar incident a few months previously. It was T's failure to act promptly which caused the damage suffered by the property owners. Therefore, since the damage suffered by the property owners was caused by T and was not "the same damage" within the meaning of s.1 (1) of the 1978 Act as the damage caused by D, T was not entitled to a contribution.

THAMES WATER UTILITIES LTD v. DIGGINWELL PLANT & CONSTRUCTION LTD, [2002] EWHC 1171, [2002] E.H.L.R. 20, Judge Richard Seymour Q.C., QBD (T&CC).

3258. Contributory negligence–road traffic accidents–failure to place infant in child restraint seat–late instruction of expert

F, Part 20 defendant to proceedings arising from a road traffic accident, applied for permission to bring a Part 20 claim against B. F had collided with an unlit tractor towing a trailer on an unlit road at night, causing the trailer to be lifted into the air and crash into a vehicle driven by B. B's wife, a front seat passenger, was killed and his three minor children were injured. The tractor driver, M, was subsequently convicted of road traffic offences. B issued proceedings against M, who brought a counterclaim against B for alleged negligent driving and Part 20 proceedings against F. F filed a defence to the Part 20 proceedings but made no allegations against B. M, F and B subsequently reached an agreement whereby judgment would be entered for B and his children, the counterclaim against B would not be pursued and F would contribute 75 per cent toward M's liability to B and his children. One year later, F and M instructed new solicitors who, in turn, instructed a seat belt expert. The expert advised that the injuries sustained by one of B's children were due to the failure to wear a seat belt but that the use of a seat belt would probably have caused different, but equally serious, injuries. The expert also advised that a child restraint seat would have prevented any injuries. F sought permission to bring a counterclaim against B for failure to put the child in a seat belt or child restraint seat.

Held, refusing the application, that (1) F had failed to explain the delay of over a year in instructing a seat belt expert; (2) whether or not there was an enforceable agreement not to pursue a claim against B, it was reasonable for B to have formed an expectation that no claim would be brought against him; (3) the allegation of negligence relating to the failure to put the child in a seat belt was bound to fail because the expert evidence showed that the use of a seat belt would not have prevented serious injuries, *Froom v. Butcher* [1976] Q.B. 286, [1975] C.L.Y. 2295 and *Traynor v. Donovan* (Unreported, October 20, 1978), [1978] C.L.Y. 2612 applied, *J (A Child) v. Wilkins* [2001] R.T.R. 19, [2001] C.L.Y. 4447 distinguished. Failure to strap a child into a child restraint seat was not negligent, and (4) if F was allowed to bring the counterclaim it was likely that B would suffer emotional distress and there would be further delay. Therefore the balance of prejudice favoured the refusal of the application.

BAROT v. MORLING, January 29, 2002, District Judge Eaton, CC (Leicester). [*Ex rel.* Sunil Iyer, Barrister, King Charles House, Nottingham].

3259. Crown immunity–personal injury–service personnel–compatibility of state's statutory immunity from tortious liability with right to public hearing

[Crown Proceedings Act 1947 s.10, s.10(1)(a), s.10(2)(a); Human Rights Act 1998 s.3, Sch.1 Part I Art.6(1).]

The Ministry of Defence appealed against a finding ([2002] EWHC 13, [2002] C.P. Rep. 26) that the Crown Proceedings Act 1947 s.10 was incompatible with the Human Rights Act 1998 Sch.1 Part I Art.6(1). M claimed that the MOD was vicariously liable for asbestos related injuries arising from alleged breaches of statutory duty and negligence in exposing him to asbestos fibres during his service with the Royal Navy. The MOD claimed that M was prevented from making the claim as s.10 granted state immunity from tortious liability in cases involving servicemen. In response, M contended (1) that s.10 should be declared incompatible with Art.6(1) as the statutory immunity prevented him from asserting a civil right, or (2) pursuant to s.3 of the 1998 Act, s.10 should be interpreted so as to achieve compatibility with his Convention rights.

Held, allowing the appeal, that (1) the existence of a civil right was a matter of substantive law in the contracting states. Although Art.6 was applicable in cases involving procedural rules, it had no impact on substantive rules delimiting rights and liabilities under civil law, *Pinder v. United Kingdom* (1985) 7 E.H.R.R. CD464 and *Dyer v. United Kingdom* (1985) 7 E.H.R.R. CD469 doubted. The court below had erred in finding that the substitution of a potential entitlement to a pension for a cause of action in negligence imparted a procedural aspect into s.10 which brought Art.6 into play. The effect of s.10 was substantive and thus, where the circumstances set out in s.10(1)(a) or s.10(2)(a) applied, a serviceman had no effective cause of action. It followed that M's Art.6 rights had not been breached, and (2) as Art.6 was not engaged on the facts of the case, s.3 of the 1998 Act had no application.

MATTHEWS v. MINISTRY OF DEFENCE, [2002] EWCA Civ 773, [2002] 1 W.L.R. 2621, Lord Phillips of Worth Matravers, M.R., CA.

3260. Duty of care–administrative decision making–medical research–delay in issuing warning as to dangers of administering aspirin to children

See HEALTH: Smith v. Secretary of State for Health. §1886

3261. Duty of care–ambulance service–manual handling of patients by ambulance technicians–injury to ambulance technician

[Manual Handling Operations Regulations 1992 (SI 1992/2793) Reg.4(1); Council Directive 90/269 on the minimum health and safety requirements for the manual handling of loads Art.3(2).]

S, appealed against a finding that it had breached Council Directive 90/269 Art.3(2) when K, one of its ambulance technicians, had suffered injuries carrying an elderly patient down the stairway of his home. K and a colleague had taken the patient down the stairway, which was narrow and steep, in a carry chair. He had been injured when forced for a brief moment to bear the full weight of the chair. K issued a respondent's notice upholding the judge's finding. K also argued that there had been a breach of the Manual Handling Operations Regulations 1992 Reg.4(1)(a) and Reg.4(1)(b) and that S had acted negligently by discouraging employees, in circumstances such as those in the instant case, from calling the fire brigade to take patients from their homes.

Held, allowing the appeal, that (1) S was not liable either under the Directive or under the Regulations. There was nothing to suggest that calling the fire brigade would have been appropriate in the instant case. The evidence showed that such an option was rarely used because it had to be carefully planned, took a long time and caused distress to the patient. There might be circumstances in which calling the fire brigade would be appropriate; that would depend on the seriousness of the problem, the urgency of the case and the actual or likely response of the patient or his carers and the fire brigade. Moreover, K had failed to show that giving more emphasis in training would have avoided K's injuries, and (2) an ambulance service owed the same duty of care to its employees as did any other employer, *Ogwo v. Taylor* [1988] A.C. 431, [1988] C.L.Y. 2445, *Stokes v. Guest Keen & Nettlefold (Bolt & Nuts) Ltd* [1968] 1 W.L.R. 1776, [1968] C.L.Y. 2701 and *Watt v. Hertfordshire CC* [1954] 1 W.L.R. 835, [1954] C.L.Y. 1340 considered. However, the question of what was reasonable for it to do might have to be judged in the light of its duties to the public and the resources available to it when performing those duties, *Kent v. Griffiths (No.3)* [2001] Q.B. 36, [2000] C.L.Y. 4204 and *Walker v. Northumberland CC* [1995] 1 All E.R. 737, [1995] C.L.Y. 3659 considered. While the risk to K had not been negligible, the task that he had been carrying out was of considerable social utility. Furthermore, S had limited resources as far as equipment was concerned. There was no evidence of any steps that S could have taken to prevent the risk and the only suggestion made was that it should have called on a third party to perform the task for it. Since calling the fire brigade was not appropriate or reasonably practicable for the purposes of the Directive and the Regulations, S had not shown a lack of reasonable care. Accordingly, S had not acted negligently.

KING v. SUSSEX AMBULANCE NHS TRUST, [2002] EWCA Civ 953, [2002] I.C.R. 1413, Hale, L.J., CA.

3262. Duty of care–banks–loan for refurbishment of property–assumption by bank of role of insurance broker

See BANKING AND FINANCE: Frost v. James Finlay Bank Ltd. §247

3263. Duty of care–buses–extent of duty of care owed to passengers

G, aged 72 at the time of the accident on one of A's buses, brought an action against A for damages for personal injuries. G had been about to sit down on a rear facing seat when the bus pulled away with an unexpected or sudden jerk, throwing G to the ground and causing him to sustain facial injuries. G had been carrying a shopping bag in each hand, neither of which was particularly heavy or bulky, and he had been able to carry them both in one hand whilst paying his fare. The driver knew nothing of the fall and it was not reported to him at the time by G or any other passenger. About four other passengers boarded after G, but there was no evidence of any inconvenience to them.

Held, granting judgment for A, that no breach of duty had been established because (1) the driver was not required to wait until all passengers were safely seated, as this was too high a duty and would slow bus services down unnecessarily; (2) there was a higher duty if any passengers were particularly vulnerable or encumbered for example in terms of frailty or difficulty with mobility; (3) there was no duty on the driver to examine each passenger minutely, but simply to be aware, for example, of walking sticks, disabilities or babes in arms, *Fletcher v. United Counties Omnibus Co Ltd* [1998] P.I.Q.R. P154, [1998] C.L.Y. 3992 followed; (4) there was no persuasive evidence that the jerk was abnormal or negligent in terms of passenger outrage or assistance offered to G, and (5) it would have been prudent for G, who was relatively unencumbered, to hold on to the supports provided with one hand, whilst keeping bags in the other hand.

GLARVEY v. ARRIVA NORTHWEST LTD, October 1, 2001, District Judge Osborne, CC (Altrincham). [*Ex rel.* John G Baldwin, Barrister, Oriel Chambers, 14 Water Street, Liverpool].

3264. Duty of care—forseeability—psychiatric illness—employer's liability for employee's illness caused by stress at work

In four joined cases the issue before the Court of Appeal concerned the liability of an employer for an employee's psychiatric illness caused by stress at work.

Held, allowing the appeals of S, SCC and B and dismissing the appeal of SMBC, that the threshold question was whether the kind of harm to the particular employee was reasonably foreseeable and not whether psychiatric injury was foreseeable in a person of "ordinary fortitude". By its very nature a psychiatric disorder would be more difficult to foresee than a physical injury. It was necessary to ask whether a harmful reaction to the pressures of the workplace was reasonably foreseeable in the relevant employee; a harmful reaction was made up of two components: (a) an injury to health, which (b) was attributable to stress at work. The determination of the question of foreseeability would depend on the inter relationship between the individual characteristics of the relevant employee and the requirements made of him by his employer. Relevant factors included: (1) the nature and extent of the work being undertaken. An employer was required to be more alert if an employee was being overworked in a job which was intellectually or emotionally demanding, and (2) signs exhibited by the employee himself. It was necessary to distinguish between signs of stress and signs of impending harm to health. Even where an employer had not received express warning from an employee, harm to health could become foreseeable where an employee uncharacteristically took regular or prolonged absences from work. However, an employer was entitled to assume, unless he was made aware of a particular problem or vulnerability, that an employee could cope with the normal pressures of his job; in general, there was no requirement to make searching and intrusive inquiries. What an employee told his employer could be taken at face value. When an employee returned to work following an absence for sickness, it was implied that in returning the employee considered himself fit to return. An employer had a duty to act only when the indications were plain enough for any reasonable employer to realise that it was necessary to do something. When considering what it was reasonable for an employer to do, the size and scope of the business together with the availability of resources were relevant. The employer only had to take steps which were likely to be of some benefit. For the purposes of proving causation, an employee merely had to show that the employer's breach of duty had materially contributed to his ill health.

SUTHERLAND v. HATTON; SOMERSET CC v. BARBER; SANDWELL MBC v. JONES; BAKER REFRACTORIES LTD v. BISHOP; *sub nom.* HATTON v. SUTHERLAND; JONES v. SANDWELL MBC; BARBER v. SOMERSET CC;

BISHOP v. BAKER REFRACTORIES LTD, [2002] EWCA Civ 76, [2002] 2 All E.R.1, Hale, L.J., CA.

3265. Duty of care-holidays-games-personal injury arising from organised game at holiday camp

B, a guest at one of R's holiday camps, brought a claim against R after suffering head and spinal injuries while participating in a party game organised by R. The game was based on a "Tarzan and Jane" scenario and involved a number of male contestants carrying female contestants from a chair at one side of a stage across to the other side. All the contestants were volunteers. B, who had played the game at another holiday camp the previous year, was successfully carried by three male contestants before being dropped on her head by the fourth. R's employees had explained the nature of the game but had given no instructions as to how the female contestants were to be carried. In fact all the male contestants used the fireman's lift. B contended that the game gave rise to a foreseeable risk of injury such that R ought not to have encouraged or permitted it, or at least not without proper instruction in lifting techniques or the provision of safety mats.

Held, dismissing the claim, that in the circumstances the mere foreseeability of injury was not enough to establish a breach of R's duty of care to B. The game had been played many times before at R's and other holiday camps without any history of injuries. Such risks as the game involved were obvious and B was both an adult and a willing participant.

BURTON v. RANK GROUP PLC, July 12, 2002, Recorder Woodward Q.C., CC (Lincoln). [*Ex rel.* Langleys Solicitors, Insurance Claims Department, Newporte House, Doddington Road Business Park, Lincoln].

3266. Duty of care-prisons-liability of prison authorities for loss of personal possessions

K, a prisoner, temporarily exchanged his hi-fi unit with that of another prisoner in breach of prison regulations. The hi-fi subsequently went missing and K brought a claim against the prison authorities, P. K had signed a form which listed his personal possessions and included an acknowledgment of the regulations. K claimed that prison officers ignored such regulations at times and that he suspected discrimination against himself. He acknowledged that a further regulation provided for approval of such an exchange of personal belongings to be obtained on written application, and that he had made no such application.

Held, giving judgment for P, that there was no liability on P's part for the disappearance of the hi-fi, as there was no adequate evidence of K's compliance with the regulations despite the fact that he was well aware of them. Any claim which K may have had was against his fellow prisoner, and not P.

KING v. PREMIER PRISON SERVICES LTD, September 12, 2001, District Judge Turner, CC (Preston). [*Ex rel.* Lupton Fawcett Solicitors, Yorkshire House, Greek Street, Leeds].

3267. Duty of care-prisons-liability of prison officers for loss of personal possessions-disclaimers-public policy considerations

N, a prisoner, brought a claim against the prison authorities, P, in connection with various items of his personal property which he alleged went missing as a consequence of the removal of N and his possessions to the segregation unit of the prison. The property had been put into bags and recorded by prison officers, the loss coming to light when the bags were later restored to N. N had signed a disclaimer removing from P responsibility for personal property in N's possession. N contended that the disclaimer did not apply, since in the circumstances, he had been unable to physically protect his property. P contended that, in a prison environment where personal property was at high risk, a wider approach towards the establishment of a duty of care should be adopted.

Held, granting judgment for P, that for the purposes of establishing a duty of care (1) it was foreseeable that N's property was at high risk of going missing; (2) there was sufficient proximity between N and P to create an obligation on P to safeguard N's property, and (3) in the circumstances it was not fair and reasonable that P be responsible for N's loss for reasons of public policy. If prison authorities were to be held responsible for such losses, which were a frequent occurence in a prison environment, the eventual effect would be to severely restrict the possessions which prisoners were allowed to have. N had therefore failed to establish that a duty of care existed, and further, was unable to prove on the balance of probabilities that the prison officers concerned were responsible for the loss.

NOLAN v. PREMIER PRISON SERVICES LTD, July 3, 2001, District Judge Cernik, CC (Northampton). [*Ex rel.* Lupton Fawcett Solicitors, Yorkshire House, Greek Street, Leeds].

3268. Duty of care–prisons–liability of prison officers for recovery of personal possessions–disclaimers

M, a prisoner, suffered an assault, during the course of which property belonging to him was stolen from his cell. M claimed compensation for the loss from the prison authorities, P, contending that they had failed to undertake appropriate searches for recovery of the property, although he acknowledged that they were not liable for preventing the actual loss. M had signed a disclaimer form accepting that any personal property in his possession was held at his own risk. M also claimed that P had failed to effect a proper removal of property from his cell, by comparing items removed from it with the prison record of property retained.

Held, granting judgment for P, that having regard to the fact that the property was in M's possession at the time of the loss, the disclaimer operated to remove from P any liability in respect of such property. Notwithstanding a report by the Prisons Ombudsman which criticised P's handling of the search procedure, there was no evidence to substantiate a claim in negligence in connection with the loss.

MERRICK v. PREMIER PRISON SERVICES LTD, May 4, 2001, District Judge Handley, CC (York). [*Ex rel.* Lupton Fawcett Solicitors, Yorkshire House, Greek Street, Leeds].

3269. Duty of care–road traffic accidents–agricultural vehicles–duty to take exceptional steps

M brought an action against B for damages arising from a road traffic accident in which he sustained personal injuries. M, who had been riding a motorcycle along a major trunk road, collided with the offside rear of a tractor pulling a trailer driven by B as B emerged onto the trunk road. M contended, inter alia, that B had been negligent in that he should have used an alternative access route to the trunk road where visibility of the junction was better. B argued that the choice of access route had been reasonable and that the accident had been caused by M's excessive speed.

Held, granting judgment in favour of B, that there was nothing unusual or abnormal about the tractor and trailer driven by B, nor was the junction unusual or abnormal when compared to other similar junctions in rural areas, *Arnot v. Sprake* [2001] EWCA Civ 341 applied. M had been driving too fast, he knew the area and was aware of the likely presence of agricultural vehicles; accordingly, M was to blame for the accident.

MacKLIN v. BAIRD, April 26, 2002, Recorder Bromilow, CC (Taunton). [*Ex rel.* Bond Pearce, Solicitors, London Court, 64 London Road, Southampton].

3270. Duty of care–schools–accidents–school skiing trips–extent and nature of duty

W appealed against a finding ([2002] P.I.Q.R. P13) that it was liable in negligence for injuries sustained by a pupil, C, on a school skiing holiday. W submitted that the judge at first instance had been wrong to hold that a teacher, J, had failed to adequately discipline C for a second incident of skiing off piste thereby allowing C to continue skiing, albeit on piste, and resulting in an accident which had left C paralysed. W contended that in finding J in breach of duty, the judge had failed to apply the reasonable teacher/parent test, and that the finding of breach ran contrary to the weight of the evidence.

Held, allowing the appeal, that the teachers on the skiing trip had owed C a duty to show him the same care as would have been exercised by a reasonably careful parent with experience of skiing and school trips but also having regard to C's level of skiing competence, the conditions at the resort and the teachers' responsibilities for the group. The decision by J to issue a severe reprimand and accept assurances from C that he would not ski off piste again, had not fallen outside the range of reasonable responses for a teacher in his position in the circumstances. It had never been disputed that C did not need supervision whilst skiing and although J could have insisted after the off piste skiing incidents that supervision be imposed, that would not have been an obvious response in the circumstances, *G v. G (Minors: Custody Appeal)* [1985] 1 W.L.R. 647, [1985] C.L.Y. 2594 applied.

CHITTOCK v. WOODBRIDGE SCHOOL; *sub nom.* WOODBRIDGE SCHOOL v. CHITTOCK, [2002] EWCA Civ 915, [2002] E.L.R. 735, Auld, L.J., CA.

3271. Duty of care–schools–children–tripping accidents–uneven school playground surface–foreseeability

C appealed against a finding that it had breached its duty of care to B, aged 6, who had suffered personal injuries after tripping in the school playground. B had successfully contended that C's failure to lay the tarmac surface to the level of the concrete edging, on premises where young primary schoolchildren played, amounted to a breach of its duty of care.

Held, allowing the appeal, that there was no evidence that the change in level of the surface presented any significant or extraordinary hazards for the users of the playground and there was no reasonable foresight of harm, *Mills v. Barnsley MBC* [1992] P.I.Q.R. P291, [1993] C.L.Y. 2967 and *Littler v. Liverpool Corp* [1968] 2 All E.R. 343, [1968] C.L.Y. 1747 applied.

B (A CHILD) v. CARDIFF CC; *sub nom.* B (A CHILD) v. CARDIFF CITY COUNCIL, [2001] EWCA Civ 703, [2002] E.L.R. 1, Pill, L.J., CA.

3272. Duty of care–schools–supervision–injury caused by sharpened pencil–primary school pupils' use of pencils not negligent

R brought an action against the local authority for damages for personal injuries arising from an accident which had occurred whilst R was at school. R, aged five years and two months at the time of the incident, had been in a class taken by an experienced teacher. The incident occurred when R's friend, who had been holding R's arm back, suddenly released it resulting in the HB pencil, being held by R and which had recently been sharpened to a fine point, entering R's right eye causing serious injury. R had suffered a 70 per cent loss of visual field in his right eye. R alleged that the local authority were negligent in permitting young children to use and be freely able to sharpen standard HB pencils when safer alternative writing materials were available and that there had been a failure to closely supervise the sharpening and use of the pencils by young children. The local authority denied negligence.

Held, granting judgment for the local authority, that it was accepted practice that in the interests of education, a range and variety of materials should be provided for pupils of R's age. The policy of providing HB pencils to be sharpened for full development of handwriting was also an accepted practice in the field of primary school education. There were strong educational benefits in the provision of HB pencils and R had used them both at school and at home. The accident happened in class, but the teacher had been unaware of it because neither R nor his friend had made any noise and no-one was aware of the injury until later in the evening. The local authority, through its teacher, had provided adequate supervision of the class to the appropriate standards and the teacher/pupil ratio was appropriate. The teacher had been diligent and had ensured that her pupils applied the school rule of sharpening pencils over a bin and carrying the pencils with the blunt end pointing out and the sharp end in the palm.

RAVEN v. SUFFOLK CC, November 23, 2001, Judge Curl, CC (King's Lynn). [*Ex rel.* Prettys Solicitors, Elm House, 25 Elm Street, Ipswich, Suffolk].

3273. **Foreseeability–intervening events–children–foreseeability of accident involving petrol removed from garage**

In February 1996 a group of five boys, including the three claimants, had entered disused garage premises which had been tenanted by A up to and including December 1995. Whilst on the premises, the boys discovered a quantity of petrol in a large plastic drum and they proceeded to remove an amount of it in a separate container, taking it to a disused changing block on a recreation field approximately 400 yards away. The following day, the three claimants returned to the changing block and ignited the petrol, causing an explosion. The two youngest claimants sustained severe burns, which ultimately caused the death of the youngest. The eldest claimant suffered nervous shock. A argued that the chain of events involving removal of the petrol to a place remote from the garage and the subsequent ignition of it, was an unlikely consequence of the breach of duty such as to amount to a mere possibility and therefore the chain of causation was broken.

Held, giving judgment in favour of the claimants, that the petrol had been stored inappropriately on the premises and A had abandoned the petrol at a time when they knew, or ought to have known, that children were gaining access to the premises. It was reasonably foreseeable that children would either ignite the petrol on the premises or alternatively remove the petrol elsewhere and ignite it. The judge rejected the defence of novus actus interveniens. The petrol had been taken to a place remote from from the garage and was there subject to the conduct on the part of the children leading to its ignition and explosion. The judge found that to allow petrol to come into the hands of children must expose them to a risk of injury, which was foreseeable because it could be reasonably anticipated that the petrol would be used for a dangerous purpose. The fact that the explosion took place on premises other than the yard itself, and on a subsequent day, was found to be immaterial.

S (A CHILD) v. A & E AUTOS, November 16, 2001, Judge Hawksworth, CC (Bradford). [*Ex rel.* Armstrongs Solicitors, Kipling House, 24 Otley Street, Skipton, North Yorkshire].

3274. **Foreseeability–schools–pupil injured sliding down bannister**

M, aged eight and a pupil at the defendant school, U, climbed onto a bannister intending to slide down it. He fell 12 feet and sustained serious injuries. There were no reports of previous accidents on the stairs and bannister, which had been in place since 1936. Shortly after the accident the school fitted studs into the bannister to prevent others from sliding down it. M, through his mother, sued U for damages.

Held, giving judgment for U, that the school had not been negligent in failing to take steps to prevent the risk. Although the possibility of a pupil sliding down the bannister was foreseeable, the school had carried out a risk assessment and no one thought the risk of injury sufficiently serious to require special safety measures. The risk of a pupil sliding down a staircase bannister and sustaining injury was no more likely than other risks which could be encountered at school. If there had been a finding of negligence against the school there would have been a finding of substantial contributory negligence against M, as, despite his age, he had known that what he was doing was dangerous.

GOUGH v. UPSHIRE PRIMARY SCHOOL [2002] E.L.R. 169, Judge Grenfell, QBD.

3275. Forseeability–psychiatric harm–communication mistakenly advising death of newborn child

F sought to recover damages for nervous shock after being informed that his newborn son had died. F had attended at the hospital after receiving a telephone call from the child's mother, with whom he no longer had a relationship, informing him that she had given birth to a son. F attended at the hospital where he was informed by staff that the baby had just died and was given a baby's corpse to hold. F was subsequently informed that there had been a mistake and that his son was in fact alive. F contended that the shock occasioned as a result of this incident had led him to develop post traumatic stress disorder. F asserted that since grief at the death of a child was a reasonably foreseeable occurrence, he was entitled to recover damages for a reasonably unforeseeable but recognised psychiatric disorder if this subsequently developed. A maintained that the public policy limitation whereby grief could not normally found an action for damages was embraced within the actual foreseeability test itself.

Held, giving judgment for F, that (1) as F was clearly a primary victim the relevant test was whether A ought reasonably to have foreseen that its conduct would expose F to the risk of a recognised psychiatric disorder, *McLoughlin v. O'Brian* [1983] 1 A.C. 410, [1982] C.L.Y. 2153 applied and *Page v. Smith* [1996] A.C. 155, [1995] C.L.Y. 3682 considered. Furthermore foreseeability depended on the precise facts known to A at the time. If A had been aware of F's lack of involvement with the child in utero and its mother, that matter would have been properly in their contemplation. However, A was unaware of F's lack of involvement and accordingly A's degree of foreseeability of risk had to be assessed on the basis of an ordinary paternal relationship with the unborn child, and (2) having regard to the unique circumstances pertaining in the instant case it was appropriate to assess risk on the basis of expert psychiatric opinion. On the basis of the available psychiatric evidence F had established that his post traumatic stress disorder, whilst delayed in onset, had been caused by the incident in question.

FARRELL v. AVON HA [2001] Lloyd's Rep. Med. 458, Judge Bursell Q.C., QBD.

3276. Misrepresentation–accountants–economic loss not established

LG, accountants and third defendants to proceedings issued by D, applied for summary dismissal of the claim against them. D sought to recover losses arising from an alleged negligent misrepresentation in accounts prepared by LG. LG contended that D had not suffered any loss and, in the alternative, that if a loss had been incurred it could not be attributed to any misrepresentation by them.

Held, granting the application and dismissing the claim against LG, that the appropriate starting point to assess the level of damages to be awarded to a claimant who alleged negligent misrepresentation was to compare the position in which the claimant found himself having entered into the transaction with the position the claimant would have been in had he not done so, *Nykredit Mortgage Bank Plc v. Edward Erdman Group Ltd (Interest on Damages)* [1997] 1 W.L.R. 1627, [1998] C.L.Y. 1432 followed. In the instant case, D alleged losses in respect of the provision of a bond to secure potential liabilities to its customers and in respect of payments made to fund the activities of ST, a tour operator. No claim had in fact been made under the bond and the sum paid by D by way of security was likely to be repaid with interest. Therefore, D had sustained no loss arising from the bond, *Forster v. Outred & Co* [1982] 1 W.L.R. 86, [1982] C.L.Y. 1849 distinguished. Similarly, N had failed to prove any losses in relation to the funding of ST; thus D's claim had been brought prematurely and should be dismissed.

DENHAM v. NOWMAN [2001] Lloyd's Rep. P.N. 623, John Martin Q.C., Ch D.

3277. Negligent misstatement–causes of action–employment references–no reliance on reference–right to seek employment–peaceful enjoyment of possessions

[Human Rights Act 1998 Sch.1 Part II Art.1.]

In the course of debt recovery proceedings, K, a financial consultant, appealed against a decision to uphold an order striking out certain paragraphs of his amended defence and counterclaim. The relevant paragraphs alleged that D's employer, L, an insurance company, had made false and negligent statements to the effect that K owed money to it in the form of unpaid commission with the result that he had been prevented from gaining other employment as a financial products' salesman. K contended that (1) he had a cause of action for negligent misstatement despite the fact that no actual reference had been sought since, having regard to the relevant regulatory bodies' rules, such a reference would have inevitably resulted in his rejection as a candidate, and (2) L, in preventing K from gaining relevant employment, had contravened his right to peaceful enjoyment of his possessions under the Human Rights Act 1998 Sch.1 Part II Art.1.

Held, dismissing the appeal, that the order to strike out the relevant paragraphs had been correct as both the defence and counterclaim had been bound to fail. Neither paragraph disclosed a cause of action as (1) the facts pleaded did not give rise to a cause of action for negligent misstatement based on the principles established in *Hedley Byrne & Co Ltd v. Heller & Partners Ltd* [1964] A.C. 465, [1963] C.L.Y. 2416 and *Spring v. Guardian Assurance Plc* [1995] 2 A.C. 296, [1994] C.L.Y. 1918. No reference had been sought and therefore there could be no reliance on it and in the absence of reliance, there was no resulting damage, *Hedley Byrne* and *Spring* applied, and (2) a right to seek a specific category of employment could not constitute a "possession" for the purposes of Art.1. Moreover, the instant case concerned the determination of private law rights, *Tre Traktorer AB v. Sweden (A/159)* (1991) 13 E.H.R.R. 309 distinguished.

LEGAL & GENERAL ASSURANCE CO LTD v. KIRK; *sub nom.* LEGAL & GENERAL ASSURANCE LTD v. KIRK, [2001] EWCA Civ 1803, [2002] I.R.L.R. 124, Jonathan Parker, L.J., CA.

3278. Occupiers liability–local authorities powers and duties–repairs–responsibility of tenant to report disrepair

[Occupiers Liability Act 1984 s.2.]

J brought a claim against the local authority when he tripped over a flagstone forming part of a forecourt area leading from the highway to a block of flats owned by the local authority. The trip measured up to 1.5cm in height. Prior to the accident, the local authority had operated a trial inspection system of land within their housing department ownership but not forming part of the adopted highway. However, this system had been discontinued due to cost. J contended that it was the local authority's responsibility to replace or repair the flags.

Held, giving judgment for the local authority, that it was reasonable for the local authority to rely upon tenants to report disrepair for which it was responsible. Under the tenancy agreement, it was the tenants responsibility to report all such repairs. It was not unreasonable for the local authority to fail to have in place a system of inspection of housing department land linking the highway and flats. Accordingly, there had been no breach of the duty of care imposed by the Occupiers Liability Act 1984 s.2 or in negligence.

JEFFERS v. WEST LANCASHIRE DC, May 23, 2002, District Judge Donnelly, CC (Wigan). [*Ex rel.* Paul Brant, Barrister, Oriel Chambers, 14 Water Street, Liverpool].

3279. Personal injury–causation–negligent medical advice

[Civil Liability (Contribution) Act 1978.]

P, an NHS Trust, appealed against the decision that it should pay a 40 per cent contribution under the Civil Liability (Contribution) Act 1978 in relation to damages claimed by W, a polio sufferer who, due to an injury sustained after a fall whilst on B's, her employers, premises, had had an above the knee amputation. The amputation had been advised by J, a doctor in the employment of P. The judge had approached the issue as one of the "loss of chance" of W avoiding amputation. B cross appealed against the judge's finding that there was not sufficient evidence to establish causation. W had not given evidence at the trial.

Held, making no order on the appeal and allowing the cross appeal, that (1) the judge had erred in awarding damages for the loss of chance, *Tahir v. Haringey HA* [1998] Lloyd's Rep. Med. 104, [1998] C.L.Y. 3966 applied; (2) a claim brought by a patient would not fail if that patient did not give evidence in person as to what might have occurred if they had been properly advised, *Chappel v. Hart* [1999] Lloyd's Rep. Med. 223, [1999] C.L.Y. 3987 considered. In the instant case, J had been negligent in failing to inform himself and accordingly advise W as to the alternatives to amputation. It was apparent that W would not have given her consent to the amputation had J provided proper advice. It followed that her claim against P would have succeeded, and (3) the chain of causation had not been broken by the intervening negligence of J. The negligence of B had been the causative force, it having increased W's vulnerability and reduced her mobility beyond the consequences of amputation. Moreover, it had been foreseeable that medical intervention would occur and that W's pre-existing vulnerability would result in its own risks. Whilst J's conduct had been negligent it had not been grossly negligent. Accordingly, it was not just and equitable to remove all liability from B.

WEBB v. BARCLAYS BANK PLC; WEBB v. PORTSMOUTH HOSPITALS NHS TRUST, [2001] EWCA Civ 1141, [2002] P.I.Q.R. P8, Henry, L.J., CA.

3280. Personal injury—football—leg—late tackle in football match

G, an aspiring professional footballer sought to recover damages when he sustained a serious leg injury during an Under 19s association football match between the youth teams of two professional football clubs. G alleged that he was kicked high on his leg by C, one of B's players, after the referee had blown his whistle for an earlier infringement and after the ball had rolled out of play. C, who was shown a red card by the referee following the incident, contended that he had challenged G for a "50-50" ball close to the touchline while the ball was still in play. C further submitted that he had not heard the whistle being blown and that G had injured himself when he lunged at the ball, kicking C high on the knee.

Held, giving judgment for G, that G's version of events was to be preferred. C's tackle on G was extremely late, continuing after the whistle and after the ball was out of play. It was unnecessary and carried a high risk of injury. It was executed in such a way that C kicked G hard enough to break his leg even though G was wearing shin pads, *Caldwell v. Maguire* [2001] EWCA Civ 1054, [2002] P.I.Q.R. P6, [2002] 1 C.L. 404 applied.

GAYNOR v. BLACKPOOL FC, November 8, 2001, Judge Armitage Q.C., CC (Oldham). [*Ex rel.* Craig Moore, Barrister, Park Lane Chambers, 19 Westgate, Leeds].

3281. Personal injury—horse racing—jockeys—duty of care

C, a jockey, appealed against the dismissal of his claim for personal injuries which he had instituted after being injured in a race during which the horse in front of him shied causing him to fall from his mount. C contended that the accident had been caused by M negligently bringing his horse too close in front of the horse which shied. The judge in the court below found that M's actions, whilst careless, did not breach his duty of care to C within the context of the race. On appeal, C argued that the judge had set the threshold of liability too high.

Held, dismissing the appeal, that the judge had applied the right test appropriately to the facts. He had correctly identified that C had to show "something more serious" by M than a lapse in care or skill or an "error of judgment", *Smoldon v. Whitworth* [1997] E.L.R. 249, [1997] C.L.Y. 3856 applied. The judge properly recognised that a horse race was a fast moving sport involving split second decision making and inherent risk. Within that context, M's carelessness and failure to follow to the letter the rules of the sport did not amount to negligence.

CALDWELL v. MAGUIRE; CALDWELL v. FITZGERALD, [2001] EWCA Civ 1054, [2002] P.I.Q.R. P6, Tuckey, L.J., CA.

3282. Professional negligence–accountants–advice on gift to fiancee–failure to advise of risk of challenge by Revenue

See TAX: Grimm v. Newman. §4498

3283. Professional negligence–accountants–sale of business–limits of retainer–area of competence

S brought an action for professional negligence against C, his accountants. C had acted as accountants for both S and N, a limited company managed by S. S had entered into negotiations to purchase the company, retaining C to advise on the sale. S contended that C had been negligent in the advice given as regards the purchase price and the structure of the sale agreement with the result that he paid too much for the business and incurred losses through avoidable tax liabilities and penalties. In response, C argued that because they acted for both parties they had limited their role to that of "facilitator" and, having specifically advised S to obtain an independent valuation and to consult tax counsel, these matters fell outside the retainer.

Held, giving judgment for the claimant, that despite C's assertion that they acted only as "facilitator", the retainer did give rise to a duty of care. The advice as to price had not been negligent. S had not requested a detailed or careful assessment and had failed to follow C's advice as to the obtaining of an independent valuation. However, C had been negligent in failing to advise S to adopt the "TopCo" structure for the sale agreement. Such advice was within C's area of competence. A general practitioner could not absolve themselves from responsibility for providing such advice by advising that a specialist be consulted.

SAYERS v. CLARKE WALKER; *sub nom.* SAYERS v. CLARKE-WALKER [2002] 2 B.C.L.C. 16, Buckley, J., QBD.

3284. Professional negligence–accountants–takeovers–overvaluation of company–measure of damages–Australia

D launched the takeover of a company, U, on the basis of financial projections prepared by P, a firm of accountants. The purchase was funded partly by a new share issue and partly by a case payment to U's shareholders. However, U had been grossly overvalued with the result that D became insolvent. It was found at first instance that P was liable in contract, tort and for breach of its fiduciary duty for giving highly optimistic projections. Damages were awarded on the basis of the cash payment to U's shareholders, with a deduction to reflect the true value of U's shares, plus an amount for loss of use of the money. P unsuccessfully appealed against the findings of breach of contract and duty of care but the court held that the value of the shares issued by D should have been calculated by reference to the value of D's shares immediately before the allocation of new shares. P appealed.

Held, dismissing the appeal, that D's loss differed from those made by its shareholders in respect of the allotment of new shares which were now worth less than their issued value. The loss that D had suffered was a reduced standing with lenders and in the market for future share issues. Therefore D was only entitled to recover damages reflecting the loss of the money paid to U's shareholders, plus its administrative expenses.

PILMER v. DUKE GROUP LTD (IN LIQUIDATION) [2001] 2 B.C.L.C. 773, McHugh, J., HC (Aus).

3285. **Professional negligence–architects–damage arising from defective guttering–chain of causation broken by opportunity to discover defect**

S, a firm of architects, appealed against a decision that they were liable for the flood damage suffered by B, the occupiers of premises designed by S, which was consequent upon the defective design of a valley roof gutter. Experts agreed that the gutter's lack of overflows was a fundamental defect and that the design criteria adopted in relation to anticipated rainfall intensity were also deficient. There was evidence from surveyors' and engineers' reports that B had been alerted to the existence of an unresolved problem having caused previous flood damage, although the absence of overflows had not been noticed. B claimed that the gutter had two latent defects, the lack of overflows and a flawed design. S claimed that there was only one defect, the lack of overflows, which was a patent defect for which they were not liable.

Held, allowing the appeal, that (1) the absence of overflows was a patent defect which should have been discovered by B's surveyors had they exercised reasonable care, and (2) it followed that had the defect been discovered and remedial measures taken the flood damage would not have occurred. The absence of overflows was the sole effective cause of the flood and it was not possible to say that the under-design of the gutter, which it was accepted could not reasonably have been discovered by the surveyors, was an additional contributory cause. There had therefore been a break in the chain of causation between the architect's error in design and the damage caused.

BAXALL SECURITIES LTD v. SHEARD WALSHAW PARTNERSHIP; *sub nom.* BLAXHALL SECURITIES LTD v. SHEARD WALSHAW PARTNERSHIP, [2002] EWCA Civ 9, [2002] B.L.R. 100, David Steel, J., CA.

3286. **Professional negligence–auditors–duty of care–negligent misstatement–auditors–"purpose or transaction" test**

Auditors, D, applied to strike out claims brought by B and another party, BSL, in the context of actions brought against D for negligence. B and BSL claimed that audits carried out by D for their subsidiary company were negligent and that as a result the activities of a rogue trader were not discovered and halted. B and BSL claimed that they were owed a duty of care by D amongst other things in the provision of its audit report to the directors. D argued that the claims did not satisfy the purpose or transaction test and that B and BSL could not claim for reflective loss.

Held, granting the application, that B and BSL had failed the purpose test because they had failed to plead that D had in contemplation that the audit would be relied upon when the decision was made to grant the loans requested by the rogue trader. The pleading also failed to define a transaction which had caused B to lose the value of its group and which had been embarked upon by B in reliance on D's audit. In any event, the claims would also have failed on the basis of reflective loss as the loss would be made good if recovered by BSL. *Johnson v. Gore Wood & Co (No.1)* [2001] 2 W.L.R. 72, [2001] C.L.Y. 410 applied.

BARINGS PLC (IN LIQUIDATION) v. COOPERS & LYBRAND (NO.4); BARINGS FUTURES (SINGAPORE) PTE LTD (IN LIQUIDATION) v. MATTAR (NO.3) [2002] 2 B.C.L.C. 364, Evans-Lombe, J., Ch D.

3287. **Professional negligence–auditors–loss–striking out–existence of triable issue**

KPMG, which had acted as auditor for SF, applied to strike out or summarily dispose of SF's negligence claim. The Court of Appeal had previously found ([2000] 1 All E.R. 676) that SF had an arguable case as to the causative link between KPMG's alleged negligence and SF's alleged losses. The application to strike out related to the proceeds from the sale of shares in a third party which SF alleged had been improperly diverted from it. KPMG maintained that the proceeds had been received by H, of which SF was a wholly owned subsidiary, and set against the indebtedness of SF to H on intercompany account with the result that SF had received value for the shares and not suffered any loss. SF argued that there had been no intercompany indebtedness as dividends declared by SF, which had never been paid, and a loan from H had not been genuine transactions.

Held, refusing the application, that it was not appropriate to strike out the claim since there was a triable issue as to whether the relevant transactions had given rise to genuine indebtedness. Moreover, having regard to the factors for and against, it would not be appropriate for the questions as to loss to be dealt with as preliminary issues.

SASEA FINANCE LTD (IN LIQUIDATION) v. KPMG (FORMERLY KPMG PEAT MARWICK McLINTOCK) (NO.3) [2002] B.C.C. 574, Hart, J., Ch D.

3288. Professional negligence–auditors–solicitors' trust accounts–duty owed to clients on public policy grounds–New Zealand

PW were appointed to audit the trust accounts of a firm of solicitors, ST. Some of ST's trust clients, including K, had incurred substantial losses as the result of investments made through ST's nominee company. It was alleged that the losses had been caused by PW's negligent audit of the trust accounts. PW sought to strike out the claims on the basis that it did not owe a duty of care to ST's clients. The application was dismissed at first instance and PW appealed.

Held, dismissing the appeal, that it could not be said at the strike out stage that K did not have a tenable argument as to the existence of a duty of care, *Attorney General v. Prince* [1998] 1 N.Z.L.R. 262 considered. On the contrary, given the scope of the New Zealand Law Society's rules pertaining to trust account audits there were sound policy reasons why auditors could owe a duty of care to solicitors' clients. To have allowed PW's application would have meant that K was restricted to a contractual claim against ST, a position that was no longer borne out by the authorities, *South Pacific Manufacturing Co Ltd v. New Zealand Security Consultants and Investigations Ltd* [1992] 2 N.Z.L.R. 282, *Kavanagh v. Continental Shelf Cp (No.46) Ltd* [1993] 2 N.Z.L.R. 648 and *Esanda Finance Corp Ltd v. Peat Marwick Hungerfords* [2000] Lloyd's Rep. P.N. 684, [2000] C.L.Y. 4246 distinguished.

PRICE WATERHOUSE v. KWAN (1999-2000) 2 I.T.E.L.R. 611, Tipping, J., CA (NZ).

3289. Professional negligence–barristers–failure to give proper advice on acceptance of offer to settle

PS, a firm of solicitors appealed against a decision that they were solely liable for the negligent conduct of M's clinical negligence claim. The relevant health authority had admitted liability and, prior to the commencement of the hearing, indicated that it would allow M to take £150,000 which had been paid into court. However, M's counsel, P, advised him to decline that offer and sought to persuade the judge to admit further medical evidence in support of a claim for continuing disability and financial loss. In the light of subsequent indications given by the trial judge, P considered that M should accept the best possible offer obtainable from the health authority. M was persuaded to accept an offer of £120,000. M commenced proceedings against PS alleging that it had acted in breach of its duty of care in failing to obtain further appropriate medical evidence. PS denied breach of duty and blamed P in both its defence and in its Part 20 proceedings. M then joined P as the second defendant. PS alleged that P had been negligent in advising M to refuse the offer of £150,000 in that she had fundamentally misjudged the chances of successfully persuading the judge to admit further medical evidence and that she had failed to advise M fully and properly so as to allow him to make an informed decision as to whether to accept the offer.

Held, allowing the appeal, that in the light of authority, P's assessment of the chances of adducing further medical evidence were, at best, over optimistic but, it was difficult for the instant court to say that judge had erred in his assessment of P's evidence *Beachley Property Ltd v. Edgar* [1997] P.N.L.R. 197,

[1996] C.L.Y. 943, *Letpak Ltd v. Harris* [1997] P.N.L.R. 239, [1997] C.L.Y. 784 and *Mortgage Corp Plc v. Sandoes* [1997] P.N.L.R. 263, [1997] C.L.Y. 783 considered. However, the advice that P had given in respect of accepting the first offer was negligently wrong. When the offer was made, M had been entitled to a proper assessment of the prospects of obtaining more, were the trial to proceed. The reasonable inference to be drawn from all the material before the court was that, given proper advice, M would have accepted the offer. In apportioning responsibility for M's loss, the court focused on the relative blameworthiness of the parties. As P had given its advice in circumstances which had been wholly created by the fault of PS, P's liability was apportioned at 25 per cent.

MOY v. PETTMAN SMITH (A FIRM), [2002] EWCA Civ 875, [2002] C.P.L.R. 619, Latham, L.J., CA.

3290. **Professional negligence–barristers–liability for advice on settlement–limitations**

[Limitation Act 1980 s.32(2); Civil Procedure Rules 1998 (SI 1998 3132) Part 20.]

R, a barrister who had represented C in an unsuccessful claim concerned with property rights, sought summary judgment in proceedings commenced by C for professional negligence. C had initiated proceedings under the Civil Procedure Rules 1998 Part 20 against R, contending that R had negligently failed to advise him to accept an offer of settlement made during the course of the trial.

Held, granting the application for summary judgment, that (1) whilst C maintained that he had not been advised to accept an offer of £75,000 plus costs, the contemporaneous attendance notes made by C's then solicitors revealed that R had suggested, on the basis of an indication from the judge, a figure of £80,000 for the main head of claim with a possibility of nominal damages only. The same attendance note recorded that C was "perturbed" by the advice and indicated that he would settle for a sum of £200,000. This evidence was supported by the recollections of R himself, R's pupil at the time and C's then solicitor. The evidence was consistent with R attempting to persuade C to consider settlement at around £100,000 but it appeared that C had been bullish and unreceptive, and (2) the claim was in any event statute barred and C was unable to take advantage of the Limitation Act 1980 s.32(2), *Foreman v. O'Driscoll & Partners* [2000] Lloyd's Rep. P.N. 720, [2000] C.L.Y. 4254 followed, *Liverpool Roman Catholic Archdiocesan Trustees Inc v. Goldberg (No.1)* [2001] 1 All E.R. 182, [2000] C.L.Y. 534 doubted and *Sheldon v. RHM Outhwaite (Underwriting Agencies) Ltd* [1996] A.C. 102, [1995] C.L.Y. 3159 considered.

PRETTYS v. CARTER [2002] P.N.L.R. 11, Judge Playford Q.C., QBD.

3291. **Professional negligence–engineers–economic loss–design and build contracts–defective foundations–extent of duty**

[Defective Premises Act 1972 s.1.]

P brought an action against J, structural engineers, alleging negligence and breach of statutory duty regarding the advice given in relation to the construction and design of four cottages which were owned by the claimants. J had been retained by the original owner of the land on which the cottages were constructed to conduct a ground investigation and advise upon the appropriate foundations. After the properties had been sold it was discovered that the foundations for the buildings were not suitable for supporting the dwelling houses constructed thereon and that the finished buildings would require substantial remedial work. P contended that J was in breach of the Defective Premises Act 1972 s.1 and further, or in the alternative, that J was in breach of its common law duty of care. A number of preliminary issues arose concerning the existence, nature and scope of the duty of care.

Held, determining the preliminary issues, that (1) the extent of the engineers' duty at common law was to exercise reasonable professional skill, care and judgment to avoid causing physical injury, loss or damage to the property; (2) as a matter of policy it had been established by a string of authorities that it was not possible, in the absence of any physical damage to other property or any risk to health and safety, to recover damages for economic loss, such as the cost of remedial work necessary to correct inherent defects in buildings resulting from a breach of duty, *Murphy v. Brentwood DC* [1991] 1 A.C. 398, [1991] C.L.Y. 2661 and *Department of the Environment v. Thomas Bates & Sons Ltd* [1991] 1 A.C. 499, [1991] C.L.Y. 2660 applied, and (3) since all four cottages were built on the same foundation slab it was not possible to argue that the cottages could be treated as separate entities such as to constitute "other property" and there was no basis for any other exception based upon the existence of a complex structure, *Warner v. Basildon Development Corp* (1991) 7 Const. L.J. 146, [1992] C.L.Y. 3197 considered.

PAYNE v. JOHN SETCHELL LTD [2002] B.L.R. 489, Judge Humphrey Lloyd Q.C., QBD (T&CC).

3292. Professional negligence–insurance brokers–duty of care–reinsurance–scope of duty when obtaining cover–extent of liability

J, insurance brokers, appealed against a decision ([2000] 1 All E.R. (Comm) 129, [2000] C.L.Y. 4252) that the scope of its duty of care to A, who had entered into a treaty of reinsurance with a Lloyds underwriter, was not limited to obtaining reinsurance cover for A but extended to an obligation to advise on the availability of such cover within the market. J had failed to advise A that outwards reinsurance was not available on the market despite having been aware that A would not proceed if it had known that outwards reinsurance was not available. A sought to recover $35 million, being the total losses suffered by it on the transaction rather than simply $11 million, being the reinsurance cover which it had lost. J contended that, in accordance with the principle established by *South Australia Asset Management Corp v. York Montague Ltd* [1997] A.C. 191, [1996] C.L.Y. 4519, it was not liable for all the foreseeable consequences of its negligence

Held, dismissing the appeal (Lord Millett dissenting), that J was liable for the entire loss since it had assumed a duty to advise A on the availability of reinsurance cover in the market, without which the transaction would not have proceeded, *South Australia Asset Management Corp* distinguished. It was commercially artificial to distinguish between reporting on the availability of reinsurance cover and reporting on the assessment of the market of the reinsurance risks.

ANECO REINSURANCE UNDERWRITING LTD (IN LIQUIDATION) v. JOHNSON & HIGGINS LTD; *sub nom.* ANECO REINSURANCE UNDERWRITING LTD v. JOHNSON & HIGGS LTD, [2001] UKHL 51, [2001] 2 All E.R. (Comm) 929, Lord Steyn, HL.

3293. Professional negligence–solicitors–advice on restrictive covenant–failure to warn of ambiguity

QE, a school, appealed against a decision that BW, a firm of solicitors, had not been negligent in providing advice in relation to a restrictive covenant. The covenant, which had been negotiated with the vendor of a property that adjoined the school, limited the height of any building constructed to that of the existing buildings on the site. E, a partner at BW, had provided advice to the effect that for the purposes of the covenant the height of the existing buildings included the chimney pots. The judge had concluded that under the covenant, development was permitted to a height which included the chimneys and that accordingly E had not been negligent in giving his advice. It was submitted that the covenant was not free from ambiguity and that E should, therefore, have provided advice to that effect.

Held, allowing the appeal, that the judge had erred in finding that there was no real scope for dispute as to the meaning of the restrictive covenant. E had been under a duty to warn QE that there was a risk that the construction of the covenant was open to question. Moreover, it was apparent that E was aware of a potential threat of litigation from the vendor of the property adjoining the site at the time he had provided the advice.

QUEEN ELIZABETH'S GRAMMAR SCHOOL BLACKBURN LTD v. BANKS WILSON (A FIRM); *sub nom.* QUEEN ELIZABETH'S SCHOOL BLACKBURN LTD v. BANKS WILSON SOLICITORS, [2001] EWCA Civ 1360, [2002] P.N.L.R. 14, Arden, L.J., CA.

3294. Professional negligence–solicitors–conveyancing–completion on basis of seller's solicitor's undertaking to discharge mortgage

P appealed against a finding ([2000] Lloyd's Rep. P.N. 844) that his solicitors, D, had not acted negligently in completing the purchase of a sports ground and pavilion on the basis of an undertaking by the seller's solicitor to discharge the outstanding mortgage on the land and provide Land Registry form 53. The mortgagee had failed to supply form 53 following a misunderstanding on the seller's solicitor's part as to the amount that was required to discharge the relevant charge. P argued that the practice of completing purchases of land on the basis of an undertaking of the kind given would constitute negligence on the part of the buyer's solicitor unless additional precautions were taken.

Held, dismissing the appeal, that if a professional practice gave rise to a foreseeable and avoidable risk, it might not be capable of being upheld on rational grounds, and the fact that it was commonly followed would not exclude liability for negligence, *Edward Wong Finance Co Ltd v. Johnson Stokes & Master* [1984] A.C. 296, [1984] C.L.Y. 3624 applied. Completing on the basis of an undertaking led to the risk that form 53 might not be provided, either because of the seller's solicitor's dishonesty or because of a late dispute or misunderstanding as to the amount required to redeem the mortgage. No alternative practice had, however, been adopted by a significant number of conveyancing solicitors. Accordingly, the practice, which had been approved by the Law Society and the Council of Mortgage Lenders, was one in respect of which, in the words of Lord Browne-Wilkinson in *Bolitho (Deceased) v. City and Hackney HA* [1998] A.C. 232, [1997] C.L.Y. 3789, "the experts [had] directed their minds to the question of comparative risks and benefits and [had] reached a defensible conclusion on the matter". It was observed that it would normally be part of the buyer's solicitor's duty to his client, once he became aware that there had been a breach of the seller's solicitor's undertaking, to take speedy action to enforce the undertaking.

PATEL v. DAYBELLS, [2001] EWCA Civ 1229, [2002] P.N.L.R. 6, Robert Walker, L.J., CA.

3295. Professional negligence–solicitors–conveyancing–failure to register transfer–date of assessment of damage

A appealed against the grant of summary judgment to T in proceedings commenced by A alleging professional negligence. A's husband had obtained a loan of £1 million secured on a London property which he later sold to A for £1.8 million in 1990. Unknown to A the lender obtained a possession order and subsequently resold the property for £1.3 million in 1993. The purchaser sold the property in 1994 for £1.9 million. A brought an action against T, the solicitors who acted for her and her husband on the property transfer between them. A claimed that T had failed to advise that there was a caution against the property, failed to register the transfer, failed to notify A that the lender had refused to extend the loan secured on the property, and failed to alert A to the possession proceedings. A maintained that, had she known of the possession proceedings, she herself would have refinanced the loan with a view to development and future sale. A consequently claimed for loss of profits. At first instance T successfully contended that A's losses were not reasonably foreseeable and that the claim disclosed no reasonable prospect of success. On appeal, A (1) contended that the judge had erred by using the date of breach as the date for assessment of loss, and (2) sought to adduce further evidence as to US tax losses incurred as a result of the failure to register the property in her name.

Held, dismissing the appeal, that (1) the date at which A's loss materialised was the date when the lender resold the property in 1993. At that date A lost an asset with development potential and the market value at that date reflected its actual value, bearing in mind the collapse in London property prices at that time; there was no suggestion that it had been resold at an undervalue. However, A could not claim for the loss of the opportunity to develop the property at some future date since A had the funds available to reinvest in some other property and it had not been shown that the property was in any way unique, and (2) the new evidence which A sought to adduce could have been put forward at an earlier stage in the proceedings. Furthermore, there was doubt as to the credibility of the new evidence since it did not show in what way, if any, T had committed any breach of duty which resulted in the tax losses which A claimed.

AYLWEN v. TAYLOR JOYNSON GARRETT (A FIRM), [2001] EWCA Civ 1171, [2002] P.N.L.R. 1, Arden, L.J., CA.

3296. **Professional negligence–solicitors–conveyancing–fiduciary relationship–conflict of interest**

[Limitation Act 1980.]

L issued proceedings against A, solicitors, in November 1998 seeking damages for professional negligence and compensation for breach of fiduciary duty in relation to the conveyance and mortgage of property in June 1990. A admitted acting negligently and in breach of contract in failing to report to L that no deposit had been paid on exchange of contracts, that the deposit had been paid direct to the vendor and that its amount had varied during the course of the transaction. L submitted that there had been a breach of fiduciary duty which removed the need to determine the issue of contributory negligence, citing *Nationwide Building Society v. Balmer Radmore* [1999] Lloyd's Rep. P.N. 241, [1999] C.L.Y. 4037. AC submitted that the claim was statute barred under the Limitation Act 1980.

Held, dismissing the claim, that the relationship of solicitor and client created the fiduciary obligation of loyalty and fidelity. If a solicitor was instructed by two parties to a transaction, he owed that obligation to each. L did not have to establish that A had acted dishonestly during the transaction. It was sufficient for L to show that A consciously and intentionally preferred his duty to the purchaser to that of L. However, L had failed to establish on a balance of probabilities that A did not disclose matters which he ought to have done, intentionally and consciously, knowing at the time that he should have disclosed them, *Nationwide* considered. Furthermore the claimant could, with reasonable diligence, have discovered all the facts relevant to his right of action by, at the very latest, the end of June 1992. That being so the case was also statute barred.

LEEDS AND HOLBECK BUILDING SOCIETY v. ARTHUR & COLE [2001] Lloyd's Rep. P.N. 649, Morland, J., QBD.

3297. **Professional negligence–solicitors–duty of care owed to beneficiaries–measure of damages based on value of farm and business assets–Canada**

Several years before his death, T incorporated a business to take over his farm and all the business assets were sold to the company. He instructed W to draw up his will in 1986 by which T believed he was leaving his land to his mother, H, his sister, ME, and her husband TE, to his other sister, RB, and her husband AB, to his niece, MH, and her husband WH, and to his hired hand, VH, and his wife, LH. In fact, the company was the beneficial owner of the land so that the gifts failed and ME and RB took the entire estate as residual legatees. The disappointed beneficiaries sued W and the judge at first instance awarded them damages, but refused to include the value of standing crops in the award. He also refused claims by TE and AB, as they held all assets jointly with their wives, the residual legatees. The award to T's estate was reduced by 25 per cent as he was found to have been contributorily negligent. All the parties appealed.

Held, dismissing the appeals of TE and W, and allowing those of MH, WH, VH and LH, that (1) the responsibility assumed by a solicitor toward his client in the preparation of a will extended to the client's intended beneficiaries as they could be deprived of their intended bequests in a situation where neither the testator nor his estate had a remedy against the solicitor, *White v. Jones* [1995] 2 A.C. 207, [1995] C.L.Y. 3701 applied; (2) a claim that the losses were attributable to an error made by the judge below was a collateral attack on a valid court order and would not be permitted as the order was final unless successfully appealed, *Wilson v. R* [1983] 2 S.C.R. 594 followed; (3) there was no contributory negligence on T's part as he did not owe his beneficiaries a duty of care and they had not contributed to any loss that had been sustained, and (4) the judge had misinterpreted expert evidence about the value of the land, which should have been greater than his award and also have included the value of the standing crops growing on the land. He had also erred in deducting the sale costs of the land because the intended beneficiaries would have received the land without such deductions if T's testamentary bequests had been carried out as he had intended.

EARL v. WILHELM; WILHELM v. HICKSON [2001] W.T.L.R. 1275, Sherstobitoff, J., CA (Sask).

3298. Professional negligence–solicitors–failure to apply for renewal of lease– measure of damages

See DAMAGES: Aran Caterers Ltd v. Stepien Lake Gilbert & Paling (A Firm). §945

3299. Professional negligence–solicitors–former client alleging lack of capacity at date of settlement

[Mental Health Act 1983.]

In 1980 M, then aged 17, sustained brain damage following a road traffic accident for which J was liable. Following legal advice from a partner in B, a firm of solicitors, and from counsel, M accepted £76,000 in settlement of his claim in 1987. In 1996, M served a statement of claim on B, alleging negligence and breach of contract. In its defence, B asserted that the claim was statute barred. However, a consultant neuropsychiatrist subsequently found that M was a "patient" within the meaning in terms of the Mental Health Act 1983 and therefore lacked capacity during the period when the settlement was being discussed. M's parents also argued that his lifestyle since the accident showed that he could not manage his own affairs. The question whether M was a patient under the Act fell to be determined on a trial of preliminary issues.

Held, ruling on the preliminary issue, finding that M was not a patient. The evidence showed that M was capable of looking after himself and had played a full part in a number of voluntary organisations, including elected positions, since the accident. Further, his ability to live independently of his parents showed that he had not been a patient in terms of the Act since at least 1983.

MASTERMAN-LISTER v. JEWELL; MASTERMAN-LISTER v. BRUTTON & CO, [2002] EWHC 417, [2002] Lloyd's Rep. Med. 239, Wright, J., QBD.

3300. Professional negligence–solicitors–intentional act–absence of knowledge of breach of duty–limitation defence

See CIVIL PROCEDURE: Cave v. Robinson Jarvis & Rolf. §466

3301. Professional negligence–solicitors–interpleader–challenge to interpleader verdict–abuse of process

G appealed against a decision in a professional negligence case brought by him against his solicitors, L. L had been instructed by G in respect of his sale of land to P, a prospective purchaser. By agreement, P had paid a deposit which was held by L, as stakeholder, on the basis that it was non returnable, save in the event that no contract was entered into by reason of G's default. No contract having been signed by the date specified in the agreement, both parties claimed the deposit. In interpleader proceedings, initiated by L, it had been determined that, the agreement being unenforceable for lack of consideration, the deposit was returnable. G had consequently issued proceedings against L in professional negligence. The court at first instance having found in favour of L, G, in his appeal, contended that in the negligence action L could not ask the court to reach a conclusion different to that of the judge in the interpleader proceedings.

Held, allowing the appeal, that whilst L was not, by virtue of the interpleader action, bound by issue estoppel, as he was not party to the dispute there litigated, it was an abuse of process for him to seek to defeat the negligence action by challenging the decision in the interpleader action which he initiated, *Hunter v. Chief Constable of the West Midlands* [1982] A.C. 529, [1982] C.L.Y. 2382 applied.

GRIBBON v. LUTTON, [2001] EWCA Civ 1956, [2002] Q.B. 902, Laddie, J., CA.

3302. Professional negligence–solicitors–legal professional privilege–duty to disclose confidential information obtained during previous retainer

H appealed against the dismissal of his claim for negligence and breach of duty against E, a firm of solicitors, in which he alleged that the firm had failed to disclose information about one of its former clients B. B had previously retained the firm to conduct his defence to offences of participation in the management of a company whilst an undischarged bankrupt, fraudulent trading and obtaining credit whilst a bankrupt, of which he was convicted. B had subsequently approached H with a proposal relating to the acquisition of land and the two parties had sought advice on the matter from the partner at E who had previously acted for B. The partner advised H that he could not act for both parties, suggesting that H instruct a junior member of the firm. The transaction was entered into and as a result H sustained considerable losses owing to B's failure to fulfil his financial obligations under the contract. H maintained that E had a duty to disclose the information relating to B's previous convictions.

Held, dismissing the appeal, that a solicitor was under no duty to disclose to a later client confidential information obtained during a previous retainer from a former client. If the solicitor was acting for both parties to a transaction then there might be a duty to disclose information obtained in the transaction from one of them to the other but in those circumstances any breach of duty to either party could not be excused by reference to the duty owed to the other. When a solicitor was retained to act for a client it was on the basis that the solicitor would not disclose confidential information obtained during the course of the retainer. Given this, the solicitor in the instant case should have informed H that he was unable to properly carry out his instructions. In any event, since H could not show that he would have discovered B's previous convictions had he instructed different solicitors, he could not establish any loss.

HILTON v. BARKER BOOTH & EASTWOOD; *sub nom.* HILTON v. BAKER BOOTH & EASTWOOD; HILTON v. BARIKER BOOTH & EASTWOOD, [2002] EWCA Civ 723, [2002] Lloyd's Rep. P.N. 500, Sir Andrew Morritt V.C., CA.

3303. Professional negligence–solicitors–limitations–defective fire certificate–relevant date of knowledge

[Limitation Act 1980 s.14A(4)(b), s.14A(7).]

R, solicitors, appealed against a preliminary determination that a claim by B against it was not time barred. R had advised B during the purchase of premises to be used as an hotel. It was subsequently discovered that the fire certificate was defective, no planning permission had been obtained and building regulations had been contravened. B failed to issue proceedings until some 10 years after the alleged negligence and R maintained that B was out of time because the relevant date of knowledge was the date in 1989 of receipt of the fire certificate as that was "the starting date" within the meaning of the Limitation Act 1980 s.14A(4)(b).

Held, dismissing the appeal, that the receipt of an inaccurate fire certificate would not necessarily lead one to the conclusion that there may not be adequate planning permission or a lack of adherence to building regulations. The judge had been entitled to make the decision that he had as he had adopted the approach specified in s.14A(7) of the Act, having come to a factual conclusion as to the way in which a reasonable person would respond when in possession of the material facts. Therefore the decision that the starting date was in 1995 when B had been made aware of other pertinent facts could not be impugned.

BABICKI v. ROWLANDS, [2001] EWCA Civ 1720, [2002] Lloyd's Rep. P.N. 121, Lord Woolf of Barnes, L.C.J., CA.

3304. Professional negligence–solicitors–limitations–failure to obtain deed of release–date of accrual of cause of action

M, a former director and principal shareholder of CGL, a company which owned and operated a gravel pit, brought a claim for damages against W, a firm of solicitors instructed to deal with the reconveyance of two parcels of land to H pursuant to an agreement made in 1974. The transaction remained uncompleted, and in 1988 CGL entered into an option agreement with R in respect of the parcels, which could only be exercised upon completion of the 1974 agreement, which in turn was dependent on CGL's bank releasing the parcels from the security it held over the whole of CGL's land. CGL subsequently went into liquidation. M's claim was based on W's alleged failure to comply with its instructions to secure the deed of release from the bank. W's defence stated that, inter alia, M's claim was statute barred because the causes of action had arisen more than six years before the issue of the writ. The limitation defence was ordered to be tried as a preliminary issue, and in order to determine that issue it fell to the court to decide (1) the date of the termination of any retainer between M and W; (2) the date on which the option agreement had lapsed; (3) whether W's failure to obtain a deed of release had been a continuing breach, and (4) the date on which M's loss had been sustained.

Held, determining the preliminary issues in favour of W, that (1) W's retainer had been terminated on the date on which CGL had gone into liquidation, since at that point, by M's own admission, it became impossible for W to fulfill its instructions by obtaining the deed of release. Alternatively, the retainer had terminated on the date when the option expired, at which point to obtain the deed of release would have been futile; (2) the option had lapsed on the expiry of the six week period provided for giving notice of the exercise of the option at the end of the three year duration of the option. The two year extension of the option provided for in the agreement had not come into effect because the option had never in fact been exercised; (3) W's instructions had been to obtain the deed of release "as soon as possible"; the breach had occurred at the point when it was possible for it to obtain the deed and it was not obtained, *Bell v. Peter Browne & Co* [1990] 2 Q.B. 495, [1991] C.L.Y. 2343 applied. This had therefore been a single breach and not a continuing one, *Midland Bank Trust Co Ltd v. Hett Stubbs & Kemp* [1979] Ch. 384, [1978] C.L.Y. 2822 distinguished. After that point, any efforts to obtain the deed had been made in order to minimise the consequences of the breach which had already occurred rather than to avoid a breach altogether, and (4) M's loss had been sustained on the date on which CGL had gone into liquidation. At that point, M became irrevocably disadvantaged in that he required the cooperation of the liquidators to proceed with the transaction, which cooperation was not forthcoming.

MORFOOT v. WF SMITH & CO [2001] Lloyd's Rep. P.N. 658, Judge Havelock-Allan Q.C., Ch D.

3305. Professional negligence–solicitors–local authority building licence–failure to advise on terms

F claimed damages against C, her former solicitors, for breach of contract and negligence arising out of a property development carried out by F's company, FL, from whom F had taken an assignment of the cause of action. F contended that C had negligently failed to advise that the terms of a building licence granted to FL by the local authority permitted FL to change the nature of the development proposal without payment of a premium to the local authority. FL had paid such a premium when it changed the development proposal from hotel to residential use. A term of the building licence stated that amendments could be made to the works with the local authority's consent, such consent not to be unreasonably withheld. C submitted that (1) the degree of change involved meant that the proposed change did not constitute an amendment of the scheme as envisaged by the terms of the licence so that a premium would be payable for consent to the change, and (2) that even if the proposed change constituted an "amendment" to the scheme, the commercial reality was that a sum would have been required to be paid to the local authority to procure their consent to the change of use.

Held, giving judgment for the claimant, that (1) the licence did not require a premium to be payable upon the change in the nature of the development proposal and, in particular, the nature of the change was an "amendment" for the purposes of the licence, and (2) whilst the commercial reality was that a sum would have been required to be paid to procure the local authority's consent to the proposed change, it would not have been as great as the sum actually paid, with the result that F had suffered loss as a result of C's negligent omission.

FINLEY v. CONNELL ASSOCIATES [2002] Lloyd's Rep. P.N. 62, Ouseley, J., QBD.

3306. **Professional negligence–solicitors–nature of retainer–failure to advise that clause amounted to time critical condition precedent–assignment of corporate lawyer to property case**

C sought damages for professional negligence against a firm of solicitors, R, which it had retained in connection with a property matter. C was the lessee of certain premises and wished to exercise a break option under the terms of the lease. The exercise of the break option was dependent upon compliance with a number of conditions, including the service in advance of six months' written notice and a payment of £11,500. Whilst the notice was served within the requisite timescale, the payment was not made within the time required. C contended that R were in breach of their duty of care by failing to warn C that the payment required by the lease was a condition precedent which was time critical.

Held, giving judgment for C, that a solicitor was not to be taken as a general insurer against his client's problems but rather his duties were determined by the scope of his agreed retainer. If, in the course of his work on the matters in respect of which he had been retained, a solicitor became aware of a risk or potential risk to his client, it would be his duty to inform the client of that risk. In so doing the solicitor would not be going beyond the scope of his instructions nor could he be deemed to be doing any extra work for which he was not to be paid. On the facts of the instant case R had erred by assigning the case to a corporate lawyer who, whilst capable and competent, did not appreciate, as an expert property lawyer would have done, that the payment of the necessary monies was a time critical condition precedent.

CREDIT LYONNAIS SA v. RUSSELL JONES & WALKER, [2002] EWHC 1310, [2003] Lloyd's Rep. P.N. 7, Laddie, J., Ch D.

3307. **Professional negligence–solicitors–psychiatric illness–foreseeability–consequence of negligent preparation of client's defence in criminal proceedings**

M appealed against a determination of a preliminary issue that a psychiatric illness he had suffered as a consequence of his solicitors' conduct of his defence in criminal proceedings had not been reasonably foreseeable. M, a businessman who had no prior convictions, had been sentenced to four years' imprisonment for offences of robbery and assault but was acquitted at a retrial in the light of new evidence, by which time he had spent approximately three months in prison. M contended that his solicitors, G, had been negligent in the preparation of his defence and that the reactive depression which followed his conviction was a foreseeable consequence.

Held, allowing the appeal, that the test to be applied was to consider whether G owed M a duty of care to assist him in avoiding psychiatric illness and then to consider whether psychiatric illness was a foreseeable consequence of the breach of such a duty. The judge had erred by focusing on the question of foreseeability as a separate topic. The adoption by the judge of the "person of reasonable fortitude test" and "foreseeability with the benefit of hindsight test" was not appropriate. It was arguable that M had assumed responsibility for ensuring that the risk of conviction and consequent distress or illness was minimised. There was no authority to the effect that damages for psychiatric illness could not be recovered in such circumstances, *Page v. Smith* [1996] A.C. 155, [1995] C.L.Y. 3682, *White v. Chief Constable of South Yorkshire* [1999] 2 A.C. 455, [1999] C.L.Y. 4059 considered. Damages could be recovered if it was foreseeable that psychiatric illness would be suffered by M, given those features of his personal life and disposition of which G was aware, *Overseas Tankship (UK) Ltd v. Morts Dock & Engineering Co (The Wagon Mound)* [1961] A.C. 388, [1961] C.L.Y. 2343 applied.

McLOUGHLIN v. GROVERS; *sub nom.* McCLOUGHLIN v. GROVERS; McLOUGHLIN v. JONES, [2001] EWCA Civ 1743, [2002] Q.B. 1312, Brooke, L.J., CA.

3308. Professional negligence–solicitors–wasted costs orders–proceedings brought in wrong form and in conflict of interest

See CIVIL PROCEDURE: Sherman v. Perkins. §408

3309. Professional negligence–stockbrokers–trustee investment monitoring–breach of duty of care–Jersey

V hired M to act as investment adviser and stockbroker for trust investments. M knew that V wanted a higher return on trust investments than it could obtain from gilts, but was risk adverse. A pattern emerged that stock would be switched if potential problems were discovered. M purchased a bond for V that became worthless following a downgrading and credit warning issued by a leading credit rating agency and V claimed that M had been negligent in not monitoring the bond's performance properly. At first instance it was held that, although V would have sold if notified by M of the downgrading, M's monitoring system was reasonable, given its size. V appealed, contending that M owed a duty of care that had been breached by its failure to monitor the bond properly between the time of its purchase and its subsequent collapse.

Held, allowing the appeal, that (1) M had placed a high degree of reliance on an informal arrangement between itself and the market maker as a means of obtaining information which did not amount to an adequate level of monitoring; (2) M was negligent in relying on casual exchanges of information between dealers in the market and failing to monitor market information systems, and (3) stockbrokers offered portfolio monitoring of portfolios as a means of generating fees and transaction commissions. M had offered such services and had failed to meet its attendant responsibilities.

VOISIN v. MATHESON SECURITIES (CI) LTD (1999-2000) 2 I.T.E.L.R. 907, Sir John Nutting Q.C. (President), CA (Jer).

3310. Professional negligence–surveyors–misrepresentation of valuation–directors–reflective loss

E appealed against the summary dismissal of his claim against P. E alleged that P's surveyor, T, had given a fraudulent valuation of a building site, and that E had suffered substantial financial losses as a result of purchasing the site in reliance of that valuation. The judge in the lower court agreed with P's contention that the losses had been suffered by companies of which E was a director and that E had had no personal loss over and above those losses. On appeal, E argued that the judge had erred in finding that the losses claimed matched those of E's companies.

Held, dismissing the appeal, that the judge had correctly found that the valuation had been given to, and the site purchased and financed by, E's companies and not E personally. The pleaded loss was therefore a "reflective loss" which E was not entitled to claim, *Johnson v. Gore Wood & Co (No.1)* [2002] 2 A.C. 1, [2001] C.L.Y. 410 applied.

ELLIS v. PROPERTY LEEDS (UK) LTD, [2002] EWCA Civ 32, [2002] 2 B.C.L.C. 175, Mantell, L.J., CA.

3311. Professional negligence–surveyors–reports–requirement for repair following acquisition of property–appropriate measure of damages

S appealed against a judgment determining the appropriate measure of damages in advance of the trial of their claim against P, a firm of surveyors, arising from an allegedly negligent survey upon which they had relied when purchasing a residential property. S had incurred approximately £130,000 repairing the property but a valuation report from a jointly instructed expert found that the value of the property at the date of its purchase was £10,000 more than the purchase price, and that the value of the property at the date of purchase was the same as the value of the property in the condition set out in P's report. The judge had ruled that the correct measure of damages was the diminution in value measure rather than the cost of repairs measure. S contended that the cost of repairs measure was the appropriate measure, in particular, since P had been instructed specifically to report on repairs and that the property was to be used in part for commercial activities.

Held, dismissing the appeal, that the appropriate measure of damages was not the cost of the repairs undertaken but the difference between the market value of the property at the date of purchase and its actual value. The application of the cost of repairs measure would place S in a much better position than they would have been had the survey revealed the need for repairs, which offended against the compensatory principle underlying the payment of damages in contract. Moreover, P had been instructed solely to report on the condition of the property, had given no warranty that no repairs would be required, and had not been instructed to advise on its commercial viability, *Watts v. Morrow* [1991] 1 W.L.R. 1421, [1992] C.L.Y. 1548 and *Philips v. Ward* [1956] 1 W.L.R. 471, [1956] C.L.Y. 936 applied.

SMITH v. PETER NORTH & PARTNERS, [2001] EWCA Civ 1553, 82 Con. L.R. 126, Jonathan Parker, L.J., CA.

3312. Standard of care–road traffic accidents–low speed approaching ice cream van insufficient

M, a child aged five at the date of the accident, sought to recover damages for personal injuries sustained when she was struck by a vehicle driven by R. M's father had taken her to an ice cream van to purchase an ice cream; he gave M the ice cream and she had gone around the front of the van whilst he was paying for it. The issue before the court in respect of liability was the standard of care to be expected by R in the circumstances.

Held, giving judgment for M, that the speed of R's vehicle at impact was no more than 15mph and the evidence indicated that M had run into the side of R's vehicle rather than the front. R had seen M with her father purchasing the ice cream and recognised that there might have been other people in front of the van and he had therefore slowed down. R had given no audible warning of his approach and had not steered his car further away from the van. Whilst it was not generally negligent to pass a vehicle at 15mph, consideration had to be given to the fact that the vehicle in question was an ice cream van and that the van carried a warning at the rear which stated "people should drive with care". Even absent a warning, R should have been driving slowly. Any reasonable person should have been aware of the hazard and it was clear that 15mph was not slow enough to avoid the impact. In addition, the accident had occurred in a residential area and R had passed the van on the near side. In all of the circumstances, R had not been sufficiently careful and he was liable to M in damages.

M (A CHILD) v. ROLLINSON, March 14, 2002, Judge Ibbotson, CC (York). [*Ex rel.* Hartley and Worstenholme, Solicitors, 20 Bank Street, Castleford].

3313. Statutory duty–local authorities–defective underpinning–decision to inspect after completion of work–Canada

[Building Code Act 1994 (Canada).]

I employed a contractor, T, to carry out underpinning work. T persuaded I to let it commence work before TCC had issued a permit. By the time that TCC inspected the premises for the purposes of granting a permit, the underpinning had been completed and was covered by other works. The inspector issued the certificate, relying on T's assurances. However, the work was defective in that it was inadequate in terms of both its width and depth and the requirements of the Building Code Act 1994 and had to be made good. I succeeded against T and TCC on the ground that TCC owed I a duty of care. On appeal it was held that by allowing the work to proceed without the permit, I was not owed a duty of care by TCC. I appealed to the Supreme Court.

Held, allowing the appeal, that the test was whether there was a sufficiently close relationship between I and TCC, so that carelessness by TCC would cause damage to I, subject to any considerations that could limit the scope of that duty or the class to whom it was owed, *Anns v. Merton LBC* [1978] A.C. 728, [1977] C.L.Y. 2030 and *Kamloops v. Nielsen, Hughes and Hughes* [1984] 5 W.W.R. 1, [1985] C.L.Y. 2303 applied. On the facts, a duty of care arose from the proximate nature of the relationship between I and TCC so that it was foreseeable that deficient inspection would cause damage. The Act imposed construction safety standards and a TCC had made a policy decision to inspect the underpinning even though work had started without a permit. The duty of care came into existence once TCC decided to act. Although I had been negligent, TCC's liability could only be negatived if I's conduct meant that it was the sole cause of the loss.

INGLES v. TORONTO CITY CORP (2001) 17 Const. L.J. 540, Bastarache, J., Sup Ct (Can).

3314. Statutory duty–local authorities–highway maintenance–personal injury– duty to maintain fabric of highway not extending to removal of deposits upon it

D brought a claim against the local authority when he sustained a knee injury after slipping on moss which was on steps between two roads. There was a handrail alongside the steps.

Held, dismissing the claim, that the steps were part of the highway and maintained at the public expense. Moss was not part of the fabric of the highway, but grew in silt which had been deposited on the highway. There was a duty to maintain the fabric of the highway, but this did not extend to removing accumulations upon it, *Goodes v. East Sussex CC* [2000] 1 W.L.R. 1356, [2000] C.L.Y. 4237 applied.

DRAKE v. TORBAY DC, July 12, 2002, Judge Meredith, CC (Torquay & Newton Abbot). [*Ex rel.* Veitch Penny Solicitors, 1 Manor Court, Dix's Field, Exeter].

3315. Statutory duty–local authorities–road signs–marking of hazard

[Highways Act 1980 s.41; Road Traffic Act 1988 s.39.]

A local authority, C, appealed against a decision giving judgment for G in her claim for damages for personal injury following a road accident. The accident had occurred on the crest of a hill of a road for which C was the responsible highway authority. The stretch of road on which the accident had occurred was known by local residents to pose a hazard. The issue before the court concerned the statutory liability of a highway authority under the Highways Act 1980 s.41 and the extent of its common law duty arising in parallel with the statutory duty to promote road safety under the Road Traffic Act 1988 s.39. G maintained that the local authority as highway authority had been under a duty to warn drivers of hazards. In particular, she argued that an "uneven road" sign should have been positioned prominently 50-60 metres before the crest of the hill and that the road should have been painted with a "Slow" road marking.

Held, allowing the appeal (Potter, L.J. dissenting in part), that (1) the duty under s.41 of the 1980 Act to maintain a highway did not extend to a duty to paint warning signs on the surface of the road. The decision of the Court of Appeal in *Lavis v. Kent CC* 90 L.G.R. 416, [1993] C.L.Y. 2949 had established that the duty did not cover the erection of signs warning traffic; it followed that the position in relation to painted signs on the road had to be the same. Accordingly, the local authority had not acted negligently in failing to paint warning markings on the road in the instant case, *Lavis* applied, and (2) a common law duty of care, parallel to the statutory duty under s.39 of the 1988 Act, would arise if there was evidence that, prior to an accident, the stretch of road should have been regarded as an accident blackspot and the local authority had irrationally failed to act appropriately in order to prevent accidents on that stretch of road, *Larner v. Solihull MBC* [2001] R.T.R. 32, [2001] C.L.Y. 4483 considered. In the instant case that common law duty had not been established.

CALDERDALE MBC v. GORRINGE; *sub nom.* GORRINGE v. CALDERDALE MBC, [2002] EWCA Civ 595, [2002] R.T.R. 27, Potter, L.J., CA.

3316. **Statutory duty–local authorities–staffing requirements at care homes– economic loss**

[Registered Homes Act 1984.]

The local authority appealed against the refusal of its application for summary judgment of a negligence claim brought by D, the owners of three residential care homes, for overpayment of wages. The action had been brought against the local authority in its capacity as the local regulatory authority responsible for, inter alia, the level of staffing in local residential care homes. D maintained that the local authority had negligently construed the Registered Homes Act 1984 as permitting or requiring staffing to capacity notwithstanding occupancy levels and that, as a consequence of the insistence on such staffing levels until 1996, a substantial overpayment of wages had been made which were recoverable.

Held, dismissing the appeal, that it was appropriate that the matters go to trial. The issues involved related to an uncertain area of developing jurisprudence, the facts were disputed, and there was a prospect of oral evidence affecting the court's assessment of the facts, *S v. Gloucestershire CC* [2001] Fam. 313, [2000] C.L.Y. 4212 considered.

DOUCE v. STAFFORDSHIRE CC, [2002] EWCA Civ 506, (2002) 5 C.C.L. Rep. 347, Sir Denis Henry, CA.

3317. **Statutory duty–local authority inquiries–roads–duties of local authority in relation to inquiries**

G appealed against the dismissal ([2000] N.P.C. 90) of his claim for negligence against the local authority in relation to its response to part of the Form of Enquiry, Form LLZ, submitted by his solicitors. G was considering the purchase of a property for redevelopment as flats and had made inquiries to the council about the property and vehicular access to it over a piece of land which fronted it. Based on the response to the enquiry about whether the highway was maintainable at the public expense, G purchased the property only to find that the land was subject to a dispute as to its ownership. As a result, one of his proposed developments did not proceed.

Held, dismissing the appeal (Sir Andrew Morritt dissenting), that whilst the local authority owed a duty of care to G in relation to his making a decision as to whether or not to purchase the land, the duty was specific only to that and to provide an accurate reply for that purpose. The local authority could not have known that G proposed to develop the property. The local authority's main duty was to provide information which could have been obtained by anyone inspecting the statutory list. On receipt of the inquiry, the appropriate step was for the local authority to consult the list. The fact that, in the instant case, the statutory list was apparently incorrect did not make the local authority's reply to the enquiry negligent.

GOODEN v. NORTHAMPTONSHIRE CC, [2001] EWCA Civ 1744, [2002] P.N.L.R. 18, Arden, L.J., CA.

3318. Subsidence caused by street trees—liability in negligence and nuisance of local authority responsible for maintenance under agency agreement

The local authority, P, appealed against a decision ([2002] B.L.R. 244) finding them liable in nuisance and negligence for damage caused to L's property as a result of tree root desiccation. The roots which had caused the damage belonged to street trees for which Hampshire County Council, H, had been the maintaining highway authority; however, under an agency agreement, P had been responsible for providing arboricultural services in respect of such trees. P contended that, as the relevant highway authority, H was the correct defendant in actions concerning the trees. It was further argued that, in respect of the negligence action, P owed a duty only to H with whom the agency agreement had been concluded.

Held, dismissing the appeal, that P could be held liable for the damage caused by the trees. Potential liability for nuisance was not dependant on occupation of the relevant land but was attached to the right and duty to maintain the road. The agency agreement had placed P under a duty to maintain the trees and, in the absence of ownership, this control made P responsible for preventing or eliminating the nuisance. Potential liability in negligence was likewise not dependant on ownership or occupation of the land. P's negligent liability was not restricted to H by way of their contractual relationship and was not negated by the possibility that H could also be held negligently liable for damage caused by the trees.

LE JONES (INSURANCE BROKERS) LTD v. PORTSMOUTH CITY COUNCIL, [2002] EWCA Civ 1723, [2003] 1 W.L.R. 427, Dyson, L.J., CA.

3319. Books

Hannabuss, Stuart—Information Liability and Negligence: Legal and Ethical Issues for Library and Information Professionals. Paperback: £29.95. ISBN 1-85604-423-8. Library Association Publishing.

Khan, Malcolm; Robson, Michelle—Clinical Negligence. 2nd Ed. Paperback: £52.95. ISBN 1-85941-492-3. Cavendish Publishing Ltd.

Kinzie, Mark; Hart, Christine—Product Liability for the Professional. Paperback: £29.99. ISBN 0-7668-2035-1. Delmar.

Lloyd's Law Reports: Professional Negligence: 2001. Hardback: £107.00. ISBN 1-84311-137-3. LLP Professional Publishing.

Powell, John; Stewart, Roger; Jackson, The Honourable Mr Justice—Jackson and Powell on Professional Negligence. 5th Ed. Common Law Library. Hardback: £225.00. ISBN 0-421-82600-2. Sweet & Maxwell.

Tettenborn, Andrew; Jackson, Justice; Asif, Jalil; Plunkett, Christopher; Goodman, Andrew—Professional Negligence and Liability Reports 2001. Hardback: £195.00. ISBN 0-421-82750-5. Sweet & Maxwell.

NUISANCE

3320. Abatement-trees-removal of tree blown down in high winds-tenant also owner of adjoining property-covenant to use property in tenant like manner

D owned a property, C, which he let to B, which also owned the adjoining property, W. A tree situated in C's grounds blew down in high winds with part of it landing on W's roof. B cut away the portion on the roof and also cut down the remainder of the tree in C's grounds, leaving a one metre tall stump. Cracks later appeared in the walls of C and D alleged that these were due to sub soil heave, due to B cutting down the tree. D claimed against B in negligence, nuisance and for breach of the covenant to use C in a tenant like manner.

Held, giving judgment for B, that B's action in felling the tree was a completely justified means of abating the nuisance caused the encroaching tree, *Lagan Navigation Co v. Lambeg Bleaching Dyeing and Finishing Co Ltd* [1927] A.C. 226 applied. B's rights as the owner of W did not conflict with its rights as tenant of C. The obligation to use C in a tenant like manner did not exclude B's obligation to abate a serious nuisance to the neighbouring property, W.

DAYANI v. BROMLEY LBC (NO.2) [2001] B.L.R. 503, Robert Moxon-Browne Q.C., QBD (T&CC).

3321. Abatement notices-noise-lack of sufficient judicial reasoning

[Environmental Protection Act 1990 s.80(1)(b).]

H applied for judicial review of a decision of the Crown Court to dismiss his appeal against conviction for failure to comply with a number of noise abatement notices, after the local authority had helped him to install equipment intended to reduce noise levels emanating from the public house he owned. H contended that (1) the notices were invalid since the means for abating the nuisance were not sufficiently identified, and (2) the judge had failed to provide adequate reasons for reaching his decision.

Held, granting the application, that (1) since the notices required abatement but had not required steps to be taken for the purposes of the Environmental Protection Act 1990 s.80(1)(b), they were not invalid for lack of specificity, however (2) the judge had failed to adequately set out the reasons for his decision, and therefore the decision had to be quashed.

R. (ON THE APPLICATION OF HOWSON-BALL) v. CANTERBURY CROWN COURT [2001] Env. L.R. 36, Rose, L.J., QBD (Admin Ct).

3322. Public nuisance-obstruction of highway-wheeled bin kept outside shop-magistrates' discretion to make removal order

[Highways Act 1980 s.149.]

EHDC brought a complaint against I under the Highways Act 1980 s.149 seeking the removal of a 1100 litre wheeled bin which had been kept on the highway outside I's shop. The magistrates dismissed the complaint. Their decision was upheld on appeal by the Crown Court which, in the light of the fact that there was no complaint that anybody had been physically inconvenienced, found that (1) the presence of the wheeled bin on the highway did not constitute a nuisance, and (2) if the presence of the wheeled bin did amount to a nuisance, the court's intervention was not justified, since the nuisance was of a "piffling nature". EHDC appealed.

Held, allowing the appeal, that (1) for the purpose of deciding whether the wheeled bin constituted a nuisance, it was necessary to determine (a) whether the bin amounted to an obstruction, and (b) if it did amount to an obstruction, whether it was permanent or temporary in nature. Since the bin obstructed part of the highway, it constituted an obstruction, and the fact that people could pass and repass by using other parts of the highway was irrelevant. Furthermore, the authorities revealed that obstructions which were neither de minimis nor ancillary to passage and repassage on a highway were not likely to be reasonable, and that obstructions of a more transitory nature than the obstruction in the instant case had been held to constitute a nuisance, *Seekings v. Clarke* 59 L.G.R. 268, [1961] C.L.Y. 3850 applied and *Harper v. GN Haden & Sons Ltd* [1933] Ch. 298, *Hirst v. Chief Constable of West Yorkshire* (1987) 85 Cr. App. R. 143, [1988] C.L.Y. 809, *Nagy v. Weston* [1965] 1 W.L.R. 280, [1965] C.L.Y. 1778 and *Torbay BC v. Cross* (1995) 159 J.P. 682, [1996] C.L.Y. 5124 considered, and (2) once a nuisance had been established, the magistrates had, by virtue of s.149(4) of the Act, a discretion when deciding whether or not to authorise the removal of the relevant object. While the magistrates might decide not to make a removal order on various grounds, hardship being an example, they could not decline to make an order on the de minimis ground, since that would be inconsistent with a finding that a nuisance had been committed in the first place, it being a prerequisite to such a finding that the relevant obstruction was more than de minimis.

EAST HERTFORDSHIRE DC v. ISABEL HOSPICE TRADING LTD; *sub nom.* EAST HERTFORDSHIRE DC v. ISOBEL HOSPICE TRADING LTD [2001] J.P.L. 597, Jack Beatson, Q.C., QBD.

3323. Rylands v Fletcher liability–locus standi–common law requirement that claimant had proprietary interest in affected land–impact of Human Rights Act 1998

[Human Rights Act 1998.]

B applied to strike out an action brought by M and over 30 others claiming damages allegedly caused, inter alia, by emissions emanating from B's property. M based her claim on strict liability and nuisance. Given that some of the claimants had no proprietary interest in the affected land, B maintained that they had no locus standi to bring the action.

Held, dismissing the application, that prior to the inception of the Human Rights Act 1998, only those with an interest in the affected land could sue in nuisance. The rule in *Rylands v. Fletcher* effectively amounted to an extension of the law of nuisance and accordingly, claimants wishing to rely on this principle were required to overcome a similar restriction on locus standi, *Cambridge Water Co Ltd v. Eastern Counties Leather Plc* [1994] 2 A.C. 264, [1994] C.L.Y. 3410 followed and *British Celanese Ltd v. AH Hunt (Capacitors) Ltd* [1969] 1 W.L.R. 959, [1969] C.L.Y. 2403 considered. However, as M had an arguable case that this restrictive aspect of the common law should be extended in the light of the 1998 Act, the application to strike out was dismissed.

McKENNA v. BRITISH ALUMINIUM LTD; *sub nom.* McKENNA v. BRITISH ALUMINUM LTD [2002] Env. L.R. 30, Neuberger, J., Ch D.

3324. Statutory nuisance–trees–objective test for statutory nuisance

[Environmental Protection Act 1990 s.79.]

A applied for judicial review of the Council's decision not to serve an abatement notice because no statutory nuisance existed. A owned a thatched cottage in an area covered by the Council. A complained that a lime tree growing in a neighbouring property was producing honeydew, mould and mould spores which adversely affected A. A applied unsuccessfully for a felling order in respect of the tree but a tree preservation order was subsequently made. A then made a number of general complaints to the Council concerning the impact on health and property which was supported by medical and other expert reports. A had alleged that the tree constituted a statutory nuisance under the Environmental Protection Act 1990 s.79 in respect of which the defendant should serve an abatement notice. The Council's officer had visited the site and produced a report which said that there was insufficient evidence to justify a conclusion that there was a statutory nuisance.

Held, refusing the application for judicial review, that (1) the steps taken by the council to investigate A's complaint were all that were reasonably practicable in the circumstances of the case. The investigations were in accordance with the requirements of the 1990 Act and had been conducted in a proper manner. The Council's officer had provided adequate reasons for conclusions which she was entitled to reach on the evidence available; (2) the test for statutory nuisance was an objective one. It was not just a question of whether the claimants' health subjectively had been prejudiced by the accumulated fall out from the tree but whether the average person would be so prejudiced, *Cunningham v. Birmingham City Council* [1998] Env. L.R. 1, [1997] C.L.Y. 2377 applied, and (3) in the circumstances there was no basis upon which the conclusions reached by the Council's officer could properly be categorised as irrational or *Wednesbury* unreasonable.

R. (ON THE APPLICATION OF ANNE) v. TEST VALLEY BC, [2001] EWHC Admin 1019, [2002] Env. L.R. 22, Forbes, J., QBD (Admin Ct).

3325. Books

Pointing, John; Malcolm, Rosalind–Statutory Nuisance: Law and Practice. Hardback: £45.00. ISBN 0-19-924246-1. Oxford University Press.

PARTNERSHIPS

3326. Partners–Limited Liability Partnerships–confidentiality orders

LIMITED LIABILITY PARTNERSHIPS (NO.2) REGULATIONS 2002, SI 2002 913; made under the Limited Liability Partnerships Act 2000 s.15, s.16, s.17. In force: April 2, 2002; £1.75.

The Criminal Justice and Police Act 2001 inserted s.723B to s.723F into the Companies Act 1985 with the intention of setting up a structure under which a confidentiality order could be obtained in relation to a company director so that there could be provided to the Registrar of Companies a service address rather than a usual residential address in respect of that director. These Regulations apply the specified sections so that a confidentiality order may also be available for a member of a limited liability partnership.

3327. Partners–Limited Liability Partnerships–confidentiality orders

LIMITED LIABILITY PARTNERSHIPS (PARTICULARS OF USUAL RESIDENTIAL ADDRESS) (CONFIDENTIALITY ORDERS) REGULATIONS 2002, SI 2002 915; made under the Companies Act 1985 s.723B, s.723C, s.723D, s.723E, s.723F. In force: April 2, 2002; £2.50.

The Criminal Justice and Police Act 2001 inserted s.723B to s.723F into the Companies Act 1985 which provide for a system of granting confidentiality orders to directors and secretaries of companies formed under the 1985 Act and directors, secretaries and permanent representatives of overseas companies with a place of business, or a branch, in the UK within the meaning of the 1985 Act. Confidentiality orders are granted to individuals on application to the Secretary of State when she is satisfied that the availability for inspection of the usual residential address of that individual in the records of the registrar of companies creates, or is likely to create, a serious risk that the individual, or a person who lives with him, will be subjected to violence or intimidation. The effect of the order is that all notifications to the registrar of companies subsequent to the granting of the order in respect of the usual residential address of the beneficiary of an order are kept in confidential records by the registrar which do not form part of his records available for public inspection. These Regulations make further provision for the implementation of the system and for supplemental and consequential amendments to the 1985 Act as applied to limited liability partnerships.

3328. Partners—Limited Liability Partnerships—fees

LIMITED LIABILITY PARTNERSHIPS (COMPETENT AUTHORITY) (FEES) REGULATIONS 2002, SI 2002 503; made under the Companies Act 1985 s.708. In force: April 2, 2002; £1.75.

The Limited Liability Partnerships (Particulars of Usual Residential Address) (Confidentiality Orders) Regulations 2002 (SI 2002 915) make provision for the keeping by the registrar of companies of confidential records, containing the usual residential address of those members of a limited liability partnership in respect of whom a confidentiality order has been made. They also provide for a competent authority to be able to inspect and take copies of the confidential record and these Regulations prescribe the fees payable by such a competent authority.

3329. Partners—Limited Liability Partnerships—fees

LIMITED LIABILITY PARTNERSHIPS (FEES) (AMENDMENT) REGULATIONS 2002, SI 2002 2895; made under the Companies Act 1985 s.708. In force: January 1, 2003; £1.50.

These Regulations amend the Limited Liability Partnerships (Fees) (No.2) Regulations 2001 (SI 2001 969), which require the payment of fees in respect of functions performed by the registrar of companies in relation to limited liability partnerships under the Companies Act 1985 and the Limited Liability Partnership Act 2000. As a result the fee for a paper copy of a document relating to a limited liability partnership delivered by post is now £3.00.

3330. Partners—Limited Liability Partnerships—forms

LIMITED LIABILITY PARTNERSHIPS (FORMS) REGULATIONS 2002, SI 2002 690; made under the Companies Act 1985 s.363, s.288A, s.706. In force: April 2, 2002; £2.00.

These Regulations prescribe new forms 723SR and 723(change), for the purposes of the Companies Act 1985 s.288A for use in respect of a member of a limited liability partnership who is a beneficiary of a confidentiality order made under the 1985 Act. They also prescribe an additional Form LLP 363, which is the annual return for a limited liability partnership, together with continuation sheets. This form must be used so that the particulars of a service address will be given rather than of a usual residential address in the case where a member has obtained a confidentiality order under s.723 of the 1985 Act.

3331. Partners—size of partnership—20 member limit—removal

REGULATORY REFORM (REMOVAL OF 20 MEMBER LIMIT IN PARTNERSHIPS ETC.) ORDER 2002, SI 2002 3203; made under the Regulatory Reform Act 2001 s.1. In force: December 21, 2002; £1.75.

This Order amends the Limited Partnerships Act 1907, the Companies Act 1985 and the Trade Union and Labour Relations (Consolidation) Act 1992 in relation to the law relating to the maximum limit of 20 on the numbers of persons who can be members of partnerships, and of certain companies or associations, which has the effect of imposing burdens on people carrying out certain activities with a view to reducing those burdens in respect of the formation of such bodies.

3332. Partners—unrestricted size of partnership—exemptions—investment companies

LIMITED PARTNERSHIPS (UNRESTRICTED SIZE) NO.4 REGULATIONS 2002, SI 2002 376; made under the Companies Act 1985 s.717, s.744. In force: March 22, 2002; £1.50.

The Limited Partnerships Act 1907 provides that a limited partnership shall not consist of more than 20 persons. These Regulations exempt from that prohibition partnerships which are collective investment schemes the operator of which, or manager of the investments of which, is authorised under the Financial Services and Markets Act 2000 to operate the scheme or manage the investments.

3333. Books

Blackett-Ord, Mark–Blackett-Ord: Partnership-the Modern Law of Partnership and Limited Liability Partnership. Hardback: £195.00. ISBN 0-406-94644-2. Butterworths Law.

Lindley, Nathaniel; Banks, R.C.–Lindley and Banks on Partnership. 18th Ed. Hardback: £210.00. ISBN 0-421-67390-7. Sweet & Maxwell.

Morse, Geoffrey–Palmer's Limited Liability Partnership Law. Hardback: £125.00. ISBN 0-421-74000-0. Sweet & Maxwell.

Sacker, Tony–Practical Partnership Agreements. Hardback: CD-ROM: £60.00. ISBN 0-85308-640-0. Jordans.

Tolley's Professional Partnership Handbook. 4th Ed. Paperback: £59.95. ISBN 0-7545-1200-2. Tolley Publishing.

Young, Simon–Limited Liability Partnerships Handbook. Paperback: £55.00. ISBN 0-7545-1181-2. Tolley Publishing.

PENOLOGY AND CRIMINOLOGY

3334. Bail–electronic monitoring–responsible officer

BAIL (ELECTRONIC MONITORING OF REQUIREMENTS) (RESPONSIBLE OFFICER) ORDER 2002, SI 2002 844; made under the Bail Act 1976 s.3AA. In force: April 22, 2002; £2.00.

This Order specifies the descriptions of persons who are to be made responsible for the electronic monitoring of a child or young person's compliance with a requirement imposed on the child or young person as a condition of bail. It deals with the situation where an electronic monitoring requirement is imposed in respect of more than one bail condition and provides that the curfew requirement takes precedence in determining the responsible officer. It also provides that if there is no curfew requirement, then the court must choose one of the police areas to which the requirements relate and the responsible officer must be a person of a description who would ordinarily be responsible for electronic monitoring in that police area.

3335. Bail–electronic monitoring–responsible officer

LOCAL AUTHORITY REMANDS (ELECTRONIC MONITORING OF CONDITIONS) (RESPONSIBLE OFFICER) ORDER 2002, SI 2002 845; made under the Children and Young Persons Act 1969 s.23AA. In force: April 22, 2002; £2.00.

This Order specifies the descriptions of persons who are to be made responsible for the electronic monitoring of a child or young person's compliance with a condition imposed on the child or young person by a court remanding him to local authority accommodation. It deals with the situation where an electronic monitoring requirement is imposed in respect of more than one bail condition and provides that the curfew requirement takes precedence in determining the responsible officer. It also provides that if there is no curfew requirement, then the court must choose one of the police areas to which the requirements relate and the responsible officer must be a person of a description who would ordinarily be responsible for electronic monitoring in that police area.

3336. Criminal record–disclosure–exemptions

REHABILITATION OF OFFENDERS ACT 1974 (EXCEPTIONS) (AMENDMENT) ORDER 2002, SI 2002 441; made under the Rehabilitation of Offenders Act 1974 s.4, s.7, s.10. In force: in accordance with Art.1 (2); £1.75.

This Order amends the Rehabilitation of Offenders Act 1974 (Exceptions) Order 1975 (SI 1975 1023) which provides exceptions to the Rehabilitation of Offenders Act 1974. It adds certain classes of air traffic workers and National Lottery Commission personnel to that exception and adds to the list of professions, offices, employments, work and occupations in relation to which exceptions from the rehabilitative provisions of the Act apply. Added to the list of excepted offices, employments and work are the Crown Prosecution Service, work for the Royal Society for the Prevention of Cruelty to Animals that involves the killing of animals, the Serious Fraud Office, the National Crime Squad, the National Criminal Intelligence Service and Her Majesty's Customs and Excise. In addition, the Order exempts work concerned with the provision of care services to vulnerable adults and that is of such a kind as to enable the holder to have access to vulnerable adults in the course of his normal duties. It also exempts work concerned with the monitoring of internet communications for the purposes of child protection.

3337. Discretionary life imprisonment–prisoners rights–extent of disclosure to prisoners seeking recategorisation–entitlement to oral hearing before review committee–risk to public safety

W appealed against the dismissal of his application for judicial review ([2001] EWHC Admin 516) of the decision of the Director of High Security Prisons that his classification as a category A prisoner should continue. W who had had five discretionary life sentences imposed on him and who had made two escape attempts, one of which had been successful, had been categorised as a "high risk" prisoner. In rejecting his referral for parole on the ground that he continued to represent a risk to the public, the Discretionary Lifer Panel of the Parole board, DLP, recognised that he had made as much progress in addressing his offending behaviour as had been possible in category A conditions. W sought recategorisation, submitting that his continued classification as a category A prisoner would prevent any future DLP concluding he was fit for release. A request for an oral hearing before the category A review committee and for full disclosure of reports had been denied.

Held, allowing the appeal, that there were exceptional cases where a prisoner who sought recategorisation was entitled to an oral hearing before the category A review committee and to full disclosure of the reports on which his categorisation was based subject to the requirements of public interest immunity. Such cases would occur where the differing approach taken by the DLP and the review committee to public safety issues would, as in the instant case, result in the possibility of inconsistent decisions.

R. (ON THE APPLICATION OF WILLIAMS) v. SECRETARY OF STATE FOR THE HOME DEPARTMENT; *sub nom.* WILLIAMS v. SECRETARY OF STATE FOR THE HOME DEPARTMENT, [2002] EWCA Civ 498, [2002] 1 W.L.R. 2264, Judge, L.J., CA.

3338. Life imprisonment–prisoners rights–release–Secretary of State's discretion to refuse to release mandatory life prisoner despite recommendation of Parole Board–right to liberty and security

[Criminal Justice Act 1991 s.35(2); European Convention on Human Rights 1950 Art.5(1), Art.5(4).]

S applied to the European Court of Human Rights alleging that his continued detention subsequent to recall on a life licence breached the European Convention on Human Rights 1950 Art.5. S had been convicted of murder in 1967 and was released on licence in 1979. Following a breach of the licence conditions, he was detained again in 1989. In 1990, the Parole Board recommended that S be released on a life licence. Subsequently, in 1994, S was convicted of cheque fraud and received a six year custodial sentence. His life licence was revoked by the Secretary of State. When S became eligible for release from the fraud sentence, the Secretary of State refused to follow the Parole Board's recommendations and decided to continue S's detention on the ground that he presented a risk of committing further non violent imprisonable offences. The House of Lords found ([1999] 2 A.C. 38) that the Secretary of State had acted within the wide discretion conferred by the Criminal Justice Act 1991 s.35(2). On the instant application, S contended that the Secretary of State had breached his rights under Art.5(1) and Art.5(4) as the continued detention was no longer justified by his original sentence for murder and that he had been deprived of the opportunity to review the lawfulness of the decision in court.

Held, granting the application, that S must be regarded as having exhausted the punishment element of his offence of murder. When his sentence for the later fraud offence expired, his continued detention could not be regarded as justified by his punishment for the murder. The Secretary of State had not relied on any evidence of mental instability or a risk to the public of further violence. Instead he expressly relied on the risk of further non violent offending. In so doing, the Secretary of State breached S's rights under Art.5(1) as there was no sufficient causal connection, as required by the notion of lawfulness in Art.5(1)(a), between the possible commission of other non violent offences and the original sentence for murder. With regard to Art.5(4), the court reminded itself that the tariff comprised the punishment element of a mandatory life sentence and the Secretary of State's role in fixing that tariff was a sentencing exercise. Upon the expiry of the tariff, continued detention depended upon assessment of elements of risk associated with the original sentence for murder. Those elements were liable to change over time and thus, new issues of lawfulness requiring determination by a body satisfying the requirement of Art.5(4) had arisen. The original trial and appeal could not satisfy issues pertaining to the compatibility of S's subsequent detention with Art.5(1). The lawfulness of S's continued detention had not been reviewed by a body with the power to release or with a procedure containing the necessary judicial safeguards and thus, his rights under Art.5(4) had been breached.

STAFFORD v. UNITED KINGDOM (46295/99) (2002) 35 E.H.R.R. 32, L Wildhaber (President), ECHR.

3339. **Life imprisonment–prisoners rights–tariff periods–delay in Parole Board's determination as to continued detention–right to liberty and security**

[Crime (Sentences) Act 1997; Human Rights Act 1998 Sch.1 Part I Art.5(4).]

N, sentenced to an automatic life sentence under the Crime (Sentences) Act 1997, appealed against the dismissal ([2001] EWHC Admin 345, Independent, July 2, 2001 (C.S.)) of his application for judicial review of the Parole Board's refusal to bring forward the date of his discretionary lifer panel hearing. The tariff period for N's sentence had been fixed at 30 months. The Parole Board hearing to determine whether he should continue to be detained had taken place two months after the expiry of the tariff. In the event, the board determined that his detention should continue. It was custom that Parole Board hearings took place after the expiry of a prisoner's tariff period. N had challenged the delay in affording him a hearing. He submitted that the lawfulness of his detention under the Human Rights Act 1998 Sch.1 Part I Art.5(4) expired with the expiry of the tariff period and that the delay in determining the lawfulness of his continued detention meant that the decision regarding his detention had not been taken speedily.

Held, allowing the appeal in part, that detention in the interim between the expiry of tariff periods and the Parole Board's determination of a prisoner's continued detention needed to be justified under Art.5(4), and it was the state's duty to organise its legal system so as to comply with that requirement. The delay in holding the Parole Board hearing could not be excused by arguing lack of resources provided by other areas of government. The system in place for determining the status of discretionary and automatic life prisoners infringed Art.5(4), given that it envisaged a delay of up to three months, and Art.5(4) was infringed in the instant case by the delay of two months before the Board's determination. It seemed necessary, therefore, that arrangements be made whereby Parole Board hearings took place before the expiry of tariff periods .

R. (ON THE APPLICATION OF NOORKOIV) v. SECRETARY OF STATE FOR THE HOME DEPARTMENT (NO.2), [2002] EWCA Civ 770, [2002] 1 W.L.R. 3284, Buxton, L.J., CA.

3340. **Mental patients–discretionary life imprisonment–right to liberty and security–procedure for challenging continued detention**

See HUMAN RIGHTS: Benjamin v. United Kingdom (28212/95). §2485

3341. **Parole–mental patients–absconding from hospital–recall to prison– necessary prior consultation**

[Mental Health Act 1983 s.3; Criminal Justice Act 1991 s.39(2).]

S, a mental patient, sought judicial review of a decision of the Secretary of State to revoke his licence and recall him to prison. S, who had a 30 year history of offending and had been sentenced to 18 months' imprisonment for breach of a restraining order, was released on licence. He was admitted to hospital prior to the expiry of the licence period but refused to remain there voluntarily; accordingly an order was made under the Mental Health Act 1983 s.3 for his detention for treatment. Between his release from prison and admission to hospital, S had displayed unusual behaviour which led his probation officer to request revocation of the licence. The Secretary of State duly revoked S's licence and recalled him to prison under the Criminal Justice Act 1991 s.39(2). In his reasons the Secretary of State made no reference to S's presence in hospital or his status under s.3 of the 1983 Act. S absconded from hospital, was arrested by police the next day and returned to prison. S argued that, until his arrest, he had had no knowledge of the decision to revoke his licence and recall to prison and that, absent that knowledge, he could not have been unlawfully at large. The Secretary of State submitted that S's knowledge was irrelevant.

Held, granting the application, that it was normal practice for a detention order under s.3 of the 1983 Act to take precedence over an order for recall made under s.39(2) of the 1991 Act. The Secretary of State had erred in departing from this practice without consulting the hospital doctors who were treating S. Further, there was no statutory basis for the Secretary of State's assertion that a person could be unlawfully at large if that person was unaware of the revocation of their licence. Accordingly the orders of the Secretary of State were quashed, enabling S's immediate release from prison.

R. (ON THE APPLICATION OF S) v. SECRETARY OF STATE FOR THE HOME DEPARTMENT, [2002] EWHC 2424, *The Times*, November 13, 2002, Maurice Kay, J., QBD (Admin Ct).

3342. **Prison discipline–prisoners rights–disciplinary proceedings–right to fair trial–legal representation**

[Human Rights Act 1998 Sch.1 Part I Art.6(1), Art.6(3)(c).]

E and C applied to the European Court of Human Rights contending that the refusal to grant them legal representation in prison disciplinary proceedings had breached their right to a fair trial under the Human Rights Act 1998 Sch.1 Part I Art.6(3)(c). They had both been charged with disciplinary offences and found guilty after adjudication hearings at which neither were legally represented. E and C had sought leave to apply for judicial review of the refusal of legal representation, on the grounds that statutory and regulatory changes had made adjudication in prison disciplinary matters almost indistinguishable from matters of summary jurisdiction and that therefore legal representation should be granted as a right. However, leave was refused on the grounds that there was no right to be represented in adjudication proceedings and the prison governor's refusal to allow such representation was neither irrational or perverse in the circumstances.

Held, upholding the complaint, that the refusal of prison governors to allow prisoners to be legally represented in disciplinary proceedings had breached the prisoners' rights to a fair trial. The nature of the charges levied against E and C, which had included assault and threatening to kill, and the severity of the penalties they had faced, led to the conclusion that they were both subject to criminal charges within Sch.1 Part I Art.6(1) of the 1998 Act, and therefore Art.6 applied to the subsequent disciplinary proceedings. A person charged with a criminal offence who did not want to conduct his own defence had to be able to have access to legal assistance. Any consideration of legal representation had to be based on the criteria as outlined in *R. v. Secretary of State for the Home Department, ex p. Tarrant (James)* [1985] Q.B. 251, [1984] C.L.Y. 2755, which excluded the right to legal representation for adjudications. Accordingly, in the instant case, E and C had been denied a right to legal representation, in line with domestic law, in violation of their rights under Art.6(3)(c), *Tarrant* considered.

EZEH v. UNITED KINGDOM (39665/98); CONNORS v. UNITED KINGDOM (40086/98) (2002) 35 E.H.R.R. 28, J-P Costa (President), ECHR.

3343. Prison discipline–punishment–adjudicator

PRISON (AMENDMENT) RULES 2002, SI 2002 2116; made under the Prison Act 1952 s.47. In force: August 15, 2002; £1.75.

These Rules amend the Prison Rules 1999 (SI 1999 728) by providing for an adjudicator, approved by the Secretary of State, investigate charges of serious offences against discipline set out in those Rules. They also remove from the governor the power to impose any additional days as a punishment on a prisoner found guilty by him, and add to his powers in certain other respects.

3344. Prisoners–death–inappropriate medical attention–duty to hold independent investigation

[Fatal Accidents Act 1976; Human Rights Act 1998 Sch.1 Part I Art.2, Art.3.]

The mother of W, a prisoner who had died after suffering a severe asthma attack whilst in his prison cell, sought judicial review of the Secretary of State's continued failure to hold an independent investigation into her son's death. She had previously brought an action under the Fatal Accidents Act 1976 over the treatment her son had received for his asthma whilst in prison, and liability and damages had been agreed. It was submitted that there had been an infringement of the Human Rights Act 1998 Sch.1 Part I Art.2 and Art.3 and that as the state was under an obligation to protect a person's right to life, an official investigation should have been held.

Held, granting the application, that the Secretary of State was in breach of Art.2 and Art.3 through his continued failure to hold an independent investigation into the death of W. The right to life contained in Art.2 was fundamental and when it was breached by the death of someone at the hands of the state or where the state bore some responsibility for the death, it had a duty to provide an independent and reasonably prompt investigation, which should be open to public scrutiny and involve the deceased's next of kin. There were no rules as to the form the investigation had to take, which would be dependent on the circumstances surrounding the death. In the instant case, Art.2 and Art.3 had arguably been breached given the fact that there was evidence that W's asthma condition worsened because of inappropriate medical attention, and the fact that the conditions in his cell were such that he did not have access to prompt medical attention.

R. (ON THE APPLICATION OF WRIGHT) v. SECRETARY OF STATE FOR THE HOME DEPARTMENT, [2001] EWHC Admin 520, [2002] H.R.L.R. 1, Jackson, J., QBD (Admin Ct).

3345. Prisoners–legal representation–Italian avvocato denied access to client prisoner–right to fair trial

See HUMAN RIGHTS: R. (on the application of Van Hoogstraten) v. Governor of Belmarsh Prison. §2448

3346. Prisoners–marriage–remand prisoner seeking to marry prosecution witness–public policy considerations

See ADMINISTRATION OF JUSTICE: R. (on the application of CPS) v. Registrar General of Births, Deaths and Marriages. §35

3347. Prisoners—release—requisite period

RELEASE OF SHORT-TERM PRISONERS ON LICENCE (AMENDMENT OF REQUISITE PERIOD) ORDER 2002, SI 2002 2933; made under the Criminal Justice Act 1991 s.34A. In force: December 16, 2002; £1.50.

This Order amends the definition of "the requisite period" contained in the Criminal Justice Act 1991 s.34A(4) so that prisoners with terms of imprisonment of four months or more but less than twelve months serve one-quarter of their term before becoming eligible for release on licence. For those short-term prisoners with terms of imprisonment of twelve months or more, the requisite period is amended by this Order to be a period that is 90 days less than one-half of their term.

3348. Prisoners rights—death—prisoner killed by mentally ill cell mate—right to life—right to effective remedy

[Fatal Accidents Act 1976; Human Rights Act 1998; European Convention on Human Rights 1950 Art.2, Art.13.]

The parents of E, a prisoner who had been killed by a cell mate with a history of violence and mental illness, brought an application to the court alleging (1) that there had been a breach of E's right to life under the European Convention on Human Rights 1950 Art.2, and (2) that they had been denied an effective remedy contrary to Art.13 of the Convention. After E's death a private inquiry had been held which found that ideally neither E nor his cell mate should have been in prison and that they should not have been placed in the same cell. The inquiry also concluded that there had been limited cooperation between the agencies that had dealt with E's cell mate.

Held, ruling in favour of E's parents, that (1) E's cell mate's mental illness, his violent record and his behaviour at the time of and after his arrest showed that he had posed a real and serious risk to E when placed in the same cell. E's right to life under Art.2 had been breached by the failure of the relevant agencies, namely the medical profession, the police, the prosecution and the court, to pass on information about E's cell mate to the prison authorities and by the inadequate nature of the prison's screening process. Furthermore, the private nature of the proceedings before the inquiry and the fact that the inquiry had lacked the power to compel the attendance of witnesses amounted to a breach of the requirement under Art.2 to conduct an effective investigation into E's death, and (2) E's parents had been denied the right to an effective remedy under Art.13. A claim in negligence or under the Fatal Accidents Act 1976 would not have been a practical option since it was not clear that non pecuniary damages would have been awarded or that legal aid would have been available. What was more, any claim under the Human Rights Act 1998 could only have been made in respect of a continuing breach of the obligation under Art.2 taking place after October 2, 2000 and would not have given rise to damages relating to the period before the coming into force of the Act. Accordingly, E's parents had not had the means of obtaining a determination of their allegations that the authorities had failed to protect E's right to life or of obtaining an enforceable award of compensation for the damage that they had suffered. E's parents would be awarded £20,000 for non pecuniary damage and the same amount in respect of their legal costs and expenses.

EDWARDS v. UNITED KINGDOM (46477/99) (2002) 35 E.H.R.R. 19, Judge Cabral Barreto (President), ECHR.

3349. Prisoners rights—right to fair trial—revocation of licence—decision on issue of re release not determination of criminal charge

[Human Rights Act 1998 Sch.1 Part I Art.6.]

W appealed a decision ([2002] EWHC 769) upholding the Parole Board's refusal of his application for an oral hearing in respect of deliberations on the question of whether to recommend his immediate release on licence. W had been sentenced to three years' imprisonment for affray. He had been automatically released on licence after serving half his sentence but was then recalled to prison following revocation of the licence for alleged breaches of its conditions. W contended that the board, when making the decision whether or not to release a prisoner whose licence had been revoked, was determining criminal charges within the meaning of the Human Rights Act 1998 Sch.1 Part I Art.6. Thus, he argued, he had been entitled to the procedural safeguards which ensured a fair trial for those facing criminal charges including the right to an oral hearing with legal representation.

Held, dismissing the appeal (Hale L.J. dissenting), that a decision whether to recommend the release of prisoners whose licences had been revoked did not involve determination of a criminal charge, *Engel v. Netherlands (No.1) (A/22)* (1979-80) 1 E.H.R.R. 647 applied, *Ezeh v. United Kingdom (39665/98)* (2002) 35 E.H.R.R. 28, [2002] 9 C.L. 367 distinguished. Consequently, Art.6 was not invoked. The decision to recall to prison and the recommendation not to re release were based on prevention of risk and protection of the public and were not intended to be a punishment. The court took the view that it had not been asked to consider whether, if the board's determination had not amounted to a determination of a criminal charge, W would nonetheless have been entitled to an oral hearing with legal representation. In its view this issue remained open.

R. (ON THE APPLICATION OF WEST) v. PAROLE BOARD, [2002] EWCA Civ 1641, [2003] 1 W.L.R. 705, Simon Brown, L.J., CA.

3350. **Prisoners rights—right to family life—refusal to allow visits by nephew of convicted sex offender—lawfulness**

[Human Rights Act 1998 Sch.1 Part I Art.8; Prison Rules 1999 (SI 1999 728) r.4(1).]

B, a discretionary life sentence prisoner, sought judicial review of the prison governor's refusal to grant permission for visits from his young nephew, and the Secretary of State's policy which introduced child protection measures for prison visits. B had a previous conviction for the gross indecency of an eight year old boy and one for the indecent assault of a boy in a detention centre. B contended that both the governor's decision and the policy contravened his right to family life as guaranteed by the Human Rights Act 1998 Sch.1 Part I Art.8. Further, he submitted that the policy was ultra vires the Prison Rules 1999 r.4(1) and the governor's decision was irrational as no account had been taken both of the impact upon B of banning his nephew's visits and of the fact that social workers had stated that they had no objection to the visits.

Held, refusing the application for judicial review, that r.4(1) did not purport to prevent the application of a policy such as that implemented by the Secretary of State. Further, the weight to be attached to factors under consideration was a matter for the decision maker. The governor's decision was not irrational and he had been entitled to conclude that B's sister's child care difficulties should not outweigh considerations of her son's welfare and to attach limited weight to the observations of the social workers. As regards Art.8, it was for B to show that his relationship with his nephew amounted to "family life" and he had failed to do this, *R. (on the application of L) v. Secretary of State for Health* [2001] 1 F.L.R. 406, [2000] C.L.Y. 3242 considered. The underlying purpose of the policy was to protect the interests of children and as such was a legitimate and proportionate response to an area of public concern; therefore even if there had been an interference with B's family life, it was justifiable in all of the circumstances.

R. (ON THE APPLICATION OF B) v. WAKEFIELD PRISON GOVERNOR, [2001] EWHC Admin 917, [2002] 1 F.C.R. 445, Harrison, J., QBD (Admin Ct).

3351. **Prisoners rights—telecommunications—ban on telephone interviews with media—matters of legitimate public interest**

[Human Rights Act 1998 Sch.1 Part I Art.10.]

H, a serving prisoner who actively campaigned for prisoners rights, challenged the policy set out in Prison Service Order 4400 para.6.10 whereby prisoners were denied permission to call the media except in exceptional circumstances. H contended that he had a right pursuant to the Human Rights Act 1998 Sch.1 Part

I Art.10 to be entitled, in certain circumstances, to contact the media by telephone to discuss matters of legitimate public interest pertaining to prisons and prisoners.

Held, granting the application in part, that the policy that permission to contact the media by telephone would only be granted in exceptional circumstances, was one which the prison authorities were entitled to make. However it was insufficiently flexible, and was therefore unlawful. Unless a prisoner could not correspond with the journalist in writing or he was wanting to establish a miscarriage of justice, it was unlikely that he would be granted permission to telephone the media. In a democratic society prisoners would not be wholly prevented from expressing their views to the media about matters affecting them. Concerns as to the monitoring and control of what would be published as a result of prisoners speaking to journalists did not justify imposing a total ban on media interviews.

R. (ON THE APPLICATION OF HIRST) v. SECRETARY OF STATE FOR THE HOME DEPARTMENT (CONTACT WITH MEDIA), [2002] EWHC 602, [2002] 1 W.L.R. 2929, Elias, J., QBD (Admin Ct).

3352. Prisons–closure–H.M. Prison Haslar

CLOSURE OF PRISONS (H.M. PRISON HASLAR) ORDER 2002, SI 2002 77; made under the Prison Act 1952 s.37. In force: February 8, 2002; £1.50.

This Order provides for the closure of H.M. Prison Haslar.

3353. Prisons–closure–H.M. Young Offender Institution Dover

CLOSURE OF PRISONS (H.M. YOUNG OFFENDER INSTITUTION DOVER) ORDER 2002, SI 2002 78; made under the Prisons Act 1952 s.37. In force: February 8, 2002; £1.50.

This Order provides for the closure of H.M. Young Offender Institution Dover.

3354. Young offender institutions–disciplinary offences–punishment

YOUNG OFFENDER INSTITUTION (AMENDMENT) RULES 2002, SI 2002 2117; made under the Prison Act 1952 s.47. In force: August 15, 2002; £1.75.

These Rules amend the Young Offender Institution Rules 2000 (SI 2000 3371) by providing for an adjudicator, approved by the Secretary of State, investigate charges of serious offences against discipline set out in those Rules. They also remove from the governor the power to impose any additional days as a punishment on an inmate found guilty by him, and add to his powers in certain other respects.

3355. Books

Abbell, Michael–International Prisoner Transfer. Looseleaf/ring bound: £120.99. ISBN 1-57105-217-8. Transnational Publishers, Inc.

Braithwaite, John–Restorative Justice and Responsive Regulation. Studies in Crime and Public Policy. Book (details unknown): £37.95. ISBN 0-19-513639-X. Oxford University Press Inc, USA.

Doherty, Michael–Criminology. 2nd Ed. Sourcebook. Paperback: £11.95. ISBN 1-85836-450-7. Old Bailey Press.

Leech, Mark; Cheney, Deborah–Prisons Handbook: 2002. 6th Ed. Paperback: £62.50. ISBN 1-872870-16-3. Waterside Press.

Raynor, Peter; Vanstone, Maurice–Understanding Community Penalties. Crime and Justice. Hardback: £50.00. ISBN 0-335-20626-3. Paperback: £16.99. ISBN 0-335-20625-5. Open University Press.

PENSIONS

3356. Armed forces–disablement or death in service

NAVAL, MILITARY AND AIR FORCES ETC. (DISABLEMENT AND DEATH) SERVICE PENSIONS AMENDMENT ORDER 2002, SI 2002 792; made under the Naval and Marine Pay and Pensions Act 1865 s.3; the Pensions and Yeomanry Pay Act 1884 s.2; the Air Force (Constitution) Act 1917 s.2; and the Social Security (Miscellaneous Provisions) Act 1977 s.12, s.24. In force: April 8, 2002; £3.00.

This Order amends the Naval, Military and Air Forces Etc. (Disablement and Death) Service Pensions Order 1983 (SI 1983 883) which makes provision for pensions and other awards in respect of disablement or death due to service in the naval, military and air forces.

3357. Magistrates courts–Greater London Magistrates' Courts Authority–occupational pensions

GREATER LONDON MAGISTRATES' COURTS AUTHORITY (PENSIONS) ORDER 2002, SI 2002 2143; made under the Justices of the Peace Act 1997 s.50; and the Access to Justice Act 1999 Sch.14 para.36. In force: September 13, 2002; £1.50.

This Order applies the Superannuation Act 1972 s.1 to employees of the Greater London Magistrates' Courts Authority, and to any other members of the Metropolitan Civil Staffs Superannuation Scheme who have been employees of the inner London court staffs.

3358. Occupational pensions–benefits–revaluation percentages

OCCUPATIONAL PENSIONS (REVALUATION) ORDER 2002, SI 2002 2951; made under the Pension Schemes Act 1993 Sch.3 para.2. In force: January 1, 2003; £1.50.

This Order specifies revaluation percentages for the purpose of the revaluation on or after January 1, 2003 of benefits under occupational pension schemes.

3359. Occupational pensions–contracting-out

OCCUPATIONAL AND PERSONAL PENSION SCHEMES (CONTRACTING-OUT) (MISCELLANEOUS AMENDMENTS) REGULATIONS 2002, SI 2002 681; made under the Pension Schemes Act 1993 s.8, s.9, s.11, s.21, s.28, s.28A, s.32, s.32A, s.34, s.55, s.56, s.57, s.156, s.181, s.182, s.183; the Pension Schemes (Northern Ireland) Act 1993 s.38A, s.51, s.52, s.53, s.177, s.178; and the Pensions Act 1995 s.40, s.67, s.91, s.92, s.124, s.174. In force: April 6, 2002; £3.00.

These Regulations amend the Occupational Pension Schemes (Contracting-out) Regulations 1996 (SI 1996 1172), the Protected Rights (Transfer Payment) Regulations 1996 (SI 1996 1461), the Personal and Occupational Pension Schemes (Protected Rights) Regulations 1996 (SI 1996 1537), the Occupational Pension Schemes (Modification of Schemes) Regulations 1996 (SI 1996 2517), the Occupational Pension Schemes (Investment) Regulations 1996 (SI 1996 3127), the Occupational Pension Schemes (Contracting-out) Regulations (Northern Ireland) 1996 (SR 1996 493), the Personal Pension Schemes (Appropriate Schemes) Regulations 1997 (SI 1997 470), the Occupational Pension Schemes (Assignment, Forfeiture, Bankruptcy etc.) Regulations 1997 (SI 1997 785) and the Occupational Pension Schemes (Contracting-out) (Payment and Recovery of Remaining Balances) Regulations 2000 (SI 2000 750). The Regulations make amendments to these various instruments which govern the arrangements whereby occupational and personal pension schemes are contracted-out of the state additional retirement pensions, and associated matters including those relating to transfer payments, benefits for widows and widowers, contributions equivalent premiums and the provision of information relating to pension schemes and state scheme rights and duties.

3360. Occupational pensions–contributions–levels during employee secondment–power of Ombudsman to give directions to parties

[Pension Schemes Act 1993 s.151 (5).]

A, an employee of the NUS, latterly the RMT, was seconded to work for the International Transport Federation, ITF, at a pay rate higher than his previous RMT salary grade. He was informed, however, that his pension contributions would remain based on his lower RMT grade. A queried this decision, as it was contrary to the pension provisions that had been in force during a previous ITF secondment. Negotiations on the issue proved to be inconclusive and A accepted the higher pay rate and pension contributions from RMT. He complained to the Pensions Ombudsman, alleging that there had been maladministration by the fund trustees. The Ombudsman decided that, because A had not agreed to the terms governing his pension contributions, he was entitled to receive contributions commensurate with the higher pay rate and he directed the parties to make increased contributions accordingly. The trustees appealed.

Held, allowing the appeal, that (1) RMT had offered to increase A's pay and there were no new terms which operated to his disadvantage, only a limit on the pension contribution. Therefore it could be inferred that he had accepted RMT's offer, and (2) under the Pension Schemes Act 1993 s.151 (5) the Ombudsman's directions were equivalent to a county court order and such orders could not require parties to agree to something so that the Ombudsman's direction was invalid.

NUS OFFICIALS AND EMPLOYEES SUPERANNUATION FUND TRUSTEES v. PENSIONS OMBUDSMAN; *sub nom.* NUS SUPERANNUATION FUND v. PENSIONS OMBUDSMAN [2002] O.P.L.R. 17, Lightman, J., Ch D.

3361. Occupational pensions–disclosure of information

OCCUPATIONAL AND PERSONAL PENSION SCHEMES (DISCLOSURE OF INFORMATION) AMENDMENT REGULATIONS 2002, SI 2002 1383; made under the Pension Schemes Act 1993 s.113, s.181, s.182, s.183. In force: April 6, 2003; £2.50.

These Regulations amend the Personal Pension Schemes (Disclosure of Information) Regulations 1987 (SI 1987 1110), the Occupational Pension Schemes (Disclosure of Information) Regulations 1996 (SI 1996 1655) and the Stakeholder Pension Schemes Regulations 2000 (SI 2000 1403). The effect of these amendments is that the information which has to be sent to members of schemes with money purchase benefits must include an illustration of the amount of future pension that might become payable under the scheme. The amount is to be determined by reference to guidance.

3362. Occupational pensions–equal treatment–exclusion of part time non teaching staff–compatibility with EC law

[EC Treaty Art.141.]

U appealed against a decision of the Pensions Ombudsman that it had indirectly discriminated against S on grounds of sex by excluding her from its pension scheme. S had been employed by a school between June 1984 and November 1996. During that time, she worked part time for around 20 hours per week. She had applied to join U's occupational retirement benefits scheme for non teaching staff, but her application had been refused. S complained to the Pensions Ombudsman, who found that her exclusion from the scheme was contrary to the EC Treaty Art.141, since its terms operated so as to exclude more women than men, and the requirements of the scheme could not be objectively justified on economic grounds.

Held, allowing the appeal, that (1) pension rights fell within the definition of "pay" in Art.141 (1), and Art.141 was capable of having direct effect. Art.141 did not however make it clear whether or not a male comparator was required in pensions cases; (2) there was no mandatory method for the calculation of pay laid down by Art.141. The only requirement was that any method adopted should not be discriminatory, *Barry v. Midland Bank Plc* [1999] 1 W.L.R. 1465, [1999]

C.L.Y. 2117 applied. In the present case, the rule which excluded S from membership of the scheme was not artificial and applied to all employees equally, and (3) U had sought to justify its scheme objectively as seeking to achieve a broad integration with the State pension scheme. The integration of an occupational pension scheme with the State pension scheme might, but would not always, objectively justify even a discriminatory policy, *Birds Eye Walls Ltd v. Roberts (C132/92)* [1993] E.C.R. I-5579, [1994] C.L.Y. 4823 and *Bestuur van het Algemeen Burgerlijk Pensioenfonds v. Beune (C7/93)* [1995] All E.R. (EC) 97, [1995] C.L.Y. 1996 considered. In the present case, the Ombudsman had made an inaccurate and too restrictive interpretation of U's scheme's objective. It was not open to S to criticise U's scheme simply on the basis that she would have been better off if the scheme had been different or better. U's policy whereby all employees had the opportunity to accrue a State pension rather than a pension under U's scheme on earnings below the lower earnings limit was not an illegitimate policy.

TRUSTEES OF UPPINGHAM SCHOOL RETIREMENT BENEFITS SCHEME FOR NON-TEACHING STAFF v. SHILLCOCK, [2002] EWHC 641, [2002] 2 C.M.L.R. 39, Neuberger, J., Ch D.

3363. **Occupational pensions—equal treatment—widower's pension entitlement—obligations on pension fund not party to contract of employment**

[EC Treaty Art.141.]

M, a widower whose late wife had been employed by B, claimed a widower's pension from B and E, a pension fund which was liable to pay a supplementary pension to B's employees under a collective insurance agreement. M's claim succeeded against E at first instance and on appeal. E appealed to the Federal Labour Court which stayed the proceedings and sought a preliminary ruling as to whether the EC treaty Art.141 was to be interpreted as meaning that E had to ensure equal treatment even where employees were protected against discriminatory acts by their employers.

Held, giving a preliminary ruling, that (1) M as a surviving spouse could rely on Art.141 to protect his entitlement to a survivor's pension; (2) pension trustees and funds, such as E, although not a party to the contract of employment, had to comply with the principle of equal treatment in paying benefits which had the character of pay under Art.141, and (3) E's obligations under Art.141 applied even where employees were protected against discriminatory acts by their employers.

PENSIONSKASSE FUR DIE ANGESTELLTEN DER BARMER ERSATZKASSE VVAG v. MENAUER (C379/99) [2001] Pens. L.R. 297, F Macken (President), ECJ.

3364. **Occupational pensions—guaranteed minimum pensions—increase**

GUARANTEED MINIMUM PENSIONS INCREASE ORDER 2002, SI 2002 649; made under the Pension Schemes Act 1993 s.109. In force: April 6, 2002; £1.50.

This Order, which is made in consequence of review under the Pension Schemes Act 1993 s.109, specifies 1.7 per cent as the percentage by which that part of any guaranteed minimum pension attributable to earnings factors for the tax years 1988-89 to 1996-97 and payable by occupational pension schemes is to be increased.

3365. **Occupational pensions—ill health—rule governing early retirement—interpretation in light of provision allowing for termination if able to undertake other duties**

O, a command supervisor employed by U, sought a declaration as to his eligibility for an early pension on the ground of ill health under the rules of the British Coal Staff Superannuation Scheme. Rule 23 provided that contributors were eligible for a pension on the ground of ill health if they were unlikely to return to duties that could "reasonably" be assigned to them, subject to r.48, which provided that the pension would cease to be payable if contributors subsequently became able to carry out the duties of "some other office or employment" with U. O contended that the assignment of duties had to be commensurate with his present status and the duties he carried out under his existing contract of employment. I, the scheme trustee, argued, however, that duties could be assigned that were beyond the scope of O's existing contract, as expressly provided for by r.48.

Held, giving judgment for I, that the issue fell to be determined by reference to the inter relationship between r.23 and r.48. Whereas the former governed the grant of a pension on ill health grounds, the latter set out the grounds on which such a pension could be terminated. The test for determining the "reasonableness" of an offer of re engagement for the purposes of r.48 was analogous to the test for the loss of a right to redundancy. Therefore the offer had to be suitable in relation to the range of tasks involved, pay rate, hours of work, travelling time and job status.

O'NEILL v. INDUSTRY WIDE COAL STAFF SUPERANNUATION SCHEME TRUSTEES LTD Etherton, J., Ch D.

3366. Occupational pensions–incapacity benefit–entitlement–medical evidence of extent of incapacity

K was a member of B's staff pension scheme, which provided a permanent incapacity benefit of four times pensionable salary and early retirement pension if further employment with B proved impossible. K claimed incapacity benefit following a heart attack in 1974. Both the insurer then underwriting the scheme and T rejected the claim, despite supporting medical evidence. T's determination was based on an oral paraphrasing of this evidence. K obtained a declaration at first instance that his claim should have been allowed and the judge ordered a pension to be paid. T appealed.

Held, allowing the appeal in part, that T had failed to give K's case the informed consideration it required and the matter was remitted for reconsideration, based on the opinion of the doctor who had examined K that it was possible he could undertake light work in the future if his symptoms improved and he lost weight. However, T's failure to consider the matter properly did not entitle the court below to substitute its own view. If T decided to admit K's claim following the reconsideration, the date of K's permanent incapacity should be decided as this could affect K's entitlement to benefits.

KERR v. BRITISH LEYLAND (STAFF) TRUSTEES LTD [2001] W.T.L.R. 1071, Fox, L.J., CA.

3367. Occupational pensions–insurance premiums–withdrawal of guaranteed annuity rates–interpretation of "increase in insurance"

S appealed against a determination of the Pensions Ombudsman that it was not permitted to withdraw guaranteed annuity rates in respect of increases to premiums paid by existing members of an occupational pension scheme under a policy of insurance issued by it. The issue for determination on appeal was what was meant by an "increase in insurance". S contended that an increase in insurance arose when a premium was increased which, under the rules of the policy, enabled it to withdraw the guaranteed annuity rates in respect of such increase.

Held, allowing the appeal, that an increase in premiums must involve an increase in insurance so that S was entitled to withdraw the guaranteed annuity rate in respect of the insurance payment attributable to the increased element of the premium.

SUN ALLIANCE & LONDON ASSURANCE CO LTD v. PENSIONS OMBUDSMAN [2001] O.P.L.R. 63, Sir Robert Andrew Morritt V.C., Ch D.

3368. Occupational pensions–judiciary–office holders

JUDICIAL PENSIONS AND RETIREMENT ACT 1993 (CERTAIN QUALIFYING JUDICIAL OFFICES) (AMENDMENT) ORDER 2002, SI 2002 3083; made under the Judicial Pensions and Retirement Act 1993 s.1. In force: January 15, 2003; £1.50.

This Order amends the Judicial Pensions and Retirement Act 1993 in order to remove the limitation that members of appeal tribunals constituted under the Social Security Act 1998 s.6 (1) and the Social Security (Northern Ireland) Order 1998 (SI 1998 1506) Art.7 (1) must serve full-time in order to qualify as judicial office holders for the purposes of Part I of the Act.

3369. Occupational pensions–local government pension scheme

LOCAL GOVERNMENT PENSION SCHEME (AMENDMENT) REGULATIONS 2002, SI 2002 206; made under the Superannuation Act 1972 s.7, s.12. In force: in accordance with Reg.1 (2); £1.75.

These Regulations amend the Local Government Pension Scheme Regulations 1997 (SI 1997 1612) which comprise the Local Government Pension Scheme. They extend provisions to allow admission agreement bodies approved by the Secretary of State to enter into admission agreements where they contract out the performance of a function, add a payment made under a School Achievements Award Scheme to the list of payments which are excluded from an employee's pensionable pay and exclude rights under a non-Scheme additional voluntary contributions scheme from the list of relevant pension rights which may count as membership in the Scheme. They also add housing management companies set up by local authorities to the list of Scheme employers and substitute the fund administered by Rhondda, Cynon, Taff County Borough Council as the appropriate fund for employees of the National Probation Service local board for the South Wales area in place of the fund administered by Swansea County Council.

3370. Occupational pensions–local government pension scheme

LOCAL GOVERNMENT PENSION SCHEME (MISCELLANEOUS) REGULATIONS 2002, SI 2002 819; made under the Superannuation Act 1972 s.7, s.12. In force: April 16, 2002; £2.00.

These Regulations amend or make certain provisions in connection with the Local Government Pension Scheme which is an occupational pension scheme established under regulations made under the Superannuation Act 1972 s.7. The Local Government Pension Scheme (Her Majesty's Chief Inspector of Schools in England) (Transfers) Regulations 2001 (SI 2001 2866) are amended by extending the period within which information must be given to members and the date by which a member must agree if a transfer is to be made. The Local Government Pension Scheme Regulations 1997 (SI 1997 1612) are amended to allow persons to remain members of the Local Government Pension Scheme after the transfer of their employment to a Care Trust, in which employment they are entitled to membership of the National Health Service Pension Scheme for England and Wales. Provision is made for the calculation and payment of transfer payments for active members of the Local Government Pension Scheme who transfer on April 1, 2002 from local government employment to employment with the Care Standards Inspectorate for Wales, a division of the National Assembly for Wales, as a consequence of the provisions of the Care Standards Act 2000 s.79. Provision is also made for members who transfer from the Local Government Pension Scheme to the Principal Civil Service Pension Scheme and for members who remain as active members of the Local Government Pension Scheme as admission agreement employees but whose appropriate fund changes.

3371. Occupational pensions–local government pension scheme–management and investment of funds

LOCAL GOVERNMENT PENSIONS SCHEME (MANAGEMENT AND INVESTMENT OF FUNDS) (AMENDMENT) REGULATIONS 2002, SI 2002

1852; made under the Superannuation Act 1972 s.7. In force: August 9, 2002; £1.75.

These Regulations, which amend the Local Government Pension Scheme (Management and Investment of Funds) Regulations 1998 (SI 1998 1831), add provisions to the regulation requiring each administering authority to publish a written statement of investment principles. The new provision requires that such statement must set out the extent to which the administering authority complies with the ten principles of investment practice contained in the document published in April 2002 by the Chartered Institute of Public Finance and Accountancy.

3372. Occupational pensions–Metropolitan Police Authority–civil staff

METROPOLITAN POLICE AUTHORITY (CIVIL STAFF PENSIONS) ORDER 2002, SI 2002 2468; made under the Greater London Authority Act 1999 s.411. In force: October 31, 2002; £1.75.

This Order, which has effect from September 1, 2002, transfers to the principal civil service pension scheme certain members and beneficiaries of the pension arrangements having effect by virtue of the Superannuation (Miscellaneous Provisions) Act 1967, which are known as the Metropolitan Civil Staffs Superannuation Scheme. The members and beneficiaries covered by the Order are persons employed or formerly employed by the Metropolitan Police Authority (or one of its predecessors) otherwise than as constables and their dependants.

3373. Occupational pensions–minimum funding requirement

OCCUPATIONAL PENSION SCHEMES (MINIMUM FUNDING REQUIREMENT AND MISCELLANEOUS AMENDMENTS) REGULATIONS 2002, SI 2002 380; made under the Pensions Act 1995 s.56, s.57, s.58, s.59, s.61, s.73, s.75, s.120, s.124, s.125, s.174, s.175. In force: March 19, 2002; £2.00.

These Regulations amend the Pensions Act 1995, the Occupational Pension Schemes (Minimum Funding Requirement and Actuarial Valuations) Regulations 1996 (SI 1996 1536), the Occupational Pension Schemes (Deficiency on Winding Up etc.) Regulations 1996 (SI 1996 3126) and the Occupational Pension Schemes (Winding Up) Regulations 1996 (SI 1996 3128). The amendments provide for the calculation of liabilities in respect of any pension or other benefit (including any increase in a pension) which has become payable under a scheme in circumstances where the scheme winds up and the employer is not insolvent at the time the winding up commenced. They also provide that, where a scheme is in the process of winding up and the employer is not insolvent, the scheme's liabilities are to be calculated so as to include the actual cost of winding up and the cost of securing pensions or other benefits in payment by way of annuities.

3374. Occupational pensions–National Health Service–additional voluntary contributions

NATIONAL HEALTH SERVICE PENSION SCHEME (ADDITIONAL VOLUNTARY CONTRIBUTIONS) AMENDMENT REGULATIONS 2002, SI 2002 610; made under the Superannuation Act 1972 s.10, Sch.3. In force: April 12, 2002; £1.75.

These Regulations amend the National Health Service Pension Scheme (Additional Voluntary Contributions) Regulations 2000 (SI 2000 619) which provide for the payment of additional voluntary contributions by persons who are members of the pension scheme constituted by the National Health Service Pension Scheme Regulations 1995 (SI 1995 300). The Regulations provide that an election shall be treated as not having ceased to have effect in circumstances where a contributor is in receipt of pension benefits under the Pension Scheme Regulations, or where he has left pensionable employment and he wishes to switch his AVC investments or future contributions to another authorised fund and provide that persons making contributions may transfer the value of investments made under those Regulations to another form of pension arrangement, including a free-standing additional voluntary contributions scheme, without having also to transfer the value of their rights held in the NHS pension scheme. They also raise the limit for retirement pensions in cases where the member retires after the age of 60 and is entitled to a greater pension because of its postponement.

3375. Occupational pensions–National Health Service–compensation–premature retirement

NATIONAL HEALTH SERVICE (COMPENSATION FOR PREMATURE RETIREMENT) REGULATIONS 2002, SI 2002 1311; made under the Superannuation Act 1972 s.24, Sch.3 para.8, Sch.3 para.9, Sch.3 para.13. In force: May 31, 2002; £2.50.

These Regulations, which revoke the National Health Service (Compensation for Premature Retirement) Amendment Regulations 1985 (SI 1985 1659), amend the National Health Service (Compensation for Premature Retirement) Regulations 1981 (SI 1981 1263), the National Health Service Superannuation, Premature Retirement and Injury Benefits (Amendment) Regulations 1991 (SI 1991 584) and the National Health Service (Pension Scheme and Compensation for Premature Retirement) Amendment Regulations 2000 (SI 2000 605). They provide for the payment of compensation to or in respect of a person who was employed in the National Health Service in England and Wales and has prematurely retired from that employment by reason of redundancy or in the interests of the efficiency of the service.

3376. Occupational pensions–National Health Service–transfer of undertakings

NATIONAL HEALTH SERVICE PENSION SCHEME (AMENDMENT) REGULATIONS 2002, SI 2002 561; made under the Superannuation Act 1972 s.10, s.12, Sch.3. In force: in accordance with Art.1 (1); £2.00.

These Regulations amend the National Health Service Pension Scheme Regulations 1995 (SI 1995 300), which provide for the superannuation of persons engaged in the National Health Service, so as to introduce various definitions relating to practitioners who are required as a result of the amendments enabling locums to belong to the Scheme. They also make amendments so as to entitle members to a transfer payment where they leave after reaching 60 as a result of a transfer of an undertaking, and to enable special terms to be applied where one member so transfers.

3377. Occupational pensions–National Ports Council Pension Scheme–excess statutory surplus

NATIONAL PORTS COUNCIL PENSION SCHEME (EXCESS STATUTORY SURPLUS) ORDER 2002, SI 2002 346; made under the Pensions Act 1995 s.72, s.174. In force: March 13, 2002; £1.75.

This Order amends the National Ports Council Pension Scheme, following the wind up of the National Ports Council, to enable the excess statutory surplus to be utilised in accordance with proposals agreed between the Secretary of State and the trustees of the Scheme and subsequently made by the administrator of the Scheme to, and approved by, the Inland Revenue.

3378. Occupational pensions–Parliament–Members of Parliament

PARLIAMENTARY PENSIONS (AMENDMENT) REGULATIONS 2002, SI 2002 1807; made under the Parliamentary and other Pensions Act 1987 s.2. In force: August 5, 2002; £2.00.

These Regulations, which amend the Parliamentary Pensions (Consolidation and Amendment) Regulations 1993 (SI 1993 3253), make various amendments to the Parliamentary Pension Scheme. They increase the accrual rate from fiftieths to fortieths and the contribution rate from 6 per cent to 9 per cent of salary; provide an exception to the abatement requirements in respect of pension. Former Members of the House of Commons who become paid office holders in the

House of Lords will not have their pension abated; provide that service in the Scottish Parliament, the National Assembly for Wales or the Northern Ireland Assembly counts towards the qualifying period for an early retirement pension, except where the service is concurrent with membership of the House of Commons; provide that in the case of members dying on or after April 1, 2001, all dependant children will receive equal treatment in respect of benefits; and increase the lump sum death in service payment from three times annual basic salary to four times annual basic salary.

3379. Occupational pensions–Parliament–Members of Parliament

PARLIAMENTARY PENSIONS (AMENDMENT) (NO.2) REGULATIONS 2002, SI 2002 1887; made under the Parliamentary and other Pensions Act 1987 s.2. In force: August 5, 2002; £1.75.

These Regulations, which amend the Parliamentary Pensions (Consolidation and Amendment) Regulations 1993 (SI 1993 3253), make amendments to the Parliamentary Pension Scheme to correct drafting errors made in the Parliamentary Pensions (Amendment) Regulations 2002 (SI 2002 1807). The Regulations provide for an office holder who opts after his appointments not to pay contributions at the increased rate of 9 per cent of salary to receive a refund of excess contributions paid since the date of his appointment; and clarifies one of the conditions subject to which the adopted child of a former husband or wife of a deceased participant is eligible for a pension by providing that at the time of the death the child should have been wholly or mainly dependant on the deceased.

3380. Occupational pensions–pensionable age–normal retirement date–request for directions by scheme trustee

B applied for directions to determine the normal retirement date, NRD, of a pension scheme of which it was trustee in relation to four periods, first, prior to May 17, 1990; second, May 17, 1990 to April 25, 1994; third, April 16, 1994 to May 22, 1996, and fourth, after May 23, 1996. The Scheme had been set up under a deed which allowed for amendment by the trustees provided certain conditions were met. Following judgment in the case of *Barber v. Guardian Royal Exchange Assurance Group (C262/88)* [1991] 1 Q.B. 344, [1990] C.L.Y. 1915, amendments were proposed to equalise the NRD of men and women to 65 years, and a purported amendment was announced on April 26, 1994. On May 23, 1996 new rules were introduced to the Scheme, which were stated to take effect retrospectively from April 6, 1994. They allowed for retirement after 50 years with the consent of the trustees and employer, such consent not being required after "state pension age", which was defined as 65 years for men and 60 years for women.

Held, giving directions, that in the first period the NRD was 65 years for men and 60 years for women as set out in the original deed; in the second period, the NRD became equalised at 60 years because of the effect of *Barber*. In the third period, the announcement of the amendments did not fully comply with the conditions of the deed as it was worded in such a way as to be ambiguous, with the effect that the announcement itself could not constitute notification as required by the deed. The amendments did not therefore take effect and so the NRD remained at 60 years for both men and women. In the fourth period, as much effect as possible should be given to the variation to the extent permitted by *Barber* and thus the 1996 rule amendments should be treated as valid despite being tainted by the flaws of the 1994 amendment and by the references to state pension age, *Coloroll Pension Trustees Ltd v. Russell (C200/91)* [1995] All E.R. (EC) 23, [1995] C.L.Y. 2001 applied. To that end, NRD would be 65 for men and women, with retirement possible at 60 with the consent of the employer.

BESTRUSTEES v. STUART [2001] O.P.L.R. 341, Neuberger, J., Ch D.

3381. Occupational pensions–personal pensions–bankruptcy

OCCUPATIONAL AND PERSONAL PENSION SCHEMES (BANKRUPTCY) (NO.2) REGULATIONS 2002, SI 2002 836; made under the Bankruptcy (Scotland) Act 1985 s.36C, s.36F; the Insolvency Act 1986 s.342C, s.342F; and the Welfare Reform and Pensions Act 1999 s.11, s.12, s.83. In force: April 6, 2002; £3.00.

These Regulations, which revoke the Occupational and Personal Pension Schemes (Bankruptcy) Regulations 2002 (SI 2002 427), make provision for the treatment of rights under certain pension arrangements in the event of a person's bankruptcy.

3382. Occupational pensions–police pension scheme–divorce–pension sharing

POLICE PENSIONS (PENSION SHARING) REGULATIONS 2002, SI 2002 3202; made under the Police Pensions Act 1976 s.1, s.2, s.3, s.4, s.5, s.6, s.7. In force: February 1, 2003; £2.50.

These Regulations amend the Police Pensions Regulations 1987 (SI 1987 257), the Police Pensions (Purchase of Increased Benefits) Regulations 1987 (SI 1987 2215) and Police Pensions (Additional Voluntary Contributions) Regulations 1991 (SI 1992 1304) to make provision for the implementation of pension sharing on divorce and nullity in accordance with the Welfare Reform and Pensions Act 1999.

3383. Occupational pensions–Polish Forces–time extension

PENSIONS (POLISH FORCES) SCHEME (EXTENSION) ORDER 2002, SI 2002 671; made under the Polish Resettlement Act 1947 s.1. In force: March 27, 2002; £1.50.

The Pension (Polish Forces) Scheme, which makes provision for payment of pensions to former members of the Polish Forces who served under British command during World War II, or in the Polish Resettlement Forces, is of limited duration because it was originally envisaged that the Polish Government would at some time assume responsibility for payment of the pensions. This still remains unlikely and the present Scheme, which expires on March 26, 2002, is extended by this Order for a further period of five years from March 27, 2002 to March 26, 2007.

3384. Occupational pensions–surplus–distribution–entitlement of former members to participate

B operated a pension scheme which was substantially in surplus. A distribution was proposed. The rules required that the funds be maintained for the benefit of members and their dependants. During the life of the long established scheme some members had retired taking their benefits. The question arose whether former members were entitled to participate in the distribution, or whether the distribution should be limited to present members.

Held, that the distribution should be limited to present members and that (1) rule changes should be approached in a practical and purposive rather than detached and literal manner; (2) the rules contained no power to back date amendments and therefore amendment to the scheme could not be retrospective; (3) the rules of the scheme required that it be operated for the benefit of present members and former members were not mentioned. There were therefore no special rules of construction to be applied to a pension scheme *Courage Group's Pension Schemes, Re* [1987] 1 W.L.R. 495, [1987] C.L.Y. 2822 applied, and (4) it was not appropriate to apply discretionary trust principles to the scheme where the rights of the members were defined by the scheme itself and questions of fairness were unfounded.

BANK OF NEW ZEALAND OFFICERS PROVIDENT FUND ASSOCIATION MANAGEMENT BOARD v. McDONALD; BANK OF NEW ZEALAND v. BANK OF NEW ZEALAND OFFICERS PROVIDENT FUND ASSOCIATION MANAGEMENT BOARD; *sub nom.* BANK OF NEW ZEALAND OFFICERS

PROVIDENT ASSOCIATION MANAGEMENT BOARD v. McDONALD [2002] Pens. L.R. 479, Williams, J., HC (NZ).

3385. Occupational pensions–teachers

TEACHERS' PENSIONS (AMENDMENT) REGULATIONS 2002, SI 2002 3058; made under the Superannuation Act 1972 s.9, s.12, Sch.3. In force: January 10, 2003; £1.75.

These Regulations amend the Teachers' Pensions Regulations 1997 (SI 1997 3001) to provide that the closing balance in the Teachers' Pension Account for the financial year ending on March 31, 2001 to be an amount determined by the Government Actuary by reference to the value of the scheme assets mentioned in Reg. G4(6); provide that the value of the scheme assets are equal to the value of the scheme liabilities on March 31, 2001; to require the Government Actuary with the agreement of Secretary of State to specify a funding methodology for each actuarial review; to provide that the formula for calculating the employer contribution rate from April 1, 2003 will not include the addition of 0.2 per cent; and reduce the interest rate on late payments of employer contributions from 12 per cent to 8 per cent for periods of pensionable employment on or after April 1, 2003.

3386. Occupational pensions–transfer of assets–improper transfer–trustee company's personal liability

A appealed against the dismissal of his claim against R, a company which had acted as a pension scheme trustee, for breach of trust. A was a director and shareholder of a company which had gone into administrative receivership. He held two valuable pension policies under a small self administered scheme of which he was a trustee. In order to access the funds within those policies he had joined another scheme operated by a company, B. In doing so, A had falsely signed a form stating that he was, or was about to be, employed by B. Assets from his two pension policies had subsequently been transferred to the new scheme. A had sought to argue before the judge that as he had never been an employee of B, a resulting trust had occurred in favour of the original policies. The judge had found that R had not initially known that A was not an employee of B and had only been put on enquiry at a date after funds from the original policies had been mixed with those in the new scheme. In such circumstances, the judge held that the funds belonging to the new scheme could not be separately identified and that, therefore, no resulting trust had occurred.

Held, dismissing the appeal, that notwithstanding the absence of the trust deed and rules of the original scheme, it could be assumed that the trustees had a fiduciary power to transfer assets to another pension scheme. That power had to be exercised in good faith and for the purposes for which it was intended, namely the transfer from one genuine employment to another. A had known, however, that the transfer was improper. It followed that, contrary to the judge's conclusion, while the legal interest in the policies had been transferred, the beneficial interest had remained in the original scheme, *Westdeutsche Landesbank Girozentrale v. Islington LBC* [1996] A.C. 669, [1996] C.L.Y. 4149 considered. A trustee had a proprietary right to recover money subject to one express trust that had been paid improperly to another trust. However, R was not personally liable for such a breach of trust since it had not had actual knowledge that the transfer had been invalid and should be returned nor had it had the means to find out what sum should be returned to the original scheme or of raising the sum. Further, A had not shown any actionable breach for which he was entitled to a remedy on the basis of R's personal liability.

ALLAN v. NOLAN; *sub nom.* ALLAN v. REA BROS TRUSTEES LTD, [2002] EWCA Civ 85, [2002] Pens. L.R. 169, Robert Walker, L.J., CA.

3387. Occupational pensions–trustees and directors–appointments–alternative arrangements

OCCUPATIONAL PENSION SCHEMES (MEMBER-NOMINATED TRUSTEES AND DIRECTORS) AMENDMENT REGULATIONS 2002, SI 2002 2327; made under the Pensions Act 1995 s.17, s.19, s.21, s.124. In force: October 6, 2002; £1.75.

These Regulations amend the Occupational Pension Schemes (Member-nominated Trustees and Directors) Regulations 1996 (SI 1996 1216) in relation to the selection and appointment of member-nominated trustees and directors. The Regulations extend the approval of alternative arrangements for selecting the trustees or directors of a scheme, and of appropriate rules for that same purpose, so that the approval ceases after a period of ten rather than six years. Where an employer seeks fresh approval of alternative arrangements on or after October 6, 2002 that approval will cease after four years.

3388. Occupational pensions–trustees powers and duties–compromise of statutory debt due from employer

[Trustee Act 1925 s.15; Pensions Act 1995 s.75.]

T, the trustee of an occupational pension scheme, sought directions in circumstances where the scheme, which was subject to the statutory minimum funding requirements imposed by the Pensions Act 1995, was in substantial debt. G, the employers, were unable to bring the scheme up to its fully funded state and would be forced into liquidation unless the deficit could be compromised. Section 75 of the 1995 Act would come into operation if the scheme was wound up or G went into liquidation, creating an unsecured non preferential debt owed by G for the shortfall. Owing to G's financial position, T would only receive a small proportion of the deficit, and a compromise was thus negotiated between T and G under which the scheme would be wound up and the s.75 debt would be simultaneously compromised by an immediate cash payment plus deferred consideration.

Held, approving the deed of compromise, that there was no reason why trustees exercising their powers under the Trustee Act 1925 s.15 should not be able to compromise a s.75 debt. By doing so effect was given to the legislation in the best practical way consistent with the exercise of the trustees' general powers. There was no overriding statutory purpose or public interest to require trustees to enforce a claim to a s.75 debt to the point of forcing an employer into liquidation, regardless of the recovery.

BRADSTOCK GROUP PENSION SCHEME TRUSTEES LTD v. BRADSTOCK GROUP PLC, [2002] EWHC 651, [2002] I.C.R. 1427, Charles Aldous Q.C., Ch D.

3389. Occupational pensions–trustees powers and duties–duty to advise on alternative options

SP, the trustee of an occupational pension scheme, appealed against a determination of the Pensions Ombudsman following a complaint by a company, S, whose employees were offered the opportunity to become members of the scheme. The ombudsman held that a failure by SP to notify S of the introduction of a new scheme with lower charges had amounted to a breach of its reasonable duty of care to members. SP maintained that as a trustee it had been under no obligation to inform S about the new policy and that its duties were limited to ensuring that contributions received were applied properly under the terms of the existing policy.

Held, allowing the appeal, that under the scheme the individual employer was responsible for choosing the particular contract to be offered to its employees. It was clear that when a new member wished to subscribe to the scheme, S as the relevant employer would inform SP and identify the relevant policy in which contributions were to be invested. Accordingly, SP had no additional duty to advise S that another policy might constitute a better prospect for an individual member. The fact that S did not receive proper information as to all the potentially available products was a result of a shortcoming in the sales process rather than any default on the part of those responsible for the administration of the scheme.

SAVE & PROSPER GROUP LTD v. SCOOT LTD [2001] O.P.L.R. 273, Hart, J., Ch D.

3390. Occupational pensions–trustees powers and duties–power to deal with disposable surplus

B appealed against a decision ([2001] Pens.L.R. 99) concerning the interpretation of the trustees' powers with respect to surplus under a pension scheme for BA's staff. Among the issues to be determined were: (1) the permissible scope of a scheme for disposing of surplus under clause 11 (b) of the trust deed; (2) whether under the clause the trustees were permitted to create reserves, and (3) whether the clause permitted refunds to be made to BA. B submitted that the balance of any disposable surplus not required to be otherwise applied was required to be used to augment members' benefits. BA contended that this interpretation of the scheme was impractical, as it did not allow for any flexibility which might be required if financial or other considerations made it prudent to apply some of the surplus to reserves, increasing the possibility of a deficiency arising. S submitted that the trustees could decide what part of the distributable surplus should be applied to reserves.

Held, allowing the appeal in part, that (1) the judge had correctly applied a wide construction to clause 11 (b). The word "scheme" was of wide import and covered arrangements of a very wide nature. The surplus to which clause 11 (b) applied was the "disposable" surplus; the scheme was the vehicle for disposing of "the" disposable surplus, which meant the entirety of it. Furthermore, clause 11 (b) imposed a duty to dispose of the surplus and the words "make a scheme" conferred the power necessary to implement a scheme. Contrary to the finding of the judge, it was not necessary to imply an amendment power into the trustees' powers under clause 11 (b). Having regard to the decision of the House of Lords in *National Grid Co Plc v. Mayes* [2001] UKHL 20, [2001] 1 W.L.R. 864, [2001] C.L.Y. 4626, it was necessary, in addition to the two limitations to the powers conferred by clause 11 (b) identified by the judge, to add the limitation that clause 11 (b) was subject to other provisions of the trust deed which excluded or qualified powers which would otherwise be implied, and that any power on the part of the trustees to amend the trust deed was so excluded; (2) having regard to the nature of the surplus, it was apparent that the type of disposals the trustees could make under clause 11 (b) included those that just regulated the position until the time of the next valuation. It was open to the trustees to take the view that the right course to take was to allocate the surplus or part of it to a particular reserve. However, contrary to the conclusion of the judge, the trustees were required to reach an affirmative decision as to the application of the surplus. It was within the power of the trustees to allocate surplus to reserves even where the actuary had already made a provision in relation to the same matter, and (3) the judge had erred in his conclusion that clause 11 (b) conferred the power to make refunds to BA, *National Grid Co Plc v. Mayes* considered.

STEVENS v. BELL; *sub nom.* AIRWAYS PENSION SCHEME, RE; BRITISH AIRWAYS PENSION TRUSTEES LTD v. BRITISH AIRWAYS PLC, [2002] EWCA Civ 672, [2002] Pens. L.R. 247, Arden, L.J., CA.

3391. Occupational pensions–warrant enforcement staff

WARRANT ENFORCEMENT STAFF PENSIONS ORDER 2002, SI 2002 1043; made under the Greater London Authority Act 1999 s.411, s.420. In force: May 15, 2002; £1.50.

This Order provides for warrant enforcement staff to continue to be eligible to be members of the Metropolitan Civil Staffs Superannuation Scheme despite their ceasing to be members of the metropolitan civil staffs as a result of the transfer of their employment to the Greater London Magistrates' Courts Authority. The

Order has retrospective effect as permitted by the Greater London Authority Act 1999 s.411 (7).

3392. Occupational pensions–winding up notices and reports

OCCUPATIONAL PENSION SCHEMES (WINDING UP NOTICES AND REPORTS ETC.) REGULATIONS 2002, SI 2002 459; made under the Pension Schemes Act 1993 s.113; and the Pensions Act 1995 s.10, s.23, s.26B, s.26C, s.49A, s.71A, s.72A, s.72B, s.118, s.124, s.174. In force: April 1, 2002; £2.50.

These Regulations, which amend the Occupational Pension Schemes (Disclosure of Information) Regulations 1996 (SI 1996 1655), supplement amendments of the Pensions Act 1995 made by the Child Support, Pensions and Social Security Act 2000 and designed to speed up the winding up of occupational pension schemes. The Regulations require the trustees of a scheme which is being wound up to give members copies of reports given to the Occupational Pensions Regulatory Authority about winding up if they request them and prescribe the period within which insolvency practitioners must appoint independent trustees of trust schemes where the employer is insolvent.

3393. Pension contributions–income tax–lawfulness of prohibition on deductibility of contributions paid to foreign pension provider

[EC Treaty Art.49.]

D was a doctor with Finnish and German nationality who had lived and worked in Germany until his return to Finland in 1977. Whilst in Germany, and subsequently on his return to Finland, D made contributions to two German pension institutions. Under Finnish tax rules introduced in 1996 the deduction of contributions for voluntary pension insurance taken out with foreign finance institutions was excluded. Such contributions would have been deductible had they been made to a Finnish institution or to a foreign institution with an establishment in Finland. D applied to the tax authorities claiming that his pension insurance contributions should be deducted in their entirety. The tax authorities refused and D appealed to Kuopio Administrative Court, Finland. The Court referred a question to the European Court of Justice for a preliminary ruling.

Held, giving a ruling, that tax law provisions of a Member State that restricted or precluded the deductibility for income tax purposes of voluntary pension contributions paid to pension providers in other Member States whilst allowing the deductibility of contributions to equivalent voluntary pension schemes operated by pension providers in the first Member State were contrary to the EC Treaty Art.49. The contested measures could not be justified by the need to preserve the coherence of the Finnish tax system, the need to ensure the effectiveness of fiscal supervision, the need to prevent tax evasion or the need to preserve the integrity of the tax base.

DANNER (C136/00), Re [2002] Pens. L.R. 153, Advocate General Jacobs, AGO.

3394. Pension funds–dissolution–no provision in substitute pension fund for distribution of surplus to members–entitlement to surplus–Australia

Pension fund trustees sought directions from the court in respect of a company pension fund that was set up by deed in 1966. The deed contained a power to amend or substitute the fund but not so as to prejudice any benefits already accrued to members. A substitute fund was set up by deed in 1974. The 1966 fund provided by rule 15 that on dissolution the trustees could pay the surplus to members. The 1974 fund contained no such provision. In 1998 the company ceased trading. By 1999 all the members of the fund had received all the benefits to which they were entitled as members. Accordingly there were no new members and no prospect of new members, and there were no pensioners and no prospect of pensioners. The fund had a surplus.

Held, giving directions, that (1) on the facts the fund had been dissolved notwithstanding that there was no formal dissolution or winding up; (2) the right to receive the discretionary benefit was an accrued benefit, notwithstanding that it was contingent, which should have been preserved, and accordingly the 1974 scheme was ultra vires insofar as it deprived the members of that benefit, and (3) rule 15 was severable and was restored. It followed that the terms of the 1966 fund applied and the trustees had a discretion whether to make payments of the remaining fund to the members, *Harwood-Smart v. Caws* [2000] O.P.L.R. 227, [2000] C.L.Y. 4355, *Asea Brown v. Asea Brown Boveri* [1999] V.R. 144 and *Air Jamaica Ltd v. Charlton* (1999-2000) 2 I.T.E.L.R. 244, [1999] C.L.Y. 4958 applied; *Lock v. Westpac Banking Corp* (1991) 25 N.S.W.L.R. 593 distinguished, and *Schmidt v. Air Products of Canada Ltd* [1995] O.P.L.R. 283, [1996] C.L.Y. 4642 and *UEB Industries v. Brabant* [1992] 1 N.Z.L.R. 294 considered.

BHLSPF PTY LTD v. BRASHS PTY LTD; *sub nom.* BHLSPF PTY LTD (TRUSTEE OF BRASHS PTY LTD STAFF PROVIDENT FUND) v. BRASHS PTY LTD [2002] O.P.L.R. 1, Warren, J., Sup Ct (Vic).

3395. **Pension schemes–compromise–approval by court–notification of beneficiaries**

[Civil Procedure Rules 1998 (SI 1998 3132) Part 8 r.8.2A.]

O, the trustee of an occupational pension scheme, made an application under the Civil Procedure Rules 1998 seeking the court's approval of a compromise agreement relating to claims against the main employer and its parent company in respect of contributions to the scheme. Permission was granted under Part 8 r.8.2A of the Rules to issue the claim form without naming defendants.

Held, approving the compromise agreement, that where a claim for the approval of a compromise agreement was issued and an application was made to issue the claim form without naming defendants, it was preferable to inform the beneficiaries or their representatives both of the proposed compromise and of the Part 8 application so that they would have the opportunity to make representations to the court. Given the urgency of the matter and other factors, it was appropriate in the instant case to approve the compromise agreement and not to grant an adjournment.

OWENS CORNING FIBERGLAS (UK) PENSION PLAN LTD, *Re; sub nom.* OWENS CORNING FIBREGLASS (UK) LTD, *Re* [2002] Pens. L.R. 323, Neuberger, J., Ch D.

3396. **Pensionable earnings–overtime–meaning of "non contractual overtime"**

[Local Government Pension Scheme Regulations 1995 (SI 1995 1019) Part C Reg.2(2)(a).]

The local authority appealed against a determination of the Pensions Ombudsman that overtime worked by S, a school caretaker, prior to his retirement was contractual overtime, and therefore remuneration for the overtime was included in his final earnings for the purpose of calculating S's pension. Payments for "non contractual overtime" were expressly excluded from the calculation of pension entitlement, pursuant to the Local Government Pension Scheme Regulations 1995 Part C Reg.2(2)(a). S's contract of employment stated an agreed rate for overtime but there was no compulsory overtime. The local authority contended that the Pensions Ombudsman's reasoning, that the overtime was contractual because the contract included an overtime rate, was wrong. The local authority submitted that "non contractual overtime" meant overtime not required by the contract and that the provision for a rate of pay for optional overtime did not make the overtime contractual.

Held, allowing the appeal, that the Pensions Ombudsman had erred in his construction of the Regulations. S had worked "non contractual overtime" and therefore his overtime payments were excluded from his final earnings for the computation of his pension, pursuant to Reg.2(2)(a). "Non contractual overtime" meant overtime that was not "called for by the contract" and was therefore voluntary. The provision for an overtime rate did not affect the status of the overtime.

NEWHAM LBC v. SKINGLE, [2002] EWHC 1013, [2002] 3 All E.R. 287, Jacob, J., Ch D.

3397. Pensions Appeal Tribunals—judicial offices—Deputy President

JUDICIAL PENSIONS (PENSIONS APPEAL TRIBUNALS) ORDER 2002, SI 2002 1347; made under the Judicial Pensions and Retirement Act 1993 s.1. In force: June 7, 2002; £1.50.

This Order adds the office of Deputy President of the Pensions Appeal Tribunals to the list of qualifying judicial offices specified in the Judicial Pensions and Retirement Act 1993.

3398. Pensions Ombudsman—appeals—liability for costs

M and R, who had successfully appealed against the determination of the Pensions Ombudsman, applied for an order for costs against him. The Ombudsman had been represented at the appeal by solicitors and counsel. The issues to be determined were (1) whether and to what extent an order of costs should be made where the Ombudsman had chosen to appear on an appeal but had not succeeded, and (2) if an order for costs was appropriate, whether it should be made in respect of both M and R or only one of them.

Held, ruling the Ombudsman pay M's costs, that (1) where the Ombudsman had "made himself a party to the lis" he put himself at risk of an order for costs if unsuccessful, *Providence Capitol Trustees Ltd v. Ayres* [1996] 4 All E.R. 760, [1997] C.L.Y. 517 applied and *Elliott v. Pensions Ombudsman* [1998] O.P.L.R. 21, [1997] C.L.Y. 518 and *University of Nottingham v. Eyett (No.2)* [1999] 1 W.L.R. 594, [1999] C.L.Y. 373 not followed. While it was often the case that the Ombudsman's participation in an appeal was of considerable assistance to the court, particularly where he had ruled in favour of a complainant who did not have the means to appear on any appeal himself, such assistance did not justify departing from the general rule that the unsuccessful party pay the costs of the successful, *R. (on the application of Touche) v. HM Coroner for Inner North London District* [2001] EWCA Civ 383, [2001] Q.B. 1206, [2001] C.L.Y. 27 considered. The practice adopted in *Elliott* and *Eyett* of ordering the Ombudsman to pay only such costs as had been caused by him appearing on an appeal ought not to be continued, and (2) M, which had been directly affected by the Ombudsman's decision, had been fully justified in appealing against it and accordingly it was appropriate to order that the Ombudsman pay its costs. However, given that R had not been directly affected by the decision and had sought to argue against it on much the same ground as M, it was not appropriate to order the Ombudsman to pay its costs.

MOORE'S (WALLISDOWN) LTD v. PENSIONS OMBUDSMAN (COSTS); ROYAL & SUN ALLIANCE LIFE & PENSIONS LTD v. PENSIONS OMBUDSMAN (COSTS) [2002] 1 W.L.R. 1649, Ferris, J., Ch D.

3399. Pensions Ombudsman—maladministration—error of law as distinct from maladministration—jurisdiction to make decision

[Pension Schemes Act 1993 s.151 (4); EC Treaty Art.119 (now, Art.141).]

G appealed under the Pension Schemes Act 1993 s.151 (4) against a determination by the Pensions Ombudsman in relation to a complaint by C that the trustees of a pension scheme were guilty of maladministration. C, a part-time employee, had been granted retrospective membership of an occupational pension scheme but her contributions were subsequently returned to her pending clarification of the law on retrospective membership from the ECJ. The Pensions Ombudsman concluded that C's exclusion from the scheme amounted to indirect discrimination under the EC Treaty Art.119 (now, Art.141), failure to comply with which amounted to maladministration. G contended that (1) there was no conduct amounting to maladministration, and (2) C had not, in any event, complained of maladministration in the respect found.

Held, allowing the appeal, that (1) the decision of the Pensions Ombudsman was wrong in law, because it failed to identify any act on G's part which amounted to maladministration. An error of law in itself did not necessarily amount to maladministration, *Miller v. Stapleton* [1996] 2 All E.R. 449, [1997] C.L.Y. 4000, *Westminster City Council v. Haywood (No.1)* [1998] Ch. 377, [1997] C.L.Y. 4010 and *Swansea City and County Council v. Johnson* [1999] Ch. 189, [1999] C.L.Y. 4149 applied. The decision of the Pensions Ombudsman was therefore wrong in law, and (2) C had never complained of the matter upon which the Pensions Ombudsman's decision was founded, and indeed had agreed to await the findings of the ECJ.

GLOSSOP v. COPNALL [2001] O.P.L.R. 287, Sir Andrew Morritt (Vice Chancellor), Ch D.

3400. Pensions Ombudsman–maladministration–jurisdiction to investigate complaint

[Pension Schemes Act 1993 Part X; Personal and Occupational Pension Schemes (Pensions Ombudsman) Regulations 1996 (SI 1996 2475) Reg.2(1).]

The Pensions Ombudsman appealed against a decision ([2001] EWHC 441, Times, April 16, 2002) allowing B's application for judicial review of the Pensions Ombudsman's decision that he had jurisdiction to investigate a complaint of maladministration against B. Following requests by the trustees of a pension scheme to whom B had issued two long term insurance policies, B had surrendered part of an insurance policy linked to the schemes. The issue arising on appeal was whether B had acted as "administrators" of the pension scheme for the purposes of the Personal and Occupational Pension Schemes (Pensions Ombudsman) Regulations 1996 Reg.2(1) in paying out the monies at the request of the trustees. Unless B had been "concerned with the administration of the scheme", the Ombudsman did not have the jurisdiction to investigate a complaint against them.

Held, dismissing the appeal, that the Pensions Ombudsman had no jurisdiction to investigate the complaint of maladministration against B. There was a distinction between doing an administrative act in connection with a pension scheme and being concerned with the administration of a pension scheme. In the instant case, B's administration of the assets of the pensions managed fund could not be regarded as administration of the scheme itself. A comparison was drawn with an insurance company which did no more than administer its own assets and occasionally calculate the amount it was liable to pay under a unit linked policy which it had issued. In such a case, the insurance company was no more concerned in the administration of the scheme than others who had contracted to make payments to the trustees or scheme beneficiaries on demand. In considering this issue, it was significant that the ombudsman's investigative powers under the Pension Schemes Act 1993 Part X had not been extended to cover those concerned only with the provision of benefits under a scheme. It followed that B was not concerned with the administration of the scheme and was outside the ombudsman's jurisdiction.

R. (ON THE APPLICATION OF BRITANNIC ASSET MANAGEMENT LTD) v. PENSIONS OMBUDSMAN; *sub nom*. R. (ON THE APPLICATION OF BRITTANNIC ASSET MANAGEMENT LTD) v. PENSIONS OMBUDSMAN; BRITANNIC ASSET MANAGEMENT LTD v. PENSIONS OMBUDSMAN, [2002] EWCA Civ 1405, [2002] 4 All E.R. 860, Chadwick, L.J., CA.

3401. Personal pensions–premiums–contract terms–application of contra proferentem rule

R sought to quash a decision of P that a retirement policy it had issued to G was a single premium policy rather than an annual premium policy. P had found the wording of the policy to be ambiguous and had applied the contra proferentem principle against R, as the party having produced the wording of the policy. R submitted that the policy was not ambiguous but that upon proper construction, was a single premium policy.

Held, granting the application for judicial review, that the wording of the policy was not ambiguous and was an annual premium policy, rejecting the P's construction that the policy was a single premium policy with an option to make subsequent annual payments.

R. v. PERSONAL INVESTMENT AUTHORITY OMBUDSMAN BUREAU LTD, *ex p.* ROYAL & SUN ALLIANCE LIFE & PENSIONS LTD [2002] Lloyd's Rep. I.R. 41, Langley, J., QBD (Comm Ct).

3402. Public service–pensions–increase in rates

PENSIONS INCREASE (REVIEW) ORDER 2002, SI 2002 699; made under the Social Security Pensions Act 1975 s.59. In force: April 8, 2002; £1.75.

Under the Social Security Pensions Act 1975, the Treasury is required to provide by order for increases in the rates of public service pensions. For pensions which began before April 9, 2001 the increase is 1.7 per cent and for pensions which began on or after April 9, 2001 the increases are specified in this Order.

3403. Stakeholder pensions–annual declaration

STAKEHOLDER PENSION SCHEMES (AMENDMENT) REGULATIONS 2002, SI 2002 1480; made under the Welfare Reform and Pensions Act 1999 s.1, s.8, s.83. In force: July 4, 2002; £1.50.

These Regulations amend the Stakeholder Pension Schemes Regulations 2000 (SI 2000 1403) which provide for an annual declaration as to the arrangements made by the trustees or manager of a stakeholder scheme for ensuring the proper administration of the scheme and for those trustees or that manager to obtain statements from the scheme's reporting accountant as to the reasonableness of the annual declaration. The trustees or manager are, prior to the coming into force of these Regulations, not required to make an annual declaration or obtain reporting accountant's statements before July 5, 2002. These Regulations provide that the trustees or manager of a scheme must make an annual declaration within three months of each reporting date, set out how the reporting date is to be ascertained and extends to December 31, 2002 the time limit for the trustees or manager of a scheme to make their annual declaration, where the declaration relates to a reporting date ending on or before September 30, 2002. In addition, they extend to December 31, 2002 the time limit for the trustees or manager of a scheme to obtain the required statements from the reporting accountants, where these would otherwise have had to have been obtained prior to this date.

3404. Stakeholder pensions–annual declaration

STAKEHOLDER PENSION SCHEMES (AMENDMENT NO.2) REGULATIONS 2002, SI 2002 2098; made under the Welfare Reform and Pensions Act 1999 s.1, s.8, s.83. In force: September 9, 2002; £2.00.

These Regulations amend the Stakeholder Pension Schemes Regulations 2000 (SI 2000 1403) which require the trustees or manager of a stakeholder scheme to appoint a reporting accountant and set out the eligibility requirements for appointment as a reporting accountant; provide for an annual declaration as to the arrangements made by the trustees or manager of a stakeholder scheme for ensuring the proper administration of the scheme and for those trustees or that manager to obtain statements from the scheme's reporting accountant as to the reasonableness of the declaration; and set out the conditions for the assets of a scheme to be invested in with-profits funds. The Regulations remove certain eligibility requirements for appointment as a reporting accountant; require the trustees or manager of the scheme to make a declaration and obtain a reporting accountant's statement within 6 months of the reporting date; set out how the reporting date is to be calculated; require the trustees or manager to send copies of the declaration and reporting accountant's statement to members and beneficiaries on request; provide that any statement obtained from a reporting accountant ineligible for such an appointment will not be regarded as a statement obtained in accordance with the Regulations; and require an insurance company managing with-profits funds for a scheme to pass various certificates to the trustees or manager.

3405. State retirement pensions–inflation–exclusion of non resident UK pensioner from annual uprating–right to peaceful enjoyment of possessions

[Human Rights Act 1998 Sch.1 Part I Art.14, Part II Art.1.]

C sought judicial review of the Secretary of State's decision to exclude her as a non resident United Kingdom pensioner from the annual uprating of the state retirement pension. C, who was resident in South Africa, contended that her pension, or alternatively the uprating, were pecuniary rights and therefore constituted possessions within the meaning of the Human Rights Act 1998 Sch.1 Part II Art.1. C further argued that she had been discriminated against on the grounds of her residence in South Africa as compared with UK pensioners living in the UK and that such discrimination was contrary to Art.14 particularly in view of the fact that pensioners living in EU countries and the United States received the uprated pensions.

Held, refusing the application, that UK legislation had never conferred a right upon C to the uprating of her pension whilst she was resident in South Africa and since she never had that right there could be no question of her having been deprived of such. Accordingly, there was no infringement of her right to peaceful enjoyment of possession. On the discrimination issue, it was within the scope of Art.14 to impose residence criteria for the differential treatment of citizens since it was an aspect of personal status. The European Commission had rejected as inadmissible similar complaints to that of C on the basis that it was impossible to simply draw a comparison between the actual amount of pounds sterling received by pensioners resident in the UK and that received by UK pensioners in different countries, owing to the varied social and economic circumstances and tax regimes operating in those other countries. In any event, given the wide margin of discretion afforded to governments it was perfectly legitimate for a government to restrict the payment of benefits to those who were within its jurisdiction leaving the care and support of those living elsewhere to be provided by the government of the country in which they lived. The remedy for persons such as C was political not judicial since the government was entitled to consider the payment of uprated pensions to those living abroad on a country by country basis having regard to the UK's interests in each case.

R. (ON THE APPLICATION OF CARSON) v. SECRETARY OF STATE FOR WORK AND PENSIONS, [2002] EWHC 978, [2002] 3 All E.R. 994, Stanley Burnton, J., QBD (Admin Ct).

3406. State retirement pensions–miscellaneous amendments

STATE PENSION CREDIT (CONSEQUENTIAL, TRANSITIONAL AND MISCELLANEOUS PROVISIONS) (NO.2) REGULATIONS 2002, SI 2002 3197; made under the Social Security Contributions and Benefits Act 1992 s.3, s.175; the Social Security Administration Act 1992 s.5, s.15A, s.189, s.191; the Jobseekers Act 1995 s.26, s.35, s.36; the Child Support Act 1995 s.10, s.26; the Social Security Act 1998 s.10, s.79, s.84; and the State Pension Credit Act 2002 s.2, 12, s.13, s.15, s.16, s.17. In force: in accordance with Reg.1 (1); £2.50.

These Regulations amend the State Pension Credit Regulations 2002 (SI 2002 1792) to amend the definition of "care home" and insert a new definition of "voluntary organisation"; provide that persons who are not habitually resident in the UK, the Channel Islands, the Isle of Man or the Republic of Ireland or who are subject to immigration control within the meaning of the Immigration and Asylum Act 1999 s.115(9) are not to be treated as being members of the same household as the claimant; add a new category of retirement pension income; remove otiose rules in relation to the treatment of capital derived from personal injury payments; prescribe how the transitional amount is to be calculated where a person's applicable amount in respect of housing costs in income support and jobseeker's allowance include an amount for housing costs calculated on a transitional basis; prescribe rules as to when amounts of loans used to calculate housing costs shall be recalculated; make changes to the rules on disregarded income and capital; and correct minor errors and make certain other clarifications.

3407. Superannuation–civil service pension scheme–additional employments

SUPERANNUATION (ADMISSION TO SCHEDULE 1 TO THE SUPERANNUATION ACT 1972) ORDER 2002, SI 2002 1913; made under the Superannuation Act 1972 s.1. In force: August 12, 2002; £1.50.

This Order amends the Superannuation Act 1972 s.1 by adding the office of the Chairman of the Forestry Commission to those listed in Sch.1 of the Act. It also adds employment by the Arts and Humanities Board, SITPRO Limited, the National Criminal Intelligence Service Authority, the National Crime Squad Service Authority and the Sector Skills Development Agency to those listed in that Schedule and removes employment by the Local Government Commission from those listed in that Schedule.

3408. War pensions–payments to civilians

PERSONAL INJURIES (CIVILIANS) AMENDMENT SCHEME 2002, SI 2002 672; made under the Personal Injuries (Emergency Provisions) Act 1939 s.1, s.2. In force: April 8, 2002; £2.00.

This Scheme amends the Personal Injuries (Civilians) Scheme 1983 (SI 1983 686), which makes provision for the payment of pensions and allowances to or in respect of civilians killed or injured during the World War II, to increase the amounts of allowances, pensions and awards payable and increase the amounts of income to be disregarded for the purposes of certain parts of the Scheme.

3409. Books

Cann, Simon; Churchill, Philip; Fallon, Liz; Head, Simon–Tolly's Basic Guide to Pensions. Paperback: £26.99. ISBN 0-7545-0745-9. Tolley Publishing.

Hayward, John; Ure, Alec–Tolley's SSAS-SIPPS-FURBS: Directors' Retirement Benefits. 5th Ed. Paperback: £54.95. ISBN 0-7545-1225-8. Tolley Publishing.

Meeks, Alastair–Tolley's Pensions Cases. Paperback: £64.95. ISBN 0-7545-1273-8. Tolley Publishing.

Quarrell, John; Beaumont, Sue–Tolleys Pension Scheme Investment: a Practical Guide to the Law. Hardback: £55.00. ISBN 0-7545-1268-1. Tolley Publishing.

Salter, David–Pensions and Insurance on Family Breakdown. 3rd Ed. Hardback: Floppy disk: £45.00. ISBN 0-85308-698-2. Family Law.

Self, Roger–Tolley's Pension Fund Trustee Handbook. 7th Ed. Paperback: £29.95. ISBN 0-7545-1648-2. Tolley Publishing.

Tolley's Pensions Law Handbook. 4th Ed. Paperback: £49.95. ISBN 0-7545-1257-6. Tolley Publishing.

Tolley's Stakeholder Pensions. Paperback: £45.00. ISBN 0-7545-1618-0. Paperback: £45.00. ISBN 0-7545-1618-0. Tolley Publishing.

Ure, Alex; Firth, John; Templeton, Andrew; Sleziak, Douglas–Taxation of Retirement Benefits: 1999. Paperback: £85.00. ISBN 0-7545-0134-5. Tolley Publishing.

PERSONAL INJURY

3410. Asbestosis–employers liability–exposure while working for more than one employer–entitlement to damages

See HEALTH AND SAFETY AT WORK: Fairchild v. Glenhaven Funeral Services Ltd (t/a GH Dovener & Son). §2225

3411. Carers–loss of earnings–loss of ability to provide gratuitous care– entitlement to recovery–pre accident earning capacity

L appealed against a decision that he was not entitled to recover damages in respect of a lost ability to provide care to his severely disabled brother or for loss of employment capacity. L had sustained personal injuries in a road traffic accident. Prior to the accident he had provided 77 hours per week gratuitous care to his brother. Following the accident he had been obliged to limit the care that he provided to the minimum amount necessary to maintain his entitlement to invalid care allowance. Included in his schedule of loss were claims for (1) the value of the care services which he could no longer provide, and (2) loss of earning capacity. In respect of the latter, L contended that as he no longer provided full time care for his brother he would have been available for remunerative work, but for his injuries, and that the consequent loss should be assessed without reference to the fact that he would have continued to provide full time care had he not been injured.

Held, allowing the appeal in part, that L's loss of ability to provide gratuitous care for his disabled brother over and above that which was necessary for the purposes of entitlement to invalid care allowance was a recoverable loss. However, when considering his claim for loss of earning capacity the court was entitled to take into account the fact that he would have continued as his brother's full time carer had he not been injured, *Hunt v. Severs* [1994] 2 A.C. 350, [1994] C.L.Y. 1530 and *Swain v. London Ambulance Service NHS Trust* (Unreported, March 12, 1999) considered.

LOWE v. GUISE, [2002] EWCA Civ 197, [2002] Q.B. 1369, Rix, L.J., CA.

3412. Clinical negligence–brain damage–negligent post operative care–future accommodation calculation and appropriate general damages

M, aged 11 years old at the date of assessment, suffered a cardiac arrest leading to brain damage during post operative care following an operation on a hole in her heart. L admitted negligence. M was severely intellectually impaired, and with significant movement disorder on her right side. Although defined neurologically as self feeding, she was doubly incontinent and could not stand, though she could sit unaided. M would never work, and would require constant care and attention. She had some insight into her condition. The outstanding issues with regard to quantum were the way in which M's accommodation costs should be calculated and the appropriate level of general damages.

Held, assessing damages, that it was not appropriate in this case to make deductions for the value that M's parents derived from having a house for their entire family or to allow for the investment M would have made in acquiring a home for herself. While M lived at home, she did not differ from any other child, who could not reasonably be expected to purchase accommodation. Thereafter, some allowance should be made to reflect the fact that M would probably have left home and bought her own property. It was also necessary to assess the extra cost of buying a house specially adapted to her needs, *Roberts v. Johnstone* [1989] Q.B. 878 and *Lamey v. Wirral HA* Unreported, September 22, 1993 considered. M's condition was between moderately severe and very severe brain damage in terms of categories 2(A)(a) and 2(A)(b) of the Judicial Studies Board Guidelines. General damages were accordingly assessed at £150,000.

M (A CHILD) v. LEEDS HA [2002] P.I.Q.R. Q4, Sullivan, J., QBD.

3413. Clinical negligence–causation–wrongful evaluation of cervical smear test– refusal to undergo further tests–contributory negligence

See NEGLIGENCE: Pidgeon v. Doncaster HA. §3250

3414. Clinical negligence–delay–referral for biopsy–concessions by claimant's expert–submission of no case

See CIVIL PROCEDURE: Nur Saed v. Ealing Hospital NHS Trust. §428

3415. Leg−football−late tackle−liability

See NEGLIGENCE: Gaynor v. Blackpool FC. §3280

3416. Measure of damages−clinical negligence−knee operation−loss of earnings

C, a 41 year old former police officer, sought damages from the national health trust following following a negligent operation to his right knee which meant that he was only able to carry out light work for the remainder of his working life.

Held, assessing the level of damages, that C was entitled to general damages of £37,500 and special damages in excess of £26,000. However, he was not entitled to an award for loss of earnings as it was clear from the evidence that he had conspired with his family to defraud the trust by seeking to create a false impression of a reduction in wages from the family business. In view of the seriousness of the conspiracy involving a claim of £300,000 the matter was referred to the DPP for consideration.

COTTRELL v. REDBRIDGE HEALTHCARE NHS TRUST (2001) 61 B.M.L.R. 72, Judge Richard Seymour Q.C., QBD.

3417. Measure of damages−discounts−departure from Lord Chancellor's rate of 2.5 per cent−entitlement to adduce expert evidence as to appropriate discount rate

[Damages Act 1996 s.1 (1), s.1 (2).]

The appellant, the defendant in a personal injury claim brought by the respondent, appealed against a decision to allow evidence from expert accountants as to the proper discount rate for a quantification of future losses to be adduced at trial. The respondent had sustained severe brain damage in a road traffic accident and consequently had a life expectancy of 46 years. The appellant contended that (1) the respondent was not entitled to seek to prove that the rate of 2.5 per cent fixed by the Lord Chancellor pursuant to the Damages Act 1996 s.1 (1) for the determination of the investment return on damages for future pecuniary loss was wrong; (2) the rate was law and had to be applied until such time as it was lawfully changed, the only exception to that rule being where the rate was not appropriate in a particular case under s.1 (2) of the 1996 Act, and (3) in the instant case, the respondent's life expectancy of 46 years was not exceptional and did not justify a departure from the set rate.

Held, allowing the appeal, that the rate of 2.5 per cent had been prescribed by the Lord Chancellor in the interests of certainty, to facilitate settlements and to save the expense of adducing expert evidence at trial. This was the first occasion on which the court had been required to consider the 1996 Act, and guidance was required in relation to the phrase "more appropriate in the case in question" in s.1 (2). Giving that guidance, a departure from the Lord Chancellor's rate would only be justified if the case fell into a category that he had not taken into account and/or the case had special features which (1) were material to the choice of rate of return, and (2) were shown not to have been taken into account in the Lord Chancellor's reasons for arriving at the rate. In the instant case, it could not be said that the Lord Chancellor had not had in mind claimants with life expectancies of between 30 and 50 years when setting the rate and on the facts there was nothing which made it "more appropriate" to apply a different rate.

WARRINER v. WARRINER; *sub nom.* W v. W (DAMAGES), [2002] EWCA Civ 81, [2002] 1 W.L.R. 1703, Dyson, L.J., CA.

3418. Measure of damages−mesothelioma−relevant date for assessment of damages

[Fatal Accidents Act 1976.]

W claimed damages following the death of her husband from mesothelioma due to exposure to asbestos in the course of his employment. Liability was admitted but the method of assessing damages was disputed. W claimed that damages should be assessed at the date of trial. E claimed that damages should be assessed at the date of death.

Held, awarding damages on the conventional basis, that the multiplier in a Fatal Accidents Act 1976 case both for pre trial loss and future loss should be calculated as at the date of death, *Cookson v. Knowles* [1979] A.C. 556, [1978] C.L.Y. 713 followed and *Graham v. Dodds* [1983] 1 W.L.R. 808, [1979] C.L.Y. 979 disapproved. Although the Law Commission had recommended that the multiplier in respect of post trial losses in a fatal claim should be calculated as at the date of trial rather than the date of death, the court was bound by authority to follow the date of death calculation rule.

WHITE v. ESAB GROUP (UK) LTD [2002] P.I.Q.R. Q6, Nelson, J., QBD.

Personal Injuries or Death—Quantum

Details have been received of the following cases in which damages for personal injuries or death were awarded. The classification and sequence of the classified awards follows that adopted in Kemp and Kemp. *The Quantum of Damages,* Vol.2. Unless there is some statement to the contrary, the age of the applicant is his age at the time of the court hearing. Unless specified the damages are stated on the basis of full liability, *ie.* ignoring any deduction made for contributory negligence. The sum is the total amount of the damages awarded unless otherwise stated. For a cumulative guide to *quantum* of damages cases reported in Current Law during 2000, see the *Quantum* of Damages table. We must stress that we are entirely dependent on the contributor of an unreported case for the accuracy of his or her report; it is impracticable for us independently to check the facts stated to us. We welcome contributions and are most grateful for all the reports received. We would appreciate reports of any alterations to awards noted here, either in, or in anticipation of, appeal.

Scars

3419.   G, female, aged seven at the date of the road traffic accident and 10 at the settlement approval hearing, suffered glass lacerations to the right side of her face and bruising to the right arm and shoulder as a result of a collision. G was taken to hospital and the facial lacerations were explored, cleaned and the glass particles were removed under general anaesthetic. One deep 3cm laceration and three smaller lacerations were repaired in layers. G was reviewed six days later when the stitches were removed. She made one further visit to the hospital for review. As the wounds were healing well and there were no functional problems, G was discharged to her GP. The scars were on the right side of her face and neck. The major facial scar was on the lower right cheek. That scar was 2.7cm by 0.6cm and it stood out from the surrounding skin because of its pink colour. On the right side of the neck there were three scars. Those scars measured 1cm by 0.3cm, 2cm by 0.6cm and 0.8cm by 0.2cm and were slightly raised. The position and size of G's scarring was permanent. The appearance of them upset G. They stood out by their raised contour and colour discrepancy. The prognosis was for the scars to take up to five years to settle. Medical opinion was that the scarring could be improved by three sessions of laser treatment under general anaesthetic. *General Damages*: £5,100. Award for cost of future cosmetic surgery treatment: £2,400.

G (A CHILD) v. HUGHES, August 15, 2001, District Judge Sehdev, CC (Dudley). [*Ex rel.* Stephen Garner, Barrister, No 8 Chambers, Fountain Court, Steelhouse Lane, Birmingham].

Pre existing disability or condition–aggravated by whiplash–psychiatric damage

3420. M, female, a part time nurse, right hand dominant, aged 52 at the date of the road traffic accident and 55 at the hearing, sustained a soft tissue strain to her neck, minor abrasions to her left forearm, a spraining injury to her right shoulder and psychological injury. M attended her local hospital immediately after the accident. She was supplied with a soft collar which she wore for three days. M also attended her own GP within a week of the accident and she was advised to rub anti-inflammatory drugs into the area of her injured right shoulder. Upon examination 30 months after the accident, M was still presenting with pain along the upper border of her right shoulder extending from her neck to the right shoulder joint. The pain in the shoulder and neck caused M difficulty with housework, lifting her grandchildren and swimming. M also had difficulty practising her hobby of calligraphy as the fingers in her right hand felt puffy. M's failure to recover completely from her neck and shoulder injuries was attributed to her pre-existing cervical spondylosis, which had been aggravated in the accident. The prognosis was that M would always have some pain and discomfort in her neck and right shoulder which would restrict her activities. She also suffered a persistent mild to moderate degree of phobic anxiety for car travel. As a passenger she became hypervigilant. She felt extremely tense after the accident and clung to the car's grab handles. She would also brake with her foot. She suffered some sleep disturbance and flashbacks to the accident. M underwent an intense course of cognitive therapy treatment, which helped to return her to her pre-accident position by the date of the hearing. There was a small risk that her symptoms of travel phobia may recur. *General Damages*: £6,500

McEVOY v. MAW, October 26, 2001, District Judge Morton, CC (Dudley). [*Ex rel.* Stephen Garner, Barrister, 8 Fountain Court, Steelhouse Lane, Birmingham].

Multiple injuries

3421. B, male, a roof tiler, aged 25 at the date of the assault and 31 at the hearing, sustained injuries when he was assaulted and hit about his head with a sledge hammer. He suffered a Le Fort 2 fracture, right zygomatic fracture, left antral wall fracture, right orbital roof fracture, a severe optic nerve injury resulting in loss of vision in the right eye, severe complex extensive craniofacial injuries involving the anterior skull with associated right temporal lobe contusion, pneumocephalous (air within the skull), haemorrhage contusions of the brain, moderate generalised brain swelling, a deep fracture to the base of the skull and fractures of both maxillary sinuses. The facial fractures were surgically repaired by bicornal scalp flap (an ear incision to roll down the skin of the face), and metallic bone plates were inserted between the frontal bone and nasal skeleton on both sides of the upper jaw to stabilise the bony injuries. A tracheostomy was performed because it was not possible to insert a tube into the mouth due to the severity of the injuries. Two further operations were later carried out to remove the bone plates securing the upper jaw and to correct drooping of the right upper eyelid. After discharge from the hospital, B was cared for by his wife and was unable to return to work. He suffered ongoing memory loss, lack of concentration, personality change as a result of organic brain change, a depressive disorder, irritability and lack of vitality. He became bored and frustrated, was committing acts of self harm such as cutting himself, and he become socially withdrawn with a tendency to isolate himself from his wife and children. He suffered extensive facial scarring and his right eye was permanently in an almost closed position. B required ongoing care assessed at 37.25 hours a week and the award for this was based on commercial cost less one-third to reflect the fact his wife was likely to provide the care. *General Damages*: £115,000. Past loss of earnings award: £53,000. Past care award: £35,822. Future loss of earnings award: £220,000 (multiplicand: £11,000 per annum; multiplier 20). Future care award: £173,781 (multiplicand: £6,224 per annum; multiplier 27.92). Award for future decorating costs: £5,000 (multiplicand: £250 per annum, multiplier 20). Total award: £607,103.

BROOKES (CICA: QUANTUM: 2001), *Re* [2002] 4 Q.R. 6, Lowther (Chairman), CICA (Birmingham).

Multiple injuries

3422.   S, male, a self employed roofer and carpenter, aged 30 at the date of the accident and 37 at trial, suffered a severe degloving injury of the right dominant shoulder, spinal injuries and psychological injury. The shoulder injury was extremely painful and required extensive debridement and subsequent skin grafting. A further revision of one scar was carried out two years after the accident. At trial, the shoulder was adequate for normal living but not for sustained work above shoulder height. There was some minor restriction of movement in the shoulder and upper limb. There was also significant cosmetic deformity with additional scarring on the right forearm and discolouration at the donor site on the left thigh. There was a loss of sensation over the area of scarring over the arm and a sense of phantom itching. S was very self conscious of his arm which ached continuously, but was worse in cold and damp weather. No further improvement was expected. S complained of spinal pain in the neck and lower back. The judge accepted that the pain and disability from the shoulder injury had deflected attention from the spinal pain until three months after the accident when S was mobilised in a rehabilitation unit, whereupon psychological symptoms also manifested themselves. The spinal problems were exacerbated by lifting, bending, twisting or any sudden or jarring movement. S suffered from post traumatic stress disorder which was initially severe for two years, then severe to moderate, becoming moderate six years after the accident. After rehabilitation he developed a chronic pain syndrome. The judge found that S would have worked to age 65 as a carpenter and that he retained a very minor earning capacity as a cabinet maker. The Ogden approach was followed in calculating pension loss, *Page v. Sheerness Steel Co Plc* [1996] P.I.Q.R. Q26, [1996] C.L.Y. 2133 and *Phipps v. Brooks Dry Cleaning Services Ltd* [1996] P.I.Q.R. Q100, [1996] C.L.Y. 2126 followed. It was no exaggeration to say that S's life had been ruined. He had lost his trade, his hobbies and pastimes and his marriage had come under intense strain. He had permanent physical and psychological problems and would never come to terms with his cosmetic injury. *General Damages*: £35,000. Future loss of earnings award: £303,180 (multiplier at 2.5 per cent: 18.6). Award for other future losses: £76,207. Total award: £573,876.

SHERGOLD v. SMITH [2002] 2 Q.R. 10, Judge Bursell Q.C., QBD.

Multiple injuries

3423.   T, male, an HGV driver, aged 38 at the date of the accident and 41 at trial, sustained an injury to his pelvis in the form of a disrupion to the pubic symphis which resulted in splaying. He also sustained three rib fractures, resulting in a flail segment, a soft tissue injury to the right shoulder and an injury to the left knee. He was initially off work for nine months and thereafter required to take some eight and a half weeks off between 13 and 16 months after the accident. T's wife was required to care for him during the nine months following the accident. T was in hospital for some five weeks and made a generally quick recovery from his injuries. T had had a laminectomy some eight years prior to the accident and the evidence was that he had been asymptomatic in this regard until the date of the accident. Despite a history of low back pain, the accident was causative in bringing his symptoms forward by a period of five years. It was expected that, by age 55, T would have to retire from his current job, although he was expected to be able to work until the normal retirement age. The shoulder and chest injuries resolved within four to five months of the accident and at the hearing the knee injury continued to cause problems of instability. There was the prospect of the need for an arthroscopy to repair meniscal damage. The pelvic injury healed well but left T with permanent numbness in the region of his right thigh and groin. T had been hopeful of competing at national level in the sport of power lifting but after his accident he was no longer able to do this. This was assessed as being a significant incursion into a hobby. T had attempted to take his life and his marriage had been threatened after the accident when financial difficulties arose. In determining T's net monthly wage loss, the judge rejected the submission that an average should be taken over a period of 10 months to a year and instead chose a figure which appeared to fall somewhere between the highest and lowest monthly net wage. At the disposal hearing, T continued to suffer from headaches at least once a week, also bruising and dizziness. He also felt the need to take some 50 pain killers a month. He was aware of a throbbing pain in his head and his teeth tended to bleed upon brushing. *General Damages*: £30,000. Smith v. Manchester award: £5,000.

TRUSTRAM v. D'AMERY [2002] 4 Q.R. 5, Judge Ansell, CC (Watford).

Multiple injuries

3424.   S, male, a delivery driver, aged 32 at the date of the accident and 35 at trial, suffered multiple injuries when he was thrown off his motorcycle. He sustained lacerations to the face, head and right dominant hand, fractures to the second and third metacarpal bases in the right hand and injury to his abdomen. He was taken to hospital where he underwent an abdominal laparotomy. The laceration to his face and right hand were sutured. The fractures in his right hand were manipulated and fixated. He was an in-patient for seven days. He developed headaches and pain in his neck and lower back. Initially he was totally dependant on his partner to care for him. The pain in his neck and lower back settled for the most part, after a few months, although two years after the accident he was still suffering some neck stiffness in the morning and occasional twinges of pain in his lower back. The headaches began to clear after 14 months. He suffered giddiness for about two months. The abdominal wall discharged pus and a small stitch abscess was incised and drained. That surgery left a scar. The fractures in his hand became deformed and surgery was performed four months after the accident to fuse the base of the third metacarpal and the capito-metacarpal joint. The fixation metalwork was removed by further surgery two years after the accident. S was left with noticeable scarring to his face, the back of his right wrist and abdomen. The surgical scar to the abdomen was 19cm long and varied between 1cm and 5mm in width.

It was a considerable cosmetic disability. The scarring to the face and hand, although noticeable, was not obvious. He was left with a 50 per cent reduction in gripping and lifting strength in his right hand and a shortened middle finger. Wrist movement was restricted. The disability in his right hand was permanent. S could no longer play rugby. He no longer went swimming because his abdominal scar embarrassed him. Pain and stiffness in his right hand prevented him from undertaking DIY and gardening. S became severely depressed. His mood improved after he returned to work seven months post accident. He subsequently gave up his job because the disability in his right hand meant that he could not perform his duties. He became phobic and self-conscious about his scars and no longer took his shirt off in summer. He was anxious about riding a motorbike and had not done so since the accident. He was more vigilant when driving. The general damages award was a global assessment. *General Damages* (agreed and approved): £29,800. Smith v. Manchester Award: £5,000.

SOAR v. CLAYTON, August 2, 2001, District Judge Collis, CC (Nottingham). [*Ex rel.* Jinder Boora, Barrister, 24, The Ropewalk, Nottingham].

Multiple injuries

3425.   SR, female, aged nine at the date of the accident and 12 at the child settlement approval hearing, was a passenger in the rear of a car travelling with her father, sister and mother. SR's mother was killed and the others injured. SR sustained a closed fracture of the shaft of the left humerus, a fracture of the right lower third of the femur, a closed fracture of the shaft of the right tibia, an open fracture of the shaft of the left tibia and fractured ribs with left tension pneumothorax. Each of the limb fractures were fixed with nails. The right leg was put in traction. SR underwent two operations followed by intensive physiotherapy. She left hospital more than two months after the accident, but by then she was fully mobile. The fractures healed three months after the accident except for a discharging abscess on the lower right femur. The removal of the metalwork took place in a third operation eight months after the accident. SR made a full recovery from the fractures within about a year. Residual scarring remained including a 3cm scar to her chest, a 4cm thickened scar to the left arm, multiple scars around both knees including, on the right, a 3cm by 2cm scar on the outer knee, a 3cm medial scar and a 3cm proximal tibia scar on the left, a 4cm by 3.5cm proximal tibia scar and a 5cm by 4cm lower tibia scar. She was conscious of the scar to the outer right knee which looked like a small round indentation. It was anticipated that some slight improvement could be achieved by surgery to this. Otherwise most other scars, which did not bother her, would fade but not completely. *General Damages* (agreed and approved): £16,000. Award for future cosmetic surgery: £1,850. Fatal Accidents Award (proportion of family's total award): £13,000.

SR (A CHILD) v. LEE [2002] 2 Q.R. 11, Judge Sennitt, CC (Cambridge).

Multiple injuries

3426.   C, male, aged 32 at the date of the accident and 35 at trial was knocked off his motorcycle sustaining a laceration to his left thigh, a fracture of his left wrist and other soft tissue injuries. C was left with an L shaped scar 18cm in length and a longitudinal shaped scar 12cm in length of which he was conscious. He also suffered from numbness on the front of his lower thigh which would be permanent. The fracture was to the lower end of the left radius at the wrist which left him with a permanent slight weakness of grip. C complained of pain in his leg and wrist on very cold days or at the end of a particularly hard day at work. The symptoms were likely to be permanent. He also suffered soft tissue injuries to his left ring and middle finger, his left shoulder, left ankle and left elbow and a sprain to his lumbar spine. He was initially in hospital for six days. He was discharged on crutches. Four days after being discharged from hospital, C suffered a pulmonary embolism which was extremely frightening for him. He was in hospital for a further six days. He was prescribed Warfarin for about five months. C required crutches for six weeks after his discharge. He then used a stick for a further six weeks. He was off work for five weeks. C was heavily reliant on his girlfriend for three weeks after his discharge. She washed him, cooked for him and she did the housework. Prior to the accident, C cycled a round trip of 16 miles to work each day. He was able to return to cycling to work on some days about a year after the accident occurred and only started riding to work every day again almost two years after the accident. He put on a stone and a half in weight because of his lower level of activity. C was also diagnosed as suffering from Post Traumatic Stress Disorder, although the judge described the diagnosis as "borderline". C suffered from flashbacks of the accident for about nine months and his sleep was disturbed for about 18 months. *General Damages*: £15,000 (apportioned £9,000 for the injuries to the leg including the pulmonary embolism, £4,000 for the injuries to the wrist and £2,000 for the Post Traumatic Stress Disorder.)

BEATON v. BUSUULWA [2003] 1 Q.R. 12, Judge Sleeman, CC (Guildford).

Multiple injuries

3427.   S, male, a company director, aged 52 at the date of the accident and 55 at the hearing, sustained injuries when he fell from a working platform having knelt on a stray bolt left lying there by a fellow employee. He sustained soft tissue injuries to his neck, left shoulder, and to his head. He also suffered an undisplaced fracture to his left elbow. He was taken by ambulance to hospital. Bruising to his face lasted for one to two weeks. He suffered a cut to his face which required four stitches. He was left with a residual scar that was small but visible at conversational distance. Dizziness and poor concentration were experienced for a period of a month. The shoulder and elbow injuries both aggravated pre-existing conditions such that the symptoms attributable to the accident were aggravated for six months. The neck injury showed bad prognostic features and at the date of hearing left S with some permanent residual pain which was described as minor and irritating rather than disabling. *General Damages*: £6,500.

SULLIVAN v. HWF LTD (QUANTUM) [2002] 2 Q.R.11, Judge Hawksworth, CC (Bradford).

Multiple injuries–psychiatric damage

3428.   R, male, a proprietor of a windscreen business, aged 48 at the date of injury and 56 at the hearing, sustained multiple injuries in a serious assault. During the assault, R, who was right-hand dominant, was severely beaten and thrown through a window. His injuries included fracture dislocation of the left elbow, soft tissue injuries to the neck and lumbar spine and a traumatic spondylolisthesis of the axis (a "hangman's" fracture). R had continuing pain and weakness in his back and neck which required ongoing treatment. He suffered with chronic pain and weakness in his left hand which rendered him unable to do manual work, DIY or to play guitar, a former hobby. R also suffered with tinnitus, dizzy spells and slight hearing loss as a result of his injuries. The tinnitus was a particular loss of amenity owing to R's love of music. R's injuries gave rise to marked post traumatic stress disorder that became chronic and continued to require treatment. In addition, R underwent a personality change. He became very anxious and lost any feeling of pleasure in his life. He could not return to his former work or undertake any heavy work. *General Damages*: £60,000.

RANSON (CICA: QUANTUM: 2001), *Re*, May 3, 2001, Not specified, CICA (London). [*Ex rel.* Blake Lapthorn, Solicitors, Harbour Road, Compass Road, Portsmouth].

Multiple injuries–psychiatric damage

3429.   D, male, aged 25 at the date of injury and 32 at the hearing, was seriously injured in 1994 when he was set upon by bouncers at a nightclub. After obtaining psychiatric and neurological evidence, it was established that D had sustained serious orthopaedic and psychiatric injuries. Psychiatrically, he suffered a loss of self confidence, a tendency to be anxious, particularly in crowded places and in town centres and he had suffered an adjustment disorder. Following counselling, his self confidence improved significantly. Neurological opinion was to the effect that he had sustained some degree of sub clinical brain damage responsible for automatic behaviour or temper tantrums together with memory problems and poor concentration. His left wrist and hand had been stamped upon in the assault and he had sustained a cut to his chin as well as having his second left upper tooth kicked out. The injuries to his left wrist meant that his grip strength was reduced and led to his dismissal from his pre-incident occupation as fitter's mate. Although the counselling was beneficial, the psychiatric prognosis in terms of the depression was guarded and the symptoms arising from the sub clinical brain injury, particularly the temper outbursts, were considered likely to be permanent. At the hearing D had recovered confidence sufficiently to enable him to set up his own business. The evidence was that he would be able to return to his pre-incident employment. *General Damages*: £25,000. Past loss of earnings award: £62,595. Smith v. Manchester award: £20,000. Future loss of earnings award: £17,600.

DICKINSON (CICAP: QUANTUM: 2001), *Re* [2002] 4 Q.R. 5, Mr. Roberts (Chairman), CICAP (Liverpool).

Very severe brain damage

3430.   A, male, aged four months at the date of the injury and nine years at the child settlement approval hearing, suffered numerous fractures and devastating head injuries whilst in the care of his natural parents, resulting in severe brain damage and epilepsy. A was subsequently adopted. He had severe learning difficulties and as an adult his achievements were likely to be those of a child aged three to four. He was severely visually impaired, with unusual activity between 6/36 and 6/60. He was not toilet trained, nor likely to become so. He had mobility problems, although did not require a wheelchair or walking sticks. He suffered from asthma and eczema. He was totally dependent upon his adoptive parents, particularly the mother. He required specialist education and attended an RNIB school. He would be incapable of living independently and unemployable. He had very poorly socialised behaviour and tantrums, with no concept of danger. His behaviour was obsessive and repetitive and he required constant attention. His life expectancy was 60. His developmental progress would be limited and he would go into residential care at the age of 19. The future loss of earnings award was calculated by multiplying £13,855, being the net average earnings of male manual workers, by a multiplier of 22.69 less five per cent reduction for uncertainties. *General Damages*: £180,000. Past care award: £45,042. Future loss of earnings award: £298,652. Future care award: £2,044,750. Total award: £2,494,653.

A (CICA: QUANTUM: 2002), *Re* [2002] 6 Q.R. 6, Michael Brent Q.C. (Chairman), CICA (London).

Very severe brain damage

3431.   G, male, aged 18 months at the date of the assault and 11 years at the appeal hearing, suffered a serious traumatising head injury which left him with profound physical and cognitive disabilities. He developed cerebral palsy which affected his trunk, both legs and his left arm. His mobility and manual dexterity were gravely impaired and he had further visual and linguistic impairments, behavioural difficulties and was doubly incontinent. G required 24 hour supervision and would never be able to live independently. Loss of earnings and lifetime multipliers were assessed at 20 and 26.34 respectively. The award for future care was based on a sliding scale of need to age 19 and assessed thereafter at £95,000 per year. *General Damages*: £175,000. Past care award: £91,000. Future loss of earnings award: £311,000. Future care award: £1,813,550. Future housing award: £200,000. Total award: £3,313,068.

G (A CHILD) (CICAP: QUANTUM: 2002), *Re* [2003] 1 Q.R. 6, John Cherry Q.C. (Chairman), CICAP.

Very severe brain damage

3432.   P, male, aged 10 at the date of the assessment hearing, experienced oxygen starvation to his brain during his birth and was diagnosed as suffering from dystonic cerebral palsy when he was one year old. All four limbs were affected and there was some additional spasticity. He was able to move by rolling or crawling, but was unable to sit unaided. He could operate a powered wheelchair, but would lose control if excited. He was able to feed himself with his hands, but needed assistance to drink. He had a normal understanding of language and he could communicate using basic speech and symbols, although strangers had difficulty understanding him. P's life expectancy was 60 years; he was unlikely to find employment and would need full-time care assistance. P was cared for by his parents. The cost of the purchase of a house was allowed on the basis that it was incurred on behalf of P and when and where P's parents would otherwise have moved was speculative. The cost of replacement automatic garage doors was allowed as they enabled P to gain access to his equipment. The judge refused to allow the withdrawal of the admission of the sum claimed for future care to age 16, as it had been admitted on the basis of full disclosure and, in any event, any allowance for care undertaken by P's parents was countered by there being no claim for respite, overnight and weekend help. Although P received various pieces of equipment free of charge, the judge found that he did not have to depend on that situation; however, as that was likely to continue, only a proportion of the claim was allowed. The claim for future housing costs was not reduced to reflect a rent saving for P's parents who had moved from rented premises into their own home because, had they not cared for P, carers would have had to be employed at a cost which would have included accommodation. A claim for a contingency fund for future technical aids agreed by experts, was rejected on the grounds it was too speculative. The sum of £13,408 was agreed as the multiplicand to be used to calculate the award for loss of future earnings claimed from the age of 19 for full life expectancy. The multiplier was determined at 23.32, with a discount for contingencies of five per cent. *General Damages*: £170,000 (agreed and approved). Award for future loss of earnings: £297,040. Future care award (agreed and approved): £1,047,232. Award for cost of future clothing and equipment: £30,000.

PARKHOUSE v. NORTH DEVON HEALTHCARE NHS TRUST; *sub nom.* PARKHOUSE v. NORTHERN DEVON HEALTHCARE TRUST [2002] Lloyd's Rep. Med. 100, Gage, J., QBD.

Very severe brain damage

3433.   S, male, a general labourer, aged 31 at the date of the accident and 38 at trial, suffered catastrophic head injuries when he was struck by a vehicle travelling at high speed. He was taken to hospital, where his Glasgow Coma scale score was four, indicating a severe brain injury. S remained unconscious for six weeks. The result of a CT scan showed small haemorrhages and diffuse axonal injury. S developed severe behavioural problems and he was treated by a consultant in rehabilitation medicine and by a neurobehavioural surgeon. S also became a patient for the purposes of Mental Health legislation. The prognosis was that the severe physical and mental damage, which he had suffered would be permanent. His condition would not improve and might deteriorate without appropriate supervision and nursing care. He also suffered from fits and was considered to be at significant risk of development of pressure sores. Medical opinion was that S would require weekly input from a psychologist, regular intervention from a senior occupational therapist and from a clinical specialist in learning disabilities, and regular physiotherapy. There was an increased risk of pre-senile dementia and it was likely that S's care needs would increase in and beyond his sixties. He was assessed as requiring supervision and care by two suitably trained staff in respect of most activities. S had not been in regular employment at the time of the accident and had only ever engaged in unskilled or very semi skilled work. *General Damages*: £150,000. Award for past loss of earnings: £20,000. Award for future loss of earnings: £50,000. Award for past care: £30,000. Award for future care: £2,365,200. Award for equipment costs: £130,000. Award for additional recurring costs: £130,000. Award for cost of adapted vehicle: £80,000. Award for Court of Protection fees: £30,000. Total award: £3.25 million.

S (A PATIENT) v. TAYLOR, September 10, 2001, Judge Nichol, QBD. [*Ex rel.* Amery-Parkes, Solicitors, Civic House, 156 Great Charles Street Queensway, Birmingham].

Very severe brain damage

3434.   L, male, aged 42 at the date of the accident and 52 at the approved settlement, was struck by ladders projecting from a vehicle driven by S. L suffered severe head injuries, with a substantial period of amnesia and unconsciousness combined with sub-arachnoid hemorrhage and a fracture at the base of the skull. As a result of his injuries, L suffered major problems with memory, learning and slow thought processes, and he underwent a personality change rendering him irritable, threatening, aggressive and suspicious. He required 24 hour care and support and high levels of medication. L was initially hyperactive and abusive with delusions and hallucinations. His behaviour was tempered by powerful sedatives but L became insecure, fearful, demanding, childish and distressed if left alone. He became increasingly violent and, approximately six years after the accident, his wife was no longer able to cope. L was admitted to a care home for periods of respite care, and was moved into residential care on a permanent basis seven years after the accident. L remained volatile and emotionally disturbed. It was ultimately agreed that L would return to his home with 24 hour care provision, which arrangement was likely to remain in place for the duration of L's life. It was agreed that L's life expectancy was reduced by two to three years as a result of the brain injury but his life had been reduced by between seven and 12 years as L had been a life long smoker. *General Damages*: £125,000 (agreed and approved). Past loss of earnings award: £62,440. Past gratuitous care award: £76,654. Past paid care award: £235,246. Award for past accommodation costs: £58,186. Future care award: £1,130,078. Award for future accommodation costs: £37,222. Total award: £1,957,044.

L v. SPARKS [2002] 2 Q.R. 10, Jack, J., QBD.

Severe brain damage

3435.   K, female, aged 20 at the date of injury and 26 at settlement, underwent a subtotal colectomy and ileostomy as treatment for severe ulcerative protocolitis, as a result of which she became septicaemic with associated hypoxia leading to a respiratory cardiac arrest. Despite resuscitation, she developed hypoxic brain injury. As a result of her injuries, K developed psychotic thoughts and depression and was childish in her behaviour, with low concentration and clear vulnerability. Her memory, both long and short term, was impaired, with some incontinence and a loss of intellectual ability. K remained incapable of managing her own affairs, or living independently. An overall settlement of £2 million was agreed and approved. *General Damages*: £100,000 (agreed and approved). The breakdown advanced by leading counsel for K for other elements was as follows: Past care award: £74,880. Future care award (including total case management): £1,619,680. Future loss of earnings award (multiplier 14.63): £55,594. Total award: £2 million.

KILBRIDE v. LEEDS NHS TRUST [2002] 4 Q.R. 6, Judge Cockroft, QBD.

Moderate brain damage

3436.   E, male, aged 22 at the date of the assault and 31 at the hearing, suffered serious head injuries when his head was repeatedly banged against iron railings. E required neurosurgery to remove a subdural haematoma. He then suffered significant speech disturbance and right hemiparesis; marked change in personality and behaviour; shifts of mood from depression to irritability or anxiety and periodic outbursts of temper to minimal frustration. There was a disregard of personal hygiene and a worsening of intellectual function. E's condition was diagnosed as Organic Personality Disorder. An initial assessed risk of post traumatic epilepsy of 15 per cent was reduced to five per cent by the date of the hearing. E had never held down a full time job on the open labour market before the assault. At school he had been listed as requiring special needs education and, after school, he had received a number of short term work placements. After the assault, E required support and assistance with house keeping, the management of his affairs and shopping. It was determined that eight hours care per week was appropriate. A Court of Protection fixed annual fee of £205 was awarded, together with a sum, to be assessed, representing the cost of administration of the fund by, or on behalf of, the receiver. *General Damages*: £90,000. Loss of earnings award (past and future): £50,000. Past care award: £5,000. Future care award: £42,000.

EMERY (CICA: QUANTUM: 2001), *Re*, August 9, 2001, Not specified, CICA (Birmingham). [*Ex rel.* Peter Buckley, Barrister, Queens Chambers, 5 John Dalton Street, Manchester].

Moderate brain damage

3437.   C, male, aged 15 at the date of the accident and 24 at the hearing, was injured at school when he was lifted up by other pupils above their heads and dropped onto his head. He suffered a severe head injury. He was admitted to hospital but not properly investigated for five hours. Eventually a CT scan was performed, indicating acute extra dural haematoma in the right parietal region and a fracture to the right temporal bone. A right tempore parietal craniotomy was performed and an extra dural haematoma was evacuated. At the assessment of damages hearing, C was suffering from substantial neurological disabilities including impaired vision, left facial weakness, impaired coordination on his left side, loss of dexterity and power in his left hand, limp and drag of his left foot, epilepsy with ongoing partial seizures, personality change, fatigue, distorted smell, difficulty with memory and concentration, organisational and motivational difficulties and word finding and linguistic problems. He was unable to drive as a result of ongoing partial epileptic seizures occurring up to six times a day. C's ambition had been to work as a forensic scientist. Since the accident he had unsuccessfully tried to complete a teacher training course and was unable to pursue a psychology course. He had been employed in sporadic menial jobs and since six and a half years after the accident had worked as a part time operations controller. C's claim for loss of congenial employment was rejected on the basis that he would not have been employed as a forensic scientist, but an additional award was made for "loss of fulfilling employment". The award for past care was subject to a 25 per cent reduction to reflect the fact that care had been provided by the family and the award for future care was based on three hours a week. A multiplier of 24.63 was used for the award for future loss of earnings award reflecting earnings to age 65, but credit was given for actual earnings as an operations controller taken only to age 60 with a corresponding multiplier of 22.91 to reflect a Smith v. Manchester award of about £15,515 in the event of C losing his job. *General Damages*: £75,000. Past loss of earnings award: £40,919. Award for loss of fulfilling employment: £50,000. Future loss of earnings award: £293,352. Future care award (full life multiplier 29.81): £54,455.

CORRIE v. EAST GLOUCESTERSHIRE NHS TRUST [2002] 6 Q.R. 6, Judge Bursell Q.C., QBD.

Moderate brain damage

3438.   J, female, aged 17 at the date of the road traffic accident and 22 at trial, sustained brain damage and orthopaedic injuries. The brain injury involved a left peri orbital haematoma and two or three minor haemorrhages in the left parieto occipital region. J's initial Glasgow Coma Score was 4/15, which, together with post traumatic amnesia was sufficient for the injury to be classed as severe. However, J made a remarkable recovery such that, at the date of trial, she was able to live independently but suffered chronic fatigue, unpredictable temper control, concentration difficulties and memory problems. Prior to the accident, J had been taking an NVQ course in horse management, but she was unable to return to her studies after the accident. She had been able to undertake part time jobs for approximately 16 hours per week assisting at riding stables, but it would not fulfil her original ambition of running her own stables. The prognosis was poor so far as working was concerned. As a result of her improvement from the original diagnosis, the award for general damages was assessed towards the top of the lowest category in the JSB guidelines for moderate brain damage. For the award for loss of earnings, a multiplier of 24.32 was adopted based on Ogden Table 24 and a discount rate of 2.5 per cent was applied. The multiplicand was assessed at £11,585 per year. *General Damages*: £42,500. Future loss of earnings award: £209,930. Future care award: £11,991.

JAMES v. STARBUCK [2002] 6 Q.R. 6, Recorder Maxwell Q.C., QBD.

Moderate brain damage

3439. S, male, aged 21 at the date of the assault and 28 at the hearing, received a heavy blow to the back of the head from an unknown assailant outside a nightclub. He suffered an occipital fracture to the head and contusion to the frontal area of the brain. An MRI scan and various CT scans were carried out. The head injuries were described as severe, although no neurosurgical intervention was required. S suffered reasonably significant post traumatic amnesia (five days) and continued to experience short term memory loss. He spent 14 days in hospital. He suffered a loss of taste and smell, in particular finding it difficult to distinguish between smells. He suffered a total of four post traumatic epileptic seizures and there remained a risk of further fits. To control his epilepsy, S changed his lifestyle instead of taking anti-convulsion medication. He socialised less, avoided drinking, took early nights and rested when tired. He also avoided looking at television and computer screens for too long. He experienced severe headaches once a week and found it difficult to concentrate. Before the assault, S was confident, sociable and even-tempered with good prospects for his future. However, after the assault he experienced a change in personality. He became irritable and bad tempered as well as finding it increasingly difficult to concentrate. He also found himself feeling increasingly tired. He subsequently took employment within the family business but would have been at a disadvantage on the open labour market. The Board assumed that the risk of further epileptic fits was minimal but made a direction that the papers be preserved so that further consideration could be given to the award in the event that further fits occurred. *General Damages*: £35,000. Smith v. Manchester award: £25,000.

RIGDEN (CICA: QUANTUM: 2001), *Re* [2002] 2 Q.R. 11, Peter Weitzman (Chairman), CICA (London).

Psychiatric damage

3440. T, female, a temporary bank clerk aged 23 at the date of the incident and 30 at the hearing, had been drinking with a male friend who assaulted her and tried to remove her trousers, preparatory to raping her. In the course of a violent struggle, in which she received some soft tissue injuries, T stabbed her attacker with a knife that she was carrying. The medical evidence was that T had a borderline personality disorder prior to the assault but she was coping with life and obtaining good work. Following the assault she developed post traumatic stress disorder which destroyed her previous fragile but successful coping capacity. Though the previous personality disorder had lowered T's threshold for the development of PSTD it did not in itself explain the occurrence. The PSTD manifested in flashbacks, panic attacks particularly associated with things that reminded her of her assailant, sleep disturbance, agoraphobia and she attempted suicide. Though she did some work after the incident, sometimes holding down a job for several months at a time, she never achieved the level of work she was doing before it. Two years and six months after the assault T was working in a public house where she was the victim of a second assault. This was very much more minor in nature but shortly afterwards T ceased work and there was little foreseeable prospect of a return to work. At the hearing, T was having almost weekly counselling from a psychologist and was a frequent attender at her local MIND centre and mental health user group. The prognosis for recovery was very poor. *General Damages*: £30,000.

T (CICA: QUANTUM: 2002), *Re* [2002] 6 Q.R. 7, Sir Julian Clarke (Chairman), CICA (London).

Psychiatric damage

3441. W, female, a school teacher, aged 50 at the date of the incident and 54 at trial, was assaulted by a pupil. She sustained mild lacerations to her face and was shocked. She took the remainder of that day and the following day off work. She then returned to work but left the school and teaching at the end of that week. She was diagnosed as suffering from moderate to moderately severe post traumatic stress disorder, depression, agoraphobia and panic attacks. Other elements independent of the assault had exacerbated W's psychiatric illness. For some time prior to the incident she had attended counselling. Initially that had been in regard to her relationship with her partner but it then continued in respect of work related stress. The counsellor had written to W's GP stating that W was on the verge of a "burnout". W had, in fact, been suffering from mild depression and had been highly stressed at the date of the assault. It was likely that she would have suffered from depression and would have needed to retire from teaching at some time even if the incident had not occurred. W's condition had been aggravated by an undiagnosed thyroid condition which had intensified her depression. *General Damages*: £20,000

WAUGH v. NEWHAM LBC, [2002] EWHC 802, [2003] 1 Q.R. 6, Cooke, J., QBD.

Psychiatric damage

3442. AR, male, aged six at the date of the accident and nine at the child settlement approval hearing, was a passenger in the rear seat of a car travelling with his father, sister and mother. The car was in a collision with a vehicle travelling in the opposite direction. AR's mother was killed and all the others injured. AR sustained two broken ribs and two incisors loosened which were removed a few days later. He made a swift recovery from his injuries. AR was awake at the time of the accident, heard his mother call out and saw the physical injuries to her. He was diagnosed as having post traumatic stress disorder based on symptoms such as flashbacks, nightmares, sleep difficulties, diminished interest in activities which he had enjoyed previously, poorer concentration and clinginess. There was some evidence that his personality had altered for a time. At school, he was reported as awkward and belligerent, and disruptive at football. However, his father reported significant improvement by the date of the hearing. It was considered that AR was likely to be vulnerable to recurrences after experiencing further trivial trauma. *General Damages*: £8,000. Fatal Accidents Award (proportion of family's total award): £13,000.

AR (A CHILD) v. LEE [2002] 2 Q.R. 12, Judge Sennitt, CC (Cambridge).

Psychiatric damage

3443. D, male, a postman, aged 34 at the date of the accident and 37 at the date of the disposal hearing, was injured when a car door was opened in front of the bicycle he was riding causing him to be thrown to the ground. He was taken to hospital by ambulance. He suffered a 4cm puncture wound to the left, non dominant, shoulder which was sutured under general anaesthetic and he was kept in hospital overnight. He wore a sling for five days and was off work for three weeks. The shoulder pain resolved over three months, leaving a scar measuring 4cm by 1cm by which D was untroubled. He had other unrelated scarring to his chest. He also suffered pain in his back for six weeks, abrasions to his forehead which lasted for a month, a lump on his left shin which lasted three months and a scab to his right knee which resolved over four months leaving a minor scar roughly 1cm in diameter. In addition, D suffered from post traumatic stress disorder for six months after the accident and mood disturbances beyond that, although the accident was only partly causative of the latter symptom. Psychological symptoms, including flashbacks to the accident, persisted for four to five months. All symptoms, save the scarring, had resolved by trial. *General Damages*: £4,000.

DARE v. HEATON [2002] 6 Q.R. 7, District Judge Frenkel, CC (Bristol).

Psychiatric damage–neck

3444. M, female, a meals on wheels delivery driver, aged 44 at the date of the accident and 48 at trial, suffered minor tissue injuries to the neck and significant psychological injury after a water skier collided with her jet ski, throwing her into the sea. The medical evidence showed that M had suffered a soft tissue sprain from which she had fully recovered within a month. The major injury was psychological. M had substantial pre existing psychological problems. She had thought she would drown after being pulled under the water by the skier's rope. She developed a fear of water and thought of the accident constantly. She suffered nightmares of being trapped under water. The symptoms were particularly severe during the first 12 months, during which time her sexual activity was reduced. Her symptoms began to improve and she resumed swimming two years after the accident. M's symptoms did not impact on her ability to work. The medical evidence supported a diagnosis of post traumatic stress disorder. At trial, the only psychological symptoms attributable to the accident were occasional nightmares which were reducing in frequency. The judge found that M would make a full recovery in the near future and he held that the appropriate award for general damages lay in the JSB bracket for moderate post traumatic stress disorder. *General Damages*: £6,500.

MUNDEN v. BUNTEN [2003] 1 Q.R. 7, District Judge Wharton, CC (Peterborough).

Psychiatric damage–neck–whiplash type injury

3445. R, male, a food production operative, aged 26 at the date of the road traffic accident and 29 at trial, suffered a whiplash injury to his neck, a bruised chest caused by his seat belt and minor grazing to the knees. Pain and stiffness in the neck and pain in the chest was acute during the first four months. He was unable to work for four weeks. His physical symptoms improved and within 12 months there remained only minor stiffness in his neck, a "popping" sensation in his right shoulder and intermittent pain in his chest, particularly when stretching or lifting. His symptoms were aggravated by his work, household chores and by his main hobby of kite flying. There were marked psychological sequelae diagnosed as an adjustment disorder. R suffered nightmares. The psychological symptoms were severe for a month and moderately severe for a further two months. One year after the accident he was still a very nervous driver, particularly at junctions. The psychological symptoms returned to their pre accident level approximately two years after the accident. The agreed medical evidence was that the minor continuing neck symptoms were attributable to the accident and would be permanent. There was no causal link between the continuing chest and shoulder symptoms and the accident. The judge found that the permanent neck symptoms were slightly above nuisance level. *General Damages*: £6,000.

RIDER v. HALL [2003] 1 Q.R. 7, District Judge Hudson, CC (Lincoln).

Psychiatric damage–digestive organs

3446. M, female, aged 40 at the date of the negligent surgery and 45 at trial, underwent a laparoscopic cholecystectomy following the diagnosis of gallstones. This involved the removal of the gall bladder using minimal access surgical techniques. The operation proved difficult and M's subsequent progress was poor. For two days after the procedure M experienced severe abdominal pain, a post operative bile leak and developed peritonitis. Three days later the decision was taken to operate again, initially by way of laparoscopy, but ultimately by open surgery. On this occasion the bile leak was repaired and M's progress was good notwithstanding the inevitable pain and discomfort associated with the open surgery. M spent three days in a high dependency unit but she was keen to leave hospital and was discharged after a further two days. She had a drainage bag in situ for seven days following her discharge from hospital and she was attended by a community nurse during that period. M lost a great deal of weight and strength and was unable to perform many of her former domestic chores. She was reliant upon her friends and family. She finally approached her former levels of strength and mobility some four months after the surgery. However, the operation sites remained tender and lumpy and, as a result of her experience, M had a great fear of future hospitalisation. *General Damages*: £7,500.

M v. UNIVERSITY OF LEICESTER HOSPITALS NHS TRUST [2003] 1 Q.R. 7, Judge Harris Q.C., CC (Northampton).

Post traumatic stress disorder

3447. S, female, aged 69 at the road traffic accident and 70 at the trial, sustained soft tissue injuries to her left shoulder and upper arm and to her right knee. A short course of physiotherapy commenced three weeks after the accident. Recovery from the physical injuries was complete between six to nine months after the accident. However, S also sustained a degree of post traumatic stress disorder. Six months after the accident S still thought about it regularly, had lost her confidence to go out and developed symptoms of anxiety and panicked when travelling as a passenger in a vehicle. S also displayed a lack of interest in previously enjoyed activities and had suffered recurring dreams for approximately three months after the accident. Six months after the accident S had frequent episodes of low moods which occurred two of three times per week. The prognosis at trial was that the low moods, irritability and social avoidance would improve significantly within nine to twelve months of the accident, the travel anxieties would progress within 15 to 18 months of the accident and that the travel phobia would remain for a further two and a half to three and a half years from the accident. *General Damages*: £12,000 (£11,000 for the psychological injury and £1,000 for the shoulder and knee injuries).

SHENTON v. WOOLLEY [2003] 1 Q.R. 8, Deputy District Judge Collis, CC (Telford).

Post traumatic stress disorder

3448. G, male, a lorry driver and electrician, aged 34 at the date of accident and 39 at trial, suffered post-traumatic stress disorder following an incident where the brakes failed on the vehicle he was driving, resulting in a serious collision with a car and the death of a child passenger in that car. G was initially held personally responsible and faced charges of manslaughter. Those charges were later dropped and the case proceeded against G's employer. G received death threats from the deceased's father which were so serious as to warrant the installation by the police of an alarm at G's home. G was subsequently moved into a safe house which was described as a "hell hole". G suffered from nightmares and flashbacks of the accident; his concentration deteriorated and he became irritable. His relationship with his girlfriend broke down, although the couple were later reconciled. G was unable to work for two years after the accident. At trial, five years after the accident, G had fully recovered, save that he would be more vulnerable, after the accident, to future life stressors. *General Damages*: £10,000. Award for past loss of earnings: £40,275. Smith v. Manchester award: £7,500.

GARDEN v. MORGAN, September 19, 2001, Judge Bray, CC (Northampton). [*Ex rel.* Robert Weir, Barrister, Devereux Chambers, Devereux Court, London].

Epilepsy – psychiatric damage

3449. S, male, aged 19 at the date of the incident and 26 at trial, was assaulted, suffering a blow near the left ear and a linear fracture of the skull causing cerebro spinal fluid discharge. As a result of his injuries, S suffered grand mal epilepsy and had approximately four fits per year. He also developed tinnitus in his ear following the assault. This was mild and intermittent, but would be permanent. S also suffered a depressive illness for six months and from agoraphobia thereafter. After counselling, S was fit to return to work approximately four years and six months after the assault and made a virtually full psychological recovery. In calculating the *Smith v. Manchester* award, a claim for disadvantage in promotion was included, as S would not be able to hold a driving licence until three years after cessation of the epileptic fits, if they ceased to occur. At the hearing, the fits were not regulated by medication and occurred approximately four times per year. General damges: £60,000. Smith v. Manchester award: £15,000.

SMITH (CICA: QUANTUM: 2002), *Re* [2002] 6 Q.R. 7, Lord Carlisle Q.C. (Chairman), CICAP.

Teeth–facial scars

3450.   G, male, aged 10 at the date of the accident and 14 at trial, suffered injuries to three of his front incisor teeth as a result of a road traffic accident. The upper right, upper left central and upper right central incisors were all knocked out and had to be replanted temporarily. The upper right incisor was lost entirely at the age of 11. G had temporary restorations to the other two teeth, was required to wear a brace for two years and needed a bridge replacement until attaining his majority. The evidence demonstrated that, when G was 22, all three teeth would need replacement with titanium implants and post crowns, and that a bone graft was likely to be needed to enable implants. The crown would then need replacement at 15 year intervals. G endured prolonged orthodontic treatment, including two root canal treatments, entailing constant monitoring of the damaged teeth. The missing tooth embarrassed G for one to two years and the brace was uncomfortable. In addition, there were two scars to the face. The first measured 2cm by 0.5cm and was on the upper lip, running beneath the nostril. The second measured 1.5cm and extended down to the chin. Both scars were permanent, could not be improved and the one on the top of the lip was prominent at a conversational distance. The wounds needed sutures under a general anaesthetic but healed without infection or breaking down subsequently. Damages were assessed at a level above that given in the 5th edition of the JSB guidelines as the judge held that £5,000 was inadequate for protracted, unpleasant dental treatment. *General Damages*: £12,500 (apportioned £7,500 for the dental damage and £5,000 for the scarring).

GOLAS (A CHILD) v. GOLAS [2003] 1 Q.R. 8, Judge Holman, CC (Manchester).

Facial scars

3451.   M, male, aged 25 at the date of the incident and 29 at trial, was attacked by another remand prisoner using a broken glass jar. M sustained a complex series of lacerations on the left side of his face. These were repaired under general anaesthetic and a flap of skin on the left nostril, which had been almost completely severed, was replaced as a free graft. The wounds healed, leaving visible scars which remained a significant cosmetic disfigurement. In particular, there was (1) a 17cm angulated and branched scar extending from the left naso labial fold across the left cheek to just above the left ear and extending into the hairline on the left side of the head above the left ear; (2) a 1.2cm by 0.3cm oblique raised scar on the left side of the forehead, and (3) a 2.0cm by 0.1cm inverted U shaped depressed scar, enclosing a raised flap of skin on the posterior part of the margin of the left nostril. M remained embarassed by his appearance to the extent that he was reluctant to make social or work contact and had not found employment a year after his release from prison. M failed to establish liability but, had he done so, the award would have been assessed as follows: *General Damages*: £9,000. Smith v. Manchester award: £500.

MYRIEL v. HOME OFFICE [2003] 1 Q.R. 8, Judge Brandt, CC (Colchester).

Facial scars

3452.　P, female, aged five at the date of the incident and eight at the child settlement hearing, was attacked by M's Alsatian dog. P sustained a bite injury to her right cheek and scratches to her chin, behind her right ear and along her left thigh. The bite was the most serious injury; it was 3cm long and required suturing as did the injury behind her right ear. The cheek injury healed leaving a scar 2.3cm long by 4mm at its widest and there was a contour defect of 1mm. There was light pink discolouration within the scar and it was readily apparent to casual inspection at conversational distance and beyond. Medical evidence was that the scar could be improved by revision surgery, but not until P was fully grown. The scar behind P's ear was only apparent on close inspection. P also developed a psychological reaction. Her sleep was disturbed for approximately six months with nightmares lasting two to three months. P developed a general phobia of dogs which largely resolved within a year. However, she remained phobic about Alsatians for considerably longer and, at the hearing, she displayed a phobic avoidance of M's shop and an extreme anxiety reaction whenever she saw M's dog. *General Damages* (agreed and approved): £7,500.

PEARSON (A CHILD) v. MAID MARIAN FOOD STORES [2002] 6 Q.R. 8, District Judge Reeson, CC (Nottingham).

Facial scars

3453.　K, male, a draughtsman, aged 34 at the date of the road traffic accident and 36 at trial, sustained multiple injuries when, as a pedestrian, he was hit by a car. The principal injury was a curved soft tissue laceration to his head that ran from the middle of the forehead and into his scalp above the left eye. The laceration was 15cm long. K also sustained bruising around the left eye, bruising to the left shoulder and an abrasion below the left knee. He was admitted to hospital for two days where the laceration was cleaned and sutured. K suffered from intermittent headaches for a period after the accident. He was left with a permanent, well healed scar measuring 15cm in length. The scar was easily visible at conversational distance but was not pink, lumpy or raised. K was embarrassed by the scar and was concerned that it would become more noticeable as his hair reduced. There was also a scar to the front of the lower left leg measuring 3cm by 0.5cm. K had given up his hobby playing football because he was fearful of heading the ball. *General Damages*: £6,250.

KAY v. SMITH [2003] 1 Q.R. 9, Recorder Lewis, CC (Middlesborough).

Facial scars

3454.　D, female, aged three at the date of the road traffic accident and six at the child settlement approval hearing, suffered a momentary loss of consciousness after the collision, which resulted in concussion. She was detained in hospital overnight for observation. In the weeks following the accident, D suffered from headaches for which she took Calpol. The headaches settled after one month. D also suffered some minor neck ache during this time and sleep disturbance, including nightmares, over a period of six weeks. She was absent from nursery school for a period of one week. The most serious part of D's injuries were lacerations to her ear, face and the outer side of her right leg. The cut to D's ear required three stitches, which were removed one week later. D was left with a scar measuring 1cm by 0.5cm, which was tender for a period of three months. The scar to D's ear would fade away in a couple of years. D also suffered three glass cuts to her face which did not require suturing and healed within one week. However, each of the three cuts left scars measuring 3mm on D's face: a textured scar on her cheek, a scar above her left eyebrow and one on her forehead. The scar on the forehead was white in colour and remained white when D was exposed to the sun. It was found that the facial cuts would be an embarrassment to D at intimate distances as she got older. The cut to D's right leg healed within one week, leaving a scar measuring 1cm. *General Damages*: £4,000.

D (A CHILD) v. SEVERN TRENT WATER LTD [2002] 6 Q.R. 8, District Judge Morton, CC (Stourbridge).

Ear

3455.   H, female, aged 12 at the date of the incident and 15 at trial, attended a local jewellers shop to have the upper part of her left ear pierced for an earring. Shortly afterwards, H developed an infection in her left ear resulting in three operations under general anaesthetic in order to incise the posterior aspect of her left ear and drain off accumulated pus. H was left with a shrivelled up and cosmetically unattractive left ear. H was embarrassed by her ear and was forced to wear her hair long to disguise it. A report from a reconstructive surgeon confirmed the condition was permanent although surgery was possible to reconstruct the ear taking cartilage from H's rib cage. Special damages were awarded to cover the cost of future reconstructive surgery. *General Damages* (agreed and approved): £10,000. Special Damages: £3,900.

HEALEY (A CHILD) v. WARNERS (JEWELLERS) LTD (T/A H WARNER & SONS) [2002] 6 Q.R. 8, District Judge Babbington, CC (Barnsley).

Hearing and speech

3456.   P, male, a care worker aged 50 at the date of the injury and 58 at the hearing, was assaulted by a patient while at work. The patient boxed P's ears several times causing P to sustain a perforated tympanic membrane which remained despite three attempts to close it surgically. In addition, P suffered from tinnitus and hearing loss in the left ear. Tinnitus was described as a continuing constant loud ringing/scratching noises in the left ear. Attempts had been made to relieve the tinnitus at the time of the appeal to no avail and it was found that the tinnitus was likely to be permanent. The tinnitus induced a moderate depressive illness leaving an undercurrent of anger, emotionality, desperation and pessimism. P stopped working in 1996 due to the depression and tinnitus and was formally dismissed a year later. *General Damages*: £17,500. Past loss of earnings award: £22,419. Future loss of earning award: £9,998.

POMARES (CICAP: QUANTUM: 2001), *Re* (2002) 3 Q.R. 5, J Cherry Q.C. (Chairman), CICA (London).

Hearing and speech

3457.   W, male, retired, aged 65 at the date of the accident and 68 at trial, sustained injury when a firework that was intended to rise into the air exploded on the ground, a short distance away from W, just after ignition. W was immediately aware of a loud ringing in his ears and found that he was unable to hear his family speaking to him. Nine months before the accident, W had become aware of intermittent tinnitus in his left ear. Audiometric testing over 1kHz, 2kHz and 3kHz had revealed an average binaural hearing loss of 24 per cent, with loss in the left ear being greater than in the right. Five days after the accident testing over the same range revealed an average binaural loss of about 49dB with the loss in each ear being roughly the same. The increase, entirely due to the accident, meant that W's hearing loss had increased by a factor of one half. The agreed medical evidence was that this increased loss would be permanent and that hearing loss would continue to deteriorate due to age but that the rate of deterioration would be unaffected by the accident. When W was examined 19 months after the accident his average binaural loss was about 55.5dB or 45 per cent. W also experienced continuous tinnitus in the left ear and intermittent tinnitus in the right after the accident. The medical expert categorised the post accident situation as moderate to severe, whereas it had previously been moderate. W's main problem after the accident was his inability to distinguish sounds; he reported his hearing as "distorted". Prior to the accident, W had been able to hold conversations on the telephone and in social situations where there was background noise. After the accident he had difficulty with conversation that was not face to face and when there was background noise. He could no longer turn up the volume on the television without causing more distortion of the sound. W felt unable to take part in social activities and felt increasingly frustrated. The judge held that the increase in hearing loss, the increase in tinnitus and the poor discrimination were all factors relevant to the level of general damages with the last factor being an important consideration which meant that reported cases and the JSB Guidelines were of limited use. *General Damages*: £10,000.

WARNE v. OCTAVIUS HUNT LTD [2002] 6 Q.R. 9, Judge Simpson, CC (City of London).

Hearing and speech–neck

3458. B, female, aged three at the date of the accident and eight at trial, was a rear seat passenger when she was involved in a road traffic accident. She was taken by ambulance to hospital and discharged with analgesics. B required no time off nursery school but she did not participate in sporting activity for one week. As a result of the collision, B suffered neck pain, bed wetting and tinnitus. The neck pain persisted for a period of three months. The bed wetting, which occurred initially several times a night, persisted for two years, occurring once or twice per week. B initially complained that she suffered a continual humming or buzzing noise which disturbed her both during the day and at night. Four years after the accident, B described the buzzing as being audible only when it was quiet and as being worse when she closed her eyes. She said that she could not hear it at school or when watching television. B had no previous hearing deficiency and no hearing deficit as a result of the tinnitus. Although the tinnitus persisted, it was found not to have affected B's performance at school and it did not interfere with her daily activities. The diagnosis was that B was suffering from intermittent tinnitus and the prognosis was that the tinnitus would probably subside completely in the future and would not affect her performance in public examinations or her choice of future employment. The district judge indicated that the tinnitus fell at the top end of the B(iv) bracket for injuries affecting the senses in the JSB guidelines. *General Damages* (agreed and approved): £10,000 (apportioned as to £6,500 for the tinnitus and £3,500 for the neck injury).

BLAKE (A CHILD) v. WILLIAMS [2003] 1 Q.R. 9, District Judge Silverman, CC (Central London).

Neck

3459. R, female, aged 70 at the date of the road traffic accident and 73 at the hearing, was a passenger in a car. She developed severe neck pain which prevented her from lifting or turning her neck. The pain radiated to the left arm and hand. Sudden movement aggravated the symptoms. R bought a neck brace the following day and attended a local physiotherapist for treatment over the next three days. R was unable to continue with her holiday and returned home where she attended a physiotherapist regularly for nearly four months. During that time she purchased a heat lamp, special pillow and heat pads in an attempt to alleviate her symptoms. Five months after the accident there was much improvement in the range of movement but quite significant symptoms persisted in the neck and arm. R was unable to do any heavy physical house work or carry heavy things in her left dominant hand. She also had disturbed sleep. The symptoms occurred everyday. R had a relapse of pain around ten months after the accident for which she was prescribed further physiotherapy, but this did not particularly improve the range of movement. She continued with self applied heat treatment and exercise. She then had a onset of severe neck pain approximately 32 months after the accident which were so intense that she attended hospital. She then recommenced physiotherapy for another two months and purchased a tens machine which assisted the symptoms slightly. The symptoms significantly restricted R from gardening and painting which she particularly enjoyed. She avoided any heavy work if possible but would wear a neck brace if the work had to be done, for example when gardening. R became very nervous when travelling and was no longer able to drive on long journeys, which she has previously enjoyed. She felt unsafe when she was towing her caravan and no longer went on lengthy caravanning holidays. R had pre existing degenerative changes in her neck but these were asymptomatic for the five years prior to the accident. Medical evidence concluded that symptoms persisting more than three years after the accident were likely to be related to R's preexisting problems. The judge accepted that R's injuries fell within the top end of bracket 6(A)(b)(ii) of the JSB guidelines and that R had lost a great deal at a most important time of her life. *General Damages*: £5,250.

ROBINSON v. SAYERS [2002] 4 Q.R. 7, Judge Barry, CC (Harrogate).

Neck

3460.　　C, female, aged 64 at the date of the accident and 69 at trial was involved in a road traffic accident which caused her car to be shunted from side to side. She suffered immediate pain in her neck and shoulder and experienced aggravation of osteo-arthritic symptoms in her knee and hip. Her mobility, which had been poor before the accident, was very much worsened afterwards and C had to rely upon the care of a friend for 16 to 18 months post accident. Medical evidence established that the symptoms in the neck and shoulder were referable to the accident and likely to last for 16 months. The aggravated symptoms in the knee and hip lasted one year. *General Damages*: £4,000. Care award: £2,500 (assessed as covering a 16 month period).

CRUTCHLEY v. STAGECOACH (2002) 3 Q.R. 6, Judge Eaglestone, CC (Manchester).

Neck–pre existing disability or condition–aggravated by whiplash

3461.　　R, female, a legal executive, aged 47 at the date of the road traffic accident and 51 at the hearing, struck her knees on the dashboard and suffered a whiplash injury to the neck. Pain developed in the neck during the course of the day. R visited her GP the following day and again a month later. She had no specific treatment beyond self-help exercises performed at home as suggested by a friend who was a physiotherapist. She did not require any time off work although she did experience pains and aches during the course of her work especially when speaking on the telephone and on bending her head forwards. She would stretch her neck to relieve symptoms. R had adapted to the continuing symptoms. There were no real amenity losses beyond the cessation of heavy gardening and DIY. Four years after the accident R took painkillers occasionally and was aware of occasional crepitus in the neck. There was a 20 per cent restriction of movement of the neck after two years. The continuing signs and symptoms were due to the effects of underlying cervical spondylosis which had been diagnosed some eight years before the accident, although R had been previously asymptomatic. She reported a subjective sense of loss of power in her left, non-dominant hand. The joint medical evidence was that the accident had brought the onset of the symptoms forward by about seven and half years. R noticed occasional aches in her knees at the date of disposal hearing. The Judge remarked that he suspected R was an uncomplaining lady who simply got on with her life and had adapted to her situation. *General Damages*: £8,500.

RALLEY v. READ [2002] 2 Q.R. 12, Judge Clarke, CC (Birmingham).

Neck–pre existing disability–aggravated by whiplash

3462.   H, female, unemployed, aged 44 at the date of the accident and 48 at trial, was pushed off a bus when the driver had a scuffle with another passenger. She hit her head on the pavement. At first she thought she was all right but later, during her journey, she felt unwell and was taken to hospital in an ambulance. She had sustained a contusion over her left parieto-occipital region, bruising to her left knee and hip, and a neck sprain. H began to suffer with headaches and dizziness which were still present at the date of the hearing. She also needed considerable ongoing voluntary help from her daughter in carrying out household tasks. The medical evidence was that the accident had advanced a pre existing deteriorating neck condition by some three to five years. *General Damages*: £6,500.

HADJIKTORI v. ARRIVA LONDON LTD, September 5, 2001, District Judge Cohen, CC (Edmonton). [*Ex rel.* John Fox, Barrister, Lamb Building, Temple, London].

Neck–pre existing disability or condition–aggravated by whiplash

3463.   S, male, a teacher, aged 60 at the date of the road traffic accident and 63 at the disposal hearing, suffered injuries when struck by a vehicle causing his vehicle to mount the pavement and collide with a metal fence. He attended his GP later that day complaining of neck and shoulder pain. He had limited movement in the shoulder, radiating to the elbow, and tenderness over the trapezius muscle. He had 10 days off work. Seven months after the accident his elbow pain had resolved but S continued to have pain in his neck which was described as sharp and severe and which required him to take painkillers. He undertook a course of physiotherapy whilst in India some three months after the accident. His hobby of yoga was affected and he struggled to keep up with his exercise regime. He had previously suffered a whiplash injury which had left him susceptible to degenerative changes. An element of this flared up as a result of the relevant accident, accounting for 15 per cent of S's overall disability. S was diagnosed with a mid myofascial syndrome two and a half years after the accident caused by scar tissue, muscle spasm and sensitivity in the muscle fibres. These symptoms troubled him four times a week and he used a Tens machine. He was restricted in his ability to meditate, which mainly involved him standing on his head, and this caused a great deal of frustration. A course of treatment from an osteopath was recommended. The prognosis was that S's symptoms would not be permanent and a full recovery would be made within three and a half years to four and a half years after the accident. *General Damages*: £4,750.

SHARMA v. JAYAWARDENA [2003] 1 Q.R. 9, Deputy District Judge Lettall, CC (Bury).

Neck–pre existing disability or condition–aggravated by whiplash

3464.   C, male, aged 42 at the date of the road traffic accident and 44 at trial, suffered a whiplash injury to his neck. He had pre accident symptoms of cervical spondylitis which were significantly aggravated by the accident, which caused severe neck pain and headaches. For six months he had difficulty sleeping, could not drive and required help with personal care and housework. After six months his neck pain had improved considerably and the headaches resolved. He had physiotherapy at eight months after the accident. C had returned to his pre accident state 10 months after the accident and there would be no long-term sequelae resulting from the accident. *General Damages*: £4,000.

CERIKAN v. NAISMITH [2002] 4 Q.R. 7, Deputy District Judge Reed, CC (Cheltenham).

Neck–pre existing disability or condition–aggravated by whiplash

3465. T, male, aged 35 at the date of the road traffic accident and 37 at trial, sustained a whiplash injury to the neck and a soft tissue injury to the lower back. T had suffered from back and neck pain prior to the accident, but both were initially made considerably worse by the accident itself. As a result of the symptoms, physical activities, including domestic chores, were extremely difficult. Without the pre existing problems, the accident would have led to intrusive symptoms lasting for one to two years. At the date of the examination, 12 months after the accident, T was suffering from the effects of the accident and from pre existing degenerative disease. The prognosis was that as time passed, the effect of the accident would recede, but T was expected to experience back and neck pain at a greater level than prior to the accident, due to the natural progression of the pre existing disease. T would experience a level of symptoms from the pre existing condition, one to two years sooner than he would have done but for the accident. However, the progression rate of the pre existing disease was otherwise unaffected by the accident. The judge found that there was a period of acceleration/aggravation of 18 months and that the effect of the accident was that T would continue to suffer worse symptoms indefinitely, albeit to a minor degree. The judge considered the injury to fall within bracket 6(A)(b)(ii) of the Judicial Studies Board Guidelines. *General Damages*: £4,000.

TURFORD v. MEYER INTERNATIONAL PLC [2003] 1 Q.R. 9, Recorder Adams, CC (Leeds).

Neck–back–whiplash type injury

3466. W, female, a nurse aged 36 at the date of the accident and 40 at trial, suffered soft tissue injuries to her neck and lower back when a lorry collided with the rear of her stationary vehicle. She attended hospital on the day of the accident and the following day attended her GP, where she was provided with a soft collar which she wore for two weeks. W was a full time student at the date of the accident so she took no time off work but she suffered considerable discomfort initially when studying. Her neck symptoms largely improved within three months of the accident but continued thereafter when aggravated, particularly by driving. At trial, W suffered constant dull pain in her lower back which was easily inflamed, in particular by prolonged sitting, standing and heavy activities. The prognosis was that the symptoms would be permanent but no long term degenerative change was expected. W underwent osteopathic and chiropractic treatment and physiotherapy. Prior to the accident she had been a keen sports woman and had participated in cycling, weight lifting and swimming. She was unable to resume these activities after the accident and this was likely to be permanently the case. W was employed as a community children's nurse at trial, in a position equivalent to sister. She had been a nurse since she was 17 but was unable to return to ward nursing because of her injuries. She would have to apply for a new position in the near future as a result of reorganisation and she was concerned that her back condition would be held against her. Medical evidence suggested that she might ultimately have to give up nursing in the future. Handicap on the labour market was assessed at the equivalent of six months' earnings. The award for future losses included the cost of assistance with gardening, cleaning and chiropractic treatment. *General Damages*: (agreed and approved) £8,000. Smith v. Manchester award: £10,000. Award for future losses: £11,680. Total award: £32,670.

WINFIELD v. VASS [2002] 6 Q.R. 9, Judge Bishop, CC (Kingston upon Thames).

Neck–whiplash type injury

3467. B, female, a scientist, aged 37 at the date of two road traffic accidents and 42 at trial, sustained a whiplash type injury to her neck and injury to her left shoulder. The first accident was more serious than the second, which occurred some five months later, but both involved a rear end shunt. B was taken by ambulance to hospital after the first accident; X-rays revealed no bone injury. B was discharged with a soft collar. She suffered from pins and needles in her left arm and the left side of her face but these reduced in frequency as B avoided activities which might precipitate pain. She was away from work for five and a half months before returning on a part time basis. She returned to full time work seven months after the first accident. B underwent around 120 sessions of physiotherapy. She was much improved after two years but continued to avoid activities which might cause pain. She continued to experience significant pain if she "overdid things". She was unable to return to her hobby of horse riding for two years and, when she did return, she was able only to walk or trot with an elderly horse. She was unable to return to the dressage, jumping and cross country riding that she had enjoyed prior to the accidents. B returned to swimming approximately one year after the accident but participated at a much lower level than before. She had to give up her hobby of gardening as this caused significant pain in both her neck and shoulder. The prognosis was that the neurological problems were of a long term nature and, whilst the neck pain might improve, the prospects of further resolution of the paraesthesiae and numbness were slender. The medical expert described B's symptoms as debilitating and restricted B in housework, gardening, sport and when making long journeys. There was a 10 per cent chance of arthritis developing. The judge, who found that the symptoms and the necessity to avoid pain at home, at work and at leisure had had a significant effect on B, awarded total damages to reflect the combined effect of both road traffic accidents. *General Damages*: £10,000.

BARRETT v. HARRIS, July 5, 2001, District Judge Pelley, CC (Harlow). [*Ex rel.* Rebecca Tuck, Barrister, Old Square Chambers, 1 Verulam Buildings, London].

Neck–whiplash type injury

3468.   E, female, aged 61 at the date of the road traffic accident and 64 at trial, was a passenger in a vehicle struck from behind. She was immediately aware of neck pain. She attended her GP later that day, who advised her to take analgesics. Pain was at its most severe for the first week, then continued at a moderate but persistent level. Neck pain and headaches were brought on by sitting in one position, movement of the head to right or left or bending the head forwards. This severely curtailed her hobbies of sugarcraft, line dancing, dog walking and the amount of administrative work she could do for her husband's business. E had travelled extensively prior to the accident, but gave evidence that the longest journey she could now undertake was about 30 miles because sitting in the car brought on severe neck pain. At the date of the trial, three years and six months after the accident, she was taking painkillers daily. Medical evidence was that the accident had triggered symptoms from degenerative change in the cervical spine and the period of acceleration was five to seven years. *General Damages*: £8,000.

EDWARDS v. FORD (2002) 3 Q.R. 6, Deputy District Judge Brookes, CC (Poole).

Neck–whiplash type injury

3469.   C, female, a beauty therapist, aged 32 at the date of the road traffic accident and 35 at trial, suffered a whiplash injury to her neck and a strain to her left shoulder. C was shaken following the accident, but did not lose consciousness. She did not seek immediate treatment as there was no apparent injury, but two days later she developed an aching discomfort on the left side of her shoulder radiating through her neck and down her left arm as far as the elbow. She also experienced parasthesia in her left hand. She sought help from her GP. As the symptoms did not improve, she was referred for physiotherapy treatment commencing six weeks after the accident which she underwent for approximately one month. On discharge, she had a full range of neck movement and was symptom free except for a light twinge on rotation of the left upper limb. With time, there was deterioration in C's condition. She was re referred for physiotherapy about 18 months after the accident and received treatment, including traction. At the time of the medical examination approximately two years after the accident, C continued to have residual symptoms, including an ache on the left side of her neck radiating into the left shoulder and left arm. It was found that C had suffered an acute neck strain principally affecting the left trapezius muscle group. The prognosis was that C was one of a relatively small group of patients who remain consistently symptomatic and her condition was unlikely to improve or deteriorate with time. There was no suggestion that C would benefit from further treatment. She would be able to undertake her normal activities of daily living, but with some degree of limitation. There was no disadvantage on the labour market and C was able to continue in her pre accident employment, albeit with some discomfort. Her sports and hobbies were affected by discomfort. *General Damages*: £7,500.

COATES v. OAKMERE CARS LTD [2002] 4 Q.R. 8, District Judge O'Leary, CC (Northwich).

Neck–whiplash type injury

3470.   C, female, a human resources manager, aged 21 at the date of the road traffic accident and 25 at trial, suffered a whiplash injury. She began to feel a burning pain in her neck and back and some stiffness. The next morning she felt pain all along her spine. She attended her GP who prescribed analgesics. She took a week off from her work. C found it difficult to lie on her back, turn her head when driving, when getting in and out of bed and when sitting for long periods. She also felt a cracking sensation in her neck. The pain continued despite the prescription of stronger analgesics. She was referred for physiotherapy and underwent 10 sessions but she felt that the treatment was not helpful. Nine months after the accident, C underwent chiropractic treatment which led to rapid improvement to the extent that she no longer required analgesics. However, intermittent neck and back symptoms remained at a residual level. Carrying a shoulder bag would trigger neck pain. Heavy lifting and some housework, such as ironing and vacuuming, would cause neck ache. Occasionally she felt a cracking sensation in her neck. Sitting for prolonged periods or driving long distances caused back pain and those symptoms were likely to be permanent. *General Damages*: £6,500.

SPRIGGS v. SPRIGGS [2002] 4 Q.R. 8, District Judge Sanghera, CC (Coventry).

Neck–whiplash type injury

3471.   H, male, aged 51 at the date of accident and 53 at the hearing, was injured in a road traffic accident. There were no obvious symptoms for the first 14 days. Thereafter H began to develop a stiff neck which gradually deteriorated into spasm. It was at its worst each morning on walking and towards the end of each day, and interfered with his sleep pattern. It was aggravated by work which involved sitting at a VDU or at a work bench and by driving. At examination seven months after the accident, there was a reduction in movement in all directions of about 50 per cent. X-rays revealed pre-existing anomaly of the spine at C3, 4 and 5, together with osteoarthritic change, both of which had been asymptomatic. H gave up his principal leisure activity of playing golf. The medical evidence suggested that symptoms beyond two years after the accident may have been the result of a pre-existing condition, which might have been accelerated by five to 10 years. *General Damages* (agreed and approved by the district judge): £6,500.

HOUGHTON v. CLARK-ABDULLAH (2002) 3 Q.R. 6, District Judge Burgess, CC (Reading).

Neck–whiplash type injury

3472.   L, female, a factory worker, aged 28 at the date of the accident and 30 at trial, suffered a soft tissue injury to her neck when she was involved in a road traffic accident. She attended hospital some two to three days after the incident and was prescribed a soft collar. She suffered severe pain and stiffness for the first four to six weeks before making a gradual recovery. When seen nine months after the accident, L complained of intermittent pain in her neck provoked by any activity requiring her to bend or lift heavy objects. Although able to undertake most domestic and leisure activities, tasks such as vacuuming could be painful. She had not required any time off work. Clinical examination revealed significantly restricted movement in the cervical spine. L was examined again some 27 months after accident and continued to complain of intermittent neck pain precipitated by strenuous activity. She had undergone physiotherapy which provided only temporary relief. There had, however, been a significant improvement in her neck movement. The prognosis was that L had a 50 per cent chance of remaining asymptomatic after 10 years and that she would have residual neck pain for a long time, possibly permanently. The pain was categorised as mild and intermittent and L was able to undertake all activities. No deterioration was anticipated. *General Damages*: £6,000.

LARKIN v. MEEHAN [2002] 4 Q.R. 8, District Judge Gaskell, CC (Cardiff).

Neck–whiplash type injury

3473.   M, male, aged 30 at the date of the road traffic accident and 34 at the date of the assessment of damages hearing, suffered immediate pain and stiffness in his neck and attended hospital. He was advised to take analgesia. His symptoms continued and he attended his GP who referred him back to hospital for an X-ray. No bony injury was revealed. M wore a collar for two weeks and was off work for the same period (although part of this was the Christmas holiday). Thereafter he sought treatment from an osteopath. He continued to have osteopathy treatment whenever his symptoms flared up, particularly after playing sport. By the date of the hearing, he had undergone a total of 49 sessions of treatment (although some of that treatment was in respect of an unrelated back condition). The medical experts of both parties had prepared a joint statement, in which it was agreed that M would be left with some minor persistent symptoms. M's expert had noted slight restriction of movement on examination but E's expert had not. Prior to the accident M was a keen sportsman, playing football to a high level as well as golf, tennis and squash. Following the accident he could not play any sport for a period of two months and thereafter was unable to play to an "aggressive" level. He also suffered discomfort carrying out heavier domestic chores such as vacuuming and ironing and he had difficulty with the heavier gardening tasks. The judge accepted that the case fell within the middle bracket "(b)(ii) Moderate Neck Injuries" of the JSB guidelines. *General Damages*: £5,500.

MARKS v. EWING, August 7, 2001, Deputy District Judge Shaw, CC (Luton). [*Ex rel.* William Latimer-Sayer, Barrister, Cloisters, 1 Pump Court, Temple, London].

Neck–whiplash type injury

3474.   D, female, aged 35 at the date of the accident and 36 at trial, was injured when her vehicle was struck in the rear, causing a whiplash-type injury affecting her neck and lower back. She went to hospital the same day and an acute neck strain was diagnosed, D was given a pain killing injection. She had one and a half days off work. She also had headaches and seat belt bruising, both of which resolved within a few days. The pain in her neck and back was at its worst for the first seven to 10 days. The back pain became intermittent and gradually resolved by about twelve months after the accident. The neck pain reduced to a level described by D as "moderate" and remained at that level at trial some 19 months after the accident. D underwent a course of physiotherapy. She modified her activities to accommodate her neck symptoms. There was some restriction of movement during activities such as gardening and ironing. D had also suffered some psychological sequelae from the accident in that she had become more nervous in traffic and had nightmares on two occasions. The medical evidence was that her neck symptoms would resolve within 24 months of the accident. *General Damages*: £4,850.

DEAS v. GOODHAND, November 28, 2001, District Judge Glentworth, CC (Great Grimsby). [*Ex rel.* Andrew Granville Stafford, Barrister, 4 King's Bench Walk, Temple, London].

Neck–whiplash type injury

3475. D, female, aged 32 at the date of the road traffic accident and 33 at trial, suffered a whiplash type injury that led to severe symptoms for two weeks before beginning to improve. Symptoms resolved almost completely within five months of the accident, save for pain when she carried out housework for more than 30 minutes. D had two young children. At the hearing, eighteen months after the accident, D still experienced problems when ironing, carrying shopping and heavy domestic tasks which lasted for more than 30 minutes. These symptoms were likely to continue for the foreseeable future. The judge considered that the injury fell within the Judicial Studies Board Guidelines bracket 6(A)(b)(ii). *General Damages*: £4,750.

DURRANI v. MacDONALD, October 23, 2001, Judge Walsh, CC (Leeds). [*Ex rel.* Sean D Yates, Barrister, Zenith Chambers, 10 Park Square, Leeds].

Neck–whiplash type injury

3476. W, female, aged 56 at the date of the road traffic accident and 58 at the hearing, suffered a whiplash type injury to her neck. She was immediately aware of pain across her neck and shoulders, which increased over the next 24 hours. W did not seek any medical advice but took painkillers. She had a history of frontal headaches but after the accident she developed occipital headaches. Symptoms in her neck were at their worst for one month after the accident. They resolved partly thereafter. W took no time off work but her hobby of yoga was affected. Nine months after the accident W was diagnosed as having a sprain to the ligaments of the neck, plus moderate driving anxiety and psychological disturbance lasting two months. The neck injury was likely to resolve within two years but there was a 20 per cent chance that symptoms might persist beyond that time. At the hearing, the judge accepted W's evidence that she was still experiencing restricted neck movements and headaches which were attributable to the accident. *General Damages*: £4,600.

WHITTINGHAM v. DOBOULAY [2002] 2 Q.R. 13, District Judge Rutherford, CC (Bath).

Neck–whiplash type injury

3477. K, female, aged 50 at the date of the road traffic accident and 52 at trial, suffered a whiplash injury to her neck. She did not seek any treatment on the day of the accident, but was awoken the following morning by neck pain. She consulted her GP, who prescribed painkillers and signed her off work for a week. The pain spread to her right shoulder. She had two sessions of osteopathy and five or six sessions of physiotherapy. Her symptoms diminished but they did not completely resolve. Nine months after the accident she was still experiencing intermittent neck pain and was unable to lift her right arm above the horizontal. At trial, 21 months after the accident, she was continuing to experience pain, principally in her right shoulder. She could only drive for a limited amount of time and was reliant on her left hand to perform tasks ordinarily performed with her right hand. Medical opinion was that her symptoms would completely resolve within two years of the accident. *General Damages*: £4,100.

KELLY v. SHAH, August 10, 2001, District Judge Hewitson-Brown, CC (Luton). [*Ex rel.* Andrew Granville Stafford, Barrister, 4 King's Bench Walk, Temple, London].

Neck–whiplash type injury

3478. A, female, aged 63 at the date of the road traffic accident and 65 at the disposal hearing, suffered a whiplash injury. The symptoms included pain in the neck and shoulders, together with headaches. A court appointed expert stated that A would have low grade symptoms persisting indefinitely. There were pre existing asymptomatic degenerative changes in the cervical spine and the acceleration period was approximately 10 years. At the disposal hearing, A said that she could "go days without a problem" and would then suffer pain and headaches along with restriction of movement. All of this interfered with driving, particularly reversing and twisting her head, gardening and washing her hair. She attended an osteopath for several months, which provided some assistance. The court paid particular attention to the actual extent of the symptoms as they related to A's everyday activities, *Diamond v. Whylie* [2000] 6 Q.R. 7, [2000] C.L.Y. 1560 and *Lucas v. Lacey* (Unreported, March 24, 1997), [1997] C.L.Y. 1908 considered. *General Damages*: £4,000.

ATKINSON v. HEESOM [2002] 6 Q.R. 9, District Judge Harrison, CC (Manchester).

Spine–back

3479. S, male, an RAF engineer, aged 22 at the date of the accident and 24 at trial, suffered injury to his cervical spine and lower back when he was thrown off his motorbike. He was taken to hospital where examination revealed pain on spinal movements in all directions and substantial bruising. During the first week he suffered severe stiffness and pain along the entire length of his spine causing him difficulties walking and moving. His mobility improved after the first week but he continued to take strong painkillers and his activities were significantly curtailed. He was unable to perform domestic chores for about three months. The pain affected his sleep for about six months and he was unable to work. He took anti inflammatory medication for six months. He was unable to exercise in the gymnasium or undertake team sports for six months. He suffered anxiety and depression resulting from his restricted activities, for which he received five sessions of counselling from a community psychiatric nurse. Upon his return to work, S found many activities difficult. His symptoms continued to improve, although his back condition deteriorated approximately 12 months after the accident. By 18 months after the accident he was left with residual symptoms. A full recovery was achieved 26 months after the accident. *General Damages*: £4,000.

SMITH v. HOBAN [2003] 1 Q.R. 10, Recorder Burrows, CC (Derby).

Spine below neck

3480. P, female, a cleaner, aged 56 at the date of the accident and 60 at trial, slipped on a patch of oil and landed heavily on her buttocks. Her lower back became very painful. She was unable to continue work that day and left early. The following day her pain increased. Her GP referred her to hospital where an X-ray revealed a fracture of the distal sacrum without gross displacement and a soft tissue sprain of the lumbar spine. The pain persisted and P resigned from her job. After six months the pain around the sacral area eased. However P's lower back remained painful and stiff, particularly when standing. She had difficulty sleeping and getting in and out of bed. Strenuous activity aggravated the pain but analgesics alleviated it. She could no longer undertake her hobbies of gardening and DIY because of the difficulty in lifting and bending. Housework, such as vacuum cleaning and ironing, caused her pain. The continuing symptoms were likely to be permanent. A second X-ray showed degenerative change at the lumbo-sacral junction. The accident accelerated symptoms that P would have suffered in any event by a period of about two years. *General Damages*: £4,750.

POTTER v. LINCOLNSHIRE CC [2002] 4 Q.R. 9, Deputy District Judge Thomas, CC (Lincoln).

Spine below neck–pre-existing disability or condition–aggravated by whiplash

3481. Y, male, a manual worker, aged 47 at the date of the incident and 50 at trial, sustained injury to his spine when a stacking crane he was operating failed to stop at ground level and continued travelling at speed to strike the buffers. Y had clear signs of pre-existing degeneration of the spine which had produced two minor episodes of pain some years before the accident. Apart from those episodes he had been pain-free. The accident aggravated the condition of his spine and he endured two years' continuous severe pain, including sciatic pain, when an operation to fuse L5 and S1 was carried out. This operation was a success and the experts agreed that it was reasonable to regard him as capable of working again, but in sedentary employment only, one year after the operation. He would never be able to return to manual work. But for the accident, he would have been able to continue in the same manual employment or similar employment for a further seven years or so. Y also suffered from severe depression and anxiety, including nightmares, panic attacks and agoraphobia. These symptoms too were greatly improved as a result of the fusion operation. There had been signs of improvement before that. There was however a real danger of relapses and it was agreed between the experts that he would still benefit from therapy. The award for future loss of earnings was based on an acceptance that (1) but for the accident, Y could have continued in his pre-accident manual employment until about 2008; (2) he was likely to suffer a reduction in earnings of £2,000 per annum, and (3) he would probably find difficulty in obtaining and keeping jobs and would therefore experience periods of unemployment, *Blamire v. South Cumbria HA* [1993] P.I.Q.R. Q1, [1993] C.L.Y. 1403 applied. *General Damages*: £18,000. Past loss of earnings award: £29,046. Past care award: £2,800. Future loss of earnings award: £17,500.

YOUNISS v. SALVESEN LOGISTICS LTD (T/A SALSTREAM) [2002] 2 Q.R. 12, Judge Critchlow, CC (Uxbridge).

Spine below neck–psychiatric damage

3482. S, female, a police officer, aged 22 at the date of the assault, in January 1985, and 38 at the hearing, sustained damage to the invertebral discs and facet joints at L4/5. Spinal fusion between the fourth and fifth lumbar vertebrae with a Hartshill loop and wires and bone grafting of the fact joints was carried out in July 1990. The procedure left a 13cm surgical scar in the midline of her lumbar region. S received a chymopapain injection into her spine in 1993, eight years after the assault. In December 1994, S underwent a discectomy and in June and September of that year, discograms were carried out under general anaesthetic. S attended numerous sessions of osteopathy and physiotherapy. Constant low back pain remained, which S compared to toothache. The pain was aggravated by bending, lifting and reaching. S could stand for 15 to 20 minutes and sit for 20 minutes before she had to change her position. Walking was restricted to 500 yards. She had taken to using a stick shortly before the hearing. S's symptoms were likely to continue at their then current level permanently. She had experienced bouts of sciatica since the assault. These had abated by the time of the hearing. S continued to receive physiotherapy treatment and used painkillers every day. She could manage light housework. She was prevented from engaging in her pre accident activities of hockey, netball, judo and weight training. Her fitness reduced and she put on weight. She looked after her two young children, but with difficulty. She could not wear high heeled shoes. The injuries led to S's medical retirement in May 1994 some years after the assault. Thereafter she had some secretarial type work and she could return to that type of work in the future. S had suffered from a recurrent depression disorder since 1991. This stemmed from her chronic back pain and the premature end of her police career. The symptoms did not prevent her working, but probably had an aggravating influence on her back pain. The prognosis relating to those symptoms reflected the further evolution of her back symptoms and her future employment path. *General Damages*: £25,000. Past loss of earnings award: £55,000. Smith v. Manchester award: £5,000. Loss of pension award: £22,339. Further loss of earnings award: £78,100. Total award: £185,439.

SMITH (CICA: QUANTUM: 2002), *Re* [2003] 1 Q.R. 10, D Bradbeer (Chairman), CICA (Durham).

Back–psychiatric damage

3483. H, male, aged 59 at the date of the road traffic accident and 61 at trial, sustained multiple injuries, the most serious of which was an exacerbation of low back pain with pins and needles in both legs. The back pain improved after three months and returned to its pre-accident state within two years of the date of the accident. He also suffered soft tissue injuries to his neck which resolved after one year. H suffered from marked aching all over his body for a few days after the accident. H feared for his life at the time of the accident and subsequently suffered from serious flashbacks and nightmares associated with post traumatic stress disorder which lasted in a severe form for two weeks. H also suffered from situational anxiety at the accident scene. The psychological symptoms persisted for a period of one year and had resolved by the time of trial. As a result of the injuries, H was unable to perform repairs to his patio and terracing walls and therefore had to employ a builder to do the repairs. H was awarded the cost of labour for the repairs to his patio and terracing walls in addition to general damages. *General Damages*: £6,250.

HOCKEDY v. BESSELL & EXEL LOGISTICS (2002) 3 Q.R. 7, District Judge Rutherford, CC (Bath).

Back–neck

3484. R, male, a security officer, aged 27 at the date of the road traffic accident and 31 at trial, initially felt dazed and shaken. The following morning he was aching all over his body. He took a week off work. He suffered right shoulder discomfort for two days, chest pain for a week and cuts and abrasions to his hands and knees which settled over two weeks. R's main problem was the neck and back symptoms. His neck was severely painful for the first week. Thereafter, it began to settle, although it would still ache every day, particularly after long periods of looking down, when standing at the sink washing dishes, when washing his hair or when driving long distances. There were occasional headaches. His back was initially very painful but began to settle, becoming an ache after the first two weeks. The symptoms were situated in the lumbar sacral area. The ache radiated into the right leg just above the knee. It was particularly acute on prolonged sitting, driving or standing. His back symptoms restricted his ability to perform housework and undertake his hobbies of keep fit and football. an MRI scan showed degenerative changes in R's lumbar spine. The neck and back symptoms were expected to resolve within six to nine months if R returned to some exercise activity. The back problems were expected to persist at the level described. The accident most likely accelerated, by a period of between five and 10 years, lumbar symptoms which R would have suffered in the future in any event. *General Damages*: £6,750.

ROSE v. SHIELDS [2002] 6 Q.R. 10, District Judge Eaton, CC (Leicester).

Back–whiplash type injury

3485. J, female, a sales supporter aged 26 at the date of the accident and 30 at the disposal hearing, suffered injuries in a side impact road traffic accident. The steering wheel struck her chest in the collision and her head rebounded against the headrest. She was taken to casualty and diagnosed as having sustained a soft tissue injury to her chest wall, whiplash to the neck and a soft tissue injury to her lower back. J attended her GP the day after the accident and was prescribed painkillers and told to undertake deep breathing exercises. She was absent from work for one week. She attended a two month course of physiotherapy which helped to alleviate the symptoms in the lower back. The injury to her chest wall and to the neck resolved completely within four weeks of the accident but the lower back symptoms improved more slowly. At the date of the hearing, J still experienced lower back pain after long car journeys or when she had been sitting down for two hours or more. She also suffered pain in her lower back when menstruating for which she had to take painkillers three or four times per month. These continuing symptoms were likely to be permanent. The judge held that J's case fell within the JSB guidelines 6(B)(b)(ii) moderate bracket for back injuries. *General Damages*: £8,000.

JOGI v. GILL [2002] 6 Q.R. 10, Recorder Cousins Q.C., CC (Birmingham).

Back–whiplash type injury

3486. G, male, a steel erector aged 35 at the date of the accident and 39 at trial, was the driver of a vehicle involved in a head on collision. He sustained a low back strain, an acute neck sprain and soft tissue injury to the right knee. He was taken to hospital where whiplash was diagnosed. Next morning he was unable to move. The pain was severe for two weeks and then moderate to severe for six weeks. During this eight week period he was off work and needed assistance from his partner with personal and domestic tasks. On his return to work he was on light duties for a number of weeks. His neck and knee symptoms disappeared between the date of the first medical report six months after the accident and the second one which was 15 months after the accident. Aching and stiffness in the lower back, particularly provoked by his work, remained at the date of trial, over three years after the accident. It was found on the basis of the medical evidence that the accident had caused symptoms in the back for a period of six months. Any symptoms thereafter were constitutional; however the onset of those constitutional symptoms had been accelerated by a period of three to four years by the accident. *General Damages*: £7,000.

GUISE v. PLP MOTORS LTD (2002) 3 Q.R. 7, District Judge Perry, CC (Warrington).

Back–whiplash type injury

3487. D, male, a post clerk, aged 19 at the date of the road traffic accident and 23 at the disposal hearing, sustained a ruptured annulus fibrosis of one of the lumbar discs in his lower back and a whiplash injury to his cervical spine. He also suffered from travel anxiety as a result of the accident. D attended his local hospital on the day of the collision complaining of pain in his lower back and neck. He was prescribed painkillers. D was subsequently advised by his GP to attend a course of physiotherapy. He attended a total of 22 sessions over a two month period. He was absent from work for six weeks and upon his return to work was put on light duties for about nine weeks. D's whiplash injury resolved after a period of two weeks. His travel anxiety, which constituted a general fear of travelling by car, settled within six months of the accident. D's lower back symptoms, however, were acute and intrusive for a period of two months after the accident. As a result he could not play football for approximately six months. Thereafter he suffered minor residual back symptoms, which plateaued after a period of 18 months. Medical opinion was that D would continue to suffer minor residual symptoms in his back on a recurring basis indefinitely, particularly after driving long distances. Such symptoms would not, however, interfere with D's daily activities. *General Damages*: £4,000.

DUDGEON v. SHAW [2002] 6 Q.R.10, District Judge Ganghera, CC (Nuneaton).

Shoulder

3488. K, male, a telecommunications engineer, aged 40 at the date of the accident and 43 at trial, sustained a dislocation of the left shoulder and minor bruising injuries as a result of a road traffic accident. Damage was caused to the acromio-clavicular joint and the coraco-clavicular ligaments. His left, dominant, arm was placed in a sling which he wore for four weeks after the accident, but he returned to work after only one day and a weekend recovery period. K suffered constant pain for two weeks and thereafter acute symptoms remained for about three months. K used Ibuprofen on a daily basis for 18 months after the accident and thereafter on an occasional basis. His sleep was disturbed on a regular basis for approximately two years following the accident but thereafter this was reduced to approximately a twice monthly occurrence. The effect of the injury to his dominant arm did not cause any loss of range of movement but there was initial difficulty in performing household tasks and personal grooming. At trial, K reported a general loss of strength in his left arm and he continued to experience problems, particularly when carrying heavy objects. A further feature of the injury was the permanent physical deformity of the clavicle. He was unable to return to his pre-accident hobbies of swimming and running as a result of the injury. K's change in character and reluctance to return to motorcycling and long distance competitive cycling were not held to be relevant for the award of general damages due to his failure to seek psychological treatment after advice to do so. The risk of degenerative arthritis was slightly increased. *General Damages*: £7,500.

KNOTT v. BROWN, October 22, 2001, District Judge Tennant, CC (Southampton). [*Ex rel.* Stuart McGhee, Barrister, College Chambers, 19 Carlton Crescent, Southampton].

Arm

3489. W, female, a receptionist, aged 55 at the date of the accident and 59 at trial, tripped on a defective pavement and sustained a soft tissue injury to her right, dominant, forearm. Initially, W went home but was in too much pain even to lift a kettle. The next day, her son took her to hospital. X-rays were taken and a fracture of the radius was suspected. A full arm plaster cast was applied which remained in situ for five weeks. W experienced severe pain, rather than discomfort, as a result of the injury. In addition, she suffered reduced grip strength. She was off work six to seven weeks, suffered sleep disturbance and took Coproxamol for a period of around eight weeks. It was three months before W started to recover during which time she needed assistance with domestic chores, personal care, dressing and gardening. When examined 10 months after the accident, W suffered occasional pain only. However she continued to have reduced grip strength, some stiffness and occasional pins and needles when driving. At the trial some three years and nine months after the accident, the stiffness had resolved. However, while matters had improved, W still felt her right hand was weaker than before the accident and she continued to suffer from pins and needles when driving. The initial prognosis had been for full recovery within two years of the accident. *General Damages*: £4,000.

WILKINSON-ROUTLEDGE v. BEDFORDSHIRE CC [2002] 4 Q.R. 9, District Judge Davis, CC (Watford).

Arm–psychiatric damage

3490. M, female, a police constable, aged 24 at the date of the assault and 31 at the hearing, suffered a soft-tissue shoulder injury while restraining a suspect. She developed a complex regional pain syndrome, with some constant pain in the right arm/shoulder, and severe shooting pains if the arm was exerted or knocked, requiring her to take to her bed often for up to three days. She had weakness of the arm, and shaking, and tended to protect it in a sling or jacket pocket. She could not lift more than half a cup of coffee and could not use the arm for any domestic or personal tasks or writing. There was no observable muscle wasting. Physiotherapy and stellate ganglion blocks had failed to make any improvement and her condition was expected to be permanent. M also suffered post traumatic stress disorder with moderate depression and mild anxiety. The depression lowered her pain threshold, which amplified the pain and in turn exacerbated the depression. Anti-depressants and cognitive behavioural therapy had failed. The award for general damages included an element for loss of her career. M had been a police officer for three years at the date of the assault. The multiplier of 17.37 was reduced to 15.5 to take account of the possibility of improvement and a smaller possibility of finding any gainful employment. The future care award was based on British Nursing Association rates reduced by one third for gratuitous care, and a further one third deduction from M's estimate of needing one and a half hours care per day plus two hours' housework. Her estimate of 48 hours' assistance per week with her baby to age four was accepted. A further five per cent discount was applied to a multiplier to age 70 to provide for a small possibility of improvement. *General Damages*: £27,000. Past loss of earnings award: £67,715. Future loss of earnings award: £160,325. Past care award: £9,000. Future care award: £60,552. Award for loss of pension: £82,585. Total award: £407,827.

M (CICA: QUANTUM: 2001), *Re* [2002] 2 Q.R. 13, Michael Brent Q.C. (Chairman), CICA (London).

Arm–non facial scars

3491.   D, male, aged nine at the date of the accident and 13 at the hearing, was injured whilst on holiday with his family when a stable hand assisted him to mount his horse in order to go pony trekking. D was propelled over the saddle and onto the floor at the other side of the horse. He sustained a minor head injury, a median nerve injury and fractures of the shafts of the right dominant radius and ulna with angulation and shortening. He underwent open reduction and internal fixation with plates and screws to both bones. He was in hospital for three days. The plaster was removed after three months. The plates and screws were removed 10 months later under general anaesthetic. D was off school for five weeks. D experienced difficulties in writing, playing sports and riding a bicycle, which caused the forearm to ache. He was left with aching in the forearm following activity, which was expected to resolve 18 months after the accident but in fact continued for much longer, although it was not permanent and D made a full recovery aside from the scarring to his arm. D was left with noticeable scars, measuring 9cm on the radius and 10cm on the ulna, described by the medical expert as "horrible". The scars itched and required protection from the sun. There was a possibility that the appearance of the scarring would be improved by further revision surgery, which the judge considered it would be reasonable for D to undergo at a later date if he wished. *General Damages*: £8,000. Award for cost of future revision surgery: £1,000.

DODD (A CHILD) v. BAILEY MILL HOLIDAY COMPLEX [2003] 1 Q.R. 11, District Judge Wood, CC (Harrogate).

Elbow

3492.   D, female, retired, aged 64 at the date of the accident and 69 at trial, tripped on a paving slab which was about 3 cm proud. D sustained a major injury to her right elbow in the form of a severely comminuted fracture of the olecranon and fracture dislocation of the radial head (Monteggia fracture), grazes on her face and bruises on both arms. She was admitted to hospital and the following day she had open reduction and internal fixation of the fracture with plate and screws. A bone graft was obtained from the right iliac crest. She was in hospital for five days and then discharged into her daughter's care. She was obliged to remain with her daughter for eight months given her disability and lack of confidence to go out. D had nightmares following the accident and was concerned because of her heart condition. She had 41 sessions of physiotherapy which she found painful. As a result of the elbow injury, D began to suffer from pain and stiffness in her right wrist, arm and shoulder. Consequently, being right hand dominant, she found it difficult to look after herself properly. By about 15 months after the accident D had developed osteoarthritis to the elbow and it was anticipated that this would worsen. Movement of the elbow was grossly restricted with a flexion range of 30 to 90 degrees and supination and pronation were very limited. Movements of the right wrist were equally limited with diminished grip in the hand, the little finger being unable to participate in the gripping process. D's social life was severely curtailed. She was unable to go out for walks as she used to, or to pursue her hobby of cake making. By the trial it was thought that she would benefit from total elbow replacement, at which time the metal work could be removed. Because of D's heart condition there was some uncertainty as to whether she could undergo the necessary operation although D's evidence that she intended to do so was accepted. *General Damages*: £22,000. Award for future medical treatment: £10,000.

DAVEY v. THURROCK BC [2002] 2 Q.R. 14, Judge Dedman, CC (Southend).

Elbow

3493. The claimant, female, a clerical assistant, aged 21 at the date of the accident and 24 at trial, suffered an undisplaced fracture to the left non dominant radial head when she slipped and fell whilst at the defendant's public house premises. She attended hospital where she was provided with a sling which she wore for two weeks. The claimant was in significant pain during that period and suffered ongoing pain and discomfort for two months after the accident. She received intensive physiotherapy treatment over the same period. Thereafter, she suffered intermittent aching, particularly at the end of the working day. When examined one year after the accident she complained of sporadic discomfort but had sought no further medical treatment. There was no functional disability. The prognosis was that there would be continued improvement such as that within a further year the claimant would be symptom free. At trial, the claimant continued to complain of occasional aching in cold weather. There was no risk of osteoarthritis developing. *General Damages*: £4,000.

CHAPMAN v. CARROLL [2002] 4 Q.R. 9, Judge Roach, CC (Bristol).

Elbow–spine

3494. E, male, a roofer, aged 28 at the date of the accident and 34 at the hearing, was injured when he fell from the roof on which he was working. He suffered injuries to his elbow comprising a fracture of the radius bone and head, and also an injury to his right brachial plexus. E subsequently suffered severe pain and muscle wasting in the arm and also headaches and neck pain. He had serious limitation of movement in the cervical spine. A spinal cord stimulator was implanted. E was diagnosed as suffering from reflex sympathetic dystrophy. As a result of his injuries, E suffered extremely severe depression. He suffered pain with every movement and he would never recover, nor work again. He required constant care from his wife or carer and this need would remain indefinitely, *Housecroft v. Burnett* [1986] 1 All E.R. 332, [1986] C.L.Y. 989 considered. *General Damages*: £100,000. Future loss of earnings award (multiplier 16): £208,000. Past care award (discounted by 25 per cent to take account of gratuitous care provided by wife): £107,390. Future care award: £378,840.

EVANS v. PONTYPRIDD ROOFING LTD, [2001] EWCA Civ 1657, [2002] P.I.Q.R. Q5, May, L.J., CA.

Wrist

3495. M, male, a quality control officer aged 24 at the date of the accident and 27 at trial, suffered a major fracture dislocation to his non dominant left wrist when knocked from his motorcycle in a road traffic accident. He was rendered unconscious and was transferred to hospital. A plaster cast was applied and this remained in situ for six weeks. Thereafter the left wrist continued to ache. It was likely that he would continue to suffer symptoms with his wrist. There was a slightly increased risk of degenerative changes taking place within the wrist and he was at risk on the open labour market for heavy strenuous manual work if the degenerative changes developed. He also suffered soft tissue injuries to his left leg and neck and bruising to his testicles. He suffered a concussive head injury. For two years after the accident he complained of headaches, which were continuing, were constitutional in nature. M was absent from work for three weeks and on his return he was put on light work for several weeks. He had not returned to riding a motorcycle. *General Damages*: £8,000. Smith v. Manchester award: £1,000.

MOSS v. PILKINGTON (2002) 3 Q.R. 7, District Judge Talbot, CC (Chorley).

Wrist

3496.   T, male, a carpenter, aged 22 at the date of the road traffic accident and 24 at trial, suffered a fracture of the left, non-dominant scaphoid, which was treated conservatively. The fracture united satisfactorily but with a degree of sclerosis. Three months after the accident T was still suffering constant pain, discomfort and restriction of movement in the wrist. Seventeen months post accident, there had been some improvement but T was still tender over the scaphoid bone, and movement of his left wrist was reduced by a third when compared to the right limb. His symptoms were likely to be permanent and they were aggravated by some aspects of his work. T also suffered a haematoma in his scrotal area, which was painful for about two weeks, and a two day soft tissue injury to his neck. *General Damages*: £7,500.

TIERNEY v. KOH, August 6, 2001, District Judge Humphreys-Roberts, CC (Southport). [*Ex rel.* Tim Grover, Barrister, 7 Harrington Street, Liverpool].

Wrist

3497.   L, female, a sales representative, aged 54 at the date of the accident and 56 at the assessment, suffered an impacted, undisplaced fracture to the lower end of the radius of her right, dominant arm. L was in plaster for six weeks and absent from work for 17 weeks. Thereafter she returned to light duties and remained dependant upon the assistance of family and friends. She had four dogs and a large house which she also ran as a small bed and breakfast property. L gave evidence that she suffered significant difficulties in running that establishment as a result of ongoing weakness in her wrist. Although the fracture had healed soundly, underlying and previously asymptomatic degenerative change was accelerated by the accident, advancing the onset of symptoms and loss of amenity by a period of two years. The judge found that L required help with washing, bathing, dressing and personal hygiene together with some assistance in respect of transport, shopping, cleaning and cooking. An award for care and assistance was made at three hours per day for the first six weeks, two hours per day from the removal of the plaster cast until L resumed driving and half an hour per day for a period of six months thereafter. The total number of hours was therefore 357, for which the rate of £4.50 per hour was held to be appropriate. *General Damages*: £6,750. Award for past care: £1,606.

LANGFORD v. SCOTTISH POWER PLC [2002] 6 Q.R. 11, District Judge Brown, CC (Telford).

Hand

3498.   H, female, retired, aged 73 at the date of the accident and 75 at trial, slipped and fell at shop premises. She landed upon her left non dominant hand. At hospital, X-rays revealed a fracture to the distal end of the radius bone within the left forearm adjacent to the wrist joint. A plaster cast was applied which she wore for six weeks. H's wedding ring had to be cut off as a result of swelling. H gradually recovered mobility in the wrist after removal of the cast but she continued to suffer pain and stiffness in the wrist each morning some three months after the accident. She had difficulty with domestic tasks such as washing, dressing and brushing her hair. Clinical examinations revealed some small deviation in the wrist bone which amounted to a minimal cosmetic deficit. The prognosis was that all symptoms would resolve between 18 months to two years after the accident. H gave evidence that her symptoms had resolved within that timescale although the slight, bony abnormality remained and would be permanent, although it did not constitute a functional impairment. *General Damages*: £4,000.

HARVEY v. TESCO PLC [2002] 6 Q.R. 11, District Judge Doel, CC (Pontypridd).

Hand–foot

3499. H, male, a member of the Royal Engineers, aged 22 at the date of the injury and 27 at the assessment, was on active service in Bosnia and on duty in the mountains when he was stranded in heavy snow without his heavy weather equipment. In consequence, H had to spend two nights in sub freezing temperatures in a Land Rover vehicle before he was rescued. H suffered what was described as a moderate to severe non freezing cold injury to his hands and feet. The resulting neuropathy affected the blood circulation to his hands and feet. Small variations in temperature could have a significantly adverse effect on his symptoms. The hands and feet also tended to suffer from recurring blistering, or pompholyx. Intermittently H lost substantial use of his hands and feet and in addition suffered marked pain and parathesiae. Conversely, in warmer conditions H's feet and hands sweated profusely, which could not be readily controlled. His condition was permanent, but would not deteriorate. H was medically discharged from the army but was unable to pursue his career as a carpenter in civilian life to full capacity because he could not work outside or in cold conditions. He consequently suffered a substantial loss of future earnings. *General Damages*: (agreed and approved) £25,000.

HOPE v. MINISTRY OF DEFENCE [2003] 1 Q.R. 11, Judge Sennitt, CC (Cambridge).

Fingers

3500. B, male, a sheet metal worker, aged 58 at the date of the accident and 60 at the disposal hearing, was operating a machine when a blade on it came down onto the index finger of his dominant right hand, cutting off the tip obliquely through the distal phalanx. He was taken to hospital where, under local anaesthetic, the finger was surgically amputated through the distal interphalangeal joint. B's finger was reduced in length by 2.8cm and his nail was missing. He had about six weeks off work and then returned to his original job. B was left with a permanent cosmetic deformity. The end of his finger was numb, resulting in loss of manual dexterity. He had particular difficulty with small objects and had to learn how to perform various tasks using his middle finger. The numbness was increased in cold weather, but there was no pain. B's grip strength was initially reduced to 55 per cent of normal, but was expected to return to 75 per cent of normal. It was not expected that neuroma would develop. The expert assessed B's disability at seven per cent from the American Medical Association's guide to evaluation of impairment of hand function. *General Damages*: £6,500.

BLAZAR v. CROSSKILL VENTILATION [2002] 4 Q.R. 9, District Judge Rogers, CC (Norwich).

Fingers

3501. H, female, aged 58 at the date of the accident and 61 at trial, was injured when she slipped and fell on a bridge owned by B. H, who was right hand dominant, sustained fractures of the metacarpals of the middle and ring fingers of her left hand. A plaster slab was applied and remained in place for one month. After the plaster was removed, H had some discomfort and a restricted range of movement which improved over the following two months. Two years after the accident she was still unable to lift or carry anything heavy in her left hand, the finger tips remaining 1.5cm away from the palm and she could not make a full fist. She was not prevented from carrying out any activities, but had adapted her approach to certain tasks. The contour of the hand was not normal and the knuckle of the ring finger was lost. On examination two years after the accident, the fingers of the left hand had a full range of movement individually, but the fingers could not all be flexed at the same time. It was found that the fracture had healed with no rotation or deformity, but with a minor degree of shortening, which would not result in any significant mechanical problem. The ongoing problems appeared to arise from adhesion to the soft tissues of the dorsum of the hand preventing full flexion of the fingers sufficiently to allow for a strong grip. No further improvement or deterioration was expected. It was found to be significant that H would have less confidence in the left hand than the right as a result of the injury but the permanent loss of function was described as a minor inconvenience, not limiting her activities in any way. *General Damages*: £5,000.

HEPPINSTALL v. BLACKPOOL PLEASURE BEACH [2002] 6 Q.R. 11, Judge Barr-Young, CC (Pontefract).

Thumb

3502.   R, female, a housewife aged 30 at the date of the accident and 33 at trial, tripped over a raised paving slab and fell forward onto her hands and knees. Her left non dominant thumb was immediately painful, but at the time she thought she had merely bruised and sprained it. However it remained painful and swollen over the next week until she attended a function where she caught it in the back of a chair. She went to hospital where exploration under general anaesthetic revealed the ulnar collateral ligament had been avulsed and it was then reinserted. She had an overnight stay in hospital following the operation and was discharged wearing a splint. She wore the splint for three months before being supplied with another which she wore at night for a further period of about 18 months. She was also referred for a course of occupational therapy. For about four weeks after the operation, R was restricted in what she could do about the house and needed the help of her eldest children and her parents. She had made a substantial recovery after about four months but was left with a permanent restriction in flexion of about 20 degrees and an operation scar measuring 4cm which the judge referred to as a "significant blemish that she does not make much of". R experienced some discomfort or aching in the thumb in cold weather or after prolonged activity such as computer games with her children and this was also expected to be permanent. At the time of the accident, R had been attending the last two weeks of a computer course, which she was unable to complete. This was a considerable disappointment to her especially when she learnt that to earn the qualification she had been seeking she would have to repeat the whole 30 week course. *General Damages*: £4,500.

REED v. BARKING & DAGENHAM LBC [2002] 4 Q.R.10, Judge Paynter-Reece, CC (Romford).

Thumb—non facial scars

3503.   K, female, aged 11 at the date of the accident and 14 at trial, sustained injury when using a defective netball inflation pump. The thumb on K's right, dominant, hand was partially amputated. She underwent four operations and, although the thumb was almost functionally normal at trial, it was disfigured and scarred. The thumb was very misshapen and K was embarrassed by it. It hurt in cold weather. K's handwriting had suffered as a result of the injury. The scarring and disfigurement were permanent and the judge found that K would become more conscious of her thumb as she grew older. *General Damages*: £6,500.

K (A CHILD) v. CHADWELL PRIMARY SCHOOL GOVERNORS [2003] 1 Q.R.11, Judge Hornby, CC (Bow).

Sacrum, pelvis and hips–post traumatic stress disorder

3504. A, female, aged 61 at the date of the injury and 64 at the date of the hearing, was struck by a piece of boarding measuring three feet by four feet which was blown from Z's premises. A suffered a fractured pelvis, cuts to the face, elbow and leg, two black eyes, a sprain to the neck and a closed head injury, although there was no loss of consciousness. The most disabling physical injury was the pelvic fracture. A remained in hospital for one week and, upon discharge, she had very restricted mobility. She used crutches for eight weeks and suffered from bad pain in the pelvis for 10 weeks. A could not go to the shops at all for two months. She received extensive help from members of her family with household chores and shopping. She also suffered psychological injury including post traumatic stress disorder of mild severity and associated depressive symptoms. She became socially withdrawn and gave up her hobbies of gardening and going out to the local club. She suffered disturbed sleep, reduced appetite and irritability. She became fearful of high winds and would not go out in such weather. She took anti depressant medication for one year. Medical opinion was that the symptoms arising from the physical injuries were limited to a period of about six months. Any further physical disability was attributable to A's pre existing arthritic condition. The psychological condition had largely resolved written six months of the accident but a degree of continuing care was required for up to three years. *General Damages*: £8,000.

ADAMS v. ZAHEER [2003] 1 Q.R. 13, Judge Taylor, CC (Leeds).

Leg

3505. S, male, a manager, aged 38 at the date of the road traffic accident and 42 at trial, suffered injury in a head on collision. He sustained a mid-shaft fracture to the right femur, four fractured ribs, cuts, bruising and psychological trauma. He was admitted to hospital for three weeks. The femur was treated with a steel pin retained by two nails. There were complications with a pulmonary embolus resulting from the fracture, but problems resolved after a few days. A right chest drain was inserted. Three days after the accident S suffered a breakdown, crying uncontrollably. He was able to dispense with walking crutches eight to nine weeks after the accident but he could only walk short distances. At trial, his right leg was fixed in 20 degrees external rotation. He had ongoing difficulties around the home but received assistance from his wife. Prior to the accident, S used to do his own DIY but his range of tasks was restricted due to his injuries. He had difficulty driving for long distances. He was unable to do heavy manual work but was able to return to his own job. There was a 20 per cent chance that he would require a total hip replacement within 10 years. The psychological trauma had been effectively treated with psychotherapy about two years after the accident. *General Damages*: £17,500. *Smith v. Manchester* award: £8,226. Award for past care: £2,244. Award for future care: £11,750. Award for future treatment: £1,200. Award for future DIY: £10,000. Total award including interest: £54,576.

SEAWARD v. SHEPHERD [2002] 2 Q.R. 14, District Judge Strachan, CC (Milton Keynes).

Leg

3506. S, male, a school teacher, aged 47 at the date of the accident and 49 at trial, sustained injuries when his motorcycle was struck by F's car. S suffered an open fracture of the lower third of his left tibia. He attended hospital, where the fracture was stabilised with a locked intra-medullary nail. S spent three weeks in hospital. On discharge, he was non weight bearing on crutches. Approximately one month later the proximal locking screw was removed under general anaesthetic and S subsequently progressed to full weight bearing. X-rays confirmed satisfactory alignment of the fracture. Approximately six months later S was discharged from the fracture clinic. S's residual disabilities included difficulty when kneeling, walking with a slight limp and a reduced walking distance. His enjoyment of visiting art galleries was reduced, he tired easily and his enjoyment of swimming was reduced because of pain in his leg when in cold water. He had a 10 per cent reduction of movement in the left ankle and the ankle gave way when he was lifting his young children. It was accepted that the situation was unlikely to improve. S was left with unsightly scars on his leg caused by a burn from the motorcycle silencer and by surgery at the fracture site. *General Damages*: £14,000. Award for past care: £3,475.

SHIRES v. FORD [2002] 4 Q.R. 15, District Judge Derbyshire, CC (Guildford).

Leg

3507. K, female, aged five at the date of the accident and seven at the hearing, was walking along a footpath when she tripped over a broken concrete post. K became partly impaled on a protruding metal reinforcing rod and, as she struggled to release her leg, she tore the skin of her left thigh. K was taken to hospital where she was x-rayed. No bone injury or foreign bodies were identified. K was diagnosed as suffering an L shaped laceration to the medial aspect of her left thigh, measuring 4cm. There was no neuro-vascular deficit and there was normal movement in the leg, the knee and the hip.The wound was cleaned and closed using absorbable stitches and adhesive strips over the skin. K was upset and suffered three nights of disturbed sleep. She was absent from school for one week. At examination six months after the accident, K was diagnosed as having suffered a large laceration to the inner left thigh which had left a large and obvious scar.The scar was unlikely to improve in appearance, nor was it likely to improve with plastic surgery. *General Damages*: £6,000.

K (A CHILD) v. DONCASTER MBC, September 6, 2001, District Judge Stocken, CC (Doncaster). [*Ex rel.* Hodgkinsons, Solicitors, The Old Manse, 14 Lumley Avenue, Skegness].

Leg

3508. R, male, aged six at the date of the injury and seven at the child settlement hearing, suffered an angulated fracture to the left tibia and fibula whilst taking part in a game of football organised by H. R underwent manipulation under anaesthesia and was in a plaster cast for approximately nine weeks. It took a considerable amount of persuasion for R to begin walking again and the help of a physiotherapist was enlisted. Some four months after the accident R was walking satisfactorily and he had made a full recovery six months after the accident. There was no risk of development of osteoarthritis arising from the injury. *General Damages*: £5,500.

R (A CHILD) v. HULL CITY AFC [2002] 2 Q.R. 14, Deputy District Judge Wildsmith, CC (York).

Leg–post traumatic stress disorder

3509. C, male, a quality assurance manager, aged 38 at the date of the road traffic accident and 42 at trial, sustained a fracture to the right femur, four fractured ribs, a head injury resulting in a brief period of unconsciousness, a soft tissue injury to the left shin requiring stitches, and post traumatic stress disorder. The fracture to the femur was secured with an intramedullary nail. C remained in hospital for three weeks. A chest drain was inserted. He developed blood clots in both lungs, necessitating a six month course of Warfarin. C relied on crutches for 10 weeks and could not drive for two months. He returned to work after three months, thereafter working part time for two months. He required continuous medication for pain relief for 12 months and attended physiotherapy for 18 months. Symptoms of PTSD, including flashbacks, nightmares, driving anxiety and claustrophobia, resolved within two years. The intramedullary nail was removed two years post accident. The femur united with 30 degrees of external rotation. There was a 20 per cent increased risk of C requiring hip replacement surgery. He walked with limp and used shoe inserts. Although dependent upon a walking stick, he could manage a distance of three miles. The surgical scars were prone to irritation. After bathing, his wife would dress them and would help C to dry himself. A claim for care was raised in relation to this and other additional household chores with which she was burdened. C could no longer enjoy golf, his main leisure interest. Whilst his job in a large international company was secure for the moment, there had been a programme of rationalisation in recent years. It was found that there was a real danger that he would need to seek alternative employment in 10 years. Disadvantage in the labour market was assessed at one year's net salary, discounted for early receipt. On appeal, the judge commented that the fractured femur alone would have attracted an award of £14,000. *General Damages*: £17,750. Smith v. Manchester award: £8,226. Award for past gratuitous care: £2,243. Award for future gratuitous care: £11,750. Award for future DIY: £10,000. Award for risk of future surgery: £1,200.

SEAWARD v. SHEPHARD [2003] 1 Q.R. 12, Judge Serota, CC (Milton Keynes).

Knee

3510.   C, male, aged 40 at the date of the accident and 44 at trial, was struck on the foot when a door, which had been sticking, opened suddenly causing him to lose his balance. His right knee was badly twisted in the resulting fall. Immediately after the accident the knee became swollen and painful. Attempts to walk resulted in severe pain and the knee giving way. C attended hospital as an outpatient on a number of occasions. He was treated with painkillers and physiotherapy. He was initially discharged 11 months after the accident but was readmitted to hospital as an outpatient after a further 16 months when the condition of his knee failed to improve. There was an increased laxity in the joint and MRI scans revealed complex tearing to the medial meniscus. Surgery was not attempted. C had suffered from athetoid cerebral palsy from birth but prior to the accident had been able to live a relatively normal life. He could walk considerable distances with the aid of a stick and only required the use of a wheelchair occasionally. He had a particularly keen love of motor sports, he was a member of the Institute of Advanced Motorists and had participated on several occasions as a course marshal at various motoring events. The judge described C as having triumphed over adversity by determination. He also found that C required all his resources to maintain his independence and mobility and that the accident, which would be minor to some, had taken its toll. After the accident C was unable to walk more than short distances and required the use of a wheelchair and electric buggy to travel any further. He was unable and unwilling to attend motor sports and social events and he became clinically depressed. The judge found that C's pre existing condition would have resulted in abnormal wear and tear and subsequent damage to the knee. The accident had brought forward the effects of that damage by 10 years. The prognosis was that the deterioration would continue, albeit slowly. It was not thought that surgery would be appropriate given C's cerebral palsy. *General Damages*: £17,500. Award for cost of future care: £6,750.

COTTRELL v. HALIFAX PLC [2002] 6 Q.R. 12, Judge Nash, CC (Medway).

Knee

3511.   R, male, a control panel builder, aged 41 at the date of the accident and 44 at the hearing, was struck by B's van while riding his motorcycle. The impact caused a compound comminuted fracture to the left tibia and fibula, and a comminuted crack fracture to the left tibial plateau. The shaft of the tibia was nailed and R remained in hospital for seven days. He wore a cast and knee brace for six weeks and remained on crutches, unable to work for three months. The shaft healed uneventfully, but the tibial plateau healed slightly displaced. R undertook intensive physiotherapy twice a week for around 18 months. Nevertheless, he continued to complain of a fairly constant background pain in the knee, stiffness, inability to kneel due to pain, and a tendency to limp. The intramedullary nail was removed around two years post accident. Following this procedure the pain became intermittent and R no longer limped. At disposal, around three years and six months post accident, R complained of pain on knocking or jarring the knee, which tended to ache towards the end of the day. He remained unable to kneel. As a result of this he had to adapt his method of work. When fitting control panels he had to sit sideways in front of machines, whereas before he would kneel. As a result, he suffered from backache. As a result of the displaced union in the knee there was a 20 per cent increased risk of premature osteoarthritis, although this was only likely to develop more than 10 years after the accident. As a result of the two operations and the bone end piercing the skin, R was left with noticeable scarring. He was unconcerned by it, but was aware that other people would look when he was wearing shorts. The judge considered that the injury fell between brackets 6(L)(b)(iv) and (c)(i) of the JSB Guidelines. *General Damages*: £14,000. Smith v. Manchester award: £19,000.

RHODES v. BRAGG [2002] 4 Q.R. 11, District Judge Marston, CC (Worcester).

Knee

3512.   W, male, a prison officer aged 48 at the date of the injury and 56 at the assessment, was assaulted at work. He was kicked and punched by a prisoner and fell to the floor, injuring his right knee. W had a history of problems with his right knee for some 12 years prior to the assault. The effect of the assault was to exacerbate the pre-existing knee injury, and bring forward symptoms by a period of five to ten years. W was unable to walk for more than about 50 yards, was unable to climb stairs without difficulty and could not drive for long periods of time. He suffered from daily pain and took painkillers. The medical evidence suggested that his symptoms were severe, in proportion to the radiological and arthroscopic findings. He was assessed by the Benefits Agency as being 30 per cent disabled, of which 19 per cent was due to the assault. W was medically retired from the prison service at the age of 49, and though he was considered by the medical experts to be fit for light sedentary work he had been unable to find employment. He would have retired from the prison service at the age of 55 but for the assault. *General Damages*: £7,500.

WEBB (CICA: QUANTUM: 2001), *Re* (2002) 3 Q.R. 7, Clark Q.C, CICA (London).

Knee

3513.   G, female, a writer, aged 22 at the date of the road traffic accident and 24 at trial, struck the steering wheel causing bruises and laceration to her lip. G experienced severe headaches for some weeks, which abated to mild weekly headaches at 12 months. Bruising to her abdomen and chest settled in about one month. There was severe bruising to both knees, which settled after about three weeks, during which time G suffered swelling and crepitus from time to time. G's neck was stiff, with pain radiating to both shoulders. G did not go to hospital but did consult her GP about her neck and knees. Although physiotherapy was recommended, G did not undertake any active management of her symptoms save for taking pain relief. The only continuing symptoms at 13 months post accident were in the neck and knees. The symptoms were described as "mild" and the prognosis was for a full recovery at about 19 months with the help of physiotherapy. G also suffered a period of travel anxiety and depression for which she sought no treatment. At trial, some 21 months post accident, G gave evidence that she continued to experience symptoms but it was noted that she had not undertaken the recommended physiotherapy. *General Damages*: £4,500.

GIBBON v. PULLAN [2002] 2 Q.R. 15, District Judge Weston, CC (Telford).

Knee

3514.   S brought an action of damages in respect of injuries sustained to his left knee in the course of his employment as a prison officer. The injury was sustained when he fell awkwardly whilst crossing a field in pursuit of an absconding young offender. S claimed that (1) the Scottish Prison Service had a duty to provide officers with instructions and training regarding precautions for their own safety during searches for and when chasing absconders, and (2) the search manager had failed to take reasonable care for the safety of the officers under his control where the field they were about to enter was uneven and the absconder had obtained a pair of scissors which could be used as a weapon.

Held, granting decree of absolvitor, that (1) the fact that S was about to enter and give chase across a field did not give rise to a duty on the search manager where no inherent dangers existed in the field; (2) the existence of the scissors was unconnected with S's injury and was therefore not relevant; (3) the Scottish Prison Service ought to have given instructions to prison officers regarding their safety during search and chase manoeuvres and were according in breach of their duty by failing to do so, and (4) given that S did not perceive the ground in the field to be particularly uneven, it was unlikely that any instructions by the Scottish Prison Service, to the effect that prison officers were to give up pursuit where they perceived that they might be at risk from continuing, would have resulted in S taking the decision not to enter the field and thus S had failed to show that the breach of duty by the Scottish Prison Service had resulted in his injury. Opinion, that had S been successful in his claim; (1) damages had been agreed at £22,290 in respect of solatium inclusive of interest and £60,000 in respect of lost pension rights, and (2) damages would also have been awarded for past wage loss of £18,705 inclusive of interest and £140,000 in respect of future wage loss.

SNEDDON v. SCOTTISH MINISTERS 2002 Rep. L.R. 52, Lord Menzies, OH.

Knee–psychiatric damage

3515.   F, male, a chemical process worker aged 33 at the date of the injury and 38 at trial, was injured when a sack of chemicals fell from a hoist and struck him. F remained trapped for 15 minutes before being found by colleagues. He was admitted to hospital for surgery to his right knee and he remained there for a week. His leg remained in plaster for a further eight weeks, and he required crutches for several months. F received intensive physiotherapy and underwent a further operation 21 months after the accident, which required him to spend a week in hospital and wear a knee brace for the following two months. Apart from nine months of "light duties" F had not worked since the accident. As a result of the accident and consequential instability of the joint, F developed Osteo-arthritis in the knee, which continued to deteriorate. He was left with a permanent weakness and instability in his knee joint and would require a knee replacement within 10 to 15 years. F would not return to active sports he previously enjoyed, but the knee became sufficiently stable for most day to day activities. He was no longer able to perform DIY work and his knee was painful after prolonged periods of driving. F suffered persistent swelling to the knee area and although he was able to return to his pre-accident employment, the range of jobs open to him in the future would be severely restricted. F suffered nightmares and flashbacks every night for five to six weeks after the accident, which then reduced in frequency over a period of 18 months. Thereafter, he suffered from depression which was treated with counselling and anti-depressant medication and was continuing at the date of the trial. The psychological effects contributed to the failure of his marriage. A multiplier of 14.82 was applied for the future loss of earnings award. *General Damages*: £38,000 (apportioned: £29,000 for the knee injury and £9,000 for the psychological injury). Past loss of earnings award: £38,437. Future loss of earnings award: £82,264. Smith v. Manchester award: £20,000. Award for future DIY expenses: £4,500.

FARRINGTON v. BASF PLC (2002) 3 Q.R. 8, Mr Recorder Cenedd Howells, CC (Chester).

Knee–psychiatric damage

3516.   B, male, a police officer aged 46 at the date of injury and 53 at the hearing, was assaulted at work by a prisoner causing him injury to his right knee. B also stubbed the middle toe of his right foot, and felt pain in his right hip and lower back. He was seen by the prison doctor, and referred to his own GP. B suffered a horizontal tear of the posterior horn of the medial meniscus; he underwent two arthroscopies and a menisectomy. The asymmetrical gait caused by the knee in turn led to symptoms in his lower back and hip deterioration. After six months of being at home, and in pain, B began to develop symptoms of anxiety. He was diagnosed as suffering from post traumatic stress disorder with symptoms of avoidance of anything associated with trauma, increased arousal, broken sleep, early morning waking, irritability, temper outbursts and a sense of nervousness. He underwent therapeutic intervention but it was found to be unlikely that he would improve before proceedings had come to an end. B did not work after the assault and was medically retired at the age of 48. *General Damages* £25,000.

BEARD (CICA: QUANTUM: 2001), *Re* (2002) 3 Q.R. 8, Clark Q.C, CICA (London).

Knee–psychiatric damage

3517.   G, male, a postman aged 34 at the date of the incident and 41 at the hearing, was shot in both legs with a hand gun by an unknown assailant. He sustained a soft tissue injury to his right knee and a compound tibial fracture at his left knee. Under general anaesthetic, both legs were debrided and under a second anaesthetic he had secondary suturing of his wounds. He spent eight days in hospital. An above knee plaster back slab was applied to his left leg which remained in plaster for approximately three and a half months while the fracture healed, followed by a period of partial weight bearing with crutches. Four months after the incident he had a full range of movement in his left knee, ankle and toes, and was able to walk without crutches. Three years after the incident he was experiencing intermittent pain in his left knee, and regular cramp in both legs, feet and ankles. Those symptoms were expected to be permanent. There was a risk of infection around the shrapnel in his left upper leg and of his developing episodes of chronic osteomyelitis in his left upper tibia. Following the incident, his wife left him with their son. He lost his job as a postman which he had been doing for 10 years. Two houses he owned were repossessed. He suffered post traumatic stress disorder, the features of which included: nightmares, flashbacks, irritability, anxiety, panic attacks, lack of impulse control, poor sleep and avoidance. He also had clear features of moderate to severe depression: low mood, lack of interest and enjoyment in the things he used to enjoy, poor sleep, agitation, irritability, anxiety, panic attacks and suicidal thoughts. He also abused alcohol. Six and a half years after the accident, he no longer depended on alcohol and no signs of major depression were noted. His cognitive functions were within normal limits and he was engaging with psychotherapy. *General Damages*: £17,500. Smith v. Manchester award: £15,500. Award for loss of pension: £40,000.

GEORGE (CICA: QUANTUM: 2001), *Re,* July 9, 2001, Lord Carlisle Q.C. (Chairman), CICA (London). [*Ex rel.* Julien Foster, Barrister, Goldsmith Chambers, Goldsmith Building, Temple, London].

Knee–psychiatric damage

3518.   A, female, aged 49 at the date of injury and 56 at the hearing, a residential care officer based in a hostel for adults with learning disabilities, was kicked on the outer side of the right knee when attempting to intervene in a fight between two male residents in December 1993.

Despite initial bruising and swelling, she managed to complete her normal sleep-in duty but was forced to return home first thing in the morning prior to completing her shift. Notwithstanding increasing pain in her right knee she struggled on at work for several weeks. From January 1994, she was forced to take 17 weeks off work. She went off sick again from June 1997 until March 1998, a total of 41 weeks, at which point she retired on grounds of ill health. It was agreed that her retirement from work was entirely related to the injuries suffered in the assault. Initially, neurapraxia of the lateral popliteal nerve (dead leg) was diagnosed. It was originally anticipated that this condition would resolve spontaneously within 24 to 36 months of the incident. However, A began to suffer increasing levels of back pain, probably on account of her tendency to limp. She also began to develop multiple joint pains, or polyarthralgia, mainly affecting her right leg and lower back. The orthopaedic expert concluded that ongoing polyarthralgia was probably connected to her depressive state. There had been little or no improvement in this condition by the date of the hearing. Following referral to a consultant clinical psychologist, A was diagnosed as suffering from a major depressive disorder together with significant symptoms of anxiety which met the DSM IV criteria for panic disorder with agoraphobia. The prognosis was guarded, although at the date of the hearing, the Board recognised some room for optimism, provided A underwent further psychological treatment as recommended. During the seven year period, A suffered regular sleep disturbance, her ability to walk distances was markedly reduced and she also developed an increased tendency to fall over. She complained of feeling permanently tired and suffered a total loss of drive. There had been a profound impact upon her ability to carry out her daily domestic routine. She was reluctant to go outside, let alone travel long distances. She was dependent upon analgesia and anti-depressant medication. There was no evidence that A had exaggerated her symptoms or malingered in any way. *General Damages*: £15,000. Past loss of earnings award: £27,189. Future loss of earnings award: £51,009. Award for loss of pension: £30,580. Total award: £123,778.

ACKROYD (CICA: QUANTUM: 2001), *Re* (2002) 3 Q.R. 8, Robertson Q.C, CICA (York).

Knee–facial scars

3519.   B, female, a computer aided design operator, aged 16 at the date of the road traffic accident and 21 at the hearing, immediately suffered serious pain in both legs as well as cuts and abrasions to her forehead, a cut to her right cheek and bruising to the right thigh. B later developed headaches, a painful left knee, backache and travel anxiety. The primary injury was to B's left knee. The experts agreed that B had suffered soft tissue traumatic chondromalacia patellae. Her knee troubled her if she played sport for between 15 and 30 minutes. She had difficulty sitting in one position for very long without experiencing discomfort. It was accepted that B had been a very keen sportswoman. She had a provisional place at university to train as a PE teacher, but had to pursue an alternative career as a CAD operator. An award was made for future loss of earnings, comparing the potential income as a graduate teacher with the income that could be secured as a CAD operator, the shortfall being £2,000 which was taken as the multiplicand. The multiplier was assessed at 13. The headaches declined gradually. At the hearing, B was still suffering from travel anxiety although at a considerably reduced level. Scarring to the forehead had receded and was not noticeable. B was left with a scar measuring 2.5cm on her right cheek, which was permanent but only noticeable upon close inspection, unless the weather was cold or particularly hot, when the scar became more apparent, and during those times B was often asked about the scar and became embarrassed about its appearance. *General Damages*: £13,000 (apportioned £9,000 for the knee, £3,000 for the scar to the cheek and £1.000 for the remaining symptoms, particularly the travel anxiety). Future loss of earnings award: £26,000.

BAYLISS v. LUNT [2003] 1 Q.R. 12, Judge McKenna, CC (Birmingham).

Foot

3520. C, male, a HGV driver, aged 46 at the date of the accident and 50 at trial, fell whilst closing a defective side gate on an HGV trailer. He suffered a closed comminuted fracture of the right calcaneus ("os calcis") and a cut to the base of the left thumb. The fracture was reduced under anaesthetic and fixed with three cancellous screws. C remained in hospital until discharged on crutches after six days. He required the crutches for several months and thereafter used a stick. He was off work for 22 months. The cut thumb healed uneventfully, leaving a small scar. By the date of the trial C no longer required a stick, but was left with permanent discomfort and stiffness in the right hind foot and difficulty negotiating uneven ground. The discomfort increased on prolonged standing, walking or driving. It was probable that he would develop arthritis. There was a possibility, although less than 10 per cent, that the arthritis would require a fusion operation. C was not fit, and never would be fit, to return to his pre accident employment pulling "TILT" trailers, which required manual dismantling for loading and unloading, or to undertake "sheet & roping" on open-backed trailers. He had been fit to return to HGV driving alone after six months. C's evidence was that around 60 to 70 per cent of all HGV vacancies involved "TILT" trailers or "sheeting & roping" and were therefore not open to him. The judge held that on the evidence adduced at the trial C's 22 month period off work after the accident was reasonable and he had not failed to mitigate his loss. The Smith v. Manchester award was equivalent to four and a half months net earnings. *General Damages*: £14,000. Smith v. Manchester award: £7,500. Total award (including interest): £47,445.61.

SIMPSON v. SPECTRANS [2003] 1 Q.R. 13, Judge Marr-Johnson, MCLC.

Non facial scars

3521. E, female, aged 13 at the date of the accident and 15 at trial, suffered a 10cm laceration to her left buttock while attending a friend's birthday party at a dry ski centre. An employee of Y had pushed E towards the side of the ski slope where she collided with a metal projection. E was taken to hospital where the wound was cleaned and steri strips were applied. She took three days off school and was unable to take part in sport activities for two months. At trial E was left with a oblique raised pink/purple scar measuring 8cm in length and 1cm in width at its widest point and described by an expert plastic surgeon as a "conspicuous deformity". The scar was visible at conversational distances and was not amenable to surgical revision, although there was a possibility that the colour would fade over time. Prior to the accident E had enjoyed swimming with her friends but discontinued the activity because she was self conscious about her appearance. The judge accepted that the scar caused embarrassment to E. However, he found that the scar was not particularly serious and could not be considered a significant cosmetic disability on the basis that it would only be seen when E was wearing swim wear or short summer clothes. *General Damages*: £5,000.

EVANS (A CHILD) v. YEOVIL SKI CENTRE [2002] 4 Q.R. 11, District Judge Gist, CC (Yeovil).

Non facial scars

3522. W, female, aged eight at the date of the accident and 11 at the child settlement approval hearing, cut her left leg on a protruding metal fence, sustaining a laceration to the lateral lower leg from the malleolus upwards. She was treated at hospital with butterfly sutures. The cut took two weeks to heal. W was absent from school for one day. The injury had no detrimental effect on her participation in sporting activities.

Two years after the accident there was visible but pale narrow scar at the side of the laceration measuring 15cm in length. Further surgery was not thought likely to improve the appearance of the scar and medical opinion was that it would be permanent. *General Damages*: £4,500.

W (A CHILD) v. COVENTRY CITY COUNCIL, September 24, 2001, District Judge Waterworth, CC (Coventry). [*Ex rel.* Stephen Garner, Barrister, No.8 Chambers, Fountain Court, Steelhouse Lane, Birmingham].

Skin conditions

3523.   E, male, a production line operator aged 23 at date of trial, was employed inserting rubber grommets and other components into apertures in windscreen wash bottles for cars and other vehicles using a rubber lubricant known as P80. He commenced work in 1996. In mid 1997 he developed a rash on the dorsal aspect of his left index finger which then spread over a matter of weeks to affect both the palms and dorsal aspects of both hands and fingers. His fingers and hands were cracked and sore and there were a number of vesicles present in the skin which tended to split. E attended his GP in December 1997 and was signed off work until February 1998, and prescribed creams. In December 1998, the condition of his hands flared up again and he required a further period off work. He was prescribed further treatment by his GP and remained reasonably well until May 2000. In May 2000, his hands became worse and required further time off work. He continued to have problems with his fingers and his hands but was then able to continue working. He had difficulty in playing his guitar, washing his hair and washing his car. The medical evidence was that if he could avoid contact with the P80 lubricant the dermatitis would settle within two to three months with continued appropriate treatment. *General Damages*: £5,000.

EVANS v. TEXTRON AUTOMOTIVE LTD (2002) 3 Q.R. 9, District Judge Wyn, CC (Cardiff).

Skin conditions–psychiatric damage

3524.   K, female, aged 36 at the date of treatment and 41 at trial, a part time care assistant, sought treatment from the hospital in respect of alopecia which began in the early 1990's and by 1995 had developed to alopecia universalis, a condition causing the complete loss of all body hair. The treatment adopted by the hospital was the application of Diphencyprone to K's scalp. Diphencyprone was a contact allergen intended to stimulate a reaction causing re-growth of hair. In fact, after several applications of the solution, no hair growth was produced and instead K's scalp developed large patches of vitiligo, or bleaching of the skin, on the areas of her scalp where the solution had been applied. That condition would be permanent. At the time the vitiligo occurred, K had reached a point where she had adjusted herself to her alopecia. Although she initially sought treatment for depression when she first began to lose her hair, her depression had never become so severe as to cause her to take time off work. She had learned to accept her appearance in a mirror and had socialised without wearing a wig. Upon the development of vitiligo, her depression became severe and she ceased working. By the date of the trial K had recovered sufficiently from her depression to be able to return to work. *General Damages*: £10,500 (apportioned £6,000 for the depressive illness and £4,500 for the physical injury to the scalp).

KENNEDY v. QUEEN'S MEDICAL CENTRE UNIVERSITY HOSPITAL NHS TRUST, January 12, 2001, Judge O'Rourke, CC (Leicester). [*Ex rel.* Nelsons, Solicitors, Pennine House, 8 Stanford Street, Nottingham].

Respiratory organs and chest

3525.   B, male, a chartered surveyor, aged 45 at the date of injury and 48 at trial, suffered a fractured sternum and an associated soft tissue injury to the chest in a road traffic accident. He was kept in hospital overnight and was bedridden for 10 to 14 days.

Eight weeks after the accident, he was beginning to work normally but still experienced intense pain on the right side of his chest. The pain eased in the following 18 months. At the hearing, B had a permanent palpable step in his sternum and experienced pain after exercise. There was a reasonable hope that this pain would settle eventually. *General Damages*: £7,000.

BAKER v. LONDON [2002] 2 Q.R. 13, District Judge Fink, CC (Croydon).

Respiratory organs and chest

3526.   S, female, a sales executive, aged 47 at the date of the road traffic accident and 50 at trial, suffered a broken sternum with slight displacement which was "very sore indeed" for three months. S was taken to hospital and detained overnight. She was allowed to leave the next morning so that she could look after her two daughters. An exponential recovery was made, so that six months after the accident S felt that she had made a good recovery. S then felt odd twinges of discomfort following severe exertion only. S noticed pain in the cervical spine after two months when the pain in the sternum started to lessen. At the time of examination, approximately one year after the accident, she continued to suffer from twinges of discomfort but they were not considered to be causing significant disability. S was unable to work as a sales executive for a period of two weeks and for the first two weeks back at work she had to be chauffeured around. After this time she drove herself, albeit with a lot of discomfort. S also taught aerobics and was described as "super fit". She was unable to teach classes for a period of four months after the accident but was back to normal six months post accident. *General Damages*: £6,100.

BROWN v. SOMERFIELD [2002] 2 Q.R. 13, Deputy District Judge Powell, CC (Nottingham).

Respiratory organs and chest–spine below neck

3527.   L, male, aged 41 at the date of the accident and 44 at trial, was injured in a road traffic accident. He suffered soft tissue injuries to the left wrist, right knee and to left side of his neck, all of which resolved within two months of the accident. A chest injury involving the costo chondral junction of the upper ribs resolved after 18 months. Damage to the lateral cutaneous nerve of the thigh, from the lap part of the seat belt, caused meralgia paraesthetica i.e. permanent numbness of the left lateral thigh. The soft tissue injury to the upper lumbar spine settled after 18 months. L had a long history of lower lumbar back pain, the progression of which was accelerated by two years as a result of the accident. *General Damages*: £6,500.

LOMAS v. LEEBETTER [2002] 6 Q.R. 12, Judge Peter Jones, CC (Sheffield).

Respiratory organs and chest–asthma

3528.   C, male, aged four at the hearing, suffered asthma contracted or exacerbated as a consequence of living in damp and mouldy premises let to the family for an eight month period when C was four weeks old. C's symptoms, which had appeared when he was five months old, comprised wheezing and coughing and regular and recurrent chest infections. At the hearing C continued to suffer chest infections every few weeks and had difficulty sleeping due to nocturnal wheezing and a worsening of chest problems in the winter months even though the family had moved house. He continued to take medication daily, including four courses of oral steroids in the 12 months prior to the hearing. Given the family history, it was said that C would probably have developed asthma due to some other provoking factor in later life, his maternal uncles having developed asthma in their late teens and early twenties. It was anticipated that C would continue to suffer mild to moderate recurring episodes of asthmatic attacks requiring the use of an inhaler. *General Damages*: £8,500.

C (A CHILD) v. EMPIRE ESTATES [2002] 6 Q.R. 13, District Judge Ackroyd, CC (Bury).

Respiratory organs and chest–asbestos related injury and disease

3529.   B, male, aged 61 at the date of the hearing, was exposed to asbestos dust between 1969 and 1983. He was 57 when first diagnosed as having asymptomatic pleural plaques and suffering from respiratory disability due to bilateral diffuse pleural thickening. He took early retirement when aged 58 as a result of his respiratory disability. The experts agreed that his overall respiratory disability was in the range of 30 to 40 per cent, but that one quarter of this was referable to chronic obstructive airways disease caused by smoking. The respiratory disease referable to asbestos exposure was therefore in the range of 22.5 to 30 per cent. The court found that B would have had to retire at 60 in any event by reasons of unrelated non-respiratory disability. As a result of his respiratory disability, B had to give up his hobbies of DIY, gardening and keeping pets. He could no longer walk long distances or climb stairs easily and had to move his bedroom downstairs. There was a 20 per cent risk of further pleural thickening causing increased disablement, a one to two per cent risk of asbestosis, a 15 to 20 per cent risk of suffering lung cancer by reason of asbestos exposure and his previous smoking of cigarettes, and an eight to 15 per cent risk of mesothelioma. His life expectancy had been reduced by three years by unrelated chronic obstructive airways disease and by a further two to four years by reason of the asbestos-related disease. In assessing the award, the judge took into account B's anxiety at the asbestos-related deaths of two of his workmates and his inability in the period between diagnosis and trial to perform DIY. The general damages award was discounted by one-quarter from £27,500 which would have been the award on a non-provisional basis. A multiplicand of £1,000 was used for the incapacity award. *General Damages*: (provisional award) £20,625. Past loss of earnings award: £32,984. Past care award: £2,500. Award for incapacity for DIY work: £10,000.
    BAHARDO v. MAYER NEWMAN & CO LTD (2002) 3 Q.R. 5, Judge Hunt, QBD.

Respiratory organs and chest–asbestos related injury and disease

3530.   B, male, aged 16 to 58 during the period of exposure and 76 at trial, developed asbestosis and bilateral calcified pleural plaques as a result of his employment with BRB's predecessor. Before the onset of asbestosis, B had been unable to do heavy work in connection with gardening and decorating because of his arthritis and because he was overweight. After the onset of asbestosis, his disability was 25 per cent, 20 per cent of which was attributed to the asbestosis and 5 per cent to his being overweight. He had a further 10 per cent disability from arthritis. There was a 50 per cent chance that the asbestosis would progress and a 10 per cent chance of diffuse pleural thickening developing. It was not likely that B would require personal care or need to move house. It was accepted that B had had friends who had died painfully from similar conditions and that consequently B was likely to have persistent thoughts about this. There was a 10 per cent risk of mesothelioma and an increased risk of lung cancer of five to seven point four from a base line of four per cent from smoking. The award was made on a provisional basis to allow for B to reapply in the event of his developing lung cancer, mesothelioma or pleural thickening. *General Damages* (Provisional Award): £20,000.
    BLACKMORE v. BRB (RESIDUARY) LTD [2002] 6 Q.R. 12, District Judge Simons, CC (Swindon).

Respiratory organs and chest–asbestos related injury and disease

3531.   H, male, aged 58 at the date of the trial, was exposed to asbestos while in C's employment between 1959 and 1962. As a result he developed bilateral calcified pleural plaques which caused underlying physical damage and anxiety, although no symptoms. H's condition led to a 1 per cent risk of developing diffuse pleural thickening sufficient to cause shortness of breath and disablement, a one per cent risk of developing asbestosis, a three per cent risk of malignant mesothelioma and a one per cent risk of lung cancer. These risks were excluded from the award of provisional damages. *General Damages*: £6,000.

HEATH v. CAPE DISTRIBUTION LTD [2003] 1 Q.R. 13, Judge Armitage Q.C., CC (Oldham).

Excretory organs

3532.   J, male, aged 36 at the date of the injury and 45 at the assessment hearing, was admitted to hospital with extreme abdominal pain. An exploratory Laparotomy was carried out the next day, but a mesenteric vein thrombosis interrupting the blood supply to the small bowel was missed. Nine days later, the majority of the small bowel had to be removed. Thereafter, J received total parenteral nutrition. Three months after the injury, J underwent an unsuccessful reanastamosis of the remaining small bowel. He remained in hospital for nine months. As a result of the injury, J's marriage failed and he was divorced and moved into a one bedroom flat. Eighteen months after the injury, J developed migrating arthropathy as a result of TPN. He was again admitted to hospital, where he developed pneumonia and a hickman line infection. The infection included candida and J suffered candida Opthalmitis and iritis in his right eye and temporary visual loss for which he was successfully treated. Three years after the injury, J developed an infected granuloma with deep involvement of the muscles. The granuloma was excised. J then suffered multiple compression fractures of the lumbar vertebrae as a result of osteoporosis caused by TPN. Four years after the injury, J received a small bowel transplant from his triplet brother, and TPN ceased three months later. J continued to suffer from diarrhoea and uncontrollable flatulence. He continued to suffer back and hip pain and remained at greatly increased risk of further fractures as a result of Osteoporosis. He had not worked in the nine years between the injury and the assessment. There was a 30 per cent chance of J redeveloping active short bowel syndrome during a normal life-span. *General Damages*: £75,000.

JONES v. SOUTHAMPTON AND SOUTH WEST HAMPSHIRE HA [2002] 4 Q.R. 10, District Judge Wade, CC (Salisbury).

Toxicosis–food poisoning

3533.   P, female, unemployed aged 28 at the date of the incident and 31 at trial, contracted a Giardia Lamblia parasitic bowel infection as a result of poor hygiene conditions whilst on a package holiday. The parasite was stubbornly resistant to treatment for 18 months and P suffered severe abdominal pain, up to 10 loose bowel movements per day and two at night, persistent flatulence, nausea, vomiting, haemorrhoids and intermittent incontinence. She lost a stone and a half in weight. Post infectious irritable bowel syndrome was diagnosed and it was thought that the parasite was harboured in the gall bladder. P underwent four invasive surgical procedures including the removal of her gall bladder 18 months after the original infection. Thereafter her condition improved moderately but she continued to suffer severe pain, flatulence, up to 12 loose bowel movements per day and episodes of incontinence. Her social life was seriously curtailed. She continued to wear panty liners and, on occasions, incontinence pants. Her plans to start a family were delayed. Her diet was strictly controlled. The prognosis was guarded and it was not known when P would feel well enough to start raising a family. *General Damages*: £26,000.

POTTER v. AIRTOURS PLC [2002] 6 Q.R. 13, Recorder Blair Q.C., CC (Swindon).

Minor injuries

3534.   J, female, aged 10 at the date of the accident and 14 at the hearing, was cycling along a road when the front wheel of her bicycle fell into a pot hole causing her to be thrown from her bicycle to the ground below. J suffered cuts and abrasions to her left shoulder, left hip and left knee. She did not lose consciousness but was upset and tearful. She sought treatment from hospital and was diagnosed as suffering from scuff mark abrasions to the shoulder, hip and knee. The wounds were cleaned and steri-strip closures were applied. J was unable to take a bath for three weeks because her wounds were raw and her sleep was disturbed for two weeks. She did not miss any schooling. The abrasion to her left shoulder healed quickly, leaving no scarring, deformity or disability. The wound to the left hip left a small and faint but permanent scar to the lower abdomen. The wound to the kneecap had also left a small but indiscernible faint scar with no disability. *General Damages*: £3,500.

J (A CHILD) v. GWYNEDD CC, September 3, 2001, District Judge Williams, CC (Caernafon). [*Ex rel.* Hodgkinsons, Solicitors, The Old Manse, 14 Lumley Avenue, Skegness].

Minor injuries

3535. W, female, aged 37 at the date of incident and 38 at trial, swallowed a piece of cheese containing fragments of either glass or plastic. Her husband examined her mouth and was able to remove a white opaque foreign body. However another piece of material had lodged on the right side of her throat localised at hyoid bone level. After two days, she attended her GP and was immediately referred to hospital. Over the next six months W underwent a series of X-rays, one of which involved a barium swallow and CT scans which confirmed the fragment in the right para-pharyngeal region. The medical evidence supported the view that W was unlikely to have suffered or would suffer from any serious medical consequences of having this foreign body embedded in her throat. Removal of the fragment by either internal or external means would not only be difficult but would also bring with it potential complications since it was sited very close to the main artery and was not recommended. Not withstanding the positive prognosis, W had instinctively altered her diet to soft foods, felt that her throat became tickly and raising her voice was more difficult. W's anxiety was an acknowledged contributor to the damages awarded. *General Damages*: £2,500.

WATTS v. J SAINSBURY PLC [2002] 4 Q.R. 11, Judge Bishop, CC (Staines).

Minor injuries

3536. H, male, aged 13 at the date of the accident and 16 at the child settlement approval hearing, was involved in a side impact road traffic accident. H suffered bruising to his forehead, a minor whiplash injury to his neck and a soft tissue injury to his knees. H was thrown forwards by the impact of the collision. He struck the right hand side of his forehead against the car's passenger window. H's forehead was bruised and tender. He suffered associated headaches. The bruising resolved within one week of the accident. Initially, H suffered no symptoms in his neck but within a few hours of the collision he experienced pain at the back of his neck radiating across the top of his shoulders. H's neck felt stiff and restricted. Those symptoms persisted for two weeks, but then improved. The neck injury resolved completely within three weeks. H had a pre-existing problem with both of his knees, which was exacerbated by the instant injury. The knee symptoms gradually improved and resolved to their pre-accident level within one to two months after the accident. He took the painkillers for one week. H was absent from school for one day. He could not play cricket or football for three weeks. *General Damages* (agreed and approved): £2,000.

H (A CHILD) v. AHMED, September 25, 2001, District Judge Ellery, CC (Birmingham). [*Ex rel.* Stephen Garner, Barrister, No.8 Chambers, Fountain Court, Steelhouse Lane, Birmingham].

Minor injuries

3537. Q, male, aged 52 at the date of the accident and 54 at trial was knocked off his moped by a motor car. He slid along the road for a short distance and suffered cuts and bruises to his right hand and leg. He was unable to drive and refrained from work for a period of one week. For some months after the accident he experienced swelling over the knuckle of the right middle finger. On examination around six months after the accident he suffered occasional numbness in the hand, particularly at night, together with some pain. The skin of the right leg was slightly discoloured as a result of the abrasions and there was a residual hematoma above the ankle. The leg had been painful for around one month. All symptoms resolved within 12 months of the accident. The judge indicated the appropriate level of damages had liability been established. *General Damages*: £1,100.

QUENDOLO v. PATEL [2002] 2 Q.R. 18, District Judge Taylor, CC (Central London).

Minor injuries

3538.   M, female, aged 12 at the time of the incident and 14 at the hearing, was prescribed an antihistamine by her GP to treat her hayfever symptoms. M's mother collected the prescription from MDC. Inadvertently, MDC placed in the same bag together with the prescribed antihistamine a container of Clomipramine tablets, an antidepressant. Not realising that these tablets had been given in error, M's mother gave to M all but one of the approximately 28 tablets in the container. Over the next three to four weeks, M exhibited typical side effects of antidepressant medication, in particular headaches and nausea, occasional dizziness, extreme thirst, loss of appetite and constipation. She also became generally quiet and subdued in mood, but was subject to sudden bursts of violent temper and irritability. Once she stopped taking the antidepressant tablets, these symptoms resolved without further complication. *General Damages*: £1,000.

M (A CHILD) v. MISTRY DISPENSING CHEMISTS [2002] 2 Q.R. 18, District Judge Wrigley, CC (Nottingham).

Minor injuries

3539.   P1, male, and P2, a female, aged 13 and seven respectively at the date of the road traffic accident and 14 and eight respectively at the child settlement approval hearing, were injured when the vehicle in which they were travelling was struck from behind. P1 sustained a whiplash injury which lasted for four weeks during which time he was unable to participate in extracurricular activities at school. He also suffered travel sickness for about one year. P2, suffered episodes of odd sounds in her head which she described as a musical triangle. The sounds persisted over a 10 minute period and were often followed by a headache which was eased by paracetamol. She missed two days of school. Six months after the accident, the episodes occurred two or three times a week. The symptoms resolved within one year of the accident. *General Damages*: P1 £850, P2 £600 (agreed and approved).

P (A CHILD) v. ELLIOT (2002) 3 Q.R. 9, Deputy District Judge Parker, CC (Horsham).

Minor injuries

3540.   [Defective Premises Act 1972 s.4.]
A, female, aged four at the assessment of damages hearing, and J, a boy, aged two at the hearing, had suffered from persistent coughs and colds over a period of six months as a result of residing in rented property affected by severe damp and related mould growth. Damages were sought under the Defective Premises Act 1972 s.4 in respect of their landlord's failure to carry out adequate repairs. There had

been no attendance by either of the children at hospital or their GP's surgery for treatment and no diagnosis of asthma. *General Damages*: £650 for each child.

CONROY v. HIRE TOKEN LTD, May 29, 2001, Judge Holman, CC (Manchester). [*Ex rel.* Adam Fullwood, Barrister, Garden Court North, 5 Cooper Street, Manchester].

Minor injuries–pre existing disability or condition–aggravated by whiplash

3541.   P, male, unemployed, aged 50 at the date of the road traffic accident and 52 at trial, suffered minor soft tissue injuries to his neck and lower back. He developed symptoms of pain and stiffness in his neck, radiating into one shoulder, and pain in his lower back, for which he attended once at hospital and once at his GP, where he was prescribed painkillers. On examination seven weeks after the accident, he reported continuing pain and stiffness in his neck, which was disturbing his sleep, and some minor continuing pain in his lower back, although he did not exhibit any restriction in his range of neck or lower back movement. The lower back symptoms settled within 10 months of the accident. The neck symptoms became intermittent within six months of the accident, with spasms of neck pain radiating into one shoulder, each lasting around a day. He suffered these with diminishing frequency, and at 17 months after the accident they were occurring twice a month. At trial, 20 months after the accident, they occurred three times every two months. Medical evidence established that the accident had caused a minor exacerbation of lower back symptoms from a pre existing lower back condition over a 10 month period, and neck symptoms which would probably resolve completely within 18 to 24 months, with any continuing symptoms thereafter being due to an unrelated pre existing cervical degenerative change. *General Damages*: £2,800.

PITCHER v. STEWART [2002] 6 Q.R. 18, District Judge Hill, CC (Sheffield).

Minor injuries–psychiatric damage

3542.   J, female, a housewife aged 30 at the date of the road traffic accident and 34 at trial, sustained bruising to her ribs and suffered a mildly depressive reaction. J was heavily pregnant at the time and for some five hours after the accident she was anxious about the health of her unborn baby who had, unusually, not moved. After the accident J was reluctant to drive and would swerve severely to one side of the carriageway in order to avoid any risk of collision. She also suffered flashbacks when passing close by other vehicles. Her symptoms were in the form of nausea, muscle tension, choking and palpitations. Those symptoms persisted at trial. For a period of three months post accident J suffered from mild depression and sleep disturbance. She also felt suicidal and was easily moved to tears. Her driving phobia prevented her from driving to see her family which heightened her sense of isolation. J's husband, being in the RAF, often worked abroad. J had a pre-existing psychological vulnerability and had, shortly prior to her examination by the expert psychiatrist witness, taken an overdose of tablets. Cognitive behavioural therapy was indicated as likely to effect an improved condition and while that head of damage was not pleaded the judge allowed an amendment at trial to include the cost of the therapy sessions. In considering the appropriate level of award the judge considered the case of *Kemp v. Burden (No1)* (Kemp & Kemp C4-128) but determined that the award should be increased slightly to take account of the fact that J's symptoms were still continuing at trial. *General Damages*: £3,300 (apportioned £3,000 for the psychiatric injury; £300 for the bruised ribs). Award for cognitive behavioural therapy costs: £1,100.

JONES v. BENNETT, August 1, 2001, District Judge Suckling, CC (Worcester). [*Ex rel.* Nigel Brockley, Barrister, Bracton Chambers, Bell House, 8 Bell Yard, London].

Minor injuries–psychiatric damage

3543. M, male, a refuse collector, aged 24 at the date of the accident and 28 at trial, suffered personal injury whilst in the course of his employment. He sustained a penetrative injury to his right leg in the area of his thigh from an unseen hypodermic needle that was protruding from a household waste bag. M's physical injury was minor. However, M was anxious and distressed about the possibility of contracting the AIDS virus or Hepatitis B. He immediately became depressed, irritable and short-tempered. He began to drink more alcohol than before for comfort. M's five year relationship with his girlfriend broke down for three months. M's anxiety began to settle approximately nine to 10 months after the accident, following several blood tests, when he was finally informed by his GP that he had not contracted any disease. *General Damages*: £2,625.

MEEK v. LEWIS [2002] 4 Q.R. 12, District Judge Ing, CC (Gloucester).

Minor injuries–psychiatric damage

3544. S, male, aged three at the date of the accident and seven at the date of the infant settlement approval hearing, was involved in a side impact road traffic accident. S was shocked after the collision. He was taken to his local hospital where he was diagnosed as having suffered a seat belt restraining injury consisting of bruising to his chest wall and abdomen. The bruising settled within two weeks of the accident. S also suffered psychological symptoms. He experienced travel anxiety and became nervous when travelling by car. He refused to sit in the front of the car and advised his parents to put their seat belts on before a journey. The prognosis which had been given was for the psychological injury to resolve within six to nine months of the accident. S also suffered from sleep disturbance for the first few weeks after the accident. He was absent from nursery for one week. At the date of the hearing, S was symptom free, his psychological symptoms settled in accordance with the prognosis. *General Damages*: £1,100.

S (A CHILD) v. ADAM [2002] 6 Q.R. 13, Deputy District Judge Sutton, CC (Birmingham).

Minor injuries–psychiatric damage

3545. F, female, aged 10 at the date of the road traffic accident and 11 at the assessment hearing, suffered a whiplash injury to her neck causing discomfort and restriction of movement which lasted two weeks. Additionally she was acutely distressed with disturbed sleep and tearfulness over that period. F had been taken to the hospital and she had paracetamol for about 10 days. Thereafter she was diagnosed as being reluctant to travel in a motor car for just over three months and her mother testified that she had to take F with her in her car in connection with her business as a seamstress and this sometimes required three trips daily as there was nobody to look after F at home. From time to time, F's mother found she almost had to force her daughter into the car. The judge found that this aspect was something more than a natural consequence of the accident and that the medical report indicated a phobia as it affected F's behaviour pattern which would sound in damages. *General Damages*: £1,000.

FOSTER (A CHILD) v. LEA [2002] 6 Q.R. 13, District Judge McCullagh, CC (Birkenhead).

Minor injuries–psychiatric damage–leg

3546. F, male, aged 33 at the date of the incident and 37 at trial, was injured when a neighbour dispute with D culminated in D driving his motorcar at the open driver's door of F's vehicle. A very low speed collision ensued, causing F's right leg to become trapped in between his car door and the side of his vehicle. F suffered pain and bruising that settled within three months. In addition, F suffered a period of phobic travel anxiety whenever he saw a vehicle of the same make and colour as D's. It was found that F was prone to exaggerate and that the injuries were de minimis. *General Damages*: £500 (apportioned £350 for the exacerbation of his anxiety and £150 for the bruising).

FRANKLIN v. DEVINE [2003] 1 Q.R. 14, Judge Coates, CC (Brighton).

Minor injuries–head

3547. S, male, a former computer programmer, aged 23 at the date of the accident and 25 at trial, was injured when travelling as a passenger on one of W's trains. As he walked along a railway carriage, a light fitting collapsed and struck him on the head. He was not rendered unconscious but suffered diffuse cerebral concussion. He received a small cut to the head not requiring stitches. S, who had a history of sinusitis and migraine, suffered powerful debilitating headaches for the first six months. These occasionally lasted up to one day. To begin with they were as frequent as three or four times a week. The court found that debilitating headaches and some neck restriction lasted for six months, gradually improving after nine months. After nine months the headaches were occurring once a week and were controllable with pain killers. S had almost fully recovered within 18 months. Two years after the accident S had fully recovered with only occasional headaches. There was no scarring and no other symptoms. At the date of the accident S was unemployed; however he had a good work history. The court held that, but for the head injury, S would probably have found work within one month, was unable to work at all for four months and thereafter was able to work part time for three months. *General Damages*: £3,500.

SMITH v. WEST COAST TRAINS LTD [2002] 4 Q.R. 12, District Judge Hassan, CC (Central London).

Minor injuries–head

3548. A, male, a lorry driver aged 53 at the date of the road traffic accident and 57 at trial was struck at the back of his head by his rear cab window which was dislodged in a collision. A sustained a blunt trauma to the back of his head. Immediately after the accident, A felt concussed. Bruising developed, which was tender and sore for six weeks. A suffered a continuous headache at the back of his head for 10 days, which he found painful and restrictive. He was unable to work for that period. Thereafter, A suffered similar headaches every week or two which lasted three to four hours. Although A complained of headaches at trial, the judge held that the symptoms had resolved three years post accident. There was no risk of post-traumatic epilepsy. A was considerably shocked and shaken for a period of two to three days following the accident, thereafter remaining nervous when driving. Prior to the accident, A had enjoyed driving and enjoyed his work as a light haulier. However, since the accident, his symptoms were such that he wished he could give up driving altogether. He was unable to do so because of his business and age. He became particularly stressed after witnessing accidents or potential accidents while driving and would have to stop his vehicle to regain his composure. Those symptoms had continued unabated since the accident. *General Damages*: £2,500. Past loss of earnings: £2,200.

ALLUM v. NICHOLAS ANTHONY LTD (2002) 3 Q.R. 9, Judge Brendt Q.C., CC (Colchester).

Minor injuries–head

3549. P, male, aged 11 days at the date of the accident and six years at the child settlement approval hearing, was a front seat passenger in a rear facing child seat when the vehicle in which he was travelling was struck from behind. P's seat was thrown forwards and his head struck the back of the seat in which his child seat was secured. P sustained an abrasion with swelling to the forehead of approximately one inch in diameter. The injury resolved completely within one week. *General Damages* (agreed and approved): £300.

P (A CHILD) v. MOHAMMED, October 26, 2001, District Judge Lingard, CC (Bradford). [*Ex rel.* Ian Miller, Barrister, Broadway House, 9 Bank Street, Bradford].

Minor injuries-teeth

3550.   D, male, a market trader aged 49 at the date of the road traffic accident and 53 at trial, suffered a broken tooth in the right side of his lower jaw, neck pain and pain in his lower back. D attended hospital where the back pain was diagnosed as a soft tissue injury. He was prescribed painkilling tablets. D's damaged tooth was capped by a dentist several days after the accident. His neck pain gradually improved and, after several days, was no longer a problem. Upon examination 10 months after the accident, D still experienced pain throughout the lumbar spine at the limit of all movements. The prognosis was that he was likely to make a full recovery from his back injury within 18 months of the accident. D was absent from work for six weeks and was unable to go on a pre-arranged holiday with his wife. *General Damages*: £3,750 (apportioned £1,000 for the tooth and neck injury and £2,750 for the back injury).

DYER v. BUGLER TRANSPORT, August 13, 2001, District Judge O'Regan, CC (Birmingham). [*Ex rel.* Stephen Garner, Barrister, No. 8 Chambers, Fountain Court, Steelhouse Lane, Birmingham].

Minor injuries-teeth

3551.   L, male, aged 11 at the date of the accident and 13 at the child settlement hearing, suffered dental injuries at school when he slipped on ice and fell onto the ground. L badly damaged his upper front teeth. His mother took him to his local dentist who repositioned L's upper left central incisor and diagnosed a root fracture. Six days later the tooth was splinted to the adjacent teeth with dental cement. Subsequently the nerve was removed from inside the tooth and a metal post inserted in an attempt to splint the fragments. The injury cast a cloud over L's Christmas holidays and his food choice was severely limited. He experienced no pain but could not eat hard food or bite hard on the tooth because he felt that would make it wobble slightly. As a result of the break in the root of the upper left central incisor, there was persistent infection around the root. In addition, L had a small chip in the crown of the upper right central incisor, the filling of which had discoloured. The prognosis for the upper left central incisor was poor and it was likely to last only a year or two after the accident before falling out. Consequently further treatment would be required to replace that tooth and the use of small denture would be necessary until L stopped growing. Thereafter L would require osteointegrated implants at the cost of £2,000, together with the cost of their maintenance at £85 annum with a multiplier of 26.86, giving a total of £2,283.10. The remaining special damage comprised the cost of replacement of the white filling in the crown of the upper right central incisor, namely £30. Because liability was in dispute an offer of £7,000 in full and final settlement was considered acceptable which included an element for pain, suffering and loss of amenity. Total Award (agreed and approved): £7,000 (split *General Damages*: £2,700 and Cost of future dental treatment £4,300).

LODGE (A CHILD) v. KIRKLEES MBC [2002] 4 Q.R. 12, District Judge Harrison, CC (Huddersfield).

Minor injuries-teeth

3552.   W, female, a nurse, aged 39 at the date of the negligent dental treatment and 44 at trial, suffered severe and continuous pain in her upper left pre molar tooth for a period of 18 months. W had a pre existing problem, namely a dental drill fragment embedded in this tooth, but this was not the result of the negligent treatment and she would have suffered from some symptoms and required corrective surgery in any event. However, the negligent failure to refer W for expert surgical treatment prolonged the symptoms by 18 months. Throughout this period, W suffered severe, continuous pain in this back tooth which was exacerbated by hot or cold food or liquid. She was unable to chew at all on one side of her mouth. She was woken by pain each night and became tired and bad tempered which caused difficulties at work, in carrying out household duties and looking after her two children. W had to take the maximum recommended daily dose of non prescription painkillers. Her social life was restricted as a result of pain and tiredness. In addition, W suffered minor swelling on one side of her face of which she was self conscious. *General Damages*: £2,500.

WILLIAMS v. VERHAERT [2003] 1 Q.R. 14, District Judge Peters, CC (Sheffield).

Minor injuries–facial scars

3553. F, male, aged two years and three months at the date of the accident and five years and six months at trial, tripped and fell whilst ascending a set of steps leading from a council house. He struck his head against a wall suffering a laceration of some 2 cm. He was conveyed to hospital where the wound was sutured with internal and external stitches. The stitches were removed approximately one week later by which time a scab had formed over the site of injury. F's face remained swollen for several weeks after the accident and he was upset and tearful over a similar timescale. When examined for the purposes of a medical report 15 months after the accident there was a noticeable scar measuring 2cm by 3mm at a position directly between the eyebrows. It was stretched and faded remaining visible from conversational distances and constituted a noticeable cosmetic deficit. The prognosis was that the appearance of the scar would not alter significantly but that cosmetic revision was not necessary or recommended. The scarring had not improved at trial although there were no functional effects and F was not particularly concerned about the residual appearance. Liability was not established. *General Damages* (valued by the judge): £3,000.

F (A CHILD) v. BLAENAU GWENT CBC [2002] 4 Q.R. 12, District Judge John, CC (Cardiff).

Minor injuries–facial scars

3554. D, female, aged four at the date of the accident and five at the child settlement approval hearing, was injured when a volleyball post fell on her at a lido. A laceration to the left side of her forehead required five sutures and glue. D suffered a sleepless night and had a headache the following day. Over the next three or four days she was unusually quiet but then improved so that, within one week, she had made a good recovery and was able to swim again. The laceration healed normally but D was left with a linear scar measuring 2cm along the front edge of her hairline The scar had faded to the colour of the surrounding skin and was under her hair so was not a cosmetic blemish. It would be almost unnoticeable by the time D reached adulthood. *General Damages* (agreed and approved): £1,000.

DIDCOTE (A CHILD) v. SANDFORD LIDO LTD [2002] 6 Q.R. 15, District Judge Carron, CC (Cheltenham).

Minor injuries–neck

3555. S, male, a mechanic, aged 42 at the date of the road traffic accident and 44 at trial, sustained soft tissue injuries to the neck and lower back. He attended his GP three or four days after the accident and was prescribed pain relief and certified as unfit for work for a period of one week. Upon his return to work S found that he was unable to cope and was absent for a further three weeks. He was advised to undergo physiotherapy and to perform a series of back strengthening exercises which were effective in restoring a full range of spinal movement. The back symptoms were at their worse for a period of 10 days. Thereafter S was left with a permanent dull ache in the back. By about nine or 10 months post accident the symptoms of both neck and back pain had reached a plateau. S, who also rode a motor cycle, found he was unable to wear a crash helmet due to the discomfort. He also found that he could not pursue his hobby of swimming. S felt a sensation of grinding when moving his neck and had difficulty in looking up. Pre-accident degenerative changes were found to be responsible for any symptoms which were continuing after 24 months post accident. The judge accepted S's evidence that he had suffered continuing symptoms affecting both neck and back for a period of between 20 to 24 months for the neck and 18 to 20 months for the back, but that after nine or 10 months post accident the symptoms had become less severe. *General Damages*: £3,500.

SMITH v. GRAHAM, July 23, 2001, District Judge Rank, CC (Stoke-on-Trent). [*Ex rel.* Nigel Brockley, Barrister, Bracton Chambers, Bell House, 8 Bell Yard, London].

Minor injuries—neck

3556. S, female, aged 22 at the date of the road traffic accident and 24 at disposal, sustained a whiplash injury to her cervical spine. She was taken to hospital and subsequently saw her GP. She was off work for one week and suffered "niggling" symptoms of pain for four weeks. S underwent 16 sessions of chiropractic treatment. She remained symptomatic 22 months after the accident, feeling a pulling sensation in the left side of her neck if she turned her head to the right. She had stopped attending the gym as a result of the neck pain and unrelated knee pain. Further improvement was expected up to 34 months after the accident with ongoing symptoms beyond that time expected to be of nuisance value only. S also suffered from episodes of vivid recall for one month and situation specific anxiety for two months. *General Damages*: £3,000.

SOUTHWAITE v. OPEN COMPUTERS & FINANCE PLC, September 25, 2001, District Judge Stewart-Brown, CC (Bristol). [*Ex rel.* Matthew White, Barrister, St John's Chambers, Small Street, Bristol].

Minor injuries—neck

3557. P, male, aged 14 at the date of the accident and 16 at the child settlement approval hearing, was accidentally shot in the left side of the neck by an air rifle pellet whilst playing with L's two sons and two other friends. Immediately, P felt pain in the neck and he was shocked. He was taken to hospital and a small open wound was revealed upon examination. An X ray showed the pellet lodged in soft tissue. P was kept in hospital overnight. The following day, it was decided not to remove the pellet. The wound was dressed and P was discharged. He was off school for two days. One year after the accident, P still experienced minor discomfort in the left side of the neck and in the left shoulder but these symptoms had resolved by the date of the hearing. *General Damages* (agreed and approved): £1,500.

PAYNE (A CHILD) v. LUKE [2003] 1 Q.R. 14, District Judge Ainsworth, CC (Southampton).

Minor injuries—neck

3558. M, female, a nursery nurse, aged 20 at the date of the road traffic accident and 21 at trial, suffered a whiplash injury to the neck. She experienced symptoms of pain and restriction of movement in the neck the day after the accident and took painkillers. Following continuing symptoms of discomfort, she attended her GP 10 days after the accident. Some tenderness was noted over the neck muscles but there was no restriction in movement. Painkillers were prescribed. M had no time off work. At the medical examination just over 2 months after the accident, tenderness was noted over the right upper trapezius muscle, but without muscle spasm. At that stage M experienced symptoms of pain approximately three per week, for a few hours at a time. Those symptoms were eased with paracetamol. During the six to nine months after the accident, M became easily tired and was conscious of discomfort in her neck, particularly when lifting children at work, which she avoided as much as possible. M had made a full recovery by nine months after the accident. *General Damages*: £1,500.

MILLER v. DAVIES, September 14, 2001, Deputy District Judge Grosscurth, CC (Liverpool). [*Ex rel.* Andrew Lawson, Barrister, 24A St John Street, Manchester].

Minor injuries–neck

3559.   N, male, aged five at the date of the road traffic accident and six at the assessment of damages hearing was a rear seat passenger, wearing a seat belt in a car, which was struck from behind by another vehicle. N was in a distressed condition and crying following the accident. He complained of pain in his neck. He was able to attend school without taking any time off, but he experienced discomfort whilst playing games. He did not experience any anxiety or nightmares. Cervical spine symptoms improved over a period of one month before completely resolving, and a full recovery was made. His enjoyment of Easter had been reduced. *General Damages*: £850.

N (A CHILD) v. SUMMERBY, August 6, 2001, District Judge Davies, CC (Chichester). [*Ex rel.* Marcus Baldwin, Barrister, Stone Buildings, Lincoln's Inn, London].

Minor injuries–neck

3560.   A, female, aged nine at the date of the accident and 12 at the child settlement approval hearing, was involved in a side impact road traffic accident. Immediately after the accident, A felt an aching across her neck. It spread across the top of her shoulders and A found it painful when she moved her neck from side to side. A was taken to the local hospital where a soft tissue whiplash injury to her cervical spine was diagnosed. She was prescribed paracetamol and a cream to apply to her neck. A's neck symptoms improved gradually and had resolved completely within one week of the accident. A was absent from school for one day. She missed one lesson of PE. *General Damages* (agreed and approved): £300.

A (A CHILD) v. AHMED, September 25, 2001, District Judge Ellery, CC (Birmingham). [*Ex rel.* Stephen Garner, Barrister, No.8 Chambers, Fountain Court, Steelhouse Lane, Birmingham].

Minor injuries–neck–psychiatric damage

3561.   K, male, unemployed, aged 44 at the date of the road traffic accident and 46 at the trial, suffered from a constitutional disability known as rheumatoid arthritis. He also suffered from disc degeneration of the lumbar spine. The day after the accident, K developed neck pain and attended his GP who referred him for physiotherapy. At trial, K was still on a waiting list for physiotherapy but felt by that stage that he no longer needed treatment. His neck pain was acute for one month but thereafter he recovered such that he suffered only intermittently. At examination 10 months after the accident, K suffered from creaking and aching in his neck. Discomfort occurred two to three times a week and was mainly when he went to bed. As a result of the accident his back pain had become more severe and he required more painkillers. K had no hobbies and could not partake in any sports due to his pre existing disabilities. K had no new limitations on his activities as a result of the accident. Recovery from the neck symptoms was expected to be made within 18 to 22 months post accident with no persisting residual symptoms. Low back pain had been exacerbated by the trauma and would resolve to the previous pre injury level within 18 months. Following the accident, K suffered from an acute anxiety reaction. He initially suffered from nightmares and intrusive thoughts. K also developed a driving phobia. Fourteen months after the accident the prognosis was that K would become symptom free within a few months if he confronted his phobia and commenced driving more regularly. *General Damages*: £3,000 (apportioned as to £2,000 for the physical injuries and £1,000 for the psychological injury).

KEEGAN v. REECE [2003] 1 Q.R. 14, District Judge Hendicott, CC (Cardiff).

Minor injuries–neck–whiplash type injury

3562.   C, male, aged 30 at the date of the road traffic accident and 33 at trial, was aware of a burning sensation in his neck a few hours after the accident, but managed to carry on working that day. He arranged an appointment with his GP who advised him to continue taking painkillers. C took no time off work but was on annual leave from the day after the accident and his symptoms interfered with his holiday plans. Neck pain was constant for three weeks, during which time C was unable to walk his dog, and then partially resolved to an intermittent level. Six months after the accident he had only very minor ongoing symptoms and these fully resolved within 21 months. However, C remained apprehensive in traffic and became tense when vehicles approached from the rear. *General Damages*: £3,200 (apportioned £2,750 for the physical injuries and £450 for psychiatric damage).

CORKISH v. HARRISON [2002] 2 Q.R. 15, District Judge Turner, CC (Preston).

Minor injuries–neck–whiplash type injury

3563.   S, female, a student nurse, aged 29 at the date of the accident and 30 at the hearing, suffered a whiplash injury to her neck and a blow to her head as a result of a road traffic accident. She was immediately aware of pain over the right side of her head and experienced severe headaches for several days. A short time after the accident she developed severe neck pain which radiated into her right shoulder. The pain remained severe for approximately four weeks before gradually starting to improve. As a result of her injuries S was absent from college for four weeks. She returned after this time but only because she was worried about the amount of study she was missing. Approximately seven weeks after the accident S's financial circumstances forced her to return to her part time bar job in a local theatre. Both the return to college and return to work aggravated S's symptoms. Three months after the accident S was still complaining of moderate neck symptoms on a daily basis and was noted to have a 25 per cent to 35 per cent reduction of normal neck movement. By approximately 12 months after the accident she had achieved a full recovery. In addition to her physical symptoms S was also very shocked and shaken by the accident. She felt generally anxious and was very reluctant to travel by car for many weeks. When she did return to driving she remained excessively nervous and it took approximately 15 months for her driving confidence to return. *General Damages*: £3,000.

SUMMERS v. K BLAKEMORE LTD [2002] 4 Q.R. 13, Deputy District Judge Ingram, CC (Dudley).

Minor injuries–neck–whiplash type injury

3564.   N, male, a private taxi driver, aged 26 at the date of injury and 26 at the trial, suffered a whiplash injury to the neck, mid lower back, right knee, head, chest and wrist. He attended his GP. His chest pain settled over two weeks and the wrist pain over four weeks. N took two weeks off from work and then restricted his working hours for a further three weeks. A medical report two months after the accident confirmed that the neck pain would settle within 10 months, the back pain within nine months, the knee pain within nine months, the shoulder pain within eight months and the elbow pain within seven months. N symptoms of anxiety and cautiousness would also settle within seven months of the accident. A more or less full resolution of all symptoms was therefore expected within seven to nine months of the accident. *General Damages*: £3,000.

NOBLE v. FRASER [2003] 1 Q.R. 15, District Judge Ewing, CC (Chester).

Minor injuries–neck–whiplash type injury

3565. L, male, an internet programmer, aged 20 at the date of the road traffic accident and 22 at the disposal hearing, sustained a soft-tissue whiplash injury to his neck. At the time of the accident L had just started a new job, was keen to avoid taking time off work and did not take time off. He was unable to resume his hobbies of football, going to the gym', tenpin bowling and break dancing. Other areas of his life that were affected included going to the cinema, driving and socialising. L had suffered a neck strain in a similar accident in December 1997; however the medical evidence was that he had made a good recovery from the symptoms of injury by the time of the second accident and that 90 per cent of his subsequent symptoms were due to the second accident. The residual disability was assessed as slight. Although there was no major handicap on L's day to day activities, his continuing intermittent neck pain was an annoying nuisance which interfered with his concentration at work and prevented him from returning to his former leisure activities. L's medical expert considered that his symptoms were likely to linger until 16 to 19 months after the accident. L gave evidence that he had made a full recovery within 18 months of the second accident. Ten per cent was deducted from the award of £3,350 which was considered appropriate in respect of the totality of L's symptoms to take account of the effects of L's previous accident. *General Damages*: £2,925.

LEE v. MARLEY [2002] 6 Q.R. 15, District Judge Girlis, CC (Barnet).

Minor injuries–neck–whiplash type injury

3566. C, female, aged 33 at the date of the accident and 34 at the hearing, was sitting in her motor vehicle when R's van reversed out of a side road and collided with the rear of C's vehicle. C was initially shaken and shocked. Within two hours of the accident she started to feel pain to her neck and therefore attended her local hospital and was prescribed a soft collar. C subsequently obtained treatment from her GP two weeks after the accident. C did not take any time off work and did not suffer any psychological consequences following the collision. C wore the surgical collar intermittently over a two week period, during which time she suffered sleepless nights and difficulties driving any distance. Upon examination four months after the accident, C was diagnosed as suffering from a classical whiplash type injury to her cervical spine. At that date C was suffering intermittent pain in her neck going towards both shoulders. C was still having difficulty driving any great distance and the opinion was that a full recovery would take place within 12 to 18 months after the accident. At the hearing the parties agreed that this claim fell within the JSB Guidelines Section 6 A(c). *General Damages*: £2,750.

COOPER v. ROMAN BANK BAKERY [2002] 2 Q.R. 15, District Judge Maw, CC (Skegness).

Minor injuries–neck–whiplash type injury

3567. A, male, a windscreen fitter, aged 33 at the date of the road traffic accident and 35 at trial, sustained a whiplash injury to his neck. The symptoms worsened the day after the accident and A attended his GP who prescribed medication. A visited his GP again two weeks later but then sought no further treatment although he continued to take analgesics regularly. A suffered pain in his neck which radiated into his right shoulder and was severe for a week or so. A was not working at the time owing to an unrelated complaint but he would have been unable to do his job for a period after the accident due to the symptoms caused by it. Two weeks after the accident, A had a full range of movement. One month after the accident, the symptoms were at a mild intermittent level and they gradually diminished until resolving completely approximately 22 months after the accident. Whilst the symptoms persisted, A had been restricted from undertaking certain activities such as heavy lifting, vacuuming with his right arm and driving for long periods because they provoked pain. He was also more wary in traffic, particularly of vehicles approaching from behind. However this had not stopped him from driving and the anxiety had diminished over time. *General Damages*: £2,700.

ANDREWS v. MURPHY [2002] 6 Q.R. 15, District Judge Wainwright, CC (Exeter).

Minor injuries–neck–whiplash type injury

3568. S, female, aged 26 at the date of the road traffic accident and 27 at trial, sustained a whiplash injury to her neck and a bump to her right shoulder. She attended hospital and her GP and had approximately 20 sessions of physiotherapy. The whiplash injury caused severe stiffness and pain for two weeks, but after physiotherapy the neck symptoms gradually subsided over a period of six months and the shoulder pain improved by 50 per cent. Ten months after the accident, S had virtually completely recovered from her shoulder injuries. It was found that S would almost certainly fully recover with her remaining shoulder symptoms disappearing within a year to 14 months of the accident. *General Damages*: £2,500.

SPICKNELL v. ARDEN CLOTHING [2002] 6 Q.R. 16, District Judge Martin, CC (Leicester).

Minor injuries–neck–whiplash type injury

3569. H, female, aged 57 at the date of the accident and 58 at the disposal hearing, was a front seat passenger in a road traffic accident. She suffered a whiplash injury to her neck and lower back, frontal headaches which persisted for two months after the accident and difficulty sleeping for two weeks after the accident. H had pre existing arthritis in her knees, for which she took painkillers, but she increased the dose due to her neck and back pain. The neck symptoms resolved within one year of the accident but there were still residual symptoms in her back 15 months after the accident, which affected H's social and domestic activities to a minor extent. *General Damages*: £2,500.

HODKINSON v. CRUTCHLEY [2002] 6 Q.R. 16, District Judge Shannon, CC (Manchester).

Minor injuries–neck–whiplash type injury

3570. M, female, aged 37 at the date of the accident and 38 at the hearing, was driving her motor car when a collision occurred. The airbag of M's vehicle immediately deployed and she was restrained by her seatbelt. M was initially shocked and dazed. She was aware that she had sustained grazing to the right side of her face, head and left lower arm. M became aware of redness and a slight blue tinge over the upper half of her chest where she had been restrained by her seatbelt. She sought hospital treatment. She was diagnosed as suffering from superficial abrasions, bruising to the chest and a whiplash type injury to the back of the neck, together with aggravated pain to the lower lumbar region. She suffered from a pre-existing back problem in the form of a degenerative disc disease. In the days following the accident, M suffered with mild stiffness of the lumbar spine and neck. The bruising and abrasions settled within a six week period. Six months after the accident, the only ongoing symptoms were related to the right side of the neck. Medical opinion was that if M performed a course of exercise herself the symptoms would resolve within 12 months of the accident. It was determined that the ongoing pain suffered in the lumbar spine was predominately the result of her pre-existing injury and any aggravation to the back would also settle within 12 months of the accident. At the hearing, M gave evidence that the pain to the lower back had settled to pre-accident levels and there was still some residual pain and stiffness to the neck which was not disabling in any way. *General Damages*: £2,500.

MEEDS v. HAMILTON, October 17, 2001, District Judge Cawood, CC (Portsmouth). [*Ex rel.* Hodgkinsons, Solicitors, The Old Manse, 14 Lumley Avenue, Skegness].

Minor injuries—neck—whiplash type injury

3571. G, male, aged 13 at the date of the accident and 16 at the child settlement approval hearing, was involved in a rear end shunt road traffic accident. G suffered initial shock, a whiplash injury to the neck, headaches and travel anxiety. He developed pain at the back of his neck and head within 15 minutes of the collision. The muscles at the back of the neck tightened and G suffered a reduction in movement. The acute symptoms in G's neck persisted for a period of two weeks and then gradually eased. G developed a headache after the accident at the back of his head. The headache settled over his eyes. The headaches continued for a few weeks before resolving. G also suffered travel anxiety. He had two nightmares in the week following the collision. Pictures of the accident replayed themselves over in his mind for one week. G found that he was regularly checking the mirror every time he travelled by car and he was more wary about other vehicles on the road. G underwent four sessions of physiotherapy on his neck after the collision. The prognosis was for G's whiplash injury to resolve within 14 to 17 months of the accident. The prognosis was for the travel anxiety to settle within 20 months. Upon examination nearly two years after the accident, G was still describing some symptoms in his neck, especially if he held his neck in a sustained position when doing his homework; however these residual symptoms were attributed to poor posture rather than to the accident. G's travel anxiety had settled in accordance with the original prognosis. G was absent from school for three days after the accident and was unable to participate in sport or PE for two months. *General Damages:* £2,500.

G (A CHILD) v. EKLADIOS, October 8, 2001, District Judge Davies, CC (Birmingham). [*Ex rel.* Stephen Garner, Barrister, 8 Fountain Court, Birmingham].

Minor injuries—neck—whiplash type injury

3572. S, male, a self employed painter and decorator, aged 37 at the date of the road traffic accident and 39 at trial, suffered a soft tissue whiplash injury to his neck. S's neck became stiff and painful within two days of the accident and he visited his GP, who referred him for x-rays which showed no bone injury. He remained off work for eight days, during which period the neck pain was acute, such that he could "do little else but sit and watch TV" and his sleep was affected. Activities such as dressing were difficult and S relied on non prescription analgesics which gave some pain relief. The district judge accepted that S had returned to work "before he was really ready" as he was self employed and "had a family to feed". For two months after the accident he suffered significant pain when lifting and carrying objects and when working with his arms above shoulder level. During that period he was he was unable to drive for longer than 20 minutes without experiencing discomfort. S's main ongoing complaint related to his hobby of weight lifting which he had previously enjoyed three to four times per week and about which much of his social life revolved. He was unable to return to this for two months and thereafter was limited to leg exercise for a further 10 months, when the lingering neck symptoms finally resolved. S lost two stones in weight during the period after the accident and it took him a further five months to regain that weight. *General Damages:* £2,400.

STOKES v. MERRITT, September 12, 2001, District Judge Field, CC (Salisbury). [*Ex rel.* Toby Halliwell, Barrister, Unity Street Chambers, 5 Unity Street, College Green, Bristol].

Minor injuries—neck—whiplash type injury

3573. R, male, a university student aged 19 at the date of the accident and 21 at the disposal hearing, suffered a whiplash type injury to the neck. He was taken to hospital where he was examined and discharged into the care of his GP, having been provided with analgesia. The next day R's neck was markedly stiff and painful.

R's neck was particularly stiff and sore during the first four weeks after the accident, during which time he treated the symptoms with analgesia. As a result of continuing symptoms, R attended his GP approximately two weeks after the accident and was prescribed Intralgin gel which he applied to the neck for a further two weeks. R experienced difficulties getting comfortable in bed and some sleep disturbance. His injuries caused him to miss lectures in the last two weeks of the University term. He was unable to meet assignment deadlines. The assignments counted towards his final degree. Four weeks after the accident R's symptoms improved. By 12 months after the accident he was able to return to his normal activities, including driving the car and playing keyboards. Examination revealed no abnormalities in the neck, which displayed a full range of movement. However, R continued to suffer from residual stiffness and intermittent sharp pains in the neck upon sudden movements. The residual symptoms were thought likely to resolve within 18 months of the accident. At the hearing, some 25 months after the accident, they had improved, but R continued to experience occasional slight sharp pains in the neck upon sudden movements. *General Damages*: £2,250.

ROBINSON v. MORGAN [2002] 6 Q.R. 16, District Judge Robertson, CC (Hartlepool).

Minor injuries–neck–whiplash type injury

3574.   F, female, aged 11 at the date of the road traffic accident and 13 at the child settlement approval hearing, sustained a musculo-ligamentous soft tissue whiplash injury to her neck and situation specific travel anxiety. F attended hospital on the day of the collision and was prescribed paracetamol. The pain in F's neck was acute for the first two weeks after the accident. During this time her neck was very stiff and painful and she was unable to turn her head from side to side or up and down. F was absent from school for six days as a result of the accident. She missed PE for two weeks. F had a nightmare about the accident on the night of the collision. She had further flashbacks. She became a nervous and over-vigilant passenger when travelling by car, particularly if she was conveyed past the area of the accident. Upon examination six months after the collision F had recurrent discomfort in her neck. If she attempted any physical exercise or moved her head in an unguarded manner this caused her pain. The prognosis was for F's neck pain and psychological travel anxiety to resolve within nine to 12 months after the accident. At the hearing F confirmed that her symptoms had settled in accordance with the prognosis. *General Damages*: £2,150.

F (A CHILD) v. ASGHAR, October 19, 2001, District Judge Cochrane, CC (Burton on Trent). [*Ex rel.* Stephen Garner, Barrister, 8 Fountain Court, Steelhouse Lane, Birmingham].

Minor injuries–neck–whiplash type injury

3575.   D, male, a proof reader, aged 36 at the date of road traffic accident and 38 at the trial, developed stiffness and tenderness in his neck and shoulders. He was taken to hospital where a full range of movement of the head and neck was noted. He wore a soft collar for five days. He did not attend his GP but had one session of physiotherapy where he was shown some exercises to carry out. D was able to return to driving after three days but had difficulty turning his neck. Activities of daily living was affected for one week. He had significant discomfort in the evening after work for about one month. He had some continuing neck discomfort and stiffness after work. The medical evidence suggested a full recovery within 10 to 11 months. However, at trial, 22 months after the accident, D still complained of discomfort at the end of a working day. He spent much of his working time looking down and the judge accepted that this was likely to exacerbate the symptoms and that those symptoms were caused by the accident. *General Damages*: £2,100.

DAWSON v. HARGREAVES [2002] 4 Q.R. 13, Judge Adams, CC (Leeds).

Minor injuries—neck—whiplash type injury

3576. T, female, a data inputter aged 35 at the date of the road traffic accident and 37 at the hearing, banged her head on the windscreen causing bruising and severe headaches for a week. Immediately after the collision she was driven to hospital by her husband where she was given a collar which she wore for about 10 days. She was also prescribed Ibuprofen which she took in large doses for approximately one week. She was absent from work for 10 days. T discovered one week after the accident that she was 14 weeks pregnant and she was extremely concerned that the painkillers she had taken following the accident may have harmed her baby. She stated that this had spoilt her pregnancy, which was her first, and had affected her emotionally for the entire term. She was only relieved of her concerns following the birth of her baby which proceeded without difficulty. Her pregnancy meant that she was unable to take painkillers for more than a week after the accident which increased the level of the pain she suffered. Medical evidence suggested that the neck symptoms arising out of the accident would last approximately eight and a half months. The judge expressed that this was a classic whiplash injury that was aggravated by the effect that the taking of painkillers had on her pregnancy. *General Damages*: £2,000.

TUBEY v. FLETCHER [2002] 6 Q.R. 16, District Judge Reeson, CC (Derby).

Minor injuries—neck—whiplash type injury

3577. M, male, a self employed manufacturer, aged 35 at the date of the road traffic accident and 36 at the assessment, sustained a whiplash injury. He experienced pain immediately after the collision in his neck and lower back. He also experienced pain in his left leg. M attended his GP the same day whereupon he was examined and a diagnosis of whiplash was made. He was not given specific treatment but was advised to take painkillers. The symptoms were acute for a period of two to three weeks before improving. During that period he had disturbed sleep for about a week due to the discomfort caused by his injuries and was unable to participate in sports due to the leg and neck discomfort. In total M was absent from work for two days but returned because he could not afford to take any more time off. When examined some nine weeks after the accident, M no longer experienced symptoms in the back or leg but there was tenderness over the neck, coupled with minimal restrictions of movement. M's symptoms resolved within 11 months of the accident. *General Damages*: £2,000.

MOHER v. PEACH, November 22, 2001, Deputy District Judge Magaw, CC (Salford). [*Ex rel.* Kiril Waite, Barrister, Kings Bench Chambers, Wellington House, 175 Holdenhurst Rd, Bournemouth, Dorset].

Minor injuries—neck—whiplash type injury

3578. M, male, a personnel manager aged 28 at the date of the road traffic accident and 30 at the disposal hearing, sustained a soft tissue whiplash injury to his neck, a soft tissue contusion to his right elbow, a soft tissue contusion to the left hip and situation specific travel anxiety. For the first three days after the accident, M was generally very stiff and his sleep was disturbed. Gradually, over the next two to three weeks, M experienced improvements in his neck symptoms and the ability to move his neck progressively improved. Upon examination two months after the accident, M continued to feel symptoms in his neck when sitting watching television, working at his computer or driving. The bruising to M's right elbow settled after one week and the hip bruising resolved within one day. M became a hesitant and over cautious driver and experienced symptoms of anxiety whilst travelling by car. He was absent from work one day. The prognosis was for M to recover fully from his neck symptoms and travel anxiety within six to nine months after the accident. In fact, M did not fully recover from his neck symptoms until 10 months after the accident and the award was made on that basis. *General Damages*: £2,000

MANNING v. GILLESPIE (2002) 3 Q.R.10, District Judge Martin, CC (Leicester).

Minor injuries–neck–whiplash type injury

3579.   W, male, a warehouseman, aged 16 at the date of injury and 18 at the disposal hearing, suffered personal injury in a rear end shunt road traffic accident. W sustained nervous shock, a whiplash injury to his cervical spine and a soft tissue jarring injury to his lower back in the accident. W was emotionally very upset by the accident, feeling physically sick and trembly for one day. He had moderately severe pain and stiffness in his neck. His symptoms remained constant for three to four weeks before improving. They largely resolved after four weeks. The prognosis was for W's whiplash symptoms to settle completely within six to seven months after the accident. W also suffered moderately severe pain and stiffness in his low back, which persisted at that level for two to three weeks. The prognosis was for W's low back symptoms to resolve completely within seven to nine months after the accident. W was absent from work for four weeks. *General Damages*: £1,850 (agreed and approved).

W (A CHILD) v. HUNT [2002] 2 Q.R.16, Judge McKenna, CC (Birmingham).

Minor injuries–neck–whiplash type injury

3580.   P, female, an agency worker, aged 52 at the date of the accident and 53 at the disposal hearing, was the driver of a vehicle involved in a rear-end shunt. She experienced pain in her neck the day after the accident. Her symptoms of whiplash were initially severe and persisted at that level for approximately three months. Following the accident she was not required to take any time off work as her hours were flexible. P took painkillers as and when required. Her domestic life, including tasks such as ironing and cleaning, was affected for two months. Her psychological symptoms included initial shock and increased anxiety as a driver. Both her physical and psychological symptoms were expected to resolve within eight to nine months from the date of the accident. *General Damages*: £1,750

PHILLIPS v. MONK [2002] 2 Q.R.16, District Judge Horan, CC (Altrincham).

Minor injuries–neck–whiplash type injury

3581.   D, male, aged 15 at the date of the accident and 17 at the child settlement approval hearing, was involved in a rear end shunt road traffic accident. D did not feel any pain immediately after the collision. However, within one day, he started to suffer from discomfort on the right side of his neck and on the top of his right shoulder. He attended hospital after the accident where he was diagnosed as having suffered a soft tissue whiplash injury to his cervical spine. D was prescribed Ibuprofen medication. He was absent from school for two days. The neck symptoms were particularly intrusive for a few months after the accident. Initially D also suffered from nightmares and intrusive thoughts about the collision. His symptoms gradually improved and had finally resolved within twelve months of the accident. *General Damages*: £1,750.

D (A CHILD) v. BERNARD SHENTON LTD [2003] 1 Q.R. 15, District Judge Cooke, CC (Birmingham).

Minor injuries–neck–whiplash type injury

3582.   T, female, aged 10 at the date of the accident and 11 at the hearing, sustained a whiplash type injury to the cervical spine. She was taken to hospital and attended her GP some days later. T was immediately aware of pain and stiffness in the neck, which was described as moderate and constant for two weeks. She further complained of moderate chest pain, which remained constant for two weeks before resolving. T was absent from school for one week and did not return to PE lessons for two weeks. T continued to experience some neck pain and stiffness four months after the accident when examination revealed mild tenderness over the cervical spine and a reduced range of movements. The prognosis was for a complete recovery within five to six months of the accident although, at the disposal hearing, T reported that her residual symptoms lasted slightly longer. In addition to the physical injuries, T was shaken for five days and continued to experience occasional flashbacks four months after the accident. *General Damages*: £1,700.

TURNER v. GRIFFITHS (2002) 3 Q.R.10, District Judge Jackson, CC (Romford).

Minor injuries—neck—whiplash type injury

3583. R1, male, a warehouseman, and R2, female, a retail manager, aged 31 and 28 respectively at the date of the road traffic accident and 33 and 30 respectively at the disposal hearing, each sustained a whiplash type injury to their necks. R1 attended hospital the following day and, upon examination, was prescribed anti-inflammatory medication. He was absent from work for two days. Symptoms were severe for the first three weeks, but they moderated themselves over the next three weeks. R1, attended upon his GP who referred him for two sessions of physiotherapy. During the initial six week period during which time the pain was controlled by ibuprofen, R1 experienced continued sleep disturbance, difficulties driving and discomfort at work with the heavier aspects of his duties. Upon examination three months post accident, a full and pain free range of movement of the cervical spine was noted. However, R1 still complained of continuing minor intermittent symptoms in his neck which were expected to and did resolve completely over the next one to two months. R2 did not need attention from her GP or the hospital. She had one day off work. She experienced moderate discomfort for the first two weeks, which was controlled by ibuprofen. She had difficulty bathing and also suffered from a disrupted sleep pattern. She transferred to desk duties at work during that initial period. Thereafter, her symptoms continued to improve until four weeks post accident when she had completely recovered. *General Damages*: R1 £1,650; R2 £800.

ROYLE v. SMITH, August 7, 2001, Deputy District Judge Cooke, CC (Salford). [*Ex rel.* Andrew Lawson, Barrister, 24A St John Street, Manchester].

Minor injuries—neck—whiplash type injury

3584. W, female, aged 34 at the date of the road traffic accident and 36 at trial, began to notice neck discomfort and stiffness, which increased thereafter, together with headaches, four to five hours after the accident. W also suffered double vision, nausea and vomiting. She was admitted to hospital for one night. The visual disturbance and vomiting settled within a few days although the headaches, nausea and neck symptoms persisted for a couple of weeks. W was on one week's annual holiday at the time of the accident and could not take a short planned trip to Scotland because of her injuries. She was unable to return to work until two weeks after the accident. On her return to work she still had intermittent headaches and nausea. The neck symptoms settled after three weeks and the residual symptoms of headache and nausea after a further four weeks. *General Damages*: £1,500.

WAKE v. BULLOUGH CONTRACT SERVICES [2002] 4 Q.R.13, District Judge Edwards, CC (Keighley).

Minor injuries—neck—whiplash type injury

3585. T, female, an accounts assistant, aged 22 at the date of the road traffic accident and 25 at the date of the disposal hearing, suffered a soft tissue whiplash injury to her cervical spine and seatbelt bruising to her chest. On the day of the accident she attended her local hospital. She was prescribed painkillers and a soft collar. She wore the surgical collar for a few days. Her sleep was disturbed for two nights and she was absent from work for two days. T suffered from moderate pain and stiffness in the centre of the back of her neck, which spread to her left shoulder. The neck and shoulder pain was acute for three days. It became mild and episodic on the left side of her neck. She could not drive for one and a half weeks after the collision. T also experienced a slight ache across the front of her chest for the first 10 days after the accident, especially upon taking a deep breath. The ache was aggravated by stooping. T's neck symptoms resolved completely within two to three months after the accident. *General Damages*: £1,400.

TWEED v. SAMRA (QUANTUM) [2003] 1 Q.R. 15, District Judge Savage, CC (Birmingham).

Minor injuries–neck–whiplash type injury

3586.   W, male, unemployed, aged 32 at the date of the road traffic accident and 34 at the hearing sustained a whiplash injury to his neck. He suffered severe symptoms for two days. These gradually improved and one month after the accident he suffered only one to two hours of symptoms each day. There was a full recovery within four months of the accident. *General Damages*: £1,350.

WEBSTER v. CENTRAL SELF DRIVE [2002] 2 Q.R. 16, Judge Marshall-Evans Q.C., CC (Liverpool).

Minor injuries–neck–whiplash type injury

3587.   K, male, an electrical engineer aged 30 at the date of the accident and 31 at the assessment of damages hearing, was injured in a road traffic accident. He suffered a whiplash injury to the neck. Acute symptoms consisting of pain at the back of the neck and restricted movement of the head persisted for 10 days. Symptoms progressively improved thereafter and a complete recovery was made after four weeks. K was absent from work for 12 hours and had difficulty entering confined spaces at work for three weeks. He was unable to do any gardening or lift anything heavy around the home for three weeks. *General Damages*: £1,250

KIRK v. BICKERDIKE [2002] 2 Q.R. 16, District Judge Wilby Q.C., CC (Bury).

Minor injuries–neck–whiplash type injury

3588.   B1, female, aged 30 at the date of the accident and 31 at the hearing, and B2, male aged 33 at the date of the accident and 34 at the hearing, driver and passenger, respectively, were involved in a road traffic accident. B1 sustained a whiplash injury to her neck. She was also shaken and in shock for three days after the accident. She had difficulty sleeping and had recurring thoughts about the accident. Her neck pain was severe for the first two weeks and she took painkillers for 10 days. She recovered fully from all her symptoms within six months of the accident. Her injuries made it difficult for her to do her household chores and to pick up her young son. She was unable to take part in her hobby of playing netball. B2 sustained a whiplash injury to his neck. He also had a pins and needles sensation in his left arm for the first week. He did not attend his GP as he had difficulty in obtaining an appointment. He took painkillers for two weeks and suffered severe discomfort in his neck for one week. After two months the majority of his symptoms had settled and he was completely recovered within six months. His daily activities were affected in that he had problems lifting his young son and he could not participate in his hobby of playing golf. He also took a week off work due to the accident. *General Damages*: B1 £1,250. B2 £1,250.

BROUGHTON v. WHITE, September 28, 2001, Deputy District Judge Blythe, CC (Birkenhead). [*Ex rel.* Percy Hughes & Roberts Solicitors, 19 Hamilton Square, Birkenhead].

Minor injuries–neck–whiplash type injury

3589. P, male, a mechanic, aged 23 at the date of the road traffic accident and 24 at trial, sustained a whiplash soft tissue injury to his lower back. Within a few hours of the accident P began to experience increasing pain in his low back with radiation of pain down the legs. He only took four days off his work, returning because he could not afford to miss out on bonus payments. However, he continued to suffer from discomfort during his work over the following month. P had one week of quite intensive discomfort in his lower back followed by a general resolution of symptoms over a further month. During that time he took painkillers, his sleep was disturbed by the back pain and he had difficulties with personal hygiene, in particular getting in and out of the bath and with dressing himself, in particular putting on pullovers. P's domestic duties were also limited and he had difficulties caring for his young children, particularly because he could not pick them up. Prior to the accident, which occurred in the middle of the rugby season, P had played rugby at a relatively high level on a weekly basis. He could not play rugby for five weeks after the accident, nor could he work out at the local gym, which he had previously enjoyed. P made a full recovery from his injuries after five weeks. *General Damages*: £1,100.

PADDOCK v. WILD [2002] 6 Q.R. 16, District Judge Wildsmith, CC (Scarborough).

Minor injuries–neck–whiplash type injury

3590. T, female, an ice skating coach, aged 57 at the date of the road traffic accident and 60 at the disposal hearing, sustained a whiplash injury to her neck and cervical spine. After the collision she was shocked, shaking, dizzy and nauseous. She had pain in her right trapezius muscle. She consulted her GP the following morning and was advised to take one week off work and to avoid lifting. She was prescribed a week's supply of ibuprofen tablets for pain relief. Thereafter she took paracetamol intermittently for a period of two weeks. T had stiffness and aching in her cervical spine towards the right shoulder, which worsened in the 36 hours immediately after the accident. T's sleep was disturbed for a few nights. Her neck pain was aggravated by bending. The neck symptoms began to ease after five days and had almost resolved three weeks after the collision. T was absent from work for a week immediately after the accident and, upon her return, felt occasional twinges in her neck when assisting clients with dance moves for a further three to five weeks. T confirmed that her neck did not become completely asymptomatic until six to eight weeks after the accident. T also suffered throbbing headaches for one to two hours per day; these had resolved completely by three weeks after the injury, *Dopson v. Oscar Faber Group Ltd* (Unreported, July 13, 1998), [1998] C.L.Y. 1737 was distinguished, the judge considering T's injuries to be more serious. *General Damages*: £1,100.

TURNER v. POULTON [2003] 1 Q.R. 15, Judge Oliver-Jones Q.C., CC (Birmingham).

Minor injuries–neck–whiplash type injury

3591. H, male, aged 45 at the date of the road traffic accident and 45 at trial, suffered a minor whiplash injury to his neck. An hour or so after the accident, mild pain and stiffness developed in the centre of the back of the neck spreading into the left and right posterio-lateral regions which persisted for a week and then diminished. Some seven weeks post accident, the continuing symptoms were described as neck discomfort occurring on rapid movement of the head and neck. There was palpable tenderness in the muscles supporting the left and right posterio-lateral regions on examination. A full recovery was expected to be made between five and six months post accident. H also suffered very minor psychological symptoms that persisted for a few days post accident. No medical treatment was sought nor any time lost from work. *General Damages*: £1,000.

HOLDEN v. DE ASHA [2002] 2 Q.R. 16, Deputy District Judge Brookes, CC (Birkenhead).

Minor injuries–neck–whiplash type injury

3592.   D, female, aged 54 at the date of the accident and 55 at the assessment, suffered a whiplash type injury to her neck. She attended hospital and was advised to take analgesia. Her symptoms were severe for two to three days but a full recovery was made within two weeks of the accident. D took painkillers for two weeks. However, she was shocked and shaky and continued to feel wary and anxious when travelling either as a driver or a passenger. She tried to avoid the scene of the accident when driving. It was accepted that these residual symptoms had continued until the date of assessment, 21 months from the date of the accident, but would not continue thereafter. *General Damages*: £1,000.

DENNY v. BENGE [2003] 1 Q.R. 16, District Judge Loomba, CC (Newcastle).

Minor injuries–neck–whiplash type injury

3593.   B, male, aged 56 at the date of the road traffic accident and 60 at trial, sustained a cervical whiplash injury. He suffered immediate pain in his neck and shoulder which worsened over the next few days, such that even slight movements caused him pain and difficulty. He rested at home for one week and took painkillers for his physical injuries, which gradually resolved within four to six weeks. B also suffered from psychological symptoms which manifested themselves as increased nervousness when driving, a hypervigilant state and increased startle responses. The psychological symptoms improved within three to four months *General Damages*: £800.

BOURNE v. GOLDING [2003] 1 Q.R. 16, District Judge Hudson, CC (Lincoln).

Minor injuries–neck–whiplash type injury

3594.   L, female, aged nine at the date of the accident and 11 at the hearing, suffered a whiplash injury to her neck when the car in which she was a rear seat passenger was struck from behind. She attended her GP on the day of the accident, complaining of a headache and a pain in her neck. She was prescribed painkillers. Pain and stiffness in the neck appeared 24 hours after the accident and remained for the following three days. The pain was aggravated by rotational movements, although L was not absent from school. After three days the symptoms began to improve and had settled fully within seven days. *General Damages*: £500.

L (A CHILD) v. CRAWFORD, October 1, 2001, District Judge Arnold, CC (Portsmouth). [*Ex rel.* Katherine Huyton, Barrister, College Chambers, 19c Carlton Crescent, Southampton].

Minor injuries–spine below neck

3595.   A, male, a factory worker aged 26 at the date of the road traffic accident and 29 at the disposal hearing, suffered a micro tearing and stretching of the ligamentous, muscular and tendinous structures of the cervical spine. He also suffered a soft tissue injury to his lumbar sacral spine and a jarring injury to his hips. With the exception of some intermittent tingling in his neck, A's neck had more or less settled within nine months of the accident. A's lumbar pain resolved within a period of three months. The pain and discomfort in his hips had resolved completely within 12 to 15 months of the accident. As A's factory job was of a sedentary nature, he did not have to take any time off work. He was reluctant to drive or cycle for six months after the collision. *General Damages*: £2,400.

AHMED v. HUSSAIN [2002] 6 Q.R. 17, Judge Durman, CC (Birmingham).

Minor injuries–spine below neck–psychiatric damage

3596.　　C, female, aged 66 at the date of the road traffic accident and 69 at trial, sustained soft tissue injuries to her sternum, ribcage, trunk and thoracic and upper lumbar spines. After one month, she was still in severe pain and required help around the house. Her hobbies of dancing, walking and cycling were curtailed. She made a full physical recovery by the first anniversary of the accident, but psychologically she had been irritable and become a nervous passenger. Her anxiety persisted at the two years and nine month stage and the help of a clinical psychologist was recommended but not taken up. Although there was no expert psychological evidence, the judge accepted that the orthopedic expert had some mental health experience and that there was a compensable psychological injury. *General Damages*: £3,250 (apportioned as to £2,500 for the physical injuries and £750 for the psychological injury).

DERBYSHIRE v. DERBYSHIRE [2003] 1 Q.R. 16, District Judge Wright, CC (Liverpool).

Minor injuries–spine below neck–whiplash type injury

3597.　　D, male, a schoolboy aged 14 at the date of the accident and 15 at the child settlement approval hearing, was involved in a rear end shunt road traffic accident. D suffered a mild whiplash injury to his neck, an injury to his upper lumbar spine and shock. The day after the collision D became aware of pain in his upper lumbar spine and a headache. Due to the persistence of the symptoms in his spine D saw a nurse at his GP's surgery five days after the accident and she prepared him analgesics. During the first week after the accident, although D attended school, he was excused from PE lessons. D's lumbar pain settled fully within six months of the accident. D was also shocked for a day or two after the collision. *General Damages*: £1,500.

D (A CHILD) v. GURNANI [2002] 6 Q.R. 17, District Judge Waterworth, CC (Coventry).

Minor injuries–spine below neck–whiplash type injury

3598.　　S, male, a schoolboy, aged 11 at the date of the accident and 12 at the child settlement hearing, was involved in a rear end shunt traffic accident. S suffered a mild whiplash injury to his neck. A few hours after the collision he became aware of pain in his lower thoracic spine. He experienced intermittent pain over the next few days in both his neck and lower thoracic spine. S saw a nurse at his GP's surgery four days after the accident and she provided him with analgesics. The pain in S's neck and spine gradually resolved within two months of the accident. The pain was occasionally severe enough to need to take painkillers but it did not otherwise restrict S's activities. He was not absent from school. *General Damages*: £1,100.

S (A CHILD) v. GURNANI [2002] 6 Q.R. 17, District Judge Waterworth, CC (Coventry).

Minor injuries–back

3599.　　M, male, aged 46 at the date of the road traffic accident and 48 at trial, sustained a soft tissue injury, diagnosed as a sacroiliac joint sprain, to his lower back. He also struck his head, sustaining bruising which resolved in two weeks and caused headaches for six to eight weeks. M attended hospital on the day of the accident, where he was given advice and discharged. He had only one day off work. M continued to suffer back pain and attended his GP three weeks after the incident, and was advised to take pain killers. His pain was provoked by standing for long periods. His job involved attending trade exhibitions in the summer months, where he had to stand up all day. By the end of the day he would be in pain from his back. Driving for long distances caused problems, as did the heavier domestic activities. However, he was relatively pain free in the winter months when he was not attending exhibitions. M had physiotherapy just over two years after the accident, which largely resolved his problems. The medical evidence was that any symptoms beyond two years from the date of the accident were not accident related. *General Damages*: £3,450.

MORRISON v. FULFORD [2002] 2 Q.R. 17, Judge Brandt, CC (Colchester).

Minor injuries–back–whiplash type injury

3600.   C, female, aged 15 at the date of the road traffic accident and 17 at the child settlement approval hearing, suffered a whiplash injury to the neck, a soft tissue injury to her lower spine and travel anxiety. She attended her GP six days after the accident and was prescribed Ibuprofen. C was very shaken up by the collision. The next morning she became aware of an aching in her neck, particularly on the right side. The neck ache worsened over the next two days, was constantly present and acute for three weeks and then became intermittent. C's neck pain had fully resolved within eight months of the accident. C also suffered right sided lower back pain, which radiated into her right buttock. Initially this pain occurred every time C stood up but eased after two weeks and only recurred two to three times per week. The lumbar pain lasted for a few minutes at a time only. C's lumbar spine pain had improved significantly within 10 months of the accident. By 17 months after the accident C still suffered from occasional low lumbar pain on turning on her right side. This occurred every couple of weeks and lasted a few seconds. C took no time off school, but could not participate in PE lessons for a few weeks. She was a very keen and competent netball player. Medical opinion was that she would not be able to return to playing county level netball until two years after the accident. C's travel anxiety settled within two months of the accident. *General Damages*: £3,000.

C (A CHILD) v. PRICE [2002] 6 Q.R. 18, District Judge Wartnaby, CC (Birmingham).

Minor injuries–back–whiplash type injury

3601.   S, male, a taxi driver, aged 36 at the date of the accident and 39 at trial, sustained a whiplash injury affecting his neck and back. He attended hospital immediately after the accident and was prescribed anti-inflammatories, which he took for a period of about two weeks. Neck pain was experienced on a daily basis along with headaches. He experienced pain radiating from the low back into the right thigh. Generally the symptoms were at their worst for the first two weeks after the accident. S's low back region was stiff for approximately 30 minutes on waking. Sharp movement, driving, sitting for long periods and bending all exacerbated S's symptoms. S was undergoing physiotherapy in addition to performing daily exercises to alleviate pain and strengthen the back. As a consequence of his accident, S was unable to work. However, at trial he did not seek to pursue a claim for loss of earnings. Upon examination four months after the accident, S exhibited tenderness in the area of the trapezius muscles. Flexion and rotation was full and normal save that full right hand movement caused discomfort. Tenderness was also present at L3/4 and L4/5. The symptoms had completely resolved within 18 months of the accident. *General Damages*: £2,000 (agreed and approved).

SHABIAR v. IQBAL [2002] 2 Q.R. 17, Recorder Cardinal, CC (Birmingham).

Minor injuries–back–whiplash type injury

3602.   F, female, a teacher, aged 37 at the date of the road traffic accident and 39 at trial, suffered a whiplash injury and lower back pain. During the first week she wore a collar and took analgesics for her neck symptoms. Within the first month she had made a more or less full recovery from her neck symptoms. Her back symptoms deteriorated about one month after the accident, improving thereafter. Back pain caused her difficulties in sitting, standing and washing for a few weeks. She took two months off work. Upon her return she could not initially participate in physical instruction. For the first two months she could not perform domestic chores. With the assistance of physiotherapy she made a reasonable recovery within four months of the accident but her symptoms persisted. F had a history of back problems and the judge found that any symptoms extending beyond four months were constitutional and not related to the accident. *General Damages*: £2,000.

FRENCH v. EDWARDS, February 14, 2002, District Judge Cooke, CC (Birmingham). [*Ex rel.* Jinder Boora, Barrister, 24 The Ropewalk, Nottingham].

Minor injuries–back–whiplash type injury

3603. B, female, a housewife, aged 20 at the date of the accident and 22 at the disposal hearing, suffered personal injuries in a side impact road traffic accident. B attended her GP immediately after the collision. She was diagnosed as having suffered micro tearing and stretching of the ligamentous, muscular and tendinous structures of the lower back. She also suffered a whiplash injury to her cervical spine. B had difficulty pursuing her hobby of sewing after the accident as she found it uncomfortable sitting at a sewing machine. B's back injury and her whiplash injury settled gradually over a 12 month period after the collision. *General Damages*: £1,900.

BIBI v. HUSSAIN [2002] 6 Q.R. 18, Judge Durman, CC (Birmingham).

Minor injuries–shoulder

3604. B, male, a driver, aged 54 at the date of the road traffic accident and 57 at the hearing, was aware of the impending impact and gripped the steering wheel bracing himself for the impact. Consequently, B developed stiffness and tenderness in his neck and right shoulder. The symptoms worsened overnight. He was taken to hospital the following morning where any bony injury was excluded but he was given painkilling tablets and cream. The neck symptoms resolved after three to four weeks. However the right shoulder symptoms, consisting of a burning type pain and significant discomfort continued, occurring on a daily basis but gradually reducing in intensity over time. B had to refrain from working for two weeks and only returned after that time due to financial pressure. He had significant difficulty driving his minibus as it did not have power assisted steering and he did not drive it at all for two or three months and thereafter avoided driving it where possible. B had difficulty lifting his arm above his shoulder and the grip in his right dominant hand was affected. B was in the process of landscaping his gardening and was unable to carry out any heavy digging or lifting for about two months. Thereafter he avoided any heavy work as much as possible. His injuries also prevented him from pursuing his hobby of fortnightly fishing. Twenty months after the accident, B was able to take a holiday, following which his residual symptoms significantly resolved. The medical evidence did not support the continuation of any symptoms beyond that period. *General Damages*: £3,300.

BAKIN v. WALL [2002] 4 Q.R. 14, District Judge Toombs, CC (Worksop).

Minor injuries–shoulder

3605. H, male, a body repair mechanic, aged 62 at the date of the accident and 64 at trial, suffered a minor injury to his right ankle, from which he made recovery within three days, and a soft tissue injury to his dominant right shoulder when he fell from a platform at work. The shoulder injury became worse over the following few days. There was significant pain and disability for a period of two weeks. Thereafter, the symptoms improved slightly. A course of physiotherapy was followed and a number of steroid injections were administered. He took nine weeks off work. Four months after the accident, H complained of a dull ache in the shoulder, giving rise to problems sleeping. The injury effected H's ability to enjoy his hobbies of tennis, swimming and caravanning. At trial, H complained of a constant nagging pain. X-rays revealed some degenerative change and it was found that H had previously had problems in the shoulder, notably what was described as "rotator cuff syndrome". The medical evidence was that the symptoms were wholly attributable to the accident for three months; thereafter, the accident had a progressively diminishing contribution to the symptoms so that twelve months after the accident, the symptoms were wholly attributable to the pre-existing problems. It was noted that at H's age such injuries were particularly difficult to recover from and that the appropriate JSB bracket was that for minor shoulder injuries. *General Damages*: £3,250.

HARRISON v. MONTRACON (REFRIGERATED VEHICLES) LTD [2002] 4 Q.R. 14, Judge Cracknell, CC (Kingston upon Hull).

Minor injuries–shoulder

3606.   A, female, aged nine at the date of the road traffic accident and 11 at the date of the settlement approval hearing, suffered a fractured left clavicle, a minor head injury, a superficial cut to the right dominant hand and travel anxiety as a result of a collision. A was not absent from school, as the accident occurred during the school holidays. A's fractured clavicle was supported by a sling fitted at the hospital. A wore the sling for six weeks and her collarbone was very painful for that period. She could not sleep properly during that time. After the sling was removed A's shoulder was still painful and the pain continued for a further three to four months. Upon examination 18 months after the accident A's collarbone and shoulder were virtually pain-free. The prognosis was for the residual discomfort in the collarbone to gradually resolve within 21 to 22 months of the accident. A also sustained a small haematoma on the back of her head which resolved spontaneously a couple of weeks after the accident. She had a minor cut to her right hand on the dorsum. Steristrips were applied. The cut healed within a couple of weeks, leaving a tiny scar of less than 0.5cm. A suffered some minor travel anxiety after the accident, including nightmares. *General Damages*: £3,000.

A (A CHILD) v. HUGHES, August 15, 2001, District Judge Sehdev, CC (Dudley). [*Ex rel.* Stephen Garner, Barrister, No 8 Chambers, Fountain Court, Steelhouse Lane, Birmingham].

Minor injuries–shoulder

3607.   B, male, aged 34 at the time of the accident and 39 at trial, suffered injury when he slipped on a patch of oil on the floor of his workplace, falling heavily onto his right shoulder. He was taken to hospital where X-rays demonstrated no sign of bony injury. B suffered pain in his shoulder capsule and in the sub-scapular muscles. He took anagesics to alleviate the pain. He had a full range of movement within six weeks. However, pain in the infra-scapular region continued. The only treatment he received was physiotherapy. He was off work for about four months. B made a full recovery from all symptoms attributable to the accident within about six months. *General Damages*: £2,000.

BIRKHEAD v. FLETCHERS BAKERIES [2002] 2 Q.R. 16, Deputy District Judge Anderson, CC (Sheffield).

Minor injuries–shoulder

3608.   A, male, aged 30 at the date of the road traffic accident and 32 at the disposal hearing, sustained a hyperextension/flexion injury to his neck, a bruising trauma to the left shoulder and shock. He did not attend hospital, but saw his GP several days after the accident, when he was given some painkillers. He received no other form of treatment. The symptoms to his neck manifested after a short period of time, but were described as being intermittent from the very outset. They slowly but steadily improved, disappearing completely within four weeks of the date of the accident. The symptoms resulting from the shoulder injury continued, causing A difficulties with heavy housework for a period of five weeks. On examination some three and a half months after the accident, A complained of trouble with his left shoulder at a frequency of about once per week. The prognosis was that the left shoulder pain would spontaneously improve, with a full and lasting recovery from all residual symptoms and disability within 12 months of the date of the report, being 15 and a half months from the date of the accident. At the date of the disposal hearing, some 11 months post accident, his symptoms had improved and only troubled him infrequently. He took no time off work from his laundry business, but this was found to reflect his stoicism rather than lack of symptoms. *General Damages*: £1,850.

ASGAR v. BUNYAN (2002) 3 Q.R. 10, District Judge Chrispin, CC (Romford).

Minor injuries – collar bone

3609.   T, male, a student aged 21 at the date of the accident and 24 at trial, right hand dominant, sustained a fracture to the right clavicle in a road traffic accident. A sling was used for the first three weeks and pain killers were taken for five weeks after the accident to alleviate problems with sleeping. Seven months after the accident, and continuing at trial, T noticed a pain free clicking sensation at the sterno clavicular joint. The clavicle healed and was undisplaced but with a callus formation resulting in a minor visible deformity which hindered T's hiking activities, causing discomfort in carrying a backpack. He was unable to return to his summer employment as a waiter for several weeks after the incident. *General Damages*: £2,800.

TOLFREE v. MAGUIRE [2002] 6 Q.R. 17, District Judge Tennant, CC (Newport).

Minor injuries – arm

3610.   H, male, aged 11 at the date of the accident and 13 at the child settlement approval hearing, tripped and landed on his left, non dominant, hand when walking on a pathway. He suffered a minimally displaced fractured distal radius and ulna. This was treated in a back slab, which H wore for approximately five weeks. After removal of the slab, H was able to move his wrist and hand well and, after a further four weeks he was able to return to full normal activities. There were no deformities or residual problems. *General Damages* (agreed and approved): £3,250.

HAMPTON (A CHILD) v. CALDERDALE BC, February 11, 2002, District Judge Slim, CC (Halifax). [*Ex rel.* Rhodes Thain & Collinson, Solicitors, 27 Harrison Road, Halifax].

Minor injuries – arm

3611.   H, female, aged 12 at the date of the accident and 14 at trial, suffered a greenstick fracture of the distal radius in her left, non dominant arm, close to the wrist, when she slipped and fell outside a shopping arcade. Her arm was in plaster for three weeks and she was off sports for five weeks but had made a complete recovery after six weeks. H was unable to undertake various planned activities in her Easter school holidays which had just begun at the date of the accident. The judge felt unable to award the minimum of £3,250 as stated in the JSB Guidelines for orthopaedic injuries class F(d) for simple fractures of the forearm because she felt that may not apply to greenstick fractures. She did however consider that the damages should be higher than were awarded in the similar case of *Murray (A Minor) v. Knowsley BC* [1998] C.L.Y 1649, particularly in view of the loss of amenity during the school holidays, *Murray* considered. *General Damages*: £2,750.

H (A CHILD) v. CB HILLIER PARKER (A FIRM) [2002] 4 Q.R. 14, District Judge Exton, CC (Cheltenham).

Minor injuries – arm

3612.   KY, female, a care assistant, aged 50 at the date of the road traffic accident and 52 at trial, sustained blunt bruising trauma to her left non-dominant forearm, and to the anterior aspect of both knees. KY, a pedestrian, described seeing the vehicle approach and believed that she would be crushed. Although shocked and tearful, she was able to attend work for a few hours before attending her GP the same afternoon, complaining of bruising and swelling to her left forearm for which she was prescribed Ibruprofen. Pain in the forearm was acute and constant for two days, subsequently becoming "mild and intermittent". Bruising to the anterior of both knees appeared within two days and resolved without complication after about two weeks. Five months after the accident KY's forearm continued to cause her short-lived discomfort when lifting patients at work. The forearm had fully recovered 15 months after the accident. KY reported sleeping difficulties, nightmares and flashbacks for some months, with occasional nightmares still occurring at the trial date. She continued to suffer situational anxiety when climbing in and out of her vehicle, although that anxiety was gradually diminishing. *General Damages*: £1,500.

KELLY v. KENDRICK, September 13, 2001, District Judge Raskin, CC (Bath). [*Ex rel.* Toby Halliwell, Barrister, Unity Street Chambers, 5 Unity Street, College Green, Bristol].

Minor injuries—elbow—leg

3613.   T, female, a clerical assistant aged 27 at the date of the accident and 29 at the disposal hearing, suffered personal injuries in a side impact road traffic accident. Immediately after the accident, T felt as if her right side was numb. She saw her GP the same day and presented with pain on the right side of her body, especially in her neck, right arm and right leg. T also started to get tingling sensations over the right elbow and the whole of her right leg. T, who was right hand dominant, was absent from work for five days. She found it difficult to type upon her return to work. Upon examination five months after the accident T still found typing difficult. She had pain and numbness in her right elbow, which made lifting objects difficult at work and domestically. She also had pain in her right knee upon driving. A diagnosis of soft tissue injury to T's right elbow and right knee was made. The prognosis was for T's symptoms to settle within 18 to 24 months from the accident. At the disposal hearing, the judge accepted that T was still having difficulty driving because of occasional pain in her right knee and elbow, but he felt such symptoms would resolve within 24 months of the accident. *General Damages*: £2,750.

THIND v. CHILDS [2002] 2 Q.R. 17, District Judge Rank, CC (Wolverhampton).

Minor injuries—fingers

3614.   N, male, a machine press operator aged 20 at the date of the accident and 24 at the assessment, crushed the index finger of his left non dominant hand whilst operating a press. He suffered a partial amputation of the pulp of the tip of the finger resulting in the nail being only partially attached and an undisplaced fracture of the terminal tuft of the distal phalanx. He suffered immediate pain and some blood loss and was taken to hospital where a nerve block was applied and an attempt made to stitch the nail back. Three weeks later, the wound was not healing and he was admitted for an operation under anaesthetic, kept overnight and the nail reinserted. He was away from work for eight weeks and did not return to his previous employment. A slight deformity remained with pointing and shortening of the finger and some cold sensitivity. The judge accepted that the injury impacted upon N's ability to undertake fine detailed work including his hobbies of pool playing, fishing and model building. The judge commented that the JSB Guidelines had not been particularly helpful, counsel for N having submitted that the case fell within a lacuna in the Guidelines. *General Damages*: £3,750.

NORTH v. PEREI GROUP PLC [2002] 6 Q.R. 18, District Judge Newman, CC (Chester).

Minor injuries—fingers

3615. H, female, aged 12 at the date of the accident and 14 at the child settlement approval hearing, caught the fingers of her right dominant hand in the hinges of a door at school. She suffered fractures to the distal phalanges of the right middle and ring fingers, together with a broken nail on the ring finger and lacerations. The lacerations were sutured and the fractures immobilised. The fractures had united approximately five weeks after the accident. H was left with two very small scars in both fingers. She made a full functional recovery. She was away from school for six weeks. *General Damages*: (agreed and approved) £2,000.

H (A CHILD) v. S [2002] 6 Q.R. 19, District Judge Harrison, CC (Halifax).

Minor injuries—fingers

3616. E, male, a construction worker, aged 37 at the date of the accident and 39 at trial, sustained injury during the course of his employment when a heavy beam of pre stressed concrete fell onto the little finger of his left, non dominant, hand. As a result E sustained a traumatic rupture to the central tendon extensor slip. The finger was immediately painful and very bruised. That evening his wife, a paramedic, bandaged the finger and applied a splint. E took no time off work. The judge found that the pain had settled within a few weeks of the accident. E sought no further medical treatment until he was seen at hospital four months after the accident and was then referred to the orthopaedic department for physiotherapy. E was treated with a dynamic splint, which he wore for six weeks. When examined 21 months after the accident, an obvious hooking of the finger was noted such that he was unable to straighten the interphalangeal joint, leading to a permanent flexion deformity around the joint of 30 to 40 degrees. As a result his ability to perform fine manipulative tasks was adversely affected. The obvious deformity caused E embarrassment. Functionally he was able to use the hand for most day to day or work related activities. No further improvement was to be anticipated. The medical expert described the ongoing disability as being of "minor inconvenience". *General Damages*: £1,900.

EWING v. FLOORSPAN CONTRACTS [2002] 6 Q.R. 19, District Judge Wharton, CC (Peterborough).

Minor injuries—fingers

3617. P, female, a packer, aged 24 at the date of injury and 26 at trial, sustained a crush injury of the index and middle fingers of her left, non dominant hand. The fingers became swollen and the injury was treated with strapping. P suffered pain, discomfort and inconvenience for some six to eight weeks and was off work for the first two weeks. The diagnosis was that P had sustained a soft tissue injury of the distal phalanges of the index and middle fingers. P suffered cold hypersensitivity for about 10 to 12 months, with a full recovery after this period. *General Damages*: £1,325.

PICKIN v. RPC CONTAINERS LTD, January 29, 2002, Deputy District Judge Foden, CC (Blackburn). [*Ex rel.* Whittles Solicitors, 23 Princess Street, Albert Square, Manchester].

Minor injuries—fingers

3618. R, male, aged 40 at the date of the accident and 41 at trial, was at his place of work when his foot fell into a six inch deep hole in the floor, causing him to lose his balance and fall to the ground below and onto his left hand. R, who was right hand dominant, suffered immediate pain to the little finger of his left hand. The pain was ongoing for two weeks after the accident. R was examined by a joint expert nine months after the accident. He was diagnosed as suffering from a bruising injury to the little finger of the left hand which had caused him pain for two weeks, but had resolved within a six to eight week period. He was said to have made a good recovery with no long term problems. *General Damages*: £900.

RICKUS v. TXU EUROPE GROUP PLC [2002] 6 Q.R. 19, District Judge Hudson, CC (Boston).

Minor injuries–sacrum, pelvis and hips

3619. S, female, aged 10 at the date of the accident and 13 at the child settlement approval hearing, was involved in a side impact road traffic accident. S was very shocked and upset by the collision. She felt the immediate onset of significant pain in the region of her left hip where the seatbelt buckle had restrained her. S's hip hurt when she walked. S was taken to hospital where she was diagnosed as having sustained a soft tissue contusion injury to her left hip. S's hip was treated by application of ice packs. S's physical symptoms improved over the 14 day period following the collision. The symptoms in her left hip had completely resolved after two weeks. S was very frightened by the accident and she became a nervous passenger. The prognosis was for S's psychological travel symptoms to settle between 15-21 months after the accident. At the hearing, S no longer suffered from travel anxiety. S was absent from school because of her injuries for one day. She could not do PE for two weeks. *General Damages*: £1,000.

S (A CHILD) v. AHMED, September 25, 2001, District Judge Ellery, CC (Birmingham). [*Ex rel.* Stephen Garner, Barrister, No.8 Chambers, Fountain Court, Steelhouse Lane, Birmingham].

Minor injuries–leg

3620. M, male, aged nine at the date of the accident and 12 at the assessment, suffered a laceration to the shin when he struck his leg on a sharp metal bar whilst descending the steps of a minibus. He was conveyed to hospital where the wound was sutured. On the following day, he fell over and the wound re-opened. On that occasion the injury was not re-sutured but was dressed and allowed to heal itself. M required the dressings be changed over the following three weeks and was absent from school for five weeks. The wound healed completely within approximately six to seven weeks of the accident. M was left with a residual scar measuring 3.5cm by 1.5cm. There were no functional restrictions but M complained that the scar was painful when it was knocked or during cold weather. The scar was a cosmetic deficit and it would not be possible to improve the appearance through surgery. *General Damages*: £3,000.

M (A CHILD) v. HUGHES [2002] 4 Q.R. 15, District Judge McCay, CC (Merthyr Tydfil).

Minor injuries–leg

3621. E, male, a traffic clerk, aged 41 at the date of the accident and 45 at trial, suffered an abrasion to his right lower leg after his motorcycle skidded when its wheels entered a depression on the highway. Initially he treated the abrasion himself. However it was slow to heal and became infected. He saw his GP five weeks after the accident and was prescribed antibiotics. Thereafter, E attended his GP on five occasions to have the abrasion dressed. The leg was painful and sore for about three months, after which full recovery was achieved. The only psychological symptom was slight shock immediately after the accident. He required no time off from work although he moved shifts when his leg was particularly sore and in order to attend his GP. He was not able to undertake his main hobby of driving for about three months after the accident. *General Damages*: £1,250.

ECCLES v. LINCOLNSHIRE CC, January 23, 2002, Deputy Circuit Judge Krickler, CC (Barnsley). [*Ex rel.* Jinder S Boora, Barrister, 24 The Ropewalk, Nottingham].

Minor injuries–knee

3622.   L, female, an auxiliary nurse aged 64 at the date of the accident and 67 at trial, suffered multiple injuries after slipping on copper pipes lying on the floor. She suffered a 2cm laceration to her right ankle, bruising to her right knee, a 0.5cm laceration to the left thigh and pain in her left shoulder and right hip. She felt extremely shocked and shaken. For the first two weeks she felt aching all over her body. She made a good recovery from her injuries within four weeks, save for the injury to her knee. She suffered pain, restricted movement and had difficulty bearing weight and walking. She required care from her son and brother assessed at one hour per day for seven weeks. After undertaking physiotherapy, her main knee symptoms began to improve after four weeks, with the remaining symptoms improving over six months. She was unable to engage in her hobby of ballroom dancing. She did not return to work and retired on medical grounds six months later. The judge did not take into account the length of time she took off work because she was so close to retirement in any event and because her failure to return to work was precautionary rather than a reflection on her ability to perform her duties. When medically examined nine months after the accident, L was suffering only occasional aching in her knee when squatting or kneeling. At trial the judge accepted that she was still suffering residual symptoms of an extremely minor nature. *General Damages*: £2,500

LAMB v. EAST YORKSHIRE NHS TRUST [2002] 2 Q.R. 18, Deputy District Judge Beavers, CC (Kingston upon Hull).

Minor injuries–knee

3623.   A, male, unemployed, aged 25 at the date of the accident and 28 at the disposal hearing, suffered personal injuries in a side impact road traffic accident. His left knee struck against the side of the front passenger car door in the collision. A attended his GP and was diagnosed as having sustained a soft tissue bruising injury to the his left knee and an aggravation of a pre existing whiplash injury to his cervical spine. The bruising to his left knee resolved within two months of the accident. Medical opinion was that A's pre existing whiplash injury had been aggravated by a period of two months. A was unable to assist his wife with the household shopping and with jobs about the house for a period of two months after the collision. *General Damages*: £1,650.

ASGHAR v. HUSSAIN [2002] 6 Q.R. 19, Judge Durman, CC (Birmingham).

Minor injuries–knee

3624.   S, female, aged 77 at the date of the road traffic accident and 78 at trial, sustained soft tissue injuries to both knees, a strain to the ankles, injury to the lumbar spine and injury to her upper arms. The knee and ankle injuries caused exacerbation of pre-existing conditions including pain and discomfort. For four months following the accident, S felt anxious and tearful. The pain to her upper arms lasted six weeks, during which time she had difficulty using her arms and found dressing and brushing her hair painful. During the week following the accident S suffered with increasing stiffness of the lumbar spine and her back remained painful for three weeks, after which her lumbar spine returned to its normal state. The knees were bruised and S suffered an exacerbation of pain in her knees for two months following the accident, after which they appeared to return to their normal state. During this two month period, S had difficulty walking without a stick and was unable to walk her dog as normal. S made a complete recovery within three months of the accident. *General Damages*: £1,500.

SHONE v. BROOKS [2002] 6 Q.R.20, District Judge Weston, CC (Telford).

Minor injuries—knee

3625.   N, male, a student, aged 17 at the date of the road traffic accident and 18 at the hearing, suffered soft tissue injuries resulting in mild to moderate pain in the right knee. The symptoms improved after two weeks and resolved two months after the accident. N also suffered mild pain for two days in the right ankle which fully resolved one week after the accident. He felt slightly shaky for two days. No medical treatment was sought. N missed a week's work at his part-time job at a fast food outlet. For three weeks, N was unable to play football but gradually resumed training thereafter and was playing three times a week after a further three weeks. There was no effect upon his domestic life. *General Damages*: £850.
    NIZIOLEK v. WHITEMAN [2002] 4 Q.R. 15, Judge Milligan, CC (Southampton).

Minor injuries—knee

3626.   S, female, a hairdresser, aged 18 at the date of the road traffic accident and 21 at the hearing, suffered a badly bruised knee caused by contact with the dashboard of the vehicle in which she was travelling. Examination at the accident and emergency department revealed no bony injury and S was advised to take analgesics when necessary. S took a few days off work as she could not stand for long periods. Maximum discomfort persisted for one week, followed by a further two or three weeks during which S's social life was restricted and certain activities of daily living were uncomfortable. She complained of disturbed sleep for three weeks but did not seek any medical advice for those symptoms. Thereafter she made a full recovery. *General Damages*: £800
    KELLARD v. SMITH [2002] 2 Q.R. 18, District Judge Siverwood-Cope, CC (Chelmsford).

Minor injuries—knee—neck

3627.   E, female, a sales assistant, aged 22 at the date of the accident and 25 at the disposal hearing, suffered injury in a side impact road traffic accident. She was initially shocked and, as she got out of her car, her knees collapsed underneath her. She saw her GP the following morning and was diagnosed as having suffered a soft tissue whiplash injury to her neck and cervical spine and soft tissue bruising to both knees. She took one day off work. E experienced some cracking and crunching noises in her neck which gradually settled and the pain and discomfort in her neck had resolved within 12 months of the accident. The initial bruising of the knees began to improve within a few days but E continued to suffer persistent pain in her left knee and across the anterior of both kneecaps. She had difficulty bending her knees and she found it difficult to walk for more than one hour. Her knees sometimes "seized up" if she tried to kneel down. E could not participate in her hobbies of dancing and aerobics. E had an underlying constitutional condition in both of her knees and only six to eight months of her knee symptoms were attributed to the road traffic accident. *General Damages* (agreed and approved): £2,600.
    IKON OFFICE SOLUTIONS LTD v. EDWARDS, February 5, 2002, Recorder Pittaway Q.C., CC (Birmingham). [*Ex rel.* Stephen Garner, Barrister, 8 Fountain Court, Steelhouse Lane, Birmingham].

Minor injuries—ankle

3628.   W, male, a factory worker, aged 21 at the date of the accident and 24 at trial, fell upon steps. He suffered an oblique fracture of the right lateral malleolus. He was treated by the application of a below knee plaster cast that he wore for eight weeks. He was absent from work during this time. After the removal of the cast W gradually recovered mobility in the ankle and there were no episodes of the joint giving way. W also injured his right knee in the fall. He had suffered from a sub standard cruciate ligament prior to the accident. He subsequently underwent reconstructive surgery.

When examined some two years after the accident, he complained only of intermittent and occasional aching of the ankle. Clinical examination was normal. It was not anticipated that long-term consequences would result. W's knee remained symptomatic notwithstanding corrective surgery. The medical evidence identified the fracture to the ankle as a consequence of the subject fall but the symptoms of discomfort in the knee and the requirement for surgery were caused by the pre existing condition and could not be connected with the accident. Damages were assessed upon the basis of the fracture to the ankle and upon the accident having caused several weeks of pain in the knee. *General Damages*: £3,750.

WILSON v. BLAENAU GWENT CBC [2002] 4 Q.R.15, District Judge Carson, CC (Cardiff).

Minor injuries—ankle

3629.   M, male, a waiter, aged 22 at the date of the accident and 25 at trial, was knocked off his motorcycle by G's van. He was shaken, but not immediately aware of any pain or injury. He went home and within one hour became aware of pain in his left ankle and noticed a cut to his right hip. He attended hospital where an X-ray of the ankle revealed no bony injury. The following morning he awoke with pain and stiffness in his neck. The cut to the hip caused minor discomfort for a week before healing leaving a small scar. M suffered moderate discomfort and restriction in the neck for one week and minor symptoms for a further two weeks before resolution. The ankle was severely painful for a week and moderately painful for a further week. Thereafter the symptoms in the ankle became intermittent. He took painkillers and was unable to sleep comfortably for two weeks. He took four weeks off work. On examination two months after the accident, M complained of intermittent pain in the ankle brought on by prolonged standing or walking, and loss of confidence as a motorcyclist. All symptoms resolved within 18 months of the accident. *General Damages*: £2,500.

MOUSER v. GROSSMAN, October 17, 2001, Judge Medawar Q.C., CC (Central London). [*Ex rel.* Richard Menzies, Barrister, 8 Stone Buildings, Lincoln's Inn, London].

Minor injuries—ankle

3630.   C, male, a warehouse operative aged 33 at the date of the accident and 36 at trial, tripped in a pot hole, sustaining severe strain to left ankle. He attended hospital and a plaster cast was applied to the ankle for a period of six weeks. C was on crutches thereafter. Eight months later, C was generally symptom-free but left with some remedial swelling, discoloration and pain on extremes. It was found that the symptoms would resolve completely by 12 months after the accident. *General Damages*: £1,750.

CHAPPELL v. UNITED BRISTOL HEALTHCARE (2002) 3 Q.R.11, District Judge Jones, CC (Manchester).

Minor injuries—respiratory organs and chest

3631.   B, female, a primary school teacher, aged 44 at the date of the road traffic accident and 45 at trial, sustained a bruising injury to the sternum, minor seat belt bruising to the right side of her neck, trapezius muscle and shoulder area and superficial grazes to the right foot, together with flashbacks and driving related anxiety. She was admitted to hospital and discharged with advice to take analgesics. The right foot healed uneventfully and the bruising to the neck, trapezius muscle and shoulder caused pain and discomfort over a period of two weeks. The major injury was the bruising to the sternum and, for the first few days, the pain from this caused B to be confined to bed. During this period, trunk movements caused pain and B required assistance from her husband to move around. B suffered sleep disturbance for approximately two weeks and discomfort when breathing and shortness of breath upon heavy activity for one month. She took analgesics for two months. She took two weeks off work and, upon her return, could not participate in physical education lessons for a further six to eight weeks. She required assistance bathing and was unable to do any housework for the first week. She was unable to go to the gym or swim for three months. Seven months after the accident, the only remaining symptom was tenderness in the midline of the sternum, which was expected to settle by 21 months after the accident. B suffered from flashbacks for one month after the accident. She returned to driving after two weeks but was very anxious. Seven months after the accident she was still a little anxious but this residual anxiety was expected to resolve by 21 months after the accident. *General Damages*: £2,500.

BOLTON v. ELLIS, March 1, 2002, District Judge Greenwood, CC (Leeds). [*Ex rel.* Tom Nossiter, Barrister, Park Lane Chambers, 19 Westgate, Leeds].

Minor injuries–respiratory organs and chest–asthma

3632. L, female, aged six at the hearing, was diagnosed with asthma in the year prior to moving into damp and mouldy premises when she was 18 months old. L lived at the property for eight months during which time her asthma became more frequent, especially at night. It was said that the prevailing conditions were directly responsible for a worsening or exacerbation of an existing asthmatic condition. L's condition improved dramatically when the family moved to better maintained accommodation. *General Damages*: £1,750.

L (A CHILD) v. EMPIRE ESTATES [2002] 6 Q.R. 20, District Judge Ackroyd, CC (Bury).

Minor injuries–headaches

3633. R, female, aged 11 at the date of the accident and 13 at the hearing, was injured when the car in which she was a passenger was involved in a collision. She sustained injuries to her head, neck, back and chest. The neck injury was a whiplash type injury which caused moderate pain and discomfort for two weeks and improved thereafter. The head injury gave rise to headaches which were frequent initially and settled after five months. The back and chest discomfort settled fully within eight weeks of the accident. R was absent from school for one day and could not take part in physical education for eight weeks. In addition, she was tearful for three days after the accident and suffered occasional nightmares. *General Damages*: £1,750.

R (A CHILD) v. HARFIELD [2002] 4 Q.R. 16, Deputy District Judge Guppy, CC (Southampton).

3634. Books

Burton, Frank; Nelson-Jones, Rodney–Nelson-Jones and Burton: Clinical Negligence Case Law 3rd Ed. Hardback: £120.00. ISBN 0-406-91959-3. Butterworths Law.

Exall, Gordon–APIL Guide to Fatal Injury Claims. Paperback: £30.00. ISBN 0-85308-757-1. Jordans.

Harvey, Mark–APIL Guide to Conditional Fee Agreements. Paperback: £30.00. ISBN 0-85308-754-7. Jordans.

Herbert, Rebecca–Personal Injury Claims Manual. Looseleaf/ring bound: £225.00. ISBN 0-421-79990-0. Sweet & Maxwell.

Kevan, Tim; Adamson, Dominic–Sports Personal Injury. Paperback: £70.00. ISBN 0-421-77840-7. Sweet & Maxwell.

McQuater, John–APIL Model Letters for Personal Injury Lawyers. Paperback/Floppy disk: £47.00. ISBN 0-85308-766-0. Paperback: Floppy disk: £40.00. ISBN 0-85308-766-0. Jordans.

Tomkins, Nigel; Edwards, Claire–CFAs and Risk Assessment in Practice. Hardback: £75.00. ISBN 0-421-78620-5. Sweet & Maxwell.

Whalan, Mark–Limitation in Personal Injury Actions. Paperback: £42.00. ISBN 1-85811-273-7. EMIS Professional Publishing.

PERSONAL PROPERTY

3635. Books

Freedman, David; Walden, Ian–Walden and Freedman: Information Law. Looseleaf/ring bound: £175.00. ISBN 0-406-91623-3. Butterworths Law.
Property Disputes in Practice. 5th Ed. Paperback: £22.95. ISBN 1-84174-318-6. Blackstone Press.
Pugh-Smith, John; Sinclair, Graham; Upton, William–Neighbours and the Law. 3rd Ed. Hardback: £55.00. ISBN 0-421-69320-7. Sweet & Maxwell.
Terrell, Martin–Practitioner's Guide to the Court of Protection. Paperback: £45.00. ISBN 0-7545-1623-7. Tolley Publishing.

PLANNING

3636. Advertisements–deemed consent–deemed consent to display advertisements–dependence on planning permission for change of use

[Town and Country Planning (Control of Advertisements) Regulations 1992 (SI 1992 666) Sch.3 Part 1 Class 8; Town and Country Planning (General Permitted Development) Order 1995 (SI 1995 418).]

C sought judicial review to quash a notice issued by H requiring C to remove advertisement hoardings from a protective fence surrounding building works. The building works in progress on the site in question were for the conversion of a former bank and restaurant into shops. C claimed to have deemed consent to display the advertisements within the meaning of the Town and Country Planning (Control of Advertisements) Regulations 1992 Sch.3 Part 1 Class 8 in so far as the hoardings partially enclosed land on which building operations were taking place and for which planning permission had been granted.

Held, refusing the application for judicial review, that planning permission for the change of use in the present case was granted pursuant to the Town and Country Planning (General Permitted Development) Order 1995. However, planning permission for change of use did not include permission to carry out building or other work incidental to that change of use. Since the 1995 Order did not authorise the building work the work was therefore not being carried out in compliance with the planning permission for the purposes of the 1992 Regulations. Accordingly, C did not have deemed consent to display advertisements under Class 8.

R. (ON THE APPLICATION OF CAL BROWN LTD (T/A CB ADVERTISING LTD)) v. HOUNSLOW LBC, [2001] EWHC Admin 864, [2002] 2 P. & C.R. 22, Goldring, J., QBD (Admin Ct).

3637. Advertisements–deemed consent–scaffolding–digital display contained within safety screen–fabric of building

[Town and Country Planning Act 1990 s.336; Town and Country Planning (Control of Advertisements) Regulations 1992 (SI 1992 666) Sch.2 Class D.]

H appealed against a decision granting injunctive relief against it and ordering that a shroud advertisement, erected on a PVC sheet attached to scaffolding outside their department store, be removed. H had obtained planning permission for the scaffolding which was necessary for renovations to the store, and for the safety screen, but had not sought further permission for the advertisement digitally displayed on that screen. H contended that express permission for the advert was unnecessary since the scaffolding was a building for the purposes of the

Town and Country Planning Act 1990 s.336, and the advertisement had been incorporated into the fabric of that building pursuant to the Town and Country Planning (Control of Advertisements) Regulations 1992 Sch. 2 Class D.

Held, dismissing the appeal, that, irrespective of whether the scaffolding constituted a building for statutory purposes, the screen on which the advertisement had been displayed was not incorporated into the fabric of the scaffold as it lacked the requisite degree of permanence. The fabric of a building were those parts such as the structural components, into which category the safety screen did not fall. The display of the advertisement on a screen for which permission had been given for safety purposes was a change of use and therefore the grant of the injunctive relief was justified.

KENSINGTON AND CHELSEA RLBC v. HARVEY NICHOLS & CO LTD, [2001] EWCA Civ 702, [2002] 1 P. & C.R. 29, Dyson, L.J., CA.

3638. **Appeals–permission–application made under Town and Country Planning Act 1990 s.289–Court of Appeal**

[Town and Country Planning Act 1990 s.289; Civil Procedure Rules 1998 (SI 1998 3132) Part 52.]

P sought permission to appeal against a High Court decision refusing permission to appeal under the Town and Country Planning Act 1990 s.289.

Held, refusing the application, that the Civil Procedure Rules 1998 Part 52 established a single set of rules which applied to all appeals and PD 52 para.4.8 stipulated that there was no appeal against a decision made by the first appeal court following an oral hearing, *Clark (Inspector of Taxes) v. Perks (Permission to Appeal)* [2001] 1 W.L.R. 17, [2002] 2 C.L. 50, [2002] 1 C.L. 50 applied.

PRASHAR v. SECRETARY OF STATE FOR THE ENVIRONMENT, TRANSPORT AND THE REGIONS, [2001] EWCA Civ 1231, [2001] 3 P.L.R. 116, Kay, L.J., CA.

3639. **Appeals–remedies–third party challenge to planning inspectors decisions– applicability of Human Rights Act**

[Human Rights Act 1998 s.7 (1) (b), s.22 (4).]

A, a third party in planning proceedings, sought to appeal against the decision of a planning inspector to allow V's appeal against the refusal of planning permission for the siting of a mobile telephone reception mast in an area of outstanding natural beauty close to A's home. A number of the appeal grounds were dependent upon the applicability of the Human Rights Act 1998. A contended that she was entitled to have the grounds of appeal adjudicated upon, by virtue of s.6 (1) of the Act which made it unlawful for a public authority to act in a way which was incompatible with Convention rights, maintaining that a refusal to adjudicate upon them would wrongly deprive her of a remedy.

Held, dismissing the appeal, that the inspector's decision which formed the substance of the appeal, had been taken before the Act came into force and since the present proceedings had not been instigated by a public authority, the court were not obliged to apply the provisions of the Act by virtue of s.7 (1) (b) and s.22 (4), *Mabey v. Secretary of State for the Environment, Transport and the Regions* (Unreported, December 13, 2000) applied.

R. (ON THE APPLICATION OF ANSCOMB) v. SECRETARY OF STATE FOR THE ENVIRONMENT, TRANSPORT AND THE REGIONS; *sub nom.* ANSCOMB v. SECRETARY OF STATE FOR THE ENVIRONMENT, TRANSPORT AND THE REGIONS, [2001] EWHC Admin 100, [2001] 2 P.L.R. 34, Turner, J., QBD (Admin Ct).

3640. **Appeals–statements–fairness of a written representation procedure**

M, a disabled man, appealed against a decision of a planning inspector dismissing his appeal against an enforcement notice in respect of an extension to his property. M contended that it was unfair for the appeal to have been conducted by written representations, in circumstances where M had only agreed to the procedure because of his ill health, as the evidence was therefore untested and limited weight had been assigned to it. As a result the inspector had failed to give adequate or proper reasons for his conclusion because the untested evidence had not been assessed, analysed and the relative strengths weighed.

Held, allowing the appeal, that the matter be remitted to the Secretary of State for further consideration as M had been prejudiced by the inadequacy of the reasons provided by the inspector. A written representation procedure was not unfair in principle. However, in the circumstances of the instant case, fairness necessitated that there was a careful examination of the untested written material and a consideration of its relative merit rather than according it limited undifferentiated weight just because it was untested. The inspector should have given reasons for the conclusions reached in the light of the written material. There was uncertainty in the absence of proper reasons as to whether the inspector had carried out such an exercise but, if he had, M had not been given adequate reasons as to why the written material was rejected.

MAHAJAN v. SECRETARY OF STATE FOR TRANSPORT, LOCAL GOVERNMENT AND THE REGIONS, [2002] EWHC 33, [2002] J.P.L. 928, Ouseley, J., QBD (Admin Ct).

3641. **Caravan sites−mobile homes−porch extension−relevance of need for "mobility"**

[Caravan Sites and Control of Development Act 1960 s.29; Mobile Homes Act 1983.]

H, the owner of a licensed caravan site, appealed against the rejection of her claim that C, the occupier of a plot on the site, had, by attaching a porch extension to her mobile home and therefore was not entitled to the statutory protection afforded by the Mobile Homes Act 1983. In 1991, C had acquired and begun to reside in a purpose built caravan on the site further to a standard form written agreement. The following year, she had attached the bolt on porch extension having obtained planning permission. H had acquired the site in 1999.

Held, dismissing the appeal, that although the judge had correctly determined that the extension had not changed the mobility aspect of C's home within the Caravan Sites and Control of Development Act 1960 s.29, the correct question to be determined, was whether there had been a valid termination of the agreement by which C's home was situated on the site. The agreement was for the stationing of a mobile home within the definitions of the 1983 Act. The caravan was still on the site and the extension was within the scope of the agreement, therefore there was no valid termination.

HOWARD v. CHARLTON; *sub nom*. CHARLTON v. HOWARD, [2002] EWCA Civ 1086, [2003] 1 P. & C.R. 21, Carnwath, L.J., CA.

3642. **Change of use−development−certificates of lawfulness−limitations on future use**

[Town and Country Planning Act 1990 s.192.]

T appealed against a decision ([2001] P.L.C.R. 2) dismissing his application for judicial review of two certificates of lawfulness of proposed use or development obtained by the MOD pursuant to the Town and Country Planning Act 1990 s.192. The local planning authority had certified as lawful the proposed use of a military airfield for civilian purposes. T contended that the trial judge had been wrong to conclude that the planning authority were under no duty to impose limitations as to the future use of the proposed development.

Held, dismissing the appeal, that whilst it might, in some instances, be appropriate that certificates set out in detail the proposed development certified as lawful, it was outside the intention of s.192 to require a local authority to provide details as to what type of future use would be lawful. In the instant case, the planning authority could not be required to investigate the proposed aircraft movements and types of aircraft that would be in use at the airport. Protection against intensification of use was provided by the necessity of planning permission should further building be proposed. Moreover, any intensification which amounted to a change of use would give rise to enforcement action by the planning authority and the certificate of lawfulness would provide no advantage to the developers in such circumstances.

R. (ON THE APPLICATION OF TAPP) v. THANET DC; *sub nom*. R. v. THANET DC, *ex p*. TAPP; R. v. THANET DC, *ex p*. BRITTON, [2001] EWCA Civ 559, [2002] 1 P. & C.R. 7, Buxton, L.J., CA.

3643. Change of use–helicopters–landing pad–ordinarily incidental usage–appropriate test

[Town and Country Planning Act 1990 s.192.]

H appealed against a decision ([2001] EWHC Admin 600) upholding the refusal of its application for a certificate of lawfulness in relation to the proposed use of the roof of its London premises for helicopter landing.

Held, dismissing the appeal, that where an application was made for a certificate of lawfulness of proposed use or development under the Town and Country Planning Act 1990 s.192, the test to be applied was whether the proposed use was "ordinarily incidental" or ancillary to the primary use of the planning unit. The introduction of a helicopter landing pad to the roof of H's shop amounted to a change of use which was not ordinarily incidental to its primary retail use.

HARRODS LTD v. SECRETARY OF STATE FOR THE ENVIRONMENT, TRANSPORT AND THE REGIONS, [2002] EWCA Civ 412, *The Times*, April 3, 2002, Schiemann, L.J., CA.

3644. Change of use–houses–comparison between present and proposed use–meaning of "lawful"

[Town and Country Planning Act 1990 s.192; Town and Country Planning (Use Classes) Order 1987 (SI 1987 764).]

The Secretary of State appealed against the decision that a planning inspector had erred in concluding that a class C3 dwelling house, defined under the Town and Country Planning (Use Classes) Order 1987 as a single dwelling house for not more than six residents living as a single household, did not require planning permission for use by six persons recovering from mental health problems living in a single household with care because there would be no material change of use. An application for a certificate of lawfulness had been made under the Town and Country Planning Act 1990 s.192 for the proposed use. The local authority had refused the application on the grounds that along with the proposed occupancy by six persons, a minimum of one carer would also be needed at all times, and therefore the use would not be lawful. The inspector concluded that, although the contention that the proposed use fell within class C3 use was ill founded because there would be a minimum occupancy of seven, the character and nature of the proposed use would not be materially different from the previous use. In its successful appeal, the local authority submitted that the inspector had erred in comparing the proposed use against use of the house by a large family, given that there was no evidence that at the time of the application the house was being used by a large family.

Held, dismissing the appeal, that the word "lawful" in s.192 of the 1990 Act, meant lawful in the context of planning legislation, and in deciding whether a proposed change of use was a material change of use, a comparison had to be made between the present use and the proposed use. In deciding whether a change of use was a material change of use, the fact that no further permissions were needed to move from an existing use to the notional use, and from the notional use to the use applied for, was potentially relevant to the issue of whether planning permission should be granted for the use applied for. However, the interposition of notionally permitted use between existing use and use applied for was a complication which was not relevant to the exercise under s.192. The proposed use of the dwelling house as a residence for six persons and relevant carers was a material change of use and planning permission was required.

WALTHAM FOREST LBC v. SECRETARY OF STATE FOR TRANSPORT, LOCAL GOVERNMENT AND THE REGIONS; *sub nom.* WALTHAM FOREST LBC v. SECRETARY OF STATE FOR THE ENVIRONMENT, TRANSPORT AND THE REGIONS; SECRETARY OF STATE FOR TRANSPORT, LOCAL GOVERNMENT AND THE REGIONS v. WALTHAM FOREST LBC, [2002] EWCA Civ 330, *The Independent*, March 22, 2002, Schiemann, L.J., CA.

3645. Change of use–immunities–mixed use–fluctuation of uses

[Town and Country Planning Act 1990 s.171B (3).]

B appealed against a decision of the planning inspector to amend an enforcement notice served on the grounds of change of use. The land was primarily agricultural but during B's occupation, it had been used for a variety of uses including storage and business. B contended that the inspector had erred by finding that a material change had occurred within the previous 10 years. It had been held that the land was in mixed use and that, during the previous 10 years, various individual uses had intensified whilst others had lapsed, to the extent that there was a material difference in the overall mix of uses and that a material change had taken place. B argued that the uses referred to had been in place for a period exceeding 10 years and were accordingly immune from enforcement under the Town and Country Planning Act 1990 s.171B (3). It was also argued that the notice was invalid in view of its wording in relation to the specification of the uses. The Secretary of State resisted the appeal, arguing that the point was technical and unmeritorious.

Held, dismissing the appeal, that the individual uses could not be treated separately in law regardless of the fluctuations in the level of the uses that existed alongside them, *Lynch v. Secretary of State for the Environment, Transport and the Regions* [1999] J.P.L. 354, [1999] C.L.Y. 4176 applied. The inspector had correctly considered the effect of the additional uses on those uses subsisting at the start of the 10 year period. The inspector had however erred in the drafting of the notice as it referred only to a limited range of uses, which was a good, albeit technical, point. However, B had failed to raise the issue before the inspector and was therefore precluded from advancing it as a ground of appeal.

BEACH v. SECRETARY OF STATE FOR THE ENVIRONMENT, TRANSPORT AND THE REGIONS, [2001] EWHC Admin 381, [2002] J.P.L. 185, Ouseley, J., QBD (Admin Ct).

3646. Change of use–use classes–hostels–multiple occupation–accommodation for persons requiring care–correct approach to concept of single household

[Housing Act 1985 s.345; Town and Country Planning (Use Classes) Order 1987 (SI 1987 764) Sch.1 Part 3 para.3.]

K, a local authority, appealed against a decision ([2002] EWHC 493, Times, April 22, 2002) that three properties, used to provide temporary accommodation for young homeless persons, required planning permission for material change of use from dwelling houses to a hostel. The judge held that the residents could not be classed as living together as a single household within the meaning of the Town and Country Planning (Use Classes) Order 1987 Sch.1 Part 3 para.3. H, who lived next door to the premises concerned, had argued that the properties were houses "in multiple occupation" for the purposes of the Housing Act 1985 s.345 and that planning permission was therefore necessary.

Held, allowing the appeal, that a group of residents only living in the same house because of "a common need for accommodation, support and resettlement" could not necessarily be regarded as a single household. The judge had been too prescriptive in his approach to the concept of a single household which had led him to conclude that there was insufficient relationship between the occupants of the premises for them to be regarded as living together as a single household. Circular 13/87, issued with the 1987 Order, stated that Class

C3 within Sch.1 Part 3 para.3 was intended to include small care homes of up to six people living together for care and support in the community as in the instant case, *Simmons v. Pizzey* [1979] A.C. 37, [1977] C.L.Y. 1520, *Barnes v. Sheffield City Council* (1995) 27 H.L.R. 719, [1996] C.L.Y. 3104 and *Islington LBC v. Rogers* [2000] E.H.L.R. 3, [1999] C.L.Y. 3704 considered.

R. (ON THE APPLICATION OF HOSSACK) v. KETTERING BC, [2002] EWCA Civ 886, [2003] R.V.R. 63, Simon Brown, L.J., CA.

3647. Compensation–interest–contaminated land

PLANNING AND COMPENSATION ACT 1991 (AMENDMENT OF SCHEDULE 18) (ENGLAND) ORDER 2002, SI 2002 116; made under the Planning and Compensation Act 1991 s.80. In force: February 22, 2002; £1.50.

This Order amends the Planning and Compensation Act 1991 Sch.18 Part I, which specifies or describes the date from which interest is payable on compensation arising under statutory provisions which do not themselves provide for the payment of interest, by adding provisions relating to the payment of compensation under the Environmental Protection Act 1990 s.78G. Compensation is payable under that section where a person has been granted, or joined in granting, rights to enable the person on whom a works notice is served to carry out such anti-pollution works or operations as are specified in the notice. The amount of compensation is assessed in accordance with the Contaminated Land (England) Regulations 2000 (SI 2000 227).

3648. Compulsory purchase–compensation–assessment–interest rate

[Arbitration Act 1950 s.19A; Town and Country Planning Act 1971 s.51, s.170; Lands Tribunal Rules 1996 (SI 1996 1022) r.32.]

The Court of Appeal had already determined the substantive appeal ([2001] R.V.R. 65) in favour of A and had given the parties an opportunity to see if agreement could be reached about the rate of interest and the period for which it should be awarded. A was entitled to compensation for the compulsory acquisition of his land. The effective date of entry was August 7, 1989. The valuation had been by the discounted cash flow method assessed at June 24, 1989. A had been kept out of his money for about 10 years. No agreement was reached.

Held, that the applicable interest rate was the commercial court rate where compensation was payable as a consequence of a discontinuance order made pursuant to the Town and Country Planning Act 1971 s.51 prior to September 25, 1991. Compensation was payable under the Town and Country Planning Act 1971 s.170 and (2) the court had power to award simple interest at such rate as it thought fit pursuant to the Arbitration Act 1950 s.19A and the Land Tribunal Rules 1996 r.32.

ASLAM v. SOUTH BEDFORDSHIRE DC (RATE OF INTEREST), [2001] EWCA Civ 515, [2002] R.V.R. 16, Chadwick, L.J., CA.

3649. Compulsory purchase–compensation–expiry of limitation period

[Compulsory Purchase (Vesting Declarations) Act 1981 s.10(3).]

B sought compensation for the compulsory purchase of his property, which he occupied as a doctor's surgery. A general vesting declaration was made in December 1987 and the vesting date was January 1988. The reference to the Lands Tribunal was made in February 1999 and the council argued that the claim was outside the six year time limit laid down by the Compulsory Purchase (Vesting Declarations) Act 1981 s.10(3) and was therefore statute barred. B argued that the council had waived its right to rely on a limitation defence and that it was estopped from doing so. B's argument was based on discussions that were carried out after the vesting order was made. Provisional agreement was reached on the value of the premises and B's solicitors submitted a claim for an advance payment of £36,000 being 90 per cent of the minimum anticipated compensation figure which was paid by the council to B in March 1994 after the expiry of the time limit. The council's housing department noted that "B's ability to refer the matter to Lands Tribunal has now lapsed". B's solicitors subsequently wrote in April 1997 submitting details of patients lost by B's practice as a result of moving. Further correspondence in March 1997 suggested compensation of three times the annual loss in patient revenue.

Held, giving judgment for the defendant, that the claim was statute barred and B could not claim compensation. There had been a waiver by the council when it paid the £36,000 to B but that waiver could not be taken to have disabled the council from ever relying on the limitation defence. The waiver was not for all time but it was necessarily implied that any claim would be made within a reasonable time thereafter. That time was when B was able to assess the loss of patients to his practice, which was some time in 1994. There was no evidence of any waiver by the council of its right to rely upon a limitation defence thereafter. A limitation of an action was not of itself a breach of the European Convention on Human Rights as the Convention recognised the need for reasonable time limits on the pursuit of claims.

BHATTACHARJEE v. BLACKBURN WITH DARWEN BC [2002] R.V.R. 55, George Bartlett Q.C. (President), Lands Tr.

3650. **Compulsory purchase–compensation–leasehold riding stables–valuation on relocation basis–no loss of goodwill or client base**

[Land Compensation Act 1961 s.5.]

P referred an assessment of compensation for the compulsory acquisition of his riding stables business in the sum of £51,400 under the Land Compensation Act 1961 s.5 r.2. The assessment was made on the basis of £51,400 for total extinguishment and £49,000 on a relocation basis. P leased the property under a 14 year lease and sought compensation of £286,475 for equivalent reinstatement under s.5 r.5 with £358,942 for disturbance on the ground that, although the business would have continued but for the compulsory acquisition, there was no market for land for that purpose.

Held, assessing compensation at £119,438, that equivalent reinstatement did not apply for the purposes of s.5 r.5 as the evidence showed that there was a demand for land to be used for that purpose and P had effectively relocated nearby with no loss to his client base. Calculating compensation on the relocation basis with an allowance for consequent loss was reasonable and reflected the sum that a business man would reasonably expect to pay in the circumstances. No loss of goodwill was allowable on this basis as P had relocated the business in the same location and retained his existing customers.

PRIELIPP v. SECRETARY OF STATE FOR THE ENVIRONMENT, TRANSPORT AND THE REGIONS [2002] 3 E.G.L.R. 143, PR Francis FRICS, Lands Tr.

3651. **Compulsory purchase–compensation–loss on forced sale of business assets**

In a claim for compensation for the compulsory purchase of their premises, W claimed for repayment of a bank loan on the basis that the bank loan would have been amortised over a period of eight years and linked the repayment of the loan to the loss on forced sale of business assets as part of the loan had been used to finance the purchase of those assets.

Held, dismissing the claim and holding that there was no additional compensation payable, that business debts would only generally come into the reckoning if there was a penalty for their early discharge or if any loan was at an advantageous interest rate so that a purchaser of the business might pay more for the business because of it. Neither applied here. There was no evidence of any penalty attaching to the early discharge of the loan and the rate was not particularly advantageous. The loss on forced sale of the assets was a matter included within agreed compensation and was irrelevant to the question of the bank loan. The evidence did not support a conclusion that the loan would have been amortised over eight years or that it would have been repaid out of profits over that period.

WEYMEDE LITHO PRINTERS LTD v. RUNNYMEDE BC [2002] R.V.R. 61, George Bartlett Q.C. (President), Lands Tr.

3652. Compulsory purchase–compensation–mortgagees–entitlement

[Housing Act 1985 Sch.24 Part I para.2(1).]

FNB, the holder of a charge on a property purchased by F, appealed against the compensation determined as payable on the compulsory purchase of the freehold interest of the property by S. The tribunal found that the requirements of the Housing Act 1985 Sch.24 Part I para.2(1) had not been satisfied, in that FNB had failed to establish that F had the necessary interest in the property throughout the qualifying period.

Held, allowing the appeal, that the tribunal had erred in law in that, although it acknowledged that there was no evidence of default on the part of F during the material period, it had proceeded to decide that he may have defaulted because he had failed to make payments under the mortgage, yet that failure had occurred after the period of occupation in dispute. Furthermore, the court had erred in attaching weight to documents which were of no evidential value.

FARRELL v. SANDWELL MBC; *sub nom.* FARRELL v. FIRST NATIONAL BANK PLC, [2001] EWCA Civ 1107, [2002] R.V.R. 11, Robert Walker, L.J., CA.

3653. Compulsory purchase–compensation–negotiations continuing after end of limitation period–no agreement as to waiver

[Land Compensation Act 1973 s.52; Limitation Act 1980 s.9.]

In July 1991, W had obtained the freehold of land subject to a notice to treat for compulsory purchase compensation purposes, dated July 1990. In June 1991, W's agents had commenced correspondence with the local authority, requesting information so that compensation negotiations could commence. In June 1995, W's agents had quantified the claim in the sum of £6,290, plus a claim for a further £10,500 for alternative accommodation. The local authority made an advance payment of £5,660 in October 1998, pursuant to a 1995 agreement, which W had accepted "without prejudice" to his continued compensation claim. W had given notice of reference to the tribunal in 2001 pursuant to the Limitation Act 1980. The local authority sought a determination, as a preliminary issue, as to whether W's claim was barred.

Held, giving rulings on preliminary issues, that W's compensation claim was dismissed. Although the advance payment in October 1998 was made after the expiry of the six year limitation period under s.9 of the 1980 Act, there was no agreement to waive limitation and the negotiations had not proceeded on the basis that limitation did not apply. Therefore W could not rely on an estoppel to defeat the local authority's limitation defence, *Hillingdon LBC v. ARC Ltd (No.2)* [2001] C.P. Rep. 33, [2000] C.L.Y. 518 applied. W's claim was therefore limited to the agreed sum of £6,290 and he could not seek any further compensation under the Land Compensation Act 1973 s.52 owing to the expiry of the statutory limitation period, *Bhattacharjee v. Blackburn with Darwen BC* [2002] R.V.R. 55, [2002] 7 C.L. 477 distinguished.

WIBERG v. SWANSEA CITY AND COUNTY COUNCIL [2002] R.V.R. 143, George Bartlett Q.C., Lands Tr.

3654. Compulsory purchase–compensation–property located in conservation and approved renewal area–underlying scheme of compulsory purchase order–regeneration grants

T, freeholders, sought compensation from the local authority for the compulsory purchase of a row of five terraced houses containing 26 flats and vacant land to the rear, with planning permission for a further 12 flats. The total site, which comprised 0.285 of a hectare, was located within a conservation area and an approved renewal area. Subsequent to the compulsory purchase the site had been refurbished, funded substantially by grants. T submitted valuations based on refurbishment, with the assumption of grants, and on demolition and redevelopment. The local authority contended that compensation should not be increased as a result of a scheme underlying the compulsory purchase order. Therefore, the local authority argued, refurbishment grant aid should be excluded from the assessment of compensation as it had been provided for refurbishment because the site was in a renewal area and the renewal area was the underlying scheme.

Held, assessing compensation, that £50,000 for the houses and £47,500 for the vacant land was payable on the basis that demolition of the houses would not have been allowed. Grants for regeneration were disregarded and the availability of grant funding for refurbishment was not considered in determining the level of compensation. The regeneration of private sector housing within the renewal area was the compulsory purchase order's underlying scheme and should be disregarded from the assessment of compensation.

TAKHAR v. WOLVERHAMPTON MBC [2002] R.V.R. 96, M St J Hopper FRICS, Lands Tr.

3655. **Compulsory purchase–compensation–valuation–land acquired for road to serve development area–real world market value basis**

[Land Compensation Act 1961 s.5, s.9.]

Held, that the compensation payable following the service of a purchase notice in respect of a holding of about 0.15 of a hectare at Burnham on Sea, Somerset, lying on the line of a proposed road to serve a development area was to be assessed at its real world market value pursuant to the Land Compensation Act 1961 s.5 without adjustment for the fact that the proposed development had been referred to in a s.9 acquisition indication.

RICHARDS v. SOMERSET CC (NO.1); *sub nom.* RICHARDS v. SOMERSET CC [2001] 2 E.G.L.R. 135, PH Clarke, FRICS, Lands Tr.

3656. **Compulsory purchase–compensation–valuation–purchase of land for nature reserve–integral part of barrage project**

W appealed against a decision of the Lands Tribunal ([2001] 1 E.G.L.R. 185). LWA, the predecessor of the Welsh Development Agency, had compulsorily acquired land owned by the claimants in order to create a wetland nature reserve and thereby mitigate the environmental effects consequent upon the construction of a large scale barrage project. The Tribunal held, basing its decision on the "no scheme" rule given in *Pointe Gourde Quarrying & Transport Co v. Sub-Intendent of Crown Lands* [1947] A.C. 565, that compensation for compulsory purchase could not include an increase in value which was entirely due to the scheme underlying the acquisition namely, the barrage project. It followed that W was not entitled to a higher valuation based on the land's indispensability to the barrage project, "the barrage inhibition value". However, the claimant argued that *Gajapatiraju v. Revenue Divisional Officer Vizagaptam* [1939] A.C. 302, the *Indian* case, provided authority for an approach to the assessment of compensation that took LWA's purpose in acquiring the land into account, in so far as it would have led a purchaser to offer a higher price in "friendly negotiations". Thus, W submitted that, regardless of the no scheme rule, the acquiring authority was required take the added value given by the barrage project into account in assessing the proper level of compensation. The Tribunal had refuted this argument and stated that the *Indian* case conflicted with the "no scheme" rule and was no longer authoritative.

Held, dismissing the appeal, that the apparent conflict between the *Indian* case and *Pointe Gourde* could be reconciled if the cases were seen as turning on their own particular facts. It was not necessary to treat the *Indian* case as wrong. However, the Tribunal's conclusions on the nature of the scheme presented an insurmountable obstacle to the claim. The Tribunal had been entitled to find, on the facts of the case, that the creation of the nature reserve was an integral part of the barrage project. W was accordingly entitled to an increased value based on the use of the land as nature reserve, but not to the barrage inhibition value, *Pointe Gourde* applied, the *Indian* case considered.

WATERS v. WELSH DEVELOPMENT AGENCY; *sub nom.* MELVILLE v. WELSH DEVELOPMENT AGENCY, [2002] EWCA Civ 924, [2003] Env. L.R. 15, Carnwath, L.J., CA.

3657. Compulsory purchase–compensation–valuation–road scheme involving mineral extraction

R sought compensation for the compulsory acquisition of 1.6 ha of land in connection with the Avon Ring Road pursuant to a planning permission granted in 1988. The construction of the ring road through the land required the extraction of 123,450 tonnes of materials including topsoil and a mixture of clay, silt sandstone and bedded laminated sandstone. The excavated material was partly used on site to create a land bridge and the remainder removed from site. A certificate of appropriate alternative development was sought for uses to include mineral excavation but permission for mineral extraction was not forthcoming and was unlikely ever to be granted. The parties agreed in principle that, if minerals were extracted from the land as part of a scheme and they had a value then that value ought to be taken into account when calculating the compensation payable. However the council argued that, even if planning permission did exist for the extraction of minerals the extraction had no value given the low quality of the extraction, the lack of demand, the problems of access and the costs of spoil disposal. R argued that the value of the quantities actually extracted was £200,000.

Held, giving judgment for the claimant in part, that R was entitled to compensation in the sum of £17,000. The award was based only on the value of the land for agricultural purpose and horse grazing. The planning permission in existence was for a road and not for the extraction of minerals as a discrete and commercial operation. Extraction of minerals other than for the purpose of building the road would not have been permitted and would have been unlawful. Accordingly any increase in value from such use must be left out of account.

ROBERTS v. SOUTH GLOUCESTERSHIRE DC [2002] R.V.R. 63, PR Francis FRICS, Lands Tr.

3658. Compulsory purchase–compensation–valuation–shopping centres–development restricted to actual development scheme

Held, that the compensation payable for the compulsory acquisition of seven shops on the outskirts of Birmingham was limited to a total of £84,650 varying between £7,600 and £37,800 per unit since there was no possibility of any development other than the development scheme.

RANK LEISURE v. CASTLE VALE HOUSING ACTION TRUST [2001] R.V.R. 313, PH Clarke FRICS, Lands Tr.

3659. Compulsory purchase–compensation–valuation basis and ransom value of access land

B claimed compensation for land adjacent to a shopping centre owned by M. Part of the land provided access to adjoining land with development potential. Access to part of the land required improvement involving land owned by M. The issues which the Lands Tribunal was asked to resolve were whether (1) retail values or B1 business values did apply to all or part of the subject land; (2) M was a special purchaser for part of the land, and (3) what were the ransom values of the relevant access lands.

Held, awarding compensation, that M was not a special purchaser because there was other suitable adjacent land available. The proper basis of valuation was B1 industrial and the ransom values of the access lands was one third.

BRB (RESIDUARY) LTD v. SOUTH YORKSHIRE PASSENGER TRANSPORT EXECUTIVE [2002] R.V.R. 18, PR Francis FRICS, Lands Tr.

3660. Development plans–harbours–judicial review in respect of proposed development of Littlehampton harbour

M sought judicial review of the Board's decision to sell land at Littlehampton Harbour and of the Council's decision to grant planning permission for development of the harbour. The Board, to which the Council appointed four members, had statutory duties to maintain and improve the harbour. Both defendants owned land at the Harbour. The Local Planning Brief set out the policies to guide future development on the east bank of the river, including the Harbour, provided for a mix of residential, commercial and marine related leisure and recreation development proposals. The defendants decided to pursue separate and independent development proposals. The Board decided to sell land to developers whilst the Council granted planning permission for redevelopment of its land. There were concerns that the development did not adequately provide for the needs of commercial fishermen or maritime businesses. M sought judicial review on the grounds that the proposed development did not accord with the development plan, the objections to the development had not been taken into account, and the members of the planning committee were biased. The defendants opposed the application on the ground of delay.

Held, refusing the applications for judicial review, that taken overall the parties were acting at arm's length. The proposals had been given proper consideration and there was no legitimate expectation of further consultation. Both local knowledge and planning judgment were required for the interpretation of planning policy in a development plan. It was not merely a linguistic or legalistic exercise. There was no breach of statutory duty by the Board. Although the application for judicial review of the Council's decision had been issued just within the three months outside time limit, there was no prior notice to the defendants and the delay was prejudicial and therefore unreasonable. The application in respect of the Board's decision was issued significantly outside the three month time limit.

R. (ON THE APPLICATION OF MILLS) v. LITTLEHAMPTON HARBOUR BOARD; R. (ON THE APPLICATION OF MILLS) v. ARUN DC, [2001] EWHC Admin 588, [2002] P.L.C.R. 13, Sullivan, J., QBD (Admin Ct).

3661. **Development plans–local plans–docks–land available for expansion–rejection of inspector's recommendations**

F, owners of the Port of Bristol, sought an order quashing part of a local plan, contending that N had (1) wrongly refused to follow the recommendations of an inspector that insufficient land had been allocated to accommodate the necessary expansion of a dock and to accord with the relevant structure plan, and (2) had failed to give adequate reasons for its decision.

Held, refusing the application, that (1) the inspector's conclusions had been founded on an erroneous basis which N had been entitled to reject, and (2) adequate reasons for the decision had been provided, *Braithwaite v. Doncaster MBC* [2000] E.G.C.S. 42 applied.

FIRST CORPORATE SHIPPING LTD (T/A BRISTOL PORT CO) v. NORTH SOMERSET COUNCIL [2001] J.P.L. 1209 (Note), Forbes, J., QBD (Admin Ct).

3662. **Development plans–local plans–material considerations–resolution passed five years prior to planning decision–change in government planning policy–reconsideration of application**

[Town and Country Planning Act 1990 s.70(2).]

K appealed against a refusal ([2001] EWHC Admin 839, [2002] J.P.L. 832) to grant permission to move for judicial review of S's decision granting outline planning permission for a large residential development and the construction of a bypass. In 1995 S had resolved in principle to grant permission for the development, but, owing to a protracted negotiating process, outline permission was not forthcoming until 2000. K submitted that, in dealing with the application, S had failed to discharge its statutory duty under the Town and Country Planning Act 1990 s.70(2) to have regard to all material considerations. S argued that changes in government planning policy, concerning the provision of affordable housing, amounted to a change in material considerations after 1995 and contended that to discharge the duty under s.70(2) the authority was obliged to formally reconsider the 1995 application.

Held, dismissing the appeal, that there was no requirement for applications to be referred back to the planning committee when circumstances had changed following the passing of a resolution. Section 70(2) imposed a wide duty on a planning authority to consider any factor which might influence the final decision. That duty did not require formal consideration of all new material and was discharged by the authority having had regard to all material considerations by the date on which a decision notice was issued. If, prior to signing a decision notice, the delegated officer was aware of factors which might constitute new material considerations then it was prudent for the application to be referred back to the committee; however, in circumstances where it was clear that the authority was aware of the new factor, had considered the factor with the planning application in mind, and would have reached the same conclusion if matters had been referred back to the committee, then a decision notice could be issued without specific reconsideration. In the instant case it was apparent that S was aware of government planning policy and had fully accounted for it in reaching its decision pursuant to the 1995 resolution.

R. (ON THE APPLICATION OF KIDES) v. SOUTH CAMBRIDGESHIRE DC, [2002] EWCA Civ 1370, [2003] 1 P. & C.R. 19, Jonathan Parker, L.J., CA.

3663. **Development plans–local plans–planning policy–relevant considerations justifying departure from policy protecting small dwellings**

[Town and Country Planning Act 1990 s.54A, s.70(2).]

G applied to quash a decision allowing an appeal against its refusal of planning permission for the demolition of a single storey extension and erection of a two storey extension. The Council's refusal was on the basis that the proposal conflicted with the policy in its local plan to protect small dwellings. There was no amenity objection. The inspector, whilst accepting that the proposals were contrary to the local plan policy, took the view that the policy should not be applied inflexibly where, as in the instant case, material considerations justified departure. The proposals were modest and merely designed to adapt an older property to meet the needs of modern life. G contended that the Inspector had taken account of irrelevant considerations and had failed to take account of the suitability of the appeal house for small households of one or two persons.

Held, refusing the application, that the Inspector had acted in accordance with the Town and Country Planning Act s.54A and s.70(2) in considering whether, notwithstanding the breach of policy, other considerations indicated that planning permission should be granted. In applying the Council's Small Dwellings Policy it was relevant to consider the historical origins of the plan and whether the appeal property (i) was affordable to those entering the housing market; (ii) being constructed to meet the needs of families, was able to provide for the modern needs of families, and (iii) was near the margins of the size of a "small dwelling" in the plan. The plan did not limit small households to those comprising one or two persons.

GUILDFORD BC v. SECRETARY OF STATE FOR THE ENVIRONMENT, TRANSPORT AND THE REGIONS, [2001] EWHC Admin 819, [2002] J.P.L. 733, Sullivan, J., QBD (Admin Ct).

3664. **Development plans–local plans–planning policy guidance–green belt boundary revision**

C, developers, appealed against the dismissal of their application to quash W's decision to adopt a local plan, the effect of which was to alter the green belt boundary to include C's development site within the metropolitan green belt for the first time. C contended that according to PPG2 the green belt boundary should be altered only exceptionally and that the planning inspector had erred when considering both the test of exceptional circumstances and its second fork of necessity and had also wrongly considered the objectives of the green belt under PPG para.1.6, which was expressly prohibited by the guidelines. The main circumstances relied upon were the refusal of planning permission for the site in earlier decisions of the Secretary of State which C contended had been specific to the particular applications, rather than establishing principles against development for all time in that area.

Held, allowing the appeal and quashing the decision, that the correct test under para.2.7 was a very stringent one but it was not a two pronged test as circumstances surrounding the proposed boundary revision could not be exceptional unless the movement of the boundary was necessary and the inspector had correctly considered that test. However, the Secretary of State's previous decision that development should not be allowed on the land could not of itself create the requisite necessity for green belt boundary revision particularly as there were sufficient planning controls in situ. Further, the inspector had erred by considering the role which the land could play in fulfilling policy objectives which was contrary to para.1.7 of PPG2.

COPAS v. WINDSOR AND MAIDENHEAD RBC, [2001] EWCA Civ 180, [2002] 1 P. & C.R. 16, Simon Brown, L.J., CA.

3665. **Development plans–local plans–planning policy guidance–residential developments–Secretary of State's direction not to grant planning permission–application of policy guidance provisions on prematurity**

[Town and Country Planning (General Permitted Development) Order 1995 (SI 1995 418) Art.14.]

H sought judicial review of a decision of the Secretary of State upholding a direction given to the local authority not to grant planning permission to H for residential development in a village. The Secretary of State had taken the view that it would not be appropriate for the local authority to grant the permission until the inspector's report into the local plan had been received. H contended that the decision determined the merits of H's planning application and constituted a decision that the application was "premature" thereby depriving H of any effective right of appeal without indicating in what way determination of H's application would prejudice the local plan process.

Held, refusing the application for judicial review, that there was no requirement for the Secretary of State to give reasons when issuing directions under the Town and Country Planning (General Development) Order 1995 Art.14. Although "premature" was an ordinary English word it had a particular meaning in relation to planning law. Under PPG 1 para.47 and para.48, planning permission could justifiably be refused on the grounds of prematurity where a development plan was in preparation and the effect of the development would be so significant as to prejudice the outcome of the development plan process by predetermining issues which ought properly to be taken in the development plan context. Under para.49, where planning permission was refused on grounds of prematurity, the planning authority had to indicate clearly how the grant of permission for the development concerned would prejudice the outcome of the development plan process. However, in the instant case the Secretary of State's decision to maintain the Art.14 direction could not be regarded as a decision on prematurity. The Secretary of State had not said that determination of the application had to await the completion of the local plan process but had merely stated that he needed the information in the inspector's report in relation to concerns about the development in the light of PPG 3. Accordingly, the Secretary of State's decision was not based on prematurity and had not determined the merits of H's application.

R. (ON THE APPLICATION OF HARTLEY PROPERTY TRUST LTD) v. SECRETARY OF STATE FOR THE ENVIRONMENT, TRANSPORT AND THE REGIONS, [2001] EWHC Admin 935, [2002] P.L.C.R. 21, Gibbs, J., QBD (Admin Ct).

3666. **Development plans–local plans–planning procedures–planning inspector's recommendations–failure to give adequate reasons for rejection**

J, the director of E, applied to quash the Great Yarmouth Local Plan on the basis that inadequate reasons had been given for rejecting the recommendation of the Plans inspector that a site owned by E be allocated for residential development. The consultation draft of the Plan had prompted various objections such that its housing allocation and other provisions went through various alterations. The Local Plan inspector recommended particular modifications relating to the use of various plots, agricultural land quality and housing use. The Councils Local Plan Working Party rejected the inspector's modifications, producing a text of its decision preceded by some partial minutes of the meeting at which that decision was made.

Held, granting the application, that the local authority had failed to give proper, adequate and intelligible reasons for its rejection of an independent planning inspector's recommendation that land owned by E be allocated for residential development. Accordingly, the decision was quashed and the matter remitted for fresh consideration. It was required not only that reasons be proper, adequate and intelligible but also that they must deal with all of the substantive points raised. It would be sufficient that they be presented in the form of minutes of a meeting at which the decision was made, provided that, in the circumstances, they were sufficiently detailed. The court was entitled to look at the documentation and at the context to see whether or not the reasons had been sufficiently spelled out.

JONES v. GREAT YARMOUTH BC, [2001] EWHC Admin 938, [2002] J.P.L. 852, Gibbs, J., QBD (Admin Ct).

3667. **Development plans–planning policy–structure plans–amendments–plan used to designate new forests–inadequate reasons–failure to address land use issue**

[Town and Country Planning Act 1990 s.287; Town and Country Planning (Development Plan) Regulations 1991 (SI 1991 2794) Reg.16.]

The Hampshire Structure Plan 1996-2011 review designated two new forests. Following a public examination of the review, the review panel suggested certain amendments to the plan on the basis that the forest designations were countryside management matters, not land use policy. H made some changes to the plan but declined to follow the panel's other recommendations. T sought the quashing of the designations under the Town and Country Planning Act 1990 s.287, contending that H had not given adequate reasons for declining to follow the panel's recommendations.

Held, allowing the application, that the reasons H had given for rejecting the alterations to a structure plan concerning the development of forests suggested it had failed to give adequate consideration to the question of countryside management as opposed to land use. Inadequate reasons had been given for not following the panel's recommendations in breach of the Town and Country Planning (Development Plans) Regulations 1991 Reg.16.

TEST VALLEY BC v. HAMPSHIRE CC [2002] P.L.C.R. 2, Jack Beatson, Q.C., QBD (Admin Ct).

3668. **Development plans–structure plans–validity–policy for housing development included in structure plan**

[Town and Country Planning Act 1990 s.31, s.36(2), s.287; Planning and Compensation Act 1991 s.27, Sch.4 Part I.]

B challenged under the Town and Country Planning Act 1990 s.287 the validity of the Wiltshire Structure Plan 2011, adopted by the local planning authority, and which included policy DP10, a policy which provided for the development of an area of land for housing. B contended that the policy was not a general policy, and as such its inclusion in the structure plan was outside the powers of the 1990 Act, and that as a detailed policy, it should have been dealt with through the local plan process. B further submitted that the issue as to whether a policy was a general or detailed policy was a matter to be determined by the courts.

Held, refusing the application, that s.31(2) of the 1990 Act as substituted by the Planning and Compensation Act 1991 s.27 and Sch.4 Part I, required that a structure plan contain a written statement setting out the planning authority's "general policies" in regard to the use and development of land in its area, and s.36(2) of the 1990 Act required the authority to make a similar statement in respect of "detailed policies". Once a court had determined the scope of the phrase "general policy", it was for the decision maker, correctly directing himself, to decide whether a particular policy fell within the scope. It was therefore a matter first of statutory interpretation and then of application. A policy could be a general policy, not only because of impact across district boundaries, but because the general location of the major developments of the county within a certain district, could be regarded as significant strategically or structurally. The general location of the development in DP10 and the direction of growth of the town which would result from the development, could be seen as a structural and strategic issue, and therefore the planning authority were entitled to conclude that DP10 was general policy falling within s.31 of the 1990 Act.

JS BLOOR LTD v. SWINDON BC; KING v. SWINDON BC, [2001] EWHC Admin 966, [2002] P.L.C.R. 22, Ouseley, J., QBD (Admin Ct).

3669. **Enforcement notices–appeals–locus standi of applicants–date of "bringing appeal"–relevant occupation**

[Town and Country Planning Act 1990 s.174(1).]

B, the tenants of a farm business, challenged a decision of an inspector refusing to determine their appeals against an enforcement notice following the alleged carrying out of engineering works to two farm tracks. The enforcement notice was dated October 13, 1998 and the appeals were made on November 17, 1998 and received the next day. The lease of the land occupied by B and part of which formed the subject of the enforcement notice had expired on October 28, 1998. The inspector had found that, for the purposes of the Town and Country Planning Act 1990 s.174, the date when an appeal was brought was the date it was received by the Planning Inspectorate, namely November 18, 1998 by which time B had no interest in the land and were not relevant occupiers for the purposes of s.174(6) with the result that they had no locus standi to bring the appeal. B contended that that there was no evidential basis to support the finding that they did not have an interest in the land or were relevant occupiers at the time the appeal was brought as they were either holding over the lease or were licensees of the property, which they had continued to farm.

Held, refusing the application, that s.174(1) required an interest in land to subsist at the time which the appeal was brought, which was the date the appeal was received by the Planning Inspectorate. The nature of the interest must be a legal or equitable interest in the land rather than a contractual right. A relevant occupier could only bring an appeal if he remained in occupation of the land at the date the appeal was brought and the inspector had been entitled to find, on the evidence before him, that B had no interest in the land in question and were not relevant occupiers at that date.

R. (ON THE APPLICATION OF BENHAM-CROSSWELL) v. SECRETARY OF STATE FOR THE ENVIRONMENT, TRANSPORT AND THE REGIONS; *sub nom.* R. v. SECRETARY OF STATE FOR THE ENVIRONMENT, TRANSPORT AND THE REGIONS EX. P BENHAM-CROSSWELL, [2001] EWHC Admin 146, [2001] J.P.L. 1405, Penry-Davey, J., QBD (Admin Ct).

3670. **Enforcement notices–breach–extent of authority of prosecuting solicitor–agreement to withdraw**

[Town and Country Planning Act 1990 s.187B.]

F appealed against a decision ([2001] 4 P.L.R. 110) allowing an appeal by the local authority from a judgment in which it had been found to be estopped from bringing proceedings against F under the Town and Country Planning Act 1990 s.187B. F, relying on the finding of fact by the trial judge that the local authority's solicitor had agreed to withdraw two enforcement notices, contended that he had a legitimate expectation that the local authority would not seek compliance with the notices by way of an injunction.

Held, dismissing the appeal, that a legitimate expectation in respect of a representation said to have been made on behalf of a public body could only arise where the person making the representation had had actual or ostensible authority to make such representations on behalf of the public body. In light of the fact that enforcement notices were important public documents which ran with the land and were enforceable against subsequent owners or occupiers, authority to withdraw them could not reasonably be regarded as attaching to those who had conduct of prosecutions for breach. In the instant case, the local authority's solicitor lacked the requisite authority to agree to withdraw the enforcement notices, therefore the local authority were not prevented from seeking an injunction.

SOUTH BUCKINGHAMSHIRE DC v. FLANAGAN; *sub nom.* FLANAGAN v. SOUTH BUCKS DC, [2002] EWCA Civ 690, [2002] 1 W.L.R. 2601, Keene, L.J., CA.

3671. Enforcement notices—change of use—validity of enforcement notice

[Town and Country Planning Act 1990 s.289.]

H appealed under the Town and Country Planning Act 1990 s.289 against the dismissal of his appeal against an enforcement notice served by the local planning authority. The enforcement notice stated that he had breached planning control by changing the use of land at his farm without planning permission, and required him to remedy the breach. H submitted that the enforcement notice as varied was a nullity on the grounds that the requirement that the land cease to be used for residential purposes as part of a garden as opposed to agricultural purposes was uncertain, and that the inspector had failed to specify in the notice which operational steps needed to be taken to remedy the breach.

Held, dismissing the appeal, that in order for an enforcement notice to be rendered invalid it had to be hopelessly ambiguous and uncertain and in the present case there was no uncertainty in the notice's requirement, *Hounslow LBC v. Secretary of State for the Environment and Indian Gymkhana Club* [1981] J.P.L. 510, [1981] C.L.Y. 2680 applied. H was required to stop using the land as as extension of his garden, and the terms of that requirement were clear.

HATTINGH v. SECRETARY OF STATE FOR THE ENVIRONMENT, TRANSPORT AND THE REGIONS, [2001] EWHC Admin 539, [2002] P.L.C.R. 10, Harrison, J., QBD (Admin Ct).

3672. Enforcement notices—estoppel—injunction to demolish premises—impact of estoppel upon obligation to enforce planning regulation

[Town and Country Planning Act 1990 s.187B; Human Rights Act 1998 Sch.1 Part I Art.8.]

L appealed against the enforcement of an injunction obtained by the local planning authority, S, under the Town and Country Planning Act 1990 s.187B, requiring him to demolish a barn which he had built without planning permission, originally for farming purposes but which he had subsequently adapted for residential use. S had obtained an order to commit L to prison for failure to comply with the injunction and L had unsuccessfully applied to vary the injunction in relation to the demolition of the barn. L contended that (1) he had relied on verbal advice from a planning officer that planning permission was not required and that S should therefore have been estopped from seeking the injunction, and (2) S were precluded from taking enforcement action in respect of L's residential use of the barn by reason of the Human Rights Act 1998 Sch.1 Part I Art.8, on the basis that such action was in breach of his right to respect for family life.

Held, dismissing the appeal, that (1) a local authority obliged by statute to enforce planning regulation was not subject to estoppel, *Western Fish Products Ltd v. Penwith DC* [1981] 2 All E.R. 204, [1981] C.L.Y. 2732 applied. However, it was possible for an authority to delegate either actual or ostensible authority to an officer to make decisions on its behalf, but in the instant case even if the officer's advice did found an estoppel, it would be against enforcement of planning control and not against the granting of planning permission as in *Western Fish Products*; (2) in reality, L's application to vary the injunction had amounted to a request that it be reversed, and it was an abuse of process for an application to be made to discharge an injunction which had been granted by a judge of the same court, and (3) it was possible for a claim under Art.8 to defeat a planning enforcement action, but in the instant case L was not currently occupying the premises and had from the outset denied any intention to reside there. Therefore he could not show that to demolish the barn would deprive him and his family of accommodation.

SALISBURY DC v. LE ROI; *sub nom.* SALISBURY DC v. WILLIAMS, [2001] EWCA Civ 1490, [2002] 1 P. & C.R. 39, Buxton, L.J., CA.

3673. **Enforcement notices–land registration–ownership of land following transfer**

[Town and Country Planning Act 1990 s.179, s.336(1).]

E appealed against a decision of the magistrates to acquit T of being in breach of an enforcement notice, contending that the justices had erred in finding that T was not the owner of the land for the purposes of the Town and Country Planning Act 1990 s.179. E submitted that, although the land had been conveyed by T to a third party between the date of issue of the enforcement notice and the expiry of the period for compliance, the legal estate in fee simple remained vested in T because the transfer had not been registered at the Land Registry. E maintained that it was the legal title which should be relied upon in order to ensure certainty in the enforcement of planning legislation.

Held, remitting the matter to the magistrates, that T remained the owner of the land until registration had taken place. It was clear from the wording of s.179 of the Act that the legislature had envisaged that the owner of the land for the purposes of enforcement need not be in possession or control of the land. Further, pursuant to the definition in s.336(1), the owner of the land was deemed to be the person entitled to receive the rack rent in respect of the land whether for himself or in the capacity of trustee, a definition apt to cover the status of T in the interim period prior to registration, *Smith v. Express Dairy Co* [1954] J.P.L. 45, [1954] C.L.Y. 1835 considered.

EAST LINDSEY DC v. THOMPSON; *sub nom.* EAST LINDSAY DC v. THOMPSON; EAST LINDSEY DC v. THOMSON, [2001] EWHC Admin 81, [2001] 2 P.L.R. 26, Keene, L.J., QBD (Admin Ct).

3674. **Enforcement notices–mobile homes–ambit of defence for non-compliance–defendant's inaction**

[Town and Country Planning Act 1990 s.179(3).]

W appealed against his convictions for non-compliance with two enforcement notices which had required him to remove a concrete base and a mobile home from his land. The mobile home was occupied by W and his family and, as with the concrete base, was placed on the land without planning permission. W submitted that the judge had erred by ruling that, on the facts, the defence under the Town and Country Planning Act 1990 s.179(3) was not available and therefore he would have had no alternative but to direct the jury to convict. As a result, W had pleaded guilty.

Held, allowing the appeal, that the issue of whether a defendant had done "everything he could be expected to do to secure compliance" for the purposes of the defence in s.179(3) was for the tribunal of fact to consider. It was also clear that magistrates or juries were to apply an objective test of "reasonableness" having regard to the defendant's circumstances which could, for example, be other people occupying the land or alternatively, the defendant's personal circumstances. Further, as in the instant case, the defence was available in cases where the defendant had done nothing, provided, as always, the statutory test was satisfied, *R. v. Beard (John)* [1997] 1 P.L.R. 64, [1996] C.L.Y. 4719 and *Kent CC v. Brockman* [1996] 1 P.L.R. 1, [1996] C.L.Y. 4712 applied. Given that the judge had ruled on the unavailability of the defence before hearing any evidence on W's inability to persuade his family to move elsewhere, there was a possibility, albeit a slight possibility, that the jury could have found in W's favour. Accordingly, the convictions were quashed and a retrial ordered.

R. v. WOOD (DAVID), [2001] EWCA Crim 1395, [2002] J.P.L. 219, Mantell, L.J., CA (Crim Div).

3675. Enforcement notices—remedial works—lack of precision in notice—consideration of documents directly referred to in notice

[Human Rights Act 1998 Sch.1 Part I Art.8; Town and Country Planning Act 1990 s.187B.]

The local authority applied for injunctive relief under the Town and Country Planning Act 1990 s.187B to prevent alleged breaches of planning control by N, the owners of the relevant land. N contended, inter alia, that those enforcement notices which were based on breach of a condition of the original planning permission did not indicate with sufficient precision the remedial action which N was required to take, and thus that the court should refuse to enforce the notice for lack of precision.

Held, granting the applications, that the true construction of an enforcement notice could legitimately involve considering the content of another document to which the notice referred. Thus, the court was permitted to use the original planning permission and any accompanying drawings as an aid to the construction of an enforcement notice which itself cross referred to a condition of the planning permission, *Miller-Mead v. Minister of Housing and Local Government* [1963] 2 Q.B. 196, [1963] C.L.Y. 3406 applied. Furthermore, where a case involved a conflict between a defendant's rights under the Human Rights Act 1998 Sch.1 Part I Art.8 and the local authority's right to enforce planning control, the court was required to look at all the circumstances in balancing the competing claims. However, mere planning considerations were unlikely to provide a sufficient counterweight to the right to enforce. In order to mount a successful challenge to an enforcement notice, infringement of positive rights, such as those protected under Art.8, would need to be established, *South Buckinghamshire DC v. Porter* [2001] EWCA Civ 1549, [2002] 1 W.L.R. 1359, [2001] C.L.Y. 4729 applied.

BUCKINGHAMSHIRE CC v. NORTH WEST ESTATES PLC; *sub nom.* BUCKINGHAM CC v. NORTH WEST ESTATES PLC, [2002] EWHC 1088, *The Times*, June 24, 2002, Jacob, J., Ch D.

3676. Enforcement notices—time limits—lack of development within time limit

[Town and Country Planning Act 1990 s.56(4)(d), s.91(1).]

C appealed against an inspector's decision to uphold an enforcement notice in relation to the erection of a dwelling on the basis that the development had been carried out without planning permission, as it had not been commenced within five years of the grant of permission as required by the Town and Country Planning Act 1990 s.91(1). C contended that work on the access to the site constituted "an operation in the course of laying out or constructing a road" as defined by the s.56(4)(d) of the Act, and that the inspector had erred in law in her approach because she had considered whether there had been substantial development rather than whether any development had begun.

Held, dismissing the appeal, that the inspector had been entitled to conclude that the work carried out, namely the scooping out of a hedge, was de minimis when considering whether the work fell within the scope of s.56(4)(d).

R. (ON THE APPLICATION OF CONNAUGHT QUARRIES LTD) v. SECRETARY OF STATE FOR THE ENVIRONMENT, TRANSPORT AND THE REGIONS, [2001] EWHC Admin 76, [2001] 4 P.L.R. 18, Elias, J., QBD (Admin Ct).

3677. Enforcement notices–time limits–point at which operations "substantially completed"

[Town and Country Planning Act 1990 s.55(1), s.171B.]

S, who had been served with an enforcement notice alleging a breach of planning control by "the partial erection of a dwelling house", appealed against a finding that the four year period for the taking of enforcement action under the Town and Country Planning Act 1990 s.171B did not begin to run until the whole operation of creating the dwelling house, including the internal finishing, had been substantially completed. The inspector had found that substantial completion of a dwelling house would probably involve "finishing the external wall, tiling, woodwork, glazing and guttering". The Secretary of State argued that for limitation purposes it was necessary to consider the building activities as a whole and determine whether they had been substantially completed.

Held, allowing the appeal, that, for the purposes of s.171B of the Act the operations that had to be substantially completed where building operations which amounted to "development" as defined by s.55(1), with the result that works affecting the interior of a building were not to be taken into account. The advice set out in Circular 10/97 para.2.80 was misleading and placed reliance, with regard to assessing substantial completion of a single operation, on *Ewen Developments v. Secretary of State for the Environment and North Norfolk DC* [1980] J.P.L. 404, [1980] C.L.Y. 2645 which had no application. Building operations would be complete when activities needing planning permission were completed. A building would only remain exempt from enforcement proceedings where it remained substantially completed at all times during the four year period. In the event of damage, such as that caused by fire, which resulted in a building ceasing to be substantially completed, the four year period would end and a new one only start running upon the building being returned to a substantially completed state, *Ewen Developments* considered.

SAGE v. SECRETARY OF STATE FOR THE ENVIRONMENT, TRANSPORT AND THE REGIONS; *sub nom.* SAGE v. MAIDSTONE BC [2001] J.P.L. 986, Duncan Ouseley Q.C., QBD (Admin Ct).

3678. Enforcement notices–variation–Secretary of State's powers–scope of enforcement notices

[Town and Country Planning Act 1990 s.173(4), s.174(2), s.176(1)(b).]

Rulings of the judge ([2001] P.L.C.R. 10) in relation to the findings of the inspector concerning three enforcement notices served on a developer were the subject of an appeal by the Secretary of State and a cross appeal by the developer. The issues to be determined were (1) whether an enforcement notice could set out steps aimed at remedying both a breach of planning control and any injury to amenity caused by the breach; (2) the extent of the evidence which could be adduced where the appellant argued, pursuant to the Town and Country Planning Act 1990 s.174(2)(f), that the enforcement notice set out steps that exceeded what was necessary to remedy a breach of planning control or any injury to amenity which had been caused by the breach, and (3) the extent of the Secretary of State's power to vary the terms of an enforcement notice under s.176(1)(b) of the 1990 Act.

Held, allowing the appeal and dismissing the cross appeal, that (1) despite the use of the word "or" in s.173(4) of the Act, an enforcement notice could set out steps aimed at remedying both a breach of planning control and any injury to amenity caused by the breach; (2) s.174(2)(f) would only be considered where a breach of planning control had been established and planning permission ought not to be granted. In those circumstances, it could not be construed so as to enable the appellant to adduce evidence and arguments as to planning merits which should have been presented in support of an argument under s.174(2)(a) that planning permission ought to be granted in respect of the breach of planning control set out in the enforcement notice, and (3) the power given to the Secretary of State under s.176(1)(b) was a wide power to correct and a generously expressed slip rule. It was not, however, a power which could properly be used to challenge the substance of an enforcement notice.

WYATT BROS (OXFORD) LTD v. SECRETARY OF STATE FOR THE ENVIRONMENT, TRANSPORT AND THE REGIONS; *sub nom.* SECRETARY OF STATE FOR THE ENVIRONMENT, TRANSPORT AND THE REGIONS v. WYATT BROS (OXFORD) LTD, [2001] EWCA Civ 1560, [2002] P.L.C.R. 18, Kennedy, L.J., CA.

3679. Enforcement notices–variation–unauthorised change of use for business purposes–use of conditions introduced by variation

H issued enforcement notices alleging unauthorised change of use of land by the owners, A, who had moved a residential caravan, market trader's caravan and a refrigeration unit on to the land from which they wanted to run a free range egg business. A's appeals against the notices were allowed by the inspector because he found that there was a sound financial basis for the business that did not conflict with the local plan. He also found that a residential presence was required. Further, the inspector imposed a timetable for A to erect housing for 5,500 chickens on the land. H appealed on the grounds that the inspector had had no basis to determine that the business had secure funding, that there was no evidence before the inspector as to other available properties for sale or rent, that the timetable was unenforceable. As to the second notice, it was also asserted that the variation allowed by the inspector was irrational, given that he had already determined that the grant of permission should not be subject to conditions.

Held, allowing the appeal and remitting the matter to the inspector for rehearing, that although there was evidence of adequate financial planning for the business, the inspector did not know whether other accommodation was available in the area. The condition setting out a timetable could be complied with in terms of the developing business and such compliance was conditional on retaining the residential caravan. Varying the second notice by allowing the trader's caravan and refrigeration unit was irrational, however, as the inspector had already decided that it would be inappropriate to impose conditions on the permission in the instant case. Further, the decision had failed to give A proper guidance as to the duration of temporary use permitted on appeal by the inspector.

HAMBLETON DC v. SECRETARY OF STATE FOR THE ENVIRONMENT, TRANSPORT AND THE REGIONS [2002] P.L.C.R. 1, Hallett, J., QBD (Admin Ct).

3680. Footpaths–diversions–footpath diversion order application–reference to Secretary of State for confirmation–local authority's discretion

[Highways Act 1980 s.119.]

H appealed against a decision ([2001] EWHC Admin 1128, Times, December 19, 2001) that the local authority, having received an application for a footpath diversion order which satisfied the condition of expediency laid down in the Highways Act 1980 s.119(1), was not, despite having resolved to make an order under s.119 of the Act, obliged to submit the order to the Secretary of State for confirmation. H contended that the local authority had no discretion to refuse to refer the matter to the Secretary of State.

Held, dismissing the appeal, that the local authority had a discretion to refuse to refer a s.119 order to the Secretary of State. It was a condition precedent to the making of an order under s.119(1) that the local authority was to make a diversion order only where it was expedient to do so in the interests of the owner or the public. However, the fulfilment of the condition precedent did not give rise to a duty to make the order. Where sustained objections to the diversion had been received, the local authority had no power to confirm the order and was under no duty to refer the matter to the Secretary of State.

R. (ON THE APPLICATION OF HARGRAVE) v. STROUD DC; *sub nom.* HARGRAVE v. STROUD DC, [2002] EWCA Civ 1281, [2003] 1 P.& C.R. 1, Schiemann, L.J., CA.

3681. Footpaths–reclassification–objections–matters to be dealt with at planning inquiries–fairness–jurisdiction

[Hampshire (Basingstoke and Deane Borough No 13) (Parish of Candovers) Public Path Reclassification Order 1989; Wildlife and Countryside Act 1981 Sch.15 para.7, Sch.15 para.8(2).]

M applied for judicial review of the Hampshire (Basingstoke and Deane Borough No.13) (Parish of Candovers) Public Path Reclassification Order 1989 which reclassified various roads used as public paths. A public inquiry had been called in 1995 under the Wildlife and Countryside Act 1981 Sch.15 para.7 in response to objections from M about the Order. Modifications to the Order were proposed, to which further objections were raised by M, resulting in a second inquiry being held in 1997 under para.8(2). At that inquiry the inspector chose, in accordance with unpublished guidelines from the Planning Inspectorate, to reopen all the issues from the first inquiry rather than restricting evidence to the modifications only. The inspector proposed further modifications, which were again objected to by M, and a third inquiry was held under para.8(2) before a different inspector, who warned at the beginning of the hearing that he would not accept any evidence relating to old matters, but did then take all matters into account in reaching his decision. M argued that the inspector at the second inquiry had had no jurisdiction to reopen the whole matter and that the procedure at both the 1997 and 1999 inquiries had been unfair.

Held, allowing the application, that in order to be procedurally fair, an inquiry held under para.7 had to deal with all the issues, whereas one held under para.8(2) had to deal with issues relating only to modifications proposed following the first inquiry. The fact that the guidelines were unpublished meant that the public had had no warning that the inspector might decide to proceed by widening the scope of the para.8(2) inquiry, and to do so only on the day of the hearing had had the effect of denying interested parties a proper opportunity to present their case. If issues had arisen relating to matters beyond the proposed modifications, the appropriate procedure would have been for the inspector to have called for a fresh para.7 inquiry. The inspector at the second and third inquiries had therefore not had jurisdiction to act as he did, and the procedure at both inquiries had been unfair.

MARRIOTT v. SECRETARY OF STATE FOR THE ENVIRONMENT, TRANSPORT AND THE REGIONS [2001] J.P.L. 559, Sullivan, J., QBD (Admin Ct).

3682. Gypsies–caravan sites–order to vacate plot–right to fair trial

[Criminal Justice and Public Order Act 1994 s.77; Human Rights Act 1998 Sch.1 Part I Art.6(2).]

W, a gypsy, challenged a removal order issued by H under the Criminal Justice and Public Order Act 1994 s.77 requiring him to vacate a plot on a designated gypsy caravan site occupied by him and his family. W had occupied the plot after it became vacant without waiting for the plot to be allocated by H. W contended that H had failed to make sufficient enquiries regarding his family's needs, that the decision was unreasonable, and that s.77 was incompatible with the Human Rights Act 1998 Sch.1 Part I Art.6.2.

Held, refusing the application for judicial review, that adequate enquiries had been made by the H and that the decision was not unreasonable as there were other families with a greater need of the vacant plot and the decision had not unduly interfered with W's right to family life. Further, the court stated that it was not appropriate to form conclusions as to the compatibility of s.77 with Art.6.2 without hearing further argument and, in view of H's decision not to prosecute W under s.77, such argument was not necessary.

R. (ON THE APPLICATION OF WARD) v. HILLINGDON LBC; *sub nom.* WARD v. HILLINGDON LBC; R. v. HILLINGDON LBC, *ex p.* WARD, [2001] EWHC Admin 91, [2002] E.H.L.R. 4, Stanley Burnton, J., QBD (Admin Ct).

3683. Gypsies–caravan sites–refusal of application for pitch allocation–previous trespass

P, a gypsy, applied for judicial review of the decision of the local authority to reject her application for a pitch allocation at a caravan site. The local authority had rejected P's application on the sole basis that she had previously entered the site without gaining authorisation and had sited a caravan without permission. An alternative site had been offered to P.

Held, granting the application, that the local authority had been wrong to reject P's application on the basis that she was a trespasser. It was necessary for a local authority to consider the needs of an applicant against the needs of the community in general and the needs of other potential occupants of the site who had not behaved improperly. While the behaviour of P could have justified her being given a lower priority it was not, of itself, a conclusive factor, *R. (on the application of Ward) v. Hillingdon LBC* [2001] EWHC Admin 91 considered.

R. (ON THE APPLICATION OF PIGGOTT) v. BEDFORDSHIRE CC, [2002] EWHC 77, *The Times*, January 29, 2002, Burton, J., QBD (Admin Ct).

3684. Gypsies–caravan sites–refusal to grant permission in green belt–right to family life

[Human Rights Act 1998 Sch.1 Part I Art.8.]

B challenged the decision of S, by his planning inspector, to dismiss her appeal against the refusal of planning permission to site caravans on land in the green belt. The inspector held that B's needs as a gypsy did not amount to "very special circumstances" capable of outweighing the need to preserve the green belt, and that other suitable sites were available in the locality. B argued that (1) the inspector had failed to give proper consideration to her rights under the Human Rights Act 1998 Sch.1 Part I Art.8, and (2) had failed to take into account the fact that local development plans did not accord with national policy regarding gypsies.

Held, dismissing the application, that (1) the inspector had properly considered all relevant matters and had reached a decision he was entitled to reach. He had considered Art.8 and had properly weighed up B's rights and needs against the wider policy issues, and it was not necessary or appropriate for the court to go behind that balancing exercise, *Chapman v. United Kingdom (27238/95)* 10 B.H.R.C. 48, [2001] C.L.Y. 4744 applied, and (2) it was quite common for local plans to be out of step with national policy given the lengthy process by which local plans were produced, but experienced planning officers, such as the inspector, were able to look at the broader picture and apply the essence of current policy. This the inspector had done competently and thoroughly.

BUCKLAND v. SECRETARY OF STATE FOR THE ENVIRONMENT, TRANSPORT AND THE REGIONS; SMITH (THOMAS) v. SECRETARY OF STATE FOR THE ENVIRONMENT; EVANS (JOHN) v. SECRETARY OF STATE FOR THE ENVIRONMENT; WYCHAVON DC v. SMITH (SITING OF CARAVANS), [2001] EWHC Admin 524, [2001] 4 P.L.R. 34, Sullivan, J., QBD (Admin Ct).

3685. Gypsies–caravan sites on green belt land within AONB–balancing exercise–special considerations favouring grant of permission

[Town and Country Planning Act 1990 s.54A.]

B's application for planning permission for two gypsy caravans was refused by the local authority, S, on the grounds that the location on green belt land in an area of outstanding national beauty was contrary to the provisions of S's rural areas local plan. B appealed and a public inquiry was held. The inspector recommended that permission should be refused and B appealed to the Secretary of State. The Secretary of State dismissed the appeal. Although he found that, contrary to the inspector's view, special circumstances justified siting the caravans in the green belt, as provided for in the local plan, the same special circumstances were not sufficient to overcome objections on the basis of the site's location within the AOND and highway safety considerations. B appealed, contending that the

Secretary of State's reasoning in relation to the green belt should also have applied to the AONB and highways issues and that by failing to treat them as such, the Secretary of State had not carried the balancing exercise in the Town and Country Planning Act 1990 s.54A correctly.

Held, dismissing the appeal, that the Secretary of State had given appropriate weight to the special circumstances that had been found to exist in B's case. In doing so, he was entitled to find that, although they outweighed the green belt considerations contained in S's rural areas local plan, they did not outweigh the area of outstanding natural beauty and highway safety considerations. Whilst the effect of special considerations could be considered together in relation to green belt and AONB issues, whether they actually outweighed such considerations could be determined separately and by doing so the Secretary of State had not carried out the s.54A balancing exercise incorrectly. In carrying out the exercise, the Secretary of State had accepted the inspector's recommendations in relation to the AONB and highway safety issues and balanced them against B's personal circumstances forming the basis of the special considerations.

BUTLER v. SECRETARY OF STATE FOR THE ENVIRONMENT, TRANSPORT AND THE REGIONS, [2001] EWHC Admin 590, [2002] J.P.L. 428, Ouseley, J., QBD (Admin Ct).

3686. **Gypsies—right to respect for private and family life—objections to living in conventional housing**

[Human Rights Act 1998 Sch.1 Part I Art.8.]

The local authority appealed against a decision ([2001] EWHC Admin 800, Times, November 9, 2001) upholding an appeal brought by C, a Romany gypsy, against the decision of an inspector. The inspector had dismissed C's appeal against the refusal to grant planning permission in relation to the continued use of certain land for the stationing of a caravan for residential use. The planning decision had involved consideration of the desire and wish of C to live in a caravan, his opposition to living in a conventional home and the obligations of the local authority to apply and enforce planning control. The judge had found that for the purposes of the Human Rights Act 1998 Sch.1 Part I Art.8 it was necessary for a person to satisfy an inspector that living in conventional housing was contrary to his and his family's cultural values or beliefs. The judge had concluded that it was unclear from the inspector's decision whether C had a "settled and immutable antipathy to conventional housing" derived from gypsy culture and that accordingly it was necessary to remit the matter to the inspector.

Held, dismissing the appeal, that the judge had not erred in his approach, which was entirely consistent with the decision of the European Court of Human Rights in *Chapman v. United Kingdom (27238/95)* (2001) 33 E.H.R.R. 18, [2001] C.L.Y. 4744. Where Art.8 of the Convention was engaged and it had been shown that a person held certain cultural values or beliefs such that he was opposed to living in conventional housing, it was not sufficient for a local authority to rely on the fact that conventional housing had been offered but refused; it was necessary that the personal circumstances of the individual concerned be considered and weighed against planning considerations. In the instant case the judge, in remitting the case, had correctly directed the inspector to carry out a detailed examination of C's objections to living in conventional housing in order to determine the extent to which Art.8 was engaged, *Chapman* considered.

CLARKE v. SECRETARY OF STATE FOR TRANSPORT, LOCAL GOVERNMENT AND THE REGIONS; *sub nom.* CLARKE v. SECRETARY OF STATE FOR THE ENVIRONMENT, TRANSPORT AND THE REGIONS, [2002] EWCA Civ 819, [2002] J.P.L. 1365, Buxton, L.J., CA.

3687. Inquiries-fees-examination in public

TOWN AND COUNTRY PLANNING (COSTS OF INQUIRIES ETC.) (STANDARD DAILY AMOUNT) (ENGLAND) REGULATIONS 2002, SI 2002 452; made under the Town and Country Planning Act 1990 s.303A. In force: March 31, 2002; £1.75.

These Regulations apply where the Secretary of State is authorised to recover costs borne by him in connection with unitary development plan, local plan or simplified planning zone inquiries or other hearings or examinations in public in respect of structure plans. They specify a standard daily amount which may be charged for each day the person appointed to hold it is engaged in the conduct of the inquiry or other hearing or is otherwise engaged on work connected with it. The amount is £516 per day in relation to qualifying inquiries opening on or after the date these Regulations come into force. This is an increase of approximately 10.5 per cent of the previous standard daily amount of £467.

3688. Inquiries-fees-standard daily amount-Wales

FEES FOR INQUIRIES (STANDARD DAILY AMOUNT) (WALES) REGULATIONS 2002, SI 2002 2780 (W.264); made under the Housing and Planning Act 1986 s.42. In force: November 29, 2002; £1.75.

These Regulations apply where the National Assembly for Wales is authorised under or by virtue of specified provisions to recover its costs in connection with the holding of an inquiry under certain enactments, namely: the Local Government Act 1972; the Road Traffic Regulation Act 1984; and the Land Drainage Act 1991. They specify a standard amount of £566 before April 1, 2003 and £645 after April 1, 2003 which may be charged for each day on which the inquiry sits or the person appointed to hold it is otherwise engaged on work connected with it.

3689. Inquiries-fees-standard daily amount-Wales

TOWN AND COUNTRY PLANNING (COSTS OF INQUIRIES ETC.) (STANDARD DAILY AMOUNT) (WALES) REGULATIONS 2002, SI 2002 2801 (W.269); made under the Town and Country Planning Act 1990 s.303A. In force: April 1, 2003; £1.75.

These Regulations apply where the National Assembly for Wales is authorised to recover costs borne by it in connection with inquiries or other hearings relating to unitary development plans, local plans or simplified planning zones. They specify a standard daily amount which may be charged for each day the person appointed to hold it is engaged in the conduct of the inquiry or other hearing or is otherwise engaged on work connected with it. The amount specified is £520 if it opens on or after April 1, 2003 but before April 1, 2004; and £618 if it opens on or after April 1, 2004.

3690. Lawful development certificates-planning procedures-permitted development-temporary land use-physical changes

[Town and Country Planning (General Permitted Development) Order 1995 (SI 1995 418) Sch.2 Part 4 Class B.]

R appealed against a decision ([2001] EWHC Admin 277, [2001] C.L.Y. 4723) dismissing their appeal against a refusal to grant a lawful development certificate in relation to the use of agricultural land for vehicular sports and leisure activities for a period not exceeding 28 days in any calendar year. R contended that deemed planning permission had been granted pursuant to the Town and Country Planning (General Permitted Development) Order 1995 Sch.2 Part 4 Class B because the land did not have a permanent mixed use as it reverted to its normal use after each occasion of temporary use and the physical changes made to the land for the purpose of the temporary use were only relevant if they prevented reversion of use. There was not permanent use as long as the duration of use did not exceed 28 days.

Held, allowing the appeal, that the court was wrong to attach the weight it did to physical changes to the land. Character or appearance of land was not a criterion in Sch.2 Part 4 Class B and there was no justification for its addition as a test. Changes could be relevant if reversion to a previous normal use was obstructed. The duration of the proposed use and the reversion to normal use were the critical issues in determining whether a proposed use of land was permanent or temporary. Providing that the land was returned to its normal use within 28 days, such use was permitted.

RAMSEY v. SECRETARY OF STATE FOR THE ENVIRONMENT, TRANSPORT AND THE REGIONS; *sub nom.* RAMSAY v. SECRETARY OF STATE FOR THE ENVIRONMENT, TRANSPORT AND THE REGIONS, [2002] EWCA Civ 118, *The Times*, March 4, 2002, Keene, L.J., CA.

3691. **Lawful development certificates–use classes–proposed use of rugby stadium as concert venue**

[Town and Country Planning Act 1990 s.192(2); Town and Country Planning (Use Classes) Order 1987 (SI 1987 764) Sch.1 Part 4 para.2.]

R appealed against the refusal ([2001] EWHC Admin 927, Times, November 8, 2001) of its application to quash the decision of a planning inspector upholding the refusal by Richmond London Borough Council to grant a certificate of lawfulness of proposed use under the Town and Country Planning Act 1990 s.192(2) for the use of Twickenham rugby football stadium for music concerts. R argued that (1) the use of the stadium for music concerts fell within Class D2(e) of the Town and Country Planning (Use Classes) Order 1987 Sch.1 Part 4 para.2 as it constituted recreational use, or (2) the proposed use of the stadium for concerts would fall within Class D2(b) as use as a concert hall, and therefore within the same class as a rugby football stadium.

Held, dismissing the appeal, that a certificate of lawfulness of proposed use could not be granted in respect of the proposed use of a rugby football stadium as a concert venue. The 1987 Order had to be looked at to see if a proposed land use could fall within the same class as an existing use. (1) The holding of concerts did not fall within Class D2(e) as other sport or recreation. Class D2(e) was focused on physical recreation, not other activities. Although the word "recreation" was capable of having a wide meaning, which could include concerts, it was right to restrict Class D2(e) to physical or sporting activity. Twickenham stadium fell within Class D2(e) because it was used for sport, not because of the presence of spectators, and (2) an open air concert could not be classified as use as a concert hall within Class D2(b) given that a concert hall had to be enclosed by a roof and walls.

RUGBY FOOTBALL UNION v. SECRETARY OF STATE FOR TRANSPORT, LOCAL GOVERNMENT AND THE REGIONS; *sub nom.* RUGBY FOOTBALL UNION v. SECRETARY OF STATE FOR THE ENVIRONMENT, TRANSPORT AND THE REGIONS, [2002] EWCA Civ 1169, *The Times*, August 13, 2002, Schiemann, L.J., CA.

3692. **Listed buildings–development–proposed extension obstructing view of listed building–view part of setting**

[Planning (Listed Buildings and Conservation Areas) Act 1990 s.66(1), s.72.]

R applied to quash the decision of a planning inspector to allow an appeal against the refusal of planning permission in respect of a proposed extension to a building. R owned a listed building and claimed that the proposed extension would obscure his view of the River Thames and also the view that the general public had of the listed building from the river. R claimed that the inspector had failed in his duty under the Planning (Listed Buildings and Conservation Areas) Act 1990 s.66(1) to have special regard to preserving the listed building or its setting.

Held, granting the application, that the planning inspector had specifically referred to s.66(1) but had done so by way of noting only that the building under appeal was a listed building itself and lay within a conservation area. He had considered the loss of the view of R's listed building from the river although he had done so in the context of the desirability of preserving the character of the conservation area under s.72. That would, on the facts of the instant case, have also satisfied the test under s.66(1) but for the fact that the inspector had not applied the test in relation to the loss of the view of the river from R's listed building. The inspector had referred to R's loss of his view of the river in terms of there being no right to a view from any house. It did not appear that he had paid special regard to the loss of the view in terms of the preservation of the setting of R's listed building. Since the view from the house could properly be regarded as part of the setting of R's listed building within the meaning of s.66(1), the inspector should have considered how the proposed development would affect that view. Accordingly, the inspector's decision would be quashed.

RYAN v. SECRETARY OF STATE FOR THE ENVIRONMENT, TRANSPORT AND THE REGIONS, [2001] EWHC Admin 722, [2002] J.P.L. 711, Judge Rich Q.C., QBD (Admin Ct).

3693. Listed buildings—enforcement notices—building operations—purpose of annexation test

[Town and Country Planning Act 1990 s.55 (1A); Planning (Listed Buildings and Conservation Areas) Act 1990 s.1 (5).]

WCC appealed against a decision of the Secretary of State to quash a planning enforcement notice and a listed building enforcement notice requiring the removal of a wooden kiosk from an external site in Covent Garden. The kiosk was situated outside the second defendant's cafe and was used for the preparation of drinks for customers. The Secretary of State had concluded that planning permission and listed building consent were not required. WCC contended that (1) the inspector had failed to apply *Skerritts of Nottingham Ltd v. Secretary of State for the Environment, Transport and the Regions (No.2)* [2000] 2 P.L.R. 102, [2000] C.L.Y. 4415 with the result that he had erroneously focused his attention on whether or not the placing of the kiosk constituted a "building operation" for the purposes of the Town and Country Planning Act 1990 s.55(1A) rather than considering whether or not the end product was a building, and (2) in concluding that the kiosk was not a fixture for the purposes of the Planning (Listed Buildings and Conservation Areas) Act 1990 s.1 (5), the inspector had misapplied the purpose of annexation test by attaching weight to the fact that the kiosk could be removed during the winter months.

Held, allowing the appeal and remitting the matter for reconsideration that (1) the failure to apply *Skerritts* had resulted in the inspector misdirecting himself in law, and (2) the inspector had considered an irrelevant factor when determining that listed building consent was not necessary, *Skerritts* applied.

R. (ON THE APPLICATION OF WESTMINSTER CITY COUNCIL) v. SECRETARY OF STATE FOR THE ENVIRONMENT, TRANSPORT AND THE REGIONS, [2001] EWHC Admin 270, [2002] 1 P. & C.R. 8, Jackson, J., QBD (Admin Ct).

3694. Listed buildings—enforcement notices—outbuildings not within curtilage of listed building

[Planning (Listed Buildings and Conservation Areas) Act 1990 s.1 (5).]

M appealed against the upholding of a listed building enforcement notice requiring him to remove and replace certain roofing works carried out on outbuildings to a listed building. The listed building itself was under separate ownership to the outbuildings which were owned by M. M contended that the outbuildings did not come "within the curtilage" of the listed building and therefore were not themselves a listed building for the purposes of the Planning (Listed Buildings and Conservation Areas) Act 1990 s.1 (5).

Held, allowing the appeal and remitting the case for rehearing, that a building was "within the curtilage" of another building if the two buildings were sufficiently close and accessible to one another, and in terms of function, the first building was ancillary to the second, *Debenhams v. Westminster City Council* [1987] A.C. 396, [1987] C.L.Y. 3195, *Attorney General ex rel Sutcliffe v. Calderdale MBC* [1983] 46 P. & C.R. 399, [1984] C.L.Y. 3451 and *Skerritts of Nottingham Ltd v. Secretary of State for the Environment, Transport and the Regions (No.1)* [2001] Q.B. 59, [2000] C.L.Y. 4473 considered. The inspector had erred in focusing his attention on the time when the main listed building and the outbuildings were under single ownership and occupancy. He should have focused on the date when the main building was actually given listed status, at which time the outbuildings were no longer ancillary to the main building. Furthermore, although in physical terms the main building was relatively close to the outbuildings, the outbuildings were not easily accessible from the main building. Therefore the outbuildings did not come "within the curtilage" of the main listed building,

MORRIS v. WREXHAM CBC, [2001] EWHC Admin 697, [2002] 2 P. & C.R. 7, Jackson, J., QBD (Admin Ct).

3695. Planning applications–change of use–lack of formal application–estoppel

[Town and Country Planning Act 1990 s.64.]

E, a local authority, appealed against a finding ([2001] Env. L.R. 14) that R had obtained a determination from it under the Town and Country Planning Act 1990 s.64, now repealed, that electricity could be generated on a waste treatment site without further planning permission despite the fact that no application had been made by R under s.64. R argued that a resolution by E to vary a condition attached to an existing planning permission amounted to a valid determination and that even if there had been no determination under s.64, E was estopped by representation or convention from denying that electricity could be generated on the site without further planning permission.

Held, allowing the appeal, that (1) a determination under s.64 of the Act was a juridical act which gave rise to legal consequences. The relevant legislation showed that a determination was a matter which concerned the general public interest and which required other planning authorities, the Secretary of State on behalf of the national interest and the public itself to be able to take part; it was not just a matter between the applicant and the planning authority where they could agree to follow whatever procedure they liked. Accordingly, there had been no determination in the instant case, and (2) the private law concepts of estoppel should not be introduced into planning law, and public law should absorb no more than it had already from the moral values which underpinned those concepts, *Newbury DC v. Secretary of State for the Environment* [1981] A.C. 578, [1980] C.L.Y. 2667 applied. In any event, an estoppel could not be established on the facts of the case.

R. (ON THE APPLICATION OF REPROTECH (PEBSHAM) LTD v. EAST SUSSEX CC; *sub nom.* REPROTECH (PEBSHAM) LTD v. EAST SUSSEX CC; EAST SUSSEX CC v. REPROTECH (PEBSHAM) LTD; R. v. EAST SUSSEX CC, *ex p.* REPROTECH (PEBSHAM) LTD, [2002] UKHL 8, [2003] 1 W.L.R. 348, Lord Hoffmann, HL.

3696. Planning applications–environmental impact assessments–lack of public inquiry into grant of permission–right to fair trial–suitability of judicial review

[Human Rights Act 1998 Sch.1 Part I Art.6.]

BT sought judicial review of a decision of the local planning authority, G, to grant outline planning permission with related consents for a city centre development, and further sought a declaration that the legislation governing G's decision was incompatible with its right to a fair trial as guaranteed by the Human Rights Act 1998 Sch.1 Part I Art.6. BT contended, inter alia, that (1) the planned development was significantly different from that in the first application such that G should not have permitted an amendment but rather required a fresh application to be made; (2) G did not consider whether an environmental impact statement was required or in the alternative erred in its approach to the issue, and (3) G was not an impartial and independent tribunal within the meaning of Art.6.

Held, granting the application in part and quashing the outline planning consent, that (1) it had been open to the planning officer to conclude that the proposed change was not substantial and accordingly to deal with it by way of amendment. Whilst the public interest had to be fully protected, it had been protected in the instant case by the detailed consultation which had taken place, *Inverclyde DC v. Lord Advocate* (1982) 43 P. & C.R. 375, [1982] C.L.Y. 3191 applied; (2) G had clearly considered the need for an environmental impact assessment, albeit in an informal manner and at a late stage. However, G had applied the wrong test as it had considered the assessment to be necessary only where there were significant adverse effects. The correct approach was to seek an assessment in instances where there were any significant effects, whether adverse or beneficial, and (3) on the facts of the instant case, and notwithstanding the lack of a public inquiry into the grant of permission, the availability of judicial review as a remedy avoided an infringement of BT's right to a fair trial, *R. (on the application of Holding & Barnes Plc) v. Secretary of State for the Environment, Transport and the Regions* [2001] UKHL 23, [2001] 2 W.L.R. 1389, [2001] C.L.Y. 4761 considered.

BRITISH TELECOMMUNICATIONS PLC v. GLOUCESTER CITY COUNCIL; *sub nom.* BT PLC v. GLOUCESTER CITY COUNCIL, [2001] EWHC Admin 1001, [2002] 2 P. & C.R. 33, Elias, J., QBD (Admin Ct).

3697. **Planning applications–general development procedure**

TOWN AND COUNTRY PLANNING (GENERAL DEVELOPMENT PROCEDURE) (AMENDMENT) (ENGLAND) ORDER 2002, SI 2002 828; made under the Town and Country Planning Act 1990 s.59, s.69, s.333. In force: July 1, 2002; £1.75.

This Order amends the Town and Country Planning (General Development Procedure) Order 1995 (SI 1995 419) so as to require the local planning authority in addition to the detail already recorded in the register of applications to include details of any planning obligation, agreement entered into or proposed in respect of an application for planning permission or application for the approval of reserved matters and of any other relevant planning obligation or agreement in respect of the land the subject of the application.

3698. **Planning applications–general development procedure–Wales**

TOWN AND COUNTRY PLANNING (GENERAL DEVELOPMENT PROCEDURE) (AMENDMENT) (WALES) ORDER 2002, SI 2002 1877; made under the Town and Country Planning Act 1990 s.59, s.61, s.65, s.69, s.71, s.73, s.74, s.77, s.78, s.79, s.188, s.193, s.196, s.333, Sch.1 para.5, Sch.1 para.6, Sch.1 para.7, Sch.1 para.8. In force: August 1, 2002; £1.75.

This Order amends the Town and Country Planning (General Development Procedure) Order 1995 (SI 1995 419) in relation to Wales so as to require any application to a local planning authority in Wales for planning permission for development which involves the construction or installation of one or more antennas for the purpose of operating a telecommunications system to be accompanied by a written declaration that the equipment and installation to which the application relates is so designed that it will, when constructed or installed, operate in full compliance with the requirements of the radio frequency public exposure guidelines of the International Commission on Non-ionising Radiation Protection.

3699. **Planning applications–right to fair trial–local authorities powers and duties–planning permission sought for local authority project–impartial decision maker**

[Human Rights Act 1998 Sch.1 Part I Art.6.]

K sought judicial review of a decision of R, a local authority, to consider a planning application for a project promoted by R on land which it also owned. The project was a major development which included schools, a cultural centre and sports facilities. K, who lived close to the proposed site, contended, inter alia, that, (1) the decision of R to determine the application was a breach of his right to have the matter decided by "an independent and impartial tribunal" under the Human Rights Act 1998 Sch.1 Part I Art.6; (2) that R had effectively already decided that planning permission should be granted and that proper consideration would not be given to the application, and (3) R had erred in its decision to seek tenders for the project via the method of competitive negotiated procedure.

Held, refusing the application, that (1) whilst R was not an impartial decision maker in this matter, it could not be said that R's decision to consider its own planning application would "inevitably" lead to a breach of Art. 6. Having regard to the procedure involved in the decision-making process of a local planning authority, there was a possibility that where a dispute as to issues of fact arose, judicial review would not provide sufficient judicial control such as to ensure compliance with Art. 6. However, the court could only determine whether the availability of judicial review was sufficient to cure any such defect when the actual planning decision had been made and the grounds for review raised. *R. (on the application of Holding & Barnes Plc) v. Secretary of State for the Environment, Transport and the Regions* [2001] UKHL 23, [2001] 2 W.L.R. 1389 considered; (2) the initial development work and promotion of the project carried out by R had been no more than would normally be done by a developer and did not mean that R was "closing its mind" to the proper consideration of the planning application on its merits, and (3) granting permission to apply for review on this ground, that whilst the decision making process adopted by R had been flawed, such deficiencies had not rendered the decision invalid.

R. (ON THE APPLICATION OF KATHRO) v. RHONDDA CYNON TAFF CBC, [2001] EWHC Admin 527, [2002] Env. L.R. 15, Richards, J., QBD (Admin Ct).

3700. Planning applications—right to fair trial—refusal of Secretary of State to call in application for determination

[Town and Country Planning Act 1990 s.77; Human Rights Act 1998 s.6(1), Sch.1 Part I Art.6.]

FP applied for judicial review of a decision of the Secretary of State not to direct that a planning application submitted by LL to the local authority for a retail shopping development be determined by him pursuant to the Town and Country Planning Act 1990 s.77. FP was the freehold owner of a successful city centre development and had formally objected to LL's proposal for a retail development in the same area. Part of the site on which LL sought to develop was owned by the local authority. FP argued that as the determination of the application by the local authority would constitute a breach of the Human Rights Act 1998 Sch.1 Part I Art.6, the decision of the Secretary of State not to determine the application himself meant that he would be acting in a way that was incompatible with FP's rights under Art.6, contrary to s.6(1) of the 1998 Act. It was submitted by LL, inter alia, that Art.6 was not engaged.

Held, refusing the application, that (1) the scope of Art.6 of the 1998 Act did extend, in appropriate cases, to the administrative decision making process concerning the objection of a third party to the grant of planning permission, provided the third party's civil rights were affected. In the instant case Art.6 had been engaged since FP had a civil right to use and enjoy their retail shopping development, *R. (on the application of Holding & Barnes Plc) v. Secretary of State for the Environment, Transport and the Regions* [2001] UKHL 23, [2001] 2 W.L.R. 1389, [2001] C.L.Y. 4761 and *Ortenberg v. Austria (A/295-B)* (1995) 19 E.H.R.R. 524 applied, and (2) the determination of the application by the local authority, which would be subject to review by the High Court, was compatible with FP's rights under Art.6. The High Court had "full jurisdiction" to deal with, and thereby ensure compliance with Art.6, those decisions which were (a) dependent on the administrative decision maker reaching a conclusion in relation to the progress or outcome of a future event or events, or (b) a decision which had been made on purely planning grounds, *Bryan v. United Kingdom (A/335-A)* (1996) 21 E.H.R.R. 342, [1996] C.L.Y. 4707 considered. In circumstances where a decision was dependent on the decision maker determining a current or future fact, an inquiry before an independent inspector was likely to be necessary to ensure, together with the High Court's power of review, that the process was compliant with Art.6. In the instant case, the potential impact of the proposed development was essentially a question of planning judgment.

R. (ON THE APPLICATION OF FRIENDS PROVIDENT LIFE OFFICE) v. SECRETARY OF STATE FOR THE ENVIRONMENT, TRANSPORT AND THE REGIONS; *sub nom.* FRIENDS PROVIDENT LIFE OFFICE v. SECRETARY OF STATE FOR THE ENVIRONMENT, TRANSPORT AND THE REGIONS; R. (ON THE APPLICATION OF FRIENDS PROVIDENT LIFE & PENSIONS LTD) v. SECRETARY OF STATE FOR TRANSPORT, LOCAL GOVERNMENT AND THE REGIONS; FRIENDS PROVIDENT LIFE & PENSIONS LTD v. SECRETARY OF STATE FOR TRANSPORT, LOCAL GOVERNMENT AND THE REGIONS, [2001] EWHC Admin 820, [2002] 1 W.L.R. 1450, Forbes, J., QBD (Admin Ct).

3701.　Planning applications—wind farms—fees

TRANSPORT AND WORKS (APPLICATIONS AND OBJECTIONS PROCEDURE) (ENGLAND AND WALES) (AMENDMENT) RULES 2002, SI 2002 1965; made under the Transport and Works Act 1992 s.6. In force: August 22, 2002; £1.75.

These Rules amend the Transport and Works (Applications and Objections Procedure) (England and Wales) Rules 2000 (SI 2000 2190) to make specific provision for the fees payable for applications relating to wind farms.

3702.　Planning control—use classes—radioactive material—Wales

TOWN AND COUNTRY PLANNING (USE CLASSES) (AMENDMENT) (WALES) ORDER 2002, SI 2002 1875; made under the Town and Country Planning Act 1990 s.55, s.333. In force: ; £1.75.

This Order amends the Town and Country Planning (Use Classes) Order 1987 (SI 1987 764), to exclude from Class B8 (Storage or distribution) use of a building or other land for the storage of or as a distribution centre for radioactive material or radioactive waste (as defined in the Radioactive Substances Act 1993), if the building or other land is situated in Wales.

3703.　Planning permission—agricultural land—errection of barn and mobile home—fairness of appeal

[Town and Country Planning Act 1990 s.288(1).]

D, an ostrich farmer, appealed under the Town and Country Planning Act 1990 s.288(1) against a planning inspector's decision to uphold both the refusal to grant planning permission for a two storey barn on his agricultural land and the refusal to permit a mobile home to be used for residential purposes. D contended that the inspector had not conducted the appeal fairly and, in particular, had failed to have regard to (1) expert evidence; (2) the existence of a comparable barn in the area for which planning permission had been granted, and (3) the fact that there was a need for a worker to live on his farm in order to deal with emergencies.

Held, dismissing the appeal, that the power of the court under s.288(1) of the Act to quash the inspector's decision was limited, *Ashbridge Investments Ltd v. Minister of Housing and Local Government* [1965] 1 W.L.R. 1320, [1965] C.L.Y. 522 followed. In the instant case, the inspector had considered all material issues and had followed the guidance in PPG 7 Annexe 1. The inspector had been entitled to refuse D's appeal on the evidence before him and, accordingly, there had been no unfairness to D.

R. (ON THE APPLICATION OF DYASON) v. SECRETARY OF STATE FOR THE ENVIRONMENT, TRANSPORT AND THE REGIONS (NO.3), [2001] EWHC Admin 4, [2001] J.P.L. 1109 (Note), Scott Baker, J., QBD (Admin Ct).

3704.　Planning permission—applications—fees—Wales

TOWN AND COUNTRY PLANNING (FEES FOR APPLICATIONS AND DEEMED APPLICATIONS) (AMENDMENT) (WALES) REGULATIONS 2002, SI 2002 1876;

made under the Town and Country Planning Act 1990 s.303. In force: August 1, 2002; £1.75.

These Regulations increase the fee payable for an application to a local planning authority for a determination as to whether prior approval will be required for proposed telecommunications development under the General Permitted Development Order 1995 SI (1995 418). The fee is increased from £35 to £190 in order to reflect the increased notification and consultation requirements imposed on local planning authorities in relation to such developments by the Town and Country Planning (General Permitted Development) (Amendment) (Wales) Order 2002 (SI 2002 1878).

3705. Planning permission–applications and deemed applications–fees

TOWN AND COUNTRY PLANNING (FEES FOR APPLICATIONS AND DEEMED APPLICATIONS) (AMENDMENT) (ENGLAND) REGULATIONS 2002, SI 2002 768; made under the Town and Country Planning Act 1990 s.303. In force: April 1, 2002; £2.00.

These Regulations, which amend the Town and Country Planning (Fees for Applications and Deemed Applications) (Amendment) Regulations 1997 (SI 1997 37), amend the Town and Country Planning (Fees for Applications and Deemed Applications) Regulations 1989 (SI 1989 193) so that all fees are increased by 14 per cent.

3706. Planning permission–applications and deemed applications–fees

TOWN AND COUNTRY PLANNING (FEES FOR APPLICATIONS AND DEEMED APPLICATIONS) (AMENDMENT NO.2) (WALES) REGULATIONS 2002, SI 2002 2258; made under the Town and Country Planning Act 1990 s.303. In force: September 4, 2002; £2.00.

These Regulations amend the Town and Country Planning (Fees for Applications and Deemed Applications) Regulations 1989 (SI 1989 193) so that all fees payable are increased by 15 per cent.

3707. Planning permission–caravans–planning history–personal circumstances–material considerations

CBC challenged the decision of a planning inspector to allow the appeal of B against an enforcement notice issued by CBC. B had been living in a residential caravan, purportedly since 1985. In 1996, on the advice of CBC, B had made an application for planning permission for the caravan and was granted temporary permission for one year. When he did not remove the caravan following the expiration of the permission, an enforcement notice was issued. The inspector granted B's appeal against the notice on the ground that B's long use of the site, and the fact that if he had been properly advised he could have obtained a Certificate of Existing Lawful Use, together amounted to a significant material consideration which outweighed the green belt issues in the case. The inspector granted personal planning permission to B. CBC argued that the inspector had taken into account an immaterial consideration.

Held, dismissing the application, that the inspector had applied the correct approach. Both the planning background of the site and factors having an impact on B's personal circumstances were material considerations, as was the issue of fairness, *Ayres v. Secretary of State for the Environment* (1997) 74 P. & C.R. 246, [1997] C.L.Y. 4117 applied. The inspector's decision was therefore not irrational or perverse.

CHRISTCHURCH BC v. SECRETARY OF STATE FOR THE ENVIRONMENT, TRANSPORT AND THE REGIONS (NO.2); CHRISTCHURCH BC v. BILLINGTON [2001] J.P.L. 1265, Ouseley, J., QBD (Admin Ct).

3708. Planning permission—conditions—abuse of power—statutory time limit on mining rights—local authority's variation of conditions

[Town and Country Planning (Minerals) Act 1981 s.7(5); Planning and Compensation Act 1991 s.22, Sch.2.]

The second defendant local authority, appealed against a judgment ([2002] EWHC 161, [2002] 6 E.G.C.S. 153) ordering it to relax the conditions it had imposed on a planning permission concerning the mining rights of certain land. Mining permission on the land, now owned by E, had been granted in 1946 and was determined to expire in 2042 as a result of the mandatory time limit imposed by the Town and Country Planning (Minerals) Act 1981 s.7(5). However, when E's predecessor in title had been granted registration of the mining right, pursuant to the Planning and Compensation Act 1991 s.22 and Sch.2, the local authority had determined that the mining should cease by September 2000. E had sought to have the condition altered but this application was rejected by the Planning Inspector. Subsequent to the Inspector's decision being overturned on appeal the local authority conceded that it had not had the right to impose a more stringent time limit than that specified in the 1981 Act. In the current appeal the local authority submitted that E should not have been entitled to challenge the validity of the condition given that E's predecessor in title had failed to appeal against the determination.

Held, dismissing the appeal, that E had been entitled to challenge the validity of the local authority's determination. Notwithstanding the time that had passed since the determination had been registered, the judge below had been correct to exercise his discretion, pursuant to the Town and Country Planning Act s.288, to quash the Planning Inspector's decision. The courts attention was drawn to past authority making it clear that, on some occasions, a party to a planning matter would be precluded from challenging an action taken by a local authority but it was held that this did not apply to the provisions of the 1991 Act, *R. v. Wicks (Peter Edward)* [1998] A.C. 92, [1997] C.L.Y. 4065 and *Boddington v. British Transport Police* [1999] 2 A.C. 143, [1998] C.L.Y. 89 distinguished. Given the clear statutory intent that the landowners should enjoy mining rights until 2042 it would need further clear statutory language to bar the landowners successors in title from challenging the local authority's misuse of power.

EARTHLINE LTD v. SECRETARY OF STATE FOR TRANSPORT, LOCAL GOVERNMENT AND THE REGIONS; *sub nom*. EARTHLINE LTD v. SECRETARY OF STATE FOR THE ENVIRONMENT, TRANSPORT AND THE REGIONS, [2002] EWCA Civ 1599, [2003] 1 P. & C.R. 24, Brooke, L.J., CA.

3709. Planning permission—conditions—coal—approval—effect of local authority's failure to determine valid application

[Environment Act 1995 s.96, Sch.13 para.9.]

P sought judicial review of the local authority's decision on his application for the approval of conditions on planning permissions relating to former coal mining land. The planning permissions dated back to 1955 and 1961 and permitted the disposal of colliery rubbish and the removal of a tip. The 1961 permission had been subject to a time limit which had expired. The local authority returned P's application, concluding that the 1961 permission was not a relevant planning permission within the meaning of the Environment Act 1995 s.96 and Sch.13 para.9 and that new conditions relating to the 1955 permission would permit only the disposal of colliery rubbish on the site. P claimed that by virtue of Sch.13 para.9(6) and (9) the local authority was required to determine his application and that the effect of its failure to do so was that it was deemed to have allowed the application.

Held, granting the application in part, that (1) although Sch.13 para.9(1) did not specifically refer to extant relevant planning permissions, it had to be assumed that Parliament did not intend that para.9(1) should apply to mineral planning permissions that were no longer extant. The purpose of para.9 was to enable applicants to invite mineral planning authorities to determine the conditions which should be attached to relevant planning permissions so as to reflect modern environmental concerns. Furthermore, the advice given in MPG 14 referring to extant permissions was sound, even though it did not have the force of statute, and mineral planning authorities were entitled to consider the validity of permissions in the context of their duty to determine conditions under para.9(6), *R. v. Oldham MBC, ex p. Foster* [2000] Env. L.R. 395, [2000] C.L.Y. 4510 approved. Accordingly, the local authority was entitled to reject P's application in respect of the 1961 planning permission on the ground that it was no longer extant, and (2) it was not disputed that the 1955 permission was a relevant permission for the purposes of the 1995 Act. P's application had been properly made under para.9(1) and satisfied the requirements of para.9(2). Although P's application related to both the 1961 and the 1955 permissions, the fact that the local authority was entitled to reject the application in respect of the 1961 permission did not mean that it was invalid in respect of the 1955 permission. Paragraph 9(6) required the local authority to determine the conditions to which each relevant planning permission relating to the site was to be subject. It was not entitled simply to return the application without a determination. Accordingly, by virtue of para.9(9), since the authority had not notified P of its decision within the prescribed time limit, the authority was deemed to have determined that the 1955 planning permission should be subject to the conditions proposed by P.

R. (ON THE APPLICATION OF PAYNE) v. CAERPHILLY CBC, [2002] EWHC 866, [2002] P.L.C.R. 25, Sullivan, J., QBD (Admin Ct).

3710. **Planning permission—conditions—motor dealers—display of vehicles other than inside premises—meaning of "display"**

[Town and Country Planning Act 1990 s.187A.]

M appealed against convictions for an offence under the Town and Country Planning Act 1990 s.187A. M operated a motor cycle dealership with planning permission containing a condition that "the display or sale of vehicles....shall not take place on any part of the site except inside the proposed building." M had placed motorcycles on the forecourt between the dealership building and the road, and the local authority contended that this constituted a display in contravention of the planning condition. The parties had based their contentions for the definition of "display" on alternative definitions given in "The Shorter Oxford Dictionary". M had contended that "display" was to be defined as "to exhibit ostentatiously; to make a show of..." but the justices had accepted the local authority's submission that it meant "to open up to view; to exhibit to the eyes." On appeal, M argued that the mere opening up of a motorcycle to view, irrespective of the purpose, was not sufficient to constitute display.

Held, allowing the appeal against conviction, that the meaning of a word must be derived from the context in which it appeared. It was vital to determine the purpose of placing a motorcycle on the forecourt when considering whether or not it was displayed within the meaning of the planning condition. To display an object was to put it on show or to exhibit it in order to attract people's attention to it, not necessarily for commercial purposes. The matter was remitted to the justices for them to consider on an objective basis whether the reasons for putting the motorcycles on the forecourt came within the meaning of "display" as defined in the instant judgment, such consideration to be based on the available evidence.

McGAHAN v. WINDSOR AND MAIDENHEAD RBC, [2002] EWHC 1551, *The Times*, July 30, 2002, Harrison, J., QBD (Admin Ct).

3711. **Planning permission—conditions—removal—rationality of decision—legitimate expectations of local residents**

[Town and Country Planning Act 1990 s.73.]

WBC and BAE appealed against an order quashing WBC's decision to remove a condition attached to BAE's planning permission in respect of an aerodrome site, which stated that the land would revert to agricultural use following BAE's cessation of use, of which notice had been given. WBC's decision was quashed following an appeal by B, the local residents, on the grounds that an immaterial consideration had been taken into account, the removal of the condition was irrational, and that B had a legitimate expectation that the condition would continue on account of the length of time it had been in place.

Held, allowing the appeal, that the potentially immaterial consideration was only referred to in one paragraph of the planning officer's report and it was unlikely that it had influenced members, given that it was their role to consider planning issues. Further, the removal of the condition was not irrational because it was not beyond the responses of a reasonable decision maker given the considerations highlighted in the planning officer's report, *R. v. Ministry of Defence, ex p. Smith* [1996] Q.B. 517, [1996] C.L.Y. 383 applied. The planning authority had to consider BAE's application in accordance with the Town and Country Planning Act 1990 s.73 and take into account all material considerations. Any legitimate expectation B may have had did not override the council's duty.

R. (ON THE APPLICATION OF BARKER) v. WAVERLEY BC, [2001] EWCA Civ 566, [2002] 1 P. & C.R. 6, Pill, L.J., CA.

3712.   Planning permission–conditions–size of structure included in design conditions

CBC applied to quash a decision of a planning inspector allowing an appeal against CBC's refusal of planning permission for the construction of two bungalows on a site. The inspector, having regard to the proximity of the proposed accommodation to the two dwellings on either side, granted permission subject to approval by CBC of the siting and design of the bungalows. CBC contended that the inspector had erred in that, having concluded that the harm was to be avoided by smaller dwellings, he had failed to impose a condition specifically limiting the size of the two bungalows.

Held, dismissing the application, that the result that the inspector had sought to achieve was capable of being achieved through the imposition of the standard condition in relation to the design of the site, since there was no reason why the size of a building should not be included within the meaning of design, *R. v. Newbury DC, ex p. Chieveley Parish Council* (1998) 10 Admin. L.R. 676, [1998] C.L.Y. 4226 considered.

CHRISTCHURCH BC v. SECRETARY OF STATE FOR THE ENVIRONMENT, TRANSPORT AND THE REGIONS (NO.2) [2001] J.P.L. 606, George Bartlett Q.C., QBD.

3713.   Planning permission–delegated responsibility–conflict of application with planning policies–proper exercise of delegated powers

C appealed against the dismissal (2001 EWHC Admin 873, [2001] 46 E.G.C.S. 179) of his application to quash a decision of the chief planning officer granting planning permission for a residential extension at a property neighbouring his own. C contended that (1) the planning decision was one which ought to have been made by the local authority's committee and should not have been delegated to the planning officer under the scheme of delegation set out in the Local Government Act 1972 s.101, and (2) the planning officer could not, in the circumstances, reasonably decide that the case fell within the exception in the 1972 Act enabling him to exercise the functions of the local authority in the absence of any conflict between the application and the local authority's policies.

Held, allowing the appeal, that (1) neither the local authority's policies nor the facts of the particular application were clear, therefore it was not possible to determine whether the application conflicted with the authority's planning policies. A material misdescription in the grant of planning permission had resulted in an obvious difficulty in determining which of the detailed policies of the local authority was applicable. Since it was not always a straightforward matter to decide whether a particular application conflicted with the policies, it was important that planning officers were circumspect in exercising their delegated powers and had regard to the complexity of the policies, and (2) this was not the type of case which was contemplated by the exception in the 1972 Act and as a matter of public policy it should have been referred to the planning committee.

R. (ON THE APPLICATION OF CARLTON-CONWAY) v. HARROW LBC, [2002] EWCA Civ 927, *The Times*, July 11, 2002, Pill, L.J., CA.

3714. **Planning permission–environmental impact assesment–right to light– residential dwellings overshadowed by sports stadium**

[Human Rights Act 1998 Sch.1 Part I Art.8; Town and Country Planning (Environmental Impact Assessment) (England and Wales) Regulations 1999 (SI 1999 293).]

M, a local resident, sought judicial review of the grant of planning permission for the redevelopment of the north stand at Ipswich Town Football Club. M's home formed part of a terrace of Victorian houses close to the stadium. Construction of the new stand would result in a degree of loss of sunlight to certain properties in the road. M maintained that (1) the failure to commission an environmental impact assessment was an error of law; (2) the plans had been formulated in contravention of the development plan which stated that non residential use in residential areas would only be permitted in circumstances where the proposed use was compatible with the size and scale of the housing in the surrounding area and would not have an adverse effect on that area in terms of [inter alia] illumination, and (3) the severity of the loss of light resulted in an infringement of M's rights under the Human Rights Act 1998 Sch.1 Part I Art.8.

Held, refusing the application for judicial review, that (1) the Town and Country Planning (Environmental Impact Assessment) (England and Wales) Regulations 1999 were not concerned with the amenity of individual properties and, whilst there might be a significant impact upon an individual property, that did not necessarily mean that there had been a "significant impact upon the environment". On the facts of the instant case, there was a severe but highly localised loss of sunlight affecting a small number of properties which was not capable of constituting a significant effect upon the environment such as to require the commissioning of an assessment; (2) there had been no contravention of planning policy as the relevant policy was plainly inapplicable since the area comprised mixed residential and commercial use whereas the policy was directed at areas solely consisting of residential usage, and (3) there was no breach of Art.8. Whilst it was possible for a breach to occur in cases of severe environmental pollution, M's case was unlikely to meet that threshold test, *Lopez Ostra v. Spain (A/303-C)* (1995) 20 E.H.R.R. 277, [1996] C.L.Y. 3118 and *Guerra v. Italy* (1998) 26 E.H.R.R. 357, [1998] C.L.Y. 3096 considered. Even if the threshold had been crossed interference could be justified under Art.8(2) provided that the appropriate balancing exercise had been performed. On the facts the local authority had carefully weighed the loss of amenity to M against the benefits likely to accrue to the public as a whole in renovating the stand and had been entitled to reach the conclusion that it had.

R. (ON THE APPLICATION OF MALSTER) v. IPSWICH BC, [2001] EWHC Admin 711, [2002] P.L.C.R.14, Sullivan, J., QBD (Admin Ct).

3715. **Planning permission–environmental impact assessments–assessment deemed unnecessary–no duty to reconsider decision**

[Town and Country Planning (Environmental Impact Assessment) (England and Wales) Regulations 1999 (SI 1999 293).]

F challenged H's decision to grant planning permission for a residential development on a former RAF site. F submitted that (1) H had erred in its approach to the issue of increased traffic congestion as a result of its belief that traffic congestion could not be a valid reason for opposing the application; (2) H's decision that an environmental impact assessment, EIA, was unnecessary should have been reconsidered in the light of new material regarding traffic congestion, and (3) the application had not been considered fairly and impartially, given that there was a belief among labour committee members that it had been predetermined in the applicant's favour following a meeting of the ruling labour majority.

Held, refusing the application, that (1) F had viewed H's approach narrowly, and when the planning officer's report was read in a wider context, as opposed to being subjected to minute textual scrutiny, the overall effect of it made sense; (2) H was not under a duty to reconsider its conclusion that an EIA was unnecessary. The issue had been adequately considered and there was no express duty imposed by virtue of the Town and Country Planning (Environmental Impact Assessment) (England and Wales) Regulations 1999. There had been no request that the matter be reconsidered, nor any submission made that the development was of a type requiring an EIA. Further the circumstances were not materially different to those prevailing at the stage when a negative screening opinion had been made, and (3) there was no factual evidence to support the submission that voting councillors had held a belief that there had been a predetermination.

R. (ON THE APPLICATION OF FERNBACK) v. HARROW LBC; *sub nom.* FERNBACK v. HARROW LBC, [2001] EWHC Admin 278, [2002] Env. L.R. 10, Richards, J., QBD (Admin Ct).

3716. Planning permission–environmental impact assessments–duty to consider need for assessment when considering reserved matters–proper implementation of EC directive

[Town and Country Planning (Assessment of Environmental Effects) Regulations 1988 (SI 1988 1199); Council Directive 85/337 on the assessment of the effects of certain public and private projects on the environment.]

B appealed against the refusal ([2001] Env. L.R.1) of her application for judicial review of BLBC's decision to grant planning permission for a development in Crystal Palace Park. BLBC had granted outline planning permission but did not consider that an environmental assessment, EA, pursuant to Council Directive 85/337, was appropriate. The Directive had been implemented into domestic law by the Town and Country Planning (Assessment of Environmental Effects) Regulations 1988, under which an EA was only necessary, if appropriate, at the time that planning permission or outline planning permission was being considered. The issue before the court was whether the Directive required BLBC to assess the need for an EA at the time it considered the reserved matters, and the question arose as to whether the Directive had been properly implemented into domestic law. B argued that the Directive required the consideration of the need for an EA at both the stage at which outline planning permission was granted, and at the stage at which the reserved matters were considered.

Held, dismissing the appeal, that the Regulations required a planning authority to consider the environmental impact of a proposed development at the outline planning stage. The Regulations had properly implemented the Directive into domestic law and there was no need, under the Regulations, for an EA when reserved matters were being considered. A reference to the European Court of Justice was neither necessary nor appropriate.

R. (ON THE APPLICATION OF BARKER) v. BROMLEY LBC; *sub nom.* R. v. BROMLEY LBC, *ex p.* BARKER, [2001] EWCA Civ 1766, [2002] Env. L.R. 25, Latham, L.J., CA.

3717. Planning permission–environmental impact assessments–motorway service areas–failure to consider environmental statement

[Town and Country Planning (Assessment of Environmental Effects) Regulations 1988 (SI 1988 1199) Reg.4(2), Reg.25; Town and Country Planning (Inquiries Procedure) Rules 1992 (SI 1992 2038).]

Following a change in government policy in 1992, eight proposals were submitted to develop motorway service areas in the western sector of the M25. The proposals were the subject of public inquiries between 1994 and 1998. Only one of the applications was successful and four of the unsuccessful developers challenged the decision to grant outline planning permission. All the applications were the subject of separate inquiries and the main issues considered by the inspectors had been impact on the Green Belt and other policies relating to countryside and the effect of the proposed development on traffic safety and flow. It was contended that the unsuccessful applicants had not had the opportunity to comment on highways evidence produced after the close of the inquiry and technical highway issues. Further, that the environmental impact assessment carried out on the successful site did not adequately address the proposed development and that the separate inquiries meant that no proper comparative exercise had been carried out.

Held, allowing the application and quashing the decision to grant outline planning permission and the decisions refusing planning permission in respect of the other sites, that (1) although there had been no breach of the Town and Country Planning (Inquiries Procedure) Rules, the Secretary of State had failed to comply with representations that objectors would have the opportunity to respond to post inquiry highways evidence and so had reached his decision in substantial breach of legitimate expectation and procedural fairness; (2) the holding of separate inquires was not a reasonable basis for the assessment of the competing proposals. The Secretary of State had failed adequately to explain how the exercise had been carried out to show that it could withstand scrutiny on rational grounds, and (3) the environmental statement accompanying the plans did not adequately describe the proposed development and there was nothing to tie the outline permission to the development as the conditions on which it had been granted meant that most of the application was subject to reserved matters approval. By granting permission without considering the environmental statement, the Secretary of State had acted ultra vires Town and Country Planning (Assessment of Environmental Effects) Regulations 1988 Reg.4(2) and Reg.25, *Berkeley v. Secretary of State for the Environment, Transport and the Regions (No.1)* [2001] 2 A.C. 603, [2000] C.L.Y. 4460 and *R. v. Rochdale MBC, ex p. Milne (No.1)* [2000] Env. L.R. 1 applied.

R. (ON THE APPLICATION OF ELMBRIDGE BC) v. SECRETARY OF STATE FOR THE ENVIRONMENT, TRANSPORT AND THE REGIONS; TOTALFINA GREAT BRITIAN LTD v. SECRETARY OF STATE FOR THE ENVIRONMENT, TRANSPORT AND THE REGIONS; HADMERE LTD v. SECRETARY OF STATE FOR THE ENVIRONMENT, TRANSPORT AND THE REGIONS; AVALON ENTERPRISES LTD v. SECRETARY OF STATE FOR THE ENVIRONMENT, TRANSPORT AND THE REGIONS; *sub nom.* ELMBRIDGE BC v. SECRETARY OF STATE FOR THE ENVIRONMENT, TRANSPORT AND THE REGIONS; R. v. SECRETARY OF STATE FOR THE ENVIRONMENT, TRANSPORT AND THE REGIONS, *ex p.* ELMBRIDGE BC [2002] Env. L.R. 1, Richards, J., QBD (Admin Ct) Administrative Court.

3718. Planning permission–extension of licensed premises–opening hours–material considerations

C, who operated a nightclub in a conservation area, appealed against the refusal of planning permission for an extension of the nightclub's opening hours beyond midnight. C contended that the planning inspector had failed to give consideration to the results of a planning inquiry and subsequent appeal decision concerned with neighbouring premises which had permission to open until 2 am and which had been granted an increase in capacity on appeal. C submitted that the planning appeal of the neighbouring premises had been a material consideration which the planning inspector in the instant case had failed to consider, and that by not obtaining a copy of the decision, the inspector had failed in his duty to take reasonable steps to obtain all relevant information.

Held, dismissing the appeal, that the planning inspector had been aware that a decision was pending in relation to the neighbouring premises, but that case had related to capacity not opening hours. It had been reasonable for the inspector to proceed to determine the appeal given the substantial delay that had already occurred coupled with the fact that the issue was not the same and neither party had suggested that he await the decision. Accordingly, he had not failed in his obligation to inform himself of relevant facts or failed to take into account a material consideration.

CLUB AIRLOCK/PLANET STUDIOS v. SECRETARY OF STATE FOR THE ENVIRONMENT, TRANSPORT AND THE REGIONS; *sub nom.* CLUB AIRLOCK v. SECRETARY OF STATE FOR THE ENVIRONMENT, TRANSPORT AND THE REGIONS, [2001] EWHC Admin 700, [2002] P.L.C.R. 16, David Pannick Q.C., QBD (Admin Ct).

3719. Planning permission–houses–size of replacement dwelling–material considerations

Y appealed against the refusal of planning permission for the replacement of a single storey 25 square metre property with a proposed dwelling of 316 square metres on two floors. Planning permission had been granted for a smaller single storey replacement building of 50 square metres. Y submitted that the inspector had erred in testing the proposals put forward on appeal against the size of the existing dwelling, instead of against the size of the proposed dwelling with the benefit of the extant planning permission, and had also misconstrued Structure Plan Strategic Policy 4.

Held, dismissing the appeal, that the inspector had been correct to consider the proposed change in size from the existing building and she had properly taken into account as a material consideration the fall back position of the existing planning permission. Although Strategic Policy 4 was at first glance ambiguous, both the memorandum to the structure plan and national policy guidance PPG7 clearly endorsed the inspector's interpretation.

YEATES v. SECRETARY OF STATE FOR THE ENVIRONMENT, TRANSPORT AND THE REGIONS, [2001] EWHC Admin 34, [2001] P.L.C.R. 28, Sullivan, J., QBD (Admin Ct).

3720. Planning permission–housing development–methane contamination

D applied for judicial review of a decision of C, the local ombudsman, that Colchester Borough Council, CBC, had not been guilty of maladministration. D had purchased a property which had been built in 1986 on a former landfill site. In 1994 high levels of methane were discovered on the site and D suffered a loss in the potential sale value of his property. He complained to C, who found that although there had been government guidance available to local authorities at the time on the risks of methane on landfill sites, CBC's planning department had not been aware of it, and that omission whilst regrettable did not amount to maladministration as other authorities were similarly unaware at the time. D argued that C's decision was perverse as he had misinterpreted the meaning of maladministration and had been wrong to excuse CBC's incompetence through comparison with other equally incompetent authorities.

Held, dismissing the application, that C's decision was not one which no reasonable ombudsman would have reached and was therefore not perverse. His comparison with other authorities was permissible in that it shed light on the general state of knowledge of methane risk at the time. C's decision was a methodical and thorough one that could not be disturbed.

R. (ON THE APPLICATION OF DOY) v. COMMISSIONER FOR LOCAL ADMINISTRATION, [2001] EWHC Admin 361, [2002] Env. L.R. 11, Morison, J., QBD (Admin Ct).

3721. Planning permission–judicial review–delay–application made 11 weeks after grant of permission

M sent a letter of objection to the chair of K's planning committee when his neighbours applied for planning permission to build an extension to their home. The committee granted planning permission on November 30, 2000 and later denied ever receiving M's letter. M informed his legal expenses insurer on December 5 that he wanted to challenge the decision, but the insurer did not instruct a solicitor until January 12, 2001. The solicitor then sent a letter before action and waited for K's response before commencing judicial review proceedings on February 16, just over 11 weeks after the decision M wanted to challenge.

Held, refusing the application, that M's case was weak and he had not proceeded with the application for judicial review promptly. The insurer's delay in instructing the solicitor was excessive in the circumstances. Further, in view of the need for promptness when challenging a planning decision by way of judicial review, there was no need for a letter before action to be sent.

R. (ON THE APPLICATION OF McCALLION) v. KENNET DC, [2001] EWHC Admin 575, [2002] P.L.C.R. 9, Jackson, J., QBD (Admin Ct).

3722. Planning permission–judicial review–time limits–jurisdiction of House of Lords to hear appeal on refusal to grant permission to apply for judicial review

See ADMINISTRATIVE LAW: R. (on the application of Burkett) v. Hammersmith and Fulham LBC. §53

3723. Planning permission–major infrastructure projects–inquiries procedure

TOWN AND COUNTRY PLANNING (MAJOR INFRASTRUCTURE PROJECT INQUIRIES PROCEDURE) (ENGLAND) RULES 2002, SI 2002 1223; made under the Tribunals and Inquiries Act 1992 s.9. In force: June 7, 2002; £3.50.

These Rules regulate the procedure to be followed in connection with local inquiries relating to major infrastructure projects in England held by the Secretary of State before he determines applications referred to him, or appeals made to him, in relation to planning permission, listed building consent and consent for the demolition of unlisted buildings in conservation areas required in respect of a major infrastructure project.

3724. Planning permission–material considerations–safeguarding land for future use as school–proposals for change of use

N applied to quash the dismissal by the Secretary of State of its appeal against the refusal of planning permission for housing development on a site previously allocated for future use as a primary school. No school had been built on the site and there were no plans to build one, but the district council wished the site to be preserved for that purpose. The inspector had found that the site was suitable for use as a school and that, although there was no definitive evidence that a school would be required in the near future and housing development would fit with the local development plan, on balance the potential need for a school outweighed other factors. In so determining, the inspector had concluded that a new primary school might be required for the local area on the balance of probability. N argued that its application should only have been rejected if a school would be built on the site if their application failed.

Held, dismissing the application, that the inspector's decision had been correct. The test was not a simplistic one in which the likelihood of an existing proposed use being manifested was the only factor capable of justifying the refusal of an application for a different use, *Bloomsbury & Solington HA v. Secretary of State for the Environment* [1992] E.G.C.S. 111, [1993] C.L.Y. 3822 and *Jackson Projects Ltd v. Secretary of State for the Environment* (Unreported, December 9, 1997) not followed. Such a test would restrict the breadth of the statutory discretion. The relative merits of preserving an existing proposed use, including the likelihood of manifestation of that use, was a factor to be weighed in the balance. In the instant case, the inspector had not specifically put his mind to the likelihood of manifestation, but his decision would have been the same had he done so.

NOTTINGHAMSHIRE CC v. SECRETARY OF STATE FOR THE ENVIRONMENT, TRANSPORT AND THE REGIONS, [2001] EWHC Admin 293, [2002] 1 P. & C.R. 30, Christopher Lockhart-Mummery Q.C., QBD (Admin Ct).

3725. Planning permission–minerals–soils–implementation of planning permission–removal of topsoil

[Agricultural Land (Removal of Surface Soil) Act 1953.]

R appealed against a ruling that the implementation of planning permission for the removal of marl had not been accomplished by the removal of topsoil from a site. R contended that the judge had erred by holding that the removal of the topsoil was simply a preparatory act, rather than an act in accordance with the planning permission. R maintained that the removal of the topsoil was a necessary part of working the marl in accordance with the permission and was not de minimis.

Held, dismissing the appeal, that an objective, rather than subjective, approach was required to determine the issue. Accordingly, the intent of those responsible for removing the topsoil was irrelevant, *East Dunbartonshire Council v. Secretary of State for Scotland* [1999] S.L.T. 1088, [1999] C.L.Y. 6410 applied. The removal of the topsoil was an ambivalent act and did not begin, or form part of, the operation of "winning and working" the marl since only 12 inches of topsoil had been removed and it was unknown to what extent the marl had been rendered accessible as a result, *English Clays Lovering Pochin & Co v. Plymouth Corp* [1974] 1 W.L.R. 742, [1974] C.L.Y. 3727 applied. The validity of such a conclusion was reinforced by the public interest in the preservation of topsoil as exemplified by the Agricultural Land (Removal of Surface Soil) Act 1953.

STAFFORDSHIRE CC v. RILEY, [2001] EWCA Civ 257, [2002] P.L.C.R. 5, Pill, L.J., CA.

3726. Planning permission–mobile homes–replacement by permanent dwelling house

FBC challenged the decision of a planning inspector granting planning permission for the erection of a dwelling house in replacement of a mobile home. The mobile home had under building, plumbing and was connected to a cesspit. The local planning policy stated that permission for domestic dwellings in the countryside would only be granted where an "existing permanent dwelling house" would be replaced. FBC argued that the mobile home, which had lawfully stood on the site for 14 years, did not meet that requirement. Moreover, it was submitted that the inspector had made an error of fact in his determination.

Held, allowing the application and quashing the decision, that (1) the inspector had been entitled to reach his conclusion that a mobile home came within the definition of a permanent dwelling house. Having regard to the surrounding circumstances, there was an existing residential unit which was permanent and lawful and could reasonably be replaced by a new dwelling. The fact that the unit was potentially mobile did not affect its permanence, and (2) the inspector had made an error of fact when determining the consequences of the proposed development on the site. Given that it was not possible to conclude that he would have reached the same determination if he had not taken into account the error of fact, it was appropriate to remit the issue back to the Secretary of State for redetermination, *Jagendorf and Trott v. Secretary of State and Krasucki* [1987] J.P.L. 771, [1987] C.L.Y. 3687 and *GE Simplex (Holdings) v. Secretary of State for the Environment* (1989) 57 P. & C.R. 306, [1988] C.L.Y. 3578 applied.

FAREHAM BC v. SECRETARY OF STATE FOR THE ENVIRONMENT, TRANSPORT AND THE REGIONS; *sub nom.* FAREHAM BC v. BARTON, [2001] EWHC Admin 462, [2002] P.L.C.R. 8, Sir Oliver Popplewell, QBD (Admin Ct).

3727. Planning permission–mobile homes–right to family life–failure to comply with time limits–compliance of time limits with Convention right

[Town and Country Planning Act 1990 s.288(3); Human Rights Act 1998 s.7(5), Sch.1 Part I Art.8.]

M sought to challenge a planning inspector's decision dismissing his appeal against the local planning authority's refusal of an application to retain a mobile home on agricultural land on the basis that the inspector had failed to give sufficient weight to his Convention rights under the Human Rights Act 1998 Sch.1 Part I Art.8. The application was lodged more than six weeks after the dismissal of his appeal. M, who was illiterate and had been living on the land in a caravan since 1984 subject to a series of temporary planning permissions and enforcement notices, contended that (1) a rigid application of the time limits stipulated by the Town and Country Planning Act 1990 s.288(3) was contrary to his Convention rights under Art.8 and, further, that it conflicted with the provisions of s.7(5) of the 1998 Act, and in the alternative (2) that s.288(3) of the 1990 Act should be read in a manner that was compatible with his Convention rights and that if the court found this was not possible then a declaration of incompatibility should be made.

Held, refusing the application, that even if a challenge had been brought within the six week time limit it would not have succeeded. Although Art.8 had not expressly been raised before the inspector, he was under a duty to consider it. However, M had advanced only very limited information on which the inspector could base his considerations and it was accepted in Convention cases that claimants were responsible for the conduct and direction of proceedings, *G v. United Kingdom (Children: Right of Contact) (32346/96)* [2001] 1 F.L.R. 153, [2000] C.L.Y. 3232 considered. The inspector had discharged his duty by a proper consideration of M's personal circumstances as well as policy considerations. The time limit in s.288(3) pursued a legitimate aim in terms of ensuring legal certainty and finality in planning matters and was proportionate given the nature of those aims, *Perez de Rada Cavanilles v. Spain* (2000) 29 E.H.R.R. 109, [2000] C.L.Y. 3232 applied. Even though M was illiterate, he was expecting a decision and could have obtained legal advice sooner than he had. Accordingly, he had suffered no injustice by reason of the strict application of the time limits. Further, although s.7(5) of the 1998 Act provided for a one year time limit for bringing a challenge on Convention grounds, this was subject to the proviso that shorter time limits could be imposed in relation to a given procedure.

MATTHEWS v. SECRETARY OF STATE FOR THE ENVIRONMENT, TRANSPORT AND THE REGIONS, [2001] EWHC Admin 815, [2002] 2 P. & C.R. 34, Sullivan, J., QBD (Admin Ct).

3728. Planning permission—open spaces—status of alternative open spaces

G applied for judicial review of a decision by L to grant planning permission to extend a school playground which would result in the loss of some public open parkland space. In accordance with its own development plan, L was required to designate alternative open space, and proposed to do so by converting "waste ground" adjoining the park into parkland. G argued that L had failed to take into account the relevant fact that the alternative land was effectively already being used as open space, the loss of which would also require replacement.

Held, granting the application and quashing the decision, that L had failed to take into account a material consideration. The nature and status of the replacement land in terms of its planning history had not been properly understood by L before it took its decision.

R. (ON THE APPLICATION OF GLOSBY) v. LAMBETH LBC, [2001] EWHC Admin 680, [2002] P.L.C.R. 15, Judge Rich Q.C., QBD (Admin Ct).

3729. Planning permission—permitted development—telecommunications development—Wales

TOWN AND COUNTRY PLANNING (GENERAL PERMITTED DEVELOPMENT) (AMENDMENT) (WALES) ORDER 2002, SI 2002 1878; made under the Town and Country Planning Act 1990 s.59, s.60, s.61, s.333. In force: August 1, 2002; £2.50.

This Order, which applies to Wales, amends the Town and Country Planning (General Permitted Development) Order 1995 (SI 1995 418), the Town and Country Planning (General Permitted Development) (Amendment) Order 1999 (SI 1999 1661) and and the Town and Country Planning (General Permitted Development) (Amendment) Order 1998 (SI 1998 462) in relation to permitted development rights for certain forms of telecommunications development. Where such rights apply no specific application for planning permission is needed.

3730. Planning permission—planning policy—failure to allow applicant to deal with issue not raised on enquiry—breach of natural justice

C challenged a non-determination by an inspector of its application for planning permission for a residential development. C contended that the inspector had erred by finding that the absence on-site of a children's play area constituted a failure to comply with the development plan and, alternatively, that such finding constituted a breach of natural justice as the issue of on-site provision had not been raised at the enquiry.

Held, granting the application, that notwithstanding that the inspector had not misinterpreted the policy C ought to have been allowed to address the question of the adequacy of on-site provision since it had not been reasonably apparent that objections would be raised on this ground. Consequently, C had been unfairly deprived of an opportunity to deal with the issue which amounted to a breach of natural justice.

CASTLEFORD HOMES LTD v. SECRETARY OF STATE FOR THE ENVIRONMENT, TRANSPORT AND THE REGIONS; *sub nom.* CASTLEFORD HOMES v. SECRETARY OF STATE FOR ENVIRONMENT, TRANSPORT AND THE REGIONS, [2001] EWHC Admin 77, [2001] P.L.C.R. 29, Ouseley, J., QBD (Admin Ct).

3731. Planning permission—planning policy guidance—permission for residential development on greenfield site—brownfield site available

An inspector granted outline planning permission for residential development comprising 81 dwellings on a greenfield site. Mitigation measures were agreed which partially addressed W's concerns as to the negative impact of the development on nature conservation and the risk of flooding. However, W continued to oppose the development and applied to have the decision quashed on the grounds that the inspector (1) should have followed PPG 3 as there were brownfield sites available, and (2) had failed to consider the underlying harm that development would cause to nature conservation as part of the site was a habitat for water voles and kingfishers.

Held, refusing the application, that (1) the inspector was entitled to conclude that the presumption against greenfield development had been outweighed in the instant case as the objections had been overcome by reference to nature conservation and flood protection issues, and (2) the inspector had addressed the measures that W had argued for as being essential to mitigate the effects of the development in nature conservation terms. The parts of the site concerned had been properly identified and the inspector had then gone on to decide on the evidence that the water vole and kingfisher populations would not be adversely affected by the development in the central part of the site.

WIGAN MBC v. SECRETARY OF STATE FOR THE ENVIRONMENT, TRANSPORT AND THE REGIONS, [2001] EWHC Admin 587, [2002] J.P.L. 417, Sullivan, J., QBD (Admin Ct).

3732. Planning permission—waste disposal—environmental statements—air pollution—residents' concerns—right to family life

[Human Rights Act 1998 Sch.1 Part I Art.6(1), Art.8.]

V applied for judicial review of HCC's decision to grant HW planning permission for an energy recovery facility and waste transfer station. V contended that (1) the planning officer's report inaccurately summarised issues detailed in the environmental statement and misled planning committee members to believe that there was no existing breach of the applicable guidelines concerning the emission of nitrogen dioxide; (2) the grant of planning permission breached the local residents' right to respect for private and family life under the Human Rights Act 1998 Sch.1 Part I Art.8, given the link between the pollution and quality of life, and (3) given that there had been no public inquiry, the residents' right to a "fair and public" hearing under Sch.1 Part I Art.6(1) of the Act had been breached.

Held, refusing the application, that (1) the planning officer's report had accurately summarised the environmental statement; (2) the grant of planning permission did not engage the local residents' rights under Sch.1 Part I Art.8 of the Act, given that their concern regarding the increase in pollution levels was only a general environmental concern, and (3) given the conclusions on the first two grounds of appeal and the fact that the residents' connection with the planning decision and the environmental consequences was remote, the issue of whether there should have been a fair and public hearing did not arise, and even if it did, the procedure implemented by HCC afforded them such an opportunity.

R. (ON THE APPLICATION OF VETTERLEIN) v. HAMPSHIRE CC, [2001] EWHC Admin 560, [2002] Env. L.R. 8, Sullivan, J., QBD (Admin Ct).

3733. Planning policy guidelines–local plans–implementation of supplementary policies

[Town and Country Planning Act 1990 s.54A.]

J sought judicial review of O's decision to amend its policy relating to the provision of affordable housing by way of supplementary planning guidance, G. J contended that O was under a duty to proceed by way of a review of the existing local plan and that there had been a failure to take material considerations into account, including the lack of opportunity for independent scrutiny and the degree of non-compliance with the relevant guidance given by the Secretary of State in PPG12.

Held, refusing the application, that where a local planning authority had adopted a local plan pursuant to the Town and Country Planning Act 1990 s.54A, it could proceed with any supplementary policies by relying on non-statutory G and was not bound to proceed by way of a statutory local plan review. The requirement for a statutory review would impose a significant fetter upon a local planning authority with the result that it would be unable to respond effectively to changed circumstances, *Westminster City Council v. Great Portland Estates Plc* [1985] A.C. 661, [1984] C.L.Y. 3413 and *Kingsley v. Secretary of State for the Environment, Transport and the Regions* (2001) 82 P. & C.R. 9, [2001] C.L.Y. 4762 considered. In the instant case, C had reasonably concluded that the G was consistent with both the local plan and PPG12 and there was no evidence to suggest that there had been any failure in the consultation process, *Bolton MBC v. Secretary of State for the Environment* (1991) 61 P. & C.R. 343, [1991] C.L.Y. 94 applied.

R. (ON THE APPLICATION OF JA PYE (OXFORD) LTD) v. OXFORD CITY COUNCIL, [2001] EWHC Admin 870, [2002] 2 P. & C.R. 35, Ouseley, J., QBD (Admin Ct).

3734. Planning procedures–enforcement notices–appeals

TOWN AND COUNTRY PLANNING (ENFORCEMENT NOTICES AND APPEALS) (ENGLAND) REGULATIONS 2002, SI 2002 2682; made under the Town and Country Planning Act 1990 s.173, s.174, s.175; the Planning (Listed Buildings and Conservation Areas) Act 1990 s.39; and the Town and Country Planning Act 1990 s.40, s.42, s.91. In force: December 23, 2002; £2.00.

These Regulations, which revoke with saving the Town and Country Planning (Enforcement Notices and Appeals) Regulations 1991 (SI 1991 2804) and the Town and Country Planning (Enforcement Notices and Appeals) (Amendment) Regulations 1992 (SI 1992 1904), contain provisions relating to the contents of enforcement notices issued under the Town and Country Planning Act 1990 s.172 and the information to be provided by local planning authorities when serving copies of such notices; and the procedure to be followed in relation to appeals against such notices and against listed building and conservation areas enforcement notices issued under the Planning (Listed Buildings and Conservation Areas) Act 1990 s.38(1). In addition they contain an additional requirement for the local planning authority to specify details of all policies and proposals in the development plan relevant to the decision to issue an enforcement notice; set out what matters should be dealt with in the explanatory note accompanying the enforcement notice. Additional matters to be included are the fee payable for a deemed application for planning permission and a list of names and addresses on whom a copy of the enforcement notice has been served; contain an additional requirement for the Secretary of State to notify the local planning authority that an appeal has been made against the enforcement notice and to copy the appellant statement of appeal to them; and require the local planning authority to serve a copy of their statement on all persons on whom a copy of the enforcement notice was served.

3735. Planning procedures–enforcement notices–appeals–determination by inspectors

TOWN AND COUNTRY PLANNING (ENFORCEMENT) (DETERMINATION BY INSPECTORS) (INQUIRIES PROCEDURE) (ENGLAND) RULES 2002, SI 2002 2685; made under the Tribunals and Inquiries Act 1992 s.9. In force: December 23, 2002; £3.00.

These Rules set out the procedure to be followed in connection with local inquiries in England held by inspectors appointed by the Secretary of State to determine appeals against enforcement notices under the Town and Country Planning Act 1990 s.174; the refusal or non-determination of an application for a certificate of lawful use or development under s.195 of the 1990 Act; and listed building enforcement notices and conservation area enforcement notices under the Planning (Listed Buildings and Conservation Areas) Act 1990 s.39.

3736. Planning procedures–enforcement notices–appeals–hearings

TOWN AND COUNTRY PLANNING (ENFORCEMENT) (HEARINGS PROCEDURE) (ENGLAND) RULES 2002, SI 2002 2684; made under the Tribunals and Inquiries Act 1992 s.9. In force: December 23, 2002; £2.50.

These Rules regulate the procedure to be followed for hearings in England caused by the Secretary of State to be held before he or an inspector determine appeals made to him against enforcement notices, listed building and conservation area consent enforcement notices and non-determination of applications for a certificate of lawful use development on or after December 23, 2002. They provide for the preliminary procedure to be followed, in particular the information to be provided by the local planning authority, on receipt by it of a notice that a hearing is to be held; provide which documents are to be sent to the Secretary of State before a hearing and for the documents to be copied by him to the appellant, the local planning authority and the inspector; provide for the date of the hearing to be fixed and notified to the parties; provide for an inquiry to be held in place of the hearing; prescribe those entitled to appear at a hearing; and provide for the procedure where a decision is remitted by the court to the Secretary of State for rehearing and redetermination.

3737. Planning procedures–enforcement notices–appeals–local inquiries

TOWN AND COUNTRY PLANNING (ENFORCEMENT) (INQUIRIES PROCEDURE) (ENGLAND) RULES 2002, SI 2002 2686; made under the Tribunals and Inquiries Act 1992 s.9. In force: December 23, 2002; £3.00.

These Rules, which revoke the Town and Country Planning (Enforcement) (Inquiries Procedure) Rules 1992 (SI 1992 1903), set out the procedure to be followed in connection with local inquiries held for the purposes of appeals against enforcement notices under the Town and Country Planning Act 1990 s.174; the refusal or non-determination of an application for a certificate of lawful use or development under s.195 of the 1990 Act; and listed building enforcement notices and conservation area enforcement notices under the Planning (Listed Buildings and Conservation Areas) Act 1990 s.39.

3738. Planning procedures–enforcement notices–appeals–written representations

TOWN AND COUNTRY PLANNING (ENFORCEMENT) (WRITTEN REPRESENTATIONS PROCEDURE) (ENGLAND) REGULATIONS 2002, SI 2002 2683; made under the Town and Country Planning Act 1990 s.175, s.323. In force: December 23, 2002; £2.00.

These Regulations lay down the procedure and time limits in connection with appeals against enforcement notices which are to be disposed of on the basis of written representations.

3739. Planning procedures–public inquiries–adequate, proper and intelligible reasons–reasonableness of not holding further inquiry

[Town and Country Planning (Development Plan) Regulations 1991 (SI 1991 2794) Reg.16(4), Reg.17(1).]

B challenged the validity of H's local plan in relation to its failure to allocate an area of 1.86 hectares of agricultural land for housing purposes. Following B's objection to the sites initial omission from the local development plan as housing land a public inquiry had been held, subsequent to which the local plan inspector recommended that the site be allocated for residential development of up to ten dwellings, a decision supported by the local plan sub-committee. The full planning committee rejected the inspector's recommendation on the grounds that any development would be visually intrusive, potentially cause an inappropriate urbanising effect on the local community and increase immigration into the district. The local authority dismissed B's objection to its decision and indicated that no further inquiry would be held publishing its reasons for dismissing B's objections. B contended that (1) the council had failed to give proper, adequate and intelligible reasons for not adopting the specific recommendations of the inspector on the issues of visibility, access and potential immigration caused by the proposed development as required by the Town and Country Planning (Development Plan) Regulations 1991 Reg.16(4) and Reg.17(1), and (2) the council had been *Wednesbury* unreasonable not to hold a further inquiry.

Held, dismissing the application, that (1) the inspector's recommendations had been findings of evaluation and not fact from which the council were entitled to differ, *Oxford Diocesan Board of Finance v. West Oxfordshire DC* [1998] P.L.C.R. 370, [1999] C.L.Y. 4226 applied. The planning authority had dealt with B's objections in an intelligible manner. There was no evidence that the authority had acted without an open mind, *Stirk v. Bridgnorth DC* (1997) 73 P. & C.R. 439, [1997] C.L.Y. 4071 and *Alfred McAlpine Homes Northumbria Ltd v. Darlington BC* [1999] J.P.L. 53, [1999] C.L.Y. 4225 distinguished, and (2) the onus was on the authority to consider whether an inquiry should be re-opened. Considering the relatively small area of land concerned, the lack of complexity in the issues raised, and the fact that no new issues had arisen, the authority had not acted unreasonably by deciding not to hold a further inquiry, *Warren v. Uttlesford DC* [1997] J.P.L. 1130, [1997] C.L.Y. 4092 considered.

BAINBRIDGE v. HAMBLETON DC (2000) 80 P. & C.R. 61, Sullivan, J., QBD.

3740. Planning procedures–public inquiries–right to fair trial–right to make oral representations–obligation to call in

[Human Rights Act 1998 Sch.1 Part I Art.6.]

A and others appealed against the refusal in judicial review proceedings ([2002] EWHC 7, Daily Telegraph, January 24, 2002) to quash the Secretary of State's decision not to call in the grant of planning permission for a new sports stadium for Fulham Football Club. A contended that because of the Secretary of State's refusal to call in the application, (1) the failure to allow him and other protesters to make oral representations at the planning committee stage had been a breach of their rights under the Human Rights Act 1998 Sch.1 Part I Art.6, and (2) therefore the Secretary of State was now obliged to call the application in either because of that breach or in the exceptional circumstances.

Held, dismissing the appeal, that (1) where an administrative decision was discretionary, there was no requirement that a statutory scheme should provide a right to an oral hearing at the initial proceedings. The remedy of judicial review was available and sufficient to counteract any individual injustice, *Begum (Runa) v. Tower Hamlets LBC* [2002] EWCA Civ 239, [2002] 2 All E.R. 668, [2002] 4 C.L. 254 considered, and (2) the Secretary of State was obliged only to ensure that his own acts were not incompatible with Convention rights not the acts of others and he had not acted incompatibly by refusing to call in an application. It was the role of the High Court to exercise the power of review. The Secretary of State could give consideration to exceptional circumstances but he was not bound to adjust his decisions to allow third party objections to be vocalised at a public enquiry.

R. (ON THE APPLICATION OF ADLARD) v. SECRETARY OF STATE FOR TRANSPORT, LOCAL GOVERNMENT AND THE REGIONS; *sub nom.* R. (ON THE APPLICATION OF ADLARD) v. SECRETARY OF STATE FOR THE ENVIRONMENT, TRANSPORT AND THE REGIONS, [2002] EWCA Civ 735, [2002] 1 W.L.R. 2515, Simon Brown, L.J., CA.

3741. Rural areas–countryside access–local access forums

See REAL PROPERTY. §3854

3742. Tree preservation orders–appeals–Secretary of State refusing to follow inspector's recommendation–irrationality and failure to give reasons

A larch tree, the subject of a tree preservation order, was located in the grounds of property A. H, the owner of an adjoining property, applied for consent for the tree to be pruned so as to remove the risk overhanging branches posed to his conservatory. R refused the application and H appealed to the Secretary of State. An inspector recommended that H's appeal should be dismissed. The inspector's report stated that the tree contributed to the general amenity of the area. Further, that it was situated so close to the boundary that removing the overhanging branches would not prevent debris falling onto H's conservatory. The inspector concluded that the amenity benefit of the tree outweighed the inconvenience involved in removing its debris from the conservatory. The Secretary of State refused to accept the inspector's findings and allowed H's appeal. R appealed.

Held, allowing the appeal and remitting the matter to the Secretary of State, that the Secretary of State's decision was irrational, and the consent itself was inadequate because it was impossible to determine precisely which operations could be lawfully carried out. The permitted work had not been identified clearly and insufficient reasons had been given for disagreeing with the inspector's recommendations.

RICHMOND UPON THAMES LBC v. SECRETARY OF STATE FOR THE ENVIRONMENT, TRANSPORT AND THE REGIONS (TREE PRESERVATION ORDER), [2001] EWHC Admin 205, [2002] J.P.L. 33, Richards, J., QBD (Admin Ct).

3743. Tree preservation orders–exemptions–questions of fact–need for appropriate jury direction

[Town and Country Planning Act 1990 s.210; Town and Country Planning (Tree Preservation Order) Regulations 1969 (SI 1969 17) Sch.2 Reg.3(d).]

A local authority appealed against a interlocutory decision that fruit trees, which were subject to a preservation order and had been cut down, were exempt from the requirement of consent under the Town and Country Planning Act 1990 s.210 by virtue of the Town and Country Planning (Tree Preservation Order) Regulations 1969 Sch.2 Reg.3(d). The judge had ruled that whether the trees were fruit trees within the meaning of the words in Reg.3d was a question of law and not of fact. The local authority contended otherwise, and that therefore it was for the jury to decide if the exemption was applicable.

Held, allowing the appeal, that it was for the jury to decide whether the trees were exempt from the requirement of consent under the Act as it was a question of fact and not law, and the judge had erred in failing to provide the jury with an appropriate direction on the matter.

R. v. CLEARBROOK GROUP PLC; *sub nom.* R. v. HAVERING LBC, [2001] EWCA Crim 1654, [2001] 4 P.L.R. 78, Rose, L.J., CA (Crim Div).

3744. Waste land–local authorities powers and duties–Combe Down Stone Mines, Bath

DERELICT LAND CLEARANCE AREA (COMBE DOWN STONE MINES, BATH) ORDER 2002, SI 2002 2053; made under the Derelict Land Act 1982 s.1. In force: August 30, 2002; £1.50.

This Order specifies a locality in the wards of Bathavon South, Combe Down and Lyncombe in the district of Bath and North East Somerset as a derelict land clearance area. It is a locality where underground stone mining has caused actual and apprehended collapse of land. In derelict land clearance areas, the Secretary of State can pay grant under the Derelict Land Act 1982 at the higher rates applicable to development and intermediate areas under that Act.

3745. Books

Beaumont, C.H.–Planning Appeal Decisions: 2001. Hardback: £405.00. ISBN 0-421-75660-8. Sweet & Maxwell.

Duxbury, R.M.C.–Telling and Duxbury: Planning Law and Procedure. 12th Ed. Paperback: £23.95. ISBN 0-406-94796-1. Butterworths Law.

Gaunt, Jonathan; Morgan, Paul–Gale on the Law of Easements. Property and Conveyancing Library. Hardback: £195.00. ISBN 0-421-77960-8. Sweet & Maxwell.

Moore, Victor–Practical Approach to Planning Law. 8th Ed. A Practical Approach. Paperback: £28.95. ISBN 0-19-925595-4. Oxford University Press.

Party Wall Legislation and Procedure. Paperback: £23.00. ISBN 1-84219-073-3. RICS Books.

Sara, Colin–Boundaries and Easements. 3rd Ed. Hardback: £155.00. ISBN 0-421-75840-6. Sweet & Maxwell.

POLICE

3746. Best value–police authorities powers and duties–performance indicators

POLICE AUTHORITIES (BEST VALUE) PERFORMANCE INDICATORS ORDER 2002, SI 2002 694; made under the Local Government Act 1999 s.4. In force: April 1, 2002; £1.75.

The Local Government Act 1999 imposes requirements on police authorities, and other authorities, to secure continuous improvement in the way in which their functions are exercised, having regard to a combination of economy, efficiency and effectiveness. This Order specifies that the performance indicators set out are to be included in the indicators by which a police authority's performance can be measured.

3747. Confiscation–retention and disposal of items seized

POLICE (RETENTION AND DISPOSAL OF ITEMS SEIZED) REGULATIONS 2002, SI 2002 1372; made under the Criminal Justice and Public Order Act 1994 s.60A. In force: June 10, 2002; £1.75.

These Regulations revoke in relation to England and Wales the Police (Retention and Disposal of Items seized under Criminal Justice and Public Order Act 1994)

Regulations 1999 (SI 1999 269) s.60 in consequence of the amendment of the Criminal Justice and Public Order Act 1994 by the Anti-terrorism, Crime and Security Act 2001. The Regulations make provision for the retention, safe-keeping, disposal and destruction of items seized under the Criminal Justice and Public Order Act 1994 s.60 and s.60AA.

3748. Criminal Justice and Police Act 2001 (c.16)–Commencement No.8 Order

CRIMINAL JUSTICE AND POLICE ACT 2001 (COMMENCEMENT NO.8) 2002, SI 2002 3032 (C.100); made under the Criminal Justice and Police Act 2001 s.138. Commencement details: bringing into force various provisions of the 2001 Act on January 1, 2003; £1.75.

This Order brings into force on January 1, 2003 the provisions set out in Art.2.

3749. National Crime Squad–objectives

NATIONAL CRIME SQUAD (SECRETARY OF STATE'S OBJECTIVES) ORDER 2002, SI 2002 779; made under the Police Act 1997 s.71. In force: April 1, 2002; £1.50.

This Order, which revokes the National Crime Squad (Secretary of State's Objectives) Order 1999 (SI 1999 821), sets out the Secretary of State's objectives for the National Crime Squad.

3750. National Criminal Intelligence Service–objectives

NATIONAL CRIMINAL INTELLIGENCE SERVICE (SECRETARY OF STATE'S OBJECTIVES) ORDER 2002, SI 2002 778; made under the Police Act 1997 s.26. In force: April 1, 2002; £1.50.

This Order, which revokes the NCIS (Secretary of State's Objectives) Order 1999 (SI 1999 822), sets out the Secretary of State's objectives for the National Criminal Intelligence Service.

3751. PACE codes of practice–identification parades–use of make up

See CRIMINAL EVIDENCE: R. v. Marrin (Keith Ian). §741

3752. Police Act 1997 (c.50)–Commencement No.9 Order–England and Wales

POLICE ACT 1997 (COMMENCEMENT NO.9) ORDER 2002, SI 2002 413; made under the Police Act 1997 s.135. Commencement details: bringing into force various provisions of the 1997 Act on March 1, 2002; £1.50.

This Order brings into force those provisions of the Police Act 1997, except s.112, which are not already in force together with an associated repeal.

3753. Police authorities–objectives

POLICE (SECRETARY OF STATE'S OBJECTIVES) ORDER 2002, SI 2002 695; made under the Police Act 1996 s.37. In force: April 1, 2002; £1.50.

This Order, which revokes the Police (Secretary of State's Objectives) (No.3) Order 1999 (SI 1999 3424), sets out the Secretary of State's objectives for the policing of the areas of all police authorities established under the Police Act 1996 and of the Metropolitan Police Authority.

3754. Police authorities–recruitment–selection panel–requirements

POLICE AUTHORITIES (SELECTION PANEL) (AMENDMENT) REGULATIONS 2002, SI 2002 1282; made under the Police Act 1996 Sch.3 para.11. In force: June 10, 2002; £1.50.

These Regulations amend the Police Authorities (Selection Panel) Regulations 1994 (SI 1994 2023) removing the requirement for advertisements for persons willing to be appointed as members of a police authority to specify that the maximum age for appointment is 70 years. They also extend the circumstances in which a selection panel can act by a majority of its members.

3755.   Police authorities–strategy plans

POLICE AUTHORITIES (THREE-YEAR STRATEGY PLANS) REGULATIONS 2002, SI 2002 2526; made under the Police Act 1996 s.6A. In force: November 1, 2002; £1.50.

The Police Act 1996 requires a police authority to prepare a three-year strategy plan for the authority's medium and long term strategies. The 1996 Act enables the first period for which a plan has to be submitted to be less than three years. These Regulations provide that the first period for which a plan is to be submitted is the two year period ending on March 31, 2005.

3756.   Police officers–conditions of employment–terms of appointment

POLICE (AMENDMENT) (NO.2) REGULATIONS 2002, SI 2002 2529; made under the Police Pensions Act 1976 s.1; and the Police Act 1996 s.50. In force: November 1, 2002; £1.50.

These Regulations amend the Police Pensions Regulations 1987 (SI 1987 257) and the Police Regulations 1995 (SI 1995 215) to permit the extension of an officer's term of appointment to a date not later than the end of the maximum term for which he could have originally been appointed. They also allow an extension to an officer's term of appointment, with the consent of the Secretary of State, for a period not exceeding three years where it would be in the interests of the efficiency and effectiveness of the police force.

3757.   Police officers–new appointments–DNA profiles and information

POLICE (AMENDMENT) REGULATIONS 2002, SI 2002 1758; made under the Police Act 1996 s.50. In force: August 1, 2002; £1.75.

These Regulations amend the Police Regulations 1995 (SI 1995 215) to insert a Regulation requiring members of a police force to provide a sample of hair or saliva upon appointment (other than in cases of transfer between police forces) from which a DNA profile can be derived. The sample and information derived from the sample will be stored separately from samples and information derived from samples provided in accordance with the provisions of the Police and Criminal Evidence Act 1984 s.63. The Regulations also allow a member of a police force who, on or after September 1, 1994, joined or rejoined that force from the British Transport Police Force to reckon his service with the British Transport Police Force as service. If the member of the police force is of the rank of chief inspector or higher then a contrary agreement can be reached. In addition, they provide for the payment of a replacement allowance to a member of a police force who has transferred to that force on or after September 1, 1994 from the British Transport Police Force and who was in receipt of a housing allowance prior to the transfer; increase from 14 weeks to 18 weeks the period of maternity leave that can be reckoned for the purposes of probation and pay; and make it clear that any period of service in a higher rank counts as a period that can be reckoned for the purposes of pay at the lower rank.

3758.   Police officers–promotion–development scheme

POLICE (PROMOTION) (AMENDMENT) REGULATIONS 2002, SI 2002 767; made under the Police Act 1996 s.50. In force: April 12, 2002; £1.50.

These Regulations amend the Police (Promotion) Regulations 1996 (SI 1996 1685) as the existing accelerated promotion courses are to be replaced with a new scheme from April 2002. The new scheme, to be known as the High Potential Development Scheme, will allow police officers participating in it to be promoted to the ranks of sergeant, inspector and chief inspector as soon as the chief officer of police determines that they are competent to carry out the duties of that rank. The Regulations allow the sergeants participating in the High Potential

Development Scheme to be promoted to inspector after 1 year's service in the rank of sergeant and allow up to 18 weeks of maternity leave to be treated as service or a period in a rank.

3759. Police officers–race discrimination–liability of Chief Constable for acts of discrimination committed by one officer against another

[Race Relations Act 1976 s.16, s.32, s.33; Race Relations (Amendment) Act 2000.]

The Chief Constable, CC, appealed against the refusal of an employment tribunal to strike out L's claim against him for race discrimination. L had presented a claim in August 1999, alleging that CC was liable for the conduct of police officers who had made abusive comments about her.

Held, allowing the appeal, that a Chief Constable was neither vicariously nor constructively liable to a police officer who, prior to the coming into force of the Race Relations (Amendment) Act 2000, had brought proceedings alleging racial discrimination by a constable. Before April 2, 2001, when the 2000 Act came into force, the Race Relations Act 1976 s.16 applied with the result that a police constable was treated as an employee in relation to acts done to him by the police force but was not considered an employee in respect of acts done by one police constable to another. Further, neither s.32 nor s.33 of the 1976 Act imposed such liability upon a Chief Constable. Accordingly, L had no cause of action against CC. The purpose of the 2000 Act was to address this lacuna in the law and to make a Chief Constable vicariously liable for acts of racial discrimination committed by an officer.

CHIEF CONSTABLE OF BEDFORDSHIRE v. LIVERSIDGE [2002] I.R.L.R. 15, Lindsay, J. (President), EAT.

3760. Police officers–special constables–terms of appointment

SPECIAL CONSTABLES (AMENDMENT) REGULATIONS 2002, SI 2002 3180; made under the Police Act 1996 s.50, s.51. In force: Reg.2(2): February 3, 2003; remainder: January 10, 2003; £1.75.

These Regulations repeal the Special Constables (Amendment) Regulations 1992 (SI 1992 1526) and amend the Special Constables Regulations 1965 (SI 1965 536) which set out the qualifications for appointment as a special constable. These Regulations require candidates for appointment to pass assessments, determined by the Secretary of State, in written and spoken English and numeracy. Candidates who are not nationals of a Member State of the European Economic Area must have indefinite leave to enter or remain in the UK. The minimum age for appointment as a special constable is raised from 18 years to 18.5 years to be consistent with the minimum age for appointment as a regular constable.

3761. Police powers–anti social behaviour orders–delegation by Chief Constable of power to seek orders

[Crime and Disorder Act 1998 s.1.]

The Chief Constable sought judicial review of the dismissal by a district judge of his applications, made through his officers, under the Crime and Disorder Act 1998 s.1 for anti social behaviour orders against five young boys. The applications had been dismissed as null and void on the grounds that the power of a Chief Constable to make applications for such orders could not be delegated to an officer of lower rank than superintendent and that consultation under s.1 (2) of the Act had to be carried out by an officer of the same rank as superintendent.

Held, granting the application, that a Chief Constable was entitled to delegate to his officers his power under s.1 of the Act to consult a local authority and bring an application for an anti social behaviour order. A Chief Constable was not the employer of the officers under his command, although he was legally answerable for them; the principle that a ministerial departmental head was responsible for things done under his authority was applicable, *Carltona Ltd v. Commissioners of Works* [1943] 2 All E.R. 560 applied. There were two qualifications to this principle in that delegation had to be to someone suitable and there would be occasions when delegation would not be appropriate. A Chief Constable's powers were likely to be delegable save for the most important functions. It was for the Chief Constable to decide who was the person most appropriate to carry out consultation and apply for anti social behaviour orders and the court could not interfere with his choices unless they were irrational or beyond his powers.

R. (ON THE APPLICATION OF CHIEF CONSTABLE OF WEST MIDLANDS) v. BIRMINGHAM MAGISTRATES COURT; *sub nom.* R. (ON THE APPLICATION OF CHIEF CONSTABLE OF WEST MIDLANDS) v. BIRMINGHAM JUSTICES, [2002] EWHC 1087, *The Times*, June 5, 2002, Sedley, L.J., QBD (Admin Ct).

3762. Police powers—codes of practice—police detention—drug testing

POLICE AND CRIMINAL EVIDENCE ACT 1984 (CODES OF PRACTICE) (MODIFICATIONS TO CODE C AND CODE D) (CERTAIN POLICE AREAS) ORDER 2002, SI 2002 1150; made under the Police and Criminal Evidence Act 1984 s.67. In force: May 20, 2002; £1.75.

This Order repeals the Police and Criminal Evidence Act 1984 (Codes of Practice) (Modification) Order 2001 (SI 2001 2254). The Police and Criminal Evidence Act 1984 s.63B gives police officers the power to undertake tests for the presence of specified Class A drugs in relation to certain persons in police detention. This Order puts in place further modifications to the Police and Criminal Evidence Act 1984 codes of practice to provide for drug testing within police detention.

3763. Police powers—codes of practice—police detention—drug testing

POLICE AND CRIMINAL EVIDENCE ACT 1984 (CODES OF PRACTICE) (MODIFICATIONS TO CODE C AND CODE D) (CERTAIN POLICE AREAS) (AMENDMENT) ORDER 2002, SI 2002 1863; made under the Police and Criminal Evidence Act 1984 s.67. In force: September 2, 2002; £1.50.

The Police and Criminal Evidence Act 1984 s.63B gives police officers a new power to undertake tests for the presence of specified Class A drugs in relation to certain persons in police detention. The Act also provides that codes in connection with those powers must be in place before the powers are exercised. The Police and Criminal Evidence Act 1984 (Codes of Practice) (Modifications to Code C and Code D) (Certain Police Areas) Order 2002 (SI 2002 1150) put such code provisions in place in respect of the police areas listed. This Order makes amendments to the 2002 Order by adding four further police areas to the list of those areas in which the modified codes apply.

3764. Police powers—codes of practice—police interviews—visual recordings

POLICE AND CRIMINAL EVIDENCE ACT 1984 (CODES OF PRACTICE) (VISUAL RECORDING OF INTERVIEWS) ORDER 2002, SI 2002 1266; made under the Police and Criminal Evidence Act 1984 s.67. In force: May 7, 2002; £1.50.

This Order appoints May 7, 2002 as the date on which the code of practice for the visual recording for police interviews under the Police and Criminal Evidence Act 1984 s.60A will come into operation. The Order will apply to the visual recording of police interviews in any area where visual recording is required by virtue of an order under the 1984 Act.

3765. Police powers—codes of practice—police interviews—visual recordings

POLICE AND CRIMINAL EVIDENCE ACT 1984 (VISUAL RECORDING OF INTERVIEWS) (CERTAIN POLICE AREAS) ORDER 2002, SI 2002 1069; made under the Police and Criminal Evidence Act 1984 s.60A. In force: May 8, 2002; £1.50.

This Order requires the visual recording of interviews held by police officers at Basingstoke, Portsmouth, Southampton, Chatham, Gravesend, Tonbridge, Bromley, Colindale, Edmonton, Redditch, Telford and Worcester police stations.

3766. Police powers–codes of practice–police interviews–visual recordings

POLICE AND CRIMINAL EVIDENCE ACT 1984 (VISUAL RECORDING OF INTERVIEWS) (CERTAIN POLICE AREAS) (NO.2) ORDER 2002, SI 2002 2527; made under the Police and Criminal Evidence Act 1984 s.60A. In force: October 30, 2002; £1.50.

This Order requires the visual recording of interviews held by police officers at Harlow, Colchester and Southend police stations.

3767. Police powers–codes of practice–stop and search

POLICE AND CRIMINAL EVIDENCE ACT 1984 (CODES OF PRACTICE) (STATUTORY POWERS OF STOP AND SEARCH) ORDER 2002, SI 2002 3075; made under the Police and Criminal Evidence Act 1984 s.67. In force: April 1, 2003; £1.50.

This Order appoints April 1, 2003 as the date on which a revised code of practice under the Police and Criminal Evidence Act 1984 will come into operation. When the Order is in operation, it will apply in England and Wales to the exercise by police officers of statutory powers to search persons and vehicles without first making an arrest.

3768. Police powers–detention–breach of the peace–justification for continued detention

[Human Rights Act 1998 Sch.1 Part I Art.5.]

The Chief Constable appealed against a decision that M's continued detention by the police for causing or being likely to cause a breach of the peace had been unjustified. It was common ground that there had been reasonable grounds for M's initial arrest and detention when a police officer had responded to a complaint that a man was attacking a woman. M and the woman had previously been involved in domestic arguments and both were known, or believed to be, heroin addicts. M's conduct whilst in custody had been violent and it was not disputed that the police had had reasonable grounds for believing that if allowed his liberty it was very likely that he would return to the woman and that a breach of peace would occur. The judge had found, however, in respect of a final period of detention that there was no longer a real apprehension based on reasonable grounds that if M were released he would again cause a breach of the peace. The judge had found that the power to detain a person in order to prevent a further breach of the peace was limited to circumstances where there was a real, rather than a fanciful, apprehension that if released that person would commit or renew his breach of the peace within a short time. The Chief Constable submitted that while the judge had set out the correct test, he had erred in applying it.

Held, allowing the appeal, that the judge had formulated the correct test but had erred in his conclusion. In particular the judge had not given sufficient weight to the fact that the woman had expressed concern that M would return and assault her, that the woman's house was within walking distance of the police station and was therefore a place where M was likely to go. Moreover, when released, M would be given some of his belongings, which had been gathered together by the woman and given to the police to demonstrate that her relationship with M was at an end, an act which was likely to inflame his emotions. It was unnecessary for the court to provide guidance in relation to the detention of a person for breach of the peace; the circumstances in which an arrest for an actual or anticipated breach of the peace could occur were set out in the decision of *R. v. Howell (Errol)* [1982] Q.B. 416, [1982] C.L.Y. 151. Detention for breach of the peace was not contrary to the Human Rights Act

1998 Sch.1 Part I Art.5, *Steel v. United Kingdom* (1999) 28 E.H.R.R. 603, [1998] C.L.Y. 3068, *Foulkes v. Chief Constable of Merseyside* [1998] 3 All E.R. 705, [1998] C.L.Y. 4258 and *Howell* considered.

CHIEF CONSTABLE OF CLEVELAND v. McGROGAN; *sub nom.* McGROGAN v. CHIEF CONSTABLE OF CLEVELAND, [2002] EWCA Civ 86, [2002] 1 F.L.R. 707, Wall, J., CA.

3769. Police powers–fingerprints–lawfulness of power to retain fingerprints and DNA samples of acquitted persons

[Police and Criminal Evidence Act 1984 s.64; Human Rights Act 1998 Sch.1 Part I Art.8, Art.14; Criminal Justice and Police Act 2001 s.82.]

S, who had been acquitted of attempted robbery, appealed against a finding ([2002] EWHC 478, Times, April 4, 2002) that the decision of the Chief Constable to retain, in accordance with the Criminal Justice and Police Act 2001 s.82, his fingerprints and DNA samples did not infringe either his right to privacy under the Human Rights Act 1998 Sch.1 Part I Art.8 or his right not to be discriminated against under Art.14. As to Art.14, S argued that individuals who had been investigated for a crime but who were no longer the subject of proceedings were discriminated against when their position was compared with that of members of the public who had not been investigated.

Held, dismissing the appeal, that (1) the retention of fingerprints and DNA samples infringed an individual's right to privacy under Art.8(1), *Attorney General's Reference (No.3 of 1999), Re* [2001] 2 A.C. 91, [2001] C.L.Y. 973 considered. The interference with that right was, however, justified under Art.8(2); the amendment to the Police and Criminal Evidence Act 1984 s.64 that was enacted in s.82 of the 2001 Act had a lawful purpose, namely "the prevention or detection of crime, the investigation of an offence or the conduct of a prosecution", language that was very similar to that used in Art.8(2). Furthermore, the retention of fingerprints and DNA samples was proportionate in that any adverse consequences to the individual were not out of proportion to the benefit gained by the public; (2) once fingerprints and samples had been lawfully obtained, there was a perfectly clear objective distinction between individuals from whom fingerprints and samples had been taken and those from whom they had not been taken. That distinction justified different treatment. In any event, the discrimination alleged did not fall within the categories of discrimination referred to in Art.14, and (3) by s.64 of the 1984 Act, as amended by s.82 of the 2001 Act, the Chief Constable had a discretion when deciding whether or not to retain fingerprints or samples. The policy of the Chief Constable to normally insist on retention but to allow exceptions to be made in exceptional circumstances was a perfectly appropriate one, *British Oxygen Co Ltd v. Minister of Technology* [1971] A.C. 610, [1970] C.L.Y. 2809 considered.

R. (ON THE APPLICATION OF S) v. CHIEF CONSTABLE OF SOUTH YORKSHIRE; R. (ON THE APPLICATION OF MARPER) v. CHIEF CONSTABLE OF SOUTH YORKSHIRE, [2002] EWCA Civ 1275, [2002] 1 W.L.R. 3223, Lord Woolf of Barnes, L.C.J., CA.

3770. Police powers–motor vehicles–retention and disposal

POLICE (RETENTION AND DISPOSAL OF MOTOR VEHICLES) REGULATIONS 2002, SI 2002 3049; made under the Police Reform Act 2002 s.60, s.105. In force: January 1, 2003; £1.75.

Under the Police Reform Act 2002 s.59 the police have certain powers to seize and remove motor vehicles. These Regulations provide for the retention, safe keeping and disposal by the police or persons authorised by them, of vehicles seized under those powers.

3771. Police powers—real property

POLICE (PROPERTY) (AMENDMENT) REGULATIONS 2002, SI 2002 2313; made under the Police (Property) Act 1897 s.2, s.2A. In force: October 1, 2002; £1.50.

These Regulations amend the Police (Property) Regulations 1997 (SI 1997 1908) by replacing references to the Powers of Criminal Courts Act 1973 with references to the Powers of Criminal Courts (Sentencing) Act 2000 which repealed and consolidated the 1973 Act.

3772. Police powers—serious arrestable offences—investigations

POLICE AND CRIMINAL EVIDENCE ACT 1984 (DEPARTMENT OF TRADE AND INDUSTRY INVESTIGATIONS) ORDER 2002, SI 2002 2326; made under the Police and Criminal Evidence Act 1984 s.114A. In force: October 14, 2002; £1.75.

This Order vests in an investigator appointed by the Secretary of State for Trade and Industry, when investigating a serious arrestable offence or anything which there are reasonable grounds for suspecting has involved the commission of a serious arrestable offence, the powers set out in the Police and Criminal Evidence Act 1984 for a constable to apply to a circuit judge for an order requiring production of or access to "special procedure material" or a warrant for one or more constables together with one or more Department of Trade and Industry investigators to search for and seize such material.

3773. Police powers—surveillance—authorisations

See HUMAN RIGHTS. §5869, §5870

3774. Police powers—surveillance—tape recordings of telephone conversations—meaning of "interception"

[Police and Criminal Evidence Act 1984 s.78; Regulation of Investigatory Powers Act 2000 s.2(2), s.26(1)(c).]

BH and DH appealed against their convictions for conspiracy to supply a Class B controlled drug. At their trial, the judge had ruled that tape recordings of face to face conversations and telephone conversations between the appellants and two undercover police officers were admissible. The issues raised by their appeals included (1) whether the recordings amounted to telephone tapping and (2) whether the conduct of the police officers amounted to surveillance and, if so, whether proper authorisation had been given.

Held, dismissing the appeals, that (1) for one party to a telephone conversation to make a tape recording of that conversation did not amount to the interception of a communication in the course of its transmission by means of a telecommunication system within the meaning of the Regulation of Investigatory Powers Act 2000 s.2(2), and (2) whilst the conduct of the police officers did amount to surveillance within the meaning of s.26(1)(c) of the Act, proper authorisation had been given.

R. v. HARDY (BRIAN); R. v. HARDY (DANNY), [2002] EWCA Crim 3012, [2003] 1 Cr. App. R. 30, Hughes, J., CA (Crim Div).

3775. Police Reform 2002 (c.30)

This Act makes new provision about the supervision, administration functions and conduct of police forces, police officers and other persons serving with, or carrying out functions in relation to, the police; amends police powers and provides for the exercise of police powers by persons who are not police officers; and amends the law relating to sex offender orders.

This Act received Royal Assent on July 24, 2002.

3776. Police Reform Act 2002 (c.30)–Commencement No.1 Order

POLICE REFORM ACT 2002 (COMMENCEMENT NO.1) ORDER 2002, SI 2002 2306; made under the Police Reform Act 2002 s.108. Commencement details: bringing into force various provisions of the 2002 Act on October 1, 2002 and November 1, 2002; £1.75.

This Order brings into force specified provisions of the Police Reform Act 2002.

3777. Police Reform Act 2002 (c.30)–Commencement No.3 Order

POLICE REFORM ACT 2002 (COMMENCEMENT NO.3) ORDER 2002, SI 2002 2750 (C.85); made under the Police Reform Act 2002 s.108. Commencement details: bringing into force various provisions of the 2002 Act on December 2, 2002, January 1, 2003 and February 3, 2003; £1.75.

This Order brings into force specified provisions of the Police Reform Act 2002.

3778. Welsh language–forms–attestation of constables

ATTESTATION OF CONSTABLES (WELSH LANGUAGE) ORDER 2002, SI 2002 2312; made under the Welsh Language Act 1993 s.26. In force: October 1, 2002; £1.50.

This Order specifies the form of words in Welsh which may be used in police areas in Wales for the attestation of constables or special constables as an alternative to the words in the Police Act 1996 Sch.4.

3779. Witness statements–human rights–complaints against police officers– disclosure of witness statements prior to conclusion of police investigation

[Human Rights Act 1998 Sch.1 Part I Art.2, Art.3.]

The Police Complaints Authority appealed against an order ([2001] EWHC Admin 1160, [2002] U.K.H.R.R. 293) for the disclosure of documents relating to an accident involving a police driver. G had sustained severe injuries as a result of being hit by an unmarked police car driven by L, a police sergeant. He subsequently made a formal complaint to the Authority alleging that L had been trying to kill him. Following the completion of the investigation into G's complaint the Authority had refused G's request for disclosure of the eyewitness accounts and expert reports. The order for disclosure had been made in judicial review proceedings brought by G on the basis that it was required by the Human Rights Act 1998 Sch.1 Part I Art.2 and Art.3 in order to secure G's right to an effective independent inquiry. The Authority had opposed disclosure on the grounds of witness contamination and confidentiality.

Held, allowing the appeal and setting aside the order for disclosure, that the refusal by the Authority to disclose to G witness statements concerning his complaint had not breached his rights under the Human Rights Act 1998 Sch.1 Part I Art.2 and Art.3. The Convention requirement that a complainant in a public law case should be involved in the investigation into his complaint to the extent necessary to safeguard his legitimate interests did not require witness statements to be disclosed to him during the course of the investigation itself, *Jordan v. United Kingdom (24746/94)* 11 B.H.R.C. 1, [2001] C.L.Y. 3575 applied. A complainants' Convention rights were appropriately and adequately safeguarded by his entitlement to be involved in the investigation process by contributing evidence, being kept informed of the progress of the investigation and by being provided with reasoned conclusions on its completion. It followed that as a general rule disclosure of witness statements should not occur before the conclusion of the police investigation, if at all.

R. (ON THE APPLICATION OF GREEN) v. POLICE COMPLAINTS AUTHORITY, [2002] EWCA Civ 389, [2002] U.K.H.R.R. 985, Simon Brown, L.J., CA.

3780. **Books**

Johnston, David; Hutton, Glenn-Blackstone's Police Manual: Evidence and Procedure 2003. Blackstone's Police Manual. Paperback: £10.99. ISBN 0-19-925488-5. Oxford University Press.

Sampson, Fraser-Blackstone's Police Manual: General Police Duties 2003- (Human Rights Ed). Blackstone's Police Manual. Paperback: £10.99. ISBN 0-19-925491-5. Blackstone Press.

Sampson, Fraser-Preparing for Police Duty. Paperback: £8.99. ISBN 0-19-925556-3. Oxford University Press.

POSTAL SERVICES

3781. **Licences-infringement-breach of exclusive privilege to convey post-existence of civil remedy**

[British Telecommunications Act 1981 s.66(1); Postal Services Act 2000.]

In proceedings brought by C, the successor in title to the Post Office, seeking damages from H for the alleged infringement of C's exclusive privilege to distribute post, the question of law arose as to whether the British Telecommunications Act 1981 s.66(1), which conferred the exclusive privilege, provided a civil right of action. C alleged that H had been operating a business which consisted of the conveying of letters. The instant proceedings related to C's claim for past damages running from around 1995, when the alleged infringement had started, and March 25, 2001, when the relevant provisions of the Postal Services Act 2000 came into force. C argued that given its duty to provide a universal postal service for which, because of the need to finance loss making operations from profitable ones, it had been given an exclusive privilege, it must have been intended that damages could be recovered through civil proceedings where the privilege had been infringed.

Held, giving judgment for H, that C did not have the right to bring civil proceedings against a party who had infringed its exclusive privilege to convey post. Having regard to the 1981 Act and its predecessors, it was clear that in using the term "exclusive privilege" Parliament had not intended to create a civil right. The statutory provisions provided a complete code. It was of significance that the word "privilege" had been used rather than the word "right"; the use of the word "privilege" suggested an entitlement to carry out something rather than an entitlement to exclude others. In circumstances where the privilege had been infringed, the available remedy was in the criminal courts, *Lonrho Ltd v. Shell Petroleum Co Ltd (No.2)* [1982] A.C. 173, [1981] C.L.Y. 2649 distinguished.

CONSIGNIA PLC v. HAYS PLC *The Times*, January 24, 2002, Jacob, J., Ch D.

3782. **Supply of services-licences**

POSTAL SERVICES ACT 2000 (MODIFICATION OF SECTION 7) ORDER 2002, SI 2002 200; made under the Postal Services Act 2000 s.8. In force: February 5, 2002; £1.50.

The Postal Services Act 2000 prevents any person from conveying a letter from one place to another unless that person holds a licence authorising that conveyance or the person is acting as an employee or agent of a person so authorised. It also sets out exceptions to this and provides that a licence is not required for the conveyance of an overseas letter out of the UK, but does not allow a person to make a collection of letters for that purpose. The Postal Services Commission (Postcomm) has recommended that this restriction should be removed. This Order achieves that effect by amending s.7 of the 2000 Act so that a licence is no longer required to do this.

3783. Supply of services–licences–penalties–determination of turnover

POSTAL SERVICES ACT 2000 (DETERMINATION OF TURNOVER FOR PENALTIES) (AMENDMENT) ORDER 2002, SI 2002 125; made under the Postal Services Act 2000 s.30. In force: January 26, 2002; £1.50.

This Order amends the Postal Services Act (Determination of Turnover for Penalties) Order 2001 (SI 2001 1135) which specifies the way to determine the turnover of a licence holder for the purposes of the Postal Services Act 2000 s.30(2). The 2001 Order does so by reference to the licence holder's annual turnover and a multiplier based on the length of time the Commission is satisfied the contravention has lasted. This Order introduces a multiplier of two where the Commission is satisfied that the contravention has lasted for exactly two years.

PUBLIC PROCUREMENT

3784. Public works contracts–tenders–equal treatment of tenderers–transparent and uniform application of award criteria–EC law

[Council Directive 71/305 concerning the coordination of procedures for the award of public works contracts Art.29.]

M advertised for tenders for a public works contract and S submitted the lowest tender. The contract notice stipulated that the contract would be awarded to the tender that was most advantageous to M in terms of cost and technical merit. A consulting engineer advised M that the three lowest tenders were of equal technical merit, but that the second lowest in cost would give better value for money. M accepted that advice and S brought proceedings, claiming that the decision to award the contract on that basis breached Council Directive 71/305 Art.29. The national court referred the matter to the ECJ for a preliminary ruling as to whether Art.29 of the Directive was to be interpreted as allowing M to award the contract on the basis of lowest ultimate cost in the professional opinion of an expert.

Held, ruling on the preliminary issue, that M could award the contract on the lowest ultimate cost basis, provided that all tenderers had been treated equally. The principle of equal treatment was central to the Directive. Therefore, tenderers had to be treated equally when they formulated their tenders and when their tenders were being assessed by M. Unrestricted freedom of choice as to the award of the contract was incompatible with Art.29. Equal treatment for tenderers implied that transparency would be guaranteed so that compliance with the award criteria could be verified, and the award criteria had to be formulated in a way that they could be uniformly interpreted by all the tenderers and the criteria had to be applied objectively and equally when assessing the tenders.

SIAC CONSTRUCTION LTD v. MAYO CC (C19/00) [2002] All E.R. (EC) 272, Jann (President), ECJ.

3785. Public works contracts–tenders–requirement to use specified products–compatibility with EC law

[EC Treaty Art.12, Art.28; Council Directive 93/37 concerning the co-ordination of procedures for the award of public works contracts.]

A Danish court referred to the ECJ questions relating to the interpretation of the EC Treaty Art.12 and Art.28. The questions arose in proceedings challenging the compatibility with Community law of a clause in the general conditions of the contract documents of a public works contract relating to the construction of a number of housing units requiring the use of particular products. V, a master carpenter, complained that, by requiring in the call for tenders the use of a specified product, the public body had infringed Art.12 and Art.28. The value of the contract did not exceed the threshold laid down by Council Directive 93/37.

Held, giving a preliminary ruling, that (1) even though the works contract fell outside the scope of Directive 93/37, the lawfulness of a clause in the contract had to be assessed by reference to the fundamental rules of the Treaty, which included the free movement of goods set out in Art.28; (2) the failure to add the words "or equivalent" after the designation in the contract documents of a particular product might not only deter economic operators using systems similar to that product from tendering for the contract, but might also impede the flow of imports in intra Community trade. This was contrary to Art.28 as it reserved the contract exclusively to suppliers intending to use the product specified, *Commission of the European Communities v. Netherlands (C359/93)* [1995] E.C.R. I-157, [1995] C.L.Y. 3266 followed, and (3) accordingly, Art.28 precluded a contracting authority from including in the contract for a public works contract which did not exceed the threshold laid down in Directive 93/37, a clause requiring the use of a product of a specified make, where that clause did not include the words "or equivalent".

VESTERGAARD v. SPOTTRUP BOLIGSELSKAB (C59/00) [2002] 2 C.M.L.R. 42, Colneric (President), ECJ.

RATES

3786. Council tax–demand notices

COUNCIL TAX AND NON-DOMESTIC RATING (DEMAND NOTICES) (ENGLAND) (AMENDMENT) REGULATIONS 2002, SI 2002 180; made under the Local Government Finance Act 1988 s.143, Sch.9 para.1, Sch.9 para.2. In force: February 22, 2002; £2.00.

These Regulations amend the Council Tax and Non-Domestic Rating (Demand Notices) (England) Regulations 1993 (SI 1993 191 as amended by SI 1995 121, SI 1997 394, SI 1998 47) and revoke, with savings, the Council Tax and Non-Domestic Rating (Demand Notices) (England) (Amendment) (No.2) Regulations 2000 (SI 2000 534). They amend the Explanatory Notes which billing authorities in England are required to include in rate demand notices with respect to any financial year beginning on or after April 1, 2002 to take account of changes to the rating system.

3787. Non domestic rates–alteration of lists–appeals

NON-DOMESTIC RATING (ALTERATION OF LISTS AND APPEALS) (AMENDMENT) (ENGLAND) REGULATIONS 2002, SI 2002 498; made under the Local Government Finance Act 1988 s.55, s.143, Sch.7A para.10, Sch.7A para.11, Sch.7A para.12. In force: April 1, 2002; £1.75.

These Regulations, which amend the Non-Domestic Rating (Alteration of Lists and Appeals) Regulations 1993 (SI 1993 291), provide for the alteration of lists by the valuation officers, proposals by other persons for alterations and appeals to valuation tribunals where there is a disagreement about a proposal between a valuation officer and the proposer.

3788. Non domestic rates–alteration of lists–appeals–Wales

NON-DOMESTIC RATING (ALTERATION OF LISTS AND APPEALS) (AMENDMENT) (WALES) REGULATIONS 2002, SI 2002 1735; made under the Local Government Finance Act 1988 s.55, s.143, Sch.7A para.10, Sch.7A para.11, Sch.7A para.12. In force: July 23, 2002; £2.00.

These Regulations amend the Non-Domestic Rating (Alteration of Lists and Appeals) Regulations 1993 (SI 1993 291) which govern the alteration of non-domestic rating lists. They provide for the alteration of lists by the valuation officers, proposals by other persons for alterations, and appeals to valuation tribunals where there is a disagreement about a proposal between a valuation officer and the proposer. The Regulations make amendments to include a new ground for making a proposal to alter a list, to extend the period in which a proposal may be made, and to extend the period in which an appeal against a certification may be made.

3789. Non domestic rates—calculation of contributions—amendment of rules

NON-DOMESTIC RATING CONTRIBUTIONS (ENGLAND) (AMENDMENT) REGULATIONS 2002, SI 2002 3021; made under the Local Government Finance Act 1988 s.143, Sch.8 para.4, Sch.8 para.6. In force: December 31, 2002; £1.75.

Under the Local Government Finance Act 1988, billing authorities are required to pay amounts to the Secretary of State. Payments in respect of a provisional amount of the contributions are made during the financial year, final calculations and any adjustments of payments being made after the year ends. These Regulations amend the rules for calculation of contributions contained in the Non-Domestic Rating Contributions (England) Regulations 1992 (SI 1992 3082) by altering certain figures used in the calculations.

3790. Non domestic rates—calculation of contributions—amendment of rules—Wales

NON-DOMESTIC RATING CONTRIBUTIONS (WALES) (AMENDMENT) REGULATIONS 2002, SI 2002 3054 (W.289); made under the Local Government Finance Act 1988 s.140, s.143, Sch.8 para.4, Sch.8 para.5, Sch.8 para.6. In force: December 31, 2002; £2.00.

Under the Local Government Finance Act 1988 Sch.8 Part II billing authorities in Wales are required to pay amounts (called non-domestic rating contributions) to the National Assembly for Wales. Rules for the calculation of those amounts are contained in the Non-Domestic Rating Contributions (Wales) Regulations 1992 (SI 1992 3238). These Regulations amend the 1992 Regulations by substituting a new multiplier in Sch.2 para.2(12) (assumptions as to gross amount) and a new Schedule 4 (adult population figures).

3791. Non domestic rates—exemptions—clinic providing counselling for drug and alcohol addiction—meaning of "training" for purposes of statutory exemption

[Local Government Finance Act 1988 Sch.5 para.16.]

H appealed against a valuation tribunal decision that parts of a clinic used for the detoxification and counselling of persons addicted to alcohol or drugs were exempt from rating as counselling was to be equated with "training" for the purposes of the exemption in the Local Government Finance Act 1988 Sch.5 para.16(1)(a).

Held, allowing the appeal, that training in terms of Sch.5 para.16(1)(a) was such as would permit a disabled person or someone who had been ill to undertake an occupation commensurate with their condition. It did not include training in the general sense of allowing the resumption of a normal life.

HALLIDAY (VALUATION OFFICER) v. PRIORY HOSPITAL GROUP OF THE NOTTINGHAM CLINIC [2001] R.A. 355, George Bartlett Q.C. (President), Lands Tr.

3792. Non domestic rates—flats—alteration of non domestic rating lists—identification of hereditaments—correction of lists

[Local Government Finance Act 1988 s.66(2C); Non-Domestic Rating (Alteration of Lists and Appeals) Regulations 1993 (SI 1993 291) Reg.4A.]

C applied for judicial review of the decision of B, a valuation officer, to alter the 1995 and 2000 Non Domestic Rating, NDR, lists for Westminster City Council. C owned buildings at two addresses which were made up of apartments, some of which were let on long leases and some of which were serviced by C as short let self contained apartments. C owned the freeholds on a long lease. In March 2001 B decided that the self contained apartments should be included in the NDR lists and amended the lists accordingly. C contended that the amendment was incurably invalid as B had not identified in the lists the parts of the buildings which were hereditaments in C's rateable ownership or occupation. C submitted that the hereditament was not a composite hereditament and therefore the hereditament could not be all the apartments without distinction. C argued that as it was the freehold owner of Hill Street it could not be the "relevant person" within the

Local Government Finance Act 1988 s.66(2C) for the purpose of identifying non domestic property. B contended that there was a drafting error in s.66(2C) and that the court should insert extra words.

Held, granting the application for judicial review in part, that (1) although B had failed to properly identify the relevant parts of the buildings, that did not render the amendment to the lists a nullity, as it was capable of correction by the Valuation Tribunal, pursuant to the Non-Domestic Rating (Alteration of Lists and Appeals) Regulations 1993 Reg.4A. Any hereditament, including a composite hereditament, had to be in single rateable occupation or ownership and could not be described so as to include parts of a building which were in different ownership or occupation, and (2) section 66(2C) of the Act was clearly wrongly drafted, but as the Act related to taxation, there was a strong constitutional convention which prevented the courts from giving anything other than a strict interpretation to the words of the statute, *Inco Europe Ltd v. First Choice Distribution* [2000] 1 W.L.R. 586, [2000] C.L.Y. 220 applied. The inclusion of Hill Street in the NDR lists was quashed.

R. (ON THE APPLICATION OF CURZON BERKELEY LTD) v. BLISS (VALUATION OFFICER); *sub nom.* R. (ON THE APPLICATION OF CURZON BERKLEY LTD) v. BLISS (VALUATION OFFICER), [2001] EWHC Admin 1130, [2002] R.A. 45, James Goudie Q.C., QBD (Admin Ct).

3793. **Non domestic rates–golf courses–rateable value–golf course site under construction**

E purchased the subject site in 1996 and were granted planning permission for a golf course the same year. J, occupied the land with its own site office and store under a verbal agreement with E to build the golf course. J brought waste material on site for which it was either paid by third parties or which came from its other construction sites, thus saving it disposal costs. By 1999 the golf course was far from completed. The valuation tribunal was asked to decide whether the site had two purposes, tipping and golf course construction, one of which was rateable.

Held, rejecting the rate payers appeals, that (1) a rateable hereditament existed namely a tipping site *Wimborne DC v. Brayne Construction Co* [1985] 2 E.G.L.R. 175, [1985] C.L.Y. 2924 followed; (2) the site was in the sole and exclusive occupation of J; (3) J was receiving a financial benefit from the occupation of the site; (4) the royalty method was the appropriate method of valuation, and (5) the effective date was the date when tipping commenced.

EARLROSE GOLF & LEISURE v. RAINE (VALUATION OFFICER) [2002] R.V.R. 7, PLG Chittenden (Chairman), Valuation Tribunal.

3794. **Non domestic rates–holiday lettings–rateable value–reduction for semi detached properties–proximity to tourist attraction**

A appealed against a valuation tribunal decision which had determined the 1995 rating list assessment of two semi detached holiday cottages situated in the Vale of Glamorgan at £2,800. A contended that the assessment should be reduced to £1,520, based on eight single bed spaces at £200 each with a five per cent reduction for being semi detached.

Held, allowing the appeal, that A's valuation was accepted, subject to a 20 per cent increase to reflect the proximity of the cottages to a vineyard which was an added attraction, giving a total valuation of £1,825.

ANDREWS v. RUSSELL (VALUATION OFFICER) [2001] R.A. 333, NJ Rose, Lands Tr.

3795. **Non domestic rates–leases–surrender by operation of law–incorrect analysis by magistrates**

T, a business tenant, finding himself physically excluded from his leased premises following the acquisition of his business by another company, A, some months previously, wrote to his landlord, stating that if he was not allowed to re occupy the premises within 28 days he would consider the lease null and void. T did not gain re-entry nor was rent demanded of him, but rather A continued in possession paying rent to the landlord. Subsequently, R, the local authority, brought proceedings against T for non payment of non domestic rates on the property. The magistrates concluded on the evidence that the lease had been surrendered by operation of law and found that T was not liable to pay the rates. R appealed by way of case stated, submitting that there had been no acceptance by the landlord that the lease was surrendered and that the magistrates' reasoning was flawed when they found that, although T's letter to S was insufficient on its own to surrender the lease, the combined effect of T's letter and the landlord's acceptance of rent from A instead of T had been sufficient to complete the surrender.

Held, allowing the appeal, that in order to ascertain whether any act by the landlord could amount to an acceptance of the surrender of the lease, it was essential to analyse the facts at each material stage, to reach conclusions on those facts and to identify precisely when it was that the surrender occurred. The magistrates had neither done so nor appreciated the need to do so and had arrived at a blanket finding, without appropriate evidence. The fact that the landlord had not pursued T for rent, which the magistrates' had considered as justification for their conclusion, was a fact cited by T as being behaviour indicative of surrender having occurred earlier and not as an incident completing the surrender. The magistrates' had failed to appreciate that distinction and their reasoning was consequently flawed; accordingly the case was remitted.

RUNNYMEDE BC v. TROTT [2002] R.V.R. 91, Kay, J., QBD.

3796. Non domestic rates–liability orders–validity of complaint encompassing more than one financial year

[Non-Domestic Rating (Collection and Enforcement) (Local Lists) Regulations 1989 (SI 1989 1058) Reg.4, Reg.10(2).]

T appealed against the dismissal of its complaint against M for failure to pay non domestic rates over a three year period. The judge at first instance had accepted a submission by M that it was not open to the authority to apply for a single liability order in respect of the liability for more than one financial year pursuant to the Non-Domestic Rating (Collection and Enforcement) (Local Lists) Regulations 1989. M argued that Reg.10(2) should be construed in light of Reg.4. On appeal, T argued that the Regulations did permit such a construction and that the judge had been wrong to find unfairness in the procedure.

Held, allowing the appeal, that the judge had erred in his decision. Reg.10(2) allowed claims for more than one financial year to be brought before the court at the same time and therefore there was no reason why applications for liability orders for more than one period should not be permitted.

TOWER HAMLETS LBC v. MERRICK, [2001] EWHC Admin 799, [2001] R.V.R. 305, Stanley Burnton, J., QBD (Admin Ct).

3797. Non domestic rates–occupancy–administrative receivership–liability for non domestic rates of company's premises

[Insolvency Act 1986 s.44(1)(a); Local Government Finance Act 1988 s.43(1).]

The local authority appealed against a decision ([2001] 2 B.C.L.C. 663) that R and B, receivers appointed to BF, were not personally liable for the payment of non domestic rates in respect of BF's commercial premises. R and B had been appointed to run the business prior to its liquidation and the local authority had demanded payment under the Local Government Finance Act 1988 s.43(1) for their occupancy during the seven months between BF's liquidation and sale. The local authority contended that the occupancy prior to liquidation was enough to constitute rateable occupation and that the only reason they were not liable for that period was that at that time they had been acting as BF's agents. The local authority submitted that after liquidation, by reason of the Insolvency Act 1986 s.44(1)(a), they were no longer agents of the company and there was therefore no reason to conclude they were not in rateable occupation.

Held, dismissing the appeal, that a receiver's actions in managing a company did not amount on its own to rateable occupation of company premises; any occupation by a receiver as agent for the company was occupation by the company, *Ratford and Hayward v. Northavon DC* [1987] Q.B. 357, [1986] C.L.Y. 2813 applied. BF had remained in rateable occupation of the premises at all times. After BF had gone into liquidation, the correct analysis of the situation was not that R and B were agents of the company, but that they were not in rateable occupation at all.

REES v. BOSTON BC; *sub nom.* BECK FOODS LTD, RE; BOSTON BC v. REES; BECK FOODS LTD v. BOSTON TAX, [2001] EWCA Civ 1934, [2002] 1 W.L.R. 1304, Jonathan Parker, L.J., CA.

3798. Non domestic rates—offices qualifyication as hereditament—building in poor state of repair and hazardous to health

H appealed against a local valuation tribunal decision determining the 1995 rating list assessment for office premises in south east London at a rateable value of £810. The office was situated in a building in a poor state of repair which had sustained serious fire damage in 1993 and presented a health hazard. S reconsidered the rateable value on that basis and gave a revised assessment of £585.

Held, confirming the revised assessment, that the premises were liable to be entered on the list as they comprised a hereditament which had some form of independent use at the material date.

HENRIQUES v. STEPHENS (VALUATION OFFICER) [2001] R.A. 366, PR Francis FRICS, Lands Tr.

3799. Non domestic rates—sports facilities—local authority leisure centres—valuation basis to take into account local authority management and financing

EBC appealed against rateable value assessments for two leisure centres having gross floor areas of 6,877 square metres and 2,526 square metres respectively. The largest, S, had a sea front location and the smaller, G, was situated in a residential area and both received local authority subsidies. EBC contended that local authority financial constraints militated against the use of the hypothetical rent basis and also rejected the contractor's basis, opting instead for a receipts based approach on the grounds that it took both trading potential and EBC's finances into account. A argued that the assessment of 297 leisure centres in the 1990 list had all been agreed on the contractor's basis, however EBC asserted that the actual settlements showed large reductions on the list figures, thereby allowing a reduction in local authority subsidies.

Held, allowing the appeals, that EBC's valuation method was rejected because the receipts basis only showed the centres' outgoings. Although the contractor's basis had some limitations, its use for a wide range of local authority premises where rental evidence was lacking and profits based valuations could not be made meant that it could be adapted to take into account local authority construction and operation and the use of subsidies to finance continued running.

EASTBOURNE BC v. ALLEN (VALUATION OFFICER) [2001] R.A. 273, George Bartlett Q.C., Lands Tr.

3800. Non domestic rates—valuation date—Wales

RATING LISTS (VALUATION DATE) (WALES) ORDER 2002, SI 2002 3186 (W.302); made under the Local Government Finance Act 1988 Sch.6 para.2. In force: March 1, 2003; £1.75.

This Order, which revokes the Rating Lists (Valuation Date) Order 1998 (SI 1998 93), specifies April 1, 2003 as the day by reference to which the rateable value of a non-domestic hereditament is to be determined for the purposes of the local and central non-domestic rating lists which are to be compiled on April 1, 2005.

3801. Rateable value–valuation officers–retrospective alteration–duty to maintain accurate list–no evidence of discriminatory treatment

[General Rate Act 1967; Local Government Finance Act 1988.]

A valuation officer made an alteration in the list in respect of a large and complex hereditament whereby he retrospectively entered a reduced value on March 29, 2001 from April 1, 1990. Regulations empowered the retrospective alteration of the list until March 31, 2001. By reason of certain transitional provisions connected with the change from the rating system under the General Rate Act 1967 to that under the Local Government Finance Act 1988 the net effect of the alteration would be to leave the ratepayer worse off by about £9 million. The rate payer sought to challenge the decision to alter the list, by way of judicial review, arguing that the decision was an abuse of power because of delay and discrimination.

Held, dismissing the application, that (1) the valuation officer was under a duty to compile and maintain an accurate list and if an inaccuracy was drawn to his attention he was duty bound to correct it. The reduced rateable value in this case was an agreed valuation; (2) the valuation officer was under a duty to act fairly but there was no evidence of discriminatory treatment by the valuation officer, and (3) there was no unfair delay since the parties had agreed to wait until another case had been heard in order to ascertain the proper principles of valuation of such large and complex hereditaments.

R. (ON THE APPLICATION OF CORUS UK LTD) v. VALUATION OFFICE AGENCY, [2001] EWHC Admin 1108, [2002] R.A. 1, Sullivan, J., QBD (Admin Ct).

REAL PROPERTY

3802. Access–business tenancies–estoppel or positive right over landlord's property–adequacy of damages

See LANDLORD AND TENANT: Rock Garden Ltd v. Covent Garden Market LP. §3017

3803. Adverse possession–right to peaceful enjoyment of possessions–compatibility with human rights

[Human Rights Act 1998 s.4, Sch.1 Part I Art.6, Sch.1 Part II Art.1.]

D appealed against a decision to allow F to amend its particulars of claim so as to raise arguments alleging breach of its Convention rights under the Human Rights Act 1998. D occupied property owned by F. F commenced possession proceedings. D pleaded the defence of adverse possession. F contended that Art.1 of the First Protocol and Art.6 of the Convention should be read so it was not deprived of its property or, if they could not be so read, that the court should make a declaration of incompatibility under s.4 of the Act. In particular, F contended that to lose its property by adverse possession would be a deprivation within the meaning of the second sentence of Art.1. D contended that the second sentence referred only to expropriations by, or on the authority of, the state and not to deprivations under private law.

Held, allowing the appeal, that (1) D's interpretation of the second sentence of Art.1 of the Convention was the correct one, *Bramelid v. Sweden (8588/79, 8589/79))* [1983] 5 E.H.R.R. 249 and *James v. United Kingdom (A/98)* [1986] 8 E.H.R.R. 123, [1986] C.L.Y. 1650 followed. Art.1 did not impinge on the adverse possession provisions of the Limitation Act 1980, *JA Pye (Oxford) Ltd v. Graham* [2001] EWCA Civ 117, [2001] C.L.Y. 4840, and (2) rules enabling the acquisition of title by adverse possession were not inherently incompatible with Art.6 of the Convention.

FAMILY HOUSING ASSOCIATION v. DONNELLAN; *sub nom.* FAMILY HOUSING ASSOCIATION v. DONELLAN [2002] 1 P. & C.R. 34, Park, J., Ch D.

3804. Adverse possession–squatting–acknowledgement of title

[Limitation Act 1980 s.29, s.31.]

B, a squatter, appealed against the grant of an order for possession of the flat which he occupied in favour of L. The premises in question formed part of a block of flats which had been purchased by L in 1979. From 1983 the premises had been occupied by a shifting population of squatters. L commenced proceedings in 1997. The court at first instance granted possession orders in favour of L in respect of the majority of the flats. On appeal, B contended that the possession proceedings were statute barred and that he had obtained lawful title to his flat as a result of adverse possession. L cross appealed in relation to those flats which had not been made subject to an order for possession, submitting that there had been acknowledgement of L's title during the relevant period of occupation such as to defeat any claim to adverse possession.

Held, dismissing the appeal and allowing the cross appeal, that determination of the appeal hinged upon the issue of acknowledgement pursuant to the Limitation Act 1980 s.29 and s.31. On the facts, a petition delivered to L in 1989 and signed by at least one resident in each of the flats had amounted to an acknowledgement under the 1980 Act, since it formed part of a campaign by the occupiers to prevent the sale of the block to a housing association and therefore implicitly acknowledged that L had the power to sell.

LAMBETH LBC v. BIGDEN; *sub nom.* BIGDEN v. LAMBETH LBC (2001) 33 H.L.R. 43, Mummery, L.J., CA.

3805. Adverse possession–squatting–requisite degree of custody and control

A squatter, G, appealed against a ruling ([2001] EWCA Civ 117, [2001] Ch. 804) granting possession of 25 hectares of agricultural land to J, the freehold owner of the land. J had permitted G to occupy the land for grazing purposes by means of a written agreement in 1983. The agreement expired in December 1983. J declined to renew it and requested that G vacate the land. Although permitted to take a cut of hay in 1984, G's continued occupation and use of the land thereafter lacked permission. At first instance the judge had held that from 1984 G had been in factual possession with the necessary intention to possess the land with the effect that J's title had been extinguished.

Held, allowing the appeal, that the question to be posed was whether the squatter had dispossessed the paper owner of the land by ordinary possession of the land for the relevant period in the absence of consent from the owner. In order to be in possession of land the squatter had to exercise the necessary degree of physical custody and control and to show an intention to possess the land. The squatter had to intend to exclude the world at large, including the paper title owner so far as was reasonably practicable. The requisite degree of physical control was dependent, inter alia, on the nature of the land and the manner of its usage. It was also necessary to demonstrate that the squatter had been treating the land in the manner of an occupying owner and that no other individual had done so. It was immaterial that the squatter would have been willing to pay to occupy the land if requested to do so. Furthermore, it was not necessary to demonstrate an intention to own or acquire ownership of the land. In the instant case, the judge had been correct to conclude that G had established possessory title to the land, *Powell v. McFarlane* (1979) 38 P. & C.R. 452, [1979] C.L.Y. 2248 and *Buckinghamshire CC v. Moran* [1990] Ch. 623, [1989] C.L.Y. 449 applied and *Leigh v. Jack* (1879-80) L.R. 5 Ex. D. 264 overruled.

JA PYE (OXFORD) LTD v. GRAHAM, [2002] UKHL 30, [2003] 1 A.C. 419, Lord Browne-Wilkinson, HL.

3806. Commonhold and Leasehold Reform Act 2002 (15)

This Act makes provision for commonhold land and gives leaseholders a no fault right to manage their block of flats.

This Act received Royal Assent on May 1, 2002.

3807. Commonhold and Leasehold Reform Act 2002 (c.15)–Commencement No.1, Savings and Transitional Provisions Order–Wales

COMMONHOLD AND LEASEHOLD REFORM ACT 2002 (COMMENCEMENT NO.1, SAVINGS AND TRANSITIONAL PROVISIONS) (WALES) ORDER 2002, SI 2002 3012 (W.284; C.96); made under the Commonhold and Leasehold Reform Act 2002 s.181. Commencement details: bringing into force various provisions of the 2002 Act on January 1, 2003; £2.50.

This Order brings into force provisions of the Commonhold and Leasehold Reform Act 2002.

3808. Contract for sale of land–implied terms–planning condition to develop shop–operation of overage clause

C sought rectification of a contract for the sale of land to imply terms releasing it from an obligation to pay overage. C had purchased a former RAF base from M with the intention of building 300 houses on the site. M now sought payment of approximately £1 million pursuant to a clause obliging C to pay overage should planning permission be granted, and development take place, on that part of the site referred to as the "hatched area". A separate clause provided C would be released from the payment of overage should it demolish the 37 properties that lay within the hatched area. To comply with a condition of the residential planning permission granted over the entire site C converted two properties within the hatched area to a retail premises. The remaining properties within the hatched area were demolished in order to make way for the building of new homes, albeit at a lower density than originally envisaged. It was argued that the condition of the planning consent, resulting in two of the original properties remaining, should not result in C being liable to pay overage. Moreover, C submitted that there was an implied term, reflecting the purpose of the overage conditions, that whilst the total number of houses on the site remained below 300 the hatched area should be overage free.

Held, giving judgment for the claimant, that C was liable to pay the overage sum due under the contract. Whilst C had made various representations as to why the overage clause was not intended to come into effect in the present situation, the question of whether a term should be implied into the contract was one of law and not of fact. The contract transferring the land made it clear that overage was due should C develop the hatched area without having demolished all the original properties and, although these terms were basic, they wholly provided for the current circumstances. Given that the contract worked in its original form there was no obvious inference or requirement for business efficacy that terms should be implied to release C from the overage payment.

MINISTRY OF DEFENCE v. COUNTRY & METROPOLITAN HOMES (RISSINGTON) LTD, [2002] EWHC 2113, *The Times*, November 7, 2002, Rimer, J., Ch D.

3809. Contract for sale of land–mortgagees powers and duties–rights of way–construction of access road necessary to effect grant

JB, a firm of solicitors appealed against a ruling on preliminary issues concerning the interpretation of contracts for the sale of land in a claim for negligence, breach of contract and breach of fiduciary duty brought by N, the mortgagee of 10 plots in a self build scheme. JB contended that the judge (1) was wrong to find that N had no common law right to construct an estate road beyond base course standard, and

(2) had erred in holding that there was no obligation on the mortgagors to construct the road in the event of default by W, a holding company formed by the borrowers.

Held, allowing the appeal, that the grant of a right of way carried with it the ancillary and incidental rights necessary to make the grant effective, *Newcomen v. Coulson* (1877) L.R. 5 Ch. D. 133 and *Mills v. Silver* [1991] Ch. 271, [1991] C.L.Y. 1508 considered. The transfer was to be construed as granting an immediate right of way to the borrowers since the words suggested that there was a right of way over roads and footpaths prior to construction and because it would not make commercial sense for the mortgagors to purchase plots of land to which they would have no access. Accordingly, if the mortgagors had an immediate right to complete the road to adoption standard, N had a similar right on taking possession of the plots.

NATIONWIDE BUILDING SOCIETY v. JAMES BEAUCHAMP (A FIRM), [2001] EWCA Civ 275, [2001] 3 E.G.L.R. 6, Peter Gibson, L.J., CA.

3810. Contract for sale of land–options to buy–ambiguity between plan and description–requirement to construe contract in commercial context

S, trustees, appealed against a decision that an option to repurchase two parcels of land, A and B, which had been sold to R's predecessors in title, had not been triggered by the grant of planning permission over part of both parcels of land. Although the conveyance had been lost, the parties' agreed that S had been granted an option to repurchase any part of parcel A if planning permission were granted in favour of it. No mention was made of parcel B. The file plan referred to a piece of land etched in pink, but both A and B were so etched. There was therefore an ambiguity between the wording of the option and the form of the plan: the former suggesting it covered only one portion whereas the latter indicated that it covered both. Permission was granted in part over both A and B. S contended that they were entitled to exercise options over both parcels of land.

Held, allowing the appeal, that the option to repurchase land included parcel B which, although not expressed in the conveyance, was evidenced by the plan and commercial common sense. For development purposes it made no commercial sense to exclude parcel B since without it, parcel A was effectively landlocked. The judge had erred in failing to construe the conveyance in its commercial context. The granting of planning permission triggered S's right to exercise that option.

SMITH v. ROYCE PROPERTIES LTD, [2001] EWCA Civ 949, [2002] 2 P. & C.R. 5, Tuckey, L.J., CA.

3811. Conveyancing–completion–conditions of sale–validity of notice to complete

H appealed against the dismissal of his claim for a declaration that a notice to complete a property purchase served by S had been invalid. S had entered into a written agreement with H to sell him a dwelling house. Following a dispute over certain works required at the property S served a notice to complete. H subsequently submitted a completion statement to S having made deductions in respect of disputed items of work upon which an adjudication of the court was still awaited. When S failed to agree the revised statement H failed to tender any monies on the date fixed for completion. S treated the contract as terminated. On appeal, H contended that (1) S had not been entitled to serve the notice to complete since it had not fulfilled its outstanding obligations under the contract as required by condition 22(1) of the National Conditions of Sale, namely compliance with an implied term to complete the outstanding items of work in a proper manner, and (2) the submission of the statement was sufficient performance to entitle him to complete and to preclude S from terminating the contract.

Held, dismissing the appeal, that (1) whilst a failure to properly perform the outstanding works could amount to a breach of the implied term and form the basis for a claim for breach of contract, it could not constitute a breach of condition 22(1) so as to prevent S from serving a valid notice to complete. Condition 22 related solely to the primary obligation of the agreement to perform the works in question, which had clearly been complied with. An obligation to pay damages for breach of the implied term that the work should be performed properly was secondary and not relevant to the issue of completion, and (2) H had failed to comply with his obligation to tender monies on completion. Providing a letter prior to completion setting out the amount that he thought was due on completion certainly did not fulfil that obligation.

HANSON v. SOUTH WEST ELECTRICITY BOARD; *sub nom.* HANSON v. SWEB PROPERTY DEVELOPMENTS LTD, [2001] EWCA Civ 1377, [2002] 1 P. & C.R. 35, Dyson, L.J., CA.

3812. **Conveyancing–completion–validity of notice requiring completion**

A appealed against the dismissal of its application for specific performance of seven contracts. Five of the contracts were concerned with the purchase of certain flats. The remaining two contracts were concerned with the purchase of the shares in two companies. The contractual completion date for all seven contracts passed without completion occurring. On the assumption that A was taking no steps to complete the purchases, C served notice pursuant to condition 22 of the National Conditions of Sale requiring completion of each of the contracts within 10 working days. The 10 day deadline expired and C accordingly rescinded the contract and declared the deposit forfeited. A subsequently initiated proceedings seeking a declaration that the notices were invalid and that the contracts remained valid and subsisting. A contended that the notices were invalid since C had not been in possession of certain charge certificates as at the date upon which the notices were served and accordingly C had not been "ready and willing" to complete its outstanding obligations as required by National Condition 22(1). The court at first instance dismissed the claim having concluded that there had been nothing to prevent C from completing on the date in question.

Held, dismissing the appeal, that the obtaining of the relevant charge certificates or the offering of an undertaking in lieu fell within the scope of the necessary administrative arrangements for completion and was not a matter of title such as to preclude contractual completion. Accordingly C had been entitled to serve the notices when it had, *Edwards v. Marshall Lee* (1975) 235 E.G. 901, [1975] C.L.Y. 2217 and *Cole v. Rose* [1978] 3 All E.R. 1121, [1979] C.L.Y. 2778 considered.

AERO PROPERTIES LTD v. CITYCREST PROPERTIES LTD [2002] 2 P. & C.R. 21, Blackburne, J., Ch D.

3813. **Conveyencing–completion–interest–request for vendor to deduce title–interest accruing from date of completion**

[Land Registration Act 1925 s.37, s.110(5).]

R, the purchaser, appealed against a decision to grant summary judgment in favour of P, the vendor, for specific performance of an agreement for the sale of land in which the judge had ruled that the interest on the balance of the purchase price accrued from the contractual completion date. R contended that interest only began to accrue once P complied with R's request to deduce title in accordance with the Land Registration Act 1925 s.110(5) which occurred some four months after the contractual completion date.

Held, dismissing the appeal, that the balance of the purchase price with interest became payable on the contractual completion date, notwithstanding non compliance with the s.110(5) request and the fact that the transfer had not been stamped, since the seller was, on that date capable of transferring the title he had contracted to give pursuant to s.37 of the Act. According to the particular terms of the contract, the obligation to stamp did not have to be performed before the completion date. Furthermore, the obligation to pay interest was separate and distinct from the s.110(5) request and was triggered by the completion date rather than the s.110(5) request, *Urban Manor Ltd v. Sadiq* [1997] 1 W.L.R. 1016, [1997] C.L.Y. 1026 applied.

P&O OVERSEAS HOLDINGS LTD v. RHYS BRAINTREE LTD, [2002] EWCA Civ 296, [2002] 2 P. & C.R. 27, Sir Andrew Morritt V.C., CA.

3814. Conveyencing–searches–mistake–error in certificate of official search of index map–Land Registrar's liability to indemnify against loss

[Land Registration Act 1925 s.83.]

P, a property company, claimed against R, the Chief Land Registrar, for an indemnity in respect of a loss allegedly arising from an error in the certificate issued following an official search of the index map. The error in the certificate had reflected an error in the filed plan, whereby a parcel of apparently unregistered land had been shown to be part of a property owned by P, when in fact part of the parcel had not been included in that property. The purchasers of the property in question, S, had refused to pay P £450,000 retention moneys because it had been unable to register title to the entirety of the parcel. P sought indemnity against that loss pursuant to the Land Registration Act 1925 s.83. R resisted the claim, contending that the loss had resulted from P's lack of proper care in limiting its investigation of title to obtaining the search certificate.

Held, giving judgment for P, that a certificate issued by the Land Registry following an official search of the index map could be relied upon in respect of that which it certified and was not to be taken as a signpost to other inquiries. It had been R's error which had created the problem which led to P's loss of retention moneys and thus R was liable to indemnify P against that loss.

PRESTIGE PROPERTIES LTD v. SCOTTISH PROVIDENT INSTITUTION; *sub nom.* PRESTIGE PROPERTIES LTD v. CHIEF LAND REGISTRAR, [2002] EWHC 330, [2003] Ch. 1, Lightman, J., Ch D.

3815. Countryside and Rights of Way Act 2000 (c.37)–Commencement No.2 Order

COUNTRYSIDE AND RIGHTS OF WAY ACT 2000 (COMMENCEMENT NO.2) ORDER 2002, SI 2002 2833 (C.89); made under the Countryside and Rights of Way Act 2000 s.103. Commencement details: bringing into force various provisions of the 2000 Act on November 21, 2002; £1.75.

This Order brings into force provisions of the Countryside and Rights of Way Act 2000 which require every local highway authority, other than an inner London authority, to prepare and publish a rights of way improvement plan within five years after the commencement of the Act; and contain supplemental provisions including provision requiring a local highway authority to consult before preparing or reviewing a rights of way improvement plan.

3816. Countryside and Rights of Way Act 2000 (c.37)–Commencement No.3 Order–Wales

COUNTRYSIDE AND RIGHTS OF WAY ACT 2000 (COMMENCEMENT NO.3) (WALES) ORDER 2002, SI 2002 2615; made under the Countryside and Rights of Way Act 2000 s.103. Commencement details: bringing into force various provisions of the 2000 Act on November 1, 2002; £1.75.

This Order brings into force on November 1, 2002, in relation to Wales, the Countryside and Rights of Way Act 2000 s.60 which requires every local highway authority to prepare and publish a plan (known as a "rights of way improvement plan") within five years of the coming into force of that section and to review the plan at intervals of not more than 10 years and which empowers the National Assembly for Wales to direct the authority as to the content of a plan and as to the matters to be assessed by the authority at the time a plan is prepared; and s.61, which requires the authority to consult with specified bodies (and such other persons as the National Assembly for Wales prescribes by regulations) and which requires the authority to consider representations made to them on a draft plan and to have regard to guidance given by the National Assembly for Wales.

3817. Easements–gardens–use of land as communal garden–scope of rights created by easement

G, the trustees of the owner of a piece of land, appealed against a declaration that M, the owner of a cottage adjacent to the land who had used the land as part of a communal garden, was entitled to reinstate a flower bed destroyed by G. The conveyance for M's cottage had included a right of way over the disputed land. M had contended however that the right was more extensive by reason of use of the land over years. M had tended a garden on the land which included a grassed area and a flower bed. M had returned home one day to find that G, exercising what they believed to be their right over the land, had removed the flower bed in a bid to create a driveway across the land. M had commenced proceedings for, and was granted, a declaration that she was entitled to freehold rights over the land. G's subsequent appeal was dismissed on the grounds that the facts of the case were sufficient to found an easement known to law. G argued that the easement was so wide as to be tantamount to a claim to use the land to the exclusion of the trustees, and was an attempt to pass off a claim for adverse possession, which could not succeed because of the communal use of the land, as a claim for an easement. G contended that such an extensive use could not be justified as an easement even if the subject of an express grant, and could not be created by way of prescription.

Held, allowing the appeal in part, that M was entitled to use the land as a communal garden but the right did not justify excluding the trustees from any use they may wish to make of the land, *Ellenborough Park, Re* [1956] Ch. 131 considered. Although G had not created or maintained the communal garden, the land had been used as such since the sale of the cottages. G had been content to allow the owners of the cottages to determine the layout of the garden and maintain it, facts which did not derogate from the conclusion that the trustees had been prepared to set aside the land for use as a communal garden. The declaration granted in favour of M went beyond what was necessary to reflect the right which had been established on the evidence. The restriction on the trustees could only be insofar as was necessary to ensure that the rights of M to use the land as a communal garden for recreational and amenity purposes were protected. In removing M's flower bed without notice, G interfered with M's rights. However, they were entitled to create a driveway over the land, as it would not necessarily interfere with the rights to use the land as a communal garden, but in carrying out works on the land, G had to ensure that the use of the land as a communal garden for recreational and amenity purposes was maintained.

MULVANEY v. GOUGH; *sub nom.* MULVANEY v. JACKSON; JACKSON v. MULVANEY, [2002] EWCA Civ 1078, [2003] 1 W.L.R. 360, Latham, L.J., CA.

3818. Easements–prescription–acquirement by conduct amounting to a crime–court's duty to follow binding authority

See LEGAL METHODOLOGY: Bakewell Management Ltd v. Brandwood. §3096

3819. Easements–prescription–right to park

B appealed against a decision that M had acquired an exclusive prescriptive right to park up to six cars on Mondays to Fridays between the hours of 9.30 am and 6.00 pm, on a strip of land owned by B ([2001] R.T.R. 12, [2000] C.L.Y. 4630). B contended that the right was incapable of being a valid easement and that the judge's findings of fact did not justify a conclusion that such a right had been acquired. B submitted that his ownership of the land had become illusory as a result because (1) the right asserted was exclusive of all others, including his own, and (2) the parking on the land was so intrusive as to prevent any other use of the land being possible during periods when cars were parked. M contended that B had 120 hours of use of the land per week and that in that time he could use it for parking or charging others to park, or alternatively he could sell the land.

Held, allowing the appeal, that B had no reasonable use of the land for parking because he was unable to use it during the periods when parking spaces were most likely to be needed. His right to use the land for other purposes was restricted by the times during the week when he could not use the land, and therefore his ownership of the land was illusory. Accordingly the judge had erred in his conclusion since such a right was incapable of being an easement.

BATCHELOR v. MARLOW, [2001] EWCA Civ 1051, [2003] 1 W.L.R. 764, Tuckey, L.J., CA.

3820. Easements–rights of way–access to parking space–uses ancillary to dominant tenement

C, owners of two mews properties, appealed against the grant of injunctions preventing them driving along the mews carriageway for the purpose of gaining access to land they owned and used for parking. L, a limited company formed by two residents of the mews, owned the freehold of the carriageway. L contended that whilst C had the right to use the carriageway to access their properties and to load or unload a vehicle they had no right to use it to gain access to adjacent garden ground for parking purposes.

Held, allowing the appeal in part, that it was not possible to extend an easement in order to accommodate any use ancillary to use of the dominant tenement. C had extended the dominant tenement by using the carriageway to gain vehicular access to land used for parking rather than for merely gaining access to their properties, *Harris v. Flower & Sons* (1905) 74 L.J. Ch. 127 applied and *National Trust for Places of Historic Interest or Natural Beauty v. White* [1987] 1 W.L.R. 907, [1987] C.L.Y. 1233 considered. Nevertheless the judge had erred in exercising his discretion to grant injunctive relief and accordingly the matter was remitted for reconsideration of whether there should be an award of damages in lieu of the injunction.

DAS v. LINDEN MEWS LTD; *sub nom.* CHAND v. LINDEN MEWS LTD, [2002] EWCA Civ 590, [2002] 2 E.G.L.R. 76, Buxton, L.J., CA.

3821. Easements–rights of way–access to petrol station–commercial efficacy

M, the owner of a petrol station, appealed against a ruling ((2000) 97(18) L.S.G. 38) that it did not possess rights of way over land owned by B which separated the petrol station from the highway. M maintained that a 1959 deed of exchange contained either an express or implied grant of a right of way. The land in question had been earmarked to form part of a road widening scheme which, if carried into effect, would have meant that M's freehold abutted directly onto the highway thus obviating the need for any right of way. Under the 1959 deed, the freehold in the land upon which the petrol station was to be constructed was conveyed to a company, NB, who originally constructed and operated the petrol station. The adjoining land was retained by B. Clause 3 of the deed imposed an obligation upon B to make available access "for the purposes of the company's trade and/or business and customers by the time the new premises to be constructed by the company are open for trading". M maintained that this obligation was effective to confer rights of way. The deputy judge had concluded that the words were meaningless in the context of the deed and should be ignored. M submitted that such rights of way were necessary in order to give commercial efficacy to the deed, particularly since both parties were aware at the time that the proposed road widening works were not likely to be concluded for many years to come.

Held, allowing the appeal in part (Sedley, L.J. dissenting), that it was only possible to ignore contractual wording in extreme circumstances. The words were likely to have been intended by the parties to carry a meaning and accordingly the court should endeavour to ascertain it, *Investors Compensation Scheme Ltd v. West Bromwich Building Society (No.1)* [1998] 1 W.L.R. 896, [1997] C.L.Y. 2537 applied. The only conclusion that was consistent with the wording of the clause and the commercial intent as evidenced by the context in which the deed was concluded was that advanced by M but such an easement would determine if the widening scheme was implemented at any stage, *Stafford v. Lee* (1993) 65 P. & C.R. 172, [1993] C.L.Y. 1615 applied.

MOBIL OIL CO LTD v. BIRMINGHAM CITY COUNCIL, [2001] EWCA Civ 1608, [2002] 2 P. & C.R. 14, Aldous, L.J., CA.

3822. **Easements–rights of way–dedication of land as public highway–evidence of unrestricted public use**

[Finance (1909-10) Act 1910; Highways Act 1980 s.31, s.32.]

R sought a declaration that an easement or quasi easement of right of way over certain land had been abandoned or extinguished. A sought to rely on a variety of historical material dating back to the 18th century to establish that the land in question was a public highway since, under the Highways Act 1980 s.31, use for 20 years by the public as of right and without interruption was sufficient to establish a piece of land as a dedicated public highway.

Held, refusing R's application, that the evidence in relation to a part of the land in question overwhelmingly supported the inference of dedication to and acceptance by the public as a highway, since a telephone box, post box and parish notice board had all been accessed via the land in dispute by the public without restriction for over 40 years. The evidence as to the use of the rest of the land, the "blue land", had to be balanced against evidence of ownership and control by R and its predecessors. A Finance (1909-10) Act 1910 map which showed the blue land as an untaxed public road was the most powerful indication that the blue land was at that time thought to be in public ownership and vested in and maintainable by the district council. Furthermore, notwithstanding the various matters upon which the claimant sought to rely to undermine such an inference, s.32 of the 1980 Act specifically provided that a court when determining whether a way had been dedicated as a highway, should take into consideration any map, plan or history of the locality. The fact that R and its predecessors had from time to time treated the blue land as private property which was not subject to public rights could not remove the legal status of the land as a public highway, *Dawes v. Hawkins* 141 E.R. 1399 applied.

ROBINSON WEBSTER (HOLDINGS) LTD v. AGOMBAR [2002] 1 P. & C.R. 20, Etherton, J., Ch D.

3823. **Equitable interests–vesting–payment of deposit and mortgage instalments by spouse of bankrupt legal owner–extent of beneficial interest created**

F's trustee in bankruptcy sought a declaration that all or part of the beneficial ownership of a property vested in F, the legal owner, and hence in the trustee. F was unmarried when she purchased the flat in her sole name by way of a mortgage and her replies to a subsequent insolvency questionnaire and a letter to a chargee indicated that she was the sole owner of the flat and that she made the monthly mortgage repayments. At trial F stated in evidence that she had acted purely as a nominee and that she had always intended that she would hold the property on trust for her husband.

Held, refusing the application, that the entire beneficial ownership of the flat vested in F's spouse. Documentary evidence established that he had provided the initial purchase monies and had made the subsequent mortgage repayments, *Lloyds Bank Plc v. Rosset* [1991] 1 A.C. 107, [1990] C.L.Y. 706 applied.

TRUSTEE OF THE ESTATE OF SHARE (A BANKRUPT) v. FISHER; *sub nom.* SHARE (LORRAINE), *Re* [2002] 2 F.L.R. 88, Patten, J., Ch D.

3824. **Greenham and Crookham Commons Act 2002 (i)**

This Act restores land at and in the vicinity of the Greenham and Crookham Commons as common land open to the public; makes provision for the conservation of the natural beauty of that land; grants public access over that land in perpetuity and makes provision with respect to that public access; restores and extends commoners' rights over that land; constitutes the Greenham and Crookham Common Commission for the management of that land and confers powers on the West Berkshire District Council and on that Commission with respect to that land.

This Act received Royal Assent on May 1, 2002.

3825. Land at Palace Avenue, Kensington (Acquisition of Freehold) Act 2002 (ii)

This Act authorises the trustees of the Imperial Tobacco Pension Fund to acquire the freehold of land forming part of the Royal Garden Hotel, Kensington.

This Act received Royal Assent on June 25, 2002.

3826. Land registration–rules

LAND REGISTRATION RULES 2002, SI 2002 2539; made under the Land Registration Act 1925 s.54, s.112, s.144; and the Land Registration and Land Charges Act 1971 s.4. In force: December 2, 2002; £2.50.

These Rules amend the Land Registration Rules 1925 (SR & O 1925 1093), the Land Registration (Souvenir Land) Rules 1972 (SI 1972 985) and the Land Registration (Open Register) Rules 1992 (SI 1992 122). They remove an obsolete reference to the Land Registry General Map; remove the obligation to provide evidence of non-revocation of powers of attorney that are more than 12 months old unless so required by the Registrar and to introduce a standard form of statutory declaration or certificate as evidence of such non-revocation; remove the obligation to provide evidence in support of a power delegating trustees' functions to a beneficiary unless required by the Registrar and to introduce a standard form of statutory declaration or certificate as supporting evidence; relax the provisions relating to the retention of original documents by the Registry where a copy is retained in an electronic or other non-documentary form; and remove the requirement that the certificate required under the Land Registration Act 1925 s.99(1)(i) be given under seal of the Church Commissioners. They also extend the provisions allowing specified persons to inspect (and to obtain copies of and extracts from) documents in the custody of the registrar and to make searches in the index of proprietors' names, to include Department of Trade and Industry senior investigators; remove references to the Drug Trafficking Offences Act 1986 and the Prevention of Terrorism (Temporary Provisions) Act 1989; and provide that provisions relating to compulsory first registration introduced by the Land Registration Act 1997 do not apply to souvenir land.

3827. Land Registration Act 2002 (c.9)

This Act makes provision about land registration.

This Act received Royal Assent on February 26, 2002.

3828. Lands Tribunal–costs–compulsory purchase–appellant successful in compensation action–reduction in award of costs–applicability of CPR to Lands Tribunal

[Land Compensation Act 1961 s.4(1); Civil Procedure Rules 1998 (SI 1998 3132) Part 44 r.44.3.]

P appealed against a decision of the Lands Tribunal awarding him only three quarters costs following his successful action relating to a compulsory purchase of his land. Following the acquisition of his land, P had brought proceedings before the Tribunal in which he sought compensation in the sum of £12,260,000. The Secretary of State contended that the land was worth £3,750,000 but had made P an offer of £5,000,000. The Tribunal determined the compensation at £6,660,000 and, having regard to the Civil Procedure Rules 1998 Part 44 r.44.3, exercised its discretion to reduce the costs award in favour of P, as P's valuation of the land had been exaggerated. On appeal P contended that under the Land Compensation Act 1961 s.4(1) a successful claimant, granted a higher amount of compensation than a sum previously offered, should receive a full award of costs unless there was a special reason not to do so. Moreover, P argued that, in accordance with the *Practice Direction (Lands Tr) (2001)* (Unreported, April 5, 2001), the CPR had no application in the Lands Tribunal.

Held, dismissing the appeal, that it was a legitimate exercise of the tribunal's discretion to reduce the costs awarded to P. The Lands Tribunal should approach its decisions with a view to acting justly and this could include having regard to the principles of the CPR. However, if regard to the principles would result in the Tribunal readily departing from an approach which it had previously adopted then the CPR should not be applied to the issue before them. The proper approach of the Tribunal should be that a successful claimant was entitled to his costs in the absence of some 'special reason' to the contrary, *Emslie & Simpson Ltd v. City of Aberdeen DC* 1995 S.L.T. 355, [1994] C.L.Y. 5474, applied. Section 4(1) of the 1961 Act reflected this underlying principle of "equivalence" and should not be extended by reference to the CPR. However, notwithstanding the fact that the CPR was inapplicable, P's evidence failed to demonstrate that he had not exaggerated his claim, thus warranting a reduction under the 1961 Act.

PURFLEET FARMS LTD v. SECRETARY OF STATE FOR TRANSPORT, LOCAL GOVERNMENT AND THE REGIONS; *sub nom.* PURFLEET FARMS LTD v. SECRETARY OF STATE FOR THE ENVIRONMENT, TRANSPORT AND THE REGIONS, [2002] EWCA Civ 1430, [2003] 1 P. & C.R. 20, Potter, L.J., CA.

3829. Lands tribunal—fees

LANDS TRIBUNAL (FEES) (AMENDMENT) RULES 2002, SI 2002 770; made under the Lands Tribunal Act 1949 s.3; and the Finance Act 1990 s.128. In force: May 1, 2002; £1.75.

These Rules, which amend the Lands Tribunal (Fees) Rules 1996 (SI 1996 1021), provide for the reduction or remission of fees in exceptional circumstances involving undue financial hardship and for refunding a fee where it would have been reduced or remitted if all the circumstances had been known at the time the fee was paid.

3830. Leaseholds—collective enfranchisement—counter notices

LEASEHOLD REFORM (COLLECTIVE ENFRANCHISEMENT) (COUNTER-NOTICES) (ENGLAND) REGULATIONS 2002, SI 2002 3208; made under the Leasehold Reform, Housing and Urban Development Act 1993 s.99. In force: April 10, 2003; £1.50.

These Regulations require a person who receives a notice for a claim for collective enfranchisement to respond by giving a counter-notice admitting or opposing the claim.

3831. Leaseholds—enfranchisement—notices—forms

LEASEHOLD REFORM (NOTICES) (AMENDMENT) (NO.2) (ENGLAND) REGULATIONS 2002, SI 2002 3209; made under the Landlord and Tenant Act 1954 s.66. In force: April 10, 2003; £1.75.

These Regulations, which amend the Leasehold Reform (Notices) Regulations 1997 (SI 1997 640), provide a new form to be used by landlords replying to claims for enfranchisement and extension of long leaseholds under the Leasehold Reform Act 1967. The new Form is to be used for notices in reply given on or after the date these Regulations come into force. Forms which are substantially to the same effect as those prescribed may also be used.

3832. Licences—implied terms—rule preventing licensees bringing dogs onto mobile home park—exemption for guide dogs

M was the owner of a mobile home park. The licence agreement between M and each occupant prohibited the keeping of dogs as pets, although an exception was provided for guide dogs and those dogs used to assist the deaf or disabled in what were termed "special circumstances", for which M was required to give written permission. In addition, M also allowed a terminally ill resident to keep a dog as a companion. A new licensee was however allowed to bring six dogs onto the site, on condition that they would be kept within the licensee's mobile home, exercised only on a lead and not replaced when they died. S, another licensee, obtained a declaration at first instance to the effect that M was in breach of an implied term of the licence agreement not to allow licensees to breach the rules, but it was held that there had been no breach of the covenant of quiet enjoyment. M appealed.

Held, dismissing the appeal, that M had breached the implied term by allowing the dogs to be brought on to the site. The exceptional circumstances allowed for in the agreement included dogs that were depended upon by their owners so that they could enjoy an accepted quality of life. This did not extend to dogs kept only as pets and by allowing them on to the site M had effectively destroyed the purpose for the rule in the licence agreement.

SAVORY v. MORRISON (T/A PARK HOME ESTATES), [2001] EWCA Civ 1225, [2002] 1 P. & C.R. 11, Astill, J., CA.

3833. Local land charges–non registration–compensation–date at which compensation to be assessed

[Local Land Charges Act 1975 s.10.]

S appealed against the decision that compensation payable by the local authority under the Local Land Charges Act 1975 s.10 for the loss S suffered after purchasing a property and subsequently discovering that an agricultural occupancy condition attached to the property which the local authority had failed to register, was to be assessed as at the date they learnt of the occupancy condition and not at the date of the compensation hearing. The court had found the local authority liable to pay compensation, the amount to reflect the difference in the amount between the value of the property without the occupancy condition and its value subject to the condition, as at the date when the condition was discovered.

Held, allowing the appeal, that the date at which the compensation was to be assessed was the date of the compensation hearing rather than the date on which S discovered the charge. Entitlement to compensation under s.10 of the 1975 Act was the equivalent of a cause of action in tort, the general rule in tort being that damages were assessed as at the date of the breach of duty. The local authority had however conceded that the compensation be assessed as at the date of discovery. The issue was whether the facts of the case entitled S to have their compensation assessed as at the date of the compensation hearing. If by adopting the breach date rule an injustice would be created to the claimants, the court had a discretion to take some other date. In the instant case, when S learnt of the occupancy condition they ceased renovations and sought the advice of a planning consultant and solicitor. All those steps were reasonable as was seeking not to sell the property before they had received adequate compensation. Looking at the question as one of principle, the only just remedy was for compensation to be assessed as at the date of the hearing, and to increase the award accordingly, *Alcoa Minerals of Jamaica Inc v. Broderick* [2002] 1 A.C. 371, [2000] C.L.Y. 1467 applied

SMITH v. SOUTH GLOUCESTERSHIRE DC; *sub nom.* SMITH v. SOUTH GLOUCESTER COUNCIL, [2002] EWCA Civ 1131, [2002] 3 E.G.L.R. 1, Sir Martin Nourse, CA.

3834. Mortgagees powers and duties–power of sale–duty owed to owner as well as mortgagor

F appealed against a decision to strike out her claim against R in which she alleged that R had breached its duty of care towards her when it exercised its power of sale over a property owned by F but charged to R by the previous owner. F contended that in selling the property at an under value, R had breached its duty of care towards her as the owner of the property, notwithstanding the fact that she was not the mortgagor. F's claim had been struck out on the basis that in law, the bank did not owe F a duty of care.

Held, allowing the appeal, that the mortgagee owed a duty not only to the mortgagor but also to any subsequent encumbrancer such as someone in F's position and indeed anybody with an interest in the equity of redemption. Since F had a interest which was subject only to a prior right, in this case a legal charge, she would therefore suffer damage if R breached its duty of care and accordingly her claim should not have been struck out, *Downsview Nominees Ltd v. First City Corp Ltd* [1993] A.C. 295, [1993] C.L.Y. 2881 and *Medforth v. Blake* [2000] Ch. 86, [1999] C.L.Y. 3286 applied.

FREEGUARD v. ROYAL BANK OF SCOTLAND PLC *The Times*, April 25, 2002, Simon Berry Q.C., Ch D.

3835. Mortgages – fraud – equitable interests – subrogation – effect of past illegality

M appealed against an order for possession of the property in which she had lived with her husband, H, and brother, B. The property had been bought jointly by M, H and B in 1988 but was registered in the sole name of B. It had been funded by a mortgage loan from Midland Bank and the proceeds of sale from two properties which H had obtained through fraud. In 1990, with the help of a dishonest solicitor who was subsequently struck off, B remortgaged the property with ME without the knowledge of M and H. He defaulted on the repayments and ME sought possession. The judge found that M and H could not claim an equitable interest because of the past illegality and made a possession order. In her appeal, M argued that it was irrelevant that some of the purchase money for the property had been from an "unlawful source". It was money belonging to M and H and therefore gave them an equitable interest.

Held, allowing the appeal, that the purchase money did belong to M and H and its source was not to the point, *Tinsley v. Milligan* [1994] 1 A.C. 340, [1993] C.L.Y. 1839 applied. A possession order was still appropriate as ME had acquired the rights of the Midland Bank under the doctrine of subrogation, but M and H were entitled to a share of the equity. If this could not be agreed, the matter should be remitted to the county court.

MORTGAGE EXPRESS v. McDONNELL; *sub nom.* MORTGAGE EXPRESS v. ROBSON, [2001] EWCA Civ 887, [2001] 2 All E.R. (Comm) 886, Robert Walker, L.J., CA.

3836. Mortgages – joint and several liability – interpretation of payment covenant

G appealed against the dismissal ([2000] 2 All. E.R. (Comm) 686) of his appeal against a decision that he was liable to A for personal debts incurred by M, his business partner. Under a joint mortgage taken out by G and M they had agreed to be liable to A for personal debts incurred by either partner. G contended for a "distributive" construction of the payment clause, given that, because "the mortgagor" as defined in the clause included more than one person, G and M, it should be interpreted as referring first to both of them, next to one of them, and then to the other of them. Accordingly, G submitted, he was not liable for sums advanced to M. G submitted that there was no reason why he should have been expected to undertake liability for M's personal debts and that his interpretation of the agreement was therefore preferable to that argued for by A.

Held, dismissing the appeal, that the payment covenant was a single joint covenant, and the liability of the partners was joint and several. The important issue was what G and M had covenanted to pay, and under the clause they had covenanted to pay "all sums of money... advanced to the mortgagor by the bank". The mortgagor was the two of them and/or each of them. Accordingly, the payment clause was a covenant by G and M to pay their joint debts to A, to pay G's debts to A, and to pay M's debts to A.

AIB GROUP (UK) PLC (FORMERLY ALLIED IRISH BANKS PLC AND AIB FINANCE LTD) v. MARTIN; AIB GROUP (UK) PLC (FORMERLY ALLIED IRISH BANK PLC AND AIB FINANCE LTD) v. GOLD; *sub nom.* AIB GROUP (UK) LTD v. MARTIN; AIB GROUP (UK) PLC (FORMERLY ALLIED IRISH BANK PLC AND AIB FINANCE LTD) v. MARTIN, [2001] UKHL 63, [2002] 1 W.L.R. 94, Lord Scott of Foscote, HL.

3837. Mortgages–non registration–failure to register–proprietary interest of mortgagee in proceeds of sale

B, the borrower, appealed against a decision that P, the lender, had a proprietary interest in the proceeds of sale of a property held under a constructive trust. B had granted a second charge to P, and although P had given notice of the charge to the prior lender, it had failed to properly register the charge, having entered the charge on the land charges register with the wrong address. Following the sale of the property, the proceeds, which were paid out of B's solicitors' client account, were used to discharge the prior mortgage and other creditors of B. P successfully contended at first instance that the proceeds of sale were held upon trust for it, subject to the prior mortgage. On appeal, B contended that (1) P did not obtain a proprietary interest in the proceeds of sale by virtue of its unregistered charge over the property; (2) P did not obtain a beneficial interest in the proceeds of sale by means of an equitable charge over the proceeds of sale, and (3) P did not have an equitable interest in the proceeds of sale by means of a constructive trust arising on the sale of the property.

Held, dismissing the appeal, that P had a proprietary interest in the proceeds of sale, those being held under a constructive trust notwithstanding its failure to properly register the charge. In particular, (1) the failure to register the charge correctly meant that the charge was void against a purchaser but it did not affect the position between the borrower and lender, *Samuel Keller Holdings Ltd v. Martins Bank Ltd* [1971] 1 W.L.R. 43, [1971] C.L.Y. 7451 distinguished; (2) where a borrower made an unauthorised disposition of the mortgaged property in a manner which destroyed the lender's interest in the mortgaged property, a security interest in the proceeds of the disposition automatically arose, and (3) B's solicitors were liable as constructive trustee.

BUHR v. BARCLAYS BANK PLC, [2001] EWCA Civ 1223, [2002] B.P.I.R. 25, Arden, L.J., CA.

3838. Mortgages–power of sale–shortfall on mortgage debt after sale of property–appropriate limitation period on action for recovery

[Land Registration Act 1925 s.34, s.35; Limitation Act 1980 s.5, s.20(1), s.20(5).]

In conjoined appeals the court was required to determine the limitation period applicable to a mortgagee's action for recovery of the shortfall on a mortgage debt. In the lead case, the mortgagees, BW, had taken possession of mortgaged property following the default of the mortgagor, B, and then sold it at a price that yielded a substantial shortfall in the amount due under the mortgage at the date of sale. B mounted a limitation defence to the action to recover the shortfall and claimed that the effect of the sale and/or the Land Registration Act 1925 s.35 was to discharge the liability arising under the covenant to pay in the mortgage deed. Accordingly, B argued that his only obligation to pay the remainder of the mortgage debt arose as an implied term under a simple contract and thus BW's action was time barred being outside the six year period provided by the Limitation Act 1980 s.5.

Held, dismissing B's appeal except in relation to the granting of permission to advance arguments concerning interest, that the fact of the sale did not discharge the clear obligation to pay that arose under the covenant to pay contained in the mortgage deed. The mortgage debt became payable on B's breach of that covenant and the fact that the power of sale was later exercised did not affect that position. Sections 34 and 35 of the 1925 Act did not affect the accrued rights to sue on the covenant in the mortgage. Even where there was an express provision in the mortgage deed that the borrower would pay any shortfall to the lender the cause of action was still that for the mortgage debt arising on default under the terms of the deed, and no separate cause of action arose in relation to the deficiency when it was ascertained, *McHenry, Re* [1894] 3 Ch. 290 applied. Thus, as BW's action concerned the recovery of money secured by a mortgage, the appropriate time limit was to be determined by reference to s.20 of the 1980 Act. The 12 year time limit provided by s.20(1) applied to any action to recover any principal sum of money secured by a mortgage which existed when the right to recover accrued and did not require the principal still to be secured by the mortgage when the action was brought. Given that s.20(1) applied to claims for principal it followed that claims for interest were governed by s.20(5) which contained a six year limitation period.

BRISTOL & WEST PLC v. BARTLETT; PARAGON FINANCE PLC v. BANKS; HALIFAX PLC v. GRANT, [2002] EWCA Civ 1181, [2003] 1 W.L.R. 284, Longmore, L.J., CA.

3839. Mortgages–undue influence–constructive notice–failure to advise borrower

C appealed against a decision that a mortgage secured over W's home was unenforceable on grounds of undue influence of which C was deemed to have constructive knowledge. W's daughter, S, had asked W to let her house be used as the security for a loan to finance S's husband's share purchase in a company of which he was to become a director. The money was subsequently used by S's husband to discharge certain monies owed by him under various judgment debts. C contended that (1) the undue influence relied upon did not justify setting aside the mortgage; (2) C did not have constructive knowledge of the undue influence, and (3) C had dispelled the effect of constructive notice by producing various documents for W to sign which suggested that W seek independent advice and that there was a possibility of W losing her home in the event of default.

Held, dismissing the appeal, that (1) given that W had been recently widowed prior to which she had relied completely on her husband in respect of all financial affairs, there was sufficient evidence to point to undue influence; (2) for a recently widowed lady to mortgage the house in which she lived which was her only asset, for no sensible reason, put her at a manifest disadvantage in the transaction. This coupled with the fact that the loan was at an extravagant rate of interest was sufficient to have put C on inquiry, and (3) notwithstanding that W had signed the various documents presented to her by C, she had not read them and C had not explained the position to her in a private interview. C had therefore not done what was required of it to dispel the effect of the constructive notice, *Barclays Bank Plc v. O'Brien* [1994] 1 A.C. 180, [1994] C.L.Y. 3300 followed.

WRIGHT v. CHERRY TREE FINANCE LTD, [2001] EWCA Civ 449, [2001] 2 All E.R. (Comm) 877, Sir Christopher Staughton, CA.

3840. Mortgages–undue influence–fraudulent misrepresentation–ability to reach a free and informed decision

W appealed against the decision of a judge, in proceedings brought by U, to order possession of a residential property. U had provided finance to a garage partnership, of which W's husband was a partner. The loans had been secured on three business properties owned by the partnership and on the homes of the partners, including the property at issue. By her defence, W had alleged that she had been induced to execute the charge because of the undue influence of her husband and that U had been put on enquiry as to her state of knowledge or ability to reach a free and informed decision in relation to whether or not to execute the charge. The judge had found that while W's husband had committed an equitable fraud on her in terms of both undue influence and misrepresentation, she would have signed the charge of her own free will even if she had known all the relevant facts and risks.

Held, allowing the appeal in part, that it was clear that the judge had found that W had executed the charge because of the undue influence and misrepresentations of her husband. Such a fraud had deprived W of the opportunity of making a free and informed choice; the fact that W had not had the opportunity to make a free and informed choice founded her equity, as against her husband, to set aside the transaction, *CIBC Mortgages Plc v. Pitt* [1994] 1 A.C. 200, [1994] C.L.Y. 3293 applied. Furthermore, in the instant case the undue influence had included fraudulent misrepresentation. W had been told lies in order to induce her to execute the charge; those lies had been "material and successful" in that W had been induced to act to her detriment in executing the charge, *Royal Bank of Scotland Plc v. Etridge (No.2)* [2001] UKHL 44, [2001] 3 W.L.R. 1021, [2001] C.L.Y. 4880 and *Downs v. Chappell* [1997] 1 W.L.R. 426, [1996] C.L.Y. 5689 considered. It was appropriate, in claims for damages for misrepresentation, to distinguish between two separate questions (1) whether the claimant had been induced to act to his detriment by the misrepresentation, and (2) if so, what loss had been suffered as a consequence. It was not relevant when considering whether a party had been induced by misrepresentation to enter into a charge that that party would have entered into the transaction anyway. In the instant case, given the finding of undue influence and misrepresentation, W was entitled to have the charge set aside.

UCB CORPORATE SERVICES LTD v. WILLIAMS; *sub nom.* WILLIAMS v. UCB CORPORATE SERVICES, [2002] EWCA Civ 555, [2002] 3 F.C.R. 448, Jonathan Parker, L.J., CA.

3841. Mortgages-undue influence-legal advice-non English speaker

A appealed against a decision of the Court of Appeal ((1999) 77 P. & C.R. D35) that she had no reasonable prospect of defending possession proceedings brought by the mortgagee, N. A, who did not speak, read or write English, had alleged in her defence to the possession proceedings that the mortgage should be avoided because of undue influence exerted by her son, the debtor, for whose benefit the mortgage had been entered into. She maintained that N had failed to advise her, in the absence of her husband and the debtor, of the amount of her potential liability and of the risks she was undertaking, and that she had not been advised to obtain independent legal advice. The Court of Appeal had applied the principles set out by Stuart-Smith, L.J. in *Royal Bank of Scotland Plc v. Etridge (No.2)* [1998] 4 All E.R. 705, [1998] C.L.Y. 4358, a decision which had subsequently been affirmed in part by the House of Lords.

Held, allowing the appeal, that it was appropriate that the case go to trial. A number of features were present that raised the issue of whether something more might be required of N before it could claim to be free of constructive notice of undue influence or of some other impropriety of the debtor, namely (1) an allegation that N had been aware that A and her husband could not speak English and were in a vulnerable position; (2) a letter from N to a firm of solicitors which had indicated that no special care was necessary when advising A and her husband and which had not stressed the importance that the couple should receive proper advice about the consequences of the proposed transaction, and (3) a letter from the solicitors to N which had not stated that A and her husband had understood what had been explained to them, *Royal Bank of Scotland Plc v. Etridge (No.2)* [2001] UKHL 44, [2001] 3 W.L.R. 1021, [2001] C.L.Y. 4880 considered. The issue of whether the solicitors were in fact acting for A or for N was a matter which ought properly to be determined at trial.

NATIONAL WESTMINSTER BANK PLC v. AMIN, [2002] UKHL 9, [2002] 1 F.L.R. 735, Lord Scott of Foscote, HL.

3842. Overriding interests-bare trusts-tenancy carved out of bare trust-meaning of "land" for purposes of Land Registration Act 1925 s.3(viii)

[Land Registration Act 1925 s.70(1)(g), s.3(viii), s.3(xxv).]

U appealed against the dismissal of its application for summary judgment in the context of proceedings in which it sought to vacate a caution registered against property subject to a charge in U's favour. The sole registered proprietor of the property, H, had granted a first charge to U in 1991. In 1997 H's wife, W, had registered a caution against the property. Both parties accepted that as at the date of the charge, H had held the property upon a bare trust for W and that she had been in receipt of weekly payments from him pursuant to a tenancy that she had granted in her capacity as beneficial owner.

Held, allowing the appeal, that W was not, as at the date of the charge, in receipt of "rents" in respect of the property for the purposes of the Land

Registration Act 1925 s.70(1)(g). A beneficial interest under a bare trust of registered land was not a registrable estate but took effect in equity as a minor interest which was capable of protection on the register by means of a caution and accordingly the interest did not constitute "land" within the meaning of s.3(viii). Rent payable under a tenancy by estoppel granted by the owner of such an interest was not "rent" "issuing out of" the land within the definition prescribed by s.3(xxv) since the expression "issuing out of" was instead intended to refer to rent payable in respect of a tenancy arising from the legal estate in the land.

UCB GROUP LTD v. HEDWORTH; *sub nom.* UCB BANK LTD v. HEDWORTH, [2002] EWCA Civ 708, [2002] 3 E.G.L.R. 76, Jonathan Parker, L.J., CA.

3843. **Overriding interests–proprietary estoppel–extent of rights accruing to managing director of company in occupation**

[Land Registration Act 1925 s.70(1)(g).]

L appealed against an order compelling him to execute a lease in favour of D. L's predecessor in title, I, orally agreed to execute a sub-lease of business premises in favour of D and subsequently allowed D's company, J, to occupy the premises. J paid for repairs to a part of the unit but the sub-lease was never executed. I later instituted possession proceedings against both D and J. Following I's death, his executors purchased the freehold title of the premises and then transferred the property to L, the parties agreeing that a deed of assignment of the possession proceedings would be executed in L's favour. L maintained that D and J were separate legal entities and thus (1) D had no claim in proprietary estoppel as material representations regarding the execution of the lease had only been made to J and, moreover, as J had paid for the repair work, D had suffered no detrimental reliance; (2) J was in actual occupation of the property and thus, D could not have acquired a personal overriding interest in accordance with the Land Registration Act 1925 s.70(1)(g), and (3) the circumstances of the case did not merit the imposition of a constructive trust.

Held, allowing the appeal, that (1) immediately prior to the transfer of the premises to L, D would have had recourse to the doctrine of proprietary estoppel as the relevant representations had been made to him personally and, in relying on those representations, he had suffered detriment as he had been deprived of the opportunity of purchasing another property and thereby enjoying the advantages of ownership, *Gillett v. Holt* [2001] Ch. 210, [2000] C.L.Y. 2321 followed; (2) however, once the transfer to L had been effected, D could only resist L's claim by demonstrating an overriding interest. D was unable to do this since he had occupied the property in his capacity as managing director of J rather than in his personal capacity, *Tunstall v. Steigmann* [1962] 2 Q.B. 593 followed, and (3) whilst the deed assigning the possession proceedings to L demonstrated that he took the property with knowledge of D's interest, L had not taken on any new obligation to give effect to D's equitable rights and hence, the special conditions for the creation of a constructive trust had not been fulfilled, *Ashburn Anstalt v. WJ Arnold & Co (No.1)* [1989] Ch. 1, [1988] C.L.Y. 2061 followed.

LLOYD v. DUGDALE, [2001] EWCA Civ 1754, [2002] 2 P. & C.R. 13, Sir Christopher Slade, CA.

3844. **Rectification–sale of land–fraudulent alteration to charges register– overriding interests–retrospective rectification**

[Land Registration Act 1925 s.70(1)(g), s.82.]

C, the purchaser of certain development land from U, appealed against a ruling that the original owner of the land, E, was entitled to retrospective rectification of the Land Charges Register pursuant to the Land Registration Act 1925 s.82. U had, by means of fraudulent conduct, secured the alteration of the register and then sold the land on to C, which had subsequently partly demolished the structure on the land. C contended that (1) the judge had erred in his conclusion that E had an overriding interest in the land pursuant to s.70(1)(g) of the 1925 Act. C maintained that the jurisdiction to rectify was entirely discretionary and that E did not have a legal or beneficial interest in the land prior to rectification merely a hope of recovering something which it had lost. C submitted that E's right to invoke s.82 in the absence of any legal interest in the land could not accordingly be regarded as a right capable of binding the land by way of an overriding interest, and (2) the court lacked jurisdiction to make a retrospective order for rectification.

Held, dismissing the appeal but varying the order to remove the retrospective effect of the rectification, that (1) if a claimant was in actual occupation of land then neither the discretionary nature of the right to seek rectification nor the concept that a claim to rectification was an overriding interest under s.82(3) precluded the existence of an overriding interest under s.70(1)(g). The fact that E had maintained fences, boarded up windows, and used the land for storage, amounted to actual occupation of the land for the purposes of s.70(1)(g), and (2) observed, obiter, that whilst it was not necessary to determine the issue in order to resolve the appeal, it was not possible to make rectification of the register retrospective, *Kingsalton Ltd v. Thames Water Developments Ltd* [2001] EWCA Civ 20, Times, February 27, 2001, [2001] C.L.Y. 4861 applied.

MALORY ENTERPRISES LTD v. CHESHIRE HOMES (UK) LTD, [2002] EWCA Civ 151, [2002] Ch. 216, Arden, L.J., CA.

3845. Remedies—negative equity—claim for refund of monies spent on home improvements by estate of cohabiting partner—no restitutionary remedy available

M formed a relationship with G. The couple agreed to sell their respective properties in order to purchase a home together. G sold her property realising a substantial capital sum but M was unable to find a purchaser for his property. The couple agreed that G and her son F would move in with M and that G would expend some of her savings on home improvements and alterations. The property market declined and G and M came to appreciate that they were in negative equity situation. Subsequently G was diagnosed with a terminal brain tumour and the relationship suffered. M left the property, and G and F also later left in order that G might be cared for by a friend during the terminal stages of her illness. After G's death, F commenced an action as her personal representative claiming an equitable interest in the property on the basis that a constructive trust existed. Before the claim reached trial, the property was sold but the proceeds failed to clear the mortgage debt of which £25,000 remained outstanding. At the trial of the action the case was presented by F on the basis of unjust enrichment rather than a constructive trust. He successfully obtained judgment in the sum of £12,370 representing the value of the improvements paid for by G prior to her death. M appealed, contending that there was no legal basis for awarding a restitutionary remedy in favour of the estate. M maintained that the monies expended were not a loan or gift to M but rather part of G's efforts towards establishing a home for herself and her son together with M to enjoy for the future. M accepted that, by investing in the property in this manner, G might well have obtained an equitable interest in the property on the basis of a constructive trust, but that such an interest could be of no possible benefit to the estate where the property had in fact been sold for less than the mortgage debt outstanding. F contended that an implied contractual agreement resulted from the arrangements for improvement to the property whereby G would either acquire a beneficial interest or the right to a refund of all monies spent on the sale of the property or alternatively at the end of the relationship whichever was to her greater benefit, *Hussey v. Palmer* [1972] 1 W.L.R. 1286, [1972] C.L.Y. 3167 relied on.

Held, allowing the appeal, that the monies expended by G were for the joint benefit of herself and M. A constructive trust establishing a beneficial interest in the property accrued as a result, and, if the property had been sold for a sum well in excess of the mortgage debt outstanding, a claim by G for a proportionate share would have been virtually impossible to contest. But where the sale had not resulted in a surfeit, it would be unconscionable for M to be required to discharge the whole of the mortgage debt outstanding without contribution from G's estate and further to repay those monies spent by G to G's estate. The principle of unjust enrichment had no application on the facts of the instant case and neither was there any basis for the suggested contractual arrangement argued for by F, *Hussey v. Palmer* distinguished.

FIRTH v. MALLENDER [2001] W.T.L.R. 1109, Jonathan Parker, J., CA.

3846. Rentcharges–freeholds–industrial units–provision of services–payments made to estate management company for the benefit of the land

[Rentcharges Act 1977 s.2(4), s.2(5).]

J appealed against a decision that a rentcharge payable to O, an estate management company, was valid. The owners of an industrial estate had transferred to O certain parts of the estate needed for the provision of services to the owners and occupiers of the units, namely, the roadways, private sewage system and a service area. In consideration of the payment of a nominal and a variable rentcharge, O had covenanted to pay all rates charged to the estate. The estate owner had transferred two units to J subject to an apportioned part of the rentcharge. Subsequently, the sewage system had broken down and O had incurred considerable expense in making alternative disposal arrangements and replacing the old system. Over the next three years O had presented certificates to J purporting to specify the variable rentcharge payable but, on each occasion, J had refused to pay. J maintained that (1) the variable rentcharge was not an "estate rentcharge" within the meaning of the Rentcharges Act 1977 s.2(4) as the payment of rates was not made "for the benefit of the land", and (2) the absence of any reasonable limitation on the variable rentcharge contravened s.2(5) of the 1977 Act.

Held, dismissing the appeal, that (1) the roadways, service area and sewage works had been transferred to O so as to enable O to carry out its obligations for the benefit of the units. The rates charged would form part of the costs incurred by O in holding areas which served to provide amenities for the units and thus, the variable rentcharge fell within s.2(4) of the Act, and (2) the variable rentcharge was measured and limited by the expense incurred by O in performing its covenants and accordingly, the absence of an express limitation of reasonableness did not render the rentcharge void.

ORCHARD TRADING ESTATE MANAGEMENT LTD v. JOHNSON SECURITY LTD; *sub nom.* JOHNSON SECURITY LTD v. ORCHARD TRADING ESTATE MANAGEMENT LTD, [2002] EWCA Civ 406, [2002] 2 E.G.L.R. 1, Peter Gibson, L.J., CA.

3847. Restrictive covenants–houses–modification–planning permission for change of use to nursing home–detrimental effect on low density housing situated in building scheme

[Law of Property Act 1925 s.84.]

A sought the modification of a restrictive covenant under the Law of Property Act 1925 s.84(a) and (aa). The covenant stipulated that the land, which formed part of a building scheme covering a residential suburb of Birmingham, could only be used for dwellinghouses with suitable outbuildings. Further, that each house had to have a minimum of a quarter of an acre of land attached and that no more than two attached houses could be built on a larger parcel. A had planning permission for change of use to a nursing home that would increase the gross floor area from 346.9 square metres to 853.96 square metres.

Held, dismissing the application, that (1) the covenant was not obsolete given that the continued character of the area was one of low density housing. The covenant therefore gave real protection to those entitled to enforce it; (2) although the contemplated change of use was reasonable, there being a need for nursing homes in the area, there was no evidence that the public interest required the siting of a nursing home on the subject land; (3) the restriction was an advantage to those living in the vicinity, since the land was part of a wider building scheme; (4) the intended change of use would have a substantial adverse impact in terms of traffic, parking, access to neighbouring properties and the unsightliness of a large extension, and (5) the proposed development would lead to substantial reductions in the value of adjoining properties for which a monetary payment would not be adequate compensation.

AZFAR'S APPLICATION, Re [2002] 1 P. & C.R. 17, NJ Rose, Lands Tr.

3848. Restrictive covenants—multiple occupation—use restricted to "single private dwelling"—letting to four students—occupation by genuine social unit for academic year

R sought to enforce a covenant not to use a neighbouring freehold property other than as a "single private dwelling". H, the owner of the property, let it to four students. The group were friends, each having their own study bedroom and sharing the lounge and dining room for communal purposes. R asserted that this use breached the covenant, as H was letting it at a profit, and that the students were not using it as a single dwelling.

Held, dismissing the claim, that (1) the covenant did not require H to reside at the property in person and it had not been breached by letting it out, and (2) the students formed a genuine social unit by their occupation of the property, whose period of occupation over an academic year was not transitory under modern conditions, even though they returned to their parental homes during vacation periods. The house was, accordingly, used as a "single private dwelling" and did not breach the covenant.

ROBERTS v. HOWLETT [2002] 1 P. & C.R. 19, Judge Langan Q.C., Ch D.

3849. Restrictive covenants—residential developments—discharge and modification of restrictive covenants—residential development with benefit of planning permission

M, a company, sought the discharge or modification of restrictive covenants to permit the redevelopment of a site currently occupied by a two storey block of flats. The redevelopment, for which planning permission had been obtained, comprised detached houses and garages and two three storey blocks of flats with car parking. The covenants, imposed by conveyances dating from 1923 and 1925, restricted development to a residential use with frontage and building line controls. Objections had been raised by eight local residents and the local authority, B. M contended that the restrictions were obsolete.

Held, granting the application, that the frontage restriction was obsolete in terms of the proposed development and its original purpose could no longer be fulfilled given the character and location of the site. The building line restriction could not be met as the frontage assumed as at the date of the conveyances could no longer be achieved. The use restriction did not refer to density or design and the proposed development matched the character of the area as it had evolved since the covenants were imposed. Compensation of £2,500 was awarded to each of the local resident objectors for personal disadvantages caused. No compensation was due to B as its rights under the covenants did not confer any practical benefit of substantial value or advantage.

MARCELLO DEVELOPMENTS LTD'S APPLICATION, Re [2002] R.V.R. 146, George Bartlett Q.C., Lands Tr.

3850. Rights of way—bridleways—burden of rebutting statutory presumption—consequence of unknown ownership

[Highways Act 1980 s.31; Wildlife and Countryside Act 1981 s.53, Sch.15 para.12.]

A made a challenge, pursuant to the Wildlife and Countryside Act 1981 Sch.15 para.12, to an assertion by the local authority that a strip of land which formed the principal route of access to his property was a public bridleway. It was common ground that A enjoyed certain vehicular rights over the strip of land. The local authority had made a modification order under s.53(2)(b) of the 1981 Act adding, if confirmed by the Secretary of State, the strip of land to the definitive map and statement and showing it as a public bridleway. An inspector had confirmed the order having found that the requirements under the Highways Act 1980 s.31 (1) for deemed dedication of a highway had been met and that there had been an "event" for the purposes of s.53(3)(b) such as to justify the modification order. A argued, inter alia, that the inspector had erred in applying s.31 (1) of the 1980 Act given that he was not the owner of the strip of land for the purposes of s.31 (7), and should also have considered whether or not the unknown owner had possessed an intention to dedicate the strip of land to public use.

Held, refusing the application, that the inspector had not been required to determine whether or not the unknown owner had intended to dedicate the strip of land to public use. The burden of rebutting the statutory presumption of dedication under s.31 (1) of the 1980 Act was on the person who needed to do so in order for his case to prevail and that burden was not removed where the owner of the land could not be identified, *Ward v. Durham CC* (1995) 70 P. & C.R. 585, [1995] C.L.Y. 4975 considered. Accordingly, it had been for A to show that the owner of the strip of land, whoever that was, had not intended to dedicate it as a public highway. He had not been able to do so and therefore the presumption had not been rebutted.

APPLEGARTH v. SECRETARY OF STATE FOR THE ENVIRONMENT, TRANSPORT AND THE REGIONS, [2001] EWHC Admin 487, [2002] 1 P. & C.R. 9, Munby, J., QBD (Admin Ct).

3851. **Rights of way—common and other land—vehicular access**

VEHICULAR ACCESS ACROSS COMMON AND OTHER LAND (ENGLAND) REGULATIONS 2002, SI 2002 1711; made under the Countryside and Rights of Way Act 2000 s.68. In force: July 4, 2002; £2.00.

These Regulations regulate the procedure to be followed by persons wishing to apply for an easement subsisting at law for the benefit of premises and giving a right of way for vehicles over common or other land. They state who is entitled to make an application, prescribe the date for the purposes of the Countryside and Rights of Way Act 2000, state the nature of an easement created and set out how to make an application for an easement and the subsequent procedure. The Regulations also provide for the Lands Tribunal to determine any matters in dispute between the applicant and the land owner except for the value of the premises; provide for the compensation sum payable to the land owner in return for the easement, to be calculated by reference to a percentage of the value of the premises; set out how, where no agreement can be reached on the value of the premises, this is determined by a chartered surveyor who is chosen by the parties or specially appointed; stipulate how the compensation sum is to be paid to the land owner or into court; and provide that the applicant shall be responsible for the costs incurred by the land owner if the application is withdrawn or abandoned.

3852. **Rights of way—prescription—acquiescence—lost modern grant**

[Prescription Act 1832 s.2, s.4.]

S brought an action claiming a right of way over a track on land owned by trustees. S had been in dispute with LC, one of the trustees, in respect of building works carried out to a cottage on land that the trustees had conveyed to S, and a further dispute had arisen between the parties in relation to land owned by S which the trustees wished to purchase. LC subsequently sent a letter to S, stating that the track across the trustees' land was closed to all members of S's household. S contended that he had a right of way over the track either by prescription or by the doctrine of lost modern grant. LC argued that S's user of the land had been no different from the user of the general public and that S's user did not give rise to the acquisition of a right of way.

Held, giving judgment for the claimant in part, that whilst S had enjoyed a right of way over the track without interruption for a period in excess of the 20 years stipulated in the Prescription Act 1832 s.2, there had been no user as of right in the year immediately prior to commencement of the instant proceedings as required by s.4 of the Act and the claim in prescription therefore failed. On the evidence it had been shown that the trustees and LC had tolerated S's user but that there had been no deliberate grant to S of a right of way. However, S's user of the land was more intensive than that of the general public because he had used the track more frequently and for vehicular access as well as for access on foot. Accordingly S had acquired a right of way over the track to the cottage by virtue of the doctrine of lost modern grant, *Dalton v. Henry Angus & Co* (1880-81) L.R. 6 App. Cas. 740 applied.

SMITH v. BRUDENELL-BRUCE [2002] 2 P. & C.R. 4, Pumfrey, J., Ch D.

3853. Rural areas–countryside access–appeals procedures–Wales

COUNTRYSIDE ACCESS (APPEALS PROCEDURES) (WALES) REGULATIONS 2002, SI 2002 1794 (W.169); made under the Countryside and Rights of Way Act 2000 s.11, s.32, s.38, s.44. In force: August 1, 2002; £6.00.

Under the Countryside and Rights of Way Act 2000, the National Assembly for Wales has the power to make regulations to provide the procedures to be followed in determining appeals brought under Part I of the Act. These Regulations will initially have effect in relation to appeals brought under s.6 of the Act which relates to appeals by persons against the showing of land, in which they have an interest, on a provisional map as open country or registered common land. The Regulations will also form the basis of the procedures in determining other appeals brought under Part I of the Act, including those under s.30 of the Act which relates to an appeal against a decision of an authority where that authority has decided not to grant an application for a direction under s.24 or s.25 of the Act or has acted otherwise than in accordance with representations made under s.27(5) of the Act.

3854. Rural areas–countryside access–local access forums

LOCAL ACCESS FORUMS (ENGLAND) REGULATIONS 2002, SI 2002 1836; made under the Countryside and Rights of Way Act 2000 s.94, s.95. In force: August 7, 2002; £2.00.

The Countryside and Rights of Way Act 2000 requires local highway authorities and National Park authorities to establish advisory bodies to be known as local access forums. The forums are required to advise about improvement of public access to land in their area for open-air recreational purposes. These Regulations make provision for the establishment and conduct of local access forums.

3855. Rural areas–countryside access–maps

ACCESS TO THE COUNTRYSIDE (PROVISIONAL AND CONCLUSIVE MAPS) (ENGLAND) REGULATIONS 2002, SI 2002 1710; made under the Countryside and Rights of Way Act 2000 s.11, s.44, s.45. In force: July 29, 2002; £6.00.

The Countryside and Rights of Way Act 2000 established a new regime for access to the Countryside under which maps prepared by the Countryside Agency will show registered common land and open country. These Regulations make provision in respect of the publication of maps issued in provisional and conclusive form. They contain provisions relating to the scale of provisional and conclusive maps, the informing of the public of the issue of such maps and of where they may be inspected, the obtaining by the public of "reduced scale maps" and for these maps to be made available by the Agency for inspection on the Internet, in local authority offices, libraries and at locations where they can be compared with registers of common land.

3856. Sale of land–rectification–transfer failing to record agreement that vendor was to retain flats

F appealed against a decision granting rectification of a transfer. F agreed to purchase from S a block of 39 flats, 37 of which were let on long leases and two of which were to be retained by S for eventual disposal on long leases at premiums. Long leases were never granted and the transfer failed to reserve any rights. On becoming aware of the omission, S sought rectification on the grounds that there had been a mistake common to the parties and that the sale had been contrary to their common intention. The trial judge ordered rectification of the transfer so as to provide for the grant to S of leases in the flats.

Held, dismissing the appeal, that the transfer did not give effect to the clear common intention of the parties. Although there had never been any common intention as to how their intentions would be effected, that did not prevent rectification in an appropriate manner.

SWAINLAND BUILDERS LTD v. FREEHOLD PROPERTIES LTD, [2002] EWCA Civ 560, [2002] 2 E.G.L.R. 71, Peter Gibson, L.J., CA.

3857. Tenancies in common–equitable interests–availability of estoppel–requirement for reliance

J appealed against an order compelling her to sell a property which she had originally bought with W and that the proceeds of sale be divided equally between J and W. W and J were unmarried and acquired the property in 1966, taking the transfer in joint names. J moved out of the house in 1971, leaving W. W emigrated to the USA in 1976 at which time J moved back into the property with the children of the relationship. In 1984 W wrote a letter stating that he wanted nothing from the house. W continued to pay the mortgage until it was redeemed in 1992. A copy of the transfer was unavailable but the Register contained an entry to the effect that no disposition was to be made by any one proprietor except with the consent of the court. W's beneficial interest claim was resisted by J who claimed estoppel and waiver based on the 1984 letter.

Held, allowing the appeal in part and dismissing the cross appeal, that at the date of purchase it appeared that the intention of the cohabiting parties was that the property should belong to them in equal shares as tenants in common, particularly given the entry in the Register which suggested separate interests. The letter did not give rise to an estoppel in the absence of reliance placed upon it nor could it be construed as an assignment of W's beneficial interest to J or the children. On these facts, the parties' subsequent conduct did not justify any equitable accounting to accommodate W's payment of mortgage payments or J's contributions to improvement of the property, *Bernard v. Josephs* [1982] Ch. 391, [1982] C.L.Y. 2675 considered. Furthermore, W could be construed to have been content that J and the children continued to reside rent free in the property, which was a complete bar to any relief against J for an occupation rent.

WRIGHT v. JOHNSON, [2001] EWCA Civ 1667, [2002] 2 P. & C.R. 15, Sir Martin Nourse, CA.

3858. Treasure–designation

TREASURE (DESIGNATION) ORDER 2002, SI 2002 2666; made under the Treasure Act 1996 s.2. In force: January 1, 2003; £1.50.

This Order extends the definition of "treasure" in the Treasure Act 1996 by designating two classes of objects as being of outstanding historical, archaeological or cultural importance. The first class of object is one of at least two base metal objects (other than coins), from the same find which are of prehistoric date. The second class of object is any object (other than a coin) of prehistoric date, any part of which is gold or silver.

3859. Books

Abbey, Robert; Richards, Mark–Blackstone's Guide to the Land Registration Act 2002. Blackstone's Guide Series. Paperback: £29.95. ISBN 0-19-925796-5. Oxford University Press.

Bell, Cedric D.–Land. 150 Leading Cases. Paperback: £11.95. ISBN 1-85836-457-4. Old Bailey Press.

Bell, Cedric D.–Real Property: Cases and Statutes. Cracknell's Companion Cases and Statutes. Paperback: £11.95. ISBN 1-85836-301-2. Old Bailey Press.

Bell, Cedric D.–Land: the Law of Real Property. Revision Workbook. Paperback: £9.95. ISBN 1-85836-376-4. Old Bailey Press.

Bray, Judith; Martin, Jacqueline; Turner, Chris–Key Facts: Land Law. Key Facts for Law. Paperback: £4.99. ISBN 0-340-84585-6. Hodder & Stoughton Educational.

Bridge, Michael–Personal Property Law. 3rd Ed. Clarendon Law Series. Paperback: £15.99. ISBN 0-19-925476-1. Oxford University Press.

Cannon, Patrick–Practical Guide to Stamp Duty and E-conveyancing. Paperback: £19.95. ISBN 0-7545-1485-4. Tolley Publishing.

Clarke, David–Commonhold-The New Law. Paperback: £35.00. ISBN 0-85308-774-1. Jordans.

Clarke, David; Wells, Andrew–Leasehold Enfranchisement. 2nd Ed. Paperback: £32.50. ISBN 0-85308-426-2. Jordans.

Clarke, Ian–Land Registration Act 2002-a Practical Guide. Paperback: £35.00. ISBN 0-421-78690-6. Sweet & Maxwell.

Clayden, Paul–Law of Allotments. 5th Ed. Paperback: £18.95. ISBN 0-7219-0143-3. Shaw & Sons.

Cockburn, David–Commercial Leases. Paperback: £40.00. ISBN 0-406-94712-0. Butterworths Law (Scotland).

Cole, Robin–Cole on Property Finance. Paperback: £125.00. ISBN 0-406-90519-3. Butterworths Law.

Dixon, Martin–Q&A Land Law. 4th Ed. Questions and Answers. Paperback: £10.95. ISBN 1-85941-627-6. Cavendish Publishing Ltd.

Dixon, Martin–Principles of Land Law. 4th Ed. Principles of Law Series. Paperback: £19.95. ISBN 1-85941-472-9. Cavendish Publishing Ltd.

Driscoll, James; Williams, Del; Boston, Charles–Handbook of Residential Tenancies. Looseleaf/ring bound: £195.00. ISBN 0-421-70310-5. Sweet & Maxwell.

Elvin, David; Karas, Jonathan–Unlawful Interference with Land-Nuisance, Trespass, Covenants and Statutes. 2nd Ed. Hardback: £145.00. ISBN 0-421-72730-6. Sweet & Maxwell.

Flushman–Demystifying Land Boundaries Adjacent to Tidal or Navigable Water: Practical Rules for Establishing the Location of Property Boundaries of Lands Adjacent to Tidal or Navigable Water Bodies. Hardback: £74.50. ISBN 0-471-40391-1. John Wiley & Sons Inc.

Goo, S.H.–Land Law. 3rd Ed. Sourcebook Series. Paperback: £32.95. ISBN 1-85941-188-6. Cavendish Publishing Ltd.

Gravells, Nigel P.–Property Law. Statutes Series. Paperback: £12.95. ISBN 0-421-78090-8. Sweet & Maxwell.

Haley, Michael–"Which?" Way to Buy, Own and Sell a Flat. Which? Consumer Guides. Paperback: £10.99. ISBN 0-85202-900-4. Which? Books.

Harpum, Charles; Bignell, Janet–Registered Land-the New Law-A Guide to the Land Registration Act 2002. Paperback: £35.00. ISBN 0-85308-759-8. Jordans.

Hewitson, Russell–Conveyancer's Yearbook 2002. Paperback: £21.00. ISBN 0-7219-1564-7. Shaw & Sons.

Ibusuki, Makoto–Transnational Cyberspace Law. Hardback: £65.00. ISBN 1-84113-163-6. Hart Publishing.

Jourdan, Stephen–Adverse Possession. Hardback: £55.00. ISBN 0-406-98251-1. Butterworths Law.

Land Lawcards. 3rd Ed. Law Cards Series. Paperback: £6.00. ISBN 1-85941-715-9. Cavendish Publishing Ltd.

Lawson, F.H.; Rudden, Bernard–Law of Property. Revised Ed. Clarendon Law Series. Paperback: £18.99. ISBN 0-19-829993-1. Oxford University Press.

Lawson, Virginia–Contracts for the Real Estate Professional. Paperback: £9.99. ISBN 0-324-15373-2. South Western College Publishing.

MacKenzie, Judith-Anne; Phillips, Mary–Textbook on Land Law. Textbook. Paperback: £19.99. ISBN 0-19-925537-7. Oxford University Press.

McAuslan, Patrick–Bringing the Law Back in. Hardback: £50.00. ISBN 0-7546-2060-3. Dartmouth.

Oakley, A.J.–Megarry's Manual of the Law of Real Property. 8th Ed. Paperback: £27.95. ISBN 0-421-71790-4. Sweet & Maxwell.

Pawlowski, Mark; Brown, James–Undue Influence and the Family Home. Hardback: £65.00. ISBN 1-85941-720-5. Cavendish Publishing Ltd.

Reynolds, Kirk; Clark, Wayne–Renewal of Business Tenancies. 2nd Ed. Hardback: £175.00. ISBN 0-421-74030-2. Sweet & Maxwell.

Rotherham, Craig–Proprietary Remedies in Context. Hardback: £35.00. ISBN 1-84113-165-2. Hart Publishing.

Scamell, E.H.–Butterworths Property Law Handbook. 5th Ed. Paperback: £49.00. ISBN 0-406-94327-3. Butterworths Law.

Scott, M.–Conveyancing Factfinder. Paperback: £11.95. ISBN 0-85308-797-0. Paperback: £11.95. ISBN 0-85308-797-0. Jordans.

Taggart, Michael–Abuse of Property Rights and Industrialisation. Oxford Studies in Modern Legal History. Hardback: £45.00. ISBN 0-19-925687-X. Oxford University Press.

Thomas, Meryl–Statutes on Property Law. Blackstone's Statutes Series. Paperback: £12.99. ISBN 0-19-925546-6. Oxford University Press.

Veale Wasbrough; J Bradford–Property Development and Investment. Paperback: £95.00. ISBN 0-406-94517-9. Butterworths Law.

Walker, Andrew–Conveyancing Lso Leading Cases. Old Bailey Press Leading Cases. Paperback: £11.95. ISBN 1-85836-421-3. Old Bailey Press.

Wasbrough, Veale–Property Development. Paperback: £95.00. ISBN 0-406-94517-9. Butterworths Law.

Webber, Gary; Dovar, Daniel–Residential Possession Proceedings. 6th Ed. Practitioner Series. Paperback: £85.00. ISBN 0-421-76410-4. Sweet & Maxwell.

RESTITUTION

3860. Books

Hedley, Steve–Law of Restitution. Butterworths Common Law Series. Hardback: £195.00. ISBN 0-406-98261-9. Butterworths Law.

Jones, Gareth–Law of Restitution. Common Law Library. Hardback: £225.00. ISBN 0-421-82820-X. Sweet & Maxwell.

SALE OF GOODS

3861. Weights and measures–EC law–relationship with domestic legislation–doctrine of implied repeal

[Weights and Measures Act 1985; Units of Measurement Regulations 1994 (SI 1994 2867); European Communities Act 1972 s.2(2); Council Directive 80/181 on the approximation of the laws of the Member States relating to units of measurement Art.1; Council Directive 80/181 on the approximation of the laws of the Member States relating to units of measurement Chapter IV; Council Directive 89/617 amending Directive 80/181 on the approximation of the laws of the Member States relating to units of measurement.]

In four appeals the issue before the court concerned the introduction in accordance with the policy of the European Union of compulsory systems of metric weights and measures. In three of the appeals the appellants had been convicted for selling produce using non metric measures. In the fourth appeal the appellant challenged the imposition of conditions on his street trading licence relating to his use of metric weights and measures. By virtue of Council Directive 80/181 Art.1, as amended by Council Directive 89/617, together with Chapter IV of the Annex, the continued use of imperial measures for trade in goods loose in bulk was only permitted until December 31, 1999. Prior to the amendment, the Weights and Measures Act 1985 had permitted the continued use of imperial and metric measures for such goods. The Units of Measurement Regulations 1994 had amended the 1985 Act so that the use of imperial measures was permitted in relation to such goods as either a primary or a supplementary indicator until January 1, 2000. However, thereafter the use of the pound as a primary indicator of weight was forbidden. The arguments before the court related to the doctrine of implied repeal and, in particular, whether the 1985 Act had impliedly repealed the European Communities Act 1972 s.2(2) to the extent that the latter empowered the provision of subordinate legislation which was inconsistent with it.

Held, dismissing the appeals, that the 1985 Act, as originally enacted, had not impliedly repealed s.2(2) of the 1972 to the extent that the latter empowered the provision of subordinate legislation which was inconsistent with it. The appropriate analysis of the relationship between EC and domestic law required regard to four propositions: (1) each specific right and obligation provided under EC law was by virtue of the 1972 Act incorporated into domestic law and took precedence. Anything within domestic law which was inconsistent with EC law was either abrogated or had to be modified so as to avoid inconsistency; (2) the 1972 Act was a constitutional statute which could not be impliedly repealed; (3) the common law recognised a category of constitutional statutes, and (4) the fundamental legal basis of the United Kingdom's relationship with the EU rested with domestic rather than European legal powers. In the instant case, since the amendments to the 1985 Act no longer permitting the use of the pound as a primary indicator had been lawful, the four appeals had to be dismissed.

THOBURN v. SUNDERLAND CITY COUNCIL; HARMAN v. CORNWALL CC; COLLINS v. SUTTON LBC; HUNT v. HACKNEY LBC; *sub nom*. THORBURN v. SUNDERLAND CITY COUNCIL, [2002] EWHC 195, [2003] Q.B. 151, Laws, L.J., QBD (Admin Ct).

3862. Books

Guest, A.G.–Benjamin's Sale of Goods. Common Law Library. Hardback: £310.00. ISBN 0-421-72950-3. Sweet & Maxwell.

Singleton, Susan; Lawson, Richard–Tolley's Sale & Purchase Agreements. Paperback: CD-ROM: £59.95. ISBN 0-7545-1948-1. Tolley Publishing.

SCIENCE

3863. Embryology–assisted reproduction–limit on number of embryos implanted–susceptibility to judicial review

A clinic, A, sought permission to seek judicial review of a decision by HFEA not to authorise the implantation of more than three embryos in a particular patient. The HFEA code of practice stipulated that no more than three embryos were to be implanted in a woman in any single fertilisation cycle. A contended that, whilst the general prescription on the numbers of embryos to be transferred was reasonable, it was nevertheless appropriate to authorise a departure from the normal rule in the case of a patient who had undergone eight previous unsuccessful attempts at in vitro fertilisation.

Held, refusing the application, that the court had no authority to intervene to quash the decision of HFEA in circumstances where careful and thorough consideration had been given to the matter and an opinion provided that was plainly rational. The subject matter under consideration formed part of a rapidly developing area of scientific knowledge and debate. It was not the function of the court to enter into scientific debate nor to adjudicate upon the merits of the decisions made by the authority or any advice that it might give. Whilst the decisions of the authority were open to judicial review, they were only amenable to such scrutiny in circumstances where the authority had either exceeded or abused its powers.

R. (ON THE APPLICATION OF ASSISTED REPRODUCTION AND GYNAECOLOGY CENTRE) v. HUMAN FERTILISATION AND EMBRYOLOGY AUTHORITY, [2002] EWCA Civ 20, [2003] 1 F.C.R. 266, Wall, J., CA.

3864. **Medical research—embryology—cell nuclear replacement organisms—meaning of "embryo"**

[Human Fertilisation and Embryology Act 1990 s.1 (1); Human Rights Act 1998.]

The Secretary of State appealed against a decision ([2001] EWHC Admin 918) that an organism created by the cloning technology known as cell nuclear replacement, CNR, fell outside the definition of "embryo" in the Human Fertilisation and Embryology Act 1990 s.1 (1). At the time when the Act had been passed, the only way known of producing an embryo was through fertilisation. Under s.1 (1) of the 1990 Act an embryo was defined as "a live human embryo where fertilisation [was] complete". The Secretary of State submitted that it was appropriate to apply a purposive construction to the definition in s.1 (1) so as to include an embryo produced by CNR.

Held, allowing the appeal, that an organism created by CNR fell within the definition of "embryo" in s.1 (1) of the 1990 Act. Having regard to the consequence of the Human Rights Act 1998 that the ambit of purposive construction should be extended where necessary, it was possible for the construction submitted by the Secretary of State to be applied if it was clear that that would be necessary in order to give effect to Parliament's intention when passing the 1990 Act. The court was required to determine whether embryos created by CNR fell within the genus of the 1990 Act and whether the clear purpose of the Act would be defeated if it was not extended to cover such embryos. It was apparent that an embryo created through CNR was of the same genus as an embryo which had been created through fertilisation. It followed that an embryo created through CNR had to fall within the ambit of the Act so as to give effect to the intention of Parliament, *Royal College of Nursing of the United Kingdom v. Department of Health and Social Security* [1981] A.C. 800, [1981] C.L.Y. 1722 considered.

R. (ON THE APPLICATION OF QUINTAVALLE) v. SECRETARY OF STATE FOR HEALTH, [2002] EWCA Civ 29, [2002] Q.B. 628, Lord Phillips of Worth Matravers, M.R., CA.

3865. Books

Cook, Trevor—Cook: Pharmaceuticals, Biotechnology and the Law. Hardback: £125.00. ISBN 0-406-91441-9. Butterworths Law.

Kayser, Valerie—Launching Space Objects: Issues of Liability and Future Prospects. Space Regulations Library Series, 1. Hardback: £91.00. ISBN 1-4020-0061-8. Kluwer Academic Publishers.

SENTENCING

3866. **Actual bodily harm—arrest—head butting police officer**

B was involved in a disturbance outside a night club. Police officers who attended found B being restrained by the door staff of the night club. He was allowed to get to his feet but when a police officer attempted to talk to him, he threatened to hit the officer. He was arrested after a short struggle and escorted to a police vehicle. As the officers attempted to place him in the vehicle he head butted the arresting officer with his forehead. The blow split the officer's lip and chipped one of his teeth. B was sentenced to nine months imprisonment and appealed.

Held, dismissing the appeal, that a sentence of nine months' imprisonment following a guilty plea to assault occasioning actual bodily harm, was not excessive.

R. v. BROYD (MICHAEL PAUL), [2001] EWCA Crim 1437, [2002] 1 Cr. App. R. (S.) 47, Butterfield, J., CA (Crim Div).

3867. Actual bodily harm−nurses−assault by patient

E appealed against a sentence of 21 months' imprisonment for assault occasioning actual bodily harm on a nurse. E had been taken to hospital after being found beaten up and drunk. After an initial examination it was considered advisable for him to have an ECG test. When a nurse asked him to turn on to his back so that the test could take place, he grabbed the nurse's finger and squeezed it tightly. He pulled her finger back sharply, causing her pain. He then let go. The nurse's finger was X-rayed; it was found to be swollen with torn ligaments. The nurse was off work for several months and it was thought that she may require surgery. E contended that the sentence was manifestly excessive.

Held, allowing the appeal, that the need to pass a severe sentence for this type of offence was obvious. Nurses were particularly vulnerable; if drunks assaulted staff in hospitals, leniency was not appropriate. The offence caused a considerable measure of suffering and distress and serious injury. In the court's view, the starting point after a trial would have been between 21 and 24 months' imprisonment. Giving E's credit for a timely plea of guilty, the court substituted a sentence of 15 months' imprisonment.

R. v. EASTWOOD (JOHN), [2002] EWCA Crim 155, [2002] 2 Cr. App. R. (S.) 72, Mitchell, J., CA (Crim Div).

3868. Actual bodily harm−prison officers−sustained assault on prisoner−breach of trust−custodial sentence

Three prison officers appealed against the sentences imposed following their conviction for assaulting a prisoner. N, the senior officer, had been sentenced to four years' imprisonment; L, whom the judge had found to be the ringleader, had also been sentenced to four years' imprisonment; F had been sentenced to three years and six months. The officers had punched and kicked the prisoner during a sustained assault which had taken place in the segregation unit. The officers had subsequently made false complaints against the prisoner alleging that he had committed an assault and that they had been required to take action to restrain him. As a result of the complaints, the prisoner had been sentenced to seven days' solitary confinement, had lost 28 days of remission and had been marked on the papers as a prisoner who was violent to prison officers. The trial of the officers had taken place three years after the events giving rise to the complaint.

Held, dismissing the appeals, that the injuries suffered by the prisoner had not been slight. Whilst the nature of the assault could have been much worse, it had been sustained and repeated after an interval, and the officers had attempted to escape the consequences of their actions, the sentences imposed were entirely justified. A prison officer who assaulted a prisoner committed a breach of trust both against the prisoner and against society itself. Such a breach of trust resulted in damage to the fabric of the prison system, the proper administration of justice, to the needs of prisoners, and to the confidence of individuals in the social role of the prison system.

R. v. FRYER (DARREN); R. v. NICHOL (JOHN); R. v. LAWRIE (ROBERT ANDREW), [2002] EWCA Crim 825, [2002] 2 Cr. App. R. (S.) 122, Newman, J., CA (Crim Div).

3869. Actual bodily harm—unlawful wounding—sentence length—extended sentences—protection of public—reviewability of determinate sentences

[Criminal Justice Act 1991 s.2(2)(b); Human Rights Act 1998 Sch.1 Part I Art.5(4); Powers of Criminal Courts (Sentencing) Act 2000 s.80(2)(b).]

The Secretary of State appealed against a declaration ([2001] EWHC Admin 834, [2002] 1 W.L.R. 654) that G's continuing period of detention was subject to the Human Rights Act 1998 Sch.1 Part I Art.5(4) and therefore reviewable periodically to determine whether the continued detention remained necessary to protect the public from serious harm. G had pleaded guilty to unlawful wounding and to assault occasioning actual bodily harm and had been sentenced to a total of seven years expressly imposed under the Criminal Justice Act 1991 s.2(2)(b), now the Powers of Criminal Courts (Sentencing) Act 2000 s.80(2)(b), although the judge had not indicated what sentence he would have otherwise imposed. The Secretary of State contended that determinate sentences could not exceed the statutory maximum and were justified for the purposes of Art.5(4) by the sentencing judge's decision. The Secretary of State submitted that in the case of a determinate sentence a court did not hand over to the executive the decision as to the timing of an offender's release.

Held, allowing the appeal, that the lower court's declaration was set aside. A sentence imposed under the Criminal Justice Act 1991 s.2(2)(b) was determinate and the product of a judicial decision, every part of which was subject to appeal. Therefore the supervision required by Art.5(4) was incorporated in the decision, *De Wilde v. Belgium (No.1) (A/12)* (1979-80) 1 E.H.R.R. 373 applied, and a sentence was not intended to be reviewed outside the appeal process. A sentence could not exceed the statutory maximum for the index offence. A sentencing judge was not handing over to the executive the decision as to the timing of an offender's release when imposing such a longer sentence, but rather was precisely fixing a period that he considered necessary to protect the public from serious harm from an offender even though the risk to the public could fluctuate over time.

R. (ON THE APPLICATION OF GILES) v. PAROLE BOARD, [2002] EWCA Civ 951, [2003] 2 W.L.R. 196, Kennedy, L.J., CA.

3870. Aggravated burglary—dwelling house—elderly victim threatened—unduly lenient sentence

[Criminal Justice Act 1988 s.36.]

The Attorney General referred as unduly lenient under the Criminal Justice Act 1988 s.36 a sentence of three years and six months' imprisonment for aggravated dwelling house burglary. The offence had been committed at night against a 72 year old victim who was threatened with a knife. The offender had pleaded guilty in response to scientific evidence which placed him at the scene.

Held, allowing the reference, that considering the aggravating features including the emotional effect of the offence on the victim, the use of the knife, the offender's previous convictions and the probation order which had been in place at the time, a sentence of no less than six years' imprisonment would have been appropriate at first instance. However, in view of the element of double jeopardy, a sentence of four years and six months' imprisonment was substituted, *Attorney General's Reference (Nos.19 and 20 of 1990), Re* (1990) 12 Cr. App. R. (S.) 490, [1991] C.L.Y. 1027, *R. v. Brewster (Alex Edward)* [1998] 1 Cr. App. R. 220, [1997] C.L.Y. 1423 and *R. v. Brady (Derek)* [2000] 1 Cr. App. R. (S.) 410, [2000] C.L.Y. 1149 considered.

ATTORNEY GENERAL'S REFERENCE (NO.35 OF 2001), *Re; sub nom.* R. v. GIRT (STUART BARRY), [2001] EWCA Crim 1271, [2002] 1 Cr. App. R. (S.) 44, Mantell, L.J., CA (Crim Div).

3871. Aggravated burglary–dwelling house–knives–victim attacked in own home by gang–undue leniency

The Attorney General referred to the court as unduly lenient sentences of 30 months' imprisonment for aggravated burglary imposed on P, J and M. Following a dispute between S, the brother of P and J, and W, the three, along with at least one other person, had gone to W's girlfriend's parents' house armed with knives and an axe. Although W was not there, the girlfriend's father was attacked. He suffered injuries to his face, chest, right forearm and right hand which required stitching. Following positive identification evidence, P, J and M entered guilty pleas on the basis of the Crown's case against them and the judge below had sentenced them by treating their role in the offence by reference to the lesser part played by M in the attack.

Held, allowing the reference, that the judge below had misdirected himself as to the correct basis for the sentence. Although he been correct to consider the respective ages of P, J and M and the fact that this was their first custodial sentence, by treating them on the basis of M's part in the attack, he had passed sentences that were unduly lenient. Taking into account the element of double jeopardy involved, along with the positive response each had shown to their custodial sentence, a sentence of four years' imprisonment was substituted.

ATTORNEY GENERAL'S REFERENCE (NOS.144, 145 AND 146 OF 2001), *Re*; *sub nom.* R. v. POTTS (PETER); R. v. POTTS (JAMES WILLIAM); R. v. McPHAIL (TERENCE ANTHONY), [2002] EWCA Crim 708, [2002] 2 Cr. App. R. (S.) 108, Judge, L.J., CA (Crim Div).

3872. Aggravated burglary–dwelling house–violence–victims tied up and attacked with crowbar–effect on victims–undue leniency

The Attorney General referred to the court as unduly lenient a sentence of three years' imprisonment imposed on B following his conviction for aggravated burglary. B had entered the victims' home while they were asleep in the early hours of the morning, tied up the victims, attacked one of them with a crowbar and had taken money from the safe. The aggravating features identified by the Attorney General were that B had entered the premises while the victims were asleep, had threatened and used violence and had tied the victims up. B had a number of previous convictions. In mitigation, B had eventually confessed to the police, pleaded guilty at the first opportunity, and had shown what appeared to be genuine remorse.

Held, allowing the reference, that the sentence was unduly lenient. This was a very serious offence which had involved a deeply traumatic and distressing experience for the victims and had lasting impact on them. Taking into account double jeopardy and the fact that B would become a long term prisoner, a sentence of six years' imprisonment was substituted.

ATTORNEY GENERAL'S REFERENCE (NO.5 OF 2002), *Re*; *sub nom.* R. v. BRIODY (PAUL JOHN) [2002] EWCA Crim 1510, Judge, L.J., CA (Crim Div).

3873. Aggravated burglary–firearms offences–use of imitation firearm to rob service station–undue leniency

The Attorney General referred as unduly lenient a sentence of two years and sixth months' detention imposed upon K following his conviction for aggravated burglary and use of an imitation firearm with intent to resist arrest. K had broken into a service station and had stolen cash, phone cards and stamps. Upon being confronted by a police officer K had fired a replica revolver and a chase ensued. K was eventually arrested and the revolver found to contain five blank firing cartridge cases, three of which had been fired. The Attorney General contended that the offence was aggravated by the fact that the offences had been planned over a considerable period. The service station was vulnerable as small business premises and K had worked in the service station and had made use of his knowledge of the work practices there in order to commit the offences K had taken a loaded blank firing pistol in order to assist his escape and he had fired the pistol at the police three times and had repeatedly pointed it at the police. Further, K had been equipped with gloves, a balaclava and dark clothing.

Held, allowing the reference, that whilst the gun used was not capable of inflicting any physical injury it did have blank cartridges in it, the noise of which would have necessarily have resulted in greater alarm than that which would have resulted from the use of a gun with no blanks in it. The use of the gun to frighten had obviously been anticipated in the planning of the offence and it had been fired more than once and used persistently during the chase. The intention behind K's possession and use of the firearm had clearly been to resist arrest and further the commission of a serious criminal offence. At first instance on a guilty plea a sentence of five years detention would have been merited. Having regard to the element of double jeopardy a sentence of four years' detention was substituted, *R. v. Avis (Tony)* [1998] 1 Cr. App. R. 420, [1998] C.L.Y. 1214 applied.

ATTORNEY GENERAL'S REFERENCE (NO.120 OF 2001), *Re; sub nom.* R. v. KUCZYNSKI (TOMEK) [2002] EWCA Crim 368, Kay, L.J., CA (Crim Div).

3874. Aggravated burglary–weapons–threats against elderly occupant–early guilty plea–remorse at scene of offence

H appealed against a seven year sentence of imprisonment imposed for aggravated burglary. H had forced his way into the home of a 61 year old man armed with a knife. The occupant, who cared for his 93 year old bedridden mother at the premises, was pushed by H causing him to break a window with his elbow. No injuries were sustained. The occupant was forced to hand over money by H, who was thereafter detained at the scene by a neighbour hearing the disturbance. H contended that the sentence was excessive and that the circumstances of the offence were mitigated by the facts that (1) he had pleaded guilty at the earliest opportunity; (2) he had demonstrated remorse at the scene before being detained and thereafter; (3) the offence had not been planned, and (4) although used to threaten, the knife had been taken with the aim of opening windows and no injuries had been sustained.

Held, allowing the appeal, that having regard to the circumstances surrounding the offence the appropriate sentence was five years' imprisonment.

R. v. HARRISON (SIMON), [2001] EWCA Crim 2117, [2002] 1 Cr. App. R. (S.) 107, Nelson, J., CA (Crim Div).

3875. Arson–community rehabilitation orders–fire started by husband in matrimonial home–undue leniency

The Attorney General referred as unduly lenient a three year community rehabilitation order for two counts of arson being reckless as to endangering life. H, a 46 year old male, was convicted after setting fire to his terraced house while he, his wife and daughter were inside. The marriage was in difficulties and there had recently been domestic violence. The following aggravating features were among those relied on by the Attorney General: H had started the fire in three places, one being outside the room where his wife and daughter were hiding thus blocking their only means of escape and forcing them to jump from the window; the two of them had suffered injuries jumping out of the window; those who had entered the house attempting to rescue the occupants had been put in danger; the fire had been started at night and the smoke alarm had been tampered with; the fire could have harmed the occupants of the neighbouring terraced property, and H had made no attempt to extinguish the fire or to unlock the front door to enable others to do so. In mitigation it was said that H was of good character and that he was suffering from ill health.

Held, allowing the reference, that the trial judge had overemphasised H's medical condition. Furthermore, the fact that H had served seven months' imprisonment was not a sufficient reason for deciding against the imposition of a custodial sentence. Despite H's good character, he had continued to deny all responsibility for starting the fire. The appropriate starting point was at least six years' imprisonment but, in the circumstances and taking double jeopardy into account, four years' imprisonment was substituted for the community rehabilitation order, *Attorney General's Reference (No.1 of 1997), Re* [1998] 1 Cr. App. R. (S.) 54, [1997] C.L.Y. 1402 considered.

ATTORNEY GENERAL'S REFERENCE (NO.98 OF 2001), *Re; sub nom.* R. v. HUSSAIN (MANZOOR), [2001] EWCA Crim 3068, [2002] 2 Cr. App. R. (S.) 25, Mance, L.J., CA (Crim Div).

3876. Arson—extended sentences—offender setting fire to property when intoxicated

[Powers of Criminal Courts (Sentencing) Act 2000 s.80(2)(b).]

J appealed against a total sentence of nine years' imprisonment imposed for arson, offences which were committed whilst under the influence of alcohol. The sentences comprised two concurrent sentences of three years' imprisonment and an extended sentence of six years' imprisonment imposed under the Powers of Criminal Courts (Sentencing) Act 2000 s.80(2)(b). J contended that whilst three years' imprisonment and an extended sentence was justified, the length of the extended sentence was excessive.

Held, allowing the appeal, that given that the offences had involved items of property such as cars, sheds and garages and not household or occupied premises, the extended sentence was excessive and was reduced to three years, making a total sentence of six years' imprisonment.

R. v. JONES (DONAN LANGFORD), [2001] EWCA Crim 1524, [2002] 1 Cr. App. R. (S.) 52, Sir Richard Tucker, CA (Crim Div).

3877. Arson—mental health—extended sentences—imposition in view of criminal record and risk of re offending

[Powers of Criminal Courts (Sentencing) Act 2000 s.80(2)(b).]

F appealed against a sentence of ten years' imprisonment imposed following his guilty plea to an offence of arson being reckless as to whether life was endangered. Despite F's assertions that the act had been prompted by a mental disorder, a pre sentence report had not recommended the imposition of a hospital order but had stated that there was a high risk of reoffending, particularly owing to the fact that F had previously served a custodial sentence for a like offence.

Held, dismissing the appeal, that whilst ten years' imprisonment was excessive and thus not commensurate with the gravity of the offence, in order to protect the public, it was appropriate for the court to exercise its powers under the Powers of Criminal Courts (Sentencing) Act 2000 s.80(2)(b) to impose a longer than normal sentence. In such circumstances, ten years was an appropriate term.

R. v. FIRTH (JOHN), [2001] EWCA Crim 1570, [2002] 1 Cr. App. R. (S.) 73, Jack, J., CA (Crim Div).

3878. Arson—recklessness—offender with learning disabilities—no risk to others

T appealed against a sentence of life imprisonment, with a recommendation that he serve a minimum of two years in custody, imposed on conviction following a guilty plea to a count of arson being reckless as to whether life was endangered. T, who was of previous good character and suffered from learning disabilities, had thrown petrol over a police officer who had forced entry into T's maisonette following a disturbance. T lit the petrol, but the officer escaped injury. Although the expert providing the psychiatric report initially recommended that T should be admitted to hospital for assessment as to his suitability for a probation order with a treatment condition, both the expert and the probation officer who prepared T's pre sentence report stated that his non cooperation and marked antipathy towards the wider community meant that a custodial sentence was inevitable.

Held, allowing the appeal, that although the offence had had potentially serious consequences, T's actions had been reckless, as opposed to intentional. He was of previous good character and the offence had been caused by his sense of social isolation, not by his mental instability. He had not, therefore, posed a risk to other persons following the offence for which he had been sentenced so that a life sentence was not justified, *R. v. Hodgson (Rowland Jack)* (1968) 52 Cr. App. R. 113, [1968] C.L.Y. 848 and *R. v. Chapman (Jamie Lee)* [2000] 1 Cr. App. R. 77, [1999] C.L.Y. 1250 applied and *Attorney General's Reference (No.32 of 1996), Re* [1997] 1 Cr. App. R. (S.) 261, [1996] C.L.Y. 1912 considered. The life sentence was quashed and replaced by a term of four years' imprisonment to reflect the period that T had already served prior to his release on licence.

R. v. TROWBRIDGE (GEORGE), [2001] EWCA Crim 2984, [2002] 2 Cr. App. R. (S.) 38, Leveson, J., CA (Crim Div).

3879. Assault—robbery—intention—gratuitous violence and use of bottle as weapon—undue leniency

The Attorney General referred to the court as unduly lenient a sentence of two years' detention in a young offender institution imposed on M following his convictions for assault with intent to rob, to run concurrently with a three month term for attempting to pervert the course of justice. M had entered the canteen area of a supermarket and attacked a female employee with a glass bottle, attempting to pull out of her grasp the till contents that she was checking. He gave a false name and date of birth following his arrest and continued to maintain the false identity. The aggravating features identified by the Attorney General were that this was an unprovoked attack involving gratuitous violence and the use of a weapon. The victim sustained significant injuries and suffered lasting detriment. The mitigating features were M's youth, being aged 18 at the date of the offence, and his guilty plea.

Held, allowing the reference, that this was a very serious offence committed against a defenceless woman. Although the offence of robbery remained uncompleted, the assault and wounding were completed offences and a dangerous weapon was used. Several blows had been struck. The offender was under the influence of drugs at the time of the attack. He had many previous convictions and could be classed as a habitual criminal. Taking into account the element of double jeopardy, the sentence for assault with intent to rob was increased from two years to four years' detention, with the sentence for attempting to pervert the course of justice running concurrently. The Court also observed that its sentencing decisions normally reflected the specific facts and circumstances of a case. Therefore, those decisions should not usually be cited by counsel in argument unless the case has been reported in an authoritative and recognised series.

ATTORNEY GENERAL'S REFERENCE (NO.17 OF 2002), *Re; sub nom.* R. v. MULHALL (LEE JAMES) [2002] EWCA Crim 1292, Judge, L.J., CA (Crim Div).

3880. Blackmail—explosives—devices mailed to supermarket

D appealed against a sentence of 14 years' imprisonment imposed following his plea of guilty to nine offences of blackmail and one offence of common assault. D had made repeated demands to a supermarket for payment of £200,000. He had sent in the post four explosive devices, one of which had exploded upon being opened. He had made threats that customers of the supermarket would received similar devices. D had pleaded guilty at the first opportunity.

Held, allowing the appeal, that D had received a sentence that was equivalent to the maximum available for a single count of blackmail. While the offences had been serious, insufficient weight had been given to the fact that D had pleaded guilty at the first opportunity. A total sentence of 12 years was substituted, *R. v. Witchelo (Rodney Francis)* (1992) 13 Cr. App. R. (S.) 371, [1993] C.L.Y. 1020 considered.

R. v. DYER (ROBERT EDWARD), [2002] EWCA Crim 567, [2002] 2 Cr. App. R. (S.) 105, Butterfield, J., CA (Crim Div).

3881. Blackmail–letters–false assertions of homosexual activity

D, aged 52 and of previous good character, appealed against a sentence of three years' imprisonment imposed on a single count of blackmail after he had written to the victim threatening to disclose false information in the event that a specified sum of money was not paid. The threat of disclosure was made to the victim's wife and to his work colleagues and had involved accusations of sexual impropriety with other males in public lavatories. D contended that the sentence was manifestly excessive given that, according to previous authorities, the fact that the accusations were false was a mitigating feature and as such, the sentencing judge failed to give sufficient weight to that factor.

Held, allowing the appeal and reducing the sentence to two years' imprisonment, that notwithstanding the gravity of the offence and the effect on the victim, given the fact that D was being treated for depression when the offence was committed and in view of sentences passed in similar cases, a reduction in sentence was appropriate, *R. v. Christie (Paul Andrew)* (1990) 12 Cr. App. R. (S.) 540, *R. v. Smith (Jonathan David)* (1993) 14 Cr. App. R. (S.) 786, [1994] C.L.Y. 1175 and *R. v. Read (David Jonathan)* [1996] 2 Cr. App. R. (S.) 240, [1997] C.L.Y. 1409 considered.

R. v. D (JOHN WILLIAM), [2001] EWCA Crim 1843, [2002] 1 Cr. App. R. (S.) 100, Crane, J., CA (Crim Div).

3882. Burglary–criminal record–elderly victims

C was convicted of burglary. A lady who arrived home at 4.20 am one morning saw C walk up the drive of her house and found him standing in the hall. When questioned he said he was with the postman delivering a parcel. He left, having taken nothing. C was sentenced to four years' imprisonment and appealed.

Held, allowing the appeal, a sentence of four years' imprisonment for burglary was excessive and was accordingly reduced to three years.

R. v. COMER (EDWARD JOHN), [2001] EWCA Crim 1281, [2002] 1 Cr. App. R. (S.) 34, Rose, L.J., CA (Crim Div).

3883. Burglary–dwelling house–sentencing guidelines

J, aged 56, appealed against a sentence of eight years' imprisonment imposed for the burglary of a house in which property in excess of £70,000 was stolen. J, who had 20 previous convictions for like offences, was on licence when the offence was committed. He contended that the sentence was manifestly excessive.

Held, dismissing the appeal, that although the sentence was severe, it was not excessive. It was apparent that J was a professional burglar and having denied the instant offence, was not entitled to any discount for a plea of guilty. The seriousness of the offence and J's previous convictions demanded a substantial term of imprisonment notwithstanding the fact that the householder was absent and there was no ransacking, *R. v. Brewster (Alex Edward)* [1998] 1 Cr. App. R. 220, [1997] C.L.Y. 1423 applied.

R. v. JENKINS (ROGER DAVID), [2001] EWCA Crim 1181, [2002] 1 Cr. App. R. (S.) 7, Scott Baker, J., CA (Crim Div).

3884. Burglary–threatening to kill–threat to former girlfriend and parents– assaults inflicted in victims' home–undue leniency

The Attorney General referred a sentence of two and half years' imprisonment for L on the basis of undue leniency. L had been convicted on a guilty plea and sentenced to two concurrent six month terms for threatening to kill with a two year consecutive term for burglary with intent to inflict grievous bodily harm and 12 months' imprisonment concurrent for assault occasioning actual bodily harm. Following the breakdown of his relationship with a woman, A, L threatened to kill her when he saw her in a bar. Later that same evening he also telephoned A's mother and threatened to kill A. L was arrested the next day and released on bail on condition that he was not to contact A or her mother. Seven days later, however, L went to the house where A lived with her parents. He broke through the front door and struggled with A and her father. In the course of the struggle, L waved a knife in the air and inflicted injuries upon both A and her father. The Attorney General contended that the offences were aggravated by the fact that A believed that the threats made against her were genuine and L had previously used violence against A. Further the Attorney General submitted that L believed himself to possess a legitimate grievance against A as a result of the failure of their relationship, there had been an attack within a home against the occupants, and the offence of burglary had been committed whilst A was subject to a specific condition not to contact A.

Held, allowing the reference, that the consecutive sentences were correct but the total period of two and a half years was unduly lenient. Having regard to the element of double jeopardy, the two and a half year term was substituted for four years' imprisonment, comprising two 12 month concurrent terms for threatening to kill and three years' imprisonment for the burglary consecutive to the two 12 month terms but concurrent to the 12 months imposed at first instance for assault occasioning actual bodily harm, *Attorney General's Reference (No.84 of 1999), Re* [2000] 2 Cr. App. R. (S.) 213, [2000] C.L.Y. 1438, *R. v. Brown (Stephen Graham)* (1992) 13 Cr. App. R. (S.) 239, [1993] C.L.Y. 1296 and *Attorney General's Reference (No.47 of 1997), Re* [1998] 2 Cr. App. R. (S.) 68, [1998] C.L.Y. 1127 considered.

ATTORNEY GENERAL'S REFERENCE (NO.94 OF 2001), *Re*; *sub nom*. R. v. LAMBERT (RONALD PETER) [2002] EWCA Crim 95, Rose, L.J., CA (Crim Div).

3885. Carriage by air–dangerous goods–fines–act of revenge by company employee–financial penalties

[Air Navigation (Dangerous Goods) Regulations 1994 (SI 1994 3187) Reg.4 (2), Reg.6 (e).]

T, a company engaged in shipping goods by air, appealed against the imposition of a fine of £20,000 and prosecution costs of £18,000 in relation to its contravention of the Air Navigation (Dangerous Goods) Regulations 1994. T pleaded guilty to causing to be delivered for loading on an aircraft dangerous goods which it knew, or ought to have known or suspected to be, goods capable of posing a significant risk to health, safety or property when carried by air, contrary to Reg.4 (2) and consigning packages of dangerous goods for carriage by air without ensuring that the relevant documentation had been completed and signed, contrary to Reg.6 (e). T contended that the sentence was manifestly excessive owing to (1) the fact that the sole explanation for the commission of the offences was that a disgruntled employee, whose cigarette smuggling activities had been discovered, deliberately dealt with the consignment as an act of revenge; (2) the fact that T reported the employee's activities to Customs and Excise officials and cooperated with the ensuing investigation and prosecution, and (3) the potentially serious effects of the monetary penalties on T's business.

Held, allowing the appeal, that whilst the offences would normally attract substantial financial penalties, in the exceptional circumstances of the instant case, the penalty was manifestly excessive. In the circumstances, the fine was reduced to £5,000 and an order was made that the prosecution costs be taxed and not exceed £17,500.

R. v. TROPICAL EXPRESS LTD, [2001] EWCA Crim 1182, [2002] 1 Cr. App. R. (S.) 27, Kay, L.J., CA (Crim Div).

3886. Child abduction–care proceedings–appropriate sentences–requirement for deterrence

[Child Abduction Act 1984 s.2; Children Act 1989 s.49.]

JA appealed against her sentence of nine months' imprisonment imposed for aiding and abetting the unlawful detention of her daughter N, contrary to the Child Abduction Act 1984 s.2. DA, N's father, appealed against his sentence of six months' imprisonment in respect of the same offence. ET, the child's grandmother, appealed against her sentence of nine months' imprisonment imposed for conspiring to abduct N. The offences had occurred following the placement of N's brother, C, in local authority accommodation. JA and DA had suspected that C had been abused whilst in care and, following the commencement of care proceedings in respect of N, had removed her from the jurisdiction of the English courts and had then contravened a recovery order obliging N to be delivered to the home address of JA and DA. The defendants contended that there had been an abuse of process on the grounds that their offending had been equivalent to that proscribed by the Children Act 1989 s.49 for which the maximum punishment on summary conviction would have been six months' imprisonment. They also argued that given their previous good character and the fact that their behaviour had been influenced by third parties pursuing their own agenda, the sentences were manifestly excessive. Alternatively, it was argued that given the exceptional circumstances of the case, their sentences should have been suspended.

Held, dismissing the appeals, that the defendants had been properly charged under the 1984 Act. Further, the commission of such an offence or to conspire to aid and abet the offence was a grave matter, particularly when its motivation was to hinder proceedings in relation to a child. In such circumstances, taking account of the requirements to punish and deter others, custodial sentences were inevitable. In the light of those observations and having regard to the mitigation, the judge had been right not to suspend the sentences and the length of the sentences properly reflected the roles of each defendant in the offences.

R. v. JA; R. v. DA; R. v. ET, [2001] EWCA Crim 1974, [2002] 1 Cr. App. R. (S.) 108, Kay, L.J., CA (Crim Div).

3887. Child cruelty–poverty–prior warning of danger–appropriateness of custodial sentence

[Children and Young Persons Act 1933 s.1 (1) (a).]

L, aged 33, appealed against a sentence of four months' imprisonment imposed following her plea of guilty to an offence of cruelty to a child, contrary to the Children and Young Persons Act 1933 s.1 (1) (a). L had asked her seven year old son to hold the broken door of a washing machine shut. He had slipped and his arm had entered the exposed drum resulting in him sustaining multiple fractures that had required internal and external fixation. When sentencing, the judge had given consideration to the fact that the incident had been an isolated one which had arisen to a large extent from impoverishment.

Held, allowing the appeal, that whilst L had suffered greatly as a result of the offence with her children being taken into care, she had received a warning in the past from a social worker concerning the danger of allowing her son to perform such tasks. It was not always appropriate for an immediate custodial sentence to be imposed in such cases but L's non regard for the warning she had been given amounted to serious neglect and warranted an immediate custodial term. Having regard to her guilty plea and her genuine remorse it was permissible to reduce her sentence from four to three months' imprisonment.

R. v. LAUT (CAROLINE ANN), [2001] EWCA Crim 2474, [2002] 2 Cr. App. R. (S.) 7, Poole, J., CA (Crim Div).

3888. Computer crime–breach of trust–act of revenge by former employee–unauthorised access into company's websites

[Computer Misuse Act 1990 s.3(1), s.3(7).]

L appealed against a sentence of nine months' imprisonment imposed following his guilty pleas to three counts of causing unauthorised modification to the contents of a computer contrary to the Computer Misuse Act 1990 s.3(1) and s.3(7). L had been employed as a computer consultant on a short term contract by a computer company but had been dismissed, leaving him with a sense of grievance. He had subsequently gained unauthorised access, using confidential passwords, into three of the company's websites relating to three different clients and had tampered with them causing much inconvenience to the company and its clients. L argued that the mitigating features of the case had not been fully taken into account, and that further regard should have been had of the effect that a custodial sentence would have on both him and his teenage daughter.

Held, dismissing the appeal, that the sentence was not excessive. L had taken advantage of his knowledge and his skill to exact unwarranted revenge by causing work and inconvenience to the company which had amounted to a breach of trust. The custodial term reflected his criminality appropriately.

R. v. LINDESAY (VICTOR), [2001] EWCA Crim 1720, [2002] 1 Cr. App. R. (S.) 86, Judge Beaumont Q.C., CA (Crim Div).

3889. Confiscation orders–criminal conduct–qualifying offences

[Criminal Justice Act 1988 s.72AA; Criminal Justice Act 1993; Proceeds of Crime Act 1995.]

S appealed against a confiscation order of £712,645.50 imposed together with a total sentence of three years' imprisonment on his guilty pleas to possession of a document with intent to deceive, in that he had used a forged document to obtain property which was used for prostitution, and living on the earnings of prostitution. R submitted that the offence of possession of the false document could not be one of the two qualifying offences required before a confiscation order could be made under the Criminal Justice Act 1988 s.72AA because it was not a truly separate offence in that it had merely facilitated the commission of the second offence. The result was therefore that the benefit was not obtained as a result of or in connection with the commission of that offence.

Held, dismissing the appeal, that the reference to "at least two qualifying offences" in s.72AA of the 1988 Act, as amended by the Criminal Justice Act 1993 and the Proceeds of Crime Act 1995, did not mean that the respective offences had to have separate origins or be based on separate allegations. Accordingly, the decision to make the confiscation order was upheld; however the order was reduced to £692,747 as the original order had been too high.

R. v. SMITH (JOHN), [2002] EWCA Crim 2561, *The Times*, November 13, 2002, Longmore, L.J., CA (Crim Div).

3890. Confiscation orders–Newton hearings–findings of fact in relation to order inconsistent with findings at hearing

[Drug Trafficking Act 1994.]

J appealed against a confiscation order of £92,039 imposed after conviction on charges of drug offences. He had pleaded guilty at the earliest opportunity to the offences with which he was charged. His case was that he was the minder of drugs for another and that he was paid a small fee for minding the drugs. A Newton hearing was conducted by the sentencing judge, followed by an investigation for the purposes of the Drug Trafficking Act 1994. The judge reminded himself that in the Newton hearing the burden of proof lay on the prosecution. The judge found that J was a trusted participating custodian or minder of drugs which had a wholesale price of £99,000 and the he had minded other consignments for a significant amount of money. The judge then found in the proceedings under the 1994 Act that J had benefited in the sum £102,540, and made the confiscation order. J challenged the confiscation order on the grounds that the findings made to support the confiscation order were inconsistent with the facts found in the Newton hearing.

Held, allowing the appeal, that the sentencing judge did not consider whether in the light of his findings in the Newton hearing, the assumption that the drugs represented a benefit had been shown to be incorrect and therefore displaced. Had he done so, it seemed to the court that he would have found the assumption was displaced since the second finding by a logical imperative must have followed the first. In the absence of any evidence to the contrary, the inference could be drawn that the drugs had been paid for. In the instant case the sentencing judge drew the inference that J had been entrusted with the drugs in question, and it was questionable whether it was proper to draw the inference that they had been paid for. In the court's view J's submissions were well founded. The court determined the benefit received by J to be £3,475, being the sums found in bank accounts held by J and a confiscation order in that amount was substituted, *R. v. J (Drug Trafficking: Sentencing)* [2001] 1 Cr. App. R. (S.) 79, [2001] C.L.Y. 1290 considered.

R. v. JOHANNES (KARL CHRISTOPHER), [2001] EWCA Crim 2825, [2002] 2 Cr. App. R. (S.) 30, Pitchford, J., CA (Crim Div).

3891. Confiscation orders–postponement–drug trafficking–adjournments of confiscation hearings were within judge's discretion

[Drug Trafficking Act 1994 s.3.]

Z, S and H appealed against confiscation orders which had been made following their conviction of conspiracy to import Class A drugs. The hearings at which the confiscation orders were made had been adjourned under the Drug Trafficking Act 1994 s.3 on several occasions, mostly at the behest of counsel, but one adjournment had been instigated by the judge and it was submitted that the judge should have provided the parties with an opportunity to be heard.

Held, dismissing the appeals, that the hearings had been properly postponed beyond the six month period under s.3 of the Act, and no purpose would have been served by permitting the parties to be heard in respect of the judge's adjournment in view of the particular circumstances which had compelled him to take that course of action. The judge had acted completely within his jurisdiction, *R. v. Shevki (Lutfiyf)* [2001] 2 Cr. App. R. (S.) 40, [2001] C.L.Y. 1242 considered.

R. v. ZELZELE (BEHCET); R. v. SLOWEY (PETER); R. v. HALIL (GURSEL), [2001] EWCA Crim 1763, [2002] 1 Cr. App. R. (S.) 62, Tomlinson, J, CA (Crim Div).

3892. Confiscation orders–postponement–drug trafficking–postponement of hearing–validity of extension beyond six months after date of conviction

[Drug Trafficking Act 1994 s.3(1), s.3(3); Human Rights Act 1998 Sch.1 Part I Art.6.]

J appealed against a confiscation order made on April 9, 2001 in the sum of £56,168.03 imposed following his conviction on July 14, 2000 for conspiracy to supply class A drugs, in respect of which he was also sentenced to 11 years' imprisonment. The confiscation order hearing was postponed a number of times under the Drug Trafficking Act 1994 s.3(1), and eventually until March 5, 2001, to await decisions in *HM Advocate v. McIntosh (Robert) (No.1)* [2001] UKPC D1, [2001] 3 W.L.R. 107, [2001] C.L.Y. 6327 and *R. v. Benjafield (Karl Robert) (Confiscation Order)* [2001] 3 W.L.R. 75, [2001] C.L.Y. 1237, which were expected to address the issue of whether the assumptions and reverse burden of proof provided for in the 1994 Act complied with the Human Rights Act 1998 Sch.1 Part I Art.6. That postponement was made on the basis that it amounted to an exceptional circumstance within the meaning of s.3(3) of the 1994 Act. J contended that the judge had no power to postpone the hearing to a date beyond the statutory six month period after his conviction, submitting that (1) the term "further information" in s.3(1) was restricted to financial and not legal matters; (2) the court's duty was to apply the law as it then stood, and (3) a potential development in the law could not amount to exceptional circumstances.

Held, allowing the appeal in part, that in the circumstances the judge was entitled to hold that the content of the expected judgments was capable of constituting further information which she would require and could therefore amount to exceptional circumstances. Only J could benefit from a postponement, which was expected to be for only a short period, and there was a real prospect that the hearing might be wasted if the case was heard before the decisions were available. The purpose of the provision was to enable a hearing to be postponed in circumstances where this was desirable to reach a fair conclusion on the confiscation issue. The judge's exercise of her power under s.3 of the 1994 Act was therefore valid. However, the appropriate term of imprisonment to be imposed in default of payment was 18 months, rather than two years, consecutive to the sentence of 11 years.

R. v. JAGDEV (MENOHAR SINGH); R. v. DHILLON (JHALMAL), [2002] EWCA Crim 1326, [2002] 1 W.L.R. 3017, Hedley, J., CA (Crim Div).

3893. Confiscation orders–postponement–exceptional circumstances–postponement beyond six months from date of conviction

[Customs and Excise Management Act 1979 s.170(2).]

C, appealed against a confiscation order imposed after his conviction for conspiring to contravene the Customs and Excise Management Act 1979 s.170(2). C was involved in an alcohol diversion fraud. He was convicted in October 1998, and was sentenced on October 30, 1998 to three years' imprisonment; confiscation proceedings were postponed for a period of four months. In February 1999, on or about the date to which the confiscation proceedings were postponed, they were adjourned administratively without a court hearing until March 19, 1999. On March 19, 1999, the judge who had tried C and sentenced him was not available due to illness, and the matter came before another judge. The confiscation application was then adjourned to a date in June 1999, which was more than six months after the relevant conviction. The case was again listed in June 1999 before the original judge who had by then recovered from illness. The matter was further adjourned until September 1999 when a further application for an adjournment was granted. The confiscation order was eventually made in December 1999, 14 months after the conviction. C challenged the confiscation order on the ground that the proceedings had been unlawfully adjourned on March 19, 1999. It was submitted that the judge who adjourned the matter on March 19, 1999 did not address his mind to the provisions of the Act relating to the necessity for exceptional circumstances for postponing a confiscation inquiry beyond the six month time limit.

Held, dismissing the appeal, that where a sentencing judge postponed confiscation proceedings for a period more than six months from the date of conviction, it was not essential for him to refer expressly to "exceptional circumstances" so long as a real judicial decision was made on good grounds and those grounds were capable of and did amount to "exceptional circumstances". The complication of the instant case and the illness of the trial judge were matters capable of amounting to "exceptional circumstances". The three factors combined, the consent of C, the complexity of the case and the illness of the trial judge, justified the second judge's decision to postpone the matter beyond the six month period. Accordingly, the confiscation order was lawful, *R. v. Shergill (Sukdev Singh)* [1999] 1 W.L.R. 1944, [1999] C.L.Y. 1106 considered.

R. v. CHUNI (NARINDER NATH), [2002] EWCA Crim 453, [2002] 2 Cr. App. R. (S.) 82, Gibbs, J., CA (Crim Div).

3894. Confiscation orders–postponement–failure to specify period of postponement–lawfulness of subsequent order

[Drug Trafficking Act 1994 s.3(1).]

P appealed against a confiscation order imposed following his conviction on guilty pleas to being concerned in the supply of cannabis and possession of cannabis. The making of the order had been postponed by the judge in order for information to be gathered under the Drug Trafficking Act 1994 s.3(1). P submitted that the judge had not had the power to make the order following the postponement given that he had failed to comply with the statutory procedure under s.3(1) stating that if the Crown Court decided to postpone a determination it must specify the period of postponement.

Held, allowing the appeal, that the failure of the judge to specify the period of postponement of the determination rendered the order unlawful. There was a conflict of authority on the interpretation of s.3(1), which centred on the use of the word "may" in "...postpone making the determination for such a period as it [the court] may specify". The use of "may" was not to be interpreted as meaning that the court had a choice as to whether or not it specified the period of postponement, but rather that the court had a discretion as to the length of the postponement, the maximum being six months, *R. v. Davies (Steven)* [2001] EWCA Crim 2902, [2002] 1 W.L.R. 1806 applied and *R. v. Copeland (Alphonso)* [2002] EWCA Crim 736, [2002] Crim. L.R. 507 not followed. The penal nature of the 1994 Act justified such a strict interpretation of s.3 and indicated why Parliament considered it necessary that the period of postponement be specified.

R. v. PISCIOTTO (FRANK), [2002] EWCA Crim 1592, [2003] 1 Cr. App. R. 4, Keene, L.J., CA (Crim Div).

3895. Confiscation orders—procedure—correct approach where defendant could have been convicted on alternative bases

[Criminal Justice Act 1988 Part VI, s.71, s.72(5)(b).]

T, who had been convicted of corruptly giving a bribe to a council employee, appealed against a costs order made against him. He also sought leave to appeal against a confiscation order which had been made after his conviction. T argued that the judge had erred by (1) making the costs order before the confiscation order, and (2) failing, when making the confiscation order, to approach the case on the basis of the more favourable of the two factual bases on which the jury could have convicted him.

Held, quashing the order for costs but refusing the application for leave to appeal against the confiscation order, that (1) since the Criminal Justice Act 1988 s.72(5)(b) required the court to take account of the confiscation order itself before "making any order involving any payment by him", the judge had erred in making the order for costs before the confiscation order, and (2) when making a confiscation order, the judge was not obliged to proceed on the basis of the version of the facts put before the jury which most favoured the defendant. The determinations which the court had to make under s.71(1A), (1B) and (6) of the Act, namely whether the defendant had benefited from criminal conduct, the amount of that benefit and the amount that might be realised at the time of making the order, were to be made, in the case of the Crown Court, by the trial judge, not by the jury. Those determinations were separate from the trial process, a fact emphasised by s.71(7A), which provided that the standard of proof required to determine questions arising under Part VI of the Act was the civil standard. In the instant case, the judge had made the relevant determinations and had not been obliged to consider the factual basis on which T had been convicted.

R. v. THREAPLETON (MICHAEL) (COSTS: CONFISCATION ORDER), [2001] EWCA Crim 2892, [2002] 2 Cr. App. R. (S.) 46, Stanley Burnton, J., CA (Crim Div).

3896. Confiscation orders—right to fair trial—burden of proof—removal of presumption of innocence

[Criminal Justice Act 1988 Part IV, s.71; Human Rights Act 1998 Sch.1 Part I Art.6, Part II Art.1.]

R, who had pleaded guilty to two counts of theft and against whom a confiscation order had been made, appealed against the decision of the Court of Appeal ([2001] 3 W.L.R. 75) that the making of a confiscation order under the provisions of the Criminal Justice Act 1988 was not incompatible with the right to fair trial under Human Rights Act 1998 Sch.1 Part I Art.6 or the right to peaceful enjoyment of possessions under Sch.1 Part II Art.1 of the 1998 Act. R's trial had been concluded before the 1998 Act had come into force and therefore following the decision of the House of Lords in *R. v. Kansal (Yash Pal) (Change of Law)* [2001] UKHL 62, [2001] 3 W.L.R. 1562, [2002] 1 C.L. 110 that the 1998 Act was not relevant to such cases, R's Convention rights were deemed not to have been engaged. Nevertheless, due to the importance of the issues, the House considered, inter alia, the question of whether a person against whom a confiscation order was sought under s.71 of the 1988 Act was charged with a criminal offence for the purposes of Art.6(2) of the Convention.

Held, dismissing the appeal, that confiscation proceedings formed part of the sentencing process that followed a conviction and accordingly did not amount to a further criminal charge, *HM Advocate v. McIntosh (Sentencing)* [2001] UKPC D1, [2001] 3 W.L.R. 107, [2001] C.L.Y. 6327 applied. Further, it was apparent that Part IV of the 1988 Act was a proportionate response to the problem which it aimed to address, namely depriving offenders of the proceeds of their criminal conduct, *Phillips v. United Kingdom (41087/98)* 11 B.H.R.C. 280, [2001] C.L.Y. 3537 applied. Given such a conclusion, it followed that the interference with the property rights provided under Sch.1 Part II Art.1 of the 1998 Act was justified. *Kansal* applied.

R. v. REZVI (SYED), [2002] UKHL1, [2002] 2 W.L.R. 235, Lord Steyn, HL.

3897. Confiscation orders–right to fair trial–compatibility of confiscation legislation with European Convention on Human Rights

[Drug Trafficking Act 1994 s.2, s.4; Human Rights Act 1998 Sch.1 Part I Art.6.]

B, who had pleaded guilty to conspiring to supply Class A and B drugs and against whom a confiscation order had been made, appealed against the decision of the Court of Appeal ([2001] 3 W.L.R. 75) that the making of a confiscation order under the Drug Trafficking Act 1994 s.2 was not incompatible with the right to fair trial under the Human Rights Act 1998 Sch.1 Part I Art.6. B's trial had been concluded before the 1998 Act had come into force and therefore following the decision of the House of Lords in *R. v. Kansal (Yash Pal) (Change of Law)* [2001] UKHL 62, [2001] 3 W.L.R. 1562, [2002] 1 C.L. 110 that the 1998 Act was not relevant to such cases, B's Convention rights were deemed not to have been engaged. Nevertheless, due to the importance of the issues, the House considered, inter alia, the question of whether a person against whom a confiscation order was sought under s.4 of the 1994 Act was charged with a criminal offence for the purposes of Art.6(2) of the Convention.

Held, dismissing the appeal, that confiscation proceedings formed part of the sentencing process that followed a conviction and accordingly did not amount to a further criminal charge, *HM Advocate v. McIntosh (Sentencing)* [2001] UKPC D1, [2001] 3 W.L.R. 107, [2001] C.L.Y. 6327 applied. Given the public interest objective of the 1994 Act and that the legislative measures were rationally connected with the furtherance of such an objective, the procedure that had been adopted by Parliament was a fair and proportionate response to the necessity of protecting the public interest. It was the responsibility of the trial judge to avoid injustice when determining whether to impose a confiscation order; where there was a risk of injustice, a confiscation order should not be made. *Kansal* applied.

R. v. BENJAFIELD (KARL ROBERT) (CONFISCATION ORDER), [2002] UKHL 2, [2002] 2 W.L.R. 235, Lord Steyn, HL.

3898. Confiscation orders–smuggling–evasion of duty on cigarettes–forfeiture before disposal–existence of derivation of benefit

[Customs and Excise Management Act 1979 s.170(2); Criminal Justice Act 1988 s.71, s.74.]

The Crown appealed against a decision allowing S's appeal ([2001] 1 Cr. App. R. (S.) 61, [2000] C.L.Y. 1162) against a confiscation order imposed following his conviction for the fraudulent evasion of excise duty contrary to the Customs and Excise Management Act 1979 s.170(2). S had smuggled cigarettes past customs posts at the mouth of a river only to be stopped further up the river before he had had the opportunity of disposing of the cigarettes. He had been sentenced on the basis that by evading payment of the duty he had obtained a pecuniary advantage for the purposes of the Criminal Justice Act 1988 s.71. S contended that he had not derived a benefit under s.74 of the Act since the cigarettes had been forfeited before he had realised their value.

Held, allowing the appeal, that the confiscation order had been properly imposed. S had derived a pecuniary advantage by evading the payment of duty at the customs posts, notwithstanding that the cigarettes had been forfeited before their disposal. The evasion of a debt fell within the scope of the ordinary meaning of deriving a "pecuniary advantage". In determining the measure of the benefit derived by the offender, the court was required by s.74(5) and s.74(6) of the 1988 Act to consider simply the value of the property at the time it was obtained. What happened to the property thereafter was irrelevant.

R. v. SMITH (DAVID CADMAN); *sub nom.* R. v. CADMAN-SMITH (DAVID), [2001] UKHL 68, [2002] 1 W.L.R. 54, Lord Rodger of Earlsferry, HL.

3899. Conspiracy–confiscation orders–evasion of duty payable in respect of dutiable goods–validity of order

[Proceeds of Crime Act 1995.]

M appealed against a confiscation order requiring him to pay £10 million following his conviction on charges of conspiracy and evading duty payable in respect of dutiable goods mainly beers, wines and cigarettes. The conspiracy consisted of a diversion fraud in the course of which dutiable goods were obtained in the United Kingdom for export to the continent. As they were being exported, the goods did not attract duty in the UK. Once the goods had been landed on the continent they were swiftly returned to the UK accompanied by documents designed to show that the goods had been purchased by a customer and were destined for a bonded warehouse. Over the period of the conspiracy, an estimated total of £18 million was lost to the Revenue. M challenged the confiscation order on the grounds that the Proceeds of Crime Act 1995 was not in force at the material time and therefore the court had no power to make the confiscation order.

Held, allowing the appeal, that the court had acted without jurisdiction in making a confiscation order because the Proceeds of Crime Act 1995 was not in force at the material time and therefore had no power to initiate the confiscation proceedings.

R. v. BROWN (PETER JOHN) (APPEAL AGAINST SENTENCE); R. v. WALTON (BRIAN JOHN); R. v. WENT (GRAHAM JOHN); R. v. MARTIN (ELLIS ANTHONY) (APPEAL AGAINST SENTENCE); R. v. MacLEOD (ALASTAIR); R. v. AARONS (MAURICE); R. v. GARDNER (JOHN PHILLIP), [2001] EWCA Crim 2761, [2002] 2 Cr. App. R. (S.) 34, Mantell, L.J., CA (Crim Div).

3900. Conspiracy–handling stolen goods–motor vehicles–aggravating features– undue leniency

The Attorney General referred as unduly lenient custodial sentences imposed on M1, M2 and E for their roles in a conspiracy to handle stolen cars. The Attorney General submitted that the sentences were unduly lenient given the various aggravating features which included the sophisticated and well organised nature of the activity and the fact that the scheme had been run as a commercial enterprise for substantial reward.

Held, allowing the references, that the sentences had been unduly lenient in light of the numerous and serious aggravating features, including the fact that the defendants had been in direct contact with car thieves who in turn had been in contact with burglars and robbers, *R. v. Webbe (Bernard)* [2001] EWCA Crim 1217, [2002] 1 Cr. App. R. (S.) 22, [2001] C.L.Y. 1340 applied. Taking into consideration the element of double jeopardy, a sentence of three years and six months' imprisonment was substituted for that of two years imposed on M1, who had pleaded guilty, and sentences of four years' imprisonment were substituted for those of two years and six months imposed on both M2 and E.

ATTORNEY GENERAL'S REFERENCE (NOS.1, 2 AND 3 OF 2002), *Re*; R. v. MacDONALD (DON ANGUS); R. v. McGEOGH (THOMAS GERRARD); R. v.

EGAN (JOHN JOSEPH); *sub nom.* ATTORNEY GENERAL'S REFERENCE (NOS 1, 2 AND 3 OF 2001), *Re* [2002] EWCA Crim 1170, Rose, L.J., CA (Crim Div).

3901. **Conspiracy–illegal entrants–change in law during currency of conspiracy–custodial sentences**

[Criminal Law Act 1977 s.1 (1); Immigration and Asylum Act 1999 s.29; Immigration and Asylum Act 1999 (Commencement No.2 and Transitional Provisions) Order 2000 (SI 2000 168).]

SH, JH, DH and C appealed against sentences of nine years, seven years and six months, three years, and three years' imprisonment respectively, imposed following their conviction for conspiracy to facilitate the illegal entry into the United Kingdom of illegal entrants contrary to the Criminal Law Act 1977 s.1 (1). SH and JH each owned road haulage businesses. Upon both returning from a trip to Germany, illegal immigrants had been observed being driven from JH's yard. On a subsequent trip, JH had been stopped by Customs at Dover and 37 illegal immigrants had been found in his lorry. He had denied knowledge of them. On a later date, DH and C had driven lorries to France. On their return, one lorry had been found to contain 33 illegal immigrants and the other 26. Both lorries had been accompanied by a third lorry, which the prosecution alleged to be a decoy, in which SH and JH were travelling. The judge had found SH and JH to be the moving forces behind the conspiracy, with SH playing a central role and establishing contacts. The judge had found that DH and C had been brought into the conspiracy at a later stage and had taken part in a single trip. It was submitted that the sentences imposed on SH and JH had been beyond the powers of the court as the judge had relied on a change in the law, which had increased the power to sentence, during the period of the conspiracy.

Held, allowing the appeal, that while the sentences imposed would have been justified under the legislative scheme as altered by the Immigration and Asylum Act 1999 s.29 and the Immigration and Asylum Act 1999 (Commencement No.2 and Transitional Provisions) Order 2000, the judge had erred in finding that he had the power to impose such sentences. A defendant should not be adversely affected in relation to the powers of sentence by a change in the law that had occurred during the currency of a conspiracy entered into prior to the change, *R. v. Ahmed (Khurshid)* (Unreported, February 8, 2000) and *R. v. Brown (Peter John) (Appeal against Sentence)* [2001] EWCA Crim 2761, [2002] Crim. L.R. 228 followed. The offences in the instant case were very serious. The relevant maximum sentence had been seven years' imprisonment. Taking into account the size and persistence of the venture, it was appropriate that the maximum penalty be imposed on SH. SH's sentence was therefore reduced to seven years. A sentence of six years was appropriate for JH and sentences of 30 months were appropriate for DH and C.

R. v. HOBBS (STEPHEN PAUL); R. v. HOBBS (JOHN WILLIAM); R. v. HOBBS (DARREN WAYNE); R. v. CHARGE (WARREN JAMES), [2002] EWCA Crim 387, [2002] 2 Cr. App. R. 22, Pill, L.J., CA (Crim Div).

3902. **Conspiracy–pleas–imposition of maximum sentence for substantive offence of corruption–absence of written basis of plea**

D, a police officer, and H, a convicted drug trafficker, appealed against their respective sentences of seven years and five years' imprisonment imposed following their guilty pleas to a conspiracy which had involved a corrupt relationship between the two to give and accept a gift or consideration. S and C sought leave to appeal against their sentences of four years' imprisonment imposed for a related offence of kidnapping. D contended that owing to the fact that the maximum available sentence for the substantive offence that D had conspired to commit was seven years' imprisonment, the judge had erred by failing to give him credit for his guilty plea notwithstanding that it had been entered late. He further argued that in the light of the judge's sentencing remarks, he had been dealt with on a greater level of criminality than he had admitted. H argued that, by making his sentence consecutive to an existing term of eight years' imprisonment imposed for drug trafficking, the judge had failed to take into account the fact that the conspiracy was related to his drug trafficking activities and thus, on the principle of totality, was excessive. S and C argued that the in the light of the delay between their prosecution and guilty pleas, their sentences were also too long.

Held, allowing the appeals of D and H, granting C's application and making a provisional order in relation to S, that (1) whilst the absence of a written basis of plea was unsatisfactory, owing to the fact that D's guilty plea had saved the witnesses from giving evidence and that a lengthy trial had been avoided, D was entitled to a reduction in his sentence. Accordingly, the period of imprisonment was reduced to six years; (2) in respect of H, whilst finding that his argument on the totality of his sentence had no merit, taking account of the reduction in D's term, his sentence was reduced to four years and six months, and (3) in relation to S and C, as there was merit in their submissions, leave to appeal was granted. C's sentence was reduced to three years' imprisonment and subject to S pursuing his substantive appeal, his sentence was also reduced to three years.

R. v. SMITH (PAUL KEVIN); R. v. CONROY (CRAIG HENRY); R. v. DEOL (MICHAEL SINGH); R. v. HAYRE (KULDIP SINGH), [2001] EWCA Crim 1812, [2002] 1 Cr. App. R. (S.) 90, Burton, J., CA (Crim Div).

3903. **Criminal charges—indictments—indictment containing several allegations of misconduct—sentencing approach**

[Mental Health Act 1983 s.127(1).]

S, a registered mental nurse, appealed against the imposition of two concurrent sentences of 12 months' imprisonment on two counts of ill treating a patient, contrary to the Mental Health Act 1983 s.127(1). In relation to the one of the counts, the Crown had alleged a total of six acts of misconduct by S against one of his patients. The other count had been an alternative to an allegation of assault occasioning actual bodily harm. In respect of the first count, S contended that the judge, when sentencing, had erroneously formed his own view of what the jury had found proved, given that because the indictment had been drafted in general terms, the jury had not had to return separate verdicts in respect of each of the six allegations. In relation to the second count, S argued that the judge appeared from his sentencing remarks, to have dealt with him for the assault offence, rather than the alternative count.

Held, allowing the appeal in part, that although the indictment could have been drafted in more specific terms by isolating the specific matters to be relied upon, the outcome of the instant appeal was academic in terms of the sentence S would serve. Therefore, taking the pragmatic approach, the sentence in relation to the first count was quashed and a concurrent sentence of nine months' imprisonment substituted. That was not to be interpreted as making any comment on the approach a judge should take when sentencing in a matter involving an indictment covering a number of issues, namely whether the judge should form his own decision on what the jury must have decided in relation to each issue based on the verdict, or whether he should sentence in the way most favourable to the defendant. In relation to the second count, the judge's sentencing remarks had made it clear that S was not being sentenced for assault. Accordingly, the sentence on that count was ordered to remain with the result that the overall sentence to be served remained at 12 months' imprisonment.

R. v. SPEDDING (STEFFAN ANTHONY), [2001] EWCA Crim 2190, [2002] 1 Cr. App. R. (S.) 119, Tomlinson, J, CA (Crim Div).

3904. **Criminal damage—offences triable either way—totality of sentence—sentencing powers of Crown Court**

[Magistrates Courts Act 1980 s.22(2).]

A, aged 18 at the time of the offences, appealed against a total sentence of 18 months' detention, having pleaded guilty on a re arraignment to assault occasioning actual bodily harm, criminal damage, common assault and a public order offence. The issue arose as to whether the total consecutive sentence of eight months' detention for the offences, other than assault occasioning actual bodily harm, was within the sentencing powers of the Crown Court, or whether that court remained subject to the maximum six months term available to the justices.

Held, dismissing the appeal, that an offence of criminal damage was an offence triable either way if the magistrates had not categorised it as one in which the value of the damage caused was less than £5,000 under the Magistrates Courts Act 1980 s.22(2). It followed that the Crown Court could impose a maximum sentence of 10 years' imprisonment, irrespective of the value of the damage caused. Where the Crown Court was additionally dealing with two summary offences, in contrast to the sentencing powers of the justices, it was not required to limit the sentence to six months, *R. v. Fennell (Peter)* [2000] 1 W.L.R. 2011, [2001] C.L.Y. 1049 followed.

R. v. ALDEN (PAUL STUART), [2002] EWCA Crim 421, [2002] 2 Cr. App. R. (S.) 74, Rose, L.J., CA (Crim Div).

3905. Dangerous driving–death–accident resulting from fatigue

P appealed against a sentence of five years' imprisonment imposed for causing death by dangerous driving. P was driving an articulated lorry on a motorway when his lorry struck the rear of a mobile crane. The lorry then left the carriageway on its near side, crashed through a crash barrier and overturned. The impact caused the crane to go out of control and travel through the central crash barrier into the opposite carriageway where it collided with two other vehicles. The drivers of all three vehicles died as a result of the collision. The evidence indicated that P had not braked before the impact and that the lorry had been travelling at about 60 mph. The tachograph in P's lorry appeared to have been interfered with and parts of the charts recording P's journey were missing. The sentencing judge passed sentence on the basis that the accident was caused by the fact that P had driven far too long without a break and that he was aware of the risks in doing so. P contended that if the sentencing judge intended to pass sentence on a basis inconsistent with that of P's plea, he should have held a Newton hearing.

Held, dismissing the appeal, that it was increasingly common for a basis of plea to be put forward which was inconsistent with the prosecution evidence, and where a judge proposed to sentence a defendant on a basis of fact at variance with the basis of plea but contained in the prosecution evidence, it was important that counsel was given an opportunity to deal with that matter, and if necessary for the issue to be resolved by a Newton hearing. The court would deal with the matter on the basis of the incontrovertible facts and the basis of plea. Anyone who while suffering fatigue, drove a heavy goods vehicle had in his hands a highly dangerous weapon capable of killing numbers of people. Anyone who did so must expect a substantial sentence; this was a very serious offence which well deserved the sentence passed, *R. v. Kallaway (Ronald)* [1998] 2 Cr.App. R. (S.) 228, [1998] C.L.Y. 1367 considered.

R. v. PORTER (WILBERT) (NO.2), [2002] EWCA Crim 1121, [2002] 2 Cr. App. R. (S.) 50, Judge Richard Brown, CA (Crim Div).

3906. Dangerous driving–death–driver suffering from hypoglycaemia–similar previous incident

[Road Traffic Act 1988 s.1.]

D, a 67 year old driver of an articulated lorry, appealed against a sentence of three years' imprisonment imposed following his conviction on three counts of causing death by dangerous driving, contrary to the Road Traffic Act 1988 s.1. D had been driving his lorry down a relatively straight main road when it was seen to veer across the lane and into oncoming traffic. The lorry collided with a vehicle carrying four occupants, three of whom were killed. The Crown maintained that D had lost control of the lorry owing to a hypoglycaemic attack. It had been submitted that D was responsible for the accident because he had previously missed medical reviews, had not taken his medication the evening before the accident and had not eaten an adequate breakfast on the day of the accident. D had been in a similar but non fatal accident previously after which he had received medical advice on how to treat hypoglycaemia.

Held, dismissing the appeal, that notwithstanding D's age, good character and genuine remorse, the accident had resulted in three deaths and, more seriously, D had been involved in a similar incident previously. Accordingly the sentence could not be described as manifestly excessive.

R. v. DAVIES (JOHN WATKIN), [2001] EWCA Crim 2319, [2002] 1 Cr. App. R. (S.) 136, Davis, J., CA (Crim Div).

3907. Dangerous driving–death–HGV driver in motorway collision

C, a long distance lorry driver, appealed against a sentence of three years' imprisonment imposed following his plea of guilty to three offences of causing death by dangerous driving. C, who was a French national, had been driving in the late afternoon on the inner lane of a motorway at a constant speed. He had failed to notice that there was a queue of traffic ahead of him and had collided with another vehicle and then several others. C could provide no explanation for the accident; he had not been drinking, had had adequate rest periods and there were no defects in his vehicle.

Held, allowing the appeal, that drivers of heavy goods vehicles had a particular responsibility to other road users due to the nature of their vehicles and the potentially catastrophic consequences if they were involved in an accident. It was apparent that C had not been looking properly at the traffic ahead and that the accident had not resulted from a momentary error of judgment. However, having regard to the circumstances it was appropriate to reduce the sentence to one of two years.

R. v. CAUCHETEUX (LUDOVIC), [2001] EWCA Crim 2960, [2002] 2 Cr. App. R. (S.) 41, Penry-Davey, J., CA (Crim Div).

3908. Dangerous driving–death–multiple deaths caused by drunken driver–offences arising out of single incident–consecutive sentences

N appealed against sentences totalling 15 years' imprisonment and disqualification from driving for life for six offences of causing death by dangerous driving. N had killed six people after drink driving on what was described as a "motorised pub crawl". The total sentence of imprisonment was made up of three concurrent terms of five years with three concurrent terms of 10 years to run consecutively to the terms of five years. N had previous drink driving convictions and was disqualified from driving at the time of the offences. N had fled the scene of the accident. N contended that (1) consecutive sentences were inappropriate where all the offences arose out of one incident; (2) the total length of imprisonment was excessive as the maximum penalty was 10 years, and (3) the life disqualification was wrong as it was contrary to the public interest because it would impair his rehabilitation.

Held, allowing the appeal in part, that (1) it was wrong in principle to impose consecutive sentences for each death caused by one piece of dangerous driving. The number of deaths should be considered in determining the total sentence to be imposed, but should not, of itself, determine the total sentence because, ultimately, the number of fatalities was a matter of chance, *R. v. France (Brian)* [2002] EWCA Crim 1419 followed; (2) the dangerousness of the driving was the main concern in sentencing and all the circumstances of the driving, including the consequences, had to be considered. The statutory maximum sentence was 10 years and the instant case was at the very top of the range of sentences because most of the aggravating features referred to in *R. v. Boswell (James Thomas)* [1984] 1 W.L.R. 1047, [1985] C.L.Y. 770 were present. The instant case equalled the highest number of deaths to have arisen from one piece of dangerous driving. Accordingly, a total sentence of 10 years' imprisonment reflected the total criminality involved, *Boswell* applied, and (3) although lengthy disqualifications were to be avoided, the disqualification from driving for life was necessary to protect the public in view of N's previous convictions and his failure to recognise that his driving ability had been impaired by drunkenness.

R. v. NOBLE (PETER), [2002] EWCA Crim 1713, [2003] 1 Cr. App. R. (S.) 65, Keene, L.J., CA (Crim Div).

3909. **Dangerous driving—death—poor driving record—undue leniency**

The Attorney General referred as unduly lenient a sentence of three years' detention imposed upon A for causing death by dangerous driving, driving without due care and burglary with intent to cause grievous bodily harm. A had entered a property with the intention of locating another man whom he believed had been responsible for driving in such a way so as to put his mother and younger brother in danger. He admitted breaking into the same property on three occasions but had never located the individual that he sought. On a subsequent occasion A had struck and injured a pensioner as he drove a motor cycle in excess of the speed limit. On a further occasion A had collided with a 12 year old cyclist as he drove a vehicle at speed. The child subsequently died from the injuries inflicted. The Attorney General contended that the offences were aggravated by the fact that the offence of burglary had been committed at night and A had lain in wait for his intended victim. In relation to the driving offences, the Attorney General submitted that A had not passed his driving test, had a poor driving record having been awaiting trial on other driving charges and had inflicted fatal injuries on a cyclist having been involved in an accident causing personal injuries only 13 days previously. Further, A had fled the scene of the fatal accident.

Held, allowing the reference, that at first instance on a guilty plea a sentence of six years' detention for the offence of causing death by dangerous driving would have been merited. Having regard to the element of double jeopardy and the fact that A had now attained the age of 21, a sentence of five years' imprisonment was substituted to be served concurrently with the 18 month sentence imposed in relation to the burglary offence, *R. v. Boswell (James Thomas)* [1984] 1 W.L.R. 1047, [1985] C.L.Y. 770 and *Attorney General's Reference (No.58 of 2000), Re* [2001] 2 Cr. App. R. (S.) 19, [2001] C.L.Y. 1264 considered.

ATTORNEY GENERAL'S REFERENCE (NO.126 OF 2001), *Re; sub nom.* R. v. ASHTON (RYAN PAUL) [2002] EWCA Crim 560, Kennedy, L.J., CA (Crim Div).

3910. **Dangerous driving—death—reckless manoeuvre at excessive speed—good character**

W, aged 21, appealed against a sentence of three years' imprisonment imposed following his guilty plea to causing death by dangerous driving. A passenger in a car driven by W had died after W lost control of the vehicle while overtaking at an excessive speed. W contended that the sentence was excessive in view of his personal mitigation and in the light of relevant authorities.

Held, allowing the appeal and reducing the sentence to two years' imprisonment, that the sentence was excessive in the light of W's age, previous good character and relevant authorities, *R. v. Richards (Lee)* [1998] 2 Cr. App. R. (S.) 346, [1998] C.L.Y. 1364 applied.

R. v. WARD (GARY), [2001] EWCA Crim 1565, [2002] 1 Cr. App. R. (S.) 55, Mance, L.J., CA (Crim Div).

3911. **Dangerous driving—disqualification—causing injury to traffic warden**

J got into an argument with T, a traffic warden, who was about to issue a ticket to him in respect of an illegally parked vehicle. J got into the vehicle, and drove it at T. T slid onto the bonnet of the vehicle and was carried down the road for 150 yards. T got off the vehicle and J drove off. T received a cut finger and suffered some pain in the back and ribs, but did not require hospital treatment. J was sentenced to 15 months imprisonment and disqualified from driving for two years. J appealed.

Held, allowing the appeal, that a sentence of 15 months' imprisonment imposed after J was convicted of deliberately driving at a traffic warden and continuing to drive with the warden on the bonnet of the car, was reduced to 10 months in view of the dramatic personal consequences of the sentence, which had caused J's business to go into bankruptcy, *R. v. Charlton (Raymond David)* (1995) 16 Cr. App. R. (S.) 703, [1996] C.L.Y. 1693 considered.

R. v. JOSEPH (FABIAN ROBERT), [2001] EWCA Crim 1195, [2002] 1 Cr. App. R. (S.) 20, Leveson, J., CA (Crim Div).

3912. Dangerous driving—grievous bodily harm—custodial sentences—appropriate counts on indictment

[Offences against the Person Act 1861 s.20, s.35.]

B appealed against a sentence of four years and six months' imprisonment for causing grievous bodily harm contrary to the Offences against the Person Act 1861 s.20 and against a concurrent term of 21 months' imprisonment and a disqualification for 15 years in respect of a count of dangerous driving. B had borrowed a car which he drove at 50 mph in a 30 mph zone and had struck a 16 year old male who suffered extensive head injuries. B contended that the sentence was both manifestly excessive and wrong in principle as the prosecution had added the s.20 count to increase the available maximum length of imprisonment from two years to five years.

Held, allowing the appeal, that there was force in B's submissions. There was no offence of causing grievous bodily harm by dangerous driving presumably because Parliament did not intend that such an offence should exist. There was also an offence of causing bodily harm by wanton or furious driving pursuant to s.35 of the 1861 Act and this carried a maximum term of two years' imprisonment. The sentence was manifestly excessive and was reduced to 21 months on each count concurrent, with a disqualification period of six years.

R. v. BRIDLE (STEVEN CHARLES), [2002] EWCA Crim 908, [2003] 1 Cr. App. R. (S.) 3, McKinnon, J., CA (Crim Div).

3913. Dangerous driving—grievous bodily harm—revenge attack

E sought leave to appeal against a sentence of eight years' imprisonment imposed for causing grievous bodily harm with intent and dangerous driving. E spent some time in a public house with a friend. Following an incident a fight developed outside the public house and E was attacked and knocked to the ground by two other men. E went home, got into his pickup truck and drove back to the place where the men were walking along the pavement in company with another. He drove his truck onto the pavement and straight into the three men. One of the men got out of the way, a second who was struck a glancing blow was not seriously injured, but the third was carried on the truck for 20 metres. He fell to the ground and sustained fractures to the spinal column which were thought likely to make him totally paraplegic. He later recovered the use of his legs but the use of his arms and hands was gravely impaired and it was not thought likely that he would recover further. E contended that the sentence was excessive and out of line with others for similar offences.

Held, refusing the application, that the offence was aggravated by the fact that E had used a relatively heavy truck as a weapon of revenge. Ample time had occurred between the attack on him and the offence for reason to reassert itself. One of his victims had suffered severe and permanent disabling injuries. The court could not consider the sentence manifestly excessive, *R. v. Mitchell (Kevin Stephen)* [1988] 10 Cr. App. R. (S.) 471, [1989] C.L.Y. 1074 considered.

R. v. EVANS (BRADLEY), [2001] EWCA Crim 2631, [2002] 2 Cr. App. R. (S.) 12, Rougier, J., CA (Crim Div).

3914. Dangerous driving–multiple injuries–lorry overtaking slow vehicle–custodial sentences

S appealed against a sentence of four months' imprisonment imposed for dangerous driving. S was driving a lorry on a single carriageway road when he attempted to overtake a slow moving JCB digger on a bend. A car being driven in the opposite direction was forced to take evasive action, but it skidded and collided head on with the lorry. The driver of the car sustained multiple injuries and extensive bruising and swelling. The tachograph on S's lorry indicated that it had come up behind the digger at about 30 mph. S contended that none of the aggravating features identified in, *R. v. Boswell (James Thomas)* [1984] 1 W.L.R. 1047, [1985] C.L.Y. 770 were present and that the sentence was excessive.

Held, dismissing the appeal, that the sentence was neither wrong in principle nor manifestly excessive. S was a man aged 40 of previous good character who had been a lorry driver for 15 years, and was now finding it difficult to find employment. However, the sentencing judge stated that he considered S had taken risks with other people's lives which he had no right to take. In the court's view, the sentencing remarks and the sentence passed reflected the aggravating and mitigating features of the case. It was a bad case which had resulted in serious injuries.

R. v. SMITH (GRANT ANTHONY), [2001] EWCA Crim 2822, [2002] 2 Cr. App. R. (S.) 28, Judge Maddison, CA (Crim Div).

3915. Death penalty–murder–inhuman and degrading treatment–consistency with constitutional rights–St Christopher and Nevis

[Offences Against the Person Act 1873 (St Christopher and Nevis) s.2; St Christopher and Nevis Constitution Order 1983 (SI 1983 881) s.7.]

F appealed against the imposition of the death penalty following his conviction for the murder of his fiancee and her mother. F contended that the imposition of the death penalty pursuant to the Offences Against the Person Act 1873 (St Christopher and Nevis) s.2 was inconsistent with the right not to be subjected to inhuman or degrading punishment or treatment under the Constitution of St Christopher and Nevis s.7. F maintained that since s.2 of the 1873 Act was accordingly void the death penalty imposed upon him was unlawful and should be quashed.

Held, allowing the appeal, that s.2 of the 1873 Act was inconsistent with s.2 of the Constitution to the extent that it required the court to impose the death penalty whenever an individual was convicted of murder, *Reyes (Patrick) v. Queen, The* [2002] UKPC 11, [2002] 2 W.L.R. 1034, [2002] 4 C.L. 123 and *Queen, The v. Hughes (Peter)* [2002] UKPC 12, [2002] 2 W.L.R. 1058 applied. A provision which simply authorised the imposition of the death penalty in the case of murder and effectively left the choice of punishment to the judge having considered all the circumstances of the case, would however be consistent with the Constitution.

FOX (BERTHILL) v. QUEEN, THE (APPEAL AGAINST SENTENCE), [2002] UKPC 13, [2002] 2 A.C. 284, Lord Rodger of Earlsferry, PC (StC).

3916. Death penalty–murder–mandatory death penalty unconstitutional–St Lucia

[Constitution of Saint Lucia s.5; Criminal Code of Saint Lucia s.178, s.1284; Saint Lucia Constitution Order 1978 (SI 1978 1901) Sch.2 para.10.]

The Crown appealed against the decision of the Eastern Caribbean Court of Appeal that the mandatory death sentence for murder under the Criminal Code of Saint Lucia s.178 amounted to inhuman or degrading punishment or treatment under the Constitution of Saint Lucia s.5. In the light of that decision, the Court of Appeal had quashed the sentence of death that had been imposed on H following his conviction for murder. It had also held that the decision whether to impose the death penalty should be left to the jury. H argued that s.178 of the Criminal Code did not in fact provide that the death penalty was mandatory in the case of murder. The

Crown argued that the Saint Lucia Constitution Order 1978 Sch.2 para.10 prevented the court from holding that the mandatory death penalty was inconsistent with s.5 of the Constitution.

Held, dismissing the appeal, that (1) it had been intended that s.178 of the Criminal Code would make the death penalty mandatory in the case of murder. Furthermore, a consideration of other provisions in the Criminal Code showed that the words "liable indictably to suffer death" meant "exposed or subject to" suffering death. Section 178 did therefore make the death penalty mandatory for murder; *Jones v. Attorney General of the Bahamas* [1995] 1 W.L.R. 891, [1995] C.L.Y. 2613 applied, (2) since s.178 required rather than merely authorised the imposition of the death penalty on a defendant convicted of murder, the exception in Sch.2 para.10 of the 1978 Order did not apply, *Minister of Home Affairs (Bermuda) v. Fisher* [1980 A.C. 319, [1979] C.L.Y. 178 applied, and H was entitled to persuade the court that s.178 was inconsistent with s.5 of the Constitution. Section 178 was in fact inconsistent with s.5 of the Constitution to the extent that it required the imposition of the death penalty on a defendant convicted of murder, *Reyes (Patrick) v. Queen, The* [2002] UKPC 11, [2002] 2 W.L.R. 1034, [2002] 4 C.L. 123 applied. Section 1284 of the Criminal Code should, however, be construed so that it applied to s.178 with the result that s.178 would no longer be inconsistent with s.5 of the Constitution. Under s.178 the court would therefore be able to impose the death sentence or a lesser sentence, and (3) the decision as to whether the death penalty should be imposed should be made by the judge rather than by the jury. Judges had the requisite training and expertise and could set out the reasons for imposing a particular sentence. In addition, redress could be sought in the Court of Appeal if the sentence imposed was excessive.

QUEEN, THE v. HUGHES (PETER), [2002] UKPC 12, [2002] 2 A.C. 259, Lord Rodger of Earlsferry, PC (StL).

3917. **Death penalty–murder–mandatory sentence for murder by shooting–compatibility with constitutional rights–Belize**

[Constitution of Belize 1981 s.2, s.7; Criminal Code (Belize) s.102; .]

R appealed against the decision of the Court of Appeal of Belize upholding the imposition of a mandatory sentence of death following his conviction on two counts of murder by shooting. Under the Criminal Code (Belize) s.102(1), as amended in 1994, a person who had committed a Class A murder was subject to a sentence of death. Class A murder included murder by shooting. The Constitution of Belize 1981 s.7 provided protection against inhuman or degrading punishment or treatment. By virtue of s.2 of the Constitution, any law that was inconsistent with Constitutional law was, to the extent of that inconsistency, void. It was submitted that the mandatory death sentence was contrary to the protection afforded under s.7.

Held, allowing the appeal, that the mandatory nature of the sentence was incompatible with the protection afforded under s.7 of the Constitution in that it precluded any judicial consideration of the humanity of condemning a person to death. The denial of the opportunity, before the sentence was passed, of persuading the court that the imposition of a sentence of death was not appropriate, or was disproportionate, was to treat a defendant inhumanely. It followed that the requirement under s.102 of the Criminal Code that "any murder by shooting" would be punishable by death was void for inconsistency with s.7 of the Constitution. The decision as to what was the appropriate punishment to be imposed was a judicial rather than an executive function.

REYES (PATRICK) v. QUEEN, THE, [2002] UKPC 11, [2002] 2 A.C. 235, Lord Bingham of Cornhill, PC (Bze).

3918. Detention and training orders–age–defendant who attained age of 18 prior to conviction

[Children and Young Persons Act 1963 s.29; Powers of Criminal Courts (Sentencing) Act 2000 s.100.]

A appealed against the magistrates' decision to impose an 18 month detention and training order in respect of offences of wounding with intent and common assault. A had first appeared before the youth court when he was aged 17 but, due to delays, he had reached the age of 18 by the time of his trial. The magistrates had decided to try A summarily and had applied the Children and Young Persons Act 1963 s.29 which provided that where a young person reached the age of 18 prior to the conclusion of proceedings against him, the court was entitled to pass sentence in accordance with the powers available should he not have attained that age. A contended that s.29 of the 1963 Act had been impliedly repealed by the Powers of Criminal Courts (Sentencing) Act 2000 s.100 which specifically stated that detention and training orders were only applicable to those under the age of 18.

Held, dismissing the appeal, that as s.29 of the 1963 Act provided the sole basis on which the summary trial was able to proceed, it could not then have been irrational to impose a sentence on a similar basis. Though s.100 of the 2000 Act was in mandatory terms, there was no conflict between the two provisions and thus, the principle of implied repeal could not have applied. It was not irrational to apply s.29 to those situations where a young person attained the age of 18 prior to conviction and Parliament's intention was to be construed so as to allow s.100 to be interpreted subject to s.29.

A v. DPP, [2002] EWHC 403, [2002] 2 Cr. App. R. (S.) 88, Goldring, J., DC.

3919. Discounts–pleas–refusal to give discount for guilty plea

[Powers of Criminal Courts (Sentencing) Act 2000 s.101.]

M, who was aged 16 at the time of the offence, appealed against a two year detention and training order imposed following his plea of guilty to counts of conspiracy to cause actual bodily harm, assault occasioning actual bodily harm, threats to kill and incitement to steal. M, with two others, had subjected two adults with learning difficulties and their children to a horrific ordeal which had included forcing the two adults to perform oral sex under threat that the father would be killed if they did not and cutting the father 60 times with kitchen knives until he agreed to steal for them. The two year sentence was the maximum possible under the Powers of Criminal Courts (Sentencing) Act 2000 s.101. The judge had refused to give any discount for M's guilty plea on the basis that the Crown had wrongly decided to accept his pleas of not guilty to two counts of indecent assault.

Held, allowing the appeal, that the judge had erred in not giving some discount for M's guilty plea. A judge could not pass a sentence which reflected charges which the Crown had chosen not to pursue. In the instant case the appropriate discount had been six months. It followed that an 18 month detention and training order would be substituted. It was observed that a prosecutor should have careful regard to whether the limited matters to which pleas of guilty were to be accepted would unreasonably limit the ability of the judge to pass an appropriate sentence.

R. v. MARCH (WAYNE ROBIN), [2002] EWCA Crim 551, [2002] 2 Cr. App. R. (S.) 98, Gross, J., CA (Crim Div).

3920. Dishonesty–mobile telephones–"chipping" to enable free calls

[Telecommunications Act 1984 s.42A.]

S appealed against a sentence of 18 months' imprisonment for telecommunications offences. He pleaded guilty before a magistrates court to having items in his custody or control with the intention of dishonestly obtaining a service, contrary to the Telecommunications Act 1984 s.42A. He was committed to the Crown Court for sentence. S was involved in "chipping" mobile telephones whereby mobile telephones were modified to enable the user to make calls free of charge.

Held, allowing the appeal, that it had not been possible to discover accurately the extent of the loss to the company providing the call facilities. The system potentially enabled the company to be defrauded of an enormous amount. S claimed that he had probably made a profit of about £500. The court agreed with the sentencing judge that the offence warranted a term of imprisonment. In the light of the fact that the appellant had indicated his intention to plead guilty in the magistrates court, the sentence was reduced to 12 months' imprisonment.

R. v. STEPHENS (BRIAN ANDREW), [2002] EWCA Crim 136, [2002] 2 Cr. App. R. (S.) 67, Judge Fawcus, CA (Crim Div).

3921. Drug offences–supply of drugs–Class A drugs

N pleaded guilty to possessing a Class A drug with intent to supply. Police officers on mobile patrol stopped a car being driven by the appellant. In the boot they found a large padlocked suitcase. N said that she did not know what it contained and that a man had asked her to pick it up and take it to Manchester. The suitcase was found to contain 50 kilograms of heroin at 79 per cent purity. During police interview, N claimed that she had been asked to collect and deliver the package and that she did not know that the package contained heroin. N was sentenced to six years' imprisonment and appealed.

Held, dismissing the appeal, that a sentence of six years' imprisonment imposed for the possession of heroin, a Class A drug, with intent to supply was not manifestly excessive and correctly reflected the fact that N had incorrectly thought that the locked suitcase, which was found in her car, contained cannabis, *R. v. Bilinski (Edward)* (1988) 86 Cr. App. R. 146, [1988] C.L.Y. 930 considered.

R. v. NGIAM (GENA), [2001] EWCA Crim 1332, [2002] 1 Cr. App. R. (S.) 35, Penry-Davey, J., CA (Crim Div).

3922. Drug offences–supply of drugs–Class A drugs–heroin–sentencing guidelines

U appealed against concurrent sentences of six years' imprisonment for supplying heroin and possessing heroin with intent to supply. He submitted that the sentence was excessive given the low level of dealing involved, his lack of relevant previous convictions, the fact that he had not previously had a custodial sentence and in the light of sentencing guidelines.

Held, allowing the appeal, that in the circumstances, the sentence was excessive and was reduced to five years' imprisonment, *R. v. Twisse (Michael James)* [2001] Crim. L.R. 151, [2001] C.L.Y. 1282 applied.

R. v. UNDERDOWN (GARY JOHN), [2001] EWCA Crim 1088, [2002] 1 Cr. App. R. (S.) 14, Rose, L.J., CA (Crim Div).

3923. Drug offences–supply of drugs–Class A drugs–imposition of minimum sentences–procedure on plea of guilty

[Crime (Sentences) Act 1997 s.3, Sch.4 para.17; Powers of Criminal Courts (Sentencing) Act 2000 s.110, s.152.]

H appealed against a sentence of seven years' imprisonment imposed for being concerned in the supply of heroin, a Class A drug, and possession of a Class A drug with intent to supply. The sentence, which the judge considered to be the minimum he could impose, was passed under the Crime (Sentences) Act 1997 s.3 (now the Powers of Criminal Courts (Sentencing) Act 2000 s.110) owing to the fact that H had two previous convictions for drug trafficking offences. H contended that the judge's belief as to the minimum sentence was erroneous owing to the provisions contained in Sch.4 para.17 (now s.152 of the 2000 Act) regarding reductions in sentences following guilty pleas.

Held, allowing the appeal, that in relation to the imposition of a minimum sentence following a guilty plea to a trigger offence, a court was to have regard to the stage in proceedings and the circumstances in which the plea was entered and decide whether those factors entitled a defendant to any credit. Having concluded that credit was to be given, Sch.4 para.17 (now s.152) then operated to permit the court to impose a sentence which was not less than 80 per cent of the appropriate minimum sentence. In the instant case, had the relevant provisions relating to guilty pleas been brought to the judge's attention, he would have given full credit for H's guilty pleas and reduced the seven year sentence by 80 per cent. In the absence of any particular circumstances to render such a sentence unjust, the term of imprisonment was reduced to five years and seven months.

R. v. HICKSON (JEFFREY), [2001] EWCA Crim 1595, [2002] 1 Cr. App. R. (S.) 71, Waller, L.J., CA (Crim Div).

3924. Drug offences—supply of drugs—community punishment and rehabilitation orders—supply of ecstasy tablets to juvenile for distribution at school—undue leniency

The Attorney General referred as unduly lenient a community punishment and rehabilitation order of 100 hours with a two year supervision order for B who had pleaded guilty to two offences of supplying ecstasy and one offence of possessing the drug. B, aged 18 at the date of the offences, had obtained ecstasy from an unknown source and supplied nine tablets to his 14 year old girlfriend who distributed them to her school friends. Three ecstasy tablets were also found in B's bedroom and he was subsequently found to have supplied approximately 50 tablets in the months preceding his arrest.

Held, finding the sentence to be unduly lenient but not varying it, that given the scale of the supply and the involvement of school pupils an appropriate sentence would have been one of four years' detention, *R. v. Asquith (Martyn Arthur)* (1995) 16 Cr. App. R. (S.) 453 considered. Account had to be taken not only of the element of double jeopardy involved but also of the fact that B's original trial had not been heard, a matter of which he was only informed at the last minute; therefore he had had the anxiety of attending court on two previous occasions. Further, B had now completed the 100 hours unpaid community work under order and a report, written during the time he was carrying out the order, stated that a custodial sentence could cause damage to B in both the short and longer term. Therefore it was not appropriate to substitute a term of detention.

ATTORNEY GENERAL'S REFERENCE (NO.89 OF 2001), *Re; sub nom.* R. v. BARROW (JAMES DAVID) [2002] EWCA Crim 329, Mantell, L.J., CA (Crim Div).

3925. Drug offences—supply of drugs—conspiracy—low risk of re offending—fines

B appealed against a sentence of two years' imprisonment imposed after he pleaded guilty to conspiracy to supply cannabis and to being concerned in the supply of amphetamine sulphate.

Held, allowing the appeal, that (1) B was capable of gaining and maintaining steady employment; (2) there was no likelihood of him preying upon the public again, and (3) he had already served the equivalent of a sentence of over 12 months' imprisonment. In those circumstances, and taking into account the problem of overcrowded prisons, it was preferable to impose a fine rather than a custodial sentence. Accordingly B's sentence was reduced so as to allow his immediate release and he was fined the sum of £5,000.

R. v. BALDWIN (PETER), [2002] EWCA Crim 2647, *The Times*, November 22, 2002, Lord Woolf of Barnes, L.C.J., CA (Crim Div).

3926. Drug offences–supply of drugs–criminal record–supplying cocaine to undercover police officer while on licence–undue leniency

The Attorney General referred to the court as unduly lenient a total sentence of two years' imprisonment imposed on B for two offences of supplying cocaine. The sentence included 12 months' imprisonment representing part of an unexpired sentence for importing cocaine, in respect of which B was in breach of licence. B had supplied cocaine to an undercover police officer 17 days after his release from prison on licence. The aggravating features identified by the Attorney General were that the offences were committed so soon after B's release on licence and B had a serious history of offences in relation to the same class A drug. In mitigation, it was submitted on B's behalf that he was not a principal in the chain of supply and that he had pleaded guilty after receiving advice from counsel.

Held, allowing the reference, that the sentence was unduly lenient. In most cases, the starting point for offences of supplying class A drugs was to impose a sentence of less than five years' imprisonment where the defendant had pleaded not guilty, *R. v. Aramah (John Uzu)* (1983) 76 Cr. App. R. 190, [1983] C.L.Y. 764.19 considered. Clearly, a proper discount was to be made for a guilty plea. In the instant case, there was no basis for considering that a starting sentence of less than at least five years was appropriate. A proper sentence would have been to order the remaining 12 months of the previous sentence to be served, together with a sentence of four years' imprisonment for the instant offence, totalling five years. Given the inherent element of double jeopardy, a total sentence of four years' imprisonment was substituted, including the 12 month unexpired period of the previous offence.

ATTORNEY GENERAL'S REFERENCE (NO.27 OF 2002), Re; sub nom. R. v. BARNETT (REUBEN), [2002] EWCA Crim 1572, [2003] 1 Cr. App. R. (S.) 24, Kay, L.J., CA (Crim Div).

3927. Drug offences–supply of drugs–custodial sentences–large scale production of cannabis with intent to supply

J appealed against a sentence of five years' imprisonment for producing cannabis on a large scale in an industrial unit adapted for the purpose. J pleaded guilty to one count of producing cannabis and one count of possessing cannabis with intent to supply. J rented an industrial unit in March 2000. In June 2000 the unit was found to contain a sophisticated system for the cultivation of cannabis. It was estimated that the project had a potential income of between £151,000 and £190,000. J admitted that he was the sole lessee of the unit and had constructed the hydroponic system, but claimed that he was not a principal in the enterprise and received no direct share in the proceeds of the sale of the drugs.

Held, dismissing the appeal, that in the court's judgment, the sentence of five years' imprisonment could not be said to be manifestly excessive.

R. v. JUBB (ALAN JAMES), [2001] EWCA Crim 2567, [2002] 2 Cr. App. R. (S.) 8, Davis, J., CA (Crim Div).

3928. Drug offences–supply of drugs–female offenders–sophisticated commercial operation–undue leniency

The Attorney General referred a sentence of three years' imprisonment on the basis of undue leniency. The sentence had been imposed upon a 64 year old woman following conviction upon four counts of the supply of Class A drugs, namely diamorphine and cocaine. Undercover officers had purchased drugs from the defendant on various occasions at her home which was equipped with metal gates, laminated windows, CCTV cameras and a radio scanner attuned to police frequencies. The Attorney General contended that the offence was aggravated by the fact that the defendant ran a sophisticated commercial operation solely for commercial gain since she was not herself an addict.

Held, finding the sentence unduly lenient but not varying it, that whilst the starting point of six years' imprisonment identified by the sentencing judge had not been unreasonable, the discount given to the defendant in the absence of a guilty plea had been grossly excessive. Having regard to the principle of double jeopardy, however, it was not appropriate to interfere with the sentence imposed at first instance, *R. v. Djahit (Turkesh)* [1999] 2 Cr. App. R. (S.) 142, [1999] C.L.Y. 1137 and *R. v. Williams (Derek Anthony)* [2000] 2 Cr. App. R. (S.) 308, [2000] C.L.Y. 1225 considered.

ATTORNEY GENERAL'S REFERENCE (NO.135 OF 2001), *Re; sub nom.* R. v. MANN (ROSE) [2002] EWCA Crim 411, Kennedy, L.J., CA (Crim Div).

3929. Drug offences–supply of drugs–low level supply to fund addiction–offences committed during currency of community rehabilitation order–undue leniency

The Attorney General referred to the court as unduly lenient a sentence of 18 months' imprisonment imposed on M, who had pleaded guilty to three counts of supplying heroin and one count of possession of heroin with intent to supply. M had supplied silver foil wraps containing heroin to several people in exchange for payment of £20. Following a search of his home, seven grammes of powder containing heroin had been found together with £645 in cash, a roll of silver foil and a knife with powder traces on its blade. When interviewed by the police, M had admitted supplying heroin from his home for the previous two or three months. At the time of the offences, M had been subject to a community rehabilitation order and a conditional discharge, both of which had been made in relation to offences of heroin possession.

Held, allowing the reference, that whilst M had pleaded guilty at the first opportunity he was not a man of good character in so far as drugs were concerned having been subject to a community rehabilitation order and a conditional discharge at the time when the offences were committed. In the circumstances, a sentence of four years' imprisonment would have been appropriate at first instance. Having regard to double jeopardy, a sentence of three years and six months was substituted.

ATTORNEY GENERAL'S REFERENCE (NO.142 OF 2001), *Re; sub nom.* R. v. MARSTON (SCOTT LEE) [2002] EWCA Crim 450, Rose, L.J., CA (Crim Div).

3930. Drug offences–supply of drugs–pleas–permitting use of premises for supply of heroin

S appealed against a sentence of four years' imprisonment imposed for permitting his premises to be used for the supply of heroin and obstructing a constable. S, a long standing heroin addict, occupied a room in a hostel for homeless people. Police officers tried to search his room and S physically blocked the door. The officers found six people in the room and various small quantities of heroin, consistent with personal use by the occupants. It was conceded that the people in the room had all used heroin and were accustomed to supplying each other by way of exchange or gift. S submitted that there was no element of widening the distribution of heroin or of corrupting others.

Held, allowing the appeal, that on a plea of guilty at the first opportunity, the sentence imposed was excessive. A sentence of three years was substituted, consecutive to the order for return to custody, *R. v. Bradley (Andrew)* [1997] 1 Cr.App. R. (S.) 59, [1997] C.L.Y. 1506 considered.

R. v. SYKES (JOHN PAUL), [2001] EWCA Crim 2781, [2002] 2 Cr. App. R. (S.) 24, Hughes, J., CA (Crim Div).

3931. Drug offences–supply of drugs–possession of ecstasy with intent to supply for profit–undue leniency

[Criminal Justice Act 1988 s.36.]

The Attorney General sought permission to refer a sentence to the Court of Appeal for the possession of ecstasy with intent to supply. The Attorney General contended that the imposition of a 200 hour community punishment order and a fine of £1000 had been unduly lenient. W had been apprehended in a nightclub in possession of 48 ecstasy tablets. The basis of his guilty plea was that he had intended only to supply his friends and that the supply had not been intended to make a profit but simply to cover his costs.

Held, refusing the application, that counsel advising the Attorney General had suggested that this was a case of a defendant supplying friends in order to achieve a modest profit yet that was not the basis upon which W had been sentenced; accordingly the Attorney General had erred in the exercise of his discretion.

ATTORNEY GENERAL'S REFERENCE (NO.131 OF 2001), *Re*; *sub nom*. R. v. WATKINS (LUKE MICHAEL) [2002] EWCA Crim 371, Kay, L.J., CA (Crim Div).

3932. Drug offences—supply of drugs—repeated heroin supplies to undercover police officers—undue leniency

The Attorney General referred a sentence of three years' imprisonment to the Court of Appeal on the basis of undue leniency. The offender, S, had pleaded guilty to eight counts of supplying, and one of possessing, heroin, following an undercover police operation. He was sentenced to 18 months' imprisonment concurrently for each offence. The Attorney General argued that the sentence was unduly lenient since S had supplied undercover officers on repeated occasions and had previous convictions for possession.

Held, allowing the reference, that the sentence was unduly lenient. A sentence of four years six months was more appropriate, *R. v. Twisse (Michael James)* [2001] 2 Cr.App.R.(S.) 9, [2001] C.L.Y. 1282 applied. This was reduced, to take account of double jeopardy and the fact that S had already completed his original sentence, to three years and six months' imprisonment.

ATTORNEY GENERAL'S REFERENCE (NO.121 OF 2001), *Re*; *sub nom*. R. v. SMITH (ANDREW) [2002] EWCA Crim 145, Rose, L.J., CA (Crim Div).

3933. Drug trafficking—confiscation orders—property acquired with mortgage—correct approach to valuation

[Drug Trafficking Act 1994 s.4(3)(c), s.4(4)(a), s.7(1).]

W appealed against a confiscation order imposed following his conviction for conspiring to supply a controlled drug. He argued that when assessing the value of his realisable assets, the judge had erred by valuing his home by reference to its market value rather than by reference to the equity in the home.

Held, allowing the appeal, that by virtue of the Drug Trafficking Act 1994 s.7(1) the value of W's home was the equity therein. The mortgage debt represented the residue of the original "clean" money advanced by the building society. Section 4(4)(a) of the Act operated to displace the statutory assumption in s.4(3)(c) that W had "received the property free of any other interests in it", *R. v. Johnson (Julie)* [1991] 2 Q.B. 249, [1991] C.L.Y. 1091 followed.

R. v.WALLS (ANDREW), [2002] EWCA Crim 2456, [2003] 1 W.L.R. 731, Judge David Clarke Q.C., CA (Crim Div).

3934. Drug trafficking—sentence length—discounts—offenders knowledge as to nature of goods carried—undue leniency

The Attorney General referred as unduly lenient a custodial sentence of three years and six months' imprisonment imposed on F, a Brazilian national, for being knowingly concerned in the fraudulent importation of a class A drug. In a search made following her arrival in the United Kingdom, F was found to be carrying just over a kilogram of cocaine at 70 per cent purity. She contended that she had been mistaken as to the nature of that which she carried, and unaware that it was something which it was prohibited to import.

Held, allowing the reference, that the sentence had been unduly lenient, the extent of the discount afforded by the trial judge being too great. Moreover, the judge had erred in treating F as having pleaded guilty in light of the jury's rejection of her account. Taking into consideration the element of double jeopardy, a sentence of five years' imprisonment was substituted. An appropriate sentence for such an offence would otherwise have been a minimum of six years' imprisonment.

ATTORNEY GENERAL'S REFERENCE (NO.14 OF 2002), Re; sub nom. R. v. FIETOSA (MARIA DAS DORES); R. v. FLORES (MARIA DAS DORES FIETOSA), [2002] EWCA Crim 1163, [2003] 1 Cr. App. R. (S.) 17, Rose, L.J., CA (Crim Div).

3935. **Environmental protection–incineration–fines–disposal of carcasses–controls on use of incinerator exceeded**

[Environmental Protection Act 1990 s.23(1)(a).]

C owned three incinerators used for the disposal of animal carcasses. Under the scheme to eradicate BSE from cattle, C was allowed to destroy a set number of carcasses at the rate of 250 kilogrammes per hour and for which they were required to account to the Intervention Board. To reduce emissions, the local authority restricted operation of the site so that only one incinerator could be used at a time. C had unsuccessfully sought permission to use all three incinerators at once and an appeal was pending when it was discovered that C was in fact using all three incinerators simultaneously and had also exceeded the hourly throughput limit. C was convicted of offences under the Environmental Protection Act 1990 s.23(1)(a), for which fines totalling £50,000 were imposed. C sought permission to appeal against sentence.

Held, refusing the application, that C had acted in a dishonest manner as a means of increasing its profits and there was nothing to suggest that the trial judge had exercised his judgment improperly. The judge below had been able to form a view during the trial that C had acted dishonestly with a view to maximising its profits by ignoring the terms of its authorisation. The fines were therefore fully justified, even though no environmental damage or threat to human health had ensued.

R. v. CLUTTON AGRICULTURE LTD, [2001] EWCA Crim 2710, [2002] Env. L.R. 19, Judge Openshaw Q.C., CA (Crim Div).

3936. **Explosions–endangering life–aggravating features–intent to endanger life–high degree of planning and sophistication–undue leniency**

The Attorney General referred as unduly lenient a sentence of five years' imprisonment for W's offence of possessing an explosive substance with intent to endanger life. W had constructed nine fragmentation bombs, each consisting of three kilogrammes of metal nuts packed around a pipe bomb. The Attorney General identified serious aggravating features which included the sophistication and lethal potential of each device, the presence of anti handling mechanisms, W's attempts to conceal his actions, the implication that W planned to conduct a campaign as opposed to an isolated explosion and, in spite of the absence of terrorist or extremist motives, the intention to cause terror and anxiety to the public.

Held, allowing the reference, that the sentence was unduly lenient as, in the light of the serious aggravating features and the clear intention to endanger life, the judge had erred in failing to place W's offences in the appropriate category of gravity. A sentence of at least 12 years' imprisonment would have been appropriate in the court below. However, taking into account the element of double jeopardy, a nine year term was substituted.

ATTORNEY GENERAL'S REFERENCE (NO.13 OF 2002), Re; sub nom. R. v. WILKES (JONATHAN PETER), [2002] EWCA Crim 1050, [2003] 1 Cr. App. R. (S.) 12, Rose, L.J., CA.

3937. **Explosions–endangering life–bomb placed beneath vehicle**

M appealed against a sentence of 10 years' imprisonment imposed following his plea of guilty to a single count of causing an explosion likely to endanger life. M had placed a bomb beneath the driver's seat of a vehicle belonging to W, the husband of a woman with whom he had been having an affair. As a diversionary tactic prior to this action, M had written to W's employer, whose work included animal testing research, purporting to threaten its employees. Evidence suggested that the bomb, which was packed with screws and could be set off by remote control, could have been triggered by a number of innocent actions such as a radio taxi operating its radio as it passed. M had changed his mind at the last minute and had not detonated the bomb whilst W was in the vehicle. He had, however, subsequently detonated the bomb, the explosion from which had caused some danger.

Held, dismissing the appeal, that in the circumstances a sentence of 10 years had been appropriate. M had carefully planned his attack and had attempted to divert blame by sending threatening letters to W's employer, an action which had caused considerable anxiety. Furthermore, whilst M had changed his mind at the last minute, the bomb had been sophisticated and powerful.

R. v. McDONALD (WILLIAM), [2001] EWCA Crim 2842, [2002] 2 Cr. App. R. (S.) 31, Judge Tilling, CA (Crim Div).

3938. False accounting–theft–non custodial sentence appropriate for economic crimes by offender of previous good character

K, a former cashier, appealed against a sentence of 12 months' imprisonment imposed, following guilty pleas, for theft and false accounting. K contended that the sentence was excessive because the starting point of 18 months was too high.

Held, allowing the appeal, that the sentence was excessive and was reduced to four months as a starting point of 12 months would have been appropriate. A sentence of imprisonment should only be imposed when necessary and only for as long as was necessary in view of the overcrowded prison system. For economic crimes, especially where the offender was of previous good character, alternative sentences to imprisonment could be appropriate punishment.

R. v. KEFFORD (MARK JAMES), [2002] EWCA Crim 519, [2002] 2 Cr. App. R. (S.) 106, Lord Woolf of Barnes, L.C.J., CA (Crim Div).

3939. False imprisonment–life imprisonment–conduct amounting to a violent offence–criteria governing determinate and specified period

[Powers of Criminal Courts (Sentencing) Act 2000 s.161 (3).]

S appealed against the imposition of a discretionary life sentence, with a determinate period of 11 years and a specified period of six years, for the offence of false imprisonment. S had broken into the home of L, a 71 year old widow, sprayed hair spray into her face, squeezed her throat with his hand and threatened her with a walking stick, screwdriver and his fist, before leaving with money, jewellery and other items stolen from her. He pleaded guilty to offences of false imprisonment and burglary. S contended that the offence of false imprisonment should not have been characterised as a violent offence within the meaning of the Powers of Criminal Courts (Sentencing) Act 2000 s.161 (3), on the basis that there must be a probability of injury rather than a mere risk of injury. He further contended that the judge had erred in setting the determinate term at 11 years and the notional specified period at more than half that term.

Held, allowing the appeal against sentence in part, that in order to establish that a "violent offence" within the meaning of s.161 (3) of the 2000 Act had been committed, it was not necessary to show that injury had been a necessary or probable result of the offence. In the instant case, S's conduct presented more than the mere risk of injury. His squeezing L's throat had been likely to lead to marks and his threats to kill her could well have lead to cardiac arrest or vagal inhibition. Whilst the imposition of a discretionary life sentence was inevitable, the notional determinate sentence had been set too high and was consequently reduced from 11 years to nine years. As a general rule the specified period should not exceed half the determinate period save in exceptional circumstances, and where a judge specified a greater period he must state his reasons for so doing. In the instant case there had been no exceptional circumstances justifying departure from the general rule and accordingly the specified period was reduced from six to four years and six months.

R. v. SZCZERBA (IAN MICHAEL), [2002] EWCA Crim 440, [2002] 2 Cr. App. R. (S.) 86, Rose, L.J., CA (Crim Div).

3940. False imprisonment–offensive weapons–holding former partner at gun point for 12 hours

W appealed against a sentence of seven years' imprisonment imposed for false imprisonment and possession of a prohibited weapon, with intent to commit an indictable offence. W, aged 44, became involved in a relationship with a woman and moved into her home. When the relationship deteriorated, the woman told W to leave the home. W left but made repeated efforts to see the woman. He went to her place of work one afternoon, armed with a loaded pistol containing two live rounds. He pointed the gun at the woman from a short distance, and forced her to remain at her place of work for about 12 hours, for most of the time holding the gun with his finger on the trigger. After 12 hours, W dismantled the gun and left the parts and bullets on the table together with a knife and surrendered to the police. W contended that the sentence was manifestly excessive.

Held, dismissing the appeal, the total sentence of seven years' imprisonment was not manifestly excessive.

R. v. WHEELER (ALLEN JOHN), [2002] EWCA Crim 65, [2002] 2 Cr. App. R. (S.) 61, Davis, J., CA (Crim Div).

3941. Firearms offences–criminal record–possession of sawn-off shotgun–gun discharged in street–previous convictions–undue leniency

[Firearms Act 1968 s.5(1), s.16A, s.19; Powers of Criminal Courts (Sentencing) Act 2000 s.116.]

The Attorney General referred to the court as unduly lenient a sentence of four years' imprisonment imposed on S following his conviction for possession of a firearm with intent to cause fear of unlawful violence contrary to the Firearms Act 1968 s.16A, having a firearm in a public place contrary to s.19 of the Act, and possession of a prohibited weapon contrary to s.5(1) of the Act. The judge had also ordered that S serve 632 days of an outstanding sentence pursuant to the Powers of Criminal Courts (Sentencing) Act 2000 s.116. S, who had been released on licence and had previous convictions for robbery and possession of a firearm with intent to rob, had pursued the ex-boyfriend of his stepdaughter along a busy street. He had been carrying a loaded sawn-off shot gun which he had discharged once during the chase. There was no evidence that the shot had been fired at anyone. When his home had subsequently been searched by the police the sawn-off shotgun with four live cartridges had been found.

Held, allowing the reference, that the sentence imposed had been unduly lenient. Having regard to the guideline case of *R. v. Avis (Tony)* [1998] 1 Cr. App. R. 420, [1998] C.L.Y. 1214, the appropriate sentence would have been one of seven years' imprisonment. When considering whether to order S to serve the outstanding sentence of 625 days, it was necessary to look at the question of totality, *R. v. Secretary of State for the Home Department, ex p. Probyn* [1998] 1 W.L.R. 809, [1997] C.L.Y. 1654 considered. In the instant case it would have been appropriate, had the judge imposed the correct sentence, to have ameliorated the order and to have ordered that one year be served prior to the new sentence being imposed. Having regard to the element of double jeopardy, a sentence of five years and six months would be substituted in respect of each count on the indictment together with one year in respect of the outstanding period of sentence.

ATTORNEY GENERAL'S REFERENCE (NO.133 OF 2001), *Re*; *sub nom. R. v. STAGGS (GARY)* [2002] EWCA Crim 455, Kennedy, L.J., CA (Crim Div).

3942. Firearms offences–discharge of starting pistol in public place–community service order–undue leniency

[Criminal Justice Act 1988 s.36.]

The Attorney General referred a sentence of 100 hours community service imposed upon N to the Court of Appeal pursuant to the Criminal Justice Act 1988 s.36 on the basis of undue leniency. N had pleaded guilty to possessing an imitation firearm with intent to cause fear of violence. N had repeatedly fired a starting pistol from the window of a car in which he was travelling, on one occasion aiming the gun at a workman on the street. Later the same day, N discharged the pistol in the presence of three men with the intention of creating an apprehension of violence. The Attorney General contended that consideration of the relevant authorities indicated that the sentence handed down to N was unduly lenient.

Held, allowing the reference, that it was not appropriate for the sentencing judge to have imposed a sentence of less than two years' imprisonment, *Attorney General's Reference (No.49 of 1999), Re* [2000] 1 Cr. App. R. (S.) 436, [2000] C.L.Y. 1244 followed. However, given that N had already served two thirds of the community service order and accounting for the element of double jeopardy, a discount on the two year starting point was warranted. Accordingly, a sentence of one year imprisonment was substituted.

ATTORNEY GENERAL'S REFERENCE (NO.71 OF 2001), *Re*; *sub nom.* R. v. NIXON (TYRONE CARLOS); ATTORNEY GENERAL'S REFERENCE (NO.7 OF 2001), *Re*, [2001] EWCA Crim 2838, [2002] 2 Cr. App. R. (S.) 23, Mantell, L.J., CA (Crim Div).

3943. Firearms offences–life imprisonment–unexpired period of licence–determination of specified period

M appealed against a determinate sentence of ten years' imprisonment and a specified period of six years' imprisonment imposed in respect of his life sentence for possession of a firearm with intent. M and his co-accused entered the home of a couple through an unlocked door. The couple parted with a sum in cash after M brandished a sawn-off shotgun at them. Prior to being arrested and charged M had been remanded in custody following the revocation of an outstanding licence as a result of the fact that he had been charged with a murder of which he was subsequently acquitted. On being sentenced for the firearms charge it was agreed by the parties and accepted by the judge that the unexpired period of the licence, having been largely accounted for by the remand in custody, would not be taken into account in deciding the appropriate specified period. M contended that the judge had nevertheless taken this into account.

Held, allowing the appeal in part, that the determinate sentence of 10 years was not excessive. However the judge had erred by having regard to irrelevant considerations when imposing a specified period of six years. The correct approach to take in determining the length of a specified sentence was to first decide the determinate sentence. Having done that the court had a general discretion to fix the specified sentence at between one-half and two-thirds of the determinate period. The specified period should be fixed at one-half of the determinate sentence unless there were circumstances in the particular case justifying it being exceeded, *R. v. O'Connor (Michael Joseph)* (1994) 15 Cr. App. R. (S.) 473 and *R. v. M (Young Offender: Time in Custody on Remand)* [1999] 1 W.L.R. 485, [1998] C.L.Y. 1269 applied. In the instant case there were no such circumstances. The only possible reason for exceeding half the determinate period was the unexpired portion of the licence, a matter which the judge had agreed to disregard. Accordingly the appropriate specified period was five years.

R. v. McQUADE (KEITH JOSEPH), [2001] EWCA Crim 2398, [2002] 1 Cr. App. R. (S.) 128, Sir Swinton Thomas, CA (Crim Div).

3944. Firearms offences–mitigation–appellant in danger due to feud

M, a traveller, appealed against a sentence of 10 years' imprisonment imposed following his guilty plea to two offences of possessing a firearm with intent to endanger life. Two attempts to murder M had been made previously, arising from a feud. He maintained that his possession of the relevant firearms was as a consequence of the feud and its related dangers. It was submitted that the judge had failed to have proper regard to the exceptional circumstances that had given rise to the offences.

Held, allowing the appeal, that whilst M had not been justified in arming himself as he had, it was apparent that the exceptional circumstances that had led him to take such action amounted to mitigation. M had been warned by the police that his life was in danger. It followed that the sentence imposed had been manifestly excessive, and it was substituted with one of eight years' imprisonment.

R. v. MARNEY (WILLIAM HENRY), [2001] EWCA Crim 2111, [2002] 1 Cr. App. R. (S.) 118, Butterfield, J., CA (Crim Div).

3945. Firearms offences–motor vehicles–possession of imitation firearm with intent to cause fear–undue leniency

[Firearms Act 1968 s.16A.]

The Attorney General referred as unduly lenient the imposition of a fine of £250 on H, a French lorry driver, for possession of an imitation firearm with intent to cause fear of violence, contrary to the Firearms Act 1968 s.16A. H had been travelling on a motorway when he became involved in an altercation with the driver of another vehicle. The driver of the other vehicle had made an offensive hand gesture which had provoked H to point an imitation hand gun out of his cab in the direction of the other driver.

Held, allowing the reference, that brandishing a firearm, albeit an imitation one, so as to threaten another road user whilst travelling at speed on a motorway was a serious example of the use of a firearm with the intention of causing fear, contrary to s.16A of the 1968 Act. Having regard to the fact that H was a foreign national and that a United Kingdom custodial sentence would have a greater impact upon him than it would on a UK citizen, a sentence of 12 to 15 months' imprisonment would have been appropriate. However, in view of the element of double jeopardy, a sentence of eight months' imprisonment was substituted.

ATTORNEY GENERAL'S REFERENCE (NO.75 OF 2001), *Re; sub nom.* R. v. HOCHARD (DAVID GASTON), [2001] EWCA Crim 1928, [2002] 1 Cr. App. R. (S.) 103, Rose, L.J., CA (Crim Div).

3946. Firearms offences–robbery–good character–undue leniency

The Attorney General referred a three year sentence of imprisonment to the Court of Appeal on the basis of undue leniency. A had pleaded guilty to robbing a bank using an imitation firearm as a result of which he obtained some £700 in cash. He was of good character and had been depressed prior to commission of the offence.

Held, allowing the reference, that the sentence was unduly lenient. Although there was evidence of the offence being out of character for A it was nevertheless a serious offence requiring a sentence with an appropriate deterrence factor, *R. v. Ward-Lee (Jonathan)* (1994) 15 Cr. App.R. (S.) 427 applied. An appropriate sentence would be five years reduced to four years to take into account double jeopardy.

ATTORNEY GENERAL'S REFERENCE (NO.95 OF 2001), *Re; sub nom.* R. v. ASHLEY (LESLIE) [2002] EWCA Crim 328, Mantell, L.J., CA (Crim Div).

3947. Firearms offences–siege of matrimonial home–undue leniency

The Attorney General referred to the court a sentence of two and a half years' imprisonment that had been imposed on S following his conviction of various firearms offences, two offences of making threats to kill and an offence of assault occasioning actual bodily harm. Armed with a pistol, stun gun, handcuffs and cable ties and in breach of a non-molestation order, S had broken into the matrimonial home, culminating in an eighteen hour siege which ended only when he was overpowered by police officers.

Held, allowing the reference, that the initial sentence failed to reflect the serious psychological effects that the incident had had on S's wife and the adult relations of hers who had been present in the home. Having regard to the element of double jeopardy, a sentence of four years' imprisonment was imposed on S, *R. v. Avis (Tony)* [1998] 1 Cr. App. R. 420, [1998] C.L.Y. 1214, *Attorney General's Reference (No.40 of 1996), Re* [1997] 1 Cr. App. R. (S.) 357, [1997] C.L.Y. 1540 and *R. v. Hewitt (Gary)* [1999] 1 Cr. App. R. (S.) 256, [1999] C.L.Y. 1161 considered.

ATTORNEY GENERAL'S REFERENCE (NO.26 OF 2001), *Re*; *sub nom.* R. v. SPAHN (RICHARD), [2001] EWCA Crim 919, [2002] 1 Cr. App. R. (S.) 2, Lord Woolf of Barnes, L.C.J., CA (Crim Div).

3948. Firearms offences–threats–brandishing firearm with intent to cause fear–undue leniency

[Firearms Act 1968 s.16A.]

The Attorney General referred a sentence imposed on G of a community punishment and rehabilitation order requiring 12 months' supervision and 80 hours' work on the basis that it was unduly lenient following his conviction for an offence contrary to the Firearms Act 1968 s.16A. After making several telephone calls in the course of one evening to DG, his former co habitee, G had appeared at her house brandishing a compressed air pistol capable of firing a pellet propelled by a gas canister. G had threatened to discharge the gun at DG's car unless DG agreed to accompany G back to his house and to bring their three year old son. When DG refused, G had fired the gun, although he had missed the car. The air pistol, containing pellets and having a full gas canister, was found in G's car when he was arrested later the same night. G had admitted making the phone calls to DG and going to her house, but denied having the pistol in his possession at the time. G was already subject to a community penalty which he was completing and had an old conviction for a firearm offence.

Held, allowing the reference but not varying the sentence, that the only appropriate sentence in the circumstances was a custodial one, *R. v. Avis (Tony)* [1998] 1 Cr. App. R. 420, [1998] C.L.Y. 1214 considered. A sentence of at least 12 months would have been appropriate. However, G had already completed the community punishment element of his sentence and must have suffered anxiety awaiting the outcome of the instant review; therefore a custodial sentence would be unjust in the circumstances and the original sentence would stand.

ATTORNEY GENERAL'S REFERENCE (NO.96 OF 2001), *Re*; *sub nom.* R. v. GOODCHILD (CHRISTOPHER ANDREW) [2001] EWCA Crim 2666, Gibbs, J., CA (Crim Div).

3949. Forgery–conspiracy–relevance of counterfeiting cases in sentencing for forgery of passports and driving licences

M and a codefendant appealed against respective sentences of five years' and seven years and six months' imprisonment respectively for their roles in a conspiracy to process paper and materials designed or adapted for making false instruments namely, passports and driving licences. M contended that, in determining the appropriate sentence, the judge below erred in relying upon authorities which concerned money counterfeiting. Moreover, the judge should not have referred to the potential for M's offence, in a context of recent inter racial violence, to increase public anxiety over the issue of immigration control.

Held, allowing the appeal, that it had been appropriate to consider those authorities which involved the forgery of other types of documents especially where the cases involved counterfeiting, *R. v. Barry (Patrick Valentine)* (1983) 5 Cr. App. R. (S.) 11, [1984] C.L.Y. 862 and *R. v. Allyson (Paul Louis)* (1989) 11

Cr. App. R. (S.) 60, [1990] C.L.Y. 1271 considered. However, events of recent racial conflict were too remote from M's conduct to have properly influenced the sentencing process and thus, terms of four years and six months and six years for M and six months for his codefendant were substituted.

R. v. MUNIR (BASIT); R. v. KHONDU (AMPRITPAL), [2002] EWCA Crim 1555, [2003] 1 Cr. App. R. (S.) 27, Kay, L.J., CA (Crim Div).

3950. **Forgery–passports–appellant acting as courier of false passports**

[Forgery and Counterfeiting Act 1981 s.5.]

C appealed against a sentence of four years' imprisonment imposed for having custody or control of 12 false passports, contrary to the Forgery and Counterfeiting Act 1981 s.5. C arrived at an airport on a flight from Amsterdam and was found to be in possession of four envelopes containing 12 counterfeit passports. C claimed that he had agreed to bring the passports into the United Kingdom as a favour to another man and that the passports would be collected from his home.

Held, allowing the appeal, that the sentencing judge passed sentence on the basis that C had gone to Amsterdam for the sole purpose of obtaining the passports. In the court's view, a person acting as a courier of false passports was not to be treated in the same light as a person using a false passport to gain entry. Couriers were a necessary element in the unlawful trade; a considerable number of passports were involved. The sentence needed to be sufficiently severe to deter others from taking part in a lucrative but obnoxious trade. However, having regard to C's age and his role in the offence, a sentence of three years imprisonment was sufficient, *R. v. Singh (Daljit)* [1999] 1 Cr. App. R. (S.) 490, [1998] C.L.Y. 1227 and *R. v. Siliavski (Boyan Yossifov)* [2000] 1 Cr. App. R. (S.) 23, [2000] C.L.Y. 1255 considered.

R. v. CHEEMA (GURMIT SINGH), [2002] EWCA Crim 325, [2002] 2 Cr. App. R. (S.) 79, Pill, L.J., CA (Crim Div).

3951. **Fraud–custodial sentences–relevance of sentence length given imposition of confiscation order**

[Criminal Justice Act 1988 s.72(5).]

R appealed against a sentence of seven years' imprisonment for defrauding the Inland Revenue in a scheme involving building contractors and sub-contractors in which rebates were fraudulently claimed in respect of tax that had not been paid. R contended that in view of the circumstances of the case, and the fact that he had also been ordered to pay a confiscation order of £900,000, the sentence of seven years was excessive, *R. v. Andrews (Daniel Thomas)* [1997] 1 Cr. App. R. (S.) 279, [1997] C.L.Y. 1710 cited.

Held, dismissing the appeal, that taking into account all the aggravating features in respect of R's role in the scheme and that, by virtue of the Criminal Justice Act 1988 s.72(5), a confiscation order was not to be taken into consideration when determining sentence, the sentence of seven years' imprisonment was not excessive, *Andrews* not followed.

R. v. ROGERS (SIMON), [2001] EWCA Crim 1680, [2002] 1 Cr. App. R. (S.) 81, Judge Beaumont Q.C., CA (Crim Div).

3952. **Fraud–dishonesty–disparate sentences between codefendants–disparate levels of criminality**

B appealed against a sentence of five years' imprisonment for conspiracy to defraud, and A appealed against a total sentence of three years and eight months' imprisonment for offences relating to fraud and dishonesty, imposed after they defrauded investors in a company they had established of large sums of money. Both were extradited from New Zealand to face trial and they submitted that the judge was wrong in only granting a discount of six months for the time spent in custody in New Zealand rather than the full 11 months. A further contended that her sentence was manifestly excessive and unfairly disparate to that of B, given the differing roles they had played in the offences, her guilty plea and her good character. B contended that the judge erred in taking into account criminal behaviour which she had not admitted.

Held, allowing A's appeal and dismissing B's appeal, that the judge did not err in the exercise of his discretion relating to the time spent in custody awaiting extradition, given that they went to New Zealand to escape arrest in the United Kingdom. A's sentence was reduced to a total sentence of three years' imprisonment to account for the disparity between her, as a woman of essentially good character, and B, who had significant previous convictions for dishonesty. B's sentence was upheld given that the criminal conduct she pursued demanded a significant sentence.

R. v. BURTON (EVELYN); R. v. ANDRE (LYLA), [2001] EWCA Crim 1206, [2002] 1 Cr. App. R. (S.) 24, Steel, J., CA (Crim Div).

3953. Fraud–solicitors–expression of strong views by jurors during trial–use of solicitors or solicitors' clerks as police informants

See CRIMINAL PROCEDURE: R. v. Robinson (Timothy Morgan). §876

3954. Fraudulent trading–directors–company winding up with losses of £374,000

M pleaded guilty to fraudulent trading and to acting as an insolvency practitioner without qualification. M was the director of a company which was eventually wound up with losses of £374,000. The company held itself out as employing chartered accountants and indicated that monies recovered on behalf of its clients would be deposited in an insured indemnity account. There was no such account. M made various false representations potential clients. Monies collected on behalf of clients were not paid over. M also acted as an insolvency practitioner without a qualification, and made false statements in that connection. M was sentenced to a total of three years' imprisonment and appealed.

Held, dismissing the appeal, that a sentence of three years for fraudulent trading and acting as an insolvency practitioner without qualification was appropriate, *R. v. Gibson (Terence Michael)* [1999] 2 Cr. App. R. (S.) 52, [1999] C.L.Y. 1174 considered.

R. v. McHUGH (DAVID), [2001] EWCA Crim 1857, [2002] 1 Cr. App. R. (S.) 79, Silber, J., CA (Crim Div).

3955. Grievous bodily harm–affray–striking victim's head repeatedly with metal bar

L pleaded guilty to causing grievous bodily harm with intent and to affray. L then armed himself with a hollow metal bar, went to V's house and attacked him striking a number of blows to his face and head. V was taken to hospital with serious injuries. L returned home, changed his clothing and concealed the weapon. When a police officer approached L he pretended that he had a gun and threatened the officer with it. L was eventually overpowered and arrested. L was sentenced to eight years' imprisonment and appealed.

Held, dismissing the appeal, that a total sentence of eight years' imprisonment for causing grievous bodily harm with intent and affray was not manifestly excessive given the serious nature of the offences, *R. v. Moseley (Christopher)* [1999] 1 Cr. App. R. (S.) 452, [1999] C.L.Y. 1183 considered.

R. v. LAKER (MICHAEL DAVID), [2001] EWCA Crim 1070, [2002] 1 Cr. App. R. (S.) 18, Sachs, J., CA (Crim Div).

3956. Grievous bodily harm–children–intention–sentencing guidelines

M, aged 25, appealed against his sentence of 10 years' imprisonment imposed for inflicting grievous bodily harm with intent. The victim, a two year old child, was his girlfriend's daughter with whom he had been living. The offence occurred when M's girlfriend had left their house for no more than 15 or 20 minutes. A medical examination revealed that she had sustained bruising to her face and back, a cut inside her mouth, tearing of the ligament attached to the tongue and head injuries which included a long fracture of the occipital bone. The child subsequently made a full physical recovery and M contended that his sentence was manifestly excessive and was out of line with sentencing guidelines for like offences.

Held, allowing the appeal, that although the attack was particularly serious and that M was not entitled to a discount given his plea of not guilty, it was appropriate to reduce the sentence to eight years' imprisonment to bring it in line with the authorities, *R. v. Lowther (Jeffrey Ian)* (1990) 12 Cr. App. R. (S.) 299, [1992] C.L.Y. 1286, *Attorney General's Reference (No.13 of 1991), Re* (1992) 13 Cr. App. R. (S.) 650, [1993] C.L.Y. 1180, *R. v. Goodwin (Philip)* (1981) 3 Cr. App. R. (S.) 214 and *R. v. Bricklebank (Scott Norman)* [1996] 2 Cr. App. R. (S.) 410, [1997] C.L.Y. 1441 considered.

R. v. EOM, [2001] EWCA Crim 1250, [2002] 1 Cr. App. R. (S.) 40, Hughes, J., CA (Crim Div).

3957. Grievous bodily harm—intention—unprovoked attack—victim kicked while lying on ground—undue leniency

The Attorney General referred as unduly lenient a sentence of six months' imprisonment imposed on L following his conviction for attempting to cause grievous bodily harm with intent. L had been the instigator of an attack upon another man as he left a nightclub. L ran towards the victim, punched him and dragged him onto the floor. Six or seven other men joined in the attack and had stamped on and punched the victim as he lay upon the ground. The victim was detained overnight in hospital where he was found to have sustained bruising together with cuts and grazes to the head, two black eyes, bruising to the legs and a deviation of the nasal septum which required corrective surgery. The Attorney General contended that the offence was aggravated by the fact that it had been unprovoked, L had instigated the attack and he had kicked the victim as he lay upon the ground.

Held, refusing the reference, that at first instance, following a plea of guilty, a sentence of 18 months' imprisonment could have been expected. Having regard to the element of double jeopardy and the fact that L had already been released from prison, a sentence of 12 months' imprisonment would have been appropriate. However, it would not be appropriate to return L to prison in circumstances where he would only be obliged to serve half of the remaining six month term and accordingly the reference was refused, *Attorney General's Reference (No.22 of 1996), Re* [1997] 1 Cr. App. R. (S.) 191, [1997] C.L.Y. 1570 and *Attorney General's Reference (No.33 of 1997), Re* [1998] 1 Cr. App. R. (S.) 352, [1997] C.L.Y. 1551 considered.

ATTORNEY GENERAL'S REFERENCE (NO.138 OF 2001), *Re; sub nom. R. v. LAUD (ANDREW JAMES)* [2002] EWCA Crim 430, Rose, L.J., CA (Crim Div).

3958. Grievous bodily harm—joint enterprise—other assailant remaining unapprehended—undue leniency

The Attorney General referred to the court as unduly lenient a sentence of three years' imprisonment imposed on T following his conviction for causing grievous bodily harm with intent. T had attacked the victim with a makeshift blade or point and had hit her with his mobile telephone causing bruising and lacerations which required stitching. The aggravating features identified by the Attorney General were that this was an attack on a lone woman by four assailants, a makeshift weapon was used and the attack was sustained despite efforts to stop it. In mitigation it was argued that T had no previous convictions for violence, this was a private argument which had led to public violence and that the principal assailant, T's girlfriend, remained unapprehended.

Held, allowing the reference, that without the element of double jeopardy and following a contested trial, this was a case which would have merited a sentence of approximately five years' imprisonment. The court took into account the fact that T had made excellent progress while in prison and a submission by T's counsel that T should not be made a long term prisoner. The original sentence was quashed and one of three years and nine months' imprisonment was substituted.

ATTORNEY GENERAL'S REFERENCE (NO.140 OF 2001), *Re*; *sub nom*. R. v. TERRELONGE (KERON) [2002] EWCA Crim 1341, McKinnon, J., CA (Crim Div).

3959. Grievous bodily harm–knives–purpose of Attorney General's references–undue leniency

[Offences Against the Person Act 1861 s.18.]

The Attorney General referred to the court as unduly lenient a sentence of fours years' imprisonment imposed on J, who had pleaded guilty to an offence under the Offences Against the Person Act 1861 s.18. J had, while drunk, made an unprovoked attack on M, whom J believed to be responsible for his imminent eviction. J had punched and kicked M until he was unconscious or semi conscious. He had then gone to fetch a knife and upon his return had inflicted upon M several stab wounds, causing life threatening injuries. The aggravating features identified by the Attorney General were that this was an unprovoked attack on a defenceless victim involving the use of a knife as a weapon, the fact that J interrupted the attack to fetch a knife and then renewed the assault, and the severity and lasting consequences of the injuries. In mitigation, J had pleaded guilty, had expressed remorse and had previously been of good character.

Held, allowing the reference, that J had been fortunate to avoid trial for attempted murder. The basis of his plea was an intention only to cause serious harm. The attack was premeditated and unprovoked, and the starting point for the judge should have been nine years' imprisonment. An appropriate sentence following J's plea would have been one of at least six years' imprisonment. Bearing in mind the purpose of the Attorney General's references, namely to avoid gross error, allay widespread concern at what may appear to be an unduly lenient sentence and preserve public confidence, and also having regard to the principle of double jeopardy, the sentence was quashed and substituted by one of five years' imprisonment.

ATTORNEY GENERAL'S REFERENCE (NO.132 OF 2001), *Re*; *sub nom*. R. v. JOHNSON (BRYN DORIAN), [2002] EWCA Crim 1418, [2003] 1 Cr. App. R. (S.) 41, Potter, L.J., CA (Crim Div).

3960. Grievous bodily harm–knives–violent criminal record–undue leniency

[Offences against the Person Act 1861 s.18.]

The Attorney General referred as unduly lenient a sentence of 30 months' imprisonment for causing grievous bodily harm with intent, contrary to the Offences against the Person Act 1861 s.18. H had stabbed a 16 year old schoolboy with a knife and had pleaded guilty to the offence. The Attorney General contended that the sentence should be increased in view of the aggravating features, namely that the offence had involved an unprovoked knife attack on a young victim who was a complete stranger, and that H had a considerable criminal record involving violence.

Held, allowing the reference, that the sentence was unduly lenient. Taking into account H's violent criminal record, a sentence of six years' imprisonment was appropriate. However, having regard to double jeopardy, a sentence of five years' imprisonment was substituted.

ATTORNEY GENERAL'S REFERENCE (NO.18 OF 2002), *Re*; *sub nom*. R. v. HUGHES (CHRISTOPHER SIMON), [2002] EWCA Crim 1127, [2003] 1 Cr. App. R. (S.) 9, Rose, L.J., CA (Crim Div).

3961. Grievous bodily harm–provocation–loss of sight–unduly lenient sentence

[Offences Against the Person Act 1861 s.18, s.20.]

The Attorney General applied to refer as unduly lenient a sentence of three years and six months' imprisonment imposed on S for an offence of causing grievous bodily harm. S had without provocation attacked D with a pool cue which had resulted in severe injuries, including the loss of the sight in one eye. S had pleaded guilty to a charge under the Offences Against the Person Act 1861 s.20, but had pleaded not guilty to a s.18 offence.

Held, allowing the reference, that the sentence had been unduly lenient and had failed to reflect the severity of the offence. Taking into consideration the element of double jeopardy, a sentence of five years' imprisonment was substituted. An appropriate sentence for such an offence would otherwise have been a minimum of six years' imprisonment, *R. v. Davies (David William)* (1986) 8 Cr. App. R. (S.) 97, [1987] C.L.Y. 1077, *R. v. Di Palma (Paul)* (1989) 11 Cr. App. R. (S.) 329, *Attorney General's Reference (No.19 of 1994), Re* (1995) 16 Cr. App. R. (S.) 541 and *Attorney General's Reference (No.43 of 2000), Re* [2001] 1 Cr. App. R. (S.) 110, [2001] C.L.Y. 1321 considered.

ATTORNEY GENERAL'S REFERENCE (NO.102 OF 2001), *Re; sub nom.* R. v. SKELTON (LEE) [2001] EWCA Crim 2837, Mantell, L.J., CA (Crim Div).

3962. Grievous bodily harm–sportspersons–injuries inflicted during rugby match

B appealed against a sentence of eight months' imprisonment imposed following conviction for grievous bodily harm. The offence had been committed in the course of a rugby union match, off the ball, and the victim's jaw had been fractured in two places. B had maintained his not guilty plea through two aborted trials prior to conviction and had challenged the identification evidence at all stages. The sentencing recorder had described the offence as "off the ball thuggery". B contended that the recorder had overstated the seriousness of the offence and that the sentence was excessive.

Held, dismissing the appeal, that the sentence was due and appropriate. B had failed to show a shred of remorse throughout the proceedings for the gratuitous violence, which could not be tolerated on the playing field.

R. v. BOWYER (DAVID JAMES), [2001] EWCA Crim 1853, [2002] 1 Cr. App. R. (S.) 101, Wright, J., CA (Crim Div).

3963. Handling stolen goods–burglary–residential premises–antiques

G appealed against a sentence of five years' imprisonment imposed for handling stolen property. G and a codefendant were involved in handling property stolen in the course of residential burglaries. The stolen property consisted for the most part of antiques which were subsequently sold at auction. G and his accomplice were shown to have been in possession of the stolen items of property within a short time after the burglaries had taken place. The prices paid for the property handled by G amounted to £16,160, but the sentencing judge was satisfied that the replacement value of the items was in most cases substantially in excess of this price. The sentencing judge expressed himself to be satisfied that when G and his accomplice received the articles, they knew that they had been stolen in residential burglaries, and that the burglars knew that G and his accomplice would be willing to receive the stolen goods. The judge was satisfied that G and his accomplice were professional receivers.

Held, allowing the appeal, that a sentence of five years was too long, in view of the delay of two and a half years between G's arrest and his conviction. A total sentence of four years was substituted, *R. v. Webbe (Bernard)* [2001] EWCA Crim 1217, [2002] 1 Cr. App. R. (S.) 22, [2001] C.L.Y. 1340 considered.

R. v. GWYER (BARRY JOHN), [2002] EWCA Crim 102, [2002] 2 Cr. App. R. (S.) 56, Keith, J., CA (Crim Div).

3964. Handling stolen goods–custodial sentences–undercover police officer posing as burglar

C appealed against a sentence of 15 months' imprisonment imposed for attempting to handle stolen goods. C was a jeweller who operated two shops. Following information that stolen jewellery was being received at his premises, an undercover police officer began to visit the shop offering to sell jewellery. Eventually the police officer indicated that the goods he was offering to sell were stolen and that he, the police officer, was a burglar. The goods offered for sale had been recovered over a period of years by the police but had not been claimed by members of the public. Subsequently, various items were sold to C. It was argued on behalf of C that the offences were committed as a result of police targeting and that there was no actual victim.

Held, allowing the appeal, that the court began its analysis with the guidelines for offences of handling stolen goods and also identified a number of the aggravating features set out in, *R. v. Webbe (Bernard)* [2001] EWCA Crim 1217, [2002] 1 Cr.App. R. (S.) 22, [2001] C.L.Y. 1340. These were (1) the closeness of the handler to the primary offence; (2) the fact that C must have appreciated that he was discussing the acquisition of stolen goods from the burglar; (3) the fact that the goods were represented to be the proceeds of domestic burglaries, and (4) the high level of profit made and expected by the handler. Accordingly the sentence was reduced to a 10 month term, *Webbe* considered.

R. v. CHALCRAFT (JAMES WILLIAM); R. v. CAMPBELL (NEIL DAVID), [2001] EWCA Crim 2931, [2002] 2 Cr. App. R. (S.) 42, Leveson, J., CA (Crim Div).

3965. Harassment—malicious communications—threatening and abusive letters

J appealed against a sentence of five years' imprisonment imposed following his guilty plea to two counts of making threats to kill and one count of causing fear of violence. J had written threatening and abusive letters to two victims. At the time of his arrest J had informed the police that he had sent a further letter to the second victim and she had consequently been warned. It was apparent that both victims had been put in genuine fear and had thought it likely that the threats would be carried out. A pre-sentence report had found that J had expressed some remorse but that he had placed a significant amount of blame on the victims. A psychiatric report had found that he was likely to repeat his actions in the future.

Held, allowing the appeal, that having regard to the fact that no actual violence had been used, the fact that no breach of any court order had occurred and the admission that J had made to the police upon his arrest, it was appropriate to make the sentence on the third count run concurrent with that of the other two with the result that the total sentence was reduced to four years' imprisonment.

R. v. JONES (JONATHAN NIGEL), [2001] EWCA Crim 2235, [2002] 1 Cr. App. R. (S.) 127, Hooper, J., CA (Crim Div).

3966. Harassment—recidivists—causing fear of violence

[Protection from Harassment Act 1997 s.4(1).]

P pleaded guilty before a magistrates court to harassment causing fear of violence, contrary to the Protection from Harassment Act 1997 s.4(1). P, who had a criminal record, was released from a custodial sentence and within a few weeks began to make series of menacing phone calls to the victim. P was sentenced to two and a half years' imprisonment and appealed.

Held, dismissing the appeal, that P had a history of disobedience to court orders in the past and his behaviour towards the victim was both persistent and threatening, and had unpleasant effects on the victim. The sentence was not wrong in principle or manifestly excessive, *R. v. Cox (Allan)* [2000] 2 Cr. App. R. (S.) 57, [2000] C.L.Y. 1192 considered.

R. v. PRESTON (AMANDA LOUISE) [2002] 1 Cr. App. R. (S.) 96, Judge Beaumont Q.C., CA (Crim Div).

3967. Harassment—restraining orders—breach

[Protection from Harassment Act 1997 s.5.]

K appealed against a sentence of 12 months' imprisonment imposed for breach of a restraining order imposed under the Protection from Harassment Act 1997 s.5. K had a relationship with a young woman which broke down after about a year and a half in about 1995 or 1996. Following the breakdown of the relationship, K parked his car outside the woman's place of work. When she married another man, the appellant constantly followed her from work to her home, with the result that her relationship with her husband was disrupted and ended in separation. K was convicted of assaulting the woman in 2000 and subjected to a community service order. He was subsequently convicted of harassment, sentenced to imprisonment and subjected to a restraining order.

Held, dismissing the appeal, that the sentence, although severe, was wholly justified in the context of the history of the case, *R. v. Liddle (Mark) (Appeal against Sentence)* [1999] 3 All E.R. 816, [1999] C.L.Y. 1188 considered.

R. v. KASOAR (JAYESING), [2002] EWCA Crim 12, [2002] 2 Cr. App. R. (S.) 60, Judge Fawcus, CA (Crim Div).

3968. Health and safety at work—risk assessment—failure to carry out resulting in serious injury—fines

[Health and Safety at Work etc. Act 1974 s.2(1); Provision and Use of Work Equipment Regulations 1998 (SI 1998 2306) Reg.11.]

C, a company, appealed against a fine of £350,000 after pleading guilty before a magistrates court to contravening the Health and Safety at Work etc. Act 1974 s.2(1), and the Provision and Use of Work Equipment Regulations 1998 Reg.11. C was committed to the Crown Court for sentence. C specialised in the manufacture of carton board. The board was produced on a large machine which contained two hundred points known as "in running nips". A Health and Safety inspector visited the company's premises and issued an improvement notice requiring the company to carry out a programme of risk assessment. C did not complete the assessment by the due date, and the inspector granted an extension of time. An experienced employee went to the machine and attempted to clean it or remove an obstruction. His arm was pulled through the "nip" and he sustained a serious crush injury to his hand and arm. He was admitted to hospital for four weeks and underwent four operations. The charges arose out of that incident. C was also ordered to pay about £5,000 prosecution costs.

Held, allowing the appeal in part, that the total fine was reduced to £200,000. The order for payment of prosecution costs was not disturbed, *R. v. F Howe & Son (Engineers) Ltd* [1999] 2 All E.R. 249, [1999] C.L.Y. 2839 considered.

R. v. COLTHROP BOARD MILLS LTD, [2002] EWCA Crim 520, [2002] 2 Cr. App. R. (S.) 80, Gibbs, J., CA (Crim Div).

3969. Hijacking—aircraft—attack upon flight attendant—threats to blow up aircraft—communicating false information

[Criminal Law Act 1977 s.51 (2).]

M, aged 62, sought leave to appeal against a sentence of four years' imprisonment imposed for communicating false information, contrary to the Criminal Law Act 1977 s.51 (2). M, who was a passenger aboard a flight from Zurich to London, wandered into the business class area carrying a briefcase. As a flight attendant approached him, he lurched forward, grabbed the back of her neck, pulled her into the front galley and held a pair of scissors to her throat. As another crew member entered the galley, M shouted out that he was hijacking the aircraft and that he would kill the flight attendant. He made several demands and indicated that he wanted political asylum in the United Kingdom. He held what appeared to be a dictaphone in his hand and indicated to all on board that he had a bomb and was prepared to blow up the aircraft if his demands were not met. Having persuaded M to release the flight attendant, the captain remained with M leaving the co-pilot to land the aircraft on his own. Police officers boarded the aircraft and M was arrested. In interview, M stated that the had been politically active in Trinidad and Tobago and that the opposition party was persecuting him and plotting to kill him. He contended that his sentence was manifestly excessive.

Held, refusing the application, that in view of the fact that M had terrified both the passengers and crew and had exposed them to danger, the offence was very serious. The co-pilot had had to land the aircraft on his own without the assistance of the pilot and this had meant that a layer of safety checks had been taken out of the system. It was unreal to think that the aircraft had not been placed in danger. Further, the flight attendant had been traumatised by the whole incident. The sentence had to punish M and deter others and could not be said to be excessive.

R. v. MASON (AUBURN), [2001] EWCA Crim 1138, [2002] 1 Cr. App. R. (S.) 29, Butterfield, J., CA (Crim Div).

3970. Immigration–deception–asylum seekers–provision of false details about country of origin

[Immigration Act 1971 s.24A (1).]

A, a Pakistani national, appealed against a sentence of 18 months' imprisonment imposed following his plea of guilty to an offence of seeking to obtain leave to enter the United Kingdom by deception, contrary to the Immigration Act 1971 s.24A (1). A had provided false details, claiming to be from Afghanistan. He had been served with an illegal entry notice and granted temporary asylum. Subsequent checks revealed that he had submitted a claim for political asylum. An anonymous letter had been received by the immigration authorities stating that A was in fact a Pakistani national and in an interview with the police he had admitted the deception.

Held, allowing the appeal, that given the prevalence of such offences it was necessary that they be treated seriously by the courts. Section 24A of the Act was a relatively new amendment and had a maximum sentence, on indictment, of two years' imprisonment. Whilst a plea of guilt would attract a discount, personal mitigation and previous good character were of little consequence. The sentence had to contain a deterrent factor. Having regard to the circumstances of the instant case, which was not the most serious that could be imagined, a term of 12 months' imprisonment was appropriate.

R. v. ALI (NASIR), [2001] EWCA Crim 2874, [2002] 2 Cr. App. R. (S.) 32, May, L.J., CA (Crim Div).

3971. Immigration–illegal entrants–facilitating illegal entry of immigrants into UK

[Immigration Act 1971 s.25 (1) (a); Immigration and Asylum Act 1999; Powers of Criminal Courts (Sentencing) Act 2000 s.155.]

W, a lorry driver, appealed against a sentence of six years' imprisonment imposed for facilitating the entry into United Kingdom of illegal entrants, contrary to the Immigration Act 1971 s.25 (1) (a). W was stopped while driving a lorry when he was about to enter the Channel Tunnel control area. He stated that the lorry contained quartz sand but a search of the lorry revealed that it contained 35 people. W claimed to have no knowledge of the people in his lorry. W was initially sentenced to five years' imprisonment, on the assumption that the maximum sentence for the offence was seven years; he was disqualified from driving for five years and an order was made forfeiting his unit. Shortly after sentence had been passed, the judge was advised that the maximum sentence had been increased from seven years to 10 years by the Immigration and Asylum Act 1999, which came into force about one year before the date of the offence. Within an hour, W was brought back before the sentencing judge who stated that he had to give full effect to the intention of Parliament, and increased the sentence from five years to six years, under the Powers of Criminal Courts (Sentencing) Act 2000 s.155. On appeal, it was argued that it was wrong of the judge to vary the sentence. It was noted that the test identified in *Hadley* had not been put forward as a definitive test for all cases and that the judge could usefully adopt it.

Held, allowing the appeal, that the approach identified in *Hadley* was not the appropriate approach to adopt in the circumstances of the present case; however, it was an approach which could usefully be adopted when the interval was measured in days. The court accordingly rejected the argument that because the sentence of five years originally imposed was not outside the bracket of sentence which the judge could reasonably have imposed on the facts, the sentencing judge was obliged by the decision in *Hadley* to take no further action. It was accepted that a lengthy period of imprisonment was inevitable, even for a man of previous good character. Sentences in cases of this kind were heavy and were intended to deter. The court had to ask itself whether, given the maximum sentence of 10 years, a sentence of six years for this particular offence was manifestly excessive. In light of *Winn* the sentence of six years was too long. The court would substitute a sentence of five years' imprisonment. The disqualification from driving was reduced to three years, *R. v. Hadley (Shaun Patrick)* (1995) 16 Cr. App. R. (S.) 358, [1994] C.L.Y. 1295 and *R. v. Winn (James Derrick)* [1999] 1 Cr. App. R. (S.) 154, [1999] C.L.Y. 1191 considered.

R. v. WOOP (MICHAEL THOMAS), [2002] EWCA Crim 58, [2002] 2 Cr. App. R. (S.) 65, Mitchell, J., CA (Crim Div).

3972. Incest–fathers–daughter aged over 16 years–sentencing guidelines

M, aged 38 and of previous good character, appealed against his sentence of five years' imprisonment imposed following trial on three counts of incest. The offences had been committed over some 21 months, when M and his daughter had engaged in regular acts of sexual intercourse which had commenced when she was nearly 17 years old. He contended that his sentence was manifestly excessive and that the term exceeded sentencing guidelines.

Held, allowing the appeal, that having regard to the sentencing guidelines, the fact that M's daughter only became aware of his existence when she was 14, that they had not shared the same household but taking into consideration M's plea of not guilty which had necessitated his daughter giving evidence, a reduction to a term of three years and six months' imprisonment was appropriate, *Attorney General's Reference (No.1 of 1989), Re* [1989] 1 W.L.R. 1117, [1991] C.L.Y. 1138 applied and *R. v. Harrison (Robert Malcolm)* (1987) 9 Cr. App. R. (S.) 292, [1989] C.L.Y. 1039, *R. v. McDonald (Peter George)* (1989) 11 Cr. App. R. (S.) 6, [1990] C.L.Y. 1332 and *R. v. T (David)* (1994) 15 Cr. App. R. (S.) 871, [1995] C.L.Y. 1402 considered.

R. v. GM, [2001] EWCA Crim 1107, [2002] 1 Cr. App. R. (S.) 26, Hughes, J., CA (Crim Div).

3973. Indecency–photographs–pornographic images of children–sentencing guidelines

W appealed against a sentence of four months' imprisonment for 15 offences of making an indecent photograph or pseudo photograph, after pornographic images of children aged between infancy and pre pubescence were recovered from the hard drive of his computer. It was submitted that (1) the judge should not have treated as an aggravating feature the fact that W said that he had distributed indecent photographs, given that he had never been charged with such activity, and (2) the judge should not have relied on W's sexually explicit internet conversations as an aggravating feature. It was further contended that the images were relatively small in number, were sent unsolicited to W and were for W's personal use rather than for commercial gain.

Held, allowing the appeal, that (1) the distribution of indecent material had to be reflected in a specific count before it could be treated as an aggravating feature, and (2) as there was no evidence of a link between the conversations and the instant offences, the judge should not have relied on them as aggravating features. The offences did not cross the custody threshold and could have been effectively dealt with by a substantial fine, *R. v. Toomer (Martin Charles)* [2001] Crim. L.R. 149, [2000] C.L.Y. 1381 followed. However, given the two months W had spent in custody, his sentence was quashed and a conditional discharge for 12 months substituted.

R. v. WILD (MICHAEL KEITH) (NO.1), [2001] EWCA Crim 1272, [2002] 1 Cr. App. R. (S.) 37, Rose, L.J., CA (Crim Div).

3974. Indecency–pornography–children–downloading images from internet–absence of distribution

[Protection of Children Act 1978 s.1 (1) (a).]

T, aged 29, appealed against a sentence of eight months' imprisonment following his guilty plea to making indecent photographs of children, contrary to the Protection of Children Act 1978 s.1 (1) (a). T contended that a custodial sentence was inappropriate as the offence was an isolated one without a commercial element or element of distribution and in view of his previous good character and guilty plea.

Held, allowing the appeal, that notwithstanding the high level of obscenity of the images, the custody threshold had not been reached and a community rehabilitation order of one year was appropriate, *R. v. Wild (Michael Keith) (No.1)* [2001] EWCA Crim 1272 applied.

R. v. TURPIN (NICHOLAS VICTOR), [2001] EWCA Crim 1600, [2002] 1 Cr. App. R. (S.) 77, Grigson, J., CA (Crim Div).

3975. Indecent assault–actual bodily harm–attempted rape–complainant and offender in relationship–unnecessary violence–undue leniency

The Attorney General referred to the court as unduly lenient a total sentence of two years' imprisonment imposed on C following his conviction for attempted rape, indecent assault and assault occasioning actual bodily harm. C and the complainant had been in a relationship for a number of years. Initially the relationship had been happy but it had deteriorated after three years. C had started to drink and had become possessive. The incident giving rise to the offences had occurred at the home shared by C and the complainant. C had demanded sex and had seized the complainant from behind and pulled her upstairs. He had forced her to take his penis in her mouth and had subsequently attempted anal intercourse. C had thrust his fist into the complainant's vagina and had slapped her face. The following aggravating features were identified (1) the attempted rape had been followed by an act of grave indecency which had caused severe pain; (2) unnecessary and gratuitous violence had accompanied the attempted rape and indecent assault, and (3) as a consequence of the incident, the complainant had suffered physical and psychological harm.

Held, allowing the reference, that having regard to the aggravating features, the sentence imposed had been unduly lenient. A sentence of at least four years' imprisonment would have been expected. Taking into account the element of double jeopardy and the fact that C's release date was close, it was appropriate that a total sentence of three years be substituted, *R. v. H (Michael)* [1997] 2 Cr. App. R. (S.) 339, [1998] C.L.Y. 1353 and *Attorney General's Reference (No.7 of 1989), Re* (1990) 12 Cr. App. R. (S.) 1, [1991] C.L.Y. 1194 considered.

ATTORNEY GENERAL'S REFERENCE (NO.26 OF 2002), Re; sub nom. R. v. C, [2002] EWCA Crim 1300, [2003] 1 Cr. App. R. (S.) 29, Rose, L.J., CA (Crim Div).

3976. Indecent assault–children–assaults on four step grandchildren aged from five to 11 years–undue leniency

The Attorney General referred a sentence of three years and six months' imprisonment with an extended licence period of five years on the basis of undue leniency. M had pleaded guilty to five offences of indecent assault and four of gross indecency. The offences had concerned four of M's step grandchildren and had been committed when the children were variously aged from five to 11 years of age. The Attorney General submitted that the offences were aggravated by the fact that M had abused a position of trust, he had moved from one child to another and the abuse had been committed on approximately 100 occasions over a four year period. Further, the Attorney General argued that the ages of the children were relevant and M had a previous conviction for indecently assaulting a boy and had been on life licence for offences of murder, attempted murder and in relation to firearms.

Held, allowing the reference, that taking into account the number and age of the children involved, the judge's starting point of six years following a trial had been too low. At first instance a total sentence of five to six years in relation to the offences of indecent assault should have been passed and accordingly the sentence of three years and six months' imprisonment had been unduly lenient and was substituted by one of four years and six months' to run concurrently with the three year and six month sentence imposed for gross indecency, resulting in a total term of eight years' imprisonment.

ATTORNEY GENERAL'S REFERENCE (NO.141 OF 2001), *Re; sub nom.* R. v. M (DAVID); R. v. MCD (DAVID), [2002] EWCA Crim 960, [2003] 1 Cr. App. R. (S.) 7, Rose, L.J., CA (Crim Div).

3977. Indecent assault–children–breach of trust–unduly lenient sentence

The Attorney General referred as unduly lenient a sentence of 18 months' imprisonment imposed upon R following his conviction for eleven counts of indecent assault and one count of indecency with a child. Over a period of six months, R had committed the offences against friends of his daughter who were aged between nine and ten years old at the relevant time. The offences had involved touching the children's vaginal areas over and beneath their clothing and R exposing himself to three of the children.

Held, allowing the reference, that the aggravating features of the offences, namely the length of the course of conduct, the breach of trust involved and the fact that there had been six young victims, warranted a lengthier term than that which had been imposed. Any personal mitigation on the part of R was outweighed by the number of victims and a sentence of three years' imprisonment would have been expected in a case of this nature. Accordingly, having regard to the principle of double jeopardy, the sentence was quashed and substituted with a sentence of 27 months' imprisonment.

ATTORNEY GENERAL'S REFERENCE (NO.27 OF 2001), *Re; sub nom.* R. v. R (MALCOLM JAMES), [2001] EWCA Crim 1283, [2002] 1 Cr. App. R. (S.) 42, Rose, L.J., CA (Crim Div).

3978. Indecent assault–children–community rehabilitation orders–offender of low intellect and previous good character–undue leniency

[Sex Offenders Act 1997.]

The Attorney General referred to the court as unduly lenient a three year community rehabilitation order imposed on B for nine counts of indecent assault on his two nieces. B was also ordered to accept psychiatric treatment and register for five years under the Sex Offenders Act 1997. B had committed the offences at the girls' grandparents' house over a period of seven years from when the girls were aged about 10 years. The aggravating features identified by the Attorney General were that B was in a position of trust in relation to the girls, the age of the girls at the time when the offending started, the fact that they had been "groomed", the persistent and repeated nature of the offences and the impact of the offences on the victims. In mitigation, B had pleaded guilty and was of previous good character, the offences had taken place more than 14 years prior to their being dealt with by the court and B was of low intellect.

Held, finding the sentence unduly lenient but not varying it, that a more appropriate sentence would have been one of at least two years' imprisonment. However, the sentencing judge had approached the matter with great care and had fully recognised the importance of protecting the public from such conduct. He had identified the risk of repeat offending as fairly limited, taking into account the length of time which had elapsed since the offences with no suggestion of any subsequent offence. The judge had also noted that the offences were opportunistic rather than predatory and did not involve the general public. In all the circumstances, it was not appropriate to interfere with the sentence passed.

ATTORNEY GENERAL'S REFERENCE (NO.29 OF 2002), *Re*; *sub nom.* R. v. B (ROBERT) [2002] EWCA Crim 1283, Rose, L.J., CA (Crim Div).

3979. Indecent assault–community rehabilitation orders–courts' duty to protect the public–undue leniency

The Attorney General referred as unduly lenient concurrent sentences of two year community rehabilitation orders imposed on M for six offences of indecent assault on two boys. M had pleaded guilty. The offences had been committed in the 1970s.

Held, refusing the reference, that although the sentences were lenient they were not unduly so. The public had to understand that sentencing judges faced a very difficult task in cases of the present nature. They had to balance the effect of the offences on the victim with a responsibility to protect the public at large from similar re offending. A sensible approach would have been to sentence such an offender to a short term of imprisonment coupled with participation in a sex offender's training programme. Unfortunately, at the date of sentencing, the courts did not have such options open to them. The sentencing judge had correctly considered all the facts of the case and the sentencing options open to him at the time. It was true to say that the sentence imposed had done little, if anything, to satisfy the needs of the victims, but it was impossible to say that the sentence was wrong in principle, *R. v. Willis (Peter Charles)* [1975] 1 W.L.R. 292, [1975] C.L.Y. 714 applied.

ATTORNEY GENERAL'S REFERENCE (NO.39 OF 2002), *Re*; *sub nom.* R. v. M (PETER), [2002] EWCA Crim 1980, *The Times*, July 11, 2002, Kay, L.J., CA (Crim Div).

3980. Indecent assault–community rehabilitation orders–victims put in fear–undue leniency

The Attorney General referred to the court as unduly lenient a three year community rehabilitation order imposed on D, who had a history of mental illness, following his conviction on two counts of indecent assault. On separate occasions within the space of four days, D had persuaded two young women to accompany him to his flat. Once inside neither had been permitted to leave. In the first assault, D had requested that the victim perform oral sex upon him, a request which she had complied with out of fear. In the second incident, D had again requested oral sex but was eventually persuaded to masturbate in front of the victim having been informed by her that he ran the risk of contracting a sexually transmitted disease. A report by a consultant psychiatrist indicated that there was no causal link between D's mental condition and the commission of the offences.

Held, allowing the reference, that the sentence imposed had been unduly lenient. The maximum sentence imposed for indecent assault had increased from two to ten years since 1989 which was suggestive of it being Parliament's intention that the courts treat the offence with greater seriousness. Following a trial, the minimum appropriate sentence would have been five years' imprisonment. Having regard to the element of double jeopardy inherent in the process, a term of four years' imprisonment was substituted, *Attorney General's Reference (No.4 of 1989), Re* [1990] 1 W.L.R. 41, [1990] C.L.Y. 1207 considered.

ATTORNEY GENERAL'S REFERENCE (NO.97 OF 2001), *Re*; *sub nom.* R. v. DORSETT (IAN ANTHONY) [2001] EWCA Crim 2798, Mantell, L.J., CA (Crim Div).

3981. Indecent assault–convictions–change of plea during trial–status of conviction entered without jury verdict

P appealed against her conviction for indecent assault. P had entered a plea of not guilty at the plea and directions stage of the proceedings but had altered her plea to guilty during the course of the trial. The judge did not invite the jury to return a verdict and discharged them. Subsequently, P sought to vacate the guilty plea but her application was refused. P contended that the conviction was a nullity in the absence of a guilty verdict from the jury.

Held, dismissing the appeal, that there was no relevant principle capable of rendering a conviction obtained in such circumstances a nullity. Where P had voluntarily pleaded guilty in open court, the trial judge's discretion to discharge the jury was not limited by the formality of asking for a verdict, *R. v. Drew (Patrick John)* [1985] 1 W.L.R. 914, [1985] C.L.Y. 608 followed. Moreover, P had not suffered any procedural disadvantage as her plea had been treated in the same manner as a guilty plea entered before the jury was sworn and consequently, the court refused to exercise its discretion to order a venire de novo.

R. v. P (LOUISE), [2001] EWCA Crim 2664, [2002] 1 W.L.R. 1528, Judge, L.J., CA (Crim Div).

3982.   Indecent assault–custodial sentences–assault of female work colleague

S, a married man aged 31, appealed against a sentence of eight months' imprisonment for indecent assault. S and the complainant were employed as security guards at a pleasure beach. While the complainant was on duty at an entrance to the pleasure beach, S spent some time in her company and made a number of remarks of a sexual nature to her. S pleaded guilty on the basis that there had been banter throughout the working day between him and the complainant and that S had gripped her arm and placed his hand inside her trousers.

Held, dismissing the appeal, that in the court's view, the sentencing judge was entitled to include a deterrent element in the sentence. A degree of force was used by S, and the assault took place in a room where the complainant was alone with him. The sentence imposed was therefore not manifestly excessive.

R. v. SHORTHOUSE (JULIAN DOMINIC), [2001] EWCA Crim 2580, [2002] 2 Cr. App. R. (S.) 10, Bell, J., CA (Crim Div).

3983.   Indecent assault–extended sentences–attack on female cyclist–sentencing guidelines

P appealed against his sentence of four years and six months' imprisonment with an extended licence period of three years and six months for indecent assault, after he dragged a female cyclist from her bicycle on a country lane and a struggle ensued in which he grabbed the victim's breast. He submitted that the sentence was excessive in the light of his guilty plea, good character and character references. He further argued that he should not have been sentenced on the basis of an intended rape given that the only sexual element of the attack was the squeezing of the victim's breast.

Held, allowing the appeal, that notwithstanding the fact that the attack was very frightening for the victim and it had had a considerable affect on her, the sentence was excessive in the light of case authorities and was reduced to three years and six months' imprisonment with an extended licence period of two years, *R. v. Currie (James)* (1988) 10 Cr. App. R. (S.) 85, [1990] C.L.Y. 1334 and *Attorney General's Reference (No.39 of 1997), Re* [1998] 2 Cr. App. R. (S.) 336, [1998] C.L.Y. 1264 considered.

R. v. PULLEN (KEITH ALEXANDER), [2001] EWCA Crim 1071, [2002] 1 Cr. App. R. (S.) 17, Steel, J., CA (Crim Div).

3984.   Indecent assault–extended sentences–length of extension period

[Powers of Criminal Courts (Sentencing) Act 2000 s.85.]

C appealed against a custodial term of two years and an extended period of five years under the Powers of Criminal Courts (Sentencing) Act 2000 s.85 for indecent assault. C approached a woman who was walking along a road with her boyfriend. He lunged forward and placed one hand on each of the woman's breasts, squeezing and holding them. The woman's boyfriend pulled him away, and the woman was caused to fall to the ground. C admitted the offence in interview, and stated that he had planned to commit an indecent assault. He had been walking around the area looking for women and had selected the victim for the purpose. C indicated an intention to plead guilty before a magistrates' court to indecent assault. He was committed to the Crown Court for sentence. C contended that the extension period was manifestly excessive.

Held, allowing the appeal, that C had previous convictions for similar indecent assaults, and was subject to a probation order for an indecent assault at the time of the offences. The sentencing judge referred to the element of premeditation and the distress caused to the victim. Therefore the length of the custodial term could be criticised. The sentencing judge had given no reason for choosing the period of five years as the extension period. It was accepted in principle that an extended sentence was justified. The principles which emerged from *Nelson* in relation to the length of the extension period were that it was not designed to reflect the seriousness of the offence, but to protect the public and secure the rehabilitation of the offender by preventing his re offending; a relatively short custodial term and a long extension period might be the right response to a low level offence with a high risk of re offending. While it might be necessary for the offender to have to serve the whole or part of the extension period, strict proportionality between the length of the extension period and the seriousness of the offence was not a primary consideration, but the principle of proportionality had to be observed. The sentencing judge had given no reason for selecting the term of the extension period. He had evidence of long standing mental health problems for which C had previously been treated. The principle of proportionality was of considerable importance in the case; the extension period was manifestly too long, looking at the totality of sentence which it produced. In the circumstances, the court substituted an extension period of two years, *R. v. Nelson (Patrick Alan)* [2001] EWCA Crim 2264, [2002] 1 Cr. App. R. (S.) 134, [2001] C.L.Y. 1369 considered.

R. v. CORNELIUS (ALAN), [2002] EWCA Crim 138, [2002] 2 Cr. App. R. (S.) 69, Mackay, J., CA (Crim Div).

3985. **Indecent assault–extended sentences–persistent offending against children–breach of trust–undue leniency**

The Attorney General referred as unduly lenient a sentence of five years' imprisonment, with an extended licence period of three years, for offences of indecent assault. W, aged 50 on appeal, was convicted on 10 counts in relation to boys and one in relation to a girl. The victims were all under the age of 13 and the offences spanned a period of four years. The assaults involved touching the boys' penises, in one case W performed oral sex on the boy and, in two cases, W had used force to simulate anal intercourse to the point of ejaculation. The Attorney General submitted that there were a number of aggravating features justifying an increased sentence including the gravity of the offences and the use of force, the fact that they constituted a course of predatory conduct, the obtaining and subsequent breach of the boys' parents' trust, the use of threats and emotional blackmail to force the boys to conceal the offences, and the real possibility of emotional or psychological damage to the victims. W had previous convictions for similar behaviour and there were no mitigating features.

Held, allowing the reference, that the three principal aggravating features in cases of this kind were all present in W's case: namely emotional damage, moral corruption and breach of trust, *R. v. Willis (Peter Charles)* [1975] 1 W.L.R. 292, [1975] C.L.Y. 714 applied. W posed a very substantial risk to young people which was likely to continue after his release. It was therefore correct to impose an extended sentence including an extended licence period, but the original sentence imposed had been unduly lenient. Accordingly, a custodial term of eight years was imposed with an extended licence period of two years.

ATTORNEY GENERAL'S REFERENCE (NO.112 OF 2001), Re; *sub nom*. R. v. WOOD (WINSTON), [2002] EWCA Crim 94, [2002] 2 Cr. App. R. (S.) 57, Rose, L.J., CA (Crim Div).

3986. Indecent assault—indictments—age of juvenile complainant not stated in each count—jurisdiction of court to impose custodial sentence in excess of two years

[Sexual Offences Act 1985 s.3(3).]

G appealed against the sentence imposed following his conviction on an indictment alleging indecent assault of his stepdaughter between 1977 and 1980 when she was aged between nine and 11 years. The particulars of the indecent acts were specifically stated in each count but the victim's age was not. G was sentenced to three years' imprisonment on each count concurrent to each other but consecutive to a nine year sentence for the rape of the same victim between 1980 and 1983. G contended that the three year sentences for the indecent assaults were not within the jurisdiction of the court.

Held, dismissing the appeal, that the court had jurisdiction to impose such a sentence on G. The Sexual Offences Act 1985 s.3(3) increased the maximum penalty for the indecent assault of a female under 10 years as from September 1985. Prior to that date, the maximum sentence was two years imprisonment unless the complainant was under 13 years old and her age was stated in the indictment; in such circumstances the maximum sentence was five years. In the instant case, the Crown had submitted a schedule of the victim's age and the acts complained of in relation to each count on the indictment. This was to be read in conjunction with the indictment. The complainant's age had been apparent to the judge, jury and the parties throughout the proceedings and accordingly the conditions in s.3(3) had been met.

R. v. G (BARRY) [2002] EWCA Crim 1257, Pill, L.J., Nelson, J., Pitchers, J., CA (Crim Div).

3987. Indecent assault—pleas—attempted unlawful intercourse with girl aged 15

R aged 60, was staying in a flat belonging to his son, S. C went to the flat to take S's dog for a walk. C returned to the flat alone and watched television together with R. An incident occurred about which R and C gave different accounts. R was charged with rape and indecent assault. It was accepted by the prosecution that lack of consent on the part of the complainant could not be proved to the required standard and that the sentence must be passed on the basis that she consented to the sexual activity. R was sentenced to two years' imprisonment and appealed.

Held, allowing the appeal, a sentence of two years' imprisonment imposed for indecently assaulting a 15 year old girl was reduced to 18 months to provide R with a discount for his plea of guilty, *R.v Hinton (Roy)* (1995) 16 Cr. App. R. (S.) 523 considered.

R. v. REEVES (ROYSTON CEDRIC), [2001] EWCA Crim 1053, [2002] 1 Cr. App. R. (S.) 15, Mitting, J., CA (Crim Div).

3988. Indecent assault—probation orders—young semi conscious victim—undue leniency

The Attorney General referred to the court as unduly lenient a three year probation order imposed on G for an offence of indecent assault. The order had a condition attached requiring attendance at a sex offenders' programme. The victim, aged 18, had attended a barbeque at the home of G. She had consumed some alcohol and smoked cannabis during the evening. Upon becoming unwell, she retired to a bedroom where she lay fully clothed and drifted in and out of a deep sleep. G had visited her on a number of occasions during which he had indecently assaulted her, culminating in ejaculation causing semen to enter her mouth. G maintained that the victim had consented.

Held, allowing the reference but not varying the sentence, that the appropriate sentence for a serious indecent assault such as had occurred in the instant case was one of two years' to 30 months' imprisonment. G had shown no remorse for the offence and the circumstances had not been sufficiently exceptional to warrant a custodial sentence not being imposed. However, given that G had conformed with the conditions of his probation order and that imprisonment would not make him less likely to commit such an offence, it was not appropriate or in the public interest to impose a custodial sentence.

ATTORNEY GENERAL'S REFERENCE (NO.17 OF 2001), *Re; sub nom*. R. v. GILMOUR (STEPHEN) [2001] EWCA Crim 2662, Waller, L.J., CA (Crim Div).

3989. Indecent assault–stepchildren–course of conduct over 10 year period– appropriateness of community punishment and rehabilitation order–undue leniency

The Attorney General referred the imposition of a three year community punishment and rehabilitation order on the basis of undue leniency. The offender, DC, had pleaded guilty to three offences of indecent assault on a child. The offences concerned his stepdaughter commencing when she was six years of age and continuing until she was 15.

Held, allowing the reference, that the sentence was unduly lenient. These were specimen charges which were part of a "course of conduct" over a period of more than ten years which had had grave effects on the child concerned. Consecutive custodial sentences of 12 months for each offence were therefore appropriate, which would be reduced to eight months for double jeopardy, making a total of two years.

ATTORNEY GENERAL'S REFERENCE (NO.130 OF 2001), *Re; sub nom*. R. v. DC [2002] EWCA Crim 331, Mantell, L.J., CA (Crim Div).

3990. Indecent assault–suspended sentences–assault by nurse upon mental patient–gross breach of trust–undue leniency

The Attorney General referred as unduly lenient a sentence of 12 months' imprisonment, suspended for two years, and a suspended supervision order for the same period, imposed in respect of an offence of indecent assault. H, a team leader and night staff nurse at a private nursing home, pleaded guilty to the offence committed against a paranoid schizophrenic resident in his care during a night shift. H was of previous good character. The Attorney General contended that the sentence should be increased in view of the aggravating features including the vulnerability of the victim and H's position of utmost trust. H argued that a suspended sentence was reasonable due to the exceptional circumstances of the case and in particular the consequential ruination of H's professional career.

Held, allowing the reference, that the sentence was unduly lenient. A sentence of six months' imprisonment was substituted, every allowance having been given for previous good character, the guilty plea and double jeopardy. Imprisonment was inevitable having regard to the gross breach of trust. The circumstances of the instant case and the consequence to H's career did not amount to exceptional circumstances justifying a suspended sentence, *R. v. Lowery (James)* (1993) 14 Cr. App. R. (S.) 485, [1994] C.L.Y. 1363 applied.

ATTORNEY GENERAL'S REFERENCE (NO.115 OF 2001), *Re; sub nom*. R. v. HEMMUTH (RASHID), [2002] EWCA Crim 1129, [2003] 1 Cr. App. R. (S.) 11, Poole, J., CA (Crim Div).

3991. Indecent assault–suspended sentences–offences committed against girl aged under 16 over three year period–undue leniency

The Attorney General referred as unduly lenient concurrent sentences of 15 months' imprisonment suspended for two years, imposed following guilty pleas by I to seven counts of indecent assault. I, aged 49 on appeal, met a 13 year old girl in 1992 and commenced a sexual relationship with her. The girl denied that she had had sexual intercourse with I until the end of their relationship, which included a period of cohabitation that commenced after her sixteenth birthday in 1995. The Attorney General, although accepting that 15 months' imprisonment was the appropriate tariff sentence, contended that there were no exceptional circumstances to warrant suspension given the age difference involved and the prolonged period during which the offences had taken place prior to the girl's sixteenth birthday.

Held, allowing the reference, that there were no exceptional circumstances on the facts of the instant case to justify a suspended sentence, *R. v. Murti (Palo Kaur)* [1996] 2 Cr. App. R. (S.) 152, [1996] C.L.Y. 2088 and *R. v. Weston (Arnold)* [1996] 1 Cr. App. R. (S.) 297, [1996] C.L.Y. 1786 considered. Although I was of previous good character and unlikely to offend again, the serious nature of the offences called for a custodial term. I was therefore required to serve a term of nine months' imprisonment following an immediate surrender to the police.

ATTORNEY GENERAL'S REFERENCE (NO.134 OF 2001), Re; *sub nom. R. v. ISOM (PAUL)* [2002] EWCA Crim 295, Kennedy, L.J., CA (Crim Div).

3992. Informers—discounts—effect of information given after sentence

R appealed against a sentence of seven years and six months' imprisonment which had been imposed on him following his plea of guilty to possessing a controlled Class A drug with intent to supply. R relied on the fact that, both before and after being sentenced, he had supplied information which was helpful to the police, notwithstanding the fact that the information supplied prior to sentence had related to a different case.

Held, allowing the appeal, that a defendant could rely on the fact that he had supplied information concerning his offence to the police after the date of his sentence provided that the information was given within a reasonable time of the sentence, that he had pleaded guilty and that he had supplied significant information to the authorities, albeit in relation to a different case, before being sentenced. However, information given after sentence would not carry the same potential for discount that it would have carried had it been supplied before sentence. R's case involved circumstances which had not been specifically anticipated by *R. v. A (Informer: Reduction of Sentence)* [1999] 1 Cr. App. R. (S.) 52, [1998] C.L.Y. 1267, which set out the principles to be applied when determining the sentence of a defendant who had supplied information which was helpful to the authorities. R's sentence would be reduced to five years' imprisonment, *R. v. A* considered.

R. v. R (INFORMER: REDUCTION OF SENTENCE) *The Times*, February 18, 2002, Mitchell, J., CA (Crim Div).

3993. Intimidation—witnesses—verbal threats to witnesses of common assault

[Criminal Justice and Public Order Act 1994 s.51 (1).]

C appealed against a sentence of six months' imprisonment imposed for two offences of intimidating witnesses contrary to the Criminal Justice and Public Order Act 1994 s.51 (1). An altercation had taken place in the ladies' lavatory at a nightclub between C's partner and his former wife. The altercation was witnessed by three other women. Following the altercation, C's partner was charged with common assault. A few days later, when the three witnesses were again in the night club, C approached one of the women and made a threatening statement. One of the women telephoned the police next day and said that she wished to withdraw her statement about the earlier incident. The other woman made a statement about both incidents. The appellant denied threatening either of the women. The question was whether the total sentence of six months was manifestly excessive.

Held, dismissing the appeal, that the sentencing judge was entitled to pass consecutive sentences. The offences were not committed on precisely the same occasion and involved different victims. The offences of which C was convicted were very serious. Witnesses to criminal offences were indispensable to the conviction of the guilty and the acquittal of the innocent. They should not be pressurised into not giving evidence. In particular, witnesses should not be intimidated through threats that they might be subjected to physical violence. C threatened two witnesses in succession, and the effect of the threat on one witness was that she communicated to the police that she wished to withdraw her statement. Offences of intimidating witnesses involved sentences containing an element of deterrence. The sentence passed was therefore not manifestly excessive.

R. v. CHINERY (ANDREW JOHN), [2002] EWCA Crim 32, [2002] 2 Cr. App. R. (S.) 55, Bennett, J., CA (Crim Div).

3994. Juvenile offenders—aggravated burglary—knives used in burglary of home of disabled man—undue leniency

The Attorney General sought leave to refer sentences of six years' detention in respect of B's offences of aggravated burglary and robbery, and three years' detention for C and O for offences of aggravated burglary and dwellinghouse burglary. B, aged 19, C, aged 16, and O, aged 17, together committed the offence of aggravated burglary at the house of a 62 year old disabled man. They had targeted the victim in advance, had threatened him with knives taken from his kitchen, and had worn scarves to conceal their faces. C and O pleaded guilty and B was convicted. C and O were jointly charged with the burglary of the dwelling house of an 83 year old man for which they were sentenced to two years' detention to run concurrently. B pleaded guilty to the robbery of a pizza shop during which he threatened the shop assistant with a knife and demanded money. All three defendants had previous convictions for similar offences, and C and O were members of a team which targeted the homes of the elderly.

Held, refusing the application for leave to refer the sentences, that the appropriate sentence in the cases of O and C would have been four years, taking account of their young age, and B should have received seven years. However, although the sentences passed were lenient, they were not unduly lenient given the youth of the offenders and the court in its discretion would not interfere with them.

ATTORNEY GENERAL'S REFERENCE (NOS.105,106, AND 107 OF 2001), *Re*; *sub nom.* R. v. O (ANDREW) (A JUVENILE); R. v. C (JASON ANDREW) (A JUVENILE); R. v. BENNETT (GRAEME TONY) [2002] EWCA Crim 190, Rose, L.J., CA (Crim Div).

3995. Juvenile offenders—arson—offender setting fire close to propane cylinder

H appealed against a sentence of four years' detention in a young offenders institution for arson. He had purchased some lighter fuel at 2 am. He then went to a camp site where travellers were camping in caravans and set light to an object, and then placed the object next to a propane gas cylinder beside a caravan, having previously poured lighter fuel over the cylinder. A passer by saw H acting suspiciously and called the police, who were able to extinguish the fire which caused only slight damage. H contended that insufficient account was taken of his age, antecedents and personal mitigation.

Held, dismissing the appeal, that although there was strong personal mitigation, the offence had extremely serious aspects including the element of planning, selection of a caravan that was likely to be occupied and setting a fire in a position where it was likely to cause an explosion. The sentence was justified, *R. v. Thomas (Derek)* (1988) 10 Cr. App. R. (S.) 386, [1990] C.L.Y. 1193 considered.

R. v. HOLLIMAN (MICHAEL), [2001] EWCA Crim 2983, [2002] 2 Cr. App. R. (S.) 36, Penry-Davey, J., CA (Crim Div).

3996. Juvenile offenders—detention and training orders—consecutive sentences exceeding six months imposed for summary offences

[Powers of Criminal Courts (Sentencing) Act 2000 s.101 (2), s.101 (3).]

C appealed against detention and training orders imposed by magistrates following his convictions for seven offences including driving whilst disqualified and affray together with breach of a combination order. The orders totalled 10 months, the justices having imposed consecutive terms of four months and six months for two offences of driving whilst disqualified. C argued that those sentences were unlawful under the Powers of Criminal Courts (Sentencing) Act 2000 s.101 (2) as they exceeded the maximum sentence which could be imposed on an adult offender, which, in the case of two summary offences would be limited to six months' imprisonment. It was also contended that s.101 (2) should, in line with the Interpretation Act 1978 s.6 (c), be read as if the singular included the plural, on which basis the total sentence was limited to six months.

Held, dismissing the appeal, that s.101 (2) of the 2000 Act was not to be read in plural and although the individual terms were not able to exceed the sentence available in the adult courts, the aggregate sentence was not so restricted. Under s.101 (3) the court was empowered to order that one term should commence upon the expiry of another and that power was not subject to the restrictions in s.101 (2). Although this resulted in juvenile offenders receiving potentially longer sentences than their adult counterparts, that outcome was permissible to reflect the special nature and objectives of detention and training orders.

C (A CHILD) v. DPP, [2001] EWHC Admin 453, [2002] 1 Cr. App. R. (S.) 45, Bell, J., QBD (Admin Ct).

3997. **Juvenile offenders–detention and training orders–discount for guilty plea**

K, aged 15 at the time of sentence, appealed against the imposition of a 24 month detention and training order for grievous bodily harm. The attack which had been lengthily sustained was committed with a codefendant and resulted in serious injury to the victim. It was argued that as 24 months was the statutory maximum for the order, no discount had been given for K's guilty plea despite the fact that the judge had said he would do so.

Held, allowing the appeal, that it was important to protect the principle that a discount would be given for a plea, *R. v. Sharkey (Bernard Lee)* [1995] 16 Cr. App. R. (S.) 257, [1996] C.L.Y. 1717 considered. Therefore, as a result of the statutory regime applicable to detention and training orders, the only available sentence was an order for a period of 18 months.

R. v. K (GARY FRANCIS) (A JUVENILE), [2001] EWCA Crim 1030, [2002] 1 Cr. App. R. (S.) 11, Mackay, J., CA (Crim Div).

3998. **Juvenile offenders–detention and training orders–guilty plea and time spent on remand**

[Powers of Criminal Courts (Sentencing) Act 2000 s.91.]

P, aged 17 at the date of conviction, appealed against the imposition of an 18 months' detention and training order for unlawful wounding. He contended that the sentence failed to reflect the fact that he had served a period of four months on remand prior to sentence and that he had pleaded guilty.

Held, allowing the appeal, that in view of P's mitigation, a reduction in sentence was appropriate. However, it was observed that the rigidity of the statutory provisions governing detention and training orders dictated that whilst a period of 15 months was an appropriate sentence, the court was bound to reduce P's sentence to 12 months. Further, it was noted that the sentencing judge may have erroneously concluded that he had power to pass a period of long term detention under the Powers of Criminal Courts (Sentencing) Act 2000 s.91 but given that the maximum sentence for unlawful wounding was five years and not 14 years, as required by s.91 (1) (a), that power was not available.

R. v. P (CHRISTOPHER) (A JUVENILE), [2001] EWCA Crim 1295, [2002] 1 Cr. App. R. (S.) 46, Butterfield, J., CA (Crim Div).

3999. **Juvenile offenders–detention and training orders–obligatory reduction for time spent in custody on remand**

[Powers of Criminal Courts (Sentencing) Act 2000 s.91, s.101 (8).]

E appealed against the imposition of a 24 month detention and training order following his guilty pleas to robbery, racially aggravated threatening behaviour, possession of an imitation firearm and threats to kill. It was argued that by imposing the maximum possible term the judge had failed to take into account the time he had already spent on remand. When the matter had been raised before the sentencer, he had held that the time served had been taken account of as mitigation preventing the imposition of a term under the Powers of Criminal Courts (Sentencing) Act 2000 s.91, which would have otherwise enabled a lengthy term of detention to be passed.

Held, allowing the appeal, that once the judge had decided to impose a detention and training order, it was obligatory for him in determining the length of that order to take account of any period spent in custody on remand, under s.101 (8). The order was therefore reduced to 18 months.

R. v. E (TERRY JAMES) (A JUVENILE), [2001] EWCA Crim 943, [2001] 2 Cr. App. R. (S.) 103, Sir Richard Tucker, CA (Crim Div).

4000. Juvenile offenders—grievous bodily harm—failure to impose extended licence on release—undue leniency

[Powers of Criminal Courts (Sentencing) Act 2000 s.85, s.91.]

The Attorney General referred a sentence of four years' detention imposed under the Powers of Criminal Courts (Sentencing) Act 2000 s.91 following a guilty plea to causing grievous bodily harm with intent, wounding with intent and two counts of affray. All the offences took place during a single evening in a public park and involved F, along with a group of others, verbally abusing and then assaulting passers by and culminating in F stabbing P in the chest, causing a collapsed lung. The Attorney General contended that the period on licence F would serve following the four years' detention would be inadequate for rehabilitation purposes and the prevention of further offending, with the result that an extended licence period should have been imposed under s.85 of the Act.

Held, allowing the reference, that F's record and psychiatric report demonstrated that he would represent a continued danger following his release so that the judge below should have exercised his powers under s.85 in addition to passing a commensurate sentence. The four year sentence would therefore be substituted with an extended sentence comprising four years' detention and an extended four year licence period.

ATTORNEY GENERAL'S REFERENCE (NO.16 OF 2001), *Re; sub nom.* R. v. F (THOMAS) [2002] EWCA Crim 92, Rose, L.J., CA (Crim Div).

4001. Juvenile offenders—grievous bodily harm—unprovoked knife attack causing serious injuries

[Powers of Criminal Courts (Sentencing) Act 2000 s.109.]

R was convicted of wounding with intent to cause grievous bodily harm. R and a friend conducted a gay chatline through which they met M. He invited R and his friend to stay with him, agreed to pay their train fares and arranged for them to travel from London to Swansea. M met R and his friend in Swansea, took them to his house and had sexual relations with both of them. R without any apparent cause attacked the man with a knife, cutting him across the throat. R and two others then left the house. M was found to have multiple stab wounds to the head and a deep laceration to the neck. R had previous convictions for robbery committed while in possession of an imitation firearm and qualified for an automatic life sentence under the Powers of Criminal Courts (Sentencing) Act 2000 s.109. R was sentenced to 12 years' detention in a young offender institution and appealed.

Held, dismissing the appeal, that a sentence of 12 years' detention for wounding with intent, imposed after R cut his victims' throat, repeatedly stabbed him and then fled from the scene, was not excessive given the circumstances of the offence, *R. v. Beaumont (Steven)* (1992) 13 Cr. App. R. (S.) 270, [1993] C.L.Y. 193 considered.

R. v. RICHARDS (SCOTT), [2001] EWCA Crim 1244, [2002] 1 Cr. App. R. (S.) 36, Steel, J., CA (Crim Div).

4002. Juvenile offenders—incest—offences committed 14 years before trial

A pleaded guilty to two counts of indecent assault on a female and two counts of incest. B pleaded guilty to five counts of incest. A and B were brothers who had sexual relations with their younger sisters. The offences took place over a period of about 30 months between May 1983 and February 1986. They both appealed against their three year sentence.

Held, allowing the appeal, that a sentence totalling three years' imprisonment for incest committed by brothers against their younger sisters when all parties were juveniles was excessive and was reduced to eight months in view of the period of time which had elapsed since the offences had been committed and the effect of the sentences on A and B's families.

R. v. C (MARTIN JOHN); R. v. C (PAUL DAVID), [2001] EWCA Crim 916, [2002] 1 Cr. App. R. (S.) 5, Lord Woolf of Barnes, L.C.J., CA (Crim Div).

4003. Juvenile offenders—manslaughter—shaking baby syndrome—severe learning disabilities—inappropriate custodial sentence

T, who had severe learning difficulties, appealed against a sentence of 30 months' detention in a young offenders institution imposed for an offence of manslaughter. The victim had been T's daughter, who was approximately one month old at the time of the offence. T had been convicted following the finding that her death had been attributable to shaking baby syndrome. Whilst T admitted to having shaken his daughter, he maintained that he had never intended to cause her harm. It was submitted that the sentence was excessive given his poor mental development, a condition which was supported by medical reports.

Held, allowing the appeal, that T's custodial sentence was both excessive and inappropriate given the exceptional circumstances of the case. T lacked the mental capacity to comprehend either his actions or the consequences and he was in obvious need of the protection of the court. Accordingly, the sentence would be substituted with a three year community rehabilitation order with a condition of medical treatment attached.

R. v. T (PAUL) (A JUVENILE), [2001] EWCA Crim 1331, [2002] 1 Cr. App. R. (S.) 50, Hallett, J., CA (Crim Div).

4004. Juvenile offenders—murder—determination of tariff term

[Crime (Sentences) Act 1997 s.28; Powers of Criminal Courts (Sentencing) Act 2000 s.82A.]

M appealed against the imposition of a 14 year tariff for murder. Shortly before his 18th birthday M had shot and killed a shopkeeper during a robbery. He pleaded guilty to murder and was sentenced to be detained during Her Majesty's pleasure. An order was made under the Powers of Criminal Courts (Sentencing) Act 2000 s.82A stipulating that parole would not be available under the the Crime (Sentences) Act 1997 s.28 until M had served 14 years. On appeal, M argued that the tariff term imposed was excessive.

Held, allowing the appeal, that orders made under s.82A should be based on judicial guidance and recommendations in respect of detention during Her Majesty's pleasure given prior to the coming into force of the 2000 Act, the starting point for which was the *Practice Statement (CA (Crim Div): Juveniles: Murder Tariff)* [2000] 1 W.L.R. 1655, [2000] C.L.Y. 1095. The aggravating features of the offence, including the shooting at point blank range of a "vulnerable victim", taken with the mitigating factors of a guilty plea and M's youth, required that the tariff should be reduced to 12 years.

R. v. MCBEAN (ISA), [2001] EWCA Crim 1891, [2002] 1 Cr. App. R. (S.) 98, Bell, J., CA (Crim Div).

4005. Juvenile offenders—pre sentence reports—value of pre appeal prison reports

A, aged 20 years at the time of the offence, appealed against a sentence of 30 months' detention imposed for affray. Whilst drunk, A assaulted his victim, biting him and causing other injuries. He pleaded guilty on the day of the trial. He had a number of previous convictions for various offences, including offences of violence. The judge took the view that a pre sentence report was unnecessary as a custodial sentence was inevitable. A contended that the judge had, in imposing a sentence near to the maximum for the offence, failed to take into account mitigating factors and the basis of the plea entered and had given insufficient credit for his guilty plea.

Held, allowing the appeal, that when viewed against the maximum available sentence, the sentence imposed was excessive given the circumstances of the offence, as pleaded, and A's guilty plea. In appeals against sentence by young offenders or persons just over that age, a report from the institution at which the sentence was being served, setting out the progress made by the offender, was valuable in determining the appropriate sentence. This was particularly so where no pre sentence report had been prepared. In the instant case, having taken into account matters disclosed in the report from the prison, the appropriate sentence was one of 21 months' detention.

R. v. ATKINS (LEE GERARD), [2001] EWCA Crim 2804, *The Times*, January 14, 2002, Thomas, J., CA (Crim Div).

4006. Juvenile offenders–public order offences–unlawful sentences–criteria for sentencing offender where offence committed as juvenile

See SENTENCING: R. v. Ghafoor (Imran Hussain). §4047

4007. Juvenile offenders–rape–child victim

W, aged 17 at the date of the offence, appealed against a sentence of eight years' detention imposed for rape. W was the friend of two young men who lived on a farm with their father. The father's partner had a 12 year old daughter. W persuaded the daughter to come outside the farmhouse with him, to recapture horses which had got out. He took her to some woods and raped her. He threatened her with violence if she told anyone. The girl immediately complained to her mother. In interview W denied the offence and absconded before the date on which his trial had been fixed. He was subsequently arrested and changed his plea to guilty.

Held, dismissing the appeal, that the facts disclosed seriously aggravating features. W was a friend and well known to the victim; he had lured her out of the house and into the woods by a combination of lies and threats. He had used violence prior to the rape and subjected the victim to further sexual indignities. The effect on the victim must have been devastating. W's character was only of minor relevance in a case such of this. W had entered a late plea of guilty. It could not be too strongly emphasised that in cases involving sexual abuse where children were complainants, a plea of guilty either before venue or at the plea and directions hearing in the Crown Court would have the most effect on the type and length of sentence. A change of plea to one of guilty thereafter would have less impact on the sentence. In the instant case, W had no option but to plead guilty in view of the forensic evidence. His plea of guilty was in reality a recognition of the inevitable outcome of the trial. In the court's judgment, the sentence did take into account all relevant factors. Although severe it could not be said to be manifestly excessive.

R. v. WOODING (CLIVE), [2002] EWCA Crim 406, [2002] 2 Cr. App. R. (S.) 73, Bennett, J., CA (Crim Div).

4008. Juvenile offenders–robbery–community punishment and rehabilitation orders–undue leniency

[Powers of Criminal Courts (Sentencing) Act 2000 s.91.]

The Attorney General referred as unduly lenient community punishment and rehabilitation orders of 80 hours' community punishment and two years' rehabilitation imposed on L and C following their guilty pleas to a count of robbery. L and C, together with another juvenile, J, had stolen a jacket and a watch from a youth in the street. The victim had been badly injured. The Attorney General submitted that, in the light of the guidelines given in *Attorney General's*

Reference (Nos.4 and 7 of 2002), Re [2002] EWCA Crim 127, [2002] 2 Cr. App. R. (S.) 77, [2002] 3 C.L. 143, a custodial sentence was appropriate. In mitigation it was argued that the youth of the offenders, their guilty pleas and the fact that the attack was not pre planned and no weapon had been used were factors to be taken into account.

Held, finding the sentences to be unduly lenient and varying C's sentence but not that imposed on L, that the appropriate sentence in a case such as this, where a plea of guilty had been entered, was a custodial term of three years, Attorney Generals's Reference (Nos.4 and 7 of 2002), Re applied. J had entered a guilty plea to a charge of assault occasioning actual bodily harm rather than to robbery. Accordingly, the powers under the Powers of Criminal Courts (Sentencing) Act 2000 s.91 had not been available to the judge when dealing with J. The judge had gone on to deal with all three defendants similarly and therefore had erred in not applying the s.91 provisions to L and C. Given L's plea, good progress and the low risk of his reoffending his sentence was not varied. However, in the light of C's persistent offending, an 18 month detention and training order was substituted.

ATTORNEY GENERAL'S REFERENCE (NOS.31 AND 32 OF 2002), Re; sub nom. R. v. LPG; R. v. CRM, [2002] EWCA Crim 1606, (2002) 166 J.P. 557, (2002) 166 J.P.N. 611, Kennedy, L.J., CA (Crim Div).

4009. **Juvenile offenders—robbery—indecent assault—appropriateness of rehabilitation order and community based penalty—undue leniency**

The Attorney General referred the imposition of a two year rehabilitation order and 90 hours community service on the basis of undue leniency. B, 17, had pleaded guilty to six counts of robbery, one of indecent assault and one of gross indecency. The incidents involved the targeting of young men travelling on trains. B obtained money from them by threatening that he had a gun and a knife, and forced one victim to perform oral sex on him. The Attorney General argued that the sentence placed too much weight on B's rehabilitation and ignored the aggravating factors.

Held, allowing the reference, that the sentence was unduly lenient. These were serious offences requiring a real deterrent effect, which was a factor to which the sentencing judge had failed to give due weight, Attorney General's Reference (Nos.44 and 46 of 1995), Re [1996] 2 Cr. App. R. (S.) 128, [1996] C.L.Y. 2058 applied and Attorney General's Reference (Nos.7, 8, 9 and 10 of 2000), Re [2001] 1 Cr. App. R. (S.) 48, [2000] C.L.Y. 1339 considered. A sentence of five years detention at a youth offender institute was appropriate, which would be reduced to three years six months to take account of double jeopardy and B's good record of rehabilitation to date.

ATTORNEY GENERAL'S REFERENCE (NO.104 OF 2001), Re [2001] EWCA Crim 3069, Mance, L.J., CA (Crim Div).

4010. **Juvenile offenders—robbery—inflicting grievous bodily harm on elderly victim**

[Powers of Criminal Courts (Sentencing) Act 2000 s.91.]

F, aged 14, appealed against a sentence of four years' detention, imposed under the Powers of Criminal Courts (Sentencing) Act 2000 s.91, for robbery and causing grievous bodily harm with intent. F approached a 75 year old man who was walking home. F asked the man where he lived and then snatched a plastic bag which the man was carrying. The man tried to prevent F from doing so and a struggle followed in which the man fell or was pushed to the ground. In the course of the struggle, F punched the man in the face and when the man was on the ground, F kicked him on the head a number of times. The man was taken to hospital where he was found to have swellings to his face, a broken nose and fractures to the left cheekbone and both orbital rims which required surgery. F contended that the sentence was excessive.

Held, dismissing the appeal, that the deliberate and repeated kicking to the head was as serious as using a weapon held in the hand. F was responsible for the appalling injuries and despite F's youth, the sentence was fully justified.

R. v. ISLAM (FOKRUL), [2001] EWCA Crim 2950, [2002] 2 Cr. App. R. (S.) 33, Sir John Blofeld, CA (Crim Div).

4011. Juvenile offenders-robbery-manslaughter occurring during robbery-no use of weapon

L and T appealed against sentences of three and six years' imprisonment respectively imposed after their conviction for manslaughter. Both appellants had pleaded guilty to robbery. L and T attacked a 32 year old man who was on his way to his sister's home. Two bottles of cider which he was carrying were stolen. The victim was taken to hospital where he was found to be suffering from various injuries including cuts and a broken nose. The victim died two weeks later due to multiple organ failure resulting from bleeding from the facial injuries. L and T, both 19, had various previous convictions.

Held, dismissing the appeal, that a sentence of six years' detention imposed was not excessive even though no weapon had been used and the attack on the victim had not been sustained.

R. v. LAPPIN (DANIEL); R. v. CLARK (STEVEN TERENCE) [2002] EWCA Crim 222, [2002] 2 Cr. App. R. (S.) 78, Tuckey, L.J., CA (Crim Div).

4012. Juvenile offenders-robbery-victim travelling alone on underground train

D, aged 19, appealed against a sentence of three years' imprisonment imposed for robbery. D approached a woman who was travelling alone on an underground train. D made the woman empty her purse and took her cash and bank cards and asked for the PIN number of her card. D then got off the train and withdrew £400 in cash from a bank, using her cash card. D contended that the sentence was manifestly excessive.

Held, dismissing the appeal, that the sentencing judge correctly identified the entitlement of the public to travel unaccompanied in safety. The sentence of three years' detention was justified.

R. v. DIKKO (JOHN), [2002] EWCA Crim 292, [2002] 2 Cr. App. R. (S.) 83, Rafferty, J., CA (Crim Div).

4013. Juvenile offenders-supply of drugs-possession of cocaine with intent to supply

[Powers of Criminal Courts (Sentencing) Act 2000 s.91.]

C appealed against a sentence of two years and six months' detention imposed under the Powers of Criminal Courts (Sentencing) Act 2000 s.91. C aged 15 was seen by a police officer in a street acting in a suspicious manner. When the officer searched him, he found a plastic bag containing nine packages containing 913 milligrammes of heroin powder at 44 per cent purity, and seven packages containing the 801 milligrammes of crack cocaine at 56 per cent purity. A further bag was found in his coat pocket; this contained 118 milligrammes of heroin at 46 per cent purity. C contended that the sentence passed failed adequately to take into account the mitigating features.

Held, allowing the appeal, that the sentence passed failed adequately to take into account the mitigating factors, in particular the age of C. A detention and training order of 18 months was therefore substituted.

R. v. COUDJOE (SIMON PHILLIP), [2001] EWCA Crim 3015, [2002] 2 Cr. App R. (S.) 47, Judge Maddison, CA (Crim Div).

4014. Life imprisonment–grievous bodily harm–risk to public–power to impose life sentence

[Crime (Sentences) Act 1997 s.2; Powers of Criminal Courts (Sentencing) Act 2000 s.109(2).]

K appealed against a sentence of life imprisonment imposed under the Crime (Sentences) Act 1997 s.2, (now the Powers of Criminal Courts (Sentencing) Act 2000 s.109(2)), following a conviction for causing grievous bodily harm with intent, the trigger offence having been committed 18 years earlier. K submitted that, in the light of *R. v. Offen (Matthew Barry) (No.2)* [2001] 1 W.L.R. 253, [2000] C.L.Y. 1347 which held that s.2 was not intended to apply to an offender from whom there was no need for the public to be protected, the court had had no power to impose a life sentence.

Held, allowing the appeal, quashing the sentence of life imprisonment and substituting a sentence of five years' imprisonment, that a court had no power to impose a life sentence pursuant to s.2 where there was no need for the public to be protected from the offender, *Offen* applied. It was for the offender to displace the statutory presumption imposed by s.2 that the commission of two serious offences warranted a sentence of life imprisonment. A psychiatric report showed to the court's satisfaction that K did not represent a risk to the public, so that the sentence of life imprisonment could not be supported.

R. v. KELLY (EDWARD) (NO.2), [2001] EWCA Crim 1751, [2002] 1 Cr. App. R. (S.) 85, Buxton, L.J., CA (Crim Div).

4015. Life imprisonment–grievous bodily harm–robbery–assessment of dangerousness prior to imposition of custody for life

[Crime (Sentences) Act 1997 s.2.]

C appealed against the imposition of a sentence of custody for life made pursuant to the Crime (Sentences) Act 1997 s.2 for causing grievous bodily harm and possession of a firearm with intent to commit an indictable offence, committed when he was 20 years old. C submitted that the judge had erred by failing to make an assessment of dangerousness prior to passing the sentence.

Held, dismissing the appeal, that notwithstanding the fact that the judge had not made an assessment of C's dangerousness, in the light of his previous convictions and the pre sentence reports, had an assessment been made, the judge would have concluded that C posed a significant risk to the public. In the circumstances, the sentence of custody for life was correctly imposed.

R. v. CRAIG (ROBERT), [2001] EWCA Crim 1641, [2002] 1 Cr. App. R. (S.) 74, Bell, J., CA (Crim Div).

4016. Life imprisonment–kidnapping–prolonged robbery and false imprisonment– appropriate determinate sentence

P appealed against the imposition of a discretionary life sentence which included a determinate sentence of 18 years' imprisonment and a specified period of 12 years following his convictions for false imprisonment, kidnapping and robbery. P's codefendant, H, appealed against his sentence of 12 years' imprisonment imposed following his guilty pleas to the same offences. The victims of the offences were four female family members, one of whom had had a relationship with P. P contended that the imposition of a life sentence was inappropriate because, despite the gravity of the offences, there were no grounds for believing that he was a danger to the public. He further submitted that the determinate sentence was manifestly excessive and that the judge failed to give any reasons for specifying that he was to serve over half of the determinate sentence prior to his eligibility for parole. H contended that his sentence failed to reflect the fact that his role in the incident was significantly less than P's, that unlike P, the victims were not known to him and that the judge failed to give an adequate discount for his guilty plea.

Held, allowing P's appeal in part, that the seriousness of the offences merited the imposition of a life sentence. In addition, given P's criminal record, the judge had been entitled to conclude that he was a danger to the public. However, having found that the determinate sentence was excessive, the court reduced the sentence to 15 years' imprisonment and fixed the specified period at half that sentence with a reduction of 327 days for time spent on remand in custody prior to sentence, *R. v. Adams (David Anthony)* [2000] 2 Cr. App. R. (S.) 274, [2000] C.L.Y. 1352 applied. Further, in relation to H, having regard to his secondary role, the element of coercion by P, his remorse and his less substantial criminal record, his sentence was reduced to eight years' imprisonment.

R. v. POWELL (MARK); R. v. HORSFORD (HARLAND), [2001] EWCA Crim 1362, [2002] 1 Cr. App. R. (S.) 48, Penry-Davey, J., CA (Crim Div).

4017. Life imprisonment–robbery–relevance of previous custodial term in avoiding automatic life sentence

[Powers of Criminal Courts (Sentencing) Act 2000 s.109.]

F, aged 29, appealed against the imposition of an automatic life sentence made pursuant to the Powers of Criminal Courts (Sentencing) Act 2000 s.109. The sentence had followed F's conviction on two counts of robbery and two counts of possessing an imitation firearm and had been triggered by F's previous conviction for wounding with intent. He contended that the judge had been wrong not to find exceptional circumstances so as to avoid the imposition of the automatic life sentence in view of (1) the fact that F had received a relatively short custodial term of 18 months for the wounding offence, and (2) the contents of a psychiatric report and a pre appeal report which did not suggest that F was a serious danger to the public.

Held, dismissing the appeal, that (1) owing to the mens rea required for a conviction for wounding with intent and in view of F's subsequent convictions, the judge had been right to conclude that F was a serious danger to the public, and (2) neither the contents of the psychiatric report or the pre appeal report assisted F in persuading the court that he did not represent a serious danger to the public.

R. v. FAULKNER (LEE), [2001] EWCA Crim 2436, [2002] 1 Cr. App. R. (S.) 133, Burton, J., CA (Crim Div).

4018. Life imprisonment–wounding with intent–mental health–life sentence not in breach of mentally ill defendant's human rights

[Mental Health Act 1983; Human Rights Act 1998 Sch.1 Part I Art.3, Art.5; Powers of Criminal Courts (Sentencing) Act 2000 s.109.]

D, who was mentally ill, appealed against the imposition of a life sentence following his pleas of guilty to wounding with intent to do grievous bodily harm and to possession of an offensive weapon. D had two previous convictions for "serious offences" for the purposes of the Powers of Criminal Courts (Sentencing) Act 2000 s.109(5). The judge had found that no exceptional circumstances existed for the purposes of s.109(2) of the Act. D argued that as it was accepted that he was suffering from a mental illness for the purposes of the Mental Health Act 1983 and that suitable orders were available under that Act, the imposition of a life sentence had been contrary to his rights under the Human Rights Act 1998 Sch.1 Part I Art.3 and Art.5.

Held, dismissing the appeal, that the imposition of a life sentence had not been contrary to D's rights under Art.3 and Art.5 of the 1998 Act. Notwithstanding previous practice, it had been open to Parliament to stipulate that in defined cases there was a rebuttable presumption that an offender posed such a serious and continuing danger to the public that a hospital order or restriction order would not provide sufficient protection. A life sentence provided the public with greater protection and it could not be said that an offender subject to such a sentence would not receive necessary medical treatment.

R. v. DREW (ANTHONY JAMES), [2001] EWCA Crim 2861, [2002] 2 Cr. App. R. (S.) 45, Kennedy, L.J., CA (Crim Div).

4019. Life imprisonment–wounding with intent–second serious offence–danger to public–exception to statutory norm

[Offences against the Person Act 1861 s.18; Crime (Sentences) Act 1997 s.2.]

C appealed against his sentence of life imprisonment imposed under the Crime (Sentences) Act 1997 s.2 for wounding with intent to do grievous bodily harm against his former girlfriend, the sentence being triggered by C's previous conviction for a like offence. C submitted that since the attack, he had resumed a relationship with the victim and had reformed his character through his attendance on a number of behaviour courses.

Held, allowing the appeal, that notwithstanding the fact that the offences were both under the Offences against the Person Act 1861 s.18, C did not represent and had never represented a danger to the general public and in the circumstances, he was an exception to the norm of offenders who usually invoked s.2 of the Act, *R. v. Offen (Matthew Barry) (No.2)* [2001] 1 W.L.R. 253, [2000] C.L.Y. 1347 considered. The sentence was therefore quashed and a sentence of four years and six months' imprisonment substituted.

R. v. CLOSE (CRAIG), [2001] EWCA Crim 1066, [2002] 1 Cr. App. R. (S.) 16, Leveson, J., CA (Crim Div).

4020. Life imprisonment–wounding with intent–substantial gap between qualifying offences–exceptional circumstances

[Crime Sentences Act 1997 s.2.]

S appealed against the imposition of an automatic life sentence pursuant to the Crime Sentences Act 1997 s.2, (now the Powers of Criminal Courts (Sentencing) Act 2000 s.109), following conviction for wounding with intent and possession of a firearm with intent to endanger life. The trigger offence of causing grievous bodily harm with intent had been committed over 30 years previously. S contended that the court should have concluded that exceptional circumstances existed such as to render the passing of an automatic life sentence inappropriate, *R. v. Offen (Matthew Barry) (No.2)* [2001] 1 W.L.R. 253, [2000] C.L.Y. 1347 cited.

Held, allowing the appeal, that the instant case had been decided before the decision in *Offen* had been promulgated. Having regard to the fact that the trigger offence had been committed in response to an assault upon S's mother and there had been no further serious violence in the 31 years thereafter, exceptional circumstances did exist. In making his sentencing remarks the judge had not made any assessment of the degree of risk that S posed to the public and on the basis of the material available it appeared that S did not pose any significant danger. Accordingly the automatic life sentence was set aside and a determinate term of seven years imprisonment substituted, *Offen* applied.

R. v. SMITH (RUBEN); R. v. FLETCHER (FRANCIS ROYSTON), [2001] EWCA Crim 1700, [2002] 1 Cr. App. R. (S.) 82, Holman, J., CA (Crim Div).

4021. Manslaughter–actual bodily harm–single unprovoked punch to head–street violence–undue leniency

The Attorney General referred to the court as unduly lenient a sentence of three years' imprisonment imposed on W, who had pleaded guilty to manslaughter. Prior to the incident giving rise to the offence, W, who had been drinking heavily, had struck two men without provocation. He had subsequently called the victim over to the vehicle in which he was a passenger and delivered a single punch to his head. The victim had been knocked backwards and struck his head against the pavement, rendering him unconscious. He had died due to profound and irreversible brain damage which had occurred immediately after sustaining the head injury. W had immediately left the scene and when, ten days later, he attended a police station, he had falsely claimed that the victim had punched him first. The aggravating features identified by the Attorney General were premeditation, deliberation and the wholly unprovoked nature of the attack.

Held, allowing the reference, that the sentence imposed had been unduly lenient. It was necessary to take a serious view of gratuitous street violence against innocent members of the public. The fact that W had been drunk was not a mitigating factor. A sentence of five years' imprisonment would have been appropriate on a guilty plea. Having regard to double jeopardy, which in the instant case had included prolonged uncertainty as a consequence of the case having been taken out of the list at short notice, it was appropriate to substitute a sentence of four years' imprisonment, *Attorney General's Reference (No.63 of 2001), Re* [2001] EWCA Crim 1652, [2002] 1 Cr. App. R. (S.) 78, [2001] C.L.Y. 1429 and *R. v. Matthews (Warren Jay)* [2001] EWCA Crim 1421, [2002] 1 Cr. App. R. (S.) 66 considered.

ATTORNEY GENERAL'S REFERENCE (NO.100 OF 2001), *Re; sub nom.* R. v. WELCH (ALFRED ROBERT), [2002] EWCA Crim 294, [2002] 2 Cr. App. R. (S.) 81, Pill, L.J., CA (Crim Div).

4022. Manslaughter – babies – severe "bonding disorder" between mother and child

W appealed against a sentence of life imprisonment, with a recommendation that a minimum of five years be served before release, imposed for the manslaughter of her nine month old baby. W's baby had been grossly underweight and the cause of death had been severe malnutrition and dehydration. At trial, W's basis of plea had been that she was suffering from a severe "bonding disorder" which had resulted in her hatred and rejection of the baby. Such a disorder was not accepted in the international classification on mental disorders and expert evidence had cast doubt on the medical opinion that she was suffering from it, attributing W's actions solely to a psychopathic disorder.

Held, allowing the appeal, that since W did not pose a grave risk to the public, the judge had erred in imposing a sentence of life imprisonment. It was apparent that he had accepted that W was suffering from a "bonding disorder" and that in setting a recommendation that she serve a minimum of five years' imprisonment he had had in mind that the determinate sentence would otherwise be one of 10 years' imprisonment. The instant case represented one of manslaughter by neglect of a very serious nature. It was not appropriate, on the facts, to give consideration to W's "bonding disorder" as mitigation. Accordingly, it was appropriate to quash the sentence of life imprisonment and replace it with a sentence of ten years' imprisonment, notwithstanding that W had entered a plea.

R. v. WATTS (SAMANTHA JOANNE), [2001] EWCA Crim 1427, [2002] 1 Cr. App. R. (S.) 56, Hooper, J., CA (Crim Div).

4023. Manslaughter – drug addiction – administration of heroin injection to drug addict

A appealed against a sentence of six years' imprisonment for manslaughter. A had been resident at a hostel for the homeless and had injected another resident, R, with heroin. R, who was an alcoholic and heroin addict, later died as a result of multiple drug toxicity. A contended that the sentence imposed had been excessive having regard to A's guilty plea and expression of remorse.

Held, allowing the appeal, that having regard to the guilty plea the sentence imposed was excessive and a term of five years' imprisonment would be substituted. No further reduction was justified as the plea had been given late and the judge had been right to seek to achieve a high level of deterrence given the particular problem of drug related deaths in the locality.

R. v. ATHERTON (KRISTIAN STEPHEN), [2001] EWCA Crim 2109, [2002] 1 Cr. App. R. (S.) 115, Rose, L.J., CA (Crim Div).

4024. Manslaughter – intoxication – lump of wood used as weapon – public interest issue where violent offence resulted in death of victim – undue leniency

The Attorney General referred a sentence of 27 months' imprisonment on the basis of undue leniency. W had pleaded guilty to an offence of manslaughter on an indictment of murder. The plea had been made on the basis that W lacked the specific intent for the offence of murder, owing to his drunken state. Whilst drunk, W had struck the victim, G, his friend and flatmate, at least two blows with a piece of wood from which a nail protruded. The nail had pierced an artery, which caused G to bleed to death. The Attorney General submitted that the offence was aggravated by the fact that W had used a heavy lump of wood as a weapon, the weapon had been used to inflict at least two blows, G was aged 67 and of slighter build than W and W had left G unconscious and bleeding and had not summoned medical assistance. The mitigating features were that W had pleaded guilty, had no previous convictions, had surrendered himself to the police and had shown remorse.

Held, allowing the reference, that there were public interest issues concerning violent offences, particularly those resulting in the death of the victim. Those issues ought to have prevented the sentencing judge from adopting a sympathetic approach and setting the sentence as low as he had done. The proper sentence in a case of this nature was in the range of four to five years' imprisonment. The fact that W was due to be released at the end of the month in which the appeal was heard did not amount to exceptional circumstances justifying the exercise of judicial discretion not to interfere with the sentence. Taking into account the normal discount on resentencing, the sentence of 27 months' imprisonment was quashed and substituted by one of three years' imprisonment.

ATTORNEY GENERAL'S REFERENCE (NO.118 OF 2001), *Re*; *sub nom*. R. v. WARNER (ROBERT FREDERICK), [2002] EWCA Crim 958, [2002] 2 Cr. App. R. (S.) 119, Kay, L.J., CA (Crim Div).

4025. Manslaughter—negligence—farm owners permitting untrained person to drive farm machine resulting in death

C appealed against a sentence of 15 months' imprisonment imposed after conviction for manslaughter on the grounds of gross negligence. C and his father were the owners of a farm at which several farm workers were employed. The deceased, D, was a 16 year old student who was present at the farm on a work placement from an agricultural college. He was driving a JCB telescopic loadall with a brush attachment to clear mud from the surface of a road alongside fields from which crops had recently been harvested. D parked the machine off the road surface, but with the raised bucket protruding about one and a half metres into the road. A passing lorry collided with the bucket, causing the JCB to roll on to D, causing him crush injuries from which he died. C and his father were charged with manslaughter on the basis that they had failed to heed warnings from the Health and Safety Executive that D should not be permitted to drive the JCB until he had undergone a course of training, which he did not. It was shown that D had used the machine regularly on the instructions of C's father. C contended that the court failed to take into consideration the exceptional circumstances which could have caused his sentence to be suspended.

Held, allowing the appeal, that the jury by their verdict had found that a significant cause of D's death was the reckless disregard for his safety demonstrated by C and his father over a period of months. The sentencing judge had identified three aggravating features, namely (1) a high degree of recklessness; (2) the foreseeability of serious injury or death, and (3) a failure to heed explicit warnings. C was not entitled to any discount for plea of guilty. However, after the sentence was imposed, C's father's health had deteriorated and the farm was now in a precarious situation in the absence of C. For that reason, there now existed exceptional circumstances enabling the court to suspend C's sentence for 12 months.

R. v. CROW (ALISTAIR), [2001] EWCA Crim 2968, [2002] 2 Cr. App. R. (S.) 49, Pitchford, J., CA (Crim Div).

4026. Manslaughter—perverting the course of justice—uninsured driver with defective vision—failure to stop—undue leniency

[Criminal Justice Act 1988 s.36.]

The Attorney-General referred as unduly lenient under the Criminal Justice Act 1988 s.36 a sentence of three years' imprisonment imposed on E for manslaughter and a concurrent sentence of nine months' imprisonment imposed for doing an act intending to pervert the course of justice. E, who had severely defective eyesight, had been driving at night without his glasses and without insurance, having been warned not to do so by a work colleague, when he struck an 18 year old woman, carried on driving to a field a few miles away, and proceeded to remove his registration plates and set fire to his vehicle. The woman later died of the injuries sustained as a result of the impact.

Held, allowing the reference, that manslaughter should have attracted a sentence of five to six years' imprisonment, and so, taking into account the element of double jeopardy, a sentence of four years and three months' imprisonment was imposed for the manslaughter, and the sentence of nine months' imprisonment for perverting the course of justice was ordered to run consecutively to that, *R. v. Boswell (James Thomas)* [1984] 1 W.L.R. 1047, [1985] C.L.Y. 770, *Attorney General's Reference (Nos.14 and 24 of 1993), Re* [1994] 1 W.L.R. 530, [1994] C.L.Y. 1193, *R. v. Atkinson (John Cameron)* (1990) 12 Cr. App. R. (S.) 245, [1992] C.L.Y. 1356, applied.

ATTORNEY GENERAL'S REFERENCE (NO.14 OF 2001), *Re; sub nom.* R. v. EMM (MICHAEL JOHN), [2001] EWCA Crim 1235, [2002] 1 Cr. App. R. (S.) 25, Kennedy, L.J., CA (Crim Div).

4027. Manslaughter–pleas–death resulting from fight

H appealed against a sentence of five years' imprisonment imposed for manslaughter. H and the victim were part of a family of travellers who lived at a caravan site. Following a family celebration at which many of the participants drank heavily, H and his brother began to fight. H kicked him in the mouth before jumping on his stomach with both feet. The victim was taken to hospital where he died as a result of a massive intra abdominal haemorrhage which was thought to be the result of the stamping.

Held, allowing the appeal, that the offence of manslaughter varied enormously in its gravity. This was not the case of a victim with an abnormally thin skull which was fractured by falling to the ground and hitting his head. The case had serious features, in particular the stamping on the victim. Bearing in mind H's age, his guilty plea, the fact that he had to live with the knowledge that he killed his own brother, and his evident remorse, the sentence was reduced to four years' detention.

R. v. HARTY (MICHAEL FRANCIS), [2002] EWCA Crim 90, [2002] 2 Cr. App. R. (S.) 58, Cresswell, J., CA (Crim Div).

4028. Manslaughter–provocation–extended sentences

[Powers of Criminal Courts (Sentencing) Act 2000 s.85.]

D was convicted of manslaughter by reason of provocation on an indictment charging murder. D and V were known to each other and they were on friendly terms until a dispute arose between them. D found V in a public house and stabbed him twice in the lower back with a knife. V died the following morning. D was sentenced to an extended sentence with a custodial term of nine years and an extension period of four years, under the Powers of Criminal Courts (Sentencing) Act 2000 s.85 and appealed.

Held, allowing the appeal, that in the absence of any evidence that D was a danger to the public and given the circumstances of the case, his sentence of nine years' imprisonment for manslaughter by reason of provocation was reduced to seven and an extended licence period of four years was quashed, *Attorney General's Reference (No.33 of 1996), Re* [1997] 2 Cr. App. R. (S.) 10, [1997] C.L.Y. 1622 considered.

R. v. DILLON (JAMES MILLER), [2001] EWCA Crim 1342, [2002] 1 Cr. App. R. (S.) 41, Penry-Davey, J., CA (Crim Div).

4029. Manslaughter–rape–nurses–administration of drug for purposes of sexual assault–imposition of life sentence

C appealed against a sentence of life imprisonment imposed following his conviction for manslaughter and multiple rape. C had been employed as a nurse in a hospital accident and emergency department and had administered the stupefying drug Midazolam to three female patients. The drug resulted in almost total memory loss of recent events. Whilst the women were under the influence of the drug C raped two of them. Prior to the instances of rape, a fellow nurse had died after C had mixed the drug Midazolam with alcohol, a toxic combination which the victim had been unaware that she was consuming. C contended that in the light of an assessment carried out prior to sentence which concluded that he was at low to medium risk of re-offending and that he did not suffer from mental illness or any form of personality disorder, a life sentence had not been justified.

Held, dismissing the appeal, that the judge passing sentence had been entitled to conclude that P represented a serious ongoing threat to women. The assessment provided by a doctor to the court had contained no explanation of his conclusion that C represented a medium to low risk of future offending. Having regard to the extremely serious nature of the conduct in question, the judge had been fully entitled to reach a conclusion that it was only by passing an indeterminate sentence that the court would be fulfilling its obligation to protect other women from similar assaults, *Attorney General's Reference (No.32 of 1996), Re* [1997] 1 Cr. App. R. (S.) 261, [1996] C.L.Y. 1912 considered.

R. v. COBB (KEVIN NASH), [2001] EWCA Crim 1228, [2002] 1 Cr. App. R. (S.) 19, Kay, L.J., CA (Crim Div).

4030. Manslaughter–robbery–attempts–death caused by victim's heart condition aggravated by stress induced by robbery

G appealed against a sentence of 12 years' imprisonment for manslaughter, following his conviction for attempted robbery and manslaughter. G and another man entered the office of a firm engaged in the distribution of frozen foods. The partners in the firm were H, who had had a triple heart bypass, and W, who was partly paralysed. One of the men produced a knife with a 10 inch blade and held it against the throat of H. There was a scuffle, in the course of which the man prodded H in the ribs with the knife. H collapsed and was taken to hospital where he was pronounced dead. A post mortem established that the cause of his death was degeneration of the arteries of the heart. Death could have occurred at any time but the pathologist's opinion was that the immediate cause of death had been a fatal heart attack precipitated by the trauma and excitement of the struggle. G submitted that the sentence of 12 years was manifestly excessive for a man aged 21 with no previous convictions for violence.

Held, dismissing the appeal, that offences of manslaughter varied very much in their seriousness and each one had to be addressed on its own particular facts. The correct approach was to consider what sentence would have been appropriate for the serious planned robbery even if no death had occurred, and then to ask whether an increase, and if so what increase, should be made to reflect the serious factor that a life had been lost as a result. The sentencing judge had been correct to consider that a sentence of nine years appropriate for a planned robbery of this kind. It was then necessary to consider whether there should be a further element to reflect the fact that there was a death. It was regularly recognised in a variety of cases that serious consequences, albeit not anticipated, would in themselves give rise to a further element in the sentence. The public would consider that the court should mark with a further significant element the fact that this particular robbery had resulted in the death of a man. It was wholly impossible to say that the increase considered appropriate by the sentencing judge, was manifestly excessive. Public confidence demanded an increase of that magnitude and the resulting sentence of 12 years was wholly appropriate for an offence which involved serious criminal behaviour resulting in the death of one of the victims.

R. v. GINLEY (MICHAEL), [2002] EWCA Crim 209, [2002] 2 Cr. App. R. (S.) 64, Kay, L.J., CA (Crim Div).

4031. **Manslaughter–robbery–death of elderly victim as result of dangerous act**

S appealed against a sentence of 10 years' imprisonment imposed for manslaughter and robbery. S accosted a lady aged 89 as she was returning to her flat after collecting her pension. S pulled her shopping bag as she was walking upstairs to her flat; when she tried to resist, S gave a further heavy pull which caused the lady to fall backwards and slide down the concrete stairs. S ran off with the bag. The victim was assisted by neighbours and taken to hospital. She was found to have a fracture to the neck of the femur in her right hip which necessitated an operation. Following the operation she suffered two consequential chest infections and died in the course of the second infection, about a month after the robbery. The second robbery took place shortly after the first. S approached a lady aged 76 as she was making her way home after collecting her pension. S thumped her in the back and pulled her shopping bag. The lady held on but she eventually let go. S got into the driver's seat of a car and drove away with the bag and its contents. S, aged 40, had a lengthy record of previous convictions; he had been sentenced in 1995 for similar robberies of elderly people. S submitted that the sentence of 10 years' imprisonment for manslaughter was manifestly excessive and that it failed to take account of S's early plea of guilty. It was submitted that the pleas of guilty were more commendable because the evidence against the appellant was limited and there was some medical evidence which questioned the necessary causal link between S's actions and the death of the victim.

Held, dismissing the appeal, that these offences were easy to commit, highly prevalent and dangerous both to life and limb of the elderly victims. When they were committed by a dangerous act which did result in death, severe sentences were called for. What the sentencing judge legitimately did was pass an overall sentence to reflect the appellant's overall criminality that day and the overall sentence of 10 years could not be faulted, *R. v. Buck (Cameron)* [2000] 1 Cr. App. R. (S.) 42, [2000] C.L.Y. 1415 considered.

R. v. SIMPSON (TREVOR JOHN), [2002] EWCA Crim 25, [2002] 2 Cr. App. R. (S.) 53, Mitchell, J., CA (Crim Div).

4032. **Manslaughter–robbery–street attacks on elderly persons–undue leniency**

[Criminal Justice Act 1988 s.36.]

The Attorney General referred as unduly lenient under the Criminal Justice Act 1988 s.36 a sentence of seven years' imprisonment imposed for an offence of manslaughter and a concurrent term of five years for attempted robbery. The first victim, a 59 year old man, who was on his own, was kicked to the head and body by B, aged 35, and two other men in an attempt to rob him. The group fled when witnesses ran to the help of the victim. About 90 minutes later, B and one of the men approached the second victim, a 60 year old man, who was walking home from a night out and from whom money and a ring were taken. The victim staggered home where his wife called for an ambulance. He collapsed and died before the emergency services arrived. The post mortem revealed that he had sustained seven fractured ribs, four of which had penetrated the chest cavity and subsequent respiratory problems had caused his death. In interview B admitted that he had been present at the time of the attacks but claimed that he had pulled the others off the victims. The plea to manslaughter was tendered on the basis that the chest injuries had been caused by a codefendant sitting on the victim to restrain him whilst his property was stolen. The Attorney General argued that owing to the prevalence of street robberies in society, public concern and expectation demanded longer sentences.

Held, allowing the reference, that in view of the aggravating features which were (1) the fact that death was caused to one of the victims; (2) that the robbery was planned; (3) that elderly and vulnerable victims were targeted, and

(4) the offences were intended to be committed by more than one person, a sentence of 11 to 12 years' imprisonment was appropriate for the manslaughter offence following B's guilty plea. However, in view of the element of double jeopardy, a sentence of nine years' imprisonment with a consecutive year for the attempted robbery was substituted. The court noted that the sentence for the latter offence was artificially low to reflect the impact of double jeopardy.

ATTORNEY GENERAL'S REFERENCE (NOS.19, 20 AND 21 OF 2001), Re; sub nom. R. v. BYRNE (ALAN EDWARD); R. v. FIELD (JASON); R. v. C (CRAIG) (A JUVENILE), [2001] EWCA Crim 1432, [2002] 1 Cr. App. R. (S.) 33, Kay, L.J., CA (Crim Div).

4033. Manslaughter–violence–consumption of drugs and alcohol prior to stabbing–undue leniency

[Offences Against the Person Act 1861 s.20.]

The Attorney General referred as unduly lenient a sentence of three years and six months' imprisonment for L for manslaughter. L, aged 29 on appeal, had been observed acting strangely in a public house and had later followed and stabbed in the heart a man with whom he had been drinking. L was charged with murder, having admitted to regularly carrying a kitchen knife, but expert evidence showed that his consumption prior to the stabbing of a combination of sleeping tablets, methadone and alcohol meant that it was unlikely that he was capable of forming the necessary intent for murder. L had a history of drug abuse and was a "binge drinker". The Attorney General submitted that the aggravating features of the case were that there had been no justification for the attack, L had sought the confrontation despite the victim's attempts to placate him, L regularly carried a weapon, and L had rendered himself incapable of anticipating the effects of the drugs he had taken. In mitigation it was claimed that L was a registered drug addict and he had a long term relationship with the mother of his two children. L had previous convictions for burglary and drugs related offences.

Held, allowing the reference, that the appropriate tariff was between four and seven years for an offence of this type. The trial judge had misdirected himself in law as to his sentencing powers by apparently taking the view that he was confined by the maximum sentence of five years for an offence of unlawful wounding contrary to the Offences Against the Person Act 1861 s.20. It was inappropriate to disregard the consequence of death from violent behaviour, *R. v. Ruby (Kenneth)* (1988) 86 Cr. App. R. 186, [1988] C.L.Y. 952 applied. The appropriate sentence in the present case would have been five years but, taking into account double jeopardy and the effect on L of converting his sentence from a short term to a long term sentence, a sentence of four years was substituted.

ATTORNEY GENERAL'S REFERENCE (NO.82 OF 2001), Re; sub nom. R. v. LYONS (JASON JOHN) [2002] EWCA Crim 93, Rose, L.J., CA (Crim Div).

4034. Manslaughter–violence–nightclub doorman–two blows to victim's head–undue leniency

[Powers of Criminal Courts (Sentencing) Act 2000 s.109.]

The Attorney General referred to the court as unduly lenient a sentence of 18 months' imprisonment imposed on D, who had pleaded guilty to manslaughter. D, an amateur boxer with a previous conviction for causing grievous bodily harm, had been employed as an unofficial doorman at a nightclub. The victim, who was in a state of considerable intoxication, had been causing a nuisance in the toilet of the nightclub. A confrontation between D and the victim had occurred during which D had inflicted two blows to the victim's head. The victim had fallen to the floor. A post mortem showed that two arteries adjacent to the brain stem had been torn either due to the movement of the victim's head when hit or due to his fall to the floor. In addition to his submission that the sentence imposed had been unduly lenient, the Attorney General argued that the sentencing judge had erred in finding exceptional circumstances such as to justify not imposing a life sentence under the Powers of Criminal Courts (Sentencing) Act 2000 s.109.

Held, refusing the reference, that there being insufficient evidence before the court concerning whether D posed a serious risk to the public, it had been appropriate to obtain the views of a probation officer. Given his view that D did not pose a risk, it was apparent that exceptional circumstances existed such that it was not right to impose an automatic life sentence under s.109 of the Act, *R. v. Offen (Matthew Barry) (No.2)* [2001] 1 W.L.R. 253, [2000] C.L.Y. 1347 applied. While the sentence imposed had been lenient it would be unduly harsh to impose a longer one given that D had served it and been released.

ATTORNEY GENERAL'S REFERENCE (NO.124 OF 2001), Re; sub nom. R. v. DAVIES (AARON BRUCE) [2002] EWCA Crim 197, Lord Woolf of Barnes, L.C.J., CA (Crim Div).

4035. Manslaughter–wounding with intent–life imprisonment–failure to displace assumption of significant future risk

[Powers of Criminal Courts (Sentencing) Act 2000 s.109.]

R appealed against his sentence of life imprisonment imposed under the automatic provisions of the Powers of Criminal Courts (Sentencing) Act 2000 s.109. The two relevant offences were wounding with intent and manslaughter. The facts of the later offence were that R had prepared a syringe and passed it to the victim, who had used it to inject heroin, which had caused his death and R had pleaded guilty on that basis. The determinate period applied by the judge was four years. R argued that because there were "exceptional circumstances" under s.109(2), the sentence should not have been passed.

Held, dismissing the appeal, that the risk posed by R to the public was significant. R had failed to displace the assumption that offenders who committed two serious offences posed a significant risk and therefore the sentence imposed had been appropriate, *Attorney General's Reference (No.53 of 1998), Re* [2000] Q.B. 198, [1999] C.L.Y. 1249, *R. v. Buckland (Andrew)* [2000] 1 W.L.R. 1262, [2000] C.L.Y. 1359 and *R. v. Offen (Matthew Barry) (No.2)* [2001] 1 W.L.R. 253, [2000] C.L.Y. 1347 applied.

R. v. RICHARDS (DARRELL) (NO.1), [2001] EWCA Crim 2712, [2002] 2 Cr. App. R. (S.) 26, Keith, J., CA (Crim Div).

4036. Money laundering–evasion–factual basis of plea–relationship of sentence with that imposed for original antecedent offence

B appealed against a sentence of five years' imprisonment imposed following conviction for an offence of assisting another person to obtain the benefit of criminal conduct. B had exchanged large sums of sterling into foreign currency representing the proceeds from the sale of jewellery smuggled into the United Kingdom from Uganda, thus evading VAT, Excise Duty and other taxes. B contended that the sentence was manifestly excessive on the basis that the judge had given insufficient credit for his guilty plea and had failed to pay sufficient regard to the undisputed factual basis of the plea. B maintained that in consequence he ought to have been sentenced on the basis of the guidelines in *R. v. Dosanjh (Barjinder)* [1998] 3 All E.R. 618, [1998] C.L.Y. 1390.

Held, allowing the appeal, that there was no necessarily direct relationship between the sentence for the laundering offence and the original antecedent offence. Nevertheless the sentence for laundering the proceeds of crime should not be wholly disproportionate to the sentence imposed for the original antecedent offence in circumstances where the retention of the proceeds of criminal conduct, amounting in the instant case to £215,000, was facilitated by the defendant. The sentence of five years' imprisonment was manifestly excessive on a guilty plea suggesting that a sentence of seven years' imprisonment would have followed on from a contested trial. Accordingly a sentence of three years and six months' imprisonment was substituted, *Dosanjh* and *R. v. Greenwood (Wayne Miles)* [1995] 16 Cr. App. R. (S.) 614 considered.

R. v. BASRA (AJAIB SINGH), [2002] EWCA Crim 541, [2002] 2 Cr. App. R. (S.) 100, Cooke, J., CA (Crim Div).

4037. Murder–attempts–attempt to suffocate partner using pillow wrapped in cling film–undue leniency

The Attorney General referred to the court as unduly lenient a sentence of five years' imprisonment imposed on P for an offence of attempted murder. P had attempted to suffocate his partner using a pillow wrapped in cling film. He had abandoned his attempt after his partner had screamed and her daughter had entered the room. Evidence given at the trial indicated that P had never previously been violent or aggressive. There was no explanation for his actions and a psychiatrist's report suggested that P was not a danger to the public and a repetition of the attack was unlikely.

Held, refusing the reference, that while the sentence had been lenient it had not been unduly so. Five years' imprisonment was within the range of sentences which could be considered appropriate.

ATTORNEY GENERAL'S REFERENCE (NO.117 OF 2001), *Re; sub nom.* R. v. PANKHURST (JOHN STEPHEN), [2002] EWCA Crim 144, [2002] 2 Cr. App. R. (S.) 63, Rose, L.J., CA (Crim Div).

4038. Obtaining by deception–elderly persons–carers–proprietor of residential home–use of pension books of former residents

H appealed against a sentence of two years' imprisonment imposed for 11 offences of obtaining property by deception with a further 68 similar offences taken into consideration. H, who had been responsible for the running of a residential care home, had been entrusted with the pension books of 11 residents and after the home had closed owing to H's rent arrears, continued to withdraw monies. The total amount taken was estimated to be £13,000. H contended that, given his guilty plea, his sentence unjustifiably exceeded sentencing guidelines.

Held, dismissing the appeal, that in view of the aggravating features of the offences, in particular, the breach of trust, and given H's previous convictions, the sentence was appropriate notwithstanding that it exceeded the guideline sentence of 21 months' imprisonment, *R. v. Clark (Trevor)* [1998] 2 Cr. App. R. 137, [1998] C.L.Y. 1392 considered.

R. v. HALE (ROBERT WINTER), [2001] EWCA Crim 1329, [2002] 1 Cr. App. R. (S.) 49, Hallett, J., CA (Crim Div).

4039. Obtaining by deception–elderly persons–carers–unlawfully transferring money from bank account of lady aged 80

R, a care worker, pleaded guilty to three counts of obtaining a money transfer by deception. R worked for a firm supplying carers to elderly and infirm people. Over a period of about two years, R cared for L aged about 80. L was housebound, and able to walk only with the aid of carers. Among the tasks performed by R was collecting the lady's pension, doing her shopping and paying her bills. Over a period of 15 months, R completed 26 cheques by making them payable to herself. The total amount obtained was £2,875. R was sentenced to 18 months' imprisonment and appealed.

Held, dismissing the appeal, that a sentence of 18 months' imprisonment imposed for obtaining money transfers by deception was not excessive. R, a care worker for the elderly, had completed the blanks on 26 cheques to make them payable to herself and during that period was convicted of a separate offence of fraudulently obtaining social security benefits, *R. v. Clark (Trevor)* [1998] 2 Cr. App.R. 137, [1998] C.L.Y. 1392 considered.

R. v. ROACH (JUANITA AMANDA), [2001] EWCA Crim 992, [2002] 1 Cr. App. R. (S.) 12, Holman, J., CA (Crim Div).

4040. Obtaining by deception–mitigation–organising collection on behalf of non existent charity

P appealed against a sentence of two years' imprisonment imposed for conspiring to obtain property by deception. P set up a scheme to collect money for a non existent charity called "Helping Kids". P created identification badges and used the signature of the secretary of a local branch of a genuine charity on the literature designed to induce potential contributors to believe that the charity was genuine. Collectors were recruited to make collections in public houses on behalf of the bogus charity. P contended the sentence was excessive and that insufficient account was taken of his previous good character and impeccable service history.

Held, dismissing the appeal, that the sentence passed was consistent with the court's public duty to stamp out dishonesty of this kind. It was therefore not excessive.

R. v. PIPPARD (NEIL EDWARD); R. v. HARRIS (EDWARD PAUL), [2001] EWCA Crim 2925, [2002] 2 Cr. App. R. (S.) 40, Gross, J., CA (Crim Div).

4041. Obtaining by deception–mothers–appropriateness of custodial term for offences of dishonesty where no violence involved

M appealed against concurrent terms of eight months' imprisonment imposed in relation to two offences of obtaining by deception. M had successfully applied for credit after supplying false details of her employment status. Subsequently, she ran up debts of approximately £15,000 knowing that she had no chance of making the repayments. On appeal, M submitted that given that she was the sole carer of her young children, there was no commercial element to the offences and in the light of her previous good character the sentence was excessive.

Held, allowing the appeal, that in borderline cases which did not involve violence and where the financial consequences only involved a commercial concern, the court would have to consider the following factors in assessing the appropriateness of a custodial term namely (1) whilst the "clang of the prison gates" was an important deterrent factor, there were limitations on the beneficial impact the prison service could hope to effect in a short time period; (2) where the offender was the sole carer of young children, the court had to consider how the imposition of a custodial term would affect the children, and (3) since 1993 there had been a marked undesirable increase in the female prison population and, as a consequence, the prison service faced difficulties in accommodating short sentences and in imprisoning mothers close to their homes. Though the instant case involved a substantial sum of money, the offences were out of character and the likelihood of reoffending low. Therefore it was wrong to conclude that prison was the only alternative. In such circumstances, the minimum sentence should be imposed. Accordingly, the eight month term was quashed and substituted with a six month community rehabilitation order.

R. v. MILLS (JOANNE), [2002] EWCA Crim 26, [2002] 2 Cr. App. R. (S.) 52, Lord Woolf of Barnes, L.C.J., CA (Crim Div).

4042. Offensive weapons–possession–sentencing guidelines

[Children and Young Persons Act 1933 s.44; Prevention of Crime Act 1953 s.1; Criminal Justice Act 1988 s.139; Crime and Disorder Act 1998 s.37.]

P appealed against a sentence of three years' imprisonment and a concurrent term of 12 months imposed after she pleaded guilty to offences of attempted robbery and having an offensive weapon in a public place contrary to the Prevention of Crime Act 1953 s.1. C appealed against his sentences of 12 months' imprisonment on his plea of guilty to having an offensive weapon and six months' imprisonment for dangerous driving.

Held, issuing sentencing guidelines and allowing the appeals, that it was not easy to issue sentencing guidelines when the maximum sentence for having an offensive weapon in a public place contrary to s.1 of the 1953 Act, had been increased from two to four years' imprisonment, yet the maximum sentence for having a bladed article in a public place contrary to the Criminal Justice Act 1988 s.139 remained two years. The court therefore concentrated on the s.1 offence. In cases where a weapons offence was carried out in conjunction with another offence, the usual totality considerations would apply. In ascertaining the seriousness of an offence it was necessary to consider the intention behind the offence, the circumstances in which it was committed, and the nature of the weapon involved. There were three factors in relation to intention which could aggravate the offence, namely (1) if it had been planned that the weapon would be used to commit violence or threaten others; (2) if hostility to a minority group motivated the offence, and (3) if the offender was under the influence of alcohol or drugs whilst in possession of the weapon. The circumstances of the offence would be aggravated by the offence being committed in a vulnerable place, such as a school or hospital, or at a large public gathering or on public transport or in licensed premises. Some weapons were more dangerous than others but the nature of the weapon would not be the main determinant of the offence, given that a less dangerous weapon such as a knuckle duster could be used to create fear and such an offence may be as serious as that involving a more obviously dangerous weapon. A defendant's intention could be gauged if the weapon he was carrying had been adapted in such a way as to cause serious injury. The offence was mitigated if the weapon was only carried on a temporary basis. Further mitigation could be provided by personal factors, cooperation with the police and a timely guilty plea. A defendant who had previous convictions for violence with an offensive weapon, and who was convicted of carrying a particularly dangerous weapon, could expect to receive at or near the maximum sentence for the offence. An adult offender of previous good character would pass the custody threshold if there was a combination of dangerous circumstances and the weapon had actually been used to threaten or cause fear. Custody could still be appropriate in cases where there had been no threatening use of the weapon. There would be cases where none of the aggravating features applied, where no threat had been made and where the weapon had not been particularly dangerous, and therefore the custody threshold may not have been passed and community punishment at the top end of the range might be appropriate. In the case of young offenders, the courts would have regard to their statutory duty under the Crime and Disorder Act 1998 s.37 and the Children and Young Persons Act 1933 s.44 and it would invariably be appropriate to have the benefit of pre sentence reports before sentencing. In the instant case, P had served the equivalent of 22 months' imprisonment and therefore a 12 month probation order was substituted for the remainder of the term. C's sentence of 12 months for having the offensive weapon was reduced to nine months.

R. v. POULTON (SARAH JANE); R. v. CELAIRE (MARIO ROLANDO), [2002] EWCA Crim 2487, [2003] 1 Cr. App. R. (S.) 116, Rose, L.J., CA (Crim Div).

4043. **Perverting the course of justice–conspiracy–implicating innocent person in drug offence–involvement of police officer–undue leniency**

The Attorney General referred to the court as unduly lenient sentences of six years' imprisonment for J and R following a jury trial for an offence of conspiracy to commit acts tending and intended to pervert the course of public justice and a sentence of four years' imprisonment imposed on W following a guilty plea for the same offence. J, R and W, a serving police officer at the time of the offence, had conspired to plant a large quantity of a Class A drug on an innocent person, thereby exposing her to the risk of a substantial prison sentence. J had financed the conspiracy and stood to gain most from it, while W had entered into the conspiracy at a later stage. The trial judge took a starting point of eight years' imprisonment with a discount of two years to reflect the fact that it had not been established that the drugs had been planted.

Held, allowing the reference, that the starting point was too low since a bracket of 10 to 12 years would have applied if it had been proved that the intended quantity of the drug had been planted, so that the appropriate lower bracket was eight to 10 years. The fact that a police officer was involved added an increased element of seriousness to the matter as it served to undermine the administration of justice. Therefore W could only be distinguished from J and R because of his plea. It would be appropriate to increase each sentence by two years, reduced to one year to reflect the element of double jeopardy, giving sentences of seven years in the case of J and R and five in the case of W.

ATTORNEY GENERAL'S REFERENCE (NOS.6, 7 AND 8 OF 2000), *Re; sub nom.* R. v. REES (JONATHAN); R. v. WARNES (AUSTIN); R. v. JAMES (SIMON), [2002] EWCA Crim 264, [2002] 2 Cr. App. R. (S.) 76, Lord Woolf of Barnes, L.C.J., CA (Crim Div).

4044. Perverting the course of justice—false statements—innocent victim imprisoned—undue leniency

The Attorney General referred to the court as unduly lenient a 180 hour community punishment order imposed on M, who had been convicted of doing acts tending and intended to pervert the course of public justice. M had given false statements to the police and had made complaints of burglary and harassment against TM. On the basis of such complaints, TM had been charged with burglary and harassment and had been remanded in custody for 18 days. It had subsequently emerged that TM and M had been lovers and that M's allegations had been false. M's trial had taken place approximately three years after the events giving rise to the offence, during which period she had remarried and started in new employment.

Held, refusing the reference, that the sentencing judge had been entitled to consider, given the passage of time, whether a custodial sentence was appropriate. The sentence could not be said to be unduly lenient and, having regard to the fact that M had done a substantial amount of the required community service, it was not appropriate to vary it. It was, however, necessary to stress that a false complaint which resulted in the arrest of an innocent person was an offence of the utmost gravity which, even with a guilty plea, warranted an immediate term of imprisonment. Where the allegation was that the innocent victim had committed a grave offence, the offence was made even more serious. Further, it was an aggravating circumstance if the innocent victim spent a long period of time in custody.

ATTORNEY GENERAL'S REFERENCE (NO.85 OF 2001), *Re; sub nom.* R. v. MATTHEWS (ALISON JANE), [2001] EWCA Crim 2518, [2002] 2 Cr. App. R. (S.) 4, Kennedy, L.J., CA (Crim Div).

4045. Perverting the course of justice—murder—defendant coerced into assisting in disposal of victim's body

L appealed against a sentence of eight years' imprisonment for perverting the course of justice and a consecutive sentence of 12 months' imprisonment for two counts of supplying a Class A drug, namely cocaine. L's uncle had shot dead a fellow criminal and L had helped him to bury the deceased's body in the garden of the uncle's home. L was implicated in the crime by fingerprint evidence, and he pleaded guilty to the offence and to the drugs offences. L argued that (1) some allowance should have been made for his fear of his uncle, who was violent, disturbed and unpredictable; (2) the trial judge had identified aggravating features, in particular the fact that the offence bore "all the hallmarks of professional organised crime", which were attributable more to his uncle than to him, and (3) the sentence of eight years for the offence of perverting the course of justice was excessive in any event.

Held, allowing the appeal, that although L had chosen to associate with his uncle at the time of the offence, the trial judge should have made allowance for the fact that there was no sound basis for rejecting his account that he had been called to his uncle's home without warning and that he had been put in fear by his uncle when he arrived. Furthermore, there appeared to be no reliable evidence that L had known what had caused his uncle to kill the deceased. In all the circumstances, the sentence was excessive. The appropriate sentence in the instant case after a plea of guilty was six years. L's sentence for the drugs offences was disturbed, making the total sentence one of seven years' imprisonment, *R. v. Skinner (Vincent Patrick)* (1993) 14 Cr. App. R. (S.) 115, [1993] C.L.Y. 1245 considered.

R. v. LANG (JACK THOMAS), [2001] EWCA Crim 2690, [2002] 2 Cr. App. R. (S.) 15, Bell, J., CA (Crim Div).

4046. Prisoners—escape—lawfulness of order requiring escaped prisoner serve part of unexpired previous sentence

[Criminal Appeal Act 1968 s.11 (3); Criminal Justice Act 1991; Powers of Criminal Courts (Sentencing) Act 2000 s.116.]

M appealed against a sentence of seven years' imprisonment and J appealed against a sentence of nine years' imprisonment imposed for an offence of aggravated burglary. At the trial, M had also pleaded guilty to an offence of escaping from lawful custody and a sentence of three months had been imposed, running concurrent with his seven year sentence. The two appellants, as well as a third man, had forced their way into a house. They had been armed with an imitation firearm and two knives. The two occupants had been beaten and a small sum of money together with two necklaces had been taken. In the case of M, the judge had additionally ordered that he serve 360 days of a sentence which had been imposed on a previous occasion at the Crown Court. In so doing, the judge had purportedly been exercising the power conferred under the Powers of Criminal Courts (Sentencing) Act 2000 s.116. The issue arose as to whether the judge's order was a nullity.

Held, allowing the appeals, that since s.116 of the 2000 Act related to prisoners who had been released on licence under the provisions of the Criminal Justice Act 1991, the judge had erred in ordering that M serve 360 days of the unexpired previous sentence; M was an escapee and had not been released on licence. It followed that the order made under s.116 was a nullity. Having regard to the Criminal Appeal Act 1968 s.11 (3), which concerned the powers of the Court of Appeal in relation to sentence where it was of the opinion that an appellant should be sentenced differently for an offence for which he was dealt with by the court below, it was apparent that an order made under s.116 did not, of itself, constitute "a sentence" and accordingly the court had no power to substitute an order that would achieve what the sentencing judge had intended. While the sentences imposed on both M and J could not be regarded as manifestly excessive, it was appropriate to reduce J's sentence from nine years to eight in light of the nullity of the s.116 order made in relation to M.

R. v. MATTHEWS (JONATHAN EDWARD); R. v. JACOBS (DARREN RODNEY), [2002] EWCA Crim 677, [2002] 1 W.L.R. 2578, Johnson, J., CA (Crim Div).

4047. Public order offences—unlawful sentences—criteria for sentencing offender where offence committed as juvenile

[Public Order Act 1986 s.1 (1); Human Rights Act 1998 Sch.1 Part I Art.7.]

G appealed against the imposition of a sentence of four years and six months' detention in a young offenders' institution following conviction for an offence of riot contrary to the Public Order Act 1986 s.1 (1). G had been 17 at the date of the offence, but was 18 by the time he came to be sentenced. On appeal, G argued that by sentencing him as an 18 year old the judge had been in breach of the Human Rights Act 1998 Sch.1 Part I Art.7 because he had imposed a heavier penalty than would have been applicable at the time the criminal offence was committed.

Held, allowing the appeal, that where a relevant age threshold was crossed between commission of an offence and conviction, the base line for sentencing had to be the sentence most likely to have been imposed at the time of commission, *R. v. Danga (Harbeer Singh)* [1992] Q.B. 476, [1992] C.L.Y. 1450 applied. This could be departed from but only with good reason. In the instant case there had only been a few months between commission and conviction and therefore the appropriate sentence was that which would have been applied at the date of commission, being a maximum of 24 months' detention and training with six months' credit for a guilty plea. Given the decision it was not necessary to consider whether there had been a breach of Art.7.

R. v. GHAFOOR (IMRAN HUSSAIN), [2002] EWCA Crim 1857, [2003] 1 Cr. App. R. (S.) 84, Dyson, L.J., CA (Crim Div).

4048. Racially aggravated offences—harassment—mitigation—repeatedly shouting racial abuse outside victim's home

S pleaded guilty to racially aggravated harassment. S and the victim were neighbours both white but the victim's partner was Afro-Caribbean origin. The victim heard S standing outside her flat shouting racial remarks on a number of occasions. S was sentenced to 15 months' imprisonment and appealed.

Held, dismissing the appeal, that the court took account of the personal mitigating factors and S's plea, but could only say that his conduct was disgraceful. The sentence was therefore not excessive.

R. v. SHAND (ARTHUR), [2001] EWCA Crim 1582, [2002] 1 Cr. App. R. (S.) 69, Judge Goddard Q.C., CA (Crim Div).

4049. Rape—indecent assault—aiding and abetting of offences upon five month old baby—undue leniency

The Attorney General referred as unduly lenient a total sentence of four years' imprisonment imposed on H for aiding and abetting the rape and indecent assault of a five month old baby. H and her co accused S were babysitting when the baby was raped and sexually assaulted by S. The Attorney General contended that the offences were aggravated by the fact that (1) H had participated in taking indecent photographs of the baby; (2) she had aided and abetted the rape, and (3) the degree of depravity of the offence was extreme.

Held, finding the sentence to be unduly lenient but not varying it, that a sentence of six years' imprisonment may have been appropriate. However, given the inherent element of double jeopardy the sentence was not varied.

ATTORNEY GENERAL'S REFERENCE (NO.12 OF 2001), *Re; sub nom.* R. v. H (JOYCE), [2002] EWCA Crim 353, [2002] 2 Cr. App. R. (S.) 84, Rose, L.J., CA (Crim Div).

4050. Rape—indecent assault—rape of child by stepfather—undue leniency

The Attorney General referred to the court as unduly lenient a total sentence of seven years' imprisonment imposed on W following his conviction, after a trial, on 11 counts of rape and four counts of indecent assault on a girl, W's stepdaughter, aged under 13. The aggravating features identified by the Attorney General were that W was in a position of responsibility towards the victim, most of the offences were committed when the victim was very young, the offences were repeated and went on over a period of time, and the victim had been subjected to various sexual indignities. In mitigation, W had no relevant previous convictions and produced testimonials as to his good character.

Held, allowing the reference, that the sentence was unduly lenient. The authorities clearly showed that a longer sentence was appropriate in view of the offences committed, *Attorney General's Reference (No.71 of 1999), Re* [2000] 2 Cr. App. R. (S.) 83, [2000] C.L.Y. 1392 considered. The appropriate range would have been in the region of 10 to 12 years' imprisonment. Taking into account the element of double jeopardy and the factors put forward on behalf of W in mitigation, the sentence was increased to nine years' imprisonment in the respect of each of the rapes, to run concurrently.

ATTORNEY GENERAL'S REFERENCE (NO.143 OF 2001), *Re; sub nom.* R. v. W (PAUL KELVIN) [2002] EWCA Crim 1574, Kay, L.J., CA (Crim Div).

4051. Rape–intoxication–previous convictions for indecent assault–undue leniency

The Attorney General referred to the court as unduly lenient a sentence of five years' imprisonment imposed on R, aged 21, for an offence of rape. The victim, who was drunk, had been walking home in the early hours. R had approached her and had asked her for a kiss. The victim had declined. As they had entered a pedestrian tunnel, R had pushed the victim against a wall and raped her, ejaculating inside her. At his trial, R had maintained that the victim had consented to intercourse. The Attorney General identified the following aggravating features (1) R had sought out the victim at night when, because of her drunkenness, she was vulnerable; (2) R had ejaculated inside the victim and had not been wearing any protection; (3) the victim had been frightened by the attack and had suffered psychological damage; (4) R had not pleaded guilty, and (5) at the time of the offence, R had recently completed a probation order imposed for five offences of indecent assault, an offence for which he had also been cautioned previously.

Held, allowing the reference, that having regard to the aggravating features, the sentence imposed had been unduly lenient. An appropriate sentence would have been one of eight years' imprisonment. Having regard to double jeopardy, a sentence of six years and six months' would be substituted.

ATTORNEY GENERAL'S REFERENCE (NO.137 OF 2001), *Re*; *sub nom*. R. v. REYNOLDS (DEAN) [2002] EWCA Crim 562, Kennedy, L.J., CA (Crim Div).

4052. Rape–life imprisonment–exceptional circumstances–no significant risk to public

[Crime (Sentences) Act 1997 s.2; Powers of Criminal Courts (Sentencing) Act 2000 s.109.]

S appealed against a sentence of automatic life imprisonment, imposed under the Crime (Sentences) Act 1997 s.2, now reenacted as the Powers of Criminal Courts (Sentencing) Act 2000 s.109, following his conviction on one count of rape. S had previously been convicted of causing grievous bodily harm with intent. The trial judge concluded that there were no exceptional circumstances so as to permit the imposition of a sentence other than life imprisonment.

Held, allowing the appeal, that following the approach in *R. v. Offen (Matthew Barry) (No.2)* [2001] 1 W.L.R. 253, [2000] C.L.Y. 1347, it was necessary to begin with the assumption that the defendant did present a significant risk to the public, an assumption which was however capable of rebuttal by evidence. Having considered the facts of the offences in question it was possible to be satisfied that S was not a significant risk to the public in terms of either violent or sexual offences. Accordingly exceptional circumstances did exist pursuant to s.109 of the 2000 Act, such as to justify the quashing of the automatic life sentence and the substitution of a sentence of six years' imprisonment, *Offen* applied.

R. v. STARK (BARRY JOHN), [2002] EWCA Crim 542, [2002] 2 Cr. App. R. (S.) 104, Keene, L.J., CA (Crim Div).

4053. Rape–spouses–repeated rape of estranged wife at knifepoint–undue leniency

The Attorney General referred as unduly lenient a sentence of four years' imprisonment imposed upon Y for the rape of his estranged wife. Y had been invited to the victim's home but after she rejected his request for a reconciliation he raped her at knifepoint on two occasions. The Attorney General contended that the offences were aggravated by the fact that Y had used a knife to compel submission, the rape was repeated, a pillow was used to smother the victim's face during the second rape and the victim was in fear of her life. Further the children of the family were in the house and awake whilst the offences were being committed, the victim was unable to summon assistance or escape, and the offences lasted for a considerable period of time.

Held, allowing the reference, that a sentence of four years' imprisonment was unduly lenient. At first instance following a trial a sentence of eight years imprisonment would have been appropriate. Having regard to the element of double jeopardy, Y's prior good character and the violence to which he had been subjected in prison, a sentence of six years' imprisonment was appropriate, *R. v. W (Stephen)* (1993) 14 Cr. App. R. (S.) 256, [1994] C.L.Y. 1337, *R. v. Malcolm (George)* (1995) 16 Cr. App. R. (S.) 151, [1996] C.L.Y. 2047 and *R. v. K (Edward James)* [1997] 1 Cr. App. R. (S.) 251, [1997] C.L.Y. 1647 considered.

ATTORNEY GENERAL'S REFERENCE (NO.128 OF 2001), *Re*; *sub nom. R. v. Y (MARTIN)*, [2002] EWCA Crim 388, [2002] 2 Cr. App. R. (S.) 66, Kay, L.J., CA (Crim Div).

4054. Rape–violence–sustained and sadistic attack–undue leniency

The Attorney General sought leave to refer to the court as unduly lenient a sentence of eight years' imprisonment imposed on B, who had pleaded guilty to rape. B had escorted the victim, who was extremely drunk, home. B had then left the victim's home but subsequently returned, gained access to the victim's house and raped her. The attack had lasted two hours and involved considerable violence, including the use of a lamp as a weapon.

Held, refusing the application, that while the sentence was lenient it was not unduly lenient. It was necessary to distinguish between campaigns of rape, which attracted higher sentences, and single offences of rape however serious. The aggravating features in the instant case included the fact that excessive violence had been used and that the rape had been part of a sustained and sadistic attack which was repeated over a two hour period. The starting point in such a case was a sentence of the order of 12 years' imprisonment. However, B had entered a guilty plea one month before trial and some discount was therefore appropriate. Therefore a sentence of between nine and 10 years would have been expected. Given the inherent element of double jeopardy, it was not appropriate to interfere with the sentence imposed, *R. v. Billam (Keith)* [1986] 1 W.L.R. 349, [1986] C.L.Y. 868, *Attorney General's Reference (No.28 of 1993), Re* (1995) 16 Cr. App. R. (S.) 103, [1996] C.L.Y. 2048, *Attorney General's Reference (No.10 of 1995), Re* [1996] 2 Cr. App. R. (S.) 122, [1996] C.L.Y. 2052 and *Attorney General's Reference (No.29 of 1996), Re* [1997] 1 Cr. App. R. (S.) 224, [1997] C.L.Y. 1648 considered.

ATTORNEY GENERAL'S REFERENCE (NO.119 OF 2001), *Re*; *sub nom. R. v. BARNFIELD (ALAN)* [2002] EWCA Crim 177, Rose, L.J., CA (Crim Div).

4055. Road traffic offences–dangerous driving–causing death–vehicle taken by unqualified driver without owner's consent–undue leniency

[Powers of Criminal Courts (Sentencing) Act 2000 s.116.]

The Attorney General referred to the court as unduly lenient a sentence of two years and six months' detention and a period of disqualification of two years that had been imposed on M, who was now aged 20, for causing death by dangerous driving. M had taken a vehicle belonging to his girlfriend's mother without her authority and, after ignoring a give way sign, had collided with a taxi, killing a female passenger. Prior to the offence he had consumed alcohol. Among the aggravating features of the offence relied on by the Attorney General were that M had merely held a provisional licence at the time of the offence, he had been charged with offences of driving while unqualified, committed only three weeks before the instant offence, and he had delayed in surrendering to the police so as to avoid being tested for the presence of alcohol. It was also argued that the recorder at M's trial had failed to make an order under the Powers of Criminal Courts (Sentencing) Act 2000 s.116 in relation to the balance of a sentence of three years' detention that had previously been imposed on M for offences of robbery and burglary. As to mitigation, the court's attention was drawn to M's age, the fact that he had surrendered to the police and his plea of guilty.

Held, allowing the reference, that, taking all factors into account, a sentence of five years' detention together with an order under s.116 of the 2000 Act would have been appropriate. Having regard to the principle of double jeopardy, however, a period of four years' detention was imposed. In addition, M should serve, pursuant to s.116, a consecutive term of 12 months in relation to the unexpired period of his three year sentence. Finally, the period of disqualification was increased to five years.

ATTORNEY GENERAL'S REFERENCE (NO.32 OF 2001), *Re; sub nom.* R. v. McCLAREN (ABIJAH), [2001] EWCA Crim 2120, [2002] 1 Cr. App. R. (S.) 121, Rose, L.J., CA (Crim Div).

4056. Robbery–attempts–knives used in attack on small shop premises–undue leniency

The Attorney General referred to the court as unduly lenient a sentence of two years and nine months' imprisonment imposed on RH for offences of robbery and breach of a community rehabilitation order, and sentences of two years' imprisonment imposed on W and NH for attempted robbery. The Attorney General drew attention to authority suggesting that, given the fact that small shop premises were particularly vulnerable to crime of this kind and should be protected by the imposition of substantial custodial sentences for such attacks, a sentence of the order of five years was appropriate. In mitigation it was accepted that the offenders had entered guilty pleas and had not previously served custodial sentences. It was relevant that W and NH had no previous convictions for offences of violence. It was submitted that the offenders had made progress in dealing with drug addiction, which had been a contributing factor leading to the commission of the offences.

Held, allowing the reference, that the sentences imposed were unduly lenient given that the offences were planned, attacked vulnerable shops and involved the carrying of knives and threat of violence. NH's offence was further aggravated by the use of violence, the crime having been committed whilst on bail and subject to a conditional discharge. A sentence in the region of five years' imprisonment would have been appropriate for each count. Accordingly, having regard to the element of double jeopardy, RH's sentence was quashed and a sentence of three years and nine months substituted for the robbery offence with a three month term to be served consecutively for breach of the community order. Moreover, contrary to the approach of the judge below, the offence of RH merited a lesser sentence than that of W and NH, as he had acted alone and did not use violence. Accordingly W and NH had their sentences quashed and terms of four years substituted.

ATTORNEY GENERAL'S REFERENCE (NOS.52, 53 AND 54 OF 2002), *Re*; R. v. HUNTER (ROBERT); R. v. WILLIAMS (SARA JANE); R. v. HELLIER (NICOLA LOUISE) [2002] EWCA Crim 2077, Rose, L.J., CA (Crim Div).

4057. Robbery–attempts–theft of mobile telephone–possession of imitation firearm and issue of threats to kill–undue leniency

The Attorney General referred to the court as unduly lenient a total sentence of four years' imprisonment imposed on D who had been convicted of theft, having an imitation firearm with intent to commit an indictable offence, attempted robbery, possessing an imitation firearm with intent to cause fear and making threats to kill. D, who had substantial previous convictions, had stolen a mobile telephone, from a taxi office, which had later been recovered by the victim. D had subsequently returned to the vicinity of the taxi office and had attempted to rob a second victim of his mobile phone at gunpoint. He had then entered the taxi office brandishing the gun and had made threats to kill. It was submitted that the sentence imposed had not reflected the serious nature of the offences, the aggravating features, or the need to deter others.

Held, allowing the reference, that the sentence imposed was unduly lenient. It would have been open to the judge to impose consecutive sentences in relation to the three separate criminal activities that had occurred. A total sentence of seven years' imprisonment would have been expected. Having regard to double jeopardy, a sentence of six years' imprisonment was substituted, *Attorney General's Reference (Nos.4 and 7 of 2002), Re* [2002] EWCA Crim 127, [2002] 2 Cr. App. R. (S.) 77, [2002] 3 C.L. 143 and *R. v. Avis (Tony)* [1998] 1 Cr. App. R. 420, [1998] C.L.Y. 1214 considered.

ATTORNEY GENERAL'S REFERENCE (NO.28 OF 2002), *Re; sub nom.* R. v. DONAGHY (PETER STEPHEN) [2002] EWCA Crim 1285, Rose, L.J., CA (Crim Div).

4058. Robbery–confessions–small off-licence–offender suffering from mental illness–undue leniency

[Theft Act 1968 s.8(1).]

The Attorney General referred as unduly lenient a two year community rehabilitation order imposed on F, a 25 year old man with mental health problems, following his plea of guilty to an offence of robbery, contrary to the Theft Act 1968 s.8(1). F had entered a small off-licence wearing a mask and had demanded money, alcohol and cigarettes. He was holding a chrome object which the manageress maintained he had held to her cheek. Shortly after the incident, F had voluntarily entered a local hospital and had confessed to a doctor about the robbery. The sentencing judge had concluded that a community rehabilitation order was appropriate given F's mental health problems but had observed that a sentence of between three and five years' imprisonment would have normally been passed.

Held, refusing the reference, that having regard to the fact that F had voluntarily disclosed his involvement in the offence before suspicion had fallen upon him and had allowed those treating him to alert the police, and to the fact that he had pleaded guilty at the earliest opportunity, the sentence passed had not been unduly lenient. It was appropriate for a sentencing judge whilst giving consideration to sentencing guidelines to also reflect upon the individual circumstances of an offender. In the instant case, it was apparent that the judge had been aware of the normal tariff for the offence.

ATTORNEY GENERAL'S REFERENCE (NO.83 OF 2001), *Re; sub nom.* R. v. FIDLER (STEPHEN DAVID), [2001] EWCA Crim 2443, [2002] 1 Cr. App. R. (S.) 139, Judge, L.J., CA (Crim Div).

4059. Robbery–elderly persons–street robbery upon 88 year old victim–serious injuries–undue leniency

The Attorney General referred a sentence of 18 months' detention in a young offender's institution to the Court of Appeal on the basis of undue leniency. T, a woman who had been 19 at the time of the offence, had pleaded guilty to the robbery of an 88 year old woman. The victim had sustained head and shoulder injuries in the incident, which took place in the street, and had been unable to continue living independently afterwards. The Attorney General submitted that those factors, together with the victim's age, were sufficiently aggravating to render the sentence unduly lenient.

Held, allowing the reference, that the sentence was unduly lenient. Given the seriousness of the offence and its effect on the victim, and the need for an effective deterrent to street robberies by young people, a sentence of 3 years six months was appropriate, which would be reduced to two years six months to take account of double jeopardy.

ATTORNEY GENERAL'S REFERENCE (NO.108 OF 2001), *Re; sub nom.* R. v. TULLIUS (KELLY LOUISE), [2002] EWCA Crim 193, [2002] 2 Cr. App. R. (S.) 68, Rose, L.J., CA (Crim Div).

4060. Robbery–elderly persons–threatening to kill

D entered a house occupied by an elderly couple. He was searching cupboards and drawers when they entered the room where he was and told him to leave. D demanded money threatening to kill them if they refused to comply with his demand. D was sentenced to 10 years' imprisonment and appealed.

Held, dismissing the appeal, that a sentence of 10 years' imprisonment imposed for robbery and attempted robbery, although severe, was not manifestly excessive given that the incidents involved elderly people whose homes were entered during the night in circumstances which must have left them very traumatised, *R. v. Swanson (Stephen Leslie)* (1979) 1 Cr. App. R. (S.) 99 considered.

R. v. DUNN (CRAIG NIGEL), [2001] EWCA Crim 1146, [2002] 1 Cr. App. R. (S.) 23, Penry-Davey, J., CA (Crim Div).

4061. Robbery–firearms–violence–use of imitation firearm on person delivering takeaway food–sentencing guidelines

H, aged 37, appealed against a sentence of 12 years' imprisonment imposed for the armed robbery of a person delivering takeaway meals. The offence, which had been planned, was committed with the use of an imitation firearm and occurred within six weeks of H's release on licence from a sentence of seven years' imprisonment for a like offence. H contended that his sentence was manifestly excessive and out of line with sentencing guidelines.

Held, allowing the appeal, that in view of the aggravating features, a severe sentence was appropriate, *Attorney General's Reference (Nos.20 and 21 of 1992), Re* (1994) 15 Cr. App. R. (S.) 152 applied. However, having regard to a number of other authorities, particularly in relation to the robbery of taxi drivers, a shorter sentence was appropriate and the term was reduced to eight years, *R. v. Jackson (Christopher Anthony)* [1998] 1 Cr. App. R. (S.) 259, [1998] C.L.Y. 1376, *R. v. Wright (Richard Arthur)* [2000] 2 Cr. App. R. (S.) 459, [2001] C.L.Y. 1474 considered and *Attorney General's Reference (Nos.22 and 23 of 1991), Re* (1992) 13 Cr. App. R. (S.) 592, [1993] C.L.Y. 1281 distinguished.

R. v. HARVEY (GEORGE), [2001] EWCA Crim 1200, [2002] 1 Cr. App. R. (S.) 31, Curtis, J., CA (Crim Div).

4062. Robbery–firearms offences–planned attack on Securicor van with loaded gun–undue leniency

The Attorney General applied to refer as unduly lenient a total sentence of three years' imprisonment imposed upon K for offences of attempted robbery and possession of a firearm upon arrest. K had targeted a Securicor cash delivery at a central London bank and, armed with a loaded revolver, had confronted the driver as he transferred monies from the van to the bank. The Attorney General highlighted three aggravating features namely, that a Securicor vehicle containing a substantial amount of money had been specifically targeted, a loaded firearm had been employed and lastly that a degree of planning had been evident.

Held, allowing the reference, that K could have expected a sentence of at least 8 years' imprisonment at first instance following a guilty plea. However, taking into account the element of double jeopardy and the progress that he appeared to have been making whilst in custody, a total term of six years was substituted.

ATTORNEY GENERAL'S REFERENCE (NO.84 OF 2001), *Re; sub nom.* R. v. KATIISA (KENNETH), [2002] EWCA Crim 7, [2002] 2 Cr. App. R. (S.) 51, Rose, L.J., CA (Crim Div).

4063. Robbery–hijacking–planned hijacking of cars on public highway–aggravated by further actual and threatened violence

S appealed against a sentence of seven years and six months' imprisonment imposed for offences of handling stolen goods, theft, robbery and going equipped for theft and a further 18 month consecutive term for an offence, on a separate indictment, of possessing a firearm with intent. The two offences of robbery related to the planned hijacking of cars on the public highway. S maintained that the seven years and six months' sentence for the robberies was excessive given that he had pleaded guilty and that the 18 month term imposed for the firearms offence was, of itself, too long.

Held, dismissing the appeal, that the pre planned hijacking of a car on the highway, usually involving ramming from behind, was a particularly serious type of robbery. Such offences almost always involved at least two criminals acting together thereby increasing the victim's fear and sense of helplessness. The offence would be aggravated where the impact from behind was followed by personal violence to the victim or the threat or use of a knife or other such weapon. The penalty imposed should reflect the fact that, where the car taken was particularly valuable, the proceeds received might make the offence as serious as robbing a bank or building society. A defendant, even of good character, who on several separate occasions committed an offence of this type, aggravated by the use or threat of additional violence, could expect a sentence of at least 10 years' imprisonment following a trial. The sentence of 18 months' imprisonment for the firearms offence, viewed in isolation, might have been too high. However, in all other respects, the individual sentences for each offence had been tailored impeccably to reflect the relative seriousness of the different offences. It was impossible to say that the total sentence of nine years' imprisonment was manifestly excessive. In the circumstances of the case it was entirely appropriate, *R. v. O'Boyle (Gerald Martin)* [2001] EWCA Crim 968 distinguished.

R. v. SNOWDON (ALEXANDER), [2002] EWCA Crim 2347, *The Times*, November 11, 2002, Rose, L.J., CA (Crim Div).

4064. Robbery–knives–premeditated violent attack on lone shop assistant– previous good character–undue leniency

[Criminal Justice Act 1988 s.36.]

The Attorney General referred as unduly lenient under the Criminal Justice Act 1988 s.36, a sentence imposed on D, a man aged 20, of a combination order comprising of a two year probation order and 100 hours' community service for the robbery of a shop assistant who had been working alone. It was contended that (1) the premeditated nature of the offence; (2) the fact that D had been armed with a knife, and (3) the degree of violence used against the victim were aggravating features.

Held, allowing the reference, quashing the combination order and substituting a sentence of eighteen months' detention, that the judge had failed to give adequate reasons for imposing the combination order and a clear tariff existed for offences like the one in the instant case. Notwithstanding D's good character, an appropriate sentence would have been three years' detention but this was reduced to eighteen months' detention to take into account the element of double jeopardy and the fact that D had made appropriate efforts to comply with the combination order.

ATTORNEY GENERAL'S REFERENCE (NO.22 OF 2001), Re; *sub nom.* R. v. DOSANJH (HARPEET); R. v. DOSANJH (HARPREET), [2001] EWCA Crim 1174, [2002] 1 Cr. App. R. (S.) 13, Kay, L.J., CA (Crim Div).

4065. Robbery–mobile telephones–homosexual victims–undue leniency

The Attorney General referred to the court as unduly lenient concurrent sentences of eight months' imprisonment imposed on O for each of two counts of robbery. O had attacked and robbed two men in the street. The aggravating features identified by the Attorney General were that the incident had taken place at night and had involved repeated threats to the victims and homophobic abuse as well as an attempt to rob the victims of their mobile phones. In mitigation, O had pleaded guilty at the first opportunity and made full admissions, he was genuinely remorseful, had no previous convictions for similar offences and had a good employment record.

Held, allowing the reference, that the sentence was unduly lenient having regard to the circumstances of the offences and the persistence of O's behaviour towards the victims. A sentence in the region of three years' imprisonment would have been appropriate for each count. However, having regard to the element of double jeopardy, the sentences were quashed and substituted by two concurrent terms of two years and six months' imprisonment.

ATTORNEY GENERAL'S REFERENCE (NO.22A OF 2002); *sub nom.* R. v. O'GRADY (RIKKI MICHAEL) [2002] EWCA Crim 1126, Rose, L.J., CA (Crim Div).

4066. Robbery—mobile telephones—sentencing guidelines—undue leniency

The Attorney General referred to the court as unduly lenient two sentences; one of six months' detention imposed on L following his conviction for robbery and assault with intent to rob and the other a rehabilitation order of 18 months combined with 60 hours' community punishment imposed on S following his plea of guilty to three robberies and two thefts. Q appealed a sentence of four years' detention imposed on him following his conviction for robbery. All three cases involved the theft of mobile phones and small amounts of money in public places.

Held, allowing the references and Q's appeal, that given the effect that the theft of mobile phones had on the public, the fact that such thefts often involved victims who were young or elderly and the fact that Home Office research showed a marked increase in the incidence of such thefts, the court should adopt a robust approach to defendants who committed them. Custodial sentences should be imposed save in very exceptional circumstances irrespective of the offender's age and whether he had previous convictions or not; those factors would, however, be important when determining the length of the sentence. The authorities seemed to show that sentences ranged from 18 months to five years and that the upper limit was three years where no weapon was used. Those guidelines were appropriate save that the upper limits could be exceeded where the defendant had a number of previous convictions, where a substantial degree of violence had been used or where a particularly large number of offences had been committed. The fact that the offence had been committed by a team of offenders would also affect the length of the sentence. The sentences imposed on L and S were increased to three years and six months' detention and to two years and six months' detention respectively, whereas Q's sentence was reduced to three years' detention.

ATTORNEY GENERAL'S REFERENCE (NOS.4 AND 7 OF 2002), *Re*; R. v. Q (STEVEN JAMES) (A JUVENILE); *sub nom.* R. v. LOBBAN (ADRIAN MICHAEL); R. v. SAWYERS (CHRISTOPHER), [2002] EWCA Crim 127, [2002] 2 Cr. App. R. (S.) 77, Lord Woolf of Barnes, L.C.J., CA (Crim Div).

4067. Robbery—pleas—doing an act with intent to impede arrest

T appealed against a sentence of 18 months' imprisonment for doing an act with intent to impede the apprehension of another. T gave his friend a lift to a supermarket car park, where they were going to purchase heroin. T's friend got out of his car and robbed a woman of her handbag. The friend then ran back to the vehicle and T drove off. Members of the public attempted to stop the vehicle and a police car followed it until T was stopped. The Crown accepted that T was unaware of the robbery; his plea was accepted on the basis that he believed his friend had committed a theft.

Held, allowing the appeal, that in the court's view the sentence was longer than necessary. A sentence of nine months' imprisonment was substituted.

R. v. TAYLOR (MARK), [2002] EWCA Crim 243, [2002] 2 Cr. App. R. (S.) 85, Gage, J., CA (Crim Div).

4068. Robbery–pleas–policy of courts to grant discounts to defendants pleading guilty

[Powers of Criminal Courts (Sentencing) Act 2000 s.152.]

K appealed against a sentence of six years' imprisonment imposed after pleading guilty to robbery. The plea was entered on re arraignment on the day fixed for trial. Prior to that date, he maintained a plea of not guilty. The appeal was based on a comment made by the sentencing judge to the effect that as K had entered his plea of guilty at the very last possible moment, he would give him no credit for the plea, because in the sentencing judge's judgment, the case against him was overwhelming. It was submitted that the sentencing judge was wrong to withhold all credit for the plea of guilty and that the Powers of Criminal Courts (Sentencing) Act 2000 s.152 made it mandatory for the sentencing judge to give some credit for the plea of guilty.

Held, allowing the appeal, that the case was not overwhelming as to make it appropriate to deprive K of all discount for his plea. It remained the strong policy of the courts to encourage guilty pleas and to reflect that policy by giving a discount in an appropriate case. That was particularly so in a case where the complainant had been spared the ordeal of giving evidence at trial. The discount in this case should be less than it otherwise might be because of the lateness of the plea, but in the court's view some discount should have been allowed. In the court's judgment, the appropriate sentence would have been five years' imprisonment.

R. v. HUSSAIN (ALTAF), [2002] EWCA Crim 67, [2002] 2 Cr. App. R. (S.) 59, Davis, J., CA (Crim Div).

4069. Robbery–threatening to kill–serious street robbery–use of loose blade– undue leniency

The Attorney General referred to the court as unduly lenient a sentence of three years' imprisonment imposed on C for an offence of robbery. C and his brother had held a student at knife point. They had forced him to walk to a cash machine, under threat that his throat would be cut, and withdraw £300. A "Sony Walkman" had also been stolen. The following aggravating features were identified (1) there had been an element of premeditation; (2) the offence had been carried out by two people acting in concert; (3) C had carried a loose blade; (4) the victim had been forced to walk to a cash machine under threat from the blade and the maximum sum possible had been withdrawn; (5) threats had repeatedly been made that the victim's throat would be cut, and (6) C and his brother had alleged, in their defence, that the victim had been seeking to buy drugs.

Held, allowing the reference, that the offence had amounted to a serious street robbery. While C's background had been an unhappy one and he was doing well in prison, having regard to the aggravating features of the offence, the sentence imposed had been unduly lenient. A sentence of six years' imprisonment would have been expected following a trial. Accordingly, taking into account double jeopardy, a sentence of five years' imprisonment would be substituted.

ATTORNEY GENERAL'S REFERENCE (NO.127 OF 2001), *Re*; *sub nom.* R. v. CREAMER (ALAN PAUL), [2002] EWCA Crim 1230, [2003] 1 Cr. App. R. (S.) 20, Rose, L.J., CA (Crim Div).

4070. Robbery–violence–elderly victims living alone–appropriateness of discretionary life sentence–undue leniency

[Powers of Criminal Courts (Sentencing) Act 2000 s.80(2)(b), s.161(3).]

The Attorney General referred to the court as unduly lenient a sentence of nine years and six months' imprisonment imposed on C, who had pleaded guilty to five counts of robbery. The robberies had been committed on two separate nights and all the victims had been elderly women who lived alone. In each case the victim had been attacked in her own home. Approximately six months prior to committing the robberies, C had been released from prison having served 12 years of an 18 year term imposed for offences of robbery and rape, which had been committed against two elderly women in their homes. C had a significant history of previous convictions and a pre-sentence report had described him as posing an exceptionally high risk of harm to the community. The judge in sentencing C had concluded that the evidence did not show that C's conduct had been likely to lead to physical injury within the meaning of the Powers of Criminal Courts (Sentencing) Act 2000 s.161(3) and that accordingly he could not impose a longer than commensurate sentence under s.80(2)(b) of the Act, or a discretionary life sentence.

Held, allowing the reference, that the judge had erred in not finding the offences to be violent offences for the purposes of s.161(3) of the Act. The fact that the victims had all been elderly, and that C's conduct had created a real possibility of fractures, asphyxia and cardiac arrest was sufficient to render each offence a violent offence, *R. v. Cochrane (Robert Brian)* (1994) 15 Cr. App. R. (S.) 708, [1995] C.L.Y. 1425 applied. Given that the offences were violent offences, the sentence passed by the judge had been unduly lenient. Accordingly, it was appropriate to impose a discretionary life sentence in relation to each of the five counts. The notional determinate sentence was one of twelve years and a period of six years should be served.

ATTORNEY GENERAL'S REFERENCE (NO.113 OF 2001), *Re; sub nom.* R. v. CONNORS (LAWRENCE), [2002] EWCA Crim 143, [2002] 2 Cr. App. R. (S.) 62, Rose, L.J., CA (Crim Div).

4071.   Robbery–violence–use of weapons–offending on bail–undue leniency

[Criminal Justice Act 1988 s.36.]

The Attorney General referred as unduly lenient under the Criminal Justice Act 1988 s.36 a sentence of a drug treatment and testing order for a period of two years imposed for four offences of robbery. The first offence, which was committed by M and two accomplices, occurred on a bus. The victim was punched in the face and his property stolen. The subsequent offences, which were committed whilst M was on bail, occurred in similar circumstances and involved threats to use a knife or firearm.

Held, allowing the reference, that notwithstanding the fact that M was aged only 21, had pleaded guilty and had no previous convictions for similar offences, given that the later offences were committed whilst on bail and involved the use of weapons, a sentence of three years' imprisonment should have been imposed. However, in view of the element of double jeopardy and given that M had already served a period of four months, the sentence was increased to two years and six months.

ATTORNEY GENERAL'S REFERENCE (NO.28 OF 2001), *Re; sub nom.* R. v. McCOLLINS (DANIEL), [2001] EWCA Crim 1373, [2002] 1 Cr. App. R. (S.) 59, Judge, L.J., CA (Crim Div).

4072.   Sex offenders orders–breach–offensive threats to female police officer

Held, dismissing the appeal, that a sentence of 12 months' imprisonment for the breach of a sex offenders order, following offensive threats made by B to a woman police officer, was not excessive in view of the imminent release of B, and the need to protect the public from his antisocial behaviour, even though a sentence of a different nature would normally have been regarded as appropriate.

R. v. BEECH (STEPHEN JOHN), [2001] EWCA Crim 915, [2002] 1 Cr. App. R. (S.) 3, Lord Woolf of Barnes, L.C.J., CA (Crim Div).

4073.   Sex offenders orders–breach–speed and intensity of acts following release

[Criminal Justice Act 1991 s.2(2)(b).]

B appealed against his concurrent sentence of three years' imprisonment imposed following three contested breaches of a sex offenders order committed within 48 hours following his release from prison. B contended that (1) the judge had not been entitled to sentence on the lines similar to those under the Criminal Justice Act 1991 s.2(2)(b), and with the protection of the public in mind; (2) this was effectively a sentence imposed for breach of a civil injunction, and (3) the sentence should have taken account of the minor nature of the incidents.

Held, dismissing the appeal, that (1) s.2(2)(b) of the Act did not specify when a judge was entitled to consider the public's protection, it was used as a general sentencing tool; (2) whilst the order was a civil injunction, it was one of criminal origin, and (3) the quality of the acts committed were not the only consideration when determining the seriousness of the breach, as the speed at which they were committed, and their intensity were also important considerations.

R. v. BROWN (GRAHAM), [2001] EWCA Crim 724, [2002] 1 Cr. App. R. (S.) 1, Rougier, J., CA (Crim Div).

4074. Sexual offences–children–breach of trust–unlawful intercourse with 12 year old girl

M, aged 20, appealed against a sentence of three years and six months' imprisonment for unlawful sexual intercourse with a girl aged 12. M was present with other young people at a house; the parents of one of the young people had gone out. Beer and cider were drunk. During the course of the evening, M and a girl aged 12 were alone in an upstairs bedroom and he asked the girl whether she wished to lose her virginity. Sexual intercourse then took place briefly. The girl subsequently told her parents what had happened. M denied that sexual intercourse had taken place. Following the trial, the sentencing judge found that M knew that if the girl had been sober she would not have agreed. M submitted that the offence did not involve any breach of trust on his part and that the sentence was excessive.

Held, dismissing the appeal, that the judge had been entitled and right to take a serious view of what occurred. There was no mistake about the victim's age and there was a considerable element of taking advantage of the state of the victim in alcohol as she was. M did not have the benefit of any remorse, admission or plea of guilty, *R. v. Fiddler (Mark Anthony)* [2001] 1 Cr.App. R. (S.) 100, [2001] C.L.Y. 1485 considered.

R. v. M (JOHN C); *sub nom.* R. v. JCM, [2001] EWCA Crim 2971, [2002] 2 Cr. App. R. (S.) 27, Mance, L.J., CA (Crim Div).

4075. Sexual offences–children–pornography–unlawful intercourse with girl aged 13

G aged 30, pleaded guilty before a magistrates court to unlawful sexual intercourse with a girl aged 13. He was committed to the Crown Court for sentence. G befriended X only just over 13 years of age and offered her money and drinks. X and several of her friends went to G's home. A pornographic video tape was played on a television set. G then had intercourse with X. He was sentenced to 12 months' imprisonment and appealed.

Held, dismissing the appeal, that a sentence of 12 months' imprisonment for unlawful sexual intercourse with a girl under 16 was not manifestly excessive given the aggravating features of the case including the use of alcohol, pornography and the fact that another young girl was present, *R. v. H* [2000] 1 Cr. App. R. (S.) 82, [2000] C.L.Y. 1429 considered.

R. v. GARRITY (STEPHEN JOHN), [2001] EWCA Crim 953, [2002] 1 Cr. App. R. (S.) 10, Eady, J., CA (Crim Div).

4076. Sexual offences–sex offender orders–meaning of "relevant date" in Crime and Disorder Act 1998 s.3(2)

[Crime and Disorder Act 1998 s.2, s.3(2).]

H appealed against a sex offender order made against him under the Crime and Disorder Act 1998 s.2. He had a number of convictions for sexual offences, the earliest having occurred in 1994 and the latest in October 2001. Under s.2 a sex offender order could be sought where it appeared that the offender had acted, since the "relevant date", in such a way as to give reasonable cause for believing that an order was necessary to protect the public from serious harm. H argued that the "relevant date" was the date of an offender's latest conviction and that there had been no relevant acts since the date of his latest conviction.

Held, allowing the appeal, that for the purposes of an application for a sex offender order, the "relevant date" was the date of the offender's latest conviction or, if later, December 1, 1998, being the date of the commencement of the provisions relating to sex offenders in the 1998 Act. The language of s.3(2) of the Act, which defined the "relevant date", clearly supported such a conclusion.

HOPSON v. CHIEF CONSTABLE OF NORTH WALES, [2002] EWHC 2430, *The Times*, November 1, 2002, Davis, J., QBD (Admin Ct).

4077. Suspended sentences – ill health – exceptional circumstances of appellant

G was convicted of conspiring to cheat the Inland Revenue. He was involved in a fraudulent scheme by which income tax repayments were made both to existing and to fictitious taxpayers. The loss incurred by the Inland Revenue was of the order of £76,000 and G received a personal benefit of about £6,000. G contended that there were "exceptional circumstances" which would have permitted the sentencing judge to suspend the sentence. The matters said to constitute "exceptional circumstances" were the medical problems of G and the behavioural and learning difficulties experienced by his 10 year old son. G was sentenced to 12 months' imprisonment and appealed.

Held, dismissing the appeal, that the ill health of G and the learning disabilities of his son, did not constitute exceptional circumstances so as to justify a suspension of sentence.

R. v. GORASIA (DHANJI), [2001] EWCA Crim 1718, [2002] 1 Cr. App. R. (S.) 84, Holman, J., CA (Crim Div).

4078. Theft – attempts – recidivists – sentencing guidelines

[Powers of Criminal Courts (Sentencing) Act 2000 s.80(2).]

G appealed against a sentence of three years' imprisonment for the attempted theft of a woman's handbag. He submitted that under the Powers of Criminal Courts (Sentencing) Act 2000 s.80(2) the sentence did not equate with the offence, and that the tariff ceiling for the offence was approximately 12 months' imprisonment.

Held, dismissing the appeal, that in the light of the relevant authorities, in the case of persistent offenders like G, the tariff ceiling was one of several years' imprisonment, and therefore G's sentence was permissible and was not manifestly excessive in the circumstances, *R. v. Glide (David)* (1989) 11 Cr. App. R. (S.) 319 and *R. v. O'Rourke (John)* (1994) 15 Cr. App. R. (S.) 650, [1995] C.L.Y. 1482 and *R. v. Spencer (Warren Anthony)* (1995) 16 Cr. App. R. (S.) 482 considered.

R. v. GWILLIM-JONES (JOHN), [2001] EWCA Crim 904, [2002] 1 Cr. App. R. (S.) 6, Holman, J., CA (Crim Div).

4079. Violent disorder – conspiracy – football – terms of severance agreed by prosecution – undue leniency

[Criminal Law Act 1997 s.1 (1).]

The Attorney General referred to the court as unduly lenient a sentence of four years' imprisonment imposed on R following his conviction for conspiracy to commit violent disorder contrary to the Criminal Law Act 1997 s.1 (1). The other offenders tried with R had been sentenced to custodial terms ranging from four to 18 months. R had engaged in public violence in a football related incident, involving the use of weapons, in full view of local residents. One man sustained a permanent brain injury. The aggravating features identified by the Attorney General were that the violent disorder had been planned, a variety of weapons had been used, the incident had been preceded by aggressive behaviour which terrified onlookers and there had been a real risk of injury to innocent bystanders. R appealed against his sentence. It was submitted that R was not solely responsible for the incident and would have a legitimate sense of grievance if his sentence was increased in view of the sentences passed on other offenders involved in the incident.

Held, finding the sentence unduly lenient but not varying it and dismissing R's appeal, that it was not appropriate to interfere with the sentence because the prosecution had indicated at the plea and directions hearing that they would not seek to distinguish between the roles of those who were not shown to have actually participated in any violence. The large numbers of offenders had been split into batches for convenience at trial but this was not a division which ought to result in any different treatment of those who had played similar parts. Accordingly, to increase the sentence passed on these offenders would be contrary to the basis on which the matters had proceeded.

ATTORNEY GENERAL'S REFERENCE (NOS.148-155 OF 2001), *Re; sub nom.* R. v. RUSSELL (GRAHAM); R. v. BURWOOD (JAMES); R. v. JARY (STEPHEN); R. v. TAPKEN (CHRISTOPHER); R. v. BATTY (CHRISTOPHER ANDREW); R. v. MILLER (CHRISTOPHER RICHARD); R. v. CLEMENTS (PAUL); R. v. WILSON (MARK); R. v. LENG (DARREN SHAUN); R. v. SHARP (JOHN WILSON) [2002] EWCA Crim 1313, Rose, L.J., CA (Crim Div).

4080. Wounding with intent–combination orders–glassing–permanent scarring– undue leniency

[Offences Against the Person Act 1861 s.18.]

The Attorney General referred to the court as unduly lenient the imposition of a combination order for a period of 12 months on M, who had pleaded guilty to an offence of wounding with intent contrary to the Offences Against the Person Act 1861 s.18. A dispute had arisen outside a night club between M and the victim, a woman aged 19. The victim had pushed M to the ground and had been shepherded away. M had smashed a bottle which she had found on the ground and had attacked the victim. The medical evidence was consistent with there having been a single blow to the victim, the impact taking place between the ear and left eye. The victim had required 30 stitches to various wounds and was likely to be permanently scarred. M had met all the requirements of the sentence imposed.

Held, allowing the reference but not varying the sentence imposed, that the sentence imposed had been unduly lenient and should never have been contemplated. It had not taken into consideration the interests of the victim or the need for the courts to make it clear that offences of such a kind were not acceptable. An appropriate sentence would have been one of three years' imprisonment. However, it was appropriate to take into account the fact that M had successfully completed the requirements of her sentence and that her mother was in need of her support. In such exceptional circumstances, it was not appropriate to interfere with the sentence imposed, *R. v. Harwood (Paul John)* (1979) 1 Cr. App. R. (S.) 354, [1980] C.L.Y. 571.92 considered.

ATTORNEY GENERAL'S REFERENCE (NO.109 OF 2001), *Re; sub nom.* R. v. McINTYRE (SARA) [2002] EWCA Crim 554, Kennedy, L.J., CA (Crim Div).

4081. Wounding with intent–knives–attack resulting in permanent scarring– undue leniency

The Attorney General referred to the court as unduly lenient a sentence of three years and six months' imprisonment imposed on Z, following his conviction for wounding with intent to cause grievous bodily harm. Z had approached the victim, A, at work and had then gone away and returned a short time later armed with a knife. Z accused A of having made an obscene telephone call to his wife and then attacked A with the knife, causing a facial wound resulting in permanent scarring and a puncture wound to the right hand. The aggravating features identified by the Attorney General were that this was a premeditated attack, apparently unprovoked, involving the use of a knife as a weapon, the attack had continued after the facial wound had been inflicted and the resulting facial injury was serious with permanent effects. In mitigation, Z was of positive good character and his prison report was commendable. There was also a delay in the matter coming to trial, not attributable to Z's conduct.

Held, allowing the reference, that the sentence was unduly lenient. Having regard to the mitigating features and the element of double jeopardy, the sentence of three years and six months was quashed and substituted by one of four years and six months' imprisonment.

ATTORNEY GENERAL'S REFERENCE (NO.11 OF 2002), *Re; sub nom.* R. v. ZEB (AQURANG) [2002] EWCA Crim 1440, Judge, L.J., CA (Crim Div).

4082. Wounding with intent–knives–police officer in riot gear stabbed in thigh– respondent heavily intoxicated–undue leniency

The Attorney General referred as unduly lenient a sentence of 27 months' imprisonment for wounding with intent imposed on W on a late guilty plea. Whilst heavily intoxicated, W had gone into a street armed with a lock knife, which he waved in the air, and had shouted threats. The police attended. The officers wore protective vests and carried shields but W stabbed one officer causing a deep wound to the thigh. W said that he had no recollection of the events and entered a late guilty plea following receipt of a psychiatric report. The report stated that, although W was of previous good character and did not have a severe or long lasting personality disorder, he suffered from an adjustment disorder making him prone to anxiety and depression and which affected his behaviour and led to alcohol abuse which genuinely affected his memory.

Held, refusing the reference, that a sentence of five years' imprisonment would be appropriate in a contested case where a police officer was stabbed while attending an incident that required riot gear to be worn, *Attorney General's Reference (No.86 of 1998), Re* [2000] 1 Cr. App. R. (S.) 10, [1999] C.L.Y. 1372 and *Attorney General's Reference (No.79 of 2000), Re* Unreported, July 10, 2001 considered, *Attorney General's Reference (No.37 of 1995), Re* [1996] 2 Cr. App. R. (S.) 38, [1996] C.L.Y. 1908 doubted. However, in the instant case, there was a good reason for the late plea because the psychiatric report was essential. In addition, W's difficult upbringing, personality disorder and satisfactory military service mitigated against the imposition of a tariff sentence.

ATTORNEY GENERAL'S REFERENCE (NO.129 OF 2001), *Re; sub nom.* R. v. WARDLE (KARL DAVID) [2002] EWCA Crim 297, Kennedy, L.J., CA (Crim Div).

4083. Wounding with intent–knives–victim stabbed in back–undue leniency

The Attorney General referred to the court as unduly lenient a sentence of 18 months' detention imposed on B, aged 19, following her conviction for wounding with intent to cause grievous bodily harm. B had stabbed the victim in the back during an argument in the street outside her flat, having rushed out of the flat armed with a kitchen knife. The aggravating features identified by the Attorney General were the use of the knife, the fact that the stab was to the victim's back and that the victim suffered serious injuries requiring emergency medical treatment. It was submitted that the sentence passed failed to reflect the seriousness of the offence, the need for retribution and deterrence and the need to protect the public from offences of this nature.

Held, allowing the reference, that the sentence was unduly lenient. An appropriate sentence at first instance would have been one of three years and six months' detention, notwithstanding the fact that the instant case involved a single stab wound and did not involve the carrying of a knife, but rather the use of a knife which happened to be to hand in the home. Allowing for the element of double jeopardy, the sentence was increased to one of 30 months' detention.

ATTORNEY GENERAL'S REFERENCE (NO.19 OF 2002), *Re; sub nom.* R. v. BADBY (EMMA LORRAINE) [2002] EWCA Crim 1556, Kay, L.J., CA (Crim Div).

4084. Wounding with intent—robbery—elderly victims attacked in their own homes—violence—undue leniency

[Powers of Criminal Courts (Sentencing) Act 2000 s.80(2)(b).]

The Attorney General referred an extended sentence of eight years' imprisonment with an extended period of three years on licence concurrent on each of three counts of wounding with intent to do grievous bodily harm, robbery and aggravated burglary, on the basis of undue leniency. C had stabbed an 83 year old man in his own home and then demanded money following a forced entry. He also slashed a married couple in their sixties with a razor blade while demanding money having called at their home. The Attorney General contended that the sentence was unduly lenient and that the judge below should have taken the more realistic course of imposing a discretionary life sentence, a longer than normal sentence under the Powers of Criminal Courts (Sentencing) Act 2000 s.80(2)(b) or a custodial sentence commensurate with the offences.

Held, allowing the reference, that the sentence was unduly lenient, given that violent attacks on elderly victims in their own homes deserved sentences in double figures, *Attorney General's Reference (Nos.32 and 33 of 1995), Re* [1996] 2 Cr. App. R. (S.) 346, [1997] C.L.Y. 1421 considered. Taking the element of double jeopardy into account, a commensurate sentence would be one of of 10 years' imprisonment. However, for public protection purposes a longer than commensurate term of 14 years' imprisonment was appropriate.

ATTORNEY GENERAL'S REFERENCE (NO.101 OF 2001), *Re* [2002] EWCA Crim 86, Rose, L.J., CA (Crim Div).

4085. Wounding with intent—undue leniency—victim kicked in head with shod feet—seriousness of offences—undue leniency

[Criminal Justice Act 1988 s.36.]

The Attorney General referred under the Criminal Justice Act 1988 s.36 sentences of three years' detention and four years' imprisonment imposed on G and S respectively, contending that they were unduly lenient. G had pleaded guilty to an offence of wounding with intent and S was convicted of wounding with intent and affray. They had both been part of a group of at least three people who had viciously attacked their victim, knocking him to the ground and kicking and punching him to the head up to 15 times each, using shod feet. The victim would have died but for the fortuitous presence of a former soldier, who had been trained in resuscitation and was able to provide assistance. The victim, nevertheless, required treatment in intensive care and suffered long term physical and psychological difficulties.

Held, allowing the references, that the sentences were unduly lenient by a substantial margin and did not reflect the seriousness of the offences, public concern regarding such offences, or the requirement for an effective deterrent. Whilst respective sentences of five and seven years' custody would have been appropriate at first instance, in view of the element of double jeopardy, G's term was increased to three years and nine months' detention and S's term to six years' imprisonment, *Attorney General's Reference (No.47 of 1994), Re* (1995) 16 Cr. App. R. (S.) 865, [1996] C.L.Y. 1910, *R. v. Coles (Barrie)* [1997] 2 Cr. App. R. (S.) 95, [1997] C.L.Y. 1559 and *R. v. Richards (Jake)* [1998] 1 Cr. App. R. (S.) 87, [1998] C.L.Y. 1236 considered.

ATTORNEY GENERAL'S REFERENCE (NOS.44 AND 45 OF 2001), *Re*; R. v. SMITH (ALFRED); *sub nom.* R. v. G (ADRIAN DAVID), [2001] EWCA Crim 1483, [2002] 1 Cr. App. R. (S.) 67, Tomlinson, J, CA (Crim Div).

4086. Wounding with intent—weapons—use of glass as a weapon—unprovoked attack—undue leniency

The Attorney General referred to the court as unduly lenient a sentence of two years' imprisonment imposed on M for an offence of wounding with intent. M and a number of others had been drinking at a bar. Two women had become involved in a scuffle. The victim had attempted to intervene but had been attacked by M who had smashed a glass into her face. The victim had suffered a wound of about 6cm over the bridge of her nose, extending down onto both her cheeks. There were also two smaller wounds. The following aggravating features were identified (1) the attack was unprovoked and the weapon used had resulted in some scarring, albeit faint, and (2) the offence had been committed when M was subject to a probation order which had been imposed for an offence of affray. M was the sole carer of her two year old daughter.

Held, allowing the reference, that having regard to the fact that a glass had been used as a weapon, albeit that it had not been broken for use as such, to the lack of mitigation in M's record, to concerns about M's behaviour when drunk and to the fact that the sentence had followed a trial rather than a plea of guilty, the sentence imposed had been unduly lenient. A sentence of four years would have been expected. Accordingly, taking into account the element of double jeopardy, a sentence of three years was substituted.

ATTORNEY GENERAL'S REFERENCE (NO.25 OF 2002), *Re; sub nom.* R. v. MENTLAK (FAYE ALICE), [2002] EWCA Crim 1297, [2003] 1 Cr. App. R. (S.) 28, Hunt, J., CA (Crim Div).

4087. Books

Banks, Robert – Banks on Sentencing. Paperback: £38.00. ISBN 0-406-95130-6. Paperback: £38.00. ISBN 0-406-95130-6. Butterworths Law.

Mitchell, Barry; Farrar, Salim – Statutes on Criminal Justice and Sentencing. Blackstone's Statute Series. Paperback: £14.99. ISBN 0-19-925485-0. Oxford University Press.

Thomas, David – Sentencing Referencer: 2002. Paperback: £20.00. ISBN 0-421-78610-8. Sweet & Maxwell.

SHIPPING

4088. Arrest – costs – appraisement and sale of vessel – priority for costs – impact upon other creditors

F sought an order that it should be awarded the costs incurred since the making of an order for the appraisement and sale of a vessel, OG, and they were to rank in priority, after the Admiralty Marshal's costs in the matter. Although OG's owners agreed that the costs of the parties obtaining the vessel's arrest and the order for appraisement and sale should be accorded priority on the ground that such actions produced a fund from which all claimants could benefit, they argued that this did not extend to costs incurred by either of those parties which only indirectly benefited the other claimants.

Held, dismissing the application, that it was appropriate for the court to exercise its equitable jurisdiction to grant costs and accord priority. The evidence did not show that the disputed costs had been incurred in a way that benefited all the claimants or the preservation of funds as a whole. Allowing F's claim would therefore mean that the fund was being expended in a disproportionate manner to the detriment of the other claimants.

FESTIVE HOLIDAYS LTD v. DEMISE CHARTERERS OF THE OCEAN GLORY 1 [2002] 1 Lloyd's Rep. 679, Aikens, J., QBD (Adm Ct).

4089. Bermuda – local legislation

MERCHANT SHIPPING (CONFIRMATION OF LEGISLATION) (BERMUDA) ORDER 2002, SI 2002 3132; made under the Merchant Shipping Act 1894 s.735. In force: in accordance with Art.1; £1.50.

This confirms the Merchant Shipping Act 2002 enacted by the Legislature of Bermuda, which repeals the Merchant Shipping Act 1894 as it applies to Bermuda and replaces it with local legislation.

4090. Bills of lading–carriers liabilities–limit of liability–application of Hague Visby Rules to contract of carriage–limitation of liability under Art.IV r.5

[Hague Visby Rules Art.I(b), Art.III, Art.X, Art.IV r.5.]

P appealed against the determination as a preliminary issue, ([2002] 1 All E.R. (Comm) 176), that the Hague Visby Rules did not apply to the contract of carriage under which three reactors were carried by sea from Italy to Saudi Arabia. The claim for $2.4 million arose from the damage caused to one reactor when it was dropped whilst being loaded after a hook on one of the vessel's cranes broke. An additional issue raised on appeal was whether the carriers had successfully limited their liability by reference to Art.IV r.5. P submitted that, as a matter of construction of the contract of carriage and the bill of lading incorporated into it, the Rules governed the contract in all trades where the Rules applied. As this included voyages from contracting states, of which Italy was one, the Rules applied. Further, it was unnecessary to consider whether the contract of carriage fell within Art.I(b) of the Rules because the parties had made their intention clear in the bill of lading, and if necessary the Rules or the contract should be manipulated to reflect that intention, *Adamastos Shipping Co Ltd v. Anglo Saxon Petroleum Co Ltd* [1959] A.C. 133, [1958] C.L.Y. 565 cited. Further, P submitted that if the damage was caused by the carrier's failure to fulfill the overriding obligation under Art.III to make the vessel seaworthy before beginning the voyage, the limitation of liability under Art.IV r.5 could not be relied upon, as it was in the nature of an exemption because it exempted the carrier from liability in excess of the amount stated, *Maxine Footwear Co v. Canadian Government Merchant Marine* [1959] A.C. 589, [1959] C.L.Y. 3034 cited.

Held, allowing the appeal, that the Rules were not applied compulsorily by the proper law of the contract. Although under Art.X of the Rules their provisions were stated to apply to "every bill of lading relating to the carriage of goods", Art.X must be subject to Art.I(b). Therefore, the instant contract was still one which had to be covered by a bill of lading or similar for the Rules to apply. It was not possible to manipulate the wording of the contract, as it would not have reflected the intention of the parties. However, the judge had been wrong in deciding that the question was whether the bill of lading to be issued would contain the terms of the contract of carriage. The Rules simply required a bill to have been issued or for the contract to provide for its issue. As the instant contract did so provide, the Rules applied. The words "in any event" contained in Art.IV r.5 meant what they said and were unlimited in scope. Limitation of liability was different from an exemption and none of the other Art.IV exemptions contained the words "in any event". As a matter of construction, they were not intended to refer only to those events giving rise to the Art.IV exemptions. As a result, P's claim was subject to the limitation of liability imposed by Art.IV r.5.

PARSONS CORP v. CV SCHEEPVAARTONDERNEMING HAPPY RANGER (THE HAPPY RANGER), [2002] EWCA Civ 694, [2002] 2 All E.R. (Comm) 24, Tuckey, L.J., CA.

4091. Bills of lading–carriers liabilities–package limitation–incorporation of Hague Rules into contract–gold value figure

[Hague Rules Art.IV r.5, Art.IX.]

D, holders of a bill of lading, sought recovery of NZD 613,667 from carrier T, the latter having accepted liability for damage to 55 coils of electrolytic tin plates incurred during carriage. The bill of lading stipulated at cl.6(B)(b)(i) that liability would be determined by reference to the Hague Rules, but that the package limitation was "deemed to be £100 Sterling, lawful money of the United Kingdom". T claimed that its liability was limited to £5,500. However, cl.8(2) of the bill purported to nullify any contractual provision repugnant to any international law or convention. It fell to the court to determine (1) whether the phrase "lawful money of the United Kingdom" in cl.6(B)(b)(i) was nullified on the grounds of inconsistency with the liability limitation of "£100 per package or unit or the equivalent of that sum in other currency" provided by the Art.IV r.5 of the

Rules, and (2) in the event that Art.IV r.5 supervened, what meaning was to be assigned to "£100" in this context.

Held, giving judgment for the plaintiffs, that cl.7 of the contract made it clear that liability was to be ascertained by the reference to the Hague Rules as stated in cl.6(B)(b)(i). Therefore the effect was to incorporate all of the Rules into the bill of lading. Since cl.8(2) of the contract had the effect of nullifying cl.6(B)(b)(i), Art. IV r.5 of the Rules supervened. Thus, the phrase "£100 Sterling lawful money of the United Kingdom" was supervened by the package limitation provided by Art.IV r.5. Further, Art.IX of the Rules provided that "the monetary units mentioned in this convention are taken to be gold value". This phrase had been introduced so as to qualify the reference to "£100" in Art.IV r.5. The two articles combined to provide a measure of T's obligation and not an indication as to the mode of payment, *Rosa S, The* [1989] Q.B. 419 and *Brown Boveri (Australia) Pty v. Baltic Shipping Co (The Nadezhda Krupskaya)* [1989] 1 Lloyd's Rep. 518, [1990] C.L.Y. 4063 followed. Thus, the package limitation was determined to be the gold value of £100 Sterling in 1924.

TASMAN DISCOVERER, THE; *sub nom.* DAIRY CONTAINERS LTD v. TASMAN ORIENT LINE CV [2001] 2 Lloyd's Rep. 665, Williams, J., HC (NZ).

4092. Bills of lading−carriers liability−order and condition of cargo when loaded−duty imposed upon carrier−qualification in bill of lading

[Hague Visby Rules Art.III r.3.]

The claimants, cargo owners, brought an action against the defendants, owners of the vessel which carried the cargo, claiming damages for breach of the duty to issue a bill of lading accurately describing the cargo's apparent condition. The cargo had been sold on to G, payment to be by letter of credit upon presentation of a clean bill of lading. Shortly after loading commenced, the master had expressed his concern at the cargo's condition. Ultimately, a mate's certificate was issued stating "Cargo discoloured also foreign materials eg plastic, rust, rubber, stone, black particles found in cargo". Bills of lading, claused using the same wording, were eventually signed, but were rejected by G. Delivery was eventually taken on reduction of the price. On inspection, the cargo's condition was found to be normal with minor stains, contamination and discolouration. The Hague Visby Rules had been incorporated. The claimants submitted that it was not sufficient for the bill of lading to show what the master honestly believed. To limit the duty to one of honesty would decrease the utility of a bill of lading, *The Trade Star Line Corp v. Mitsui & Co Ltd (The Arctic Trader)* [1996] 2 Lloyd's Report 449 and *Compania Naviera Vasconzada v. Churchill & Sim* [1906] 1 K.B. 237 cited.

Held, giving judgment for the defendants, that although the master had failed in his duty under Art.III r.3 of the Hague Visby Rules by misrepresenting the condition of the cargo, the claimants had failed to establish that this had caused their loss because a reasonably observant master would have claused the bill of lading, albeit by quantifying the extent of the problem. The carrier was under a duty to decide whether the cargo appeared to satisfy its description in the bill. If the master honestly considered the cargo not to be in good order and that was a view that a reasonably observant master could hold, then he was entitled to qualify the statement in the bill. It was for the master to decide the extent of any qualification, but the words used had to reflect reasonably closely the actual condition of the cargo and the extent of any apparent defect. In the instant case, the cargo only contained minimal contamination. Therefore, although a reasonable master might have considered it appropriate to refer to it in the bill, some indication of its extent should have been given. The description actually used was therefore misleading in that respect.

OWNERS OF CARGO LATELY LADEN ON BOARD THE DAVID AGMASHENEBELI v. OWNERS OF THE DAVID AGMASHENEBELI, [2002] EWHC 104, [2002] 2 All E.R. (Comm) 806, Colman, J., QBD (Adm Ct).

4093. Bills of lading–carriers liability–package limitation–meaning of "apply compulsorily"

[Hague Rules; Hague Visby Rules; Carriage of Goods by Sea Act 1936 (United States).]

H, a carrier, sought determination of preliminary issues concerning the interpretation of contractual clauses, evidenced in the bill of lading, relating to the applicable law under which package limitation was to be determined. T had brought an action to recover compensation for damage to cargo sustained whilst being carried by H from the USA to Hong Kong. The clause paramount of the contract, cl.2(a), stated that the bill of lading would be subject to the Hague Rules as enacted in country of shipment unless the the Hague Visby Rules or the Carriage of Goods by Sea Act 1936 (United States) applied compulsorily. If those enactments were not in force in the country of shipment, cl.2(b) provided that the corresponding convention or legislation of the destination country should apply. The questions before the court were (1) whether the contract of carriage incorporated and/or was subject to the US legislation, and (2) if so, the extent of H's liability.

Held, determining the preliminary issues in favour of the defendant, that (1) that the phrase "apply compulsorily" as found in cl.2(a) was clearly directed towards the status of the relevant legislation in the country of shipment. Therefore cl.2(b) was only triggered where those legislative provisions covered in cl.2(a) were not in force in the country of shipment. As the country of shipment was undoubtedly the US and the 1936 US Act was clearly in force, applying compulsorily to outward carriage from US ports, the obligations under the contract were governed by the provisions of that Act, *Nelson Pine Industries Ltd v. Seatrans New Zealand Ltd (The Pembroke)* [1995] 2 Lloyd's Rep. 290, *Balli Trading Ltd v. Afalona Shipping Ltd (The Coral)* [1993] 1 Lloyd's Rep. 1, [1993] C.L.Y. 3573 and *Lauritzen Reefers v. Ocean Reef Transport Ltd SA (The Bukhta Russkaya)* [1997] 2 Lloyd's Rep. 744, [1998] C.L.Y. 4412 considered, and (2) accordingly, H's liability in respect of T's claim was limited to $500.

TRANE CO v. HANJIN SHIPPING CO LTD (THE HANJIN MARSEILLES) [2001] 2 Lloyd's Rep. 735, Stone, J., CFI (HK).

4094. Bills of lading–delivery–locus standi of carrier to sue where consignee named as foreign bank–nature and extent of delivery obligation

[Carriage of Goods by Sea Act 1992 s.2(1), s.5(2)(a); Hamburg Rules Art.4.]

U sought to recover damages in respect of a cargo shipped by P to Chile and wrongly released to the agent of the nominated consignee without presentation of the relevant accompanying bill of lading. The consignment in question had been shipped on terms of cash against delivery. U had made arrangements for the relevant shipping documents to be remitted to Chilean banks in order that the documents could only be released upon payment. The consignee in each case on the bill of lading was the relevant bank and the notifying party was named as G. Upon arrival, the goods were placed in a customs warehouse and thereafter released to G's agent without presentation of the original bills of lading and ultimately handed over to G. G subsequently failed to meet its payment obligations. P defended U's claim on the basis that (1) U lacked title to sue having regard to the provisions of the Carriage of Goods by Sea Act 1992 whereby the lawful holder of a bill of lading became the individual entitled to sue upon it; (2) once the goods had been delivered to the customs warehouse, P's obligations under the contract of carriage came to an end; (3) P was exempted from liability by virtue of the Hamburg Rules Art.4 which were in force in Chile; (4) even if wrong as to their interpretation of Chilean law and the application of the Hamburg Rules, P was exempted from liability by virtue of the express terms of the bills of lading, and (5) P had not been negligent in delivering the goods in the absence of the bills of lading.

Held, giving judgment for U, that (1) the consignees identified in the bills of lading were the Chilean banks within the ordinary meaning of those words in the

1992 Act. Upon receipt of the bills, the banks held possession of them and became the lawful holders for the purposes of s.5(2)(a). By virtue of s.2(1) of the 1992 Act, the lawful holder of a bill of lading had transferred to him all rights of suit under the contract of carriage and accordingly U did not possess title to sue. U's contention that it retained title to sue as an undisclosed principal could not succeed, having regard to the clear statutory definitions in the 1992 Act. Nevertheless, U were entitled to bring a claim in negligence on the basis that P's actions had deprived U of its proprietary interest in the goods; (2) as a matter of the customs law of Chile, an ocean carrier was not obliged to deliver goods to the physical possession of customs but only to a duly authorised customs warehouse. A carrier was not precluded from entering into a contract with the customs warehouse operator, requiring such an operator only to deliver against presentation of an original bill of lading, and P should either have done so or, in the alternative, contracted with the container operators to ensure that they would not issue a Title for the Temporary Admission of Containers form without presentation of the relevant bill of lading; (3) Art.4 was of no assistance to P since there had been no "delivery " to customs, rather the goods had been placed with a customs warehouse operator subject to the jurisdiction of customs; (4) there had been no relevant qualification to the normal obligation as to delivery by virtue of the express clauses in the bills of lading, and (5) P had clearly been negligent having regard to the fact that it could have contracted with the customs warehouse operator to ensure that the goods were not released without presentation of the original bill of lading or alternatively could have instructed its port agents to demand sight of an original bill of lading before issuing a TATC form as container operators.

EAST WEST CORP v. DKBS 1912; UTANIKO LTD v. P&O NEDLLOYD BV (NO.1); *sub nom.* EAST WEST CORP v. DAMPSKIBSSELSKABET AF 1912 A/S (NO.1), [2002] EWHC 83, [2002] 1 All E.R. (Comm) 676, Thomas, J., QBD (Comm Ct).

4095. Bills of lading – forwarding agents – vehicle demurrage

C, a freight forwarder, brought proceedings against A, another freight forwarder, claiming, inter alia, vehicle demurrage. C had operated a combined transportation service, namely ocean carriage followed by on carriage by truck to the point of delivery, between the United Kingdom and various destinations in Russia and Finland. Under that service C had a contract whereby it could book space on vessels owned or operated by T, with on carriage being handled by N. When giving quotes to customers, C would provide all in rates which were not related to what it was paying to T or N. C would procure the issue of a "Conlinebill" liner bill of lading covering, where appropriate, pre carriage, ocean carriage and on carriage. C entered into negotiations with A with a view to arranging for consignments belonging to S, one of A's customers, to be transported to Russia. N's vehicle containing one such consignment was detained in Moscow for 35 days and C claimed vehicle demurrage for that period at the rate of $350 per day. A argued, inter alia, (1) that C did not have title to sue, and (2) that no demurrage had been incurred.

Held, giving judgment for C, that (1) it was clear from the communications between the parties that as far as monetary rights and obligations were concerned C and A had been acting as principals. The tenor of the negotiations was that terms were being agreed between C and A, no matter what dealings were taking place between C and T and between A and S. Furthermore, there were clear arrangements between C and A, the invoicing of A for example, under which it was established that C would seek payment from A and that A accepted liability for payment. The relationship between C and T, on the other hand, was that of independent contractors. Accordingly, C did have title to sue, and (2) the terms of the bill of lading made it clear that in the case of delay at the point of delivery to the consignees, demurrage would be payable at the rate sought by C.

COLI SHIPPING (UK) LTD v. ANDREA MERZARIO LTD [2002] 1 Lloyd's Rep. 608, Judge Hallgarten Q.C., CC (Central London).

4096. Bills of lading–misdelivery–release of goods without production of relevant documents–liability of forwarding agent

C, an exporter, submitted claims against J, a freight forwarder based in China, for recovery in contract and conversion arising from the wrongful misdelivery of goods. C's action related to two consignments of spectacle frames and sunglasses manufactured in China by W and exported to a third party buyer in Miami, H. C had collected the goods from W and delivered them to J in Shangai for direct shipment to the US. The original bills of lading were issued by J under the name of "Dynamic Container Line", DCL, naming C as shipper, the consignee as "to order" and the notify party as H. In the subsequent bills, J was named as shipper and the third party in this action, P, as consignee and notify party. Earlier shipments had been consensually released to H in the US without production of the relevant documents. However, the two consignments in suit were not to be released until payment had been made, thus enabling H to present the original bill of lading for each shipment. In the event, the two shipments were erroneously released from storage by P to H without production of the original bills of lading. C subsequently failed to secure payment for the goods. J contended that (1) W was the correct entity to sue on the contract of carriage and that C had no locus to bring the action; (2) J was not the contracting carrier under the original bill of lading as it had acted merely as an agent for DCL; (3) a contractual clause limited J's liability by expressly alerting C to the fact that if, upon discharge, the goods were not taken, storage would be arranged by J's agent at C's risk, and (4) the release of the containers in the absence of the bills of lading was not causative of C's loss.

Held, giving judgment for C, that (1) on the evidence, it was difficult to see how C, named as shipper on the original bill of lading did not possess sufficient locus to bring the action; (2) it was clear that J was the principal under the DCL bills and that it used DCL as a trade name. Moreover, if J was indeed acting as an agent for DCL as J contended, it was acting as agent for an unnamed principal. Therefore, liability accrued to the alleged agent where the name of the principal had not been disclosed, *Cory Brothers Shipping Ltd v. Baldan Ltd* [1997] 2 Lloyd's Rep. 58, [1997] C.L.Y. 4507 followed, (3) the wording of the relevant clause was not sufficiently clear to displace J's central obligation, namely delivery of the cargo to the owner or his agent only upon the production of the original bill of lading, *Motis Exports Ltd v. Dampskibsselskabet AF 1912 A/S (No.1)* [2000] 1 All E.R. (Comm) 91, [2000] C.L.Y. 4680 and *Glebe Island Terminals Pty v. Continental Seagram Pty (The Antwerpen)* [1994] 1 Lloyd's Rep. 213 considered, and (4) the wrongful release had clearly been causative of C's loss.

CENTER OPTICAL (HONG KONG) LTD v. JARDINE TRANSPORT SERVICES (CHINA) LTD [2001] 2 Lloyd's Rep. 678, Stone, J., CFI (HK).

4097. Bills of lading–title to goods–displacement of presumption that seller reserved right of disposal

[Sale of Goods Act 1979 s.19.]

T, the owner of a vessel, applied for interpleader relief in a dispute as to ownership of goods forming the subject of a free alongside ship, FAS, contract while the goods remained on board the ship. V, the seller had entered into a contract for the sale of a cargo of soya to S who had in turn entered into a contract for the sale of the cargo to K. V was named on the bills of lading as the shipper and contended that this demonstrated that the intention of the parties was that title to the goods would not pass until full payment was made, by virtue of the Sale of Goods Act 1979 s.19. K argued that the presumption under s.19 had been displaced by the fact that the contract in the instant case was an FAS contract, with S named on the mate's receipts as consignee indicating that the intention of the parties was that property should pass at the time that the cargo was unloaded. In the alternative K submitted that the goods had been paid for in advance by S under a running account.

Held, granting a declaration that the cargo was the property of V, that the presumption under s.19 was applicable to the contract and there was no substance to K's arguments to the contrary, *Mitsui & Co Ltd v. Flota Mercante Grancolombiana SA (The Ciudad de Pasto and The Ciudad de Neiva)* [1988] 1 W.L.R. 1145, [1989] C.L.Y. 3330 applied. So far as K's arguments concerning pre-payment were concerned there was no evidence of pre-payment and, in any event, there would have been no reason for K to establish a letter of credit if payment had already been made.

TRANSPACIFIC ETERNITY SA v. KANEMATSU CORP (THE ANTARES III) [2002] 1 Lloyd's Rep. 233, David Steel, J., QBD (Comm Ct).

4098. **Charterparties–breach of contract–wrongful carriage of cargo on deck– loss and damage–applicability of Hague Rules**

[Hague Rules Art.IV r.2(c), r.2(n), Art.5.]

The court was concerned to determine a number of preliminary issues arising from the partial loss of and damage to a cargo of 34 excavators carried on board a vessel from Korea to Turkey pursuant to a charterparty between D, cargo owners, and K, the defendant charterers. The cargo had been carried on deck in breach of the terms of the charterparty. During the course of the voyage eight of the excavators were lost overboard and others sustained minor rusting/wetting damage. D contended that in view of the fundamental breach of contract arising from the on deck stowage, K was not entitled to rely upon the limitation provisions or other defences in the Hague Rules in order to limit its liability.

Held, giving judgment on the preliminary issues, that (1) K was not precluded from relying on the limitation provisions in Art.5 of the Hague Rules by virtue of the unauthorised deck carriage. The "repugnancy" principle was not an appropriate basis for rejection of a limitation clause applicable "in any event" unless there was something in that phrase which would justify giving the words a restricted meaning and there was no basis for such a submission, *Parsons Corp v. CV Scheepvaartonderneming Happy Ranger (The Happy Ranger)* [2002] EWCA Civ 694, [2002] 2 All E.R. (Comm.) 24 considered and *Wibau Maschinefabrik Hartman SA v. Mackinnon Mackenzie (The Chanda)* [1989] 2 Lloyd's Rep. 494, [1989] C.L.Y. 3350 distinguished, and (2) the availability of other defences under the Hague Rules would depend on the facts but it was unlikely that K could take advantage of them. A charterer who contracted to carry goods under deck but wrongfully proceeded to carry them on deck could not rely upon the exemptions covering "perils at sea" or "insufficiency of packing" in Art.IV r.2(c) and r.2(n) to exclude liability if the damage in question would not have occurred had the goods been carried below deck, *Photo Production Ltd v. Securicor Transport Ltd* [1980] A.C. 827, [1980] C.L.Y. 353 considered.

DAEWOO HEAVY INDUSTRIES LTD v. KLIPRIVER SHIPPING LTD (THE KAPITAN PETKO VOIVODA), [2002] EWHC 1306, [2002] 2 All E.R. (Comm) 560, Langley, J., QBD (Comm Ct).

4099. **Charterparties–demurrage–interruption of laytime–owners using vessel for own purpose**

S, ship owners, appealed against an arbitration decision disallowing part of its demurrage claim against L, charterers of one of its vessels. On reaching its discharge port, the vessel had been unable to berth due to congestion. After laytime had begun to run, the vessel twice left her anchorage in order to discharge and load cargoes carried under other charterparties. S contended that as these operations were carried out during a time when the berth was unavailable the arbitrators had erred in holding that laytime and time on demurrage had been interrupted during the periods the vessel had been away from the anchorage.

Held, dismissing the appeal, that the arbitrators had correctly concluded that laytime and time on demurrage had been interrupted while the owners had used the vessel for their own purposes. That was the case even though, during the relevant times, L could not have discharged its cargo due to the unavailability of a berth. Demurrage could only be claimed for the period when the vessel was ready and able to give discharge in accordance with the contract; when the ship was proceeding from one port to another for whatever reason, it was on a voyage and not in detention by the charterers. There was accordingly no liability upon the charterers to pay compensation, *Navico AG v. Vrontados Naftiki Etairia PE* [1968] 1 Lloyd's Rep. 379, [1968] C.L.Y. 3633 applied.

STOLT TANKERS INC v. LANDMARK CHEMICALS SA [2002] 1 Lloyd's Rep. 786, Andrew Smith, J., QBD (Comm Ct).

4100. Charterparties–formation of contract–contract terms contained in telex

W sought a declaration that no arbitration agreement had been incorporated into a contract of carriage contained in or evidenced by a bill of lading between itself as consignee/receiver and R, the owner of the relevant vessel. Before the bill of lading had been issued, a recap telex had been sent by the charterers to R. Among other things, the telex provided details of the vessel and set out requirements for the terms of bills of lading and payment of freight. It was accompanied by a standard form which provided that arbitration was to take place in London. R had replied to the telex by stating that it was "in order". The issue before the court was whether the recap telex and the accompanying form amounted to the charterparty for the purposes of a clause in the bill of lading which provided for the incorporation in the bill of the terms and conditions of the charterparty.

Held, giving judgment for R, that a contract for chartering a ship could be set out in telex exchanges, *Partenreederei M/S Heidberg v. Grosvenor Grain & Feed Co Ltd (The Heidberg) (No.2)* [1994] 2 Lloyd's Rep. 287, [1995] C.L.Y. 4501 distinguished. In the instant case, the terms of the contract could be easily identified from the contents of the recap telex and the accompanying standard form. Accordingly, the charterparty referred to in the bill of lading was the agreement contained in the recap telex and the standard form which accompanied it. Such a conclusion accorded with the court's duty to give an intelligent meaning to documents surrounding the commercial transaction in the instant case.

WELEX AG v. ROSA MARITIME LTD (THE EPSILON ROSA) (NO.1), [2002] EWHC 762, [2002] 1 All E.R. (Comm) 939, David Steel, J., QBD (Comm Ct).

4101. Charterparties–warranties–breach–engine failure–inability to complete voyage

B, charterers, appealed against a decision of the arbitrators that S, owners of a vessel which had been unable to complete its voyage owing to engine failure, had not breached an express warranty of speed which was contained in the charterparty. B contended that the warranty was absolute, subject only to exceptions of weather and safe navigation.

Held, dismissing the appeal, that the arbitrators had been correct to read the charterparty as a whole as it would not have made commercial sense for S to have bound itself to a set speed for the entire voyage, *Marifortuna Naviera SA v. Government of Ceylon* [1970] 1 Lloyd's Rep. 247, [1971] C.L.Y. 10860 and *Seven Seas Transportation Ltd v. Pacifico Union Marina Corp (The Satya Kailash and The Oceanic Amity)* [1984] 2 All E.R. 140, [1984] C.L.Y. 3171 not followed.

BAYOIL SA v. SEAWIND TANKERS CORP (THE LEONIDAS) [2001] 1 All E.R. (Comm) 392, Langley, J., QBD (Comm Ct).

4102. Choice of forum–bills of lading–subcontractors–permissive nature of jurisdiction clause

S, ocean carrier and second defendant, sought to dismiss the plaintiffs' claim for recovery of damages sustained to a shipment of furniture during an ocean voyage from Spain to New York, and further to dismiss the cross claim of co defendant, U. In contracting to carry the furniture, N, a non vessel common carrier, had issued three bills of lading stating that any dispute would be governed by US law and determined in the US courts. N subcontracted the ocean carriage of the cargo to S and a bill of lading was issued containing a clause which stipulated that "the contract would be governed by German law and any dispute determined in the courts of Bremen". S's vessel carried further cargo, namely a motor vehicle, under a bill of lading issued by U pursuant to a United Alliance agreement. U's bill of lading stated that the US was the selected forum for dispute resolution. However, the United Alliance agreement, to which both U and S were parties, provided that any dispute that could not be resolved within a specified time limit would be submitted for arbitration in London. During the course of the voyage, the vehicle shifted and fell onto the container carrying the furniture. Given that the claim and cross claim were issued in the US, S submitted motions to dismiss on the grounds that, in each case, the appropriate forum had not been selected.

Held, denying the motions to dismiss, that the forum selection clauses invoked by S would only be interpreted as excluding jurisdiction elsewhere where the parties employed the specific language of exclusion, *John Boutari & Son, Wines and Spirits, SA v. Attiki Importers and Distributors Inc* [1995] I.L.Pr. 488 and *City of New York v. Pullman Inc.* 477 F. Supp. 438 (S.D.N.Y. 1979) applied. Neither forum selection clause contained mandatory exclusions and thus, the US courts had the jurisdiction to hear both the plaintiffs' claim and U's cross claim. The plaintiffs' case was further strengthened by the fact they had contracted with N and, not having been signatories to S's bill of lading, could not have foreseen that they would be required to submit to the jurisdiction of the German court.

HARTFORD FIRE INSURANCE CO v. NOVOCARGO USA INC (THE PACIFIC SENATOR) (NO.1) [2001] 2 Lloyd's Rep. 674, District Judge Pauley, US Court.

4103. **Choice of forum–jurisdiction clauses–motion for reconsideration–United States**

S, whom N had sub-contracted for the ocean carriage of a cargo of furniture, moved for reconsideration of the order of the court ([2001] 2 Lloyd's Rep. 674) denying the following two motions (1) a motion for the dismissal of plaintiffs' complaint on the basis of a clause in the bill of lading pursuant to which the cargo had been carried specifying Bremen, Germany as the appropriate forum for any dispute, and (2) a motion for the dismissal of a cross-claim brought by U on the basis of a London arbitration clause in an agreement between S and U.

Held, denying the motion for reconsideration, that (1) a party bringing a motion for reconsideration had to show that the court had not considered "controlling decisions or factual matters that were put before it on the underlying motion" and which, if they had been considered, might reasonably have produced a different outcome. The grounds by which S sought to challenge the court's determination on the issue of the Bremen clause lacked merit. While the clause had stated that any dispute that arose "shall be governed by German law", the use of the word "shall" did not establish that jurisdiction was conferred on only one forum at the exclusion of other jurisdictions. Furthermore, specific language of exclusion had not been used in the forum selection clause and therefore it could not be construed so as to oust jurisdiction where it otherwise existed, and (2) the court had not overlooked controlling authority in relation to the motion to dismiss U's cross-claim; the new arguments before the court were without merit. The arbitration clause merely granted an option to resolve any dispute outside the courts.

HARTFORD FIRE INSURANCE CO v. NOVOCARGO USA INC (THE PACIFIC SENATOR) (NO.2) [2002] 1 Lloyd's Rep. 485, Judge William H Pauley III, US Court.

4104. **Collisions at sea–apportionment–use of VHF radio as means of exchanging information**

[International Regulations for Preventing Collisions at Sea 1972 r.15, r.17, r.19.]

The owners of HM, a vessel which had come into collision with MD, appealed against a decision ([2000] 1 All E.R. (Comm) 870) that its vessel was 80 per cent to blame. As a result of the collision, MD had sunk with the loss of all 27 crew. It was common ground that until the vessels had been three miles apart they had been navigating in restricted visibility within the meaning of the International Regulations for Preventing Collisions at Sea 1972 r.19. There had been two VHF radio conversations between the vessels prior to the collision, one before and one after they had come into sight of one another. During the second conversation HM had told MD to keep its current course and speed. The judge had found that neither vessel had been to blame for what she had or had not done prior to each coming in sight of the other at approximately three miles apart. Further, the judge had found that at such time no blame was to be attached to the fact or content of the first VHF conversation. The judge did, however, attach blame to HM's officer of the watch for failing to keep a proper radar lookout. The judge also concluded that after the vessels had come into visual contact when they were about two miles apart, MD should have realised, in accordance with r.17(b), that the position of HM was "so close that collision [could not] be avoided by the action of the give way vessel alone". The judge determined that the reason no action had been taken had been the second VHF conversation. HM submitted, inter alia, that the judge should have concluded that before both vessels came into sight of each other they should have taken action under r.19.

Held, dismissing the appeal, that having regard to the views of the assessors, the judge had been correct in finding that neither vessel had been in breach of r.19 of the Regulations by not taking action prior to their coming into sight of one another. The nature of the visibility was an important consideration. Given what both vessels reasonably thought to be the actual visibility and the fact that there had been sufficient time to take action under r.15 and r.17, it could not be said that there had been a breach of r.19, *Maloja II, The* [1993] 1 Lloyd's Rep. 48, [1993] C.L.Y. 3601 considered. The judge had, however, erred in finding that MD had breached r.17(b). Previous statements of the Admiralty Court concerning the use of VHF communications about navigation between two vessels passing at, or approaching, a close quarters situation were not to be read as an embargo on such. In certain circumstances VHF conversations could be useful as a means of exchanging information between vessels. However, before following any information received it was essential that there be no doubt as to which vessel had sent the information. Where two vessels were approaching one another, it might in some circumstances be useful if the vessel required to give way informed the other vessel of the action being taken to comply with the Regulations. In circumstances where visibility was restricted and two vessels were approaching, the vessel taking avoiding action pursuant to r.19 might assist the other vessel if it informed it by VHF of the action being taken.

OWNERS AND/OR DEMISE CHARTERERS OF THE MINERAL DAMPIER v. OWNERS AND/OR DEMISE CHARTERERS OF THE HANJIN MADRAS, [2001] EWCA Civ 1278, [2001] 2 All E.R. (Comm) 805, Lord Phillips of Worth Matravers, M.R., CA.

4105. Collisions at sea—causation—total loss of vessel due to ingress of water—inability to discharge burden of proof

As the result of a collision at sea between F and S, for which liability was subsequently agreed at 50 per cent, F sustained damage to her forepeak, which flooded. Nine days later it was discovered that two holds, commencing 79 metres aft of the collision site were also flooded. As a result, a cargo of cement in one of the flooded holds led to F becoming a constructive total loss. F asserted that a badly corroded plate had failed as a result of the collision, leading to flooding in both holds. This was challenged by S and the matter fell to be determined as a preliminary issue.

Held, determining the preliminary issue in favour of S, that expert evidence as to the amount of water found in the holds did not show that the ingress had occurred as a result of a failure due to the collision. Expert evidence as to the state of F's drafts in the period up to and immediately after the collision did not allow a reliable determination to be made as to when the ingress commenced. Therefore F could not show that the loss and damage to the hold was caused by the collision.

OWNERS OF THE SEAFARER 1 v. OWNERS OF THE FEDRA [2002] 1 Lloyd's Rep. 453, Aikens, J., QBD (Adm Ct).

4106. Conservation–vessels–designation–protected places

PROTECTION OF MILITARY REMAINS ACT 1986 (DESIGNATION OF VESSELS AND CONTROLLED SITES) ORDER 2002, SI 2002 1761; made under the Protection of Military Remains Act 1986 s.1. In force: September 30, 2002; £1.75.

This Order designates various vessels as vessels to which the Protection of Military Remains Act 1986 applies meaning that the places containing the remains of those vessels are protected places.

4107. Fishing vessels–detention–claim for indemnity under mortgagees interest insurance policy–impact of exclusion clause in owners was risks policy– meaning of "trading regulations"

[Fisheries Management Act 1991 (Australia).]

H, a Norwegian bank and mortgagee of the vessel "Aliza Glacial" had insured the vessel under a mortgagees interest insurance policy, MII. The owners of the vessel had insured the vessel under a War Risks policy which contained an express term "Warranted no illegal fishing". Following the seizure and detention of the vessel for illegal fishing by the Australian Navy pursuant to the Fisheries Management Act 1991, a claim by the owners under the War Risks policy was rejected by the underwriters for breach of the "no illegal fishing" warranty. H accordingly claimed an indemnity under the MII policy in respect of the owner's outstanding indebtedness. At first instance the claim was dismissed on the basis that the exclusions contained in the War Risks Cover were effective to exclude all liability. The clauses in question precluded cover in the instance of "arrest, restraint, detainment, confiscation or expropriation under quarantine regulations or by reason of infringement of any customs or trading regulations". The judge at first instance concluded that since the 1991 Act had the purpose of regulating commercial fishing the exclusion was effective since commercial fishing undoubtedly constituted a "trade" and, a fortiori, the vessel had been detained pursuant to a trading regulation. H submitted that the term "trade" should be interpreted as the process of buying, selling or otherwise dealing in goods or services, and that accordingly regulations forbidding, controlling or otherwise regulating the sale or importation of goods into a country would constitute trading regulations but that the regulation of fishing for conservation purposes, as in the case of the 1991 Act, would not.

Held, allowing the appeal, that the exception in question had been introduced in the aftermath of the Iran-Iraq war and the effect upon trading vessels of the sanctions operated at that time. It formed part of a longstanding regime of clauses designed for inclusion in policies relating to vessels of all types, the majority of which would be trading vessels concerned with the carriage of goods by sea in furtherance of international trading transactions and it was appropriate to interpret the exclusion with that in mind. The question as to whether a regulation was a trading regulation or not would depend upon its own nature and purpose and not upon the fact that it might affect a shipowner in the course of his business. The aims of the 1991 Act were ecological and environmental and in that context it regulated fishing within Australian waters whether for pleasure or as a commercial activity. On that basis the regulations were not "trading regulations" for the purposes of the exclusion, *Panamanian Oriental Steamship Corp v. Wright (The Anita)* [1970] 2 Lloyd's Rep. 365 and *Ikerigi Compania Naviera SA v. Palmer (The Wondrous)* [1991] 1 Lloyd's Rep. 400 considered.

HANDELSBANKEN ASA v. DANDRIDGE (THE ALIZA GLACIAL); *sub nom.* SVENSKA HANDELSBANKEN AB v. DANDRIDGE, [2002] EWCA Civ 577, [2002] 2 All E.R. (Comm) 39, Potter, L.J., CA.

4108. Fishing vessels–ship safety–code of practice

FISHING VESSELS (SAFETY OF 15-24 METRE VESSELS) REGULATIONS 2002, SI 2002 2201; made under the European Communities Act 1972 s.2; and the Merchant Shipping Act 1995 s.43, s.85, s.86, s.307. In force: November 23, 2002; £2.50.

These Regulations amend the Fishing Vessels (Safety Provisions) Rules 1975 (SI 1975 330), the Merchant Shipping (Crew Accommodation) (Fishing Vessels) Regulations 1975 (SI 1975 2220), the Fishing Vessels (Life-Saving Appliances) Regulations 1988 (SI 1988 38), the Merchant Shipping (Radio) (Fishing Vessels) Regulations 1999 (SI 1999 3210) and the Fishing Vessels (Code of Practice for the Safety of Small Fishing Vessels) Regulations 2001 (SI 2001 9). They provide for fishing vessels of at least 15 metres length overall but less than 24m registered length to comply with the requirements of the "Code of Safe Working Practice for the Construction and Use of 15m to less than 24m Fishing Vessels" published by the Maritime and Coastguard Agency. The Regulations also provide that if a vessel proceeds or attempts to proceed on any voyage without complying with the Code of Practice, that is an offence on the part of the owner or the skipper, and provide for penalties and for the inspection and detention of vessels.

4109. Harbours–pilotage functions–Port of Larne

PORT OF LARNE (PILOTAGE FUNCTIONS) ORDER 2002, SI 2002 3037; made under the Pilotage Act 1987 s.1. In force: December 31, 2002; £1.50.

This Order provides that Larne Harbour Ltd is to be a competent harbour authority for the port of Larne for the purposes of the Pilotage Act 1987.

4110. Harbours–revision–constitution–Brightlingsea

BRIGHTLINGSEA HARBOUR REVISION (CONSTITUTION) ORDER 2002, SI 2002 2476; made under the Harbours Act 1964 s.14. In force: September 18, 2002; £2.00.

This Order, which revokes the Brightlingsea Harbour Revision Order 1981 (SI 1981 1096), reconstitutes the Brightlingsea Harbour Commissioners and provides for the Commissioners to consist of a body of eight Commissioners with experience in relevant matters. Six persons will be appointed by the Commissioners and the chief executive and the harbour master will also hold office as Commissioners. Under the terms of the Order the appointed Commissioners will retire in rotation. The Order includes other provision with respect to the Commissioners' constitution and provision for the protection of the Commissioners from personal liability in the discharge of their functions.

4111. Harbours–revision–constitution–Dart Harbour and Navigation

DART HARBOUR AND NAVIGATION HARBOUR REVISION (CONSTITUTION) ORDER 2002, SI 2002 2730; made under the Harbours Act 1964 s.14. In force: November 4, 2002; £2.50.

This Order, which reconstitutes the Dart Harbour and Navigation Authority and amends the Dart Harbour and Navigation Authority Act 1975, provides for the Authority to consist of a body of not less than eight and not more than eleven members with experience in relevant matters. It also includes other provisions with respect to the Authority's constitution including provisions for the protection of members from personal liability in the discharge of their functions and increases the Authority's borrowing powers, amends existing statutory requirements as to the Authority's accounts and repeals certain statutory provisions.

4112. Harbours–revision–constitution–Gloucester

GLOUCESTER HARBOUR REVISION (CONSTITUTION) ORDER 2002, SI 2002 3268; made under the Harbours Act 1964 s.14. In force: December 16, 2002; £2.50.

This Order amends An Act for the making navigable the Rivers Wye and Lugg, and the Rivers and Brooks running into the same, in the Counties of, Hereford,

Gloucester and Monmouth 1662, An Act for making navigable the Rivers of Wye and Lugg in the County of Hereford 1665, An Act for explaining and amending any Act passed in the Seventh and Eighth Years of the Reign of His Majesty King William the Third, intituled, An Act for making navigable the Rivers Wye and Lugg, in the County of Hereford, and for making the same more effectual 1727, An Act for amending several Acts for making navigable the Rivers Wye and Lugg, in the County of Hereford; and for making a Horse Towing-path on certain Parts of the Banks of the said River Wye 1809, Pier and Harbour Orders Confirmation (No.3) Act 1889, Pier and Harbour Orders Confirmation (No 3) Act 1890, the Gloucester Harbour Revision Order 1988 (SI 1988 1040) and the Gloucester Harbour Revision Order 1994 (SI 1994 3162). This Order alters the constitution of the Gloucester Harbour Trustees by providing that the new constitution provides for a body of 10 trustees of whom nine are to be appointed by the Trustees. The remaining trustee is to be the principal operational officer thereby securing executive representation on the Trustees. Provision is included to enable a gradual transition to the new appointment arrangements and to govern the selection and terms of appointment of trustees and the manner in which they are to conduct business. The Order also extends the seaward limits of the harbour and repeals ancient legislation relating to the River Wye.

4113. Harbours−revision−constitution−Lymington

LYMINGTON HARBOUR REVISION (CONSTITUTION) ORDER 2002, SI 2002 2586; made under the Harbours Act 1964 s.14. In force: October 15, 2002; £2.50.

This Order, which amends the Pier and Harbour Order (Lymington) Confirmation Act 1951, reconstitutes the Lymington Harbour Commissioners. It provides for the Commissioners to consist of a body of 10 Commissioners with experience in relevant matters and nine persons will be appointed by the Commissioners. The Chief Executive will also hold office as a Commissioner and under the terms of the Order, the appointed Commissioners will retire in rotation. The Order also includes other provisions with respect to the Commissioners' constitution including provisions for the co-option of up to two additional Commissioners and for the protection of the Commissioners from personal liability in the discharge of their functions. In addition, the Order confers on the Commissioners power to make temporary borrowings, amends existing statutory requirements as to the Commissioners' accounts and repeals certain statutory provisions.

4114. Harbours−revision−constitution−Whitehaven Harbour Commissioners

WHITEHAVEN HARBOUR COMMISSIONERS (CONSTITUTION) HARBOUR REVISION ORDER 2002, SI 2002 306; made under the Harbours Act 1964 s.15. In force: March 4, 2002; £2.50.

This Order, which revokes the Borough and Harbour of Whitehaven Scheme 1894 and the Whitehaven Harbour Revision Order 1991 (SI 1991 238), reconstitutes the Whitehaven Harbour Commissioners, provides for the appointment of Commissioners with experience in relevant matters and lays down procedures for their meetings with transitional arrangements.

4115. Harbours−revision−Felixstowe Dock and Railway

FELIXSTOWE DOCK AND RAILWAY HARBOUR REVISION ORDER 2002, SI 2002 2618; made under the Harbours Act 1964 s.14. In force: October 31, 2002; £2.50.

This Order, which amends the Haven Act 1974 and the Felixstowe Dock and Railway Act 1988, authorises the Felixstowe Dock and Railway Company to construct and maintain a specified work at Felixstowe and to carry out subsidiary works.

4116. Harbours–revision–Mersey Docks and Harbour Company

MERSEY DOCKS AND HARBOUR COMPANY (LANGTON RIVER BERTH) HARBOUR REVISION ORDER 2002, SI 2002 3127; made under the Harbours Act 1964 s.14. In force: December 31, 2002; £2.00.

This Order authorises the Mersey Docks and Harbour Company to construct a rock berm and twin deck linkspan together with berthing dolphins adjoining Langton Dock and a bridge to the new linkspan.

4117. Harbours–revision–transfer of undertaking–Port of Ipswich

PORT OF IPSWICH (TRANSFER OF UNDERTAKING) HARBOUR REVISION ORDER 2002, SI 2002 3269; made under the Harbours Act 1964 s.14. In force: December 30, 2002; £1.75.

This Order, which amends the British Transport Commission Act 1949, the Ipswich Dock Act 1950, the British Transport Commission Act 1961, the British Transport Docks Act 1964 and the Ipswich Dock Act 1971, designates Associated British Ports (A.B. Ports) as the harbour authority for the Port of Ipswich in place of Ipswich Port Limited and transfers the undertaking of that company to A.B. Ports. Provision is made for byelaws and contracts made or entered into by Ipswich Port Limited to remain in force as if they had been made or entered into by A.B. Ports and for legal and other proceedings to be carried on by or in relation to A.B. Ports.

4118. Harbours–revision–Yarmouth

YARMOUTH (ISLE OF WIGHT) HARBOUR REVISION ORDER 2002, SI 2002 311; made under the Harbours Act 1964 s.14. In force: March 4, 2002; £1.75.

The Order authorises the Yarmouth (Isle of Wight) Harbour Commissioners to borrow upon the security of their assets or their revenues or both such sums as they think necessary not exceeding three million pounds for capital purposes and with the consent of the Secretary of State such further sums as they may require. It also authorises the Commissioners to borrow temporarily by way of overdraft or otherwise such sums of money as they require not exceeding £300,000.

4119. Indemnities–cargo discharged in error–forged letters of indemnity

C, shipowners, sought to recover the value of a cargo of palm oleate which it contended had been discharged in error to a third party against letters of indemnity provided by S, a bank, in the absence of receipt of the relevant bills of lading.

Held, giving judgment for S, that the expert handwriting witnesses had concluded that the signature and stamps on the letters of indemnity had been forged with the result that C had no arguable case, and it was not open to C to advance fresh allegations against S without proper notice in an attempt to salvage the claim.

CHINA SHIPPING DEVELOPMENT CO LTD v. STATE BANK OF SAURASHTRA [2001] 2 Lloyd's Rep. 691, Thomas, J., QBD (Comm Ct).

4120. Laytime–voyage charterparties–invalid notice of readiness–commencement of discharge–waiver of reliance on invalidity of original notice

F, shipowners, appealed against a decision ([2001] 1 All E.R. (Comm) 659) overturning an interim final arbitration award which had been made in favour of F in relation to its claim for, inter alia, demurrage under a voyage charterparty. Upon arrival off the discharge port the Master gave a notice of readiness which, although valid in form, was invalid for prematurity. The issue for decision before the instant court was whether laytime could commence under a voyage charterparty, the terms of which required service of notice of readiness, when no valid notice of readiness had ever been served.

Held, allowing the appeal, that laytime could commence where (1) a notice of readiness which was valid in form had been served upon the charterers as required under the charterparty prior to the arrival of the vessel; (2) the vessel thereafter arrived and was, or was accepted to be, ready to discharge to the knowledge of the charterers, and (3) discharge thereafter commenced to the order of the charterers or receivers without either having given any intimation of rejection or reservation in respect of the notice of readiness which had been previously served or any indication that any further notice of readiness was required before laytime was to commence. In such circumstances, the charterers may be deemed to have waived reliance upon the invalidity of the original notice as from the time of the commencement of discharge and laytime would commence in accordance with the regime provided for in the charterparty as if a valid notice of readiness had been served at that time, *Transgrain Shipping BV v. Global Transporte Oceanico SA (The Mexico 1)* [1990] 1 Lloyd's Rep. 507, [1991] C.L.Y. 3234 and *TA Shipping Ltd v. Comet Shipping Ltd (The Agamemnon)* [1998] 1 Lloyd's Rep. 675, [1998] C.L.Y. 4443 considered, *Sofial SA v. Ove Skou Rederi (The Helle Skou)* [1976] 2 Lloyd's Rep. 205, [1976] C.L.Y. 2544 and *Surrey Shipping Co v. Compagnie Continentale (France) SA (The Shackleford)* [1978] 1 W.L.R. 1080, [1978] C.L.Y. 2720 applied.

GLENCORE GRAIN LTD v. FLACKER SHIPPING LTD (THE HAPPY DAY); *sub nom.* FLACKER SHIPPING LTD v. GLENCORE GRAIN LTD (THE HAPPY DAY), [2002] EWCA Civ 1068, [2002] 2 All E.R. (Comm) 896, Potter, L.J., CA.

4121. Liner conferences–competition agreements–price fixing–compatibility with EC law

See COMPETITION LAW: Compagnie Generale Maritime v. Commission of the European Communities (T86/95). §582

4122. Marine insurance–evidence–destination of ship at time of sailing–determination of when insurance risk attached to cargo

[Marine Insurance Act 1906 s.44.]

D, an insurance company, appealed against the dismissal of its application to set aside service of a claim form against it in Thailand. The claim related to a cargo of rice which was lost when a vessel went missing after commencing her voyage from Thailand to Senegal.

Held, allowing the appeal, that D was not liable for the loss of the cargo under the Marine Insurance Act 1906 s.44. Where s.44 was invoked, the authorities showed that the court would investigate the actual destination of the ship at the time of departure rather than its contractual destination and the findings would take into account the acts and intentions of the owner or master at the relevant time. If it was found that, at the time of departure, the ship was bound for a destination other than that identified in the policy as the insured voyage, s.44 would apply and no risk would be held to have attached to the goods on leaving the warehouse.

NIMA SARL v. DEVES INSURANCE PUBLIC CO LTD (THE PRESTRIOKA); *sub nom.* NIMA SARL v. DEVES INSURANCE PLC (THE PRESTRIOKA), [2002] EWCA Civ 1132, [2002] 2 All E.R. (Comm) 449, Potter, L.J., CA.

4123. Marine insurance–salvage–insurers plead no positive case–limits on evidential challenge as to causation

In proceedings commenced by S to recover salvage payments from underwriters, P, it fell to the court to determine whether evidence relating to alleged defects in the ballast system of vessel, V, could be led and relied upon by each side or by P alone. V had been stable when she left port but soon developed an increasing starboard list. Ultimately the vessel had to be abandoned and salvage services rendered. S sought recovery of payments made to the salvors under a hull and machinery policy issued by P. S claimed that the losses incurred arose from inferred acts of negligence on the part of V's chief engineer and master. In the pleadings, P refrained from submitting any positive case on the issue of causation but, in written questions to S's expert witness, raised the possibility that the list had been caused by a defective ballast system. P maintained that, as S's claim rested upon the inference that negligence was the proximate cause of the loss and that there could have been no other cause, P should be entitled to adduce evidence disproving the evidence called by S.

Held, ruling on the preliminary issue, that, as P had not pleaded a positive case, S did not have to plead and prove that other states of affairs did not exist. Therefore S was under no obligation to lead any evidence relating to the condition of the ballast system, *Rhesa Shipping Co SA v. Edmunds (The Popi M)* [1985] 1 W.L.R. 948, [1985] C.L.Y. 3207 followed. However, P would be allowed put forward evidence relating to defects in the ballast system in order to challenge S's case in accordance with authorities, *Regina Fur Co v. Bossom* [1958] 2 Lloyd's Rep. 425, [1958] C.L.Y. 1631, *Palamisto General Enterprises SA v. Ocean Marine Co Ltd (The Dias)* [1972] 2 Q.B. 625, [1972] C.L.Y. 3252, *Lamb Head Shipping Co Ltd v. Jennings (The Marel)* [1994] 1 Lloyd's Rep. 624, [1995] C.L.Y. 4534 and *Roselodge Ltd (formerly Rose Diamond Products Ltd) v. Castle* [1966] 2 Lloyd's Rep. 113, [1966] C.L.Y. 6353 considered. Therefore P could not put a positive case on the condition of the ballast system and documents could not be employed in support of such a positive case. However evidence could be adduced disproving negligence as opposed to any positive assertion of a defect. P was entitled to ask S's expert whether he had considered defects in the ballast system as a possible cause of the list. Further, P could use S's witness statements in order to disprove negligence and would be allowed to cross examine S's witnesses by suggesting the possibility, through documents, that the defective ballast system was causative of the list.

SEASHORE MARINE SA v. PHOENIX ASSURANCE PLC (THE VERGINA) (NO.1) [2001] 2 Lloyd's Rep. 719, Aikens, J., QBD (Comm Ct).

4124. Maritime arbitration–bills of lading–challenging awards–failure to deal with all issues

See ARBITRATION: Ascot Commodities NV v. Olam International Ltd. §213

4125. Maritime arbitration–time charterparties–choice of forum for dispute resolution–enforceability of clause in sub charter

F, a company incorporated in Japan, sought an order staying S's claim against it arising from a time charter. F had chartered the vessel from M, also incorporated in Japan, and had sub chartered it to S. The head charter contained a clause to the effect that the disputes had to be referred to arbitration in Japan but the equivalent provision in the sub charter was amended to give jurisdiction to the English courts. S sought to recover monies it alleged were owed to it by F for, inter alia, breach of speed and fuel consumption warranty. F contended that all claims by S should be referred to arbitration in Japan but S argued that the claims fell outside the choice of forum clause or, in the alternative, that the clause was unenforceable for uncertainty.

Held, granting the application, that, as a matter of construction, only disputes totally separate from the head charter were subject to English law and jurisdiction. This was consistent with F's contention and with commercial reality. The clause did not require all disputes between F and S to be governed by English law, as contended for by S. The meaning of the arbitration and jurisdiction clause in the sub charter was clear and it purported to match the proper law to the venue depending on the nature of the dispute, with the result that a breach of the contract had to occur before the parties knew which law applied. That clause was therefore unenforceable for uncertainty. However, the unenforceable method of proper law selection did not necessarily mean that the choice of forum clause was also void as the latter was free standing, *Armar Shipping Co v. Caisse Algerienne d'Assurance et de Reassurance (The Armar)* [1981] 1 W.L.R. 207, [1981] C.L.Y. 2483 considered and *Dubai Electricity Co v. Islamic Republic of Iran Shipping Lines (The Iran Vojdan)* [1984] 2 Lloyd's Rep. 380, [1984] C.L.Y. 2712 applied. In the instant case the choice of forum clause was enforceable and F was entitled to a stay as all claims by S would be passed onto M by F and so fell within the scope of the arbitration provision.

SONATRACH PETROLEUM CORP (BVI) v. FERRELL INTERNATIONAL LTD [2002] 1 All E.R. (Comm) 627, Colman, J., QBD (Comm Ct).

4126. Milford Haven Port Authority Act 2002 (c.v)

This Act alters the constitution of and confers further powers upon the Milford Haven Port Authority.

4127. Navigation–safety at sea

MERCHANT SHIPPING (SAFETY OF NAVIGATION) REGULATIONS 2002, SI 2002 1473; made under the Merchant Shipping Act 1995 s.77, s.85, s.86. In force: July 1, 2002; £3.00.

These Regulations revoke the Merchant Shipping (Automatic Pilot and Testing of Steering Gear) Regulations 1981 (SI 1981 571), the Merchant Shipping (Passenger Ships of Classes IV, V, VI, & VI(A)-Bridge Visibility) Regulations 1992 (SI 1991 2357), the Merchant Shipping (Navigational Equipment) Regulations 1993 (SI 1993 69), the Merchant Shipping (Mandatory Ship Reporting) Regulations 1996 (SI 1996 1749), the Merchant Shipping (Navigational Warnings) Regulations 1996 (SI 1996 1815), the Merchant Shipping (Mandatory Ships' Routing) Regulations 1997 (SI 1997 1341), the Merchant Shipping (Master's Discretion) Regulations 1997 (SI 1997 2886), the Merchant Shipping (Navigation Bridge Visibility) Regulations 1998 (SI 1998 1419), the Merchant Shipping (Co-operation with Search and Rescue Services) Regulations 1998 (SI 1998 1692), the Merchant Shipping (Carriage of Nautical Publications) Regulations 1998 (SI 1998 2647) and the Merchant Shipping (Pilot Transfer Arrangements) Regulations 1999 (SI 1999 17). They also amend the Merchant Shipping (Official Log Books) Regulations 1981 (SI 1981 569), the Merchant Shipping (Official Log Books) (Fishing Vessels) Regulations 1981 (SI 1981 570), the Merchant Shipping Act 1995, the Merchant Shipping (Survey and Certification) Regulations 1995 (SI 1995 1210), the Merchant Shipping (Distress Messages) Regulations 1998 (SI 1998 1691), the Merchant Shipping (Vessels in Commercial Use for Sport or Pleasure) Regulations 1998 (SI 1998 2771), the Merchant Shipping (Life-Saving Appliances for Ships Other Than Ships of Classes III to VI(A)) Regulations 1999 (SI 1999 2721) and the Merchant Shipping (Passenger Ships on Domestic Voyages) Regulations 2000 (SI 2000 2687). These Regulations, which give effect to provisions of Chapter V of the International Convention for the Safety of Life at Sea 1974, provide for the granting of exemptions and permission, granting of approvals and for contravention of various requirements to be offences, and subject to criminal penalties.

4128. Navigational aids–light dues–fees

MERCHANT SHIPPING (LIGHT DUES) (AMENDMENT) REGULATIONS 2002, SI 2002 504; made under the Merchant Shipping Act 1995 s.205. In force: April 1, 2002; £1.50.

These Regulations amend the Merchant Shipping (Light Dues) Regulations 1997 (SI 1997 562) by reducing the amounts of the annual payment for tugs and fishing vessels from £202 to £190, and from £21 to £20 for each metre of length in excess of 10 metres. The Regulations also reduce the light dues payable per voyage in respect of ships other than tugs, fishing vessels and pleasure vessels.

4129. Safety at sea–diving safety–duty of care

MERCHANT SHIPPING (DIVING SAFETY) REGULATIONS 2002, SI 2002 1587; made under the Merchant Shipping Act 1995 s.88, Sch.2. In force: September 1, 2002; £2.50.

These Regulations, which revoke the Merchant Shipping (Diving Operations) Regulations 1975 (SI 1975 116) and the Merchant Shipping (Diving Operations) (Amendment) Regulations 1975 (SI 1975 2062), apply to diving within UK territorial waters in the circumstances specified. The Regulations place duties on the owner and master of a craft from which certain diving projects are undertaken, on the diving contractor or diving supervisor for such a diving project, and on the persons diving in such projects; certain powers are also conferred on masters and diving supervisors. They make provision for the Secretary of State to grant exemptions, for transitional provisions, inquiries and investigations into accidents, and create criminal offences for contravention of the Regulations.

4130. Safety at sea–miscellaneous amendments

MERCHANT SHIPPING (MISCELLANEOUS AMENDMENTS) REGULATIONS 2002, SI 2002 1650; made under the Merchant Shipping Act 1995 s.85, s.86. In force: August 1, 2002; £1.75.

These Regulations amend the Merchant Shipping (Passenger Ship Construction: Ships of Classes I, II and II(A)) Regulations 1998 (SI 1998 2514) to correct a reference to a published code of practice, clarify the offence in Reg.91(5) and alter the penalty for contravention of Reg.42(1). They also amend the Merchant Shipping (Passenger Ship Construction: Ships of Classes III to VI(A)) Regulations 1998 (SI 1998 2515) to alter a manoeuvring requirement, clarify a reference to a Merchant Shipping Notice, correct a reference to a published code of practice, create an offence where a door is reported closed and locked but is not closed and locked, and alter the penalty for contravention of Reg.34(4)(a) of those Regulations.

4131. Safety at sea–seamen–medical fitness certificates

MERCHANT SHIPPING (MEDICAL EXAMINATION) REGULATIONS 2002, SI 2002 2055; made under the Merchant Shipping Act 1995 s.85, s.86. In force: September 1, 2002; £2.00.

These Regulations, which revoke the Merchant Shipping (Medical Examination) Regulations 1983 (SI 1983 808), the Merchant Shipping (Medical Examination) (Amendment) Regulations 1985 (SI 1985 512) and the Merchant Shipping (Medical Examination) (Amendment) Regulations 1990 (SI 1990 1985), remove the previous restriction on application based on tonnage and apply to sea-going ships, irrespective of tonnage and also make new provision in relation to the period of validity of medical fitness certificates and in relation to seafarers on watchkeeping duties. The Regulations give effect to Convention 147 of the Merchant Shipping (Minimum Standards) Convention 1976 which requires provisions to be made substantially equivalent to those of the Medical Examinations (Seafarers) Convention 1946 which is in force but has not been ratified by the UK. They apply to sea-going UK ships other than fishing vessels, pleasure vessels and offshore installations whilst on their working stations; prohibit the employment of seafarers in such a ship unless they hold a valid medical fitness certificate and provide for certain other medical certificates to be treated as equivalent; provide for the issue of medical fitness certificates, on payment of the prescribed fee, by medical practitioners approved by the Secretary of State; provide for the period of validity of medical fitness certificates, for the suspension or cancellation of certificates in specified circumstances, and for the review of a refusal of a medical fitness certificate, or the suspension or cancellation of a certificate, by a medical referee appointed by the Secretary of State; and provide for the transfer to day work of seafarers with health problems due to performing work at night.

4132. Salvage–insurance–recovery sought under Institute Time Clause (Hulls) terms

S, the owner of a vessel salvaged off the coast of West Africa, brought an insurance claim for its share of the salvage liabilities. The vessel had been insured under hull and machinery policies that were subject to the terms of the Institute Time Clauses (Hulls), ITC. The claim was made under clauses 11.1 and 11.4 of the ITC on the ground that if the vessel had not been salvaged it would have been lost either by the perils of the sea or by the negligence of the master, officers or crew within clauses 6.1.1 and 6.2.3. P, the insurers, disputed liability, arguing that the salvage liabilities had been incurred in relation to the avoidance of a loss which would not have been proximately caused by an insured peril.

Held, giving judgment for S, that S had to prove a proximate link between the clause 11 loss and a clause 6 insured peril. Accordingly, it had to prove that the salvage liabilities had been incurred to avoid a loss caused by a clause 6 peril or in relation to the avoidance of a loss so caused. Having regard to the events leading up to the crew abandoning the vessel, it was apparent that the chief engineer had been negligent and therefore S had shown that, but for the salvage operations, the vessel would have been lost as a result of the negligence of the master, officers and crew for the purposes of clause 6.2.3. Moreover, the entry of sea water into the upper scupper valve would also have been a proximate cause, constituting a peril of the seas for the purposes of clause 6.1.1.

SEASHORE MARINE SA v. PHOENIX ASSURANCE PLC (THE VERGINA) (NO.2) [2002] 1 All E.R. (Comm) 152, Aikens, J., QBD (Comm Ct).

4133. Seafarers–hours of work

MERCHANT SHIPPING (HOURS OF WORK) REGULATIONS 2002, SI 2002 2125; made under the European Communities Act 1972 s.2; the Merchant Shipping Act 1995 s85; and the Merchant Shipping Act 1995 s.86. In force: September 7, 2002; £2.50.

These Regulations amend the Merchant Shipping Act 1995 c.21, the Merchant Shipping (Local Passenger Vessels) (Masters' Licences and Hours, Manning and Training) Regulations 1993 (SI 1993 1213), the Merchant Shipping (Safe Manning, Hours of Work and Watchkeeping) Regulations 1997 (SI 1997 1320) and the Merchant Shipping and Fishing Vessels (Health and Safety at Work) (Employment of Young Persons) Regulations 1998 (SI 1998 2411). These Regulations, which implement the majority of the provisions of Council Directive 1999/63 ([1993] OJ L167/33) concerning the Agreement on the organisation of working time of seafarers and the European Parliament and Council Directive 1999/95 ([1995] OJ L014/29) concerning the enforcement of provisions in respect of seafarers' hours of work on board ships calling at Community ports, require employers to ensure seafarers have at least the specified minimum hours of rest and keep records of seafarers' daily hours of rest. They further prohibit the employment on a ship of a person under 16 years of age, establish seafarers' entitlement to annual leave and provision for the enforcement of these Regulations.

4134. Seaworthiness–due diligence–extent and nature of duty

G, vessel owners, brought an action against S, the cargo insurers, under guarantees given by S concerning delivery of the cargo to the consignees against customary average bonds. S argued that no payment was due under the guarantees as the general average expenditure was due to G's own failure to exercise due diligence to ensure that the vessel was seaworthy before the start of the voyage contrary to the terms of the contract of carriage contained in the bills of lading.

Held, giving judgment for S, that (1) G had not satisfied the burden of proving that they had exercised due diligence. The risk of breakdown could have been avoided by adhering to the cylinder service interval set by both the engine builders and the vessel managers. There was nothing to justify the extension of that period. Although the damage to the vessel was caused by the fitting of an incompatible spare piston rather than the cracking of the original piston, the presence on board of the incompatible piston constituted unseaworthiness, *Smith Hogg & Co Ltd v. Black Sea & Baltic General Insurance Co Ltd* [1940] A.C. 997 applied, and (2) the duty to exercise due diligence to make the ship seaworthy under the Hague Rules was a contractual promise by the carrier that due diligence had been exercised by any person concerned in making the ship seaworthy. G had failed to show that the piston suppliers had exercised due diligence in respect of the supply of the incompatible spare piston or that they had satisfied the burden under the Hague Rules. Accordingly, the general average expenditure was caused by G's actionable fault, precluding recovery from the insurers under the average guarantees.

GUINOMAR OF CONAKRY v. SAMSUNG FIRE & MARINE INSURANCE CO LTD (THE KAMSAR VOYAGER) [2002] 2 Lloyd's Rep. 57, Judge Dean Q.C., QBD (Comm Ct).

4135. Shipbuilding–contracts–nature of refund guarantees

Ten Spanish banks appealed against a decision giving summary judgment for G under the terms of refund guarantees which those banks had given in relation to a shipbuilding contract. The issue before the court concerned whether the guarantees were "on demand" guarantees which were independent of the shipbuilding contract or true guarantees dependent upon the liability of the principal debtor.

Held, dismissing the appeal, that the refund guarantees were on demand guarantees.

CAJA DE AHORROS DEL MEDITERRANEO v. GOLD COAST LTD; *sub nom.* GOLD COAST LTD v. CAJA DE AHORROS DEL MEDITERRANEO, [2001] EWCA Civ 1806, [2002] 1 All E.R. (Comm) 142, Tuckey, L.J., CA.

4136. Wrecks–protection–restricted area designation

PROTECTION OF WRECKS (DESIGNATION) ORDER 2002, SI 2002 1858; made under the Protection of Wrecks Act 1973 s.1. In force: July 18, 2002; £1.50.

This Order designates as a restricted area for the purposes of the Protection of Wrecks Act 1973 the area within a distance of 300 metres from the site believed to be the wreck of the Bonhomme Richard, which the Secretary of State is satisfied ought to be protected from unauthorised interference on account of its historical, archaeological and artistic importance.

4137. Books

Acer, Yucel–Aegean Maritime Disputes and International Law. Hardback: £55.00. ISBN 0-7546-2273-8. Dartmouth.

Al-Azzawi, Ayad H.A.–Crime of International Maritime Fraud. Hardback: £50.00. ISBN 0-7546-2101-4. Ashgate Publishing Limited.

Annuaire: 2000, Vol 4. Paperback: £50.00. ISBN 90-411-1761-X. Kluwer Law International.

Coles, Richard; Ready, Nigel–Ship Registration: Law and Practice. Lloyd's Shipping Law Library. Hardback: £185.00. ISBN 1-84311-119-5. Lloyd's List.

Lloyd's Law Reports: Vol 2. 2001. Hardback: £120.00. ISBN 1-84311-132-2. LLP Professional Publishing.

Lloyd's Maritime & Commercial Law Quarterly: 2001. Hardback: £96.00. ISBN 1-84311-138-1. LLP Professional Publishing.

Pallis, Athanasios A.–Common EU Maritime Transport Policy: Policy Europeanisation in the 1990s. Transport and Mobility. Hardback: £45.00. ISBN 0-7546-1913-3. Ashgate Publishing Limited.

Rose, Francis–Kennedy and Rose on Law of Salvage. British Shipping Laws. Hardback: £215.00. ISBN 0-421-60230-9. Sweet & Maxwell.

Thomas, D. Rhidian–Modern Law of Marine Insurance: Vol 2. Hardback: £140.00. ISBN 1-84311-120-9. LLP Professional Publishing.

Turner; Goldrein–Ship Sale and Purchase. 4th Ed. Hardback: £170.00. ISBN 1-84311-145-4. LLP Professional Publishing.

Yearbook: 2000, Vol 4. Paperback: £50.00. ISBN 90-411-1762-8. Kluwer Law International.

SOCIAL SECURITY

4138. Attendance allowance–disability living allowance–cost of accommodation

SOCIAL SECURITY (ATTENDANCE ALLOWANCE AND DISABILITY LIVING ALLOWANCE) (AMENDMENT) (NO.2) REGULATIONS 2002, SI 2002 1406; made under the Social Security Contributions and Benefits Act 1992 s.67, s.72, s.175. In force: July 1, 2002; £1.50.

These Regulations amend the Social Security (Attendance Allowance) Regulations 1991 (SI 1991 2740) and the Social Security (Disability Living Allowance) Regulations 1991 (SI 1991 2890). They provide that the cost of the accommodation for the purposes of the Attendance Allowance Regulations Reg.7 and Reg.8(6) and the Disability Living Allowance Regulations Reg.9 and Reg.10(8) does not include the cost of nursing care provided by a local authority for which the local authority is not to charge by virtue of the Community Care and Health (Scotland) Act 2002 s.1. These Regulations do not impose a charge on business.

4139. Attendance allowance–disability living allowance–service costs

SOCIAL SECURITY (ATTENDANCE ALLOWANCE AND DISABILITY LIVING ALLOWANCE) (AMENDMENT) REGULATIONS 2002, SI 2002 208; made under the Social Security Contributions and Benefits Act 1992 s.67, s.72, s.175. In force: March 1, 2002; £1.50.

These Regulations amend the Social Security (Attendance Allowance) Regulations 1991 (SI 1991 2740) and the Social Security (Disability Living Allowance) Regulations 1991 (SI 1991 2890). They provide that the cost of the accommodation for the purposes of the Attendance Allowance Regulations Reg.7 and Reg.8(6) and the Disability Living Allowance Regulations Reg.9 and Reg.10(8) does not include the cost of services provided pursuant to the National Health Service Act 1977 or the National Health Service (Scotland) Act 1978. These Regulations do not impose a charge on business.

4140. Benefits–child care charges–computation of earnings

SOCIAL SECURITY BENEFIT (COMPUTATION OF EARNINGS) (CHILD CARE CHARGES) REGULATIONS 2002, SI 2002 842; made under the Social Security Contributions and Benefits Act 1992 s.3, s.175. In force: April 1, 2002; £1.50.

These Regulations amend the Social Security Benefit (Computation of Earnings) Regulations 1996 (SI 1996 2745) which provide for the calculation of the earnings of employed and self-employed persons, to whom benefit is or may be payable, and of such a person's dependants, for the purposes of those provisions of the Social Security Contributions and Benefits Act 1992. The 1996 Regulations also provide that certain specified childcare charges are to be deducted when determining a person's earnings for those purposes. These Regulations extend and update the category of childcare charges, which are to be deducted from a person's earnings.

4141. Benefits–child support maintenance–deductions

SOCIAL SECURITY (CLAIMS AND PAYMENTS) AMENDMENT (NO.2) REGULATIONS 2002, SI 2002 1950; made under the Child Support Act 1991 s.43; and the Social Security Administration Act 1992 s.5, s.189. In force: in accordance with Reg.1 (2); £1.50.

These Regulations, which amend the Social Security (Claims and Payments) Regulations 1987 (SI 1987 1968), provide that where the amount of maternity allowance payable includes any fraction of a penny it shall be rounded up to the next whole penny. They also provide that deductions from benefit may be made in respect of arrears of child support maintenance calculated under the Child Support Act 1991 or assessed under that Act prior to its amendment by the Child Support, Pensions and Social Security Act 2000 or both such arrears, including arrears of maintenance payable at a transitional rate under the latter Act.

4142. Benefits–children and young persons–personal allowance–increase

SOCIAL SECURITY AMENDMENT (PERSONAL ALLOWANCES FOR CHILDREN AND YOUNG PERSONS) REGULATIONS 2002, SI 2002 2019; made under the Social Security Contributions and Benefits Act 1992 s.123, s.135, s.137, s.175; and the Jobseekers Act 1995 s.4, s.35, s.36. In force: October 14, 2002; £1.75.

These Regulations amend the Income Support (General) Regulations 1987 (SI 1987 1967), the Housing Benefit (General) Regulations 1987 (SI 1987 1971), the Council Tax Benefit (General) Regulations 1992 (SI 1992 1814) and the Jobseeker's Allowance Regulations 1996 (SI 1996 207). They increase by £3.50 the amounts of the weekly personal allowance applicable in respect of children and young persons in income support, jobseeker's allowance, housing benefit and council tax benefit.

4143. Benefits–claims and information–housing and council tax benefit

SOCIAL SECURITY (CLAIMS AND INFORMATION) (HOUSING BENEFIT AND COUNCIL TAX BENEFIT) REGULATIONS 2002, SI 2002 1132; made under the Social Security Administration Act 1992 s.7A, s.189, s.191. In force: May 17, 2002; £1.75.

These Regulations permit the Secretary of State for Work and Pensions or persons providing services to him to collect information relating to housing benefit and council tax benefit and forward this information to the local authority.

4144. Benefits–claims and payments

SOCIAL SECURITY (CLAIMS AND PAYMENTS AND MISCELLANEOUS AMENDMENTS) REGULATIONS 2002, SI 2002 428; made under the Social Security Administration Act 1992 s.5, s.191; and the Social Security Act 1998 s.9, s.10, s.84. In force: April 2, 2002; £1.75.

These Regulations, which amend the Social Security (Claims and Payments) Regulations 1987 (SI 1987 1968) and the Social Security and Child Support (Decisions and Appeals) Regulations 1999 (SI 1999 991), provide for certain claims to take effect earlier when entitlement is affected by benefit awarded to a partner or child or where entitlement to income support or jobseeker's allowance is affected by a qualifying benefit, and makes minor amendments relating certain provisions to the award rather than the payability of a benefit. They also provide for an extension of the time for claiming income support, jobseeker's allowance, working families' tax credit and disabled person's tax credit in specified circumstances.

4145. Benefits–claims and payments

SOCIAL SECURITY (CLAIMS AND PAYMENTS AND MISCELLANEOUS AMENDMENTS) (NO.2) REGULATIONS 2002, SI 2002 2441; made under the Social Security Administration Act 1992 s.5, s.15A, s.71, s.189, s.191. In force: in accordance with Reg.1 (1); £1.75.

These Regulations amend the Social Security (Claims and Payments) Regulations 1987 (SI 1987 1968) and the Social Security (Payments on account, Overpayments and Recovery) Regulations 1988 (SI 1988 664) to make further provision as to the payment of social security benefits.

4146. Benefits—claims and payments

SOCIAL SECURITY (CLAIMS AND PAYMENTS AND MISCELLANEOUS AMENDMENTS) (NO.3) REGULATIONS 2002, SI 2002 2660; made under the Social Security Contributions and Benefits Act 1992 s.138, s.175; and the Social Security Administration Act 1992 s.5, s.189. In force: in accordance with Reg.1; £1.50.

These Regulations, which amend the Social Security (Claims and Payments) Regulations 1987 (SI 1987 1968) and the Social Fund Winter Fuel Payment Regulations 2000 (SI 2000 729), extend the period for claiming a bereavement payment from three to 12 months and provide for the extended period to apply in respect of deaths occurring on or after April 1, 2003. They provide for a winter fuel payment to be paid, alternatively, to the partner of the person entitled despite the partner being aged under 60 if the partner receives income support or an income-based jobseeker's allowance.

4147. Benefits—claims and payments—administration fees

SOCIAL SECURITY (CLAIMS AND PAYMENTS) AMENDMENT REGULATIONS 2002, SI 2002 355; made under the Social Security Administration Act 1992 s.15A, s.189. In force: April 1, 2002; £1.50.

These Regulations amend the Social Security (Claims and Payments) Regulations 1987 (SI 1987 1968) by increasing from £0.54 to £0.66 the fee which qualifying lenders pay for the purpose of defraying administrative expenses incurred by the Secretary of State in making payments in respect of mortgage interest direct to qualifying lenders.

4148. Benefits—employment programmes—New Deal Scheme—employment option

SOCIAL SECURITY AMENDMENT (EMPLOYMENT PROGRAMME) REGULATIONS 2002, SI 2002 2314; made under the Social Security Contributions and Benefits Act 1992 s.123, s.136, s.137, s.175; and the Jobseekers Act 1995 s.12, s.19, s.35, s.36, Sch.1 para.3. In force: October 14, 2002; £1.75.

These Regulations amend the Jobseeker's Allowance Regulations 1996 (SI 1996 207), the Income Support (General) Regulations 1987 (SI 1987 1967), the Housing Benefit (General) Regulations 1987 (SI 1987 1971) and the Council Tax Benefit (General) Regulations 1992 (SI 1992 1814). They amend the definition of the Employment Option of the New Deal in the Jobseeker's Allowance Regulations 1996 (SI 1996 207) Reg.75 so that the employed earner's Employment Option of the New Deal becomes subject to sanctions of discretionary length and is omitted from the linking provisions set out in Reg.48; and provide that mandatory top-up payments made under the Employment and Training Act 1973 s.2 in relation to the Full-Time Education and Training Option of the New Deal shall be disregarded in the calculation of income or capital for jobseeker's allowance, income support, housing benefit and council tax benefit

4149. Benefits—fraud

SOCIAL SECURITY (LOSS OF BENEFIT) (AMENDMENT) REGULATIONS 2002, SI 2002 486; made under the Social Security Fraud Act 2001 s.7, s.11. In force: April 1, 2002; £1.50.

These Regulations amend the Social Security (Loss of Benefit) Regulations 2001 (SI 2001 4022) so as to make special arrangements as regards the disqualification period for housing benefit and council tax benefit and corrects a drafting error. They are made in connection with the coming into force of provisions of the Social Security Fraud Act 2001 which relate to restrictions in payment of certain benefits where a person has been convicted of one or more benefit offences in each of two separate proceedings and one offence is committed within three years of the conviction for another such offence.

4150. Benefits–hospital in-patients

SOCIAL SECURITY (HOSPITAL IN-PATIENTS) AMENDMENT REGULATIONS 2002, SI 2002 685; made under the Social Security Administration Act 1992 s.73, s.189, s.191. In force: April 8, 2002; £1.50.

A person who receives free in-patient treatment in a hospital or similar institution for between 6 and 53 weeks has his entitlement to receive incapacity benefit, widow's allowance, widowed mother's allowance, widow's pension, bereavement allowance, widowed parent's allowance, age addition, severe disablement allowance, retirement pension, unemployability supplement, industrial death benefit widow's and widower's pensions, reduced. These Regulations, which amend the Social Security (Hospital In-Patients) Regulations 1975 (SI 1975 555), decrease the reduction which would otherwise apply in certain circumstances, from 39 per cent to 38 per cent of the basic retirement pension.

4151. Benefits–income related benefits–personal injury payments

SOCIAL SECURITY AMENDMENT (PERSONAL INJURY PAYMENTS) REGULATIONS 2002, SI 2002 2442; made under the Social Security Contributions and Benefits Act 1992 s.123, s.136, s.137, s.175; and the Jobseekers Act 1995 s.12, s.35, s.36. In force: October 28, 2002; £1.75.

These Regulations amend the Income Support (General) Regulations 1987 (SI 1987 1967), the Housing Benefit (General) Regulations 1987 (SI 1987 1971), the Council Tax Benefit (General) Regulations 1992 (SI 1992 1814) and the Jobseeker's Allowance Regulations 1996 (SI 1996 207). They require periodical payments received by virtue of any agreement or court order to make personal injury payments to the claimant to be treated as income and provide that payments of income received from all trusts whose funds derive from personal injury payments to a claimant, from an annuity purchased with such funds and those received by virtue of any agreement or court order to make personal injury payments to the claimant, are to be disregarded in their entirety when used for items other than everyday living expenses and £20 of such income disregarded when used for such expenses.

4152. Benefits–income support–job seekers allowance

SOCIAL SECURITY AND CHILD SUPPORT (DECISIONS AND APPEALS) (MISCELLANEOUS AMENDMENTS) REGULATIONS 2002, SI 2002 1379; made under the Vaccine Damage Payments Act 1979 s.4; the Child Support Act 1991 s.20; the Jobseekers Act 1995 s.31, s.35, Sch.1 para.4; the Social Security (Recovery of Benefits) Act 1997 s.11; the Social Security Act 1998 s.6, s.9, s.10A, s.12, s.14, s.16, s.24A, s.28, s.79, s.84, Sch.1 para.12, Sch.2 para.9, Sch.5 para.1, Sch.5 para.2, Sch.5 para.3, Sch.5 para.4, Sch.5 para.6, Sch.5 para.7; and the Child Support, Pensions, and Social Security Act 2000 s.68, Sch.7 para.3, Sch.7 para.6, Sch.7 para.10, Sch.7 para.19, Sch.7 para.20, Sch.7 para.23. In force: May 20, 2002; £3.00.

These Regulations, which amend the Social Security and Child Support (Decisions and Appeals) Regulations 1999 (SI 1999 991), make further provision for the revision of decisions and provide for the interaction of awards of income support and jobseeker's allowance. They add an appointee after the death of a claimant to the list of prescribed persons who may appeal, clarify the limits for making an appeal, provide for the Secretary of State or the Board to grant an extension of time for an appeal in specified circumstances, provide for the clerk to an appeal tribunal to reinstate an appeal if he has struck it out because the appellant failed to comply with a direction concerning an oral hearing and provide for oral hearings to be in public except in specified circumstances and for participation in an oral hearing by a live television link. The Regulations also remove rules about the constitution of an appeal tribunal after an adjournment, require applications for statements of appeal tribunals' reasons to be sent to the clerk and provide that the death or serious illness of the appellant's partner is a reason for granting further time for the appellant to take procedural steps. In addition, these

Regulations amend the Housing Benefit and Council Tax Benefit (Decisions and Appeals) Regulations 2001 (SI 2001 1002) to provide for the correction of accidental errors in a decision of a relevant authority and for a relevant authority to grant an extension of time for an appeal in specified circumstances.

4153. Benefits—industrial diseases—entitlement

SOCIAL SECURITY (INDUSTRIAL INJURIES) (PRESCRIBED DISEASES) AMENDMENT REGULATIONS 2002, SI 2002 1717; made under the Social Security Contributions and Benefits Act 1992 s.109, s.122, s.175, Sch.6 para.1. In force: July 29, 2002; £1.50.

These Regulations amend the Social Security (Industrial Injuries) (Prescribed Diseases) Regulations 1985 (SI 1985 967) so as to remove the provision for assessing, for the purposes of industrial injuries benefit, the extent of disablement arising from diffuse mesothelioma and to prescribe impaired function of the pleura, pericardium or peritoneum caused by diffuse mesothelioma as a loss of faculty from which the resulting disabilities are to be taken as amounting to 100 per cent disablement.

4154. Benefits—intercalating students

SOCIAL SECURITY AMENDMENT (INTERCALATING STUDENTS) REGULATIONS 2002, SI 2002 1763; made under the Social Security Contributions and Benefits Act 1992 s.123, s.131, s.137, s.175; and the Jobseekers Act 1995 s.6, s.35, s.36. In force: August 1, 2002; £1.50.

These Regulations, which amend the Housing Benefit (General) Regulations 1987 (SI 1987 1971), the Council Tax Benefit (General) Regulations 1992 (SI 1992 1814) and the Jobseeker's Allowance Regulations 1996 (SI 1996 207), make a change to the period during which students, who have taken a break from their courses due to illness or caring responsibilities, may claim housing benefit, council tax benefit and jobseeker's allowance.

4155. Benefits—invalid care allowance—carer premium

SOCIAL SECURITY AMENDMENT (CARER PREMIUM) REGULATIONS 2002, SI 2002 2020; made under the Social Security Contributions and Benefits Act 1992 s.123, s.135, s.137, s.175; and the Jobseekers Act 1995 s.4, s.35, s.36. In force: October 28, 2002; £1.75.

These Regulations amend the Income Support (General) Regulations 1987 (SI 1987 1967), the Housing Benefit (General) Regulations 1987 (SI 1987 1971), the Council Tax Benefit (General) Regulations 1992 (SI 1992 1814) and the Jobseeker's Allowance Regulations 1996 (SI 1996 207). They provide that the period for which a carer premium is payable shall be extended for eight weeks from either the death of the person in respect of whose care invalid care allowance has been awarded or, in any other case, until eight weeks after the entitlement to invalid care allowance ceases.

4156. Benefits—loss of benefits

SOCIAL SECURITY (LOSS OF BENEFIT) (CONSEQUENTIAL AMENDMENTS) REGULATIONS 2002, SI 2002 490; made under the Social Security Contributions and Benefits Act 1992 s.22, s.122, s.123, s.124, s.135, s.137, s.175; the Jobseekers Act 1995 s.5, s.26, s.35, s.36; the Social Security Act 1998 s.9, s.10, s.79, s.84; and the Child Support, Pensions and Social Security Act 2000 s.62, s.65, s.69, Sch.7 para.3, Sch.7 para.4, Sch.7 para.23. In force: April 1, 2002; £2.00.

These Regulations make amendments to the Social Security (Credits) Regulations 1975 (SI 1975 556) to ensure that those whose invalid care allowance or jobseeker's allowance is restricted through the application of the loss of benefit provisions do not lose credits and the Income Support (General) Regulations 1987 (SI 1987 1967) to ensure that those whose invalid care allowance is restricted through the application of the loss of benefit provisions are still treated as carers. They amend the Housing Benefit (General) Regulations 1987 (SI 1987 1971) and the Council Tax Benefit (General) Regulations 1992 (SI 1992 1814) to ensure that those whose jobseeker's allowance is restricted through the application of the loss of benefit provisions do not lose their housing benefit or council tax benefit as a result and amend the Jobseeker's Allowance Regulations 1996 (SI 1996 207) to ensure that days where contribution-based jobseeker's allowance is not payable because of the loss of benefit provisions are treated as days of entitlement to that allowance. The Regulations make a consequential amendment to the Social Security (Back to Work Bonus) (No.2) Regulations 1996 (SI 1996 2570) and amend the Social Security and Child Support (Decisions and Appeals) Regulations 1999 (SI 1999 991) and the Housing Benefit and Council Tax Benefit (Decisions and Appeals) Regulations 2001 (SI 2001 1002) respectively to ensure that the decision-making and appeals mechanisms apply to decisions to restrict payment of benefit as a result of the loss of benefit provisions. In addition, the Regulations amend the Discretionary Financial Assistance Regulations 2001 (SI 2001 1167) to provide that discretionary housing payments shall not be made where the requirement for financial assistance arises as a consequence of the application of the loss of benefit provisions and the Social Security (Breach of Community Order) Regulations 2001 (SI 2001 1395) so as to provide that a reduction in income support imposed for breach of a community order shall not take effect where a reduction of income support under the loss of benefit provisions is in operation.

4157. Benefits–maternity and funeral–expenses–entitlement

SOCIAL FUND MATERNITY AND FUNERAL EXPENSES (GENERAL) AMENDMENT (NO.2) REGULATIONS 2002, SI 2002 470; made under the Social Security Contributions and Benefits Act 1992 s.138, s.175. In force: March 30, 2002; £1.50.

These Regulations amend the Social Fund Maternity and Funeral Expenses (General) Amendment Regulations 2002 (SI 2002 79) to correct an error in a transitional provision.

4158. Benefits–maternity expenses–entitlement

SOCIAL FUND MATERNITY AND FUNERAL EXPENSES (GENERAL) AMENDMENT REGULATIONS 2002, SI 2002 79; made under the Social Security Contributions and Benefits Act 1992 s.138, s.175; and the Social Security Act 1998 s.9. In force: March 31, 2002; £1.75.

These Regulations, which amend the Social Fund Maternity and Funeral Expense (General) Regulations 1987 (SI 1987 481), increase the amount of a Sure Start Maternity Grant from £300 to £500.

4159. Benefits–miscellaneous amendments

CHILD SUPPORT (MISCELLANEOUS AMENDMENTS) REGULATIONS 2002, SI 2002 1204; made under the Child Support Act 1991 s.14, s.16, s.17, s.20, s.28B, s.28E, s.28G, s.46, s.51, s.52, s.54, s.57, Sch.1 para.5, Sch.1 para.10, Sch.1 para.11, Sch.4B para.3, Sch.4B para.4, Sch.4B para.5; and the Child Support, Pensions and Social Security Act 2000 s.29. In force: in accordance with Reg.1 (3); £2.50.

These Regulations amend the Child Support (Information, Evidence and Disclosure) Regulations 1992 (SI 1992 1812), the Child Support (Maintenance Assessments and Special Cases) Regulations 1992 (SI 1992 1815), the Child Support Departure Direction and Consequential Amendments Regulations 1996 (SI 1996 2907), the Social Security and Child Support (Decisions and Appeals) Regulations 1999 (SI 1999 991), the Child Support (Variations) (Modification of Statutory Provisions) Regulations 2000 (SI 2000 3173), the Child Support (Transitional Provisions) Regulations 2000 (SI 2000 3186), the Child Support (Maintenance Calculations and Special Cases) Regulations 2001 (SI 2001 155), the Child Support (Variations) Regulations 2001 (SI 2001 156) and the Child Support (Maintenance Calculation Procedure) Regulations 2001 (SI 2001 157).

4160. Benefits–miscellaneous amendments

SOCIAL SECURITY (MISCELLANEOUS AMENDMENTS) REGULATIONS 2002, SI 2002 841; made under the Social Security Contributions and Benefits Act 1992 s.123, s.135, s.136, s.137, s.175; the Social Security Administration Act 1992 s.134, s.139; and the Jobseekers Act 1995 s.4, s.12, s.35, s.36. In force: April 8, 2002; £1.75.

These Regulations amend the Income Support (General) Regulations 1987 (SI 1987 1967), the Housing Benefit (General) Regulations 1987 (SI 1987 1971), the Council Tax Benefit (General) Regulations 1992 (SI 1992 1814) and the Jobseeker's Allowance Regulations 1996 (SI 1996 207). They provide for income disregards in respect of war widowers' pensions and extend the 52 week linking provisions to claimants whose housing costs are met in part.

4161. Benefits–miscellaneous amendments

SOCIAL SECURITY (MISCELLANEOUS AMENDMENTS) (NO.2) REGULATIONS 2002, SI 2002 2380; made under the Social Security Contributions and Benefits Act 1992 s.123, s.136, s.137, s.175; and the Jobseekers Act 1995 s.4, s.12, s.35, s.36. In force: in accordance with Reg.1; £2.00.

These Regulations amend the Income Support (General) Regulations 1987 (SI 1987 1967), Housing Benefit (General) Regulations 1987 (SI 1987 1971), the Council Tax Benefit (General) Regulations 1992 (SI 1992 1814) and the Jobseeker's Allowance Regulations 1996 (SI 1996 207). They clarify the date from which the condition for the award of carer premium shall be treated as satisfied and amend the capital disregard provisions that apply when ascertaining entitlement to those benefits so that the disregard of specified arrears and concessionary payments will apply for either 52 weeks or, where large payments are made to rectify an official error and are paid during the benefit award, for the remainder of that award if that is a longer period. They also provide that any payment made to a claimant in respect of the repayment of a student loan shall be disregarded in the calculation of income.

4162. Benefits–paternity and adoption–entitlement

SOCIAL SECURITY (PATERNITY AND ADOPTION) AMENDMENT REGULATIONS 2002, SI 2002 2689; made under the Social Security Contributions and Benefits Act 1992 s.123, s.124, s.136, s.137, s.175; and the Jobseekers Act 1995 s.1, s.12, s.35, s.36, Sch.1 para.1. In force: in accordance with Reg.1 (1); £2.00.

These Regulations amend the Support (General) Regulations 1987 (SI 1987 1967), the Housing Benefit (General) Regulations 1987 (SI 1987 1971), the Council Tax Benefit (General) Regulations 1992 (SI 1992 1814) and the Jobseeker's Allowance Regulations 1996 (SI 1996 207). They extend entitlement to income support, where a woman is or has been pregnant and has an expected week of confinement beginning on or after April 6, 2003, to a period commencing 11 weeks before her expected week of confinement and ending fifteen weeks after the date on which her pregnancy ends and extend entitlement to income support to a person who is entitled to and taking paternity leave by virtue of the Employment Rights Act 1986 and who satisfies the prescribed conditions. They also provide that a person on statutory paternity leave or statutory adoption leave shall not be treated as engaged in remunerative work; and add statutory adoption pay and statutory paternity pay to those payments in respect of which prescribed sums are to be disregarded in the calculation of income.

4163. Benefits—paternity and adoption leave—computation of earnings

SOCIAL SECURITY BENEFIT (COMPUTATION OF EARNINGS) (AMENDMENT) REGULATIONS 2002, SI 2002 2823; made under the Social Security Contributions and Benefits Act 1992 s.3. In force: in accordance with Art.1; £1.75.

These Regulations amend the Social Security Benefit (Computation of Earnings) Regulations 1996 (SI 1996 2745) so that earnings for benefit purposes include not only remuneration paid to a claimant during a period of maternity leave or sick absence but also any payment of remuneration during a period of adoption leave or paternity leave under the Employment Rights Act 1996.

4164. Benefits—statutory maternity pay—statutory sick pay

SOCIAL SECURITY, STATUTORY MATERNITY PAY AND STATUTORY SICK PAY (MISCELLANEOUS AMENDMENTS) REGULATIONS 2002, SI 2002 2690; made under the Social Security Contributions and Benefits Act 1992 s.35, s.35A, s.153, s.163, s.164, s.165, s.166, s.171, s.171ZP, s.171ZS, s.175, Sch.11 para.1, Sch.11 para.1A, Sch.13 para.2; and the Social Security Administration Act 1992 s.5, s.132, s.189, s.191. In force: in accordance with Reg.1; £2.50.

These Regulations amend the Statutory Sick Pay (General) Regulations 1982 (SI 1982 894), the Statutory Maternity Pay (General) Regulations 1986 (SI 1986 1960), the Social Security (Maternity Allowance) Regulations 1987 (SI 1987 416), the Statutory Maternity Pay (National Health Service Employees) Regulations 1991 (SI 1991 590), the Social Security (Incapacity Benefit) Regulations 1994 (SI 1994 2946) and the Social Security (Maternity Allowance) (Earnings) Regulations 2000 (SI 2000 688). They provide for a woman's maternity pay period (MPP) to commence where she gives notice to her employer that she expects his liability to pay her statutory maternity pay to begin and she ceases work in conformity with that notice; extends the MPP to 26 consecutive weeks; provides for a woman's MPP to commence where she is confined before the eleventh week before the expected week of confinement (EWC); provide that where a woman is absent from work wholly or partly because of pregnancy or confinement, on or after the fourth week before her EWC that her MPP will commence on the day after the first day on which she is so absent; and add references to statutory paternity, statutory adoption and statutory parental leave to the circumstances in which a woman may be treated as employed and makes other minor drafting changes.

4165. Benefits—up rating

SOCIAL SECURITY BENEFITS UP-RATING ORDER 2002, SI 2002 668; made under the Social Security Administration Act 1992 s.150, s.151, s.189. In force: in accordance with Art.1 (2); £7.50.

This Order amends the National Insurance Act 1965, the Child Benefit and Social Security (Fixing and Adjustment of Rates) Regulations 1976 (SI 1976 1267), the Social Security (Graduated Retirement Benefit) (No.2) Regulations 1978 (SI 1978 393), the Statutory Maternity Pay (General) Regulations 1986 (SI 1986 1960), the Income Support (General) Regulations 1987 (SI 1987 1967), the Income Support (Transitional) Regulations 1987 (SI 1987 1969), the Housing Benefit (General) Regulations 1987 (SI 1987 1971), the Social Security (Disability Living Allowance) Regulations 1991 (SI 1991 2890), the Social Security Contributions and Benefits Act 1992, the Council Tax Benefit (General) Regulations 1992 (SI 1992 1814), the Pension Schemes Act 1993, the Social Security (Incapacity Benefit) Regulations 1994 (SI 1994 2946), the Social Security (Incapacity Benefit) (Transitional) Regulations 1995 (SI 1995 310), the Jobseeker's Allowance Regulations 1996 (SI 1996 207) and revokes the Social Security Benefits Up-rating (No.2) Order 2000 (SI 2000 207). The Order is made as a consequence of a review under the Social Security Administration Act 1992 and alters and increases specified benefits.

4166. Benefits—up rating—child dependency

SOCIAL SECURITY BENEFITS UP-RATING REGULATIONS 2002, SI 2002 684; made under the Social Security Contributions and Benefits Act 1992 s.30E, s.90, s.113, s.122, s.171D, s.171G, s.175, Sch.7 para.2; and the Social Security Administration Act 1992 s.155, s.189, s.191. In force: April 8, 2002; £1.50.

These Regulations, which amend the Social Security Benefit (Dependency) Regulations 1977 (SI 1977 343) and the Social Security Benefits Up-rating Regulations 2001 (SI 2001 910), provide that where a question has arisen about the effect of the Social Security Benefits Up-rating Order 2002 (SI 2002 668) on a benefit already in payment, the altered rates will not apply until that question is determined by the Secretary of State, an appeal tribunal or a Commissioner. They also raise from £150 to £155 one of the earnings limits for child dependency increases payable with an invalid care allowance.

4167. Benefits—work focused interviews

SOCIAL SECURITY (JOBCENTRE PLUS INTERVIEWS) REGULATIONS 2002, SI 2002 1703; made under the Social Security Administration Act 1992 s.2A, s.2B, s.5, s.6, s.7A, s.189, s.191; and the Child Support, Pensions and Social Security Act 2000 s.68, Sch.7 para.3, Sch.7 para.4, Sch.7 para.6, Sch.7 para.20, Sch.7 para.23. In force: September 30, 2002; £3.00.

These Regulations amend the Social Security (Claims and Payments) Regulations 1987 (SI 1987 1968), the Housing Benefit (General) Regulations 1987 (SI 1987 1971), the Child Support (Maintenance Assessment Procedure) Regulations 1992 (SI 1992 1813), the Council Tax Benefit (General) Regulations 1992 (SI 1992 1814), the Child Support Departure Direction and Consequential Amendments Regulations 1996 (SI 1996 2907), the Social Security and Child Support (Decisions and Appeals) Regulations 1999 (SI 1999 991) and the Security (Work-focused Interviews) Regulations 2000 (SI 2000 897). They impose a requirement on persons who claim, or are entitled to, certain benefits to take part in a work-focused interview.

4168. Benefits—work focused interviews—lone parents

SOCIAL SECURITY (WORK-FOCUSED INTERVIEWS FOR LONE PARENTS) AMENDMENT REGULATIONS 2002, SI 2002 670; made under the Social Security Administration Act 1992 s.2A, s.189, s.191. In force: April 8, 2002; £1.75.

These Regulations, which amend the Social Security (Work-focused Interviews for Lone Parents) and Miscellaneous Amendments Regulations 2000 (SI 2000 1926), impose a requirement for additional work-focused interviews on certain lone parents making claims for income support on or after April 8, 2002. For lone parents claiming income support on or after this date, the requirement to participate in work-focused interviews will arise when their youngest child is aged three years. Lone parents already claiming income support will be required to take part in work-focused interviews when their youngest child reaches five years three months. Also, an additional work-focused interview will be required six months after lone parents have taken part, or were treated as having taken part, in an initial interview.

4169. Carers—carers allowance

SOCIAL SECURITY AMENDMENT (CARER'S ALLOWANCE) REGULATIONS 2002, SI 2002 2497; made under the Child Support Act 1991 Sch.1 para.4; the Social Security Contributions and Benefits Act 1992 s.22, s.70, s.79, s.90, s.113, s.124, s.135, s.136, s.138, s.175, Sch.3 para.2; the Social Security Administration Act 1992 s.2A, s.5, s.7A, s.73, s.78, s.107, s.189; the Social Security (Consequential Provisions) Act 1992 s.5, Sch.4 para.12; the Jobseekers Act 1995 s.26, s.40; the Child Support Act 1995 s.10, s.26; the Welfare Reform and Pensions Act 1999 s.72, s.83; and the Immigration and Asylum Act 1999 s.115. In force: in accordance with Reg.1; £2.00.

This Order amends the Social Security Benefit (Persons Abroad) Regulations 1975 (SI 1975 563), the Social Security (Credits) Regulations 1975 (SI 1975 1483), the Social Security (Invalid Care Allowance) Regulations 1976 (SI 1976 409), the Social Security Benefit (Dependency) Regulations 1977 (SI 1977 343), the Social Security (Overlapping Benefits) Regulations 1979 (SI 1979 597), the Social Security (Widow's Benefit and Retirement Pensions) Regulations 1979 (SI 1979 642), the Income Support (General) Regulations 1987 (SI 1987 1967), the Social Security (Claims and Payments) Regulations 1987 (SI 1987 1968), the Housing Benefit (General) Regulations 1987 (SI 1987 1971), the Social Fund (Recovery by Deductions from Benefits) Regulations 1988 (SI 1988 35), the Income Support (Liable Relatives) Regulations 1990 (SI 1990 1777), the Council Tax Benefit (General) Regulations 1992 (SI 1992 1814), the Social Security (Incapacity Benefit) Regulations 1994 (SI 1994 2946), the Jobseeker's Allowance (Transitional Provisions) Regulations 1996 (SI 1996 2567), the Social Security (Back to Work Bonus) (No.2) Regulations 1996 (SI 1996 2570), the Social Security (Invalid Care Allowance) Amendment Regulations 1996 (SI 1996 2744), the Social Security (Child Maintenance Bonus) Regulations 1996 (SI 1996 3195), the Social Security (Claims and Information) Regulations 1999 (SI 1996 3108), the Social Security (Immigration and Asylum) Consequential Amendments Regulations 2000 (SI 2000 636), the Child Support (Maintenance Calculations and Special Cases) Regulations 2001 (SI 2001 155) and the Social Security (Jobcentre Plus Interviews) Regulations 2002 (SI 2002 1703). It makes amendments as a consequence of the change of the name of the allowance from invalid care allowance to carer's allowance.

4170. Carers–carers allowance–disabled people

REGULATORY REFORM (CARER'S ALLOWANCE) ORDER 2002, SI 2002 1457; made under the Regulatory Reform Act 2001 s.1. In force: in accordance with Art.1 (1); £1.75.

This Order, which amends the Social Security Contributions and Benefits Act 1992, provides for an allowance for those caring for severely disabled people. It provides that a carer may continue to receive an allowance for a specified period after the death of the severely disabled person for whom he has been caring and revokes certain provisions which restricted the circumstances in which a person may be entitled to the allowance, and provides for an enabled provision to be made for such a person to continue to be entitled to the allowance despite his not satisfying all of the conditions of entitlement.

4171. Child benefit–EC law–refugees–statelessness–entitlement whilst resident in Member State

[EC TreatyArt.51 (now, after amendment, Art.42 EC); Council Regulation 1408/71 on the application of social security schemes to employed persons and their families moving within the Community.]

The national court referred to the ECJ for a preliminary ruling questions as to the validity and interpretation of Council Regulation 1408/71 that had arisen in proceedings concerning the right of stateless persons and refugees to claim child benefit and child raising allowances. The applicants in the proceedings were regarded as stateless persons under German law whose entitlement to child benefit had been discontinued on the ground that only foreigners with either a residence entitlement or a residence permit could receive child benefit under national law. The national court questioned (1) the validity of the Regulation in so far as it included stateless persons or refugees residing within a Member State given that the EC TreatyArt.51 (now, after amendment, Art.42 EC) included stateless persons and refugees resident in a Member State as a means of meeting the international legal obligations of the Member States, and (2) whether workers who were stateless persons or refugees could rely on the Regulation where they had travelled directly to a Member State from outside the Community and remained there.

Held, that, (1) the inclusion of stateless persons or refugees in the Regulation was valid where they resided in a Member State, and (2) workers who were stateless persons or refugees residing in a Member State with their families could not rely on the rights conferred by the Regulation where they had travelled to and remained in one Member State from a non Community country.

KHALIL v. BUNDESANSTALT FUR ARBEIT (C95/99); CHAABAN v. BUNDESANSTALT FUR ARBEIT (C96/99); OSSEILI v. BUNDESANSTALT FUR ARBEIT (C97/99); NASSER v. LANDESHAUPTSTADT STUTTGART (C98/99); ADDOU v. LAND NORDRHEIN WESTFALEN (C180/99) [2001] 3 C.M.L.R. 50, Rodriguez Iglesias (President), ECJ.

4172. Child benefit—electronic communications

SOCIAL SECURITY (ELECTRONIC COMMUNICATIONS) (CHILD BENEFIT) ORDER 2002, SI 2002 1789; made under the Electronic Communications Act 2000 s.8, s.9. In force: October 28, 2002; £2.00.

This Order, which amends the Social Security (Claims and Payments) Regulations 1987 (SI 1987 1968), the Child Benefit (General) Regulations 1976 (SI 1976 965), the Social Security (Guardian's Allowances) Regulations 1975 (SI 1975 515) and the Social Security (Notification of Change of Circumstances) Regulations 2001 (SI 2001 3252), makes provision for claims for child benefit to be made electronically.

4173. Child benefit—parents—discrimination—sharing of benefit between separated parents

[Social Security Contributions and Benefits Act 1992 s.144; Human Rights Act 1998 s.3, Sch.1 Part I Art.14; Social Security (Claims and Payments) Regulations 1987 (SI 1987 1968) Reg.34.]

B challenged the decision by the Secretary of State to decline to exercise his powers under the Social Security (Claims and Payments) Regulations 1987 Reg.34 to divide the child benefit in respect of his son between himself and his former wife. B submitted that the approach adopted by the United Kingdom statutory scheme was an all or nothing approach, whereby the parent who was not in receipt of child benefit was regarded as an absent parent and was not eligible for pension support or other welfare benefits. B argued that Reg.34 should be construed with regard to the Human Rights Act 1998 s.3 so as to authorise payment of part of the child benefit to him, and that other provisions governing the payment of benefits should also be construed in the light of s.3 so as to provide entitlement on receipt of monies under Reg.34 or remove the absent parent status.

Held, refusing the application for judicial review, that Reg.34 of the 1987 Regulations could not be interpreted in such a way as to give the Secretary of State power to split or rotate child benefit. The purpose behind Reg.34 was to enable a person other than the parent of a child to receive the child benefit where it was necessary to protect the interests of the parent or child. There was no breach of Sch.1 Part I Art.14 of the 1998 Act. The Secretary of State's approach did not amount to B being given less favourable treatment. The approach applied across the board regardless of a person's status under Reg.34. The fact that B was a parent not receiving child benefit did not amount to a personal characteristic or represent a status forming the basis of any discrimination. There was insufficient evidence before the court for there to be an assessment of the claim of indirect discrimination on the ground of sex. The Secretary of State was justified in reaching his decision and there was no justification for altering the present system as contained in the Social Security Contributions and Benefits Act 1992 s.144 whereby only one parent was entitled to child benefit in respect of the same child, and furthermore the system worked well and was cost efficient.

R. (ON THE APPLICATION OF BARBER) v. SECRETARY OF STATE FOR WORK AND PENSIONS; *sub nom.* BARBER v. SECRETARY OF STATE FOR WORK AND PENSIONS, [2002] EWHC 1915, [2002] 2 F.L.R. 1181, Sir Richard Tucker, QBD (Admin Ct).

4174. Child support–maintenance orders–jurisdiction of courts–appeals

CHILD SUPPORT APPEALS (JURISDICTION OF COURTS) ORDER 2002, SI 2002 1915; made under the Child Support Act 1991 s.45. In force: July 20, 2002; £1.50.

This Order revokes the Child Support Appeals (Jurisdiction of Courts) Order 1993 (SI 1993 961) which provides for child support appeals to be made to a court instead of an appeal tribunal where the issue in the appeal is parentage of the qualifying child in relation to whom an application for child support maintenance has been made under the Child Support Act 1991. It makes provision for the application of provisions of the Social Security and Child Support (Decision and Appeals) Regulations 1999 (SI 1999 991) in relation to the appeals to which this Order applies.

4175. Child support–temporary compensation scheme–recovery of arrears

CHILD SUPPORT (TEMPORARY COMPENSATION PAYMENT SCHEME) (MODIFICATION AND AMENDMENT) REGULATIONS 2002, SI 2002 1854; made under the Child Support, Pensions and Social Security Act 2000 s.27. In force: July 17, 2002; £1.50.

These Regulations amend the Child Support, Pensions and Social Security Act 2000 and the Child Support (Temporary Compensation Payment Scheme) Regulations 2000 (SI 2000 3174) in relation to the temporary compensation payment scheme. The scheme makes provision for certain cases where there has been a delay in the making of a maintenance assessment under the Child Support Act 1991 leading to arrears of child support maintenance.

4176. Contributions–business travel–Class 1 contributions

SOCIAL SECURITY (CONTRIBUTIONS) (AMENDMENT NO.2) REGULATIONS 2002, SI 2002 307; made under the Social Security Contributions and Benefits Act 1992 s.3, s.4; and the Social Security Contributions and Benefits (Northern Ireland) Act 1992 s.3, s.4. In force: April 6, 2002; £2.00.

These Regulations, which amend the Social Security (Contributions) Regulations 2001 (SI 2001 1004), insert a definition of "business travel" and brings into charge to Class 1 contributions the cash equivalent for car fuel provided for use by an employee if the cash equivalent is charged to tax under the Income and Corporation Taxes Act 1988.

4177. Contributions–earnings period

SOCIAL SECURITY (CONTRIBUTIONS) (AMENDMENT NO.3) REGULATIONS 2002, SI 2002 2366; made under the Social Security Contributions and Benefits Act 1992 s.3, s.17, s.119, Sch.1 para.2, Sch.1 para.4, Sch.1 para.8; the Social Security Contributions and Benefits (Northern Ireland) Act 1992 s.3, s.17, s.119, Sch.1 para.2, Sch.1 para.4, Sch.1 para.8; the Social Security Contributions and Benefits (Transfer of Functions etc.) Act 1999 s.8, s.25; the Social Security Contributions and Benefits (Transfer of Functions etc.) (Northern Ireland) Order 1999 (SI 1999 671) Art.7; and the Social Security Contributions and Benefits (Transfer of Functions etc.) (Northern Ireland) Order 1999 Art.23. In force: October 8, 2002; £2.50.

These Regulations amend the Social Security (Contributions) Regulations 2001 (SI 2001 1004), the Social Security (Crediting and Treatment of Contributions, and National Insurance Numbers) Regulations 2001 (SI 2001 769) and the Social Security (Crediting and Treatment of Contributions, and National Insurance Numbers) Regulations (Northern Ireland) 2001 (SR 2001 102). The Regulations provide for decisions to be taken by officers of the Board and accordingly appeallable to the tax appeal Commissioners. They set out the basic rule as to earnings periods in respect of earnings paid, or treated as paid, at regular intervals and provide a specific rule in relation to periods of the same length where the first such earnings period begins at the start of the year. The Regulations also enable an officer of the Commissioners of Inland Revenue to decide whether to issue a notice to a secondary contributor specifying a longer earnings period if he is satisfied that the employer's practice is to pay the greater part of the earnings from the employment at longer intervals.

4178. Contributions–employers

SOCIAL SECURITY (CONTRIBUTIONS) (AMENDMENT NO.5) REGULATIONS 2002, SI 2002 2929; made under the Social Security Contributions and Benefits Act 1992 Sch.1 para.6; and the Social Security Contributions and Benefits (Northern Ireland) Act 1992 Sch.1 para.6. In force: November 28, 2002; £1.75.

These Regulations amend the Social Security (Contributions) Regulations 2001 (SI 2001 1004) to amend the definition of "employer" to be the same as the secondary contributor and to provide that where a payment of emoluments is made by an intermediary of an employer, it is attributed to the employer for the purposes of collection provisions. They also provide for the employer to reimburse himself for contributions paid on behalf of employees, out of earnings, to cover such attributed payments.

4179. Contributions–intermediaries

SOCIAL SECURITY CONTRIBUTIONS (INTERMEDIARIES) (AMENDMENT) REGULATIONS 2002, SI 2002 703; made under the Social Security Contributions and Benefits Act 1992 s.4A, s.122, s.175. In force: April 6, 2002; £1.75.

These Regulations, which amend the Social Security Contributions (Intermediaries) Regulations 2000 (SI 2000 727), make amendments following the consolidation of regulations relating to national insurance contributions in the Social Security (Contributions) Regulations 2001 (SI 2001 1004). The Regulations extend the calculation of worker's attributable earnings so as to cater for cases where expenses are met by the worker and reimbursed by the intermediary, and cases involving mileage allowance relief and mileage allowance payments. They also amend the worker's attributable earnings so as to provide, in a case where the intermediary is a company which ceases to trade in the course of a year of assessment, that the deemed payment of worker's attributable earnings is treated as made on the date that the company ceases to trade and not on the later date of April 5, in that year.

4180. Contributions–payments to be disregarded

SOCIAL SECURITY (CONTRIBUTIONS) (AMENDMENT NO.4) REGULATIONS 2002, SI 2002 2924; made under the Social Security Contributions and Benefits Act 1992 s.3. In force: December 17, 2002; £1.50.

The Education (Teacher Student Loans) (Repayment etc.) Regulations 2002 (SI 2002 2086) make provision for the repayment or reduction of amounts payable in respect of student loans of newly qualified teachers. These Regulations amend the Social Security (Contributions) Regulations 2001 (SI 2001 1004) by specifying payments in respect of such loans and payments discharging any income tax liability relating to such payments, as payments which are to be disregarded in the calculation of earnings from employed earner's employment for the purpose of earnings-related contributions.

4181. Contributions–statutory sick pay and statutory maternity pay

SOCIAL SECURITY CONTRIBUTIONS (DECISIONS AND APPEALS) (AMENDMENT) REGULATIONS 2002, SI 2002 3120; made under the Social Security Contributions (Transfer of Functions, etc.) Act 1999 s.9, s.11, s.13, s.24, s.25; and the Social Security Contributions (Decisions and Appeals) Regulations 1999 (SI 1999 1027) Art.8, Art.10, Art.12, Art.23. In force: January 7, 2003; £1.50.

These Regulations amend the Social Security Contributions (Decisions and Appeals) Regulations 1999 (SI 1999 1027) by replacing all references to statutory sick pay or statutory maternity pay with references to statutory sick pay, statutory maternity pay, statutory paternity pay or statutory adoption pay. Statutory paternity pay and statutory adoption pay are introduced, for employees whose place of employment is in Great Britain, by the Employment Act 2002 Part 1 Ch.1 and, for those whose place of employment is in Northern Ireland, by the corresponding provisions of the Employment (Northern Ireland) Order 2002 (SI 2002 2836 (NI.2)).

4182. Disability living allowance–attendance allowance–residential care homes and nursing homes

SOCIAL SECURITY AMENDMENT (RESIDENTIAL CARE AND NURSING HOMES) REGULATIONS 2002, SI 2002 398; made under the Social Security Contributions and Benefits Act 1992 s.123, s.135, s.137, s.175; the Social Security Administration Act 1992 s.5, s.189; the Jobseekers Act 1995 s.4, s.35, s.36; and the Social Security Act 1998 s.10, s.84. In force: April 8, 2002; £1.75.

These Regulations amend the Social Security (Claims and Payments) Regulations 1987 (SI 1987 1968), the Social Security and Child Support (Decisions and Appeals) Regulations 1999 (SI 1999 991) and the Security Amendment (Residential Care and Nursing Homes) Regulations 2001 (SI 2001 3767) so as to make further provision and consequential amendments in connection with the cessation, from April 8, 2002, of the payment of special amounts applicable to recipients of income support and jobseeker's allowance who are in residential care homes and nursing homes.

4183. Disability living allowance–conditions of entitlement–mental disability

SOCIAL SECURITY (DISABILITY LIVING ALLOWANCE) (AMENDMENT) REGULATIONS 2002, SI 2002 648; made under the Social Security Contributions and Benefits Act 1992 s.73, s.175. In force: April 8, 2002; £1.50.

These Regulations amend the Social Security (Disability Living Allowance) Regulations 1991 (SI 1991 2890) in relation to the conditions of entitlement to the mobility component of a disability living allowance. They provide that a person does not meet the condition of the Social Security Contributions and Benefits Act 1992 s.73 if the reason he or she does not take advantage of the faculty of walking out of doors unaccompanied is fear or anxiety. This provision does not apply where the fear or anxiety is a symptom of a mental disability and so severe as to prevent the person from taking advantage of the faculty of walking out of doors unaccompanied.

4184. Earnings factors–calculation of additional pension

SOCIAL SECURITY REVALUATION OF EARNINGS FACTORS ORDER 2002, SI 2002 519; made under the Social Security Administration Act 1992 s.148, s.189. In force: April 6, 2002; £1.75.

This Order directs that the earnings factors relevant to the calculation of the additional pension in the rate of any long-term benefit or of any guaranteed minimum pension, or to any other calculation required under the Pension Schemes Act 1993, are to be increased for specified tax years. In addition, this Order provides for the rounding of fractional amounts for earnings factors relevant to the calculation of the additional pension in the rate of any long term benefit.

4185. Electronic communications–statutory payment schemes

STATUTORY PAYMENT SCHEMES (ELECTRONIC COMMUNICATIONS) REGULATIONS 2002, SI 2002 3047; made under the Finance Act 1999 s.132, s.133. In force: January 1, 2003; £1.75.

These Regulations provide for the delivery by electronic means of information in respect of statutory maternity pay, statutory paternity pay and statutory adoption pay and the making of payments in connection with those forms of statutory pay either to or by the Board of Inland Revenue.

4186. Employees rights–statutory paternity and adoption pay

STATUTORY PATERNITY PAY AND STATUTORY ADOPTION PAY (GENERAL) REGULATIONS 2002, SI 2002 2822; made under the Social Security Contributions and Benefits Act 1992 s.171ZA, s.171ZB, s.171ZC, s.171ZD, s.171ZE, s.171ZG, s.171ZJ, s.171ZL, s.171ZM, s.171ZN, s.171ZP, s.171ZS, s.175; and the Social Security Administration Act 1992 s.5. In force: December 8, 2002; £3.50.

These Regulations make provision relating to statutory paternity pay and statutory adoption pay.

4187. Fraud–request for information–specified organisations

SOCIAL SECURITY ADMINISTRATION ACT 1992 (AMENDMENT) ORDER 2002, SI 2002 817; made under the Social Security Administration Act 1992 s.109B, s.189. In force: April 1, 2002; £1.75.

The Social Security Fraud Act 2001 provides for officers authorised under the Social Security Administration Act 1992 to require information about individuals from specified private and public sector organisations. This Order amends s.109B of the 1992 Act by adding to the list of organisations the Director of National Savings, gas distributors and electricity distributors.

4188. Guardians allowance–custodial sentences

SOCIAL SECURITY (GUARDIAN'S ALLOWANCES) AMENDMENT REGULATIONS 2002, SI 2002 492; made under the Social Security Contributions and Benefits Act 1992 s.77, s.122, s.175. In force: April 1, 2002; £1.75.

These Regulations amend the Social Security (Guardian's Allowances) Regulations 1975 (SI 1975 515) in relation to the circumstances in which a person is to be treated as being in prison for the purposes of Social Security Contributions and Benefits Act 1992. The Regulations reduce the minimum length of custodial sentence from five to two years and include persons who are ordered by a court to be detained in hospital under the Mental Health Act 1983 or the Criminal Procedure (Scotland) Act 1995 following conviction and under the Criminal Procedure (Insanity) Act 1964 or the Criminal Appeal Act 1968 following a verdict of not guilty by reason of insanity or a finding that the accused was under a disability or under the Criminal Procedure (Scotland) Act 1995 following an acquittal on the grounds of insanity or a finding of insanity.

4189. Housing benefit–council tax benefit–childcare charges

HOUSING BENEFIT AND COUNCIL TAX BENEFIT (CHILD CARE CHARGES) REGULATIONS 2002, SI 2002 499; made under the Social Security Contributions and Benefits Act 1992 s.123, s.136, s.137, s.175. In force: April 1, 2002; £1.50.

These Regulations amend the Benefit (General) Regulations 1987 (SI 1987 1971) and the Council Tax Benefit (General) Regulations 1992 (SI 1992 1814) which stipulate that for Housing Benefit and Council Tax Benefit purposes, certain specified "relevant child care charges" shall be deducted from the income of a claimant when calculating entitlement to benefit. These Regulations enlarge and update the category of "relevant child care charges" to take account of changes to the Children Act 1989 brought in by the Care Standards Act 2000, in respect of England and Wales and provisions in the Regulation of Care (Scotland) Act 2001, which replace the relevant provisions in the Children Act 1989 in respect of Scotland.

4190. Housing benefit–entitlement–human rights–father of child also landlord of parent with care–validity of regulation

[Human Rights Act 1998 Sch.1 Part I Art.8, Art.14; Housing Benefit (General) Amendment (No.2) Regulations 1998 (SI 1998 3257) Reg.7(1) (d).]

T appealed against a ruling ([2001] EWHC Admin 260, [2001] A.C.D. 74) dismissing her challenge to the validity of the Housing Benefit (General)

Amendment (No.2) Regulations 1998 Reg.7(1)(d) whereby a tenant who was responsible for a child of the landlord was treated as not liable to make payments in respect of the dwelling. T contended that (1) the Secretary of State's decision to amend the Regulations as he did was *Wednesbury* unreasonable and disproportionate since there was no basis for the underlying assumption that a parent should be responsible for providing accommodation for his child; (2) there should have been a reverse burden of proof provision and that it was unreasonable not to provide transitional provisions excluding T, who was a recipient of housing benefit under the previous Regulations, and who would have ordered her life accordingly, and (3) the Regulations contravened the Human Rights Act 1998 Sch.1 Part I Art.8 and Art.14.

Held, dismissing the appeal, that (1) the judge was correct in finding that irrationality was not proved and that assumption underlying Regulation 7(1)(d)'s was based on a rational belief that where the tenant was a parent and carer of the landlord's child, the landlord would not generally consider the tenancy in the usual commercial manner; (2) the absence of a reverse burden of proof was not unreasonable as it was hard to refute evidence of a tenancy provided by the tenant or landlord. The lack of transitional provisions could not form a successful basis of challenge having regard to the need to prevent significant abuse of the housing benefit system, and (3) there was no contravention of T's rights pursuant to the Human Rights Act 1998 Sch.1 Part I Art.8 and Art.14 since the provision was in pursuit of a legitimate aim, namely the prevention of abuse, and was not disproportionate.

R. (ON THE APPLICATION OF TUCKER) v. SECRETARY OF STATE FOR SOCIAL SECURITY; *sub nom.* TUCKER v. SECRETARY OF STATE FOR SOCIAL SECURITY, [2001] EWCA Civ 1646, [2002] H.L.R. 27, Waller L.J., CA.

4191. **Housing benefit–Housing Benefit Review Board–presence of local councillors on Board–risk of bias–right to review by independent tribunal**

[Social Security Administration Act 1992 s.63; Human Rights Act 1998 Sch.1 Part I Art.6.]

B challenged a decision of N's Housing Benefit Review Board to refuse him housing benefit. The Board had held that B had not proven that he was liable for rent at the property where he lived as there were a number of inconsistencies and unanswered questions in the evidence presented by him. B argued that, as the Board consisted of N's councillors, it was not an independent and impartial tribunal and that his rights under the common law and under the Human Rights Act 1998 Sch.1 Part I Art.6 had therefore been infringed.

Held, granting the application for judicial review, that B did have a common law right for his case to be heard by an independent tribunal and that right had been infringed. B had a right to a review of the determination of his application for housing benefit under the Social Security Administration Act 1992 s.63. Such a right to review was essentially no different from a right of access to a court; accordingly the Board was required to act with procedural fairness and impartiality. It was therefore not necessary to consider B's rights under the 1998 Act but authorities relating to the application of that statute were relevant to the common law right. Although there were safeguards in place sufficient to ensure procedural fairness in hearings before the Board, the councillors were so closely aligned to the interests of N that their presence on the Board meant that there was a real risk of bias which, given the fact finding nature of Board hearings, was not capable of cure by an appellate court, *R. (on the application of Holding & Barnes Plc) v. Secretary of State for the Environment, Transport and the Regions* [2001] UKHL 23, [2001] 2 W.L.R. 1389, [2001] C.L.Y. 4761 applied.

R. (ON THE APPLICATION OF BEWRY) v. NORWICH CITY COUNCIL, [2001] EWHC Admin 657, [2002] H.R.L.R. 2, Moses, J., QBD (Admin Ct).

4192. Housing benefit–ill health–dependency of applicant on carer–commercial basis of living arrangement–findings of fact

[Housing Benefit (General) Regulations 1987 (SI 1987 1971).]

T applied for judicial review of the dismissal of his appeal against the refusal of his claim for housing benefit. It was contended for T, who suffered from Alzheimer's disease, that the Housing Benefit Review Board had failed to give adequate reasons for its decision that T did not reside with his carer on a commercial basis with the result that he was not eligible for housing benefit, and that the decision was irrational.

Held, granting the application for judicial review, that although it was not irrational for the board to have found that T's residence was not on a commercial basis, material findings of fact both supporting and against the decision were required to be set out pursuant to the Housing Benefit (General) Regulations 1987 and it was not sufficient for the Board to provide only the reasons for its conclusions.

R. (ON THE APPLICATION OF T) v. RICHMOND UPON THAMES LBC; *sub nom.* R. v. RICHMOND UPON THAMES LBC, *ex p.* T (2001) 33 H.L.R. 65, Elias, J., QBD (Admin Ct).

4193. Housing benefit–landlords–overpayment of benefits–recovery of overpayment from landlord

[Housing Benefit (General) Regulations 1987 (SI 1987 1971) Reg.82(2)(c), Sch.6 para.14(2)(c).]

G appealed against the dismissal of his claim for the recovery of housing benefit payable to him as landlord in respect of a tenant. The local authority had deemed that housing benefit had been overpaid to G because the tenant had not actually been in occupation of G's premises. The local authority had therefore set off the overpayment against rent payable to G by another tenant. G contended that the local authority had failed to comply with the statutory procedure governing the recovery of housing benefit. G submitted that (1) pursuant to the Housing Benefit (General) Regulations 1987 Reg.82(2)(c) he should not have been deprived of attending a Review Board hearing of the authority's decision whilst the other witnesses were giving evidence; (2) the Review Board had been under a statutory obligation to give reasons for its decision and that the reasons it gave were inadequate, and (3) the procedure followed in recovering the overpayment was defective so as to cause him such prejudice that the council could not be allowed to retain the money they had obtained through set off.

Held, dismissing the appeal, that (1) although G should not have been excluded from the Review Board hearing save in exceptional circumstances, the fact that he was excluded from attending the hearing had not prejudiced his case in any way; (2) there could have been no doubt in G's mind as to why the Review Board had reached its decision, and the Chairman did not need to give a detailed explanation of the reasons, and (3) a local authority recovering overpayments of housing benefits by deducting it from housing benefits payable to a landlord in respect of other tenants, was obliged to notify affected persons by a further notice of determination which conferred a right of appeal. That right of appeal only applied to a decision referred to in Sch.6 para.14(2)(c) of the Regulations. However, any prejudice caused to G by a notice of determination not being given before the actual recovery of the overpayment, was minimal, given that the overpayment was recoverable and the time period, short.

GODWIN v. ROSSENDALE BC; *sub nom.* GODWIN v. ROSENDALE BC, [2002] EWCA Civ 726, [2003] H.L.R. 9, Peter Gibson, L.J., CA.

4194. Housing benefit–local authorities powers and duties–criteria relevant to restriction of benefit

[Housing Benefit (General) Regulations 1987 (SI 1987 1971) Reg.10(6B).]

L challenged a decision of the Housing Benefit Review Board to restrict his eligible rent for housing benefit purposes pursuant to the Housing Benefit

(General) Regulations 1987 Reg.10(6B). Following an increase in the rent due in respect of the premises which L occupied, the local authority, W, conducted a review as a result of which it was maintained that there were cheaper properties in the locality which L could occupy. A decision was subsequently taken to restrict L's rent on the basis that to do so would not cause exceptional hardship to L and his family. L contended that in reaching its decision the Board had failed to take into account certain relevant information concerning his personal and financial situation.

Held, granting the application for judicial review, that on the plain wording of the statute it was clear that Reg.10(6B) conferred a wide discretion upon a local authority to take into account all relevant circumstances, *R. v. Macclesfield BC Housing Benefit Review Board, ex p. Temsamani* (Unreported, February 24, 1999) considered, and the Board had been wrong not to take into account matters such as L's personal financial circumstances before invoking Reg.10(6B).

R. (ON THE APPLICATION OF LAALI) v. WESTMINSTER HOUSING BENEFIT REVIEW BOARD; *sub nom.* R. (ON THE APPLICATION OF LAALI) v. WESTMINSTER CITY COUNCIL [2002] H.L.R. 8, Silber, J., QBD (Admin Ct).

4195. **Housing benefit–rent–apportionment to include full time student**

[Housing Benefit (General) Regulations 1987 (SI 1987 1971) Reg.10(5); Housing Benefit (General) Regulations 1987 Reg.48A.]

N appealed against the decision ([2001] EWHC Admin 813) that in assessing his entitlement to housing benefit, the local authority had correctly apportioned the rent payable on his property. N lived with his wife, mother in law, daughter and son, who was a student. The local authority had assessed them as each being liable for one fifth of the rent. N had argued that his son, as a full time student, should not have been included in the calculation. The Housing Benefit (General) Regulations 1987 Reg.10(5) provided that where more than one person was liable to make payments on a dwelling, the payments "should be apportioned for the purpose of calculating the eligible rent for each such person". It was not disputed that the son was not entitled to claim housing benefit by virtue of Reg.48A, which stated that in apportioning rent for the purposes of housing benefit a full time student should be treated as if not liable to make any payments for the dwelling. N contended that the deeming provision in Reg.48(A) applied to any part of the Regulations where his son's liability to make payment was in issue, and that accordingly his son did not fall within Reg.10(5).

Held, dismissing the appeal, that in apportioning rent amongst those persons liable to pay rent on an individual property pursuant to Reg.10(5) of the 1987 Regulations for the purposes of assessing entitlement to housing benefit, a full time student should not be excluded from the apportionment. The scope of deeming provisions should be limited to what was necessary in order to achieve their statutory purpose. The deeming provision in Reg.48A was limited to ensuring that full time students did not usually receive housing benefit, in line with the policy that students obtained their financial support from the educational maintenance system. A broader application of Reg.48A would lead to unjust results.

R. (ON THE APPLICATION OF NAGHSHBANDI) v. CAMDEN LBC; *sub nom.* NAGHSHBANDI v. CAMDEN LBC, [2002] EWCA Civ 1038, [2003] H.L.R. 21, Schiemann, L.J., CA.

4196. **Housing benefit–tenancies–referrals**

HOUSING BENEFIT (GENERAL) AMENDMENT REGULATIONS 2002, SI 2002 2322; made under the Social Security Contributions and Benefits Act 1992 s.123, s.130, s.137, s.175; and the Housing Act 1996 s.122. In force: October 7, 2002; £1.50.

These Regulations further amend the Housing Benefit (General) Regulations 1987 (SI 1987 1971) which provide for a scheme whereby housing benefit is payable to persons liable to make certain payments in respect of a dwelling occupied as their home. They make amendments so that a tenancy in respect of a dwelling whose ownership has been transferred on or after October 7, 2002, with the consent of the Secretary of State, Scottish Ministers or the National Assembly for Wales, or to a person approved by the Housing Corporation, must be referred to a rent officer only where the rent payable under the tenancy has been increased since the transfer and the local authority considers the rent to be unreasonably high. Such a tenancy need no longer be referred to the rent officer on the ground that the local authority considers the dwelling to be larger than the claimant reasonably requires.

4197. Housing benefit–voluntary workers–recovery of over payment–legal liability to pay rent

[Social Security Contributions and Benefits Act 1992 s.130 (1) (a); Housing Benefit (General) Regulations (SI 1987 1971) 1987 r.6 (1) (a).]

TW sought to challenge two decisions of the Housing Benefit Review Board that G, an Austrian voluntary worker and TW's licensee, was not eligible for housing benefit pursuant to the Social Security Contributions and Benefits Act 1992 s.130(1) (a) and the Housing Benefits General Regulations 1987 r.6 (1) (a), as she was not liable to pay rent in respect of the dwelling house in which she lived and that housing benefit that had been paid directly to TW, on behalf of G, be recovered as an overpayment. TW, who housed a number of volunteers participating in the European Voluntary Service Scheme, submitted that the review board (1) had erred in its approach to the question of whether there was a legal liability upon G to pay rent as it was unnecessary for TW to demonstrate that they would commence proceedings to recover unpaid charges in order to establish a legally enforceable obligation; (2) had erred in exercising its discretion to recover benefits already paid, as TW had acted in good faith and had sought prior confirmation of the volunteers' eligibility for housing benefit, and (3) had failed to provided adequate reasons for its decision and had failed to refer to the evidence of TW's directors in its written reasons.

Held, dismissing the application, that (1) the board, having considered the material before it, particularly G's understanding of her obligations, had been entitled to concluded that TW had no intention of creating a legal obligation in relation to the payment of rent; (2) the board's decision to recover benefits could not be regarded as either perverse or wrong, and (3) the board had considered all the relevant evidence, correctly concluding that the evidence of TW's directors was marginal. Moreover, the finding was not made inadequate by a failure to make specific reference to that evidence within their reasons.

R. v. DERBY CITY COUNCIL, *ex p.* THIRD WAVE HOUSING LTD (2001) 33 H.L.R. 61, Gibbs, J., QBD.

4198. Incapacity benefit–allowances

SOCIAL SECURITY (INCAPACITY) (MISCELLANEOUS AMENDMENTS) (NO.2) REGULATIONS 2002, SI 2002 2311; made under the Social Security Contributions and Benefits Act 1992 s.30A, s.30E, s.122, s.171D, s.171G, s.175, Sch.7 para.2. In force: Reg.3(2): January 1, 2003; remainder: October 1, 2002; £1.50.

These Regulations amend the Social Security (General Benefit) Regulations 1982 (SI 1982 1408), the Social Security (Incapacity Benefit) Regulations 1994 (SI 1994 2946) and the Social Security (Incapacity for Work) (General) Regulations 1995 (SI 1995 311) so as to increase the amount which can be earned before disqualification from unemployability supplement to £3,510; to increase the earnings limit for councillor's allowance to £67.50; and to increase to £67.50 the weekly limit for earnings from work which may be undertaken by a person without his being treated as being capable of work.

4199. **Incapacity benefit–EC law–industrial injuries–migrant workers–eligibility for occupational disability pension–qualifying periods**

[EC Treaty Art.39, Art.42; Council Regulation 1408/71 on the application of social security schemes to employed persons and their families moving within the community; Council Regulation 118/97 on the application of social security schemes to employed persons, to self employed persons and to members of their families moving within the Community; General Law on Social Security (Austria) para.235(3)(a); General Law on Social Security (Austria) para.235(2)(b.]

The Austrian Supreme Court sought a preliminary ruling on the interpretation of EC Treaty Art.39 and Art.42 and also Council Regulation 1408/71. The reference followed proceedings brought by D, who suffered an industrial accident in 1968 while he was working in Germany, against PA, the Austrian Salaried Employees' Pension Insurance Institution. D's initial application for an Austrian occupational disability pension with effect from January 1, 1994 was rejected by PA. His appeal against the decision was rejected by the Supreme Court, on the grounds, that he had not completed the qualifying period of 60 months during the reference period of 120 months and that he was not covered by the exceptions laid down in the General Law on Social Security para.235(3)(a) para.236(3) and para.234(1)(2)(b). A further application with a different start date of January 1, 1998 was also rejected on the same grounds. D eventually returned to the Supreme Court on a point of law and the court decided to stay proceedings and seek a preliminary ruling as to the applicability of the Regulation to events before the accession of Austria to the EU and whether Art.9a of the Regulation was compatible with Art.39 and Art.42 given that it appeared to make the position of migrant workers less favourable than that of settled workers.

Held, giving a preliminary ruling, that (1) the situation of a national of a Member State who, before that State's accession to the EU, was employed in another Member State where he was the victim of an accident at work, and who, after the accession of his home State, applied to the authorities in that State for a pension for incapacity for work as a result of that accident fell within the scope of application of the Regulation; (2) Art.94(3) of the Regulation, as amended and updated by Council Regulation 118/97 read in conjunction with Art.39(2), had to be interpreted as precluding a national provision such as para.235(3)(a), which restricted rights to an occupational disability pension by excluding consideration of work in other Member States; (3) Art.39(2) and Art.42 had to be interpreted as meaning that they precluded a provision such as para.234(1)(2)(b), read in conjunction with para.236(3), because in its consideration of reference periods for benefits it took no account of benefits paid in another Member State, and (4) Art.9a of the Regulation, as amended, was incompatible with Art.39 and Art.42 insofar as it disregarded periods during which industrial accident benefits were paid under the legislation of another Member State and was therefore invalid.

DUCHON v. PENSIONSVERSICHERUNGSANSTALT DER ANGESTELLTEN (C290/00) [2002] 2 C.M.L.R. 23, P Jann (President), ECJ.

4200. **Incapacity benefit–entitlement**

SOCIAL SECURITY (INCAPACITY) (MISCELLANEOUS AMENDMENTS) REGULATIONS 2002, SI 2002 491; made under the Social Security Contributions and Benefits Act 1992 s.171D, s.171G, s.175; the Social Security (Incapacity for Work) Act 1994 s.4; and the Welfare Reform and Pensions Act 1999 s.85. In force: Reg.4: April 5, 2002; remainder: April 8, 2002; £2.00.

These Regulations, which amend the Social Security (Incapacity Benefit) Regulations 1994 (SI 1994 2946) and the Social Security (Incapacity for Work) (General) Regulations 1995 (SI 1995 311), amend the Social Security (Incapacity Benefit) (Transitional) Regulations 1995 (SI 1995 310) as they relate to the circumstances in which a person is to be treated as capable of work for the purposes of entitlement to certain social security benefits. The Regulations make amendments in connection with the categories of work which may be undertaken by a person without his being treated as being capable of work. In particular, the requirement that some categories of work may be undertaken only on medical advice has been replaced with a requirement that notice must be given to the Secretary of State that the work is being done.

4201. Incapacity benefit–entitlement–amendment to regulation–statutorily prescribed procedure–Social Security Advisory Committee

[Social Security Administration Act 1992 s.172; Social Security (Incapacity for Work) (General) Regulations 1995 (SI 1995 311) Reg.27; Social Security (Incapacity for Work and Miscellaneous Amendments) Regulations 1996 (SI 1996 3207) Reg.2(27).]

H, who suffered from a heart condition, appealed against the finding that he was no longer entitled to receive incapacity benefit pursuant to the Social Security (Incapacity for Work) (General) Regulations 1995 Reg.27. The 1995 Regulations had been amended by the Social Security (Incapacity for Work and Miscellaneous Amendments) Regulations 1996 Reg.2(27) which removed Reg.27(b) under which H had previously been entitled to benefit. H argued that the 1996 amendments were invalid as the Secretary of State had failed to comply with the statutory provisions governing the procedure for making and amending Regulations. Under the Social Security Administration Act 1992 s.172 the Secretary of State was obliged to refer Regulation amendments to the Social Security Advisory Committee unless, under s.173 of the Act, the Committee had agreed that the matter should not be referred. The Advisory Committee had been incorrectly informed that the amended Reg.27 would continue to provide support to those who were entitled to benefit under the old Reg.27(b) and S submitted that they had therefore been misled into agreeing that a referral was unnecessary.

Held, allowing the appeal, that the new Reg.27 was invalid and H should continue to be assessed under the provisions of the original Reg.27(b). The 1992 Act introduced procedural rules which reflected Parliament's intention that the Secretary of State should not enact substantive changes to Regulations without having first referred the matter to the Advisory Committee and received their report. Where the Secretary of State had misled the Committee, and the provision of the correct information would have led to a referral, then it was manifest that procedure had not been complied with. The subordinate legislation enacted pursuant to the 1992 Act was of general application and it was clear that the court had jurisdiction to declare Regulations invalid in cases where specific procedure was not followed, *Boddington v. British Transport Police* [1999] 2 A.C. 143, [1998] C.L.Y. 89 followed.

HOWKER v. SECRETARY OF STATE FOR WORK AND PENSIONS, [2002] EWCA Civ 1623, [2003] I.C.R. 405, Peter Gibson, L.J., CA.

4202. Incapacity benefit–equal treatment–males qualifying at age 57 and females at 55–compatibility with Council Directive 79/7 Art.7(1)(a)

[Council Directive 79/7 on equal treatment for men and women in matters of social security Art.7.]

B's application for an incapacity pension was refused on the basis that he had not yet reached 57 years of age, as required by the relevant national legislation, whereas women qualified on reaching 55 years of age. The refusal was upheld at first instance and B appealed to the Supreme Court, which referred a number of questions to the ECJ for a preliminary ruling on the interpretation of Council Directive 79/7 Art.7(1)(a).

Held, giving a preliminary ruling, that (1) the incapacity pension claimed by B was not an old age pension in terms of Art.7(1)(a), *Secretary of State for Social Security v. Thomas (C328/91)* [1993] Q.B. 747, [1993] C.L.Y. 4368 followed; (2) the discriminatory effect was not intended to preserve the balance of the social security system and its removal would not therefore upset that balance; (3) there was no exact correlation between the qualifying ages for the incapacity pension and statutory retirement ages, so that the discriminatory effect of the age differential was not required to preserve coherence between various social security schemes and therefore did not come within the derogation permitted by Art.7(1)(a), and (4) there were no grounds for limiting the temporal effects of the judgment as the compatibility of the national legislation in question with Art.7(1)(a) could have been assessed as at the date it came into force.

BUCHNER v. SOZIALVERSICHERUNGSANSTALT DER BAUERN (C104/98) [2002] 1 C.M.L.R. 39, Rodriguez Iglesias (President), ECJ.

4203. Income–capital–assessment

NATIONAL ASSISTANCE (ASSESSMENT OF RESOURCES) (AMENDMENT) (ENGLAND) REGULATIONS 2002, SI 2002 410; made under the National Assistance Act 1948 s.22. In force: April 8, 2002; £1.50.

These Regulations amend the National Assistance (Assessment of Resources) Regulations 1992 (SI 1992 2977), which concern the assessment of the ability of a person to pay for accommodation arranged by local authorities under the National Assistance Act 1948, by increasing specified capital limits. They also amend the National Assistance (Assessment of Resources) (Amendment) (No.2) (England) Regulations 2001 (SI 2001 1066).

4204. Income–capital–assessment–Wales

NATIONAL ASSISTANCE (ASSESSMENT OF RESOURCES) (AMENDMENT) (WALES) REGULATIONS 2002, SI 2002 814; made under the National Assistance Act 1948 s.22. In force: April 8, 2002; £1.75.

These Regulations amend the National Assistance (Assessment of Resources) Regulations 1992 (SI 1992 2977) which concern the assessment of the ability of a person to pay for accommodation arranged by local authorities under the National Assistance Act 1948 Part III. The 1992 Regulations also provide that no resident shall be assessed as unable to pay for Part III accommodation at the standard rate if that resident's capital calculated in accordance with the principal Regulations, exceeds £18,500 and provide for the calculation of a resident's income to take account of capital which is treated as equivalent to income. These Regulations increase the capital limit to £19,000 and amend the upper and lower limits of such capital between which each complete £250, or any part which is not a complete £250 is treated as to a weekly income of £1.

4205. Income–residential accommodation–assessment of resources

NATIONAL ASSISTANCE (ASSESSMENT OF RESOURCES) (AMENDMENT) (NO.2) (ENGLAND) REGULATIONS 2002, SI 2002 2531; made under the National Assistance Act 1948 s.22. In force: in accordance with Reg.1; £1.75.

These Regulations amend the National Assistance (Assessment of Resources) Regulations 1992 (SI 1992 2977) which concern the assessment of the ability of a person to pay for accommodation arranged by local authorities under the National Assistance Act 1948 Part III. They allow all periodical payments received by virtue of any agreement or court order to make personal injury payments to the resident, to the extent that they are not a payment of income, to be treated as income; provide that payments of income received from all trusts whose funds derive from personal injury payments to a resident, from an annuity purchased with such funds and those received by virtue of any agreement or court order to make personal injury payments to the resident be disregarded in their entirety when intended and used for any item not taken into account when the standard rate was fixed for the accommodation provided; and maintain the current position regarding the treatment of arrears of various social security benefits in the financial assessment of a resident's capital and removes a reference to a paragraph of the Income Support (General) Regulations 1987 (SI 1987 1967).

4206. Income related benefits—subsidy to authorities

INCOME-RELATED BENEFITS (SUBSIDY TO AUTHORITIES) AMENDMENT ORDER 2002, SI 2002 1859; made under the Social Security Administration Act 1992 s.140B, s.140F, s.189. In force: August 17, 2002; £6.00.

This Order, which amends the Income-Related Benefits (Subsidy to Authorities) Order 1998 (SI 1998 562), provides that the additional subsidy payable to Scottish Homes is not to exceed £682,145 and provides a new schedule of figures to be used in calculating the subsidy payable in respect of rent allowances. It also provides a new table of figures to be used in calculating thresholds for a reduced subsidy in respect of rent allowances, amends the method by which the benefit savings threshold is calculated and makes a small remedial amendment to the subsidy due to Sefton Council for the year commencing on April 1, 2000.

4207. Income related benefits—subsidy to authorities

INCOME-RELATED BENEFITS (SUBSIDY TO AUTHORITIES) AMENDMENT (NO.2) ORDER 2002, SI 2002 3116; made under the Social Security Administration Act 1992 s.140B, s.104F, s.189. In force: January 13, 2003; £1.75.

This Order amends the Income-related Benefits (Subsidy to Authorities) Order 1998 (SI 1998 562) which provides for subsidy to be payable to authorities administering housing benefit and council tax benefit by making further provision for subsidy payments in relation to a scheme which introduces new terms, including incentives and rewards, relating to local authorities' anti-fraud activities.

4208. Income support—EC law—meaning of "habitually resident"

[Income Support (General) Regulations 1987 (SI 1987 1967) Reg.21 (3); Council Regulation 1408/71 on the application of social security schemes to employed persons and their families moving within the Community Art.1 (h).]

G, a British citizen originally resident in Cyprus, appealed against the decision of the Commissioner that she was not "habitually resident" in the United Kingdom four weeks after her arrival and was therefore a "person from abroad" for the purposes of the Income Support (General) Regulations 1987 Reg.21 (3). The Commissioner, applying the decision of the House of Lords in *Nessa v. Chief Adjudication Officer* [1999] 1 W.L.R. 1937, [1999] C.L.Y. 4564, had found that habitual residence required a person to have lived in the UK for an appreciable period. The issue before the court was whether the interpretation of the term "residence" by the ECJ in the case of *Swaddling v. Adjudication Officer (C90/97)* [1999] All E.R. (EC) 217, [1999] C.L.Y. 4565, which differed from that of the House of Lords in *Nessa*, could be applied to the instant case. The decision in *Swaddling* related to Council Regulation 1408/71. By virtue of Art.1 (h) of that Regulation, the term "residence" meant "habitual residence".

Held, dismissing the appeal, that the Commissioner had not erred in applying *Nessa*, the authority of which had not been altered or eroded by the conclusion of the ECJ in *Swaddling*. The decision in *Swaddling* related to the free movement of migrant workers within the Community and there was no basis for applying the reasoning of the ECJ to the circumstances of the instant case. Moreover, the decision in *Swaddling* had not established a rule of Community law in relation to the interpretation of the term "habitual residence" and accordingly there was no requirement to transpose the ECJ's findings into all domestic law containing that term, *Swaddling* and *ICI Plc v. Colmer (Inspector of Taxes) (C264/96)* [1999] 1 W.L.R. 108, [1998] C.L.Y. 4620 considered and *Nessa* applied.

GINGI v. SECRETARY OF STATE FOR WORK AND PENSIONS, [2001] EWCA Civ 1685, [2002] 1 C.M.L.R. 20, Buxton, L.J., CA.

4209. Income support–jobseekers allowance–lone parents–self employment route

INCOME SUPPORT (GENERAL) AND JOBSEEKER'S ALLOWANCE AMENDMENT REGULATIONS 2002, SI 2002 1411; made under the Social Security Contributions and Benefits Act 1992 s.123, s.136, s.137, s.175; and the Jobseekers Act 1995 s.12, s.35, s.36. In force: June 17, 2002; £1.50.

These Regulations amend the Income Support (General) Regulations 1987 (SI 1987 1967) and the Jobseeker's Allowance Regulations 1996 (SI 1996 207) so as to amend the definition of "self-employment route" to include assistance in pursuing self-employed earner's employment whilst participating in the New Deal for Lone Parents.

4210. Income support–loans–interest rate

INCOME SUPPORT (GENERAL) (STANDARD INTEREST RATE AMENDMENT) REGULATIONS 2002, SI 2002 105; made under the Social Security Contributions and Benefits Act 1992 s.123, s.135, s.137, s.175. In force: February 17, 2002; £1.50.

These Regulations amend the Income Support (General) Regulations 1987 (SI 1987 1967) with respect to the standard rate of interest applicable to a loan which qualifies for income support. The new rate is 5.74 per cent. In addition, the Regulations revoke Income Support (General) (Standard Interest Rate Amendment) (No.3) Regulations 2001 (SI 2001 3721) which made the previous amendment to that standard rate of interest.

4211. Income support–loans–interest rate

INCOME SUPPORT (GENERAL) (STANDARD INTEREST RATE AMENDMENT) (NO.2) REGULATIONS 2002, SI 2002 338; made under the Social Security Contributions and Benefits Act 1992 s.123, s.135, s.137, s.175. In force: March 17, 2002; £1.50.

These Regulations amend the Income Support (General) Regulations 1987 (SI 1987 1967) with respect to the standard rate of interest applicable to a loan which qualifies for income support under that Schedule to those Regulations. The new rate is 5.34 per cent. They also revoke the Income Support (General) (Standard Interest Rate Amendment) Regulations 2002 (SI 2002 105), with a saving provision, which made the previous amendment to that standard rate of interest.

4212. Industrial injuries–compensation–adjustments to lower rate of incapacity benefit

WORKMEN'S COMPENSATION (SUPPLEMENTATION) (AMENDMENT) SCHEME 2002, SI 2002 718; made under the Social Security Contributions and Benefits Act 1992 Sch.8 para.2; and the Social Security Administration Act 1992 Sch.9 para.1. In force: April 10, 2002; £1.75.

This Scheme amends the Workmen's Compensation (Supplementation) Scheme 1982 (SI 1982 1489) by making adjustments to the rate of lesser incapacity allowance consequential upon the increase in the maximum rate of that allowance made by the Social Security Benefits Up-rating Order 2002 (SI 2002 668).

4213. Industrial injuries–dependants–permitted earnings limits

SOCIAL SECURITY (INDUSTRIAL INJURIES) (DEPENDENCY) (PERMITTED EARNINGS LIMITS) ORDER 2002, SI 2002 683; made under the Social Security Contributions and Benefits Act 1992 s.175, Sch.7 para.4. In force: April 8, 2002; £1.50.

Where a disablement pension with unemployability supplement is increased in respect of a child or children and the beneficiary is one of two persons who are spouses residing together or an unmarried couple, the Social Security Contributions and Benefits Act 1992 provides that the increase shall not be payable in respect of the first child if the other person's earnings are £150 a week or more and in respect of a further child for each complete £20 by which the earnings exceed £150. This Order, which amends the Social Security (Industrial Injuries) (Dependency) (Permitted Earnings Limits) Order 2001 (SI 2001 911), increases the amount of £150 to £155.

4214. Invalid care allowance–carers–meaning of "severely disabled person"

[Social Security Contributions and Benefits Act 1992 s.70(2), s.70(8).]

The Secretary of State appealed against the decision of the Social Security Commissioner that P was entitled to invalid care allowance during a period of 12 weeks when his elderly mother had been in hospital. P had failed to disclose to the Department of Social Security that his mother had been admitted to hospital and had continued to claim and be paid invalid care allowance. Upon it being discovered that his mother had been hospitalised, proceedings had been brought seeking to recover the sums paid. The Commissioner had found that, in respect of a certain period of her hospitalisation, P's mother had remained a "severely disabled person" for the purposes of the Social Security Contributions and Benefits Act 1992 s.70(2) even though attendance allowance was no longer payable to her. The Secretary of State had filed a notice of appeal seven months after the grant of permission.

Held, granting an extension of time and allowing the appeal, that (1) given the lack of prejudice to P and the importance of the legal issue to be determined, it was appropriate to grant the necessary extension of time, and (2) s.70(2) of the Act provided the exclusive definition of a "severely disabled person". To be regarded as a "severely disabled person", the disabled person had to be entitled to attendance allowance and attendance allowance was only payable for 28 days after the disabled person's admission to hospital. Invalid care allowance was payable only for as long as attendance allowance was payable to the disabled person. It followed that the Commissioner had erred in his conclusion.

PRIDDING v. SECRETARY OF STATE FOR WORK AND PENSIONS, [2002] EWCA Civ 306, [2002] C.P.L.R. 315, Keene, L.J., CA.

4215. Invalid care allowance–students–full time education–disentitlement– meaning of "supervised study"

[Social Security Contributions and Benefits Act 1992 s.70(3); Social Security (Invalid Care Allowance) Regulations 1976 (SI 1976 409) Reg.5(1), Reg.5(2).]

A student, F, appealed against the ruling of a social security commissioner to the effect that time engaged in private study away from university premises could be taken into account when assessing whether or not an individual was in full time education for the purposes of the Social Security Contributions and Benefits Act 1992 s.70(3) and the Social Security (Invalid Care Allowance) Regulations 1976 Reg.5(1). Prior to embarking on a university course, F had been in receipt of invalid care allowance in respect of the care of her mother. After the course commenced an adjudication officer concluded that F was no longer entitled to the allowance on the basis that she was in receipt of full time education. F's first instance appeal was dismissed and a subsequent appeal to a social security commissioner resulted in the decision under appeal. F contended that (1) under Reg.5(1) the phrase "attends a course of education" required physical presence at the educational establishment in question; and (2) that time spent studying away from the university premises should not be taken into account when calculating the hours spent in study for the purposes of Reg.5(2) since such study was not "supervised".

Held, dismissing the appeal, that (1) for the purposes of Reg.5, "attends a course at university" required enrolment upon a university course. Time spent studying away from the educational institution in question was capable of falling within the period of attendance; and (2) work done to meet the reasonable requirements of the course could usually be regarded as "supervised" study and it also required a degree of direction by, and answerability to, a supervisor although it was not necessary for the supervisor to be present at the time,

Wright-Turner v. Department for Social Development (Unreported, January 11, 2002) applied.

FLEMMING v. SECRETARY OF STATE FOR WORK AND PENSIONS, [2002] EWCA Civ 641, [2002] 1 W.L.R. 2322, Pill, L.J., CA.

4216. Jobseekers allowance–appeals–jurisdiction of tribunal following withdrawal of appeal

[Social Security (Adjudication) Regulations 1995 (1995 1801) Reg.3, Reg.6.]

R appealed against a decision of a social security commissioner to the effect that he did not have jurisdiction to overturn a decision of the Social Security Appeal Tribunal dismissing R's appeal against an adjudication officer's decision to disallow his claim for jobseeker's allowance. R had withdrawn his appeal to the Tribunal by letter in accordance with the Social Security (Adjudication) Regulations 1995 Reg.6 but notwithstanding this, the appeal had been heard and dismissed. The social security commissioner found that he had no jurisdiction to overturn the tribunal's decision, since the tribunal itself had had no such jurisdiction by virtue of the appeal having been withdrawn. R contended that as he had been unaware that he could not appeal in the first instance to the tribunal because of the withdrawal, he had not been in a position to seek permission to bring a fresh appeal out of time under Reg.3 of the 1995 Regulations, and had thereby suffered an injustice, *R. v. Secretary of State for the Home Department, ex p. Jeyeanthan* [2000] 1 W.L.R. 354, [1999] C.L.Y. 3162 cited.

Held, dismissing the appeal, that the instant case concerned lack of jurisdiction rather than procedural irregularities, *Jeyeanthan* distinguished. Any suggestion that jurisdictional requirements could be waived in the same way as procedural requirements would prove potentially hard to reconcile with established law, *Essex CC v. Essex Incorporated Congregational Church Union* [1963] A.C. 808, [1963] C.L.Y. 3432 considered.

RYDQVIST v. SECRETARY OF STATE FOR WORK AND PENSIONS, [2002] EWCA Civ 947, [2002] 1 W.L.R. 3343, Peter Gibson, L.J., CA.

4217. Jobseekers allowance–equal treatment–pregnant student's leave of absence–refusal of claim

[Jobseeker's Allowance Regulations 1996 (SI 1996 207) Reg.1 (3), Reg.4, Reg.15(a); Council Directive 79/7 on the progressive implementation of the principle of equal treatment for men and women in matters of social security.]

The Secretary of State appealed against the social security commissioner's finding that the Jobseeker's Allowance Regulations 1996 Reg.15(a) discriminated against pregnant students and thus breached the Council Directive 79/7. W, a full time university student, had been granted a leave of absence from her studies during her pregnancy. She had made a claim for jobseeker's allowance, but was refused on the grounds that she still held student status. The Secretary of State refuted the sexual discrimination claim, maintaining that the refusal had been based solely on W's student status.

Held, allowing the appeal, that Reg.15(a), read in conjunction with the definitions provided in Reg.1 (3) and Reg.4, defined student status so as to disqualify all full-time students, including those who interrupted their studies, from claiming jobseeker's allowance until the last day of the course or at such a time as the student either abandoned or was dismissed from the course. No specific distinction was made between male and female applicants, nor was there any reference to the possibility that a female applicant might be pregnant. Consequently, W's status as a student had been the only operating factor in the refusal of her claim and hence, the Regulations did not breach the principle of equal treatment. The court rejected W's further submission that the application of the Regulations imposed a financial hardship consequent upon her pregnancy

as no principle of EC law equated detriment with discrimination, *Webb v. EMO Air Cargo (UK) Ltd (C32/93)* [1994] Q.B. 718, [1994] C.L.Y. 4825 considered.
WALTER v. SECRETARY OF STATE FOR SOCIAL SECURITY; *sub nom.* SECRETARY OF STATE FOR SOCIAL SECURITY v. WALTER, [2001] EWCA Civ 1913, [2002] 1 C.M.L.R. 27, Keene, L.J., CA.

4218. Jobseekers allowance—joint claims

JOBSEEKER'S ALLOWANCE (JOINT CLAIMS) AMENDMENT REGULATIONS 2002, SI 2002 1701; made under the Jobseekers Act 1995 s.1, s.35, s.36. In force: October 28, 2002; £1.50.

These Regulations amend the Jobseeker's Allowance Regulations 1996 (SI 1996 207) by prescribing that a joint-claim couple shall include those childless couples where at least one member was born after October 28, 1957. They also allow one member of such a couple to continue to claim a jobseeker's allowance where that member was entitled to that allowance on October 27, 2002, but only until the member of the couple who is not entitled to an allowance on that day is notified that he or she is required to attend at a time and place specified by an employment officer.

4219. Jobseekers allowance—voluntary workers—available for employment

JOBSEEKER'S ALLOWANCE (AMENDMENT) REGULATIONS 2002, SI 2002 3072; made under the Jobseekers Act 1995 s.6, s.8, s.35, s.36. In force: in accordance with Reg.1; £1.75.

These Regulations amend the Jobseeker's Allowance Regulations 1996 (SI 1996 207) to provide that a person who is engaged in voluntary work shall be treated as available for employment if he is available to commence employment on receipt of one week's notice and is available for interview in connection with the opportunity of any such employment on receipt of 48 hours' notice; and that a person on statutory paternity leave or ordinary adoption leave shall not be regarded as being available for employment for the purposes of those regulations.

4220. National insurance—compulsory payments—non salaried workers—social function of scheme

[EC Treaty Art.81, Art.82, Art.86(2), Art.234.]

N, the body charged with operating a compulsory insurance scheme for non salaried craft workers in respect of accidents at work and occupational diseases, obtained an order against V, requiring the payment of contributions in respect of B, V's managing partner, for the period from 1992 to 1996. V appealed, contending that B had been covered by private insurance during the period in question and that the compulsory insurance scheme operated by N breached Community competition law. The national court stayed the proceedings and referred questions to the ECJ for a preliminary ruling, asking whether N was an economic undertaking, given the monopoly nature of the insurance scheme and the automatic payment of benefits for employed persons. N contended that the reference was inadmissible as the automatic payment of benefits had been abolished from January 1, 1998 and that the ECJ was not competent to give a ruling on the reference as only the Commission had the power to monitor and ensure compliance with EC Treaty Art.86(2).

Held, giving a preliminary ruling, that the reference was admissible as it was for the national court to determine the need for and scope of a reference under EC Treaty Art.234 and Art.86(2) could be relied upon in cases brought before the national courts which required a review of compliance with the conditions set out therein. The scheme operated by N pursued a social objective that was intended to protect workers against the economic effects of accidents at work and industrial diseases. The scheme was also subject to the principle of solidarity in that it was financed by contributions which were not proportionate to the risks covered, thereby providing a link between better paid workers and those who would otherwise be deprived of cover because of their low earnings. N was also subject to State supervision in terms both of its liability to pay benefits and the amount of contributions it levied, which were subject to ministerial approval. N therefore fulfilled a completely social function and was not an economic undertaking for the purposes of EC Treaty Art.81 and Art.82.

CISAL DI BATTISTELLO VENANZIO & CO SAS v. ISTITUTO NAZIONALE PER L'ASSICURAZIONE CONTRO GLI INFORTUNI SUL LAVORO (INAIL) (C218/00) [2002] 4 C.M.L.R. 24, S Von Bahr (President), ECJ.

4221. National insurance–contributions

SOCIAL SECURITY (CONTRIBUTIONS) (RE-RATING AND NATIONAL INSURANCE FUNDS PAYMENTS) ORDER 2002, SI 2002 830; made under the Social Security Administration Act 1992 s.141, s.142, s.143, s.144, s.189; the Social Security Administration (Northern Ireland) Act 1992 s.129, s.165; the Social Security Act 1993 s.2; and the Social Security (Northern Ireland) Order 1993 (SI 1993 592 (NI.2)) Art.4. In force: April 6, 2002; £1.75.

This Order, which amends the Social Security Contributions and Benefits Act 1992 and the Social Security Contributions and Benefits (Northern Ireland) Act 1992, reduces the rate of secondary Class 1 contributions from 11.9 per cent to 11.8 per cent. It increases from £3,955 to £4,025 the amount of earnings below which an earner may be excepted from liability for Class 2 contributions and amends the amount of a Class 3 contribution. The Order amends, from £4,535 to £4,615 and from £29,900 to £30,420 respectively, the lower and upper limits of profits or gains.

4222. National insurance–contributions–earning limits and threshold

SOCIAL SECURITY (CONTRIBUTIONS) (AMENDMENT) REGULATIONS 2002, SI 2002 238; made under the Social Security Contributions and Benefits Act 1992 s.5, s.175; and the Social Security Contributions and Benefits (Northern Ireland) Act 1992 s.5, s.171. In force: April 6, 2002; £1.50.

These Regulations amend the Social Security (Contributions) Regulations 2001 (SI 2001 1004) to combine the relevant annual changes to National Insurance Contributions for Great Britain and Northern Ireland in a single instrument. The Regulations specify the lower earnings limit, upper earnings limit, primary threshold and secondary threshold for the tax year beginning on April 6, 2002 and provide for the equivalents of the primary threshold and secondary threshold where an employed earner's earnings period is other than a week.

4223. National insurance contributions–employment status–computer consultant providing services to bank through service company

[Social Security Contributions and Benefits Act 1992; Social Security Contributions (Intermediaries) Regulations 2000 (SI 2000 727) Reg.6(1).]

B, a computer consultant, appealed against the Revenue's decision that he was to be treated as employed by a bank to which he supplied his services through a limited company which he had set up to act as a service company. The service company was an intermediary within the Social Security Contributions (Intermediaries) Regulations 2000 Reg.6(1). In 1994 B started supplying his services to a bank through the company, initially for six month periods and later for 12 months at a time. It was agreed that B would devote his time, attention, skill and ability full-time to the bank's requirements at such location as the bank might reasonably require. It was expressly stated that the agreement did not create an employer/employee relationship. In April 2001 B accepted a permanent position with the bank. The Revenue took the view that under the Social Security Contributions and Benefits Act 1992, as amended, payments to the service company from May 31, 2000 to November 29, 2000 should be treated as B's earnings on which the service company was liable to pay national insurance contributions (NIC).

Held, dismissing the appeal, that the label given by the parties to their relationship was not conclusive and the arrangement between B and the bank pointed to the existence of a contract of service. In particular B worked only for the bank for a given number of hours and any absence had to be agreed by the bank. He was supervised by a manager employed by the bank and his performance was controlled by the bank. He had no opportunity of profit and no risk of loss and was integrated into the bank's structure, Accordingly, B would be regarded for the purposes of the 1992 Act as employed by the bank so that his service company was liable to pay Class 1 NIC in respect of his earnings attributable to the engagement.

BATTERSBY v. CAMPBELL (INSPECTOR OF TAXES) [2001] S.T.C. (S.C.D.) 189, Nuala Brice, Sp Comm.

4224. National insurance contributions—employment status—computer consultant providing services to bank through service company

See SOCIAL SECURITY: Battersby v. Campbell (Inspector of Taxes). §4223

4225. National insurance contributions—employment status—EC law—simultaneous employment and self employment in different Member States—effect on social security rights and liabilities

[EC Treaty Art.39, Art.42, Art.43; Council Regulation 1408/71 on the application of social security schemes to employed persons and their families moving within the Community Art.14.]

The Belgian Labour Court referred questions to the ECJ for a preliminary ruling on the validity of Council Regulation 1408/71 Art.14c and the interpretation of the terms "employed" and "self employed". H was a resident of France and was a director of companies in both France and Belgium. Under French law, H was regarded as an employee, and paid social security contributions in France under the scheme applicable to employees. Under Belgian law, company directors were regarded as self employed. I accordingly brought proceedings seeking payment by H of social security contributions in Belgium. Article 14c(a) provided that a person who was simultaneously in employment within one Member State, and self employed within another Member State, was, for the purpose of liability for social security contributions, deemed subject to the law of the Member State where he was in employment. However, Art.14c(b) provided that in the cases set out in Annex VII, which included cases where a person was self employed in Belgium and employed at the same time in any other Member State, such a person was subject to the law of the Member State where the self employment was carried on.

Held, giving a ruling, that the validity of Art.14c(b) and Annex VII fell to be considered in the light of the EC Treaty Art.39 and Art.42 in relation to freedom of movement for employees, and Art.43 in relation to freedom of establishment for self employed persons. Those provisions were intended to enable Community citizens to pursue occupational activities throughout the Community and precluded national legislation which disadvantaged Community citizens who wished to extend their activities beyond the territory of a single Member State. Therefore national legislation could not exempt persons principally employed in that Member State from the obligation to pay social security contributions in respect of secondary self employment while withholding the exemption from persons principally employed in another Member State. Similarly a Member State could not require social security contributions to be paid by self employed persons who were resident in another Member State and making contributions in that Member State. However, the EC Treaty provided for the coordination rather than the harmonisation of the social security legislation of Member States. Therefore the Treaty did not guarantee that social security rights would not be affected by movement of workers between Member States. It followed that any disadvantage experienced by a person extending or transferring his occupational activities into another Member State arising from becoming subject to additional social security legislation there was not necessarily contrary to Art.39 and Art.43, provided that the legislation did not disadvantage that person as compared with a worker who carried out his activities entirely within that Member State. Regulation 1408/71 simply determined which legislation was applicable in various situations, it did not define the content of national social security legislation. It was for Member States to ensure that such legislation was compatible with Art.39 and Art.43. It could not be said that Art.14c(b) was incompatible with Art.39, Art.42 and Art.43.

INSTITUT NATIONAL D'ASSURANCES SOCIALES POUR TRAVAILLEURS INDEPENDANTS (INASTI) v. HERVEIN (C393/99); INSTITUT NATIONAL D'ASSURANCES SOCIALES POUR TRAVAILLEURS INDEPENDANTS (INASTI) v. LORTHIOIS (C394/99) [2002] 2 C.M.L.R. 16, Rodriguez Iglesias (President), ECJ.

4226. National insurance contributions–employment status–EC law–simultaneous employment and self employment in different Member States–effect on social security rights and liabilities

See SOCIAL SECURITY: Institut National d'Assurances Sociales pourTravailleurs Independants (INASTI) v. Hervein (C393/99). §4225

4227. National insurance contributions–employment status–worker supplied by service company through agency–meaning of "arrangements involving an intermediary"

[Social Security Contributions and Benefits Act 1992; Social Security Contributions (Intermediaries) Regulations 2000 (SI 2000 727) Reg.6(1).]

A company, F, appealed against a decision of the Revenue that S, the sole director and shareholder of F, who provided his services to F, which then provided them to an agency, which in turn provided them to another company, B, came within the scope of the arrangements covered by the Social Security Contributions (Intermediaries) Regulations 2000. S was a specialist computer consultant. B paid the agency, which paid a smaller sum to F, which in turn paid S. The Revenue took the view that the arrangements were such that had they taken the form of a contract between S and B, S would have been regarded for the purposes of the Social Security Contributions and Benefits Act 1992 as having been employed by B. Therefore the company was to be treated as liable to pay primary and secondary Class I national insurance contributions in respect of the worker's attributable earnings from his engagements.

Held, dismissing the appeal, that (1) the fact that the arrangements in the instant case involved a non-intermediary, namely the agency, as well as an intermediary, namely F, did not prevent Reg.6(1)(b) of the 2000 Regulations from applying. That provision covered "arrangements involving an intermediary" rather than "arrangements with an intermediary"; (2) when applying Reg.6(1)(c), the question was whether the circumstances were such that had the arrangements (involving the company as intermediary and the non-intermediary agency) taken the form of a contract between the worker, S, and the client, B, the worker would be regarded as employed in employed earner's employment by B. That meant that although B paid the agency and not F or S, the payment of the remuneration was still part of the arrangements to be considered, and (3) in the instant case, S would have been regarded as employed by B under a contract of service. He worked for B for a standard 37.5 hour week as part of a team consisting mainly of employees of B. There was a project manager who controlled what was to be done. The contract between F and the agency provided that S would take his instructions from B and comply with its rules and procedures. S used the mainframe computer provided by B. He had no opportunity of profit and no risk of loss. The working relationship between S and B had lasted for over two years and while working for B, S did not work for anyone else.

FS CONSULTING LTD v. McCAUL (INSPECTOR OF TAXES) [2002] S.T.C. (S.C.D.) 138, Nuala Brice, Sp Comm.

4228. National insurance contributions–employment status–worker supplied by service company through agency–meaning of "arrangements involving an intermediary"

See SOCIAL SECURITY: FS Consulting Ltd v. McCaul (Inspector of Taxes). §4227

4229. National insurance contributions–exemptions–school fees–habitual payment by company for director's children

[Social Security (Contributions) Regulations 1979 (SI 1979 591) Reg.19(1)(d).]

A appealed against an assessment for national insurance contributions in respect of school fees paid for the children of two of its directors. A argued that the payment of school fees was a payment in kind and therefore exempt from contributions by virtue of the Social Security (Contributions) Regulations 1979 Reg.19(1)(d), now repealed.

Held, dismissing the appeal, that the liability for the school fees was that of the directors themselves, notwithstanding that they had been habitually discharged by A. It followed that the payments had been equivalent to payments in cash and had not been payments in kind, with the result that national insurance contributions should have been made in respect of them.

ABLEWAY LTD v. INLAND REVENUE COMMISSIONERS; *sub nom.* ABLEWAY LTD v. CUSTOMS AND EXCISE COMMISSIONERS [2002] S.T.C. (S.C.D.) 1, N Brice, Sp Comm.

4230. National Insurance Contributions Act 2002 (19)

This Act makes provision for, and in connection with, increasing national insurance contributions and for applying the increases towards the cost of the National Health Service.

This Act received Royal Assent on July 8, 2002.

4231. Pensions–state pension credit–income

STATE PENSION CREDIT REGULATIONS 2002, SI 2002 1792; made under the Social Security Contributions and Benefits Act 1992 s.175; the Social Security Fraud Act 2001 s.7, s.9, s.11; and the State Pension Credit Act 2002 s.1, s.2, s.3, s.4, s.5, s.6, s.7,, s.9, s.12, s.15, s.16, s.17. In force: October 6, 2003; £6.50.

These Regulations, which amend the Social Security (Loss of Benefit) Regulations 2001 (SI 2001 4022) and the State Pension Credit Act 2002, contain provisions relating to claimant's absent from Great Britain and relate to the amounts of the guarantee credit and savings credit. They specify the income to be taken into account in determining the amount of any savings credit and make provision for the calculation of income and capital. They also contain a separate provision relating to the reduction in state pension credit in a case where the claimant has been convicted of benefit offences on at least two separate occasions.

4232. Pensions–state pension credit–miscellaneous provisions

STATE PENSION CREDIT (CONSEQUENTIAL, TRANSITIONAL AND MISCELLANEOUS PROVISIONS) REGULATIONS 2002, SI 2002 3019; made under the Social Security Administration Act 1992 s.5, s.7A, s.15A, s.159B, s.189; the Social Security Contributions and Benefits Act 1992 s.3, s.138, s.175; the Social Security Act 1998 s.10, s.18, s.79; and the State Pension Credit Act 2002 s.1, s.2, s.3, s.3, s.7, s.12, s.13, s.15, s.17, Sch.1 para.13. In force: Part I: April 7, 2003; Part II: April 7, 2003; Part III: April 7, 2003; Part VII: April 7, 2003; remainder: October 6, 2003; £6.50.

These Regulations amend the Social Fund Maternity and Funeral Expenses (General) Regulations 1987 (SI 1987 481), the Income Support (General) Regulations 1987 (SI 1987 1967), the Social Security (Claims and Payments) Regulations 1987 (SI 1987 1968), the Social Security (Payments on account, Overpayments and Recovery) Regulations 1988 (SI 1988 664), the Community

Charges (Deductions from Income Support) (Scotland) Regulations 1989 (SI 1989 507), the Community Charges (Deductions from Income Support) (No.2) Regulations 1990 (SI 1990 545), the Social Security (Attendance Allowance) Regulations 1991 (SI 1991 2740), the Social Security (Disability Living Allowance) Regulations 1991 (SI 1991 2890), the Child Support (Arrears, Interest and Adjustment of Maintenance Assessments) Regulations 1992 (SI 1992 1816), the Fines (Deductions from Income Support) Regulations 1992 (SI 1992 2182), the Council Tax (Deductions from Income Support) Regulations 1993 (SI 1993 494), the Jobseeker's Allowance Regulations 1996 (SI 1996 207), the Social Security and Child Support (Decisions and Appeals) Regulations 1999 (SI 1999 991), the Child Support (Maintenance Calculations and Special Cases) Regulations 2001 (SI 2001 155) and the State Pension Credit Regulations 2002 (SI 2002 1792). The Regulations make separate provision for claims for, and payment of, state pension credit; provide information as to the likelihood of future changes in their circumstances; provide for the date on which entitlement to state pension credit is to begin; and add specified provisions.

4233. Residential accommodation—sums for personal requirements

NATIONAL ASSISTANCE (SUMS FOR PERSONAL REQUIREMENTS) (ENGLAND) REGULATIONS 2002, SI 2002 411; made under the National Assistance Act 1948 s.22. In force: April 8, 2002; £1.50.

These Regulations, which revoke the National Assistance (Sums for Personal Requirements) (England) Regulations 2001 (SI 2001 1005), set out the weekly sum which local authorities in England are to assume, in the absence of special circumstances, that residents in accommodation arranged under the National Assistance Act 1948 will need for their personal requirements. Residents will be assumed to need £16.80 per week for their personal requirements.

4234. Social fund—cold weather payments—weather stations and postcode districts

SOCIAL FUND COLD WEATHER PAYMENTS (GENERAL) AMENDMENT REGULATIONS 2002, SI 2002 2524; made under the Social Security Contributions and Benefits Act 1992 s.138, s.175. In force: November 1, 2002; £1.75.

These Regulations amend the Social Fund Cold Weather Payments (General) Regulations 1988 (SI 1988 1724) in relation to the list of weather stations and applicable postcode districts to take account of an additional weather station and changes to postcodes.

4235. Social fund—crisis loans—applications

SOCIAL FUND (MISCELLANEOUS AMENDMENTS) REGULATIONS 2002, SI 2002 2323; made under the Social Security Contributions and Benefits Act 1992 s.138, s.175; and the Social Security Administration Act 1992 s.12, s.189, s.191. In force: October 1, 2002; £1.75.

These Regulations amend the Social Fund (Applications) Regulations 1988 (SI 1988 524) by allowing applications for crisis loans to be made otherwise than in writing and making consequential amendments relating to when such applications are to be treated as made. They also amend the Social Fund Maternity and Funeral Expenses (General) Regulations 1987 (SI 1987 481) so that persons may be entitled to a funeral payment only under those Regulations where they are entitled to a qualifying benefit in respect of the date of claim for a funeral payment.

4236. Social Security Commissioners—appeals—permission—appropriate threshold test

[Access to Justice Act 1999 s.55.]

C applied for permission to appeal against a decision of a social security commissioner dismissing her appeal against a decision of a Disability Appeal

Tribunal. C's application had been adjourned to enable a full hearing to take place so as to allow the court to decide whether her appeal had a real prospect of success which was the threshold test under the Access to Justice Act 1999 s.55. The issue of whether that test was applicable fell to be decided by the court.

Held, granting permission to appeal and dismissing the appeal, that when considering an application for permission to appeal against a decision of a social security commissioner, the court should take into account s.55 of the Act and adopt a robust attitude. Notwithstanding that the wording of the section did not apply to the application before the court, many of its underlying reasons applied with equal or stronger force. Social security was a highly specialised area, and the decision making structure which involved legally qualified specialists in the field, was sufficiently expert to enable the court to take a robust view when a government agency had allegedly erred. Accordingly, an application for permission to appeal should be approached with caution since social security commissioners were best placed to make the correct decisions regarding technical issues.

COOKE v. SECRETARY OF STATE FOR SOCIAL SECURITY; *sub nom.* COOKE v. SOCIAL SECURITY COMMISSIONER, [2001] EWCA Civ 734, [2002] 3 All E.R. 279, Hale, L.J., CA.

4237. Social Security Commissioners–tax credits–appeals

SOCIAL SECURITY COMMISSIONERS (PROCEDURE) (TAX CREDITS APPEALS) REGULATIONS 2002, SI 2002 3237; made under the Social Security Act 1998 s.14, s.15, s.16, s.28, s.39, s.79, s.84, Sch.4, Sch.5. In force: January 1, 2003; £2.50.

These Regulations regulate the procedure of the Social Security Commissioners in determining appeals and applications arising from decisions of appeal tribunals in relation to tax credits.

4238. Social Security Fraud Act 2001 (c.11)–Commencement No.3 Order

SOCIAL SECURITY FRAUD ACT 2001 (COMMENCEMENT NO.3) ORDER 2002, SI 2002 117; made under the Social Security Fraud Act 2001 s.20. Commencement details: bringing into force various provisions of the 2001 Act on January 28, 2002; £1.50.

This Order provides for the coming into force of the Social Security Fraud Act 2001 s.3 which makes provision in relation to a code of practice about the use of information powers.

4239. Social Security Fraud Act 2001 (c.11)–Commencement No.4 Order

SOCIAL SECURITY FRAUD ACT 2001 (COMMENCEMENT NO.4) ORDER 2002, SI 2002 403; made under the Social Security Fraud Act 2001 s.20. Commencement details: bringing into force various provisions of the 2001 Act on February 26, 2002; £1.50.

This Order provides for the coming into force of the Social Security Fraud Act 2001 s.1 (4), order-making power to amend list of persons who may be required to provide information, and s.1 (9), order adding any person to that list to be subject to affirmative Parliamentary procedure, on February 26, 2002.

4240. Social Security Fraud Act 2001 (c.11)–Commencement No.5 Order

SOCIAL SECURITY FRAUD ACT 2001 (COMMENCEMENT NO.5) ORDER 2002, SI 2002 1222; made under the Social Security Fraud Act 2001 s.20. Commencement details: bringing into force various provisions of the 2001 Act on April 30, 2002; £1.50.

This Order provides for the coming into force of further provisions of the Social Security Fraud Act 2001 on April 30, 2002.

4241. State Pension Credit Act 2002 (c.16)

This Act makes provision for and in connection with a new social security benefit called state pension credit and amends the Pension Schemes Act 1993 s.47(1).
This Act received Royal Assent on June 25, 2002.

4242. State Pension Credit Act 2002 (c.16)–Commencement No.1 Order

STATE PENSION CREDIT ACT 2002 (COMMENCEMENT NO.1) ORDER 2002, SI 2002 1691; made under the State Pension Credit Act 2002 s.22. Commencement details: bringing into force various provisions of the 2002 Act on July 2, 2002; £1.50.
This Order brings into force certain provisions of the State Pension Credit Act 2002.

4243. State Pension Credit Act (c.16)–Commencement No.2 Order

STATE PENSION CREDIT ACT (COMMENCEMENT NO.2) ORDER 2002, SI 2002 2248; made under the State Pension Credit Act 2002 s.22. Commencement details: bringing into force various provisions of the 2002 Act on September 3, 2002; £1.50.
This Order appoints September 3, 2002 as the day for the coming into force of the State Pension Credit Act 2002 s.18 which amends the Pension Schemes Act 1993 to provide for equal treatment for widows and widowers in connection with the treatment of their guaranteed minimum pensions.

4244. State retirement pensions–EC law–failure to take into account periods of child rearing–Austria

[Council Regulation 1408/71 on the application of social security schemes to employed persons and their families moving within the Community; Agreement on a European Economic Area 1992.]
K, an Austrian national with three children, worked in Austria until August 1964. Her first child was born in July 1966. She moved to Belgium in April 1970, with her family, where she did not work. She returned to Austria and resumed work there from September 1975. At K's request, the relevant national institution confirmed in April 1998 that she had accumulated 355 months of old age insurance under national legislation. That period included 46 months recognised by the institution as qualifying periods spent child rearing, which corresponded to the period from July 1966, when her first child was born, to April 1970, when she moved to Belgium. K challenged the decision, claiming that the institution should have recognised a total of 82 months' child rearing, including time spent in Belgium. The national court seised of the issue made a reference to the ECJ, asking whether Austria had to recognise such a period spent in another Member State of the EEA where it had occurred before the entry into force of the Agreement on a European Economic Area 1992, on January 1, 1994.
Held, giving a preliminary ruling, that Austrian social security provisions were in conflict with Community law to the extent that they did not allow periods of child rearing to be taken into account for the purposes of calculating periods of old age insurance where they had been completed in another Member State of the EEA, unless they were completed after the entry into force of the EEA Agreement and the mother had been in receipt of Austrian maternity allowance, whereas such periods were taken into account unconditionally if they were completed in Austria. Under Council Regulation 1408/71 Art.94(1), that Regulation could not have the effect of creating a right in respect of a period prior to its entry into force. However, Art.94(2) required that, for determining future rights, periods of insurance, employment or residence completed before the Regulation's entry into force had to be taken into account. Similarly, Art.94(3) required account to be taken of any contingency that had materialised before that date.
KAUER v. PENSIONSVERSICHERUNGSANSTALT DER ANGESTELLTEN (C28/00) [2002] 1 C.M.L.R. 51, S Von Bahr (President), ECJ.

4245. State retirement pensions–low earnings threshold

SOCIAL SECURITY PENSIONS (LOW EARNINGS THRESHOLD) ORDER 2002, SI 2002 36; made under the Social Security Administration Act 1992 s.148A. In force: April 6, 2002; £1.50.

This Order is made following a review by the Secretary of State under the Social Security Administration Act 1992 s.148A of the general level of earnings in Great Britain with a view to determining whether, and if so by how much, the amount of the low earnings threshold for the purposes of the Social Security Contributions and Benefits Act 1992 be increased for any future tax years. As a result of that review, it appears to the Secretary of State that the general level of such earnings during the period from October 1, 1998 to September 30, 2001 be increased by 10 per cent. This Order directs that the low earnings threshold for the tax years following 2001 to 2002 shall be £10,800. The low earnings threshold is the amount by reference to which the three surplus earnings bands are determined for the purpose of calculating the additional pension in a state retirement pension.

4246. Statutory maternity pay–compensation of employers–reduction

STATUTORY MATERNITY PAY (COMPENSATION OF EMPLOYERS) AMENDMENT REGULATIONS 2002, SI 2002 225; made under the Social Security Contributions and Benefits Act 1992 s.167, s.171, s.175; and the Social Security Contributions and Benefits (Northern Ireland) Act 1992 s.163, s.171. In force: April 6, 2002; £1.75.

These Regulations amend the Statutory Maternity Pay (Compensation of Employers) and Miscellaneous Amendment Regulations 1994 (SI 1994 1882) and the Statutory Maternity Pay (Compensation of Employers) and Miscellaneous Amendment Regulations (Northern Ireland) 1994 (SR 1994 271). They substitute the amount of an employer's contributions payments to define the expression "small employer", to £40,000; reduce the additional amount an employer can recover payments of statutory maternity pay from 5 per cent to 4.5 per cent which takes effect from April 6, 2002.

4247. Students–income related benefits

SOCIAL SECURITY AMENDMENT (STUDENTS AND INCOME-RELATED BENEFITS) REGULATIONS 2002, SI 2002 1589; made under the Social Security Contributions and Benefits Act 1992 s.123, s.130, s.136, s.137, s.175; and the Jobseekers Act 1995 s.12, s.35, s.36. In force: in accordance with Reg.1 (1); £2.00.

These Regulations amend the Income Support (General) Regulations 1987 (SI 1987 1967), the Housing Benefit (General) Regulations 1987 (SI 1987 1971), the Council Tax Benefit (General) Regulations 1992 (SI 1992 1814) and the Jobseeker's Allowance Regulations 1996 (SI 1996 207) in relation to students. They amend the definitions of "access funds", "periods of experience" and of "sandwich course", increase the amounts of grant and loan income to be disregarded in respect of books and equipment and for travel costs and provide for the disregard of childcare grants payable under Northern Ireland legislation and of the child care component of the National Assembly for Wales Learning Grants. The Regulations provide for both grant income and student loans to be apportioned over complete benefit weeks, clarify the position as regards the apportionment of amounts in grants intended for the maintenance of dependents and abolish the student rent deduction.

4248. Students–income related benefits

SOCIAL SECURITY AMENDMENT (STUDENTS AND INCOME-RELATED BENEFITS) (NO.2) REGULATIONS 2002, SI 2002 2207; made under the Social Security Contributions and Benefits Act 1992 s.123, s.136, s.137, s.175; and the Jobseekers Act 1995 s.12, s.35, s.36. In force: September 2, 2002; £1.50.

These Regulations amend the Income Support (General) Regulations 1987 (SI 1987 1967), the Housing Benefit (General) Regulations 1987 (SI 1987 1971), the

Council Tax Benefit (General) Regulations 1992 (SI 1992 1814) and the Jobseeker's Allowance Regulations 1996 (SI 1996 207) in so far as those Regulations apply to students. They increase the disregard for grants paid for an eldest or dependent child and in respect of expenditure on travel, books and equipment under the Education (Student Support) Regulations 2002 (SI 2002 195).

4249. Tax credits—disabled persons tax credit—working families tax credit

TAX CREDITS (MISCELLANEOUS AMENDMENTS NO.4) REGULATIONS 2002, SI 2002 1696; made under the Social Security Contributions and Benefits Act 1992 s.128, s.136, s.137, s.175; the Tax Credits Act 1999 s.2, Sch.2 para.1 Tax Credits Act 1999 Sch.2 para.7, Sch.2 para.20 Social Security Administration Act 1992 s.1; and the Social Security Administration Act 1992 s.5, s.189. In force: July 23, 2002; £1.75.

These Regulations amend the Family Credit (General) Regulations 1987 (SI 1987 1973), the Disability Working Allowance (General) Regulations 1991 (SI 1991 2887) and the Social Security (Claims and Payments) Regulations 1987 (SI 1987 1968) to enable Crown servants posted overseas and their partners to make claims for working families' tax credit with effect from July 23, 2002.

4250. Tax credits—disabled persons tax credit and working families tax credit—miscellaneous amendments

TAX CREDITS (MISCELLANEOUS AMENDMENTS) REGULATIONS 2002, SI 2002 14; made under the Social Security Contributions and Benefits Act 1992 s.128, s.129, s.136, s.137, s.175; and the Tax Credits Act 1999 s.2, Sch.2 para.1, Sch.2 para.20. In force: January 29, 2002; £1.75.

These Regulations amend the Disability Working Allowance (General) Regulations 1991 (SI 1991 2887) and the Family Credit (General) Regulations 1987 (SI 1987 1973) with effect for award periods of working families' tax credit and disabled person's tax credit commencing on or after January 29, 2002. They provide for citation, commencement and effect and Reg.2 for interpretation; amend Reg.51A of the Disability Working Allowance Regulations and Reg.46A of the Family Credit Regulations so as to extend the definition of "relevant childcare charges" to include charges for childcare provided by persons registered by OFSTED under the Children Act 1989 Part XA, by persons to whom the requirement to register under Part XA of that Act does not yet apply by virtue of the Care Standards Act 2000 (Commencement No.7 (England) and Transitional, Transitory and Savings Provisions) Order 2001 (SI 2001 2041 (C.68), or in schools or establishments exempted from registration under Part XA of that Act; amend the Disability Working Allowance Regulations Sch.3 para.25 and the Family Credit Regulations Sch.2 para.25 so as to add to the list of payments by local authorities to be disregarded as income in computing entitlement to working families' tax credit and disabled person's tax credit payments under the Children Act 1989 s.23C, 24A and 24B; and makes a similar amendment as that made by the Disability Working Allowance Regulations Reg.4 to Sch.4 para.18 and the Family Credit Regulations Sch.3 para.18.

4251. Welfare Reform and Pensions Act 1999 (c.30)—Commencement No.13 Order

WELFARE REFORM AND PENSIONS ACT 1999 (COMMENCEMENT NO.13) ORDER 2002, SI 2002 153; made under the Welfare Reform and Pensions Act 1999 s.89. Commencement details: bringing into force various provisions of the 1999 Act on April 6, 2002; £2.00.

This Order, which amends the Welfare Reform and Pensions Act 1999 (Commencement No.12) Order 2001 (SI 2001 4049), brings into force provisions of the Welfare Reform and Pensions Act 1999.

4252. Welfare Reform and Pensions Act 1999 (c.30)–Commencement No.14 Order

WELFARE REFORM AND PENSIONS ACT 1999 (COMMENCEMENT NO.14) ORDER 2002, SI 2002 381; made under the Welfare Reform and Pensions Act 1999 s.89. Commencement details: bringing into force various provisions of the 1999 Act on March 19, 2002; £2.00.

This Order brings into force provisions of the Welfare Reform and Pensions Act 1999 which relate to occupational pension schemes and certificates etc. relating to the minimum funding requirement.

4253. Welfare Reform and Pensions Act 1999 (c.30)–Commencement No.15 Order

WELFARE REFORM AND PENSIONS ACT 1999 (COMMENCEMENT NO.15) ORDER 2002, SI 2002 818; made under the Welfare Reform and Pensions Act 1999 s.89. Commencement details: bringing into force various provisions of the 1999 Act on March 26, 2002 and April 6, 2002; £2.00.

This Order amends the Welfare Reform and Pensions Act 1999 (Commencement No.13) Order 2002 (SI 2001 153) so as to revoke the day appointed for the coming into force of specified provisions of the Welfare Reform and Pensions Act 1999.

4254. Widows benefits–equal treatment–settlement reached between widower and UK government

[Human Rights Act 1998 Sch.1 Part I Art.8, Art.14, Part II Art.1; Welfare Reform and Pensions Act 1999.]

F, a widower whose claim for bereavement tax allowance and for the equivalent of widowed mother's allowance and a widow's payment had been turned down, brought an application against the United Kingdom Government alleging that the relevant tax and social security legislation discriminated against him on the ground of his sex contrary to the Human Rights Act 1998 Sch.1 Part I Art.14 taken in conjunction with Sch.1 Part I Art.8 and Sch.1 Part II Art.1. Prior to the application being heard, F had arrived at a settlement with the Government whereby he was paid, in addition to his legal costs and the amount which the bereavement tax allowance would have been worth to him, an amount equating to the widow's benefits that he would have received had he enjoyed the same social security rights as a widow prior to April 9, 2001, when the Welfare Reform and Pensions Act 1999 came into force, making bereavement benefits available to both women and men.

Held, striking out F's application, that the settlement would be noted, the court being satisfied that it respected F's human rights.

FIELDING v. UNITED KINGDOM (36940/97) *The Times*, February 25, 2002, J-P Costa (President), ECHR.

4255. Widows benefits–government departments–conflicting findings of fact–legitimate expectation of consistent treatment–issue estoppel

N appealed against the dismissal ([2001] EWHC Admin 1049, [2002] 1 F.L.R. 670) of her application for judicial review of a prior refusal to grant permission to appeal a decision of the Benefits Directorate. N was a citizen of Bangladesh who married K. K subsequently became a British citizen. N had sought to enter the United Kingdom as K's widow and claimed entitlement to a widow's pension. Her application for a pension was rejected by the Benefits Directorate on the basis that her marriage was not valid, although an immigration adjudicator separately considering N's immigration status had concluded that the marriage was valid. N contended that issue estoppel operated in her favour as a result of the inconsistent decisions by separate government departments and relied upon the fact that, although the first immigration adjudicator's decision had been set aside, a second immigration adjudicator had subsequently reached the same conclusion on validity.

Held, dismissing the appeal, that the argument on issue estoppel was misguided. The fact that a second immigration adjudicator had reached the same decision on the validity of the marriage as the first adjudicator was immaterial in light of the fact that the second decision had been made in reliance on inaccurate information and after a decision on N's pension entitlement had been reached.

R. (ON THE APPLICATION OF NAHAR) v. SOCIAL SECURITY COMMISSIONERS; *sub nom.* R. (ON THE APPLICATION OF NAHAR) v. SECRETARY OF STATE FOR WORK AND PENSIONS, [2002] EWCA Civ 859, *The Times*, June 5, 2002, Robert Walker, L.J., CA.

4256. Books

Bonner, David; Hooker Ian–Social Security Legislation 2002: Non-means Tested Benefits, Vol 1. Paperback: £63.00. ISBN 0-421-79120-9. Sweet & Maxwell.

Puttick, Keith–Welfare Benefits: 200-2001. Welfare Benefits. Paperback: £14.99. EMIS Professional Publishing.

Robinson, Alan–Tolley's Social Security and Family Benefit Law: a Practical Guide. Paperback: £39.95. ISBN 0-7545-1895-7. Tolley Publishing.

Rowland, Mark; White, Robin–Social Security Legislation: Administration, Adjudication and the European Dimension, Vol 3. Paperback: £63.00. ISBN 0-421-79140-3. Sweet & Maxwell.

Tonge, Kate–Social Security and State Benefits: a Practical Guide. 2nd Ed. Paperback: £40.00. ISBN 0-7545-1657-1. Tolley Publishing.

Tonge, Kate–Tolley's Practical Guide to State Benefits and Personal Injury Awards. Paperback: £45.00. ISBN 0-7545-1625-3. Tolley Publishing.

Wikeley, N.J.–Wikely, Ogus & Barendt: the Law of Social Security. Paperback: £35.95. ISBN 0-406-98585-5. Butterworths Law.

Wood, Penny; Wikeley, Nick; Paynter, Richard; Bonner, David–Social Security Legislation 2002: Income Support, Jobseeker's Allowance, Tax Credits and the Social Fund, Vol 2. Paperback: £64.00. ISBN 0-421-79130-6. Sweet & Maxwell.

SOCIAL WELFARE

4257. Accommodation–mental health–duties arising from community care assessment–relevance of availability of resources

[National Assistance Act 1948 s.21; National Health Service and Community Care Act 1990 s.47(1).]

B, who had severe mental health problems, challenged the failure of ILBC to provide suitable accommodation pursuant to its duties under the National Health Service and Community Care Act 1990 s.47(1) and the National Assistance Act 1948 s.21 following assessments of his community care needs and the needs of his wife and four children. The assessments concluded that B required larger, ground floor accommodation but the waiting lists were such that, three months later, suitable accommodation had still not been provided. B submitted that ILBC had failed to comply with its duty under s.21 of the 1948 Act which arose as a result of the assessments pursuant to s.47(1) of the 1990 Act. ILBC contended that they were entitled to take into account lack of resources when deciding how to meet accommodation needs.

Held, allowing the application, that once ILBC had concluded under s.21 of the 1948 Act that B had specific needs which were not met by the accommodation otherwise available to him it was under a duty to provide accommodation so as to meet his lawfully assessed needs, which in this case was safe, secure, accessible and larger ground floor accommodation, *R. v. Kensington and Chelsea RLBC, ex p. Kujtim* [1999] 4 All E.R. 161, [1999] C.L.Y. 3052 applied. There were four stages when lack of resources might fall to be considered by a local authority; when considering whether to carry out an assessment under s.47(1)(a) of the 1990 Act, during the assessment itself, when deciding whether to comply with their duty under s.21 of the 1948 Act or when considering a range of suitable accommodation available to meet an applicant's needs. It was only at this final stage that lack of resources could be taken into account, *R. v. Sefton MBC, ex p. Help the Aged* [1997] 3 F.L.R. 392 applied. In the instant case, nine months had passed since the assessment without any material change of circumstance, despite ILBC's recognition of its duty to provide accommodation. In the view of the urgency of the situation, a mandatory order was justified, requiring ILBC to identify a suitable property within three months, followed by a further three month period within which the property had to be made available to B and his family.

R. (ON THE APPLICATION OF BATANTU) v. ISLINGTON LBC; *sub nom.* R. v. ISLINGTON LBC, *ex p.* BATANTU (2001) 33 H.L.R. 76, Henriques, J., QBD (Admin Ct).

4258. Care–child protection–standards–Wales

CHILDREN ACT 1989 AND THE CARE STANDARDS ACT 2000 (MISCELLANEOUS REGULATIONS) (AMENDMENT) (WALES) REGULATIONS 2002, SI 2002 2622 (W.254); made under the Children Act 1989 s.79C, s.79E, s.104; and the Care Standards Act 2000 s.12, s.16, s.22, s.118. In force: October 18, 2002; £3.00.

These Regulations, which revoke the Child Minding and Day Care (Wales) (Amendment) Regulations 2002 (SI 2002 2171), amend the Care Homes (Wales) Regulations 2002 (SI 2002 324), the Private and Voluntary Health Care (Wales) Regulations 2002 (SI 2002 325), the Children's Homes (Wales) Regulations 2002 (SI 2002 327), the Child Minding and Day Care (Wales) Regulations 2002 (SI 2002 812) and the Registration of Social Care and Independent Health Care (Wales) Regulations 2002 (SI 2002 919). The Regulations make amendments to omit the requirement for a police check to be available in respect of the individuals specified; and require that a criminal record certificate or (as the case may be) an enhanced criminal record certificate is to be available in respect of such individuals.

4259. Care–children–local authority assistance–Wales

CHILDREN (LEAVING CARE) (AMENDMENT) (WALES) REGULATIONS 2002, SI 2002 1855; made under the Children Act 1989 s.23A, s.104, Sch.2 para.19B. In force: August 1, 2002; £1.75.

These Regulations amend the Children (Leaving Care) Regulations 2001 (SI 2001 2189) which make provision about support for children and young people aged 16 and over, who are, or have been, looked after by a local authority. They provide that children placed with a parent, a person with parental responsibility or someone with a residence order in their favour under the Children Act 1989 and who are subject to a care order, are eligible for local authority assistance. The Regulations also provide that children who have spent six months or more living with a parent, a person with parental responsibility or someone with a residence order in their favour, will still be eligible for local authority assistance if the placement subsequently breaks down.

4260. Care–social and health care–registration–fees–Wales

REGISTRATION OF SOCIAL CARE AND INDEPENDENT HEALTHCARE (FEES) (WALES) REGULATIONS 2002, SI 2002 921; made under the Children Act 1989 s.79F, s.104, Sch.9A para.7; and the Care Standards Act 2000 s.12, s.15, s.16, s.118. In force: April 1, 2002; £2.00.

These Regulations prescribe the fees payable by certain establishments under the Care Standards Act 2000 Part II on an application for registration and on an application for the variation or removal of any condition in force in relation to a registration. They also prescribe the fee for applications for registration in relation to certain providers of day care under the Children Act 1989 Part XA and prescribe the annual fee to be paid by certain establishments and providers of day care.

4261. Care—social and health care—registration—Wales

REGISTRATION OF SOCIAL CARE AND INDEPENDENT HEALTH CARE (WALES) REGULATIONS 2002, SI 2002 919; made under the Children Act 1989 s.79E, s.104, Sch.9A para.6; and the Care Standards Act 2000 s.12, s.14, s.15, s.16, s.25, s.118. In force: April 1, 2002; £4.00.

These Regulations make provision in relation to the registration of care homes, children's homes, independent hospitals and independent clinics, child minders and providers of day care. They specify the information and documents to be provided by an applicant for registration; require the responsible person to attend an interview; require the applicant to give notice of certain changes that take place, or details of staff engaged, after the application for registration is made and before it is determined; specify the particulars that any certificate of registration is to contain; require a person registered in respect of an establishment to return the certificate to the National Assembly if the registration is cancelled; and make provision in respect of an application by the registered person to apply for the variation or removal of a condition in relation to his or her registration. In addition, the Regulations require the registered person to report the relevant circumstances to the National Assembly if it appears that the establishment or agency is likely to cease to be financially viable, specify certain grounds on which the National Assembly may cancel a person's registration, provide for the registered person to apply for his or her registration to be cancelled and make provision in relation to registration of child minders and providers of day care for children under eight.

4262. Care—standards—establishments and agencies—miscellaneous amendments

CARE STANDARDS ACT 2000 (ESTABLISHMENTS AND AGENCIES) (MISCELLANEOUS AMENDMENTS) REGULATIONS 2002, SI 2002 865; made under the Children Act 1989 s.23, s.59, Sch.2 para.12; and the Care Standards Act 2000 s.12, s.22, s.25, s.36, s.48, s.118. In force: April 18, 2002; £2.00.

These Regulations amend the Care Homes Regulations 2001 (SI 2001 3965), the Children's Homes Regulations 2001 (SI 2001 3967), the Fostering Services Regulations 2002 (SI 2002 57), the Private and Voluntary Health Care (England) Regulations 2001 (SI 2001 3968) and the National Care Standards Commission (Registration) Regulations 2001 (SI 2001 3969) which relate respectively to the conduct and management of care homes, children's homes, fostering agencies and independent hospitals, independent clinics and independent medical agencies, and to the fitness of persons who carry on, manage or work at those establishments or agencies; and the registration of persons who carry on or manage establishments or agencies defined in Part II of the Act consequential on the coming into force of most of the relevant provisions of the Police Act 1997.

4263. Care plans—local authorities powers and duties—proposal to send child to residential school 350 miles from mother—right to respect for private and family life

[Human Rights Act 1998 Sch.1 Part I Art.8.]

D, the mother of an eight year old boy, K, sought to challenge a proposal within the local authority's revised care plan to the effect that K should be placed in a residential school, E, which was 350 miles away from her, for 50 weeks of the year. D contended that the proposal breached both her own and K's rights under the Human Rights Act 1998 Sch.1 Part I Art.8. K had been placed in the care of the local authority following a history of instability and neglect. K was currently accommodated in a small children's unit and continued to attend an infant school. Contact with D took place on a monthly basis. D contended that placement in a residential school was inappropriate for an eight year old child and that the significant distance involved would imperil her relationship with K. D further maintained that there had been no consideration given to alternative schools and that there was a lack of clarity as to whether K was to remain at the school for most of the year or whether he would go to foster parents.

Held, refusing the application, that (1) on the basis of the available evidence the move to E, if established to be a suitable placement for K, was a lawful interference by the local authority in relation to a child in their care which was necessary to protect the best interests of K and proportionate to the obvious needs of K; (2) whilst it was not ideal to place a small boy of eight in a residential placement, the local authority had now revised their plans from arranging for K to stay at E for the full year to seeking a foster placement for weekends and holidays. Such a proposal was sensible having regard to the fact that K could not presently be accommodated even within a specialised foster placement due to his behavioural difficulties. In opting to place K at E with a view to part time and ultimately full time foster placement, the local authority were acting appropriately and accordingly there had been no breach of Art.8 in respect of either K or D, *S (Children) (Care Order: Implementation of Care Plan), Re* [2001] EWCA Civ 757, [2001] 2 F.L.R. 582, [2001] C.L.Y. 2562, *S (Children) (Care Order: Implementation of Care Plan), Re* [2002] UKHL 10, [2002] 2 W.L.R. 720, [2002] 4 C.L. 194, *M (Care: Challenging Decisions by Local Authority), Re* [2001] 2 F.L.R. 1300, [2002] 3 C.L. 232 and *A (A Patient) v. A Health Authority* [2002] EWHC 18, [2002] 3 W.L.R. 24, [2002] 4 C.L. 46 considered, and (3) the local authority had agreed to fund the cost of D's journeys for contact with K. Those journeys should continue at the rate of one per month having regard to the close nature of the relationship between K and his mother.

DC v. B MBC; *sub nom.* C v. B MBC, [2002] EWHC 1438, [2002] 2 F.L.R. 868, Dame Elizabeth Butler-Sloss (President), Fam Div.

4264. **Care standards–social care worker–extension of meaning–Wales**

CARE STANDARDS ACT 2000 (EXTENSION OF MEANING OF "SOCIAL CARE WORKER") (WALES) REGULATIONS 2002, SI 2002 1176; made under the Care Standards Act 2000 s.55, s.118. In force: April 30, 2002; £1.75.

These Regulations provide that for the purposes only of the functions of the Care Council for Wales under the Care Standards Act 2000 s.54 certain persons are to be treated as social care workers. They include persons engaged in work for the purposes of a local authority's social services functions; persons engaged in the provision of personal care for any person; certain persons involved with social work agencies; persons employed in day centres; and certain social work students.

4265. **Care Standards Act 2000 (c.14)–Commencement and Transitional Provisions Order–England**

CARE STANDARDS ACT 2000 (COMMENCEMENT AND TRANSITIONAL PROVISIONS) (AMENDMENT) (ENGLAND) ORDER 2002, SI 2002 2001; made under the Care Standards Act 2000 s.118, s.122. Commencement details: bringing into force various provisions of the 2000 Act on various dates; £2.50.

This Order makes amendments to the Care Standards Act 2000 (Commencement No.9 (England) and Transitional and Savings Provisions) Order 2001 (SI 2001 3852) and the Care Standards Act 2000 (Commencement No.10 (England) and Transitional, Savings and Amendment Provisions) Order 2001 (SI 2001 4150). The day appointed for the coming into force of certain provisions of the Care Standards Act 2000, in respect of the registration under that Act of residential family centres, domiciliary care agencies and nurses agencies, is altered from September 1, 2002 to January 1, 2003. The Order also makes amendments to provisions in respect of a residential care home or nursing home under the Registered Homes Act 1984, or those who are authorised to carry on a nurses agency under the Nurse Agencies Act 1957.

4266. **Care Standards Act 2000 (c.14)–Commencement and Transitional Provisions Order–England**

CARE STANDARDS ACT 2000 (COMMENCEMENT AND TRANSITIONAL PROVISIONS) (AMENDMENT NO.2) (ENGLAND) ORDER 2002, SI 2002 3210 (C.109); made under the Care Standards Act 2000 s.118, s.122. Commencement details: bringing into force various provisions of the 2000 Act in accordance with Art.2; £2.50.

This Order amends the Care Standards Act 2000 (Commencement No.9 (England) and Transitional and Savings Provisions) Order 2001 (SI 2001 3852) and the Care Standards Act 2000 (Commencement No.10 (England) and Transitional, Savings and Amendment Provisions) Order 2001 (SI 2001 4150). The day appointed for the coming into force of certain provisions of the Care Standards Act 2000, in respect of the registration under that Act of residential family centres, domiciliary care agencies and nurses agencies, is altered from January 1, 2003 to April 1, 2003.

4267. Care Standards Act 2000 (c.14)–Commencement No.8 and Transitional, Savings and Consequential Provisions Order–Wales

CARE STANDARDS ACT 2000 (COMMENCEMENT NO.8 (WALES) AND TRANSITIONAL, SAVINGS AND CONSEQUENTIAL PROVISIONS) ORDER 2002, SI 2002 920; made under the Care Standards Act 2000 s.118, s.119, s.122. Commencement details: bringing into force various provisions of the 2000 Act on April 1, 2002; £4.00.

This Order, which amends the National Health Service (Functions of Health Authorities and Administration Arrangements) Regulations 1996 (SI 1996 708), commences certain specified provisions of the Care Standards Act 2000.

4268. Care Standards Act 2000 (c.14)–Commencement No.9–Wales

CARE STANDARDS ACT 2000 (COMMENCEMENT NO.9) (WALES) ORDER 2002, SI 2002 1175; made under the Care Standards Act 2000 s.118, s.122. Commencement details: bringing into force various provisions of the 2000 Act on April 30, 2002; £2.00.

This Order brings into force certain provisions of the Care Standards Act 2000 Part IV which relate to the registration of social care workers; the use of the title "social worker"; codes of practice about standards of conduct and practice expected of social care workers and their employers; social work qualifications obtained outside Wales; and post-registration training of social care workers.

4269. Care Standards Act 2000 (c.14)–Commencement No.11 Order

CARE STANDARDS ACT 2000 (COMMENCEMENT NO.11) ORDER 2002, SI 2002 629; made under the Care Standards Act 2000 s.118, s.122. Commencement details: bringing into force various provisions of the 2000 Act on March 18, 2002 and April 1, 2002; £2.00.

This Order brings into force certain provisions of the Care Standards Act 2000 which relate to criminal record certificates.

4270. Care Standards Act 2000 (c.14)–Commencement No.12 Order–England

CARE STANDARDS ACT 2000 (COMMENCEMENT NO.12) (ENGLAND) ORDER 2002, SI 2002 1245; made under the Care Standards Act 2000 s.118, s.122. Commencement details: bringing into force various provisions of the 2000 Act on March 25, 2002 and April 1, 2002; £2.00.

This Order brings into force, in relation to England only, the Care Standards Act 2000 s.54(2), s.55, s.62, s.63, s.66, s.67, s.113(1)(3)(4) on March 25, 2002, and s.70(1) on April 1, 2002.

4271. Care Standards Act 2000 (c.14)–Commencement No.13 Order–England

CARE STANDARDS ACT 2000 (COMMENCEMENT NO.13) (ENGLAND) ORDER 2002, SI 2002 839; made under the Care Standards Act 2000 s.118, s.122. Commencement details: bringing into force various provisions of the 2000 Act on April 1, 2002; £2.00.

This Order brings into force the Care Standards Act 2000 s.79 to give effect to specified provisions of the Children Act 1989 Part XA.

4272. Care Standards Act 2000 (c.14)–Commencement No.14–England

CARE STANDARDS ACT 2000 (COMMENCEMENT NO.14 (ENGLAND) AND TRANSITIONAL, SAVINGS AND AMENDMENT PROVISIONS) ORDER 2002, SI 2002 1493; made under the Care Standards Act 2000 s.118, s.122. Commencement details: bringing into force various provisions of the 2000 Act on April 1, 2002; £2.50.

This Order, which amends the Care Standards Act 2000 (Commencement No.9 (England) and Transitional and Savings Provisions) Order 2001 (SI 2001 3852) and the Care Standards Act 2000 (Commencement No.10 (England) and Transitional, Savings and Amendment Provisions) Order 2001 (SI 2001 4150), brings into force certain provisions of the Care Standards Act 2000 which amend the Protection of Children Act 1999 to allow certain authorities to refer persons for inclusion in the list of individuals considered unsuitable to work with children. They also amend the provisions in the Children Act 1989 concerning persons disqualified from carrying on or being employed in children's homes and related appeals.

4273. Care Standards Act 2000 (c.14)–Commencement No.15 and Transitional Provisions Order–England

CARE STANDARDS ACT 2000 (COMMENCEMENT NO.15 (ENGLAND) AND TRANSITIONAL PROVISIONS) (AMENDMENT) ORDER 2002, SI 2002 1790; made under the Care Standards Act 2000 s.118, s.122. Commencement details: bringing into force various provisions of the 2000 Act on various dates; £2.00.

This Order amends the Care Standards Act 2000 (Commencement No.9 (England) and Transitional and Savings Provisions) Order 2001 (SI 2001 3852) and the Care Standards Act 2000 (Commencement No.10 (England) and Transitional, Savings and Amendment Provisions) Order 2001 (SI 2001 4150). The day appointed for the coming into force of provisions of the Care Standards Act 2000 is altered from July 1, 2002 to September 1, 2002 in respect of the registration under that Act of residential family centres, domiciliary care agencies and nurses agencies. The day appointed for the purpose of giving effect to determinations of certain applications made under the Children Act 1989 is brought forward to June 1, 2002.

4274. Care Standards Act 2000 (c.14)–Commencement No.16 Order–England

CARE STANDARDS ACT 2000 (COMMENCEMENT NO.16) (ENGLAND) ORDER 2002, SI 2002 2215; made under the Care Standards Act 2000 s.118, s.122. Commencement details: bringing into force various provisions of the 2000 Act on September 2, 2002; £2.00.

This Order brings into operation various provisions of the Care Standards Act 2000 relating to the register of nursery education inspectors.

4275. Child Support, Pensions and Social Security Act 2000 (c.19)–Commencement No.11 Order

CHILD SUPPORT, PENSIONS AND SOCIAL SECURITY ACT 2000 (COMMENCEMENT NO.11) ORDER 2002, SI 2002 437; made under the Child Support, Pensions and Social Security Act 2000 s.86. Commencement details: bringing into force various provisions of the 2000 Act on March 1, 2002, April 1, 2002 and April 6, 2002; £2.00.

This Order, which amends the Child Support, Pensions and Social Security Act 2000 (Commencement No.9) Order 2001 (SI 2001 2295), brings into force further provisions of the Child Support, Pensions and Social Security Act 2000.

4276. Children–care–accommodation

CHILDREN ACT (MISCELLANEOUS AMENDMENTS) (ENGLAND) REGULATIONS 2002, SI 2002 546; made under the Children Act 1989 s.23, s.23A, s.25, s.26, s.51, s.59, s.104, Sch.2 para.12, Sch.2 para.13, Sch.2 para.14, Sch.4 para.4, Sch.5 para.7, Sch.6 para.10; and the Care Standards Act 2000 s.119. In force: April 1, 2002; £2.00.

These Regulations make miscellaneous amendments to the Arrangements for Placement of Children (General) Regulations 1991 (SI 1991 890), the Placement of Children with Parents etc. Regulations 1991 (SI 1991 893), the Representations Procedure (Children) Regulations 1991 (SI 1991 894), the Review of Children's Cases Regulations 1991 (SI 1991 895), the Children (Secure Accommodation) Regulations 1991 (SI 1991 1505), the Refuges (Children's Homes and Foster Placements) Regulations 1991 (SI 1991 1507), the Children (Secure Accommodation) (No.2) Regulations 1991 (SI 1991 2034) and the Children (Leaving Care) (England) Regulations 2001 (SI 2001 2874) which govern the placement, care and accommodation of children looked after by local authorities in the exercise of their functions under the Children Act 1989. The Regulations make amendments to reflect the implementation of Part I and Part II of the Care Standards Act 2000 in respect of children's homes and care homes.

4277. Children–care–accommodation–Wales

CHILDREN ACT 1989 AND THE CARE STANDARDS ACT 2000 (MISCELLANEOUS REGULATIONS) (AMENDMENT) (WALES) (NO.2) REGULATIONS 2002, SI 2002 2935 (W.277); made under the Children Act 1989 s.23, s.23A, s.25, s.26, s.51, s.59, s.104, Sch.2 para.13, Sch.2 para.14, Sch.4 para.4, Sch.5 para.7, Sch.6 para.10; and the Care Standards Act 2000 s.3, s.12, s.16, s.22, s.118. In force: December 31, 2002; £2.00.

These Regulations amend the Arrangements for the Placement of Children (General) Regulations 1991 (SI 1991 890), Placement of Children with Parents etc. Regulations 1991 (SI 1991 893), Representations Procedure (Children) Regulations 1991 (SI 1991 894), Review of Children's Cases Regulations 1991 (SI 1991 895), Children (Secure Accommodation) Regulations 1991 (SI 1991 1505), Refuges (Children's Homes and Foster Placements) Regulations 1991 (SI 1991 1507), Children (Secure Accommodation) (No. 2) Regulations (SI 1991 2034), Children (Leaving Care) (Wales) Regulations 2001 (SI 2001 2189), Care Homes (Wales) Regulations 2002 (SI 2002 324), Registration of Social Care and Independent Health Care (Wales) Regulations 2002 (SI 2002 919), Registration of Social Care and Independent Health Care (Fees) (Wales) Regulations 2002 (SI 2002 921), which govern the placement, care and accommodation of children looked after by local authorities.

4278. Childrens welfare–foreign nationals–destitute mother suffering from HIV– local authority's power to provide financial assistance–acquisition of accommodation

[National Assistance Act 1948 s.21; Children Act 1989 s.17; Human Rights Act 1998 s.4, Sch.1 Part I Art.8; Local Government Act 2000 s.2.]

J, a HIV positive Ghanaian citizen with a two year old child, sought judicial review of a local authority's decision that it had no power to provide her with accommodation or to provide financial assistance to enable her to acquire accommodation. J and her daughter had over stayed their permitted period for remaining in the United Kingdom. They were reliant on the charity of others and were living in accommodation that was both overcrowded and inadequate. J contended that the local authority should have provided her with accommodation pursuant to the National Assistance Act 1948 s.21 or provide her with financial assistance pursuant to the Children Act 1989 s.17. The local authority whilst maintaining that it did not have power to assist her under either statutory provision, accepted that its failure to provide assistance infringed her rights under the Human Rights Act 1998 Art.8. The Secretary of State, who had been joined in the proceedings because of the possibility of a declaration of incompatibility under s.4 of the 1998 Act, contended that the local authority had power to provide the financial assistance sought under the Local Government Act 2000 s.2.

Held, granting the application for judicial review, that a local authority had a discretionary power to grant financial assistance for the acquisition of accommodation pursuant to the Local Government Act 2000 s.2. In circumstances where there was a potential for the infringement of a claimant's human rights, that power became a duty. However there was no liability upon local authorities under the Children Act 1989 s.17 to provide financial assistance to enable a mother and child to find such accommodation.

R. (ON THE APPLICATION OF J) v. ENFIELD LBC, [2002] EWHC 432, [2002] 2 F.L.R. 1, Elias, J., QBD (Admin Ct).

4279. Executive agencies–domiciliary care agencies–quality of services

DOMICILIARY CARE AGENCIES REGULATIONS 2002, SI 2002 3214; made under the Care Standards Act 2000 s.4, s.22, s.25, s.34, s.35, s.118. In force: April 1, 2003; £3.00.

These Regulations except certain agencies from being a domiciliary care agency, require each agency to prepare a statement of purpose in relation to the matters set out in Sch.1 and a service user's guide to the agency. The agency must be carried on in a manner consistent with the statement of purpose. These Regulations also make provisions in relation to the fitness of the persons carrying on and managing an agency, requiring satisfactory information to be obtained and make provision in relation to the conduct of agencies, in particular about the quality of services to be provided by an agency.

4280. Executive agencies–National Care Standards Commission–fees and frequency of inspections–registration

NATIONAL CARE STANDARDS COMMISSION (FEES AND FREQUENCY OF INSPECTIONS) AMENDMENT (NO. 3) REGULATIONS 2002, SI 2002 3211; made under the Care Standards Act 2000 s.12, s.16, s.31, s.118. In force: January 1, 2003; £1.75.

These Regulations amend the National Care Standards Commission (Fees and Frequency of Inspections) Regulations 2001 (SI 2001 3980) in relation to the registration of nurses agencies, domiciliary care agencies and residential family centres, so that a "new provider", in the case of a residential family centre, a nurses agency or a domiciliary care agency will be a person who carries on such an establishment or agency for the first time on or after April 1, 2003 and not January 1, 2003 and providing that where an application for registration is made by a person who manages an existing undertaking which is a licensed nurses agency, then provided that application is made before April 1, 2003, no registration fee will be payable.

4281. Executive agencies–National Care Standards Commission–inspection of schools and colleges

NATIONAL CARE STANDARDS COMMISSION (INSPECTION OF SCHOOLS AND COLLEGES) REGULATIONS 2002, SI 2002 552; made under the Children Act 1989 s.87, s.104. In force: April 1, 2002; £1.75.

These Regulations, which revoke the Inspection of Premises, Children and Records (Independent Schools) Regulations 1991 (SI 1991 975), make provision relating to the inspection of schools and colleges providing accommodation for children. The Children Act 1989 confers power on a person authorised by the National Care Standards Commission to enter the premises of a school or college accommodating children, in order to determine whether the welfare of the children is being adequately safeguarded and promoted. A person so authorised may inspect the premises of the school or college, its records, and the children accommodated there, as provided for by these Regulations.

4282. Executive agencies–National Care Standards Commission–registration fees

NATIONAL CARE STANDARDS COMMISSION (FEES AND FREQUENCY OF INSPECTIONS) AMENDMENT (NO.2) REGULATIONS 2002, SI 2002 2070; made under the Care Standards Act 2000 s.12, s.16, s.31, s.118. In force: September 1, 2002; £1.50.

These Regulations amend the National Care Standards Commission (Fees and Frequency of Inspections) Regulations 2001 (SI 2001 3980) in consequence of nurses agencies, domiciliary care agencies and residential family centres being deferred until January 1, 2003. They make amendments so that a "new provider", in the case of a residential family centre, a nurses agency or a domiciliary care agency will be a person who carries on such an establishment or agency after January 1, 2003 and not September 1, 2002; so that where an application for registration is made by a person who manages an existing licensed nurses agency, then provided that that application is made before January 1, 2003, no registration fee will be payable; and so that in the case of a nurses agency which is an existing provider, the first annual fee is due on the anniversary first occurring after January 1, 2003. They also make amendments so that for the purposes of a residential family centre, a nurses agency or a domiciliary care agency, the first "12 month period" is to be treated as commencing on January 1, 2003 and ending on March 31, 2004.

4283. Executive agencies–National Care Standards Commission–registration fees

NATIONAL CARE STANDARDS COMMISSION (FEES AND FREQUENCY OF INSPECTIONS) (AMENDMENT) REGULATIONS 2002, SI 2002 1505; made under the Care Standards Act 2000 s.12, s.16, s.31, s.118. In force: July 1, 2002; £1.50.

These Regulations amend the National Care Standards Commission (Fees and Frequency of Inspections) Regulations 2001 (SI 2001 3980) in consequence of the registration of nurses agencies, domiciliary care agencies and residential family centres under the Care Standards Act 2000 being deferred until September 1, 2002. They make amendments so that a "new provider", in the case of a residential family centre, a nurses agency or a domiciliary care agency will be a person who carries on such an establishment or agency after September 1, 2002, and not July 1, 2002; so that where an application for registration is made by a person who manages an existing undertaking which is a licensed nurses agency, then provided that that application is made before September 1, 2002, no registration fee will be payable; and to provide that in the case of a residential family centre, a nurses agency or a domiciliary care agency, the "12 month period" ending on March 31, 2003 is to be treated as commencing on September 1, 2002 and not July 1, 2002.

4284. Executive agencies–National Care Standards Commission–residential family centres–registration and inspection

RESIDENTIAL FAMILY CENTRES REGULATIONS 2002, SI 2002 3213; made under the Care Standards Act 2000 s.4, s.22, s.25, s.34, s.35, s.118. In force: April 1, 2003; £4.00.

These Regulations establish, in relation to England, the National Care Standards Commission and provide for the registration and inspection of establishments and agencies, including residential family centres, by the Commission. It also provides powers for regulations governing the conduct of establishments and agencies.

4285. Food–milk

WELFARE FOOD (AMENDMENT) REGULATIONS 2002, SI 2002 550; made under the Social Security Act 1988 s.13; and the Social Security Contributions and Benefits Act 1992 s.175. In force: April 1, 2002; £1.50.

These Regulations, which amend the Welfare Food Regulations 1996 (SI 1996 1434) by increasing the purchase price of 900 grammes of dried milk to £4.10 and increase to £72.20 the amount of the reduction in the appropriate maximum not to be exceeded to establish entitlement to working families' tax credit, revoke the

Welfare Food (Amendment) Regulations 1997 (SI 1997 857), the Welfare Food (Amendment) Regulations 1998 (SI 1998 691), the Welfare Food (Amendment) Regulations 1999 (SI 1999 2561) and the Welfare Food (Amendment) Regulations 2001 (SI 2001 758).

4286. Health care–private and voluntary health care–Wales

PRIVATE AND VOLUNTARY HEALTH CARE (WALES) REGULATIONS 2002, SI 2002 325; made under the Care Standards Act 2000 s.2, s.22, s.25, s.34, s.35, s.118. In force: April 1, 2002; £6.50.

These Regulations provide that "listed services" includes treatment using the prescribed techniques and technology specified and exclude certain techniques and technology from being listed services. They also exclude certain establishments from the definition of an independent hospital and include establishments providing medical or psychiatric treatment but which have no overnight beds for patients, plus establishments which are service hospitals under the Armed Forces Act 1981, or which cater for offenders under the Prison Act 1952. The Regulations modify the definition of cosmetic surgery, define the meaning of the term "independent clinic" and exempts certain establishments from being an independent medical agency. In addition, they make provision about the fitness of the persons carrying on and managing an establishment or agency and require satisfactory information to be obtained and make provision about the conduct of establishments or agencies, in particular about the quality of the services to be provided in an establishment or agency, including matters relating to privacy, dignity and religious observance, the staffing of the establishment or agency and the fitness of workers and about complaints and record keeping.

4287. Residential accommodation–asylum seekers–community financial assistance–need caused by destitution

[National Assistance Act 1948 s.21 (1) (a), s.21 (1A); Immigration and Asylum Act 1999 s.115; Local Government Act 2000 s.2, s.3.]

K applied for judicial review of the local authority's decision that she did not satisfy the assistance criteria pursuant to the National Assistance Act 1948 s.21 (1) (a). K was subject to immigration control.

Held, granting the application for judicial review, that the local authority's decision was unreasonable. However, the local authority had applied the correct test. As K was subject to immigration control under the Immigration and Asylum Act 1999 s.115, her options for pursuing state support were limited. She could either seek the provision of residential accommodation under s.21 (1) (a) of the 1948 Act or financial assistance under the Local Government Act 2000 s.2. People subject to immigration control under s.115 of the 1999 Act were not eligible for state support under s.21 (1) (a) of the 1948 Act if their need was caused only by destitution, pursuant to s.21 (1A) of the 1948 Act. This limitation also constituted a prohibition for the purpose of s.3 of the 2000 Act thus preventing a local authority from providing financial assistance under s.2.

R. (ON THE APPLICATION OF KHAN) v. OXFORDSHIRE CC, [2002] EWHC 2211, [2003] H.L.R. 23, Moses, J., QBD (Admin Ct).

4288. Residential accommodation–asylum seekers–destitute and infirm asylum seekers–local authorities obligations

[National Assistance Act 1948 s.21, s.21 (1A); Immigration and Asylum Act 1999 s.95; Asylum Support Regulations 2000 (SI 2000 704) Reg.6 (4).]

W, a local authority, appealed against the refusal to quash N's decision not to provide accommodation and support for an infirm destitute asylum seeker, Y. The Court of Appeal ([2001] EWCA Civ 512) held that W was obliged to provide support and accommodation to Y, owing to her infirmity, under the National Assistance Act 1948 s.21, and since Y had this recourse to assistance from W, N was not obliged to provide support pursuant to the Immigration and Asylum Act 1999 s.95. Had Y been able bodied and destitute, she would have been excluded from assistance under s.21 (1A) of the 1948 Act and would have qualified for support from N under the 1999 Act. W contended that Parliament should not have confined itself to merely excluding the able-bodied destitute, but should have excluded the infirm destitute from local authorities duty to provide care under s.21.

Held, dismissing the appeal, that it was clear that the intention of the 1999 Act had been to remove the burden of funding the housing of asylum seekers from local authorities and give it to the Secretary of State, but the inescapable conclusion of the new s.21 (1A) was that local authorities still had a duty to afford assistance where asylum seekers were destitute and infirm. Although s.95 appeared prima facie to give N the power to accommodate all destitute aslyum seekers, whether able bodied or infirm, the Asylum Support Regulations 2000 Reg 6 (4) made it clear that when assessing under s.95 whether a person applying for support was destitute, account had to be taken of other support available to him. As support for infirm destitute asylum seekers was available under s.21, they could not be deemed destitute under s.95. There was thus no overlap in responsibilities, *R. v. Hammersmith and Fulham LBC, ex p. M* (1998) 30 H.L.R. 10, [1997] C.L.Y. 2885 considered.

R. (ON THE APPLICATION OF WESTMINSTER CITY COUNCIL) v. NATIONAL ASYLUM SUPPORT SERVICE; *sub nom.* WESTMINSTER CITY COUNCIL v. NATIONAL ASYLUM SUPPORT SERVICES; R. (ON THE APPLICATION OF WESTMINSTER CITY COUNCIL) v. SECRETARY OF STATE FOR THE HOME DEPARTMENT, [2002] UKHL 38, [2002] 1 W.L.R. 2956, Lord Hoffmann, HL.

4289. **Residential accommodation–asylum seekers–disabled persons–offer of assistance from National Asylum Support Service**

[National Assistance Act 1948 s.21; Asylum Support Regulations 2000 (SI 2000 704) Reg.6 (3), Reg.23 (1).]

M, a destitute asylum seeker, applied for judicial review of the decision of the local authority that he was not entitled to residential accommodation pursuant to the National Assistance Act 1948 s.21, as amended, since his disability did not justify such provision and as he had been offered accommodation by the National Asylum Support Service, NASS. M suffered from a physical disability which necessitated care and attention but which did not give rise to a need for managed residential accommodation. The local authority contended that in order to satisfy the requirements of s.21, the need for care and attention arising from a particular disability had to be such that it could only be met by the provision of residential accommodation.

Held, granting the application, that the nature of the need arising under s.21 of the Act was for care and assistance which was not "otherwise available". In most cases such care and attention was available from friends, family or public authorities. If such care and attention was not available then whatever the need s.21 permitted its provision. Accordingly, M was entitled to assistance under s.21 by virtue of his disability. Moreover, it was not the case that such an applicant was only entitled to care and attention if he would still require such assistance even if no longer destitute, *R. v. Wandsworth LBC, ex p. O* [2000] 1 W.L.R. 2539, [2000] C.L.Y. 4895 considered. Since by virtue of the Asylum Support Regulations 2000 Reg.6 (3) and Reg.23 (1) local authorities were obliged to disregard the prospect of asylum support from any external source when assessing destitution under s.21 (1A), the availability or otherwise of support from NASS could not impact upon the obligation arising under s.21.

R. (ON THE APPLICATION OF MANI) v. LAMBETH LBC; R. (ON THE APPLICATION OF TASCI) v. ENFIELD LBC; R. (ON THE APPLICATION OF J) v. ENFIELD LBC, [2002] EWHC 735, (2002) 5 C.C.L. Rep. 486, Wilson, J., QBD (Admin Ct).

4290. Residential accommodation–sums for personal requirements–Wales

NATIONAL ASSISTANCE (SUMS FOR PERSONAL REQUIREMENTS) (WALES) REGULATIONS 2002, SI 2002 815; made under the National Assistance Act 1948 s.22. In force: April 8, 2002; £1.75.

These Regulations, which revoke the National Assistance (Sums for Personal Requirements) (Wales) Regulations 2001 (SI 2001 1408), set out the weekly sum which local authorities in Wales are to assume, in the absence of special circumstances, that residents in accommodation arranged under the National Assistance Act 1948 Part III will need for their personal requirements. From April 8, 2002 all such residents will be assumed to need £16.80 per week for their personal requirements.

4291. Residential care–care homes and nursing homes–Wales

CARE HOMES (WALES) REGULATIONS 2002, SI 2002 324; made under the Care Standards Act 2000 s.3, s.22, s.25, s.33, s.34, s.35, s.118. In force: April 1, 2002; £6.50.

These Regulations, which replace the regulatory system provided for in relation to residential care homes and nursing homes by the Registered Homes Act 1984, exclude from the definition of a care home under the Care Standards Act 2000 family care settings, establishments that provide accommodation for less than 28 days in a year, certain NHS facilities providing nursing and certain education institutions. Under the Regulations, each home must have a statement of purpose and supply a guide to the home of each service user. The Regulations make provision about the fitness of the persons carrying on and managing the home, and require satisfactory information to be available in relation to certain specified matters. In addition, they prescribe the circumstances where a manager must be appointed for the home, impose general requirements in relation to the proper conduct of the home, make provision about the conduct of care homes and about the suitability of premises and fire precautions to be taken.

4292. Residential care–disabled persons–provision of accommodation by voluntary sector–performance of public function

[National Assistance Act 1948 s.21 (1), s.26(1); Local Government Act 1972 s.195(6), Sch.23; Human Rights Act 1998 Sch.1 Part I Art.8, s.6; Civil Procedure Rules 1998 (SI 1998/3132) Part 54.]

H, residents of a home for the disabled, owned and run by L, a charity, appealed against the dismissal of their application for judicial review of L's decision to redevelop the home. As a consequence of the redevelopment, H would no longer be accommodated at the home. The local authority had exercised its statutory powers in placing H at the home and funding the placements pursuant to the National Assistance Act 1948 s.21 (1) and s.26(1), as amended by the Local Government Act 1972 s.195(6) and Sch.23. H contended that the loss of their home was an infringement of their rights under the Human Rights Act 1998 Sch.1 Part I Art.8. H argued that the provision of accommodation by L constituted the performance of a public function within the definition in s.6 of the 1998 Act and therefore its decision to redevelop the home was amenable to judicial review. The court considered whether judicial review proceedings were appropriate for disputes as to whether a body was performing a public function.

Held, dismissing the appeal, that the role performed by L did not amount to the exercise of a public function. However, bona fide disputes as to whether bodies were performing a public function were appropriate matters for judicial review proceedings under the Civil Procedure Rules 1998 Part 54. Although the local authority had exercised its powers under s.26 of the 1948 Act to use L as a provider of residential accommodation, the local authority had not divested itself of its duties under s.21 of the 1948 Act and under Art.8 of the 1998 Act. The provision of funding by itself was not decisive as to whether functions were public and, in the instant case, there was no other material difference in the services provided to privately funded residents of the home as opposed to publicly funded residents.

R. (ON THE APPLICATION OF HEATHER) v. LEONARD CHESHIRE FOUNDATION, [2002] EWCA Civ 366, [2002] 2 All E.R. 936, Lord Woolf of Barnes, L.C.J., CA.

4293. Residential care—elderly persons—closure of home—relevant considerations

[Local Authority Social Services Act 1970; National Health Service and Community Care Act 1990 s.47; Local Government Act 1999.]

B sought judicial review of C's decision to close W, a residential care home for the elderly, in order to permit building work to develop a new facility for "frail older people" on the same site. B contended that C had failed to take into account all material considerations as it had not assessed the needs of the individual residents as required by the National Health Service and Community Care Act 1990 s.47, or had due regard to documents promising the residents a "home for life". C submitted that the decision had been lawful as group consultation had taken place which obviated the need for individual assessment of the residents and that, in any event, a decision in principle had to be taken before any needs assessment could be carried out.

Held, granting the application for judicial review, that the decision for closure had not been taken "in principle" but had been a final decision. Consequently, C were in breach of their assessment obligations under the 1990 Act. The provisions of the Local Authority Social Services Act 1970 required that residential care for the elderly should be provided on a "needs led" basis. Therefore, C had not been entitled to change the basis of care provision in the way that it had such as to defer the interests of individual residents to C's concern to carry out a "Best Value Review" under the Local Government Act 1999. Moreover, the handbook and letter previously issued to the residents gave rise to a substantive legitimate expectation that they would have a home for life at W, *R. v. North and East Devon HA, ex p. Coughlan* [2001] Q.B. 213, [1999] C.L.Y. 2643 applied.

R. (ON THE APPLICATION OF B) v. CAMDEN LBC, [2001] EWHC Admin 271, (2001) 4 C.C.L. Rep. 246, Turner, J., QBD (Admin Ct).

4294. Residential care—transfer of assets—assessment of means—independence of review panel—right to fair trial

[Human Rights Act 1998 Sch.1 Part I Art.6 (1); National Assistance (Assessment of Resources) Regulations 1992 (SI 1992 2977).]

The personal representatives of B, challenged the local authority's decision that B had intentionally deprived himself of his house for the purposes of the National Assistance (Assessment of Resources) Regulations 1992 and that the value of the house fell to be taken into consideration when assessing his ability to pay for the residential care arranged for him by the local authority. B had transferred the property to his son soon after suffering a stroke, however he had later been assessed as requiring residential care, and his son applied, on his father's behalf, for financial assistance towards the placement. The representatives submitted that the local authority had misdirected itself as to the relevant test under the Regulations and that the statutory procedure was incompatible with, among other things, the Human Rights Act 1998 Sch.1 Part I Art.6.1, and that the decision was therefore unlawful.

Held, granting the application for judicial review, that the correct test under the 1992 Regulations was a subjective test, *Yule v. South Lanarkshire Council (No.2)* 2001 S.C. 203, [2000] C.L.Y. 6693 applied. It was not clear that the review panel had understood the test given that there was no evidence it had rejected the evidence of B's son regarding intention at the time of transfer. The decision was one based on means testing and therefore a wrong decision could result in serious economic consequences, and Art.6.1 applied given that the statutory scheme was a measure of welfare assistance falling within the reasoning of *Schuler-Zgraggen v. Switzerland (A/263)* [1994] 1 F.C.R. 453,

[1995] C.L.Y. 2667 and *Salesi v. Italy (A/257-E)* (1998) 26 E.H.R.R. 187, [1998] C.L.Y. 3139. The decision had also not been made by an independent and impartial tribunal under Art.6.1 given that the chairperson had been the only independent member of the panel and the final decision had rested with the council's director of social services. The failings behind the decision could only be remedied by the decision being quashed and the issue being referred to an totally independent panel. *Schuler-Zgraggen* and *Salesi* considered.

R. (ON THE APPLICATION OF BEESON) v. DORSET CC, [2001] EWHC Admin 986, [2002] H.R.L.R. 15, Richards, J., QBD (Admin Ct).

4295. **Social work–education and training–transfer scheme–abolition of Central Council**

ABOLITION OF THE CENTRAL COUNCIL FOR EDUCATION AND TRAINING IN SOCIAL WORK ORDER 2002, SI 2002 797; made under the Care Standards Act 2000 s.70, s.118. In force: April 1, 2002; £1.50.

This Order amends the Health and Social Services and Social Security Adjudications Act 1983, the Government of Wales Act 1998, the Freedom of Information Act 2000 and the Central Council for Education and Training in Social Work (Transfer Scheme) Order 2001 (SI 2001 2561). The functions of the Central Council for Education and Training in Social Work are abolished. Any remaining assets and liabilities of the Central Council for Education and Training in Social Work are transferred to the Secretary of State or the successor bodies established under the specified Acts.

4296. **Social workers–child protection–defective investigation procedure in relation to sexual abuse allegations against social worker–appropriate forum for appeal**

[Protection of Children Act 1999.]

M, a social worker, appealed against the refusal of his application for judicial review ([2002] EWHC 351) of a local authority's decision to put his name on the Consultancy Index following allegations that he had sexually abused children. M contended that the local authority's investigation procedure had been flawed.

Held, dismissing the appeal, that the Care Standards Tribunal established under the Protection of Children Act 1999 was the most suitable forum for hearing M's appeal. Whilst judicial review provided an alternative remedy, the annulment of the investigative procedure may have caused unfairness to those under M's care. The overriding consideration was the danger to disadvantaged children under M's care if M was wrongly cleared and his name removed from the Index. The Tribunal had expertise in dealing with evidence from handicapped people and accordingly could determine whether M was unfit even if it found that the investigation procedure was defective.

R. (ON THE APPLICATION OF M) v. BROMLEY LBC; *sub nom.* M v. BROMLEY LBC, [2002] EWCA Civ 1113, [2002] 2 F.L.R. 802, Buxton, L.J., CA.

4297. **Social workers–disciplinary procedures–alleged breach of duty of care–holding of disciplinary proceedings in advance of public inquiry**

A and M, social workers employed by the local authority, H, challenged the decision of H to proceed with disciplinary proceedings for alleged misconduct in advance of a government appointed inquiry into the circumstances surrounding the death of C, who had died at the hands of her aunt and her aunt's partner, and to whom it was alleged A and M had owed the duty of care. A and M contended that the implied term in their contract of employment was that disciplinary proceedings could not proceed before a public inquiry, dealing on the same matter, if there was a risk of inconsistent findings.

Held, granting the application for judicial review in part, that it was not unlawful per se for H to hold disciplinary proceedings in advance of a public inquiry, given that the implied term in A and M's contracts of employment was that disciplinary proceedings would not proceed before a public inquiry if there was a real risk that the proceedings would prevent the employee from participating properly in the inquiry. It was important that H was able to take disciplinary action against staff where appropriate. However, an order restraining H from holding the disciplinary hearings until A and M had given evidence at the inquiry was justified having regard to the evidence concerning the impact of events since C's death upon A and M's health, which gave rise to a real risk that disciplinary proceedings in advance of the inquiry might prevent them from participating fully in it. Accordingly, on the particular facts, if the disciplinary proceedings were to proceed at this time H would be acting in breach of the implied contractual term.

R. (ON THE APPLICATION OF ARTHURWORREY) v. HARINGEY LBC; *sub nom.* R. (ON THE APPLICATION OF ARTHURWORRY) v. HARINGEY LBC, [2001] EWHC Admin 698, [2002] I.C.R. 279, Jackson, J., QBD (Admin Ct).

4298. Books

Ashton, District Judge Gordon R.–Ashton: Elderly People and the Law. Paperback: £40.00. ISBN 0-406-94152-1. Butterworths Law.

Brammer, Alison–Social Work Law. Paperback: £19.99. ISBN 0-582-43831-4. Longman.

Cooper, Jeremy–Care Homes Legal Handbook. Paperback: £13.95. ISBN 1-84310-064-9. Jessica Kingsley Publishers.

Gilliom, John–Overseers of the Poor-Surveillance, Resistance, and the Limits of Privacy. Hardback: £25.00. ISBN 0-226-29360-2. University of Chicago Press.

Gilliom, John–Overseers of the Poor. Paperback: £10.50. ISBN 0-226-29361-0. University of Chicago Press.

Jaeger, Paul T.; Bowman, Cynthia Ann–Disability Matters. Hardback: £51.95. ISBN 0-89789-909-1. Praeger Publishers.

Luba, Jan; Davies, Liz–Homelessness Act 2002. Paperback: £30.00. ISBN 0-85308-825-X. Family Law.

Ridout, P.–Care Standards. Paperback: £45.00. ISBN 0-85308-823-3. Jordans.

Williams, Lucy A.–Welfare Law. International Library of Essays in Law and Legal Theory (second Series). Hardback: £100.00. ISBN 0-7546-2096-4. Dartmouth.

SPORT

4299. Sporting organisations–membership–existence of contractual relationship

See CONTRACTS: Modahl v. British Athletic Federation Ltd (No.2). §704

4300. Sporting organisations–restrictive trade practices–restrictions on members' activities–abuse of dominant position

See COMPETITION LAW: Hendry v. World Professional Billiards & Snooker Association Ltd. §598

4301. Sports–football–football grounds–seating

FOOTBALL SPECTATORS (SEATING) ORDER 2002, SI 2002 1755; made under the Football Spectators Act 1989 s.11. In force: July 31, 2002; £1.75.

This Order directs the Football Licensing Authority to include in any licence to admit spectators to the specified football ground a condition imposing certain requirements as respects the seating of spectators at designated football matches at that premises, which are those association football matches designated by the Secretary of State in the Football Spectators (Designation of Football Matches in England and Wales) Order 2000 (SI 2000 3331), including all association football matches played at the specified premises.

4302. Sports−football−spectators−world cup control period

FOOTBALL SPECTATORS (WORLD CUP CONTROL PERIOD) (NO.2) ORDER 2002, SI 2002 1143; made under the Football Spectators Act 1989 s.14. In force: May 15, 2002; £1.50.

This Order describes the control period under the Football Spectators Act 1989 for the 2002 FIFA (Fdration Internationale de Football Associations) World Cup Korea/Japan. The control period begins on May 26, 2002, being five days before the first match in the tournament, and ends when the last match in the tournament is finished or cancelled. The last match is due to be played on June 30, 2002. During the period powers contained in the Football Spectators Act 1989 s.19, s.21A and s.21B are exercisable.

4303. Sports facilities−safety certificates

SAFETY OF SPORTS GROUNDS (DESIGNATION) ORDER 2002, SI 2002 1754; made under the Safety of Sports Grounds Act 1975 s.1, s.18. In force: July 31, 2002; £1.50.

This Order designates the Walker's Stadium in Leicester as a sports ground requiring a safety certificate under the Safety of Sports Grounds Act 1975.

4304. Sports grounds−safety certificates

SAFETY OF SPORTS GROUNDS (DESIGNATION) (NO.2) ORDER 2002, SI 2002 2893; made under the Safety of Sports Grounds Act 1975 s.1, s.18. In force: December 16, 2002; £1.50.

This Order designates Kingston Communications Stadium in Kingston upon Hull as a sports ground requiring a safety certificate under the Safety of Sports Ground Act 1975.

4305. Books

Beloff, Michael−International Sports Law Review: 2000. Hardback. ISBN 0-421-78700-7. Sweet & Maxwell.

Reeb, Matthieu−Digest of CAS Awards II, 1998-2000. Digest of "CAS" Awards Series, 2. Hardback: £82.00. ISBN 90-411-1730-X. Kluwer Law International.

Taylor, Jonathan; Lewis, Adam−Taylor and Lewis: Sport: Law and Practice. Hardback: £120.00. ISBN 0-406-94592-6. Hardback: £120.00. ISBN 0-406-94592-6. Butterworths Law.

Weiler, Paul−Leveling the Playing Field. Paperback: £12.50. ISBN 0-674-00687-9. Harvard University Press.

Wong, Glenn M.−Essentials of Sports Law. Hardback: £54.50. ISBN 0-275-97121-X. Praeger Publishers.

SUCCESSION

4306. Administration of estates−administrators−no evidence of wilful default− estate comprising land subject to disputes amongst members of family farming partnership

S's will divided his estate between his grandchildren. The main asset was a beneficial interest in land used in a farming partnership comprising S and his children, who all had beneficial interests in the land. A number of legal disputes remained outstanding between S and his children on his death in 1997. The executors named in the will declined to act and T, who had obtained the grant of letters of administration to act in relation to the land, was in the process of obtaining counsel's advice as to how best to proceed when I, S's grandson, sought an order that T was liable to account to him on the basis of their wilful default. I contended that T should have sold the land occupied by the partnership or recovered rents due from its continued occupation.

Held, refusing the application, that I had failed to make out his claim of wilful default. T had correctly exercised their judgment before seeking counsel's opinion and were anxious not to involve the estate in expensive litigation.

ILIFFE v. TRAFFORD; *sub nom*. ILLIFFE v. TRAFFORD [2002] W.T.L.R. 507, Hart, J., Ch D.

4307. Administration of estates–breach of trust–joint and several liability–purported resignation of administrator–continuing liability under implied indemnity

[Trustee Act 1925 s.61.]

A, the administrator of the estate of K, which comprised assets in both Ghana and England, appealed against a decision that he was in breach of duty for acts carried out by the other three administrators after his purported resignation. Owing to the nature of the estate, guarantors were appointed in respect of K's English assets. However, A found that he was unable to continue as an administrator. At first instance he was held to be liable to indemnify the guarantors for acts done after his resignation. Relief against claims by the guarantors under the Trustee Act 1925 s.61 was refused on the basis that they had not been notified of the resignation. A contended that the implied indemnity under the guarantee did not include liability for acts done by the other administrators.

Held, dismissing the appeal, that A was in default as his resignation did not mean that he had ceased to be an administrator. Although he had not taken part in the breach of trust, he had neglected his position by allowing them to occur. A's liability to the guarantors under the implied indemnity was contractual in nature and was not limited only to his own defaults. The joint and several nature of the guarantee meant that A could not base his defence to a claim for indemnity on the ground that he was not liable for the breach of trust which were a matter for contribution proceedings between A and the other administrators.

SEGBEDZI (MINORS) v. SEGBEDZI [2002] W.T.L.R. 83, Jonathan Parker, J., CA.

4308. Beneficiaries–public policy–validity of condition subsequent deterring challenges to a will's validity–applications for "reasonable financial provision"

[Inheritance (Provision for Family and Dependants) Act 1975.]

The court considered as a preliminary issue the validity of a condition contained in a codicil to a will, that provided that if a beneficiary mounted a challenge to the will the whole estate would go to the first and second defendants. N, the son of the testator, made an application under the Inheritance (Provision for Family and Dependants) Act 1975, thereby triggering the condition.

Held, determining the preliminary issue in favour of N, that the fact that a condition subsequent to a will would deter a beneficiary from challenging it for fear of losing his benefit thereunder, did not, of itself, render the condition void on grounds of public policy. Any loss of benefit resulting from a challenge made by way of an application for financial provision under the 1975 Act, would be taken into account by the court when considering that application. In the instant case the condition was void for uncertainty.

NATHAN v. LEONARD, [2002] EWHC 1701, [2003] 1 W.L.R. 827, John Martin Q.C., Ch D.

4309. Family provision–time limits–application for reasonable financial provision out of time–criteria for extension

[Inheritance (Provision for Family and Dependants) Act 1975 s.4.]

MM, wife of the deceased testator, TM, brought an application for reasonable financial provision pursuant to the Inheritance (Provision for Family and

Dependants) Act1975. She also sought permission to bring the proceedings out of time having regard to the fact that the originating summons had not been issued until more than three years and seven months after the expiry of the six month time limit prescribed by s.4 of the 1975 Act. Under the terms of TM's will, MM was entitled to an annuity paid out of TM's business interests together with the residue of the estate. The business itself had been bequeathed to the testator's sons from whom MM was estranged. MM contended that the court's discretion to extend the time limit should be exercised in her favour having regard to the fact that the estate had not been distributed and that there had been no identifiable prejudice caused to the remaining beneficiaries. MM further maintained that part of the delay was explicable on the basis that she had possessed no idea of the true value of certain land forming part of the testator's business which had had a low value attributed to it for probate purposes but which had subsequently been sold to developers for a vastly increased sum.

Held, granting the application and giving judgment for MM, that it would be disproportionate and unfair to prevent MM from advancing a sound claim for reasonable financial provision when the period of delay had resulted in no prejudice to the remaining beneficiaries of the estate. The applicable time limit should not be viewed as a disciplinary provision to be enforced for its own sake. The will had not made reasonable financial provision for MM, who ought to be entitled to share in the realised value of the business. Having regard to the potential position on divorce and taking into account the fact that the competing beneficiaries were not only comfortably provided for but had already extracted significant value from the estate, an appropriate award would be a lump sum of £175,000.

McNULTY v. McNULTY, [2002] EWHC 123, [2002] W.T.L.R. 737, Launcelot Henderson Q.C., Ch D.

4310. **Family provision–void marriages–Hindu ceremony–absence of good faith**

[Marriage Act 1949; Inheritance (Provision for Family and Dependants) Act 1975 s.25(4).]

HG brought a claim under the Inheritance (Provision for Family and Dependants) Act 1975 seeking provision from the estate of JG. HG and JG had partaken in a Hindu marriage in 1989. The ceremony, which had taken place at an Indian restaurant and been presided over by a Brahmin priest, had not complied with the requirements of the Marriage Act 1949. Moreover, at the time of the ceremony JG had still been married to another woman. HG maintained that she should, nevertheless, be regarded for the purposes of the 1975 Act as "the wife of the deceased". The issue before the court related to whether HG was "a person who in good faith [had] entered into a void marriage" within the meaning of s.25(4) of the 1975 Act.

Held, giving judgment for JG's executors, that the Hindu marriage ceremony had not resulted in a "void marriage" but, for the purposes of English law, "no marriage at all". It was apparent that in many respects the ceremony had not complied with the 1949 Act. In such circumstances, it could not be said that the marriage was void; rather it had amounted to a "non marriage", *M v. M (Divorce: Jurisdiction: Validity of Marriage)* [2001] 2 F.L.R. 6, [2001] C.L.Y. 2615 applied. Moreover, even if the ceremony had amounted to a void marriage, it was apparent that HG had not entered into it in good faith. On the balance of probabilities, HG had been aware that the marriage was not valid at the time that she had entered into it. Furthermore, she had known that JG was still married at the time of the ceremony.

GANDHI v. PATEL; *sub nom.* GHANDI v. PATEL [2002] 1 F.L.R. 603, Park, J., Ch D.

4311. Family provision—widows—interest in matrimonial home following severance of joint tenancy

[Inheritance (Provision for Family and Dependants) Act 1975.]

G and her husband, R, married in 1987. R had two children from his previous marriage, P and N. In 1991, G and R instructed a solicitor, B, to draw up wills disposing of the couple's shares separately, subject to a qualified right for the survivor to remain in the matrimonial home. They also severed the joint tenancy, with P and N taking R's share. R died in 1996 and G sought rectification of his will, contending that it had not evidenced his actual intention, or, in the alternative, provision under the Inheritance (Provision for Family and Dependants) Act 1975.

Held, refusing the rectification claim but allowing the claim for financial provision, that the evidence was inadequate to show that R's will had failed to carry out his intentions, *Walker v. Geo H Medlicott & Son* [1999] 1 W.L.R. 727, [1998] C.L.Y. 4584 applied. However, R's will did not make reasonable provision for G. Therefore the assets in R's estate would be used to discharge the mortgage remaining in the matrimonial home and G's right to remain would be varied to allow her to cohabit in the future. Discharging the mortgage would ensure that P and N each received a 50 per cent unencumbered half share and also relieve G of the need to make further mortgage payments. Further, G was to take the residuary estate absolutely with a £5,000 legacy each to P and N.

GRATTAN v. McNAUGHTON; *sub nom.* GRATTAN (ROBIN FRANCIS), IN THE ESTATE OF [2001] W.T.L.R. 1305, Judge Behrens Q.C., Ch D.

4312. Family provision—widows—reasonable provision—likelihood marriage would have ended in divorce

[Inheritance (Provision for Family and Dependants) Act 1975 s.1 (1) (a), s.2, s.3 (2).]

S applied pursuant to the Inheritance (Provision for Family and Dependants) Act 1975 s.1 (1) (a) for relief under s.2 on the ground that the dispositions in the will of her late husband, A, did not make reasonable provision for her. S was 60 years old and both S and A had been married previously. She married A in 1988 and they were married for 11 years before he died in 1999. A had two adult children. Although S regarded the marriage as happy, A had commenced divorce proceedings and had memoranda drawn up to explain changes to his wills arising from his belief that the marriage would end in divorce, however the proceedings were not carried into effect due to A's final illness. S contended that the income from a £10,000 fund, left to her under A's will was insufficient, given that his net estate was worth £1.5 million.

Held, allowing the application, that S was entitled to an additional lump sum of £225,000, taking into account her age, the length of the marriage and her contribution to it. Regard also had to be paid to the settlement S could have expected to receive had the marriage ended in divorce rather than death, as set out in s.3(2), *Krubert (Deceased), Re* [1997] Ch. 97, [1996] C.L.Y. 5547 considered. S could have expected £900,000 on divorce, equal to the matrimonial home, which actually passed to S by survivorship, and a further £290,000 allowing for sale of the property. Reasonable provision in terms of the Act had to be determined objectively and not by asking whether A believed the provision made by his will was reasonable. On the facts, A's children did not require provision to be made for them to S's detriment. The memoranda were largely self serving as they attempted to justify A's actions in terms of the changes to his wills, but the factors set out therein could explain the provision he had made.

SINGER v. ISAAC [2001] W.T.L.R. 1045, Master Bowles, Ch D.

4313. Gifts—inheritance tax—exempt transfers—discretionary beneficiaries—gift of life interest to settlor's spouse

See TAX: Inland Revenue Commissioners v. Eversden. §4454

4314. Gifts–inter vivos–presumption of undue influence–absence of wrongful act by donee insufficient to rebut

H appealed against a decision that the presumption of undue influence in respect of a large gift made to O by P had been successfully rebutted. P, H's cousin, was an elderly man in poor health who had come to rely upon the care and friendship provided by O, his neighbour. The gift was in the sum of £297,005, which represented more than 90 per cent of P's liquid assets and exposed him to a substantial tax liability. These facts were not drawn to P's attention by O, nor did he receive any form of independent advice as regards the nature and effect of the proposed gift. O contended that in order to rebut the presumption of undue influence it was sufficient to show that her conduct had been unimpeachable or that there had been nothing sinister in it.

Held, allowing the appeal, that the presumption of undue influence raised by a substantial gift being made in circumstances where there was a relationship of trust and confidence between donor and donee could only be rebutted by the donee proving the gift had been made after full, free and informed thought by the donor. It was insufficient for the donee to show there had been no wrongdoing on their part, *Allcard v. Skinner* (1887) L.R. 36 Ch. D. 145 and *Zamet v. Hyman* [1961] 1 W.L.R.1442, [1961] C.L.Y. 3704 applied. In the instant case O had failed to discharge the burden of proof and thus the gift was set aside.

HAMMOND v. OSBORN, [2002] EWCA Civ 885, [2002] W.T.L.R. 1125, Sir Martin Nourse., CA.

4315. Gifts–inter vivos–setting aside–lifetime gift intended to defeat provision for widow–Canada

[Family Law Act 1990 (Ontario); Fraudulent Conveyances Act 1990 (Ontario).]
The children of H appealed the court's finding that the Fraudulent Conveyances Act 1990 applied to certain transactions made by H prior to his death. H and W both had children by previous marriages. After being diagnosed with terminal cancer H made certain dispositions of property without W's consent or knowledge. After his death W sought an equalisation payment rather than the provision made for her by H under his will. Under Canadian law a widow could seek an "equalisation" payment rather than accept the provision made in the deceased spouse's will. On W's application the judge set aside the inter vivos transactions.

Held, dismissing the appeal, that the Family Law Act 1990 was not a self contained code and accordingly the judge had rightly invoked the provisions of the Fraudulent Conveyances Act 1990.

STONE v. STONE (2001-02) 4 I.T.E.L.R. 671, Feldman, J.A., CA (Ont).

4316. Inheritance tax–legacies–disclaimers–interest in possession–property left to spouse–presumption in favour of acceptance not rebutted

See TAX: Cook v. Inland Revenue Commissioners. §4456

4317. Intestacy–constructive trusts–joint tenants–facilitating purchase of property–agreements for beneficial ownership of property

W, as administrator of her late mother's estate, claimed that a property, sole title to which was vested in P, was held by P on trust for the estate or for himself and the estate. The property, a lease of a flat in a retirement home for the elderly, had been purchased in the joint names of M and P, M's nephew. P provided the monies to purchase the lease but was subsequently reimbursed in a sum equal to 68 per cent of the purchase costs by M. M and P's mother, I, had lived together in a property owned jointly by them. On her death, I had devised her share in that property to M. M had used less than half of the proceeds of sale of that property to finance her share of the purchase costs of the lease. On the death of M legal title to the lease had vested in P by the doctrine of survivorship. In the absence of an express written agreement between M and P as to beneficial title, the issue to be decided was whether M and P had held the property as joint tenants. W contended that they had not.

Held, giving judgment for P, that facilitating the purchase of a property by paying the deposit or contributing to the purchase price was a sufficient detriment to invoke the doctrine of constructive trusts under which a party is deemed to have a beneficial interest in a property if they have acted to their detriment in reliance on an agreement made with another that the property would be shared beneficially, *Lloyds Bank Plc v. Rosset* [1991] 1 A.C. 107, [1990] C.L.Y. 706 applied. In light of the evidence given by P and the solicitor acting in the purchase, the close bond between M and P, and the fact that P stood to recover a sum representing less than half his mother's interest in the property she had owned jointly with M, the judge found that there had been an agreement between M and P that in return for P contributing to the purchase price they would hold the lease as joint tenants in equity. Accordingly P was solely beneficially entitled to the flat.

WINSPER v. PERRETT [2002] W.T.L.R. 927, Kim Lewison Q.C., ChD (Chancery Division).

4318. Intestacy–family provision–advancement of capital for benefit of child– New Zealand

[Trustee Act 1956 (New Zealand) s.41.]

G's long term partner died as a result of an accident. He died intestate, leaving an infant daughter. G made an application under the Trustee Act 1956 (New Zealand) s.41 for an order approving payment to her outright of the funds and property in the estate held by her on trust for the child. The grounds for the application were that such an order would best provide for the maintenance, education, advancement and benefit of the child within the meaning of s.41.

Held, granting the application, that an advancement was the payment to a beneficiary of part of the capital of a bequest before the time had come at which the capital fell into the beneficiary's hands. An advancement was neither a loan or a debt to be repaid. In the form put forward, the application secured a substantial percentage of the estate to the intended beneficiary. The recasting of the estate in the form sought was for the benefit of the child.

GERBICH, *Re* (2001-02) 4 I.T.E.L.R. 589, Hammond, J., HC (NZ).

4319. Intestacy–proprietary estoppel–promises made to gardener–quantifying equity–detriment and expectation

The intestate died in 1997. She had been dependent for some years before her death on the services of J who had begun working for her as a gardener and handyman in 1970, but over the years had taken increasing care for her. From the late 1980s onwards, however, she had ceased paying J, telling him instead that he would have the house and furniture on her death, which were then worth £435,000 and her total estate was valued at £1.3 million. J appealed against a decision ([2001] W.T.L.R. 871, [2001] C.L.Y. 5158) that his equity would be satisfied with an award of £200,000, taking into account a series of factors, including the payments J had foregone. J contended that he had expected at least the value of the house and furniture. R, the administrator of the estate, submitted that J's expectation represented the maximum award but the award had to be proportionate to detriment experienced and expectation.

Held, dismissing the appeal, that proportionality was essential between expectation and detriment in deciding how to satisfy an equity based on proprietary estoppel. The detriment to J was more difficult to establish than his expectation. Courts must consider unconscionability. By considering the circumstances and focusing on the payment J had foregone, the judge below had taken all relevant factors into account, *Campbell v. Griffin* [2001] EWCA Civ 990, [2001] W.T.L.R. 981, [2001] C.L.Y. 4859, *Crabb v. Arun DC (No.1)* [1976]

Ch. 179, [1975] C.L.Y. 1191 and *Gillett v. Holt* [2001] Ch. 210, [2000] C.L.Y. 2321 considered.
    JENNINGS v. RICE, [2002] EWCA Civ 159, [2003] 1 F.C.R. 501, Aldous, L.J., CA.

4320. Mutual wills–burden of proof–spouses making wills on same day–subsequent change to disposition by survivor–New Zealand

[Family Protection Act 1955 (New Zealand).]
    LC and his wife, DC, executed wills on the same day in 1983. Under LC's will, DC was to receive a life income, one daughter, S, was to receive a beach house and a legacy of NZD 25,000, a second daughter, GL, obtained the option of purchasing land and stock on payment of NZD 25,000, and their son, GC, took the residue. Under DC's will, LC received a life interest and the whole estate was left to GC. DC predeceased LC in 1987 and he went on to make several more wills before his death in 1997. LC's final will varied the shares granted to the children, in particular by granting GL the forgiveness of a debt of NZD 100,000. GL and her husband had net assets of NZD 1.28m at the time LC died. Nevertheless, GL contested the will, claiming that LC and DC had made mutual wills in 1983. She also claimed for provision to be made for her under the Family Protection Act 1955. Her claims were dismissed at first instance and she appealed.
    Held, dismissing the appeal, that (1) the revocable nature of a will could be affected by a contractual promise against revocation, so that the executors and trustees of a subsequent will held the assets on a constructive trust under the terms of the revoked will; (2) the standard of proof for the existence of mutual wills was the balance of probabilities, but such claims called for very careful scrutiny; (3) GL's assertion that LC and DC had made mutual wills was not borne out by the evidence, and (4) GL also failed to establish a case under the 1955 Act. A will was not to be effectively rewritten merely because it proved unfair to a family member who did not need provision owing to their existing financial situation.
    LEWIS v. COTTON [2001] W.T.L.R. 1117, Richardson (President), CA (NZ).

4321. Mutual wills–spouses–survivor changing disposition to children–lack of agreement to make irrevocable mutual will–Canada

P and S were brothers who prospered in legal practice and property development. They each had children, one of whom on each side of the family was involved in the management of the family business. P's daughter, J, was married. She was not involved in the business. P and his wife, G, made wills that were not quite identical in their provisions. The wills were made with a view to providing for their children and to preserving the family business in the most tax efficient manner. After the wills had been made the family business was restructured. After G's death, P and S executed new wills and there was a further major restructuring of the business. P and J subsequently fell out and P made yet another will excluding J from his estate. He also exercised a power of appointment of capital whereby shares held on trust for J were removed and placed in trust for P's other child, M. J commenced proceedings against P, alleging that the wills of P and G were mutual, alternatively that all P's assets were held on trust for J and M.
    Held, dismissing the action, that for wills to be enforceable as mutual wills the party asserting mutuality had to show that there was an agreement between the testators that the survivor would not alter their will at any time during their lifetime. The mere making of corresponding wills, without more, did not amount to an agreement never to alter the will. On the evidence, there was no such contract between P and G. Further, there was no estoppel raised on the facts, and there was nothing that could be construed as a declaration of trust.
    EDELL v. SITZER; *sub nom.* SITZER v. EDELL (2001-02) 4 I.T.E.L.R. 149, Cullity, J., CJ (Gen Div) (Ont).

4322. Options–sale of land–tenant's option to purchase property–valuation criteria

L brought an action claiming that he was entitled under the will of B to an option to buy a property. B had converted the property into two flats in 1974 and L had become the tenant of the ground floor flat on a low rent, B living in the top flat. In 1997, B made a will in contemplation of marriage granting her future husband a right to live in her flat after her death. After her marriage she added a codicil requiring her executor, N, to give L an option to buy the entire property, or either of the flats. B died in March 1998. Her husband continued to live in the top flat for a short period and then moved into a nursing home. L was not offered an option and initiated proceedings against N.

Held, allowing the application, that N was required to offer to L a single option to buy the whole property or either flat. The offer would have to be made forthwith as it should have been made shortly after B's death as part of the administration of the estate. The date for valuation should therefore be the date of death and the valuer should look at the situation as it then was and only take into account matters known at that time, *Mackay v. McSparran* [1974] N.I. 136, [1976] C.L.Y. 1998 applied.

LAYTON v. NEWCOMBE [2002] W.T.L.R. 541, Ferris, J., Ch D.

4323. Practice directions–grants of representation–estates of those killed in United States on September 11, 2001

The Senior District Judge of the Principal Registry of the Family Division has issued a Practice Direction pertaining to applications for grants of representation for the estates of those who died in the United States on September 11, 2001.

All personal applications are to be supported by a death certificate issued by the relevant US authority. If no certificate is available, application for leave to swear death will have to be made supported by an explanation as to why there is no death certificate. Such applications should be made to the Principal Registry of the Family Division and applications lodged elsewhere should be transferred accordingly.

PRACTICE DIRECTION (FAM DIV: DEATHS IN USA ON 11 SEPTEMBER 2001) [2002] 1 F.C.R. 96, District Judge Angel, Fam Div.

4324. Practice directions–probate–excepted estates–wording on face of grant of representation

With effect from April 15, 2002 *Practice Direction (Fam Div: Probate Records: Grants of Representation) (No.1)* [1998] 1 W.L.R. 1699, [1999] C.L.Y. 4643 was revised.

The revisions related to the information which appeared on grants of representation in probate records and were as follows (1) in respect of the addresses referred to in sub paragraph (b) of the Practice Direction the post code should be stated, if known; (2) in respect of excepted estates referred to in sub paragraph (f) of the Practice Direction the net value of the estate should be rounded up to the nearest thousand and stated as "not exceeding £".

PRACTICE DIRECTION (FAM DIV: PROBATE RECORDS: GRANTS OF REPRESENTATION) (NO.2); *sub nom.* PRACTICE DIRECTION (FAM DIV: PROBATE RECORDS: EXCEPTED ESTATES) [2002] 1 W.L.R. 1303, Dame Elizabeth Butler-Sloss (President), Fam Div.

4325. Probate–costs–departure from normal rule–applicable factors

[Civil Procedure Rules 1998 (SI 1998 3132) Part 44 r.44.3.]

In a probate action the issue arose as to the factors to be taken into account when departing from the general rule as to costs under the Civil Procedure Rules 1998 Part 44 r.44.3. In the action, C had shown that the deceased had known and approved of the contents of the will. C had been successful in defending an allegation made of undue influence.

Held, ordering that G pay one half of C's costs, that when taking into account "all the circumstances" for the purposes of r.44.3 of the Rules, a judge could have regard to the principles laid down in *Spiers v. English* [1907] P. 122 namely, that it might be appropriate to make an alternative costs order where the testator or those interested in the residue had caused the litigation or if the circumstances led reasonably to an investigation. In the instant case, while there had been grounds for suspecting undue influence and therefore G had been entitled to their case, C had had to endure the consequences of defending that charge. *Spiers v. English* considered.

GOOD (DECEASED) (COSTS), *Re*; *sub nom.* CARAPETO v. GOOD; BRENNAN v. GOOD, [2002] EWHC 640, [2002] W.T.L.R. 1305, Rimer, J., Ch D.

4326. Probate–foreign jurisdictions–validity of revocation clause–Jersey

A and B, the only surviving relatives of the deceased, V, applied for V's will to be admitted to probate. V, was a citizen of the United Kingdom who had resided and died in Portugal. V made a will in 1990 dealing with her worldwide estate but excluding her property in Portugal and in New Zealand. She subsequently made a New Zealand will which stated that it revoked all former wills, but dealt only with property in New Zealand. She also made a will relating to her Portuguese property, revoking any previous Portuguese will. The person to whom the Portuguese property was left predeceased the testator, so that she died intestate in respect of the Portuguese property. It fell to be determined whether New Zealand will revoked the 1990 will.

Held, admitting the 1990 will to probate, that where a testator had executed a will a revocation clause was a grave and weighty circumstance to be taken into account but there was no presumption of law in favour of the clause. If the obvious facts militated against an intention expressed in a will, the court could act upon the real intention as found by the court, *Phelan (Deceased), Re* [1972] Fam. 33, [1971] C.L.Y. 12165 applied. In the instant case, neither of the later wills intended to revoke the 1990 will dealing with worldwide property other than that in New Zealand and Portugal. It was clear that all three wills were intended to stand separately.

VICKERS, IN THE ESTATE OF (2001-02) 4 I.T.E.L.R. 584, Hamon (Commissioner), Royal Ct (Jer).

4327. Testators–capacity–elderly persons–knowledge and approval of contents of will

B had sought to have admitted to probate the will of her grandmother, M, more than 20 years after M's death. The validity of the will was challenged by J, M's grandson, on the grounds that she had lacked testamentary capacity when making the will, and that she had neither known of nor approved its contents. M's demeanour at the time she gave her instructions had been such as to cause her solicitor, P, to be concerned about her testamentary capacity. Despite her doctor being unable to state that she possessed the requisite capacity, P, having formed the view M had lucid intervals, made arrangements for her to attend his office in order to execute the will.

Held, dismissing the claim, that far from supporting a conclusion that M had had the requisite capacity the evidence from M's doctors, contemporaneous documents, her solicitor and her family painted a picture of an often confused woman and cast doubts on her testamentary capacity both before and after the signing of the will. B having failed to discharge the burden of proof, her application to have the will admitted to probate was refused.

BROWN v. DEACY [2002] W.T.L.R. 781, Kim Lewison Q.C., Ch D.

4328. Testators–capacity–elderly testatrix prone to periods of confusion–lack of knowledge and capacity

O died on July 31, 1995. On May 13, 1994, she signed a will appointing A as her sole executrix, which was subsequently challenged by those who would have been entitled on an intestacy. At the time of the execution, O was 84 years old, prone to periods of confusion and in poor health due to non insulin dependent diabetes. A had suggested that O should make a will and had approached T, her solicitor brother in law, who drew up the will for O.

Held, declaring the will to be invalid, that A had failed to discharge the burden of proving that O had the requisite capacity to execute a will, *Banks v. Goodfellow* (1870) L.R. 5 Q.B. 549 applied. It was particularly important for A to prove that O had given the requisite knowledge and approval, given the circumstances surrounding the drawing up and execution of the will and her position as sole beneficiary under it. O's condition meant that she had moments of lucidity, interspersed between periods of confusion and although she had appeared to understand what she was doing when the will was executed, her GP had found her to be confused earlier in the day. Following the execution, she was subsequently admitted to hospital having been found in a collapsed state and in hospital it was noted that O was confused for part of the time.

RICHARDS v. ALLAN [2001] W.T.L.R. 1031, Anthony Mann Q.C., Ch D.

4329. Testators–capacity–execution by elderly incapacitated testator–burden of proof in respect of validity of will

An elderly and physically incapacitated testator had instructed L, a licensed conveyancer, to prepare a new will. The will had been drafted and engrossed. At L's request the testator, who was in hospital, had been examined by a doctor, who considered that he had testamentary capacity. The testator had executed the will by using his thumb as a mark and it had been witnessed by the doctor and L's secretary. The same day the testator had a stroke. B, beneficiaries under an earlier will and to a lesser extent under this will, claimed that this will had not been properly executed because L's secretary was not present and, alternatively, L had not proved that the testator had the necessary testamentary capacity. L counterclaimed that the will had been duly executed and that the testator had testamentary capacity.

Held, dismissing the claim and giving judgment for L on the counterclaim, that the will was valid. In the circumstances, the burden of proof in respect of the validity of the will, both with regard to due execution and testamentary capacity, was on L who sought to propound the will. On the evidence, L had discharged the burden. However, the court commented that in circumstances where a would be testator was elderly or incapacitated, a solicitor with experience of wills should take instructions and supervise execution of a will.

BORMAN v. LEL; *sub nom.* PARSONS, IN THE ESTATE OF [2002] W.T.L.R. 237, Nigel Davis Q.C., Ch D.

4330. Testators–capacity–relationship between elderly employer and housekeeper–presumption of undue influence

GOSH, residuary beneficiaries under the will of M, deceased, sought preliminary determinations as to the validity of transactions transferring the bulk of M's estate to R, her housekeeper. These transactions included a contract for sale of M's house, gifts and a loan of monies to purchase cars and the gift of monies in an account in M's name. It was contended that there was evidence of senile dementia, that M lacked the capacity to enter the transactions and that R had exerted undue influence over M. The court's determination was sought regarding (1) whether M had the mental capacity to effect the transactions; (2) whether the relationship was one in which the presumption of undue influence arose, and (3) whether R had provided evidence to rebut that presumption.

Held, giving determination in favour of the hospital, that (1) there was overwhelming evidence that M was suffering from serious dementia in the form of Alzheimers' disease during the months prior to her death and therefore lacked the capacity to make the decisions concerning her will; (2) in the event that she was shown to have capacity, the relationship was one in which the presumption arose due to M's complete dependence on R and her daughter; (3) R had failed to show that M had the requisite understanding of the true effects and implications of the sale of the house, *Beaney (Deceased), Re* [1978] 1 W.L.R. 770, [1978] C.L.Y. 1538 applied. The transaction itself was so unlikely that it alone was evidence of M's delusional state and it was declared void; (4) as a result of the findings regarding M's capacity, the gifts of monies for the purchase of cars and of the monies in the account were void, although the loan was allowed to stand pending counsels' submissions as to the appropriate way in which it should be discharged.

SPECIAL TRUSTEES FOR GREAT ORMOND STREET HOSPITAL FOR CHILDREN v. RUSHIN; *sub nom.* MORRIS, IN THE ESTATE OF; MORRIS (DECEASED), *Re* [2001] W.T.L.R 1137, Rimer, J., Ch D.

4331. Testators–inheritance trusts–beneficiaries–grandchildren born after testatrix's death–meaning of phrase "as shall survive me"

B died in 1977 having made a will in 1975 that left her estate on trust for her three children. B also executed a codicil at the same time that established a trust for the children of her son, R, that survived B and reached 21 years of age, with equal shares if more than one child qualified. At the date of B's will, R had two children. However, he divorced after B died and had two further children, B and E, to his second wife. R sought summary judgment as to the meaning of the phrase "as shall survive me" and whether it precluded the children born after B died.

Held, giving judgment in favour of B and E, that the circumstances showed that B intended to make a gift in favour of R's children. Given the age of R's children born at the date of B's will, there was a period of 17 years before the eldest reached 21 and B could be taken to have assumed that R might have further children during that time, *Allsop, Re* [1968] Ch. 39, [1967] C.L.Y. 4099 applied.

BLECH v. BLECH [2002] W.T.L.R. 483, Patten, J., Ch D.

4332. Trusts–deeds of variation–Texan domiciled testator–will governed by English law–variaton governed by English law

[Hague Convention on the Law Applicable to Trusts and on their Recognition 1985 Art.6, Art.8.]

B, who was domiciled in Texas, made two wills, the first disposing of his United States property to his wife, L. The second, stated as taking effect under English law, left all remaining property to a charity, C, subject to an annuity to B's son, W, payable when he reached 65. Following B's death, C and W executed a deed of variation that converted the annuity into a lump sum and terminated the trust fund. L and T, trustees of B's Texan will, challenged the variation on the ground that it was ineffective in Texan law, which they contended applied in the instant case, and was contrary to B's wishes.

Held, upholding the variation, that the express provision in favour of English law meant that the variation was governed by English law by virtue of the Hague Convention on the Law Applicable to Trusts and on their Recognition 1985 Art.6 and Art.8. Therefore the deed was effective even though it was contrary to B's wishes and W and C could terminate the trust and direct the trustees to hand over the trust property to fulfil the terms of the variation, *Saunders v. Vautier* (1841) 4 Beav. 115 applied.

BARTON (DECEASED), *Re; sub nom.* TOD v. BARTON, [2002] EWHC 264, [2002] W.T.L.R. 469, Lawrence Collins, J., Ch D.

4333. Trusts of land–schools–reversion capable of being devised–statutory fiction under Schools Sites Act 1841 s.2

[Wills Act 1837 s.3; Schools Sites Act 1841 s.2; Reverter of Sites Act 1987.]

The trustee applied for directions as to who was beneficially entitled to the proceeds of sale of land originally conveyed under the Schools Sites Act 1841 by the Fourth Duke of Cleveland to a local rector to use as a site for a church school. Under s.2 of the 1841 Act once the land ceased to be used for a school it reverted to the Fourth Duke's estate and that reverter was purportedly devised by him under the Wills Act 1837 s.3 on his death. All that land was later sold by the Fourth Duke's beneficiary to an estate company but the land was never legally transferred. The school use subsequently ceased and in 1990 the trustees sold the site under the Reverter of Sites Act 1987 and held the proceeds of sale on trust. Although it was common ground that the rights of the reverter had become vested in the Crown as bona vacantia, the Crown agreed to vest its rights in the defendants who were beneficial owners of the estate company subject to the establishment that (1) the rights of the reverter could be devised under the Fourth Duke's will, and (2) a statutory fiction existed in relation to the Schools Sites Act 1841 s.2 so that the school site had remained part of the Fourth Duke's estate at his death as if it had never been conveyed.

Held, giving directions in favour of the defendant, that (1) the rights of the reverter were devised under the Fourth Duke's will since a wider interpretation of s.3 of the 1837 Act gave effect to its manifest purpose without offending the draughtsman's language, and (2) those entitled to the land immediately following the reverter were to be traced as if the land had never been conveyed under the 1841 Act, *Cawston's Conveyance, Re* [1940] Ch. 27 and *Fraser v. Canterbury Diocesan Board of Finance* [2001] Ch. 669, [2001] C.L.Y. 5534 followed and *Dennis v. Malcolm* [1934] Ch. 244 applied.

BATH AND WELLS DIOCESAN BOARD OF FINANCE v. JENKINSON; *sub nom.* RECTOR OF WRINGTON v. JENKINSON, [2002] EWHC 218, [2003] Ch. 89, Etherton, J., Ch D.

4334. Undue influence–burden of proof–knowledge and approval of contents of will

C, as executor, sought to prove the will of G under which she and her husband were the principal beneficiaries. The only provision made for G's family was the gift of specific legacies, the bulk of G's substantial estate passing to the Cs as residuary legatees. C had been G's housekeeper for more than 20 years, during which time she and her family had lived with G. A close and mutual affection had developed between G and the C family over the years. G had made a number of previous wills in which she had demonstrated that she felt a strong moral obligation to make testamentary provision for C. The provision made had been increasingly generous with each successive will. Latterly she had expressed concern as to where the C family were to live following her death, and her later wills had made provision for their accommodation. G's family, whilst conceding that she had had testamentary capacity at the time the will was made, nonetheless challenged its validity. They contended that G had neither known of nor approved the contents of the will, and that it had been induced by undue influence. They maintained that the C family had manipulated and controlled G for their own financial ends.

Held, allowing the claim and dismissing the counterclaim, that where the circumstances surrounding the making of a will were such as to raise suspicions the burden of proving that the testator knew of and approved its contents would not be satisfied merely by establishing due execution and that the testator had testamentary capacity, *Fuller v. Strum* [2001] EWCA Civ 1879, [2002] 1 W.L.R. 1097, [2002] 2 C.L. 555 applied. In the instant case the burden of proof had been discharged. G was a highly intelligent woman who had received legal advice prior to executing her will. She knew the contents of the will and understood its financial consequences, the full extent of her estate having been explained to her a few weeks prior to her making the will. There had been no evidence on which the court could conclude that the Cs had coerced G into making the will. She had demonstrated herself to be an intelligent, strong minded woman, capable of making her own decisions regarding the disposition of her estate.

GOOD (DECEASED), Re; sub nom. CARAPETO v. GOOD; BRENNAN v. GOOD, [2002] EWHC 640, [2002] W.T.L.R. 801, Rimer, J., Ch D.

4335. Wills–beneficiaries–intention–grandson as beneficiary under grandfather's will in place of deceased father–no contrary intention in will to exclude Wills Act 1837 s.33(2)

[Wills Act 1837 s.33(2).]

VL, the surviving child of M and A, sought a declaration that she was solely entitled to M's estate on the basis of his will. The will provided that if A died less than one month after M, the residue of his estate would be held on trust for any of his children aged 21 alive at his death and who survived for a month afterwards. M's son, R, died in 1989, leaving a son, AL, born in 1984. Although VL argued that the will excluded the Wills Act 1837 s.33(2), AL contended that the requirement that M's children had to survive him by one month did not limit the class of beneficiaries only to those who had fulfilled that contingency as the will did not contain an intention contrary to s.33(2).

Held, refusing the application, that AL qualified as a beneficiary under M's will in the absence of an intention that M's grandchildren would not benefit in the place of their deceased parent contrary to s.33(2). AL could not qualify until he reached 21, however, as his interest was subject to the same contingencies that applied to his late father's gift.

LING v. LING [2002] W.T.L.R. 553, Etherton, J., Ch D.

4336. Wills–beneficiaries–representation orders–approval of compromise settlement between beneficiaries

[Civil Procedure Rules 1998 (SI 1998 3132) Part 19 r.19.7(2)(d).]

A testatrix had died having made two wills. A dispute arose between the respective beneficiaries, Mu and Mc, as to the validity of each will. Mu was the sole surviving executor and was a beneficiary of the first will. There had also been another executor and beneficiary who had died leaving a son but his whereabouts were unknown. There was no formal evidence of his succession and little evidence of efforts to trace him so as to give him notice in accordance with the Practice Direction relating to contentious probate proceedings. Mu and Mc agreed a settlement on the basis of the first will. Mu applied for a representation order under the Civil Procedure Rules 1998 Part 19 r.19.7(2)(d) to appoint her to represent all persons who might be interested under the first will, and court approval for the settlement. Mu submitted that the representation order would meet the overriding objective under the Rule.

Held, granting the application, that the first will was pronounced valid on the basis of affidavit evidence and the compromise was approved as it was for the benefit of all those represented by Mu. In view of the relatively small size of the estate the overriding objective of the Civil Procedure Rules was fulfilled by appointing Mu as representative as it was proportionate and reduced the expense involved in finding out the son's position.

MURPHY v. McGLYNN [2002] W.T.L.R. 231, Lloyd, J., Ch D.

4337. Wills–equitable interests–testatrix with half share in land and life interest in remainder–undivided share insufficient for conveyance under Settled Land Act 1925

[Settled Land Act 1925.]

Under her late husband's will D held a half share in an estate and was the life tenant of the other half share. D's will purported to direct the ultimate beneficiary, H, to permit P and P's husband to live in a property on the land for the survivor's lifetime. By way of an originating summons, P claimed that this constituted a strict settlement, entitling her to a conveyance on D's death by virtue of the Settled

Land Act 1925. P divorced and remarried after D died and a secondary issue was whether the reference to P's husband meant only her husband at the date D's will was executed.

Held, that (1) on a proper construction of D's will D had settled her equitable interest in the property on P and her husband for their lives. As co-owner after D's death, H had a notional right of occupation which it had agreed to postpone so as to prevent it exercising a concurrent right of occupation; (2) P was not entitled to a conveyance as she only had an interest in an undivided share which did not satisfy the requirements for a settlement under the Act, and (3) the reference in D's will to P's husband meant her husband on the date that the will was executed, *Coley, Re* [1903] 2 Ch. 102 followed.

PEASLEY v. GOVERNORS OF HAILEYBURY AND IMPERIAL SERVICE COLLEGE [2001] W.T.L.R. 1365, Rimer, J., Ch D.

4338. Wills–intention–person instrumental in procuring will in receipt of benefit– standard of proof for establishing testator's intentions

F, the executor of the deceased, appealed against an order of the deputy judge ([2001] W.T.L.R. 677) whereby he pronounced for the force and validity of a will only in relation to certain standard directions and one of five pecuniary legacies. F had been instrumental in procuring the will and had taken a benefit under it. S, the adopted son of the deceased, had challenged the will, alleging, inter alia, that the deceased had not known or approved of its contents. The deputy judge had found that F had failed to remove the suspicion of the court as to his role in the procurement of the will.

Held, allowing the appeal, that it was apparent that the deputy judge had erred in his findings. In circumstances where a person had been instrumental in procuring a will under which he took a benefit, it was required that the court be satisfied on the balance of probabilities that the contents of the will did represent the testator's intentions. The burden of proof was on the person propounding the will, *Barry v. Butlin* (1838) 2 Moo. P.C. 480 and *Wintle v. Nye (No.2)* [1959] 1 W.L.R. 284, [1959] C.L.Y. 3451 considered. In the opinion of Chadwick, L.J., the use of the phrase "the righteousness of the transaction" when describing the burden was not helpful given its suggestion of the requirement of a moral judgment. Having regard to the evidence and, in particular, to the improbability that the deceased had not read the will, it was apparent that the will did reflect the deceased's true intentions.

FULLER v. STRUM, [2001] EWCA Civ 1879, [2002] 1 W.L.R. 1097, Peter Gibson, L.J., CA.

4339. Wills–interpretation–meaning of words "demise together with me"–wife predeceasing testator–residue passing by way of intestacy

[Administration of Justice Act 1982 s.21 (1).]

T drafted a home made will that gave all his estate to his wife, L. The will also provided that, should L "demise together with me", the estate was to be shared equally between C and M. L died seven years before T. H contended that the words used referred to T and L dying together, as opposed to L predeceasing T. C and M argued that the words referred to L predeceasing T, so that they were to take the estate in equal shares.

Held, giving judgment for H, that T's estate was to pass by way of the intestacy rules. The words used were intended to provide for the contingency of T and L dying together. The interpretation put forward by C and M did not accord with the meaning of the words, which were not ambiguous in terms of the Administration of Justice Act 1982 s.21 (1), therefore no extrinsic evidence was admissible to assist with interpretation.

HODGSON v. CLARE; *sub nom.* OWEN (DECEASED), *Re* [2002] W.T.L.R. 619, Stanley Burnton Q.C., Ch D.

4340. Wills–joint tenancies–severance–agreement not to sell half share in house during survivor's life time

W and his sister, E, owned a house as joint tenants. In 1981, W and E made wills that stipulated that the survivor of either of them was to have the income from the other's half share of the house for life. On the survivor's death, the residue was to go to another sister, D, with a gift over to her children. After D's death, W made another will leaving all his estate to E, with a gift over to S, D's granddaughter. In 1993, W made a final will, appointing P as his executrix and giving her and her son £500 pecuniary gifts with the residue being divided between two charities. In response to S's queries as to the validity of W's final will, P sought an order certifying that B had no interest in W's estate.

Held, refusing to grant the order in the form sought and finding that P held a half share on trust for E's estate, that the evidence showed that W and E had instructed their solicitor to grant a life interest in the house. The 1981 will specifically provided that the half share of the first to die should not be sold during the survivor's lifetime. The element of agreement present in their instructions was sufficient to severe the joint tenancy. Costs were ordered to be paid out of the proceeds of sale of the house before division of E and W's shares.

PERKINS v. BORDEN; *sub nom.* WOOLNOUGH (DECEASED), *Re* [2002] W.T.L.R. 595, Master Moncaster, Ch D.

4341. Wills–mistake–rectification–husband executing wife's will–evidence as to actual intention–Jersey

L and S, a husband and wife, executed each other's wills, which were in reciprocal terms, by mistake, which was not discovered until after S had died. L sought a declaration that either (1) the will purporting to be S's should be admitted to probate, or (2) that the will S had signed by mistake should be rectified so that it could be admitted to probate, as she had intended.

Held, refusing to admit the will not signed by S to probate but allowing rectification of the other will, that (1) the will not signed by S could not be admitted to probate, and (2) as there was overwhelming evidence as to the nature of the mistake, rectification would be granted so as to alter words of the will to reflect S's intention.

VAUTIER'S ESTATE, *Re* (2000-01) 3 I.T.E.L.R. 566, Deputy Bailiff Birt, Royal Ct (Jer).

4342. Wills–mutual wills–constructive trusts–formalities of contract for disposition of land–undivided shares in property

[Law of Property (Miscellaneous Provisions) Act 1989 s.2.]

H sought an order for the transfer of a property to her by B. The property had been the matrimonial home of H's aunt, A, and B's father, F, who had been beneficial joint tenants. A and F had made mutual, non revocable wills under which each would receive the entirety of the other's estate if they were the survivor and H would receive the matrimonial home on the death of the survivor. Following the death of A, F transferred the property from his sole name into the joint names of himself and B by way of an inter vivos gift. On the death of F, sole title to the property vested in B by the doctrine of survivorship. Neither A nor F had revoked their wills prior to death. H contended that in circumstances where F had breached the agreement between himself and A as regards the disposition of the property and thereby committed a fraud on A, B held the property on trust for her absolutely.

Held, giving judgment in part for H, that B held the property on trust for himself and H in equal shares. The declarations contained in the mutual wills of F and A had no legal effect as a contract for the disposition of land because of a failure to satisfy the requirements of the Law of Property (Miscellaneous Provisions) Act 1989 s.2, and therefore the doctrine of mutual wills did not apply, *Goodchild v. Goodchild* [1997] 1 W.L.R. 1216, [1997] C.L.Y. 4726 applied.

F's actions in making the inter vivos gift to his son had been designed to defeat the intention of the compact and thus deprive H of the intended bequest. It had been unconscionable for F having accepted the benefit of the compact, to then attempt to avoid his obligations under it. In such circumstances equity would intervened to impose a constructive trust. In the absence of a binding legal contract, such a trust could not be imposed in respect of F's original share in the property but only in respect of A's one half undivided share, *Yaxley v. Gotts* [2000] Ch. 162, [1999] C.L.Y. 848 referred to and *Lloyds Bank Plc v. Rosset* [1991] 1 A.C. 107, [1990] C.L.Y. 706 distinguished. This was so despite the fact that because A had never severed the joint tenancy, her interest in the property had not passed to F under her will but had vested in him by operation of the doctrine of survivorship.

HEALEY v. BROWN [2002] W.T.L.R. 849, David Donaldson Q.C., Ch D.

4343. Books

Barnes, David; Stone, Tim—Practitioner's Guide to Legacies. Paperback: £45.00. ISBN 0-7545-1454-4. Tolley Publishing.

Bridges, Mark; Way, David—Tolley's Guide to International Succession Laws. Looseleaf/ring bound: £115.00. ISBN 0-7545-1246-0. Looseleaf/ring bound: £145.00. ISBN 0-7545-1447-1. Tolley Publishing.

Hayton, David—European Succession Laws. Hardback: £99.00. ISBN 0-85308-816-0. Jordans.

Keating, Albert—Probate Law and Practice. Brehon Library. Hardback. ISBN 1-85800-300-8. Round Hall Ltd.

Keating, Albert—Construction of Wills. Hardback: £78.00. ISBN 1-85800-231-1. Round Hall Ltd.

Kerridge, R.—Parry and Clark: the Law of Succession. Paperback: £29.95. ISBN 0-421-74110-4. Sweet & Maxwell.

Ray, Ralph—Wills and Post-death Tax Planning. 3rd Ed. Paperback: £38.00. ISBN 1-858-11286-9. EMIS Professional Publishing.

Rovati, Veena Kanda—Succession. Revision Workbook. Paperback: £9.95. ISBN 1-85836-469-8. Old Bailey Press.

Sherrin, C.H.; Barlow, R.F.D.; Wallington, R.A.; Meadway, Susannah L.; Waterworth, Michael—Williams on Wills. Hardback: £295.00. ISBN 0-406-93391-X. Butterworths Law.

Sunnucks, James H.G.—Williams, Mortimer & Sunnucks-executors, Administrators and Probate: 1st Supplement to the 18th Edition. Property and Conveyancing Library. Paperback: £40.00. ISBN 0-421-77000-7. Sweet & Maxwell.

Thurston, John—Practitioner's Guide to Inheritance Claims. Paperback: £37.00. ISBN 0-7545-1247-9. Tolley Publishing.

Thurston, John—Practitioner's Guide to Executorship and Administration. Paperback: £42.00. ISBN 0-7545-1697-0. Tolley Publishing.

Tristram and Cootes: Probate Practice. Hardback: £285.00. ISBN 0-406-94720-1. Butterworths Law.

Walker, Andrew—Administration of Estates. Paperback: £30.00. ISBN 0-85297-604-6. Financial World Publishing.

TAX

4344. Aggregates levy

AGGREGATES LEVY (GENERAL) REGULATIONS 2002, SI 2002 761; made under the Finance Act 1997 s.51; the Finance Act 1999 s.132; and the Finance Act 2001 s.17, s.23, s.25, s.30, s.31, s.37, s.38, s.39, s.45, Sch.6 para.9, Sch.7

para.2, Sch.8 para.1, Sch.8 para.9, Sch.8 para.10, Sch.8 para.11. In force: April 1, 2002; £3.50.

These Regulations, which amend the Distress for Customs and Excise Duties and Other Indirect Taxes Regulations 1997 (SI 1997 1431), make further provision for aggregates levy. They contain provisions relating to the determination of the weight of any quantity of aggregate levy (AL), require relevant traders to make returns and pay the AL due from them in accordance with their allocated accounting periods and cover representation in the case of death, incapacity or insolvency and the transfer of a business as a going concern.

4345. Aggregates levy–imports–free movement of goods–compatibility with EC law

[Finance Act 2001; EC Treaty Art.25, Art.87, Art.90.]

B, an incorporated association representing independent quarrying companies, applied for judicial review of the Treasury's imposition of an aggregates levy, pursuant to the Finance Act 2001. B contended that (1) EC Treaty Art.25 had been breached, as the chargeable event giving rise to the duty was different for the imposition of the levy on imported aggregate and the relevant provision of Art.25 could not apply to imports, with the result that the chargeable events were not identical for the purposes of Art.25 para.8; (2) Art.90 had been breached because the levy amounted to an additional tax burden on importers who had exported from an EC member state where a similar levy had been imposed; (3) exemptions for certain products and processes constituted state aid within Art.87, for which there was no environmental justification. The result was a distortion of competition which enabled one kind of damaging waste to be sold as aggregate instead of another, and (4) the implementation of the levy was premature.

Held, refusing the application for judicial review, that (1) Art.25 had not been breached as the mere fact that one of the chargeable events could not apply to imported aggregate and that the event occurred later in relation to imports did not mean that the levy applied different criteria to the charge on imports as opposed to domestic aggregate, *Commission of the European Communities v. Belgium (314/82)* [1984] E.C.R. 1543 applied. The charge was imposed on identical products, whether imported or domestic, and the chargeable events were identical; (2) there was no obligation to take into account any similar charges levied in other member states on aggregate exported to the United Kingdom as the harmonisation rules did not apply to charges regulated by independent national legislation, *Firma Herbert Scharbatke Gmbh v. Germany (C72/92)* [1993] E.C.R. I-5509 applied; (3) an analysis of the scheme and of the justification for the exemptions based on it was required. Exemptions were justified and reflected the environmental basis of the scheme, which was aimed at discouraging the extraction of aggregate from natural rock whilst encouraging the use of alternative supplies. The levy was not a tax on aggregates but a tax on rock, sand or gravel extracted for use as aggregate. The differentiation between non aggregate and its waste and primary aggregate and its waste did not constitute state aid, and (4) implementation of the levy was not premature, as the applicable test was whether it was reasonably practicable for those affected to prepare for implementation of the essential features of the levy, and in the instant case that test had not been fulfilled.

R. (ON THE APPLICATION OF BRITISH AGGREGATES ASSOCIATES) v. CUSTOMS AND EXCISE COMMISSIONERS; *sub nom.* R. (ON THE APPLICATION OF BRITISH AGGREGATES ASSOCIATION) v. HM TREASURY; BRITISH AGGREGATES ASSOCIATES v. HM TREASURY, [2002] EWHC 926, [2002] 2 C.M.L.R. 51, Moses, J., QBD (Admin Ct).

4346. Anti dumping duties–imports–computer diskettes–partial assembly in Macau–determination of place of origin

[Council Regulation 2913/92 establishing the Community Customs Code Art.24; Council Regulation 920/93 imposing provisional anti-dumping duty on certain imports into the Community from Japan, Taiwan and China.]

The components of 3.5 inch computer diskettes were manufactured in China, the US and Japan then assembled partly in Macau before being imported into the UK. Following an EU mission of enquiry to Macau, Customs decided that the diskettes originated in China and were therefore liable to antidumping duty under Council Regulation 920/93. Customs accepted that the processing was carried out in Macau in a factory equipped for that purpose in terms of Council Regulation 2913/92 Art.24. However, they contended that the processing was not such as to confer origin status, or, alternatively, that the processing did not result in a new product or amount to a key manufacturing stage. D appealed.

Held, allowing the appeal, that (1) place of origin was to be determined in accordance with Art.24 of Regulation 2913/92, *Brother International GmbH v. Hauptzollamt Giessen (C26/88)* [1989] E.C.R. 4253, [1990] C.L.Y. 2032 applied, and (2) applying both the economical and technical tests from Art.24 the diskettes were deemed to have originated in Macau.

DYSAN MAGNETICS LTD v. CUSTOMS AND EXCISE COMMISSIONERS; HANNY MAGNETICS (EUROPE) LTD v. CUSTOMS AND EXCISE COMMISSIONERS [2000] V. & D.R. 422, RK Miller CB (Chairman), V&DTr.

4347. Anti dumping duties–imports–fertilisers arranged between group members–excess stock purchased for sale in falling market

[Council Regulation 2913/92 establishing the Community Customs Code Art.29(1); Council Regulation 2238/2000 amending Regulation 384/96 on protection against dumped imports from countries not members of the European Community Art.2B.9.]

F imported Russian ammonium nitrate, urea and other fertilisers into the UK having purchased the fertiliser from another group member. Following is liquidation, F appealed against anti dumping duty in relation to those imports. Many of F's sales had been made at prices below that which it had bought the fertiliser, either because excess stock had been purchased for sale in a falling market or due to deterioration from poor storage conditions. The Commissioners contended that they were entitled to impose anti dumping duty on the basis of onward sales relying on Council Regulation 384/96 Art.2B.9.

Held, allowing the appeal, that (1) The Commissioners could not rely on Art.2B.9 as that was limited either to where imports were not the result of a sale involving the importing purchaser because the exporter had consigned the goods to himself, or where transactions had not been conducted at arm's length or were subject to a compensatory agreement, neither of which applied on the facts of the instant case, and (2) for the purposes of Council Regulation 2913/92 Art.29(1) the Commissioners had not established that the prices declared by F were not the net c.i.f. prices. There was evidence of continued downward movement in prices during the relevant period and the liquidator had found nothing to show that the invoice prices were not those of the actual transactions.

VTI FERTASCO (UK) LTD v. CUSTOMS AND EXCISE COMMISSIONERS [2000] V. & D.R. 110, Stephen Oliver Q.C., V&DTr.

4348. Appeals–assessment–inspector's exercise of discretion under Taxes Management Act 1970 s.30–General Commissioners' jurisdiction on appeal

[Taxes Management Act 1970 s.30.]

The Revenue appealed against a ruling by General Commissioners quashing an assessment raised by an inspector pursuant to the Taxes Management Act 1970 s.30. The assessment related to a refund of tax which the inspector concluded had been made in error. The Commissioners concluded that the inspector's discretion had been exercised either wrongly or unreasonably. The Revenue contended that the Commissioners did not possess any jurisdiction to review the inspector's decision.

Held, allowing the appeal, that the Commissioners did not possess any jurisdiction to substitute their own view as to the appropriate way in which the discretion should have been exercised nor did they possess any power to review the decision on the basis that it was *Wednesbury* unreasonable. Accordingly the assessment had been properly made and could not be interfered with, *Steibelt (Inspector of Taxes) v. Paling* [1999] S.T.C. 594, [1999] C.L.Y. 4660 considered.

GUTHRIE (INSPECTOR OF TAXES) v. TWICKENHAM FILM STUDIOS LTD, [2002] EWHC 1936, [2002] S.T.C. 1374, Lloyd, J., Ch D.

4349. Appeals—time limits—litigants in person—failure to submit appeal notice—application to appeal out of time refused—no action taken to correct error for three months

[Civil Procedure Rules 1998 (SI 1998 3132) Part 52.]

G, a litigant in person, sought permission to appeal out of time from a general commissioner's decision. G had submitted a case stated on the advice of a clerk to the commissioners but not a notice of appeal. The court wrote to G, stating that a notice was needed by virtue of Civil Procedure Rules 1998 Part 52 PD 52 para.23.4. In fact, the letter referred to the wrong paragraph, but G took no further action for another three months.

Held, refusing the application, that time limits had to be enforced even where the applicant was a litigant in person. Further, G's application would be refused as it could adversely affect third party rights and he had been unable to show that he had any real interest in appealing.

GURNEY v. SPENCE (INSPECTOR OF TAXES) [2002] S.T.C. 758, Jacob, J., Ch D.

4350. Appeals—time limits—no excuse given for delay in appealing against notice of determination

[Taxes Management Act 1970 s.49(1).]

C sought permission to appeal out of time against a notice of determination issued on October 7, 1997. The notice was correctly addressed but for an incorrect post code. C contended that it had not received the notice and its accountants, N, asserted that they had not received a copy either, although their copy was correctly addressed. On October 8, 1997 the inspector wrote to N stating that a formal loss determination would be served. C was experiencing financial difficulties at the time and instructed N not to handle anything other than immediate tax matters. C's difficulties were settled in February 2001 and on April 5, N purported to give formal notice of a late appeal under the Taxes Management Act 1970 s.49(1). The Revenue contended that the notice was ineffective because of the length of the delay for which no excuse had been given.

Held, refusing the application, that although the letter of April 5, 2001 was a proper application in terms of s.49, N, as C's agent, was deemed to have received notice of the determination by the letter dated October 8, 1997. This meant that C could have instructed N to appeal, notwithstanding its financial difficulties. Therefore, C did not have sufficient excuse for the three and a half years' delay.

CONSULTANTS LTD v. INSPECTOR OF TAXES [2002] S.T.C. (S.C.D.) 162, John F Avery Jones, Sp Comm.

4351. Business expansion scheme—reliefs—directors—investments—effect of remuneration from connected company

[Income and Corporation Taxes Act 1988 s.300.]

F appealed against a decision of the General Commissioners in litigation concerning T's tax affairs. T had been granted business expansion scheme relief,

BES, under the Income and Corporation Taxes Act 1988 in relation to his investments in companies incorporated by him. Work was carried out for those companies by another company, C, of which T was a paid director. F had allowed BES relief but then withdrew it because of the connection between C and the companies. T appealed successfully to the General Commissioners. On appeal, F argued that the payments made to T as director of C fell within s.300(2)(h) of the Act and therefore had to be offset fully against the value of T's investment in the companies, thus cancelling out BES relief.

Held, allowing the appeal, that C was connected to the companies for the purposes of the Act and therefore "value received" by T from C was the equivalent of value received from the companies. Looking at all the categories under s.300, it was clear that the most appropriate category for the payment to T as director was that of "any other payment" under s.300(2)(h) and not that of "benefit" under s.300(2)(f) as contended by T.

FLETCHER (INSPECTOR OF TAXES) v. THOMPSON; R. (ON THE APPLICATION OF THOMPSON) v. FLETCHER (INSPECTOR OF TAXES), [2002] EWHC 1447, [2002] EWHC 1448, [2002] S.T.C. 1149, Lawrence Collins, J., Ch D.

4352. **Capital allowances–contracts for hire–motor vehicles–hire payments subject to deductibility of expenditure**

[Capital Allowances Act 1990 s.35(2), s.36(1)(c).]

B appealed against a finding ([2001] S.T.C. 1652) that the Capital Allowances Act 1990 s.35(2) applied to all rental payments, made by the company which it had originally owned, under finance leases granted in respect of "expensive" motor cars. The company had acquired the rights to enable it to carry on the business of hiring motor vehicles to members of the public under finance leases, granted by a funder who had acquired and retained ownership of the vehicles. B contended that the restriction on the deductibility of expenditure contained in s.35(2) was limited to hire contracts where the hirer was the end user.

Held, dismissing the appeal, that s.35(2) of the Act applied to all contracts of hire in respect of "expensive motor cars" including those where the hirer had entered into a contract of sub hire to a third party end user. Had Parliament intended intermediate hirings to be excluded from the operation of s.35(2) it could have done so expressly. Moreover, the express exemption of certain categories of short term sub hire to members of the public by s.36(1)(c) of the Act strongly suggested that it had been the intention of Parliament that s.35(2) should apply to long term, intermediate, hirings, *Macniven (Inspector of Taxes) v. Westmoreland Investments Ltd* [2001] UKHL 6, [2001] 2 W.L.R. 377, [2001] C.L.Y. 5199 considered.

LLOYDS UDT FINANCE LTD v. CHARTERED FINANCE TRUST HOLDINGS PLC; *sub nom.* BRITAX INTERNATIONAL GmbH v. INLAND REVENUE COMMISSIONERS, [2002] EWCA Civ 806, [2002] S.T.C. 956, Jonathan Parker, L.J., CA.

4353. **Capital allowances–energy conservation–machinery**

CAPITAL ALLOWANCES (ENERGY-SAVING PLANT AND MACHINERY) (AMENDMENT) ORDER 2002, SI 2002 1818; made under the Capital Allowances Act 2001 s.45A, s.45C. In force: August 5, 2002; £1.50.

This Order, which amends the Capital Allowances (Energy-saving Plant and Machinery) Order 2001 (SI 2001 2541), adds further technology classes to those for which the plant and machinery must be specified in, or accepted for inclusion in, the Energy Technology Product List in order to qualify for the 100 per cent first-year allowance scheme and extends the rules for components to compressed air equipment.

4354. Capital allowances–leasing–circular network of agreements–object of expenditure

See BANKING AND FINANCE: Barclays Mercantile Business Finance Ltd v. Mawson (Inspector of Taxes). §261

4355. Capital gains–allowances–state aids–100 per cent allowance for gains on investments in companies located in former GDR

[EC Treaty Art.87; Commission Decision 98/476; Income Tax Act (Germany) Art.52(8).]

Germany sought the annulment of Commission Decision 98/476, which stated that the 100 per cent capital gain allowance permitted under the Income Tax Act (Germany) s.52(8) for gains made on investments in capital companies with fewer than 250 employees located in the former GDR was incompatible with the common market in breach of the E C Treaty Art.87(1). Germany contended that the allowance was permitted under Art.87(2) as it was aid to parts of the Germany which had been adversely affected by the former division of the country. Alternatively, that it was a measure intended to encourage economic development in areas affected by a low standard of living and high unemployment in terms of Art.87(3)(c).

Held, refusing the application, that (1) the allowance conferred advantageous tax treatment on investments that was intended to reduce costs in a way that distorted competition by strengthening the position of Germany companies. The allowance amounted to State aid for the purposes of Art.87(1) in that it rewarded investors by way of a reduction in State revenue; (2) the derogation permitting State aid in Art.87(2) was to be interpreted narrowly and did not include compensation for the disadvantages suffered by companies located in the former GDR, and (3) there was no evidence that the Commission had exceeded its discretion when deciding that the allowance did not fulfil the requirements of Art.87(3).

GERMANY v. COMMISSION OF THE EUROPEAN COMMUNITIES (C156/98) 3 I.T.L. Rep. 159, Rodriguez Iglesias (President), ECJ.

4356. Capital gains–foreign exchange–loan made under forward contract with currency swap–rate of interest allowed for capital gains purposes–Canada

[Income Tax Act 1985 (Canada) s.20(1)(c)(i).]

As a way of financing its business, S borrowed NZD150 million at 15.4 per cent in 1988 which it then used to purchase $100 million under a forward contract, with payment due in 1993. The US dollar rate was only 9.1 per cent at the time. The transaction allowed S to use the capital for business purposes which it could repay with only $79.5 million. S sought to deduct the 15.4 per cent interest against its profits and declared the saving it made on repaying the loan as a capital gain, against which it could offset certain capital losses. The Minister for National Revenue assessed S to tax on the basis of the lower US interest rate, however, and contended that the lower sum paid at the repayment date was an income profit, not a capital gain. S's appeal against this decision succeeded before the Tax Court of Canada but the Minister's appeal was allowed in part by the Court of Appeal. S appealed and the Minister cross appealed.

Held, allowing the appeal and dismissing the cross appeal, that the Income Tax Act 1985 (Canada) s.20(1)(c)(i) allowed interest payments to be deducted from income where the loan capital had been used to earn income, as long as the amount, which had to be "reasonable", was paid in the same year for which the deduction was sought and the repayment was made under a legal obligation. On the facts, S satisfied all those requirements, with "reasonableness" being established by reference to the arm's length nature of the loan. By limiting the interest rate to the lower US dollar rate, the Minister and the Court of Appeal had wrongly applied an "economic reality" approach in a way that undermined both the legal relationships that S had entered into and the clear meaning of s.20(1)(c)(i). The cross appeal against the Court of Appeal's decision that the gain was capital in nature could not succeed as, although s.20(1)(c)(i) allowed deductions to be made from income, this did not mean that the gain was income and the way in which it was recorded for ordinary accounting purposes was not determinative of the matter for tax purposes.

SHELL CANADA LTD v. QUEEN, THE; *sub nom.* R. v. SHELL CANADA LTD 2 I.T.L. Rep. 241, McLachlin, J., Sup Ct (Can).

4357. Capital gains tax–assessment–sale of company–contractual liability to pay percentage of sale proceeds to third party

B appealed against the decision of a Special Commissioner upholding an assessment of capital gains tax arising from the sale of a company of which he held 98 per cent of the issued share capital. Prior to the sale, B had entered into a loan agreement with his parents who were resident abroad. Under the terms of the agreement, B was required to pay his parents 60 per cent of the net proceeds from the sale of the company if it was sold within two years. The company having been sold, capital gains tax had been assessed on the entire proceeds of the sale. B maintained that he should only have been liable to capital gains tax on 40 per cent of the purchase price, that being the amount left to him once his parent's rights under the agreement had been taken into account.

Held, dismissing the appeal, that capital gains tax was chargeable on the whole of the sale proceeds and any contractual obligation of B to his parents was to be disregarded. There had been a single disposal by B alone. The fact that B was contractually bound to make a payment from the sale proceeds to his parents did not result in that amount being excluded from the consideration for his disposal of the asset, *Garner (Inspector of Taxes) v. Pounds Shipowners & Shipbreakers Ltd* [2000] 1 W.L.R. 1107, [2000] C.L.Y. 4922 applied. B's obligation to his parents was one in contract alone.

BURCA v. PARKINSON (INSPECTOR OF TAXES) [2001] S.T.C. 1298, Park, J., Ch D.

4358. Capital gains tax–disposals–shares–company divided into two–meaning of "reconstruction"

[Capital Gains Tax Act 1979 s.86.]

F, the executor of M, appealed against a capital gains tax assessment of £448,020, payable from M's estate. M had owned shares in a company, X, which had two areas of business, locks and enamelling. In 1979, X's business was split into two companies and its shares were divided into A and B shares. X was then put into liquidation and two new companies, L and R, were created. Holders of A shares, which included M, were transferred to L, and holders of B shares to R. M subsequently disposed of his shares and the Revenue raised an assessment on chargeable gains of £1.5 million, contending that the division of X and re-issue of shares was a reconstruction in terms of the Capital Gains Tax Act 1979 s.86. F argued that there had not been a reconstruction within the meaning of s.86. The special commissioners dismissed F's appeal against the assessment ([2001] S.T.C. (S.C.D.) 45) and F appealed.

Held, allowing the appeal, that (1) for the purposes of determining whether an arrangement amounted to a "reconstruction" within s.86, the concept of reconstruction did not include the partition of a business between two groups of shareholders who each held separate parts of the original business following the restructuring, *Brooklands Selangor Holdings v. Inland Revenue Commissioners* [1970] 1 W.L.R. 429, [1970] C.L.Y. 2715 applied. The 1979 restructuring was a partition rather than a reorganisation since the shareholders in M did not all own shares in the successor companies. The fact that the share capital had been reorganised by attaching streaming rights to new classes of share prior to the transfer of the businesses to the successor companies did not affect the position because it had been carried out as a part of the scheme, *Swithland Investments v. Inland Revenue Commissioners* [1990] S.T.C. 448, [1991] C.L.Y. 3390 applied; (2) it was immaterial whether a company was reconstructed into one or more companies for the purposes of s.86, and (3) as s.86 did not apply, the value of M's shares equalled their 1980 market value for capital gains tax purposes.

FALLON (MORGAN'S EXECUTORS) v. FELLOWS (INSPECTOR OF TAXES); *sub nom.* MORGAN'S EXECUTORS v. FELLOWS (INSPECTOR OF TAXES) [2001] S.T.C. 1409, Park, J., Ch D.

4359. Capital gains tax—exempt amount—2002-2003

CAPITAL GAINS TAX (ANNUAL EXEMPT AMOUNT) ORDER 2002, SI 2002 702; made under the Taxation of Chargeable Gains Act 1992 s.3. In force: March 15, 2002; £1.50.

This Order specifies £7,700 as the amount which, under the Taxation of Chargeable Gains Act 1992 s.3, is the exempt amount for the year 2002-03 and above which an individual's capital gains for a year of assessment are chargeable to capital gains tax.

4360. Capital gains tax—gilt edged securities—exemptions

CAPITAL GAINS TAX (GILT-EDGED SECURITIES) ORDER 2002, SI 2002 2849; made under the Taxation of Chargeable Gains Act 1992 Sch.9 para.1. In force: November 18, 2002; £2.00.

This Order specifies gilt edged securities disposals of which are exempt from tax on chargeable gains in accordance with the Taxation of Chargeable Gains Act 1992 s.115.

4361. Capital gains tax—reduction of capital—cancellation of class of share capital—meaning of "reorganisation"

[Taxation of Chargeable Gains Act 1992 s.126(1), s.127, s.128(3).]

U appealed against a decision of the special commissioners upholding a corporation tax assessment on the basis that there had been neither a reduction of share capital nor a reorganisation for the purposes of the Taxation of Chargeable Gains Act 1992 s.126(1). In 1992 U disposed of its ordinary stock in B. On April 29, 1965 B's share capital had been subject to a scheme of arrangement approved by the court involving the cancellation of all B's preference capital of £3,652,124, leaving only the £6 million ordinary stock held by U. The authorised and issued share capital was reduced to the extent of the cancellation of the preference stock but the authorised capital was increased to the same nominal value, although none of the newly authorised ordinary shares was in fact issued. U had paid the former holders of the preference capital a total of £6,924,773. The Revenue raised an assessment on its profits chargeable to corporation tax for 1998. U sought to set against its chargeable gains a loss made on the disposal of the stock in 1992. It appealed against the assessment, challenging the method of calculating the chargeable gain and the base cost of the stock. The special commissioners dismissed the appeal.

Held, dismissing the appeal, that when interpreting s.126(1) in the context of Chapter II of the Act, a reduction of a company's share capital did not include cancellation of an entire class of share capital. In the event of such a cancellation, there was no new holding in respect of those shares and the statutory framework, for which s.126 provided the definition, depended upon, and did not work without, a new holding. There was no way of taxing the consideration received by the outgoing preferential shareholder, who would not be treated as having made a disposal by virtue of s.127 of the Act if such cancellation of share capital were a reorganisation. There was no way to tax him under s.128(3) if there was no new holding. Accordingly where nothing other than the cancellation of a class of share capital was relied upon, there was no reorganisation.

UNILEVER (UK) HOLDINGS LTD v. SMITH (INSPECTOR OF TAXES) [2002] S.T.C. 113, Burton, J., Ch D.

4362. Capital gains tax–sale of assets–inclusion of public authority grant in calculation of expenditure on new asset–roll over relief

[Taxation of Chargeable Gains Act 1992 s.50, s.152.]

The Revenue appealed against a determination upholding P's claim to defer capital gains liabilities on the sale of assets. Following the sale of a portion of its land, P constructed a new clubhouse. The sports council assisted in meeting the costs of the project by way of a substantial grant. The parties agreed that the land had been an "old asset" within the meaning of the Taxation of Chargeable Gains Act 1992 s.152 and that the expenditure on the club house had been employed in the acquisition of new assets. However, the Revenue contended that s.50 of the Act, which excluded expenditure met by public bodies from the computation of a gain, applied to both the expenditure associated with acquisition of the new asset and in respect of the acquisition and disposal of the old asset. Thus, it was argued, the Sports Council grant was to be subtracted from P's expenditure in acquiring the new asset when calculating P's entitlement to roll over relief.

Held, dismissing the appeal, that s.50 and s.152 of the Act were concerned with entirely different aspects of the ascertainment of liability to tax on capital gains. Whilst s.50 precluded deductions in respect of expenditure which had been met by a public authority, s.152 related to the temporal deferral of tax liability on a realised gain. The s.152(10) requirement that provisions in the Act "fixing the amount of consideration deemed to be given" were to be applied prior to any application of s.152 did not extend to those provisions relating to the non deductability of acquisition expenditure. Thus, the Revenue had erred in considering that s.50 was to be applied before giving effect to s.152, *Watton (Inspector of Taxes) v. Tippett* [1997] S.T.C. 893, [1997] C.L.Y. 339 applied.

WARDHAUGH (INSPECTOR OF TAXES) v. PENRITH RUGBY UNION FOOTBALL CLUB, [2002] EWHC 918, [2002] S.T.C. 776, Ferris, J., Ch D.

4363. Capital gains tax–sale of land–assignment of beneficial interests prior to completion–date of disposal

[Capital Gains Tax Act 1979 s.27(1); Taxation of Chargeable Gains Act 1992 s.28(1).]

J appealed a decision ([2001] S.T.C. (S.C.D.) 170) upholding an assessment to capital gains tax. J and his wife had entered into a contract for the sale of land beneficially owned by them and other members of their family, as tenants in common. Before the sale had been completed they each assigned one half of their respective beneficial interests to a settlement in Bermuda. Following completion, the Bermudian settlements received a share of the proceeds of the sale of the land. The Revenue contended that J was liable to capital gains tax in respect of that part of the proceeds received by the Bermudian trustees. J contended that the disposal for the purposes of the Capital Gains Tax Act 1979 s.27(1), now the Taxation of Chargeable Gains Act 1992 s.28(1)) had taken place at the date of completion and not at the date of the contract of sale and thus J had been liable for tax only on the actual sum received on completion.

Held, allowing the appeal, that notwithstanding that the deeming provisions of s.27(1) might deem a disposal actually made at one time to have been made at another time, it could not be used to justify one person being assessed to tax in respect of a disposal of property which had been made by another. Accordingly, on the facts, there had been no deemed disposal by J and his wife of their undivided shares in the land under the contract of sale. To interpret s.27 in the manner contended for by the Revenue would mean that a person would incur a capital gains tax liability on a gain which he did not make, whilst a person who made the actual gain from an arm's length transaction between unconnected parties would incur no tax liability.

JEROME v. KELLY (INSPECTOR OF TAXES), [2002] EWHC 604, [2002] S.T.C. 609, Park, J., Ch D.

4364. Capital gains tax—sale of land—valuation—five bedroom detached property let for multiple occupation—use of comparables

Held, that the value of a half share of a five bedroom detached house in Ashford let for multiple occupation was assessed at £29,250 as at March 31, 1982 for capital gains tax purposes. The valuation was based on sales of comparable properties derived from Inland Revenue Particulars Delivered forms and presented in anonymised form.

NEWMAN (INSPECTOR OF TAXES) v. HATT [2002] 1 E.G.L.R. 89, NJ Rose, FRICS, Lands Tr.

4365. Capital gains tax—share option schemes—meaning of "bargain at arm's length"—computation of cost of acquisition of shares

[Capital Gains Tax Act 1979 s.29A(1)(a), s.29A(1)(b); Taxation of Chargeable Gains Act 1992 s.17.]

The Revenue appealed against a decision of the commissioner, on an assessment to capital gains tax in respect of J, that the base value of shares that J had acquired when exercising options granted to him by his employer was their market value when he had exercised the options. J had been granted options by his employer, M, in 1983, 1984 and 1985 to purchase shares in M at the market price of those shares. In 1989 and 1991 J had exercised the options and had quickly sold the shares acquired. It was common ground that J had acquired the options by reason of his employment and that accordingly the Capital Gains Tax Act 1979 s.29A(1)(b), now the Taxation of Chargeable Gains Act 1992 s.17, applied to the acquisitions. Furthermore, the Revenue conceded that the acquisition of the shares was the acquisition of an asset "otherwise than by way of a bargain made at arm's length" with the result that s.29A(1)(a) of the 1979 Act also applied. The issue for determination was the impact, if any, of the fact that J had acquired the options by reason of his employment "otherwise than by way of a bargain made at arm's length" had on the character of the acquisition of the underlying assets acquired on the exercise of the options, in the instant case the shares, and whether for the purposes of s.29A(1)(a) and (b), by reason of that fact not only the options but also the shares were to be treated as acquired by reason of J's employment "otherwise than by way of a bargain made at arm's length".

Held, dismissing the appeal, that the statutory language was clear. The words "by way of a bargain made at arm's length" suggested more than a transaction; they indicated a transaction between two parties each of which had separate and distinct interests and both of whom had agreed terms with a mind to their own respective interests. Where there had been a grant of options to purchase shares and a subsequent acquisition of those shares, s.29A of the 1979 Act focused on the entirety of the process of acquisition of the shares as single transactions. The character of the grant of the option was of essential importance when determining whether the acquisition of the shares fell within s.29A(1)(a) or (b). In the instant case s.29A applied in respect of J's acquisition of the shares. It followed that in the computation of the cost of acquisition of the shares, the cost of acquisition had to equate to the market value at the date when the options had been exercised.

MANSWORTH (INSPECTOR OF TAXES) v. JELLEY, [2002] EWHC 442, [2002] S.T.C. 1013, Lightman, J., Ch D.

4366. Childcare—tax credits—new category

TAX CREDIT (NEW CATEGORY OF CHILD CARE PROVIDER) REGULATIONS 2002, SI 2002 1417; made under the Tax Credits Act 1999 s.15. In force: June 20, 2002; £2.00.

These Regulations make a scheme for establishing a new category of persons whose charges for providing child care outside the UK are to be taken into account for the purposes of determining working families' tax credit or disabled person's tax credit. The persons whose charges can be taken into account for these purposes must be approved by an organisation that has been accredited by the Secretary of State. The scheme establishes the criteria to be met by an organisation seeking accreditation to approve child care providers; the matters to be included in the system operated by an accredited organisation for approving child care providers and assessing the quality of child care they provide; the information to be provided by an organisation making or renewing an application for accreditation; the procedure for renewing accreditation; the procedure for withdrawing accreditation or varying the conditions of accreditation; the requirements on an accredited organisation during the period of accreditation; the requirements on an approved child care provider during the period of his approval to give access to the Secretary of State and the Inland Revenue; the consequences for child care providers approved by an organisation whose accreditation is withdrawn or expires; the criteria for approval of a child care provider; and the ability for the Secretary of State to make payments to accredited organisations.

4367. Childrens tax credit—qualifying person—entitlement

CHILD TAX CREDIT REGULATIONS 2002, SI 2002 2007; made under the Tax Credits Act 2002 s.8, s.9, s.65, s.67. In force: in accordance with Reg.1; £2.00.

The Tax Credits Act 2002 introduces the child tax credit and working tax credit which will be available from April 6, 2003. These Regulations determine the circumstances in which a person is or is not responsible for a child or qualifying young person, for child tax credit purposes. The Regulations provide for a person who has attained the age of 16 years to remain a "child" for the purposes of child tax credit and working tax credit until September 1 following their sixteenth birthday; provide for the maximum age for a qualifying young person; prescribe the circumstances in which a person is entitled to child tax credit for a child or qualifying young person who has died; prescribe the maximum rate at which a person or persons may be entitled to child tax credit; and define "disabled" and "severely disabled".

4368. Climate change levy

CLIMATE CHANGE LEVY (GENERAL) (AMENDMENT) REGULATIONS 2002, SI 2002 1152; made under the Finance Act 2000 s.30, Sch.6 para.41. In force: June 1, 2002; £1.75.

These Regulations amend The Climate Change Levy (General) Regulations 2001 (SI 2001 838) to make provision for an annual accounting scheme. They introduce a scheme which provides, subject to certain conditions, for registered traders to be authorised to account for and pay climate change levy (CCL) on an annual basis; contain definitions of expressions used elsewhere in the new regulations; provide for registered traders to be authorised to use the scheme on application to Customs and Excise; prescribe conditions for eligibility for the scheme; make provision for the cessation and termination of authorisation to use the scheme; specify how registered traders should account for and pay CCL when they cease to be authorised to use the scheme; and enable Customs and Excise to vary, by means of publication in a notice, the various monetary thresholds prescribed in these regulations (which have all been set at fl2,000 initially).

4369. Corporation tax—advance corporation tax—tax planning—payment of dividends—meaning of "transactions in securities"

[Income and Corporation Taxes Act 1988 s.709(2).]

The Revenue appealed against a decision ([2001] S.T.C. 689) dismissing its appeal against the discharge of a notice and assessment. The Revenue contended that the payment of an interim dividend constituted a transaction in securities as defined in the Income and Corporation Taxes Act 1988 s.709(2). The Revenue submitted that the definition of transaction in securities was unambiguous.

Held, allowing the appeal, that the declaration or payment of a dividend was a transaction in securities as defined in s.709(2). The lower court was wrong to determine that a declaration and payment of a dividend merely gave effect to pre existing rights and therefore did not constitute a transaction in securities. A shareholder had no right to a dividend until it was declared or paid. The definition of transaction in securities was not to be limited by reference to any supposed mischief at which the legislation was aimed or by reference to the specific transactions detailed in the definition. It was applicable in accordance with its wide terms, *Inland Revenue Commissioners v. Parker* [1966] A.C. 141, [1966] C.L.Y. 6179 and *Greenberg v. Inland Revenue Commissioners* [1972] A.C. 109, [1971] C.L.Y. 5718 applied, and to a unilateral act which related to securities. The definition was not ambiguous. Further, a fear that a wide interpretation would lead to injustice was no reason to limit its ambit. The Act clearly set out the conditions which had to be present before it could be applied.

INLAND REVENUE COMMISSIONERS v. LAIRD GROUP PLC; *sub nom.* LAIRD GROUP PLC v. INLAND REVENUE COMMISSIONERS, [2002] EWCA Civ 576, [2002] S.T.C. 722, Sir Andrew Morritt V.C., CA.

4370. Corporation   tax–assessment–postponement   pending   appeal– documentation of tax avoidance schemes

[Taxes Management Act 1970 s.55(6).]

S, a property investment business belonging to a group which owned and leased a number of shop premises, applied under the Taxes Management Act 1970 s.55(6) to postpone the tax charged under a corporation tax assessment raised in respect of rental income on the ground that it had no liability to tax in the relevant period. Rents from some of the properties were paid directly or indirectly to S. In 1996 S entered into a series of transactions which were part of a tax avoidance scheme which included a zero coupon note with the nominal value of £1,765.5 million issued at a discount of seven per cent and a forward share purchase agreement under which the consideration payable by S was £1.65 billion. It was designated to eliminate the liability to tax on that rental income. In December 2000, S was assessed to corporation tax on estimated profits of £115 million on the basis that tax was due on the rentals received by S.

Held, dismissing the application, that (1) the court did not have to decide at this stage whether the scheme would be found to be effective but had to have regard to the evidence adduced and consider whether it supported S's representations that it was overcharged to tax by the assessment. There were no reasonable grounds for believing that an overseas bank had offered S an unsecured loan of £1.65 billion. There was considerable doubt whether S ever in fact had the sum of £1.65 billion to make payment under the agreement and there was no evidence that the agreement was ever completed. In all the circumstances there were no reasonable grounds for believing that S was overcharged to tax and so no tax would be postponed apart from the sum of £688,008 already agreed by the Revenue.

PUMAHAVEN LTD v. WILLIAMS (INSPECTOR OF TAXES); *sub nom.* SPARROW LTD v. INSPECTOR OF TAXES [2001] S.T.C. (S.C.D.) 206, Nuala Brice, Sp Comm.

4371. Corporation tax–controlled foreign companies–exemptions

CONTROLLED FOREIGN COMPANIES (EXCLUDED COUNTRIES) (AMENDMENT) REGULATIONS 2002, SI 2002 1963; made under the Income and Corporation Taxes Act 1988 s.748. In force: October 1, 2002; £1.50.

These Regulations amend the Controlled Foreign Companies (Excluded Countries) Regulations 1998 (SI 1998 3081) in consequence of the repeal of specified provisions of the Finance Act 1993 by the Finance Act 2002 s.79(1)(b) and the repeal of provisions of the Finance Act 1994 by the Finance Act 2002 s.83(2).

4372. Corporation tax–controlled foreign companies–exemptions–Republic of Ireland

CONTROLLED FOREIGN COMPANIES (EXCLUDED COUNTRIES) (AMENDMENT NO.2) REGULATIONS 2002, SI 2002 2406; made under the Income and Corporation Taxes Act 1988 s.748. In force: October 11, 2002; £1.50.

These Regulations amend the Controlled Foreign Companies (Excluded Countries) Regulations 1998 (SI 1998 3081) by omitting the entry in respect of Ireland with the effect that the Income and Corporation Taxes Act 1988 s.748(1) (e) will not apply to a controlled foreign company resident in the Republic of Ireland.

4373. Corporation tax–deductions–expenditure incurred in replacing cast iron pipes by gas supplier–expenditure as revenue or capital

T appealed against a decision by the Revenue to disallow its claim to deduct expenditure on the insertion of pipes of polyethylene in certain iron and steel pipes from its profits for the years 1995 to 1998. T operated an integrated gas transportation system across Great Britain with gas transmitted through an interconnected network of steel pipes. In 2001 the Health and Safety Executive required the replacement of all cast iron mains within 30 metres of any property over the next 30 years to comply with health and safety legislation. T sought to deduct the cost of inserting new pipes from its profits for tax purposes. The Revenue took the view that the expenditure was in connection with a long-term policy of renewal and improvement of the entire system and was of a capital nature. T argued that the whole expenditure was incurred to repair parts of the system and was of a revenue nature.

Held, allowing the appeal, that whether there had been a repair or an improvement depended on whether the character of the fixed asset had been changed by the work. Repair occurred when part of a complex whole was renewed or replaced and renewal occurred when substantially the whole was reconstructed or when the character of the subject matter changed. In the instant case the evidence supported the conclusion that only small parts of the complex whole were renewed each year. The expenditure in question had merely restored the pipeline to its original condition. It had not rendered the pipeline capable of giving a greater service than the original. There had been no improvement and no new asset was created. In the circumstances the expenditure was in respect of repairs rather than improvements and was of a revenue rather than a capital nature; such a conclusion was supported by the ordinary principles of commercial accountancy.

TRANSCO PLC v. DYALL (INSPECTOR OF TAXES) [2002] S.T.C. (S.C.D.) 199, AN Brice (Chairman), Sp Comm.

4374. Corporation tax–exemptions–foreign companies–assets invested in shares of companies established in taxing Member State–exemption from tax on investments

[EC Treaty Art.43.]

The Dutch Wealth Tax Law 1964 provided that investments by Dutch nationals and by nationals from other countries residing in the Netherlands in the assets of a Dutch company were exempt from tax. B, a Dutch national, applied for an exemption concerning his investment in the capital of an Irish company of which he was the sole shareholder. His request was rejected on the basis that the exemption only applied to assets held in Dutch companies. He argued that the Dutch provisions were contrary to the principle of freedom of establishment under EC Treaty Art.43. The national court referred the question to the ECJ.

Held, giving a preliminary ruling, that the area of direct taxation remained largely within the Member States discretion but the Member States had to exercise that discretion in a manner compatible with Community law and refrain from any discrimination based on nationality. Article 43 EC was applicable to a situation where an individual had a 100 per cent shareholding in a company established in another Member State. An individual who owned all the shares in a company could be assimilated to the company to the extent that the individual was exercising his right of establishment. Article 43 precluded the Member States from treating EU nationals differently from their own nationals, from placing obstacles to the exercise by their nationals of their freedom of establishment and from placing obstacles to the exercise by EU nationals resident in their territory of their right of establishment in a third Member State. The unavailability of the exemption in question to assets held in companies based in another Member State constituted a restriction on the right of establishment of Dutch nationals and other EU nationals residing in the Netherlands, which was incompatible with Art.43. The objections that the provisions at issue were intended to avoid double taxation and to maintain the cohesion of the tax system were ill founded. The exemption under the Wealth Tax Law related to an individual as a separate entity, not to the undertaking which was taxed separately as a taxable person distinct from its shareholders. In addition, the tax applied irrespective of whether or not the company made a profit.

BAARS v. INSPECTEUR DER BELASTINGDIENST PARTICULIEREN/ ONDERNEMINGEN GORINCHEM (C251/98) [2002] 1 C.M.L.R. 49, Edward (President), ECJ.

4375. Corporation tax–intangible assets–finance leasing

CORPORATION TAX (FINANCE LEASING OF INTANGIBLE ASSETS) REGULATIONS 2002, SI 2002 1967; made under the Finance Act 2002 Sch.29 para.104. In force: August 15, 2002; £1.75.

These Regulations apply the Finance Act 2002 Sch.29 to a company that is the finance lessor of an intangible asset which is the subject of a finance lease.

4376. Corporation tax–investment companies–loans used to finance cost of Eurobond and securities issues–deductibility of costs of loans

[Income and Corporation Taxes Act 1988 s.75(1), s.77, s.130.]

C, a investment company under the Income and Corporation Taxes Act 1988 s.130, appealed against a Revenue decision refusing to allow it to claim the full costs of loans used to finance a Eurobond issue and an issue of preferential securities by a group company. C contended that the costs should be allowed as management costs under s.77 in the year they were incurred. However, the costs were treated as written off over the life of the issues, as required by Financial Reporting Standard 4 and the Revenue determined that the longer period applied by virtue of s.75(1).

Held, allowing the appeal, that s.77 referred to the period in which the finance was obtained and the matter did not fall to be decided by reference to FRS 4, which dealt with the accounting treatment of the entire loan, as opposed to the costs of the issue.

CADBURY SCHWEPPES PLC v. WILLIAMS (INSPECTOR OF TAXES) [2002] S.T.C. (S.C.D.) 115, John F Avery Jones, Sp Comm.

4377. Corporation tax–life insurance–reinsurance contracts made in respect of non resident policy holders

[Income and Corporation Taxes Act 1988 s.431C, s.431D(1)(b)(i); Finance Act 1995 Sch.8 para.55(2).]

R, a United Kingdom resident life insurer, appealed against a corporation tax assessment in relation to three reinsurance contracts made in respect of non resident policy holders on December 22 and 23, 1993 and November 25, 1994. The Revenue contended that all three contracts were liable to be treated as life reinsurance business under the Income and Corporation Taxes Act 1988 s.431C. Alternatively, that the contract dated November 25, 1994 was overseas life assurance business for the purposes of s.431D.

Held, allowing the appeal except for policies reinsured after November 1, 1994, that s.431C did not apply to the instant case as s.431D(1)(b)(i) provided that the phrase "life reinsurance business" did not include policies held by non UK residents. However, the Finance Act 1995 Sch.8 para.55(2) provided that s.431D(1)(b)(i) only applied to overseas reinsurance business that was subject to underlying policies which were written after November 1, 1994, with the result that only a small part of the final contract came within s.431D(1)(b)(i).

ROYAL LONDON MUTUAL INSURANCE SOCIETY LTD v. BARRETT (INSPECTOR OF TAXES) [2002] S.T.C. (S.C.D.) 61, Nuala Brice, Sp Comm.

4378. Corporation tax—losses—freedom of establishment—entitlement to offset loss against profit made in another Member State

[EC Treaty Art.43.]

A, a Belgian company with a permanent establishment in Luxembourg, sustained a loss in Belgium in 1981, whereas its Luxembourg permanent establishment made a profit in the same period. A made a profit in Belgium the following year. As Luxembourg law prevented A from offsetting the Belgian loss against the profits made in Luxembourg, A sought to deduct the 1981 Belgian loss against the profits it made there in 1982. This was refused by the Belgian tax authorities, on the ground that national legislation prevented losses incurred in one tax year from being offset against the following year's profits. A challenged this refusal in the national court. The court stayed the matter and referred the question to the ECJ for a preliminary ruling as to whether Belgian law, which only allowed losses in one tax year to be offset against profits made in a later tax year if they could not be attributed to profits made in the earlier period by a permanent establishment resident in another Member State, was compatible with the EC Treaty Art.43.

Held, ruling on the preliminary issue, that Art.43 precluded national legislation which made A's right to offset the losses it had sustained in Belgium in 1981 from the profits it made there in 1982 conditional on the fact that the losses could not be set against the profits made by its Luxembourg permanent establishment in 1981. The effect of the provision in issue was to prevent taxable income made in either Member State from being deducted when a right of deduction would have existed if A had operated only within Belgium.

ALGEMENE MAATSCHAPPIJ VOOR INVESTERING EN DIENSTVERLENING NV (AMID) v. BELGIUM (C141/99) [2003] S.T.C. 356, Judge Gulmann (President), ECJ.

4379. Corporation tax—reliefs—availability where associated investment company carried on business during relevant period

[Income and Corporation Taxes Act 1988 s.13.]

L appealed against a decision refusing its application for a reduction in corporation tax under the Income and Corporation Taxes Act 1988 s.13(1) on the ground that S, an associated investment company, had carried on in business during the relevant accounting periods for which the deduction was sought. S had taken part in investment activity, let property and paid dividends during the accounting periods, but L argued that these were not business activities for the purposes of s.13(4).

Held, dismissing the appeal, that "business" had a wider interpretation than "trade" with the result that investment activity conducted by a company incorporated for that purpose, including the receipt of rents, was a business activity in terms of s.13(4), *American Leaf Blending Co Sdn Bhd v. Director General of Inland Revenue* [1979] A.C. 676, [1979] C.L.Y. 270 applied.

LAND MANAGEMENT LTD v. FOX (INSPECTOR OF TAXES) [2002] S.T.C. (S.C.D.) 152, Nuala Brice, Sp Comm.

4380.   Corporation tax—reliefs—group relief—deductible losses

[Income and Corporation Taxes Act 1988 s.403(8) (now repealed); Taxation of Chargeable Gains Act 1992 s.8(1).]

M, an investment company liable to corporation tax, appealed against a decision of the judge ([2002] S.T.C. 430) rejecting its claim that it had an amount of £48.3 million available for surrender by way of group relief for its 1994 accounts. The special commissioners had accepted M's argument that "losses" and "allowances" in the Income and Corporation Taxes Act 1988 s.403(8) (now repealed) meant only trading losses and capital allowances and did not include allowable losses which fell to be deducted under the Taxation of Chargeable Gains Act 1992 s.8(1). Overruling that decision, the judge held that, properly construed, s.403(8) provided that in calculating the profits of the surrendering company, no account should be taken of any deduction in respect of any losses, including allowable losses, that would otherwise fall to be made in the course of calculating those profits.

Held, dismissing the appeal, that the judge had been correct to find that s.403(8) prevented any deduction from the taxpayer's chargeable gains from being made in respect of the allowable losses of a previous accounting period.

TAYLOR (INSPECTOR OF TAXES) v. MEPC HOLDINGS LTD; *sub nom.* MEPC HOLDINGS LTD v. TAYLOR (INSPECTOR OF TAXES), [2002] EWCA Civ 883, [2002] S.T.C. 997, Chadwick, L.J., CA.

4381.   Corporation tax—transfer pricing—employee share schemes—UK resident parent company providing business facilities for foreign subsidiaries

[Income and Corporation Taxes Act 1988 s.770(1), s.773(4).]

W sought a decision in principle as to the applicability of the Income and Corporation Taxes Act 1988 s.770(1) and s.773(4), both of which had now been repealed, to an employee share option scheme established by W and intended to provided share options for employees of W's overseas subsidiaries. W made interest free loans to the scheme trustee for the purchase of shares and the making of options to selected employees. The Revenue issued directions to the effect that the scheme was a form of business facility given at an undervalue for the purposes of s.773(4), which fell to be valued on an arm's length basis under s.770(1). The Revenue also issued corporation tax assessments on W and two subsidiaries, E and P, showing an increased corporation tax liability. W, P and E appealed against the assessments.

Held, giving a decision in principle and adjourning the appeal so that the assessment could be agreed, that the giving of employee benefits in the form of share options satisfied the wide meaning of "business facilities" in s.773(4). Reading s.770(1) in the light of s.773(4), the facilities supplied by W to its foreign subsidiaries, including the services of the trust, amounted to expenditure by a UK resident company that was intended to benefit foreign companies in its control. The cost of those facilities fell to be determined on an arm's length basis under s.773(4) and s.770(1) by reference to the borrowing, management and administrative costs that would have been incurred if they had been supplied by a third party. The arm's length price determined on that basis could then be used to compute W's corporation tax liability.

WATERLOO PLC v. INLAND REVENUE COMMISSIONERS [2002] S.T.C. (S.C.D.) 95, Nuala Brice, Sp Comm.

4382.   Corporation tax—voluntary winding up—expenses—meaning of "necessary disbursement"

See INSOLVENCY: Toshoku Finance UK Plc (In Liquidation), *Re.* §2718

4383. Corporation tax, capital gains–derivative products purchased to meet obligations under life insurance guaranteed equity bonds

[Finance Act 1996 s.81, s.103.]

H appealed against corporation tax assessments which sought to treat certain derivative products purchased to enable H to meet its liabilities to guaranteed equity bond holders as being subject to the loan relationships provisions of the Finance Act 1996 s.81 and s.103. H contended that s.81 (1) did not apply as the products in issue did not give rise to a "money debt" in terms of s.81 (2), neither did they constitute money lending, pursuant to s.81 (1) (b).

Held, allowing the appeal, that (1) a "money debt" under s.81 (2) was a debt that was settled by the payment of cash. Examining the matter from the point that the transactions were entered into, only those derivatives allowing for settlement in cash, or with an option to receive cash as opposed to shares, were money debts for the purposes of s.81 (2), and (2) for the loan relationship rules to apply there had to be both a lender and a borrower. On the facts of the instant case, however, H and the derivatives providers had been careful not to adopt such positions with the result that they had not concluded contracts for the lending of money.

HSBC LIFE (UK) LTD v. STUBBS (INSPECTOR OF TAXES); NATIONWIDE LIFE LTD v. CRISP (INSPECTOR OF TAXES); ABBEY LIFE ASSURANCE CO LTD v. COLCLOUGH (INSPECTOR OF TAXES); TSB LIFE LTD v. COLCLOUGH (INSPECTOR OF TAXES); LLOYDS TSB LIFE ASSURANCE CO LTD v. COLCLOUGH (INSPECTOR OF TAXES) [2002] S.T.C. (S.C.D.) 9, Malachy Cornwell-Kelly, Sp Comm.

4384. Double taxation–Malaysia–Australia–government pension received by Australian resident–interpretation of agreement

[Australia-Malaysia Double Tax Treaty Art.18(2).]

N was resident in Australia. He received a Malaysian pension that was taxed at source in Malaysia. C assessed him to tax on the pension and applied a tax credit in the same sum as the tax deducted in Malaysia. N asserted that his Malaysian pension was not taxable in Australia by virtue of the Australia-Malaysian Double Taxation Convention Art.18(2). N's claim was dismissed at first instance and he appealed.

Held, dismissing the appeal, that Australia had not abrogated its right to tax under the Convention, but rather Malaysia had asserted its right to tax. The Convention did not restrict Australia's right to tax N's pension and the domestic provisions governing the issuing of tax credits did not assist in the interpretation of the Convention.

NGEE HIN CHONG v. COMMISSIONER OF TAXATION 2 I.T.L. Rep. 707, Goldberg, J., Fed Ct (Aus).

4385. Double taxation–reliefs–Lithuania

DOUBLE TAXATION RELIEF (TAXES ON INCOME) (LITHUANIA) ORDER 2002, SI 2002 2847; made under the Income and Corporation Taxes Act 1988 s.788. In force: November 20, 2002; £1.75.

This Order amends the Double Taxation Relief (Taxes on Income) (Lithuania) Order 2001 (SI 2001 3925) by substituting a new Art.31 to the Convention set out in the Schedule to that Order to provide that the Convention will take effect in the UK for any financial year beginning on or after April 1, 2002, in respect of corporation tax, and for any year of assessment beginning on or after April 6, 2002, in respect of income tax and capital gains tax and will take effect in Lithuania from January 1, 2002.

4386. Double taxation–reliefs–South Africa

DOUBLE TAXATION RELIEF (TAXES ON INCOME) (SOUTH AFRICA) ORDER 2002, SI 2002 3138; made under the Income and Corporation Taxes Act 1988 s.788. In force: December 17, 2002; £3.50.

The Convention with South Africa, which is set out in the Schedule to this Order and replaces the Convention set out in the Double Taxation Relief (Taxes on Income) (South Africa) Order 1969 (SI 1969 864), provides for business profits not arising through a permanent establishment to be taxed only in the country of the taxpayer's residence; profits attributable to a permanent establishment may be taxed in the country in which the permanent establishment is situated; income from immovable property and gains derived from the alienation of such property may be taxed in the country in which the property is situated; and shipping and air transport profits are generally to be taxed only in the country of residence of the operator.

4387. Double taxation–reliefs–Taiwan

DOUBLE TAXATION RELIEF (TAXES ON INCOME) (TAIWAN) ORDER 2002, SI 2002 3137; made under the Income and Corporation Taxes Act 1988 s.788. In force: December 17, 2002; £3.50.

The Agreement with Taiwan, set out in this Order, provides for business profits not arising through a permanent establishment to be taxed only in the territory of the taxpayer's residence; profits attributable to a permanent establishment may be taxed in the territory in which the permanent establishment is situated; income from immovable property may be taxed in the territory in which the property is situated and international shipping and air transport profits are generally to be taxed only in the territory of residence of the operator.

4388. Double taxation–reliefs–United States

DOUBLE TAXATION RELIEF (TAXES ON INCOME) (THE UNITED STATES OF AMERICA) ORDER 2002, SI 2002 2848; made under the Income and Corporation Taxes Act 1988 s.788. In force: November 20, 2002; £6.50.

The Convention between the government of the UK and the government of the United States of America for the avoidance of double taxation and the prevention of fiscal evasion with respect to taxes on income and on capital gains, which replaces the Convention set out in the Schedule to the Double Taxation Relief (Taxes on Income) (The United States of America) Order 1980 (SI 1980 568), is set out in this Order. It provides for business profits to be taxed only in the country of the taxpayer's residence unless they are profits attributable to a permanent establishment maintained by the taxpayer in the other country. Profits attributable to a permanent establishment may be taxed in the country in which the permanent establishment is situated but the attributable profits may include only the profits derived from the assets used, risks assumed and activities performed by the permanent establishment. It also provides income from real property and gains derived from the alienation of such property may be taxed in the country in which the property is situated, and shipping and air transport profits of an enterprise of one country operating in international traffic shall be taxable only in that country.

4389. Double taxation–United States–Canada–permanent establishment–US resident providing training services to Canadian resident company–meaning of "fixed base"–Canada

[Canada-US Income Tax Convention 1980 Art.V, Art.XIV; Model Tax Convention (OECD) Art.14.]

D, a resident and citizen of the United States, appealed against Canadian income tax assessments relating to a period he spent providing training services to a Canadian resident business. During the contract, D was provided with an office on the company's premises. D argued that his earnings from his work in Canada were exempt from Canadian tax under the Canada-US Income Tax Convention 1980 Art.XIV. He contended that he did not have "a fixed base" in Canada, as required by Art.XIV. The Crown argued that the provision of services from a fixed location amounted to a fixed base, which had a wider meaning than "permanent establishment", as defined in Art.V.

Held, allowing the appeal, that the OECD Model Convention Art.14 and its associated commentary showed that there was no real distinction between the concept of a "fixed base" and a "permanent establishment". D was not liable to Canadian income tax as he had no control of any part of the company's premises. Therefore his income fell to be taxed in the US.

R. v. DUDNEY; *sub nom.* DUDNEY v. R. 1 I.T.L. Rep. 371, Judge EA Bowie, Tax Court of Canada (Canada).

4390. Double taxation–United States–Canada–US resident radio sports reporter–liability to Canadian income tax–Canadian baseball game commentary

[Canada United States Income Tax Convention 1980 Art.XVI; Model Tax Convention (OECD) Art.17; Income Tax Act (Canada) s.110(1) (f) (i).]

C, a US resident, provided exclusive radio commentary for a Toronto baseball team playing in the American League. He filed Canadian income tax returns but deducted the income earned from this activity under Income Tax Act (Canada) s.110(1) (f) (i). This was disallowed by the Canadian authorities however, on the ground that C was liable to income tax on his Canadian income as he was an "entertainer" for the purposes of the Canada United States Income Tax Convention 1980 Art.XVI. C appealed.

Held, allowing the appeal, that C did not attract an audience in his own right, as would be the case with an entertainment artiste. The 1980 Convention was to be given a liberal construction with reference also to the corresponding OECD Model Convention Art.17 and commentary. On this basis, C fulfilled the role of a reporter commentating on the game and providing commentary to fill in for moments of inactivity on the field.

CHEEK v. R. 4 I.T.L. Rep. 652, Mogan, J., Tax Ct (Can) Tax Court of Canada (Canada).

4391. Employee Share Schemes Act 2002 2002 (34)

This Act makes provision relating to employee share schemes.
This Act received Royal Assent on November 7, 2002.

4392. Excise duty–beer–reduced rates–small breweries

BEER AND EXCISE WAREHOUSING (AMENDMENT) REGULATIONS 2002, SI 2002 1265; made under the Customs and Excise Management Act 1979 s.93, s.118A; and the Alcoholic Liquor Duties Act 1979 s.49. In force: June 1, 2002; £1.75.

These Regulations amend the Beer Regulations 1993 (SI1993 1228) and the Excise Warehousing (Etc.) Regulations 1988 (SI 1988 809) reflecting the amendments to the Alcoholic Liquor Duties Act 1979 in relation to charging reduced rates of excise duty on beer from small breweries. These Regulations support the introduction of these reduced rates by requiring a certificate of production to accompany beer eligible for reduced rates when moved in duty suspension, additional information regarding "co-operated breweries", and the keeping of additional records regarding production and certificates of production. They also prohibit the carrying out of certain operations on beer eligible for reduced rates, including mixing with beer subject to a different rate of duty.

4393. Excise duty–beer and tobacco products

EXCISE GOODS, BEER AND TOBACCO PRODUCTS (AMENDMENT) REGULATIONS 2002, SI 2002 2692; made under the Finance (No.2) Act 1992 s.1. In force: December 1, 2002; £2.00.

These Regulations implement the requirements of Council Directive 92/12 ([1992] OJ L76/1) on the general arrangements for products subject to excise duty and on the holding, movement and monitoring of such products, in respect of the right of individuals to import excise goods which they have acquired duty-paid in another Member State for their own use and which they have transported to the UK. They amend the Excise Goods (Holding, Movement, Warehousing and REDS) Regulations 1992 (SI 1992 3135), the Beer Regulations 1993 (SI 1993 1228) and the Tobacco Products Regulations 2001 (SI 2001 1712) to provide for an excise duty point where such goods are held or used in the UK for a commercial purpose; and make other ancillary amendments.

4394. Excise duty–excise duty points–movement of excise goods–accompanying documents

EXCISE GOODS (ACCOMPANYING DOCUMENTS) REGULATIONS 2002, SI 2002 501; made under the European Communities Act 1972 s.2; the Customs and Excise Management Act 1979 s.93, s.100G, s.100H, s.118A; and the Finance (No.2) Act 1992 s.1. In force: April 1, 2002; £4.00.

These Regulations amend the Excise Warehousing (Etc.) Regulations 1988 (SI 1988 809), the Excise Goods (Holding, Movement, Warehousing and REDS) Regulations 1992 (SI 1992 3135), the Beer Regulations 1993 (SI 1993 1228) and the Warehousekeepers and Owners of Warehoused Goods Regulations 1999 (SI 1999 1278). They implement the requirements of Council Directive 92/12 ([1992] OJ L76/1) in respect of the documentation required to accompany commercial movements of excise goods within the European Union, provide for the creation of excise duty points, and identify the persons liable to pay, where there is a failure to comply with specified requirements.

4395. Excise duty–fuel–rates

OTHER FUEL SUBSTITUTES (RATES OF EXCISE DUTY ETC.) (AMENDMENT) ORDER 2002, SI 2002 3042; made under the Hydrocarbon Oil Duties Act 1979 s.6A. In force: January 1, 2003; £1.75.

This Order amends the Other Fuel Substitutes (Rates of Duty etc.) Order 1995 (SI 1995 2716) which prescribes the rates of the excise duty charged on certain liquids. The Order makes amendments such that where the rate previously prescribed in respect of a liquid was the rate specified by the Hydrocarbon Oil Duties Act 1979 for heavy oil, the rate now prescribed is the rate specified by the 1979 Act for ultra low sulphur diesel. Where the rate specified by the 1979 Act for light oil less any rebate specified for unleaded petrol, the rate now prescribed is the rate specified for ultra low sulphur petrol.

4396. Excise duty–gambling–gaming duty rates

GAMING DUTY (AMENDMENT) REGULATIONS 2002, SI 2002 2310; made under the Finance Act 1997 s.12, s.14. In force: October 1, 2002; £1.50.

These Regulations, which revoke the Gaming Duty (Amendment) Regulations 2000 (SI 2000 2408), amend the Gaming Duty Regulations 1997 (SI 1997 2196) by substituting a new Table reflecting changes to gaming duty made by the Finance Act 2002 s.10 which will apply in the case of payments on account of gaming duty for any quarter that ends on or after October 31, 2002.

4397. Excise duty–hydrocarbon oil–relief

HYDROCARBON OIL (INDUSTRIAL RELIEFS) REGULATIONS 2002, SI 2002 1471; made under the Hydrocarbon Oil Duties Act 1979 s.24, Sch.4. In force: Reg.5: July 1, 2002; Reg.6: July 1, 2002; remainder: September 1, 2002; £1.75.

These Regulations, which amend the Hydrocarbon Oil Regulations 1973 (SI 1973 1311), regulate how persons are to be approved for specified purposes, define specified terms and enable the Commissioners of Customs and Excise to approve persons for specified purposes individually or by reference to a class, in relation to particular descriptions of oil or generally and subject to conditions. It also enables the Commissioners to revoke such approval and vary the conditions of approval for reasonable cause. They prescribe the method of application for individual approval, impose the restriction that tied oil may be supplied only to an approved tied oil trader, require claims by an approved repayment user for repayment of duty to be made within a prescribed time limit and impose the restriction that no drawback of duty is allowed where an approved repayment user can make a claim for repayment of duty on oil used in industrial processes.

4398. Excise duty–hydrocarbon oil–relief

HYDROCARBON OIL (MARKING) REGULATIONS 2002, SI 2002 1773; made under the European Communities Act 1972 s.2; and the Hydrocarbon Oil Duties Act 1979 s.24, s.24A, Sch.4. In force: August 1, 2002; £2.50.

These Regulations, which amend the Hydrocarbon Oil Regulations 1973 (SI 1973 1311) and the Hydrocarbon Oil (Designated Markers) Regulations 1996 (SI 1996 1251), revoke the Hydrocarbon Oil (Amendment) Regulations 1985 (SI 1986 1033) and the Hydrocarbon Oil (Amendment) (No.2) Regulations 1994 (SI 1994 694). The Regulations require the marking of gas oil, kerosene and light oil with one or more chemical markers and colouring substance as a condition of allowing specified rebates of, and, in the case of gas oil and kerosene, relief from, excise duty on that oil under specified provisions of the Hydrocarbon Oil Duties Act 1979. They also prescribe the time and manner of marking and impose requirements as to the storage and labelling of containers of markers and marked oil and prohibit certain activities in relation to markers and marked oil.

4399. Excise duty–personal reliefs–revocation

EXCISE DUTIES (PERSONAL RELIEFS) (REVOCATION) ORDER 2002, SI 2002 2691; made under the Customs and Excise Duties (General Reliefs) Act 1979 s.13. In force: December 1, 2002; £1.50.

This Order revokes the Excise Duties (Personal Reliefs) Order 1992 (SI 1992 3155) and the Duties (Personal Reliefs) (Amendment) Order 1999 (SI 1999 1617).

4400. Excise duty–personal reliefs–revocation

EXCISE DUTIES (PERSONAL RELIEFS) (REVOCATION) ORDER 2002, SI 2002 2691; made under the Customs and Excise Duties (General Reliefs) Act 1979 s.13. In force: December 1, 2002; £1.50.

This Order revokes the Excise Duties (Personal Reliefs) Order 1992 (SI 1992 3155) and the Excise Duties (Personal Reliefs) (Amendment) Order 1999 (SI 1999 1617).

4401. Excise duty–relief–alcohol and tobacco products–France

CHANNEL TUNNEL (ALCOHOLIC LIQUOR AND TOBACCO PRODUCTS) (AMENDMENT) ORDER 2002, SI 2002 2693; made under the Channel Tunnel Act 1987 s.11, s.13. In force: December 1, 2002; £1.50.

The Excise Duties (Personal Reliefs) (Revocation) Order 2002 (SI 2002 2691) and the Excise Goods, Beer and Tobacco Products (Amendment) Regulations 2002 (SI 2002 2692) create new arrangements for individuals who acquire for their own use excise goods duty-paid in another Member State and transport them to the UK. This Order amends the Channel Tunnel (Alcoholic Liquor and Tobacco Products) Order 2000 (SI 2000 426) to enable the new arrangements to apply to relevant alcohol and tobacco taken into a shuttle train control zone in France.

4402. **Excise duty—tobacco products—calculation of national tax on cigarillos—interpretation of Council Directive 92/80**

[EC Treaty Art.234; Council Directive 92/80 on the approximation of taxes on manufactured tobacco other than cigarettes Art.3(1).]

The Finance Court in Dusseldorf made a reference for a preliminary ruling under EC Treaty Art.234 seeking guidance on the interpretation of Council Directive 92/80. The issue arose in a dispute between BT and HB over the assessment of excise duty on tobacco. BT ran a tobacco factory which made "semi-finished cigarillos" and other tobacco products. BT had made regular tax declarations in 1996 and 1997 and had assessed the level of tax payable itself. It had also complained that the tax ought to have been calculated by HB so as to take into account the minimum levy of DM 0.031 in accordance with Art.3(1) of the Directive. When HB refused to deal with the complaints, BT took the matter to the Finance Court which, in turn, made a reference to the ECJ for a preliminary ruling. The first part of the question referred involved a consideration of whether an ad valorem tax on cigars or cigarillos which was subject to a minimum amount was contrary to Art.3(1) under the Directive. The second part of the question involved a consideration of whether Art.3(1) could be relied on in a national court by a taxable person to challenge a method of calculating tax which was believed to be contrary to the Directive.

Held, giving a preliminary ruling, that (1) Council Directive 92/80 Art.3(1) laid down three tax formulae: ad valorem, specific by quantity and mixed, which was a combination of ad valorem and specific. The German tax could only be a mixed excise duty. Article 3(1) provided that the mixed duty involved the cumulative application of an ad valorem and a specific element, whereby they were combined to form the duty. Under the German system, the two elements were not applied cumulatively and could not therefore be said to constitute a mixed formula. The duty did not work to the disadvantage of taxable persons and was not in contravention of Art.3(1); (2) Member States had a certain amount of discretion as there was a choice of three different tax formulae in Art.3(1). If Member States had been obliged to pursue a particular course of conduct pursuant to a directive, that course of conduct would be rendered less effective if individuals could not rely on the directive in national proceedings, or if national courts were not able to take it into account as a matter of Community law in deciding if the national legislature had exercised its discretion properly when implementing the directive, *World Wildlife Fund (WWF) v. Autonome Provinz Bozen (C435/97)* [1999] E.C.R. I-5613, [1999] C.L.Y. 2162 applied. The German authorities had opted for a tax formula which was not provided for in Art.3(1) and taxable persons could therefore rely on that provision to ensure that any tax formula did not involve an abuse of the discretion left to the national legislature; (3) the tax formula as a whole, rather than merely the minimum specific duty, involved an abuse of the discretion under Art.3(1). As the ad valorem formula was only one of the options available under the Directive, it could not be interpreted as requiring that a national court take the place of the national legislature, which was the only body with the option of choosing the tax formula in accordance with Art.3(1). Taxable persons could not therefore rely on Art.3(1) to challenge the minimum specific duty in favour of an ad valorem duty, and (4) Member States were under an obligation to ensure that the substance of the Directive was achieved and the obligation under EC Treaty Art.10 to take appropriate measures covered all national bodies, including the courts, *Marleasing SA v. La Comercial Internacional de Alimentacion SA (C106/89)* [1990] E.C.R. I-4135 applied. National courts were required to interpret national law in the light of the wording and purpose of the Directive regardless of whether the national law had been adopted before or after the Directive, *Marleasing* applied.

BRINKMANN TABAKFABRIKEN GmbH v. HAUPTZOLLAMT BIELEFELD (C365/98) [2002] 2 C.M.L.R. 36, Moitinho de Almeida (President), ECJ.

4403. Finance Act 2001 (c.9)–Appointed Day Order–s.16

FINANCE ACT 2001, SECTION 16, (APPOINTED DAY) ORDER 2002, SI 2002 809; made under the Finance Act 2001 s.16. Commencement details: bringing into force various provisions of the 2001 Act on April 1, 2002; £1.50.

This Order appoints April 1, 2002 as the commencement date of the purpose of the Finance Act 2001 s.16 which contains the charging provisions for aggregates levy.

4404. Finance Act 2002 (c.23)

This Act grants certain duties, alters other duties; amends the law relating to the National Debt and the Public Revenue and makes further provision in connection with finance.

This Act received Royal Assent on July 24, 2002.

4405. Finance Act 2002 (c.23)–Appointed Day Order–s.5(6)

FINANCE ACT 2002, SECTION 5(6), (APPOINTED DATE) ORDER 2002, SI 2002 1926; made under the Finance Act 2002 s.5. Commencement details: bringing into force various provisions of the 2002 Act on July 25, 2002; £1.50.

The Finance Act 2002 s.5 makes provision in respect of two new duties of excise to be charged on biodiesel and bioblend under the provisions of the Hydrocarbon Oil Duties Act 1979. This Order determines the date from which the charges to duty under the new provisions apply as July 25, 2002.

4406. Finance Act 2002 (c.23)–Appointed Day Order–s.6

FINANCE ACT 2002, SECTION 6, (APPOINTED DAY) ORDER 2002, SI 2002 3056 (C.103); made under the Finance Act 2002 s.6. Commencement details: bringing into force various provisions of the 2002 Act on April 1, 2003; £1.50.

This Order brings into force the Finance Act 2002 s.6(1) insofar as it is not already in force, giving effect to Sch.3 of the Act which makes provision for regulating trade in certain heavy oil on which rebate of excise duty has been allowed.

4407. Finance Act 2002 (c.23)–Appointed Day Order–s.22

FINANCE ACT 2002, SECTION 22, (APPOINTED DAY) ORDER 2002, SI 2002 3028 (C.99); made under the Finance Act 2002 s.22. Commencement details: bringing into force various provisions of the 2002 Act on January 1, 2003; £1.50.

This Order provides that the Finance Act 2002 s.22, which inserts s.26A into the Value Added Tax Act 1994, shall have effect in relation to supplies made on or after January 1, 2003.

4408. Foreign exchange–gains and losses

EXCHANGE GAINS AND LOSSES (TRANSITIONAL PROVISIONS AND SAVINGS) REGULATIONS 2002, SI 2002 1969; made under the Finance Act 2002 s.81. In force: October 1, 2002; £2.00.

These Regulations amend the Exchange Gains and Losses (Transitional Provisions) Regulations 1994 (SI 1994 3226), the Exchange Gains and Losses (Alternative Method of Calculation) Regulations 1994 (SI 1994 3227), the Exchange Gains and Losses (Insurance Companies) Regulations 1994 (SI 1994 3231) and the Exchange Gains and Losses (Miscellaneous Modifications) Regulations 2000 (SI 2000 3315). The Regulations are intended to make transitional provision in respect of the change of tax treatment of exchange gains and losses which will be governed in future by the provisions relating to loan relationships in the Finance Act 1996 Ch.2 Part 4 and to derivative contracts in the Finance Act 2002 Sch.26.

4409. Foreign exchange–gains and losses–bringing into account

EXCHANGE GAINS AND LOSSES (BRINGING INTO ACCOUNT GAINS OR LOSSES) REGULATIONS 2002, SI 2002 1970; made under the Finance Act 1996 s.84A; and the Finance Act 2002 Sch.23 para.26, Sch.26 para.16. In force: October 1, 2002; £2.00.

Following the repeal of the Finance Act 1996 Sch.9 para.4, the tax treatment of exchange gains and losses will be governed by the provisions relating to loan relationships in the Finance Act 1996 Ch.2 Part 4 and derivative contracts in the Finance Act 2002 Sch.26. The Finance Act 1996 s.84A provides that any profits, gains and losses arising to a company from its loan relationships and related transactions include gains and losses arising to the company. The Finance Act 2002 Sch.26 provides for a new regime under which the taxation of profits arising to a company from certain derivative contracts are chargeable to tax as income. These Regulations, which provide for the bringing into account of amounts, prescribe the circumstances in which amounts are to be brought into account and provide for a general rule for bringing amounts into account. They also provide for a different rule for bringing amounts into account in the case of assets representing certain loan relations and ships or aircraft; provide for a special rule for bringing into account amounts where the disposal is a no gain or no loss disposal under the Taxation of Chargeable Gains Act 1992; and provide for a special rule for bringing into account amounts where there is no disposal of the asset for the purpose of the 1992 Act. In addition, the Regulations provide for a special rule for bringing into account amounts where, but for the 1992 Act s.116, s.127 would apply in relation to a transaction involving original shares; provide for a special rule for bringing into account amounts where there is no disposal of the asset for the purpose of the 1992 Act; provide for a special rule for bringing into account amounts where the 1992 Act s.127 applies in relation to a transaction involving original shares which are or include an asset; and provide for a special rule for bringing into account amounts where exchange gains or losses have fallen within s.84A(4) of the 1992 Act.

4410. Free zones–designation–Port of Tilbury

FREE ZONE (PORT OF TILBURY) DESIGNATION ORDER 2002, SI 2002 1418; made under the Customs and Excise Management Act 1979 s.100A. In force: June 2, 2002; £1.50.

This Order, which replaces the Free Zone (Port of Tilbury) Designation Order 1992 (SI 1991 1282), designates an area at the Port of Tilbury, Essex, as a Free Zone, appoints the responsible authority and imposes obligations upon that authority relating to the operation of the zone.

4411. General Commissioners–Special Commissioners–jurisdiction and procedure

GENERAL COMMISSIONERS AND SPECIAL COMMISSIONERS (JURISDICTION AND PROCEDURE) (AMENDMENT) REGULATIONS 2002, SI 2002 2976; made under the Taxes Management Act 1970 s.46A, s.56B; the Social Security Contributions (Transfer of Functions etc.) Act 1999 s.13; and the Social Security Contributions and Benefits (Transfer of Functions etc.) (Northern Ireland) Order 1999 (SI 1999 671) Art.12. In force: December 31, 2002; £2.00.

These Regulations amend the Special Commissioners (Jurisdiction and Procedure) Regulations 1994 (SI 1994 1811) and the General Commissioners (Jurisdiction and Procedure) Regulations 1994 (SI 1994 1812) to change definitions of proceedings under the Social Security Contributions (Transfer of Functions, etc.) Act 1999 and to transfer from the Secretary of State to the Commissioners of Inland Revenue or the Treasury certain functions relating to social security contributions, statutory sick pay or pension schemes and certain associated functions relating to benefits. These Regulations similarly include appeals under the Working Tax Credit (Payment by Employers) Regulations 2002 (SI 2002 2172) within the definition of proceedings in the Special

Commissioners Regulations and also amend that definition in the Special Commissioners Regulations to include within it preliminary proceedings.

4412. Income–tax credits–calculation of income

TAX CREDITS (DEFINITION AND CALCULATION OF INCOME) REGULATIONS 2002, SI 2002 2006; made under the Tax Credits Act 2002 s.7, s.65, s.67. In force: in accordance with Reg.1; £4.00.

These Regulations, which define what is income for the purposes of working tax credit and child tax credit under the Tax Credits Act 2002, sets out the steps to be taken to calculate the income of a claimant, or in the case of a joint claim, of the claimants for an award of either of the tax credits payable under Part 1 of the 2002 Act. The Regulations also set out the extent to which a claimant's employment income, pension income, trading income, social security income, student income, property income and foreign income will be taken into account and provides that if a person is treated as having income for income tax purposes under specified provisions of the Income and Corporation Taxes Act 1988 or Finance Act 1996. In addition, they provide that a claimant depriving himself or herself of income in order to secure entitlement to or increasing the amount of a tax credit is to be treated as having it; provide that a claimant to whom income would become available upon the making of an application for it to be treated as having that income; and provide that income chargeable to income tax is to be taken into account in calculating the claimant's income.

4413. Income–tax credits–relevant income–income thresholds

TAX CREDITS (INCOME THRESHOLDS AND DETERMINATION OF RATES) REGULATIONS 2002, SI 2002 2008; made under the Tax Credits Act 2002 s.8, s.13, s.65, s.67. In force: in accordance with Reg.1; £2.00.

The Tax Credits Act 2002 provides that the entitlement of a person or persons to a tax credit is dependent on "the relevant income" not exceeding an income threshold or exceeding the income threshold by only so much as will result in there being a rate of the tax credit in his or her case. These Regulations prescribe the manner in which the income threshold is to be determined and also prescribe amounts in relation to the definition of "the relevant income", prescribe social security benefits for the purposes of the 2002 Act s.7(2) and provide for the manner of determining the rate at which a person, or persons are, entitled to working tax credit and/or child tax credit. In addition, the Regulations also provide for the manner of determining the rate of working tax credit in such a way that any child care element of the tax credit is reduced last; provide for the manner of determining the rate of child tax credit in such a way that the tax credit is reduced only after the rate of any working tax credit to which a person is, or persons are, entitled has been reduced to nil; and provide that in cases where the rate of tax credit would be less than £26, or the rates of tax credits would total less than £26, there is no rate for either or both tax credits.

4414. Income tax–allowances–courses held in tourist resorts outside member state–refusal of permission to deduct expenses from taxable income

[EC Treaty Art.49.]

Danish tax law allowed the cost of professional training courses held in Denmark as a deductible expense but presumed that training courses held in foreign tourist resorts involved such a significant element of tourism that the cost could not automatically be treated as deductible. V, a Danish auditor, attended a training course in Crete and claimed his expenses were tax deductible. The tax authorities applied the Danish law. V appealed and the Danish court sought a preliminary ruling by the ECJ on the interpretation of EC Treaty Art.49 concerning the deduction of expenses from taxable income.

Held, that because the Danish law required the rebuttal of the presumption regarding courses held in tourist resorts outside Denmark but not where courses were held in tourist resorts in Denmark different tax arrangements applied making it more difficult to deduct costs of participation in training courses abroad than to deduct costs relating to courses held in Denmark. The difference in treatment could not be justified in terms of the cohesion of the tax system nor by the effectiveness of fiscal supervision. The law was based on the place where the service was provided and was not compatible with the freedom to provide services under Art.49.

SKATTEMINISTERIET v. VESTERGAARD (C55/98) [2001] 3 C.M.L.R. 65, R Schintgen (President), ECJ.

4415. Income tax–allowances–widowers–refusal to pay equivalent of widow's bereavement allowance by way of extra statutory concession

[Taxes Management Act 1970 s.1; Income and Corporation Taxes Act 1988 s.262; Human Rights Act 1998 s.6(1), Sch.1 Part I Art.14, Sch.1 Part II Art.1.]

W, a widower, sought judicial review of the Revenue's refusal to pay him the equivalent of a widow's bereavement allowance under the Income and Corporation Taxes Act 1988 s.262 on the same basis as that afforded to another widower, C, by way of a friendly settlement to a complaint to the European Commission on Human Rights. W contended that the Revenue had the power to make the payment under an extra statutory concession which it was obliged to exercise under the Human Rights Act 1998 s.6(1). Further, that a refusal to do so would be contrary to the Human Rights Act 1998 Sch.1 Part I Art.14, in conjunction with Part II Art.1.

Held, refusing the application but making a declaration of incompatibility with regard to s.262 of the 1988 Act, that tax matters came within Part II Art.1 and it was a breach of Art.14 to accord different treatment to men and women in the absence of an objective justification. The Revenue had the power to grant extra statutory concessions under the Taxes Management Act 1970 s.1. However, under s.6 of the 1998 Act, the Revenue's power to grant such a concession could not be converted into a duty which ran contrary to a statutory provision. The Revenue had not acted unlawfully in refusing the allowance to W. Further, there was a difference in bringing proceedings before the European Court of Human Rights, as C had done, and seeking to impose a duty on the Revenue, as W had sought to do in domestic proceedings.

R. (ON THE APPLICATION OF WILKINSON) v. INLAND REVENUE COMMISSIONERS; *sub nom.* WILKINSON v. INLAND REVENUE COMMISSIONERS, [2002] EWHC 182, [2002] S.T.C. 347, Moses, J., QBD (Admin Ct).

4416. Income tax–assessment–out of time assessment for loss of tax attributable to negligent or fraudulent conduct–burden of proof

M appealed against out of time assessments raised by the Revenue on the ground that there had been a loss of tax attributable to his negligent conduct. M was involved in a number of accountancy businesses and was investigated for alleged tax fraud in relation to accounting periods from 1976 to 1994. M failed to cooperate with the investigation and out of time tax assessments were raised against which he appealed. After a number of delays the special commissioners decided to go ahead with the hearing of M's appeal in his absence. The Revenue argued that the evidence supported their view that M had knowingly understated his income as an accountant and tax practitioner and asked the commissioners to confirm, reduce or increase the assessment in accordance with the schedule put before them.

Held, dismissing the appeal, that the Revenue had shown that, on the balance of probabilities, there had been a loss of tax attributable to M's negligent conduct in that he had understated his income and had refused to furnish the Revenue with relevant information. Such conduct could be inferred from M's status as an accountant and tax practitioner and his failure to make full and frank disclosure. Furthermore it was for M to prove that the out of time assessments carried out by the Revenue were too high and given that no evidence had been put forward to that effect, the assessments would be confirmed, increased or reduced as requested by the Revenue.

MASHOOD v. WHITEHEAD (INSPECTOR OF TAXES) [2002] S.T.C. (S.C.D.) 166, AN Brice (Chairman), Sp Comm.

4417. Income tax–capital–annual surrender payments under single premium policy–liability to tax

[Income and Corporation Taxes Act 1988 s.18(3), s.539-s.554.]

The Revenue raised assessments against S on the full value of partial annual surrender payments he received from a single premium insurance policy he had entered into with a Luxembourg insurance company. The Revenue stated that such payments were foreign source income and liable to income tax under Sch.D Case V by virtue of the Income and Corporation Taxes Act 1988 s.18(3). S appealed, contending that the single premium of £200,000 and the partial repayments were capital in nature.

Held, allowing the appeal, that the single premium was a capital investment that S had opted to have repaid by way of part annual payments not exceeding £20,000. As a result, only £10,000 was liable to tax as a gain chargeable to income tax under s.539 to s.554 with the remainder being tax free *Perrin v. Dickson (Inspector of Taxes)* [1930] 1 K.B. 107, [1994] C.L.Y. 5928 applied.

SUGDEN v. KENT (INSPECTOR OF TAXES) [2001] S.T.C. (S.C.D.) 158, Nuala Brice, Sp Comm.

4418. Income tax–car fuel benefits

INCOME TAX (CASH EQUIVALENTS OF CAR FUEL BENEFITS) ORDER 2002, SI 2002 706; made under the Income and Corporation Taxes Act 1988 s.158. In force: April 6, 2002; £1.50.

This Order which amends Income and Corporation Taxes Act 1988, substitutes new tables of flat rate cash equivalents in the Income and Corporation Taxes Act 1988 s.158(2) which provides that directors and employees earning £8,500 or more a year for whom fuel is provided for private use in a company car are chargeable to income tax on an amount equal to the appropriate cash equivalent of the benefit.

4419. Income tax–construction industry–subcontractors

INCOME TAX (SUB-CONTRACTORS IN THE CONSTRUCTION INDUSTRY) (AMENDMENT) REGULATIONS 2002, SI 2002 2225; made under the Income and Corporation Taxes Act 1988 s.566. In force: September 20, 2002; £1.50.

These Regulations amend the Income Tax (Sub-contractors in the Construction Industry) Regulations 1993 (SI 1993 743) to allow for the renewal of sub-contractors' temporary registration cards and extension of the period of validity of temporary registration cards from three to twelve months; allow for the use of system identifiers on sub-contractors' gross payment certificates; and allow such certificates to be prepared by any authorised officer of the Commissioners of Inland Revenue or by any person nominated by the Board.

4420. Income tax–consultants–liability of one man service companies–state aids–freedom of establishment–compatibility of IR 35 legislation with EC law

[Welfare Reform and Pensions Act 1999 s.75, s.76; Finance Act 2000 s.60; Social Security Contributions (Intermediaries) Regulations 2000 (SI 2000 727); EC Treaty Art.39, Art.43, Art.49, Art.87, Art.88.]

P, an organisation of some 11,000 members who provided knowledge based skills via one man service companies, particularly in information technology, appealed against the refusal of its application for judicial review ([2001] EWHC Admin 236) of composite legislation known as IR 35. The legislation, contained in the Finance Act 2000 s.60, Welfare Reform and Pensions Act 1999 s.75 and s.76, and Social Security Contributions (Intermediaries) Regulations 2000, was enacted as an anti avoidance measure under which fees paid to contractors were to be treated as remuneration liable to income tax as opposed to company revenue liable to corporation tax. P contended that IR 35 (1) amounted to unnotified state aid contrary to the EC Treaty Art.87 and Art.88 and (2) unlawfully impeded the free movement of workers, freedom of establishment and the freedom to provide services contrary to Art.39, Art.43 and Art.49 respectively.

Held, dismissing the appeal, that (1) the judge had been correct in his finding that IR 35 was a general measure which sought to ensure that individuals who provided employee type services paid the income tax and national insurance appropriate for an employee and should not be permitted to avoid that system by the interposition of an intermediary. Hence, IR 35 was not an unnotified state aid contrary to Art.87 and Art.88, *R. v. Customs and Excise Commissioners, ex p. Lunn Poly Ltd* [1999] S.T.C. 350, [1999] C.L.Y. 4743 and *Ferring SA v. Agence Centrale des Organismes de Securite Sociale (ACOSS) (C53/00)* (Unreported, November 22, 2001) followed, and (2) P's arguments relating to Art.39 and Art.43 had been correctly dismissed. However, the judge had erred in concluding that IR 35 was a relevant restriction on the freedom to provide services contrary to Art.49. The composite legislation did not provide a direct and demonstrable inhibition on the establishment of a business within the United Kingdom or upon the provision of services without establishment. Legitimate self employed activities would not be affected, as only those providing employee like services would be taxed in accordance with a real employment situation, *Syndesmos ton en Elladi Touristikon kai Taxidiotikon Grafeion v. Ergasias (C398/95)* [1997] E.C.R. I-3091, [1998] C.L.Y. 2139 considered.

R. (ON THE APPLICATION OF PROFESSIONAL CONTRACTORS GROUP LTD) v. INLAND REVENUE COMMISSIONERS; *sub nom.* R. v. INLAND REVENUE COMMISSIONERS, *ex p.* PROFESSIONAL CONTRACTORS GROUP LTD; PROFESSIONAL CONTRACTORS GROUP LTD v. INLAND REVENUE COMMISSIONERS, [2001] EWCA Civ 1945, [2002] S.T.C. 165, Robert Walker, L.J., CA.

4421. Income tax−corporation tax−payments−exemptions

INCOME AND CORPORATION TAXES ACT 1988, SECTION 349B(3), ORDER 2002, SI 2002 2931; made under the Income and Corporation Taxes Act 1988 s.349B. In force: December 1, 2002; £1.50.

The Income and Corporation Taxes Act 1988 s.349A provides that a company or local authority may make certain payments gross if it reasonably believes one of the conditions in s.349B is satisfied. This Order amends the Income and Corporation Taxes Act 1988 so as to widen the condition to cover payments to a nominee of UK tax exempt bodies.

4422. Income tax−deductions−business expenses not incurred "wholly and exclusively for business"

[Income and Corporation Taxes Act 1988 s.74(1)(a); Capital Allowances Act 1990 s.137(1)(a) (now repealed), s.139 (now repealed).]

S appealed against an amended income tax assessment raised to deny claims for a deduction of expenses on the basis that they had not been incurred wholly and exclusively for business purposes. S claimed that he was carrying on three businesses as author, researcher and publisher. In his self assessment tax return, he claimed expenses totalling £4,400 under the Income and Corporation Taxes Act 1988 s.74(1)(a) and an allowance for capital expenditure on scientific research under the Capital Allowances Act 1990 s.137(1)(a). The Revenue was not satisfied that the expenses claimed had been laid out wholly and exclusively for business purposes and raised an amended income tax assessment to deny those claims.

Held, dismissing the appeal, that (1) there was no evidence that the expenses payments had been made. But even if they had, to be deductible, they had to be "wholly and exclusively" made for the purposes of the payer. In that regard, S had adduced no evidence to show that they were so made and the only conclusion was that they were not. Any claim that agency arrangements existed could only be justified if the businesses traded at arm's length, which they did not, but that was not to say that the claim would have been successful, and (2) as regards the claim for scientific research allowance, even if S had carried out the separate trade of publishing, which on the evidence he had not, there was nothing to suggest that any research carried out by him related to his trade of publishing within s.137 and s.139 of the 1990 Act.

SALT v. BUCKLEY (INSPECTOR OF TAXES) [2001] S.T.C. (S.C.D.) 262, JD Demack, Sp Comm.

4423. Income tax–deductions–cost of psychotherapy sessions required as part of training and condition of contract of employment

[Income and Corporation Taxes Act 1998 s.198(1).]

S, a psychiatrist employed by an NHS trust, claimed a deduction for the cost of personal psychotherapy sessions that he was required to attend as part of his training to become a psychotherapist. The Revenue refused his claim on the ground that the expenditure was not required for S to carry out his employment duties. S appealed, arguing that the sessions were part of his employment and a requirement of his psychotherapy training.

Held, dismissing the appeal, that although S was required to incur the expense of psychotherapy sessions under his contract of employment, he was not entitled to tax relief under the Income and Corporation Taxes Act 1988 s.198(1) as the expense he incurred enabled him to obtain further qualifications and had not arisen in the performance of his duties, *Smith (Inspector of Taxes) v. Abbott* [1994] 1 W.L.R. 306, [1994] C.L.Y. 5928 applied.

SNOWDON v. CHARNOCK (INSPECTOR OF TAXES); *sub nom.* SNOWDON v. INLAND REVENUE COMMISSIONERS (SPC 282) [2001] S.T.C. (S.C.D.) 152, Nuala Brice, Sp Comm.

4424. Income tax–deductions–dividends from taxable profits–dividends paid to non resident companies–Solomon Islands

[Income Tax Act, Cap 123 (Solomon Islands) s.14(2)(m), s.33.]

The appellant company, situated in the Solomon Islands, paid dividends to a UK resident company and sought to deduct those dividends in computing its liability to income tax under the Income Tax Act, Cap 123 (Solomon Islands) s.14(2)(m). That section provided that in computing the gains or profits of any person there could be deducted the amount of any dividends paid by a company resident in the Islands from which tax had been deducted in accordance with the s.33 of the Act. Section 33 stated that tax should be deducted at the rate of 35 per cent on dividends paid to non resident companies. However, no such tax had been deducted in the instant case by virtue of Art.6(4) of the United Kingdom-Solomon Islands double taxation arrangement of 10 May 1950. The appellant company was disallowed the deduction it claimed and that disallowance was upheld by Palmer J. Accordingly the company appealed to the Solomon Islands Court of Appeal.

Held dismissing the appeal, that since tax had not been deducted from the dividends paid by virtue of the provisions of the double taxation arrangement, they were not deductible by the appellant company under s.14(2)(m) whose provisions should be given their ordinary meaning.

SOLOMON ISLANDS PLANTATION LTD v. INLAND REVENUE COMMISSIONER 1 I.T.L. Rep. 751, Mason (President), CA (Sol) Court of Appeal (Solomon Islands).

4425. Income tax–deductions–homeworkers–expenses incurred travelling from home to office

[Income and Corporation Taxes Act 1988 s.198(1), s.198(1A)(b)(ii), Sch.12A.]

The Revenue appealed against a decision by general commissioners that E was entitled to deduct expenses of travelling to and from his home in Norfolk to Leeds and the cost of keeping an office at his home, in computing his Schedule E income tax liability. E, a civil servant employed under a home working scheme, had been required under the terms of the scheme to provide his own office facilities at home and to visit his department's office in Leeds one day a week. The commissioners had found that the fact that E had two places of work and that he had to travel between them, was enough to bring his expenses within the Income and Corporation Taxes Act 1988 s.198(1).

Held, allowing the appeal, that the general commissioners had erred in law in concluding that E's expenses were deductible. The expenses could only have been incurred in the performance of E's duties if E was uniquely qualified for the job or that the job could only be done by him working at home and at the Leeds office. The scope of s.198(1) of the Act had been broadened and included a requirement of "qualifying travelling expenses". Therefore the travelling expenses had to be not only incurred in the performance of employment duties but also be attributable to necessary attendance at any place in the performance of those duties and not excluded by the definition of ordinary commuting in Sch.12A of the Act. E's travel from home to Leeds was a permanent and continuing part of his employee duties but amounted to "ordinary commuting" within S.198(1A)(b)(ii). Office expenses were only deductible if incurred "wholly, exclusively and necessarily in the performance of" employment duties. The costs incurred by E in lighting and heating his home were non deductible because the homeworking scheme was optional. Furthermore, E was not required to maintain a separate room for work and therefore the cost of heating and lighting the work space in his home were not wholly, exclusively and necessarily in the performance of his employment duties, given that they were equally attributable to the maintenance of his home.

KIRKWOOD (INSPECTOR OF TAXES) v. EVANS, [2002] EWHC 30, [2002] 1 W.L.R. 1794, Patten, J., Ch D.

4426. Income tax–deductions–insurance premiums–life assurance companies– interest on late premiums–New Zealand

[Income Tax Act 1976 (New Zealand) s.204.]

C, a mutual insurance company, charged policyholders interest on overdue insurance premiums. In accordance with the Income Tax Act 1976 (New Zealand) s.204 an insurance company paid tax on its investment income but its premium income was exempt. The Commissioner treated the interest as investment income subject to tax. C appealed successfully to the Court of Appeal. The Commissioner appealed to the Privy Council.

Held, dismissing the appeal, that the interest in this case was part of the consideration payable by the policyholder and were therefore deductible.

INLAND REVENUE COMMISSIONER v. COLONIAL MUTUAL LIFE ASSURANCE SOCIETY LTD, [2001] UKPC 54, [2002] S.T.C. 13, Lord Nicholls of Birkenhead, PC (NZ).

4427. Income tax–deductions–legal fees not deductible from taxpayer's emoluments

[Taxes Management Act 1970 s.33; Income and Corporation Taxes Act 1988 s.198(1)(b).]

B, a stock exchange dealer, appealed against the refusal of his claim under the Taxes Management Act 1970 s.33 for error or mistake relief in relation to an income tax assessment. The alleged error or mistake had been the failure to deduct a certain sum, which had been paid as legal fees, from the emoluments of the appellant's employment. B had incurred the legal costs in order to rebut allegations made by a previous employer which were preventing him from fully performing the duties of his new employment. The issue for determination concerned whether for the purposes of the Income and Corporation Taxes Act 1988 s.198(1)(b) B had been necessarily obliged to spend the sum "wholly, exclusively and necessarily" in the performance of the duties of his employment.

Held, dismissing the appeal, that B could not rely on s.198(1)(b) of the 1988 Act. The decisive issue was whether the expenditure on legal advice had been incurred "in the performance of [B's] duties". It was apparent that the expenditure had been incurred to put B in a position to perform, or qualify himself to perform, the duties which he had originally been employed to undertake, *Humbles v. Brooks* 40 T.C. 50, [1962] C.L.Y. 15230 applied. Further, B had not been "necessarily obliged" to incur the expenditure, it being personal to him, nor had it been "wholly, exclusively and necessarily" incurred in the performance of the duties of his employment.

BEN NEVIS v. INLAND REVENUE COMMISSIONERS (SC-281); *sub nom.* X v. INLAND REVENUE COMMISSIONERS (SC-281) [2001] S.T.C. (S.C.D.) 144, N Brice, Sp Comm.

4428. Income tax–delivery of notices–electronic communications

INCOME TAX (EMPLOYMENTS AND ELECTRONIC COMMUNICATIONS) (MISCELLANEOUS PROVISIONS) REGULATIONS 2002, SI 2002 680; made under the Income and Corporation Taxes Act 1988 s.203; and the Finance Act 1999 s.132. In force: April 8, 2002; £1.75.

These Regulations, which amend the Tax (Employments) Regulations 1993 (SI 1993 744), provide for the electronic delivery of notices by the Inland Revenue in connection with the recovery of student loans under the Education (Student Loans) (Repayment) Regulations 2000 (SI 2000 944). They provide that notices may be given, either to the employer or a person acting on his behalf, by an approved means of electronic communications, amends the definition of "electronic communications" to make it explicit that that expression does not include electronic transmission of information by the system known as Electronic Data Interchange and permits electronic delivery of code authorisations to employers' agents. They also enable the employer of an employee on fixed pay to notify the cessation of employment by means of an approved method of electronic communications.

4429. Income tax–deposit takers–interest payments

INCOME TAX (PRESCRIBED DEPOSIT-TAKERS) ORDER 2002, SI 2002 1968; made under the Income and Corporation Taxes Act 1988 s.481, s.482. In force: October 1, 2002; £1.50.

The Income and Corporation Taxes Act 1988 s.481 (2) defines "deposit-taker" and includes any person or class of person who receives deposits in the course of his business or activities and which is for the time being prescribed by order made by the Treasury. This Order prescribes persons authorised for the purposes of the Financial Services and Markets Act 2000 and whose business consists wholly or mainly of dealing in financial instruments as principal for the purposes of the 1988 Act in relation to all relevant deposits, so that interest paid to individual depositors by such persons will be subject to the rules regulating deduction of tax at source.

4430. Income tax–directors–change from executive to unpaid non executive status–payment from occupational pension scheme not made on retirement

[Income and Corporation Taxes Act 1970 s.26 (1); Income and Corporation Taxes Act 1988 s.600; Income Tax (Employments) Regulation 1993 (SI 1993 744) Reg.49.]

The Revenue appealed against an order ([2001] S.T.C. 1221, [2001] C.L.Y. 5263), allowing an appeal against a special commissioner's decision ([2001] Pens. L.R. 17) upholding an income tax assessment against V under the Income and Corporation Taxes Act 1988 s.600 and a determination against the trustees of the F pension scheme that they were liable to tax on payments made to V under the Income Tax (Employments) Regulation 1993 Reg.49. V was a director of a company that participated in the F scheme. V retired as an executive director in June 1994 on health grounds and became an unpaid non executive director. Between July 7 and August 4, 1994, V received the sum of £580,591 from the F scheme, which the Revenue contended was liable to income tax under s.600 as the payments were not made on his retirement from employment. V argued that if the payments were not properly made under the terms of the scheme, then they were paid in breach of trust and, as he was also a trustee of the scheme, were liable to be repaid, with the result that no payment had actually been made for the purposes of s.600.

Held, allowing the appeal, that "retirement" was to be construed in light of the meaning of "service" contained in the F trust deed and the Income and Corporation Taxes Act 1970 s.26(1) and required a cessation of service. As a director, V was also an employee and his service included all periods when he held office as a director. Therefore the payment was given in connection with a change to his conditions of service, not his retirement. V's argument as to the payment being made in breach of trust was contrary to the intention of Parliament, as evidenced by the wording of s.600, as deeming the unauthorised payment as a non payment for the purposes of s.600 would mean that the section was self defeating, *Hillsdown Holdings Plc v. Inland Revenue Commissioners* [1999] S.T.C. 561, [1999] C.L.Y. 4679 distinguished.

VENABLES v. HORNBY (INSPECTOR OF TAXES); *sub nom.* TRUSTEES OF THE FUSSELL PENSION SCHEME v. HORNBY (INSPECTOR OF TAXES), [2002] EWCA Civ 1277, [2002] S.T.C. 1248, Chadwick, L.J., CA.

4431. Income tax–emoluments–foreign nationals–payment by firm of tax incurred by US citizen whilst working in UK

[Income and Corporation Taxes Act 1988 s.203C.]

P, a US citizen, appealed against the treatment of amounts of UK income tax paid by her firm, which was established in the US, on account of taxable emoluments that she received while resident and working in the UK. P was based in London from July 1997, when she became resident in the UK. However she worked abroad for nearly half the time so that emoluments while based in the UK fell to be apportioned between those "in respect of duties performed in the UK" and those which were not. The UK tax was deducted by the associated UK firm under the Income and Corporation Taxes Act 1988 s.203C. A dispute arose as to whether the payments of tax should be apportioned between P's duties performed in the UK and those performed abroad in the same way as her other emoluments. The Revenue contended that the payment of UK tax pursuant to the tax equalisation scheme was "in respect of duties performed in the UK" both on the wording of the documents and as a matter of law and that the whole amount of the emoluments was taxable without apportionment. P contended that the payments were indistinguishable from her other emoluments. They were not attributed either expressly or by implication to UK duties and they were to be apportioned along with the other emoluments.

Held, dismissing the appeal, that the relevant documents made no specific reference to UK tax as opposed to "foreign taxes" generally and did not attribute the UK tax paid to the performance of UK duties. In that sense it was correct to say that the payments were not expressly in respect of duties performed in the UK. It was quite another matter to say that they were not impliedly or in fact "in respect of" such duties. The tax was only payable because of the performance of duties in the UK and the amount of the tax depended on the proportion of P's emoluments that was attributable to those duties. There was no logical case for distinguishing between payments to enable duties to be performed in the UK and payments resulting from the performance of duties in the UK.

PERRO v. MANSWORTH (INSPECTOR OF TAXES) [2001] S.T.C. (S.C.D.) 179, Theodore Wallace, Sp Comm.

4432. Income tax–employee benefits–exemptions–employment costs due to disability

INCOME TAX (BENEFITS IN KIND) (EXEMPTION FOR EMPLOYMENT COSTS RESULTING FROM DISABILITY) REGULATIONS 2002, SI 2002 1596; made under the Income and Corporation Taxes Act 1988 s.155ZB. In force: July 9, 2002; £1.50.

The Income and Corporation Taxes Act 1988 s.155ZB gives the Treasury power to exempt such minor benefits as are specified in these Regulations, and are made available to the employer's employees generally on similar terms. These Regulations exempt hearing aids and other equipment, services or facilities made available to disabled employees, to enable them to fulfil the duties of their employment.

4433. Income tax—exemptions—refusal of exemption on share dividends paid by company established in another Member State

[EC Treaty Art.58(1)(a); Council Directive 88/361 for the implementation of Art.67 of the Treaty Art.1 (1).]

The Dutch Supreme Court made a reference for a preliminary ruling seeking guidance on the interpretation of Council Directive 88/361. The issue arose during a dispute between the Dutch Finance Minister, F, and V, a Dutch national, when F refused to grant him an exemption from income tax on share dividends from a company established in another Member State. V had lived in the Netherlands and had worked for Fina Nederland BV, a company which distributed petroleum products which was controlled indirectly by Petrofina NV, a public limited company established in Belgium and quoted on the stock exchange. V had acquired shares in Petrofina NV in 1991 as part of an employees' savings plan. Twenty five per cent had been deducted at source from the dividend in Belgium and V had made a declaration to that effect on his Dutch tax return for 1991. V was informed that he should have included the entire dividend as part of his taxable income and he filed an objection with F. The Dutch court asked the ECJ whether it was contrary to Art.1 (1) of the Directive, for national legislation to make the granting of an exemption from income tax on dividends paid to natural persons who were shareholders subject to the proviso that the dividends were paid by a company whose seat was in that Member State. In addition, the court asked whether the answer to that question would be different if the taxpayer requesting the exemption was an ordinary shareholder or an employee who held the shares under an employees' saving plan.

Held, giving a preliminary ruling, that (1) Council Directive 88/361 covered the situation where a resident national of one Member State was in receipt of dividends from a company whose seat was in another Member State; (2) if dividends were exempt from tax provided that the seat of the company was in the same State as the shareholder, that situation amounted to a restriction on capital movement subject to Art.1 of the Directive; (3) Member States were permitted to treat taxpayers differently according to where they lived or where their capital was invested in accordance with EC Treaty Art.58(1)(a). However, such distinctions could only be applied to situations that were not objectively comparable, *Finanzamt Koln-Altstadt v. Schumacker (C279/93)* [1996] Q.B. 28, [1995] C.L.Y. 2773 applied, or could be justified by overriding reasons in the public interest, especially in relation to the cohesion of the tax system, *Commission of the European Communities v. Belgium (C300/90)* [1992] E.C.R. I-305 applied. Economic reasons did not constitute an overriding reason, *Decker v. Caisse de Maladie des Employes Prives (C120/95)* [1998] All E.R. (EC) 673, [1998] C.L.Y. 4517 applied. There was no direct link between granting shareholders resident in the Netherlands an exemption from income tax for dividends received and taxing dividends from companies in another State because they were two separate taxes levied on different taxpayers; (4) even if there were a tax advantage for taxpayers in the Netherlands in receipt of dividends from companies in other States, unfavourable tax treatment, which ran contrary to a fundamental freedom, could not be justified by other tax advantages, *Asscher v. Staatssecretaris van Financien (C107/94)* [1996] All E.R. (EC) 757, [1996] C.L.Y. 3341 applied. Dutch law was therefore in breach of Art.1 (1) of the Directive and (5) Dutch law amounted to a restriction on the free movement of capital regardless of the status of the shareholder.

STAATSSECRETARIS VAN FINANCIEN v. VERKOOIJEN (C35/98) [2002] S.T.C. 654, GC Rodriguez Iglesias (President), ECJ.

4434. Income tax–exemptions–"service in a foreign country" not including time at sea–Australia

[Income Tax Assessment Act 1936 (Australia) s.23AG.]

C, an Australian resident, appealed against a decision that by spending more than 91 days at sea as a merchant navy officer on board a Panamanian vessel, he had not been operating in the "service in a foreign country" for the purposes of the income tax exemption under the Income Tax Assessment Act 1936 (Australia) s.23AG.

Held, dismissing the appeal, that a foreign country for the purposes of s.23AG meant a legal or political capable of imposing its own revenue law. Giving the word its ordinary meaning, *CIC Insurance Ltd v. Bankstown Football Club Ltd* (1997) 187 C.L.R. 384 applied, and did not include time spent at sea on a vessel flying another country's flag.

CHAUDHRI v. COMMISSIONER OF TAX 4 I.T.L. Rep. 215, Hill, J., Fed Ct (Aus) (Full Ct).

4435. Income tax–home workers–payment of salary and commission–provision of home office–office user incidental to employment

[Income and Corporation Taxes Act 1988 s.19.]

A appealed against a decision of the Revenue that payments of salary and commission made to him by his employer were wholly attributable to his employment. A was an auctioneer and valuer employed by a firm of chartered surveyors under an agreement which required him to work from home. He was paid monthly with commission on a sliding scale based on sales. He was paid under the PAYE system and no payments were attributed to the provision by him of an office at home. A submitted his self assessment tax return on the basis that part of the payments he received each year were in respect of the provision of office accommodation which was taxable under Sch.A rather than Sch.E. Since the house was owned jointly with his wife, he claimed that she was assessable in respect of one half of that amount. The Revenue amended the return on the basis that the whole of the payments received were in respect of the emoluments of his employment taxable under Sch.E with a small deduction for expenses.

Held, dismissing the appeal, that under the Income and Corporation Taxes Act 1988 s.19, tax was charged under Sch.E "in respect of any office or employment on the emoluments therefrom" falling under any of Cases I to III. The crucial word was "therefrom". A payment was assessable if it had been paid to the taxpayer in return for his acting as or being an employee. The office user was incidental to A's employment and no separate consideration was attributed to it. Accordingly the payments arose from the employment and were properly taxable under Sch.E.

AINSLIE v. BUCKLEY (INSPECTOR OF TAXES) [2002] S.T.C. (S.C.D.) 132, Theodore Wallace, Sp Comm.

4436. Income tax–indexation

INCOME TAX (INDEXATION) ORDER 2002, SI 2002 707; made under the Income and Corporation Taxes Act 1988 s.1, s.257C. In force: March 15, 2002; £1.50.

This Order specifies the relevant amounts for the purposes of the Income and Corporation Taxes Act 1988 s.1 (2), starting rate and basic rate limits, s.257AA, children's tax credit and s.265(1) blind person's allowance, for the year 2002-03. The amounts are increased by this Order in accordance with the percentage increase in the retail prices index for September 2001 over that for September 2000.

4437. Income tax—indexation

INCOME TAX (INDEXATION) (NO.2) ORDER 2002, SI 2002 2930; made under the Income and Corporation Taxes Act 1988 s.257C. In force: November 27, 2002; £1.50.

The Income and Corporation Taxes Act 1988 s.257C operates to provide that the Treasury shall by order made by statutory instrument before April 6, 2003 specify the amounts which by virtue of that section shall, unless Parliament otherwise determines, be treated as specified for the purposes of s.257 (personal allowances), s.257A (married couple's allowances for those born before April 6, 1935) and s.265 (blind person's allowance) of the Act for the year of assessment 2003/04. This Order increases the amounts of basic personal allowance, age related personal allowances and blind person's personal allowances in accordance with the percentage increase in the retail prices index for September 2002 over that for September 2001.

4438. Income tax—investigations—information powers of revenue authorities—legal professional privilege—Australia

[Income Tax Assessment Act 1936 (Australia) s.264(1).]

The Commissioner sought a declaration that legal professional privilege did not apply to information about clients of a law firm requested in notices issued to C under the Income Tax Assessment Act 1936 (Australia) s.264(1). C was a tax partner who advised on the establishment and operation of employee benefit trusts and share plans. He objected to the notices, arguing that the identity of his clients was protected by legal professional privilege.

Held, refusing the application, that the disclosure of the names and addresses of C's clients could disclose confidential information that was subject to legal professional privilege where the client had discussed with C whether to enter into a benefit trust or share plan.

COMMISSIONER OF TAXATION v. COOMBES (NO.2) 1 I.T.L. Rep. 397, Heerey, J., Fed Ct (Aus) (Sgl judge).

4439. Income tax—minor benefits—exemption

INCOME TAX (EXEMPTION OF MINOR BENEFITS) REGULATIONS 2002, SI 2002 205; made under the Income and Corporation Taxes Act 1988 s.155ZB. In force: April 6, 2002; £1.75.

These Regulations, which have effect for the year 2002/03 and subsequent years of assessment, exempt certain minor benefits from the Income and Corporation Taxes Act 1988 s.154. They provide for an exemption in respect of certain food or drink provided to employees in recognition of their cycling to work and provide for an exemption in respect of the provision to employees of a bus or a minibus for the purpose of making certain journeys on working days.

4440. Income tax—pension contributions—lawfulness of prohibition on deductibility of contributions paid to foreign pension provider

See PENSIONS: Danner (C136/00), *Re.* §3393

4441. Income tax—pension schemes—funds of approved scheme exported offshore—decision to remove approved status

[Income and Corporation Taxes Act 1988 s.591B.]

M sought judicial review of a Revenue decision under the Income and Corporation Taxes Act 1988 s.591B to withdraw approval for a company directors pension scheme, JML, of which M owned one per cent and his wife, E, 99 per cent. JML had been created by deed in 1987 and obtained Revenue approval in 1993. In 1994, however, the Revenue approved trustee, J, was replaced and in 1996 M and E were replaced as trustees by L, a Guernsey based trustee company.

DJT and L then authorised the transfer of funds to a scheme with non UK resident trustees of which M and E were members.

Held, refusing the application, that the changes brought about in 1996 amounted to a pre planned scheme to export funds from JML into an offshore scheme beyond the control of the Revenue. M and E had maintained their controlling interest throughout, with the result that the Revenue was fully entitled to remove approval, *R. v. Inland Revenue Commissioners, ex p. Roux Waterside Inn Ltd* [1997] S.T.C. 781, [1997] C.L.Y. 2975 applied.

R. (ON THE APPLICATION OF MANDER) v. INLAND REVENUE COMMISSIONERS [2002] S.T.C. 631, Sullivan, J., QBD (Admin Ct).

4442. Income tax–personal portfolio bonds

PERSONAL PORTFOLIO BONDS (TAX) (AMENDMENT) REGULATIONS 2002, SI 2002 455; made under the Income and Corporation Taxes Act 1988 s.553C. In force: April 6, 2002; £1.75.

These Regulations amend the Personal Portfolio Bonds (Tax) Regulations 1999 (SI 1999 1029) in consequence of the restructuring of the Income and Corporation Taxes Act 1988 s.552.

4443. Income tax–profits–stockbrokers–apportionment of profits–commissions earned by offshore group companies acting as agent for principal–Hong Kong

I, a Hong Kong resident stockbroker, acted as regional headquarters for other group members which in turn acted as its agents in carrying out share purchases for Hong Kong resident clients in other South East Asian states. IRC assessed I to income tax in respect of commission earned by other group members on those transactions. I successfully appealed against the assessments to the Board of Review on the basis that there was no express statutory power of apportionment. IRC appealed by way of case stated.

Held, allowing the appeal and remitting the case to the Board, that Hong Kong was I's main place of business and the Board had erred by not determining that the execution of orders for I's Hong Kong resident clients in the other markets was performed for I by the other group members acting as its agents. The profit on the commission earned from those clients could be apportioned for Hong Kong taxation purposes, even though there was no express statutory power to do so, *Inland Revenue Commissioners v. Hang Seng Bank* [1991] 1 A.C. 306, [1991] C.L.Y. 596 applied and *Inland Revenue Commissioner v. Hong Kong & Whampoa Dock Co Ltd* [1960] H.K.L.R. 166 not followed.

INLAND REVENUE COMMISSIONER v. INDOSUEZ WI CARR SECURITIES LTD 4 I.T.L. Rep. 604, Deputy Judge Longley, CFI (HK).

4444. Income tax–residence–Canadian national working in Kuwait–family living in Canada owing to aftermath of Gulf War

[Income Tax Act 1998 (Canada) s.250(1)(a), s.250(3).]

K appealed against income tax assessments for the years 1992, 1993 and 1994 on the basis that he was a not a Canadian resident during that period. K was a Canadian citizen, but between 1977 and the end of 1994 he had been employed in Kuwait. During 1992, 1993 and 1994 he had spent between 40 and 70 days in Canada. The rest of the time he resided and worked in Kuwait. However, his family was in Canada as his wife, a Jordanian national, was not allowed to live in Kuwait after the Gulf War. K contended that as he was not resident in Canada during 1992, 1993 and 1994 he was not eligible to pay income tax.

Held, allowing the appeal, that the Income Tax Act 1998 (Canada) s.250(1)(a) provided that a person was resident in Canada if they spent more than 183 days there in a single year. Under s.250(3) "resident" those who were "ordinarily resident" in Canada. Someone was ordinarily resident in the place where they usually lived as opposed to special, intermittent or casual residence, *Thomson v. Minister of National Revenue* (Unreported, January 26, 1946) applied. On the facts, K was not ordinarily resident in Canada during 1992, 1993 or 1994.

KADRIE v. R. 4 I.T.L. Rep. 263, Bowman, A.C.J.,Tax Court of Canada (Canada).

4445. Income tax–retirement benefits scheme–indexation of earnings cap

RETIREMENT BENEFITS SCHEMES (INDEXATION OF EARNINGS CAP) ORDER 2002, SI 2002 700; made under the Income and Corporation Taxes Act 1988 s.590C. In force: March 15, 2002; £1.50.

The Income and Corporation Taxes Act 1988 s.590C(1) provides that in arriving at an employee's final remuneration for the purposes of s.590(3)(a) or (d) of that Act any excess over the permitted maximum figure for the year of assessment in which the employee's participation in the scheme ceases shall be disregarded. This Order specifies £97,200 as the earnings cap for the year of assessment 2002-03.

4446. Income tax–state aids–exempt companies and qualifying companies–operating aid

See COMPETITION LAW: Gibraltar v. Commission of the European Communities (T195/01). §613

4447. Indirect taxes–company incorporation–notarial act recording company formation–classification of charges levied as tax–European Community

[Council Directive 69/335 concerning indirect taxes on the raising of capital Art.10(c); Council Directive 85/303 amending Council Directive 69/335.]

A German court sought a preliminary ruling from the ECJ on the interpretation of Council Directive 69/335, as amended by Council Directive 85/303. G, a company with limited liability, challenged a notice of assessment of the charges payable to L in respect of the drawing up of a notarial act recording its formation as a capital company. It claimed that the charges were in fact a tax, the amount of which was disproportionate to the service rendered and that their imposition was contrary to Directive 69/335.

Held, giving a preliminary ruling, that (1) charges constituted taxes for the purposes of the Directive where they were payable for the drawing up of a notarially attested act recording a transaction where the notaries were civil servants, and the charges were paid in part to the public authority which employed them and used for the financing of its official business, *Modelo SGPS SA v. Director-Geral dos Registros e Notariado (C56/98)* [2001] S.T.C. 1043, [2001] C.L.Y. 5189 applied; (2) where such charges amounted to a tax, they were prohibited by Art.10(c) of the Directive; and (3) the fact that the charges could not exceed a specified maximum was not sufficient, without more, to render them duties paid by way of fees or dues within the Directive, where the maximum bore no relation to the costs of the service for which the charges constituted consideration.

GRUNDERZENTRUM BETRIEBS GmbH v. LAND BADEN-WURTTEMBERG (C264/00) [2002] 2 C.M.L.R. 46, Macken (President), ECJ.

4448. Inheritance tax–agricultural property relief–orchard used for fruit growing and grazing–use incidental to rural residential property

[Inheritance Tax Act 1984 s.115(2), s.116.]

D was given a 40 per cent interest in a property by B, who retained 60 per cent. The property comprised a cottage with a garden and orchard totalling 0.6 acres. Fruit with an approximate sale value of £70 was grown in the orchard, which was also used to keep hens and as occasional grazing for sheep. On D's death, the Revenue issued a notice of determination for inheritance tax which stated that the property was not "agricultural property" pursuant to the Inheritance Tax Act 1984 s.115(2). D appealed.

Held, dismissing the appeal, that the question as to whether land qualified for agricultural property relief under s.116 was a matter of fact and degree.

Although agricultural activities were carried out on the land, they were merely incidental to the residential use of a rural property.

DIXON v. INLAND REVENUE COMMISSIONERS [2002] S.T.C. (S.C.D.) 53, Nuala Brice, Sp Comm.

4449. Inheritance tax–delivery of accounts–excepted estates–specified transfers

INHERITANCE TAX (DELIVERY OF ACCOUNTS) (EXCEPTED ESTATES) REGULATIONS 2002, SI 2002 1733; made under the Inheritance Tax Act 1984 s.256. In force: August 1, 2002; £2.00.

These Regulations revoke the Capital Transfer Tax (Delivery of Accounts) Regulations 1981 (SI 1981 880), the Capital Transfer Tax (Delivery of Accounts) (Scotland) Regulations 1981 (SI 1981 881), the Capital Transfer Tax (Delivery of Accounts) (Northern Ireland) Regulations 1981 (SI 1981 1441), the Capital Transfer Tax (Delivery of Accounts) (No.3) Regulations 1983 (SI 1983 1039), the Capital Transfer Tax (Delivery of Accounts) (Scotland) (No.2) Regulations 1983 (SI 1983 1040), the Capital Transfer Tax (Delivery of Accounts) (Northern Ireland) (No.2) Regulations 1983 (SI 1983 1911), the Inheritance Tax (Delivery of Accounts) Regulations 1987 (SI 1987 1127), the Inheritance Tax (Delivery of Accounts) (Scotland) Regulations 1987 (SI 1987 1128), the Inheritance Tax (Delivery of Accounts) (Northern Ireland) Regulations 1987 (SI 1987 1129), the Inheritance Tax (Delivery of Accounts) Regulations 1989 (SI 1989 1078), the Inheritance Tax (Delivery of Accounts) (Scotland) Regulations 1989 (SI 1989 1079), the Inheritance Tax (Delivery of Accounts) (Northern Ireland) Regulations 1989 (SI 1989 1080), the Inheritance Tax (Delivery of Accounts) Regulations 1990 (SI 1990 1110), the Inheritance Tax (Delivery of Accounts) (Scotland) Regulations 1990 (SI 1990 1111), the Inheritance Tax (Delivery of Accounts) (Northern Ireland) Regulations 1990 (SI 1990 1112), the Inheritance Tax (Delivery of Accounts) Regulations 1991 (SI 1991 1248), the Inheritance Tax (Delivery of Accounts) (Scotland) Regulations 1991 (SI 1991 1249), the Inheritance Tax (Delivery of Accounts) (Northern Ireland) Regulations 1991 (SI 1991 1250), the Inheritance Tax (Delivery of Accounts) Regulations 1995 (SI 1995 1459), the Inheritance Tax (Delivery of Accounts) (Northern Ireland) Regulations 1995 (SI 1995 1460), the Inheritance Tax (Delivery of Accounts) Regulations 1995 (SI 1996 1461), the Inheritance Tax (Delivery of Accounts) Regulations 1996 (SI 1996 1470), the Inheritance Tax (Delivery of Accounts) (Scotland) Regulations 1996 (SI 1996 1472), the Inheritance Tax (Delivery of Accounts) (Northern Ireland) Regulations 1996 (SI 1996 1473), the Inheritance Tax (Delivery of Accounts) (Northern Ireland) Regulations 1998 (SI 1998 1429), the Inheritance Tax (Delivery of Accounts) (Scotland) Regulations 1998 (SI 1998 1430), the Inheritance Tax (Delivery of Accounts) Regulations 1998 (SI 1998 1431), the Inheritance Tax (Delivery of Accounts) (Northern Ireland) Regulations 2000 (SI 2000 965), the Inheritance Tax (Delivery of Accounts) (Scotland) Regulations 2000 (SI 2000 966) and the Inheritance Tax (Delivery of Accounts) Regulations 2000 (SI 2000 967). The Regulations, which provide that a person is not required to deliver an account of the property comprised in an excepted estate for inheritance tax purposes, increases the limit on the aggregate of the gross value of the deceased's estate and of the value transferred by any "specified transfers" made by the deceased to £220,000. They also increase to £100,000 the limit on the aggregate value of chargeable transfers that are specified transfers made during the period of seven years ending with the deceased's death and the limit on the value of property situated outside the UK which may form part of the deceased's estate is raised to £75,000. In addition, the Regulations extend the definition of "specified transfers" to include a transfer of an interest in land and furnishings and chattels disposed of at the same time to the same person which is intended to be enjoyed with the land save to the extent that the property transferred is property subject to a reservation to which Finance Act 1986 applies or becomes settled property and introduces a new category of excepted estates for person who have never been domiciled in the UK.

4450. Inheritance tax–delivery of accounts–excepted settlements

INHERITANCE TAX (DELIVERY OF ACCOUNTS) (EXCEPTED SETTLEMENTS) REGULATIONS 2002, SI 2002 1732; made under the Inheritance Tax Act 1984 s.256. In force: August 1, 2002; £1.75.

These Regulations dispense with the need to deliver an account of the property comprised in a limited class of small discretionary trusts where a chargeable event occurs on or after April 6, 2002. These trusts are defined as "excepted settlements". In order to fall within this definition no interest in possession must subsist in the settled property which can only comprise cash, the trustees must be resident in the UK, the settlor must not have provided any additions to the settled property following commencement of the settlement or have created any other settlements on the same day and the value of the settled property at the time of the chargeable event must not exceed £1,000.

4451. Inheritance tax–delivery of accounts–excepted transfers and terminations

INHERITANCE TAX (DELIVERY OF ACCOUNTS) (EXCEPTED TRANSFERS AND EXCEPTED TERMINATIONS) REGULATIONS 2002, SI 2002 1731; made under the Inheritance Tax Act 1984 s.256. In force: August 1, 2002; £1.75.

These Regulations, which revoke the Capital Transfer Tax (Delivery of Accounts) (No.2) Regulations 1981 (SI 1981 1440), dispense with the need to deliver an account of lifetime transfers where the total value of an individual's transfers made in any one year does not exceed £10,000, and where the cumulative total does not exceed £40,000. The Regulations, which have effect in relation to lifetime transfers made on or after April 1, 1981, also dispense with the delivery of an account by trustees and discharge them from any liability to inheritance tax where the termination of an interest in possession in settled property is wholly covered by an annual or marriage gift exemption made available to the trustees.

4452. Inheritance tax–discretionary trusts–creation of five separate but identical trusts at same time–invoking "associated operations" definition

[Inheritance Tax Act 1984 s.43, s.64, s.268(1).]

Trustees appealed to the High Court against a decision of a special commissioner that the creation of five identical discretionary settlements on overseas trusts were to be treated as a single settlement for the purposes of calculating the inheritance tax charge applied every 10 years to a discretionary settlement created by UK domiciled settlors. The settlor made the five settlements within the space of a month. The Revenue took the view that the creation of the settlements and the transfers of shares to the trustee in each case were all associated operations within the Inheritance Tax Act 1984 s.268(1) (a) and s.268(1) (b). Therefore there was a single settlement within the meaning of s.43 so that at the 10 year anniversary tax was chargeable under s.64 at the rate applicable to the total value of the property in all five settlements. The trustees argued that s.268(1)(a) was inapplicable as the operations in connection with each settlement did not affect the same property and that s.268(1)(b) was inapplicable because the operations had not been effected with reference to each other. Moreover each of the five settlements had to be looked at separately as in trust law each was a separate settlement.

Held, allowing the appeal, that (1) the question was whether there was property comprised in a settlement within s.64 (the charging provision), read together with s.43, which explained the concepts of settlement and property comprised in a settlement. If there was property comprised in a settlement without the need to rely on the extended meaning of "disposition" to cover a disposition by associated operations, the associated operations provision was not relevant. Sections 43 and 64 applied without the need to invoke the definition of associated operations, and (2) in the instant case, all the parcels of shares were property comprised in settlements for the purposes of s.64. In respect of each settlement the parcel of shares was held by the trustee on discretionary trust by virtue of a disposition effected by a single operation. It was neither necessary nor appropriate to invoke or apply the extended statutory definition in order to conclude that the parcel of shares was property comprised in a settlement at the time when the 10 yearly charge fell to be applied.

RYSAFFE TRUSTEE CO (CI) LTD v. INLAND REVENUE COMMISSIONERS; *sub nom.* RYSAFFE TRUSTEE CO (CI) LTD v. CUSTOMS AND EXCISE COMMISSIONERS, [2002] EWHC 1114, [2002] S.T.C. 872, Park, J., Ch D.

4453. **Inheritance tax–domicile–failure to acquire Hong Kong domicile of choice when transfers made to offshore discretionary and charitable trusts**

E appealed against a notice of determination to inheritance tax in respect of transfers to a Guernsey discretionary trust and a Jersey charitable foundation in April 1990. E was born in England but between 1960 and 1989 he lived and worked in Hong Kong, making irregular return visits to England until 1990, when he returned, stating that he intended to remain permanently. E contended that he had obtained a Hong Kong domicile of choice, which he retained as at the date of the transfers. Alternatively, that the Guernsey trust was a life interest trust.

Held, dismissing the appeal, that there was no evidence to show that E had either acquired a Hong Kong domicile of choice or relinquished his English domicile of origin, but if he had, the former would have terminated when he returned to the UK, stating his intention to remain permanently. The notice had been validly issued, therefore, as E was domiciled in England when the transfers were made. The Jersey foundation did not qualify as a charity in English law as none of the trustees were resident in the jurisdiction. Further, the wide discretionary powers conferred on the trustees of the Guernsey trust and the fact that E was in receipt of monthly payments militated against it being a life interest trust.

CIVIL ENGINEER v. INLAND REVENUE COMMISSIONERS [2002] S.T.C. (S.C.D.) 72, Dr JF Avery Jones, Sp Comm.

4454. **Inheritance tax–exempt transfers–reservation of benefit–discretionary beneficiaries–gift of life interest to settlor's spouse**

[Inheritance Tax Act 1984 s.18; Finance Act 1986 s.102.]

The Revenue appealed against a determination by a special commissioner ([2002] S.T.C. (S.C.D.) 39) upholding a challenge to notices determining liability for inheritance tax issued to E, executors of the will of G, a deceased settlor. G had settled a property on trust to be held as to five per cent for herself absolutely and as to 95 per cent on the settlement trusts. G's husband had occupied the property, along with G, as a life tenant until his death in 1992 and thereafter the property had been sold and the proceeds partly applied in the purchase of a new property. G occupied the new property until her death in 1998. The notices were issued on the basis that the trust fund formed part of G's estate, pursuant to the Finance Act 1986 s.102(3), because it was held on discretionary trusts in respect of which G was a beneficiary and she had occupied the property. The commissioner found that s.102(5)(a) of the 1986 Act operated to prevent any charge to tax arising under s.102(3) because of the gift of the interest in possession by G to her husband. On appeal, the issues to be decided were whether G's entitlement as a discretionary beneficiary constituted a reservation of benefit within s.102(3), whether the occupation of the property gave rise to such reservation and whether the gift of the life interest to G's husband exempted the trust fund from the provisions of s.102 indefinitely or for only so long as the life interest subsisted.

Held, dismissing the appeal, that s.102(5)(a) operated to prevent a charge to tax arising at any time and not only for the duration of G's husband's life interest, thus the exemption given by the Inheritance Tax Act 1984 s.18 applied. The fact that G was one of the discretionary beneficiaries capable of receiving benefit from the fund precluded a finding that G was entirely excluded from enjoyment of the fund. Under s.102(5), a gift constituting an exempt transfer under s.18 of the 1984 Act did not give rise to the consequences provided for in s.102(3). Whether the gift constituted an exempt transfer had to be determined at the date of the gift and not at the date of the donor's death. For the purposes of s.18, the duration of G's husband's life interest was irrelevant.

INLAND REVENUE COMMISSIONERS v. EVERSDEN; *sub nom.* ESSEX (SOMERSET'S EXECUTORS) v. INLAND REVENUE COMMISSIONERS, [2002] EWHC 1360, [2002] S.T.C. 1109, Lightman, J., Ch D.

4455. Inheritance tax-indexation

INHERITANCE TAX (INDEXATION) ORDER 2002, SI 2002 701; made under the Inheritance Tax Act 1984 s.8. In force: March 15, 2002; £1.50.

This Order substitutes a new table of rate bands and rates in the Inheritance Act 1984 Sch.1 for the table which was substituted by the Inheritance Tax (Indexation) Order 2001 (SI 2001 639) in relation to chargeable transfers made in the year beginning April 6, 2001. The new table will apply in relation to chargeable transfers on or after April 6, 2002 unless Parliament otherwise determines.

4456. Inheritance tax-legacies-disclaimers-interest in possession-property left to spouse-presumption in favour of acceptance not rebutted

C, the executors of W's estate, appealed against a notice of determination that T, W's husband, had not acquired an interest in possession of a house left by W in her will. W's will directed that C was to hold the house on trust, but that T could live there if he paid all the outgoings and insured the property. On T ceasing to live there, the house was to become part of W's residuary estate. When W died, T went to stay with his daughter, D, but returned to the property on several occasions. D considered that T was living with her. T later went into hospital and his family went to the house and removed some personal effects. C believed that some household property forming part of W's estate had also been taken and changed the locks. Whilst T was in hospital he told F, W's daughter to a previous marriage, that he would need a carer and did not want to burden D when he came out. F understood this to mean that T wanted to return to the property when he left hospital. T died shortly afterwards, without leaving hospital, and the Revenue issued the notice on the ground that T's conduct amounted to a disclaimer of interest in the property.

Held, allowing the appeal, that T's conduct did not amount to a disclaimer. He had continued to pay the outgoings on the property and had made occasional use of it, albeit without living there, until he was admitted to hospital for the last time. There was a presumption in favour of accepting a gift and this had not been rebutted on the evidence of the instant case.

COOK v. INLAND REVENUE COMMISSIONERS [2002] S.T.C. (S.C.D.) 318, John F Avery Jones, Sp Comm.

4457. Inheritance tax-offshore trusts-transfer of Hong Kong property to Manx discretionary trusts-valid nature of intermediate steps-Hong Kong

P owned substantial assets in Hong Kong. By a series of complex transactions the assets were transferred to SW, an Isle of Man company. SW was itself owned by two further Isle of Man companies, F and SK. P had seven children. His wife, M, and three children were directors of F and the other four children were directors of SK. M and the seven children were also all directors of SW. Each of the three Manx companies was sole trustee of a number of different discretionary or unit trusts. Following P's death, SW, F and SK obtained declarations that no estate duty was due as the result of the transactions. CED successfully appealed, however, and SW, F and SK appealed to the Court of Final Appeal, where CED, although accepting that the transactions were not shams, contended that the intermediate steps should be disregarded so that the transfers could be recharacterised as gifts to P's family in Hong Kong.

Held, allowing the appeal, that P had lawfully disposed of his property by transferring it to SW, F and SK. If the steps taken to achieve the transactions were ignored, it was still clearly P's intention that the Hong Kong property was to be transferred to the Manx companies for them to hold on discretionary and unit trusts. The transactions did not therefore come within the *Ramsay* principle,

WT Ramsay Ltd v. Inland Revenue Commissioners [1982] A.C. 300, [1981] C.L.Y. 1385 considered and *Ensign Tankers (Leasing) Ltd v. Stokes (Inspector of Taxes)* [1992] 1 A.C. 655, [1992] C.L.Y. 611 not followed.
SHIU WING LTD v. COMMISSIONER OF ESTATE DUTY 2 I.T.L. Rep. 794, Li, C.J., CFA (HK).

4458. **Inheritance tax–reliefs–application to amend probate values of real property–requirement for "appropriate person"**

[Inheritance Tax Act 1984 s.190, s.191.]

S, the executors of a deceased taxpayer, appealed against the Revenue's refusal to accept the sale values of certain properties as the amended probate values under the Inheritance Tax Act 1984 s.190 and s.191. The deceased died in 1996 leaving the residue of her estate to three charities. The remainder of the estate did not exceed the nil band rate so that no inheritance tax was payable on the death. The estate included 10 freehold properties valued at £582,000 at the date of death and they were sold for substantially higher sums within a year. The executors' claim for the sale values to be accepted as the amended probate values was refused.

Held, dismissing the appeal, that (1) the purpose of s.191 was to grant relief from inheritance tax where there had been a fall in the value of land after death. The expectation was that if values increased after a death no claim would be made as it would increase the amount of inheritance tax payable, and (2) the appropriate person to make the claim under s.191 was the person liable for inheritance tax attributable to the value of the interest in the land. Each interest had to be identified separately. The person liable for inheritance tax under s.190(1) was the person who either had paid the tax or had an obligation to pay it. There was no such person if no tax was payable. Consequently there was no appropriate person under s.191 and no claim could be made under that section.
STONOR (EXECUTOR OF DICKINSON'S ESTATE) v. INLAND REVENUE COMMISSIONERS [2001] S.T.C. (S.C.D.) 199, Nuala Brice, Sp Comm.

4459. **Inheritance tax–valuation–deceased's husband died intestate–no grant of letters of administration–value of deceased's interest in husband's estate**

[Inheritance Tax Act 1984 s.5(1), s.272.]

The administrator of D's estate appealed against a decision of the Revenue that D was entitled to the whole of her deceased husband's property immediately before her death. The husband died intestate in 1994. He and D held their home in trust for themselves as beneficial tenants in common. No application was made for the grant of letters of administration of his estate. D died in 2000 and the Revenue took the view that her interest in the deceased husband's estate formed part of her own estate immediately before her death as it was then property to which she was beneficially entitled under the Inheritance Tax Act 1984 s.5(1) and s.272 for inheritance tax purposes.

Held, dismissing the appeal, that since prior to her death D had had a statutory right to apply for the grant of letters of administration of her husband's estate, she had had a right to the whole of that estate; such rights were "rights and interests of any description" and so amounted to "property" as defined by s.272. Accordingly D's interest in her husband's estate, including his half share in the family home, formed part of her estate immediately before her death under s.5(1) even though no letters of administration in respect of his estate had ever been applied for.
DAFFODIL v. INLAND REVENUE COMMISSIONERS [2002] S.T.C. (S.C.D.) 224, AN Brice (Chairman), Sp Comm.

4460. Inheritance tax–valuation–solicitor executor delivering account containing estimated valuation–no negligence where acting in accordance with accepted practice

[Inheritance Tax Act 1984 s.216(3), s.247.]

The Revenue brought proceedings before the special commissioners alleging negligence by an executor of a will, R, in delivering the inventory of the deceased's estate by entering estimated values. R, a solicitor, was executor of the will of S, who died in 1999 owning properties in England and Scotland. Tenants occupied the English property, but R and his co-executor were anxious that the Scottish property should be sold as soon as possible to avoid retaining it during the slow period in the housing market and deterioration in its condition over the winter. However it was R's practice not to advertise executory properties for sale until confirmation of the executors' title had been applied for. He submitted an inventory to the Capital Taxes Office, CTO, with estimated values for both properties to obtain confirmation at the earliest opportunity. When accurate valuations were subsequently obtained, an additional sum of inheritance tax was found to be due. The CTO advised R that they considered that the executors had not fulfilled their obligations under the Inheritance Tax Act 1984 s.216(3) to make the fullest enquiries that were reasonably practicable in the circumstances to ascertain values for the properties. Therefore a penalty of £9,000 was to be imposed under s.247. R believed that the penalty was excessive and refused to agree the Revenue's proposal.

Held, declaring that R was not liable to any penalty, that R had made the fullest enquiries that were reasonably practicable in the circumstances and was therefore not liable to penalties. It had been prudent to lodge the inventory so that the Scottish house could be sold as soon as possible; to have obtained professional valuations in the circumstances would have caused considerable delay. R had acted in accordance with accepted practice and the Revenue had failed to show what a prudent executor would have done in the circumstances.

ROBERTSON v. INLAND REVENUE COMMISSIONERS (NO.1) [2002] S.T.C. (S.C.D.) 182, J Gordon Reid Q.C., Sp Comm.

4461. Insurance companies–overseas insurers–tax representatives–information requirements

OVERSEAS INSURERS (TAX REPRESENTATIVES) (AMENDMENT) REGULATIONS 2002, SI 2002 443; made under the Income and Corporation Taxes Act 1988 s.552A; and the Finance Act 1999 s.133. In force: April 6, 2002; £1.75.

These Regulations, which amend the Overseas Insurers (Tax Representatives) Regulations 1999 (SI 1999 881), vary the terms of the undertaking the insurer is required to give in the light of changes made to the information requirements for UK insurers by the Finance Act 2001.

4462. Insurance premium tax–state aids–supply of domestic appliances–imposition of higher rate for insurance

[EC Treaty Art.92 (now, after amendment, Art.87 EC), Art.93 (now Art.88 EC) Sixth Council Directive 77/388 on a common system for VAT Art.13B; Sixth Council Directive 77/388 on a common system for VAT Art.27, Art.33.]

G, a supplier of insurance for domestic appliances sold or rented to consumers by its parent, appealed against the rejection of its claim for the repayment of higher rate insurance premium tax, IPT. The goods supplied were standard rated for VAT purposes and the insurance itself was exempt by virtue of the Sixth Council Directive 77/388 Art.13B. The higher rate of IPT was introduced for insurance supplied by connected insurers in the same position as G in 1997, based on a belief that VAT was being avoided by suppliers increasing exempt charges and reducing standard rate charges on the supply of domestic appliances. G claimed that the imposition of the higher rate was contrary to Community law in the absence of a derogation under Art.27 of the Sixth Directive. Alternatively, that the higher rate was a turnover tax contrary to Art.33 of the Directive or an illegal State aid contrary to the EC Treaty Art.92 (now, after amendment, Art.87 EC) and Art.93 (now Art.88 EC).

Held, staying the proceedings pending a preliminary ruling from the ECJ, that (1) IPT was not a single progressive tax where the rate increased in relation to the volume of supplies as the standard and the higher rates applied to entirely different types of supply. The higher rate of IPT could therefore be seen as a special measure requiring authorisation under Art.27 of the Directive; (2) G's insurance services were commercially priced, based on a fiscally attractive option which mitigated its liability to tax; (3) the higher rate of IPT was not a turnover tax in terms of Art.33 since it did not apply to all transactions relating to goods or services, and (4) the differential between the higher and standard rates of IPT was a State aid granted through state resources within the meaning of Art.87 which distorted competition in a way that was not objectively justifiable, *R. v. Customs and Excise Commissioners, ex p. Lunn Poly Ltd* [1999] S.T.C. 350, [1999] C.L.Y. 4743 applied. The issue whether the higher rate affected trade between Member States was referred to the ECJ, along with the question whether repayment of overpaid tax was the appropriate remedy.

GIL INSURANCE LTD v. CUSTOMS AND EXCISE COMMISSIONERS [2001] Eu. L.R. 401, AN Brice (Chairman), V&D Tr.

4463. International taxation–transfer of assets–exemptions–jurisdiction of ECJ in respect of domestic transfer

[Council Directive 90/434 on the common system of taxation applicable to mergers Art.2(c), Art.2(i); Fusionsskattelov (Denmark) para.15(c); Fusionsskattelov (Denmark) para.15(d).]

The shareholders of a Danish limited company, A, had set up a new company, N, to which A's business was to be transferred. The intention was to protect the existing capital within A. A took out a loan and was to retain the proceeds, with the liability transferred to N. N's cash flow was to be met by a line of credit from a bank which was to have a lien over N's shares. A had applied to the Ligningsrad, the Danish tax authority, for authorisation to carry out the planned transfer of assets taking advantage of the tax exemption in the Fusionsskattelov para.15(c) and para.15(d). These provisions were intended to be of identical effect to Council Directive 90/434 Art.2(c) and Art.2(i), so that the same law applied to all such transfers, whether domestic or involving another Member State. The Ligningsrad granted the application subject to the proceeds and liability of the debt either remaining with A or being transferred wholly to N, and limitations on the provision of security for the benefit of N. A brought proceedings against S, the Danish Ministry of Fiscal Affairs, and sought to review the conditions imposed. The Danish court referred the matter to the ECJ for a preliminary ruling on the meaning of the Directive.

Held, determining the preliminary issue in favour of S, that the transfer did not qualify for tax exemption. Although the ECJ had jurisdiction to interpret the provisions of the Directive, even though it was a domestic transfer, given the alignment of domestic legislation with EC law, *Leur-Bloem v. Inspecteur der Belastingdienst/Ondernemingen Amsterdam 2 (C28/95)* [1998] Q.B. 182, [1997] C.L.Y. 1083 applied; there was no qualifying transfer under the Directive as the proposed transfer did not involve the entire transfer of assets and liabilities relating to a branch of activity. The issue of whether a transferee business was an independent operation was to be assessed primarily by reference to whether the assets transferred were capable of operating as an independent undertaking without further transfers of assets. The fact that a transferee business took out a loan did not preclude it from being independent. The issue of whether a transferee was independent was a question for the trial court.

ANDERSEN & JENSEN APS v. SKATTEMINISTERIET (C43/00); *sub nom.* ANDERSEN OG JENSEN APS v. SKATTEMINISTERIET (C43/00) 4 I.T.L. Rep. 523, Jann (President), ECJ.

4464. Investigations–disclosure–claim by accountant that documents lost–accountant's duties

[Taxes Management Act 1970 s.20(3), s.98(1).]

F, an accountant, appealed against a penalty imposed on him under the Taxes Management Act 1970 s.98(1) for failing to comply with a notice issued under s.20(3) of the Act requiring the production of certain documents believed to be in his possession relating to the preparation of accounts and other documents for a client under investigation by the Revenue. Following receipt of the s.20(3) notice, F had written to the Revenue, stating that a large number of files had been placed in storage and that although a visit had been made to the depository, none of the documents referred to in the notice had been found. On the appeal F raised the question of the Commissioners' power under s.98(1)(ii) to impose a daily penalty for a continuing failure to produce documents.

Held, dismissing the appeal, that the documents were of a type that would have been retained by an accountant and the onus lay on F to show that he did not in fact have them. To do that, F had to demonstrate that they had either been destroyed or could not be found after a thorough search. The Commissioners had been entitled to reject F's assertion that the documents could not be located as he had not given an adequate explanation of the type of search that had been carried out. As to the Commissioners' power to impose a daily penalty for a continuing failure to produce documents, a person on whom a penalty had been imposed could avoid liability by proving that he did not have the relevant documents within his possession or power at the material time.

FOX v. UXBRIDGE GENERAL COMMISSIONERS; *sub nom.* FOX v. McKAY (INSPECTOR OF TAXES) [2002] S.T.C. 455, Jacob, J., Ch D.

4465. Landfill tax–taxable disposals

LANDFILL TAX (AMENDMENT) REGULATIONS 2002, SI 2002 1; made under the Finance Act 1996 s.51, s.53, s.62. In force: February 1, 2002; £1.75.

These Regulations amend the Landfill Tax Regulations (SI 1996 1527) to provide that the temporary holding of material pending its use for site restoration purposes at the landfill site at which the disposal was made, or pending it being sorted, is not a taxable disposal. They also correct a drafting error.

4466. Landfill tax–waste disposal–meaning of "waste"

[Finance Act 1996 s.40(2), s.64.]

C appealed against a ruling ([2002] E.H.L.R. Dig. 2) that material deposited at a landfill site did not give rise to any liability to landfill tax. C contended that P, a landfill site operator, was liable for landfill tax in respect of the deposit of material at the site following recycling because material did not have to be useless to qualify as a taxable disposal.

Held, allowing the appeal, that a liability to landfill tax had arisen because a disposal of material as waste had taken place for the purposes of the Finance Act 1996 Part III s.40(2). Pursuant to s.64 of the Act, material did not have to be useless but the individual making the disposal had to possess an intention to discard it. It was irrelevant whether benefit was derived from recycling the material before disposal by way of landfill.

PARKWOOD LANDFILL LTD v. CUSTOMS AND EXCISE COMMISSIONERS; *sub nom.* CUSTOMS AND EXCISE COMMISSIONERS v. PARKWOOD LANDFILL LTD, [2002] EWHC 47, [2002] S.T.C. 417, Sir Robert Andrew Morritt V.C., Ch D.

4467. Lottery duty–national lottery

LOTTERY DUTY (AMENDMENT) REGULATIONS 2002, SI 2002 2355; made under the Finance Act 1993 s.24, s.38. In force: October 17, 2002; £1.50.

These Regulations, which amend the Lottery Duty Regulations 1993 (SI 1993 3212), provide that the time when a ticket or chance is taken in a lottery that is part of the National Lottery shall be treated as the day on which the lottery takes place. This does not apply to a ticket or chance where, before it is taken, it has been determined whether or not it will win.

4468. **Lottery duty—national lottery—instant chances—excise duty**

LOTTERY DUTY (INSTANT CHANCES) (AMENDMENT) REGULATIONS 2002, SI 2002 2354; made under the Finance Act 1993 s.24, s.28, s.38. In force: October 17, 2002; £1.50.

An instant lottery chance in a lottery that forms part of the National Lottery is treated as being taken for the purposes of payment of lottery duty when the batch of which it forms part is settled. These Regulations amend one of the rules in the Lottery Duty (Instant Chances) Regulations 1995 (SI 1995 2815) which determines the time when a batch is settled from 15 days after it was first activated to 30 days.

4469. **Mortgages—relief—remortgages—refusal of lender to accept self certification—loan for qualifying purpose**

[Finance Act 1972 Sch.9 Part I para.1.]

A appealed against a decision that C, the mortgagee of a property owned by A, was not obliged to adjust his mortgage account to reflect the failure to allow for MIRAS. The original purchase price for the property had been financed partly by a mortgage advance and partly by drawing down on an overdraft facility, which was later converted into a fixed loan secured by a second charge. The property was remortgaged in favour of P, whose undertaking was later transferred to C. C operated a policy, which it applied in A's case, whereby loans made on a remortgage were treated as not qualifying for MIRAS since it was probable that the loan would not be used, in whole, to discharge an existing qualifying loan under the Finance Act 1972 Sch.9 Part I para.1 and accordingly C did not accept self-certification in such cases. If a borrower believed that the loan qualified for MIRAS he was asked to notify the Inland Revenue on the relevant form. A had failed to complete the relevant form.

Held, dismissing the appeal, that C was not obliged to adjust the mortgage account. C was entitled to believe that the remortgage would not be used to discharge an existing qualifying loan and was entitled to refuse to accept self-certification and to require its customers to obtain the necessary approval from the Inland Revenue. Unless the loan were split into two parts, the first of which would be used to discharge the mortgage and thus constitute a qualifying loan, the second to discharge the bank borrowing and thus constitute a non qualifying loan, self-certification would, in any event, not have entitled A to MIRAS since the loan being discharged was for a mixed purpose and, as such, was not a qualifying loan.

CHELTENHAM & GLOUCESTER PLC v. ASHFORD, [2001] EWCA Civ 1713, [2002] B.T.C. 81, Chadwick, L.J., CA.

4470. **Registration—aggregates levy—notification**

AGGREGATES LEVY (REGISTRATION AND MISCELLANEOUS PROVISIONS) (AMENDMENT) REGULATIONS 2002, SI 2002 1929; made under the Finance Act 2001 Sch.4 para.6. In force: August 15, 2002; £1.50.

These Regulations, which amend the Aggregates Levy (Registration and Miscellaneous Provisions) Regulations 2001 (SI 2001 4027), remove the provision relating to the manner of notification in the case of persons exempted from the requirement of registration.

4471. Self assessment–reliefs–error and mistake relief–amendments to self assessment return following inquiry by tax inspector–no agreement as to effect of changes

[Taxes Management Act 1970 s.33(1).]

W appealed against a Revenue decision refusing his claim for error or mistake relief under the Taxes Management Act 1970 s.33(1). As the result of an inquiry into W's tax affairs, W and his father attended a meeting with the tax inspector where the inspector refused a claim for 75 per cent business use for a car. The car was eventually excluded altogether and W, who was dyslexic, signed the amended tax return. Records were subsequently discovered that proved 72 per cent business use for the car. W contended that he had not understood what the inspector was proposing at the meeting and that he had been pressurised into agreeing to the amendment.

Held, allowing the appeal, that error or mistake relief was available as the amendment to W's self assessment return had the same effect as the original return and the appeal had been made within the time limit in s.33(1)(a). W had been under stress at the meeting and had not realised the effect of the inspector's decision, with the result that there had been no actual agreement as to the amendment he had signed.

WALL v. INLAND REVENUE COMMISSIONERS [2002] S.T.C. (S.C.D.) 122, Nuala Brice, Sp Comm.

4472. Shipping–tonnage tax companies–training commitment

TONNAGE TAX (TRAINING REQUIREMENT) (AMENDMENT) REGULATIONS 2002, SI 2002 2265; made under the Finance Act 2000 Sch.22 para.29, Sch.2 para.31, para.36. In force: October 1, 2002; £1.50.

These Regulations further amend the Tonnage Tax (Training Requirement) Regulations 2000 by increasing the amount of the payments in lieu of training. In respect of a relevant four month period falling on or after October 1, 2002, the figure by which the number of months is to be multiplied is increased from £562 to £573. In the case of the higher rate of payment where there has been failure to meet the training requirement, the basic rate to be used in the calculations is increased from £512 to £522

4473. Single currency–amendment

EUROPEAN SINGLE CURRENCY (TAXES) (AMENDMENT) REGULATIONS 2002, SI 2002 1971; made under the Finance Act 1998 s.163. In force: October 1, 2002; £1.50.

These Regulations amend the European Single Currency (Taxes) Regulations 1998 (SI 1998 3177) in consequence of the repeal of specified sections of the Finance Act 1993 by the Finance Act 2002.

4474. Small self administered schemes–exemptions–entitlement of Revenue to withdraw approval

[Finance Act 1970; Income and Corporation Taxes Act 1988 s.591C, s.591D (5); Retirement Benefits Schemes (Restriction on Discretion to Approve) (Small Self-administered Schemes) Regulations 1991 (SI 1991 1614) Reg.2(1).]

L, the trustees of a pension fund, appealed against the Revenue's decision to withdraw its approval of a retirement benefits scheme as an exempt approved scheme for the purposes of the Finance Act 1970. Approval had been given on the understanding that the Revenue would be informed of any alterations to the rules or other terms of the scheme. The other trustees became dissatisfied with the performance of the pensioner trustee and he resigned. The Revenue was not informed of the resignation nor of the failure to appoint a replacement contrary to the provisions of the trust deed and approval was withdrawn. An income tax assessment was then issued under the Income and Corporation Taxes Act 1988 s.591C. L argued that the criteria adopted by the Revenue for approval were unlawful and that approval could only be withdrawn where the pension fund was being operated otherwise than for the purposes intended, for example if the fund was being used for tax avoidance or evasion or for criminal activities such as money laundering.

Held, dismissing the appeal, that (1) the Revenue had an unqualified power to decide who should and who should not be granted approval as a pensioner trustee by virtue of the Retirement Benefits Schemes (Restriction on Discretion to Approve) (Small Self-administered Schemes) Regulations 1991 Reg.2(1) and the Income and Corporation Taxes Act 1988 s.591D(5); (2) the decision to withdraw approval was within the Revenue's powers since there was no cogent evidence that the criteria were irrational or otherwise unlawful under the 1988 Act; (3) the trustees had failed to comply with the requirements of their own trust deed which was a matter which the Revenue was entitled and obliged to take into account when considering whether to continue or withdraw approval. There were no exceptional circumstances to prevent the conclusion that the Revenue was legally entitled to withdraw approval of the scheme even though it was bona fide established and administered for the sole purpose of providing retirement benefits; and (4) the provisions of s.591C were mandatory and the fact that the scheme administrator had not evaded or avoided tax nor distributed the funds improperly was irrelevant. Payment of the tax was in effect the automatic sanction for withdrawal of approval and accordingly L had a personal liability to pay 40 per cent of the funds by way of tax under Sch.D.

LAMBERT (ADMINISTRATORS OF CID PENSION FUND) v. GLOVER (INSPECTOR OF TAXES) [2001] S.T.C. (S.C.D.) 250, THK Everett, Sp Comm.

4475. Sport—clubs—tax relief;

RELIEF FOR COMMUNITY AMATEUR SPORTS CLUBS (DESIGNATION) ORDER 2002, SI 2002 1966; made under the Finance Act 2002 Sch.18 para.14. In force: August 15, 2002; £1.50.

This Order designates as eligible sports the sports appearing in the list of recognised activities which is maintained by the National Sports Councils.

4476. Stamp duties—loan agreements—foreign loans—discrimination in treatment of loans recorded in accounts—Austria

See EUROPEAN UNION: Sandoz GmbH v. Finanzlandesdirektion fur Wien, Niederosterreich und Burgenland (C439/97). §1560

4477. Stamp duties—sale of land—avoidance of stamp duty on sale of land using redemption of unit trust as vehicle for sale—Australia

[Stamp Duties Act 1920 (NSW) Pt.3, Div.3A; Stamp Duties Act 1920 (NSW) s.44 (2)(d).]

P, a company, agreed to sell two shopping centres to I, a company using the following transactions to avoid stamp duty. P had subscribed the purchase price of the properties by cheque to a unit trust, T, to purchase all the units in the trust. T then endorsed the cheque back to P in exchange for the real estate which it agreed to hold as bare trustee for P. I using associated trusts had then subscribed the purchase price to acquire further units in T. T used the subscription money from I to redeem P's units. Thus I became the effective owner of the real estate. The Commissioner deemed that there had been a transfer of beneficial ownership of real estate to which stamp duty was chargeable under the anti avoidance provisions of the Stamp Duties Act 1920 (NSW) Pt.3, Div.3A. I had appealed contending that the moneys had been paid to P for redemption of unit trusts, which was exempt under the Stamp Duties Act 1920 s.44(2)(d). The Supreme Court had upheld the contention of I and the Commissioner appealed.

Held, dismissing the appeal by majority, that the change in beneficial ownership occurred when the unit trusts were redeemed and no stamp duty was payable.

CHIEF COMMISSIONER OF STAMP DUTIES v. ISPT PTY LTD (1999-2000) 2 I.T.E.L.R. 1, Mason (President), Sup Ct (NSW).

4478. Stamp duties–stamp duty reserve tax–exemptions

STAMP DUTY AND STAMP DUTY RESERVE TAX (EXTENSION OF EXCEPTIONS RELATING TO RECOGNISED EXCHANGES) REGULATIONS 2002, SI 2002 1975; made under the Finance Act 2002 s.117. In force: July 26, 2002; £1.50.

These Regulations extend the stamp duty and stamp duty reserve tax exemptions for sales of stock to intermediaries and for repurchases and stock lending to the market known as OFEX.

4479. State retirement pension–information powers–electronic delivery

RETIREMENT BENEFITS SCHEMES (INFORMATION POWERS) (AMENDMENT) REGULATIONS 2002, SI 2002 3006; made under the Income and Corporation Taxes Act 1988 s.605; and the Finance Act 1999 s.133. In force: April 6, 2003; £2.00.

These Regulations amend the Retirement Benefits Schemes (Information Powers) Regulations 1995 (SI 1995 3103) to remove the obligation on the prescribed person in respect of a small self-administered scheme to furnish information to the Commissioners of the Inland Revenue about investments in unlisted companies which are open-ended investment within the meaning of the Financial Services and Markets Act 2000 s.236. They also provide that information required to be furnished to the Board may be delivered electronically and make a drafting amendment so that the time within which the payment of a special contribution falls to be reported is computed by reference to the end of the scheme year, in which falls the end of the chargeable period, in the course of which it is paid.

4480. Tax credits–administrative arrangements

TAX CREDITS (ADMINISTRATIVE ARRANGEMENTS) REGULATIONS 2002, SI 2002 3036; made under the Tax Credits Act 2002 s.58, s.65. In force: January 1, 2003; £1.75.

The Tax Credits Act 2002 s.58 applies where regulations permit or require a claim of notification relating to a tax credit to be made or given to a relevant authority. Where the 2002 Act applies, regulations may make provision as to the administrative arrangements between a relevant authority and the Commissioners of the Inland Revenue who have the care and management of tax credits. These Regulations provide for administrative arrangements in relation to claims and notifications made or given to a relevant authority in accordance with the Tax Credits (Claims and Notifications) Regulations 2002 (SI 2002 2014).

4481. Tax credits–appeals

TAX CREDITS (APPEALS) REGULATIONS 2002, SI 2002 2926; made under the Tax Credits Act 2002 s.63, s.65. In force: December 17, 2002; £2.00.

The Taxes Credit Act 2002 s.63 provides that appeals against decisions relating to tax credit shall lie for a temporary period to the appeal tribunal constituted under the Social Security Act 1998 and not to the General or Special Commissioners. The 2002 Act also provides that regulations may apply with modifications any provision of the 1998 Act or the Taxes Management Act 1970 s.54 in relation to such appeals. These Regulations accordingly make such provision.

4482. Tax credits–appeals–procedure

TAX CREDITS (APPEALS) (NO.2) REGULATIONS 2002, SI 2002 3196; made under the Social Security Act 1998 s.7, s.12, s.14, s.16, s.28, s.39, s.79, s.84, Sch.1 para.11, Sch.1 para.12, Sch.5. In force: January 1, 2003; £3.50.

These Regulations, which are made in consequence of the application and modification of the Social Security Act 1998 by the Tax Credits (Appeals) Regulations 2002 (SI 2002 2926), contain provisions relating to commencement, citation and interpretation and service of notices or documents.

They concern rights of appeal and the procedure for bringing appeals; make provision for additional persons to have a right of appeal, or to make an application for a direction to close down an enquiry; set out the procedure for dealing with a dispute in relation to time limits; deal with late appeals; provide for the manner in which an application for an extension of time must be made; and make provision for appeal tribunals for tax credits.

4483. Tax credits—claims and notification

TAX CREDITS (CLAIMS AND NOTIFICATIONS) REGULATIONS 2002, SI 2002 2014; made under the Tax Credits Act 2002 s.4, s.6, s.14, s.15, s.16, s.17, s.19, s.22, s.65, s.67. In force: August 12, 2002; £3.00.

These Regulations, which provide for the way in which claims for a tax credit are to be made and processed, provide for the use of electronic communications to make claims or to give notices or notifications. They also provide for a standard rule for a claim to be "backdated" by up to three months; for the date of a claim for working tax credit including the disability element of that tax credit; for claims to be made before the beginning of the tax year to which they relate; for claims for working tax credit to be made in advance in certain circumstances; for circumstances in which claims made by one member of a couple are to be treated as made by the other member of the couple; for circumstances in which claims made before April 6, 2003 can be made; how a claim is to proceed after the person or persons die after making it; for circumstances where one person may act for another in making a claim; that increases of the maximum rate of entitlement to a tax credit as a result of changes of circumstances are to be dependent on notification; and for the date of notification in cases where the change of circumstances may increase the maximum rate of entitlement to a tax credit.

4484. Tax credits—disabled persons tax credit—working families tax credit

TAX CREDITS (MISCELLANEOUS AMENDMENTS NO.2) REGULATIONS 2002, SI 2002 525; made under the Social Security Contributions and Benefits Act 1992 s.123, s.128, s.129, s.136, s.137, s.175; and the Tax Credits Act 1999 s.2, Sch.2 para.1, Sch.2 para.20. In force: April 2, 2002; £1.75.

These Regulations amend the Family Credit (General) Regulations 1987 (SI 1987 1973) and the Disability Working Allowance (General) Regulations 1991 (SI 1991 2887) in relation to award periods of working families' tax credit and disabled person's tax credit commencing on or after April 2, 2002. They extend the definition of "relevant childcare charges" so as to include care service consisting of child minding and day care of children which is registered under the Regulation of Care (Scotland) Act 2001 and provide for armed forces pensions for widows to be disregarded so that the Regulations also cover corresponding pensions for widowers.

4485. Tax credits—disabled persons tax credit—working families tax credit

TAX CREDITS (MISCELLANEOUS AMENDMENTS NO.3) REGULATIONS 2002, SI 2002 1333; made under the Social Security Contributions and Benefits Act 1992 s.128, s.129, s.136, s.137, s.175; and the Tax Credits Act 1999 s.2, Sch.2 para.1, Sch.2 para.20. In force: in accordance with Reg.1 (1); £1.75.

These Regulations, which amend the Family Credit (General) Regulations 1987 (SI 1987 1973) and the Disability Working Allowance (General) Regulations 1991 (SI 1991 2887), amend amounts to be disregarded in calculating a student's income for the purposes of determining his entitlement to working families' tax credit or disabled person's tax credit. They enable persons receiving the higher rate of attendance allowance to receive the enhanced disability credit and amend the adult credit figures for working families' tax credit and disabled person's tax credit.

4486. **Tax credits—disabled persons tax credit—working families tax credit**

TAX CREDITS (PRESCRIBED PERIODS OF AWARDS) REGULATIONS 2002, SI 2002 1334; made under the Social Security Contributions and Benefits Act 1992 s.128, s.129, s.137, s.175; and the Tax Credits Act 1999 s.2, Sch.2 para.1, Sch.2 para.20. In force: June 4, 2002; £1.50.

These Regulations provide that where an award of working families' tax credit or disabled person's tax credit becomes payable on or after June 4, 2002, the period for which that award shall be payable is the period that begins on the date on which it becomes payable and ends on April 7, 2003 rather than the period of 26 weeks specified in Social Security Contributions and Benefits Act 1992. The purpose of these Regulations is to facilitate the transition to the new tax credits to be introduced from April 2003 under the Tax Credits Bill currently before Parliament.

4487. **Tax credits—disabled persons tax credit—working families tax credit—claims and payments**

TAX CREDITS (CLAIMS) (TRANSITIONAL PROVISION) (AMENDMENT) ORDER 2002, SI 2002 2158; made under the Tax Credits Act 2002 s.62. In force: August 20, 2002; £1.50.

This Order corrects an error in Tax Credits Act 2002 (Commencement No.1) Order 2002 (SI 2002 1727 (C.52)) Art.3 which makes transitional provision in relation to claims for tax credit for the tax year 2003-04, by substituting a new Art.3. The correction makes clear that such claims are income for the tax year 2001-02.

4488. **Tax credits—dividends—purchase of own shares—abnormal dividend received by approved pension scheme on buy back—tax credit amounting to tax advantage**

[Income and Corporation Taxes Act 1988 s.592(2), s.709(4).]

S, an exempt approved occupational pension scheme, obtained a tax credit under the Income and Corporation Taxes Act 1988 s.592(2) on the purchase price it obtained from participating in a buy back of shares it held in P. The Revenue assessed S to income tax under s.703 on the basis that the amount received was an abnormal dividend under s.709(4). S succeeded on appeal to the special commissioners ([2001] Pens. L.R. 305), where it was held that, although the tax credit amounted to a tax advantage, S had not received an abnormal dividend, as the amount paid on the buy back was determined by market conditions.

Held, allowing the appeal, that abnormality was to be determined by reference to the level of return normally to be expected on the shares. The level of dividend paid to S on the buy back was not the normal form of regular dividend payment, but rather a one off sum paid by P to S and its other participating shareholders. Although the authorities were unclear on the point, the most recent decision showed that the tax credit amounted to a tax advantage, *Colchester Estates (Cardiff) v. Carlton Industries Plc* [1986] Ch. 80, [1984] C.L.Y. 2588 applied and *Inland Revenue Commissioners v. Universities Superannuation Scheme Ltd* [1997] S.T.C. 1, [1997] C.L.Y. 2980 followed.

TRUSTEES OF THE SEMA GROUP PENSION SCHEME v. INLAND REVENUE COMMISSIONERS; *sub nom.* INLAND REVENUE COMMISSIONERS v. TRUSTEES OF THE SEMA GROUP PENSION SCHEME; TRUSTEES OF THE OMEGA GROUP PENSION SCHEME v. INLAND REVENUE COMMISSIONERS, [2002] EWHC 94, [2002] S.T.C. 276, Lightman, J., Ch D.

4489. **Tax credits—up rating**

TAX CREDITS UP-RATING ORDER 2002, SI 2002 829; made under the Social Security Administration Act 1992 s.150, s.189; the Social Security Administration

(Northern Ireland) Act 1992 s.132; and the Tax Credits Act 1999 s.2, Sch.2 para.2, Sch.2 para.4, Sch.2 para.20. In force: April 9, 2002; £1.75.

This Order is made in consequence of a review under the Social Security Administration Act 1992 s.150 in awards of working families' tax credit and disabled person's tax credit commencing on or after April 9, 2002. It specifies the applicable amount for working families' tax credit and the amount of credits for an adult, child or young person which determines a family's maximum working families' tax credit and specifies the applicable amount for disabled person's tax credit and the amount of credit for an adult, child or young person which determines the appropriate maximum disabled person's tax credit.

4490. Tax credits—working tax credit—child tax credit—notice of appeal

TAX CREDITS (NOTICE OF APPEAL) REGULATIONS 2002, SI 2002 3119; made under the Tax Credits Act 2002 s.39, s.65, s.67. In force: January 7, 2003; £1.50.

These Regulations prescribe the manner of giving notice of appeal under the Tax Credits Act 2002 against decisions relating to working tax credit or child tax credit.

4491. Tax credits—working tax credit—child tax credit—payments by the Inland Revenue

TAX CREDITS (PAYMENTS BY THE BOARD) REGULATIONS 2002, SI 2002 2173; made under the Tax Credits Act 2002 s.24, s.65, s.67. In force: April 6, 2003; £2.00.

These Regulations, which make provision in relation to the payment of tax credits by the Board of Inland Revenue, prescribe the member of a married couple or an unmarried couple to whom payment is to be made where an award of a tax credit is made to such a couple. They relate to child tax credit and the child care element of working tax credit; deal with cases where one member of such a couple dies; prescribe the person to whom payment is to be made where a claim for a tax credit was made by one person on behalf of another; prescribe circumstances in which payments may continue to be made for any period, after the tax year for which an award of tax credit has been made to a person or persons, within which the person is or the persons are entitled to make a claim for the tax credit for the next tax year; and provide for the time when a tax credit is to be paid. In addition, the Regulations provide for the manner of payments and provide for entitlement to a tax credit to be dependent on a bank account or other account having been notified to the Board.

4492. Tax credits—working tax credit—entitlement

WORKING TAX CREDIT (ENTITLEMENT AND MAXIMUM RATE) REGULATIONS 2002, SI 2002 2005; made under the Tax Credits Act 2002 s.10, s.11, s.12, s.65, s.67. In force: in accordance with Reg.1; £3.50.

These Regulations prescribe the conditions of entitlement for the elements of working tax credit introduced by the Tax Credits Act 2002.

4493. Tax credits—working tax credit—payments by employers

WORKING TAX CREDIT (PAYMENT BY EMPLOYERS) REGULATIONS 2002, SI 2002 2172; made under the Tax Credits Act 2002 s.25, s.65, s.67. In force: March 1, 2003; £2.50.

These Regulations, which make provision in relation to the payment of working tax credit by employers to their employees from April 6, 2003, define "relevant employer" and provide for the issue of start notices to employers by the Board of Inland Revenue notifying them to commence paying working tax credit. They also provide for the issue of amendment notices by the Board to an employer where the amount of working tax credit to which his employee is entitled changes; specify the obligation of employers to whom start notices or amendment notices are issued to calculate and pay working tax credit to employees in accordance with the notices; set out how payment of working tax credit is to be funded by the employer; enable the employer to apply to the Board for funding in order to pay working tax credit; provide for renewal of funding by the Board for each income tax year; and enable the employer to notify the Board in the course of an income tax year if, as a result of a change of circumstances, any of the details recorded on an application form for funding.

4494. Tax Credits Act 2002 (21)

This Act makes provision for tax credits and amends the law about child benefit and guardian's allowance.

This Act received Royal Assent on July 8, 2002.

4495. Tax credits Act 2002 (c.21)–Commencement No. 1 Order

TAX CREDITS ACT 2002 (COMMENCEMENT NO.1) ORDER 2002, SI 2002 1727; made under the Tax Credits Act 2002 s.61, s.62. Commencement details: bringing into force various provisions of the 2002 Act in accordance with Art.2; £3.00.

This Order brings into force the majority of the provisions of the Tax Credits Act 2002.

4496. Tax planning–accountants–power to obtain information from accountants– Australia

[Income Tax Assessment Act 1936 (Australia) s.264(1)(a).]

M, an accountancy firm, applied for judicial review of notices issued in Australia by the Commissioner under the Income Tax Assessment Act 1936 s.264(1)(a). The notices required members of M to identify clients for whom they had provided services. The members were selected on the basis that it was suspected that they had been connected with mass marketed tax planning. M applied for judicial review on the ground that the notices were not issued bona fide for the purposes of the statutory power.

Held, refusing the application for judicial review, that the only limitation on the power to issue notices was that it had to be exercised to enable the Commissioner to perform his functions under the Act. Accordingly the notices had been issued to ascertain the proper taxable income of taxpayers. Notices overrode any duty of confidence and normal limitations on discovery in litigation did not apply.

McCORMACK v. DEPUTY COMMISSIONER OF TAX (LARGE BUSINESS & INTERNATIONAL) 4 I.T.L. Rep. 447, Sackville, J., Fed Ct (Aus) (Sgl judge).

4497. Tax planning–losses–company in liquidation transferring losses–sale of share in partnership–Canada

[Income Tax Act (Canada) s.245(3), s.248(10).]

As part of the liquidation of S a partnership was formed with a subsidiary. The intention was to create a loss when S's share in the partnership was sold. O subsequently acquired S's share and sought to offset the loss against its profits. This was refused on the ground that the scheme had only been entered into for avoidance purposes and was therefore to be disregarded under the Income Tax Act (Canada) s.245 and s.248(10). O appealed.

Held, dismissing the appeal, that s.248(10) increased the common law definition of a tax avoidance scheme comprising a series of pre determined steps to include other related transactions and steps that could have been within the contemplation of the scheme's planners, *Furniss (Inspector of Taxes) v. Dawson* [1984] A.C. 474, [1984] C.L.Y. 270 applied. The facts showed that O had only entered into the transaction to obtain a tax advantage, which far outweighed the earnings it could have expected from the assets purchased. The policy behind the Act was to prevent trading in losses for tax avoidance purposes, which had been the intended outcome in the instant case where S's losses were to be transferred to O by use of the partnership.

OSFC HOLDINGS LTD v. R. 4 I.T.L. Rep. 68, Stone, J.A., CA (Can).

4498. **Tax planning–professional negligence–accountants–gifts from husband to wife–foreign emoluments**

[Income and Corporation Taxes Act 1988 s.19.]

N, a chartered accountant, appealed against a decision ([2002] S.T.C. 84) whereby he was held to have been negligent in advising G that a transaction would not give rise to United Kingdom tax liability. G was domiciled in the US but resident in the UK and had intended transferring US held investments to his wife, W, to enable her to apply the proceeds of sale from such assets to the purchase of a house in England. The Income and Corporation Taxes Act 1988 s.19, commonly known as Schedule E, classified foreign investments as emoluments taxable upon their remittance to the UK; however, N had advised that, if the transfer were perfected as a gift overseas G would incur no tax liability when the proceeds were applied in the UK. Subsequent to W purchasing a half share in the house the Revenue claimed that the transaction effected a remittance of G's foreign emoluments and was taxable under Schedule E. N argued that the advice he had given was correct and/or was consistent with the advice which a reasonably competent accountant would have given.

Held, allowing the appeal, that the advice given by N was correct. In the absence of the Revenue as a party to proceedings the court was reluctant to rule as to whether the transfer was correctly classified as a taxable remittance of foreign emoluments; however, a decision had to be reached on the correctness in law of N's advice. When analysing the scheme the court was to have regard to the legal nature of the transactions that had taken place and was not entitled to look into the underlying substance or agreements to classify the transaction as a sham, *Macniven (Inspector of Taxes) v. Westmoreland Investments Ltd* [2001] UKHL 6, [2001] 2 W.L.R. 377, [2001] C.L.Y. 5199 considered. In the instant case the gift was to be perfected in the US with G failing to retain any beneficial interest in the investments or benefitting from a monetary equivalent in the UK; moreover, the legislation dealing with constructive remittances did not allow the court to treat a husband and wife as the same person. Given these facts, and in the light of supporting authority, N had been correct to advise that the application of funds by the wife would not result in a tax liability for G, *Carter v. Sharon* [1936] 1 All E.R. 720 applied, *Harmel v. Wright (Inspector of Taxes)* [1974] 1 W.L.R. 325 distinguished. It was further held that the judge below had been wrong to allow G to support his claim on the basis of a late submission that an alternative scheme could have been instigated to successfully avoid tax.

GRIMM v. NEWMAN, [2002] EWCA Civ 1621, [2003] 1 All E.R. 67, Sir Andrew Morritt V.C., CA.

4499. **Tax planning–share sales–company with group tax losses–offsetting–New Zealand**

[Income Tax Act 1976 (New Zealand) s.25(2), s.30, s.99(2).]

O appealed against a refusal to quash assessments to income tax. O had taken part in a scheme for tax avoidance which was held to be contrary to the Income Tax Act 1976 (New Zealand) s.99(2) and O's assessable income was consequently increased to offset the tax advantage he had gained. The scheme involved the selling of shares in a trading company to a company which had group tax losses to offset and which was controlled by an accountant, and as a result tax was avoided by the shareholders, including O, and the accountant. O contended that (1) the assessments were time-barred; (2) the thorough analysis required by the Revenue's policy statement had not been carried out making the assessment ultra vires; (3) "an error of principle" had taken place in that a tax advantage could not have been gained by both the trading company and O, and it was an abuse of process that the commissioner had turned his attention to O merely because he was solvent; (4) the assessments were inconsistent in that an assessment of O had been made before the assessment of the trading company had been completed, and so they had both been assessed on the same income and the assessment of O was therefore invalid, and (5) the assessments were only tentative because of the fact that two different parties were being assessed.

Held, dismissing the appeal, that: (1) the commissioner had been correct to apply the s.25(2) which negated the time-bar if a tax return had omitted to mention income; (2) the commissioner had done all that was required by the policy statement; (3) the commissioner had been within his rights in assessing both parties to tax as they had each benefited from the scheme; (4) while an objection might be made under s.30, the assessment itself was valid; and (5) the assessments had been strongly defended, and held to be valid, in court and could hardly be said to be tentative.

O'NEIL v. INLAND REVENUE COMMISSIONER, [2001] UKPC 17, [2001] 1 W.L.R. 1212, Lord Hoffmann, PC (NZ).

4500. **Tax planning—swap agreements—composite transaction creating capital gain—no recharacterisation as tax avoidance scheme—Canada**

[Income Tax Act 1990 (Canada) s.245.]

CP raised capital by entering into a swap agreement under which it borrowed Australian dollars that it then sold for Japanese yen. CP then entered into forward contracts to buy Australian dollars with the yen. Australian dollars had a higher interest rate than Canadian dollars and CP deducted the higher rate of interest from its taxable income as a capital gain. The Revenue decided that CP had entered into the transactions for avoidance purposes and disallowed the deduction of interest under the Income Tax Act 1990 (Canada) s.245. CP successfully appealed against this decision in the Tax Court (3 I.T.L. Rep. 238). The Revenue appealed, contending that the fact that the loan was denominated in Australian dollars meant it had been entered into for avoidance purposes.

Held, dismissing the appeal, that CP had entered into a composite transaction on arm's length terms. The borrowing element of the agreement could not be isolated from the fact that foreign currencies were involved. The transaction could not be reinterpreted as being entered into for avoidance purposes when there was no evidence to show that CP had made repayments of principle, rather than interest. The nature of the transaction in the instant case would have to be ignored before it could be recharacterised as being entered into for avoidance purposes, *OSFC Holdings Ltd v. R.* 4 I.T.L. Rep. 68, [2002] 8 C.L. 523 applied.

CANADIAN PACIFIC LTD v. R.; *sub nom.* R. v. CANADIAN PACIFIC LTD 4 I.T.L. Rep. 588, Strayer, J.A., CA (Can).

4501. **Tax planning—takeovers—nature of special dividend payment and inter company loans—Australia**

[Income Tax Assessment Act 1936 (Australia) s.79D, s.177D(b), s.177E.]

C, A and M were part of an Australian group of companies involved in a takeover bid for a UK company, B. A complex scheme was devised involving companies in Singapore and the Bahamas, and certain inter company borrowings, share transfers and the payment of a special dividend. COT assessed C, A and M to income tax under the Income Tax Assessment Act 1936 (Australia) s.79D and s.177E on the grounds that the scheme involved an element of dividend stripping, contrary to s.177E, and that the inter company loans were subject to the quarantine provisions of s.79D. The assessments were overturned on appeal and COT appealed.

Held, allowing the appeal in part, that (1) the scheme, which had been structured and entered into on the basis of professional advice, was designed to avoid s.79D, therefore s.177D(b) applied, *Federal Commissioner of Taxation v. Spotless Services Ltd* (1996) 186 C.L.R. 404 applied, and (2) the special dividend did not come within the accepted definition of "dividend stripping" and did not have tax avoidance as a main purpose with the result that s.177E did not apply.

COMMISSIONER OF TAXATION v. CONSOLIDATED PRESS HOLDINGS LTD 2 I.T.L. Rep. 165, French, J., Fed Ct (Aus) (Full Ct).

4502. Tax rates–supply of services–rest home subsidy schemes–New Zealand

[Goods and Services Act 1985 s.78(2).]

K, the former proprietor of a rest home, appealed against the dismissal of its claim under the Goods and Services Act 1985 s.78(2). K had been a participant in a rest home subsidy scheme whereby a rest home proprietor agreed to provide a set level of accommodation and services in return for a fee which did not exceed the maximum "fee for service rate" prescribed by the Department of Social Welfare. When the fee for service rate was first established, the calculation of labour and non labour operating costs took into account the fact that rest homes were liable to pay goods and services tax, GST, on the fees charged at a discounted rate of 8.2 per cent. Immediately after K had signed the agreement, the general rate of GST was increased to 12.5 per cent and the rate for rest homes to 10.25 per cent. The unchallenged evidence from the Department of Social Welfare was that this increase was taken into account at the time of the first adjustment of the fee for service rate in 1990. K maintained that the sums paid to it by the department should have been subject to an increase representing the difference between the lower and higher rate of GST during the currency of the contract. The court at first instance dismissed the claim on the basis that the proviso to s.78(2) precluded an increase in the case of a public authority making a payment in respect of any goods and services where the consideration for the supply was in the nature of a grant or subsidy. K contended that the payment was a subsidy to the residents of the home and not the home itself and that the words "in the nature of a grant or subsidy" should be construed to mean a grant or subsidy to the other party to the contract.

Held, dismissing the appeal, that it was not possible to restrict the application of the proviso to grants or subsidies of which the beneficiary was the other party to the contract, since most such grants or subsidies would be made to public, charitable or private bodies in order to confer benefits upon third parties. It was instead appropriate to ask whether the character and quality of the payment was in the nature of a grant or subsidy. The question of whose benefit the payment was for was accordingly immaterial, *Director General of Social Welfare v. De Morgan* [1996] 3 N.Z.L.R. 677 applied.

KENA KENA PROPERTIES LTD v. ATTORNEY GENERAL OF NEW ZEALAND, [2001] UKPC 51, (2001) 145 S.J.L.B. 270, [2002] 1 A.C. 362, Lord Hoffmann, PC (NZ).

4503. Taxation administration–investigations–disclosure–TMA s.20 notice issued to serving prisoner–previous failure to co-operate–validity of notice given alternative means of obtaining disclosure

[Taxes Management Act 1970 s.20(1); General Commissioners (Jurisdiction and Procedure) Regulations 1994 (SI 1994 1812) Reg.10.]

W sought permission to appeal against the refusal of his application for judicial review of the decision to issue a notice under the Taxes Management Act 1970 s.20(1). W was serving a prison sentence when he was asked for information by the Revenue. Although he initially agreed to cooperate, he later said he would only do so after his release on licence. Therefore the Revenue issued the s.20(1) notice, requiring disclosure. W's application was refused on the grounds that he could have complied with the notice even though he was in prison and that he had failed to cooperate with the Revenue previously.

Held, refusing the application, that there was no arguable basis for the appeal. There was no evidential basis upon which the Revenue could be required to prove that the s.20 notice had been properly authorised. Further, it could not be accepted that the decision to issue the notice was irrational. The fact that there was an alternative method of obtaining the information under the General

Commissioners (Jurisdiction and Procedure) Regulations 1994 Reg.10 did not affect the validity of the decision to issue the s.20 notice.

R. (ON THE APPLICATION OF WERNER) v. INLAND REVENUE COMMISSIONERS, [2002] EWCA Civ 979, [2002] S.T.C. 1213, Hart, J., CA.

4504. Taxation administration–investigations–notices for delivery up of information–IRS relying on information subject to legal professional privilege and in breach of confidence–Bermuda

[European Convention for the Protection of Human Rights and Fundamental Freedoms 1950; USA-Bermuda Tax Convention Act 1986 (Bermuda) s.5.]

B sought an order setting aside notices for the delivery up of information issued against him by the Bermudan Minister of Finance under the USA-Bermuda Tax Convention Act 1986 s.5. The United States' Internal Revenue Service, IRS, commenced an investigation into B's activities in reliance upon information given by two of B's former employees, P and O, based on documents they had retained from their employment which were subject to legal professional privilege. B argued that the notices were invalidated where they were obtained by the use of information gained as the result of a breach of confidence or professional privilege. The Minister contended that he only had to be satisfied that the procedure used to obtain the notices was correct and that the issue legal professional privilege was a matter for the US courts.

Held, allowing the application, that valid notices could not be issued where they had been obtained in reliance upon either a breach of confidence or legal professional privilege. Legal professional privilege was protected in Bermuda by the European Convention on Human Rights 1950, *R. v. Derby Magistrates Court, ex p. B* [1996] A.C. 487, [1996] C.L.Y. 1402 applied. Privilege could not be abrogated by the 1986 Act. The IRS had failed to make full disclosure as to how the information on which the request depended was received with the result that the application was incorrectly made.

BRASWELL, *Re* 4 I.T.L. Rep. 226, Meerabux, J., Sup Ct (Ber).

4505. Taxation administration–notices–disclosure–documents in hands of taxpayer–notice issued by tax inspector–legal professional privilege

[Taxes Management Act 1970 s.20(1).]

M, a bank, appealed against the dismissal of its appeal ([2001] EWCA Civ 329, [2002] 2 W.L.R. 255) following the refusal of its application for judicial review ([2001] 1 All E.R. 535) of a decision of a Special Commissioner. The Commissioner had approved a tax inspector's issue of a notice pursuant to the Taxes Management Act 1970 s.20(1) requiring M to disclose documents relating to a tax avoidance scheme that it had operated for its customers. M contended that the documents, which contained the advice given to M by counsel as to the potential for success of the scheme, were protected by legal professional privilege. The Revenue maintained that if the intention of Parliament in passing the 1970 Act had been to preserve privilege generally then it would not have enacted specific provisions that preserved the fundamental rights of the taxpayer, including privilege in relation to documents in the hands of lawyers.

Held, allowing the appeal and quashing the notice, that there was no express reference in s.20(1) of the Act to legal professional privilege and that section could not be construed as necessarily implying that a tax inspector could, by the issue of a notice, require the disclosure of documents which were subject to legal professional privilege, *R. v. Secretary of State for the Home Department, ex p. Simms* [2000] 2 A.C. 115, [1999] C.L.Y. 4105 applied. There were specific safeguards, totally distinct from legal professional privilege, incorporated into other sections of the Act that meant that it was impossible to imply that legal professional privilege was intended to be excluded from the measures designed to protect taxpayers, *Parry-Jones v. Law Society* [1969] 1 Ch.1, [1968] C.L.Y. 3703 applied.

R. (ON THE APPLICATION OF MORGAN GRENFELL & CO LTD) v. SPECIAL COMMISSIONER OF INCOME TAX; *sub nom.* R. v. INLAND REVENUE

COMMISSIONERS, *ex p.* MORGAN GRENFELL & CO LTD; R. v. SPECIAL COMMISSIONERS OF INCOME TAX, *ex p.* MORGAN GRENFELL & CO LTD, [2002] UKHL 21, [2003] 1 A.C. 563, Lord Hoffmann, HL.

4506. **Taxation administration—notices—tribunals—General Commissioners— penalties—small businesses—notices to produce analyses of balance sheets**

[Companies Act 1985 s.248; General Commissioners (Jurisdiction and Procedure) Regulations 1994 (SI 1994 1812) Reg.10(3).]

S appealed against continuing penalties imposed under the General Commissioners (Jurisdiction and Procedure) Regulations 1994 Reg.10(3) by the General Commissioners, arising from S's failure to comply with notices to produce analyses of items in the companies' balance sheets.

Held, dismissing the appeal, that when hearing a tax appeal the General Commissioners could require a small company within the meaning of the Companies Act 1985 s.248 to disclose more detailed information and analyses than were required for production of their abbreviated accounts to the Registrar of Companies if they had reason to believe that such information was necessary for their assessments. It was not sufficient to allow the Commissioners access to the company records; they were entitled to request a profit and loss account in statutory form. Penalties were justified in the instant case and found to be proportionate.

SLATER LTD v. BEACONTREE GENERAL COMMISSIONERS [2002] S.T.C. 246, Lightman, J., Ch D.

4507. **Taxation administration—search and seizure—computers—lawfulness of removal from searched premises to copy entire hard drive**

[Taxes Management Act 1970 s.20C, s.20CC.]

H applied for judicial review of the Revenue's decision to seize two computers from his home. Revenue officers had entered the premises pursuant to a warrant issued under the Taxes Management Act 1970 s.20C. The officers found it impossible to copy the contents of the hard drives at H's home and therefore removed the computers from the premises before copying the entire contents of both hard drives. H contended, inter alia, that the officers had no authority under s.20C to copy the entire contents of the hard drives and that they merely had the power to examine the contents during the search of his home and copy the incriminating files only.

Held, refusing the application, that a Revenue officer executing a warrant under s.20C who reasonably believed that the computer data might be needed as evidence could seize and remove the computer even though it contained irrelevant material. A hard drive could not be regarded as a container of separate files visible to the computer's operating system; rather it was a single "thing" that could be required as evidence for the purposes of s.20C(3)(b). The subsequent making of a copy was impliedly authorised by s.20CC of the Act, *R. v. Chesterfield Justices, ex p. Bramley* [2000] Q.B. 576, [1999] C.L.Y. 900 distinguished and *R. (on the application of Paul Da Costa & Co) v. Thames Magistrates Court* [2002] EWHC 40, [2002] S.T.C. 267, [2002] 4 C.L. 129 applied.

R. (ON THE APPLICATION OF H) v. INLAND REVENUE COMMISSIONERS, [2002] EWHC 2164, [2002] S.T.C. 1354, Stanley Burnton, J., QBD (Admin Ct).

4508. **Vehicle excise duty—small islands—designation**

VEHICLE EXCISE DUTY (DESIGNATION OF SMALL ISLANDS) (AMENDMENT) ORDER 2002, SI 2002 1072; made under the Vehicle Excise and Registration Act 1994 Sch.1 para.18. In force: June 1, 2002; £1.50.

This Order amends the Vehicle Excise Duty (Designation of Small Islands) Order 1995 (SI 1995 1397) and designates Shapinsay, Orkney Mainland, Harris and Lewis and Shetland Mainland as small islands for the purposes of Vehicle Excise and Registration Act 1994 Sch.1 para.18 which defines the expression "island goods vehicle".

4509. Vehicle excise duty–unlicensed vehicles–removal from public roads
VEHICLE EXCISE DUTY (IMMOBILISATION, REMOVAL AND DISPOSAL OF VEHICLES) (AMENDMENT) REGULATIONS 2002, SI 2002 745; made under the Vehicle Excise and Registration Act 1994 s.57, Sch.2A para.3. In force: April 9, 2002; £1.75.
These Regulations amend the provisions of the Vehicle Excise Duty (Immobilisation, Removal and Disposal of Vehicles) Regulations 1997 (SI 1997 2439) which provide for the removal and disposal of unlicensed vehicles found stationary on a public road. The Regulations distinguish between vehicles of no economic value and other vehicles.

4510. Withholding tax–commission–payments to foreign associated companies– Canada
[Income Tax Act 1998 (Canada) s.212(1)(d).]
H appealed against income tax assessments raised in response to its failure to withhold tax under the Income Tax Act 1988 (Canada) s.212(1)(d) on commission payments to associated companies in Hong Kong for locating supplies and negotiating prices. H argued that (1) the payments were not rents or royalties for the purposes of s.212(1)(d); (2) s.212(1)(d) did not apply as the payments were for the provision of services, as opposed to know how, and (3) the payments were excluded by s.212(1)(d)(iii) as they were made in connection with contract negotiations.
Held, allowing the appeal, that (1) a payment coming within s.212(1)(d) did not also have to be a rent or royalty to be liable to tax, *R. v. Farmparts Distributing Ltd* (Unreported, February 28, 1980) applied. The payments were not rental in nature as they were not made for the use of property; (2) royalties were not dependent on profit or sales, as occurred in the instant case, *Grand Toys Ltd v. Minister of National Revenue* (Unreported, December 13, 1989) applied, and (3) part of the payments were made in connection with contract negotiations and were therefore exempt under s.212(1)(d)(iii), *R v. Farmparts Distributing Ltd* applied.
HASBRO CANADA INC v. R. 1 I.T.L. Rep. 341, Judge PR Dussault, Tax Court of Canada (Canada).

4511. Withholding tax–derogations–dividends paid by Portuguese resident subsidiary to non resident parent–liability to succession and donation tax
[Council Directive 90/435 on the common system of taxation applicable in the case of parent companies and subsidiaries of different Member States Art.5(4); Municipal Tax Code (Portugal) Art 182; Municipal Tax Code (Portugal) Art184.]
Portugal levied corporation tax at 15 per cent on dividend distributions paid to E, a non resident parent, by its Portuguese subsidiary for the years 1992 to 1996 in reliance upon a derogation under Council Directive 90/435 Art.5(4). Succession and donation tax was also levied at 10 per cent for the years 1997 to 1999 under the Municipal Tax Code (Portugal) Art 182 and Art.184. E brought proceedings to recover the succession and donation tax. The application was allowed at first instance, on the ground that the levy charged under Art.5(4) of the Directive meant that succession and donation tax did not apply. On appeal, the court doubted whether the Directive included succession and donation tax. Therefore it stayed proceedings pending a preliminary ruling from the ECJ as to whether the derogation in Art.5(4) of the Directive, limiting the amount of withholding tax, was restricted to corporation tax or included any tax on share income and dividends.
Held, ruling on the preliminary issue, that the limit on withholding tax in Art.5(4) applied to all taxes on dividends distributed by subsidiaries and was not restricted to corporation tax. Succession and donation tax was a withholding tax which applied to the payment of dividends to a non resident parent and

could be levied in combination with corporation tax, if it did not exceed the limits in Art.5(4).

MINISTERIO PUBLICO v. EPSON EUROPE BV (C375/98) [2002] S.T.C. 739, DAO Edward (President), ECJ.

4512. Books

Andersen–Tolley's Guide to the UK/US DoubleTaxTreaty. Paperback: £75.00. ISBN 0-7545-1723-3. Tolley Publishing.

Antczak, Gina–Tolley's Tax Essentials: Employment and Benefits. Tolley's Tax Essentials. Paperback: £35.00. ISBN 0-7545-1329-7. Tolley Publishing.

Baker, Philip–Transfer Pricing and Taxation. Hardback. ISBN 0-421-49910-9. Sweet & Maxwell.

Barcroft, Charles; Jenney, Hugo–BDO Stoy Hayward's Orange Tax Guide 2002-03. Paperback: £47.95. ISBN 0-406-95033-4. Butterworths Tolley.

Bohan, Brian–Bohan: Capital Acquisitions Tax. Reissued 2nd Ed. Hardback: £70.18. ISBN 1-85475-762-8. Butterworths Law (Ireland).

Bramwell, Richard; James, Alun; Hardwick, Mike; Lindsay, John–Taxation of Companies and Company Reconstructions. 8th Ed. Looseleaf/ring bound: £295.00. ISBN 0-421-82720-3. Sweet & Maxwell.

Brieger, N.–TestYour Professional English Law. PENG. Paperback: £6.00. ISBN 0-582-46898-1. Longman.

BudgetTaxTables 2002. Paperback: £9.95. ISBN 0-406-95032-6. Butterworths Tolley.

Butler, Julie M.–Tax Planning for Agriculture and Land Diversification. Paperback: £49.95. ISBN 0-7545-1769-1. Tolley Publishing.

Cannon, Patrick–Tolley's Stamp Duties and Stamp Duty Reserve Tax 2002-03. Paperback: £74.95. ISBN 0-7545-1677-6. Tolley Publishing.

Cannon, Patrick–Tolley's Tax Essentials: Stamp Duties. Tolley's Tax Essentials. Spiral/comb bound: £35.00. ISBN 0-7545-1295-9. Tolley Publishing.

Clarke, Giles–Clarke: Offshore Tax Planning. Paperback: £89.95. ISBN 0-406-95039-3. ButterworthsTolley.

Cochrane, F. Michael–Tolley's Accounting Principles for Tax Purposes. Paperback: £53.95. ISBN 0-7545-0260-0. Tolley Publishing.

Cochrane, Mike–Tolley'sTaper Relief. 2nd Ed. Paperback: £64.95. ISBN 0-7545-1299-1. Tolley Publishing.

Craig, William–Taxation of E-commerce. Paperback: £71.95. ISBN 0-7545-1213-4. Tolley Publishing.

Curtis, Richard; Donnelly, Tracy–Tax Office Directory 2002: Six Monthly. Spiral/comb bound: £19.95. ISBN 0-7545-1433-1. Tolley Publishing.

Davies, Rt Hon Denzil–Booth: Residence, Domicile and UK Taxation. Paperback: £89.95. ISBN 0-7545-1685-7. Tolley Publishing.

Davis, Anthony C.R.–Tolley'sTaxation in Corporate Insolvency. 5th Ed. Spiral/comb bound: £61.95. ISBN 0-7545-1211-8. Tolley Publishing.

Davis, Colin; Sutherland, Mike; Eastaway, Nigel–BDO Stoy Hayward's Yellow Tax Guide 2002-03. Paperback: £67.95. ISBN 0-406-95036-9. Butterworths Tolley.

Dixon, John C.–Tolley's Trading in the European Union: a Guide to Business and Taxation. 4th Ed. Paperback: £65.00. ISBN 0-7545-1157-X. Tolley Publishing.

Dolton, Alan; Saunders, Glyn–Tolley'sTax Cases 2002. Paperback: £69.00. ISBN 0-7545-1783-7. Tolley Publishing.

Donnelly, Aileen; Walsh, Majella–Enforcement of Revenue. Paperback: £57.97. ISBN 1-85475-687-7. Butterworths Law.

Foreign Exchange Tax Team–Tolley's Taxation of Foreign Exchange Gains and Losses. Paperback: £79.95. ISBN 0-7545-1221-5. Tolley Publishing.

Gibraltar-international Finance Centre. Paperback: £55.00. ISBN 0-7545-1340-8. Tolley Publishing.

Gravestock, Peter; Hear, William–Tolley's Guide to Self-assessment 2001-02. Paperback: £45.95. ISBN 0-7545-1204-5. Tolley Publishing.

Homer, Arnold; Burrows, Rita–Tolley's Tax Guide 2002-03. Hardback: £44.95. ISBN 0-7545-1686-5. Tolley Publishing.

Homer, Arnold; Burrows, Rita; Deeks, Sarah—Tolley's PartnershipTaxation. 5th Ed. Paperback: £56.95. ISBN 0-7545-1199-5. Tolley Publishing.

Homer, Arnold; Burrows, Rita; Gravestock, Peter—Tolley's Taxwise II 2002-03. Paperback: £39.95. ISBN 0-7545-1681-4. Tolley Publishing.

Hutton, Matthew—Tolley's Tax Essentials: Trusts and Estates 2001. Tolley's Tax Essentials. Paperback: £39.00. ISBN 0-7545-1393-9. Tolley Publishing.

Hutton, Matthew—Tolley's UK Taxation of Trusts. Paperback: £89.95. ISBN 0-7545-1675-X. Tolley Publishing.

Hutton, Matthew—Tolley's Tax Essentials: Trusts and Estates 2002-03. Spiral / comb bound: £39.00. ISBN 0-7545-1707-1. Tolley Publishing.

Hyatt—Law of Tax-exempt Healthcare Organizations: 2002 Supplement. Nonprofit Law, Finance, and Management Series. Paperback: £66.95. ISBN 0-471-41942-7. John Wiley & Sons Inc.

Kirkbride, James; Olowofoyeku, Abimbola A.; Butler, Debbie—Revenue Law. Hardback: £60.00. ISBN 1-903499-05-4. Paperback: £24.95. ISBN 1-903499-09-7. Liverpool Academic Press.

Lawson, R.G.; Bertram, A.D.W.—Business Tax and Law Handbook. Zurich. Hardback: £29.99. ISBN 0-273-66216-3. Financial Times Prentice Hall.

Maas, Robert—Tolley's Taxation of Employments. 8th Ed. Paperback: £65.95. ISBN 0-7545-1220-7. Tolley Publishing.

Maas, Robert W.—Tolley's Property Taxes 2001-02. Paperback: £65.95. ISBN 0-7545-1201-0. Tolley Publishing.

Matthews, Jan; Eastaway, Nigel—Corporation Tax Self-assessment. 3rd Ed. Paperback: £65.95. ISBN 0-7545-1288-6. Tolley Publishing.

Matthews, Jan; Eastaway, Nigel—Tolley's Self-assessment 2001-02. Paperback: £69.95. ISBN 0-7545-1203-7. Tolley Publishing.

Maugham, Jolyon; Peacock, Jonathan—Taxation for Personal Injury Specialists. Paperback: £49.95. ISBN 0-406-94802-X. Butterworths Tolley.

Mumford, Ann—Taxing Culture: Towards a Theory of Tax Collection Law. Socio-legal Studies. Hardback: £55.00. ISBN 1-84014-710-5. Dartmouth.

Murphy, Liam; Nagel, Thomas—Myth of Ownership-Taxes and Justice. Hardback: £17.99. ISBN 0-19-515016-3. Oxford University Press Inc, USA.

Orange Tax Handbook 2002-03. Paperback: £51.95. ISBN 0-406-95034-2. Butterworths Tolley.

Parrington, Sheila—Whillans Tax Tables 2001-02. Paperback: £13.95. ISBN 0-406-94457-1. Butterworths Tolley.

Parrington, Sheila; Antczak, Gina—Whillan's Tax Tables 2002-03. Paperback: £15.95. ISBN 0-406-95028-8. Butterworths Tolley.

Parrington, Sheila; Antczak, Gina—Whillans's Tax Tables 2002-03. 63rd Ed. Paperback: £15.95. ISBN 0-406-95027-X. Butterworths Tolley.

Personalised Client Publications-tax Facts Cards. Printed stationery. ISBN 0-7545-1649-0. Butterworths Law.

Price, John—Tolley's Taxation 2001: VAT. Spiral/comb bound: £35.00. ISBN 0-7545-1294-0. Tolley Publishing.

Racheter, Donald P.; Wagner, Richard E.—Politics, Taxation, and the Rule of Law. Hardback: £78.00. ISBN 1-4020-7154-X. Kluwer Academic Publishers.

Ray, Ralph; Hitchmough, Andrew; Wilson, Elizabeth—Ray's Practical Inheritance Tax Planning. 6th Ed. Paperback: £69.95. ISBN 0-406-94284-6. Butterworths Tolley.

Rayney, Peter—Tolley's Tax Planning for Family and Owner-managed Companies. Paperback: £59.95. ISBN 0-7545-1683-0. Tolley Publishing.

Rayney, Peter; Cave, Rebecca—Tolley's Tax Planning for Family and Owner-managed Companies. 5th Ed. Paperback: £54.95. ISBN 0-7545-1215-0. Tolley Publishing.

Ridgway, Philip—Principles of Revenue Law. 2nd Ed. Principles of Law. Paperback: £27.95. ISBN 1-85941-385-4. Cavendish Publishing Ltd.

Rohatgi, Roy—Basic International Taxation. Hardback: £138.60. ISBN 90-411-9852-0. Kluwer Law International.

Salter, David; Snape, John—Easson: Cases and Materials on Revenue Law. Paperback: £40.00. ISBN 1-85941-726-4. Cavendish Publishing Ltd.

Saunders, Glyn; Antczak, Gina–Tolley's Corporation Tax 2002-03: Main Annual. Paperback: £59.95. ISBN 0-7545-1711-X. Tolley Publishing.

Saunders, Glyn; Smailes, David; Antczak, Gina–Tolley's Income Tax 2002-03: Main Annual. Paperback: £59.95. ISBN 0-7545-1710-1. Tolley Publishing.

Saunders, Glyn; Smailes, David; Walton, Kevin–Tolley's Capital Gains Tax Workbook 2001-02. Paperback: £24.95. ISBN 0-7545-1285-1. Tolley Publishing.

Saunders, Glyn; Smailes, David; Walton, Kevin–Tolley's Income Tax Workbook 2001-02. Paperback: £24.95. ISBN 0-7545-1286-X. Tolley Publishing.

Schwarz, Jonathan–Law of UK Tax Treaties. Hardback: £120.00. ISBN 0-421-72490-0. Sweet & Maxwell.

Smailes, David K.; Walton, Kevin–Tolley's Capital Gains Tax Workbook 2001-02. Paperback: £24.95. ISBN 0-7545-1284-3. Tolley Publishing.

Smailes, David; Walton, Kevin–Tolley's Tax Losses. Paperback: £59.95. ISBN 0-7545-1745-4. Tolley Publishing.

Southern, David–Taxation of Corporate Debt and Financial Instruments. Paperback: £65.95. ISBN 0-7545-1219-3. Tolley Publishing.

Tax Annuals Set 2001-02. Paperback: £180.00. ISBN 0-406-94116-5. Butterworths Tolley.

Tax Annuals Set 2002-03. Paperback: £199.00. ISBN 0-406-95046-6. Butterworths Tolley.

Taylor, Rodney–Tolley's Double Taxation Relief. 4th Ed. Paperback: £85.00. ISBN 0-7545-0261-9. Tolley Publishing.

The Tolley Editorial Team–Tolley's Tax Computations 2001-02. Paperback: £59.95. ISBN 0-7545-1206-1. Tolley Publishing.

Tingley, K.R.–Tolley's Roll-over, Hold-over and Retirement Reliefs. 11th Ed. Paperback: £68.95. ISBN 0-7545-1202-9. Tolley Publishing.

Tingley, K.R.–Tolley's Roll-over, Hold Over and Retirement Reliefs. Paperback: £69.95. ISBN 0-7545-1676-8. Tolley Publishing.

Tolley's Capital Gains Tax 2001-02. Tolley's Tax Annuals. Paperback: £54.95. ISBN 0-7545-1390-4. Tolley Publishing.

Tolley's Dictionary of Tax and Accountancy. Paperback: £14.95. ISBN 0-7545-1009-3. Tolley Publishing.

Tolley's Inheritance Tax 2001-02. Tolley's Tax Annuals. Paperback: £53.95. ISBN 0-7545-1188-X. Tolley Publishing.

Tolley's International Handbook of Corporate and Personal Taxes. 6th Ed. Paperback: £79.95. ISBN 0-406-94627-2. Butterworths Tolley.

Tolley's International Tax Planning. 5th Ed. Paperback: £195.00. ISBN 0-7545-1510-9. Tolley Publishing.

Tolley's Leasing in the UK 2001. Paperback: £59.95. ISBN 0-7545-1198-7. Tolley Publishing.

Tolley's Tax Essentials: Family Taxation 2001. Tolley's Tax Essentials. Spiral/comb bound: £35.00. ISBN 0-7545-1297-5. Tolley Publishing.

Tolley's Tax Investigations. Paperback: £56.95. ISBN 0-7545-1212-6. Tolley Publishing.

Tolley's Tax Planning 2001-02. Paperback: £139.00. ISBN 0-7545-1214-2. Tolley Publishing.

Tolley's Tax Planning 2002-03. Paperback: £145.00. ISBN 0-7545-1732-2. Tolley Publishing.

Tolley's Taxation in the Channel Islands and the Isle of Man 2001-02. Paperback: £55.00. ISBN 0-7545-1281-9. Tolley Publishing.

Tolley's Taxation of Lloyd's Underwriters. Hardback: £89.95. ISBN 0-7545-1678-4. Tolley Publishing.

Tookey, Michael–Revenue Law: Textbook. 3rd Ed. Old Bailey Press Textbooks. Paperback: £14.95. ISBN 1-85836-417-5. Old Bailey Press.

Tunkel, Daniel; Auger, David–Butterworths Compliance Series: Managed Funds. Butterworths Compliance Series. Paperback: £45.00. ISBN 0-406-93749-4. Butterworths Law.

Voller, Mike–Tolley's Taxation of Lloyds Underwriters. 10th Ed. Hardback: £89.95. ISBN 0-7545-1282-7. Tolley Publishing.

Walton, Kevin; Smailes, David−Tolley's Capital Allowances 2001-02. Paperback: £54.95. ISBN 0-7545-1193-6. Tolley Publishing.

Ward, John−Judge Irish Income Tax 2002. Butterworth's Irish Tax Library. Paperback: £79.33. ISBN 1-85475-648-6. Butterworths Law (Ireland).

Wareham, Robert; Dolton, Alan−Tolley's Value Added Tax 2002. 2nd Ed. Paperback: £69.00. ISBN 0-7545-1706-3. Tolley Publishing.

Wareham, Robert; Smailes, David; Antczak, Gina−Tolley's Tax Data 2002-03 (six-monthly) Budget/Finance Act Editions-Budget 2002 Ed. Spiral/comb bound: £29.95. ISBN 0-7545-1699-7. Tolley Publishing.

White, Jeremy−Customs Duties Handbook 2002. Paperback: £99.00. ISBN 0-406-95114-4. Butterworths Tolley.

Whiteman, Peter; Goy, David; Sandison, Francis; Sherry, Michael−Whiteman on Income Tax: 12th Supplement to the 3rd Edition. British Tax Library. Paperback: £110.00. ISBN 0-421-76790-1. Sweet & Maxwell.

Whiteman, Peter; Gammie, Malcolm; Herbert, Mark−Whiteman on Capital Gains Tax: 12th Supplement to the 4th Edition. British Tax Library. Paperback: £95.00. ISBN 0-421-76780-4. Sweet & Maxwell.

Whiteman, Peter; Gammie, Malcolm; Herbert, Mark−Whiteman on Capital Gains Tax: 13th Supplement to the 4th Edition. British Tax Library. Paperback: £115.00. ISBN 0-421-79050-4. Sweet & Maxwell.

Wilson, Martin−Tolley's Capital Allowances: Transactions and Planning 2001-0.2. 4th Ed. Paperback: £71.95. ISBN 0-7545-1194-4. Tolley Publishing.

Yellow Tax Handbook 2002-03. Paperback: £57.95. ISBN 0-406-95035-0. Butterworths Tolley.

TELECOMMUNICATIONS

4513. Broadcasting−television licences−increase in fees

WIRELESS TELEGRAPHY (TELEVISION LICENCE FEES) (AMENDMENT) REGULATIONS 2002, SI 2002 641; made under the Wireless Telegraphy Act 1949 s.2. In force: April 1, 2002; £1.75.

These Regulations amend the Wireless Telegraphy (Television Licence Fees) Regulations 1997 (SI 1997 290) by increasing the amount of basic fee for television licences from £36.50 to £37.50 in the case of black and white and from £109 to £112 in the case of colour. The fee is also increased in the case of licences for hotels and hospitality areas and mobile units, where the fee is calculated by reference to "the relevant amount". In the cases of installment licences the issue fee and subsequent instalments for the premium instalment licence are increased to £29.25 with the amount payable being £117 and amendments are made in relation to the budget instalment licence and the "Easy entry" licence so that in every case the total amount payable is £112.

4514. Broadcasting−wireless telegraphy−licence fees

WIRELESS TELEGRAPHY (LICENCE CHARGES) REGULATIONS 2002, SI 2002 1700; made under the Wireless Telegraphy Act 1998 s.1. In force: July 26, 2002; £6.00.

These Regulations, which revoke the Wireless Telegraphy (Licence Charges) Regulations 1999 (SI 1999 1774), the Wireless Telegraphy (Licence Charges) (Amendment) Regulations 1999 (SI 1999 3243), the Wireless Telegraphy (Licence Charges) (Amendment) Regulations 2000 (SI 2000 1678) and the Wireless Telegraphy (Licence Charges) (Amendment) Regulations 2001 (SI 2001 2265), provide for fees to be paid in relation to wireless telegraphy licences granted under the Wireless Telegraphy Act 1949. They limit the issue or renewal of licences for periods of less than a year to licences with fees in excess of £75 per annum; rename the Maritime Radio (Navigational Air and Radar) and the Ship Fixed Radio licence classes in the Maritime sector as the Maritime Navigational Aids and Radar and the Ship Radio licence classes; introduce the Commercial

(5-Year) Ship Radio Licence in the Maritime sector and also the Private Business Radio IR 2008 Data and the Private Business Radio UK General licence classes in the Private Business Radio sector; rename request channels as multi-use type; rename the Public Telecommunication Networks sector as the Public Wireless Networks sector; and replace the Very Small Aperture Terminal Licence with the Network Licence in the Satellite Services sector.

4515. Broadcasting—wireless telegraphy—licences

WIRELESS TELEGRAPHY (PUBLIC FIXED WIRELESS ACCESS LICENCES) REGULATIONS 2002, SI 2002 1911; made under the Wireless Telegraphy Act 1998 s.3, s.6. In force: August 12, 2002; £2.00.

These Regulations make provision for a procedure for the grant in each of the regions of the UK described in Part I of the Schedule by reference to their post codes of wireless telegraphy licences authorising the use of apparatus at specified frequencies for the provision by means of a wireless communications system of Public Fixed Wireless Access wireless communications links over which data may be transmitted and received on demand and whereby end users gain access to other telecommunication systems. The Regulations provide that applications for the grant of the licences shall only be made in accordance with a procedure which is set out in a notice issued by the Secretary of State. They also provide for the matter which such notice shall contain, including: a procedure for a body corporate to make an application to participate in a bidding procedure; criteria for determining whether an applicant is qualified to participate in a bidding procedure; criteria for determining whether a qualified applicant is associated with any other qualified applicants and if so whether they may participate in a bidding procedure; provision for payment of deposits and the circumstances in which such deposits may not be refunded; procedures for submitting bids for the licences, including the determination of reserve prices and minimum bids; further conditions which, following completion of the bidding procedures, must be satisfied before a licence is issued; payment for the licences; an option to successful qualified applicants to renew the licences for two successive periods of five years; provision for other terms, provisions and limitations subject to which the licences are to be issued; and provision for the other conditions with which participants must comply to participate, or continue to participate, in the procedures specified in the notice. In addition, the Regulations provide for publication of the notice on the Radiocommunications Agency's internet website and provide that the Secretary of State may, in such cases as she thinks fit, refund fees paid to her for one or more of the licences.

4516. Broadcasting—wireless telegraphy—licensing—exemptions

WIRELESS TELEGRAPHY (EXEMPTION) (AMENDMENT) REGULATIONS 2002, SI 2002 1590; made under the Wireless Telegraphy Act 1949 s.1. In force: July 8, 2002; £1.50.

These Regulations amend the Wireless Telegraphy (Exemption) Regulations 1999 (SI 1999 930) which exempt "relevant apparatus" from the requirement to be licensed under the Wireless Telegraphy Act 1949. These Regulations remove "relevant apparatus" operating in the frequency band 2400.0 to 2483.5 MHz from the exclusion, so that it is exempt from licensing.

4517. Electronic mail—interception—telecommunications companies—lawful authority to act to preserve emails pending court order for production of special procedure material

[Police and Criminal Evidence Act 1984 s.9, Sch.1; Regulation of Investigatory Powers Act 2000 s.1.]

N, a telecommunications company, sought judicial review of the decision to grant an application by the Chief Constable of Suffolk under the Police and Criminal Evidence Act 1984 s.9 and Sch.1 for an order for the production of special procedure material in the form of email information from an email address over a specified period. N had a computer system whereby emails from an internet service provider were automatically stored. The emails were automatically deleted one hour after they were read by the recipient and the only way to keep a customer's emails was to transfer them to a different address. N submitted that any order made on an application under s.9 of the 1984 Act could not apply to information in the system prior to the order being made, given that if it took the steps to preserve the information pending the court hearing, as contemplated by Sch.1 para.2, it would be committing an offence under the Regulation of Investigatory Powers Act 2000 s.1.

Held, refusing the application, that a telecommunications company would not commit the criminal offence of unlawfully intercepting a communication in the course of its transmission, in intercepting emails the subject of an application for the production of special procedure material under the 1984 Act. It was implicit within the wording of Sch.1 para.2 of that Act, when read in conjunction with s.9, that a body which was subject to an application under s.9 had the power to take any action necessary to preserve emails within the system pending the court's decision as to whether or not to make the order.

R. (ON THE APPLICATION OF NTL GROUP LTD) v. IPSWICH CROWN COURT, [2002] EWHC 1585, [2003] Q.B. 131, Lord Woolf of Barnes, L.C.J., QBD (Admin Ct).

4518. Licences–AT&T Global Network Services (UK) B.V.

PUBLIC TELECOMMUNICATION SYSTEM DESIGNATION (AT&T GLOBAL NETWORK SERVICES (UK) B.V.) ORDER 2002, SI 2002 1376; made under the Telecommunications Act 1984 s.9. In force: June 14, 2002; £1.50.

The Secretary of State has granted a licence to AT&T Global Network Services (UK) B.V. under the Telecommunications Act 1984 s.7 to run specified telecommunication systems. This Order designates those telecommunication systems as public telecommunication systems.

4519. Licences–Companhia Portuguesa Radio Marconi SA

PUBLIC TELECOMMUNICATION SYSTEM DESIGNATION (COMPANHIA PORTUGUESA RADIO MARCONI SA) ORDER 2002, SI 2002 1560; made under the Telecommunications Act 1984 s.9. In force: July 12, 2002; £1.50.

The Secretary of State has granted a licence to Companhia Portuguesa Radio Marconi SA under the Telecommunications Act 1984 to run specified telecommunication systems. This Order designates those telecommunication systems as public telecommunication systems.

4520. Licences–Econet Satellite Services Ltd

PUBLIC TELECOMMUNICATION SYSTEM DESIGNATION (ECONET SATELLITE SERVICES LIMITED) ORDER 2002, SI 2002 2657; made under the Telecommunications Act 1984 s.9. In force: November 26, 2002; £1.50.

The Secretary of State has granted a licence to Econet Satellite Services Ltd under the Telecommunications Act 1984 to run specified telecommunication systems. This Order designates those telecommunication systems as public telecommunication systems.

4521. Licences–Eurocall Ltd

PUBLIC TELECOMMUNICATION SYSTEM DESIGNATION (EUROCALL LIMITED) ORDER 2002, SI 2002 1071; made under the Telecommunications Act 1984 s.9. In force: May 17, 2002; £1.50.

The Secretary of State has granted a licence to Eurocall Ltd under the Telecommunications Act 1984 s.7 to run specified telecommunication systems. This Order designates those telecommunication systems as public telecommunication systems.

4522. Licences–Fibernet UK Ltd

PUBLIC TELECOMMUNICATION SYSTEM DESIGNATION (FIBERNET UK LIMITED) ORDER 2002, SI 2002 1070; made under the Telecommunications Act 1984 s.9. In force: May 17, 2002; £1.50.

The Secretary of State has granted a licence to Fibernet UK Ltd under the Telecommunications Act 1984 s.7 to run specified telecommunication systems. This Order designates those telecommunication systems as public telecommunication systems.

4523. Licences–France Telecom Network Services-UK Ltd

PUBLIC TELECOMMUNICATION SYSTEM DESIGNATION (FRANCE TELECOM NETWORK SERVICES-UK LTD) ORDER 2002, SI 2002 400; made under the Telecommunications Act 1984 s.9. In force: March 26, 2002; £1.50.

The Secretary of State has granted a licence to France Telecom Network Services-UK Ltd under the Telecommunications Act 1984 s.7 to run specified telecommunication systems. This Order designates those telecommunication systems as public telecommunication systems. Consequently, by virtue of s.9(3) of that Act, France Telecom Network Services-UK Ltd will be a public telecommunications operator when the Order comes into force.

4524. Licences–Gamma Telecommunications Ltd

PUBLIC TELECOMMUNICATION SYSTEM DESIGNATION (GAMMA TELECOMMUNICATIONS LIMITED) ORDER 2002, SI 2002 2658; made under the Telecommunications Act 1984 s.9. In force: November 26, 2002; £1.50.

The Secretary of State has granted a licence to Gamma Telecommunications Ltd under the Telecommunications Act 1984 to run specified telecommunication systems. This Order designates those telecommunication systems as public telecommunication systems.

4525. Licences–Severn Trent Retail Services Ltd

PUBLIC TELECOMMUNICATION SYSTEM DESIGNATION (SEVERN TRENT RETAIL SERVICES LIMITED) ORDER 2002, SI 2002 1947; made under the Telecommunications Act 1984 s.9. In force: August 22, 2002; £1.50.

The Secretary of State has granted a licence to Severn Trent Retail Services Limited under the Telecommunications Act 1984 s.7 to run specified telecommunication systems. This Order designates those telecommunication systems as public telecommunication systems.

4526. Licences–state aids–auction of licences for operation of mobile telephone network

BT and OO, telecommunications companies, appealed against the refusal ([2001] Eu. L.R. 325) of their application for judicial review of decisions of the Secretary of State concerned with the auction of licences for the "third generation" of mobile telephones, also known as the "Universal Mobile Telecommunications System" or UMTS. Under the auction rules, each licence had to be paid for as soon as it was granted. OO and BT were each granted a licence and paid the required fee. Other applicants, V and O, were associated companies and whilst their licence bids were accepted, the rules required that as a precondition of the grant of a licence they must cease to be associated. The resultant delay whilst V divested itself of O, meant that the licences were not granted for approximately four months which resulted in a saving to V and O on the substantial cost of financing the licence fee when compared with BT and OO. BT and OO contended that the consequent increase in interest that they had been obliged to bear when compared with V and O was a result that the Secretary of State could and should have avoided, and that his failure to do so was (1) in breach of the relevant European law concerning state aid, and (2) discriminatory, irrational and unfair, contrary to established public law principles.

Held, dismissing the appeal, that (1) no state aid had arisen as a result of the application of the auction rules. There had been no complaint about the rules prior to the auction and they appropriately reflected the Secretary of State's dual commercial and regulatory role. Whilst the Secretary of State had possessed the power to prevent any financial advantage accruing to V and O, he possessed an objective justification for refusing to do so, namely that it would detract from his paramount objective of ensuring a lack of association between successful bidders, and (2) no discrimination could have existed between BT and OO when compared with V and O, since their respective positions were not comparable. Any bidder could have become subject to a precondition at any stage in the bidding process and the auction rules would have been applied in exactly the same way to any such bidder. Having regard to the Secretary of State's paramount concern to ensure that there should be no association between licence holders, his conduct could not be regarded as in any way irrational or unfair.

R. (ON THE APPLICATION OF BT3G LTD) v. SECRETARY OF STATE FOR TRADE AND INDUSTRY; R. (ON THE APPLICATION OF ONE 2 ONE PERSONAL COMMUNICATIONS LTD) v. SECRETARY OF STATE FOR TRADE AND INDUSTRY; *sub nom.* BT3G LTD v. SECRETARY OF STATE FOR TRADE AND INDUSTRY, [2001] EWCA Civ 1448, [2001] 3 C.M.L.R. 61, Lord Phillips of Worth Matravers, M.R., CA.

4527. Licences–T-Systems Ltd

PUBLIC TELECOMMUNICATION SYSTEM DESIGNATION (T-SYSTEMS LIMITED) ORDER 2002, SI 2002 1562; made under the Telecommunications Act 1984 s.9. In force: July 12, 2002; £1.50.

The Secretary of State has granted a licence to T-Systems Ltd under the Telecommunications Act 1984 to run specified telecommunication systems. This Order designates those telecommunication systems as public telecommunication systems.

4528. Licences–Telekom Malaysia (UK) Ltd

PUBLIC TELECOMMUNICATION SYSTEM DESIGNATION (TELEKOM MALAYSIA (UK) LIMITED) ORDER 2002, SI 2002 399; made under the Telecommunications Act 1984 s.9. In force: March 26, 2002; £1.50.

The Secretary of State has granted a licence to Telekom Malaysia (UK) Limited under the Telecommunications Act 1984 s.7 to run specified telecommunication systems. This Order designates those telecommunication systems as public telecommunication systems. Consequently, by virtue of s.9(3) of that Act, Telekom Malaysia (UK) Limited will be a public telecommunications operator when the Order comes into force.

4529. Licences–Tweedwind Ltd

PUBLIC TELECOMMUNICATION SYSTEM DESIGNATION (TWEEDWIND LIMITED) ORDER 2002, SI 2002 1949; made under the Telecommunications Act 1984 s.9. In force: August 22, 2002; £1.50.

The Secretary of State has granted a licence to Tweedwind Ltd under the Telecommunications Act 1984 to run specified telecommunication systems. This Order designates those telecommunication systems as public telecommunication systems.

4530. Licences–United Networks Ltd

PUBLIC TELECOMMUNICATION SYSTEM DESIGNATION (UNITED NETWORKS LIMITED) ORDER 2002, SI 2002 1561; made under the Telecommunications Act 1984 s.9. In force: July 12, 2002; £1.50.

The Secretary of State has granted a licence to United Networks Ltd under the Telecommunications Act 1984 to run specified telecommunication systems. This Order designates those telecommunication systems as public telecommunication systems.

4531. Licences–VTL (UK) Ltd

PUBLIC TELECOMMUNICATION SYSTEM DESIGNATION (VTL (UK) LIMITED) ORDER 2002, SI 2002 1948; made under the Telecommunications Act 1984 s.9. In force: August 22, 2002; £1.50.

The Secretary of State has granted a licence to VTL (UK) Ltd under the Telecommunications Act 1984 to run specified telecommunication systems. This Order designates those telecommunication systems as public telecommunication systems.

4532. Management–Channel Islands–termination of agreements

TELECOMMUNICATION SERVICES (CHANNEL ISLANDS) ORDER 2002, SI 2002 799; made under the Post Office Act 1969 s.87. In force: March 29, 2002; £1.50.

This Order revokes the Telecommunication Services (Jersey) Order 1972 (SI 1972 1814), the Telecommunication Services (Guernsey) Order 1972 (SI 1972 1815) and the Telecommunication Services (Channel Islands Consequential Provisions) Order 1972 (SI 1972 1816) which gave the force of law to two Agreements made in 1972 between the Minister of Posts and Telecommunications and the States of Jersey and the States of Guernsey respectively. They handed over to Jersey and Guernsey the Post Office's statutory privilege over the administration of telecommunications services in the Channel Islands. The effect of the revocation of the earlier Orders is that the Agreements are terminated.

4533. Mobile Telephones (Re-progamming) Act 2002 (c.31)–Commencement Order

MOBILE TELEPHONES (RE-PROGAMMING) ACT 2002 (COMMENCEMENT) ORDER 2002, SI 2002 2294; made under the Mobile Telephones (Re-progamming) Act 2002 s.3. Commencement details: bringing into force various provisions of the 2002 Act on October 4, 2002; £1.50.

This Order brings into force the Mobile Telephones (Re-progamming) Act 2002, sections 1 and 2.

4534. Mobile Telephones (Re-programming) Act 2002 (c.31)

This Act creates offences in respect of unique electronic equipment identifiers of mobile wireless communications devices.

This Act received Royal Assent on July 24, 2002.

4535. OFCOM–membership

OFFICE OF COMMUNICATIONS (MEMBERSHIP) ORDER 2002, SI 2002 2956; made under the Office of Communications Act 2002 s.1. In force: December 24, 2002; £1.50.

This Order amends the Office of Communications Act 2002 by increasing the maximum membership of the Office of Communications from six to nine.

4536. Office of Communications Act 2002 (c.11)–Commencement No.1 Order

OFFICE OF COMMUNICATIONS ACT 2002 (COMMENCEMENT NO.1) ORDER 2002, SI 2002 1483; made under the Office of Communications Act 2002 s.7. Commencement details: bringing into force various provisions of the 2002 Act on July 1, 2002; £1.50.

This Order brings into force all the provisions of the Office of Communications Act 2002 not yet in force.

4537. Office of Communications Act 2002 (c.11)–Commencement No.2 Order

OFFICE OF COMMUNICATIONS ACT 2002 (COMMENCEMENT NO.2) ORDER 2002, SI 2002 2955 (C.94); made under the Office of Communications Act 2002 s.7. Commencement details: bringing into force various provisions of the 2002 Act on November 29, 2002; £1.50.

This Order brings into force specified provisions of the Office of Communications Act 2002.

4538. Telecommunications networks–access–national law requiring operator dominant in market to offer interconnections–compatibility with Council Directive 97/33–European Community

[Council Directive 97/33 on harmonisation of the telecommunications network Art.4(2), Art.9(2); Royal Decree 1651/1998.]

The Spanish Supreme Court sought a preliminary ruling on the interpretation of Council Directive 97/33 Art.4(2) and Art.9(2) following a challenge to the validity of Royal Decree 1651/1998, the domestic legislation giving effect to the Directive, by T, a telecommunications operator dominant in the market. The Decree required T to offer interconnection at local and higher level switching centres and access to the local subscriber loop. T argued that this contravened Annex VII Part 2 of the Directive, which provided that the location of interconnection points was to be determined by negotiation between the parties concerned.

Held, that the Directive was intended to provide a framework for achieving harmonisation of the telecommunications network. Although Art.4(2) required operators holding major positions in the market to meet reasonable requests for interconnection, that did not prevent Member States from imposing access conditions in relation to the matters contained in Annex VII Part 2.

TELEFONICA DE ESPANA SA v. ADMINISTRACION GENERAL DEL ESTADO (C79/00) [2002] 4 C.M.L.R. 22, Macken (President), ECJ.

4539. Books

Gillies, David; Roger, Marshall–Telecommunications Law. Hardback: £210.00. ISBN 0-406-95129-2. Butterworths Law.

Rennie, Michele T.; et al–Computer and Telecommunications Law Review 2002. Hardback. ISBN 0-421-83300-9. Sweet & Maxwell.

TORTS

4540. Conversion–wrongful interference with goods–aircraft–validity of Iraqi resolution–public policy considerations

In proceedings relating to ten commercial aircraft belonging to K which had been seized by Iraqi forces after their invasion of Kuwait, both parties appealed against the decision of the Court of Appeal ([2001] 3 W.L.R.1117). The Court of Appeal had upheld the decision of a judge ([1999] C.L.C. 31) that I had wrongly interfered with the aircraft and was therefore liable but had allowed in part K's appeal against the decision of a judge ([2000] 2 All E.R. (Comm) 360) in relation to damages, finding that while K's claims in respect of four of the aircraft failed, its claims in respect of the other six succeeded. K had issued a writ seeking delivery up of the aircraft and damages resulting from their conversion or, in the alternative, payment of the value of the aircraft. Following its invasion of Kuwait, the Iraqi government had passed Resolution 369 by which it purported to dissolve K and transfer its assets to I.

Held, dismissing the appeal (Lord Scott dissenting), that (1) Resolution 369 had amounted to a gross breach of the established rules of international law and accordingly, as a matter of public policy, the court would decline to recognise it. It was appropriate to consider the acceptability of a provision of foreign law by having regard to contemporary standards. Resolution 369 had been adopted as part of Iraq's attempt to destroy Kuwait as a separate state. It followed that to enforce or recognise the Resolution would be contrary to public policy and would, furthermore, be contrary to the obligations of the United Kingdom under the UN Charter. A national court could decline to give effect to legislation or the acts of a foreign state where that state was in violation of international law, and (2) under the English tort of conversion, every person through whose hands certain goods passed in a series of conversions was himself guilty of conversion and liable to the owner for the loss caused by the misappropriation of the goods. The wrongful acts of a previous possessor did not reduce the owner's claim in relation to the wrongful acts of a later possessor. In the instant case the Court of Appeal had not erred in its conclusion.

KUWAIT AIRWAYS CORP v. IRAQI AIRWAYS CO (NO.6), [2002] UKHL 19, [2002] 2 A.C. 883, Lord Nicholls of Birkenhead, HL.

4541. Deceit–fraudulent misrepresentation–meaning of "fault"–contributory negligence not a defence to action in deceit

[Law Reform (Contributory Negligence) Act 1945 s.1 (1).]

S, a bank, appealed against a decision of the Court of Appeal ([2000] 1 All E.R. (Comm) 1) in relation to damages to be assessed in their action for deceit against P, a shipping company. M, the managing director of O, the beneficiary under a letter of credit which had been issued by I, a Vietnamese bank and confirmed by S, had fraudulently backdated bills of lading to a date before the goods had been shipped in order to obtain payment under the letter of credit. It was agreed that if S had known of the false date, payment would not have been made. S decided to waive late presentation of the credit documentation after the expiry date for negotiations, and authorised payment. S then sought reimbursement from I, stating falsely that the documents had been presented before the expiry date. P appealed against the decision ([2001] Q.B. 167) that S had made out its claim for damages to be assessed, contending that S's loss had resulted from its own "fault" as defined by the Law Reform (Contributory Negligence) Act 1945 s.1 (1) and its damages should be reduced accordingly. The Court of Appeal held that contributory negligence was not a common law defence to an action in deceit, and that M had made the fraudulent representations on behalf of O and was therefore not personally liable.

Held, allowing S's appeal and dismissing P's appeal, that the definition of "fault" applied to claimants and defendants in different ways. "Fault" was defined as "negligence, breach of statutory duty or other act or omission" which gave rise to a liability in tort in the case of a defendant and a defence of contributory negligence in the case of a claimant. It followed that conduct by the claimant could not amount to "fault" within the 1945 Act unless it gave rise to a common law defence of contributory negligence. S had suffered damage, namely the loss of the money it had paid to O, and it was established that reliance upon fraudulent representation was in itself sufficient irrespective of other matters, *Edgington v. Fitzmaurice* (1885) L.R. 29 Ch. D 459 approved, therefore it was irrelevant that S would not have paid if they had not also mistakenly and negligently believed that they could obtain reimbursement. There was no common law defence of contributory negligence in the case of fraudulent misrepresentation, therefore no apportionment could be made under the 1945 Act. In relation to M's liability for deceit, although S had relied upon the representation being attributable to O as the beneficiary under the letter of credit, M could not escape personal liability by asserting that he had made it on

O's behalf. His liability arose from having committed fraud, not by virtue of his position as a director.

STANDARD CHARTERED BANK v. PAKISTAN NATIONAL SHIPPING CORP (NO.2); STANDARD CHARTERED BANK v. MEHRA, [2002] UKHL 43, [2002] 3 W.L.R. 1547, Lord Hoffmann, HL.

4542. Deceit–negligent misstatement–inducement to become a Lloyds Name

P, the former chairman of an insurance agency, now in liquidation, and his brother, a non-executive director of the company, sought summary judgment of a claim brought against them by N, an underwriting Name at Lloyds. N, who had become liable for losses on a number of syndicates, claimed that she had been deliberately misled by P into becoming, and remaining, a Name. She sought damages in negligence and in deceit.

Held, granting the application, that (1) any statements made by P to N had been made by him in his capacity as chairman on behalf of the company and he had not assumed any additional personal responsibility to N, *Hedley Byrne & Co Ltd v. Heller & Partners Ltd* [1964] A.C. 465, [1963] C.L.Y. 2416,, *Williams v. Natural Life Health Foods Ltd* [1998] 1 W.L.R. 830, [1998] C.L.Y. 3920, applied, and (2) liability in deceit for a negligent misstatement did not require the existence of a special relationship between the parties, but the claimant had to establish that the defendant either knew that the statement was false or that he was reckless as to its truthfulness, *Lloyd v. Grace Smith & Co* [1912] A.C. 716 considered. Such conduct would be sufficient to establish liability on the part of the agent's company as well as personal liability in deceit. On the facts, in the absence of evidence as to P's state of mind when the statements were made, there was no real prospect of N's claim in deceit succeeding.

NOEL v. POLAND [2001] 2 B.C.L.C. 645, Toulson, J., QBD (Comm Ct).

4543. False imprisonment–mistake–erroneous warrant–liability of prison governors and Registrar

[Crown Proceedings Act 1947 s.2(5.]

Q appealed against the decision of the district judge to strike out his claim for damages against two prison governors and the Lord Chancellor's department for false imprisonment. Q had been convicted of blackmail and burglary. In addition to imposing a sentence for those offences, the sentencing judge had also had to deal with certain other matters. In accordance with the judge's sentencing remarks, a total sentence of two years and three months' imprisonment should have been imposed. However, the judge had wrongly indicated a total sentence of six years and six months and the order of the court and the warrant of commitment had been drawn up in accordance with the erroneous total. Q had sought leave to appeal against his sentence and the single judge had given leave restricted to the correction of the arithmetical error if it was found to be so. Due to administrative errors, Q's appeal was not brought before the full court until after his release, by which time he had served the period appropriate for a sentence of two years and six months. The district judge had struck out Q's claim on the grounds that (1) he had been detained in accordance with the warrant and the prison governors could not have acted contrary to that warrant, and (2) the Registrar was protected from litigation by virtue of the Crown Proceedings Act 1947 s.2(5).

Held, dismissing the appeal, that (1) until an order of a court was set aside it justified detention; imprisonment pursuant to that order was not tortious. In the instant case the two prison governors had had no other option than to obey the warrant, *Olotu v. Secretary of State for the Home Department* [1997] 1 W.L.R. 328, [1997] C.L.Y. 1299 and *R. v. Governor of Brockhill Prison, ex p. Evans (No.2)* [2001] 2 A.C. 19, [2000] C.L.Y. 5113 applied, and (2) the Registrar in failing to put Q's papers before the full court had been acting "in connection with the execution of the judicial process" and was accordingly protected from litigation by virtue of s.2(5) of the Act, *Wood v. Lord Advocate* 1994 S.C.L.R 1034, [1995] C.L.Y. 6386 approved and *Welsh v. Chief Constable of Merseyside* [1993] 1 All E.R. 692, [1993] C.L.Y. 2943 considered. In the opinion of Clarke,

L.J., the word "execution" within s.2(5) meant something more than the execution of judgments and orders and referred to any act in connection with the implementation of the judicial process within the meaning of the sub section. He expressed doubt that Tudor-Evans, J. in *Welsh* had been correct in concluding that the language of the sub section was directed to judicial and not administrative functions.

QUINLAND v. GOVERNOR OF SWALESIDE PRISON; *sub nom.* QUINLAND v. GOVERNOR OF BELMARSH PRISON, [2002] EWCA Civ 174, [2003] Q.B. 306, Kennedy, L.J., CA.

4544. Joint tortfeasors–directors liabilities–copyright–procuring infringements pursuant to common design

Y appealed against a decision ([2000] E.M.L.R. 743) that he was personally liable, as joint tortfeasor, for infringements of copyright by C, a music company operating in the re-issue market. Y, who had been engaged in the music industry for a number of years, was an employee, and had previously been a director, of C. C released recordings taken from certain master recordings under a licence purportedly granted to it by R. In proceedings issued in California it was established that title in the recordings in question rested with M and not R. Proceedings were issued in the UK against C and Y, in which it was successfully alleged that Y was personally liable as joint tortfeasor with C for the infringements of M's copyright.

Held, dismissing the appeal, that a director or officer might be liable with the company as joint tortfeasor for acts committed by the company. Whether a director or officer was so liable was determined not by the fact of his being a director or officer but by considering whether his acts would have rendered him so liable if he were not a director or officer. For a director or officer of a company to be personally liable, as joint tortfeasor, for infringements of copyright by the company in circumstances in which he was not himself a person who had committed or participated directly in those acts, it was necessary and sufficient to find that he had procured or induced those acts to be done by the company or that, in some other way, he and the company had joined together in concerted action to secure that those acts were done, *CBS Songs Ltd v. Amstrad Consumer Electronics Plc* [1988] A.C. 1013, [1988] C.L.Y. 503, *Unilever Plc v. Gillette (UK) Ltd (Joinder)* [1989] R.P.C. 583, [1989] C.L.Y. 2805 and *PLG Research Ltd v. Ardon International Ltd* [1993] F.S.R 197, [1993] C.L.Y. 3041 applied. On the facts of the present case, Y was personally liable with C as a joint tortfeasor. Y had induced C to copy M's recordings and to issue copies to the public and furthermore he and C had joined together in concerted action to ensure that those unlawful acts were done.

MCA RECORDS INC v. CHARLY RECORDS LTD (NO.5), [2001] EWCA Civ 1441, [2002] B.C.C. 650, Chadwick, L.J., CA.

4545. Malicious prosecution–jury trial–presentation of bankruptcy petition not included in tort

[Supreme Court Act 1981 s.69.]

W had leased properties during the 1970s and 1980s but had not submitted tax returns for the rents received. In 1992 W was served with a statutory demand on the basis of two county court judgments and income tax assessments for the tax years 1983-84 and 1987-88. The Revenue obtained a bankruptcy order in 1993, but this was rescinded by consent in 1999. In November 1998, W brought a claim against the Revenue, on the basis that the bankruptcy proceedings had been negligently or maliciously brought. He subsequently applied for the case to be heard by a jury in the QBD. W also sought disclosure of the file of C, a third party, whom W alleged had been subjected to the same negligent or malicious treatment by the Revenue officers that had handled his own case.

Held, refusing the applications, that the provision for a jury trial under the Supreme Court Act 1981 s.69 was restricted only to malicious prosecution in criminal matters and did not include the tort of malicious presentation of a bankruptcy petition. The discretion to allow a jury trial under s.69(3) did not apply because W had not applied when commencing his action in 1998. No order for disclosure could be made as W had not adduced any evidence in support of his claims. Further, disclosure could not be used to attack the credit of the Revenue's witnesses, *Thorpe v. Chief Constable of Greater Manchester* [1989] 1 W.L.R. 665, [1989] C.L.Y. 2965 applied.

WOODWARD v. INLAND REVENUE COMMISSIONERS 73 T.C. 516, Jacob, J., Ch D.

4546. Misfeasance in public office–personal injury–death–victims having locus standi

A, the administrators of the estate of L, appealed against an order striking out a personal injury claim brought against the Secretary of State and the Metropolitan Police Commissioner. L had been murdered by D, a man with a record of violent crime in Jamaica. Shortly after entering the country using false papers D had been arrested and charged with drug and firearms offences. His true identity having been ascertained, a decision was made by the police and immigration authorities that he should be released on bail in order that he could act as a police informer. It was in the period following his release that D murdered L. All parties had agreed that the judge at first instance had erred in concluding that an action for misfeasance in public office resulting in death or personal injury could not lie because the risk created by D's release had been to the public at large rather than to L specifically. The issue raised was whether an action for misfeasance in public office was excluded where the victim had not been an identifiable individual or an identifiable group of individuals likely to be at risk from the harm contemplated.

Held, allowing the appeal, that where it was alleged that death or personal injury had occurred as a consequence of misfeasance in public office, it was not necessary that the victim be known prior to the expected harm happening, *Three Rivers DC v. Bank of England (No.3)* [2000] 2 W.L.R. 1220, [2000] C.L.Y. 270 considered. It was sufficient for the claimant to plead that harm had been contemplated to a known victim or to a victim or victims who would be unknown unless and until the harm was done. It had been predictable that D would kill someone in circumstances such had arisen in the present case.

AKENZUA v. SECRETARY OF STATE FOR THE HOME DEPARTMENT, [2002] EWCA Civ 1470, [2003] 1 W.L.R. 741, Sedley, L.J., CA.

4547. Misfeasance in public office–striking out–abuse of position as public officer–exploration of the facts

C appealed against the striking out of his claim against the local authority, H. C had been employed by H as an accountant. He had been dismissed for disclosing documents relating to frauds and other corrupt irregularities by a former senior employee of H to the chairman of the committee investigating those irregularities. Following his dismissal the chief executive had published letters stating that C was, inter alia, "unfit to hold a post requiring complete professional integrity". C brought a claim in misfeasance in public office against H. H contended that the claim should be struck out as the chief officer had not been exercising a power when he published the letters.

Held, allowing the appeal, that a claim of misfeasance in public office could be founded upon an allegation that the public officer had abused his position as a public officer, *Elliott v. Chief Constable of Wiltshire* Times, December 5, 1996, [1997] C.L.Y. 4867 applied. In the instant case, the question as to whether or not the chief executive and other members of H had abused their public office could only be answered by a full exploration of the facts and thus it had not been appropriate to strike out the claim.

CORNELIUS v. HACKNEY LBC, [2002] EWCA Civ 1073, *The Times*, August 27, 2002, Waller, L.J., CA.

4548. **Occupiers liability–foreseeability–personal injury sustained by falling against glass panel–compliance with building regulations in force at date of construction**

[Occupiers Liability Act 1957 s.2(2).]

M slipped while descending stairs in a block of flats owned by G, he then reached forward and his hand went through a glass door panel. M claimed damages against G for personal injury, contending that G was in breach of the Occupiers Liability Act 1957 s.2(2). It was accepted that the glass used complied with the building regulations in force at that time, but that it did not meet current safety regulations. M argued that G had failed to take reasonable care in the circumstances by failing to replace the glass. At first instance it was held that, although it was reasonably foreseeable that a person could lose their footing, it was not reasonably foreseeable that they would then be propelled forward into the glass pane. Further, that the accident was a remote and unlikely occurrence that G could not be expected to guard against. M appealed on the basis that the judge's reasoning was not logical in finding that an accident was foreseeable but this particular outcome was not.

Held, dismissing the appeal, that the judge was entitled to come to the view, as a matter of common sense, that M's accident was not foreseeable. Further, s.2(2) provided that the relevant standard of care was one that was reasonable in all the circumstances and it could not be said that G had breached that duty by failing to replace the original pane with one that complied with current regulations.

McGIVNEY v. GOLDERSLEA LTD (2001) 17 Const. L.J. 454, Swinton Thomas, L.J., CA.

4549. **Occupiers liability–independent contractors–occupier's duty to enquire into insurance position of independent contractor**

[Occupiers' Liability Act 1957 s.2(2).]

G appealed against a finding that W, a hospital, had owed her no duty in respect of which damages could be recovered for injuries which she had sustained while using a "splat wall" operated by C, who had been engaged by W to provide entertainment at a fair being held in W's grounds. At the time of G's accident, C's insurance had expired.

Held, dismissing the appeal (Sedley, L.J. dissenting as to whether a duty had been owed), that W had owed G a duty under the Occupiers' Liability Act 1957 s.2(2) to take such care as in all the circumstances was reasonable to see that she would be reasonably safe in using the premises to which she had been invited. To establish that it had discharged that duty, W had to show that it had employed an appropriate and competent independent contractor. In deciding whether the contractor was competent, W had to take into account the nature of the task that the contractor was required to perform. In the instant case, that entailed satisfying itself that C was sufficiently experienced and reliable to be entrusted with ensuring that members of the public would be reasonably safe when using the splat wall. The question whether C had insurance was relevant for the purpose of his competence. On the facts of the instant case, W had been under an obligation to enquire into C's insurance position so as to confirm his suitability to be entrusted with the operation of the splat wall. Since W had made such an enquiry, it had discharged its duty of care. W had not been under a duty to check the terms of C's insurance policy.

GWILLIAM v. WEST HERTFORDSHIRE HOSPITALS NHS TRUST; *sub nom.* GWILLIAM v. WEST HERTFORDSHIRE HOSPITAL NHS TRUST, [2002] EWCA Civ 1041, [2003] Q.B. 443, Lord Woolf of Barnes, L.C.J., CA.

4550. **Occupiers liability–signs–injuries resulting from slipping accident at bowling alley–adequacy of warning signs**

D sustained personal injuries at a bowling alley when she crossed the foul line, slipped and fell, fracturing her left humerus. The only warning sign, which measured

22cm by 15cm, was situated on the gutter of the alley and depicted a figure slipping with the words "Danger slippery surface. Do not proceed beyond foul line." D contended that she did not know the bowling alley was slippery and that the warning sign was inadequate.

Held, granting judgment in favour of D, that A had failed to discharge its common duty of care. The warning sign was present but inadequate due to the fact that it was not sufficiently prominent. Further, the positioning of the sign at the end of the alley did not afford any or any adequate opportunity for D to see the content of the sign in any event.

D v. AMF BOWLING, July 31, 2002, District Judge Peters, CC (Sheffield). [*Ex rel.* Dermot Hughes, Barrister, 26 Paradise Square, Sheffield].

4551. Occupiers liability–supermarkets–shopper injured slipping on produce

D brought a claim against A after she slipped on a cherry in A's produce department. D contended that A had been negligent in failing to place slip mats in the produce department and in failing to have an adequate system for maintaining a safe floor in that department. D accepted that the cherry was near the cherry display but had been dropped by a customer. A conceded that there had not been an anti slip mat in front of the cherry display, but gave evidence that cleaning had taken place every half hour and that employees were trained to deal with spillages on the floor.

Held, giving judgment for A, that there was a risk that cherries would fall to the floor and that such risk ought to have been guarded against. Although anti slip mats should have been placed in front of the cherry display, it was not necessary to place them in areas any further than the relevant display and that it was a question of assessing the extent of the risk. A's cleaning system was excellent and there had been only four accidents recorded that year despite the 1.3 million customers that had used the store. The cleaning system had not failed on the date of D's accident as the cherry had been on the floor for only a short time, the accident having happened only 10 minutes after the last clean in the department, *Ward v. Tesco Stores Ltd* [1976] 1 W.L.R. 810, [1976] C.L.Y. 1866 applied.

DOBSON v. ASDA STORES LTD, March 19, 2002, Recorder Lewis, CC (Middlesborough). [*Ex rel.* Eversheds Solicitors, Central Square South, Orchard Street, Newcastle upon Tyne].

4552. Occupiers liability–supermarkets–shopper injured tripping over post

H brought a claim against A after tripping over a freezer protector post while shopping in A's store. H contended that A was in breach of design, construction and maintenance requirements in relation to the posts, that they stood proud of the general line of cabinets that they protected and that they constituted a tripping hazard. A gave evidence that there had been only three similar incidents in the five year period prior to the index accident, that there was a total of some 1.4 million people using their store each year and that the posts were universally used in all its supermarkets. A maintained that the posts were required for the protection of the freezer units and to prevent potentially dangerous jagged edges being created on the freezers themselves.

Held, granting judgment for A, that the posts or bollards were substantial items which were plainly visible. They were not such a hazard as to amount to a breach of the common duty of care or negligence, and that the safety of those visiting A's premises had not been significantly compromised. It could not be said that they were not reasonably safe for those using the premises when taking into account the low number of incidents relating to the bollards compared to the number of customers using the store. Further, it was common practice to install such proprietary protection as the use of these bollards.

HEYS v. ASDA STORES LTD, May 13, 2002, Judge Armitage, CC (Oldham). [*Ex rel.* Eversheds Solicitors, Central Square South, Orchard Street, Newcastle upon Tyne].

4553. Occupiers liability—trespassers—lake in park—applicable standard of care

[Occupiers' Liability Act 1984 s.1.]

T, who had suffered paralysis as a result of a diving accident in a lake, appealed against the decision of a judge that the local authority, which owned and occupied the park containing the lake, had not been in breach of its duty under the Occupiers' Liability Act 1984 s.1. The local authority had posted notices prohibiting swimming in the lake but had been aware that the notices were ineffectual and that there was a history of accidents in the lake. T had been a trespasser because he had entered the water in breach of the prohibition. Shortly before the accident, the local authority had commenced works to deter people from swimming in the lake. T contended that (1) the judge had been wrong to identify the risk as the specific risk of injury from diving rather than the general risk of injury from entering the water, and (2) the local authority, as an occupier, had a duty of care to do what was practicable to prevent accidents, not only to warn of their occurrence.

Held, allowing the appeal (Longmore, L.J. dissenting), that the local authority had been in breach of the duty to take reasonable care. The risk of injury was the risk from entering the water, although this included diving. The local authority owed a duty of care to T, pursuant to s.1 (3) (c) of the Act, to provide some protection against the risk given the gravity of the risk of injury, the frequency of exposure to the risk, the failure of the warning signs, and the attraction of the lake to swimmers. That duty had not been discharged by the posting of ineffective notices. The standard of care required the carrying out of relatively inexpensive and simple deterrent works to the lake.

TOMLINSON v. CONGLETON BC, [2002] EWCA Civ 309, [2003] 2 W.L.R. 1120, Ward, L.J., CA.

4554. Trespass to the person—strip searches—retrospective application of legislation—infringement of right to privacy

[Human Rights Act 1998 s.3.]

The Secretary of State appealed against the decision to award basic and aggravated damages to MW and her son AW for the way in which they were strip searched by prison officers in 1997 after they were suspected of bringing drugs on a prison visit. The court had found that a tort of trespass to the person had been committed against them in the form of wilfully causing each of them to do something to themselves which infringed their right to privacy. It further found that the tort of trespass to the person had been committed against AW by wilfully causing him to do something calculated to cause him harm by infringing his legal right to personal safety. MW and AW submitted that the rule that the Human Rights Act 1998 could not be applied retrospectively to conduct complained of before the coming into force of the Act did not apply to s.3 of the Act, given that it was clear from s.3(1) that the judge had to comply with the Act even if the conduct complained of took place before the coming into force of the Act.

Held, allowing the appeal, that the 1998 Act could not change the rule at common law that there was no tort of invasion of privacy, by introducing a retrospective right to privacy. Furthermore, there had been no intended harm or recklessness in the prison officers' conduct, *Wilkinson v. Downton* [1897] 2 Q.B. 57 distinguished, and therefore the judge's decision could not be upheld.

SECRETARY OF STATE FOR THE HOME DEPARTMENT v. WAINWRIGHT; *sub nom.* WAINWRIGHT v. SECRETARY OF STATE FOR THE HOME DEPARTMENT; WAINWRIGHT v. HOME OFFICE, [2001] EWCA Civ 2081, [2002] Q.B. 1334, Lord Woolf of Barnes, L.C.J., CA.

4555. Vicarious liability—employees—assault by ticket inspector on passenger

F appealed against a finding that an assault committed on him by a ticket inspector, S, was not an act carried out during the course of S's employment for which, C, his employer, was vicariously liable. The judge had found that the task which C had authorised S to do consisted of checking tickets to protect C's revenue and preventing anyone without a ticket from proceeding, therefore his authorised duties were concluded just before the assault took place. It was submitted that the judge had erred in placing too narrow an emphasis on the concept of authorisation and what S was employed to do.

Held, allowing the appeal, that a broader approach was necessary to the question of authorisation and the altercation during which the assault occurred followed immediately from S carrying out the duties of his employment. It was artificial to say that the assault was divorced from what S was employed to do, which was to challenge whether F had a ticket, on behalf of his employer and the series of events comprised a single incident. There was nothing to suggest that S carried out the assault for his own purposes, *Daniels v. Whetstone Entertainments and Allender* [1962] 2 Lloyd's Rep. 1, [1962] C.L.Y. 1140 distinguished and *Vasey v. Surrey Free Inns Plc* [1996] P.I.Q.R. P373, [1995] C.L.Y. 3735 considered.

FENNELLY v. CONNEX SOUTH EASTERN LTD [2001] I.R.L.R. 390, Schiemann, L.J., CA.

4556. Books

Bermingham, Vera – Nutcases-tort. 3rd Ed. Nutcases. Paperback: £5.95. ISBN 0-421-76740-5. Sweet & Maxwell.

Cracknell, D.G. – Obligations. 150 Leading Cases. Paperback: £11.95. ISBN 1-85836-459-0. Old Bailey Press.

Dugdale, Anthony – Clerk & Lindsell on Torts: 1st Supplement. 18th Ed. Common Law Library. Paperback: £38.00. ISBN 0-421-76250-0. Sweet & Maxwell.

Dugdale, Anthony – Clerk & Lindsell on Torts: 2nd Supplement to the 18th Edition. Common Law Library. Paperback: £40.00. ISBN 0-421-79580-8. Sweet & Maxwell.

Exall, Gordon – Practice Notes on Personal Injury. 3rd Ed. Practice Notes. Paperback: £19.95. ISBN 1-85941-577-6. Cavendish Publishing Ltd.

Grubb, Andrew – Law of Tort. 2nd Ed. Butterworths Common Law. Hardback: £195.00. ISBN 0-406-89672-0. Butterworths Law.

Hedley, Steve – Butterworths Core Text: Tort. 3rd Ed. Butterworths Core Text. Paperback: £12.95. ISBN 0-406-95002-4. Butterworths Law.

Hodge, Sue – Tort Law. 2nd Ed. Paperback: £14.99. ISBN 1-903240-87-5. Willan Publishing.

Jervis, Nick; Dawson, Judy – Jervis & Dawson: a Practical Guide to Motor Accident Claims. Paperback: £65.00. ISBN 0-406-91780-9. Butterworths Law.

Jones, Michael – Textbook on Torts. 8th Ed. Textbook. Paperback: £19.99. ISBN 0-19-925533-4. Oxford University Press.

Krishnan, Vickneswaren – Obligations. Revision Workbook. Paperback: £9.95. ISBN 1-85836-354-3. Old Bailey Press.

McMahon, Bryan M.E.; Binchy, William – McMahon and Binchy: Casebook on Irish Law of Torts. 3rd Ed. Paperback: £39.66. ISBN 1-85475-203-0. Butterworths Law.

Rogers, W.V.H. – Winfield and Jolowicz on Tort. 16th Ed. Paperback: £30.00. ISBN 0-421-76850-9. Sweet & Maxwell.

Tiernan, Ralph – Nutshells-tort. 6th Ed. Nutshells. Paperback: £5.95. ISBN 0-421-76530-5. Sweet & Maxwell.

Tort Law. 3rd Ed. LawCards Series. Paperback: £6.00. ISBN 1-85941-718-3. Cavendish Publishing Ltd.

Weinrib, Ernest Joseph – Tort Law. International Library of Essays in Law and Legal Theory (second Series). Hardback: £100.00. ISBN 0-7546-2142-1. Hardback: £110.00. ISBN 0-7546-2142-1. Dartmouth.

TRANSPORT

4557. **Air transport–freedom of establishment–lawfulness of air services agreement between UK and US**

See EUROPEAN UNION: Commission of the European Communities v. United Kingdom (C466/98). §1572

4558. **Bus services–bus service operators–grants**

BUS SERVICE OPERATORS GRANT (ENGLAND) REGULATIONS 2002, SI 2002 1015; made under the Transport Act 2000 s.154. In force: May 1, 2002; £1.75.

These Regulations describe "eligible bus services" for the purposes of the Transport Act 2000 s.154. Under that section grants may be made to operators of eligible bus services towards their costs in operating the service. These Regulations re-enact the previous eligibility rules for fuel duty rebates under the Finance Act 1965 s.92 and extend eligibility to services provided by a range of non-profit making community transport bodies whose services do not follow a fixed route or timetable and are for use by particular categories of passengers, rather than the general public.

4559. **Bus services–bus service operators–grants–Wales**

BUS SERVICE OPERATORS GRANT (WALES) REGULATIONS 2002, SI 2002 2022; made under the Transport Act 2000 s.154. In force: August 14, 2002; £2.00.

These Regulations define "eligible bus services" for the purposes of the Transport Act 2000 s.154 under which grants may be made to operators of eligible bus services towards their costs in operating the service. These Regulations re-enact the eligibility rules for fuel duty rebates under the Finance Act 1965 s.92 but also extend eligibility to services provided by a range of non-profit making community transport bodies whose services do not follow a fixed route or timetable and are primarily for use by particular categories of passengers, rather than the general public.

4560. **Bus services–fares–travel concessions**

TRAVEL CONCESSIONS (ELIGIBLE SERVICES) ORDER 2002, SI 2002 1016; made under the Transport Act 1985 s.94; and the Transport Act 2000 s.146. In force: May 1, 2002; £1.50.

This Order prescribes bus services which are eligible for the purposes of the mandatory half fare travel concessions under the Transport Act 2000 and the provisions of the Transport Act 1985 Part IV relating to participation in travel concession schemes, and reimbursement arrangements.

4561. **Bus services–fares–travel concessions–Wales**

TRAVEL CONCESSIONS (ELIGIBLE SERVICES) (WALES) ORDER 2002, SI 2002 2023; made under the Transport Act 1985 s.94; and the Transport Act 2000 s.146. In force: August 14, 2002; £2.00.

This Order prescribes bus services which, when the Finance Act 1965 s.92 ceases to have effect as a result of the coming into force of the Transport Act 2000 s.154(6), are eligible for the purposes of the mandatory travel concessions under the Transport Act 2000 s.145 and the provisions of the Transport Act 1985 Part IV relating to participation in travel concession schemes, and reimbursement arrangements.

4562. Buses–community bus permit–fees

COMMUNITY BUS (AMENDMENT) REGULATIONS 2002, SI 2002 2537; made under the Public Passenger Vehicles Act 1981 s.52, s.60. In force: November 1, 2002; £1.50.

These Regulations, which amend the Community Bus Regulations 1986 (SI 1986 1245), increase the fee for a community bus permit granted under the Transport Act 1985 to £39.

4563. Buses–permits–fees

MINIBUS AND OTHER SECTION 19 PERMIT BUSES (AMENDMENT) REGULATIONS 2002, SI 2002 2534; made under the Public Passenger Vehicles Act 1981 s.52, s.60. In force: November 1, 2002; £1.50.

These Regulations, which amend the Minibus and Other Section 19 Permit Buses Regulations 1987 (SI 1987 1230), increase the fee for a permit granted under the Transport Act 1985 s.19 in respect of the use of a large bus to £15 and in respect of a small bus to £8.

4564. Carriage by road–dangerous goods–radioactive material

RADIOACTIVE MATERIAL (ROAD TRANSPORT) REGULATIONS 2002, SI 2002 1093; made under the Radioactive Material (Road Transport) Act 1991 s.2. In force: June 7, 2002; £9.50.

These Regulations, which revoke the Radioactive Material (Road Transport) (Great Britain) Regulations 1996 (SI 1996 1350), implement regulations made by the International Atomic Energy Agency in its safety standards series for the Safe Transport of Radioactive Material and additional requirements contained in the European Agreement concerning the international carriage of dangerous goods by road up to July 1, 2001. The Regulations also implement provisions of Council Directive 96/29 ([1996] OJ L159/1) laying down basic safety standards for the protection of the health of workers and the general public against the dangers arising from ionizing radiation and Commission Directive 2001/7 ([2001] OJ L30/43) adapting for the third time to technical progress Council Directive 94/55 ([1994] OJ L319/7) on transport of dangerous goods by road.

4565. Carriage by road–dangerous goods–radioactive material

RADIOACTIVE MATERIAL (ROAD TRANSPORT) (DEFINITION OF RADIOACTIVE MATERIAL) ORDER 2002, SI 2002 1092; made under the Radioactive Material (Road Transport) Act 1991 s.1. In force: June 7, 2002; £1.50.

The Radioactive Material (Road Transport) Act 1991 provides that "radioactive material" means any material having a specific activity in excess of 70 kilobecquerels per kilogram or such lesser specific activity as is specified in an Order. This Order specifies the level of activity at 0.1 kilobecquerels per kilogram, thus lowering it from 70 kilobecquerels per kilogram and widening the definition of "radioactive material" for the purposes of that Act.

4566. Carriage of goods–motor vehicles–type approval–fees

INTERNATIONAL TRANSPORT OF GOODS UNDER COVER OF TIR CARNETS (FEES) (AMENDMENT) REGULATIONS 2002, SI 2002 539; made under the Finance Act 1973 s.56. In force: April 1, 2002; £1.50.

These Regulations amend the International Transport of Goods under Cover of TIR Carnets (Fees) Regulations 1988 (SI 1988 371) which prescribe the fees payable in connection with the approval of a vehicle design-type and with the issue by the Secretary of State of a certificate of approval for a road vehicle following the inspection of the road vehicle in pursuance to the Customs Convention on the International Transport of Goods under Cover of TIR Carnets. The fee for an inspection of a vehicle design-type in connection with the grant of TIR design-type approval is increased to £72 where the inspection of a design-type which is a variation of a design-type for which a TIR design-type approval has been granted and to £446 in any other case. The fee for the issue of a TIR vehicle approval certificate for a vehicle which is a design-type for which TIR design-type approval has been granted is increased to £11 and the fee for the issue of a duplicate of such certificate is also increased to £11. The fee for an inspection of a vehicle in connection with the issue of a TIR vehicle approval certificate is increased to £48 where the inspection is carried out following refusal of such a certificate for the vehicle and to £72 in any other case.

4567. Driving licences–designation–Guernsey

DRIVING LICENCES (DESIGNATION OF RELEVANT EXTERNAL LAW) ORDER 2002, SI 2002 2590; made under the Road Traffic Act 1988 s.89. In force: November 1, 2002; £1.50.

This Order designates the law of Guernsey as one which makes satisfactory provision for the granting of licences to drive goods and passenger-carrying vehicles.

4568. Driving licences–exchangeable licences–Kenya–removal from list

DRIVING LICENCES (EXCHANGEABLE LICENCES) (AMENDMENT) ORDER 2002, SI 2002 1593; made under the Road Traffic Act 1988 s.108. In force: June 21, 2002; £1.50.

This Order amends the Driving Licences (Exchangeable Licences) Order 1984 (SI 1984 672) which designates various countries and territories as countries and territories who have satisfactory provision for the issue of driving licences. The Order, which also amends the Road Traffic Act 1988, removes Kenya from the list of countries and territories so designated. The holder of a Kenyan driving licence will therefore no longer be able to exchange that licence for a corresponding British one.

4569. Driving licences–exchangeable licences–Korea and Monaco

DRIVING LICENCES (EXCHANGEABLE LICENCES) ORDER 2002, SI 2002 2379; made under the Road Traffic Act 1988 s.108. In force: September 20, 2002; £1.75.

This Order designates the Republic of Korea and the Principality of Monaco under the Road Traffic Act 1988 s.108(2)(b) as making satisfactory provision for the issue of certain classes of driving licence thus enabling a person holding one of these licences to exchange it for a corresponding British licence. The licences affected are those authorising the driving of mopeds, motor cars and small goods vehicles up to 3.5 tonnes maximum authorised mass, tractors, pedestrian controlled vehicles and mowing machines.

4570. Heavy goods vehicles–carriage by road–community authorisations

GOODS VEHICLES (COMMUNITY AUTHORISATIONS) (MODIFICATION OF THE ROAD TRAFFIC (FOREIGN VEHICLES) ACT 1972) REGULATIONS 2002, SI 2002 1415; made under the European Communities Act 1972 s.2. In force: July 1, 2002; £1.50.

These Regulations amend the Road Traffic (Foreign Vehicles) Act 1972 in order to provide an express power to examiners to prohibit goods vehicles which do not conform with the requirements of the Goods Vehicles (Community Authorisations) Regulations 1992 (SI 1992 3077) which gave effect to Council Regulation 881/92 ([1992] OJ L95/1) on access to the market in the carriage of goods by road within the community.

4571. Heavy goods vehicles–licensing–fees

GOODS VEHICLES (LICENSING OF OPERATORS) (FEES) (AMENDMENT) REGULATIONS 2002, SI 2002 2778; made under the Goods Vehicles

(Licensing of Operators) Act 1995 s.45, s.57, s.58. In force: December 1, 2002; £1.50.

These Regulations amend the Goods Vehicles (Licensing of Operators) (Fees) Regulations 1995 (SI 1995 3000) to increase specified fees which have not been increased since the 1995 Regulations came into force on January 1, 1996.

4572. International carriage by road–dangerous goods–fees

INTERNATIONAL CARRIAGE OF DANGEROUS GOODS BY ROAD (FEES) (AMENDMENT) REGULATIONS 2002, SI 2002 537; made under the Finance Act 1973 s.56; and the Department of Transport (Fees) Order 1988. In force: April 1, 2002; £1.50.

These Regulations, which amend the International Carriage of Dangerous Goods by Road (Fees) Regulations 1988 (SI 1988 370), increase the fee payable where a first inspection in relation to an application for an ADR certificate is carried out on the same day as an examination under the Goods Vehicles (Plating and Testing) Regulations 1988 (SI 1988 370) from £66 to £68. The additional fee payable where a vehicle fails to pass an inspection and arrangements are made for a further inspection to be carried out not more than 14 days after the first inspection is increased to £34, and fees are also increased for the issue of a copy of an ADR certificate which has been lost or destroyed and for an application for an ADR certificate.

4573. London–service permits–appeals procedure

LONDON SERVICE PERMITS (APPEALS) REGULATIONS 2002, SI 2002 614; made under the Greater London Authority Act 1999 s.189. In force: April 1, 2002; £1.50.

The Greater London Authority Act 1999 prohibits any person from operating a London local service, where that service will not be part of the London bus network, unless they have been granted a London service permit by the Transport for London. Section 189 of the Act provides for an Appeal Panel to determine appeals brought by applicants for permits who have had their applications refused or granted subject to conditions or who have had a permit revoked or suspended. These Regulations prescribe the procedure for making an appeal.

4574. Motor vehicles–construction and use–emissions

ROAD VEHICLES (CONSTRUCTION AND USE) (AMENDMENT) REGULATIONS 2002, SI 2002 227; made under the Road Traffic Act 1988 s.41. In force: March 1, 2002; £1.50.

These Regulations amend the Road Vehicles (Construction and Use) Regulations 1986 (SI 1986 1078) in compliance with Commission Directive 2001/9 ([2001] OJ L48/18) in relation to in-service exhaust emissions tests. They delete the specification of 0.3 per cent for fast idling speeds and to allow the manufacturer to set the specification for the relevant vehicle.

4575. Motor vehicles–construction and use–emissions

ROAD VEHICLES (CONSTRUCTION AND USE) (AMENDMENT) (NO.2) REGULATIONS 2002, SI 2002 1474; made under the Road Traffic Act 1988 s.41. In force: Reg.4: August 1, 2002; remainder: July 1, 2002; £1.75.

These Regulations amend the Road Vehicles (Construction and Use) Regulations 1986 (SI 1986 1078) to add a reference to Commission Directive 2001/27 ([2001] OJ L107/10) adapting to technical progress Council Directive 88/77 ([1988] OJ L36/33) on the approximation of the laws of the Member States relating to measures to be taken against the emission of gaseous and particulate pollutants from compression-ignition engines for use in vehicles, and the emission of gaseous pollutants from positive-ignition engines fuelled with natural gas or liquefied petroleum gas for use in vehicles. They also amend the definition of "the emissions publication" so as to refer to the most recent edition of the publication entitled "In-Service Exhaust Emission Standards for Road Vehicles".

4576. Motor vehicles–construction and use–radio interference

ROAD VEHICLES (CONSTRUCTION AND USE) (AMENDMENT) (NO. 3) REGULATIONS 2002, SI 2002 2126; made under the Road Traffic Act 1988 s.41. In force: September 4, 2002; £1.75.

These Regulations amend the Road Vehicles (Construction and Use) Regulations 1986 (SI 1986 1078) in relation to the suppression of radio interference in compliance with Commission Directive 95/54 ([1995] OJ L266/1) adapting to technical progress Council Directive 72/245 relating to the suppression of radio interference produced by spark-ignition engines fitted to motor vehicles and amending Directive 70/156 relating to the type-approval of motor vehicles and their trailers.

4577. Motor vehicles–driving instruction–hazard perception tests

MOTOR CARS (DRIVING INSTRUCTION) (AMENDMENT) REGULATIONS 2002, SI 2002 2640; made under the Road Traffic Act 1988 s.125, s.132. In force: November 14, 2002; £1.75.

These Regulations amend the Motor Cars (Driving Instruction) Regulations 1989 (SI 1989 2057) by adding a new element to the test of driving ability and fitness; a requirement to take a test of hazard perception as part of the test of driving ability and fitness, this test to be taken and passed on the same day as the written examination and before the remaining elements of the driving ability and fitness test.

4578. Motor vehicles–driving tests–fees

MOTOR VEHICLES (DRIVING LICENCES) (AMENDMENT) REGULATIONS 2002, SI 2002 2641; made under the Road Traffic Act 1988 s.89, s.105. In force: November 14, 2002; £1.75.

These Regulations amend the Motor Vehicles (Driving Licences) Regulations 1999 (SI 1999 2864) by replacing the theory test currently taken by those wishing to obtain a driving licence with a two-part theory test. They increase the amount that may be charged by the Secretary of State to those applying to take the theory test to £18; increase the amount the Secretary of State may charge examiners not employed by the Driving Standards Agency for the supply of theory test pass certificates to £7.50; and increase the amount that the Secretary of State may charge examiners appointed by the Secretary of State for Defence for the supply of practical or unitary test pass certificates to £2.75.

4579. Motor vehicles–EC type approval

MOTOR VEHICLES (EC TYPE APPROVAL) (AMENDMENT) REGULATIONS 2002, SI 2002 1835; made under the European Communities Act 1972 s.2. In force: August 7, 2002; £1.75.

These Regulations amend the Motor Vehicles (EC Type Approval) Regulations 1998 (SI 1998 2051) by changing the definition of the Framework Directive to include Commission Directive 2001/116 ([2002] OJ L18/1) adapting to technical progress Council Directive 70/156 ([1970] OJ L42/174) on the approximation of the laws of the Member States relating to the type-approval of motor vehicles and their trailers which consolidates certain amendments to the Framework Directive. They also provide new annexes for use by manufacturers and approval authorities in applying for and granting type approvals.

4580. Motor vehicles—EC type approval

MOTOR VEHICLES (EC TYPE APPROVAL) (AMENDMENT) (NO.2) REGULATIONS 2002, SI 2002 2743; made under the European Communities Act 1972 s.2. In force: November 27, 2002; £1.50.

These Regulations amend the Motor Vehicles (EC Type Approval) Regulations 1998 (SI 1998 2051) by inserting a reference to Commission Directive 2002/78 ([2002] OJ L267/23) adapting to technical progress Council Directive 71/320 relating to the braking devices of certain categories of motor vehicles and their trailers.

4581. Motor vehicles—goods vehicles—plating and testing—fees

GOODS VEHICLES (PLATING AND TESTING) (AMENDMENT) REGULATIONS 2002, SI 2002 487; made under the Road Traffic Act 1988 s.49, s.51, s.53. In force: April 1, 2002; £1.75.

These Regulations, which amend the Goods Vehicles (Plating and Testing) Regulations 1988 (SI 1988 1478), amend the fees payable for first examinations, periodical tests or retests, alterations of plated weights and plating certificates.

4582. Motor vehicles—registration documents—replacement

ROAD VEHICLES (REGISTRATION AND LICENSING) (AMENDMENT) REGULATIONS 2002, SI 2002 2382; made under the Vehicle Excise and Registration Act 1994 s.22, s.22A, s.57. In force: in accordance with Reg.1 (2); £1.75.

These Regulations amend the Road Vehicles (Registration and Licensing) Regulations 1971 (SI 1971 450) in order to make examination of the vehicle or other evidence mandatory in specified circumstances before a replacement registration document is issued. The Regulations also make amendments to require the surrender or the destruction by an insurance company of the registration document on a change of ownership where there is substantial bodywork damage and either the owner's insurance does not cover that damage or the owner is an insurer.

4583. Motor vehicles—registration marks

ROAD VEHICLES (DISPLAY OF REGISTRATION MARKS) (AMENDMENT) REGULATIONS 2002, SI 2002 2687; made under the Vehicle Excise and Registration Act 1994 s.57. In force: November 22, 2002; £1.75.

These Regulations amend the Road Vehicles (Display of Registration Marks) Regulations 2001 (SI 2001 561) to prohibit the use of a number plate on which the background is patterned or textured, or gives that appearance and so that references to "relevant character height" do not apply in specified circumstances. They also make special provision in relation to the size and spacing of characters in the registration mark of certain imported vehicles.

4584. Motor vehicles—registration marks

ROAD VEHICLES (REGISTRATION AND LICENSING) REGULATIONS 2002, SI 2002 2742; made under the Vehicle Excise and Registration Act 1994 s.7, s.10, s.11, s.12, s.14, s.21, s.22, s.22A, s.23, s.25, s.33, s.52, s.57, s.59, s.61A, s.61B, s.62, Sch.1 para.1, Sch.1 para.3, Sch.1 para.5, Sch.2, para.2A, Sch.2 para.24. In force: Reg.15(3): April 7, 2003; Reg.20(4)(5): April 7, 2003; remainder: November 30, 2002; £6.50.

These Regulations, which amend the Vehicle and Driving Licence Records (Evidence) Regulations 1970 (SI 1970 1997), revoke the Road Vehicles (Registration and Licensing) Regulations 1971 (SI 1971 450), the Road Vehicles (Registration and Licensing) (Amendment) Regulations 1972 (SI 1972 1865), the Vehicle Licences Records (Evidence) Regulations (Northern Ireland) 1973 (SR & O 1973 352), the Road Vehicles (Registration and Licensing) Regulations (Northern Ireland) 1973 (SR & O 1973 490), the Road Vehicles (Registration and Licensing) (Amendment) Regulations 1973 (SI 1973 870), the Road Vehicles (Registration and Licensing) (Amendment) (No.2) Regulations 1975 (SI 1975 1342), Road Vehicles (Registration and Licensing) (Amendment) Regulations 1976 (SI 1976 1680), the Road Vehicles (Registration and Licensing) (Amendment) Regulations (Northern Ireland) 1976 (SI 1976 2088), the Road Vehicles (Registration and Licensing) (Amendment) (No.2) Regulations 1976 (SI 1976 2089), the Road Vehicles (Registration and Licensing) (Amendment) (No.2) Regulations (Northern Ireland) 1976 (SI 1976 2180), the Road Vehicles (Registration and Licensing) (Amendment) Regulations 1977 (SI 1977 230), the Road Vehicles (Registration and Licensing) (Amendment) Regulations (Northern Ireland) 1977 (SI 1977 231), the Road Vehicles (Registration and Licensing) (Amendment) Regulations 1978 (SI 1978 1536), the Road Vehicles (Registration and Licensing) (Amendment) Regulations (Northern Ireland) 1978 (SI 1978 1541), the Road Vehicles (Registration and Licensing) (Amendment) Regulations 1981 (SI 1981 366), the Road Vehicles (Registration and Licensing) (Amendment) Regulations (Northern Ireland) 1981 (SI 1981 367), the Road Vehicles (Excise) (Prescribed Particulars) Regulations 1981 (SI 1981 931), the Road Vehicles (Registration and Licensing) (Amendment) Regulations 1982 (SI 1982 1802), the Road Vehicles (Registration and Licensing) (Amendment) Regulations 1983 (SI 1983 1248), the Road Vehicles (Registration and Licensing) (Amendment) Regulations 1986 (SI 1986 607), the Road Vehicles (Registration and Licensing) (Amendment) Regulations (Northern Ireland) 1986 (SI 1986 706), the Road Vehicles (Registration and Licensing) (Amendment) (No.2) Regulations 1986 (SI 1986 1177), the Road Vehicles (Registration and Licensing) (Amendment) (No.2) Regulations (Northern Ireland) 1986 (SI 1986 1178), the Road Vehicles (Exemptions from Duty) Regulations 1986 (SI 1986 1467), the Road Vehicles (Excise) (Prescribed Particulars) (Amendment) Regulations 1986 (SI 1986 2100), the Road Vehicles (Registration and Licensing) (Amendment) (No.3) Regulations 1986 (SI 1986 2101), the Road Vehicles (Registration and Licensing) (Amendment) (No.3) Regulations (Northern Ireland) 1986 (SI 1986 2102), the Road Vehicles (Prescribed Regulations for the Purposes of Increased Penalties) Regulations 1987 (SI 1987 2085), the Road Vehicles (Prescribed Regulations for the Purposes of Increased Penalties) (Northern Ireland) Regulations 1987 (SI 1987 2086), the Road Vehicles (Excise) (Prescribed Particulars) (Amendment) Regulations 1987 (SI 1987 2122), the Road Vehicles (Registration and Licensing) (Amendment) Regulations 1987 (SI 1987 2123), the Road Vehicles (Registration and Licensing) (Amendment) Regulations (Northern Ireland) 1987 (SI 1987 2124), the Road Vehicles (Excise) (Prescribed Particulars) (Amendment) Regulations 1988 (SI 1988 847), the Road Vehicles (Registration and Licensing) (Amendment) Regulations (Northern Ireland) 1988 (SI 1988 1130), the Recovery Vehicles (Prescribed Purposes) Regulations 1989 (SI 1989 1376), the Recovery Vehicles (Prescribed Purposes) Regulations (Northern Ireland) 1989 (SI 1989 1377), the Road Vehicles (Registration and Licensing) (Amendment) Regulations 1990 (SI 1990 2185), the Road Vehicles (Registration and Licensing) (Amendment) Regulations (Northern Ireland) 1990 (SI 1990 2186), the Road Vehicles (Registration and Licensing) (Amendment) Regulations (Northern Ireland) 1993 (SI 1993 1759), the Road Vehicles (Registration and Licensing) (Amendment) Regulations 1993 (SI 1993 1760), the Road Vehicles (Registration and Licensing) (Amendment) Regulations 1994 (SI 1994 1364), the Road Vehicles (Registration and Licensing) (Amendment) (No.2) Regulations 1994 (SI 1994 1911), the Road Vehicles (Registration and Licensing) (Amendment) Regulations (Northern Ireland) 1994 (SI 1994 2735), the Road Vehicles (Registration and Licensing) (Amendment) (No.3) Regulations 1994 (SI 1994 3296), the Road Vehicles (Registration and Licensing) (Amendment) (No.2) Regulations (Northern Ireland) 1994 (SI 1994 3297), the Road Vehicles (Registration and Licensing) (Amendment) Regulations 1995 (SI 1995 1470), the Road Vehicles (Registration and Licensing) (Amendment) Regulations (Northern Ireland) 1995 (SI 1995 1471), the Vehicle Registration (Sale of Information) Regulations 1996 (SI 1996 2800), the Road Vehicles (Registration and Licensing) (Amendment) Regulations 1997 (SI 1997 401), the Road Vehicles (Statutory Off-Road

Notification) Regulations 1997 (SI 1997 3025), the Road Vehicles Registration Fee Regulations 1998 (SI 1998 572), the Road Vehicles Registration Fee (Amendment) Regulations 1998 (SI 1998 995), the Vehicle Excise Duty (Reduced Pollution) Regulations 1998 (SI 1998 3094), the Road Vehicles (Statutory Off-Road Notification) (Amendment) Regulations 1999 (SI 1999 713), the Road Vehicles (Registration and Licensing) (Amendment) Regulations (Northern Ireland) 2000 (SI 2000 1369), the Vehicle Excise Duty (Reduced Pollution) (Amendment) Regulations 2000 (SI 2000 3274), the Road Vehicles (Registration and Licensing) (Amendment) Regulations (Northern Ireland) 2002 (SI 2002 2381) and the Road Vehicles (Registration and Licensing) (Amendment) Regulations 2002 (SI 2002 2382). They make amendments so as to provide a single set of Regulations for the whole of the UK.

4585. Motor vehicles–roadworthiness–disclosure of information

ROAD VEHICLES (TESTING) (DISCLOSURE OF INFORMATION) (GREAT BRITAIN) REGULATIONS 2002, SI 2002 2426; made under the European Communities Act 1972 s.2. In force: October 15, 2002; £1.50.

These Regulations complete the transposition in Great Britain of Council Directive 2000/30 ([2000] OJ L203/1) on the technical roadside inspection of the roadworthiness of commercial vehicles circulating in the Community, allowing the Secretary of State as competent authority in Great Britain to give information obtained in the course of testing and inspecting commercial vehicles for their roadworthiness to be passed to the competent authorities in other Member States and in Northern Ireland and Gibraltar.

4586. Motor vehicles–testing–fees

MOTOR VEHICLES (TESTS) (AMENDMENT) REGULATIONS 2002, SI 2002 488; made under the Road Traffic Act 1988 s.45, s.46. In force: April 1, 2002; £2.00.

These Regulations amend the Motor Vehicles (Tests) Regulations 1981 (SI 1981 1694) to make provision for certain motor vehicles to be examined by persons authorised by the Secretary of State, for test certificates to be issued for vehicles found to meet certain requirements and amend the fees for examinations.

4587. Motor vehicles–testing–fees

MOTOR VEHICLES (TESTS) (AMENDMENT) (NO.2) REGULATIONS 2002, SI 2002 1698; made under the Road Traffic Act 1988 s.45, s.46. In force: August 1, 2002; £1.75.

These Regulations amend the Motor Vehicles (Tests) Regulations 1981 (SI 1981 1694), which make provision for certain motor vehicles to be examined by persons authorised by the Secretary of State and for test certificates to be issued for vehicles found to meet certain requirements, by prescribing the fees payable for examinations of vehicles. They also increase the fees payable for specified test examinations of vehicles.

4588. Parking–disabled persons–fines–power of parking adjudicator to consider mitigating circumstances

[Road Traffic Act 1991 Sch.6 para.2 (4) (f).]

A local authority sought judicial review of a decision by a parking adjudicator that no penalties could be imposed on W in respect of 11 parking fine notices issued against him. As a result of his disabilities W could walk no more than a limited distance and then only with the aid of crutches. On the occasions when the tickets had been issued he had been aware that W had parked where he was not supposed to, but no disabled parking spaces had been available. W contended that by virtue of the words "the amount applicable in the circumstances of the case", found in the Road Traffic Act 1991 Sch.6 para.2 (4) (f), the adjudicator had been required to have regard to all mitigating circumstances in determining the amount payable.

Held, granting the application for judicial review, that the parking adjudicator had possessed no power to take mitigating circumstances into account when determining the amount of any payment payable by a person adjudged to be in contravention of parking regulations. The phrase "the amount applicable in the circumstances of the case" referred to the amount of the penalty specified by law as the appropriate penalty for the offence under review. It had been the local authority and not the adjudicator who possessed the power to decide whether or not the penalties should have been waived in the light of extenuating circumstances. All the adjudicator had been empowered to do was to ensure that the penalty imposed had been the correct one.

R. (ON THE APPLICATION OF WESTMINSTER CITY COUNCIL) v. PARKING ADJUDICATOR, [2002] EWHC 1007, [2003] R.T.R. 1, Elias, J., QBD (Admin Ct).

4589. Parking–special parking areas–Basingstoke and Deane

ROAD TRAFFIC (PERMITTED PARKING AREA AND SPECIAL PARKING AREA) (COUNTY OF HAMPSHIRE) (BOROUGH OF BASINGSTOKE AND DEANE) ORDER 2002, SI 2002 2187; made under the Road Traffic Act 1991 Sch.3 para.1, para.2, para.3. In force: October 1, 2002; £2.00.

This Order, which amends the Road Traffic Regulation Act 1984 and the Road Traffic Act 1991, designates the Borough of Basingstoke and Deane, excluding specified roads, as both a permitted parking area and a special parking area.

4590. Parking–special parking areas–Brentwood

ROAD TRAFFIC (PERMITTED PARKING AREA AND SPECIAL PARKING AREA) (COUNTY OF ESSEX) (BOROUGH OF BRENTWOOD) ORDER 2002, SI 2002 2183; made under the Road Traffic Act 1991 Sch.3 para.1, para.2, para.3. In force: October 1, 2002; £2.00.

This Order, which amends the Road Traffic Regulation Act 1984 and the Road Traffic Act 1991, designates the Borough of Brentwood, excluding specified roads, as both a permitted parking area and a special parking area.

4591. Parking–special parking areas–Brentwood

ROAD TRAFFIC (PERMITTED PARKING AREA AND SPECIAL PARKING AREA) (COUNTY OF ESSEX) (BOROUGH OF BRENTWOOD) (AMENDMENT) ORDER 2002, SI 2002 2440; made under the Road Traffic Act 1991 Sch.3 para.1, para.2, para.3. In force: September 30, 2002; £1.50.

This Order amends the Road Traffic (Permitted Parking Area and Special Parking Area) (County of Essex) (Borough of Brentwood) Order 2002 (SI 2002 2183) for the purpose of changing the area to which that Order applies. It substitutes for the words "the Borough of Chelmsford" the words "the Borough of Brentwood".

4592. Parking–special parking areas–Bury

ROAD TRAFFIC (PERMITTED PARKING AREA AND SPECIAL PARKING AREA) (METROPOLITAN BOROUGH OF BURY) ORDER 2002, SI 2002 2188; made under the Road Traffic Act 1991 Sch.3 para.1, para.2, para.3. In force: October 14, 2002; £2.00.

This Order, which amends the Road Traffic Regulation Act 1984 and the Road Traffic Act 1991, designates the Borough of Bury, excluding specified roads, as both a permitted parking area and a special parking area.

4593. Parking–special parking areas–Chelmsford

ROAD TRAFFIC (PERMITTED PARKING AREA AND SPECIAL PARKING AREA) (COUNTY OF ESSEX) (BOROUGH OF CHELMSFORD) ORDER 2002, SI 2002

2184; made under the Road Traffic Act 1991 Sch.3 para.1, para.2, para.3. In force: October 1, 2002; £2.00.

This Order, which amends the Road Traffic Regulation Act 1984 and the Road Traffic Act 1991, designates the Borough of Chelmsford, excluding specified roads, as both a permitted parking area and a special parking area.

4594. Parking–special parking areas–Colchester

ROAD TRAFFIC (PERMITTED PARKING AREA AND SPECIAL PARKING AREA) (COUNTY OF ESSEX) (BOROUGH OF COLCHESTER) ORDER 2002, SI 2002 2186; made under the Road Traffic Act 1991 Sch.3 para.1, para.2, para.3. In force: October 1, 2002; £2.00.

This Order, which amends the Road Traffic Regulation Act 1984 and the Road Traffic Act 1991, designates the Borough of Colchester, excluding specified roads, as both a permitted parking area and a special parking area.

4595. Parking–special parking areas–East Dorset

ROAD TRAFFIC (PERMITTED PARKING AREA AND SPECIAL PARKING AREA) (COUNTY OF DORSET) (DISTRICT OF EAST DORSET) ORDER 2002, SI 2002 1485; made under the Road Traffic Act 1991 Sch.3 para.1, para.2, para.3. In force: July 1, 2002; £2.00.

This Order amends the Road Traffic Regulation Act 1984 and the Road Traffic Act 1991 to designate specific roads to be used for permitted parking areas and as special parking areas.

4596. Parking–special parking areas–Eden

ROAD TRAFFIC (PERMITTED PARKING AREA AND SPECIAL PARKING AREA) (COUNTY OF CUMBRIA) (DISTRICT OF EDEN) ORDER 2002, SI 2002 2520; made under the Road Traffic Act 1991 Sch.3 para.1, para.2, para.3. In force: January 20, 2003; £2.00.

This Order, which amends the Road Traffic Regulation Act 1984 and the Road Traffic Act 1991, designates the district of Eden, excluding the M6 motorway and the A66 trunk road for the whole of their lengths in the district, as both a permitted parking area and a special parking area.

4597. Parking–special parking areas–Epping Forest

ROAD TRAFFIC (PERMITTED PARKING AREA AND SPECIAL PARKING AREA) (COUNTY OF ESSEX) (DISTRICT OF EPPING FOREST) ORDER 2002, SI 2002 2185; made under the Road Traffic Act 1991 Sch.3 para.1, para.2, para.3. In force: October 1, 2002; £2.00.

This Order, which amends the Road Traffic Regulation Act 1984 and the Road Traffic Act 1991, designates the District of Epping Forest, excluding specified roads, as both a permitted parking area and a special parking area.

4598. Parking–special parking areas–Harrogate

ROAD TRAFFIC (PERMITTED PARKING AREA AND SPECIAL PARKING AREA) (COUNTY OF NORTH YORKSHIRE) (BOROUGH OF HARROGATE) ORDER 2002, SI 2002 1621; made under the Road Traffic Act 1991 Sch.3 para.1, para.2, para.3. In force: July 15, 2002; £2.00.

This Order, which amends the Road Traffic Regulation Act 1984 and the Road Traffic Act 1991, designates the borough of Harrogate, excluding specified roads as both a permitted parking area and a special parking area.

4599. Parking–special parking areas–Hart

ROAD TRAFFIC (PERMITTED PARKING AREA AND SPECIAL PARKING AREA) (COUNTY OF HAMPSHIRE) (DISTRICT OF HART) ORDER 2002, SI 2002 1351;

made under the Road Traffic Act 1991 Sch.3 para.1, para.2, para.3. In force: June 5, 2002; £2.00.

This Order modifies the Road Traffic Regulation Act 1984 and the Road Traffic Act 1991 to designate specific roads to be used for permitted parking areas and as special parking areas.

4600. Parking–special parking areas–Liverpool

ROAD TRAFFIC (PERMITTED PARKING AREA AND SPECIAL PARKING AREA) (CITY OF LIVERPOOL) ORDER 2002, SI 2002 1353; made under the Road Traffic Act 1991 Sch.3 para.1, para.2, para.3. In force: July 1, 2002; £2.00.

This Order modifies the Road Traffic Regulation Act 1984 and the Road Traffic Act 1991 to designate specific roads to be used for permitted parking areas and as special parking areas.

4601. Parking–special parking areas–Milton Keynes

ROAD TRAFFIC (PERMITTED PARKING AREA AND SPECIAL PARKING AREA) (BOROUGH OF MILTON KEYNES) ORDER 2002, SI 2002 421; made under the Road Traffic Act 1991 Sch.3 para.1, para.2, para.3. In force: March 25, 2002; £2.00.

This Order modifies the Road Traffic Regulation Act 1984 and the Road Traffic Act 1991 to designate specific roads to be used for permitted parking areas and as special parking areas.

4602. Parking–special parking areas–North Dorset

ROAD TRAFFIC (PERMITTED PARKING AREA AND SPECIAL PARKING AREA) (COUNTY OF DORSET) (DISTRICT OF NORTH DORSET) ORDER 2002, SI 2002 1504; made under the Road Traffic Act 1991 Sch.3 para.1, para.2, para.3. In force: July 1, 2002; £2.00.

This Order amends the Road Traffic Regulation Act 1984 and the Road Traffic Act 1991 to designate specific roads to be used for permitted parking areas and as special parking areas.

4603. Parking–special parking areas–Norwich

ROAD TRAFFIC (PERMITTED PARKING AREA AND SPECIAL PARKING AREA) (COUNTY OF NORFOLK) (CITY OF NORWICH) ORDER 2002, SI 2002 37; made under the Road Traffic Act 1991 Sch.3 para.1, para.2, para.3. In force: February 4, 2002; £2.00.

This Order, which amends the Road Traffic Regulation Act 1984 and the Road Traffic Act 1991, designates the City of Norwich as both a permitted parking area and a special parking area.

4604. Parking–special parking areas–Nottingham

ROAD TRAFFIC (PERMITTED PARKING AREA AND SPECIAL PARKING AREA) (CITY OF NOTTINGHAM) ORDER 2002, SI 2002 2012; made under the Road Traffic Act 1991 Sch.3 para.1, para.2, para.3. In force: October 1, 2002; £2.00.

This Order, which amends the Road Traffic Regulation Act 1984 and the Road Traffic Act 1991, designates the City of Nottingham, with the exception of the MI motorway for the whole of its length in the City, as both a permitted parking area and a special parking area.

4605. Parking—special parking areas—Poole

ROAD TRAFFIC (PERMITTED PARKING AREA AND SPECIAL PARKING AREA) (BOROUGH OF POOLE) ORDER 2002, SI 2002 422; made under the Road Traffic Act 1991 Sch.3 para.1, para.2, para.3. In force: April 2, 2002; £2.00.

This Order modifies the Road Traffic Regulation Act 1984 and the Road Traffic Act 1991 to designate specific roads to be used for permitted parking areas and as special parking areas.

4606. Parking—special parking areas—Purbeck

ROAD TRAFFIC (PERMITTED PARKING AREA AND SPECIAL PARKING AREA) (COUNTY OF DORSET) (DISTRICT OF PURBECK) ORDER 2002, SI 2002 1484; made under the Road Traffic Act 1991 Sch.3 para.1, para.2, para.3. In force: July 1, 2002; £2.00.

This Order, which amends the Road Traffic Regulation Act 1984 and the Road Traffic Act 1991, designates the district of Purbeck, excluding certain roads and parking places, as both a permitted parking area and a special parking area.

4607. Parking—special parking areas—Rushmoor

ROAD TRAFFIC (PERMITTED PARKING AREA AND SPECIAL PARKING AREA) (COUNTY OF HAMPSHIRE) (BOROUGH OF RUSHMOOR) ORDER 2002, SI 2002 1352; made under the Road Traffic Act 1991 Sch.3 para.1, para.2, para.3. In force: June 5, 2002; £2.00.

This Order modifies the Road Traffic Regulation Act 1984 and the Road Traffic Act 1991 to designate specific roads to be used for permitted parking areas and as special parking areas.

4608. Parking—special parking areas—South Lakeland

ROAD TRAFFIC (PERMITTED PARKING AREA AND SPECIAL PARKING AREA) (COUNTY OF CUMBRIA) (DISTRICT OF SOUTH LAKELAND) ORDER 2002, SI 2002 276; made under the Road Traffic Act 1991 Sch.3 para.1, para.2, para.3. In force: March 4, 2002; £2.00.

This Order modifies the Road Traffic Regulation Act 1984 and the Road Traffic Act 1991 to designate specific roads to be used for permitted parking area and as special parking area.

4609. Parking—special parking areas—Southampton

ROAD TRAFFIC (PERMITTED PARKING AREA AND SPECIAL PARKING AREA) (CITY OF SOUTHAMPTON) ORDER 2002, SI 2002 126; made under the Road Traffic Act 1991 Sch.3 para.1, para.2, para.3. In force: February 25, 2002; £2.00.

This Order, which amends the Road Traffic Regulation Act 1984 and the Road Traffic Act 1991, designates the City of Southampton, excluding the M27 motorway and the M271 motorway, together with all its on and off slip roads, from its junction with the Redbridge Roundabout for the whole of its entire length in the City of Southampton, as both a permitted parking area and a special parking area.

4610. Parking—special parking areas—Sunderland

ROAD TRAFFIC (PERMITTED PARKING AREA AND SPECIAL PARKING AREA) (CITY OF SUNDERLAND) ORDER 2002, SI 2002 3266; made under the Road Traffic Act 1991 Sch.3 para.1, Sch.3 para.2, Sch.3 para.3. In force: February 3, 2003; £2.00.

This Order which amends the Road Traffic Regulation Act 1984 and the Road Traffic Act 1991, designates the City of Sunderland, with specified exceptions, as both a permitted parking area and a special parking area in accordance with the Road Traffic Act 1991 Sch.3.

4611. Parking—special parking areas—West Dorset

ROAD TRAFFIC (PERMITTED PARKING AREA AND SPECIAL PARKING AREA) (COUNTY OF DORSET) (DISTRICT OF WEST DORSET) ORDER 2002, SI 2002 1486; made under the Road Traffic Act 1991 Sch.3 para.1, para.2, para.3. In force: July 1, 2002; £2.00.

This Order amends the Road Traffic Regulation Act 1984 and the Road Traffic Act 1991 to designate specific roads to be used for permitted parking areas and as special parking areas.

4612. Parking—special parking areas—Weymouth and Portland

ROAD TRAFFIC (PERMITTED PARKING AREA AND SPECIAL PARKING AREA) (COUNTY OF DORSET) (BOROUGH OF WEYMOUTH AND PORTLAND) ORDER 2002, SI 2002 2705; made under the Road Traffic Act 1991 Sch.3 para.1, para.2, para.3. In force: November 25, 2002; £2.00.

This Order, which amends the Road Traffic Regulation Act 1984 and the Road Traffic Act 1991, designates the Borough of Weymouth and Portland as both a permitted parking area and a special parking area.

4613. Parking—special parking areas—Worcester

ROAD TRAFFIC (PERMITTED PARKING AREA AND SPECIAL PARKING AREA) (COUNTY OF WORCESTERSHIRE) (CITY OF WORCESTER) ORDER 2002, SI 2002 3265; made under the Road Traffic Act 1991 Sch.3 para.1, Sch.3 para.2, Sch.3 para.3. In force: February 3, 2003; £2.00.

This Order, which amends the Road Traffic Regulation Act 1984 and the Road Traffic Act 1991, designates the City of Worcester as a permitted parking area and as a special parking area in accordance with the Road Traffic Act 1991 Sch.3.

4614. Passenger vehicles—accessibility requirements—disabled persons

PUBLIC SERVICE VEHICLES ACCESSIBILITY (AMENDMENT) REGULATIONS 2002, SI 2002 2981; made under the Disability Discrimination Act 1995 s.40, s.67. In force: December 31, 2002; £1.50.

These Regulations amend the Public Service Vehicles Accessibility Regulations 2000 (SI 2000 1970) to put back the date on which specified requirements come into effect. They also increase the angle of slope of a fitted wheelchair ramp to a maximum of 8 degrees.

4615. Passenger vehicles—accessibility requirements—disabled persons

PUBLIC SERVICE VEHICLES (CONDITIONS OF FITNESS, EQUIPMENT, USE AND CERTIFICATION) (AMENDMENT) REGULATIONS 2002, SI 2002 335; made under the Public Passenger Vehicles Act 1981 s.6, s.10, s.60; and the Road Traffic Act 1988 s.41. In force: March 18, 2002; £2.50.

These Regulations amend the Public Service Vehicles (Conditions of Fitness, Equipment, Use and Certification) Regulations 1981 (SI 1981 257) which imposed new accessibility requirements for disabled persons to single-deck and double-deck buses and coaches, and partly in order to apply certain provisions to all public service vehicles on account of the fact that on a voluntary basis more vehicles are being made accessible to disabled persons. The amendments are made to update certain provisions and to provide certain alternative provisions in line with the Public Service Vehicles Accessibility Regulations 2000 (SI 2000 1970) so as to provide for consistency between the requirements under the 1981 Regulations and the provisions that now apply to and regulate new public service vehicles under the 2000 Regulations.

4616. Passenger vehicles–accessibility requirements–disabled persons–conduct of drivers and conductors

PUBLIC SERVICE VEHICLES (CONDUCT OF DRIVERS, INSPECTORS, CONDUCTORS AND PASSENGERS) (AMENDMENT) REGULATIONS 2002, SI 2002 1724; made under the Public Passenger Vehicles Act 1981 s.24, s.25, s.60. In force: October 1, 2002; £2.00.

These Regulations, which amend the Public Service Vehicles (Conduct of Drivers, Inspectors, Conductors and Passengers) Regulations 1990 (SI 1990 1020), are consequent upon the introduction by the Public Service Vehicles Accessibility Regulations 2000 (SI 2000 1970) of accessibility requirements for disabled persons to single-deck and double-deck buses and coaches. The Regulations make provisions setting out additional duties for drivers and conductors with respect to passengers who are disabled, add new duties towards wheelchair users of regulated public service vehicles required to comply with the wheelchair accessibility requirements and add new duties towards disabled persons using regulated public service vehicles required to comply with the general accessibility requirements for single-deck and double-deck buses and single-deck and double-deck coaches. The Regulations also contain provisions relating to duties in the deployment of boarding lifts and ramps and, when it is requested, in the providing of assistance to wheelchair users and other disabled persons to board or to alight.

4617. Passenger vehicles–buses–guided busway–Chester

CHESTER GUIDED BUSWAY ORDER 2002, SI 2002 412; made under the Transport and Works Act 1992 s.1, s.5, Sch.1 para.1, Sch.1 para.2, Sch.1 para.3, Sch.1 para.4, Sch.1 para.5, Sch.1 para.7, Sch.1 para.8, Sch.1 para.9, Sch.1 para.10, Sch.10 para.11, Sch.1 para.12, Sch.1 para.13, Sch.1 para.15, Sch.1 para.16, Sch.1 para.17. In force: March 14, 2002; £6.50.

This Order, which amends the Compulsory Purchase Act 1965 and the Land Compensation Act 1973, authorises Cheshire County Council to construct, operate and maintain a guided busway, mainly along part of the former Mickle Trafford to Shotton railway between a site at Hoole, Chester, adjacent to the junction of the M53 and the A55 and the A56, and Northgate Avenue Chester. For this purpose the Order also authorises the Council compulsorily or by agreement to acquire land and rights in land.

4618. Passenger vehicles–goods vehicles–tachographs–fees

PASSENGER AND GOODS VEHICLES (RECORDING EQUIPMENT) (APPROVAL OF FITTERS AND WORKSHOPS) (FEES) (AMENDMENT) REGULATIONS 2002, SI 2002 538; made under the Finance Act 1973 s.56. In force: April 1, 2002; £1.50.

These Regulations amend the Passenger and Goods Vehicles (Recording Equipment) (Approval of Fitters and Workshops) (Fees) Regulations 1986 (SI 1986 2128) so as to increase the fees for the approval of fitters or workshops for the installation or repair of recording equipment. The fee for the issue of an approval is increased to £259 and for the renewal of an approval to £105.

4619. Passenger vehicles–local services–compulsory registration

PUBLIC SERVICE VEHICLES (REGISTRATION OF LOCAL SERVICES) (AMENDMENT) (ENGLAND AND WALES) REGULATIONS 2002, SI 2002 182; made under the Transport Act 1985 s.6. In force: March 1, 2002; £1.50.

These Regulations further amend the Public Service Vehicles (Registration of Local Services) Regulations 1986 (SI 1986 1671) in respect of England and Wales. The Regulations replace the 42 day period of notice, as prescribed by Reg.5 of the 1986 Regulations for registering or applying to vary or cancel a registration of a local service, with a period of notice of 56 days. The Regulations further revoke Reg.9(2)(c) of the 1986 Regulations, which permitted a registered service to be varied to a time either 5 minutes earlier or 5 minutes later than the registered time without the need to vary the prescribed particulars of the service.

4620. Passenger vehicles–local services–compulsory registration–fees

PUBLIC SERVICE VEHICLES (REGISTRATION OF LOCAL SERVICES) (AMENDMENT) (NO.2) (ENGLAND AND WALES) REGULATIONS 2002, SI 2002 2536; made under the Public Passenger Vehicles Act 1981 s.52, s.60. In force: November 1, 2002; £1.50.

These Regulations, which amend the Public Service Vehicles (Registration of Local Services) Regulations 1986 (SI 1986 1671), increase the fee for the registration of, or the variation of the registration of, a local bus service other than a community bus service to £40.

4621. Passenger vehicles–roadworthiness–fees

PUBLIC SERVICE VEHICLES (CONDITIONS OF FITNESS, EQUIPMENT, USE AND CERTIFICATION) (AMENDMENT) REGULATIONS 2002, SI 2002 489; made under the Public Passenger Vehicles Act 1981 s.10, s.52, s.60. In force: April 1, 2002; £1.50.

These Regulations, which amend the Public Service Vehicles (Conditions of Fitness, Equipment, Use and Certification) Regulations 1981 (SI 1981 257), increase the fee payable for a certificate of initial fitness from £169 to £174 in respect of a public service vehicle which, when equipped with seat belts, is not of a type of vehicle in respect of which the Secretary of State is satisfied that the vehicle manufacturer holds certain approvals relating to seat belt anchorage points. The fee payable for a certificate of initial fitness is increased from £135 to £139 on the first application in any other case and from £135 to £139 on any subsequent application when the test which that application will require includes a test of stability. Fees payable for type approvals are also increased.

4622. Private Hire Vehicles (Carriage of Guide Dogs etc.) Act 2002 (37)

This Act makes provision for the carriage of disabled persons accompanied by guide dogs, hearing dogs or other assistance dogs by drivers and operators of private hire vehicles.

This Act received Royal Assent on November 7, 2002.

4623. Public transport–operators licences–fees

PUBLIC SERVICE VEHICLES (OPERATORS' LICENCES) (FEES) (AMENDMENT) REGULATIONS 2002, SI 2002 2535; made under the Public Passenger Vehicles Act 1981 s.52, s.60. In force: November 1, 2002; £2.00.

These Regulations amend the Public Service Vehicles (Operators' Licences) (Fees) Regulations 1995 (SI 1995 2909) to increase specified fees. They also contain transitional provisions in respect of fees for the grant and continuation in force of standard and restricted operators' licences, and make minor changes to the provisions about vehicle discs issued for a period of one year or less under the Public Service Vehicles (Operators' Licences) Regulations 1995 (SI 1995 2908).

4624. Rail network–Merseyrail Electrics–passenger services

MERSEYRAIL ELECTRICS NETWORK ORDER 2002, SI 2002 1946; made under the Railways Act 1993 s.24, s.49, s.151. In force: July 20, 2003; £1.75.

This Order relating to the Merseyrail Electrics railway network exempts railway passenger services provided exclusively on the network from the requirement of the Railways Act 1993 s.23 to be subject to franchise agreements and disapplies in relation to the Network 1993 Act s.37 which regulates the discontinuance of non-franchised and other railway passenger services; s.39 which regulates the closure of operational passenger networks; and s.41 which regulates the closure of stations and light maintenance depots used in connection with railway passenger services.

4625. Railways-accessibility-disabled persons

RAIL VEHICLE ACCESSIBILITY (C2C CLASS 357/0 VEHICLES) EXEMPTION (AMENDMENT) ORDER 2002, SI 2002 3002; made under the Disability Discrimination Act 1995 s.47. In force: January 1, 2003; £1.50.

This Order amends the Rail Vehicle Accessibility (C2C Class 357/0 Vehicles) Exemption Order 2001 (SI 2001 3955) by extending the time limit until December 31, 2011 on the exemption granted from the Rail Vehicle Accessibility Regulations 1998 (SI 1998 2456) because priority seats are not fitted with a table.

4626. Railways-accessibility-disabled persons

RAIL VEHICLE ACCESSIBILITY (CROYDON TRAMLINK CLASS CR4000 VEHICLES) EXEMPTION (AMENDMENT) ORDER 2002, SI 2002 3001; made under the Disability Discrimination Act 1995 s.47. In force: January 1, 2003; £1.50.

This Order amends the Rail Vehicle Accessibility (Croydon Tramlink Class CR4000 Vehicles) Exemption Order 2001 (SI 2001 3952) by extending the time limit until March 31, 2005 on the exemption granted from the Rail Vehicle Accessibility Regulations 1998 (SI 1998 2456) because the wheelchair space does not have a structure or fitting to prevent a wheelchair moving or tipping.

4627. Railways-accessibility-disabled persons-exemptions

RAIL VEHICLE ACCESSIBILITY (CAIRNGORM FUNICULAR RAILWAY) EXEMPTION ORDER 2002, SI 2002 657; made under the Disability Discrimination Act 1995 s.47. In force: April 3, 2002; £1.75.

This Order authorises the use of two specified rail vehicles on the Cairngorm Funicular Railway although they do not conform with certain provisions of the Rail Vehicle Accessibility Regulations 1998 (SI 1998 2456) because the colour of the exterior doors does not contrast with that of the vehicle body and there is no system for visual announcements on the front exterior of the vehicles. The Order also requires the floor surface of the passenger apartments to contrast with the platform surface at Base and Ptarmigan stations.

4628. Railways-accessibility-disabled persons-exemptions

RAIL VEHICLE ACCESSIBILITY (EAST HAYLING LIGHT RAILWAY VEHICLES) EXEMPTION ORDER 2002, SI 2002 285; made under the Disability Discrimination Act 1995 s.47. In force: March 7, 2002; £2.00.

This Order authorises the use of any rail vehicle known as CoachType A, B, C, D or E which complies with a specified design, on the East Hayling Light Railway, although the vehicles do not comply with certain requirements of the Rail Vehicle Accessibility Regulations 1998 (SI 1998 2456) because no audible warning device is fitted to passenger doorways; priority seats and the space they occupy are not of the required size; there is no passenger information system; some vehicles do not meet the wheelchair space specifications; some doorways are not of the required width; and some passageways are not of the required width.

4629. Railways-accessibility-disabled persons-exemptions

RAIL VEHICLE ACCESSIBILITY (ISLE OF WIGHT RAILWAY LCDR NO.2515 VEHICLE) EXEMPTION ORDER 2002, SI 2002 1694; made under the Disability Discrimination Act 1995 s.47. In force: July 31, 2002; £1.75.

This Order authorises the use of the vehicle known as the London, Chatham and Dover Railway, 4 wheel, 5 compartment, 3rd Class Carriage, Southern Railway No.2515 on the Isle of Wight Railway between Smallbrook Junction and Wootton even though it does not comply with certain requirements of the Rail Vehicle Accessibility Regulations 1998 (SI 1998 2456) because the colour of the exterior doors does not contrast with that of the vehicle body; no audible warning device is fitted to passenger doorways; the treads of the steps for use by passengers at the external doorways are not covered in slip-resistant material and do not have a band of colour on the front edge; the rear of the steps used by passengers at the external doorways is not closed by a vertical riser; the steps used by passengers at external doorways are not illuminated; the floor across the width of the doorways is not appropriately marked; requirements for the provision of priority seats have not been fully satisfied; there is no handrail on the interior side of the external passenger doorways; the external handrails are not of the required diameter; the radius of the surface of the external handrails inside the curves is less than is permitted; there is no passenger information system; the wheelchair space is not fitted with a communication device of the required specification; and the wheelchair symbol is not displayed as required next to the wheelchair space or beside the wheelchair compatible doorway.

4630. Railways—accessibility—disabled persons—exemptions

RAIL VEHICLE ACCESSIBILITY (MIDDLETON RAILWAY DREWRY CAR) EXEMPTION ORDER 2002, SI 2002 1188; made under the Disability Discrimination Act 1995 s.47. In force: May 22, 2002; £1.75.

This Order authorises the use of the vehicle known as the Drewry Car DB998901 on the Middleton Railway in Leeds even though it does not comply with certain requirements of the Rail Vehicle Accessibility Regulations 1998 (SI 1998 2456).

4631. Railways—accessibility—disabled persons—exemptions

RAIL VEHICLE ACCESSIBILITY (SOUTH CENTRAL CLASS 375/3 VEHICLES) EXEMPTION ORDER 2002, SI 2002 1617; made under the Disability Discrimination Act 1995 s.47. In force: July 16, 2002; £1.75.

This Order authorises the use by South Central Ltd of specified rail vehicles forming Class 375/3 electrical multiple units, even though they do not comply with one of the requirements of the Rail Vehicle Accessibility Regulations 1998 (SI 1998 2456) because some letters and numbers on the visual display screens at the front of the vehicle cannot be displayed at the required size.

4632. Railways—accessibility—disabled persons—exemptions

RAIL VEHICLE ACCESSIBILITY (SOUTH WEST TRAINS CLASS 458 VEHICLES) EXEMPTION ORDER 2002, SI 2002 656; made under the Disability Discrimination Act 1995 s.47. In force: April 3, 2002; £1.75.

This Order, which revokes the Rail Vehicle Accessibility (South West Trains Class 458 Vehicles) Exemption Order 2001 (SI 2001 848), authorises the use of specified rail vehicles forming Class 458 electrical multiple-units although they do not conform with certain requirements of the Rail Vehicle Accessibility Regulations 1998 (SI 1998 2456).

4633. Railways—accessibility—disabled persons—exemptions

RAIL VEHICLE ACCESSIBILITY (SOUTH WEST TRAINS CLASS 458 VEHICLES) EXEMPTION (AMENDMENT) ORDER 2002, SI 2002 1762; made under the Disability Discrimination Act 1995 s.47. In force: July 31, 2002; £1.75.

This Order amends the Rail Vehicle Accessibility (South West Trains Class 458 Vehicles) Exemption Order 2002 (SI 2002 656) which authorises the use of specified rail vehicles even though they do not conform with the Rail Vehicle Accessibility Regulations 1998 (SI 1998 2456). The Order extends the expiry date for the exemption given in respect of the amount of force required to operate door control devices inside an exempted vehicle and sets different time limits and conditions on the authorisation depending on the location of the door control device concerned.

4634. Railways–accessibility–disabled persons–exemptions

RAIL VEHICLE ACCESSIBILITY (SUMMERLEE TRAMCAR NO.392) EXEMPTION ORDER 2002, SI 2002 2873; made under the Disability Discrimination Act 1995 s.47. In force: December 15, 2002; £1.75.

This Order authorises the use of the vehicle known as the Summerlee Tramcar number 392 in the Summerlee Heritage Park near Glasgow even though it does not comply with certain specified requirements of the Rail Vehicle Accessibility Regulations 1998 (SI 1998 2456).

4635. Railways–accessibility–disabled persons–exemptions

RAIL VEHICLE ACCESSIBILITY (VIRGIN WEST COAST CLASS 390 VEHICLES) EXEMPTION ORDER 2002, SI 2002 1699; made under the Disability Discrimination Act 1995 s.47. In force: July 22, 2002; £1.75.

This Order authorises the use for carriage of specified rail vehicles forming part of the fleet of Class 390 electrical multiple units even though they do not conform with certain provisions in the Rail Vehicle Accessibility Regulations 1998 (SI 2000 3215) because the step illumination is inadequate; more force than is permitted is required to operate a refrigerator door handle; and the tables fitted in the wheelchair spaces can be fixed at a level lower than the minimum specified by the Regulations.

4636. Railways–administration orders–meaning of "other proceedings"–Rail Regulator's power to direct Railtrack to enter into access contract

See INSOLVENCY: Railtrack Plc (In Administration) (No.2), *Re.* §2647

4637. Railways–Bitton–maintenance and operation

BITTON RAILWAY ORDER 2002, SI 2002 366; made under the Transport and Works Act 1992 s.1, s.5, Sch.1 para.1, Sch.1 para.7, Sch.1 para.16, Sch.1 para.17. In force: February 12, 2002; £2.50.

This Order authorises the Avon Valley Railway Heritage Trust to construct, maintain and operate a railway (380m in length) in the areas of the Councils of South Gloucestershire and of Bath and North East Somerset consisting of an extension of the railway authorised by the Bitton Light Railway Order 1991 (SI 1991 134). It also contains provisions for the maintenance and operation of the railway and authorises the undertaker to transfer the railway and the existing railway.

4638. Railways–Channel Tunnel Rail Link–Thames Tunnel Approach

CHANNEL TUNNEL RAIL LINK (THAMES TUNNEL APPROACH) ORDER 2002, SI 2002 1943; made under the Transport and Works Act 1992 s.1, s.5, Sch.1 para.1, Sch.1 para.2, Sch.1 para.3, Sch.1 para.4, Sch.1 para.7, Sch.1 para.8, Sch.1 para.10, Sch.1 para.11, Sch.1 para.15, Sch.1 para.16, Sch.1 para.17. In force: August 12, 2002; £2.00.

This Order, which makes provision for the compulsory acquisition of land within the limit of land to be acquired shown on the deposited plan, the raising of land within the limit of earth works shown on that plan and the temporary use of land within the limit of land to be temporarily used shown on that plan at West Thurrock Marshes between Burnley Road and the river Thames in the borough of Thurrock in connection with the construction of Work No.10 authorised by the Channel Tunnel Rail Link Act 1996.

4639. Railways–Heathrow Express–exemptions

RAILWAYS (HEATHROW EXPRESS) (EXEMPTIONS) (AMENDMENT) ORDER 2002, SI 2002 2703; made under the Railways Act 1993 s.49, s.143, s.151. In force: December 1, 2002; £1.50.

This Order amends the Railways (Heathrow Express) (Exemptions) Order 1994 (SI 1994 574) so that the Railways Act 1993 s.37 shall not apply to railway passenger services provided on any extension to the Heathrow Express Railway to any part of Heathrow Airport.

4640. Railways–Heathrow Express Railway–extension

HEATHROW EXPRESS RAILWAY EXTENSION ORDER 2002, SI 2002 1064; made under the Transport and Works Act 1992 s.1, s.5, Sch.1 para.1, Sch.1 para.2, Sch.1 para.3, Sch.1 para.4, Sch.1 para.5, Sch.1 para.7, Sch.1 para.8, Sch.1 para.9, Sch.1 para.10, Sch.1 para.11, Sch.1 para.13, Sch.1 para.15, Sch.1 para.16. In force: April 30, 2002; £4.50.

This Order authorises Heathrow Airport Ltd to construct works and compulsorily to acquire and use land for the purpose of making an extension to the Heathrow Express Railway from the Central Terminal Area of Heathrow Airport to the proposed site of the new Terminal 5 building. This Order also confers ancillary powers in connection with the construction and operation of that extension.

4641. Railways–interoperability–high speed

RAILWAYS (INTEROPERABILITY) (HIGH-SPEED) REGULATIONS 2002, SI 2002 1166; made under the European Communities Act 1972 s.2; and the Transport Act 2000 s.247. In force: May 16, 2002; £6.50.

These Regulations, which amend the Railways and Other Transport Systems (Approval of Works, Plant and Equipment) Regulations 1994 (SI 1994 157) and revoke, with savings, the Railways (Interoperability) (Notified Bodies) Regulations 2000 (SI 2000 1674), implement Council Directive 96/48 on the interoperability of the trans-European high-speed rail system ([1996] OJ L235/6), which has the purpose of bringing about the inter-working (interoperability) of rolling stock on the trans-European high-speed rail system and introduces common standards of construction across the EC.

4642. Railways–light railways–Docklands Light Railway

DOCKLANDS LIGHT RAILWAY (SILVERTOWN AND LONDON CITY AIRPORT EXTENSION) ORDER 2002, SI 2002 1066; made under the Transport and Works Act 1992 s.1, s.5, Sch.1 para.1, Sch.1 para.2, Sch.1 para.3, Sch.1 para.4, Sch.1 para.7, Sch.1 para.8, Sch.1 para.10, Sch.1 para.11, Sch.1 para.15, Sch.1 para.16, Sch.1 para.17. In force: April 30, 2002; £7.50.

This Order authorises Docklands Light Railway Limited (DLRL) to construct an extension to the Docklands Light Railway from Canning Town in the London Borough of Newham to North Woolwich in the London Borough of Newham, passing through Silvertown and alongside London City Airport and, for that purpose, compulsorily or by agreement to acquire land and rights in land.

4643. Railways–light railways–East Lancashire–Heywood extension

EAST LANCASHIRE (HEYWOOD EXTENSION) LIGHT RAILWAY ORDER 2002, SI 2002 1384; made under the Light Railways Act 1896 s.7, s.10, s.11, s.12; and the Transport Act 1968 s.121. In force: May 16, 2002; £2.00.

This Order authorises the extension of a railway approximately 6.9 kilometres in length commencing in the Metropolitan Borough of Rochdale at the junction with the railway of Railtrack at a point 470 metres east of Green Lane level crossing and terminating in the Metropolitan Borough of Bury at a junction with the light railway authorised by the East Lancashire Light Railway Order 1986 (SI 1986 277) at a point 28 metres east of the bridge carrying Knowsley Street over that light railway. It also authorises in the Metropolitan Borough of Bury a railway being a branch of the said light railway running 306 metres in a north-westerly direction before terminating in a junction with that railway and a railway 140 metres in length curving in a south-westerly direction before terminating in a junction with the said light railway.

4644. Railways–light railways–Greater Manchester–Trafford depot

GREATER MANCHESTER (LIGHT RAPID TRANSIT SYSTEM) (TRAFFORD DEPOT) ORDER 2002, SI 2002 1327; made under the Transport and Works Act 1992 s.1, s.5, Sch.1 para.1, Sch.1 para.2, Sch.1 para.3, Sch.1 para.4, Sch.1 para.7, Sch.1 para.8, Sch.1 para.9, Sch.1 para.10, Sch.1 para.11, Sch.1 para.12, Sch.1 para.13, Sch.1 para.15, Sch.1 para.16, Sch.1 para.17. In force: May 31, 2002; £4.00.

This Order, which amends the Compulsory Purchase Act 1965, the Land Compensation Act 1973 and the Land Act 1981, authorises Greater Manchester Passenger Transport Executive to construct a servicing and maintenance depot for its Metrolink system at a site in and adjoining Elsinore Road in the borough of Trafford.

4645. Railways–London Underground–Piccadilly Line–extension

PICCADILLY LINE (HEATHROW T5 EXTENSION) ORDER 2002, SI 2002 1065; made under the Transport and Works Act 1992 s.1, s.5, Sch.1 para.1, Sch.1 para.2, Sch.1 para.3, Sch.1 para.4, Sch.1 para.5, Sch.1 para.7, Sch.1 para.10, Sch.1 para.11, Sch.1 para.15, Sch.1 para.16, Sch.1 para.17. In force: April 30, 2002; £4.50.

This Order authorises London Underground Ltd to construct works and compulsorily to acquire land for the purpose of making an extension to its Piccadilly Line from the Central Terminal Area of Heathrow Airport to the proposed site of the new Terminal 5 building. The Order also confers ancillary powers in connection with the construction and operation of that extension including the power to enter into agreements with Heathrow Airport Ltd.

4646. Railways–Strand Road, Preston–transfer of ownership

STRAND ROAD, PRESTON RAILWAY ORDER 2002, SI 2002 2398; made under the Transport and Works Act 1992 s.1, s.5, Sch.1 para.1, Sch.1 para.3, Sch.1 para.8, Sch.1 para.15, Sch.1 para.17. In force: September 24, 2002; £2.00.

This Order relates to a portion of the Preston Dock branch railway in the vicinity of, and including, the Strand Road, Preston level crossing which at the date of the Order is owned jointly by Preston City Council and Railtrack Plc. The Order authorises the owners to transfer the railway to Steamport Southport Ltd and makes other provisions in relation to it.

4647. Railways–Wear Valley–safety provisions

WEAR VALLEY RAILWAY ORDER 2002, SI 2002 1997; made under the Transport and Works Act 1992 s.1, s.5, Sch.1 para.1, Sch.1 para.15. In force: August 12, 2002; £2.00.

This Order authorises the transfer to Weardale Railways Ltd of the railway line between Bishop Auckland and Eastgate, County Durham, together with certain statutory and other rights and liabilities. It places responsibility on Durham County Council for bridges carrying highways over the railway and makes provision for the safety of works and equipment and for the safe operation of level crossings.

4648. Road safety–school crossing patrol sign

SCHOOL CROSSING PATROL SIGN (ENGLAND AND WALES) REGULATIONS 2002, SI 2002 3020; made under the Road Traffic Regulation Act 1984 s.28. In force: January 9, 2003; £1.75.

These Regulations, which amend the Traffic Signs Regulations and General Directions 1994 (SI 1994 1519), prescribe the size, colour and type of the sign which a school crossing patrol may exhibit so as to require traffic to stop when approaching a place where a person is crossing or seeking to cross a road.

4649. Road safety–traffic signs

TRAFFIC SIGNS REGULATIONS AND GENERAL DIRECTIONS 2002, SI 2002 3113; made under the Road Traffic Regulation Act 1984 s.64, s.65, s.85; and the Road Traffic Act 1988 s.36. In force: January 31, 2003; £40.00.

These Regulations revoke the Traffic Signs Regulations 1994 (SI 1994 1519), the Signs General (Amendment) Directions 1995 (SI 1995 2769), the Traffic Signs (Amendment) Regulations 1995 (SI 1995 3107) and the Traffic Signs General (Amendment) Directions 1999 (SI 1999 1723). They prescribe traffic signs for the purposes of of the Road Traffic Act 1988 s.36 and provide that the sign for conveying information or a warning, requirement, restriction, prohibition or speed limit of the description specified in the caption to a diagram illustrated in these Regulations must be of the size, colour and type shown in the diagram. The Regulations also provide for particular warning and regulatory signs with provisions for permitted variants of the prescribed signs, including variants which are required to be made in particular circumstances.

4650. Service contracts–subsidies–tendering requirements

SERVICE SUBSIDY AGREEMENTS (TENDERING) (ENGLAND) REGULATIONS 2002, SI 2002 2090; made under the Transport Act 1985 s.90, s.91, s.134. In force: September 2, 2002; £2.00.

These Regulations, which revoke the Service Subsidy Agreement (Tendering) Regulations 1985 (SI 1985 1921), the Service Subsidy Agreements (Tendering) (Amendment) Regulations 1989 (SI 1989 464), the Service Subsidy Agreements (Tendering) (Amendment) Regulations 1994 (SI 1994 1227) and the Service Subsidy Agreements (Tendering) (Amendment) Regulations 1998 (SI 1998 2197), excludes from the tendering requirements of the Transport Act 1985 s.89 various agreements that provide for the payment of subsidies as part of the provision of a local service.

4651. Service contracts–subsidies–tendering requirements–Wales

SERVICE SUBSIDY AGREEMENTS (TENDERING) (AMENDMENT) (WALES) REGULATIONS 2002, SI 2002 520; made under the Transport Act 1985 s.91. In force: April 1, 2002; £1.75.

These Regulations, which amend the Service Subsidy Agreements (Tendering) Regulations 1985 (SI 1985 1921), provide for exceptions to the requirement of the Transport Act 1985 s.89 for tendering where local authorities enter into agreements for the provision of local bus services subject to a service subsidy. The 1985 Regulations provide for an exemption from the tendering requirement where the agreement provides for payments of less than £12,000 in any 12-month period unless the aggregate which a service operator receives from that local authority under such agreements exceeds £70,000. These Regulations provide for the exception to apply to any agreement or agreements under which payments do not exceed 40 per cent of the budgeted total expenditure of an authority on such agreements in that financial year.

4652. Traffic wardens–functions

FUNCTIONS OF TRAFFIC WARDENS (AMENDMENT) ORDER 2002, SI 2002 2975; made under the Road Traffic Regulation Act 1984 s.95, s.96. In force: December 2, 2002; £1.50.

This Order, which amends the Functions of Traffic Wardens Order 1970 (SI 1970 1958) in consequence of the Police Reform Act 2002, provides that references to a constable are to include references to a traffic warden. It also adds two functions to those prescribed as appropriate for discharge by traffic wardens. These are stopping vehicles for vehicle testing purposes and escort of abnormal loads. It also removes the prohibition on a traffic warden directing traffic from a moving vehicle.

4653. Transport Act 2000 (c.38)–Commencement No.2 Order–Wales

TRANSPORT ACT 2000 (COMMENCEMENT NO.2) (WALES) ORDER 2002, SI 2002 2024; made under the Transport Act 2000 s.275. Commencement details: bringing into force various provisions of the 2000 Act on August 14, 2002; £2.00.

This Order brings into force provisions of the Transport Act 2000 Part II which provides that the Finance Act 1965 s.92, which relates to grants towards duty charged on bus fuel, and the Transport Act 1985 s.111, which relates to unregistered and unreliable local services, are to cease to have effect.

4654. Transport Act 2000 (c.38)–Commencement No.8 and Transitional Provisions Order–amendment

TRANSPORT ACT 2000 (COMMENCEMENT NO.8 AND TRANSITIONAL PROVISIONS) (AMENDMENT) ORDER 2002, SI 2002 846; made under the Transport Act 2000 s.275. In force: March 27, 2002; £1.50.

This Order amends the Transport Act 2000 (Commencement No.8 and Transitional Provisions) Order 2002 (SI 2002 658) by substituting, for references to the repeal of certain provisions of the Road Traffic Act 1988 and the Road Traffic (Driver Licensing and Information Systems) Act 1989, references to the repeal of provisions in the Road Traffic Act 1988 s.130, relating to revocation of trainee instructor's licences, and s.131 (5), relating to appeals against decisions of the Registrar of Approved Driving Instructors. Those repeals are brought into force on April 1, 2002.

4655. Transport Act 2000 (c.38)–Commencement No.8 Order

TRANSPORT ACT 2000 (COMMENCEMENT NO.8 AND TRANSITIONAL PROVISIONS) ORDER 2002, SI 2002 658; made under the Transport Act 2000 s.275, s.276. Commencement details: bringing into force various provisions of the 2000 Act on April 1, 2002; £2.00.

This Order brings into force those parts of the Transport Act 2000 s.144 not already in force which enable provision to be made for, and in connection with, the imposition of penalty charges in respect of contravention of bus lane restrictions on roads in Greater London and the payment, notification, adjudication and enforcement of such charges. It brings into force provisions which amend the Road Traffic Act 1998 as regards the date when decisions by the Registrar of Approved Driving Instructors come into effect and also amends the Greater London Authority Act 1999 by removing the power of the Mayor to determine appeals brought by applicants for a London service permit and transferring this function to an independent appeals panel.

4656. Transport Act 2000 (c.38)–Commencement No.9 and Transitional Provisions Order–England

TRANSPORT ACT 2000 (COMMENCEMENT NO.9 AND TRANSITIONAL PROVISIONS) ORDER 2002, SI 2002 1014; made under the Transport Act 2000 s.275, s.276. Commencement details: bringing into force various provisions of the 2000 Act on May 1, 2002; £2.00.

This Order brings into force specified provisions of the Transport Act 2000 which repeal all the statutory provisions relating to bus fuel duty grant and provide for the enforcement of bus service registrations, quality partnerships, quality contracts and bus information obligations through the imposition of new financial penalties and provide for the making of regulations under which a person is required to undertake a prescribed training course as a condition of being permitted to take a test of competence to drive, being permitted to obtain a licence authorising the driving of, or (having passed a test) being permitted to drive on a road a specified class of motor vehicle.

4657. Transport policy–quality partnership schemes–Wales

QUALITY PARTNERSHIP SCHEMES (EXISTING FACILITIES) (WALES) REGULATIONS 2002, SI 2002 3017 (W.287); made under the Transport Act 2000 s.119. In force: December 20, 2002; £1.75.

These Regulations make provision for existing facilities which may form part of a quality partnership scheme. They provide that existing facilities may not form part of a quality partnership scheme where they were first provided more than ten years before notice of the proposed scheme is given. If an existing facility was provided more than five years but less than ten years before notice of the proposed scheme is given, it may form part of a quality partnership scheme providing no objection, which has not been withdrawn, is made by any person who is relying on that facility in providing a local service. In addition they provide that any objection must be made in writing or by electronic means and must be served on the appropriate authority within the time specified and provide that an authority must, when it gives notice of a proposed scheme, specify the date on which it believes each relevant facility was first provided and the date by which any objection may be made, which may not be less than 42 days after the date on which the notice is published.

4658. Travel Concessions (Eligibility) Act 2002 (c.4)

This Act amends the law relating to the age at which certain persons become eligible to receive travel concessions on journeys on public passenger transport services.

This Act received Royal Assent on February 26, 2002.

4659. Travel Concessions (Eligibility) Act 2002 (c.4)–Commencement Order– England

TRAVEL CONCESSIONS (ELIGIBILITY) ACT 2002 (COMMENCEMENT) (ENGLAND) ORDER 2002, SI 2002 673; made under the Travel Concessions (Eligibility) Act 2002 s.2. Commencement details: bringing into force various provisions of the 2002 Act on April 1, 2003; £1.50.

This Order brings into force all of the substantive provisions of the Travel Concessions (Eligibility) Act 2002.

4660. Travel Concessions (Eligibility) Act 2002 (c.4)–Commencement Order– Wales

TRAVEL CONCESSIONS (ELIGIBILITY) ACT 2002 (COMMENCEMENT) (WALES) ORDER 2002, SI 2002 3014 (W.286, C.97); made under the Travel Concessions (Eligibility) Act 2002 s.2. Commencement details: bringing into force various provisions of the 2002 Act on April 1, 2003; £1.75.

This Order brings into force all the substantive provisions of the Travel Concessions (Eligibility) Act 2002 in relation to Wales which equalise at 60 the ages at which men and women are entitled to concessionary travel on local bus services.

4661. Vehicle tests–supply of goods–return of unroadworthy vehicle to customer following repairs–meaning of "supply"

[Road Traffic Act 1988 s.75.]

The local authority appealed against a decision that DB had not supplied an unroadworthy vehicle to W. DB, which operated a vehicle repair garage, had taken possession of a car with a view to carrying out repairs so as to enable it to pass an MOT test. The car was then returned to W and the rear suspension subsequently collapsed. The court held that the return of the vehicle to W did not constitute a supply for the purposes of the Road Traffic Act 1988 s.75.

Held, allowing the appeal, that DB had supplied the vehicle to W by returning it after the repairs had supposedly been carried out. The word "supply" involved the transfer of physical control of goods from one person to another in order to provide something that the recipient wanted or required, *R. v. Maginnis (Patrick Terrance)* [1987] A.C. 303, [1987] C.L.Y. 797 applied. Physical control of the vehicle had been transferred to W, thus providing W with the repaired vehicle that he wanted.

DEVON CC v. DB CARS LTD, [2001] EWHC Admin 521, (2002) 166 J.P. 38, Forbes, J., QBD (Admin Ct).

4662. Books

Blackstone's Police Manual: Road Traffic 2003. Blackstone's Police Manual. Paperback: £10.99. ISBN 0-19-925490-7. Blackstone Press.

Burton, Nicholas-Highway Law: a Practical Guide. Paperback: £28.00. ISBN 1-85811-267-2. EMIS Professional Publishing.

Clarke-Contracts of Carriage by Air. Transport Law Series. Hardback: £180.00. ISBN 1-84311-148-9. LLP Professional Publishing.

Proceedings of the 43rd Colloquium on the Law of Outer Space. AIAA Conference Proceedings. Hardback: £67.50. ISBN 1-56347-488-3. AIAA American Institute of Aeronautics and Astronautics.

Wallis, Peter; McCormac, Kevin; Niekirk, Paul-Road Traffic Offences: 2nd Supplement to the 20th Edition. Paperback: £57.00. ISBN 0-421-79720-7. Sweet & Maxwell.

TRUSTS

4663. Accumulation and maintenance settlements-variation-infant beneficiaries-avoidance of capital gains tax-Jersey

[Trusts (Jersey) Law 1984 Art.43.]

An application was made to the Jersey Royal Court, under the Trusts (Jersey) Law 1984 Art.43, to approve on behalf of minor beneficiaries a proposed variation of a Jersey trust. The trust was an accumulation and maintenance settlement under which the beneficiaries would become entitled to capital at age 25. The variation was proposed as a consequence of 1998 changes to the United Kingdom tax law under which a charge to capital gains tax might arise when beneficiaries became entitled to a share of capital. That charge would fall upon the settlors, who could then seek reimbursement from the trustees. The settlors were resident in the UK, as were three of the beneficiaries. One beneficiary was only temporarily not resident in the UK and the other resided in Israel. All the beneficiaries were children of the settlors. At the time of the application for variation, three of the children were under 18, S was 19 and the other was 22. Before the court was a proposal to appoint the trust assets to a new settlement under which the beneficiaries would become entitled to a life interest only at age 25 and the entitlement to capital was to be deferred indefinitely. It was further proposed that the trustees of the new settlement would be resident in the UK. A further question before the court was whether S was to be regarded as a minor. He was an adult under UK law, his domicile and Israel law where he was temporarily resident.

Held, granting the application and approving the variation, that the proposed variation benefited the minor beneficiaries since it avoided the charge to tax and avoided a dispute between parents and trustees. S was to be regarded as a minor since that was his status under Jersey law.

N'S 1989 SETTLEMENT, *Re* (1998-99) 1 I.T.E.L.R. 803, FC Hamon (Deputy Bailiff), Royal Ct (Jer).

4664. Beneficiaries-life tenants-trust deed requiring trustee to pay income to life tenant-duty to balance interests of all beneficiaries-Bahamas

[Trustee Act 1998 (Bahamas) s.89.]

J, a life tenant, brought proceedings against M, the trustee, claiming that M had failed to keep a fair balance between those interested in income and those interested in capital within the meaning of the Trustee Act 1998 (Bahamas) s.89(2). Under a trust settlement it was specified that J was to be paid either the net annual income of the trust fund or $800,000 per annum, whichever was the greater. with such The payments being could be made from income to the extent available, but otherwise from principal if insufficient income were available. J claimed that the annual value of $800,000 gradually diminished and therefore he should be entitled to receive all profits and gains on the investments made by the investment company set up and controlled by M. It was unlikely that the principal would produce such a sum from investment income. Discretion was also given to the trustee to meet medical emergencies and certain other needs of the life tenant or the remaindermen from trust capital. Investments were made on behalf of the trust by a company which reported as income the gains from the investments and the gains from the sale of those investments. The trustee accounted for the gains realised as capital. J claimed to be aggrieved within the Trustee Act 1998 s.89(3) by the trustee's failure to keep a balance under s.89(2) of the 1998 Act between those interested in income and those interested in capital.

Held, dismissing J's claim, that (1) trustees were expected to consider total return on trust assets as the yardstick for their investment performance without prejudicing the position of a life tenant or a remainderman, and have to strike a fair balance between fixed interest securities, favouring the life tenant, and stocks and shares which, with their potential for capital growth, favoured the remainderman interested in capital where there is a low dividend policy, and (2) both the settlor and M would have known that the trust fund of $10 million would have been unlikely to produce an annual income of $800,000 without incurring a detriment to the remaindermen whose interests as capital beneficiaries the settlor wished to promote as well as those of J as income beneficiary. If M had acted in accordance with J's wishes and paid J all the profits and gains on the investments of the trust fund, J would have received over $3 million while the trust fund would have diminished in value. The settlor could not have intended such unfair treatment of the fund's capital beneficiaries. In the circumstances, the trustee had acted properly in employing trust accounting principles, and had kept a fair balance between those interested in income and those interested in income capital.

J W v. MORGAN TRUST CO OF THE BAHAMAS LTD (2001-02) 4 I.T.E.L.R. 541, Hayton, A.J., Sup Ct (Bah).

4665. Beneficiaries–trust funds–assignment of interest–entitlement to inspect trust documents–Australia

A number of investors established a fighting fund to which they each contributed. The fund were held under a trust deed. S and G contributed to the fund and assigned all their interests in the trust to G. G sought a declaration that it was entitled to inspect the books of account of the trust fund.

Held, dismissing the application, that a beneficiary of a trust could not assign a right of action against the trustees to have the trust fund properly administered. The only rights which they were able to assign to the assignee were their proprietary rights in the trust property.

GLOBAL CUSTODIANS LTD v. MESH (1999-2000) 2 I.T.E.L.R. 327, Young, J., Sup Ct (NSW).

4666. Breach of trust–constructive trusts–company incorporated and operated by accountant–share purchase moneys paid out on instructions of fraudster–knowing assistance–Vanuatu

K engaged B, a firm of accountants, to incorporate a company, M, which K stated was to be the Vanuatu resident subsidiary of a similarly named overseas company. M's directors were nominee companies owned by B, and M was operated by B's staff. B believed that M was selling shares in foreign real estate. The funds supplied by intending share purchasers were distributed immediately on receipt on K's instructions to persons that had no apparent connection with M. The scheme was subsequently found to be fraudulent and entirely unconnected to the supposed overseas parent company. A, one of the victims of the fraud, sued B for the return of his purchase money, contending that the sum was the subject of a constructive trust. A succeeded at first instance and B appealed.

Held, dismissing the appeal, that the purchase money was held on a constructive trust for the purpose for which it had been paid. However, because of the fraud, there was no consideration for A's payment, *Westdeutsche Landesbank Girozentrale v. Islington LBC* [1996] A.C. 669, [1964] C.L.Y. 4149 applied. Once it was established that the purchase money was held on trust, its disbursement was a breach of the trust as the scheme was fraudulent from its inception and any payments made under it were in breach of trust. B's actions amounted to assistance in the breach. Given the facts of the instant case, B had chosen to ignore obviously fraudulent facets of the scheme, thereby rendering dishonest assistance to the breach, *Royal Brunei Airlines Sdn Bhd v. Tan* [1995] 2 A.C. 378, [1995] C.L.Y. 2193 considered.

BARRET v. McCORMACK (2001-02) 4 I.T.E.L.R. 1, Lunabek, A.C.J., CA (Van).

4667. Breach of trust–dishonesty–payments made by trustees out of deceased's estate–restitution by way of summary judgment

[Financial Services Act 1986.]

G, who was incapacitated, was a resident in a care home run by W until her death in 1992, at which point her estate was worth £2.2 million, £1.8 million of which was invested in a bond. This was surrendered in 1997, incurring a £98,000 penalty, by M, who was the home's bookkeeper and trustee of G's estate, along with W, the home's owner. The proceeds were paid into a trustee account from where payments were made to W and M and his wife. Payments of £74,000, £550,000 and £1.12 million were also made to S and V, a married couple who were associates of W. The first payment went to V, with the two larger sums being paid into a Swiss bank account, ostensibly for investment purposes to be managed by S. A payment of £422,000 was also made to a company, E, which was wholly owned by S and V, £247,000 of which was used to purchase a house in V's name. The Public Trustee sought orders for either summary judgment or interim payments against S, V, M, W and E.

Held, allowing the applications, that W and M's conduct had been dishonest throughout and amounted to a serious breach of trust. M, W and S had acted together to deceive the bank into making the payments to the Swiss bank account. In addition, S, a discharged bankrupt, had been carrying on unauthorised investment activities contrary to the Financial Services Act 1986. Summary judgment was granted against S in respect of all payments made to him for the supposed investment, which was a sham, and he was further held to have dishonestly assisted in a breach of trust in relation to payments made to V. Furthermore, S's knowledge was imputed to E, so that all sums it had received were to be repaid to G's estate, *El Ajou v. Dollar Land Holdings Plc (No.1)* [1994] 2 All E.R. 685, [1994] C.L.Y. 416 considered. An order for sale was made for the house purchased by V. None of the parties were bona fide purchasers for value without notice of G's assets. However, judgment would not be entered against V in respect of the £74,000 as it was arguable that she did not have knowledge as to the source of that sum and could not have been expected to be on enquiry, given that S had other Swiss business interests, *Lipkin Gorman v. Karpnale Ltd* [1991] 2 A.C. 548, [1991] C.L.Y. 502 applied.

PUBLIC TRUSTEE (GORDON'S EXECUTOR) v. WILLIAMS [2002] W.T.L.R. 45, Neuberger, J., Ch D.

4668. Breach of trust–knowing assistance–state of mind required to establish dishonest assistance

See BANKING AND FINANCE: Twinsectra Ltd v. Yardley. §249

4669. Charitable trusts-education-advancement of children overseas-choice of law based on closest connection to settlor and trustee

[Hague Convention on the Law Applicable to Trusts and on their Recognition 1985 Art.7.]

M sought the determination of four questions arising from the interpretation of a settlement created by C's will. C was born in Iraq but acquired an Indian domicile of dependency through marriage. She subsequently went to live in Italy, but frequently visited London, where she maintained an address. N, the trustee named in the settlement was a London registered bank. The settlement provided that after C's death, M was to receive the income from the trust to be applied for "the purpose of education and advancement in life of Armenian children or for such other charitable purpose" he considered was "allied thereto". The questions set out to determine (1) the law applicable to the settlement; (2) whether it was charitable; (3) if its purpose was to pay income of the trust to M, and (4) the number and identity of the trustees.

Held, that (1) the trust was most closely connected with the law of England and Wales for the purposes of the Hague Convention on the Law Applicable to Trusts and on their Recognition 1985 Art.7, given that both C and N had strong links with London; (2) The trust had charitable status as it satisfied the educational purpose in *Special Commissioners of Income Tax v. Pemsel* [1891] A.C. 531; (3) although the purpose took effect outside the jurisdiction, this did not prevent the trust being charitable as the presumption of charitable purpose was not defeated on public policy grounds. The clause was to be read conjunctively, therefore the education was limited to that which would advance the children in their future lives *Pemsel* applied, and (4) N was the single trustee with M's position being similar to that of a life tenant under a strict settlement.

CARAPIET'S TRUSTS, *Re*; *sub nom.* MANOOGIAN (ARMENIAN PATRIARCH OF JERUSALEM) v. SONSINO; HIS BEATITUDE ARCHBISHOP TORKOM MANGOONIAN, ARMENIAN PATRIARCH OF JERUSALEM v. SONSINO, [2002] EWHC 1304, [2002] W.T.L.R. 989, Jacob, J., Ch D.

4670. Charitable trusts-Guernsey-jurisdiction of Royal Court to confirm status of trust

[Trusts (Guernsey) Law 1989.]

T was the trustee of the FDS Charitable Trust established in Guernsey by a pharmaceutical company under the terms of a deed of charitable trust. The objects of the trust were the advancement of education and research in the fields of medicine, ecology and pharmaceutics. T sought a declaration that the trust was a charity but the Royal Court held that it had no jurisdiction under the Trusts (Guernsey) Law 1989 to grant such a declaration. T appealed.

Held, allowing the appeal, that there being no register of charities in Guernsey and no special body to administer or regulate charities in Guernsey, the regulation of charities was a matter for the Guernsey courts. Before the passing of the 1989 Law, all trusts were governed by Guernsey customary law and, thereafter, the statutory framework came into play. The power to declare that the trust was a charitable trust arose both under Guernsey customary law and under the terms of the 1989 Law.

INSIGER TRUST (GUERNSEY) LTD, *Re* (1999-2000) 2 I.T.E.L.R. 154, RC Southwell Q.C. (President), CA (Gue).

4671. Charitable trusts-purpose trusts-interpretation of trust-Bahamas

The court was required to decide whether K was a trust for beneficiaries or a pure purpose trust and, if so, whether charitable or non charitable.

Held, giving judgment for the plaintiff, that the trust was a valid purpose trust for charitable purposes. The existence of a perpetuity period and the nomination of an incorporated non profit making body as a beneficiary indicated a trust for beneficiaries, and the presumption in favour of validating a clause rather than invalidating a clause supported the view that this was a charitable trust.

KRISHNA BOOKS PUBLISHING TRUST, *Re*; *sub nom.* SUTTON v. FEDOROWSKY (2001-02) 4 I.T.E.L.R. 665, Hayton, A.J., Sup Ct (Bah).

4672. Charitable trusts–shares–unincorporated associations–sale of assets to satisfy damages claim–Canada

VC and STM were two schools operated in Canada by the Christian Brothers, CBIC, an unincorporated association created by statute. The beneficial ownership of the shares in both schools was called into question in the course of claims for damages arising from abuse suffered by the residents of a home run by CBIC ((2000-01) 3 I.T.E.L.R. 34, [2001] C.L.Y. 387). CBIC was put into liquidation so that its assets could be disposed of to meet the claims and the liquidator wanted to sell the shares in VC and STM for the same purpose.

Held, finding the shares to be held for the specific charitable purpose of operating the schools and dismissing the liquidator's petition, that (1) evidence showed that the donors had intended to establish the schools and not to further the general charitable objects of CBIC, and (2) the absence of a trust deed did not prevent a determination of the donors' intention as the surrounding circumstances could be construed in deciding the issue.

ROWLAND v. VANCOUVER COLLEGE LTD; ST THOMAS MORE COLLEGIATE LTD v. BURNELL; BURNELL v. CHRISTIAN BROTHERS OF IRELAND IN CANADA (IN LIQUIDATION); CHRISTIAN BROTHERS OF IRELAND IN CANADA (IN LIQUIDATION) v. ROWLAND (2000-01) 3 I.T.E.L.R. 182, Levine, J., Sup Ct (BC).

4673. Constructive trusts–contribution made during period of cohabitation–Australia

B and G lived together for about 13 years. There were no children of the relationship, but B had two children by a prior relationship to whom G was generous. G increased his wealth by about AUD 700,000 during the period of the cohabitation. He refused to marry B. At the end of the cohabitation, B claimed a one third share in the assets that G had acquired during that period. Her claim was refused at first instance as the judge found that B had not made a significant contribution to the couple's standard of living and that she had not contributed to the acquisition of property. B appealed against the refusal to impose a constructive trust.

Held, dismissing the appeal, that the facts showed that B had made only a limited contribution to G's business activities and her efforts had benefited herself as much as G. It would not be unconscionable, therefore, for G to retain the property acquired during the cohabitation.

BROWN v. GEORGE (1999-2000) 2 I.T.E.L.R. 669, Miles, J., Fed Ct (Aus) (Full Ct).

4674. Constructive trusts–legitimate expectation–equal distribution of superannuation funds–New Zealand

H and G lived in New Zealand and had a relationship which lasted for 22 years. H had previously been married, and the religious beliefs of both H and G meant that they could not marry or have a sexual relationship while H's former wife remained alive. Otherwise they were a couple who lived as husband and wife in all but name. G acted as step-mother to H's children. They planned for their joint retirement and made various investments in that regard. When H was seconded to Australia by his employer in 1998 the parties continued to act jointly in connection with all their business and personal affairs until shortly after arriving in Australia H met another lady and advised G that their relationship was at an end. The news had a devastating effect on G and her health. The parties agreed to divide equally all the property they owned except that H declined to share his non-contributory superannuation. The

High Court divided all their property including their respective interests in their superannuation funds equally. H appealed.

Held, dismissing the appeal, that (1) although H's contention that the facts found by the judge did not truly amount to an express agreement or formal declaration of trust was correct, his findings of fact were ample to evidence the common intention of the parties; (2) the court could and would impose a constructive trust to give effect to the reasonable expectation of G that she should share in the superannuation provisions equally, and (3) she had contributed indirectly to H's acquisition of that provision notwithstanding that it was an employer funded pension, by assisting H to meet his work commitments, running his household and looking after his children, and accordingly he would be unjustly enriched if he were to retain the whole of it.

HORSFIELD v. GILTRAP (2001-02) 4 I.T.E.L.R. 393, Blanchard, J., CA (NZ).

4675. **Constructive trusts–moneylending–inducement to remortgage on basis of fraud**

N, a company, proposed to develop a shopping centre using loans from mortgagees, M and MK. The loans had been obtained on the basis of pre leasing information, which turned out to be fraudulent. M had decided to continue with the project but MK had demanded repayment. F had replaced MK as second mortgagee but had been induced by N to lend on the same fraudulent information about pre leasing. F's money had been used to repay MK. When IF discovered the fraud, it sued MK on the basis of money had and received, tracing and on the basis of liability as constructive trustee for knowing receipt of the money.

Held, giving judgment for MK, that (1) it was a prerequisite to the operation of the equitable remedy of tracing that there was a fiduciary relationship which did not exist here; (2) the constructive trust argument failed as MK had no actual or constructive knowledge of the fact that N had received funds from F pursuant to any fraud committed by N, and (3) F had failed to make adequate enquiry of MK.

FIRST ISLAND FINANCIAL SERVICES LTD v. NOVASTAR DEVELOPMENTS (KELOWNA ORCHARD GARDENS) LTD (1998-99) 1 I.T.E.L.R. 877, Melvin, J., Sup Ct (BC).

4676. **Constructive trusts–transfer of assets–presumption of resulting trust**

W acquired a farm which he placed in the names of both of his sons. W and one of his sons, T, became partners in the business of repairing mowing machines, subsequently incorporating the business as a company in return for shares in that company. The business was later sold to a larger company. The sale proceeds were paid by allocation of shares in the acquiring company and in loan notes. T was unhappy with this arrangement. W therefore agreed to pay T cash on the basis that T holds the loan notes and shares for W. Further, as part of this same arrangement, W paid one further cash amount for the son's half interest in the farm and another by way of gift. T son contended that the transfer of his interest in the farm was made on the basis of representations from W that this was necessary for tax purposes, that T could continue to occupy the farm, and that W would leave the farm to T on death. The court at first instance found that T's half interest in the farm had been transferred to W for full consideration, that W's representations had not been made to induce T to transfer the half interest in the farm and that T had not paid over the proceeds of the loan notes. T appealed.

Held, dismissing the appeal, that (1) W and T had agreed to the sale of the interest in the farm for full consideration and therefore there could be neither a resulting nor a constructive trust over the property in favour of T; (2) the representations made by W had not been sufficient to constitute an inducement to transfer rights to him. This was particularly so given that W had paid full consideration for T's interest in the farm. Those representations merely indicated

W's future intentions with regards to the farm, and (3) that the trial judge had rightly found that T had not paid over the proceeds of the loan notes.

WINSTANLEY v. WINSTANLEY (NO.1) (1999-2000) 2 I.T.E.L.R. 269, Rattee, J. Buxton L.J., CA.

4677. **Constructive trusts–transfer of assets–transfer out of jurisdiction awarding judgment debt–discretionary nature of remedy–New Zealand**

CR purchased stocks in a US investment scheme run by C through companies C controlled. The scheme was found to be fraudulent and a US court awarded CR damages by way of a judgment debt. These were not paid, however, and CR brought an action in New Zealand, on the basis that C's only identifiable assets were situated there. Mareva injunctions were obtained over the assets. Subsequently, V, a Cayman Islands registered company and S, a New Zealand family trust, were joined in the proceedings as they contended that they were the actual owners of the New Zealand situated assets. CR sought declarations that the assets were held on trust for them and an enquiry into C, V and S's handling of the assets.

Held, allowing the application and imposing a remedial constructive trust, that (1) a remedial constructive trust differed from an institutional constructive trust as the latter was the mandatory consequence of certain events, whereas the former was discretionary in nature; (2) an institutional constructive trust existed from the time the events complained of occurred, while a remedial constructive trust only became effective on the making of a court order where unjust enrichment was found to exist and all other equitable remedies were inadequate, and (3) in the instant case, C, V and S had conducted themselves in a manner likely to prevent CR from enforcing the judgment debt. Therefore it was appropriate for the court to exercise its discretionary jurisdiction by imposing a remedial constructive trust.

COMMONWEALTH RESERVES v. CHODAR (2000-01) 3 I.T.E.L.R. 549, Glazebrook, J., HC (NZ).

4678. **Constructive trusts–trustees powers and duties–trustee's suspicions about trust fund following intervention of financial regulatory body–Bahamas**

C, the trustee of a settlement created by M in the Bahamas, sought directions from the court as to whether it could properly pay out sums to the beneficiaries, including M, as required by the trust deed. C was concerned, following action against M by the United States Federal Trade Commission, to avoid any allegation of dishonestly assisting in the breach of a constructive trust in favour of third parties imposed on the trust fund.

Held, granting leave to distribute the trust funds, that suspicions arising from unsubstantiated claims were not sufficient to prevent a banker or trustee from carrying out its contractual or equitable duties to a client or beneficiary. There had to be positive evidence of misfeasance or breach of trust. In the present case, there were no claims against M that could be traced to C. Therefore any suspicions C might have had could be said to have been dispelled.

C v. M (2001-02) 4 I.T.E.L.R. 548, Hayton, A.J., Sup Ct (Bah).

4679. **Constructive trusts–unjust enrichment–defence of change of position–Australia**

G was murdered. His solicitor R proved a will giving substantial legacies to F and H, which were paid. R had forged the will and the probate was revoked. HG was entitled on G's intestacy and applied to the court for repayment of the legacies claiming that (1) F and H held the legacies on constructive trusts and (2) for restitution on the grounds of unjust enrichment and (3) that he was entitled to trace that part of the legacy to H which had been used to repay her mortgage. F and H claimed change of position.

Held, that (1) since F believed that there might have been a subsequent will a constructive trust could arise but as there was not in fact any will and therefore no identifiable beneficiary no such trust arose but (2) F could only rely on change of position in relation to expenditure which would not have been incurred had he not received the legacy and (3) H had acted honestly and therefore no constructive trust could arise; (4) she was entitled to claim change of position against the claim for tracing but (5) she would have incurred ordinary living expenses and would have reduced her mortgage in any event and therefore was liable to repay those amounts.

GERTSCH v. ASPASIA (1999-2000) 2 I.T.E.L.R. 342, Foster, A.J., Sup Ct (NSW).

4680. **Creation–agreements lacking certainty of subject and object–Canada**

IG, a motor vehicle warranty supplier, entered into arrangements with C which were referred to as trusts in the relevant documentation. Subsequently, interlocutory orders were made in the course of IG's insolvency proceedings which assumed that the funds under consideration were trust funds. However, documents and material relating to related proceedings raised the possibility that the funds were not held on trust and C sought to argue that point. E argued that the status of the funds in fact and law had been determined in the earlier proceedings so that C was estopped from arguing at a later stage that the funds were not trusts and that such an argument was an abuse of process.

Held, that some of the arrangements were not valid as trusts, that (1) res judicata or abuse of process could not be raised in relation to the existence of the trusts as the matter had not been considered in the earlier proceedings; (2) it was not sufficient that IG and C believed they were setting up a series of trusts as a valid trust required the three certainties of intention, subject matter and object to exist at the time the trust was formed, and (3) on the facts of the instant case, although IG and C had evidenced sufficient certainty of intention to create a trust, certainty of subject matter and object were lacking as there was no identifiable trust property or shares on which it was to be held by the beneficiaries. Further, there was no evidence of a fiduciary relationship existing between C and those who had purchased warranties from IG.

ERNST & YOUNG INC v. CENTRAL GUARANTY TRUST CO (2000-01) 3 I.T.E.L.R. 605, Wilson, J., QB (Alta).

4681. **Deeds–rectification–evidence of mistake–failure to give effect to settlor's intention–Jersey**

An application was made to rectify an error in a deed of settlement which, if uncorrected, would exclude the beneficiaries whom the settlor intended to benefit.

Held, allowing the application, that rectification should be allowed where (1) there was enough evidence that an error had occurred; (2) the mistake was shown to exist on the highest application of the civil burden of proof; (3) complete and frank disclosure had been made, and (4) no other remedy was available, *Smouha Family Trust, Re* [2000] W.T.L.R. 133, [2000] C.L.Y. 5261 applied.

WESTBURY SETTLEMENT, *Re* (2000-01) 3 I.T.E.L.R. 699, Sir Peter Crill (Commissioner), Royal Ct (Jer).

4682. **Discretionary trusts–compromise agreements–surrender of trustee's discretion to the court–Jersey**

A trustee sought the sanction of the court to a compromise of various actions concerning trust assets. The deceased had settled his estate on discretionary trust and had left letters indicating his wish that the trustee should exercise its discretion in favour of his widow in her lifetime. In three sets of proceedings after the death of the deceased, the widow and the two children of the deceased each challenged the financial arrangements made on the death of the deceased and each other's various claims. All three actions were heard together and after a number of days the widow and the children agreed a compromise which effectively gave the widow a life interest in most of the assets.

Held, granting the application, that the proper test was whether the compromise was in the best interests of the trust and the beneficiaries. Where the trustee surrendered his discretion to the court, that test would be applied by the court acting as if it was the trustee. Here there was good reason to accept the trustee's surrender of its discretion since the court was better placed to make a judgment on the prospects and effect of the litigation. The compromise was within the power of the trustee in any event, and it would clearly be beneficial to prevent the continuance of the extremely expensive proceedings which were eating up the assets of the trust and which had already lasted for five years, *Cowan v. Scargill* [1985] Ch. 270, [1984] C.L.Y. 3135 and *Marley v. Mutual Security Merchant Bank & Trust Co Ltd* [1991] 3 All E.R. 198, [1991] C.L.Y. 1730 applied.

ABACUS (CI) LTD v. HIRSCHFIELD (2001-02) 4 I.T.E.L.R. 686, Smith (Commissioner), Royal Ct (Jer).

4683. **Discretionary trusts—employee share schemes—entitlement to earmarked shares—admissible evidence for interpretation of documents**

C applied for a declaration that a trustee company held certain shares on trust for him. C had been employed in a senior position by a company. The company had an employee share scheme in which he was a participant. He was told that a large number of shares had been "earmarked" for him. The scheme was so constructed that for tax reasons the shares were held on discretionary trust by the trustee company before being transferred to the employee. C resigned his employment about two years after the shares had been earmarked for him, and sought to have the shares transferred to him. The trustee company had refused to do so.

Held, refusing the application, that (1) it was a principal of general application that in construing a document evidence of subjective intention at the time that the document was created was inadmissible, but that all the relevant extrinsic circumstances concerning the creation of the document will be taken into account, *Investors Compensation Scheme Ltd v. West Bromwich Building Society (No.1)* [1998] 1 All E.R. 98, [1997] C.L.Y. 2537 considered and *Perrin v. Morgan* [1943] A.C. 399 applied, and (2) on the facts the word "earmark" as used by the trustee company was intended to indicate that they retained the shares in the discretionary trust so that beneficial ownership had not been transferred. This was consistent with the intended tax effects of the scheme, which would only remain effective if there was no transfer of beneficial ownership of the shares, the fact that no dividends were paid to the employee and no voting rights could be exercised by him in respect of the shares so "earmarked".

CAMERON v. M&W MACK (ESOP) TRUSTEE LTD [2002] W.T.L.R. 647, Jonathan Gaunt, Q.C., Ch D.

4684. **Discretionary trusts—Isle of Man—refusal to accept trusts—interpretation of settlor's instructions by legal advisors**

Questions arose as to whether an Isle of Man trust was established in accordance with the instructions given and whether assets had been correctly transferred to that trust. In 1989, a Liechtenstein anstalt was being wound up and it became necessary to transfer its assets to a new vehicle. Acting on advice, R established two British Virgin Islands trusts ("the BVI trusts"). Those trusts named the beneficiary as the Red Cross and such other persons as the trustees might appoint. Companies with bearer shares held the assets of those trusts. The bearer shares were placed in a bank in Jersey to which R and his son, RH, had access. RH, acting on behalf of R, sought advice on establishing in the Isle of Man a trust similar to the BVI trusts. The advice given was that such a trust would not be acceptable in the Isle of Man. Instead, it was suggested, that a broad discretionary settlement should be established, together with a letter of wishes. A draft settlement along those lines was drawn up. Just such a trust was set up in 1990 with an initial trust fund of £5, the settlor being a clerk at the offices of the law firm, which had given the advice. Two partners of that firm were the trustees. Subsequently, certain valuable properties were transferred to those partners or to the law firm. Here R and RH contended that the assets never became subject to the trust provisions, and alleged that they had never agreed to the establishment of the trust. The Acting Deemster found that the trust was established on R's instructions and that it was to be a standard discretionary trust. He further found that substantial assets were comprised in the trust fund. R, RH and RH's wife appealed against that decision.

Held, dismissing the appeal, that the Acting Deemster had not erred in relation to the facts found to answer the questions raised by the appellants. R's initial wish was that arrangements in the Isle of Man should mirror those made in Jersey. It was clear that no such arrangements would have been acceptable in the Isle of Man. It was clear why advice was given to pursue the alternative course of a discretionary settlement with a protector and a letter of wishes indicating how the settlor wished the settlement to be administered. Such a course was appropriate to give effect to the wishes of R and RH. At no time had either expressed any written criticism of the proposed form of settlement.

HOLMAENGEN TRUST, *Re* (1998-99) 1 I.T.E.L.R. 901, Tattersall Q.C., J.A., HC (IoM).

4685. **Discretionary trusts–trustees powers and duties–power to distribute trust assets direct to judgment creditor of beneficiary–Jersey**

G appealed against a decision that a payment by trustees out of trust assets to G as the beneficiary's judgment creditor would not be for the benefit of the beneficiary, S. A discretionary trust settled by S was expressed to be for the benefit of S and other members of his family. G applied for proprietary remedies against the trust assets. The trustees applied to the court for directions on whether they should, in exercise of their discretionary powers, distribute the trust funds in whole or in part to the beneficiary's judgment creditor. S had written to the trustees objecting to any such distribution, saying that he did not wish any payments to be made to himself at any time. G was joined as a party to the action, since it had a proprietary claim against the trust assets. It was held that the trustees, and therefore the court, could make a distribution for the benefit of a beneficiary even if that beneficiary objected to such a distribution. However, it concluded that a distribution to G in reduction of S's debt would not have been a payment for the benefit of S, and that such a payment of all or most of the trust funds would materially disadvantage the other discretionary beneficiaries.

Held, dismissing the appeal, that there could be no interference with the decision of the lower court unless that court had erred in law, had misdirected itself, or it appeared that the decision would, on other grounds, have resulted in injustice. The lower court was entitled to reach its decision as it was clear, on the facts, that a distribution from the trust would have still left a very large sum payable to G and the position between S and G would not have been materially altered. The lower court was entitled to reject the claim made by G that the distribution would benefit S by his being confronted by his dishonesty. It remained a matter within the discretion of the trustee, in this case the court, to weigh the interests of S and those of the other discretionary beneficiaries in deciding whether or not such a distribution should be made.

GRUPO TORRAS SA v. AL-SABAH (NO.6); *sub nom.* ABACUS (CI) LTD v. AL-SABAH; ESTEEM SETTLEMENT, *Re* [2002] W.T.L.R. 337, Gloster, J.A. (President), CA (Jer).

4686. **Discretionary trusts–trustees powers and duties–settlor's children as beneficiaries–protection of unborn child's interests–Australia**

Y was the settlor of a discretionary family trust. The primary beneficiaries were Y's children that were either alive at the date of the trust's creation or born in the future. The subject matter of the trust was the wholly owned shareholding in a group of companies with a turnover of AUD 30 million per annum. Y was divorced from the mother of his two living children, D and S, and he had fallen out with them to the extent that there was substantial litigation between them or between entities they controlled. The trustee, C, was a corporation wholly controlled by D and S. Y had remarried and his second wife was pregnant. He was concerned that D and S would cause C to exercise its wide powers so as to exclude the unborn child from the class of primary beneficiaries. Y therefore sought an order that would allow him to represent the unborn child's interests and an interlocutory injunction to restrain C from altering the terms of the trust until the child was born, at which point the child could be made a party to proceedings for a permanent injunction.

Held, allowing the application, that (1) the unborn child was a person for the purpose of proceedings where a right that was for its benefit was in issue and in circumstances where it could institute proceedings regarding that right if it survived birth, *Watt v. Rama* [1972] V.R. 353, [1972] C.L.Y. 2408 considered; (2) Y was the appropriate person to appoint to protect the unborn child's interests, and (3) there was a serious issue to be tried and on a balance of convenience the unborn child could suffer a greater hardship if the injunction was not granted than C might suffer if the injunction was granted.

YUNGHANNS v. CANDOORA NO 19 PTY LTD (NO.1) (1999-2000) 2 I.T.E.L.R. 589, Gillard, J., Sup Ct (Vic).

4687. Fees–public trustee

PUBLIC TRUSTEE (FEES) (AMENDMENT) ORDER 2002, SI 2002 2232; made under the Public Trustee Act 1906 s.9. In force: September 27, 2002; £1.50.

This Order amends the Public Trustee (Fees) Order 1999 (SI 1999 855) which prescribes fees to be charged by the Public Trustee. It provides that the Public Trustee's power to compromise disputes in relation to fees or remit fees in simple or exceptional cases will no longer be subject to the approval of the Treasury and for the purposes of calculating the administration fee the estate will be valued as at September 30, 2002 instead of September 30, 1998.

4688. Jurisdiction–exclusive jurisdiction clause in trust deed stipulating trust governed by Guernsey law–factors determining grant of stay–Jersey

E, a trustee company resident in Malta, brought proceedings in Jersey on behalf of beneficiaries against C, a former trustee resident in Jersey. A jurisdiction clause in the trust deed stated that the trust was subject to the law of Guernsey and the exclusive jurisdiction of the Guernsey court. C sought a stay, contending that the matter should be litigated in Guernsey.

Held, refusing the application, that an exclusive jurisdiction clause in a trust instrument was not to be treated on the same footing as a similar clause in a contract because the trust beneficiaries had not consented to its imposition. Although the court would normally uphold the jurisdictional directions of the trust, there was a discretion not to order a stay if sufficient reasons were shown. However, the burden of doing so was not as onerous as in contract cases. All the circumstances had to be examined, including availability of witnesses, applicable law, whether there was any linked litigation, costs, security, enforceability of the judgment, time bars, and whether a trial could be held fairly. The facts of the instant case showed that a linked contractual case was to be heard in Jersey involving the same evidence; the non overseas witnesses were in Jersey; the relevant Guernsey law was similar to Jersey law; and there would be costs savings if only one set of legal advisors was engaged on each side, *Aratra Potato Co Ltd v. Egyptian Navigation Co (The El Amria)* [1981] 2 Lloyd's Rep. 119, [1981] C.L.Y. 2198 applied.

EMM CAPRICORN TRUSTEES LTD v. COMPASS TRUSTEES LTD [2001] W.T.L.R. 997, Deputy Bailiff Birt, Royal Ct (Jer).

4689. Public Trustee (Liability and Fees) Act 2002 (35)

This Act amends the Public Trustee Act 1906 in respect of the liability and fees of the Public Trustee.

This Act received Royal Assent on November 7, 2002.

4690. Resulting trusts—foreign property—German property transferred to children—father rebutting presumption of advancement—refusal to enforce German revenue law—Australia

W transferred properties he owned in Germany to his two children, O and N, prior to the family's emigration to Australia. The family later split up and O and N claimed that the properties had been outright gifts. W, however, asserted that O and N held the properties on trust for him as the transfers had only been made to avoid capital gains tax in Germany. O and N argued that any trusts were rendered unenforceable due to illegality. At first instance it was held, on the assumption that German and Australian revenue law were the same, that the properties had not been gifts but that the trusts they were held under were unenforceable. W appealed.

Held, allowing the appeal, that (1) the evidence adduced before the court below showed that W had not intended to make outright gifts to O and N with the result that the properties were held on resulting trusts; (2) W had rebutted the presumption of advancement by showing that he intended to keep the properties for his own benefit by carrying out work on them after they were transferred to O and N; (3) as no evidence of German revenue law had been given, it could not be assumed that it was the same as Australian law. O and N could not, therefore avoid the resulting trusts, and (4) for O and N's claim to succeed, they would have to pay German tax and by granting an order in their favour, the court would be indirectly enforcing German revenue law, *Nelson v. Nelson* (1995) 185 C.L.R. 538 considered.

DAMBERG v. DAMBERG (2001-02) 4 I.T.E.L.R. 65, Heydon, J.A., CA (NSW).

4691. Resulting trusts—mortgagors—joint mortgages—no contribution to purchase price of property

C, a joint owner and mortgagor of a property, appealed against an order declaring that she held the property on a resulting trust for the estate of the father of G absolutely. C had assisted G's father in obtaining a joint mortgage on the strength of their joint total income in order to purchase a property for his sole use and occupation. However, while he was alive she had made no contribution to the deposit or mortgage repayments and had not lived at the property. The property was transferred into their joint names and there had been no agreement as to beneficial interests. There had been an understanding that she would be removed from the mortgage, but this had not happened. C contended that the resulting trust was for herself and G's father in unequal shares. She maintained that her beneficial interest arose from her deemed contribution towards the purchase of the property by her execution of the mortgage as security for a loan which paid a substantial part of the purchase price. She submitted that her contribution was the mortgage liabilities.

Held, dismissing the appeal, that C had not made a contribution to the purchase price of the property so as to give rise to a resulting trust in her favour. Her contribution to the purchase price at the date of acquisition of the property was the vital consideration. Any subsequent contributions resulting from enforcement of the mortgage would have been a contribution to the discharge of the mortgage liabilities and not to the purchase price. C was entitled as a trustee to be indemnified out of the trust property for any such mortgage repayments made. Therefore mortgage repayments made by C did not rebut the resulting trust to G's father as sole contributor to the purchase price and did not give C a beneficial interest in the property, *Dyer v. Dyer* (1788) 2 Cox Eq. Cas. 92 applied. It was observed that conveyancers should explain to clients the difference between a joint tenancy and a tenancy in common, determine what the client wanted, and expressly declare in the conveyance or transfer how the beneficial interest was to be held.

CARLTON v. GOODMAN; *sub nom.* GOODMAN v. CARLTON, [2002] EWCA Civ 545, [2002] 2 F.L.R. 259, Mummery, L.J., CA.

4692. **Settlements–sham transactions–validity–Jersey**

In 1977, R created a settlement under Jersey law and appointed C as trustee. R was substantially entitled as a beneficiary of the settlement and settlement terms gave him effective control over the trustee. R treated the trust funds as his own. On his death R's widow applied to set aside the settlement.

Held, allowing the application, that the settlement was wholly invalid and of no effect because the trust was a sham. The terms of the settlement were such that the settlor could revoke it or bring it to an end for the benefit of himself or at his direction, thereby infringing the rule of law in Jersey known as donner et retenir ne vaut.

RAHMAN v. CHASE BANK (CI) TRUST CO LTD [2002] B.P.I.R. 129, Deputy Bailiff Tomes, Royal Ct (Jer).

4693. **Settlements–variation–scheme to circumvent capital gains tax–benefit conferred on unborn beneficiaries–Jersey**

[Trusts Law (Jersey) Art.43.]

D was the UK resident settlor of a Jersey trust. He was potentially liable to capital gains tax on gains made by the trust, with a statutory right of reimbursement from the trustees. A scheme was devised to circumvent D's CGT liability by creating a new trust with a wider class of potential beneficiaries, to which the assets of the existing trust would be transferred. D and the trustee sought approval for the variation under the Trusts (Jersey) Law Art.43.

Held, allowing the application, that the variation meant that unborn beneficiaries could have access to the sum that would have been payable in tax. The fact that such benefits were achieved by way of tax mitigation was not a reason for consent to be refused, *N's 1989 Settlement, Re* (1998-99) 1 I.T.E.L.R. 803, *Osias Settlement, Re* 1987-88 Jer. L.R. 389, *Weston's Settlements, Re* [1969] 1 Ch. 223, [1968] C.L.Y. 3603 and *Whitehead's Will Trusts, Re* [1971] 1 W.L.R. 833, [1971] C.L.Y. 10704 considered.

DOUGLAS 1990 SETTLEMENT, Re (1999-2000) 2 I.T.EL.R. 682, Deputy Bailiff Birt, Royal Ct (Jer).

4694. **Settlements–variation–tax planning purposes–Jersey**

[Trusts (Jersey) Law 1984 Art.43.]

The trustees of a Jersey trust sought the variation of a settlement under the Trusts (Jersey) Law 1984 Art.43 to allow them the flexibility necessary to engage in legitimate tax avoidance of UK taxes.

Held, approving the variation, that the variation (1) would not automatically avoid UK taxation but instead allowed the trustees to plan for the future benefit of the settlor and the beneficiaries in reliance upon counsel's advice, and (2) did not infringe any undertakings given by the Jersey authorities to the UK Government regarding taxation, *Douglas 1990 Settlement, Re* (1999-2000) 2 I.T.E.L.R. 682 applied.

PETER HYND (H) SETTLEMENT, Re [2001] W.T.L.R. 1027, Sir Peter Crill (Commissioner), Royal Ct (Jer).

4695. **Trust corporations–Freezing injunctions–Bahamas–absence of substantive cause of action**

See CIVIL PROCEDURE: Meespierson (Bahamas) Ltd v. Grupo Torras SA. §438

4696. Trust funds-bankruptcy-beneficial interest in retirement plan-pre emptive costs orders

[Supreme Court Act 1981 s.51; Insolvency Act 1986 s.306.]

N, a bankrupt who was engaged in litigation to determine whether or not his benefits under a retirement plan had vested in his trustees in bankruptcy, sought an order that his costs in the action be paid out of his interest in the plan. The retirement plan had been amended to appoint TCL as trustee and N's rights under the plan had passed to the trustees pursuant to the Insolvency Act 1986 s.306. N contended that a change in the trust fund rules took precedence over the statutory vesting of his property with the result that it could be held on protective trust and applied to himself in the event of his suffering hardship.

Held, refusing the application, that the court's jurisdiction to make a preemptive costs order pursuant to the Supreme Court Act 1981 s.51 could not be extended to a hostile claim made by a single beneficiary as the financial ramifications for the trust fund would be considerable even in the event that N lost the claim, *McDonald v. Horn* [1995] 1 All E.R. 961, [1995] C.L.Y. 3836 applied. Further, this was not an appropriate case for making a costs order as there was no evidence that the deed introducing the new trust fund rules was to have retrospective effect, nor was there reason to believe that it could take precedence over vested statutory rights, *Imperial Foods Ltd Pension Scheme, Re* [1986] 1 W.L.R. 717, [1986] C.L.Y. 2514 considered.

TRUSTEE CORP LTD v. NADIR [2001] B.P.I.R. 541, Lawrence Collins, J., Ch D.

4697. Trust funds-freezing injunctions-foreign jurisdictions-claim for breach of contract and unjust enrichment-Bahamas

T applied to discharge a Mareva injunction freezing her assets in the Bahamas. A trust fund in the Bahamas had been divided into three separate trusts for the benefit of B and T. Disputes arose as to the construction and validity of the original trust and were resolved by the execution of an agreement between B and T releasing each other from any claims or actions relating to the Bahamian trust assets. T subsequently obtained a judgment in France which took into account, on T's request, the value of the Bahamian trust assets. B obtained the Mareva injunction against T claiming that by bringing the French action relating to the Bahamian trust assets T was in breach of contract, and was unjustly enriched by the French judgment. T sought to have the injunction discharged on the basis that the principle of unjust enrichment was not applicable to a judgment creditor who having obtained but not enforced a judgment had not yet been enriched.

Held, refusing the application, that the French judgment was a chose in action and it was clear that T would continue to try to enforce it. On the evidence, B's claims for damages for breach of contract and for unjust enrichment were made out, and therefore it would be just and equitable to maintain the injunction pending trial.

B v. T (NO.2) (2001-02) 4 I.T.E.L.R. 535, Longley, J., Sup Ct (Bah).

4698. Trust funds-receivers-appointment of receiver to protect trust property-Australia

In 1992, Y set up a discretionary trust for the benefit of his adult children, D and S, and future issue. Following his divorce and remarriage, Y had another son, W. D and S controlled C, the company that acted as trustee, but their relationship with Y deteriorated and a number of court cases had ensued, funded by C from the trust funds. Y became concerned that the trust funds were being dissipated and sought the appointment of a receiver to safeguard W's interest in the trust property.

Held, allowing the application, that a receiver could be appointed to protect trust property where there was evidence to show that it was at risk due to misconduct or breach of duty by the trustees. A strong case had to be made in favour of such an appointment, subject also to a quantitative assessment of the risks posed to the trust property. The situation that existed between Y and his adult children was such as to favour the appointment, given that trust funds had been used to fund the ongoing litigation. Further, C was reluctant to provide information on trust affairs. Taken together, the facts of the instant case showed that W's interests were at risk and a receiver could be appointed, subject to an undertaking in damages in favour of D and S.

YUNGHANNS v. CANDOORA NO 19 PTY LTD (NO.2) (2000-01) 3 I.T.E.L.R. 154, Warren, J., Sup Ct (Vic).

4699. Trustees–breach of trust–delay in prosecution of action–Isle of Man

[Trusts (Guernsey) Law 1989 s.70.]

S was a beneficiary of a settlement. The settlement was established under the laws of Guernsey. E and H were sole directors and shareholders of the corporate trustee. On September 6, 1996 S brought an action against the defendant trustees, E and H, alleging breach of trust. In February 1997, E and H filed notice of payment in. Two years and five months later S served notice of intention to proceed. E and H applied by notice of motion to dismiss the claim for want of prosecution, to strike out the action as disclosing no reasonable cause of action, and to strike out the claim as being frivolous, vexatious and an abuse of process of the court. S filed an affidavit explaining the reasons for the delay in the prosecution of the action.

Held, dismissing the notice of motion, that (1) the delay was excusable because of the need to prepare complex reports; (2) even if the delay was not excusable it had not been shown that the delay had been seriously prejudicial to the defendants, the evidence in question being largely documentary, and (3) there was an arguable case against E and H as corporate trustees because the Trusts (Guernsey) Law 1989 s. 70 provided that a director of a corporate trustee was deemed to be a guarantor of the trustee in respect of any damages for breach of trust.

SEGAL v. EDWARDS (1999-2000) 2 I.T.E.L.R. 575, Deemster Cain, HC (IoM).

4700. Trustees–indemnity–fraudulent transfer of assets–Australia

[Law of Property Act 1936 (Australia) s.86; Bankruptcy Act 1966 (Australia) s.121.]

Issues arose in relation to the termination of a trust and alleged sham transactions connected to that termination. RFP was a company which acted as trustee of a family trust. RFP sought an indemnity against liabilities it had incurred to banks while acting as trustee. The directors of RFP were C and her sons R, S and A. RFP had been trustee of the trust from its creation in 1981 until 1993 when it was replaced in that office by another company, BP which was similarly under the control of members of C's family. In September 1998, RFP was placed into provisional liquidation. By 1993 the liabilities owed by RFP as trustee to two banks had exceeded the assets of the trust. That was the reason for the replacement of RFP as trustee with BP. The directors of BP were members of the extended C's family. Further, after sequestration orders were made against C, R and S in 1998, an attempt was made to terminate the trust and to vest all of its assets in A. Yet further, valuable trust assets were then purportedly sold by A at an undervalue to an agent of the C'S family trust. Therefore, RFP claimed an indemnity in relation to its debts to banks and it also sought to repudiate all three of those transactions as having been made to defraud creditors or otherwise as shams.

Held, upholding the trustee's right to an indemnity, that the indemnity was operative in spite of the purported change of trustee and the transfers of the trust's assets. Furthermore, the indemnity applied to interests acquired subsequent to the company ceasing to be trustee. The replacement of the trustee was an act intended to defraud creditors and was therefore void under the Bankruptcy Act 1966 s.121. The vesting of the assets in A and the sale at an undervalue were acts intended to defeat or delay creditors and were therefore voidable under the Law of Property Act 1936 s.86.

ROTHMORE FARMS PTY LTD (IN LIQUIDATION) v. BELGRAVIA PTY LTD (1999-2000) 2 I.T.E.L.R. 159, Mansfield, J., Fed Ct (Aus) (Sgl judge).

4701. Trustees–indemnity–property development funded by unit trust–failure of venture leading to insolvency of beneficiaries–personal liability of beneficiaries–Australia

C brought an action against B, the director of an insolvent company, G, which owed debts to C. A syndicate, taking the form of a unit trust, had been set up to purchase and develop land owned by C. Difficulties arose with the planning process and G put up additional funds to support the trust. The trust deed vested beneficial ownership of the trust property in the unit holders. Subsequently, the trustee company went into liquidation, followed by G and other investor companies, and C sought to recover the money owing to it from the directors of G, including B. C claimed that by making the additional investment G had incurred liabilities at a time when it was reasonable to expect that it was unable to pay its debts.

Held, dismissing the action, that a beneficiary getting the benefit of a trust should also bear its burdens unless some good reason could be shown why the trustee should bear the burden. The beneficiaries of a trust being sui juris and absolutely entitled were personally bound to indemnify the trustee against liabilities incurred when carrying out the trust. In the case of multiple beneficiaries, in order to establish personal liability on the part of the beneficiaries, there had to be something more than the mere fact that the beneficiaries were sui juris and absolutely entitled. It might be sufficient that the beneficiary was a settlor of the trust, or had contributed funds which were managed, or that the beneficiaries requested that expenditure be incurred, or that the trustee was carrying on a business established for the benefit of the beneficiaries. In the present case, B was not aware that the trustee had a right of indemnity from the unit holders. G did not, by making an additional investment become liable to indemnify the trustee in respect of expenses previously paid or incurred by the trustee. That transaction did not amount to the adoption and approval of all that had previously occurred, but was no more than the raising of a modest sum aimed at overcoming some of the problems then faced by the venture. No principle of trust law or of the law of unjust enrichment required that G be held liable for the debts incurred before the additional payment was made.

COUNTRYSIDE (NO.3) PTY LTD v. BEST (2001-02) 4 I.T.E.L.R. 600, Davies, A.J., Sup Ct (NSW).

4702. Trustees–indemnity costs orders–indemnification from trust funds

There were competing claims against two trusts, one of which the Privy Council had already found to be non-charitable. One of the claimants was the Norwegian Revenue. Acting on an order of the Governor General, apparently on foreign policy grounds, the Attorney General declined to continue to represent the interests of the charity after appealing against the substantive action to the Privy Council. The trustees applied to represent the interests of the charity and for a pre-emptive order indemnifying their costs from the trust funds.

Held, granting the applications, that (1) where there were competing claims to the assets of the trust pre-emptive costs orders would only be made in exceptional circumstances; (2) the withdrawal of the Attorney General was an exceptional circumstance; (3) the court must be satisfied that the merits of success justified the costs expenditure; (4) rectification was not available in this case, but (5) resettlement and associated arguments were tenable.

BRIDGE TRUST CO LTD v. ATTORNEY GENERAL OF THE CAYMAN ISLANDS (2001-02) 4 I.T.E.L.R. 369, Smellie, C.J., Grand Court (Cayman Islands).

4703. Trustees–indemnity costs orders–indemnification from trust funds

S was a Gibraltar trust company and trustee of two funds created by the US settlor, which together held about US$20 million by the date of the hearing. When the trusts were established the settlor advised S of claims against him by the New York Securities and Exchange Commission. Nevertheless the settlor were registered in Gibraltar as solvent in accordance with local law. About 2 years and six months after the creation of the trusts the settlor became bankrupt in the USA. His trustee in bankruptcy sought to recover the trust moneys for the benefit of the creditors alleging fraud and negligence. S applied for directions as to whether to defend the actions and that its costs of the litigation should be borne by the trust funds. The judge gave leave for the trustee to apply to strike out the action and ordered indemnity for costs from the trust fund for the application to strike out and down to close of discovery. The trustee in bankruptcy appealed.

Held, dismissing the appeal, save on one minor point, that (1) the trustee of the bankrupt's estate was properly excluded from the hearing. Where there was to be hostile litigation against a trustee, the other party to that actual or contemplated litigation should not be a party to the hearing, *Beddoe, Re* [1893] 1 Ch.547 applied; (2) The relevant considerations were the strength of the trustee's case, whether it was clear that the judge at trial would make an order in favour of the applicant, the degree of risk that a *Beddoe* order might cause injustice, and any special circumstances, and (3) although a *Beddoe* order in favour of a trustee sued personally would be rare, it was within the scope of the judge's discretion. At the instant stage of the litigation it should be limited to the proposed application by S to strike out the claim against it, *Walters v. Woodbridge* (1877-78) L.R. 7 Ch. D. 504 followed.

STG VALMET TRUSTEES LTD v. BRENNAN [2002] W.T.L.R. 273, Sir John Waite, CA (Gib).

4704. Trustees–offshore trusts–appointment of trustee and protector–Cook Islands

In 1995 A and his wife created an asset protection trust registered in the Cook Islands. The definition of excluded persons in the trust deed included "administrative bodies" and "claimants". In 1998, on the application of the Federal Trade Commission, FTC, the settlers were committed to prison in the US for contempt. The settlers then executed a document purporting to remove the existing trustee and to appoint X, a company wholly owned by the FTC, as the new trustee. They also executed a deed, which purported to remove FTC from the definition of "excluded persons" set out in the trust deed. They executed a third deed resigning and appointing X as protector of the trust. The former trustee applied to the court for directions for the management and administration of the trust. The issues were whether the settlers were acting under duress when they executed the documents and whether the effect of the documents was to confer a benefit on an excluded person.

Held, finding the documents to be invalid, that (1) the imprisonment for contempt of court was lawful in the State of Nevada and so the documents were not executed under duress rendering them void or voidable but (2) FTC was an "excluded person" being an administrative body and claimant falling within those definitions and the effect of the documents was to confer a benefit on FTC thus rendering them invalid; (3) the appointment of X as trustee and protector was invalid; and (4) as there was no protector of the trust it would be appropriate for the court to appoint a new protector.

A IRREVOCABLE TRUST, *Re* (1999-2000) 2 I.T.E.L.R. 482, Quilliam, C.J., HC (Cook I).

4705. Trustees–personal property–requirements for valid trust of personalty

F, a father and his son, S, were both called "SS Dhingra". On the death of F's wife insurance proceeds of £33,000 were paid to F. F opened a bank account at a building society where he already held a number of accounts in his own name. The new bank account was opened in the name "Trustee for SS Dhingra". The court below issued a declaration that the account was held for S and was to be transferred to him. F appealed.

Held, dismissing the appeal, that (1) there were other accounts at a building society held in F's own name which raised a presumption on the facts that the new account was intended to operate differently; (2) by calling the account "Trustee for SS Dhingra" that raised a presumption on the facts that F was intending to be a trustee. It is not possible to hold on trust for one's self and therefore the question arose as to who was to be the beneficiary; (3) F said in evidence that the welfare of S was his "paramount consideration" at the time, and (4) F held a Masters degree in law which the court below held had worked against him because F would surely have acted to correct any error in the naming of this account understanding what it meant to be a trustee, it having been proved that F had received a statement for that account.

DHINGRA v. DHINGRA (1999-2000) 2 I.T.E.L.R. 262, Lindsay, J., CA.

4706. Trustees-trust corporations-entitlement to probate-British Virgin Islands

[Trust Corporation (Probate and Administration) Act Cap. 75 (British Virgin Islands) s.2.]

HSBC was a company incorporated in the British Virgin Islands. It was not a trust company but held a general trust. It made four applications for probate where it had been named sole executor and all were refused by the deputy registrar. HSBC applied by summons for review of the refusals.

Held, dismissing the application, that (1) as an international business company, HSBC did not fall within the definition of a trust corporation under the Trust Corporation (Probate and Administration) Act Cap. 75 s.2 and only such a trust corporation was entitled to apply for probate; (2) the general trust licence did not entitle HSBC to apply for probate; (3) under HSBC's memorandum of association it was entitled to act as an administrator or as an executor and that was not in contravention of the International Business Companies Act and (4) as a non-trust corporation, HSBC was nevertheless entitled to apply for letters of administration with will annexed.

DOONE (SYLVIA) (DECEASED), Re (1999-2000) 2 I.T.E.L.R. 425, Benjamin, J., HC (BVI).

4707. Trustees powers and duties-conflict of interest-will trust appointing spouse as beneficiary and trustee-South Africa

B was a professional adviser to J, who was the income beneficiary and trustee of her late husband's will trust. D was a capital beneficiary under the trust. The trust held shares in a holding company which in turn held shares in a quoted company, T. B mistakenly advised J to sell T shares and lend to proceeds of sale to the AJ Trust, which was actually moribund. J had also been the trustee of the AJ Trust and so used the money generated by the sale to make other investments. When the mistake was subsequently discovered, the investments were transferred to the will trust. D complained that the investment had been detrimental to his interest in the capital. His claim against D for pure economic loss was dismissed at first instance on the ground that his interest did not accrue until J died and, in any event, the will trust did not prevent the trustees from selling the T shares. D appealed.

Held, dismissing the appeal, that D could not show any actual loss. His right to the capital of the will trust was contingent upon J's death and any loss arising from the change of investment fell to be quantified in the future. There was a conflict of interest in J's position as both income beneficiary and trustee. However, there was nothing in the will to prevent her selling T shares and such a restriction could not easily be implied as to do so would prevent the trustees from ever changing the investments held by the trust.

JOWELL v. BRAMWELL-JONES [2002] W.T.L.R. 31, Scott, J., Sup Ct (SA).

4708. Trustees powers and duties-discretion-court approval for proposed course of action-Jersey

The court gave guidelines as to the approach to be taken when asked by trustees to authorise a proposed course of action.

Held, that trustees generally sought the approval of the court in four situations: (1) on a question of construction of the trust instrument or a statute; (2) where a major decision was required involving the disposal of a valuable asset, such as a family estate or company; (3) where the trustees were deadlocked or could not reach a decision for other reasons and wanted to surrender their discretion to the court, or (4) where the trustees had been attacked for acting outwith their powers or for misusing their powers. In (1) the application would be heard in open court with argument from both sides. For (2) and (3) applications should be heard in chambers and adversarial argument would not usually be required; (4) was hostile litigation that needed to be heard in open court, *Public Trustee v. Cooper* [2001] W.T.L.R. 901, [2001] C.L.Y. 5527 applied.

S SETTLEMENT (2001/154), *Re* (2001-02) 4 I.T.E.L.R. 206, Birt (Deputy Bailiff), Royal Ct (Jer).

4709. **Trustees powers and duties–discretionary powers–trustees seeking directions from court–relevant considerations–Jersey**

S was a Netherlands citizen resident and domiciled in Belgium who had established a Jersey trust. His marriage was subject to the Dutch regime of community of property, whereby all the assets of both parties to the marriage became subject to the equal ownership of both of them, subject to any countervailing ante-nuptial agreement. There was no such agreement in this case. The wife died before S and on her death he became the legal and beneficial owner of his one half of the joint assets and the owner of a life interest in the deceased wife's half. He purported to transfer all his assets, including the life interest, to the Jersey trust. On his death it became apparent that there might be liabilities to tax in either or both of Belgium and the Netherlands. The trustee sought the directions of the court on proposals made by it.

Held, granting the application, that (1) the trustee was right to seek the directions of the court on what was a serious matter involving large sums of money. It was not surrendering its discretion to the court because it was seeking approval of its suggested course of action, and so had already exercised its discretion, and (2) the court was satisfied that the trustee had formed its proposals in good faith and were reasonable. The trustee's proposals were not vitiated by any conflict of interest and therefore the trustee should pay such tax as the fund was liable to pay and divide the residue into three funds for the beneficiaries, including minors and those not yet ascertained or born.

REPRESENTATION OF I, *Re* (2001-02) 4 I.T.E.L.R. 446, Commissioner Hamon, Royal Ct (Jer).

4710. **Trustees powers and duties–discretionary trusts–statutory duty to provide information–discretionary trust established prior to entry into force of Trusts (Guernsey) Law 1989–Guernsey**

[Trusts (Guernsey) Law 1989 s.22, s.63.]

By virtue of the Trusts (Guernsey) Law 1989 s. 22 a trustee was required to provide beneficiaries or settlers with information regarding the status and value of trust property. However, s.22(2) also provided that it only applied to trusts established prior to the entry into force date of the 1989 Act where beneficiaries had a vested interest in the property at that date. SH, the beneficiary in a discretionary trust established before the Act came into force, sought an order under either s.22(2), s.63 or the inherent jurisdiction for the trustee to deliver up trust documents and accounts.

Held, dismissing the application, that (1) the Act set out all the duties and rights pertaining to the provision of information, and (2) s.22(2) clearly stipulated that beneficiaries in trusts established prior to the date the Act came into force could only obtain delivery of trust information where they also had a vested interest in trust property as at that date. As no such vested interest existed in SH's case, he could not rely on s.22(2) to obtain the information sought.

STUART-HUTCHESON v. SPREAD TRUSTEE CO LTD; *sub nom.* PETER ACATOS NO. 2 SETTLEMENT, *Re* (2000-01) 3 I.T.E.L.R. 683, Deputy Bailiff Day, Royal Ct (Gue).

4711. Trustees powers and duties–occupational pension scheme–demutualisation windfall–power to distribute to past and present members–New Zealand

The trustees of a fund M sought a direction as to whether they had power under the the trust deed to distribute the proceeds of the sale of a windfall share issued to both past and present members, as proposed by the trustees, or whether the distribution was restricted to only one of those classes. The windfall share issue arose from the demutualisation of a provident fund in which the fund held investments. The demutualisation was announced in December 1996, but entitlement to the proceeds of the windfall only occurred in January 1998, by which time many members had left the M scheme. Disputes arose as to the entitlement of the past and present members. The trustees proposed an amendment to the deed to allow distribution of the proceeds to both classes, but the present membership refused its consent.

Held, giving a direction that the trustees could make payments to both past and present members without amending the trust deed, that (1) although an express trust could be made subject to the terms of a constructive trust, this device could not be used in the instant case as the windfall was due to the conduct of others prior to receipt by the trustees; (2) the windfall share allocation resulted from the members' contributions prior to December 1996. The trustees were only the means by which the contributions were held and past members' contributions could not be dismissed on the ground that further steps were necessary before their contributions became eligible, and (3) the trustees had erred by not taking the prospective windfall into account when making distributions to members leaving the scheme after December 1996. This error could be addressed, however, without the need to amend the trust deed.

MOTOROLA NEW ZEALAND SUPERANNUATION FUND, *Re* (2000-01) 3 I.T.E.L.R. 578, McGechan, J., HC (NZ).

4712. Trustees powers and duties–unit trusts–bank acting as trustee and banker

N agreed to act as the trustee for a unit trust that was formed to purchase blocks of flats and then sell separate flats at a profit for its investors. Under the trust deed, W had sole responsibility for acquiring and selling the properties, which W was authorised to deal with as a beneficial owner. Concerns were expressed within N as to the extent of W's powers and its management abilities. Following losses caused by the downturn in the property market, G, an investor in the trust, brought an action against N, contending that it was liable to compensate investors in equity as it had failed to perform its duty as trustee.

Held, dismissing the action, that while N was acting in a fiduciary capacity there was no conflict of interest in it acting both as W's banker and trustee, as this was provided for in the trust deed. N had no obligation to make enquiries of W after the trust was constituted. Knowledge as to the concerns expressed about W by various employees of N could not be imputed to N as a whole so that it was not liable on the basis of those concerns. Further, there was no evidence that the investors had sustained losses because N had not removed W from its position as manager of the unit trust.

GALMERROW SECURITIES LTD v. NATIONAL WESTMINSTER BANK PLC [2002] W.T.L.R. 125, Harman, J., Ch D.

4713. Trustees powers and duties–variation–beneficiaries' informed consent to variation of trust–equitable jurisdiction to set aside

AP, Danish residents, were the beneficiaries of a UK family trust. C, trustees, had determined to export the trust to Jersey for inheritance tax planning purposes. AP had executed an assignment as part of the scheme to export the trust. The principal effects of the Jersey trust were not revealed to AP, but (1) ended their absolute entitlement to the income of the trust as the Jersey trust was discretionary; (2) ended their power of appointment over capital, and (3) meant that their children ceased to be the only class of beneficiary because the wide discretionary powers conferred on the trustees allowed other beneficiaries to be added. On discovering the full effect of the changes, AP applied to have the assignment set aside. C submitted that the burden of proof was upon AP to show that they would not have executed the assignment if they had been advised properly.

Held, granting the application, that the assignment deed was set aside in the exercise of the court's equitable discretion as AP had not understood the effect of the transaction when they had executed the deed, *Gibbon v. Mitchell* [1990] 1 W.L.R. 1304, [1991] C.L.Y. 1724 and *Lady Hood of Avalon v. MacKinnon* [1909] 1 Ch. 476 considered. To succeed, it was not necessary for AP to show that they would not have executed the deed if they had known the true position, but the evidence clearly showed that AP would not have done so if they had known the full extent of the changes, *Dutton v. Thompson* (1883) L.R. 23 Ch. D. 278 considered. The changes from the original trust were significant and necessitated informed consent from AP.

ANKER-PETERSEN v. CHRISTENSEN [2002] W.T.L.R. 313, Davis, J., Ch D.

4714. Books

Atherton, Rosalind F.–Papers of the International Academy of Estate and Trust Law-2000. The International Academy of Estate and Trust Law Yearbook, 2. Hardback: £69.00. ISBN 90-411-9855-5. Kluwer Law International.

Atherton, Rosalind F.–Papers of the International Academy of Estate and Trust Law: 2001. The International Academy of Estate and Trust Law Yearbook, Vol 3. Hardback: £72.00. ISBN 90-411-9880-6. Kluwer Law International.

Campbell, Emily–Campbell: Varying International Domestic Trusts. Paperback: £60.00. ISBN 0-406-94023-1. Butterworths Law.

Clayton, Nigel–Administration of Trusts. Paperback: £30.00. ISBN 0-85297-605-4. Paperback: £30.00. ISBN 0-85297-605-4. Financial World Publishing.

Dunkley, Mark–Practitioner's Guide to Drafting Trusts. Paperback: £45.00. ISBN 0-7545-1245-2. Tolley Publishing.

Eastaway, Nigel; Richards, Ian–Tax Adviser's Guide to Trusts. Paperback: £75.00. ISBN 0-7545-1223-1. Tolley Publishing.

Edwards, Richard; Stockwell, Nigel–Trusts and Equity. 5th Ed. Foundation Studies in Law. Paperback: £26.99. ISBN 0-582-43810-1. Longman.

Hayton, David J.–Extending the Boundaries of Trust and Similar Ring-fenced Funds. Hardback: £100.00. ISBN 90-411-9879-2. Kluwer Law International.

Kessler, James–Drafting Trusts and Will Trusts. Hardback: CD-ROM: £99.00. ISBN 0-421-79310-4. Sweet & Maxwell.

Lloyd, Stephen; Bleasdale, Marie-Claire–Practitioner's Guide to Powers and Duties of Trustees. Paperback: £49.00. ISBN 0-7545-1489-7. Paperback: £49.00. ISBN 0-7545-1489-7. Tolley Publishing.

Meek, Alison; Wood, John; Meadway, Susannagh; Evans, Nicola–Practitioner's Guide to Contentious Trusts and Estates. Paperback: £49.00. ISBN 0-7545-1658-X. Tolley Publishing.

Ramage, Roderick W.–Underhill and Hayton: Law Relating to Trustees. Hardback: CD-ROM: £295.00. ISBN 0-406-93884-9. Butterworths Law.

Reed, Penelope–Trust and Estates Handbook. Paperback: £49.95. ISBN 0-7545-1946-5. Butterworths Law.

Riddall, John G.–Riddall: Law of Trusts. Paperback: £23.95. ISBN 0-406-94286-2. Butterworths Law.

Sanders, Catherine–Declarations of Trust. 2nd Ed. Paperback: £49.00. ISBN 0-7520-0605-3. Sweet & Maxwell.

Stebbings, Chantal–Private Trustee in Victorian England. Cambridge Studies in English Legal History. Hardback: £45.00. ISBN 0-521-78185-X. Cambridge University Press.

Trusts Law. 3rd Ed. LawCards Series. Paperback: £6.00. ISBN 1-85941-710-8. Cavendish Publishing Ltd.

Warnock-Smith, S.; Legge, Henry; Tidmarsh Christopher–Practitioner's Guide to Variations of Trusts. Paperback: £48.00. ISBN 0-7545-1244-4. Tolley Publishing.

Whitehouse, Chris; Hassall, Nicholas—Whitehouse and Hassall: Principles of Trust and Will Drafting. Paperback: £50.00. ISBN 0-406-91444-3. Butterworths Law.

UTILITIES

4715. Electricity supply industry—connection charges

ELECTRICITY (CONNECTION CHARGES) REGULATIONS 2002, SI 2002 93; made under the Electricity Act 1989 s.19, s.60, s.64. In force: February 11, 2002; £1.75.

These Regulations, which revoke and re-enact the Electricity (Connection Charges) Regulations 1990 (SI 1990 527), provide for an electricity distributor to recover from subsequent users of electric lines and electrical plant first provided for the purpose of giving a connection to the premises or distribution system of another person an amount in respect of the expenses incurred in first providing the line or plant. Recovery provisions for connections on domestic premises are also incorporated.

4716. Electricity supply industry—determination of turnover for penalties

ELECTRICITY AND GAS (DETERMINATION OF TURNOVER FOR PENALTIES) ORDER 2002, SI 2002 1111; made under the Gas Act 1986 s.30A; and the Electricity Act 1989 s.27A. In force: April 13, 2002; £1.50.

This Order makes a provision for the determination of the turnover of a licence holder for the purposes of the Electricity Act 1989 s.27A(8) and the Gas Act 1986 s.30A(8) which provide that where the Gas and Electricity Markets Authority is satisfied that a licence holder has contravened or is contravening any licence condition or certain requirements imposed on him by the Electricity Act 1989 or the Gas Act 1986 or is failing or has failed to achieve any standard of performance, the Authority may impose on the licence holder a penalty of such amount as is reasonable in all the circumstances of the case not exceeding 10 per cent of the turnover of the licence holder.

4717. Electricity supply industry—electrical equipment—meters

ELECTRICITY (APPROVAL OF PATTERN OR CONSTRUCTION AND INSTALLATION AND CERTIFICATION) (AMENDMENT) REGULATIONS 2002, SI 2002 3129; made under the Electricity Act 1989 s.31, s.60, Sch.7 para.2, Sch.7 para.13. In force: February 1, 2003; £2.50.

These Regulations, which amend the Meters (Approval of Pattern or Construction and Manner of Installation) Regulations 1998 (SI 1998 1565) and the Meters (Certification) Regulations 1998 (SI 1998 1566), provide that a meter examiner shall not, unless asked to do so by a person submitting a meter for approval, carry out examinations or tests on a meter submitted for approval of its pattern or construction or manner of installation if the report of a nominated laboratory on the meter enables the examiner to conclude that the specified requirement will be met. The requirement is that a meter of that pattern or construction or a meter installed in that manner will be capable of accurately recording the quantity of electricity for which the meter is intended to operate. The amendments also enable the Gas and Electricity Markets Authority to use the services of a nominated laboratory in carrying out its functions and to rely on a report prepared by a nominated laboratory to satisfy itself as to the fitness of a manufacturer or repairer of meters to be authorised; to amend the conditions that apply to an examiner authorised under the regulations; to facilitate the use by an authorised manufacturer or repairer of a nominated laboratory in the arrangements they make for audit of their apparatus, processes, systems and records; and to enable a nominated laboratory to deploy authorised examiners employed by it.

4718. Electricity supply industry–renewable energy–renewables obligation

RENEWABLES OBLIGATION ORDER 2002, SI 2002 914; made under the Electricity Act 1989 s.32, s.32A, s.32B, s.32C. In force: April 1, 2002; £3.00.

This Order imposes an obligation on all suppliers licensed under the Electricity Act 1989, to supply specified amounts of electricity, generated by using renewable sources, to customers in England and Wales. The renewables obligation requires the electricity supplier to produce evidence of the supply of electricity generated from renewable sources to the Gas and Electricity Markets Authority. It provides for how the amount of an electricity supplier's renewables obligation is to be determined, determines what types of electricity generated from renewable sources are eligible to satisfy an electricity supplier's renewables obligation and provides how payments made to the Authority by electricity suppliers are to be divided amongst those electricity suppliers subject to the renewables obligation.

4719. Electricity supply industry–safety and quality

ELECTRICITY SAFETY, QUALITY AND CONTINUITY REGULATIONS 2002, SI 2002 2665; made under the Electricity Act 1989 s.29, s.30, s.60. In force: January 31, 2003; £4.50.

These Regulations which revoke the Electricity Supply Regulations 1988 (SI 1988 1057), the Electricity Supply (Amendment) Regulations 1990 (SI 1990 390), the Electricity Supply (Amendment) Regulations 1992 (SI 1992 2961) the Electricity Supply (Amendment) (No.2) Regulations 1994 (SI 1994 3021) and the Electricity Supply (Amendment) Regulations 1998 (SI 1998 2971), impose requirements regarding the installation and use of electrical networks and equipment owned or operated by generators, distributors and meter operators, and the participation of suppliers in providing electricity to consumers. They further impose duties on agents, contractors and sub-contractors of duty holders.

4720. Electricity supply industry–standards of performance

ELECTRICITY (STANDARDS OF PERFORMANCE) (AMENDMENT) REGULATIONS 2002, SI 2002 476; made under the Electricity Act 1989 s.39, s.39A, s.39B, s.40B, s.42A, s.60. In force: April 1, 2002; £1.75.

These Regulations, which amend the Electricity (Standards of Performance) Regulations 2001 (SI 2001 3265), delete regulations 9 to 12 and replace them with new regulations 13A and B which are in substantially similar form to the revoked regulations 10 and 11 but apply to all electricity suppliers. They also make amendments so that where payments are to be made by a relevant distributor to a customer, they are to be made to the electricity supplier of that customer for onward transmission to the customer.

4721. Electricity supply industry–standards of performance

ELECTRICITY (STANDARDS OF PERFORMANCE) (AMENDMENT NO.2) REGULATIONS 2002, SI 2002 742; made under the Electricity Act 1989 s.39, s.39A, s.39B, s.40B, s.42A, s.60. In force: Reg.1: March 31, 2002; Reg.2: March 31, 2002; remainder: April 1, 2002; £2.00.

These Regulations, which amend the Electricity (Standards of Performance) Regulations 2001 (SI 2001 3265), revoke the Electricity (Standards of Performance) (Amendment) Regulations 2002 (SI 2002 476). They provide that where the conveyance of electricity to a customer's premises is discontinued on more than three occasions in a year for more than three hours on each occasion, the distribution company of that customer will pay the customer the prescribed sum. They also provide that where payments are to be made by a relevant distributor to a customer, they are to be made to the electricity supplier of that customer for onward transmission to the customer.

4722. Gas supply industry—connection charges—recovery of expenses—time extension

GAS (CONNECTION CHARGES) (AMENDMENT) REGULATIONS 2002, SI 2002 1488; made under the Gas Act 1986 s.10, s.47. In force: July 1, 2002; £1.50.

These Regulations amend the Gas (Connection Charges) Regulations 2001 (SI 2001 3267) by extending the period during which expenses may be recovered from five years from the laying of the main in question to twenty years from that date.

4723. Gas supply industry—standards of performance—compensation

GAS (STANDARDS OF PERFORMANCE) REGULATIONS 2002, SI 2002 475; made under the Gas Act 1986 s.33A, s.33AB, s.33D, s.47. In force: April 1, 2002; £2.50.

These Regulations prescribe the sum which a gas supplier must pay to a domestic customer by way of compensation for failure to meet specified standards' of performance in respect of specified services to be provided by such gas suppliers. They set out the period within which a standard is to be performed and the amount of compensation payable where it is not performed.

4724. Gas supply industry—standards of performance—compensation

GAS (STANDARDS OF PERFORMANCE) (AMENDMENT) REGULATIONS 2002, SI 2002 741; made under the Gas Act 1986 s.33A, s.33AA, s.33AB, s.33D, s.47. In force: April 1, 2002; £2.00.

These Regulations amend the Gas (Standards of Performance) Regulations 2002 (SI 2002 475) by prescribing the sum which a gas transporter must pay to a customer by way of compensation for failure to meet three new standards of performance. The Regulations introduce three new standards which provide that where the conveyance of gas by a gas transporter is discontinued as a result of a fault or damage to his pipe-line system, he must pay the prescribed compensation if the conveyance of gas is not resumed within the prescribed periods, that where the gas transporter has carried out certain works on the customer's premises, he must pay the prescribed compensation if he does not reinstate the customer's premises within prescribed periods and also that where the conveyance of gas to a priority domestic customer is discontinued, either on a planned or unplanned basis, he must pay the prescribed compensation if the customer is not provided with alternative heating or cooking facilities within the prescribed periods.

4725. Gas supply industry—thermal energy calculation

GAS (CALCULATION OF THERMAL ENERGY) (AMENDMENT) REGULATIONS 2002, SI 2002 3130; made under the Gas Act 1986 s.13, s.47. In force: February 1, 2003; £1.50.

These Regulations amend the Gas (Calculation of Thermal Energy) Regulations 1996 (SI 1996 439) by removing the words "who is a member of the Director's staff" from Reg.14, which gives a right of entry onto any premises owned or occupied by a gas transporter to a gas examiner appointed under the Gas Act 1986 s.13(1).

4726. Road works—damage—telecommunications cables—compensation payable

[New Roads and Street Works Act 1991 s.82, s.96.]

Cables owned by BT were damaged by M's contractors in the course of various street works. BT claimed compensation under the New Roads and Street Works Act 1991 s.82. BT and M treated the proceedings as a test case to establish the principles under which compensation was payable under the Act. In addition to the direct repair cost, BT also claimed administrative expenses and overheads due on the basis of its internal accounting procedures. These separated running costs into categories that included both damage repair work and damage caused by identifiable parties. An issue arose as to the extent that BT could claim its administrative expenses and overheads under s.82 and s.96 and the extent to which it was required to show that those expenses were incurred as a direct result of the damage caused by M's contractors. BT further sought a declaration that the administrative expenses fell to be calculated on a full absorption costing basis.

Held, that an undertaker which damaged street apparatus was liable under s.82 to compensate the owner of that apparatus for all direct expenses, including the cost of labour, materials and a proportionate amount of administrative expenses. Such expenses were to be calculated on the basis of actual or historical costs and apportionment methods. However, the declaration was refused as this required the administrative expenses to be calculated on an absorption costing basis. While this could be valid in some cases, other calculation methods could be equally valid for the purposes of s.82 and the compensation claimed in each instance of damage, along with the method of calculating the claim, had to be considered on a case by case basis.

BRITISH TELECOMMUNICATIONS PLC v. BELL CABLE MEDIA (LEEDS) LTD [2001] B.L.R. 343, Judge McGonigal, QBD.

4727. Sewerage undertakers—water companies—requirement to provide public sewerage services—meaning of "premises in a particular locality"

[Water Industry Act 1991 s.101A(1), s.101A(7).]

EA appealed against the decision ([2001] E.H.L.R. 22, [2001] C.L.Y 5631) to quash two decisions made by it under the Water Industry Act 1991 s.101A(7). Under s.101A(7), EA was required to determine disputes between sewerage undertakers and owners or occupiers of property in relation to whether the undertaker owed a duty pursuant to s.101A(1) to provide a public sewer. The two quashed decisions concerned the finding that A, a water and sewerage undertaker, was under a duty to provide a public sewer to serve the village of Brent Hill and the village of Wretton. The issue before the court concerned, inter alia, the appropriate interpretation of s.101A(1) of the Act.

Held, dismissing the appeal, that the phrase "premises in a particular locality" as contained in s.101A(1) of the Act did not necessarily mean all the premises situated in the locality but was to be construed as meaning those premises within a particular locality being considered by the undertaker for public sewerage and, in cases of dispute under s.101A(7), those also under consideration by EA.

R. (ON THE APPLICATION OF ANGLIAN WATER SERVICES LTD) v. ENVIRONMENT AGENCY; *sub nom.* R. v. ENVIRONMENT AGENCY, *ex p.* ANGLIAN WATER SERVICES LTD; ENVIRONMENT AGENCY v. ANGLIAN WATER SERVICES LTD, [2002] EWCA Civ 5, *The Times,* February 18, 2002, Laws, L.J., CA.

4728. Sewers and drains—liability—pipe built as a culverted watercourse

[Public Health Act 1936 Part II, Part XI.]

S appealed against a finding that a pipe built as a culverted watercourse had not become a sewer and that it was liable for it under the terms of a deed made in 1961. S was the successor to the local authority which had entered into the deed under which it agreed to pay half the cost of repairs to the culvert. U was responsible for sewerage in the area. S's predecessor had carried out works of new culverting in response to increased residential development in the area. The question before the court was whether such works had been carried out in the exercise of the powers under the Public Health Act 1936 Part II or Part XI. S maintained that the works had been carried out as part of a major sewerage scheme under Part II. U, however, claimed that the scheme had been to put a natural watercourse into an underground culvert under Part XI.

Held, dismissing the appeal, that the judge had not erred in deciding that the pipe had not become a sewer and S was therefore liable.

SEFTON MBC v. UNITED UTILITIES WATER LTD, [2001] EWCA Civ 1284, [2002] E.H.L.R. 7, Robert Walker, L.J., CA.

VAT

4729. Sewers and drains–water supply–connection of converted premises– meaning of "connection" for purposes of Water Industry Act 1991 s.146(2)

[Water Industry Act 1991 s.146(2).]

T, a water and sewerage undertaker, appealed against a dismissal of its claim against H, developers, for water supply and public sewer connection charges. Two former office blocks had been converted by H into 109 flats and H had requested the connection of each flat following the conversion. However, prior to the conversion the office blocks had each been connected for domestic purposes to the public sewer and water supply. The instant case was concerned with the interpretation of the Water Industry Act 1991 s.146(2) and whether the flats were premises that had not previously been connected.

Held, allowing the appeal, that the flats were new premises which had not been previously connected to the public sewer or to a water supply. Therefore T was entitled to charge for the connection of each flat. For the purposes of s.146(2) premises were likely to include buildings with a water supply and from which sewage was removed. However, s.146(2) applied to the connection of new premises likely to make extra demands on the water and sewerage system. In the context of conversions of premises previously connected, it was a question of fact and degree whether the converted premises had retained the identity of previously connected premises.

THAMES WATER UTILITIES LTD v. HAMPSTEAD HOMES (LONDON) LTD, [2002] EWCA Civ 1487, [2003] 1 W.L.R. 198, May, L.J., CA.

4730. Weights and measures–equipment–electrical energy meters

MEASURING INSTRUMENTS (EC REQUIREMENTS) (ELECTRICAL ENERGY METERS) (AMENDMENT) REGULATIONS 2002, SI 2002 3082; made under the European Communities Act 1972 s.2. In force: February 1, 2003; £2.00.

These Regulations amend the Measuring Instruments (EC Requirements) (Electrical Energy Meters) Regulations 1995 (SI 1995 2607) to provide that the Gas and Electricity Markets Authority shall not, unless asked to do so by a person submitting a meter for EC pattern approval, carry out examinations on a meter submitted for approval if the report of a nominated laboratory on the meter enables the Authority to conclude that the pattern conforms to the requirements of the relevant EC Directive. The amendments also enable the Authority to use the services of a nominated laboratory in carrying out its functions under the 1995 Regulations.

VAT

4731. Acquisitions–imported goods

VALUE ADDED TAX (ACQUISITIONS) RELIEF ORDER 2002, SI 2002 1935; made under the Value Added Tax Act 1994 s.36A. In force: August 15, 2002; £1.50.

This Order provides that no VAT is payable on an acquisition of goods from another EU Member State where, had the goods been imported from outside the EU, relief would have been given by the Value Added Tax (Imported Goods) Relief Order 1984 (SI 1984 746). It also gives effect to Council Directive 77/388 ([1977] OJL145/1) on a common system for VAT to the extent that this exempts the intra-Community acquisition of goods the importation of which would in all circumstances be exempt under that Directive.

4732. Assessment–mistake–best judgment challenge–requirement for material inaccuracy

R appealed against a decision of the VAT and duties tribunal that the commissioners had raised VAT assessments to their best judgment. Following a visit by Customs officers to R's VAT registered restaurant a VAT assessment was raised in the sum of £17,249 plus interest. R appealed and by the time of the hearing before the tribunal Customs had conceded that there were some errors in the calculation so that only £7,683 was in dispute. The tribunal upheld the assessment on the ground that it had been made to the commissioners' best judgment. R appealed, arguing that the discrepancy in the figures as a result of the concession showed that the original assessment could not have been made to best judgment.

Held, dismissing the appeal, that (1) on a best judgment challenge a taxpayer had to show that the assessment was wrong in a material respect and that, if it was, the mistake was such that the only fair inference was that the assessment was arbitrary or dishonest, vindictive or capricious, based on a spurious estimate or guess, or wholly unreasonable, dicta of Dyson, J. in *McNicholas Construction Co Ltd v. Customs and Excise Commissioners* [2000] S.T.C. 553, [2000] C.L.Y. 5348 considered. The primary focus of the attention of the tribunal had to be on the objective evidence adduced by the taxpayer in seeking to discharge the burden of showing that the amount of VAT assessed was not due from him; (2) an assessment which turned out on the evidence to be substantially correct could not normally be attacked as contrary to best judgment and the fact that it turned out to be substantially incorrect did not necessarily mean that it was contrary to best judgment; (3) if the assessment was wrong in a material respect but the taxpayer failed to show that it was not made to best judgment, the tribunal would deal with it on the quantum aspect of the appeal, and (4) accordingly, the tribunal had correctly directed itself on the best judgment issue and its decision could not be impugned.

RAHMAN (T/A KHAYAM RESTAURANT) v. CUSTOMS AND EXCISE COMMISSIONERS (NO.2) [2002] S.T.C. 73, Lawrence Collins, J., Ch D.

4733. **Assessment–retail schemes–consideration–motor dealers–discount scheme by motor dealer on part exchanges**

[Value Added Tax Act 1994 Sch.6 para.5.]

H was a motor dealer. When it sold cars, taking customers' existing cars in part exchange, it issued discount vouchers to customers, which were used either (1) as part payment of the deposit on the purchase price when finance companies were involved, or (2) as discounts for future MOT tests. The VAT tribunal held that the vouchers formed part of the consideration on which VAT was payable. H appealed.

Held, allowing the appeal, that (1) under the Value Added Tax Act 1994 Sch.6, para.5 any consideration received on the supply of the voucher was to be disregarded in computing the turnover of the supplier for VAT purposes, and (2) the result of deciding that the supply of the vouchers was merely ancillary to the supply of the car would remove from the supplier the benefit of the double taxation provisions regardless of whether the single supply fell to be treated as standard rated or exempt. Paragraph 5 did not refer to whether the issue of the voucher was a separate supply or merely part of a larger supply to which it was ancillary; and that it could not be assumed that the supply of MOT vouchers was ancillary to the supply of the replacement car.

HARTWELL PLC v. CUSTOMS AND EXCISE COMMISSIONERS [2002] S.T.C. 22, Patten, J., Ch D.

4734. **Assessment–retail schemes–transfer of business–adjustments for zero rated stock sold below expected price**

M, an industrial and provident society, appealed against a decision upholding a VAT assessment made by the Commissioners following the transfer of a retail business to it by L, another industrial and provident society. Prior to the transfer, L had adopted Retail Scheme B to calculate its VAT liability. L submitted a VAT return for the period up to and including the date of transfer which did not make any adjustment in respect of zero rated stock sold below the expected retail price as a result of the transfer. L contended that no adjustment needed to be made as it did not continue to be a retailer following the transfer and ceased to use the scheme.

Held, dismissing the appeal, that Customs and Excise Notice 727, read as a whole, indicated that where a retailer who accounted for VAT under Retail

Scheme B simultaneously transferred his business and ceased to use the scheme the Commissioners were entitled to raise an assessment, *United Norwest Cooperatives Ltd v. Customs and Excise Commissioners* [1999] S.T.C. 686, [1999] C.L.Y. 5022 considered. In the instant case, the fact that L had sold zero rated stock below the expected price at the same time as it ceased to use the scheme triggered paragraph 22 of the notice and an adjustment had to be made.

MIDLANDS COOPERATIVE SOCIETY LTD v. CUSTOMS AND EXCISE COMMISSIONERS [2002] S.T.C. 198, Lightman, J., Ch D.

4735. **Assessment–statutory powers–notice for summary payment in default–restricted right to appeal–South Africa**

[Constitution of South Africa 1996 s.34, s.36; Value Added Tax Act 1991 (South Africa) s.36, s.40.]

C assessed M to VAT under the Value Added Tax Act 1991 (South Africa) s.36(1) following dissatisfaction with the returns submitted by M between July 1996 and June 1997. M was required to make an immediate payment under s.36(1), with any dispute being left to subsequent determination by C or on appeal to the Special Income Tax Court. C refused M's objection to the assessment and gave notice for payment with summary payment in default under s.40(2)(a), following which the assessment could not be challenged by virtue of s.40(5). M complained that s.36 and s.40 of the 1991 Act were contrary to the right of access to a court guaranteed by the Constitution of the Republic of South Africa s.34. The complaint was upheld by the High Court, which found that s.36 and s.40 were invalid and referred the matter to the Constitutional Court for confirmation.

Held, refusing to confirm the High Court decision, that s.36 did not oust the jurisdiction of the court and any VAT assessment made by C remained subject to judicial review and control even when C invoked his powers under s.36 and s.40. Any restriction on M's right of access to the court pursuant to s.40(5) of the Act was justified under s.36 of the Constitution, with reference also to the practice in other States where immediate payment with later dispute resolution was provided for under other taxation statutes.

METCASH TRADING LTD v. SOUTH AFRICAN REVENUE SERVICE COMMISSIONER 11 B.H.R.C. 497, Chaskalson (President), Const Ct (SA).

4736. **Businesses–assets–allocation of business assets for private use–input tax deducted on repair costs–liability under Art.5(6) of Sixth VAT Directive**

[Sixth Council Directive 77/388 on a common system for VAT Art.5(6), Art.11(A)(1)(b), Art.20(1)(b).]

The German court referred questions on the interpretation of the Sixth VAT Directive 77/388 in relation to the liability for VAT on the allocation by taxable persons of business assets for private use. F, a second hand car dealer, bought a vehicle from a private individual for the purpose of his taxable activities, which entailed the vehicle being resold in the course of his business. Consequently, F was unable to deduct VAT from the purchase price. F paid for extensive repairs and restoration to the car and deducted VAT on the invoice for the work as input tax. Subsequently, F ceased trading and took the vehicle into his private assets. The court was required to rule as to (1) whether F, upon allocation, was liable to pay VAT under Art.5(6) of the Directive and, if so, whether Art.5(6) was to be interpreted as meaning that VAT was payable on the goods and their "component parts" or only on the "component parts" subsequently incorporated into the goods; (2) whether the taxable amount for the purpose of Art.11(A)(1)(b) was to be determined by reference to the purchase price of the vehicle at the time of allocation plus the price of the repairs or whether it consisted solely of the price paid for the repair work upon which input tax had been deducted, and (3) whether, in the event that work carried out after the purchase of the vehicle, and on which VAT was deductible, did not give rise to liability for VAT under Art.5 (6) upon allocation, the VAT deducted in respect of that work was to be adjusted pursuant to Art.20 (1) (b).

Held, giving a preliminary ruling, that (1) assessment applied solely to the "component parts" of the goods in respect of which there was entitlement to deduct, namely those components which definitively lost their physical and economic distinctiveness when they were incorporated into the vehicle, after its purchase, following transactions involving supplies of goods which led to a lasting increase in the value of the vehicle and which had not been entirely consumed at the time of allocation; (2) the taxable amount for the purpose of Art.11 (A) (1) (b) was to be determined by reference to the price, at the time of the allocation, of the goods incorporated in the vehicle which constituted component parts of the goods allocated within the meaning of Art.5 (6), and (3) VAT was to be deducted in accordance with Art.20 (1) (b) where the value of the work in question had not been entirely consumed in the context of the business activity of the taxable person prior to the allocation of the vehicle to his private assets.

FISCHER v. FINANZAMT BURGDORF (C322/99); BRANDENSTEIN v. FINANZAMT DUSSELDORF-METTMANN (C323/99); *sub nom.* FINANZAMT BURGDORF v. FISCHER (C322/99); FINANZAMT DUSSELDORF-METTMANN v. BRANDENSTEIN (C323/99) [2002] Q.B. 704, AM La Pergola (President), ECJ.

4737. Deductions–notification–compatibility of prior notification requirement with Sixth VAT directive

[Sixth Council Directive 77/388 on a common system for VAT Art.17.]

G, along with other entrepreneurs and professional practitioners, challenged the refusal of E, the Spanish tax agency, to allow them to deduct the VAT they had incurred prior to the commencement of their respective professional or business activities, on the ground that they had not complied with the notification requirements set down in national law. The regional economic and administrative court referred the question to the ECJ for a preliminary ruling as to whether domestic provisions making the right to deduct VAT paid in such circumstances subject to a prior notification requirement were compatible with the general right to deduct VAT under the Sixth Council Directive 77/388 Art.17.

Held, ruling on the preliminary issue, that the restriction on the right to deduct VAT incurred prior to the commencement of regular trading was contrary to Art.17. Tax authorities could require objective evidence to support an intention to begin trading, *BP Supergas Anonimos Etairia Geniki Emporiki Viomichaniki Kai Antiprossopeion v. Greece (C62/93)* [1995] All E.R. (E.C.) 684, [1995] C.L.Y. 5063 and *Rompelman v. Minister van Financien (C268/83)* [1985] E.C.R. 655, [1985] C.L.Y. 1499 followed. However, the restriction imposed by the domestic legislation was disproportionate and could not be justified on the ground that it was necessary to ensure that VAT was correctly levied or for the prevention of fraud for the purposes of Art.22 (8), *Garage Molenheide BVBA v. Belgium (C286/94)* [1998] All E.R. (E.C.) 61, [1998] C.L.Y. 4931 followed.

GABALFRISA SL v. AGENCIA ESTATAL DE ADMINISTRACION TRIBUTARIA (AEAT) (C147/98) [2002] S.T.C. 535, GC Rodriguez Iglesias (President), ECJ.

4738. Exemptions–cars–dealer acquiring secondhand cars in Ireland–sham transaction constructed so that only profit on sale in UK was liable to VAT

[Value Added Tax Act 1994 s.24 (1) (b); Value Added Tax (Cars) Order 1992 (SI 1992 3122) Art.8 (2) (a); Sixth Council Directive 77/388 on a common system for VAT Art.28.]

R, a UK resident and VAT registered motor dealer, appealed against an assessment raised on the basis of underdeclared output tax on the sale to UK customers of secondhand cars obtained by R in Ireland. R argued that the purchase of such cars from private persons who had themselves obtained the vehicles from Irish dealers came within the Value Added Tax (Cars) Order 1992

Art.8 margin scheme and that the only VAT due was the profit R made on the sale in the UK. Customs contended that the reality of the situation was that the cars had been obtained directly from Irish dealers and that the documents adduced to support R's claims were shams that were to be disregarded. R claimed however that Customs' decision produced double taxation so that Art.8(2)(a) should be construed in a way that avoided that result. R also asserted that the assessment should be reduced to give effect to its right to deduct Irish acquisition tax under the Sixth Council Directive Art.28bA1 and A2.

Held, dismissing the appeal, that (1) the transactions relied on by R were false as the cars had been purchased directly from the Irish dealers, which was an exempt supply for Irish VAT purposes under Art.28cAa of the Sixth Directive; (2) Irish acquisition tax could be reclaimed as input tax in the UK under the Value Added Tax Act 1994 s.24(1)(b), and (3) under Art.28bA1, R acquired the cars in the UK not Ireland so that R could not rely on Art.28bA2 to claim a reduction in the assessment to reflect the Irish acquisition tax incurred on the transactions.

RICHMOND CARS LTD v. CUSTOMS AND EXCISE COMMISSIONERS [2000] V. & D.R. 388, Stephen Oliver Q.C. (Chairman), V&D Tr.

4739. **Exemptions–cemeteries–provision by local authority–acting as a "public authority"**

[Value Added Tax Act 1994 s.33; Sixth Council Directive 77/388 on a common system for VAT Art.4.]

R appealed against a decision refusing its claim for a refund of input tax incurred in the provision and maintenance of cemeteries and crematoria under the Value Added Tax Act 1994 s.33 on the basis that it was making exempt supplies in the course of a business. Customs contended that the Sixth Council Directive Art.4(5) did not include activities carried by public law bodies under the same legal conditions that applied to private undertakings. Further, that to allow R's claim would lead to a distortion of competition between private cemetery and crematorium operators who would remain taxable persons under Art.4(1).

Held, allowing the appeal, that in providing and maintaining its cemeteries and crematoria, R was carrying out statutory duties relating to the provision of such facilities and the disposal of human remains which did not apply to private operators. As such it was acting as a "public authority" for the purposes of Art.4(5) so that it was not a taxable person in respect of those activities. R's cemeteries and crematoria were not close to any similar privately owned facilities therefore no risk of a distortion of competition arose, *Ufficio Distrettuale delle Imposte Dirette di Fiorenzuola d'Arda v. Comune di Carpaneto Piacentino (C231/87)* [1991] S.T.C. 205, [1991] C.L.Y. 3661 applied. Article 4(5) was to be read as a whole, without undue reliance on the first indent. Taken together, the indents provided that public law bodies acting as such were not taxable persons if their activities were not liable to distort competition.

RHONDDA CYNON TAFF CBC v. CUSTOMS AND EXCISE COMMISSIONERS [2000] B.V.C. 2226, AN Brice (Chairman), V&D Tr.

4740. **Exemptions–educational institutions–profit making body supplying higher education services under partnership agreement with UK university**

[Value Added Tax Act 1994 Sch.9, Group 6, item 1, note (1); Sixth Council Directive 77/388 on a common system for VAT Art.13A.]

S provided higher education courses to fee paying overseas students under a partnership agreement with the University of Lincolnshire and Humberside. Customs determined that S was not an exempt body in terms of the Value Added Tax Act 1994 Sch.9, Group 6, on the ground that it made a profit from its activities. S contended that it was a college of a university within note (1)(b) to Group 6. This was upheld on appeal by the VAT and Duties tribunal, which found that S's main purpose was to provide education services at degree level so that it was to be considered as the college of a university. Customs appealed, arguing that to fall within the definition of a college of a university in the Act, S had to be either a public law body or come within the definition made by the UK in the exercise of its discretion under Council Directive 77/388 Art.13A(1), but that this precluded non public law bodies which operated on a profit making basis.

Held, dismissing the appeal, that the exemptions set out in Group 6 were not to be construed in such a way as to limit them to non profit making bodies in the case of institutions which were not governed by public law.

SCHOOL OF FINANCE AND MANAGEMENT (LONDON) LTD v. CUSTOMS AND EXCISE COMMISSIONERS; *sub nom.* CUSTOMS AND EXCISE COMMISSIONERS v. SCHOOL OF FINANCE AND MANAGEMENT (LONDON) LTD [2001] S.T.C. 1690, Burton, J., Ch D.

4741. Exemptions–educational institutions–supplies made by students' union

[Value Added Tax Act 1994 Sch.9 Group 6 Item 4.]

L, a university student union, appealed against a finding ([2001] S.T.C. 550) that supplies of soft drinks to students were not exempt from VAT. L had accounted for VAT on the sales but had subsequently claimed that the supplies were exempt as supplies related to the provision of education by an "eligible body" for the purposes of the Value Added Tax Act 1994 Sch.9 Group 6 Item 4. In response to Customs refusal to allow exemption, L maintained that it qualified as an eligible body as it was (1) an integral part of a United Kingdom university for the purposes of Item 4 Note 1 (b); (2) an "institution" of a UK university in accordance with the same Note 1 (b), or (3) a non profit making organisation making supplies within the Group 4 definitions under Note (1) (e).

Held, dismissing the appeal (Arden L.J. dissenting in part), that (1) consideration of the university's Charter demonstrated that L, in contrast to the other bodies such as the Court, Council and Senate, was not incorporated in the university and there was evidence supporting the view that the university and L treated each other as distinct entities. Moreover, it was clear that Note 1 (b) only applied to universities and other entities providing university education. As Note 1 (b) conferred exemptions, it was to be interpreted restrictively. Thus, in the absence of explicit Parliamentary intent to apply Note 1 (b) to entities whose function was other than the supply of education, such as student unions, L did not qualify under this exemption; (2) as L supplied no education, it could not be an institution of a UK university. Even if L qualified as an institution under Note 1 (b), it would still not fall within the Item 4 exemption as it would not have been the eligible body making the principal supply, and (3) the argument surrounding the applicability of Note 1 (e) was irrelevant as L did not make the principal supply and consequently could not bring itself within Item 4.

CUSTOMS AND EXCISE COMMISSIONERS v. LEICESTER UNIVERSITY STUDENTS UNION; *sub nom.* CUSTOMS AND EXCISE COMMISSIONERS v. UNIVERSITY OF LEICESTER STUDENTS UNION; CUSTOMS AND EXCISE COMMISSIONERS v. LEICESTER UNIVERSITY STUDENT UNION, [2001] EWCA Civ 1972, [2002] S.T.C. 147, Peter Gibson, L.J., CA.

4742. Exemptions–equal treatment–retention of international air transport exemption and non provision of equivalent for international coach travel– European Community

[Sixth Council Directive 77/388 on a common system for VAT Art.28 (3) (b).]

International air passenger transport was exempt from VAT under a Belgian law which predated the coming into force of the Sixth Council Directive 77/388. However, there was no parallel exemption for international passenger transport by coach. The Belgian tax authorities charged IT, a coach company, amounts of unpaid VAT, along with a fine for non payment. IT then brought proceedings for reimbursement of those sums, contending that the exemption in national law for international air transport breached the Community law principle of equal treatment. The national court stayed proceedings pending a preliminary ruling by the ECJ as to whether the principle of equal treatment precluded national legislation that retained the air transport exemption under Art.28(3)(b) of the Directive, while denying a similar exemption for international coach transport.

Held, giving a preliminary ruling, that (1) Art.28(3(b) permitted Member States to retain exemptions in their national legislation that predated the coming into force of the Directive; (2) although Art.28(3)(b) did not allow new exemptions, or the extension of existing ones, after the Directive entered into force, it did not prevent a reduction of existing exemptions, and (3) given the gradual harmonisation of national laws relating to VAT by the Member States, the disparate nature of the exemptions in the instant case did not breach the principle of equal treatment.

IDEAL TOURISME SA v. BELGIUM (C36/99) [2001] S.T.C.1386, JC Moitinho de Almeida (President), ECJ.

4743. Exemptions–financial services–affinity credit cards–agreement between professional institute and card issuer–marketing information sent in return for commission payment

[Value Added Tax Act 1994 Sch.9 Group 5 item 5.]

I appealed against a Customs decision that an agreement between I and B whereby I sent its members marketing information on B's affinity credit card in return for commission payments did not qualify for the exemption in the Value Added Tax Act 1994 Sch.9 Group 5 item 5. Although I accepted that the terms of the original agreement did not qualify, it contended that a change to the effect that it could give an explanation of the offer to members and that it was acting in "an intermediary capacity" brought it within the exemption.

Held, dismissing the appeal, that I did not come within the exemption by sending promotional information to its members. To qualify, I needed the ability to negotiate as an agent between B and its members, but that was not provided for in the terms of either the original or the amended agreement, *Customs and Excise Commissioners v. Civil Service Motoring Association Ltd* [1998] S.T.C. 111, [1998] C.L.Y. 4899 distinguished.

INSTITUTE OF DIRECTORS v. CUSTOMS AND EXCISE COMMISSIONERS [2002] B.V.C. 2065, JC Gort (Chairman), V&DTr.

4744. Exemptions–financial services–affinity credit cards–selection of potential applicants–mediation activities between applicant and card issuer

[Value Added Tax Act 1994 Sch.9 Group 5 item 2, Sch.9 Group 5 item 5; Sixth Council Directive 77/388 on a common system for VAT Art.13B(d)(1).]

Customs appealed against a VAT and Duties Tribunal decision ([2001] B.V.C. 2405) that the process of identifying potential applicants for an affinity credit card and the checking of completed applications for errors and omissions amounted to the "negotiation of credit" for the purposes of the exemption in the Sixth Council Directive 77/388 Art.13B(d)(1). The operations were carried out by a subsidiary of B, prior to the issue of the affinity card by a bank, S.

Held, dismissing the appeal, that the exemption in Art.13B(d)(1) was wider than the mere brokering of exempt transactions and included the mediation activities carried out by B's subsidiary prior to the issue of a card by S. The subsidiary's actions went beyond promotion, marketing and clerical support. Further, the operations satisfied the requirements of the Value Added Tax Act 1994 Sch.9 Group 5 item 2 and item 5, as they were the services of an intermediary to an exempt transaction, *Customs and Excise Commissioners v. Civil Service Motoring Association Ltd* [1998] S.T.C. 111, [1998] C.L.Y. 4899 applied.

BAA PLC v. CUSTOMS AND EXCISE COMMISSIONERS; *sub nom.* CUSTOMS AND EXCISE COMMISSIONERS v. BAA PLC, [2002] EWHC 196, [2002] S.T.C. 327, Etherton, J., Ch D.

4745. Exemptions–general practitioners–supply of pharmaceutical services to patients unable to access pharmacist

[National Health Service (Pharmaceutical Services) Regulations 1992 (SI 1992 662) Reg.19, Reg.20.]

B, a GP, supplied drugs to patients who did not have access to a pharmacy under the National Health Service (Pharmaceutical Services) Regulations 1992 Reg.20. Such supplies were zero rated. B appealed against a VAT and Duties Tribunal decision ([2001] B.V.C. 2331) that drugs which B personally administered to such patients formed part of an exempt supply under Reg.19.

Held, dismissing the appeal, that B was acting as a pharmacist when supplying drugs to Reg.20 patients and the tribunal had correctly found that such supplies were zero rated. However, when administering drugs personally to such patients, B was making part of a larger exempt supply of medical services under Reg.19, *Card Protection Plan Ltd v. Customs and Excise Commissioners (C349/96)* [1999] 2 A.C. 601, [1999] C.L.Y. 4972 applied.

BEYNON v. CUSTOMS AND EXCISE COMMISSIONERS, [2002] EWHC 518, [2002] S.T.C. 699, Lawrence Collins, J., Ch D.

4746. Exemptions–holding companies–supply of auditing legal and tax services

[Sixth Council Directive 77/388 on a common system for VAT Art.4.]

C was a holding company for three subsidiaries and had sought to deduct VAT for the supply of auditing, legal and tax services in connection with the acquisition of shares in its subsidiaries. C claimed that it was involved in the management of its subsidiaries and therefore the relevant expenditure fell within the scope of VAT as general expenses. This was disputed by the French tax authorities who claimed that C derived the majority of its turnover from dividends and that the relevant expenditure had no connection with the supply of services but related only to C's ownership of shares and receipt of dividends. The French court sought a preliminary ruling from the ECJ on the interpretation of the Sixth Council Directive 77/388 Art.4 on the question whether a holding company could deduct VAT charged on services purchased in the context of the acquisition of shareholdings in its subsidiaries.

Held, giving a preliminary ruling, that (1) the mere acquisition and holding of shares in a company was not an economic activity within the meaning of Art.4 and did not confer on the holder the status of a taxable person unless the holding was accompanied by direct or indirect involvement in the management of the company; (2) direct or indirect involvement in the management of a company included the supply of administrative, financial, commercial and technical services; (3) in order to give rise to the right to deduct VAT the goods or services acquired must have a direct and immediate link with the output transactions in respect of which VAT is deductible. Expenditure incurred by a holding company for the various services purchased in connection with the acquisition of shares in its subsidiaries formed part of its general costs and therefore had a direct and immediate link with its business as a whole, and (4) the receipt of dividends was not the consideration for any economic activity and did not therefore fall within the scope of VAT. Dividends paid by subsidiaries to their holding company which was a taxable person in respect of other activities and which supplied management services to those subsidiaries must be excluded from the calculation of the deductible proportion of VAT.

CIBO PARTICIPATIONS SA v. DIRECTEUR REGIONAL DES IMPOTS DU NORD PAS DE CALAIS (C16/00) [2002] S.T.C. 460, Wathelet (President), ECJ.

4747. Exemptions–imports–second hand car bought in Cyprus–VAT paid on export from UK–double taxation

[Customs and Excise Duties (Personal Reliefs for Goods Permanently Imported) Order 1992 (SI 1992 3193) Art.11 (1); Value Added Tax Regulations 1995 (SI 1995 2518) Reg.124.]

D, a civil servant returning to the UK from a posting to the Sovereign Base Areas in Cyprus, was charged VAT on a car he had bought from a work colleague there. D appealed, contending that he had not intended to benefit financially from the importation and that as VAT had already been levied on the vehicle it should not be charged on it a second time. D also argued that he had been subject to UK taxation throughout his time in Cyprus and should not therefore be liable to import tax. Customs argued that the car was liable to VAT because it had been imported from outside the European Union.

Held, dismissing the appeal, that D could not benefit from the exemption from taxes and duties in the Customs and Excise Duties (Personal Reliefs for Goods Permanently Imported) Order 1992 Art.11 (1) (c) as the car had not been in his possession for six months prior to his return. Neither had it been exported by him from the UK, so that he could not claim remission of VAT under the VAT Regulations 1995 Reg.124 (b). Furthermore, the principle that double taxation was contrary to Community law did not apply to goods imported into the EU from non Member States and the Sovereign Base Areas did not form part of the territory of the EU.

DULLAGHAN v. CUSTOMS AND EXCISE COMMISSIONERS [2000] V. & D.R. 189, Paul Heim CMG (Chairman), V&DTr.

4748. **Exemptions–insurance companies–pension misselling review conducted by insurance agent–related services**

[Sixth Council Directive 77/388 on a common system for VAT Art.13B (a).]

The Commissioners appealed against a decision ([2000] S.T.C. 276, [2000] C.L.Y. 5294) that the services provided by CL to LA, a pension policy provider, of reviewing pension policies and aiding in the provision of redress where misselling had occurred were exempt from VAT pursuant to the Sixth Council Directive 77/388 Art.13B (a). The Commissioners contended that (1) a purposive interpretation of the Directive, having regard to its spirit and intention, meant that exempt services had to be performed by an insurance agent acting in that capacity and although CL was an insurance agent, it had not acted as an agent; (2) exemptions under European legislation had to be construed strictly, and (3) there was an insufficient connection between the services provided by CL and the original insurance transaction for CL's services to be considered "related services". The nature of the services related to compliance with the need to review policies and provide redress where misselling had occurred rather a commercial one and could not be related to the pension transactions because they were past transactions.

Held, dismissing the appeal, that (1) the exemption under Art.13B could not be interpreted with regard to its spirit or intent owing to the absence of express guidance; (2) the principle that exceptions to a general rule should be interpreted strictly did not justify attributing to an exception a meaning that was not apparent from the relevant words or legislative purpose, and (3) in order to qualify as a "related service", a close nexus had to exist between that service and the relevant insurance transaction. In the present case, ensuring that a policy complied with regulations was a service which was intimately connected to that policy, since continuing obligations attached to the policy after its execution.

CUSTOMS AND EXCISE COMMISSIONERS v. CENTURY LIFE PLC; *sub nom.* CENTURY LIFE PLC v. CUSTOMS AND EXCISE COMMISSIONERS [2001] S.T.C. 38, Jacob, J., CA.

4749. **Exemptions–leases–assignment–consideration paid to assignee**

[Sixth Council Directive 77/388 on a common system for VAT Art.13B (b).]

C, as the assignee of a lease of commercial property, accepted a payment of £1.5 million from the original tenant, W, as consideration for the assignment and agreeing to indemnify W in respect of all obligations or losses arising under the lease. C accounted for VAT on the sum but subsequently appealed to the VAT and Duties Tribunal, which held that the transaction was exempt from VAT. Customs appealed to the High Court which referred to the ECJ for a preliminary ruling as to whether the Sixth Council Directive 77/388 Art.13B (b) was to be interpreted, in the light of the decision in *Lubbock Fine & Co v. Customs and Excise Commissioners (C63/92)*

[1994] Q.B. 571, [1994] C.L.Y. 4961, as meaning that C had made an exempt supply to W when accepting the payment for taking the assignment of the lease.

Held, giving a preliminary ruling, that C had not made an exempt supply to W for the purposes of Art.13B(b) as C did not have any interest in the property at the time it was made. The payment was rather consideration for the assignment. This interpretation was unaffected by the fact that W and C could have structured the assignment in such a way that no VAT was incurred, *Lubbock Fine* distinguished.

CUSTOMS AND EXCISE COMMISSIONERS v. CANTOR FITZGERALD INTERNATIONAL (C108/99); CUSTOMS AND EXCISE COMMISSIONERS v. MIRROR GROUP PLC (C409/98); *sub nom*. CANTOR FITZGERALD INTERNATIONAL v. CUSTOMS AND EXCISE COMMISSIONERS [2001] 3 C.M.L.R. 56, F Macken (President), ECJ.

4750. Exemptions–opticians–supply of services–dispensing services and sale of spectacles forming separate exempt and standard rated supplies

[Sixth Council Directive 77/388 on a common system for VAT Art.13A(1)(c).]

S appealed against a decision by Customs that the sale of spectacles and contact lenses was a single standard rated supply. S contended, in reliance upon *Commission of the European Communities v. United Kingdom (C353/85)* [1988] 2 All E.R. 557, [1988] C.L.Y. 1574, that the supply of dispensing services, which accounted for more than half the total cost of the spectacles, was a separate exempt supply by virtue of Council Directive 77/388 Art.13A(1)(c).

Held, allowing the appeal, that it was necessary first to identify the essential features of the transaction before going on to identify whether the supply of dispensing services was ancillary to the supply of goods. Where patients wanted S to supply dispensing services and spectacles or contact lenses appropriate to their needs, there were two distinct supplies. The cost of the dispensing services meant that they were not ancillary to the supply of goods, with the result that there were two separate supplies for VAT purposes. That analysis accorded with the Art.13A(1)(c) exemption, *Card Protection Plan Ltd v. Customs and Excise Commissioners (C349/96)* [1999] 2 A.C. 601, [1999] C.L.Y. 4972 and *Commission of the European Communities v. United Kingdom (C353/85)* applied.

SOUTHPORT VISIONPLUS LTD v. CUSTOMS AND EXCISE COMMISSIONERS [2002] B.V.C. 2047, AN Brice, V&DTr.

4751. Exemptions–partial exemption–company making taxable and exempt supplies

[Value Added Tax Regulations 1995 (SI 1995 2518) Reg.101(3); Council Directive 77/388 relating to turn over taxes Art.19(2).]

J, a company retailing motor cars, was required, under its franchise agreements, to have "demonstrator" cars for the purpose of test and trial drives. When J had no further use for those cars they were sold. These cars were depreciated in the books of the company and treated as capital items for VAT. The Value Added Tax Regulations 1995 Reg.101(3) provided that there should be attributable to taxable supplies such proportion of the input tax attributable to such of those goods and services as were used in making both taxable and exempt supplies as bore the same ratio to the total of such input tax as the value of such taxable supplies made by the taxable person bore to the value of all supplies made. Council Directive 77/388 Art.19(2) excluded from the calculation of the deductible proportion amounts of turnover attributable to the supplies of capital goods used by the taxable person for the purposes of his business. The Commissioners treated them as stock in trade sold in the ordinarily course of its business. On appeal against assessment, the tribunal found that the demonstrators were not acquired for the purpose of sale, but for the purpose of use by J in the carrying out of its taxable activities and were sold off only at the end of their useful life. The Commissioners appealed.

Held, dismissing the appeal, that (1) neither the United Kingdom legislation on VAT or the EC case law laid down a general definition of what constitutes capital goods; (2) there was no justification for limiting capital goods to goods which differed from those sold in the course of the taxpayer's business, and (3) whether or not an item was a capital good was essentially a question to be determined by the tribunal. In this instance the tribunal had asked itself the right questions and had been entitled to come to its conclusion on the evidence before it.

JDL LTD v. CUSTOMS AND EXCISE COMMISSIONERS; *sub nom.* CUSTOMS AND EXCISE COMMISSIONERS v. JDL LTD [2002] S.T.C. 1, Lawrence Collins, J., Ch D.

4752. **Exemptions–partnerships–transaction between partner and partnership– independent economic activity–European Community**

[Sixth Council Directive 77/388 on a common system for VAT Art.4(1).]

A farmer, H, formed a partnership in the Netherlands with his wife (the H partnership). Netherlands law provided that partnerships governed under it had the de facto independence of companies and could carry on economic activities independently. H leased immoveable property to the H partnership and the parties requested that they be excluded from exemption for VAT. The tax authorities refused the request. On appeal the Dutch Court referred to the ECJ the question whether the letting could be considered to be an an independent economic activity for the purpose of Sixth Council Directive 77/388 on a common system for VAT Art.4(1).

Held, giving a preliminary ruling, that a bona fide letting between A and a legally constituted partnership of which he was a partner was an independent economic activity within the provisions of Art.4(1).

STAATSSECRETARIS VAN FINANCIEN v. HEERMA (C23/98) [2001] S.T.C. 1437, Judge Kapteyn (President), ECJ.

4753. **Exemptions–residential care–homes operated on profit making basis–no supply of medical services**

[Value Added Tax Act 1994 Sch.9 Group 7; Sixth Council Directive 77/388 on a common system for VAT Art.13A(1).]

Customs appealed against a VAT and Duties Tribunal decision ([2001] B.V.C. 2326) allowing K's appeal against a decision by Customs that the operation of a residential home for adults with learning difficulties and a residential home for children in local authority care was exempt from VAT under the Value Added Tax Act 1994 Sch.9 Group 7. K argued that the exemption in Group 7 item 4 and item 9 was restricted to medical care, such as that supplied by a hospital or medical centre, by virtue of Council Directive 77/388 Art.13A(1)(b), and did not apply in the case of a profit making partnership that did not supply medical care in either of its homes.

Held, dismissing the appeal, that item 4 defined a narrow range of medical supplies and did not apply on the facts of the instant case. To come within the exemption, K would have had to be operating on a non profit making basis for the purposes of item 9. That construction accorded with the activities and services detailed in Art.13A(1), which were referred to as being carried out by public bodies or charitable organisations. K was neither of those, *Gregg v. Customs and Excise Commissioners (C216/97)* [1999] All E.R. (EC) 775, [1999] C.L.Y. 4986 considered.

KINGSCREST ASSOCIATES LTD v. CUSTOMS AND EXCISE COMMISSIONERS; *sub nom.* KINGSCREST RESIDENTIAL CARE HOMES v. CUSTOMS AND EXCISE COMMISSIONERS; CUSTOMS AND EXCISE COMMISSIONERS v. KINGSCREST ASSOCIATES LTD, [2002] EWHC 410, [2002] S.T.C. 490, Pumfrey, J., Ch D.

4754. Exemptions–residential tenancies–national law imposing VAT on all leaseholds with exemption for residential property–Spain

[EC Treaty Art.249(3); Sixth Council Directive 77/388 on a common system for VAT Art.13B(b), Art.13C.]

M, the landlord of commercial premises, evicted his brother, J, as the latter had failed to pay VAT on the rent. The Spanish national court stayed proceedings between M and J and sought a preliminary ruling from the ECJ as to whether Law 37/1992 Art.4(2)(b) and Art.11(2) correctly transposed Council Directive 77/388 Art.13B as it imposed VAT on all leases with an exemption for residential tenancies.

Held, giving a ruling, that Member States had a discretion when deciding how they achieved the intended result of Directives under the EC Treaty Art.249(3). Under Art.13B(b) and Art.13C of the Council Directive it was for Member States to decide which transactions were exempt from or liable to VAT, with the result that Art.13B(b) allowed a blanket imposition of VAT for leases with an exemption for residential tenancies.

FAR v. FAR (C12/98) [2002] S.T.C. 382, Schintgen (President), ECJ.

4755. Exemptions–securities–financial services–information provided by call centre on behalf of financial institutions–applicability of sixth Council Directive 77/388–EC law

[Sixth Council Directive 77/388 on a common system for VAT Art.13B(d)(5).]

A question relating to the interpretation of the Sixth Council Directive 77/388 Art.13B(d)(5) was referred to the ECJ for a preliminary ruling. On behalf of certain financial institutions, CSC provided a call centre service which involved the provision of information to potential investors relating to specific financial products and the processing of application forms. CSC had received fees from one such institution, SA, for providing the service in relation to one of SA's personal equity plans although the execution of the issue and transfer of the securities involved in the plan was carried out by a separate firm. CSC contended that under Art.13B(d)(5) of the Directive the services were VAT exempt.

Held, giving a preliminary ruling, that the services provided by CSC were not exempt from VAT, *Sparekassernes Datacenter (SDC) v. Skatteministeriet (C2/95)* [1997] All E.R. (EC) 610, [1997] C.L.Y. 4987 applied. For the purposes of the exemption permitted under Art.13B for "transactions, including negotiation...in securities", "transactions" meant transactions liable to create, alter or extinguish parties' rights and obligations in respect of securities. "Negotiation" did not cover services limited to providing information about a financial product or processing applications for securities without issuing them. It was a necessary ingredient of negotiation that the negotiator took the role of mediator occupying a different stance from that which was occupied by the parties to the contract. In the present case, CSC had in effect only acted as a subcontractor for SA.

CUSTOMS AND EXCISE COMMISSIONERS v. CSC FINANCIAL SERVICES LTD (C235/00); *sub nom.* CSC FINANCIAL SERVICES LTD v. CUSTOMS AND EXCISE COMMISSIONERS (C235/00) [2002] 1 W.L.R. 2200, P Jann (President), ECJ.

4756. Exemptions–sporting organisations–meaning of "non profit making organisations" within Sixth Council Directive 77/388

[Sixth Council Directive 77/388 on a common system for VAT Art.13A(1)(m).]

The Supreme Court of the Netherlands referred to the ECJ certain questions relating to the interpretation of the phrase "non profit making" within the Sixth Council Directive 77/388 Art.13A(1)(m). K, a golf club, received the majority of its funding from annual membership subscriptions with the remainder being provided by day fees from visitors. The club made an operating surplus which was treated as a provisional reserve for non annual expenditure. K did not pay VAT on the day fees claiming an entitlement to an exemption under national legislation implementing the Directive, Art.13A(1)(m) of which referred to services closely linked to sport education supplied by "non-profit-making" organisations. The national tax authorities imposed however, an additional assessment to VAT on the ground that K was aiming to systematically make a profit. K challenged that decision before its national courts.

Held, giving a preliminary ruling that, the categorisation of an organisation as "non-profit-making" should be based on all the organisation's activities. The purpose of the exemptions was to provide more favourable VAT treatment for certain organisations whose activities were directed towards non-commercial purposes. Therefore, classification of an organisation as "non-profit-making" should depend on its aim which, unlike a commercial undertaking, should not be to achieve profits for its members. This assessment, which was for the competent national authorities to make, was not affected by the fact that the organisation achieved profits used for the provision of its services, even if it sought to make them or made them systematically. Indeed, Article 13A(1)(m) of the Directive did not prohibit "non-profit-making" organisations from finishing their accounting year with a positive balance. Accordingly "non-profit-making" organisations could systematically achieve surpluses used for providing their services.

KENNEMER GOLF & COUNTRY CLUB v. STAATSSECRETARIS VAN FINANCIEN (C174/00); *sub nom.* KENNEMER GOLF & COUNTRY CLUB v. INSPECTEUR BELASTINGDIENST PARTICULIEREN/ONDERNEMINGEN HAARLEM (C174/00) [2002] Q.B.1252, P Jann (President), ECJ.

4757. **Exemptions–supply of services–meaning of "aims of a civic nature"**

[Value Added Tax Act 1994 Sch.9 Group 9 item 1 (e); Sixth Council Directive 77/388 on a common system for VAT Art.13A(1)(l).]

Customs appealed against a decision ([2001] 1 W.L.R. 1658, [2001] C.L.Y. 5566) that E was exempt from VAT. E was a non profit making body whose main aim was "the support of the proper administration of justice and the early resolution of disputes through fair and unbiased expert evidence". Toward that end it provided training and education, gave names of experts to solicitors, assisted members with insurance cover, established a library, sent out an annual newsletter and organised various conferences and events for members and solicitors. The judge had found that E's aims were "of a civic nature" and that accordingly its services were exempt from VAT under the provisions of the Sixth Council Directive 77/388 Art.13A(1)(l). Customs contended that the phrase "aims of a civic nature" was intended to denote aims of a municipal significance as opposed to aims relating to citizenship nationwide.

Held, dismissing the appeal, that the supply of services by E were exempt from VAT since they were of a "civic nature" within Art.13A(1)(l) of the Directive and the Value Added Tax Act 1994 Sch.9 Group 9 item 1 (e). The phrase "aims of a civic nature" was to be construed strictly so as to mean "pertaining, or proper to citizens" and the purposes of E fell within that meaning.

EXPERT WITNESS INSTITUTE v. CUSTOMS AND EXCISE COMMISSIONERS, [2001] EWCA Civ 1882, [2002] 1 W.L.R.1674, Chadwick, L.J., CA.

4758. **Exemptions–voluntary organisations–zoos–meaning of "body administered on an essentially voluntary basis" within Sixth Council Directive 77/388**

[Sixth Council Directive 77/388 Art.13A(2)(a).]

The High Court referred to the ECJ questions relating to the interpretation of the phrase "body administered on an essentially voluntary basis" within the Sixth Council Directive 77/388 Art.13A(2)(a). Z, a non profit making society, consisted of a governing body whose members were not remunerated, and a paid staff including various directors who attended meetings of the governing body and played a significant part in the running of the society. Z's claim for a refund of VAT paid on admission charges to zoos owned by it was rejected by the UK tax authorities on the basis that Z did not meet the requirement of being managed and administered on an essentially voluntary basis within the meaning of the Art.13A(2)(a), since paid staff of the society were involved in its management and administration. The national tax authorities appealed against a ruling which overturned their decision at first instance.

Held, giving a preliminary ruling, that the condition requiring a body to be "managed and administered on an essentially voluntary basis" applied only to persons directly associated with the management and administration of a body and not to all persons working for reward in one way or another in its administration. Accordingly, there was nothing in the Directive to prohibit the bodies referred to in Art.13A from taking on paid staff, *Kennemer Golf & Country Club* v. *Staatssecretaris van Financien (C174/00)* Times, April 11, 2002 followed. In determining who was directly associated with the management and administration of the body reference should be made to the body's constitution in order to identify the members of the directing organs and their specific tasks and also to the persons who actually carried out the management and administration of the body. These would be the persons who, like the directing members of a commercial undertaking, would take the decisions of last resort concerning the policy of the body, particularly in the financial area, and carry out the higher supervisory tasks. The words "on an essentially voluntary basis" referred to the members who composed the organs entrusted with the management and administration of a body of the kind referred to in Art.13A(2)(a) and those persons who, without being designated by the constitution, did in fact direct it, and referred also to the reward which the latter might receive, habitually or exceptionally, from that body.

ZOOLOGICAL SOCIETY OF LONDON v. CUSTOMS AND EXCISE COMMISSIONERS (C267/00); *sub nom.* CUSTOMS AND EXCISE COMMISSIONERS v. ZOOLOGICAL SOCIETY OF LONDON (C267/00) [2002] Q.B.1252, P Jann (President), ECJ.

4759. **Gambling–cheques–presumption of conditional acceptance when exchanged for gambling chips–duty payable on value of cheque when dishonoured**

[Gaming Duties Act 1981.]

A, a Kuwaiti, had a "cheque cashing facility" at L's casino whereby he exchanged his personal cheques for gambling chips. Following delays in receiving payment on some of these cheques, the service was withdrawn and A went on to use bankers drafts or similar. A presented four cheques to L, up to a value of £6.5 million, which purported to have been drawn by International Holding Company, IHC, on the Bank of Kuwait. A stated that IHC was an exchange company and despite being unable to verify the credit worthiness of IHC, L accepted the cheques. A gambled and lost the full amount. The cheques were never honoured and A returned to Kuwait where he was untraceable. CEC assessed the sum as forming part of L's gross gaming yield, even though it was never received, so that gaming licence duty of £2.24 million was payable. L applied to the VAT and Duties Tribunal who upheld the assessment. L appealed, arguing that the cheques had been accepted as absolute payment for the chips and therefore L was not able to pursue A for the loss and it should not be assessed as part of its gross gaming yield.

Held, dismissing the appeal, that the Tribunal had applied the right test in holding that there was a presumption that a cheque exchanged for cash, or its equivalent in chips, was accepted by the payee on condition that the cheque would be honoured, and there was therefore a loan contract between payor and payee, *Crockfords Club Ltd* v. *Mehta* [1992] 1 W.L.R. 355, [1992] C.L.Y. 2191 applied. The Tribunal had been entitled to find that L had not discharged that presumption. L's argument was effectively inviting the court to imply bad debt relief into the Gaming Duties Act 1981, which the court would not do.

LYDIASHOURNE LTD v. CUSTOMS AND EXCISE COMMISSIONERS [2000] V. & D.R.127, Lloyd, J., QBD.

4760. Input tax–deductions–allowances–employees use of own car in connection with employer's business–European Community

[Sixth Council Directive on a common system for VAT 77/388 Art.4, Art.17(2)(a), Art.18(1)(a), Art.22(3)(a).]

The Commission sought a declaration that the Netherlands had failed to fulfil its obligations under the Sixth VAT Directive 77/388 Art.17(2)(a) and 18(1)(a). Dutch legislation provided that where an employee used his own car in connection with his employer's business and received an allowance from his employer for that purpose, a percentage of the allowance could be deducted by the employer as input tax, in so far as the allowance did not fall within income for income tax purposes. The percentage that could be deducted corresponded to the weighted average of VAT included in the various cost components relating to possession and use of a car.

Held, giving a declaration, that the right to deduct conferred on a taxable person by Art.17(2)(a) concerned VAT paid in respect of goods and services supplied to that taxable person by another taxable person. Art.4(1) and Art.4 of the Sixth Directive expressly stated that an employee acting for his employer could not have the status of a taxable person. It followed that the fact that an employee used his own vehicle in connection with his employer's business could not transform the employee into a taxable person, even if the costs linked with such use gave rise to reimbursement by the employer. Moreover, it was clear that an employee's use of his own vehicle in connection with his employer's business could not constitute a supply to his employer. Consequently, the Commission's complaint was well founded as regards Art.17(2)(a). It was also apparent from Art.18(1)(a), together with Art.22(3)(a), that, in order to make a deduction, the taxable person was required to hold an invoice or a document considered to be an invoice, issued to him by another taxable person. In the absence of any supply of goods or services between two taxable persons and, therefore, of any possibility of an invoice or a document considered to be an invoice being delivered by one such taxable person to another, the deduction of VAT authorised by the Netherlands legislation at issue could, by definition, only occur in breach of Article 18(1)(a).

COMMISSION OF THE EUROPEAN COMMUNITIES v. NETHERLANDS (C338/98) *The Times*, December 10, 2001, S Von Bahr (President), ECJ.

4761. Input tax–deductions–assessment–settlement–failure to pay sum as agreed–commencement of possession proceedings–alleged infringement of human rights

[Value Added Tax Act 1994 s.60; Human Rights Act 1998 Sch.1 Part I Art.6, Art.8, Art.14.]

A was one of five partners in a business. They were all subject to VAT assessments and to a civil penalty. An appeal and a further appeal were rejected and permission to appeal further was refused. The Commissioners served statutory demands and bankruptcy petitions. In due course A agreed a settlement figure of £520,000 and entered into a deed securing payment on the business premises. The agreed sum was not paid and the Commissioners commenced possession proceedings. A opposed the possession proceedings and counterclaimed on the basis that there had been infringements of his human rights under the Human Rights Act 1998 Sch.1 Part I Art.6, Art.8 and Art.14.

Held, ordering possession within 28 days, striking out alleged breaches of Art.6 and Art.14 and refusing to stay possession notwithstanding that the allegation under Art.8 stood pending trial that (1) there was no evidence that the tribunal was anything other than independent; (2) VAT Act 1994 s.60 placed the burden of proof on the Commissioners, not on the taxpayer and the presumption of innocence was maintained *Han (t/a Murdishaw Supper Bar) v. Customs and Excise Commissioners* [2001] EWCA Civ 1048, [2001] 1 W.L.R. 2253, [2001] C.L.Y. 5557 considered; (3) there was no basis for arguing inequality of arms; (4) A had only limited allegations under Art. 8 which could not amount to an equitable set-off or other defence *Esso Petroleum Co Ltd v.*

Milton [1997] 1 W.L.R. 938, [1997] C.L.Y. 799 considered and (5) in any event the existence of a cross-claim did not defeat the right to possession, *National Westminster Bank Plc v. Skelton* [1993] 1 W.L.R. 72 considered.

AKBAR (T/A MUMTAZ PAAN HOUSE) v. CUSTOMS AND EXCISE COMMISSIONERS (HUMAN RIGHTS) [2002] B.P.I.R. 62, Judge Behrens Q.C., Ch D.

4762. Input tax–deductions–entertainment–film distributor holding premiere parties to launch film

[Value Added Tax (Input Tax) Order 1992 (SI 1992 3222) Art.5.]

E, a film distributor, incurred expenditure on holding premiere parties to launch a film. Customs disallowed E's claim to deduct input tax on the ground that it had been incurred on business entertainment so that it was excluded from credit under the Value Added Tax (Input Tax) Order 1992 Art.5. E appealed.

Held, dismissing the appeal, that E was not required to host premiere parties under the terms of the film marketing agreement. The entertainment was a benefit to E and those attending did not come within Art.5. with the result that the claim was disallowed.

ENTERTAINMENT GROUP OF COMPANIES LTD v. CUSTOMS AND EXCISE COMMISSIONERS [2000] B.V.C. 2369, Angus Nicol (Chairman), V&DTr.

4763. Input tax–deductions–holding companies–extent of participation in management of subsidiaries necessary to amount to economic activity–EC law

[Sixth Council Directive 77/388 on a common system for VAT Art.2, Art.4(2).]

W was a holding company which held shares in manufacturing companies resident in a number of Member States. During the relevant period, W employed no staff, but its board of directors was actively engaged in giving guidance to its subsidiaries. W did not charge remuneration for this, but it did receive dividends from its subsidiaries and it claimed input tax credits on the expenses it incurred. The Netherlands tax authorities sought recovery of the input tax credits on the ground that W was not engaged in an economic activity that carried an entitlement to deduct VAT. W appealed, and the national court asked the ECJ to determine as a preliminary issue whether the mere involvement by W in the management of its subsidiary companies amounted to an economic activity within the meaning of the Sixth Council Directive 77/388 Art.4(2).

Held, giving a preliminary ruling, that the mere acquisition of shares in a company did not amount to an economic activity for the purposes of Art.4(2). Similarly, such shareholdings did not constitute an exploitation of property for the purpose of obtaining income on a continuing basis, since the resulting dividends were only the result of owning the property. However, a shareholding accompanied by direct or indirect involvement in the management of subsidiary companies was as an economic activity in terms of Art.4(2) where it entailed the carrying out of transactions that were subject to VAT under Art.2, *Floridienne SA v. Belgium (C142/99)* [2001] All E.R. (EC) 37, [2001] C.L.Y. 5578 followed.

WELTHGROVE BV v. STAATSSECRETARIS VAN FINANCIEN (C102/00) [2001] 3 C.M.L.R. 43, Wathelet (President), ECJ.

4764. Input tax–deductions–Spain–compatibility with EC law

See VAT: Gabalfrisa SL v. Agencia Estatal de Administracion Tributaria (AEAT) (C147/98). §4737

4765. Input tax–falsification–search warrants–failure to disclose to court proposal to use questionnaires

See CUSTOMS: R. (on the application of Paul Da Costa & Co) v. Thames Magistrates Court. §924

4766. Input tax—motor vehicles—high value sports car acquired solely for business use—availability for private use

[Value Added Tax (Input Tax) Order 1992 (SI 1992 3222) Art.7 (2).]

U, a taxable person, appealed against a decision ([2001] S.T.C. 912) that he was liable under the Value Added Tax (Input Tax) Order 1992 Art.7 (2G) (b) for tax incurred on his acquisition of a Lamborghini Diablo motor car. U, who carried on a business supplying and servicing cigarette machines in clubs, contended that he was entitled to have the input tax in respect of the car offset against his liability to pay output tax. This contention was based upon his assertion that the car was used exclusively for business purposes. The car was insured for both business and private use. The provision by Art.7 (2E) of the Order that a taxable person could claim such credit if he intended "to use the car exclusively for the purposes of a business carried on by him" was made subject to Art.7 (2G). Art.7 (2G) (b) provided that the taxable person would not be taken to have such an intention if he intended to make the car available for the private use of any person, including himself.

Held, dismissing the appeal, that the test of intention for the purpose of Art.7 (2E) (a) was not synonymous with the test of intention under Art.7 (2G) (b). The fact that a taxable person intended to use a car exclusively for business purposes did not preclude him from having an intention to make it "available" for private use. Such availability was a necessary consequence of ownership unless the taxpayer took positive steps to exclude it. In the instant case the fact that U had insured his car for private as well as business use was indicative of an intention that it would be available for private use.

CUSTOMS AND EXCISE COMMISSIONERS v. UPTON (T/A FAGOMATIC), [2002] EWCA Civ 520, [2002] S.T.C. 640, Peter Gibson, L.J., CA.

4767. Input tax—repayments—no claims made since VAT registration—application of Value Added Tax Regulations 1995 Reg.29

[Value Added Tax Act 1994 s.80 (4); Value Added Tax Regulations 1995 (SI 1995 2518) Reg.29; Sixth Council Directive 77/388 on a common system for VAT Art.17, Art.18.]

U appealed against a VAT and Duties Tribunal decision ([2001] B.V.C. 2003) rejecting a claim for the repayment of previously unclaimed input tax to the extent that the claim related to any period prior to November 25, 1996, as provided for in the Value Added Tax Act 1994 s.80 (4). It appeared that, during the period between U's registration for VAT in 1973 and 1996, U had consciously decided not to make claims to deduct input tax. U contended that, rather than being governed by s. 80, its claim was made under the Value Added Tax Regulations 1995 Reg.29 so that no time limit applied in respect of repayments. Additionally, U argued that the right to deduct input tax under the Sixth Council Directive 77/388 Art.17 and Art.18 could not be removed by domestic law and that the difference in time limits for late claims for input tax between "payment traders" and "repayment traders" under Reg. 29 constituted unlawful State aid contrary to the EC Treaty Art.92 (1) (now, after amendment, Art.87 (1)).

Held, allowing the appeal, that (1) Art.17 and Art.18 of the Sixth Directive did not mean that U could claim input tax repayments whenever it wanted. However, its failure to do so did not mean that VAT had been overpaid so that U's claim was covered by Reg.29 of the 1995 Regulations and not s.80 of the 1994 Act; (2) printed guidance for taxpayers for the period including November 1996 stated that all claims due to inaccurate returns would be allowed by Customs and there was no requirement for underpayment claims to be in a prescribed form, and (3) Art.92 (1) EC cold not be used to justify an input tax repayment claim and the only remedy open to U, had it succeeded on the State aid point before the tribunal, would have been for an order for the aid to be discontinued or that the beneficiary was liable to repay it.

UNIVERSITY OF SUSSEX v. CUSTOMS AND EXCISE COMMISSIONERS [2001] S.T.C. 1495, Neuberger, J., Ch D.

4768. National Health Service–VAT reliefs–disabled persons

VALUE ADDED TAX (DRUGS, MEDICINES, AIDS FOR THE HANDICAPPED AND CHARITIES ETC) ORDER 2002, SI 2002 2813; made under the Value Added Tax Act 1994 s.30, s.96. In force: December 5, 2002; £1.50.

This Order amends the Value Added Tax Act 1994 to maintain the present scope of VAT reliefs available to the National Health Service.

4769. Partnerships–spouses–joint and several liability–failure to notify Customs of dissolution following marital breakdown

[Value Added Tax Act 1994 s.45(2).]

Customs appealed against a decision setting aside a statutory demand for unpaid VAT that had been served on J in January 2001. Until August 1999, when her marriage broke down, J ran a pub and restaurant in partnership with her husband. In the county court, J successfully contended that the partnership had ended when she left her husband. Customs argued, however, that J retained her VAT liability under the Value Added Tax Act 1994 s.45(2) as she had not informed them that the partnership had been dissolved and that she was liable for VAT up to the end of the August 1999 accounting period in any event.

Held, allowing the appeal, that it was not necessary to decide whether the partnership had been dissolved because partners had the responsibility of notifying Customs of changes to a partnership under s.45(2). Customs were therefore entitled to continue treating J and her former husband as partners until the partnership was deregistered in February 2000. Further, J had joint and several liability for the VAT payment due at the end of August 1999, subject to any contribution she could obtain from her former husband.

JAMIESON v. CUSTOMS AND EXCISE COMMISSIONERS; *sub nom.* CUSTOMS AND EXCISE COMMISSIONERS v. JAMIESON [2002] S.T.C. 1418, Peter Leaver Q.C., Ch D.

4770. Payments–delay–late payments under credit transfer scheme–surcharges imposed without warning following change to computer system

R appealed against a default surcharge imposed for the three month period to April 30, 2000. The tax due had been paid two days late under the credit transfer scheme. R's director explained that payments were made at the end of the period allowed by the scheme as it understood this was acceptable to Customs. Customs contended that R could not rely on the previous practice of refraining from imposing surcharges where payments were only two to three days late. Customs claimed that surcharge notices had not been sent because of a computer problem that had since been rectified.

Held, allowing the appeal, that R's consistent payment arrangements were based on Customs' practice of not imposing default surcharges. R was therefore entitled to rely on the fair operation of the penalty regime given its established arrangements. At the least, Customs should have warned R that surcharges would be imposed following changes to its computer system.

RENLON LTD v. CUSTOMS AND EXCISE COMMISSIONERS [2000] V. & D.R. 442, Stephen Oliver Q.C. (Chairman), V&DTr.

4771. Penalties–right to fair trial–pre trial disclosure

[Value Added Tax Act 1994 s.60; Human Rights Act 1998 Sch.1 Part I Art.6; Value Added Tax Tribunals Rules 1986 (SI 1986 590).]

Six applications relating to pre-trial disclosure were made following the decision of the Court of Appeal in *Han (t/a Murdishaw Supper Bar) v. Customs and Excise Commissioners* [2001] EWCA Civ 1048, [2001] S.T.C. 1188, [2001] C.L.Y. 5557 that penalty proceedings under the Value Added Tax Act 1994 s.60 were "criminal" proceedings for the purposes of the Human Rights Act 1998 Sch.1 Part I Art.6(1).

Held, refusing the applications, that the applications were premature. It was apparent that the Commissioners had not withheld or sought to withhold any documents on public interest grounds. Moreover, the Value Added Tax Tribunals Rules 1986, if duly complied with, provided for the orderly, speedy and just determination of issues and for the purposes of Art.6(3) of the Convention informed the relevant person "of the nature and cause of the accusation against him" and provided "adequate time and facilities for the preparation of [a] defence".

NENE PACKAGING LTD v. CUSTOMS AND EXCISE COMMISSIONERS [2001] V. & D.R. 286, Stephen Oliver Q.C., V&DTr.

4772. **Registration–VAT groups–application for retrospective registration–impact of existing registration**

[Value Added Tax Act 1994 Sch.1 Para.9; Sixth Council Directive 77/388 on a common system for VAT Art.24(6).]

Customs appealed against a tribunal decision allowing E's appeal against a decision to cancel its VAT registrations. In 1995 E, five subsidiaries within the same group of companies, had applied voluntarily for a group registration to cover themselves and the parent company effective from August 1, 1995. The following year E applied for individual registrations for the three year period from 1992 to 1995. The applications for individual registrations were granted but were cancelled as soon as Customs became aware of the existence of the group registration. The tribunal held that the Sixth Council Directive 77/388 Art.24(6) conferred on E the right to opt for retrospective individual registrations irrespective of the existence of the group registration and, to the extent that such a right was precluded by the wording of the Value Added Tax Act 1994 Sch.1 Para.9, then the 1994 Act contravened the express provisions of the Sixth Directive.

Held, allowing the appeal, that (1) the Directive contained no requirement to grant an application for voluntary registration to a person who was already registered; (2) the Directive envisaged the making of a prospective rather than a retrospective choice, and (3) the wording of Art.24(6) was insufficiently precise to be capable of being intended to have direct effect.

EASTWOOD CARE HOMES (ILKESTON) LTD v. CUSTOMS AND EXCISE COMMISSIONERS; EASTWOOD CARE HOMES (MANSFIELD) LTD v. CUSTOMS AND EXCISE COMMISSIONERS; EASTWOOD CARE HOMES (NOTTINGHAM) LTD v. CUSTOMS AND EXCISE COMMISSIONERS; EASTWOOD CARE HOMES (BURTON) LTD v. CUSTOMS AND EXCISE COMMISSIONERS; EASTWOOD CARE HOMES (WALSALL) LTD v. CUSTOMS AND EXCISE COMMISSIONERS; *sub nom.* CUSTOMS AND EXCISE COMMISSIONERS v. EASTWOOD CARE HOMES LTD (ILKESTON) LTD [2001] S.T.C. 1629, Lloyd, J., Ch D.

4773. **Reliefs–residential developments–conversion of building used for partly residential and partly non residential purposes into dwelling house**

[Value Added Tax Act 1994 s.35(1), s.35(1D); Finance Act 1996 s.30.]

Customs appealed against a decision of the Value Added Tax and Duties Tribunal that B's conversion of public house premises including residential accommodation into a single family dwelling amounted to a residential conversion within the meaning of the Value Added Tax Act 1994 s.35(1D) and that relief was consequently available under s.35(1) on the basis that the works had been carried out by a person otherwise than in the course of their business. Customs contended that the term "residential conversion" in s.35(1D) was only applicable where the whole of the resulting dwelling house was developed from the non residential part of the building, and in the instant case the new conversion comprised both residential and non residential parts of the original building.

Held, dismissing the appeal, that there was no basis upon which to conclude that s.35(1D) was intended to be limited in the way suggested by Customs and such a finding could lead to absurd outcomes. It followed that B's conversion works amounted to a residential conversion within s.35(1D) and the relief was available.

BLOM-COOPER v. CUSTOMS AND EXCISE COMMISSIONERS; *sub nom.* CUSTOMS AND EXCISE COMMISSIONERS v. BLOM-COOPER, [2002] EWHC 1421, [2002] S.T.C.1061, Peter Smith, J., Ch D.

4774. Repayments–grants–private sector housing–local authority acting as agent for property owners–entitlement to VAT refund

[Value Added Tax Act 1994 s.33; Housing Grants, Construction and Regeneration Act 1996.]

A, a local housing authority, administered grants for improving private sector housing under the Housing Grants, Construction and Regeneration Act 1996 via an agency it established to supervise the works, C. A paid the building contractors directly and sought to reclaim the VAT it was charged under the Value Added Tax Act 1994 s.33. The claim was refused by the Revenue and the decision was upheld on appeal to the VAT and Duties Tribunal ([2001] S.T.I. 983). A appealed, contending that it was the party that paid the contractors and to whom they supplied their services. Further, that by completing the works to private houses, A obtained a benefit in terms of the discharge of its obligations under the 1996 Act and the improvements to the quality of life for the local community.

Held, dismissing the appeal, that A's liability remained with the owner of the property throughout once the grant application had been approved and neither C nor A had any liability to the contractors, notwithstanding the fact that the contractors invoiced A for the work. C acted as the property owners' agent, so that the owners were liable to the contractor under the contracts entered into between the contractors and C on behalf of the owners, *Customs and Excise Commissioners v. Redrow Group Plc* [1999] 1 W.L.R. 408, [1999] C.L.Y. 4994 applied. As no services were therefore supplied to A it could not claim a refund of VAT under s.33 of the 1994 Act.

ASHFIELD DC v. CUSTOMS AND EXCISE COMMISSIONERS [2001] S.T.C.1706, Sir Andrew Morritt V.C., Ch D.

4775. Repayments–limitations–retrospective reduction of limitation period– compatibility with Community law principles

[Finance Act 1997 s.47; Sixth Council Directive 77/388 on a common system for VAT.]

Questions relating to validity of the Finance Act 1997 s.47 which purported to retrospectively reduce to three years, the six year limitation period in which it was possible to obtain repayment of VAT paid in breach of Community law, were referred to the ECJ for a preliminary ruling. By virtue of s.47(2) the reduction was deemed to have come into force in July 1996. M&S sold gift vouchers at less than their face value, to corporate purchasers who passed the vouchers onto third parties who could then redeem them for goods to the face value of the vouchers. M&S believed it had to account for VAT on the amount it received when it sold the vouchers and not on their face value. The Commissioners ruled that in accordance with the Sixth Council Directive 77/388 Art.11 (A)(1)(a) M&S had to account for VAT on the face value of the vouchers. M&S paid VAT on that basis until it became apparent as a result of the ECJ's judgment in *Argos Distributors Ltd v. Customs and Excise Commissioners (C288/94)* [1997] Q.B. 499, [1996] C.L.Y. 5909 that the regime applied by the Commissioners was incorrect.

Held, giving a preliminary ruling, that it was incompatible with the principle of effectiveness and the principle of legitimate expectation for domestic legislation to remove an individual's opportunity to obtain repayment of VAT levied in breach of Community law, by reason of the retrospective reduction of the period within which repayment could be sought. Although in the absence of Community rules providing for repayment in these circumstances it was for the domestic legal system to lay down detailed rules to safeguard individuals' Community rights, the retrospective effect of the legislation at issue deprived individuals of the possibility of exercising a right which they had previously enjoyed. It was however, open to domestic legal systems to reduce the limitation period for the repayment of incorrectly levied sums only as long as the new limitation period was reasonable and there was a transitional period allowing persons to lodge repayment claims which they would have been entitled to under the previous legislation. The Court of Appeal had considered that individuals could only rely on the direct effect of sufficiently precise and unconditional Community law provisions if, and in so far as, the provision had not been properly implemented in national law, so that if a Directive had been properly implemented, as in the present case, it could not be relied on in that way. However, the ECJ held that it would be inconsistent with the legal order of the Community if individuals were able to rely on a Directive which had been incorrectly implemented but not to be able to rely on it where the national authorities applied the implementing legislation in a way which was incompatible with the Directive, *Argos Distributors* applied.

MARKS & SPENCER PLC v. CUSTOMS AND EXCISE COMMISSIONERS (C62/00) [2003] 2 W.L.R. 665, P Jann (President), ECJ.

4776. Repayments–overpayments–agreement with Customs before imposition of three year repayment cap

[Value Added Tax Act 1994 s.80(4A), s.85.]

D sought judicial review of a refusal by Customs to repay the proceeds of an assessment made under the Value Added Tax Act 1994 s.80(4A), which represented a sum Customs was liable to repay D resulting from a voluntary over declaration made by D following the announcement of the three year repayment cap in July 1996. Customs initially refused to repay until after the cap was introduced. D made a written request for repayment and commenced an appeal before the tribunal. D later withdrew the appeal when Customs agreed to make the repayment, but Customs warned D that it would have to repay the amount if the cap received Parliamentary approval. Following that approval, Customs sought repayment under s.80(4A). D argued that Customs was liable to repay on the basis of the agreement to settle the appeal.

Held, allowing the application, that an objective consideration of the facts showed that Customs had agreed to D's offer to make the repayment in return for the appeal being withdrawn. The warning that D would be liable to repay if the cap was approved did not constitute a counter offer as no agreement was sought by D. D had made it clear in writing that repayment would settle its claim and this fulfilled the requirements for a valid settlement under s.85(3), *Scorer (Inspector of Taxes) v. Olin Energy Systems Ltd* [1985] A.C. 645, [1985] C.L.Y. 449 and *R. (on the application of Building Societies Ombudsman Co Ltd) v. Customs and Excise Commissioners* [2000] S.T.C. 892 applied.

R. (ON THE APPLICATION OF DFS FURNITURE CO PLC) v. CUSTOMS AND EXCISE COMMISSIONERS; *sub nom.* CUSTOMS AND EXCISE COMMISSIONERS v. DFS FURNITURE CO PLC, [2002] EWHC 807, [2002] S.T.C. 760, Moses, J., QBD (Admin Ct).

4777. Repayments–time limits–VAT incurred on rent and service charges–recovery of inputs deriving from period prior to election to waive exemption

[Value Added Tax Regulations 1995 (SI 1995 2518) Reg.109.]

The Commissioners appealed against an order ([2000] S.T.C. 933) allowing RSA to recover input tax incurred on the payment of rent and service charges under business leases. RSA had vacated the premises in the early 1990's and then attempted, unsuccessfully, to find subtenants. Consequently, the properties remained unoccupied for VAT purposes until RSA made an election to waive exemption from VAT on November 21, 1995. RSA subsequently sought repayment of the VAT charged by the lessors in the vacant period prior to the election. In response, the Commissioners maintained that the inputs relating to each separate and successive supply of the premises for rent had been used up by RSA in the unsuccessful attempts to make exempt supplies by subletting the properties and, moreover, that there was no sufficient direct and immediate link between the inputs and RSA's business as a whole.

Held, dismissing the appeal (Arden LJ dissenting), that RSA was entitled to recover the inputs as the requirements of the Value Added Tax Regulations 1995 Reg.109 had been satisfied. Thus, RSA (1) had incurred input tax through payments to the lessor; (2) the inputs were not attributable to a taxable supply as any supply made was an exempt supply; (3) the input tax was not attributed to taxable supplies because RSA had intended to make either exempt supplies or taxable supplies depending on the terms agreed with any prospective sublicensee; (4) that intention was not fulfilled as RSA had not granted any leases and thus, no exempt supply had been made, and (5) in electing to opt to tax, RSA formed and then acted upon the intention to use the services in making taxable supplies. Moreover, Reg.109 allowed a six year period in respect of a change of use and thus, where the relevant supply was the grant of the lease, and where RSA sought to make that supply in the period before election, there was a direct and immediate link between the VAT charged by the lessors and that charged by RSA after it opted to tax.

ROYAL & SUN ALLIANCE INSURANCE GROUP PLC v. CUSTOMS AND EXCISE COMMISSIONERS; *sub nom.* ROYAL SUN ALLIANCE GROUP PLC v. CUSTOMS AND EXCISE COMMISSIONERS, [2001] EWCA Civ 1476, [2001] S.T.C. 1476, Arden, L.J., CA.

4778. Sale of goods–hire purchase agreements–conditional sale agreements– margin scheme

VALUE ADDED TAX (SPECIAL PROVISIONS) (AMENDMENT) (NO.2) ORDER 2002, SI 2002 1503; made under the Value Added Tax Act 1994 s.50A. In force: July 1, 2002; £1.75.

This Order amends the Value Added Tax (Special Provisions) Order 1995 (SI 1995 1268) in order to prevent the sale of goods being taxed under the margin scheme following certain assignments of rights in hire purchase or conditional sale agreements, if the assignors could not themselves have used the scheme to sell the goods. It further amends the conditions which must be met in order for taxable persons to be able to opt to use the margin scheme to account for VAT on the sale of works of art, antiques, collectors' items and other second-hand goods and introduces the concepts of "de-supplied transaction" and "article 5 transaction".

4779. Sale of goods–hire purchase and conditional sale agreements–margin scheme–cars

VALUE ADDED TAX (CARS) (AMENDMENT) ORDER 2002, SI 2002 1502; made under the Value Added Tax Act 1994 s.50A. In force: July 1, 2002; £1.75.

This Order, which amends the Value Added Tax (Cars) Order 1992 (SI 1992 3122), prevents car sales being taxed under the margin scheme following certain assignments of rights in hire purchase or conditional sale agreements if the assignors could not themselves have used the scheme to sell the cars. It further amends the conditions which must be met for taxable persons to be able to opt to use the margin scheme to account for VAT on the sale of used motor cars and introduces new concepts of "de-supplied transaction" and "article 5 transaction".

4780. Small businesses–flat rate scheme

VALUE ADDED TAX (AMENDMENT) (NO.2) REGULATIONS 2002, SI 2002 1142; made under the Value Added Tax Act 1994 s.25, s.26B, Sch.11 para.2. In force: April 25, 2002; £2.50.

These Regulations amend the Value Added Tax Regulations 1995 (SI 1995 2518) but the annual accounting scheme continues to have effect in the case of persons who are already operating the annual accounting scheme only from the beginning of their relevant accounting periods starting after 24th April. They amend the definitions of "the agreed quarterly sum", "the quarterly sum", and "the monthly sum" and make amendments so that persons using annual accounting will make payments of the monthly sum or the agreed monthly sum, unless the Commissioners agree that payment may be made of the quarterly sum or the agreed quarterly sum instead. The Regulations, which establish the flat-rate scheme (FRS) for small businesses, provide that the Commissioners may authorise a taxable person to commence using the FRS, or may refuse to do so for the protection of the revenue, prescribe the date of entry, including provision that the Commissioners and a taxable person may agree the date of his entry to the FRS, which date may be earlier or later than the taxable person's application and define what are to be considered "relevant purchases" and "relevant supplies" for the purposes of the FRS.

4781. Social services–health and welfare

VALUE ADDED TAX (HEALTH AND WELFARE) ORDER 2002, SI 2002 762; made under the Value Added Tax Act 1994 s.31. In force: March 21, 2002; £1.75.

This Order amends the Value Added Tax Act 1994 which makes provision for the exemption of the supply of health and welfare services. It specifies the types of organisations that are entitled to exemption, provides for a consistent interpretation of what is now termed a "state-regulated" institution, ensures legislative references are consistent and comprehensive and removes the requirement that supplies be made otherwise than for profit. It also inserts a reference to care within the exemption for services directly connected with children and young persons.

4782. Supplies–banks–personalised stationery supplied by bank for use by customers

[Value Added Tax (Special Provisions) Order 1995 (SI 1995 1268) Art.11 (1) (a).]

N supplied cheque books, statements and other personalised stationery to its customers as part of its banking service. N accounted for VAT during 1995 and 1996 on the basis that the inhouse production of such material was a self supply under the Value Added Tax (Special Provisions) Order 1995 Art.11 (1) (a). Subsequently, N sought repayment of the tax paid under that provision on the ground that the stationery had been supplied beyond the bank or incorporated into other goods in terms of Art.11 (1) (a). This was refused by Customs on the basis that the stationery was part of a single supply of banking services and was goods in which N retained ownership. N appealed.

Held, allowing the appeal, that N's supply of stationery was ancillary to its supply of banking services, *Card Protection Plan Ltd v. Customs and Excise Commissioners (C349/96)* [1999] 2 A.C. 601, [1999] C.L.Y. 4972 applied. The fact that the stationery was a supply of services did not prevent if from being incorporated into other goods in the case of personalised statements and cheque books produced by overprinting base stocks held in pre printed sheet form.

NATIONAL WESTMINSTER BANK PLC v. CUSTOMS AND EXCISE COMMISSIONERS (V&DTR 17000) [2000] V. & D.R. 484, Stephen Oliver Q.C. (Chairman), V&DTr.

4783. Supplies–consideration–agreement to replace golf clubs–liability on non monetary consideration

[Value Added Tax Act 1994 s.19; Sixth Council Directive 77/388 on a common system for VAT Art.11A.]

The Commissioners appealed against a decision that non monetary consideration received by P through the implementation of an exchange policy whereby P supplied a new golf club to its customers in return for a payment of £22 and the surrender of the customer's old golf club did not attract VAT liability as the old club was of no value to P. The exchange policy was introduced after the Royal and Ancient Golf Club ruled that the "Ping Eye 2" clubs did not comply with its rules. The Commissioners submitted that by supplying the replacement club at less than the wholesale price, P had attributed a value to the old clubs equivalent to the wholesale price of the new club minus the payment of £22. Accordingly, it was submitted that P was liable for VAT on that attributed value.

Held, dismissing the appeal, that the tribunal and judge had not erred in finding that the monetary value of the consideration was nil. The value of the non-monetary consideration taxable under the Value Added Tax Act 1994 s.19 and the Sixth VAT Directive 77/388 Art.11A was to be determined by reference to an express or implied understanding between the supplier and recipient. In the instant case no such understanding could be shown between recipient and supplier, nor could the transaction be characterised as P selling clubs at a discount, *Empire Stores Ltd v. Customs and Excise Commissioners (C33/93)* [1994] 3 All E.R. 90, [1995] C.L.Y. 5084 and *Littlewoods Organisation Plc v. Customs and Excise Commissioners* [2001] EWCA Civ 1542, [2001] C.L.Y. 5556 considered.

CUSTOMS AND EXCISE COMMISSIONERS v. PING (EUROPE) LTD; *sub nom.* PING (EUROPE) LTD v. CUSTOMS AND EXCISE COMMISSIONERS, [2002] EWCA Civ 1115, [2002] S.T.C. 1186, Robert Walker, L.J., CA.

4784. **Supplies–firearms–compensation for surrender of handguns– compensation as consideration**

[Value Added Tax Act 1994 Sch.4 para.1 (1); Firearms (Amendment) Act 1997.]

S appealed against a decision of the VAT and Duties Tribunal ([2001] S.T.I. 1122) that the surrender of firearms to the state under the large calibre handgun compensation scheme constituted a supply for the purposes of VAT. S carried on business selling and repairing guns. The Firearms (Amendment) Act 1997 made it an offence to own, make or sell most handguns. A scheme was set up whereby the owners of prohibited firearms were required to surrender them to the police in return for compensation. S surrendered firearms and ancillary equipment under the scheme and received compensation. Customs took the view that the surrender of firearms and ammunition constituted the making of a taxable supply and issued a VAT assessment. S argued that VAT was a tax on consumption and that the Government was not a consumer in respect of the guns surrendered, which were rendered worthless by the 1997 Act.

Held, dismissing the appeal, that the surrender of firearms under the scheme was a transfer of the whole of the property in the goods under the Value Added Tax Act 1994 Sch.4 para.1 (1) and so constituted a supply for VAT purposes. In the context of VAT, consumption meant the acquisition of the right to dispose of the goods as owner. The fact that the Government had acquired the firearms for destruction was irrelevant. There was the necessary mutuality or direct link and a legal relationship between the supplier and the recipient so that the payment of compensation constituted consideration for the supply of the firearms.

STEWART (T/A GT SHOOTING) v. CUSTOMS AND EXCISE COMMISSIONERS; *sub nom.* STEWARD (T/A GT SHOOTING) v. CUSTOMS AND EXCISE COMMISSIONERS, [2001] EWCA Civ 1988, [2002] S.T.C. 255, Laws, L.J., CA.

4785. **Supplies–mail order–consideration–treatment of postage element of supplier's charges**

Customs appealed against a finding ([2000] S.T.C.137) that P, a company which supplied goods by mail order, was not liable to account for output tax on the postage element of the postage and packing charge which it made to its customers. P had argued that it had entered into an arrangement with Parcelforce whereby the latter would act as its agent for its customers, that it would receive the postage and pass it on to Parcelforce as its agent, that the services rendered by Parcelforce were rendered as principal to the customer, and that the consideration for the postage charges moved from the customer to Parcelforce.

Held, allowing the appeal (Lord Mackay dissenting), that if the appropriate question was whether one act, which in the instant case was arranging the delivery of the goods, was "ancillary or incidental to another", in the instant case the supply of the goods, or was "a distinct supply", the arrangements between P and the customer amounted to a single supply. What the customer wanted and what P agreed to provide were goods delivered to the home. There was a separate supply comprising the delivery of the goods by P to Parcelforce under a separate contract. However, under the contract between the customer and P, arranging the delivery was ancillary to the making available of the goods, and one total sum was paid for one supply of delivered goods. On the basis, however, that there were two supplies, the question was whether the money received by P for postage could amount to consideration received by P or whether it was simply money that was channelled through P so that it could not amount to consideration passing to P. There was nothing in the agreement between P and Parcelforce to suggest that the two parties were not acting as principals. There was no link between Parcelforce and the customer, P rather than the customer was liable to pay Parcelforce and no consideration passed from the customer to Parcelforce. It had not been shown that the postage charge became the property of Parcelforce on payment to P. It was not earmarked for Parcelforce; instead, it was part of P's receipts forming part of its turnover. In the circumstances, P was liable to account for output tax on the postage element of the postage and packing charge which it made to its customers, *Customs and Excise Commissioners v. British Telecommunications Plc* [1999] 1 W.L.R. 1376, [1999] C.L.Y. 4993 applied.

CUSTOMS AND EXCISE COMMISSIONERS v. PLANTIFLOR LTD; *sub nom.* PLANTIFLOR LTD v. CUSTOMS AND EXCISE COMMISSIONERS, [2002] UKHL 33, [2002] 1 W.L.R. 2287, Lord Slynn of Hadley, HL.

4786. **Supplies–property rights–grant of usufructuary right over immoveable property–interpretation of Sixth Council Directive**

[Sixth Council Directive 77/388 on a common system for VAT Art.5(3), Art.13B(b), Art.13C(a).]

The Dutch court referred to the ECJ for a preliminary ruling as to (1) whether the Sixth Council Directive 77/388 Art. 5(3)(b) permitted Member States to treat the grant of rights in rem giving the holder a right of use over immovable property, as the supply of goods only on condition that the consideration was at least equivalent to the value of the immovable property concerned, and (2) whether Arts. 13B(b) and 13C(a) of the Directive precluded the adoption of a national provision which treated the grant of an usufructuary right over immovable property as the leasing or letting of immovable property. A housing association had granted to its successor in title, S, a usufructuary right over its newly constructed dwellings. S then commissioned the association to manage the dwellings, including collecting rent and carrying out maintenance. Tax inspectors employed amendments made to the Dutch VAT laws to refuse the association's attempt to claim a net repayment after it had accounted for output tax on the grant of the usufruct and then sought to deduct input tax on the construction of the dwellings.

Held, giving a preliminary ruling, that (1) Art. 5(3)(b) the Directive did not preclude a national provision whereby classification of the grant, transfer, modification, waiver or termination of rights in rem over immovable property as a supply of goods, was made subject to the condition that the total consideration had to be at least equal to the economic value of the immovable property to which those rights related, and (2) a national provision which allowed the grant, for an agreed period and for payment, of a right in rem entitling the holder to use immovable property, such as the usufructuary right in the present case, to be treated as the leasing or letting of immovable property was not incompatible with Arts. 13B(b) and 13C(a) of the Directive.

STICHTING GOED WONEN v. STAATSSECRETARIS VAN FINANCIEN (C326/99) [2001] 3 C.M.L.R. 54, AM La Pergola (President), ECJ.

4787. Supplies–tax planning–claim for recovery of input tax by subsidiary companies–entitlement to claim

H appealed against a decision of the VAT and Duties Tribunal ([2001] B.V.C. 2240) that a scheme relating to the recovery of input tax incurred on the construction of four call centres was entered into solely for tax mitigation purposes. H needed to construct the centres for business purposes, but was concerned that it would be unable to recover the input tax as most of its business was exempt from VAT. It therefore devised a scheme using three subsidiary companies. The first company, L, which was subject to VAT on a partial exemption basis, took an interest in the sites from H and then engaged the second company, C, to carry out the construction works. C was to be paid in a prescribed accounting period falling shortly before the end of L's partial exemption year. During that accounting period, L would make a small value standard rated supply so that when the period ended it would be able to recover the excess of input tax over output tax for that period. C would discharge its contractual obligations by engaging professional builders on arm's length terms and then account for the VAT charged on the invoice issued to L and in due course recover the VAT charged by the builders. In L's next partial exemption year it would transfer its interest in the sites to a third subsidiary company that would lease them back to H.

Held, allowing the appeal and remitting the matter for reconsideration by the same tribunal, that taken as a whole the tribunal's decision failed to show that it had considered L and C's subjective reasons for entering into the transactions and whether the only reason for doing so was VAT mitigation or avoidance. Given that the sum in issue was nearly £7 million, the cost of remitting the matter was justified and H was entitled, as the appellant, to have a definitive ruling.

HALIFAX PLC v. CUSTOMS AND EXCISE COMMISSIONERS (INPUT TAX ON BUILDING WORKS) (NO.1) [2002] S.T.C. 402, Neuberger, J., Ch D.

4788. Supplies–zero rating–equipment in lifeboats

VALUE ADDED TAX (EQUIPMENT IN LIFEBOATS) ORDER 2002, SI 2002 456; made under the Value Added Tax Act 1994 s.30. In force: April 1, 2002; £1.50.

This Order amends the Value Added Tax Act 1994, which makes provision for the supply of certain goods at the zero rate, zero-rates the supply to sea rescue charities of equipment that is to be installed, incorporated or used in a lifeboat and is of a kind ordinarily installed, incorporated or used in a lifeboat. It also zero-rates the making of arrangements for such a supply. In addition, the Order gives effect to Council Directive 77/388 ([1977] OJ L145/1) in so far as this relates to the supply of equipment that is to be incorporated or used in a vessel used for rescue or assistance at sea.

4789. Supply of services–competitions–obligations of service provider unenforceable–taxable amount

[Sixth Council Directive 77/388 on a common system for VAT Art.2(1).]

A reference was made to the ECJ for a preliminary ruling as to whether VAT was payable on the entry fees for a Spot the Ball competition, and if so, the amount payable. T, the competition organiser, contended that VAT was not payable as it was under no legal obligation to award prizes, being only honour bound to do so. T also argued that if VAT was payable, the taxable amount was the total of the fees received less the value of the prizes awarded.

Held, giving a preliminary ruling, that (1) for the purpose of the Sixth Council Directive 77/388 Art.2(1) the supply of services for consideration constituted a transaction subject to VAT even where the provider's obligations were not enforceable such as in the instant case where T was only honour bound to provide the relevant services. A legal relationship existed between T and each entrant despite the fact that T's obligations as service provider were unenforceable, and (2) where, as in the instant case, the full amount of the entry fees paid to the organiser of a competition were freely at his disposal, VAT was payable on that full amount.

TOWN & COUNTY FACTORS LTD v. CUSTOMS AND EXCISE COMMISSIONERS (C498/99) [2003] All E.R. (EC) 33, Colneric (President), ECJ (6th Chamber).

4790. **Supply of services–grants–consideration–link between grant payment and improvement to school premises–EC law**

[Value Added Tax Act 1994; Sixth Council Directive 77/388 on a common system for VAT.]

C, a company incorporated for charitable purposes only, appealed against the decision of a judge ([2000] S.T.C. 651, [2000] C.L.Y. 5347) that a grant given to it by its parent company, T, had amounted to a supply of services for VAT purposes and was therefore subject to tax under the Value Added Tax Act 1994. C managed and leased various properties as church schools. T, which was also incorporated for charitable purposes only, had made a grant to C of £1 million. C had used the money for building improvements on the properties. The judge had found that the grant was consideration for a supply of services, namely the execution of the improvements, and that there was sufficient reciprocity and a legal relationship between the parties.

Held, allowing the appeal (Buxton, L.J. dissenting), that the judge had erred in finding that a contractual relationship existed between C and T; such a finding had not been open to him. It was clear that a legal relationship existed, *Tolsma v. Inspecteur der Omzetbelasting, Leeuwarden (C16/93)* [1994] E.C.R. I-743, [1994] C.L.Y. 4962 and *Town & County Factors v. Customs and Excise Commissioners (C498/99)* (Unreported, September 27, 2001) considered. Under the Act and the Sixth Council Directive 77/388, a taxable supply was required to be "for" consideration. Accordingly, the question was whether the improvements undertaken had been done "for" the grant, or "with" the grant. It was apparent that C had made improvements to the properties with finance from various sources, of which the grants were but one. It followed that grant had not been made "for" a supply and did not therefore amount to consideration for a supply.

CHURCH SCHOOLS FOUNDATION LTD v. CUSTOMS AND EXCISE COMMISSIONERS; *sub nom.* CUSTOMS AND EXCISE COMMISSIONERS v. CHURCH SCHOOLS FOUNDATION LTD, [2001] EWCA Civ 1745, [2001] S.T.C. 1661, Sir Andrew Morritt V.C., CA.

4791. **Supply of services–prostitution–"escort agency"–liability for VAT**

[Sixth Council Directive 77/388 on a common system for VAT Art.2.]

Customs appealed against a decision of the VAT and Duties tribunal (Unreported, June 13, 2001) that the activities of P's business, which P described as an "escort agency", were unlawful and therefore exempt from VAT. The tribunal had found that P's business consisted entirely, or very substantially, of the procurement of women for the purposes of their becoming common prostitutes.

Held, allowing the appeal, that P's business fell within the scope of the Sixth Council Directive 77/388 Art.2 and accordingly was not exempt from VAT. The tribunal had failed to have proper regard to three principles established by the decisions of the ECJ: the principle of fiscal neutrality, the principle of the inherent nature of the service and the principle of sufficient proximity. As to the principle of fiscal neutrality, the tribunal had not enquired as to whether P's business was unlawful throughout the European Union. Further, as to the principle of the inherent nature of the service, the tribunal had overlooked the fact that prostitution, as such, was not unlawful. It followed that P's procurement "service" was in competition with a lawful service, *Lange v. Finanzamt Furstenfeldbruck (C111/92)* [1997] S.T.C. 564, [1997] C.L.Y. 4985, *Fischer v. Finanzamt Donaueschingen (C-283/95)* [1998] All E.R. (EC) 567, [1998] C.L.Y. 4911 and *R. v. Goodwin (John Charles) (C3/97)* [1998] Q.B. 883, [1998] C.L.Y. 4966 considered. Finally, in relation to the principle of sufficient proximity,

P's activity in supplying the time of their escorts was a lawful and autonomous activity; the activities of the escorts and their customers were separable from the service that P provided, *Staatssecretaris van Financien v. Coffeeshop Siberie vof (C158/98)* [1999] All E.R. (EC) 560, [1999] C.L.Y. 5014 applied.

POLOK v. CUSTOMS AND EXCISE COMMISSIONERS; *sub nom.* CUSTOMS AND EXCISE COMMISSIONERS v. POLOK, [2002] EWHC 156, [2002] S.T.C. 361, Jacob, J., Ch D.

4792. Supply of services–subsidies–subsidies paid to energy adviser not excluded from taxable amount

[Home Energy Efficiency Grants Regulations 1992 (SI 1992 483); Sixth Council Directive 77/388 on a common system for VAT Art.11A(1)(a).]

A reference was made to the European Court of Justice for a preliminary ruling whether a sum paid to a network installer for energy advice given under the Home Energy Efficiency Scheme constituted part of the consideration for the supply of services and part of the taxable amount for VAT purposes. K was a company limited by guarantee registered under the Home Energy Efficiency Grants Regulations 1992. Its main object was the promotion of the efficient use of energy and in particular to undertake appropriate works to improve the energy efficiency of the homes of people in need and to give advice and education relating to energy efficiency. A question arose as to the treatment of a grant of £10 paid by the Energy Action Grants Agency, E, each time K gave energy advice under the Home Energy Grants Action Scheme for VAT purposes. K paid VAT on the grants received, but applied for a refund on the basis that the grant was not directly linked to the price of the supply within the Sixth Council Directive 77/388 Art.11A(1)(a). The VAT and Duties Tribunal decided that the grants were part of the taxable amount as they constituted consideration for supplies. K appealed to the High Court.

Held, giving a ruling, that Art.11A(1)(a) dealt with situations involving three parties: the authority granting the subsidy, the body benefiting from it and the purchaser of the goods or services delivered or supplied by the subsidised body. The sum paid by a public authority such as E to an economic operator such as K in connection with the service of energy advice supplied by K to certain categories of householders might constitute a subsidy within Art.11A(1)(a). It was clear that the sum paid by E to K was received by the latter in consideration for the services supplied by it to certain categories of recipient. As consideration in respect of a supply, that sum formed part of the taxable amount within Art.11A(1)(a).

KEEPING NEWCASTLE WARM LTD v. CUSTOMS AND EXCISE COMMISSIONERS (C353/00) [2002] All E.R. (EC) 769, Macken (President), ECJ.

4793. Supply of services–tour operators–change to calculation method–requirement for notification

[Value Added Tax Act 1994 s.30, Sch.8 Group 8 item 12; Value Added Tax (Tour Operators) Order 1987 (SI 1987 1806) Art.7.]

Customs appealed against a VAT and duties tribunal's decision that S was entitled to elect to change the basis of its VAT calculation retrospectively. Under the Value Added Tax Act 1994 s.30 and Sch.8 Group 8 item 12 the supply of a designated travel service to be enjoyed outside the EU was zero-rated. Pursuant to the Value Added Tax (Tour Operators) Order 1987 Art.7 the value of a designated travel service was determined by reference to the difference between sums paid to and sums paid by the tour operator in respect of the service. Customs Notice 709/5/96 para.13(c) provided that if a taxpayer made supplies which were enjoyed wholly outside the EU, he could elect to do a separate annual calculation at the end of the year in respect of those supplies, so long as permission was obtained from the VAT Business Advice Centre. However permission would not be granted retrospectively. S applied to revert from an EC/non-EC calculation back to a single worldwide Tour Operators Margin Scheme calculation and Customs refused.

Held, allowing the appeal, that (1) the tribunal had erred in law in its interpretation of para.13(c) since the only permissible construction, giving it its plain and ordinary meaning, was that notification should be given at the start of the relevant financial year when the taxpayer wished to change from the single calculation method to the separated calculation method or vice versa. It was not for the tribunal to override, or decline to give effect to, the language used in a statutory instrument because it disapproved of the policy to which the instrument gave effect.

SIMPLY TRAVEL LTD v. CUSTOMS AND EXCISE COMMISSIONERS; *sub nom.* CUSTOMS AND EXCISE COMMISSIONERS v. SIMPLY TRAVEL LTD [2002] S.T.C. 194, Lightman, J., Ch D.

4794. **Tax rates—free movement of goods—reduced VAT rate levied on books in Icelandic—disparate treatment not compatible with EFTA Agreement Art.14**

[Agreement between the EFTA States on the Establishment of a Surveillance Authority and a Court of Justice Art.34; Agreement on a European Economic Area 1992 Art.14(2).]

The Reykjavik District Court sought an advisory opinion under the EFTA Surveillance Agreement Art.34. In Iceland, VAT was levied at a general rate of 24.5 per cent. However, books written in or translated into Icelandic were only liable to VAT at 14 per cent. E brought proceedings in the District Court, complaining of the disparate VAT treatment and the court sought the opinion of the EFTA Court of Justice as to whether the domestic VAT regime was compatible with the EFTA Agreement Art.14.

Held, that (1) Member States had the power to fix disparate VAT rates on the basis of objective criteria, but only where these were compatible with the Agreement, *Norway v. EFTA Surveillance Authority (E6/98)* [1999] 2 C.M.L.R. 1033, [2000] C.L.Y. 729 followed; (2) Icelandic VAT legislation came within Art.14 of the Agreement, the purpose of which was to ensure free movement of goods between EEA countries by providing that internal taxation had a neutral effect on competition between national and imported merchandise, *Societe Critouridienne de Distribution (SOCRIDIS) v. Receveur Principal des Douanes (C166/98)* [1999] E.C.R. I-3791, [2000] C.L.Y. 2382 followed; (3) books in Icelandic and those in other languages were in partial competition with each other, and the lower rate of VAT levied on the former was intended to support Iceland's own book industry in a way that contravened Art.14(2) of the Agreement, *Commission of the European Communities v. Italy (C184/85)* [1987] E.C.R. 2013 followed, and (4) the public interest in promoting the Icelandic language did not justify the difference in treatment allowed under national law.

EINARSSON v. ICELAND (E1/01) [2002] 2 C.M.L.R 2, Vilhjalmsson (President), EFTA.

4795. **Taxation—amendment**

VALUE ADDED TAX (AMENDMENT) REGULATIONS 2002, SI 2002 1074; made under the Value Added Tax Act 1994 s.26. In force: April 18, 2002; £1.75.

These Regulations amend the Value Added Tax Regulations 1995 (SI 1995 2518) in order to counter avoidance schemes based on the partial exemption method specified in those regulations and to deal with situations where the result of the method is clearly unreasonable.

4796. Taxation—amendment

VALUE ADDED TAX (AMENDMENT) (NO.3) REGULATIONS 2002, SI 2002 2918; made under the Value Added Tax Act 1994 s.6. In force: November 28, 2002; £1.75.

These Regulations amend the Value Added Tax Regulations 1995 (SI 1995 2518) by restricting the application of regulation 84(2).

4797. Taxation—bad debt relief—input tax

VALUE ADDED TAX (AMENDMENT) (NO.4) REGULATIONS 2002, SI 2002 3027; made under the Value Added Tax Act 1994 s.26A, s.36. In force: January 1, 2003; £1.75.

These Regulations amend the Value Added Tax Regulations 1995 (SI 1995 2518) so that the requirement for a person who has claimed bad debt relief to send a notice to his customer notifying him of the claim only applies where the supply upon which the claim is based was made before January 1, 2003. They make provision which applies where a person makes a supply of goods and an associated supply of credit under a hire purchase, conditional sale or credit sale agreement; for the restoration of an entitlement to credit for input tax where a person has repaid input tax and, after the end of the relevant period, pays the whole or part of the consideration for the supply in relation to which the repayment was made.

4798. Taxation—buildings and land—calculation method

VALUE ADDED TAX (BUILDINGS AND LAND) ORDER 2002, SI 2002 1102; made under the Value Added Tax Act 1994 s.51. In force: June 1, 2002; £1.50.

This Order amends the Value Added Tax Act 1994 Sch.10 in relation to the method of calculating the value of supplies relating to buildings which are intended for use solely for a relevant charitable or residential purpose but the use of the building is changed to use for other purposes within 10 years of its completion. Whereas at present the calculation method gives a value which means that all of the original VAT saved by zero-rating has to be accounted for, the new formula allows a reduction in the value (and the corresponding VAT) by one tenth for each complete year of relevant charitable or relevant residential use before the change of use occurs.

4799. Taxation—construction of buildings

VALUE ADDED TAX (CONSTRUCTION OF BUILDINGS) ORDER 2002, SI 2002 1101; made under the Value Added Tax Act 1994 s.30. In force: June 1, 2002; £1.50.

This Order amends the Value Added Tax Act 1994 Sch.8 so that, providing the other conditions in Group 5 Note 17 are met, the construction of an annexe can be regarded as the construction of a building when only part of it is intended to be used solely for a relevant charitable purpose.

4800. Taxation—fuel—rates

VALUE ADDED TAX (CONSIDERATION FOR FUEL PROVIDED FOR PRIVATE USE) ORDER 2002, SI 2002 1099; made under the Value Added Tax Act 1994 s.57. In force: May 1, 2002; £1.50.

VAT is payable if road fuel of a business is used for private motoring. The VAT due must be calculated using flat-rate values related to engine type and size. This Order reduces those flat-rates by an average of 6 per cent for diesel vehicles and 7 per cent for those using other fuels. The new rates apply to any relevant accounting period starting after April 30, 2002.

4801. Taxation—heating systems—reduced rate

VALUE ADDED TAX (REDUCED RATE) ORDER 2002, SI 2002 1100; made under the Value Added Tax Act 1994 s.29A. In force: June 1, 2002; £2.00.

This Order amends the Value Added Tax Act 1994 Sch.7A to extend the reduced rate to the installation, maintenance or repair of renewable source heating systems and the definition of "central heating systems" to include those systems that generate electricity as well as heat, such as micro combined heat and power systems.

4802. Taxation—printed matter—special provisions

VALUE ADDED TAX (SPECIAL PROVISIONS) (AMENDMENT) ORDER 2002, SI 2002 1280; made under the Value Added Tax Act 1994 s.5, s.43. In force: June 1, 2002; £1.50.

This Order amends the Value Added Tax (Special Provisions) Order 1995 (SI 1995 1268) by removing the definition of "printed matter" and abolishing the requirement that, in certain circumstances, where a person who is not a fully taxable person produces printed matter for use in his business (otherwise than by way of supplying it or incorporating it in other goods) the printed matter shall be treated as both supplied to him and by him.

4803. Taxation—registration—acquisitions and cancellations—increase in limits

VALUE ADDED TAX (INCREASE OF REGISTRATION LIMITS) ORDER 2002, SI 2002 1098; made under the Value Added Tax Act 1994 Sch.1 para.15, Sch.3 para.9. In force: April 25, 2002; £1.50.

This Order increases the VAT registration limits for taxable supplies and for acquisitions from other Member States from £54,000 to £55,000, the limit for cancellation of registration in the case of taxable supplies from £52,000 to £53,000, and in the case of acquisitions from other Member States from £54,000 to £55,000.

4804. VAT and duties tribunals—appeals—costs—hearing length affected by misleading or incorrect evidence of Customs officers

[Value Added Tax Act 1994 s.60.]

S, a partnership, appealed against a VAT assessment and a civil penalty under the Value Added Tax Act 1994 s.60. The assessment was later withdrawn against two partners that joined the partnership during the investigation but prior to the assessment being made. S sought the costs of the appeal in respect of the two new partners, contending that Customs should pay 25 per cent of the costs incurred up to the date that Customs conceded the two were not liable. Customs argued that only the costs of the new partners taking part in the appeal were recoverable. The appeal took 26 days and a large part of Customs' evidence was either misleading of or little probative value.

Held, allowing the appeal in part, that (1) the new partners were entitled to the costs attributable to their participation in the appeal; (2) a large part of the hearing had been taken up with misleading or incorrect evidence from Customs officers which increased the length of the hearing so that Customs' costs would be reduced by 15 per cent, and (3) apart from those reductions, S was liable for Customs remaining costs of the appeal.

STANDARD TANDOORI NEPALESE RESTAURANT v. CUSTOMS AND EXCISE COMMISSIONERS (NO.2) [2000] V. & D.R. 105, Angus Nicol (Chairman), V&D Tr.

4805. VAT and duties tribunals—appeals—dismissal—jurisdiction to dismiss appeal for want of prosecution—appellant's whereabouts unknown

[Value Added Tax Tribunal Rules 1986 (SI 1986 590) r.18(2).]

In September 1998 P appealed against a decision that his business had been transferred to him as a going concern. Various communications then followed between P and the tribunal in an attempt to determine unsuitable dates for the hearing. The last letter from P was sent from an address in Wells in March 1999, however letters subsequently sent to that address were returned with notes to the effect that P had never lived there. Customs applied for the appeal to be struck out under either the Value Added Tax Tribunals Rules 1986 r.18(2) or the tribunal's inherent jurisdiction.

Held, allowing the application and dismissing the appeal under r.18(2) for want of prosecution, that although it would have been possible to give an unless order and then dismiss for failure to comply, dismissal under r.18(2) reflected the circumstances of the instant case. It was uncertain whether the tribunal had an inherent jurisdiction to dismiss an appeal as an abuse of process. Further, it would be a misuse of its resources to hear the appeal in P's absence.

POWER v. CUSTOMS AND EXCISE COMMISSIONERS [2001] B.V.C. 2082, Nuala Brice, V&DTr.

4806. VAT and duties tribunals–appeals–dismissal where neither party appeared– appellant able to seek reinstatement within 14 days

[Company Directors Disqualification Act 1986; Value Added Tax Tribunal Rules 1986 (SI 1986 590) r.26(1).]

H appealed against a decision by Customs refusing its input tax repayment claim. The appeal was stood over on several occasions before H's solicitor informed the tribunal that H's sole director was resident in Zimbabwe and that his two UK representatives had been disqualified under the Company Directors Disqualification Act 1986 so that there was no one that could give instructions within the jurisdiction. Customs wrote to the tribunal, asking whether it was necessary to attend the hearing and stating that the appeal could be dismissed under the Value Added Tax Tribunals Rules 1986 r.26(1). The appeal was called for hearing but neither party attended, although Customs' representative was present in the building.

Held, dismissing the appeal, that although it was anomalous to dismiss an appeal without considering the issues when neither party appeared, H had been given plenty of time to give instructions for the hearing. In the circumstances the appeal was dismissed under r.26(1) as H had 14 days to apply for reinstatement if there were proper grounds.

HAZELACRE LTD v. CUSTOMS AND EXCISE COMMISSIONERS [2000] V. & D.R. 185, Theodore Wallace (Chairman), V&DTr.

4807. VAT and duties tribunals–appeals–jurisdiction–extra statutory concession as basis for appeal

[Value Added Tax Act 1994 s.83(b), s.84(10) Value Added Tax Tribunal Rules 1986 (SI 1986 590) r.6(1).]

GP granted a long lease of student residential accommodation to a university. The university gave GP a certificate in reliance upon an extra statutory concession, termed a concordat, that had been entered into between Customs and the Committee of University Vice Chancellors and Principals of the UK, which allowed GP to treat the grant of the lease as zero rated. Customs subsequently decided, however, that the certificate had been wrongly issued and assessed GP to input tax. GP appealed and Customs sought to have the appeal struck out under the Value Added Tax Tribunal Rules 1986 r.6(1), which provided that the tribunal had no jurisdiction to determine an appeal relating to an extra statutory concession. GP argued that the tribunal had jurisdiction as the appeal was against an assessment under the Value Added Tax Act 1994 s.83(b). Further, that the appeal came within s.84(10) of the Act as the question of whether the concordat applied was a matter upon which the assessment depended.

Held, dismissing the application under r.6(1) and determining the s.84(10) point as a preliminary issue, that the words "prior decision" in s.84(10) meant a decision by Customs which formed an integral part of the tax system and came within Customs' statutory discretionary powers. On the facts, there was no such decision in the instant case as the concordat did not confer any legal rights on GP. The tribunal did not, therefore, have jurisdiction to review Customs' application of the concordat.

GREENWICH PROPERTY LTD v. CUSTOMS AND EXCISE COMMISSIONERS (RIGHT OF APPEAL) [2000] V. & D.R. 167, Stephen Oliver Q.C. (Chairman), V&DTr.

4808. VAT and duties tribunals–costs–appeal against review of assessment–extent of recoverable costs

[Finance Act 1994 s.12, s.15, s.16; Value Added Tax Tribunals Rules 1986 (SI 1986 590) r.29(1)(a).]

Following the compromise of an appeal brought by D against an assessment of liability to hydrocarbon duty and possible penalties, the issue arose as to what costs were payable. By virtue of the Value Added Tax Tribunals Rules 1986 r.29(1)(a), a tribunal could direct that a party pay to the other party to the appeal or application "within such period as it may specify such sum as it may determine on account of the costs of such other party of and incidental to and consequent upon the appeal or application". In the instant case the costs incurred fell into three categories (1) those incurred from the notification of the proposed assessment up until the notification of the assessment; (2) those incurred from the notification of the assessment up until the notification of the review decision, and (3) those incurred subsequent to notification of the review decision. Customs denied liability for the costs incurred in the first two categories. The issue to be determined was whether the costs in the first two categories were "incidental" to the appeal.

Held, allowing the appeal, that having regard to the Finance Act 1994 s.12, s.15 and s.16, those being the statutory provisions under which an assessment, review and appeal were made, it was apparent that a review under s.15 was an administrative decision rather than the first stage of an appeal and that an appeal lay against the review decision. Accordingly, the costs incurred "incidental" to the appeal were those incidental to the appeal against the review decision, *Gibson's Settlement Trusts, Re* [1981] Ch. 179, [1981] C.L.Y. 2136 considered. Such a conclusion was consistent with the wording of the Act, the intention of Parliament and the normal practice of the courts where an appeal was brought against a first instance decision. It followed that, in the instant case, only the costs incurred in the third category were recoverable.

DAVE v. CUSTOMS AND EXCISE COMMISSIONERS (COSTS); *sub nom.* CUSTOMS AND EXCISE COMMISSIONERS v. DAVE (COSTS), [2002] EWHC 969, [2002] S.T.C. 900, Burton, J., Ch D.

4809. VAT and Duties Tribunals–jurisdiction–appeals

VALUE ADDED TAX TRIBUNALS (AMENDMENT) RULES 2002, SI 2002 2851; made under the Value Added Tax Act 1994 Sch.12 para.9. In force: December 9, 2002; £1.50.

These Rules amend the Value Added Tax Tribunals Rules 1986 (SI 1986 590) to provide for a new jurisdiction, covering appeals relating to the aggregates levy, given to the VAT and duties tribunals by the Finance Act 2001. In addition the opportunity has been taken to correct an anomaly and provide a time limit for the filing of a notice of appeal where the Commissioners have failed to review a decision within the time required by the relevant statute.

4810. Zero rating–air transport–carriage by ship

VALUE ADDED TAX (TRANSPORT) ORDER 2002, SI 2002 1173; made under the Value Added Tax Act 1994 s.30, s.96. In force: June 1, 2002; £1.50.

This Order amends the Value Added Tax Act 1994 Sch.8 so that services provided for the handling or storage of goods carried in a ship or aircraft are zero-rated if they are supplied in an airport, in a port or on land adjacent to a port. This Order also zero-rates such services if they are supplied in a place approved by the Commissioners of Customs and Excise for the storage of goods in temporary storage, no matter where that place is.

4811. Zero rating–charities–building constructed by charity and leased to second charity for use by playgroup

[Value Added Tax Act 1994 s.94, Sch.8 Part II Group 5 Item 2 Note 6; Sixth Council Directive 77/388 on a common system for VAT Art.4(2).]

Y, a charity, sought to treat as zero rated the costs it had incurred in the supply of a building leased to another charity which ran a playgroup. Customs refused the claim on the ground that the leasing was an economic activity so that the building was not therefore used for a charitable purpose in terms of the Value Added Tax Act 1994 Sch.8 Group 5 item 2 Note 6. On appeal to the VAT and Duties Tribunal ([2001] B.V.C. 2307) it was held that the supply was eligible for zero rating, as the hall came within the village hall exception in Note 6(b). Customs appealed.

Held, dismissing the appeal, that the definition of "charitable purpose" in Note 6 excluded buildings that were exploited for business purposes by virtue of the Sixth Council Directive 77/388 Art.4(2) and s.94(1) of the Act. However, this did not serve to exclude premises used by charities that had some business use but which were intended to benefit a final consumer in a defined social sense. In the instant case, although rent was charged, the letting did not amount to an economic activity under s.94(2), so that the use came within Group 5 Note 6. The village hall exception did not apply, however, as the building was not made generally available to the local community, as required by Note 6(b).

YARBURGH CHILDRENS TRUST v. CUSTOMS AND EXCISE COMMISSIONERS; *sub nom.* CUSTOMS AND EXCISE COMMISSIONERS v. YARBURGH CHILDREN'S TRUST [2002] S.T.C. 207, Patten, J., Ch D.

4812. Zero rating–charities–goods exported to be given away for no consideration in non Member States

[Value Added Tax Act 1994 s.26(2)(b), s.30(5).]

I, a registered charity with headquarters in London, distributed goods free of charge in developing countries. The goods were purchased both within and outside the European Union from I's London headquarters but were distributed from its warehouse in the Netherlands and never entered the UK. Customs assessed I to VAT on the basis that the input tax was incurred by I on goods that were given away for no consideration. I appealed, contending that the goods were supplies that were exported beyond the European Union and that the Value Added Tax Act 1994 s.30(5) deemed them to have been made in the course of I's business and that they should be zero rated as they were made to non Member States.

Held, dismissing the appeal, that as "export" was not defined in the Act it was to be accorded its usual meaning of goods that were sent from one country to another. In the instant case, the goods were not removed from the UK and so had not been exported from here. As the goods were given away for no consideration they did not constitute supplies made by I in the course of its business so that I was not entitled to an input tax credit under s.26(2)(b).

INTERNATIONAL PLANNED PARENTHOOD FEDERATION v. CUSTOMS AND EXCISE COMMISSIONERS [2000] V. & D.R. 396, AN Brice (Chairman), V&D Tr.

4813. Zero rating–charities–sirens supplied by registered charity–provision of rescue services

[Value Added Tax Act 1994 Sch.8 Group 15.]

S, a registered charity having as its main object the provision of sirens as an early warning system, appealed against a decision by Customs that this activity was not liable to zero rating under the Value Added Tax Act 1994 Sch.8 Group 15. Customs based its decision on the ground that providing sirens was not intended to rescue people in the accepted sense of the word.

Held, allowing the appeal, that the addition of the word "services" to rescue and first aid in Group 15 Item 5 Note (3)(g) and Note (4) meant that "rescue" was to be given a wider interpretation than that relied on by Customs. Further, the sirens were "aural equipment" supplied by a charity as a rescue service for the purposes of Note (3)(g).

SEVERNSIDE SIREN TRUST LTD v. CUSTOMS AND EXCISE COMMISSIONERS [2000] B.V.C. 2381, Angus Nicol (Chairman), V&DTr.

4814. Zero rating–food products–sports energy drinks–nutritional supplements not liable to standard rating

[Value Added Tax Act 1983 Sch.5 Group 1 Excepted Item 4; Finance Act 1985s.25; Value Added Tax Act 1994 Sch.8 Group 1 Excepted Item 4.]

S manufactured sports energy drinks. As the result of an earlier appeal Customs had accepted in a letter of November 1993 that the drinks were eligible for zero rating under the Value Added Tax Act 1983 Sch.5 Group 1 Excepted Item 4. That appeal did not proceed to a hearing but it was never withdrawn. By a further letter dated August 1998, Customs ruled that the sports energy drinks were standard rated from December 1, 1997. S appealed against that decision and the subsequent VAT assessment. S contended that the present appeal merely reconsidered a previously resolved matter and, secondly, that its products were entitled to be zero rated as food products that did not come under the Value Added Tax Act 1994 Sch.8 Group 1 Excepted Item 4.

Held, allowing the appeal, that (1) the November 1993 letter did not constitute a written agreement between S and Customs so that the earlier appeal had been settled by an oral agreement under the Finance Act 1985 s.25(1) for which no there was no written notice of confirmation; (2) the decision in August 1998 that the goods were standard rated was a reconsideration by Customs of its earlier decision which had not given rise to an estoppel, and (3) the products were nutritional supplements for those using large amounts of energy which were liable to zero rating.

SIS (SCIENCE IN SPORT) LTD v. CUSTOMS AND EXCISE COMMISSIONERS (NO.1) [2000] B.V.C. 2277, MS Johnson (Chairman), V&DTr.

4815. Zero rating–residential care–incontinence pads supplied to named residents

[Value Added Tax Act 1994 s.47(2A), Sch.8 Group 12 Item 2(g); Sixth Council Directive 77/388 on a common system for VAT Art.5.4(c), Art.6.4.]

E appealed against a decision by Customs that incontinence pads supplied to nursing homes for use by individual named residents were liable to VAT at the standard rate by virtue of the Value Added Tax Act 1994 s.47(2A). E contended that the pads should be zero rated under Sch.8 Group 12 Item 2(g). Customs argued, however, that the homes acting as agents so that s.47(2A) treated goods supplied by them as both a supply to the agent and a supply by them, which brought the domestic provisions into line with the Sixth Council Directive 77/388 Art.5.4(c) and Art.6.4.

Held, allowing the appeal, that the homes were acting on behalf of their residents and not as agents in their own names, as required by s.47(2A). There was a discrepancy between s.47(2A), which treated goods and services equally, and Art.5.4(c) of the Directive.

EXPRESS MEDICARE LTD v. CUSTOMS AND EXCISE COMMISSIONERS [2001] B.V.C. 2152, Theodore Wallace (Chairman), V&DTr.

4816. Zero rating–supply of services–alterations to listed building–meaning of "protected building"

[Planning (Listed Buildings and Conservation Areas) Act 1990 s.1(5); Value Added Tax Act 1994 s.30, Sch.8 Part II Group 6.]

Z appealed against an order ([2001] S.T.C. 585) allowing an appeal by Customs against a finding ([2001] B.V.C. 2059) that alterations to an outbuilding of a listed building qualified for zero rating. Z contended that the outbuilding was a "protected building" by virtue of falling within the curtilage of a listed house, and that therefore the cost of any work carried out upon it was zero rated pursuant to the Value Added Tax Act 1994 s.30. The Commissioners cross appealed, contending that the outbuilding was not a listed building within the meaning of the Planning (Listed Buildings and Conservation Areas) Act 1990 s.1 (5).

Held, allowing the appeal (Aldous, L.J. dissenting) and dismissing the cross appeal, that when interpreting Sch. 8 Part II Group 6 of the 1994 Act it was appropriate to take a holistic approach rather than a step by step approach. By adopting this approach the building which fell within the definition of a "protected building" was the main building, namely the house, and not the outbuilding which was secondary to it. In the instant case, the approved alterations to the outbuilding qualified for zero rating because the outbuilding formed part of a building which was both a listed building and a dwelling, despite the fact that the outbuilding itself was not a dwelling.

CUSTOMS AND EXCISE COMMISSIONERS v. ZIELINSKI BAKER & PARTNERS LTD; *sub nom.* ZIELINSKI BAKER & PARTNERS LTD v. CUSTOMS AND EXCISE COMMISSIONERS; ZIELINSKY BAKERS & PARTNERS LTD v. CUSTOMS AND EXCISE COMMISSIONERS, [2002] EWCA Civ 692, [2002] S.T.C. 829, Aldous, L.J., CA.

4817. Books

Dolton, Alan; Wareham, Robert–Tolley's VAT Cases 2002. Paperback: £89.95. ISBN 0-7545-1688-1. Tolley Publishing.

Glaser, Maric–Tolley's VAT Business by Business Guide 2001-02. Paperback: £79.95. ISBN 0-7545-1290-8. Tolley Publishing.

Hamilton, Penny–Hamilton on VAT and Duty Appeals. Paperback: £74.95. ISBN 0-7545-1484-6. Tolley Publishing.

Jordan, David–Understanding VAT on Property. Paperback: £39.95. ISBN 1-85328-860-8. Law Society Publications.

Soares, Patrick–VAT Planning for Property Transactions. 8th Ed. Hardback: £120.00. ISBN 0-421-77460-6. Sweet & Maxwell.

Somerville, Ian; Lewis, Susan–VAT for Retailers and E-tailers. Paperback: £49.95. ISBN 0-7545-0991-5. Butterworths Law.

Turczynowicz, Antoni; O'Reilly, Toby; Sherratt, Antonia–VAT in Central and Eastern Europe. Paperback: £49.95. ISBN 0-7545-0838-2. Tolley Publishing.

Wareham, Robert–Tolley's VAT Planning 2001-02. Paperback: £74.95. ISBN 0-7545-1291-6. Tolley Publishing.

Wareham, Robert–Tolley's VAT Planning 2002-03. Paperback: £84.95. ISBN 0-7545-1689-X. Tolley Publishing.

WATER LAW

4818. Land drainage–planning control–discretion of justices in issuing warrants to sewerage undertakers–protection of sites of special scientific interest

[Water Industry Act 1991 Sch.6 Part II para.7.]

ST appealed by way of case stated against the refusal of a warrant to enable them to enter onto S's land in order to carry out sewerage works in accordance with their statutory duty as sewerage undertakers. B, property developers, obtained planning permission for a residential development subject to certain drainage works being carried out, including the replacement of a sluice which protected an adjoining site of special scientific interest. ST having been requisitioned by B to carry out the drainage work, undertook to carry out the work on the sluice although that was not part of their statutory duty. S, owners of the land, refused to allow ST to enter on the land to carry out the necessary works. Despite finding that the requirements of the Water Industry Act 1991 Sch.6 Part II para.7 (1) (a) and para 7 (1) (b) had been met, the justices refused the warrant because they could not accept the goodwill of ST to replace the sluice as they had not entered into negotiations for the work to be carried out. ST contended that this had been an immaterial consideration by the justices in relation to the exercise of their discretion.

Held, allowing the appeal and remitting the application for reconsideration, that where a warrant was sought pursuant to the Water Industry Act 1991 Sch.6 Part II para.7, if the conditions in para.7(1)(a) and para.7(1)(b) have been satisfied then, subject to the relevant procedural requirements also having been met, the justices have no discretion to refuse to issue the warrant. In the instant case, whether or not B, a third party who was not party to the application, had complied with the requirement of the planning permission by ensuring the provision of a sluice was not a material consideration to the exercise of the justices discretion. However, it would have been open to the justices to have refused the warrant by reason of non compliance with para.7(1)(a), if they had taken the view that a site of special scientific interest would have been damaged by the sewerage works being carried out without the sluice being replaced at or about the same time.

SEVERN TRENT WATER LTD v. SLACK, [2001] EWHC Admin 1094, [2002] E.H.L.R. 12, Elias, J., QBD (Admin Ct).

4819. Land drainage–powers of entry–local authority's right to carry out new drainage works

[Land Drainage Act 1991 s.14, s.64; Human Rights Act 1998 Sch.1 Part II Art.1.]
M challenged the lawfulness of a notice of intended entry served on it by the local authority under the Land Drainage Act 1991 s.64 giving the local authority the power to enter onto M's land in order to carry out drainage works to alleviate a long standing flooding problem. M contended that (1) s.64 of the Act did not confer an independent right of entry on the local authority to carry out new drainage works since they did not have a right of entry under s.14 of the Act. Furthermore, any such right of entry would infringe M's proprietary rights under the Human Rights Act 1998 Sch.1 Part II Art.1, and (2) the local authority's actions were disproportionate in seeking to resolve the flooding in that area.

Held, refusing the application for judicial review, that notwithstanding that it was agreed between the parties that s.14 of the 1991 Act did not give the authority the right to enter the claimant's land to carry out new drainage works, s.64(8) of the 1991 Act did however create a right to enter land in connection with the construction of new drainage channels. On these facts, there was no disproportionate interference with M's human rights.

R. (ON THE APPLICATION OF MWH&H WARD ESTATES LTD) v. MONMOUTHSHIRE CC, [2002] EWHC 229, [2002] E.H.L.R. 14, Richards, J., QBD (Admin Ct).

4820. Water quality–crops–damage to crops caused by herbicide contaminated water supply–drinking water standards–New Zealand

[Sale of Goods Act 1908 (New Zealand) s.16(a).]
H appealed against a decision of the Court of Appeal of New Zealand ([2000] 1 N.Z.L.R. 265) upholding the dismissal of their claim for damages against P and W for the alleged damage caused to their cherry tomato crops by the hormone herbicide triclopyr, present in the town water supply. H had purchased the water from P who had obtained it from W, the main bulk water supplier for the area. H had brought a claim in contract and negligence against P and in negligence and nuisance against W. They claimed that the spraying of gorse by W's contractors had contaminated a lake from which the water supply was obtained, and that it, in turn, had caused H's crops to be contaminated. The Court of Appeal rejected the claim on the basis that although the damage was caused by triclopyr contamination of the range of up to 10 parts per billion, 100 parts per billion was the maximum triclopyr permitted by the New Zealand Drinking Water Standards 1995. H contended that (1) pursuant to the Sale of Goods Act 1908 (New Zealand) s.16(a), P had breached an implied term that the water it supplied was suitable for horticultural use in circumstances where H had relied upon P's skill and judgment; (2) P and W had breached their duty of care to supply water fit for the

purposes for which it was intended, to monitor its quality and to notify them that the water might not be fit for its intended purpose, and (3) W were liable in nuisance and under *Rylands v. Fletcher* given that it had brought a hormonal herbicide onto land, which if it escaped was likely to cause damage.

Held, dismissing the appeal (Lord Hutton and Lord Roger dissenting), that a local authority which complied with its statutory duty to provide drinking water to the requisite standard was not under an implied duty to meet the special requirements of individual users who required water of a higher quality for horticultural purposes. Accordingly, (1) P's objective was to provide water fit for human use in accordance with the drinking water standards, and it had not breached those standards. It would not have occurred to P that H were relying on it to supply water of a higher quality, and there was no evidence that H ever thought that drinking water would not be suitable for their crops, *Ashington Piggeries Ltd v. Christopher Hill Ltd* [1972] A.C. 441, [1971] C.L.Y. 10517 distinguished; (2) to impose such a duty on P and W as that contended for by H, would extend beyond the duty met by those authorities which supplied bulk water, a duty which had been founded on drinking water standards compiled from the World Health Organisation guidelines and established through consultation. Imposing a broader duty on suppliers would mean extra costs for general users. In addition, it had not been reasonably foreseeable to W or P that the water would damage H's tomato crop, and (3) although no longer contested by H, foreseeability was essential in order to establish liability under *Rylands v. Fletcher* and nuisance.

HAMILTON v. PAPAKURA DC, [2002] UKPC 9, *The Times*, March 5, 2002, Sir Kenneth Keith, PC (NZ).

4821. Water quality—fines—method of calculation

[Water Industry Act 1991 s.70(1).]

YW appealed against fines totalling £119,000 imposed following its guilty pleas to 17 counts of supplying water unfit for human consumption contrary to the Water Industry Act 1991 s.70(1). The charges stemmed from incidents in which households were supplied with discoloured or foul smelling water as a result of work being carried out by YW.

Held, allowing the appeal, that in determining the level of fines, the court had to have regard to, among other things, the degree of culpability and the damage caused, the defendants previous record of offending and the attitude and actions of the water authority following the incidents. A balance also had to be struck between the level of the fine and its effect on the supplier carrying out necessary works in connection with the water supply. Furthermore, the number of complaints should not be used as a multiplier in determining the level of the fine to be imposed. Accordingly, in the instant case the penalty imposed on YW was too high and was reduced to £80,000.

SECRETARY OF STATE FOR THE ENVIRONMENT, TRANSPORT AND THE REGIONS v. YORKSHIRE WATER SERVICES LTD; *sub nom.* R. v. YORKSHIRE WATER SERVICES LTD, [2001] EWCA Crim 2635, [2002] 2 Cr. App. R. (S.) 13, Rougier, J., CA (Crim Div).

NORTHERN IRELAND

ADMINISTRATION OF JUSTICE

4822. Access to justice–state security–issue of Section 42 certificate–disproportionate restriction on access to Fair Employment Tribunal

[Fair Employment (Northern Ireland) Act 1976 s.42; European Convention on Human Rights 1950 Art.6(1).]

D, an Irish citizen, brought an application against the United Kingdom in relation to the decision of the Secretary of State to issue a certificate under the Fair Employment (Northern Ireland) Act 1976 s.42 preventing him from pursuing a complaint of unfair discrimination before the Fair Employment Tribunal. D, who had been dismissed from his employment at a hotel, maintained that he had been the only Roman Catholic employee and that he had been discriminated against on the grounds of religious belief or political opinion. The Section 42 certificate had been put before the tribunal stating that D's employment had been terminated in order to protect public safety and public order, and his complaint had been dismissed. D submitted that the issuing of the certificate had deprived him of his right to access to the tribunal and had accordingly violated his rights under the European Convention on Human Rights 1950 Art.6(1).

Held, allowing the application, that D had had a statutory right to access to the tribunal and, although limitations could legitimately be applied to that right, they could not restrict the access remaining in such a way that the essence of the right was impaired. Limitations would not be compatible with Art.6(1) if they did not pursue a legitimate aim or if there was a lack of reasonable proportionality between the means used and what the limitation sought to achieve. Accordingly, although national security constituted a legitimate aim, it was necessary to consider whether there was reasonable proportionality between the concerns as to national security and the impact which the means employed to protect that security had on an applicant's right to access to court, *Tinnelly & Sons Ltd v. United Kingdom* (1999) 27 E.H.R.R. 249, [1998] C.L.Y. 3147 applied. In the instant case therefore, although mindful of the security considerations regarding establishments such as hotels, the dismissal had also to be considered in the light of the effect it had had upon D and the fact that s.42 of the Act left him unable to challenge his dismissal or seek financial recompense. D had not been told on what grounds the certificate had been issued. Moreover, the Government had not identified new elements to persuade the court to depart from the conclusion reached in *Tinnelly* that the severity of a Section 42 certificate was not mitigated by other means of complaint. The issuing of the certificate had amounted to a disproportionate restriction on D's right of access to court and had accordingly breached his rights under Art.6(1) of the Convention. Damages of £10 000 were awarded for loss of opportunity.

DEVENNEY v. UNITED KINGDOM (24265/94) (2002) 35 E.H.R.R. 24, J-P Costa (President), ECHR.

4823. Coroners–practice and procedure–witnesses

CORONERS (PRACTICE AND PROCEDURE) (AMENDMENT) RULES (NORTHERN IRELAND) 2002, SR 2002 37; made under the Coroners Act (Northern Ireland) Act 1959 s.36. In force: February 11, 2002; £1.50.

These Rules, which amend the Coroners (Practice and Procedure) Rules (Northern Ireland) 1963 (SR & O 1963 199), allow a person suspected or charged with causing death to be compellable as a witness at the inquest into the death and provide that witness at an inquest may decline to answer any question tending to incriminate himself or his spouse.

4824. County courts–fees

COUNTY COURT FEES (AMENDMENT) ORDER (NORTHERN IRELAND) 2002, SR 2002 342; made under the Judicature (Northern Ireland) Act 1978 s.116. In force: in accordance with Art.1; £2.00.

This Order amends the County Court Fees Order (Northern Ireland) 1996 (SR 1996 103) so as to increase a number of court fees to be taken in proceedings in county courts; and allow fees to be taken by a range of payment methods including credit or debit card.

4825. County courts–rules

COUNTY COURT (AMENDMENT) RULES (NORTHERN IRELAND) 2002, SR 2002 255; made under the County Courts (Northern Ireland) Order 1980 (SI 1980 397 (NI.3)) Art.47. In force: November 4, 2002; £3.00.

These Rules amend the County Court Rules (Northern Ireland) 1981 (SR 1981 225) to implement specified recommendations of the Final Report of the Civil Justice Reform Group; take account of the recent increases in the small claims and the district judges' defended civil bill jurisdiction; and delete the provisions relating to applications for declarations of legitimacy and legitimation.

4826. Intervenors–Human Rights Commission–power to make submissions before courts and tribunals

[Northern Ireland Act 1998 s.68, s.69.]

The Northern Ireland Human Rights Commission, which had been established under the Northern Ireland Act 1998 s.68, appealed against a decision ([2001] N.I. 271) upholding a ruling of the Greater Belfast Coroner that the Commission had no power to intervene in and make submissions at the inquest into the deaths of victims of the bomb explosion that had occurred in Omagh in August 1998.

Held, allowing the appeal (Lord Hobhouse dissenting), that s.69 of the 1998 Act indicated that the Commission had been granted general powers to promote an understanding of human rights law and practice and to review its adequacy and effectiveness together with an incidental power to make, but not insist on making, submissions to courts and tribunals. It would be for the court or tribunal to decide whether the Commission should be allowed to intervene or act as amicus curiae. The Commission should show caution when deciding whether a case was sufficiently important to justify its intervention and whether there was a risk that one party would feel unfairly treated if it took a particular stance on a legal argument; those matters would ultimately be determined by the court or tribunal.

R. (ON THE APPLICATION OF NORTHERN IRELAND HUMAN RIGHTS COMMISSION) v. GREATER BELFAST CORONER; *sub nom.* NORTHERN IRELAND HUMAN RIGHTS COMMISSION'S APPLICATION FOR JUDICIAL REVIEW, RE; NORTHERN IRELAND HUMAN RIGHTS COMMISSION, *Re*, [2002] UKHL 25, [2002] N.I. 236, Lord Slynn of Hadley, HL (NI).

4827. Judgments and orders–magistrates courts

MAGISTRATES' COURTS (CIVIL JURISDICTION AND JUDGMENTS ACT 1982) (AMENDMENT) RULES (NORTHERN IRELAND) 2002, SR 2002 159; made under the Magistrates' Courts (Northern Ireland) Order 1981 (SI 1981 1675 (NI.26)) Art.13; and the Civil Jurisdiction and Judgments Act 1982 s.48. In force: May 20, 2002; £1.75.

These Rules amend the Magistrates' Courts (Civil Jurisdiction and Judgments Act 1982) Rules (Northern Ireland) 1986 (SR 1986 3929) in consequence of the coming into force of Council Regulation 44/2001 ([2001] OJ L12/1) on jurisdiction and the recognition and enforcement of judgments in civil and commercial matters.

4828. Judiciary—bias—indication that damages would not be awarded for whiplash injuries in absence of predisposition

M was one of a number of passengers injured in a bus when it collided with a car. The bus operator, U, admitted liability and claims were heard on the issue of quantum. The judge, R, heard several claims arising from the accident. At the end of those cases, R stated that on the evidence heard as to the minor impact caused by the collision he would not be inclined to award damages for whiplash type injuries allegedly suffered by bus passengers in the absence of a predisposition to such injury. M's claim came before R two weeks after that pronouncement. M's counsel asked R to discharge himself because of the indication he had given. R refused and M sought judicial review of that decision.

Held, allowing the application and quashing the decision, that the indication meant that later claimants, such as M, had not had the chance to be heard as to the impact needed to cause whiplash injury and gave rise to the danger of bias. Therefore R should have acceded to the application to discharge himself from hearing M's case, *Hauschildt v. Denmark (A/154)* (1990) 12 E.H.R.R. 266, *R. v. Gough (Robert)* [1993] A.C. 646, [1993] C.L.Y. 849 and *Locabail (UK) Ltd v. Bayfield Properties Ltd (Leave to Appeal)* [2000] Q.B. 451, [1999] C.L.Y. 38 considered.

McCAFFERY'S APPLICATION FOR JUDICIAL REVIEW, *Re* [2001] N.I. 378, Kerr, J., QBD (NI).

4829. Justice (Northern Ireland) Act 2002 (c.26)

This Act makes provision about the judiciary in Northern Ireland and amends section 6 of the Appellate Jurisdiction Act 1876; makes provision about the law officers and other legal officers and the courts in Northern Ireland; establishes a Public Prosecution Service for Northern Ireland, a Chief Inspector of Criminal Justice in Northern Ireland and a Northern Ireland Law Commission; amends the law of youth justice in Northern Ireland; makes provision for making available to victims of crime information about the release of offenders in Northern Ireland; makes provision about community safety in Northern Ireland; and amends the law of legal aid in Northern Ireland.

This Act received Royal Assent on July 24, 2002.

4830. Justice (Northern Ireland) Act 2002 (c.26)—Commencement No.1 Order

JUSTICE (NORTHERN IRELAND) ACT 2002 (COMMENCEMENT NO.1) ORDER 2002, SR 2002 319; made under the Justice (Northern Ireland) Act 2002, s.87. In force: bringing into operation various provisions of the 2002 Act on October 15, 2002; £1.75.

This Order brings into operation on October 15, 2002 the Justice (Northern Ireland) Act 2002 s.9(4)(5)(6)(14), s.17, s.18(1) to (9), s.19, s.21, s.46(6)(7), s.79, s.80, s.81, part of s.85(1), part of s.86, Sch.6, part of Sch.12 and part of Sch.13.

4831. Justice (Northern Ireland) Act 2002 (c.26)—Commencement No.2 Order

JUSTICE (NORTHERN IRELAND) ACT 2002 (COMMENCEMENT NO.2) ORDER 2002, SR 2002 405 (C.33); made under the Justice (Northern Ireland) Act 2002 s.87. In force: bringing into operation various provisions of the 2002 Act on January 6, 2003; £1.50.

This Commencement Order, which is the second to be made under the Justice (Northern Ireland) Act 2002, brings into operation section 66 of the 2002 Act on January 6, 2003.

4832. Magistrates courts–fees

MAGISTRATES' COURTS FEES (AMENDMENT) ORDER (NORTHERN IRELAND) 2002, SR 2002 343; made under the Judicature (Northern Ireland) Act 1978 s.116. In force: in accordance with Art.1; £2.00.

This Order amends the Magistrates' Courts Fees Order (Northern Ireland) 1996 (SR 1996 102) to increase a number of the fees payable in respect of proceedings in Magistrates' Courts; and allow fees to be taken by a range of payment methods, including credit or debit cards.

4833. Supreme Court–fees

SUPREME COURT FEES (AMENDMENT) ORDER (NORTHERN IRELAND) 2002, SR 2002 341; made under the Judicature (Northern Ireland) Act 1978 s.116. In force: in accordance with Art.1; £2.50.

This Order amends the Supreme Court Fees Order (Northern Ireland) 1996 (SR 1986 100) to increase a number of fees to be taken in proceedings in the Supreme Court; and allow fees to be taken by a range of payment methods, including credit or debit card.

4834. Supreme Court–rules

RULES OF THE SUPREME COURT (NORTHERN IRELAND) (AMENDMENT NO.2) 2002, SR 2002 202; made under the Judicature (Northern Ireland) Act 1978 s.55. In force: June 21, 2002; £2.00.

These Rules amend the Rules of the Supreme Court (Northern Ireland) 1980 (SR 1980 346) to make provision for existing procedures relating to the re-opening of extortionate agreements; to prevent default judgments being obtained in writ actions without the leave of the Court in circumstances where that would appear to be inconsistent with the scheme of protection for consumers under the Consumer Credit Act 1974; to prescribe procedures to facilitate debtors or sureties in bringing applications for time orders; to prescribe for the joinder of parties; and to simplify the procedure requiring notices of hearing to occupiers of mortgaged property so that a single notice must be addressed to the occupier(s) and only in dwelling house cases. The amendments also confer power on the court to direct an account and inquiry as to all mortgages and to make an order for delivery of possession conditional on the result of such an account and inquiry and make it possible for samples to be taken of bodily fluid and tissues, rather than simply blood, and for scientific tests to be used to determine whether a person is the mother of the person whose parentage falls to be determined, as well as whether a person is the father.

4835. Supreme Court–rules–terrorism

RULES OF THE SUPREME COURT (NORTHERN IRELAND) (AMENDMENT) 2002, SR 2002 15; made under the Judicature (Northern Ireland) Act 1978 s.55. In force: February 15, 2002; £2.00.

These Rules amend the Rules of the Supreme Court (Northern Ireland) 1980 (SR 1980 346) in consequence of the Terrorism Act 2000 and the Anti-terrorism, Crime and Security Act 2001. They substitute any reference to the Prevention of Terrorism (Temporary Provisions) Act 1989 with the appropriate reference under the Terrorism Act 2000, provide for the procedure to be followed in relation to applications for an order and take account of the extended circumstances in which a prosecutor may apply to the High Court for a restraint order, by providing that such an application may be made where a criminal investigation has been started in Northern Ireland with regard to a suspected offence

ADMINISTRATIVE LAW

4836. Criminal injuries compensation–discretionary powers–refusal on basis of victims' terrorist involvement–duty to give reasons

[Criminal Injuries (Compensation) (Northern Ireland) Order 1998 (SI 1988 73) Art.5(9), Art.10(2).]

M, L and A, were the widows of men killed as the result of either sectarian violence or feuds between republican groups. They sought judicial review of the Secretary of State's decision refusing to exercise his discretion under the Criminal Injuries (Compensation) (Northern Ireland) Order 1998 Art.10(2) to disapply the bar on compensation in Art.5(9) in the public interest. Factors taken into account for the purposes of applications under Art.10(2) included previous convictions for terrorist offences and the extent to which victims had been involved in illegal organisations. The decisions taken in all three cases were based on information supplied by the Contributions Agency which showed that the husbands of M, L and A had all been engaged in terrorist activities or been republican sympathisers.

Held, allowing the applications by L and A but refusing M's application, that M, L and A should have been informed of factors adverse to their applications under Art.10(2) unless they could reasonably have been expected to have been aware of such matters. L and A had not been made aware of evidence adverse to their claims and it was therefore unfair to deny them the opportunity to make representations on such matters. However there were no such adverse factors in M's case. Where a decision was reached on the basis of matters unknown to the applicant, this should be explained on enquiry in the absence of public interest requirements to the contrary.

McCALLION'S APPLICATION FOR JUDICIAL REVIEW, *Re* [2001] N.I. 401, Kerr, J., QBD (NI).

4837. Ombudsmen–salaries

SALARIES (ASSEMBLY OMBUDSMAN AND COMMISSIONER FOR COMPLAINTS) ORDER (NORTHERN IRELAND) 2002, SR 2002 320; made under the Ombudsman (Northern Ireland) Order 1996 (SI 1996 1298 (NI.8)) Art.5; and the Commissioner for Complaints (Northern Ireland) Order 1996 (SI 1996 1297 (NI.7)) Art.4. In force: November 21, 2002; £1.50.

This Order which provides for an increase in the annual salaries payable to the Assembly Ombudsman for Northern Ireland and the Northern Ireland Commissioner for Complaints with a retrospective effect from April 1, 2002, revokes the Salaries (Assembly Ombudsman and Commissioner for Complaints) Order (Northern Ireland) 2001 (SR 2001 302)

4838. Registration–fees–births, deaths and marriages

BIRTHS, DEATHS AND MARRIAGES (FEES) (NO.2) ORDER (NORTHERN IRELAND) 2002, SR 2002 242; made under the Registration of Births, Deaths and Marriages (Fees, etc.) Act (Northern Ireland) 1955 s.1. In force: August 1, 2002; £2.00.

This Order, which revokes the Births, Deaths and Marriages (Fees) Order (Northern Ireland) 1998 (SR 1998 330) and the Births, Deaths and Marriages (Fees) Order (Northern Ireland) 2002 (SR 2002 224), provides for the various fees payable under the Births, Deaths and Marriages enactments relating to licences and other preliminary proceedings for marriages; registration for marriage purposes of meeting houses and other places of worship; and registration of births, deaths and marriages. It makes provision for the person by whom and to whom fees are payable for services under the Marriage Act 1983 and exempts any person in receipt of income support from payment for those services.

AGRICULTURE

4839. Agricultural produce–agricultural processing and marketing–grants

AGRICULTURAL PROCESSING AND MARKETING GRANT REGULATIONS (NORTHERN IRELAND) 2002, SR 2002 30; made under the European Communities Act 1972 s.2. In force: March 14, 2002; £2.50.

These Regulations, which revoke the Agricultural Processing and Marketing Grant Regulations (Northern Ireland) 1996 (SR 1996 196), supplement in respect of Northern Ireland the Community legislation listed in the Schedule to the Regulations which provides for support to be paid from the Guidance Section of the European Agricultural Guidance and Guarantee Fund towards investment for the improvement of the processing and marketing of agricultural products. These Regulations operate within the scope of these provisions to enable Community support to be paid towards expenditure incurred in connection with operations involving such improvements. They implement a part of the Northern Ireland Programme for Building Sustainable Prosperity (BSP) as approved by the European Commission and provide for the payment of Community support by the Department of Agriculture and Rural Development in respect of any expenditure it has approved. The Regulations also provide for the making of claims for, and the payment of, grants following approval and also contain provisions creating obligations on those in receipt of grants concerning the provision of information and record keeping. In addition, the Regulations confer powers of entry on certain authorised persons, introduce a system of penalties to be imposed in the event of a breach of obligations by granting the Department various powers to take action, up to and including termination of approval in the event of breaches of the conditions of an approval and in a number of other cases, provide power to recover interest on sums recovered and that these be classified as a debt and create offences in respect of the furnishing of false information for the purpose of obtaining financial assistance and in respect of obstruction.

4840. Agricultural produce–marketing–grants

MARKETING OF QUALITY AGRICULTURAL PRODUCTS GRANT REGULATIONS (NORTHERN IRELAND) 2002, SR 2002 29; made under the European Communities Act 1972 s.2. In force: March 14, 2002; £2.50.

These Regulations supplement in respect of Northern Ireland the Community legislation listed in the Schedule to the Regulations which provides for support to be paid from the Guidance Section of the European Agricultural Guidance and Guarantee Fund towards investment relating to the marketing of quality agricultural products. The Regulations operate within the scope of these provisions by enabling Community support to be paid by the Department of Agriculture and Rural Development in respect of any expenditure it has approved. They also provide for the making of claims for, and the payment of, grants following approval and also contain provisions creating obligations on those in receipt of grants concerning the provision of information and record keeping. In addition, the Regulations confer powers of entry on certain authorised persons, introduce a system of penalties to be imposed in the event of a breach of obligations by granting the Department various powers to take action, up to and including termination of approval in the event of breaches of the conditions of an approval and in a number of other cases, provide power to recover interest on sums recovered and that these be classified as a debt and create offences in respect of the furnishing of false information for the purpose of obtaining financial assistance and in respect of obstruction.

4841. Animal products–beef–premiums

BEEF SPECIAL PREMIUM (AMENDMENT) REGULATIONS (NORTHERN IRELAND) 2002, SR 2002 335; made under the European Communities Act 1972 s.2. In force: January 1, 2003; £1.75.

These Regulations amend the Beef Special Premium Regulations (Northern Ireland) 2001 (SR 2001 363) which lay down implementing measures for the beef special premium scheme provided for in Council Regulation 1254/1999 ([1999] OJ L160/21) on the common organisation of the market in beef and veal. They also update references to Commission Regulation 2342/1999 ([1999] OJ L281/30) to take account of amendments effected since the date of making of the 2001 Regulations and provide for an increase in the number of applications an applicant is entitled to make from 10 to 18 applications for second premium during any one calendar year.

4842. Animal products–diseases and disorders–TSE

TRANSMISSIBLE SPONGIFORM ENCEPHALOPATHY REGULATIONS (NORTHERN IRELAND) 2002, SR 2002 225; made under the European Communities Act 1972 s.2. In force: July 18, 2002; £9.00.

These Regulations revoke the Fertilisers (Mammalian Meat and Bone Meal) Regulations (Northern Ireland) 1998 (SR 1998 187), the Fertilisers (Mammalian Meat and Bone Meal) (Conditions of Manufacture) Regulations (Northern Ireland) 1998 (SR 1998 188), the Diseases of Animals (Modification) Order (Northern Ireland) 1998 (SR 1998 365), the Sheep and Goats (Spongiform Encephalopathy) Order (Northern Ireland) 1998 (SR 1998 366), the Sheep and Goats (Spongiform Encephalopathy) Regulations (Northern Ireland) 1998 (SR 1998 367), the Diseases of Animals (Modification) (No.2) Order (Northern Ireland) 1998 (SR 1998 442), the Bovine Spongiform Encephalopathy Order (Northern Ireland) 1999 (SR 1999 322), the Bovine Spongiform Encephalopathy (Feedingstuffs and Surveillance) Regulations (Northern Ireland) 1999 (SR 1999 323), the Restriction on Pithing Regulations (Northern Ireland) 2001 (SR 2001 292). They also amend the Diseases of Animals (Northern Ireland) Order 1981 (SI 1981 1115), the Specified Risk Material Order (Northern Ireland) 1997 (SR 1997 551), the Specified Risk Material Regulations (Northern Ireland) 1997 (SR 1997 552), the Restriction on Pithing Regulations (Northern Ireland) 2001 (SR 2001 186) and the Processed Animal Protein Regulations (Northern Ireland) 2001 (SR 2001 405). The Regulations make provision for the administration and enforcement of Council Regulation 999/2001 ([2001] OJ L147/1) laying down rules for the prevention, control and eradication of certain transmissible spongiform encephalopathies; Commission Regulation 1248/2001 ([2001] OJ L173/12) amending Annexes III, X and XI to Regulation 999/2001 as regards epidemio-surveillance and testing of transmissible spongiform encephalopathies; Commission Regulation 1326/2001 ([2001] OJ L177/61) laying down transitional measures to permit the changeover to the European Parliament Council Regulation 999/2001 laying down rules for the prevention, control and eradication of certain transmissible spongiform encephalopathies, and amending Annexes VII and XI to that Regulation; Commission Regulation 270/2002 ([2002] OJ L45/4) amending Annex XI to Regulation 999/2001 of the European Parliament and of the Council as regards bovine vertebral column and amending Regulation 1326/2001 as regards animal feeding and the placing on the market of ovine and caprine animals and products thereof; and continuing the implementation of Council Decision 2000/766 ([2000] OJ L306/32) concerning certain protection measures with regard to transmissible spongiform encephalopathies and the feeding of animal protein, and Commission Decision 2001/9 ([2001] OJ L2/32) concerning control measures required for the implementation of Council Decision 2000/766 in accordance with Commission Regulation 1326/2001 Art.1 (2).

4843. Animal products–feedingstuffs–import controls–China

FOOD AND ANIMAL FEEDINGSTUFFS (PRODUCTS OF ANIMAL ORIGIN FROM CHINA) (EMERGENCY CONTROL) REGULATIONS (NORTHERN IRELAND) 2002 2002, SR 2002 226; made under the European Communities Act 1972 s.2. In force: June 28, 2002; £2.00.

These Regulations, which revoke the Animal Feedingstuffs (Products of Animal Origin from China) (Control) Regulations (Northern Ireland) 2002 (SR 2002 183) and amend the Food Safety (Northern Ireland) Order 1991 (SI 1991 762 (NI.7)), implement Commission Decision 2002/69 ([2002] OJ L30/50) concerning certain protective measures with regard to the products of animal origin imported from China. The Regulations define "relevant product of animal origin", prohibit their importation, specify the enforcement authorities and apply with modifications certain provisions of the 1991 Order.

4844. Animal products–identification–sterilisation and staining–carcases

ANIMAL BY-PRODUCTS (IDENTIFICATION) (AMENDMENT) REGULATIONS (NORTHERN IRELAND) 2002, SR 2002 238; made under the Food Safety (Northern Ireland) Order 1991 (SI 1991 762 (NI.7)) Art.15, Art.25, Art.47, Sch.1 para.3. In force: August 19, 2002; £2.50.

These Regulations, which amend the Animal By-Products (Identification) Regulations (Northern Ireland) 1999 (SR 1999 418), define "animal by-product premises" and "game processing facility" to exclude cold stores and cutting premises and "occupier" to include the occupier of a cold store or cutting premises. The Regulations make amendments by changing specified definitions and provide that the only whole carcases which have to be sterilised or stained are whole poultry carcases which are dead on arrival at a slaughterhouse or which are rejected following pre-slaughter or post-mortem health inspections carried out at such premises. The Regulations also make amendments to specified exemption provisions and impose requirements with respect to the storage of unsterilised animal by-products in the same room as products intended for human consumption and in cold stores, cutting premises, game processing facilities and slaughterhouses.

4845. Animal products–waste disposal–animal feed

ANIMAL BY-PRODUCTS ORDER (NORTHERN IRELAND) 2002, SR 2002 209; made under the Diseases of Animals (Northern Ireland) Order 1981 (SI 1981 1115 (NI.22)) Art.2, Art.5, Art.19, Art.29, Art.44, Art.46, Art.60. In force: July 8, 2002; £6.00.

This Order revokes the Diseases of Animals (Animal Protein) (No.2) Order (Northern Ireland) 1989 (SR 1989 347), the Diseases of Animals (Animal Protein) (No.2) (Amendment) Order (Northern Ireland) 1992 (SR 1992 62), the Diseases of Animals (Animal Protein) (No.2) (Amendment) Order (Northern Ireland) 1993 (SR 1993 193) and the Catering Waste (Feeding to Livestock) Order (Northern Ireland) 2001 (SR 2001 286). It implements Council Directive 90/667 ([1990] OJ L363/51) laying down the veterinary rules for the disposal and processing of animal waste, for its placing on the market and for the prevention of pathogens in feedingstuffs of animal or fish origin and amending Directive 90/425; Commission Decision 92/562 ([1992] OJ L359/23) on the approval of alternative heat treatment systems for processing high-risk material; Commission Decision 94/382 ([1994] OJ L172/25) on the approval of alternative heat treatment systems for processing animal waste of ruminant origin, with a view to the inactivation of spongiform encephalopathy agents; Commission Decision 95/29 ([1995] OJ L38/17) amending Decision 94/382 on the approval of alternative heat treatment systems for processing animal waste of ruminant origin, with a view to the inactivation of spongiform encephalopathy agents; and Commission Decision 96/449 ([1996] OJ L184/43) on the approval of alternative heat treatment systems for processing animal waste with a view to the inactivation of spongiform encephalopathy agents. It also implements Council Decision 95/348 ([1995] OJ L202/8) laying down the veterinary and animal health rules applicable in the UK and Ireland to the treatment of certain types of waste intended to be marketed locally as feedstuffs for certain animal categories. It prohibits the feeding to livestock of certain categories of catering waste, whether processed or unprocessed. In addition, it removes the possibility of non-mammalian animal by-products being rendered for the production of swill for feeding to pigs or poultry.

4846. Animal products—waste disposal—animal feed—revocation

ANIMAL BY-PRODUCTS (REVOCATION) REGULATIONS (NORTHERN IRELAND) 2002, SR 2002 210; made under the European Communities Act 1972 s.2. In force: July 8, 2002; £1.50.

These Regulations, which revoke the Animal By-Products Regulations (Northern Ireland) 1993 (SR 1993 192) and the Animal By-Products (Amendment) Regulations (Northern Ireland) 1998 (SR 1998 108), re-enact with amendments in the Animal By-Products Order (Northern Ireland) 2002 (SR 2002 209).

4847. Animals—feedingstuffs

FEEDING STUFFS (AMENDMENT) REGULATIONS (NORTHERN IRELAND) 2002, SR 2002 263; made under the Agriculture Act 1970 s.66, s.68, s.69, s.74A, s.75, s.76, s.77, s.78, s.79, s.84; and the European Communities Act 1972 s.2. In force: September 16, 2002; £2.00.

These Regulations amend the Feeding Stuffs (Sampling and Analysis) Regulations (Northern Ireland) 1999 (SR 1999 296), the Feeding Stuffs (Establishments and Intermediaries) Regulations 1999 (SI 1999 1872), the Feeding Stuffs (Enforcement) Regulations 1999 (SI 1999 2325) and the Feeding Stuffs Regulations (Northern Ireland) 2001 (SR 2001 47). They implement Commission Directive 2001/79 ([2001] OJ L267/1) amending Council Directive 87/153 fixing guidelines for the assessment of additives in animal nutrition; Council Directive 2001/102 ([2001] OJ L6/45) amending Directive 1999/29 on the undesirable substances and products in animal nutrition; and Commission Directive 2002/1 ([2002] OJ L5/9) amending Directive 94/38 as regards animal feedingstuffs for the support of liver function in case of chronic liver insufficiency. In addition, these Regulations also provide for the enforcement of Commission Regulation 2013/2001 ([2001] OJ L272/24) concerning the provisional authorisation of a new additive use and the permanent authorisation of an additive in feedingstuffs; Commission Regulation 2200/2001 ([2001] OJ L299/1) concerning provisional authorisation of additives in feedingstuffs; and Commission Regulation 256/2002 ([2002] OJ L41/6) concerning the provisional authorisation of an additive and the permanent authorisation of an additive in feedingstuffs. The Regulations modify the provisions in the 2001 Regulations which specify the procedure to be followed in relation to the assessment of feed additives for which marketing authorisation has been sought and as regards applications for such authorisation; modify the provisions in the 2001 Regulations provide for the enforcement of the provisions of those Regulations which are made under the European Communities Act 1972; modify the controls of the 2001 Regulations regulating the presence of undesirable substances in animal feed by specifying new maximum levels for dioxin in feed; and modify the provisions of the 2001 Regulations regulating dietetic feeds as regards the required nutritional characteristics and labelling of feeds intended for the support of liver function in case of chronic liver insufficiency in dogs or cats.

4848. Animals—feedingstuffs—zootechnical products

FEEDINGSTUFFS (ZOOTECHNICAL PRODUCTS) (AMENDMENT) REGULATIONS (NORTHERN IRELAND) 2002, SR 2002 162; made under the European Communities Act 1972 s.2. In force: April 25, 2002; £1.75.

These Regulations amend the Feedingstuffs (Zootechnical Products) Regulations 1999 (SI 1999 1871). The 1999 Regulations as amended continue to implement, in relation to zootechnical additives and products with those additives in them, a number of Community instruments including in particular Council Directive 95/69 ([1995] OJ L332/15) laying down the conditions and arrangements for approving and registering certain establishments and intermediaries operating in the animal feed sector. They provide for new fees for approval of, and official checks carried out at, premises manufacturing zootechnical additives, premixtures and/or feedingstuffs incorporating zootechnical additives or premixtures and set out the fees payable for Northern Ireland carrying out certain specified functions in connection with the application for the European Community authorisation of zootechnical feed additives.

4849. Animals–feedingstuffs–zootechnical products

MEDICATED FEEDINGSTUFFS (AMENDMENT) REGULATIONS (NORTHERN IRELAND) 2002, SR 2002 161; made under the European Communities Act 1972 s.2. In force: April 25, 2002; £1.75.

These Regulations amend the Medicated Feedingstuffs Regulations 1998 (SI 1998 1046) which continue to implement Council Directive 90/167 ([1990] OJ L92/42) laying down the conditions governing the preparation, placing on the market and use of medicated feedingstuffs in the Community. They provide for new fees for application for approval or renewal of premises manufacturing authorised intermediate products, premises which manufacture medicated feedingstuffs incorporating medicated pre-mixes and distributors of medicated feedingstuffs.

4850. Infectious disease control–foot and mouth disease–controlled areas

FOOT-AND-MOUTH DISEASE (CONTROLLED AREA) ORDER (NORTHERN IRELAND) 2002, SR 2002 44; made under the Foot-and-Mouth Disease Order (Northern Ireland) 1962 (SR & O (NI) 1962 209 Art.29; and the Diseases of Animals (Northern Ireland) Order 1981 (SI 1981 1115 (NI.22)) Art.5, Art.10, Art.12, Art.14, Art.19, Art.20, Art.60. In force: February 15, 2002; £1.75.

This Order repeals and replaces the Foot-and-Mouth Disease (Controlled Area) (No.6) Order (Northern Ireland) 2001 (SR 2001 424) which imposed the restrictions contained in the Foot-and-Mouth Disease Order (Northern Ireland) 1962 (SR & O 1962 209) Part III. It varies the controls set out in the fifth Schedule to the 1962 Order and removes the prohibition on the hunting of animals with horses and/or dogs and the prohibition on the movement of horses except under the authority of a licence.

4851. Pesticides–residue levels in crops, food and feeding stuffs

PESTICIDES (MAXIMUM RESIDUE LEVELS IN CROPS, FOOD AND FEEDING STUFFS) REGULATIONS (NORTHERN IRELAND) 2002, SR 2002 20; made under the European Communities Act 1972 s.2; and the Food and Environment Protection Act 1985 s.16. In force: March 4, 2002; £15.00.

These Regulations revoke the Pesticides (Maximum Residue Levels in Crops, Food and Feeding Stuffs) (National Limits) Regulations (Northern Ireland) 1995 (SR 1995 32), the Pesticides (Maximum Residue Levels in Crops, Food and Feeding Stuffs) (EEC Limits) Regulations (Northern Ireland) 1995 (SR 1995 33), the Pesticides (Maximum Residue Levels in Crops, Food and Feeding Stuffs) (EEC Limits) (Amendment) Regulations (Northern Ireland) 1995 (SR 1995 460), the Pesticides (Maximum Residue Levels in Crops, Food and Feeding Stuffs) (EEC Limits) (Amendment) Regulations (Northern Ireland) 1995 (SR 1995 461), the Pesticides (Maximum Residue Levels in Crops, Food and Feeding Stuffs) (National Limits) (Amendment) Regulations (Northern Ireland) 1996 (SR 1996 526), the Pesticides (Maximum Residue Levels in Crops, Food and Feeding Stuffs) (EEC Limits) (Amendment) Regulations (Northern Ireland) 1996 (SR 1996 527), the Pesticides (Maximum Residue Levels in Crops, Food and Feeding Stuffs) (National Limits) (Amendment) Regulations (Northern Ireland) 1997 (SR 1997 243), the Pesticides (Maximum

Residue Levels in Crops, Food and Feeding Stuffs) (National Limits) (Amendment) Regulations (Northern Ireland) 1997 (SR 1997 244), the Pesticides (Maximum Residue Levels in Crops, Food and Feeding Stuffs) (EEC Limits) (Amendment) Regulations (Northern Ireland) 1 (SR 1 320) and the Pesticides (Maximum Residue Levels in Crops, Food and Feeding Stuffs) (EEC Limits) (Amendment No.2) Regulations (Northern Ireland) 1 (SR 1 321). The Regulations specify maximum levels of pesticide residues which crops, food and feedingstuffs may contain in implementation of Council Directive 86/362 ([1986] OJL221/37) and Council Directive 86/363 ([1986] OJL22/43) as regards cereals and products of animal origin, and Council Directive 90/642 ([1990] OJL350/71) as regards products of plant origin. In particular, these Regulations specify for the first time maximum residue levels for the pesticide Azoxystrobin in implementation of Commission Directive 1/71.

4852. Pesticides–residue levels in crops, food and feeding stuffs

PESTICIDES (MAXIMUM RESIDUE LEVELS IN CROPS, FOOD AND FEEDING STUFFS) (AMENDMENT) REGULATIONS (NORTHERN IRELAND) 2002, SR 2002 27; made under the European Communities Act 1972 s.2; and the Food and Environment Protection Act 1985 s.16. In force: March 11, 2002; £4.00.

These Regulations, which amend the Pesticides (Maximum Residue Levels in Crops, Food and Feeding Stuffs) Regulations (Northern Ireland) 2002 (SR 2002 20), specify maximum levels which crops, food and feeding stuffs may contain in implementation of Commission Directive 2000/81 ([2000] OJ L326/56), Commission Directive 2000/82 ([2001] OJ L3/18), Commission Directive 2001/39 ([2001] OJ L148/70), Commission Directive 2001/48 ([2001] OJ L180/26) and Commission Directive 2001/57 ([2001] OJ L208/36). The maximum level for iprodione on spring onions is amended to reflect Commission Directive 1998/82 ([1982] OJ L290/25) and the maximum level for methamidophos on cottonseed is corrected to that set out in Commission Directive 1993/58 ([1993] OJ L211/6).

4853. Pesticides–residue levels in crops, food and feedingstuffs

PESTICIDES (MAXIMUM RESIDUE LEVELS IN CROPS, FOOD AND FEEDING STUFFS) (AMENDMENT) (NO.2) REGULATIONS (NORTHERN IRELAND) 2002, SR 2002 250; made under the European Communities Act 1972 s.2; and the Food and Environment Protection Act 1985 s.16. In force: September 1, 2002; £2.00.

These Regulations, which amend the Pesticides (Maximum Residue Levels in Crops, Food and Feeding Stuffs) Regulations (Northern Ireland) 2002 (SR 2002 20), specify maximum levels of pesticides which crops, food and feeding stuffs may contain in implementation of Commission Directive 2002/5 ([2002] OJ L34/7) amending Annex II to Council Directive 90/642 as regards the fixing of maximum levels for pesticide residues in and on certain products of plant origin, including fruit and vegetables, and Commission Directive 2002/23 ([2002] OJ L64/13) amending the Annexes to Council Directives 86/36, 86/363 and 90/642 as regards the fixing of maximum levels for pesticide residues in and on cereals, foodstuffs of animal origin and certain products of plant origin, including fruit and vegetables respectively.

4854. Plant varieties–seeds–fees

SEEDS (FEES) REGULATIONS (NORTHERN IRELAND) 2002, SR 2002 257; made under the Seeds Act (Northern Ireland) 1965 s.1, s.2. In force: September 2, 2002; £3.00.

These Regulations, which revoke the Seeds (Fees) Regulations (Northern Ireland) 1999 (SR 1999 379), prescribe fees for certain initial applications, crop inspection fees, seed lot fees, seed testing fees and fees in relation to licensed seed testing establishments.

4855. Plant varieties–seeds–fees

SEEDS (FEES) (NO.2) REGULATIONS (NORTHERN IRELAND) 2002, SR 2002 407; made under the Seeds Act (Northern Ireland) 1965 s.1, s.2. In force: January 29, 2003; £2.50.

These Regulations, which revoke the Seeds (Fees) Regulations (Northern Ireland) 2002 (SR 2002 257), prescribe fees for certain initial applications, crop inspection fees, seed lot fees, seed testing fees and fees in relation to licensed seed testing establishments. Fees are also prescribed in relation to the making of written representations by, and hearings involving, seed merchants, processors or packers. They also provide that the same fees shall be payable in relation to breeders' confirmations as are payable in relation to official certificates.

4856. Plants–plant health–Phytophthora ramorum

PLANT HEALTH (PHYTOPHTHORA RAMORUM) ORDER (NORTHERN IRELAND) 2002, SR 2002 269; made under the Plant Health Act (Northern Ireland) 1967 s.2, s.3, s.4. In force: September 9, 2002; £2.00.

This Order implements measures to prevent the introduction and spread of the pest Phytophthora ramorum, a fungus not established in the UK, regulates the importation and movement into and within Northern Ireland of plant material identified as susceptible to the pest, believed to cause Sudden Oak Death syndrome in certain species of oak in the USA, and harm to Rhododendron, Viburnum and other plants.

4857. Plants–plant health–protected zones

PLANT HEALTH (AMENDMENT) ORDER (NORTHERN IRELAND) 2002, SR 2002 273; made under the Plant Health Act (Northern Ireland) 1967 s.2, s.3, s.3A, s.3B, s.4. In force: September 23, 2002; £1.75.

This Order amends the Plant Health Order (Northern Ireland) 1993 (SR 1993 256) so as to implement certain elements of Commission Directive 2002/28 ([2002] OJ L77/23) amending certain annexes to Council Directive 2000/29 on protective measures against the introduction into the Community of organisms harmful to plants or plant products and against their spread within the Community; and Commission Directive 2002/29 ([2002] OJ L77/26) amending Directive 2001/32 as regards certain protected zones exposed to particular plant health risks in the Community. The Order removes Great Britain from the protected zone in respect of Beet necrotic yellow vein virus and redefines the Italian and Austrian protected zones in respect of the bacterium Erwinia amylovora (Burr) Winsl et al.

4858. Plants–plant health–protected zones

PLANT HEALTH (WOOD AND BARK) (AMENDMENT) ORDER (NORTHERN IRELAND) 2002, SR 2002 285; made under the Plant Health Act (Northern Ireland) 1967 s.2, s.3, s.3A, s.3B, s.4. In force: September 23, 2002; £1.75.

This Order, which revokes the Plant Health (Wood and Bark) Order (Northern Ireland) 1993 (SR 1993 460), implements certain elements of Commission Directive 2002/28 ([2002] OJ L77/23) amending certain annexes to Council Directive 2000/29 on protective measures against the introduction into the Community of organisms harmful to plants or plant products and against their spread within the Community and Commission Directive 2002/29 ([2002] OJ L77/26) amending Directive 2001/32 as regards certain protected zones exposed to particular plant health risks in the Community. The Order makes amendments to remove the protected zone in respect of the pest Pissodes spp. which is present in Great Britain and which has now spread to Northern Ireland and Ireland, and modify the protected zone within England in respect of the pest Dendroctonus micans.

4859. **Plants–plant protection products–marketing**

PLANT PROTECTION PRODUCTS (AMENDMENT) REGULATIONS (NORTHERN IRELAND) 2002, SR 2002 21; made under the European Communities Act 1972 s.2. In force: March 4, 2002; £2.00.

These Regulations amend the Plant Protection Products Regulations (Northern Ireland) 1995 (SR 1995 371) which implements Council Directive 91/414 ([1991] OJ L230/1) concerning the placing of plant protection products on the market and revoke the Plant Protection Products (Amendment) Regulations (Northern Ireland) 2001 (SR 2001 280). The Regulations amend the definition of the Directive provided in the 1995 Regulations in consequence of Commission Directive 2000/80 ([2000] OJ L309/14), Commission Directive 2001/21 ([2001] OJ L69/17), Commission Directive 2001/28 ([2001] OJ L113/5), Commission Directive 2001/47 ([2001] OJ L175/21, Commission Directive 2001/49 ([2001] OJ L176/61) which add fenhexamid, amitrole, diquat, pyridate, thiabendazole, Paecilomyces fumosoroseus and flupyrsulfuron-methyl to Annex I to the Directive and Commission Directive 2001/36 ([2001] OJ L164/1) which substantially amends the Annex II dossier requirements for inclusion of an active substance in Annex I, and Annex III dossier requirements for approval of plant protection products.

4860. **Plants–plant protection products–marketing**

PLANT PROTECTION PRODUCTS (AMENDMENT) (NO.2) REGULATIONS (NORTHERN IRELAND) 2002, SR 2002 125; made under the European Communities Act 1972 s.2. In force: April 15, 2002; £1.75.

These Regulations, which revoke the Plant Protection Products (Amendment) Regulations (Northern Ireland) 2002 (SR 2002 21), amend the Plant Protection Products Regulations (Northern Ireland) 1995 (SR 1995 371) which implement Council Directive 91/414 ([1991] OJ L230/1) concerning the placing of plant protection products on the market. The Regulations amend the definition of the Directive provided in the principal Regulations in consequence of Commission Directive 2001/87 ([2001] OJ L276/17) which adds acibenzolar-s-methyl, cyclanilide, ferric phosphate, pymetrozine and pyraflufen-ethyl to Annex I of the Directive.

4861. **Plants–plant protection products–marketing**

PLANT PROTECTION PRODUCTS (AMENDMENT) (NO.3) REGULATIONS (NORTHERN IRELAND) 2002, SR 2002 289; made under the European Communities Act 1972 s.2. In force: October 22, 2002; £1.75.

These Regulations, which revoke the Plant Protection Products (Amendment) (No.2) Regulations (Northern Ireland) 2002 (SR 2002 125), amend the Plant Protection Products Regulations (Northern Ireland) 1995 (SR 1995 371) which implement in Northern Ireland Council Directive 91/414 ([1991] OJ L230/1) concerning the placing of plant protection products on the market. The Regulations amend the definition of the 1991 Directive so as to implement Commission Directive 2001/99 ([2001] OJ L304/14) amending Annex I to Council Directive 91/414 concerning the placing of plant protection products on the market to include glyphosate and thifensulfuron-methyl as active substances. It also makes amendments to add Commission Directive 2001/103 ([2001] OJ L313/37) amending Annex 1 to Council Directive 91/414 concerning the placing of plant protection products on the market to include 2,4-dichlorophenoxy acetic acid (2,4-D) as an active substance and Commission Directive 2002/18 ([2002] OJ L55/29) amending Annex 1 to Council Directive 91/414 concerning the placing of plant-protection products on the market to include isoproturon as an active substance.

4862. Potatoes–import controls–notice–Germany

POTATOES ORIGINATING IN GERMANY (NOTIFICATION) ORDER (NORTHERN IRELAND) 2002, SR 2002 7; made under the Plant Health (Northern Ireland) Act 1967 s.2, s.3, s.3B, s.4. In force: February 11, 2002; £1.75.

This Order places certain notification requirements upon persons importing potatoes from Germany which have been grown after 2000. It requires importers bringing such potatoes into Northern Ireland on or after February 11, 2002 to give at least two days' notice in writing to an inspector of the Department of Agriculture and Rural Development, providing specified details as to the landing and intended use of potatoes. In addition, it also requires importers of German potatoes which arrived in Northern Ireland between January 14, 2002 and the coming into operation of the Order to provide specified information of a similar nature no later than February 28, 2002. The Order provides that an inspector who has reasonable grounds for suspecting a contravention of its provisions may exercise in respect of German potatoes certain enforcement powers conferred by the Plant Health Order (Northern Ireland) 1993 (SR 1993 256).

4863. Potatoes–imports–infectious disease control–Egypt

POTATOES ORIGINATING IN EGYPT (AMENDMENT) REGULATIONS (NORTHERN IRELAND) 2002, SR 2002 246; made under the European Communities Act 1972 s.2. In force: August 12, 2002; £2.50.

These Regulations, which amend the Potatoes Originating in Egypt Regulations (Northern Ireland) 1998 (SI 1998 107), implement Commission Decision 2001/664 ([2001] OJ L233/49) amending Commission Decision 96/301 ([1996] OJ L115/47) authorising Member States temporarily to take emergency measures against the dissemination of Pseudomonas solanacearum (Smith) Smith as regards Egypt. They do so by adding to the list of instruments amending the Decision contained in the 1998 Regulations. Pseudomonas solanacearum Smith (Smith) is now referred to as Ralstonia solanacearum Smith (Yabuuchi) et al albeit that the reference to it in the Decision has not been amended. Decision 2001/664 renews the framework within which potatoes may be imported from Egypt into the territory of the European Community during the 2001/2002 season. In addition, these Regulations clarify the basis on which powers of inspectors under the Plant Health Order (Northern Ireland) 1993 (SR 1993 256) may be used and increase the fee payable by importers from whose potatoes samples are taken for testing for the presence of Ralstonia solanacearum Smith (Yabuuchi) et al.

4864. Potatoes–seed potatoes–certification of crops–fees

SEED POTATOES (CROP FEES) REGULATIONS (NORTHERN IRELAND) 2002, SR 2002 169; made under the Seeds Act (Northern Ireland) Act 1965 s.1. In force: May 30, 2002; £1.75.

These Regulations prescribe the fees payable to the Department of Agriculture and Rural Development in respect of the certification of seed potato crops arising under the Seed Potatoes Regulations (Northern Ireland) 2001 (SR 2001 188).

4865. Reorganisation–Milk Marketing Board

MILK MARKETING BOARD (RESIDUARY FUNCTIONS) (AMENDMENT) REGULATIONS (NORTHERN IRELAND) 2002, SR 2002 151; made under the Agriculture (Northern Ireland) Order 1993 (SI 1993 2665 (NI.10)) Art.17, Art.30. In force: May 15, 2002; £1.75.

These Regulations amend the Milk Marketing Board (Residuary Functions) Regulations (Northern Ireland) 1995 (SR 1995 25) so as to facilitate the winding up of the affairs of the residuary Milk Marketing Board. The Regulations allow the Board to proceed to a winding-up where sums it has distributed in accordance with its obligations remain unclaimed and where certain other liabilities remain outstanding and certain assets remain unrecovered, dissolve the Board and transfer any remaining property, rights or liabilities of the Board to the Department of Agriculture and Rural Development.

4866. Rural areas–less favoured areas–compensatory allowances

LESS FAVOURED AREA COMPENSATORY ALLOWANCES REGULATIONS (NORTHERN IRELAND) 2002, SR 2002 72; made under the European Communities Act 1972 s.2. In force: March 6, 2002; £2.50.

These Regulations, which amend the Farm Subsidies (Review of Decisions) Regulations (Northern Ireland) 2001 (SR 2001 391), implement Commission Regulation 1750/1999 ([1999] OJ L214/31) laying down detailed rules for the application of Council Regulation 1257/1999 ([1999] OJ L160/80) on support for rural development from the European Agricultural Guidance and Guarantee Fund. In addition, they implement Measure 2 of the Northern Ireland Rural Development Programme. They implement Articles which deal with support for less favoured areas by defining the conditions of eligibility for less favoured area compensatory allowance and the rates at which it is to be paid. They provide for the exclusion of forage area in respect of claimants who held milk quota at March 31, 2001, confer powers of entry and inspection on persons authorised by the Department of Agriculture and Rural Development, provide for the recovery of interest on sums recovered and create offences of making false or misleading statements and of obstructing persons authorised by the Department.

4867. Sheep–premiums

SHEEP ANNUAL PREMIUM (AMENDMENT) REGULATIONS (NORTHERN IRELAND) 2002, SR 2002 368; made under the European Communities Act 1972 s.2. In force: December 3, 2002; £1.75.

These Regulations amend the Sheep Annual Premium Regulations (Northern Ireland) 1992 (SR 1992 476) to provide for the period in which to apply for sheep annual premium in respect of any marketing year.

ANIMALS

4868. Animal welfare–farmed animals–laying hens

WELFARE OF FARMED ANIMALS (AMENDMENT) REGULATIONS (NORTHERN IRELAND) 2002, SR 2002 259; made under the Welfare of Animals Act (Northern Ireland) 1972 s.2; and the European Communities Act 1972 s.2. In force: in accordance with Reg.1 (2) (3) (4); £2.00.

These Regulations amend the Veterinary Surgery (Exemptions) Order 1962 (SI 1962 2557) and the Welfare of Farmed Animals Regulations (Northern Ireland) 2000 (SR 2000 270) to give effect to the provisions of Council Directive 99/74 ([1999] OJ L203/53) laying down minimum standards for the protection of laying hens, in establishments with 350 or more laying hens.

4869. Animal welfare–slaughter

WELFARE OF ANIMALS (SLAUGHTER OR KILLING) (AMENDMENT) REGULATIONS (NORTHERN IRELAND) 2002, SR 2002 304; made under the European Communities Act 1972 s.2. In force: November 8, 2002; £1.75.

These Regulations amend the Welfare of Animals (Slaughter or Killing) Regulations (Northern Ireland) 1996 (SI 1996 558) so as to permit a new gas mixture for killing birds at a slaughterhouse.

4870. Fur Farming (Prohibition) (Northern Ireland) Order 2002 (SI 2002 3151 (NI.5))

This Order prohibits the keeping of animals solely or primarily for slaughter for the value of their fur and provides for the making of payments in respect of the related closure of certain businesses.

4871. Game Preservation (Amendment) Act (Northern Ireland) 2002 (2)

This Act amends the Game Preservation Act (Northern Ireland) 1928 and amends the law relating to the killing, taking or destroying of rabbits and hares.

This Act received Royal Assent on February 13, 2002.

4872. Game Preservation (Amendment) Act (Northern Ireland) 2002 (c.2)– Commencement Order

GAME PRESERVATION (AMENDMENT) (2002 ACT) (COMMENCEMENT) ORDER (NORTHERN IRELAND) 2002, SR 2002 130; made under the Game Preservation (Amendment) Act (Northern Ireland) 2002 s.4. In force: bringing into operation various provisions of 2002 Act on April 1, 2002; £1.50.

This Order provides for the coming into force of the Game Preservation (Amendment) Act (Northern Ireland) 2002 s.1 and s.2 from April 1, 2002.

AVIATION

4873. Airports–designation–Belfast International Airport and Belfast City Airport

AIRPORTS BYELAWS (DESIGNATION) ORDER (NORTHERN IRELAND) 2002, SR 2002 396; made under the Airports (Northern Ireland) Order 1994 (SI 1994 426 (NI.1)) Art.18. In force: February 3, 2003; £1.50.

Under the Airports (Northern Ireland) Order 1994 Art.18(2) the operator of an airport to which the Article applies may make byelaws for regulating the use and operation of the airport and the conduct of persons while within the airport. Art.18(1) of that Order provides that any airport other than an airport managed by a district council must be designated for the purposes of Art.18. This Order designates Belfast International Airport and Belfast City Airport for the purposes of Art.18.

BANKING AND FINANCE

4874. Deeds–variation–borrower granting bank power of sale over shares–effect of unilateral variation by lender

L had used an overdraft facility granted by N to purchase 53,000 shares in an Israeli technology company. L provided security for the overdraft by depositing shares subject to a memorandum that entitled N to sell those shares at any time. The shares pledged as security became worthless and L transferred the 53,000 shares along with another 30,000 shares to N. L stated that he would clear his debt to N by March 31, 1999 and contended that N had agreed not to sell the shares until that date. L signed blank share transfer forms so that N could sell the shares. In November 1998, N requested immediate repayment from L and sold the shares at a considerable loss. Subsequently, N found that the wrong transfer form had been used but L refused to sign the correct form. N was forced to purchase 83,000 shares at a higher price to meet its contractual obligations and N sought the full amount outstanding to it from L and the loss it had made on the share purchase. L argued that N had no authority to sell the shares. He further contended that N's actions in unilaterally altering the memorandum meant that it only had an equitable mortgage of the shares so that a court order was needed before they could lawfully be sold.

Held, giving judgment for N, that L had agreed to give N a mortgage over the 53,000 shares purchased with the overdraft and to lodge to 30,000 shares with N as security. Further, L had also agreed to the memorandum and had signed the incorrect transfer form. By doing so he had done all that was necessary to allow N to exercise its power of sale. As the memorandum required L to sign all documents necessary to effect the transfer, he had granted an equitable mortgage of the 53,000 shares and was therefore bound to enable the sale to be completed. N's unilateral alteration of the memorandum had not prejudiced L's rights, *Pigot's Case* [1558-1774] All E.R. Rep. 50 and *Raiffeisen Zentralbank Osterreich AG v. Crossseas Shipping Ltd* [2000] 1 W.L.R. 1135, [2000] C.L.Y. 278 considered.

NORTHERN BANK LTD v. LAVERTY [2001] N.I. 315, Girvan, J., Ch D (NI).

CIVIL EVIDENCE

4875. **Admissibility – video evidence – interviews with children in care proceedings – admissibility as hearsay evidence – right to fair trial**

[Children (Admissibility of Hearsay Evidence) Order (Northern Ireland) 1996 (SR 1996 301) Art.50; Civil Evidence (Northern Ireland) Order 1997 (SI 1997 2983) Art.3(3)(a); Human Rights Act 1998 Sch.1 Part I Art.6.]

In an application for a care order under the Children (Admissibility of Hearsay Evidence) Order (Northern Ireland) 1996 Art.50, T, a health and social services trust, tendered video evidence of interviews with the children in which they made allegations of ill treatment. This was the only substantial evidence of ill treatment. Their mother, M, contested the application. The judge ruled that the videotapes were admissible as hearsay evidence, thereby obviating the right to cross examination by M's counsel. M appealed, contending that video taped interviews should not be treated as hearsay. Further, that admitting such evidence would breach her right to a fair trial under the Human Rights Act 1998 Sch.1 Part I Art.6.

Held, dismissing the appeal, that the taped interviews were hearsay as they amounted to oral evidence in the proceedings that had been given as evidence of matters alleged to have occurred, as provided for in the Civil Evidence (Northern Ireland) Order 1997 Art.3(3)(a), *R. v. Sharp (Colin)* [1988] 1 W.L.R. 7, [1988] C.L.Y. 547 and *R. v. Kearley (Alan Robert)* [1992] 2 A.C. 228, [1992] C.L.Y. 852 applied. The judge could accord such weight to the recorded interviews as he though proper, taking into account the demeanour of each child and any hints of coaching or hesitation. Although Art.6 gave an absolute right to a fair trial, this did not automatically apply to constituent parts of the trial process and limited qualification was permitted where necessary in the public interest. M was not on trial in the instant case and she could use expert evidence to comment on the children's evidence or argue that the weight to be accorded to it should be reduced.

APPEAL (NO. 2000/11) (CHILDREN: VIDEO EVIDENCE), Re [2001] N.I. 358, Carswell, L.C.J., CA (NI).

CIVIL PROCEDURE

4876. **Limitations – professional negligence – surveyors – date of accrual of cause of action**

[Limitation (Northern Ireland) Order 1989 (SI 1989 1339) Art.11.]

M appealed against a decision on a trial of preliminary issues which determined that a claim against R, a firm of surveyors, was statute barred by virtue of the Limitation (Northern Ireland) Order 1989 Art.11. In April 1989, M purchased a house and garage relying on a report and valuation by R. In June 1989, M discovered defects in the garage and instructed T, a firm of solicitors, who found that improvements had been carried out to the garage in 1984 without Buildings Regulations consent. T advised M that, subject to proving negligence, he could recover the diminution in value from R. That claim was settled in November 1990 for £700. In 1997, while attempting to sell the property, M discovered that works had also been carried out to the house in breach of Building Regulations, with the result that the property was unsellable.

Held, dismissing the appeal, that (1) time had begun to run from the date when M had suffered some loss as a result of R's negligence and had become aware of facts which justified the taking of proceedings against R, who admitted liability; the latest date that time had begun to run was the date of the November 1990 settlement, and (2) M's action against R was a unitary claim for diminution in the value of the property arising out of the report and valuation; the subsequent discovery of further heads of loss did not mean that there were any further causes of action, *Hamlin v. Edwin Evans (A Firm)* 80 B.L.R. 85, [1996] C.L.Y. 822 followed.

McKILLEN v. RUSSELL; *sub nom.* McKILLEN v. RUSSELL BROS [2002] N.I. 35, Kerr, J., CA (NI).

COMMERCIAL LAW

4877. Weights and measures—equipment—fees

MEASURING INSTRUMENTS (EEC REQUIREMENTS) (VERIFICATION FEES) REGULATIONS (NORTHERN IRELAND) 2002, SR 2002 309; made under the Finance Act 1973 s.56. In force: November 4, 2002; £1.75.

These Regulations prescribe the fees to be paid in respect of EC verification under the Measuring Instruments (EEC Requirements) Regulations 1988 (SI 1988 186) and the Non-automatic Weighing Instruments Regulations 2000 (SI 2000 3236). They revoke with savings the Measuring Instruments (EEC Requirements) (Verification Fees) Regulations (Northern Ireland) 1993 (SR 1993 470) to rationalise and simplify the fee structure previously prescribed by reducing the number of test categories to four. These Regulations increase the fees in those categories by an average of 10 per cent, prescribe the fees to be paid in respect of EEC initial verification of measuring instruments, and prescribe the fees to be paid in respect of EC verification of non-automatic weighing instruments.

4878. Weights and measures—fit for use—fees

WEIGHTS AND MEASURES (PASSING AS FIT FOR USE FOR TRADE AND ADJUSTMENT FEES) REGULATIONS (NORTHERN IRELAND) 2002, SR 2002 308; made under the Weights and Measures (Northern Ireland) Order 1981 (SI 1981 231 (NI.10)) Art.9, Art.43. In force: November 4, 2002; £2.00.

These Regulations, which revoke the Weights and Measures (Testing and Adjustment Fees) Regulations (Northern Ireland) 1992 (SR 1992 483), prescribe the fees to be paid in having certain weighing or measuring equipment passed as fit for use for trade by inspectors of weights and measures and for the adjustment by them of weights and measures.

4879. Weights and measures—metrication

WEIGHTS AND MEASURES (METRICATION AMENDMENTS) REGULATIONS (NORTHERN IRELAND) 2002, SR 2002 71; made under the Weights and Measures (Northern Ireland) Order 1981 (SI 1981 231 (NI.10)) Art.13. In force: April 8, 2002; £1.75.

These Regulations amend the Measuring Equipment (Liquid Fuel by Road Tanker) Regulations (Northern Ireland) 1984 (SR 1984 117), the Measuring Equipment (Intoxicating Liquor) Regulations (Northern Ireland) 1984 (SR 1984 188), the Weighing Equipment (Beltweighers) Regulations (Northern Ireland) 1985 (SR 1985 319), the Measuring Equipment (Measures of Length) Regulations (Northern Ireland) 1986 (SR 1986 308), the Weighing Equipment (Filling and Discontinuous Totalising Automatic Weighing Machines) Regulations (Northern Ireland) 1986 (SR 1986 311), the Weighing Equipment (Non-automatic Weighing Machines) Regulations (Northern Ireland) 1991 (SR 1991 266), the

Capacity Serving Measures (Intoxicating Liquor) Regulations (Northern Ireland) 1993 (SR 1993 441), the Measuring Equipment (Capacity Measures) Regulations (Northern Ireland) 1998 (SR 1998 48) and the Measuring Equipment (Liquid Fuel and Lubricants) Regulations (Northern Ireland) 1998 (SR 1998 113). The Regulations implement in part the amendments made by European Parliament and Council Directive 1/103 ([2000] OJ L34/17) to Council Directive 80/181 ([1980] OJ L39/40) which relates to the use of units of measurement for economic, public health, public safety or administrative purposes so as to permit the use of non-metric units of measurement as "supplementary indications" until December 31, 2009.

4880. Weights and measures–units of measurement

UNITS OF MEASUREMENT REGULATIONS (NORTHERN IRELAND) 2002, SR 2002 70; made under the European Communities Act 1972 s.2. In force: April 8, 2002; £1.50.

These Regulations, which amend the Weights and Measures (Northern Ireland) Order 1981 (SI 1981 231) by inserting a deadline of December 31, 2009 for the end of the authorised use of supplementary indications in conjunction with metric units, implement in part the amendments made by Directive 1/103 ([2000] OJ L34/17) to Council Directive 80/181 ([1980] OJ L39/40) which relates to the use of units of measurement for economic, public health, public safety or administrative purposes.

COMPANY LAW

4881. Company Directors Disqualification (Northern Ireland) Order 2002 (SI 2002 3150 (NI.4))

This Order amends the Insolvency Act 1986, the Criminal Justice Act 1993, the Deregulation and Contracting Out Act 1994, the Youth Justice and Criminal Evidence Act 1999, the Judgments Enforcement (Northern Ireland) Order 1981 (SI 1981 226 (NI.6)), the Companies (Northern Ireland) Order 1986 (SI 1986 1032 (NI.6)), the Insolvency (Northern Ireland) Order 1989 (SI 1989 2404 (NI.18)), the Insolvency (Northern Ireland) Order 1989 (SI 1989 2405 (NI.19)), the Companies (Northern Ireland) Order 1990 (SI 1990 593 (NI.5)), the Companies (No.2) (Northern Ireland) Order 1990 (SI 1990 1504 (NI.10)), the Electricity (Northern Ireland) Order 1992 (SI 1992 231 (NI.1)), the Airports (Northern Ireland) Order 1994 (SI 1994 426 (NI.1)), the Pensions (Northern Ireland) Order 1995 (SI 1995 3213 (NI.22)) and the Deregulation and Contracting Out (Northern Ireland) Order 1996 (SI 1996 1632 (NI.11)). The Order amends and consolidates provisions relating to the disqualification of persons for being directors of companies in Northern Ireland, and for otherwise being concerned with a company's affairs and will permit the Department of Enterprise, Trade and Investment in specified circumstances to accept a disqualification undertaking from a director, instead of applying to a court for a disqualification order.

4882. Open-Ended Investment Companies Act (Northern Ireland) 2002 (c.13)

This Act makes provision for facilitating the carrying on of collective investment by means of open-ended investment companies and for regulating such companies.

CONSTITUTIONAL LAW

4883. Northern Ireland Arms Decommissioning (Amendment) Act 2002 (6)

This Act provides for the extension of the amnesty period fixed by the Northern Ireland Arms Decommissioning Act 1997 s.2.

This Act received Royal Assent on February 26, 2002.

4884. Northern Ireland Assembly–suspension of devolved government–members salaries

NORTHERN IRELAND ACT 2000 (MODIFICATION) ORDER 2002, SI 2002 2587; made under the Northern Ireland Act 2000 s.6. In force: October 15, 2002; £1.50.

This Order which modifies the Northern Ireland Act 2000 in consequence of provision made under s.2 of that Act, suspending devolved government in Northern Ireland, on October 14, 2002, provides that during suspension expenditure incurred by the Secretary of State in exercising the functions of the Assembly Commission and in relation to members' salaries etc. is to be defrayed from the Consolidated Fund of Northern Ireland.

4885. Northern Ireland Assembly–suspension of devolved government;

NORTHERN IRELAND ACT 2000 (SUSPENSION OF DEVOLVED GOVERNMENT) ORDER 2002, SI 2002 2574; made under the Northern Ireland Act 2000 s.2. In force: October 15, 2002; £1.50.

This Order which revokes the Northern Ireland Act 2000 (Restoration of Devolved Government) (No.2) Order 2001 (SI 2001 3231) brings into force again Northern Ireland Act 2000 s.1 which suspends devolved government.

4886. Territorial waters–boundaries

ADJACENT WATERS BOUNDARIES (NORTHERN IRELAND) ORDER 2002, SI 2002 791; made under the Northern Ireland Act 1998 s.98. In force: March 28, 2002; £2.50.

This Order describes the boundary between the parts of the territorial sea of the UK which are to be treated as adjacent to Northern Ireland and the parts which are not to be so treated and the boundary between the parts of the sea within British fishery limits which are to be treated as adjacent to Northern Ireland and the parts which are not to be so treated.

CONSTRUCTION LAW

4887. Construction industry–Construction Industry Training Board–levy on employers

INDUSTRIAL TRAINING LEVY (CONSTRUCTION INDUSTRY) ORDER (NORTHERN IRELAND) 2002, SR 2002 245; made under the Industrial Training (Northern Ireland) Order 1984 (SI 1984 1159 (NI.9)) Art.23, Art.24. In force: August 31, 2002; £2.00.

This Order gives effect to proposals submitted by the Construction Industry Training Board to the Department for Employment and Learning for the imposition of a further levy upon employers in the construction industry for the purpose of raising money towards the expenses of the Board. The levy is to be imposed in respect of the 38th levy period, commencing on September 1, 2003 and ending on August 31, 2003. The levy will be assessed by the Board and will be payable in two instalments with a right of appeal against an assessment to an industrial tribunal. An employer will be exempt from levy in the 38th levy period where the relevant emoluments are less than £15,000.

CONSUMER LAW

4888. Consumer protection—hazardous substances—packaging and labelling

CHEMICALS (HAZARD INFORMATION AND PACKAGING FOR SUPPLY) REGULATIONS (NORTHERN IRELAND) 2002, SR 2002 301; made under the European Communities Act 1972 s.2; and the Health and Safety at Work (Northern Ireland) Order 1978 (SI 1978 1039 (NI.9)) Art.17, Health and Safety at Work (Northern Ireland) Order 1978 (SI 1978 1039 (NI.9)) Art.55, Sch.3 para.1, Sch.3 para.2, Sch.3 para.14, Sch.3 para.15. In force: November 14, 2002; £6.00.

These Regulations, which amend the Use of Transportable Pressure Receptacles Regulations (Northern Ireland) 1997 (SR1997 247), revoke the Chemicals (Hazard Information and Packaging for Supply) Regulations (Northern Ireland) 1995 (SR 1995 60), the Chemicals (Hazard Information and Packaging for Supply) (Amendment) Regulations (Northern Ireland) 1996 (SR 1996 276), the Chemicals (Hazard Information and Packaging for Supply) (Amendment) Regulations (Northern Ireland) 1997 (SR 1997 398), the Chemicals (Hazard Information and Packaging for Supply) (Amendment) Regulations (Northern Ireland) 1998 (SR 1998 459), the Chemicals (Hazard Information and Packaging for Supply) (Amendment) Regulations (Northern Ireland) 1999 (SR 1999 303) and the Chemicals (Hazard Information and Packaging for Supply) (Amendment) Regulations (Northern Ireland) 2001 (SR 2001 168). They implement Council Directive 1992/32 ([1992] OJ L154/1) relating to a reduction in the sulphur content of certain liquid fuels and amending Directive 93/12; Council Directive 1999/45 ([1999] OJ L200/1) relating to the classification, packaging and labelling of dangerous preparations; Council Directive 76/769 ([1976] OJ L262/201) relating to restrictions on the marketing and use of certain dangerous substances and preparations; and Commission Directive 91/155 ([1991] OJ L76/39) defining and laying down the detailed arrangements for the system of specific information relating to dangerous preparations in implementation of Article 10 of Directive 88/379. The Regulations also implement a number of Directives which adapt to technical progress. They describe the procedures for classifying dangerous substances and dangerous preparations; describe the safety data sheets required to be provided when dangerous substances, dangerous preparations and certain other preparations are supplied; and require that advertisements for dangerous substances and dangerous preparations must refer to the hazards presented by that dangerous substance or dangerous preparation.

4889. Weights and measures—prescribed stamp

WEIGHTS AND MEASURES (PRESCRIBED STAMP) (AMENDMENT) REGULATIONS (NORTHERN IRELAND) 2002, SR 2002 36; made under the Weights and Measures (Northern Ireland) Order 1981 (SI 1981 231 (NI.10)) Art.9. In force: March 25, 2002; £1.75.

These Regulations amend the Weights and Measures (Prescribed Stamp) Regulations (Northern Ireland) 1969 (SR & O 1969 11) which prescribe the stamp for the stamping of weighing and measuring equipment which has been passed as fit for use for trade for use by certain persons. The Regulations provide that certain persons who are not inspectors of weights and measures may now be authorised to use the stamp and the stamp used may now be made of plastic as well as glass, earthenware or enamelled metal.

CRIMINAL EVIDENCE

4890. **Expert evidence–voice identification–acoustic and auditory analysis**

O appealed against his conviction for aggravated burglary and causing grievous bodily harm with intent. The court heard fresh evidence concerning the identification of the voice of a male speaker who had made a 999 call. The Crown argued that the evidence linked O with the offences.

Held, allowing the appeal, that as a general rule where one of the issues was voice identification, it was necessary for there to be expert evidence of acoustic analysis as well as of auditory analysis. The exceptions to the general rule were: (1) where the voices being listened to were of a known group and the issue was which voice had spoken which words; (2) where the speaker was identifiable because of rare characteristics, and (3) where the issue concerned the accent or dialect of the speaker. Where the prosecution relied on voice recognition and the jury had heard the accused giving evidence, it was appropriate for the jury to be allowed to listen to a tape recording on which the recognition had been based. A specific warning should be given to the jurors relating to the danger of relying on their untrained ears. In the instant case, there was a reasonable possibility that the voice of the speaker who had made the 999 call was not that of O and therefore the convictions were unsafe.

R. v. O'DOHERTY (ANTHONY) [2002] N.I. 263, Nicholson, L.J., CA (Crim Div) (NI).

CRIMINAL LAW

4891. **Drugs–controlled drugs–exemptions**

MISUSE OF DRUGS REGULATIONS (NORTHERN IRELAND) 2002, SR 2002 1; made under the Misuse of Drugs Act 1971 s.7, s.10, s.22, s.31. In force: February 1, 2002; £5.50.

These Regulations revoke the Misuse of Drugs (Northern Ireland) Regulations 1986 (SI 1986 52), the Misuse of Drugs (Amendment) Regulations (Northern Ireland) 1987 (SI 1987 68), the Misuse of Drugs (Amendment) Regulations (Northern Ireland) 1988 (SI 1988 206), the Misuse of Drugs (Amendment) Regulations (Northern Ireland) 1989 (SI 1989 346), the Misuse of Drugs (Amendment) Regulations (Northern Ireland) 1991 (SI 1991 1), the Misuse of Drugs (Amendment) Regulations (Northern Ireland) 1995 (SI 1995 305), the Misuse of Drugs (Amendment) (No.2) Regulations (Northern Ireland) 1995 (SI 1995 480), the Misuse of Drugs (Amendment) Regulations (Northern Ireland) 1996 (SI 1996 353), the Misuse of Drugs (Amendment) Regulations (Northern Ireland) 1998 (SI 1998 128) and the Misuse of Drugs (Amendment) Regulations (Northern Ireland) 1 (SI 1 251). The Regulations provide certain exemptions from the provisions of the Misuse of Drugs Act 1971 which prohibit the production, importation, exportation, possession and supply of controlled drugs. In addition, they make provision in relation to prescriptions, records and the furnishing of information concerning controlled drugs and for the supervision of the destruction of such drugs.

4892. **Explosives–fireworks–prohibition**

EXPLOSIVES (FIREWORKS) REGULATIONS (NORTHERN IRELAND) 2002, SR 2002 147; made under the Explosives Act (Northern Ireland) 1970 s.1, s.3. In force: May 6, 2002; £2.00.

These Regulations revoke the Explosives (Fireworks) Regulations (Northern Ireland) 1999 (SR 1999 392) which are largely re-enacted and make provisions to prohibit the possession, purchase, sale, acquisition, handling or use of certain categories of fireworks except under licence, issued by the Secretary of State to whom application shall be made in writing. The Regulations prohibit the possession, purchase, sale, acquisition, handling or use of fireworks of erratic flight, mini-rockets, bangers or certain air bombs but provide an exception for any person for use, in the course of a trade or business of his, for special effects purposes in the theatre, on film or on television and also require specified fireworks and assemblies to be marked with the words "This device must not be sold to, or used by, a member of the general public". In addition, they provide a sliding scale of fees for the issue of fireworks licences.

CRIMINAL PROCEDURE

4893. **Drink driving offences–blood tests–amount of sample to be taken where accused does not request division of sample**

[Human Rights Act 1998 Sch.1 Part I Art.6; Road Traffic Offenders (Northern Ireland) Order 1996 (SI 1996 1320) Art.18(5).]

M was charged with drink driving after an accident in which he was injured and taken to a hospital. When he recovered consciousness, a police officer, K, carried out the procedure for obtaining a blood sample from a hospital patient. The doctor in charge had no objection. K recorded that M did not object. Because of tubes attached to M's elbows it was decided to take a specimen from M's left hand. This yielded only a small amount of blood which could not be divided into two parts. M was asked to permit a specimen from his right hand but refused. The specimen was sealed without being divided and sent for forensic analysis in accordance with the Road Traffic Offenders (Northern Ireland) Order 1996 Art.18. The resident magistrate refused to admit evidence of the analysis and dismissed the summonses against M on the ground that Art.18(5) required the sample to be capable of being divided. The police appealed by way of case stated.

Held, allowing the appeal and remitting the matter with instructions to the resident magistrate to admit the evidence, that M had a statutory right to be given a part of the specimen and it was an essential part of his right to a fair trial under the Human Rights Act 1998 Sch.1 Part I Art.6 that he should be fully aware of his rights with regard to sample taking and testing. However, there was no evidence that M had asked for a part of the specimen so that only the minimum amount necessary for the analysis needed to be taken. M had been informed of his right to request part of the sample by K and there was no further need for him to have had further legal advice.

McCLENAGHAN (CHIEF INSPECTOR OF THE ROYAL ULSTER CONSTABULARY) v. McKENNA [2001] N.I. 327, McCollum, L.J., CA (Crim Div) (NI).

4894. **Drink driving offences–blood tests–validity of conviction where sample taken at medical centre as opposed to hospital or police station**

[Road Traffic (Northern Ireland) Order 1995 (SI 1995 2994) Art.13(2), Art.15(1), Art.18(4).]

D appealed by way of case stated against a resident magistrate's decision that a blood sample taken by a doctor at a health centre had been taken at a "hospital" for the purposes of the Road Traffic (Northern Ireland) Order 1995 Art.18(4). D had been arrested on suspicion of drink driving but the doctor available to take a blood sample was unable to leave the medical centre and go to the police station where D was taken following his arrest. The sample showed D was over the limit and he was convicted under Art.15(1) of the Order.

Held, dismissing the appeal, that the health centre was not a hospital for the purposes of Art.18(4) or Art.13(2) as it lacked in patient facilities and was not the type of medical facility to which a driver would usually be taken following an accident. However, it was not essential that the blood specimen was taken in a hospital as Art.18(4) was concerned with the place where the requirement to give a specimen was made, which could be either a hospital or a police station, and not the place where it was actually taken, with the result that D had been properly convicted, *Pascoe v. Nicholson* [1981] 1 W.L.R. 1061, [1981] C.L.Y. 2330 applied.

RUSSELL (SUPERINTENDENT OF THE ROYAL ULSTER CONSTABULARY) v. DEVINE [2001] N.I. 385, Carswell, L.C.J., CA (Crim Div) (NI).

4895. Magistrates courts–rules–terrorist assets–detention and forfeiture

MAGISTRATES' COURTS (DETENTION AND FORFEITURE OF TERRORIST CASH) RULES (NORTHERN IRELAND) 2002, SR 2002 12; made under the Magistrates' Courts (Northern Ireland) Order 1981 (SI 1981 1675 (NI.26)) Art.13. In force: February 11, 2002; £4.00.

These Rules, which revoke and replace the Magistrates' Courts (Terrorism Act 2000) Rules (Northern Ireland) 2001 (SR 2001 65), prescribe the procedure to be followed for applications to a magistrates' court for the detention, further detention, forfeiture or release of cash seized by a constable, customs officer, or immigration officer under the Anti-terrorism, Crime and Security Act 2001 Sch.1 on reasonable suspicion of a connection to terrorism. They also prescribe the procedure to be followed for applications to a magistrates' court for compensation where no forfeiture order is made and prescribe the forms to be used in connection with the application and hearings.

4896. Police–powers of inspection

JUSTICE (NORTHERN IRELAND) ACT 2002 (AMENDMENT OF SECTION 46(1)) ORDER 2002, SR 2002 414; made under the Justice (Northern Ireland) Act 2002 s.46. In force: December 20, 2002; £1.50.

This Order amends the Justice (Northern Ireland) Act 2002 by adding to the list of organisations which the Chief Inspector of Criminal Justice in Northern Ireland is under a duty to inspect. It also makes a consequential amendment to the Police (Northern Ireland) Act 1998 with the effect that disclosure of documents or information by the Ombudsman or a member of staff of the Ombudsman to an inspector under the Justice (Northern Ireland) 2002 Act, in relation to an inspection of the Ombudsman, will not constitute a criminal offence.

DAMAGES

4897. Bereavement–variation of sum

DAMAGES FOR BEREAVEMENT (VARIATION OF SUM) (NORTHERN IRELAND) ORDER 2002, SI 2002 645; made under the Fatal Accidents (Northern Ireland) Order 1977 (SI 1977 1251 (NI.18)) Art.3A. In force: April 1, 2002; £1.50.

This Order amends the Accidents (Northern Ireland) Order 1977 (SI 1977 1251) by increasing the sum which may be awarded as damages for bereavement in Northern Ireland from £7,500 to £10,000.

EDUCATION

4898. Disabled persons–grants–postgraduate students

EDUCATION (GRANTS FOR DISABLED POSTGRADUATE STUDENTS) (AMENDMENT) REGULATIONS (NORTHERN IRELAND) 2002, SR 2002 272;

made under the Education (Student Support) (Northern Ireland) Order 1998 (SI 1998 1760 (NI.14)) Art.3. In force: September 1, 2002; £1.50.

These Regulations amend the Education (Grants for Disabled Postgraduate Students) Regulations (Northern Ireland) 2001 (SR 2001 285) to increase the maximum amount of grant payable to £5,245.

4899. Grants–students–eligibility

EDUCATION (STUDENT SUPPORT) REGULATIONS (NORTHERN IRELAND) 2002, SR 2002 224; made under the Education (Student Support) (Northern Ireland) Order 1998 (SI 1998 1760 (NI.14)) Art.3, Art.8. In force: July 24, 2002; £7.00.

These Regulations, which revoke the Education (Student Support) Regulations (Northern Ireland) 2001 (SR 2001 277) and the Education (Student Support) (Amendment) Regulations (Northern Ireland) 2002 (SR 2002 111) on September 1, 2002, provide for support for students attending higher education courses in respect of the academic year beginning on or after September 1, 2002. They make a number of changes, principally in relation to the introduction of bursaries for living costs for certain students from low-income backgrounds, the reduction in the amounts of the loans for living costs for students from high-income backgrounds and the closer alignment of the parental and spouse contribution scales.

4900. Grants–students–eligibility

EDUCATION (STUDENT SUPPORT) (AMENDMENT) REGULATIONS (NORTHERN IRELAND) 2002, SR 2002 111; made under the Education (Student Support) (Northern Ireland) Order 1998 (SI 1998 1760 (NI.14)) Art.3, Art.8. In force: April 8, 2002; £1.75.

These Regulations amend the Education (Student Support) Regulations (Northern Ireland) 2001 (SR 2001 277) so that where a student's academic year begins in the autumn he or she shall be eligible for 85 per cent of the grant for dependants for childcare costs for a period of 40 weeks beginning on the first day of the first term of that year. Where a student's academic year begins in the winter, spring or summer he or she shall be eligible for 85 per cent of the dependant's requirement for childcare costs for each week of each term of the year and Christmas and Easter vacations. For any other week of the academic year a student shall be eligible for 70 per cent of the dependant's requirement for childcare costs, except for any week that falls between the end of his course of study and the end of the academic year in which the course ends.

4901. School admissions–discrimination–extra curricular activity sub criteria– subjective basis did not discriminate against lower socio economic groups

[Human Rights Act 1998 s.6, Sch.1 Part 1 Art.14; Education (Northern Ireland) Order 1997 (SI 1997 866) Art.16(6).]

A appealed against a decision refusing judicial review of a decision by a school, LC, subsequently affirmed on appeal to the relevant education and library board admissions appeal tribunal, refusing a place to A. A had achieved an A grade in his 11 plus examination, but was refused admission on the basis of LC's admission sub criteria which provided for admission on the basis of extra curricular activities, as evidenced by certificates issued by the extra curricular body concerned. A contended that the sub criteria amounted to a test or examination imposed by LC contrary to the Education (Northern Ireland) Order 1997 Art.16(6). Further that such a requirement indirectly discriminated against pupils from lower social economic groups in breach of the Human Rights Act 1998 s.6 and Sch.1 Part 1 Art.14.

Held, dismissing the appeal, that selection by reference to extra curricular achievement did not constitute an examination or test of a pupil's ability as Art.16(6) referred to the examination of a pupil's ability. The use of the disputed sub criteria did not amount to a performance test but sought instead to determine the extent of a pupil's involvement in out of school activities. Use of the sub criteria did not discriminate against lower socio-economic groups as extra curricular activities were not restricted to predominantly middle class interests. Further, the requirement for such achievements to be evidenced by certificates issued by the extra curricular body concerned was a legitimate means of objectively assessing such achievements. Although there was a degree of subjectivity in assessing performance in this way, this was legitimate in that it furthered the objective of enhancing LC by admitting pupils who had attained individual success in non academic fields.

A (A CHILD) (APPLICATION FOR JUDICIAL REVIEW), *Re*; O (A CHILD) (APPLICATION FOR JUDICIAL REVIEW), *Re* [2001] N.I. 454, Carswell, L.C.J., CA (NI).

4902. Students–educational awards

STUDENTS AWARDS REGULATIONS (NORTHERN IRELAND) 2002, SR 2002 265; made under the Education and Libraries (Northern Ireland) Order 1986 (SI 1986 594 (NI.3)) Art.50, Art.134. In force: September 1, 2002; £6.00.

These Regulations, which revoke the Students Awards Regulations (Northern Ireland) 2001 (SR 2001 298), replace the definitions of "higher cost country" and "high cost country" with one definition of "high cost country" and amend the definition of "independent student" so that there will be no assessment of parental contribution where a student has been married before the academic year in respect of which the contribution would have applied. The Regulations provide that where a student attends another course at another institution with the consent of that institution's academic authority he can request that the Board transfer his award in relation to that course and also remove the provision which authorised a Board to refuse, after consulting the academic authority concerned, to transfer a student's award in certain specified circumstances.

4903. Students–educational awards

STUDENTS AWARDS (AMENDMENT) REGULATIONS (NORTHERN IRELAND) 2002, SR 2002 112; made under the Education and Libraries (Northern Ireland) Order 1986 (SI 1986 594 (NI.3)) Art.50, Art.134. In force: April 8, 2002; £1.75.

These Regulations amend the Students Awards Regulations (Northern Ireland) 2001 (SR 2001 298) so that where a student's academic year begins in the autumn he or she shall be eligible for 85 per cent of the grant for dependants for childcare costs for a period of 40 weeks beginning on the first day of the first term of that year. Where a student's academic year begins in the winter, spring or summer he or she shall be eligible for 85 per cent of the dependants requirement for childcare costs for each week of each term of the year and Christmas and Easter vacations. For any other week of the academic year a student shall be eligible for 70 per cent of the dependants requirement for childcare costs, except for any week that falls between the end of his course of study and the end of the academic year in which the course ends.

4904. Students–loans–mortgage style repayment loans

EDUCATION (STUDENT LOANS) (AMENDMENT) REGULATIONS (NORTHERN IRELAND) 2002, SR 2002 241; made under the Education (Student Loans) (Northern Ireland) Order 1990 (SI 1990 1506 (NI.11)) Art.3, Sch.2 para.1. In force: August 1, 2002; £1.50.

These Regulations amend the Education (Student Loans) Regulations (Northern Ireland) 1998 (SR 1998 58) which govern loans made under the Education (Student Loans) (Northern Ireland) Order 1990 (SI 1990 1506 (NI.11)), which are mortgage style repayment loans and are for the most part made to students who began their courses before August 1, 1998. The Regulations increase in line with inflation the maximum amounts which may be lent to students in relation to an academic year.

ELECTORAL PROCESS

4905. **Elections–Northern Ireland Assembly–time limits–lawfulness of elections outside statutory time limit**

[Northern Ireland Act 1998 s.16(8), s.32(3).]

R, an MP, appealed against a decision ([2002] N.I. 206) upholding the refusal of his application for judicial review ([2002] N.I. 64) of (1) the election of T and D as First Minister and Deputy First Minister respectively, and (2) the Secretary of State's decision, following that election, to propose May 1, 2003 as the date for the poll for the election of the next Assembly. T and D had been elected outside the six week period referred to in the Northern Ireland Act 1998 s.16(8).

Held, dismissing the appeal (Lords Hutton and Hobhouse dissenting), that while Parliament had intended the Assembly to adhere to the six week time limit in s.16(8), it had not intended that on a failure to elect within that time the Secretary of State should immediately dissolve the Assembly and instigate an early poll. The time limit had been introduced to prevent the possibility of indefinite deadlock but had not been intended to restrict the Assembly's power to elect otherwise than by subjecting it to the Secretary of State's power and duty to intervene. Under s.32(3) of the Act the Secretary of State had a duty, where no election had taken place within the six week time limit under s.16(8), to propose a date for the poll for the election of the next Assembly, but the section imposed no temporal limitation. If there seemed to be no prospect of an imminent and effective election under s.16(8), he would undoubtedly be expected to propose a very early date for a poll. If, however, an effective election seemed to be imminent, he would be expected to wait so that the political process might take effect and, if it did, to propose a date in the future which would take that effective election into account. The 1998 Act was in effect a constitution whose provisions had, consistently with the language used, to be construed generously and purposively. Where constitutional arrangements retained scope for the exercise of political judgment, they allowed a flexible response to differing and unpredictable events in a way that the application of strict rules would not.

ROBINSON v. SECRETARY OF STATE FOR NORTHERN IRELAND; *sub nom.* ROBINSON'S APPLICATION FOR JUDICIAL REVIEW, *Re*, [2002] UKHL 32, [2002] N.I. 390, Lord Bingham of Cornhill, HL (NI).

4906. **Elections–parliamentary election rules and registers**

REPRESENTATION OF THE PEOPLE (NORTHERN IRELAND) (AMENDMENT) REGULATIONS 2002, SI 2002 1873; made under the Representation of the People Act 1983 s.10A, s.13C, s.53, s.201, Sch.1 rule.24, Sch.1 rule.37, Sch.2 para.1, Sch.2 para.10, Sch.2 para.11, Sch.2 para.12, Sch.2 para.13. In force: in accordance with Reg.2; £4.00.

These Regulations, which amend the Representation of the People Act 1983, the Representation of the People (Northern Ireland) Regulations 2001 (SI 2001 400) and the Representation of the People (Northern Ireland) (Amendment) Regulations 2001 (SI 2001 1877), revoke the People (Form of Canvass) (Northern Ireland) Regulations 2001 (SI 2001 2725). They prescribe the form of annual canvass; amend the parliamentary elections rules to add the travel pass specified in it to the list of documents that may be presented at a polling station in order to receive a ballot paper; provide free supply and the sale of the register of electors; and provide for a version of the register of electors which does not contain the names of those persons who have requested the exclusion of their names from this version of the register.

4907. Elections–postal votes–Northern Ireland Assembly

NORTHERN IRELAND ASSEMBLY (ELECTIONS) (AMENDMENT) ORDER 2002, SI 2002 1964; made under the Northern Ireland Act 1998 s.34. In force: December 1, 2002; £1.50.

This Order, which amends the Northern Ireland Assembly (Elections) Order 2001 (SI 2001 2599), makes an amendment to the rules for elections to the Northern Ireland Assembly which corresponds to the amendment which the Electoral Fraud (Northern Ireland) Act 2002 made to the parliamentary elections rules. In the case of an elector who votes by post, the returning officer is required to be satisfied that the date of birth and signature on the declaration of identity that is returned with a postal ballot paper correspond with the date and signature provided on registration.

4908. Electoral Fraud (Northern Ireland) Act 2002 (c.13)

This Act provides for the supply to the Chief Electoral Officer for Northern Ireland of the signatures and dates of birth of electors and persons seeking registration as electors in Northern Ireland; for the use of that information in connection with elections; for the issue of electoral identity cards and for the modification in relation to voters with disabilities of certain rules about voting procedure in Northern Ireland.

This Act received Royal Assent on May 1, 2002.

4909. Electoral Fraud (Northern Ireland) Act 2002 (c.13)–Commencement Order

ELECTORAL FRAUD (NORTHERN IRELAND) ACT 2002 (COMMENCEMENT) ORDER 2002, SI 2002 1648; made under the Electoral Fraud (Northern Ireland) Act 2002 s.8. Commencement details: bringing into force various provisions of the 2002 Act on July 1, 2002; September 1, 2002 and December 1, 2002; £1.50.

This Order brings into force all of the provisions of the Electoral Fraud (Northern Ireland) Act 2002 not already in force.

4910. Local elections–prevention of fraud

LOCAL ELECTIONS (NORTHERN IRELAND) (AMENDMENT) ORDER 2002, SI 2002 2835; made under the Northern Ireland Act 1998 s.84. In force: in accordance with Art.2; £2.00.

This Order amends the Local Elections (Northern Ireland) Order 1985 (SI 1985 454), the Local Elections (Northern Ireland) (Amendment) Order 1990 (SI 1990 595) and the Local Elections (Northern Ireland) (Amendment) Order 1991 (SI 1991 1715). It makes amendments to the provisions relating to local elections in Northern Ireland corresponding to the amendments made in respect of parliamentary elections by the Electoral Fraud (Northern Ireland) Act 2002. The Order allows staff at polling stations to ask the date of birth of an elector and to check against the date provided on registration; adds the electoral identity card to the list of specified documents which may be presented at a polling station in order to receive a ballot paper; adds the travel card to the description of documents in the list; and removes the entitlement to an absent vote on a change in a person's qualifying address.

EMPLOYMENT

4911. Arbitration–Labour Relations Agency Arbitration Scheme

LABOUR RELATIONS AGENCY ARBITRATION SCHEME ORDER (NORTHERN IRELAND) 2002, SR 2002 120; made under the Industrial Relations (Northern Ireland) Order 1992 (SI 1992 807 (NI. 5)) Art.84A. In force: April 28, 2002; £6.00.

This Order, which amends the Arbitration Act 1996, sets out a Scheme submitted to the Department for Employment and Learning by the Labour Relations Agency.

It sets out details of the Scheme, providing for arbitration in the case of disputes involving proceedings, or claims which could be subject of proceedings, before an industrial tribunal arising out of a contravention of or alleged contravention of the Employment Rights (Northern Ireland) Order 1996 (SI 1996 1919 (NI.16)). In addition, the Order provides for certain provisions of the 1996 Act to apply to arbitration conducted in accordance with the Scheme, for industrial tribunals to enforce re-employment orders made in such arbitration and for the award of a basic amount in such an arbitration to be treated as a basic award of compensation for unfair dismissal for the purposes of debts which the Department for Employment and Learning must satisfy if the employer has become insolvent.

4912. Benefits—paternity and adoption—entitlement

SOCIAL SECURITY (PATERNITY AND ADOPTION AMENDMENT) REGULATIONS (NORTHERN IRELAND) 2002, SR 2002 363; made under the Social Security Contributions and Benefits (Northern Ireland) Act 1992 s.122, s.123, s.132, s.133, s.171; and the Jobseekers (Northern Ireland) Order 1995 (NI 15) (SI 1995 2705) Art.14, Art.23, Art.36, Sch.1 para.1. In force: December 8, 2002; £2.00.

These Regulations amend the Income Support (General) Regulations (Northern Ireland) 1987 (SR 1987 459), the Housing Benefit (General) Regulations (Northern Ireland) 1987 (SR 1987 461) and the Jobseeker's Allowance Regulations (Northern Ireland) 1996 (SR 1996 198). They insert definitions of "adoption leave" and "paternity leave"; provide that a person on statutory paternity leave or statutory adoption leave shall not be treated as engaged in remunerative work; provide that remuneration received while on statutory paternity or statutory adoption leave is not counted as earnings for the purposes of calculating entitlement to income support or jobseeker's allowance; extends entitlement to income support to a person who is entitled to and taking paternity leave by virtue of the Employment Rights (Northern Ireland) Order 1996 (SI 1996 1919); and adds statutory adoption pay and statutory paternity pay to those payments in respect of which prescribed sums are to be disregarded in the calculation of income.

4913. Codes of practice—disciplinary and grievance procedures

CODE OF PRACTICE (DISCIPLINARY AND GRIEVANCE PROCEDURES) (APPOINTED DAY) ORDER (NORTHERN IRELAND) 2002, SR 2002 347; made under the Industrial Relations (Northern Ireland) Order 1992 (SI 1992 807 (NI.5)) Art.90, Art.107. In force: December 1, 2002; £1.50.

This Order appoints December 1, 2002 as the day upon which the Code of Practice on Disciplinary and Grievance Procedures issued by the Labour Relations Agency shall come into effect. The Code can be admitted in evidence in any proceedings before an industrial tribunal or the Industrial Court and if any provision of it appears to the tribunal or Court to be relevant to any question arising in the proceedings it shall be taken into account in determining that question.

4914. Codes of practice—industrial action ballots

CODE OF PRACTICE (INDUSTRIAL ACTION BALLOTS AND NOTICE TO EMPLOYERS) (APPOINTED DAY) ORDER (NORTHERN IRELAND) 2002, SR 2002 345; made under the Industrial Relations (Northern Ireland) Order 1992 (SI 1992 807 (NI.5)) Art.95, Art.107. In force: December 1, 2002; £1.50.

This Order brings into operation the Code of Practice on Industrial Action Ballots and Notice to Employers. It shall be admissible in evidence in any proceedings before a court or industrial tribunal or the Industrial Court and any provision of the Code which appears to the court, industrial tribunal or Industrial Court to be relevant to any question arising in those proceedings shall be taken into account in determining that question.

4915. Codes of practice–redundancy consultation and procedures

CODE OF PRACTICE (REDUNDANCY CONSULTATION AND PROCEDURES) (APPOINTED DAY) ORDER (NORTHERN IRELAND) 2002, SR 2002 346; made under the Industrial Relations (Northern Ireland) Order 1992 (SI 1992 807 (NI.5)) Art.90, Art.107. In force: December 1, 2002; £1.50.

This Order appoints December 1, 2002 as the date upon which the revised Code of Practice on Redundancy Consultation and Procedures issued by the Labour Relations Agency shall come into effect. The Code can be admitted in evidence in any proceedings before an industrial tribunal or the Industrial Court and although failure on the part of any person to observe any provision of it shall not of itself render him liable to any proceedings, if any provision of it appears to the tribunal or Court to be relevant to any question arising in the proceedings it shall be taken into account in determining that question.

4916. Conditions of employment–annual leave

WORKING TIME (AMENDMENT) REGULATIONS (NORTHERN IRELAND) 2002, SR 2002 93; made under the European Communities Act 1972 s.2. In force: April 14, 2002; £1.75.

These Regulations amend the Working Time Regulations (Northern Ireland) 1998 (SI 1998 386) which implement Council Directive 93/104 ([1993] OJ L307/18) concerning certain aspects of the organisation of working time. The Regulations provide that the amount of leave to which a worker is entitled in a leave year is four weeks and limit the extent to which a worker is able to exercise his entitlement to leave during the course of his first year of employment.

4917. Discrimination–politics–difference in methods advocated by job applicants

[Fair Employment (Northern Ireland) Act 1976 s.16, s.17.]

G and Y were shortlisted for the post of N's coordinator. Y's application was successful and G claimed that he had been discriminated against on the basis of his political opinion, contrary to the Fair Employment (Northern Ireland) Act 1976. G argued that he favoured an anti racist approach in furthering N's objectives, whereas Y advocated cultural sensitivism. The Fair Employment Tribunal found that G had been discriminated against on the grounds of political opinions. N appealed by way of case stated, contending that G's views were not a political opinion for the purposes of the Act, with the result that there had been no discrimination.

Held, allowing the appeal, that it could not be said that G was the better candidate and so the argument that he had been discriminated against failed. In any event, G's views did not amount to a political opinion in terms of the Act, which sought to protect opposing or minority views relating to government and public policy. The differences in the instant case amounted to different methods to be used to attain the same goal, not different political opinions.

GILL v. NORTHERN IRELAND COUNCIL FOR ETHNIC MINORITIES [2002] I.R.L.R. 74, Sir Robert Carswell, L.C.J., CA (NI).

4918. Employees rights–increase of limits

EMPLOYMENT RIGHTS (INCREASE OF LIMITS) ORDER (NORTHERN IRELAND) 2002, SR 2002 24; made under the Employment Relations (Northern Ireland) Order 1 (SI 1 2790 (NI.9)) Art.33, Art.39. In force: March 10, 2002; £2.00.

This Order, which revokes the Employment Rights (Increase of Limits) Order (Northern Ireland) 2001 (SR 2001 54), increases the limits applying to certain awards of industrial tribunals, and other amounts payable under employment legislation. The increases reflect the increase in the retail prices index from September 2000 to September 2001.

4919. Employees rights–statutory paternity and adoption leave

PATERNITY AND ADOPTION LEAVE REGULATIONS (NORTHERN IRELAND) 2002, SR 2002 377; made under the Employment Rights (Northern Ireland) Order 1996 (SI 1996 1919 (NI.16)) Art.70C, Art.107A, Art.107B, Art.107C, Art.107D, Art.112A, Art.112C, Art.112D, Art.112E, Art.131. In force: December 8, 2002; £3.50.

These Regulations relate to the new rights to paternity and adoption leave provided for in the Employment Act 2002. The right to take paternity leave is conferred in connection with the birth of a child and in connection with the adoption of a child. In each case, the right is available to employees with 26 weeks' qualifying service, and is exercisable for the purpose of caring for the child or supporting the child's mother or adopter. An employee has the option of taking either one week's leave or two consecutive weeks' leave, and also options concerning the date on which the employee's period of leave will begin; however, leave may only be taken within 56 days of the child's birth or placement with the adopter. An employee is required to notify his employer of his intention to take leave and of his choices in respect of the options available. An employee is entitled during his absence on leave to the benefit of all of his terms and conditions of employment apart from the right to remuneration and is subject to all of the obligations under those terms and conditions except in so far as they are inconsistent with the right to leave. The Regulations provide for an employee's right to return to work after taking leave, distinguishing the case where the leave was an isolated period of absence from the case where it followed another period of statutory leave; confer rights to ordinary and additional adoption leave which are analogous to the right to ordinary and additional maternity leave; and set out the conditions of entitlement to ordinary adoption leave.

4920. Employees rights–statutory paternity and adoption pay

STATUTORY PATERNITY PAY AND STATUTORY ADOPTION PAY (GENERAL) REGULATIONS (NORTHERN IRELAND) 2002, SR 2002 378; made under the Social Security Contributions and Benefits Act (Northern Ireland) 1992 s.167ZA, s.167ZB, s.167ZC, s.167ZD, s.167ZE, s.167ZG, s.167ZJ, s.167ZL, s.167ZM, s.167ZN, s.167ZP, s.167ZS; and the Social Security Administration (Northern Ireland) Act 1992 s.5. In force: December 8, 2002; £4.00.

These Regulations make provision relating to statutory paternity pay and statutory adoption pay. They specify that statutory paternity pay is payable in connection with a birth if the entitlement conditions as regards the relationship with the newborn child and the child's mother; provide for a modification of the entitlement conditions in the case of early birth; specify the period of payment; set out additional notice requirements, the period within which the statutory paternity pay period must occur; set out the evidence of entitlement that is required; and provide for exceptional circumstances in which statutory paternity pay is payable to a person even though he is working for another employer. The Regulations also make provision relating to statutory paternity pay payable in connection with an adoption which include provisions for the termination of statutory paternity pay where a person has commenced work, for there to be no liability for payment of statutory paternity pay where there is entitlement to statutory sick pay, where the person claiming it has died, or where he has been detained in legal custody or imprisoned.

4921. Employees rights–statutory paternity and adoption pay–employers liabilities

STATUTORY PATERNITY PAY AND STATUTORY ADOPTION PAY (ADMINISTRATION) REGULATIONS (NORTHERN IRELAND) 2002, SR 2002 379; made under the Employment (Northern Ireland) Order 2002 (SI 2002 2836 (NI.2)) Art.8, Art.9, Art.11, Art.16; and the Social Security Contributions

(Transfer of Functions, etc.) (Northern Ireland) Order 1 (SI 1 671) Art.7, Art.23. In force: December 8, 2002; £2.00.

These Regulations provide for the funding of employers' liabilities to make payments of statutory paternity or statutory adoption pay and also impose obligations on employers in connection with such payments and confer powers on the Commissioners of Inland Revenue. These Regulations provide an employer is entitled to an amount equal to 92 per cent of payments made by him of statutory paternity pay or statutory adoption pay, or the whole of such payments if he is a small employer. They also provide for employers to be reimbursed through deductions from income tax, national insurance and other payments that they would otherwise make to the Board, and for the Board to fund payments to the extent that employers cannot be fully reimbursed in this way.

4922. Employees rights–statutory paternity and adoption pay–Health and Personal Social Services employees

STATUTORY PATERNITY PAY AND STATUTORY ADOPTION PAY (HEALTH AND PERSONAL SOCIAL SERVICES EMPLOYEES) REGULATIONS (NORTHERN IRELAND) 2002, SR 2002 381; made under the Social Security Contributions and Benefits (Northern Ireland) Act 1992 s.167ZJ, s.167ZS. In force: December 8, 2002; £1.75.

These Regulations make provision for certain cases where an employee of the Health and Personal Social Services has two or more contracts of employment for that employee to elect to treat those contracts as one contract. They provide for employees, whose contract of employment has been divided into two or more contracts with different bodies, to elect to have those contracts treated as one contract for the purposes of entitlement to statutory paternity pay or statutory adoption pay. They also provide for the manner in which, and the time within which, such an election is to be made; the information that is to be provided by a person to his employers, for one of a person's employers under the two or more contracts to be regarded for the purposes of statutory paternity pay; and statutory adoption pay as his employer under the one contract and for the time within which an election is to have effect.

4923. Employees rights–statutory paternity and adoption pay–persons abroad

STATUTORY PATERNITY PAY AND STATUTORY ADOPTION PAY (PERSONS ABROAD AND MARINERS) REGULATIONS (NORTHERN IRELAND) 2002, SR 2002 382; made under the Social Security Contributions and Benefits (Northern Ireland) Act 1992 s.167ZI, s.167ZR. In force: December 8, 2002; £2.00.

These Regulations amend the Social Security Contributions and Benefits (Northern Ireland) Act 1992 in relation to provisions on statutory adoption pay and statutory paternity pay in respect of persons abroad, persons who work as mariners and persons who work on the continental shelf. These Regulations are limited in their application in to cases where the person would be treated as an employee under the Act if the employment were in Northern Ireland. They also provide for a person employed in another State of the European Economic Area but subject to the legislation of the UK to be treated as an employee for the purposes of statutory paternity pay and statutory adoption pay and for a person who is absent from Northern Ireland but in respect of whom an employer has secondary Class 1 national insurance contribution liability to be treated as an employee for the purposes of statutory paternity pay and statutory adoption pay.

4924. Employees rights–statutory paternity and adoption pay–weekly rates

STATUTORY PATERNITY PAY AND STATUTORY ADOPTION PAY (WEEKLY RATES) REGULATIONS (NORTHERN IRELAND) 2002, SR 2002 380; made under the Social Security Contributions and Benefits Act (Northern Ireland)

1992 s.167ZE, s.167N; and the Social Security Administration (Northern Ireland) Act 1992 s.5. In force: December 8, 2002; £1.75.

These Regulations set out the weekly rates payable in relation to statutory paternity pay and statutory adoption pay payable under the Social Security Contributions and Benefits (Northern Ireland) Act 1992 Part XIIZA and Part XIIZB, as inserted by Art.5 and 6 respectively of the Employment (Northern Ireland) Order 2002. The weekly rate of payment of statutory paternity pay is set at £75 where the paternity pay period begins before April 6, 2003, and at the smaller of £100 and 90 per cent of the employee's normal weekly earnings where the paternity pay period begins on or after April 6, 2003. The weekly rate of payment of statutory adoption pay is set at the smaller of £100 and 90 per cent of the employee's normal weekly earnings.

4925. Employment Relations (Northern Ireland) Order 1999 (SI 1999 2790 (NI.9))– Commencement No.5 and Transitional Provision Order

EMPLOYMENT RELATIONS (1999 ORDER) (COMMENCEMENT NO.5 AND TRANSITIONAL PROVISION) ORDER (NORTHERN IRELAND) 2002, SR 2002 214; made under the Employment Relations (Northern Ireland) Order 1999 (SI 1999 2790 (NI.9)) Art.1, Art.39. Commencement details: bringing into force various provisions of the 1999 Order on June 2, 2002; £1.75.

This Order brings into operation specified provisions of the Employment Relations (Northern Ireland) Order 1999 (SI 1999 2790 (NI.9)) which provide for the right of a worker to be accompanied at disciplinary and grievance hearings by a single companion and that the only workers who may avail themselves of the right to be accompanied are those required or invited on or after June 2, 2002 to attend a disciplinary or grievance hearing.

4926. Employment Relations (Northern Ireland) Order 1999 (SI 1999 2790 (NI.9))– Commencement No.6 and Transitional Provisions Order

EMPLOYMENT RELATIONS (1999 ORDER) (COMMENCEMENT NO.6 AND TRANSITIONAL PROVISIONS) ORDER (NORTHERN IRELAND) 2002, SR 2002 317; made under the Employment Relations (Northern Ireland) Order 1999 (SI 1999 2790 (NI.9)) Art.1, Art.39. In force: bringing into operation various provisions of the 1999 Order on October 13, 2002; £1.75.

This Order brings into operation specified provisions of the Employment Relations (Northern Ireland) Order 1999 (SI 1999 2790) which require trade unions to hold a ballot before organising industrial action and relate to ballots and notices.

4927. Employment (Northern Ireland) Order 2002 (SI 2002 2386 (NI.2))– Commencement, Transitional and Savings Provisions Order

EMPLOYMENT (2002 ORDER) (COMMENCEMENT AND TRANSITIONAL AND SAVINGS PROVISIONS) ORDER (NORTHERN IRELAND) 2002, SR 2002 356 (C.29); made under the Employment (Northern Ireland) Order 2002 (SI 2002 2386 (NI.2)) Art.1. In force: bringing into operation various provisions of the 2002 Order on November 23, 2002, December 8, 2002 and April 6, 2003; £1.75.

This Order brings into operation the provisions of the Employment (Northern Ireland) Order 2002 (SI 2002 2366) specified in Sch.1 Part I, which relate to rights during and after maternity leave, on November 23, 2002; provisions specified in Sch.1 Part II, relating to Paternity and Adoption and administration and enforcement of statutory paternity pay and statutory adoption pay, on December 8, 2002; and provision specified in Employment (Northern Ireland) Order 2002 .1 Part III, relating to funding of employers' liabilities, power to confer rights on individuals; amendment, and flexible working subject to the transitional and saving provisions, on April 6, 2003.

4928. Employment (Northern Ireland) Order 2002 (SI 2002 2836 (NI.2))

This Order amends the Social Security Contributions and Benefits (Northern Ireland) Act 1992, the Social Security Administration (Northern Ireland) Act 1992, the Industrial Relations (Northern Ireland) Order 1992 (SI 1992 807 (NI.5)), the Employment Rights (Northern Ireland) Order 1996 (SI 1996 1919 (NI.16)), the Industrial Tribunals (Northern Ireland) Order 1996 (SI 1996 1921 (NI.18)), the Social Security Contributions (Transfer of Functions, etc.) (Northern Ireland) Order 1999 (SI 1999 671) and the Employment Relations (Northern Ireland) Order 1999 (SI 1999 2790 (NI.9)). It makes provision for statutory rights to paternity and adoption leave and pay, amends the law relating to statutory maternity leave and makes provision about flexible working.

4929. Equal opportunities–public bodies–specification

FAIR EMPLOYMENT (SPECIFICATION OF PUBLIC AUTHORITIES) (AMENDMENT) ORDER (NORTHERN IRELAND) 2002, SR 2002 367; made under the Fair Employment and Treatment (Northern Ireland) Order 1998 (SI 1998 3162 (NI.21)) Art.50, Art.51. In force: January 1, 2003; £2.00.

This Order amends the Fair Employment (Specification of Public Authorities) (No.2) Order (Northern Ireland) 2000 (SR 2000 371) which specifies a number of persons or bodies as public authorities for certain purposes and provides for the persons who are to be treated for such purposes as the employees of some of those authorities. The Order adds a number of persons or bodies as public authorities for certain purposes.

4930. Equal treatment–fixed term employees

FIXED-TERM EMPLOYEES (PREVENTION OF LESS FAVOURABLE TREATMENT) REGULATIONS (NORTHERN IRELAND) 2002, SR 2002 298; made under the Employment Act 2002 s.46. In force: October 1, 2002; £3.00.

These Regulations amend the Social Security Contributions and Benefits (Northern Ireland) Act 1992, the Employment Rights (Northern Ireland) Order 1996 (SI 1996 1919) and the Industrial Tribunals (Northern Ireland) Order 1996 (SI 1996 1921). They implement Council Directive 99/70 ([1999] OJ L244/64) concerning the framework agreement on fixed-term work concluded by ETUC, UNICE and CEEP and give fixed-term employees the right in principle not to be treated less favourably than permanent employees of the same employer doing similar work. The right, which is exercisable by complaint to an employment tribunal, applies where the less favourable treatment is on the ground that the employee is fixed-term and is not justified on objective grounds. The Regulations also make provision about what constitutes objective justification and provide that where a fixed-term employee continuously employed on fixed-term contracts for four years or more is re-engaged on a fixed-term contract without his continuity being broken, the new contract has effect under the law as a permanent contract unless the renewal on a fixed-term basis was objectively justified

4931. Equal treatment–part time employees

PART-TIME WORKERS (PREVENTION OF LESS FAVOURABLE TREATMENT) (AMENDMENT) REGULATIONS (NORTHERN IRELAND) 2002, SR 2002 286; made under the Employment Relations (Northern Ireland) Order 1999 (SI 1999 2790 (NI.9)) Art.21. In force: October 1, 2002; £1.75.

These Regulations amend the Part-time Workers (Prevention of Less Favourable Treatment) Regulations (Northern Ireland) 2000 (SR 2000 219) to secure that, consistent with Council Directive 1999/70 ([1999] OJ L175/43) concerning the framework agreement on fixed-term work concluded by ETUC, UNICE and CEEP, there is no longer a distinction between fixed-term and open ended contracts, for the purposes of ascertaining what are different types of contract for the purposes of the 2000 Regulations. They also provide that the compensation that can be awarded in cases involving occupational pension schemes is no longer limited to the two years before the date on which the complaint was presented.

4932. Maternity leave—period of leave

MATERNITY AND PARENTAL LEAVE ETC. (AMENDMENT NO.3) REGULATIONS (NORTHERN IRELAND) 2002, SR 2002 355; made under the Employment Rights (Northern Ireland) Order 1996 (SI 1996 1919 (NI.16)) Art.70C, Art.103, Art.105, Art.106, Art.107, Art.108, Art.131. In force: November 24, 2002; £2.00.

These Regulations amend provisions relating to maternity leave in the Maternity and Parental Leave etc. Regulations (Northern Ireland) 1999 (SR 1999 471) and also provisions in those Regulations concerning the right to return from parental leave. Some of the amendments concern provisions which implement provisions of Council Directive 92/85 ([1992] OJ L348/1) on the safety and health at work of pregnant workers and workers who have recently given birth, and provisions of Council Directive 96/34 ([1996] OJ L145/4) on the framework agreement on parental leave. The Regulations extend ordinary maternity leave from 18 to 26 weeks and additional maternity leave so as to end 26 weeks from the end of ordinary maternity leave rather than 29 weeks after the week of childbirth. They also make amendments to provide for notification of the date on which an employee intends her ordinary maternity leave period to start to be given to the employer before the end of the fifteenth week before the expected week of childbirth, rather than 21 days before the intended start date as previously; however, there is a new provision for the employee to change the date subsequently provided that her employer is given 28 days' notice. They also insert a new requirement for an employer notified of the commencement of an employee's maternity leave to notify the employee of the date on which it will end and make provision for all of the rights and obligations in an employee's contract of employment, apart from the right to remuneration, to continue during an employee's ordinary maternity leave period.

4933. Parental leave—period of leave

MATERNITY AND PARENTAL LEAVE ETC. (AMENDMENT) REGULATIONS (NORTHERN IRELAND) 2002, SR 2002 110; made under the Employment Rights (Northern Ireland) Order 1996 (SI 1996 1919 (NI.16)) Art.108. In force: April 21, 2002; £1.75.

These Regulations, which amend the provisions relating to parental leave in the Maternity and Parental Leave etc. Regulations (Northern Ireland) 1999 (SR 1999 471), implement in Northern Ireland Council Directive 96/34 ([1996] OJ L145/4) on the framework agreement on parental leave. They revoke the provision which restricted the right to parental leave so as to be exercisable only in respect of children born or placed for adoption on or after December 15, 1999 and allow parents of children born or placed for adoption up to five years before that date the period up until July 20, 2005 in which to take up parental leave. They enable these parents to rely on a period of service with a previous employer in order to satisfy the one-year qualifying service requirement to which the right to take parental leave is subject and require parents seeking to take advantage of this provision to give their current employer notice of, and if the employer reasonably requires it, evidence of, the relevant period of service. In addition, the Regulations extend the period of leave to which a parent is entitled from 13 to 18 weeks in the case of a child who is entitled to a disability living allowance, provide that the notice period in respect of parental leave required to be given to the employer by the employee is 21 days instead of 13 weeks and provide that an employer may not postpone a period of parental leave in respect of a child beyond the date of the child's 18th birthday.

4934. Parental leave—period of leave

MATERNITY AND PARENTAL LEAVE ETC. (AMENDMENT NO.2) REGULATIONS (NORTHERN IRELAND) 2002, SR 2002 135; made under the Employment Rights (Northern Ireland) Order 1996 (SI 1996 1919 (NI.16)) Art.108. In force: April 21, 2002; £1.75.

These Regulations, which revoke the Maternity and Parental Leave etc. (Amendment) Regulations (Northern Ireland) 2002 (SR 2002 110), amend the provisions relating to parental leave in the Maternity and Parental Leave etc. Regulations (Northern Ireland) 1999 (SR 1999 471) and implement Council Directive 96/34 ([1996] OJ L145/4) on the framework agreement on parental leave. The Regulations allow parents of children born or placed for adoption up to five years before that date the period up until July 20, 2005 in which to take parental leave, enable these parents to rely on a period of service with a previous employer in order to satisfy the one-year qualifying service requirement to which the right to take parental leave is subject and extend the period of leave to which a parent is entitled from 13 to 18 weeks in the case of a child who is entitled to a disability living allowance. They also provide that the notice period in respect of parental leave required to be given to the employer by the employee is 21 days instead of 13 weeks and that an employer may not postpone a period of parental leave in respect of a child beyond the date of the child's 18th birthday.

4935. Police officers—local recruitment

POLICE (RECRUITMENT) (NORTHERN IRELAND) (AMENDMENT) REGULATIONS 2002, SR 2002 385; made under the Police (Northern Ireland) Act 1998 s.25, s.26, s.41, s.43, s.44. In force: January 17, 2003; £1.75.

These regulations amend the Police (Recruitment) (Northern Ireland) Regulations 2001 (SR 2001 140). In particular, they provide for recruitment to the Police Service of Northern Ireland Reserve to be carried out on a local basis, as recommended by the Independent Commission on Policing for Northern Ireland in its report A New Beginning: Policing in Northern Ireland.

4936. Teachers—compensation for redundancy and retirement

TEACHERS' (COMPENSATION FOR REDUNDANCY AND PREMATURE RETIREMENT) REGULATIONS (NORTHERN IRELAND) 2002, SR 2002 393; made under the Superannuation (Northern Ireland) Order 1972 (SI 1972 1073 (NI.10)) Art.19, Sch.3 para.9. In force: March 1, 2003; £2.00.

These Regulations amend the Teachers' (Compensation for Redundancy and Premature Retirement) Regulations (Northern Ireland) 1991 (SR 1991 132) to introduce changes necessitated by the incorporation of institutions of further education and provide for the Department for Employment and Learning rather than the education and library board to be the compensating authority in the case of such institutions; reduces the amount of added years which may be granted to a person retiring on grounds of redundancy or in the interests of the efficient discharge of his employer's functions; and clarify that additional years purchased for a past period shall not be counted as qualifying years in determining the amount of added years to be granted as compensation for early retirement.

ENERGY

4937. Electricity industry—applications for consent—fees

ELECTRICITY (APPLICATIONS FOR CONSENT) (FEES) (AMENDMENT) REGULATIONS (NORTHERN IRELAND) 2002, SR 2002 364; made under the Electricity (Northern Ireland) Order 1992 (SI 1992 231 (NI.1)) Art.39, Sch.8 para.1. In force: January 1, 2003; £1.50.

These Regulations amend the Electricity (Applications for Consent) (Fees) Regulations (Northern Ireland) 1992 (SI 1992 178) to revise upwards the fees which are payable on applications to the Department of Enterprise, Trade and Investment for its consent to the construction, extension or operation of a generating station or to the installation or keeping installed of an overhead line.

4938. Energy conservation–grants

DOMESTIC ENERGY EFFICIENCY GRANTS REGULATIONS (NORTHERN IRELAND) 2002, SR 2002 56; made under the Social Security (Northern Ireland) Order 1990 (SI 1990 1511 (NI.15)) Art.17. In force: April 1, 2002; £2.00.

These Regulations, which revoke the Domestic Energy Efficiency Grants Regulations (Northern Ireland) 1994 (SR 1994 306) and the Domestic Energy Efficiency Grants (Amendment) Regulations (Northern Ireland) 1996 (SR 1996 417), enable the Department for Social Development to make or arrange for the making of grant for the improvement of energy efficiency in dwellings occupied by persons on low incomes with children, elderly persons on low incomes or persons in receipt of benefit relating to ill health. They provide for the introduction of new grants entitled Warm Homes and Warm Homes Plus, for a restriction on the categories of person who may apply for grant and on the tenure of applicants, for a wider set of purposes for which grant may be made and for an increase in the maximum amount of grant payable.

4939. Gas supply industry–internal market–licence conditions

GAS ORDER 1996 (AMENDMENT) REGULATIONS (NORTHERN IRELAND) 2002, SR 2002 291; made under the European Communities Act 1972 s.2. In force: October 16, 2002; £2.00.

These Regulations amend the Gas (Northern Ireland) Order 1996 (SI 1996 275) to ensure that it conforms with the requirements of Council Directive 98/30 ([1998] OJ L204/1) concerning common rules for the internal market in natural gas. They ensure consistency with the Directive as regards exclusive rights to carry on certain activities conferred by licence by making provision so as to automatically limit any exclusivity granted to a period of ten years; allowing for an extension of exclusivity by consent beyond the period of ten years where it is requisite or expedient to do so in the interests of the efficient operation of the activities in question; and providing for the granting of a licence authorising supply to certain customers through a direct line even though such supply would otherwise contravene the exclusive rights given to another licence holder. The Regulations require the inclusion of appropriate conditions in licences to ensure that the authorised activities comply with the requirements of the Directive and provide that no condition of a licence shall be modified in a manner inconsistent with the Directive.

ENVIRONMENT

4940. Air pollution–air quality reviews

AIR QUALITY LIMIT VALUES REGULATIONS (NORTHERN IRELAND) 2002, SR 2002 94; made under the European Communities Act 1972 s.2. In force: May 1, 2002; £4.00.

These Regulations, which revoke the Air Quality Standards Regulations (Northern Ireland) 1990 (SR 1990 145), are made in the implementation of Council Directive 96/62 ([1996] OJ L296/55) on ambient air quality assessment and management, and Council Directive 99/30 ([1999] OJ L163/41) relating to limit values for sulphur dioxide, nitrogen dioxide and oxides of nitrogen, particulate matter and lead in ambient air. They place a duty upon any relevant government department to ensure that in each zone in Northern Ireland concentrations of relevant pollutants do not exceed the limit values, require the Department of the Environment to assess ambient air quality in each zone and require the Department to classify each zone in relation to each of the relevant pollutants in accordance with the method required to assess air quality in that zone. The Regulations place a duty on the Department to review the classification of zones every five years or in the event of significant changes affecting levels of any of the relevant pollutants, require the Department to ensure that specified methods are used for assessing air quality for each pollutant in each zone and require the Department to draw up, after consultation with other relevant government departments, action plans indicating measures to be taken in the short term where there is a risk that limit values for any of the relevant pollutants, or alert thresholds for sulphur dioxide or nitrogen dioxide, will be exceeded. They also require the Department to draw up lists of zones where the levels of one or more of the relevant pollutants is above the limit value, or between the limit value and any margin of tolerance specified and require the Department to list zones where levels of the relevant pollutants are below limit values. In addition, the Regulations require the Department to ensure that up-to-date information on ambient concentrations of each of the relevant pollutants is routinely made available to the public.

4941. Air pollution–air quality reviews

AIR QUALITY LIMIT VALUES (AMENDMENT) REGULATIONS (NORTHERN IRELAND) 2002, SR 2002 357; made under the European Communities Act 1972 s.2. In force: December 13, 2002; £2.50.

These Regulations, which amend the Air Quality Limit Values Regulations (Northern Ireland) 2002 (SR 2002 94), are made in implementation of European Parliament and Council Directive 2000/69 ([2000] OJ L313/12) relating to limit values for benzene and carbon monoxide in ambient air and Council Directive 1996/62 ([1996] OJ L296/55) on ambient air quality assessment and management. They designate competent authorities for various air quality assessment and management functions and add benzene and carbon monoxide as "relevant pollutants".

4942. Air pollution–liquid fuels–sulphur content

SULPHUR CONTENT OF LIQUID FUELS REGULATIONS (NORTHERN IRELAND) 2002, SR 2002 28; made under the European Communities Act 1972 s.2. In force: March 11, 2002; £2.00.

These Regulations, which revoke the Marketing of Gas Oil (Sulphur Content) Regulations 1994 (SI 1994 2249), implement Council Directive 1/32 ([1] OJ L121/13) relating to a reduction in the sulphur content of certain liquid fuels and amending Directive 93/12. The Regulations make it an offence to use heavy fuel oil on or after January 1, 2003 with a sulphur content exceeding 1 per cent, subject to certain exceptions and make it an offence to use gas oil or marine gas oil on or after March 11, 2002 with a sulphur content exceeding 0.2 per cent by mass and to use such oil on or after January 1, 2008 with a sulphur content exceeding 0.1 per cent by mass. They require the Department to check by sampling that the sulphur content of fuels used complies with these requirements, provide for the granting of permits to enable an operator of a combustion plant who would not otherwise require a permit to operate the plant to apply for a permit so that he can take advantage of the exemptions to the restriction on the use of heavy fuel oil and set out requirements for the analysis of samples taken.

4943. Environment (Northern Ireland) Order 2002 (SI 2002 3153 (NI.7))

This Order amends the Public Health (Ireland) Act 1878, the Land Development Values (Compensation) Act (Northern Ireland) 1965, the Pollution Control and Local Government (Northern Ireland) Order 1978 (SI 1978 1049 (NI.19)), the Clean Air (Northern Ireland) Order 1981 (SI 1981 158 (NI.4)), the Nature Conservation and Amenity Lands (Northern Ireland) Order 1985 (SI 1985 170 (NI.1)), the Nature Conservation and Amenity Lands (Amendment) (Northern Ireland) Order 1989 (SI 1989 492 (NI.3)), the Environmental Protection Act 1990, the Planning (Northern Ireland) Order 1991 (SI 1991 1220 (NI.11)), the Merchant Shipping Act 1995, the Finance Act 1996, the Road Traffic Regulation (Northern Ireland) Order 1997 (SI 1997 276 (NI.2)), the Waste and Contaminated Land (Northern Ireland) Order 1997 (SI 1997 2778 (NI.19)), the Northern Ireland Act 1998, the Water (Northern Ireland) Order 1999 (SI 1999 662 (NI.6)) and revokes the Industrial Pollution Control (Northern Ireland) Order 1997 (SI 1997

2777 (NI.18)). The Order makes provision for the implementation of Council Directive 96/61 ([1996] OJ L257/26) concerning integrated pollution prevention and control.

4944. Environmental impact assessments–forestry projects–summary offences

ENVIRONMENTAL IMPACT ASSESSMENT (FORESTRY) (AMENDMENT) REGULATIONS (NORTHERN IRELAND) 2002, SR 2002 249; made under the European Communities Act 1972 s.2. In force: September 27, 2002; £1.50.

These Regulations correct two errors in the Environmental Impact Assessment (Forestry) Regulations (Northern Ireland) 2000 (SR 2000 84) so as to remove an erroneous reference and to correct the provision relating to fines in accordance with the terminology used for offences which are summary only.

4945. Environmental protection–biocidal products

BIOCIDAL PRODUCTS (AMENDMENT) REGULATIONS (NORTHERN IRELAND) 2002, SR 2002 302; made under the European Communities Act 1972 s.2; and the Health and Safety at Work (Northern Ireland) Order 1978 (SI 1978 1039 (NI.9)) Art.17, Art.40, Art.55, Sch.3 para.1, , Sch.3 para.3, Sch.3 para.12, Sch.3 para.14, Sch.3 para.15. In force: November 14, 2002; £1.75.

These Regulations amend the Biocidal Products Regulations (Northern Ireland) 2001 (SR 2001 422) to define the duty on any person using a biocidal product containing certain active substances; and to introduce a new provision explicitly to make a breach of that duty an offence. The Regulations clarify that, in any prosecution for breach of the duty under Reg.8(5), the onus lies on the prosecution to prove that the use of the product was not in accordance with the requirements of the duty.

4946. Environmental protection–waste–packaging

PRODUCER RESPONSIBILITY OBLIGATIONS (PACKAGING WASTE) (AMENDMENT) REGULATIONS (NORTHERN IRELAND) 2002, SR 2002 239; made under the Producer Responsibility Obligations (Northern Ireland) Order 1998 (SI 1998 1762 (NI.16)) Art.3, Art.4. In force: September 2, 2002; £1.75.

These Regulations amend the Producer Responsibility Obligations (Packaging Waste) Regulations (Northern Ireland) 1999 (SR 1999 115), which impose on producers obligations to recover and recycle packaging waste, and related obligations, by increasing from the year 2002 onwards, the recovery target used to calculate recovery obligations, to 59 per cent and the recycling target, used to calculate recycling obligations, to 19 per cent.

4947. Navigation–river Bann

RIVER BANN NAVIGATION ORDER (NORTHERN IRELAND) 2002, SR 2002 395; made under the Harbours Act (Northern Ireland) 1970 s.1, Sch.1 Part I, Sch.2. In force: February 17, 2003; £2.50.

This Order amends the Commissioners Clauses Act 1847, the Harbours, Docks and Piers Clauses Act 1847, the River Bann Navigation Act 1879, River Bann Navigation Act (Northern Ireland) 1927; the River Bann Navigation Act (Northern Ireland) 1938 the River Bann Navigation Act 1956 and the Local Government (Modification and Repeal of Transferred Provisions relating to Harbours) Order (Northern Ireland) 1973 (SR&O 1973 313) and revokes the River Bann Navigation Act 1879 (Amendment) Order (Northern Ireland) 1988 (SR 1988 286). It provides new limits of jurisdiction of the Coleraine Harbour Commissioners.

4948. Pollution control–noise pollution–codes of practice–construction works

CONTROL OF NOISE (CODES OF PRACTICE FOR CONSTRUCTION AND OPEN SITES) ORDER (NORTHERN IRELAND) 2002, SR 2002 303; made under the

Pollution Control and Local Government (Northern Ireland) Order 1978 (SI 1978 1049 (NI.19)) Art.51, Art.86. In force: November 1, 2002; £1.75.

Under the Pollution Control and Local Government (Northern Ireland) Order 1978 (SI 1978 1049 (NI.19)), the Department of the Environment may give guidance on appropriate methods for minimising noise, including vibration, by approving Codes of Practice. It is required to approve a Code for the carrying out of works to which Article 40 of the 1978 applies including building and roadworks, demolition, dredging and other works of engineering construction. This Order, which revokes the Control of Noise (Code of Practice for Construction Sites) Order (Northern Ireland) 1978 (SR 1978 349), approves four codes of practice.

4949. Waste and Contaminated Land (Northern Ireland) Order 1997 (SI 1997 2778 (NI.19))–Commencement No.6 Order

WASTE AND CONTAMINATED LAND (1997 ORDER) (COMMENCEMENT NO.6) ORDER (NORTHERN IRELAND) 2002, SR 2002 185; made under the Northern Ireland Act 1998 Sch.12 para.11; and the Waste and Contaminated Land (Northern Ireland) Order 1997 (SI 1997 2778 (NI.19)) Art.1. In force: bringing into operation various provisions of the 1997 Order on June 3, 2002; £1.75.

This Order brings into force a provision of the Waste and Contaminated Land (Northern Ireland) Order 1997 (SI 1997 2778 (NI.19)) which imposes a duty of care on anyone who imports, produces, carries, keeps, treats or disposes of controlled waste or, as a broker, has control of such waste and which enables the Department to make regulations in relation to the duty of care and issue a code of practice for the purpose of providing practical guidance on how to discharge the duty.

4950. Waste management–controlled waste–duty of care

CONTROLLED WASTE (DUTY OF CARE) REGULATIONS (NORTHERN IRELAND) 2002, SR 2002 271; made under the Waste and Contaminated Land (Northern Ireland) Order 1997 (SI 1997 2778 (NI.19)) Art.2, Art.5. In force: October 1, 2002; £1.75.

These Regulations, which amend the Controlled Waste Regulations (Northern Ireland) 2002 (SR 2002 248), require the transferor and the transferee to complete and sign a transfer note at the same time as the written description of the waste is transferred and require the transferor and the transferee to keep that description and the transfer note, or copies of them, for two years from the transfer. The Regulations impose a duty on a person who is under a duty to keep any document to furnish a copy of that document to the Department if he is required by notice to do so within the period specified in the notice.

4951. Waste management–controlled waste–household, industrial and commercial

CONTROLLED WASTE REGULATIONS (NORTHERN IRELAND) 2002, SR 2002 248; made under the Litter (Northern Ireland) Order 1994 (SI 1994 1896 (NI.10)) Art.17; and the Waste and Contaminated Land (Northern Ireland) Order 1997 (SI 1997 2778 (NI.19)) Art.2,, Art.4, Art.20. In force: August 27, 2002; £2.50.

The Waste and Contaminated Land (Northern Ireland) Order 1997 (SI 1997 2778 (NI. 19)) defines three sorts of controlled waste: household, industrial and commercial waste. These Regulations, which amend the Waste Collection and Disposal Regulations (Northern Ireland) 1992 (SR 1992 254), enable regulations to be made whereby waste of any description is to be treated for the purposes of the provisions of Part II as being of one or other of those categories. They provide for descriptions of waste to be treated as household waste; prescribe certain types of waste not to be treated as household waste; prescribe a number of cases where a charge may be made for the collection of household waste; prescribe certain types of waste to be treated as industrial waste; prescribe certain types of waste to be treated as commercial waste; and provide for certain types of litter to be treated as controlled waste

FAMILY LAW

4952. Adoption–intercountry adoption–rules

ADOPTION OF CHILDREN FROM OVERSEAS REGULATIONS (NORTHERN IRELAND) 2002, SR 2002 144; made under the Adoption (Northern Ireland) Order 1987 (SI 1987 2203 (NI.22)) Art.10, Art.58ZA. In force: May 13, 2002; £1.75.

These Regulations impose requirements with which a person who is habitually resident in the British Islands must comply before and after bringing a child who is habitually resident outside those Islands into the UK for the purpose of adoption. The prospective adopter is required to undergo assessment by an adoption agency, be approved as suitable to be an adoptive parent and have received notification from the Secretary of State for Health that he is willing to issue a certificate confirming that the prospective adopter has been assessed and approved and that the child will be authorised to reside permanently in the British Islands if entry clearance is granted and an adoption order is made. The prospective adopter is required to notify his Health and Social Services Trust of his intention to apply for an adoption order or, alternatively, that he does not intend to give the child a home, within 14 days after bringing the child into the UK. The Regulations also specify the procedure to be followed by an adoption agency and adoption panel in relation to assessment and approval of a person wishing to adopt a child from overseas, and require the provision of certain information to the Department of Health, Social Services and Public Safety.

4953. Adoption (Intercountry Aspects) Act (Northern Ireland) 2001 (c.11)–Commencement No.2 Order

ADOPTION (INTERCOUNTRY ASPECTS) ACT (NORTHERN IRELAND) 2001 (COMMENCEMENT NO.2) ORDER (NORTHERN IRELAND) 2002, SR 2002 22; made under the Adoption (Intercountry Aspects) Act (Northern Ireland) 2001 s.16. In force: bringing into operation various provisions of the 2001 Act on February 1, 2002; £1.50.

This Order brings into operation provisions of the Adoption (Intercountry Aspects) Act (Northern Ireland) 2001 and makes it an offence in Northern Ireland for anyone habitually resident in the British Islands other than a parent, relative or guardian to bring a child into the UK unless they meet the specified requirements.

4954. Adoption (Intercountry Aspects) Act (Northern Ireland) 2001 (c.11)–Commencement No.3 Order

ADOPTION (INTERCOUNTRY ASPECTS) ACT (NORTHERN IRELAND) 2001 (COMMENCEMENT NO.3) ORDER (NORTHERN IRELAND) 2002, SR 2002 45; made under the Adoption (Intercountry Aspects) Act (Northern Ireland) 2001 s.16. In force: bringing into operation various provisions of the 2001 Act on February 22, 2002; £1.75.

This Order brings into operation the remaining provisions of the Adoption (Intercountry Aspects) Act (Northern Ireland) 2001 not already in operation.

4955. Child support–maintenance orders–jurisdiction of courts–appeals

CHILD SUPPORT APPEALS (JURISDICTION OF COURTS) ORDER (NORTHERN IRELAND) 2002, SR 2002 391; made under the Child Support (Northern Ireland) Order 1991 (SI 1991 2628 (NI.23)) Art.42. In force: in accordance with Art.1 (2) (3); £1.75.

This Order, which amends the Child Support Appeals (Jurisdiction of Courts) Order (Northern Ireland) 1993 (SR1993104), provides for child support appeals to be made to a court of summary jurisdiction, rather than an appeal tribunal, where the issue in the appeal is the parentage of the qualifying child in relation to whom an application for child support maintenance. This Order further provides for the application of certain provisions of the Social Security and Child Support (Decisions and Appeals) Regulations (Northern Ireland) 1 (SR 1 162), to those appeals that are made to a court of summary jurisdiction.

4956. Children–secure accommodation–absconding–relevant considerations

[Children (Northern Ireland) Order 1995 (SI 1995 755) Art.44(7); Human Rights Act 1998 Sch.1 Part I Art.5, Art.6.]

N applied for a secure accommodation order in respect of DH, who was aged 16 years and five months. DH had been the subject of previous secure accommodation orders because he had a history of absconding and there was also a likelihood of significant harm due to drug and solvent abuse and his association with an older female. DH had absconded three times since he was placed in secure accommodation and was still absent on the day of the hearing, although his legal representative and guardian ad litem attended. N submitted that the circumstances of the instant case were exceptional as DH would lose his secure accommodation place without the order. The guardian supported the application on the basis that it would assist DH's transition from care.

Held, adjourning the application with liberty to apply in the future, that the fact of DH's absconding did not amount to an exceptional circumstance. The Children (Northern Ireland) Order 1995 Art.44(7) required that children should be available to give instructions such an application and there was nothing in the Order that allowed the court to proceed on the basis of findings made at previous hearings. Proceeding in DH's absence would be contrary to the Human Rights Act 1998 Sch.1 Part I Art.6, as well as raising issues concerned with his right to liberty under Art.5.

NORTH AND WEST BELFAST HEALTH AND SOCIAL SERVICES TRUST v. DH [2001] N.I. 351, Higgins, J., Fam Div (NI).

4957. Children (Leaving Care) Act (Northern Ireland) 2002 (c.11)

This Act makes provision about children and young persons who are being, or have been, looked after by an authority within the meaning of the Children (Northern Ireland) Order 1995; and replaces Art.35 of that Order.

4958. County courts–proof of parentage–blood tests

COUNTY COURT (BLOOD TESTS) (AMENDMENT) RULES (NORTHERN IRELAND) 2002, SR 2002 240; made under the County Courts (Northern Ireland) Order 1980 (SI 1980 397 (NI.3)) Art.47. In force: August 12, 2002; £1.75.

These Rules amend the County Court (Blood Tests) Rules (Northern Ireland) 1978 (SR 1978 378) to take account of recent amendments made to the Family Law Reform (Northern Ireland) Order 1977 (SI 1977 1250 (NI.17)) Part III, by the Family Law Act (Northern Ireland) 2001. The amendments make it possible for samples to be taken of bodily fluid and bodily tissue rather than simply blood, and for scientific tests to be used to determine whether a person is the mother of the person whose parentage falls to be determined, as well as whether a person is the father.

4959. Family Law Act (Northern Ireland) 2001 (c.12)–Commencement Order

FAMILY LAW (2001 ACT) (COMMENCEMENT) ORDER (NORTHERN IRELAND) 2002, SR 2002 138; made under the Family Law Act (Northern Ireland) 2001 s.4. In force: bringing into operation various provisions the 2001 Act on April 8, 2002 and April 15, 2002; £1.50.

This Order provides for the coming into force of the Family Law Act (Northern Ireland) 2001 s.3, concerning the taking and testing of bodily samples in civil proceedings where a child's parentage is in dispute, to coincide with the commencement of specified provisions of the Child Support, Pensions and

Social Security Act (Northern Ireland) 2000 which also makes provision in relation to declarations of parentage.

4960. Family proceedings–allocation of proceedings

DECLARATIONS OF PARENTAGE (ALLOCATION OF PROCEEDINGS) ORDER (NORTHERN IRELAND) 2002, SR 2002 119; made under the Children (Northern Ireland) Order 1995 (SI 1995 755 (NI.2)) Art.164, Sch.7. In force: April 15, 2002; £2.00.

This Order provides for the commencement and transfer of proceedings under the Matrimonial and Family Proceedings (Northern Ireland) Order 1989 (SI 1989 677 (NI.4)) Art.31B. That Article combines proceedings under the 1989 Order and proceedings under the former Child Support (Northern Ireland) Order 1991 (SI 1991 2628 (NI.23)) Art.28. It will be possible to begin proceedings under the 1989 Order Article 31B in a court of summary jurisdiction.

4961. Family proceedings–allocation of proceedings–juvenile courts

CHILDREN (ALLOCATION OF PROCEEDINGS) (AMENDMENT) ORDER (NORTHERN IRELAND) 2002, SR 2002 350; made under the Children (Northern Ireland) Order 1995 (SI 1995 755 (NI.2)) Art.164, Sch.7. In force: December 9, 2002; £1.50.

This Order, which amends the Children (Allocation of Proceedings) Order (Northern Ireland) 1996 (SR 1996 300), provides for the allocation of proceedings by designating the juvenile court for the petty sessions district of East Tyrone as a family proceedings court, in place of the juvenile court for the petty sessions district of Omagh.

4962. Family proceedings–declarations of parentage–magistrates courts

MAGISTRATES' COURTS (DECLARATIONS OF PARENTAGE) RULES (NORTHERN IRELAND) 2002, SR 2002 158; made under the Magistrates' Courts (Northern Ireland) Order 1981 (SI 1981 1675 (NI.26)) Art.13. In force: May 20, 2002; £3.50.

These Rules prescribe the procedure to be followed in magistrates' courts on applications for declarations of parentage under the Matrimonial and Family Proceedings (Northern Ireland) Order 1989 (SI 1989 677 (NI.4)).

4963. Family proceedings–fees

FAMILY PROCEEDINGS FEES (AMENDMENT) ORDER (NORTHERN IRELAND) 2002, SR 2002 344; made under the Judicature (Northern Ireland) Act 1978 s.116. In force: in accordance with Art.1; £2.00.

This Order amends the Family Proceedings Fees Order (Northern Ireland) 1996 (SR 1996 495) to increase a number of the fees to be taken in family proceedings in the High Court and county courts; and allow fees to be taken by a range of payment methods, including credit or debit card.

4964. Family proceedings–fees

See FAMILY LAW. §4963

4965. Family proceedings–proof of parentage–blood tests

BLOOD TESTS (EVIDENCE OF PATERNITY) (AMENDMENT) REGULATIONS (NORTHERN IRELAND) 2002, SR 2002 150; made under the Family Law Reform (Northern Ireland) Order 1977 (SI 1977 1250 (NI.17)) Art.10. In force: May 7, 2002; £1.75.

These Regulations amend the Blood Tests (Evidence of Paternity) Regulations (Northern Ireland) 1978 (SR 1978 379), to make it possible for samples to be taken of bodily tissue and bodily fluid other than blood and for scientific tests to be used to establish whether a person is the mother of the person whose parentage falls to be determined, as well as whether a person is the father. They provide that tests are to be carried out by an accredited body, rather than a named individual and lay down the conditions which a body must meet if it is to be accredited. They also reflect the courts' new jurisdiction to order that a sample be taken from a person under 16, where it would be in his best interests for the sample to be taken, even though the person with care and control of him does not consent.

4966.   Family proceedings–rules–applications procedure

FAMILY PROCEEDINGS (AMENDMENT) RULES (NORTHERN IRELAND) 2002, SR 2002 137; made under the Family Law (Northern Ireland) Order 1993 (SI 1993 1576 (NI.6)) Art.12. In force: May 6, 2002; £3.00.

These Regulations, which amend the Family Proceedings Rules (Northern Ireland) 1996 (SR 1996 322), prescribe the procedure for applications under the Matrimonial and Family Proceedings (Northern Ireland) Order 1989 (SI 1989 677 (NI.4)) and give effect to Council Regulation 1347/2000 ([2000] OJ L160/19) on jurisdiction and the recognition and enforcement of judgments in matrimonial matters and in matters of parental responsibility for children of both spouses.

4967.   Magistrates courts–proof of parentage–blood tests

MAGISTRATES' COURTS (BLOOD TESTS) (AMENDMENT) RULES (NORTHERN IRELAND) 2002, SR 2002 163; made under the Magistrates' Courts (Northern Ireland) Order 1981 (SI 1981 1675 (NI.26)) Art.13. In force: May 20, 2002; £1.75.

These Rules amend the Magistrates' Courts (Blood Tests) Rules (Northern Ireland) 1978 (SR 1978 376) to give effect to amendments made to the Family Law Reform (Northern Ireland) Order 1977 (SI 1977 1250 (NI.17)) by the Child Support, Pensions and Social Security Act (Northern Ireland) 2000 and the Family Law Act (Northern Ireland) 2001. The amendments make it possible for samples to be taken of bodily tissue and bodily fluid other than blood and for scientific tests to be used to establish whether a person is the mother of the person whose parentage falls to be determined as well as whether a person is the father.

FISHERIES

4968.   Fishing–byelaws–amendments

FISHERIES (AMENDMENT) BYELAWS (NORTHERN IRELAND) 2002, SR 2002 11; made under the Fisheries Act (Northern Ireland) 1966 s.26. In force: March 1, 2002; £1.75.

These Byelaws amend the Fisheries Byelaws (Northern Ireland) 1997 (SR 1997 425) by inserting a new Part XIX requiring any person who takes a salmon whilst angling during the period from March 1 to May 31 to return it immediately to the water from which it was taken without avoidable injury. The Regulations also require any person who takes a salmon in excess of two on any day during the period from June 1 to the start of the annual close season to return it immediately to the water from which it was taken without avoidable injury.

4969.   Fishing–byelaws–amendments

FISHERIES (AMENDMENT NO.2) BYELAWS (NORTHERN IRELAND) 2002, SR 2002 274; made under the Fisheries Act (Northern Ireland) 1966 s.26, s.37, s.70. In force: October 1, 2002; £1.75.

These Byelaws amend the Fisheries Byelaws (Northern Ireland) 1997 (SR 1997 425) by prohibiting the Fisheries Conservancy Board for Northern Ireland issuing a drift net licence in a case where a person who held a drift net licence has undertaken, in consideration of compensation paid or payable by the Department of Culture, Arts and Leisure to make no further applications for a fishing licence to use a drift net to fish for salmon or sea trout; and reducing the maximum number of tidal draft net licences which may be issued in any calendar year from six to two. They also make amendments by requiring the Board to revoke a fishing licence or to refuse to renew a fishing licence where, in consideration of compensation paid or payable by the Department, the person who held it consented to its revocation.

4970. Fishing–byelaws–amendments

FISHERIES (AMENDMENT NO.3) BYELAWS (NORTHERN IRELAND) 2002, SR 2002 371; made under the Fisheries Act (Northern Ireland) 1966 s.26, s.37. In force: January 1, 2003; £1.75.

These Byelaws amend the Fisheries Byelaws (Northern Ireland) 1997 (SR 1997 425) to introduce a concessionary season fishing rod licence for disabled anglers, women who have attained the age of 60 years and men who have attained the age of 65 years, and a juvenile season fishing rod licence for persons who have attained the age of 12 years but not 19 years.

4971. Fishing–enforcement of Community quotas

See FISHERIES. §1740

4972. Fishing–gill tags–logbooks–byelaws

FISHERIES (TAGGING AND LOGBOOK) (AMENDMENT) BYELAWS (NORTHERN IRELAND) 2002, SR 2002 372; made under the Fisheries Act (Northern Ireland) 1966 s.26, s.37. In force: January 1, 2003; £1.75.

These Byelaws amend the Fisheries (Tagging and Logbook) Byelaws (Northern Ireland) 2001 (SR 2001 291) by amending the definition of "game fishing rod licence" so that it also includes concessionary and juvenile season fishing rod licences, deleting the definition of "one day angling logbook", and inserting a definition of "three day angling logbook"; replacing references to "one day angling logbook" with references to "three day angling logbook"; and replacing the format of the one day angling logbook.

4973. Fishing–transfer of functions

SEA FISHERIES (NORTHERN IRELAND) ORDER 2002, SI 2002 790; made under the Northern Ireland Act 1998 s.6, s.86. In force: March 28, 2002; £2.50.

This Order amends the Sea Fish Industry Act 1962, the Fisheries Act (Northern Ireland) 1966, the Sea Fisheries Act 1968, the Fishery Limits Act 1976, the Fisheries Act 1981, the Fisheries Amendment Order (Northern Ireland) 1981 (SI 1981 227) and the British Fishing Boats Act 1983. It transfers to the Department of Agriculture and Rural Development functions relating to sea fishing in the Northern Ireland zone and sea fishing by Northern Ireland fishing boats.

4974. Fishing industry–grants

FISHERIES AND AQUACULTURE STRUCTURES (GRANTS) REGULATIONS (NORTHERN IRELAND) 2002, SR 2002 6; made under the European Communities Act 1972 s.2. In force: February 25, 2002; £3.00.

These Regulations provide for and regulate the payment of grants and Community aid by the Department of Agriculture and Rural Development and the Department of Culture, Arts and Leisure towards expenditure in respect of relevant operations. The grants and Community aid are payable by the Department of Culture, Arts and Leisure in the case of aquaculture investments in inland waters and by the Department of Agriculture and Rural Development in the case of all other relevant operations approved in accordance with these Regulations and the Community legislation.

4975. Infectious disease control–fish

DISEASES OF FISH (CONTROL) (AMENDMENT) REGULATIONS (NORTHERN IRELAND) 2002, SR 2002 53; made under the European Communities Act 1972 s.2. In force: March 10, 2002; £2.00.

These Regulations amend the Diseases of Fish (Control) Regulations (Northern Ireland) 1996 (SR 1996 16) in implementation of Council Directive 2000/27 ([2000] OJ L114/28) amending Council Directive 93/53 ([1993] OJ L175/23) introducing minimum Community measures for the control of certain fish diseases. They allow fish on a farm which has been confirmed as having infectious salmon anaemis (ISA) to be withdrawn in accordance with the scheme and enable the vaccination of fish against ISA if so authorised by the Minister.

4976. Shellfish–emergency prohibitions–amnesic shellfish poisoning–scallops

See FOOD. §4983

4977. Shellfish–emergency prohibitions–diarrhetic shellfish poisoning–scallops

See FOOD. §4984

FOOD

4978. Animal products–feedingstuffs–import controls–China

FOOD AND ANIMAL FEEDINGSTUFFS (PRODUCTS OF ANIMAL ORIGIN FROM CHINA) (CONTROL) REGULATIONS (NORTHERN IRELAND) 2002, SR 2002 33; made under the European Communities Act 1972 s.2. In force: February 8, 2002; £2.00.

These Regulations implement Commission Decision 2002/69 ([2002] OJ L30/50) concerning certain protective measures with regard to products of animal origin imported from China. The Regulations define "relevant product of animal origin", prohibit their importation, specify the enforcement authorities and apply with modifications certain provisions of the Food Safety (Northern Ireland) Order 1991 (SI 1991 762).

4979. Food composition–food for particular nutritional uses–specific nutritional purposes

FOOD FOR PARTICULAR NUTRITIONAL USES (ADDITION OF SUBSTANCES FOR SPECIFIC NUTRITIONAL PURPOSES) REGULATIONS (NORTHERN IRELAND) 2002, SR 2002 264; made under the Food Safety (Northern Ireland) Order 1991 (SI 1991 762 (NI.7)) Art.15, Art.16, Art.25, Art.26, Art.47. In force: in accordance with Reg.1 (2)(3); £2.50.

These Regulations, which amend the Tryptophan in Food Regulations (Northern Ireland) 1990 (SR 1990 329), implement Commission Directive 2001/15 ([2001] OJ L52/19) on substances that may be added for specific nutritional purposes in foods for particular nutritional uses. The Regulations concern food for most particular nutritional uses where there has been added to that food for a specific nutritional purpose a substance falling within one of the following categories: vitamins; minerals; amino acids; carnitine and taurine; nucleotides, choline and inositol. They prohibit the sale of such food unless the substance is listed under the relevant category in Sch.1 or, in the case of foods for special medical purposes, is listed under the relevant category in either Sch.1 or Sch.2. The Regulations impose general restrictions on the sale of designated PNU foods in the manufacture of which any substances have been used for specific nutritional purposes and require the manufacturer or importer to supply the Food Standards Agency with information on request to verify that those restrictions are met. They also make provision as to responsibility for enforcement; create offences and penalties; apply certain provisions of the Food Safety (Northern Ireland) Order 1991 (SI 1991 762 (NI.7)); and provide a defence in relation to exports in accordance with Council Directive 89/397 ([1989] OJ L186/23) on the official control of foodstuffs.

4980. Food safety–additives–sweeteners

SWEETENERS IN FOOD (AMENDMENT) REGULATIONS (NORTHERN IRELAND) 2002, SR 2002 39; made under the Food Safety (Northern Ireland) Order 1991 (SI 1991 762 (NI.7)) Art.15, Art.16, Art.25, Art.26, Art.47, Sch.1 para.1. In force: March 8, 2002; £2.00.

These Regulations amend the Sweeteners in Food Regulations (Northern Ireland) 1996 (SR 1996 48) by bringing up to date the definition of "Directive 95/31" so as to cover its amendment by Directive 2000/51 ([2000] OJ L198/41) in so far as that Directive substituted new specifications for maltitol syrup and by Directive 2001/52 ([2001] OJ L1190/18) to substitute new purity criteria for mannitol and acesulfame K. They also grant provisional authorisation for the marketing and use as a sweetener of sucralose, as permitted by Directive 89/107 ([1989] OJ L140/27) on the approximation of the laws of Member States concerning food additives authorised for use in foodstuffs intended for human consumption.

4981. Food safety–contaminants–maximum levels

CONTAMINANTS IN FOOD REGULATIONS (NORTHERN IRELAND) 2002, SR 2002 219; made under the Food Safety (Northern Ireland) Order 1991 (SI 1991 762 (NI.7)) Art.15, Art.16, Art.25, Art.26, Art.47. In force: July 29, 2002; £2.50.

These Regulations, which revoke the Lead in Food Regulations Northern Ireland) 1979 (SR 1979 407), the Lead in Food (Amendment) Regulations (Northern Ireland) 1985 (SR 1985 163), the Contaminants in Food Regulations (Northern Ireland) 1997 (SR 1997 338) and the Contaminants in Food (Amendment) Regulations (Northern Ireland) 1999 (SR 1999 302), amend the Food (Revision of Penalties and Mode of Trial) Regulations (Northern Ireland) 1987 (SR 1987 38), the Food Safety (Northern Ireland) Order 1991 (Consequential Modifications) Order (Northern Ireland) 1991 (SR 1991 203), the Food Safety (Exports) Regulations (Northern Ireland) 1991 (SR 1991 344), the Flavourings in Food Regulations (Northern Ireland) 1992 (SR 1992 416), the Colours in Food Regulations (Northern Ireland) 1996 (SR 1996 49) and the Food (Miscellaneous Revocations and Amendments) Regulations (Northern Ireland) 1996 (SR 1996 53). They make provision for the enforcement of Commission Regulation 466/2001 ([2001] OJ L77/1) setting maximum levels for certain contaminants in foodstuffs; implement Commission Directive 98/53 [1998] OJ L201/93) laying down sampling and analysis methods for the official control of the levels for certain contaminants of foodstuffs; Commission Directive 2001/22 ([2001] OJ L77/14) laying down the sampling methods and the methods of analysis for the official control of the levels of lead, cadmium, mercury and 3-MPCD in foodstuffs; Commission Directive 2002/26 ([2002] OJ L75/38) laying down the sampling methods and the methods of analysis for the official control of the levels of ochratoxin A in foodstuffs; and Commission Directive 2002/27 ([2002] OJ L75/44) amending Directive 98/53 laying down the sampling methods and the methods of analysis for the official control of the levels for certain contaminants in foodstuffs. The Regulations provide that it is an offence to place on the market certain foods if they contain contaminants of any kind specified in the Commission Regulation at levels exceeding those specified; to use foods containing such contaminants at such levels as ingredients in the production of certain foods; to mix foods which comply with the maximum levels referred to above with foods which do not; to mix foods to which the Commission Regulation relates and which are intended for direct consumption with foods to which the Commission Regulation relates and which are intended to be sorted or otherwise treated prior to consumption; and to detoxify by chemical treatments, food not complying with the limits specified in the Commission Regulation. In addition, the Regulations specify the enforcement authorities.

4982. Food safety–contaminants–maximum levels

CONTAMINANTS IN FOOD (AMENDMENT) REGULATIONS (NORTHERN IRELAND) 2002, SR 2002 262; made under the Food Safety (Northern Ireland) Order 1991 (SI 1991 762 (NI.7)) Art.15, Art.16, Art.25, Art.26, Art.47. In force: August 8, 2002; £1.75.

These Regulations amend the Contaminants in Food Regulations (Northern Ireland) 2002 (SR 2002 219), which make provision for the execution and enforcement of Commission Regulation 466/2001 ([2001] OJ L77/1) setting maximum levels for certain contaminants in foodstuffs. They also amend the definition of the "Commission Regulation" correcting the error made in Commission Regulation 563/2002 ([2002] OJ L155/63) amending Regulation 466/2001 setting maximum levels for certain contaminants in foodstuffs.

4983. Food safety–emergency prohibitions–amnesic shellfish poisoning–scallops

FOOD PROTECTION (EMERGENCY PROHIBITIONS) ORDER (NORTHERN IRELAND) 2002, SR 2002 339; made under the Food and Environment Protection Act 1985 s.1, s.24. In force: November 6, 2002; £1.75.

This Order contains emergency prohibitions restricting various activities in order to prevent human consumption of scallops or food which is derived from scallops originating in the specified area. It designates areas of sea within which fishing for or taking scallops is prohibited and prohibits the movement of scallops out of these areas.

4984. Food safety–emergency prohibitions–diarrhetic shellfish poisoning–scallops

FOOD PROTECTION (EMERGENCY PROHIBITIONS) (REVOCATION) ORDER (NORTHERN IRELAND) 2002, SR 2002 370; made under the Food and Environment Protection Act 1985 s.1, s.24. In force: December 2, 2002; £1.50.

This Order revokes the Food Protection (Emergency Prohibitions) Order (Northern Ireland) 2002 (SR 2002 339) which contains emergency prohibitions restricting various activities to prevent human consumption of scallops or food derived from scallops originating in that part of ICES (International Council for the Exploration of the Sea) Area VIIA within British fishery limits and adjacent to Northern Ireland.

4985. Food safety–food hygiene–meat products–hazard analysis and critical control point

MEAT (HAZARD ANALYSIS AND CRITICAL CONTROL POINT) REGULATIONS (NORTHERN IRELAND) 2002, SR 2002 217; made under the European Communities Act 1972 s.2; and the Food Safety (Northern Ireland) Order 1991 (SI 1991 762 (NI.7)) Art.15, Art.16. In force: in accordance with Reg.2; £2.50.

These Regulations, which amend the Poultry Meat, Farmed Game Bird Meat and Rabbit Meat (Hygiene and Inspection) Regulations (Northern Ireland) 1995 (SR 1995 396) and the Fresh Meat (Hygiene and Inspection) Regulations (Northern Ireland) 1997 (SR 1997 493), implement Commission Decision 2001/471 ([2001] OJ L165/48) laying down rules for the regular checks on the general general hygiene carried out by the operators in establishments according to Directive 64/433 on health conditions for the production and marketing of fresh meat and Directive 71/118 ([1971] OJ L55/23) on health problems affecting the production and placing on the market of fresh poultry meat.

4986. Food safety–imports–star anise–emergency controls

FOOD (STAR ANISE FROM THIRD COUNTRIES) (EMERGENCY CONTROL) ORDER (NORTHERN IRELAND) 2002, SR 2002 82; made under the Food Safety (Northern Ireland) Order 1991 (SI 1991 762 (NI.7)) Art.12, Art.26, Art.47. In force: March 7, 2002; £2.00.

This Order is made in consequence of it appearing to the Department of Health, Social Services and Public Safety that the importation of certain Star Anise consigned from countries which are not Member States of the European Community may involve imminent risk of injury to health. The Order, which implements Commission Decision 2002/75 ([2002] OJ L33/31) laying down special conditions on the import from third countries of Star Anise, prohibits the importation of "Star Anise for human consumption" consigned from countries which are not Member States of the European Community except where it is accompanied by health certificates completed by the competent authority of the exporting third country and a report on the results of official sampling and analysis undertaken in that country, the importation takes place only through specified points of entry and the consignment is identified with a code corresponding with that specified on the health certificate and in the sampling and analysis results. It also prohibits the importation of "Japanese Star Anise" intended for human consumption or which is not labelled to the effect that it is unfit for such use.

4987. Food safety–packaging–plastics

PLASTIC MATERIALS AND ARTICLES IN CONTACT WITH FOOD (AMENDMENT) REGULATIONS (NORTHERN IRELAND) 2002, SR 2002 316; made under the Food Safety (Northern Ireland) Order 1991 (SI 1991 762 (NI.7)) Art.15, Art.16, Art.25, Art.32, Art.47. In force: November 30, 2002; £5.50.

These Regulations, which amend the Plastic Materials and Articles in Contact with Food Regulations (Northern Ireland) 1998 (SR 1998 264), implement Commission Directive 2001/62 ([2001] OJ L221/18) amending Directive 90/128 relating to plastic materials and articles intended to come into contact with foodstuffs; Commission Directive 2002/16 ([2002] OJ L51/27) on the use of certain epoxy derivatives in materials and articles intended to come into contact with foodstuffs; and Commission Directive 2002/17 ([2002] OJ L58/19) amending Directive 90/128 relating to plastic materials and articles intended to come into contact with foodstuffs. They also reflect the revocation of Commission Directive 90/128 ([1990] OJ L75/19) relating to plastic materials and articles intended to come into contact with foodstuffs and add a provision declaring that, in addition to regulating the contact with food of certain types of plastic materials and articles, the 1998 Regulations now also include provisions which regulate the contact with food of certain other types of food contact materials, namely adhesives and materials or articles covered by surface coatings.

4988. Imports–emergency controls–figs, hazelnuts and pistachios from Turkey

FOOD (FIGS, HAZELNUTS AND PISTACHIOS FROM TURKEY) (EMERGENCY CONTROL) REGULATIONS (NORTHERN IRELAND) 2002, SR 2002 140; made under the European Communities Act 1972 s.2. In force: April 11, 2002; £2.00.

These Regulations, which implement Commission Decision 2002/80 ([2002] OJ L34/26) imposing special conditions on the import of figs, hazelnuts and pistachios and certain products derived thereof originating in or consigned from Turkey, prohibit the importation of any controlled Turkish products except where they are accompanied by a Turkish Government health certificate and the results of official sampling and analysis, the importation takes place only through a specified point of entry, and the consignment is identified with a code corresponding with that specified on the health certificate and on the accompanying report containing the sampling and analysis results or if they left Turkey before March 11, 2002. They also specify the enforcement authorities and apply, with modifications, provisions of the Food Safety (Northern Ireland) Order 1991 (SI 1991 762 (NI.7)).

4989. Imports–emergency controls–figs, hazelnuts and pistachios from Turkey

FOOD (FIGS, HAZELNUTS AND PISTACHIOS FROM TURKEY) (EMERGENCY CONTROL NO.2) REGULATIONS (NORTHERN IRELAND) 2002, SR 2002 307; made under the European Communities Act 1972 s.2. In force: October 4, 2002; £2.00.

These Regulations, which revoke the Food (Figs, Hazelnuts and Pistachios from Turkey) (Emergency Control) Regulations (Northern Ireland) 2002 (SR 2002 140), implement Commission Decision 2002/80 ([2002] OJ L34/26) imposing special conditions on the import of figs, hazelnuts and pistachios and certain products derived thereof originating in or consigned from Turkey. They prohibit the importation of any controlled Turkish products except where they are accompanied by a Turkish Government health certificate and the results of official sampling and analysis, the importation takes place only through a specified point of entry, and the consignment is identified with a code corresponding with that specified on the health certificate and on the accompanying report containing the sampling and analysis results or if they left Turkey before March 11, 2002. They also specify the enforcement authorities and apply with modifications certain provisions of the Food Safety (Northern Ireland) Order 1991 for the purposes of the Regulations and provide for sampling and analysis. These Regulations amend the definition of Turkish figs, hazelnuts and pistachios to remove fresh figs and include fig paste and hazelnut paste; provide that the previous requirement that consignments of Turkish figs, hazelnuts and pistachios be subjected random sampling and analysis in order to ensure compliance with Commission Decision 2002/80 is modified; provide that the sampling procedure for hazelnuts is modified; and an authorised officer of a food authority is empowered to issue a notice ordering the re-dispatch or destruction of illegal imports of Turkish figs, hazelnuts and pistachios.

4990. Imports–emergency controls–jelly confectionery

FOOD (JELLY CONFECTIONERY) (EMERGENCY CONTROL) REGULATIONS (NORTHERN IRELAND) 2002, SR 2002 141; made under the European Communities Act 1972 s.2. In force: April 11, 2002; £2.00.

These Regulations, which implement Commission Decision 2002/24 ([2002] OJ L84/69) suspending the placing on the market and import of jelly confectionery containing the food additive E425: Konjac, prohibit the carrying out of commercial operations with regard to jelly confectionery which contains the food additive E425: Konjac and which is intended for human consumption and also the use of that additive in the manufacture of jelly confectionery intended for human consumption. The Regulations also specify the enforcement authority and make consequential provisions relating to the execution and enforcement of the Regulations by that authority and apply, with modifications, provisions of the Food Safety (Northern Ireland) Order 1991 (SI 1991 762 (NI.7)).

4991. Imports–emergency controls–peanuts from China

FOOD (PEANUTS FROM CHINA) (EMERGENCY CONTROL) REGULATIONS (NORTHERN IRELAND) 2002, SR 2002 293; made under the European Communities Act 1972 s.2. In force: September 23, 2002; £2.00.

These Regulations, implement Commission Decision 2002/79 ([2002] OJ L34/21) imposing special conditions on the import of peanuts and certain products derived from peanuts originating in, or consigned from China. The Regulations prohibit the importation of "Chinese peanuts" except where they are accompanied by a Chinese Government health certificate and the results of official sampling and analysis, the importation takes place only through a specified point of entry and the consignment and each of its constituent bags or other containers are identified with a code corresponding with that specified on the health certificate and on the accompanying report containing the sampling and analysis results; or they left China before March 11, 2002; specify the enforcement authority and its duties; and apply certain provisions of the Food Safety (Northern Ireland) Order 1991 (SI 1991 762 (NI.7)).

4992. Marketing—food for particular nutritional uses

NOTIFICATION OF MARKETING OF FOOD FOR PARTICULAR NUTRITIONAL USES REGULATIONS (NORTHERN IRELAND) 2002, SR 2002 35; made under the Food Safety (Northern Ireland) Order 1991 (SI 1991 762 (NI.7)) Art.16, Art.25, Art.26, Art.47. In force: March 8, 2002; £1.75.

These Regulations implement Council Directive 89/398 ([1989] OJ L186/27) Article 9 on the approximation of the laws of the Member States relating to foodstuffs intended for particular nutritional uses. The Regulations concern foods which, owing to their special composition or manufacturing process, are clearly distinguishable from foods for normal consumption, and which are marketed as suitable for categories of consumers with disturbed digestive processes or metabolism or in a special physiological condition, or for infants or young children in good health, but which are neither covered nor to be covered by other Directives on specific types of foodstuffs for particular nutritional uses.

FORESTRY

4993. Forests—reproductive material—marketing

FOREST REPRODUCTIVE MATERIAL REGULATIONS (NORTHERN IRELAND) 2002, SR 2002 404; made under the Seeds Act (Northern Ireland) 1965 s.1, s.2; and the European Communities Act 1972 s.2. In force: January 1, 2003; £6.00.

These Regulations, which revoke the Forest Reproductive Material Regulations 1977 (SR 1977 194) and the Forest Reproductive Material (Amendment) Regulations (SI 1993 197), implement Council Directive 1/105 ([2002] OJ L11/17) on the marketing of forest reproductive material.

4994. Environmental impact assessments—forestry projects—summary offences

See ENVIRONMENT. §4944

GOVERNMENT ADMINISTRATION

4995. Assembly members—winding up allowances

ALLOWANCES TO MEMBERS OF THE ASSEMBLY (WINDING UP ALLOWANCE) (AMENDMENT) ORDER (NORTHERN IRELAND) 2002, SR 2002 230; made under the Allowances to Members of the Assembly Act (Northern Ireland) 2000 s.3. In force: June 26, 2002; £1.50.

This Order, which amends the Allowances to Members of the Assembly Act (Northern Ireland) 2000, increases the maximum ceiling of the Winding Up allowance from £11,617 to £16,000.

4996. Ministerial functions—transfer and modification

NORTHERN IRELAND ACT 1998 (MODIFICATION OF ENACTMENTS) ORDER 2002, SI 2002 2843; made under the Northern Ireland Act 1998 s.86. In force: November 21, 2002; £2.00.

This Order, which amends the Plant Varieties and Seeds Act 1964, provides for the transfer of functions and the modification of certain enactments in consequence of the Northern Ireland Act 1998.

4997. Ministers–nomination–refusal to nominate Sinn Fein ministers to sit on North-South Ministerial Council–wrongful exercise of discretionary power

[Northern Ireland Act 1998 s.52.]

T, the First Minister of the Northern Ireland Assembly, refused to nominate D and M, respectively the Minister for Health, Social Services and Public Safety and the Minister for Education as members of the North-South Ministerial Council so that they could take part in discussions relating to their portfolios. T's purpose in refusing to nominate D and M was to put pressure on SF, the party to which D and M belonged, to use its best efforts to secure arms decommissioning, as provided for by the Belfast Agreement. The Northern Ireland Act 1998 s.52 required T and S, the deputy First Minister, to nominate the ministers they considered necessary to ensure proper cross community participation in the Council and the Ministerial Code, as approved by the Assembly, stipulated that T and S would usually nominate the minister with executive responsibility that corresponded to the matter to be discussed by the Council. D and M were successful in challenging T's decision by way of judicial review and T appealed against the first instance decision that his refusal to nominate them was unlawful.

Held, dismissing the appeal, that the wording of the Ministerial Code showed that T was not obliged to nominate the actual minister with corresponding executive responsibility in every case. However, the judge below had correctly determined that T's refusal was a wrongful exercise of his discretion under s.52 as arms decommissioning was not an overriding objective of the Act which T could seek to further in this way.

DE BRUN'S APPLICATION FOR JUDICIAL REVIEW, *Re* [2001] N.I. 442, Carswell, L.C.J., CA (NI).

4998. Northern Ireland–modification

NORTHERN IRELAND ACT 1998 (MODIFICATION) ORDER 2002, SI 2002 265; made under the Northern Ireland Act 1998 s.87. In force: March 15, 2002; £1.50.

This Order amends the Northern Ireland Act 1998 by adding the Social Security Fraud Act 2001 and the Social Security Fraud Act (Northern Ireland) 2001 to the legislation listed in s.87 the 1998 Act. The effect of this amendment will be to render those Acts subject to the provisions in that section concerning consultation and co-ordination between the Secretary of State and the Northern Ireland Minister having responsibility for social security.

HEALTH

4999. Dentistry–general dental services–general anaesthesia

GENERAL DENTAL SERVICES (AMENDMENT) REGULATIONS (NORTHERN IRELAND) 2002, SR 2002 2; made under the Health and Personal Social Services (Northern Ireland) Order 1972 (SI 1972 1265 (NI.14)) Art.61, Art.106, Art.107. In force: February 1, 2002; £1.75.

These Regulations amend the Health and Personal Social Services General Dental Services Regulations (Northern Ireland) 1993 (SR 1993 326) which regulate the terms on which general dental services are provided under the Health and Personal Social Services (Northern Ireland) Order 1972 (SI 1972 1265). The Regulations remove references to general anaesthesia which may no longer be provided under general dental services.

5000. Dentistry–general dental services–maximum charge

GENERAL DENTAL SERVICES (AMENDMENT NO.2) REGULATIONS (NORTHERN IRELAND) 2002, SR 2002 171; made under the Health and

Personal Social Services (Northern Ireland) Order 1972 (SI 1972 1265 (NI.14)) Art.61, Art.106, Art.107. In force: June 1, 2002; £1.50.

These Regulations amend the Health and Personal Social Services General Dental Services Regulations (Northern Ireland) 1993 (SR 1993 326) which regulate the terms on which general dental services are provided under the Health and Personal Social Services (Northern Ireland) Order 1972 (SI 1972 1265). The Regulations increase from £260 to £270 the amount specified as the maximum cost, or likely cost, of care and treatment which a dentist may undertake without seeking the prior approval of the Dental Committee.

5001. Health and Personal Social Services—medical treatment—civil penalty for failure to pay

HEALTH AND PERSONAL SOCIAL SERVICES (PENALTY CHARGE) REGULATIONS (NORTHERN IRELAND) 2002, SR 2002 181; made under the Health and Personal Social Services (Northern Ireland) Order 1972 (SI 1972 1265 (NI.14)) Art.98, Art.106, Art.107, Sch.15 para.6. In force: June 10, 2002; £1.75.

These Regulations make provision for a civil penalty to be imposed where a person fails to pay a Health Service (HS) charge in respect of the provision of drugs and medicines, dental treatment and appliances, optical services, or any other appliances, or receives a payment or benefit towards the cost of an HS charge or service to which he is not entitled, such as HS spectacle vouchers or free HS sight tests.

5002. Health and Personal Social Services—travelling expenses—remission of charges—capital limits

TRAVELLING EXPENSES AND REMISSION OF CHARGES (AMENDMENT NO.2) REGULATIONS (NORTHERN IRELAND) 2002, SR 2002 172; made under the Health and Personal Social Services (Northern Ireland) Order 1972 (SI 1972 1265 (NI.14)) Art.45, Art.98, Art.106, Art.107, Sch.15 para.1, Sch.15 para.1B. In force: June 1, 2002; £1.75.

These Regulations amend the Travelling Expenses and Remission of Charges Regulations (Northern Ireland) 1989 (SI 1989 348) which provide for remission and repayment of certain charges otherwise payable under the Health and Personal Social Services (Northern Ireland) Order 1972 (SI 1972 1265) and for the payment by the Department of travelling expenses incurred in attending a hospital. The Regulations uprate the capital limits used in remission and repayment calculations relating to people living permanently in residential care or nursing homes. It brings those limits into line with those used by Boards under the 1972 Order to determine such people's liability to pay for their care.

5003. Health and Personal Social Services Act (Northern Ireland) 2002 (c.9)

This Act amends the Health and Personal Social Services (Northern Ireland) Order 1972 in relation to charges for nursing care in residential accommodation; and provides for the establishment and functions of the Northern Ireland Practice and Education Council for Nursing and Midwifery.

This Act received Royal Assent on October 4, 2002.

5004. Health and Personal Social Services (Northern Ireland) Act 2002 (c.9)— Commencement Order

HEALTH AND PERSONAL SOCIAL SERVICES (2002 ACT) (COMMENCEMENT) ORDER (NORTHERN IRELAND) 2002, SR 2002 311; made under the Health and Personal Social Services (Northern Ireland) Act 2002 s.4. In force: bringing into operation various provisions of the 2002 Act on October 7, 2002; £1.50.

This Order brings into force specified provisions of the Health and Personal Social Services Act (Northern Ireland) 2002 which provide that the cost of nursing care for people in nursing homes will not be recoverable from the resident and provides for the establishment of the Northern Ireland Practice and Education Council for Nursing and Midwifery.

5005. Health services–dentistry–dental services–fees

DENTAL CHARGES (AMENDMENT) REGULATIONS (NORTHERN IRELAND) 2002, SR 2002 84; made under the Health and Personal Social Services (Northern Ireland) Order 1972 (SI 1972 1265 (NI.14)) Art.98, Art.106, Sch.15. In force: April 1, 2002; £1.50.

These Regulations amend the Dental Charges Regulations (Northern Ireland) 1989 (SR 1989 111) which relate to charges for dental treatment provided and dental appliances supplied as part of health service general dental services or under a pilot scheme. They increase to £366 the maximum charge which a patient may be required to pay towards the cost of his treatment or appliance under general dental services or under a pilot scheme and provide that these new charges shall apply only where the arrangements for treatment or supply of a dental appliance are made on or after April 1, 2002. In addition, the Regulations amend the Dental Charges (Amendment) Regulations (Northern Ireland) 2001 (SR 2001 124).

5006. Health services–general medical services–doctors–Hepatitis B

GENERAL MEDICAL SERVICES (AMENDMENT) REGULATIONS (NORTHERN IRELAND) 2002, SR 2002 213; made under the Health and Personal Social Services (Northern Ireland) Order 1972 (SI 1972 1265 (NI.14)) Art.56, Art.106, Art.107. In force: July 1, 2002; £1.50.

These Regulations amend the General Medical Services Regulations (Northern Ireland) 1997 (SR 1997 380) which regulate the terms on which doctors provide general medical services under the Health and Personal Social Services (Northern Ireland) Order 1972 (SI 1972 1265 (NI.14)). They ensure that doctors confirm at quinquennial review that they continue to follow the Departmental Guidance regarding protection of health care workers and patients from Hepatitis B.

5007. Health services–general medical services–prescription of drugs

GENERAL MEDICAL SERVICES (AMENDMENT NO.2) REGULATIONS (NORTHERN IRELAND) 2002, SR 2002 266; made under the Health and Personal Social Services (Northern Ireland) Order 1972 (SI 1972 1265 (NI.14)) Art.56, Art.106, Art.107. In force: October 1, 2002; £1.75.

These Regulations amend the General Medical Services Regulations (Northern Ireland) 1997 (SR 1997 380) which regulate the terms on which doctors provide general medical services under the Health and Personal Social Services (Northern Ireland) Order 1972 (SI 1972 1265 (NI.14)). The Regulations remove two products from Reg.2(b) and add five products to Sch.10 of the 1997 Regulations so that they may not be prescribed for supply in the course of pharmaceutical services.

5008. Medical profession–nurses, midwives and health visitors–professional conduct

NURSES, MIDWIVES AND HEALTH VISITORS (PROFESSIONAL CONDUCT) (AMENDMENT) RULES 2002, APPROVAL ORDER (NORTHERN IRELAND) 2002, SR 2002 43; made under the Nurses, Midwives and Health Visitors Act 1997 s.19, s.22, Sch.3. In force: February 18, 2002; £1.75.

This Order, which amends the Nurses, Midwives and Health Visitors (Professional Conduct) Rules 1993 (SR 1993 313), approves Rules set out in the Schedule which amend the Professional Conduct Rules of the United Kingdom Central Council for Nursing, Midwifery and Health Visiting so as to remove the requirement for the deputy chairman of, respectively, the Preliminary Proceedings Committee, the Professional Conduct Committee and the Health Committee to be Council members and to reduce from two to one the number of

Council members necessary to constitute a quorum of each of the said Committees.

5009. Medical profession–nurses, midwives and health visitors–professional conduct

NURSES, MIDWIVES AND HEALTH VISITORS (PROFESSIONAL CONDUCT) (AMENDMENT) (NO.2) RULES 2002, APPROVAL ORDER (NORTHERN IRELAND) 2002, SR 2002 117; made under the Nurses, Midwives and Health Visitors Act 1997 s.19, s.22, Sch.3. In force: March 31, 2002; £2.00.

This Order amends the Nurses, Midwives and Health Visitors (Professional Conduct) Rules 1993 (SR 1993 313) so as to reduce the number of medical examiners who are required to examine the practitioner from two to one in cases concerning the practitioner's fitness to practice and to make further provision with respect to any medical practitioner instructed by the practitioner.

5010. Medical profession–services–pharmaceutical services and general medical services

PHARMACEUTICAL SERVICES AND GENERAL MEDICAL SERVICES (AMENDMENT) REGULATIONS (NORTHERN IRELAND) 2002, SR 2002 92; made under the Health and Personal Social Services (Northern Ireland) Order 1972 (SI 1972 1265 (NI.14)) Art.56, Art.63, Art.64, Art.106, Art.107. In force: April 1, 2002; £2.00.

These Regulations amend the General Medical Services Regulations (Northern Ireland) 1997 (SR 1997 380) and the Pharmaceutical Services Regulations (Northern Ireland) 1997 (SR 1997 381) to take account of the fact that certain appliances may be available for prescription within the health services only in circumstances specified by the Department of Health, Social Services and Public Safety.

5011. National Health Service–drugs and appliances–fees

CHARGES FOR DRUGS AND APPLIANCES (AMENDMENT) REGULATIONS (NORTHERN IRELAND) 2002, SR 2002 91; made under the Health and Personal Social Services (Northern Ireland) Order 1972 (SI 1972 1265 (NI.14)) Art.98, Art.106, Sch.15. In force: April 1, 2002; £1.75.

These Regulations amend the Charges for Drugs and Appliances Regulations (Northern Ireland) 1997 (SI 1997 382) which provide for the making and recovery of charges for drugs and appliances supplied by doctors and chemists providing pharmaceutical services, and by hospitals and HSS trusts to out-patients. They increase the charge for each item on prescription from £6.10 to £6.20. The sums prescribed for the grant of pre-payment certificates of exemption from prescription charges are increased from £31.90 to £32.40 for a 4 month certificate and from £87.60 to £89.00 for a 12 month certificate. In addition, they increase charges for certain fabric supports and wigs.

5012. National Health Service–pharmaceutical services–prescriptions–nurses

PHARMACEUTICAL SERVICES AND CHARGES FOR DRUGS AND APPLIANCES (AMENDMENT) REGULATIONS (NORTHERN IRELAND) 2002, SR 2002 397; made under the Health and Personal Social Services (Northern Ireland) Order 1972 (SI 1972 1265 (NI.14)) Art.63, Art.64, Art.98, Art.106, Art.107, Sch.15. In force: February 1, 2003; £1.75.

These Regulations amend the Pharmaceutical Services Regulations (Northern Ireland) 1997 (SR 1997 381) and the Charges for Drugs and Appliances Regulations (Northern Ireland) 1997 (SR 1997 382) to extend the categories of nurse, midwife or health visitor who may prescribe under the Health Service in Northern Ireland.

5013. Nursing-midwifery-appointments and procedure

NORTHERN IRELAND PRACTICE AND EDUCATION COUNCIL FOR NURSING AND MIDWIFERY (APPOINTMENTS AND PROCEDURE) REGULATIONS (NORTHERN IRELAND) 2002, SR 2002 386; made under the Health and Personal Social Services Act (Northern Ireland) 2002 s.2, Sch.1 para.5, Sch.1 para.22. In force: January 27, 2003; £2.00.

These Regulations make provision concerning the membership and procedure of the Northern Ireland Practice and Education Council for Nursing and Midwifery. They provide for the appointment and tenure of office of the chairman and members of the Council, for the disqualification for appointment, for resignations, for the termination of appointments by the Department and for the appointment of a deputy chairman. Provision is also made for the establishment of committees and sub-committees, the conduct of meetings and the exclusion from meetings of those with a pecuniary interest in matters under discussion.

5014. Opticians-fees and payments

OPTICAL CHARGES AND PAYMENTS AND GENERAL OPHTHALMIC SERVICES (AMENDMENT) REGULATIONS (NORTHERN IRELAND) 2002, SR 2002 85; made under the Health and Personal Social Services (Northern Ireland) Order 1972 (SI 1972 1265 (NI.14)) Art.62, Art.98, Art.106, Art.107, Sch.15. In force: Reg.3: April 9, 2002; Reg.6: April 9, 2002: remainder April 1, 2002; £2.00.

These Regulations amend the General Ophthalmic Services Regulations (Northern Ireland) 1986 (SR 1986 163), which provide for the arrangements under which ophthalmic medical practitioners and ophthalmic opticians provide General Ophthalmic Services, and the Optical Charges and Payments Regulations (Northern Ireland) 1997 (SR 1997 191), which provide for payments to be made, by means of a voucher system, in respect of costs incurred by certain categories of persons in connection with the supply, replacement and repair of optical appliances. The Regulations increase charges for glasses and contact lenses supplied by an HSS trust, increase the income level at which recipients of tax credit are entitled to health service optical vouchers, increase the redemption value of two categories of vouchers, namely, vouchers for replacement and vouchers for repair and increase the value of vouchers issued towards the cost of the supply and replacement of glasses and contact lenses. They also increase the additional values for vouchers in respect of prisms, tints, and special categories of appliances, increase the value of vouchers issued towards the cost of repair and replacement of optical appliances and increase the income level used in determining eligibility to free health service sight tests for recipients of tax credits.

5015. Opticians-fees and payments

OPTICAL CHARGES AND PAYMENTS (AMENDMENT) REGULATIONS (NORTHERN IRELAND) 2002, SR 2002 5; made under the Health and Personal Social Services (Northern Ireland) Order 1972 (SI 1972 1265 (NI.14)) Art.62, Art.98, Art.106, Art.107, Sch.15 para.2A. In force: February 1, 2002; £1.75.

These Regulations amend the Health and Personal Social Services (Optical Charges and Payments) Regulations (Northern Ireland) 1997 (SR 1997 191) which provide for payments to be made, by means of a voucher system, in respect of costs incurred by certain categories of persons in connection with eye sight tests and the supply, replacement and repair of optical appliances. They amend the definition of "health service sight test fee" to reflect the values of the two levels of fees for Health Service sight tests payable to ophthalmic medical practitioners and opticians. These amounts are relevant to the determination of eligibility for, and the redemption value of, a voucher towards the cost of a sight test.

5016. Opticians-fees and payments-National Health Service sight test

OPTICAL CHARGES AND PAYMENTS (AMENDMENT NO.2) REGULATIONS (NORTHERN IRELAND) 2002, SR 2002 221; made under the Health and

Personal Social Services (Northern Ireland) Order 1972 (SI 1972 1265 (NI.14))
Art.62, Art.98, Art.106, Art.107, Sch.15 para.2A. In force: July 9, 2002; £1.50.

These Regulations amend the Health and Personal Social Services (Optical
Charges and Payments) Regulations (Northern Ireland) 1997 (SR 1997 191)
which provide for payments to be made, by means of a voucher system, in
respect of costs incurred by certain categories of persons in connection with eye
sight tests and the supply, replacement and repair of optical appliances. They
amend the definition of "health service sight test fee" to reflect the values of the
two levels of fees for Health Service sight tests payable to ophthalmic medical
practitioners and opticians. These amounts are relevant to the determination of
eligibility for, and the redemption value of, a voucher towards the cost of a sight test.

**5017. Pharmaceutical industry–Pharmaceutical Society of Northern Ireland–
members' registration fees**

PHARMACEUTICAL SOCIETY OF NORTHERN IRELAND (GENERAL)
(AMENDMENT) REGULATIONS (NORTHERN IRELAND) 2002, SR 2002 206;
made under the Pharmacy (Northern Ireland) Order 1976 (SI 1976 1213 (NI.22))
Art.5. In force: July 1, 2002; £1.50.

These Regulations amend the Pharmaceutical Society of Northern Ireland
(General) Regulations (Northern Ireland) 1994 (SR 1994 202) by increasing
fees payable in respect of registration as a pharmaceutical chemist and as a
student; retention fees payable in respect of members of the Society; penalty for
default in payment of the retention fee.

5018. Public health–fund holding practices–transfer of assets

HEALTH AND PERSONAL SOCIAL SERVICES ACT (NORTHERN IRELAND)
2001 (FUND-HOLDING PRACTICES) (TRANSFER OF ASSETS, RIGHTS AND
LIABILITIES AND TRANSITIONAL PROVISIONS) ORDER (NORTHERN
IRELAND) 2002, SR 2002 66; made under the Health and Personal Social
Services Act (Northern Ireland) 2001 s.58. In force: April 1, 2002; £2.50.

This Order makes provisions in connection with the abolition of the Health and
Personal Social Services Act (Northern Ireland) 2001 s.39, of the system of GP
fund-holding as established by the Health and Personal Social Services (Northern
Ireland) Order 1991 (SI 1991 194). The Order provides for the transfer of assets,
rights and liabilities connected with fund-holding to the relevant Health and
Social Services Board of the former fund-holding practice and for the use by the
Health and Social Services Board of those assets in meeting rights and liabilities
transferred to it and those retained by the former members of fund-holding
practices.

5019. Public health–travelling expenses–remission of charges

TRAVELLING EXPENSES AND REMISSION OF CHARGES (AMENDMENT)
REGULATIONS (NORTHERN IRELAND) 2002, SR 2002 46; made under the
Health and Personal Social Services (Northern Ireland) Order 1972 (SI 1972
1265 (NI.14)) Art.45, Art.98, Art.106, Art.107, Sch.15 para.1B. In force: April 9,
2002; £1.75.

These Regulations amend the Travelling Expenses and Remission of Charges
Regulations (Northern Ireland) 1989 (SR 1989 348) which provide for
remission and repayment of certain charges which would otherwise be payable
under the Health and Personal Social Services (Northern Ireland) Order 1972 (SI
1972 1265) and for the payment by the Department of travelling expenses incurred
in attending a hospital. The Regulations increase the income level at which
recipients of tax credits are entitled to remission from charges and make
amendments so that the provisions governing the period of validity of a notice of
entitlement to remission or payment of charges held by a student will relate only to
full-time students.

5020. Road traffic–health services charges

ROAD TRAFFIC (HEALTH SERVICES CHARGES) (AMENDMENT) REGULATIONS (NORTHERN IRELAND) 2002, SR 2002 52; made under the Health and Personal Social Services Act (Northern Ireland) 2001 s.23, s.25, s.32, s.37, s.57. In force: February 16, 2002; £1.75.

These Regulations, which revoke the Road Traffic (Health Services Charges) (Amendment) Regulations (Northern Ireland) 2001 (SR 2001 434), amend the Road Traffic (Health Services Charges) Regulations (Northern Ireland) 2001 (SR 2001 125) which provide for a scheme for the recovery from insurers and certain other persons of charges in connection with the health services treatment of road traffic casualties. They revoke charges applying to incidents occurring on or after January 28, 2002 and reinstate the charges that applied in respect of incidents which occurred on or after July 2, 1997. The charge where the traffic casualty received health services treatment but was not admitted to hospital is reduced from £402 to £354, the daily charge for health services treatment where the traffic casualty is admitted to hospital is reduced from £494 to £435 and the maximum charge for treatment where the traffic casualty is admitted to hospital is reduced from £30,000 to £10,000. For incidents occurring during the period January 28, 2002 to February 15, 2002 the appropriate charges for treatment are those in operation on the days on which treatment occurred.

5021. Road traffic–health services charges

ROAD TRAFFIC (HEALTH SERVICES CHARGES) (AMENDMENT NO.2) REGULATIONS (NORTHERN IRELAND) 2002, SR 2002 373; made under the Health and Personal Social Services Act (Northern Ireland) 2001 s.25, s.37, s.57. In force: January 1, 2003; £1.75.

These Regulations amend the Road Traffic (Health Services Charges) Regulations (Northern Ireland) 2001 (SR 2001 125) which provide for a scheme for the recovery from insurers and certain other persons of charges in connection with the health services treatment of road traffic casualties. They increase the charges where traffic casualty received health services treatment but was not admitted to hospital in respect of an incident which occurred on or after January 1, 2003 and before April 1, 2003.

HEALTH AND SAFETY AT WORK

5022. Hazardous substances–batteries and accumulators

BATTERIES AND ACCUMULATORS (CONTAINING DANGEROUS SUBSTANCES) (AMENDMENT) REGULATIONS (NORTHERN IRELAND) 2002, SR 2002 300; made under the European Communities Act 1972 s.2. In force: November 8, 2002; £1.75.

These Regulations, which amend the Batteries and Accumulators (Containing Dangerous Substances) Regulations (Northern Ireland) 1995 (SR 1995 122), implement Commission Directive 98/101 ([1999] OJ L1/1) amending Council Directive 91/157 on batteries and accumulators containing certain dangerous substances. The Regulations make amendments in relation to batteries and accumulators put on the market as from January 1, 1999 containing more than 0.0005 per cent of mercury by weight; batteries and accumulators put on the market as from September 18, 1992, containing more than 25mg of mercury per cell, except alkaline manganese batteries, more than 0.025 per cent of cadmium by weight, more than 0.4 per cent of lead by weight; and alkaline manganese batteries containing more than 0.025 per cent of mercury by weight.

5023. Industrial injuries–compensation–payment of claims

PNEUMOCONIOSIS, ETC., (WORKERS' COMPENSATION) (PAYMENT OF CLAIMS) (AMENDMENT) REGULATIONS (NORTHERN IRELAND) 2002, SR

2002 133; made under the Pneumoconiosos etc. (Workers' Compensation) (Northern Ireland) Order 1979 (SI 1979 925 (NI.9)) Art.3, Art.4, Art.11. In force: in accordance with Reg.1 (1); £2.00.

Under the Pneumoconiosis, etc., (Workers' Compensation) (Northern Ireland) Order 1979 (SI 1979 925) lump sum payments may be made to certain persons disabled by a disease to which the Order applies, or to dependants of persons who were so disabled immediately before they died. These Regulations amend the Pneumoconiosis, etc., (Workers' Compensation) (Payment of Claims) Regulations (Northern Ireland) 1988 (SR 1988 242) so as to increase the amount payable under the Order. The increase in each case is 3.8 percent, rounded up or down to the nearest £1 as appropriate. The diseases to which the Order applies are pneumoconiosis, byssinosis, diffuse mesothelioma, primary carcinoma of the lung (where accompanied by asbestosis or diffuse pleural thickening) and diffuse pleural thickening.

HIGHWAYS

5024. Road works—register, notices, directions and designations

STREET WORKS (REGISTER, NOTICES, DIRECTIONS AND DESIGNATIONS) REGULATIONS (NORTHERN IRELAND) 2002, SR 2002 10; made under the Street Works (Northern Ireland) Order 1995 (SI 1995 3210 (NI.19)) Art.3, Art.13, Art.14, Art.15, Art.16, Art.17, Art.18, Art.22, Art.23, Art.24, Art.54. In force: March 18, 2002; £4.00.

These Regulations prescribe the form of certain notices to be served under the Street Works (Northern Ireland) Order 1995 (SI 1995 3210) and the manner in which they are to be published or served. They prescribe the information with respect to street works which is to be held in the register the Department is required to keep, prescribe the period of notice of starting date of street works for urgent and standard works, define "substantial road works" and provide that the Department shall be the street authority for a street which is not a road for the purposes of keeping the register and receiving information from an undertaker as to the location and description of apparatus he has found.

HOUSING

5025. Housing Support Services (Northern Ireland) Order 2002 (SI 2002 3154 (NI.8))

This Order, which amends the Social Security Contributions and Benefits (Northern Ireland) Act 1992, confers on the Northern Ireland Housing Executive the function of securing the provision of housing support services to individuals with particular needs, and empowers the Executive to pay grants to eligible persons towards expenditure incurred by them in providing certain housing support services. Payments in respect of such services when determining entitlement to housing benefit are excluded from 1992 Act.

HUMAN RIGHTS

5026. Public authorities—Regulation of Investigatory Powers

REGULATION OF INVESTIGATORY POWERS ACT 2000 (AMENDMENT) ORDER (NORTHERN IRELAND) 2002, SR 2002 183; made under the

Regulation of Investigatory Powers Act 2000 s.30, s.31. In force: in accordance with Art.1; £1.75.

This Order amends the Regulation of Investigatory Powers Act 2000 by adding various Northern Ireland public authorities to the lists of public authorities in that Act.

5027. Right to life–investigations–procedural obligation to conduct proper inquiry into death which had occurred during civil disturbance

See HUMAN RIGHTS: McShane v. United Kingdom (43290/98). §2490

5028. Surveillance–authorisation by public authorities

REGULATION OF INVESTIGATORY POWERS (PRESCRIPTION OF OFFICES, RANKS AND POSITIONS) ORDER (NORTHERN IRELAND) 2002, SR 2002 292; made under the Regulation of Investigatory Powers Act 2000 s.30, s.31. In force: October 24, 2002; £2.00.

This Order prescribes offices, ranks and positions for the purposes of the Regulation of Investigatory Powers Act 2000 s.30(1), under which individuals holding such offices, ranks or positions are designated persons for the purposes of granting authorisations under s.28 and s.29 of the Act.

IMMIGRATION

5029. Books

Egan, Suzanne–Immigration and Refugee Law in Ireland. Paperback: £70.00. ISBN 1-85475-270-7. Butterworths Law (Ireland).

INDUSTRY

5030. Industrial Development Act (Northern Ireland) 2002 (1)

This Act makes provision about establishing Invest Northern Ireland to exercise certain existing functions in relation to industrial development; to dissolve the Industrial Development Board for Northern Ireland, the Local Enterprise Development Unit and the Industrial Research and Technology Unit; to abolish certain functions of the Northern Ireland Tourist Board; to amend the Industrial Development (Northern Ireland) Order 1982.

This Act received Royal Assent on February 7, 2002.

5031. Industrial Development Act (Northern Ireland) 2002 (c.1)–Commencement Order

INDUSTRIAL DEVELOPMENT (2002 ACT) (COMMENCEMENT) ORDER (NORTHERN IRELAND) 2002, SR 2002 134; made under the Industrial Development Act (Northern Ireland) 2002 s.7. In force: bringing into operation various provisions of the 2002 Act on April 1, 2002; £1.50.

The Industrial Development Act (Northern Ireland) 2002 establishes a single economic development agency, Invest Northern Ireland (Invest NI), as a Non-Departmental Public Body (NDPB). This Order provides for the coming into operation of the Industrial Development Act (Northern Ireland) 2002 s.1, s.2, s.3, s.4, s.5 and s.6 on April 1, 2002.

INSOLVENCY

5032. Corporate insolvency–insolvency proceedings–EU member states

INSOLVENCY (AMENDMENT) RULES (NORTHERN IRELAND) 2002, SR 2002 261; made under the Insolvency (Northern Ireland) Order 1989 (SR 1989 2405 (NI. 19)) Art.359. In force: September 5, 2002; £6.00.

These Rules amend the Insolvency Rules (Northern Ireland) 1991 (SR 1991 364) in light of Council Regulation 1346/2000 ([2000] OJ L160/1) on insolvency proceedings which aims to provide for the efficient and effective functioning of cross-border insolvency proceedings in the EU. The Rules provide procedures for the conversion of company and individual voluntary arrangements and administration into winding up for companies and bankruptcy for individuals on the application of a liquidator appointed in another EU Member State in main proceedings; make provision for giving notice of insolvency proceedings, and to give notice of various steps taken in such proceedings, to Member State liquidators; provide for the right of a Member State liquidator appointed in main proceedings or a temporary liquidator to be able to apply for the appointment of a provisional liquidator of a company or an interim receiver of an individual; provide a procedure allowing a liquidator of a company being wound up voluntarily to apply to court for the confirmation of the proceedings, such confirmation being a pre-requisite for recognition of a voluntary winding up in other Member States; remove conflicts between the EC Regulation and the Rules; make provision with regard to voting at creditors' meeting and proving for dividends in insolvency proceedings where the EC Regulation applies; and provide revised forms, among others forms, for petitions and orders which require petitioners and the court to consider the applicability of the EC Regulation to the proceedings in question.

5033. Corporate insolvency–insolvency proceedings–EU member states

INSOLVENCY (NORTHERN IRELAND) ORDER 1989 (AMENDMENT NO.2) REGULATIONS (NORTHERN IRELAND), SR 2002 334; made under the European Communities Act 1972 s.2. In force: December 5, 2002; £1.75.

These Regulations make amendments to the Insolvency (Northern Ireland) Order 1989 (SI 1989 2405 (NI.19)) as a result of the adoption by the Council of the European Union of Council Regulation 1346/2000 ([2000] OJ L160/1) on insolvency proceedings which aims to provide for the efficient and effective functioning of cross-border insolvency proceedings in the EU. The Regulations provide amendments to ensure that provisions of domestic law do not conflict with the EC Regulation and generally to provide for it.

5034. Corporate insolvency–Insolvency Rules Advisory Committee

INSOLVENCY (NORTHERN IRELAND) ORDER 1989 (AMENDMENT) REGULATIONS (NORTHERN IRELAND) 2002, SR 2002 223; made under the European Communities Act 1972 s.2. In force: July 15, 2002; £1.75.

These Regulations amend the Insolvency (Northern Ireland) Order 1989 (SI 1989 2405 (NI 19)) to extend existing rule-making powers under the Order to allow for making rules which are required as a result of the adoption by the Council of the European Union of Council Regulation 1346/2000 ([2000] OJ L160/1) on insolvency proceedings. They also make amendments to apply insolvency legislation to insolvent partnerships and to the insolvent estates of deceased persons to allow provision to be made in relation to the Regulation. As a result of making these amendments, rules made under the amended 1989 Order in relation to the regulation will, like rules presently made under the Order, need to be reviewed by the Insolvency Rules Advisory Committee. The Insolvency Rules Advisory Committee is consulted by the Lord Chancellor prior to making insolvency rules and consists of the Chancery Judge, the Master (Bankruptcy), and practicing insolvency professionals.

5035. Insolvency (Northern Ireland) Order 2002 (SI 2002 3152 (NI.6))

This Order, which amends the Insolvency (Northern Ireland) Order 1989 (SI 1989 2405 (NI.19)) and the Companies (No.2) (Northern Ireland) Order 1990 (SI 1990 1504 (NI.10)), provides for directors proposing to enter into a voluntary arrangement with creditors of an eligible company to obtain an initial moratorium during which the company will be protected from legal proceedings, including a petition to wind up the company.

INSURANCE

5036. Motor vehicles–insurance–records

MOTOR VEHICLES (THIRD-PARTY RISKS) (AMENDMENT) REGULATIONS (NORTHERN IRELAND) 2002, SR 2002 154; made under the Road Traffic (Northern Ireland) Order 1981 (SI 1981 154 (NI.1)) Art.103, Art.218. In force: July 15, 2002; £1.75.

These Regulations amend the Motor Vehicles (Third-Party Risks) Regulations (Northern Ireland) 1994 (SR 1994 46) by altering the requirements as to the keeping of records of policies of insurance and securities issued under the Road Traffic (Northern Ireland) Order 1981 (SI 1981 154 (NI.1)) and vehicles the use of which is exempt from the normal insurance requirement. The requirements are extended to include particulars of every person whose liability is covered by a policy or security and additional particulars of the vehicles whose use is covered. Records of old insurance policies and securities are required to be kept for a period of seven years after expiry. Copies of any records may be supplied to the Motor Insurers' Bureau or its nominated subsidiary in electronic form and kept by it on a database. In such cases the Bureau or its subsidiary must keep the copy records of expired policies and securities for the same seven-year period and disclose particulars of any record it holds to the Department or police on request.

INTERNATIONAL LAW

5037. International criminal law–fines–forfeiture–reparation orders

See INTERNATIONAL LAW. §2943

INTERNATIONAL TRADE

5038. Animal products–bone in beef–despatch to domestic market

BOVINES AND BOVINE PRODUCTS (TRADE) (AMENDMENT) REGULATIONS (NORTHERN IRELAND) 2002, SR 2002 278; made under the European Communities Act 1972 s.2. In force: September 30, 2002; £2.50.

These Regulations amend the Bovines and Bovine Products (Trade) Regulations (Northern Ireland) 1999 (SR 1999 308) which give effect to Commission Decision 98/692 ([1998] OJ L328/28) amending Commission Decision 98/256 to provide for the export from the UK of deboned beef and beef products under the strict conditions of the Date-based Export Scheme; and Commission Decision 98/564 ([1998] OJ L273/37) amending Council Decision 98/256 as regards certain emergency measures to protect against bovine spongiform encephalopathy. The effect of the amendments is to give effect to Commission Decision 2002/670 ([2002] OJ L228/22) amending Council Decision 98/256 concerning emergency measures to protect against bovine spongiform encephalopathy to enable the despatch from England of bovine embryos and bone in veal carcases from calves between six and nine months exported under the Date Based Export

Scheme. The Regulations also prohibit offering to despatch or consign goods which may not be despatched or consigned whether on the internet or otherwise and provide for the payment of expenses reasonably incurred in connection with storage by the owner of the consignment and in some circumstances the payment of compensation to the owner for any depreciation in value of the consignment.

5039. Animal products–import and export controls

ANIMALS AND ANIMAL PRODUCTS (IMPORT AND EXPORT) (AMENDMENT) REGULATIONS (NORTHERN IRELAND) 2002, SR 2002 296; made under the European Communities Act 1972 s.2. In force: October 21, 2002; £1.75.

These Regulations amend the Animals and Animal Products (Import and Export) Regulations (Northern Ireland) 2000 (SR 2000 253) to make provision to give effect to Commission Decision 2001/327 ([2001] OJ L115/12) concerning restrictions to the movement of animals of susceptible species with regard to foot-and-mouth disease. They also introduce operational agreements for assembly centres to ensure that such centres are capable of being operated in accordance with Council Directive 90/425 ([1990] OJ L224/29) concerning veterinary and zootechnical checks applicable in intra-Community trade in certain live animals and products with a view to the completion of the internal market.

5040. Animal products–origin marking–third country imports–veterinary checks

PRODUCTS OF ANIMAL ORIGIN (THIRD COUNTRY IMPORTS) REGULATIONS (NORTHERN IRELAND) 2002, SR 2002 340; made under the European Communities Act 1972 s.2. In force: December 6, 2002; £7.00.

These Regulations, which revoke the Imported Food Regulations (Northern Ireland) 1991 (SR 1991 475), amend the Fresh Meat (Import Conditions) Regulations (Northern Ireland) 1997 (SR 1997 218), the Imported Food Regulations (Northern Ireland) 1997 (SR 1997 499), the Products of Animal Origin (Import and Export) Regulations (Northern Ireland) 1998 (SR 1998 45) and the Miscellaneous Products of Animal Origin (Import Conditions) Regulations (Northern Ireland) 1999 (SR 1999 189). They implement Council Directive 97/78 ([1998] OJ L24/9) laying down the principles governing the organisation of veterinary checks on products entering the Community from third countries which applies to products of animal origin. The Regulations establish the inspection system which will apply to the generality of products, lay down special provisions which apply to particular categories of product and deal with the calculation and payment of charges for the veterinary checks.

LANDLORD AND TENANT

5041. Ground rent–leaseholds–redemption money–multiplier

GROUND RENTS (MULTIPLIER) ORDER (NORTHERN IRELAND) 2002, SR 2002 228; made under the Ground Rents Act (Northern Ireland) 2001 s.5, Sch.1 para.2, Sch.1 para.4. In force: July 29, 2002; £1.50.

The Ground Rents Act (Northern Ireland) 2001 provides that the redemption money appropriate to the redemption of a ground rent under that Act is the sum produced by multiplying the yearly amount of the ground rent by the figure fixed by an order of the Department of Finance and Personnel. It fixes nine as the number of years purchase applicable to the redemption of all ground rents under the Act and makes provision in relation to the yearly amount of ground rents which are subject to a future increase within nine years from the date of application to redeem the ground rent.

5042. Ground Rents Act (Northern Ireland) 2001 (c.5)–Commencement No.1 Order

GROUND RENTS (2001 ACT) (COMMENCEMENT NO.1) ORDER (NORTHERN IRELAND) 2002, SR 2002 251; made under the Ground Rents Act (Northern Ireland) 2001 s.32. In force: bringing into operation various provisions of the 2001 Act on July 29, 2002; £1.50.

This Order provides for the coming into operation of the Ground Rents Act (Northern Ireland) 2001 with the exception of s.2 which relates to the compulsory redemption of a ground rent.

5043. Rent–registered rents–increase

REGISTERED RENTS (INCREASE) ORDER (NORTHERN IRELAND) 2002, SR 2002 54; made under the Rent (Northern Ireland) Order 1978 (SI 1978 1050 (NI.20)) Art.33. In force: March 4, 2002; £1.50.

This Order increases the rents registered with the Department for Social Development under the Rent (Northern Ireland) Order 1978 (SI 1978 1050 (NI 20)) Part IV for dwelling houses, let under regulated tenancies, by three per cent from March 4, 2002.

LEGAL ADVICE AND FUNDING

5044. Criminal procedure–costs

LEGAL AID IN CRIMINAL PROCEEDINGS (COSTS) (AMENDMENT) RULES (NORTHERN IRELAND) 2002, SR 2002 376; made under the Legal Aid, Advice and Assistance (Northern Ireland) Order 1981 (SI 1981 228 (NI.8)) Art.36. In force: December 30, 2002; £1.50.

These Rules amend the Legal Aid in Criminal Proceedings (Costs) Rules (Northern Ireland) 1992 (SR 1992 314) to alter the date after which certain work may be remunerated at discretionary instead of prescribed rates from December 31, 2002 to December 31, 2003.

5045. Legal advice–assistance–scale of contributions

LEGAL ADVICE AND ASSISTANCE (AMENDMENT) REGULATIONS (NORTHERN IRELAND) 2002, SR 2002 62; made under the Legal Aid, Advice and Assistance (Northern Ireland) Order 1981 (SI 1981 228 (NI.8)) Art.7, Art.22, Art.27. In force: April 8, 2002; £1.75.

These Regulations, which revoke the Legal Advice and Assistance (Amendment No.2) Regulations (Northern Ireland) 2001 (SR 2001 113), amend the Legal Advice and Assistance Regulations (Northern Ireland) 1981 (SI 1981 228 (NI.8)) so as to substitute a new scale of contributions payable for legal advice.

5046. Legal advice–legal assistance–income limits

LEGAL ADVICE AND ASSISTANCE (FINANCIAL CONDITIONS) REGULATIONS (NORTHERN IRELAND) 2002, SR 2002 61; made under the Legal Aid, Advice and Assistance (Northern Ireland) Order 1981 (SI 1981 228 (NI.8)) Art.3, Art.7, Art.22, Art.27. In force: April 8, 2002; £1.50.

These Regulations, which revoke the Legal Advice and Assistance (Financial Conditions) Regulations (Northern Ireland) 2001 (SR 2001 112), amend the Legal Aid, Advice and Assistance (Northern Ireland) Order 1981 (SR 1981 228 (NI.8)) so as to increase the upper income limit to make legal advice and assistance available to those with disposable income of not more than £189 a week and increase the lower limit below which legal advice and assistance is available without payment of a contribution to £80 a week.

5047. Legal aid–financial conditions–calculation of disposable income–limit increase

LEGAL AID (FINANCIAL CONDITIONS) REGULATIONS (NORTHERN IRELAND) 2002, SR 2002 60; made under the Legal Aid, Advice and Assistance (Northern Ireland) Order 1981 (SI 1981 228 (NI.8)) Art.9, Art.12, Art.22, Art.27. In force: April 8, 2002; £1.75.

These Regulations, which revoke with savings the Legal Aid (Financial Conditions) Regulations (Northern Ireland) 2001 (SR 2001 111), amend the Legal Aid (Assessment of Resources) Regulations (Northern Ireland) 1981 (SI 1981 228 (NI.8)) so as to increase the upper income limit to make legal aid available to those with disposable incomes of not more than £8,335, or in connection with proceedings involving a personal injury £9,188, and also increase the lower limit below which legal aid is available without payment of a contribution to £2,814.

5048. Legal services–advice and assistance–prisoners

LEGAL ADVICE AND ASSISTANCE (AMENDMENT NO.2) REGULATIONS (NORTHERN IRELAND) 2002, SR 2002 212; made under the Legal Aid, Advice and Assistance (Northern Ireland) Order 1981 (SI 1981 228 (NI.8)) Art.5, Art.22. In force: June 21, 2002; £1.50.

These Regulations amend the Legal Aid, Advice and Assistance (Northern Ireland) Order 1981 (SR 1981 366) by extending assistance by way of representation to prisoners at hearings held under the Life Sentences (Northern Ireland) Order 2001 (SI 2001 2564 (NI.2)).

LEGAL PROFESSION

5049. Books

Doyle, Christopher–The Company Secretary. Hardback. ISBN 1-85800-290-7. Round Hall Ltd.

LEGISLATION

5050. Delegated legislation–discrimination–validity–regulations made by Secretary of State during suspension of Northern Ireland Assembly

[Northern Ireland Act 1998 s.75, s.76; Flags (Northern Ireland) Order 2000 (SI 2000 1347); Flags Regulations (Northern Ireland) 2000 (SR 2000 347) Reg.2.]

M, a member of the Legislative Assembly, sought judicial review of the decision by the Secretary of State to make the draft Flags (Northern Ireland) Order during the period that the Assembly was suspended between February and May 2000. The Order was subsequently approved by Parliament as the Flags (Northern Ireland) Order 2000 and the Flags Regulations (Northern Ireland) 2000 were made under the Order. The Regulations entered into force in November 2000 and Reg.2 permitted the Union flag to be flown from government offices on certain dates. M contended that the Order and the Regulations had been made as an inducement to the Ulster Unionist Party, UUP, to re-enter the Assembly and formed part of an agreement between the Secretary of State and T, the UUP leader. M argued that the Order and the Regulations were discriminatory in effect and contrary to the Northern Ireland Act 1998 s.75 and s.76, which stipulated that it was unlawful for a "public authority" to discriminate against sections of the Northern Ireland population on the grounds, inter alia, of religious or political belief.

Held, refusing the application, that neither the Order nor the Regulations made under it could be invalidated on the basis that they had been made pursuant to an agreement between the Secretary of State and T. Further, the Secretary of State was not a "public authority" in terms of s.75 of the 1998 Act. The purpose of the Order and the Regulations was to determine the constitutional position of the Union flag and its use in Northern Ireland, not to discriminate against a sector of the province's population.

MURPHY'S APPLICATION FOR JUDICIAL REVIEW, *Re* [2001] N.I. 425, Kerr, J., QBD (NI).

LOCAL GOVERNMENT

5051. Fire service–appointments–Chief Fire Officer–eligibility

FIRE SERVICES (APPOINTMENTS AND PROMOTION) (AMENDMENT) REGULATIONS (NORTHERN IRELAND) 2002, SR 2002 283; made under the Fire Services (Northern Ireland) Order 1984 (SI 1984 1821 (NI.11)) Art.9, Art.52. In force: October 1, 2002; £1.75.

These Regulations amend the Fire Services (Appointments and Promotion) Regulations (Northern Ireland) 1979 (SR 1979 167) by substituting provisions relating to eligibility for appointment of the Chief Fire Officer.

5052. Grants–central funds–calculation of grant from Department of the Environment

LOCAL GOVERNMENT (GENERAL GRANT) ORDER (NORTHERN IRELAND) 2002, SR 2002 182; made under the Local Government &c. (Northern Ireland) Order 1972 (SI 1972 1 (NI.22)) Sch.1 Part I para.3. In force: in accordance with Art.1 (2); £1.50.

This Order specifies those districts which are to be taken into account in calculating the standard penny rate products for the year ending March 31, 2003 for the purpose of computing the resources element of the grant made from central funds by the Department of the Environment to district councils.

5053. Grants–central funds–calculation of grant from Department of the Environment

LOCAL GOVERNMENT (GENERAL GRANT) ORDER (NORTHERN IRELAND) 2002, SR 2002 182; made under the Local Government &c. (Northern Ireland) Order 1972 (SI 1972 1999 (NI.22)) Sch.1 Part I para.3. In force: in accordance with Art.1 (2); £1.50.

This Order specifies those districts to be taken into account in calculating the standard penny rate products for the year ending March 31, 2003 for the purpose of computing the resources element of the grant made from central funds by the Department of the Environment to district councils.

5054. Local authorities–change of district name–Lisburn Borough

CHANGE OF DISTRICT NAME (LISBURN BOROUGH) ORDER (NORTHERN IRELAND) 2002, SR 2002 231; made under the Local Government Act (Northern Ireland) 1972 s.51. In force: August 8, 2002; £1.50.

This Order changes the name of the local government district of Lisburn Borough to Lisburn City from August 8, 2002

5055. Local Government (Best Value) Act (Northern Ireland) 2002 (4)

This Act places on district councils a general duty to make arrangements for continuous improvement in the way in which their functions are exercised.

5056. **Local Government (Miscellaneous Provisions) (Northern Ireland) Order 2002 (SI 2002 3149 (NI.3))**

This Order amends the Local Government &c. (Northern Ireland) Order 1972 (SI 1972 1999 (NI.22)), the Rates (Northern Ireland) Order 1977 (SI 1977 2157 (NI.28)), the Enterprise Zones (Northern Ireland) Order 1981 (SI 1981 607 (NI.15)), the Local Government (Miscellaneous Provisions) (Northern Ireland) Order 1985 (SI 1985 1208 (NI.15)), the Local Government (Miscellaneous Provisions) (Northern Ireland) Order 1992 (SI 1992 810 (NI.6)) and the Rates (Amendment) (Northern Ireland) Order 1994 (SI 1994 1897 (NI.11)) to make provision for the payment of general and other grants to district councils and confer new powers on district councils in relation to economic development and community safety.

PARTNERSHIPS

5057. **Limited Liability Partnerships Act (Northern Ireland) 2002 (c.12)**

This Act makes provision for limited liability partnerships.

PENSIONS

5058. Occupational pensions–disclosure of information

OCCUPATIONAL AND PERSONAL PENSION SCHEMES (DISCLOSURE OF INFORMATION) (AMENDMENT) REGULATIONS (NORTHERN IRELAND) 2002, SR 2002 410; made under the Pension Schemes (Northern Ireland) Act 1993 s.109, s.177, s.178; and the Welfare Reform and Pensions (Northern Ireland) Order 1 (NI.11) (SI 1 3147) Art.3. In force: April 6, 2003; £2.50.

These Regulations amend the Personal Pension Schemes (Disclosure of Information) Regulations (Northern Ireland) 1987 (SR 1987 288), the Occupational Pension Schemes (Disclosure of Information) Regulations (Northern Ireland) 1997 (SR 1997 98), the Stakeholder Pension Schemes Regulations (Northern Ireland) 2000 (SR 2000 262) and the Pension Sharing (Consequential and Miscellaneous Amendments) Regulations (Northern Ireland) 2000 (SR 2000 335) following the amendment of the Pension Schemes (Northern Ireland) Act 1993 by the Child Support, Pensions and Social Security Act (Northern Ireland) 2000. The effect of these amendments is that the information which has to be sent to members of schemes with money purchase benefits must include an illustration of the amount of future pension that might become payable under the scheme. The amount is to be determined by reference to guidance.

5059. Occupational pensions–guaranteed minimum pensions–increase

GUARANTEED MINIMUM PENSIONS INCREASE ORDER (NORTHERN IRELAND) 2002, SR 2002 98; made under the Pension Schemes (Northern Ireland) Act 1993 s.105. In force: April 6, 2002; £1.50.

This Order specifies 1.7 per cent as the percentage by which that part of any guaranteed minimum pension attributable to earnings factors for the tax years 1988-89 to 1996-97 and payable by occupational pension schemes is to be increased.

5060. Occupational pensions–local government pension scheme

LOCAL GOVERNMENT PENSION SCHEME (AMENDMENT) REGULATIONS (NORTHERN IRELAND) 2002, SR 2002 115; made under the Superannuation

(Northern Ireland) Order 1972 (SI 1972 1073 (NI.10)) Art.9, Art.14, Sch.3. In force: May 1, 2002; £2.00.

These Regulations, which amend the Local Government Pension Scheme Regulations (Northern Ireland) 2000 (SR 2000 177), make provision for the preparation and auditing of the financial statements of the Northern Ireland Local Government Officers' Superannuation Committee and makes amendments in relation to payments by the Committee to its members by substituting the term "attendance allowance" for "financial loss allowance". They also insert a new Schedule L2 to make provision for the form and the content of the financial statements.

5061. Occupational pensions–local government pension scheme–membership

LOCAL GOVERNMENT PENSION SCHEME REGULATIONS (NORTHERN IRELAND) 2002, SR 2002 352; made under the Superannuation (Northern Ireland) Order 1972 (SI 1972 1073 (NI.10)) Art.9, Sch.3. In force: February 1, 2003; £10.00.

These Regulations replace certain provisions of the Local Government Pension Scheme Regulations (Northern Ireland) 2000 (SR 2000 177) and constitute the occupational pension scheme for persons employed by a local authority or engaged in other employment, who are active members of the Scheme on or after the commencement date of these Regulations, and replace them in part for other members in accordance with the Local Government Pension Scheme (Amendment No.2 and Transitional Provisions) Regulations (Northern Ireland) 2002 (SR 2002 353).

5062. Occupational pensions–local government pension scheme–membership

LOCAL GOVERNMENT PENSION SCHEME (AMENDMENT NO.2 AND TRANSITIONAL PROVISIONS) REGULATIONS (NORTHERN IRELAND) 2002, SR 2002 353; made under the Superannuation (Northern Ireland) Order 1972 (SI 1972 1073 (NI.10)) Art.9, Art.14, Sch.3. In force: February 1, 2003; £4.00.

These Regulations amend the Local Government (Superannuation) (Milk Marketing Board for Northern Ireland) Regulations (Northern Ireland) 1997 (SR 1997 137), the Local Government Pension Scheme Regulations (Northern Ireland) 2000 (SR 2000 177) and the Local Government (Discretionary Payments) Regulations (Northern Ireland) 2001 (SR 2001 279). They are supplemental to the Local Government Pension Scheme Regulations (Northern Ireland) 2002 (SR 2002 352) which set out the pension arrangements of the Local Government Pension Scheme. The Regulations make provision for the transition from the Scheme arrangements in the 2000 Regulations to those set out in the 2002 Regulations. They provide for the continuation of certain provisions of the 2000 Regulations for members who are not then active members and also make amendments to those Regulations to provide for continuity of membership in periods of maternity absence or parental leave and in relation to an employee's obligations to make contributions during a period of maternity absence.

5063. Occupational pensions–minimum funding requirement

OCCUPATIONAL PENSION SCHEMES (MINIMUM FUNDING REQUIREMENT AND MISCELLANEOUS AMENDMENTS) REGULATIONS (NORTHERN IRELAND) 2002, SR 2002 64; made under the Pensions (Northern Ireland) Order 1995 (SI 1995 3213 (NI.22)) Art.56, Art.57, Art.58, Art.59, Art.61, Art.73, Art.75, Art.122, Art.166. In force: March 19, 2002; £2.50.

These Regulations amend the Pensions (Northern Ireland) Order 1995 (SI 1995 3213), the Occupational Pension Schemes (Minimum Funding Requirement and Actuarial Valuations) Regulations (Northern Ireland) 1996 (SR 1996 570), the Occupational Pension Schemes (Deficiency on Winding Up etc.) Regulations (Northern Ireland) 1996 (SR 1996 585) and the Occupational Pension Schemes (Winding Up) Regulations (Northern Ireland) 1996 (SR 1996 621). The amendments extend the deficit correction periods within which scheme underfunding must be made good, remove the requirement for annual recertifications for schemes that are fully funded and include a number of minor technical amendments and provide that, where a scheme is in the process of winding up and the employer is not insolvent, the scheme's liabilities are to be calculated so as to include the actual cost of winding up and the cost of securing pensions or other benefits in payment by way of annuities. The Regulations also amend the calculation of liabilities in respect of any pension or other benefit which has become payable under a scheme in circumstances where the scheme winds up and the employer is not insolvent at the time the winding up commenced.

5064. Occupational pensions – personal pensions – bankruptcy

OCCUPATIONAL AND PERSONAL PENSION SCHEMES (BANKRUPTCY) REGULATIONS (NORTHERN IRELAND) 2002, SR 2002 127; made under the Insolvency (Northern Ireland) Order 1989 (SI 1989 2405 (NI.19)) Art.315C, Art.315F; and the Welfare Reform and Pensions (Northern Ireland) Order 1999 (SI 1999 3147 (NI.11)) Art.12, Art.13, Art.73. In force: April 6, 2002; £2.50.

These Regulations prescribe pension arrangements for the purposes of the Welfare Reform and Pensions (Northern Ireland) Order 1999 (SI 1999 3147) to allow pension rights of a bankrupt person under such arrangements to be excluded from his estate. They prescribe pension arrangements which qualify as "unapproved pension arrangements", prescribe the person responsible for providing information for the purpose of making applications to the High Court or entering into agreements to have rights under an unapproved pension arrangement excluded from the bankrupt's estate and set out the ways in which an unapproved pension arrangement can be excluded from a bankrupt's estate. They make provision, in relation to a prescribed unapproved pension arrangement, relating to the making of an "exclusion order" excluding the rights of a bankrupt under such an arrangement from his estate, provide for the making of a "qualifying agreement" between the bankrupt and the trustee in bankruptcy excluding the rights of a bankrupt under an unapproved pension arrangement from his estate and provide for the calculation and verification of the cash equivalent of a bankrupt's rights under an approved pension arrangement. In addition, the Regulations provide that where a restoration order has been made the person responsible for the pension arrangement in question shall comply with that order within the prescribed time, provide for the calculation and verification of the cash equivalent of a person's pension rights where those rights are derived directly, or indirectly, from a pension-sharing transaction and prescribe the periods within which the person responsible for the pension arrangement in question has to comply with a request for information.

5065. Occupational pensions – police – unpaid maternity and sick leave

POLICE SERVICE OF NORTHERN IRELAND PENSIONS REGULATIONS 2002, SR 2002 100; made under the Police (Northern Ireland) Act 1998 s.25. In force: April 12, 2002; £2.00.

These Regulations amend the Royal Ulster Constabulary Pensions Regulations 1988 (SR 1988 374) with respect to unpaid maternity and sick leave. The Regulations incorporate police trainees as members, make new arrangements for making contributions to enable periods of unpaid maternity leave to count as pensionable service and make new provision for enabling periods of unpaid sick leave to count as pensionable service.

5066. Occupational pensions – police – unpaid maternity and sick leave

POLICE SERVICE OF NORTHERN IRELAND RESERVE (FULL-TIME) PENSIONS REGULATIONS 2002, SR 2002 101; made under the Police (Northern Ireland) Act 1998 s.26. In force: April 12, 2002; £2.00.

These Regulations amend the Royal Ulster Constabulary Reserve (Full-time) Pensions Regulations 1994 (SR 1994 197) with respect to unpaid maternity and sick leave. They make new arrangements for making contributions to enable periods of unpaid maternity leave to count as pensionable service, make new provision for enabling periods of unpaid sick leave to count as pensionable service and provide for part-time service under the Royal Ulster Constabulary Reserve (Full-time) (Appointment and Conditions of Service) Regulations 1996 (SR 1996 564) to be calculated for determining pensionable service.

5067. Occupational pensions—revaluation of benefits

OCCUPATIONAL PENSIONS (REVALUATION) ORDER (NORTHERN IRELAND) 2002, SR 2002 369; made under the Pension Schemes (Northern Ireland) Act 1993 Sch.2 para.2. In force: January 1, 2003; £1.50.

This Order, which corresponds to the Occupational Pensions (Revaluation) Order 2002 (SI 2002 2951), specifies appropriate revaluation percentages. The percentages specified are relevant to the revaluation of benefits under occupational pension schemes as required by the Pension Schemes (Northern Ireland) Act 1993.

5068. Occupational pensions—trustees and directors—appointments—alternative arrangements

OCCUPATIONAL PENSION SCHEMES (MEMBER-NOMINATED TRUSTEES AND DIRECTORS) (AMENDMENT) REGULATIONS (NORTHERN IRELAND) 2002, SR 2002 279; made under the Pensions (Northern Ireland) Order 1995 (SI 1995 3213 (NI 22)) Art.17, Art.19, Art.21, Art.166. In force: October 6, 2002; £2.00.

These Regulations amend the Occupational Pension Schemes (Member-nominated Trustees and Directors) Regulations (Northern Ireland) 1996 (SR 1996 431) which concern the selection and appointment of member-nominated trustees and directors. The Regulations extend the approval of alternative arrangements for selecting the trustees or directors of a scheme, and of appropriate rules for that same purpose, so that the approval ceases after a period of 10 years rather than six years.

5069. Occupational pensions—winding up notices and reports

OCCUPATIONAL PENSION SCHEMES (WINDING UP NOTICES AND REPORTS, ETC.) REGULATIONS (NORTHERN IRELAND) 2002, SR 2002 74; made under the Pension Schemes (Northern Ireland) Act 1993 s.109; and the Pensions (Northern Ireland) Order (SI 1995 3213 (NI.22)) Art.10, Art.23, Art.26B, Art.26C, Art.49A, Art.71A, Art.72A, Art.72B, Art.115, Art.121, Art.166. In force: April 1, 2002; £3.00.

These Regulations, which amend the Occupational Pension Schemes (Disclosure of Information) Regulations (Northern Ireland) 1997 (SR 1997 98), give effect to the winding up provisions of the Pensions (Northern Ireland) Order 1995 (SI 1995 3213 (NI.22)) and introduce measures designed to speed up the winding up of occupational pension schemes.

5070. Public service—pensions—increase in rates

PENSIONS INCREASE (REVIEW) ORDER (NORTHERN IRELAND) 2002, SR 2002 102; made under the Social Security Pensions (Northern Ireland) Order 1975 (SI 1975 1503 (NI.15)) Art.69. In force: April 8, 2002; £2.00.

Under the Social Security Pensions (Northern Ireland) Order 1975, the Department of Finance and Personnel is required to provide by Order for increases in the rates of public service pensions. For pensions which began before April 9, 2001 the increase is 1.7 per cent and for pensions which began on or after April 9, 2001 the increases are specified in this Order.

5071. Stakeholder pensions—annual declaration

STAKEHOLDER PENSION SCHEMES (AMENDMENT) REGULATIONS (NORTHERN IRELAND) 2002, SR 2002 216; made under the Welfare Reform and Pensions (Northern Ireland) Order1999 (SI1999 3147 (NI.11)) Art.3, Art.73. In force: July 4, 2002; £1.75.

These Regulations, which amend the Stakeholder Pension Schemes Regulations (Northern Ireland) 2000 (SR 2000 262), provide for an annual declaration as to the arrangements made by the trustees or manager of a stakeholder pension scheme for ensuring the proper administration of the scheme and for the trustees or manager to obtain statements from the scheme's reporting accountant as to the reasonableness of the annual declaration. They further provide that the trustees or manager of a scheme must make an annual declaration within 3 months of each reporting date, extend to December 31, 2002 the time limit for the trustees or manager of a scheme to make their annual declaration, where the declaration relates to a reporting date on or before September 30, 2002, and extends to December 31, 2002 the time limit for the trustees or manager of a scheme to obtain the required statements from the reporting accountants, where these would otherwise have had to be obtained prior to this date.

5072.   Stakeholder pensions–trustees powers and duties

STAKEHOLDER PENSION SCHEMES (AMENDMENT NO.2) REGULATIONS (NORTHERN IRELAND) 2002, SR 2002 268; made under the Welfare Reform and Pensions (Northern Ireland) Order 1999 (SI 1999 3147 (NI.11)) Art.3, Art.73. In force: September 9, 2002; £2.00.

These Regulations amend the Stakeholder Pension Schemes Regulations (Northern Ireland) 2000 (SR 2000 262), the Stakeholder Pension Schemes (Amendment No.2) Regulations (Northern Ireland) 2001 (SR 2001 119) and the Stakeholder Pension Schemes (Amendment) Regulations (Northern Ireland) 2002 (SR 2002 216). They remove certain eligibility requirements for appointment as a reporting accountant; require the trustees or manager of the scheme to make a declaration and obtain a reporting accountant's statement within 6 months of the reporting date; set out how the reporting date is to be calculated; set out the statements to be made by the trustees or manager in their declaration; require the trustees or manager to send copies of the declaration and reporting accountant's statement to members and beneficiaries on request; provide that any statement obtained from a reporting accountant ineligible for such an appointment will not be regarded as a statement obtained in accordance with the Regulations; and require an insurance company managing with-profits funds for a scheme to pass various certificates to the trustees or manager.

5073.   Superannuation–addition of employment–Invest Northern Ireland

SUPERANNUATION (INVEST NORTHERN IRELAND) ORDER (NORTHERN IRELAND) 2002, SR 2002 211; made under the Superannuation (Northern Ireland) Order 1972 (SI 1972 1073 (NI.10)) Art.3. In force: July 11, 2002; £1.50.

This Order adds employment in Invest Northern Ireland to the employments listed in the Superannuation (Northern Ireland) Order 1972 (SI 1972 1073 (NI.10)) for which the Department of Finance and Personnel may make pension schemes.

5074.   Superannuation–additional voluntary contributions–Health and Personal Social Services

HEALTH AND PERSONAL SOCIAL SERVICES (SUPERANNUATION) (ADDITIONAL VOLUNTARY CONTRIBUTIONS) (AMENDMENT) REGULATIONS (NORTHERN IRELAND) 2002, SR 2002 129; made under the Superannuation (Northern Ireland) Order 1972 (SI 1972 1073 (NI.10)) Art.12, Art.14, Sch.3. In force: May 9, 2002; £2.00.

These Regulations amend the Health and Personal Social Services (Superannuation) (Additional Voluntary Contributions) Regulations 1999 (SR 1999 294) which make provision for the payment of additional contributions by persons who are members of the Health and Personal Social Services

Superannuation Scheme. They make provision for members of the HPSS Superannuation Scheme who have paid additional contributions and secured additional benefits under the principal Regulations to defer the purchase of an annuity, until a time of their choosing, up to and including age 75.

5075. Superannuation–Health and Personal Social Services

HEALTH AND PERSONAL SOCIAL SERVICES (SUPERANNUATION) (AMENDMENT) REGULATIONS (NORTHERN IRELAND) 2002, SR 2002 69; made under the Superannuation (Northern Ireland) Order 1972 (SI 1972 1073 (NI.10)) Art.12, Art.14, Sch.3. In force: May 1, 2002; £2.00.

These Regulations amend the Health and Personal Social Services (Superannuation) Regulations 1995 (SR 1995 95) which provide for the superannuation of persons engaged in the Health and Personal Social Services in Northern Ireland. They make provision for a member's employment to be certified as terminated in the interests of the service only where his employing authority agrees and for the reckoning of service in part-time employment for the purposes of that pension. The Regulations also make new arrangements for members to nominate someone other than their surviving spouse as the person who is to receive the lump sum payable on their death, with transitional protection for existing arrangements.

PERSONAL INJURY

5076. Compensation–criminal injuries

CRIMINAL INJURIES COMPENSATION (NORTHERN IRELAND) ORDER 2002, SI 2002 796; made under the Northern Ireland Act 1998 s.85. In force: in accordance with Art.1 (2); £2.50.

This Order, which revokes the Criminal Injuries (Compensation) (Northern Ireland) Order 1988 (SI 1988 793 (NI.4)) and amends the Criminal Justice (Northern Ireland) Order 1991 (SI 1991 1711), replaces the arrangements for paying compensation for criminal injuries. The key features of the new arrangements are the introduction of a new statutory Scheme; the establishment of a tariff of injuries to calculate the standard amount of compensation; in certain cases payment for loss of earnings and special expenses; the introduction of a new bereavement support payment; provision for reviews of decisions; the establishment of an independent Appeals Panel to hear appeals against decisions of the Secretary of State; the introduction of funded support and assistance from a designated body to replace paid legal assistance.

5077. Criminal Injuries Compensation (Northern Ireland) Order 2002 (SI 2002 796 (NI.1))–Commencement No.1 Order

CRIMINAL INJURIES COMPENSATION (NORTHERN IRELAND) ORDER 2002 (COMMENCEMENT NO.1) ORDER 2002, SR 2002 148 (C.15); made under the Criminal Injuries Compensation (Northern Ireland) Order 2002 (SI 2002 796 (NI.1)) Art.1. In force: bringing into operation various provisions of the 2002 Order on April 9, 2002; £1.50.

This Order brings into operation the provisions of the Criminal Injuries Compensation (Northern Ireland) Order 2002 (SI 2002 796 (NI.1)) which are necessary for the Secretary of State to make the Scheme for the payment of criminal injuries compensation under the Order.

5078. Criminal Injuries Compensation (Northern Ireland) Order 2002 (SI 2002 796 (NI.1))–Commencement No.2 Order

CRIMINAL INJURIES COMPENSATION (NORTHERN IRELAND) ORDER 2002 (COMMENCEMENT NO.2) ORDER 2002, SR 2002 205 (C.20); made under the

Criminal Injuries Compensation (Northern Ireland) Order 2002 (SI 2002 796 (NI.1)) Art.1. In force: bringing into operation various provisions of the 2002 Order on May 1, 2002; £1.50.

This Order brings into operation all the remaining provisions of the Criminal Injuries Compensation (Northern Ireland) Order 2002 (SI 2002 796 (NI.1)).

5079. Northern Ireland Criminal Injuries Compensation Scheme 2002–Commencement No.1 Order

NORTHERN IRELAND CRIMINAL INJURIES COMPENSATION SCHEME 2002 (COMMENCEMENT NO.1) ORDER 2002, SR 2002 204; made under the Criminal Injuries Compensation (Northern Ireland) Order 2002 (SI 2002 796 (C.15)) Art.3. In force: bringing into operation various provisions of the 2002 Scheme on May 1, 2002; £1.50.

This Order brings into operation the Northern Ireland Criminal Injuries Compensation Scheme 2002 save for a provision relating to jurisdiction of claim.

PLANNING

5080. Planning applications–general development procedure–permitted development rights

PLANNING (GENERAL DEVELOPMENT) (AMENDMENT) ORDER (NORTHERN IRELAND) 2002, SR 2002 195; made under the Planning (Northern Ireland) Order 1991 (SI 1991 1220 (NI.11)) Art.13. In force: June 21, 2002; £1.75.

This Order amends the Planning (General Development) Order (Northern Ireland) 1993 (SR 1993 278) to remove permitted development rights previously available to telecommunications code system operators. It provides that land may be used, subject to conditions, by telecommunications code system operators for up to 6 months to provide replacement moveable apparatus in place of unserviceable apparatus. It also provides that the amendment will not apply to applications for prior approval already made to the Department before the date on which the Order comes into operation.

POLICE

5081. Conditions of employment–police support staff–recruitment

POLICE SERVICE OF NORTHERN IRELAND (RECRUITMENT OF POLICE SUPPORT STAFF) REGULATIONS 2002, SR 2002 258; made under the Police (Northern Ireland) Act 2000 s.43, s.44. In force: September 20, 2002; £1.75.

These Regulations, which make provision for the recruitment of police support staff, give effect to recommendations of the Independent Commission on Policing in Northern Ireland in its report A New Beginning: Policing in Northern Ireland published on September 9, 1999. They apply only to posts to which candidates are to be appointed under the Police (Northern Ireland) Act 2000 s.4(3). They provide for the appointment of an agent to exercise certain functions of the Chief Constable in connection with the recruitment of police support staff; make provision for the advertising of vacancies for police support staff and require the Chief Constable or the recruitment agent to have regard to the recommendations of the Patten Report in conducting advertising; set out the functions of the Chief Constable and the recruitment agent as regards information to be provided by candidates for posts in the police support staff, and as regards tests and assessments for such candidates; and make provision for vetting candidates for posts in the police support staff.

5082. Detention–place of detention–designation–Lisburn police station

POLICE (NORTHERN IRELAND) ACT 2000 (DESIGNATED PLACES OF DETENTION) 2002, SR 2002 179; made under the Police (Northern Ireland) Act 2000 s.73. In force: May 31, 2002; £1.50.

This Order specifies as a designated place of detention that part of Lisburn Police Station that is designated for the purposes of the Terrorism Act 2000 Sch.8 para.1 with the effect that the whole of Lisburn Police Station is a designated place of detention.

5083. Flags–emblems

POLICE EMBLEMS AND FLAGS REGULATIONS (NORTHERN IRELAND) 2002, SR 2002 23; made under the Police (Northern Ireland) Act 2000 s.54. In force: April 5, 2002; £2.00.

These Regulations prescribe the emblem for the police and provide that that is the only emblem for the police which may be used on equipment and property. Exceptions are made to this general rule for the emblem which is to be used on police officers' uniform buttons, for emblems in a police memorial and the police museum and for the purposes of signifying rank. They also prescribe the flag for the police which is the flag that may be flown from police buildings, except where the building is being visited by Her Majesty the Queen and the only flag that may be carried on parade by the police.

5084. Police officers–policing plan–statements and particulars

POLICE (NORTHERN IRELAND) ACT 2000 (POLICING PLAN) REGULATIONS 2002, SR 2002 76; made under the Police (Northern Ireland) Act 2000 s.26. In force: in accordance with Art.1; £1.75.

These Regulations set out the statements and particulars to be included in the annual policing plan which the Northern Ireland Policing Board is required to issue under the Police (Northern Ireland) Act 2000. The Policing Plan must set out the proposed arrangements for the policing of Northern Ireland and, in addition to the matters prescribed in these Regulations, must also include the matters specified in the 2000 Act which relate to requirements for educating and training police officers and members of the police support staff.

5085. Police officers–Royal Ulster Constabulary GC Foundation–establishment

ROYAL ULSTER CONSTABULARY GC FOUNDATION REGULATIONS 2002, SR 2002 260; made under the Police (Northern Ireland) Act 2000 s.70. In force: September 16, 2002; £1.75.

These Regulations provide for the establishment, maintenance and operation of a Royal Ulster Constabulary GC Foundation in accordance with the Police Act (Northern Ireland) 2000 s.70 for the purpose of marking the sacrifices and honouring the achievements of the Royal Ulster Constabulary.

5086. Police (Northern Ireland) Act 2000 (c.32)–Commencement No.4 Order

POLICE (NORTHERN IRELAND) ACT 2000 (COMMENCEMENT NO.4) ORDER 2002, SR 2002 146 (C.14); made under the Police (Northern Ireland) Act 2000 s.79. In force: bringing into operation vrious provisions of the 2000 Act on April 15, 2002; £1.50.

This Order brings into force specified provisions of the Police (Northern Ireland) Act 2000.

5087. Remuneration–pay scales

POLICE SERVICE OF NORTHERN IRELAND REGULATIONS 2002, SR 2002 95; made under the Police (Northern Ireland) Act 1998 s.25. In force: in accordance with Reg.1 (2); £3.00.

These Regulations, which amend the Royal Ulster Constabulary Regulations 1996 (SI 1996 473), provide for June 3, 2002 and June 4, 2002 to be public holidays. They make provision for part-time workers, including those taking part in job-share arrangements, replace the pay scales formerly set out in the 1996 Regulations, provide for the pay of a chief inspector who for 14 days in any year performs the duties of a superintendent to be determined in respect of any further days in that year in which the chief inspector performs those duties by reference to the pay range applicable to superintendents and provide for a higher rate of pay on promotion. In addition, the Regulations increase various allowances, abolish detective expenses allowances and provide and increase a single dog handler's allowance.

5088. Remuneration–pay scales

POLICE SERVICE OF NORTHERN IRELAND RESERVE (FULL-TIME) (APPOINTMENT AND CONDITIONS OF SERVICE) REGULATIONS 2002, SR 2002 96; made under the Police (Northern Ireland) Act 1998 s.26. In force: in accordance with Reg.1 (2); £2.00.

These Regulations, which amend the Royal Ulster Constabulary Reserve (Full-time) (Appointment and Conditions of Service) Regulations 1996 (SR 1996 564), make provision for the last bank holiday in May to be replaced with June 3, 2002 and June 4, 2002. They replace the pay scales formerly set out in the 1996 Regulations with a provision that the pay of members of the police force will be determined by the Secretary of State, make provision for part-time workers, including those taking part in job-share arrangements and increase the amounts of certain allowances.

RATES

5089. Non domestic rates–shops–rateable value–allowance for cost of repairs

B sought a reduction of the rating valuation placed on shop premises of £9,300 on the ground that insufficient allowance had been given to reflect the poor condition of the premises when compared with other premises in the area. The shop was situated in a secondary retail location close to the main shopping street and was one of a terrace of former dwelling houses which had been converted to retail use many years before. The main building consisted of three floors. In addition, there was a return which was mainly two storey and a single storey lean to. The ground floor was used for a dry cleaning business and the upper floors, although largely disused, were in partial use for the storage of unclaimed items. Different methods of valuation were put forward by B and the Valuation Commissioner. B used the zone A price for the parade of shops to calculate a value for the ground floor assuming it was in a refurbished condition and then made an allowance for the cost of refurbishing and partially rebuilding the property to achieve that condition. The allowance was based on estimates obtained from two builders which had been rentalised. This method arrived at a valuation of £7,500. B's valuer also gave evidence that it was his practice to value property in first class order and then make allowances for the condition of the property. The Commissioner also used a zonal approach but relied on the comparison of the property with two similar properties within the terrace. He also looked at the state of repair of the property on a block by block basis assessing its suitability for use and adjusting the pricing accordingly using a halving back approach. He made no further allowance for annual repairs.

Held, confirming the assessment, that (1) the ratepayers method of valuation was flawed in that the cost of repairs used to restrict the valuation was the cost to partially rebuild the premises to a higher standard than that of the surrounding properties, but the initial valuation had been based on the value of those properties where the repairs allowable should have been those required to maintain the property in its existing condition or to bring it up to the standard of comparable properties, and (2) the method adopted by the Commissioner was to be preferred as it was based on comparable assessments, was transparent and used a modified application of the zoning method in relation to the return an lean to, which resulted in a valuation that needed limited adjustment.

BLACK v. COMMISSIONER OF VALUATION FOR NORTHERN IRELAND [2002] R.A. 79, Michael R Curry FRICS, Lands Tr (NI).

5090. Rateable value—determination of rateable value

RATES (REGIONAL RATES) ORDER (NORTHERN IRELAND) 2002, SR 2002 26; made under the Rates (Northern Ireland) Order 1977 (SI 1977 2157 (NI.28)) Art.2, Art.7, Art.27. In force: April 1, 2002; £1.50.

This Order, which fixes the amounts of the regional rates for the year ending March 31, 2003, specifies 31.42 pence in the pound as the amount of the regional rate in respect of those hereditaments which are not dwelling houses, private garages or private storage premises and 199.29 pence in the pound in respect of those hereditaments which are. It also fixes 66.82 pence as the amount by which the normal regional rate is reduced in respect of unspecified hereditaments and hereditaments which, though not specified hereditaments, are used partly for the purposes of unspecified hereditaments.

5091. Rateable value—valuation list—2003

RATES (MAKING AND LEVYING OF DIFFERENT RATES) REGULATIONS (NORTHERN IRELAND) 2002, SR 2002 409; made under the Rates (Northern Ireland) Order 1977 (SI 1977 2157 (NI.28)) Art.6. In force: January 28, 2003; £1.75.

A new valuation list comes into effect on April 1, 2003 for the purposes of the Rates (Northern Ireland) Order 1977 (SI 1977 2157 (NI.28)) Part III which contains general revaluations of all properties in Northern Ireland other than dwelling-houses, private garages and private storage premises. These Regulations, which revoke with a saving the Rates (Making and Levying of Different Rates) (No.2) Regulations (Northern Ireland) 1997 (SR 1997 50), prescribe the rules under which different rates may be made and levied in relation to domestic property on the one hand and any other property on the other and ensure that the rate set in relation to non-domestic premises reflect the changes in the new valuation list in relation to such premises.

REAL PROPERTY

5092. Land registration—compulsory registration areas

COMPULSORY REGISTRATION OF TITLE ORDER (NORTHERN IRELAND) 2002, SR 2002 400; made under the Land Registration Act (Northern Ireland) 1970 s.25. In force: April 1, 2003; £1.75.

This Order declares Counties Fermanagh, Tyrone and Londonderry to be compulsory registration areas under the Land Registration (Northern Ireland) Act 1970. The type of property transaction which triggers a compulsory registration within that area is defined by entry 2 of Sch.2 to the 1970 Act.

5093. Land registration–compulsory registration areas

COMPULSORY REGISTRATION OF TITLE (NO.2) ORDER (NORTHERN IRELAND) 2002, SR 2002 401; made under the Land Registration Act (Northern Ireland) 1970 s.25. In force: May 1, 2003; £1.75.

This Order declares County Antrim, the County Borough of Belfast and the remaining part of County Down not already declared to be such an area to be compulsory registration areas under the Land Registration (Northern Ireland) Act 1970. The type of property transaction which triggers a compulsory registration within that area is defined by entry 2 of Sch.2 to the 1970 Act. This is the last Compulsory Registration Order which declares the remaining part of Northern Ireland to be a compulsory first registration area.

5094. Land registration–ground rents

LAND REGISTRATION (AMENDMENT) RULES (NORTHERN IRELAND) 2002, SR 2002 229; made under the Land Registration Act (Northern Ireland) 1970 s.81; the Ground Rents Act (Northern Ireland) 2001 s.4, s.5, s.6, s.7, s.23, s.26, s.31; and the Property (Northern Ireland) Order 1997 (SI 1997 1179 (NI.8)) Art.35, Art.35A. In force: July 29, 2002; £3.00.

These Rules, which amend the Land Registration Rules (Northern Ireland) 1994 (SR 1994 424), enable the Land Registry to deal with applications made by persons wishing to redeem ground rents under the Ground Rents Act (Northern Ireland) 2001 Act; provide for the making of entries and cancellations on the title register in consequence of the redemption of ground rents; provide for searches in the register kept under s.5(2) of the 2001 Act and searches in that register; and provide for the disposal of money lodged with the Land Registry.

5095. Property (Northern Ireland) Order 1997 (SI 1997 1179 (NI.8))– Commencement No.3 Order

PROPERTY (1997 ORDER) (COMMENCEMENT NO.3) ORDER (NORTHERN IRELAND) 2002, SR 2002 252; made under the Property (Northern Ireland) Order 1997 (SI 1997 1179 (NI.8)) Art.1. In force: bringing into operation various provisions of the 1997 Order on July 29, 2002; £1.50.

This Order brings into operation the provisions of the Property (Northern Ireland) Order 1997 (SI 1997 1179 (NI.8)) which deal with the enlargement of a leasehold estate subject to no or a nominal rent, and associated repeals.

SENTENCING

5096. Dangerous driving–death–driver under influence of alcohol and driving at excessive speed–suspended sentence–undue leniency

[Road Traffic (Northern Ireland) Order 1995 Art.9.]

R was sentenced to four years' imprisonment suspended for four years following a guilty plea to a charge of causing death by dangerous driving. The plea was entered on the basis that R's driving was a causative factor in an accident in which his fiancee died. In sentencing R, the judge recognised that a custodial sentence would normally be imposed, but felt that a suspended sentence was appropriate, given the relationship between R and the deceased and the fact that her father had asked for leniency and a non custodial sentence. The Attorney General for Northern Ireland sought leave to refer the sentence on the ground of undue leniency as R had been disqualified at the date of the accident. He had also driven at excess speed and been under the influence of alcohol at the time.

Held, allowing the reference and imposing a sentence of two years' imprisonment, that R's driving, which had included an attempt to evade the

police, had been dangerous and showed a total lack or responsibility. Even with the mitigating factors taken into account, a custodial sentence was required.
ATTORNEY GENERAL OF NORTHERN IRELAND'S REFERENCE (NO.3 OF 2000), *Re; sub nom.* R. v. ROGAN (GERARD JAMES); ATTORNEY GENERAL FOR NORTHERN IRELAND'S REFERENCE (NO.3 OF 2000) [2001] N.I. 367, Carswell, L.C.J., CA (Crim Div) (NI).

5097. Dangerous driving–escaped prisoner evading recapture–high speed car chase when under influence of alcohol

G escaped from custody and was later apprehended after a dangerous high speed car chase. Following his arrest, a breath test showed that G was over the permitted alcohol limit at the time. G was sentenced to 12 months' imprisonment on a count of escaping from lawful custody, 21 months' imprisonment for dangerous driving consecutive to the 12 month term and 9 months' imprisonment again consecutive for driving while disqualified, giving a total custodial sentence of three and a half years' imprisonment. G appealed, contending that the sentences were excessive and should have been concurrent. Further, G argued that a custody probation order should have been used.
Held, allowing the appeal in part, the consecutive sentences for escaping from custody and the road traffic offences committed while G was at large were within the discretion of the sentencing judge and would not be interfered with. However, the length of the sentence for dangerous driving was not justified on a guilty plea and would be reduced to 18 months' imprisonment. A one year custody probation order was justified on the ground that it would assist G to redeem himself. Therefore the total term of imprisonment would be reduced to two years with one year's probation.
R. v. GAYNOR (CHARLES JOHN) [2001] N.I. 418, Carswell, L.C.J., CA (Crim Div) (NI).

SHIPPING

5098. Harbours–Belfast

BELFAST HARBOUR ORDER (NORTHERN IRELAND) 2002, SR 2002 40; made under the Harbours Act (Northern Ireland) 1970 s.1, Sch.1, Sch.2; and the Part 1. In force: in accordance with Art.1 (1); £2.50.
This Order amends the Belfast Harbour Act 1847, the Belfast Port and Harbour Conservancy Act 1852, the Belfast Dock Act 1854, the Belfast Harbour Act 1870, the Belfast Harbour Act 1882, the Belfast Harbour Act 1898, the Belfast Harbour Act 1918, the Belfast Harbour Act 1938, the Belfast Harbour Act 1950, the Belfast Harbour Act 1956 and the Belfast Harbour Acts (Amendment) Order (Northern Ireland) 1979 (SR 1979 32). It confers on the Belfast Harbour Commissioners general powers and duties, the power of retention and disposal of land subject to arrangements made by the Department, the power of formation of wholly-owned subsidiaries for carrying on activities which the Commissioners have power to carry on, the power of regulation of borrowing of money and licensing of pleasure craft and boatmen within the port.

5099. Harbours–Londonderry

LONDONDERRY HARBOUR ORDER (NORTHERN IRELAND) 2002, SR 2002 41; made under the Harbours Act (Northern Ireland) 1970 s.1, Sch.1, Sch.2 Part 1. In force: in accordance with Art.1 (1); £2.50.
This Order amends the Londonderry Port and Harbour Act 1854, the Londonderry Port and Harbour Act 1874, the Londonderry Port and Harbour Act 1882, the Londonderry Port and Harbour Act 1919, the Londonderry Port and Harbour Act 1920, the Londonderry Port and Harbour Commissioners Acts

(Amendment) Order (Northern Ireland) 1976 (SR 1976 389) and the Londonderry Harbour Order (Northern Ireland) 1991 (SR 1991 261). It confers on the Londonderry Port and Harbour Commissioners general powers and duties, the power of retention and disposal of land subject to arrangements made by the Department, the power of formation of wholly-owned subsidiaries for carrying on activities which the Commissioners have power to carry on, the power of regulation of borrowing of money and the power of licensing of pleasure craft and boatmen within the port.

5100. Harbours–pilotage limits–Londonderry–variation

LONDONDERRY PORT AND HARBOUR (VARIATION OF PILOTAGE LIMITS) ORDER (NORTHERN IRELAND) 2002, SR 2002 394; made under the Harbours Act (Northern Ireland) 1970 s.1, Sch.1. In force: February 17, 2003; £1.75.

By virtue of the Pilotage Act 1987 s.7 (5) a direction given by a competent harbour authority for the purpose of making pilotage compulsory for ships navigating in a specified area shall not apply to any area which is outside the authority's harbour unless the limits of jurisdiction of the authority for pilotage purposes has been extended to cover that area. This Order extends the limits of jurisdiction of Londonderry Port and Harbour Commissioners for pilotage purposes under the Pilotage Act 1987 Part I to include an area outside their harbour in respect of which the Commissioners consider that pilotage should be compulsory.

5101. Harbours–Warrenpoint

WARRENPOINT HARBOUR AUTHORITY ORDER (NORTHERN IRELAND) 2002, SR 2002 42; made under the Harbours Act (Northern Ireland) 1970 s.1, Sch.1, Sch.2 Part 1. In force: in accordance with Art.1 (1); £2.50.

This Order, which amends the Warrenpoint Harbour Authority Order (Northern Ireland) 1971 (SR & O 1971 136), confers on the Warrenpoint Harbour Authority general powers and duties, the power of retention and disposal of land subject to arrangements made by the Department, the power of formation of wholly-owned subsidiaries for carrying on activities which the Commissioners have power to carry on, the power of regulation of borrowing of money and licensing of pleasure craft and boatmen within the port.

5102. Harbours (Northern Ireland) Order 2002 (SI 2002 3155 (NI.9))

This Order confers functions on the Department for Regional Development in relation to the regulation of certain harbour authorities.

SOCIAL SECURITY

5103. Attendance allowance–disability living allowance–cost of accommodation

SOCIAL SECURITY (ATTENDANCE ALLOWANCE AND DISABILITY LIVING ALLOWANCE) (AMENDMENT) REGULATIONS (NORTHERN IRELAND) 2002, SR 2002 31; made under the Social Security Contributions and Benefits (Northern Ireland) Act 1992 s.67, s.72, s.171. In force: March 1, 2002; £1.75.

These Regulations, which amend the Social Security (Attendance Allowance) Regulations (Northern Ireland) 1992 (SR 1992 20) and the Social Security (Disability Living Allowance) Regulations (Northern Ireland) 1992 (SR 1992 32), provide that the cost of the accommodation does not include the cost of health services provided pursuant to the Health and Personal Social Services (Northern Ireland) Order 1972 (SI 1972 1265).

5104. Benefits–approved work–computation of earnings

SOCIAL SECURITY BENEFIT (COMPUTATION OF EARNINGS) (AMENDMENT) (NORTHERN IRELAND) REGULATIONS 2002, SI 2002 2925; made under the Social Security Contributions and Benefits (Northern Ireland) Act 1992 s.3. In force: in accordance with Art.1; £1.75.

These Regulations amend the Social Security Benefit (Computation of Earnings) Regulations (Northern Ireland) 1996 (SR 1996 520) so that earnings for benefit purposes include not only remuneration paid to a claimant during a period of maternity leave or sick absence but also any payment of remuneration during a period of adoption leave or paternity leave under the Employment Rights Act 1996.

5105. Benefits–children and young persons–personal allowances

SOCIAL SECURITY (PERSONAL ALLOWANCES FOR CHILDREN AND YOUNG PERSONS AMENDMENT) REGULATIONS (NORTHERN IRELAND) 2002, SR 2002 267; made under the Social Security Contributions and Benefits (Northern Ireland) Act 1992 s.122, s.131, s.171; and the Jobseekers (Northern Ireland) Order 1995 (SI 1995 2705 (NI.15)) Art.6. In force: October 14, 2002; £1.75.

These Regulations amend the Income Support (General) Regulations (Northern Ireland) 1987 (SR 1987 459), the Housing Benefit (General) Regulations (Northern Ireland) 1987 (SR 1987 461) and the Jobseeker's Allowance Regulations (Northern Ireland) 1996 (SR 1996 198). They increase by £3.50 the amounts of the weekly personal allowance applicable in respect of children and young persons in income support, jobseeker's allowance and housing benefit.

5106. Benefits–claims and payments

SOCIAL SECURITY (CARER'S ALLOWANCE) (AMENDMENT) REGULATIONS (NORTHERN IRELAND) 2002, SR 2002 323; made under the Social Security Contributions and Benefits (Northern Ireland) Act 1992 s.22, s.70, s.79, s.90, s.113, s.122, s.123, s.131, s.132, s.134, s.171, s.171 (4), Sch.3 para.2(8); the Social Security Administration (Northern Ireland) Act 1992 s.2A, s.5, s.5A, s.71, s.74, s.102, s.165; the Social Security (Consequential Provisions) (Northern Ireland) Act 1992 s.5, Sch.3 para.12; the Immigration and Asylum Act 1999 s.115, ; the the Child Support (Northern Ireland) Order 1991 (SI 1991 2628) Sch.1 para 4, ; the the Child Support (Northern Ireland) Order 1995 (NI 13) Art 4; the the Child Support (Northern Ireland) Order 1995 (NI13) Art19; the the Jobseekers (Northern Ireland) Order 1995 (NI 15) (SI 1995 2705) Art.28, Art.39, Art.39; and the the Welfare Reform and Pensions (Northern Ireland) Order 1999 (NI 11) (SI 1999 3147) Art.69, Art.73. In force: in accordance with Reg.1; £2.00.

These Regulations amend the Social Security (Invalid Care Allowance) Regulations (Northern Ireland) 1976 (SR 1976 99); the Social Security (Credits) Regulations (Northern Ireland) 1975 SR 1975 (113); the Social Security Benefit (Dependency) Regulations (Northern Ireland) 1977 (SR 1977 74); the Social Security Benefit (Persons Abroad) Regulations (Northern Ireland) 1978 (SR 1978 114); the Social Security (Overlapping Benefits) Regulations (Northern Ireland) 1979 (SR 1979 242); the Social Security (Widow's Benefit and Retirement Pensions) Regulations (Northern Ireland) 1979 (SR 1979 243); the Income Support (General) Regulations (Northern Ireland) 1987 (SR 1987 459); the Housing Benefit (General) Regulations (Northern Ireland) 1987 (SR1987 461); the Social Security (Claims and Payments) Regulations (Northern Ireland) 1987 (SR 1987 465); the Social Fund (Recovery by Deductions from Benefits) Regulations (Northern Ireland) 1988 (SR 1988 21); the Income Support (Liable Relatives) Regulations (Northern Ireland) 1990 (SR 1990 375); the Child Support (Maintenance Assessments and Special Cases) Regulations (Northern Ireland) 1992 (SR 1992 341); the Invalid Care Allowance Regulations (SR 1994 370); the Social Security (Incapacity Benefit) Regulations (Northern Ireland) 1994 (SR 1994 461); the Jobseeker's Allowance Regulations (Northern Ireland) 1996 (SR 1996 198); the Jobseeker's Allowance (Transitional Provisions) (No. 2) Regulations (Northern Ireland) 1996 (SR 1996 518) the Social Security (Back to Work Bonus) (No. 2) Regulations (Northern Ireland) 1996 (SR 1996 519); the Social Security Benefit (Computation of Earnings) Regulations (Northern Ireland) 1996 (SR 1996 520); the Social Security (Invalid Care Allowance) (Amendment) Regulations (Northern Ireland) 1996 (SR 1996 521); the Social Security (Child Maintenance Bonus) Regulations (Northern Ireland) 1996 (SR 1996 622); the Social Security (Immigration and Asylum) Consequential Amendments Regulations (Northern Ireland) 2000 (SR 2000 71); the Child Support (Maintenance Calculations and Special Cases) Regulations (Northern Ireland) 2001 (SR 2001 18); the Social Security (Claims and Information) Regulations (Northern Ireland) 2001 (SR 2001 175) and the Social Security (Work-focused Interviews) Regulations (Northern Ireland) 2001 (SR 2001 176) as a consequence of changes made to the Social Security Contributions and Benefits (Northern Ireland) Act 1992 s.70 by the Deregulation (Carer's Allowance) Order (Northern Ireland) 2002 (SR 2002 321).

5107. Benefits—claims and payments

SOCIAL SECURITY (CLAIMS AND PAYMENTS) (AMENDMENT NO.2) REGULATIONS (NORTHERN IRELAND) 2002, SR 2002 254; made under the Social Security Administration (Northern Ireland) Act 1992 s.5, s.165; and the Child Support (Northern Ireland) Order SI 1991 2628 (NI.23) Art.40. In force: in accordance with Reg.1 (1) (2); £1.75.

These Regulations, which amend the Social Security (Claims and Payments) Regulations (Northern Ireland) 1987 (SR 1987 465), provide that where the amount of maternity allowance payable includes a fraction of a penny, that fraction shall be rounded up to the next whole penny; and provide that deductions from benefit may be made in respect of arrears of child support maintenance assessed under the Child Support (Northern Ireland) Order 1991 (SI 1991 2628) or calculated under the Order as amended by the Child Support, Pensions and Social Security Act (Northern Ireland) 2000 or such arrears both assessed and calculated, including arrears of maintenance payable at a transitional rate in accordance with regulations made under the 2000 Act.

5108. Benefits—claims and payments

SOCIAL SECURITY (CLAIMS AND PAYMENTS) (AMENDMENT NO.3) REGULATIONS (NORTHERN IRELAND) 2002, SR 2002 297; made under the Social Security Administration (Northern Ireland) Act 1992 s.5, s.165. In force: in accordance with Reg.1 (1); £1.75.

These Regulations amend the Social Security (Claims and Payments) Regulations (Northern Ireland) 1987 (SR 1987 465), the Social Security (Claims and Payments) (Amendment) Regulations (Northern Ireland) 1992 (SR 1992 7), the Social Security (Miscellaneous Provisions) (Amendment) Regulations (Northern Ireland) 1992 (SR 1992 83), the Social Security (Claims and Payments) (Amendment) Regulations (Northern Ireland) 1994 (SR 1994 345), the Social Security (Claims and Payments) (Amendment No. 4) Regulations (Northern Ireland) 1994 (SI 1994 484) and the Social Security (Claims and Payments Etc.) (Amendment) Regulations (Northern Ireland) 1996 (SI 1996 85). They make amendments to provide for arrangements to be made with a claimant to pay benefit by direct credit transfer into a bank or other account in his name without an application by him, into the account of another specified person or into an account in the joint names of the claimant and another specified person; provide that disability living allowance continues to be payable at four weekly intervals and other long term benefits be payable at four weekly intervals or weekly in advance; clarify the time when child benefit, guardian's allowance, incapacity benefit and severe disablement allowance is paid; provide that payment of benefit by direct credit transfer into the account of a beneficiary under age 18 or a statutory appointee shall be a good discharge to the Department for Social Development; provide that specified social fund payments may be made by direct credit transfer and if an instrument of payment is payable to a third party it may be sent to the beneficiary; and specify days for payment of retirement pension, widow's benefit and bereavement benefit.

5109. Benefits—claims and payments

SOCIAL SECURITY (CLAIMS AND PAYMENTS AND MISCELLANEOUS AMENDMENTS) REGULATIONS (NORTHERN IRELAND) 2002, SR 2002 67; made under the Social Security Administration (Northern Ireland) Act 1992 s.5; and the Social Security (Northern Ireland) Order 1998 (SI 1998 1506 (NI.10)) Art.10, Art.11. In force: April 2, 2002; £2.00.

These Regulations amend the Social Security (Claims and Payments) Regulations (Northern Ireland) 1987 (SR 1987 465), the Social Security and Child Support (Decisions and Appeals) Regulations (Northern Ireland) 1 (SR 1 162) and the Social Security and Child Support (Miscellaneous Amendments) Regulations (Northern Ireland) 2000 (SR 2000 215). They provide that where a claimant's partner or child is awarded a benefit which has the effect of making a benefit which the claimant receives payable or payable at an increased rate, the periods of entitlement to those benefits shall be the same in the circumstances specified, link certain provisions to the award rather than the payability of a benefit and provide for an extension of the time for claiming income support and jobseeker's allowance in specified circumstances.

5110. Benefits—claims and payments

SOCIAL SECURITY (CLAIMS AND PAYMENTS AND MISCELLANEOUS AMENDMENTS NO.2) REGULATIONS (NORTHERN IRELAND) 2002, SR 2002 327; made under the Social Security Contributions and Benefits (Northern Ireland) Act 1992 s.134, s.171; and the Social Security Administration (Northern Ireland) Act 1992 s.5, s.165. In force: in accordance with Reg.1 (1); £1.75.

These Regulations amend the Social Security (Claims and Payments) Regulations (Northern Ireland) 1987 (SR 1987 465) to extend the period for claiming a bereavement payment from three to 12 months; and to provide for a winter fuel payment out of the social fund to be paid, alternatively, to the partner of the person entitled despite the partner being aged under 60 where the partner is in receipt of income support or an income-based jobseeker's allowance. The extended period for claiming a bereavement payment is to apply only in respect of deaths occurring on or after April 1, 2003. A consequential amendment is made to the Social Fund Winter Fuel Payment Regulations (Northern Ireland) 2000 (SR 2000 91).

5111. Benefits—claims and payments—administration fees

SOCIAL SECURITY (CLAIMS AND PAYMENTS) (AMENDMENT) REGULATIONS (NORTHERN IRELAND) 2002, SR 2002 59; made under the Social Security Administration (Northern Ireland) Act 1992 s.13A, s.165. In force: April 1, 2002; £1.50.

These Regulations, which amend the Social Security (Claims and Payments) Regulations (Northern Ireland) 1987 (SR 1987 465) and revoke the Social Security (Claims and Payments) (Amendment) Regulations (Northern Ireland) 2000 (SR 2000 181), increase the fee which qualifying lenders pay for the purpose of defraying administrative expenses incurred by the Department for Social Development in making payments in respect of mortgage interest direct to those lenders.

5112. Benefits—employment programmes—New Deal Scheme—employment option

SOCIAL SECURITY (EMPLOYMENT PROGRAMME AMENDMENT) REGULATIONS (NORTHERN IRELAND) 2002, SR 2002 275; made under the Social Security Contributions and Benefits (Northern Ireland) Act 2002 s.122, s.132, s.171; and the Jobseekers (Northern Ireland) Order 1995 (SI 1995 2705 (NI.15)) Art.14, Art.21, Art.36, Sch.1 para.3. In force: October 14, 2002; £1.75.

These Regulations amend the Income Support (General) Regulations (Northern Ireland) 1987 (SR 1987 459), the Housing Benefit (General) Regulations (Northern Ireland) 1987 (SR 1987 461) and the Jobseeker's Allowance Regulations (Northern Ireland) 1996 (SR 1996 198). They amend the definition of the Employment Option of the New Deal so that the employed earner's Employment Option of the New Deal becomes subject to sanctions of discretionary length and is omitted from the linking provisions; and provide that mandatory top-up payments made under the Employment and Training Act (Northern Ireland) 1950 s.1 in relation to the Full-Time Education and Training Option of the New Deal shall be disregarded in the calculation of income or capital for jobseeker's allowance, income support and housing benefit.

5113. Benefits–entitlement–capital disregards

SOCIAL SECURITY (MISCELLANEOUS AMENDMENTS NO.2) REGULATIONS (NORTHERN IRELAND) 2002, SR 2002 295; made under the Security Contributions and Benefits (Northern Ireland) Act 1992 s.122, s.132, s.171; and the Jobseekers (Northern Ireland) Order 1995 (SI 1995 2705 (NI.15)) Art.14, Art.36. In force: October 14, 2002; £1.75.

These Regulations amend the Income Support (General) Regulations (Northern Ireland) 1987 (SR 1987 459), the Housing Benefit (General) Regulations (Northern Ireland) 1987 (SR 1987 461) and the Jobseeker's Allowance Regulations (Northern Ireland) 1996 (SR 1996 198). They amend the capital disregard provisions that apply when ascertaining entitlement to those benefits so that the disregard of specified arrears and concessionary payments will apply for either 52 weeks or, where large payments are made to rectify an official error and are paid during the benefit award, for the remainder of that award (as defined) if that is a longer period.

5114. Benefits–fraud

SOCIAL SECURITY (LOSS OF BENEFIT) REGULATIONS (NORTHERN IRELAND) 2002, SR 2002 79; made under the Social Security (Northern Ireland) Order 1998 (SI 1998 1506 (NI.10)) Art.74, Sch.2 para.9; and the Social Security Fraud Act (Northern Ireland) 2001 s.6, s.7, s.8, s.9. In force: April 1, 2002; £3.50.

These Regulations, which amend the Social Security and Child Support (Decisions and Appeals) Regulations (Northern Ireland) 1999 (SR 1999 162), relate to restrictions in payment of certain benefits which apply where a person has been convicted of one or more benefit offences in each of two separate proceedings and one offence is committed within three years of the conviction for another such offence. They prescribe what is to be the disqualification period for the purposes of the imposition of the loss of benefit or reduction in the amount payable, what are to be the reductions in income support or joint-claim jobseeker's allowance when the restrictions apply and make provision for an income-based jobseeker's allowance to be paid where the claimant is a person in hardship. They also make provision regarding reductions in housing benefit during the disqualification period or the relevant period and prescribe certain benefits which are to be disqualifying but not sanctionable benefits.

5115. Benefits–hospital in-patients

SOCIAL SECURITY (HOSPITAL IN-PATIENTS) (AMENDMENT) REGULATIONS (NORTHERN IRELAND) 2002, SR 2002 106; made under the Social Security Administration (Northern Ireland) Act 1992 s.71, s.165. In force: April 8, 2002; £1.75.

These Regulations, which revoke the Social Security (Hospital In-Patients) (Amendment) Regulations (Northern Ireland) 2001 (SR 2001 115), amend the Social Security (Hospital In-Patients) Regulations (Northern Ireland) 1975 (SR

1975 109) to provide for a decrease, from 39 per cent to 38 per cent of the basic retirement pension, in the percentage by which the personal rate of certain benefits is reduced in certain circumstances in respect of persons who receive continuous free in-patient treatment in a hospital or similar institution for more than six weeks but not more than 52 weeks.

5116. Benefits—income related benefits—personal injury payments

SOCIAL SECURITY (PERSONAL INJURY PAYMENTS AMENDMENT) REGULATIONS (NORTHERN IRELAND) 2002, SR 2002 299; made under the Social Security Contributions and Benefits (Northern Ireland) Act 1992 s.122, s.132, s.171; and the Jobseekers (Northern Ireland) Order 1995 (SI 1995 2705 (NI.15)) Art.14. In force: October 28, 2002; £1.75.

These Regulations amend the Income Support (General) Regulations (Northern Ireland) 1987 (SR 1987 459), the Housing Benefit (General) Regulations (Northern Ireland) 1987 (SR 1987 461) and the Jobseeker's Allowance Regulations (Northern Ireland) 1996 (SR 1996 198). They require periodical payments received by virtue of any agreement or court order to make personal injury payments to the claimant to be treated as income; and provide that payments of income received from all trusts whose funds derive from personal injury payments to a claimant, from an annuity purchased with such funds and those received by virtue of any agreement or court order to make personal injury payments to the claimant, are to be disregarded in their entirety when used for items other than everyday living expenses and £20 of such income disregarded when used for such expenses.

5117. Benefits—industrial diseases—entitlement

SOCIAL SECURITY (INDUSTRIAL INJURIES) (PRESCRIBED DISEASES) (AMENDMENT) REGULATIONS (NORTHERN IRELAND) 2002, SR 2002 237; made under the Social Security Contributions and Benefits (Northern Ireland) Act 1992 s.109, s.171, Sch.6 para.1. In force: July 29, 2002; £1.75.

These Regulations, which amend the Social Security (Industrial Injuries) (Prescribed Diseases) Regulations (Northern Ireland) 1986 (SR 1986 179), remove the provision for assessing, for the purposes of industrial injuries benefit, the extent of disablement arising from diffuse mesothelioma and to prescribe impaired function of the pleura, pericardium or peritoneum caused by diffuse mesothelioma as a loss of faculty from which the resulting disabilities are to be taken as amounting to 100 per cent disablement.

5118. Benefits—intercalating students

SOCIAL SECURITY (INTERCALATING STUDENTS AMENDMENT) REGULATIONS (NORTHERN IRELAND) 2002, SR 2002 243; made under the Social Security Contributions and Benefits (Northern Ireland) Act 1992 s.122, s.133, s.171. In force: August 1, 2002; £1.75.

These Regulations, which amend the Housing Benefit (General) Regulations (Northern Ireland) 1987 (SI 1987 461) and the Jobseeker's Allowance Regulations (Northern Ireland) 1996 (SI 1996 198), make a change to the period during which students, who have taken a break from their courses due to illness or caring responsibilities, may claim housing benefit and jobseeker's allowance.

5119. Benefits—invalid care allowance

DEREGULATION (CARER'S ALLOWANCE) ORDER (NORTHERN IRELAND) 2002, SR 2002 321; made under the Deregulation and Contracting Out (Northern Ireland) Order 1996 (SI 1996 1632 (NI.11)) Art.17. In force: in accordance with Art.1 (1); £1.75.

This Order which makes an number amendments in relation to invalid care allowance provides for the benefit to be renamed carer's allowance and makes a number of consequential amendments to the Social Security Contributions and

Benefits (Northern Ireland) Act 1992, the Social Security Administration (Northern Ireland) Act 1992 and the Social Security (Northern Ireland) Order 1998. It amends the Contributions and Benefits Act s.70 to provide that a carer may continue to receive the allowance for a specified period after the death of the severely disabled person for whom he had been caring; repeals Contributions and Benefits Act s.70(5)(6); and preserves entitlement to the allowance in the case of any person over the age of 65 who is entitled to it immediately before this Order comes into operation.

5120. Benefits—invalid care allowance—carer premium—entitlement

SOCIAL SECURITY (CARER PREMIUM AMENDMENT) REGULATIONS (NORTHERN IRELAND) 2002, SR 2002 322; made under the Social Security Contributions and Benefits (Northern Ireland) Act 1992 s.122, s.131, s.171; and the Jobseekers (Northern Ireland) Order 1995 (SI 1995 2705 (NI.15)) Art.6, Art.36. In force: October 28, 2002; £1.75.

These Regulations amend the Income Support (General) Regulations (Northern Ireland) 1987 (SR 1987 459), the Housing Benefit (General) Regulations (Northern Ireland) 1987 (SR 1987 461) and the Jobseeker's Allowance Regulations (Northern Ireland) 1996 (SR 1996 198) to provide that the period for which a carer premium is payable under the principal sets of Regulations shall be extended for eight weeks from either the death of the person in respect of whose care invalid care allowance has been awarded or, in any other case, until eight weeks after entitlement to invalid care allowance ceases.

5121. Benefits—maternity expenses—entitlement

SOCIAL FUND (MATERNITY AND FUNERAL EXPENSES) (GENERAL) (AMENDMENT) REGULATIONS (NORTHERN IRELAND) 2002, SR 2002 14; made under the Social Security Contributions and Benefits (Northern Ireland) Act 1992 s.134, s.171; and the Social Security (Northern Ireland) Order 1998 (SI 1998 1506 (NI.10)) Art.10. In force: March 31, 2002; £1.75.

These Regulations, which amend the Social Fund (Maternity and Funeral Expenses) (General) Regulations (Northern Ireland) 1987 (SI 1987 150), increase the amount of a Sure Start Maternity Grant from £300 to £500.

5122. Benefits—maternity expenses—entitlement

SOCIAL FUND (MATERNITY AND FUNERAL EXPENSES) (GENERAL) (AMENDMENT NO.2) REGULATIONS (NORTHERN IRELAND) 2002, SR 2002 90; made under the Social Security Contributions and Benefits (Northern Ireland) Act 1992 s.134, s.171. In force: March 30, 2002; £1.50.

These Regulations, which amend the Social Fund (Maternity and Funeral Expenses) (General) (Amendment) Regulations (Northern Ireland) 2002 (SR 2002 14), make in relation to Northern Ireland only provision corresponding to provision contained in Regulations made by the Secretary of State for Work and Pensions in relation to Great Britain and accordingly are not subject to the requirement of the Social Security Administration (Northern Ireland) Act 1992 for prior reference to the Social Security Advisory Committee.

5123. Benefits—miscellaneous amendments

SOCIAL SECURITY AND CHILD SUPPORT (MISCELLANEOUS AMENDMENTS) REGULATIONS (NORTHERN IRELAND) 2002, SR 2002 164; made under the Child Support (Northern Ireland) Order 1991 (SI 1991 2628 (NI.23)) Art.16, Art.18, Art.19, Art.22, Art.28B, Art.28E, Art.28G, Art.43, Art.47, Art.48, Art.50, Sch.1 para.5, Sch.1 para.10, Sch.1 para.11, Sch.4B para.3, Sch.4B para.4, Sch.4B para.5; and the Child Support, Pensions and Social

Security Act (Northern Ireland) 2000 s.28. In force: in accordance with Reg.1; £2.50.

These Regulations amend the Child Support (Information, Evidence and Disclosure) Regulations (Northern Ireland) 1992 (SR 1992 339), Child Support (Maintenance Assessment Procedure) Regulations (Northern Ireland) 1992 (SR 1992 340), the Child Support (Maintenance Assessments and Special Cases) Regulations (Northern Ireland) 1992 (SR 1992 341), the Child Support Departure Direction and Consequential Amendments Regulations (Northern Ireland) 1996 (SR 1996 541), the Social Security and Child Support (Decisions and Appeals) Regulations (Northern Ireland) 1 (SR 1 162), the Child Support (Maintenance Calculation Procedure) Regulations (Northern Ireland) 2001 (SR 2001 17), the Child Support (Maintenance Calculations and Special Cases) Regulations (Northern Ireland) 2001 (SR 2001 18), the Child Support (Transitional Provisions) Regulations (Northern Ireland) 2001 (SR 2001 19), the Child Support (Variations) Regulations (Northern Ireland) 2001 (SR 2001 20), relating to child support.

5124. Benefits−miscellaneous amendments

SOCIAL SECURITY (MISCELLANEOUS AMENDMENTS) REGULATIONS (NORTHERN IRELAND) 2002, SR 2002 128; made under the Social Security Contributions and Benefits (Northern Ireland) Act 1992 s.122, s.131, s.132, s.171; and the Jobseekers (Northern Ireland) Order 1995 (SI 1995 2705 (NI 15)) Art.6, Art.14, Art.36. In force: April 8, 2002; £2.00.

These Regulations, which amend the Income Support (General) Regulations (Northern Ireland) 1987 (SR 1987 459), the Housing Benefit (General) Regulations (Northern Ireland) (SR 1987 461) and the Jobseeker's Allowance Regulations (Northern Ireland) (SR 1996 198), provide for income disregards in respect of war widowers' pensions in the Income Support (General) Regulations (Northern Ireland) 1987 and to the Jobseeker's Allowance Regulations (Northern Ireland) 1996. They provide for a full disregard in respect of a war widower's pension in the Housing Benefit (General) Regulations (Northern Ireland) 1987. In addition they extend the 52 week linking provisions to claimants whose housing costs are met in part and do not impose any charge on business.

5125. Benefits−statutory maternity pay−statutory sick pay

SOCIAL SECURITY, STATUTORY MATERNITY PAY AND STATUTORY SICK PAY (MISCELLANEOUS AMENDMENTS) REGULATIONS (NORTHERN IRELAND) 2002, SR 2002 354; made under the Social Security Contributions and Benefits (Northern Ireland) Act 1992 s.35, s.35A, s.149, s.160, s.161, s.162, s.167, s.171, Sch.11 para.1, Sch.11 para.1A; and the Social Security Administration (Northern Ireland) Act 1992 s.5, s.124, s.165. In force: in accordance with Reg.1; £2.50.

These Regulations amend the Statutory Sick Pay (General) Regulations (Northern Ireland) 1982 (SR 1982 263), the Statutory Maternity Pay (General) Regulations (Northern Ireland) 1987 (SR 1987 30), the Social Security (Maternity Allowance) Regulations (Northern Ireland) 1987 (SR 1987 170), the Statutory Maternity Pay (Health and Social Services Employees) Regulations (Northern Ireland) 1992 (SR 1992 17), the Social Security Maternity Benefits, Statutory Maternity Pay and Statutory Sick Pay (Amendment) Regulations (Northern Ireland) 1994 (SR 1994 191), the Social Security (Maternity Allowance) (Earnings) Regulations (Northern Ireland) 2000 (SR 2000 104) and the Statutory Maternity Pay (General) (Modification and Amendment) Regulations (Northern Ireland) 2000 (SR 2000 324) in consequence of the Social Security Act (Northern Ireland) 2002. The Regulations provide that the maternity pay period (MPP) will commence when a woman gives notice to her employer that she expects his liability to pay her statutory maternity pay to begin and she stops work in conformity with that notice; extend the MPP to 26 consecutive weeks; amend the first week of the MPP for women confined before the 11th week before the expected week of confinement (EWC); provide that where a woman is absent from work wholly or partly because of pregnancy or confinement, on or after the 4th week before her EWC that her MPP will commence on the day after the first day on which she is so absent; provide a new meaning of "week"; and substitute 28 days for 21 days as the period of notice a woman must give her employer.

5126. Benefits–statutory maternity pay–statutory sick pay

SOCIAL SECURITY, STATUTORY MATERNITY PAY AND STATUTORY SICK PAY (MISCELLANEOUS AMENDMENTS NO.2) REGULATIONS (NORTHERN IRELAND) 2002, SR 2002 359; made under the Social Security Contributions and Benefits (Northern Ireland) Act 1992 s.35A, s.159, s.160, s.167, s.167ZP, s.171, Sch.13 para.2. In force: December 8, 2002; £2.00.

These Regulations amend the Statutory Sick Pay (General) Regulations (Northern Ireland) 1982 (SR 1982 263), the Statutory Maternity Pay (General) Regulations (Northern Ireland) 1987 (SR 1987 30), the Statutory Maternity Pay (General) (Amendment) Regulations (Northern Ireland) 1988 (SR 1988 128), the Statutory Maternity Pay (General) (Amendment) Regulations (Northern Ireland) 1990 (SR 1990 112), the Social Security (Incapacity Benefit) Regulations (Northern Ireland) 1994 (SR 1994 461), the Social Security (Incapacity Benefit) (Consequential and Transitional Amendments and Savings) Regulations (Northern Ireland) 1995 (SR 1995 150) and the Social Security (Maternity Allowance) (Earnings) Regulations (Northern Ireland) 2000 (SR 2000 104). They add references to paternity leave, adoption leave and parental leave to the circumstances in which a woman may be treated as employed and makes other minor drafting changes; and include references to certain sums payable by way of statutory maternity pay, statutory paternity pay and statutory adoption pay in the expression "earnings".

5127. Benefits–up rating

SOCIAL SECURITY BENEFITS UP-RATING REGULATIONS (NORTHERN IRELAND) 2002, SR 2002 108; made under the Social Security Contributions and Benefits (Northern Ireland) Act 1992 s.90, s.113, s.171; and the Social Security Administration (Northern Ireland) Act 1992 s.135, s.165. In force: April 8, 2002; £1.75.

These Regulations, which amend the Social Security Benefit (Dependency) Regulations (Northern Ireland) 1977 (SR 1977 74) and the Social Security Benefits Up-rating Regulations (Northern Ireland) 2001 (SR 2001 106), contain only provisions in consequence of an order under the Social Security Administration (Northern Ireland) Act 1992. They provide that where a question has arisen about the effect of the Social Security Benefits Up-rating Order (Northern Ireland) 2002 (SR 2002 99) on a benefit already in payment the altered rate will not apply until that question is determined. They also apply provisions of the Social Security (Persons Abroad) Regulations (Northern Ireland) 1978 (SR 1978 114) so as to restrict the application of the increases specified in the Up-rating Order in cases where the beneficiary lives abroad. In addition, they raise from £150 to £155, one of the earnings limits for child dependency increases payable with an invalid care allowance.

5128. Benefits–work focused interviews–lone parents

SOCIAL SECURITY (WORK-FOCUSED INTERVIEWS FOR LONE PARENTS AMENDMENT) REGULATIONS (NORTHERN IRELAND) 2002, SR 2002 105; made under the Social Security Administration (Northern Ireland) Act 1992 s.2A, s.165. In force: April 8, 2002; £1.75.

These Regulations, which amend the Social Security (Work-focused Interviews for Lone Parents) Regulations (Northern Ireland) 2001 (SR 2001 152), impose a requirement for additional work-focused interviews on certain lone parents making claims for income support on or after April 8, 2002. For lone parents claiming income support on or after that date the requirement to participate in work-focused interviews will arise when their youngest child is aged 3 years. Lone parents already claiming income support will be required to take part in work-focused interviews when their youngest child reaches 5 years and 3 months. Also, an additional work-focused interview will be required six months after lone parents have taken part, or were treated as having taken part, in an initial interview.

5129. Child support—decisions and appeals—miscellaneous amendments

SOCIAL SECURITY AND CHILD SUPPORT (DECISIONS AND APPEALS) (MISCELLANEOUS AMENDMENTS) REGULATIONS (NORTHERN IRELAND) 2002, SR 2002 189; made under the Child Support (Northern Ireland) Order 1991 (SI 1991 2628 (NI.23)) Art.22; the Jobseekers (Northern Ireland) Order 1995 (SI 1995 2705 (NI.15)) Art.32, Sch.1 para.4; the Social Security (Recovery of Benefits) (Northern Ireland) Order 1997 (SI 1997 1183 (NI.12)) Art.13; the Social Security (Northern Ireland) Order 1998 (SI 1998 1506 (NI.10)) Art.7, Art.10, Art.11A, Art.13, Art.15, Art.16, Art.24A, Art.28, Art.74, Sch.1 para.12, Sch.2 para.9, Sch.4 para.1, Sch.4 para.2, Sch.4 para.3, Sch.4 para.4, Sch.4 para.6, Sch.4 para.7; and the Child Support, Pensions and Social Security Act (Northern Ireland) 2000 Sch.7 para.3, para.6, para.10, para.19, para.20. In force: May 20, 2002; £2.50.

These Regulations amend the Social Security and Child Support (Decisions and Appeals) Regulations (Northern Ireland) 1999 (SR 1999 162), the Social Security and Child Support (Decisions and Appeals) and Jobseeker's Allowance (Amendment) Regulations (Northern Ireland) 1999 (SR 1999 408), the Social Security and Child Support (Miscellaneous Amendments) Regulations (Northern Ireland) 2000 (SR 2000 215) and the Housing Benefit (Decisions and Appeals) Regulations (Northern Ireland) 2001 (SR 2001 213). They provide for the correction of accidental errors in a decision of the Department for Social Development, provide for the interaction of awards of income support and jobseeker's allowance, provide for a person appointed after the death of a claimant to be added to the list of prescribed persons who may appeal, clarify the time limits for making an appeal, provide for the Department to grant an extension of time for an appeal in specified circumstances and provide for the clerk to the appeal tribunal to reinstate an appeal if he has struck it out because the appellant failed to comply with a direction concerning an oral hearing. The Regulations also provide for oral hearings to be in public except in specified circumstances and for participation in oral hearings by means of a live television link, remove rules about the constitution of an appeal tribunal after an adjournment, require an application for a statement of an appeal tribunal's reasons to be sent to the clerk to the appeal tribunal, provide that the death or serious illness of the appellant's partner is a reason for granting further time for the appellant to take procedural steps and clarify the provisions governing applications for leave to appeal to the Social Security Commissioners.

5130. Child support—reciprocal arrangements

CHILD SUPPORT (GREAT BRITAIN RECIPROCAL ARRANGEMENTS) (AMENDMENT) REGULATIONS (NORTHERN IRELAND) 2002, SR 2002 121; made under the Northern Ireland Act 1998 s.87. In force: April 16, 2002; £2.00.

These Regulations, which amend the Child Support (Great Britain Reciprocal Arrangements) Regulations (Northern Ireland) 1993 (SI 1993 117), give effect in Northern Ireland to amendments made to reciprocal arrangements relating to matters for which provision is made by the Child Support (Northern Ireland) Order 1991 (SI 1991 2628). The Regulations make provision for changes in terminology introduced by the Social Security Act 1998, the Child Support, Pensions and Social Security Act (Northern Ireland) 2000 and the Child Support, Pensions and Social Security Act 2000.

5131. Child support–reciprocal arrangements

CHILD SUPPORT (NORTHERN IRELAND RECIPROCAL ARRANGEMENTS) AMENDMENT REGULATIONS 2002, SI 2002 771; made under the Northern Ireland Act 1998 s.87. In force: April 16, 2002; £2.00.

These Regulations give effect to amendments made to reciprocal arrangements relating to matters for which provision is made by the Child Support Act 1991 and, in Northern Ireland, by the Child Support (Northern Ireland) Order 1991 (SI 1991 2628). The Regulations, which amend the Child Support (Northern Ireland Reciprocal Arrangements) Regulations 1993 (SI 1993 584), make provision for changes in terminology introduced by the Social Security Act 1998 and the Child Support, Pensions and Social Security Act 2000.

5132. Child support–temporary compensation scheme–modification of dates

CHILD SUPPORT (TEMPORARY COMPENSATION PAYMENT SCHEME) (MODIFICATION AND AMENDMENT) REGULATIONS (NORTHERN IRELAND) 2002, SR 2002 247; made under the Child Support, Pensions and Social Security Act (Northern Ireland) 2000 s.26. In force: July 20, 2002; £1.50.

These Regulations amend the Child Support, Pensions and Social Security Act (Northern Ireland) 2000 in relation to the temporary compensation payment scheme and amend the Child Support (Temporary Compensation Payment Scheme) Regulations (Northern Ireland) 2001 (SR 2001 12). They make amendments to the 2000 Act so that it has effect as if later dates were substituted in the 2000 Act, being the dates before which an agreement must be entered into and expire. They also substitute a later prescribed date for the purposes of the 2000 Act, being the date before which a maintenance assessment must be made for the scheme to apply.

5133. Child Support, Pensions and Social Security Act (Northern Ireland) 2000 c.4– Commencement No.8 Order

CHILD SUPPORT, PENSIONS AND SOCIAL SECURITY (2000 ACT) (COMMENCEMENT NO.8) ORDER (NORTHERN IRELAND) 2002, SR 2002 118; made under the Child Support, Pensions and Social Security Act (Northern Ireland) 2000 s.68. In force: bringing into operation various provisions of the 2000 Act on March 23, 2002 and April 15, 2002; £1.75.

This Order provides for the coming into operation of specified provisions of the Child Support, Pensions and Social Security Act (Northern Ireland) 2000.

5134. Contributions–intermediaries

SOCIAL SECURITY CONTRIBUTIONS (INTERMEDIARIES) (NORTHERN IRELAND) (AMENDMENT) REGULATIONS 2002, SI 2002 705; made under the Social Security Contributions and Benefits (Northern Ireland) Act 1992 s.4A, s.121, s.171. In force: April 6, 2002; £1.75.

These Regulations, which amend the Social Security Contributions (Intermediaries) (Northern Ireland) Regulations 2000 (SI 2000 728), make amendments following the consolidation of regulations relating to national insurance contributions in the Social Security (Contributions) Regulations 2001 (SI 2001 1004). The Regulations extend the calculation of worker's attributable earnings so as to cater for cases where expenses are met by the worker and reimbursed by the intermediary, and cases involving mileage allowance relief and mileage allowance payments. They also amend the worker's attributable earnings so as to provide, in a case where the intermediary is a company which ceases to trade in the course of a year of assessment, that the deemed payment of worker's attributable earnings is treated as made on the date that the company ceases to trade and not on the later date of April 5, in that year.

5135. Disability living allowance–attendance allowance–residential care homes and nursing homes

SOCIAL SECURITY (AMENDMENT) (RESIDENTIAL CARE AND NURSING HOMES) REGULATIONS (NORTHERN IRELAND) 2002, SR 2002 132; made under the Social Security Administration (Northern Ireland) Act 1992 s.5, s.165; the Social Security Contributions and Benefits (Northern Ireland) Act 1992 s.67, s.72, s.122, s.123, s.131, s.132, s.133, s.171; the Jobseekers (Northern Ireland) Order 1995 (SI 1995 2705 (NI.15)) Art.6, Art.14, Art.15, Art.23, Sch.1 para.1; and the Social Security (Northern Ireland) Order 1998 (SI 1998 1506 (NI.10)) Art.12. In force: April 8, 2002; £3.00.

These Regulations amend the Income Support (General) Regulations (Northern Ireland) 1987 (SR 1987 459), the Social Security (Claims and Payments) Regulations (Northern Ireland) 1987 (SR 1987 465), the Social Security (Attendance Allowance) Regulations (Northern Ireland) 1992 (SR 1992 20), the Social Security (Disability Living Allowance) Regulations (Northern Ireland) 1992 (SR1992 32), the Jobseeker's Allowance Regulations (Northern Ireland) 1996 (SR 1996 198) and the Social Security and Child Support (Decisions and Appeals) Regulations (Northern Ireland) 1999 (SR 1999 162) so as to provide that the special amounts which are applicable to those persons in residential care homes and nursing homes who have preserved rights, shall no longer be applicable from April 8th 2002.

5136. Disability living allowance–conditions of entitlement–mental disability

SOCIAL SECURITY (DISABILITY LIVING ALLOWANCE) (AMENDMENT) REGULATIONS (NORTHERN IRELAND) 2002, SR 2002 97; made under the Social Security Contributions and Benefits (Northern Ireland) Act 1992 s.73, s.171. In force: April 8, 2002; £1.75.

These Regulations, which amend the Social Security (Disability Living Allowance) Regulations (Northern Ireland) 1992 (SI 1992 32) in relation to the conditions of entitlement to the mobility component of a disability living allowance, provide that a person does not meet the conditions of the Social Security Contributions and Benefits (Northern Ireland) Act 1992 s.73 if the reason he does not take advantage of the faculty of walking out of doors unaccompanied is fear or anxiety. This provision does not apply where the fear or anxiety is a symptom of a mental disability and so severe as to prevent the person from taking advantage of the faculty of walking out of doors unaccompanied.

5137. Fraud–request for information–specified organisations

SOCIAL SECURITY ADMINISTRATION (NORTHERN IRELAND) ACT 1992 (AMENDMENT) ORDER (NORTHERN IRELAND) 2002, SR 2002 408; made under the Social Security Administration (Northern Ireland) Act 1992 s.103B, s.165. In force: February 24, 2003; £1.75.

The Social Security Fraud Act (Northern Ireland) 2001 provides for officers authorised by the Social Security Administration (Northern Ireland) Act 1992 s.103A and s.104A to require information about individuals from specified private and public sector organisations. This Order amends s.103B of the 1992 Act by adding to the list of organisations the Director of National Savings, gas distributors and electricity distributors and substituting the definition of "bank".

5138. Guardians allowance–custodial sentences

SOCIAL SECURITY (GUARDIAN'S ALLOWANCES) (AMENDMENT) REGULATIONS (NORTHERN IRELAND) 2002, SR 2002 87; made under the Social Security Contributions and Benefits (Northern Ireland) Act 1992 s.77, s.171. In force: April 1, 2002; £1.75.

These Regulations amend the Social Security (Guardian's Allowances) Regulations (Northern Ireland) 1975 (SR 1975 98) in relation to the circumstances in which a person is to be treated as being in prison for the purposes of the Social Security Contributions and Benefits Act (Northern

Ireland) 1992 by reducing the minimum length of custodial sentence to two years and including persons who are ordered by a court to be detained in a hospital under the Criminal Appeal (Northern Ireland) Act 1980 or Mental Health (Northern Ireland) Order 1986 (SI 1986 595) or following a verdict of not guilty by reason of insanity or a finding that the accused was under a disability.

5139. Housing benefit–tenancy–size of dwelling

HOUSING BENEFIT (GENERAL) (AMENDMENT) REGULATIONS (NORTHERN IRELAND) 2002, SR 2002 280; made under the Social Security Contributions and Benefits (Northern Ireland) Act 1992 s.122, s.129, s.171. In force: October 7, 2002; £1.75.

These Regulations amend the Housing Benefit (General) Regulations (Northern Ireland) 1987 (SR1987 461) so that rent in respect of a tenancy of a dwelling, whose ownership has been transferred from the Northern Ireland Housing Executive (NIHE) to a Housing Association does not need to be considered by NIHE on the ground that the dwelling is larger than the claimant reasonably requires.

5140. Incapacity benefit–allowances

SOCIAL SECURITY (INCAPACITY) (MISCELLANEOUS AMENDMENTS) REGULATIONS (NORTHERN IRELAND) 2002, SR 2002 86; made under the Social Security Contributions and Benefits (Northern Ireland) Act 1992 s.167D, s.171; the Social Security (Incapacity for Work) (Northern Ireland) Order 1994 (SI 1994 1898 (NI.12)) Art.6; and the Welfare Reform and Pensions (Northern Ireland) Order 1999 (SI 1999 3147 (NI.11)) Art.75. In force: in accordance with Reg.1 (1); £2.00.

These Regulations, which amend the Social Security (Incapacity Benefit) Regulations (Northern Ireland) 1994 (SR 1994 461) and the Social Security (Incapacity Benefit) (Transitional) Regulations (Northern Ireland) 1995 (SR 1995 35), amend the Social Security (Incapacity for Work) (General) Regulations (Northern Ireland) 1995 (SR 1995 41) as they relate to the circumstances in which a person is to be treated as capable of work for the purposes of entitlement to certain social security benefits. They substitute references to officers of, and persons providing services to, the Department for references to the Department of Higher and Further Education, Training and Employment and make amendments in relation to the categories of work which may be undertaken by a person without his being treated as being capable of work.

5141. Incapacity benefit–allowances

SOCIAL SECURITY (INCAPACITY) (MISCELLANEOUS AMENDMENTS NO.2) REGULATIONS (NORTHERN IRELAND) 2002, SR 2002 276; made under the Social Security Contributions and Benefits (Northern Ireland) Act 1992 s.30A, s.30E, s.167D, s.171, Sch.7 para.2. In force: in accordance with Reg.1; £1.75.

These Regulations amend the Social Security (General Benefit) Regulations (Northern Ireland) 1984 (SR 1984 92), the Social Security (Incapacity Benefit) Regulations (Northern Ireland) 1994 (SR 1994 461), the Social Security (Incapacity for Work) (General) Regulations (Northern Ireland) 1995 (SR 1995 41) and the Security (Incapacity Benefit) (Miscellaneous Amendments) Regulations (Northern Ireland) 2001 (SR 2001 316). They increase to £3,510 the amount which can be earned before disqualification from unemployability supplement; increase the earnings limit for councillor's allowance to £67.50; allow a person who was previously entitled to incapacity benefit in youth to become entitled again after returning from an unlimited absence abroad; and increase to £67.50 the weekly limit for earnings from work which many be undertaken by a person without his being treated as being capable of work.

5142. Income support-jobseekers allowance-entitlement-maternity rights

INCOME SUPPORT (GENERAL) AND JOBSEEKER'S ALLOWANCE (AMENDMENT NO.2) REGULATIONS (NORTHERN IRELAND) 2002, SR 2002 332; made under the Social Security Contributions and Benefits (Northern Ireland) Act 1992 s.122, s.123, s.171; and the Jobseekers (Northern Ireland) Order 1995 (NI. 15) (SI 1995 2705) Art.3, Art.36. In force: November 25, 2002; £1.75.

These Regulations, which amend the Income Support (General) Regulations (Northern Ireland) 1987 (SR 1987 459) and the Jobseeker's Allowance Regulations (Northern Ireland) 1996 (SR 1996 198), extend entitlement to income support, where a woman is or has been pregnant and has an expected week of confinement beginning on or after April 6, 2003, to a period commencing 11 weeks before her expected week of confinement and ending fifteen weeks after the date on which her pregnancy ends.

5143. Income support-jobseekers allowance-lone parents-self employment route

INCOME SUPPORT (GENERAL) AND JOBSEEKER'S ALLOWANCE (AMENDMENT) REGULATIONS (NORTHERN IRELAND) 2002, SR 2002 203; made under the Social Security Contributions and Benefits (Northern Ireland) Act 1992 s.122, s.132, s.171; and the Jobseekers (Northern Ireland) Order 1995 (SI 1995 2705 (NI.15)) Art.14, Art.36. In force: June 17, 2002; £1.50.

These Regulations amend the Income Support (General) Regulations (Northern Ireland) 1987 (SR 1987 459) and the Jobseeker's Allowance Regulations (Northern Ireland) 1996 (SR 1996 198) so as to amend the definition of "self-employment route" to include assistance in pursuing self-employed earner's employment whilst participating in the New Deal for Lone Parents.

5144. Income support-loans-interest rate

INCOME SUPPORT (GENERAL) (STANDARD INTEREST RATE AMENDMENT) REGULATIONS (NORTHERN IRELAND) 2002, SR 2002 16; made under the Social Security Contributions and Benefits (Northern Ireland) Act 1992 s.122, s.131, s.171. In force: February 17, 2002; £1.75.

These Regulations amend the Income Support (General) Regulations (Northern Ireland) 1987 (SI 1987 459) Sch.3 with respect to the standard rate of interest applicable to a loan which qualifies for income support. The rate is decreased from 6.19 per cent to 5.74 per cent. In addition, the Regulations revoke, with a saving provision, the Income Support (General) (Standard Interest Rate Amendment No.3) Regulations (Northern Ireland) 2001 (SR 2001 410) which made a previous amendment to the standard rate of interest.

5145. Income support-loans-interest rate

INCOME SUPPORT (GENERAL) (STANDARD INTEREST RATE AMENDMENT NO.2) REGULATIONS (NORTHERN IRELAND) 2002, SR 2002 58; made under the Social Security Contributions and Benefits (Northern Ireland) Act 1992 s.122, s.131, s.171. In force: March 17, 2002; £1.75.

These Regulations amend the Income Support (General) Regulations (Northern Ireland) 1987 (SR 1987 459) with respect to the standard rate of interest applicable to a loan which qualifies for income support under that Schedule to those Regulations. The new rate is 5.34 per cent. They also revoke the Income Support (General) (Standard Interest Rate Amendment) Regulations (Northern Ireland) 2002 (SR 2002 16), with a saving provision, which made the previous amendment to that standard rate of interest.

5146. Industrial injuries–compensation–adjustments to lower rate of incapacity benefit

WORKMEN'S COMPENSATION (SUPPLEMENTATION) (AMENDMENT) REGULATIONS (NORTHERN IRELAND) 2002, SR 2002 114; made under the Social Security Contributions and Benefits (Northern Ireland) Act 1992 s.171, Sch.8 para.2; and the Social Security Administration (Northern Ireland) Act 1992 Sch.6 para.1. In force: April 10, 2002; £2.00.

These Regulations amend the Workmen's Compensation (Supplementation) Regulations (Northern Ireland) 1983 (SR 1983 101) by increasing the lower rates of lesser incapacity allowance consequential upon the increase in the maximum rate of that allowance made by the Social Security Benefits Up-rating Order (Northern Ireland) 2002 (SI 2002 99). The Regulations also revoke the Workmen's Compensation (Supplementation) (Amendment) Regulations (Northern Ireland) 2001 (SR 2001 116).

5147. Industrial injuries–dependants–permitted earnings limits

SOCIAL SECURITY (INDUSTRIAL INJURIES) (DEPENDENCY) (PERMITTED EARNINGS LIMITS) ORDER (NORTHERN IRELAND) 2002, SR 2002 107; made under the Social Security Contributions and Benefits (Northern Ireland) Act 1992 s.171, Sch.7 para.4. In force: April 8, 2002; £1.50.

Where a disablement pension with unemployability supplement is increased in respect of a child or children and the beneficiary is one of two persons who are spouses residing together or an unmarried couple, the Social Security Contributions and Benefits Act 1992 provides that the increase shall not be payable in respect of the first child if the other person's earnings are £150 a week or more and in respect of a further child for each complete £20 by which the earnings exceed £150. This Order, which amends the Social Security (Industrial Injuries) (Dependency) (Permitted Earnings Limits) Order (Northern Ireland) 2001 (SR 2001 107), increases the amount of £150 to £155.

5148. Jobseekers allowance–voluntary workers–available for employment

JOBSEEKER'S ALLOWANCE (AMENDMENT) REGULATIONS (NORTHERN IRELAND) 2002, SR 2002 388; made under the Jobseekers (Northern Ireland) Order 1995 (SI 1995 2705 (NI.15)) Art.8, Art.10, Art.36. In force: in accordance with Reg.1; £1.75.

These Regulations amend the Jobseeker's Allowance Regulations 1996 (SR 1996 198) to provide that a person who is engaged in voluntary work shall be treated as available for employment if he is available to commence employment on receipt of one week's notice and is available for interview in connection with the opportunity of any such employment on receipt of 48 hours' notice; and that a person on statutory paternity leave or ordinary adoption leave shall not be regarded as being available for employment for the purposes of those regulations.

5149. Pensions–earnings factors–calculation of additional pension

SOCIAL SECURITY REVALUATION OF EARNINGS FACTORS ORDER (NORTHERN IRELAND) 2002, SR 2002 89; made under the Social Security Administration (Northern Ireland) Act 1992 s.130, s.165. In force: April 6, 2002; £1.75.

This Order directs that the earnings factors relevant to the calculation of the additional pension in the rate of any long-term benefit or of any guaranteed minimum pension, or to any other calculation required under the Pension Schemes (Northern Ireland) Act 1993, are to be increased for the tax years specified in the Schedule to this Order by the percentage of their amount specified in that Schedule.

5150. Social fund–cold weather payments–weather stations

SOCIAL FUND (COLD WEATHER PAYMENTS) (GENERAL) (AMENDMENT) REGULATIONS (NORTHERN IRELAND) 2002, SR 2002 315; made under the Social Security Contributions and Benefits (Northern Ireland) Act 1992 s.134, s.171. In force: November 1, 2002; £1.50.

These Regulations amend the Social Fund (ColdWeather Payments) (General) Regulations (Northern Ireland) 1988 (SR 1988 368) in relation to the list of weather stations to take account of a change of weather station.

5151. Social fund–crisis loans–applications

SOCIAL FUND (MISCELLANEOUS AMENDMENTS) REGULATIONS (NORTHERN IRELAND) 2002, SR 2002 284; made under the Social Security Contributions and Benefits (Northern Ireland) 1992 s.134, s.171; and the Social Security Administration (Northern Ireland) Act 1992 s.10, s.165. In force: October 1, 2002; £1.75.

These Regulations amend the Social Fund (Applications) Regulations (Northern Ireland) 1988 (SR 1988 130) by allowing applications for crisis loans to be made otherwise than in writing and making consequential amendments relating to when such applications are to be treated as made. They also amend the Social Fund (Maternity and Funeral Expenses) (General) Regulations (Northern Ireland) 1987 (SR 1987 150) so that persons may be entitled to a funeral payment under those Regulations only where they are entitled to a qualifying benefit in respect of the date of claim for a funeral payment

5152. Social Security Act (Northern Ireland) 2002 (c.10)–Commencement No.1 Order

SOCIAL SECURITY (2002 ACT) (COMMENCEMENT NO.1) ORDER (NORTHERN IRELAND) 2002, SR 2002 351 (C.28); made under the Social Security Act (Northern Ireland) 2002 s.9. In force: bringing into operation various provisions of the 2002 Act on November 19, 2002; £1.75.

This Order provides for the coming into operation of provisions of the Social Security Act (Northern Ireland) 2002 relating to the use of information for, or relating to, employment and training, and consequential repeals; and relating to the maternity pay period, the rate of, and entitlement to, statutory maternity pay, the rate of maternity allowance and a consequential repeal, for the purpose only of authorising the making of regulations.

5153. Social Security Act (Northern Ireland) 2002 (c.10)–Commencement No.2 and Transitional and Saving Provisions Order

SOCIAL SECURITY (2002 ACT) (COMMENCEMENT NO.2 AND TRANSITIONAL AND SAVING PROVISIONS) ORDER (NORTHERN IRELAND) 2002, SR 2002 358 (C.30); made under the Social Security Act (Northern Ireland) 2002 s.9. In force: bringing into operation various provisions of the 2002 Act on November 24, 2002 and April 6, 2003; £1.75.

This Order provides for the coming into operation of provisions of the Social Security Act (Northern Ireland) 2002 which relate to the sharing of functions as regards certain claims and information; maternity pay period, entitlement to statutory maternity pay, the rate of maternity allowance and a consequential repeal; and rate of statutory maternity pay, in so far as not already in operation, and the rate of maternity allowance and consequential amendments.

5154. Social Security Commissioners–appeals–right to fair trial–reduction in amount of income support pending outcome of appeal

[Income Support (General) Regulations (Northern Ireland) 1987 (SI 1987 459) Reg.22A; EuroHuman Rights Act 1998 Sch.1 Part I Art.6 (1).]

S, who was appealing against a decision of the Social Security Commissioner that he was fit to work, sought judicial review of a decision to reduce his income support by 20 per cent under the Income Support (General) Regulations (NI) 1987 Reg.22A pending the outcome of the appeal. S contended that Reg.22A served to discourage appeals and was contrary to the right to a fair trial under the Human Rights Act 1998 Sch.1 Part I Art.6(1).

Held, refusing the application, that the reduction allowed under Reg.22A was a proportionate method of discouraging unmeritorious appeals. Art.6(1) was not breached by the reduction as S was still able to claim income support at a reduced rate pending the determination of the appeal and he had a right to claim the backdated amount if successful.

SMYTH'S APPLICATION FOR JUDICIAL REVIEW, *Re* [2001] N.I. 393, Kerr, J., QBD (NI).

5155. Social Security Fraud Act (Northern Ireland) 2001 (c.17)–Commencement No.2 Order

SOCIAL SECURITY FRAUD (2001 ACT) (COMMENCEMENT NO.2) ORDER (NORTHERN IRELAND) 2002, SR 2002 75; made under the Social Security Fraud Act (Northern Ireland) 2001 s.17. Commencement details: bringing into force certain provisions of the 2001 Act on March 6, 2002 and April 1, 2002; £1.50.

This Order provides for the coming into operation of specified provisions of the Social Security Fraud Act (Northern Ireland) 2001.

5156. Social Security Fraud Act (Northern Ireland) 2001 (c.17)–Commencement No.3 Order

SOCIAL SECURITY FRAUD (2001 ACT) (COMMENCEMENT NO.3) ORDER (NORTHERN IRELAND) 2002, SR 2002 165; made under the Social Security Fraud Act (Northern Ireland) 2001 s.17. In force: bringing into operation various provisions of the 2001 Act on May 1, 2002; £1.50.

This Order provides for the coming into operation of provisions of the Social Security Fraud Act (Northern Ireland) 2001 which enable the Department to give directions to the Housing Executive in relation to the supply by it of housing benefit information; which relate to provision for civil penalties as an alternative to prosecution for benefit offences; and which provide for consequential repeals.

5157. Social Security Fraud Act (Northern Ireland) 2001 (c.17)–Commencement No.4 Order

SOCIAL SECURITY FRAUD (2001 ACT) (COMMENCEMENT NO.4) ORDER (NORTHERN IRELAND) 2002, SR 2002 392 (C.32); made under the Social Security Fraud Act (Northern Ireland) 2001 s.17. In force: bringing into operation various provisions of the 2001 Act on December 19, 2002; £1.50.

This Order provides for the coming into operation on December 19, 2002 of the Social Security Fraud Act (Northern Ireland) 2001 s.3.

5158. Social Security Fraud Act (Northern Ireland) 2001 (c.17)–Commencement No.5 Order

SOCIAL SECURITY FRAUD (2001 ACT) (COMMENCEMENT NO.5) ORDER (NORTHERN IRELAND) 2002, SR 2002 406 (C.34); made under the Social Security Fraud Act (Northern Ireland) 2001 s.17. In force: bringing into operation various provisions of the 2001 Act on December 23, 2002 and February 24, 2003; £1.50.

This Order provides for the coming into force of certain provisions of the Social Security Fraud Act (Northern Ireland) 2001 on December 23, 2002 and February 24, 2003.

5159. Social Security (Northern Ireland) Act 2002 (10)

This Act amends the law relating to statutory maternity pay; amends the law relating to maternity allowance; makes provision for work-focused interviews for partners of benefit claimants; makes provision about the use of information for, or relating to, employment and training; and amends the Deregulation and Contracting Out (Northern Ireland) Order 1996.

This Act received Royal Assent on October 17, 2002.

5160. State Pension Credit Act (Northern Ireland) 2002 (c.14)

This Act makes provision for and in connection with a new social security benefit called state pension credit; and amends the Pension Schemes (Northern Ireland) Act 1993 s.43 (1).

5161. State Pension Credit Act (Northern Ireland) 2002 (c.14)–Commencement No.1 Order

STATE PENSION CREDIT (2002 ACT) (COMMENCEMENT NO.1) ORDER (NORTHERN IRELAND) 2002, SR 2002 366 (C.31); made under the State Pension Credit Act (Northern Ireland) 2002 s.21. In force: bringing into operation various provisions of the 2002 Act on December 2, 2002 and January 14, 2003; £1.75.

This Order appoints specified days for the coming into operation of certain provisions of the State Pension Credit Act (Northern Ireland) 2002.

5162. State retirement pensions–low earnings threshold

SOCIAL SECURITY PENSIONS (LOW EARNINGS THRESHOLD) ORDER (NORTHERN IRELAND) 2002, SR 2002 57; made under the Social Security Administration (Northern Ireland) Act 1992 s.130A. In force: April 6, 2002; £1.50.

This Order directs that the low earnings threshold, for the purposes of the Social Security Contributions and Benefits (Northern Ireland) Act 1992, for the tax years following 2001-2002 shall be £10,800. The low earnings threshold is used for the purposes of calculating entitlement to the additional pension in a state retirement pension.

5163. Students–income related benefits

SOCIAL SECURITY (STUDENTS AND INCOME-RELATED BENEFITS AMENDMENT) REGULATIONS (NORTHERN IRELAND) 2002, SR 2002 222; made under the Social Security Contributions and Benefits (Northern Ireland) Act 1992 s.122, s.129, s.132, s.171; and the Jobseekers (Northern Ireland) Order 1995 (SI 1995 2705 (NI.15)) Art.14. In force: in accordance with Reg.1 (1); £2.00.

These Regulations amend the Housing Benefit (General) Regulations (Northern Ireland) 1987 (SR 1987 459), the Income Support (General) Regulations (Northern Ireland) 1987 (SR 1987 451) and the Jobseeker's Allowance Regulations (Northern Ireland) 1996 (SR 1996 198) in relation to students. They amend the definitions of "access funds", "periods of experience" and "sandwich course"; increase the amounts of grant and loan income to be disregarded in respect of books and equipment and for travel costs; provide for the disregard of childcare grants payable under Great Britain legislation and of the child care component of the National Assembly for Wales Learning Grants; provide for both grant income and student loans to be apportioned over complete benefit weeks; clarify the position as regards the apportionment of amounts in grants intended for the maintenance of dependants; and abolish the student rent deduction.

5164. Students–income related benefits

SOCIAL SECURITY (STUDENTS AND INCOME-RELATED BENEFITS AMENDMENT NO.2) REGULATIONS (NORTHERN IRELAND) 2002, SR 2002 270; made under the Social Security Contributions and Benefits (Northern

Ireland) Act 1992 s.122, s.132, s.171; and the Jobseekers (Northern Ireland) Order 1995 (SI 1995 2705 (NI.15)) Art.14. In force: September 2, 2002; £1.75.

These Regulations amend the Income Support (General) Regulations (Northern Ireland) 1987 (SR 1987 459), the Housing Benefit (General) Regulations (Northern Ireland) 1987 (SR 1987 461) and the Jobseeker's Allowance Regulations (Northern Ireland) 1996 (SR 1987 198). They increase the disregard for grants paid for an eldest or dependant child and in respect of expenditure on travel, books and equipment under the Education (Student Support) Regulations (Northern Ireland) 2002 (SR 2002 224).

5165. Tax credits–disabled persons and working families tax credit–period of awards

TAX CREDITS (MISCELLANEOUS AMENDMENTS NO.3) (NORTHERN IRELAND) REGULATIONS 2002, SI 2002 1697; made under the Social Security Contributions and Benefits (Northern Ireland) Act 1992 s.127; and the Tax Credits Act 1999 s.2, Sch.6 para.3, Sch.6 para.22. In force: July 23, 2002; £1.50.

These Regulations amend the Disability Working Allowance (General) Regulations (Northern Ireland) 1992 (SR 1992 78) and the Family Credit (General) Regulations (Northern Ireland) 1987 (SR 1987 463) as a consequence of the extension to April 7, 2003 of awards of disabled person's tax credit and working families' tax credit that became payable on or after June 4, 2002, by virtue of the Tax Credits (Prescribed Period of Awards) (Northern Ireland) Regulations 2002 (SI 2002 1339).

5166. Welfare Reform and Pensions (Northern Ireland) Order 1 (SI 1 3147 NI.11))– Commencement No.11 Order

WELFARE REFORM AND PENSIONS (1 ORDER) (COMMENCEMENT NO.11) ORDER (NORTHERN IRELAND) 2002, SR 2002 63; made under the Welfare Reform and Pensions (Northern Ireland) Order 1 (SI 1 3147 (NI.11)) Art.1. In force: bringing into operation various provisions of the 1 Order on March 19, 2002; £1.75.

This Order provides for the coming into operation of specified provisions of the Welfare Reform and Pensions (Northern Ireland) Order 1 (SI 1 3147).

5167. Welfare Reform and Pensions (Northern Ireland) Order 1 (SI 1 3147 (NI.11))– Commencement No.10 Order

WELFARE REFORM AND PENSIONS (1 ORDER) (COMMENCEMENT NO.10) ORDER (NORTHERN IRELAND) 2002, SR 2002 25; made under the Welfare Reform and Pensions (Northern Ireland) Order 1 (SI 1 3147 (NI.11)) Art.1. Commencement details: bringing into force various provisions of the 1 Order on April 6, 2002; £2.00.

This Order, which amends the Welfare Reform and Pensions (Commencement No.9) Order (Northern Ireland) 2001 (SR 2001 438) to revoke the day previously appointed for the coming into operation of provisions in relation to occupational pension schemes for certificates etc. relating to minimum funding requirement, provides for the coming into operation of specified provisions of the Welfare Reform and Pensions (Northern Ireland) Order 1 (SI 1 3147).

5168. Welfare Reform and Pensions (Northern Ireland) Order 1999 (SI 1999 3147 (NI.11))–Commencement No.12 Order

WELFARE REFORM AND PENSIONS (1999 ORDER) (COMMENCEMENT NO.12) ORDER (NORTHERN IRELAND) 2002, SR 2002 126; made under the Welfare Reform and Pensions (Northern Ireland) Order 1999 (SI 1999 3147 (NI.11)) Art.1. Commencement details: bringing into force various provisions of the 1999 Order on March 27, 2002 and April 6, 2002; £1.75.

This Order, which amends the Welfare Reform and Pensions (1999 Order) (Commencement No.10) Order (Northern Ireland) 2002 (SR 2002 25), provides for the coming into operation of specified provisions of the Welfare Reform and Pensions (Northern Ireland) Order 1999 (SI 1999 3147).

SOCIAL WELFARE

5169. Carers and Direct Payments Act (Northern Ireland) 2002 (c.6)

This Act makes provision about the assessment of carers' needs; provides for services to help carers and provides for the making of direct payments to persons in lieu of the provision of personal social services or carers' services.

5170. Child Support, Pensions and Social Security Act (Northern Ireland) 2000 (c.4)–Commencement No.7 Order

CHILD SUPPORT, PENSIONS AND SOCIAL SECURITY (2000 ACT) (COMMENCEMENT NO.7) ORDER (NORTHERN IRELAND) 2002, SR 2002 68; made under the Child Support, Pensions and Social Security Act (Northern Ireland) 2000 s.68. Commencement details: bringing into force various provisions of the 2000 Act on March 1, 2002 and April 1, 2002; £2.00.

This Order, which amends the Child Support, Pensions and Social Security (2000 Act) (Commencement No.6) Order (Northern Ireland) 2001 (SR 2001 249), provides for the coming into operation of specified provisions of the Child Support, Pensions and Social Security Act (Northern Ireland) 2000 relating to the winding-up of pension schemes and to investigations by the Pensions Ombudsman.

5171. Food–milk

WELFARE FOODS (AMENDMENT) REGULATIONS (NORTHERN IRELAND) 2002, SR 2002 83; made under the Social Security (Northern Ireland) Order 1988 (SI 1988 594 (NI.2)) Art.13; and the Social Security Contributions and Benefits (Northern Ireland) Act 1992 s.171. In force: April 1, 2002; £1.50.

These Regulations amend the Welfare Foods Regulations (Northern Ireland) 1988 (SR 1988 137) to increase the purchase price of 900 grammes of dried milk to £4.10 and to increase from £71 to £72.20 the amount of the reduction in the appropriate maximum, not to be exceeded to establish entitlement to working families' tax credit.

5172. Health and Personal Social Services Act (Northern Ireland) 2001 (c.3)– Commencement No.3 Order

HEALTH AND PERSONAL SOCIAL SERVICES ACT (NORTHERN IRELAND) 2001 (COMMENCEMENT NO.3) ORDER (NORTHERN IRELAND) 2002, SR 2002 73; made under the Health and Personal Social Services Act (Northern Ireland) 2001 s.61. Commencement details: bringing into force various provisions of the 2001 Act on April 1, 2002; £1.75.

This Order brings into force provisions of the Health and Personal Social Services Act (Northern Ireland) 2001 which relate to the repeal of law about fund-holding practices.

5173. Health and Personal Social Services Act (Northern Ireland) 2001 (c.3)– Commencement No.4 Order

HEALTH AND PERSONAL SOCIAL SERVICES (2001 ACT) (COMMENCEMENT NO.4) ORDER (NORTHERN IRELAND) 2002, SR 2002 180; made under the Health and Personal Social Services Act (Northern Ireland) 2001 s.61. In force: bringing into operation various provisions of the 2001 Act on June 10, 2002; £1.75.

This Order brings into operation the Health and Personal Social Services Act (Northern Ireland) 2001 s.48.

5174. **Personal Social Services (Preserved Rights) Act (Northern Ireland) 2002 (5)**

This Act makes provision in relation to persons in residential accommodation with preserved rights under the Income Support (General) Regulations (Northern Ireland) 1987.

5175. **Personal Social Services (Preserved Rights) Act (Northern Ireland) 2002 (c.5)–Commencement Order**

PERSONAL SOCIAL SERVICES (PRESERVED RIGHTS) (2002 ACT) (COMMENCEMENT) ORDER (NORTHERN IRELAND) 2002, SR 2002 131; made under the Personal Social Services (Preserved Rights) Act (Northern Ireland) 2002 s.6, s.7. In force: bringing into operation various provisions of the 2002 Act on March 28, 2002 and April 8, 2002; £1.50.

This Order brings into operation specified provisions of the Personal Social Services (Preserved Rights) Act (Northern Ireland) 2002 on specified dates.

5176. **Social services–personal social services–preserved rights**

PERSONAL SOCIAL SERVICES (PRESERVED RIGHTS) REGULATIONS (NORTHERN IRELAND) 2002, SR 2002 136; made under the Personal Social Services (Preserved Rights) Act (Northern Ireland) 2002 s.1, s.6. In force: April 8, 2002; £1.75.

These Regulations provide exceptions to the duties imposed by the Personal Social Services (Preserved Rights) Act (Northern Ireland) 2002 on the Department of Health, Social Services and Public Safety to ensure the provision of community care services for people who were preserved rights cases before the appointed day. The exceptions are cases where a person, in respect of the day before the appointed day, is not entitled to income support, or is so entitled but not at the preserved rights rate. They provide for the amount that can be recovered where the Department is responsible for payments under arrangements which existed before the appointed day and which continue until community care services are provided. They further specify the circumstances in which a person is to be treated as ordinarily resident for the purposes of the 2002 Act.

5177. **Social services–Social Care Council–appointments and procedure**

NORTHERN IRELAND SOCIAL CARE COUNCIL (APPOINTMENTS AND PROCEDURE) (AMENDMENT) REGULATIONS (NORTHERN IRELAND) 2002, SR 2002 349; made under the Health and Personal Social Services Act (Northern Ireland) 2001 s.1, s.57, Sch.1 para.5. In force: December 20, 2002; £1.75.

These Regulations amend the Northern Ireland Social Care Council (Appointments and Procedure) Regulations (Northern Ireland) 2001 (SR 2001 313) which make provision concerning the membership and procedure of the Northern Ireland Social Care Council. The Regulations provide that where a person is disqualified for appointment as chairperson or as a member of the Council because of dismissal from paid employment with a health service body or a health and social services body this disqualification does not apply where the dismissal was found to have been unfair in industrial proceedings. They also enable the Department of Health, Social Services and Public Safety to terminate the appointment of the chairperson or a member where that person fails, without the consent of the Council, to attend three consecutive meetings of the Council.

5178. **Books**

Cousins, Mel–Irish Social Welfare System. Paperback. ISBN C. Round Hall Ltd.

SPORT

5179. Admissions–Dundrod circuit–charges

DUNDROD CIRCUIT (ADMISSION CHARGES) REGULATIONS (NORTHERN IRELAND) 2002, SR 2002 167; made under the Road Races (Northern Ireland) Order (SI 1986 1887 (NI.17)) Art.3. In force: July 1, 2002; £1.50.

These Regulations, which revoke and replace the Dundrod Circuit (Admission Charges) Regulations (Northern Ireland) 1979 (SR 1979 196) increase the maximum admission charge for each person to the Dundrod Circuit on race days from £5 to £10 and remove the charge in respect of vehicles.

TAX

5180. Aggregates levy–tax credits

AGGREGATES LEVY (NORTHERN IRELAND TAX CREDIT) REGULATIONS 2002, SI 2002 1927; made under the Finance Act 2001 s.17, s.30A, s.45, Sch.7 para.2. In force: August 15, 2002; £1.75.

These Regulations make provision in respect of certain tax credits which are to apply in Northern Ireland during the period April 1, 2002 to March 31, 2007. They provide for the entitlement to the tax credit and further provide that it supplements the provisions contained in Aggregates Levy (General Regulations) 2002 (SI 2002 761) Part III, which deal with accounting, payment, records, tax credits, repayments and set-off and set out the additional records required in the case of a claim for a Northern Ireland tax credit. The Regulations also contain the requirements for a claim to be made and provide for a penalty where the additional record keeping requirement is breached.

5181. Budget Act (Northern Ireland) 2002 (3)

This Act authorises the issue out of the Consolidated Fund of certain sums for the service of the years ending 31st March 2002 and 2003; appropriates those sums for specified purposes; authorises the Department of Finance and Personnel to borrow on the credit of the appropriated sums; authorises the use for the public service of certain resources for the years ending 31st March 2002 and 2003 and revises the limits on the use of certain accruing resources in the year ending 31st March 2002.

5182. Budget (No.2) Act (Northern Ireland) 2002 (7)

This Act authorises the issue out of the Consolidated Fund of certain sums for the service of the year ending March 31 2003; appropriates those sums for specified purposes; authorises the Department of Finance and Personnel to borrow on the credit of the appropriated sums and authorises the use for the public service of certain resources (including accruing resources) for the year ending March 31 2003.

5183. Tax credits–appeals–procedure

TAX CREDITS (APPEALS) REGULATIONS (NORTHERN IRELAND) 2002, SR 2002 403; made under the Social Security (Northern Ireland) Order 1998 (SI 1998 1506 (NI.10)) Art.8, Art.13, Art.15, Art.16, Art.28, Art.74, Sch.1 para.11, Sch.1 para.12, Sch.4. In force: January 1, 2003; £3.50.

These Regulations, which are made in consequence of the application and modification of the Social Security (Northern Ireland) Order 1998 (SI 1998 1506 (NI.10)) by the Tax Credits (Appeals) Regulations 2002 (SI 2002 2926), concern rights of appeal and the procedure for bringing appeals; make provision for additional persons to have a right of appeal, or to make an application for a direction to close down an enquiry; set out the procedure for dealing with a dispute in relation to time limits; deal with late appeals; provide for the manner in which an application for an extension of time must be made; and make provision for appeal tribunals for tax credits.

5184. Tax credits–decisions and appeals

TAX CREDITS (DECISIONS AND APPEALS) (NORTHERN IRELAND) (AMENDMENT) REGULATIONS 2002, SI 2002 1378; made under the Social Security (Northern Ireland) Order 1998 (SI 1998 1506 (NI.10)) Art.2, Art.10, Art.13, Art.15, Art.16, Art.28, Art.74, Sch.2 para.9, Sch.4 para.1, Sch.4 para.2, Sch.4 para.4, Sch.4 para.6, Sch.4 para.7; and the Tax Credits Act 1999 s.2, Sch.2 para.8, Sch.2 para.9, Sch.2 para.22, Sch.2 para.36. In force: May 21, 2002; £2.50.

These Regulations, which amend the Social Security and Child Support (Decisions and Appeals) Regulations (Northern Ireland) 1999 (SR 1999 162) in relation to working families' tax credit and disabled person's tax credit, insert definitions of "official error" and "partner" and deal with the correction of accidental errors in a decision by an officer of the Board of Inland Revenue. They add any person appointed by the Board to proceed with the claim of a person who has died, clarify the time limits for making an appeal, allow the clerk to an appeal tribunal to reinstate an appeal which has been struck out for failure to comply with a direction, provide for oral hearings to be in public except in specified circumstances and for participation in an oral hearing by means of a live television link and remove rules about the constitution of an appeal tribunal after an adjournment.

5185. Tax credits–disabled persons tax credit–working families tax credit

TAX CREDITS (MISCELLANEOUS AMENDMENTS NO.2) (NORTHERN IRELAND) REGULATIONS 2002, SI 2002 1340; made under the Social Security Contributions and Benefits (Northern Ireland) Act 1992 s.127, s.128, s.132, s.133, s.171; and the Tax Credits Act 1999 s.2, Sch.2 para.3, Sch.2 para.22. In force: in accordance with Reg.1 (1); £1.75.

These Regulations which, amend the Family Credit (General) Regulations (Northern Ireland) 1987 (SR 1987 463) and the Disability Working Allowance (General) Regulations (Northern Ireland) 1992 (SR 1992 78) provide for amounts to be disregarded in calculating a student's income for the purposes of determining his entitlement to working families' tax credit or disabled person's tax credit. They also make provision for persons receiving the higher rate of attendance allowance to receive the enhanced disability credit and amend the adult credit figures for working families' tax credit and disabled person's tax credit.

5186. Tax credits–disabled persons tax credit–working families tax credit

TAX CREDITS (PRESCRIBED PERIOD OF AWARDS) (NORTHERN IRELAND) REGULATIONS 2002, SI 2002 1339; made under the Social Security Contributions and Benefits (Northern Ireland) Act 1992 s.127, s.128, s.133, s.171; and the Tax Credits Act 1999 s.2, Sch.2 para.3, Sch.2 para.22. In force: June 4, 2002; £1.50.

These Regulations, which amend the Family Credit (General) Regulations (Northern Ireland) 1987 (SR 1987 463) and the Disability Working Allowance (General) Regulations (Northern Ireland) 1992 (SR 1992 78), provide for amounts to be disregarded in calculating a student's income for the purposes of determining his entitlement to working families' tax credit or disabled person's tax credit. They also make provision for persons receiving the higher rate of attendance allowance to receive the enhanced disability credit and amend the adult credit figures for working families' tax credit and disabled person's tax credit.

5187. Tax credits-disabled persons tax credit-working families tax credit-claims and payments

TAX CREDITS (CLAIMS AND PAYMENTS AND MISCELLANEOUS AMENDMENTS) (NORTHERN IRELAND) REGULATIONS 2002, SI 2002 527; made under the Social Security Administration (Northern Ireland) Act 1992 s.5, s.167; and the Social Security (Northern Ireland) Order 1998 (SI 1998 1506 (NI.10)) Art.2, Art.10, Art.11. In force: April 2, 2002; £1.75.

These Regulations amend the Social Security (Claims and Payments) Regulations (Northern Ireland) 1987 (SR 1987 465) to provide for an extension of the time for claiming working families' tax credit or disabled person's tax credit in specified circumstances and the Social Security and Child Support (Decisions and Appeals) Regulations (Northern Ireland) 1999 (SR 1999 162) to provide the power to revise or supersede a decision.

5188. Books

Giblin, B.H.–Irish Tax Reports 2001 Cases, Cumulative Tables, Index, and Determinations of the Appeal Commissioners. Paperback: £45.76. ISBN 1-85475-217-0. Butterworths Law.

Saunders, Glyn–Tolley's Taxation in the Republic of Ireland 2002. Paperback: £59.95. ISBN 0-7545-1672-5. Tolley Publishing.

TRANSPORT

5189. Driving licences-Community driving licences

DRIVING LICENCES (COMMUNITY DRIVING LICENCE) REGULATIONS (NORTHERN IRELAND) 2002, SR 2002 374; made under the European Communities Act 1972 s.2. In force: January 20, 2003; £2.00.

These Regulations amend the Road Traffic (Northern Ireland) Order 1981 (SI 1981 154) and the Driving Licences (Community Driving Licence) Regulations (Northern Ireland) 1996 (SR 1996 426) to give effect to Council Directive 96/47 ([1996] OJ L235/1) amending Directive 91/439 on driving licences and Council Directive 97/26 ([1997] OJ L150/41) amending Directive 91/439 on driving licences. The Directives provide for the introduction of a model form of photocard driving licence as an alternative to the model paper form, amend the definition of "motor cycle" and specifies codes which Member States must include on the licences they issue to indicate, amongst other things, restrictions on the classes of vehicle which a licence holder may drive on account of physical disability or conditions which may be imposed on his driving vehicles on account of such disability.

5190. Driving licences-exchangeable licences-Kenya-removal from list

MOTOR VEHICLES (EXCHANGEABLE LICENCES) (AMENDMENT) ORDER (NORTHERN IRELAND) 2002, SR 2002 328; made under the Road Traffic (Northern Ireland) Order 1981 (SI 1981 154 (NI.1)) Art.19D. In force: December 9, 2002; £1.50.

This Order amends the Motor Vehicles (Exchangeable Licences) Order (Northern Ireland) 1994 (SR 1994 364) which designates various countries and territories as countries and territories who have satisfactory provision for the issue of driving licences. The Order removes Kenya from the list of countries and territories so designated. The holder of a Kenyan driving licence will therefore no longer be able to exchange that licence for a corresponding Northern Ireland one.

5191. Driving tests-theory tests-additional hazard perception test

MOTOR VEHICLES (DRIVING LICENCES) (AMENDMENT NO.2) REGULATIONS (NORTHERN IRELAND) 2002, SR 2002 383; made under the

Road Traffic (Northern Ireland) Order 1981 (SI 1981 154 (NI.1)) Art.5, Art.19C, Art.218. In force: January 6, 2003; £1.75.

These Regulations amend the Motor Vehicles (Driving Licences) Regulations (Northern Ireland) 1996 (SR 1996 542) by replacing the theory test currently taken by those wishing to obtain a driving licence with a two-part theory test. Part I of the new two-part theory test consists of the old theory test, consisting of a test of driving theory. Part II consists of a test of the candidate's ability to recognise hazards to driving. The fee for the theory test is increased from £18 to £20.50.

5192. Heavy goods vehicles–testing–fees

GOODS VEHICLES (TESTING) (FEES) (AMENDMENT) REGULATIONS (NORTHERN IRELAND) 2002, SR 2002 48; made under the Road Traffic (Northern Ireland) Order 1995 (SI 1995 2994 (NI.18)) Art.65, Art.67, Art.110. In force: April 1, 2002; £1.75.

These Regulations, which revoke the Goods Vehicles (Testing) (Fees) (Amendment) Regulations (Northern Ireland) 2001 (SR 2001 247), amend the Goods Vehicles (Testing) Regulations (Northern Ireland) 1995 (SR 1995 450) by increasing specified fees relating to the testing of goods vehicles.

5193. International carriage by road–dangerous goods

CARRIAGE OF DANGEROUS GOODS (AMENDMENT) REGULATIONS (NORTHERN IRELAND) 2002, SR 2002 34; made under the Health and Safety at Work (Northern Ireland) Order 1978 (SI 1978 1039 (NI.9)) Art.17, Art.40, Art.55, Sch.3 para.1, Sch.3 para.2, Sch.3 para.5, Sch.3 para.6, Sch.3 para.11, Sch.3 para.13, Sch.3 para.15. In force: April 1, 2002; £7.00.

These Regulations implement Commission Directive 96/86 ([1996] OJ L335/43) adapting to technical progress Council Directive 94/55 ([1994] OJ L319/7) with regard to regarding the transport of dangerous goods by road; Commission Directive 96/87 ([1996] OJ L335/45) adapting to technical progress Council Directive 96/49 ([1996] OJ L235/25) regarding the transport of dangerous goods by rail; Commission Directive 99/47 ([1] OJ L169/1) adapting to technical progress Council Directive 94/55 and Commission Directive 96/86 the transport of dangerous goods by road; and Commission Directive 99/48 ([1] OJ L169/58) adapting to technical progress Council Directive 96/49 and Commission Directive 96/87 regarding the transport of dangerous goods by rail, insofar as they relate to the carriage of dangerous goods other than explosives. The Regulations amend the Pressure Systems and Transportable Gas Containers Regulations (Northern Ireland) 1991 (SR 1991 471), the Carriage of Dangerous Goods (Classification, Packaging and Labelling) and Use of Transportable Pressure Receptacles Regulations (Northern Ireland) 1997 (SR 1997 247), the Carriage of Dangerous Goods by Road Regulations (Northern Ireland) 1997 (SR 1997 248), the Carriage of Dangerous Goods by Road (Driver Training) Regulations (Northern Ireland) 1997 (SR 1997 249), the Health and Safety (Fees) Regulations (Northern Ireland) 1998 (SR 1998 125), the Carriage of Dangerous Goods by Rail Regulations (Northern Ireland) 1998 (SR 1998 131) and the Packaging, Labelling and Carriage of Radioactive Material by Rail Regulations (Northern Ireland) 1998 (SR 1998 132). The amendments have the effect to align the specified Regulations with the versions of the ADR and RID agreements.

5194. Motor vehicles–authorised weight vehicles

MOTOR VEHICLES (AUTHORISED WEIGHT) (AMENDMENT) REGULATIONS (NORTHERN IRELAND) 2002, SR 2002 8; made under the Road Traffic (Northern Ireland) Order 1995 (SI 1995 2994 (NI.18)) Art.55, Art.110. In force: February 28, 2002; £2.00.

These Regulations, which amend the Motor Vehicles (Authorised Weight) Regulations (Northern Ireland) 1 (SR 1 258) to permit the use of such vehicles, give effect in Northern Ireland to the proposals in "Transport 2010, The 10 Year Plan". They also provide safeguards against the misuse of current axle lift technology and the emission of pollutants.

5195. **Motor vehicles–construction and use–exemptions**

MOTOR VEHICLES (CONSTRUCTION AND USE) (AMENDMENT NO.4) REGULATIONS (NORTHERN IRELAND) 2002, SR 2002 375; made under the Road Traffic (Northern Ireland) Order 1995 (SI 1995 2994 (NI.18)) Art.55, Art.110. In force: February 28, 2003; £2.50.

These Regulations amend the Motor Vehicles (Construction and Use) Regulations (Northern Ireland) 1999 (SR 1999 454) to require motor vehicles to comply with such design, construction and equipment requirements and limit values as apply to them by virtue of Community Directives or ECE Regulations specified. They also make amendments to Reg.16 (turning circle -articulated vehicles other than those incorporating a car transporter) to modify the categories of articulated vehicle which are exempted.

5196. **Motor vehicles–construction and use–exhaust emissions**

MOTOR VEHICLES (CONSTRUCTION AND USE) (AMENDMENT NO.3) REGULATIONS (NORTHERN IRELAND) 2002, SR 2002 294; made under the Road Traffic (Northern Ireland) Order 1995 (SI 1995 2994 (NI.18)) Art.55, Art.110. In force: November 1, 2002; £1.75.

These Regulations amend the Motor Vehicles (Construction and Use) Regulations (Northern Ireland) 1999 (SI 1999 454) in relation to the requirement that certain goods vehicles and buses must have plates fitted detailing specified particulars relating to the vehicle. They also make amendments in relation to in-service exhaust emissions tests as a result of the requirement to implement Commission Directive 2001/9 ([2001] OJ L48/18) adapting to technical progress Council Directive 96/96 on the approximation of the laws of the Member States relating to the roadworthiness tests for motor vehicles and their trailers.

5197. **Motor vehicles–construction and use–seat belts and restraint systems**

MOTOR VEHICLES (CONSTRUCTION AND USE) (AMENDMENT) REGULATIONS (NORTHERN IRELAND) 2002, SR 2002 197; made under the Road Traffic (Northern Ireland) Order 1995 (SI 1995 2994 (NI.18)) Art.55, Art.110. In force: September 1, 2002; £2.50.

These Regulations amend the Motor Vehicles (Construction and Use) Regulations (Northern Ireland) 1999 (SR 1999 454) in relation to seat belts and their anchorage points in light of Commission Directive 96/36 ([1996] OJ L178/15) adapting to technical progress Council Directive 77/541 ([1977] OJ L220/95) relating to safety belts and restraint systems of motor vehicles; Commission Directive 96/38 ([1996] OJ L187/95) adapting to technical progress Council Directive 76/115 ([1976] OJ L24/6) relating to anchorages for motor vehicle safety belts; and Commission Directive 2000/3 ([2000] OJ L53/1) adapting to technical progress Council Directive 77/541 relating to safety belts and restraint systems of motor vehicles. They substitute a new regulation which specifies what anchorage points are to be fitted to which vehicles and the technical requirements for anchorage points. In addition, they make amendments so as to enable rearward-facing seats meeting specified requirements to count towards the minimum number of forward-facing seats with seat belts that must be provided on minibuses and coaches used to carry groups of children on organised trips

5198. **Motor vehicles–construction and use–seat belts and restraint systems**

MOTOR VEHICLES (CONSTRUCTION AND USE) (AMENDMENT NO.2) REGULATIONS (NORTHERN IRELAND) 2002, SR 2002 256; made under the

Road Traffic (Northern Ireland) Order 1995 (SI 1995 2994 (NI.18)) Art.55, Art.110. In force: September 1, 2002; £2.00.

These Regulations, which revoke the Motor Vehicles (Construction and Use) (Amendment) Regulations (Northern Ireland) 2002 (SR 2002 197) to correct a number of drafting errors, amend the Motor Vehicles (Construction and Use) Regulations (Northern Ireland) 1999 (SR 1999 454) in relation to seat belts and their anchorage points in the light of Commission Directive 96/36 ([1996] OJ L178/15) adapting to technical progress Council Directive 77/541 relating to safety belts and restraint systems of motor vehicles; Commission Directive 96/38 ([1996] OJ L187/95) adapting to technical progress Council Directive 76/115 relating to anchorages for motor vehicle safety belts; and Commission Directive 2000/3 ([2000] OJ L53/1) adapting to technical progress Council Directive 77/541 relating to safety belts and restraint systems of motor vehicles. They specify what anchorage points are to be fitted to which vehicles and the technical requirements for anchorage points. In addition, they make amendments so as to enable rearward-facing seats meeting specified requirements to count towards the minimum number of forward-facing seats with seat belts that must be provided on minibuses and coaches used to carry groups of children on organised trips.

5199. Motor vehicles–driving tests–fees

MOTOR VEHICLES (DRIVING LICENCES) (AMENDMENT) (TEST FEES) REGULATIONS (NORTHERN IRELAND) 2002, SR 2002 51; made under the Road Traffic (Northern Ireland) Order 1981 (SI 1981 154 (NI.1)) Art.5, Art.218. In force: April 1, 2002; £1.75.

These Regulations, which revoke the Motor Vehicles (Driving Licences) (Amendment) (Test Fees) Regulations (Northern Ireland) 2001 (SR 2001 245), amend the Motor Vehicles (Driving Licences) Regulations (Northern Ireland) 1996 (SR 1996 542) by increasing fees for driving tests.

5200. Motor vehicles–registration documents–replacement

ROAD VEHICLES (REGISTRATION AND LICENSING) (AMENDMENT) REGULATIONS (NORTHERN IRELAND) 2002, SI 2002 2381; made under the Vehicle Excise and Registration Act 1994 s.22, s.22A, s.57. In force: in accordance with Reg.1 (2); £1.75.

These Regulations amend the Road Vehicles (Registration and Licensing) Regulations (Northern Ireland) 1973 (SR & O 1973 490) in order to make examination of the vehicle or other evidence mandatory in specified circumstances before a replacement registration is issued. They also make amendments to require the surrender or destruction by an insurance company of the registration document on a change of ownership where there is substantial bodywork damage and either the owner's insurance does not cover that damage or the owners is an insurer.

5201. Motor vehicles–testing–fees

MOTOR VEHICLE TESTING (AMENDMENT) (FEES) REGULATIONS (NORTHERN IRELAND) 2002, SR 2002 47; made under the Road Traffic (Northern Ireland) Order 1995 (SI 1995 2994 (NI.18)) Art.61, Art.62, Art.110. In force: April 1, 2002; £1.75.

These Regulations, which amend the Motor Vehicle Testing Regulations (Northern Ireland) 1995 (SR 1995 448), increase the fees payable for examinations and re-examinations of specified vehicles in specified classes.

5202. Passenger vehicles–buses and taxis–licensing–fees

PUBLIC SERVICE VEHICLES (LICENCE FEES) (AMENDMENT) REGULATIONS (NORTHERN IRELAND) 2002, SR 2002 49; made under the Road Traffic

(Northern Ireland) Order 1981 (SI 1981 154 (NI.1)) Art.61, Art.66, Art.218. In force: April 1, 2002; £1.75.

These Regulations, which revoke the Public Service Vehicles (Licence Fees) (Amendment) Regulations (Northern Ireland) 1996 (SR 1996 143) and the Public Service Vehicles (Licence Fees) (Amendment) Regulations (Northern Ireland) 2001 (SR 2001 244), amend the Public Service Vehicles Regulations (Northern Ireland) 1985 (SR 1985 123) by increasing the fees payable for certain applications and re-applications for a licence for a taxi or a bus.

5203. Passenger vehicles–goods vehicles–tachographs–fees

PASSENGER AND GOODS VEHICLES (RECORDING EQUIPMENT) (FEES) (AMENDMENT) REGULATIONS (NORTHERN IRELAND) 2002, SR 2002 50; made under the Finance Act 1973 s.56. In force: April 1, 2002; £1.75.

These Regulations amend the Passenger and Goods Vehicles (Recording Equipment) Regulations (Northern Ireland) 1996 (SR 1996 145) by increasing the fee for granting or renewing approval of a fitter or workshop for the installation or repair of recording equipment from £325 to £336 and the renewal of an approval from £99 to £102.

5204. Passenger vehicles–public hire vehicles–conditions of fitness

PUBLIC SERVICE VEHICLES (CONDITIONS OF FITNESS, EQUIPMENT AND USE) (AMENDMENT) REGULATIONS (NORTHERN IRELAND) 2002, SR 2002 384; made under the Road Traffic (Northern Ireland) Order 1981 (SI 1981 154 (NI.1)) Art.66, Art.218. In force: January 6, 2003; £1.50.

These Regulations amend the Public Service Vehicles (Condition of Fitness, Equipment and Use) Regulations (Northern Ireland) 1995 (SR 1995 447) so that all vehicles licensed for public hire in Belfast shall be upholstered in cloth, leather or good quality artificial leather.

5205. Railway Safety Act (Northern Ireland) 2002 (c.8)

This Act makes provision with respect to the safety of railways.

This Act received Royal Assent on August 13, 2002.

5206. Road safety–traffic signs

TRAFFIC SIGNS (AMENDMENT) REGULATIONS (NORTHERN IRELAND) 2002, SR 2002 143; made under the Road Traffic Regulation (Northern Ireland) Order 1997 (SI 1997 276 (NI.2)) Art.28. In force: May 20, 2002; £2.00.

These Regulations amend the Traffic Signs Regulations (Northern Ireland) 1997 (SR 1997 386) to provide a definition of "permitted taxi", to redefine the expression "bus lane", to change the minimum rate of flashing of a road danger lamp showing an intermittent light from not less than 40 to not less than 55 flashes per minute and make various amendments to specified diagrams.

TRUSTS

5207. Trustee Act (Northern Ireland) 2001 (c.14)–Commencement Order

TRUSTEE (2001 ACT) (COMMENCEMENT) ORDER (NORTHERN IRELAND) 2002, SR 2002 253; made under the Trustee Act (Northern Ireland) 2001 s.45. In force: bringing into operation the 2001 Act on July 29, 2002; £1.50.

This Order brings into operation the Trustee Act (Northern Ireland) 2001.

UTILITIES

5208. **Water quality–water supply**

WATER SUPPLY (WATER QUALITY) REGULATIONS (NORTHERN IRELAND) 2002, SR 2002 331; made under the European Communities Act 1972 s.2; and the Water and Sewerage Services (Northern Ireland) Order 1973 (SI 1973 70 (NI.2)) Art.3B, Art.3C. In force: in accordance with Reg.1 (2)-(5); £6.00.

These Regulations, which supplement the Water and Sewerage Services (Northern Ireland) Order 1973 (SI 1973 70 (NI.2)), amend for a limited time the Water Quality Regulations (Northern Ireland) 1994 (SI 1994 221) and on January 1, 2004, revoke and replace those Regulations primarily concerned with the quality of water supplied in Northern Ireland for drinking, washing, cooking and food preparation, and for food production, and with arrangements for the publication of information about water quality. These Regulations are directed at the achievement of the objective set out in Council Directive 98/83 ([1998] OJ L330/32) on the quality of water intended for human consumption, to protect human health from the adverse effects of any contamination of water intended for human consumption by ensuring that it is wholesome and clean. They also partially revoke the Private Water Supplies Regulations (Northern Ireland) 1994 (SR 1994 237) and the Surface Waters (Abstraction for Drinking Water) (Classification) Regulations (Northern Ireland) 1996 (SR 1996 603). The Regulations require the Department for Regional Development to identify annually the areas that are to be relevant for a particular year; prescribe standards of wholesomeness in respect of water supplied by the Department for Regional Development for cooking, drinking, food preparation and washing and other domestic purposes and to premises for food production purposes; provide for the monitoring of water supplies by reference to the analysis of samples; contain additional provisions relating to sampling; and provide for the investigation of every failure to satisfy a concentration, value or state prescribed and for a report to be made to the Department.

SCOTLAND

ADMINISTRATION OF JUSTICE

5209. Contempt of court—accused's mobile phone ringing in court—ignorance of phone being switched on not a defence

W was late for his appearance in court and another trial was interrupted for his case to be dealt with. W pleaded guilty but while the sheriff was addressing him during sentencing, W's mobile phone rang. The sheriff then considered whether that amounted to contempt of court. W argued that he had been unaware that the phone was switched on, was found to be in contempt and appealed to the High Court

Held, passing the bill and suspending the conviction, that the sheriff was entitled to regard the phone ringing as contempt, particularly when the ringing phone belonged to the accused in the dock and given the prominent prohibitory signs throughout the court building. The sheriff had applied the correct test to ascertain contempt; whether there was intentional disrespect or action against the court's authority. However, the sheriff might have taken more factors into account in assessing whether there had been intentional disrespect or action rather than inferring such from his lateness. Opinion of the court per Lord Cameron of Lochbroom.

WILLIAMS v. CLARK 2001 S.C.C.R. 505, Lord Cameron of Lochbroom, Lord Caplan, Lord Hamilton, HCJ Appeal.

5210. Contempt of court—advocates—solicitors—conduct—failure to arrange timeous representation

G, an advocate, was instructed by C, a solicitor, to appear on behalf of D. G appeared in Forfar on January 24, 2002 and the case was transferred to Inverness. G assumed the case would not go ahead in Inverness because some of the witnesses would not travel. G appeared for D again, on February 1 and the case was transferred back to Forfar. G had been advised that the case would not start before February 6 and he accepted instruction to appear in another case beginning February 4 for two days, it actually started on the February 5 and G made notice of his inability to appear for D. C was told of that and made no effort to find counsel until the February 6 when the case was continued until the following morning. A hearing was fixed to allow C and G to make submissions as to whether they had been in contempt or not. At the hearing G referred to a 48 hour rule whereby the Crown gave counsel 48 hours notice before calling a case for trial in sittings involving a number of cases.

Held, making no finding of contempt, that (1) the court had jurisdiction to determine issues of contempt and impose penalty in cases of contempt arising out of the conduct of counsel in the same way as solicitors; (2) G was not in contempt, having arranged to let C know that he would be unavailable; (3) serious errors had been made by C. Had he treated the case with the required urgency on February 5 he could have obtained alternate representation and the case could have gone ahead, and (4) C's conduct could be described as grossly reckless and resulted in disregard for the Court and the administration of justice, but since gross recklessness could not amount to contempt without wilful challenge or wilful failure, and the necessary inference could go either way, the Court gave C the benefit of the doubt.

Observed, that (1) it was extremely imprudent for G to plan his commitments on the basis that witnesses would not travel to Inverness given that the Crown could enforce warrants to secure attendance; (2) counsel and solicitor had a mutual obligation to ensure representation of the accused and must maintain contact with each other, and (3) if the 48 hour rule were operated in the way described by G the Court would be in danger of not sitting for a number of days.

HM ADVOCATE v. DICKIE (GRAEME GEORGE) (CONTEMPT OF COURT) 2002 S.L.T. 1083, Lord Hardie, HCJ.

5211. Contempt of court–publications–appearance on website–accessibility

[Contempt of Court Act 1981 (c.49) s.2.]

B, on trial in September 2001 on a charge of assault, sodomy and murder, moved for the "publishers" of material found in the archive sections of certain web sites to be ordained to appear before the court, arguing that the material constituted a prima facie contempt of court. The Crown argued inter alia that the "time of the publication" in the Contempt of Court Act 1981 s.2(3) referred to the moment the material first appeared on the web sites.

Held, refusing the motion, that (1) "publication" in s.2(1) signified a work of some kind that had been published rather than the action of making something publicly known, or issuing or offering something to the public, and the material contained on these web sites had to be regarded as "publications" within the definition in s.2(1); (2) the "time of the publication" referred to the whole period during which the material was accessible to the public, and (3) the material had not been shown to create a substantial risk that the course of justice would be seriously impeded or prejudiced in terms of s.2(2) and a prima facie case of contempt had not been established. The material was originally published in December 1999, was only accessible as part of an archive and was unlikely to be accessible by random search under B's name, and there was no reason to suppose the jury would not follow the direction of the trial judge to base their decision on the evidence they heard in the present proceedings and not on any extraneous material.

HM ADVOCATE v. BEGGS (NO.2) 2002 S.L.T. 139, Lord Osborne, HCJ.

5212. Contempt of court–witnesses–summary punishment–independent and impartial tribunal

[Criminal Procedure (Scotland) Act 1995 (c.46) s.155; European Convention on Human Rights 1950 Art.6.]

A witness for the prosecution in a trial for drink driving was considered to be in contempt of court after giving evidence which was contrary to a statement made to the police following the incident. The witness was told to appear later and consult a solicitor. At the hearing the witness argued that a finding of contempt would breach his rights under the European Convention on Human Rights 1950 Art.6 as the sheriff was in effect acting as complainer, prosecutor, judge and jury. Furthermore, his right under Art.6(2) to be presumed innocent, and his right under Art. 6(3)(d) to examine witnesses against him and to produce witnesses on his own behalf, had been breached.

Held, taking no action against the witness, that (1) the finding of a witness in contempt and the imposition of summary punishment was a criminal process; (2) the provisions of the Criminal Procedure (Scotland) Act 1995, s.155 and the common law power of a sheriff to punish persons in contempt of his court prima facie contravened the right to a fair trial before an independent and impartial tribunal, and (3) s.155 of the 1995 Act was not in itself incompatible with Art.6 if the action taken was immediately necessary to enforce the authority of the court or to secure the proper running of the trial.

MAIR (BRYAN), PETITIONER 2002 S.L.T. (Sh Ct) 2, Sheriff IC Simpson, Sh Ct (South Strathclyde, Dumfries and Galloway).

5213. Court of Session—fees

COURT OF SESSION ETC. FEES AMENDMENT ORDER 2002, SSI 2002 270; made under the Courts of Law Fees (Scotland) Act 1895 s.2. In force: July 1, 2002; £2.50.

This Order amends the Court of Session etc. Fees Order 1997 (SI 1997 688) to provide exemption from the fees payable under the Order for persons in receipt of certain forms of benefits and legal aid. It also specifies for fees payable to the Principal Clerk of Session, to the Accountant of Court and to the Auditor of Court of Session or to any officer acting for any of them respectively in relation to proceedings in the Court of Session, new fee levels in substitution for those applicable since the 1997 Order was last amended. In addition, the Order simplifies the fees payable in relation to recording, engrossing and copying documents and makes new provision for fees payable in connection with the cancellation of a diet of taxation or a remit to the Auditor to determine whether an additional fee should be paid.

5214. Court of Session—rules—personal injuries—procedure

ACT OF SEDERUNT (RULES OF THE COURT OF SESSION AMENDMENT NO.2) (PERSONAL INJURIES ACTIONS) 2002, SSI 2002 570; made under the Court of Session Act 1988 s.5. In force: April 1, 2003; £2.00.

This Act of Sederunt, which amends the Rules of the Court of Session 1994 (SI 1994 1443) and introduces new rules of procedure for personal injury actions, applies to personal injury actions raised on or after April 1, 2003.

5215. Court of Session—rules—powers of arrest—applications

ACT OF SEDERUNT (RULES OF THE COURT OF SESSION AMENDMENT NO.2) (APPLICATIONS UNDER THE PROTECTION FROM ABUSE (SCOTLAND) ACT 2001) 2002, SSI 2002 514; made under the Court of Session Act 1988 s.2, s.3, s.5. In force: December 1, 2002; £2.00.

This Act of Sederunt amends the Court of Session Rules 1994 (SI 1994 1443) to make provision for applications in the Court of Session in respect of a power of arrest under the Protection from Abuse (Scotland) Act 2001. It provides that an application for a power of arrest is to be made by conclusion in the summons, prayer in the petition, defences, answers or counterclaim in which the interdict to which it relates is applied for or, if made after the application for interdict, by motion in the action to which the application relates; prescribes certain documents that are to be served along with the power of arrest; prescribes certain documents that are to be delivered to a chief constable; that where the interdict to which the power of arrest is attached is varied or recalled a copy of the interlocutor varying or recalling the interdict is to be delivered to the chief constable; and that where a person is required to deliver documents to a chief constable where a power of arrest is served, extended or recalled, or the interdict is varied or recalled, he shall after compliance lodge a certificate of delivery.

5216. Court of Session—solicitors, shorthand writers and witnesses—fees

ACT OF SEDERUNT (RULES OF THE COURT OF SESSION AMENDMENT) (FEES OF SOLICITORS, SHORTHAND WRITERS AND WITNESSES) 2002, SSI 2002 301; made under the Court of Session Act 1988 s.5. In force: July 1, 2002; £2.00.

This Act of Sederunt amends the Act of Sederunt (Rules of the Court of Session) 1994 (SI 1994 1443) by increasing the fees payable to solicitors in the Court of Session by 4.3 per cent. It also increases the fees payable to shorthand writers in the Court of Session by 3.25 per cent and provides for a new table of fees for witnesses in the Court of Session.

5217. High Court of Justiciary–legal representation–right of audience–unqualified accused unable to represent co-accused

[Human Rights Act 1998 (c.42) Sch.1 Part I Art.6(3)(c).]

R and two other persons presented a joint petition to the High Court seeking recovery of certain documents. The Human Rights Act 1998 Sch.1 Part I Art.6(3)(c) provided that everyone charged with a criminal offence has the right to defend themselves in person or through legal representation. When the petition presented, R sought to represent not only himself but the absent persons. The judge refused to allow R to do so and continued the case to enable the two others to be present. R was granted leave to appeal so that the representation point could be canvassed.

Held, that R had no right of audience other than to represent his own interests. If a person chose not to represent himself only a legally qualified representative who enjoyed a right of audience in the High Court could appear in his place which fully conformed with Art.6(3)(c). Opinion of the Court per Lord Cameron of Lochbroom.

ROBBIE THE PICT v. HM ADVOCATE 2002 S.C.C.R. 213, Lord Cameron of Lochbroom, Lord Carloway, Lady Cosgrove, HCJ Appeal.

5218. Judges–bias–judge previously involved as Lord Advocate in promoting relevant legislation

[Crown Proceedings Act 1947 (10 & 11 Geo VI, c.44) s.21, s.38(2); Human Rights Act 1998 (c.42) Sch.1 Part I Art.3, Art.6(1).]

D, a prisoner, petitioned the nobile officium praying the court to set aside decisions of an Extra Division refusing his reclaiming motion for an interim order ordaining M, the Scottish Ministers, to secure his transfer to conditions of detention compliant with the Human Rights Act 1998 Sch.1 Part I Art.3, and refusing leave to appeal to the House of Lords. The question for the Division had been whether, in view of the Crown Proceedings Act 1947 s.21, D could competently obtain an order for specific performance, or only an order declaratory of his rights. D submitted that one member of the court, Lord Hardie, ought not to have participated in the determination of the issues on the basis that his advocacy of amendments to s.38(2) of the 1947 Act, while Lord Advocate, in order to include M within the class of officers of the Crown who, by reason of s.21, were not subject to coercive orders of the court, gave rise to legitimate doubts as to his objective impartiality, or that he ought at least to have declared his involvement in the promotion of the legislation. D argued that the relative interlocutors of the Extra Division were therefore vitiated, both under common law and the Human Rights Act 1998 Sch.1 Part I Art.6(1). M argued inter alia that (1) Lord Hardie had given a ministerial rather than personal view in relation to the scope of s.21; (2) in light of Lord Hardie's judicial oath, it should be assumed that he approached his decision in the reclaiming motion with an open mind, and (3) the Extra Division were concerned with the interpretation of the Crown Proceedings Act 1947 which was a different piece of legislation from the Scotland Bill, with the passage of which Lord Hardie had been involved.

Held, granting the petition and appointing the reclaiming motion to summar roll for a rehearing by a new division, that (1) it made no difference that Lord Hardie had been securing the passage of the Scotland Bill whereas the Extra Division had been concerned with the construction of the Crown Proceedings Act 1947, given the opinion he expressed in Parliament as to the effect of the proposed amendment to the 1947 Act; (2) Lord Hardie's involvement in the passage of the Scotland Bill had a material bearing on the question before the Extra Division, and when looking at the issue objectively, the fair minded and informed observer would have concluded that there was a real possibility of bias; (3) the same conclusion fell to be drawn in relation to the court's decision to refuse leave to appeal to the House of Lords and both decisions were therefore vitiated by Lord Hardie's participation in them; (4) his opinion was expressed in the formal context of the passage of the legislation and it did not matter whether he was expressing a ministerial rather than personal opinion, and

(5) it would be inappropriate to grant leave to appeal to the House of Lords as no answers had been lodged to the petition, and other questions of relevancy, not to mention the substantive human rights question, had yet to be decided at first instance.

DAVIDSON v. SCOTTISH MINISTERS (NO.2); *sub nom.* DAVIDSON, PETITIONER 2002 S.L.T. 1231, Lord Gill L.J.C., Lord Kirkwood, Lord Philip, 2 Div.

5219. Judges–Lands Valuation Appeal Court–appointments

ACT OF SEDERUNT (LANDS VALUATION APPEAL COURT) 2002, SSI 2002 340; made under the Valuation of Lands (Scotland) Amendment Act 1879 s.7. In force: August 1, 2002; £1.50.

This Act of Sederunt, which revokes the Act of Sederunt (Lands Valuation Appeal Court) 1997 (SI 1997 378), appoints the judges who may hear appeals under the Valuation of Lands (Scotland) Amendment Act 1879.

5220. Legal Services Ombudsman–compensation–prescribed amount

SCOTTISH LEGAL SERVICES OMBUDSMAN (COMPENSATION) (PRESCRIBED AMOUNT) ORDER 2002, SSI 2002 32; made under the Law Reform (Miscellaneous Provisions) (Scotland) Act 1990 s.34A. In force: February 28, 2002; £1.50.

This Order prescribes the amount which the stated amount, in terms of the Reform (Miscellaneous Provisions) (Scotland) Act 1990 s.34A, cannot exceed. The stated amount is such compensation payment as may be recommended by the Scottish legal services ombudsman. The previous prescribed amount was £1,000 and this Order raises this amount to £1,200.

5221. Messengers at arms–fees

ACT OF SEDERUNT (FEES OF MESSENGERS-AT-ARMS) 2002, SSI 2002 513; made under the Execution of Diligence (Scotland) Act 1926 s.6; and the Court of Session Act 1988 s.5. In force: January 1, 2003; £2.00.

This Act of Sederunt amends the Act of Sederunt (Fees of Messengers-At-Arms) 1994 (SI 1994 391) by increasing the fees payable to Messengers-At-Arms by 2.6 per cent.

5222. Messengers at arms–fees

ACT OF SEDERUNT (FEES OF MESSENGERS-AT-ARMS) (NO.2) 2002, SSI 2002 566; made under the Execution of Diligence (Scotland) Act 1926 s.6; and the Court of Session Act 1988 s.5. In force: December 30, 2002; £2.50.

This Act of Sederunt, which repeals the Act of Sederunt (Fees of Messengers-at-Arms) 1994 (SI 1994 391 (with savings)), the Act of Sederunt (Fees of Messengers-at-Arms) (No.2) 1994 (SI 1994 3268), the Act of Sederunt (Fees of Messengers-at-Arms) 1995 (SI 1995 3094), the Act of Sederunt (Fees of Messengers-at-Arms) 1996 (SI 1996 2855), the Act of Sederunt (Fees of Messengers-at-Arms) 1997 (SI 1997 2825), the Act of Sederunt (Fees of Messengers-at-Arms) 1998 (SI 1998 2668), the Act of Sederunt (Fees of Messengers-at-Arms) (Amendment) 1998 (SI 1998 3256), the Act of Sederunt (Fees of Messengers-at-Arms) 1999 (SSI 1999 351), the Act of Sederunt (Fees of Messengers-at-Arms) 2000 (SSI 2000 421), the Act of Sederunt (Fees of Messengers-at-Arms) 2001 (SSI 2001 440) and the Act of Sederunt (Fees of Messengers-at-Arms) 2002 (SSI 2002 513), provides for regulations to apply to the charging of fees by, and for fees of, Messengers-at-Arms and incorporates amendments following the abolition of warrant sales and poinding under the provisions of the Debt Arrangement and Attachment (Scotland) Act 2002.

5223. Non harassment orders–competency–pre existing interdict

See CIVIL PROCEDURE: McCann v. McGurran. §5338

5224. Non harassment orders–competency–pre existing interim interdict

See CIVIL PROCEDURE: McGuire v. Kidston. §5339

5225. Sheriff courts–fees

ACT OF SEDERUNT (FEES OF SOLICITORS IN THE SHERIFF COURT) (AMENDMENT) 2002, SSI 2002 235; made under the Sheriff Courts (Scotland) Act 1907 s.40. In force: June 10, 2002; £2.50.

This Act of Sederunt amends the Act of Sederunt (Fees of Solicitors in the Sheriff Court) (Amendment and Further Provisions) 1993 (SI 1993 3080) by substituting two new tables which regulate fees under the procedure for non personal injury summary causes and personal injury summary causes introduced by new summary cause rules. In addition, it increases the values of actions to which reduced fees apply and removes undefended actions for recovery of possession of heritable property from the list of actions to which reduced fees apply.

5226. Sheriff courts–fees

ACT OF SEDERUNT (FEES OF SOLICITORS IN THE SHERIFF COURT) (AMENDMENT NO.2) 2002, SSI 2002 274; made under the Sheriff Courts (Scotland) Act 1907 s.40. In force: July 1, 2002; £2.00.

This Act of Sederunt amends the Table of Fees in the Schedule to the Act of Sederunt (Fees of Solicitors in the Sheriff Court) (Amendment and Further Provisions) 1993 (SI 1993 3080) by increasing the fees payable to solicitors by 4.3 per cent.

5227. Sheriff courts–fees

ACT OF SEDERUNT (FEES OF SOLICITORS IN THE SHERIFF COURT) (AMENDMENT NO.3) 2002, SSI 2002 328; made under the Sheriff Courts (Scotland) Act 1907 s.40. In force: June 30, 2002; £2.00.

This Act of Sederunt substitutes the table set out in the Schedule, for the table in the Schedule to the Act of Sederunt (Fees of Solicitors in the Sheriff Court) (Amendment No.2) 2002 (SSI 2002 274) which contains inaccuracies which have been rectified by this Act of Sederunt.

5228. Sheriff courts–fees

SHERIFF COURT FEES AMENDMENT ORDER 2002, SSI 2002 269; made under the Courts of Law Fees (Scotland) Act 1895 s.2. In force: July 1, 2002; £2.50.

This Order amends the Sheriff Court Fees Order 1997 (SI 1997 687) to provide exemption from certain of the fees payable for persons in receipt of certain forms of benefits and legal aid. It also specifies for proceedings in the sheriff court new fee levels in substitution for those applicable since the 1997 Order was last amended and simplifies the fees payable relating to recording, engrossing and copying documents and makes new provision for payment of a fee on cancellation of a diet of taxation.

5229. Sheriff courts–sheriff officers–fees

ACT OF SEDERUNT (FEES OF SHERIFF OFFICERS) 2002, SSI 2002 515; made under the Sheriff Courts (Scotland) Act 1907 s.40; and the Execution of Diligence (Scotland) Act 1926 s.6. In force: January 1, 2003; £2.00.

This Act of Sederunt amends the Act of Sederunt (Fees of Sheriff Officers) 1994 (SI 1994 392) by increasing the fees payable to sheriff officers by 2.6 per cent.

5230. Sheriff courts—sheriff officers—fees

ACT OF SEDERUNT (FEES OF SHERIFF OFFICERS) (NO.2) 2002, SSI 2002 567; made under the Sheriff Courts (Scotland) Act 1907 s.40; and the Execution of Diligence (Scotland) Act 1926 s.26. In force: December 30, 2002; £2.50.

This Act of Sederunt repeals the Act of Sederunt (Fees of Sheriff Officers) 1994 (SI 1994 392 (with saving)), the Act of Sederunt (Fees of Sheriff Officers) (No.2) 1994 (SI 1994 3267), the Act of Sederunt (Fees of Sheriff Officers) 1995 (SI 1995 3095), the Act of Sederunt (Fees of Sheriff Officers) 1996 (SI 1996 2858), the Act of Sederunt (Fees of Sheriff Officers) 1997 (SI 1997 2824), the Act of Sederunt (Fees of Sheriff Officers) 1998 (SI 1998 2669), the Act of Sederunt (Fees of Sheriff Officers) 1999 (SSI 1999 150), the Act of Sederunt (Fees of Sheriff Officers) 2000 (SSI 2000 419), the Act of Sederunt (Fees of Sheriff Officers) 2001 (SSI 2001 439) and the Act of Sederunt (Fees of Sheriff Officers) 2002 (SSI 2002 515). This Act of Sederunt provides for regulations to apply to the charging of fees by, and for fees of, sheriff officers. The new regulations incorporate amendments following the abolition of warrant sales and poinding under the provisions of the Debt Arrangement and Attachment (Scotland) Act 2002.

5231. Sheriff courts—small claims

ACT OF SEDERUNT (SMALL CLAIM RULES) 2002, SSI 2002 133; made under the Sheriff Courts (Scotland) Act 1971 s.32. In force: June 10, 2002; £9.00.

This Order, which revokes the Act of Sederunt (Small Claim Rules) 1988 (SI 1988 1976), amends the Act of Sederunt (Amendment of Sheriff Court Ordinary Cause, Summary Cause and Small Claim, Rules) 1990 (SI 1990 661), the Act of Sederunt (Amendment of Sheriff Court Ordinary Cause, Summary Cause and Small Claim, Rules) (No.2) 1990 (SI 1990 2105), the Act of Sederunt (Amendment of Summary Cause and Small Claim Rules) 1991 (SI 1991 821), the Act of Sederunt (Amendment of Ordinary Cause, Summary Cause and Small Claim Rules) 1992 (SI 1992 249), the Act of Sederunt (Sheriff Court Ordinary Cause Rules) 1993 (SI 1993 1956) and makes rules of procedure in the sheriff court for small claims.

5232. Sheriff courts—summary causes

ACT OF SEDERUNT (SUMMARY CAUSE RULES) 2002, SSI 2002 132; made under the Sheriff Courts (Scotland) Act 1971 s.32. In force: June 10, 2002; £13.50.

This Act of Sederunt amends the Act of Sederunt (Ordinary Cause Rules, Sheriff Court) 1983 (SI 1983 747), the Act of Sederunt (Civil Jurisdiction of the Sheriff Court) 1986 (SI 1986 1946), the Act of Sederunt (Miscellaneous Amendments) 1986 (SI 1986 1966), the Act of Sederunt (Small Claim Rules) 1988 (SI 1988 1976), the Act of Sederunt (Amendment of Sheriff Court Ordinary Cause, and Summary Cause, Rules) 1988 (SI 1988 1978), the Act of Sederunt (Amendment of Ordinary Cause and Summary Cause Rules) (Written Statements) 1989 (SI 1989 436), the Act of Sederunt (Amendment of Sheriff Court Ordinary Cause, Summary Cause and Small Claim, Rules) 1990 (SI 1990 661), the Act of Sederunt (Amendment of Sheriff Court Ordinary Cause, Summary Cause and Small Claim, Rules) (No.2) 1990 (SI 1990 2105), the Act of Sederunt (Amendment of Ordinary Cause, Summary Cause and Small Claim Rules) 1992 (SI 1992 249), the Act of Sederunt (Child Support Act 1991) (Amendment of Ordinary Cause and Summary Cause Rules) 1993 (SI 1993 919) and the Act of Sederunt (Sheriff Court Ordinary Cause Rules) 1993 (SI 1993 1956). It also revokes the Act of Sederunt (Summary Cause Rules, Sheriff Court) 1976 (SI 1976 476), the Act of Sederunt (Summary Cause Rules, Sheriff Court) (Amendment) 1978 (SI 1978 112), the Act of Sederunt (Summary Cause Rules, Sheriff Court) (Amendment No.2) 1978 (SI 1978 1805), the Act of Sederunt (Summary Cause Rules, Sheriff Court) (Amendment) 1980 (SI 1980 455) and the Act of Sederunt (Amendment of Summary Cause and Small Claim Rules) 1991 (SI 1991 821). It makes rules of procedure in the sheriff court for summary cause actions except for those actions which have been prescribed as small claims.

5233. Sheriff courts—summary causes

ACT OF SEDERUNT (SUMMARY CAUSE RULES) (AMENDMENT) 2002, SSI 2002 516; made under the Sheriff Courts (Scotland) Act 1971 s.32. In force: January 1, 2003; £1.75.

This Act of Sederunt amends the Act of Sederunt (Summary Cause Rules) 2002 (SSI 2002 132) to provide power to the Sheriff or Sheriff Clerk in summary causes to allow an account of expenses to be taxed by the auditor of court.

5234. Sheriff courts—summary causes—fees

ACT OF SEDERUNT (FEES OF SOLICITORS IN THE SHERIFF COURT) (AMENDMENT NO.4) 2002, SSI 2002 568; made under the Sheriff Courts (Scotland) Act 1907 s.40. In force: January 1, 2003; £2.00.

This Act of Sederunt re-introduces the Table of Fees previously contained in the Act of Sederunt (Fees of Solicitors in the Sheriff Court) (Amendment and Further Provisions) 1993 (SI 1993 3080) which shall apply to any summary cause commenced before June 10, 2002. The Act also re-names the new Tables introduced by the Act of Sederunt (Fees of Solicitors in the Sheriff Court) (Amendment) 2002 (SSI 2002 235) as Part III of Chapter IV of the Table of Fees and provides that Part III shall apply in relation to any summary cause commenced on or after June 10, 2002.

5235. Sheriff courts—summary warrants—forms

ACT OF SEDERUNT (DEBT ARRANGEMENT AND ATTACHMENT (SCOTLAND) ACT 2002) 2002, SSI 2002 560; made under the Local Government (Scotland) Act 1947 s.247; the Taxes Management Act 1970 s.63; the Sheriff Courts (Scotland) Act 1971 s.32; the Car Tax Act 1983 Sch.1 para.3; the Court of Session Act 1988 s.5; the Local Government Finance Act 1992 Sch.8 para.2; the Local Government etc. (Scotland) Act 1994 Sch.10 para.2; the Finance Act 1996 Sch.5 para.13; the Finance Act 1997 s.52; and the Debt Arrangement and Attachment (Scotland) Act 2002 s.17, s.18, s.32, s.56, s.64. In force: December 30, 2002; £7.50.

This Act of Sederunt which makes rules of procedure in the sheriff court for applications relating to attachments and auctions amends the Act of Sederunt (Proceedings in the Sheriff Court under the Debtors (Scotland) Act 1987) 1988 (SI 1988 2013); Act of Sederunt (Form of Charge for Payment) 1988 (SI 1988 2059); Act of Sederunt (Messengers-at-Arms and Sheriff Officers Rules) 1991 (SI 1991 1397); Act of Sederunt (Sheriff Court Ordinary Cause Rules) 1993 (SI 1993 1956); Act of Sederunt (Rules of the Court of Session 1994) 1994 (SI 1994 1443); Act of Sederunt (Sheriff Court Bankruptcy Rules 1996) (SI 1996 2507); and Act of Sederunt (Child Care and Maintenance Rules) 1997 (SI 1997 291) and revokes Act of Sederunt (Proceedings in the Sheriff Court under the Debtors (Scotland) Act 1987) (Amendment) 1996 (SI 1996 2709). It provides for new forms of summary warrant, which may be granted by the sheriff for recovery of certain kinds of taxes and charges.

5236. Sheriff courts—witnesses and shorthand writers—fees

ACT OF SEDERUNT (FEES OF WITNESSES AND SHORTHAND WRITERS IN THE SHERIFF COURT) (AMENDMENT) 2002, SSI 2002 280; made under the Sheriff Courts (Scotland) Act 1907 s.40. In force: July 1, 2002; £1.75.

This Act of Sederunt, which substitutes a new table of witnesses' fees in the Act of Sederunt (Fees of Witnesses and Shorthand Writers in the Sheriff Court) 1992 (SI 1992 1878), increases the fees payable to shorthand writers in the Sheriff Court by 3.25 per cent.

5237. Sheriffs—bias—motion for leave to appeal—hearing before sheriff whose decision under challenge—independence and impartiality

[European Convention on Human Rights 1950 Art.6(1).]

In an action by F, the father of a young child, for contact, the sheriff made an order for interim contact. M, the mother, sought leave to appeal to the sheriff principal. When the motion came before the sheriff who had granted the contact order, M moved that he should decline jurisdiction, founding on the European Convention on Human Rights 1950 Art.6(1). The sheriff refused that motion and the motion for leave to appeal. M appealed to the Court of Session, arguing that while there was no ground for suggesting actual bias or lack of impartiality by the sheriff, there was a lack of the necessary appearance of independence and impartiality, as the motion for leave to appeal carried the implication that his decision was wrong.

Held, dismissing the appeal, that it was artificial to approach the application of the Convention, or of the "independent observer" test, as if the application for leave to appeal was a separate proceeding to the substantive issue, and the proper view was that the two questions were so intimately linked that there could be no breach of Art.6 in having the same judge decide both.

UMAIR v. UMAIR 2002 S.C.153, Lord Coulsfield, Lord Caplan, Lord Johnston, Ex Div.

5238. Vexatious litigants—right to fair trial—compatibility with Convention rights

[Vexatious Actions (Scotland) Act 1898 (c.35); European Convention on Human Rights 1950 Art.6.]

The Lord Advocate petitioned for an order under the Vexatious Actions (Scotland) Act 1898 in respect of B, a party litigant, who had brought a series of actions each seeking to raise essentially the same issues as previous litigations which had been decided against him. B argued, inter alia, that the order would breach his rights under the European Convention on Human Rights 1950 Art.6.

Held, making the order sought, that B's pleadings had been devoid of any statement of a comprehensible ground of action, and had become increasingly wild, as had his choice of defenders and a limitation which did not prevent B from raising actions but only required the leave of a Lord Ordinary before he did so was not incompatible with the requirements of Art.6 nor were orders to find caution made in previous actions.

HM ADVOCATE v. BELL (JAMIE) 2002 S.L.T. 527, Lord Coulsfield, Lord Cowie, Lord Marnoch, Ex Div.

ADMINISTRATIVE LAW

5239. Crown proceedings—interim orders—prisoners rights

[Crown Proceedings Act 1947 (c.44) s.21, s.38(1), s.44; European Convention on Human Rights 1950 Art.3; Act of Sederunt (Rules of the Court of Session 1994) 1994 (SI 1994 1443) Sch.2 r.58, r.58.3; Court of Session Act 1988 (c.36) s.45(b); Scotland Act 1998 (c.46) s.57(2); Human Rights Act 1998 (c.42) s.6.]

D, a prisoner, reclaimed against the Lord Ordinary's decision (2001 G.W.D. 35-1341) refusing his motion for an interim order ordaining M, the Scottish Ministers, to secure his transfer to conditions of detention compliant with the European Convention on Human Rights 1950 Art.3. A hearing was set restricted to whether in view of the Crown Proceedings Act 1947 s.21, D could competently obtain an order for specific performance, or whether his remedy was restricted to an order declaratory of his rights. D was thereafter allowed to amend his petition and sought declarator (1) that an order ordaining M to transfer him to other conditions of detention could competently be made in proceedings by way of application to the supervisory jurisdiction of the court under the Act of Sederunt (Rules of the Court of Session 1994) 1994 Sch.2 r.58, and was not precluded by operation of s.21 of the 1947 Act, and (2) that a similar order could competently be made under the Court of Session Act 1988 s.45(b). He argued, inter alia, that (1) by analogy with English law, "specific performance" under s 21.(1)(a) of the 1947 Act should be read as confined to specific implement at common law, thereby excluding any application under s.45(b) of the 1988 Act; (2) the bringing of proceedings by way of judicial review under Ch.58 elided the sort of specification which would otherwise be required; (3) reference to "civil proceedings" under s.21 of the 1947 Act should be read as excluding applications to the supervisory jurisdiction, as it did in s.44 of the 1947 Act; (4) an analogy should be drawn with the effect of s.21 of the 1947 Act in England, where "proceedings on the Crown side of the King's Bench Division" were excluded by s.38(1), and (5) that s.21 of the 1947 Act should be interpreted in a manner which was consistent with Art.3 of the Convention.

Held, refusing the reclaiming motion, that (1) the argument that s.21 (1)(a) of the 1947 Act was confined to specific implement at common law failed because the statutory duty sought to be enforced was the very general duty in the Scotland Act 1998 s.57 (2) and the Human Rights Act 1998 s.6, neither of which was the sort of precise duty in respect of which application by summary petition was envisaged by s.45 of the 1988 Act; and whether or not that application purported to be brought under r.58.3 of the 1994 Rules made no difference to the specification required; (2) the true purpose of s.44 of the 1947 Act was to equate the position of the Crown with that of the subject where, after the Act, proceedings were raised in the sheriff court, and it did not follow that "civil proceedings" in s.44 excluded applications to the supervisory jurisdiction; (3) the argument on Art.3 of the Convention overlooked the availability of the internal complaints procedure to D, with judicial review of any decision of the governor, as well as the remedy of declarator and damages, and (4) although it was difficult to express an authoritative view on what was covered by "proceedings on the Crown side of the King's Bench Division", it was clear that there was no separately identifiable department of Scots law which was capable of equating even approximately to such proceedings, and impossible to identify any analogous exclusion for Scotland.

DAVIDSON v. SCOTTISH MINISTERS (NO.1) 2002 S.C. 205, Lord Marnoch, Lord Hardie, Lord Weir, Ex Div.

5240. Fees–births, deaths, marriages and divorce

BIRTHS, DEATHS, MARRIAGES AND DIVORCES (FEES) (SCOTLAND) AMENDMENT REGULATIONS 2002, SSI 2002 390; made under the Registration of Births, Deaths and Marriages (Scotland) Act 1965 s.28A, s.37, s.38, s.40, s.43, s.47, s.54, s.56; and the Marriage (Scotland) Act 1977 s.3, s.25, s.26. In force: October 1, 2002; £1.75.

These Regulations amend the Registration of Births, Deaths, Marriages and Divorces (Fees) (Scotland) Regulations 1998 (SI 1998 643) to introduce new fees in relation to bulk particular searches, and to remove or increase certain other fees.

5241. Judicial review–competency–availability of alternative remedy–taxi licensing

[Civic Government (Scotland) Act 1982 (c.45) s.10, Sch.1 para.5(3)(d), Sch.1 para.18.]

F, holders of taxi licences, sought reduction of a decision by S, a licensing subcommittee, on December 14, 2000, inter alia, to approve 35 new applications for taxi licences and not to determine a maximum number of licences for the area. S lodged preliminary pleas to the competency of the petition, arguing that F had not exercised their statutory right of appeal, and had no title to sue. The case had been continued for adjustment. F argued that (1) S had not properly exercised its discretion at the meeting on December 14, having already decided to invite applications for licences on September 7, prior to a survey on the demand for extra taxis in the area; (2) S had acted erroneously in proceeding on the view that it was for F to supply evidence that there was no significant unmet demand in terms of the Civic Government (Scotland) Act 1982 s.10; (3) having regard to the material before S, no reasonable committee would have concluded that there was a significant and continuous unmet demand, and (4) in approaching the exercise of its discretion under s.10(3), S had erred in law in one or more respects or exercised their discretion in an unreasonable manner if it had waited for a comprehensive report on demand, it might have refused the applications under para.5(3)(d).

Held, dismissing the petition as incompetent, that (1) judicial review was not available where other means of review were provided and had not been made use of or were used without success; (2) F's complaints were matters which could have been the subject of an appeal to the sheriff under para.18 of Sch.1 to the 1982 Act, and (3) F had not relied on para.5(3)(d) at the hearing before S, and S was not bound to raise it ex proprio motu, but if it had been, its failure to do so could likewise have been appealed.

FALCONER v. SOUTH AYRSHIRE COUNCIL 2002 S.L.T. 1033, Lord Hamilton, OH.

5242. Judicial review—delay—mora, taciturnity and acquiescence—challenge to planning permission

A group of individuals sought judicial review of the decision of a local planning authority, granting outline planning permission for the erection of a single storey house on part of an area of land owned by the applicants. The applicants had previously submitted unsuccessful proposals for development at varying locations on their land. An application for outline consent was granted in March 1998 but a further application for a house in the same position was refused in 1999, the refusal being affirmed on appeal. The permission challenged, for a smaller scale house at a lower level, was granted on December 13, 2000. A report by an officer of the planning authority had recommended refusal as the application was contrary to the local plan. The planning committee members conducted a site visit but decided not to hold a hearing. The petitioners wrote to a councillor on January 25, 2001, formed an action group in May, and convened a public meeting in June, prior to raising the petition on July 31. They argued, inter alia, that the decision was Wednesbury unreasonable as being one which no local planning authority could reasonably have taken, having regard to the policy in the local plan, the planning history of the site and the officer's recommendation. In response to a plea of mora they argued that there had been a great deal of activity on their part of which the applicants must have been aware, and that the applicants had suffered no sufficient prejudice to justify any bar to the proceedings where no works had yet taken place on the site, the amount of fees incurred in preparing plans for the detailed application was not large, and it would be open to them to reapply for the outline consent which they had allowed to lapse. The petitioners also argued that the decision to grant planning permission without a hearing involved a breach of their legitimate expectations.

Held, dismissing the petition, that (1) it was necessary for an objector who wished to challenge by judicial review the validity of a decision granting planning consent, to act with alacrity; the delay by the petitioners in the present case, which was not justified by any conceivable practical consideration, fell to be regarded as unreasonable and the applicants were entitled to infer that the petitioners had acquiesced in the validity of the decision, and (2) in the absence of any indication of an intention to challenge the grant, the applicants had materially altered their position and would be prejudiced if the grant was annulled.

DEVINE v. McPHERSON; *sub nom.* DEVINE v. MORAY COUNCIL 2002 S.L.T. 213, Lord Eassie, OH.

5243. Judicial review—delay—mora, taciturnity and acquiescence—review of minister's decision

[Education (Scotland) Act 1980 (c.44) s.75A; Disability Discrimination Act 1995 (c.50); Education (Schools) Act 1997 (c.59).]

F sought judicial review of the decision of the Deputy Minister for Children and Education, not to allow her son, J, to continue to hold an assisted place under the

Education (Scotland) Act 1980. F sought (1) reduction of the decision; (2) declarator that J should have been entitled to an assisted place until completion of his secondary education; (3) declarator that J suffered from a disability, and (4) declarator that the decision was discriminatory in terms of the Disability Discrimination Act 1995 and therefore unlawful. J suffered from learning difficulties and was awarded an assisted place in September 1996. As a result of the learning difficulties J was placed in the year below his chronological age. The Education (Schools) Act 1997 ended the assisted places scheme but transitional provisions continued assisted places for those in the middle of primary or secondary education. J was in primary 6 at the end of the scheme, but had J been in primary 7 at the start of the qualifying year, his assisted place would have continued until completion of his secondary education. F argued, that (1) the Minister had failed to apply his mind to s.75A(1B)(b) of the 1980 Act; (2) the Ministers letter indicated that he felt he was excluded from using his discretion and that was wrong; (3) the decision to discontinue J's assisted place was irrational and one which no reasonable Minister would have reached, and (4) that in failing to adjust his policy to ensure that J was not disadvantaged by his disability the Minister had failed to comply with s.21 of the Disability Discrimination Act 1995. L argued that (1) the Minister was not a provider of services to J in terms of the 1995 Act, and (2) F was barred from insisting in these proceedings given that they were lodged 3 years after the decision.

Held, dismissing the petition, that (1) the delay between the end of the school year 1998 and the lodging of the petition in 2001 could be categorised as excessive and unreasonable; (2) that if F were to succeed in this petition at this stage, it would be detrimental to good administration and not achieve the result F sought and the plea of mora sustained; (3) the Ministerial correspondence did reveal an error of law but it did not follow that the court would have granted all the remedies sought. This would have, in effect substituted the court's decision for the Minister's which was not the court's function, and (4) the provider of services was required, under the 1995 Act, to not treat less favourably those who are disabled and the Minister could not be said to have done so in considering the continuation of assisted places.

MacKAY-LUDGATE v. LORD ADVOCATE 2002 S.C.L.R. 109, Lord Philip, OH.

5244. Judicial review—error of fact—social security tribunals—inevitability of result

[Social Security (Adjudication) Regulations 1995 (SI 1995 1801) Reg.10.]

A, an applicant for incapacity benefit sought reduction of the refusal by a social security appeal tribunal to reconsider the dismissal of her appeal against a determination that she did not satisfy the "all work test". A suffered from agoraphobia and certain other conditions and after she had completed an incapacity for work form she was invited to attend for a medical examination. As a result of her agoraphobia the examination took place at her home. When she initially appealed she was notified that an oral hearing had been arranged. A averred that she had written to the Independent Tribunal Service to the effect that her state of health prevented her attending but the hearing before the appeal tribunal proceeded without A being present or represented. The Secretary of State did not accept that A's letter was ever received, but accepted that the tribunal's decision was based on a material error of fact, that A had been able to attend a medical centre for examination, despite papers to the contrary before the tribunal. The Secretary of State also contended that the tribunal had not addressed the correct questions under the Social Security (Adjudication) Regulations 1995 Reg.10, but argued that had it done so, it could not properly have reached any other result and no purpose would be served by reconsideration.

Held, reducing the decision, that as the tribunal's decision had been based on a material error in fact, it was not appropriate to refuse to reduce the decision on the ground that reconsideration must inevitably reach the same result: the respondent's argument depended on a potentially disputable issue of fact, namely that A had not sent the letter, there was prejudice to her in the lack of opportunity to persuade the tribunal and it was not necessary for her to demonstrate that had she been present she would necessarily have succeeded.

ANDERSON v. SECRETARY OF STATE FOR WORK AND PENSIONS; *sub nom.* ANDERSON, PETITIONER 2002 S.L.T. 68, Lord Eassie, OH.

5245. Judicial review–identity of decision maker–all parties not called

[Police Pensions Regulations 1987 (SI 1987 257) Reg. H1 (2), Reg. H2 (2); Act of Sederunt (Rules of the Court of Session 1994) 1994 (SI 1994 1443) Sch. 2 Form 58.6.]

T, a former police inspector, sought reduction of two medical certificates granted in connection with his claim for an injury pension under the Police Pensions Regulations 1987 Reg. H1 (2). C, the chief constable, had decided T should retire on the grounds he was permanently disqualified from performing his duty. T claimed that his disability was as a result of an injury received in the execution of his duty. A certificate by a medical practitioner selected by C under Reg. H1 (2) (c) and (d) was unfavourable to T, who appealed under Reg. H2 (2), as required by the regulations. C notified the Scottish Ministers (S) who appointed a medical referee. C argued that because it was S's decision on appeal that was being challenged, they were the appropriate respondents and all parties had not been called.

Held, continuing the case to enable service to be effected on S, that (1) the method under the regulations for both the original decision and the appeal involved the decision maker appointing a medical practitioner as the means by which to make their decision. The practitioners themselves did not make the decision. At the appeal stage the decision was made by S and it was clear from Act of Sederunt (Rules of the Court of Session 1994) 1994 Sch. 2 Form 58.6 that the respondent in an action would normally be the decision maker, and (2) the question whether the first certificate could be subjected to judicial review, given C's argument that the regulations provided for a full review by way of appeal, could not be decided in isolation but required full argument as to the nature of the alleged defects and the capacity of the medical referee.

THOMSON v. CHIEF CONSTABLE OF GRAMPIAN POLICE (MEDICAL CERTIFICATES) 2001 S.C. 443, Lord Philip, OH.

5246. Judicial review–natural justice–consultation–school closure

B sought judicial review of a decision by C, a local authority to close a primary school at which a child of hers was a pupil. C had produced a consultation paper, and a detailed response (including redevelopment plans) was submitted by the school board. B argued that there had been no meaningful consultation as C's mind had already been made up. There was a lack of information and the response to the redevelopment proposals was only produced at the relevant meeting, giving the school board no adequate time to reply. B also argued that the decision was irrational in that C had failed to take into account or apply adequate weight to relevant factors.

Held, dismissing the petition, that (1) B had failed to demonstrate that any aspect of the consultation process was unfair or that C's mind had been closed; the consultation paper gave very clear reasons for the proposals advanced; the time awarded for consideration exceeded the statutory requirement, and given the nature of the discussion at the meeting the complaint relating to reaction time to the redevelopment study was not sufficient to render the whole process unfair, and (2) B's total lack of averment as to any material effect of C's alleged failure to take account of relevant factors rendered her case irrelevant on that aspect.

BUCHAN v. WEST LOTHIAN COUNCIL 2001 S.L.T. 1452, Lord Johnston, OH.

5247. Judicial review–scope–intra vires error of law

C and T, members of G, the Showmen's Guild of Great Britain, both sought judicial review of a decision of A, G's appeal tribunal. C and T, as lessees of fairground occupancy rights, had refused to allow M (other members of G) to participate in a fair for a second immediately successive year on the ground that M's previous occupation had been on a "one year only" basis. Under G's rules the relevant section committee had to give consent to a lease of ground at a fair on such a basis. No such consent had been given. M's complaints were upheld. C and T averred that (1) A had failed to give adequate, comprehensible reasons for its decision, and (2) A had erred in law in failing to appreciate a distinction between the letting of a particular fairground "position" and the letting of an area of ground; only the latter arrangement required consent for a one year let, whereas the disputes with M related to the former type. C and T argued that if a domestic tribunal of a voluntary association reached a decision involving a misconstruction of either the rules of the association or the general law, that constituted an error of law which the court would review and correct and need not be an error as to the tribunal's powers or jurisdiction.

Held, dismissing the petitions, that (1) where parties had by agreement conferred on a body the power of interpretation of the law and its application to their dispute and agreed to accept the determination as final, that agreement was a matter to be respected and was reason for the court not interfering with an intra-jurisdictional error of law; (2) in C's case it was not evident that the decision was in error having regard to G's rules; more importantly, the alleged error was not one going to the jurisdiction of A and it was not within the supervisory jurisdiction of the court to intervene on that ground: the alleged distinction between "ground" and "position" and whether the requirement of consent to a one year only letting applied to the arrangements in question were matters falling well within A's field of expertise as constituted under G's rules and upon which those rules provided for finality to be given to A's decision. Nor had A purported, as argued for C, to rule on the civil law of contract but had simply been concerned with G's internal rules, and (3) in T's case the absence of any discussion of the reason for not accepting the existence of a one year only agreement was not a ground for reducing A's decision as there was no prejudice to T where it was further found that any such agreement would have been invalid as not sanctioned by G's Scottish section.

CODONA v. SHOWMEN'S GUILD OF GREAT BRITAIN 2002 S.L.T. 299, Lord Eassie, OH.

5248. Registration—fees—births, deaths and marriages

REGISTRATION OF BIRTHS, DEATHS AND MARRIAGES (FEES) (SCOTLAND) ORDER 2002, SSI 2002 389; made under the Public Expenditure and Receipts Act 1968 s.5, Sch.3 para.1. In force: October 1, 2002; £1.75.

This Order, which revokes the Registration of Births, Deaths and Marriages (Fees) (Scotland) Order 1997 (SI 1997 717), amends the sum specified as the amount or maximum amount payable under certain statutory provisions for a certificate of birth, death or marriage issued for the purposes of certain Acts. The sum specified as the amount or maximum amount payable is increased as at that date to £8.50.

AGENCY

5249. Commercial agents—agreements—termination—expiry of contractual period—compensation

[Commercial Agents (Council Directive) Regulations 1993 (SI 1993 3053) Reg.17.]

F, a former commercial agent for E, a fashion company, sought compensation in terms of the Commercial Agents (Council Directive) Regulations 1993 Reg.17. In the terms of a written agreement the engagement ended when the pursuer was 65 or on May 31, 1997, whichever was earlier. The pursuer turned 65 on April 13, 1997 and the company ended his contract. E argued that the directive did not define "termination", but it meant being deprived of the proper performance of a contractual obligation. F's contract had expired through time, concluded of consent on his birthday and there was no "termination".

Held, allowing proof before answer, that (1) "termination" had to be interpreted in a purposive way which would protect all commercial agents, otherwise the EU Treaty objectives would not be attained, and (2) that "termination" was habile to cover contracts expiring through the effluxion of time and the pursuer was entitled to compensation, *Whitehead (Patrick Whitehead Partnership) v. Jenks & Cattell Engineering Ltd* [1999] Eu. L.R. 8277 followed.

FRAPE v. EMRECO INTERNATIONAL LTD 2002 S.L.T. 371, Lord McEwan, OH.

5250. Commercial agents–agreements–termination–sales representatives–interpretation of contract

[Commercial Agents (Council Directive) Regulations 1993 (SI 1993 3053) Reg.17.]

H was appointed to act as commercial agent for P and entered into a sales representative agreement in January 1995 which was amended in May. In September 1999, 3 months notice of termination was given to H. H sued for commission allegedly due on sales arranged prior to termination. H also sought compensation due in accordance with the Commercial Agents (Council Directive) Regulations 1993 Reg.17. P argued that the agreement, properly interpreted, provided for indemnity rather than compensation and the words "compensation after termination" in Art.10 meant no more than "termination payment". H argued that the default remedy was compensation in terms of Commercial Agents (Council Directive) 86/653 Art 17(2). This remedy would be rendered unavailable if indemnity was determined to be the intention of the agreement.

Held, granting decree of dismissal in respect of the second conclusion of the summons and allowing, quoad ultra proof before answer, that (1) notwithstanding the use of the word "compensation" there was sufficient clarity to conclude that the intention was indemnity, not compensation, and (2) on sound construction of Art.10, it had been agreed that upon termination H would be entitled to indemnity and consequently was excluded from claiming compensation.

HARDIE POLYMERS LTD v. POLYMERLAND LTD 2002 S.C.L.R. 64, Lord Macfadyen, OH.

AGRICULTURE

5251. Abattoirs–levy scheme–application of scheme to premises dealing with Over Thirty Months Scheme

[Meat and Livestock Commission Levy Scheme (Confirmation) Order 1987 (SI 1987 1303); Agriculture Act 1967 (c.22) s.13(1); Slaughter of Animals (Scotland) Act 1980 (c.13) s.22.]

K petitioned for judicial review seeking a declarator that the imposition on them of levies by M pursuant to a levy scheme established under the Agriculture Act 1967 s.13(1) and confirmed by the Meat and Livestock Commission Levy Scheme (Confirmation) Order 1987 for the period from May 1996 to January 2000, and the retention by M of such levies were unlawful and ultra vires. K also sought repayment of the total amount of the levies paid with interest. Under the levy scheme, levies were due to M in respect of buildings used for the slaughtering of animals, the flesh of which was intended for use for human consumption. It was not in dispute that until May 1996, K operated such premises and were responsible, as the persons in control and management of such premises, for payment of the levies. However, between May 1996 and January 2000, the premises operated by K were used for the slaughtering of animals over 30 months old, which, in terms of the Over Thirty Months Scheme introduced after the outbreak of bovine spongiform encephalopathy (BSE), meant that the flesh from the animals could not be used for human consumption. K argued that they had taken their premises outwith the levy scheme and that the payments made during the relevant period should be refunded. M argued that once premises were established as a slaughterhouse in terms of the 1987 Order, they remained so despite their participation in the Over Thirty Months Scheme, as they were still licensed as a slaughterhouse.

Held, finding that the premises were not a slaughterhouse subject to the levy scheme as statutorily defined and allowing a proof before answer on other matters, that (1) in order for premises to be liable for the levies to M, they had to be used for the killing of animals whose flesh was intended for human consumption, and (2) during the period where the abattoir was used solely under the Over Thirty Months Scheme, the flesh from animals killed had not been intended for use for human consumption.

J KELLY & SONS LTD v. MEAT & LIVESTOCK COMMISSION 2001 S.C.L.R. 1093, Lord Hamilton, OH.

5252. Agricultural policy—wine

COMMON AGRICULTURAL POLICY (WINE) (SCOTLAND) REGULATIONS 2002, SSI 2002 325; made under the European Communities Act 1972 s.2. In force: September 23, 2002; £4.50.

These Regulations, which revoke in relation to Scotland the Common Agricultural Policy (Wine) Regulations 1996 (SI 1996 696), the Common Agricultural Policy (Wine) (Amendment) Regulations 1997 (SI 1997 542), the Common Agricultural Policy (Wine) (Amendment) Regulations 1998 (SI 1998 453) and the Common Agricultural Policy (Wine) (Amendment) Regulations 1999 (SI 1999 482), provide for the enforcement of specified EC Regulations concerned with the production and marketing of wine and related products. They designate authorities for the purposes of enforcement; define "medium dry" for the purposes of labelling and description; specify the vine varieties classified for the production of wine in Scotland; specify conditions for the use of geographical indications for the designation of table wine; provide for powers of inspection and enforcement; authorise controls on the movement of wine-sector products; provide for reviews of prohibitions etc. on movement of wine-sector products; confer on courts before which proceedings are brought powers in relation to the analysis and examination of samples; and prescribe offences and penalties and provide defences.

5253. Agricultural produce—milk—quota arrangements

DAIRY PRODUCE QUOTAS (SCOTLAND) AMENDMENT REGULATIONS 2002, SSI 2002 228; made under the European Communities Act 1972 s.2. In force: June 5, 2002; £1.75.

These Regulations, which amend the Agricultural Subsidies (Appeals) (Scotland) Regulations 2000 (SI 2000 347) and the Dairy Produce Quotas (Scotland) Regulations 2002 (SI 2002 110), make provision for an opportunity to make representations to the Scottish Ministers before decisions are made by them involving matters of ministerial discretion and a right of representation and ultimately appeal through the 2000 Regulations against decisions made by the Scottish Ministers involving principally matters of fact.

5254. Agricultural produce—milk—quota arrangements

DAIRY PRODUCE QUOTAS (SCOTLAND) REGULATIONS 2002, SSI 2002 110; made under the European Communities Act 1972 s.2. In force: March 31, 2002; £6.00.

These Regulations, which revoke the Dairy Produce Quotas (Amendment) (Time limits) Regulations 1997 (SI 1997 733), the Dairy Produce Quotas Amendment (Scotland) Regulations 2000 (SSI 2000 52) and the Act of Sederunt (Rules of the Court of Session Amendment No.4) (Application under s.1 of the Administration of Justice (Scotland) Act 1972) 2000 (SSI 2000 319), amend the Abolition of the Intervention Board for Agricultural Produce

(Consequential Provisions) (Scotland) Regulations 2001 (SSI 2001 390). They implement Council Regulation 3950/92 ([1992] OJ L405) establishing an additional levy in the milk and milk products sector and Commission Regulation 1292/2001 ([2001] OJ L187/19) laying down detailed rules for applying Council Regulation 3950/92. Under this Community legislation, a levy continues to be payable on dairy produce sold by direct sale by a producer or delivered by him wholesale to a purchaser, unless the sales or deliveries are within a reference quantity described in that legislation. The Community legislation establishes the system of what are commonly called "milk quotas" and in these Regulations the term "quota" is used to refer to the reference quantity described in the Community legislation.

5255. Agricultural produce–seeds–fodder plant and cereal seeds–marketing

SEEDS (MISCELLANEOUS AMENDMENTS) (SCOTLAND) REGULATIONS 2002, SSI 2002 520; made under the Plant Varieties and Seeds Act 1964 s.16, s.36. In force: January 1, 2003; £1.75.

These Regulations amend the Cereal Seeds Regulations 1993 (SI 1993 2005) and the Fodder Plant Seeds Regulations 1993 (SI 1993 2009) to exempt certain types of seed marketed in bulk from the labelling and packaging requirements. They specify the conditions for the exemption, in implementation of Council Directive 2001/64 ([2001] OJ L234/60) amending Directive 66/401 on the marketing of fodder plant seed and Directive 66/402 on the marketing of cereal seed.

5256. Animal products–diseases and disorders–BSE

BSE MONITORING (SCOTLAND) AMENDMENT REGULATIONS 2002, SSI 2002 1; made under the European Communities Act 1972 s.2. In force: January 30, 2002; £1.75.

These Regulations, which make amendments to the Cattle Identification Regulations 1998 (SI 1998 871), the Cattle (Identification of Older Animals) (Scotland) Regulations 2001 (SI 2001 1) and the BSE Monitoring (Scotland) Regulations 2001 (SI 2001 231), give effect to Commission Regulation 1248/ 2001 ([2001] OJ L173/12) amending Annex III to Regulation 999/2001 ([2001] OJ L147/1) as regards epidemio-surveillance and testing of transmissible spongiform encephalopathies. These Commission Regulations require Member States to ensure that certain categories of bovine animals over 24 months of age are examined in accordance with the prescribed minimum requirements for monitoring BSE.

5257. Animal products–diseases and disorders–TSE

TSE (SCOTLAND) REGULATIONS 2002, SSI 2002 255; made under the European Communities Act 1972 s.2. In force: June 19, 2002; £10.50.

These Regulations, which amend the Fresh Meat (Hygiene and Inspection) Regulations 1995 (SI 1995 539), the Specified Risk Material Order 1997 (SI 1997 2964), the Cattle Identification Regulations 1998 (SI 1998 871), the Animal By-Products Order 1999 (SI 1999 646) and the BSE Monitoring (Scotland) Regulations 2001 (SI 2001 231), revoke specified Orders. They provide for the administration and enforcement of European Parliament and Council Regulation 999/2001 ([2001] OJ L147/1) laying down rules for the prevention, control and eradication of certain transmissible spongiform encephalopathies; Commission Regulation 1248/2001 ([2001] OJ L173/12) amending Annexes III, X and XI to Regulation 999/2001 as regards epidemio-surveillance and testing of transmissible spongiform encephalopathies; Commission Regulation 1326/2001 ([2001] OJ L177/61) laying down transitional measures to permit the changeover to the European Parliament Council Regulation 999/2001 laying down rules for the prevention, control and eradication of certain transmissible spongiform encephalopathies, and amending Annexes VII and XI to that Regulation; Commission Regulation 270/2002 ([2002] OJ L45/4) amending Annex XI to Regulation 999/2001 of the European

Parliament and of the Council as regards bovine vertebral column and amending Regulation 1326/2001 as regards animal feeding and the placing on the market of ovine and caprine animals and products thereof; and continuing the implementation of Council Decision 2000/766 ([2000] OJ L306/32) concerning certain protection measures with regard to transmissible spongiform encephalopathies and the feeding of animal protein, and Commission Decision 2001/9 ([2001] OJ L2/32) concerning control measures required for the implementation of Council Decision 2000/766 in accordance with Commission Regulation 1326/2001 Art.1 (2).

5258. Animal products–feedingstuffs–import controls–China

FOOD AND ANIMAL FEEDINGSTUFFS (PRODUCTS OF ANIMAL ORIGIN FROM CHINA) (EMERGENCY CONTROL) (SCOTLAND) AMENDMENT REGULATIONS 2002, SSI 2002 356; made under the European Communities Act 1972 s.2. In force: July 31, 2002; £1.50.

These Regulations, which amend the Food and Animal Feedingstuffs (Products of Animal Origin from China) (Emergency Control) (Scotland) Regulations 2002 (SSI 2002 300), implement Commission Decision 2002/69 ([2002] OJ L30/51) concerning certain protective measures with regard to the products of animal origin imported from China.

5259. Animal products–origin marking–third country imports

PRODUCTS OF ANIMAL ORIGIN (THIRD COUNTRY IMPORTS) (SCOTLAND) AMENDMENT REGULATIONS 2002, SSI 2002 565; made under the European Communities Act 1972 s.2. In force: January 1, 2003; £1.75.

These Regulations, which amend the Products of Animal Origin (Third Country Imports) (Scotland) Regulations 2002 (SSI 2002 445), implement Commission Decision 2002/995 ([2002] OJ L353/1) of December 9, 2002 laying down interim safeguard measures with regard to imports of products of animal origin for personal consumption amending the existing exemption from the general requirements for personal imports meeting certain criteria.

5260. Cattle–identification and registration–movement control

CATTLE IDENTIFICATION (NOTIFICATION OF MOVEMENT) (SCOTLAND) AMENDMENT REGULATIONS 2002, SSI 2002 22; made under the European Communities Act 1972 s.2. In force: February 18, 2002; £1.50.

These Regulations, which amend the Cattle Database Regulations 1998 (SI 1998 1796) and the Cattle (Identification of Older Animals) (Scotland) Regulations 2001 (SSI 2001 1), reduce from seven days to three the period within which notification of movements of cattle must be posted or made by electronic means by a keeper to the Scottish Ministers. This is in accordance with the requirements of Council Regulation 1760/2000 ([2000] OJ L204/1) establishing a system for the identification and registration of bovine animals.

5261. Cattle–infectious disease control–foot and mouth disease–artificial insemination

ARTIFICIAL INSEMINATION OF CATTLE (ANIMAL HEALTH) (SCOTLAND) AMENDMENT REGULATIONS 2002, SSI 2002 191; made under the Animal Health and Welfare Act 1984 s.10. In force: April 18, 2002; £1.75.

These Regulations amend the Artificial Insemination of Cattle (Animal Health) (Scotland) Regulations 1985 (SI 1985 1857) in order to make transitional provision relating to the expiry of emergency licences issued under the Artificial Insemination of Cattle (Emergency Licences) (Scotland) Regulations 2001 (SSI 2001 179) during the recent outbreak of foot and mouth disease. The Regulations permit the acceptance for supply of semen collected in accordance with an emergency licence from an approved bull, permit the use of semen collected in accordance with an emergency licence and enable the Scottish Ministers to recognise training courses in addition to those already recognised by the (now defunct) Agricultural Training Board.

5262. Feedingstuffs–additives–animal feed–maximum levels

FEEDING STUFFS AMENDMENT (SCOTLAND) REGULATIONS 2002, SSI 2002 285; made under the Agriculture Act 1970 s.66, s.68, s.69, s.74A, s.75, s.76, s.77, s.78, s.79, s.84; and the European Communities Act 1972 s.2. In force: July 1, 2002; £2.50.

These Regulations amend the Feeding Stuffs (Sampling and Analysis) Regulations 1999 (SI 1999 1663), the Feeding Stuffs (Enforcement) Regulations 1999 (SI 1999 2325) and the Feeding Stuffs (Scotland) Regulations 2000 (SI 2000 453). They implement Commission Directive 2001/79 ([2001] OJ L267/1) amending Council Directive 87/153 fixing guidelines for the assessment of additives in animal nutrition; Council Directive 2001/102 ([2001] OJ L6/45) on the undesirable substances and products in animal nutrition; Commission Regulation 2013/2001 ([2001] OJ L272/24) concerning the provisional authorisation of a new additive use and the permanent authorisation of an additive in feedingstuffs; Commission Regulation 2200/2001 ([2001] OJ L299/1) concerning provisional authorisation of additives in feedingstuffs; Commission Directive 2002/1 ([2002] OJ L5/9) amending Directive 94/39 as regards animal feedingstuffs for the support of liver function in case of chronic liver insufficiency; and Commission Regulation 256/2002 ([2002] OJ L41/6) concerning the provisional authorisation of an additive and the permanent authorisation of an additive in feedingstuffs. The Regulations specify the requirements for a dossier submitted in relation to the assessment of feed additives for which marketing authorisation has been sought by providing that EC legislation referred to; regulate the presence of undesirable substances in animal feed by specifying new maximum levels for dioxin in feed; and regulate dietetic feeds as regards the required nutritional characteristics and labelling of feeds intended for the support of liver function in case of chronic liver insufficiency in dogs or cats.

5263. Feedingstuffs–import controls–China

See FOOD. §5659

5264. Infectious disease control–animal movements–interim measures

DISEASE CONTROL AND ANIMAL MOVEMENTS (INTERIM MEASURES) (SCOTLAND) AMENDMENT ORDER 2002, SSI 2002 221; made under the Animal Health Act 1981 s.1, s.7, s.8. In force: May 9, 2002; £2.50.

This Order amends the 20-day standstill on the movement of animals in the Disease Control (Interim Measures) (Scotland) Order 2002 (SSI 2002 34) and the Sheep and Goats (Interim Measures) (Scotland) Order 2002 (SSI 2002 38), permits the movement of animals to premises if those animals return from slaughterhouses and permits the movement of animals from premises to shows and exhibitions to places for veterinary treatment or research or to artificial insemination centres. It further permits those animals to be returned to the holding from which they came without applying the standstill to the animals on the holding to which they are returned. The Order extends the common grazings exemption, permits the movement of pigs on the same conditions as cattle and creates a specific offence of taking unauthorised access to a stock area in regulated market premises.

5265. Infectious disease control–foot and mouth disease–controlled areas– revocation

FOOT-AND-MOUTH DISEASE DECLARATORY (CONTROLLED AREA) (SCOTLAND) AMENDMENT AND REVOCATION ORDER 2002, SSI 2002 54;

made under the Foot-and-Mouth Disease Order 1983 (SI 1983 1950) Art.30. In force: Art 2: February 11, 2002 at 3 pm; remainder: February 18, 2002; £2.00.

This Order revokes with savings the Foot-and-Mouth Disease (Scotland) (Declaratory and Controlled Area) Amendment Order 2001 (SSI 2001 66), the Foot-and-Mouth Disease (Scotland) (Declaratory and Controlled Area) Amendment (No.2) Order 2001 (SSI 2001 90), the Foot-and-Mouth Disease Declaratory (Controlled Area) (Scotland) (No.3) Order 2001 (SSI 2001 111), the Foot-and-Mouth Disease (Scotland) (Declaratory and Controlled Area) Amendment (No.3) Order 2001 (SSI 2001 146), the Foot-and-Mouth Disease Declaratory (Controlled Area) (Scotland) (No.3) Amendment (No.2) Order 2001 (SSI 2001 150), the Foot-and-Mouth Disease (Scotland) (Declaratory and Controlled Area) Amendment (No.4) Order 2001 (SSI 2001 159), the Foot-and-Mouth Disease Declaratory (Controlled Area) (Scotland) (No.3) Amendment (No.3) Order 2001 (SSI 2001 170), the Foot-and-Mouth Disease (Scotland) (Declaratory and Controlled Area) Amendment (No.5) Order 2001 (SSI 2001 187), the Foot-and-Mouth Disease (Scotland) (Declaratory and Controlled Area) Amendment (No.6) Order 2001 (SSI 2001 204), the Foot-and-Mouth Disease (Scotland) (Declaratory and Controlled Area) Amendment (No.7) Order 2001 (SSI 2001 246), the Foot-and-Mouth Disease Declaratory (Controlled Area) (Scotland) (No.3) Amendment (No.5) Order 2001 (SSI 2001 290) and the Foot-and-Mouth Disease Declaratory (Controlled Area) (Scotland) (No.3) Amendment (No.6) Order 2001 (SSI 2001 481). The Order removes the requirement that vehicles moving animals from premises to slaughter be cleansed and disinfected before moving the vehicle from those premises and revokes all controlled area restrictions remaining in Scotland which were imposed under the Foot-and-Mouth Disease Order 1983 (SI 1983 1950).

5266. Infectious disease control—foot and mouth disease—import and export restrictions

IMPORT AND EXPORT RESTRICTIONS (FOOT-AND-MOUTH DISEASE) (SCOTLAND) (NO.3) AMENDMENT REGULATIONS 2002, SSI 2002 21; made under the European Communities Act 1972 s.2. In force: January 18, 2002 at 5 pm; £1.50.

These Regulations amend the Import and Export Restrictions (Foot-and-Mouth Disease) (Scotland) (No.3) Regulations 2001 (SSI 2001 429) to remove the requirement in relation to meat originating in a restricted area for on-farm checking of farm movement records, inspection of vehicles for cleansing and disinfection and observation of the loading of the consignment.

5267. Infectious disease control—foot and mouth disease—import and export restrictions

IMPORT AND EXPORT RESTRICTIONS (FOOT-AND-MOUTH DISEASE) (SCOTLAND) (NO.3) AMENDMENT (NO.2) AMENDMENT REGULATIONS 2002, SSI 2002 169; made under the European Communities Act 1972 s.2. In force: March 29, 2002; £1.50.

These Regulations, which amend the Import and Export Restrictions (Foot-and-Mouth Disease) (Scotland) (No.3) Amendment (No.2) Regulations 2002 (SSI 2002 35), continue in force the provisions of the 2002 Regulations.

5268. Infectious disease control—foot and mouth disease—import and export restrictions

IMPORT AND EXPORT RESTRICTIONS (FOOT-AND-MOUTH DISEASE) (SCOTLAND) (NO.3) AMENDMENT (NO.2) REGULATIONS 2002, SSI 2002 35; made under the European Communities Act 1972 s.2. In force: February 1, 2002 at 12 pm; £2.00.

These Regulations amend the Meat Products (Hygiene) Regulations 1994 (SI 1994 3082), the Fresh Meat (Hygiene and Inspection) Regulations 1995 (SI 1995 539) and the Minced Meat and Meat Preparations (Hygiene) Regulations 1995 (SI

1995 3205) and revoke the Foot-and-Mouth Disease (Marking of Meat, Meat Products, Minced Meat and Meat Preparations) (Scotland) Regulations 2001 (SSI 2001 358) and the Import and Export Restrictions (Foot-and-Mouth Disease) (Scotland) (No.3) Amendment Regulations 2002 (SSI 2002 21). The Regulations implement Commission Decision 2001/938 ([2001] OJ L345/ 100), Commission Decision 2002/37 ([2002] OJ L15/34) and Commission Decision 2002/48 ([2002] OJ L21/28) amending Commission Decision 2001/ 740 concerning certain protection measures with regard to foot and mouth disease in the UK. They remove all restrictions on the export of pigs, remove all export restrictions on cattle, remove the need to provide additional health assurances for horse exports, allow the export to other Member States of fresh and frozen bovine and porcine semen produced after January 15, 2002, allow meat to be exported from foot and mouth disease susceptible animals sourced from anywhere in Great Britain, lift export restrictions on fresh meat and meat products, lift foot and mouth disease based export restrictions on milk and milk products, hides and skins and all other animal products and lift restrictions on foot and mouth disease susceptible live animals.

5269. **Infectious disease control—foot and mouth disease—import and export restrictions—revocation**

IMPORT AND EXPORT RESTRICTIONS (FOOT-AND-MOUTH DISEASE) (SCOTLAND) (NO.3) REVOCATION REGULATIONS 2002, SSI 2002 109; made under the European Communities Act 1972 s.2. In force: March 7, 2002; £1.75.

These Regulations, which revoke the Import and Export Restrictions (Foot-and-Mouth Disease) (Scotland) (No.3) Regulations 2001 (SSI 2001 429), the Import and Export Restrictions (Foot-and-Mouth Disease) (Scotland) (No.3) Amendment Regulations 2001 (SSI 2001 455) and the Import and Export Restrictions (Foot-and-Mouth Disease) (Scotland) (No.3) Amendment (No.2) Regulations 2001 (SSI 2001 483), amend the Import and Export Restrictions (Foot-and-Mouth Disease) (Scotland) (No.3) Amendment (No.2) Regulations 2002 (SSI 2002 35). They implement Commission Decision 2002/153 ([2002] OJ L50/98) concerning certain protection measures with regard to foot and mouth disease in the UK, repealing Decision 2001/740 ([2001] OJ L277/30) and amending for the eighth time Decision 2001/327 ([2001] OJ L115/12).

5270. **Infectious disease control—foot and mouth disease—movement of animals**

PIGS (RECORDS, IDENTIFICATION AND MOVEMENT) (SCOTLAND) AMENDMENT ORDER 2002, SSI 2002 540; made under the Animal Health Act 1981 s.1, s.8, s.83. In force: December 31, 2002; £1.75.

This Order, which amends the Pigs (Records, Identification and Movement) Order 1995 (SI 1995 11), implements Council Directive 2000/15 ([2000] OJ L105/34) amending Council Directive 64/432 on health problems affecting intra-Community trade in bovine animals and swine. It provides revised versions of the declarations to accompany movements of pigs so that such declarations must be sent to the appropriate local authority even if the pigs are being moved for immediate slaughter. The Order also makes revisals to the movement licence.

5271. **Infectious disease control—movement of animals—restrictions—interim measures**

DISEASE CONTROL (INTERIM MEASURES) (SCOTLAND) AMENDMENT ORDER 2002, SSI 2002 369; made under the Animal Health Act 1981 s.1, s.7, s.8. In force: August 13, 2002; £1.75.

This Order, which amends the 20 day standstill on the movement of animals in the Disease Control (Interim Measures) (Scotland) Order 2002 (SSI 2002 34), lifts the controls in relation to camelids and elephants and substitutes for the requirement that persons having access to a market shall wear rubber boots, a requirement that such persons shall wear robust footwear which is capable of being properly cleansed and disinfected. It further allows animals which are located in the areas of the Orkney Islands Council, the Shetland Islands Council or Comhairle nan Eilan Siar, and which have been marketed there, to be marketed on the Scottish mainland within the 20 day standstill period, provided they have been kept separately from other stock.

5272. Infectious disease control–movement of animals–restrictions–interim measures

DISEASE CONTROL (INTERIM MEASURES) (SCOTLAND) AMENDMENT (NO.2) ORDER 2002, SSI 2002 530; made under the Animal Health Act 1981 s.1, s.7, s.8. In force: January 1, 2003; £1.50.

This Order amends the Disease Control (Interim Measures) (Scotland) Order 2002 (SSI 2002 34) to change the 20 day standstill on the movement of animals in relation to breeding goats. It allows breeding goats of either sex to move onto a holding for breeding purposes without triggering a 20 day standstill on that holding, and to return to their holding of origin without triggering a 20 day standstill.

5273. Infectious disease control–movement of animals–restrictions–interim measures

DISEASE CONTROL (INTERIM MEASURES) (SCOTLAND) ORDER 2002, SSI 2002 34; made under the Animal Health Act 1981 s.1, s.7, s.8, s.83. In force: February 18, 2002; £3.00.

This Order, which amends the Pigs (Records, Identification and Movement) Order 1995 (SI 1995 11), principally imposes restrictions on the movement of cattle, sheep, goats and other ruminating animals, swine and elephants in Scotland. It requires that any such movement from premises must be permitted by a specific or general licence issued by the Scottish Ministers and further requires that no animal is moved onto those premises during the period of 20 days before such movement.

5274. Infectious disease control–movement of animals–sheep and goats–interim measures

SHEEP AND GOATS IDENTIFICATION (SCOTLAND) AMENDMENT REGULATIONS 2002, SSI 2002 39; made under the European Communities Act 1972 s.2. In force: February 18, 2002; £2.00.

These Regulations amend the marking requirements in the Sheep and Goats Identification (Scotland) Regulations 2000 (SSI 2000 418) to sheep and goats born on holdings in Scotland, sheep and goats moved from holdings in Scotland, sheep and goats imported to holdings in Scotland and subsequently moved, and where tags applied in accordance with such markings are replaced, to require that an individual number is inserted into the mark so applied.

5275. Infectious disease control–movement of animals–sheep and goats–interim measures

SHEEP AND GOATS MOVEMENT (INTERIM MEASURES) (SCOTLAND) ORDER 2002, SSI 2002 38; made under the Animal Health Act 1981 s.1, s.8. In force: February 18, 2002; £1.75.

This Order requires that sheep and goats moving from holdings must have a movement eartag applied bearing an "S" and the number of the flockmark or herdmark subject to certain exemptions. The Order makes provision for the maximum number of eartags, for missing movement eartags and shall be enforced by the local authority, unless the Scottish Ministers so direct, and the Scottish Ministers may direct joint enforcement.

5276. Livestock–extensification payment

EXTENSIFICATION PAYMENT (SCOTLAND) REGULATIONS 2002, SSI 2002 278; made under the European Communities Act 1972 s.2. In force: June 28, 2002; £2.00.

These Regulations lay down, in relation to holdings in respect of which the Scottish Ministers are the competent authority for IACS purposes, implementing measures for the extensification payment scheme introduced by Council Regulation 1254/1999 ([1999] OJ L160/21) on the common organisation of the market in beef and veal for beef producers who comply with certain stocking density requirements.

5277. Pesticides–residue levels in crops, food and feeding stuffs

PESTICIDES (MAXIMUM RESIDUE LEVELS IN CROPS, FOOD AND FEEDING STUFFS) (SCOTLAND) AMENDMENT REGULATIONS 2002, SSI 2002 271; made under the European Communities Act 1972 s.2. In force: September 1, 2002; £3.00.

These Regulations amend the Pesticides (Maximum Residue Levels in Crops, Food and Feeding Stuffs) (Scotland) Regulations 2000 (SSI 2000 22), the Pesticides (Maximum Residue Levels in Crops, Food and Feeding Stuffs) (Scotland) Amendment (No.2) Regulations 2001 (SSI 2001 221) and the Pesticides (Maximum Residue Levels in Crops, Food and Feeding Stuffs) (Scotland) Amendment (No.3) Regulations 2001 (SSI 2001 435). They update the definition of "Residue Directives" to incorporate Commission Directive 2002/5 ([2002] OJ L34/7) amending Annex II to Council Directive 90/642 as regards the fixing of maximum levels for pesticide residues in and on certain products of plant origin, including fruit and vegetables, and Commission Directive 2002/23 ([2002] OJ L64/13) amending the Annexes to Council Directives 86/36, 86/363 and 90/642 as regards the fixing of maximum levels for pesticide residues in and on cereals, foodstuffs of animal origin and certain products of plant origin, including fruit and vegetables respectively.

5278. Pesticides–residue levels in crops, food and feedingstuffs

PESTICIDES (MAXIMUM RESIDUE LEVELS IN CROPS, FOOD AND FEEDING STUFFS) (SCOTLAND) AMENDMENT (NO.2) REGULATIONS 2002, SSI 2002 489; made under the European Communities Act 1972 s.2. In force: November 30, 2002; £10.50.

These Regulations amend the Pesticides (Maximum Residue Levels in Crops, Food and Feeding Stuffs) (Scotland) Regulations 2000 (SSI 2000 22), the Pesticides (Maximum Residue Levels in Crops, Food and Feeding Stuffs) (Scotland) Amendment Regulations 2001 (SSI 2001 84), the Pesticides (Maximum Residue Levels in Crops, Food and Feeding Stuffs) (Scotland) Amendment (No.2) Regulations 2001 (SSI 2001 221), the Pesticides (Maximum Residue Levels in Crops, Food and Feeding Stuffs) (Scotland) Amendment (No.3) Regulations 2001 (SSI 2001 435) and the Pesticides (Maximum Residue Levels in Crops, Food and Feeding Stuffs) (Scotland) Amendment Regulations 2002 (SI 2002 271). The Regulations provide for the sampling procedure contained in the Annex to Commission Directive 2002/63 ([2002] OJ L187/30) establishing Community methods of sampling for the official control of pesticide residues in and on products of plant and animal origin and repealing Directive 79/700, to apply for the determination of pesticide residues, maximum levels for which are set by the Community. They also insert references to the pesticides bentazone, formothion, lindane, metsulfuran methyl, oxydemeton-methyl and pyridate and their residues, to reflect Commission Directive 2002/42 ([2002] OJ L134/29) for bentazone and pyridate; Commission Directive 2002/66 ([2002] OJ L192/47) for lindane, quintozene, parathion and permethrin; Commission Directive 2002/71 ([2002] OJ L225/21) for formthion, dimethoate and oxydemeton-methyl; and Commission Directive 2002/76 ([2002] OJ L240/45) for metsulfuron methyl. In addition, the Regulations remove pesticide residues, which had previously been set nationally by virtue of powers contained in the Food and Environment Protection Act 1985, from the list contained in the 2000 Regulations because they have been replaced by Community levels.

5279. Pigs–pig industry–capital grants

PIG INDUSTRY RESTRUCTURING (CAPITAL GRANT) (SCOTLAND) SCHEME 2002, SSI 2002 43; made under the Agriculture Act 1970 s.29. In force: March 29, 2002; £1.75.

This Scheme makes provision in Scotland for the payment of grants towards the cost of loans obtained in order to pay for capital expenditure incurred in the restructuring of pig production businesses. The Scheme provides that claims for payment of grant shall be made in such form as the Scottish Ministers may reasonably require.

5280. Pigs–pig industry–non-capital grants

PIG INDUSTRY RESTRUCTURING (NON-CAPITAL GRANT) (SCOTLAND) SCHEME 2002, SSI 2002 44; made under the Farm Land and Rural Development Act 1988 s.1. In force: March 29, 2002; £1.75.

This Scheme makes provision in Scotland for the payment of grants towards the cost of loans incurred in connection with the establishment or promotion of farm businesses which are ancillary to pig production businesses and relate to the products of pig production as part of the restructuring of a pig production business. The Scheme provides that claims for grant shall be made in such form as the Scottish Ministers may reasonably require and enables grant monies to be withheld or recovered in certain circumstances.

5281. Plant varieties–seeds–fees

SEEDS (FEES) (SCOTLAND) REGULATIONS 2002, SSI 2002 526; made under the Plant Varieties and Seeds Act 1964 s.16, s.36. In force: December 31, 2002; £3.00.

These Regulations, which revoke the Seeds (Fees) (Scotland) Regulations 2000 (SSI 2000 1), prescribe revised fees in respect of matters arising under the Seeds (Registration, Licensing and Enforcement) Regulations 1985 (SI 1985 980), the Cereal Seeds Regulations 1993 (SI 1993 2005), the Oil and Fibre Plant Seeds Regulations 1993 (SI 1993 2007), the Beet Seeds Regulations 1993 (SI 1993 2006) and the Vegetable Seeds Regulations 1993 (SI 1993 2008).

5282. Plant varieties–seeds–labelling and packaging

SEEDS (MISCELLANEOUS AMENDMENTS) (NO.2) (SCOTLAND) REGULATIONS 2002, SSI 2002 564; made under the Plant Varieties and Seeds Act 1964 s.16, s.36. In force: In accordance with Art.1; £1.75.

These Regulations, which revoke the Seeds (Miscellaneous Amendments) (Scotland) Regulations 2002 (SSI 2002 520), amend the Cereal Seeds Regulations 1993 (SI 1993 2005) and the Fodder Plant Seeds Regulations 1993 (SI 1993 2009) to exempt certain types of seed marketed in bulk from the labelling and packaging requirements.

5283. Plants–plant health–Phytophthora ramorum

PLANT HEALTH (PHYTOPHTHORA RAMORUM) (SCOTLAND) ORDER 2002, SSI 2002 223; made under the Plant Health Act 1967 s.2, s.3, s.4. In force· May 13, 2002; £2.00.

This Order implements measures to prevent the introduction and spread of the pest Phytophthora ramorum, a fungus which is not established in Scotland. It regulates the importation and movement into and within Scotland of plant material identified as susceptible to the pest, believed to cause Sudden Oak

Death syndrome in certain species of oak in the USA, and harm to Rhododendron, Viburnum and other plants.

5284. Plants—plant health—Phytophthora ramorum

PLANT HEALTH (PHYTOPHTHORA RAMORUM) (SCOTLAND) (NO.2) ORDER 2002, SSI 2002 483; made under the Plant Health Act 1967 s.2, s.3, s.4. In force: November 1, 2002; £2.00.

This Order, which revokes the Plant Health (Phytophthora ramorum) (Scotland) Order 2002 (SSI 2002 223), implements Commission Decision 2002/757 ([2002] OJ L252/37) on provisional emergency phytosanitary measures to prevent the introduction into and the spread within the Community of Phytophthora ramorum Werres, De Cock & Man insofar as it relates to plants other than forest trees. It prohibits the introduction and spread of the plant pest, Phytophthora ramorum, a fungus identified as causing Sudden Oak Death syndrome in certain species of oak in the USA and harm to other plant species, including Rhododendron and Viburnum. In addition it controls the importation of plants of a number of susceptible species from the USA, requiring such material to be accompanied by phytosanitary certificates which may be issued only after specific checks have been carried out during production and before consignment; or alternatively, where the material originates in a part of the USA recognised by plant health authorities as free from the pest, confirming that fact.

5285. Plants—plant health—protected zones

PLANT HEALTH (GREAT BRITAIN) (AMENDMENT) (SCOTLAND) ORDER 2002, SSI 2002 164; made under the European Communities Act 1972 s.2. In force: April 1, 2002; £1.75.

This Order amends the Plant Health (Great Britain) Order 1993 (SI 1993 1320) and the Plant Health (Great Britain) Amendment (Scotland) Order 2001 (SSI 2001 249) to implement certain elements of Commission Directive 2002/28 ([2002] OJ L77/23) amending certain annexes to Council Directive 2000/29 on protective measures against the introduction into the Community of organisms harmful to plants or plant products and against their spread within the Community and Commission Directive 2002/29 ([2002] OJ L77/26) amending Directive 2001/32 as regards certain protected zones exposed to particular plant health risks in the Community. The Order removes Great Britain from the protected zone in respect of Beet necrotic yellow vein virus and redefines the Italian and Austrian protected zones in respect of the bacterium Erwinia amylovora (Burr) Winsl et al.

5286. Plants—plant protection products—marketing

PLANT PROTECTION PRODUCTS AMENDMENT (NO.2) (SCOTLAND) REGULATIONS 2002, SSI 2002 279; made under the European Communities Act 1972 s.2. In force: July 1, 2002; £1.75.

These Regulations amend the Plant Protection Products Amendment (No.3) (Scotland) Regulations 2001 (SSI 2001 454) and the Plant Protection Products Amendment (Scotland) Regulations 2002 (SSI 2002 117). They amend the definition of "the Directive" so as to implement Commission Directive 2001/99 ([2001] OJ L304/14) amending Annex I to Council Directive 91/414 concerning the placing of plant protection products on the market to include glyphosate and thifensulfuron-methyl as active substances. It also makes amendments so as to add Commission Directive 2001/103 ([2001] OJ L313/37) amending Annex 1 to Council Directive 91/414 concerning the placing of plant protection products on the market to include 2,4-dichlorophenoxy acetic acid (2,4-D) as an active substance and Commission Directive 2002/18 ([2002] OJ L55/29) amending Annex 1 to Council Directive 91/414 concerning the placing of plant-protection products on the market to include isoproturon as an active substance.

5287. Plants–plant protection products–marketing

PLANT PROTECTION PRODUCTS AMENDMENT (NO.3) (SCOTLAND) REGULATIONS 2002, SSI 2002 537; made under the European Communities Act 1972 s.2. In force: December 31, 2002; £1.75.

These Regulations amend the Plant Protection Products Regulations 1995 (SI 1995 887) which implement Council Directive 91/414 ([1991] OJ L230/1) concerning the placing of plant protection products on the market. The Regulations allow the continuation in effect of provisional approvals containing active substances included in Annex I to the Directive beyond their expiry date. They also amend the definition of "the Directive" so as to implement Commission Directive 2002/37 ([2002] OJ L117/10) amending Council Directive 91/414 to include ethofumesate as an active substance; Commission Directive 2002/48 ([2002] OJ L148/19) amending Council Directive 91/414 to include iprovalicarb, prosulfuron and sulfsulfuron as active substances; Commission Directive 2002/64 ([2002] OJ L189/27) amending Council Directive 91/414 to include cinidon-ehyl, cyhalofop butyl, famoxadone, florasulam, metalaxyl-M and picolinafen as active substances; and Commission Directive 2002/81 ([2002] OJ L276/28) amending Council Directive 91/414 to include flumioxazine as an active substance.

5288. Plants–plant protection products–marketing

PLANT PROTECTION PRODUCTS AMENDMENT (SCOTLAND) REGULATIONS 2002, SSI 2002 117; made under the European Communities Act 1972 s.2. In force: March 30, 2002; £1.75.

These Regulations amend the Plant Protection Products Regulations 1995 (SI 1995 887) which implement Council Directive 91/414 ([1991] OJ L230/1) concerning the placing of plant protection products on the market. The Regulations, which also amend the Plant Protection Products (Amendment) Regulations 1997 (SI 1997 7), amend the definition of "the Directive" in the 1995 Regulations so as to implement Commission Directive 2001/87 ([2001] OJ L276/17) which adds the active substances acibenzolar-s-methyl, cyclanilide, ferric phosphate, pymetrozine and pyraflufen-ethyl to Annex I of the Directive.

5289. Potatoes–imports–infectious disease control–Egypt

POTATOES ORIGINATING IN EGYPT (SCOTLAND) AMENDMENT REGULATIONS 2002, SSI 2002 518; made under the European Communities Act 1972 s.2. In force: December 13, 2002; £1.50.

These Regulations, which amend the Potatoes Originating in Egypt (Scotland) Regulations 2001 (SSI 2001 421), implement Commission Decision 2002/903 ([2002] OJ L312/28) amending Decision 96/301 ([1996] OJ L115/47) by renewing the Member States' authorisation to take emergency measures against the dissemination of Pseudomonas solanacearum (Smith) Smith as regards Egypt.

5290. Poultry–breeding flocks and hatcheries–fees

POULTRY BREEDING FLOCKS, HATCHERIES AND ANIMAL BY-PRODUCTS (FEES) (SCOTLAND) ORDER 2002, SSI 2002 529; made under the Animal Health Act 1981 s.84. In force: January 1, 2003; £1.75.

This Order, which revokes the Poultry Breeding Flocks, Hatcheries and Processed Animal Protein (Fees) Order 1993 (SI 1993 1998) as it applies to Scotland, provides for fees to recover the full costs of activities specified in the Schedule to this Order in respect of breeding flocks and hatcheries, and for the purposes of the authorisation of laboratories under the Poultry Breeding Flocks and Hatcheries Order 1993 (SI 1993 1898) and the approval of laboratories under the Animal By-Products Order 1999 (SI 1999 646).

5291. Rural areas–Less Favoured Area Support Scheme

LESS FAVOURED AREA SUPPORT SCHEME (SCOTLAND) REGULATIONS 2002, SSI 2002 139; made under the European Communities Act 1972 s.2. In force: March 22, 2002; £3.50.

These Regulations, which revoke with savings the Less Favoured Area Support Scheme (Scotland) Regulations 2001 (SSI 2001 50), make provision for the purposes of implementation of Council Regulation 1257/1999 ([1999] OJ L160/80) on support for rural development from the European Agricultural Guidance and Guarantee Fund and Commission Regulation 1750/1999 ([1999] OJ L214/31) laying down detailed rules for the application of Council Regulation 1257/1999. They apply to holdings in respect of which the Scottish Ministers are the competent authority under the Integrated Administration and Control System Regulations 1993 (SI 1993 1317). The Regulations set out the maximum amount of less favoured area support to be paid by the Scottish Ministers in 2002, contain powers of enforcement and deal with an applicant's right of appeal against decisions taken by the Scottish Ministers. They also amend the Agricultural Subsidies (Appeals) (Scotland) Regulations 2000 (SSI 2000 347).

5292. Sheep–goats–identification and movement

SHEEP AND GOATS IDENTIFICATION (SCOTLAND) AMENDMENT (NO.2) REGULATIONS 2002, SSI 2002 531; made under the European Communities Act 1972 s.2. In force: January 1, 2003; £1.75.

These Regulations amend the Sheep and Goats Identification (Scotland) Regulations 2000 (SSI 2000 418) which amended the 20 day standstill on the movement of animals contained in the Disease Control (Interim Measures) (Scotland) Order 2002 (SSI 2002 34), relative to breeding goats. The Regulations make consequential amendments which make provision for the identification of goats moved from and to holdings within Great Britain.

5293. Books

Barraclough, Fraser R.–Practical Guide to Rent Review of Agricultural Holdings in Scotland. Paperback: £20.00. ISBN 0-414-01506-1. W.Green & Son.

ANIMALS

5294. Animal welfare–farmed animals–laying hens

WELFARE OF FARMED ANIMALS (SCOTLAND) AMENDMENT REGULATIONS 2002, SSI 2002 334; made under the Agriculture (Miscellaneous Provisions) Act 1968 s.2. In force: Reg.2(3): January 1, 2003; remainder: July 3, 2002; £2.00.

These Regulations, which amend the Welfare of Farmed Animals (Scotland) Regulations 2000 (SSI 2000 442), give effect to the provisions of Council Directive 99/74 ([1999] OJ L203/53) laying down minimum standards for the protection of laying hens, in establishments with 350 or more laying hens. The Regulations insert new definitions, including a new definition of laying hen and apply requirements in relation to the keeping of poultry other than those kept in the systems specified.

5295. Animal welfare–slaughter

WELFARE OF ANIMALS (SLAUGHTER OR KILLING) AMENDMENT (SCOTLAND) REGULATIONS 2002, SSI 2002 238; made under the European Communities Act 1972 s.2. In force: June 10, 2002; £1.75.

These Regulations amend the Welfare of Animals (Slaughter or Killing) Regulations 1995 (SI 1995 731), which gave effect to Council Directive 93/119

([1993] OJ L349/21) on the protection of animals at the time of slaughter or killing, so as to permit a new gas mixture for killing birds at the slaughterhouse.

5296. Conservation–seals

CONSERVATION OF SEALS (SCOTLAND) ORDER 2002, SSI 2002 404; made under the Conservation of Seals Act 1970 s.3. In force: September 4, 2002; £1.50.

This Order prohibits in the period from September 4, 2002 to September 3, 2004 the killing, injuring or taking of common seals in Scotland and adjacent territorial waters and the killing, injuring or taking of grey seals in a defined area within the Moray Firth.

5297. Fur Farming (Prohibition) (Scotland) Act 2002 (asp 10)

This Act of the Scottish Parliament prohibits the keeping of animals solely or primarily for slaughter for the value of their fur and provides for the making of payments in respect of the related closure of certain businesses.

5298. Fur Farming (Prohibition) (Scotland) Act 2002 (asp 10)–Commencement Order

FUR FARMING (PROHIBITION) (SCOTLAND) ACT 2002 (COMMENCEMENT) ORDER 2002, SSI 2002 519 (C.27); made under the Fur Farming (Prohibition) (Scotland) Act 2002 s.6. Commencement details: bringing into force various provisions of the 2002 Act on January 1, 2003; £1.50.

This Order appoints January 1, 2003 as the date for coming into force of specified sections of the Fur Farming (Prohibition) (Scotland) Act 2002.

5299. Medicated feedingstuffs–zootechnical products–fees

See AGRICULTURE. §98

5300. Protection of Wild Mammals (Scotland) Act 2002 (asp 6)

This Act of the Scottish Parliament protects wild mammals from being hunted with dogs.

This Act received Royal Assent on March 15, 2002.

5301. Protection of Wild Mammals (Scotland) Act 2002 (asp 6)–Commencement Order

PROTECTION OF WILD MAMMALS (SCOTLAND) ACT 2002 (COMMENCEMENT) ORDER 2002, SSI 2002 181; made under the Protection of Wild Mammals (Scotland) Act 2002 s.12. Commencement details: bringing into force the 2002 Act on August 1, 2002; £1.50.

This Order appoints August 1, 2002 as the date for coming into force of specified provisions of the Protection of Wild Mammals (Scotland) Act 2002.

ARBITRATION

5302. Awards–judicial review–arbiter appointed under deed of conditions–sheltered housing–award capable of implementation

H, superiors of heritable subjects used as sheltered accommodation sought judicial review of decisions reached by arbitration, following a dispute with the occupiers; namely (1) the method of payment being advocated in respect of each occupiers share of the common charge; (2) what was to be done with any excess paid towards the common charge; (3) variation of the constitution of the property council, and (4) there should be an alteration to the deed of conditions to allow special meetings to be convened by a sub committee established by the property council for the purpose of doing certain things.

Held, dismissing the petition, that (1) the whole purpose and intent of the arbiter's decision was clear and capable of implementation by H. There was no substance in the claim that H were incapable or had already done all that was required; (2) the changes in calculation and collection of the common charges were not an additional burden, rather a more efficient discharge of the present burden, nor was the procedure invalid since the minority could have been bound by a majority decision in a property council meeting, and (3) H, having already agreed to be bound by the arbiter's decision could not now object to the changes.

HANOVER (SCOTLAND) HOUSING ASSOCIATION LTD v. SANDFORD; *sub nom.* HANOVER (SCOTLAND) HOUSING ASSOCIATION LTD, PETITIONER 2002 S.C.L.R. 144, Lord Wheatley, OH.

5303. **Interdicts—interim interdict—plea of prescription—determination by arbiter**

See CIVIL PROCEDURE: Orkney Islands Council v. Charles Brand Ltd. §5332

5304. **Books**

Hunter, Robert L.—Law of Arbitration in Scotland. 2nd Ed. Paperback: £60.00. ISBN 0-406-94887-9. Butterworths Law (Scotland).

AVIATION

5305. **International carriage by air—accidents—injury resulting in psychiatric illness to passenger—meaning of "bodily injury"**

[Warsaw Convention on International Carriage by Air 1929 Art.17; Carriage by Air Act 1961 (c.27) Sch.1 Part I Art.17.]

In two appeals the issue before the House of Lords was whether a person who had suffered no physical injury but who had suffered mental injury or illness as a consequence of an accident on board an aircraft could bring a claim against the carrier under the Warsaw Convention on International Carriage by Air 1929 Art.17. In the appeal of B, the First Division had held, by a majority, that a claim could be brought ([2001] 1 Lloyd's Rep. 95, [2000] C.L.Y. 6704). In the appeal of M, the Court of Appeal ([2001] EWCA Civ 790, [2002] Q.B. 100, [2001] C.L.Y. 5385) had held that such a claim could not be brought.

Held, allowing B's appeal and dismissing M's appeal, that a psychiatric condition developed by a passenger as a result of an accident on board an aircraft did not fall within the definition of "bodily injury" for the purposes of Art.17 of the Convention. It followed that a passenger was not entitled to claim compensation for such a condition. However, if the condition could be shown to have caused an adverse physical symptom, such as a peptic ulcer, or the condition was the expression of physical changes to the brain's structure, then the requirements of Art.17 would be satisfied because a bodily injury could be shown. "Bodily injury" was a change in part or parts of the body which was sufficiently serious to be capable of being called an "injury". The definition did not extend to emotional upset such as fear, distress or mental anguish. In order to prove that a physical change had manifested itself in a psychiatric condition and that such change amounted to an injury within Art.17, the passenger had to prove, by expert evidence, that the physical changes had occurred as a result of the accident and that they had led to the psychiatric condition. The passenger would suffer a bodily injury for the purposes of Art.17 if he could prove that the accident had caused brain damage. In the case of K, it had not been argued that he had suffered a brain injury as a result of the accident and therefore the decision of the First Division could not stand. In the case of M, the Court of Appeal had applied the wrong test. However, given that M accepted that she could not prove bodily injury, it was not appropriate to remit the case. Lord Steyn and Lord Hope dissented on the construction of "bodily injury" in Art.17, concluding that bodily injury involved strict liability for manifested physical injury and that it excluded mental injury or illness.

KING v. BRISTOW HELICOPTERS LTD; MORRIS v. KLM ROYAL DUTCH AIRLINES; *sub nom.* HAMMOND v. BRISTOW HELICOPTERS LTD, [2002] UKHL 7, [2002] 2 A.C. 628, Lord Hope of Craighead, HL.

BANKING AND FINANCE

5306. Debt Arrangement and Attachment (Scotland) Act 2002 (asp 17)

This Act of the Scottish Parliament provides a scheme under which individuals may arrange for their debts to be paid under payment programmes; creates a new diligence in relation to corporeal moveable property owned by a debtor; makes special provision for the use of that diligence in relation to property kept in dwellinghouses; and abolishes poindings and warrant sales.

5307. Public expenditure–accountability

PUBLIC FINANCE AND ACCOUNTABILITY (SCOTLAND) ACT 2000 (CONSEQUENTIAL MODIFICATIONS) ORDER 2002, SSI 2002 176; made under the Public Finance and Accountability (Scotland) Act 2000 s.26. In force: April 1, 2002; £1.75.

As a consequence of the Public Finance and Accountability (Scotland) Act 2000, this Order amends the Erskine Bridge Tolls Act 1968 so that any statement of account prepared is to be sent by the Scottish Ministers to the Auditor General for Scotland for auditing and the Development of Tourism Act 1969 so that any statement of account prepared by the Scottish Tourist Board shall be sent by the Scottish Ministers to the Auditor General for Scotland for auditing. It also amends the National Health Service (Scotland) Act 1978 so that accounts prepared by the Scottish Hospital Trust are to be sent to the Scottish Ministers by such time as they may direct; and that the Scottish Ministers shall send the accounts to the Auditor General for Scotland for auditing, the National Health Service and Community Care Act 1990 in consequence of the amendment made to the 1978 Act and the Local Government Finance Act 1992 is amended so that the accounts kept shall be sent by the Scottish Ministers to the Auditor General for Scotland for auditing.

5308. Public expenditure–accountability–access to documents and information– relevant persons

PUBLIC FINANCE AND ACCOUNTABILITY (SCOTLAND) ACT 2000 (ACCESS TO DOCUMENTS AND INFORMATION) (RELEVANT PERSONS) ORDER 2002, SSI 2002 78; made under the Public Finance and Accountability (Scotland) Act 2000 s.24. In force: April 1, 2002; £1.75.

This Order specifies persons and classes of person in relation to whom the Auditor General for Scotland is entitled to have access to documents or information for the purposes of conducting an audit or an economy, efficiency and effectiveness examination under the Public Finance and Accountability (Scotland) Act 2000.

5309. Public expenditure–accountability–efficiency and effectiveness of examinations–specified bodies

PUBLIC FINANCE AND ACCOUNTABILITY (SCOTLAND) ACT 2000 (ECONOMY, EFFICIENCY AND EFFECTIVENESS EXAMINATIONS) (SPECIFIED

BODIES ETC.) ORDER 2002, SSI 2002 77; made under the Public Finance and Accountability (Scotland) Act 2000 s.23. In force: April 1, 2002; £1.75.

This Order specifies various bodies or office-holders, and classes of bodies or office-holders, in relation to which the Auditor General for Scotland may initiate examinations under the Public Finance and Accountability (Scotland) Act 2000 into the economy, efficiency and effectiveness of the use of their resources in discharging their functions.

CIVIL EVIDENCE

5310. Admissibility–disciplinary procedures–teachers–proper test

[Children and Young Persons (Scotland) Act 1937 (c.37) s.12(1).]

F was convicted of an offence in contravention of the Children and Young Persons Act 1937 s.12(1). The Disciplinary Committee of the GTC directed that F's name be removed from the register of teachers after he was declared unfit. F appealed to the Court of Session arguing that certain evidence regarding his character and conduct in school should not have been admitted. It was also argued that the Committee should have considered the question of admissibility and clearly had not.

Held, quashing the decision, that (1) the Committee had not addressed the necessary questions prior to the decision to admit the evidence and it could not be held that they would have considered it admissible. This was fundamental to the decision that F was unfit and the resultant direction to have his name removed from the register, and (2) in the circumstances of the case, it was not appropriate to remit the case to the same committee and, given the considerable public interest, it would be unlikely that any other committee could reach a decision without any prior influence.

F v. GENERAL TEACHING COUNCIL FOR SCOTLAND; *sub nom.* F, APPELLANT 2002 S.L.T. 1178, Lord Abernethy, Lord Cullen L.J.C., Lord Weir, 2 Div.

5311. Admissibility–hearsay evidence–statement by person not called as witness–compatibility with Convention rights

[Human Rights Act 1998 (c.42) Sch.1 Part I Art.6(1).]

In an action of damages for asbestos related mesothelioma, a dispute arose between A, the defenders, and the insurers, C, called as third party, as to whether C had been A's employer's liability insurers at the relevant time. C disputed the admissibility of evidence by A's current financial director of a telephone conversation with the person who had been A's company secretary at the relevant time. C argued that the evidence was hearsay and that reliance on it would be unfair in terms of the Human Rights Act 1998 Sch.1 Part I Art.6(1) whereat the request of a relative the former company secretary had not been cited for health reasons.

Held, repelling the objection, that there was no fundamental objection in Convention jurisprudence to the use of hearsay evidence, nor was there an absolute rule that all parties had to have equal access to those whose statements might figure in hearsay evidence, and the insurers had had sufficient opportunity to prepare and present their case.

IRVINE v. ARCO ATHOLL LTD 2002 S.L.T. 931 (Note), Lord Mackay of Drumadoon, OH.

5312. Books

Sheldon, David–Evidence: Cases and Materials. 2nd Ed. Paperback: £41.50. ISBN 0-414-01387-5. W.Green & Son.

CIVIL PROCEDURE

5313. Actions–count, reckoning and payment–relevancy–parties agreeing to pursue venture through new company to be formed–fiduciary duty–averments of joint venture

N raised an action for count, reckoning and payment against three other companies, T, B and A, which was later abandoned against T. N averred that N, A and B formed a joint venture or partnership in 1998 to obtain certain government training contracts. In February 1998 they decided that the venture should operate through a limited company, T, with each receiving one third of the shares in T, and nominating one member to T's board. T took over the running of the training contracts from September 1, 1998. In November 1998 A and B, following difficulties, purportedly terminated their relationship with N. N did not receive any shares in T. N, alleging breach of fiduciary duties by A and B in appropriating the benefit of the contracts to themselves, sought count, reckoning and payment by A and B of one third of all profits derived directly or indirectly by them from the implementation of the training contracts.

Held, dismissing the action, that (1) on the pursuers' pleadings it was clear that from February 1998 at least, the contractual purpose was to be pursued through the new company and it was inappropriate to use the terminology of partnership to seek to apply the consequences of the law of partnership; (2) while fiduciary duties could arise outwith partnership and there was no precise categorisation or enumeration of particular relationships in which they might arise, a principal feature was that the person on whom the duty reposed had also the task of managing, or transacting with, property or material interests belonging to another, and there was no asset or interest which A and B (as individuals) were to manage or were entrusted with protecting on N's behalf, and (3) any profits were clearly earned by T, and following abandonment against T there was no proper basis for saying that A and B had received profits from the contracts in issue.

NESS TRAINING LTD v. TRIAGE CENTRAL LTD 2002 S.L.T. 675, Lord Eassie, OH.

5314. Commission and diligence–recovery of documents–documents sought to discredit witness after completion of evidence–recovery denied

W, in an action of divorce, sought an order for payment of a capital sum. H gave evidence and was questioned as to whether he had ever been asked to provide an up-to-date consent form. H denied that he had. W lodged a motion for commission diligence with the intention of recovering documents from H's solicitor showing that he had in fact been so asked. The motion was granted; credibility being very much in issue. H appealed arguing that the documents would be covered by confidentiality and it would be inappropriate to grant an application, the sole purpose of which was to discredit evidence already given.

Held, allowing the appeal, that the sheriff was wrong to have granted commission diligence, the sole purpose of which was to test the credibility of witness evidence that had already been completed.

O'SULLIVAN v. O'SULLIVAN; *sub nom.* O'SULLIVAN v. SLATER 2001 S.C.L.R. 696, JC McInnes Q.C., Sheriff Principal, Sh Ct.

5315. Court of Session–jury trial–issues–proposed issues–amendment–issue not containing question of fault on part of defenders–competency

[Act of Sederunt (Rules of the Court of Session 1994) 1994 (SI 1994 1443) Sch.2 r.37.1.]

B, the executors and family members of D, deceased, sought damages from his employer, S, in respect of his death from mesothelioma. S admitted liability and issues were allowed, following which B lodged a document within 14 days under the Act of Sederunt (Rules of the Court of Session 1994) 1994 Sch.2

r.37.1 which listed heads of damages and the amounts claimed by each pursuer, but contained no question directed to the issue of liability. On S opposing the motion for approval of the proposed issue, B sought leave to amend at the bar to add a question whether D's death was caused by S's fault. The Lord Ordinary allowed the issue to be amended on the basis that it could properly be described as a proposed issue for consideration as it impliedly contained a series of questions for the jury as to whether the death was S's fault. S reclaimed, arguing, inter alia, that without the necessary question as to fault, the document lodged was not an issue and B had forfeited their right to jury trial.

Held, refusing the reclaiming motion, that although the form in which the proposed issue was lodged was deficient by reason of the omission of the essential question and could not be approved by the court for the purposes of r.37.1 (1), a proposed issue was always subject to the court's approval, and the Lord Ordinary had acted properly in permitting adjustment.

BENSON v. SCOTTISH LION ENGINEERING LTD; *sub nom.* BENSON'S EXECUTOR v. SCOTTISH LION ENGINEERING LTD 2002 S.C. 228, Lord Gill L.J.C., Lord MacLean, Lady Paton, 2 Div.

5316. Defences—lis alibi pendens

R, heritable creditor in possession, raised an action in the Court of Session for (1) payment from A, the infeft proprietor of £50,000, as recompense for improvements allegedly carried out on a property in Ayrshire, and (2) concluded for interdict to prevent A from succeeding in a Sheriff Court action to evict him. The Sheriff Court action was sisted awaiting the outcome of the instant action. A pled lis alibi pendens arguing that one of the questions before the Court of Session, namely whether R was entitled to continue to possess the subjects or whether A was entitled to recover possession, had already been presented before a competent court; the Sheriff Court. R argued that for the plea to succeed it must be directed against the whole case not just the question of possession. R also argued that the questions in each action were different. In the Sheriff Court the question was whether A was entitled to evict R, in the Court of Session it was whether R was entitled to recompense and interdict to protect that claim.

Held, sustaining the plea of lis alibi pendens in relation to the conclusion for interdict and quoad ultra allowing proof before answer, that (1) the requirements for lis alibi pendens had been established; (2) both actions had raised the same issue; whether R was entitled to retain possession of the property, and (3) A, having raised the action first was entitled to have the matter decided in the forum of his choice.

BAIN v. BAIN 2002 S.L.T. 1177, Lord Dawson, OH.

5317. Diligence—arrestment—arrestment on dependence—ascription of arrestments—entitlement of debtor or arrestee to ascribe arrestment of different funds

C, a Chinese state owned company, raised an action against T, a Norwegian company, seeking declarator that the credit balance on four bank accounts, (a), (b), (c) and (d), were beneficially owned by C and were held by T as trustee for them, and decree ordaining T to transfer the credit balances on each of the accounts to a designated account in C's name. C sought summary decree in relation to accounts (c) and (d). T's parent company (P) had contracted with C to manage C's semi-submersible oil drilling unit. The accounts, in T's name but with beneficial ownership of the balances in C, were set up for the purpose of the management agreement. Previous proceedings in respect of alleged breach of contract by C resulted in funds to the value of $3.7 million being arrested and account (b) being transferred to the joint control of the parties' agents. T relied on the arrestment as a defence to the claim for transfer. C argued that (1) the arrestment had been released by P to the extent that it exceeded $3.7 million, C as beneficial owner of the funds in the accounts was entitled to determine how that release was ascribed among the accounts and they had effectively ascribed the release to accounts (c) and (d); (2) under the contractual arrangements governing the parties' relationship, T were under no direct personal obligation to C and thus there was no obligation to account that was capable of arrestment, and (3) T's right to payment of the sums in the two accounts was held as a mere nominee for C, which, unlike the obligation of a trustee, was ignored for the purposes of the law of arrestment. T argued, inter alia, that (1) an arrestee had power to ascribe an arrestment and they had done so in respect of accounts (c) and (d) as well as (b); (2) as C as well as T operated account (d), T were not a mere nominee, and (3) as respects account (c), T's position in relation to C was no different from that of a bank.

Held, granting summary decree, that (1) the reasoning that applied to ascription of debt also applied to ascription of release of arrestments: C could therefore give such directions to T as were necessary to ensure that the right to payment of the credit balances in accounts (c) and (d) could be effectively made available for C's benefit; (2) in relation to account (c), it must have been agreed between C and P, expressly or impliedly, that T would open it as nominee for, and therefore in trust for, C, and the obligation to account to C was capable of arrestment in T's hands, *Heron v. Winfields* (1894) 22 R. 182 distinguished; (3) in relation to account (d), the parties to the agreement were C and T, which gave rise to a direct obligation to account; (4) the relationship between T and C was that of bare trust in relation to accounts (c) and (d), the trust was revocable and constituted solely for the benefit of C, C was entitled to terminate the trust agreement at any time and it was not competent to arrest T's liability to account to C, and (5) P's arrestment in the sum of $3.7 million remained effective against that sum in account (b).

CHINA NATIONAL STAR PETROLEUM CO v. TOR DRILLING (UK) LTD 2002 S.L.T. 1339, Lord Drummond Young, OH.

5318. Diligence–arrestment–arrestment on dependence–compatibility with right to peaceful enjoyment of possessions–bank accounts

[Human Rights Act 1998 (c.42) Sch.1 Part II Art.1.]

C, the curator bonis of I, an elderly woman suffering from dementia, raised an action alleging that S had caused her to uplift £172,496.88 from her bank accounts and distribute the funds among them. C obtained an arrestment on the dependence on the bank account of one of S. S sought recall of the arrestment as contravening their right to peaceful enjoyment of their possessions under the Human Rights Act 1998 Sch.1 Part II Art.1 and that it was unfair and inequitable where there had been no inquiry into their position and C had failed to provide any material to demonstrate a prima facie case or that they were attempting to do anything which might thwart any subsequent court order.

Held, refusing the motion, that (1) an arrestment on the dependence did not amount to a deprivation of property, being at its highest a control on the use of property; (2) assuming Art.1 applied to arrestment on the dependence, the grant of a warrant to arrest on the dependence where the tests set out in *Karl Construction Ltd v. Palisade Properties Plc* 2002 S.L.T. 312, [2002] 4 C.L. 525 had not been followed did not necessarily mean that a defender was entitled to recall of the arrestment or that the grant of the warrant was unlawful ab initio, and (3) assuming the application of the tests to the present case there was ample material to justify the retention of the arrestment.

IRVING'S CURATOR BONIS v. SKILLEN 2002 S.L.T. (Sh Ct) 119, WH Holligan, Sh Ct (Glasgow and Strathkelvin).

5319. Diligence–arrestment–arrestment on dependence–offer of alternative security

[Civil Jurisdiction and Judgments Act 1982 (c.27); Human Rights Act 1998 (c.42) Sch.1 Part I Art.6(1).]

W was ordered to pay M, a French company, FF110,101,000 with interest. The judgment of the Cour d'appel de Bordeaux was registered under the Civil Jurisdiction and Judgments Act 1982 and W appealed arguing that its right to a fair trial under the Human Rights Act 1998 Sch.1 Part I Art.6(1) had been infringed.

The interlocutor granted M warrant to arrest on the dependence and arrestments were laid against W one of which was successful but recalled on consignation of £70,000. W enrolled a motion for recall of the arrestments on the strength of a guarantee affording full security to M. The guarantee expired in 12 months but W undertook, irrevocably, to procure an immediate replacement. W argued that (1) the guarantee and letter of undertaking was sufficient security for M; (2) M and W had agreed to recall once a guarantee was in place, and (3) it was the best that W could offer. There was evidence that the guarantor would not supply guarantees that exceeded 12 months. M argued that the security was insufficient, there had not been enthusiastic compliance previously by W, there was no trust between the parties and if W was taken over or was unable to provide a replacement guarantee in 12 months M would be prejudiced.

Held, granting the motion for recall and releasing the consigned funds, that (1) the alternate security offered by W was not sufficient to warrant recall of the arrestments, even when account was taken of the facts that only one of the arrestments had funds attached, the inconvenience to W and the financial standing of W, and (2) that it was clear from the productions that the parties intended that formal documentation would implement, rather than constitute and record, the agreement between them and it was clear from the correspondence that W and M had gone further than merely forming an intention of agreeing to the recall of the arrestments once further documentation was executed and delivered.

MARIE BRIZZARD ET ROGER INTERNATIONAL SA v. WILLIAM GRANT & SONS LTD (NO.1); *sub nom.* MARIE BRIZZARD ET ROGER INTERNATIONAL SA, PETITIONER (NO.1); MARIE BRIZARD ET ROGER INTERNATIONAL SA v. WILLIAM GRANT & SONS LTD (NO.1) 2002 S.L.T. 1359, Lord Mackay of Drumadoon, OH.

5320. Diligence–arrestment–arrestment on dependence–winding up more than 60 days later–entitlement to funds arrested

In G's action of furthcoming against E (a local authority) as arrestees, N (a company) as common debtors and J (N's liquidator), G moved for summary decree. G had raised an action of payment against N on February 3, 1999. G arrested on the dependence in the hands of E on March 1, 2000. N's winding up commenced on January 18, 2001. N argued that the diligence executed by G was incomplete while the commencement of N's winding up was equivalent to a completed diligence, and the arrested sums should be paid to J: the court should not follow *Commercial Aluminium Windows v. Cumbernauld Development Corp* 1987 S.L.T. (Sh.Ct.) 91, [1987] C.L.Y. 4053, which had been doubted by certain text writers.

Held, granting summary decree, that J, as liquidator, was not automatically vested in N's property unlike a trustee in sequestration, and there was no reason at all why the funds should have to pass through J's hands *Commercial Aluminium Windows*, followed.

GRANITE PROPERTIES v. EDINBURGH CITY COUNCIL 2002 S.L.T. (Sh Ct) 79, AM Bell, Sh Ct (Lothian and Border).

5321. Diligence–arrestment–arrestment on dependence

See SHIPPING: Global Marine Drilling Co v. Triton Holdings Ltd (The Sovereign Explorer) (No.2). §6091

5322. Diligence–inhibition–inhibition on dependence–justification

[European Convention on Human Rights 1950 First Protocol, Art.1; Act of Sederunt (Rules of the Court of Session 1994) 1994 (SI 1994 1443) Sch.2 r.13.6; Human Rights Act 1998 (c.42) s.3, Sch.1 Part II Art.1.]

P sought recall of an inhibition on the dependence in K's action for payment, or alternatively damages, in respect of work done but not certified by A (the architect) in terms of a construction contract between S, then acting for K as an undisclosed principal, and P. P argued that (1) K had no title to sue, the contract being personal to P and S: this was a sophisticated building contract, it involved the design of substantial parts of the building by the main contractor and there was a prohibition on assignation and subcontracting; (2) K's claim was contingent and inhibition on the dependence was incompetent without averments of special circumstances, and (3) the automatic grant of inhibition where no particular justification was presented infringed P's rights under the Human Rights Act 1998 Sch.1 Part II Art.1. K argued, inter alia, that a claim for sums due but not certified, or damages for failure to certify, could be made; *Beaufort Developments (NI) Ltd v. Gilbert-Ash (NI) Ltd* [1999] 1 A.C. 266, [1998] C.L.Y. 5055, *Costain Building & Civil Engineering Ltd v. Scottish Rugby Union Plc* 1993 S.C. 650, [1994] C.L.Y. 6112 cited, only related to actions for payment of sums due under contract. In relation to the Convention point K argued that Act of Sederunt (Rules of the Court of Session 1994) 1994 Sch.2 r.13.6, read with the Human Rights Act 1998 s.3 could not, as contended by P, be construed that a summons could not be signeted unless special justification for the use of inhibition on the dependence was put before the court. The current law struck a fair balance between parties' competing rights and a margin of appreciation was accorded to Convention states.

Held, recalling the inhibition, that (1) K had a colourable case on title to sue: while generally a building contract involving complex work would be personal to the contracting parties, particularly where it involved detailed administrative or management work, S was closely connected with K, they had the same shareholders and K performed all management and administrative services for S. In that situation it might be a matter of indifference to an employer which company carried out the contract; (2) inhibition on the dependence was incompetent in K's action in absence of averments of special circumstances: in terms of the JCT contract and in accordance with *Costain*, no debt was due and payment could not be demanded by K until work done was certified by A. K averred no special circumstances. *Beaufort* was essentially consistent with *Costain*. On a proper analysis an action for damages would never arise, because if K required to go to court or arbitration to pursue their claim, any resulting decree would be equivalent to a certificate under the contract and the remedy was essentially enforcement of the contract. K's claim for damages was contingent and could not put K into a more favourable position than their claim for payment, and (3) the automatic right to inhibition on the dependence on raising an action conferred by Scots law was disproportionate and incompatible with P's rights under Art.1, particularly when taken with the absence of any general right to compensation for the use of the diligence in an ill founded action. Four requirements had to be met if a right of protective attachment of immovable property during litigation was to conform to Art.1: (a) the pursuer had to establish a prima facie case on the merits; (b) the pursuer had to establish a specific need for an interim remedy, demonstrating a significant risk of the defender's insolvency, that the defender was concealing or dissipating assets or that there was a significant risk that the defender would remove his assets from the jurisdiction; (c) a hearing had to take place before a judge at which (a) and (b) were discussed; and (d) if protective attachment was used without objective justification, particularly where the pursuer was unsuccessful, the defender should be entitled to damages for any loss suffered in consequence. Scots law on inhibition on the dependence was seriously out of step with the prevailing approach in Europe and North America; it went too far to fall within the principle of the margin of appreciation or its equivalent in national law. Inhibition on the dependence was an interim remedy granted as a form of judicial security and could not be granted in a manner incompatible with a defender's Convention rights, but only if specific justification was advanced.

KARL CONSTRUCTION LTD v. PALISADE PROPERTIES PLC 2002 S.C. 270, Lord Drummond Young, OH.

5323. **Diligence–inhibition–inhibition on the dependence–compatibility with right to peaceful enjoyment of possessions–disproportionate remedy**

[Act of Sederunt (Sheriff Court Ordinary Cause Rules) 1993 (SI 1993 1956) r.3.3, r.3.5, r.5.1; Human Rights Act 1998 (c.42) s.6(1), s.6(2)(a), Sch.1 Part II Art.1.]

C, a construction company, moved for recall of arrestments against them on the dependence of an action of payment. They submitted on the basis of *Karl Construction Ltd v. Palisade Properties Plc* 2002 S.L.T. 312, [2002] 4 C.L. 525, which concerned inhibition, that the automatic grant of arrestment on the dependence breached their rights under the Human Rights Act 1998 Sch.1 Part II Art.1. C argued that there were important differences between inhibition and arrestment on the dependence, and that s.6(2)(a) of the 1998 Act applied since the Act of Sederunt (Sheriff Court Ordinary Cause Rules) 1993 r.3.5 and r.5.1 were expressed in mandatory form.

Held, granting the motion, that (1) r.3.3, r.3.5 and r.5.1 were permissive and warrant could be declined where no cause had been shown for granting it; (2) s.6(2)(a) did not apply as the court could have acted differently, namely by hearing C's justification for obtaining arrestment on the dependence, thus complying with s.6(1), and (3) the same criteria relied on in relation to inhibitions were equally compelling in relation to arrestments on the dependence.

FAB TEK ENGINEERING LTD v. CARILLION CONSTRUCTION LTD 2002 S.L.T. (Sh Ct) 113, JS Forbes, Sh Ct (Tayside, Central and Fife).

5324. **Diligence–inhibition–inhibition on the dependence–compatibility with right to peaceful enjoyment of possessions–risk of insolvency**

[Human Rights Act 1998 (c.42).]

B, a construction company, raised an action of payment against L, developers, for sums allegedly due under a construction contract in terms of an interim valuation. The Lord Ordinary ex parte granted warrant to inhibit on the dependence. L moved for recall of the inhibition, arguing on the basis of *Karl Construction Ltd v. Palisade Properties Plc* 2002 S.L.T. 312, [2002] 4 C.L. 525, that the continued use of the inhibition was contrary to their rights under the Human Rights Act 1998 to peaceful enjoyment of their possessions, where they had adequate funds to meet the claim in the event the action was successful, there was no significant risk of insolvency, the action was being defended, and the result of the inhibition was to prevent them realising the heritable property that was their stock in trade, making them inevitably incapable of paying their debts.

Held, refusing the motion, that (1) what was material was the risk that L would not be able to satisfy B's claim at the conclusion of the action and it was appropriate to look not only at their present financial situation but to take account of future events, so far as they could be predicted with some degree of accuracy; (2) the audited balance sheet submitted by L showing their present state of solvency was not conclusive and on the material before the court there was a significant risk of insolvency; (3) a settlement offer from L indicated that B had a good prima facie case, it was likely that substantial sums would ultimately be due by L and the defence put forward, which related to claimed deductions against a subsequent valuation, was unlikely for the most part to be well founded, and (4) the doubts surrounding the L's solvency did not arise from difficulties caused by the inhibition and any practical difficulty caused could be solved either by their offering consignation or caution for the sum sued for or by recall of the inhibition in relation to individual properties with an appropriate condition as to disposal of the proceeds.

BARRY D TRENTHAM LTD v. LAWFIELD INVESTMENTS LTD 2002 S.C. 401, Lord Drummond Young, OH.

5325. **Expenses–abandonment of action**

[Act of Sederunt (Rules of the Court of Session 1994) 1994 (SI 1994 1443) Sch.2 r.2.1, r.29.1, r.29.1 (1) (b).]

VP raised an action against four defenders, including L, in 1993 which was remitted to the High Court in 1996 and after sundry procedure sent to the procedural roll on May 27,1997. On May 21, a minute of abandonment was lodged against L and another defender in respect of which an interlocutor was pronounced finding VP liable to those defenders in the expenses to date and remitting an account of those expenses to the Auditor of Court for taxation. L forwarded their accounts to VP, inviting them to agree them. Revisals were intimated and the revised accounts were lodged in process on September 9. A diet of taxation was fixed but discharged and a fresh diet fixed for January 28,1998. The day before the new diet, VP agreed the account and the diet did not proceed. The expenses however, remained unpaid and on April 15, 1998 L obtained decree for the agreed sum which was eventually paid on September 30, 1998. Following decree of absolvitor being granted against the remaining two defenders in the original action, L enrolled a motion for absolvitor in terms of the Act of Sederunt (Rules of the Court of Session 1994) 1994 Sch.2 r.29.1 (1) (b) claiming that the expenses not having been paid within the prescribed time limits, absolvitor was the only course of action open to the court to determine the case. The minute of abandonment had sought dismissal, but, L argued, that was no longer available as an auditor's report on the expenses had not been obtained and the agreed expenses had not been paid within 28 days of decree. VP argued that r.29.1 (1) (b) did not cover the position where the parties agreed expenses and did not go to taxation. They claimed that even where expenses had been agreed, an auditor's report as required and dismissal was the appropriate course of action. Alternatively, VP asked the court to exercise its dispensing power under r.2.1 and dismiss the action.

Held, granting the motion and assoilzing L, that (1) dismissal in terms of the Rules could only be obtained if certain conditions were met and, those having not been met, dismissal was unavailable; (2) where dismissal was not available, the only appropriate course of action was absolvitor, and (3) it was inappropriate to use the dispensing power of the court to allow VP to escape from the consequences of their failure to observe the terms of r.29.1.

Observed, that it would be inappropriate to ask the Auditor to issue a report on agreed expenses.

VP PACKAGING LTD v. ADF PARTNERSHIP 2002 S.L.T. 1224, Lord Wheatley, OH.

5326. Expenses−abandonment of action−abandonment after restoration of company to register−sheriff finding no expenses due to or by−competency

D, the sole employee and director of a company, C, which had entered into a contract with A for the provision of his services as a drilling consultant and business development manager, appealed against a sheriff's decision to grant decree of dismissal and find no expenses due to or by, following A's abandonment of an action against him. C had been struck off the register of companies and dissolved by notice following a failure to submit an annual return or accounts. D continued to work for A for a further six months, rendering invoices including VAT, and A only discovered that C had been struck off the register when they made inquiries after D handed in his notice. A then raised an action against D, inter alia, for accounting for profits, and for breach of contract in that C had charged VAT although not VAT registered. D successfully petitioned for restoration of C to the register. A then lodged a minute of abandonment and moved for dismissal, which the sheriff granted. D argued that (1) the sheriff's decision to grant dismissal instead of absolvitor was an unreasonable exercise of his discretion; (2) the sheriff had offered no justification for departing from the general rule that the pursuer in such circumstances should be found liable in expenses and that one reason given for the departure, that it could not be said that the action was bound to fail all along, was erroneous in law, as was taking into account D's conduct, and (3) the sheriff had failed to take into account relevant material including the fact that A had brought the action in the knowledge that C had been struck off and was liable to be restored, and that any restoration would have retrospective effect.

Held, dismissing the appeal, that (1) the sheriff's conclusion that he could not be satisfied that the action never had any prospect of success was not in order to support a departure from the normal rule on expenses but to reject the argument that it should be adhered to because the action had been bound to fail; (2) A could not be faulted for having instituted proceedings on the basis of the factual situation at the relevant time, and (3) it was D's inaction in allowing C to be struck off which formed the basis of the action and it was only when the action was well advanced that D took steps to undermine the factual basis upon which it was based, and in the circumstances the sheriff had not erred in his disposal of the action or in relation to the question of expenses.

ABERDEEN DRILLING SCHOOLS LTD v. DAVIS 2002 S.L.T. (Sh Ct) 147, Sir SST Young, Sheriff Principal, Sh Ct.

5327. **Expenses—abandonment of action—motion for dismissal—third party not entitled to expenses from pursuer**

[Act of Sederunt (Sheriff Court Ordinary Cause Rules) 1993 (SI 1993 1956) r.23.1 (2).]

In E's action for damages for breach of contract against C, T, a third party convened by C, appealed against the sheriff's decision that E was not liable to pay his expenses on lodging a minute of abandonment seeking dismissal. T argued that the phrase "and any third party against whom he has directed any crave" in Act of Sederunt (Sheriff Court Ordinary Cause Rules) 1993 r.23.1 (2) required E to pay his expenses as well as C's before becoming entitled to dismissal.

Held, refusing the appeal, that while at first sight "he" in r.23.1 (2) referred to the defender, it was logical to require on abandonment that E should only pay the expenses of those they had brought into the process. It remained open to the court to deal with other questions of expenses in exercise of its discretion. T's interpretation of the rule ignored certain words and would lead to the bizarre conclusion that it was only a third party convened by a defender that would be entitled to his expenses from the pursuer; in the present case T had in turn convened a second third party. These difficulties were obviated if "he" was treated as meaning a pursuer.

Observed, that there would be merit in amending r.23.1 to this effect.

EUROPOOLS LTD v. CLYDESIDE STEEL FABRICATIONS LTD 2001 S.L.T. (Sh Ct) 91, EF Bowen Q.C., Sheriff Principal, Sh Ct.

5328. **Expenses—caution for expenses—appeal—statable case**

T, former partners in a law firm, who had been found guilty of professional misconduct and struck from the solicitors' roll, appealed against the Lord Ordinary's decision to dismiss their action seeking damages against the President of the Law Society, X, the Law Society, Y, and members of the Scottish Solicitors Discipline Tribunal, Z, in respect of alleged defamatory statements made in a press release issued by Z, the findings issued by Z and in responses by X to questions in a press conference. The Lord Ordinary had stated that he might have been persuaded to allow a proof before answer but he considered that the press conference statements were made in circumstances covered by the plea of qualified privilege and T had failed to make sufficient averments to allow the court to hold that there had been such an inadequacy of inquiry prior to the press conference to enable T to prove malice. X, Y and Z enrolled a motion severally seeking caution from T as a condition precedent to the continuation of the appeal, arguing inter alia that (1) T having failed to meet previous decrees for expenses over a period of four years, there was no prospect that their liability in that respect would be met, T being to all intents and purposes bankrupt, and failure to pay expenses awarded against a pursuer in a previous action was relevant as evidence of impecuniosity or unreasonable behaviour; (2) the grounds of appeal did not reveal any statable grounds for challenging the Lord Ordinary's interlocutor, and (3) T's conclusion, seeking a joint and several decree, was incompetent, as the grounds laid against X and Y were to be distinguished from that laid against Z.

Held, refusing the motions, that (1) T's action was not so wholly devoid of merit that for that reason alone caution ought to be granted. A real and statable argument arose as to whether it was sufficient for X, as an officer representing Y at the press conference, Y having prosecuted the complaints before Z and accepted T's pleas upon which Z's decision was founded, where X was making a public statement on Y's behalf, to rely on "a failure to make proper inquiry, however reprehensible" in avoiding a charge of malice; (2) in respect of the case against Z there was little doubt that nothing in T's averments would serve to remove the absolute privilege attached to the tribunal and the utterances of its members in the course of a hearing. However in *McC (A Minor), Re* [1985] A.C. 528, [1986] C.L.Y. 2389, referred to in *Russell v. Dickson* 1997 S.C. 269, [1997] C.L.Y. 5568, the House of Lords had reserved opinion as to whether the common law liability of justices for acts done within their jurisdiction but with malice was obsolete in England; there could be merit in that area being reconsidered by a higher court; (3) there was a statable case to be put forward in support of the joint and several decree sought. In the particular circumstances, given the relationship between Y and Z and that the thrust of the case against each party was to the same effect, a joint and several decree could be appropriate, and (4) the factors relied on by X, Y and Z were not so cogent and compelling as to displace the general principle that even an impecunious litigant should be entitled to present a statable case without finding caution. Even if T were currently unable to pay the £122,000 outstanding by way of expenses to Y, the sum related to proceedings connected to the instant action *Stevenson v. Midlothian DC (Expenses)* 1983 S.C. (H.L.) 50, [1992] C.L.Y. 5191 distinguished and it was accepted that if T succeeded in securing damages those could be offset against the outstanding expenses. The time likely to be taken on appeal was not as long as suggested, taking into account the brevity and succinctness of T's arguments before the court.

THOMSON v. ROSS 2001 S.L.T. 807, Lord Cameron of Lochbroom, Lord Dawson, Lord Wheatley, Ex Div.

5329. Expenses–liability–successful joint defender

D raised an action of reparation against contractors, H, and subcontractors, R, after falling down stairs while working as a shopfitter. H intended to introduce a plea of apportionment of liability between themselves and R but, prior to proof, D accepted a tender from H. No order was made for or against R who moved for their expenses from D. D argued that it was inequitable for him to meet R's expenses; he had legitimately sued both defenders but had had to accept H's tender given its amount and thereafter he could not proceed further against R. D sought relief from H in the event an award was made.

Held, finding D liable in expenses to R, that (1) D had served proceedings on both defenders and had to bear the consequences of failing against R, and (2) the matter of relief was one of discretion but in determining entitlement to expenses, the essential question was who put whom to the litigation; D had chosen to sue both H and R from the outset, without inducement from H, and H's late attempt to admit a plea of apportionment did not alter that situation.

DONNACHIE v. HAPPIT LTD 2002 S.L.T. 1141, Lord Johnston, OH.

5330. Expenses–time–tender–time for acceptance

P sought damages from his employers, M, in respect of serious burns sustained to his face and hands in 1997. M lodged a tender of £250,000 on November 1, 2001 which was not accepted. The proof began on November 6 and about 2.30 pm, at the conclusion of the day's evidence, M lodged an increased tender of £275,000. Further evidence was heard on November 7. After the court rose P decided to accept the second tender, and on the morning of November 8 he lodged a minute of acceptance. On P's motion for decree with expenses, M sought expenses from the date of tender, on the basis that P should have been in a position to accept the revised tender on the afternoon of November 6.

Held, granting P's motion, that the importance of the decision and the sums involved made it unreasonable to force the pursuer into making an instant decision at consultation, particularly where the first formal offer had only been made a few days before, and that it was reasonable for the tender to be accepted when it was.

PAGAN v. MILLER GROUP LTD 2002 S.C. 150, Lord Carloway, OH.

5331. Expenses—witnesses—certification of skilled witnesses—competency

[Act of Sederunt (Rules of the Court of Session 1994) 1994 (SI 1994 1443) Sch.2 r.42.13(2).]

In E's action of damages for personal injury against K, E accepted K's tender before a procedure roll diet. In moving for decree E sought certification of a consultant dermatologist, T, and an employment consultant, C, for carrying out investigations and preparing reports for the purpose of giving evidence at proof. K argued that it was incompetent and inappropriate to seek certification under the Act of Sederunt (Rules of the Court of Session 1994) 1994 Sch.2 r.42.13(2) before proof or jury trial had been allowed, but did not oppose the certification of T.

Held, refusing the motion in relation to C but granting it in relation to T, that (1) there was no indication, even by ex parte statement, that C had conducted any "investigations" in terms of r.42.13(2) and no proper basis had been provided for certification of him as a skilled witness to whom r.42.13(2) applied, and (2) the meaning of "prospective" under r.42.13(2) in relation to proof or jury trial was ambiguous and might apply where proceedings had not yet reached the stage of the allowance of a proof or jury trial, and on that basis the unopposed certification of T would be granted.

EARL v. KVAERNER ENERGY LTD 2002 S.L.T. 1167, Lord Eassie, OH.

5332. Interdicts—interim interdict—arbitration—plea of prescription—determination by arbiter

[Prescription and Limitation (Scotland) Act 1973 (c.52) s.6, s.9(3).]

O, a local authority, sought to interdict contractors, X, from proceeding with an arbitration in respect of preliminary notices of arbitration issued on January 24, 1996 and January 16, 2001 in relation to a dispute over retention of liquidated damages by O, and moved for interim interdict. O argued that there was no dispute capable of resolution by an arbiter as the five year prescriptive period under the Prescription and Limitation (Scotland) Act 1973 s.6 from the date of any loss experienced by X had expired, that there had to be a dispute within the meaning of the arbitration clause in the contract for there to be a relevant and competent submission to arbitration, that there was no current dispute between the parties, and that there had been no interruption of the prescriptive period where no arbitration had followed the preliminary notice, having regard to the terms of s.9.(3) of the 1973 Act.

Held, refusing the motion for interim interdict in hoc statu, that the court required to be satisfied that there was only one resolution of the dispute that was tenable before rejecting the role of the arbiter, that there were two sides to the present issue and in general terms a prescription issue was capable of being determined by an arbiter in response to a claim which was otherwise competently before him.

ORKNEY ISLANDS COUNCIL v. CHARLES BRAND LTD; *sub nom.* ORKNEY ISLANDS COUNCIL, PETITIONERS 2002 S.L.T. 100, Lord Johnston, OH.

5333. Interdicts—interim interdict—competency—obstruction of roadway—interdict as competent method of enforcing removal of obstruction

D, the heritable proprietor of premises adjoining a private road sought recall of interim interdict granted to his superiors H, the proprietors of a nearby football stadium, in so far as it prevented him from placing or maintaining in place any obstructions in, on or near the roadway. H used the roadway as a means of access to the stadium and the registered title to D's property contained a real burden to keep the relevant area "open". Following the obstruction of the roadway by a car and the erection of bollards and a sleeping policeman, H were granted interim interdict on the basis of breaches of the real burden. D argued that as the interdict was an attempt to obtain a positive order and force the removal of the barriers, it was rendered incompetent.

Held, refusing the motion, that (1) as the fundamental nature of interdict was as a preventive or prohibitory remedy, the order sought had to be negative in substance, and (2) in the present case the obligation on D was negative in substance, the interdict reflected that prohibition, and while compliance with the order would involve incidental positive action, it was unnecessary to specify any particular act to be undertaken.

HAMPDEN PARK LTD v. DOW 2002 S.L.T. 95, Lord Drummond Young, OH.

5334. Interdicts–interim interdict–newspaper articles–alleged conflict of interest on part of solicitor–freedom of expression–likelihood of permanent order

[Human Rights Act 1998 (c.42) s.12.]

D, a firm of solicitors, moved for interim interdict in their action seeking to interdict B, newspaper publishers, from publishing a story showing, or tending to show that A (a partner in D) had acted in a conflict of interest situation. A was in a relationship with R who had a substantial interest in two companies; a third company (E, a client of D) had invested heavily in one of R's companies. D argued they had made out a prima facie case and having regard to the potential damage to their reputation, the balance of convenience favoured interim interdict

Held, refusing the motion, that (1) in terms of the Human Rights Act 1998 s.12, before the court could grant interim interdict it would have to be satisfied that D had a prima facie case, that the balance of convenience rested in their favour and also that on a final determination of their case, after proof if necessary, D would be likely to succeed; (2) D had not established that they were likely to succeed in an application for permanent interdict, even if the proposed article did allege or hint at conflict of interest. It was difficult on ex parte statements to conclude that even a hypothetical article would ultimately, after inquiry, be prohibited as defamatory against defences of veritas and/or fair comment: as solicitors, D's performance in accordance with ethical standards was a matter of public interest, and despite problems of quantification the remedy of damages was open to D, and (3) weighing the important private interest of D in protecting their professional reputation against the right of freedom of expression and its importance in maintaining a free press, the balance of convenience favoured B.

DICKSON MINTO WS v. BONNIER MEDIA LTD 2002 S.L.T. 776, Lord Carloway, OH.

5335. Interdicts–interim interdict–reasonable apprehension of direct act–interdict granted on the basis of stated aims and objectives and activities against other parties

A was contracted to install pipeline in the North Sea for BP. A sought an interim interdict against G, an environmental pressure group, from, (1) disrupting A's activities, and (2) boarding or obstructing the use of some of A's vessels. G had previously carried out actions designed to disrupt and prevent the operation of other petrol and gas companies in the North Sea. A argued that although no action had, as yet, been taken by G, G's stated opposition to North Sea oil and gas extraction and previous conduct were sufficient to warrant the granting of an interim interdict.

Held, granting the interim interdict, that the correct test where no delict or injury had yet been committed was to consider whether A were in reasonable apprehension that a serious delict or injury would be, or would be likely to be, committed against them by G. G's stated opposition and previous activities justified A's apprehension.

ALLSEAS UK LTD v. GREENPEACE LTD 2001 S.C. 844, Lord Wheatley, OH.

5336. Interdicts–variation–power of arrest–competency

[Act of Sederunt (Sheriff Court Ordinary Cause Rules) (SI 1993 1956) Chap.14; Chap.15; Chap.41; r.41.2(1); Protection from Abuse (Scotland) Act 2001 (asp 14) s.1 (1).]

A woman lodged a minute under the Ordinary Cause Rules, Chap.14 seeking the variation of a permanent common law interdict against molestation by her former husband, granted on their divorce, by the addition of a power of arrest in terms of the Protection from Abuse (Scotland) Act 2001 s.1 (1). The sheriff found her minute incompetent, as there was no provision in the rules to regulate the attachment of a power of arrest to a pre existing interdict. The pursuer appealed.

Held, allowing the appeal, that (1) there was no doubt that it was the Scottish Parliament's intention that a divorced spouse should be able to apply to the court for a power of arrest to be attached to a pre existing interdict granted in divorce proceedings, and if there was no express procedural provision it was for the court to devise or adapt a procedure which would permit the pursuer's application to be made, intimated and heard; (2) OCR, r.41.2(1) was intended to deal with both the situation where an interdict was being sought for the first time and where it was sought to attach a power of arrest to a pre existing interdict, and the appropriate procedure in the latter case was the enrolment of a motion in the process in which the interdict was granted, and (3) where Chap.41 made no further provision as to the procedure to be followed, the procedure had to be that set out in Chap.15, but as that Chapter made no provision for a supporting statement of facts or answers, the court had to proceed as best it could, possibly by analogy with minute procedure.

THOMSON v. THOMSON; *sub nom.* COPLAND v. THOMSON 2002 S.L.T. (Sh Ct) 97, CGB Nicholson Q.C., Sheriff Principal, Sh Ct.

5337. Interim orders–electricity supply industry–alleged overpayments under commercial agreement–relevant considerations

[Court of Session Act 1988 (c.36) s.47(2).]

B reclaimed against the Lord Ordinary's interlocutor (2002 G.W.D. 2-60) ordering S, under the Court of Session Act 1988 s.47(2), to deposit in a designated account the sum of £6.54 million each month, withheld from future payments to B, until a total of £52.3 million was deposited, being the sum S averred they had overpaid to B in respect of electricity supply. In the course of his decision, the Lord Ordinary determined, inter alia, that (1) the disputed sums were not "property" for the purposes of s.47(2), but the order sought was an order "regarding the subject matter of the cause"; (2) there was no justification for declining to make a s.47(2) order simply because it would innovate on the status quo, and (3) it was appropriate to make an order broadly in the terms sought by S. S argued, inter alia, that the Lord Ordinary had arrived at a fair solution after taking account of all the relevant circumstances and looking to the balance of convenience, where there was a neutral balance prima facie of the cases presented by each party.

Held, allowing the reclaiming motion, that (1) in a case of the present kind, the Lord Ordinary had to (i) identify the issues in the action, including the legal basis of the claims with which he was dealing; (ii) consider whether the party seeking the order had demonstrated a prima facie case that an obligation existed and that there was a continuing or threatened breach of that obligation which the order would address; (iii) avoid significantly innovating on the parties' contractual rights and obligations, and (iv) consider whether the balance of convenience was such as to justify the making of the interim order, bearing in mind the nature and degree of the harm likely to be suffered on either side by the grant or refusal of the interim order, and the relative strength of the cases put forward by each party, and (2) in the present case there was no basis on which any disputed funds could be identified for the purpose of securing such funds by an interim order, and the Lord Ordinary had failed to exercise his discretion in accordance with the above principles. Opinion of the Court per Lord Reed.

SCOTTISH POWER GENERATION LTD v. BRITISH ENERGY GENERATION (UK) LTD 2002 S.L.T. 870, Lord Reed, Lord Cameron of Lochbroom, Lord Emslie, Ex Div.

5338. Judgments and orders—non harassment orders—pre existing interdict—competency

[Protection from Harassment Act 1997 (c.40) s.8(5) (b) (ii).]

A woman raised an action against her former husband seeking interdict and a non-harassment order under the Protection from Harassment Act 1997 s.8(5) (b) (ii). The sheriff refused to grant a non-harassment order, expressing the view that such an order would not be competent where the defender was already subject to a permanent interdict against violent and abusive conduct toward the pursuer, granted in the divorce process. The pursuer appealed.

Held, recalling the sheriff's interlocutor, refusing in hoc statu the motion for a non-harassment order, and remitting the case to the sheriff to proceed as accords, that (1) on a proper construction of s.8(5) the restriction on the power to pronounce a non-harassment order was aimed alone at interdict orders pronounced within the framework of the action of harassment, and while the fact that the pursuer had the protection of a permanent interdict was a significant factor to be considered in determining whether to grant a non-harassment order, the application was technically competent, but (2) there were no circumstances in the instant case justifying the grant of a non-harassment order at that stage.

McCANN v. McGURRAN 2002 S.L.T. 592, Lord Caplan, Lord Cameron of Lochbroom, Lord Kingarth, Ex Div.

5339. Judgments and orders—non harassment orders—pre existing interim interdict—competency

[Protection from Harassment Act 1997 (c.40) s.8(5) (b) (ii).]

K appealed against a sheriff's decision to grant M a non harassment order in terms of the Protection from Harassment Act 1997 s.8(5) (b) (ii). An interim interdict had previously been granted, since when the conduct complained of had ceased. The sheriff considered that an interdict in the terms craved would not give sufficient protection to M and that the Act gave the court power to frame a non-harassment order in whatever terms seemed appropriate.

Held, allowing the appeal and granting interdict in the same terms as the interim interdict, that (1) a non-harassment order was a more serious order than an interdict and a court should only consider granting such an order where it considered that an interdict would be insufficient; (2) the court had no power to make an order beyond the terms craved by M, and (3) as the interim interdict appeared to have been effective in preventing any recurrence of the incidents that had happened in the past, it was not appropriate to replace it with a non-harassment order even in the same terms as the interdict.

McGUIRE v. KIDSTON 2002 S.L.T. (Sh Ct) 66, CGB Nicholson Q.C., Sheriff Principal, Sh Ct.

5340. Judgments and orders—sex offender orders—order of English court—necessity of concurrent order in Scotland

[Crime and Disorder Act 1998 (c.37) s.20; Human Rights Act 1998 (c.42) Sch.1 Part I Art.8.]

C, a chief constable, applied for an order under the Crime and Disorder Act 1998 s.20 concerning B in respect of whom an order had previously been granted under the equivalent provisions in England. The sheriff granted an interim order. B moved the court to recall the interim order, arguing inter alia that an order repeating the terms of the English order was unnecessary as it was automatically enforceable in Scotland, that if a Scottish order was granted while the English order subsisted he would suffer double jeopardy, that the actings required by s.20(2)(b) had to be of a sexual nature, that his behaviour was constantly monitored by two social workers and the police and there was already sufficient protection for the public, and further, that a prohibition on being drunk or under the influence of illicit drugs in any place, was too wide and a more restricted prohibition concerning drunkenness had been removed from the English order on appeal.

Held, continuing the interim orders, that (1) proceedings for a sex offender order were essentially civil in nature, and the English order was not automatically enforceable in Scotland; (2) the existence of two orders was not an example of double jeopardy as it would be incompetent for an English court to visit punishment on the respondent if a Scottish court had already done so, and vice versa; (3) s.20(2)(b) was aimed at conduct of a kind which gave rise to a reasonable apprehension that the respondent presented a risk to females and that conduct did not require to be of a sexual nature; (4) the court had no power to direct the social workers or the police and was entitled under the 1998 Act to put in place whatever mechanism it felt appropriate, and (5) although the prohibition regarding drink or drugs was not expressed so as to be restricted to behaviour in a public place, on the pleadings there was a greater risk of harm to females if the respondent was under the influence of either, it was not unreasonable to attempt to prevent him getting into a position where the threat was increased, and the rights of females within the court's jurisdiction had to be taken into account as well as the respondent's rights under the Human Rights Act 1998 Sch.1 Part I Art.8.

CHIEF CONSTABLE OF GRAMPIAN v. BEECH 2002 S.L.T. (Sh Ct) 106, DJ Cusine, Sh Ct (Grampian, Highland and Islands).

5341. Judgments and orders–variation of minute of agreement–interlocutor varying minute of agreement–effect of variation

P sought suspension of a charge for payment proceeding upon a decree for aliment of his two daughters. P and B had entered into a minute of agreement in 1989, which was entered into the Books of Council and Session, under which P was to pay £140 aliment per month for each child. The agreement was varied by interlocutor in 1992 and P had to pay £50 per child. A new minute of agreement was entered into which did not make provision for aliment. That agreement was varied in 1994 whereupon the requirement for aliment was reduced to nil with effect from January 1994. B did not demand or request payment between the cessation of payment in 1993 and 1999. B argued that the 1992 interlocutor was not a variation of the 1989 agreement but was in fact independent. Therefore the 1994 variation sought to vary an obligation in the 1989 agreement which no longer existed. Accordingly the aliment due under the 1992 variation was still due.

Held, granting decree suspending the charge and interdicting B from doing any further diligence on the decree, that while the 1994 interlocutor, with hindsight, could have been framed more felicitously, the clear intention had been to reduce P's alimentary liability to nil.

PEEBLES v. BOWMAN (FORMERLY PEEBLES) 2001 S.C.L.R. 712, Lord Eassie, OH.

5342. Judicial factors–appointment–accountant sequestrated at instance of professional body–interim orders granted prior to service–competency

K, a chartered accountant sought recall of interim orders granted to I, his professional body for the appointment of a judicial factor and the sequestration of his estates. I had withdrawn K's practising certificate in terms of their disciplinary rules following complaints from clients and, having been of the opinion that he had nevertheless continued to carry on business, presented the petition in which they averred that the measures sought were necessary for protection of K's clients. The motion for interim orders was not intimated to K and orders were sought prior to service. I argued that the underlying principle at common law was that a judicial factor could be appointed to protect against any potential loss or injustice.

Held, granting the motion, that the seizure of K's assets by interim sequestration and the appointment of a factor was not competent, appropriate or reasonable where I were neither creditors nor potential creditors and no colourable basis was offered relative to K's solvency.

INSTITUTE OF CHARTERED ACCOUNTANTS OF SCOTLAND v. KAY 2001 S.L.T. 1449, Lord Carloway, OH.

5343. Jury trial–awards–compatibility with right to fair trial

[Court of Session Act 1988 (c.36) s.9(b), s.11; Human Rights Act 1998 (c.42) Sch.1 Part I Art.6.]

In an action of damages in which liability was admitted, T opposed H's motion for issues, raising a question of the compatibility of jury trial with their right to a fair hearing under the Human Rights Act 1998 Sch.1 Part I Art.6. The temporary judge reported the case to the Inner House. T argued that the existing law and practice in the Court of Session in regard to jury trials did not amount to a controllable and fair judicial procedure inter alia because a jury received no meaningful guidance on levels of solatium and gave no reasons for its decision, the grounds of challenge to a jury's award on appeal had been restrictively interpreted and the preferable approach was the application of a conventional system of assessment as in England, that "special cause" in the Court of Session Act 1988 s.9(b) could be read compatibly with the Convention as meaning "substantial", which they had demonstrated or in the event the court was obliged by public general legislation to send the case to jury trial, a declaration of incompatibility should be made.

Held, remitting the case for the allowance of issues, that (1) in determining whether there was any infringement of Art.6 the procedure as a whole, including in any appeal, required to be examined; (2) the procedures followed in a civil jury trial were adequate to give the assurance that the jury were directed to the proper questions, and there was no necessary breach of Art.6 either by the jury not giving reasons or by the lack of guidance to juries as to current levels of awards; (3) as any jury award which was disproportionate to what a reasonable jury would have awarded was liable to be struck down, the appellate procedure provided a framework for ensuring that a party did not suffer the consequences of an unfair trial; (4) a system such as the English one had disadvantages as well as advantages; there was no reason to regard a judge's award as having greater intrinsic merit than a jury's award and it could not be said that remitting an action for jury trial was inconsistent with either party's rights under Art.6; (5) "special cause" in s.9(b) could not be interpreted as having the effect of sending every case involving the assessment of solatium to proof rather than jury trial, and (6) the question of a declaration of incompatibility did not arise.

HEASMAN v. JM TAYLOR & PARTNERS 2002 S.C. 326, Lord Coulsfield, Lord Hamilton, Lord Johnston, Ex Div.

5344. Limitations–conflict of laws–claim for restitution under English law introduced prior to closing of record–effect of amendment under Scottish procedure

[Prescription and Limitation (Scotland) Act 1973 (c.52) s.23A; Limitation Act 1980 (c.58) s.5, s.35.]

K sought repayment of various sums paid to G, the predecessors of a local authority, under interest rate swap contracts which were subsequently held to be ultra vires of local authorities. K pled that they were entitled to restitution under English law and an alternative claim for repetition under Scots law. The action, raised in 1992, had been sisted pending English proceedings which ultimately failed for want of jurisdiction. Thereafter K was allowed, no defences having yet been lodged, to amend in terms of a note of adjustments to introduce the claims under English law. G pled that esto English law was the proper law of the obligation to make restitution, any claim founded on an absence of consideration was time barred in terms of the Limitation Act 1980 s.5 and that any claim founded on mistake was a new claim and time barred in terms of s.35, under which a new claim could not be introduced by amendment into an existing action after the expiry of the relevant limitation period. K disputed the applicability of s.35, arguing that the Prescription and Limitation (Scotland) Act 1973 s.23A only applied the foreign rules of limitation, not rules of court procedure, which was what s.35 was truly concerned with and that on a proper application of Scottish rules of procedure, the English law claims had been effectively incorporated into the pleadings without objection having been taken at the proper time.

Held, case put out by order, that (1) the effect of s.35 was to lay down a general rule preventing a party from evading the effect of the ordinary limitation rule by bringing forward a claim based on a new cause of action in the form of an amendment to an existing action, and its provisions were an integral part of the law of limitation of actions and fell within the scope of s.23A; (2) s.23A did not exclude the operation of the Scottish procedural rules by which the cases based on English law had become part of K's case, but it required the court to address the English criteria and decide whether on a proper application the new claim should be allowed to be introduced, and (3) this required a preliminary proof before answer with evidence led as to how an English court would apply s.35.

KLEINWORT BENSON LTD v. GLASGOW CITY COUNCIL (NO.3) 2002 S.L.T. 1190, Lord Macfadyen, OH.

5345. **Limitations–personal injury–date when pursuer aware injury was "sufficiently serious"**

[Prescription and Limitation (Scotland) Act 1973 (c.52) s.17(2)(b)(i).]

F raised an action of damages against C (his former employers) in respect of an injury sustained to his back in July 1988. The action was raised on November 26, 1997. A preliminary proof was held on time bar. F argued that it was only after either an acute episode on November 27, 1994 or his being informed by his doctor on May 2, 1995 that he required surgery, that he became aware that his injury was sufficiently serious to justify bringing an action, and that it was also only on those dates that it was reasonably practicable for him to have done so under the Prescription and Limitation (Scotland) Act 1973 s.17(2)(b)(i).

Held, dismissing the action as time barred, that (1) two principles could be extracted from the case law: (a) that it was not a question of whether F had a reasonable excuse for not doing something, but whether it would have been reasonably practicable for him to do something, *Elliot v. J&C Finney (No.1)* 1989 S.L.T. 605, [1989] C.L.Y. 4554 referred to, and (b) that it was not material to the application of the test that F was not aware of the whole history or subsequent development of his condition, the determining factor being how serious the situation was when it required to be considered, *Ferla v. Secretary of State for Scotland* 1995 S.L.T. 662, [1995] C.L.Y. 6099 referred to; (2) it was not necessary to focus extensively on the perceived risks of litigation or the possible award because it would be assumed under the statutory test that liability would be admitted, and the question was whether the injuries were sufficiently serious to justify bringing an action; (3) there was no evidence to suggest that, prior to a consultation with his GP following the incident in November 1994, F had actually become aware that his injuries were sufficiently serious, however (4) it had been reasonably practicable for F to have become aware of the seriousness of his injuries by the end of July 1991, at which time F had further consulted his GP and had had his back x-rayed. That was notwithstanding the fact that F had been told after the x-ray that the inflammation might resolve itself, because he had been told that before but the injury had subsisted, *Blake v. Lothian Health Board* 1993 S.L.T. 1248, [1993] C.L.Y. 5500 and *Lowe v. Grampian Health Board* 1998 S.L.T. 731, [1997] C.L.Y. 5674 distinguished.

FORREST v. COOPERATIVE WHOLESALE SOCIETY LTD 2001 S.L.T. (Sh Ct) 59, Sheriff JA Baird, Sh Ct (Glasgow and Strathkelvin).

5346. Limitations–personal injury–identification of members of unincorporated association

[Prescription and Limitation (Scotland) Act 1973 (c.52) s.17(2)(b)(iii).]

M appealed against a sheriff's finding that her action of damages against N, a national charity, was time barred. M averred that she had sustained personal injuries while attending a barn dance organised by a local branch of N on June 14, 1996. The action was served on October 12, 1999. M argued that an unincorporated association could only be sued by convening a sufficient number of members qualified to defend the association's interests and that she had not become aware of the relevant facts in terms of the Prescription and Limitation (Scotland) Act 1973 s.17(2)(b)(iii) until she had information on a sufficient number of office holders, which was not prior to October 12, 1996.

Held, dismissing the action, that s.17(2)(b)(iii) read in the context of subparas (i) and (ii) did not require full knowledge of all the details of individual office bearers such as would be necessary to raise an action, and M had been made sufficiently aware of the identity of the persons to whom her injuries were attributable by the middle of August 1996, at which time she knew the names of the two associations involved.

MURRAY v. NATIONAL ASSOCIATION OF ROUND TABLES OF GREAT BRITAIN AND IRELAND 2002 S.L.T. 204, Lord McCluskey, Lady Cosgrove, Lord Coulsfield, Ex Div.

5347. Limitations–personal injury–psychological injury distinct from physical injury and subject to separate time scale

[Prescription and Limitation (Scotland) Act 1973 (c.52) s.17.]

C, a soldier, raised an action for damages for personal injury against the Lord Advocate as representing the Ministry of Defence. C claimed that during his training (July 1991) and time spent in Northern Ireland (February 1992), he had suffered loss and injury as a result of deliberate acts of mistreatment by non-commissioned officers and the failure of officers to deal with the bullying regime. In May 1992 he developed psychological injuries and was dismissed in July 1992. The Lord Advocate tabled a plea of time bar under the Prescription and Limitation (Scotland) Act 1973 s.17 which was repelled and a proof before answer was allowed. It was held that C's version of events in Northern Ireland indicated a regime of bullying that continued within the triennium in terms of s.17(2)(a). The Lord Advocate reclaimed, arguing that there was no basis on record for any course of conduct in Northern Ireland and that timeous objection had been made to that evidence. C cross appealed arguing that his personal circumstances should have been given more weight and that the psychological injuries were separate and distinct from the physical injuries and subject to a different time limit.

Held, allowing the reclaiming motion and cross appeal and retaining the interlocutor of the Lord Ordinary allowing proof before answer under deletion of certain averments, that (1) there was no record of the mistreatment in Northern Ireland, other than a specific allegation of assault. Timeous objection had been taken to that evidence and the Lord Ordinary was not entitled to hold that the bullying regime had extended to C's service in Northern Ireland; (2) where it might be appropriate to have regard to the gravity of an injury to a particular injured party, it would not be appropriate to go beyond that to look at the context of the environment in which the injury was sustained or to consider factors such as fear of losing one's job; (3) the claim in relation to the loss and injury sustained in 1991 and in Northern Ireland was time barred, and (4) the psychological injuries were distinct from the physical and subject to a separate triennium, *Shuttleton v. Duncan Stewart & Co Ltd* 1996 S.L.T. 517, [1996] C.L.Y. 7228 followed.

CARNEGIE v. LORD ADVOCATE (NO.3) 2001 S.C. 802, Lord Milligan, Lord Johnston, Lord Marnoch, Ex Div.

5348. Mortgages-mortgage rights-applications

ACT OF SEDERUNT (AMENDMENT OF ORDINARY CAUSE RULES AND SUMMARY APPLICATIONS, STATUTORY APPLICATIONS AND APPEALS ETC. RULES) (APPLICATIONS UNDER THE MORTGAGE RIGHTS (SCOTLAND) ACT 2001) 2002, SSI 2002 7; made under the Sheriff Courts (Scotland) Act 1971 s.32. In force: January 17, 2002; £2.50.

This Act of Sederunt amends the Sheriff Courts (Scotland) Act 1907 and the Act of Sederunt (Summary Applications, Statutory Applications and Appeals etc. Rules) 1999 (SI 1999 929) to regulate proceedings in which an order under the Mortgage Rights (Scotland) Act 2001 may be applied for by a defender. It inserts a new provision requiring the initial writ in a relevant action to include averments about those persons who appear to the pursuer to be entitled to apply for such an order and requiring such persons so far as known to the pursuer to be called as defenders for their interest and provides a procedure to be followed when a person wishes to apply for an order.

5349. Nobile officium-citation of witnesses to professional disciplinary body-Outer House petition-competency

[Act of Sederunt (Rules of the Court of Session 1994) 1994 (SI 1994 1443) Sch.2 r.14.3.]

A professional body petitioned for exercise of the court's powers under the nobile officium to cite witnesses to a discipline committee hearing. The petitioners argued that the witnesses' evidence was essential for a proper investigation into complaints against an insolvency practitioner, which was in the interests of justice, and that the remedy sought was one which could be granted in the Outer House as the situation was analogous to petitions to cite witnesses in arbitration proceedings, which were routinely dealt with there.

Held, refusing the petition, that while the remedy sought was within the powers of the nobile officium, it could not competently be granted in the Outer House, having regard to the mandatory terms of the Act of Sederunt (Rules of the Court of Session 1994) Sch.2 r.14.3.

INSTITUTE OF CHARTERED ACCOUNTANTS OF SCOTLAND, PETITIONERS 2002 S.L.T. 921, Lord Menzies, OH.

5350. Proof or jury trial-special cause-averments of loss-complexity

C raised an action for damages against his employers, R, and sought to have the case declared suitable for jury trial.

Held, allowing a jury trial, that no special cause making the matter unsuitable for jury trial had been shown. (1) C's averments that he had contributed to R's pension scheme and that he would make a specific loss were sufficient. The details of the scheme were well within R's knowledge and it was not enough for R to point to potential complexities without any suggestion as to why matters might be difficult; (2) contradictions in C's claim for services were of marginal significance, R had been given sufficient notice of the case against them and a plain reading of the averments revealed two separate claims for services which were not competing. There were no averments to support a claim that the Ogden tables might require adjustment, and (3) while different multipliers would fall to be applied in relation to different heads of claim, they all related to C himself and fell within a jury's competence, *Potts v. McNulty* 2000 S.L.T. 1269, [2000] C.L.Y. 5907 distinguished.

CRAWFORD v. RENFREWSHIRE COUNCIL 2001 Rep. L.R. 50, Lord Wheatley, OH.

5351. Right to fair trial-appeals-application for leave-motion before sheriff whose decision was under challenge

See ADMINISTRATION OF JUSTICE: Umair v. Umair. §5237

5352. Sheriff courts–appeals–sheriff principal, to–leave–competency of remit to sheriff to consider leave

[Sheriff Courts (Scotland) Act 1907 (7 Edw.VII, c.51); Court of Session Act 1988 (c.36) s.32(2).]

The wife raised an action of divorce, seeking a capital sum and the setting aside of a minute of agreement. The sheriff set aside the minute following a preliminary proof agreed to by the parties. The husband appealed. At the diet of appeal he conceded the appeal was incompetent for want of leave to appeal and moved the sheriff principal to remit the cause to the sheriff to decide on whether to grant leave to appeal.

Held, refusing the motion, that in terms of the Sheriff Courts (Scotland) Act 1907 the appeal was incompetent. The marking of the appeal removed the cause from the court below and no application could be entertained by the sheriff at that stage, *Thompson v. Lynn* 1995 S.C.L.R. 1090, [1996] C.L.Y. 7331 distinguished. The sheriff principal had no power to remit similar to the Court of Session Act 1988, s.32(2) under statute or at common law.

MacDONALD v. MacDONALD 2002 S.L.T. (Sh Ct) 144, RA Dunlop Q.C., Sheriff Principal, Sh Ct.

5353. Sheriff courts–appeals–sheriff principal, to–prior incompetent appeal to Court of Session–competency

[Sheriff Courts (Scotland) Act 1907 (7 Edw VII, c.51) s.27, s.28.]

In an action of damages the sheriff repelled C's plea of time bar and allowed a proof. C appealed to the Court of Session without seeking leave. The appeal was referred by the Deputy Principal Clerk to a single judge who refused it as incompetent. C then sought to appeal the sheriff's interlocutor to the sheriff principal and moved him to allow their appeal to be received late. They argued that the appeal to the Court of Session had not been effectually launched as there had been no hearing or opportunity to make representations in that court.

Held, refusing the motion, that the Sheriff Courts (Scotland) Act 1907 s.27 and s.28 provided alternative rights of appeal and once a party had committed himself to an appeal under one of those provisions, he had to abide by that choice; the marking of an appeal was the point at which the appellant chose his route.

SELLERS v. CALEDONIAN ALL TRADES LTD 2002 S.L.T. (Sh Ct) 110, EF Bowen Q.C., Sheriff Principal, Sh Ct.

5354. Sheriff courts–decrees–debtors–time to pay direction–relevant considerations

[Debtors (Scotland) Act 1987 (c.18) s.1 (1).]

P applied for a time to pay direction under the Debtors (Scotland) Act 1987 s.1 (1). C, a bank, had raised an action against P for delivery of a motor car and payment of £5,327.35 pursuant to a hire purchase agreement. The defender had borrowed about £6,000, with repayments of £199 a month from May 2000, and problems arose in July 2001. P did not defend the action.

Held, granting decree, that (1) once an application was made there was nothing in s.1 (1) that imposed an onus on the debtor to justify the making of a direction and it was up to the court, considering the information provided by both parties, as to how the discretion ought to be exercised; (2) the court was primarily concerned with the financial position of the defender at the time the application was heard, and should be presented with information as to the current amount of the debt, the history of any agreement constituting the debt and whether any security was taken, and (3) P's application should be granted as his offer was reasonable given his financial position and the three and a half years it would take to pay the debt was not unreasonable.

CAPITAL BANK PLC v. PATERSON 2002 S.L.T. (Sh Ct) 100, Sheriff WH Holligan, Sh Ct (Glasgow and Strathkelvin).

5355. Sheriff courts–decrees–decree by default–non appearance of defender who admitted liability–third party minuters

[Road Traffic Act 1988 (c.52) s.151.]

M raised an action for damages against T for losses incurred as a result of a road traffic accident, for which T had admitted being at fault. The second and third pursuers in the action were claiming damages in respect of personal injuries suffered in the accident. T was not covered by insurance. A policy of insurance had been issued by the third party minuters who would be liable to settle any judgment obtained, in terms of the Road Traffic Act 1988 s.151. A proof was set for January 13 and 14, 2000, however T's solicitors withdrew from acting before then. A peremptory diet was fixed for January 12 and then continued to February 11. At that diet the proof was discharged, but T indicated that he intended to continue defending the action and a new proof was fixed for May 30, 2000. At the proof T was absent and the second and third pursuers moved for decree, M's case having already been settled. The sheriff granted decree and the third party minuters appealed. They argued that the sheriff should have found T as having confessed by his absence, but then given the third party minuters a chance to defend the action in respect of the quantum claimed.

Held, allowing the appeal, that (1) the granting of the motion for decree had defeated the object of the minuters being sisted to the action and having entered the process, the minuters were entitled to a proof on the quantum of the claims; (2) T should be held to have confessed by his failure to appear at the proof, and (3) as neither party to the appeal was responsible for the appeal, no expenses would be due to or by either party.

McGONIGAL v. TAYLOR 2001 S.C.L.R. 1070, EF Bowen Q.C., Sheriff Principal, Sh Ct.

5356. Sheriff courts–decrees–decree by default–suspension

The husband petitioner, H, sought suspension and interdict against his former wife, W, to prevent the enforcement of decree awarding W a share of the matrimonial property. H had allowed the sheriff court proceedings to continue undefended.

Held, refusing the petition, that (1) the circumstances leading to the action becoming undefended were entirely of H's own making and the sheriff was entitled to take account of that fact; (2) once the action became undefended, the sheriff was bound to disregard the terms of the defences and any productions lodged on H's behalf; (3) the sheriff's failure to require affidavit evidence in support of the claim for a capital sum did not invalidate the decree, but was a factor to be taken into account by the court in determining whether to exercise its discretion in relation to the decree; (4) having regard to all the information which was or should reasonably have been before the sheriff, the award, although at the top end of the range, could not be described as extravagant, and (5) no miscarriage of justice or fraud had occurred, nor anything which would allow the court to interfere with the sheriff's decision

ALI v. ALI (NO.3) 2002 S.C.L.R. 264, Lord Nimmo Smith, OH.

5357. Sheriff courts–diets–peremptory diet–failure to appear

K, a firm of solicitors, raised an action seeking to recover professional fees relating to a divorce action from M, their former client. M instructed another firm of solicitors to act for him but they withdrew before the continued options hearing. There was no need for a peremptory diet at that time as M contacted K and it was agreed that K should appear for both parties at the continued options hearing and have the action sisted. K maintained that the intention of the sist was for M to make an agreed payment for £2,500 in settlement or to suggest other payment terms. M disputed that but agreed that his solicitor had withdrawn from acting on account of M's inability to pay their fees. In due course, K enrolled a motion to recall the sist which was unopposed and a new options hearing was assigned for May 28, 2001. M received intimation but failed to appear at the options hearing and K asked the court to appoint a peremptory diet which was fixed for June 19. Again intimation was given to M, who failed to appear. The court pronounced interlocutor holding that M was no longer insisting on his defences and continued the case to allow K's account of expenses to be taxed by the Auditor of Court. M appealed against that interlocutor explaining that he had been in hospital from June 5 and, although he had received intimation on May 31, he had been unable to arrange representation before the onset of his sudden illness and had been unable, during his stay in hospital, to indicate to the court that he would be unable to attend. K, whilst agreeing that M had been in hospital, could not agree that his lack of representation had been justified and submitted that no proper explanation had been offered for his failure to attend the hearing on May 28. M's defence of the action had been that K had unreasonably withdrawn from acting and had, as a result, caused difficulties in M's divorce action which resulted in a duplication of fees to his new solicitors.

Held, allowing the appeal, allowing 21 days for M to amend his pleadings and directing that a new options hearing be fixed, that (1) it was possible, given the claims made by M, for a relevant defence to be made to the action and, taking account of the circumstances which prevented M from attending court on June 19, it would be unreasonable not to afford him the opportunity to amend his pleadings and advance the defence put forward, and (2) M's unexplained failure to appear at the diet on May 28 had resulted in the requirement for the hearing on June 19 and the appeal and as such M was liable to K for the expenses of both the appeal and the diets on May 28 and June 19.

KERR & CO v. McALOON 2002 S.C.L.R. 374, RA Dunlop Q.C., Sheriff Principal, Sh Ct.

5358. Sheriff courts–expenses–certification of counsel–counsel not appearing in court–competency

M sought damages in respect of personal injury sustained while crossing a bridge, the land on one side being owned by the first defender, and on the other by the second defenders. M moved the sheriff to certify the proof as suitable for employment of junior counsel. The defenders opposed the motion, arguing first that it was incompetent where counsel had not appeared at the proof, and, secondly, that it was not justified on the merits.

Held, sanctioning the employment of junior counsel, that (1) there was no reason why counsel need appear before certification was given, and (2) the legal issue raised in the case, relating to title position and occupiers' liability where M was crossing a bridge on either side of which there were public footpaths, was one of some nicety.

McDOUGALL v. TAWSE 2002 S.L.T. (Sh Ct) 10, DJ Cusine, Sh Ct (Grampian, Highland and Islands).

5359. Sheriff courts–pleadings–amendment–amendement to take accout of differing evidence

J raised an action for damages in respect of injuries he sustained after a motorcycle accident. J averred that a rabbit ran out in front of him and when he braked, the loose stones on the road, as a result of a failed treatment, caused him to lose control of the bike. The action was raised on the basis of those claims but when giving evidence J denied the existence of loose stones and maintained that the road had been rutted but smooth. Counsel for J moved to amend J's pleadings to take account of J's evidence regarding the state of the road. The sheriff concluded that the evidence did not support the allegations and that J had failed to prove the case on record. J appealed to the sheriff principal.

Held, refusing the appeal, that (1) the ground of appeal being that "the sheriff erred in failing to allow the pursuer's proposed amendment" was defective and an unacceptable formulation of a ground of appeal, and (2) J had failed to establish that the sheriff's decision was an unreasonable exercise of his discretion, that the defenders would have been prejudiced was a proper conclusion.

JOHNSTON v. PERTH AND KINROSS COUNCIL 2002 S.C.L.R. 558, RA Dunlop Q.C., Sheriff Principal, Sh Ct.

5360. Sheriff courts–pleadings–amendment–change in law after expiry of limitation period

[Prescription and Limitation (Scotland) Act 1973 (c.52) s.19A.]

G claimed damages as a result of sexual abuse which was allegedly perpetrated by a member of the teaching staff at St Joseph's College, Dumfries. The abuse was said to have occurred between 1972 and 1976. G was 18 in 1978 and raised the action in 1999. G's claim, under the Prescription and Limitation (Scotland) Act 1973, would have become time barred in 1981, but G pled that it was equitable to allow the action to proceed in terms of s. 19A. M appealed to the sheriff principal. G's case was one of negligence on the basis that M had had a duty of reasonable care in employing a fit and proper person within a teaching capacity. No case was made that M were vicariously liable, however the House of Lords subsequently restated the law in *Lister v. Hesley Hall Ltd* [2001] UKHL 22, [2002] 1 A.C. 215, [2001] C.L.Y. 5359 and at appeal the question was raised as to whether the record should be amended to take account of those developments. M opposed any amendment arguing that it changed the whole basis of the case and was only possible because the action had been brought 25 years after the fact. The action had been raised against M, an unincorporated voluntary association, in a descriptive name, Marist Brothers, the effect of which would be to effectively call all brothers as defenders. M argued that there were no reasonable grounds for suing those who had no connection with St Joseph's. G argued that it was not necessary to identify the persons who were in control of the college at the material time, it was sufficient to identify the body by whom the duty of care was owed. M also argued that the action was time barred, but G argued that he had delayed by reason of psychological distress. This accounted for the delay until 1997 and beyond that G had been awaiting the prosecution of the individual.

Held, allowing the amendment, that (1) when an unincorporated voluntary association was called as a defender, it was called as a continuing entity. There was no Scottish authority to the effect that, where a party sued such an association, that it must sue the association as it was at the date of the loss or must sue only those members, or that part of it that was averred to be responsible for the loss; (2) the question of whether liability fell only on those who were members at the date of delict or those who were members at date of action could be resolved in the context of a proof to determine the merits of G's claim, not a proof relating to time bar; (3) that G had pled a relevant case in relation to s. 19A and it was necessary to balance the arguments for and against allowing him to proceed and that could only be carried out by a court in full possession of the material facts, accordingly, the appeal relating to a preliminary proof on time bar and liability of current members was refused, and (4) that although the minute of amendment was made a long time after expiry of the limitation period, it amounted to a reformulation of the basis of the case which had been made against M and it was not suggested that allowing the amendment would cause prejudice by requiring further investigations or more witnesses and nor would the factual basis of the case be materially altered.

GORRIE v. MARIST BROTHERS 2002 S.C.L.R. 436, JC McInnes Q.C., Sheriff Principal, Sh Ct.

5361. Sheriff courts–power of arrest–applications–Protection from Abuse (Scotland) Act 2001

ACT OF SEDERUNT (ORDINARY CAUSE RULES) AMENDMENT (APPLICATIONS UNDER THE PROTECTION FROM ABUSE (SCOTLAND) ACT 2001) 2002, SSI 2002 128; made under the Sheriff Courts (Scotland) Act 1971 s.32; and the Protection from Abuse (Scotland) Act 2001 s.2, s.3. In force: March 8, 2002; £2.00.

This Act of Sederunt amends the Sheriff Courts (Scotland) Act 1907 by inserting a new Chapter to make provision for applications in the sheriff court in respect of a power of arrest under the Protection from Abuse (Scotland) Act 2001. The new Chapter provides an application for a power of arrest is to be made by crave in the initial writ, defences or counterclaim in which the interdict to which it relates is applied for or, if made after the application for interdict, by motion in the action or application to which the application relates and prescribes certain documents that are to be served along with the power of arrest. It also provides an application to extend or recall a power of arrest is to be made by minute in the application or action to which the application relates and provides that where the interdict to which the power of arrest is attached is varied or recalled a copy of the interlocutor varying or recalling the interdict is to be delivered to a chief constable. In addition, it provides that where a person is required to deliver documents to a chief constable where a power of arrest is served, extended or recalled, or the interdict is varied or recalled, he shall after compliance lodge a certificate of delivery in Form PA1 in process.

5362. Sheriff courts—rules—applications—detention and forfeiture of terrorist cash

ACT OF SEDERUNT (SUMMARY APPLICATIONS, STATUTORY APPLICATIONS AND APPEALS ETC. RULES) AMENDMENT (DETENTION AND FORFEITURE OF TERRORIST CASH) 2002, SSI 2002 129; made under the Sheriff Courts (Scotland) 1971 s.32. In force: March 8, 2002; £1.75.

This Act of Sederunt amends the Act of Sederunt (Summary Applications, Statutory Applications and Appeals etc. Rules) 1999 (SI 1999 929) by inserting Ch.3 which contains specific provision in relation to the Anti-Terrorism, Crime and Security Act 2001. It provides for applications to the sheriff for an order for extended detention of cash to be made by summary application, and for further applications to be made by minute in the process and provides for applications to the sheriff Act to be made by summary application. It also provides for applications to the sheriff to be made by summary application, except where the court has already made an order in which case the application is to be made by minute in the original process. This rule further provides for notice of any such applications to be given to any persons who the sheriff considers might be affected by the granting of such an application.

5363. Sheriff courts—rules—applications—warrants for appeals

ACT OF SEDERUNT (SUMMARY APPLICATIONS, STATUTORY APPLICATIONS AND APPEALS ETC. RULES) AMENDMENT (NO.2) (LOCAL GOVERNMENT (SCOTLAND) ACT 1973) 2002, SSI 2002 130; made under the Sheriff Courts (Scotland) Act 1971 s.32. In force: March 8, 2002; £2.00.

This Act of Sederunt amends the Act of Sederunt (Summary Applications, Statutory Applications and Appeals etc. Rules) 1999 (SI 1999 929) to make a further exception to the requirement for warrants citation to be in Form 2. It inserts a new Part XVIII containing specific provision in relation to appeals against findings and imposition of sanctions or suspensions by the Accounts Commission under the Local Government (Scotland) Act 1973 and provides for appeals to the sheriff principal under s.103J of the 1973 Act to be made by summary application, and further provides for such summary applications to include certain statements in the grounds of appeal and to be accompanied by certain documents. It also prescribes the form of warrant for citation, and form of citation in respect of such warrants for any appeals.

5364. Sheriff courts—summary applications—suspension of charge—whether timeously brought

[Act of Sederunt (Summary Suspension) 1993 (SI 1993 3128) Art.2; Act of Sederunt (Summary Applications, Statutory Applications and Appeals etc Rules) 1999 (SI 1999 929) r.2.6.]

W, a driving instructor, appealed against a decision of the sheriff dismissing his application, under the Act of Sederunt (Summary Suspension) 1993 Art.2 for suspension of a charge served by a driving school, D, on March 23, 2001, as out of time in terms of the Act of Sederunt (Summary Applications, Statutory Applications and Appeals etc Rules) 1999, r.2.6. The charge proceeded on an "instructor's franchise agreement" between the parties, which along with a statement of indebtedness was presented for registration on March 2, 2001. The application was warranted by the sheriff clerk on August 8, 2001. W sought to withdraw a concession made before the sheriff that the application was governed by the 1999 Rules, arguing that they did not apply to an application of the present type. D argued that the terms of r.2.6 were clear and there was no authority to justify making an exception.

Held, remitting the case to the sheriff to determine W's application in terms of the 1993 provisions, that the time limit in r.2.6 applied only to statutory appeals and applications in the nature of appeals, and not to statutory applications, or to an application at common law for suspension of a charge.

WARD v. DRM DRIVER TRAINING CENTRE (GLASGOW) 2002 S.L.T. (Sh Ct) 108, EF Bowen Q.C., Sheriff Principal, Sh Ct.

5365. **Sheriff courts–writ–initial writ drafted by English firm of solicitors–unqualified person–legality**

[Solicitors (Scotland) Act 1980 (c.46) s.32(2)(a).]

A hearing was held on an application by G, an English firm of solicitors, for a warrant for service in respect of an initial writ at the instance of B, a bank, against M, a debtor resident in Scotland. The writ was said to have been drafted by G and revised by a Scottish firm of solicitors. It was intended that the warranted writ be returned to the Scottish firm for service but that G would prepare the minute for decree if the action was undefended. It was argued that the system adopted did not disclose any impropriety such as to prevent the granting of a warrant as, in terms of the Solicitors (Scotland) Act 1980 s.32(2)(a), drafting could be carried out by anyone provided that they did not receive a direct reward for doing so.

Held, refusing the warrant, that any person who was not admitted as a solicitor in terms of the Act and holding a current practising certificate, or a registered European lawyer, was by implication an unqualified person, the qualification in s.32(2)(a) referred to unqualified staff employed by persons currently qualified and the writ had been illegally drafted by an unqualified person operating under the auspices of G and illegally assisted by the Scottish firm.

BANK OF SCOTLAND v. MITCHELL 2002 S.L.T. (Sh Ct) 55, RA Davidson, Sh Ct (Tayside, Central and Fife).

5366. **Sist–choice of forum–proceedings in another jurisdiction–motion after record closed**

[Civil Jurisdiction and Judgments Act 1982 (c.27) s.49; Rome Convention on the law applicable to contractual obligations 1980 Art.8; Brussels Convention on Jurisdiction and Enforcement of Judgments in Civil and Commercial Matters 1968.]

An Italian company raised an action of payment against the Norwegian owners of a vessel flying the Panamanian flag, in respect of bunker fuel obtained by the charterers of the vessel. The pursuers arrested the vessel *ad fundandam jurisdictionem* at Aberdeen. The defenders admitted the jurisdiction of the Scottish court. After the record closed the pursuers moved to sist the action pending determination of the dispute by the Italian courts. They argued that Italy was the more appropriate forum where, by application of the Rome Convention on the law applicable to contractual obligations 1980 Art.8 the question of the existence of the contract, which was disputed, fell to be determined by Italian law and that the Civil Jurisdiction and Judgments Act 1982 s.49 permitted a sist and there was no inconsistency with any of the Conventions.

Held, refusing the motion, that (1) the pursuers having invoked the jurisdiction of the Scottish court and litigated to the closed record stage without challenge by the defenders, it would require some extraordinary feature to entitle the court, against the defenders' wishes, to permit the pursuers to "forum shop", and (2) so long as the action remained before the Scottish court, no other action could be raised elsewhere since the Brussels Convention on Jurisdiction and Enforcement of Judgments in Civil and Commercial Matters

1968 would require it to be dismissed, *Owners of Cargo Lately Laden on Board the Tatry v. Owners of the Maciej Rataj (C406/92)* [1999] Q.B. 515, [1995] C.L.Y. 704.

MARODI SERVICE DE D MIALICH v. MIKKAL MYKLEBUSTHAUG REDERI A/S 2002 S.L.T. 1013, Judge TG Coutts Q.C., OH.

5367. Sist–defenders–partial sist against one defender only–competence

[Insolvency Act 1986 (c.45) s.8, s.11 (3) (d).]

B, an asbestosis sufferer, sought damages from three former employers, claiming his condition was a result of negligent exposure to asbestos during the course of his employment. In October 2001 an administration order under the Insolvency Act 1986 s.8 was made in respect of the first defenders in the English High Court. B sought to sist the action so far as directed against the first defenders only. The defenders submitted that the entire action required to be sisted, arguing that it was incompetent to sist proceedings against one of three defenders against whom a single joint and several conclusion was directed while proceedings continued against the remaining two, that the second and third defenders would be unable to proceed with their claims for contribution against the first defenders, and that there was a risk that the first defenders' position would be prejudiced if the actions against the remaining defenders were allowed to proceed while the action against the first defenders was sisted.

Held, sisting all proceedings against the first defenders and quoad ultra allowing proof before answer, that (1) whether a particular form of partial sist should be granted in a given set of circumstances was not a matter of competency but a matter for the proper exercise of judicial discretion; (2) in light of s.11 (3) (d) of the 1986 Act, it was necessary to sist all proceedings against the first defenders, including the second and third defenders' claims for contribution, but s.11 (3) (d) had no direct effect on the proceedings against the second and third defenders; (3) any practical impact on subsequent litigation against the first defenders did not amount to the sort of prejudice which would make it inappropriate to proceed as B proposed, and it had not been shown that such a course would operate to the prejudice of any of the defenders, and (4) to sist the action as a whole would clearly be prejudicial to B due to the effect in delaying pursuit of his claim, and in the absence of prejudice to the defenders the motion should be granted.

BEE v. T&N SHELF TWENTY SIX LTD; *sub nom.* BEE v. T&N TWENTY SIX LTD 2002 S.L.T. 1129, Lord Macfadyen, OH.

COMMERCIAL LAW

5368. Debts–delay–interest

LATE PAYMENT OF COMMERCIAL DEBTS (SCOTLAND) REGULATIONS 2002, SSI 2002 335; made under the European Communities Act 1972 s.2. In force: August 7, 2002; £1.75.

These Regulations, which amend the Late Payment of Commercial Debts (Interest) Act 1998, partially implement Council Directive 2000/35 ([2000] OJ L200/35) on combating late payment in commercial transactions. They specify by order categories of contracts as excepted contracts, in relation to which late payment interest is not to be payable; introduce a provision that the 1998 Act shall apply to Advocates' fees; repeal provisions that debts do not carry interest if they are specified in an order made by the Scottish Ministers; and introduce a right to a fixed sum by way of compensation for the costs suffered by suppliers arising from late payment, such sum being based on the size of the debt. In addition, the Regulations provide that a representative body may bring proceedings in the Court of Session on behalf of small and medium-sized enterprises where standard terms put forward by a purchaser in contracts to which the 1998 Act applies include a term purporting to oust or vary the right to statutory interest in relation to debts created by those contracts.

5369. Debts–delay–interest rates

LATE PAYMENT OF COMMERCIAL DEBTS (RATE OF INTEREST) (SCOTLAND) ORDER 2002, SSI 2002 336; made under the Late Payment of Commercial Debts (Interest) Act 1998 s.6. In force: August 7, 2002; £1.75.

This Order, which revokes the Late Payment of Commercial Debts (Rate of Interest) (No.2) Order 1998 (SI 1998 2765), sets the rate of statutory interest which may be claimed under the Late Payment of Commercial Debts (Interest) Act 1998 providing qualifying creditors with a statutory right to claim interest on qualifying debts from qualifying debtors.

5370. Late Payment of Commercial Debts (Interest) Act 1998 (c.20)–Commencement No.6 Order

LATE PAYMENT OF COMMERCIAL DEBTS (INTEREST) ACT 1998 (COMMENCEMENT NO.6) (SCOTLAND) ORDER 2002, SSI 2002 337; made under the Late Payment of Commercial Debts (Interest) Act 1998 s.17. Commencement details: bringing into force various provisions of the 1998 Act on August 7, 2002; £1.50.

This Order brings into force the Late Payment of Commercial Debts (Interest) Act 1998 for all remaining commercial contracts for the supply of goods or services not already covered by the preceding four commencement orders. In addition, the Order partially implements Council Directive 2000/35 ([2000] OJ L200/35) on combating late payment in commercial transactions.

5371. Tobacco Advertising and Promotion Act 2002 (c.36)–Commencement Order

TOBACCO ADVERTISING AND PROMOTION ACT 2002 (COMMENCEMENT) (SCOTLAND) ORDER 2002, SSI 2002 512 (C.26); made under the Tobacco Advertising and Promotion Act 2002 s.22. Commencement details: bringing into force various provisions of the 2002 Act on November 20, 2002, February 14, 2003 and May 14, 2003; £1.75.

This Order brings into force all the provisions of the Tobacco Advertising and Promotion Act 2002 except for provisions relating to any tobacco advertisement which is, or is to be, published, printed, devised or distributed solely for the promotion of a tobacco product in a place or on a website where tobacco products are offered for sale; or in circumstances in which the tobacco advertisement uses the name, emblem or other feature of a tobacco product in connection with a product (other than a tobacco product) which has a function in addition to that of carrying advertising and the advertisement is not published in a newspaper, periodical or other electronic or paper publication or carried on a billboard, wall or other fixed or moveable surface which serves a function similar to that of a billboard.

5372. Books

Cockburn, David–Commercial Leases. Paperback: £40.00. ISBN 0-406-94712-0. Butterworths Law (Scotland).

Cusine, Douglas J., NP; Forte, A.D.M.–Scottish Cases and Materials in Commercial Law. Paperback: £35.00. ISBN 0-406-04658-1. Butterworths Law (Scotland).

COMPANY LAW

5373. Company registration—restoration of company to register—relevance of delay by petitioner in seeking restoration to calculation of limitation period

WHL brought a petition for an order that the name of W be restored to the register. WHL had issued proceedings against W in England alleging negligence and breach of contract. When such proceedings had been issued, WHL had not been aware of the prior dissolution of W. WHL requested the court to decree, for the purposes of the limitation period, that the period of time between W's dissolution and its restoration to the register should not be taken into account. W argued, inter alia, that if the period was ignored it, together with its insurers, would be deprived of the protection afforded under the limitations statutes which would have been enjoyed had the company not been dissolved.

Held, granting the petition in part, that delay on the part of the petitioner in making an application to restore a company to the register could be taken into account for the purposes of limitation or prescription. In the instant case, it was apparent that no reason existed as to why WHL should not suffer the consequences of its failure to act in the period between W's dissolution and the bringing of the proceedings. Moreover, it was not appropriate that other creditors who had been inactive in the same period should have any benefit conferred on them. The period between dissolution and the petition should not be discounted, *Huntington Poultry, Re* [1969] 1 W.L.R. 204, [1969] C.L.Y. 399 applied and *Kenyon (Donald), Re* [1956] 1 W.L.R. 1397, [1956] C.L.Y. 1193 considered.

WHITBREAD (HOTELS) LTD v. WALKMORE (95) LTD; *sub nom.* WHITBREAD (HOTELS) LTD, PETITIONERS 2002 S.L.T. 178, Lord Eassie, OH.

5374. Directors—property transactions—valid approval—sufficiency of information before shareholders

[Companies Act 1985 (c.6) s.263, s.320, s.322(3)(b), s.346.]

C owned a football club and raised an action against R, seven former directors. A and B, the first and second defenders, were the original shareholders and directors, and were members of the same family (F). In 1994-95 C began to experience financial difficulties and by then C's stadium (S) no longer met acceptable safety criteria. In April 1996 C acquired land for £75,000 for the purpose of building a new stadium. C entered a conditional contract with a development company (V) in June 1996 to sell S. As part of the deal, V lent £600,000 to C, secured on S, and S was thereafter given a valuation for the purposes of C's financial statements of £600,000, duly approved by C's auditors. In January 1997 a company (H) approached B with the intention of acquiring C's playing interests, but not C's heritable property. A company (D) in which members of F held controlling shares, held 87 per cent of C's shares. In June 1997 B formed a new company (L) to acquire C's heritable property against the prospect of a sale to H of C's shares once the assets had been acquired. All the directors were in agreement with the plan. B called an extraordinary general meeting of C in July 1997 to seek members' approval of the proposal. The resolution was passed by majority. D abstained in order not to determine the outcome of the vote. Thereafter, shares in L were allotted to members proportionately to their respective holdings in C. The share purchase agreement with H went ahead in September 1997, and D's whole shareholding in C was transferred to H. R resigned and new directors were appointed. H exercised its statutory powers to acquire remaining shares; C became a wholly owned subsidiary of H. In December 1997 the conditions attached to V's purchase of S came to fruition and L realised a net sum of £1.7 million. C argued inter alia (1) that the disposal of C's heritable property to L constituted "distributions" which were unlawful in terms of s.263, which allowed distribution only out of profits available for that purpose, and that each of R who had participated in the decision to make such distributions were liable for C's loss as a result; and (2) that R were liable to the same extent by contravening the Companies

Act 1985 s.320, and each director was personally liable as a consequence in terms of s.322(3)(b).

Held, assoilzing R, that (1) the s.320 argument failed as, where the shareholders of L were proportionately the same as those of C, no prejudice to their financial interests could arise and the consideration for the transfer was not a central aspect; the shareholders of C had had sufficient information before them in considering the proposals and the passing of the resolution at the extraordinary general meeting constitued a valid approval by them of the arrangement carried through; (2) taking the whole relevant circumstances into account S might reasonably have been expected to achieve on an unconditional bargain struck as at the valuation date, a price in excess of but not substantially in excess of £600,000, namely £700,000; £65,000 correctly reflected the value of the land purchased for a new stadium, as initially agreed by parties. Thus the disposals in September 1997 involved their transfer at a cumulative sum of £165,000 less than their aggregate value, and (3) "distribution" in terms of s.263 would generally be a transfer without consideration given by the recipient. It was clear from the authorities that it was necessary first to consider the character of the transaction and determine whether there was a "dressed up return of capital", *Aveling Barford Ltd v. Perion* [1989] B.C.L.C. 626, [1990] C.L.Y. 549 applied. If the transaction was genuinely conceived of and effected as an exchange for value and the difference ultimately found did not give rise to an exchange at "gross undervalue" and was not unreasonably large, there would not to any extent be a "dressed up return of capital". The transaction between C and L was genuinely conceived of and effected by R for value, put together in order to facilitate H injecting substantial funds into C's footballing activities, which H offered to do only if C was stripped of heritable assets. It was always intended that L would give consideration for the property. In the circumstances the disposals of heritable property to L did not constitute a "distribution".

CLYDEBANK FOOTBALL CLUB LTD v. STEEDMAN 2002 S.L.T. 109, Lord Hamilton, OH.

5375. **Shareholders−unfairly   prejudicial   conduct−directors−unauthorised redundancy payment−competence and appropriateness of petition**

[Companies Act 1985 (c.6) s.459.]

A brought a reclaiming motion following the dismissal (2000 S.L.T. 634) of his petition against H under the Companies Act 1985 s.459. Following an agreement by members to cease trading and to sell off the assets of an informally run company, H made an unauthorised payment to himself in respect of redundancy or the termination of his employment. A had not tried to persuade the company itself to take action to recover the payment. The Lord Ordinary dismissed the petition on the basis that A had failed to show that the payment to H was unfair as well as being unlawful, and further held that it was inappropriate to proceed by way of a petition under s.459 in circumstances where a remedy was available in an ordinary, derivative action.

Held, allowing the reclaiming motion (Lord Prosser dissenting), that the existence of circumstances which justified the commencement of a derivative action to recover monies from a company director and shareholder a petition did not necessarily act as a bar to proceedings brought under s.459. In general it was possible for a petitioner to succeed if he could show that an action, or proposed action, of the company satisfied the test of unfairness in s.459, notwithstanding that the action might be lawful in that the company had acted or was acting within its powers. The test of unfairness to be applied was not a subjective test but was based upon equitable principles of good faith, *O'Neill v. Phillips* [1999] 1 W.L.R. 1092, [1999] C.L.Y. 634 and *Guidezone Ltd, Re* [2001] B.C.C. 692 applied. In the instant case, H had maintained that the redundancy payment, although unlawful, was not unfair. However the refusal of a s.459 petition on that basis could not be justified because such a refusal, of necessity, required the court to apply a subjective test of fairness and to consider whether the actions of a shareholder were reasonable.

ANDERSON v. HOGG 2002 S.C. 190, Lord Coulsfield, Lord Hamilton, Lord Prosser, Ex Div.

5376. Shareholders—unfairly prejudicial conduct—proposed amendment concerning rights of petitioners as landlords of company—scope of inquiry

[Companies Act 1985 (c.6) s.459, s.461.]

B, minority shareholders in a company, S, producing mineral water, brought a petition seeking reduction of an assignation of an option agreement granted by B in favour of S. The agreement gave C an option to purchase B's farm from which water bottled and sold by S was taken. B submitted that the granting of the assignation was a discriminatory abuse of power, and relying on the Companies Act 1985 s.459 and s.461, argued that an assignation of the option was getting rid of a valuable company asset and was contrary to a shareholders' agreement and that the lease, option and shareholders' agreement all had to be looked at together and it was artificial and unworkable for the court to consider whether the assignation was valid without considering the construction and effect of the option agreement. S opposed a motion by B to amend the pleadings to add an averment that on a proper construction, the option agreement was not assignable, and argued inter alia that the amendment was extraneous to the interests of S's members, having introduced a civil dispute between landlord and an option holder, and could not be disguised as a members' dispute.

Held, refusing the motion to amend, that the amendment raised issues which were not appropriate to s.459, it raised a pure question of construction of a document entered into between B and C, and the fact that B were also shareholders was not in point, *JE Cade & Son Ltd, Re* [1991] B.C.C. 360, [1992] C.L.Y. 423 followed.

BROWN v. SCOTTISH BORDER SPRINGS LTD 2002 S.L.T. 1213, Lord McEwan, OH.

5377. Shareholders—unfairly prejudicial conduct—share allotment at undervalue

[Companies Act 1985 (c.6) s.459.]

P, shareholders, brought a petition against T, a company, under the Companies Act 1985 s.459 on the basis that T's actions in allotting shares to other shareholders at par and substantially below their proper value, were unfairly prejudicial to P's interests because they reduced the value of P's shareholding. Prior to the allotment, P had 43 per cent of the shares; following the allotment that was reduced to 22 per cent. P argued that, T having put forward no coherent explanation for issuing at par, any inquiry should be confined to questions of remedy. T argued that (1) even if there had been unfairly prejudicial conduct, the court had a discretion as to whether or not to grant a remedy and, if they did so, the form which that remedy might take; (2) although failure to allocate shares at a premium might be a breach of a duty, it was not necessarily unfairly prejudicial conduct, and the actions of P, who had been given the chance to subscribe, might be relevant, as might T's need for capital and their existing practice of making new allotments at par when raising capital.

Held, allowing proof on the question of remedy, that (1) P's complaint was not directed at the diminution in their voting power but simply at the reduction in value of their shares by the new allotment at par. The disputed allotment was indeed prejudicial to P and T were in prima facie breach of their duties, not having considered the existing value of the shares, and (2) the court was not required to hear evidence prior to exercising its discretion or assessment. A hearing was only required where facts relevant to that assessment were disputed; there were no relevant averments to dispute P's claim regarding value and none of T's contentions, if proved, amounted to a proper justification for inflicting a reduction in the value of P's shareholding: (a) one prior instance of issuing at par did not amount to a consistent practice, particularly where that had been by agreement; (b) it was not sufficient that P had been given the opportunity to subscribe, because where a minority contested the allotment an insistence by the majority to proceed effectively amounted to coercing the provision of further funds, T not having previously paid dividends, under the threat of the minority being penalised by suffering a relative diminution in their capital value, and (c) there were no averments that there was any commercial reason for allotting the shares at par, and it was accepted that the original purpose for seeking capital (an acquisition) no longer existed.

PETTIE v. THOMSON PETTIE TUBE PRODUCTS LTD 2001 S.C. 431, Lord Eassie, OH.

5378. Books

Grier, Nicholas—Company Law. Greens Concise Scots Law. Paperback: £32.00. ISBN 0-414-01496-0. Paperback: £32.00. ISBN 0-414-01496-0. W.Green & Son.

Stewart, Andrew F.—Cautionary Obligations. Greens Practice Library. Hardback: £80.00. ISBN 0-414-01311-5. W.Green & Son.

COMPETITION LAW

5379. Competition Commission Appeals Tribunal—hearings—location of tribunal—appeal by company resident in Scotland

See COMPETITION LAW: Aberdeen Journals Ltd v. Director General of Fair Trading (Preliminary Hearing: Jurisdiction). §583

CONFLICT OF LAWS

5380. Choice of forum—contracts—exclusive jurisdiction clauses—interpretation

A, a Spanish shipbuilding company, raised an action against M, a firm of Scottish solicitors, seeking an order requiring them to release deposited funds being part of the price under a shipbuilding contract between A and clients of M. Article 15(a) provided for the governing of any disputes in connection with the contract exclusively by the High Court in London according to English law, and Art.19 provided that any further agreement signed by both parties to the contract should be deemed as embodied in the contract. M pled no jurisdiction. A argued (1) that an undertaking by M to release the deposited funds on the occurrence of certain events was a personal obligation independent of the shipbuilding contract, and (2) that there had been no clear and precise demonstration of the parties' consent to the operation of the prorogation clause in a question between them, such as was necessary for it to be given effect.

Held, dismissing the action, that (1) Art.19 was capable of introducing additional parties to the contract and placing ancillary obligations on them, and M's obligations were mere machinery for implementation of a supplementary agreement between the original parties to the contract, to which Art.15(a) could apply, and (2) there was no good reason to look for direct evidence of consensus concerning the application of Art.15(a) where M, strangers to the original contract, evinced their consent by seeking to rely on it and A as original parties had to be taken to have consented to it and to its application to any further agreement which became part of the original contract.

ASTILLEROS ZAMAKONA SA v. MacKINNONS 2002 S.L.T. 1206, Lord Macfadyen, OH.

5381. Choice of forum–contracts–exclusive jurisdiction clauses–interpretation

[Civil Jurisdiction and Judgments Act 1982 (c.27) Sch.4 Art.17; Civil Jurisdiction and Judgments Order 2001 (SI 2001 3929) Sch.2 Part II para.4.]

S, an insurer, appealed against a decision of the Paisley Sheriff Court that it had jurisdiction to determine an action brought by M, one of its insured. S had argued that the insurance policy contained a clause conferring exclusive jurisdiction on the English courts. The clause provided as follows: "This document shall be governed by the laws of England, whose courts shall have jurisdiction in any dispute arising hereunder".

Held, dismissing the appeal, that (1) the Civil Jurisdiction and Judgments Act 1982 Sch.4 Art.17 (now the Civil Jurisdiction and Judgments Order 2001 Sch.2 Part II para.4) did not prevent parties to a contract from agreeing to confer exclusive jurisdiction on the courts of one part of the United Kingdom, and (2) the question whether a clause conferred exclusive jurisdiction on a particular court was to be decided by applying the normal rules of contractual interpretation. It was important to read the contract as a whole, and the surrounding circumstances might have a bearing on the interpretation of the words used, *S&W Berisford Plc v. New Hampshire Insurance Co Ltd* [1990] 2 Q.B. 631, [1990] C.L.Y. 3721 applied and *Cannon Screen Entertainment Ltd v. Handmade Films (Distributors) Ltd* (Unreported, July 11, 1989) considered. Certain factors might indicate that the parties had agreed that a particular court would have exclusive jurisdiction, while other factors might show that there had been no such agreement. In the former category were the fact that a clause selecting a jurisdiction had been specifically agreed and the fact that the clause could be invoked by either party to the contract; in the latter category were the fact that the clause was contained in a printed form issued by one party to the other and the fact that exclusivity would in practice impose an obligation falling substantially on the party to whom such a form had been issued. The clause in the instant case did not confer exclusive jurisdiction on the English courts. The natural meaning of the clause did not go that far. Furthermore, the clause appeared in a printed form of policy issued to M, and the main relevance of the clause had to be to actions brought by M against S or the underwriters.

McGOWAN v. SUMMIT AT LLOYDS 2002 S.L.T. 1258, Lord Reed, Lady Cosgrove, Lord Marnoch, Ex Div.

5382. Choice of forum–sist–proceedings in another jurisdiction–motion after record closed

See CIVIL PROCEDURE: Marodi Service de D Mialich v. Mikkal Myklebusthaug Rederi A/S. §5366

5383. Choice of forum–trade marks–domain names–test for establishing jurisdiction

[Brussels Convention on Jurisdiction and the Enforcement of Judgments in Civil and Commercial Matters 1968 Art.5(3).]

S issued a motion for the recall of an order for interim interdict awarded to B. B, the owner of a newspaper, had registered a trade mark which included the words "business a.m.". It provided an online service at its website under the domain name www.businessam.co.uk. It had argued that S had a history of using domain names with the aim of passing himself off as other organisations and that he would establish or have established websites which would pass themselves off as its website. S, who was domiciled in Greece, had argued that (1) the Brussels Convention 1968 Art.5(3) applied only to completed delicts, and (2) B's contentions did not raise a prima facie case in relation to jurisdiction

Held, refusing the motion, that (1) Art.5(3) applied to threatened delicts as well as to completed delicts. It was vitally important that the courts of a country should be able to take effective action in respect of any civil wrong of a delictual nature that was threatened within that country without having to resort to a foreign court. In addition, it was often difficult to draw a clear distinction between a threatened delict and a completed one, and (2) the court had jurisdiction over S to interdict a threatened wrong that was likely to produce a harmful event within Scotland. The crucial issue was the location of the wrong that was said to have been committed by way of the internet. Jurisdiction could be established if it could be shown that the infringer's website was intended to be of significant interest in the country in which jurisdiction was claimed. In the instant case, an inference might readily be drawn that S intended to do the acts contemplated by B and since it was obvious that those acts were intended to have their main effect in Scotland, the Scottish courts had jurisdiction.

BONNIER MEDIA LTD v. SMITH; *sub nom.* BONNIER MEDIA LTD v. KESTREL TRADING CORP 2002 S.C.L.R. 977, Lord Drummond Young, OH.

5384. Choice of law—contracts—factors to be considered in establishing governing law of a contract

[Rome Convention on the law applicable to contractual obligations 1980 Art.4.]

M reclaimed against the decision by the Lord Ordinary (2001 S.C. 716) that it was subject to the jurisdiction of the Court of Session in an action brought against it by C.

Held, refusing the reclaiming motion, that the place of business of the main performer of a contract was crucial in establishing the governing law of a contract in circumstances where the Rome Convention 1980 Art.4 applied, and it was only to be disregarded where there were clear factors in favour of another country's law. It was clear that the 1980 Convention had been intended to change the way in which courts in a number of countries determined the law which governed a contract. Under Art.4 para.2, the appropriate country was ascertained not by reference to where performance took place but by reference to the performer's place of business "at the time of conclusion of the contract". However, Art.4 para.5 stated that the presumption in para.2 was to be disregarded if it appeared from all the circumstances that the contract was more closely connected with another country. There are two distinct schools of thought as to the interrelationships of para.2 and para.5 which have been the subject of discussion and objection, *Definitely Maybe (Touring) Ltd v. Marek Lieberberg Konzertagentur GmbH (No.2)* [2001] 1 W.L.R. 1745, [2001] C.L.Y. 797 and *Credit Lyonnais v. New Hampshire Insurance Co Ltd* [1997] 2 Lloyd's Rep. 1, [1997] C.L.Y. 873 considered. The purpose of Art.4 had been to make the place of business of the performer a crucial factor in determining the country with which the contract had the closest connection. If it had been intended that special significance was to be attached to the place where performance took place it could have been readily incorporated into Art.4, but this was not done, which therefore suggested a move away from this approach. One had to give consideration to the social and economic factors mentioned in the Report on the Convention on the law applicable to contractual obligations by Mario Giuliano, Professor, University of Milan, and Paul Lagarde, Professor, University of Paris I (1980 OJ C282/1). Although the place of performance of the contract was of relevance, it may be only one of a number of considerations under Art.4 para.5. The presumption in Art.4 para.2 was not to be disregarded unless consideration of para.5 demonstrated clear factors favouring the law of another country.

CALEDONIA SUBSEA LTD v. MICOPERI SRL 2002 S.L.T. 1022, Lord Cullen L.P., Lord Cameron of Lochbroom, Lord Marnoch, 1 Div.

5385. Domicile—acquisition of domicile of choice—intention

A Thai citizen living in Aberdeen raised an action for, inter alia, divorce against her husband, a UK citizen living in Kuala Lumpur. The husband lodged a preliminary plea to the jurisdiction, arguing that his wife had not established domicile in Scotland. The sheriff repelled the preliminary plea, finding that the wife had accepted her husband's domicile and her domicile of choice was Scotland. The husband appealed to the sheriff principal, arguing, as was conceded by his wife, that there was insufficient evidence before the sheriff to support the finding that he was Scottish.

Held, refusing the appeal, that (1) it appeared that the sheriff's conclusion that the pursuer was domiciled in Scotland was based to some extent on that erroneous finding and the matter was at large for the appeal court, and (2) on the balance of probabilities, by the time the action began the pursuer had decided to reside in Scotland without limit of time, having, inter alia, chosen to give the child of the marriage UK citizenship and chosen on the parties' separation to return to Aberdeen rather than return to Thailand.

MARSH v. MARSH 2002 S.L.T. (Sh Ct) 87, Sir Stephen ST Young, Sheriff Principal, Sh Ct.

5386. Domicile—acquisition of domicile of choice—intention

In R's action for declarator that certain holograph writings of D were valid testamentary writings, a preliminary proof was held on D's domicile at his death in December 1999, aged 95. D's domicile of origin was Scotland, he had travelled extensively during his working life as a marine engineer and retired to live in Falkirk in 1964. In 1978 he moved with his wife (W) to Bournemouth. The evidence for the defenders, principally from one H, was that the climate there suited D's health better, that some of W's family moved with them, that D said on various occasions that he would not move again, that he purchased a grave there capable of holding four caskets of remains and W was buried there when she died in 1987, and that while D was proud of being Scottish, he only visited Scotland once or twice after his move south and never expressed a desire to return. R led evidence that D kept a bank account in Scotland and continued to instruct Scottish solicitors, who drew up a will in 1996 in which D declared his Scottish domicile, that D missed Scotland and that his visits were more frequent than claimed by H.

Held, finding that D had acquired a domicile of choice in England, that the most significant evidence was D's stated intention never to move again, and the lack of any contrary indication. It was also significant that he did not return after W's death and declared in his will that he was to be buried beside her. The declaration as to domicile had been carried over from previous wills and it was not clear whether it had originally been made when D was living in Scotland, in any event such declarations were not by themselves conclusive. The question was whether, having regard to the evidence, it could be said that D intended his home in Bournemouth to be his permanent home where, all other things being equal, he would end his days, *Inland Revenue Commissioners v. Bullock* [1976] 1 W.L.R. 1178, [1976] C.L.Y. 1414, *Udny v. Udny* (1866-69) L.R. 1 Sc. 441 applied, and at least by the time of W's death, that was D's intention.

REDDINGTON v. RIACH'S EXECUTOR 2002 S.L.T. 537, Lord Clarke, OH.

5387. Foreign judgments—enforcement—declarator that foreign decree fraudulently obtained—competency

[Civil Jurisdiction and Judgments Act 1982 (c.27) Sch.6, Art.18.]

C, a director of D, sought declarator and interdict against F, a merchant bank, enforcing a decree obtained against C in a US court, on grounds that decree had been obtained through a conspiracy to unseat C from the board of D and through the perjury of A and H, witnesses before the court. Subsequent attempts to raise the matter before the US courts had failed and an action before the English courts was rejected. F argued that (1) C's action was simply an attempt to reopen matters dealt with before the US courts and rejected in England and a failed litigant should not be permitted to continue to raise the same issue before the courts; (2) there was no legal wrong capable of being interdicted where all F were doing was enforcing a foreign decree by action conform and in the absence of a legal wrong there was no jurisdiction in the Scottish courts. While the plea of no jurisdiction had not been led at the outset it could still be taken as a matter of competency also; (3) the declarators sought were incompetent since they sought to challenge the validity of foreign decrees, and (4) if the court had any jurisdiction to entertain as a matter of competency and relevancy an attack on a foreign decree by reason of fraud, that fraud had to be extrinsic and not intrinsic, see *Mackintosh's Trustee v. Stewart's Trustees* 8 F. 467, and C's averments of perjury at best instructed a case of intrinsic fraud and were irrelevant. C argued that jurisdiction had been admitted in the original record of the action and then withdrawn.

Held, allowing proof before answer under deletion of certain of F's pleas, that (1) jurisdiction was established by reason of the threatened wrong in Scotland of the manifest injustice to be suffered by C if he was correct that the US decree was fraudulently obtained. The question was also settled by F's initial admission, which had been withdrawn improperly; F could be taken to have consented to or prorogated jurisdiction, and while in terms of the Civil Jurisdiction and Judgments Act 1982 Sch.6, Art.18 it was legitimate to plead both no jurisdiction and a substantive defence, it would create manifest unfairness to allow F to plead a substantive defence and then take up a plea to jurisdiction later; (2) both Scots and English law recognised it was a relevant defence to an attempt to enforce a decree in a foreign court to allege extrinsic fraud or other deceit directly linked with obtaining the decree (*Mackintosh's Trustee*), and assuming C's averments disclosed a relevant case of extrinsic fraud capable of yielding an inference of conspiracy or collusion they would constitute a relevant defence; (3) the declarators sought were competent: the authorities supported the use of declarator in a positive or a negative sense to assert a matter that could competently be a defence to another action, which was precisely what C was attempting; (4) C had made out a relevant case: it was not possible at this stage to hold C's averments of perjury on the part of A and H, which referred to evidence apparently not available earlier, incapable of yielding an inference of collusion and conspiracy, and (5) where the whole case was perilled on a question of injustice for the reasons pled, and where the enforcement being challenged was being threatened in Scotland, it would be wholly inequitable to deny in principle the remedy of interdict to prevent that enforcement.

CLARKE v. FENNOSCANDIA LTD (NO.2) 2001 S.L.T. 1311, Lord Johnston, OH.

5388. **Jurisdiction–contracts–consumer contracts–jurisdiction–purpose outside trade or profession**

[Civil Jurisdiction and Judgments Act 1982 (c.27) Sch.8 r.3.]

S, a firm of solicitors, raised an action of payment in Glasgow sheriff court for services rendered to a client for whom they had acted in proceedings concerning his disqualification as a company director. The defender had recently moved to England and argued that the court did not have jurisdiction because the contract between the parties was a consumer contract and required to be raised in the court in which he was domiciled.

Held, putting the case out by order, that (1) the applicable test when considering the Civil Jurisdiction and Judgments Act 1982 Sch.8 rule 3 was whether the purpose of the contract was to satisfy the needs in terms of private consumption of the person being supplied with the goods and services (*Benincasa v. Dentalkit Srl (C269/95)* [1997] E.C.R. I-3767, [1997] C.L.Y. 888 followed; *Chris Hart (Business Sales) Ltd v. Niven* 1992 S.L.T. (Sh. Ct.) 53, [1992] C.L.Y. 5931 and *BJ Mann (Advertising) Ltd v. ACE Welding & Fabrications Ltd* 1994 S.C.L.R. 763, [1994] C.L.Y. 5958 not followed) and evidence would be required to establish whether S had been instructed in that connection or in furtherance of the defender's business interests, and (2) the defender was entitled to fair notice of the case against him and to be told how S's account was made up, even where the matter had to go to taxation, but S had failed to provide the necessary specification.

SEMPLE FRASER WS v. QUAYLE 2002 S.L.T. (Sh Ct) 33, JA Taylor, Sh Ct (Glasgow and Strathkelvin).

CONSTITUTIONAL LAW

5389. Devolution issues–incompatibility of legislation under which minuter prosecuted–incompatibility as devolution issue

See HUMAN RIGHTS: Stevens (Andrew) v. HM Advocate. §5843

5390. Public authorities–ethical standards–stipulated time limit

ETHICAL STANDARDS IN PUBLIC LIFE ETC. (SCOTLAND) ACT 2000 (STIPULATED TIME LIMIT) ORDER 2002, SSI 2002 55; made under the Ethical Standards in Public Life etc. (Scotland) Act 2000 s.3. In force: March 11, 2002; £1.50.

This Order stipulates the time limit within which devolved public bodies are required to submit draft codes of conduct for their members for consideration by the Scottish Ministers. In terms of this Order all such bodies are required to submit their draft Code within the period ending on July 11, 2002.

5391. Scottish devolution–cross border public authorities

SCOTLAND ACT 1998 (CROSS-BORDER PUBLIC AUTHORITIES) (ADAPTATION OF FUNCTIONS ETC.) (AMENDMENT) ORDER 2002, SI 2002 2636; made under the Scotland Act 1998 s.89, s.113. In force: October 23, 2002; £1.75.

This Order amends the Scotland Act 1998 Cross-Border Public Authorities) (Adaptation of Functions etc.) Order 1999 (SI 1999 1747) in relation to the Meat and Livestock Commission. It provides for part of the levy raised under a levy scheme confirmed under the Agriculture Act 1967 s.13 to be determined as a Scottish levy by the Secretary of State, the National Assembly for Wales and the Scottish Ministers acting jointly, that the function of giving directions to the Commission in respect of spending the Scottish levy will fall to the Scottish Ministers alone, and the function of giving directions in respect of the spending of the remainder of the levy will fall to the Secretary of State and the National Assembly for Wales acting jointly.

5392. Scottish devolution–legislative competence

SCOTLAND ACT 1998 (MODIFICATIONS OF SCHEDULE 5) ORDER 2002, SI 2002 1629; made under the Scotland Act 1998 s.30. In force: June 27, 2002; £1.75.

This Order amends the Scotland Act 1998 Sch.5 which is concerned with matters outwith the legislative competence of the Scottish Parliament. The Order permits the Scottish Parliament to legislate in relation to the promotion and construction of railways, which start, end and remain in Scotland.

5393. Scottish devolution–Scottish Ministers–transfer of functions

SCOTLAND ACT 1998 (TRANSFER OF FUNCTIONS TO THE SCOTTISH MINISTERS ETC.) ORDER 2002, SI 2002 1630; made under the Scotland Act 1998 s.63, s.113, s.124. In force: June 27, 2002; £1.75.

This Order, which amends the Scotland Act 1998, provides for specified functions of a Minister of the Crown so far as they are exercisable by that Minister in or as regards Scotland, to be exercisable by the Scottish Ministers concurrently with the Minister of the Crown. It provides that the functions of providing financial assistance conferred on a Minister of the Crown by the Industrial Development Act 1982 shall be exercisable in or as regards Scotland by the Scottish Ministers concurrently with a Minister of the Crown. The exercise of the functions is subject to the restriction specified in the Schedule to the Order that the functions may be exercised only in respect of shipping services carrying passengers between the Highlands and Islands of Scotland and Northern Ireland.

5394. Scottish Parliamentary Standards Commissioner 2002 (asp 16)

This Act of the Scottish Parliament establishes a Scottish Parliamentary Standards Commissioner who investigates complaints about the conduct of members of the Parliament and then reports upon the outcome of such investigations to the Parliament.

5395. Secretary of State–directions–national security

WATER INDUSTRY (SCOTLAND) ACT 2002 (DIRECTIONS IN THE INTERESTS OF NATIONAL SECURITY) ORDER 2002, SI 2002 1264; made under the Scotland Act 1998 s.104, s.112, s.113. In force: May 31, 2002; £1.75.

This Order makes provision consequential on the Water Industry (Scotland) Act 2002 which established Scottish Water and repealed the Local Government etc. (Scotland) Act 1994 s.117 which enabled the Secretary of State to give directions to the new water and sewerage authorities in the interests of national security or for mitigating the effects of any civil emergency. The purpose of this Order is to confer on the Secretary of State and the Scottish Ministers the power to give directions to Scottish Water in the interests of national security or for mitigating the effects of any civil emergency. The Order enables the Secretary of State, after consultation with Scottish Water, to give it directions in the interests of national security or for mitigating the effects of any civil emergency which may occur or directions to do or omit to do a specified thing, in the interests of national security or for mitigating the effects of any civil emergency which has or may occur. It also makes provision as regards the disclosure of directions. Any person who contravenes the disclosure provision is guilty of an offence and liable on conviction on indictment to imprisonment for up to 2 years and/or a fine.

5396. Separation of powers–challenge to decision following Lord Advocate's reference–complaint that Lord Advocate and court acted ultra vires

H, who was charged with rape, lodged a devolution minute arguing that the Lord Advocate and the court in *Lord Advocate's Reference (No.1 of 2001)* 2002 S.L.T. 466, [2002] 5 C.L. 765, had acted as legislatures, because between the two the law relating to rape in Scotland was changed, and this could only be done by the Scottish Ministers and the Scottish Parliament.

Held, refusing the minute, that what H was complaining against was the court's majority decision in response to a point of law raised by the Lord Advocate's reference and the decision did not fall, even remotely, within the definition of a devolution issue.

HM ADVOCATE v. H 2002 S.L.T. 1380, Lord Maclean, HCJ.

CONSTRUCTION LAW

5397. Adjudication–awards–enforcement–error of law–decision within adjudicator's jurisdiction

[Housing Grants, Construction and Regeneration Act 1996 (c.53) s.110, s.111.]

S supplied timber to C under three contracts. S applied for payment under the terms of the contracts but C did not pay. S therefore took the disputes to adjudication and the adjudicator ruled that C had failed to give adequate notice under the Housing Grants Construction and Regeneration Act 1996 s.110 and s.111 in time, with the result that he did not need to examine the merits of the dispute provided that S had demanded payment as provided for by the contracts. The adjudicator awarded S the sums claimed and S sought to enforce the decision. C defended the enforcement proceedings on the ground, inter alia, that the adjudicator had been wrong in law when refusing to examine the merits of the dispute.

Held, giving judgment for S, that errors of fact or law by an adjudicator were not grounds for refusing enforcement unless the error meant that the decision was beyond the adjudicator's jurisdiction. On the facts of the instant case, although the adjudicator had been wrong in law in his interpretation of the notice requirements of s.110 and s.111, in that failure to give a notice on time did not prevent him from looking at the merits of the dispute, or mean that S did not have to prove its entitlement to payment, those errors were within the adjudicator's jurisdiction. The decision reached was therefore intra vires and valid as against C.

SL TIMBER SYSTEMS LTD v. CARILLION CONSTRUCTION LTD 2002 S.L.T. 997, Lord Macfadyen, OH.

5398. Adjudication–jurisdiction–consideration of more than one dispute in single adjudication

On a contract for road improvement works, disputes arose between the parties that were referred to an adjudicator under the terms of the contract. The adjudicator ordered payment by B to L. B then brought proceedings to enforce the award. L challenged the adjudicator's decision, arguing that he had exceeded his jurisdiction by considering more than one dispute in a single adjudication, that he had decided questions that only arose after rescission of the contract and that he had failed properly to deal with the submission that there was no entitlement to payment without certification.

Held, granting a summary decree to B, that the question of whether there was one single or several separate disputes was a question of fact for the adjudicator and, in deciding that all of the matters referred to him amounted to one single dispute he had not exceeded his jurisdiction. The adjudicator could not have jurisdiction over matters that had arisen after the contract had been rescinded. It was necessary for him therefore to decide whether the contract had been rescinded and when that had happened. The adjudicator could decide that there had been no rescission and then go on to decide all disputes but in the present case he had made no decision on the question of a rescission. That was an error since such a decision was necessary to decide whether there was jurisdiction or not. L had conceded that this issue did not affect B's entitlement to the amount awarded by the adjudicator. A letter from the engineer providing that payment for work was to be 30 days after certification had varied the contractual provision for certification and payment. L argued that this did not comply with the statutory provisions. The adjudicator's decision to reject this argument, although one that might be wrong in law, was one that he was entitled to make and there was no question that his decision exceeded his jurisdiction.

BARR LTD v. LAW MINING LTD 2003 S.L.T. 488, Lord Macfadyen, OH.

5399. Adjudication–summary decree–action for payment of adjudicator's award– competency

[Housing Grants, Construction and Regeneration Act 1996 (c.53) s.108, s.111.]

C raised an action against H for payment of £245,469.24 awarded by an adjudicator, A, in a dispute under a construction contract. C moved for summary decree. H argued that (1) C's motion was incompetent as the arbitration provisions of the contract did not allow the arbiter to take account of a final decree of the court pronounced in accordance with A's decision; (2) H were entitled to withhold payment as they had a claim in liquidate damages against C for £420,000 and had a right of retention, and (3) they had served a valid notice of intention to withhold payment under the Housing Grants, Construction and Regeneration Act 1996 s.111 in respect of A's determination, as that represented a "sum due under the contract".

Held, granting summary decree, that (1) there was no incompatibility between any decree in C's favour pronounced in the present action and the provisional character of A's award where the whole point of adjudication under a construction contract in terms of s.108 of the 1996 Act was to obtain payment of money on a provisional basis, C was seeking recognition that the parties were contractually bound to implement A's decision, and any decision of the court had no effect on the final determination of the dispute by the arbiter other than taking into account any payments that had been made in giving effect to his determination; (2) H's alleged right of retention could have been raised before A and the fact that they did not do so did not entitle them to raise it now for the purpose of depriving the award of its enforceability, and (3) s.111 was intended to apply only to the withholding of payments in respect of which the contract provided a final date for payment and did not apply to payments due in consequence of an adjudicator's decision.

CONSTRUCTION CENTRE GROUP LTD v. HIGHLAND COUNCIL 2002 S.L.T. 1274, Lord Macfadyen, OH.

5400. Building regulations–fire precautions–energy conservation

BUILDINGS STANDARDS (SCOTLAND) AMENDMENT REGULATIONS 2001 AMENDMENT REGULATIONS 2002, SSI 2002 40; made under the Building (Scotland) Act 1959 s.3, s.24, s.29, Sch.4. In force: March 3, 2002; £1.75.

These Regulations, which make amendments to the transitional provisions of the Building Standards (Scotland) Amendment Regulations 2001 (SSI 2001 320), provide that the 2001 Regulations shall not apply to conservatories where the contract has been entered into before those Regulations come into force on March 4, 2002 providing that the construction work begins on or before May 31, 2002 and is completed on or before July 1, 2002.

5401. Construction contracts–arbitration–further reference after award– jurisdiction of arbiter

S and D, parties to a building contract, appointed J, an arbiter, in terms of a joint deed of appointment to hear disputes which had arisen. J pronounced final decree arbitral in S's favour on August 26, 1999. In March 2001 D intimated a claim against S arising out of the contract and sought J's appointment under the deed. J accepted the appointment. S sought interdict against him from proceeding with any further arbitrations in terms of the deed, arguing that he was functus and had no jurisdiction. D argued that the deed of appointment placed no limit on the disputes which could be referred to J, and that the action was incompetent as review of the actings of an arbiter required to be sought by judicial review proceedings where there was a bona fide dispute as to jurisdiction.

Held, granting interdict, that J's power to resolve disputes between the parties ended on the issue of the decree arbitral in 1999, at which point he was functus officio, and in purporting thereafter to make the orders that he did, he was not subject to the supervisory jurisdiction of the court but was someone who could be prevented from acting unlawfully by means of ordinary procedures, *Naylor v. Greenacres Curling Ltd* 2001 S.L.T. 1092 distinguished.

SIM GROUP LTD v. JACK 2002 S.L.T. 847, Lord Clarke, OH.

5402. Construction contracts–breach of contract–defective performance by subcontractor–contractor's voluntary assumption of repair expenses– contractor's entitlement to compensation

In S's action seeking compensation for costs incurred by repairing latent defects in four retaining walls built by A, A appealed against the sheriff principal's decision, reversing the sheriff, to allow a proof before answer. S's predecessor had entered into an environment improvement agreement with a landowner, X, in respect of works which included the construction of the walls, the contract for which was let by S to A. X subsequently intimated to S that the brickwork in the walls was spalling and S instructed repairs and sought damages for the cost. A argued that as S had undertaken the work voluntarily, there was no loss.

Held, dismissing the appeal, that S were suing on the original building contract in respect of defective performance which they were fully entitled to do, and their assumption of the responsibility for the expenditure at the instigation of X was simply a short cut approach to what otherwise could have happened, namely X suing S for repairs to the wall who in turn would have founded on breach of the building contract by A in order to claim relief in damages.

SCOTTISH ENTERPRISE v. ARCHIBALD RUSSEL OF DENNY LTD 2002 S.L.T. 519, Lord Johnston, Lord Cameron of Lochbroom, Lord Wheatley, Ex Div.

5403. Construction contracts—breach of contract—liquidate damages—whether penalty clause

C was the employer and S the building contractor under a building contract for the construction of an hotel. The contract provided that the date for completion of the contract was January 25, 1999. The dispute between the parties centred on whether, as argued by C, that the contractual date remained the completion date or whether, as argued by S, they were entitled to an extension of time. If an extension of time was allowed, S argued that they were entitled to a four-week extension as certified by the architect and also to a further five-week extension awarded by the adjudicator to whom the matter was originally referred. C made monetary claims for liquidate and ascertained damages in respect of the extension period granted by the architect, repayment of a payment made by them to S which would not have been made if the adjudicator had not awarded the additional five-week extension and for repayment of a sum of direct loss and expense certified by the architect as a consequence of the extension period that he had granted. C maintained that S was not entitled to an extension of time as they had not complied with the procedures set out in cl.13.8 of the contract which required S to give adequate notice to C in the event that an architect's instruction would be likely to result in delay in the completion of the contract. S argued that cl.13.8 amounted to a penalty clause and as such was unenforceable. They argued that its terms deprived them of extensions of time that they would otherwise be entitled to and left them exposed to claims for liquidate and ascertained damages. S argued that in order for the clause to operate, S would have had to have formed an opinion that the extension of time would be required and that no such averments had been made by C. S further pled acquiescence by C in the failure to meet the contracted completion date. C pled that S's averments were irrelevant and that the clause was not a penalty clause. C argued that the necessity for S to have formed such an opinion for the operation of the clause to take effect would be to deprive the clause of its intended use.

Held, putting the case out by order for a discussion of further procedure, if any, before allowing proof before answer under certain exclusions that (1) for a contractual provision to be regarded as a penalty, it must stipulate for the payment by one party to the contract to another of a sum of money in respect of a breach of the contract, which sum must not constitute a genuine pre-estimate of the losses likely to result from such a breach, but should rather act oppressively or punitively; (2) the liquidate damages arising from cl.13.8 were for the delay in completion of the works and not for S's failure to follow the procedures under the clause, albeit that by complying with the procedures under the clause, S would have avoided liability for the liquidate damages and been entitled to an extension of time; (3) the effect of the clause was to require S to apply their mind, upon receipt of instructions from the architect, as to whether the implementation of such instructions would affect the price or time involved in completing the contract, and that S, having failed to relevantly aver that they had so applied their mind and reached the opinion that such an extension was not required, C could be considered as having relevantly averred that S had breached their obligations under the clause; (4) cl.13.8 could not be deemed to be inapplicable to architect's instructions for the expenditure of provisional sums, and (5) it was appropriate for the averments relating to acquiescence, personal bar and waiver to be remitted to proof before answer.

CITY INN LTD v. SHEPHERD CONSTRUCTION LTD 2002 S.L.T. 781, Lord Macfadyen, OH.

5404. **Construction contracts–causation–elements required to establish global claim for loss and expense**

L sought the dismissal of a claim for loss and expense instituted by J arising out of the alleged breach of a construction contract.

Held, repelling L's plea for dismissal and allowing J a proof before answer, that in circumstances where a global claim for loss and expense was advanced, it was necessary to demonstrate that all aspects contributing to the loss claimed were occurrences for which the defender was liable. A failure to establish that a specific event previously found to have contributed to the global loss was an event for which the defender was liable would undermine the global claim. Whilst the global claim would fail in such circumstances it did not follow that no claim would succeed at all. It might prove possible to establish a causal connection between particular losses and particular events or to make some logical apportionment of an element of the global loss with respect to those causative events for which the defender had been held liable. In such a case causation had to be approached in a common sense manner, *John Holland Construction & Engineering Pty Ltd v. Kvaerner RJ Brown Pty Ltd* 82 B.L.R. 81, [1997] C.L.Y. 932 considered.

JOHN DOYLE CONSTRUCTION LTD v. LAING MANAGEMENT (SCOTLAND) LTD [2002] B.L.R. 393, Lord Macfadyen, OH.

5405. **Construction contracts–novation–nature of party suffering alleged loss under tripartite agreement**

T and C entered into an agreement for the design and construction of a leisure development. A deed of appointment between T and B expressly stated to run from the date upon which B started to provide services. The deed empowered T to instruct B to enter into a novation agreement. B, C and T subsequently entered into the agreement. B then brought an action against C for payment of fees. C counterclaimed in respect of alleged breaches of contract by B, raising issues as to the meaning and effect of the novation agreement. C argued that B was in breach of the agreement with T and that C's losses were to be treated as those that would have been suffered by T prior to the date of the novation agreement.

Held, giving judgment for B, that C's argument meant that the novation agreement produced a tripartite relationship by which C engaged B to render services and give advice to T. T was therefore the party that had sustained the losses as the effect of the novation agreement was that B had agreed to perform the appointment for the future with C as its client so that C could not claim that it had sustained losses arising from an alleged breach by B before the date of the novation agreement.

BLYTH & BLYTH LTD v. CARILLION CONSTRUCTION LTD 2002 S.L.T. 961, Lord Eassie, OH.

5406. **Construction contracts–payments–division of payment between parties to consortium agreement**

[Court of Session Act 1988 (c.36) s.47(2).]

V, a company, raised an action against another M, with whom it was in a construction consortium agreement for the construction under a separate contract of a sludge treatment centre for a third company, S. The consortium agreement provided in Art.6.3 that each party would be liable for the provision and performance of any ancillary supplies and services necessary to complete its part of the installation of the centre, in Art.6.4 for a provisional rule for the allocation of the cost of such supplies and services in the event of disagreement, in Art.6.5 for the proportion of the contract price due to each party to be subject to any adjustments in respect of variations to the price pursuant to the provisions of the contract, and in Art.14.1 that payments under the construction contract should be promptly distributed to the parties, subject only to such adjustments as were provided for in the consortium agreement. V and M had a joint bank account into which payments under the construction contract were transferred. S issued two payment certificates in November and December 2001 stating that certain moneys were due to V and M respectively. M refused to consent to the release from the joint account of the moneys due to V, submitting claims against V for certain ancillary services provided by M which M argued properly fell under V's part of the project. V obtained ex parte interim interdict to stop M or those acting on M's behalf from preventing or otherwise hindering the release of the moneys. At a further hearing M sought recall and V sought an order under the Court of Session Act 1988 s.47(2) of ordaining M to consent to the transfer of the moneys. M argued inter alia that "adjustments" in Art.14 did not have the same meaning as in Art.6.5 and was sufficiently wide to cover division of the cost of ancillary services under Art.6.4, and, in relation to balance of convenience, that V could have referred the dispute to adjudication for a quick decision.

Held, refusing the motion for recall of interim interdict and granting an order under s.47(2), that (1) under Art.14.1 the moneys received from S had to be distributed as quickly as possible in accordance with the certificates issued, apart from the exception covered by Art.6.5 which did not apply in this case, Art.6.3 and Art.6.4 dealt with the cost of ancillary supplies and services as between V and M and were not concerned with the contract price, and accordingly fell outwith the exception to Art.14, and V had a clear prima facie case for interdict; (2) the balance of convenience also favoured V, having regard to the relative strength of the parties' cases and the maintenance of the status quo, which in a case involving payments due under a commercial contract, especially a construction contract, should be understood as the making of payments under the contract as they fell due according to its terms; (3) the further order sought by V related to the subject matter of the cause in terms of s.47(2), and for the same reasons as related to interim interdict V had made out a prima facie case, and (4) the same dynamic concept of the status quo applied and granting the order did not foreclose the disputed issue between the parties.

VA TECH WABAG UK LTD v. MORGAN EST (SCOTLAND) LTD 2002 S.L.T. 1290, Lord Drummond Young, OH.

5407. Construction contracts–payments–interim certificates issued by architect–sums due under contract

[Housing Grants, Construction and Regeneration Act 1996 (c.53) s.111.]

C, contractors, sought payment from B, its employers, under a construction contract of a sum due in terms of an interim certificate issued by A, the architect. B argued (1) that A's view was indicative, not authoritative, and what was due was not necessarily what the architect said was due, and (2) it was not necessary for them to serve a notice of intention to withhold payment in terms of the Housing Grants, Construction and Regeneration Act 1996 s.111 as the sum sued for was not "due under the contract", as the interim certificate was conclusive and C had not given notice of what works they said entitled them to payment.

Held, putting the case out for a case management conference, that (1) the sum due in terms of the certificate was due under the contract, as to reach that sum required use of the contractual mechanism, and while A's certificate was not conclusive evidence that the works for which the contractors sought payment were in accordance with the contract, this did not preclude the sum being due under the contract, *SL Timber Systems Ltd v. Carillion Construction Ltd* 2002 S.L.T. 997, [2002] 3 C.L. 674 distinguished, and (2) if B wished to withhold payment because the works did not conform to contract they should have served a notice under s.111, and C had pled all that was required of them given that failure, *Beaufort Developments (NI) Ltd v. Gilbert-Ash (NI) Ltd* [1999] 1 A.C. 266, [1998] C.L.Y. 5055 distinguished.

CLARK CONTRACTS LTD v. BURRELL CO (CONSTRUCTION MANAGEMENT) LTD (NO.1); *sub nom.* CLARK CONTRACTS LTD v. BURRELL COLLECTION CO (CONSTRUCTION MANAGEMENT) LTD 2002 S.L.T. (Sh Ct) 103, JA Taylor, Sh Ct (Glasgow and Strathkelvin).

5408. Construction contracts–subcontracts–subsequent actings of parties irrelevant in determining terms

M were the main contractors working on a development called "The Lighthouse". C were employed as subcontractors. A dispute arose under the subcontract and C raised an action seeking £400,000 from M. The main contract contained an arbitration clause and M argued that the same clause also applied to the subcontract. M argued that C's post-contractual conduct indicated that C also considered the contract to be governed by those conditions.

Held, putting the case out by order for discussion of further procedure, that all that could be concluded from C's post-contractual conduct was that they believed that at least some of the main contract terms were incorporated into the subcontract. That belief was erroneous and it could not be suggested that C, in acting upon it, had altered their position nor would it preclude them from arguing that arbitration was not a contractual term.

CAMERON (SCOTLAND) LTD v. MELVILLE DUNDAS LTD 2001 S.C.L.R. 691, Lord Hamilton, OH.

5409. Construction contracts–subcontracts–title to sue–undisclosed principal

See CIVIL PROCEDURE: Karl Construction Ltd v. Palisade Properties Plc. §5322

5410. Books

Hamilton, W.; Kennedy, P.; Kilpatrick, A.; Mclaughlin, R.–Scottish Building Regulations. Paperback: £27.50. ISBN 0-632-04945-6. Blackwell Science (UK).

Ramsey, Lynn; Macaulay, Mark–Construction Law. Greens Practice Library. Paperback: £65.00. ISBN 0-414-01348-4. W. Green & Son.

Ramsey, Lynn; Macaulay, Mark–Construction and Procurement Law. Greens Practice Library. Paperback: £85.00. ISBN 0-414-01348-4. W. Green & Son.

CONSUMER LAW

5411. Consumer credit–credit hire agreement–enforceabilty–exempt agreement

[Consumer Credit Act 1974 (c.39) s.16(5), s.127(3); Consumer Credit (Agreements) Regulations 1983 (SI 1983 1553) Art.3(1); Unfair Terms in Consumer Contracts Regulations 1994 (SI 1994 3159) Reg.7.]

In L's action for damages against M arising from a road accident, M accepted liability and agreement was reached on quantum save for the cost of hire by L of a replacement vehicle. L had entered into an agreement with H, a hire company, under which H agreed to pursue M for the cost of the hire. It was agreed that this was a consumer credit agreement and that unless it was an exempt agreement it was unenforceable by H as it did not comply with the Consumer Credit Act 1974. M argued inter alia that it was not exempt as it was envisaged that the period during which the claim was being pursued could exceed 12 months, and it did not expressly provide that the number of payments was not to exceed four. M also argued that the elements in the costs beyond the basic hire, for delivery of the vehicle and uplifts for financing the claim and legal services, were not recoverable as they were unreasonable, and that L had made no payments to H who had a policy not to pursue payments and that averments concerning an insurance policy were irrelevant. L argued that the rate charged was comparable with the National Hire tariffs and that the legal services were financed by a separate insurance policy and not through the hire agreement.

Held, allowing proof before answer, that (1) the agreement had to be read as a whole and was exempt under s.16(5) and the Consumer Credit (Agreements) Regulations 1983 Art.3(1). Condition 14 clearly stated that after 26 weeks H would "become liable to pay" and it did not matter whether H actually demanded payment. Condition 9(vi), which required any hire charges paid to L to be paid to H, did not entitle H to be paid twice and it was clear that condition 14 provided for a long stop date when payment would be due no matter what had gone before or that the pursuit of recovery from the third party had not reached a conclusion. The agreement did not fall foul of the number of payments condition in Art.3(1). The agreement provided for one payment of all the hire charges, and the fact that the number of payments in fact made exceeded that did not cause the agreement to cease to be exempt. The status of the agreement was determined at its commencement and its exempt status could not be lost. As the terms of the agreement were clear on the issue of exemption, the Unfair Terms in Consumer Contracts Regulations 1994 Reg.7 did not apply; (2) without proof, it was not possible to hold that L was only entitled to payments on the local spot rate and both sides had made sufficient averments for proof to be allowed, and (3) the question to be answered was not whether payments had been made but whether loss had been sustained, and there was nothing to prevent M asserting that notwithstanding the terms of the hire and credit agreement, L would never be called upon to make a payment and would have sustained no loss. M had failed to make relevant averments to support his belief that H would not demand payment. It was not enough to aver that was usual practice for hirers such as H. M's averments that L's solicitors had asserted that L was insured against any requirement to pay the hire charges were irrelevant where M accepted that he could not plead the existence of the agreement against L or his insurers, and L did not aver that his entitlement to recover hire charges arose from such insurance arrangements nor sought recovery of any premium paid.

LARG v. MOORE 2001 S.L.T. (Sh Ct) 147, DCW Pyle, Sh Ct (Tayside, Central and Fife).

CONTRACTS

5412. Assignation—debt—transfer of liability under counterclaim

A, factors, raised an action of payment against M, a company, under a contract between M and N, painters, N having assigned their rights to benefit under the contract to A. M argued that works carried out by N did not conform to contract and that as a result they had suffered loss and damage, the amount of which exceeded the contract value of the works, and pled a right of retention as a defence. M also counterclaimed against A for loss and damage, arguing that by virtue of the assignation they had taken on the liabilities under the contract. It was agreed that there was no binding authority, that the assignation ex facie on its terms transferred only the benefit, and that M were entitled to plead retention or compensation in the defences to the extent that A's claim might be extinguished.

Held, dismissing M's counterclaim and putting the case out by order, that A had no better right than N. If N's entitlement could be extinguished by retention or compensation, A's rights assigned from N would be similarly qualified, but that did not mean that A was exposed to the same liabilities as N. If M were correct, they could have initiated proceedings against A, a possibility which would cause considerable problems for factoring businesses generally, and the common law in Scotland would be different from its English counterpart, something not argued for by M in debate.

Observed, that (1) the decision would not lead to an inequitable result. M could bring in N as a third party or raise a separate action and have the proofs conjoined to gain the excess, and (2) it was assumed that M was proceeding on the basis that N retained no rights or liabilities, but if that was wrong and what had been argued was that liabilities could reside in both N and A, then M could have chosen which party to go against.

ALEX LAWRIE FACTORS LTD v. MITCHELL ENGINEERING LTD 2001 S.L.T. (Sh Ct) 93, Sheriff JA Taylor, Sh Ct (Glasgow and Strathkelvin).

5413. Breach of contract–construction contracts–defective performance by subcontractor–contractor's voluntary assumption of repair expenses

See CONSTRUCTION LAW: Scottish Enterprise v. Archibald Russel of Denny Ltd. §5402

5414. Breach of contract–construction contracts–penalty clause–liquidated damages

See CONSTRUCTION LAW: City Inn Ltd v. Shepherd Construction Ltd. §5403

5415. Formation of contract–contract induced by fraud

See REPARATION: Barry v. Sutherland (Damages). §6066

5416. Formation of contract–director acting on behalf of company–conditions imposing personal liability on director

Solicitors sought payment of fees for professional services rendered to a company in an action against the directors personally. The solicitors averred that their conditions letter, addressed to the directors personally, gave fair notice that the directors of a company would be liable for any fees and outlays incurred by the company, and that the defenders by having then instructed the pursuers had accepted these conditions. The sheriff, dismissing the action as irrelevant, held that the relevant clause was unusual and onerous and that while fair notice had been given to the defenders, it was not enough to infer acceptance from the company's subsequent instruction to carry out legal services, and that where the clause sought to impose an obligation on a third party it would be reasonable and fair to require acceptance by the third party at least verbally but preferably in writing. The pursuers appealed to the sheriff principal.

Held, allowing the appeal and a proof before answer, that (1) the question of whether the clause was either unusual or onerous could only be determined after proof; (2) the directors had been given fair notice of the clause, and (3) if the pursuers' averments, that each of the defenders were sent copies of the conditions letter and that they thereafter instructed the pursuers to carry out legal services for the company, were proved it would be open to infer acceptance by the directors as individuals of the terms of the letter.

BUDGE v. DONALD; *sub nom.* DONALD & BUDGE (A FIRM) v. DONALD 2002 S.L.T. (Sh Ct) 18, Sir SST Young, Sheriff Principal, Sh Ct.

5417. Formation of contract–offer and acceptance–time for acceptance–reasonableness

F, fishermen, reclaimed against the Lord Ordinary's decision (2001 S.L.T. 897) to dismiss their action for declarator that they were entitled under the terms of two separate contracts constituted by correspondence with I during 1997 and 1998, to payment of compensation for oil pollution damage following the grounding of the Braer oil tanker on the basis that they had failed to accept the offers within a reasonable time. F argued principally that a paragraph in the first letter stating that I would contact them as soon as they had accurate information as to the value of outstanding claims and how these should be progressed, meant that more information would be forthcoming to help F to decide whether to proceed, and made it reasonable for them to wait nine months before purportedly accepting the offer.

Held, refusing the reclaiming motion, that it was clear that when the letter was read as a whole, the paragraph related not to the provision of further information about the total value of unassessed claims, but to giving the pursuers an indication of the extent of any pro rata restriction and when they might expect actual payment, and envisaged a certain urgency in response.

FLAWS v. INTERNATIONAL OIL POLLUTION COMPENSATION FUND 2002 S.L.T. 270, Lord Marnoch, Lord Kingarth, Lord McCluskey, Ex Div.

5418. **Illegality–supply of labour–foreign workers without legal authority–enforceability of contract**

[Asylum and Immigration Act 1996 (c.49).]

D, employment contractors, raised an action of payment against A for sums allegedly due under a contract to supply labour to A's factory, which was defended on the basis of illegality (2000 G.W.D. 12-412). A counterclaimed for losses from decreased production caused by alleged breach of contract by D, as the labour was withdrawn prior to the end of the contract period. It was found after proof that following an approach in 1996 D in turn approached S, a company run by two persons (C), who managed the importation of foreign labour. A were under the impression that C were part of D's organisation. Rates were agreed and foreign workers (W) were supplied to work in A's factory. S settled the sums for payment of W, and A were then invoiced by D for the sums paid in wages and for D and S's fees. W did not have legal authority to work in the UK in terms of the Asylum and Immigration Act 1996 and were detained in October 1997 with a view to deportation. A argued that (1) while knowledge, actual or constructive, by D of the existence of illegality was necessary before the contract could be set aside or declared unenforceable, it was possible for a person to be only an accessory to the illegal act and still be barred from suing on the contract if it was germane to it; (2) a contract would also not be enforced for illegality where it was contrary to public policy and it was clear from the 1996 Act that the public policy was not to allow foreign workers to work in the UK without the necessary documentation; (3) illegality would render a contract unenforceable if there was an express or implied statutory prohibition affecting its performance, and (4) despite the fact that actual knowledge had not been established in D as to W's lack of documentation, on the evidence D and C were engaged in a joint venture and D's evidence that they were innocent or in ignorance of W's lack of documentation should not be accepted. In relation to the counterclaim A argued that the contract had an express or implied term as to duration, admitting a claim for failure to provide labour for the relevant period, and on the evidence that period was one year; alternatively, there was an implied termination clause of reasonable notice or that losses for one month should be allowable due to withdrawal of labour.

Held, granting decree and assoilzing D in the counterclaim, that (1) it was established that D had been unaware that the workers did not have the necessary documentation; (2) the issue of illegality was one of equitable remedy, in that a person seeking to rely knowingly on his own illegal act could not gain by it, but should not lose if the illegal act was committed by someone else completely outwith his knowledge, actual or constructive; (3) statutory illegality raised a separate issue from common law illegality in that it was necessary to analyse the extent to which the contract was affected, or governed, by the illegal act, including considerations of inadvertence, irrelevance, immateriality and innocence, in the present case the most important consideration was that the contract was perfectly legal for a legal purpose and in the circumstances it would not be equitable to deny D the right to sue, and (4) on the evidence there was no express term as to duration and no reason to imply one, or to imply a term of reasonable notice, as this was a contract for provision of labour on a day to day basis which either side could bring to an end in any way they liked.

DOWLING & RUTTER v. ABACUS FROZEN FOODS LTD (NO.2) 2002 S.L.T. 491, Lord Johnston, OH.

5419. **Indemnities–contractors–contractual indemnity overrode indemnity under insurance policy**

N, a contractor, appealed against a finding (2000 S.L.T. 1123) that it was liable to indemnify C, the operator of the Piper Alpha oil platform in the North Sea, for payments made in settlement of death and personal injury claims made by or on behalf of the employees of N who had been killed or injured as a result of an explosion on the platform in 1988. The issues to be decided were whether (1) N's contractual liability to indemnify C had been extinguished by payments which C had recovered under its own insurance policy; (2) C was entitled to be indemnified by N, and (3) the contract between N and C prevented C from recovering from N settlement monies paid in excess of the Scottish level of damages.

Held, dismissing the appeal, that (1) as there was no provision in the contract between N and C which required C to take out insurance, it could not be argued that N's indemnity was limited to indemnifying C if and to the extent that C's insurers failed to do so. Clauses in the contract supported the conclusion that the indemnities provided therein were to be primary obligations and that any other insurance available to C was to be secondary, *Mason v. Sainsbury* (1782) 3 Doug. K.B. 61 applied; (2) properly construed, the contract required N to indemnify C in respect of claims arising from the deaths of and injuries to N's employees despite the fact that N would not be liable at common law or for breach of statutory duty in respect of such claims, and (3) the relevant clause in the contract excluding N from liability did not cover liability to the victims or victims' relatives in respect of injury or death claims so that N was liable to indemnify C in respect of the full amount of the settlement monies which had been paid.

CALEDONIA NORTH SEA LTD v. LONDON BRIDGE ENGINEERING LTD; *sub nom.* CALEDONIA NORTH SEA LTD v. BT PLC; CALEDONIA NORTH SEA LTD v. BRITISH TELECOMMUNICATIONS PLC; CALEDONIA NORTH SEA LTD v. NORTON (NO.2) LTD (IN LIQUIDATION), [2002] UKHL 4, [2002] 1 All E.R. (Comm) 321, Lord Bingham of Cornhill, HL.

5420. Interpretation–obligation of payment or accounting

L, a firm of solicitors, appealed against the sheriff's dismissal of their action of count, reckoning and payment against M, a former partner, in respect of fees received from S, the Scottish Legal Aid Board, for work done while a partner of L. A letter settling M's earlier action of count, reckoning and payment against L, provided for payment to M of a sum representing her agreed balance after deduction of sums paid to M by S in error, and by cl.2(g) M undertook to account to L for all sums received by way of fees from S after that date (June 4, 1996) for work done while a partner of L, and to pay L within seven days. The sheriff's note stated that he had come to the view that the action fell to be dismissed by reference to matters not discussed at debate, and decided to issue a proposed interlocutor and draft note allowing parties the opportunity to make further submissions, but that the sheriff principal, having learned of the proposed course, had advised him extrajudicially that a clear expression of views having been given, further procedure would be inappropriate and the interlocutor should be issued. L argued that the sheriff had erred in that course of action and in concluding L's averments were insufficient where he accepted that M had been in receipt of fees from S admittedly due to L. On appeal L amended their crave to apply to the period after June 4, 1996 in terms of cl.2(g). M argued that L had not established a relationship of the type giving rise to a duty to account, and that the terms of cl.2(g) disclosed an obligation to pay, not an obligation to "account" enforceable by action of count, reckoning and payment, and extinguished any pre-existing obligation to account.

Held, allowing the appeal and remitting the case to the sheriff to proceed as accords, that (1) it was plainly appropriate to afford parties the chance to make submissions on the undiscussed considerations and, having regard to the fact that counsel, the solicitors and sheriff were not locally based, issuing the proposed interlocutor with a note in draft, giving parties an opportunity for further submissions, was eminently sensible. Dismissing the action deprived the parties of an opportunity to make submissions on these unargued considerations which they should have had; (2) M's argument was unsound. In the context of the pre-existing situation and the whole terms of the letter, cl.2(g) had to be read as acknowledging and preserving in relation to future receipts the pre-existing relationship and obligation to account. The fact that the obligation was expressed as a term of a contract did not mean that it had to be one of simple debt, and (3) an averment by L that M received and kept a payment from S which was at least in part partnership moneys was an averment of intromission, and there was a proper basis for ordering an accounting.

Observed, that the question of whether further procedure was appropriate was for the sheriff. It would be inappropriate for a sheriff principal who might have to hear an appeal to advise a sheriff extrajudicially that further procedure could be dealt with in the event of an appeal and to direct a sheriff to issue an interlocutor in a matter where the sheriff principal had no locus.

LYONS LAING v. LAND 2001 S.L.T. 1246, Lord Prosser, Lord Eassie, Lord McCluskey, Ex Div.

5421. Misrepresentation–negligent misrepresentation–representation relied upon–no requirement for "special relationship"

H were shareholders in G, a company that produced mineral water. The company required access to a distribution network for further development which A could supply. A's director, B, represented that the distribution arrangements would be made available to G. H and A entered into an agreement whereby G became, effectively, a subsidiary of A with H a minority shareholder. Thereafter the distribution network was not made available to G, whose profitability suffered. G was placed under administration and there was a resultant "destruction of the value" of H's shareholding. H sought reparation from A in respect of negligent misrepresentation. A argued that there was no "special relationship" of the type required to establish liability for negligence for pure economic loss in terms of *Hedley Byrne & Co Ltd v. Heller & Partners Ltd* [1964] A.C. 465, [1963] C.L.Y. 2416 because; (1) the nature of the statement was not clear from the proceedings and in any case related to the future actings of a third party which could not be relied upon; (2) B was not portrayed as having special skill; (3) there were no averments as to what H would have done but for the representation; (4) the transaction to which the statements related was purely the choice of a suitable investor; (5) the action was purely that choice and the pursuers did not make further investment or change their position, and (6) no loss flowed from H becoming a minority shareholder. H argued that; (1) the representation B made, was one of fact not intention; (2) B was a director of the distribution company and capable of bringing about that which he represented; (3) it was not necessary to show what H would have done otherwise; (4) the reliance induced the choice of investor, and (5) the action taken was to enter into the shareholders' agreement and the loss flowed from H ceasing to be majority shareholders and A having control of the company.

Held, allowing proof before answer, that (1) the terms of the representation were clear from the pleadings; (2) under Scots law there exists a remedy for negligent misrepresentation, accordingly, the establishment of a "special relationship" was not required; (3) it was sufficient for H to show that they had an asset, the value of which was destroyed by the contract, and (4) H was not bound to aver their alternate courses of action but for the contract.

HAMILTON v. ALLIED DOMECQ PLC 2001 S.C. 829, Lord Carloway, OH.

5422. Novation–construction contracts

See CONSTRUCTION LAW: Blyth & Blyth Ltd v. Carillion Construction Ltd. §5405

5423. Books

Huntley, John a K–Contract. Cases & Materials. Paperback: £45.00. ISBN 0-414-01281-X. W. Green & Son.

Huntley, John a K–Contract-Cases and Materials. 2nd Ed. Cases & Materials. Paperback: £45.00. ISBN 0-414-01281-X. W. Green & Son.

CRIMINAL EVIDENCE

5424. Admissibility—evidence deriving from search—search warrants—civilian employee of police assisting in search

[Civic Government (Scotland) Act 1982 (c.45) s.52, s.52A.]

An accused person was charged with being in possession of indecent photographs of children in contravention of the Civic Government (Scotland) Act 1982 s.52 and s.52A. At trial the accused objected to evidence deriving from a search of his home on the basis that a civilian employee, C, attached to the police computer forensic unit had been actively involved in the search and not being a police officer, was not authorised to carry out the search. C had assisted the head of the unit in tagging and removing computing equipment, in particular a computer and 10 zip disks. The accused was acquitted after the sheriff upheld his objection. The Lord Advocate referred to the High Court, inter alia, the question whether in doing so the sheriff erred.

Held, answering the question in the affirmative, that (1) where a warrant authorised a search of premises by police officers, other people might assist them in their search, the assistance that could legitimately be provided depending on the circumstances of each individual case, and (2) the fact that C accompanied the forensic unit did not render the search irregular where he was present to assist the police officer who was head of the forensic unit and who was authorised to tag and remove the equipment, C was acting under directions and had not been conducting a search himself.

LORD ADVOCATE'S REFERENCE (NO.1 OF 2002) 2002 S.L.T. 1017, Lord Kirkwood, Lord Cameron of Lochbroom, Lord Caplan, HCJ.

5425. Admissibility—evidence irregularly obtained—tracking device on vessel

[Criminal Law (Consolidation) (Scotland) Act 1995 (c.39) s.24; Human Rights Act 1998 (c.42) Sch.1 Part I Art.6, Art.8.]

Four Dutch nationals (H) appealed against conviction for being concerned in the importation of three tonnes of cannabis resin. H argued inter alia that (1) the use of a tracking device attached to a ship (I) on which H had allegedly carried the drugs to a rendezvous point with a second ship (O), was illegal and contrary to the Human Rights Act 1998 Sch.1 Part I Art.8 and any evidence flowing from it was inadmissible; no justification had been put forward for the Crown's failure to disclose the existence of the device in advance of the trial, which constituted a breach of Art.6 and denied H the opportunity of producing records to show that the ships were not close enough for long enough to transfer three tonnes of drugs; (2) the appeal court at an earlier hearing had misunderstood information given as to the opportunity to examine evidence prior to trial, and the court having refused a motion that the opinion be set aside in exercise of the nobile officium, H were not able to have all their grounds of appeal considered as a whole and a miscarriage of justice had occurred; (3) in relation to a site visit to inspect O and I that (a) the judge denied H the opportunity to inspect their vessel at the same time as the jury; and (b) the judge had encouraged the jury to speculate among themselves by indicating that they could discuss with each other what they saw, though they were not to engage in conversation with others; (4) the trial judge misdirected the jury in fact by misleading them in regard to the presence of a smell of cannabis resin and the period of time for which I and O might have been in contact, failed to give adequate directions in law as to how to treat the prosecution evidence of surveillance, having regard to the issues concerning the tracking device, and failed to present H's case to the jury adequately; (5) he misdirected the jury by failing to distinguish between interviews conducted by Customs officers under the Criminal Law (Consolidation) (Scotland) Act 1995 s.24 and judicial examination, and (6) he was also in error in stating that the jury could take it into account in assessing credibility if an accused "chose not to mention certain allegations" at interview, the truth of which he now maintained, contrary to the right to silence in s.24(8); (7) the instruction as advocate depute for a procedural hearing of senior counsel who previously represented two of H and acted as adviser to one, was contrary to natural justice, professional conduct, and Art.6, and (8) there was delay in the proceedings, contrary to Art.6.‹F:Held›Held, refusing the appeals, that (1) while it had to be assumed that the tracking device had been planted deliberately, and that weighed heavily against the admission of any evidence arising from its use, the device had played a very limited role in the proceedings. No evidence directly derived from it had been relied on against H and the irregularity could be excused; (2) Art.6 did not necessarily require the exclusion of illegally obtained evidence. In the present case the fairness of the proceedings had not been affected by the introduction of the evidence; the defence had not raised the matters they now sought to, which therefore could not qualify as new evidence. The device had not played such a central part in the prosecution as to taint the later observations. It was impossible to state that the fairness of the proceedings was affected by introducing this evidence; (3) there might well have been a misunderstanding on the part of the appeal court at the earlier hearing, and in the circumstances the court would look at that decision for the limited purpose of determining whether the error affected the outcome; but having done so, the fact that H chose at trial to explore matters relating to the tracking device only to a limited extent and purpose meant that the decision that the evidence could not constitute new evidence was unaffected by the error; (4) the trial judge had made it clear to the jury that the visit to the vessels was not an investigatory exercise but simply an opportunity to look at them to understand the evidence better, a perfectly legitimate purpose; H had suffered no prejudice in not being present and jurors were permitted to discuss a case among themselves once empanelled, and (5) the reference to smell was such that no particular emphasis was placed on that consideration; the admissibility of the surveillance evidence depended only on issues of law and the circumstances considered by the judge, apart from the evidence itself, were not matters for the legitimate consideration of the jury; the judge had adequately presented the defence case; the complaints of misdirection were therefore unfounded; (6) the trial judge had dealt with the Customs interviews and judicial examination in close proximity but clearly kept them separate and no reasonable jury would have been likely to have been confused; (7) there had been a misdirection having regard to H's rights under s.24(8), but no miscarriage of justice arose as it only affected the two of H who gave evidence; (8) in considering directions to a jury prior to October 2, 2000, those should be evaluated by reference to the requirements of Scots law and procedure rather than against the Convention; (9) the court having heard evidence concerning senior counsel's involvement as advocate depute, was satisfied that no devolution issue arose: he withdrew once realising the error, and was replaced before the members of the court entered, and (10) while there had been a longer delay than normal, much of which could not be laid at H's door, neither could it blamed on the prosecution or the court.

HOEKSTRA v. HM ADVOCATE (NO.7); VAN RIJS (JAN) v. HM ADVOCATE (NO.7); VAN RIJS (RONNY) v. HM ADVOCATE (NO.7); VAN RIJS (HENDRIK) v. HM ADVOCATE (NO.7) 2002 S.L.T. 599, Lord Cullen L.J.G., Lord Coulsfield, Lord Osborne, HCJ Appeal.

5426. Admissibility–expert evidence–credibility and reliability of complainers in child abuse cases

G was charged on indictment with two offences of sodomy against two young boys. The boys had initially reported acts of indecent behaviour by G, who was tried and convicted of those offences on summary complaint. After the conviction, and following an incident at school, one of the boys revealed the full extent of the acts which G had allegedly perpetrated against both boys. The other boy corroborated the allegations and G was charged. Both boys gave evidence of the sodomy in court. The Crown then attempted to lead evidence from a clinical psychologist who worked in cases of child sexual abuse. Although she had not had any direct contact with the boys, she had studied material relevant to the case and had compiled a clinical psychology report in order to assess the credibility and reliability of the boys statements given the two stage revelations. She concluded that the statements given by the boys were both credible and reliable. The defence objected to her evidence as inadmissible arguing that the credibility and reliability of a witness was a matter for the jury. The Crown maintained that the only evidence that they sought to lead from the psychologist was in relation to how common the pattern of two stage revelations of child sexual abuse was as that information would not be within common public knowledge and might assist the jury in their determinations of credibility and reliability. The Crown indicated that they did not intend to lead evidence on that part of the report where the psychologist had reached her own conclusions on the boys' credibility or reliability.

Held, sustaining the objection and declaring the evidence inadmissible, that (1) evidence of facts affecting the credibility or reliability of a witness was generally inadmissible in Scotland unless those facts were also relevant to the questions at issue in the case, and (2) psychiatric evidence would be relevant if it had been established that the witness suffered from a mental illness raising questions on the quality of the evidence which would be obtainable from that witness, but those circumstances did not prevail in the instant case, *R. v. Turner (Terence Stuart)* [1975] Q.B. 834, [1975] C.L.Y. 562, approved.

HM ADVOCATE v. GRIMMOND (DAVID) 2002 S.L.T. 508, Lord Osborne, HCJ.

5427. Admissibility–hearsay evidence–admission of deceased's statements–deceased not precognosced

[Criminal Procedure (Scotland) Act 1995 (c.46) s.259.]

B was charged with murder. Before the trial the Crown tendered a notice under the Criminal Procedure (Scotland) Act 1995 s.259 applying for particular statements to be admitted as evidence. The statements had been given by H, who died before the defence could precognosce him. No objection was taken nor was the application granted. The Crown sought to lead evidence of the deceased's statement at trial and B raised a devolution issue arguing that its admission would be contrary to his right under the European Convention on Human Rights 1950 Art.6(3)(d) to examine, or have examined, witnesses against him. The Crown argued that, in terms of the Act of Adjournal (Criminal Procedure Rules) 1996 r.40.5, the decolution issue was raised too late. B argued that H's evidence was manifestly crucial to the Crown case and that, on the basis of a prior contradictory ststement, it was manifestly suspect. The Crown argued that they had other evidence implicating B and that H's statement was not crucial to their case.

Held, refusing the application to have the evidence excluded and repelling the objection to the admission of that evidence, that (1) it was doubtful wether the court could have granted the application under s.259 prior to the jury being sworn, the application was to have evidence admitted rather than to rule on its admissibility; (2) the issue had not been raised late, the question was whether it had been raised too early. Although there was no reason why a judge could not reach a conclusion on the effect certain evidence would have on the fairness of a trial, in practice it might be difficult to reach a conclusion until all the evidence had been heard; (3) there was no absolute rule that an accused had a right to question a witness. The European Convention was concerned with the fairness of a trial as a whole and not the fairness of its individual parts; (4) the significance of H's statements would be affacted by the way the case was presented and the way it was challenged. It was not clear that H's statement would be the only significant evidence. In any case it could not stand alone and the requirement of corroboration was itself an important safeguard against unfairness; (5) the defence had the opportunity to precognosce the police officers that had taken H's statement and could cross examine the officer so as to undermine H's credibility. The jury would be directed as to how to apporach H's evidence and the question of its credibility was one for the jury, and (6) the only question raised by s.259 was wether B's inability to cross examine H would prejudice his right to a fair trial, that did no appear to be the case.

Observed, that the defence submission could be renewed at a later stage as the overall case became clearer.

HM ADVOCATE v. BAIN (DAVID) 2002 S.L.T. 340, Lord Reed, HCJ Appeal.

5428. Admissibility—hearsay evidence—pretrial notice wrongly attached to statement—entitlement of Crown to lead correct statement

[Criminal Procedure (Scotland) Act 1995 (c.46) s.259, s.259(5).]

M was charged on indictment with a variety of charges including reset, fraud and attempted fraud. He was convicted of one charge of reset, one of attempted fraud and 15 charges of fraud involving a total of £78,150. He was sentenced to four years' imprisonment and appealed against both conviction and sentence. The charges of fraud were in relation to bogus workman incidents. The appeal was advanced only in relation to charge 16, that M had defrauded a 91 year old woman out of £20,100. The victim had made two statements to the police, one concerning repairs to her driveway, which did not relate to any of the charges on the indictment, and one concerning repairs to her roof, which were the subject of the charge. As the complainer was unfit to attend court the fiscal decided to make use of the provisions of the Criminal Procedure (Scotland) Act 1995 s.259. In preparing the papers for trial an error was made on the part of the fiscal's office in that the notice in terms of s.259(5) was attached to the statement concerning the driveway rather than the one concerning the roof. When the police officer came to give evidence in relation to the statement, the error was discovered and the Crown moved the court to allow the correct statement to be lodged. The defence objected, but the sheriff repelled the objection and allowed the hearsay evidence to be led and the correct statement to be lodged. The sheriff took the view that M would not be prejudiced provided the defence were given time to the content of the statement. M was subsequently convicted and appealed.

Held, allowing the appeal and quashing the conviction on the charge, that (1) the sheriff had erred in considering whether there was good reason for the correct evidence to be led and whether M would suffer any prejudice as a result of his decision and the correct question to be considered was whether there had been good reason why the crown had failed to give notice in terms of s.259(5) in respect of the correct statement; (2) no reason had been put forward by the Crown as to why notice had not been given on the correct statement other that an unexplained mistake, and (3) with the failure of the Crown to give the appropriate notice under s.259(5), the conditions for admissibility of the hearsay evidence had not been met and the evidence was inadmissible. Opinion of the court per Lord Rodger LJ-G.

McPHEE (WILLIAM McALLISTER) v. HM ADVOCATE 2002 S.L.T. 90, Lord Rodger L.J.G., Lord Cowie, Lord Marnoch, HCJ Appeal.

5429. Admissibility—hearsay evidence—statement by witness who had since died

[Criminal Procedure (Scotland) Act 1995 (c.46) s.259(1)(b); European Convention on Human Rights 1950 Art.6.]

B was charged on indictment with assault, sodomy and murder. During his trial the Crown sought to lead a witness statement made by P, who had died before the trial commenced. In the statement P described how he was gay and had met B through the Edinburgh gay scene; where and how B had said he liked to pick up men; and a comment by B that he liked to "cruise early morning in an attempt to pick up young guys in his car". B objected, contending that the passages relied on were general material irrelevant to any issues arising in the trial, would not have been admissible if P had been alive to give direct oral evidence in terms of the Criminal Procedure (Scotland) Act 1995 s.259(1)(b), and the final passage was not relevant to what had occurred in the present case. B also argued that the statement was inadmissible being a precognition. The trial judge held a trial within a trial into the issue. B also raised, as a devolution issue, that to lead evidence of the statement would infringe his right to a fair trial and to examine or have examined witnesses against him under the European Convention on Human Rights 1950 Art.6(1) and Art.6(3)(d).

Held, repelling the objections, that (1) had P been alive, evidence of the passages in question would have been admissible in the proceedings if he had given direct oral evidence in terms of s.259(1)(b), as they described habitual behaviour on B's part which could be seen as indicating his sexual interests and preferences at the time of the alleged crime, and the charge alleged a homosexual assault on the victim, who had been seriously affected by drink; (2) P's statement was not a precognition: it was taken as a result of the pursuit of a line of inquiry, and had not been taken on the instructions of the procurator fiscal; apart from the formal opening words of the statement the words were P's; and P had been given the chance to check the statement on completion and had approved it subject to additions, and (3) the leading of evidence of the contents of P's statement would not contravene Art.6(1) or Art.6(3)(d) of the Convention given the safeguards of the requirement for corroborated evidence of the crimes charged, the provisions of s.259(4) and the special directions which would require to be given to the jury, and given that B had not contended that anything in P's statement was untrue.

HM ADVOCATE v. BEGGS (NO.3) 2002 S.L.T. 153, Lord Osborne, HCJ.

5430. Admissibility—statement by accused—fairness—burden of proof

J was accused of attempting to murder and of murdering his two infant sons. The Crown sough to lead in evidence a statement made to police by J. J objected, arguing that the statement had been unfairly obtained and a trial within a trial was held. The circumstances in which the interview took place where that (1) J had attended the police station voluntarily; (2) J had declined a solicitor; (3) the interview lasted for five hours, with breaks; (4) all questions were asked by one police officer, and (5) the interview was, on the whole, a calm exchange.

Held, repelling the objection and admitting the statement, that it was for the Crown to prove, beyond reasonable doubt, that the statement had been fairly obtained. Unless the police and clearly broken the rules of fairness the court would be reluctant to rule the statement inadmissible. Given that, the interview was conducted in a low key, measured and polite fashion; J had been able to stand up for himself; J's incriminating remarks had been made spontaneously; J was 29 and in good health the interview had been conducted during the day with breaks; there was one questioner who had not rushed, led or threatened J, the statement could not be said to have been unfairly obtained.

HM ADVOCATE v. JENKINSON (DARREN JOHN) 2002 S.C.C.R. 43, Lord McEwan, HCJ Appeal.

5431. Admissibility—statement by accused—incriminating and exculpatory material

[European Convention on Human Rights 1950 Art.6.]

M appealed against his conviction for murder, based on the trial judge's refusal to allow cross examination of a police officer in relation to a mixed statement by M four days after his arrest following a Crown objection, arguing that the second rule in *Morrison v. HM Advocate (Evidence)* 1990 J.C. 299, [1991] C.L.Y. 4552, should be reformulated to remove the reference to lack of objection by the Crown so that evidence as to the contents of a mixed statement could be led by the Crown or the defence. The case was remitted to a bench of nine judges (2001 GWD 1-22). M argued that the Crown's "power of veto" in regard to leading such evidence was inconsistent with fairness and the principle of equality of arms under the European Convention on Human Rights 1950 Art.6. It was a tactical question for the defence and the Crown's objection compromised M's right to silence, because if he was to put his account before the jury he would require to enter the witness box.

Held, dismissing the appeal, that (1) to deny the defence the opportunity to use such evidence was not unfair and did not compromise M's right to silence: his argument ran counter to the general rule against the admission of hearsay, and there was no inconsistency with the position where evidence of the statement was led by the Crown since in that case it was necessary in order to secure fairness; (2) there was no basis in principle for any practice of the Crown of conceding the admissibility of a mixed statement of which they had not led evidence, and no duty on the Crown to lead such evidence or to refrain from objecting if the defence sought to do so, and the rule in *Morrison* fell to be disapproved to that extent, and (3) it followed that the judge had been correct to sustain the Crown objection.

McCUTCHEON (GEORGE) v. HM ADVOCATE 2002 S.L.T. 27, Lord Cullen L.J.G., Lord Clarke, Lady Cosgrove, Lord Coulsfield, Lord Kingarth, Lord Macfadyen, Lord Nimmo Smith, Lord Penrose, Lord Wheatley, HCJ Appeal.

5432. Admissibility–surveillance–evidence deriving from police surveillance operation–right to respect for private and family life

[European Convention on Human Rights 1950 Art.8(1).]

C was charged on indictment with being concerned in the supply of diamorphine. At trial he raised as a devolution issue the admissibility of evidence to be given by a police officer, which he submitted had been obtained in a manner which violated his rights under the European Convention on Human Rights 1950 Art.8(1). C alleged that his home had been subject to systematic surveillance beyond mere observation for seven and a half hours, during which some people entering and leaving the building were detained and questioned, and their identity and other observations noted. A search warrant had been obtained on the basis of the observations. The sheriff dismissed the devolution minute and C appealed, arguing, inter alia, that the monitoring of the identity of persons entering and leaving, and the recording of observations made, was akin to interference by telephone tapping and interfered with the right to respect for private life.

Held, refusing the appeal, that the procedures involved in speaking to those entering and leaving involved third parties and did not breach C's rights under Art.8; furthermore, neither the search warrant nor its execution had been directly impugned and there had been no intrusion into C's private life.

CONNOR (NEIL PATRICK) v. HM ADVOCATE 2002 J.C. 255, Lord Cameron of Lochbroom, Lord Carloway, Lord Kingarth, HCJ Appeal.

5433. Corroboration–identification–person giving accused's name making similar threat to second witness–mutual corroboration

[Telecommunications Act 1984 (c.12) s.43(1)(a).]

F was convicted of an offence under the Telecommunications Act 1984 s. 43(1)(a) after making offensive phone calls. Four witnesses gave evidence that a person giving F's name had called and threatened to "knee cap" someone. One of those witnesses positively identified the caller as F. The sheriff repelled a plea of no case to answer and F appealed to the High Court.

Held, refusing the appeal, that there had been sufficient evidence in law for the sheriff to conclude that F had been the caller. Two of the calls were made to the same place, the positive identification was made subsequent to the first call and the threats were the same or similar. Opinion of the Court per Lord Cameron of Lochbroom.

FORD v. RITCHIE 2002 S.C.C.R. 395, Lord Cameron of Lochbroom, Lord Hamilton, Lord MacLean, HCJ Appeal.

5434. Corroboration–Moorov doctrine–course of conduct

D appealed against his conviction on four charges of rape of which he was found guilty, out of seven such charges which went to the jury. Charge 1 related to rape on two occasions between August 22, 1969 and July 25, 1970, charge 2 to rape on one occasion between June 29, 1972 and February 26, 1973, charge 10 to rape on one occasion between July 18 and October 18, 1977 or February 18, 1978 and November 30, 1979, and charge 15 to repeated rape between February 19 and August 31, 1978. D argued that the judge had misdirected the jury in relation to the application of the *Moorov* doctrine as (1) the jury should have been directed that a more rigorous approach to the application of the doctrine was appropriate than in cases where charges were more recent, and in cases like the present where the Crown had taken considerable latitude the jury should have been directed that the benefit of the maximum latitude should be given to D, and (2) the jury should have been directed that there could be no application of the doctrine as between the offences under charges 1 and 15 and the directions given could be seen as authorising such an application. The Crown argued that D had made no plea of no case to answer and presumably considered the multiplicity of charges against him were capable of amounting to a course of criminal conduct to which the doctrine could apply, that four rapes in eight years in the same area of Edinburgh had been established, and that there was sufficient similarity between the offences for *Moorov* to apply.

Held, allowing the appeal, that (1) the question was whether the criterion for application of the doctrine was satisfied, whether or not the charges were of antiquity; (2) to take a more rigorous approach in cases such as the present, or to afford the accused the benefit of maximum latitude, would constitute a wholly unwarranted judicial interference with the jury's fact finding function and had no support in authority; (3) the judge could not be criticised for deciding not to give detailed directions on the application of the doctrine to different combinations of cases given the number of charges faced by D and the risk of confusing the jury; (4) it was impossible for the court to lay down any maximum period of time in relation to the application of the doctrine and whether any period of time was or was not too great for its application depended on the circumstances of the case and the force of the other elements in the criterion for its application, and (5) considering the character and circumstances of the offences of which D was convicted and the lapses of time between them, the jury were not entitled to hold that they were part of a systematic course of criminal conduct.

DODDS (BRIAN) v. HM ADVOCATE 2002 S.L.T. 1058, Lord Osborne, Lord Gill L.J.C., Lord Kirkwood, HCJ Appeal.

5435. Corroboration–road traffic offences–speeding–proof–accuracy of measured distance

[Criminal Procedure (Scotland) Act 1995 (c.46) s.280.]

H appealed against conviction for speeding at 87 mph, measured by police officers using speed check equipment in a patrol car. H argued that the justice had no foundation for the finding that the equipment was calibrated by driving the police vehicle at set speeds between two marked points on a road, marking out half a mile. Neither police officer spoke in evidence to having measured the half mile, although H had notified the Crown of his objection to a certificate of accuracy of the equipment lodged in terms of the Criminal Procedure (Scotland) Act 1995 s.280. The justice had relied on evidence from a police officer that both the police pilot system and the speedometer of the vehicle indicated that the distance was half a mile and concluded that it was unlikely that both would be inaccurate at the same time.

Held, allowing the appeal, that the distance between the two painted marks was not shown to have been measured as half a mile, and could not be inferred from past use of that marked distance when calibrating other equipment or speedometers.

Observed, that with the available procedures in relation to uncontroversial evidence, and the possibility of confirmatory measurement before trial, it was not the case that the instant decision amounted to a requirement that police measure out the half mile in every case.

HOGG v. MacNEILL 2001 S.L.T. 873, Lord Prosser, Lord Johnston, Lord Allanbridge, HCJ Appeal.

5436. Corroboration–road traffic offences–speeding–proof–accuracy of measured distance

P appealed against conviction for speeding at between 86 and 90 mph in a 70 mph area. Police officers had followed P, travelling at the same speed, using the police car speedometer to gauge P's speed. P argued that the justice had not been entitled to hold that the police speedometer was accurate, given the evidence in relation to the prior checking of its accuracy over a distance between two marked fence posts on a particular road, because there had been no corroboration of the measurement of the half-mile distance. Only one of the police officers (T) gave evidence of measuring the distance in 1989 with a steel tape, and there was no evidence as to the accuracy of the tape.

Held, refusing the appeal, that the distance between the two posts was not a matter which required corroboration. T's evidence was sufficient to establish that fact, without further evidence as to the accuracy of the tape.

Observed, that past use of the same marked distance might suggest that inaccuracy might have emerged, but could not have established accuracy if T's evidence had not been available and sufficient.

PERVEZ v. CLARK 2001 S.C.C.R. 138, Lord Prosser, Lord Johnston, Lord Allanbridge, HCJ Appeal.

5437. Corroboration–road traffic offences–speeding–speed recorded on radar–accuracy of device

[Road Traffic Act 1988 (c.52) s.2.]

The offender was charged with dangerous driving contrary to the Road Traffic Act 1988 s.2, and speeding. Two police officers gave evidence that they had seen the offender's vehicle whilst operating a radar speed trap and it had registered a speed of 72mph. Only one police officer spoke as to the accuracy of the radar device, the other as to the sound and sight of the vehicle, coupled with the reading on the radar device. The sheriff repelled a submission of no case to answer based on the ground that the radar evidence had not been corroborated and convicted the offender of both charges. The offender appealed to the High Court and the Crown did not seek to uphold the conviction on the speeding charge since there was duplication between the two charges.

Held, refusing the appeal against conviction on the charge of dangerous driving, that (1) if proof of the precise speed were necessary to prove commission of an offence and such proof was offered by a radar device then corroborative evidence of the accuracy of the device would be required, and (2) that proof of actual speed was not necessary for a charge under s. 2(3) and although the second police officer's description of the speed was perhaps capable of ambiguity, it was for the sheriff to interpret the evidence. In the whole circumstances the sheriff was entitled to interpret his evidence as supporting the conclusion that the speed was excessive in the appropriate sense relative to the charge. Opinion of the Court per Lord Coulsfield.

McLEAN v. McLEOD 2002 S.C.C.R. 127, Lord Coulsfield, Lord Caplan, Lord Philip, HCJ Appeal.

5438. Corroboration–special knowledge of accused

M appealed against conviction and sentence of seven months' imprisonment for robbing a 75 year old woman, L, in the street by snatching her shopping bag from behind, causing her to fall and injure herself. The Crown case depended on a statement said to be a special knowledge admission, in which M admitted grabbing a woman's bag from behind at a locus similar in description to that in the attack on L, the bag containing a purse with about £30, some reading books and various cards. The bag was a leather one, quite big, which she had in her hand. In a joint minute it was agreed that L was carrying a blue nylon shopping bag over her shoulder and had a carrier bag in her hand when her shopping bag was snatched; it contained a purse with about £30, a travel pass, two bank cards, her house keys and three library books. M argued that there were clear differences in regard to the description of the bag; that the whole affair had been reported in the press before M's interview; and it could not be said that the only reasonable explanation was that he was the perpetrator; *Wilson (Brian) v. HM Advocate* 1987 J.C. 50 considered.

Held, refusing the appeal, that contrary to the Crown's argument, the question of sufficiency was one of law and not simply one for the court of first instance, and the court should consider the statement as a whole rather than simply look at the points of agreement with the established facts. However, the sheriff was entitled to conclude, having regard to the nature and manner of commission of the crime, the location and the contents of the bag, that the test in *Wilson* was met, despite the discrepancies; and further, sentence was not excessive where M, who had needed money for heroin, had a record of persistent offending since the early 1980s including many convictions for theft.

McLAUGHLIN v. CLARK 2002 S.L.T. 332, Lord Philip, Lord Caplan, Lord Coulsfield, HCJ Appeal.

5439. Cross examination–statements–previous inconsistent statement by witness–examination on different version of statement

[Criminal Procedure (Scotland) Act 1995 (c.46) s.263(4).]

L appealed against his conviction for the assault of C, a 16 year old boy, on the ground that there had been a miscarriage of justice when the trial judge had sustained an objection by the Crown to cross examination. The solicitor advocate for L, in cross examining C by reference to his police statement, used a copy made by a police officer of C's statement to the officer, which was based on and not materially different to that which the officer recorded in his notebook. The solicitor advocate subsequently attempted to put to the officer certain parts of C's statement as recorded in the notebook. The Crown objected, arguing that for that matter to be put to the officer it would have been necessary to put to C the content of the statement as actually recorded in the notebook "line by line". L argued that preventing him from exploring apparent inconsistencies between what C had told the officer when giving his statement and what C had said in the witness box had given rise to a miscarriage of justice. The Crown accepted that it was not necessary to put the whole of the written record to C, but argued that as a matter of fairness, where a written record existed, the record of those parts of the statement relied on should have been put to him.

Held, allowing the appeal, that (1) in terms of the Criminal Procedure (Scotland) Act 1995 s.263(4), there was nothing to prevent, in principle, parts of a statement being put to a witness to prove he said something different on another specified occasion from the evidence given by him at trial, and (2) since it was not suggested that what C said to the officer was in substance any different to what the officer had recorded or materially different to what was recorded in the copy, there was no basis for holding that fairness required the notebook to be put to C line by line, and the refusal to allow the evidence to be taken from the officer amounted to a miscarriage of justice.

LECKIE (DENNIS) v. HM ADVOCATE 2002 S.L.T. 595, Lord Clarke, Lord Bonomy, Lord Marnoch, HCJ Appeal.

5440. Identification–similar fact evidence–sufficiency

G appealed against conviction for the assault and robbery of B, while acting with another, by holding a syringe and hypodermic needle at B's neck and threatening him with violence. G had also been convicted of assault to injury of R by holding a syringe and needle to his neck, having been positively identified by two witnesses. There was no direct evidence of the offences against B other than B's account and he was unable to identify the perpetrators except to say that G was not one of them. The Crown relied on the principle in *Howden (John) v. HM Advocate* 1994 S.C.C.R. 19, [1994] C.L.Y. 5531 applied in *Townsley v. Lees* 1996 S.L.T. 1182, [1996] C.L.Y. 6722, to support the conviction for assault on B, there being similarities in the locus, timing and commission of the two offences. G argued, inter alia, that these cases were wrongly decided as *Howden* infringed the general principle that on a criminal charge there had to be identification of the accused as the perpetrator from two independent sources and should be reconsidered by a larger court and the evidence in relation to the offence against R did not justify conviction of the offence against B where there was no identification of G in that respect.

Held, allowing the appeal and quashing the convictions, that (1) *Howden* and *Townsley* were correctly decided in relying on circumstantial evidence that the perpetrator on one charge was the same person who was identified as having been the perpetrator on the other, and (2) the evidence as to the similarities between the two offences was insufficient to support the application of the *Howden* principle as the similarities did not go to the identification of either alleged assailant on B, *Howden* and *Townsley* considered.

GILLAN (SHAUN CHRISTOPHER) v. HM ADVOCATE 2002 S.L.T. 551, Lord Gill L.J.C., Lord Kingarth, Lord Marnoch, HCJ Appeal.

5441. Sufficiency–drug offences–slang reference to cannabis and cannabis resin– no forensic evidence–prior charge of rape but no conviction–no entitlement to statutory defence

[Misuse of Drugs Act 1971 (c.38) s.4(3)(a); Criminal Law (Consolidation) (Scotland) Act 1995 (c.39) s.5(3), s.14; European Convention on Human Rights 1950 Art.6(3)(a).]

M was charged with (1) supplying cannabis resin to VS contrary to the Misuse of Drugs Act 1971 s.4(3)(a), and (2) having unlawful sexual intercourse with VS, who was aged 15 at the time, in contravention of the Criminal Law (Consolidation) (Scotland) Act 1995 s.5(3). The drug had been smoked and there was no material remaining for forensic analysis. The witnesses made reference to "blow" and "hash" and the jury were directed that those were slang terms for cannabis or cannabis resin. M had been previously indicted for rape but not convicted of that or any lesser offence. The jury were directed that the defence under s.5(5)(b) was not available to M. M was convicted of both offences and appealed to the High Court arguing that (1) there had not been sufficient evidence to prove the existence of cannabis resin and the sheriff had misdirected the jury, and (2) the offence of rape was not a listed offence and as such he should have been afforded the s.5(5)(b) defence. M also argued that the situation was in breach of his right to be informed in detail of the nature and cause of an accusation against him in terms of the European Convention on Human Rights 1950 Art.6(3)(a).

Held, refusing the appeal, that (1) the trial had clearly proceeded upon the basis that "hash" and "blow" were references to cannabis resin and the sheriff had not erred in directing the jury as such; (2) the s.5(5)(b) of the 1995 Act defence was to be afforded once, but denied thereafter: the accused having received unequivocal notice of the rules; (3) M had, at the time of his trial for rape, intimation of s.14 of the 1995 Act whereby the accused could be acquitted of rape but convicted of a lesser offence, and would also have understood that the s.5(5)(b) defence could be relied upon. If M had been convicted of that charge he could not have argued a breach of his Convention rights, and (4) the European Court of Human Rights accepted that any court had the power to depart slightly from the original classification of offence provided that the criminal intent was essentially the same, no different facts were considered, the sentence imposed would be lesser and the new legal classification might involve the finding of aggravating circumstances that were implicit in the original finding. Such circumstances existed in the instant case and the judge was correct in holding that M had been given notice of a charge which included the possibility of a lesser charge when he was originally tried for rape. *De Salvador Torres v. Spain* (1997) 23 E.H.R.R. 601, [1997] C.L.Y. 2813 applied. Opinion of the court per Lord Cameron of Lochbroom.

McMASTER (ROSS CHARLES) v. HM ADVOCATE 2001 S.C.C.R. 517, Lord Cameron of Lochbroom, Lord Macfadyen, Lord Morison, HCJ Appeal.

5442. Witnesses–expert witnesses–entitlement of Crown to call defence expert

[Criminal Procedure (Scotland) Act 1995 (c.46) s.67; European Convention on Human Rights 1950 Art.6(1).]

W and five other accused were charged on indictment on a number of charges involving serious sexual abuse of two young children which included allegations of rape and anal penetration. The indictment was set down for trial at a sitting commencing on June 25, 2001. On May 11, 2001, the Lord Advocate gave notice under the Criminal Procedure (Scotland) Act 1995 s.67, that he intended to examine two witnesses, with the leave of the court, who had not been included on the list of witnesses attached to the indictment. The witnesses were both consultant paediatricians who had examined the complainers. W and the other co-accused lodged devolution minutes in which they sought orders to prevent the Lord Advocate proceeding in terms of the s.67 notice. The minutes were discussed at a preliminary diet who refused the orders sought by the accused. They appealed against the refusal. The witnesses in question had originally been instructed by agents for the appellants to examine the complainers with a view to their reports assisting in the preparation of defences. The doctors had been given access to defence precognitions and documents and, it was claimed, they were instructed purely as advisers. They were told to treat the information obtained and findings reached as confidential, which they had accepted. Although a consultation had taken place between one of the doctors and a senior counsel for the appellants, no decision had been made to cite the doctors as witnesses and they had not, therefore, been added to the list of defence witnesses. The Crown had been aware that the two doctors were acting for the defence as the Crown's co-operation had been sought in arranging the examination with the consent of the children and their parents. Following the examinations, the procurator fiscal wrote requesting copies of the reports which led to the s.67 notice being issued. The appellants argued that allowing the doctors to be added to the list of prosecution witnesses would breach defence rights of confidentiality and would contravene the European Convention on Human Rights 1950 Art.6(1) by interfering with the defence right to prepare for trial freely and confidentially.

Held, allowing the appeal, that (1) the fact that the defence had instructed a particular witness did not allow them to put an absolute veto on the use of that expert's findings and opinions without first having regard to the interests of justice and the real issue was what circumstances would allow the Crown to examine a defence expert given that allowing the Crown to list and call such an expert might inhibit the conduct of the defence; (2) it was not necessary for the defence to prove that they were likely to suffer serious repercussions, but simply that it would fetter or hinder them in the preparation of their case; (3) whilst respecting the interests of the accused, the court, in a criminal prosecution, should, where necessary, have the benefit of all available expert evidence, but in the circumstances, the Crown had not put forward any sufficient explanation as to why it was necessary to call the two witnesses; (4) the fact that the expert evidence existed, although its exact nature was unknown, was insufficient to reason to justify its inclusion in the interests of justice, and (5) the court would have to be satisfied that such evidence could be made available without the disclosure of confidential information and without the risk of prejudice to the accused, neither of which prevailed in the instant case.

HM ADVOCATE v. WILSON; *sub nom.* WALES v. HM ADVOCATE 2001 S.C.C.R. 633, Lord Coulsfield, Lady Paton, Lord Sutherland, HCJ Appeal.

CRIMINAL LAW

5443. **Breach of the peace–accused resisting arrest and telling police to "fuck off"– no basis for lawful arrest**

[Police (Scotland) Act 1967 (c.77) s.41.]

K was charged with breach of the peace and resisting arrest, contrary to the Police (Scotland) Act 1967 s.41. K had been approached by two police officers who believed that there was a warrant for his arrest and was asked to wait while the existence of the warrant was checked. K replied "fuck off" and tried to walk away three times. K was arrested for breach of the peace and pushed one of the officers. K was acquitted of breach of the peace and there was no finding that K had shouted or that his behaviour had caused or was likely to cause alarm or distress. K was convicted of the statutory offence and appealed to the High Court.

Held, allowing the appeal and quashing the conviction, that it could not be said that the police officer had any basis upon which to reasonably conclude that a breach of the peace had been or was about to be committed. There was, therefore, no lawful basis for the arrest.

KINNAIRD v. HIGSON 2001 S.C.C.R. 427, Lord Prosser, Lord Eassie, Lord Kingarth, HCJ Appeal.

5444. Breach of the peace–police powers–reasonableness of suspicion

M was charged with a breach of the peace occurring after he had been taken hold of by a police officer. The officer had received a report of a breach of the peace and investigated. The area was clear but M was spotted, drunk and with an injured arm, trying to avoid the police and coming from the disturbance area. The police officer had reason to believe that M was the cause of the reported disturbance and tried to catch up with him. M became aggressive and the police officer took hold of M's uninjured arm, whereupon M threatened him. M was convicted and appealed, arguing that the police officer's conduct had been unlawful

Held, refusing the appeal, that the police officer's suspicions, which led to him taking hold of M's arm, were reasonable in the circumstances, *Cardle v. Murray* 1993 S.L.T. 525, [1993] C.L.Y. 5059 distinguished.

McDONALD (RYAN) v. HEYWOOD 2002 S.C.C.R. 92, Lord Cullen L.J.C., Lord Caplan, Lord Philip, HCJ Appeal.

5445. Defences–coercion–accused lacking reasonable firmness–objective test

C, 17, was charged on indictment with assault and robbery. H lodged a special defence of coercion by his co-accused. Following a trial, he was convicted by the jury of assault and robbery with a rider added to say "under pressure" and he was sentenced to two years' detention. C appealed against his conviction and sentence on two grounds: (1) that the sheriff had misdirected the jury on the law of coercion and in particular advising them to consider whether the threats made by the co-accused would have been sufficient to overcome the will of an ordinary person of the same age and sex. The complainer had given evidence that C had entered her house whilst she was asleep. She had awoken to find him standing over her with a candlestick in his hand. He demanded her purse threatening to hit her if she did not comply. When she refused, he had struck her several times on the head with the candlestick and stolen her wages from her purse. She did not mention the co-accused as being present in the house or taking part in the assault against her. C gave evidence that his co-accused had initiated the idea for the crime and had selected the house. He had then threatened C with physical violence and that he would blow up C's house if he did not carry out the attack. C stated in evidence that he believed that even if he had run away from the scene, his co-accused would have caught up with him later and carried out his threats. During the trial, the defence had led evidence from a chartered psychologist to the effect that C was in the bottom 4 per cent of the population in terms of intelligence and was a highly compliant individual. As such he was on the borderline of mental handicap. On appeal, the defence argued that the sheriff should have directed the jury to consider whether the threats levelled against C were sufficient to overcome a person displaying the same characteristics as the accused of low intelligence and high compliance.

Held, refusing the appeal against conviction, that (1) the test adopted in Scottish law was an objective one to prevent people, who would otherwise be responsible for their actions, avoiding that responsibility as a result of some failing in their character which they should be striving to overcome, (2) the test required the jury to consider whether an ordinary person of reasonable firmness and sharing the same characteristics as the accused would have been overcome in the circumstances and any attempt to require the jury to consider less than reasonable firmness must be rejected, (3) nothing in the test prevented the jury from having regard to characteristics resulting from mental illness, mental impairment or a recognised psychiatric condition, which were not present in the instant case, and (4) although not applicable when considering matters for conviction, failings in the accused's character were relevant to the sheriff in determining the appropriate sentence.

COCHRANE v. HM ADVOCATE (ASSAULT) 2001 S.C.C.R. 655, Lord Rodger L.J.G., Lord Cowie, Lord Marnoch, HCJ Appeal.

5446. **Defences–insanity–amnesia resulting from incident giving rise to charge**

[Road Traffic Act 1988 (c.52) s.1; Criminal Procedure (Scotland) Act 1995 (c.46) s.54(1).]

H was charged on indictment with causing death by dangerous driving contrary to the Road Traffic Act 1988 s.1. H tendered a plea in bar of trial on the grounds that he was suffering from amnesia as a result of the accident from which the charges arose and, as a result, was unable to properly instruct counsel in his defence. The sheriff repelled the plea and H appealed under the Criminal Procedure (Scotland) Act 1995 against the refusal by the sheriff to make a finding of insanity in terms of s.54(1). H argued that being affected by amnesia to the extent that he was resulted in his being insane in terms of s.54(1).

Held, refusing the appeal, that (1) amnesia did not afford a plea in bar of trial, *Russell v. HM Advocate* 1946 J.C. 37, followed, and (2) an inability to properly instruct counsel did not prevent H from testing the Crown's case against him or from leading witnesses who could speak to the events in question. Opinion of the Court per Lord Rodger LJG.

HUGHES (BRIAN ANDREW) v. HM ADVOCATE 2002 J.C. 23, Lord Rodger L.J.G, Lord Cameron of Lochbroom, Lady Paton, HCJ Appeal.

5447. **Drink driving offences–breath test–driving while unfit through drink– whether suspect under prior unlawful arrest**

[Road Traffic Act 1988 (c.52) s.5(1)(a).]

G was charged with driving with excess alcohol contrary to the Road Traffic Act 1988 s.5(1)(a). An off duty police constable had seen G on the stairs in a car park, smelt alcohol on his breath, and seen him drive in the wrong direction and narrowly avoid a collision. She alerted a cashier to stop G's car from leaving the car park and phoned the police. She waved down his car, advised him to wait for the police and asked him to give her his car keys, which he did. When uniformed police arrived G took a breath test, which was positive, and they arrested him. G argued that the off duty officer had made a citizen's arrest, which she had not been entitled to do as the circumstances did not justify such an action, and the subsequent breath test procedure was tainted with illegality.

Held, refusing the appeal, that G had not been under arrest, having been under no restraint and having voluntarily complied with the officer's requests, unaware of the request to the cashier, and the subsequent breath test procedure was untainted by any illegality.

GOODSON v. HIGSON 2002 S.L.T. 202, Lord Philip, Lord Caplan, Lord Cullen L.J.C., HCJ Appeal.

5448. **Drink driving offences–specimen tests–failure to provide without reasonable excuse**

M appealed against conviction for failing to to provide a specimen of urine without reasonable excuse following a positive roadside breath test. The Camic machine at police headquarters was found to be malfunctioning and M agreed to provide a urine specimen. After providing his first specimen, M repeatedly stated when asked that he was unable to produce the required second specimen and did not do so or attempt to do so. M argued that where the police evidence raised the issue of reasonable excuse, it was for the Crown to lead evidence to prove its absence .

Held, refusing the appeal, that if the evidence showed unwillingness or a refusal to provide a sample, there could be no question of a reasonable excuse. The sheriff was entitled where M did not suffer from any relevant medical condition or physical incapacity to prevent him at least attempting to pass urine during the specified period, to conclude M was refusing to provide a sample when required to do so, *McGregor v. Jessop* 1988 J.C. 98, [1988] C.L.Y. 4818 distinguished.

McGUCKIN v. O'DONNELL; *sub nom.* McGUCKIAN v. O'DONNELL 2000 J.C. 629, Lord Cameron of Lochbroom, Lord Caplan, Lord Dawson, HCJ Appeal.

5449. Electronic monitoring–restriction of liberty orders–additional devices

RESTRICTION OF LIBERTY ORDER (SCOTLAND) AMENDMENT REGULATIONS 2002, SSI 2002 119; made under the Criminal Procedure (Scotland) Act 1995 s.245A, s.245C. In force: Reg.4(a): April 16, 2002; remainder: May 1, 2002; £1.75.

These Regulations amend the Restriction of Liberty Order (Scotland) Regulations 1998 (SI 1998 1802) which regulate aspects of the monitoring, by electronic and radio devices, of the compliance of offenders with requirements of restriction of liberty orders. They extend the courts which may make restriction of liberty orders to include the High Court of Justiciary, all sheriff courts and any district court when constituted by a stipendiary magistrate and specify additional devices which may be used for the purpose of remotely monitoring. In addition, the Regulations remove all devices manufactured by Care Electronics, Geografix and Premier Geografix and one device manufactured by Elmo-tech from the list of specified devices.

5450. Entrapment–accused charged with conspiracy to steal–undercover police officers posing as buyers–conspiracy

Four men appealed against conviction for conspiracy to steal motor vehicles. Evidence was led from undercover police officers who had posed as prospective buyers. The appellants argued that (1) by the time evidence had concluded it should have been apparent to the trial judge that this was, or might have been, a case of entrapment by the police and it should have been removed from the jury, and (2) the trial judge's direction that "as a matter of law the police operation here was quite within the bounds of the law", had the effect of telling the jury that the police activities were legitimate, effectively withdrawing the critical issue from determination, which had not been cured by a subsequent direction that fairness was an issue for the jury.

Held, refusing the appeals, that (1) police entrapment had never properly been raised as an issue in the case, the defence having been that the apparent conspiracy was a pretence to extract money from persons interested in acquiring the cars, and there was no evidence from which it could be inferred that the police had instigated a crime that would not otherwise have been committed, and (2) the judge's direction was, on the approach being adopted, the very question the jury had to determine in terms of the careful directions they had been given on the question of fairness, but since it had not been necessary to leave entrapment to the jury at all, there had been no miscarriage of justice.

BROWN (ROBERT BARR) v. HM ADVOCATE; BOWMAN (SAMUEL WATSON) v. HM ADVOCATE; BRAUN (ALEXANDER) v. HM ADVOCATE; ROONEY (DAVID) v. HM ADVOCATE 2002 S.L.T. 809, Lord Marnoch, Lord Clarke, Lord Philip, HCJ Appeal.

5451. Indecent photographs of children–not necessary to prove accused knew photograph was of child

[Civic Government (Scotland) Act 1982 (c.45) s.52A.]

A was convicted of a contravention of the Civic Government (Scotland) Act 1982 s. 52A. A had been found to be in possession of an indecent photograph and expert testimony placed the child's age as under 15 years and six months. A appealed to the High Court arguing that the Crown had failed to prove that he knew the person had been a child, nor had it been proved by the best evidence.

Held, refusing the appeal, that (1) there was nothing within the Act that required the Crown to prove that A knew the picture was of a child, and (2) the best evidence rule was a generalisation; better evidence would not have been essential given that the date of the photograph was unknown.

ARNOTT (NEIL PATERSON) v. McFADYEN; *sub nom.* ARNOT v. McFADYEN 2002 S.C.C.R. 96, Lord Marnoch, Lord Bonomy, Lord Dawson, HCJ Appeal.

5452. Murder—mens rea—concert

B, S, R, N and J were charged with the murder of X and the assault of Y and Z. The principal Crown case against all five was based on concert. B was convicted on the two charges of assault and the other four were convicted on all three charges. The five appealed. B had claimed self defence, having assaulted Y in attempting to protect S. In B's case the Crown accepted that although the judge had adequately and correctly defined self defence, the conditions applicable had not been appropriately applied to the case of defence of another and more should have been said. N, 17 at the time, argued that it had been unfair to allow incriminating answers from an interview to be admitted in evidence given his age, the fact he had been interviewed originally as a witness before he became a suspect and that he had specifically asked whether he could have access to his lawyer. The Crown argued that N had given a full account without prompting, the procedure of detention and intimation had been properly carried out and the judge had properly directed the jury to consider the question of fairness. S, R and J submitted that the trial judge erred in removing culpable homicide from the consideration of the jury. Further by using the term "liable to be used" (of knives) in relation to what a member of the group might have anticipated, the judge had erred in introducing a civil law concept into a criminal law issue: mere foreseeability did not supply the necessary basis for inferring the mens rea of murder in relation to someone who did not participate in the actual stabbing.

Held, allowing B's appeal, dismissing N's appeal and referring the appeal based on concert to a larger court, that (1) while it was not necessarily incumbent on a judge when dealing with a plea of self defence in the form of the present case to analyse the conditions applicable in great detail, the judge made only a very passing reference to defence of another person and, although a jury might reasonably be expected to allow for the specialities of the situation, so long as the general position was put clearly to them, they were not given adequate directions as to how they should deal with B's defence; (2) there was no sufficient ground for holding the evidence of N's interview inadmissible, and (3) in the interests of clarification of the law on a frequently occurring situation it was desirable to remit the matter of concert, murder and mens rea to a larger court.

BARRIE (LEON) v. HM ADVOCATE; McKINNON (STEPHEN) v. HM ADVOCATE; McKAY (ROSS) v. HM ADVOCATE; NORWOOD (ALLAN) v. HM ADVOCATE; JACKSON (JOHN) v. HM ADVOCATE 2002 S.L.T. 1053, Lord Coulsfield, Lord Hamilton, Lord McCluskey, HCJ.

5453. Obstruction of police—failure to cooperate by remaining motionless

[Police (Scotland) Act 1967 (c.77) s.41 (1) (a).]

W appealed against his conviction under the Police (Scotland) Act 1967 (c.77) s.41 (1) (a) for hindering two police officers in the execution of their duty. Having been detained in his home in connection with an assault on his wife, W refused to cooperate by remaining motionless when requested to dress, rise and walk and he had to be physically removed from the premises. W argued that mere passivity was not enough to constitute a breach of the section.

Held, refusing the appeal, that a person who deliberately performed an action with their body so as to place difficulty in the way of the police trying to take a detainee to a police station, especially if the police were required to resort to force, was clearly hindering the police in the execution of their duty; if a physical element was required under the section, that was provided by W's decision to remain inert thus rendering it necessary for the police to use force.

WALSH v. McFADYEN 2002 J.C. 93, Lord McCluskey, Lord Cameron of Lochbroom, Lord Marnoch, HCJ Appeal.

5454. Offences–sale of goods–offensive weapons

CRIMINAL JUSTICE ACT 1988 (OFFENSIVE WEAPONS) AMENDMENT (SCOTLAND) ORDER 2002, SSI 2002 323; made under the Criminal Justice Act 1988 s.141. In force: June 22, 2002; £1.50.

The Criminal Justice Act 1988 provides that any person who manufactures, sells or hires, or offers for sale or hire, exposes or has in his or her possession for the purpose of sale or hire, or lends or gives to any other person, a weapon to which that section applies shall be guilty of an offence and liable on summary conviction to imprisonment for a term not exceeding six months or to a fine not exceeding level 5 on the standard scale or both. The import of any such weapon is prohibited by the 1988 Act. This Order amends the Criminal Justice Act 1988 (Offensive Weapons) Order 1988 (SI 1988 2019) to add a new description of weapon, the disguised knife, to the list of weapons specified.

5455. Rape–actus reus–consent–use of force

[Criminal Procedure (Scotland) Act 1995 (c.46) s.123.]

The Lord Advocate referred points of law to the High Court further to the Criminal Procedure (Scotland) Act 1995 s.123 in respect of the acquittal of W for rape. The trial judge withdrew the case from the jury on the basis that there was no evidence that W had used force and, applying the decision in *HM Advocate v. Sweenie* (1858) 3 Irv. 109, it was essential that the complainer was subjected to some degree of force, or the threat of force, and insufficient for a conviction that sexual intercourse took place without her consent. The Lord Advocate invited the court to hold that the actus reus of rape consisted of sexual intercourse by a man with a woman who at the time of intercourse did not consent to it. W argued that the court was being asked to reconsider what had been long accepted and followed, that the decision in *William Fraser, Re* (1847) 1 Ark. 280, founded on by the Crown, had been overtaken by legislation in that provision had been made where it was perceived that the common law offered inadequate protection, and that the present case was not a suitable one to review the law of rape, since the Crown had failed to seek any alternative conviction.

Held, answering the questions in the affirmative (Lords Marnoch and McCluskey dissenting) that (1) the instant case was an appropriate occasion to review the law, the question raised not being new and the matter being one of continuing public concern; (2) there was no impediment to the court reconsidering *Sweenie*, which was not properly to be regarded as a decision of the whole court, and was unsatisfactory in applying a general rule which looked only at those who were adult and who but for the conduct of the man, would have had an unimpaired ability to withhold consent, *Sweenie* overruled; (3) the actus reus of rape was constituted by a man having sexual intercourse with a woman without her consent; in the case of females under 12, or who for any other reason were incapable of giving such consent, the absence of consent should, as at present, be presumed, and (4) mens rea on the part of the man was present where he knew that the woman was not consenting or was at any rate reckless as to whether she was consenting, "reckless" as the law currently stood being understood in the subjective sense.

LORD ADVOCATE'S REFERENCE (NO.1 OF 2001) 2002 S.L.T. 466, Lord Cullen L.J.G., Lady Cosgrove, Lord Marnoch, Lord McCluskey, Lord Menzies, Lord Nimmo Smith, Lord Wheatley, HCJ.

5456. Recklessness–arrest–detained accused failing to disclose presence of hypodermic syringe in clothing prior to search–police officer sustaining injury–duty of disclosure

[Criminal Procedure (Scotland) Act 1995 (c.46) s.14.]

M was charged with culpably and recklessly concealing a used syringe on his person and failing to disclose that fact to police officers when being searched, whereby an officer, F, was injured. Following trial the sheriff found that while at the police station M had been asked if he was in possession of any "sharps" and replied he did not know; that despite taking precautions F felt a pricking on his hand when searching M's jacket; and that M subsequently produced a syringe from his shirt pocket which F assumed had caused the injury. There was no finding that any legal warrant for taking M to the station or searching him was in effect. The sheriff convicted M, who appealed.

Held, allowing the appeal, that on the particular facts and the terms of the charge, no proper basis for a duty of disclosure on M had been established *Kimmins v. Normand* 1993 S.L.T. 1260, [1993] C.L.Y. 5069 distinguished. Assuming the intention of the officers was to exercise their powers under the Criminal Procedure (Scotland) Act 1995, s.14 no information as mentioned in s.14(9) was given to M and the circumstances did not give rise to a positive duty on him to volunteer information, particularly pertaining to possible involvement in criminal activity.

MALLIN v. CLARK 2002 S.L.T. 1202, Lord McCluskey, Lord Cullen L.J.G., Lord Hamilton, HCJ.

5457. Road traffic offences–dangerous driving–72 mph in 30 mph area–speed recorded on radar–accuracy of device

See CRIMINAL EVIDENCE: McLean v. McLeod. §5437

5458. Road traffic offences–dangerous driving–causing death–mobile phone in vehicle

M was convicted for causing death by dangerous driving. M had failed to stop at a junction and had crashed a large goods vehicle into a car, which then crashed into another vehicle. It was established that M was speeding and the vehicle's braking system was defective. However, in relation to an allegation that M had been using a mobile phone at the time, the other evidence did not support a remark M was said to have made at the time, that he had been called by a female colleague (F) from his office. F denied that, and no phone records supported the claim. At the trial, M submitted that reference to the mobile phone should be withdrawn from the indictment, but that was opposed by the fiscal (P), who had suggested to the jury that F could be believed but that M had been speaking to someone else, and refused by the sheriff, who considered that was a matter which the jury required to assess. M appealed and the Crown accepted that the conviction could not be sustained on the allegation of phone use, but argued that had no bearing on the conviction as the phone was not a handheld one and using it would not necessarily have affected the manner of driving.

Held, quashing the conviction, substituting a conviction of careless driving, and continuing the appeal for a hearing on sentence, that, whether the correct test was that a reasonable jury would "necessarily" still have convicted, as submitted for the Crown, or would "without doubt" have returned the same verdict (the pre-1980 law), the question had to be answered in the negative; it could not be said that the finding in relation to the mobile phone would have been immaterial to a reasonable jury's conclusion that M had driven dangerously.

MURRAY (ROGER GEOFFREY) v. HM ADVOCATE 2001 S.L.T. 435, Lord Rodger, L.J.G., Lord Kirkwood, Lord Penrose, HCJ Appeal.

5459. Road traffic offences–dangerous driving–deliberately driving close to other vehicle and making abusive gestures

[Road Traffic Act 1988 (c.52) s.2.]

Y was charged with dangerous driving contrary to the Road Traffic Act 1988 s.2. Y had driven into a petrol station, noticed the complainer and followed him very closely, making abusive gestures and apparently in a rage; there had been previous animosity between the two. The sheriff found that Y's driving had caused concern and distress to the other driver and passenger. It had not been caused by mere inattention but had been deliberate and fell far below the standard of a competent and careful driver. Y was convicted and appealed to the High Court

Held, refusing the appeal, that, although there was some concern as to the importance the sheriff had placed on deliberation, it was part of the explanation as to what had occurred; accordingly, the sheriff had been entitled to conclude that the driving had created dangers that a competent and careful driver would not create.

YOUNG (STEVEN JAMES) v. BARBOUR 2002 S.C.C.R. 84, Lord Cullen L.J.C., Lord Caplan, Lord Philip, HCJ Appeal.

5460. Road traffic offences–driving while unfit–police observation indicated influence of drugs–medical evidence showed accused fit to drive an hour later–court entitled to convict on basis of police observation

[Road Traffic Act 1988 (c.52) s.4(1).]

M was charged with driving while unfit through drink or drugs contrary to the Road Traffic Act 1988 s.4(1). M was seen speeding and a police officer stepped into the road, raising his hand to stop the vehicle. M swerved and the officer had to step back onto the pavement to avoid being hit. M left the car and his speech was slow and slurred and pupils contracted. The police officers, trained in observing signs of influence, maintained that M was under the influence of drugs, there being no smell of alcohol. M admitted taking a betablocker. A medical examination one hour and a quarter later showed that M's driving ability was not impaired, however it was possible that it could have been impaired an hour earlier.

Held, refusing the appeal, that the sheriff had been entitled to convict after concluding that M's driving ability had been impaired.

McEWAN v. HIGSON 2001 S.C.C.R. 579, Lord Cameron of Lochbroom, Lord Osborne, Lord Sutherland, HCJ Appeal.

5461. Road traffic offences–speeding–corroboration–accuracy of measured distance

See CRIMINAL EVIDENCE: Hogg v. MacNeill. §5435, Pervez v. Clark. §5436

5462. Search and seizure–recovery of cash–code of practice

PROCEEDS OF CRIME ACT 2002 (CASH SEARCHES: CONSTABLES IN SCOTLAND: CODE OF PRACTICE) ORDER 2002, SSI 2002 569; made under the Proceeds of Crime Act 2002 s.293. In force: In accordance with Art.1; £1.75.

This Order brings into operation a code of practice which is required by the Proceeds of Crime Act 2002 s.293(1) for cash searches conducted by constables in relation to Scotland. The Code allows constables and customs officers to search for cash, which is recoverable property or is intended by any person for use in unlawful conduct.

5463. Sexual offences–procedure and evidence–rules

ACT OF ADJOURNAL (CRIMINAL PROCEDURE RULES AMENDMENT NO.3) (SEXUAL OFFENCES (PROCEDURE AND EVIDENCE (SCOTLAND) ACT 2002) 2002, SSI 2002 454; made under the Criminal Procedure (Scotland) Act 1995 s.305. In force: November 1, 2002; £2.50.

This Act of Adjournal amends the Act of Adjournal (Criminal Procedure Rules) 1996 (SI 1996 513) following provisions of the Sexual Offences (Procedure and

Evidence) (Scotland) Act 2002 which regulate procedure in pre-trial diets and further pre-trial diets held to establish whether an accused has legal representation where he is charged with a sexual offence. The Act sets out forms notifying the accused that he must be legally represented and that if he fails to appoint a solicitor, the court will do so, and prevents legal aid being withdrawn from an accused whose solicitor has been appointed by the court for these purposes. It also ensures that the Scottish Legal Aid Board is advised of the appointment of a solicitor by the court. It makes further provision in relation to applications to introduce evidence relating to sexual offences. It sets out the form for such applications and regulates the procedure for preliminary diets to hear such applications. It also makes provision to ensure that the terms of the application and decision by the court are recorded.

5464. Sexual Offences (Procedure and Evidence) (Scotland) Act 2002 (asp 9)–Commencement and Transitional Provisions Order

SEXUAL OFFENCES (PROCEDURE AND EVIDENCE) (SCOTLAND) ACT 2002 (COMMENCEMENT AND TRANSITIONAL PROVISIONS) ORDER 2002, SSI 2002 443; made under the Sexual Offences (Amendment) Act 2000 s.11. Commencement details: bringing into force various provisions of the 2002 Act on November 1, 2002; £1.75.

This Order brings into force various provisions of the Sexual Offences (Procedure and Evidence) (Scotland) Act 2002.

5465. Books

Christie, Michael G.A.; Gordon, Gerald H.–Criminal Law of Scotland: Vol 2. Scottish Universities Law Institute. Hardback: £150.00. ISBN 0-414-01399-9. W. Green & Son.

Connelly, Claire–Criminal. Greens Law Basics. Paperback: £9.95. ISBN 0-414-01231-3. W. Green & Son.

Criminal Law Statutes: 2002. A Parliament House Book. Paperback: £33.00. ISBN 0-414-01492-8. W. Green & Son.

Ferguson, Peter W.–Statutory Controlled Substance Offences. Green's Essential Legislation. Paperback: £32.00. ISBN 0-414-01491-X. W. Green & Son.

Guthrie, Tom–Statutory Sexual Offences. Green's Essential Legislation. Paperback: £28.00. ISBN 0-414-01473-1. W. Green & Son.

CRIMINAL PROCEDURE

5466. 12 month rule–extensions of time–entitlement of Crown to retrospective extension

[Criminal Procedure (Scotland) Act 1995 (c.46) s.65(1).]

H appeared, along with two others, on petition on July 19, 1999. H was fully committed and remanded in custody on July 26, 1999. The 12 month period under the Criminal Procedure (Scotland) Act 1995 s. 65(1) expired on July 19, 2000. H was released on October 7, 1999 and the proceedings against him were deferred until resolution of the proceedings against his co accused on January 8, 2001. The Crown presented a petition to the sheriff on March 8, 2001 for an extension of the 12 month period. The extension was granted and H appealed to the High Court arguing that while the 12 month period was running, the Crown should have elected to proceed against either H or the co accused.

Held, refusing the appeal, that the legislation did not create that dilemma for the Crown. Since it initially appeared that there was sufficient evidence to put J on petition it was proper for the Crown to do so and it was equally proper, in light of the investigation, to release J when it was clear there was not sufficient evidence. It had been a proper exercise of the Crown's discretion to proceed against the co accused, await the outcome and then try to precognosce them and reassess the position, all of which the Crown did with due expedition.

HOGG (STEVEN KENNETH) v. HM ADVOCATE 2002 S.L.T. 639, Lord Rodger L.J.G., Lord Carloway, Lord Hamilton, HCJ Appeal.

5467. 12 month rule – extensions of time – judge not impartial – indictment deserted pro loco et tempore – entitlement of Crown to retrospective extension

[Misuse of Drugs Act 1971 (c.38); Human Rights Act 1998 (c.42) Sch.1 Part I Art.6.]

R had been charged on indictment with a number of offences including contraventions of the Misuse of Drugs Act 1971. The 12 month period expired on May 8, 2001. R pleaded guilty to the charges on May 3, 2001 before Lord Hardie and it was discovered that Lord Hardie had been Lord Advocate when a restraint order was requested against R. Lord Hardie declined jurisdiction on May 4, despite the wishes of counsel on both sides for him to continue. R presented petition to the nobile officium seeking leave to withdraw his plea of guilty, arguing that it was contrary to the Human Rights Act 1998 Sch.1 Part I Art. 6 to have been brought before Lord Hardie rather than an impartial tribunal. The petition was granted and the indictment deserted pro loco et tempore. The Crown sought and was granted a retrospective extension of the 12 month period on May 30. R appealed arguing that it was necessary only in response to the Crown's unlawful act and the extension should have been sought between May 4 and May 8.

Held, refusing the appeal, that the breach of Art. 6 had been inadvertent on the part of the Crown. Defence counsel's reaction at the time suggested that he considered the error to have been venial. It was the kind of administrative inadvertence that could occur even in a system that was, generally speaking, operating effectively. In this particular case no great importance was attached to the fact of retrospectivity. The need for an extension depended on the outcome of the petition and had been sought when the guilty plea was withdrawn.

RIMMER (ROY WILLIAM) v. HM ADVOCATE 2002 S.C.C.R. 22, Lord Roger L.J.G., Lord Clarke, Lord Sutherland, HCJ Appeal.

5468. 12 months rule – accused arrested on non-appearance warrant – released on bail – no entitlement to resumption of protection of rule

[Criminal Procedure (Scotland) Act 1995 (c.46) s.65(1).]

K appeared on petition in August 1999 and was released on bail. The 12 month period was extended by three months. K failed to appear at the first diet and a warrant was issued and executed for his arrest. K appeared in court and was again released on bail. After further adjournments K lodged a plea in bar of trial on the ground that the proceedings were time barred under the Criminal Procedure (Scotland) Act 1995 s.65(1). The plea was repelled and K appealed to the High Court arguing that his release on bail after arrest for non appearance resulted in s.65(2) ceasing to operate and the resumption of the 12 month period.

Held, refusing the appeal, that Parliament clearly did not intend a person in K's position to benefit from the 12 month rule.

Observed that (1) where an accused could show that a non-appearance warrant had been granted improperly, he could have it suspended, even if executed, to ensure retention of the right to trial within 12 months, and (2) the court noted its awareness of the widely held view that granting a warrant would automatically bring proceedings on indictment to an end but was less clear with regard to its basis.

KELLY (PETER DAVID) v. HM ADVOCATE 2002 S.L.T. 43, Lord Rodger L.J.G., Lord Osborne, Lord Nimmo Smith, HCJ Appeal.

5469. 110 day rule – delay attributable to procurator fiscal

[Criminal Procedure (Scotland) Act 1995 (c.46) s.65(5), s.65(7).]

F was charged on indictment with assault and robbery and contraventions of the Firearms Act 1968 alleged to have taken place on May 30, 1997. Following a long procedural history, a trial was set for the sitting commencing on January 22, 2001. F appeared and the trial was adjourned until March 19. At that sitting F failed to appear and a warrant was issued for his arrest. At that time, only four days remained of the 110 day period of detention permitted under the Criminal Procedure (Scotland) Act 1995 s.65(5). No application was made at that time for a further extension of the 110 day period, a previous extension having been granted following F's failure to attend a previous diet. On April 11, F was granted bail. The Crown successfully appealed against the grant of bail on April 19. It was not, however until May 11 that the Crown applied for an extension of the 110 day period, to be granted retrospectively and to extend for a period of 95 days in order to allow F to be detained until the new trial which had been set for the sitting of the High Court commencing on June 25. No reasonable excuse was offered by the Crown for their inactivity on the case between March 28, when F had been re-arrested, and May 11 and it was confirmed that, without such a delay, it could have been possible for the case to be reindicted for the sitting commencing on May 14. F submitted that s.65(7) prevented an extension where the delay in proceeding to trial was due to any fault on the part of the prosecutor and that clearly the inactivity in the case had resulted in the trail taking place in the sitting commencing on June 25 rather than May 14. The advocate depute submitted that the real cause of the delay and the need for an extension of the 110 day period was F's failure to attend court and that, in the circumstances, the extension should be granted. A single judge of the High Court allowed the extension of 95 days and F appealed.

Held, allowing the appeal, that (1) s.65(7) clearly prohibited an extension of the 110 day period where the delay in bring the case to trial is attributable to the procurator fiscal, (2) no satisfactory explanation had been advanced by the Crown to cover the period of inactivity between March 28 and May 11 although the Crown clearly knew that F was still being detained as they had defended his action for bail, and (3) had the Crown acted promptly, the case could have been set for the earlier sitting commencing on May 14.

Observed, that (1) the trial whose commencement had been delayed in terms of s.65(7) was the one set to commence on June 25, with the delay being wholly attributable to the Crown's failure to promptly reindict F and that on that interpretation of s.65(7), the Crown's action was incompetent, and (2) had the Crown promptly applied for an extension of the 110 day period in order to fix the trial for the sitting on May 14, such an extension could competently have been granted. Opinions reserved as the whether a single judge had a discretion to grant such an application.

FARRELL (PAUL MICHAEL) v. HM ADVOCATE 2002 J.C. 50, Lord Hamilton, HCJ Appeal.

5470.   110 day rule–undue delay in execution of warrant

[Criminal Procedure (Scotland) Act 1995 (c.46) s.136.]

G was charged on summary complaint with a number of contraventions of the Road Traffic Act 1988 most of which were subject to a time limit for commencement of proceedings as set out in the Criminal Procedure (Scotland) Act 1995 s.136. The expiration of the time limit was June 18, 2000. The warrant to cite G was granted on June 16, received by the fiscal's office on June 19 but not executed until June 28. G took a plea to the competency of the statutory charges to which s.136 applied on the grounds that proceedings had not been commenced timeously due to the undue delay in executing the warrant. The sheriff repelled the plea and G appealed. The reason given by the Crown for the delay was that it had been decided that a letter should be prepared to accompany the warrant to the police advising them to invite G to attend court. Due to internal pressures within the fiscal's office, the letter was not prepared until June 24 and, having been posted on a Friday, did not arrive with the police until June 27.

Held, allowing the appeal, that (1) delay in execution of a warrant was only excusable where such a delay had been outwith the fiscal's control and could not be excused where such a delay had been caused by the actions or omissions of the fiscal or his staff, *Smith v. Peter Walker & Son (Edinburgh) Ltd* 1978 J.C. 44, [1980] C.L.Y. 3019, followed, and (2) although the warrant was granted within the time limit set out in s.136, it had arrived in the fiscal's office after the expiry of that time limit and every effort should therefore have been made to ensure that it was executed as quickly as possible; lack of typing resources being an unacceptable reason for a delay. Opinion of the court per Lord Cameron of Lochbroom.

GALLOWAY v. CLARK 2001 S.C.C.R. 734, Lord Cameron of Lochbroom, Lord Osborne, Lord Sutherland, HCJ Appeal.

5471. Committal—until liberation in due course of law—custody statement attached to petition—whether proper basis for remand

An accused person, held on remand on charges of housebreaking, lodged a bill of suspension, complaining that the sheriff erred in finding that a custody statement attached to the petition afforded sufficient basis for the grant of warrant to imprison him pending trial.

Held, refusing the bill, that (1) contrary to the sheriff's view it was necessary to examine the bill on its substantive merits, and (2) the test was that the custody statement should disclose a "proper basis" for incarcerating an accused pending trial, that test involved no more than an indication of sources of evidence from which a sufficiency might be obtained, and was satisfied in the present case.

HYND v. RITCHIE 2002 S.L.T. 984, Lord Marnoch, Lord Macfadyen, Lord Osborne, HCJ.

5472. Contempt of court—order prohibiting publication of proceedings—circumstances in which order considered necessary—recall of order

[Contempt of Court Act 1981 (c.49) s.4(2).]

BBC appealed, by way of petition, to the nobile officium against an order under the Contempt of Court Act 1981 s.4(2). The order had been pronounced in the case of D, who had lodged a special defence incriminating W in response to a charge of murder. The order prohibited publication of reports about the trial until 24 hours after the trial was concluded. The BBC sought recall or variation of the order and the judge accepted that the order was unnecessarily wide and restricted it to any matter showing or intending to show W's participation in the events leading to the death of the deceased. BBC then appealed, during the hearing of which, D was convicted of murder.

Held, allowing the appeal and recalling the order, that (1) the general rule was that trials take place in public, promoting not only the interests of the accused by ensuring that others can see the fairness or otherwise of the trial, but also the interests of the public, who could see and, if appropriate, "endorse, criticise, applaud or castigate the conduct of their courts"; (2) the general rule favoured publication, therefore any s.4(2) order was an exception and as such the court had to consider its necessity and appropriate scope; (3) in considering the necessity of an order the court had to have regard to the competing considerations of ensuring a fair trial and open justice. Consideration of those points, in the context of Convention of Human Rights jurisprudence would determine whether there was "a pressing social need" to make the order; (4) it would be relevant for the court to assess the risk of prejudice and how to deal with that, ie judicial direction to a jury. If the court was to conclude that such measures would not adequately deal with the risk of prejudice, a s.4(2) order would be considered necessary; (5) the court was prepared to accept that there was likely to be a considerable amount of evidence led that would suggest W had been involved in the offence and also to assume that potential jurors at a possible trial of W might notice the reports and recall it at the trial, and (6) the interests of justice in any proceedings against W and the public interest in having fair and accurate reports were both substantial but the court was not satisfied that an order was necessary to deal with the risk of prejudice in any trial of W. Directions by a judge could deal with the risk of prejudice and if the judge felt that the jury could not return a fair and impartial verdict the diet could be deserted. Opinion reserved as to whether proceedings against W were pending or imminent at the time the order was made. Opinion of the court per Lord Rodger, LJ-G.

BBC, PETITIONERS (NO.3) 2002 J.C. 27, Lord Rodger L.J.G., Lord Abernethy, Lord Kirkwood, HCJ Appeal.

5473. **Contempt of court–order prohibiting publication of proceedings– competence–recall**

[Contempt of Court Act 1981 (c.49) s.2(2), s.4(2).]

B, who was on trial on a charge of assault, sodomy and murder, moved for an order under the Contempt of Court Act 1981 s.4(2) postponing the publication of any report of the proceedings or any part of them until the jury's verdict had been delivered. B argued that although a plea in bar of trial on account of prejudicial publicity had been rejected, the exceptional nature of the case might result in responsible court reporting stimulating a "feeding frenzy" on the part of less responsible elements in the media, including publication of material on web sites, some of which still carried earlier prejudicial material. An order had been made at an earlier stage, following a hearing on a minute of postponement, postponing reporting of "these proceedings" (amended by the clerk of court from "today's proceedings") "until further notice".

Held, refusing the motion, that (1) it was improbable that the earlier order was intended to extend to B's trial and, in any event, the court was entitled to terminate the order and would do so having regard to the terms of the order as it was wrong to leave the reporting of the trial in a state of ambiguity, and (2) B's acceptance that fair and accurate reporting did not itself create a problem was fatal to his motion where s.4(2) was concerned with such reporting and not with material outwith that scope, to which the s.2(2) strict liability rule applied and, in any event, there was no basis for concluding that fair and accurate reports of the trial could create a substantial risk of prejudice to the administration of justice in the same proceedings.

HM ADVOCATE v. BEGGS (NO.1) 2002 S.L.T. 135, Lord Osborne, HCJ.

5474. **Contempt of court–witnesses–summary punishment–independent and impartial tribunal**

[European Convention on Human Rights 1950 Art.6.]

A witness was called by the Crown to give evidence against her boyfriend in a trial for robbery. In examination in chief she gave an account which contradicted a statement previously made in precognition. The witness admitted committing perjury but gave two further inconsistent accounts despite receiving a warning of prevarication from the sheriff. The witness received a further warning and a hearing was held to consider the matter. The witness was found guilty but released on bail to appear in court each day and on the conclusion of the trial for the purpose of being sentenced. The witness submitted that the sheriff was not entitled to make that finding as he had acted as both judge and prosecutor in his own cause and had thus failed to appear to be independent and impartial, contrary to the European Convention on Human Rights 1950 Art.6: she should have been prosecuted in respect of her admission when she could have received legal advice and have led witnesses in her defence.

Held, holding the finding justified, that the sheriff had not acted as both prosecutor and judge, but had simply assessed the evidence of the witness already before the court, and her credibility and reliability, which formed part of the normal function of a sheriff *Mair (Bryan), Petitioner*, 2001 G.W.D. 14-543 not followed.

LITTLE (CHERYL), PETITIONER 2002 S.L.T. (Sh Ct) 12, Sheriff JS Forbes, Sh Ct (Tayside, Central and Fife).

5475. **Criminal appeals–evidence–precognition of witness differing from evidence at trial–refusal to sign affidavit**

[Criminal Procedure (Scotland) Act 1995 (c.46) s.106.]

B was convicted of conspiracy to rob and assault and robbery, acting along with two others (M and D), and attempted subornation of perjury in respect of D. He appealed against conviction, inter alia, on the grounds of new exculpatory evidence in terms of the Criminal Procedure (Scotland) Act 1995 s.106(3)(a). M and D had previously pled guilty and gave evidence against him. D's evidence was accepted to be essential. B claimed that D had since admitted that his evidence against B was untrue and had been precognosced to that effect, giving an explanation why he had given the evidence he did. D then refused to sign an affidavit based on the precognition, with no explanation. B tendered affidavits from his solicitor speaking to D's change of evidence, from M that B was not the third man who assisted M and D, and from a prisoner that D had admitted to him that he lied at the trial in incriminating B.

Held, dismissing the appeal, that information in the form of a precognition of a witness was not "evidence" for the purpose of s.106(3)(a), being merely the precognoscer's account of what was said by the witness, and the consequence of the refusal to sign the affidavit, whatever the reasons, was that its contents could not be accepted as evidence under s.106.

BINNIE (WILLIAM SMART) v. HM ADVOCATE 2002 S.L.T. 994, Lord Gill L.J.C., Lord Kirkwood, Lord MacLean, HCJ.

5476. **Criminal appeals–reports–conviction by panel of judges in Netherlands–provision of report by trial judge–applicability of the Criminal Procedure (Scotland) Act 1995**

[European Convention on Human Rights 1950 Art.6; Criminal Procedure (Scotland) Act 1995 (c.46) s.110(1)(a), s.113(1); High Court of Justiciary (Proceedings in the Netherlands) (United Nations) Order 1998 (SI 1998 2251) Art.3(2).]

M, who was convicted in the Netherlands by a panel of Scottish judges sitting under Scottish procedure of the murder of the persons killed in the Lockerbie air disaster in 1988, lodged a note of appeal against conviction and petitioned the nobile officium, the prayer of which sought an order in hoc statu that "no report should be sought or furnished in terms of the Criminal Procedure (Scotland) Act 1995 s.113(1) or otherwise of said Act by the presiding judge, or other trial judges". M argued inter alia that (1) the High Court of Justiciary (Proceedings in the Netherlands) (United Nations) Order 1998, under which the court was constituted, did not allow for the provision of such a report; (2) the relevant provisions of the 1995 Act were inapplicable to the appeal; (3) a report was rendered unnecessary by reason of the written judgment which the trial judges had been under an obligation to issue, and (4) to permit a report to be provided would give the judges a second opportunity to state their reasons and might appear to prejudice the impartiality of the appeal court, contrary to the European Convention on Human Rights 1950 Art.6.

Held, refusing the petition, that (1) in terms of Art.3(2) of the Order, trial proceedings were to be conducted in accordance with the law relating to proceedings on indictment before the High Court in Scotland except insofar as special provision was made in the Order, and in the event of a conviction the same was implied in respect of appeal proceedings; (2) s.110(1)(a) and s.113.(1) of the Act therefore applied and a report should be provided to the High Court in order to assist in the consideration of the accused's appeal, it being appropriate that the trial judges should be given the opportunity to make observations on the grounds of appeal, and (3) the provision of a report would not breach the requirements of Art.6.

HM ADVOCATE v. AL-MEGRAHI (NO.5); *sub nom.* MEGRAHI v. HM ADVOCATE (NO.5); AL-MEGRAHI v. HM ADVOCATE (NO.5) 2002 J.C. 38, Lord Kirkwood, Lord Carloway, Lord Hamilton, Lord Nimmo Smith, Lord Wheatley, HCJ Appeal.

5477. Criminal Procedure (Amendment) (Scotland) Act 2002 (asp 4)

This Act of the Scottish Parliament provides, retrospectively, as to the effect on trial diets in summary proceedings of arrest warrants granted at intermediate diets. This Act received Royal Assent on March 8, 2002.

5478. Devolution issues–separation of powers–challenge to decision following Lord Advocate's reference–complaint that Lord Advocate and court acted ultra vires

See CONSTITUTIONAL LAW: HM Advocate v. H. §5396

5479. Devolution issues–time limit for raising–ultra vires

[Scotland Act 1998 (c.46) Sch.6; Criminal Procedure (Scotland) Act 1995 (c.46) s.305; Act of Adjournal (Devolution Issues Rules) 1999 (SI 1999 1346) r.40.2, r.40.5; Human Rights Act 1998 (c.42) Sch.1 Part I Art.6.]

D, charged with being concerned in the supply of cocaine, appealed against the decision of a court of the trial judge and two others that the Act of Adjournal (Devolution Issues Rules) 1999 was intra vires. At trial, D had objected to the use of a transcript of an interview because it had been obtained in a manner incompatible with the right to a fair trial under the Human Rights Act 1998 Sch.1 Part I Art.6. The Crown had replied that the matter could be a devolution issue and, if so, written notice should have been given within seven days after service of the indictment in terms of r.40.2(1) of the Act of Adjournal. D then argued that the Act of Adjournal was ultra vires in prescribing a time limit, which was rejected. On appeal D argued that (1) because the Act of Adjournal was an act of the whole Lords Commissioners of Justiciary, the High Court was precluded from hearing and determining the correctness or otherwise of a challenge to the Act or any provision within it on the ground that it was incompatible with the Convention, and should have referred the matter to the Privy Council; (2) the Act of Adjournal was a legislative act involving policy making which was for the Scottish Parliament alone and the present case raised questions as to the functions of the Scottish Ministers constituting a devolution issue; (3) the court had failed to address whether it was an independent and impartial tribunal in determining the vires of the Act of Adjournal; (4) the trial judge erred in refusing to allow a devolution issue to be raised on the leading of the interview transcript in relation to D being refused access to a solicitor, and thereafter holding the evidence admissible; (5) there was a miscarriage of justice in that the trial judge failed to direct the jury on the provisions of the Convention.

Held, refusing the appeal, that (1) the mere fact the court was required to determine whether or not the provisions of the Act of Adjournal were compatible with the Convention did not make it any less an independent and impartial tribunal; criticisms of legislative provisions were often found in judicial opinions and the court, and its individual members, were expected to bring an unbiased and impartial mind to the exercise of their judicial duties. Reference of a devolution issue, without prior determination of the issue by the court, was for the discretion of the court and whether the court should be required to refer a devolution issue to the Privy Council was for the discretion of the Lord Advocate; (2) under the Criminal Procedure (Scotland) Act 1995 s.305 and the Scotland Act 1998 Sch.6, it was for the court to make provision for the stage at which a devolution issue should be raised, and r.40.5 allowed a devolution issue to be raised at trial on cause shown, which was both practical and effective for preserving D's Convention rights; (3) there was nothing in the opinion of the court below to suggest they were addressed on their competency to adjudicate on the challenge. It was sufficient at the time of their determination for the court to indicate that the Act of Adjournal was intra vires and it could not tenably be suggested that the subsequent conduct of the trial by the defence was, or could have been, affected by present ignorance of the full reasons for the decision on vires. The court had left it open to D to show cause why the devolution issue should be received; (4) while it could be said the trial judge had accepted he misdirected himself in relation to whether a devolution issue had arisen, it had not been shown that a miscarriage of justice had resulted from allowing the evidence: neither Scots law or the Convention required that in all cases a detainee should have the opportunity to have their solicitor present and there was no suggestion that the absence of a solicitor had a decisive effect on the preparation of D's defence, and (5) there was no need to direct the jury on the Convention provisions.

DICKSON (ANNIE MULVEY) v. HM ADVOCATE; *sub nom*. GOURLAY v. HM ADVOCATE 2001 J.C. 203, Lord Cameron of Lochbroom, Lord Hamilton, Lord Macfadyen, Lord Milligan, Lord Weir, HCJ Appeal.

5480. Drink driving offences–breath tests–nature of device required to meet type approval criteria–standards of measurement

[Road Traffic Act 1988 (c.52) s.5(1), s.7(1)(a).]

B appealed against his conviction for a contravention of the Road Traffic Act 1988 s.5(1). The device used to analyse specimens of breath had been an Intoximeter EC/IR, manufactured by Alcotek Inc. The "device known as the Intoximeter EC/IR manufactured by Intoximeters Inc" had been approved by the Secretary of State by virtue of s.7(1)(a). Two issues arose for determination (1) whether the Intoximeter EC/IR manufactured by Alcotek Inc was an approved device, and (2) whether inconsistencies in the way the device responded to mouth alcohol deprived it of type approval.

Held, dismissing the appeal, that (1) Alcotek Inc had contracted with Intoximeter Inc to manufacture the device in accordance with specifications as to the parts used and assembly of the device which meant that the device in question was in all respects identical to the device which had received approval. It was accordingly not necessary for each device to have been manufactured by Intoximeter Inc in order for it to meet the type approval criteria, *Chief Constable of Northumbria v. Browne* [1986] R.T.R. 113, [1986] C.L.Y. 2878 considered, and (2) whilst the requirement to detect mouth alcohol had posed problems for the device, safeguards had been incorporated in order to remove the risk of an unreliable reading resulting in injustice. The fact that the device had been inconsistent in its reaction to mouth alcohol in tests did not merit a conclusion that it had not been operating correctly at the time when a sample had been taken from B at the police station.

BROWN (GARY JOHN) v. GALLACHER; *sub nom*. BROWN v. GALLAGHER 2002 S.L.T. 756, Lord Cameron of Lochbroom, Lord Hamilton, Lord Morison, HCJ Appeal.

5481. Drink driving offences–breath tests–provision of breath specimen–compatibility with human rights

[Road Traffic Act 1988 (c.52) s.7; Human Rights Act 1998 (c.42) Sch.1 Part I Art.6.]

B, charged with driving with excess breath alcohol, appealed against a sheriff's dismissal of his devolution minute submitting that the Crown had no power to lead and rely on evidence relating to the measured results produced by the Intoximeter device from B's breath samples. B argued (1) that he had a right not to incriminate himself under the European Convention on Human Rights 1950 Art.6 and there was no material distinction between what could be termed self incriminatory testimony and the compulsory provision of a breath sample by an accused, and (2) that even if that right was limited by the legitimate aim of the statutory regime under the Road Traffic Act 1988, the sanction imposed for failure to comply with the s.7 requirement constituted that degree of compulsion such as, in effect, destroyed B's right not to incriminate himself.

Held, dismissing the appeal, that European human rights jurisprudence recognised a distinction between material such as breath or urine specimens, provided in accordance with prescribed statutory procedures, which had an existence independent of the person concerned and was not therefore obtained by coercion, and answers obtained under compulsion, and the requirement made of B, being otherwise lawfully made, did not interfere with his implied right not to incriminate himself even though it was accompanied by notice that failure to provide the specimens might make him liable to prosecution, and did not prejudice his right to a fair trial, *Brown v. Stott* [2001] 2 W.L.R. 817, [2001] C.L.Y. 6319 considered.

BROWN (SCOTT) v. GALLACHER 2002 S.L.T. 1135, Lord Cameron of Lochbroom, Lord Gill L.J.C., Lord MacLean, HCJ.

5482. Extradition–rules–forms of notice

ACT OF ADJOURNAL (CRIMINAL PROCEDURE RULES AMENDMENT NO.4) (EXTRADITION) 2002, SSI 2002 517; made under the Extradition Act 1989 s.14A; and the Criminal Procedure (Scotland) Act 1995 s.305. In force: December 1, 2002; £1.75.

This Act of Adjournal amends the Act of Adjournal (Criminal Procedure Rules) 1996 (SI 1996 513) to provide a form of notice to consent for committal for return to be used for the purposes of the Extradition Act 1989 s.14A(3).

5483. Judges–bias–plea tendered before judge holding public office connected to case

[Human Rights Act 1998 (c.42) Sch.1 Part I Art.6.]

R was charged with drug and traffic offences. He appeared before the sheriff and was released on bail. The case called in January but was deserted due to the absence of a co accused. The case was reindicted, called before Lord Hardie and twice adjourned. The Crown sought recall of bail, concerned that R might abscond. Lord Hardie recalled bail and remanded R in custody until the adjourned date. R pleaded guilty and the case was adjourned overnight. During that time Lord Hardie realised that he had been Lord Advocate when a petition for a restraint order against R had been presented. The next day he declined to act further, adjourning the case for sentencing. R petitioned the nobile officium arguing that (1) he considered himself under pressure following recall of bail, and (2) it was unlawful in terms of the Human Rights Act 1998 Sch.1 Part I Art.6 for the case to have called before Lord Hardie since he could not be seen to be impartial. The Crown argued that the petition was incompetent given that R had had the opportunity to withdraw his guilty plea.

Held, granting the order to withdraw the plea of guilty, (Lord Marnoch dissenting) that (1) it was appropriate for the Court to hear the petition and decide whether R should be granted leave to withdraw his plea since it was not competent for the trial judge to do so; (2) R's argument that he was under pressure was not justified. R had legal advisors and was aware of the charges against him; (3) in recognising the appearance of impartiality, Lord Hardie had acted accordingly in removing himself, and (4) the High Court had a duty to ensure that each case was tried before an impartial judge and the trial judge in this case could not pass the objective test of impartiality. In the dissenting judgment, it was stated that, at worst, the fact that Lord Hardie was the presiding judge was an irregularity which did not give rise to any unfairness, real or perceived.

Observed, that the question of impartiality, real or perceived, should be judged from the moment the judge or tribunal first becomes seised of the case, not simply when the judge first acts.

RIMMER (ROY WILLIAM), PETITIONER 2002 S.C.C.R. 1, Lord Cameron of Lochbroom, Lord Clarke, Lord Marnoch, HCJ.

5484. Life imprisonment–rules

ACT OF ADJOURNAL (CRIMINAL PROCEDURE RULES AMENDMENT) (CONVENTION RIGHTS (COMPLIANCE) (SCOTLAND) ACT 2001) 2002, SSI

2002 137; made under the Criminal Procedure (Scotland) Act 1995 s.305. In force: March 4, 2002; £1.75.

This Act of Adjournal amends the Act of Adjournal (Criminal Procedure Rules) 1996 (SI 1996 513) to extend the definition of "punishment part hearing" to include transferred life prisoners and also to clarify the definition of "life prisoner".

5485. Nobile officium–competency–alternative remedy available–application to Scottish Criminal Cases Review Commission

[Prisoners and Criminal Proceedings (Scotland) Act 1993 (c.9) s.2; Criminal Procedure (Scotland) Act 1995 (c.46) Pt.XA.]

An accused person was convicted in 1997 of abduction, robbery and sexual assault. He received a discretionary life sentence, with 15 years as the designated part under the Prisoners and Criminal Proceedings (Scotland) Act 1993 s.2. He appealed against sentence but abandoned his appeal in March 1998 before it was heard. The accused petitioned the nobile officium seeking to have that appeal reinstated, seeking review of the designated part of his sentence principally in the light of *O'Neill (John) v. HM Advocate* 1999 S.L.T. 958, [1999] C.L.Y. 5949.

Held, dismissing the petition, that (1) there were no exceptional circumstances, notwithstanding the decision in *O'Neill*, the petitioner having acted on legal advice although it was now suggested that that advice was wrong, and (2) there was now a procedure available to the petitioner under the Criminal Procedure (Scotland) Act 1995 Pt.XA which might result in the Scottish Criminal Cases Review Commission referring his case to the High Court, and this was an appropriate first step before the nobile officium jurisdiction was exercised.

McWILLIAM, PETITIONER 2002 S.L.T. 972, Lord Hamilton, Lord Reed, Lord Drummond Young, HCJ Appeal.

5486. Nobile officium–competency–extension of time limit for leave to appeal

[Criminal Procedure (Scotland) Act 1995 (c.46) s.107(4); European Convention on Human Rights 1950 Art.6.]

R petitioned the nobile officium for leave to appeal against the refusal of leave to appeal against conviction for murder, theft and an attempt to defeat the ends of justice, after a breakdown in communication between her solicitors and counsel resulted in failure to comply with the 14 day time limit under the Criminal Procedure (Scotland) Act 1995 s.107(4) which provided no possibility of extension. R moved the court to reconsider *Connolly, Petitioner* 1997 S.L.T. 689, [1997] C.L.Y. 5806, arguing that it was wrongly decided, and that it conflicted with the European Convention on Human Rights Art.6(1) and Art.6(3) in respect that she had not been given a fair and proper hearing, nor received effective legal representation.

Held, refusing the petition, that no Convention case law had been cited and the court had no basis for acceding to the case presented under the Convention; that there was no other cogent reason for holding that *Connolly* was wrongly decided; and that the instants was simply a case where a statutory time limit had been missed and that was not a circumstance which could justify the use of the nobile officium.

RYAN, PETITIONER 2002 S.L.T. 275, Lord Gill L.J.C., Lady Cosgrove, Lord Marnoch, Lady Paton, Lord Reed, HCJ Appeal.

5487. Oppression–delay–execution of warrant in order to serve sentence

B, convicted of embezzlement, petitioned the nobile officium for suspension of a warrant for his apprehension dated September 25, 2001 and to quash a sentence of nine months' imprisonment imposed on May 21, 2001. B had appealed against sentence and was granted interim liberation on May 30. The appeal was formally abandoned on 13 August. Letters were written by his solicitors to the warrants officer of Strathclyde Police on three occasions in August and September explaining the abandonment of the appeal and seeking to be advised as soon as possible when a warrant was issued for his apprehension so he could hand himself in and begin his sentence. The warrant was issued on September 25. Letters were written to the procurator fiscal at Paisley and to B's Edinburgh agents in an attempt to ensure prompt execution of the warrant. No action was taken by the police, and the Crown offered no explanation for the delay. B argued that the delay was oppressive and that had the warrant been executed promptly, his sentence would by then have been served.

Held, granting the prayer of petition, that in the absence of a satisfactory explanation the failure to execute the warrant was oppressive where the petitioner had been attempting to rebuild his life and had endured almost a year of anxiety and uncertainty.

BEGLAN, PETITIONER 2002 S.L.T. 1175, Lord Gill L.J.C., Lord Kingarth, Lord MacLean, HCJ.

5488. Pleas–plea in bar of trial–delay–conviction not incompatible with convention rights

[Scotland Act 1998 (c.46) s.57; Human Rights Act 1998 (c.42) s.6, Sch.1 Part I Art.6(1).]

R charged on indictment with six offences of indecent behaviour towards children, raised an issue under the Human Rights Act 1998 as to whether he had been brought to trial within a reasonable time in terms of Human Rights Act 1998 Sch.1 Part I Art.6(1). The trial judge refused his plea in bar of trial, holding that failure to bring a person to trial within a reasonable time did not in itself render further prosecution a breach of Convention rights. R appealed, arguing, inter alia, that (1) it would be wrong to make too sharp a distinction between the right to a trial within a reasonable time and other rights comprised in Art.6, breach of which resulted in the quashing of proceedings; (2) the European jurisprudence related only to cases where the proceedings had already been concluded before a breach of the time guarantee became apparent and did not support the Crown's position; (3) the only true and effective protection for accused persons and the only real compulsitor on prosecutors to comply with the Convention requirement was the risk that proceedings would be stopped or annulled; (4) the court was acting incompatibly with R's Convention rights within s.6(1) of the 1998 Act if it allowed a prosecution to proceed after a reasonable time had expired, and (5) whatever the position under the Act, the court was not able to provide any redress short of discontinuance by reason of the provisions of the Scotland Act 1998 s.57. The Crown argued, inter alia, that "acts" of the Lord Advocate for the purposes of s.57 did not include every act taken in relation to criminal proceedings.

Held, refusing the appeal, that (1) the right to trial within a reasonable time could properly be distinguished from the other rights in Art.6 in terms of the possible consequences on breach of the right; (2) there were limits to the assistance that could be derived from European jurisprudence, as the European Court was primarily concerned with the question whether the member state had complied with its obligations under the Convention and the question of the appropriate remedy was of no practical importance to it, but it was sufficiently clear that annulment was not a necessary consequence of a breach of Art.6(1) as regards reasonable time, and it was not incompatible with the rights of R to proceed with the prosecution; (3) the right to have proceedings concluded within a reasonable time was one which required the balancing of different interests, and the best way for that to be done was for the court to exercise a judgment, when necessary, according to the particular circumstances of the case: it was not the case that the only effective sanction was the risk that proceedings would be stopped or annulled; (4) s.6(1) of the 1998 Act should be construed not as meaning that an action was incompatible with a Convention right if it involved any infringement of that right, however minor, but that the action was incompatible with a Convention right if it was of such character as to entitle the holder to require that it should not be taken at all; (5) s.57(2) should be interpreted in the same manner as Art.6(1): a conviction was not incompatible with a breach of the reasonable time requirement provided certain quite stringent conditions were met, and it was the length of the proceedings, not the proceedings themselves, which contravened Art.6(1), and (6) "acts" of the Lord Advocate for the purposes of s.57(2) beyond those of bringing a prosecution initially before the court, but where the issue was brought before the court for determination it could not be said that the Lord Advocate had acted unlawfully until the court had determined that it could give no effective redress for the alleged violation short of ordering that proceedings at his instance should be discontinued.

HM ADVOCATE v. R; *sub nom.* R v. HM ADVOCATE 2002 S.L.T. 834, Lord Coulsfield, Lord Cameron of Lochbroom, Lord Caplan, HCJ Appeal.

5489. Pleas−plea in bar of trial−extradition−irregularity and illegality of extradition proceedings

See EXTRADITION: HM Advocate v. Vervuren. §5598

5490. Pleas−plea in bar of trial−fixed payments for criminal legal aid−right to legal representative of own choice−chosen representative withdrawing due to lack of funds

[European Convention on Human Rights 1950 Art.6; Criminal Legal Aid (Fixed Payments) (Scotland) Regulations 1999 (SI 1999 491).]

V, charged on summary complaint with drug offences, appealed against the sheriff's decision repelling her plea in bar of trial that the fixed payment scheme under the Criminal Legal Aid (Fixed Payments) (Scotland) Regulations 1999 breached her rights under the European Convention on Human Rights 1950 Art.6. She argued that her right to a representative of her own choosing was breached where the particular solicitor she had selected was unable to act by virtue of the 1999 Regulations which did not provide fair or adequate remuneration where the trial was to be heard in Fort William and that solicitor practised from Glasgow.

Held, refusing the appeal, that the Convention had to be read reasonably in regard to the actual functioning of the courts and the legal profession so that the accused was entitled to select from among the practitioners available, qualified and willing to act in the particular circumstances and could not insist on the services of a particular individual. There was nothing in V's argument which took the instant case outwith the ambit of the decision in *McLean v. Buchanan* [2001] UKPC D3, [2001] 1 W.L.R. 2425, [2001] C.L.Y. 6760, and it would be premature to hold that there must be a breach of her Convention rights.

VICKERS v. BUCHANAN 2002 S.L.T. 686, Lord Coulsfield, Lord MacLean, Lord Sutherland, HCJ Appeal.

5491. Pleas−withdrawal of guilty plea−refusal to accept−no miscarriage of justice

The Scottish Criminal Cases Review Commission (S) referred the case of C, convicted of fraudulent evasion of betting duty and fined £500, on the basis that there had been a possible miscarriage of justice, and the court ordained C to lodge a bill of suspension. C had pled guilty by written intimation and the diet was adjourned to allow him to obtain legal advice. On November 21, 1991 C had appeared before the sheriff court and the matter was again adjourned to obtain a social inquiry report. On December 12, 1991 C appeared again, represented by a solicitor (Y) and the court deferred sentence for further reports. On January 23, 1992 C, represented by a different solicitor, sought to withdraw the plea of guilty, which was refused. C was allegedly advised that he had no grounds for appeal. C argued that the plea of guilty was tendered without advice or representation and that when visiting Y before the December 12 diet he had told Y that he disputed the amount. That was also referred to in the social inquiry report.

Held, refusing the bill, that (1) the court had to consider the bill rather than the reasons given by S in making the reference, but it was useful to note that S had concentrated on Y's failure to seek to have the guilty plea withdrawn and apparently ignored C's stated position that he disputed the amount of tax. C's averments supported this and though it was suggested that C was not guilty at all during submissions, this was not supported by the bill and not considered; (2) it was material that C had engaged a solicitor in May 1991 to deal with the outstanding Customs and Excise claim, but had not told him about the complaint or sought his advice before pleading guilty and did not dispute the figure either when he pled guilty in writing or when he appeared on 21 November, after a continuation which he was expressly told was to enable him to seek legal advice; (3) C's averments of his instructions to Y were vague, there was no evidence of any material that Y could have put before the court to justify a withdrawal, and even the current bill contained no indication that C had any defence or that the figure was wrong or inaccurate; the figure was merely "not accepted" without an indication of any basis upon which C could dispute it, and (4) C had failed to satisfy the court that there had been any miscarriage of justice. There was no basis for concluding, given the unspecific averments, that Y had failed in his duty on December 12, but also having regard to the whole background there was no basis for concluding that if C had been "given his voice" at any point the eventual outcome of conviction and sentence would have been any different.

CROMBIE v. CLARK (PROCURATOR FISCAL); *sub nom.* CROMBIE v. GUILD 2001 S.L.T. 635, Lord Prosser, Lord Bonomy, Lord Cowie, HCJ Appeal.

5492.   Prosecutions—publicity—previous convictions disclosed

[Contempt of Court Act 1981 (c.49); European Convention Extradition Order 1990 (SI 1990 1507) Art.14; European Convention on Human Rights 1950 Art.6.]

B was charged on indictment with murder. Following the discovery of dismembered body parts, the police obtained a warrant to search B's house and subsequently a petition warrant for B's arrest. A week later, B surrendered himself to Dutch police in Amsterdam and, was extradited to Scotland. Following indictment, B presented two minutes to the court; the first sought to have the Lord Advocate's right to prosecute him revoked on the grounds that publicity given to the case and to B personally prior to the trial had made it impossible for him to receive a fair trial. He argued that, although the facts of each case had to be examined in detail, it was enough to demonstrate that there was an appearance of unfairness. He further argued that the right to a fair trial had supremacy over all other rights including the right of the Crown to prosecute a criminal offence. The second minute challenged the validity of the extradition procedures and sought to have allegations of dismemberment and disposal of the body removed from the indictment. In support of that proposition, B argued that the extradition proceedings had been granted by the Dutch court in terms of the first petition warrant against him which alleged assault and dismemberment causing death. The extradition was refused in respect of the second petition warrant which included a charge of dismemberment in an attempt to pervert the course of justice. B argued that such inclusion was contrary to the terms of the European Convention Extradition Order 1990 Art.14. B appealed against Lord Wheatley's refusal of the minutes, on the basis that B had failed to meet the test in *HM Advocate v. Stuurman (Pre-trial)* 1980 J.C. 111, [1980] C.L.Y. 3010 and on the ground that the competence of the indictment was a matter for the Scots courts.

Held, refusing the appeal, that (1) the test was not whether a fair trial was impossible but whether it could be reasonably expected; (2) the Contempt of Court Act 1981 confined the application of strict liability when proceedings were active which in the instant case was when the petition warrant had been granted and the court had no jurisdiction over the material published about the case or about B prior to that date either under statute or common law; (3) it was impossible for the court to study the investigative procedures adopted by the police in detail to determine whether a petition warrant could have been sought at an earlier stage thereby restricting the amount of adverse publicity, and although such delay could give rise to a complaint by B against the police, such a complaint would only succeed in the most extreme cases; (4) the pretrial publicity was extensive and prejudicial and included allegations in relation to previous convictions, for both assault and murder and, had the trial been likely to proceed under the 110 day rule, it would be unlikely that it could proceed and ensure a fair trial and the Crown would have to give consideration to releasing B from custody and attempting to bring the case to trial within the 12 month time limit; (5) the prejudicial nature of the information had to be balanced against the lapse of time and the process of the trial and having weighed up the various factors the court could not differ from the conclusions reach by Lord Wheatley, *Stuurman*, followed, and (6) in relation to the minute on the extradition issue, the court agreed with the findings of Lord Wheatley.

Observed, that (1) the court's duty did not extend to an investigation of complaints into police procedures and resultant delays particularly before the trial had begun and where the court was satisfied that B had not been deprived of his right to protection; (2) from the court's review of material published, some may well have come from police sources; (3) the risk of prejudicial pretrial publicity was not only an issue in relation to the potential jurors, but also to the recollections and opinions of witnesses, and (4) refusal of the minute did not affect B's right to claim a breach of the European Convention on Human Rights 1950 Art.6 in relation to the trial proceedings. Opinion of the Court per Lord Coulsfield.

BEGGS v. HM ADVOCATE (PRELIMINARY DIET) 2001 S.C.C.R. 836, Lord Coulsfield, Lord Mackay of Drumadoon, Lord Penrose, HCJ Appeal.

5493. Right to fair trial–acquiescence–hearing by independent and impartial tribunal–delay in challenging conviction

[Misuse of Drugs Act 1971 (c.38) s.5(2); European Convention on Human Rights 1950.]

L was convicted of contravening the Misuse of Drugs Act 1971 s.5(2) following trial on April 12, 30 and May 24, 1999. He was ultimately admonished on October 24, 2000 after sentence was deferred on two occasions for good behaviour. In October 2001 L brought a bill of suspension relating to his conviction on the basis that his trial was heard before a temporary sheriff, who was not an independent and impartial tribunal in terms of the European Convention on Human Rights 1950, and argued that he did not have full knowledge that he was entitled to challenge his conviction until the Privy Council decision of *Millar v. Dickson* [2001] UKPC D4, [2002] 1 W.L.R. 1615, [2001] C.L.Y. 6372 was issued on July 24, 2001. The Crown contended that the bill was barred by acquiescence.

Held, dismissing the bill, that (1) a complainer could be barred by the lapse of time from challenging a conviction or sentence, even where the ground of challenge was one of competence; (2) if waiver was not, in appropriate circumstances, incompatible with the Convention, the application of a principle of acquiescence, in appropriate circumstances, equally should not be incompatible, and (3) the fact that L was not aware that a challenge would be unopposed, or that it would succeed, did not excuse the failure to raise a challenge promptly, once the grounds were clearly established as they had been by the decision in *Starrs v. Ruxton* 2000 J.C. 208, [1999] C.L.Y. 5884.

LOCHRIDGE v. MILLER (PROCURATOR FISCAL); *sub nom.* LOCHRIDGE v. GILCHRIST 2002 S.L.T. 906, Lord Coulsfield, Lord MacLean, Lord Sutherland, HCJ Appeal.

5494. Right to fair trial–delay–reasonableness of 23 months delay

[European Convention on Human Rights 1950 Art.6(1).]

Following an incident on May 15, 1999, V and two others were questioned by police regarding the alleged offences. The fourth accused was not questioned until October 1999 and all were subsequently charged with three charges of assault and a breach of the peace. The trial diet was set for a sitting commencing on April 30, 2001. V and the other accused lodged devolution minutes on the ground of unreasonable delay resulting in unfairness contrary to the European Convention on Human Rights 1950 Art.6(1), which were repelled by the sheriff. They appealed to the High Court. The Crown explained that the delay between May and October 1999 had been attributable to the police officer in charge of the investigation also being responsible for a number of other time consuming and complicated investigations. The case had been passed to another police officer in October who proceeded to question the fourth accused. There was a further delay whilst a suitable police officer was found who could prepare the file for passing to the procurator fiscal's office. The file was finally submitted in February 2000 and by April 2000 had been examined by a procurator fiscal depute. She determined that certain evidential concerns were of such a complexity that the case required to be reviewed by her superior. In June 2000, however, it was decided that the matter could not wait and the case was marked for petition proceedings. A petition warrant was granted and, following a petition hearing in August 2000, the accused was admitted to bail. Due to pressure of business passed to the Crown Office and instructions to indict were not received by the procurator fiscal until January 3, 2001. The indictment was served on March 29 for trial in the sitting commencing on April 30.

Held, refusing the appeal, that (1) a delay due to pressure of business did not result in liability under the Convention where such a delay had been caused merely by pressures peculiar to a particular time or circumstance and were not systematic, long standing or indicative of inadequate resourcing given past and anticipated future workloads in the police or fiscal's office; (2) the sheriff was correct in declining to criticise to procurator fiscal depute's decision to refer the case to her superiors, and (3) the time taken for the case to reach trial, although longer than normal, was not outwith the acceptable range of times taken to reach trial in similar cases.

Observed, that (1) the court would occasionally be called upon to comment on a particular course of action taken by the police or a procurator fiscal, but they should be circumspect about doing so and any attempt to apply the Convention to encourage criticism of the conscientious work of procurators fiscal would be wrong. Opinion of the court per Lord Rodger LJ-G.

VALENTINE (ALAN) v. HM ADVOCATE; WELLS (PHILIP) v. HM ADVOCATE; MURPHY (THOMAS) v. HM ADVOCATE; MURPHY (MICHAEL) v. HM ADVOCATE 2002 J.C. 58, Lord Rodger, L.J.G., Lord Carloway, Lady Cosgrove, HCJ Appeal.

5495. Right to fair trial–delay–unreasonable delay–summary complaint changed to petition after nine months–total time not unreasonable

[European Convention on Human Rights 1950 Art.6(1).]

W was charged on summary complaint in October 1999 with assaults allegedly committed in May 1999. The trial was fixed for March 2000. In February 2000, the summary complaint was changed to petition in light of medical reports that indicated the injuries inflicted during the assault were more serious than originally thought. An indictment was served for trial in December 2000 and W lodged devolution minutes raising pleas in bar of trial on the grounds of unreasonable delay, a breach of W's right under the European Convention on Human Rights 1950 Art.6(1). W submitted that the time between petition and trial was not in itself unreasonable but was made so by the addition of the nine months summary period. The sheriff held that the case, because of the earlier period, was exceptional and should have been reported without precognition of the witnesses or "fast tracked". The pleas in bar were upheld and indictment dismissed. The Crown appealed.

Held, allowing the appeal and remitting the case to the sheriff, that it was not reasonable that the case be reported without precognition of the witnesses. The total time was prima facie not unreasonable and "fast tracking", was not the only reasonable course of action. To fast track merely meant prioritisation and that was a discretionary process based on the relevant facts, *Gibson (David Blair) v. HM Advocate* 2001 J.C. 125, [2001] C.L.Y. 6361 applied. The question to be answered was whether the actual course of events would result in W being deprived of the right to trial within a reasonable time and there was no ground for holding that that would be the case. Opinion of the court per Lord Prosser.

HM ADVOCATE v. WRIGHT (KAREN HALLIDAY) (OTHERWISE SKILBECK) 2001 S.C.C.R. 509, Lord Prosser, Lord Cowie, Lord MacLean, HCJ Appeal.

5496. Rules—notes of appeal

ACT OF ADJOURNAL (CRIMINAL APPEALS) 2002, SSI 2002 387; made under the Criminal Procedure (Scotland) Act 1995 s.305. In force: in accordance with para.1 (2); £2.00.

This Act of Adjournal, which amends the procedure relating to Criminal Appeals, amends the Act of Adjournal (Criminal Appeal Rules) 1996 (SI 1996 513) and the Criminal Procedure (Scotland) Act 1995 to extend the period within which a note of appeal may be lodged from six weeks to eight.

5497. Sentencing—child offence—pre sentence reports

See SENTENCING: Ross (Scott Andrew) v. HM Advocate (Sentencing). §6073

5498. Sentencing—competency—second offence inferring personal violence—relevant date

[Criminal Procedure (Scotland) Act 1995 (c.46) s.5(3).]

M appealed against five months' detention for assault by seizing his sister and pouring hot water on her back and shoulders to her severe injury on March 20, 2002. He was convicted in April 2002. On March 25 the accused had been convicted of an act of violence committed on September 28, 2000. M argued that the sentence was incompetent where the schedule of previous convictions did not disclose any earlier analogous offences.

Held, dismissing the appeal, that the relevant dates for the operation of the Criminal Procedure (Scotland) Act 1995 s.5(3) were those of the commission of the offences *Sim v. Lockhart* 1994 S.L.T. 1063, [1994] C.L.Y. 5704 distinguished, and the present assault being later in date, the requirements of s.5(3) were satisfied.

MARSHALL v. STOTT 2002 S.L.T. 1353, Lord Hardie, Lord MacLean, HCJ.

5499. Sentencing—variation—accused sentenced to imprisonment but recalled for imposition of driving disqualification—competency

[Criminal Procedure (Scotland) Act 1995 (c.46) s.198(1).]

S appealed against a five year disqualification from driving for assaulting a couple by driving a car at them, striking the woman on the body to her severe injury. S had been convicted and the trial judge imposed a sentence of four years' imprisonment. Shortly after leaving court, the judge realised that disqualification was appropriate, the court was reconvened and S was then disqualified from driving for five years. Thereafter the clerk of court entered the details of the prison sentence and the disqualification in the record of proceedings. S argued that the judge had been functus officio at the time the second order was made and that the moment the panel left the courtroom after being sentenced ought to be seen as the time when proceedings were finally determined.

Held, dismissing the appeal, that further to the Criminal Procedure (Scotland) Act 1995 s.198(1), for a valid sentence to be pronounced, it required to be announced in open court and entered in the record in the form prescribed, which was what had taken place.

STEELE (ROBERT) v. HM ADVOCATE 2002 S.L.T. 868, Lord Osborne, Lord Kirkwood, Lord Sutherland, HCJ Appeal.

5500. Sexual Offences (Procedure and Evidence) (Scotland) Act 2002 (asp 9)

This Act of the Scottish Parliament prohibits persons charged with certain sexual offences from conducting their own defence at the trial; provides for the appointment of solicitors to defend those persons where they do not make those appointments themselves; prevents those persons from personally precognoscing or taking statements from alleged victims; requires those persons to give notice of defences of consent; makes new provision about the admissibility of certain evidence bearing on the character, conduct or condition of alleged victims at trials of those persons for those offences and provides for disclosure of those persons' previous convictions of sexual offences where such evidence is allowed.

5501.　Sheriff courts–summary proceedings–recovery of cash–procedure

ACT OF SEDERUNT (SUMMARY APPLICATIONS, STATUTORY APPLICATIONS AND APPEALS ETC. RULES) AMENDMENT (NO.5) (PROCEEDS OF CRIME ACT 2002) 2002, SSI 2002 563; made under the Sherrif Courts (Scotland) Act 1971 s.32. In force: December 30, 2002; £1.75.

This Act of Sederunt amends the Act of Sederunt (Summary Applications, Statutory Applications and Appeals etc. Rules) 1999 (SI 1999 929) by setting out the procedure for the recovery of cash in summary proceedings as provided for by the Proceeds of Crime Act 2002 and revoking provisions relating to drug trafficking subject to exceptions.

5502.　Summary　procedure–citations–defective　citation–appearance　by accused–time limits

[Criminal Procedure (Scotland) Act 1995 (c.46) s.136, s.144(8).]

S appealed against the refusal of his preliminary plea in his prosecution for speeding. A purported citation dated January 17, 2001 requiring S to appear on March 1, 2001 was sent to his father in error. A solicitor appeared on S's behalf at the diet and tendered a plea in bar of trial on the basis that the execution of the citation could not, and did not, establish that the proceedings had been commenced against S within six months in terms of the Criminal Procedure (Scotland) Act 1995 s.136. The justice refused the plea on the ground that any defect in the manner of citation was deemed to have been cured as at the date of the defective citation in terms of s.144(8) of the 1995 Act.

Held, dismissing the appeal, that (1) it was not a necessary implication of s.144(8) of the 1995 Act that any defect in the manner of citation was deemed to have been cured at the date of citation, but (2) its effect was that the appearance for S on the date specified in the citation meant that he had to be taken to have received the complaint at some previous date, there was at least some onus on him to set up his preliminary defence of time bar and S had made no attempt to discharge that onus.

SHAW v. DYER 2002 S.L.T. 826, Lord Marnoch, Lord Macfadyen, Lord Osborne, HCJ Appeal.

5503.　Summary procedure–district court–court officials prevented from reaching court–power to adjourn by telephone

[Criminal Procedure (Scotland) Act 1995 (c.46) s.6(1), s.151.]

C pled guilty in the district court to a speeding charge and a proof was fixed to determine whether there was exceptional hardship sufficient to avoid disqualification under the totting up procedure. On the date of the proof very heavy snowfalls prevented, inter alia, the procurator fiscal, the clerk of the court and the justice from reaching the court. By agreement between the justice and the clerk proceedings were conducted by telephone and the proof purportedly adjourned. C presented a bill of advocation seeking recall of that decision. The Crown argued that the local authority powers to determine where a district court sat were generally delegated to the clerk of the court, and having had those powers delegated to him the clerk had fulfilled the requirements of the Criminal Procedure (Scotland) Act 1995 s.6(1) and s.151, expediency and the very unusual circumstances justifying any irregularity which had occurred in relation to the public's right to be present.

Held, passing the bill, that it was clear that the district court had not in any way been convened at a place within s.6(1), nor had the clerk properly convened the court and adjourned the diet in the absence of the presiding judge under s.151.

CLARKE v. FRASER 2002 S.L.T. 745, Lord Marnoch, Lord Macfadyen, Lord Osborne, HCJ.

5504. Summary procedure–intermediate diet–warrant to apprehend on failure to appear–whether trial diet discharged by implication

[Criminal Procedure (Scotland) Act 1995 (c.46) s.150(3).]

S, charged on summary complaint with theft, appealed against the sheriff's decision that the grant of a warrant for his apprehension for failure to appear at an intermediate diet had the effect of discharging a trial diet. S failed to appear at an intermediate diet on June 7 and the sheriff granted warrant to apprehend S under the Criminal Procedure (Scotland) Act 1995 s.150(3). The trial diet set for June 30 did not take place. The Crown argued that the grant of the warrant had discharged the trial diet by necessary implication as it could not be known when an accused would be apprehended.

Held, allowing the appeal, that the discharge of a trial diet, which was a peremptory diet, should not be left to implication, and the granting of a warrant at an intermediate diet did not per se discharge a trial diet. As the case did not call on June 30 the instance fell.

REYNOLDS v. DYER 2002 S.L.T. 295, Lord Kirkwood, Lord Nimmo Smith, Lord Weir, HCJ Appeal.

5505. Summary procedure–miscarriage of justice–sheriffs–sheriff asking improper questions of witness

W was tried on summary complaint and called D as a witness. W's defence was that D had committed the offence, and D admitted the offence. The sheriff asked D what his response would be if charged and D replied that he would plead guilty. The procurator fiscal was asked by the sheriff and decided that she would serve a complaint on D and he was remanded in custody during lunch. When the court was reconvened she intimated she no longer wished to serve the complaint and D was released. W was convicted and appealed to the High Court arguing that the sheriff's actions had been oppressive and in contravention of natural justice.

Held, refusing the bill, that there was no miscarriage of justice. Although it would have been better if D had not been detained and the sheriff had not asked the procurator fiscal whether she wished to serve a complaint, there was nothing in the sheriff's conduct that would have caused a reasonable onlooker to believe that the sheriff had formed a concluded view of the credibility of D before all the evidence had been led.

WEBLEY (DON LEE) v. McFADYEN 2002 S.C.C.R. 78, Lord Kirkwood, Lord Caplan, Lord Philip, HCJ Appeal.

5506. Summary procedure–previous convictions–disclosure to sheriff

[Criminal Procedure (Scotland) Act 1995 (c.46) s.166, s.166(3).]

C was charged with committing an offence whilst on bail. He pled not guilty, challenging the fact that he was on bail. In an attempt to prove that fact, the depute fiscal handed the sheriff a bundle of papers opened to the page showing the bail warrant. Inadvertently, the depute fiscal had included amongst the papers, a list of C's previous convictions. Upon the papers being passed to the sheriff, C's solicitor immediately requested an adjournment to consider the papers, which were passed to him. Following the adjournment, the depute fiscal deleted the bail aggravation charge and moved that the papers be withdrawn. C's solicitor opposed the motion arguing that the sheriff should acquit C due to unfair prejudice arising from the lodgement in court of C's previous convictions in contravention of the Criminal Procedure (Scotland) Act 1995 s.166 (3). The sheriff refused to acquit and granted the motion for the papers to be withdrawn. The sheriff did not consider that C had suffered any prejudice as he had not actually seen the list of previous convictions. He was satisfied that the depute fiscal had lodged the list of previous convictions in error rather than as a result of the procedure under s.166. He was also satisfied that he could put his knowledge of the existence of previous convictions out of his mind when deciding the case. C appealed.

Held, refusing the appeal, that (1) the sheriff had been entitled to consider the reason why the list of previous convictions had been placed before the court and, in finding that it was in error on the part of the depute fiscal rather than part of the procedure set out in s.166, was entitled to find that no breach of the prohibition contained in s.166(3) had taken place; (2) it had been open to C's solicitor to simply consent to the withdrawal of the papers without bringing to the court's attention the inclusion of the list of previous convictions, or if he required the papers to remain in court, to request that the contents not be referred to in the course of further evidence, and (3) given all the circumstances, the sheriff's knowledge of the existence of the list could not be considered by the reasonable man sufficient as to render the sheriff unable to act impartially. Opinion of the Court per Lord Cameron of Lochbroom.

CLAMPETT v. STOTT 2002 J.C. 89, Lord Cameron of Lochbroom, Lord Marnoch, Lord McCluskey, HCJ Appeal.

5507. Summary procedure–previous convictions–negligent disclosure to sheriff

[Criminal Procedure (Scotland) Act 1995 (c.46) s.166(3); European Convention on Human Rights 1950 Art.6.]

P was charged on summary complaint with driving without insurance. P was seen driving his motor car by two police officers who followed him and later detained him on suspicion of driving whilst disqualified. P satisfied the police that his disqualification had expired but admitted that his car was not insured. In the course of giving evidence against P, one of the police officers revealed to the court that P had a previous conviction for a Road Traffic Act offence. P objected arguing that the fiscal depute had deliberately elicited the revelation from the police officer and the court should therefore find that a breach of the Criminal Procedure (Scotland) Act 1995 s.166 (3) had taken place. P additionally argued that, in light of that breach, he could no longer receive a fair trial in terms of the European Convention on Human Rights 1950 Art.6. The fiscal depute denied that the revelation had been elicited deliberately. The sheriff found that the revelation had been accidental and that he could be sufficiently objective in dealing with P by ignoring the reference to a previous Road Traffic Act conviction. P appealed by way of stated case.

Held, refusing the appeal, that (1) the stated case failed to specify the questions posed by the fiscal depute and it was therefore impossible to establish whether the information had been either deliberately or negligently elicited from the police officer; (2) in the absence of such a determination, the previous convictions could not be held to have been laid before the could under the procedure set out in s.166(3), and (3) whether the sheriff was entitled to conclude that the evidence revealed to the court could be ignored by him depended on the nature of the evidence and, given that it did not involve any element of dishonesty, it could not be held to be relevant to any determination the sheriff was required to make on the P's credibility and the sheriff was therefore entitled to ignore it without any miscarriage of justice resulting. Opinion of the Court per Lord Kirkwood.

PENMAN v. STOTT 2001 S.C.C.R. 911, Lord Kirkwood, Lord Caplan, Lord Philip, HCJ Appeal.

5508. Summary procedure–sheriffs–miscarriage of justice–expression of impatience during witness examination

M was charged, summarily, with assault. During witness examination M's solicitor was asked by the sheriff how much longer he was going to take. The sheriff then remarked on his case load for the next day, the preparatory work involved, and his desire to get home that evening and not be in Court until 6.00 pm or 7.00 pm in the evening. M's solicitor did not continue. M was convicted and appealed to the High Court by bill of suspension.

Held, passing the bill and quashing the conviction, that the sheriff's remarks went beyond mere impatience. The intemperate nature of the language was such as to create suspicion in the mind of a reasonable observer as to whether the sheriff had already made his mind up before all the evidence had been presented. Justice, in this case, had not been seen to be done and accordingly there had been a miscarriage of justice.

MURRAY (WILLIAM BURNS) v.WATT 2002 S.C.C.R.122, Lord Kirkwood, Lord Caplan, Lord Philip, HCJ Appeal.

5509. Summary procedure–sheriffs–miscarriage of justice–sheriff indicating concluded view of evidence following examination in chief

M was tried on charges of maliciously damaging a car and assaulting its owner to severe injury. At the end of M's evidence he said that he had beaten the victim badly, but had not kicked the car. The sheriff asked M's solicitor whether M's statement was intended to mitigate or exonerate, and if an adjournment was required. No adjournment was taken, M was convicted and appealed to the High Court arguing that the sheriff had reached a concluded view at the end of his evidence and therefore the trial was unfair and oppressive.

Held, allowing the appeal and quashing the conviction, that a sheriff should not express any view until all evidence had been heard. In the instant case, although the intention was otherwise, the sheriff had given the impression of a concluded view. Opinion of the Court per Lord Cameron of Lochbroom.

McDONALD v. CRAIGEN 2002 S.C.C.R. 405, Lord Cameron of Lochbroom, Lord Hamilton, Lord Weir, HCJ Appeal.

5510. Summary procedure–trials–delay–trial not brought within reasonable time

B was charged with reset and obtaining goods by fraud. He raised a preliminary plea requesting dismissal of the charges on the ground of failure to bring the case to a hearing within a reasonable time, there being a 10 month gap between caution and charge and the case coming to court.

Held, dismissing the complaint, that (1) the starting date for consideration was the date of "charge" (ie. the official notification of an allegation that the accused had committed a criminal offence) which might be the date when preliminary investigations were opened (December 3, 1998) as contended by B, but in the instant case was clearly May 20, 1999, when B was cautioned and charged; (2) the test was whether B had received a hearing within a reasonable time, and not, as contended by the fiscal, whether the delay had been inordinate, and (3) given that the instant case was a summary prosecution with simple facts, that the police had taken three months to report it to the fiscal, that three months later the fiscal had asked for supplementary information, and that the complaint first called more than three months after that information was provided, the delay was unreasonable and the Crown had not explained it satisfactorily.

HIGSON v. BOYLE 2001 S.L.T. (Sh Ct) 49, Sheriff Brian A Lockhart, Sh Ct (Glasgow and Strathkelvin).

5511. Summary procedure–trials–trial within a trial–whether evidence required to be led again

C was charged on complaint with theft. At trial C objected to the admissibility of a police officer's evidence of statements made by him during interview. The sheriff heard the evidence in a trial within a trial and also heard C's evidence in that context before repelling the objection. At an adjourned diet C argued in support of a submission of no case to answer that the officer's evidence could not be taken as evidence on the substantive issue as it had not been led again before the

Crown case closed. The sheriff repelled the submission and convicted C, who appealed.

Held, refusing the appeal, that in general, no useful purpose was served by requiring that evidence given in the course of a trial within a trial in summary proceedings should be repeated after the judge had determined the question of admissibility, and that there was no prejudice to C in the procedure followed.

CROOKS v. RUSSELL 2002 S.L.T. 221, Lord Coulsfield, Lord Dawson, Lady Paton, HCJ Appeal.

5512. Terrorism–rules–High Court applications

ACT OF ADJOURNAL (CRIMINAL PROCEDURE RULES AMENDMENT NO.2) (ANTI-TERRORISM, CRIME AND SECURITY ACT 2001) 2002, SSI 2002 136; made under the Criminal Procedure (Scotland) Act 1995 s.305. In force: March 4, 2002; £1.50.

This Act of Adjournal amends the Act of Adjournal (Criminal Procedure Rules) 1996 (SI 1996 513) in relation to applications to the High Court of Justiciary under the Anti-Terrorism, Crime and Security Act 2001 in connection with terrorist cash.

5513. Trials–coaccused–counsel's comment on coaccused's case

S appealed against conviction of murder and assault to severe injury, permanent disfigurement and danger of life. S and his co-accused, R, who gave evidence at trial, incriminated one another. S remained silent at judicial examination and trial. Two witnesses gave evidence that near the scene of the incidents and shortly after they took place S did not deny responsibility when accused. In his speech to the jury counsel for R repeatedly referred to S's silence and commented, in particular, that "in his silence there [was] the most eloquent statement of admitted guilt as you would ever wish to hear". S argued that there was a miscarriage of justice: since the judge and prosecutor could only comment on an accused's failure to speak at judicial examination or to give evidence at trial in special circumstances and only sparingly, the same rule should apply to counsel for a co-accused; there were no such circumstances in this case and in any event the comments were repeated, excessive and seriously prejudicial to S to the extent that the damage was not remediable by any direction from the trial judge and he had been deprived of a fair trial.

Held, refusing the appeal, that (1) it was appropriate in the presentation of the case for one accused for his counsel to comment on a co-accused's case, in particular, where his client might be adversely affected by that case. Counsel had to be able to present the defence fully and was entitled to comment on the content and quality of any evidence led in support of the accused's case and on the absence of potentially important supporting evidence by reason of the accused's silence at judicial examination or trial. The approach in *R. v. Wickham (Anthony John)* (1971) 55 Cr. App. R. 199, [1971] C.L.Y. 2171 was consistent with Scots law and ought to be applied; (2) while a judge was impartial and a prosecutor impartial as between the accused, defence counsel had a duty to present the case as strongly as possible to his client's best advantage and was entitled to comment on the silence of a co-accused subject only to the normal restraints of professional propriety and courtesy and provided that where he commented on a co-accused's silence in circumstances where he had a right to be silent, he acknowledged that the co-accused had that right; (3) counsel for R's comments were undisciplined and lacked the necessary care and precision required but, given the state of the transcript which referred to certain words as inaudible, it was not possible to conclude that they constituted an impropriety, and (4) even if they did constitute an impropriety, they did not prejudice S's defence irremediably where the trial judge reasonably and correctly exercised his judgment in not intervening during the speech and his strong direction to the jury sufficiently set out the proper approach to be taken to the right to silence.

SHEVLIN (STEVEN JASON) v. HM ADVOCATE 2002 S.L.T. 739, Lord Gill L.J.C., Lord Hamilton, Lord McCluskey, HCJ Appeal.

5514. Trials–delay–compatibility with right to fair trial

[Human Rights Act 1998 (c.42) Sch.1 Part I Art.6.]

M, charged with the murder of S (M's son, born August 5, 1998) on October 7, 1998 by repeatedly and violently shaking him causing his death, appealed against the trial judge's refusal on October 15, 2001 of M's plea in bar of trial that his prosecution was incompatible with the Human Rights Act 1998 Sch.1 Part I Art.6 where his case had not been determined within a reasonable time. It was agreed that the relevant period began on October 14, 1998 when M and W (his wife) were interviewed by police under caution. W did not positively agree to give evidence until September 13, 2000 and was precognosced on October 6 when she confirmed her willingness to give evidence. A petition warrant was granted on November 7 and M appeared on it on November 22. M argued (1) that there was unreasonable delay in furthering the investigation of causation prior to November 2000, particularly between November 1998 and July 1999, where a post mortem, including neuropathological examination, was available from late 1998, and between July 1999 and June 2000 in obtaining further medical reports; (2) that there was an unacceptable delay between June and September 2000 in addressing the availability of W's evidence, where it was unreasonable and unfounded for the trial judge to take the view that W's evidence was crucial to bringing the case against M; (3) that there was an unreasonable delay from October 2000 as standing the period of time which had elapsed from October 1998 it was incumbent on the Crown to proceed to trial as quickly as possible and no priority had been accorded M's case, and (4) that the delay from October 1998 to September 2001 would prejudice M through problems with precise recollection of witnesses.

Held, dismissing the appeal, that (1) the trial judge was fully entitled to look at the expert medical opinion obtained in the context of an ongoing investigation and consider the issue on that basis, the post mortem report had been considered to provide insufficient evidence on which to proceed, and while it was unfortunate that obtaining further medical opinion took so long, that was not the Crown's responsibility; (2) the trial judge was correct in identifying the wife's evidence as crucial; (3) there was no unreasonable delay in the period since October 2000 and the Crown had done all that would be expected in a complex case like the present, and (4) the risk of prejudice could be offset by reference to statements to police at the time of the alleged offence and to contemporary written records, and there was nothing that took the present case out of the ordinary.

MORRISON (ALLAN) v. HM ADVOCATE 2002 S.L.T. 795, Lord Cameron of Lochbroom, Lord Mackay of Drumadoon, Lord McCluskey, HCJ Appeal.

5515. Trials–delay–criminal appeals–reduction in sentence appropriate remedy

[Human Rights Act 1998 (c.42) Sch.1 Part I Art.6(1).]

M appealed against a determination ([2001] S.L.T. 1359) that a nine month reduction in his sentence of eight years and six months' detention was the appropriate remedy to apply in respect of an unreasonable delay in the hearing of his appeal against conviction. The delay had been caused by an act of the prosecutor. The respondent had not disputed the finding that there had been a breach of M's right to a hearing within a reasonable time under the Human Rights Act 1998 Sch.1 Part I Art.6(1). M's appeal against conviction had been found to be without merit. M contended that the only and inevitable remedy available for such a breach was the quashing of his conviction.

Held, dismissing the appeal, that in determining the appropriate remedy in respect of a breach of an appellant's right under Art.6(1) the court should first identify the remedy that would be appropriate under domestic law and then consider whether that remedy would achieve just satisfaction for the breach by reference to the jurisprudence of the European Court. In the instant case, where the effect of the delay had been that M had to wait an additional 12 months to discover that his appeal against conviction had been unsuccessful, the quashing of his conviction would have been regarded as unjustified under domestic law. The jurisprudence of the European Court made it clear that a reduction in sentence could provide an adequate remedy for an unreasonable delay in hearing an appeal, *Bunkate v. Netherlands (A/248-B)* (1995) 19 E.H.R.R. 477 and *Eckle v. Germany (A/51)* (1983) 5 E.H.R.R. 1 applied. In the circumstances of the instant case, the reduction in sentence had adequately compensated M for the breach of his right under Art.6(1), *Dyer v. Watson* 2002 S.L.T. 229, [2002] 3 C.L. 683 applied.

MILLS (KENNETH ANTHONY PATON) v. HM ADVOCATE (NO.2); COCHRANE (JOHN) v. HM ADVOCATE, [2002] UKPC D2, [2002] 3 W.L.R.1597, Lord Hope of Craighead, Privy Council (Scotland).

5516. Trials–delay–period of 25 months between charge and trial–compatibility with Convention rights

[Human Rights Act 1998 (c.42) Sch.1 Part I Art.6(1); Mental Health (Scotland) Act 1984 (c.36).]

S was charged with lewd and libidinous practices and behaviour against C, born July 2, 1989, whilst acting with T, this was later reduced to a charge on summary procedure without T. S appealed against the sheriff's refusal of his plea in bar of trial. T argued that there had been a failure to bring him to trial within a reasonable time in breach of his rights under the Human Rights Act 1998 Sch.1 Part I Art.6(1). S was arrested, cautioned and charged on May 28, 1999 but not brought to trial for a further 25 months. The Crown conceded that there had been periods of relative inactivity, that T had been brought to trial prior to S and that the case should have been given priority in view of C's age, but argued, inter alia, that there was significant pressure on the fiscal's office, there was originally insufficient evidence in relation to the more serious charge and a prosecution could only be mounted against S when T's evidence became available, and that some of the delay was due to the fact that T had been detained in hospital in terms of the Mental Health (Scotland) Act 1984.

Held, allowing the appeal, that (1) the delay was particularly undesirable when a child was the complainer, and the period in the present case gave rise to real concern, and (2) the case was not inherently complex, the fact that there was an insufficiency of evidence against S unless T gave evidence had been known from the outset, there had been an apparent lack of urgency throughout and the lapse of 25 months was, in the circumstances, unreasonable.

SMITH v. ANGIOLINI; *sub nom.* SMITH v. ANGIOLIONI 2002 S.L.T. 934, Lord Kirkwood, Lord Abernethy, Judge EF Bowen Q.C., HCJ.

5517. Trials–delay–right to trial within a reasonable time

[Human Rights Act 1998 (c.42) Sch.1 Part I Art.6(1); Convention on the Rights of the Child 1989 (United Nations).]

In two appeals, the issue before the Privy Council concerned the right to a trial within a reasonable time as provided under the Human Rights Act 1998 Sch.1 Part I Art.6(1). The appeals concerned the prosecution of a 13 year old boy, K, for serious sexual offences and the prosecution of two police officers for perjury. The delay between the bringing of charges and the proposed trials was 28 months and 20 months respectively. The High Court of Justiciary had found in both cases (2001 S.L.T. 751 and 2001 S.L.T. 1261) that such delay had breached Art.6(1).

Held, allowing D's appeal and dismissing the Crown's appeal, that (1) the delay of 28 months in prosecuting K did amount to a breach of Art.6(1) of the Convention. It was necessary to have regard to the time requirements of the Convention on the Rights of the Child 1989 (United Nations) and the Beijing Rules when considering the reasonable time requirement within Art.6(1). While cases involving children required careful and sensitive handling, there had been no satisfactory explanation provided for the delay, *HM Advocate v. P* 2001 S.L.T. 924, [2001] C.L.Y. 6351 considered, and (2) while it was desirable that there be a shorter period between the bringing of charges and the proposed trial, the 20 month delay between charge and trial had not infringed the rights of the two police officers under Art.6(1). Save in *Mansur v. Turkey (A/321)* (1995) 20 E.H.R.R. 535, [1996] C.L.Y. 3133 where special considerations existed, there appeared to be no case in which a 20 month delay had been found to infringe the reasonable time requirement. Police officers, by reason of their occupation, were susceptible to accusations of misconduct. Such accusations necessitated careful and independent investigation and such investigations took time. Per Lord Hope, there was apparent conflict between the decisions of the Board in *Darmalingum v. Mauritius* [2000] 1 W.L.R. 2303, [2000] C.L.Y. 1104 and *Bell v. DPP of Jamaica* [1985] A.C. 937, [1985] C.L.Y. 181. In circumstances where there was an alleged violation of Art.6(1) the decision of the Board in *Darmalingum* was to be preferred given that it was based on a consideration of the decisions of the European Court of Human Rights, *Darmalingum, Bell* and *Mansur* considered.

DYER v. WATSON; K (A JUVENILE) v. HM ADVOCATE; *sub nom.* HM ADVOCATE v. K (A JUVENILE); HM ADVOCATE v. JK; PROCURATOR FISCAL, LINLITHGOW v. WATSON; DYER (PROCURATOR FISCAL, LINGLITHGOW) v. WATSON; K v. LORD ADVOCATE, [2002] UKPC D1, [2002] 3 W.L.R. 1488, Lord Bingham of Cornhill, Lord Hope of Craighead, Lord Hutton, Lord Millett, Lord Rodger of Earlsferry, PC (Sc).

5518. Trials–desertion–evidence allegedly tainted

[Criminal Procedure (Scotland) Act 1995 (c.46) s.263, s.268.]

K appealed against conviction for assaulting C to his injury, with a co-accused, by punching, kicking, and hitting his head and body with a wooden slab. C identified K as being one of his assailants, but in the course of the Crown evidence, one witness (W) conceded after identifying K that he had identified a stand-in at an identification parade, and his girlfriend (S), who had also not identified K at the time, said she had been told that the person she had identified had not played the role she thought. It then emerged that W and S were informed of their mistake by an unidentified person (X) from the procurator fiscal's office, and that a further witness (P), a police officer, was informed by another officer that he had also chosen a stand-in. K argued that (1) W and S's evidence had become tainted as a result of X's remarks, and the only remedy was to desert the trial pro loco et tempore as there had been deliberate interference by persons in the service of the criminal authorities; (2) the Crown had erred in declining to allow X to be identified and precognosced, as the general rules preserving the confidentiality of the precognition process were not strict and universal, *Wotherspoon (William) v. HM Advocate (No.1)* 1999 S.L.T. 664, [1999] C.L.Y. 5819, *McLeod (Alistair) v. HM Advocate (No.2)* 1998 J.C. 67, [1998] C.L.Y. 5607, and an inquiry into X's conduct could not be protected in a criminal trial by confidentiality; (3) the sheriff erred in refusing a motion under the Criminal Procedure (Scotland) Act 1995 s.263 to recall C to allow an opportunity to cross examine him regarding his meeting at the procurator fiscal's office in light of the subsequent evidence, and had erred in refusing a motion under s.268 to allow the leading of additional evidence from a member of the fiscal's staff, and (4) the sheriff's directions were inadequate: although drawing the jury's attention to the allegedly tainted evidence of W, S and P, he failed to remind them that they had been deprived of evidence that might have shown that the identification by C was similarly tainted.

Held, refusing the appeal, that (1) the court was left in doubt as to the correctness of the Crown's decision to refuse to co-operate in assisting to identify, or allow access to X. Although the confidentiality of matters passing between a procurator fiscal and the head of the criminal department was a paramount consideration *Arthur v. Lindsay* (1894) 1 Adam 582, there was an important difference between allowing the investigation of the whole precognition process if its purpose was to reveal what a witness said to the precognoscer, and allowing an investigation in circumstances such as this, where someone was said to have made a remark which might have caused the witness to adjust his evidence. The Crown had discretion in such matters and more openness would have been more in line with the new approach in *McLeod*; (2) evidence of identification which was subject to serious criticism, including alleged irregularities preceding the appearance in court of identified witnesses, should be assessed by a jury, and the question whether the accused was truly identified by a witness was one of fact for the jury, not of law for the court *Howarth v. HM Advocate* 1992 S.C.C.R. 364, [1992] C.L.Y. 5361, *McAvoy (Thomas) v. HM Advocate* 1991 J.C. 16, [1991] C.L.Y. 4744; *Adams (John) v. HM Advocate* 1999 J.C. 139, [1999] C.L.Y. 5816; (3) the decision to desert a trial pro loco et tempore should only be taken in exceptional circumstances, and fell within the discretion of the judge. The sheriff in the present case was correct not to do so given that there was more evidence to come. The motion to recall C (who had also identified K at the parade) was also a matter of discretion for the judge. The motion based on s.268 was inept as K was not able to inform the sheriff what the evidence might be, and therefore show that it was prima facie material in terms of s.268(b); furthermore, the sheriff also had a discretion even when all statutory conditions were met, and it had not been shown that he erred in exercising his discretion, and (4) the sheriff's directions followed a detailed speech by K's solicitor and were appropriate.

KERR v. HM ADVOCATE (IDENTIFICATION EVIDENCE) 2002 S.L.T. 582, Lord McCluskey, Lord Cameron of Lochbroom, Lord Cullen L.J.G, HCJ.

5519. Trials—interviews—evidence of statement of co accused incriminating accused

[Customs and Excise Management Act 1979 (c.2) s.170(2).]

B appealed against his conviction for being concerned in importing cannabis, contrary to the Customs and Excise Management Act 1979 s.170(2). B had gone to trial along with two co-accused, N and L. When the Crown case concluded, the libel in toto was withdrawn against both N and L. At the trial both B and L's tape recorded interviews with the police were played and the transcripts provided to the jury. L's interview contained material which was incriminatory of B. B was not able to object when L's interview was placed before the jury as, so far as he was aware, L was still standing trial for the offences. However, prior to the playing of L's taped interview the Crown had decided and intimated to L and N that they no longer sought convictions against them. The trial judge clearly directed the jury to disregard any material incriminatory of B from L's tape. The Crown accepted that this evidence should never have been led, but argued that there was no miscarriage of justice since there was no material difference between what was contained in L's interview and what B himself had said in his interview which had been played before L's.

Held, allowing the appeal and quashing the conviction, that there was absolutely no justification for placing before the jury the co-accused's taped interview, it was improper for it to have been led in view of the Crown's intention not to seek the co-accused's conviction, the accused's position at trial was undeniably prejudiced and there had been a miscarriage of justice.

BEACOM (MICHAEL) v. HM ADVOCATE 2002 S.L.T. 349, Lord Clarke, HCJ Appeal.

5520. Trials—judge's charge—misdirection—evidence relating to charges withdrawn

D was charged on an indictment libelling eight charges of shameless indecency and lewd, libidinous and indecent practices against males who had been in a Boys' Brigade company while he was captain. At trial D objected to the leading of a police officer's evidence relating to an earlier operation to catch extortionists who had sought to exploit a stolen videotape which contained footage of D inducing a complainer (P) to expose his private parts and masturbate (which formed the basis of charge 6), and of a statement in which D referred to one extortionist having called him a paedophile. The objection was repelled but charge 6 was later dropped after P, who was 18 at the time, stated that no other person had been present. D was convicted of charges 4, 7 and 8 which involved inducing T, then aged between 14 and 17, to expose his private parts and photographing him naked, at a brigade camp; inducing J, then aged between eight and 14, to expose his private parts on various occasions at a church, and handling them; and inducing J, then aged between 15 and 17, to expose his private parts at the solicitors' firm where D worked, and photographing them. D appealed, contending, inter alia, that (1) he had not been afforded a fair trial as the Crown had adduced evidence in relation to the paedophile accusation in the knowledge that they would not be able to prove that charge, and ought to have omitted any charges relating to P and all references to the extortion trial; (2) the jury should have been directed to ignore extensive press coverage of the extortion trial and of the trial with which they were concerned; (3) the jury ought to have been directed to ignore all evidence relating to charges which had been withdrawn, and (4) there was insufficient evidence of the necessary link between the charges to apply the *Moorov* doctrine and the sheriff's directions on the rule were inadequate.

Held, refusing the appeal, that (1) the evidence of the statement was relevant to the proof of charge 6, which the Crown were entitled to pursue on P's statement in precognition that another person had been present, and there was no unfairness to D in using it at trial where it contained no statement of wrongdoing by D, the jury learned that the videotape referred to concerned an adult complainer and the charge was dropped; (2) there was no need to direct the jury expressly to disregard the statement given that they had been directed on how to approach the evidence on the remaining charges; (3) the sheriff was entitled to take the view that no express direction was required in relation to press reports; (4) there was no general principle that a jury had to disregard evidence relating to a charge which had been withdrawn and no special circumstances necessitating such a direction existed in this case, and (5) there were sufficient similarities in the evidence on the charges concerning T and J to justify application of the *Moorov* principle, and the sheriff's directions on the principle, while brief, sufficiently explained what it involved in a case like the present.

DANSKIN v. HM ADVOCATE 2002 S.L.T. 889, Lord Carloway, Lord Hamilton, Lord Rodger L.J.G., HCJ Appeal.

5521. Trials–judge's charge–misdirection–failure to summarise evidence led

Three accused persons went to trial charged with repeatedly raping a woman. Each gave evidence, consistent with earlier statements to the police, that the complainer consented to, and encouraged, what took place. In the course of charging the jury, the judge deliberately chose not to summarise the evidence, on the basis that many aspects had been covered in the defence and Crown speeches, and instead directed them in relation to "relevant" legal matters which included the issues of consent and corroboration. The accused were convicted and appealed on the basis that the directions amounted to a material misdirection, in particular that (1) the trial judge failed to give any account of their evidence; (2) she failed to give standard directions on how the jury should approach that evidence, and in particular directions that if they believed their evidence, or if it raised a reasonable doubt in their minds, they should acquit; (3) her reference to the evidence was unbalanced in that the emphasis was on the Crown case alone, and (4) if each of the individual criticisms on their own was insufficient, the cumulative effect was such that a miscarriage of justice had occurred.

Held, refusing the appeals, that (1) it was well recognised that there was no general obligation on a trial judge to attempt to summarise the evidence, and the decision not to do so in the present case could not be criticised where the jury had heard evidence of the appellants' police statements and from the appellants themselves, and speeches for each, in which their position would have been made clear; (2) although the standard directions on exculpatory evidence should have been given in the present case, the jury had not been misdirected in their absence where the position of each accused was straightforward, the judge had given clear directions regarding consent and corroboration, and as to the onus and standard of proof on the Crown, and the jury could not have been in any real doubt that if they believed the evidence of an accused, or were left with a reasonable doubt, they would be bound to acquit; (3) the judge had chosen to give legal directions arising from certain aspects of the evidence, which were balanced and fair, and while a reference to the accused's statements could have been better expressed, it was not illustrative of a general lack of balance, and (4) this was not a case in which the cumulative effect of a number of criticisms led to the conclusion that there had been a misdirection overall.

MEIGHAN (BRIAN JAMES) v. HM ADVOCATE; KANE (KEVIN JAMES) v. HM ADVOCATE; PUGH (DAVID SUTHERLAND) v. HM ADVOCATE 2002 S.L.T. 914, Lord Kingarth, Lord Cullen L.J.G., Lord Hamilton, HCJ Appeal.

5522. Trials—judge's charge—misdirection—hearsay evidence wrongly admitted

G was charged with a breach of the peace and malicious damage to property at a club. During the trial the sheriff allowed hearsay evidence of a witness (A), that G had spoken to A's daughter B, who was not a witness, asked her what she had seen of events at the club and told her to keep quiet. G was convicted and appealed, arguing that there had been a miscarriage of justice in that the sheriff had failed to direct the jury in relation to hearsay evidence.

Held, refusing the appeal, that while the sheriff was wholly wrong to repel the objection to the evidence, he had a discretion whether or not to give a direction on the evidence, and having regard to the fact that A's evidence, while undoubtedly prejudicial, had been given two days before and had not been referred to in the speeches to the jury, the sheriff's decision not to give a direction, whether of a general or a specific nature, was not one which no reasonable sheriff could have reached and there had been no miscarriage of justice.

GARDINER (IAN) v. HM ADVOCATE (HEARSAY EVIDENCE) 2002 S.L.T. 667, Lord Cameron of Lochbroom, Lady Cosgrove, Lord Kingarth, HCJ Appeal.

5523. Trials—judge's charge—misdirection—judicial examination—comments on failure to state defence

H appealed against his conviction for murder on the ground of misdirection. At judicial examination, H had not advanced a defence but he later lodged a special defence of self defence. In evidence at trial H explained that his failure to do so at judicial examination was on the advice of his lawyer. The trial judge in directing the jury commented on the purpose of judicial examination, saying that if a defence had been stated at that time it would be "more difficult to conclude that the special defence has been fabricated at a later date", and that the jury might think it "astonishing" if H had been advised, as he claimed in evidence, to remain silent.

Held, dismissing the appeal, that the opportunity presented by judicial examination was one which an accused was entitled to decline, but while the trial judge's comments were inappropriate, they were deprived of weight by other passages in what was an otherwise accurate and thorough charge and did not constitute a material misdirection amounting to a miscarriage of justice.

HICKS (GARY ROBERT) v. HM ADVOCATE 2002 S.L.T. 523, Lord Gill L.J.C., Lord Hamilton, Lord McCluskey, HCJ Appeal.

5524. Trials—jury directions—majority verdict—unnecessary elaboration not resulting in miscarriage of justice

S was charged on indictment and in the course of her direction to the jury the sheriff detailed the requirements for a majority verdict, whether the verdict was guilt or acquittal. S was convicted and appealed to the High Court on the basis of misdirection with regard to the available verdicts.

Held, refusing the appeal, that (1) there was no doubt that in dealing with majority verdicts the sheriff had gone further than was required. A jury did not require direction in relation to any verdict other than guilty, and to give one might lead to confusion. In the instant case the Court was satisfied that the unnecessary elaboration did not result in a miscarriage of justice, and (2) although the sheriff's concluding observations on the available verdicts were open to the argument that a restriction had been placed on the circumstances under which a not guilty verdict could be returned and should not have been made, the Court was satisfied that there had been no miscarriage of justice.

Observed, that unless and until the High Court reviewed the matter, sheriff's ought to follow the advice issued repeatedly over a decade. Opinion of the Court per Lord Hamilton.

SWEENEY (ALISON) v. HM ADVOCATE 2002 S.C.C.R.131, Lord Hamilton, Lord Caplan, Lord McEwan, HCJ Appeal.

5525. Trials – retrial – murder conviction of accused set aside on appeal – subsequent retrial – indictment charged offences of which previously acquitted

[Criminal Procedure (Scotland) Act 1995 (c.46) s.118(1)(c), s.119, s.119(6), s.119(7).]

H was originally charged in 1995 on indictment with six charges, one of which was for murder. H was found guilty of murder. The other five charges were withdrawn by the Crown and H was according acquitted. In April 2001, the guilty verdict was set aside and authority granted in terms of the Criminal Procedure (Scotland) Act 1995 s.118(1)(c) and s.119 for a new prosecution. H was subsequently charged on indictment with nine charges including the charge of murder. The remaining charges included the five charges of which H had been acquitted and three new charges. In the original trial evidence had been led in relation to the subject matter of one of the new charges. Evidence in relation to the other two new charges would have been inadmissible in the original trial. H sought a preliminary hearing that the charges, other than the murder charge, were incompetent. The defence emphasised that they were only challenging the competency of including the charges on the indictment and not whether evidence could competently be led on those charges in a subsequent trial. The Crown indicated that the five charges, of which H had already been acquitted, had been included purely to enable the Crown to lead evidence at the trial in relation to those charges in accordance with the principles set out in *Boyle (Daniel), Petitioner (No.2)* 1993 S.L.T. 1085, [1993] C.L.Y. 4963, and that they would not be seeking conviction on those charges. The defence submitted that *Boyle* could be distinguished from the present case as the verdict of the jury had been set aside on all charges in *Boyle*. Furthermore, the ability to lead evidence of that kind was dealt with by s.119(7). In relation to the additional charges, the defence argued that their inclusion was oppressive, having not been included in the original indictment when the facts relating to them had been known to the prosecution at that time.

Held, upholding the plea to the competency, that (1) it was incompetent to include on indictment charges in relation to which an accused has already been acquitted and where such verdicts had not been set aside; (2) even if the verdicts had been set aside, there was still no justification for including the charges on indictment where there was no intention to obtain convictions rather than using the procedures set out in s.119(6) and s.119(7), and (3) the inclusion of new charges in the indictment was oppressive.

HM ADVOCATE v. HEMPHILL (JOHN) 2002 S.L.T. 754, Lord Prosser, HCJ.

5526. Trials – right to fair trial – conduct of defence case – failure to explore reliability of child complainers

[Criminal Procedure (Scotland) Act 1995 (c.46) s.106(3)(b).]

E appealed against his conviction for the rape of his two young daughters, then aged between three and five, on the grounds that a substantial line of defence for which there was supporting medical evidence and which could have led to the conclusion that there was a reasonable doubt, was not presented to the jury and that the verdict was one which no reasonable jury, properly directed, could have returned, in terms of the Criminal Procedure (Scotland) Act 1995 s.106(3)(b). E had denied the charges, claiming the complainants had been manipulated by their mother, M, who had instigated a false case of sexual abuse. At trial the Crown relied for corroboration on the Moorov doctrine. The defence attempted to highlight inconsistencies in statements provided by the complainants at various times and the lack of clearly supportive medical evidence, but did not directly challenge their credibility in naming E as their abuser or advance a case of instigation by M.

Held, allowing the appeal, and quashing the conviction, that (1) the conduct of E's defence had been inadequate because (per the Lord Justice Clerk and Lord McCluskey) his consistent denials of any sexual interference with either child left the defence no alternative but to challenge the compainants' credibility in relation to the identity of their abuser, which would have necessitated a thorough investigation into the medical evidence, the possible manipulation by M and the introduction of evidence to demonstrate how young children's evidence might be manipulated in sexual abuse cases. The failure to do so affected the conduct of the trial to such an extent that E was denied a fair trial; (per Lord Hamilton) the defence's subtle approach to M did not amount to a failure on their part, but the failure to challenge the inferences sought to be drawn from the complainers' medical examinations, or to instruct expert evidence as to the reliability of their statements obtaied at interview, denied E the opportunity to have his defence properly presented; (2) (per the Lord Justice Clerk and Lord McCluskey) s.106(3)(b), as amended, set an objective test under which issues of credibility and reasonable doubt could no longer be regarded as being at all times within the exclusive preserve of the jury, and the court could alter a verdict if it was satisfied on the basis of its experience of criminal trials that, on any view, a verdict of guilty beyond reasonable doubt was one that no jury could reasonably have returned; (3) (Lord Hamilton dissenting) given the contradictions in the evidence and statements given by the younger complainant, her age and the lack of medical evidence that she had been sexually interefered with at any time, no reasonable jury could have found that the evidence that she had been sexually penetrated was reliable, and (4) the Crown's motion for leave to bring a new prosecution would be refused, given the complainants' ages, the nature of the charges on which they would be required to give evidence, the lapse of time and the four and a half years of a seven year sentence already served by E.

E v. HM ADVOCATE; *sub nom.* AJE v. HM ADVOCATE 2002 J.C. 215, Lord Gill L.J.C., HCJ Appeal.

5527. Warrants–search warrants–validity–misuse of drugs–information justifying warrant

[Misuse of Drugs Act 1971 (c.38) s.23(3).]

G, charged with offences under the Misuse of Drugs Act 1971, sought suspension of a warrant to search his premises granted on July 14, 2000 under s.23(3) of that Act. G obtained a statement on precognition from the justice (J) who had granted the warrant to the effect that in general he did not ask any questions when such a warrant was sought. However, in response to an interlocutor from the court, J produced a report in which he stated that he did not recall anything about the signing of the warrant but that he would put the applicant for a warrant on oath and ask them questions about it before signing. G argued that given the contradiction between the precognition and the report, it was impossible to know what J's invariable practice had been.

Held, refusing the bill, that it could not be inferred from the report, the terms of which were accepted by the court, that J had failed to act as an independent judicial officer in granting the search warrant, notwithstanding that he could not recall the particular circumstances of this application; that a precognition was not equivalent to such a report; and that it was clear that the warrant would only have been signed after questioning of G.

GRAHAM v. HIGSON 2002 S.L.T. 1382, Lord Cameron of Lochbroom, Lord Caplan, Lord Marnoch, HCJ.

5528. Warrants—search warrants—validity—sheriffs—warrant granted by temporary sheriff

[European Convention on Human Rights 1950; Misuse of Drugs Act 1971 (c.38).]

M, charged with offences under the Misuse of Drugs Act 1971, sought suspension of a warrant to search his flat granted under the Act by a temporary sheriff on December 1, 1998. M argued that a warrant required to be granted by an independent judicial figure, and if a temporary sheriff could not conduct a trial he was equally disqualified from any part in the determination of a charge. While the warrant predated the implementation of the European Convention on Human Rights 1950, it was a basic principle of Scots law that there should be an independent and impartial judicial figure.

Held, refusing the bill, that in the absence of discussion in argument of the common law prior to the importation of the Convention, or analysis of Convention decisions on the "objective guarantees" requirements as compared with the common law, it would be taking a large step and one unjustified by the argument presented to hold that the temporary sheriff was disqualified at common law when it was not suggested that he in any way lacked impartiality.

McFARLANE v. GILCHRIST 2002 S.L.T. 521, Lord Coulsfield, Lord Carloway, Lord Wheatley, HCJ Appeal.

5529. Warrants—search warrants—validity—time—warrant containing incomplete date

Following the indictment of F and Y for forming a fraudulent scheme to steal and reset motor vehicles, the Crown appealed against the sheriff's decision at preliminary diet to sustain F's objection to the validity of a search warrant on the basis that the warrant was invalid through failure to insert a precise date, the warrant being dated "November 2000". F argued, inter alia, that a full and precise date was an essential requirement of a warrant granted at common law, being necessary in order to determine whether by the time of its execution a search under it had become oppressive.

Held, allowing the appeal, that (1) the warrant was a common law warrant and neither the right of the prosecutor to seek such a warrant nor the power of the sheriff to grant it was prescribed or restricted by any statutory provision concerning a time limit for its execution, and (2) the date which appeared on the warrant was sufficient for its validity, and while it would be preferable that the full date was inserted when such a warrant was signed by a sheriff, the warrant was not ex facie invalid.

HM ADVOCATE v. FOULIS (DEAN ROBERT); HM ADVOCATE v. YOUNG (GRANT) 2002 J.C. 262, Lord Cameron of Lochbroom, Lord Carloway, Lord Kingarth, HCJ Appeal.

5530. Warrants—search warrants—validity—warrant relating to accused's dwellinghouse bearing handwritten additions relating to lockup or garage—state of warrant on execution

B was charged on indictment with assault, sodomy and murder. During his trial B objected to the leading of evidence in relation to a search warrant produced by the Crown. While the printed type of the warrant related to B's dwellinghouse it bore a variety of handwritten words and phrases including a reference to a lockup or garage rented by him. The Crown stated that these were the result of mistaken use of the warrant subsequent to its grant by the sheriff and use in relation to B's dwellinghouse, to prepare a draft of a new warrant relating to the lockup, and that when the warrant was executed it did not bear the handwritten additions. The trial judge held that the presumption in favour of regularity was displaced by the handwritten material and the composite document could not be viewed as an ex facie valid warrant. He allowed a trial within a trial to establish the state of the warrant when the search of B's dwellinghouse commenced, while holding it incompetent to inquire into the circumstances surrounding the granting of the warrant by the sheriff. The Crown then led evidence. B moved the court to adjourn the trial to seek suspension of the warrant, arguing that sufficient inquiries had not been made in obtaining the information necessary to support an application for a warrant, and inaccurate or misconstrued information had been relied on.

Held, repelling the objection and refusing the motion to adjourn, that (1) on the evidence the warrant as executed did not contain the writings complained of and constituted a valid warrant, and (2) material had been placed before the sheriff supporting the procurator fiscal's application for the search warrant and B had not demonstrated a prima facie case of invalidity of the warrant; in any event, adjournment was a matter of discretion, and given the disruption to the trial and the jury and the fact that the validity of the warrant could be raised in any appeal following conviction, refusal of the motion created no injustice.

HM ADVOCATE v. BEGGS (NO.4) 2002 S.L.T. 163, Lord Osborne, HCJ.

5531. **Books**

Brown, Alastair N.—Regulation of Investigatory Powers in Scotland. Green's Essential Legislation. Paperback: £39.00. ISBN 0-414-01490-1. W.Green & Son.

DAMAGES

5532. **Expenses–tender–award exceeding tender when interest added–award below tender at date of lodging**

[Interest on Damages (Scotland) Act 1958 (c.61) s.1 (1B).]

S appealed against the sheriff principal's decision to award full expenses to M in her action for personal injuries. M was awarded damages of £2,800 and as at the date of decree the principal award with interest amounted to £3,047. S had lodged a tender of £3,000 along with the defences. As at that date the value of the award with interest amounted to £2,992. The sheriff awarded expenses to M up to the date of the tender and thereafter to S. On M's appeal the sheriff principal upheld the award of solatium, but held that the Interest on Damages (Scotland) Act 1958 s.1 (1B) gave the court a discretion as to expenses in such circumstances.

Held, allowing the appeal and finding S entitled to expenses from the date of tender, that the general rule that a pursuer who ultimately obtained an award in excess of a tender was entitled to expenses incurred both before and after the date of tender, was abridged by s.1 (1B) which was clearly aimed at a case like the present where an award only exceeded the tender amount due to the accrual of interest and M's refusal of the tender had unnecessarily extended the proceedings to no purpose.

MANSON v. SKINNER 2002 S.L.T. 448, Lord Gill, Lord Maclean, Lord Weir, 2 Div.

5533. **Loss of society–children–death of eldest son in Muslim family**

T, a trainee pilot, was killed in a flying accident. He was the eldest son in a Muslim family and S, his parents, sought, inter alia, loss of society in respect of his death.

Held, awarding each parent £35,000 less discount for contributory negligence, that there were particular bonds of affection in this case and the death of their eldest son had a special significance for S.

SHAHER v. BRITISH AEROSPACE FLYING COLLEGE LTD 2002 S.L.T. 833 (Note), Lord Wheatley, OH.

5534. **Loss of support–specification of loss–extent of financial support– appropriate amount of deceased's earnings to be allocated to widow**

In an action by S, family members of W, for damages from J, W's employer, in respect of W's death from mesothelioma, S reclaimed against the Lord Ordinary's interlocutor excluding from probation certain averments relating to loss of support of W's widow (X), as lacking in specification where it was simply averred that X was supported by W and that the earnings of each would be vouched and a schedule of damages produced. Their respective earnings and ages had been vouched by productions. The Lord Ordinary considered that given the variations in families' financial arrangements in modern times, J should not have to investigate the value of S's claims when the information was within S's knowledge

Held, allowing the reclaiming motion, that it was not necessary to require further specification, as loss of support was assessed on a broad basis and in the absence of averments supporting a different basis of calculation, the normal approach would be applied of adding the respective incomes and deducting 25 per cent as being for the maintenance of the deceased, the loss of dependency comprising the net figure less the earnings of the surviving spouse.

SMITH'S EXECUTRIX v. J SMART (CONTRACTORS) PLC; *sub nom.* SMITH v. SMART; SMITH v. J SMART (CONTRACTORS) PLC 2002 S.L.T. 779, Lord Cullen L.P., Lord Cameron of Lochbroom, Lord Hamilton, 1 Div.

5535. **Measure of damages–loss of earnings–loss of earning capacity and loss of services–injury preventing active involvement in restaurant business**

S, a restaurant owner, sought damages following a road accident on December 5, 1997. She suffered chest, neck and back pain which resolved within a year, and a knee injury for which she attended physiotherapy for some months in 1998 but from which the pain persisted. Following proof, the Lord Ordinary found that that injury was sufficiently disabling that she could not meet the physical demands of working in the restaurant, and that her decision to sell it as from April 2000 and find an alternative business in which her disability would not prevent her active involvement was reasonable.

Held, granting decree, that (1) solatium was properly valued at £5,500, £4,000 to the past; (2) in the absence of accurate figures from S's accountant a fair assessment of loss of income to the date of sale of the restaurant business was £30,000; (3) as the restaurant had still been making some profit and the business purchased was unlikely to make a profit for at least three years, H did not have to meet the full cost of the sale and purchase; (4) loss of earnings was calculated as £11,000 for the period from May 2000 to date and £5,000 for loss of future earning capacity, and (5) £2,500 was awarded for S's inability to provide certain personal services, on a lump sum rather than a multiplier basis in the absence of evidence as to value.

SMITH v. HASTIE 2002 S.L.T. 1183, Lord Menzies, OH.

5536. **Personal injuries–damages–rate of return**

DAMAGES (PERSONAL INJURY) (SCOTLAND) ORDER 2002, SSI 2002 46; made under the Damages Act 1996 s.1. In force: February 8, 2002; £1.50.

This Order prescribes 2.5 per cent as the rate of return which, under the Damages Act 1996 s.1, courts are required to take into account when calculating damages for future pecuniary loss in an action for personal injury.

5537. **Remoteness–loss sustained through limited company–recoverability of investment**

See REPARATION: Barry v. Sutherland (Damages). §6066

EDUCATION

5538. **Disabled persons–accessibility strategies**

EDUCATION (DISABILITY STRATEGIES) (SCOTLAND) REGULATIONS 2002, SSI 2002 391; made under the Education (Disability Strategies and Pupils'

Educational Records) (Scotland) Act 2002 s.1, s.2, s.3, s.5. In force: October 1, 2002; £1.75.

The Education (Disability Strategies and Pupils' Records) (Scotland) Act 2002 provides that bodies responsible for schools shall prepare accessibility strategies at prescribed intervals. In the case of education authorities providing school education to pupils under school age and to children educated outwith schools, strategies will also be prepared for each place where such education is provided. These Regulations prescribe the intervals at which such strategies should be prepared and the alternative forms in which responsible bodies should make their accessibility strategies available on request.

5539. Duty of care–local education authorities–supervision of pupils leaving school

See NEGLIGENCE: Hunter v. Perth and Kinross Council. §6005

5540. Education (Disability Strategies and Pupils' Educational Records) (Scotland) Act 2002 (asp 12)

This Act of the Scottish Parliament requires bodies responsible for schools to prepare and implement strategies relating to the accessibility of school education for pupils with a disability and makes provision in respect of the educational records of school pupils.

This Act received Royal Assent on April 30, 2002.

5541. Education (Disability Strategies and Pupils' Educational Records) (Scotland) Act 2002 (asp 12)–Commencement Order

EDUCATION (DISABILITY STRATEGIES AND PUPILS' EDUCATIONAL RECORDS) (SCOTLAND) ACT 2002 (COMMENCEMENT) ORDER 2002, SSI 2002 367; made under the Education (Disability Strategies and Pupils' Educational Records) (Scotland) Act 2002 s.7. Commencement details: bringing into force various provisions of the 2002 Act on August 15, 2002; £1.50.

This Order brings into force those provisions of the Education (Disability Strategies and Pupils' Educational Records) (Scotland) Act 2002 which did not come into force on Royal Assent. These provisions relate to the requirement for bodies responsible for schools to prepare and implement accessibility strategies designed to improve access for pupils with disabilities to the curriculum and to the physical environment of the school, and to improve communication with and to those pupils.

5542. Grants–assisted places–remission of fees–qualifying income levels

EDUCATION (ASSISTED PLACES) (SCOTLAND) AMENDMENT REGULATIONS 2002, SSI 2002 249; made under the Education (Scotland) Act 1980 s.75A, s.75B. In force: August 1, 2002; £1.75.

These Regulations amend the Education (Assisted Places) (Scotland) Regulations 2001 (SSI 2001 222) to uprate the qualifying income levels for the remission of fees and charges and the making of grants under the assisted places scheme. The deduction made from relevant income for dependent children and relatives has been increased to £1,463 and the level of income at or below which fees are to be wholly remitted is increased to £11,368 with corresponding increases in the extent of remission where the relevant income exceeds that figure. The qualifying income levels for school travel grants and clothing grants are also uprated, with clothing grants being increased by either £2 or £1.

5543. Grants–nurses and midwives

NURSING AND MIDWIFERY STUDENT ALLOWANCES (SCOTLAND) AMENDMENT REGULATIONS 2002, SSI 2002 423; made under the Education (Scotland) Act 1980 s.73, s.74. In force: October 4, 2002; £2.00.

These Regulations amend the Nursing and Midwifery Student Allowances (Scotland) Regulations 1992 (SI 1992 580) which govern allowances paid to persons attending courses of education in Colleges of Nursing and Midwifery in Scotland, and prescribe the conditions and requirements subject to which allowances may be paid. The Regulations make provision as to when a person is to be treated as ordinarily resident in a place for or at a particular time and provide a definition of the phrase "relevant day". They also allow the Ministers to pay allowances to students on distance learning courses as well as students attending courses of education and make amendments so that an application for an allowance may be made by electronic means.

5544. Listed bodies–recognition

EDUCATION (LISTED BODIES) (SCOTLAND) ORDER 2002, SSI 2002 406; made under the Education Reform Act 1988 s.216. In force: September 26, 2002; £3.00.

This Order, which revokes the Education (Listed Bodies) Order 2000 (SSI 2000 293), lists the names of each body which is not a recognised body within the Education Reform Act 1988 s.214(2)(a)(b), but which either provides any course which is in preparation for a degree to be granted by such a recognised body and is approved by or on behalf of that body; or is a constituent college, school, hall or other institution of a university which is such a recognised body.

5545. Nursery education–prescribed children

PROVISION OF SCHOOL EDUCATION FOR CHILDREN UNDER SCHOOL AGE (PRESCRIBED CHILDREN) (SCOTLAND) ORDER 2002, SSI 2002 90; made under the Education (Scotland) Act 1980 s.1. In force: April 1, 2002; £1.75.

The Standard in Scotland's Schools Act 2000 amends the Education (Scotland) Act 1980 by imposing a duty on an education authority to secure the provision of school education for categories of children as may be prescribed by the Scottish Minister. This Order describes eligible children, deals with the situations where children do not attend primary school when they are first eligible to do so, applies to children who have their fifth birthday after the start of the school year and whose parents opt to defer entry to primary school to the following school year and excludes from the scope of an education authority's duty children who may not be educated at a primary school on reaching 5 years old, or who may seek to defer entry for second or subsequent years. The Order also provides that eligible children are to receive 412.5 hours of school education during the school year.

5546. Qualifications–committee–establishment–Advisory Council

ADVISORY COUNCIL (ESTABLISHMENT) (SCOTLAND) REGULATIONS 2002, SSI 2002 293; made under the Scottish Qualifications Authority Act 2002 s.3. In force: August 7, 2002; £1.75.

These Regulations provide for the establishment of a committee, to be known as the Advisory Council, for the purposes of considering matters relating to qualifications devised or awarded by the SQA, and its functions, and procedure. The Council will provide advice to the SQA or to Scottish Ministers in relation to those matters, and also on other matters as the Council thinks appropriate.

5547. School Education (Amendment) (Scotland) Act 2002–Commencement Order

SCHOOL EDUCATION (AMENDMENT) (SCOTLAND) ACT 2002 (COMMENCEMENT) ORDER 2002, SSI 2002 74; made under the School Education (Amendment) (Scotland) Act 2002 s.3. Commencement details:

bringing into force various provisions of the 2002 Act on February 26, 2002 and March 22, 2002; £1.50.

This Order brings into force provisions of the School Education (Amendment) (Scotland) Act 2002 which amend the law on placing requests for children under school age and relate to the abolition of the post of assistant headteacher.

5548. Schools–aided places–St Mary's Music School

ST MARY'S MUSIC SCHOOL (AIDED PLACES) (SCOTLAND) AMENDMENT REGULATIONS 2002, SSI 2002 248; made under the Education (Scotland) Act 1980 s.73, s.74. In force: August 1, 2002; £1.75.

These Regulations amend the St Mary's Music School (Aided Places) (Scotland) Regulations 2001 (SSI 2001 223) to uprate the qualifying income levels for the remission of fees and charges and the making of grants under the aided places scheme. The deduction from relevant income for dependent children and relatives has been increased to £1,463; the level of income at or below which fees are to be wholly remitted is increased to £9,772 for boarders and to £12,310 for day pupils, with corresponding increases in the extent of fee remission where the relevant income exceeds these sums; the qualifying income levels for clothing grants and school travel grants are increased; and the school clothing grants are increased by either £2 or £1 depending on the income level.

5549. Schools–placings–placing request–refusal–proper approach by sheriff on appeal

[Education (Scotland) Act 1980 (c.44) s.28A, s.28C, s.28E, s.28F.]

A, a local authority, sought reduction of a sheriff's decision (2002 G.W.D. 2-72) allowing W's appeal against A's refusal of a placing request in respect of her child, and declarator that the Education (Scotland) Act 1980 s.28F should be read as containing a reference to s.28A(3A). A argued (1) that the sheriff had acted ultra vires in holding that the decision of an education authority based on s.28A(3A) could be the subject of an appeal to him under s.28F, and (2) that the sheriff had erred in holding that he could not interpret s.28F(5) as if it contained a reference to s.28A(3A) as well as s.28A(3). W withdrew a concession before the sheriff that s.28F(5) contained a drafting error, and argued that a further reason for refusing reduction was that A's prioritisation process for placing requests was ultra vires: in A's final category, priority was determined by distance between the school and a pupil's home without regard to other reasons, which failed to take individual pupils' circumstances into account and amounted to a fettering of A's discretion.

Held, granting reduction and declarator, that (1) the sheriff had not acted ultra vires where the right to refer a decision to an appeal committee under s.28C(1) and the corresponding right of an appeal to a sheriff in s.28F(1) were both expressed in general terms; (2) s.28E(1) and s.28F(5) should each be construed as including a reference to refusals under s.28A(3A) as well as under subs.(3), as both contained an obvious drafting error and there was no sensible reason for distinguishing the grounds in s.28A(3A) and s.28A(3), there was a manifest failure to give effect to the purpose of the provision which could be easily corrected, and the requirements for correction in *Inco Europe Ltd v. First Choice Distribution* [2000] 1 W.L.R. 586, [2000] C.L.Y. 220 were clearly established, and (3) if the sheriff had erred, the proper course was to reduce the decision and remit the matter to the sheriff for reconsideration, W's motion to amend to seek declarator that A's prioritisation policy was unlawful would be refused where such a direct challenge would be an important matter on which A's counsel would require to take detailed instructions.

WOKOMA v. ABERDEEN CITY COUNCIL; *sub nom.* ABERDEEN CITY COUNCIL v. WOKOMA 2002 S.C. 352, Lord Drummond Young, OH.

5550. Schools–self governing status–compatibility with ECHR

[Self Governing Schools etc. (Scotland) Act 1989 (c.39); Human Rights Act 1998 (c.42) Sch.1 Part II Art.2.]

D, parents of pupils at M, the only school in Scotland still holding self governing status under the Self Governing Schools etc. (Scotland) Act 1989, reclaimed against the Lord Ordinary's dismissal (2002 S.L.T. 640, [2002] 6 C.L. 745) of their petition for judicial review of orders seeking to effect the reversion of M to the management of the local authority and refusal of an application for grant aided status. D's petition, as amended, claimed (1) that the orders violated their child's right to education under the Human Rights Act 1998 Sch.1 Part II Art.2 and in any event their own rights as parents to respect for their philosophical convictions relating to their child's education and teaching, and (2) that the orders discriminated against them within the ambit of their Art.2 rights in that M would be treated differently from another school, J, which would continue to be self managed outwith the control of a local authority. D argued that the Lord Ordinary had adopted an overly restrictive approach to the scope or ambit of the Art.2 right, which was concerned, inter alia, with standards and quality, that D were entitled to respect for their philosophical convictions that self governing status with its particular ethos was of greater educational benefit, and that discrimination could exist where states without an objective and reasonable justification failed to treat differently persons whose situations were significantly different.

Held, refusing the reclaiming motion, that (1) pluralism in education, which was supported by the case law, guaranteed the right to exist of fee paying independent schools but did not entail the right to obtain from public authorities the creation of a particular kind of educational establishment, and the orders complained of, which were concerned only with management and administration and not the curricula or teaching at the school, did not fall within the scope or ambit of the Art.2 right to education; (2) refusal of grant aided status could not itself be regarded as constituting any disadvantage to the exercise by D's child of any of the "modalities" of the right to education, nor could it be linked to any discrimination in the exercise of the right by way of access to education, and (3) that D's averments were insufficient to constitute philosophical convictions within the meaning of Art.2 and amounted at best to no more than individual opinions relating to the running of the school.

DOVE v. SCOTTISH MINISTERS 2002 S.L.T. 1296, Lord Cameron of Lochbroom, Lord Macfadyen, Lord Sutherland, Ex Div.

5551. Scottish Education (Amendment) (Scotland) Act 2002 (asp 2)

This Act of the Scottish Parliament makes provision in respect of education for children under school age for whom placing requests have been made; and makes provision relating to the abolition of the post of assistant headteacher.

This Act received Royal Assent on January 22, 2002.

5552. Scottish Qualifications Authority Act 2002 (asp 14)

This Act of the Scottish Parliament makes provision in relation to the members of the Scottish Qualifications Authority; confers power on the Scottish Ministers to regulate the procedure of that Authority; provides for the establishment of a committee to consider and advise on matters relating to qualifications awarded by, and the functions and procedures of, that Authority.

This Act received Royal Assent on June 6, 2002.

5553. Scottish Qualifications Authority Act 2002 (asp 14)–Commencement No.1 Order

SCOTTISH QUALIFICATIONS AUTHORITY ACT 2002 (COMMENCEMENT NO.1) ORDER 2002, SSI 2002 355; made under the Scottish Qualifications

Authority Act 2002 s.6. Commencement details: bringing into force various provisions of the 2002 Act on August 7, 2002 and August 19, 2002; £1.50.

This Order brings into force the remaining provisions of the Scottish Qualifications Authority Act 2002, with the exception of s.1 (7) (b) relating to repeal of the Education (Scotland) Act 1996 Sch.1 para.9(2)(3), which makes provision for the payment of pension, and compensation, to the chairman of the Scottish Qualifications Authority.

5554. Special educational needs−records−right of appeal against part of record− competence of judicial review

[Education (Scotland) Act 1980 (c.44) s.62(3).]

E opened a record of needs with regard to G, an autistic child. Part IV of the record was a statement of G's needs, Part V was E's proposed measures and Part VI was the nominated school for attendance on day placement. G sought judicial review, contending that E had failed in its statutory duty to provide appropriate provision for his special educational needs under the Education (Scotland) Act 1980 s.62(3). G challenged E's proposed measures (Part V), choice of school (Part VI) and E's unwillingness to provide funding for home educating G. The principal issue was whether G had a statutory right of appeal in relation to Parts V and VI. E maintained that such a right did exist, and therefore the petition should be dismissed. E conceded that G had no right of appeal with regard to Parts V and VI but did in relation to Part IV. E argued that the success of an appeal against Part IV could alter Parts V and VI, regardless of a direct right of appeal and failure to follow this route of appeal was fatal to the petition for judicial review.

Held, rejecting E's challenge as to the competency of the petition, that given G's acceptance of Part IV of the record, it would have been an abuse of procedure to allow G a Part IV appeal with the actual intention of reviewing Parts V, VI or E's unwillingness to fund home education for G.

G (A CHILD) v. EDINBURGH CITY COUNCIL (EDUCATIONAL NEEDS: JUDICIAL REVIEW) 2002 S.C.L.R. 92, Lord Emslie, OH.

5555. Standards in Scotland's Schools etc. Act 2000 (asp 6)−Commencement No.5 Order

STANDARDS IN SCOTLAND'S SCHOOLS ETC. ACT 2000 (COMMENCEMENT NO.5) ORDER 2002, SSI 2002 72; made under the Standards in Scotland's Schools etc. Act 2000 s.61. Commencement details: bringing into force various provisions of the 2000 Act on March 4, 2002 and April 1, 2002; £1.75.

This Order brings into force specified provisions of the Standards in Scotland's Schools etc. Act 2000.

5556. Students−loans

EDUCATION (STUDENT LOANS) AMENDMENT (SCOTLAND) REGULATIONS 2002, SSI 2002 282; made under the Education (Scotland) Act 1990 s.1, Sch.2 para.1. In force: August 1, 2002; £1.75.

These Regulations amend the Education (Student Loans) Regulations 1998 (SI 1998 211) by increasing the maximum amounts which may be lent to students in relation to an academic year in line with inflation.

5557. Teachers−disciplinary procedures−admissibility of evidence

See CIVIL EVIDENCE: F v. General Teaching Council for Scotland. §5310

5558. University of St. Andrews (Postgraduate Medical Degrees) 2002 (asp 15)

This Act of the Scottish Parliament permits the University of St. Andrews to grant postgraduate research degrees in medicine to qualified medical practitioners.

This Act received Royal Assent on July 30, 2002.

ELECTORAL PROCESS

5559. Elections–candidates–sex discrmination–jurisdiction of employment tribunal

See EMPLOYMENT: Secretary of State for Scotland v. Mann. §5571

5560. Elections–Scottish Parliament–conduct of elections

SCOTTISH PARLIAMENT (ELECTIONS ETC.) ORDER 2002, SI 2002 2779 (S.11); made under the Scotland Act 1998 s.12, s.113. In force: in accordance with Art.1; £13.50.

This Order, which amends the Act of Sederunt (Rules of the Court of Session 1994) 1994 (SI 1994 1443), revokes the Scottish Parliament (Elections etc.) Order 1999 (SI 1999 787), the Scottish Parliament (Elections etc.) (Amendment) Order 2001 (SI 2001 1399), the Scottish Parliament (Elections etc.) (Amendment (No.2) Order 2001 (SI 2001 1748) and the Scottish Parliament (Elections etc.) (Amendment) (No.3) Order 2001 (SI 2001 1750). It sets out provisions as to the conduct of elections for, and the return of members to, the Scottish Parliament, established by the Scotland Act 1998.

5561. Local elections–Scottish local authorities

SCOTTISH LOCAL GOVERNMENT ELECTIONS AMENDMENT RULES 2002, SSI 2002 522; made under the Representation of the People Act 1983 s.42. In force: December 19, 2002; £1.75.

These Regulations amend the Scottish Local Government Elections Rules 2002 (SSI 2002 457), which apply in respect of the election of councillors in Scotland, to correct errors or omissions in those Rules.

5562. Local elections–Scottish local authorities

SCOTTISH LOCAL GOVERNMENT ELECTIONS RULES 2002, SSI 2002 457; made under the Representation of the People Act 1983 s.42. In force: in accordance with r.1 (2); £7.50.

These Rules, which revoke the Scottish Local Elections Rules 1986 (SI 1986 2213) and the Scottish Local Elections Amendment (No.2) Rules 1999 (SI 1999 492), provide for the conduct of elections of members of local authorities.

5563. Local elections–Scottish local authorities–postal ballot papers

SCOTTISH LOCAL GOVERNMENT ELECTIONS REGULATIONS 2002, SSI 2002 561; made under the Representation of the People Act 1983 s.53, Sch.2. In force: In accordance with Art.1; £2.50.

These Regulations provide for revised procedures on the issue and receipt of postal ballot papers for local government elections and provide that the proceedings on the issue of ballot papers may be taken together where there is a combined poll.

EMPLOYMENT

5564. Contract of employment–conflict of interest–breach of duty of fidelity– knowledge of damage

R, a light engineering and manufacturing company, employed S in 1984 and promoted him to the position of senior buyer in 1995. His employment was terminated in September 1999. The third defender was employed by T, with whom R had extensive commercial dealings between 1995 and 1999. In addition to his work for T, the third defender also traded on his own account under the name of Alloy & Metal. In April 1999, Alloy & Metal was taken over by Alloy & Metal Ltd, A, in which the third defender had an interest. A were the second defenders to the action. The action was a claim for damages in respect of losses allegedly incurred by R as a result of agreements between S and the third defender between 1995 and April 1999 and between S and A between April and September 1999, for the supply of machine parts by the third defenders and latterly by A to R which would then be used by R in the manufacturing of tail lifts and wheelchairs. R argued that the price at which S agreed to purchase the parts was grossly inflated on the price at which those parts could have been obtained directly form the suppliers. R claimed that S was in breach of an express term in his contract of employment which required him not to engage in any activity which involved a conflict of interest with R. R further argued that S was also in breach of his implied fiduciary duty. R argued that the loss incurred should be quantified as the difference between the price actually paid for the parts and the price at which the suppliers sold the parts to the third defenders and A. R claimed that S was aware of the additional cost of the arrangements he had made for the supply of the parts as the manager of one of the supply firms had faxed S in April 1999 to advise him of the gross inflation of prices. Finally, R claimed that the third defenders and A had induced S to breach his contract of employment. S argued that the case against him was irrelevant as there were no averments to the effect that the suppliers would have sold the parts directly to him at the prices and on the same terms as had been obtained by the third defenders and A, nor were there any averments that S had been aware that the prices being paid were grossly inflated. R argued that the existence of the fax from the manager of one of the suppliers was sufficient evidence to prove knowledge from April 1999.

Held, dismissing the action against the third defender, dismissing the action against S in respect of the period up to April 1999 and allowing a proof in respect of the period from April to September 1999, that (1) in order to prove a breach of the implied fiduciary duty in a contract of employment, it was necessary to prove knowledge on S's part that his dealings with the third defender were to the detriment of R and that, at the time S entered into the agreements, S was also aware that the parts could be purchased from an alternative source at a materially cheaper price; (2) R's failure to specify the basis for such knowledge in their averments resulted in the case against S in respect of the period to April 1999 being irrelevant; (3) there were no averments that the third defender had offered any inducement to S to enter the agreements and there was no duty on the third defender to inform S or R that the prices paid by R for the parts were grossly inflated when compared to the prices charged by the suppliers, and (4) the existence of the fax sent to S was sufficient to allow a proof before answer in relation to the claims against S for the period from April to September 1999.

ROSS & BONNYMAN LTD v. SMALL 2001 S.C.L.R. 900, Lord Hamilton, OH.

5565. Contract of employment–termination–disciplinary procedures–employers duties–trust and confidence

K, an employee, sought damages from U in respect of the termination of his contract of employment following a hearing on disciplinary charges. K argued, inter alia, that U had breached an implied duty of trust and confidence in the course of their investigation into the charges against him. U disputed the relevancy of K's case standing the decision in *Johnson v. Unisys Ltd* [2001] UKHL 13, [2001] 2 W.L.R. 1076.

Held, putting the case out by order, that *Johnson* made it clear that once a decision to dismiss had been made, there was no room for an implied term of trust and confidence but while an employer was carrying out investigative procedures which might not necessarily culminate in dismissal, an employee was entitled to rely on the implied duty of trust and confidence as subsisting,

Johnson distinguished, particularly where K's contract envisaged the establishing before a hearing of good cause for dismissal.

KING v. UNIVERSITY COURT OF THE UNIVERSITY OF ST ANDREWS; *sub nom.* KING v. UNIVERSITY OF ST ANDREWS 2002 S.L.T. 439, Lady Smith, OH.

5566. Criminal record–applications for certificates–fees

POLICE ACT 1997 (CRIMINAL RECORDS) (SCOTLAND) REGULATIONS 2002, SSI 2002 143; made under the Police Act 1997 s.112, s.113, s.114, s.115, s.116, s.118, s.125. In force: in accordance with Reg.1 (2); £2.50.

These Regulations make detailed provisions in relation to applications for criminal conviction certificates, criminal record certificates and enhanced criminal record certificates. They require an application for the issue of a criminal conviction certificate, criminal record certificate or an enhanced criminal record certificate to be made on the specified form, specify the fee for such an application as £13.60, prescribe the details of convictions which appear on criminal conviction certificates and the details of convictions and cautions which appear on criminal record certificates and enhanced criminal record certificates. They also prescribe the sources of information comprising central records for the purposes of certificates, define "relevant police force" for the purposes of enhanced criminal record certificates, make provision in relation to the taking of fingerprints from applicants where the Scottish Ministers require them for the purposes of ascertaining the identity of an applicant and prescribe the fees to be paid to police authorities who maintain police forces that have been requested to supply information in relation to an application for an enhanced criminal record certificate.

5567. Criminal record–certificates–protection of vulnerable adults

POLICE ACT 1997 (ENHANCED CRIMINAL RECORD CERTIFICATES) (PROTECTION OF VULNERABLE ADULTS) (SCOTLAND) REGULATIONS 2002, SSI 2002 217; made under the Police Act 1997 s.115. In force: May 3, 2002; £1.75.

The Police Act 1997 s.115 provides for the issue by the Scottish Ministers of an enhanced criminal record certificate. Application for such a certificate must be accompanied by a statement by a person registered under the Act that the certificate is required for the purpose of an exempted question in the course of considering the applicant's suitability for a position or for a purpose relating to any of the matters specified. These Regulations provide that a position is within s.115 if it is of a kind which enables a person to have regular contact with a vulnerable adult.

5568. Criminal record–registration–fees

POLICE ACT 1997 (CRIMINAL RECORDS) (REGISTRATION) (SCOTLAND) REGULATIONS 2002, SSI 2002 23; made under the Police Act 1997 s.120. In force: February 18, 2002; £1.75.

These Regulations provide for the information to be included in the register maintained by the Scottish Ministers, the removal, subject to prescribed safeguards, of persons from that register and the payment of a fee of £150 for inclusion in that register and £10 for each additional signature recorded in the register for the purposes of counter-signing applications for criminal record and enhanced criminal record certificates.

5569. Disability discrimination–meaning of "disability"–employee's ability to perform day to day activities relevant

[Disability Discrimination Act 1995.]

R, a staff nurse at Law Hospital, injured her back in 1984 and was absent from work for 14 months. R took painkillers daily, her mobility was affected and she had difficulty lifting anything with her right hand. Her disability was assessed at 7 per cent for life and she continued to work. R later injured her neck, shoulders and chest while lifting a patient and was dismissed in 1999. R complained that she had been discriminated against, contrary to the Disability Discrimination Act 1995. L argued that R had completed her nursing duties for many years despite her back injury and was not disabled in terms of the Act. The EAT held that R was disabled and L appealed to the Court of Session arguing that the EAT had erred in stating that the nature and extent of R's nursing duties were not a matter for the tribunal.

Held, refusing the appeal, that (1) the EAT had erred if it had intended to imply that evidence of R's duties and her discharge of them at work could not be a relevant consideration in the question of R's disability. If an employee has given evidence that he could not do Y at home, evidence that Y was done at work could have a bearing on the witness's credibility. The relevance of any such evidence was entirely reliant upon the circumstances of each case, and (2) the EAT's decision that R was disabled was correct. The fact that R had continued to work did not refute the evidence about her difficulties at home, nor had L provided evidence relating to R's performance at work that was contrary to R's in relation to her physical difficulties.

LAW HOSPITAL NHS TRUST v. RUSH 2002 S.C. 24, Lord Kirkwood, Lord Cowie, Lord Nimmo Smith, Ex Div.

5570. Employment agencies—contract to supply labour—illegality—foreign workers without legal authority

See CONTRACTS: Dowling & Rutter v. Abacus Frozen Foods Ltd (No.2). §5418

5571. Employment tribunals—jurisdiction—electoral matters

[Scottish Parliament Election Order 1999 (SI 1999 787) para.16(7).]

AG appealed against a determination that the employment tribunal had jurisdiction to adjudicate upon a claim for sex discrimination by M, a prospective candidate to the Scottish Parliament. The application to the tribunal had been filed following the refusal of a returning officer to respond to an application by M's party to field candidates for elections to the Scottish Parliament on a job share basis. AG contended that, pursuant to the Scottish Parliament Election Order 1999 para.16(7), the decision of a returning officer could not be challenged in any proceedings except where jurisdiction to do so had been specifically conferred upon a body or organisation.

Held, allowing the appeal, that in the absence of express provision to the contrary, and by the creation of criminal sanctions, it had been the intention of the Westminster Parliament to remove any right to challenge decisions of the returning officer within the civil justice system.

SECRETARY OF STATE FOR SCOTLAND v. MANN; *sub nom.* ADVOCATE GENERAL FOR SCOTLAND v. MANN [2001] I.C.R. 1005, Lord Johnston, EAT.

5572. Employment tribunals—jurisdiction—right of executors to commence claim for breach of contract and disability discrimination on behalf of deceased

[Law Reform (Miscellaneous Provisions) Act 1934 (c.41) s.1 (1).]

Executors appealed against the refusal of the employment tribunal to accept jurisdiction to hear complaints of breach of contract and disability discrimination on behalf of S. The executors argued that the fact that there was no Scottish equivalent to a tribunal in England and Wales which could entertain the claim under the Law Reform (Miscellaneous Provisions) Act 1934, was irrelevant in the light of the Scottish common law which allowed an executor to vindicate rights vested in the deceased at the time of death. J resisted the appeal, contending that S himself was the only "person" within the Disability Discrimination Act 1975 s.8 who could have brought the action, not his representatives.

Held, allowing the appeal, that the apparent anomaly could have been resolved by the commencement of the claim in England. However, as it fell for the Scottish tribunal to decide, it was found that the common law of Scotland had admitted the right of an executor to pursue claims on behalf of the deceased. Furthermore, as S had argued, the statutory silence on the subject was significant as it reiterated the lack of need for any additional legislation.

SOUTAR'S EXECUTORS v. JAMES MURRAY & CO (CUPAR) LTD [2002] I.R.L.R. 22, Lord Johnston, EAT.

5573. Employment tribunals—jurisdiction and judgments

EMPLOYMENT TRIBUNALS (ENFORCEMENT OF ORDERS IN OTHER JURISDICTIONS) (SCOTLAND) REGULATIONS 2002, SI 2002 2972 (S.12); made under the Civil Jurisdiction and Judgments Act 1982 s.18, Sch.6 para.2, Sch.6 para.4; and the Employment Tribunals Act 1996 s.7. In force: December 24, 2002; £2.00.

These Regulations revoke the Employment Tribunals (Enforcement of Orders under the Civil Jurisdiction and Judgments Act 1982) (Scotland) Regulations 1995 (SI 1995 1717) which provided for the issue of copies of, and certificates in connection with, orders for the payment of a sum of money issued by employment tribunals in Scotland, in order to enable an interested party to secure the recognition and enforcement of that order in another state which is a contracting state under the Convention on Jurisdiction and Enforcement of Judgments in Civil and Commercial Matters signed at Brussels on September 27, 1968 or the Convention on Jurisdiction and Enforcement of Judgments in Civil and Commercial Matters opened for signature at Lugano on September 16, 1988. The Regulations provide for the form of application for a copy of the money order.

5574. Equal pay—comparators—teachers—collective agreement governing pay and conditions

[Equal Pay Act 1970 (c.41); Education (Scotland) Act 1980 (c.44).]

The local authority appealed against a decision of the Employment Appeal Tribunal ([2001] I.R.L.R. 28, [2002] 1 C.L. 615) upholding the decision of an employment tribunal to allow M, a primary school head teacher who alleged a breach of the equal pay legislation, to use as a comparator a head teacher employed by another education authority. M maintained that while 75 per cent of primary school head teachers were female, the same percentage of secondary school head teachers were male and that the disparity in salary scales between primary and secondary school head teachers amounted to discrimination. Under the Education (Scotland) Act 1980, a committee had been established with the purpose, inter alia, of, if it thought fit, formulating a settlement in relation to the appropriate remuneration payable to teachers employed by education authorities in Scotland. The local authority argued that the Equal Pay Act 1970 required that the comparator be employed by the same employer as the applicant or by an associated employer.

Held, dismissing the appeal, that the settlement amounted to a national collective agreement. It was logical and reasonable in a uniform statutory regime governing pay and conditions in the education sector for comparisons to be made between teachers working for the different authorities that were statutorily obliged to give effect to the regime, *Defrenne v. SABENA (C43/75)* [1981] 1 All E.R. 122, [1976] C.L.Y. 1164 applied.

SOUTH AYRSHIRE COUNCIL v. MORTON; *sub nom.* MORTON v. SOUTH AYRSHIRE COUNCIL 2002 S.L.T. 656, Lord Gill L.J.C., Lord Caplan, Lord MacLean, 2 Div.

5575. Minimum wage—night workers—nightwatchman permitted to sleep when not attending duties—time work for purpose of Regulations

S, construction contractors, appealed against the decision of an employment appeal tribunal ([2001] I.R.L.R. 589, [2001] C.L.Y. 6472), sustaining W's claim that the terms of his employment entitled him to the application of the National Minimum Wage Regulations 1999. W had been employed by S as a nightwatchman and he was required to attend S's office premises from 5 pm each evening until 7 am. the following day, seven days a week. A mattress was provided and W was permitted to sleep when he was not required to carry out work. The employment tribunal found that Reg.15(1) of the 1999 Regulations applied and that the relevant period of time for the purposes of time work was the period of four hours when W was required to be awake. The EAT reversed those findings, concluding that the essential requirement was that W required to be on the premises for the 14 hour period and Reg.15(1) did not apply where there was not a specific allocation of time during which a worker was permitted to sleep. S submitted that Reg.3 fell to be read along with Reg.15(1) and the period in which a worker was allowed to sleep did not qualify as "time work" unless he was awake for the purpose of working.

Held, dismissing the appeal, that under the terms of his contract the work for which W was paid, for the purposes of Reg.3, was the whole 14 hours he was required to be in attendance at the premises and the whole period fell to be regarded as "time work" even though he had little or nothing to do during certain hours, Reg.15(1) applied only to workers who were on call waiting to work and did not apply in the present case, *British Nursing Association v. Inland Revenue (National Minimum Wage Compliance Team)* [2002] EWCA Civ 494, [2002] I.R.L.R. 480, [2002] 6 C.L. 190 applied.

SCOTTBRIDGE CONSTRUCTION LTD v. WRIGHT; *sub nom.* WRIGHT v. SCOTTBRIDGE CONSTRUCTION LTD 2002 S.L.T. 1356, Lord Cullen L.P., Lord Osborne, Lord Wheatley, 1 Div.

5576. Sex discrimination–female associate minister–dismissal for misconduct– status as employee

[Church of Scotland Act 1921 (c.29); Sex Discrimination Act 1975 (c.65) s.63(1), s.82(1); Council Directive 76/207 on equal treatment for men and women as regards access to employment.]

P, an associate minister, appealed against the decision of the EAT, to refuse her appeal against dismissal by the board of the church (B), on the grounds of sex discrimination. P was initially ordained as a minister in 1991 and became an associate in a parish in 1994 under an agreement with the presbytery (R). Following allegations of misconduct in June 1997, B suspended P on full salary until R accepted P's demission of status as a minister from December 3, 1997. In 1998 the employment tribunal (T) dismissed P's submissions that similar action had not been taken against male ministers having extra-marital affairs and was affirmed by EAT, who held that P's claim of sex discrimination fell outside the jurisdiction given to them under the Sex Discrimination Act 1975 s.63(1), and that the arrangement between P and R did not constitute a contract of employment within the meaning of s.82(1): P's appointment was spiritual and should be dealt with by the church, not the civil courts. P submitted that the EAT had erred in law and argued (1) that on the ordinary principles of construction, her claim was not a spiritual matter within the terms of the Church of Scotland Act 1921, and even if it was to be so classified, the provisions of the 1975 and 1921 Acts, by virtue of the Council Directive 76/207, had to be interpreted in such a way as to affirm the jurisdiction of T, even if it meant that the civil authority was entering into an area where Parliament had been concerned in 1921 to declare the autonomy of the church courts; (2) that the position of associate minister should be distinguished from parish minister: an associate's rights derived from contract entered into with the church as opposed to rights deriving from office which applied to parish ministers, and in P's case, terms and conditions were incorporated into a contract constituted on April 26, 1994 and in the terms of subsequent correspondence.

Held, refusing the appeal, that (1) as an associate minister, P held a position recognised in the legislation of the church and which could properly be regarded as an office. However, a parish minister and an associate entered office in different ways, a minister being elected, whilst an associate was appointed, and they had different tenures of appointment and different functions. Consequently, it should not be too readily assumed that the two positions fell to be treated in the same way for present purposes. However, against the special pre-existing legal framework of the church, the law required clear evidence of an intention to create a contractual relationship in addition to that pre-existing framework, *Diocese of Southwark v. Coker* [1998] I.C.R. 140, [1997] C.L.Y. 2293 applied; there was a rebuttable presumption that there was no such intention; (2) the formal language used in the agreement and subsequent correspondence demonstrated that B had regulated the appointment with precision, but within the framework of ecclesiastical, as opposed to civil, law, and the fact that R, as the court of the church having jurisdiction, had dealt with the allegations of P's misconduct reinforced that view.

PERCY v. BOARD OF NATIONAL MISSION OF THE CHURCH OF SCOTLAND 2001 S.C. 757, Lord Rodger L.P., Lord Cameron of Lochbroom, Lord Caplan, 1 Div.

5577. Trade unions–recognition–determination of membership by employees–compliance with natural justice

[Trade Union and Labour Relations (Consolidation) Act 1992 (c.52) Sch.A1 para.22.]

F, a company, sought reduction of certain decisions of C in a dispute arising from an attempt by a trade union to gain recognition. F had announced possible redundancies in October/November 2000 and when it did not respond to an application from the union for recognition, the union applied to C in December 2000 for recognition in respect of a bargaining unit under the Trade Union and Labour Relations (Consolidation) Act 1992 Sch.A1 para.22. C established a panel and appointed a case manager. No agreement was reached between the union and F and in February 2001, C decided that the appropriate bargaining unit at the relevant plant was that proposed by the union. In order to ascertain whether a majority of the relevant employees were union members, the case manager carried out a comparison exercise between a list of employees and a list of union members. The percentage initially arrived at was 49.3, but following a request from the union to reconsider the figures, was redetermined at 51.3 and C then decided against holding a ballot. F argued (1) that the decision as to a majority had clearly been taken by the case manager and where para.22 required C to be satisfied, such delegation was ultra vires; (2) that the decision had been unfair: the original decision was overturned on the union submitting information on an additional 12 employees, yet in the result a further 15 members were found, and F had no way of ascertaining how this conclusion was reached, and (3) that C's ballot decision was irrational as it had failed to take properly into account the qualifying conditions in para.22(4) or the marginal nature of the majority decision against the changing numbers of employees.

Held, dismissing the petition, that (1) taking a practical view of the situation, the delegation to the case manager had been a perfectly legitimate way for C to conduct their work and the decision had not been taken by the case manager alone; (2) while the principle of natural justice could be breached if the opportunity existed for injustice to occur even if in practical terms it had not occurred, the position was different when the evidence disclosed that the complaint had positively had no substantive effect, and as F had conceded they would have been bound to accept the reconsideration of the decision as to whether a majority existed, there was no material issue to be determined on its lawfulness; (3) the scheme of the process was that, generally, the need for a ballot depended on there being no majority vote in favour of recognition, and where there was such a majority, para.22(4) provided exceptions by way of a let out in appropriate circumstances by reference to either good industrial relations or the attitude of the membership, which the employer could be expected to raise, and (4) the ballot decision was not flawed because C had applied their minds to the right test in relation to each of the three exceptions and had reached decisions they were entitled to reach without manifest error on the face of the record.

FULLARTON COMPUTER INDUSTRIES LTD v. CENTRAL ARBITRATION COMMITTEE 2002 S.L.T. 13, Lord Johnston, OH.

5578. Unfair dismissal–disclosure–public interest–disclosure made prior to commencement of statutory protection

[Employment Rights Act 1996 (c.18) s.43F; Public Interest Disclosure Act 1998 (c.23).]

A company, S, appealed against a decision of the EAT, remitting M's application to an employment tribunal for a full hearing on all aspects of the case. S had dismissed M in 1993 following his disclosure to the Inland Revenue of an attempt to reclassify him as self employed when that was inaccurate, which after further proceedings by the revenue resulted in fines totalling £3 million against S. Following a transfer of undertaking, S again became M's employer in 1998. M alleged that he was subject to victimisation for his earlier disclosure and that was the reason for his dismissal in September 2000. S averred that M's employment had been terminated by reason of redundancy. On M's application for interim relief, the tribunal held that it did not have jurisdiction to hear M's complaint as his disclosure had occurred prior to the amendments to the 1996 Act introduced by the Public Interest Disclosure Act 1998. The EAT held the crucial aspect to be that dismissal took place after that Act came into force. S argued that T was entitled to find as it did where the revenue did not become prescribed persons under the Employment Rights Act 1996 s.43F until it came into force on 2 July 1999, and if s.43F did not apply to the 1993 disclosure the 1998 Act should be construed to mean no disclosure before that date could be protected.

Held, dismissing the appeal, that it was immaterial when M's disclosure was made as his dismissal occurred after July 2, 1999. The point in time with the greatest significance for the purposes of the legislation was the time of dismissal, the making of the disclosure required to be considered at that time and provided a person to whom a disclosure was made had been prescribed under s.43F by the date of dismissal, the criteria for unfair dismissal were satisfied.

MIKLASZEWICZ v. STOLT OFFSHORE LTD; *sub nom.* MIKLASEWICZ v. STOLT OFFSHORE LTD; STOLT OFFSHORE LTD v. MIKLASEWICZ; STOLT OFFSHORE LTD v. MIKLASZEWICZ 2002 S.C. 232, Lord Nimmo Smith, Lord Marnoch, Lord Weir, Ex Div.

5579. Books

Mackay, Malcolm R.; Simon, Shona–Employment Law. 2nd Ed. Greens Concise Scots Law. Hardback: £95.00. ISBN 0-414-01402-2. W. Green & Son.

ENERGY

5580. Electricity generation–non fossil fuel sources

ELECTRICITY FROM NON-FOSSIL FUEL SOURCES (LOCATIONAL FLEXIBILITY) (SCOTLAND) ORDER 2002, SSI 2002 92; made under the Utilities Act 2000 s.67. In force: March 31, 2002; £1.75.

This Order, which modifies the Electricity Act 1989 s.33 as it has effect in Scotland, relates to arrangements made by public electricity suppliers under the Electricity Act 1989 s.32 relating to the securing of generating capacity from non-fossil fuel generating stations. The Order allows such arrangements to continue to attract the fossil fuel levy in circumstances where the location of the generating station has changed.

5581. Electricity generation–wind and water generating stations–requirements for consent

ELECTRICITY ACT 1989 (REQUIREMENT OF CONSENT FOR OFFSHORE GENERATING STATIONS) (SCOTLAND) ORDER 2002, SSI 2002 407; made under the Electricity Act 1989 s.36, s.111. In force: September 26, 2002; £1.75.

This Order modifies the Electricity Act 1989 s.36(2) to specify that any generating station constructed in Scottish territorial waters (and wholly or mainly driven by water or wind) with a permitted capacity of 1 megawatt or above requires the consent of the Scottish Ministers. This allows for more control over developments in territorial waters and brings these generating stations within the Electricity Works (Environmental Impact Assessment) (Scotland) Regulations 2000 (SSI 2000 320).

ENVIRONMENT

5582. Air pollution–air quality reviews

AIR QUALITY LIMIT VALUES (SCOTLAND) AMENDMENT REGULATIONS 2002, SSI 2002 556; made under the European Communities Act 1972 s.2. In force: January 19, 2003; £2.00.

These Regulations amend the Air Quality Limit Values (Scotland) Regulations 2001 (SSI 2001 224) and implement provisions of Directive 2000/69 ([2000] OJ L313/12) of the European Parliament and the Council relating to limit values for benzene and carbon monoxide in ambient air.

5583. Air pollution–air quality reviews

AIR QUALITY (SCOTLAND) AMENDMENT REGULATIONS 2002, SSI 2002 297; made under the Environment Act 1995 s.87, s.91. In force: June 12, 2002; £1.75.

The Environment Act 1995 Part IV requires local authorities in Scotland to review air quality within their areas, with an assessment of whether any of the prescribed air quality objectives detailed in the associated regulations are being achieved or are likely to be achieved within the relevant period. These Regulations amend the Air Quality (Scotland) Regulations 2000 (SSI 2000 97), which prescribe the relevant periods for the purpose of that review and set the air quality objectives to be achieved by the end of those periods, by inserting a relevant period for the new air quality objectives. The Regulations also make amendments by setting new air quality objectives for benzene, carbon monoxide and PM10 and by prescribing the relevant period for their achievement.

5584. Environmental impact assessments–planning permission–applications– procedural requirements

ENVIRONMENTAL IMPACT ASSESSMENT (SCOTLAND) AMENDMENT REGULATIONS 2002, SSI 2002 324; made under the European Communities Act 1972 s.2; and the Town and Country Planning (Scotland) Act 1997 s.40. In force: September 23, 2002; £2.00.

These Regulations amend the Environmental Impact Assessment (Scotland) Regulations 1999 (SSI 1999 1) which impose procedural requirements in relation to the consideration of applications for planning permission under the Town and Country Planning (Scotland) Act 1997. The Regulations implement Council Directive 85/337 ([1985] OJ L175/40) on the assessment of the effects of certain public and private projects on the environment, as amended by Council Directive 97/11 ([1997] OJ L73/5) in relation to applications to planning authorities to determine the revised conditions to which an existing minerals planning permission should be subjected

5585. Environmental impact assessments–uncultivated land and semi-natural areas

ENVIRONMENTAL IMPACT ASSESSMENT (UNCULTIVATED LAND AND SEMI-NATURAL AREAS) (SCOTLAND) REGULATIONS 2002, SSI 2002 6; made under the European Communities Act 1972 s.2. In force: February 4, 2002; £4.00.

These Regulations implement, in relation to projects for the use of uncultivated land and semi-natural areas in Scotland, Council Directive 85/337 ([1985] OJ L175/40) on the assessment of the effects of certain public and private projects on the environment and Council Directive 1992/43 ([1992] OJ L1206/7) on the conservation of natural habitats and of wild fauna and flora insofar as it applies to such projects. The Regulations prohibit a relevant project from being carried out without consent first having been obtained from the Scottish Ministers, entitles the prospective applicant for consent to obtain an opinion from the Scottish Ministers as to the information which will be required as part of the environmental statement to accompany the application for consent and requires the specified environmental bodies referred to provide any relevant information in their possession to the applicant for consent.

5586. Environmental protection–combustion plants–emissions

LARGE COMBUSTION PLANTS (SCOTLAND) REGULATIONS 2002, SSI 2002 493; made under the Pollution Prevention and Control Act 1999 s.2, Sch.1 Part 1 para.20. In force: November 27, 2002; £1.75.

These Regulations, which amend the Pollution Prevention Control (Scotland) Regulations 2000 (SSI 2000 323), partly implement in Scotland the provisions of Council Directive 2001/80 ([2001] OJ L309/22) on the limitation of emissions of certain pollutants into the air from large combustion plants. They provide that where a new plant is subject to a permit but the plant is not put into operation before November 28, 2003, the plant will no longer be authorised to operate until the Scottish Environment Protection Agency has varied the permit to give effect to the requirements of the Directive. They also set out requirements which new plants subject to an authorisation or permit must comply with from November 27, 2002.

5587. Environmental protection–pollution control regime–emissions

POLLUTION PREVENTION AND CONTROL (DESIGNATION OF COUNCIL DIRECTIVES ON LARGE COMBUSTION PLANTS AND NATIONAL EMISSION CEILINGS) (SCOTLAND) ORDER 2002, SSI 2002 488; made under the Pollution Prevention and Control Act 1999 Sch.1 Part 1 para.20. In force: November 4, 2002; £1.50.

This Order designates Council Directive 2001/80 ([2001] OJ L309/1) on the limitation of emissions of certain pollutants into the air from large combustion plants and Council Directive 2001/81 ([2001] OJ L309/22) on national emission ceilings for certain atmospheric pollutants as relevant directives for the purposes of the Pollution Prevention and Control Act 1999 which specifies particular purposes for which provision regulating polluting activities may be made.

5588. Environmental protection–waste–packaging

PRODUCER RESPONSIBILITY OBLIGATIONS (PACKAGING WASTE) AMENDMENT (SCOTLAND) REGULATIONS 2002, SSI 2002 147; made under the Environment Act 1995 s.93, s.94. In force: March 26, 2002; £1.75.

These Regulations amend the Producer Responsibility Obligations (Packaging Waste) Regulations 1997 (SI 1997 648) which impose on producers obligations to recover and recycle packaging waste, and related obligations. The Regulations amend the recovery and recycling targets, used to calculate recovery and recycling obligations, by increasing from 56 per cent to 60 per cent the target for recovery and from 18 per cent to 19 per cent the target for recycling.

5589. Financial assistance–environmental purposes

FINANCIAL ASSISTANCE FOR ENVIRONMENTAL PURPOSES (SCOTLAND) ORDER 2002, SSI 2002 83; made under the Environmental Protection Act 1990 s.153. In force: March 26, 2002; £1.50.

This Order amends the Environment Protection Act 1990 to enable the Scottish Ministers to give financial assistance for the purposes of storing or treating any material or product prior to its disposal in an environmentally safe manner.

5590. Genetically modified organisms–deliberate release

GENETICALLY MODIFIED ORGANISMS (DELIBERATE RELEASE) (SCOTLAND) REGULATIONS 2002, SSI 2002 541; made under the European Communities Act 1972 s.2. In force: in accordance with Reg.1 (1); £6.50.

These Regulations amend the Genetically Modified Organisms (Deliberate Release and Risk Assessment-Amendment) Regulations 1997 (SI 1997 1900), the Genetically Modified Organisms (Contained Use) Regulations 2000 (SI 2000 2831) and the Scotland Act 1998 (Agency Arrangements) (Specification) (No.2) Order 2002 (SI 2002 830). In addition they repeal the Genetically Modified Organisms (Deliberate Release) Regulations 1992 (SI 1992 3280) (with saving), the Genetically Modified Organisms (Deliberate Release) Regulations 1993 (SI 1993 152) and the Genetically Modified Organisms (Deliberate Release) Regulations 1995 (SI 1995 304). The Regulations implement Directive 2001/18 ([2001] OJ L106/1) of the European Parliament and of the Council on the deliberate release of genetically modified organisms and repealing Council Directive 90/220 ([1990] OJ L117/15) which strengthens the existing control regime, particularly in respect of post marketing monitoring.

5591. National parks–Loch Lomond and the Trossachs–designation

LOCH LOMOND AND THE TROSSACHS NATIONAL PARK DESIGNATION, TRANSITIONAL AND CONSEQUENTIAL PROVISIONS (SCOTLAND) ORDER 2002, SSI 2002 201; made under the National Parks (Scotland) Act 2000 s.6, s.7, s.9, s.10, s.33, s.34, Sch.1 para.3, Sch.1 para.4, Sch.1 para.16. In force: April 25, 2002; £2.50.

This Order designates an area as the Loch Lomond and the Trossachs National Park and establishes a National Park Authority for the Park.

5592. National parks–Loch Lomond and the Trossachs–elections

LOCH LOMOND AND THE TROSSACHS NATIONAL PARK ELECTIONS (SCOTLAND) ORDER 2002, SSI 2002 202; made under the National Parks (Scotland) Act 2000 Sch.1 para.4. In force: April 25, 2002; £3.00.

This Order, which sets out the arrangements under which direct elections to the Loch Lomond and the Trossachs National Park Authority shall be conducted, designates the returning officer of Stirling Council as the returning officer for each election and provides for expenses.

5593. Pollution control–noise pollution–codes of practice–construction works

CONTROL OF NOISE (CODES OF PRACTICE FOR CONSTRUCTION AND OPEN SITES) (SCOTLAND) ORDER 2002, SSI 2002 104; made under the Control of Pollution Act 1974 s.71, s.104. In force: March 29, 2002; £1.75.

Under the Control of Pollution Act 1974, the Scottish Ministers may give guidance on appropriate methods for minimising noise (which includes vibration) by approving codes of practice. This Order, which revokes the Control of Noise (Codes of Practice for Construction and Open Sites) (Scotland) Order 1985 (SI 1985 145) and the Control of Noise (Code of Practice for Construction and Open Sites) Order 1987 (SI 1987 1730), allows the Scottish Ministers to approve codes of practice which are issued otherwise than by the Scottish Ministers as in their opinion are suitable for the purpose. It requires the Scottish Ministers to approve a code for the carrying out of works including building and roadwork's, demolition, dredging and other works of engineering construction. It also approves the four specified codes.

5594. Smoke control—authorisation of fuel

SMOKE CONTROL AREAS (AUTHORISED FUELS) (SCOTLAND) AMENDMENT REGULATIONS 2002, SSI 2002 527; made under the Clean Air Act 1993 s.20, s.63. In force: December 23, 2002; £1.75.

The Clean Air Act 1993 provides that where smoke is emitted from a chimney in a smoke control area and that chimney is either a chimney of a building; or a chimney serving the furnace of a fixed boiler or industrial plant, the occupier of the building, or as the case may be, the person having possession of the boiler or plant, is guilty of an offence. It is a defence to show that the alleged emission was caused solely by the use of an authorised fuel. These Regulations amend the Smoke Control Areas (Authorised Fuels) (Scotland) Regulations 2001 (SSI 2001 433) so that Dragonglow briquettes and Dragonbrite briquettes meeting the conditions specified are authorised fuels.

5595. Water pollution—nitrate vulnerable zones

DESIGNATION OF NITRATE VULNERABLE ZONES (SCOTLAND) REGULATIONS 2002, SSI 2002 276; made under the European Communities Act 1972 s.2. In force: July 1, 2002; £1.75.

These Regulations, which amend the Protection of Water against Agricultural Nitrate Pollution (Scotland) Regulations 1996 (SI 1996 1564), implement Council Directive 91/676 ([1991] OJ L375/1) concerning the protection of waters against pollution caused by nitrates from agricultural sources. They designate further nitrate vulnerable zones, make provision for maps of nitrate vulnerable zones to be available for public inspection and provide that the Code of Good Practice for the Prevention of Environmental Pollution from Agricultural Activity Nitrogen and Phosphorous Supplement is the code of practice established for the purposes of the Directive.

5596. Water pollution—nitrate vulnerable zones

DESIGNATION OF NITRATE VULNERABLE ZONES (SCOTLAND) (NO.2) REGULATIONS 2002, SSI 2002 546; made under the European Communities Act 1972 s.2. In force: January 15, 2003; £1.75.

These Regulations implement in Scotland the requirements of Council Directive 91/676 ([1996] OJ L 375/1) concerning the protection of waters against pollution caused by nitrates from agricultural sources. The objective of the Directive is to ensure that measures are taken to reduce and prevent nitrate pollution from agricultural sources. It provides a framework for action to reduce nitrate levels in the catchments of rivers and groundwater sources affected by such pollution, and to reduce eutrophication of freshwater bodies, estuaries, and coastal waters.

5597. Books

Brown, Vincent; Aitchison, Karen—Brown and Aitchison: Environmental Law and Commercial Property Transactions in Scotland. Paperback: £60.00. ISBN 0-406-92758-8. Butterworths Law.

EXTRADITION

5598. Pleas—plea in bar of trial—irregularity and illegality of extradition proceedings

[European Convention on Human Rights 1950 Art.5, Art.6; Scotland Act 1998 (c.46) s.57(2).]

V, a Dutch national, charged on indictment with the importation and supply of amphetamine, pled in bar of trial that his arrest and extradition from Portugal to the United Kingdom were in contravention of the European Convention on Human Rights 1950 Art.5 and Art.6. The plea stated that he had not received effective legal assistance at the extradition hearings, was not informed promptly, in a language he understood, of the reasons for his arrest and of any charge against him, and had signed the document consenting to the order under undue pressure, and that the Lord Advocate in continuing the proceedings against him was in contravention of the Scotland Act 1998 s.57(2). At a hearing V claimed that he had been represented by a trainee lawyer, that neither of the two interpreters provided understood the legal procedures or language employed, and that he had been informed by the interpreter that if he did not sign a form allowing an extradition order to be made he would be confined in a Portuguese jail under atrocious conditions until extradition proceedings were resolved. V had signed the form and added in English "under protest". V argued (1) that any signatory state to the Convention had a duty to adopt a proactive role in relation to another signatory state's extradition proceedings, including checking their regularity and legality when initiated by the UK, and (2) that once an illegality or irregularity in foreign extradition proceedings had been brought to the attention of UK authorities they could not benefit from the proceedings.

Held, refusing the minute, that *Sinclair v. HM Advocate* (1890) 17 R. (J.) 38 was technically still binding authority and on that basis the minute was irrelevant, *Sinclair* followed.

HM ADVOCATE v. VERVUREN; *sub nom.* VERVUREN v. HM ADVOCATE 2002 S.L.T. 555, Lady Paton, HCJ.

FAMILY LAW

5599. Adoption—freeing orders—consent unreasonably withheld

[Adoption (Scotland) Act 1978 (c.28) s.16(2)(b), s.16(2)(c), s.18.]

P, the natural parents of J, appealed against a decision by the sheriff, following proof, to grant A's application under the Adoption (Scotland) Act 1978 s.18 and declare J free for adoption. Both natural parents suffered some degree of mental impairment in the form of learning difficulties and the father also suffered from tunnel vision and epilepsy. The sheriff concluded that J's mother had persistently failed to fulfil her parental responsibilities and both parents were withholding their consent to the adoption unreasonably in terms of s.16(2)(b) and s.16(2)(c). He further concluded that full consideration had been given by A to the alternatives to adoption and that in all the circumstances, their consent to the adoption should be dispensed with. P argued that the sheriff (1) had failed to put forward sufficient reasoning as to how he had reached his determination to grant the order; (2) had not given proper regard to the mental impairment suffered by both parents and consider that withholding their consent had been the only course of action open to them to enable contact with J to be maintained, and (3) had not considered the alternative course of action which was to dismiss the application to enable the prospective adoptive parent to apply for residence, thereby allowing scope for continued contact between J and P, which P believed was in the best interests of J.

Held, refusing the appeal, that (1) the sheriff's judgment was deficient in that it did not make clear the reasoning which led him to the conclusion and the matter would, by agreement, be considered de novo; (2) having applied the objective test, with regard to J's welfare as the paramount consideration, a reasonable parent would not have withheld consent in all the circumstances; (3) the sheriff was justified in reaching his conclusion that there would be an unacceptable risk to J's welfare if he were to face any major disruption to his present settled environment; (4) whilst it was clearly desirable to avoid severing the links between natural parents and children, that consideration was outweighed by other considerations which were material to J's welfare, now and throughout his life, which included the provisions of a stable home life; (5) the sheriff could not be criticised for failing to deal with the option of a residence order where such a suggestion was not dealt with at proof and there was nothing to indicate that there was any substance to those submissions, and (6) given the overwhelming weight of unchallenged evidence which pointed to adoption as the desirable option, the sheriff was entitled to reach the conclusions which he had. Opinion of the Court per Lord Cameron of Lochbroom.

P v. ABERDEEN CITY COUNCIL 2001 Fam. L.R. 127, Lord Cameron of Lochbroom, Lord McCluskey, Lord Penrose, Ex Div.

5600. Adoption−freeing orders−consent unreasonably withheld−child injured by person close to mother−mother failing to cooperate with investigation

[Adoption (Scotland) Act 1978 (c.28) s.16(2).]

E petitioned to have M's child declared free for adoption on the grounds that the mother was withholding agreement unreasonably under the Adoption (Scotland) Act 1978 s.16(2)(b) and had persistently failed to safeguard and promote the child's welfare under s.16(2)(c)(i). The child had sustained an injury to the scrotum while under the care of one of three people, M did not cooperate with the investigation into the injury but did allow the child to be taken into care. Petition was granted under both grounds and M appealed to the Court of Session arguing that while she had been "persistently" uncooperative with the investigation she could not be said to have "persistently" failed to safeguard and promote the child's welfare under s.16(2)(c)(i) since she had allowed the child to be taken into care following the injury.

Held, dismissing the appeal, that the sheriff had not demonstrated a sound basis for the use of the word "persistently" and had this been the only ground under which parental consent had been dispensed with, the matter would have required reconsideration. However, the Court's decision with regard to withholding consent unreasonably negated the need for reconsideration.

EAST LOTHIAN COUNCIL v. A; *sub nom.* EAST LOTHIAN COUNCIL v. M; EAST LOTHIAN COUNCIL v. MA 2002 S.C. 106, Lord Coulsfield, Lord Cameron of Lochbroom, Lord McCluskey, Ex Div.

5601. Adoption−freeing orders−consent unreasonably withheld−failure to discharge parental responsibilities

[Children (Scotland) Act 1995 (c.36) s.4, s.6; Human Rights Act 1998 (c.42) Sch.1 Part I Art.8.]

W, a local authority, petitioned to have two boys, D and M, freed for adoption. The natural mother, G, and the respective fathers, P and F, opposed the petition. Neither father had ever been married to G but in 1999 they entered into separate minutes of agreement with G under the Children (Scotland) Act 1995 s.4. In 1998 both D and M were placed with foster carers. Since then access by G and F had been irregular. However, D saw P, who suffered from mental illness, regularly and wished to remain in contact with him. D and M were both well settled with the foster carers and it was almost certain that the foster carers would adopt them if they were freed for adoption. The sheriff found, inter alia, that G, P and F were withholding their agreement unreasonably to the making of adoption orders, that G and P had persistently failed without reasonable cause to safeguard and promote D's health, development and welfare, as had G and F in respect of M, that G had persistently failed without reasonable cause to maintain personal relations and contact with D on a regular basis and that G and F had similarly failed in respect of M. The sheriff granted the orders sought. P and F appealed, arguing, inter alia, that the sheriff erred (1) in having regard to evidence concerning their conduct prior to the acquisition of parental responsibilities under the minutes of agreement, and (2) in holding that they were withholding their agreement unreasonably, where it had been withheld on the basis that such an order would deprive them, in particular, of the right to continued contact with D and M following adoption. P further argued (1) that the sheriff had erred in exercising his discretion to dispense with P's agreement to adoption if it was in D's interests for P to retain contact rights, since a freeing order would extinguish such rights, and had failed to have regard to D's views which favoured continued contact with P, and (2) that the loss of the right to contact and of the right to seek an order for contact from the court conflicted with both P and D's rights under the Human Rights Act 1998 Sch.1 Part I Art.8.

Held, dismissing the appeals, that (1) the sheriff erred in finding that P and F had failed to fulfil their parental responsibilities, as neither father had parental responsibilities before the dates of the s.4 agreements, and they could not be said to have failed to discharge them; (2) the reasonableness of a decision to withhold agreement was to be judged objectively by the standard of a hypothetical parent who had in mind the paramount consideration in s.6 of the 1995 Act, which assumed that the parent would recognise that adoption would extinguish all parental rights and leave any future involvement in the hands of the adopters; (3) the fact that P would lose his right to contact with D if a freeing order was granted did not of itself render the order inappropriate, the sheriff was satisfied that the foster carers would ensure the continuation of contact between D and P, and considered that there was no need to deprive D of the benefits of a settled family life with the carers, F's case was weaker than P's and the sheriff was entitled, applying the objective test, to hold that both P and F had unreasonably withheld their agreement; (4) the undisputed findings amply justified the sheriff's exercise of his discretion in dispensing with agreement, and (5) the sheriff's decision predated the coming into force of the Human Rights Act 1998 and he was not obliged to give effect to the Convention rights; it had not been put to him that he should take them into account and it was too late to raise the point now.

WEST LOTHIAN COUNCIL v. M; *sub nom.* WEST LOTHIAN COUNCIL v. MCG 2002 S.C. 411, Lord Gill L.J.C., Lord Hamilton, Lord Reed, 2 Div.

5602. **Adoption – freeing orders – consent unreasonably withheld – proper test**

[European Convention on Human Rights 1950 Art.8(1).]

In the petition of C, a local authority, to free M (born January 1998) for adoption, C sought dispensation with the agreement of M's mother (D), who suffered from ataxia, and unmarried father (F) who had entered a parental rights agreement with respect to M, on the grounds that it had been unreasonably withheld. M had been placed with foster parents in April 1998 after failing to gain weight. F was violent towards D and neither D nor F had co-operated with the social work department. During supervised contact M seemed uncomfortable with D and that could not be directly attributed to D's disability, and though M's relationship with F was appropriate, F had attended only one out of four arranged visits prior to the petition. M had a good bond with her foster parents (X) who were seeking to adopt her. X were prepared to consent to two supervised contacts a year for D and F and to allow contact between M and her brother B and half sister S. It was unlikely that adoptive parents would be found for M and B together. D argued inter alia that consent was reasonably withheld because (1) the decision breached the European Convention on Human Rights 1950 Art. 8(1); (2) there was no basis for the original decision to take M into care; (3) in a number of decisions taken, D's rights had not been considered, and (4) the adoption panels were not independent. Proof began on February 7, 2000 and finished on May 5, it being impossible to hear the case on consecutive court days. In June, D indicated that she no longer wished to oppose the petition and a hearing was set for August 3, when it was revealed that, having separated from F, she had again changed her mind. A further hearing was set for September 7 by which point D and F were again living together for about half of each week.

Held, granting the petition, that (1) Art.8(1) had not been breached. Further, the ultimate test was whether a reasonable parent would withhold agreement, and even if a particular decision was in breach of the Convention, it did not follow that all that happened thereafter was invalidated; (2) it was unsatisfactory that the adoption panels included members belonging to the same team as the social worker involved in the case, and that they did not produce a written report, but the decisions reached were correct; (3) contact post-adoption was for the purpose not of developing a relationship but of preserving a link for the benefit of the child that would boost their self image, and D and F could not be said to be reasonably withholding consent simply because they were being denied the amount of contact that they sought; and in the circumstances of this case a reasonable parent would not withhold consent on the issue of contact; (4) there was no problem with sibling contact and though M and B could not be adopted together, the link between them could be maintained by contact, and this was not a reasonable ground on which to refuse consent; (5) there was no reasonable alternative to adoption. M could not be returned to a home with an undercurrent of violence; F did not put his relationship with M above antagonisms to social workers and D had indicated that her relationship with F came before that with M; no relatives had come forward; and long term fostering was not appropriate, and (6) the changes that had occurred since proof only confirmed the court's decision given D and F's relationship was not stable.

Observed, that it was wholly unacceptable that it had taken over seven months to complete this case. Opinion, that given current thinking on adoption and contact a change in the law to allow contact to be regulated at or after freeing for adoption might lessen some of the problems in this area.

EDINBURGH CITY COUNCIL v. D 2001 S.L.T. (Sh Ct) 135, Sheriff NMP Morrison Q.C., Sh Ct (Lothian and Border).

5603. Adoption–freeing orders–consent unreasonably withheld–proper test

[Adoption (Scotland) Act 1978 (c.28) s.6; Children (Scotland) Act 1995 (c.36); Act of Sederunt (Child Care and Maintenance Rules 1997) (SI 1997 291).]

A local authority applied for an order freeing a male child, W, for adoption and dispensing with the agreements of W's parents on the ground that they were withholding their consent unreasonably. W, born on June 20, 2000, was immediately made the subject of an emergency protection order and placed with foster parents. W's parents were of low intelligence and suffered learning and personality difficulties. W's maternal grandparents sought an award of parental rights and responsibilities. Before the proof, W's mother gave birth to premature twins and her sister and brother in law expressed an interest in adopting W. An adoption report stated that the paramount consideration had been to safeguard and promote W's welfare throughout his childhood. The parents submitted that there was a fundamental flaw in the application as the correct test was to consider W's welfare throughout his lifetime and not just his childhood, as required by the Adoption (Scotland) Act 1978 s.6 as amended by the Children (Scotland) Act 1995. The Sheriff sustained the submission and dismissed the application. The local authority appealed, arguing that (1) on finding that the wrong test had been applied by the local authority, the sheriff was entitled to make such inquiries at the proof so as to determine the outcome of the action based on the application of the correct test; (2) the sheriff failed to give sufficient weight to the report of the curator ad litem which was based on the correct test, and (3) the sui generis nature of adoption proceedings was underlined by the fact that the sheriff was given wider powers for the calling of additional evidence by the Act of Sederunt (Child Care and Maintenance Rules 1997).

Held, refusing the appeal, that (1) the action was not incompetent as it had been raised following the correct procedures and with the necessary documentation, however it was irrelevant; (2) there was no breach of rights by raising the action as the child was already outwith the control of the parents, however there could have been a breach of the right to fair trial had the sheriff allowed the application to proceed on the basis of the wrong statutory test; (3) the extended inquisitorial powers of the sheriff in adoption proceedings did not extend to the type of inquiry suggested by the local authority in order to rectify the situation and apply the correct test; (4) given the change of circumstances since the raising of the application with the second pregnancy, the intervention of the maternal grandparents and the interest of the sister and brother in law, it could not be certain that the local authority, if applying the correct test, would reach the same conclusion that adoption was the best course of action, and (5) the sheriff was not only entitled to reach the conclusions that she did, but was bound to do so.

Observed, that it was regrettable that the action had been allowed to proceed to proof, at some distress to the parents, where such a fundamental flaw existed and for the adoption agency to have relied on a r.8 test that had been amended some six years previously.

EDINBURGH CITY COUNCIL v. W 2002 Fam. L.R. 67, CGB Nicholson Q.C., Sheriff Principal, Sh Ct.

5604. **Adoption—freeing orders—locus standi—father with no parental rights or responsibilities—competency of appeal**

[Children (Scotland) Act 1995 (c.36) s.1, s.11; Adoption (Scotland) Act 1978 (c.28) s.18(7); Human Rights Act 1998 (c.42) Sch.1 Part I Art.8.]

E, a local authority adoption agency, petitioned for an order freeing a four and a half year old child (K) for adoption. The child's father, G, who had never been married to the mother, had raised separate proceedings for, inter alia, orders for parental responsibilities and rights under the Children (Scotland) Act 1995 s.1 and s.11. The sheriff granted the prayer of the petition, dispensing with the mother's agreement and, at the same time, refused G's motion for interim parental responsibilities and rights. G appealed to the sheriff principal against the freeing order. The sheriff principal refused his appeal as incompetent on the basis that once it was concluded that the application for parental rights and responsibilities would be refused, an unmarried father had no locus to be heard in the freeing process: this was the only possible construction of the legislation even though the result might be inconsistent with the Human Rights Act 1998. G appealed, arguing, inter alia, that his rights and interests were clearly affected by the freeing order and there had to be a locus for him to challenge the ultimate decision on appeal; and that the sheriff had erred in finding that it was likely that any application for a s.11 order would be refused, having failed properly to apply the test under the Adoption (Scotland) Act 1978 s.18(7), which was a high one, failed to give adequate reasons for her decision, taken into account irrelevant factors and omitted relevant factors, in particular giving insufficient weight to the prior contact between G and his child, and having failed to have regard to his right to respect for his family life under the Human Rights Act 1998 Sch.1 Part I Art.8.

Held, refusing the appeal, that (1) since G had a locus to be heard unless the conditions for excluding him were satisfied, he had to have a locus to appeal against any finding which had the effect of excluding him from being heard, a conclusion which was reinforced when having regard to Art.8 of the Convention; (2) the sheriff was entitled to decide the matter on the material before her without hearing evidence, where the facts were not in dispute and no request was made on behalf of G, who was legally represented throughout, that evidence should be heard; (3) the test under s.18(7) was a demanding one, but the sheriff had not failed to apply it properly or misdirected herself as to the nature of the test to be applied, nor had she confused the question of interim parental rights and the question under s.18(7), in relation to which the respective considerations were essentially the same, and (4) the essential reason for her decision, that adoption was in the child's best interests and that a satisfactory adoption required to exclude contact with G, was sufficiently clear; the weight to be attached to the other matters taken into account, all of which were relevant, was a matter for the sheriff and there was a proper foundation for her conclusion.

G v. EDINBURGH CITY COUNCIL (ADOPTION: PATERNAL RIGHTS); *sub nom.* EDINBURGH CITY COUNCIL v. G 2002 S.C. 440, Lord Coulsfield, Lord Caplan, Lady Cosgrove, Ex Div.

5605. Adoption (Intercountry Aspects) Act 1999 (c.18)–Commencement No.7 Order

ADOPTION (INTERCOUNTRY ASPECTS) ACT 1999 (COMMENCEMENT NO.7) (SCOTLAND) ORDER 2002, SSI 2002 562 (C.28); made under the Adoption (Intercountry Aspects) Act 1999 s.18. In force: Bringing into operation various provisions of the 1999 Act on Janaury 14, 2003; £1.50.

This Order provides for the coming into operation specified provisions of the Adoption (Intercountry Aspects) Act 1999.

5606. Child abduction–wrongful removal–child objecting to order to return

[Child Abduction and Custody Act 1985 (c.60) s.5; Hague Convention on the Civil Aspects of International Child Abduction 1980.]

A mother, M, and her son, A, reclaimed against a decision of the Lord Ordinary holding that M's removal of A from the United States was wrongful and ordering A's return to the United States. M and F were married in 1989 and A was born in 1990. F and M separated in 1992 following allegation of abuse being perpetrated by F against A. In 1995, F raised divorce proceedings in which he sought custody of A. Before proceedings were concluded, M removed A from the US aware that police were looking for her and A, S moved around a number of European countries with ML and A before settling in Scotland in 1998. ML's brother DL accompanied them to Scotland and resided with them. M gave birth to another child shortly thereafter, but she and ML separated in 1999. By that time, M had adopted different identities for herself and A to prevent their whereabouts becoming known. A warrant had been issued for M's detention to face an application for extradition to answer a Grand Jury indictment for international child abduction. In March 2000, M was arrested at her home and subsequently released on bail. A was taken into the care under the Child Abduction and Custody Act 1985 s.5. A petition seeking A's return to the US was raised, with A objecting to his return was granted. The Lord Ordinary found that neither M nor A were settled in Scotland.

Held, refusing the reclaiming motions, that (1) the Lord Ordinary had not erred in finding that he was compelled to grant the order for the prompt return of A to the United States in terms of the Hague Convention on the Civil Aspects of International Child Abduction 1980 unless there were compelling reasons to refuse such an application; (2) although A's views about his future had to be considered, the Lord Ordinary was within his right to find that A's views were not sufficient, when considered alongside all the other circumstances of the case, to prevent the granting of an order for his return; (3) in finding that the courts in the United States would deal quickly with A's situation on his return with his welfare as paramount, the Lord Ordinary was entitled to find that A would be unlikely to be at risk of an intolerable situation if the order for his return were made, and (4) given the fact that M had moved around Europe for several years and had only recently moved to her current location with A, and that, had she had warning of her impending arrest, she would undoubtedly have taken steps to evade the authorities further, the Lord Ordinary was entitled to find that A was not settled in his current environment, *N (Minors) (Child Abduction), Re* [1991] 1 F.L.R. 413, [1991] C.L.Y. 2530, followed. Opinion of the Court per Lord Prosser.

P v. S (CHILD ABDUCTION: WRONGFUL REMOVAL) 2002 Fam. L.R. 2, Lord Prosser, Lord Caplan, Lord Milligan, Ex Div.

5607. Child protection orders–unborn children–caveats–local authority to seek order after birth

[Human Rights Act 1998 (c.42) Sch.1 Part I Art.6, Art.8.]

C, a 15 year old mother of an unborn child, sought to lodge a caveat in the sheriff court in order to receive intimation of any application by the local authority for a child protection order in respect of her unborn child whose birth was expected imminently. C was the subject of a child protection order herself. The sheriff refused to warrant the sheriff clerk to receive the caveat and indicated that he would not hear representations by, or on behalf of, C if an application came before him for a child protection order. C petitioned the Court of Session for judicial review of the sheriff's decision.

Held, granting the petition and ordering the sheriff to instruct the sheriff clerk to accept a caveat on behalf of C and to afford her the chance to make representations, that (1) in determining whether a child protection order should be granted, it was important, within reason, for the sheriff to hear from all interested parties and given that the child was unborn, there would be no immediate urgency for a determination on the order to be made; (2) under the terms of the Human Rights Act 1998 and the European Convention on Human Rights 1950, both the mother and child had rights which had to be taken into consideration, in particular those under Art.6 and Art.8, and (3) it was unnecessary to interdict the sheriff from determining the application without hearing from C as, although possible to do so, it was doubtful whether such a determination by the sheriff would amount to a legal wrong.

C, PETITIONER 2002 Fam. L.R. 42, Lord McCluskey, OH.

5608. Child protection orders–unborn children–caveats–local authority to seek order after birth

[European Convention on Human Rights 1950 Art.6, Art.8; Act of Sederunt (Sheriff Court Ordinary Cause Rules) 1993 (SI 1993 1956) r.4.1; Children (Scotland) Act 1995 (c.36) s.58; Act of Sederunt (Child Care and Maintenance Rules) 1997 (SI 1997 291).]

The unmarried parents of an unborn child sought to lodge caveats for notice of any application for a child protection order by the local authority, who had advised that they would be seeking such an order at birth, to be given to their solicitor. The sheriff held that caveats could not competently be lodged in respect of such orders and the parents appealed, arguing, inter alia, that a child protection order was an interim order within the meaning of the Ordinary Cause Rules 1993 r.4.1, against which it was competent to lodge a caveat that the issues of the welfare of the child, which was of paramount importance, and of contact in terms of the Children (Scotland) Act 1995 s.58 could not be properly considered without their being represented at a hearing, and that to deny a parent a right to be heard on such an application might breach the European Convention on Human Rights 1950 Art.6 and Art.8.

Held, dismissing the appeal, that (1) the lodging of a caveat was competent only where provided for in the rules, and neither the Ordinary Cause Rules nor the Act of Sederunt (Child Care and Maintenance Rules) 1997 provided for the lodging of a caveat against such an order; (2) a child protection order was not an interim order within r.4.1 (b), and (3) provided a hearing within a reasonable time was guaranteed and regard was had to the welfare of others, the denial of a right to be heard at this stage did not breach the Convention.

K AND F, APPLICANTS 2002 S.L.T. (Sh Ct) 38, CGB Nicholson Q.C., Sheriff Principal, Sh Ct.

5609. Children–aliment–minute of agreement–enforceability of variation

See CIVIL PROCEDURE: Peebles v. Bowman (formerly Peebles). §5341

5610. **Children–aliment–variation–competency–application for retrospective variation after obligation to aliment ceased**

[Family Law (Scotland) Act 1985 (c.37) s.5(1).]

The parents of two children divorced in 1991. The father was ordered to pay the mother aliment for each child. When one child was aged 20 and the obligation to aliment had ceased, the father sought to reduce the payments to nil and to backdate the variation. He argued that his application was competent in the absence of any mention in the Family Law (Scotland) Act 1985, s.5(1) of a specific time limit within which it was competent to seek a variation of a decree for aliment, and that this type of court decree was not subject to prescription.

Held, refusing the application, that the provisions of the Act had to be read against the background that aliment ceased to be payable when the child reached the age of majority, even if arrears were still recoverable after the child reached that age, and an application to vary an award of aliment had to be made while the obligation to aliment still existed.

PATERSON v. PATERSON; *sub nom.* MITCHELL v. PATERSON 2002 S.L.T. (Sh Ct) 65, DJ Cusine, Sh Ct (Grampian, Highland and Islands).

5611. **Children–aliment–variation of minute of agreement–change of circumstances**

F and M applied for variation of a minute of agreement of aliment payable by F to M in respect of their two children as a result of material changes in circumstances. F sought reduction of the aliment while M sought an increase in respect of the second child, C, of the marriage. The parties had agreed the incomes and household expenditures for both F and his new wife and M and her new husband. At the time of the minute of agreement in 1996, aliment was calculated on the assumption that the two children would reside with M. Since 1997, however, their son, J, had been residing with F. F had not paid the £350 per month aliment in respect of J since that time, but no variation of the agreement had been sought. There was no dispute between the parties on that point. The dispute was over the amount of aliment payable in respect of C. F argued that it should be reduced to £200 and M that it should be increased to £450. F argued that at the time of the minute of agreement, he had been in employment, but was now in receipt of a pension, having been made redundant. His income was greatly reduced and he would still responsible for J's upkeep during his early years at university. He also argued that, at the time of the minute of agreement, M was a student with two dependant children. Since then she had obtained employment and was only supporting one child. M argued that F had received a substantial redundancy payment and had chosen to invest it for capital growth rather than to receive income, and that had F invested the money differently, he would be in a better financial position to afford suitable aliment payments. She maintained that J would be likely to obtain part time employment whilst at university and could apply for a student loan, thus reducing the financial burden on F. M also claimed that her costs in supporting C had risen significantly as she was now a teenager.

Held, varying the minute of agreement to the effect that aliment payable by F to M be reduced to nil in respect of J and to £175 in respect of C, that (1) no aliment should be paid by F to M in respect of a child who was living with and supported by F; (2) F had been entitled to use his redundancy payment to provide capital growth for his future rather than income although the existence of the redundancy payment was a factor to be considered; (3) that an allowance of £400 per month against F's income was reasonable in terms of his responsibilities to support J whilst at university, it being unreasonable to expect a first year student to feel compelled for lack of financial resources to obtain employment in addition to full-time study; (4) an allowance of £400 per month was reasonable to cover the living costs of their teenage daughter, and (5) taking all the factors into account that the allowance in respect of C, less the child benefit paid to M in respect of C, be divided equally between the parties, making F liable to M for the sum of £175 per month.

WATSON v. McLAY 2002 Fam. L.R. 20, AS Jessop, Sh Ct (Grampian, Highland and Islands).

5612. Children–contact–fostering–child subject to local authority supervision requirement

[Children (Scotland) Act 1995 (c.36) s.17, s.51 (11) (b), s.93 (2) (b); Social Work (Scotland) Act 1968 (c.49) s.94 (1); Act of Sederunt (Child Care and Maintenance Rules) 1997 (SI 1997 291).]

S, foster carers of a child A, appealed under the Children (Scotland) Act 1995 s.51 (11) (b) against the sheriff's decision allowing M, A's natural mother, limited contact rights. A was placed with S by the local authority under a supervision requirement made by the children's hearing. The hearing refused M's application for contact rights. M appealed to the sheriff. No intimation of that appeal was given to S, who were neither present nor represented at the appeal hearing. M argued that S were not "relevant persons" in terms of s.93 (2) (b) of the 1995 Act and had no right to receive intimation of or to be heard in the appeal. A child placed under the supervision of a local authority became a "looked-after child" for the purposes of s.17 and it was truly the local authority who had the charge and control of that child. S only had care and possession of A in extraordinary circumstances subject to decisions of the local authority and did not "ordinarily" have the charge of and control over A as required by s.93 (2) (b), which was worded differently from its predecessor the Social Work (Scotland) Act 1968 s.94 (1) which referred to a person with the charge of or control of a child "for the time being". Where a supervision requirement was in force, the persons with whom a child was placed did not "ordinarily" have the charge or control of the child.

Held, allowing the appeal and remitting the case to the sheriff, that S were "relevant persons" within s.93 (2) (b) and should have been notified of the appeal and given the opportunity to be heard. It was clear from the 1995 Act and the Child Care and Maintenance Rules 1997 that s.93 (2) (b) prima facie referred to a natural person and not a body such as a local authority. It would have been easy to expressly exclude persons with the charge or control of a child under a supervision requirement had this been intended by Parliament, but only charge and control by reason of employment was specifically excluded from the definition. M's argument could result in persons who might not have had any involvement with the child for many years obtaining important rights and obligations in respect of that child and conflicted with the ordinary and natural meaning of s.93 (2) (b). The former s.94 (1) concerned the de facto care and possession of a child and the use of "ordinarily" in the 1995 Act simply represented an attempt to improve the drafting.

S v. N 2002 S.L.T. 589, Lord Emslie, Lord Cameron of Lochbroom, Lord Reed, Ex Div.

5613. Children–contact–report prepared to assist court–status of report

F, a father, lodged a minute seeking contact with his three children, custody having been awarded by agreement to M. Several interim contact orders were made for specific dates, however it was alleged that M had failed to co-operate and, as a result, only three contact visits out of 16 arranged had actually taken place. Although the sheriff made no adverse findings about F as a father, or about his ability to care for and relate to the children during contact visits, he decided that F was not entitled to contact with them. His decision was based on the children's views from which he concluded that the two older children did not want contact to take place. The sheriff also found, based on evidence of the children's schoolteacher and headmistress, that the prospect of contact had had a serious effect on the youngest child which had resulted in behaviour at home and at school that was causing concern. Although the sheriff agreed that some obstruction of contact had taken place by M, he concluded that it had not been sufficient to prevent the contact visits from taking place. F appealed against on the grounds that the evidence did not support the sheriff's conclusions that any disturbance in the youngest child's behaviour had been as a result of contact visits or the anticipation of them, or that it was not in the children's best interests to have contact with their father. F argued that the sheriff had failed to give proper consideration to evidence given by professionals, R and G, who had prepared reports for the court, with one of those reports not being considered at all as it had been lodged after the case was taken to avizandum. Finally, F claimed that the sheriff had misunderstood M's obligation, as the parent with residence, to encourage contact between the children and their absent father and to give effect to the previous court orders.

Held, remitting the case to the sheriff to consider submissions on the report which was lodged late and for determination of whether any further procedure was necessary, that (1) there was no requirement for the sheriff to write a lengthy note on his findings particularly where the findings were sufficiently clear as to what course of action would be in the best interests of the children; (2) although the evidence of the schoolteachers did not fully support the sheriff's conclusions, it did not automatically follow that the court should make on order for contact where such an order might prolong or exacerbate a situation where stress levels within the family were very high; (3) the sheriff had been entitled to ignore the report prepared by R as it had been prepared at an earlier stage in the proceedings and R had not given evidence at the proof, *Whitecross v. Whitecross* 1977 S.L.T. 225, [1977] C.L.Y. 3240, followed, and (4) the report by G had been prepared to assist the court at the time of the proof and, as such, should have been considered by the sheriff when reaching his decision as it had the potential to significantly affect the decision he reached.

Observed, that reporters appointed to report to the court are independent officers of the court and should not normally be cited as witnesses at a proof, nor should their reported opinions normally be open to cross examination.

BAILEY v. BAILEY (NO.1) 2001 Fam. L.R.133, JC McInnes Q.C., Sheriff Principal, Sh Ct.

5614. Children—names—change of name—requirement of paternal consent

W raised an action of divorce against her husband, H. H sought two specific issue orders in relation to the parties' five year old son (M), first, that W could not alter M's surname and secondly, that M should not be required to attend classes in religious instruction, in each case without H's consent. W was a practising Roman Catholic and wanted M to be brought up in that faith. H had formally agreed to that at the time of the marriage and at M's baptism. After the parties separated W reverted to using her maiden name and wished M to use that name also. After a meeting between the parties to discuss the two issues, W believed, reasonably but mistakenly, that H did not actively oppose the change of surname, and enrolled him at school under the changed name. H argued (1) that it was unreasonable to insist that a child of five attend catechism classes and he should be entitled to prevent such attendance, and (2) that his position regarding the change of M's surname had been clearly set out in a solicitor's letter following the parties' meeting.

Held, granting the order in relation to the change of name only, that (1) the catechism classes were a normal part of the education of a child being brought up as a Catholic who did not attend a denominational school and H's consent was not required, and in any event, could not reasonably be withheld, and (2) the naming of a child was a parental responsibility which was shared by both parents, as a general rule it was quite inappropriate for either parent to take a unilateral decision to change a child's name, and there were no overwhelming reasons why M's surname should be changed without H's consent, even though eight months had elapsed since M was registered at school under the changed name.

M v. C (CHILDREN: CONSENT TO CHANGE OF NAME) 2002 S.L.T. (Sh Ct) 82, AL Stewart, Q.C., Sh Ct (Tayside, Central and Fife).

5615. Children–parental responsibility–supervision requirement–father not "relevant person" with regard to children's hearings–decision not made on pleadings alone

[European Convention on Human Rights 1950 Art.6, Art.8.]

T, an unmarried father of three applied to the court for parental rights and responsibilities. T's children had been subject to a supervision requirement which named their place of residence as T's. A subsequent place of safety order removed the children from T's care and T ceased to be a "relevant person" in terms of attendance and participation at the children's hearings. On two occasions T appealed decisions of the hearing but these were dismissed as incompetent. T's application was dismissed and he appealed to the sheriff principal relying on European Convention on Human Rights 1950 Art.6 and Art.8, arguing that the sheriff had failed to construe the acquisition of parental rights as a necessary element of a fair hearing in the determination of T's civil rights in the children's hearing. A argued that was not a sufficient basis for granting parental rights.

Held, recalling the interlocutor and allowing proof before answer, that (1) there was no reason in principle why a court could not impose parental rights and responsibilities even where the parent could not immediately exercise them, the question should be whether T had something to offer the children that will be of benefit to their welfare; (2) the correct approach was to permit an unmarried father to compel acceptance of his attendance at the hearing only if he had the child in his care or he could otherwise convince the court that he should be granted an order conferring particular parental rights or responsibilities, and (3) the issues in the case were a matter for inquiry and only after such inquiry would it be apparent what order, if any, was to be made.

T v. A (PARENTAL RIGHTS) 2001 S.C.L.R. 647, RA Dunlop Q.C., Sheriff Principal, Sh Ct.

5616. Children–parental responsibility orders–not in best interests of child

C, a local authority, applied for a parental responsibility order in respect of J (born October 1989). J's mother (G) had signed a form agreeing to the application, but in evidence opposed it, having entered the process as a party minuter. There had been a long and troubled history of social work involvement with J's family. Both J and H, his brother (born August 1992), had been in foster care since April 1998; there was little contact between them. A similar order had been granted in respect of H. J's sister (born September 1995) resided with G. After J's foster carers applied to care for J on a long term basis, he became unsettled, ran away twice, the placement broke down in February 2000 and J was placed in a resource centre. Evidence was led of G's long history of failed contact appointments in respect of J and H. J remained deeply attached to G and wished to return to her care. Aged 10 at proof, J met with the sheriff in chambers and expressed his concern that the order would result in him being further distanced from G.

Held, refusing the application, that (1) G's evidence confirmed that she seemed incapable of making the effort to keep a regular schedule of visits with J and blamed everyone else for her failures. Despite her professed affections, it was unlikely that she would be able to provide J with the permanent and satisfactory home background he require; (2) it was not in J's best interests that the application be granted. Despite C's expressed intention not to phase G out if the order was granted, there would be an inevitable tendency to do just that, given G's record of failures. The only point of the order would be to try to channel J's future into a further long term fostering situation, preferably outwith G's influence. That would not be effective without J's co-operation, which would not be forthcoming, J being a strong willed child who knew what he wanted. The court agreed with J's psychiatric expert witness that the granting of the order would be seen by J as victory for C, damage his relationship with his social worker, and make J feel distanced from G. That was contrary to the view of the children's hearing and the curator, but, though their views were entitled to serious consideration and respect, J's placement had broken down since the views were framed. It was intended that the order would remove the jurisdiction of the children's hearing. J did not want that to happen, he was perfectly capable of expressing his views to a hearing, and it would be advisable for any periodic regulation of contact between G and J to be overseen by a hearing. Opinion, that frequent and residential contact should be arranged for J with G, and J ought to be kept advised of such efforts and of any failures by G in that regard. Either J would realise C's long term view for his future was in his best interests or, if contact were successful, he could return to G's care.

EDINBURGH CITY COUNCIL v. H (A CHILD) 2001 S.L.T. (Sh Ct) 51, Sheriff RG Craik Q.C., Sh Ct (Lothian and Border).

5617. Children–residence–views of child–intimation to child previously dispensed with–effect of lapse of time

[Children (Scotland) Act 1995 (c.36) s.11 (2) (e); Act of Sederunt (Sheriff Court Ordinary Cause Rules) 1993 (SI 1993 1956) r.33.7.]

In an action in which both parents sought a residence order in respect of their son D (born April 1992), H appealed against the sheriff principal's decision upholding the sheriff's order granting W a residence order and a specific issue order under the Children (Scotland) Act 1995 s.11 (2) (e) to enable her to take D to Australia for three years so she could take up a job promotion. The action was raised in 1999 when D was seven and a half years old. Intimation to D was dispensed with as inappropriate given his age under the Ordinary Cause Rules 1993 r.33.7 (7) and H's notice of intention to defend similarly sought dispensation on the same grounds. The sheriff, affirmed by the sheriff principal, granted the orders sought by the mother in May 2001, by which time D was nine. H argued, inter alia, that D's views had not been taken into account. W argued that where intimation had been dispensed with it was unnecessary for the sheriff to reconsider giving a child an opportunity to indicate whether he wished to express his views unless the question later arose or there was a material change of circumstances. Further, on the evidence D had reacted favourably to the prospect of moving abroad.

Held, allowing the appeal, that (1) the duty under s.11 (7) (b) required to be discharged at the time the relevant order was made, and if necessary by the court ex proprio motu; (2) the lapse of time in the present case between intimation being dispensed with and the decision being made amounted to a material change of circumstances; (3) the existence of evidence of D's view was no substitute for a proper inquiry into his own views, and (4) the sheriff had erred in failing to ascertain whether D wished to express a view on whether he should go to Australia.

SHIELDS v. SHIELDS; *sub nom.* CUNNINGHAM v. SHIELDS 2002 S.C. 246, Lord Marnoch, Lady Cosgrove, Lord Dawson, Ex Div.

5618. Children (Scotland) Act 1995 (c.36)–Commencement No.5 Order

CHILDREN (SCOTLAND) ACT 1995 (COMMENCEMENT NO.5) ORDER 2002, SSI 2002 12; made under the Children (Scotland) Act 1995 s.105. Commencement details: bringing into force various provisions of the 1995 Act on January 22, 2002; £1.50.

This Order brings into force the repeal of the Children Act 1975 s.103 which provided for the establishment of a panel of persons from whom curators ad litem, reporting officers and safeguarders were to be appointed.

5619. Childrens hearings–fair hearing–unavailability of legal aid

[Children (Scotland) Act 1995 (c.36) s.51; Human Rights Act 1998 (c.42) s.7, s.22 (4), Sch.1 Part I Art.6.]

M appealed against the decision of a children's hearing, C, reviewing a supervision order concerning her child L and considering a proposed application to free L for adoption, not to discharge the referral, on the grounds that legal aid not being available to M, she had not had a fair hearing under the Human Rights Act 1998 Sch.1 Part I Art.6. It was agreed that the appeal would fail unless M was, under the s.7 of the 1998 Act, a victim of an unlawful act. M argued that (1) she was a victim under s.7: (a) although she had been legally represented at the specific hearing whose decision was being appealed, she had not been legally represented at previous hearings where significant decisions had been made and *Dempsey v. Ireland* E.C.H.R., 6 April 2000, could be distinguished, the proceedings being continuous; (b) she had suffered past detriment as a result of these hearings which had led to L being placed in foster care and proceeding in the direction of adoption, and past detriment could lead to unfairness; (2) that defect was not cured by the availability of an appeal under the Children (Scotland) Act 1995 s.51 because such an appeal was limited and did not amount to an appeal on the merits, and (3) in rejecting the objection, C had simply followed a guidance note issued by the Scottish Executive and had failed to exercise their discretion properly.

Held, refusing the appeal, that (1) the only hearing that was relevant was the one at which the decision appealed was made. There was not a continuous process; s.51 set a deadline for any appeal against a specific decision, and unfairness at one hearing could not found the basis of a ground of appeal against the decision at another. The scheme of the 1995 Act compelled review of any supervision requirement at regular intervals at each successive hearing; (2) M was not a victim under s.7. The right under Art.6 was to a fair hearing, not to legal aid, and there was no suggestion of any other unfairness. M had been legally represented and the decision, which led to re-establishment of contact with L, suggested that she had had some success. There was no suggestion of future prejudice leading to an unfair hearing, and any past decision could have been subject to a s.51 appeal where legal aid might be available, *Buchanan v. McLean* 2000 S.L.T. 928, [2000] C.L.Y. 6089 distinguished, and (3) C, having made it clear that they had rejected M's argument on the grounds that she had been represented and had not simply conformed with guidance, had been justified in their decision. Opinion, that (1) nothing in s.51 suggested that such an appeal could not address questions of unfairness at a children's hearing, and (2) different criteria might have applied if M's solicitor had withdrawn after the Art.6 submission had been rejected and C had made its substantive decision when M was without legal representation.

Observed, that the decision had been determined on the basis of a limited argument relating to s.7 and the court was not addressed on s.22(4) of the 1998 Act.

M v. CALDWELL 2001 S.L.T. (Sh Ct) 106, Sheriff KA Ross, Sh Ct (South Strathclyde, Dumfries and Galloway).

5620. Childrens hearings–legal representation

CHILDREN'S HEARINGS (LEGAL REPRESENTATION) (SCOTLAND) AMENDMENT RULES 2002, SSI 2002 30; made under the Children (Scotland) Act 1995 s.42. In force: February 22, 2002; £1.50.

These Rules amend the Children's Hearings (Legal Representation) (Scotland) Rules 2001 (SSI 2001 478) to correct an incorrect reference to the Panels of Persons to Safeguard the Interests of Children (Scotland) Regulations 2001 (SSI 2001 476).

5621. Childrens hearings–legal representation

CHILDREN'S HEARINGS (LEGAL REPRESENTATION) (SCOTLAND) RULES 2002, SSI 2002 63; made under the Children (Scotland) Act 1995 s.42, s.103. In force: February 23, 2002; £1.75.

These Rules, which revoke the Children's Hearings (Legal Representation) (Scotland) Rules 2001 (SI 2001 478) and the Children's Hearings (Legal Representation) (Scotland) Amendment Rules 2002 (SI 2002 30), permit legal representatives to attend Children's Hearings in certain circumstances. They specify when the business meeting and the Children's Hearing may consider the appointment of a legal representative, and the circumstances in which an appointment may be made and authorise the Principal Reporter to make copies of the relevant documentation available to legal representatives. In addition, the

Rules specify groups of persons from whom a legal representative may be appointed.

5622. Childrens hearings–supervision orders–suspension of condition by hearing–competence

[Children (Scotland) Act 1995 (c.36) s.16(1), s.51 (9), s.73(6).]

S sought declarator by judicial review that C (a children's hearing) had erred in a decision of September 14, 2001 refusing her application under the Children (Scotland) Act 1995 s.51 (9) to have a weekend and holidays residence condition of a supervision requirement suspended pending determination of an appeal to the sheriff court. The supervision requirement was imposed on August 13, 2001. C held that s.51 (9) did not allow them to suspend a condition. S argued (1) that s.16(1) required the children's hearing to construe s.51 (9) broadly, the condition was severable from the rest of the requirement and could be suspended without suspending the whole requirement; (2) that there was no explanation for difference between a sheriff's powers on appeal and the powers of C ad interim and any difference was illogical, and (3) that the power in s.73(6) to review the requirement in three months did not provide a remedy as C would be likely to reach the same conclusions.

Held, refusing the petition, that (1) s.73(6) provided an alternative remedy and from November 13, 2001 S could have availed herself of s.73(6) under which it would have been open to C to delete the condition and no material change of circumstances would have been required; (2) that the s.16(1) principle applied to any decision falling within C's discretion but was not relevant to competency, and (3) that having regard to the contrast between the powers conferred on a children's hearing under s.51 (9) and s.73(9) with the powers conferred on a sheriff under s.51 (5), C correctly determined that they had no power to suspend only one condition without suspending the whole supervision requirement.

S v. PROUDFOOT; *sub nom.* S v. STIRLING COUNCIL (SUPERVISION REQUIREMENT) 2002 S.L.T. 743, Lord Menzies, OH.

5623. Divorce–financial provision–appeal–relevant considerations–award of expenses

[Family Law (Scotland) Act 1985 (c.37) s.8(2).]

A wife, W, appealed against a sheriff's award of a £10,370 capital sum in her action of divorce, and the husband, H, appealed against an award of expenses against him. W had craved periodical allowance and a capital sum of £50,000. H twice offered, during the proceedings, to settle the claim for a capital sum at a figure higher than the £10,370 W was ultimately awarded, but not by minute of tender. The sheriff awarded expenses to W on the basis that expenses should follow success and that the offer to settle should have been by way of minute of tender. Both parties appealed. It was accepted that there had been an inadvertent double allowance made for H paying off matrimonial debts and as a matter of arithmetic W should have been awarded a further £1,950, which would give her exactly one half of the matrimonial property. H however resisted an increase in the capital award having regard to his resources in terms of the Family Law (Scotland) Act 1985, s.8(2), under reference to the sheriff's findings as to his debts and his liability to his solicitors. W argued that there were no circumstances entitling the court to review the sheriff's discretion as to expenses.

Held, allowing both appeals, that (1) it would be unrealistic of an appellate court reconsidering an award of capital sum to ignore the consequences of an award of expenses, and unrealistic for a court of first instance to ignore the amount of a capital sum it had awarded when considering expenses; (2) the sheriff could and should have had regard to H's offers: in many instances a formal minute of tender would not be appropriate in family actions, and where an offer had been made and refused a court was entitled to give that matter the appropriate weight in considering liability for expenses; (3) the principle that expenses should follow success could not be fully applied in cases of this type, and in any event it was incorrect to say that the wife had been wholly successful, and no expenses would be found due to or by either party up to and including the diet of proof; and, (4) having allowed H's appeal on expenses, it was appropriate to allow W's appeal to increase the capital sum to £12,320.

CAMERON v. CAMERON; *sub nom.* FITZSIMMONS v. CAMERON 2002 S.L.T. (Sh Ct) 23, CGB Nicholson Q.C., Sheriff Principal, Sh Ct.

5624. Divorce—financial provision—capital sum—available resources

EF raised an action of divorce against her husband AF which was undefended on the merits. EF sought a capital payment of £40,000. At the time that the parties ceased to cohabit, the only matrimonial property was AF's occupational pension valued at £105,395. AF, who had retired early, was in receipt of a pension of £520 per month and had received a lump sum of £39,099 which he had invested in a business. Since that time, he had made drawings from the capital in that business to support himself, and at the time of the proof, the lump sum had been virtually dissipated. After the parties separation, AF had cohabited with M, initially at M's property in Edinburgh. M had since sold that house and used the proceeds to purchase a property in joint names with AF where they cohabited with their respective children. The sheriff found that AF had no resources from which to pay such a sum and EF appealed to the Court of Session. EF argued that the sheriff had erred in his findings as AF had, at the time of the proof, a one half share in the property in which he cohabited with M, the equity in which was £35,000, and a one half share of £2,000 held in a joint bank account with M, which together gave AF assets of £18,500. In recognition that AF was caring for their child, EF had restricted her claim for a capital sum to £40,000 rather than claiming half the matrimonial property which would have amounted to £52,697.

Held, allowing the appeal to the extent that EF should have been awarded a capital sum of £1,000, with payment to be made within six months of decree, that (1) the sheriff misdirected himself in finding that AF had no resources as at the date of the proof, AF was entitled to half of the £2,000 held in a joint bank account, and (2) EF had failed to show that AF had a beneficial interest in the equity in the property as it had been submitted by AF that the equity had been provided by M from the proceeds of the sale of her property in Edinburgh and this evidence had not been sufficiently rebutted by EF during the proof.

FRASER v. FRASER 2002 Fam. L.R. 53, Lord Murray, Lord Brand, Lord Caplan, Ex Div.

5625. Divorce—financial provision—capital sum—husband's conduct after separation adversely affecting wife financially—conduct relevant to award

[Family Law (Scotland) Act 1985 (c.37) s.11 (7).]

W raised an action of divorce after 12 years of marriage on the basis of adultery. W sought a capital sum from H. The matrimonial property had a net value of £33,838.04 and W sought an unequal share justified by special circumstances. W also sought transfer of title to the matrimonial home into her sole name. H disputed there were no such special circumstances and, even if there were, they could not justify the extent of inequality that H had suggested.

Held, that an unequal sharing of £26,824.44 to £7,013.60 was in all the circumstances fair and reasonable; (i) W had contributed £6,000 as a deposit for the family home; (ii) W and children had continued to live in the home which was close to the children's school and W's family. Any move from there would be disruptive; (iii) H had failed to fulfil financial orders from the court; (iv) H had failed to notify the court after obtaining employment; (v) H had failed to contribute financially to the children's maintenance. In terms of the Family Law (Scotland) Act 1985 s.11 (7) "conduct" usually referred to conduct within the marriage but there was no reason why it could not also refer to H's conduct after separation that had adversely affected W's financial position.

GRAY v. GRAY 2001 S.C.L.R. 681, Sheriff AL Stewart, Sh Ct (Tayside, Central and Fife).

5626. Divorce—financial provision—fair sharing of economic burden of caring for children

W raised an action of divorce against H. The extent and value of the parties matrimonial property and the amount of the capital sum to be awarded to H was in dispute. The parties married in October 1980 when W was 19 and H was 21. They separated in May 1993 with W retaining custody of the two children of the marriage by agreement. W came from a family with a background in farming and substantial property interests and owned a farm in her own right at the time of their marriage. In return for the capital sum, H agreed to transfer his shares in two family businesses and his share of the parties' partnership to W. Following their marriage, the parties lived and worked at W's farm (farm A) they later moved to another farm (farm B) and became tenants, W's mother being the owner and landlord. In 1984, W sold farm A at a substantial profit. She used some of the money to purchase additional land, N, from her parents and made loans totalling £68,000 to a company in which her father was actively involved. The company subsequently went into receivership and W lost all but £5,000 of the loans. Following those losses, it was decided that W should become the owner of farm B. Farm B was purchased from her mother and financed partly by a monetary gift and partly by a loan, both from W's mother. Although the loan was subsequently repaid, the money was reinvested for the benefit of the parties' children. W's father subsequently negotiated the sale of grouse moors which included N and part of farm B at a price of £1,531,000 of which W received £656,549.01. Much of the proceeds and later profits from the sale of the grouse moor, after tax, were used to purchase shares in a family company. W contended that she had effectively acquired farm B by gift and that separate properties should be treated individually and in the context of the way in which the proceeds of farm A had been used to acquire land which value had risen because of general increases in land value.

Held, granting decree for payment by W to H of a capital sum of £235,000 with interest at 6 per cent per annum from the date of decree until payment, that (1) given that farm B was sold as a farm with a sitting tenant, the value at sale was not sufficiently different from the open market value so as to indicate that it was intended as a gift. However the circumstances did warrant special consideration with the value of the gift from her mother being deductible form the value of the asset as part of the parties' matrimonial property; (2) the grouse moor lease had no realisable value at the relevant date; (3) although not financial, H had made an appropriate contribution to the running of the farm B and, although that did not entitle him to a share in any gift intended for W, the origin of the assets was not sufficient in itself to deny H a share in their value; (4) the increase in the value of N was as a result of it being sold as part of a larger grouse moor; (5) given that the value of the parties' personal equity plans was roughly equal, each should be allowed to retain their respective plans with the balance of the value of the matrimonial property being divided between the parties with 75 per cent to W and 25 per cent to H, the sum payable by W to H being able to be met out of the sale of shares which she held outwith the family businesses, and (6) given that W had responsibility for the care and maintenance of the children to the marriage, it was not appropriate to backdate the interest to the date of the separation.

MacLEAN v. MacLEAN 2001 Fam. L.R. 118, Lord Rodger, OH.

5627. Divorce—financial provision—periodical allowance—serious financial hardship

[Family Law (Scotland) Act 1985 (c.37) s.9(1) (e), s.13(4).]

W, a 51 year old woman, after 27 years of marriage during which she had been in employment for short periods only, separated from her Norwegian husband (H) and returned to Scotland. Her health was poor. She had poor hearing and chronic high blood pressure and fibrositis. She was also suffering from depression which, on its own, would render her unfit for employment over the next two years. She received no aliment and was wholly reliant on state benefit. H earned about £74,000 net of tax per year and had necessary annual expenditure of, he said, £72,000. After proof in 1995 in W's action of divorce H's potential excess of income over expenditure was assessed by the Lord Ordinary at £12,000 per year, and W was awarded periodical allowance of £1,000 per month. H reclaimed. On February 12, 1997 the court allowed a minute for H seeking variation to nil to be received and allowed W to include in any answers a conclusion to convert her conclusion for periodical allowance to one for a capital sum. The minute was remitted to the temporary judge (J) to hear proof and make recommendations. J found that H had lost his job, including pension and bonus entitlement, that he was engaged periodically on contract work and might expect a free income of around £1,000 per month, but that he had debts of around £100,000. J saw no practical prospect of W regularly receiving a substantial allowance and recommended reduction to nil, backdated to February 12, 1997 when the minute was received, leaving her to try and recover arrears. W, who remained wholly reliant on needs-related social security payments, argued inter alia that H had not established a material change in circumstances since 1995. H argued that it had been incompetent for an award of periodical allowance to be made because no aliment had been paid by him following the separation, and therefore any hardship suffered was not "as a result of the divorce" in terms of the Family Law (Scotland) Act 1985, s.9(1)(e).

Held, refusing the reclaiming motion and remitting the cause to J with a direction to vary the order by reducing the periodical allowance to £500 per month, backdated to February 12, 1997, that (1) while the pattern of actual support provided prior to divorce, including during separation, was among the factors to be taken into account when assessing whether the loss of the right to aliment on divorce was likely to give rise to hardship, the presence or absence of actual support could not be determinative, and it was open to the Lord Ordinary to make an order under s.9(1)(e), and (2) H had established a material change in his financial circumstances in terms of s.13(4) where he was no longer in secure pensionable employment, but J's recommendation of variation to nil was based on the erroneous ground of W's poor prospects of enforcing any award whereas it was a matter for her whether she sought to enforce any award, and on the findings made by J on the limited material before him a reduction to £500 per month, backdated, was reasonable having regard to the resources of the parties.

HAUGAN v. HAUGAN (NO.1); *sub nom.* HAUGHAN v. HAUGHAN (NO.1) 2002 S.L.T.1349, Lord Hamilton, Lord McCluskey, Lord Menzies, Ex Div.

5628. Divorce–financial provision–periodical allowance–variation allowed in Singapore–reciprocal enforcement

[Maintenance Orders (Reciprocal Enforcement) Act 1972 (c.56) s.5(5).]

M and C divorced in 1979. C was ordered to pay to M a periodical allowance of £40 a week, increased ultimately to £125 in 1984. The relevant interlocutors were sent to Singapore, where C resided for the purposes of the Maintenance Orders (Reciprocal Enforcement) Act 1972. In February 2000 C obtained a provisional order in Singapore, purportedly reducing the periodical allowance to £50 per week as from April 1999, subject to confirmation by the Court of Session. M applied for an order refusing confirmation in terms of s.5(5). C argued that there had been a material change in his circumstances in that he had retired in June 1998 and his (part time) earnings were now $7,400 per month, having previously been $16,000 per month, and that he had married in 1990 the partner he had been living with in 1984. Further, his pension fund was a capital asset over which M had no claim. M, who suffered from various medical conditions, claimed that she was unfit for work and, apart from benefits, the maintenance payments were her only income.

Held, refusing confirmation, that (1) C's earnings were only very slightly below those he was receiving in July 1984 when the order was registered, at which time he had failed to disclose his true financial position. It was fair to compare C's earnings now with his earnings in 1984, rather than those immediately before his retirement; (2) it was reasonable to infer that C's pension fund yielded income and it could be concluded that the income declared by C was an understatement; (3) C did not seek to rely on his remarriage as a change in circumstance when it took place and it ought not to weigh heavily in any reassessment of maintenance, and (4) M's evidence was accepted.

CANDLISH v. CANDLISH 2001 Fam. L.R. 45, Lord Macfadyen, OH.

5629. **Divorce–financial provision–periodical allowance–variation to nil–non-payment over substantial period**

H, the former husband of W, sought variation to nil of an award of periodical allowance of £20 per week made on their divorce in 1982. H remarried in 1987 and had three children to this subsequent marriage. H had lost his job in 1998 and started work in partnership, and latterly as a sole trader, as a jobbing carpenter on hourly rates, and had got into debt supporting his new family. Although not receiving any payments since 1985 W, who was partially disabled and lived on benefit, though she hoped to start a university course, denied the existence of an agreement that she would not seek payment of periodical allowance. W claimed that she had not wished to go through legal aid, H had told her he did not have the money, and as long as H continued to pay aliment in respect of S, a child of their marriage, she did not want payment of periodical allowance. W had sought payment of the allowance only in January 1999, H being no longer required to pay aliment to S.

Held, varying the periodical allowance to nil, that both W and H lived on a bare subsistence basis, having no surplus income after meeting ordinary living expenses, but the order placed an unacceptable burden on H and his new family. H no longer had the revenue surplus he had at the date of the divorce and W had, whatever the reason, lived without the payment since 1985. Opinion, that W's evidence having been less than satisfactory, that H had established that there had been an agreement in 1985 that she would not receive periodical allowance; however that did not allow the court to backdate a variation, *Wilson v. Wilson* 1992 S.L.T. 664, [1992] C.L.Y. 5685 referred to, and a declaratory action would be required to recognise the agreement.

DOUGLAS v. IRELAND 2001 Fam. L.R. 42, Lord Penrose, OH.

5630. **Divorce–financial provision–res judicata–minute of agreement not implemented**

H and W were involved in a defended divorce, but matters were agreed and a minute of agreement prepared. The divorce continued undefended. W did not fulfil the requirements of the minute of agreement and H raised an action for declarator that W was in material breach and that he was entitled to resile also and insist upon division and sale of the matrimonial home. W argued that the action was res judicata, the matter of the matrimonial home had already been decided in the divorce. H argued that action for declarator involved a different media concludendi, namely the consequences of W's failure to fulfil her part of the agreement.

Held, repelling the plea of res judicata, that the action involved different media concludendi, however H would have to establish that he was entitled to resile.

CASSIDY v. CASSIDY 2002 S.C.L.R. 576, Andrew Lothian, Sh Ct (Lothian and Border).

5631. **Family proceedings–sist of proceedings–jurisdiction–father, mother and child moving to England albeit separately**

[Family Law Act 1986 (c.55) s.14, s.15.]

F, a father of a child, S, born in April 1992, successfully raised an action for contact with S, in February 1999. Contact took place in both February and March 1999, but shortly after, the child's mother, M, moved with the child to the north of England. In February 2000, the sheriff, in response to a motion by F, reduced the contact order to nil and varied all previous interlocutors in hoc statu to the effect that no contact should take place between F and the child. F appealed against that decision. By the time the case came before the Court of Session on appeal, F was resident in Devon and, although there had been no contact between him and the child for 18 months, he now intended to raise new proceedings in England. F, M and the child's curator ad litem were in agreement that a sist of the present proceedings was desirable to enable proceedings to be raised in England.

Held, sisting the action in terms of the Family Law Act 1986 s.14, that (1) the appeal proceedings could only review the sheriff's decision based on the circumstances which existed at the time that decision was made and could not take into account whether contact would be in the child's best interests given the current circumstances; (2) given the change in circumstances and lack of a live Scottish connection, fresh proceedings would be more appropriate in England, and (3) there was no requirement to recall existing interlocutors as they would be superseded in due course by the English disposal of the case in terms of s.15 of the 1986 Act. Opinion of the Court per Lord Prosser.

M v. M 2002 S.C. 103, Lord Prosser, Lord Coulsfield, Lady Paton, Ex Div.

5632. Harassment–non harassment order–competency–pre existing interim interdict

See CIVIL PROCEDURE: McGuire v. Kidston. §5339

5633. Harassment–non harassment orders–competency–pre existing interdict

See CIVIL PROCEDURE: McCann v. McGurran. §5338

5634. Marriage–irregular marriage–cohabitation with habit and repute–additional evidence on appeal

A raised an action for declarator that she was married by cohabitation with habit and repute to L from 1996 until shortly before his death in 1998. A met L in 1994 and began cohabiting with him within a few months. In February 1996, L asked A to marry him and, following her acceptance, bought her a ring, which A maintained was a wedding ring. They went on holiday together, which A claimed they treated as a honeymoon and, following their return, A averred that they lived as husband and wife. A claimed that she was introduced by L at social and business functions as his wife, and she introduced him to friends and acquaintances as her husband. A maintained that members of various organisations which they belonged to, work colleagues, friends and neighbours all regarded them as married, as did all but their close family. At the proof, the defenders, B, led contradictory evidence that neighbours, work colleagues and business associates regarded them as living together or engaged, but had not formed any view as to their marital status. B maintained that L did not regard them as married and anticipated a marriage in the future as was becoming of an elder in the local church. Following a proof, the Lord Ordinary granted absolvitor holding that L and A had agreed in February 1996 to become engaged and be married at some future time and that the evidence presented fell far shot of that required to establish habit and repute. A reclaimed, arguing that the Lord Ordinary had erred in finding that there was insufficient evidence and in failing to give satisfactory reasons for rejecting evidence supporting her claims in favour of evidence led for B. A also sought a remit for further evidence from a woman who was believed to have formed a relationship with L shortly before his death.

Held, refusing the reclaiming motion, that (1) there were no grounds for the court to exercise its discretion to hear the additional evidence where knowledge of the additional witness had been available to A in sufficient time as to allow her to follow correct procedure and lodge an appropriate minute, where the additional evidence was consistent with evidence already heard and where it had no material bearing on the reasons given by the Lord Ordinary in reaching his decision; (2) in order to establish marriage by cohabitation with habit and repute, there had to be evidence that the habit and repute was so general and widespread as to leave no substantial doubt and, that in the absence of such evidence, it was not open to the court to imply tacit consent to marriage, and (3) on the basis of the evidence before him, the Lord Ordinary had been entitled to reach the conclusions he did on the matter of repute and on the question of the parties intention. Opinion of the Court per Lord Cameron of Lochbroom.

ACKERMAN v. BLACKBURN (NO.1); *sub nom.* ACKERMAN v. LOGAN'S EXECUTORS (NO.1) 2002 S.L.T. 37, Lord Cameron of Lochbroom, Lord Mackay of Drumadoon, Lord Philip, Ex Div.

5635. Marriage—nullity—arranged marriage—lack of consent to marry

[Marriage (Scotland) Act 1977 (c.15) s.3, s.5, s.13(1)(a), s.23A.]

S, a 19 year old Muslim woman from Glasgow, sought declarator of nullity of her marriage to K, by reason of lack of consent, having allegedly entered into it under duress when aged 16; and by reason of the lack of a marriage schedule at the ceremony, although the marriage was subsequently registered. S averred that the marriage was arranged without her prior knowledge or consent between K's parents and her own, P, and she was only informed of their intention one week before the wedding. S further claimed that when she protested, P threatened to disown her and to send her to live in Pakistan, as had happened to her friend, if she refused to marry K, and that her mother threatened to commit suicide, which S took seriously. Evidence suggested that K, who resided in England, was not aware of S's lack of consent and he sought to rely on *Mahmood v. Mahmood* 1993 S.L.T. 589, [1993] C.L.Y. 5216 to show that there could be a range of consent. K, further relying on *Mahmud v. Mahmud* 1994 S.L.T. 599, [1993] C.L.Y. 5217, which showed the importance of events before and after a ceremony, claimed that there had been a courtship between him and S, and together with his family, F, stated that S had visited him in England on occasions when wedding clothes and other outfits were purchased for her. Cohabitation following the marriage in December 1998 was short, unhappy, and interrupted, with S finally leaving K on April 25, 1999. No reconciliation attempts were made thereafter. Evidence further suggested that although a marriage schedule had been submitted to the registrar following the wedding, it did not relate to the date of the ceremony between S and K.

Held, granting decree of nullity, that (1) S's evidence was credible whereas K and F's evidence in relation to events prior to the wedding was untruthful and unreliable, which affected the court's view of their evidence on other matters; (2) S had not genuinely consented to the marriage. She had been put under more pressure than a 16 year old could bear, her will had thus been broken and whatever semblance of consent was exchanged at the wedding ceremony was vitiated. None of the authorities cited compelled any different result, and (3) the need to have a schedule under the Marriage (Scotland) Act 1977 s.13(1)(a) at the solemnisation of a marriage following a notice was a requirement that could not be dispensed with even where registration followed. To conclude that it could encourage carelessness and dishonesty, would defeat the purpose of notice, and would effectively render s.3 and s.5 of the 1977 Act nugatory. The inserted s.23A of the Act did not affect such requirements.

SOHRAB v. KHAN 2002 S.C. 382, Lord McEwan, OH.

5636. Marriage (Scotland) Act 2002 (asp 8)

This Act of the Scottish Parliament amends the Marriage (Scotland) Act 1977 and enables civil marriages to be solemnised in certain places approved by local authorities.

This Act received Royal Assent on April 4, 2002.

5637. Marriage (Scotland) Act 2002 (asp 8)—Commencement Order

MARRIAGE (SCOTLAND) ACT 2002 (COMMENCEMENT) ORDER 2002, SSI 2002 184; made under the Marriage (Scotland) Act 2002 s.2. Commencement details: bringing into force various provisions of the 2002 Act on April 25, 2002; £1.50.

This Order brings into force the Marriage (Scotland) Act 2002 s.1 which makes provision for the solemnisation of civil marriages at places approved by local authorities.

5638. Matrimonial home—occupancy rights—non-entitled spouse—loss of rights due to lapse of time

[Matrimonial Homes (Family Protection) (Scotland) Act 1981 (c.59) s.1 (1), s.6(3) (f).]

S, a non-entitled spouse, who had been ejected from the matrimonial home by her husband in 1993 and had not resided there since, sought declarator against R, the purchasers of the house, that she was entitled to occupy the house in terms of the Matrimonial Homes (Family Protection) (Scotland) Act 1981 s.1 (1). S's husband had disponed the house to R in 1995. S had been asked for her consent to the transfer and had refused. She later discovered that her husband had sworn an affidavit declaring that there was no non-entitled spouse with occupancy rights. In 1997 she delivered a letter to R advising them of her intention to take up her occupancy rights in the property. R obtained interim interdict to prevent this. S subsequently raised the present action. R pled that the husband having permanently ceased to be entitled to occupy the subjects, and S thereafter not having occupied the subjects for a continuous period of five years (in terms of s.6(3) (f) of the Act), they should be assoilzied. S argued that s.6(3) (f) did not apply where the period had been interrupted by her raising a claim to assert her rights.

Held, dismissing the action, that s.6(3) (f) referred to the fact of occupation, not the right to occupy, and the five year period was not interrupted by the raising of proceedings to assert occupancy rights or by unsuccessful attempts to effect physical reoccupation.

STEVENSON v. ROY 2002 S.L.T. 445, Lord Drummond Young, OH.

5639. Matrimonial home—transfer of joint tenancy—transfer—wife caring for children and husband suffering mental health problems—tenancy transferred to wife

[Matrimonial Homes (Family Protection) (Scotland) Act 1981 (c.59) s.13.]

A wife, W, sought transfer of a joint tenancy into her sole name under the Matrimonial Homes (Family Protection) (Scotland) Act 1981 s.13. W and three children were living apart from the matrimonial home in a less attractive area. It was accepted that, if required to move, the children would have to change schools. H, who suffered mental health problems also sought transfer of the tenancy arguing that he should remain in the home, the security and established support network being desirable.

Held, granting the transfer tenancy order to W, that in balancing the interests of children and adults, the children had to come first. Transferring the tenancy to W would ensure that the children lived in better conditions and remained in the same school. Medical experts believed that, with support, H could cope with the move.

G v. G (DIVORCE: TRANSFER OF JOINT TENANCY) 2001 Fam. L.R. 99, AM Cowan, Sh Ct (Grampian, Highland and Islands).

5640. Parental rights—artificial insemination—donor seeking parental rights

[Children (Scotland) Act 1995 (c.36) s.11; Human Rights Act 1998 (c.42) Sch.1 Part I Art.8.]

X, a homosexual man living with his partner, B, sought an order for parental rights and responsibilities in respect of his son, A, born as a result of artificial insemination. X had agreed to be a donor for Y and her lesbian partner C in the belief that he would be allowed frequent access to A. The decision to become a donor had not been taken lightly by X, who had wanted to become a father for some time. During the pregnancy, X visited Y occasionally, attended an ultrasound scan and was present in the side room at birth. It was understood that he had not been informed of other antenatal appointments. X also raised the question of an agreement regarding parental rights during the pregnancy and was informed by Y that this was not possible until after the birth. X was named, and signed as the father on the birth certificate. He was told that aliment was not needed, so he bought many clothes for the child in lieu. It was later agreed that aliment of £55 per fortnight should be paid, and when Y decided that she no longer wanted to receive the money, X opened a bank account and deposited the aliment there. From around the time that A was 5 or 6 weeks old, Y and C devised strategies to exclude X and minimise his contact with A. When X raised the proceedings for parental rights, Y reduced his access the A, then 9 or 10 weeks old, to only 2 hours a week. Following a child welfare hearing, Y and C sent X an email with proposals for contact providing the action was dropped. Y and C saw themselves as a family unit and felt that C, rather than X should be given parental rights in respect of A. Y and C were critical of frequency of X's visits to A and his abilities in caring for him, however, a psychologist instructed by Y in preparation for the proof seemed reasonably impressed with X's abilities to interact with A and ensure that contact was a relaxed, happy time for A. The psychologist also gave evidence that A appeared well cared for by Y and C and that there was no evidence to suggest that being brought up in a homosexual relationship would have any detrimental effect respect for authority and Y had participated in a sham marriage to enable the homosexual partner of C's brother to remain in the United Kingdom.

Held, granting parental rights and responsibilities to X, that (1) it would be wrong for the court to chose the path of least resistance where one parent was determined to make life difficult for the other resulting in anxiety which was transmitting to the child as it was the court's duty to consider the best interests of the child; (2) the court was not bound to accept the evidence of an expert where, despite expert opinion, the court was of the opinion that the child would not receive a balanced emotional upbringing; (3) Y had not given fair notice of her intention to seek parental rights and responsibilities in respect of C and the court would therefore not make any order in that respect, particularly, as in this instance, where the point was a novel one in Scot's law; (4) it was appropriate the X should be granted parental rights and responsibilities where no attempt at anonymity had been made by Y in asking X to donate sperm, no intention had been shown during the pregnancy or during the first six weeks of A's life to exclude X; (5) as the biological father and where no intention had existed to exclude X from A's life, X did have a right to respect for family life under Human Rights Act 1998 Sch.1 Part I Art.8, and (6) C did not fall within the scope of what was envisaged as a family unit to enable an order to be made under s.11 of the Act.

X v. Y (PARENTAL RIGHTS: INSEMINATION) 2002 S.L.T. (Sh Ct) 161, ALA Duncan, Sh Ct (Glasgow and Strathkelvin).

5641. **Spouse—aliment—interim aliment—capacity to earn did not equate to actual earnings**

A husband, H, appealed, with leave of the sheriff, against his interlocutor awarding interim aliment of £412.50 per calendar month to W claiming that, although it appeared clear that W had a need for aliment at that rate, the sheriff had failed to consider whether H had the resources and/or the earning capacity to meet such an award. The evidence before the sheriff showed that H had no income, limited savings and substantial outgoings, but the sheriff found that, as a businessman of some experience, H ought, in terms of his earning resources, to be able to maintain both his own position and meet the sum required for interim aliment. On appeal, H argued that his bank statements showed a declining position and he had no equity in either his house or car. Although he was an experienced businessman, he had not been successful as was evidenced by the collapse of his business. H claimed that although he had the capacity to earn, it had not been translated into actual earnings despite all his efforts to secure employment and without that capacity being fulfilled, he had no resources to meet the award. W argued that H's bank statements had shown payments into the bank over the preceding 12 months of £23,000 and withdrawals of £10,000 with no satisfactory explanation of where the difference of £13,000 had gone. Neither had there been any signs of a slowdown in H's expenditure, which entitled the sheriff to conclude that H had means to meet the interim aliment awarded.

Held, recalling the sheriff's interlocutor and allowing W's motion for interim aliment to be heard of new, that (1) the fact that H had been able to meet his financial commitments in the past was not necessarily evidence that he would be able to meet them in the future and his bank statements had clearly shown a decline in his income in the preceding five months, and (2) a capacity to earn was not sufficient to meet a claim for aliment unless that capacity had been fulfilled.

ADAMS (ANNA) v. ADAMS (KENNETH ALEXANDER); *sub nom.* COSGROVE v. ADAMS 2002 S.C.L.R. 379, RA Dunlop Q.C., Sheriff Principal, Sh Ct.

5642. Books

Family Law Statutes 2002. A Parliament House Book. Paperback: £14.00. ISBN 0-414-01428-6. W.Green & Son.

Thomson, Joseph M.–Family Law in Scotland. Paperback: £39.00. ISBN 0-406-95567-0. Butterworths Law.

FISHERIES

5643. Conservation–enforcement of Community measures

SEA FISHING (ENFORCEMENT OF COMMUNITY CONSERVATION MEASURES) (SCOTLAND) AMENDMENT ORDER 2002, SSI 2002 81; made under the Fisheries Act 1981 s.30. In force: March 26, 2002; £2.00.

This Order, which amends the Sea Fishing (Enforcement of Community Conservation Measures) (Scotland) Order 2000 (SSI 2001 53), makes further provision for the enforcement of specified Community restrictions and obligations concerning the recovery of the stocks of cod in the Irish Sea, the North Sea and to the west of Scotland.

5644. Conservation–salmon

CONSERVATION OF SALMON (PROHIBITION OF SALE) (SCOTLAND) REGULATIONS 2002, SSI 2002 418; made under the Salmon Act 1986 s.10A. In force: October 1, 2002; £1.50.

These Regulations prohibit the sale, offer or exposure for sale in Scotland of any salmon taken using a rod and line.

5645. Fish–several fishery rights–Loch Caolisport

LOCH CAOLISPORT SCALLOPS SEVERAL FISHERY (SCOTLAND) ORDER 2002, SSI 2002 272; made under the Sea Fisheries (Shellfish) Act 1967 s.1, s.7. In force: July 1, 2002; £1.75.

This Order confers on Ormsary Farmers the right of several fishery for scallops in part of the sea at Loch Caolisport for a period of 15 years.

5646. Fish farms–escape of fish–notification to Scottish Ministers

REGISTRATION OF FISH FARMING AND SHELLFISH FARMING BUSINESSES AMENDMENT (NO.2) (SCOTLAND) ORDER 2002, SSI 2002 220; made under the Diseases of Fish Act 1983 s.7. In force: May 10, 2002; £1.50.

This Order amends the Registration of Fish Farming and Shellfish Farming Businesses Amendment (Scotland) Order 2002 (SSI 2002 193) to correct a drafting defect.

5647. Fish farms–escape of fish–notification to Scottish Ministers

REGISTRATION OF FISH FARMING AND SHELLFISH FARMING BUSINESSES AMENDMENT (SCOTLAND) ORDER 2002, SSI 2002 193; made under the Diseases of Fish Act 1983 s.7. In force: May 10, 2002; £2.00.

This Order, which amends the Registration of Fish Farming and Shellfish Businesses Order 1985 (SI 1985 1391), provides for the notification of circumstances giving rise to any escapes of fish, or of circumstances that gave rise to a significant risk of an escape of fish from fish farms registered in terms of the 1985 Order. It requires persons who carry on such businesses to notify the Scottish Ministers of such escapes in a prescribed form and also requires that details of the numbers of fish that have escaped, attempts to recover the fish and the numbers of fish recovered must also be notified within 28 days of the initial notification of the escape.

5648. Fishing–enforcement of Community quotas

SEA FISHING (ENFORCEMENT OF COMMUNITY QUOTA AND THIRD COUNTRY FISHING MEASURES) (SCOTLAND) ORDER 2002, SSI 2002 51; made under the Fisheries Act 1981 s.30. In force: March 10, 2002; £2.50.

This Order, which revokes the Sea Fishing (Enforcement of Community Quota and Third Country Fishing Measures) (Scotland) Order 2001 (SSI 2001 117) with a saving, makes provision for the enforcement of certain enforceable Community restrictions and other obligations relating to sea fishing by Community vessels and third country vessels set out in Council Regulation 2555/2001 ([2001] OJ L347/1). The Council Regulation fixes total allowable catches and the quotas of Member States for 2002 and lays down certain conditions under which they may be fished. It also authorises fishing by vessels of Norway and the Faroe Islands for specified descriptions of fish in certain specified areas within the fishery limits of Member States in 2002 and imposes requirements concerning fishing quotas and authorised zones, methods of fishing, the holding of licences and observance of licence conditions, the keeping of logbooks, the making of reports and similar matters. The Order creates offences in respect of breaches of provisions of the Council Regulation, provides for penalties in relation to an offence and for the recovery of fines imposed in respect of such offences. It confers on British sea-fishery officers powers of enforcement in relation to fishing boats and on land. These include power to enter premises, to go on board fishing boats, to stop and search vehicles transporting fish, to examine fish, to require the production of documents, to search for and seize documents, to take a boat to the nearest convenient port and to seize fish and fishing gear, and provision is also made in relation to the liability of officers for anything done in the purported exercise of powers conferred by the Order.

5649. Fishing–prohibited methods of fishing–Firth of Clyde

SEA FISH (PROHIBITED METHODS OF FISHING) (FIRTH OF CLYDE) ORDER 2002, SSI 2002 58; made under the Sea Fish (Conservation) Act 1967 s.5, s.15, s.22. In force: February 14, 2002; £2.00.

This Order prohibits, subject to certain exceptions, all methods of fishing within certain areas of the Firth of Clyde until 0000 hours on April 30, 2002. The prohibition does not apply to vessels fishing within the closed areas exclusively with creels, scallop dredges and trawls used for fishing for Norway lobsters.

5650. Fishing–Salmon fishery district–baits and lures–River Dee (Kirkcudbright)

RIVER DEE (KIRKCUDBRIGHT) SALMON FISHERY DISTRICT (BAITS AND LURES) REGULATIONS 2002, SSI 2002 11; made under the Salmon Act 1986 s.8. In force: February 1, 2002; £1.50.

These Regulations, which apply to the River Dee (Kirkcudbright) Salmon Fishery District, specify natural prawns and shrimps and any part of them, as baits and lures for the purpose of the definition of "rod and line" in the Salmon and Freshwater Fisheries (Protection) (Scotland) Act 1951 s.24(1). The effect of the Regulations is to prohibit the use of those baits or lures when fishing by rod and line for salmon or sea trout.

5651. Fishing–salmon fishery district–designation–Mull

MULL SALMON FISHERY DISTRICT DESIGNATION (SCOTLAND) ORDER 2002, SSI 2002 138; made under the Salmon Act 1986 s.1, s.2. In force: March 20, 2002; £2.00.

This Order creates a new salmon fishery district to be known as the Mull Salmon Fishery District and comprises the salmon fishery districts of Baa, Lussa and Pennygown which included the Islands of Mull, Coll, Tiree and the other islands to the west of the coast between Ardmore Point and Fidden Point. The salmon fishery districts of Baa, Lussa and Pennygown are abolished. It provides for the retention of Regulations relating to matters specified in the Salmon Fishery (Scotland) Act 1862 which applied in the superseded district.

5652. Fishing–several fishery rights–Little Loch Broom–scallops

LITTLE LOCH BROOM SCALLOPS SEVERAL FISHERY ORDER 2002, SSI 2002 186; made under the Sea Fisheries (Shellfish) Act 1967 s.1, s.7. In force: May 7, 2002; £2.00.

This Order confers on Grant Campbell the right of several fishery for scallops in part of Little Loch Broom for 15 years. It requires the harvesting of scallops under the right of several fishery to be carried out manually by divers and restricts the deposit of juvenile scallops taken from outside the fishery within the boundaries of the fishery, specifies creels as implements of fishing the use of which is permitted within the fishery, prohibits the assignation or other transfer of the right of several fishery without the prior written consent of Scottish Ministers, requires the limits of the area to be clearly marked and maintained and provides that its effect will not prejudicially affect the rights of the Crown.

5653. Fishing–several fishery rights–Loch Ewe, Isle of Ewe, Wester Ross–scallops

LOCH EWE, ISLE OF EWE, WESTER ROSS, SCALLOPS SEVERAL FISHERY (VARIATION) ORDER 2002, SSI 2002 185; made under the Sea Fisheries (Shellfish) Act 1967 s.1, s.7. In force: May 7, 2002; £2.00.

This Order amends the Loch Ewe, Isle of Ewe, Wester Ross, Scallops Several Fishery Order 1997 (SI 1997 830) by extending the period for which the right of several fishery in Loch Ewe, Wester Ross is granted to Mrs Jane Hardman or Grant; requiring the harvesting of scallops within the fishery to be carried out manually by divers; specifying a creel as an implement of fishing the use of which is permitted within the fishery; enabling the Scottish Ministers to give their consent to the assignation or other transfer of the right of several fishery in electronic form; and amending the description of the fishery.

5654. Shellfish–emergency prohibitions–amnesic shellfish poisoning

See FOOD. §5671, §5676, §5695, §5698, §5702, §5692, §5685, §5687, §5683, §5667, §5693, §5668, §5669, §5694, §5670, §5684, §5672, §5673, §5686, §5696, §5674, §5675, §5697, §5677, §5699, §5688, §5700, §5678, §5701, §5713, §5689, §5703, §5714, §5691, §5690, §5704, §5705, §5715, §5679, §5706, §5707, §5680, §5708, §5709, §5681, §5710, §5711, §5682, §5712

5655. Shellfish–emergency prohibitions–amnesic, paralytic and diarrhetic shellfish poisoning

See FOOD. §5716

5656. Shellfish—emergency prohibitions—diarrhetic shellfish poisoning
See FOOD. §5717

5657. Shellfish—emergency prohibitions—paralytic shellfish poisoning
See FOOD. §5718

FOOD

5658. Animal products—feedingstuffs—import controls—China

FOOD AND ANIMAL FEEDINGSTUFFS (PRODUCTS OF ANIMAL ORIGIN FROM CHINA) (CONTROL) (SCOTLAND) REGULATIONS 2002, SSI 2002 36; made under the European Communities Act 1972 s.2. In force: February 2, 2002; £2.00.

These Regulations implement Commission Decision 2002/69 ([2002] OJ L30/51) concerning certain protective measures with regard to the products of animal origin imported from China. They define "relevant product of animal origin", prohibit with exceptions importation of relevant products of animal origin, specify the enforcement authorities and apply with modifications certain provisions of the Food Safety Act 1990.

5659. Animal products—feedingstuffs—import controls—China

FOOD AND ANIMAL FEEDINGSTUFFS (PRODUCTS OF ANIMAL ORIGIN FROM CHINA) (EMERGENCY CONTROL) (SCOTLAND) REGULATIONS 2002, SSI 2002 300; made under the European Communities Act 1972 s.2. In force: June 20, 2002; £2.00.

These Regulations, which revoke the Food and Animal Feedingstuffs (Products of Animal Origin from China) (Control) (Scotland) Regulations 2002 (SI 2002 36), implement Commission Decision 2002/441 ([2002] OJ L151/16) amending Decision 2002/69 ([2002] OJ L30/50) concerning certain protective measures with regard to the products of animal origin imported from China. The Regulations define "relevant product of animal origin"; prohibit importation of relevant products of animal origin; specify the enforcement authorities; and apply certain provisions of the Food Safety Act 1990 and the Food Safety (Sampling and Qualifications) Regulations 1990 (SI 1990 2463).

5660. Animal products—identification—sterilisation and staining—carcases

ANIMAL BY-PRODUCTS (IDENTIFICATION) AMENDMENT (SCOTLAND) REGULATIONS 2002, SSI 2002 283; made under the Food Safety Act 1990 s.6, s.16, s.26, s.48, Sch.1 para.3. In force: July 1, 2002; £2.00.

These Regulations amend specified definitions in the By-Products (Identification) Regulations 1995 (SI 1995 614) and provide that the only whole carcases which have to be sterilised or stained are whole poultry carcases which are dead on arrival at a slaughterhouse or which are rejected following pre-slaughter or post-mortem health inspections carried out at such premises.

5661. Food composition—food for particular nutritional uses—specific nutritional purposes

FOOD FOR PARTICULAR NUTRITIONAL USES (ADDITION OF SUBSTANCES FOR SPECIFIC NUTRITIONAL PURPOSES) (SCOTLAND) REGULATIONS 2002, SSI 2002 397; made under the Food Safety Act 1990 s.6, s.16, s.17, s.26, s.48. In force: in accordance with Reg.1 (2) (3); £2.50.

These Regulations, which amend the Tryptophan in Food (Scotland) Regulations 1990 (SI 1990 1972), implement Commission Directive 2001/15 ([2001] OJ L52/19) on substances that may be added for specific nutritional purposes in foods for particular nutritional uses (PNU). The Regulations concern food for most particular nutritional uses where there has been added to that food for a specific nutritional purpose a substance falling within one of the following categories: vitamins; minerals; amino acids; carnitine and taurine; nucleotides, choline and inositol. They prohibit the sale of such food unless the substance is listed under the relevant category in Sch.1 or, in the case of foods for special medical purposes, is listed under the relevant category in either Sch.1 or Sch.2. The Regulations impose general restrictions on the sale of designated PNU foods in the manufacture of which any substances have been used for specific nutritional purposes and require the manufacturer or importer to supply the Food Standards Agency with information on request to verify that those restrictions are met. They also make provision as to responsibility for enforcement; create offences and penalties; apply certain provisions of the Food Safety Act 1990; and provide a defence in relation to exports in accordance with Council Directive 89/397 ([1989] OJ L186/23) on the official control of foodstuffs.

5662. Food composition–food safety–kava-kava

KAVA-KAVA IN FOOD (SCOTLAND) REGULATIONS 2002, SSI 2002 523; made under the Food Safety Act 1990 s.6, s.16, s.18, s.26, s.48. In force: January 1, 2003; £1.75.

These Regulations prohibit the sale, possession for sale, offer, exposure or advertisement for sale, and the importation into Scotland, of any food consisting of, or containing, Kava-kava. Any such food may be treated as being unfit for human consumption and be liable to be seized and destroyed.

5663. Food hygiene–animal products–slaughtering

POULTRY MEAT, FARMED GAME BIRD MEAT AND RABBIT MEAT (HYGIENE AND INSPECTION) AMENDMENT (SCOTLAND) REGULATIONS 2002, SSI 2002 87; made under the European Communities Act 1972 s.2; and the Food Safety Act 1990 s.16, s.17, s.19, s.26, s.48, Sch.1 para.5, Sch.1 para.6. In force: Reg.2(2)-(6): December 1, 2002; remainder: April 1, 2002; £1.75.

These Regulations amend the Meat, Farmed Game Bird Meat and Rabbit Meat (Hygiene and Inspection) Regulations 1995 (SI 1995 540) and the Products of Animal Origin (Import and Export) Regulations 1996 (SI 1996 3124). They implement in part the provisions of Council Directive 91/495 ([1991] OJ L268/41) concerning public health and animal health problems affecting the production and placing on the market of rabbit meat and farmed game bird meat and Council Directive 71/118 ([1971] OJ L55/23) on health problems affecting the production and placing on the market of fresh poultry meat, a consolidated text of which is annexed to Council Directive 92/116 ([1993] OJ L62/1). The Regulations also exempt certain local sales of small quantities of poultry meat or rabbit meat by farmers with an annual production of less than 10,000 birds or 10,000 rabbits and prohibit a person from operating a licensed low throughput slaughterhouse unless that person has notified the Food Standards Agency of the number and origin of the birds and rabbits to be slaughtered there.

5664. Food safety–additives–sweeteners

SWEETENERS IN FOOD AMENDMENT (SCOTLAND) REGULATIONS 2002, SSI 2002 61; made under the Food Safety Act 1990 s.16, s.17, s.48, Sch.1 para.1. In force: March 15, 2002; £2.00.

These Regulations amend the Sweeteners in Food Regulations 1995 (SI 1995 3123) to bring up to date the definition of "Directive 95/31" so as to cover its amendment by Directive 2001/52 ([2001] OJ L190/18) to substitute new purity criteria for two permitted sweeteners, mannitol and acesulfame K. The Regulations also grant provisional authorisation for the marketing and use as a sweetener of sucralose, as permitted by Directive 89/107 ([1989] OJ L40/27) on the approximation of the laws of the member States concerning food additives authorised for use in foodstuffs intended for human consumption. This authorisation will last for a maximum of two years, in which time EC-wide approval for sucralose must be sought.

5665. Food safety–contaminants–maximum levels

CONTAMINANTS IN FOOD (SCOTLAND) AMENDMENT REGULATIONS 2002, SSI 2002 349; made under the Food Safety Act 1990 s.6, s.16, s.17, s.26, s.48. In force: July 24, 2002; £1.75.

These Regulations, which amend the Food and Drugs (Scotland) Act 1956 (Transfer of Enforcement Functions) Regulations 1983 (SI 1983 270), the Food (Revisions of Penalties and Mode of Trial) (Scotland) Regulations 1985 (SI 1985 1068) and the Contaminants in Food (Scotland) Regulations 2002 (SSI 2002 267), revoke the Lead in Food (Scotland) Amendment Regulations 1985 (SI 1985 1438). The Regulations correct an error in the 2002 Regulations because of an error in Commission Regulation 466/2001 ([2001] OJ L155/63) setting maximum levels for certain contaminants in foodstuffs.

5666. Food safety–contaminants–maximum levels

CONTAMINANTS IN FOOD (SCOTLAND) REGULATIONS 2002, SSI 2002 267; made under the Food Safety Act 1990 s.6, s.16, s.17, s.26, s.48. In force: July 1, 2002; £2.50.

These Regulations, which revoke the Lead in Food (Scotland) Regulations 1979 (SI 1978 1641), the Contaminants in Food Regulations 1997 (SI 1997 1499), the Contaminants in Food (Amendment) Regulations 1999 (SI 1999 1603) and the Contaminants in Food Amendment (Scotland) Regulations 1999 (SSI 1999 171), amend the Food Safety Act 1990, the Food Safety (Sampling and Qualifications) Regulations 1990 (SI 1990 2463), the Food Safety Act 1990 (Consequential Modifications) (Scotland) Order 1990 (SI 1990 2625), the Food Safety (Exports) Regulations 1991 (SI 1991 1476), the Flavourings in Food Regulations 1992 (SI 1992 1971), the Colours in Food Regulations 1995 (SI 1995 3124) and the Food (Miscellaneous Revocations and Amendments) Regulations 1995 (SI 1995 3267). They make provision for the enforcement of Commission Regulation 466/2001 ([2001] OJ L77/1) setting maximum levels for certain contaminants in foodstuffs; implement Commission Directive 98/53 [1998] OJ L201/93) laying down sampling and analysis methods for the official control of the levels for certain contaminants of foodstuffs; Commission Directive 2001/22 ([2001] OJ L77/14) laying down the sampling methods and the methods of analysis for the official control of the levels of lead, cadmium, mercury and 3-MPCD in foodstuffs; Commission Directive 2002/26 ([2002] OJ L75/38) laying down the sampling methods and the methods of analysis for the official control of the levels of ochratoxin A in foodstuffs; and Commission Directive 2002/27 ([2002] OJ L75/44) amending Directive 98/53 laying down the sampling methods and the methods of analysis for the official control of the levels for certain contaminants in foodstuffs. The Regulations provide that it is an offence to place on the market certain foods if they contain contaminants of any kind specified in the Commission Regulation at levels exceeding those specified; to use foods containing such contaminants at such levels as ingredients in the production of certain foods; to mix foods which comply with the maximum levels referred to above with foods which do not; to mix foods to which the Commission Regulation relates and which are intended for direct consumption with foods to which the Commission Regulation relates and which are intended to be sorted or otherwise treated prior to consumption; and to detoxify by chemical treatments food not complying with the limits specified in the Commission Regulation. In addition, the Regulations specify the enforcement authorities.

5667. Food safety–emergency prohibitions–amnesic shellfish poisoning

FOOD PROTECTION (EMERGENCY PROHIBITIONS) (AMNESIC SHELLFISH POISONING) (ORKNEY) (NO.2) (SCOTLAND) ORDER 2002, SSI 2002 353;

made under the Food and Environment Protection Act 1985 s.1, s.24. In force: July 23, 2002 at 5 pm; £1.75.

This Order contains emergency prohibitions restricting various activities in order to prevent human consumption of food rendered unsuitable for that purpose by virtue of shellfish having been affected by the toxin which causes amnesic shellfish poisoning in human beings. It designates an area of sea around Orkney in Scotland within which taking scallops is prohibited and prohibits the movement of scallops out of the area.

5668. Food safety–emergency prohibitions–amnesic shellfish poisoning

FOOD PROTECTION (EMERGENCY PROHIBITIONS) (AMNESIC SHELLFISH POISONING) (ORKNEY) (NO.3) (SCOTLAND) ORDER 2002, SSI 2002 408; made under the Food and Environment Protection Act 1985 s.1, s.24. In force: September 4, 2002 at 5 pm; £1.75.

This Order contains emergency prohibitions restricting various activities in order to prevent human consumption of food rendered unsuitable for that purpose by virtue of shellfish having been affected by the toxins which cause amnesic, paralytic and diarrhetic shellfish poisoning in human beings. It designates an area around Orkney within which taking scallops is prohibited and prohibits the movement of scallops out of that area.

5669. Food safety–emergency prohibitions–amnesic shellfish poisoning

FOOD PROTECTION (EMERGENCY PROHIBITIONS) (AMNESIC SHELLFISH POISONING) (ORKNEY) (SCOTLAND) ORDER 2002, SSI 2002 345; made under the Food and Environment Protection Act 1985 s.1, s.24. In force: July 12, 2002 at 4 pm; £1.75.

This Order contains emergency prohibitions restricting various activities in order to prevent human consumption of food rendered unsuitable for that purpose by virtue of shellfish having been affected by the toxin which causes amnesic shellfish poisoning in human beings. It designates an area of sea around Orkney in Scotland within which taking scallops is prohibited and prohibits the movement of scallops out of the area.

5670. Food safety–emergency prohibitions–amnesic shellfish poisoning

FOOD PROTECTION (EMERGENCY PROHIBITIONS) (AMNESIC SHELLFISH POISONING) (WEST COAST) (NO.10) (SCOTLAND) ORDER 2002, SSI 2002 357; made under the Food and Environment Protection Act 1985 s.1, s.24. In force: July 30, 2002 at 4 pm; £1.75.

This Order contains emergency prohibitions restricting various activities in order to prevent human consumption of food rendered unsuitable for that purpose by virtue of shellfish having been affected by the toxin which causes amnesic shellfish poisoning in human beings. It designates areas of sea off the west coast of Scotland within which taking scallops is prohibited and prohibits the movement of scallops out of those areas.

5671. Food safety–emergency prohibitions–amnesic shellfish poisoning

FOOD PROTECTION (EMERGENCY PROHIBITIONS) (AMNESIC SHELLFISH POISONING) (WEST COAST) (NO.10) (SCOTLAND) REVOCATION ORDER 2002, SSI 2002 510; made under the Food and Environment Protection Act 1985 s.1, s.24. In force: November 19, 2002 at 5 pm; £1.50.

This Order revokes the Food Protection (Emergency Prohibitions) (Amnesic Shellfish Poisoning) (West Coast) (No.10) (Scotland) Order 2002 (SSI 2002 357) which prohibited fishing for or taking scallops within the designated area; the movement of such scallops out of the designated areas; and landing, using in the preparation or processing for supply of food of, supplying and other specified activities in relation to, such scallops from the designated areas. The Order, which also revokes the Food Protection (Emergency Prohibitions)

(Amnesic Shellfish Poisoning) (West Coast) (No.10) (Scotland) Partial Revocation Order 2002 (SSI 2002 421), removes the prohibitions in respect of the areas of sea designated.

5672. Food safety—emergency prohibitions—amnesic shellfish poisoning

FOOD PROTECTION (EMERGENCY PROHIBITIONS) (AMNESIC SHELLFISH POISONING) (WEST COAST) (NO.11) (SCOTLAND) ORDER 2002, SSI 2002 388; made under the Food and Environment Protection Act 1985 s.1, s.24. In force: August 26, 2002 at 4 pm; £1.75.

This Order contains emergency prohibitions restricting various activities in order to prevent human consumption of food rendered unsuitable for that purpose by virtue of shellfish having been affected by the toxin which causes amnesic shellfish poisoning in human beings. It designates the areas of sea off the west coast of Scotland within which taking scallops is prohibited and prohibits the movement of scallops out of those areas.

5673. Food safety—emergency prohibitions—amnesic shellfish poisoning

FOOD PROTECTION (EMERGENCY PROHIBITIONS) (AMNESIC SHELLFISH POISONING) (WEST COAST) (NO.12) (SCOTLAND) ORDER 2002, SSI 2002 430; made under the Food and Environment Protection Act 1985 s.1, s.24. In force: September 18, 2002 at 4 pm; £1.75.

This Order contains emergency prohibitions restricting various activities in order to prevent human consumption of food rendered unsuitable for that purpose by virtue of shellfish having been affected by the toxin which causes amnesic shellfish poisoning in human beings. It designates areas of sea off the west coast of Scotland within which taking scallops is prohibited and prohibits the movement of scallops out of these areas.

5674. Food safety—emergency prohibitions—amnesic shellfish poisoning

FOOD PROTECTION (EMERGENCY PROHIBITIONS) (AMNESIC SHELLFISH POISONING) (WEST COAST) (NO.13) (SCOTLAND) ORDER 2002, SSI 2002 465; made under the Food and Environment Protection Act 1985 s.1, s.24. In force: October 15, 2002 at 4 pm; £2.00.

This Order contains emergency prohibitions restricting various activities in order to prevent human consumption of food rendered unsuitable for that purpose by virtue of shellfish having been affected by the toxin which causes amnesic shellfish poisoning in human beings. It designates areas of sea off the west coast of Scotland within which taking scallops is prohibited and prohibits the movement of scallops out of these areas.

5675. Food safety—emergency prohibitions—amnesic shellfish poisoning

FOOD PROTECTION (EMERGENCY PROHIBITIONS) (AMNESIC SHELLFISH POISONING) (WEST COAST) (NO.14) (SCOTLAND) ORDER 2002, SSI 2002 482; made under the Food and Environment Protection Act 1985 s.1, s.24. In force: October 25, 2002 at 2 pm; £1.75.

This Order contains emergency prohibitions restricting various activities in order to prevent human consumption of food rendered unsuitable for that purpose by virtue of shellfish having been affected by the toxin which causes amnesic shellfish poisoning in human beings. It designates areas of sea off the west coast of Scotland within which taking scallops is prohibited and prohibits the movement of scallops out of these areas.

5676. Food safety—emergency prohibitions—amnesic shellfish poisoning

FOOD PROTECTION (EMERGENCY PROHIBITIONS) (AMNESIC SHELLFISH POISONING) (WEST COAST) (NO.15) (SCOTLAND) ORDER 2002, SSI 2002

511; made under the Food and Environment Protection Act 1985 s.1, s.24. In force: November 19, 2002 at 5 pm; £1.75.

This Order contains emergency prohibitions restricting various activities in order to prevent human consumption of food rendered unsuitable for that purpose by virtue of shellfish having been affected by the toxin which causes amnesic shellfish poisoning in human beings. The Order, which designates an area of sea off the west coast of Scotland within which taking scallops is prohibited, prohibits the movement of scallops out of those areas.

5677. Food safety—emergency prohibitions—amnesic shellfish poisoning

FOOD PROTECTION (EMERGENCY PROHIBITIONS) (AMNESIC SHELLFISH POISONING) (WEST COAST) (NO.2) (SCOTLAND) ORDER 2002, SSI 2002 65; made under the Food and Environment Protection Act 1985 s.1, s.24. In force: February 20, 2002 at 4 pm; £1.75.

This Order contains emergency prohibitions restricting various activities in order to prevent human consumption of food rendered unsuitable for that purpose by virtue of shellfish having been affected by the toxin which causes amnesic shellfish poisoning in human beings. It designates an area of water off the west coast of Scotland within which taking scallops and the movement of scallops out of the area is prohibited.

5678. Food safety—emergency prohibitions—amnesic shellfish poisoning

FOOD PROTECTION (EMERGENCY PROHIBITIONS) (AMNESIC SHELLFISH POISONING) (WEST COAST) (NO.3) (SCOTLAND) ORDER 2002, SSI 2002 80; made under the Food and Environment Protection Act 1985 s.1, s.24. In force: March 1, 2002 at 5 pm; £1.75.

This Order contains emergency prohibitions restricting various activities in order to prevent human consumption of food rendered unsuitable for that purpose by virtue of shellfish having been affected by the toxin which causes amnesic shellfish poisoning in human beings. It designates an area of sea off the west coast of Scotland within which taking scallops is prohibited and prohibits the movement of scallops out of that area.

5679. Food safety—emergency prohibitions—amnesic shellfish poisoning

FOOD PROTECTION (EMERGENCY PROHIBITIONS) (AMNESIC SHELLFISH POISONING) (WEST COAST) (NO.7) (SCOTLAND) ORDER 2002, SSI 2002 332; made under the Food and Environment Protection Act 1985 s.1, s.24. In force: July 3, 2002 at 3 pm; £1.75.

This Order, which contains emergency prohibitions restricting various activities in order to prevent human consumption of food rendered unsuitable for that purpose by virtue of shellfish having been affected by the toxin which causes amnesic shellfish poisoning in human beings, designates areas of sea off the west coast of Scotland within which taking scallops is prohibited.

5680. Food safety—emergency prohibitions—amnesic shellfish poisoning

FOOD PROTECTION (EMERGENCY PROHIBITIONS) (AMNESIC SHELLFISH POISONING) (WEST COAST) (NO.8) (SCOTLAND) ORDER 2002, SSI 2002 333; made under the Food and Environment Protection Act 1985 s.1; and the Food and Environment Protection Act 1985 24. In force: July 3, 2002 at 3 pm; £1.75.

This Order, which contains emergency prohibitions restricting various activities in order to prevent human consumption of food rendered unsuitable for that purpose by virtue of shellfish having been affected by the toxin which causes amnesic shellfish poisoning in human beings, designates areas of sea off the west coast of Scotland within which taking scallops is prohibited.

5681. Food safety–emergency prohibitions–amnesic shellfish poisoning

FOOD PROTECTION (EMERGENCY PROHIBITIONS) (AMNESIC SHELLFISH POISONING) (WEST COAST) (NO.9) (SCOTLAND) ORDER 2002, SSI 2002 350; made under the Food and Environment Protection Act 1985 s.1, s.24. In force: July 22, 2002 at 4 pm; £1.75.

This Order contains emergency prohibitions restricting various activities in order to prevent human consumption of food rendered unsuitable for that purpose by virtue of shellfish having been affected by the toxin which causes amnesic shellfish poisoning in human beings. It designates an area of sea off the west coast of Scotland within which taking scallops is prohibited and prohibits the movement of scallops out of that area.

5682. Food safety–emergency prohibitions–amnesic shellfish poisoning

FOOD PROTECTION (EMERGENCY PROHIBITIONS) (AMNESIC SHELLFISH POISONING) (WEST COAST) (SCOTLAND) ORDER 2002, SSI 2002 49; made under the Food and Environment Protection Act 1985 s.1, s.24. In force: February 7, 2002 at 5 pm; £1.75.

This Order contains emergency prohibitions restricting various activities in order to prevent human consumption of food rendered unsuitable for that purpose by virtue of shellfish having been affected by the toxin which causes amnesic shellfish poisoning in human beings. It designates an area of water off the west coast of Scotland within which taking scallops and the movement of scallops out of the area is prohibited.

5683. Food safety–emergency prohibitions–amnesic shellfish poisoning–partial revocation

FOOD PROTECTION (EMERGENCY PROHIBITIONS) (AMNESIC SHELLFISH POISONING) (ORKNEY) (NO.3) (SCOTLAND) PARTIAL REVOCATION ORDER 2002, SSI 2002 558; made under the Food and Environment Protection Act 1985 s.1, s.24. In force: 02 at 5pm1217; £1.75.

These Regulations revoke in part the Food Protection (Emergency Prohibitions) (Amnesic Shellfish Poisoning) (Orkney) (No.3) (Scotland) Order 2002 (SSI 2002 408) which prohibited the fishing for or taking scallops within the areas designated, movement of such scallops out of the designated areas and the landing, using in the preparation or processing for supply of food of, supplying and other specified activities in relation to, such scallops from the designated areas. The effect of the Order is to remove the prohibitions in respect of the area of sea designated.

5684. Food safety–emergency prohibitions–amnesic shellfish poisoning–partial revocation

FOOD PROTECTION (EMERGENCY PROHIBITIONS) (AMNESIC SHELLFISH POISONING) (WEST COAST) (NO.10) (SCOTLAND) PARTIAL REVOCATION ORDER 2002, SSI 2002 421; made under the Food and Environment Protection Act 1985 s.1, s.24. In force: September 11, 2002 at 4 pm; £1.50.

This Order is a partial revocation of the Food Protection (Emergency Prohibitions) (Amnesic Shellfish Poisoning) (West Coast) (No.10) (Scotland) Order 2002 (SSI 2002 357) which prohibited fishing for or taking scallops within the areas designated; movement of such scallops out of the designated areas; and landing, using in the preparation or processing for supply of food of, supplying and other specified activities in relation to, such scallops from the designated areas. The effect of the Order is to remove the prohibitions in respect of the sea designated.

5685. Food safety–emergency prohibitions–amnesic shellfish poisoning–partial revocation

FOOD PROTECTION (EMERGENCY PROHIBITIONS) (AMNESIC SHELLFISH POISONING) (WEST COAST) (NO.12) (SCOTLAND) PARTIAL REVOCATION

ORDER 2002, SSI 2002 552; made under the Food and Environment Protection Act 1985 s.1, s.24. In force: 02 at 5pm1216; £1.50.

This Order revokes in part the Food Protection (Emergency Prohibitions) (Amnesic Shellfish Poisoning) (West Coast) (No.12) (Scotland) Order 2002 (SSI 2002 430) which prohibited fishing for or taking scallops within the areas designated, movement of such scallops out of the designated areas and the landing, using in the preparation or processing for supply of food of, supplying and other specified activities in relation to, such scallops from the designated areas. The effect of the Order is to remove the prohibitions in respect of the area of sea designated.

5686. **Food safety–emergency prohibitions–amnesic shellfish poisoning–partial revocation**

FOOD PROTECTION (EMERGENCY PROHIBITIONS) (AMNESIC SHELLFISH POISONING) (WEST COAST) (NO.12) (SCOTLAND) PARTIAL REVOCATION ORDER 2002, SSI 2002 66; made under the Food and Environment Protection Act 1985 s.1, s.24. In force: February 20, 2002 at 4 pm; £1.75.

This Order partially revokes the Food Protection (Emergency Prohibitions) (Amnesic Shellfish Poisoning) (West Coast) (No.12) (Scotland) Order 2001 (SSI 2001 423) which prohibited fishing for or taking scallops within the area designated, movement of such scallops out of the designated area and landing, using in the preparation or processing for supply of food of, supplying and other specified activities in relation to, such scallops from the designated area.

5687. **Food safety–emergency prohibitions–amnesic shellfish poisoning–partial revocation**

FOOD PROTECTION (EMERGENCY PROHIBITIONS) (AMNESIC SHELLFISH POISONING) (WEST COAST) (NO.14) (SCOTLAND) PARTIAL REVOCATION ORDER 2002, SSI 2002 553; made under the Food and Environment Protection Act 1985 s.1), s.24. In force: 02 at 5pm1216; £1.50.

These Regulations revoke in part the Food Protection (Emergency Prohibitions) (Amnesic Shellfish Poisoning) (West Coast) (No.14) (Scotland) Order 2002 (SSI 2002 482) which prohibited the fishing for or taking scallops within the areas designated, movement of such scallops out of the designated areas and the landing, using in the preparation or processing for supply of food of, supplying and other specified activities in relation to, such scallops from the designated areas. The effect of the Order is to remove the prohibitions in respect of the area of sea designated.

5688. **Food safety–emergency prohibitions–amnesic shellfish poisoning–partial revocation**

FOOD PROTECTION (EMERGENCY PROHIBITIONS) (AMNESIC SHELLFISH POISONING) (WEST COAST) (NO.2) (SCOTLAND) PARTIAL REVOCATION ORDER 2002, SSI 2002 67; made under the Food and Environment Protection Act 1985 s.1, s.24. In force: February 21, 2002 at 2 pm; £1.75.

This Order amends the Food Protection (Emergency Prohibitions) (Amnesic Shellfish Poisoning) (West Coast) (No.2) (Scotland) Order 2001 (SSI 2001 281) which prohibited fishing for or taking scallops within the designated area, movement of such scallops out of the area and landing, using in the preparation or processing for supply of food of, supplying and other specified activities in relation to, such scallops from the designated area. The effect of this Order is to remove the prohibitions in respect of the area of sea designated.

5689. **Food safety–emergency prohibitions–amnesic shellfish poisoning–partial revocation**

FOOD PROTECTION (EMERGENCY PROHIBITIONS) (AMNESIC SHELLFISH POISONING) (WEST COAST) (NO.4) (SCOTLAND) PARTIAL REVOCATION

(NO.2) ORDER 2002, SSI 2002 19; made under the Food and Environment Protection Act 1985 s.1, s.24. In force: January 24, 2002 at 4 pm in accordance with Art.1; £1.50.

This Order is the second partial revocation of the Food Protection (Emergency Prohibitions) (Amnesic Shellfish Poisoning) (West Coast) (No.4) (Scotland) Order 2001 (SSI 2001 289) which prohibited fishing for or taking scallops within the designated areas, movement of such scallops out of these areas and the landing, using in the preparation or processing for supply of food of, supplying and other specified activities in relation to, such scallops from the designated areas. The effect of this Order is to remove the remaining prohibitions in respect of the areas of designated sea.

5690. Food safety—emergency prohibitions—amnesic shellfish poisoning—partial revocation

FOOD PROTECTION (EMERGENCY PROHIBITIONS) (AMNESIC SHELLFISH POISONING) (WEST COAST) (NO.5) (SCOTLAND) PARTIAL REVOCATION ORDER 2002, SSI 2002 383; made under the Food and Environment Protection Act 1985 s.1, s.24. In force: August 21, 2002 at 4 pm; £1.50.

This Order partially revokes the Food Protection (Emergency Prohibitions) (Amnesic Shellfish Poisoning) (West Coast) (No.8) (Scotland) Order 2002 (SSI 2002 306) which prohibited fishing for or taking scallops within the designated area, movement of such scallops out of the area and landing, using in the preparation or processing for supply of food of, supplying and other specified activities in relation to, such scallops from the designated area. The effect of this Order is to remove the prohibitions in respect of the area of sea designated.

5691. Food safety—emergency prohibitions—amnesic shellfish poisoning—partial revocation

FOOD PROTECTION (EMERGENCY PROHIBITIONS) (AMNESIC SHELLFISH POISONING) (WEST COAST) (NO.5) (SCOTLAND) PARTIAL REVOCATION (NO.2) ORDER 2002, SSI 2002 409; made under the Food and Environment Protection Act 1985 s.1, s.24. In force: September 4, 2002 at 4.30 pm; £1.50.

This Order revokes the Food Protection (Emergency Prohibitions) (Amnesic Shellfish Poisoning) (West Coast) (No.5) (Scotland) Order 2002 (SSI 2002 306) which prohibited fishing for or taking scallops within the designated area, movement of such scallops out of the area and landing, using in the preparation or processing for supply of food of, supplying and other specified activities in relation to, such scallops from the designated area. The effect of this Order is to remove the prohibitions in respect of the area of sea designated.

5692. Food safety—emergency prohibitions—amnesic shellfish poisoning—partial revocation

FOOD PROTECTION (EMERGENCY PROHIBITIONS) (AMNESIC SHELLFISH POISONING) (WEST COAST) (NO.6) (SCOTLAND) PARTIAL REVOCATION ORDER 2002, SSI 2002 551; made under the Food and Environment Protection Act 1985 s.1 (1) (2), s.24 (3). In force: 02 at 5pm1216; £1.50.

This Order revokes in part the Food Protection (Emergency Prohibitions) (Amnesic Shellfish Poisoning) (West Coast) (No.6) (Scotland) Order 2002 (SI 2002 307) which prohibited fishing for or taking scallops within the areas designated, movement of such scallops out of the designated areas and the landing, using in the preparation or processing for supply of food of, supplying and other specified activities in relation to, such scallops from the designated areas. The effect of the Order is to remove the prohibitions in respect of the area of sea designated.

5693. Food safety–emergency prohibitions–amnesic shellfish poisoning–revocation

FOOD PROTECTION (EMERGENCY PROHIBITIONS) (AMNESIC SHELLFISH POISONING) (ORKNEY) (NO.2) (SCOTLAND) REVOCATION ORDER 2002, SSI 2002 403; made under the Food and Environment Protection Act 1985 s.1. In force: August 30, 2002 at 4 pm; £1.50.

This Order revokes the Food Protection (Emergency Prohibitions) (Amnesic Shellfish Poisoning) (Orkney) (No.2) (Scotland) Order 2002 (SSI 2002 353) which prohibited fishing for or taking scallops within the designated area, movement of such scallops out of the area and landing, using in the preparation or processing for supply of food of, supplying and other specified activities in relation to, such scallops from the designated area. The effect of this Order is to remove the prohibitions in respect of the area of sea designated.

5694. Food safety–emergency prohibitions–amnesic shellfish poisoning–revocation

FOOD PROTECTION (EMERGENCY PROHIBITIONS) (AMNESIC SHELLFISH POISONING) (ORKNEY) (SCOTLAND) REVOCATION ORDER 2002, SSI 2002 402; made under the Food and Environment Protection Act 1985 s.1. In force: August 30, 2002 at 4 pm; £1.50.

This Order revokes the Food Protection (Emergency Prohibitions) (Amnesic Shellfish Poisoning) (Orkney) (Scotland) Order 2002 (SSI 2002 345) which prohibited fishing for or taking scallops within the designated area, movement of such scallops out of the area and landing, using in the preparation or processing for supply of food of, supplying and other specified activities in relation to, such scallops from the designated area. The effect of this Order is to remove the prohibitions in respect of the area of sea designated.

5695. Food safety–emergency prohibitions–amnesic shellfish poisoning–revocation

FOOD PROTECTION (EMERGENCY PROHIBITIONS) (AMNESIC SHELLFISH POISONING) (WEST COAST) (NO.11) (SCOTLAND) PARTIAL REVOCATION ORDER 2002, SSI 2002 545; made under the Food and Environment Protection Act 1985 s.1, s.24. In force: December 9, 2002 at 4 pm; £1.50.

This Order is a partial revocation of the Food Protection (Emergency Prohibitions) (Amnesic Shellfish Poisoning) (West Coast) (No.11) (Scotland) Order 2002 (SSI 2002 338) which prohibited fishing for or taking scallops within the areas designated; movement of such scallops out of the designated areas; and landing, using in the preparation or processing for supply of food of, supplying and other specified activities in relation to, such scallops from the designated areas. The effect of the Order is to remove the prohibitions in respect of the area of sea designated.

5696. Food safety–emergency prohibitions–amnesic shellfish poisoning–revocation

FOOD PROTECTION (EMERGENCY PROHIBITIONS) (AMNESIC SHELLFISH POISONING) (WEST COAST) (NO.12) (SCOTLAND) REVOCATION ORDER 2002, SSI 2002 198; made under the Food and Environment Protection Act 1985 s.1. In force: April 19, 2002 at 4 pm; £1.50.

This Order revokes the Food Protection (Emergency Prohibitions) (Amnesic Shellfish Poisoning) (West Coast) (No.12) (Scotland) Order 2001 (SSI 2001 423) which prohibited fishing for or taking scallops within the areas designated, movement of such scallops out of these areas and the landing, using in the preparation or processing for supply of food of, supplying and other specified activities in relation to, such scallops from the designated areas. It revokes the Food Protection (Emergency Prohibitions) (Amnesic Shellfish Poisoning) (West Coast) (No.12) (Scotland) Partial Revocation Order 2002 (SSI 2002 66) which partially revoked the 2001 Order and removes remaining prohibitions in respect of the designated area of sea.

5697. Food safety–emergency prohibitions–amnesic shellfish poisoning–revocation

FOOD PROTECTION (EMERGENCY PROHIBITIONS) (AMNESIC SHELLFISH POISONING) (WEST COAST) (NO.14) (SCOTLAND) REVOCATION ORDER 2002, SSI 2002 48; made under the Food and Environment Protection Act 1985 s.1. In force: February 7, 2002 at 5 pm; £1.50.

This Order revokes the Food Protection (Emergency Prohibitions) (Amnesic Shellfish Poisoning) (West Coast) (No.14) (Scotland) Order 2001 (SSI 2001 451) which prohibited fishing for or taking scallops within the designated area, movement of such scallops out of the area and landing, using in the preparation or processing for supply of food of, supplying and other specified activities in relation to, such scallops from the designated area. The effect of this Order is to remove the prohibitions in respect of the area of sea designated.

5698. Food safety–emergency prohibitions–amnesic shellfish poisoning–revocation

FOOD PROTECTION (EMERGENCY PROHIBITIONS) (AMNESIC SHELLFISH POISONING) (WEST COAST) (NO.16) (SCOTLAND) ORDER 2002, SSI 2002 544; made under the Food and Environment Protection Act 1985 s.1, s.24. In force: December 9, 2002 at 5 pm; £1.75.

This Order contains emergency prohibitions restricting various activities in order to prevent human consumption of food rendered unsuitable for that purpose by virtue of shellfish having been affected by the toxins which cause amnesic, paralytic and diarrhetic shellfish poisoning in human beings. It designates an area of sea off the West Coast of Scotland within which taking scallops is prohibited and prohibits the movement of scallops out of that area.

5699. Food safety–emergency prohibitions–amnesic shellfish poisoning–revocation

FOOD PROTECTION (EMERGENCY PROHIBITIONS) (AMNESIC SHELLFISH POISONING) (WEST COAST) (NO.2) (SCOTLAND) ORDER 2001 REVOCATION ORDER 2002, SSI 2002 182; made under the Food and Environment Protection Act 1985 s.1. In force: April 10, 2002 at 4 pm; £1.50.

This Order revokes the Food Protection (Emergency Prohibitions) (Amnesic Shellfish Poisoning) (West Coast) (No.2) (Scotland) Order 2001 (SSI 2001 281), the Food Protection (Emergency Prohibitions) (Amnesic Shellfish Poisoning) (West Coast) (No.2) (Scotland) Partial Revocation Order 2001 (SSI 2001 434) and the Food Protection (Emergency Prohibitions) (Amnesic Shellfish Poisoning) (West Coast) (No.2) (Scotland) Partial Revocation Order 2002 (SI 2002 67) which prohibited fishing for or taking scallops within the areas designated, movement of such scallops out of these areas and the landing, using in the preparation or processing for supply of food of, supplying and other specified activities in relation to, such scallops from the designated areas.

5700. Food safety–emergency prohibitions–amnesic shellfish poisoning–revocation

FOOD PROTECTION (EMERGENCY PROHIBITIONS) (AMNESIC SHELLFISH POISONING) (WEST COAST) (NO.2) (SCOTLAND) REVOCATION ORDER 2002, SSI 2002 183; made under the Food and Environment Protection Act 1985 s.1. In force: April 10, 2002 at 4 pm; £1.50.

This Order revokes the Food Protection (Emergency Prohibitions) (Amnesic Shellfish Poisoning) (West Coast) (No.2) (Scotland) Order 2002 (SSI 2002 65) which prohibited fishing for or taking scallops within the areas designated, movement of such scallops out of these areas and the landing, using in the preparation or processing for supply of food of, supplying and other specified activities in relation to, such scallops from the designated areas.

5701. Food safety–emergency prohibitions–amnesic shellfish poisoning–revocation

FOOD PROTECTION (EMERGENCY PROHIBITIONS) (AMNESIC SHELLFISH POISONING) (WEST COAST) (NO.3) (SCOTLAND) REVOCATION ORDER 2002, SSI 2002 218; made under the Food and Environment Protection Act 1985 s.1. In force: May 7, 2002 at 4 pm; £1.50.

This Order revokes the Food Protection (Emergency Prohibitions) (Amnesic Shellfish Poisoning) (West Coast) (No.3) (Scotland) Order 2002 (SSI 2002 80) which prohibited the fishing for or taking scallops within the specified area, the movement of such scallops out of that area and the landing, using in the preparation or processing for supply of food of, supplying and other specified activities in relation to, such scallops from the designated area. The effect of this Order is to remove the prohibitions in respect of the area of sea designated.

5702. Food safety–emergency prohibitions–amnesic shellfish poisoning–revocation

FOOD PROTECTION (EMERGENCY PROHIBITIONS) (AMNESIC SHELLFISH POISONING) (WEST COAST) (NO.4) (SCOTLAND) ORDER 2002 REVOCATION ORDER 2002, SSI 2002 550; made under the Food and Environment Protection Act 1985 s.1. In force: 02 at 5pm1216; £1.50.

This Order revokes the Food Protection (Emergency Prohibitions) (Amnesic Shellfish Poisoning) (West Coast) (No.4) (Scotland) Order 2002 (SSI 2002 231) which prohibited fishing for or taking scallops within the designated areas, movement of such scallops out of that area and landing, using in the preparation or processing for supply of food of, supplying and other specified activities in relation to, such scallops from the designated area. The effect of the Order is to remove the prohibitions in respect of the area of sea designated.

5703. Food safety–emergency prohibitions–amnesic shellfish poisoning–revocation

FOOD PROTECTION (EMERGENCY PROHIBITIONS) (AMNESIC SHELLFISH POISONING) (WEST COAST) (NO.4) (SCOTLAND) REVOCATION ORDER 2002, SSI 2002 160; made under the Food and Environment Protection Act 1985 s.1. In force: March 26, 2002 at 5 pm; £1.50.

This Order revokes Food Protection (Emergency Prohibitions) (Amnesic Shellfish Poisoning) (West Coast) (No.4) (Scotland) Order 2001 (SSI 2001 289), the Food Protection (Emergency Prohibitions) (Amnesic Shellfish Poisoning) (West Coast) (No.4) (Scotland) Partial Revocation Order 2001 (SSI 2001 473) and the Food Protection (Emergency Prohibitions) (Amnesic Shellfish Poisoning) (West Coast) (No.4) (Scotland) Partial Revocation (No.2) Order 2002 (SSI 2002 19) which prohibited fishing for or taking scallops within the areas designated, movement of such scallops out of these areas and the landing, using in the preparation or processing for supply of food of, supplying and other specified activities in relation to, such scallops from the designated areas.

5704. Food safety–emergency prohibitions–amnesic shellfish poisoning–revocation

FOOD PROTECTION (EMERGENCY PROHIBITIONS) (AMNESIC SHELLFISH POISONING) (WEST COAST) (NO.5) (SCOTLAND) REVOCATION ORDER 2002, SSI 2002 126; made under the Food and Environment Protection Act 1985 s.1. In force: March 8, 2002 at 2 pm; £1.50.

This Order revokes the Food Protection (Emergency Prohibitions) (Amnesic Shellfish Poisoning) (West Coast) (No.5) (Scotland) Order 2001 (SSI 2001 295) which prohibited fishing for or taking scallops within designated areas, movement of such scallops out of those areas and landing, using in the preparation or processing for supply of food of, supplying and other specified activities in relation to, such scallops from the designated areas. The Order removes the prohibitions in respect of the areas of sea designated.

5705. Food safety—emergency prohibitions—amnesic shellfish poisoning—revocation

FOOD PROTECTION (EMERGENCY PROHIBITIONS) (AMNESIC SHELLFISH POISONING) (WEST COAST) (NO.5) (SCOTLAND) REVOCATION ORDER 2002, SSI 2002 431; made under the Food and Environment Protection Act 1985 s.1. In force: September 18, 2002 at 4 pm; £1.50.

This Order revokes the Food Protection (Emergency Prohibitions) (Amnesic Shellfish Poisoning) (West Coast) (No.5) (Scotland) Order 2002 (SSI 2002 306) which prohibited fishing for or taking scallops within the designated area; the movement of such scallops out of the designated areas; and landing, using in the preparation or processing for supply of food of, supplying and other specified activities in relation to, such scallops from the designated areas. It also revokes the Food Protection (Emergency Prohibitions) (Amnesic Shellfish Poisoning) (West Coast) (No.5) (Scotland) Partial Revocation Order 2002 (SSI 2002 383) and the Food Protection (Emergency Prohibitions) (Amnesic Shellfish Poisoning) (West Coast) (No.5) (Scotland) Partial Revocation (No.2) Order 2002 (SSI 2002 409). The effect of this Order is to remove the remaining prohibitions in respect of the areas of sea designated.

5706. Food safety—emergency prohibitions—amnesic shellfish poisoning—revocation

FOOD PROTECTION (EMERGENCY PROHIBITIONS) (AMNESIC SHELLFISH POISONING) (WEST COAST) (NO.7) (SCOTLAND) ORDER 2002 REVOCATION ORDER 2002, SSI 2002 422; made under the Food and Environment Protection Act 1985 s.1. In force: September 11, 2002 at 4 pm; £1.50.

This Order revokes the Food Protection (Emergency Prohibitions) (Amnesic Shellfish Poisoning) (West Coast) (No.7) (Scotland) Order 2002 (SSI 2002 232) which prohibited fishing for or taking scallops within the areas designated; movement of such scallops out of those areas; and landing, using in the preparation or processing for supply of food of, supplying and other specified activities in relation to, such scallops from the designated areas. The effect of this Order is to remove the prohibitions in respect of the areas of sea designated.

5707. Food safety—emergency prohibitions—amnesic shellfish poisoning—revocation

FOOD PROTECTION (EMERGENCY PROHIBITIONS) (AMNESIC SHELLFISH POISONING) (WEST COAST) (NO.7) (SCOTLAND) REVOCATION ORDER 2002, SSI 2002 20; made under the Food and Environment Protection Act 1985 s.1. In force: January 24, 2002 at 4 pm; £1.50.

This Order revokes the Food Protection (Emergency Prohibitions) (Amnesic Shellfish Poisoning) (West Coast) (No.7) (Scotland) Order 2001 (SSI 2001 322) which prohibited the fishing for or taking scallops within the designated area, the movement of such scallops out of that area and the landing, using in the preparation or processing for supply of food of, supplying and other specified activities in relation to, such scallops from the designated area. This Order removes the prohibitions in respect of the area of sea designated.

5708. Food safety—emergency prohibitions—amnesic shellfish poisoning—revocation

FOOD PROTECTION (EMERGENCY PROHIBITIONS) (AMNESIC SHELLFISH POISONING) (WEST COAST) (NO.8) (SCOTLAND) REVOCATION ORDER

2002, SSI 2002 127; made under the Food and Environment Protection Act 1985 s.1. In force: March 8, 2002 at 2 pm; £1.50.

This Order revokes the Food Protection (Emergency Prohibitions) (Amnesic Shellfish Poisoning) (West Coast) (No.8) (Scotland) Order 2001 (SSI 2001 374) which prohibited fishing for or taking scallops within designated areas, movement of such scallops out of those areas and landing, using in the preparation or processing for supply of food of, supplying and other specified activities in relation to, such scallops from the designated areas. The Order removes the prohibitions in respect of the areas of sea designated.

5709. Food safety–emergency prohibitions–amnesic shellfish poisoning–revocation

FOOD PROTECTION (EMERGENCY PROHIBITIONS) (AMNESIC SHELLFISH POISONING) (WEST COAST) (NO.8) (SCOTLAND) REVOCATION ORDER 2002, SSI 2002 384; made under the Food and Environment Protection Act 1985 s.1. In force: August 21, 2002 at 4 pm; £1.50.

This Order revokes the Food Protection (Emergency Prohibitions) (Amnesic Shellfish Poisoning) (West Coast) (No.8) (Scotland) Order 2002 (SSI 2002 333) which prohibited fishing for or taking scallops within the designated area, movement of such scallops out of the area and landing, using in the preparation or processing for supply of food of, supplying and other specified activities in relation to, such scallops from the designated area. The effect of this Order is to remove the prohibitions in respect of the area of sea designated.

5710. Food safety–emergency prohibitions–amnesic shellfish poisoning–revocation

FOOD PROTECTION (EMERGENCY PROHIBITIONS) (AMNESIC SHELLFISH POISONING) (WEST COAST) (NO.9) (SCOTLAND) REVOCATION ORDER 2002, SSI 2002 401; made under the Food and Environment Protection Act 1985 s.1. In force: August 30, 2002 at 4 pm; £1.50.

This Order revokes the Food Protection (Emergency Prohibitions) (Amnesic Shellfish Poisoning) (West Coast) (No.9) (Scotland) Order 2002 (SSI 2002 350) which prohibited fishing for or taking scallops within the designated area, movement of such scallops out of the area and landing, using in the preparation or processing for supply of food of, supplying and other specified activities in relation to, such scallops from the designated area. The effect of this Order is to remove the prohibitions in respect of the area of sea designated.

5711. Food safety–emergency prohibitions–amnesic shellfish poisoning–revocation

FOOD PROTECTION (EMERGENCY PROHIBITIONS) (AMNESIC SHELLFISH POISONING) (WEST COAST) (NO.9) (SCOTLAND) REVOCATION ORDER 2002, SSI 2002 9; made under the Food and Environment Protection Act 1985 s.1. In force: January 14, 2002 at 4 pm in accordance with Art.1; £1.50.

This Order revokes the Food Protection (Emergency Prohibitions) (Amnesic Shellfish Poisoning) (West Coast) (No.9) (Scotland) Order 2001 (SSI 2001 388) and the Food Protection (Emergency Prohibitions) (Amnesic Shellfish Poisoning) (West Coast) (No.9) (Scotland) Partial Revocation Order 2001 (SSI 2001 469) which prohibited fishing for or taking scallops within the designated areas, movement of such scallops out of these areas and the landing, using in the preparation or processing for supply of food of, supplying and other specified activities in relation to, such scallops from the designated areas. The effect of this Order is to remove the remaining prohibitions in respect of the areas of designated sea.

5712. Food safety—emergency prohibitions—amnesic shellfish poisoning—revocation

FOOD PROTECTION (EMERGENCY PROHIBITIONS) (AMNESIC SHELLFISH POISONING) (WEST COAST) (SCOTLAND) REVOCATION ORDER 2002, SSI 2002 152; made under the Food and Environment Protection Act 1985 s.1. In force: March 20, 2002 at 4 pm; £1.50.

This Order revokes the Food Protection (Emergency Prohibitions) (Amnesic Shellfish Poisoning) (West Coast) (Scotland) Order 2002 (SSI 2002 49) which prohibited fishing for or taking scallops within the designated area, movement of such scallops out of that area and landing, using in the preparation or processing for supply of food of, supplying and other specified activities in relation to, such scallops from the designated area. The effect of this Order is to remove the prohibitions in respect of the area of sea designated.

5713. Food safety—emergency prohibitions—amnesic shellfish poisoning—scallops

FOOD PROTECTION (EMERGENCY PROHIBITIONS) (AMNESIC SHELLFISH POISONING) (WEST COAST) (NO.4) (SCOTLAND) ORDER 2002, SSI 2002 231; made under the Food and Environment Protection Act 1985 s.1, s.24. In force: May 14, 2002 at 4 pm; £1.75.

This Order contains emergency prohibitions restricting various activities in order to prevent human consumption of food rendered unsuitable for that purpose by virtue of shellfish having been affected by the toxin which causes amnesic shellfish poisoning in human beings. It designates an area of sea off the west coast of Scotland within which taking scallops is prohibited and prohibits the movement of scallops out of that area.

5714. Food safety—emergency prohibitions—amnesic shellfish poisoning—scallops

FOOD PROTECTION (EMERGENCY PROHIBITIONS) (AMNESIC SHELLFISH POISONING) (WEST COAST) (NO.5) (SCOTLAND) ORDER 2002, SSI 2002 306; made under the Food and Environment Protection Act 1985 s.1, s.24. In force: June 24, 2002 at 4.30 pm; £1.75.

This Order, which contains emergency prohibitions restricting various activities in order to prevent human consumption of food rendered unsuitable for that purpose by virtue of shellfish having been affected by the toxin which causes amnesic shellfish poisoning in human beings, designates three areas of sea off the west coast of Scotland within which taking scallops is prohibited. It prohibits the movement of scallops out of those areas.

5715. Food safety—emergency prohibitions—amnesic shellfish poisoning—scallops

FOOD PROTECTION (EMERGENCY PROHIBITIONS) (AMNESIC SHELLFISH POISONING) (WEST COAST) (NO.6) (SCOTLAND) ORDER 2002, SSI 2002 307; made under the Food and Environment Protection Act 1985 s.1, s.24. In force: June 24, 2002 at 4.30 pm; £1.75.

This Order, which contains emergency prohibitions restricting various activities in order to prevent human consumption of food rendered unsuitable for that purpose by virtue of shellfish having been affected by the toxin which causes amnesic shellfish poisoning in human beings, designates areas off the west coast of Scotland within which taking scallops is prohibited. It prohibits the movement of scallops out of those areas.

5716. Food safety—emergency prohibitions—amnesic, paralytic and diarrhetic shellfish poisoning—revocation

FOOD PROTECTION (EMERGENCY PROHIBITIONS) (AMNESIC, PARALYTIC AND DIARRHETIC SHELLFISH POISONING) (ORKNEY) (SCOTLAND)

REVOCATION ORDER 2002, SSI 2002 197; made under the Food and Environment Protection Act 1985 s.1. In force: April 19, 2002 at 4 pm; £1.50.

This Order revokes the Food Protection (Emergency Prohibitions) (Amnesic, Paralytic and Diarrhetic Shellfish Poisoning) (Orkney) (Scotland) Order 2001 (SSI 2001 282) which prohibited fishing for or taking scallops within the designated area, movement of such scallops out of that area and landing, using in the preparation or processing for supply of food of, supplying and other specified activities in relation to, such scallops from the designated area. It also revokes the Food Protection (Emergency Prohibitions) (Amnesic, Paralytic and Diarrhetic Shellfish Poisoning) (Orkney) (Scotland) Partial Revocation Order 2001 (SSI 2001 463) and removes remaining prohibitions in respect of scallops of the class pecten maximus in respect of the designated area of sea.

5717. Food safety—emergency prohibitions—diarrhetic shellfish poisoning—revocation

FOOD PROTECTION (EMERGENCY PROHIBITIONS) (DIARRHETIC SHELLFISH POISONING) (ORKNEY) (SCOTLAND) REVOCATION ORDER 2002, SSI 2002 57; made under the Food and Environment Protection Act 1985 s.1. In force: February 12, 2002 at 4 pm; £1.50.

This Order revokes the Food Protection (Emergency Prohibitions) (Diarrhetic Shellfish Poisoning) (Orkney) (Scotland) Order 2001 (SSI 2001 391) which prohibited fishing for or taking scallops within the area designated, movement of such scallops out of the designated area and landing, using in the preparation or processing for supply of food of, supplying and other specified activities in relation to, such scallops from the designated area.

5718. Food safety—emergency prohibitions—paralytic shellfish poisoning—revocation

FOOD PROTECTION (EMERGENCY PROHIBITIONS) (PARALYTIC SHELLFISH POISONING) (ORKNEY) (NO.3) (SCOTLAND) REVOCATION ORDER 2002, SSI 2002 82; made under the Food and Environment Protection Act 1985 s.1. In force: March 4, 2002 at 4 pm; £1.50.

This Order revokes the Food Protection (Emergency Prohibitions) (Paralytic Shellfish Poisoning) (Orkney) (No.3) (Scotland) Order 2001 (SSI 2001 255) which prohibited fishing for or taking scallops within the designated area, the movement of such scallops out of that area and landing, using in the preparation or processing for supply of food of, supplying and other specified activities in relation to, such scallops from the designated area. The effect of this Order is to remove the prohibitions in respect of the area of sea designated.

5719. Food safety—food hygiene—meat products—hazard analysis and critical control point

MEAT (HAZARD ANALYSIS AND CRITICAL CONTROL POINT) (SCOTLAND) REGULATIONS 2002, SSI 2002 234; made under the Food Safety Act 1990 s.6, s.16, s.17, s.26, s.48. In force: June 7, 2002 in accordance with Reg.3; £3.00.

These Regulations, which amend the Fresh Meat (Hygiene and Inspection) Regulations 1995 (SI 1995 539), the Poultry Meat, Farmed Game Bird Meat and Rabbit Meat (Hygiene and Inspection) Regulations 1995 (SI 1995 540) and the Products of Animal Origin (Import and Export) Regulations 1996 (SI 1996 3124), give effect to Commission Decision 2001/471 ([2001] OJ L165/48) laying down rules for the regular checks on the general hygiene carried out by the operators in establishments according to Directive 64/433 on health conditions for the production and marketing of fresh meat and Directive 71/118 ([1971] OJ L55/23) on health problems affecting the production and placing on the market of fresh poultry meat.

5720. **Food safety–imports–star anise–emergency controls**

FOOD (STAR ANISE FROM THIRD COUNTRIES) (EMERGENCY CONTROL) (SCOTLAND) ORDER 2002, SSI 2002 64; made under the Food Safety Act 1990 s.6, s.13, s.48. In force: February 16, 2002; £1.75.

This Order is made in consequence of it appearing to the Scottish Ministers that the importation into Scotland of star anise consigned from certain third countries which are not member States of the European Community may involve imminent risk of injury to health. The Order, which implements Commission Decision 2002/ 75 ([2002] OJ L33/31) laying down special conditions on the import from third countries of Star Anise, prohibits the importation of "Star Anise for human consumption" consigned from countries which are not Member States of the European Community except where it is accompanied by health certificates completed by the competent authority of the exporting third country and a report on the results of official sampling and analysis undertaken in that country, the importation takes place only through specified points of entry and the consignment is identified with a code corresponding with that specified on the health certificate and in the sampling and analysis results. It also prohibits the importation of "Japanese Star Anise" intended for human consumption or which is not labelled to the effect that it is unfit for such use.

5721. **Food safety–ionising radiation–control**

FOOD (CONTROL OF IRRADIATION) AMENDMENT (SCOTLAND) REGULATIONS 2002, SSI 2002 284; made under the Food Safety Act 1990 s.6, s.16, s.17, s.18, s.19, s.26, s.48, Sch.1 para.1, Sch.1 para.4. In force: July 1, 2002; £1.75.

These Regulations amend the Food (Control of Irradiation) Regulations 1990 (SI 1990 2490) in accordance with Council Directive 1999/2 ([1999] OJ L66/16) concerning foods and food ingredients treated with ionising radiation and Council Directive 1999/3 ([1999] OJ L66/24) on the establishment of a Community list of foods and food ingredients treated with ionising radiation. They re-enact provisions in a clarified format for the documents required to accompany foods treated with ionising radiation and clarify ambiguities in the wording of the principal Regulations.

5722. **Food safety–packaging–plastics**

PLASTIC MATERIALS AND ARTICLES IN CONTACT WITH FOOD (AMENDMENT) (SCOTLAND) REGULATIONS 2002, SSI 2002 498; made under the Food Safety Act 1990 s.6, s.16, s.17, s.26, s.31, s.48. In force: November 30, 2002; £4.50.

These Regulations, which amend the Plastic Materials and Articles in Contact with Food Regulations 1998 (SI 1998 1376), implement Commission Directive 2001/62 ([2001] OJ L221/18) amending Directive 90/128 relating to plastic materials and articles intended to come into contact with foodstuffs; Commission Directive 2002/16 ([2002] OJ L51/27) on the use of certain epoxy derivatives in materials and articles intended to come into contact with foodstuffs; and Commission Directive 2002/17 ([2002] OJ L58/19) amending Directive 90/128 relating to plastic materials and articles intended to come into contact with foodstuffs. They also reflect the revocation of Commission Directive 90/128 ([1990] OJ L75/19) relating to plastic materials and articles intended to come into contact with foodstuffs and add a provision declaring that, in addition to regulating the contact with food of certain types of plastic materials and articles, the 1998 Regulations now also include provisions which regulate the contact with food of certain other types of food contact materials, namely adhesives and materials or articles covered by surface coatings.

5723. Imports–emergency controls–figs, hazelnuts and pistachios from Turkey

FOOD (FIGS, HAZELNUTS AND PISTACHIOS FROM TURKEY) (EMERGENCY CONTROL) (SCOTLAND) REGULATIONS 2002, SSI 2002 148; made under the European Communities Act 1972 s.2. In force: March 25, 2002 at 5 pm; £2.00.

These Regulations, which implement Commission Decision 2002/80 ([2002] OJ L34/26) imposing special conditions on the import of figs, hazelnuts and pistachios and certain products derived thereof originating in or consigned from Turkey, prohibit the importation of any controlled Turkish products except where they are accompanied by a Turkish Government health certificate and the results of official sampling and analysis, the importation takes place only through a specified point of entry, and the consignment is identified with a code corresponding with that specified on the health certificate and on the accompanying report containing the sampling and analysis results or if they left Turkey before March 11, 2002. They also specify the enforcement authorities and apply, with modifications, provisions of the Food Safety Act 1990.

5724. Imports–emergency controls–figs, hazelnuts and pistachios from Turkey

FOOD (FIGS, HAZELNUTS AND PISTACHIOS FROM TURKEY) (EMERGENCY CONTROL) (SCOTLAND) (NO.2) REGULATIONS 2002, SSI 2002 424; made under the European Communities Act 1972 s.2. In force: September 13, 2002; £2.00.

These Regulations, which revoke the Food (Figs, Hazelnuts and Pistachios from Turkey) (Emergency Control) (Scotland) Regulations 2002 (SSI 2002 148), implement Commission Decision 2002/80 ([2002] OJ L34/26) imposing special conditions on the import of figs, hazelnuts and pistachios and certain products derived thereof originating in or consigned from Turkey. They prohibit the importation of any controlled Turkish products except where they are accompanied by a Turkish Government health certificate and the results of official sampling and analysis, the importation takes place only through a specified point of entry, and the consignment is identified with a code corresponding with that specified on the health certificate and on the accompanying report containing the sampling and analysis results or if they left Turkey before March 11, 2002. They also specify the enforcement authorities and apply, with modifications, provisions of the Food Safety Act 1990. These Regulations amend the definition of Turkish figs, hazelnuts and pistachios to remove fresh figs and include fig paste and hazelnut paste; provide that the previous requirement that consignments of Turkish figs, hazelnuts and pistachios be subjected to random sampling and analysis to ensure compliance with Commission Decision 2002/80 is modified; provide that the sampling procedure for hazelnuts is modified; and an authorised officer of a food authority is empowered to issue a notice ordering the re-dispatch or destruction of illegal imports of Turkish figs, hazelnuts and pistachios.

5725. Imports–emergency controls–jelly confectionery

FOOD (JELLY CONFECTIONERY) (EMERGENCY CONTROL) (SCOTLAND) REGULATIONS 2002, SSI 2002 179; made under the European Communities Act 1972 s.2. In force: April 4, 2002; £2.00.

These Regulations, which implement Commission Decision 2002/24 ([2002] OJ L84/69) suspending the placing on the market and import of jelly confectionery containing the food additive E425: Konjac, prohibit the carrying out of commercial operations with regard to jelly confectionery which contains the food additive E425: Konjac and which is intended for human consumption and also the use of that additive in the manufacture of jelly confectionery intended for human consumption. The Regulations also specify the enforcement authority and make consequential provisions relating to the execution and enforcement of the Regulations by that authority and apply, with modifications, provisions of the Food Safety Act 1990 and the Food Safety (Sampling and Qualifications) Regulations 1990 (SI 1990 2463).

5726. Imports–emergency controls–peanuts from China

FOOD (PEANUTS FROM CHINA) (EMERGENCY CONTROL) (SCOTLAND) REGULATIONS 2002, SSI 2002 149; made under the European Communities Act 1972 s.2. In force: March 25, 2002 at 5 pm; £2.00.

These Regulations implement Commission Decision 2002/79 ([2002] OJ L34/21) imposing special conditions on the import of peanuts and certain products derived from peanuts originating in, or consigned from, China. They prohibit the importation of "Chinese peanuts" except where they are accompanied by a Chinese Government health certificate and the results of official sampling and analysis. The importation takes place through a specified point of entry and the consignment is identified.

5727. Imports–emergency controls–peanuts from China

FOOD (PEANUTS FROM CHINA) (EMERGENCY CONTROL) (SCOTLAND) (NO.2) REGULATIONS 2002, SSI 2002 425; made under the European Communities Act 1972 s.2. In force: September 13, 2002; £2.00.

These Regulations, which revoke the Food (Peanuts from China) (Emergency Control) (Scotland) Regulations 2002 (SSI 2002 149), implement Commission Decision 2002/79 ([2002] OJ L34/21) imposing special conditions on the import of peanuts and certain products derived from peanuts originating in, or consigned from China. The Regulations prohibit the importation of "Chinese peanuts" except where they are accompanied by a Chinese Government health certificate and the results of official sampling and analysis, the importation takes place only through a specified point of entry and the consignment and each of its constituent bags or other containers are identified with a code corresponding with that specified on the health certificate and on the accompanying report containing the sampling and analysis results; or they left China before March 11, 2002; provide for their enforcement; apply certain provisions of the Food Safety Act 1990; and provide for the redispatch or destruction of illegal imports of controlled Chinese peanuts. These Regulations provide that the previous requirement that each consignment of controlled Chinese peanuts be identified by a code is additionally applied to each bag making up the consignment concerned; that the previous requirement that each consignment of controlled Chinese peanuts be subjected to sampling and analysis to ensure compliance with Commission Decision 2002/79 is modified; and that an authorised officer of the relevant enforcement authority is empowered to issue a notice ordering the re-dispatch of illegal imports of controlled Chinese peanuts.

5728. Labelling–food labelling–implementation of Council Directive 2001/101

FOOD LABELLING AMENDMENT (SCOTLAND) REGULATIONS 2002, SSI 2002 524; made under the Food Safety Act 1990 s.6, s.16, s.17, s.26, s.48. In force: January 1, 2003; £1.75.

These Regulations, which amend the Food Labelling Regulations 1996 (SI 1996 1489), implement Commission Decision 2001/101 ([2001] OJ L38/24) concerning the approval of an Agreement in the form of an Exchange of Letters between the Community and each of the EFTA countries that grants tariff preferences under the Generalised System of Preferences (Norway and Switzerland), providing that goods with content of Norwegian or Swiss origin shall be treated on their arrival on the customs territory of the Community as goods with content of Community origin and Commission Directive 2002/86 ([2002] OJ L305/19) amending Directive 2001/101 [2001] OJ L310/19 as regards the date from which trade in products not in conformity with Directive 2000/13 ([2000] OJ L109/29) of the European Parliament and of the Council is prohibited. They allow the use of the generic name "meat" with the name of the animal species from which it comes for skeletal muscles of mammalian and bird species in ingredients lists, subject to certain conditions and insert a transitional provision in respect of that generic name.

5729. Marketing—food for particular nutritional uses

NOTIFICATION OF MARKETING OF FOOD FOR PARTICULAR NUTRITIONAL USES (SCOTLAND) REGULATIONS 2002, SSI 2002 50; made under the Food Safety Act 1990 s.6, s.17, s.26, s.48. In force: March 8, 2002; £1.75.

These Regulations implement Council Directive 89/398 ([1989] OJ L186/27) Art.9 relating to foodstuffs intended for particular nutritional uses. The Regulations concern foods which, owing to their special composition or manufacturing process, are clearly distinguishable from foods for normal consumption, and which are marketed as suitable for categories of consumers with disturbed digestive processes or metabolism or in a special physiological condition, or for infants or young children in good health, but which are neither covered nor to be covered by other Directives on specific types of foodstuffs for particular nutritional uses.

FORESTRY

5730. Leases—woodland tenancy—delectus personae

See LANDLORD AND TENANT: Scottish Ministers v. Trustees of the Drummond Trust. §5924

GOVERNMENT ADMINISTRATION

5731. Devolution—Scottish Administration—offices

SCOTTISH ADMINISTRATION (OFFICES) ORDER 2002, SI 2002 801; made under the Scotland Act 1998 s.126. In force: in accordance with Art.1 (1); £1.50.

This Order specifies the office of the Drinking Water Quality Regulator as an office in the Scottish Administration which is not a ministerial office for the purposes of the Scotland Act 1998. This enables funds to be paid to the Regulator under the Scotland Act 1998 s.65 and places the Regulator under specific accounting obligations under the Public Finance and Accountability (Scotland) Act 2000.

5732. Freedom of Information (Scotland) Act 2002 (asp 13)—Commencement No.1 Order

FREEDOM OF INFORMATION (SCOTLAND) ACT 2002 (COMMENCEMENT NO.1) ORDER 2002, SSI 2002 437; made under the Freedom of Information (Scotland) Act 2002 s.75. Commencement details: bringing into force various provisions of the 2001 Act on September 30, 2002; £1.50.

This Order brings into force specified provisions of the Freedom of Information (Scotland) Act 2002 which specify which bodies are to be subject to the Act including machinery to have bodies removed from or added to the list of those specified, and to have the Act apply with limited application; establish the office of Scottish Information Commissioner and set out the Commissioner's functions and conditions attached to the functions; enable the Scottish Information Commissioner to make model publication schemes and enable the Scottish Ministers to issue codes of practice, and to make regulations for the purpose of implementing the information provisions of the Aarhus Convention and to replace or amend enactments prohibiting disclosure; and amend the Public Records (Scotland) Act 1937.

5733. Mental patients–public guardians–fees

ADULTS WITH INCAPACITY (PUBLIC GUARDIAN'S FEES) (SCOTLAND) AMENDMENT REGULATIONS 2002, SSI 2002 131; made under the Adults with Incapacity (Scotland) Act 2000 s.7, s.86. In force: April 22, 2002; £1.75.

These Regulations amend the Adults with Incapacity (Public Guardian's Fees) (Scotland) Regulations 2001 (SSI 2001 75) to make provision for the fees which may be charged by the Public Guardian for providing certain services under Adults with Incapacity (Scotland) Act 2000.

5734. Ministers–Scottish Ministers–agency arrangements

SCOTLAND ACT 1998 (AGENCY ARRANGEMENTS) (SPECIFICATION) ORDER 2002, SI 2002 261; made under the Scotland Act 1998 s.93, s.113. In force: March 15, 2002; £1.75.

This Order specifies functions of the Scottish Ministers for the purposes of the Scotland Act 1998 s.93 which allows a Minister of the Crown to make arrangements for any of that Minister's specified functions to be exercised on his or her behalf by the Scottish Ministers and allows the Scottish Ministers to make arrangements for any of their specified functions to be exercised on their behalf by a Minister of the Crown. The functions of the Scottish Ministers which are specified by the Order are the non-statutory functions of preparing, by means of an emissions trading scheme, for the implementation of the UK's obligations under the Kyoto Protocol adopted on December 11, 1997 to the United Nations Framework Convention on Climate Change, which was adopted on May 9, 1992 and came into force on March 21, 1994.

5735. Ministers–Scottish Ministers–agency arrangements

SCOTLAND ACT 1998 (AGENCY ARRANGEMENTS) (SPECIFICATION) (NO.2) ORDER 2002, SI 2002 800; made under the Scotland Act 1998 s.93, s.113. In force: May 3, 2002; £1.75.

This Order, which revokes the Scotland Act 1998 (Agency Arrangements) (Specification) Order 2001 (SI 2001 3917), specifies functions of the Scottish Ministers for the purposes of the Scotland Act 1998 s.93(2) which allows a Minister of the Crown to make arrangements for any of that Minister's specified functions to be exercised on his or her behalf by the Scottish Ministers and allows the Scottish Ministers to make arrangements for any of their specified functions to be exercised on their behalf by a Minister of the Crown. The functions of the Scottish Ministers which are specified by the Order relate to the public register of applications and consents to release genetically modified organisms, relate to applications for consent to release genetically modified organisms in Scotland, relate to applications for consent to market in Europe genetically modified organisms as or in a product where it is proposed that the product be marketed first in Scotland, relate to the assessment of ambient air quality and relates to the Environmental Protection (Controls on Ozone-Depleting Substances) Regulations 2002 (SI 2002 528), which make provision in relation to Council Regulation 2037/2000 ([2000] OJ L244/1) on substances that deplete the ozone layer.

5736. Public services–ombudsman–payment of expenses

SCOTTISH PUBLIC SERVICES OMBUDSMAN ACT 2002 (TRANSITORY AND TRANSITIONAL PROVISIONS) ORDER 2002, SSI 2002 469; made under the Scottish Public Services Ombudsman Act 2002 s.26. In force: October 23, 2002; £1.75.

This Order makes transitory and transitional provisions in relation to the payment of the expenses of the Scottish Public Services Ombudsman and in relation to the provision of accommodation for the Ombudsman. It provides that Audit Scotland is to pay certain expenses of the Ombudsman and make arrangements for the provision of offices and other accommodation for the Ombudsman; and that the

Order, unless it is previously revoked, shall cease to have effect on December 31, 2003

5737. Public services–ombudsman investigations–removal from list

SCOTTISH PUBLIC SERVICES OMBUDSMAN ACT 2002 (AMENDMENT) ORDER 2002, SSI 2002 468; made under the Scottish Public Services Ombudsman Act 2002 s.3. In force: October 23, 2002; £1.50.

This Order amends the Scottish Public Services Ombudsman Act 2002 Sch.2 Part 2 which specifies persons liable to investigation by the Scottish Public Services Ombudsman. The Order removes from the list of persons specified for this purpose the Traffic Commissioner for the Scottish Traffic Area.

5738. Scottish Public Services Ombudsman Act 2002 (asp 11)

This Act makes provision (including provision for the purposes of the Scotland Act 1998 s.91) for the appointment and functions of the Scottish Public Services Ombudsman.

This Act received Royal Assent on April 23, 2002.

5739. Scottish Public Services Ombudsman Act 2002 (asp 11)–Commencement and Revocation of Transitory and Transitional Provisions Order

SCOTTISH PUBLIC SERVICES OMBUDSMAN ACT 2002 (COMMENCEMENT AND REVOCATION OF TRANSITORY AND TRANSITIONAL PROVISIONS) ORDER 2002, SSI 2002 467; made under the Scottish Public Services Ombudsman Act 2002 s.27. Commencement details: bringing into force various provisions of the Act on October 23, 2002; £1.50.

This Order brings into force on October 23, 2002 the sections of the Scottish Public Services Ombudsman Act 2002 not brought into force on Royal Assent and revokes the Scotland Act 1998 (Transitory and Transitional Provisions) (Complaints of Maladministration) Order 1999 (SI 1999 1351)

HEALTH

5740. Community care–NHS and local authorities–joint working–functions

COMMUNITY CARE (JOINT WORKING ETC.) (SCOTLAND) REGULATIONS 2002, SSI 2002 533; made under the Community Care and Health (Scotland) Act 2002 s.13, s.14, s.15, s.17. In force: January 1, 2003; £2.50.

These Regulations prescribe those functions which may be the subject of payments or of delegation between local authorities and NHS bodies in accordance with the Community Care and Health (Scotland) Act 2002 Part 2 and the terms and conditions and related provisions, subject to which these arrangements take place.

5741. Community Care and Health (Scotland) Act 2002 (asp 5)–Commencement No.1 Order

COMMUNITY CARE AND HEALTH (SCOTLAND) ACT 2002 (COMMENCEMENT NO.1) ORDER 2002, SSI 2002 170; made under the Community Care and Health (Scotland) Act 2002 s.27. Commencement details: bringing into force various provisions of the 2002 Act in accordance with Art.2; £1.75.

This Order brings into force specified provisions of the Community Care and Health (Scotland) Act 2002 relating to carers and joint working arrangements between local authorities and certain NHS bodies.

5742. Health and Social Care Act 2001–Commencement No.9 Order

HEALTH AND SOCIAL CARE ACT 2001 (COMMENCEMENT NO.9) (SCOTLAND) ORDER 2002, SSI 2002 75; made under the Health and Social Care Act 2001 s.70. Commencement details: bringing into force various provisions of the 2001 Act on April 1, 2002; £1.50.

This Order brings into force specified sections of the Health and Social Care Act 2001.

5743. Medical profession–nurses, midwives and health visitors–professional conduct

NURSES, MIDWIVES AND HEALTH VISITORS (PROFESSIONAL CONDUCT) (AMENDMENT) RULES 2002 APPROVAL (SCOTLAND) ORDER 2002, SSI 2002 59; made under the Nurses, Midwives and Health Visitors Act 1997 s.19. In force: February 18, 2002; £1.75.

This Order approves the Nurses, Midwives and Health Visitors (Professional Conduct) (Amendment) Rules 2002 which are set out in the Schedule. They amend the Nurses, Midwives and Health Visitors (Professional Conduct) Rules 1993 (SI 1993 893) by enabling persons who are not members of the Council to be appointed as deputy chairpersons of the Preliminary Proceedings Committee and Professional Conduct Committee, provide that the Council will appoint persons who are not members of the Council as members of the Health Committee, and enable the appointment of a person, who is not a member of the Council, to act as chairperson of the respective committees when the chairperson and deputies are not present. The rules also amend the quorum of each of the committees to provide that they are quorate if there are three committee members present of whom one shall be a member of the Council.

5744. Medical profession–nurses, midwives and health visitors–professional conduct

NURSES, MIDWIVES AND HEALTH VISITORS (PROFESSIONAL CONDUCT) (AMENDMENT) (NO.2) RULES 2002 APPROVAL (SCOTLAND) ORDER 2002, SSI 2002 142; made under the Nurses, Midwives and Health Visitors Act 1997 s.19. In force: March 31, 2002; £2.00.

This Order, which amends the Nurses, Midwives and Health Visitors (Professional Conduct) Rules 1993 (SI 1993 893), approves the Nurses, Midwives and Health Visitors (Professional Conduct) (Amendment) (No.2) Rules 2002. It provides for the submission of information received by the Registrar of the Council, raising a question as to the fitness to practise of a practitioner, to professional screeners, the Registrar to make arrangements for the examination of a practitioner by medical examiner(s) and for any examination by a medical practitioner nominated by the practitioner and for the action to be taken following examination of a practitioner by medical examiner(s). The Order also provides for the examination of a practitioner by medical examiner(s) where a case has been referred to the professional screeners by the Preliminary Proceedings Committee, the President or the Professional Conduct Committee of the Council and for the preliminary circulation of evidence to the Health Committee of the Council. It provides for the termination of a suspension and restoration to the register and deals with the nomination of persons from a number of professional bodies to hold the position of "medical examiner" and on the role of such persons.

5745. National Health Service–charges–dental services

NATIONAL HEALTH SERVICE (GENERAL DENTAL SERVICES) (SCOTLAND) AMENDMENT REGULATIONS 2002, SSI 2002 192; made under the National Health Service (Scotland) Act 1978 s.2, s.25, s.105, s.108. In force: May 10, 2002; £1.50.

These Regulations amend the National Health Service (General Dental Services) (Scotland) Regulations 1996 (SI 1996 177) which make arrangements under which dentists provide general dental services as part of the National Health Service in Scotland. They correct a cross-referencing error and increase to £270 the amount specified as the maximum cost, or likely cost, of care and treatment which a dentist may undertake without seeking the prior approval of the Scottish Dental Practice Board.

5746. National Health Service–charges–road traffic accidents

ROAD TRAFFIC (NHS CHARGES) AMENDMENT (NO.2) (SCOTLAND) REGULATIONS 2002, SSI 2002 528; made under the Road Traffic (NHS Charges) Act 1999 s.3, s.16. In force: January 1, 2003; £1.75.

These Regulations amend the Road Traffic (NHS Charges) Regulations 1999 (SI 1999 785) which provide for a scheme for the recovery from insurers and other persons of charges in connection with the treatment of road traffic casualties by the National Health Service. They increase those charges in relation to incidents giving rise to treatment which occur on or after January 1, 2003.

5747. National Health Service–charges–road traffic accidents

ROAD TRAFFIC (NHS CHARGES) AMENDMENT (SCOTLAND) REGULATIONS 2002, SSI 2002 56; made under the Road Traffic (NHS Charges) Act 1999 s.3, s.16, s.17. In force: February 14, 2002; £1.75.

These Regulations amend the Road Traffic (NHS Charges) Regulations 1999 (SI 1999 785), which provide for a scheme for the recovery from insurers and certain other persons of charges in connection with the treatment of road traffic casualties by the National Health Service, by introducing different charges in respect of incidents occurring on or after January 28, 2002 depending on whether the treatment was received before February 14, 2002 or on or after that date.

5748. National Health Service–clinical negligence–indemnity scheme–Mental Welfare Commission

NATIONAL HEALTH SERVICE (CLINICAL NEGLIGENCE AND OTHER RISKS INDEMNITY SCHEME) (SCOTLAND) AMENDMENT REGULATIONS 2002, SSI 2002 239; made under the National Health Service (Scotland) Act 1978 s.2, s.85B, s.105, s.108. In force: June 14, 2002; £1.75.

These Regulations amend the National Health Service (Clinical Negligence and Other Risks Indemnity Scheme) (Scotland) Regulations 2000 (SSI 2000 54), which established a scheme under which members could make provision for meeting liabilities arising out of negligence in the carrying out of functions and for indemnity for other financial loss, in order to add the Mental Welfare Commission for Scotland as a member of the scheme.

5749. National Health Service–dental services–dental charges

NATIONAL HEALTH SERVICE (GENERAL DENTAL SERVICES AND DENTAL CHARGES) (SCOTLAND) AMENDMENT REGULATIONS 2002, SSI 2002 99; made under the National Health Service (Scotland) Act 1978 s.2, s.25, s.70, s.71, s.71A, s.105, s.108. In force: April 1, 2002; £1.75.

These Regulations amend the National Health Service (Dental Charges) (Scotland) Regulations 1989 (SI 1989 363), which provide for the making and recovery of charges for dental appliances supplied or repaired under the National Health Service, and for other dental treatment provided as part of NHS general dental services, and the National Health Service (General Dental Services) (Scotland) Regulations 1996 (SI 1996 177), which provide for the arrangements under which dentists provide general dental services as part of the National Health Service in Scotland. They add two new items to the statement of dental remuneration, remove the distinction between the treatment available to non-registered occasional patients and those occasional patients registered with a dentist elsewhere and increase to £366 the maximum contribution which a patient may be required to make towards the aggregate costs of dental treatment and appliances under the National Health Service (Scotland) Act 1978 Part II.

5750. National Health Service–drugs and appliances–fees

NATIONAL HEALTH SERVICE (CHARGES FOR DRUGS AND APPLIANCES) (SCOTLAND) AMENDMENT REGULATIONS 2002, SSI 2002 100; made under the National Health Service (Scotland) Act 1978 s.19, s.25, s.27, s.69, s.105, s.108. In force: April 1, 2002; £2.00.

These Regulations amend the National Health Service (Charges for Drugs and Appliances) (Scotland) Regulations 2001 (SSI 2001 430) which provide for the making and recovery of charges for drugs and appliances supplied by doctors and pharmacists providing pharmaceutical services, and by Health Boards and NHS trusts to out-patients. They extend the categories of nurse, midwife or health visitor who may prescribe under the National Health Service in Scotland, enable payment certificates to be granted by chemists and doctors, increase pre-payment certificates charges to £32.40 for a four month certificate and to £89 for a 12 months certificate and increase various charges as specified.

5751. National Health Service–education and training–postgraduates

NHS EDUCATION FOR SCOTLAND ORDER 2002, SSI 2002 103; made under the National Health Service (Scotland) Act 1978 s.2, s.105. In force: Art.7: April 1, 2002; remainder: March 31, 2002; £2.50.

This Order, which revokes the Scottish Council for Postgraduate Medical and Dental Education Order 1993 (SI 1993 577), constitutes a Special Health Board for the whole of Scotland to be known as NHS Education for Scotland. The Board will exercise functions of the Scottish Ministers in respect of providing, co-ordinating, funding and advising on education and training for persons providing services under the National Health Service (Scotland) Act 1978. It will carry out the functions formerly carried out by the Scottish Council for Postgraduate Medical and Dental Education. This Order applies to the Board various provisions in enactments which apply to Health Boards in general including provisions as to funding, the keeping and auditing of accounts, the transfer of officers and the appointment and remuneration of Board members and staff.

5752. National Health Service–general medical services–pharmaceutical services

NATIONAL HEALTH SERVICE (GENERAL MEDICAL SERVICES AND PHARMACEUTICAL SERVICES) (SCOTLAND) AMENDMENT (NO.2) REGULATIONS 2002, SSI 2002 153; made under the National Health Service (Scotland) Act 1978 s.2, s.19, s.27, s.28, s.28A, s.105, s.106, s.108, Sch.1 para.11. In force: March 31, 2002; £1.75.

These Regulations amend the National Health Service (General Medical Services and Pharmaceutical Services) (Scotland) Amendment Regulations 2002 (SSI 2002 111) in order to correct citation errors. They also substitute the correct citation of the National Health Service (Pharmaceutical Services) (Scotland) Regulations 1995 (SI 1995 414) and the National Health Service (General Medical Services) (Scotland) Regulations 1995 (SI 1995 416).

5753. National Health Service–general medical services–prescription of drugs

NATIONAL HEALTH SERVICE (GENERAL MEDICAL SERVICES) (SCOTLAND) AMENDMENT REGULATIONS 2002, SSI 2002 438; made under the National Health Service (Scotland) Act 1978 s.19, s.105, s.108. In force: October 31, 2002; £1.75.

These Regulations amend the National Health Service (General Medical Services) (Scotland) Regulations 1995 (SI 1995 416) which regulate the terms on which doctors provide general medical services under the National Health Service (Scotland) Act 1978. They remove two products and add five products to the list in Sch.10 which identifies those drugs and other substances which are not to be supplied by general medical practitioners or prescribed for supply in the course of pharmaceutical services under the National Health Service (Scotland) Act 1978.

5754. National Health Service–grants–dental services

NATIONAL HEALTH SERVICE (GENERAL DENTAL SERVICES) (SCOTLAND) AMENDMENT (NO.2) REGULATIONS 2002, SSI 2002 268; made under the National Health Service (Scotland) Act 1978 s.2, s.25, s.105, s.108. In force: August 1, 2002; £1.50.

These Regulations amend the National Health Service (General Dental Services) (Scotland) Regulations 1996 (SI 1996 177) which make arrangements under which dentists provide general dental services as part of the National Health Service in Scotland. They enable grants to be made towards practice improvements as well as the making of allowances for such improvements and provide that allowances will be payable to certain categories of practitioner in order to provide incentives for the recruitment and retention of dentists providing general dental services in Scotland.

5755. National Health Service–health boards–National Waiting Times Centre Board

NATIONAL WAITING TIMES CENTRE BOARD (SCOTLAND) ORDER 2002, SSI 2002 305; made under the National Health Service (Scotland) Act 1978 s.2, s.105. In force: June 27, 2002; £2.50.

This Order, which amends the National Health Service (Financial Provisions) (Scotland) Regulations 1974 (SI 1974 468) and the National Health Service (Scotland) Act 1978, constitutes a Special Health Board for the whole of Scotland to be known as the National Waiting Times Centre Board. It confers on the Board functions in relation to the provision of goods and services for the purpose of the Health Service, including in particular surgical, medical and related services at hospital accommodation and ancillary facilities situated at Dalmuir, Clydebank. The Order also applies provisions in enactments which apply to Health Boards in general.

5756. National Health Service–health boards–NHS Quality Improvement– establishment

NHS QUALITY IMPROVEMENT SCOTLAND ORDER 2002, SSI 2002 534; made under the National Health Service (Scotland) Act 1978 s.2, s.105. In force: in accordance with Art.1 (2) (3); £2.50.

This Order, which revokes the Clinical Standards Board for Scotland Order 1999 (SI 1999 726) and the Health Technology Board for Scotland Order 2000 (SSI 2000 47), constitutes a Special Health Board for the whole of Scotland to be known as NHS Quality Improvement Scotland. It confers on the Board functions in relation to the quality of healthcare in the National Health Service in Scotland and the evaluation and provision of advice to the National Health Service in Scotland on the clinical and cost effectiveness of health technologies.

5757. National Health Service–health boards–NHS Quality Improvement– transfer of officers

NHS QUALITY IMPROVEMENT SCOTLAND (TRANSFER OF OFFICERS) REGULATIONS 2002, SSI 2002 535; made under the National Health Service (Scotland) Act 1978 s.105, s.108, Sch.1 para.7A, Sch.5 para.7B. In force: January 1, 2003; £1.75.

These Regulations provide for the transfer of those persons employed on that date by the Clinical Standards Board for Scotland and the Health Technology Board for Scotland, to NHS Quality Improvement Scotland. They provide for those persons who on that date are employed by the Common Services Agency and engaged in duties in the bodies known as the Clinical Resource and Audit Group or the Scottish Health Advisory Service. In addition they provide that the contracts of employment transferred shall be transferred with continuation of the contracts and all rights and liabilities pertaining to those transferred.

5758. **National Health Service–pharmaceutical services–nurse prescribers–restricted availability appliances**

NATIONAL HEALTH SERVICE (GENERAL MEDICAL SERVICES AND PHARMACEUTICAL SERVICES) (SCOTLAND) AMENDMENT REGULATIONS 2002, SSI 2002 111; made under the National Health Service (Scotland) Act 1978 s.2, s.19, s.27, s.28, s.28A, s.105, s.106, s.108, Sch.1 para.11. In force: April 1, 2002; £2.00.

These Regulations amend the National Health Service (Pharmaceutical Services) Regulations 1995 (SI 1995 414) and the National Health Service (General Medical Services) Regulations 1995 (SI 1995 416) which govern the arrangements to be made by Health Boards for the provision in their area of pharmaceutical services under the National Health Service (Scotland) Act 1978 and regulate the terms on which doctors provide general medical services under the 1978 Act. They extend the definition of "nurse prescriber" to the categories of nurse, midwife or health visitor who may prescribe under the National Health Service in Scotland and introduce a new category of appliance to be known as a restricted availability appliance which is an appliance that will only be available on prescription to patients falling within limited categories and for certain limited purposes to be set out in the Drug Tariff. The Regulations enable such appliances to be added to the Drug Tariff and restrict the circumstances in which such appliances may be supplied on prescription.

5759. **National Health Service–postgraduate education and training–transfer of staff**

SCOTTISH COUNCIL FOR POSTGRADUATE MEDICAL AND DENTAL EDUCATION AND NHS EDUCATION FOR SCOTLAND (TRANSFER OF STAFF) REGULATIONS 2002, SSI 2002 105; made under the National Health Service (Scotland) Act 1978 s.105, s.108, Sch.1 para.7A. In force: March 31, 2002; £1.75.

These Regulations transfer to NHS Education for Scotland, the officers and employees of the Scottish Council for Postgraduate Medical and Dental Education.

5760. **Opticians–fees and payments**

NATIONAL HEALTH SERVICE (OPTICAL CHARGES AND PAYMENTS) AND (GENERAL OPHTHALMIC SERVICES) (SCOTLAND) AMENDMENT REGULATIONS 2002, SSI 2002 86; made under the National Health Service (Scotland) Act 1978 s.26, s.70, s.73, s.74, s.105, s.108, Sch.11 para.2, Sch.11 para.2A. In force: Reg.2(2): April 9, 2002; Reg.4: April 9, 2002; remainder: April 1, 2002; £2.00.

These Regulations amend the National Health Service (Optical Charges and Payments) (Scotland) Regulations 1998 (SI 1998 642) which provide for payments to be made by means of a voucher system, in respect of eligibility to obtain a voucher and of costs incurred by certain categories of persons in connection with the supply, replacement and repair of optical appliances. They also amend the National Health Service (General Ophthalmic Services) (Scotland) Regulations 1986 (SSI 965) which provide for arrangements under which ophthalmic medical practitioners and ophthalmic opticians provide general ophthalmic services under the National Health Service. The Regulations increase the value of an optical voucher issued towards the cost of replacing a single contact lens, and to increase the maximum contribution by way of voucher to the cost of repairing a frame and increase the value of vouchers issued towards the cost of the supply and replacement of glasses and contact lenses. They increase the value of vouchers issued towards the cost of the repair and replacement of optical appliances and increase the additional values for vouchers for prisms, tints or photochromic lenses, and special categories of appliances.

5761. Opticians–fees and payments

NATIONAL HEALTH SERVICE (OPTICAL CHARGES AND PAYMENTS) (SCOTLAND) AMENDMENT REGULATIONS 2002, SSI 2002 17; made under the National Health Service (Scotland) Act 1978 s.26, s.70, s.105, s.108, Sch.11 para.2, Sch.11 para.2A. In force: February 15, 2002; £1.50.

These Regulations amend the National Health Service (Optical Charges and Payments) (Scotland) Regulations 1998 (SI 1998 642) which provide for payments to be made by means of a voucher system, in respect of costs incurred by certain categories of persons in connection with sight tests and the supply, replacement or repair of optical appliances. The Regulations amend the definition of "NHS sight test fee" to reflect the values of the two levels of fees for National Health Service sight tests payable to ophthalmic medical practitioners and opticians. This fee is set at two levels depending on whether or not the sight test was carried out at the patient's home and the appropriate figure is used to calculate the value of assistance towards the cost of a private sight test. The fee for a test at home is increased from £42.85 to £44.39 and for tests elsewhere from £15.52 to £16.08.

5762. Opticians–fees and payments

NATIONAL HEALTH SERVICE (OPTICAL CHARGES AND PAYMENTS) (SCOTLAND) AMENDMENT (NO.2) REGULATIONS 2002, SSI 2002 224; made under the National Health Service (Scotland) Act 1978 s.26, s.70, s.105, s.108, Sch.11 para.2, Sch.11 para.2A. In force: June 3, 2002; £1.75.

These Regulations amend the National Health Service (Optical Charges and Payments) (Scotland) Regulations 1998 (SI 1998 642) which provide for payments to be made by means of a voucher system, in respect of costs incurred by certain categories of persons in connection with sight tests and the supply, replacement or repair of optical appliances. They amend the definition of "NHS sight test fee" to reflect the values of the two levels of fees for National Health Service sight tests payable to ophthalmic medical practitioners and opticians. This fee is set at two levels depending on whether or not the sight test was carried out at the patient's home and the appropriate figure is used to calculate the value of assistance towards the cost of a private sight test. In addition, they increase from £44.39 to £46.16 the fee for a test at home and from £16.08 to £16.72 for tests elsewhere.

5763. Social welfare–Community Care and Health (Scotland) Act 2002– consequential amendment

COMMUNITY CARE AND HEALTH (SCOTLAND) ACT 2002 (CONSEQUENTIAL AMENDMENT) ORDER 2002, SSI 2002 233; made under the Community Care and Health (Scotland) Act 2002 s.24. In force: June 7, 2002; £1.50.

This Order amends the Community Care and Health (Scotland) Act 2002 which is considered necessary in consequence of the Community Care and Health (Scotland) Act 2002 (Commencement No.1) Order 2002. The 2002 Act enables Regulations to be made modifying Social Work (Scotland) Act 1968 in its application to people who met certain criteria. This Order amends the Act by substituting "subsection" for "section" where it last occurs in order to remove the ambiguity as to the appropriate date to be taken as the coming into force date referred to therein.

5764. Books

Blackie, John W.G.; Patrick, Hilary–Mental Health-the Law in Scotland. Paperback (C format): £45.00. ISBN 0-406-07756-8. Butterworths Law (Scotland).

HEALTH AND SAFETY AT WORK

5765. **Employers liability–accident outwith employers' premises–safe means of access to workplace**

M sought damages from her employers, B, for injuries sustained when she slipped outside the factory premises on her way to work. M lost her footing as she crossed a stretch of wet grass, which was not part of B's property, in order to reach a gap in the fencing around the factory. She averred that the habitual means of pedestrian access was through the gap, of which B was aware, having laid four or five paving slabs in the grass between the gap and the factory entrance. B argued that there was insufficient proximity for liability in negligence to arise and that while an employer's duty of care extended to providing safe access to those premises occupied, it had already been provided by way of a road.

Held, allowing a proof before answer, that (1) an employer's duty of care to provide a safe means of access to a workplace was not restricted to access over the employer's own property or property under his control, but a relationship of proximity had nevertheless to exist, and (2) it was impossible to assert as an absolute proposition that the provision of a single safe access route would of itself discharge an employer's duty of care; an employer facilitating of the use of an informal access route might readily be considered as an invitation to employees, which was a question of fact and degree.

METHVEN v. BABYGRO LTD 2002 S.L.T. 1282, Lord Drummond Young, OH.

5766. **Employers liability–fireman slipping on polished floor**

[Workplace (Health, Safety and Welfare) Regulations 1992 (SI 1992 3004) Reg.12.]

M, a fireman, raised an action for damages against S in respect of injuries sustained when he slipped on a floor at work. M was responding to a summons to attend at the muster room when he slipped on the floor, laid with terrazzo tiles, which had been cleaned and polished between 30 minutes and an hour earlier. M averred that S were in breach of their statutory duty under the Workplace (Health, Safety and Welfare) Regulations 1992 Reg.12 arguing that the construction of the floor was not suitable for its purpose due to the tiles being worn and not of a non-slip material, in breach of Reg.12(1), which M argued was an absolute duty. M further argued that the S had failed to keep the surface free from a substance which might cause a person to slip, in breach of Reg.12(3). M maintained that, had S complied with their duties under Reg.12, the accident would not have occurred. S averred that under Reg.12(1), the fact that it might be possible to slip on a surface did not, in itself, render the surface unsafe. S, whilst admitting that M had slipped on the floor, argued that the risk of injury from slippage had to be real or material to result in a breach of the regulation. S further argued that the slip resistance of the floor in a newly polished state was within recommended levels.

Held, granting decree and awarding agreed damages in the sum of £51,300, that (1) in interpreting regulations, the Court, in the first instance, should be untrammelled by superseded legislation and the interpretation of it, *English v. North Lanarkshire Council* 1999 S.C.L.R. 310, [1999] C.L.Y. 6226, followed; (2) the requirement under Reg.12(1) was a continuing one, unable to be qualified on the grounds of reasonable practicality, where the construction of the floor at the time immediately prior to the accident would be deemed suitable only if there was no real risk of a person using it as a means of passage and thereby sustaining injury; (3) the requirements under Reg.12(3) was limited by the qualification of reasonable practicality which primarily related to practical measures which could reasonably have been taken to keep the floor free from substances which might cause a person to slip; (4) both Reg.12(1) and Reg.12(3) required a degree of foreseeability and the admission by S that M slipped and fell on the surface did not automatically result in a breach of either regulation, and (5) the surface when in a freshly polished state represented a real, albeit relatively low, risk that someone might slip on it in breach of

Reg.12(3), and the smoothness of the worn tiles were such that, by way of slipperiness, such as to expose someone to a risk to their safety in breach of Reg.12(1).

McGHEE v. STRATHCLYDE FIRE BRIGADE 2002 S.L.T. 680, Lord Hamilton, OH.

5767. Employers liability–maintenance of workplace–disused wall mounted bracket–causing injury

[Factories Act 1937 (c.67); Occupiers' Liability (Scotland) Act 1960 (c.30); Factories Acts 1961 (c.34); Workplace (Health, Safety and Welfare) Regulations 1992 (SI 1992 3004) Reg.5(1); Council Directive (89/654) on the minimum safety and health requirement for the use if work equipment in the workplace Art.6.]

M, a fork lift truck driver, raised an action for damages against his employer (T). M had been depositing a reel into a cradle and when it had rolled out he had gone to retrieve it. When returning to his truck, M had walked into a wall mounted bracket for a shelf no longer in use. M argued that T had breached the Workplace (Health, Safety and Welfare) Regulations 1992 Reg.5 in terms of which T owed an absolute duty to ensure that the workplace and equipment were in good working order. T argued that (1) M had been negligent in either depositing the reel or in not using designated walkways, and (2) there were difficulties in relying on previous case law under the Factories Acts and Reg.5 did not impose an absolute duty. T had sustained a bruised shoulder and arm and the swelling and discomfort had continued for five months. Damages were agreed at £2,250 solatium and £1,000 past loss of earnings.

Held, granting T absolvitor, that (1) whether or not M had been negligent in depositing the reel, by the time he had recovered it, as he was expected to, a novus actus had occurred. There was no evidence that M had been negligent in what was accepted to be a tricky operation. Further, the walkways were not the only areas in which employees were allowed to walk. Given that M's actions were natural and the cradle area was otherwise empty, it was hard to see what danger there was in entering the area even though it was not a designated walkway, and (2) there had been no breach of Reg.5. Regulation 5, in implementing the Council Directive (89/654) Art.6, required an employer to see that technical maintenance of the workplace was carried out to a standard which eliminated fault, which was effectively the same standard as was applied in Galashiels Gas Co Ltd v. Millar [1949] A.C. 275. The similarity between the words used in Reg.5 and those used in the Factories Act 1937 and Factories Act 1961 to define "maintained", suggested an absolute duty of compliance in Reg.5, at least so far as concerning equipment. However Millar could be distinguished on the ground that it involved equipment: a bracket could not be "technically maintained" where it did not support anything. Opinion, that (1) there was no doubt that the bracket was a hazard, and a properly pled case at common law or under the Occupiers' Liability (Scotland) Act 1960 might have been difficult to resist, and (2) although M had been distracted, given the bracket had been near eye level there had been a small degree of contributory negligence of about 25 per cent.

McNAUGHTON v. MICHELIN TYRE PLC 2001 S.L.T. (Sh Ct) 67, Sheriff Richard A Davidson, Sh Ct (Tayside, Central and Fife).

5768. Employers liability–manual handling–caretaker injuring back–reduction of risk

[Manual Handling Operations Regulations 1992 (SI 1992 2793) Reg.4.]

K raised an action for damages against N in respect of a back injury sustained at work, which, M averred, resulted from a breach by N of their statutory duties under the Manual Handling Operations Regulations 1992 Reg.4 and their common law duty to provide a safe system of work. K's duties as caretaker involved setting out tables and chairs for various functions which took place at the hall where she was employed. It was not in dispute that at the time of the accident K was moving a table weighing 13 kg. The method for moving the tables had remained unchanged between 1989, when K became caretaker, and the date of the accident, and thereafter. With the exception of K's accident, no other injuries had been reported using that method, nor complaints received. K had not been given any specific training in how to manoeuvre and lift tables and had never been told that she was handling them incorrectly. She argued that the lack of training and the system of storing tables vertically rather than horizontally had resulted in her accident. K accepted that if her claim under the Regulations failed then her claim under common law would also fail. N explained that, in pursuance of the Regulations coming into force, they had arranged courses to train supervisors in risk assessment, and, whilst not indicating whether such an assessment had been carried out in respect of the method for manoeuvring tables, indicated that they did not consider that it involved a significant risk of injury. N further maintained that there was no evidence to suggest that training would have made any practical difference, or that the storage of tables horizontally would have prevented injury. They argued that the tables in question were lightweight, portable and designed to be moved by one person and the system of always having one corner on the floor resulted in the load being reduced by half.

Held, assoilzing the defenders, that (1) there was not a foreseeable possibility of injury requiring a risk assessment to be carried out as the tables were designed to be handled manually, the loading on K's spine, were the tables to be lifted off the ground completely, was within the guidelines set by the Health and Safety Executive and, given that one corner of the tables remained on the ground, the actual loading was reduced by half, and the same tables had been manoeuvred by K in the same manner for over nine years without incident; (2) even if N had been required to carry out a risk assessment, K's case based on lack of training would have failed as she failed to show what training had been absent and what difference any training would have made to the system for moving the tables; (3) the storage of tables in a vertical position was in accordance with the guidance given by the manufacturers and N had correctly identified that storage in a horizontal position was likely to result in slippage of the tables with corresponding risk of injury, and (4) had K succeeded, the damages to be awarded had been agreed at £6,500.

Observed, that the assumption by N that K's experience as a caretaker in handling the tables was sufficient in terms of the Regulations bordered on the cavalier and the regulations imposed duties irrespective of the experience of employees or how settled the work practices were.

KERR v. NORTH AYRSHIRE COUNCIL 2002 Rep. L.R. 35, Lady Smith, OH.

5769. Employers liability–manual handling–failure to train or instruct

[Manual Handling Operations Regulations 1992 (SI 1992 2793) Reg.4 (1) (b) (i), Reg.4 (1) (b) (ii).]

S raised an action for damages against his employers, A, in respect of a shoulder injury sustained during the course of his employment as a foreman road worker. The incident occurred in early 1997 and S retired on medical grounds in October 1997. S had been instructed to lift some broken slabs. The slab, which he had been lifting with a crowbar, broke causing the crowbar to slip, which in turn caused a jerking motion in his upper body and resulted in injury to his shoulder. He was very experienced in lifting and laying slabs and was expected, by his employers, to devise the best method of doing so depending on the circumstances of each job. S alleged that the slabs in question had been wet and covered in mud, making the task of raising them more difficult. On that occasion, in order to achieve more leverage, S had placed a hammer beneath the end of the crowbar to create a makeshift fulcrum. S asserted that A was in breach of its duty to provide a safe system of work but only pursued his case under the Manual Handling Operations Regulations 1992. He submitted that A had failed to carry out an assessment of the manual handling operations involved in lifting and laying slabs and had also failed to take steps to minimise any risk to employees from such operations, contrary to Reg.4 (1) (b) (i) and Reg.4 (1) (b) (ii). A submitted that failure to carry out an assessment did not give rise to a liability for damages and that S had failed to prove how the accident had occurred; the evidence was unclear and unreliable, and the use of the hammer meant S had contributed to the accident as the increased leverage had placed too high a force on the slab causing it to break. Both S and A agreed that the lifting and laying of slabs did constitute a manual handling operation in terms of the 1992 Regulations, that the task could give rise to a risk of injury and that the task could not be avoided by use of a mechanical device.

Held, finding A liable, awarding damages of £15,000 with interest to the date of proof and putting the case out by order for submissions on any further interest due, that (1) S was a credible witness who had established the essential features of how his injury had been sustained even though he had proven unreliable in respect of dates and some minor details in relation to the incident and had established that he had received no training or instruction from, or on behalf of A, on how to approach the task, nor had he been advised that the method adopted by him was unsafe; (2) in failing to train or instruct S in order to reduce the risk of injury to the lowest possible level, A had been in breach of its obligations under Reg.4(1)(b)(i) and Reg.4(1)(b)(ii); (3) where a breach of Reg.4(1)(b)(i) and Reg.4(1)(b)(ii) had occurred, the onus was on the employer to prove that the method of carrying out the task reduced the risk of injury to the lowest possible level where no action taken by the employer could have made a difference, which A had failed to prove, and (4) the accident resulted from A's breach of the Regulations and there had been no contributory negligence by S.

SKINNER v. ABERDEEN CITY COUNCIL 2001 Rep. L.R. 118, Lady Paton, OH.

5770. **Employers liability—manual handling—risk of injury—relevancy of averments of risk**

[Manual Handling Operations Regulations 1992 (SI 1992 2793) Reg.3, Reg.4.]

T reclaimed against the Lord Ordinary's dismissal of his claim for damages from his local authority employers (G) having injured his back while moving a cupboard upstairs between two floors in a school. T averred that he was moving the cupboard, which was two metres high and weighed 35 kilograms, with J and K. G did not take appropriate steps to provide T with precise information on the heaviest side of the cupboard; T and J were at the front, and they had almost reached the top when T felt a pain in his back. T argued inter alia that he had averred sufficient for inquiry on the question of foreseeable possibility of injury. The Lord Ordinary held that on his pleadings T had not established a risk of injury in the circumstances. G argued that as T had failed to specify how a risk of injury arose from such an operation his case lacked the necessary specification. T had given no notice of what he planned to prove in support of the contention that the particular operation in the present case carried the requisite risk.

Held, allowing the reclaiming motion and proof before answer, that (1) even on the Lord Ordinary's approach, if account was taken of the ergonomics of the manoeuvre on which T was engaged it could not be said that T's averments did not warrant at least a proof before answer on the question of whether it involved a foreseeable risk of injury under the Manual Handling Operations Regulations 1992 Reg.4(1)(a); (2) per Lords Marnoch and Carloway, that although it could be so applied, Reg.4(1)(a) had to be seen not as applying to a specific task ultimately involving injury but as imposing a general duty to avoid the need for all manual handling carrying with it a risk of injury, and where a particular pursuer was injured when engaged in and as a result of such an operation, liability for breach of the regulation could only be avoided if an employer had relevantly pled the defence of lack of reasonable practicability in respect of the type of operation carried out; (3) per Lord Reed, that it was not sufficient for T to establish that the operation he undertook belonged to a wider category of operations generally involving a risk of injury: while Reg.4 might call for a generalised approach in some circumstances it was necessary in the circumstances of the present case for T to establish that the actual operation was one which involved a risk of injury under Reg.4(1)(a); (4) per Lords Marnoch and Reed, that Reg.4(1)(a) had to be understood as referring to manual handling operations at work which involved a foreseeable risk of injury, having regard to the terms of Reg.3(1) and Reg.4(1)(b), and (5) per Lord Carloway, that while agreeing with previous dicta that "foreseeable possibility" of a particular injury arising was sufficient to demonstrate that a risk of injury was present, foreseeability was not a necessary prerequisite and whether an operation carried a risk of injury was a question of fact for the court to assess at proof looking at, amongst other things, what actually happened.

TAYLOR v. GLASGOW CITY COUNCIL 2002 S.C. 364, Lord Carloway, Lord Marnoch, Lord Reed, Ex Div.

5771. Employers liability–manual handling–slip on wet magazine–breach of statutory duty–foreseeability of risk of injury

[Workplace (Health, Safety and Welfare) Regulations 1992 (SI 1992 3004); Manual Handling Operations Regulations 1992 (SI 1992 2793) Reg.4(1).]

P raised an action for damages against G in respect of personal injuries sustained in the course of his employment. P was engaged in shovelling piles of wet magazines into the shovel of a JCB when he slipped on a wet magazine, which had blown off the pile and fell injuring his back. P's action was based on alleged breaches of the duty of care owed by G under the Workplace (Health, Safety and Welfare) Regulations 1992 and the Manual Handling Operations Regulations 1992. G agreed that the action, in so far as based on the Workplace (Health, Safety and Welfare) Regulations 1992 should proceed to proof, but raised pleas to the relevancy of P's case in respect of claims under the Manual Handling Operations Regulations 1992 and the case under common law. G argued that the incident which allegedly led to the injury was a slippage rather than a manual handling and that P had failed to make relevant averments of a foreseeable risk of injury as required by the regulations. They argued that P had not been instructed to stand on the magazines and that G could not have foreseen that one would be blown under his feet. In response, P submitted that it was unnecessary to aver or prove that the employer should have foreseen the particular occurrence which had led to the injury provided that the possibility of injury arising from the task was foreseen. P argued that his averments that the task involved an element of manual handling, that the nature of the task required him to turn whilst carrying a load and that the wind had blown the magazines around so that he might stand on one, were sufficient to allow the case to go to proof. Finally P maintained that the case at common law was concerned with a different legal basis namely G's requirement to provide a safe place and system of work.

Held, allowing a proof before answer, that (1) the requirement under the Manual Handling Operations Regulations 1992 Reg.4(1) was for the foreseeability of a possibility of injury and that given the nature of the task, it was reasonable that G should have foreseen the possibility of the magazines being blown around whilst being moved and that this might result in injury, and (2) given that P had made sufficient averments to allow the statutory case to proceed to proof, the case under common law must also proceed as G had not invited the court to dispose of it on any other basis.

PURDIE v. GLASGOW CITY COUNCIL 2002 Rep. L.R. 26, Lord Hamilton, OH.

5772. Employers liability–safe place of work–employee slipping in toilet cubicle

[Workplace (Health, Safety and Welfare) Regulations 1992 (SI 1992 3004) Reg.5, Reg.10(1), Reg.11.]

B, an outpatient assistant, sought damages from her employer, G, having allegedly suffered leg and back pain after bearing the weight of a disabled patient who fell while being assisted by the pursuer and a carer in a toilet cubicle. B averred that the cubicle was unsuitable for wheelchair bound patients, inter alia, in that G had failed to maintain the workplace in an efficient state as required by the Workplace (Health, Safety and Welfare) Regulations 1992 Reg.5, that the floor area was inadequate in terms of Reg.10(1), and that they had failed to arrange workstations in a suitable manner for any work likely to be done there, in terms of Reg.11. G argued, inter alia, that (1) reg.5(1) was concerned with maintenance and not provision, and the pursuer's averments disclosed no lack of maintenance; (2) B's averments in relation to Reg.10(1) did not address the statutory test which was expressed in terms of sufficient floor area, and (3) the cubicle was not a "workstation" under reg.11.

Held, allowing proof before answer under exclusion of the case based on Reg.11, that (1) the purpose of the Regulations as disclosed in the Workplace Directive was to secure a continuing state of efficiency, and it was a relevant averment of a breach of Reg.5 to set out circumstances supporting the conclusion that the workplace was not efficient in terms of safety; (2) the sufficiency of a floor area under Reg.10(1) could not be judged without reference to the work being undertaken, and (3) although the cubicle was B's workplace at the material time, a "workstation" connoted set up items of equipment for the purpose of enabling certain categories of work to be carried on there, and not simply apparatus to enable certain natural functions to be performed, and the case based on Reg.11 was irrelevant.

BUTLER v. GRAMPIAN UNIVERSITY HOSPITALS NHS TRUST; *sub nom.* BUTLER v. GRAMPIAN UNIVERSITY HOSPITAL NHS TRUST 2002 S.L.T. 985, Lord Macfadyen, OH.

5773. Employers liability–sufficiency of instruction–vicarious liability

[Provision and Use of Work Equipment Regulations 1992 (SI 1992 2932) Reg.8, Reg.9.]

C, a shipwright aged 53 at proof, sought damages from his former employers, K, in respect of injuries sustained when he was hit by a shore, a temporary wooden support for a ship while in construction. C was in charge of its removal. C averred that he had carried out part of the usual procedure (removing wedges from around sole pieces on which the shore rested and then removing the sole pieces) when two fellow employees, X, who had watched him carrying out the full procedure on a previous shore, offered to help, and that he had told them to group and remove the staples from the loose end of the cable next to the ship being used to attach the shore to the ship. Instead, X had removed not only the staples but also the wire, with the result that the shore was not supported and it fell. X claimed that they had followed C's instructions, which had been to loosen and remove the wire. At the time they were of the view that the shore was securely in place. C argued that X were at fault and K were vicariously liable. K had been negligent in leaving training to be provided on an ad hoc basis by fellow workers such as C; that failure also breached the Provision and Use of Work Equipment Regulations 1992 Reg.8 and Reg.9. C had suffered fractures to his skull, his left little finger and a perforation of the tympanic membrane. He lost his sense of smell and taste. His hearing was affected. He lost some physical and mental capacity and his neck was painful when turned. He was unable to follow any of his previous physical pursuits and he had been retired on medical grounds. He had since suffered dizziness with occasional blackouts.

Held, granting decree on the basis of K's vicarious liability for X, that (1) C had not given sufficiently precise instructions to X, and it was likely that what he had actually said was to prepare the shore for removal, which was ambiguous in the circumstances. The person best placed to judge the position of the shore was C, and his instructions should have been more explicit; (2) there had been no breach of the regulations: (a) the incident had not warranted prosecution because either an instruction to X was wrong or X had exceeded an instruction, and in neither case would the regulations or K's personal duties arise; (b) it would not have been appropriate to make written instructions available to X in relation to such a simple task, (c) and the issue was not training, but ambiguity in instructions and X's erroneous assumption that the shore was secure; (3) X were at fault in failing adequately to inform themselves of the stability of the shore in a situation where the danger of a falling shore was obvious and great, and (4) given the ambiguity of the instructions, C was 20 per cent responsible. Solatium of £30,000, half to the past, was awarded as agreed. On the evidence, C was not precluded from all forms of employment. His loss to date of £12,387 was an adequate reflection of patrimonial loss, with no future loss. £1,000 was awarded for loss of pension benefit.

CAMERON v. KVAERNER GOVAN LTD (PERSONAL INJURY) 2001 Rep. L.R. 52, TG Coutts Q.C., OH.

5774. Employers liability–suitability and sufficiency of lighting

[Workplace (Health, Safety and Welfare) Regulations 1992 (SI 1992 3004) Reg.8(1).]

M raised an action for damages against P, her employer, in respect of injuries sustained to her left ankle at the access to the school in which she worked as a cleaner. M had been carrying out her cleaning duties when an infirm family friend arrived at the school to give a message. Given the friend's level of infirmity, M escorted her back to her car, but did not leave the school premises. At the access, which was not one previously used by M, there was a configuration of walls approximately six feet in height, through which the pavement led with a series of 90 degree bends and culminating in a slight upwards incline to meet the level of the pavement outside the school premises. On her return journey to the school, M had turned and placed a foot on the path, unaware of the downwards incline, lost her footing, fallen and broken her ankle. M raised the action under the Workplace (Health, Safety and Welfare) Regulations 1992 Reg.8(1) arguing that P had failed to provide suitable and sufficient lighting. The accident occurred at around 4.20pm and the configuration of the walls was such that the street lighting on the adjacent road cast a shadow over the incline making it difficult to see. P argued that the lighting was sufficient, either from the ambient natural light or from the street lighting, and that M had fallen as she was not paying attention to what she was doing or was looking the other way.

Held, granting decree and awarding agreed damages in the sum of £31,500 inclusive of interest to date, that (1) the incline on the path combined with the sharp right-hand turn was likely to cause someone to lose their footing if unfamiliar with the area and that risk was aggravated during the hours of darkness where artificial light was not provided to illuminate that part of the pavement; (2) as the person having control of the premises which included access areas, P were in breach of their statutory duty under Reg.8(1), and (3) although the issue was narrow, on the balance of probabilities, P's failure to provide suitable or sufficient lighting had been a material cause of the accident.

MILLER v. PERTH AND KINROSS COUNCIL 2002 Rep. L.R. 22, Lord Hamilton, OH.

5775. Statutory duty–workplace–duty to non employees–duty owed to customer visiting shop premises

[Workplace (Health, Safety and Welfare) Regulations 1992 (SI 1992 3004) Reg.12(3).]

L, a customer, sought damages from A, shopowners, for injuries sustained when she came into contact with a wooden pallet on the floor of A's premises, causing her to lose her balance. A disputed the relevancy of L's claim insofar as it was brought under the Workplace (Health, Safety and Welfare) Regulations 1992 Reg.12(3). L relied on the decision in *Banna v. Delicato* 1999 S.L.T. (Sh Ct) 84, [1999] C.L.Y. 6229 and argued that although Reg.12(3) applied to a workplace, the reference to "a person" was not restricted to employees or persons working.

Held, allowing proof before answer under exclusion of averments under the 1992 Regulations, that having regard to the enabling powers recited in the regulations, "person" in the regulations meant a person who was working, *Banna* and *O'Brien v. Duke of Argyll's Trustees* 1999 S.L.T. (Sh Ct) 88, [1999] C.L.Y. 6222 not followed.

LAYDEN v. ALDI GmbH & CO KG 2002 S.L.T. (Sh Ct) 71, KA Ross, Sh Ct (South Strathclyde, Dumfries and Galloway).

HERITABLE PROPERTY AND CONVEYANCING

5776. Crofts—resumption of grazings—prescriptive period

See PRESCRIPTION: Nicolson v. Tait & Peterson. §6054

5777. Disposition—breach of warrandice—registered title—whether rectification required

[Land Registration (Scotland) Act 1979 (c.33) s.9 (3).]

The proprietor of a public house raised an action of damages against the company from which it had been purchased for breach of warrandice. The subjects disponed to the pursuer included a right of access to entrances at the side and rear of the bar. The disposition contained a clause of absolute warrandice and was registered in the Land Register. The pursuer averred that the neighbouring proprietors informed him that he had no right to use their land as a means of access and forbade him from using the path. He negotiated a three month access period with the neighbouring proprietors while a new fire exit was built, following which they fenced off the area to prevent access. The sheriff allowed a proof before answer and the defenders appealed. The pursuer argued that the emergence of a real or threatened burden on the property was all that was required to found an action for breach of warrandice, and rectification of the register was not required. The only question was whether the neighbouring proprietor's demand was irresistible and that was a matter for proof. The pursuer was not the "proprietor in possession" of the right of access, which term related to possession of land rather than a legal interest, and could not found on the Land Registration (Scotland) Act 1979 s.9 (3).

Held, allowing the appeal and dismissing the action, that (1) while a successful claim was not dependent on rectification of the Land Register, the statutory effect of registration strengthened the need for clear averments of the unquestionable right of the competing title holder and the pursuer had made no averments of the nature of the neighbouring proprietor's competing title and had failed to make a relevant case, and (2) the pursuer's averments as to the form and effective date of the neighbouring proprietor's "unquestionable demand" lacked specification: the pursuer's cessation of use of the right of access in terms of the agreement with the neighbouring proprietors could not be said to be in consequence of eviction or the threat of eviction; any eviction took place before the agreement was entered into, and that date, which was when damages fell to be assessed, was not specified.

MUTCH v. MAVISBANK PROPERTIES LTD 2002 S.L.T. (Sh Ct) 91, EF Bowen Q.C., Sheriff Principal, Sh Ct.

5778. Land obligations—real burdens—breach—interdict competent remedy despite positive action incidental to compliance

See CIVIL PROCEDURE: Hampden Park Ltd v. Dow. §5333

5779. Land obligations—variation and discharge—compensation—proper measure in terms of Human Rights Act

[Conveyancing and Feudal Reform (Scotland) Act 1970 (c.35) s.1; Human Rights Act 1998 (c.42) s.3; European Convention on Human Rights 1950 First Protocol, Art.1.]

S, a police board, applied under the Conveyancing and Feudal Reform (Scotland) Act 1970 s.1 (3) (c) for the discharge of a land obligation under a feu contract restricting the use of a property as a police house and office. The superiors were prepared to grant a minute of waiver but only on payment of a substantial consideration. The superiors claimed compensation and argued that the tribunal had an obligation to interpret the 1970 Act in a manner compatible with the European Convention on Human Rights 1950, and its established approach to s.1 (4) (i) of the 1970 Act as not extending to the right to extract a fee for waiver, amounted to a deprivation of possessions in terms of Art.1 of the First Protocol to the Convention and a disproportionate interference with their rights.

Held, granting the application, that (1) the existence of an obligation restricting the use of a dwellinghouse to police purposes did impede reasonable use of the subjects in terms of s.1 (3) (c) of the 1970 Act; (2) the Human Rights Act 1998 s.3(1) did not require the tribunal to take an entirely fresh approach to the interpretation of s.1 (4) (i) of the 1970 Act but simply required a consideration of whether any particular interpretation was compatible with Convention rights; (3) the superior's primary right was to control the use of the dominium utile and while it was misleading to refer to that right as a right to extract money, it had a cash value and its removal by way of the tribunal's exercise of its jurisdiction could in effect amount to the deprivation of a possession, and (4) the deprivation was justifiable as the provisions of the 1970 Act served a legitimate aim in the public interest and were proportional to the needs of the situation, s.1 (4) (i) of the 1970 Act providing for the protection of benefited proprietors with real interests to protect, *McVey v. Glasgow Corporation* 1973 S.L.T. (Lands Tr.) 15, [1973] C.L.Y. 3731 and *Robertson v. Church of Scotland General Trustees* 1976 S.L.T. (Lands Tr.) 11, [1976] C.L.Y. 3179 followed.

STRATHCLYDE JOINT POLICE BOARD v. ELDERSLIE ESTATES LTD 2002 S.L.T. (Lands Tr) 2, Lord McGhie, Lands Tr (Scot).

5780. **Land obligations–variation and discharge–discharge of obligation preventing development**

[Conveyancing and Feudal Reform (Scotland) Act 1970 (c.35) s.1 (3) (c).]

I applied for discharge of a land obligation under the Conveyancing and Feudal Reform (Scotland) Act 1970 s.1 which prevented development of a plot of land. The plot had formerly formed part of the garden ground of the property owned by S. Since the deed creating the land obligation had been granted, the amenity of the area had changed dramatically, with higher residential density and the establishment of a retail and leisure park. The plot was screened from S's property by a brick wall and a line of evergreen trees and from another adjoining property by a dense beech hedge. Although the plot was identified in the local plan as suitable for leisure use, the local authority had indicated that they felt it would be more acceptable to use the land for residential purposes. I sought the discharge to enable them to sell the plot as a residential development site for more than one property on the grounds that the land obligation was unduly burdensome and impeded a reasonable use of the land. S objected on the grounds that high density development of the site would lower the amenity of the area and create an intrusion into the privacy currently enjoyed by them. An adjoining neighbour, B, also objected on the ground that removal of the obligation to allow an unlimited number of houses to be built on the land would reduce her peaceable enjoyment of the property. Neither S nor B were opposed to the possibility of the land being used for low density housing. Following an interim decision by the Lands Tribunal that the applicants had failed to offer evidence of the reasonableness of their proposed development, planning permission was obtained, enabling the tribunal to make their determination.

Held, discharging the obligation, that (1) I had owned that land for 15 years without the obligation being unduly burdensome and any burden imposed on I by the obligation was outweighed by the benefit to S as it afforded them protection against damage to their amenity; (2) the significant changes to the local area and the grant of planning permission supported the application under s.1 (3) (c) that the obligation impeded a reasonable use of the land, and (3) although the proposed development of the site was fairly dense, the arrangement of the properties on the site would minimise any effect on the privacy of the objectors.

Observed, that the density of the proposed development in relation to the local area was a matter for the local authority to consider in the granting or refusal of the change of use and planning permission.

ITELSOR LTD v. SMITH 2001 Hous. L.R. 120, AR MacLeary FRICS, Lands Tr (Scot).

5781. Land obligations—variation and discharge—discharge of obligations preventing further property being built

[Conveyancing and Feudal Reform (Scotland) Act 1970 (c.35) s.1, s.1 (3) (c), s.1 (4).]

M and S made a joint application under the Conveyancing and Feudal Reform (Scotland) Act 1970 s.1 for discharge of a land obligation which prevented the erection of a further dwellinghouse on the property in question. The application was opposed by P as feudal superiors, who indicated that in the event of the obligation being varied, they claimed compensation of £2,250 in terms of s.1 (4). M's mother, MM, had owned the property comprising of a dwellinghouse and garden. M had erected another dwellinghouse in the garden for himself and his wife to live in due to his mother's ill health. Following MM's death, M, as executor, disponed his mother's house to S. It was a condition of the sale that M make an application to vary the land obligation preventing the development which had already occurred. An application was made to P for variation and the consented subject to payment of £7,500 which represented 15 per cent of the net development gain in accordance with current practices. Following failed attempts to lower the sum sought by P, M applied to have the burden discharged on the grounds that it was unduly burdensome and prevented reasonable use of the property, the reasonableness of which was evidenced by the grant of planning permission.

Held, discharging the obligation and awarding no compensation, that (1) the application had to be considered on the assumption that the additional development had not taken place; (2) MM's death had removed the reason for the erection of the dwellinghouse, so that at the date of application, no reason existed for such development; (3) P had claimed no benefit from the continued enforcement of the obligation, which had to be balanced with the continuing burden experienced by S and M arising out of the obligation; (4) s.1 (3) (c) was not concerned with whether the use of the garden for ornamental purposes was reasonable, as suggested by the superiors, but whether the burden impeded some reasonable use of the land, and given the superiors lack of objection to the erection of a dwelling, provided sufficient compensation was paid, and the grant of planning permission, it could be concluded that the erection of an additional dwelling was a reasonable use of the land which was impeded by the condition, and (5) no evidence had been produced which would indicate that the amount paid for lot in the 1936 feu charter was less than would have been paid had the obligation not been included as the amount paid had been calculated solely on the basis of the area of the lot and, hence, no compensation was due.

MORAN'S EXECUTORS v. SHENSTONE PROPERTIES LTD 2001 Hous. L.R. 124, AR MacLeary FRICS, Lands Tr (Scot).

5782. Land obligations—variation and discharge—variation of servitude right of access—change to route of pedestrian footpath across garden

[Conveyancing and Feudal Reform (Scotland) Act 1970 (c.35) s.1 (3).]

H applied to the Lands Tribunal under the Conveyancing and Feudal Reform (Scotland) Act 1970 s.1 (3) for variation of a land obligation. B and S, the benefited proprietors under the obligation, objected to the application. The land obligation created a right of access over H's garden ground to the nearby road and clearly stated the distance that the path should be from the front of H's property. Following several incidents when a previous proprietor of one of the neighbouring properties allegedly created a nuisance in his use of the footpath, H had moved the footpath further away from her property. The right of access ran was made up of paving stones and sets. H had installed fencing around the boundary of her garden with gates allowing access to and from the road. No objection had been taken to the changes effected by H. H alleged that the right of access was infrequently exercised by B and S, with the most common use being once a month when B used the right of access to transport her wheelie bin to the road. H alleged that the noise created by the bin being moved over the sets created an intolerable nuisance and that, despite the changes effected to the footpath, visitors to the neighbouring properties still looked through H's windows causing her upset. H applied for a variation to allow the footpath to be moved to the end of her garden ground, was willing to pay for the necessary alterations and to dispone the land concerned to the benefited proprietors as a sign of her good faith. She submitted that the proposed changes would not create any inconvenience to the other proprietors as they rarely used the right of access at present and had the option of alternative access. B argued that the additional distance she would have to cover was unreasonable and less convenient.

Held, refusing the application, that (1) the opening of a second access to the rear of the B's property did not render the existing servitude right of access inappropriate or unreasonable; (2) for a variation to be allowed, the proposed route of the servitude right of access must be of equivalent or superior function to the existing one, which was not the case as (a) the proposed route was over grass and soil as opposed to the existing one over paved areas, (b) the proposed route was also longer, and (c) the proposed route involved a sharp incline or stairs making it more difficult to transport a wheelie bin; (3) there was doubt about the extent of work required to deal with the incline at the end of the proposed path and whether consent could be obtained from the neighbouring shop owner to any excavation work making the proposed route unsuitable at present, and (4) the benefit of the servitude right of access to the benefited proprietors outweighed the slight burden suffered by H as a result of the use of the right of access.

HENDERSON v. BARDEN 2001 Hous. L.R. 113, J Devine FRICS, LandsTr (Scot).

5783. **Land registration—rectification of register—boundary altered by administrative error where lying along part of river—prejudice to proprietor in possession**

[Land Registration (Scotland) Act 1979 (c.33) s.9(3).]

T, the proprietors of an area of ground bounded by a river, appealed against K's refusal to rectify the Land Register in respect of the title to the subjects on the opposite bank, which showed the boundary as closer to T's bank than the centre line of the river, which was the boundary according to T's title. The opposite proprietors, who wished to develop the site and take advantage of the overlap area in building an access bridge, opposed the application. The discrepancy arose due to an administrative error by K's staff when the title plan to the objectors' subjects was unintentionally altered consequent on digital conversion of the map base. The objectors argued that they were proprietors in possession in terms of the Land Registration (Scotland) Act 1979 s.9(3) and would be prejudiced by rectification and that the relevant interest in land was the whole interest shown by the title sheet and it was possession of that interest which had to be established, there being no need to look at the overlap area in isolation, but if proof of possession of that area was required, they had acted in reliance on that right in planning the bridge. T argued inter alia that the objectors had no proper registered interest in the overlap area.

Held, allowing the appeal and ordering rectification in the terms sought, that (1) the starting point of any question of rectification was the register as it stood and the objectors were to be treated as proprietors of the overlap area for the purposes of s.9(3); (2) what was required to establish possession was a matter of circumstances depending on the nature of the subjects, "possession" in the present context included the sense of physical use and enjoyment, embracing the concepts of mental and physical control; (3) it was essential to determine the unit which was being possessed, and where subjects were bounded by a river, when considering the physical unit in absence of the evidence of the title plan, there would be no question of the unit of possession extending beyond the centre line; (4) there was no justification in principle or authority for treating title as an element relevant to the physical as well as the mental element of possession, and evidence of occupation of the objectors' subjects as a whole did not, of itself, suffice to establish possession of the overlap area, and (5) there was no stage at which the objectors could reasonably be said to have been established as proprietors in physical possession of the relevant land.

TESCO STORES LTD v. KEEPER OF THE REGISTERS OF SCOTLAND 2001 S.L.T. (LandsTr) 23, Lord McGhie (President), LandsTr (Scot).

5784. Land Registration (Scotland) Act 1979 (c.33)–Commencement No.16 Order

LAND REGISTRATION (SCOTLAND) ACT 1979 (COMMENCEMENT NO.16) ORDER 2002, SSI 2002 432; made under the Land Registration (Scotland) Act 1979 s.30. Commencement details: bringing into force various provisions of the Act on April 1, 2003; £1.50.

This Order brings into force in the areas of the Counties of Banff; Moray, Ross and Cromarty; Caithness; Sutherland; and Orkney and Zetland provisions of the Land Registration (Scotland) Act 1979 which provide for the circumstances in which an interest in land shall be registerable and that certain persons are to obtain a real right only by registration.

5785. Sale–mineral resources–sale by heritable creditor–failure to take account of mineral deposits–duty to obtain best price

[Conveyancing and Feudal Reform Act 1970 (c.35) s.25.]

D, a debtor, raised an action of damages for £2.5 million against C, his heritable creditors. D had granted a number of standard securities over, inter alia, a farm, land and buildings. In December 1986, C obtained the right to possession and sale of the subjects. Shortly before this D had reapplied for planning permission to work sand and gravel deposits on the subjects and in March 1987 the local council indicated that they would authorise the grant of a conditional permission. D was sequestrated on October 29, 1987. C entered into possession of the subjects in early 1988 and instructed a company, H, to market the property. H instructed consulting mining engineers, R, to value the mineral deposits, following their report H marketed the property by emphasising the attractive features of the farmhouse and its location. D claimed loss in that no separate sale of the minerals had been obtained and the full price for the subjects had not been realised. He averred that had the full price been realised his creditors, including C, would have been paid off and he would have been entitled to the free proceeds remaining. C argued, inter alia, that D had no title and interest to sue as his trustee in sequestration had not been discharged at the date of raising the action and D's radical right to sue had not emerged.

Held, assoilzing C, that (1) while R's report to H was unsatisfactory, H were nonetheless made aware that there were at least 500,000 tonnes of sand and gravel available for extraction and H were not entitled to conclude that no value should be attached to the deposits but on the evidence, the deposits had a value of no more than £200,000; (2) H's marketing of the subjects fell short of taking "all reasonable steps", as required under the Conveyancing and Feudal Reform (Scotland) Act 1970 s.25, but because of detriment to the farmhouse if an active quarry were operating, no greater sum would have been obtained by selling the minerals separately; (3) although D's title could not have withstood a challenge by the trustee, he could not be prejudiced by a trustee not taking action within the prescriptive period, and it could be assumed that the trustee had abandoned or would abandon any action open to him on the claim asserted, *Whyte v. Forbes* (1890) 17 R. 895 not followed, and (4) since, had the subjects been sold to encompass the value of the mineral deposits, they would not have realised more than the sum in fact realised, there was no loss and the pursuer had no interest to sue.

DAVIDSON v. CLYDESDALE BANK PLC 2002 S.L.T.1088, JudgeTG Coutts Q.C., OH.

5786. Sale—missives—interpretation—"achievement" of planning permission

G, a local authority, sought payment from C, a development company, of a sum allegedly due in terms of missives under which C purchased two plots of land. Clause 12 provided for an increase in price in accordance with a certain formula in the event that C "achieved" planning permission for more than 49 residential units on the subjects. C successfully applied for permission for 49 residential units. Another company, S, then successfully applied for variation of the planning permission to create a further 12 residential units. S, which was incorporated after missives were concluded, was a wholly owned subsidiary of C; it currently had a sole director who was also C's sole director and one of the two persons who controlled C's holding company. G averred that C had "achieved" planning permission for more than 49 residential units. C argued (1) that there was no basis in the commercial purpose of the contract or in commercial common sense for displacing the ordinary meaning of "achieve" as "obtain"; (2) that G's construction attacked the principle of separate legal personality of related companies, and (3) that the condition had been put forward by G and should be construed contra proferentem.

Held, granting decree de plano, that (1) C could be regarded as "achieving" the grant of planning permission if they had made some material contribution to bringing the grant about; (2) C's contribution was sufficient to amount to "achievement" where they had set up S and procured that it made the relevant application for permission which, if granted to C, would undoubtedly have triggered liability to pay the increased price; (3) no piercing of the corporate veil was involved where the focus was not on whether S should be treated as if it were the same as C but on whether C could be said to have done enough to be regarded as having "achieved" the planning permission granted on S's application, and (4) there was no ambiguity such as to justify resort to the contra proferentem approach.

GLASGOW CITY COUNCIL v. CASTSTOP LTD 2002 S.L.T. 47, Lord Macfadyen, OH.

5787. Sale—missives—interpretation—non-supersession clause—effect where no settlement

In 1993, the parties entered into a contract whereby S acquired an option to purchase an area of ground. By cl.18 of the conditions annexed to S's offer, the missives would cease to be enforceable after a period of two years from the date of entry. On February 28, 1994 S exercised the option and by cl.4 of S's offer, the date of entry was 40 days after that date. Settlement of the purchase did not take place and the disposition was not delivered because of queries in regard to W's title. S eventually decided to accept the position and in 1999 they brought an action seeking to have W ordained to implement the contract. The sheriff dismissed the action, sustaining W's plea that in terms of cl.18 the contract was no longer enforceable. S appealed, arguing that the two year period was intended to commence when the right to receive a disposition in exchange for the purchase price had been satisfied and "the date of entry" should be understood as the date when settlement of the transaction was effected.

Held, refusing the appeal, that the time limit in cl.18 was independent of whether the disposition had been delivered as (per the Lord President (Cullen) and Lord Kirkwood) S's interpretation of "the date of entry" gave the expression a different meaning from that in cl.4 of the same missive, the expression had a well recognised meaning as the date when entry was to be given under the missives, and as used in cl.4 it provided an understandable starting point for the running of time with regard to the enforcement of rights under the missives; (per Lord Morison) when the clause was viewed in the context of the contract as a whole, it was impossible to construe "the date of entry" as referring to any date other than that specified in the offer to which the clause was subject.

SPENCE v. W&R MURRAY (ALFORD) LTD 2002 S.L.T. 918, Lord Cullen L.P., Lord Kirkwood, Lord Morison, 1 Div.

5788. Sale—missives—interpretation—non-supersession clause—failure to state commencement date

[Capital Allowances Act 1990 (c.1).]

The purchaser of an area of land and warehouse depot sought, inter alia, declarator that in terms of the missives the sellers had warranted that they had incurred expenditure such as to attract relief under the Capital Allowances Act 1990 and that in the event that the purchasers' claim for allowances in that connection failed on appeal, the sellers were obliged to indemnify the pursuers. The Lord Ordinary heard debate on a preliminary point for the defenders that the effect of cl.15.1 of the pursuer's offer dated March 3, 1995, by which the missives remained in force notwithstanding delivery of the disposition but for two years only, was that any warranty had lapsed by passage of time, along with any related indemnity, as no proceedings had been brought within the two year period.

Held, putting the case out by order, that cl.15.1 was unenforceable because of uncertainty, in that it did not contain a starting point from which the two year period was to run nor could one be implied.

LONERGAN v. W&P FOOD SERVICE LTD 2002 S.L.T. 908, Lord Clarke, OH.

5789. Sale—option to purchase—identification of subjects—consensus

B sought declarator that he had a valid option to purchase an area of land from F.

Held, granting decree of absolvitor, that (1) there was clear authority that the essentials of a contract for the sale of heritable property included the identification of the subjects of sale, which extended to cover options to purchase, but which did not normally permit identification by reference to the general area and location of the subjects even where part of the subjects could clearly be identified but the remainder could not, and (2) B had failed to prove that consensus in idem had been reached concerning the identification of the subjects for sale or the price to be paid on the exercise of the option, which were both essential elements of such a contract.

BOGIE (T/A OAKBANK SERVICES) v. FORESTRY COMMISSION 2002 S.C.L.R. 278, Lord Macfadyen, OH.

5790. Sale—sequestration of seller—disposition granted and delivered but not yet recorded

See INSOLVENCY: Burnett's Trustee v. Grainger. §5890

5791. Servitudes—constitution—sufficiency of averments

K sought declarator of the existence of a servitude right for water supply pipes across a field so K could connect their property to the water main. A challenged the averments and sought dismissal of the action.

Held, finding K's averments irrelevant, recalling the sheriff's interlocutor and dismissing the action, that (1) the missives did not, of themselves, grant a servitude, merely an undertaking to grant one if required to do so and there was no authority for the proposition that a right to demand a servitude could be translated into a grant of a servitude without further steps being taken; (2) K had demonstrated that they only had a right to demand a servitude and G's actions in laying the pipe could not be used to bridge the gap between that right and the declarator sought in the action, and (3) there were no averments in K's pleadings which attempted to answer the fundamental question of how the servitude, if it existed, had been created.

KAY v. ALEXANDER 2002 S.C.L.R. 203, RA Dunlop Q.C., Sheriff Principal, Sh Ct.

5792. Standard securities–calling up notice–suspension–relevancy

[Conveyancing and Feudal Reform (Scotland) Act 1970 (c.35).]

The grantors of two standard securities in respect of commercial debts petitioned for suspension of a certificate and calling up notices served by the respondent creditors. In separate proceedings raised by the respondents the parties each alleged breach of contract by the other in relation to an agreement appointing the petitioners as the respondents' distributors in Scotland. The respondents sought payment for goods delivered while the petitioners counterclaimed for damages. The Lord Ordinary granted interim suspension and the respondents reclaimed. The petitioners accepted that they could not claim a right of retention in respect of their damages claim but argued that the petitions disclosed an adequate defence to the notices in that no sum was due by them to the respondents, or at least that they disputed the sum said to be due, and their obligations to pay for the goods at that stage were extinguished because the reclaimers' alleged breaches of contract arose in relation to the same contract from which their demand for payment arose.

Held, allowing the reclaiming motions and recalling the interim orders, that (1) it was for the petitioners to challenge the calling up notices by specifying why no sum was due by them under the notices when issued, and to show that they were not in default, and no statable defence had been made out where the petitioners did not aver that they had made any payment in response to the calling up notices, or that they had paid for goods which they admitted had been delivered, and none of the figures specified in the certificates had been challenged as not being due at the relevant date; (2) the Conveyancing and Feudal Reform (Scotland) Act 1970 did not require any inquiry, validation or justification of the figure specified in the calling up notice prior to service and the reclaimers were entitled to do diligence on the basis of that figure, and (3) there was no authority to support the petitioners' argument that their obligations to pay for the goods at that stage were extinguished, and their claim did not fall within the principle of reciprocity.

GARDINER v. JACQUES VERT PLC 2002 S.L.T. 928, Lord Cameron of Lochbroom, Lord Dawson, Lord Marnoch, Ex Div.

5793. Standard securities–discharge–failure to oppose calling up of standard security–entitlement to defend subsequent action for possession

[Conveyancing and Feudal Reform (Scotland) Act 1970 (c.35) s.10(1) (a).]

F, a company, raised an action seeking declarator that G, two individuals, were in default in terms of a standard security, warrant to enter into possession of and to sell the property concerned and warrant for the ejection of G from the subjects. G counterclaimed that they were entitled to have the standard security discharged, averring that they were not in default, that at no stage had F advanced any sums to them, that no sums were due by them in terms of the personal obligation provided for in the standard security and that the sum referred to in calling up notices issued by F was owed by a company. The sheriff refused F's motion for summary decree. On appeal it was accepted that the sheriff had misappreciated the defence stated. F argued that it was not open to G to dispute liability in relation to the personal obligation, having regard to the Conveyancing and Feudal Reform (Scotland) Act 1970 s.10(1) (a), by which a clause in a security for a fixed amount undertaking to make payment to the creditor imported an acknowledgment of liability to pay that sum, that where a debtor failed to comply with a calling up notice and made no attempt to interrupt the procedure of calling up and default, there would be no defence, and that the counterclaim should not influence the decision on the motion for summary decree.

Held, dismissing the appeal, that there was no basis for granting summary decree where in the event of the counterclaim being resolved in G's favour the standard security would be discharged, and there was no authority requiring a debtor to seek judicial interruption of the default procedure in respect of a standard security as a prerequisite of stating a defence to an action such as the

SCOTLAND: HERITABLE PROPERTY AND CONVEYANCING

present, the issues raised by s.10(1)(a) requiring to be resolved, if necessary, after proof.

J SYKES & SONS (FISH MERCHANTS) LTD v. GRIEVE 2002 S.L.T. (Sh Ct) 15, JC McInnes Q.C., Sheriff Principal, Sh Ct.

5794. Standard securities–guarantees–enforcement–undue influence by debtor against co-debtor–constructive knowledge of creditor–relevancy

A bank raised an action seeking decree to enforce a standard security granted by B supporting a guarantee in respect of obligations of her husband relating to his business. B pled that the guarantee should be set aside, she having signed it under the undue influence of her husband, on whom she relied to take all financial decisions, and without being aware of its true nature. She admitted she had had independent legal advice, without admitting the content of that advice. The guarantee document emphasised the nature of the obligations being undertaken by B and that she should seek independent legal advice. The document was signed by B below that warning and bore to have been signed outwith her home in the presence of two witnesses. B averred that a document which must have been the guarantee was placed before her by her husband, at home, for her signature, no other person being present. The sheriff, affirmed by the sheriff principal, granted decree de plano. B appealed to the Court of Session, arguing that (1) the courts below had erred in holding that she had failed to plead a relevant case of undue influence, and (2) the subsequent decision in *Royal Bank of Scotland Plc v. Etridge (No.2)* [2001] UKHL 44, [2001] 3 W.L.R. 1021, [2001] C.L.Y. 4880 should be applied in Scotland to the effect of requiring a creditor to take certain particular steps before it could be held to have acted in good faith in terms of *Smith v. Bank of Scotland* 1997 S.C. (H.L.) 111, [1997] C.L.Y. 6087.

Held, refusing the appeal, that (1) (per Lords Coulsfield and Marnoch) although B's pleadings were less than frank about her knowledge of and participation in the transaction, there was sufficient in her averments for proof on the question of undue influence; (2) *Etridge* effected no change in the creditor's duties so far as Scots law was concerned, and B had no relevant averments that the pursuers had not acted in good faith at the time of the transaction, because (per Lords Coulsfield and Sutherland) the developments effected by the House of Lords were stated not to be retrospective, and the pursuers had acted in good faith in terms of the law as understood at the time of the transaction; (per Lord Marnoch) although court decisions which affected the common law were retrospective in character and little importance could be attached to the fact that the events preceded *Etridge*, the pursuers had complied with what the House of Lords required in *Smith*, which remained the applicable law.

CLYDESDALE BANK PLC v. BLACK 2002 S.L.T. 764, Lord Coulsfield, Lord Marnoch, Lord Sutherland, Ex Div.

5795. Standard securities–guarantees–misrepresentation–creditors–previous guarantee covering all debts–relevancy

K sought production and reduction of a standard security granted by her and her husband (M) in favour of a bank (C) in 1991, so far as it affected her interest in a flat. In 1992 M borrowed £30,000 from C to purchase a shop, and in August 1995, without K's knowledge, entered into a term loan agreement to restructure his business debts. The effect of that loan in conjunction with the standard security was to render K a guarantor of M's business liabilities to C. In April 1995, C had written to K asking her to sign a guarantee of M's debts, advising her that she might become liable and urging her to seek independent legal advice. K informed C that she was not willing to grant such a guarantee but C proceeded with the loan and did not warn her that her interest in the security subjects was now burdened to that extent, nor did he advise her to seek further independent advice. K argued that C had acted in bad faith. K sought to rely on *Smith v. Bank of Scotland* 1997 S.L.T. 1061, [1997] C.L.Y. 6087, arguing that a creditor should not mislead a cautioner by withholding part of the truth; that C's letter in April 1995 gave the wrong impression that K required to sign a deed in order to become guarantor; and that C ought to have corrected that erroneous impression before entering into the loan.

Held, dismissing the action, that (1) by the terms of the standard security, K had committed herself in advance to being a cautioner for M's debts and, as solicitors were acting for K and M at that time, C were entitled to suppose that K was advised as to its effect, and (2) *Smith* applied to the setting aside of cautionary obligations which a cautioner had entered into as a result of having been misled by what a creditor said or did in bad faith. K's standard security was entered into long before the alleged acts of bad faith, and if the letter had never been sent K's position would have been no different from her present position. Furthermore there was no clear averment that the loan agreement altered K's position for the worse.

AHMED v. CLYDESDALE BANK PLC 2001 S.L.T. 423, Lord Macfadyen, OH.

5796. Books

Brown, Vincent; Aitchison, Karen—Brown and Aitchison: Environmental Law and Commercial Property Transactions in Scotland. Paperback: £65.00. ISBN 0-406-92758-8. Butterworths Law.

Commercial Property. Looseleaf/ring bound. ISBN 0-414-01421-9. W. Green & Son.

Conveyancing Statutes 2002. Paperback: £29.95. ISBN 0-414-01493-6. W. Green & Son.

Pitt, M and Bowman, E—Valuation: Law and Practice. Greens Law Basics. Paperback: £25.00. ISBN 0-414-01298-4. W. Green & Son.

Reid, Kenneth—Execution of Deeds. Greens Practice Library. Hardback. ISBN 0-414-01138-4. W. Green & Son.

Reid, Kenneth G.C.; Gretton, George L.—Conveyancing 2001. Paperback: £22.00. ISBN 0-406-95703-7. Butterworths Law (Scotland).

Ross, Kenneth—Contaminated Land for Conveyancers. Paperback: £38.00. ISBN 0-414-01289-5. W. Green & Son.

Sinclair, John H.—Sinclair: Handbook of Conveyancing Practice in Scotland. 4th Ed. Paperback: £42.00. ISBN 0-406-95705-3. Butterworths Law (Scotland).

HIGHWAYS

5797. Bridges—tolls—assignation of right to collect—written consent of Secretary of State not required

[Roads (Scotland) Act 1984 (c.54) Sch.2, para.4.]

R appealed against the refusal of the Lord Ordinary (1999 S.C.L.R. 749) to grant interdict against M and their agents from demanding any toll from R in respect of the Skye Bridge. In 1991 notices appeared in the press to the effect that the Secretary of State for Scotland had decided to charge tolls in respect of the bridge and that he had made a statement assigning the right to charge and collect tolls, which detailed the person to whom the rights had been assigned. Details were given in the notice of where the draft toll order and the statement of assignation could be examined and information on how to object to it. The assignation in 1991 of the right to charge and collect tolls had been made in favour of Skye Bridge Ltd whom, it was alleged had subsequently re-assigned those rights in favour of M without the consent of the Secretary of State. R claimed that M had no authority to charge and collect tolls as consent to the assignation in their favour had not been given. He also argued that the form and content of the original assignation by the Secretary of State was invalid in terms of the enabling legislation and that the order and statement had not been properly publicised in terms of the procedure for statutory instruments.

Held, refusing the appeal, that (1) the issue of consent by the Secretary of State did not arise as the agreement between Skye Bridge Ltd and M was a form of agency and not an assignation, *Smith v. Hingston* 2000 G.W.D. 2-62, followed; (2) R's objections to the validity of the original assignation by the Secretary of State and the scheme operated pursuant to that assignation, had to fail as they were not made timeously in terms of the procedures set out in the Roads (Scotland) Act 1984 Sch.2, para.4, which acted as an ouster clause to deny jurisdiction to the court in respect of such a claim, *Pollock v. Secretary of State for Scotland* 1993 S.L.T. 1173, [1992] C.L.Y. 6511, followed; (3) the change of concessionaire was a change in name only as M had formerly been registered as Skye Bridge Ltd, and (4) the procedures for publication of statutory instruments did not apply to toll orders or assignations and the level of publicity given was sufficient. Opinion of the Court per Lord Johnston.

ROBBIE THE PICT v. MILLER CIVIL ENGINEERING LTD 2001 S.C.L.R.1103, Lord Johnston, Lord Cameron of Lochbroom, Lord Dawson, Ex Div.

5798. Disabled persons–traffic orders–exemptions

LOCAL AUTHORITIES' TRAFFIC ORDERS (EXEMPTIONS FOR DISABLED PERSONS) (SCOTLAND) AMENDMENT REGULATIONS 2002, SSI 2002 547; made under the Road Traffic Regulation Act 1984 s.124, Sch.9 Part III, Sch.9 para.21, Sch.9 para.22, Sch.9 para.25. In force: January 15, 2003; £1.75.

These Regulations, amend the Local Authorities' Traffic Orders (Exemptions for Disabled Persons) (Scotland) Regulations 2002 (SSI 2002 450) by omitting the references contained in Reg 6 and 7 to the Road Traffic Regulation Act 1984 s.6.

5799. Disabled persons–traffic orders–exemptions

LOCAL AUTHORITIES' TRAFFIC ORDERS (EXEMPTIONS FOR DISABLED PERSONS) (SCOTLAND) REGULATIONS 2002, SSI 2002 450; made under the Road Traffic Regulation Act 1984 s.124, Sch.9 Part III, Sch.9 para.21, Sch.9 para.22, Sch.9 para.25. In force: November 8, 2002; £1.75.

These Regulations, which revoke the Local Authorities' Traffic Orders (Exemptions for Disabled Persons) (Scotland) Regulations 2000 (SSI 2000 60), concern certain Traffic Orders made by local authorities in Scotland under the Road Traffic Regulation Act 1984. They provide that such Orders should include in certain cases an exemption from waiting prohibitions or restrictions for vehicles displaying a disabled person's badge issued under the Chronically Sick and Disabled Persons Act 1970 s.21

5800. Local authorities powers and duties–traffic orders

LOCAL AUTHORITIES' TRAFFIC ORDERS (PROCEDURE) (SCOTLAND) AMENDMENT REGULATIONS 2002, SSI 2002 31; made under the Road Traffic Regulation Act 1984 s.124, Sch.9 Part III. In force: March 1, 2002; £1.75.

These Regulations amend the Local Authorities' Traffic Orders (Procedure) (Scotland) Regulations 1999 (SI 1999 614), which prescribe the procedure to be followed by local traffic authorities in Scotland for making the main types of traffic and parking orders under the Road Traffic Regulation Act 1984, to clarify the operation of that provision in connection with the Local Roads Authorities' Traffic Orders (Procedure) (Scotland) Regulations 1987 (SI 1987 2245) and also corrects an erroneous cross reference to the revocation of the 1987 Regulations.

5801. Road works–inspections–fees

ROAD WORKS (INSPECTION FEES) (SCOTLAND) AMENDMENT REGULATIONS 2002, SSI 2002 13; made under the New Roads and Street Works Act 1991 s.134, s.163. In force: March 1, 2002; £1.50.

These Regulations, which revoke the Road Works (Inspection Fees) (Scotland) Amendment Regulations 1998 (SI 1998 1029), amend the Road Works (Inspection Fees) (Scotland) Regulations 1992 (SI 1992 1676) to provide for an increase to £15.50 in the fee payable by undertakers for inspections of their work by street authorities.

5802. Roads–traffic calming–installation of wheelie bins–ultra vires

[Roads (Scotland) Act 1984 (c.54) s.39A, s.40, s.54; Roads (Traffic Calming) (Scotland) Regulations 1994 (SI 1994 2488).]

M petitioned for the reduction of a decision of A (a local authority), to install permanent wheelie bins on M's street. A purported to rely on powers under the Roads (Traffic Calming) (Scotland) Regulations 1994.

Held, ordering A to remove the structures within six weeks, that (1) given that parking was permitted throughout the length of the street, and the bins occupied no more space than a parked car, the movement of vehicular and other traffic was not affected, except the prevention of parking where the bins were located, therefore the bins could not constitute traffic calming works under the Roads (Scotland) Act 1984 s.39A and s.40 and the 1994 Regulations; and (2) "road refuse" in terms of s.54 of the 1984 Act, relied on by A ex post facto as permitting the bins for the collection and temporary deposit of road refuse, was refuse deposited on the road by those using it or pedestrians using the pavement, and domestic refuse placed outside houses for collection did not become road refuse because of the location in which it was left.

McKELLER v. ABERDEEN CITY COUNCIL 2001 S.C. 729, Lord MacLean, OH.

5803. Vehicles–abandoned vehicles–disposal and removal

REMOVAL AND DISPOSAL OF VEHICLES AMENDMENT (SCOTLAND) REGULATIONS 2002, SSI 2002 538; made under the Refuse Disposal (Amenity) Act 1978 s.3, s.4; and the Road Traffic Regulation Act 1984 s.99, s.101. In force: January 15, 2003; £1.75.

These Regulations amend the Removal and Disposal of Vehicles Regulations 1986 (SI 1986 183) in two cases. The first is where an authority proposes to remove a vehicle which appears to the authority to be abandoned and in its opinion is in such a condition that it ought to be destroyed; the notice period is reduced from 7 days to 24 hours from when a notice is affixed to the vehicle. The second case is where an authority has removed a vehicle (but it is not in such condition that it ought to be destroyed) and has located the owner; the period during which the owner is required to remove the vehicle from the custody of the authority is reduced from 21 days to 7 days from when the relevant notice is served on the owner.

HOUSING

5804. Accommodation–appointment of arbiter

HOUSING (SCOTLAND) ACT 2001 (APPOINTMENT OF ARBITER) ORDER 2002, SSI 2002 413; made under the Housing (Scotland) Act 2001 s.6, s.110. In force: September 30, 2002; £1.50.

The Housing (Scotland) Act 2001 s.6(1)(c) provides that if the local authority and the landlord are unable to reach agreement within a specified period as to whether there is a good reason why the landlord has not complied with a request to provide accommodation then an arbiter must be appointed to determine the issue. This Order prescribes the specified period for the purposes of that section.

5805. Asylum seekers–secure tenancies

HOUSING (SCOTLAND) ACT 2001 (ACCOMMODATION FOR ASYLUM-SEEKERS) ORDER 2002, SI 2002 2367; made under the Scotland Act 1998 s.104, s.112. In force: September 30, 2002; £1.50.

This Order provides that a tenancy granted to asylum-seekers under the Immigration and Asylum Act 1999 Part VI is not a Scottish secure tenancy within the meaning of the Housing (Scotland) Act 2001, unless the tenant is notified otherwise by the landlord.

5806. Childrens welfare-multiple occupation-licensing

CIVIC GOVERNMENT (SCOTLAND) ACT 1982 (LICENSING OF HOUSES IN MULTIPLE OCCUPATION) AMENDMENT ORDER 2002, SSI 2002 161; made under the Civic Government (Scotland) Act 1982 s.44. In force: April 1, 2002; £1.75.

This Order makes amendment provisions to the Civic Government (Scotland) Act 1982 (Licensing of Houses in Multiple Occupation) Order 2000 (SSI 2000 177) which relate to foster and other children. It adds foster children and those brought up or treated as someone's child to the list of persons who are treated as being members of the same family for the purposes of the 2000 Order and updates terminology and statutory references now superseded by the Regulation of Care (Scotland) Act 2001.

5807. Defective premises-dampness-statutory nuisance

See NUISANCE: Robb v. Dundee City Council. §6014

5808. Demolition-right to buy-information requirements

HOUSING (RIGHT TO BUY) (HOUSES LIABLE TO DEMOLITION) (SCOTLAND) ORDER 2002, SSI 2002 317; made under the Housing (Scotland) Act 1987 s.70A. In force: September 30, 2002; £1.75.

This Order provides details of the information to be submitted to the Scottish Ministers by a landlord in support of an application for authorisation to refuse to sell a house to an applicant under the right to buy legislation where the landlord has already made a decision to demolish that house.

5809. Homelessness-advice and assistance

HOMELESS PERSONS ADVICE AND ASSISTANCE (SCOTLAND) REGULATIONS 2002, SSI 2002 414; made under the Housing (Scotland) Act 1987 s.31, s.32. In force: September 30, 2002; £1.75.

These Regulations prescribe the types of advice and assistance local authorities must provide under the Housing (Scotland) Act 1987 to homeless applicants and applicants threatened with homelessness who are not in priority need or have become homeless or threatened with homelessness intentionally. The Regulations apply only to persons assessed as homeless or threatened with homelessness after the date on which the Regulations come into force; set out the advice to be provided by local authorities to applicants found to be homeless or threatened with homelessness; and set out the assistance to be provided by local authorities to applicants found to be homeless or threatened with homelessness.

5810. Homelessness-interim accommodation

HOMELESS PERSONS INTERIM ACCOMMODATION (SCOTLAND) REGULATIONS 2002, SSI 2002 412; made under the Housing (Scotland) Act 1987 s.32A. In force: September 30, 2002; £1.75.

These Regulations prescribe the circumstances where local authorities can provide interim accommodation to homeless applicants who otherwise would be entitled to permanent accommodation in terms of the Housing (Scotland) Act 1987 s.31. The Regulations set out the prescribed circumstances which apply where a housing support services assessment has identified that an applicant for housing requires housing support services which cannot reasonably be provided within permanent accommodation.

5811. Housing associations–registered social landlords

HOUSING (SCOTLAND) ACT 2001 (REGISTERED SOCIAL LANDLORDS) ORDER 2002, SSI 2002 411; made under the Housing (Scotland) Act 2001 s.57. In force: September 3, 2002; £1.75.

This Order provides that the specified bodies are to be treated as housing associations which were, immediately before the commencement of the Housing (Scotland) Act 2001 s.57(2), registered in the register of housing associations maintained under the Housing Associations Act 1985. By virtue of the 2001 Act, such housing associations are registered as social landlords.

5812. Housing associations–support services–grants

HOUSING (SCOTLAND) ACT 2001 (HOUSING SUPPORT SERVICES) REGULATIONS 2002, SSI 2002 444; made under the Housing (Scotland) Act 2001 s.91, s.109. In force: October 31, 2002; £1.75.

These Regulations prescribe the types of support, assistance, advice or counselling services that may be provided by local authorities using grants paid by the Scottish Ministers. The purpose of the support is to assist individuals with particular needs to occupy or continue to occupy, as that person's sole or main residence, accommodation other than residential accommodation provided as part of a care home service; or accommodation provided under the Social Work (Scotland) Act 1968 for offenders and persons under supervision.

5813. Housing associations–support services–information

HOUSING (SCOTLAND) ACT 2001 (HOUSING SUPPORT SERVICES INFORMATION) ORDER 2002, SI 2002 2264; made under the Scotland Act 1988 s.104, s.112, s.113. In force: October 1, 2002; £1.75.

The Housing (Scotland) Act 2001 gives power to the Scottish Ministers to pay grants to local authorities towards spending incurred in connection with prescribed housing support services. This Order makes provision for information on income support, income based jobseeker's allowance and housing benefit to be passed to and from local authorities for purposes connected with that spending.

5814. Housing support grant–aggregate amount and apportionment

HOUSING SUPPORT GRANT (SCOTLAND) ORDER 2002, SSI 2002 171; made under the Housing (Scotland) Act 1987 s.191, s.192. In force: April 1, 2002; £2.00.

This Order fixes for the year 2002-2003 the aggregate amount of the housing support grants payable to some local authorities under the Housing (Scotland) Act 1987 s.191. It provides for the aggregate amount to be divided into general and hostel provisions, prescribes the local authorities among whom the grants for the general portion will be apportioned, provides the method of calculation and prescribes the local authorities among whom the grants for the hostel portion will be apportioned and the method of calculation.

5815. Housing (Scotland) Act 2001 (asp 10)–Commencement No.4 and Transitional Provisions Order

HOUSING (SCOTLAND) ACT 2001 (COMMENCEMENT NO.4, TRANSITIONAL PROVISIONS AND SAVINGS) ORDER 2002, SSI 2002 168; made under the Housing (Scotland) Act 2001 s.109, s.113. Commencement details: bringing into force various provisions of the 2001 Act on April 1, 2002; £2.00.

This Order, which amends the Housing (Scotland) Act 1987, the Social Security Administration Act 1992 and the Leasehold Reform, Housing and Urban Development Act 1993, brings into force various provisions of the Housing (Scotland) Act 2001 relating to homelessness, common housing registers, housing lists and allocations.

5816. Housing (Scotland) Act 2001 (asp 10)–Commencement No.5, Transitional Provisions and Savings Order

HOUSING (SCOTLAND) ACT 2001 (COMMENCEMENT NO.5, TRANSITIONAL PROVISIONS AND SAVINGS) ORDER 2002, SSI 2002 321; made under the Housing (Scotland) Act 2001 s.109, s.113. Commencement details: bringing into force various provisions of the 2001 Act on September 30, 2002; £2.00.

This Order brings into force various provisions of the Housing (Scotland) Act 2001.

5817. Housing (Scotland) Act 2001 (asp 10)–Commencement No.6 Order

HOUSING (SCOTLAND) ACT 2001 (COMMENCEMENT NO.6 AND AMENDMENT) ORDER 2002, SSI 2002 433; made under the Housing (Scotland) Act 2001 s.113. Commencement details: bringing into force various provisions of the 2001 Act on September 30, 2002; £2.00.

This Order, which amends the Housing (Scotland) Act 2001 (Commencement No.5, Transitional Provisions and Savings) Order 2002 (SSI 2002 321), brings into force various provisions of the Housing (Scotland) Act 2001 which relate to repeal of management agreements between housing cooperatives and local authorities.

5818. Local authorities powers and duties–tenant organisations–registration

HOUSING (SCOTLAND) ACT 2001 (REGISTRATION OF TENANT ORGANISATIONS) ORDER 2002, SSI 2002 416; made under the Housing (Scotland) Act 2001 s.53. In force: September 30, 2002; £2.00.

The Housing (Scotland) Act 2001 s.53(3) requires that every local authority landlord and registered social landlord must maintain a register of tenant organisations. This Order sets out the criteria for organisations seeking registration, the criteria for removal from a register and the procedure in relation to applications for registration in and removal from a register.

5819. Local government finance–housing revenue account–contribution from general fund

HOUSING REVENUE ACCOUNT GENERAL FUND CONTRIBUTION LIMITS (SCOTLAND) ORDER 2002, SSI 2002 45; made under the Housing (Scotland) Act 1987 s.204. In force: March 11, 2002; £1.50.

This Order provides that local authorities may not include in their estimates for the year 2001 to 2002 any contribution from their general fund to their housing revenue account.

5820. Public sector tenancies–repossession–anti social behaviour–husband of tenant convicted with supply of drugs

[Housing (Scotland) Act 1987 (c.26) s.48(2)(a), Sch.3, Pt1, para.2, Sch.3, Pt1, para.7.]

Following the conviction of M's husband for being concerned with supply of controlled drugs, the local authority raised proceedings under the Housing (Scotland) Act 1987 s.48(2)(a) for the recovery of possession of the property, which M occupied as a secure tenant, and for warrant for ejection. The sheriff granted decree in favour of the local authority on the grounds that the conviction was sufficient to establish that M's husband had used the property for illegal purposes under the Housing (Scotland) Act 1987 Sch.3, Pt 1, para.2 and that being concerned with the supply of controlled drugs from the premises constituted a nuisance under the Sch.3, Pt 1, para.7. The sheriff also held that, in all the circumstances, it was not reasonable to expect the local authority to make alternative accommodation available to M. M appealed by way of stated case to the sheriff principal, arguing that (1) the conviction had been for being concerned with the supply of controlled drugs and it and that it was not open to the sheriff to infer from that conviction that the property had actually been used for illegal purposes; (2) the statutory provisions required actual nuisance to have taken place, of which there was no evidence, and (3) it was unreasonable for the local authority not to offer alternative accommodation.

Held, refusing the appeal, that (1) there had been sufficient evidence during the trial that controlled drugs had been found on the premises to enable the sheriff to make his finding that the property had been used for illegal purposes; (2) a conviction for a drug related offence did not amount to evidence that nuisance had taken place and for that ground to have been established, evidence that the drug dealing had become so notorious as to have caused concern or public offence was required; (3) whether it was reasonable in the circumstances for the local authority to provide alternative accommodation had not been addressed in evidence and the sheriff should not have held that it had been established, and (4) the sheriff could not be considered to have erred in deciding that it was reasonable in the circumstances of the case to support the local authority's policy of eviction in cases of drug dealing given the risk of serious prejudice to the interests of the local community from failing to take action against that type of behaviour.

GLASGOW CITY COUNCIL v. McALINDEN 2001 Hous. L.R. 110, EF Bowen Q.C., Sheriff Principal, Sh Ct.

5821. **Public sector tenancies–repossession–anti social behaviour–no offer of alternative accommodation**

[Housing (Scotland) Act1987 (c.26) Sch.3 para.7; Crime and DisorderAct1998 (c.37) s.23(3).]

E raised proceedings for recovery of possession of a flat occupied by W and her children on the ground that W, a person residing with her at the flat or someone visiting the property had acted in an anti-social manner in terms of the Housing (Scotland) Act 1987 Sch.3 para.7 as substituted by the Crime and Disorder Act 1998 s.23(3). There was a great deal of evidence, much of which was not in dispute, as to the conduct of W, her children and, in particular, the extreme anti-social, violent and criminal behaviour of her husband. There was also sufficient evidence to allow the court to regard W's husband as residing with her at the flat, or at least visiting the property. The conduct which gave rise to the action by E, was primarily that involving W's children and young people visiting them. W admitted having parties at the property and that, on occasions, police had attended the property as a result of complaints about the noise levels. Evidence was also given of persistent dog barking, constant yelling and the use of foul language. Amongst the numerous complaints there were allegations of fireworks being set off in the common stairwell, of fuses being removed from a common fuse box leaving neighbours without power for hours, and of drug dealing from the premises. The key issue in dispute, however, was whether it was reasonable for the court to grant an order for eviction of W and her children without requiring E to make an offer of suitable alternative accommodation. The action was adjourned to allow the local authority to make an offer of suitable alternative accommodation and for W to consider such an offer. The court emphasised that W was not entitled to refuse such an offer unreasonably. An offer was duly made for a suitably sized house in another area, which W refused as she claimed it was too far for her children to travel to school.

Held, granting decree, that (1) the evidence of the housing officers who had investigated the complaints, together with the admissions made by W were sufficient to demonstrate that W, her family and their visitors had acted in an anti-social manner over a sustained period of time, evidence to the contrary being unconvincing; (2) E had made an offer of suitable alternative accommodation which had been unreasonably refused by W as her children were old enough to use public transport to travel to school, and (3) it was reasonable in all the circumstances for E to be granted possession without the requirement to provide a further offer of suitable alternative accommodation.

EDINBURGH CITY COUNCIL v. WATSON 2002 Hous. L.R. 2, AM Bell, Sh Ct (Lothian and Border).

5822. Public sector tenancies–repossession–notice–no ish in tenancy agreement–40 days notice required

[Sheriff Courts (Scotland) Act 1907 (7 Edw.7 c.51) s.37, s.38; Housing (Scotland) Act 1987 (c.43) s.47, Sch.3 para.6.]

W raised an action for recovery of possession of a property tenanted by R on the grounds that she induced W to grant the tenancy by making a false statement in her application in terms of the Housing (Scotland) Act 1987 Sch.3 para.6. It was alleged that R had failed to disclose that, at the time of the application to W, she was already the tenant of a local authority flat in another town. In terms of s.47, W served notice on R that they intended to raise proceedings, giving R 28 days notice. R, whilst admitting making the false statement, argued that the proceedings were incompetent as the tenancy agreement, having no ish date had continued by tacit relocation making the notice period 40 days under common law. R also argued that the action, if not incompetent, should fail on the ground that it would be unreasonable to evict her, her partner and their daughter due to the ill-health of R and her daughter and the lack of suitably priced private rental property in the area.

Held, dismissing the action as incompetent, that 40 days notice was required under the Sheriff Courts (Scotland) Act 1907 s.37 and s.38 as no ish had been stated in the lease and the lease had therefore continued by tacit relocation. Opinion, that in determining whether it would have been reasonable to grant the action for recovery, it would have been necessary to balance the needs of R's child and her partner, who were no party to the false statement, against the interests of the wider community and that although R's action in providing false information had been reprehensible and to the detriment of other applicants, the court would have found marginally in her favour as an eviction would have had an adverse effect on members of her family and their low income would make finding alternative accommodation difficult.

WEST LOTHIAN COUNCIL v. REAPE 2002 Hous. L.R. 58, P Gillam, Sh Ct (Lothian and Border).

5823. Public sector tenancies–repossession–reasonableness–hearing not required following sufficient admission of facts

[Act of Sederunt (Summary Cause Rules) 1976 (SI 1976 476) r.18(9).]

The local authority raised an action for recovery of possession of property tenanted by F following failure to pay rent arrears totalling £572.60. Decree was granted in absence and F lodged a minute of recall. At the hearing before the sheriff, F admitted the rent arrears but moved the sheriff to assign a proof on the question of reasonableness. F submitted that it would be unreasonable for the order for recovery to be granted as she had suffered ill health over the preceding year following a diagnosis of cervical cancer, had found it extremely difficult to cope with the recent loss of her mother, was a single parent on incapacity benefit and had recently paid £25 towards the arrears, which, by the time of the hearing had increased to £1,143. The sheriff refused the motion for a proof on the basis that the facts had been sufficiently admitted to enable him the decide the cause on its merits in terms of the Act of Sederunt (Summary Cause Rules) 1976 r.18(9). F appealed to the sheriff principal on the ground that the sheriff had erred in law in declining to assign a proof on the question of reasonableness. F submitted that the sheriff was under a duty to consider all the circumstances and a proof would have allowed a more detailed explanation of the circumstances which led to the rent arrears, which had only been stated briefly at the hearing before the sheriff. In addition, F also took issue with the comment made by the sheriff that if a proof were to be granted in every case where a defender argued unreasonableness it would produce an unacceptable workload for the court, which, F argued, was an improper consideration which should have played no part in the sheriff's decision.

Held, refusing the appeal, that (1) reasonableness was not a fact but a concept or conclusion determined by an exercise of judgment and, given that all the facts relied on by the local authority had been admitted by F and that the local authority had not taken issue with any of the personal circumstances relied on by F, the sheriff was entitled to conclude that the facts had been sufficiently admitted to enable him to exercise his judgment, and (2) the part of the sheriff's judgment relating to the court's workload was obiter, added after the decision had been made.

Observed, that the workload of the court would have been an improper consideration in deciding the question of reasonableness.

EDINBURGH CITY COUNCIL v. FORBES 2002 Hous. L.R. 61, Nicholson Q.C., Sheriff Principal, Sh Ct.

5824. Public sector tenancies–repossession–rent arrears–part payment of arrears

[Housing (Scotland) Act 1987 (c.43) s.48(2).]

A local authority raised proceedings for the recovery of possession of a property tenanted by M and an order that M should pay rent arrears of £1,093. Following proof, the sheriff granted warrant for ejecting M from the property, but no order was made for payment of the rent arrears claimed in the summons. M appealed arguing that the local authority had failed to serve notice and productions on her within the time limits set out in the rules of court, having only received the productions on a Friday for a proof diet on the following Monday. M argued that until receiving the productions, she was unaware that she had to attend court, and given the time-scale, was unable to secure the services of a lawyer. M also claimed that, on the date the action was raised, she had already paid £800 to the local authority, which had the effect of clearing the rent arrears on which the action had been based and, given that information, the sheriff should not have granted decree. She did not dispute that since the action had been raised, further rental payments had been missed and that at the time decree was granted, there was a significant amount of rent still in arrears. She claimed that the local authority were not entitled to decree on those arrears without raising a fresh action.

Held, refusing the appeal, that (1) M had been represented in court at the time that the proof diet was fixed and it was therefore not open to her to argue that she did not know when the proof was taking place; (2) there was no basis for the submission by M that, in terms of the Housing (Scotland) Act 1987 s.48(2), the arrears of rent at the time of granting decree had to be the same arrears as those at the time of commencing the action where the tenant had been continuously in arrears throughout, and (3) given that M, despite paying sums towards the arrears, never succeeded in bringing her account up to date, the sheriff had not made any error in his approach to granting decree.

STIRLING COUNCIL v. MAGAR 2002 Hous. L.R. 64, RA Dunlop Q.C., Sheriff Principal, Sh Ct.

5825. Secure tenancies–exceptions

SCOTTISH SECURE TENANCIES (EXCEPTIONS) AMENDMENT REGULATIONS 2002, SSI 2002 434; made under the Housing (Scotland) Act 2001 s.109, Sch.1 para.3. In force: September 30, 2002; £1.50.

These Regulations amend the Scottish Secure Tenancies (Exceptions) Regulations 2002 (SSI 2002 314) by replacing the descriptions of certain institutions for the provision of higher education and further education.

5826. Secure tenancies–exceptions

SCOTTISH SECURE TENANCIES (EXCEPTIONS) REGULATIONS 2002, SSI 2002 314; made under the Housing (Scotland) Act 2001 s.109, Sch.1 para.3. In force: September 30, 2002; £1.75.

The Housing (Scotland) Act 2001 provides that a tenancy is not a Scottish secure tenancy if it is a tenancy of a kind mentioned in Sch.1 to the Act. That Schedule provides that a tenancy is not a Scottish secure tenancy if it is granted to a person who is pursuing or intends to pursue a course of study provided by a specified educational institution and is granted either by that institution or by another specified institution or body. These Regulations specify the educational institutions and bodies for specified purposes.

5827. Secure tenancies—housing associations

HOUSING (SCOTLAND) ACT 2001 (SCOTTISH SECURE TENANCY ETC.) AMENDMENT ORDER 2002, SSI 2002 415; made under the Housing (Scotland) Act 2001 s.11, s.109. In force: September 30, 2002; £1.75.

This Order amends the Housing (Scotland) Act 2001 (Scottish Secure Tenancy etc.) Order 2002 (SSI 2002 318) by adding to the categories of tenancy, which will become Scottish secure tenancies, certain types of contractual tenancy granted by registered social landlords which are co-operative housing associations.

5828. Secure tenancies—notice requirements

SHORT SCOTTISH SECURE TENANCIES (NOTICES) REGULATIONS 2002, SSI 2002 315; made under the Housing (Scotland) Act 2001 s.34, s.109. In force: September 30, 2002; £2.00.

These Regulations prescribe the notice that is to be used by a prospective landlord when notifying a prospective tenant that the tenancy being offered is a short Scottish secure tenancy.

5829. Secure tenancies—possession proceedings—form of notice

SCOTTISH SECURE TENANCIES (PROCEEDINGS FOR POSSESSION) REGULATIONS 2002, SSI 2002 320; made under the Housing (Scotland) Act 2001 s.14, s.109. In force: September 30, 2002; £2.00.

These Regulations prescribe the form of notice to be used by a landlord when notifying its tenant under a Scottish secure tenancy, within the meaning of the Housing (Scotland) Act 2001 Part 2, that the landlord may commence possession proceedings in respect of the dwellinghouse which is the subject of the Scottish secure tenancy.

5830. Secure tenancies—possession proceedings—form of notice

SHORT SCOTTISH SECURE TENANCIES (PROCEEDINGS FOR POSSESSION) REGULATIONS 2002, SSI 2002 319; made under the Housing (Scotland) Act 2001 s.36, s.109. In force: September 30, 2002; £1.75.

These Regulations prescribe the form of notice to be used by a landlord when notifying a tenant under a short Scottish secure tenancy, within the meaning of the Housing (Scotland) Act 2001 Part 2, that the landlord requires possession of the house occupied by that tenant and may commence possession proceedings in respect of that house.

5831. Secure tenancies—qualifying improvement work—compensation

SCOTTISH SECURE TENANTS (COMPENSATION FOR IMPROVEMENTS) REGULATIONS 2002, SSI 2002 312; made under the Housing (Scotland) Act 2001 s.30, s.109. In force: September 30, 2002; £2.00.

These Regulations, which introduce provisions for compensation for qualifying improvement work payable at the termination of a Scottish secure tenancy, prescribe qualifying improvement work with reference to the Schedule which details improvements that are to be regarded as qualifying improvements and the notional life of those improvements. The Regulations prescribe the lower limit for compensation and specifies circumstances where no compensation is payable; provide a formula for calculating compensation and specifies the upper limit for compensation; set out the procedure to be followed in relation to compensation claims; provide that a landlord can set off against compensation sums due to it by a qualifying person; and set out the procedures for review of decisions and allows a right of appeal to the sheriff.

5832. Secure tenancies–qualifying repairs

SCOTTISH SECURE TENANTS (RIGHT TO REPAIR) REGULATIONS 2002, SSI 2002 316; made under the Housing (Scotland) Act 2001 s.27, s.109. In force: September 30, 2002; £2.00.

These Regulations specify entitlement procedures, timescales and limits applying to qualifying repairs to houses subject to Scottish secure tenancies. They specify the entitlement provisions for qualifying repairs; specify the landlords to which the Regulations apply; specify the maximum amount for a single repair; provide details of what constitutes a qualifying repair and the maximum period in which these repairs are to be completed; make provision for landlords to maintain a list of contractors; set out the procedure for notifying qualifying repairs, the details which landlords are required to provide to tenants and the procedures a landlord should follow in relation to contractors; detail what is to happen when the tenant instructing a repair fails to provide access; make provision for instructing another contractor when the primary contractor fails to carry out the work and provides for compensation to be payable to the tenant in that eventuality; set out the circumstances when the maximum period for a repair can be disregarded; and make provision for a landlord to provide tenants with information on the Regulations.

5833. Secure tenancies–repossession–abandoned property–storage and disposal

SCOTTISH SECURE TENANCIES (ABANDONED PROPERTY) ORDER 2002, SSI 2002 313; made under the Housing (Scotland) Act 2001 s.18, s.109. In force: September 30, 2002; £1.75.

This Order, which makes provision for the procedure to be followed by a landlord in respect of property found in a house which has been re-possessed under the Housing (Scotland) Act 2001 s.18, provides that the tenant will be advised by notice that if the tenant's property is not collected within a specified time it may be disposed of. It provides that property of a value sufficient to cover the cost of storage will be stored for six months and may thereafter be sold; provides that property of a value insufficient to cover the cost of storage may be disposed of; provides that, subject to the landlord's security for unpaid rent, the landlord shall, on receipt of payment of its expenses, surrender any property to which the Order applies to any person appearing to be a person entitled to delivery; provides that the landlord may deduct its expenses and the amount of any arrears of rent from the proceeds of sale of any property to which the Order applies; and provides that landlords will maintain for five years, in a register open to public inspection, information as to the houses in which property to which the Order applies has been found.

5834. Secure tenancies–right to buy

HOUSING (SCOTLAND) ACT 2001 (SCOTTISH SECURE TENANCY ETC.) ORDER 2002, SSI 2002 318; made under the Housing (Scotland) Act 1987 s.61A; and the Housing (Scotland) Act 2001 s.11, s.109, s.110. In force: September 30, 2002; £1.75.

This Order introduces the Scottish secure tenancy, makes various transitional provisions and savings in consequence of that introduction, and sets out the circumstances in which the limitation on the right to buy from a registered social landlord does not apply.

5835. Secure tenancies–right to buy–application forms

RIGHT TO PURCHASE (APPLICATION FORM) (SCOTLAND) ORDER 2002, SSI 2002 322; made under the Housing (Scotland) Act 1987 s.63. In force: September 30, 2002; £3.00.

This Order, which revokes the Right to Purchase (Application Form) (Scotland) Order 2000 (SI 2000 120), prescribes another form of notice which is to be used by any tenant with a right to purchase under a Scottish secure tenancy, within the meaning of Housing (Scotland) Act 1987 when exercising the right to purchase a dwellinghouse.

5836. Tenants rights–right to purchase–occupation in accordance with contract–occupancy retained after change in job–occupancy not necessary for better performance of duties

[Housing (Scotland) Act 1987 (c.26) Sch.2 para.1.]

S, a husband and wife, made an application for a finding that they had a right to buy the school house they occupied. H had occupied the premises in connection with janitorial duties. Access to the house had initially been through the school gates, but the house was subsequently given its own access. H was offered a new position as facilities coordinator during DCC's reorganisation and remained in the house although he had no direct responsibility for the school. DCC's policy with regard to the new position was that the facility coordinators had to live in tied houses and respond to situations at school outwith working hours. DCC argued that S were not secure tenants and had no right to buy and although S was no longer in charge of the adjacent school, an obligation to continue to live there could be inferred from DCC's policy and it was clear that, taking his duties as a whole, residence would enable better performance of his duties. DCC also argued that the house and garden were within the school curtilage, the present position of the gates not being determinative. DCC also highlighted that S received discounted rent and council tax rebate.

Held, allowing the application, that (1) for DCC to be able to rely on the Housing (Scotland) Act 1987 Sch.2, para.1 it had to be established that there was an express or implied obligation to occupy; (2) the test of better performance was a separate issue and should be assessed, not by reference to the obligation on the employee but by reference to the effect of performance in practical terms; (3) it had not been established that occupation allowed better performance of any duty which would be of any value to DCC, nor any genuine intention of DCC that an obligation of occupation be imposed for better performance of H's duties, and (4) a secure physical boundary was a strong indication of the extent of a curtilage and the house had its own clearly defined boundary.

SMITH v. DUNDEE CITY COUNCIL 2001 Hous. L.R. 78, Lord McGhie (President), Lands Tr (Scot).

5837. Tenants rights–right to purchase–secure tenancies–change in status of tenancy by transfer

[Housing (Scotland) Act 1987 (c.26) s.61, s.68(4); Housing (Scotland) Act 1988 (c.43) s.43(3).]

M applied for a finding under the Housing (Scotland) Act 1987 s.68(4) that she had a right to purchase the property occupied by her from Q, her landlords. Q had refused her application on the grounds that she was not a secure tenant and therefore did not qualify under s.61 of the 1987 Act. M had been the tenant of the flat from September 1986 until November 1991, Q were her landlords and that tenancy had been a secure tenancy under the 1987 Act. The introduction of the Housing (Scotland) Act 1988, did not affect the status of that tenancy. In November 1991, M became the tenant of a different flat; her landlords continued to be Q and there was no interruption between the cessation of one tenancy and the commencement of the other. M submitted that on the proper construction of the Housing (Scotland) Act 1988 s.43(3)(c), the fact that the tenant and landlord had remained the same and where there had been no interruption between the tenancies, M's rights as a secure tenant carried over to the new tenancy, rather than the new tenancy becoming an assured tenancy under the 1988 Act. The fact that the subjects of the tenancy had changed did not affect the transition of those rights. Q submitted that the specific intention of the 1988 Act was to remove housing associations from secure tenancies and that, by the correct interpretation of s.43(3)(c), where the new tenancy was for a different property. Q also submitted that "secure" was a status given to the tenancy and not to the tenant and was not transferable

Held, allowing the application, that (1) although the intention of the 1988 Act had been to remove housing associations from provisions relating to secure tenancies, the saving provisions of s.43(3) could be applied to housing associations as they were transitional provisions applying to secure tenancies which existed before the 1988 Act came into force; (2) a tenancy was an agreement between a landlord and a tenant and it could not have been legislative intention to place the tenant in a separate class to the tenancy; where a tenancy was secure, the tenant was also secure; (3) the natural interpretation of s.43(3)(c) was to include tenants of the instant tenancy who had also been tenants of the same landlord under a previous tenancy, with no mention of a requirement for the property to be the same and that such a requirement could easily have been incorporated into the provision if that had been Parliament's intention; (4) for secure status to pass to the new tenancy, there had to be no interruption between the tenancies, and (5) the equivalent provisions in England were not limited to tenancies of the same property and it would be inappropriate to ascribe a different legislative intention to the corresponding provisions of the Scottish Act.

McALLISTER v. QUEENS CROSS HOUSING ASSOCIATION LTD 2002 S.L.T. (Lands Tr) 13, JN Wright Q.C., Lands Tr (Scot).

5838. **Tenants rights—right to purchase—secure tenancies—no written lease—tenant not in occupation**

[Tenants' Rights etc. (Scotland) Act 1980 (c.52) s.7(3), s.10(4)(a), s.19, s.82.]

F applied for an order under the Tenants Rights Etc. (Scotland) Act 1980 s.7(3) on the basis that A, his landlord, had failed to timeously issue either an offer to sell or a notice of refusal following his application to purchase the house he tenanted. F first took occupation of the property in 1968 and vacated it in October 1980 in order to move to France. In view of his intention to travel to France, F had applied to A for permission to grant a subtenancy, which had been refused in a letter by the director of housing, which indicated that F continued to occupy his property on a normal tenancy basis. Although he had been in arrears with his rent earlier in 1980, at the time of his leaving to go to France, his rent was up to date and he had arranged for future payments through his bank. In addition, he left some furniture at the property. The rental payments for January and February 1981 had been returned by A and no further rent had been paid. As regards the application to purchase the property, F had made various calls to A's offices to obtain the necessary application form, which was finally sent to him on October 1980. He completed the form and submitted it to the council. He also indicated that future correspondence should be through his solicitor. A's housing officer had, meantime, seen an article in the local newspaper indicating that F was moving to France permanently and advised A that the house was available for reletting, preferably to the teacher who had taken over from F. A could not find any trace of a lease but claimed that, even if a lease had existed, it had been terminated under s.19 procedure for recovery of abandoned properties. They confirmed that the s.19 procedure had been carried out despite the fact that F was still paying rent, had unsuccessfully applied to sublet and had applied to purchase the property. A maintained that they felt it unnecessary, where there was no valid tenancy, to make an offer or notice in respect of the application, but that a notice of refusal had been given in February 1981 making the action under s.7(3) irrelevant. A also argued that the lands tribunal did not have jurisdiction to determine whether or not a tenancy existed.

Held, granting the order, that (1) the plea to the relevancy could be dismissed as the notice of refusal was, on A's own admission, made out of time; (2) the tribunal could make investigations prior to making any decision under s.7(3) to determine whether a secure tenancy existed and in any event it would be incorrect to interpret that Act as meaning that F would have the right to prove his entitlement had A acted timeously, but not be able to do so where they hadn't; (3) the subjects, unless brought within the exceptions specified in s.10(4)(a), were let under a secure tenancy and, in any event, it would be inappropriate for A to argue that no tenancy existed where they had indicated the opposite stance by acceptance of rent, in a letter from the director of housing and by instigating s.19 procedure against F, which only applied to the termination of secure tenancies; (4) F's reasons for leaving the property were irrelevant as F was only required to prove that the property was his only or principal home on the relevant date, which in terms of the Act was October 3, 1980, at which time F had been on his way to France to reside temporarily in a tent, and (5) F's right to purchase was not affected by the subsequent s.19 procedure.

Observed, that much of the argument was directed at showing that F was not a secure tenant under common law when the appropriate definition of a secure tenancy, which should have been applied, was the statutory definition given under s.82 of the Act, which was wider and more generous to the tenant.

FOX v. ARGYLL AND BUTE DC 2002 Hous. L.R. 52, WDC Andrews, Lands Tr (Scot).

5839. Tenants rights–right to purchase–secure tenancies–qualifying occupation–effect of interruption

[Housing (Scotland) Act 1987 (c.26) s.61 (2) (c).]

L applied to the Lands Tribunal for Scotland in April 2000 for a finding that she had a right to purchase a house from her local authority, E, of which she had been a secure tenant since July 1999. Prior to the application, L had occupied different local authority houses since August 1996 with breaks between March and September 1997, and February and April 1999. E argued that because L's period of occupation was not continuous, she did not fulfil the requirements of the Housing (Scotland) Act 1987 s.61 (2) (c). L argued that (1) as the Act did not use the word "continuous" there was no justification for including it by implication; (2) the Act had formerly made express provision under s.61 (10) (b) for interruption of occupation, but since that section's repeal there was nothing to justify the implication of continuity, and (3) the continuous occupation requirement could give rise to manifest unfairness: lengthy occupation could be interrupted by numerous things such as fire damage.

Held, dismissing the application, that (1) because occupancy of at least two years had to be established in relation to an identified two year period, unbroken occupation was required throughout the whole period if a total of two years was to be achieved, and there was no need to specify continuity; (2) it was unsafe to rely on any inferences from s.61 (10) as the tribunal did not have the benefit of detailed analysis of the relationship of that subsection to any other provisions of the Act in which a period of occupation fell to be determined, and (3) while it was accepted that a need for continuous occupation could work unfairly in certain circumstances, it was inevitable that clear criteria required lines to be drawn and as a guide to construction there was no reason to give preference to a total period of occupancy which might have been many years before, as opposed to a measured period immediately prior to the application.

LOCK v. EDINBURGH CITY COUNCIL 2001 S.L.T. (Lands Tr) 19, Lord McGhie, Lands Tr (Scot).

5840. Tenants rights–right to purchase–secure tenancies–valuation–dwellinghouse–perversity

E, a local authority, sought judicial review of the decision of the district valuer, V, in relation to valuation of a dwellinghouse owned by E, which H as secure tenants had applied to buy. The market value was determined by V, following inspection in April 1999 by a senior valuer, R, as £75,000. In February 1999 a company, B, owner of a nearby quarry site, had informed E that it wished to purchase the whole of the coastal land strip owned by E, including the site of H's house, for the purposes of access to part of their site which they wished to develop. Having been advised of H's statutory right to purchase the house, B approached H directly to discuss the possibility of buying the house from H, and verbally advised H that B would pay up to £210,000 to cover relocation costs, which offer was later withdrawn. E took no steps to serve either a notice of refusal or an offer to sell to H within the statutory time limits. An application by H to the Lands Tribunal was sisted pending the outcome of the judicial review. E argued inter alia that V's decision was perverse, in that it failed to take account of the particular location of the house and B's demand to acquire the property. H lodged affidavits by R and another valuer, attempting to explain the basis of the valuation. H argued for dismissal on the basis that (1) E had not relevantly averred that V had acted in error, E failing, inter alia, to aver that V was told about B's actual interest when instructed by E, and (2) the delay of approximately seven months between the intimation of the valuation and the date on which proceedings were raised, for which no explanation was offered, had been detrimental to good administration, and caused prejudice to H, by reason of their having to lodge an application with the Lands Tribunal, on account of E's delay in issuing an offer to sell.

Held, putting the petition out by order for discussion of further procedure, that (1) whilst it was competent for affidavits to be used in judicial review proceedings it would not be appropriate to resolve factual issues of such significance between the parties on that basis; such issues required to be resolved after the leading of oral evidence, which was subject to cross examination; (2) it could not be said at that stage that E had no chance of establishing that V's decision was perverse. It might be open to the court to infer from the nature of B's current quarrying operations, the existence of planning consent for the quarry site and the geography of the area in which the house was located, that certain matters ought to have been readily apparent to R on inspecting the property. These included the requirement for the construction of new roads in the coastal strip for the purposes of the quarry development, that occupation of the strip was of great commercial importance to B and that B's exploitation of the quarry would be restricted by the presence of residential occupiers on the strip. Such issues would require to be addressed in the light of opportunities available to R, and whether R actually addressed the questions of fact before her, whether she adopted the correct legal approach and whether she took all relevant considerations into account, and (3) H's plea of mora would be reserved pending a hearing of evidence *Singh (Gurjit) v. Secretary of State for the Home Department (No.1)* 2000 S.L.T. 533, [2000] C.L.Y. 6493, followed. Having regard to the submissions made, which had not been heralded by either party's written pleadings, as to whether or not H had been prejudiced, the court was not satisfied that the plea should be sustained. On the other hand, E had not sought to have it repelled.

EAST LOTHIAN COUNCIL v. LUMSDEN; *sub nom.* EAST LOTHIAN COUNCIL'S PETITION 2002 S.L.T. 1141, Lord Mackay of Drumadoon, OH.

5841. **Tenants rights–right to purchase–temporary let–oral agreement to occupy**

[Housing (Scotland) Act (c.26); Housing (Scotland) Act (c.26) 1987 s.68(4); Contract (Scotland) Act 1997 (c.34).]

B applied for a finding in terms of the Housing (Scotland) Act 1987 s.68(4) that he was entitled to purchase premises occupied by him from A, his landlord. B's application to purchase the property had been refused on the grounds that the property had been let as bedsit accommodation for employees at low rent and B was not a tenant of the whole premises but rather of a room within the property, that B did not have a secure tenancy and the let had been for a temporary period pending redevelopment resulting in the demolition of the property and that the part of the property rented by B did not constitute a house in terms of the 1987 Act. A argued that (1) he had been given sole occupation of the entire property by virtue of an oral agreement with the housing stock manager; (2) the provisions relating to the extent of occupation given in subsequent written leases were a sham intended to hide the low rent being paid by B for occupation of the whole house, that A were aware that B occupied the whole house, and the effect of the sham agreements was to make the only valid agreement the oral one between B and the housing stock manager; (3) the written agreements did not revoke the terms of the oral agreement between B and the housing stock manager; (4) the Contract (Scotland) Act 1997 had the effect that oral agreements were not necessarily superseded by subsequent written ones, and (5) narration of a statutory exception within a written agreement did not necessarily bring the tenancy within that exception and, both at the time of the original agreement and at the date of the application, no development had been pending on the property.

Held, refusing the application, that (1) the entire property was a house, a lease of which, if not subject to a statutory exception, could constitute a secure tenancy; (2) there was no requirement for the agreement to be in writing for a secure tenancy to exist; (3) for the written agreements to be considered shams, there had to be a mutual intention by the parties to such agreements to deceive, *Snook v. London and West Riding Investments Ltd* [1967] 2 Q.B. 786, [1967] C.L.Y. 1836, followed; (4) extrinsic evidence was admissible to prove a sham but the 1997 Act added nothing to B's case at common law; (5) whilst B had honestly come to believe his version of the conversation with the housing stock manager, the version proffered by A was more credible in that B had been let a room and use of communal areas on the understanding that for the short duration of the let, pending development work, it would be unlikely that A would move anyone else into the property, and as such, B did not have a tenancy to the whole house which were the subject of his application to purchase, and (6) A had grounds for maintaining their hope that the road improvements would proceed until the Scottish Executive indicated their final decision in October 2000, thereby making the premises only available for temporary let, the statutory exception having been made out.

BOLTON v. ABERDEEN CITY COUNCIL 2002 Hous. L.R. 40, JN Wright Q.C., LandsTr (Scot).

5842. Books

Dailly, Mike–Housing Law in Practice. Paperback: £40.00. ISBN 0-414-01500-2. W.Green & Son.

HUMAN RIGHTS

5843. Devolution issues–incompatibility of legislation under which minuter prosecuted–incompatibility as devolution issue

[Civic Government (Scotland) Act 1982 (c.45) s.58; Human Rights Act 1998 (c.42) s.4; Scotland Act 1998 (c.10) s.57(2); Criminal Procedure (Scotland) Act 1995 (c.46) s.1(5); Act of Adjournal (Criminal Procedure Rules) 1996 (SI 1996 13946) r.40.3; Human Rights Act 1998 (c.42) Sch.1 Part I Art.6(2).]

S was charged on summary complaint with a contravention of the Civic Government (Scotland) Act 1982 s.58 in that being a person with two or more convictions for theft, he had been found in possession of tools and equipment from which it could reasonably be presumed that he had either committed a further theft or was intending to commit a theft, and where he could not offer any other reasonable explanation for his possession of such equipment. He pled not guilty and, at the intermediate diet, presented a minute seeking a declaration of incompatibility under the Human Rights Act 1998 s.4. He argued that the requirement in s.58 that he prove that his possession of such equipment was not for the purposes of committing theft was incompatible with the Human Rights Act 1998 Sch.1 Part I Art.6(2). S also requested that the issue be remitted to the High Court. The sheriff refused to remit the minute to the High Court and refused leave to appeal. S lodged a new minute in application with the Justiciary Office of the High Court. Intimation was made to the Lord Justice General and the Advocate General in accordance with procedures, but neither were joined as parties to the proceedings. The Crown argued that the minute was incompetent and that even if it was competent, it should not proceed before a single Lord Ordinary, but should be heard and determined by the Court of Appeal. The advocate depute argued that the challenge that S sought to make was in fact a devolution issue and that as such, the correct procedure under the Scotland Act 1998 had not been followed, which rendered the action incompetent.

Held, dismissing the minute as incompetent, that (1) the bringing of a prosecution under s.58 of the 1982 Act was an act of the Lord Advocate in terms of the Scotland Act 1998 s.57(2); (2) an action challenging the compatibility of s.58 with Convention rights included a challenge that the Lord Advocate, in beginning and proceeding with such a prosecution, had acted in a way which was incompatible with Convention rights and accordingly a devolution issue had been raised; (3) the correct procedure for raising a devolution issue under the Act of Adjournal (Criminal Procedure Rules) 1996 r.40.3 had not been followed, and (4) given that a declaration of incompatibility could not affect the outcome of S's trial, there were no grounds for exercising the court's power to dispense with the procedures set out in r.40.3.

Observed, that (1) the proper interpretation of the Human Rights Act 1998 s.4 was that questions of incompatibility could be determined by a single judge of the High Court, and (2) had the minute been competently before the High Court, the procedure under the Criminal Procedure (Scotland) Act 1995 s.1 (5) which allowed a single judge, in cases of difficulty or importance, to invite additional judges to form a larger bench would not have been available as s.1 (5) specifically related to single judges sitting as a trial court which was not the capacity in which a judge would determine an action for a declaration of incompatibility would be heard.

STEVENS (ANDREW) v. HM ADVOCATE 2002 S.L.T. 1249, Lady Paton, HCJ.

5844. Freedom of Information (Scotland) Act 2002 (asp 13)

This Act of the Scottish Parliament makes provision for the disclosure of information held by Scottish public authorities or by persons providing services for them.

This Act received Royal Assent on May 28, 2002.

5845. Race discrimination–statutory duties–Race Equality Scheme

RACE RELATIONS ACT 1976 (STATUTORY DUTIES) (SCOTLAND) ORDER 2002, SSI 2002 62; made under the Race Relations Act 1976 s.71. In force: March 13, 2002; £2.00.

This Order imposes certain bodies and other persons subject to the general duty of the Race Relations Act 1976 to have due regard, when exercising their functions, to the need to eliminate unlawful racial discrimination and to promote equality of opportunity and good relations between persons of different racial groups. The duties are imposed for the purpose of ensuring the better performance of the general duty. The Order imposes on a body or other persons specified, a duty to publish by November 30, 2002 a Race Equality Scheme, that is a Scheme showing how it intends to fulfil the general duty and its duties under this Order. It also imposes on an educational body duties to prepare, by November 30, 2002, a statement of its race equality policy, to have arrangements in place for fulfilling duties to assess and monitor the impact of its policies on different racial groups, and to fulfil those duties in accordance with such arrangements.

5846. Race relations–statutory duties–code of practice

RACE RELATIONS ACT 1976 (GENERAL STATUTORY DUTY: CODE OF PRACTICE) (SCOTLAND) ORDER 2002, SI 2002 3111 (S.13); made under the Race Relations Act 1976 s.71C. In force: December 18, 2002; £1.50.

This Order appoints December 19, 2002 as the day on which the code of practice containing the Commission for Racial Equality's guidance in relation to the performance in Scotland of the duties under the Race Relations Act 1976 s.71 (1) and (2) is to come into effect.

5847. Right to fair trial—acquiescence—hearing by independent and impartial tribunal—delay in challenging conviction

See CRIMINAL PROCEDURE: Lochridge v. Miller (Procurator Fiscal). §5493

5848. Right to fair trial—bias—judge previously holding public office connected to case

See ADMINISTRATION OF JUSTICE: Davidson v. Scottish Ministers (No.2). §5218

5849. Right to fair trial—bias—plea tendered before judge holding public office connected to case

See CRIMINAL PROCEDURE: Rimmer (Roy William), Petitioner. §5483

5850. Right to fair trial—conduct of defence case—failure to explore reliability of child complainers

See CRIMINAL PROCEDURE: E v. HM Advocate. §5526

5851. Right to fair trial—delay—criminal appeals—reduction in sentence appropriate remedy

See CRIMINAL PROCEDURE: Mills (Kenneth Anthony Paton) v. HM Advocate (No.2). §5515

5852. Right to fair trial—delay—plea in bar of trial—conviction not incompatible with convention rights

See CRIMINAL PROCEDURE: HM Advocate v. R. §5488

5853. Right to fair trial—delay—reasonableness—10 months from charge to trial

See CRIMINAL PROCEDURE: Higson v. Boyle. §5510

5854. Right to fair trial—delay—reasonableness—23 month delay

See CRIMINAL PROCEDURE: Valentine (Alan) v. HM Advocate. §5494

5855. Right to fair trial—delay—reasonableness—period of 25 months between charge and trial

See CRIMINAL PROCEDURE: Smith v. Angiolini. §5516

5856. Right to fair trial—delay—reasonableness—summary complaint changed to petition—total time not unreasonable

See CRIMINAL PROCEDURE: HM Advocate v. Wright (Karen Halliday) (otherwise Skilbeck). §5495

5857. Right to fair trial—delay—reasonableness

See CRIMINAL PROCEDURE: Dyer v. Watson. §5517, Morrison (Allan) v. HM Advocate. §5514

5858. Right to fair trial—hearsay evidence—statement of dead witness

See CRIMINAL EVIDENCE: HM Advocate v. Bain (David). §5427

5859. **Right to fair trial–independent and impartial tribunal–contempt of court**
See ADMINISTRATION OF JUSTICE: Mair (Bryan), Petitioner. §5212

5860. **Right to fair trial–legal representation–right of audience in criminal trial**
See ADMINISTRATION OF JUSTICE: Robbie the Pict v. HM Advocate. §5217

5861. **Right to fair trial–plea in bar of trial–fixed payments for criminal legal aid–right to legal representative of own choice**
See CRIMINAL PROCEDURE: Vickers v. Buchanan. §5490

5862. **Right to fair trial–pretrial publicity–previous convictions disclosed**
See CRIMINAL PROCEDURE: Beggs v. HM Advocate (Preliminary Diet). §5492

5863. **Right to fair trial–sheriffs–application for leave–independence and impartiality**
See ADMINISTRATION OF JUSTICE: Umair v. Umair. §5237

5864. **Right to fair trial–vexatious litigants**
See ADMINISTRATION OF JUSTICE: HM Advocate v. Bell (Jamie). §5238

5865. **Right to peaceful enjoyment of possessions–application for extension of entertainment licence–refusal as interference with property rights**
See LICENSING: Catscratch Ltd v. Glasgow City Licensing Board (No.2). §5965

5866. **Right to peaceful enjoyment of possessions–hunting–controlling use of property–consideration of foxhunting as activity of private life**
[Human Rights Act 1998 (c.42) Sch.1 Part I Art.8, Art.14, Part II Art.1; Scotland Act 1998 (c.46) s.100; Protection of Wild Mammals (Scotland) Act 2002 (asp.6) s.100.]
A brought a petition for judicial review of the Protection of Wild Mammals (Scotland) Act 2002, which criminalized mounted foxhunting, on the grounds that it was partly incompatible with the Human Rights Act 1998 Sch.1 Part I Art.8 and Art.14, was beyond the legislative competence of the Scottish Parliament, and was therefore ultra vires. A, a manager of foxhounds, occupied a tied house by virtue of his employment and contended that his livelihood and the house constituted possessions for the purposes of Sch.1 Part II Art.1 of the Human Rights Act.
Held, dismissing the petition, that (1) the Scotland Act 1998 s.100 provided for only those who could claim to be victims to bring proceedings on the grounds of incompatibility of an Act with Convention rights, and the locus standi of such persons was to be established by reference to decisions of the ECHR. In the instant case, A was a member of a club which supported traditional hunting, but supporting an activity was not equivalent to being actively engaged in it, therefore their entitlement to bring proceedings was not established; (2) in principle, the prevention of cruelty to animals was capable of being regarded as a legitimate purpose of legislation and such issues involving moral judgment were more appropriate for decision by a democratically elected legislature than a court. In assessing the extent to which the court would defer to the Scottish Parliament in this respect it was necessary to consider the "discretionary area of judgment" identified in *R. v. DPP, ex p. Kebilene* [2000] 2 A.C. 326, [1999] C.L.Y. 1045 and *Brown v. Stott* [2001] 2 W.L.R. 817, [2001] C.L.Y. 6319, *Kebilene* and *Brown* considered; (3) mounted foxhunting with dogs did not amount to an activity of private life for the purposes of Art.8 of the Human Rights Act; (4) the 2002 Act operated to "control the use of property"

within the meaning of Sch.1 Part II Art.1 of the Human Rights Act in the sense that A's opportunity to make a living had been affected. However, it was open to Parliament to strike a balance between the desirability of controlling the use of property and upholding the general interest in preventing cruelty to animals without paying compensation, *Pinnacle Meat Processors Co v. United Kingdom* (1999) 27 E.H.R.R. CD217 and *Slough v. United Kingdom* (Unreported, September 26, 2000) considered, and (5) no breach of Art.14 of the Human Rights Act had been made out as A had been unable to establish that there had been discrimination against him in the enjoyment of his Convention rights without objective justification.

ADAMS v. SCOTTISH MINISTERS; *sub nom*. ADAMS, PETITIONER; ADAMS v. LORD ADVOCATE; ADAMS v. ADVOCATE GENERAL FOR SCOTLAND 2003 S.L.T. 366, Lord Nimmo Smith, OH.

5867. Right to respect for private and family life–asylum seekers–marriage to UK citizen

See IMMIGRATION: Ahmed (Saleem) v. Secretary of State for the Home Department. §5875

5868. Right to respect for private and family life–surveillance

See CRIMINAL EVIDENCE: Connor (Neil Patrick) v. HM Advocate. §5432

5869. Surveillance–covert human intelligence sources–authorisations–cancellation

REGULATION OF INVESTIGATORY POWERS (CANCELLATION OF AUTHORISATIONS) (SCOTLAND) REGULATIONS 2002, SSI 2002 207; made under the Powers (Scotland) Act 2000 s.20. In force: May 20, 2002; £1.50.

The Regulation of Investigatory Powers (Scotland) Act 2000 s.20 imposes a duty on a number of persons to cancel authorisations under the Act, provided certain conditions are met. These Regulations address the case where the duty falls on a person no longer available to perform it by providing for the duty to fall instead on the person who has taken over most of that person's responsibilities and providing a power to appoint a person for this specific purpose.

5870. Surveillance–covert human intelligence sources–authorisations–juveniles

REGULATION OF INVESTIGATORY POWERS (JUVENILES) (SCOTLAND) ORDER 2002, SSI 2002 206; made under the Regulation of Investigatory Powers (Scotland) Act 2000 s.7, s.19. In force: May 20, 2002; £1.75.

The Regulation of Investigatory Powers (Scotland) Act 2000 s.7 allows authorisations to be granted for the use or conduct of covert human surveillance sources. This Order contains special provisions for the cases of covert human intelligence sources who are under 18. It provides that no authorisation may be given for the conduct or use of a source where the source is under 16 and the conduct or use would relate to the relationship between the source and their parent or any person who has responsibility for them; makes provision for the presence of an appropriate adult at all meetings between a source under 16 and the representative of the relevant investigating authority; makes provision regarding the need for and scope of risk assessments where the source is under 18; and amends, in respect of sources under 18, the period of authorisation in s.19(3)(b) of the 2000 Act from 12 months to one month.

5871. Surveillance–covert human intelligence sources–authorisations–source records

REGULATION OF INVESTIGATORY POWERS (SOURCE RECORDS) (SCOTLAND) REGULATIONS 2002, SSI 2002 205; made under the Regulation of Investigatory Powers (Scotland) Act 2000 s.7. In force: May 20, 2002; £1.75.

Under the Regulation of Investigatory Powers (Scotland) Act 2000 s.7(2)(c) a person may not grant an authorisation for the conduct or use of a covert human intelligence source unless they are satisfied that arrangements exist that satisfy the requirements of s.7(6) of that Act which provides that the arrangements must be adequate to ensure that the records relating to the source contain particulars of certain matters as may be specified by the Scottish Ministers. These Regulations specify those matters.

5872. Books

Lord Reed; Murdoch, James L.–Guide to Human Rights Law in Scotland. Paperback: £40.00. ISBN 0-406-92320-5. Butterworths Law.

Loux, Andrea; Boyle, Alan; Himsworth, Chris; MacQueen, Hector–Human Rights and Scots Law-Comparative Perspectives on the Incorporation of the ECHR. Hardback: £40.00. ISBN 1-84113-044-3. Hart Publishing.

IMMIGRATION

5873. Asylum–deportation orders–visa issued by Italian consulate–removal to Italy for determination of application–legitimate expectation

[Dublin Convention 1990 Art.4, Art.5, Art.6, Art.7, Art.8; Immigration and Asylum Act 1999 (c.33) s.11 (2).]

I, a Turkish national, sought judicial review of a decision of the Secretary of State, to remove him to Italy to have his asylum application determined in terms of the Immigration and Asylum Act 1999 s.11 (2). I had travelled to Lebanon from Turkey and obtained a 30 day travel visa from the Italian consulate in Beirut. Following travel through the European Union, he obtained a visa extension in Germany before entering the United Kingdom and claiming asylum. At interview he claimed his Lebanese passport was forged, however inquiries disclosed that the passport and visa had been duly issued by the relevant authorities. I argued that the decision was unreasonable where he had a legitimate expectation that the Dublin Convention 1990 Art.4, Art.5, Art.6, Art.7 and Art.8 would apply, in terms of which he should only be removed to Italy if the visa was valid.

Held, refusing the petition, that (1) I was entitled to expect that the Secretary of State would abide by the procedural or administrative steps stipulated in the Convention, as ratification of the Convention even without its incorporation into domestic law could create a legitimate expectation relating to the fairness and appropriateness of procedures, at least where, as here, further steps were taken to implement its terms as a matter of stated policy or accepted practice, and (2) the Secretary of State had acted in conformity with the terms of the Convention as the visa was not forged, the Italian authorities accepted its validity and I could not successfully maintain the contrary simply on assertions that there might have been some unspecified misrepresentation made during the application process.

IBRAHIM v. SECRETARY OF STATE FOR THE HOME DEPARTMENT 2002 S.L.T. 1150, Lord Carloway, OH.

5874. Asylum–evidence–standard of proof–treatment of evidence "in the round"

S, a Bangladeshi national, entered the UK with entry clearance for a six month visit on June 18, 1992. He applied for an extension and following its refusal, applied for asylum which was refused. A special adjudicator refused S's appeal against the notice to depart. The appeal before the IAT was also refused. He sought judicial review seeking reduction of both the determination of the special adjudicator and the refusal of leave to appeal. Reductions were opposed by the Secretary of State. In relation to the determination by the special adjudicator, S argued that she had erred in her approach to the determination by considering S's case as a series of separate stages, both historically and evidentially, rather than looking at the case as a whole. S also argued that the special adjudicator had misunderstood the evidence before her to such an extent that she had acted unreasonably. The determination of the IAT was challenged by S on the ground that his application for leave to appeal had set out serious and substantial criticisms of the special adjudicator's determination and no reasonable tribunal could have reached the conclusion to refuse leave to appeal. It was agreed that, in the event that the court agreed that the special adjudicator had erred in law or acted unreasonably, the court should reduce the determination of the IAT.

Held, reducing the determination of the IAT, that (1) the special adjudicator had erred in law in adopting a multi stage approach to her determination rather than looking at S's case in the whole as was required by the authorities, *R. v. Secretary of State for the Home Department, ex p. Kaja* [1995] Imm. A.R. 1, [1995] C.L.Y. 2697 and *Karanakaran v. Secretary of State for the Home Department* [2000] 3 All E.R. 449, [2000] C.L.Y. 3307, followed; (2) the special adjudicator cast doubt on some of the claims made by S and in doing so cast doubt on his credibility without giving unambiguous reasons for doing so which could be tested by an appeal court, and (3) the special adjudicator failed to assess the evidence given by S in the careful and sensitive manner required in asylum cases, taking into account the uncertainty of such evidence in some cases, and her rejection of certain parts of S's evidence was founded on a misunderstanding of the importance of that evidence, which in turn had an adverse effect on the decision that she reached.

SATTAR v. SECRETARY OF STATE FOR THE HOME DEPARTMENT; *sub nom.* SATTAR (OTHERWISE NAZIMUDDEN), PETITIONER 2002 S.L.T. 1397, Lord Mackay of Drumadoon, OH.

5875. Asylum–Pakistan–marriage to UK citizen

[European Convention on Human Rights 1950 Art.8.]

A, a Pakistani citizen, sought judicial review of a decision of S, the Secretary of State, refusing A leave to remain in the UK. A had entered the UK illegally in October 1992 and renewed an application for political asylum, having returned to Pakistan voluntarily in October 1991 following a previous application after overstaying illegally. In March 1993 A married a UK citizen and applied for leave to remain as her spouse, requesting also that his application for asylum be deferred. In January 1995 A's application for asylum was refused, with A's subsequent appeal to the special adjudicator and leave to appeal to the immigration appeal tribunal also being refused. A's application for leave to remain was also refused and, following separation from his wife, A's petition for judicial review against that refusal was dismissed on A's motion. In January 1997 A married W, a UK citizen with custody of a child, X, from a former marriage. X had contact with her natural father who also lived in the UK. A and W had a child in October 1997. A argued S's decision was *Wednesbury* unreasonable in light of the European Convention on Human Rights 1950 Art.8. He further submitted that interference in Art.8 rights had to be proportionate to the legitimate aim of the interference and S had failed to recognise the exceptional circumstances presented by X. He contended that if A was removed while W remained to maintain contact between X and her father, A would be separated from them but if W and the family moved to Pakistan that contact would be broken and that whatever option was taken involved an interference in Art.8 rights (*Berrehab v. Netherlands* (1988) 11 E.H.R.R. 322, [1988] C.L.Y. 1816).

Held, refusing the application, that there was not such disproportion between the continuation of enforcement action in the public interest and the consequent interference with family relationships that came into existence after its commencement as to render S's decision *Wednesbury* unreasonable. While the interests of X, as a child accepted into the family, had to be taken into account, that relationship only came into existence after the commencement of enforcement action and did not constitute exceptional circumstances, *Berrehab* distinguished and *Gangadeen v. Secretary of State for the Home Department* [1998] Imm A.R. 106, [1998] C.L.Y. 3215 followed.

AHMED (SALEEM) v. SECRETARY OF STATE FOR THE HOME DEPARTMENT 2001 S.L.T. 1347, Lord Nimmo Smith, OH.

5876. Asylum—persecution—evidential discrepancy—fairness of proceedings

[Asylum and Immigration Appeals Act 1993 (c.23) Sch.2 para. 5.]

S, an Indian national, sought reduction of the decisions of the Home Secretary and special adjudicator refusing his application for political asylum. S had claimed that he had been beaten and tortured by police because of the terrorist activities of his adopted son, and that his family had been harassed and his wife had to leave their home with the children because the police were still looking for him. S had referred to visible bruising on his ribs. The Home Secretary, in refusing the application, founded on the applicant giving a false name to immigration authorities and only applying for asylum after his apprehension. He certified the application for the "fast track" procedure, being one to which the Asylum and Immigration Appeals Act 1993 Sch. 2 para.5(2), namely designation of country as one where no serious risk of persecution, applied but para.5(5), namely evidence establishing reasonable likelihood of torture, did not. S argued that the decision did not deal properly with his claim that he was still in fear of his life. A significant majority of asylum applicants did not apply at their point of entry and persons detained were often not truthful with police. Further, there was a failure to deal with any information regarding torture and a complete absence of explanation for certification under para.5(5). At interview before the adjudicator S stated that he was not a member of a political party but admitted political involvement. The adjudicator relied on a discrepancy in S's evidence as to whether he had been hiding in Uttar Pradesh or Andra Pradesh in assessing his credibility. The representatives for both sides had failed to appreciate the confusion. S argued that the adjudicator should have cleared up the discrepancy at the hearing and his failure to do so was procedurally unfair and that the adjudicator had erred in not first considering the validity of the certification for "fast track" procedure and, in any event, in upholding the certification on the evidence before him.

Held, reducing the decision and directing that any further appeal be heard before a different special adjudicator, that (1) the certification did not require to be determined at the outset as both the merits of S's claim and the propriety of the certification depended on the special adjudicator accepting his evidence of past torture and the likelihood of it if he returned, and it was therefore sensible for the adjudicator to hear the evidence before reaching a decision on either point; (2) in asylum cases administrative decisions had to be the subject of the most rigorous scrutiny and it was vital that both the applicant and the court on judicial review should be able to see clearly why asylum had been refused, particularly in certification cases; (3) the Home Secretary and the adjudicator had knowledge of, and had taken into account, the socio-political situation of S's home country, his background, the circumstances of the making of his claim, and his general credibility, and there was in general terms sufficient material before them to entitle them to reject his account, and (4) the adjudicator's failure to allow S to explain the discrepancy of whether he went to Uttar Pradesh or Andra Pradesh when assessing that as further detracting from his credibility was procedurally unfair, especially as neither representative at the hearing seemed aware of the confusion or its significance.

SINGH (JIJAR) v. SECRETARY OF STATE FOR THE HOME DEPARTMENT 2002 S.L.T. 73, Lord Dawson, OH.

5877. Asylum—refugees—meaning of "refugee"

S, an Indian national, entered the UK illegally and very quickly applied for asylum. His application was refused and he appealed. S failed to attend or be represented at the appeal before the special adjudicator, who refused his appeal. S sought leave to appeal to the Immigration Appeal Tribunal, which was also refused. S petitioned for judicial review and sought reduction of the special adjudicator's determination and the refusal of leave to appeal. S argued that the special adjudicator had failed apply the correct standard of proof and had been unreasonable in the Wednesbury sense in reaching a decision that no properly informed adjudicator, applying the law correctly, could have reached. S claimed that the special adjudicator had taken into account facts about India without indicating the source of those facts and had preferred one source over another without specifying the reasons for doing so. He argued that the special adjudicator had oversimplified the issues and had failed to take account of the whole picture as was required by the authorities. The Secretary of State sought dismissal of the petition on the grounds that S had acted unreasonably and delayed seeking judicial review. It was argued that it was impossible for the special adjudicator to record everything and that S had failed to put sufficient information before the special adjudicator and then criticised him for taking into account information within his own body of knowledge. It was further argued on behalf of the Secretary of State that the question which the special adjudicator had adequately addressed was whether S had a well founded fear of persecution should he return to India.

Held, reducing the special adjudicator's determination and the IAT's refusal to grant leave to appeal, that (1) the special adjudicator was correct in finding that a family association with a member of a terrorist organisation was sufficient to form a Convention reason for the granting of asylum and that the illegal detention, without being brought before an independent judiciary, and torture could give rise to a well-founded fear of persecution; (2) the special adjudicator was also correct in finding that there was a need, in questions relating to the S's credibility, to set out fully his reasons for disbelieving S in order that they could be reviewed by the court, particularly as a flawed decision could lead to life-threatening results; (3) the special adjudicator was also correct in finding that, in line with authorities, the question of credibility had to be viewed as a whole but had misdirected himself in setting the question of S's credibility against general improvements in the human rights situation in India without indicating why he had reached the conclusion that lapses in human rights treatment could not occur in the part of India which S originated from, *Karanakaran v. Secretary of State for the Home Department* [2000] 3 All E.R. 449, [2000] C.L.Y. 3307, followed, and *Bhatti v. Secretary of State for the Home Department* 1999 G.W.D. 9-433 and *Singh (Harjit), Re* (Unreported, July 22, 1999), distinguished, and (4) such an error on the part of the special adjudicator should have been recognised by any reasonable IAT chairman.

SINGH (GURJIT) v. SECRETARY OF STATE FOR THE HOME DEPARTMENT (NO.2); *sub nom.* SINGH (GURJIT) (NO.2), PETITIONER 2001 S.C.L.R. 776, Lady Paton, OH.

5878.   Asylum–refusal–reasons for decision–credibility

A, a Pakistani citizen who illegally remained in the United Kingdom after his leave to remain expired, sought judicial review of decisions of a special adjudicator, refusing his appeal against refusal of asylum, and of the immigration appeal tribunal, refusing leave to appeal further. His application for leave to appeal to the tribunal was on the ground that the adjudicator's decision was "against the weight of the evidence and not in accordance with the law". A did not give evidence before the adjudicator, who relied, inter alia, on the record of his interview. The Lord Ordinary refused the petition, holding, inter alia, that the adjudicator had correctly identified the issue for decision and had given sufficient reasons for not finding A to be credible. A reclaimed, presenting a different argument that in assessing credibility, attention had to be paid to cultural differences and it was acceptable for an asylum seeker not to be prepared to give a full background. No factors had been isolated as crucial, peripheral issues had dominated the question of credibility in the adjudicator's determination and the adjudicator had wholly failed to treat the question of coherence of the basic claim with conditions in Pakistan.

Held, refusing the reclaiming motion, that (1) the UK system of immigration control presupposed that the credibility of applicants had to be judged; it was a matter of everyday experience that credibility frequently had to be assessed by examination of witnesses' evidence of peripheral as well as central issues and an applicant had to be judged with reference to ordinary tests of consistency, applied with sensitivity to cultural differences and the difficult position asylum seekers often found themselves in, and (2) the adjudicator's decision was not unreasonable as there were real questions concerning A's account and given the very slight explanations available in answer to these questions the adjudicator was entitled to take into account, to the limited extent he did, that A did not give evidence.

ASIF v. SECRETARY OF STATE FOR THE HOME DEPARTMENT 2002 S.C. 182, Lord Coulsfield, Lord Kingarth, Lord Marnoch, Ex Div.

5879. Asylum seekers—refusal—applicant submitting fresh application—procedure for consideration—correct test

N, a Pakistani national sought reduction of a decision of the Home Secretary, S refusing to treat representations made by him as a fresh application for asylum. Following N's original application, a special adjudicator had concluded in 1998 that while N's claims of active involvement in the Pakistan Muslim League (PML) were credible, he had not established a well founded fear of persecution, as by that time the PML had become the party of government. Following a military coup in 1999 the PML again became an opposition party and N made further representations that the military regime had initiated action against leading PML members and as a result he had a well founded fear of persecution. N enclosed letters from his father and the vice president of the PML. S issued a decision letter dated April 19, 2000 stating that there was no realistic prospect that the conditions in the Immigration Rules, para.334 under which asylum would be granted, would be satisfied and the representations did not constitute a fresh application under para.346. The decision letter contained an assessment of the socio-political climate in Pakistan and concluded inter alia that the letters, submitted without independent corroborating material, were not significant and doubted their credibility. S argued inter alia that the tests of credibility and significance were part of para.346 and that his decision on credibility at the stage of deciding whether or not the new representations amounted to a fresh claim for asylum was only subject to review on *Wednesbury* grounds.

Held, granting reduction, that (1) it was necessary for S to keep separate the questions (a) whether representations amounted to a fresh application, and (b) if so, whether the new claim was well founded: S had to proceed, separately, to the second stage whenever the fresh claim was potentially genuine and there was a reasonable prospect that it could succeed; (2) if the representations put forward a relevant and substantial change of circumstances, that should be sufficient to amount to a fresh application and S had misdirected himself by assessing at that stage the significance of the effect of the coup as affording grounds for a well founded fear of persecution, thereby depriving N of the opportunity of having the decision on the significance and credibility of the evidence reviewed by a special adjudicator; (3) it was not appropriate to test individual aspects of S's decision by the *Wednesbury* test if those aspects involved decisions being made on issues that did not properly form part of what the decision maker had to decide; (4) the questions of credibility and reliability of the material advanced, the weight to be attached to acceptable material and whether it afforded grounds for granting asylum, were all matters properly forming part of the decision S had to take on the merits of a fresh application once he had determined that the material submitted constituted a fresh application, and (5) the test for rejection of evidence as incredible or not significant at the preliminary stage was whether no reasonable decision maker could regard the material as credible or significant, and while S had formulated a similar test he had not adhered to it.

NAZIR v. SECRETARY OF STATE FOR THE HOME DEPARTMENT 2002 S.C.134, Lord Macfadyen, OH.

5880. Asylum seekers–third countries–human rights considerations

[European Convention on Human Rights 1950.]

J, a citizen of Sierra Leone, first entered Europe in Germany where responsibility for his asylum application was accepted. J subsequently moved to Scotland and sought asylum alleging state and non state persecution. The Secretary of State sought a third country certificate and J's removal to Germany. J sought judicial review of the validity of the certificate on the ground that Germany could not be a safe country as it did not at that time, recognise non state persecution.

Held, dismissing the petition, that (1) the decision in *R. (on the application of Adan (Lul Omar)) v. Secretary of State for the Home Department* [2001] 2 A.C. 477, [2001] C.L.Y. 3639 had been superseded by the coming into force of s.11 of the 1999 Act to the effect that all EC Member States who was also parties to the Dublin Convention were automatically to be regarded as safe countries; (2) under the s.11 procedure, the only consideration was whether the Member State accepted responsibility for the claim under standing arrangements and whether the claimant was a national or citizen of that Member State, *R. (on the application of Ibrahim (Ayman)) v. Secretary of State for the Home Department* [2001] EWCA Civ 519, [2001] Imm. A.R. 430 followed, and (3) in order for the act of returning J to Germany to involve a breach of human rights, it would have to be assumed that Germany would return J to Sierra Leone in breach of its obligations under the European Convention on Human Rights 1950 and would disregard any interim measures by the European Court of Human Rights, which was not the case.

JALLOH v. SECRETARY OF STATE FOR THE HOME DEPARTMENT; *sub nom.* JALLOH, PETITIONER 2002 S.C.L.R. 248, Lord Eassie, OH.

5881. Deportation–appeals–powers of adjudicator–review of fairness of proceedings

[Immigration Act 1971 (c.77) s.3(5)(a); Immigration Act 1988 (c.14) s.5.]

K, a Pakistani citizen, who had illegally remained in the United Kingdom after the expiry of his leave to remain, sought judicial review of the decisions of the Secretary of State to deport him and of a special adjudicator and the Immigration Appeal Tribunal refusing his appeals against that decision. K had entered the UK in April 1997 on a visitor's permit lasting six months and a deportation order was made following an interview in March 1998. K argued that (1) the adjudicator had erred in determining that he could not consider an appeal based on a procedural error because of the restriction allegedly imposed by the Immigration Act 1988 s.5, and that the reasoning in *R. v. Secretary of State for the Home Department, ex p. Malhi* [1991] 1 Q.B. 194, [1990] C.L.Y. 2583 should not be followed as s.5 simply intended the termination of an adjudicator's power to review the discretion of immigration officers; (2) the Secretary of State's reasons for his decision to deport did not disclose whether all relevant factors had been considered, and (3) there was insufficient evidence for the Secretary of State to conclude that he was an overstayer.

Held, refusing the petition, that (1) the court in *Malhi* had given a clear judgment on the effect of s.5 as confining an adjudicator's appellate jurisdiction to whether the Secretary of State had power in the circumstances to make a deportation order, not to the propriety of procedures leading to the making of that order, the interpretation was expressly approved by the House of Lords in *R. v. Secretary of State for the Home Department, ex p. Oladehinde* [1991] 1 A.C. 254, [1991] C.L.Y. 1981 and there was no justification for reaching a different result in Scotland; (2) the immigration officer had concluded that the facts necessary for deportation as an overstayer under the Immigration Act 1971 s.3(5)(a) had been established based on the petitioner's own admission, and the reason given to that effect left no doubt as to which factors had been considered, and (3) it was insufficient for the petitioner to challenge a finding of fact without attempting to set out what he maintained was the true factual position.

KHALIL v. SECRETARY OF STATE FOR THE HOME DEPARTMENT 2002 S.L.T. 1039, Lord Carloway, OH.

5882. Deportation—marriage as compassionate factor

[European Convention on Human Rights 1950 Art.8.]

S brought a petition for judicial review seeking reduction of a decision by the Secretary of State to refuse him permission to remain exceptionally in the UK following his marriage to a British citizen. S entered the UK illegally and was served with a notice that he was an illegal entrant in November 1992. His marriage which took place in September 1994 following six months of cohabitation was proved to be a genuine and sustaining marriage. There was also a child of the marriage. The letter, which purported to refuse S's application to remain in the UK, stated that the decision had been made to proceed with S's removal to India and that any resultant disruption of family life, whilst regrettable, was justified in the public interest of maintaining effective immigration controls and therefore did not breach the terms of the European Convention on Human Rights 1950 Art.8. The petition came before the Lord Ordinary who, whilst accepting that it would be so disproportionate as to be unreasonable if the Home Department were to proceed with S's removal where it would result in his permanent separation from his wife and child, was not persuaded that the Home Department should have recognised permanent separation as the likely outcome for the removal action. The Home Department suggested that, in the circumstances, S would be likely to satisfy the entry requirements, making the separation temporary. Consequently, the Lord Ordinary dismissed the petition. S reclaimed arguing that the Lord Ordinary had erred in holding that the author of the decision letter had applied the policy correctly. He maintained that the decision letter repeatedly referred to the fact that his marriage post dated the date that enforcement action was taken against him in the form of the notice of illegal entrant status and that the author of the decision letter had clearly misunderstood the terms of DP2/93 which required him to consider all the material facts surrounding the marriage with its date in relation to the date of enforcement action being only one factor. The Secretary of State accepted that an error had been made in the interpretation of DP2/93, but that, when taken as a whole, the decision letter clearly showed that due consideration had been given to the compassionate factor associated with the marriage.

Held, remitting the matter for reconsideration and decision, that (1) the view expressed within the decision letter that the marriage would only avail S in his application if it predated the enforcement action was fundamentally wrong and was repeated within that letter, and (2) as S's marriage did not predate the enforcement action the question which should have been addressed was not whether there should have been deviation from the general rule stated in para.2 of DP2/93, but whether enforcement action was to be taken given the weight to be attached to the marriage as a compassionate factor in terms of para.1 of DP2/93.

Observed, that (1) where there was a material risk that S would be permanently removed from his wife and child, his rights under Art.8 would have to be considered, and (2) where it was clear that S would satisfy the entry requirements on reapplication, making the separation temporary, the question of whether it was necessary or sensible to remove S as a step towards readmitting him would have to be considered. Opinion of the court per Lord Prosser.

SAINI v. SECRETARY OF STATE FOR THE HOME DEPARTMENT 2001 S.C. 951, Lord Prosser, Lord Clarke, Lord Kingarth, Ex Div.

5883. Entry clearances–parental contact–leave to remain–proceedings for contact with child in progress–reasonableness

[European Convention on Human Rights 1950 Art.6, Art.8.]

N, a Nigerian national, sought reduction by judicial review of a decision of the Home Secretary of November 1998 refusing his application for exceptional leave to remain in the United Kingdom. N had overstayed his extended visitor's visa, which expired in February 1993, and was convicted of benefits fraud in 1995. During his incarceration he married and his application for asylum was refused. The couple had a son in February 1998. N's wife raised divorce and custody proceedings. N last had contact with his son in March 1999 and sought contact in January 2000. He wrote to the chief immigration officer informing him of a pending application for legal aid in connection with the matrimonial proceedings and submitted that any proposed removal would violate his right to respect for his family life under the European Convention on Human Rights 1950 Art.8 by preventing him exercising contact, and potentially violate Art.6 as he was in the process of litigating to ensure contact. The officer replied that there would be no breach of Art.8 as N had not seen his son since March 1999 nor lived with his wife and son as a family unit since October/November 1998, and that N's family life was not established when his presence in the UK was lawful. N subsequently obtained legal aid and raised an action for contact. N argued (1) that the letter demonstrated an error in law (a) as the officer obviously believed there was no "family life" between himself and his son in the absence of direct contact, and (b) in the assertion that there would be no interference with family life where his presence in the UK was unlawful; (2) that the officer's reasons did not demonstrate a proper consideration of all the relevant factors advanced by N; (3) that the decision was unreasonable as it involved violations of Art.6 and Art.8, which obliged the officer to justify his decision, and (4) that the decision to deport him violated his rights under Art.6 in relation to the hearing on the issue of contact.

Held, dismissing the petition, that (1) it did not have to be apparent on the face of the letter which considerations the respondent took into account: examination had to be directed toward the decision, not a textual examination of the letter communicating it; (2) the officer's approach to the circumstances of N's family life, and contact with his son, was neither unreasonable nor factually in error, as the officer was not saying there was no family life between N and his son but was referring to the quality of it in the exercise of his discretion; (3) while it was unfortunate that the letter made no mention of the alleged violation of Art.6, at the time the decision was made N had not raised contact proceedings, and it was not the case that the respondent would be bound to grant special leave to remain in favour of any litigant in contact proceedings which could not be satisfactorily conducted from outside the UK to prevent violation of Art.6 rights, and (4) it was not difficult to see what the reasons for S's decision were, albeit they were somewhat cryptically expressed in the letter, and the decision was not unreasonable.

NWOKOYE v. SECRETARY OF STATE FOR THE HOME DEPARTMENT; *sub nom.* NWOKOYE, PETITIONER 2002 S.L.T. 128, Lord MacLean, OH.

5884. Leave to remain–refusal–marriage to UK citizen

[European Convention on Human Rights 1950 Art.8.]

A, a citizen of Pakistan, sought judicial review of the decision of C, the chief immigration officer, to refuse A leave to remain in the UK, on the basis of A's marriage to R, a UK citizen. A had entered the UK as a visitor in October 1995 and in November had sought political asylum which was refused. Enforcement action commenced in September 1996. A appealed this decision but later withdrew the appeal and on May 8, 1998 applied for leave to remain on the basis of his marriage to R on March 30. A son was born to A and R on July 21. In a letter on March 31, 1999 C refused to grant A leave to remain; following an objection from A, C replied on April 27 restating his position. A argued that (1) the decision breached the European Convention on Human Rights 1950 Art.8, right to family life: R had two children by a previous marriage to whom her ex-husband was permitted contact under a residence order; R would have to seek permission of the courts to take them abroad and if refused would be unable to go with A, who would then have to apply for leave to enter, and (2) as C had stated that the Convention had been taken into account, and therefore that Art.8 had not been breached, the court could declare that C's view of the article had been wrong (*R. v. Secretary of State for the Home Department, ex p. Launder (No.2)* [1997] 1 W.L.R. 839, [1997] C.L.Y. 2433).

Held, refusing the petition, that (1) *Launder* did not support the proposition that a court should reach its own view of whether a breach of Art.8 had occurred and impose that view on the Secretary of State, which would involve a direct application of Art.8 before it had come into force; (2) the application of Art.8 in such cases as this involved balancing considerations and an exercise of discretion, and in a judicial review the question was whether the decision taker's view that it had not been infringed was one at which he might reasonably have arrived; (3) insofar as it was implied that C had not given full reasons, C had been responding to a request to exercise discretion and was under no duty to give full reasons. In cases involving the exercise of residual discretion it was the decision and not the terms of the letter communicating the decision that was under consideration; (4) nothing in the cases cited required C to reach a different conclusion on Art.8. The Commission had decided in similar cases that it had been the parent's choice to remarry someone whose immigration status was in doubt that had brought about the adverse affect, and not the state, and (5) it was a matter for C to consider whether the circumstances were sufficiently exceptional to merit departure from the published policy and as these circumstances were implicit in the decision to marry in the knowledge that enforcement action had been taken, his decision was not irrational and unreasonable.

AKHTAR v. SECRETARY OF STATE FOR THE HOME DEPARTMENT; *sub nom.* AKHTAR, PETITIONER 2001 S.L.T. 1239, Lord Eassie, OH.

5885. Refugees—refusal by part time temporary special adjudicator—right to fair trial

[European Convention on Human Rights 1950 Art.6(1).]

S entered the UK in July 1995, claiming to have left India as a result of being assaulted by members of a Khalistan independence movement and threats by the Punjab police. His application for permission to remain as a refugee was refused in September 1997 and S appealed against the decision. The special adjudicator refused the appeal in February 1998. S sought judicial review and reduction of both decisions arguing that he was entitled to have his appeal heard by an independent and impartial tribunal under common law, by way of legitimate expectation and under the terms of European Convention on Human Rights 1950 Art.6(1). He argued that the special adjudicator was not an independent and impartial tribunal as at the time of the appeal he was appointed at the sole discretion of the Lord Chancellor, who also had sole arbiter as to the merits of any complaints made against the special adjudicator. In addition, the special adjudicator had no minimum guarantee of days of engagement or therefore no guaranteed income, no security of tenure either legally or de facto, had no control over the days he was required to hear appeals and was eligible for re-appointment at the sole discretion of the Lord Chancellor. The Secretary of State accepted S's submission that the correct approach at common law was apparent bias of the adjudicator, but argued that it required such bias to be based on the conduct of the appeal rather than simply as a result of the adjudicator's appointment.

Held, reducing the decision of the special adjudicator in November 1997 and corresponding determination, refusing the appeal against the decision of the Secretary of State of September 1997 and remitting S's appeal against that decision for a fresh hearing before a different special adjudicator, that (1) an independent observer of the system of part time special adjudicators, as it existed in November 1997, could have taken the view that the special adjudicator might have been influenced in his decision by his desire for successive appointments; (2) the type of case, which the holder of a part time judicial appointment is required to conduct, was a relevant factor in determining the issue potential bias, and (3) requirements that the special adjudicator be a qualified lawyer bound to disqualify himself where a potential conflict of interest arose was insufficient to dispel a suspicion of bias from a reasonable man.

Observed, that (1) the submissions made on the grounds of legitimate expectation added nothing to the case pled at common law and, in any case, the appellate system in place in 1997 did not breach any legitimate expectation S might have held, and (2) Art.6(1) did not apply to the type of proceedings conducted by the special adjudicator.

SINGH (CHARANJIT) v. SECRETARY OF STATE FOR THE HOME DEPARTMENT 2002 S.C.119, Lord Mackay of Drumadoon, OH.

INSOLVENCY

5886. Bankruptcy–sequestration–gratuitous alienations–disposition for love, favour and affection

[Bankruptcy (Scotland) Act 1985 (c.66) s.34(4).]

A was N's accountant in bankruptcy and sought payment from N in relation to two alleged gratuitous alienations from her husband, M, who had since gone bankrupt. N argued that (1) there had been adequate consideration for the first alienation, of M's half share in a property, the disposition having erred in stating that it was for "love, favour and affection", and (2) with regard to the second alienation of photographic equipment, A should be seeking restoration of the property, not payment. N averred that the equipment had been sold but that she had not received a sale price, and there was an outstanding action against the buyer. A argued that averments concerning adequate consideration for the property were irrelevant because an action for rectification had not been raised.

Held, allowing proof before answer under deletion of certain matters, that (1) N was not prevented from arguing that there had been adequate consideration despite the terms of the disposition, and (2) A was entitled to rely on the words "or other redress as may be appropriate" in the Bankruptcy (Scotland) Act 1985 s.34(4) in choosing to seek payment when N was not seeking restoration herself but payment, had not sought to convene the purchaser as a third party, and there were no averments concerning the whereabouts of the goods; the fact that she herself had not received payment was not relevant.

NOTTAY'S TRUSTEE v. NOTTAY; *sub nom.* ACCOUNTANT IN BANKRUPTCY v. NOTTAY 2001 S.L.T. 769, Lord Clarke, OH.

5887. Bankruptcy–sequestration–recall–motion for further procedure not lodged timeously–relief not granted

[Act of Sederunt (Rules of the Court of Session 1994) 1994 (SI 1994 1443) Sch.2 r.14.8.]

VW was sequestrated in the sheriff court and petitioned the Court of Session for recall claiming she had not received the petition. VW should have enrolled a motion for further procedure in terms of the Act of Sederunt (Rules of the Court of Session 1994) 1994 Sch.2 r.14.8 but failed to do so timeously. H sought dismissal of the petition in respect of that failure. VW's lawyers withdrew and additional time was sought to instruct a new lawyer, they also withdrew and more time was sought. H intimated a further motion for dismissal for want of insistence and it was granted. VW reclaimed arguing that the issue as to whether or not she had received the petition was a genuine one and the delay in advancing the petition was attributable to her difficulties in retaining a solicitor. H argued that there was no reasonable explanation for the delay.

Held, refusing the reclaiming motion, that it was important that sequestrations proceeded with reasonable dispatch and steps in the recall procedure were taken promptly.

VAN OVERWAELE v. HACKING & PATERSON; *sub nom.* OVERWAELE, PETITIONER 2002 S.C. 62, Lord Coulsfield, Lord Johnston, Lord Prosser, Ex Div.

5888. Bankruptcy–sequestration–recall–no assets in bankrupt's estate

G, a construction firm and two individuals, petitioned for recall of sequestrations. C, a bank, were the petitioning creditors in all the sequestrations. G sought recall on the grounds that there were no assets in their estates except in an action against C and that the trustee had declined to take any action in connection with that claim and no creditor was willing to take up the action. The bank was both a secured and ordinary creditor. G offered to assign the proceeds of the action against the bank to professional persons so it could be distributed amongst the creditors. C argued that there was insufficient disclosure of G's assets and sought further clarification, they also argued that even if it was shown that there was no assets it would not be appropriate for the court to exercise its discretion in recalling the sequestration.

Held, refusing the motion for recall of the sequestration but refusing to dismiss the petition as irrelevant and allowing G a proof to persuade the court, that (1) sequestration should be recalled when its continuation was not in the interests of the creditors, and (2) C was using the sequestration as a block to the action. G's proposed assignation could not meet the essential requirement of protection for the creditors in all circumstances and nor would it be appropriate for the court to recall the sequestration in the exercise of its discretion.

GRANTLY DEVELOPMENTS v. CLYDESDALE BANK PLC (RECALL OF SEQUESTRATION) 2002 S.C.L.R. 175, TG Coutts Q.C., OH.

5889. Bankruptcy–sequestration–recall–payment of trustee's fees–interlocutor providing fees to be met out of "debtor's estate"–meaning of "debtor's estate"

[Bankruptcy (Scotland) Act 1985 (c.66) s.17.]

The trustee of a sequestrated estate sought payment from the debtor, following recall of the sequestration, of a sum which represented the shortfall of fees due to him as permanent trustee. The defender had not opposed the initial award of sequestration but later petitioned the Court of Session and was granted recall. The terms of the Lord Ordinary's interlocutor provided that the pursuer's outlays should be made out of the "debtor's estate". The sheriff granted decree on the basis that the interlocutor authorised the pursuer to satisfy his claim out of the defender's estate prior to repaying any surplus, or to seek payment from the defender at any time thereafter. The sheriff principal allowed the defender's appeal, holding that "debtor's estate" was consistently used in the Bankruptcy (Scotland) Act 1985 s.17(3) in the sense of the debtor's estate as vested in the trustee, and s.17(3) had to be construed as enabling the court to authorise the pursuer to recoup his expenses out of the funds vested in him. The pursuer appealed to the Court of Session.

Held, refusing the appeal, that taking the interlocutor in the context of the terms of the petition, which averred that funds provided were sufficient to meet the debtor's liabilities together with the fees and outlays of the interim trustee and the appellant, the Lord Ordinary had to be presumed to have granted recall on the basis that the appellant had sufficient funds in his hands at the time to cover all such claims and outlays. Per Lords Cameron of Lochbroom and Marnoch: A direction for payment of outlays and remuneration under s.17(3)(a) could not be equated with an order for payment to be made by a debtor personally; that was emphasised by the court's ability to make orders under s.17(3)(c). Per Lord Nimmo Smith (dissenting on this point): A direction under s.17(3)(a) for payment out of the debtor's estate might be apt to impose a personal obligation on the debtor: such provision might extend to the debtor's estate as was not in fact recovered by the permanent trustee and which, on recall of sequestration, by virtue of s.17(4) as well as the debtor's radical right, had to be taken to have remained vested in the debtor.

CRAWFORD'S TRUSTEE v. CRAWFORD; *sub nom.* HALL v. CRAWFORD 2002 S.L.T. 182, Lord Cameron of Lochbroom, Lord Marnoch, Lord Nimmo Smith, Ex Div (Extra Division).

5890. **Bankruptcy–sequestration–sale of heritable property–trustees in bankruptcy–rights of holder of unrecorded disposition–notice of title by trustee recorded before disposition**

[Bankruptcy (Scotland) Act 1985 (c.66) s.31(1).]

B, C's permanent trustee, appealed against the sheriff principal's interlocutor (2000 S.L.T. (Sh. Ct.) 116) allowing D's appeal and recalling a sheriff's declarator that property, which had been sold by C to D and which D had entered and occupied for over five months prior to C's sequestration, but in respect of which the disposition had only been recorded eight months after C's sequestration and one month after B's recording of notice of title for the property, vested in B under the Bankruptcy (Scotland) Act 1985 s.31(1) and that D were unlawfully occupying the property. The sheriff principal took the view that the decision of the House of Lords in *Sharp v. Thomson* 1997 S.L.T. 636, [1997] C.L.Y. 6156, was not restricted to the specific situation of receivership and that D should enjoy the same protection against B. D submitted that the logic of Lord Jauncey's view, based on *Heritable Reversionary Co Ltd v. Millar* [1892] A.C. 598 and supported by Lord Clyde's reliance on the same authority, was compelling and obliged the court to take the broader interpretation and apply the same construction to the words "the estate of the debtor" as was applied to the "property and undertaking" of the company.

Held, allowing the appeal, that (1) the ratio of *Sharp* was properly confined to the statutory provisions dealing with floating charges and receivership, and (2) to extend the decision would involve the recognition of a right of property intermediate between real and personal which was inconsistent with the underlying principles of Scots law and liable to cause difficulty and inconsistency in its application, and "the whole estate of the debtor" in s.31(1) should be construed as including everything to which the bankrupt had a real right.

BURNETT'S TRUSTEE v. GRAINGER 2002 S.L.T. 699, Lord Coulsfield, Lord Hamilton, Lord Maclean, Ex Div.

5891. **Coporate insolvency–liquidation–unfair preferences–form of remedy**

[Insolvency Act 1986 (c.45) s.243.]

M, a company in liquidation, sought to challenge a transaction between them and D, another company, on the grounds that it created an unfair preference under and in terms of the Insolvency Act 1986 s.243, and payment by D of £191,350, the amount the unsecured creditors would have received but for the transaction. At the time all shares in D were held by X, also shareholders in M. M averred that at the time of the agreement to transact, it was insolvent. X had suggested that they acquire M's assets and business for a consideration which included their payment of its trade creditors (T) but not other creditors, in order to preserve the goodwill attached to M, and in entering into the agreement, M was creating preferences to the prejudice of other creditors. D argued inter alia that the agreement alone did not create any obligation enforceable by T and if the whole transaction could be challenged, then T should have been called as defenders. M argued, inter alia, that under s.243(5) an action need not be directed against the preferred creditors and, though there was no case in which a claim for similar compensation had been made, in *Mitchell v. Rodger* (1834) 12 S. 802 the outcome was likely to have involved payment of compensation.

Held, dismissing the action, that (1) M was challenging the whole transaction which concluded with payment of the debts to T, and which therefore had the effect of creating a preference. The word "challenge" in s.243 (5) was used in a broad sense and did not equiparate with an action to reduce or set aside; (2) T did not have to be called as defenders as the action did not seek to disturb any payment to them and the proviso to s.243(5) suggested that a claim could be made against a third party; (3) although, looking at the agreement itself, M and D undertook certain reciprocal obligations, the exception in s.243(2)(c) relating to nova debita could not be relevant; and the exception in s.243(2)(b) relating to cash payments of debts due, fell to be construed in line with longstanding authority which required such payments to have been made bona fide and in the ordinary course of business; (4) the action was irrelevant because what M were seeking was not any remedy against the preferred creditor but damages from D, measured not by the whole amount paid to T but by the alleged loss to the remainder of the unsecured creditors; s.243(5) was designed to enable a company to be restored to the position it would have been in but for the preference, and the primary remedies envisaged were reduction and restoration of property. The words "or other redress as may be appropriate" meant redress of the same character and did not give the court a general equitable jurisdiction, *Short's Trustee v. Chung (No.1)* 1991 S.L.T. 472, [1991] C.L.Y. 4415, and *Cay's Trustee v. Cay* 1999 S.L.T. 321, [1998] C.L.Y. 6001 followed. There was no warrant for a claim of damages and no legal basis for such a claim had been set out; (5) it was not clear why D, who had paid full value for what was purchased, should be required to make payment in addition of a substantial proportion of sums which they paid to T while leaving those sums in T's hands, and (6) there was no clear averment of collusion and no relevant basis had been averred for the claim for compensation. As D remained a creditor it would have been acting against its own interest, and authority suggested (as did the statutory language) that collusion in this context had to involve the agreement of the preferred creditor.

BAILLIE MARSHALL LTD (IN LIQUIDATION) v. AVIAN COMMUNICATIONS LTD 2002 S.L.T. 189, Lord Kingarth, OH.

5892. **Corporate insolvency–liquidation–gratuitous alienations–assignation of lease–receipt of rental a "consideration"–adequacy of "consideration" judged at time of transaction**

[Insolvency Act 1986 (c.45) s.242.]

N, a company in liquidation, raised an action against C challenging certain transactions as gratuitous alienations. N had leased a piece of land and were to erect a building under the terms of the lease. N assigned the lease to a partnership, C, both of whom were directors of N. C argued that the assignation was not challengeable under the Insolvency Act 1986 s.242 as it had taken place five years before the winding up. N argued that if that was found to be the case, then sums made by N after the "relevant day" should be held to be gratuitous alienations being money expended on heritable property which would effeir to the land and benefit the tenant under the lease and ultimately the land owner. C averred that it had been decided that N would fund the balance of the construction costs and would, in consideration thereof, receive the rental income. N argued that there had been no adequate consideration since the rental amounted to only 48 per cent of the cost. C argued that the decision had been potentially adequate and adequacy had to be viewed at the point at which the transaction was entered into.

Held, allowing proof before answer on the whole case, that (1) a decision taken by two individuals in their dual capacities of creditors and partners creating an arrangement whereby the company would receive the future rental income was capable of constituting consideration, and (2) the adequacy of a consideration tendered for an alienation must be judged at the time of the transaction and the promise of an entitlement to future income might well, in commercial terms, constitute an adequate consideration.

NOVA GLAZE REPLACEMENT WINDOWS LTD v. CLARK THOMSON & CO 2001 S.C. 815, Lord Eassie, OH.

5893. **Corporate insolvency–winding up–guarantees–adequate consideration**

[Insolvency Act 1986 (c.45) s.127, s.242.]

J, interim liquidator of a company, M, raised an action against R, a bank, seeking reduction of a guarantee as a gratuitous alienation under the Insolvency Act 1986 s.242 and payment of the sum at credit in M's account, frozen by R after the guarantee was called up on M being wound up. X, Y and Z, three companies in the same group, were also called as defenders. R acted as bankers to all four companies who had accepted an offer of a group overdraft facility. All four granted a guarantee in favour of R, providing that they would jointly and severally guarantee to discharge on demand all the obligations of each debtor. X, Y and Z were then insolvent. R averred that the guarantee was required as a condition of the group overdraft and M made use of the facility, enjoying reduced interest. J argued that the provision and adequacy of the consideration had to be determined at the time when the guarantee obligation was undertaken, and the guarantee was granted for no, or no adequate consideration. R argued that (1) the alienation was not completed until the guarantee was called up, any challenge under s.242 had to relate to an alienation during the period specified in s.242(3), which terminated on the commencement of the winding up, and s.127 was the applicable provision, and (2) J's averments that the guarantee was granted for no consideration or no adequate consideration were irrelevant.

Held, granting reduction, allowing proof regarding the freezing of M's account and proof before answer on R's averments relating to guarantees granted by R and indemnities granted by M, that (1) s.242 could apply to any alienation taking place after the commencement of the period specified in s.242(3), including an alienation that became completely effectual after the commencement of winding up, and s.127 was wholly inapplicable to a case such as the present; (2) consideration was something which had a patrimonial worth at the time it was given; where an obligation was cautionary in nature, the consideration had to move from the party providing it and at least in part, though not exclusively, to the company making the alienation; and the adequacy of the consideration should be assumed if the transaction as a whole appeared commercial provided it was assessed strictly and full consideration in money or money's worth had moved from the creditor; (3) in all such cases it was for the creditor in the guarantee to aver and prove that consideration was provided, and that it was adequate, and (4) R's averments did not disclose that adequate consideration was provided as the guaranteeing of obligations of other companies which were already insolvent was inevitably detrimental and provided immediate benefit to the creditor distinct from the usual benefit that a guarantee conferred, and the making of future advances by the creditor in such a guarantee could never be adequate consideration for a security of that nature.

JACKSON v. ROYAL BANK OF SCOTLAND PLC 2002 S.L.T. 1123, Lord Drummond Young, OH.

5894. **Corporate insolvency–winding up–liquidators–appointment–admission that money owed–dispute as to extent of debt**

Landlords, petitioned for the winding up of C (a tenant company) and moved for the appointment of an interim liquidator. The petitioners served a charge for £24,663.66 on C in respect of service charges and served the current petition when C failed to pay. C lodged a summary application for suspension of the charge which was later sisted. On April 26, 2001 C's solicitor admitted on their behalf that they owed the petitioners £10,000. On May 2, the solicitor confirmed by fax that C owed the petitioners "in the region of £7,000 to £10,000". On May 3 the solicitor faxed the petitioners stating that a cheque would be passed the following day. No cheque was received. On May 8 the solicitor made a conditional offer of £8,500 in full and final settlement. The directors of C argued that the petition should be dismissed or sisted to await the outcome of the other proceedings. C and the petitioners were in dispute as to the amount owed and the sum due had not been established. There was no indication of how the sum in the charge had been calculated and C were under no obligation to liquidate the amount in dispute. A winding up process was not appropriate for the recovery of a disputed debt.

Held, appointing an interim liquidator, that (1) it was untenable for the respondents to say that they did not know what sum was due and to contend there was a bona fide dispute as to liability, given the unambiguous acknowledgments that a sum was due and C's statement that they had calculated the sum to be £8,500 in the letter of May 8, and (2) the petitioners were well entitled to have an interim liquidator appointed: C had failed to honour their promise to pay a sum admittedly due and the facts that the sum had not been precisely quantified by the petitioners, that there was dispute as to the balance owed and that C might appear to be solvent were nothing to the purpose.

CLOWES DEVELOPMENTS (SCOTLAND) LTD v. WHANNEL; *sub nom.* CLOWES DEVELOPMENTS (SCOTLAND) LTD v. WHANNELL 2002 S.L.T. (Sh Ct) 6, Sheriff ID Macphail Q.C., Sh Ct (Lothian and Border).

5895. Diligence–arrestment–arrestment on dependence–winding up more than 60 days later–entitlement to funds arrested

See CIVIL PROCEDURE: Granite Properties v. Edinburgh City Council. §5320

5896. Insolvency proceedings–voluntary arrangements

INSOLVENCY (SCOTLAND) AMENDMENT RULES 2002, SI 2002 2709; made under the Insolvency Act 1986 s.411. In force: January 1, 2003; £6.00.

These Rules amend the Insolvency (Scotland) Rules 1986 (SI 1986 1915) to permit the holding of the meetings of members and creditors on different days and provide that creditors with unliquidated claims are always entitled to vote for £1 unless the chairperson of the meeting agrees to put a higher value on the claim. They also provide that a voluntary arrangement is to have effect notwithstanding that the members of the company do not vote in favour of it and allow the directors of eligible companies to obtain a moratorium with a view to obtaining the approval of a proposal for a voluntary arrangement.

5897. Books

Greene, J.H.; Fletcher, I.M.–Greene & Fletcher: the Law and Practice of Receivership in Scotland. 3rd Ed. Paperback: £110.00. ISBN 0-406-94451-2. Butterworths Law (Scotland).

Higgins, Mark–Scottish Repossessions. Paperback: £55.00. ISBN 0-414-01465-0. W.Green & Son.

INSURANCE

5898. Fire insurance–repudiation–breach of policy conditions–knowledge of continuing breach

M, occupiers of a hotel, raised an action against their insurers, N, and insurance brokers, H, seeking declarator that N was obliged to indemnify them under an insurance policy for losses sustained in a fire which began in the hotel kitchens, and payment of the amount of the losses, or, alternatively, payment of that amount by H as damages for breach of their contractual duty of care. Debate was heard on M's averments that N had waived or were personally barred from relying on a "Frying and Cooking Equipment Condition", FCEC, under the policy. The FCEC provided that (a) all frying and other cooking ranges, flues and ducting had to be free from contact with combustible material, and (b) all flues, ducting, grease traps, sumps and filters had to be cleaned once a month. M averred, inter alia, that as a result of two surveys of the premises carried out on behalf of N, if ducting was in contact with combustible material N were or ought to have been aware of this, and also that N knew that it was physically impossible to clean all the internal surfaces of the ducting because access could not be obtained. Subsequent renewal of the policy and acceptance of the premium by N constituted waiver of the right to rely on breaches of the FCEC, and N were also personally barred from so relying. Their knowledge in relation to requirement (a) of the FCEC could be inferred from the surveyors having had unrestricted access to the whole premises during the surveys and possibly having taken access to the attic space through which the ducting ran, as they were at liberty to, the reference to ducts above a cooker in one of the survey reports, and N's own averments that the ducting was in contact with combustible materials at the time of the fire. In relation to requirement (b), knowledge could be inferred from what was visible to the surveyors and the surveyors' failure to inquire about the presence of grease traps or inspection hatches. M also argued that a relevant case of waiver did not require averments that they had conducted their affairs on the basis that N had abandoned the right to found on breaches of the FCEC.

Held, dismissing the action against N, that (1) renewal of the policy and acceptance of the premium were not acts inconsistent with future reliance on breaches of the FCEC, a continuing obligation, if N were only aware of past remediable breaches, and would be inconsistent with reliance on breaches of the condition in the future only if they knew the breaches would continue because they were of an unavoidable nature; (2) averments either of actual knowledge or of facts and circumstances from which it might be inferred that N actually knew of that state of affairs would be sufficient to support a case of waiver; and averments of imputed knowledge would also be sufficient but only if facts and circumstances were averred which put N on inquiry and averments made that they had deliberately refrained from inquiry to avoid the risk of acquiring such knowledge; (3) M had not averred circumstances yielding the inference that as a result of the surveys N must have known that equipment and ducting were in contact with combustible material, nor were their averments sufficient to support a case of imputed knowledge; (4) M's averments did not support the inference that N actually knew M could not comply with the cleaning requirements of the FCEC, and no case of imputed knowledge in this respect was or could be made on the averments, and (5) M's case of personal bar also failed for want of relevant averments of N's knowledge, actual or imputed.

MOODIESBURN HOUSE HOTEL LTD v. NORWICH UNION INSURANCE LTD 2002 S.L.T. 1069, Lord Macfadyen, OH.

5899. Indemnities–subrogation–contractual indemnity clause

See CONTRACTS: Caledonia North Sea Ltd v. London Bridge Engineering Ltd. §5419

5900. Insurance contracts–composite insurance–reporting requirements as condition precedent to liability–benefit of innocent insured party not forfeit as result of other insured party's fraud

B advanced money, secured by a standard security, to the owners of a hotel. Both parties were insured by I, each for their respective rights and interests in the hotel. Condition 6 made the truth of the statements in the proposal conditions precedent to I's liability; condition 7(a) required the "insured" to report anything that might lead to a claim immediately; condition 9 stated that in the event of a fraudulent claim all benefit would be forfeited. A claim would be settled under one of three heads (i) cost of rebuilding; (ii) cost of repair; (iii) "where for any reason a payment cannot be made in accordance with (i) or (ii) above the liability of the Company will be arrived at as if this Basis of Claims settlement had not been incorporated". The hotel was damaged by fire and B sought indemnity from I. On appeal after debate I argued that, (1) notification had not been timeous; (2) there were averments of fraud and, under condition 9, all benefit would be forfeit, regardless of B's innocence, and (3) the correct basis of claim was repair, but since no repairs had been carried out, there was no basis for seeking payment. B argued that, (1) on proper construction, notification by B was not precedent to liability; (2) on proper construction, conduct of one party would not forfeit the innocent parties' benefit, and (3) since there had been no repair, the claim came under head (iii). B cross appealed arguing that the owners had reported the fire timeously and at no time had I indicated that a claim would be out of time. B argued that I, by their inaction, had waived any right to repudiate the claim at a later date for want of notice. I argued that there was no such waiver.

Held, refusing B's appeal, allowing I's appeal and dismissing the action, that (1) a provision for forfeiture of normal benefits needed to be very clearly expressed, and on proper construction of condition 9, the fraud of the owners would have no effect upon the rights between B and I; (2) the observance and fulfilment of timeous notification was a condition precedent to liability; (3) the contractual requirement of reporting was both parties' responsibility. Notification by one did not relieve the other of the responsibility, accordingly I was not liable to B; (4) I had done nothing to imply that they were treating B's claim as valid, nor anything which would preclude their right to rely on lack of timeous notice, and (5) since actual expenditure could have been incurred, the relevant requirements were found in head (ii) not (iii). Rebuilding costs had not been incurred and I was not liable, *Donnison v. Employers Accident & Livestock Insurance Co Ltd* (1897) 24 R. 681 distinguished.

BASS BREWERS LTD v. INDEPENDENT INSURANCE CO LTD 2002 S.C. 67, Lord Prosser, Lord Dawson, Lord Osborne, Ex Div.

INTELLECTUAL PROPERTY

5901. **Passing off—personal bar—failure to assert rights in past did not preclude remedy against future acts**

[EC Treaty Art.29 (now, after amendment, Art.28 EC).]

The name "Grants" was associated with W's long established business, producing and marketing high quality whisky, gin and vodka. G, originally a small bottling business, acquired the business John Grant (Food and Wine) Limited and used the name "Grant" on their products. In 1984 W became aware of G's products, but waited to see what would happen. In 1989 W became concerned and in 1992 raised an action for interdict of G from passing off their alcoholic drinks as W's. After proof it was found that G had passed off gin and vodka as W's. Interdict was granted in respect of G's products but not the business. G reclaimed, not challenging the findings but arguing that (1) W were barred by acquiescence because of their delay in raising proceedings, and (2) the interdict was too wide. W cross appealed against the refusal of interdict in respect of G's business.

Held, refusing the reclaiming motion and allowing the cross appeal, that (1) it was essential to the doctrine of personal bar that G had acted in the reasonable belief that W was consenting, G accepted that they had used the name "Grant" because they believed they were entitled to do so; (2) since the only remedies W sought related to the future, to hold that W were barred by acquiescence would be to hold that they had granted an irrevocable consent or licence to passing off by G; (3) the interdict was not too wide territorially since interdict was granted on the premise that when goods were exported which were intended to deceive abroad, the wrong was committed in the United Kingdom, and (4) that where it had been found that G had taken advantage of Ws investment in their name to further their own business, it would have been appropriate to grant interdict prohibiting G from passing off their business as W's.

WILLIAM GRANT & SONS LTD v. GLEN CATRINE BONDED WAREHOUSE LTD (NO.3); *sub nom.* GRANT (WILLIAM) & SONS LTD v. GLEN CATRINE BONDED WAREHOUSE LTD 2001 S.C. 901, Lord Rodger L.P., 1 Div.

5902. Patents—assignment—verbal agreement to assign—enforceability

[Patents Act 1977 (c.37) s.31.]

R sought interim interdict against P, inter alia, using a certain invention which R claimed P was under a duty to assign to R despite there being no written agreement to that effect. R had been incorporated to exploit P's invention and pre incorporation discussions had taken place which P had failed to implement.

Held, refusing the motion for interim interdict, that (1) there was no requirement for a personal obligation to grant an assignation at some point in the future to be in probative form or holograph of the grantor in order to be enforceable; (2) although R's case appeared weak on the pleadings, a prima facie case could be said to exist concerning the alleged breach of a contractual obligation owed by P to R, and (3) on the balance of convenience, and having regard to the terms of the undertaking offered by P, it was preferable that the patent be used by P and accounted for than to be sterilised which would be the effect of the interim interdict.

ROADVERT LTD v. PITT 2002 S.C.L.R. 323, Lord Clarke, OH.

5903. Trade marks—Community trade marks—infringement—word mark "PEBBLE BEACH"—likelihood of confusion

[Council Regulation 40/94 on the Community trade mark Art.9(1)(c).]

P, owners and operators of a Californian golf course, sought interdict against L, a whisky marketing company. P were the proprietors of the European Community trade mark for "Pebble Beach" in classes 9, 28 and 41 (computer software, games and sporting activities). L held the UK trade mark in "Pebble Beach" in class 33, relating to alcoholic beverages, this being one of a new range of malt whiskies. P moved for interim interdict against L from infringing P's trade mark, and from passing themselves off as P or as associated with P's business. P argued that (1) P had made out a prima case under Council Regulation 40/94 Art.9(1)(c), P's trade mark had a reputation in the Community, and L's use of the sign would take unfair advantage of its distinctive character or repute, would be detrimental to its distinctive character or repute, and was without due cause; (2) P had made out a prima facie case of passing off, and (3) the balance of convenience favoured P, it would be difficult, if not impossible to quantify P's losses in the event interim interdict was refused whereas any losses to L if L ultimately succeeded would be readily quantifiable.

Held, refusing interim interdict, that (1) P had not made out a prima facie case of trade mark infringement, while they had a prima facie case of sufficient reputation to enable them to rely on Art.9(1)(c), they had not made out a prima facie case that L's use of the sign took unfair advantage of the distinctive character or repute of the pursuers' Community trade mark, or a prima facie case of detriment, and (2) P had not made out a prima facie case of passing off where the suggestion of confusion in the public appeared somewhat far fetched and, in any event, there was nothing to suggest that L were misrepresenting their goods as being the goods of, or otherwise connected with, P.

PEBBLE BEACH CO v. LOMBARD BRANDS LTD 2002 S.L.T. 1312, Lord Menzies, OH.

5904. Trade marks—domain names—test for establishing jurisdiction

See CONFLICT OF LAWS: Bonnier Media Ltd v. Smith. §5383

INTERNATIONAL TRADE

5905. Animal products–bone in beef–despatch to domestic market

BOVINES AND BOVINE PRODUCTS (TRADE) AMENDMENT (SCOTLAND) REGULATIONS 2002, SSI 2002 449; made under the European Communities Act 1972 s.2. In force: October 7, 2002; £2.50.

These Regulations amend the Bovines and Bovine Products (Trade) Regulations 1999 (SI 1999 1003) and the Bovines and Bovine Products (Trade) Amendment (Scotland) Regulations 2000 (SSI 2000 184) which give effect to Commission Decision 98/692 ([1998] OJ L328/28) amending Commission Decision 98/256 to provide for the export from the UK of deboned beef and beef products under the strict conditions of the Date-based Export Scheme; and Commission Decision 98/564 ([1998] OJ L273/37) amending Council Decision 98/256 as regards certain emergency measures to protect against bovine spongiform encephalopathy. The effect of the amendments is to give effect to Commission Decision 2002/670 ([2002] OJ L228/22) amending Council Decision 98/256 concerning emergency measures to protect against bovine spongiform encephalopathy to enable the despatch from England of bovine embryos and bone in veal carcases from calves between six and nine months exported under the Date Based Export Scheme. The Regulations also prohibit offering to despatch or consign goods which may not be despatched or consigned whether on the internet or otherwise and provide for the payment of expenses reasonably incurred in connection with storage by the owner of the consignment and in some circumstances the payment of compensation to the owner for any depreciation in the value of the consignment.

5906. Animal products–import and export controls

ANIMALS AND ANIMAL PRODUCTS (IMPORT AND EXPORT) (SCOTLAND) AMENDMENT REGULATIONS 2002, SSI 2002 125; made under the European Communities Act 1972 s.2. In force: March 7, 2002 at 5 pm; £1.75.

These Regulations, which amend the Animals and Animal Products (Import and Export) (Scotland) Regulations 2000 (SSI 2000 216), implement Commission Decision 2002/153 ([2002] OJ L50/98) concerning certain protection measures with regard to foot and mouth disease in the UK, repealing Decision 2001/740 ([2001] OJ L277/30) and amending for the eighth time Decision 2001/327 ([2001] OJ L115/12).

5907. Animal products–import and export controls

ANIMALS AND ANIMAL PRODUCTS (IMPORT AND EXPORT) (SCOTLAND) AMENDMENT (NO.2) REGULATIONS 2002, SSI 2002 196; made under the European Communities Act 1972 s.2. In force: April 20, 2002; £1.75.

These Regulations, which amend the Animals and Animal Products (Import and Export) (Scotland) Regulations 2000 (SSI 2000 216), implement Commission Decision 2002/242 ([2002] OJ L82/18) amending for the ninth time Decision 2001/327 ([2001] OJ L115/12) concerning restrictions to the movement of animals of susceptible species with regard to foot and mouth disease to continue the effect of the restrictions contained in Decision 2001/327 until midnight on December 31, 2002. The Regulations implement Commission Decision 2002/153 ([2002] OJ L50/98) concerning certain protection measures with regard to foot and mouth disease in the UK, repealing Decision 2001/740 ([2001] OJ L277/30) and amending for the eighth time Decision 2001/327 ([2001] OJ L115/12).

5908. Animal products—origin marking—third country imports

PRODUCTS OF ANIMAL ORIGIN (THIRD COUNTRY IMPORTS) (SCOTLAND) REGULATIONS 2002, SSI 2002 445; made under the European Communities Act 1972 s.2. In force: October 1, 2002; £7.50.

These Regulations amend the Dairy Products (Hygiene) (Scotland) Regulations 1995 (SI 1995 1372), the Products of Animal Origin (Import and Export) Regulations 1996 (SI 1996 3124), the Fresh Meat (Import Conditions) Regulations 1996 (SI 1996 3125), the Imported Food Regulations 1997 (SI 1997 2537), the Miscellaneous Products of Animal Origin (Import Conditions) Regulations 1999 (SI 1999 157) and revoke the Imported Food (Scotland) Regulations 1985 (SI 1985 913). They implement Council Directive 97/98 ([1998] OJ L24/9) laying down the principles governing the organisation of veterinary checks on products entering the Community from third countries which applies to products of animal origin. The Regulations establish the inspection system which will apply to the generality of products, lay down special provisions which apply to particular categories of product and deal with the calculation and payment of charges for the veterinary checks.

LANDLORD AND TENANT

5909. Agricultural holdings—existence of lease

[Agricultural Holdings (Scotland) Act 1949 (c.75); Agricultural Holdings (Scotland) Act 1991 (c.55).]

A sought declarator that he was tenant of lands in terms of the Agricultural Holdings (Scotland) Act 1949 now the Agricultural Holdings (Scotland) Act 1991 and that the second respondents had interfered with A's open and peaceful possession of some of the lands which comprised the agricultural tenancy. The lands were originally wholly owned by K, but part had been sold to the second respondents in 1996. The sheriff held that A had not proved that he was a tenant under the Act, nor that he was entitled to open and peaceful possession. A appealed arguing that the sheriff had been wrong to find that A had failed to establish that his occupation of the lands derived from a lease granted by K, which constituted an agricultural tenancy. A argued that the court was entitled to look beyond the wording of the contract between A and K and establish the true intention, which, A argued, had been to establish a lease of an agricultural holding. A accepted the sheriff's findings that there had been nothing in writing which constituted a lease of an agricultural holding and that, to constitute a lease, there had to be agreement between the parties as to the subjects, the rent, the parties concerned and the term of the lease. It was not in dispute that a lease of the subjects was capable of being an agricultural lease in terms of statute. A disputed the sheriff's finding that there was no agreement on the extent of the subjects, the term or the rent to be paid. The arrangement between A and K had arisen out of the fact that K's son was returning to agricultural college to study organic farming methods which would leave the land owned by K fallow for a period approaching five years. A offered to work the land in return for payment of £100 per acre where potatoes were grown and £33 per acre for oats. There was apparently no agreement as to when such an arrangement would begin or end, nor on the extent of land which would be involved. A had asked K for a written lease, which had been refused. The sums paid by A to K in consequence of their agreement had been varying in terms of amount and period between payments as had the amount of land occupied by A.

Held, refusing the appeal, that (1) the sheriff had been correct in determining that the first and essential question to be determined was whether A and K had entered into a lease; (2) the sheriff was fully entitled to find that the arrangement between the parties was not a lease and that the consideration paid by A to K in respect of the possession of the fields was not of the nature of rent, and (3) the sheriff was entitled, in reaching his decision, to have regard to the whole circumstances of the case in order to determine the true intention of the parties. Opinion of the Court per Lord Cameron of Lochbroom.

ALI v. KHOSLA 2001 S.C.L.R. 1072, Lord Cameron of Lochbroom, Lord Marnoch, Lord Philip, Ex Div.

5910. Assured shorthold tenancies–tacit relocation

[Housing (Scotland) Act 1988 (c.43) s.32, s.32(1)(a), s.33.]

C raised proceedings for recovery of possession of heritable property occupied by R. At the first calling, following agreement between the parties that there were no disputed questions of fact which warranted a diet of proof, C moved the sheriff to grant decree as craved together with expenses. The terms of the lease were that it ran from August 18, 1997 to August 18, 1998 and thereafter could be terminated by C on the 18th day of any month on at least 28 days written notice to R. R argued that the lease had tacitly relocated on August 18, 1998 and then again on August 18, 1999, which therefore made the next ish August 18, 2000. R argued that, in terms of the Housing (Scotland) Act 1988 s.33, the sheriff was not entitled to grant decree where tacit relocation of the lease was in operation. R further argued that the alternative month to month provision contained in the lease should drop out of account as it was inconsistent with the principal provision of the lease which was for a yearly let. R then argued an alternative approach that, if the lease did not continue by tacit relocation, the month to month provision was effective making each period of the lease one month, thereby excluding it from the protection afforded to short assured tenancies which had to be for a minimum period of six months in terms of s.32(1)(a) and instead became an assured tenancy, for which the provisions of s.33 were not available. Finally R argued that if the month by month clause was to be applied, then the ish was the 18th day of each month. The notice having been served on September 16, 1999 only two days before the ish and, therefore, proper notice in terms of the Act had not been given. In response, C submitted that none of the authorities cited by R post dated the 1988 Act and that s.32 specifically provided that where a short assured tenancy continued by tacit relocation, it continued to be classed as a short assured tenancy, notwithstanding that it would be for less than six months, which entitled her to the remedy contained in s.33. Finally, C contended that the four week notice required by statute was a minimum period and not a maximum period and R was not entitled to claim that the notice was invalidated by C giving her too much notice, C having given notice on September 16, 1999 that possession was required on November 18, 1999.

Held, refusing the appeal, that (1) C's replies to R's submissions were well founded and a complete answer thereto, and (2) there was no stateable defence in this case and nothing could be gained by remitting the case to proof.

CAVRIANI v. ROBINSON 2002 Hous. L.R. 67, JA Farrell, Sh Ct (Lothian and Border).

5911. Crofts–common grazings–boundaries–jurisdiction to determine

[Crofters (Scotland) Act 1993 (c.44) s.53.]

F applied to the court to determine the boundaries of Balgowan Common Grazings. As a preliminary point, F submitted that the landlord (S) had no right to challenge the extent of the common grazings when they had been incorporated into regulations by the Crofters Commission. S submitted that although the Crofters Commission had a duty to ascertain the boundaries, jurisdiction for determining the boundaries of common grazings lay with the Land Court under the Crofters (Scotland) Act 1993 s.53. As regards the boundaries of the common grazings, F submitted that an area, which had originally been woodland, was included. F maintained that even if the wood had not originally been included, it had subsequently become part of the common grazings as a result of general agreement and use. The use of the wood as part of the common grazings had taken place since at least 1946. S argued that the wood had been used under a separate seasonal lease.

Held, finding that there had, at least since 1946, been an unwritten consensual agreement for the use of the wood as part of the grazings, that (1) jurisdiction lay with the Land Court under s.53 and there was nothing untoward in the landlord's actions in defending the application; (2) there was no evidence of a separate lease having been granted for the seasonal use of the wood, and (3) had there been any dispute as to the boundaries, it would have been raised at the meeting in 1984 which led to the Crofters Commission's regulation of the grazings in 1985.

FRASER v. SPENCER 2001 S.L.C.R. 116, J Kinloch, Land Ct (Div Ct).

5912. Crofts–common grazings–resumption–use as winter feeding ground for stags reasonable

[Crofters (Scotland) Act 1993 (c.44) s.20.]

S, the landlord of common grazings, applied to the court for a resumption of part of the common grazings for the winter feeding of stags. The main income for the estate managed by S was from sporting rights in the form of stalking and fishing. The income from fishing had depleted in recent years and the estate had to look at ways to increase its revenue from stalking. In addition, the migration of red deer in the winter months was recognised by the local community as a problem due principally to the deer crossing roads in the area. In exchange for the land to be resumed, S had agreed to enlarge the common grazings by an equal area, albeit of land at a higher altitude and less accessible. The land had, however, been approved for a Forestry Commission Woodland Grant Scheme which would be transferred to the crofters at an estimated value of £78,000 over 16 years. S had also agreed to allow the crofters access over the estate land, use of the sheep fanks in the area to be resumed and to the erection of stockproof fencing on the boundaries. The area of land being resumed was less than 2 per cent of the total common grazings. The action was unopposed by the crofters entitled to a share in the grazings.

Held, granting the resumption subject to the landlord erecting and maintaining stockproof fencing on the boundary between the resumption and the common grazings enlargement, that (1) the evidence supported a finding that the purpose for the resumption was a reasonable one in terms of Crofters (Scotland) Act 1993 s.20, and (2) the crofters waiving of their right to a share in value of the land to be resumed was reasonable given the terms of the compensation package being offered by S.

SCOBIE v. MOREFIELD RHUE AND ARDMAIR CROFTERS 2001 S.L.C.R. 100, DM Macdonald, Land Ct (Div Ct).

5913. Crofts–common grazings–status of holding

[Crofters (Scotland) Act 1993 (c.44) s.12(3).]

C applied to the court for a determination of the status of land known as Suisinish Croft. The croft had originally been subdivided into five separate crofts, which had then been restructured to form three crofts. Each croft had a one third share in an area of land to be used as common grazings. On renunciation of two of the crofts by their tenants, the landlord applied to C for the right to lease the two vacant crofts to the remaining tenant of the third croft. That tenant, S, then held all rights to the common grazings. C asked the court to determine whether (1) the whole area of land was croft land within the meaning of the Crofters (Scotland) Act 1993 s.12(3); (2) whether any part of the holding was merely a right in grazing, and (3) whether any part of the land was a right in land that formed part of common grazing to which the Act applied. C argued that the amalgamation of the land into one croft had the effect of the common grazings becoming part of the croft land. S argued that there was a distinction between croft land and grazing land and that the mere amalgamation of the three areas of crofting land was insufficient to establish a change in the status of the grazing land.

Held, finding that S had rights of grazing over the land in question, but not rights to the land but that the land was no longer common grazing, that (1) the totality of shareholders' rights in common grazings was not equivalent to a right to use the land as if it had been let as croft land; (2) the statutory procedures followed which resulted in all rights to the common grazings being held by one crofter had the effect of removing the common element of the grazing rights, and (3) procedures resulting in one crofter holding all shares in the grazing rights was not equivalent at common law to an apportionment.

CROFTERS COMMISSION v. SCOTTISH MINISTERS 2002 S.L.T. (Land Ct) 19, Lord McGhie, DJ Houston, DM MacDonald, Land Ct (Full Ct).

5914. Crofts–decrofting direction–appeal against refusal–hearing de novo

[Crofters (Scotland) Act 1993 (c.44) s.20, s.24(3).]

L appealed against a decision by C to refuse to grant a decrofting direction in respect of L's croft on the Isle of Mull. It was agreed between the parties that the court should deal with the appeal by a hearing de novo. L wanted to decroft, "to free the property from crofting legislation so that if any scheme came along he would be free to take advantage of it", but intended to remain in, and work the croft after the direction was granted. C argued that there was a demand for crofts in the area and that it was not in the interests of the local crofting community for the decrofting direction to be granted where no reasonable purpose for doing so had been established. C was concerned that such a move would result in a dangerous precedent being set with L's croft being the thin edge of the wedge in the subsequent decline of the crofting community on Mull.

Held, refusing the appeal, that (1) L had failed to establish a reasonable purpose for decrofting within the terms of the Crofters (Scotland) Act 1993 s.20, the fundamental test being that the purchase should have relation to the good of the croft or of the estate or to the public interest, *Knight v. Crofters Commission* 1999 S.L.C.R. 102, [2000] C.L.Y. 6528 followed; (2) where an application was not based on a reasonable purpose, the court had to consider whether decrofting was appropriate in the circumstances under the discretion conferred by s.24(3) with the key considerations being the interests of the crofting community and the demand for a tenancy, and as the parties had agreed to the hearing de novo, on the evidence before it, and (3) in making a determination, C and the court had to assess the situation as if the croft was available.

LAMONT v. CROFTERS COMMISSION 2001 S.L.C.R. 7, Lord McGhie, DJ Houston, DM Macdonald, Land Ct (Full Ct).

5915. Crofts–removal of crofter–appeals–duty of law agent to client

C, a landlord, applied to the court for an order ordaining B, to remove from the croft on the grounds of non payment of rent and failure to maintain stockproof fencing. The court continued the case to afford B the chance to pay the arrears of rent, which was done. In addition, the court allowed B a period of three months to repair and erect stockproof fencing as required by the order of court. On expiry of that time, C inspected the property and advised the court that the work had not been carried out and moved the court to grant removal. No answers were lodged by B and the court duly granted the order for removal on January 9, 2001. On January 18, B lodged a statement of grounds of appeal challenging the contention that the work had not been carried out. B indicated that the nature of his work resulted in his being uncontactable for periods of time which had resulted in the failure to respond to the motion for removal. B maintained that the fencing work had been undertaken by contractors and all boundaries were stockproof. B however admitted that he had not been aware of the specific requirements of the court order and had merely instructed the contractors to make the boundaries stockproof. C carried out a further inspection and admitted that some of the work had been done, but that all the work required by the Divisional Court had not been completed. The court undertook an inspection of the croft boundaries.

Held, refusing the appeal, that (1) B had failed to show good reason for failure to comply with the specific requirements of the Divisional Court order as the court must assume that proper intimation of information to a party's agent was equivalent to intimation to the party themselves; (2) the work undertaken by B to improve the boundaries was insufficient to meet the requirements of the court order, and (3) the fact that B did not keep stock on the croft did not reduce the burden on him to maintain stockproof boundaries.

COWELL v. BEATON 2001 S.L.C.R. 65, Lord McGhie, DJ Houston, J Kinloch, Land Ct (Full Ct).

5916. Crofts–removal of crofter–compensation–whether deduction for grant aid

[Agricultural Holdings (Scotland) Act1991 (c.55); Crofters (Scotland) Act1993 (c.44) s.32.]

M, a crofter removed in terms of a declarator of vacancy, applied for an order fixing the amount of compensation to which he was entitled for permanent improvements. M claimed an open market value in excess of £17,000, relying on the expression of demand when the croft was advertised for assignation and the arrangement with the new tenant who was willing to meet whatever sum the court assessed. He argued inter alia that in contrast with the agricultural holdings legislation, where specific provision was made, sums paid by way of grant aid in respect of improvements did not fall to be deducted in the calculation.

Held, assessing compensation, that (1) it was established practice of the court when making such valuations to deduct the element of grant aid, there was no reason to distinguish the position from that under the Agricultural Holdings (Scotland) Act 1991 and on that basis the compensation due to the applicant under the Crofters (Scotland) Act 1993 s.32(3) was £7,088.50, and (2) on the evidence the agreement with the new tenant could not be considered as evidence of open market value and in spite of its desirable location, the croft had limited agricultural potential and the sum due in terms of s.32(2) of the 1993 Act was £11,500.

MacLEAN v. MacSWEEN'S TRUST; *sub nom.* MacLEAN v. DG MacSWEEN TRUST 2001 S.L.T. (Land Ct) 39, DM MacDonald, Land Ct.

5917. Crofts–resumption–share of development value–evidence of sales by incorporated landlord

[Crofters (Scotland) Act1993 (c.44) s.20, s.21.]

B applied to the court for an order authorising the resumption of three plots of ground, which would then be sold on as house sites. M, the crofter, accepted that the grounds for the application were acceptable under the Crofters (Scotland) Act 1993 s.20, but took issue with the value being placed on the land for the purpose of calculating the compensation due to him under s.21. M lodged a specification of documents seeking to obtain from B details of property sales in the area since B's incorporation. M had tried, unsuccessfully, to obtain the information from other sources, including the Register of Sasines, local surveyors and local estate agents. B argued that the information available to M from those sources, and in particular from the Register of Sasines, was sufficient, together with the evidence of expert witnesses for both parties, for the court to make a determination as to the value of the land. B maintained that an examination of their books was unnecessary.

Held, ordering B to produce details of all house sales on their estate since incorporation, that (1) it was essential to produce evidence of open market value and the best evidence available was that of open market sales in the locality, and (2) a search in the Register of Sasines would not produce the required information.

BORVE AND ANNISHADER TOWNSHIP v. MacLEOD 2001 S.L.C.R. 160, DM Macdonald, Land Ct (Div Ct).

5918. Crofts–right of access–burden of proof of access of necessity

DE appealed against a decision of the Divisional Court regarding access over his land to a neighbouring croft. He argued that the court had misdirected itself in regard to the burden of proof in relation to the necessity for a right of access. DE maintained that it was for the DI to prove that the access was necessary and not for him to prove the contrary. He submitted that the croft was not landlocked as there was a public road along one boundary from which vehicular access could be taken without the need for the right of access. He also maintained that the existing use by vehicles was insufficient to establish a right of access. Finally, DE argued that, in order to establish necessity, direct evidence had to be given in court and it was not open for the court to reach a decision based on a site visit where no evidence had been given. DI argued that the test for the establishment of a right of access in a non-crofting context was irrelevant and that the correct test was one of practicality. It was unreasonable to base the rights of access available on what was required over a 100 years ago. DI further argued that the requirements of modern crofting meant that vehicular access was required which could not readily be taken from the public road abutting the croft.

Held, refusing the appeal, that (1) the court was entitled to take the findings of a site visit into consideration when establishing necessity, even where direct evidence had not been given; (2) the fact that the burden of proof applied by the court was possibly inverted and weight attached to the inversion was not of itself sufficient to counter the facts that it was not practical to create an access to the public road; (3) use of the disputed access route and lack of evidence of any alternative route being used could be considered by the court when determining the question of necessity, and (4) use of the existing tarred road over the adjacent croft by DE involved little or no interference in DI's enjoyment of his croft.

DINAN v. DENNETT 2001 S.L.C.R. 55, Lord McGhie, J Kinloch, DM Macdonald, Land Ct (Full Ct).

5919. Crofts—status of holding

[Small Landholders (Scotland) Act 1911 (1 & 2 Geo V, c.49) s.17.]

H's trustees applied to the court for a determination that an area of land was not subject to crofting tenure. The area had been granted as an enlargement by an order of the court in 1917, however, no rights in respect of the land had been exercised between 1958 and the instant query which had begun in 2000. Evidence was given by B, who had purchased the land in 1957, that the land had been sold free of crofting rights and with vacant possession. She confirmed that the land had only been used during her ownership for the grazing of estate livestock. Records from the Crofters Commission suggested that the crofters who had been entitled to the common grazings had renounced their rights some time prior to 1955, probably in the 1930's, but no formal record of a resumption or renunciation existed. B sold the land to H in 1971, and H gave evidence that if there had been crofting land included there would not have been a purchase. Witnesses again gave evidence that the land had only been used for estate grazing, except in recent years when H had allowed a new farm manager to graze some of his cattle there seasonally. In opposition, it was submitted that an entry in the Register of Crofts in 1960 referred to the land as a croft occupied by the owner and the lack of any formal proof of a resumption or renunciation suggested that the land was still crofting land.

Held, finding that the land was not subject to the Crofting Acts, that (1) failure to locate any record of a resumption or renunciation in respect of a croft would lead to the court to an assumption that the croft had not been removed from crofting tenure by such means; (2) evidence pointing to a renunciation in the 1930's was to be believed, given judicial knowledge of the downturn in profitability of livestock farming at that time and the lack of tenants' interest in the land since the 1940's; (3) under the Small Landholders (Scotland) Act 1911 s.17, the Board of Agriculture were under a duty to take timely action to re-let any vacant agricultural land, and (4) failure of the Board to take such action resulted in the land falling outwith the jurisdiction of the Landholders Acts prior to 1955 and the land was therefore ineligible for inclusion in the Register of Crofts in 1960, *Highland Primary Care NHS Trust v. Thomson* 1999 S.L.T. (Land Ct) 10, [2000] C.L.Y. 6531, followed.

HORLICK'S TRUSTEES v. O'HARA 2001 S.L.C.R. 125, DM Macdonald, Land Ct (Div Ct).

5920. Crofts—status of holding

[Agricultural Holdings (Scotland) Act1991 (c.55); Crofters (Scotland) Act1993 (c.44) s.23.]

R let a croft from W, who was also the owner-occupier of another neighbouring croft. At the time of the let, R enquired with W as to whether additional land was available and it was agreed that W would allow R to use an area of land known as Top Park at no extra charge. The Crofters Commission were never formally advised of the arrangement, although W had provided letters for R to use in support of R's applications for Hill Livestock Compensatory Allowances. Since the agreement had begun, R had cultivated, seeded, fertilised and grazed the land and used it for the production of hay. R had also replaced fencing to make the land stock proof, all of which were within the W's knowledge. W had subsequently indicated to R that he wanted her to vacate the land as he had other plans for it and R, in response, raised an action asking the court to determine the legal status of the arrangement between R and W. R maintained that the land had become an extension of her croft, failing which it was an agricultural lease under the Agricultural Holdings (Scotland) Act 1991. R maintained that the principle of rei interventus should apply as R had worked the land in the genuine belief that W had obtained consent to the lease of the land from the Crofters Commission. W argued that it could not be an extension of the croft in terms of the Crofters (Scotland) Act 1993 as the Crofters Commission had not consented and neither could it be an agricultural lease as the let to R had been for an indefinite period.

Held, finding that R's occupation of the land was in the nature of a licence for the duration of R's tenancy of the principle croft from W, that the occupancy of the land had not been (1) a seasonal let as it had been continuous for at least 13 years; (2) sublet as W was an owner-occupier rather than a tenant; (3) a crofting tenancy as no consent had been obtained from the Crofters Commission in terms of the 1993 Act s.23, and rei interventus could not be used to establish a crofting tenancy, and (4) an agricultural lease was not possible as the 1991 Act did not apply to land subject to crofting law, and in any case, no rent had been paid and the term had been indefinite.

ROBERTSON v. WILLIAMSON 2001 S.L.C.R. 18, DJ Houston, Land Ct (Div Ct).

5921. Joint tenancies—transfer of matrimonial home

See FAMILY LAW: G v. G (Divorce: Transfer of Joint Tenancy). §5639

5922. Land Court—expenses—failure to find caution—appropriate order

H, the widow of an agricultural tenant, applied to the court for an order finding that she had succeeded to the agricultural holding, the lease having been bequeathed to H by her husband. The court ordained H to find caution. H failed to find caution timeously and applied to the court for an extension, arguing that she did not have sufficient means to find caution for the sum ordered, failing which, she asked for leave to withdraw the application. C moved the court to refuse H's application with a finding of expenses in their favour. C maintained that failure by the court to make a positive determination in the case could result in H raising the same issue in the sheriff court when C raised an action for vacant possession, or re-applying to the Land Court at a future date. C argued that H's husband had not been the sole tenant of the agricultural holding, which had been held in joint tenancy with his father. Following his father's death, no approval had been sought from C for the transfer of the tenancy to H's husband as sole tenant. C therefore submitted that H was not entitled to succeed to the tenancy. On the question of expenses, H argued that she had no means to meet a large award of expenses, if made against her. C submitted that an award of expenses should follow success in the action.

Held, granting order assoilzing C, that (1) an order for caution was an important matter and H's failure to treat it as such meant that the motion for further time had to be refused; (2) the evidence precluded any court from finding that H's husband had been sole tenant of the farm prior to his father's death, and (3) failure to obtain the landlord's permission for a change of tenancy following his father's death prevented H's husband from being entitled to bequeath the tenancy to H.

HUTTON v. COAL AUTHORITY 2001 S.L.C.R.1, Lord McGhie, DJ Houston, MM Macdonald, Land Ct (Full Ct).

5923. Landlords powers and duties–repairs–repairing obligations–extent of landlord's duty to inspect prior to commencement of lease

M raised an action against G, her landlord, for damages for loss suffered as a result of flooding caused by a burst pipe. Following notification by M to G of a leak in her water tank, an emergency plumber had effected a temporary repair on December 24, 1997 by connecting the mains water supply to the cold water supply, bypassing the water tank. On December 26, the cold water pipe burst causing substantial damage to the contents of the house. On inspection, it became apparent that the burst had occurred as a result of a temporary repair which had been effected some time prior to 1982 when M's family took over the tenancy of the property. That repair had taken the form of a solder wiping over a hole in a copper pipe and had not been noticed by the emergency plumber on December 24. The sheriff found that such a repair was highly likely to burst again and that, although the pipe had burst as a result of the mains pressure, it could easily have burst under normal use. The losses resulting from the flood were agreed at £17,500. The sheriff, applying *Summers v. Salford Corp* [1943] A.C. 283, held that G were liable for damages on the basis that they had failed in their duty to deliver to M, at the commencement of her tenancy, a house which was habitable and was fit for human habitation in all respects. G appealed arguing that they had complied with the test laid down in *Wolfson v. Forrester* 1910 S.C. 675, which stated that a landlord would be deemed to have fulfilled his obligations where the premises were wind and watertight against ordinary attacks of the elements and that did not include exceptional encroachments of water due to other causes. G submitted that *Summers* should be distinguished as it involved personal injury to the tenant as a result of a defect arising after the commencement of the tenancy.

Held, refusing the appeal, that (1) it was the condition of the property at the commencement of the lease which required examination as that included a pipe which was liable to burst at any moment with the likelihood of causing damage to M's possessions; (2) although *Summers* involved personal injury following a defect which occurred during the currency of a tenancy, it clearly illustrated that the definition of habitable meant more that simply a house which was capable of being lived in, and it had not been unreasonable for the sheriff to conclude that a property containing a pipe which was liable to burst at any minute was not fit for human habitation; (3) G were under a duty to inspect the property at the commencement of the tenancy, during which inspection such a defect would have been likely to be revealed, *Lamb v. Glasgow DC* 1978 S.L.T. (Notes) 64, [1978] C.L.Y. 3536, followed, and (4) even where the defect was regarded as latent, it would not be any more unjust to make the landlord liable for the resultant damage than it would be to make the tenant liable for the consequences.

Observed, that the landlord's liability for damages would have been obvious where the burst had occurred within days of the tenancy commencing and the fact that the pipe did not burst for a period of 15 years was irrelevant.

MEARNS v. GLASGOW CITY COUNCIL 2002 S.L.T. (Sh Ct) 49, EF Bowen Q.C., Sheriff Principal, Sh Ct.

5924. Leases–assignation–consent of landlord–delectus personae

S, tenants of woodland in respective of Forestry Commission (F) functions, sought declarator that they were entitled to assign their whole interest in the lease without the consent of T (trustees and landlords). T sought dismissal, arguing that (1) the lease made it clear it was for a distinct purpose, i.e. forestry, and F had been seen as the best tenant for that purpose; (2) although the lease was for 99 years, the original landlord had an unfettered power to terminate at 10-yearly intervals, albeit this had been lost on later disposition, and it was not correct to view the lease as the equivalent of alienation; (3) the normal rule in rural leases was that they were not assignable as they involved delectus personae and there was no basis for maintaining that a lease for 99 years for the purpose of growing timber was extraordinary, and (4) there was no reason why there could not be delectus personae in a body like F.

Held, granting declarator de plano, that (1) the question of whether the tenant's obligations under a lease contained an element of delectus personae could often be determined on the pleadings. There was no material factual dispute in the present case and the issue became one of applying the law to the facts averred; (2) there was no reason why delectus personae should not operate just because a natural person was not involved, (3) there was no delectus personae and S's obligations could be assigned without T's consent: (a) although of a rural nature the lease was not "agricultural", and while the original landlord no doubt considered F would make good and reliable tenants, that was insufficient to introduce delectus personae in the same way as might be perceived with a working arable or pastoral farm; (b) the lease contained a use clause limiting what could be done on the land to forestry, substantially restricting the activities of any tenant, which suggested that F would not necessarily always be the tenant, and (c) the duration of the lease at 99 years put it into the extraordinary category where, even in the case of an agricultural lease, assignation would be permitted.

Observed, that because the character of corporations, and to a lesser degree governments, could change, sometimes rapidly, over time, it might be difficult to establish delectus personae in a contract with such a person where, as in a long lease, it was to last for a number of years.

SCOTTISH MINISTERS v. TRUSTEES OF THE DRUMMOND TRUST; *sub nom.* SCOTTISH MINISTERS v. TRUSTEES OF THE DIAMOND TRUST; SCOTTISH MINISTERS v. DRUMMOND'S TRUSTEES 2001 S.L.T. 665, Lord Carloway, OH.

5925. Leases–guarantors–whether bound by missives–authority of tenant's agents–averments relating to prior correspondence

[Requirements of Writing (Scotland) Act 1995 (c.7).]

H, the landlords of a shopping centre sued the tenant (O), and P, the party alleged to be guarantors for O, in respect of rent and other charges. P disputed that they were bound as guarantors. The offer of lease had specified in cl.5.1 that O's obligations would be supported by the personal guarantee of P and acceptance of the offer would be on their behalf in respect of that guarantee. The offer also specified that in absence of the execution of an engrossed lease by the date of entry, the missives incorporating the draft lease would be binding on the parties. J, the solicitors acting for O had responded by qualified acceptance inserting reference to O's nominee, followed by a letter naming G as that nominee. H accepted this qualification. No formal lease was executed. H argued that where the qualified acceptance contained no amendment in respect of P as guarantors, it had to be taken as made on their behalf, with J having been authorised so to act. They further averred that in previous correspondence J had specifically tried to amend the guarantee obligation, and at H's request had provided P's details for inclusion in the offer; that it was invariable practice for solicitors acting on behalf of proposed tenants who required to produce a guarantor, to act also for the proposed guarantor; and that subsequent to the conclusion of missives, agents for P had described them as guarantors in the lease in a letter to H. P sought dismissal, or alternatively, that averments relating to the prior correspondence and to their agents' letter should be excluded from probation. They argued that there was no sign in the qualified acceptance that it was intended to be executed on their behalf; that the qualified acceptance fell to be construed as a rejection of the original offer, and the documents constituting the contract made no reference to them; and that the missives could not bind them because they did not bear to be subscribed by them or on their behalf, as required by the Requirements of Writing (Scotland) Act 1995.

Held, allowing proof before answer on the whole averments, that (1) cl.5.1 could only be properly construed under reference to the surrounding circumstances, and H's averments relating to the prior communings fell into the category of circumstances to which regard might be had as part of the factual background of the contract entered into; (2) H were entitled to rely on the fact that the qualified acceptance contained nothing qualifying cl.5.1, as capable of supporting the construction for which they contended; (3) the original offer did not fall out of consideration because O returned a qualified acceptance, and where the qualification was restricted to adding the possibility that the lease might be taken in the name of a nominee, its effect was to incorporate the entire original offer into the qualified acceptance; (4) the contention relating to the 1995 Act had no merit, as the question was whether J were also acting as agents of P in issuing the qualified acceptance, and (5) the relevancy of the letter describing P as guarantors was best left for determination at proof.

HOWGATE SHOPPING CENTRE LTD v. GLS 164 LTD; *sub nom.* HOWGATE SHOPPING CENTRE LTD v. PINWISE LTD 2002 S.L.T. 820, Lord Macfadyen, OH.

5926. Leases—shops—kiosk in mall selling competing goods—implied prohibition on landlord

M was the tenant of a shop in a shopping centre. C succeeded to the landlord's interests under the lease on purchasing the shopping centre. In December 2000, C granted a right of occupation of a kiosk placed on the common area of the shopping centre for the purposes of selling jewellery and other goods similar to those sold by M. The kiosk was located in the entrance hallway. M raised an action for declarator that C was bound to refrain from granting any third party a lease, licence or right of occupation over the common areas within the shopping centre and for interdict from granting such a right of occupation. Her case was based on the fact that she, along with the other tenants in the shopping centre, had rights in relation to the common areas, and that it was an implied condition in her lease that C would not grant a right of occupancy to any trader in direct competition with M. M founded on the provision within her lease that she had a right to pass on foot over the common areas and that the location of the kiosk prevented her from having access over that area of the common parts of the shopping centre, thus breaching the provisions of the lease. C argued that the rights contained in the lease were intended to provide M, and her potential customers, with access to and from her unit and had to be read in conjunction with C's general right to control the use of the common areas. C further argued that M's lease included mention of the location of barrows and stalls on the malls. Finally, C argued that there were no averments that the location of the kiosk had any tangible effect on access to and from M's unit. M referred to a condition of her lease preventing her from using the unit to carry on any business already established within the centre, and argued that the condition should be held to apply equally to the landlord's grant of rights of occupancy to competing traders.

Held, dismissing the action, that (1) the tenants' rights of access over the common parts did not extend to the ability to access every single part of those common parts at all times and was always subject to the landlord's reasonable use of the floor space provided that access was not unduly restricted, and (2) the condition of the lease preventing the tenant from setting up in competition with existing tenants contained a proviso that the landlord could override its terms by express consent, and did not imply any undertaking on the landlord not to permit a competing business to be carried on within the shopping centre, *Craig v. Miller* (1888) 15 R. 1005, followed.

MILLER v. CLERICAL MEDICAL INVESTMENT GROUP LTD 2001 S.C.L.R. 990, Lord Eassie, OH.

5927. Leases—shops—obligation to keep premises open during trading hours—underleases

[Court of Session Act 1988 (c.36) s.47(2).]

Landlords raised an action to enforce a "keep open" clause in a lease of a shop unit, seeking declarator, interdict and specific implement. Following the grant of interim interdict and an interim order under the Court of Session Act 1988, s.47(2) the tenants reopened the shop and resumed trading. The landlords advanced a proposed final order for specific implement. The tenants were willing to submit to the proposed final order but only if it included a proviso that on a lawful subletting to a party other than a wholly owned subsidiary of theirs, the court's interlocutor would cease to apply. The landlords argued that the granting of a sublease had no effect on the subsistence of the tenants' obligations under the lease.

Held, putting the case out by order, that (1) it was possible that on a sound construction of the lease, the content of an obligation on the tenant would vary according to whether the tenant was in actual occupation or there was a subtenancy in existence, and this applied to the keep open clause and, (2) so long as there was a lawful sublease in subsistence the tenants' obligation was to procure observance of the keep open clause by the subtenant, and it would be demanding more of the tenants than they were contractually obliged to do to impose an order in the form proposed.

BRITEL FUND TRUSTEES LTD v. SCOTTISH AND SOUTHERN ENERGY PLC 2002 S.L.T. 223, Lord Macfadyen, OH.

5928. Leases–student accommodation–rent review–meaning of "the other universities in Scotland"

In 1987, P leased property to UD for a period of 20 years for use as student accommodation. The lease was subsequently varied twice and at the time of the action, it was agreed that US were the landlords under the lease and UD the tenants. The lease contained a rent review clause which referred to the "average percentage increase in rental levied in the year of review by the other universities in Scotland for student accommodation". US sought declarator that term "other universities in Scotland" meant all institutions designated as a university in the year of the review. UD argued that it only referred to those institutions which were designated universities in 1987 when the lease commenced.

Held, granting decree of declarator, that (1) the clause was designed to measure increases in rent recoverable by reference to an average rate which could derived from the retail market and by restricting the clause to universities in existence in 1987, the effect would be to refer to the average rate that could be derived from a specific part of the retail market, and (2) given that the number of universities had doubled in the quarter century preceding the commencement of the lease, it would not be unreasonable to construe that the parties to the lease envisaged that additional universities would be likely to be established which would fall to be accounted in such a clause.

UNILODGE SERVICES LTD v. UNIVERSITY OF DUNDEE 2001 S.C.L.R. 1008, Lord Macfadyen, OH.

5929. Rent–retention–scope of right–tenants' retention of sums due against claim for damages for fraudulent misrepresentation–relevant defence

S, the landlord of licensed premises, raised an action of payment against B, the tenants, in respect of outstanding sums due under the lease. B did not dispute the amount but sought to withhold payment against a claim which they had against S in respect of allegedly fraudulent representations which induced them to enter into the lease.

Held, putting the case out by order, that the scope of the principle of retention was concerned with the obligations under a contract, and a claim for damages for loss suffered by reason of fraud was a claim in delict and did not offer a relevant defence to B's claim for payment of outstanding sums due under the lease.

SUTHERLAND v. BARRY (RETENTION OF RENT) 2002 S.L.T. 418, Lord Eassie, OH.

5930. Books

Mcallister, Angus—Scottish Law of Leases. Paperback: £36.00. ISBN 0-406-93238-7. Butterworths Law.

Scottish Landlord & Tenant Fact Book. Looseleaf/ring bound. ISBN 0-414-01380-8. W.Green & Son.

LEGAL ADVICE AND FUNDING

5931. Civil legal aid—capital limits for eligibility

CIVIL LEGAL AID (FINANCIAL CONDITIONS) (SCOTLAND) (NO.2) REGULATIONS 2002, SSI 2002 330; made under the Legal Aid (Scotland) Act 1986 s.36. In force: July 1, 2002; £1.50.

These Regulations amend the Legal Aid (Scotland) Act 1986 by increasing certain of the financial limits for eligibility for civil legal aid. They increase to £10,000 the upper limit of disposable capital, above which civil legal aid may be refused if it appears the applicant can afford to proceed without it, and increase to £6,000 the upper limit of disposable capital, above which a legally assisted person may be required to pay a contribution. The Regulations only apply in relation to any case where an application for civil legal aid is made to the Scottish Legal Aid Board on or after July 1, 2002. In addition, they amend the Civil Legal Aid (Financial Conditions) (Scotland) Regulations 1996 (SSI 1996 1012) which prescribed the previous disposable capital limit of £8,500.

5932. Civil legal aid—expenses—assesment of liability—modification of award—modification of liability of assisted person by Land Court

[Legal Aid (Scotland) Act 1986 (c.47) s.18(2).]

MN appealed against a decision of the Divisional Court, arguing that his liability for the expenses awarded against him should have been modified to take account of his status as an assisted person in terms of the Legal Aid (Scotland) Act 1976 s.18(2). MN had been an assisted person at the outset of the action, but his certificate had been suspended and later withdrawn as a result of his conduct during the action. MN submitted that he lived in poverty with his family on income support and would find it impossible to make any meaningful contribution by way of expenses. MD argued against such a modification on the basis that MN's defence of the action had been founded on a falsified document. Indeed, when the falsification had come to light, MN's answers in the action had been withdrawn by his agents and the action had proceeded as undefended. Moreover, it was only MN's production and reliance on a falsified document, which had resulted in the expenses which had been incurred in the action.

Held, refusing the appeal, that MN's conduct in producing and relying on a falsified document with the intention of deceiving, not on the parties to the action, but also the court, was an overriding factor in determining that he should remain liable for the expenses of the original action and also of the appeal.

MacDOUGALL v. MacNEIL 2001 S.L.C.R. 166, Lord McGhie, DJ Houston, DM Macdonald, Land Ct (Full Ct).

5933. Civil legal aid—expenses—assessment of liability

[Legal Aid (Scotland) Act 1986 (c.47) s.18(2).]

H sought a contact order in respect of the child of the marriage between himself and W. After extensive and expensive proceedings, H indicated that he did not intend to proceed and the sheriff dismissed the action. At a hearing on expenses, the sheriff found W liable in expenses to H. The decision was not appealed, however, W enrolled a motion for modification of her liability to expenses to nil. The motion was refused and W appealed. The sheriff, in his note, indicated that his refusal was based on verifiable information available to him at the time and that much of the information offered in support of the motion had not been vouched. He had refused a motion to continue to allow both parties to produce vouching. On appeal, W argued that the sheriff had failed to assess both parties' means adequately and had given too much weight to her conduct. She further argued that the sheriff's refusal to modify her liability to expenses he was preventing her from seeking a reassessment in the event of a change in either parties circumstances in the future. H argued that he had lost his job and was living with a partner who had recently had a child. He claimed that he only had sufficient funds to support himself for three months whilst he sought employment and had accrued a debt of £5000 in respect of unpaid aliment, which was being pursued by the Child Support Agency.

Held, allowing the appeal and remitting the case to the sheriff, that (1) in order for a proper assessment of the parties' means to be made, the court required to have sufficient information before it, and where insufficient information existed, the court should postpone its decision as to modification of expenses until that information is available; (2) in deciding how much a legally aided person should reasonably be required to pay, the correct approach for the court under the Legal Aid (Scotland) Act 1986 s.18(2) was that taken in *Armstrong v. Armstrong* 1970 S.C. 161, [1970] C.L.Y. 3176 which was that the court should set a reasonable figure based on the information before it, that such a figure should not be so high that the person liable would, for practical purposes, find it impossible to repay, that the court should have regard to any aliment or periodical payments being made and also the conduct of the parties, particularly ensuring that the person in receipt of legal aid had not used their position to obtain an unfair advantage, and (3) given the serious implications of his order for W, the sheriff should not have proceeded without first having full and complete information before him and there was, therefore, sufficient justification for interference with the sheriff's exercise of his discretion to the extent of remitting the case back for further consideration.

MASSON v. MASSON (ASSESSMENT OF LIABILITY) (NO.1) 2001 Fam. L.R. 138, JC McInnes Q.C., Sheriff Principal, Sh Ct.

5934. Civil legal aid—expenses—assessment of liability—modification of contribution

[Legal Aid (Scotland) Act 1986 (c.47) s.18(2).]

W enrolled a motion under the Legal Aid (Scotland) Act 1986 s.18(2) for reduction to nil of her contribution to expenses awarded to H following dismissal of his action for contact with the child of their marriage. W successfully appealed ([2001] F.L.R. 138, [2002] 4 C.L. 612) to the sheriff principal and the case was remitted to the sheriff for reconsideration. W claimed that her liability should be modified due to a change in her circumstances as she was now liable to pay rent to her parents, which had not been paid in the past. She lodged a schedule of income giving her total income as £1,592.47 per month which included payments from the Child Support Agency of £537.35, which was stated as the amount W had been advised by them that she would receive from October 2001. A letter from the CSA, however, stated that she was currently receiving £637.75. W's total outgoings were £1,561.88 per month, which included rent of £470, insurance premiums of £36.67 and a regular payment to an ISA of £55.33. Her bank records indicated that she actually paid only £250 in rent. She was also in receipt of family tax credit. She argued that (1) the only reason her income had risen since the award of expenses against her, was that her maintenance payments and tax credit had risen, (2) the rent which she was expected to pay was reasonable, but in any event, the court should take into consideration the rent that she actually paid, (3) although the insurance and ISA payments were investments, she should not be deprived of the ability to invest for the future of her and her child, and (4) her conduct in relation to the original action should not be a factor in determining the extent of her liability as it had already been the determining factor when making the award of expenses, and in any event, her conduct should be outweighed by her lack of means.

Held, allowing H to give an account of his expenses, remitting the same to the auditor of court for taxation and report and modifying W's liability for those expenses to £9,280, that (1) in determining her income, the court must rely on the letter from the CSA as accurate making her monthly income £100 more than indicated by her; (2) with regard to the insurance and ISA payments, the policies had been entered into prior to a determination on liability for expenses and could not be taken to have been entered into for the purposes of defeating such liability, and in any event, W was entitled, given the modest nature of the payments, to make some provision for her future and that of her child; (3) it would be unreasonable to expect W's parents to provide accommodation rent free to W and her son in order to allow W to repay her liability to expenses, but, given the evidence, the sum of £470 was unreasonable for property in the area and a sum of £250 would therefore be allowed against her income; (4) given the increase in income and reduction in rent, W could reasonably afford to pay £320 per month, and (5) the court was entitled to consider the parties' conduct in determining a modification of liability, particularly their conduct during the hearings on that motion where W had failed to attend court and failed to provide adequate or complete information on her means and where H had always been present and co-operated fully with requests for information.

MASSON v. MASSON (ASSESSMENT OF LIABILITY) (NO.2) 2002 S.C.L.R. 382, DJ Cusine, Sh Ct (Grampian, Highland and Islands).

5935. Civil legal aid–fees–increase–competency–proceedings relating to children's hearings

[Civil Legal Aid (Scotland) (Fees) Regulations 1989 (SI 1989 1490) Reg.5(4).]

Solicitors for several children referred by the reporter to the children's panel sought an increase in fees in terms of the Civil Legal Aid (Scotland) (Fees) Regulations 1989, reg.5(4) in respect of an application to the sheriff for a finding as to whether the grounds of referral, which had not been accepted, were established. The sheriff, considering himself bound by Sheriff Principal Cox's decision in *Caldwell v. Walker* (Unreported, September 1, 1998), refused an increase as incompetent. On appeal it was argued inter alia that the proper construction of "Ordinary Roll" in reg.5(4) meant all matters which were not summary causes, and that the decision in *L, Petitioners (No.3)* 1996 S.L.T. 928, [1996] C.L.Y. 7129, could be applied to permit an increase. The Scottish Legal Aid Board inter alia sought to distinguish other cases in which *Caldwell* had not been followed, and argued that *L, Petitioners* was limited to its particular circumstances.

Held, allowing the appeal and granting a 10 per cent increase in fees, that (1) Reg.5(4) applied to applications for the establishment of grounds of referral and to appeals from a decision of a children's hearing: the phrase "Ordinary Roll" did not mean "Ordinary Cause Roll" and its application was not restricted to such causes, and having regard to the statutory background the proceedings were properly regarded as civil proceedings, and (2) since *L, Petitioners* involved an application to the nobile officium it was not, at least to that extent, of general application but the court was entitled nonetheless to conclude that it was for the sheriff to determine what percentage increase should be allowed in such a case.

CALDWELL v. I; *sub nom.* CALDWELL v. SCOTTISH LEGAL AID BOARD 2002 S.L.T. (Sh Ct) 28, JC McInnes Q.C., Sheriff Principal, Sh Ct.

5936. Civil legal aid–income limits for eligibility

CIVIL LEGAL AID (FINANCIAL CONDITIONS) (SCOTLAND) REGULATIONS 2002, SSI 2002 145; made under the Legal Aid (Scotland) Act 1986 s.36. In force: April 8, 2002; £1.75.

These Regulations, which revoke the Civil Legal Aid (Financial Conditions) (Scotland) Regulations 2001 (SSI 2001 123), increase certain of the financial limits of eligibility for civil legal aid under the Legal Aid (Scotland) Act 1986. The income limits are increased to make eligible for civil legal aid, persons with a yearly disposable income of not more than £9,188 and to make eligible without payment of a contribution, persons with a yearly disposable income of not more than £2,814.

5937. **Civil procedure–civil legal aid–availability**

CIVIL LEGAL AID (SCOTLAND) AMENDMENT REGULATIONS 2002, SSI 2002 88; made under the Legal Aid (Scotland) Act 1986 s.36. In force: April 1, 2002; £1.50.

These Regulations amend the Civil Legal Aid (Scotland) Regulations 1996 (SI 1996 2444) so as to add certain proceedings under the Adults with Incapacity (Scotland) Act 2000 to the list of proceedings specified. The availability of civil legal aid for those proceedings is based on the resources of the incapable adult, not the applicant, where the applicant is a person claiming or having an interest in the property, financial affairs or personal welfare of that adult.

5938. **Civil procedure–civil legal aid–availability**

CIVIL LEGAL AID (SCOTLAND) AMENDMENT (NO.2) REGULATIONS 2002, SSI 2002 254; made under the Legal Aid (Scotland) Act 1986 s.36. In force: July 1, 2002; £1.50.

These Regulations amend the Civil Legal Aid (Scotland) Regulations 1996 (SI 1996 2444) so as to add certain proceedings under the Adults with Incapacity (Scotland) Act 2000 reg.14A to the specified list of proceedings. The availability of civil legal aid for the proceedings listed in that regulation is based on the resources of the incapable adult, not the applicant, where the applicant is a person having an interest in the personal welfare of that adult.

5939. **Civil procedure–civil legal aid–availability**

CIVIL LEGAL AID (SCOTLAND) REGULATIONS 2002, SSI 2002 494; made under the Legal Aid (Scotland) Act 1986 s.17, s.19, s.20, s.36, s.37, s.42. In force: December 1, 2002; £6.00.

These Regulations revoke the Civil Legal Aid (Scotland) Regulations 1996 (SI 1996 2444), the Civil Legal Aid (Scotland) Amendment Regulations 1997 (SI 1997 727), the Civil Legal Aid (Scotland) Amendment Regulations 1998 (SI 1998 725), the Civil Legal Aid (Scotland) Amendment Regulations 2000 (SSI 2000 182), the Civil Legal Aid (Scotland) Amendment Regulations 2001 (SSI 2001 82), the Civil Legal Aid (Scotland) Amendment Regulations 2002 (SSI 2002 88) and Civil Legal Aid (Scotland) Amendment (No.2) Regulations 2002 (SSI 2002 254). The provisions relating to the availability of civil legal aid in matters of special urgency are amended so that any contribution which may be payable by a person for whom special urgency work is done is paid to the Scottish Legal Aid Board; and where an application for civil legal aid is refused after a solicitor has undertaken certain work as a matter of special urgency, that solicitor may still be paid for that work, provided certain conditions are met.

5940. **Criminal legal aid–fees–witnesses**

CRIMINAL LEGAL AID (SCOTLAND) (FEES) AMENDMENT REGULATIONS 2002, SSI 2002 246; made under the Legal Aid (Scotland) Act 1986 s.33. In force: June 17, 2002; £1.50.

These Regulations amend the Criminal Legal Aid (Scotland) (Fees) Regulations 1989 (SI 1989 1491) so that the outlays which may be paid to a solicitor by the Scottish Legal Aid Board in respect of fees paid to witnesses shall not be restricted to the amount payable by the Crown for witnesses of the same category. Instead, the Board shall pay such fees as it considers to be reasonable, having regard to the amount payable to Crown witnesses.

5941. **Criminal legal aid–fixed payments–exemptions**

CRIMINAL LEGAL AID (FIXED PAYMENTS) (SCOTLAND) AMENDMENT (NO.2) REGULATIONS 2002, SSI 2002 442; made under the Legal Aid (Scotland) Act 1986 s.33, s.41A. In force: November 1, 2002; £1.50.

These Regulations amend the Criminal Legal Aid (Fixed Payments) (Scotland) Regulations 1999 (SI 1999 491) to provide that fixed payment criminal legal aid shall not apply to proceedings where a court has appointed a solicitor to act for a person accused of a sexual offence.

5942. Criminal legal aid–sex offenders–nominated solicitor

CRIMINAL LEGAL AID (SCOTLAND) AMENDMENT REGULATIONS 2002, SSI 2002 441; made under the Legal Aid (Scotland) Act 1986 s.36. In force: November 1, 2002; £1.50.

These Regulations amend the Criminal Legal Aid (Scotland) Regulations 1996 (SI 1996 2555) to provide that the duty of the Scottish Legal Aid Board to cease to make criminal legal aid available in specified circumstances shall not apply in cases where such legal aid is made available to a solicitor appointed by the court to act for a person accused of a sexual offence.

5943. Criminal legal aid–sexual offences–nominated solicitor

CRIMINAL LEGAL AID (SCOTLAND) (FEES) AMENDMENT (NO.2) REGULATIONS 2002, SSI 2002 440; made under the Legal Aid (Scotland) Act 1986 s.33. In force: November 1, 2002; £1.50.

These Regulations amend the Criminal Legal Aid (Scotland) (Fees) Regulations 1989 (SI 1989 1491) so that a "nominated solicitor" includes a solicitor appointed by the court to act for a person accused of a sexual offence.

5944. Criminal legal aid–summary proceedings–fixed payments

CRIMINAL LEGAL AID (FIXED PAYMENTS) (SCOTLAND) AMENDMENT REGULATIONS 2002, SSI 2002 247; made under the Legal Aid (Scotland) Act 1986 s.33, s.36. In force: June 17, 2002; £1.75.

These Regulations amend the Criminal Legal Aid (Fixed Payments) (Scotland) Regulations 1999 (SI 1999 491) to provide that in certain circumstances the Scottish Legal Aid Board may determine that a solicitor shall not receive fixed payments but shall instead receive payment based on the amount of time spent and work done in providing summary criminal legal aid. The Regulations prescribe the factors to be taken into account by the Board in deciding whether to determine that a solicitor should not receive fixed payments; make provision in relation to the form of application for a determination by the Board; require solicitors to keep proper records of professional services and provide for a procedure for review of the Board's decision. They also provide that, where there has been a change of solicitor in the course of proceedings, any solicitor who represented an assisted person at any time before that change shall, in certain circumstances and subject to certain conditions, receive payment based on the amount of time spent and work done. In addition, the Regulations provide for a fixed payment of £50 in respect of work done in connection with appeals under the Criminal Procedure (Scotland) Act 1995 against the refusal of bail, or against bail conditions imposed.

5945. Legal advice–assistance by way of representation

ADVICE AND ASSISTANCE (ASSISTANCE BY WAY OF REPRESENTATION) (SCOTLAND) AMENDMENT REGULATIONS 2002, SSI 2002 37; made under the Legal Aid (Scotland) Act 1986 s.9, s.37. In force: February 6, 2002; £1.75.

These Regulations amend the Advice and Assistance (Assistance by Way of Representation) (Scotland) Regulations 1997 (SI 1997 3070) so as to make assistance by way of representation available for detained persons brought before a sheriff under the Matrimonial Homes (Family Protection) (Scotland) Act 1981 and the Protection from Abuse (Scotland) Act 2001. This assistance by way of representation shall be available without reference to the provisions of the Legal Aid (Scotland) Act 1986 which relate to financial limits on the availability of advice and assistance and payment of contributions towards advice and assistance.

5946. Legal aid–advice and assistance–payment of fees–family proceedings

ADVICE AND ASSISTANCE (SCOTLAND) AMENDMENT REGULATIONS 2002, SSI 2002 495; made under the Legal Aid (Scotland) Act 1986 s.12, s.37. In force: December 1, 2002; £1.50.

These Regulations amend the Advice and Assistance (Scotland) Regulations 1996 (SI 1996 2447) to provide that a solicitor's right to prior payment of fees and outlays out of any property recovered or preserved for a client in respect of advice and assistance shall not apply to the first £4,200 recovered or preserved by virtue of certain family proceedings; and any money paid in accordance with an order made by the Social Security Commissioners or the Child Support Commissioners.

5947. Legal aid–civil legal aid

LEGAL AID (SCOTLAND) ACT 1986 AMENDMENT REGULATIONS 2002, SSI 2002 532; made under the Legal Aid (Scotland) Act 1986 s.13, s.37. In force: December 1, 2002; £1.50.

These Regulations add proceedings comprising appeals to the Social Security Commissioners and appeals to the Child Support Commissioners to the list of proceedings in the Legal Aid (Scotland) Act 1986 for which civil legal aid is available.

5948. Legal aid–civil legal aid–fees

CIVIL LEGAL AID (SCOTLAND) (FEES) AMENDMENT REGULATIONS 2002, SSI 2002 496; made under the Legal Aid (Scotland) Act 1986 s.33. In force: December 1, 2002; £1.75.

These Regulations amend the Civil Legal Aid (Scotland) (Fees) Regulations 1989 (SI 1989 1490) so that where there is an award of judicial expenses in favour of a person in receipt of civil legal aid, the Scottish Legal Aid Board may, if requested by that person's solicitor, pay those expenses to the solicitor (and any counsel who acted in the case) instead of the fees and outlays prescribed. They also provide that certain fees prescribed shall be payable to solicitors and counsel for work done in relation to proceedings before the Social Security Commissioners and the Child Support Commissioners and references to the Restrictive Practices Court.

5949. Legal representation–right of accused to chose–payment scheme contrary to rights

See CRIMINAL PROCEDURE: Vickers v. Buchanan. §5490

5950. Legal services–advice and assistance–capital limits

ADVICE AND ASSISTANCE (FINANCIAL CONDITIONS) (SCOTLAND) (NO.2) REGULATIONS 2002, SSI 2002 329; made under the Legal Aid (Scotland) Act 1986 s.36. In force: July 1, 2002; £1.50.

These Regulations amend the Legal Aid (Scotland) Act 1986 by increasing the disposable capital limit for eligibility for advice and assistance to £1,300 and amend the Advice and Assistance (Financial Conditions) (Scotland) Regulations 1992 (SI 1992 1587) which prescribed the previous disposable capital limit of £1,000.

5951. Legal services–advice and assistance–income limits

ADVICE AND ASSISTANCE (FINANCIAL CONDITIONS) (SCOTLAND) REGULATIONS 2002, SSI 2002 144; made under the Legal Aid (Scotland) Act 1986 s.11, s.36, s.37. In force: April 8, 2002; £1.75.

These Regulations, which revoke the Advice and Assistance (Financial Conditions) (Scotland) Regulations 2001 (SSI 2001 124), amend the Legal Aid (Scotland) Act 1986 in relation to any case where an application for advice and assistance is made on or after April 8, 2002. They increase the disposable income limit for eligibility for advice and assistance from £186 to £189 a week, increase the weekly disposable income above which a person is required to pay a contribution from £79 to £80 and prescribe the scale of contributions to be paid where the weekly disposable income exceeds £80 but does not exceed £189.

LEGAL METHODOLOGY

5952. Books

Current Law Statutes: Vol 1. 2001. Hardback: £130.00. ISBN 0-421-78860-7. Sweet & Maxwell.

Styles, Scott–Butterworths Glossary of Scottish and European Legal Terms. Paperback: £20.00. ISBN 0-406-94947-6. Butterworths Law (Scotland).

LEGAL PROFESSION

5953. Solicitors–professional conduct–disciplinary proceedings–hearing within reasonable time

[Human Rights Act 1998 (c.42) Sch.1 Part I Art.6(1).]

C, the Law Society Council, appealed against a decision of S, the Scottish Solicitors' Discipline Tribunal, dismissing a professional conduct complaint against H which originated from a complaint by a client of H's firm with regard to the conduct of a sheriff court action in 1992, on the ground that to prosecute the charge would breach H's right under the Human Rights Act 1998 Art.6(1) to a determination within a reasonable time. S held, inter alia, that by May 30, 1997 C should have satisfied themselves that they had all the relevant information and that it would have been open to them to proceed with a complaint of professional misconduct to S. At that date the society, ratified by C, made a finding of inadequate professional services against H following proceedings before the ombudsman the question of professional misconduct was raised for the first time in January 1999. In May 1999 it was intimated to H by the society that C had raised a complaint in that connection, which the society were obliged to investigate; the decision to prosecute was taken in February 2000 and the complaint made to S in May 2000.

Held, allowing the appeal, that (1) the distinct nature of proceedings before the tribunal and the dispute with which it was concerned meant that no dispute existed in the matter of professional misconduct when the complaint was made to the council or when the council made their finding of inadequate professional services, and (2) the correct starting point was the making of the complaint to the tribunal on May 9, 2000, which first put in issue a dispute as to professional misconduct which could affect the respondent's civil right to practise as a solicitor, and there was no breach of Art.6(1).

COUNCIL OF THE LAW SOCIETY OF SCOTLAND v. HALL 2002 S.L.T. 989, Lord Cullen L.P., Lord Cameron of Lochbroom, Lord Hamilton, 1 Div.

5954. Solicitors–professional conduct–disciplinary proceedings–penalties– applicable test for court on appeal

G, C and L, three former partners in a law firm, appealed against penalties imposed by the Scottish Solicitors' Discipline Tribunal for professional misconduct. G and C were suspended for five years in respect of 29 admitted breaches of the accounts rules, failure to record a disposition and failure to inform a client of intromissions with and interest on sums held. L was struck off the roll of solicitors in respect of inter alia misconduct relating to three breaches of the accounts rules and his lack of candour over a standard security and loan arrangement entered into with clients to prevent his sequestration by the Inland Revenue, payments being made without the clients' consent.

Held, dismissing L's appeal and directing G and C's suspensions to run from 5 September 2001, that (1) it was necessary to apply a less rigorous test than formerly in reviewing the tribunal's decisions in relation to seriousness of the offence and the appropriate penalty, and to simply look at the decision in the light of the whole circumstances, always having respect for the tribunal's expertise and giving their decision such weight as the court thought appropriate, *Ghosh v. General Medical Council* [2001] UKPC 29, [2001] 1 W.L.R. 1915, [2001] C.L.Y. 2894 applied; (2) although there was no finding of dishonesty in respect of G and C, their misconduct was serious in every respect, the tribunal had carefully considered restricting their practising certificates and concluded having regard to the public interest that that was not an option, and they were fortunate not to suffer more severe penalties; but where the petitioners' practising certificates had previously been withdrawn but the tribunal's order had not remained in force pending the appeal, the suspensions would be directed to run from the date of the tribunal's decision so as to avoid penalising them for exercising their rights of appeal, and (3) L's sentence was correct and appropriate, his conduct demonstrated not only incompetence but dishonesty with clients' money, in respect of which there could be few instances where leniency could be shown.

McMAHON v. COUNCIL OF THE LAW SOCIETY OF SCOTLAND 2002 S.L.T. 363, Lord Gill L.J.C., Lord Caplan, Lord Maclean, 2 Div.

5955. **Solicitors–professional conduct–disciplinary proceedings–striking from roll**

[Firearms Act 1968 (c.27).]

M was admitted and enrolled as a solicitor in 1983. He was the subject of a complaint to the Scottish Solicitors' Discipline Tribunal in 1998 after he had been convicted of an offence in contravention of the Firearms Act 1968 and sentenced to three years imprisonment. M appealed and the Inner House recalled the order and the complaint was remitted to a different tribunal. The new tribunal ordered M's name struck off the roll of solicitors and M sought recall arguing that in the whole circumstances no reasonable tribunal properly directing itself could have arrived at the decision. M argued that while it was inappropriate for the tribunal to review what had been done by the trial judge, it was appropriate for M, in disciplinary proceedings, to point out any way in which the tribunal misdirected itself, and if that misdirection consisted of adopting propositions from the trial judge which amounted to misdirection then the tribunal could consider it.

Held, refusing the petition, that there had been no error or misdirection. Opinion of the Court per Lord Prosser.

McINTYRE v. COUNCIL OF THE LAW SOCIETY OF SCOTLAND 2002 S.C.L.R. 169, Lord Prosser, Lord Coulsfield, Lord Hamilton, Ex Div.

5956. **Books**

Blue Book 2002: the Directory of the Law Society of Scotland. Paperback: £36.00. ISBN 0-406-94755-4. Butterworths Law (Scotland).

Scottish Law Directory: the White Book 2002. 111th Ed. Hardback: £36.00. ISBN 0-406-94888-7. Butterworths Law (Scotland).

LEGAL SYSTEMS

5957. **Books**

Green's Guide to the Sheriff Court Districts. Paperback. ISBN 0-414-01494-4. W. Green & Son.

Greens Annotated Rules of the Court of Session 2002. Paperback: £59.00. ISBN 0-414-01463-4. W. Green & Son.

Hennessy, Charles—Practical Advocacy in the Sheriff Court. Paperback: £25.00. ISBN 0-414-01503-7. W.Green & Son.

Sheriff Court Rules 2002. A Parliament House Book. Paperback: £28.00. ISBN 0-414-01495-2. W.Green & Son.

LICENSING

5958. Firearms—certificates—revocation—scope of review—relevance of antecedent incidents

[Firearms Act 1968 (c.27) s.30C; Firearms (Amendment) Act 1997 (c.5).]

C, the chief constable, appealed against the decision of a sheriff overturning his revocation of the shotgun certificate of E, a retired policeman. C argued, inter alia, that the sheriff had erred in law in regarding as essential to the test in the Firearms Act 1968 s.30C, that a shotgun be a factor in C's past conduct, and should not have ignored certain hearsay evidence. C's initial revocation was based on six incidents between E and his neighbour, X, over the closing of a gate and an incident involving F about which the only evidence produced was a copy of a written statement by F.

Held, dismissing the appeal, that (1) the sheriff had been entitled to approach the issues de novo and on their merits in the light of the amendments introduced by the Firearms (Amendment) Act 1997; (2) there was no error of law in the sheriff's approach to the statutory test and he had been entitled to take into account the lack of evidence as to the use or threatened use of a shotgun in the antecedent incidents, and (3) the sheriff had justifiably found that he could not attach significant weight to the statement, taking into account the lengthy delay in bringing it to the notice of the police and the lack of explanation as to how it was made.

EVANS v. CHIEF CONSTABLE OF CENTRAL SCOTLAND 2002 S.L.T. (Sh Ct) 152, CGB Nicholson Q.C., Sheriff Principal, Sh Ct.

5959. Gambling—applications—renewal of gaming licence—variation of restrictions regarding types of games which may be played

[Gaming Clubs (Licensing) (Scotland) Regulations 1969 (SI 1969 1115); Gaming Act 1968 (s.65) Sch.2 para.21, Sch.2 para.25.]

N operated five casinos in Glasgow under gaming licences granted by the Licensing Board. In June 2001, N applied for the annual renewal of those licences with the intention that, on renewal, Touchbet Roulette would be brought within their scope. To this end, the applications for renewal of three of the licences left the pro forma wording regarding restrictions to be placed on the licences unaltered, but, in the space left for identification of restrictions, indicated that the Licensing Board should have regard to the addendum attached to the application. That addendum sought for the licence to allow all bankers games permitted by the regulations and card room games of equal chance only. Notwithstanding the pro forma terms, the wording sought differed materially from the existing licences held by N. At the meeting of the Board, no objections were intimated in respect of the applications and the Board renewed all five licences in exactly the same terms as they had been held before, so that Touchbet Roulette was not permitted. N petitioned for review to the Board's decision on the grounds that the licence issued did not match the terms of the unopposed application as required by Gaming Clubs (Licensing) (Scotland) Regulations 1969 although N admitted that the applications would have been made clearer by the deletion of the pro forma wording.

Held, dismissing the petitions, that (1) in relation to the licences granted (a) N's claim was irrelevant as there had been a failure to delete the pro forma wording and the Board had thus been invited to renew the licences subject to the pre-existing restrictions, (b) the addendum could not oblige the Board to do something materially different to what the application form actually proposed, and (c) if the addition of Touchbet Roulette had been N's intention on renewal then their failure to specifically mention that in the application amounted to a failure to supply prescribed particulars under the 1969 Regulations, and (2) in relation to the decision intimated by letter, (a) the decision did not arise out of an application for grant or renewal of a licence but as a result of a request for approval for a new development within the currency of an existing licence and as such the Gaming Act 1968 Sch.2 paras 21 and 25 were not directly applicable, (b) the Board were entitled to take the view that Touchbet Roulette was a material addition to what was permitted by the licences as it involved different facilities and playing methods and it was therefore not unreasonable for the Board to require a fresh licence application so that all the issues surround such a proposal could be looked into, (c) it was open to the Board to require that the overall gaming facilities be maintained at their current level during the grant of an interim licence for Touchbet Roulette, (d) it was difficult for N to contend that they were entitled to additional tables when they had given a specific undertaking when one of the licences had been renewed previously that they would not do so without first seeking the Board's approval, and (e) if N were not willing to accept the restriction placed on the introduction of Touchbet Roulette as indicated in the letter, they should deal with the matter either by making an application for a new licence or raising the matter at the next renewal.

NORTH ROTUNDA CASINO LTD v. GLASGOW CITY LICENSING BOARD; *sub nom.* NORTH ROTUNDA CASINO LTD, PETITIONERS 2002 S.L.T. 974, Lord Emslie, OH.

5960. Gambling–bingo–charges

See LICENSING. §3123

5961. Gambling–licences and certificates–fees

GAMING ACT (VARIATION OF FEES) (SCOTLAND) ORDER 2002, SSI 2002 281; made under the Gaming Act 1968 s.48, s.51. In force: July 15, 2002; £1.75.

This Order, which revokes the Gaming Act (Variation of Fees) (Scotland) Order 2001 (SSI 2001 83) and the Gaming Act (Variation of Fees) (No.2) (Scotland) Order 2001 (SSI 2001 230), increases the fees to be charged in relation to the grant, renewal and transfer of gaming licences in Scotland under the Gaming Act 1968.

5962. Gambling–licences and certificates–fees

See LICENSING. §3131

5963. Licensed premises–regular extension of permitted hours–restricted grant–adequacy of reasons

[Human Rights Act 1998 (c.42) Sch.1 Part I Art.6(1), Part II Art.1.]

A, the holder of a public house licence, applied to S, the licensing authority, at their quarterly meeting in June 2001 for a regular extension of permitted hours for the sale and supply of alcohol at her premises. The extension sought was for the periods of 11.00pm to 11.45pm on Sundays to Thursdays, from 11.00pm to 1.00am on Fridays and Saturdays and from 2.30pm to 6.30pm on Sundays. The application was partially refused in respect of the extension between 11.00pm and 1.00am on Fridays and Saturdays. A sought judicial review of the partial refusal and supporting written reasons. S's statement of reasons indicated that they did not consider themselves bound by previous decisions which related to regular occasional extensions, that they were aware of differing views within the locality as to the desirability and benefit to the community of such additional opening hours and that they felt there was no need for such regular extensions on a permanent basis. They also noted the results of a newspaper poll which, they claimed, indicated that 97 per cent of those who called in were against extended hours for public houses in the area. They also expressed doubt over the reliability of a petition produced by A in support of her application. A argued that the reasons given by S were inadequate as (1) in light of S's practice of granting regular occasional extensions which had had the effect of allowing the premises to remain open until 1.00am on Fridays and Saturdays for some time, A had been left with real or substantial doubt as to why the decision had been reached, (2) S had based their decision on irrelevant or incorrect material as the survey by the newspaper had been carried out some nine months before A's application and had been in relation to regular extensions to 2.00am every night, making the conclusions drawn by S inaccurate, (3) she had a legitimate expectation that the application would be successful given her previous enjoyment of regular occasional extensions, (4) S should not have departed from existing policy without consulting with those likely to be affected, as had happened previously, and (5) the partial refusal interfered with A's right to peaceful enjoyment of her property in contravention of the Human Rights Act 1998 (c.42) Sch.1 Part II Art.1.

Held, dismissing the petition, that (1) there was no reason for doubt or confusion by A as the reasons for refusal had been clearly given in the written statement; (2) S could not be held to have fettered their discretion where sufficient reasons had been given for their application of the policy; (3) A's argument in relation to legitimate expectation was unfounded as applications for occasional and regular extensions were covered by different statutory provisions and it would be incorrect to assume that S should treat them as if they were the same; (4) S were entitled to change their policy without consultation despite the fact that consultation had occurred prior to policy changes in the past; (5) although possession of a licence was a property right and refusal of the application was a control of that property right, S had not contravened Part II Art.1 as they had not exercised their control in a disproportionate way, and (6) there were sufficient safeguards in place, including a right of appeal, to ensure that A received a fair hearing in terms of Part I Art.6(1).

Observed, that opinion had been reserved on whether S's practice of granting regular occasional extensions was ultra vires, but such a determination would have been unlikely to affect the outcome of the review.

ADAMS v. SOUTH LANARKSHIRE COUNCIL; *sub nom.* ADAMS, PETITIONER 2003 S.L.T. 145, Lord Wheatley, OH.

5964. Licensed premises—renewal of licence—landlord not a fit and proper person—failure to pay rates

[Licensing (Scotland) Act 1976 (c.66) s.17(1)(a).]

D, a licensing board, refused B's application for renewal of a public house licence, on the ground that R, the nominee responsible for the day to day running of the premises and a director of B, was not a "fit and proper person" in terms of the Licensing (Scotland) Act 1976 s.17(1)(a). D's reasons stated that B and L, another company of which R was a director, owed the local authority (A), £26,141.52 in unpaid non-domestic rates. It was further suggested that the premises had been "sublet" to C, a company of which R's husband was the sole director, and the note of objections submitted by M, A's revenue manager, stated C had unpaid liabilities in respect of rates from the premises. In B's appeal, D argued that (1) M had the authority to maintain an objection on behalf of D in terms of D's standing orders on delegation of authority from F, the director of finance, to "take all necessary actions" with regard to the recovery of non-domestic rates, because if the licence was renewed there would likely be further losses to A, and (2) the fact that members of D considering the application were also members of A's finance committee did not breach natural justice, because they played no role in the determination of the levels of non-domestic rates.

Held, reversing D's decision and ordaining D to grant B's application, that the objection was incompetent. Objecting to the fitness of a person to be a licence holder did not properly fall within the scope of M's delegated authority and did not authorise "blacklisting" potential applicants because of non-payment. In the absence of a valid objection, D would have no option but to grant the application and there was no point in remitting the case to D. Opinion, that (1) in ruling on the objection D, as members of A's finance committee, had acted contrary to the rules of natural justice; (2) there was prima facie justification for

D's conclusion that there was a deliberate policy to evade payment of rates and that R was intrinsically involved, and had the objection been taken in accordance with A's standing orders and considered in accordance with natural justice the appeal would have been refused.

BLUSINS LTD v. DUNDEE CITY LICENSING BOARD 2001 S.L.T. (Sh Ct) 176, RA Davidson, Sh Ct.

5965. Licensing boards–natural justice–applicant's right to cross examine objector–interference in property rights by reason of closing the business

[Licensing (Scotland) Act 1976 (c.66) s.64(9); European Convention on Human Rights 1950 Art.6, Protocol 1 Art.1.]

C operated premises as a nightclub under a public house licence and had enjoyed regular extensions of permitted hours until 2 am from Monday to Sunday and from 2.30 pm to 6.30 pm on Sundays. In June 2000, at the statutory meeting of the licensing board, C's annual application for a regular extension in relation to an entertainment licence was refused. The application was renewed by C at the licensing board statutory meeting in January 2001 and was again refused. Although a number of objections to the application had been lodged, none was from the police or the local authority. The licensing board also refused C's motion under the Licensing (Scotland) Act 1976 s.64(9) which would have enabled them to make a fresh application earlier then would otherwise be possible. C sought judicial review of the decision on the grounds that, (1) the proceedings at the January meeting were incompatible with the rules of natural justice; (2) the proceedings had violated C's rights under the European Convention on Human Rights 1950 Art.6; (3) lack of ability to cross examine the one objector who had appeared at the meeting had been unfair, and (4) C's property rights under European Convention on Human Rights 1950 Protocol 1 Art.1 had been violated as a refusal of the regular extensions would result in C's business having to close.

Held, dismissing the petition, that (1) fairness required an equality of arms and no element of ambush in the emergence of evidence and, given that C was legally represented at the hearing and that all the objections were given in writing and in advance of the hearing, C had ample opportunity to advise their representative of their position and accordingly the proceedings were not unfair under common law; (2) although a licensing board was an administrative body, Art.6 applied but, given that the proceedings had been deemed to be fair at common law, there was nothing to indicate that a breach of Art.6 had occurred; (3) no right to lead evidence or to cross examine witnesses existed at such a hearing, but, had it existed, it could not be implied that C's solicitor had waived such rights merely by his failure to seek such rights during the hearing; (4) failure to obtain a permitted extension leading to the closure of C's business amounted to a control of C's premises sufficient to be regarded as an interference with C's property rights. However, Protocol 1 permitted such interference where it was proportionate to the aim being achieved and in the instant circumstances, there had been sufficient evidence for the licensing board to conclude that refusal of the application was proportionate to the need to protect the environment, and (5) the refusal of the board to grant the motion under s.64(9) did not affect the question of proportionality as C could competently reapply within one year in any case.

CATSCRATCH LTD v. GLASGOW CITY LICENSING BOARD (NO.2) 2002 S.L.T. 503, Lord Johnston, OH.

5966. Taxis–licensing committee–refusal to grant licence–reasons for decision–chairman's error in law as to application of policy

B, a former taxi licence holder, appealed against the refusal by D, the local authority licensing committee, of his application for a taxi licence. B had held a taxi licence for a number of years but had failed to apply timeously for its renewal and had to apply afresh. D operated a policy of granting only 507 licences. At the hearing of the application, following a divided vote, D's chairman stated that he felt under the law that he had no discretion in the matter standing the policy, and used his casting vote for refusal. Written reasons were subsequently issued stating the application was refused on grounds that B had failed to convince D that he should be granted a licence where there was no significant unmet demand for taxi services and in light of their policy. D argued that only the written reasons could be considered and that B was seeking to found on remarks made by a member of D, which could not be taken as D's collective view.

Held, remitting the case to D for reconsideration, that (1) there was no dispute that D's chairman erred in law, or that he made the comments which were attributed to him, inferring that was the reason for how his vote was cast; (2) the written reasons could not be said to express the collective will of D, where the chairman's remarks, given that his vote was crucial to the decision, might properly be construed as giving the reason why the decision was taken, and D's decision was based on an error of law, and (3) B had not established any unreasonable exercise of discretion as in effect there was no exercise of discretion.

BLACK v. DUNDEE CITY COUNCIL 2002 S.L.T. (Sh Ct) 139, AL Stewart Q.C., Sh Ct (Tayside, Central and Fife).

5967. Taxis–refusal to renew licence–fit and proper person

R a local authority, refused an application by M for renewal of his taxi driver's licence. M appealed on the grounds that R had made an irrelevant and flawed connection between M's two convictions for dishonesty and his responsibility for the safety and wellbeing of his passengers. R had decided that M's conviction of obtaining an overdraft and taking part in managing a company while bankrupt, indicated at best weakness of character and at worst a large element of dishonesty, such that he was no longer a fit and proper person to hold a licence. The sheriff overturned R's decision. R appealed.

Held, allowing the appeal, that (1) the sheriff had erred in assuming that R was focusing on physical safety rather than the relevant consideration that passengers should have a driver whose honesty could be relied upon, and (2) R had acknowledged that there was a range of explanations for the convictions which did not necessarily entail deliberate dishonesty. The matter was one for R to weigh and they were entitled to reach the conclusion they did.

MEJURY v. RENFREWSHIRE COUNCIL 2001 S.C. 426, Lord Prosser, Lord Milligan, Lord Kingarth, Ex Div.

5968. Books

Agnew, Crispin; Baillie, Heather M.–Licensing (Scotland) Act 1976. 5th Ed. Greens Annotated Acts. Paperback: £48.00. ISBN 0-414-01488-X. W.Green & Son.

Agnew, Crispin; Baillie, Heather M.–Licensing (Scotland) Act 1976: Combined Set Of: Licensing (Scotland) Act and Scottish Civic Government Law. 5th Ed. Greens Annotated Acts. Paperback: £85.00. ISBN 0-414-01509-6. W.Green & Son.

Hadjucki, A,; Stuart, S.–Scottish Civic Government Licensing Law. Paperback: £48.00. ISBN 0-414-01497-9. W.Green & Son.

LOCAL GOVERNMENT

5969. Burials and cremation–cemeteries–petition for authority to disinter–right of lairholder

P, the holder of a certificate granting an exclusive right of burial in a particular lair, sought an order to compel the local authority managing the cemetery to disinter the remains of two people who were allegedly buried in error, and to reinter the remains in accordance with the wishes of the families of the deceased. The lair was no.906 in the cemetery and was averred to be the burial place of P's mother in law. At proof P sought to rely, inter alia, on the terms of a certificate issued by the local authority's predecessor which certified his right over the plot, supported by the cemetery records concerning the burial. Excavation had revealed that the other deceased were buried in the lair, contrary to cemetery records showing lair 609 as their resting place, which conformed with an entry in a lair owners' book that one of the deceased had purchased a right over that plot in 1929. This, however, contradicted the terms of a "duplicate certificate" issued to the respondent family by the authority in 1994, and a certificate of transfer in 1995, recording their right of burial as in lair 906. The respondent family argued that P had not proved his title, and their own certificate was valid, that sensitivities applied in relation to enforcing lairholders' rights, and potential damage to the coffins and potential consequences to third parties were relevant considerations. The authority argued, inter alia, that the remains were sacred and the court had a wide discretion in deciding whether or not to grant authority to disinter given the sensitive nature of the proposed operation, the limited number of years remaining on P's exclusive right and the lack of proof that P's mother in law was buried in the lair.

Held, granting the order to disinter, that (1) on the evidence P's mother in law was buried in lair 906; (2) on the evidence disinterment of the two coffins was practicable and could be achieved without disruption of or damage to the remains or the coffins; (3) remains were sacred but a person would normally be entitled to insist on disinterment as a matter of legal right, whether or not disturbance might result, if the proprietor of land where remains had been buried without permission or a third party held an exclusive contractual right of burial, in which cases the court would not have a discretion to refuse the remedy of specific implement except in exceptional circumstances; (4) the court also had a discretion to permit disinterment on cause shown where there was no right to be enforced but a person wished to disinter remains for practical or other reasons; (5) P had a legally enforceable exclusive contractual right of burial in lair 906, and the onus of demonstrating exceptional circumstances justifying refusal of specific implement rested on the respondents but had not been discharged, and (6) it was not necessary or appropriate for the court to specify the manner in which the remains should be disinterred, nor was there an evidential basis for imposing conditions regarding re-interment.

PATERSON, PETITIONER (NO.2); *sub nom.* PATERSON v. BUTLER 2002 S.C. 160, Lord Carloway, OH.

5970. Civil marriage–approval of places–application procedures

MARRIAGE (APPROVAL OF PLACES) (SCOTLAND) REGULATIONS 2002, SSI 2002 260; made under the Marriage (Scotland) Act 1977 s.18A. In force: June 10, 2002; £2.00.

These Regulations make provision for and in relation to the approval of places by local authorities for the solemnisation of civil marriages. They set out the parties who may apply for approval of a place for the solemnisation of a civil marriage; the application procedures which those parties must follow for the different types of approval; the requirements for notification of applications by the local authority and third party objection procedure; the considerations to be taken into account by a local authority in determining an application; the procedure for attaching standard conditions to a period approval and non-standard conditions to either period or temporary approvals, the notification of decisions and a restriction on successive applications; the duration of approvals and the procedure for renewal; the determination and charging of fees by a local authority for the approval of places and renewal of approvals and in respect of the attendance by authorised registrars at approved places; the grounds and procedures for revocation, suspension and variation of an approval; the deeming of a person who takes over the interest in a period approval as the approval holder; the requirements for the keeping of registers of approved places; and the duty on the Registrar General to issue supplementary guidance.

5971. Council tax–valuation–conveyance of dwelling to two beneficiaries by executor–conveyance between beneficiaries not a sale–meaning of "sale"–meaning of "any part of it"

[Council Tax (Alteration of Lists and Appeals) (Scotland) Regulations 1993 (SI 1993 355) Reg.4(1).]

M's executors conveyed her house equally to her two sons. The council tax banding of the house was E and when one son conveyed his share, for £35,000, to the other son, the council tax banding was increased to F; the house had been extended and had increased in value. The valuation committee, following an appeal, restored the banding to E. G appealed to the Court of Session arguing that the house had been sold, which, with its increase in value, justified an increase in the banding. M's beneficiaries argued that there had not been a sale, the conveyance had been of only one share in the house.

Held, refusing the appeal, that there had not been a sale of the whole dwelling in terms of the Council Tax (Alteration of Lists and Appeals) (Scotland) Regulations 1993 Reg.4(1), nor had there been a sale of part of it, that would normally indicate a physical part of the property as opposed to a pro indiviso share.

GRAMPIAN VALUATION JOINT BOARD ASSESSOR v. MacDONALD 2002 S.L.T. 817, Lord Hamilton, OH.

5972. Council tax–valuation–transfer of matrimonial home on separation–no sale

[Council Tax (Alteration of Lists and Appeals) (Scotland) Regulations 1993 (SI 1993 290) Reg.4(1)(a)(i).]

B and his wife jointly owned their matrimonial home which was purchased in 1994. They made several improvements to the property which resulted in an increase in its value. In 1998, in furtherance of a separation agreement, ownership of the property was transferred from joint names to sole ownership by B. In return, B paid his wife the sum of £20,000. The assessor advised B that, as a result of the sale, the property had been reassessed for council tax purposes from Band D to Band E. B appealed to the Rating Committee who upheld the appeal and the assessor appealed to the court arguing that the deed transferring the property had been granted for a consideration and was therefore a sale within the Council Tax (Alteration of Lists and Appeals) (Scotland) Regulations 1993 Reg.4(1)(a)(i).

Held, dismissing the appeal, that no sale within the meaning of Reg.4(1)(a)(i) had taken place as a sale of a severable proprietorial share did not constitute a sale of the property or any part of it.

GRAMPIAN VALUATION JOINT BOARD ASSESSOR v. ABERDEEN CITY VALUATION APPEAL COMMITTEE; *sub nom.* GRAMPIAN VALUATION JOINT BOARD ASSESSOR v. BENZIES [2002] R.A. 69, Lord Hamilton, OH.

5973. Elections–boundaries–transfer of constituencies

ABERDEEN CITY COUNCIL AND ABERDEENSHIRE COUNCIL BOUNDARIES (BLACKBURN) AMENDMENT ORDER 2002, SSI 2002 154; made under the Local Government (Scotland) Act 1973 s.17. In force: June 1, 2002; £2.00.

This Order transfers the area of land described in the Schedule to this Order between Aberdeen City Council and Aberdeenshire Council on June 1, 2002 and makes consequential changes to electoral arrangements.

5974. Elections–boundaries–transfer of constituencies

ARGYLL AND BUTE COUNCIL AND WEST DUNBARTONSHIRE COUNCIL BOUNDARIES (ARDOCH SEWAGE WORKS) AMENDMENT ORDER 2002, SSI 2002 155; made under the Local Government (Scotland) Act 1973 s.17. In force: June 1, 2002; £2.00.

This Order transfers the area of land described in the Schedule to this Order between the Argyll and Bute Council and the West Dunbartonshire Council on June 1, 2002 and makes consequential changes to electoral arrangements.

5975. Elections–boundaries–transfer of constituencies

CITY OF EDINBURGH COUNCIL AND WEST LOTHIAN COUNCIL BOUNDARIES (WEST FARM, BROXBURN) AMENDMENT ORDER 2002, SSI 2002 157; made under the Local Government (Scotland) Act 1973 s.17. In force: June 1, 2002; £2.00.

This Order transfers the area of land described in the Schedule to this Order between the City of Edinburgh Council and the West Lothian Council on June 1, 2002 and makes consequential changes to electoral arrangements.

5976. Elections–boundaries–transfer of constituencies

GLASGOW CITY COUNCIL AND RENFREWSHIRE COUNCIL BOUNDARIES (BRAEHEAD) AMENDMENT ORDER 2002, SSI 2002 156; made under the Local Government (Scotland) Act 1973 s.17. In force: June 1, 2002; £2.00.

This Order transfers the area of land described in the Schedule to this Order between Glasgow City Council and Renfrewshire Council on June 1, 2002 and makes consequential changes to electoral arrangements.

5977. Elections–fire services–appointment of board members

COMBINED FIRE SERVICES AREA ADMINISTRATION SCHEMES (VARIATION) (SCOTLAND) ORDER 2002, SSI 2002 141; made under the Fire Services Act 1947 s.36. In force: March 31, 2002; £1.75.

This Order amends the North Eastern Combined Fire Services Area Administration Scheme Order 1995 (SI 1995 2632), the Northern Combined Fire Services Area Administration Scheme Order 1995 (SI 1995 2633), the South Eastern Combined Fire Services Area Administration Scheme Order 1995 (SI 1995 2634), the Central Combined Fire Services Area Administration Scheme Order 1995 (SI 1995 2635), the Mid and South Western Combined Fire Services Area Administration Scheme Order 1995 (SI 1995 2636) and the Mid Eastern Combined Fire Services Area Administration Scheme Order 1995 (SI 1995 2637). Each of the Schemes is amended in order that the appointment of members of the board and of the convener and vice convener occurs in line with the ordinary elections of councillors irrespective of the frequency of those elections. This reflects changes made to the timing of local government elections made by the Scottish Local Government (Elections) Act 2002.

5978. Local authorities powers and duties–processions–prohibition of public procession–reasonableness

[Civic Government (Scotland) Act 1982 (c.45) s.63; Human Rights Act 1998 (c.42) Sch.1 Part I Art.11.]

O, an Orange Lodge, appealed against a notice by A, a local authority, under the Civic Government (Scotland) Act 1982 s.63, prohibiting the holding of a public procession, arguing that there were no reasonable grounds for the notice and that it was an unjustified restriction of their rights to free assembly under the Human Rights Act 1998 (c.42) Sch.1 Part I Art.11. A argued there was no right in members of the public to peacefully assemble and process on a public road, relying on local knowledge and a memorandum by a representative of their environment and property department which referred to traffic and public order considerations and that such events did not "always go off entirely problem free".

Held, amending the notice to become a permission to hold a public procession, that (1) there was a public right to pass along a public road, which was why the Act permitted the imposition of conditions on processions; (2) in exercising their powers under s.63, A had to base their decision on correct facts, exercise their discretion reasonably, act within their powers and give reasons for their decision, and (3) A had not given proper reasons for their decision insofar as they relied on the official's memorandum and unexplained local knowledge, the memo was unclear and referred to considerations which were matters for the police, and there was no factual basis for an assertion that such events were not always problem free.

ABERDEEN BON ACCORD LOYAL ORANGE LODGE 701 v. ABERDEEN CITY COUNCIL 2002 S.L.T. (Sh Ct) 52, AM Cowan, Sh Ct (Grampian, Highland and Islands).

5979. **Local authorities powers and duties–processions–prohibition of public procession–reasonableness**

[European Convention on Human Rights 1950 Art.6, Art.11; Civic Government (Scotland) Act 1982 (c.45) s.63.]

W, an Orange Lodge, appealed against notice by A, a local authority, under the Civic Government (Scotland) Act 1982 s.63 prohibiting the holding of a public procession. They argued that their rights of assembly and to a fair hearing under the European Convention on Human Rights 1950 Art.11 and Art.6 respectively had been breached as the presence and participation of two councillors, who had objected the previous year, in A's deliberations was contrary to the right to a fair hearing. Further, the statement of reasons given displayed a degree of intolerance and the reasons themselves were inadequate and A's failure to process the application as quickly as possible was contrary to their Art.6 rights. A argued that the two councillors had not made themselves party to the current proceedings and were not disqualified, that the statement of reasons had clearly identified what they had decided and why, and that their members were entitled to take into account their local knowledge in coming to their decision.

Held, granting permission for the procession, that (1) the presence and participation of the two councillors, who had proposed and seconded the prohibition, was sufficient to breach the Art.6 right to a fair and impartial hearing, where they could not be said to have displayed open minds; (2) A's statement of reasons did not justify a restriction of W's Art.11 (2) rights; (3) while A might be entitled to use their local knowledge they still had to give notice to W as to the grounds for their decision arising from such knowledge; (4) while A's timetable for their decision had not been ideal, it was fair for them to wait until they had the views of consultees and the full advice of their legal officers before calling a meeting, and this did not give rise to a breach of Art.6, and (5) there was no time to remit to A, but in any event the statement of reasons cast doubt as to whether the application could ever receive a hearing which an independent observer could regard as fair and impartial.

WISHART ARCH DEFENDERS LOYAL ORANGE LODGE 404 v. ANGUS COUNCIL 2002 S.L.T. (Sh Ct) 43, ID Dunbar, Sh Ct (Tayside, Central and Fife).

5980. **Local Government in Scotland Act 2003 (asp 1)**

This Act of the Scottish Parliament provides anew about the way in which local authorities discharge their functions and about the local provision of certain public services; gives local authorities power to do things which they consider will advance well-being; provides exemptions and reliefs from non-domestic rates in relation to certain lands and heritages; confers power on the Scottish Ministers to combine certain lands and heritages for the purposes of assessing rateable value; requires local authorities to prepare, and endeavour to implement, a plan relating to the carrying out of their waste disposal and collection functions; makes new provision about the capital expenditure of those authorities and about the making of capital grants to them; and makes some miscellaneous provisions connected with the functions of local authorities.

5981. **Local government officers–expenses–allowances**

LOCAL AUTHORITIES ETC. (ALLOWANCES) (SCOTLAND) AMENDMENT REGULATIONS 2002, SSI 2002 15; made under the Local Government

(Scotland) Act 1973 s.45, s.47, s.235; and the Local Government and Housing Act 1989 s.18, s.190. In force: February 15, 2002; £1.75.

These Regulations, which revoke the Local Authorities Etc. (Allowances) (Scotland) Amendment Regulations 1998 (SI 1998 3219), amend the Local Authorities Etc. (Allowances) (Scotland) Regulations 1995 (SI 1995 912) which make provision as to the payment of allowances of various sorts to members of Scottish local authorities and joint boards. The amendments all concern increases in the maximum amounts payable by way of allowances.

5982. Police and Fire Services (Finance) (Scotland) Act 2001 (asp 15)–Commencement Order

POLICE AND FIRE SERVICES (FINANCE) (SCOTLAND) ACT 2001 (COMMENCEMENT) ORDER 2002, SSI 2002 84; made under the Police and Fire Services (Finance) (Scotland) Act 2001 s.3. Commencement details: bringing into force various provisions of the 2001 Act on March 11, 2002; £1.50.

This Order brings into force the provisions of the Police and Fire Services (Finance) (Scotland) Act 2001 in so far as not already in force.

5983. Revenue support grant–determination for 2002/03

LOCAL GOVERNMENT FINANCE (SCOTLAND) ORDER 2002, SSI 2002 70; made under the Local Government Finance Act 1992 Sch.12 para.1, para.9. In force: February 1, 2002; £2.00.

This Order, which amends the Local Government Finance (Scotland) (No.2) Order 2001 (SSI 2001 260), determines the amount of the revenue support grant payable to each local authority in Scotland in respect of the financial year 2002-2003 and determines the amount of non-domestic rate income to be distributed to each local authority in respect of that year. It also redetermines the amount of the revenue support grant payable to each local authority in respect of the financial year 2001-2002.

5984. Revenue support grant–determination for 2002/03

LOCAL GOVERNMENT FINANCE (SCOTLAND) (NO.2) ORDER 2002, SSI 2002 230; made under the Local Government Finance Act 1992 Sch.12 para.1, para.9. In force: June 21, 2002; £2.00.

This Order, which amends the Local Government Finance (Scotland) Order 2002 (SI 2002 70), redetermines the amount of the revenue support grant payable to each local authority in respect of the financial year 2001 to 2002; redetermines the amount of the revenue support grant payable to each local authority in Scotland in respect of the financial year 2002 to 2003; and determines the amount of non-domestic rate income to be distributed to each local authority in respect of the financial year 2002 to 2003.

5985. Scottish Local Government (Elections) Act 2002 (asp 1)

This Act of the Scottish Parliament makes provision as respects the synchronisation of the polls at local government elections with the polls at elections to the Scottish Parliament; makes some minor rectifications in enactments relating to the timing of elections; and makes provision in relation to the casting and counting of votes at, and the sending of election communications in connection with, local government elections.

This Act received Royal Assent on January 22, 2002.

MENTAL HEALTH

5986. Adults with Incapacity (Scotland) Act 2000 (asp 4)–Commencement No.1 Order

ADULTS WITH INCAPACITY (SCOTLAND) ACT 2000 (COMMENCEMENT NO.1) (AMENDMENT) ORDER 2002, SSI 2002 172; made under the Adults with Incapacity (Scotland) Act 2000 s.89. In force: March 28, 2002; £1.50.

This Order amends the Adults with Incapacity (Scotland) Act 2000 (Commencement No.1) Order 2001 (SSI 2001 8) to exclude from commencement on April 1, 2002 the provisions of s.81 and s.82 of the Adults with Incapacity (Scotland) Act 2000 insofar as they relate to the managers of an authorised establishment, and to exclude from repeal on that date the Mental Health (Scotland) Act 1984 s.94.

5987. Adults with Incapacity (Scotland) Act 2000 (asp 4)–Commencement No.2 Order

ADULTS WITH INCAPACITY (SCOTLAND) ACT 2000 (COMMENCEMENT NO.2) ORDER 2002, SSI 2002 189; made under the Adults with Incapacity (Scotland) Act 2000 s.89. Commencement details: bringing into force various provisions of the 2000 Act on July 1, 2002; £1.50.

This Order brings into force the Adults with Incapacity (Scotland) Act 2000 s.47 to s.52 on July 1, 2002.

5988. Mental patients–local authorities–specified medical treatments

ADULTS WITH INCAPACITY (SPECIFIED MEDICAL TREATMENTS) (SCOTLAND) REGULATIONS 2002, SSI 2002 275; made under the Adults with Incapacity (Scotland) Act 2000 s.48. In force: July 1, 2002; £2.00.

These Regulations, which make provision in relation to the medical treatment of adults with incapacity, specify certain medical treatments to which the authority to treat shall not apply and authorise the carrying out of such treatments.

5989. Mental patients–local authorities–specified medical treatments–neurosurgery

ADULTS WITH INCAPACITY (SPECIFIED MEDICAL TREATMENTS) (SCOTLAND) AMENDMENT REGULATIONS 2002, SSI 2002 302; made under the Adults with Incapacity (Scotland) Act 2000 s.48. In force: July 1, 2002; £1.50.

These Regulations amend the Incapacity (Specified Medical Treatments) (Scotland) Regulations 2002 (SI 2002 275) which make provision in relation to the medical treatment of adults with incapacity, specify certain medical treatments to which the authority to treat shall not apply and authorise the carrying out of such treatments but only in accordance with the provisions of the Regulations. These Regulations remove neurosurgery for mental disorder from the list of medical treatments to which the authority will not apply.

5990. Mental patients–local authorities–supervision of welfare guardians

ADULTS WITH INCAPACITY (SUPERVISION OF WELFARE GUARDIANS ETC. BY LOCAL AUTHORITIES) (SCOTLAND) REGULATIONS 2002, SSI 2002 95; made under the Adults with Incapacity (Scotland) Act 2000 s.10, s.86. In force: April 1, 2002; £1.75.

These Regulations, which amend the Mental Health (Specified Treatments, Guardianship Duties etc.) (Scotland) Regulations 1984 (SI 1984 1494), prescribe the duties of the local authority in relation to supervision of welfare guardians and persons authorised under intervention orders for the purposes of the Adults with Incapacity (Scotland) Act 2000 s.10. They also prescribe the information to be provided by a welfare guardian or person authorised under an intervention order to a local authority to enable it to carry out its supervisory function.

5991. Mental patients–medical treatment certificates

ADULTS WITH INCAPACITY (MEDICAL TREATMENT CERTIFICATES) (SCOTLAND) REGULATIONS 2002, SSI 2002 208; made under the Adults with Incapacity (Scotland) Act 2000 s.47. In force: July 1, 2002; £1.75.

These Regulations prescribe the form of certificate of medical practitioner primarily responsible for the medical treatment of an adult that the practitioner is of the opinion that the adult is incapable in relation to a decision about medical treatment. Medical treatment is defined in the Adults with Incapacity (Scotland) Act 2000 s.47(4).

5992. Mental welfare–adults with incapacity–rules–applications and appeals

ACT OF SEDERUNT (SUMMARY APPLICATIONS, STATUTORY APPLICATIONS AND APPEALS ETC. RULES) AMENDMENT (NO.3) (ADULTS WITH INCAPACITY) 2002, SSI 2002 146; made under the Sheriff Courts (Scotland) Act 1971 s.32. In force: April 1, 2002; £1.75.

This Act of Sederunt, which amends the Act of Sederunt (Summary Applications, Statutory Applications and Appeals etc. Rules) 1999 (SI 1999 929), inserts a number of definitions for the purposes of applications made under the Adults with Incapacity (Scotland) Act 2000 Part 6 and makes provision for the service of an application to be effected upon the Mental Welfare Commission or the relevant local authority in appropriate cases. It also disapplies the requirement to hold the hearing within 28 days in cases where one of the persons upon whom the application is to be served is outside Europe.

5993. Mental welfare–ethics committee–membership and qualifications

ADULTS WITH INCAPACITY (ETHICS COMMITTEE) (SCOTLAND) REGULATIONS 2002, SSI 2002 190; made under the Adults with Incapacity (Scotland) Act 2000 s.51, s.86. In force: July 1, 2002; £1.75.

These Regulations constitute the Ethics Committee referred to in the Adults with Incapacity (Scotland) Act 2000 s.51. They make provision as to the membership and qualifications of certain members and length of membership of the Committee; for the appointment of a Chair and Vice-Chair of the Committee; for payment by the Scottish Ministers of expenses of members of the Committee; specify certain matters which the Committee must consider before approving research; and make certain procedural provision in relation to the conduct of the Committee.

5994. Mental welfare–guardianship and intervention orders–reports

ADULTS WITH INCAPACITY (REPORTS IN RELATION TO GUARDIANSHIP AND INTERVENTION ORDERS) (SCOTLAND) REGULATIONS 2002, SSI 2002 96; made under the Adults with Incapacity (Scotland) Act 2000 s.57, s.86. In force: April 1, 2002; £10.50.

These Regulations prescribe the forms to be used by certain persons when completing reports for the purposes of applications for guardianship orders, renewal of guardianship orders and intervention orders under the Adults with Incapacity Act 2000.

5995. Mental welfare–powers of guardians–recall

ADULTS WITH INCAPACITY (RECALL OF GUARDIANS' POWERS) (SCOTLAND) REGULATIONS 2002, SSI 2002 97; made under the Adults with Incapacity (Scotland) Act 2000 s.73, s.86. In force: April 1, 2002; £6.50.

These Regulations prescribe the forms to be completed in relation to applications to, and decisions of, the Mental Welfare Commission and local authorities in relation to recall of the powers of guardians under the Adults with Incapacity (Scotland)

Act 2000 s.73. They provide that the period within which a person may object to the recall of a guardian's powers, or to the decision of the Mental Welfare Commission or the local authority as to the recall of those powers, shall be 21 days and that the Mental Welfare Commission or a local authority shall notify each other, the applicant and the Public Guardian of any decision to recall the powers of a guardian.

5996. Mental welfare–welfare guardians–non compliance of decisions

ADULTS WITH INCAPACITY (NON-COMPLIANCE WITH DECISIONS OF WELFARE GUARDIANS) (SCOTLAND) REGULATIONS 2002, SSI 2002 98; made under the Adults with Incapacity (Scotland) Act 2000 s.70. In force: April 1, 2002; £1.75.

These Regulations, which prescribe the form of applications for warrants under the Adults and Incapacity (Scotland) Act 2002 s.70, provide that the period within which a person may object to the granting of an application in relation to non-compliance with decisions of guardian and welfare powers, shall be 21 days beginning with the date on which that person receives intimation of the application.

MINING

5997. Coal mining–breach of statutory duty–personal injury

[Administration of Justice Act 1982 (c.53) s.12; Mines (Safety of Exit) Regulations 1988 (SI 1988 1729) Reg.6.]

A mining electrician, Y, sought damages for injuries to his knee having slipped on a wooden walkway. The severity of the injury meant that Y would be unlikely to work underground for more than 15 years, so Y claimed provisional damages based on the risk of osteoarthritis.

Held, that (1) S were in breach of their statutory duty under the Mines (Safety of Exit) Regulations 1988 Reg.6 in failing to take reasonable steps to ensure that the walkway was safe to walk along and that they should have foreseen the risk to their employees caused by a slippery walkway; (2) an appropriate threshold for seeking an award of provisional damages under s.12 of the Administration of Justice Act 1982 would not be met by the circumstances outlined by Y; (3) for an award for solatium to be discounted, S would have required to prove that Y would have suffered osteoarthritis as a result of the earlier injury and that the mining accident had merely exacerbated a pre-existing condition. Medical evidence had, however, shown that there was no evidence of osteoarthritis in Y's knee at the time of the mining accident and any discounting of the award for solatium would, therefore, be inappropriate. An award of £12,000 was made, and (4) in calculating future loss of earnings, it was assumed that Y would be unable to continue to work underground in 11 years, but would secure light duties as an electrician elsewhere until retirement at 60 which gave an annual differential of £3,640. The multiplier was 8.91 and a discount for early payment by 11 years at a rate of 3 per cent gave a figure of £23,429 which was rounded up to £23,450.

YOUNG v. SCOTTISH COAL (DEEP MINING) CO LTD 2002 S.L.T. 1215, Lord Mackay of Drumadoon, OH.

MOVEABLE PROPERTY

5998. Ownership–possession–presumption arising from possession–motor vehicle

M appealed in an action of multiplepoinding raised by C, a chief constable, in relation to a Porsche motor car. The claimants were the original owner, S, who had reported the car stolen and made an insurance claim, and M, who had purchased the car from an intermediary, bearing false registration plates, without documentation and without the appropriate alarm key fob, and who had contacted the police on learning they were interested in the car. At that time S claimed the car was not his, but identified the keys provided by M as a set he had held for his vehicle. S was charged with attempted insurance fraud but no proceedings were taken. The sheriff held that it was not established that the car had been stolen, that the intermediary was aware when involved in the sale to M that lawful title could not be transferred and was not a mercantile agent in possession with ostensible authority to sell, and that M had not acted in good faith. S was preferred as the original owner.

Held, allowing the appeal, that (1) having held that it was not established that the car had been stolen, the sheriff was not entitled to find that the intermediary was aware he could not pass on good title, as the possibility remained open that it came into his possession lawfully, and (2) the sheriff having found neither party convincing, this was an open case where the presumption arising from possession of moveable property applied, and where S had failed to prove his car was stolen and had not established that his possession terminated in such a way that M could not have acquired a right of ownership, the sheriff erred in holding it necessary for M to establish bona fide possession and that the presumption only applied to such possession.

CHIEF CONSTABLE OF STRATHCLYDE v. SHARP 2002 S.L.T. (Sh Ct) 95, EF Bowen Q.C., Sheriff Principal, Sh Ct.

NEGLIGENCE

5999. Duty of care—auditors—proximity—creditor's reliance on accounts

B, a firm of chartered accountants, enrolled a motion for dismissal in the action for damages brought against it by R, a bank. B had been the auditors for a company which had been lent substantial sums of money by R. Receivers had subsequently been appointed to the company and R had been unable to recover much of the moneys lent. R argued that B, as auditors of the company, had owed it a duty of care and that the losses it had sustained had been attributable to B's breach of that duty. B denied liability, contending that it did not owe R a duty of care as it had not intended that the bank should rely upon the audited accounts when making lending decisions in respect of the company.

Held, refusing the motion for dismissal, that in the absence of a disclaimer of responsibility being attached to audited accounts the auditors of a company would owe a duty of care to a lender which they were aware might rely on the information contained in those accounts when advancing money to the company. It was not necessary that the auditors had intended the lender to rely on the audited accounts in order to establish a relationship of proximity between them. In the instant case, no disclaimer of responsibility to R having been made by B in respect of the company's accounts, there had been a sufficient relationship of proximity between them to establish that B had owed a duty to R to take reasonable care to save R from suffering loss as a result of relying on the audited accounts when making lending decisions.

ROYAL BANK OF SCOTLAND v. BANNERMAN JOHNSTONE MacLAY 2003 S.L.T. 181, Lord Macfadyen, OH.

6000. Duty of care—banks—preparation of wills—intended beneficiaries

H, a niece and nephew, sought damages from B, a bank, for losses allegedly caused by its failure to arrange timeously for the execution of their aunt's will, for which instructions had been given shortly before her death. B sought dismissal, arguing that its duties to prepare and have executed a will were no higher than those owed by solicitors and that there was binding Scots authority to the effect that, absent any special facts, no duty of care was owed to intended beneficiaries and further, that there were no relevant averments as to when B should have arranged for execution or that they should have had in contemplation the potential total loss of the legacies.

Held, allowing proof before answer, that (1) there was an authoritative indication in *Robertson v. Watt & Co* (Unreported, July 4, 1995) that a court in Scotland would not now regard itself as being bound by *Robertson v. Fleming* (1861) 4 Macq. 167 and that the principle in *White v. Jones* [1995] 2 A.C. 207, [1995] C.L.Y. 3701 would be followed in Scotland, the court having specifically acknowledged the views of the majority that an intended beneficiary could be extended a remedy under the principle in *Hedley Byrne & Co Ltd v. Heller & Partners Ltd* [1964] A.C. 465, [1963] C.L.Y. 2416, and (2) the particular duty alleged was a matter for evidence, and prima facie the loss which was reasonably foreseeable was the loss of the legacies to be provided.

HOLMES v. BANK OF SCOTLAND; *sub nom.* DAVIDSON v. BANK OF SCOTLAND 2002 S.L.T. 544, Lord Kingarth, OH.

6001.   Duty of care–causation–two factors capable of causing accident–proof

[Occupiers liability (Scotland) Act 1960 (c.30); Offshore installations (Operational safety, Health and Welfare) Regulations 1976 (SI 1976 1019).]

S sought damages from his employers, T, when he lost his footing on a stairway. S averred that T were in breach of their duty at common law, the Occupiers liability (Scotland) Act 1960 and Offshore installations (Operational safety, Health and Welfare) Regulations 1976 which averments were excluded from probation by the Sheriff. S appealed.

Held, sustaining the appeal in part and refusing the cross appeal, that (1) whilst S had to prove that it was the coincidence of sludge and smooth steps that had caused his accident, there was no requirement on him to prove that both of those factors were the attributable to a breach of T's duties under common law or statutory provisions; it was sufficient that one of the causes could be attributed in that way. Therefore only one of the causes needed to be relevantly pled for the case to proceed, and (2) given that T would only be subject to a duty under the 1976 Regulations if they were the owners of an offshore installation, their pleadings that they had fulfilled all their obligations under those Regulations could be taken as an admission on their part of the applicability of those Regulations without the need for S to make specific averments to that effect.

SIMPSON v. TRANSOCEAN OFFSHORE (UK) INC 2002 S.C.L.R. 233, Sir SST Young, Sheriff Principal, Sh Ct.

6002.   Duty of care–civil engineers–certificate of proper construction of dwellinghouse–reliance on certificate by purchaser

H raised an action of damages against C, a building consultant, in respect of defects in a house which belonged to one of C's clients. H alleged that she had relied on a letter which endorsed the local authority certification of works concerning the proper construction of that house, which C had provided to the seller.

Held, granting decree of absolvitor, that (1) the question of whether C owed a duty of care to H had to be tested on the basis of three principles (a) that it had to be reasonably foreseeable by C that if he produced the letter negligently, that the recipient of the letter would be liable to suffer loss as a result, (b) that the relationship between C and the recipient claiming loss had to be sufficiently proximate, and (c) that it was fair, just and reasonable in all the circumstances for the law to impose such a duty of care on C in respect of H, and (2) in the circumstances described, H had not demonstrated sufficient proximity in her relationship with C to make it fair, just and reasonable to impose such a duty of care on C in respect of the contents of the second letter, dissenting judgment of Denning, LJ in *Candler v. Crane Christmas & Co* [1951] 2 K.B.164, applied.

Observed, that the impression given by the surveyor and also by a consultant engineer who gave evidence for H that they saw the second letter as the equivalent of a guarantee, replacing an NHBC guarantee, was unsound.

HOWES v. CROMBIE 2001 S.C.L.R. 921, Lord Eassie, OH.

6003. Duty of care—local authorities—application of neighbourhood principle to statutory duty

See REPARATION: Morrison v. Aberdeen City Council. §6067

6004. Duty of care—local authorities—community service workers—defective system of work

W raised an action for damages against M, for injuries sustained to his right hand whilst he was carrying out work under a community service order. The work, which was supervised by M, involved painting the interior of a house. The injury was allegedly caused by a defective door catch on a van supplied by M. On attempting to close the door, the door jammed causing the catch, which had rusted to form a hook, to puncture W's hand. W averred that M had failed in their duty to provide a safe system of work by failing to ensure that machinery and equipment provided was safe for use. M submitted that W's pleadings were irrelevant and should not be admitted to probation. The sheriff, whilst accepting that W's pleadings were lacking, concluded that M had been given fair notice of the case being made against them and allowed a proof before answer. M appealed against that decision arguing that there were no averments to support a case that M did not have a safe system of work or that any system of work provided was relevant to W's accident. In addition, M maintained that it was irrelevant for W to attempt to establish a case of reasonable foreseeability on the basis of alleged similar actings by persons who had not been identified.

Held, refusing the appeal, that (1) although W had failed to establish a ground of fault based on a defective system of work, his averments, when read as a whole were sufficient to proceed to proof on the basis that M had required W to work with, and close, the rear door of the van which had a dangerous and defective catch which was likely to cause injury to those using it; (2) W's averments were sufficient to allow him to lead evidence at proof that M had allowed the catch to deform until it formed a hook which went some way to establishing reasonable foreseeability; (3) the fact that W could not name his fellow community service workers who has closed the door in the same manner on previous occasions, should not be held against him as their identity was within M's knowledge and could, therefore not surprise them at proof, *Hayward v. Edinburgh Royal Infirmary Board of Management* 1954 S.C. 453, [1954] C.L.Y. 4047, applied, and (4) W's averments that no inspection of the van was carried out was sufficient to allow proof on whether or not such a system for inspections was in place, but was insufficient to allow proof on whether any such system was adequate or effective.

WILSON v. MIDLOTHIAN COUNCIL 2002 S.C.L.R. 554, CGB Nicholson Q.C., Sheriff Principal, Sh Ct.

6005. Duty of care—local education authorities—supervision of pupils leaving school

H, a secondary school pupil, raised an action for damages against P, as the local education authority responsible for Perth Academy. H claimed that, as a result of violent horseplay, she was pushed against the side of the school bus she was about to board and sustained dental injuries. She argued that P was liable as they had failed in their duty to provide adequate supervision in the playground to children exiting the school and boarding the school buses and that, had such supervision been in place, the incident would not have occurred. P submitted that the level of supervision provided at Perth Academy was equivalent to that provided at other schools in the area. Teachers frequently passed through the area used for boarding school buses on their way to the car park, the headmaster would be present on unpredictable occasions and the driver of the school bus had the authority to report any misbehaviour to the school and, if necessary, to remove bus passes from the children concerned. In addition, P submitted that the size of the school grounds, the number of exits from the school and the numbers of children involved made it impractical to increase the levels of supervision available, that the ages of the children involved made it undesirable to have higher levels of supervision in place as they had to allow the children to begin to take some responsibility for themselves and even if higher levels of supervision were in place, it would be impossible to prevent all horseplay in the playground.

Held, dismissing the action, that (1) the evidence did not support H's claim that her injuries were caused through malicious intent; (2) H had failed to prove that the level of supervision at Perth Academy fell below that provided at other schools in the area; (3) the levels of supervision described by P appeared adequate in the circumstances; (4) there was no evidence to suggest that higher levels of supervision would have prevented the incident leading to the injury, and (5) existing authority negated the contention that the local education authority owed a duty to constantly supervise pupils in the playground.

HUNTER v. PERTH AND KINROSS COUNCIL 2001 S.C.L.R. 856, Lord Eassie, OH.

6006. **Duty of care—prison officers—back injury sustained as a result of negligence by senior officer**

See PERSONAL INJURY: Hendrie v. Scottish Ministers. §6022

6007. **Duty of care—prison officers—knee injury sustained in chasing absconder—no breach of duty**

See PERSONAL INJURY: Sneddon v. Scottish Ministers. §3514

6008. **Duty of care—surveyors—proximity of relationships—survey instructed by bank's customer—survey presented directly to bank—effect of disclaimer**

[Unfair Contract Terms Act 1977 (c.50).]

M sought a loan from B, a bank, in respect of a proposed purchase of a hotel. B required a survey of the hotel in connection with the loan application and M duly instructed F, a firm of surveyors. F forwarded a copy of the survey, by arrangement, directly to B and on the basis of its contents, B approved the loan to M. M defaulted on the loan and B consequently suffered a loss on the sale of the hotel. B alleged that the value placed on the hotel by F was higher than would have been given by a reasonably competent surveyor and that F, being negligent in the performance of their duties were liable to B for damages in respect of the loss suffered. F argued that the survey had been instructed by M and contained a clear and unambiguous disclaimer to the effect that F accepted no responsibility to anyone other than the client who had instructed them, and anyone else relying on the report, did so at their own risk. They disputed the existence of a duty of care owed by them to B, arguing that the element of proximity required to establish such a duty was negated by the existence of the disclaimer. They further argued that the requirement of reasonableness had not been met where B, given the existence of the disclaimer, could have instructed their own survey or contacted F directly to request advice on the contents of the survey with regard to B obtaining a security over the hotel. B argued that the survey had been instructed specifically for loan security purposes and that, by forwarding the report directly to the bank, F had accepted responsibility for the advice contained in it. B maintained that for the disclaimer to be effective it should have been stated on a communication addressed directly to them, rather than relying on a disclaimer contained in a communication addressed to M. B finally argued that F was a well known firm whose reputation should have been able to be relied on by B and it was therefore reasonable, given that F were insured, that they should have owed a duty of care to B.

Held, granting decree of absolvitor, that (1) the disclaimer was not obviated simply by virtue of the method in which the report was transmitted to B, which was not materially different from the situation which would have arisen had F forwarded the report to M, who had then delivered it to B; (2) the disclaimer was clear and unambiguous and told B that no reliance could be placed on its terms and was therefore, subject to the reasonableness test under the Unfair Contract Terms Act 1977 being satisfied, effective to prevent the creation of a duty of care, *Hedley Byrne & Co Ltd v. Heller & Partners Ltd* [1964] A.C. 465, [1963] C.L.Y. 2416, followed, and (3) given that B were a large, commercial entity with ready access to legal and financial advice, that they had equal bargaining power to F, that they were well able to understand the meaning and implications of the disclaimer and could have instructed a separate report and were financially able to bear any losses incurred by their reliance on a without responsibility report, the reasonableness test under the 1977 Act had been satisfied.

BANK OF SCOTLAND v. FULLER PEISER 2002 S.L.T. 574, Lord Eassie, OH.

6009. Occupiers liability–duty of care–duty to fence reservoir

[Occupiers Liability (Scotland) Act 1960 (c.30) s.2(1).]

G sought damages under the Occupiers Liability (Scotland) Act 1960 s.2(1) from the water authority for the death of her husband by drowning in Glencourse Reservoir, maintaining that the edge of the reservoir should have been fenced at the point where her husband allegedly fell in. The water authority pled that the action was irrelevant and should be dismissed. G, in response, argued that a proof before answer should be allowed. G averred that her husband, in an intoxicated state, had been driven by the son to his home on a farm at night, their route taking them along an access road to the side of the reservoir. The road was separated from the reservoir by a grass strip of approximately one metre and then by a stone wall of varying heights. For a period of approximately 70 metres, the wall height was reduced to only 30 centimetres with a 1.7 metre drop into the water. No warning signs were displayed and the access road was frequently used by farmers and tourists alike, both by day and night. G averred that her son stopped the car on the approach to the farm and her husband got out and wandered off. She alleged that he lost his footing and drowned. She claimed that the water authority should have taken steps to protect the public from the obvious dangers of such an artificial feature. There were no averments of similar accidents or complaints alleging danger being made to the water authority. The water authority argued that the action was irrelevant on two grounds. Firstly that occupiers of land owed no duty to erect fences for protection against permanent and obvious features in the environment and that established rule applied to man made features as well as to natural ones. There had been no allegation made that the danger had been concealed or that her husband, who lived nearby, had been unfamiliar with it. Secondly, they argued that G had failed to show any direct link between the alleged danger and her husband's death. There were no averments as to how he lost his footing or how he ended up in the water.

Held, dismissing the action as irrelevant, that (1) any duty on occupiers to fence off dangers did not apply to permanent, ordinary and familiar features of the landscape, whether natural or man made, and (2) G could, at best, ask the court to speculate on whether, and if so how, the alleged danger was linked to her husband's death.

GRAHAM v. EAST OF SCOTLAND WATER AUTHORITY 2002 S.C.L.R. 340, Lord Emslie, OH.

6010. Occupiers liability–landlords powers and duties–window at foot of stairs not glazed with safety glass–tenant falling through glass

[Occupiers Liability (Scotland) Act 1960 (c.30) s.2, s.3.]

M, a tenant in one of N's properties had a responsibility to replace all broken glass unless she could prove that the damage was caused by someone other than the tenant and N had a responsibility to keep the structure and exterior of the dwelling in good repair. M sought damages after she had fallen down twelve stairs in the house and put her arm through a window that was situated at the foot of the stairs. The window was not glazed with toughened safety glass. M argued that N had breached their statutory duty under the Occupiers Liability (Scotland) Act 1960 s.2 and s.3. N argued that in the absence of any damage or lack of repair for which N was responsible there could be no liability under the 1960 Act. N also argued that M had willingly accepted any danger which was obvious by occupying and using the home for 17 years.

Held, that there could be no liability because the risk was not one arising from a failure on the part of N.

McCALLIE v. NORTH AYRSHIRE COUNCIL 2002 S.C.L.R. 178, Colin G McKay, Sh Ct (North Strathclyde).

6011. Professional negligence–insurance brokers–failure to test market for insurance portfolio–loss of opportunity–measure of damages

M, a company, sought damages from W, insurance brokers, by reason of their alleged failure to test the market for M's insurance portfolio, resulting in them losing the opportunity of obtaining substantial reductions in the premiums paid over a period of two years. M had sought alternative quotes from two other brokers on which basis the damages claim had been made. W sought dismissal, arguing that (1) M's case was founded on loss of opportunity and was not relevant in the absence of averments of some loss of legal right, and (2) no proper basis had been laid for quantification as the right lost had to be of ascertainable, measurable, non-negligible value and M's averments of rates which according to their expert could have been obtained, lacked the necessary specification of the bases for the figures averred.

Held, allowing proof before answer, that (1) there was nothing in the authorities to suggest that the loss of a "right" was an essential prerequisite to a relevant claim in Scots law, and as M had offered to prove that by reason of W's fault, it had sustained actual loss in the form of the loss of a substantial chance to obtain materially lower rates than those achieved, it could not be said that their case was bound to fail, and (2) the issue as respects quantification related to lack of vouching for the evidence proposed to be led from M's expert, and not fair notice of M's case, and W were sufficiently protected by the mechanisms in existence for the disclosure of materials and would also have their own sources for assistance.

McCRINDLE GROUP LTD v. WILLIS CORROON SCOTLAND LTD 2002 S.L.T. 209, Lord Hamilton, OH.

6012. Professional negligence–solicitors–failure to raise action–nature of instructions

S sought damages from L, a firm of solicitors, in respect of losses incurred through their alleged failure to raise an action of damages in due time on S's behalf against C. C had failed to carry out building works which he had agreed to complete in missives for property purchased by S. The First Division (2000 S.L.T 287) held, inter alia, that S was left with no surviving right of action against C on the basis of the missives, contrary to L's position. S were forced to sell the property and were unable to proceed with the sale of their present home, which gave rise to an action of damages against them by the intended purchasers (Y). In 1991, S instructed V (a solicitor with L), after their solicitor withdrew, to defend Y's action and to raise proceedings against C. V claimed that his instructions were restricted to defending Y's action and that the question of acting against C was not raised until after the two year period had expired. M, who had introduced S to V, thought it unlikely that S would not have given instructions to raise proceedings against C, M himself having mentioned litigation to V. On the question of quantum, L argued that S had failed to establish that their lost right had an ascertainable, measurable, non-negligible value inter alia because S had resold the property at a higher price and because C could not have met a court award.

Held, granting decree, that (1) in considering the whole evidence, it was likely that S did, at least at the first meeting with V, ask for his advice in relation to legal action against C, S's evidence was generally credible and reliable on this point and was supported by M whilst V appeared to rely not on what he remembered, but on the documents on his file, which, it transpired during evidence, was not a careful and complete record of all that took place, and (2) the value of loss was assessed at £5,000, being the sum which C would likely have offered and S have accepted in settlement, it was likely that a defence based on the missives would not have succeeded, there having been an agreed plan, produced and spoken to by S, with only details of bathroom and kitchen fittings remaining outstanding.

SMITH v. LINDSAY & KIRK (A FIRM) (NO.2) 2002 S.L.T. 335, Lord Kingarth, OH.

NUISANCE

6013. Economic loss—claim by tenant of public house—failure to repair sewer—persistent ingress of water allegedly affecting custom—relevancy

H, the tenant of a public house under a registered lease, raised an action of damages against N, a water authority, claiming solatium and loss of revenue allegedly occurring as a result of a persistent ingress of water caused by the perforation and blocking of a sewer, following the demolition of a neighbouring church and construction of a road in 1991. N sought dismissal on the basis, inter alia, that H did not have any possessory right or title to the property such that she could claim for loss suffered to the subjects, especially as her landlords were responsible for keeping the premises wind and watertight; and that H's averments of loss were insufficient, where various figures of net profit before and after 1991 were averred, but no consistent level of profit was claimed.

Held, allowing proof before answer, that (1) while the test for title was high, H had established a possessory right to advance a claim for economic loss through her registered lease, which was not only close to ownership, but in many respects identical to the interests of that ownership; (2) the nature of the landlords' obligations had no connection with the responsibilities of a water authority to maintain and repair sewers, and (3) H's claim could have been more clearly quantified, particularly as to whether the measure of loss was to be ascertained by looking at gross as opposed to net levels of profit, but there was enough material to allow N to identify the appropriate measure of loss in the circumstances.

HAND v. NORTH OF SCOTLAND WATER AUTHORITY 2002 S.L.T. 798, Lord Wheatley, OH.

6014. Statutory nuisance—local authority housing—dampness—responsibility for nuisance

[Environmental Protection Act 1990 (c.43) s.79, s.82.]

R, the tenant of a flat, lodged an application under the Environmental Protection Act 1990 s.82 against D, her local authority landlord, seeking an order requiring them to abate an alleged nuisance of condensation dampness at the subjects. R claimed in terms of s.79(1)(a) that the state of the premises was prejudicial to health, in that she and her young son were at risk of respiratory ailments due to the dampness, and that it amounted to a nuisance, in that severe mould growth had damaged the decoration of the house and bedding, clothes and toys. This continued despite various efforts to heat, clean and ventilate the property. After proof the sheriff found that the block conformed to building standards current at the time of its construction; that it was not in need of repair; that D had provided sufficient points for electric heating plus one electric heater; and that R had other heaters but could not afford to heat the flat to a level which would reduce the dampness. He held that R had failed to establish either branch of her case under s.79(1)(a), or that D were the persons responsible since the principal cause was R's inability to afford adequate heating. This decision was upheld by the sheriff principal. R appealed to the Court of Session.

Held, refusing the appeal, that (1) on the evidence the sheriff and sheriff principal should have held it established that the state of the premises was such as to be prejudicial to health in terms of s.79(1)(a); (2) (per Lord Johnston and Lady Paton, Lord Cameron of Lochbroom dissenting) that R had established that the state of the flat also constituted a nuisance in terms of s.79(1)(a), which denoted any physical state of affairs recognised by Scots common law as something which a person should not have to suffer and it was not necessary to establish that the environment was likely to cause injury to health, or to establish any interference by a third party; (3) (per Lords Cameron of Lochbroom and Johnston, Lady Paton dissenting) that it had not been established that D were the persons responsible in terms of s.82(4)(a) for the statutory nuisance constituted by the above findings, as they had provided sources of electrical power for heating throughout the subjects and had not done anything to the premises to reduce the effect of the heating. D had satisfied the test in *Dover DC v. Farrar* (1981-82) 2 H.L.R. 32, [1983] C.L.Y. 1792 and did not have to go as far as providing heaters; (4) (per Lords Cameron of Lochbroom and Johnston, Lady Paton dissenting) that the inadequate insulation of the building was not a "defect of a structural character" in terms of s.82(4)(b).

ROBB v. DUNDEE CITY COUNCIL 2002 S.C. 301, Lord Cameron of Lochbroom, Lord Johnston, Lady Paton, Ex Div.

PENOLOGY AND CRIMINOLOGY

6015. Detention—legalised police cells—discontinuance

DISCONTINUANCE OF LEGALISED POLICE CELLS (AYR) RULES 2002, SSI 2002 472; made under the Prisons (Scotland) Act 1989 s.14, s.39. In force: November 30, 2002; £1.75.

These Rules provide for the discontinuance of the police cells in the possession of the Strathclyde Joint Police Board at Ayr as a place in which prisoners may be detained before, during or after trial for any period not exceeding 14 days.

6016. Prisons—young offender institutions—supervision levels

PRISONS AND YOUNG OFFENDERS INSTITUTIONS (SCOTLAND) AMENDMENT RULES 2002, SSI 2002 107; made under the Prisons (Scotland) Act 1989 s.39. In force: April 1, 2002; £2.50.

These Rules amend the Prisons and Young Offenders Institutions (Scotland) Rules 1994 (SI 1994 1931) to give effect to the replacement of the system of security categorisation of prisoners by a new system of prisoner supervision levels. They add supervision level to the matters to which a Governor may have regard when deciding to which part of a prison a particular prisoner or group of prisoners may be confined and set out the detailed procedures that are to govern the operation of the new prisoner supervision level system, and in particular prescribes the procedures to be followed when assigning or reviewing the supervision level of, or the imposition of special security measures on, an individual prisoner and the opportunities that a prisoner is to have to make representations in respect of such decisions.

PENSIONS

6017. Occupational pensions—local government pension scheme

LOCAL GOVERNMENT PENSION SCHEME (SCOTLAND) AMENDMENT REGULATIONS 2002, SSI 2002 311; made under the Superannuation Act 1972 s.7, s.12. In force: September 23, 2002; £1.75.

These Regulations make amendments to the Local Government Pension Scheme (Scotland) Regulations 1998 (SI 1998 366) which are necessary as a result of the creation of Careers Scotland and Scottish Water. They make amendments in relation to the employees of careers service companies, adult guidance networks, education business partnerships and lifelong learning partnerships who transferred into the employment of Scottish Enterprise and Highlands and Islands Enterprise on April 1, 2002 due to the creation of Careers Scotland. Careers Scotland is a new national careers guidance service and provide that notwithstanding their transfer, they may be members of the Local Government Pension Scheme. They also make amendments in relation to former employees of the North of Scotland Water Authority, the East of Scotland Water Authority and the West of Scotland Water Authority who transferred into the employment of Scottish Water on April 1, 2002 to allow continued access to the Local Government Pension Scheme for the former employees of the old Water Authorities who transferred to the new body on that date and to allow access to the Scheme for new employees of the body.

6018. Pension schemes—winding up—delay by independent trustee

[Pension Schemes Act 1993 (c.48) s.146.]

M, an independent trustee of a final salary pension scheme in administration, appealed the determination of the Pensions Ombudsman that M had been responsible for maladministration and should reimburse costs to the scheme.

Held, quashing the decision as to reimbursement but leaving standing his direction to wind up the scheme immediately, that (1) although delay could amount to maladministration, it had to be unjustified or culpable and in the circumstances of the instant case, much of the delay since 1995 had been outwith the M's control, being delays by the Inland Revenue and the company's auditors in responding to legitimate inquiries by M, (2) even if M could have procured the removal of EAF and JAF as trustees, which was not certain, a misunderstanding on M's part as to their power to take such an action could not be construed as maladministration, (3) the Ombudsman's view that M, as professionals, should have done more to persuade EAF and JAF that the figures were correct and had instead fostered the dispute between them had not been supported by evidence as they had declined to accept the figures even after the OPAS investigation, and, (4) M, as independent trustees faced with such an impasse, took the correct course of action in referring the matter to OPAS for a determination by the Pensions Ombudsman rather than risking protracted litigation in the courts.

MITRE PENSIONS LTD v. PENSIONS OMBUDSMAN [2000] O.P.L.R. 349, Lord Kirkwood, Lord McCluskey, Lord Weir, Ex Div.

6019. Superannuation—committees—members—consideration of superannuation fund as trust scheme

[Superannuation Act 1972 (c.11); Housing (Scotland) Act 1988 (c.43); Pensions Act 1995 (c.26) s.16; Local Government Superannuation (Scotland) Regulations 1987 (SI 1987 1850).]

B, the members of C, a superannuation committee of, H, a body corporate constituted under the Housing (Scotland) Act 1988, raised a petition seeking direction as to whether they owed fiduciary duties to the employees and former employees of H. C was established by the board of H in 1990 with the remit, inter alia, of administering their superannuation fund in terms of the Superannuation Act

1972 and regulations made thereunder. The fund was maintained by contributions from H and their employees, initially under the terms of the Local Government Superannuation (Scotland) Regulations 1987, and latterly under the Local Government Superannuation (Scotland) Regulations 1998. C's remit was later revised by board minute in 1993, and following the enactment of the Pensions Act 1995 s.16, C endorsed proposals for the introduction of member nominated committee members from 1997. C's chairman thereafter set out the function of such members in a letter dated February 14, 1997 which provided, inter alia, that they would maintain and administer the fund in accordance with the 1987 Regulations, would conduct the committee's functions within a remit determined by H, would manage the fund at all times exclusively in the best interests of all members, and would appoint suitably qualified and experienced agents to assist them in doing so. When the Scottish Ministers put forward proposals in a Housing Bill to transfer the assets, liabilities and employees of H to a new executive agency, with H becoming a residuary body and holding the fund until the creation of a new civil service pension scheme, C's members became concerned as to the proper characterisation of their position and obligations in respect of the fund. They contended that the fund was held in trust for the members, pensioners and deferred pensioners, that H stood in the position of employer, that they were trustees of the fund with a legal personality established by the minute of 1993, that the fund was a "trust scheme" for the purposes of the 1995 Act, and that as a consequence, they were subject to the duties, obligations and penalties imposed by the 1995 Act and at common law on the trustees of a trust scheme. The contention that the scheme constituted a trust was supported by a representative beneficiary of the scheme.

Held, answering the questions in the negative, that (1) nothing in the 1993 minute suggested any intention to create a trust in the sense of an act equivalent to delivery or transfer of the funds as trust funds or anything to demonstrate the irrevocable character of a trust, and (2) the scheme for which Scottish Homes were responsible as the administering authority was established under the 1972 Act, its particulars were set out in subordinate legislation, it was therefore not a trust scheme but a public service pension scheme, and s.16 of the 1995 Act provided that the statutory requirement for member nominated trustees applied only to a trust scheme.

BAIN, PETITIONER 2002 S.L.T. 1112, Lord Cameron of Lochbroom, Lord Johnston, Lord Wheatley, Ex Div.

6020. Superannuation—teachers

TEACHERS' SUPERANNUATION (SCOTLAND) AMENDMENT REGULATIONS 2002, SSI 2002 288; made under the Superannuation Act 1972 s.9, s.12, Sch.3. In force: July 1, 2002; £2.00.

These Regulations, which amend the Teachers' Superannuation (Scotland) Regulations 1992 (SI 1992 280), provide for the calculation of reckonable service where a teacher is in winding down employment. They introduce a new early retirement provision; give effect to the amount of actuarially reduced pension and lump sum to be paid; provide that the enhancement which may be paid to a teacher whose ill-health retirement benefits are calculated by reference to further employment which is pensionable is limited to the shorter of the length of the teacher's relevant service or the length of the period remaining before the teacher's 60th birthday; provide that a teacher's actuarially reduced pension will not be subject to abatement; provide that a teacher may take an actuarially reduced pension following a period of re-employment which is pensionable; increase employers' contributions by 0.25 per cent from April 1, 2002; and introduce a new Regulation whereby teachers who meet certain criteria may, with the consent of the employer, wind down by working 50 per cent of full-time service or more and receive full-time service credit.

PERSONAL INJURY

6021. Measure of damages—loss of earnings—loss of earning capacity and loss of services—injury preventing active involvement in restaurant business

See DAMAGES: Smith v. Hastie. §5535

6022. Measure of damages—prison officers—back injury sustained in workplace

H sought damages for an injury sustained to his back whilst breaking up a fight between two inmates at a young offenders' institution where he worked as a prison officer. H alleged that the incident arose out of the negligence of senior officers in either (1) re introducing one of the prisoners to the wing following an earlier separation which had resulted from fighting involving the possible use of a weapon, and where there was a real possibility that retribution would be taken, or (2) failing to separate the two prisoners following such an incident where, in both cases, the senior officers were aware of the likelihood of retribution involving the possible use of a weapon and one of the inmates was due to be transferred the following day. H alleged that the senior officers were aware that if such retribution took place, the prison officers within the wing were likely to be injured trying to break up the ensuing altercation.

Held, granting decree and awarding damages of £18,000 in respect of solatium with interest at an agreed rate of four per cent per annum from the date of the accident, £101,555 in respect of past wage loss with interest at an agreed rate of four per cent per annum from April 1, 1995, £310,020 in respect of future wage loss and a pension loss of £65,000, that (1) there was no direct evidence of a separation having taken place the previous day although there was clear evidence that there had been an altercation between the two inmates which had resulted in injury requiring medical attention; (2) the evidence supported a finding that the seriousness of the situation had been reported to senior officers who had a duty to inform officers of governor grade, who were authorised to make the decision to separate the inmates; (3) given the impending transfer of one of the inmates the following day, it was reasonable to assume that any attempt at retribution for the earlier attack would have to be made during the shift in which H was injured; (4) any separation would only have been required for one day until the permanent transfer took place; (5) a duty of care was owed to H on the basis that there was a reasonably foreseeable risk that injury would take place to prison officers who had a duty to intervene in disputes between inmates, and (6) failure to separate the inmates in the circumstances led to a breach of that duty of care for which the Scottish Ministers were liable.

HENDRIE v. SCOTTISH MINISTERS 2002 Rep. L.R. 46, Lord Kingarth, OH.

6023. Measure of damages—risk of osteoarthritis shortening career as miner

See MINING: Young v. Scottish Coal (Deep Mining) Co Ltd. §5997

Personal Injuries or Death—Quantum

Details have been received of the following cases in which damages for personal injuries or death were awarded. The classification and sequence of the classified awards follows that adopted in Kemp and Kemp. *The Quantum of Damages,* Vol. 2. Unless there is some statement to the contrary, the age of the applicant is his age at the time of the court hearing. Unless specified the damages are stated on the basis of full liability, *ie.* ignoring any deduction made for contributory negligence. The sum is the total amount of the damages awarded unless otherwise stated. For a cumulative guide to *quantum* of damages cases reported in Current Law during 2000, see the *Quantum* of Damages table. We must stress that we are entirely dependent on the contributor of an unreported case for the accuracy of his or her report; it is impracticable for us independently to check the facts stated to us. We welcome contributions and are most grateful for all the reports received. We would appreciate reports of any alterations to awards noted here, either in, or in anticipation of, appeal.

Jaw–psychiatric damage

6024.   M, male, a prisoner raised an action of damages against the Lord Advocate representing the Scottish Prison Service, in respect of injuries sustained when he was assaulted by another prisoner. Conflicting evidence was lead as to the identity of the alleged assailant, R. M claimed that the prisoner officer in charge of the hall in which he was detained failed to have regard to his safety in the face of threats issued by R. M had been attacked from behind when washing his face in a basin. He suffered a fractured jaw and a laceration to his left temple, both injuries leaving permanent scars. The jaw injury required two operations for the insertion of a metal plate. M lost sensation in his lower lip and chin resulting in an inclination to drool, bite the inside of his lip and discomfort when kissing, eating, brushing his teeth and shaving. M also claimed his mood was adversely affected.

Held, granting absolvitor, that (1) there was no evidence to establish that R was the assailant or that special steps should have been taken to observe R and M, and (2) solatium would have been awarded at £14,000, 75 per cent attributable to the past.

  McKEOWN v. LORD ADVOCATE 2002 S.L.T. 269 (Note), Lady Paton, OH.

Neck–back

6025.   L, female, a management consultant, aged 32 at the time of the accident, sought damages from R, the driver of a vehicle which had struck a parked car in which she had been sitting. L had sustained a cervical and lumbar sprain involving considerable neck pain which spread to her lower back and left leg for which she attended a physiotherapist. The sprain resolved itself within a year without further risk of deterioration but the pursuer continued to suffer twinges of leg pain from time to time which had been expected to resolve itself by proof, but had not fully done so. She was deterred from fully resuming her sporting activities and was forced to take a 15 minute break when driving for extended periods, which her job required. Solatium of £5,000 was appropriate, 90 per cent to the past.

  LEWIS v. RICHARDSON 2002 S.L.T. 272, Lord Reed, OH.

Back

6026.   [Administration of Justice Act 1982 (c.53) s.8.]

C, male, a mechanic, aged 46, suffered injury as a result of a road accident and could no longer work as a motor mechanic. C was in partnership with his brother in a garage. There was no formal partnership agreement and the profits were split 40/60 in favour of C's brother. After the accident C, by arrangement, received no profits but received similar sums in the form of a loan to be repaid out of damages from the present action. The sheriff awarded sums for past loss of earnings, solatium and necessary services, but not for future loss of earnings. C appealed for future earnings and Campbell cross appealed in relation to past earnings. The Inner House allowed the appeal and refused the cross appeal. Solatium: £15,000. Award under Administration of Justice Act 1982 s. 8 £500. Past loss of earnings: £54,101. Future loss of earnings: £74,970 plus interest at 8 per cent. Opinion of the Court per Lord Cullen LP.

  CUSICK v. CAMPBELL 2002 S.C.L.R. 581, Lord Cullen L.P., Lord MacLean, Lady Paton, 1 Div.

Leg

6027. K, aged 31 at proof, raised a successful action of damages against F, a local authority, in respect of a ruptured Achilles tendon sustained when he fell on a wet floor in F's premises. K, initially in plaster, was absent from work for 10 weeks, with intermittent absences thereafter, and had gradually to build up the range of duties (which involved climbing ladders) that he had previously carried out. He suffered continuing pain, loss of bulk in the calf muscle and slight loss of dorsiflexion in the left ankle. He would not be able to return to football, his primary recreation, and his enjoyment of other sporting interests was reduced. (1) solatium was properly valued at £10,000, two thirds to the past; (2) potential difficulty in the labour market were K to lose his job was properly valued at £5,000; (3) additional expenditure was properly valued at £180, and (4) that loss of K's domestic services together with personal and domestic services provided by his wife and driving by his brother were properly valued at £2,500.

KIRK v. FIFE COUNCIL 2002 S.L.T. 21 (Note), Lord Bonomy, OH.

Respiratory organs and chest–asbestos related injury and disease

6028. M, a former shipyard engineer, aged 61 at proof, sought damages for personal injuries from B, his former employers, in respect of his exposure to asbestos dust. M had pleural plaques, pleural thickening and asbestosis and he no longer led a normal life. He ran the risk of developing mesothelioma or cancer, about which he lived in constant fear, and was convinced he would die before the age of 65. The Lord Ordinary found that the pursuer suffered from a 50 per cent disability, half of which was attributable to asbestos related conditions. Granting decree, that solatium of £35,000 was appropriate, one half to the past.

McKENZIE v. BARCLAY CURLE LTD 2002 S.L.T. 649, Lady Paton, OH.

Minor injuries–back

6029. H, male, aged 45 at the date of the accident, sought damages from W, the driver of a vehicle which had collided with the back of his vehicle. H sustained injuries in his lower back and knees for which he attended his GP. He experienced some pain for which he was prescribed painkillers and anti inflammatory drugs but he continued to work. The Lord Ordinary found that the accident aggravated a pre existing condition of H's lower back, the effects of which did not exceed 12 months, and accelerated the onset of degenerative symptoms in his knees by some two to three years, which symptoms caused intermittent stiffness and discomfort. Granting decree, that solatium of £3,500 was appropriate, with interest at the rate of four per cent per annum from the date of the accident.

HAWKES v. WYNN 2002 S.L.T. 1227, Lord MacFadyen, OH.

Minor injuries–hand

6030. [Administration of Justice Act 1982 (c.53) s.9.]

M, a skilled shuttering joiner, had his left hand crushed in a sling which was lifting a concrete block. As a result of the accident M required nine surgical operations. Following the surgeries, the fingers would not straighten, form a fist or pinch properly. M could no longer work as a joiner nor perform any work that required a firm left hand grip. M had an extensive history of steady employment and was able to engage others as part of a squad. M was intending to work until he was 65. M also suffered from depression as a result of the injury and lengthy litigation and took medication. M expressed a desire to seek work as a software technician, but would require retraining and given the competitive nature of the field might need to retrain for clerical work. Solatium: £2,500. Past wage loss: £5,000. Future loss of earnings: £80,000. Award under Administration of Justice Act 1982 s.9 £4,000 inclusive of interest.

MURRAY v. WELDEX INTERNATIONAL OFFSHORE LTD 2002 S.C.L.R. 591, Lord Eassie, OH.

PLANNING

6031. Compulsory purchase–certificate of appropriate alternative development–planning authority justified in issuing certificate

G's land was deemed to be compulsorily purchased by S in September 1996. At that time the Secretary of State was also dealing with two other applications. G sought a certificate of appropriate alternative development in December 1997, S did not determine the application within the statutory timescale and it was deemed refused. G appealed to the Secretary of State, a reporter was appointed and a public enquiry held. The appeal was allowed in May 2000, the deemed certificate cancelled and a certificate issued that, as of 1996, planning permission would have been granted for certain classes of development, subject to conditional access. S appealed against the grant of the certificate arguing that (1) in considering the two other applications the reporter had erred in law in failing to apply the guidance given in *Fletcher Estates (Harlescott) Ltd v. Secretary of State for the Environment, Transport and the Regions* [2000] 2 A.C. 307, [2000] C.L.Y. 4427; (2) the certificate was erroneous in giving September 1996 as the date since there would have been a planning enquiry and permission would not have been granted until 1997; (3) the Scottish Ministers had erred in law in failing to have proper regard for the local development plan in that the reporter made no mention of the local plan; (4) the reporter had been wrong to grant a certificate subject to a condition in terms of *Grampian Regional Council v. City of Aberdeen DC* 1984 S.C. (H.L.) 58, [1984] C.L.Y. 4734 since, in practice, the local planning authority would have sent a letter indicating an intention to grant planning permission provided agreement was reached on access, and (5) the Scottish Ministers had erred in concluding that a solution to the access problem would present itself.

Held, refusing the appeal, that (1) the planning authority were bound only to assume that the acquisition scheme and underlying proposal were cancelled on the relevant date, not that they did not exist prior to that date, accordingly the two sites were part of the planning landscape which the reporter was bound to consider; (2) a certificate should be based on the planning authority's best estimate of what would have happened. S could not, after accepting the date at the inquiry, insist that 1997 was the planning date to be taken into consideration; (3) it was clear the reporter had considered the local plan but had found it of negligible importance; (4) the reporter was entitled to find that the matter of access would have been dealt with by means of a Grampian condition, and (5) the reporter was justified in concluding on the basis of the evidence and his expertise that no difficulty would have remained if a suspensive condition was acceptable and it was open to the Scottish Ministers to issue a conditional certificate, applying *Fletcher.*

Observed that in relation to certificates of alternative development, (1) the planning authority are to give their opinion as to whether or not planning permission, having been duly sought, would have been granted at the relevant date, and, if so, for which kind of development, and (2) the certificate might specify a date, which might be a different or later date than that specified in the application, and such a flexible approach would advance the aim of the system to assist in determining the appropriate level of compensation for the acquisition of the interest in land. Opinion of the Court per Lord Rodger, Lord President.

SOUTH LANARKSHIRE COUNCIL v. LORD ADVOCATE 2002 S.C. 88, Lord Rodger L.P., Lady Cosgrove, Lord Prosser, 1 Div.

6032. Compulsory purchase–compensation–cemeteries–value of land as open space and disturbance caused by acquisition

Held, that compensation for the compulsory acquisition of two cemeteries in Edinburgh of 3.4184 and 3.7231 hectares respectively was assessed at £8,824 for the value of the land as open space and £2,803 for disturbance caused by the acquisition.

FRESHBRIGHT CEMETERIES LTD v. EDINBURGH CITY COUNCIL [2001] R.V.R. 285, Lord McGhie, AR MacLeary, LandsTr (Scot).

6033. Compulsory purchase–compensation–evidence of value–comparables

The Lands Tribunal was asked to value land compulsorily acquired in the A8 corridor near Edinburgh. The acquiring authority argued that given the absence of any specific planning proposals or permissions for the land and a restrictive planning policy there was no realistic planning case to support hope value in the land. The claimant argued that where there was market perception of future unspecified development, there was hope value which could be estimated on the basis of professional judgment and experience.

Held, that the land should be valued taking into account an allowance for hope value notwithstanding that currently established planning policies were against development.

YOUNG v. EDINBURGH CITY COUNCIL [2002] R.V.R. 36, Lord McGhie, LandsTr (Scot).

6034. Enforcement notices–change of use–proof of date of change

[Town and Country Planning (Scotland) Act 1997 (c.8) s.124(3).]

E appealed against the decision of R, a reporter appointed by the Secretary of State, to dismiss an appeal against the granting of an enforcement order. The council (C) had served the order on the ground that E had changed the use of land occupied by him from agricultural to storage and distribution of lime without planning permission. While E maintained that the site had been used for the storage and distribution of lime since 1984, R held that the scale and intensity of the activities had materially increased in recent years. E argued that (1) there was insufficient factual material available to R to support this finding: a mere increase in activity did not give rise to a material change of use; (2) R had failed to take into account an affidavit sworn by E's landlord (F) that E had carried on the business of storage since 1984 which put C's action outwith the 10 year period in the Town and Country Planning (Scotland) Act 1997 s.124(3), and (3) R's decision was *Wednesbury* unreasonable.

Held, refusing appeal, that (1) R had relied on a statement given by a neighbour who claimed that the level of lime in the area in 1988 was minimal and that it was only in the last two years that a commercial operation had been in place; (2) R was entitled to prefer that evidence to an affidavit by F, which did not describe the intensity of E's activities at the outset and which was not entitled to any special weight in proceedings before R by being an affidavit, and (3) C's notice was therefore timeous and the proposition that R's decision was unreasonable was untenable.

Observed, that the grounds of appeal did not deal with a possible discrepancy between the notice and the breach addressed by R (increase in quantities of lime stored and distributed and associated vehicle movements), but that the notice might be construed as implicitly referring to change of use of the latter nature.

EDWARD v. SCOTTISH MINISTERS 2001 S.C.L.R. 338, Lord Hamilton, OH.

6035. Enforcement notices–licensed premises–unauthorised material change of use–validity of reporter's decision

[Town and Country Planning (Use Classes) (Scotland) Order 1997 (SI 1997 3061) Sch.1.]

The proprietors of licensed premises appealed against an enforcement notice that alleged an unauthorised material change of use from a restaurant to a bar/club. The local authority granted planning permission in 1996 for use as a class 3 restaurant in terms of the Town and Country Planning (Use Classes) (Scotland) Order 1997 Sch.1 which permitted the sale of food or drink for consumption on the premises. The local authority had a policy L5 which disallowed the change in use of subjects in the midst of housing "to a public house or similar licensed premises". The reporter appointed to determine the appeal held that although a material change of use had occurred, policy L5 had already been breached when the authority allowed a change in use to a restaurant and, as such, no longer applied, and allowed the appeal. The local authority appealed to the Court of Session, arguing that this amounted to an error in law vitiating the reporter's decision. The proprietors argued that the court could only interfere if the reporter's interpretation of the policy was one which it could not possibly bear.

Held, allowing the appeal, that (1) it was the duty of a reporter to interpret a relevant policy but her decision was open to challenge if she failed to interpret it properly or failed to have regard to a relevant policy, and (2) the wording of policy L5 was not capable of referring to a change of use to a class 3 restaurant, and was not capable of bearing the reporter's interpretation that the restaurant fell into the category of "similar licensed premises", and the reporter had accordingly reached a decision that no reasonable reporter properly directed could have reached.

EDINBURGH CITY COUNCIL v. SCOTTISH MINISTERS 2001 S.C. 957, Lord Kirkwood, Lord Abernethy, Lord Rodger L.P., 1 Div.

6036. Enforcement notices–refusal of expenses of abortive appeal–human rights

[Town and Country Planning (Scotland) Act 1997 (c.8) s.265(9), s.265(10); European Convention on Human Rights 1950 Art.6, Art.8; European Convention on Human Rights 1950, First Protocol to the Convention Art.1.]

C, the owner of a listed dwellinghouse, sought judicial review of a decision of S refusing to give an undertaking to meet C's expenses relating to an enforcement notice and subsequent public local inquiry surrounding C's removal of certain stained glass panels. The reporter in that inquiry had failed to address correctly the tests necessary to determine whether the panels were heritable fixtures and C's appeal required to be redetermined. C argued that (1) he would be unfairly burdened by the additional expense required by the redetermination; (2) on an ordinary construction of the Town and Country Planning (Scotland) Act 1997 s.265(9) and s.265(10) S were not excluded from paying C's expenses where "parties" in s.265(9) could be held to include S, and (3) S's decision breached C's rights under the European Convention on Human Rights 1950 Art.6 and Art.8 and the First Protocol Art.1 where C's appeal constituted a determination of his civil rights, and any decision on expenses was an integral part of that determination.

Held, dismissing the petition, that (1) the expenses claimed by C could not be dissociated from the general expenses of C's appeal: expenses would follow success, including any additional expense incurred as a result of an erroneous determination; (2) C's submissions on s.265(9) were ill founded: s.265 as a whole distinguished between the position of S as responsible for determining the appeal and that of the parties interested in the outcome, and (3) A claim for expenses incurred as a result of an appeal against an enforcement notice ordinarily constituted part of that appeal's determination and (contrary to S's submission) liability for expenses incurred as a result of an appeal was relevant to the question whether someone's civil rights were infringed by the notice. However in the circumstances averred, S's decision did not breach C's Convention rights: C's claim for expenses was not part of the issue to be determined in the appeal; there was no precedent or principle for a party making such a claim against S because they were the persons responsible for arranging the inquiry and determining the appeal; the European Court regarded liability for expenses as a matter exclusively for domestic law and C's claim had to be dealt with by reference to s.265(9), not any Article of the Convention.

CANNELL v. SCOTTISH MINISTERS 2002 S.L.T. 634, Lord Morison, OH.

6037. Listed buildings–consent–validity of conditions affecting visibility of alterations

E, a local planning authority, appealed against the decision of R, a reporter appointed by S, the Scottish Ministers, determining an appeal to S against a listed building enforcement notice in relation to the partitioning of a principal room in property comprising part of a B listed building to form an en suite bathroom. R held that the structure should receive listed building consent subject to a condition that "the partition walls shall be removed and the room restored to its original proportions within one month of whichever of these matters first occurs (1) the permanent cessation of the use of the room as a bedroom; (2) the removal of the net curtains from the windows [facing the street]; (3) the removal of the privet hedge at the heel of the footpath". S argued that R had not erred where the structure was removable and, due to the net curtains and privet hedge, not visible from the street. The second and third subheads of the condition related to visibility and the first subhead reflected the fact that the en suite bathroom was installed because of the intention to use the room as a bedroom. All aspects of the condition were enforceable and readily ascertainable.

Held, quashing the decision, that (1) the first subhead of the condition was flawed as there was no planning control on the use to which a householder or the owner of a guest house might put individual rooms, this was not relevant to the question whether consent should be given for the alterations and it would be difficult to know whether the use of a room within domestic premises as a bedroom had ceased permanently; (2) the second subhead was unsatisfactory as planning conditions and listed building consents ran with the land, and even assuming, in principle, that an internal alteration to a principal room within a listed building which adversely affected the character of the building might receive consent if the windows were screened to prevent view from the outside, the terms of this subhead did not admit of any alternatives like venetian blinds; (3) the third subhead was irrelevant to whether the character of the building had been adversely affected, and the extent of any such effect, and the existence and height of the hedge was not something which was subject to planning control, and (4) R had erred in that while purporting to decide whether listed building consent for the works in issue should be granted, he appeared to address the different question of whether, the works having been erected without a prior grant of listed building consent, it was reasonable that they should now be removed.

EDINBURGH CITY COUNCIL v. SCOTTISH MINISTERS; *sub nom.* CITY OF EDINBURGH v. SCOTTISH MINISTERS 2002 S.L.T. 1243, Lord Eassie, OH.

6038. Planning permission–applications and deemed applications–fees

TOWN AND COUNTRY PLANNING (FEES FOR APPLICATIONS AND DEEMED APPLICATIONS) (SCOTLAND) AMENDMENT REGULATIONS 2002, SSI 2002 122; made under the Town and Country Planning (Scotland) Act 1997 s.252. In force: April 1, 2002; £2.00.

These Regulations amend the Town and Country Planning (Fees for Applications and Deemed Applications) (Scotland) Regulations 1997 (SI 1997 10) which make provision for the payment of fees to planning authorities in respect of applications made under the Town and Country Planning (Scotland) Act 1997 for planning permission for development or for approval of matters reserved by an outline planning permission and in respect of applications for consent for the display of advertisements; applications for planning permission which are deemed to have been made in connection with an appeal against an enforcement notice; and applications for certificates of lawful use or development. The effect of these

Regulations is that all fees are increased by approximately 5 per cent from April 1, 2002.

6039. Planning permission–departure from development plan–no independent assessment of scheme required

[Urban Wastewater Treatment (Scotland) Regulations 1994 (SI 1994 2842); European Convention on Human Rights 1950 Art.6.]

S, owners of an inn at a development site, sought the annulment of conditional planning permission granted by C, a local authority, to I, a water company, for the construction of a waste water pumping station. S argued (1) that the application for planning permission should have been referred to the Scottish Ministers (M) under the Town and Country Planning (Notification of Applications) (Scotland) Direction 1997 because it constituted a significant departure from the approved structure plan. It had not been shown that the development was necessary and that no suitable alternative location existed. I's representations on those matters could not be relied on by C and assurances from an independent adviser following an independent inquiry were required, and (b) under the 1997 Direction, any application involving development on land wholly or partly owned by the planning authority, which was the case here, where there had been a substantial body of objections, had to be referred to S. A "substantial body" meant anything other than de minimis. C had to act as an independent and impartial tribunal in terms of the European Convention on Human Rights Art.6, and (2) although X, a councillor, had declared an interest and moved from the chair of the meeting of C's committee in discussing the development, it could be inferred from the circumstances that X continued to participate contrary to the requirements of natural justice. C and I argued that (1) S had no interest to insist in the petition, and (2) in the event of the court finding in favour of S it should exercise its discretion to refuse relief because, unless the development was carried out by the end of 2000, I would be in breach of the Urban Wastewater Treatment (Scotland) Regulations 1994.

Held, dismissing the petition dismissed as irrelevant, that (1) (a) the issues raised under the 1997 Direction had been dealt with expressly by C. S's contention that an independent report was required was little short of nonsense and while C might not have been entitled to accept a bare assertion by I, the extent to which their representations were treated as credible and reliable was a matter for C. It was clear that C had applied their minds to the necessity for the development and alternative locations; (b) S's argument based on Art.6 was without foundation. Assuming Art.6 applied to C, it was unclear how the 1997 Direction and the presence or absence of statutory objections could be related to Art.6 obligations and there was no guarantee that a notified application would be called in by S, and (c) the 1997 Direction lacked the clear direction justifying the purposive construction contended for by S, and C had not been unreasonable in viewing S's objection as not constituting a "substantial body", and (2) there was nothing in the circumstances advanced by S to infer actual or perceived bias in the conduct of the committee. The code was not legally binding. That X was also chairman of I, at best could only have lent colour to other suspicious conduct on his part, of which there was none. It appeared that X had withdrawn from the discussion. There was nothing to suggest that a vote by general assent was a circumstance from which it could be inferred that a councillor having declared an interest and removed himself from the immediate environs of a meeting could be deemed to have continued to take part in its deliberations. *Opinion*, that (1) S had an interest in ensuring that a sizeable number of objections were properly considered by C, and (2) the consideration advanced by I would have been insufficient justification for the exercise of the court's discretion.

SAMUEL SMITH OLD BREWERY (TADCASTER) v. EDINBURGH CITY COUNCIL (NO.2) 2001 S.L.T. 977, Lord Marnoch, OH.

6040. Planning permission-refusal-appeals-sist-pending appeal against draft local plan

B, a development company sought judicial review of a decision by a reporter, R, to refuse B's motion to sist their appeal against a deemed refusal of their application for outline planning consent for a housing development, pending determination of an appeal against the draft local plan which affected the application subjects. The inquiry was adjourned from March 29 to May 15 2001 to allow B to lodge additional material, during which time correspondence took place between B, the authority, the inquiry reporters' unit and S. On April 3, 2001 an appeal was taken to the Court of Session against the terms of the relevant local plan. When the inquiry resumed B's motion to sist the appeal was refused. B argued that (1) in a letter dated May 10, 2001, R had recognised the development plan as central to his decision, and the need to sist proceedings pending the outcome of the local plan appeal, and it was illogical for him subsequently to take a different view; (2) a proper interpretation of the structure plan housing policies was central to the proceedings before R, and as that issue also arose in the local plan appeal he had deprived himself of the Court of Session's interpretation of policy and ignored a relevant and material consideration, and (3) although R cited general public expectation that planning appeals would be duly processed, he had not identified a particular public interest in the present case.

Held, refusing the petition, that (1) the letter of May 10 should not be read as indicating that R had already formed a clear view other than that if an application were made for a sist it should be done before the inquiry closed, and even if R had reached a preliminary view on the desirability of a sist it was open to him to take a different view on hearing the parties; (2) the local plan appeal would not result in the grant or refusal of consent in relation to B's site, and R was not bound to sist the inquiry to await the outcome of the appeal, and (3) R was entitled to take account of the public interest in the efficacious administration of the planning system, and B had not considered final settlement of the new local plan a necessary precondition for their application or their appeal.

BLUE CIRCLE INDUSTRIES PLC v. SCOTTISH MINISTERS 2002 S.L.T. 894, Lord Eassie, OH.

6041. Structure and local plans-proposed structure plans-examination in public-reasonableness of refusal

[Town and Country Planning (Scotland) Act 1997 (c.8) s.10(4)(b).]

S, a company representing the interests of Scottish housebuilders raised a petition for judicial review, seeking declarator that a decision of the Scottish Ministers, M, not to cause an examination in public to be held into certain matters in connection with a proposed structure plan was ultra vires, and reduction of that decision. Following a consultation process in which S's views had not been accepted, they submitted an objection to M on outstanding issues and formally requested an EIP. M concluded that the information before them was sufficient and that an EIP was not required. S argued inter alia that where no reasons had been given the reasonableness of the decision could be judged by reference to the terms of para.4 of the relevant code of practice which set out seven factors which might need to be examined in public, six of which arose in the present case, that M had acted irrationally, and therefore ultra vires, given that an EIP was the procedure provided by statute for resolving matters of substantial unresolved controversy, such as were constituted by S's objection, that M had improperly fettered their discretion under the Town and Country Planning (Scotland) Act 1997 s.10(4)(b) where no EIP had been held in Scotland for almost 20 years whereas they were regularly held in England and Wales and M had adopted a policy of not holding them because they interfered with an administrative target timetable for approval of structure plans, and that the involvement of the Housing Statistics Division of the Scottish Executive Development Department in approving the methodology for calculating housing demand was an illegitimate delegation of M's decision making function to civil servants.

Held, refusing the petition, that (1) s.10(4)(b) conferred a discretion on M whether to cause an EIP to be held, but set out no objective criteria to be applied in making the judgment required, and while this did not exclude judicial review, it made it more difficult to make out a case of unreasonableness; (2) it could be inferred from s.10 that an EIP was intended as a means of obtaining further material to support a decision M had to make, and that it was open to them to hold an EIP not only where they thought it necessary or desirable for that purpose, but also where they thought it in the public interest and/or likely to be of assistance to them in making their decision that matters should be aired in public; (3) the factors mentioned in para.4 were truly a list of examples of reasons for holding an EIP, not a set of considerations the presence of a sufficient number of which would make a failure to order one unreasonable, and it was not a proper inference that in the absence of reasons for deciding not to hold an EIP, M must have considered that none of the para.4 factors were present; (4) the existence of issues involving substantial unresolved controversy was only a factor which might make it appropriate to hold an EIP, and neither that nor the other matters founded on made M's decision unreasonable, having regard to the material available to them; (5) M were entitled to rely on the advice and expertise of civil servants, and it was not evident that they had delegated part of the substantive decision they had to take to civil servants *Bushell v. Secretary of State for the Environment* [1981] A.C. 75, [1980] C.L.Y. 1337 applied, and (6) the fact that no EIPs had been held for a considerable time did not itself justify the inference that M had not been operating their discretion properly, and it had not been established that they had improperly fettered their discretion.

SHBA LTD v. SCOTTISH MINISTERS; *sub nom.* SCOTTISH HOUSEBUILDERS ASSOCIATION LTD v. SCOTTISH MINISTERS 2002 S.L.T. 1321, Lord Macfadyen, OH.

6042. Books

Collar, Neil–Planning and Human Rights. Paperback: £39.00. ISBN 0-414-01432-4. W.Green & Son.

Rowan-Robinson, Jeremy–Planning Law and Procedure. Scottish Universities Law Institute. Hardback: £165.00. ISBN 0-414-01430-8. W.Green & Son.

POLICE

6043. Elections–police service–appointment and removal of board members–convenor

COMBINED POLICE AREA AMALGAMATION SCHEMES 1995 AMENDMENT (NO.2) (SCOTLAND) ORDER 2002, SSI 2002 458; made under the Police (Scotland) Act 1967 s.20, s.21. In force: November 8, 2002; £2.50.

This Order, which makes the six Combined Police Area Amalgamation Amendment (No.2) Schemes 2002, amends provisions of the Central Scotland Combined Police Area Amalgamation Scheme 1995 (SI 1995 2638), the Grampian Combined Police Area Amalgamation Scheme Order 1995 (SI 1995 2639), the Lothian and Borders Combined Police Area Amalgamation Scheme Order 1995 (SI 1995 2640), the Northern Combined Police Area Amalgamation Scheme Order 1995 (SI 1995 2641), the Strathclyde Combined Police Area Amalgamation Scheme Order 1995 (SI 1995 2642) and the Tayside Combined Police Area Amalgamation Scheme Order 1995 (SI 1995 2643). The 1995 Schemes are amended in order that the appointment of the convenor may be terminated by the relevant joint police board. At present, the appointment of the convenor will terminate only at the expiry of the three year period of office unless the convenor ceases to be a member of the board. These amendments brings the position into line with that of Combined Fire Services Area Administration Schemes where such a power to remove the convenor exists.

6044. Elections–police service–appointment of board members

COMBINED POLICE AREA AMALGAMATION SCHEMES 1995 (AMENDMENT) (SCOTLAND) ORDER 2002, SSI 2002 140; made under the Police (Scotland) Act 1967 s.20, s.21. In force: March 31, 2002; £2.50.

This Order, which makes the six Combined Police Area Amalgamation (Amendment) Schemes 2002, amends the provisions of the Central Scotland Combined Police Area Amalgamation Scheme 1995 (SI 1995 2638), the Grampian Combined Police Area Amalgamation Scheme 1995 (SI 1995 2639), the Lothian and Borders Combined Police Area Amalgamation Scheme 1995 (SI 1995 2640), the Northern Combined Police Area Amalgamation Scheme 1995 (SI 1995 2641), the Strathclyde Combined Police Area Amalgamation Scheme 1995 (SI 1995 2642) and the Tayside Combined Police Area Amalgamation Scheme 1995 (SI 1995 2643). The 1995 Schemes are amended in order that the appointment of members of the board and of the convener and vice-convener occur in line with the ordinary elections of councillors irrespective of the frequency of those elections. This reflects changes made to the timing of local government elections made by the Scottish Local Government (Elections) Act 2002.

6045. Grants–police authorities and joint police boards

POLICE GRANT (SCOTLAND) ORDER 2002, SSI 2002 116; made under the Police (Scotland) Act 1967 s.32. In force: April 1, 2002; £1.75.

This Order is made under the Police (Scotland) Act 1967 which makes provision for the Scottish Ministers to make grants out of money from the Scottish Consolidated Fund for police purposes to police authorities and joint police boards. This Order determines the aggregate amount of grants to be made to all police authorities and joint police boards for the financial year 2002-2003 and the amount of such grants to be made to each police authority or joint police board. It also sets out how and when the grant is payable.

6046. Police Act 1997 (c.50)–Commencement No.10 Order

POLICE ACT 1997 (COMMENCEMENT NO.10) (SCOTLAND) ORDER 2002, SSI 2002 124; made under the Police Act 1997 s.135. Commencement details: bringing into force various provisions of the 1997 Act on March 11, 2002, April 25, 2002 and July 31, 2002; £1.75.

This Order brings into force specified provisions of the Police Act 1997.

6047. Police officers–disciplinary procedures–delay–investigation–ultra vires

[Police (Conduct) (Scotland) Regulations 1996 (SI 1996 1642) Reg.6, Reg.7.]

M, a police inspector, sought judicial review of decisions made by W, an assistant chief constable, in the course of disciplinary proceedings against him. A debate was heard on M's preliminary plea that W had acted outwith his powers under the Police (Conduct) (Scotland) Regulations 1996 in delaying an investigation into disciplinary allegations against him pending investigation into separate allegations which could have produced criminal charges. M argued that delay, under Reg.7, was only specifically provided for in a case where the same allegations might form the basis of criminal proceedings and Reg.6 excluded any interpretation that might imply a general power to delay proceedings. W, who had acted on advice from the procurator fiscal due to concern at the effect of any publicity on the criminal proceedings, argued inter alia that even if there had been a delay prohibited by the regulations he had a responsibility to complete the investigation into the complainers' allegations.

Held, repelling the preliminary plea, that on a proper construction of Reg.6, W was not excluded from delaying the investigation: there was no time limit qualifying his duty to decide whether to require M to appear before a disciplinary hearing under Reg.6(2) and a misconduct hearing would require to consider any prejudicial effect of the delay established by M in its duty to act fairly and reasonably.

McADAM v. WOOD 2002 S.L.T. 23, Lord Wheatley, OH.

6048. **Police officers–injury pensions–refusal–appropriate respondent on appeal**

See ADMINISTRATIVE LAW: Thomson v. Chief Constable of Grampian Police (Medical Certificates). §5245

6049. **Police powers–animals–lost or abandoned property–dogs–notice given to owner of disposal**

[Civic Government (Scotland) Act 1982 (c.45) s.68, s.76.]

D, the owner of 35 German shepherd dogs sought interdict against a chief constable, C, from removing or disposing of the dogs from boarding kennels where C had been caring for them in terms of the Civic Government (Scotland) Act 1982, s.68. The dogs had been moved to the kennels from D's home following his arrest and remand for a psychiatric assessment. D had been released on bail on condition that he did not return home; he now lived in a caravan at the kennels and assisted in caring for the dogs. C had given notice under s.68(3) of his intention to terminate the arrangements for the dogs' care and in the event that the dogs were not collected from the kennels, to dispose of them. Interim interdict was granted but subsequently recalled. D appealed, arguing that as the dogs were neither lost nor abandoned, the Act did not apply; and that the dogs were his property and their disposal would amount to a civil wrong.

Held, refusing the appeal, that (1) if the provisions of the Act were applicable, D had failed to avail himself of the remedy contained in s.76 of the Act and C was entitled to give notice under s.68(3), and (2) if the provisions of the Act were inapplicable, C had no responsibility for the care of the dogs and could not be considered to be committing any civil wrong, as he would be obliged to return the dogs to D who seemed to be unwilling or unable to take full responsibility for them.

DEBIDIN v. CHIEF CONSTABLE OF THE NORTHERN CONSTABULARY 2002 S.L.T. (Sh Ct) 125, JC McInnes Q.C., Sheriff Principal, Sh Ct.

6050. **Police Reform Act 2002 (c.30)–Commencement No.2 Order**

POLICE REFORM ACT 2002 (COMMENCEMENT NO.2) (SCOTLAND) ORDER 2002, SSI 2002 420; made under the Police Reform Act 2002 s.108. Commencement details: bringing into force various provisions of the 2002 Act on October 1, 2002; £1.50.

This Order brings into force specified provisions of the Police Reform Act 2002 which amend the Crime and Disorder Act 1998 in relation to when sex offender orders may be sought and granted in Scotland; makes it an offence for persons to do anything in Scotland which is an offence under a sex offender order or interim order made in England and Wales or Northern Ireland; and changes the liability of the chief constable from liability in reparation for wrongful acts or omissions of constables to liability for any unlawful conduct by them.

PRESCRIPTION

6051. **Negative–date from which time runs–reasonable awareness that loss had been suffered through negligence**

[Prescription and Limitation (Scotland) Act 1973 (c.52) s.6(4)(a)(ii), s.11(3).]

G raised an action of damages in October 1999 alleging professional negligence by a firm of solicitors, P, in relation to a settlement negotiated by a partner of the firm,

X, in a property dispute in 1992, and G's sequestration in February 1993. Following a preliminary proof on P's plea of prescription the sheriff held that (1) in terms of the Prescription and Limitation (Scotland) Act 1973, s.11 (3) G could not with reasonable diligence have become aware that they had suffered loss caused by negligence until April 1995 when P handed over their files to G's new agents, and (2) having regard to G's intellectual deficiencies, their lack of English and their awe of X as a solicitor, taken with his repeated assurances that all would be well, G had been induced to refrain from making a relevant claim in terms of s.6(4)(a)(ii) of the Act. P appealed.

Held, refusing the appeal, that (1) in light of *Glasper v. Rodger* 1996 S.L.T. 44, [1996] C.L.Y. 6667, the sheriff had applied the correct test under s.11 (3), and (2) the sheriff was entitled to find that G were entitled to rely on s.6(4)(a)(ii).

GHANI v. PETER T McCANN & CO 2002 S.L.T. (Sh Ct) 135, EF Bowen Q.C., Sheriff Principal, Sh Ct.

6052. Negative—interruption—insurance claims—interim payments

[Prescription and Limitation (Scotland) Act 1973 (c.52) s.10(1)(a).]

W, a policyholder, raised an action to enforce a claim from D, his insurance company, for the value of heritable property and its contents destroyed in a fire on December 6, 1992. The action was raised on May 22, 1998. D pled that the claim had prescribed. A preliminary proof on prescription was allowed, at which W founded on evidence of payments made by D while the claim was investigated, in response to his claim that he was homeless and required alternative accommodation, while their inquiries were continuing. In April 1993 they provided a caravan and by letter dated May 7, they confirmed that they were "prepared to meet alternative accommodation costs" in view of difficulties connecting services to the caravan. On May 27, they advised that payment would cease from May 28, having avoided the policy from inception due to alleged misstatements on the proposal form. W argued that the making of the interim payments, against the background of the communings between the parties, constituted a "relevant acknowledgment" within the Prescription and Limitation (Scotland) Act 1973 s.10(1)(a). D argued that whereas W was seeking to enforce separate obligations to indemnify in relation to the heritable property and contents, the only obligation which it could possibly be said was performed on or after May 22, 1993 was the different obligation to provide alternative accommodation and that the payments made had been ex gratia without admission of liability pending inquiries.

Held, repelling the plea of prescription, that (1) the fundamental issue in the case was whether D had any liability to pay under the policy at all, and there was no reason to distinguish the various aspects of the obligation to indemnify, in any event the obligation to provide alternative accommodation was ancillary, and (2) the payments made indicated to W, and judged objectively would have indicated to anyone in his position, that D had accepted a present liability under the policy even under reservation of the right to repudiate liability later, and constituted such performance by them towards implement of their obligation as clearly to indicate that it subsisted.

WILKIE v. DIRECT LINE INSURANCE PLC (NO.2) 2002 S.L.T. 530, Lord Kingarth, OH.

6053. Negative—long—date from which time runs—personal injury—psychiatric illness—separate cause of action

[Prescription and Limitation (Scotland) Act 1973 (c.52) s.7, s.11 (4).]

K, a former pupil, averred that he had been sexually abused by G, his form teacher, between 1955 and 1961. He sought damages from E, G's executrix, and L, the local education authority, in respect of psychiatric injuries sustained as a result. In response to a plea of prescription K argued that (1) the necessary concurrence of damnum and iniuria had not occurred until 1995 when he developed a psychiatric illness, which could properly be regarded as distinct from any physical injuries suffered and the action therefore was not time barred; (2) if the long negative prescription began to run at December 31, 1961, the plea of non valens agere cum effectu preserved his right to sue, as he could not competently have raised an action prior to 1995 to recover damages for a condition which had not yet developed, and (3) that as the court had a duty to interpret legislation compatibly with the European Convention, it should construe the Prescription and Limitation (Scotland) Act 1973 s.11 (4) as if the words disapplying subs (3) did not exist.

Held, assoilzing E and L, that (1) K had suffered some sort of loss, injury and damage within the meaning of Prescription and Limitation (Scotland) Act 1973 s.7 as soon as the sexual assaults occurred, which was sufficient to trigger the running of the long negative prescription and any obligation on the defenders' part to make reparation had been extinguished by December 31, 1981; (2) it was incorrect to characterise an inability to sue for a condition which did not yet exist as an obstacle in law such as to support the plea non valens agere cum effectu, and (3) s.7 and s.11 (4) were clear and unambiguous and it was impossible for the court to interpret the latter in the way argued for by K.

K v. GILMARTIN'S EXECUTRIX 2002 S.L.T. 801, Lady Paton, OH.

6054. Negative–long–date from which time runs–resumption of grazings

[Crofting (Scotland) Act1976 (c.21); Prescription and Limitation (Scotland) Act 1973 (c.52) s.7.]

N, a crofter, held as a pertinent to his croft, a one third share in grazings. In 1976, the local authority offered to purchase the grazings from the landlords in order to lease them to BP for a temporary village at the Sullom Voe oil terminal. A condition of the offer was that the landlords would apply for a resumption of the land and that the crofters would grant discharges upon payment of compensation for their loss of grazing rights. The agreement reached stipulated that if BP ever relinquished their lease, the local authority would re-establish the land as grazings, return it to the ownership of the landlords, and reinstate the crofters grazing rights. Both the landlords and the crofters believed that the resumption was temporary. The Land Court authorised resumption by order dated March 16, 1978, and compensation was agreed at £2,500. In 1984, BP relinquished the lease of the land and the council duly re-established it as grazings and returned it to the landlords. In 1985, N recommenced his use of the land as grazings. In 1992 a landlord raised an action for removal of N from the land. The action was sisted to allow N to apply to the Land Court for enforcement of the conditions of the 1978 order entitling him to resume use of the land as grazings following its return to the landlords' possession. The Land Court ruled that the conditions had been ultra vires as resumption of the land had the effect that the land was no longer subject to the Crofting (Scotland) Act 1976 and it had not been open to the court to impose conditions which effectively extended their jurisdiction over the land beyond the date of the order. N raised an action for damages in negligence against his solicitors, T. T pled that the claim had prescribed in terms of the Prescription and Limitation (Scotland) Act 1973 s.7.

Held, allowing time for the pursuer to lodge a minute of amendment specifying the date of implementation and appointing the case to the By Order roll, that the loss alleged by N was sustained on the date on which the resumption order took effect, which was the date that it was implemented by the landlords rather than the date that it was pronounced by the court.

NICOLSON v. TAIT & PETERSON 2001 S.C.L.R. 766, Lord Gill, OH.

6055. Negative–short–date from which time runs–construction contracts– interim certificates–enforceability–time running upon issue of final certificate

S and M concluded a contract for demolition and construction in May 1988. Disagreements arose and M made a claim on S. M and S appointed an arbiter and it was agreed that in matters relating to prescription, the relevant period would be treated as short negative prescription. M sought five declarators and three craves for payment, essentially the review of interim certificate 29 to include loss/expense incurred by M. S argued that the right had prescribed and it went to arbitration. M argued that the right had not prescribed, the date of commencement of the arbitration being within five years. S argued that in terms of cl.6 M had a right to make a written application regarding the loss/expense but was obliged to do so as soon as it had become, or should reasonably have become apparent, in this situation the right had clearly prescribed. The arbiter found that the prescriptive period would begin to run only upon issue of a final certificate or at least upon issue of interim certificate 29 and, accordingly, M's claim had not prescribed.

Held, that in the whole circumstances, the rights founded upon by M had not prescribed. Notwithstanding the terminology of clause 26.1.1 it did not appear to the Court that a claimant who refrains from making an application could properly be regarded as having departed from his right to apply.

SCOTTISH EQUITABLE PLC v. MILLER CONSTRUCTION LTD 2002 S.C.L.R. 10, Lord Prosser, Lord Kingarth, Lord Milligan, Ex Div.

6056. Pleadings–amendments–restatement of law after expiry of prescriptive period

See CIVIL PROCEDURE: Gorrie v. Marist Brothers. §5360

6057. Positive–heritable property–creditors–interruption–subjects left vacant by heritable creditor

R, a bank, raised an action of damages for professional negligence against M, a firm of solicitors, in relation to an alleged failure to obtain a valid standard security over heritable subjects. It was averred that the disposition in favour of the debtor, C, in 1989 was granted by C as the last remaining partner in W, a firm, in favour of himself as an individual. In reality there were other partners in the firm in dispute with C. R argued in response to C's plea invoking the positive prescription, that any defects in the debtor's title had not been cured, the property not having been possessed openly, peaceably and as of right for the continuous 10 year period required, where in an action of removing by R, C was ordained in 1995 by sheriff court decree to remove from the property, which then remained unoccupied in R's possession until 1997 when they entered into possession.

Held, allowing proof before answer to both parties, that (1) the sheriff court action in 1995 did not amount to judicial interruption as R's action did not challenge C's interests as owner, and no third party had done so, and (2) M's averments were sufficient for a court to hold that C retained civil possession through R's natural possession for the remainder of the prescriptive period, which was sufficient for prescription to continue to run.

ROYAL BANK OF SCOTLAND PLC v. MacBETH CURRIE 2002 S.L.T. (Sh Ct) 128, JS Forbes, Sh Ct (Tayside, Central and Fife).

6058. Positive–heritable property–habile title–requirement of fair notice–right of property previously–extinguished under pre 1973 law–revival

[Prescription and Limitation (Scotland) Act 1973 (c.52) s.1 (1) (a), Sch.3 s.8 para.(h).]

R, as executors of M, sought reduction of a disposition of land at B in favour of S, granted by S's father and recorded in May 1988, and ejection of S from B. R averred that by disposition dated September 11 and 28, 1979, the executors of M's father (F) disponed to M subjects at B which included the disputed land and which were described in a disposition and a charter of novodamus registered in 1862, to which F had title through decrees of general service of 1902 and 1922, the latter in favour of F who died in 1973. R argued (1) that even if M had no real right prior to recording the disposition in October 1979, thereafter positive prescription had begun to run in M's favour under the Prescription and Limitation (Scotland) Act 1973, s.1 (1) (a); (2) that M and her ancestors had never lost the right to complete title to the subjects conveyed under the 1979 disposition, as prior to the coming into force of the 1973 Act the right of an uninfeft proprietor to complete title to heritable subjects was imprescriptible, and (3) that in any event the right had been revived by s.8 of and para. (h) of Sch.3 to the 1973 Act.

Held, dismissing the action, that (1) R having averred that when the 1979 disposition was recorded there was no defect in title that required to be cured by positive prescription, and having made no alternative case, had not given fair notice of a case based on positive prescription; (2) any right to complete title to the subjects disponed in 1862 had been extinguished by negative prescription long before the 1979 disposition was recorded, *Pettigrew v. Harton* 1956 S.C. 67, [1956] C.L.Y. 12456 followed, and (3) nothing in the 1973 Act supported the conclusion that Parliament had intended to restore rights that had previously been extinguished, and R had no right to found on the recording of the 1979 disposition as creating, by itself, a real right of ownership in M which could provide a basis for the reduction of the 1988 disposition.

MASON'S EXECUTORS v. SMITH; *sub nom.* REDFORD v. SMITH 2002 S.L.T. 1169, Lord Mackay of Drumadoon, OH.

RATES

6059. Council tax–care home services–exemptions

COUNCIL TAX (DWELLINGS AND PART RESIDENTIAL SUBJECTS) (SCOTLAND) AMENDMENT REGULATIONS 2002, SSI 2002 102; made under the Local Government Finance Act 1992 s.72, s.99, s.116. In force: April 1, 2002; £1.75.

These Regulations amend the Council Tax (Dwellings and Part Residential Subjects) (Scotland) Regulations 1992 (SI 1992 2955) in consequence of changes made to the Local Government Finance Act by the Regulation of Care (Scotland) Act 2001 which replaces hostels, nursing homes and residential care homes with care home services. These Regulations ensure that exemptions in relation to council tax apply to accommodation in relation to care home services as they formerly did to hostels, nursing homes and residential care homes.

6060. Council tax–exempt dwellings–dwellings awaiting demolition

COUNCIL TAX (EXEMPT DWELLINGS) (SCOTLAND) AMENDMENT ORDER 2002, SSI 2002 101; made under the Local Government Finance Act 1992 s.72. In force: April 1, 2002; £1.50.

This Order amends the Council Tax (Exempt Dwellings) (Scotland) Order 1997 (SI 1997 728), which lists those classes of dwelling which are exempt from the council tax in Scotland, to extend exemption from the council tax to dwellings awaiting demolition that are owned by a registered social landlord.

6061. Non domestic rates–rate for 2002/03

NON-DOMESTIC RATE (SCOTLAND) ORDER 2002, SSI 2002 89; made under the Local Government (Scotland) Act 1975 s.7B, s.37. In force: April 1, 2002; £1.50.

This Order prescribes a rate of £0.48 as the non-domestic rate to be levied throughout Scotland in respect of financial year 2002 to 2003.

6062. Non domestic rates–rate for 2002/03

NON-DOMESTIC RATES (LEVYING) (SCOTLAND) REGULATIONS 2002, SSI 2002 91; made under the Local Government etc. (Scotland) Act 1994 s.153. In force: April 1, 2002; £2.50.

These Regulations, which revoke the Non-Domestic Rates (Levying) (Scotland) Regulations 2001 (SSI 2001 71), make provision as to the amount payable in certain circumstances as non-domestic rates in respect of property in Scotland. They apply only to financial year 2002 to 2003.

6063. Non domestic rates–rateable value–electricity lands and generators–variation

ELECTRICITY LANDS AND GENERATORS (RATEABLE VALUES) (SCOTLAND) VARIATION ORDER 2002, SSI 2002 158; made under the Local Government (Scotland) Act 1975 s.6, s.35, s.37. In force: March 31, 2002; £2.00.

This Order amends the Local Government (Scotland) Act 1975, the Electricity Generators (Rateable Values) (Scotland) Order 2000 (SSI 2000 86) and the Electricity Lands (Rateable Values) (Scotland) Order 2000 (SSI 2000 88) following changes in the electricity industry consequential on the Utilities Act 2000. The variations take account of the fact that during the course of the financial year 2001-2002, Scottish Power UK Plc and Scottish and Southern Energy Plc were required to transfer their generation, distribution and transmission activities to successor companies. In the case of Scottish Power UK Plc the successor companies are Scottish Power Generation Ltd, SP Distribution Ltd, SP Power Systems Ltd and SP Transmission Ltd. In the case of Scottish and Southern Energy Plc the successor companies are SSE Generation Ltd, Scottish Hydro-Electric Power Distribution Ltd and Scottish Hydro-Electric Transmission Ltd.

6064. Non domestic rates–rateable value–water undertakings

WATER UNDERTAKINGS (RATEABLE VALUES) (SCOTLAND) VARIATION ORDER 2002, SSI 2002 159; made under the Local Government (Scotland) Act 1975 s.6, s.35, s.37. In force: March 31, 2002; £1.75.

This Order amends the Water Undertakings (Rateable Values) (Scotland) Order 2000 (SSI 2000 90) to correct an apportionment figure used when apportioning the aggregate amount of rateable values amongst the three water authorities and amongst the local authorities with effect from April 1, 2002.

6065. Non domestic rates–valuation–exemptions

VALUATION AND RATING (EXEMPTED CLASSES) (SCOTLAND) ORDER 2002, SSI 2002 262; made under the Valuation and Rating (Exempted Classes) (Scotland) Act 1976 s.1. In force: June 1, 2002; £1.75.

This Order provides for the exemption from rating of pipelines used for transporting petroleum to any licensed area or offshore installation, there to be used solely for the purposes of the underwater exploitation of petroleum resources.

REPARATION

6066. Fraudulent misrepresentation–fraud–loss sustained through limited company–recoverability of investment–remoteness

B, the purchasers under missives concerning licensed premises sought damages from S, the vendor, in respect of allegedly fraudulent misrepresentations concerning the accounts, which B averred had induced them into entering the missives. B were sole directors of a limited company which was to carry on the business. B averred that they were initially to lease the premises but on taking entry discovered the true position and the sale provisions were never implemented. They further averred that loans provided by them to the company to enable it to operate the business were irrecoverable. S sought dismissal, arguing (1) that the averments of loss were irrelevant as the trading losses had primarily been suffered by the company and any secondary loss reflected in the irrecoverability of B's investment was too remote, and (2) that the value of any losses was the difference in value between the sum paid and the true price.

Held, putting the case out by order prior to allowing proof before answer, that (1) the decision to invest money in the company could not be considered too remote to be recovered in damages in a case based on fraudulent misrepresentation, and (2) B had been induced by the misrepresentations to embark upon the commercial venture of the licensed premises to their financial detriment and on that basis, they were entitled to recover the financial loss to them which directly flowed from that course in spite of the normal basis for assessment of damages, *Doyle v. Olby (Ironmongers) Ltd* [1969] 2 Q.B. 158, [1969] C.L.Y. 1528 followed.

BARRY v. SUTHERLAND (DAMAGES) 2002 S.L.T. 413, Lord Eassie, OH.

6067.   Local authorities powers and duties–disposal of abandoned vehicles–proper service of notice

[Removal and Disposal of Vehicles Regulations 1986 (SI 1986 183) Reg.12, Reg.13; Refuse Disposal (Amenity) Act 1978 (c.3) s.3, s.4(1)(a).]

M suffered a stroke and was taken to hospital in November 1995 where he remained for 17 weeks. During that time, he left his van parked in a public car park near his home. The tax disc on the van had expired on January 31, 1995. On January 19, 1996, A sent M a notice in terms of the Refuse Disposal (Amenity) Act 1978 s.3, advising him to remove his van from the car park within seven days or it would be disposed of. On February 16, A affixed a notice to the van advising that the van would be removed and destroyed within seven days. On February 23, a girl seeing A's employees in the vicinity of the van, advised them that M was in hospital. The van was uplifted from the car park and destroyed along with its contents on February 27. M raised an action for damages against A in respect of the loss of his van and contents based on breach of A's statutory duty and common law. M argued that A had breached their statutory duty in terms of s.3 and the Removal and Disposal of Vehicles Regulations 1986 Reg.12 and Reg.13 as they had not taken measures to ensure that the notice was properly and effectively served on the owner of the van. He further argued that A was negligent in failing to take reasonable steps to ensure that the statutory notice served had been received by M. A argued that they were under no duty under statute or common law to take further measures in terms of notice other than following the procedures laid down by the 1978 Act or the 1986 Regulations.

Held, dismissing the action, that (1) there was no additional duty under common law which required A to go beyond the terms of the statutory provisions; (2) the required notice in terms of s.3 was for a notice to be affixed to the van, which had been done, and (3) as the licence on the van had already expired, the right to dispose of the vehicle arose from s.4(1)(a), making the procedures under Reg.12 and Reg.13 irrelevant.

Observed, that even if the court had found A to be in breach of a duty, M's pleadings were lacking in specification in respect of the items allegedly lost, that averments in relation to the contents of the van would have been excluded from proof.

MORRISON v. ABERDEEN CITY COUNCIL 2001 S.C.L.R. 1067, Sheriff KA McLernan, Sh Ct (Grampian, Highland and Islands).

6068.   Books

Cameron, Gordon–Delict Law Basics. Greens Law Basics. Paperback: £9.95. ISBN 0-414-01233-X. W. Green & Son.

SENTENCING

6069.   Assault–babies–excessive custodial sentence

D, aged 23, was the father of a small baby who had pleaded guilty to assaulting the child when she was between three and 10 weeks old. The child sustained subconjuctival haemorrhages, bruising and fractures of the ribs, tibia and humerus. D admitted gripping the child too tightly, gripping her face too tightly and dropping her from a height onto a cot. D was of previous good character and appeared to the paediatric surgeon bewildered and unprepared for parenthood and completely unaware of the needs of a child of that age. A consultant clinical psychologist opined that D presented a low risk as far as future violence or child abuse was concerned. D was sentenced to two years' imprisonment and appealed to the High Court

Held, allowing the appeal, quashing the sentence and substituting a probation order for two years and a 240 hour community service order, that the sentence was excessive. It was important to ensure that D had support in the areas of stress management and parenting skills.

M v. HM ADVOCATE (SENTENCING) 2002 S.C.C.R. 29, Lord Rodger L.J.G., Lord Abernethy, Lord Sutherland, HCJ Appeal.

6070. Assault–intent to rape–undue leniency

[Sex Offenders Act 1997 (c.51) s.5(2)(a), s.5(2)(b).]

S pleaded guilty to assaulting a woman late at night by pushing her to the ground, placing his hand over her mouth and placing a hand up her skirt and touching her underpants, with intent to rape. The sentencing sheriff made a probation order for a period of two years with a condition that S make compensation of £2,000, undertake 100 hours' unpaid work, and attend a sex offenders' programme. The Lord Advocate appealed against the sentence as unduly lenient, and also sought to rectify the failure on the date of S's conviction to make a statement under the Sex Offenders Act 1997 s.5(2)(a) or certification in terms of s.5(2)(b). S, a 45 year old first offender, argued, inter alia, that the charge had been restricted; that the complainer had only sustained minor injuries and had made a full recovery; and that he had already performed a substantial part of the previous disposal.

Held, allowing the appeal and substituting 18 months' imprisonment, that (1) aggravation of intent to rape was very serious, and the sentence imposed was unduly lenient as it failed properly to reflect the need to condemn and to discourage serious sexual attacks on vulnerable women, and (2) the certification sought by the Crown had to be done by the court by which the person was convicted and on the date of conviction, and it was not competent for the court to rectify the omission.

HM ADVOCATE v. STOPPER (THOMAS) (SENTENCING) 2002 S.L.T. 885, Lord Hamilton, Lord Kingarth, Lord Drummond Young, HCJ.

6071. Assault–severe injury–glassing–victim permanently disabled–undue leniency

The Lord Advocate appealed against three years' imprisonment for H who pleaded guilty to assaulting a man in a nightclub by repeatedly striking on the neck with a glass tumbler to his severe injury, permanent impairment, permanent disfigurement and to the danger of his life. The complainer suffered a stroke due to loss of blood. H, a first offender, had become depressed, his wife of 15 years left him and six months later, he saw the complainer in the company of his wife in a nightclub. The sentencing judge accepted that the offence was out of character.

Held, allowing the appeal and substituting six years' imprisonment, that bearing in mind all the mitigating factors, the assault was both vicious and unprovoked, resulting in catastrophic injuries to the victim, and the sentence was unduly lenient.

HM ADVOCATE v. HEGARTY (JOHN JAMES) 2002 S.L.T. 1383, Lord Gill L.J.C., Lord Kirkwood, Lord Osborne, HCJ.

6072. Breach of the peace–violence–threats–community penalty

[Criminal Procedure (Scotland) Act 1995 (c.46) s.5(3)(b).]

P, who had previous convictions for violence, was convicted of two charges of breach of the peace by conducting himself in a disorderly manner, shouting, swearing, threatening the lieges with violence and brandishing knives. The sheriff sentenced him to six months' imprisonment on each charge, to run concurrently. P appealed, arguing that as a matter of fair notice a charge required to libel assault or otherwise make it clear that the Criminal Procedure (Scotland) Act 1995 s.5(3)(b) might apply, and, in any event, no violence was averred to have been perpetrated.

Held, allowing the appeal and substituting one year's probation with 200 hours' unpaid work in the community, that (1) an offence would infer personal violence if the libel, admitted or proved, disclosed that violence was actually offered by the accused to the person of a specified complainer; (2) fair notice that s.5(3)(b) would apply was to be given by the language of the charge and did not require the use of a particular nomen iuris, and (3) neither the allegation of threats nor that of brandishing knives was sufficient to infer personal violence.

PATERSON v. WEBSTER 2002 S.L.T. 1120, Lord Macfadyen, Lord MacLean, Lord McCluskey, HCJ.

6073. Child offenders—pre sentence reports—road traffic offences—hearing on evidence

[Criminal Procedure (Scotland) Act 1995 (c.46) s.207(4).]

R, a young offender, pleaded guilty to two charges of driving whilst disqualified and admitted a large number of previous convictions. The sheriff called for reports under the Criminal Procedure (Scotland) Act 1995 s. 207(4). The reports included one from the prison where R had been remanded for trial and where he had been subject to disciplinary proceedings with regard to assaults on other prisoners and an attempt to introduce drugs. R appeared for sentencing, denied the allegations in the prison report and the court ordered evidence to be led. The procurator fiscal led evidence as in a proof in mitigation. The sheriff held that the allegations had been established and R was sentenced to 27 months' detention. R appealed to the High Court, arguing that the procedure adopted by the sheriff had been unfair because any evidence given by R might prejudice a future defence should proceedings be brought against him.

Held, allowing the appeal and substituting consecutive custodial sentences of nine months for each offence, that the sentences had been excessive. The sheriff had followed a course of action that resulted in a hearing on evidence usually directed to establishing whether or not criminal offences had been committed; it was completely unlike a proof in mitigation, the truth of the allegations was strictly irrelevant to the determination of the proper sentences and was inappropriate in the circumstances.

ROSS (SCOTT ANDREW) v. HM ADVOCATE (SENTENCING) 2002 J.C. 84, Lord Coulsfield, Judge EF Bowen Q.C., HCJ Appeal.

6074. Drug offences—confiscation orders—funds in name of accused's cohabitee—failure to establish implicative gift

[Misuse of Drugs Act 1971 (c.38) s.4(3)(b); Proceeds of Crime (Scotland) Act 1995 (c.43) s.6.]

M and his cohabitee B were charged on indictment with being concerned in the supply of drugs contrary to the Misuse of Drugs Act 1971, s.4(3)(b). M pled guilty and the Crown accepted a plea of not guilty from B. As part of the arrangement B signed a disclaimer of all right and interest in her building society deposit accounts and a sum of money taken from her by police on arrest. The Crown sought the Court to infer that they were implicative gifts in terms of the Proceeds of Crime (Scotland) Act 1995 s.6 from M on the basis that B did not have sufficient income to account for the sums. The Crown relied on evidence that B had never paid income tax, that the sums exceeded her benefits and the disclaimer as an acceptance by B that the monies were not hers. At the confiscation hearing, B maintained that the monies came from sources other than M. Evidence was also led that B was found in possession of concealed heroin and that M was a heroin addict who financed his habit by drug dealing.

Held, refusing the motion for confiscation, that the Crown had to establish to the requisite criminal standard that the property held by B was conveyed by M gratuitously. While recognising the inadequacy of B's explanation and in light of her possession of drugs and money, the Court was unable to conclude that the sums could be treated as gifts from M and must assess B's proven proceeds of M's drug trafficking at nil.

HM ADVOCATE v. McINTOSH (ROBERT) (NO.2); *sub nom.* BLACK (ISOBEL), MINUTER 2002 S.C.C.R. 287, Lord Eassie, HCJ.

6075. **Drug offences—confiscation orders—oppression—accused pled guilty to acting as drugs courier on one occasion—not oppressive to seek confiscation order on basis of income over five years**

[Misuse of Drugs Act 1971 (c.38) s.4(3)(b); Proceeds of Crime (Scotland) Act 1995 (c.43) s.1, s.6; Human Rights Act 1998 (c.42) Sch.1 Part I Art.6(1).]

U pled guilty on indictment to contravention of the Misuse of Drugs Act 1971, s.4(3)(b). U's plea was tendered on the basis that U had couriered drugs on one occasion and had not obtained financial gain. U's assets were subject to a restraint order at the time of the plea and no discussion was made of a confiscation order. However the crown initiated confiscation proceedings based on income over the previous five year. U lodged answers and a devolution minute arguing that he had a legitimate expectation that the Crown would not take confiscation proceedings against him, and for the Lord Advocate to do so was oppressive at common law and incompatible with U's right to a fair trial under the Human Rights Act 1998 Sch.1 Part I Art.6(1).

Held, refusing the minute and ordering a proof, that (1) U had no basis for his legitimate expectation given the history of the proceedings; (2) it was clear that Parliament intended confiscation proceedings to proceed in respect of drug trafficking of which the accused had not been convicted. It was not necessary for the Crown to prove that the accused had benefited from the offence that triggered the confiscation proceedings and the Lord Advocate's pursuance of confiscation proceedings in the instant case could not be constituted oppressive, and (3) before U could succeed on the basis of the Convention he would have to demonstrate a real risk that he would be prejudiced if the confiscation proceedings went ahead and U could not. If it had been held that the Lord Advocate was acting unlawfully and outwith his powers that would place a significant restriction on the provisions of the Proceeds of Crime (Scotland) Act 1995 s.1 and s.6 such a restriction would be unwarranted.

HM ADVOCATE v. URQUHART (ROBERT DAVID) 2002 S.L.T. 1143, Lord Mackay of Drumadoon, HCJ.

6076. **Drug offences—drug treatment and testing orders—revocation—no reference made to breach of any requirement of order**

[Criminal Procedure (Scotland) Act 1995 (c.46) s.234G.]

T appealed against 90 days' imprisonment on charges of theft, shoplifting and a drugs offence. A drug treatment and testing order was originally imposed for two years but the magistrate subsequently revoked it and imposed the custodial sentences, giving as his reason the lack of improvement in relation to T's use of illegal drugs. The Crown accepted that the magistrate had misdirected himself and acted in excess of jurisdiction.

Held, remitting the case to the magistrate to proceed as accords, that the magistrate had erred where no reference was made to breach of any requirement of the order or proof of failure to comply with it without reasonable excuse, no consideration was given to alternatives to revocation notwithstanding the options provided by the Criminal Procedure (Scotland) Act 1995 s.234G, and T's supervising officer's report advanced positive signs of improvement following the start of methadone treatment.

TWEEDIE v. HIGSON 2002 S.L.T. 443, Lord Cameron of Lochbroom, Sir Gerald Gordon Q.C., HCJ Appeal.

6077. **Drug offences—supply of drugs—first offence—assistance given to police**

B pled guilty to being concerned with the supply of category A and category B drugs over a four month period and was sentenced to seven years' imprisonment.

He appealed against sentence arguing that he was a first offender and had a history of public service in both the Royal Marines and the Scottish Prison Service. He accepted his involvement in the distribution of drugs but argued that, as he was not operating at street level, the value placed on the drugs by the prosecution (approximately £53,000) was exaggerated. He further argued that the court had not taken into consideration that his co-operation with the police had resulted in a significant number of arrests and the seizure of category A and category B drugs worth more than £1 million.

Held, allowing the appeal and reducing the sentence to four years and six months, that (1) B's age, at 31, should have been given greater weight by the court in relation to the fact that he was a first offender and he had led a responsible adult life up to that point, and (2) the importance of his co-operation with the police could not be underestimated and such a significant degree of help should be reflected in a material reduction in the normal sentence which would otherwise have applied. Opinion of the Court per Lord Prosser.

B v. HM ADVOCATE (SENTENCING) 2001 S.C.C.R. 876, Lord Prosser, Lord McCluskey, HCJ Appeal.

6078. Murder—life imprisonment—designated period

G was charged on indictment of assault, robbery and murder as well as the lesser charges of theft and being concerned in the supply of cannabis resin. She was convicted of the assault, robbery and murder charge by a jury and sentenced to detention for life with a recommendation that she serve at least 14 years before being considered for release on licence. She appealed against both conviction and sentence. The appeal against conviction was refused. In passing sentence the trial judge had referred to the depravity of the crime and the lack of remorse shown by G. G argued that she was only 21, had no previous convictions, that the attack had not involved long planning and was not sustained. She also argued that the circumstances of the crime were sufficiently strange as to suggest the influence of some additional feature such as drugs which had not been taken into account.

Held, sustaining the appeal to the extent of quashing the recommendation, that (1) whilst the attack was horrible, there was insufficient evidence before the trial judge to enable him to conclude that the strange circumstance could only be attributable to wickedness on G's part, and (2) it would be for the parole board and the Secretary of State to determine whether the circumstances of the crime warranted psychiatric or psychological examinations to take place in order to determine G's fitness for release on licence.

GOURLAY (PAMELA ANN) v. HM ADVOCATE (SENTENCING) 2002 J.C. 81, Lord Coulsfield, Judge EF Bowen Q.C., Lord Maclean, HCJ Appeal.

6079. Murder—life imprisonment—determination of punishment part—reliance on past recommendations

[Convention Rights (Compliance) (Scotland) Act 2001 (asp.7) Sch.para.13.]

M was convicted of murder. He had stabbed five times a drunk man making a call from a telephone box. He had telephoned for an ambulance but had then left the scene. His case was referred for a determination of the punishment part of his life sentence under the Convention Rights (Compliance) (Scotland) Act 2001 Sch. para.13. The sentencing judge specified 15 years as the punishment part. M appealed on the basis that the original sentencing judge had considered it inappropriate to make a recommendation as to the minimum period to be served before he was released on licence and that in 2001 it had been recommended that he should be eligible for reference to the parole board after serving nine years.

Held, dismissing the appeal, that (1) past decisions concerning recommendations as to the minimum period to be served before a person could be released on licence could not provide a yardstick for determining the length of a punishment part; (2) no account should be taken of the prior arrangements for considering whether an accused should be released on licence since the court had to proceed as if the new provisions had been in force at the time of sentence, and (3) the punishment part was not excessive given that this was a very savage assault on a person wholly unconnected with M and at least two of the wounds must have been inflicted with the intention of causing very serious injury, if not actual death, *Stewart (William) v. HM Advocate (Sentencing)* 2002 S.L.T. 1307 followed.

McCREADDIE (DEREK ALEXANDER) v. HM ADVOCATE (APPEAL AGAINST SENTENCE) 2002 S.L.T. 1311, Lord Cullen L.J.G., Lord Hamilton, Lord Marnoch, HCJ Appeal.

6080. Murder–life imprisonment–determination of punishment part–reliance on past recommendations

[Convention Rights (Compliance) (Scotland) Act 2001 (asp.7) Sch.para.13; Criminal Procedure (Scotland) Act 1995 (c.46) s.205.]

S was convicted of murder and robbery. S had sought out the victim in his house in the middle of the night, assaulted and strangled him after he refused to give the accused the number of his bank card. Following a referral for the making of an order under the Convention Rights (Compliance) (Scotland) Act 2001 Sch. para.13, the sentencing judge specified 14 years as the punishment part of S's life sentence. S appealed, arguing, inter alia, that where no minimum period had been recommended under the previous legislation the punishment part should not be similar to a period which might have been recommended, and that prior to the coming into force of the 2001 Act, he had had a legitimate expectation that he would be released on licence after 10 years, and further, that the court should have regard to the prejudicial effect of selecting a punishment part that conflicted with that expectation.

Held, dismissing the appeal, that (1) past recommendations under the Criminal Procedure (Scotland) Act 1995 s.205 as to the minimum period to be served before a person could be released on licence could not provide a general yardstick for determining the length of a punishment part; (2) no account should be taken of the prior arrangements for considering whether an accused should be released on licence since the court had to proceed as if the new provisions had been in force at the time of sentence, and (3) the punishment part was not excessive given the deliberate and brutal nature of the assault.

STEWART (WILLIAM) v. HM ADVOCATE (SENTENCING) 2002 S.L.T. 1307, Lord Cullen L.J.G., Lord Hamilton, Lord Marnoch, HCJ Appeal.

6081. Probation orders–condition–unpaid work–period for completion exceeding duration of order

[Criminal Procedure (Scotland) Act 1995 (c.46) s.239(2), s.229(1).]

An accused person pled guilty to two charges of assault. The sheriff sentenced him to six months' probation, intended to cover the transitional period of the accused moving elsewhere, with a condition of 80 hours' unpaid work. The accused appealed, arguing that the order was incompetent having regard to the terms of the Criminal Procedure (Scotland) Act 1995 s.239(2).

Held, quashing the probation order and substituting 80 hours' community service, (the Crown conceding the order was incompetent), that if a probation order was for only six months no requirement could be made under s.229(1) that would extend beyond that period.

LYNN v. HOWDLE 2002 S.L.T. 970, Lord Kirkwood, Lord Marnoch, Lord Sutherland, HCJ.

6082. Probation orders–right to respect for private and family life–ban on visiting boyfriend in prison

[Human Rights Act 1998 (c.42) Sch.1 Part I Art.8(1).]

R pled guilty to a charge of supplying diamorphine to her boyfriend, M, while she was visiting him in prison. The sheriff sentenced R, who was then pregnant, to two years' probation subject to a condition that she did not visit M while he was in prison. R appealed, arguing that the condition was disproportionate and interfered with her right to respect for private and family life under the Human

Rights Act 1998 Sch.1 Part I Art.8(1) since preventing such visits would inhibit the maintenance and development of her relationship with M which she intended to continue after his release, and the development of a family relationship between herself, M and their child, since born.

Held, refusing the appeal, that the condition was reasonable and in R's best interests given that probation was an appropriate disposal, and having regard to her immaturity, her susceptibility to pressure from M and her own struggle against drug addiction, it was conducive to her welfare and increased the likelihood of the order succeeding.

REID v. NAPIER 2002 S.L.T. 1229, Lord Gill L.J.C., Lord Cameron of Lochbroom, Lord MacLean, HCJ.

6083. Rape–two sisters raped at age 16–14 year sentence not excessive–risk assessment encouraged even where extended sentence legislation incompetent

[Crime and Disorder Act 1998 (c.37).]

M was convicted of two charges of rape. The complainants were sisters and the stepdaughters of M's uncle. M was found to have raped the sisters, each at age 16, at knife point and was sentenced to 14 years' imprisonment. M appealed against sentence.

Held, refusing the appeal, that although the sentence was severe it was within the trial judge's discretion, particularly given the circumstances and public interest in the case.

Observed, that although the judge could not consider an extended sentence in terms of the Crime and Disorder Act 1998, he could have sought a risk assessment, the seeking of which ought to be considered in order to ensure the sentence adequately reflected the risk posed by the accused. Opinion of the court per Lady Cosgrove.

MCC v. HM ADVOCATE (SENTENCING) 2001 S.C.C.R. 576, Lord Rodger L.J.G., Lord Carloway, Lady Cosgrove, HCJ Appeal.

6084. Road traffic offences–causing death by dangerous driving–deterrent sentence

B, a male aged 21, was charged on indictment with causing death by dangerous driving. B, having undertaken another car on a dual carriageway, then approached a roundabout at such a speed that he lost control of his car which hit the kerb, spun across the other carriageway, mounted the pavement and hit two pedestrians, killing one and seriously injuring another. The surviving pedestrian was left close to a persistent vegetative state. B pled guilty and was sentenced to five years imprisonment. He appealed against the sentence arguing that the trial judge had been overly affected by the tragic outcome of the accident and the need to deter other drivers rather than looking at B as an individual and sentencing according to his circumstances. He was driving within the speed limit for the road and had also shown genuine remorse for the accident.

Held, refusing the appeal, that (1) in entering the roundabout without reducing his speed, B had been guilty of grossly irresponsible driving justifying a deterrent sentence, and (2) the trial judge had all the facts before him when deciding the sentence and it was appropriate given those circumstances.

Observed, that it was vital to make drivers understand that causing death by dangerous driving would be viewed by the courts as a very serious crime regardless of the age or previous good record of the driver. Opinion of the court per Lord Penrose.

BRUNTON v. HM ADVOCATE (SENTENCING) 2001 S.C.C.R. 689, Lord Penrose, Lord Bonomy, HCJ Appeal.

6085. **Road traffic offences–drink driving offences–back calculation of blood alcohol**

B was charged on summary complaint with drinking and driving and a breach of the peace. Following a trial, B was fined £100 in respect of the breach of the peace and £400 for the drinking and driving offence together with a two year disqualification from driving. She appealed arguing that the sentence was excessive given her means as a single mother of three children and given that she only had one and a half times the legal limit of alcohol in her blood. The sheriff, in his report, indicated that the blood sample indicating 122mg of alcohol per 100ml of blood had been taken from B at 01.00hrs following the incident of drinking and driving which had taken place at 21.30hrs the previous evening. The sheriff had concluded that B would have been considerably more intoxicated at the time of the incident than she had been at the time the sample had been taken making the sentence appropriate. He also made it clear that the fine had been considerably less that normal given B's limited means and he had allowed her to pay at the modest rate of £5 per fortnight.

Held, quashing the sentence and substituting alternative sentences of 18 months' disqualification and a £300 fine, that (1) the sheriff had erred in sentencing according to a back calculation on the level of B's intoxication as he was only entitled to sentence according to the charges brought against B by the Crown, and (2) in order to avoid unnecessary hardship for B's children, an extension of the normal time limit to pay was appropriate and instalments of £5 per fortnight were set. Opinion of the court per Lord Penrose.

BUGLASS v. STOTT 2001 S.C.C.R. 692, Lord Penrose, Lord Bonomy, HCJ Appeal.

6086. **Sexual offences–clandestine injury–custodial sentences–offender having sexual intercourse with intoxicated woman**

P, 41, pleaded guilty to having sexual intercourse with the complainer whilst she was asleep and under the influence of alcohol. The woman had been very drunk, lost her house keys and was befriended by P outside a nightclub. They returned to his flat where there was some sexual foreplay and she fell asleep sharing his bed. She then awoke to find P having intercourse with her and pushed him off. P was a first offender who had been abused by his father and had attempted suicide following a stab injury. P had also assisted society by foiling a post office robbery and recovered an elderly lady's handbag after it had been snatched. P was sentenced to two years' imprisonment and appealed.

Held, allowing the appeal, quashing the sentence and substituting an order for 300 hours of community service, that clandestine injury was an offence which might be of unusual character and might merit an unusual form of disposal. Taking account of the strong mitigating factors, the judge had erred in imposing a custodial sentence.

PATON (GLEN CHRISTIE) v. HM ADVOCATE (SENTENCING) 2002 S.C.C.R. 57, Lord Coulsfield, Lord Sutherland, HCJ Appeal.

6087. **Sexual offences–extended sentences–form of order**

[Criminal Procedure (Scotland) Act 1995 (c.46) s.210A(2).]

O appealed against a cumulo sentence of 15 months' imprisonment and the further imposition of "an extended sentence of 21 months", to commence from the same date, for two charges of sexually abusing a nine year old girl. He argued that there was no adequate basis for the imposition of an extended period, which was also incompetent as only the custodial element of the sentence had been pronounced in open court.

Held, that as neither ground had yet been considered by the sheriff the appeal would be continued to enable him to provide a report. It was clear from the Criminal Procedure (Scotland) Act 1995 s.210A(2) that an extended sentence was not added on to a custodial sentence but comprised both the custodial term and the extension period. A minute recording an extended sentence should specify the total period of the sentence followed by the period of the custodial term and the period of the extension period. The order was ambiguous and was further confused by the sheriff's reference to a supervised release order, which was no longer competent for sexual offences.

O'HARE v. HM ADVOCATE (SENTENCING) 2002 S.L.T. 925 (Note), Lord Bonomy, Lord Penrose, HCJ Appeal.

6088. Sexual offences–indecency–video recordings–children–excessive custodial sentence

G, a first offender aged 74, pled guilty to making a video recording of a naked 14 year old girl in explicit poses. G was sentenced to six months' imprisonment and appealed to the High Court.

Held, allowing the appeal, quashing the sentence and substituting a fine of £1,500, that the amount of material was small, it was for G's personal purpose not commercial gain, G was a first offender and had freely admitted his guilt. Having regard to these factors and G's health, notwithstanding the serious nature of offences like these, this was not a case where the only appropriate sentence was custodial

GAIR (WALTER) v. HM ADVOCATE (SENTENCING) 2002 S.C.C.R. 54, Lord Coulsfield, HCJ Appeal.

6089. Sexual offences–indecency–young female victims–undue leniency

[Criminal Procedure (Scotland) Act 1995 (c.46) s.76, s.210A.]

M pled guilty to 16 charges of lewd, libidinous and indecent practices against approximately 30 young girls, all strangers, aged between three and eight, committed over a period of 21 months in 2000 and 2001. M would win the confidence of each girl, take her to a secluded place and remove her clothing in order to photograph her private parts, often also exposing himself. The psychological effects on the victims were serious. The sentencing judge imposed six years' imprisonment with an extension period of 10 years under the Criminal Procedure (Scotland) Act 1995 s.210A concurrent with five years, not the subject of appeal, on charges of using lewd, indecent and libidinous practices against two young girls by forcing them to handle his private member and masturbate him, and two years for making a quantity of indecent pseudo photographs of children. The judge considered that it was essential to show a degree of leniency as there had been no penetrative sex, masturbation or ejaculation in respect of the 16 charges, and M had pled guilty by a s.76 letter, had been frequently abused as a child by his alcoholic father and several other adults of both sexes, and had expressed remorse. The Lord Advocate appealed against the sentence as unduly lenient.

Held, allowing the appeal and substituting 10 years' imprisonment, that the predominant consideration had to be the nature and effects of the offences and the need to impose a sentence that would mark the court's view of the gravity of the case, and the sentence was unduly lenient having regard to the fact that it was one of the most serious cases of its kind and reports indicated that there was a high risk of M reoffending.

HM ADVOCATE v. MILLBANK (JOSEPH) (SENTENCING) 2002 S.L.T. 1116, Lord Gill L.C.J., Lord Kirkwood, Lord MacLean, HCJ Appeal.

6090. Sexual offences–lewd and libidinous behaviour

B pled guilty to two charges of lewd, indecent and libidinous behaviour which was committed in the period between 1969 and 1972. The offences were committed against two brothers who were aged nine and seven in 1969. The conduct was serious and committed whilst B helped out at the children's home where the brothers were living. B appealed against six years' imprisonment arguing that the court should have had regard to the fact that B had pled guilty, the remorse he had shown, the length of time which had passed since the offences were committed and his apparent good behaviour in the intervening period.

Held, refusing the appeal, that (1) the age of the offence, the appellant's remorse and his intervening good behaviour did not merit alteration of the period of imprisonment imposed by the sentencing judge, and (2) the passage of time could not, in general, warrant a different sentence from that which would have been imposed had the appellant been apprehended at the time of the offences. Opinion of the Court per Lord Prosser.

BLANEY (PETER) v. HM ADVOCATE (SENTENCING) 2001 S.C.C.R. 858, Lord Prosser, Lord Weir, HCJ Appeal.

SHIPPING

6091. Arrestment—on dependence—recall—offer of guarantee

T sought recall of an arrestment of a mobile offshore drilling unit, laid on the dependence of an action by D. D raised the action to secure claims which had been advanced by arbitration in London which might not conclude until 2003. S, the former parent of T, was now prepared to grant a guarantee and T argued that this afforded acceptable alternative security in the place of arrestment. D argued that (1) the court should consider S's reputation and that they had been fined for criminal contempt in the US, and (2) the available material did not disclose what assets S had under its own control as distinct from the control of subsidiaries, or that it had assets in the UK.

Held, continuing case for the parties to consider the terms of the guarantee, that the primary question was the financial standing of the guarantor. The court would accept guarantees that were not by banks or financial institutions if it was proven that the guarantor was of sufficient financial standing. An accountant's report established this with regard to S and the material from the US did not undermine S's financial probity. As the margin between the guarantee and the guarantor's assets was considerable it was not relevant that the report related to the group's position. It was appropriate that the guarantee contain a clause prorogating jurisdiction in Scottish or English courts. The possibility that enforcement proceedings might have to be taken in other jurisdictions did not render the security inadequate.

GLOBAL MARINE DRILLING CO v. TRITON HOLDINGS LTD (THE SOVEREIGN EXPLORER) (NO.2) [2001] 1 Lloyd's Rep. 60, Lord Macfadyen, OH.

6092. Harbours—revision—Clydeport—closure of Yorkhill Basin

CLYDEPORT (CLOSURE OF YORKHILL BASIN) HARBOUR REVISION ORDER 2002, SSI 2002 121; made under the Harbours Act 1964 s.14. In force: March 12, 2002; £1.75.

This Order empowers Clydeport Operations Ltd to close Yorkhill Basin, extinguishes any right of navigation thereon and extinguishes any obligation on Clydeport Operations Ltd to maintain Yorkhill Basin for the purposes of navigation.

6093. Harbours—revision—constitution—Aberdeen

ABERDEEN HARBOUR REVISION (CONSTITUTION) ORDER 2002, SSI 2002 310; made under the Harbours Act 1964 s.14. In force: June 25, 2002; £2.50.

This Order, which amends the Aberdeen Harbour Order Confirmation Act 1960 and the Aberdeen Harbour Order Confirmation Act 1987, revokes the Aberdeen Harbour Revision Order 1972 (SI 1972 275), the Aberdeen Harbour Revision Order 1972 (SI 1972 1704), the Aberdeen Harbour Revision Order 1976 (SI 1976 817) and the Aberdeen Harbour Revision Order 1990 (SI 1990 2359). It reconstitutes the Aberdeen Harbour Board as from January 1, 2003; provides for the Board to consist of a body of twelve members with experience in relevant matters and provides nine persons to be appointed by the Board. It also includes other provisions with respect to the Board's constitution including provisions for the protection of the members from personal liability in the discharge of their functions. The Order amends the Board's borrowing powers, amends existing statutory requirements as to the Board's accounts and repeals or revokes certain statutory provisions.

6094. Harbours–revision–constitution–Inverness

INVERNESS HARBOUR REVISION (CONSTITUTION) ORDER 2002, SSI 2002 557; made under the Harbours Act 1964 s.14. In force: December 13, 2002; £2.50.
This Order, which amends the Inverness Harbour Act 1899 and the Inverness Harbour Order 1991, reconstitutes the Inverness Harbour Trustees in line with the recommendations of the Trust Ports Review, published by the Department of the Environment, Transport and the Regions in January 2002 and endorsed by the Scottish Executive.

6095. Harbours–revision–constitution–Peterhead

PETERHEAD HARBOURS REVISION (CONSTITUTION) ORDER 2002, SSI 2002 504; made under the Harbours Act 1964 s.14. In force: October 31, 2002; £2.50.
This Order reconstitutes the Peterhead Harbours Trustees in line with the recommendations of the Trust Ports Review, published by the Department of Environment, Transport and the Regions in January 2000 and endorsed by the Scottish Executive.

6096. Harbours–revision–constitution–Peterhead Bay Authority

PETERHEAD BAY AUTHORITY (CONSTITUTION) REVISION ORDER 2002, SSI 2002 294; made under the Harbours Act 1964 s.14. In force: June 10, 2002; £2.50.
This Order, which amends the Peterhead Bay Harbour Trust and Transfer Order 1983 (SI 1983 316), reconstitutes the Peterhead Bay Authority as from April 1, 2002. It provides for the Authority to consist of a body of nine members with experience in relevant matters; specifies eight persons will be appointed by the Authority; and the Chief Executive will also hold office as a member. It also includes other provisions with respect to the Authority's constitution including provisions for the protection of the members from personal liability in the discharge of their functions. The Order also amends the Authority's borrowing powers, extends the Authority's area of jurisdiction and revokes certain statutory provisions.

6097. Harbours–revision–various harbours

COMHAIRLE NAN EILEAN SIAR (VARIOUS HARBOURS) HARBOUR REVISION ORDER 2002, SSI 2002 410; made under the Harbours Act 1964 s.14. In force: September 5, 2002; £6.50.
This Order, which revokes the Western Isles Islands Council (Various Harbours Jurisdiction and Byelaws) Harbour Revision Order 1995 (SI 1995 2007) and the Comhairle nan Eilean Siar (Ardveenish) Harbour Revision Order 2000 (SSI 2000 233), amends the Pier and Harbour Orders Confirmation Act 1878 (No.2), the Lochmaddy Pier Order 1949 (SI 1949 1516), the Portnaguiran Pier Order 1951 (SI 1951 1866), the Ardveenish Harbour Order Confirmation Act 1980, the Breasclete Harbour Confirmation Act 1980, the Western Isles Islands Council (Loch Roag) Order Confirmation Act 1982, the Western Isles Islands Council (Kallin Pier, Harbour Jurisdiction) Order Confirmation Act 1984, the Lochmaddy and East Loch Tarbert (Improvement of Piers &c.) Order Confirmation Act 1984, the Western Isles Islands Council (Berneray Harbour) Order Confirmation Act 1986, the Western Isles Islands Council (Ardveenish) Harbour Revision Order 1992 (SI 1992 1975), the Western Isles Islands Council (Breasclete) Harbour Revision Order 1992 (SI 1992 1976), the Western Isles Islands Council (Brevig) Harbour Empowerment Order 1993 (SI 1993 2908), the Western Isles Islands Council

(Leverburgh) Harbour Revision Order 1995 (SI 1995 2971) and the Comhairle nan Eilean Siar (Aird Mhor, Barra) Harbour Empowerment Order 2001 (SI 2001 262). The Order relates to certain harbour areas in na h'Eileanan an Iar. It defines and in some cases alters the harbour limits, confers powers on Comhairle nan Eilean Siar as harbour authority in relation to the harbour areas and makes other related provisions.

SOCIAL SECURITY

6098. Industrial injuries benefits—personal injury—back injury from repeated lifting of patients—carers

[Social Security Contributions and Benefits Act 1992 (c.4) s.94(1).]

M, a former assistant care officer in a home for the elderly, made an application for industrial injuries benefit, having suffered back pain which made her unfit for work due to repeated lifting of patients over a number of years. An adjudication officer and a social security appeal tribunal held that her injuries had resulted from a gradual process, that there was no specific and ascertainable accident or series of accidents and that the applicant's injury was not an injury contemplated by the Social Security Contributions and Benefits Act 1992 s.94(1). That conclusion was affirmed by the Social Security Commissioner, who also refused leave to appeal, holding that M's ground of appeal did not raise a true question of law.

Held, allowing the appeal and remitting the case to the Social Security Commissioner, that (1) a genuine question of law had been raised which was dependent on the interpretation of statute and case law in the context of the facts; (2) a back injury sustained whilst handling a patient was an accident within the meaning of s.94 and where there was a series of accidents an applicant was not disqualified only because they could not identify the date of each accident and identify which one caused or contributed to the condition, and (3) the tribunal's findings sufficiently established the essential factual basis on which M was entitled to benefit.

MULLEN v. SECRETARY OF STATE FOR WORK AND PENSIONS 2002 S.C. 251, Lord Gill L.J.C., Lord Bonomy, Lord Eassie, 2 Div.

6099. Social security tribunals—error of fact—judicial review of decision based on error

See ADMINISTRATIVE LAW: Anderson v. Secretary of State for Work and Pensions. §5244

SOCIAL WELFARE

6100. Care—regulation of care—applications and provision of advice

REGULATION OF CARE (APPLICATIONS AND PROVISION OF ADVICE) (SCOTLAND) ORDER 2002, SSI 2002 113; made under the Regulation of Care (Scotland) Act 2001 s.4, s.7, s.14, s.33. In force: April 1, 2002; £2.00.

This Order specifies the information to be provided by a person who makes an application for registration of a care service under the Registration of Care (Scotland) Act 2001. It specifies the information to be provided by a person who makes an application for variation or removal of a condition of registration relating to registration of a care service or for cancellation of the registration of a care service. The Order also prescribes the Mental Welfare Commission as a body to which the Scottish Commission for the Regulation of Care is to provide advice when asked to do so.

6101. Care–regulation of care–appointments and procedure

SCOTTISH COMMISSION FOR THE REGULATION OF CARE (APPOINTMENTS AND PROCEDURE) REGULATIONS 2002, SSI 2002 106; made under the Regulation of Care (Scotland) Act 2001 Sch.1 para.7. In force: April 1, 2002; £2.50.

These Regulations make provision concerning the membership and procedure of the Scottish Commission for the Regulation of Care established under the Regulation of Care (Scotland) Act 2001. They make provision for the appointment and tenure of office of the convener and members of the Commission; for disqualification for appointment; the termination of appointments by the Scottish Ministers; and for the appointment of a deputy convener. Provision is also made for the establishment of committees and sub-committees and of a National Forum Advisory Committee; the conduct of meetings and proceedings and the exclusion from meetings of those with an interest in matters under discussion. In addition, they make provision for the payment of remuneration and allowances to the convener and members and for the delegation of the functions of the Commission.

6102. Care–regulation of care–care service requirements

REGULATION OF CARE (REQUIREMENTS AS TO CARE SERVICES) (SCOTLAND) REGULATIONS 2002, SSI 2002 114; made under the Regulation of Care (Scotland) Act 2001 s.29. In force: April 1, 2002; £2.50.

These Regulations set out requirements which must be complied with by providers of care services under the Regulation of Care (Scotland) Act 2001. A care service must be provided in accordance with the general principles specified and the provider is required to prepare a written statement of the aims and objectives of the care service. The Regulations impose requirements on providers which relate to the welfare of service users and require the provider to prepare a personal plan for each service user setting out how the service user's health and welfare needs will be met. They specify persons not fit to provide, manage or be employed in a care service and also make provision as to fitness of premises. In addition, the Regulations impose requirements as to the equipment and facilities to be provided in a care home service, prohibit any person having a financial interest in a care home service from acting as a medical practitioner for any user of that service and make as to the appointment of a manager of a care service.

6103. Care–regulation of care–excepted services

REGULATION OF CARE (EXCEPTED SERVICES) (SCOTLAND) REGULATIONS 2002, SSI 2002 120; made under the Regulation of Care (Scotland) Act 2001 s.2. In force: April 1, 2002; £1.75.

These Regulations exclude certain specified activities from the definition of care services under the Regulation of Care (Scotland) Act 2001. They except certain activities from the definition of support service, restrict the scope of the definition of a school care accommodation service and provide that activities of health bodies under the National Health Service (Scotland) Act 1978 are excepted from the definition of nurse agencies. In addition, they except certain activities from the definition of day care of children.

6104. Care–regulation of care–fees

REGULATION OF CARE (FEES) (SCOTLAND) ORDER 2002, SSI 2002 112; made under the Regulation of Care (Scotland) Act 2001 s.24. In force: April 1, 2002; £1.75.

This Order prescribes the maximum fees which may be imposed by the Scottish Commission for the Regulation of Care in respect of applications for registration or for cancellation of registration of a care service, the annual continuation of any such registration, and applications for variation or removal of a condition of registration under the Regulation of Care (Scotland) Act 2001. It also prescribes the maximum fee for issuing a new certificate of registration.

6105. Care—regulation of care—registration and registers

REGULATION OF CARE (REGISTRATION AND REGISTERS) (SCOTLAND) REGULATIONS 2002, SSI 2002 115; made under the Regulation of Care (Scotland) Act 2001 s.28. In force: April 1, 2002; £2.00.

These Regulations make provision about registration of care services by the Scottish Commission for the Regulation of Care. They require the Commission to maintain a separate register for each of the types of care service covered by the Regulation of Care (Scotland) Act 2001. They specify information to be recorded in the registers in respect of each individual care service, set out the information to be specified in a certificate of registration of a care service and specify categories of persons who may not make an application for registration of a care service. The Regulations also require the Commission to make its registers available for inspection at its offices and on the internet, and provides that a fee of £30 will payable for copies provided in the circumstances which are specified.

6106. Care—regulation of care—staff transfer scheme

SCOTTISH COMMISSION FOR THE REGULATION OF CARE (STAFF TRANSFER SCHEME) ORDER 2002, SSI 2002 108; made under the Regulation of Care (Scotland) Act 2001 s.30. In force: April 1, 2002; £2.00.

This Order provides for the transfer of the specified local authority and Health Board employees to the Scottish Commission for the Regulation of Care.

6107. Community care—additional payments

COMMUNITY CARE (ADDITIONAL PAYMENTS) (SCOTLAND) REGULATIONS 2002, SSI 2002 265; made under the Community Care and Health (Scotland) Act 2002 s.4, s.23. In force: July 1, 2002; £1.75.

These Regulations make provision for additional payments to be made so that a person who is in receipt of or is eligible for residential accommodation can choose to live in accommodation which is more expensive than the local authority would usually pay for someone with that person's assessed needs.

6108. Community care—assessment of needs—relevant person

COMMUNITY CARE (ASSESSMENT OF NEEDS) (SCOTLAND) REGULATIONS 2002, SSI 2002 304; made under the Community Care and Health (Scotland) Act 2002 s.1. In force: July 1, 2002; £1.75.

These Regulations, which amend the Social Work (Scotland) Act 1968, provide that a local authority shall regard a relevant person as being a person in need of services and the duty to carry out an assessment. They provide that a local authority, where it does not intend to exercise its power to assess needs, shall, on receipt of a request, decide that the person has needs that call for the provision of a service and those needs shall be treated as such care as the person is receiving from the care home service. A "relevant person" is defined as a person who is receiving a care home service, including the provision of care, who received that service immediately before April 1, 2002, who before July 1, 2003 requests the local authority to provide or secure provision of care and, in the case of a person receiving only personal care, personal support or care of a kind specified.

6109. Community care—deferred payment of accommodation costs

COMMUNITY CARE (DEFERRED PAYMENT OF ACCOMMODATION COSTS) (SCOTLAND) REGULATIONS 2002, SSI 2002 266; made under the Community Care and Health (Scotland) Act 2002 s.6, s.23. In force: July 1, 2002; £1.75.

These Regulations make provision concerning entering into deferred payment agreements by local authorities under the Community Care and Health (Scotland) Act 2002 s.6. A local authority may enter into such an agreement where the conditions are met. The conditions are that an assessment of the person's resources in accordance with the National Assistance (Assessment of Resources) Regulations 1992 (SI 1992 2977), disregarding the value of their home, shows that they have capital at or below the lower capital limit; the person does not wish to, or is unable to, sell their home; the person will grant a standard security against their home; the value of the person's interest in their home is such that it will meet the local authority's reasonable estimate of the amount that will become due under the deferred payment agreement; and where the home is subject to other standard securities the person is, in the opinion of the local authority, able to continue to pay those and make the payments due to the local authority for the provision of residential accommodation. The Regulations prevent the making of a deferred payment agreement (except in relation to additional payments) where the value of a person's home is disregarded, other than for the purpose of making the agreement, when assessing their need for and ability to pay for residential accommodation and set out how the amount that may be the subject of a deferred payment agreement is calculated.

6110. Community care–disregard of resources

COMMUNITY CARE (DISREGARD OF RESOURCES) (SCOTLAND) ORDER 2002, SSI 2002 264; made under the Social Work (Scotland) Act 1968 s.12, s.94. In force: July 1, 2002; £1.75.

The Community Care and Health (Scotland) Act 2002 provides that an order may specify so much of a person's resources as shall be disregarded by a local authority, or specify a way of calculating such resources as shall be disregarded, when deciding whether to make available assistance, by way of residential accommodation, to a person. This Order, which amends the National Assistance (Assessment of Resources) Regulations 1992 (SI 1992 2977), specifies the resources to be disregarded for that purpose.

6111. Community care–personal care and nursing care

COMMUNITY CARE (PERSONAL CARE AND NURSING CARE) (SCOTLAND) REGULATIONS 2002, SSI 2002 303; made under the Community Care and Health (Scotland) Act 2002 s.1, s.2, s.23. In force: July 1, 2002; £1.75.

These Regulations, which amend the Social Work (Scotland) Act 1968 and the Mental Health (Scotland) Act 1984, provide for free personal care and free nursing care to specified categories of people.

6112. Community Care and Health (Scotland) Act 2002 (asp 5)

This Act of the Scottish Parliament makes further provision as respects social care; makes provision in relation to arrangements and payments between National Health Service bodies and local authorities as respects certain of their functions and amends the law relating to the National Health Service.

This Act received Royal Assent on March 12, 2002.

6113. Local authorities–transfer of staff–consultation

SCOTTISH COMMISSION FOR THE REGULATION OF CARE (CONSULTATION ON TRANSFER OF STAFF) ORDER 2002, SSI 2002 18; made under the Regulation of Care (Scotland) Act 2001 s.30. In force: February 15, 2002; £1.75.

This Order prescribes the requirements about consultation with which the Scottish Ministers must comply before making a scheme for the transfer of staff from local authorities and Health Boards to the Scottish Commission for the Regulation of Care.

6114. Regulation of Care (Scotland) Act 2001 (asp 8)–Commencement No.2 and Transitional Provisions Order

REGULATION OF CARE (SCOTLAND) ACT 2001 (COMMENCEMENT NO.2 AND TRANSITIONAL PROVISIONS) ORDER 2002, SSI 2002 162; made under the Regulation of Care (Scotland) Act 2001 s.81. Commencement details: bringing into force various provisions of the 2001 Act on April 1, 2002; £2.50.

This Order brings into force specified provisions of the Regulation of Care (Scotland) Act 2001.

6115. Residential accommodation–sums for personal requirements

NATIONAL ASSISTANCE (SUMS FOR PERSONAL REQUIREMENTS) (SCOTLAND) REGULATIONS 2002, SSI 2002 85; made under the National Assistance Act 1948 s.22. In force: April 8, 2002; £1.75.

These Regulations, which revoke the National Assistance (Sums for Personal Requirements) (Scotland) Regulations 2001 (SSI 2001 100), set out the weekly sum which local authorities in Scotland are to assume that residents in accommodation arranged under the Social Work (Scotland) Act 1968 or the Mental Health (Scotland) Act 1984 will need for their personal requirements. All residents will be assumed to need £16.80 per week for their personal requirements.

6116. Residential care–public funding–provision of residential accommodation with nursing–capital not relevant

[Social Work (Scotland) Act 1968 (c.49) s.12, s.12(3A), s.12(3B), s.12A(1), s.13A(1).]

R appealed against a decision ([2001] S.C. 849) refusing her reclaiming motion against the dismissal of her petition for judicial review of F's refusal to enter into arrangements to provide her with residential nursing care. By reason of her suffering from senile dementia R would require nursing care in secure surroundings for the rest of her life. F's refusal to fund the provision of such care was based upon their conclusion that she had transferred ownership in her house to her children for the purpose of reducing her future liability to contribute towards the costs of residential care. In assessing her means the local authority had taken into account a notional capital figure equivalent to the value of the house. As a consequence of the local authority's decision R may have had to move out of the accommodation which best met her care needs into less appropriate accommodation. F relied upon the Social Work (Scotland) Act 1968 s.12(3A) and s.12(3B) as providing statutory authority for its decision in respect of the provision of residential accommodation, and further submitted that s.12A(1)(b) as read in conjunction with s.13A(1) permitted an authority to take into account financial resources when deciding whether to provide residential accommodation with nursing under s.13A.

Held, allowing the appeal, that F had erred in taking R's capital, including her notional capital, into account when assessing her need for residential accommodation with nursing; (1) the duty to provide residential accommodation with nursing under s.13A was separate and distinct from the duty under s.12 to provide general social and welfare services, including the provision of residential accommodation. This meant that, giving the words "for the purposes of this section" in s.12(3A) their ordinary meaning, a local authority needed to perform the exercise directed in that subsection as to a persons capital when making a determination regarding the provision of residential accommodation under s.12, but not when making a decision as to the provision of residential accommodation with nursing under s.13A; (2) the direction to disregard capital under the limit in s.12(3A) could not be interpreted as indicating that capital above the limit was to be brought into account in determining the need for the provision of accommodation. Such capital was taken into account when charges were made for the accommodation provided, and (3) the words in s.12A(1)(b) which required a local authority to decide whether the needs of a person "call for" the provision of services, were directed to the person's needs for any of the services which the local authority were able to provide, not to the question whether the person was able to pay for them.

ROBERTSON v. FIFE COUNCIL, [2002] UKHL 35, 2002 S.L.T. 951, Lord Hope of Craighead, HL.

6117. Social services–community care–accommodation

PRESERVED RIGHTS (TRANSFER TO RESPONSIBLE AUTHORITIES) (SCOTLAND) REGULATIONS 2002, SSI 2002 76; made under the Health and Social Care Act 2001 s.50. In force: April 8, 2002; £1.75.

These Regulations provide that duties that would otherwise be incumbent on responsible authorities under the Health and Social Care Act 2001 to provide community care services do not apply in the case of a person who, on the day before the appointed day, is not entitled to receive income support, is so entitled but not as a person having a preserved right to a higher rate of payment, or is being provided with after-care services under the Mental Health (Scotland) Act 1984. They also prescribe the amount of any payment made by a responsible authority which that authority may recover from the person to whom it was made and prescribe the circumstances in which a person is to be treated as ordinarily resident in premises for the purposes of the 2001 Act.

6118. Social services–Social Services Council–appointments, procedure and access to the register

SCOTTISH SOCIAL SERVICES COUNCIL (APPOINTMENTS, PROCEDURE AND ACCESS TO THE REGISTER) AMENDMENT REGULATIONS 2002, SSI 2002 60; made under the Regulation of Care (Scotland) Act 2001 Sch.2 para.7. In force: March 15, 2002; £1.50.

These Regulations amend the Scottish Social Services Council (Appointments, Procedure and Access to the Register) Regulations 2001 (SSI 2001 303) by requiring the Scottish Social Services Council to pay to its convener and to any member, such fee, and to its convener, to any member and to any person appointed to a committee or sub-committee, such allowances, as the Scottish Ministers may from time to time specify.

SPORT

6119. Recreational services–sports grounds–designation for criminal law purposes

SPORTS GROUNDS AND SPORTING EVENTS (DESIGNATION) (SCOTLAND) AMENDMENT ORDER 2002, SSI 2002 382; made under the Criminal Law (Consolidation) (Scotland) Act 1995 s.18. In force: September 21, 2002; £1.50.

This Order amends the Sports Grounds and Sporting Events (Designation) (Scotland) Order 1998 (SI 1998 2314) which designates the sports grounds, the classes of sporting events played at those grounds and the classes of sporting events outside Great Britain for the purposes of the Criminal Law (Consolidation) (Scotland) Act 1995 Part II. As a result of the amendment, Harlaw Park, Inverurie and Raydale Park, Gretna, become designated sports grounds

SUCCESSION

6120. Administration of estates–petition for directions–distribution of estate– potential liabilities of Lloyd's name

M, executors of N, a former underwriting member of Lloyd's of London, raised a petition for directions. They sought the court's approval of the distribution of N's estate to date and the final distribution thereof without any retention or further provision being made for potential claims in respect of any contract of insurance or reinsurance underwritten by him. They further sought an order relieving them from personal liability for any such potential claims or for distributing the estate in accordance with the court's direction. One syndicate of which N had been a member had not yet closed for the year 1982; under a reconstruction and renewal plan produced by Lloyd's in 1996 a reinsurance company, approved by the Department of Trade, had been formed to reinsure all liabilities in respect of 1992 and earlier years. The court remitted to a reporter who considered that the reinsurance scheme provided a very substantial level of security, and that it was most unlikely that any claims would be made against N's estate in respect of the liabilities reinsured, but that those liabilities nevertheless remained obligations of the estate.

Held, granting the petition, that (1) the present position was not precisely covered by the authorities, there being no actual claim against the estate and an enforceable claim only if two contingencies were satisfied, the emergence of a liability and the reinsurance scheme proving inadequate; (2) the possibility that a liability might emerge would be discounted by any reasonable person as so remote as to be merely speculative or hypothetical, and the court was prepared to approve the distribution of the estate since it would be wholly unreasonable to paralyse the administration given the arrangements which had been put in place, and (3) the orders sought should be granted as M would not have a defence to an action by beneficiaries and the orders could be regarded as a way of short-circuiting the procedure which might otherwise have to be followed, and of avoiding unnecessary expense.

NEILSON'S EXECUTORS, PETITIONERS; *sub nom.* NEILSON'S EXECUTORS v. BALFOUR THOMSON; McINNES, PETITIONER 2002 S.L.T. 1100, Lord Abernethy, Lord Cameron of Lochbroom, Lord Coulsfield, Ex Div.

6121. Wills—entail—trust deeds—declarator of fee simple proprietorship—date of execution—deed varied by codicil

[Entail Amendment (Scotland) Act 1848 (11 & 12 Vict. c.36) s.47, s.48.]

B appealed against the refusal of his petition (2002) S.L.T. 981) under the Entail Amendment (Scotland) Act 1848, s.48, or alternatively s.47, for declarator that he was the fee simple proprietor of the lands and barony of W. B, born on December 23, 1925, was liferenter of the estate in terms of a trust disposition and settlement of A who died in 1930. The settlement was dated January 1, 1923 but was varied by a codicil dated December 20, 1927 which changed the order of succession in respect of the first person to succeed, expressly for the purpose of minimising estate duty. A second codicil dated September 20, 1929 appointed a literary executor for A. B argued that he met the conditions of s.47 and s.48 as the 1923 deed was the final expression of A's testamentary will so far as the estate was concerned. The Extra Division held that the trust settlement was composed of the original deed and first codicil taken together and the date of the deed had to be taken as the date of the codicil.

Held, allowing the appeal, that (1) the petition, being concerned with liferents created under a trust, was more properly to be regarded as falling under s.47 than under s.48, which was directed at proper liferents; (2) s.47 was concerned not with the historic position but with the settlement by which the petitioning party was in possession of the estate, and the matter had to be considered as at the time of the application to the court *Earl of Moray, Petitioner* 1950 S.C. 281, [1950] C.L.Y. 5391, and *Watson's Trustees v. Miller* 1958 S.C. 125, [1958] C.L.Y. 4147; (3) while the trust deed by which the beneficiary first entitled to the liferent entered into possession included the first codicil, the purpose of the codicil was served and its effect spent as soon as he did so; (4) the second codicil was of no relevance to the present question, and (5) the settlement by virtue of which B became entitled to his interest in possession was therefore the 1923 trust disposition.

EARL OF BALFOUR, PETITIONER; *sub nom.* BALFOUR v. KEEPER OF REGISTERS OF SCOTLAND, [2002] UKHL 42, 2002 S.L.T. 1385, Lord Hope of Craighead, HL.

6122. Books

Chill, R.—Executry Practice. Paperback. ISBN 0-414-01386-7. W. Green & Son.

Hiram, Hilary–Scots Law of Succession. Paperback: £34.00. ISBN 0-406-90040-X. Butterworths Law (Scotland).

Meston, Michael–Succession (Scotland) Act 1964. 5th Ed. Greens Annotated Acts. Paperback: £40.00. ISBN 0-414-01453-7. W.Green & Son.

TAX

6123. Budget (Scotland) Act 2002 (asp 7)

This Act of the Scottish Parliament makes provision, for financial year 2002/03, for the use of resources by the Scottish Administration and certain bodies whose expenditure is payable out of the Scottish Consolidated Fund, for authorising the payment of sums out of the Fund, for the maximum amount of relevant expenditure for the purposes of the Local Government (Scotland) Act 1973 (c.65) s.94(5) and the maximum amounts of borrowing by certain statutory bodies and makes provision, for financial year 2003/04, for authorising the payment of sums out of the Fund on a temporary basis.

6124. Public expenditure–use of resources

BUDGET (SCOTLAND) 2002 AMENDMENT ORDER 2002, SSI 2002 542; made under the Budget (Scotland) Act 2002 s.7. In force: November 29, 2002; £1.75.

This Order amends the Budget (Scotland) Act 2002, which makes provision, for financial year 2002/03, for the use of resources by the Scottish Administration and certain bodies whose expenditure is payable out of the Scottish Consolidated Fund, for authorising the use of resources, and for limits on the capital expenditure of and borrowing of local authorities and certain other public bodies. The Order alters the maximum amount for the purposes of the Local Government (Scotland) Act 1973 (c.65) s.94(5), restates the purposes for which resources may be used in accordance with s.1 and Sch.1 to the 2002 Act, with specified changes.

6125. Public expenditure–use of resources

BUDGET (SCOTLAND) ACT 2001 (AMENDMENT) ORDER 2002, SSI 2002 134; made under the Budget (Scotland) Act 2001 s.7. In force: March 13, 2002; £2.00.

This Order amends the Budget (Scotland) Act 2001 which makes provision, for financial year 2001/02, for the use of resources by the Scottish Administration and certain bodies whose expenditure is payable out of the Scottish Consolidated Fund, for authorising the use of resources, and for limits on the capital expenditure of and borrowing of local authorities and certain other public bodies. In particular the Order alters the overall cash authorisations for the purposes of Public Finance and Accountability (Scotland) Act 2000, alters the maximum amount for the purposes of the Local Government (Scotland) Act 1973 and alters the amounts of resources which may be used by the Scottish Administration.

6126. Taxation administration–agreements–forward tax agreement to pay flat rate–power of Commissioners to enter into agreement–ultra vires

[Inland Revenue Regulation Act 1890 (c.21) s.1, s.13; Taxes Management Act 1970 (c.9).]

A, an individual ordinarily resident in the UK but with a foreign domicile, petitioned for judicial review of a decision by the Commissioners that they would not abide by the terms of a forward tax agreement. Under the terms of the agreement, A agreed to pay certain annual sums in respect of specified future years of assessment, the sums in question being accepted in lieu of income and capital gains tax liabilities to which A might otherwise have been liable.

Held, refusing the petition, that (1) the agreement had been ultra vires. Under the Inland Revenue Regulation Act 1890 s.1 and s.13, the Commissioners were appointed "for the collection and management of inland revenue" and they were obliged to "collect and cause to be collected every part of inland revenue and all money under their care and management". By virtue of the Taxes Management Act 1970, the Commissioners were responsible for income tax, corporation tax and capital gains tax. The agreement constituted a renunciation of the obligation imposed upon the Commissioners to make a full investigation of the financial circumstances of A, particularly with respect to the amount of foreign remittances that he received. Since the payment in question was unrelated to any disclosed sum by way of income or gains it could not be said to constitute a collection of inland revenue. The agreement also breached the Commissioner's duty of fairness as between taxpayers since the obligation to pay a certain sum bore no relation to the amount of any taxable transactions. In consequence, A and others like him had become a privileged group who were effectively untaxed by concession, *Vestey v. Inland Revenue Commissioners* [1980] A.C. 1148, [1980] C.L.Y. 1489 applied, and (2) the Commissioners did not retain any discretion to abide by the terms of the agreement since any decision to adhere to its terms would amount to a continuance of their previous non compliance with their statutory duties, *R. v. Inland Revenue Commissioners, ex p. Preston* [1983] 2 All E.R. 300, [1983] C.L.Y. 1981 considered.

AL-FAYED v. ADVOCATE GENERAL FOR SCOTLAND; *sub nom.* AL-FAYED v. INLAND REVENUE COMMISSIONERS; ALI FAYED v. ADVOCATE GENERAL FOR SCOTLAND; ALI FAYED v. INLAND REVENUE COMMISSIONERS [2002] S.T.C. 910, Lord Gill L.J.C., OH.

TRANSPORT

6127. Bus services—bus service operators—grants

BUS SERVICE OPERATORS GRANT (SCOTLAND) REGULATIONS 2002, SSI 2002 289; made under the Transport (Scotland) Act 2001 s.38, s.81. In force: July 1, 2002; £1.75.

These Regulations describe the "eligible bus services" for the purposes of the Transport (Scotland) Act 2001 s.38 under which grants may be made to operators of eligible bus services towards their costs in operating the service. The Regulations, which re-enact the previous eligibility rules for fuel duty rebates under the Finance Act 2001 s.38, extend eligibility to services provided by a range of non-profit making community transport bodies whose services do not follow a fixed route or timetable and are for use by particular categories of passengers, rather than the general public.

6128. Bus services—fares—travel concessions

TRAVEL CONCESSIONS (ELIGIBLE SERVICES) (SCOTLAND) ORDER 2002, SSI 2002 290; made under the Transport Act 1985 s.94. In force: July 1, 2002; £1.75.

This Order prescribes classes of bus services eligible for participation in travel concession schemes, and reimbursement arrangements.

6129. Bus services—written complaints—tribunals—establishment

BUS USER COMPLAINTS TRIBUNAL REGULATIONS 2002, SSI 2002 199; made under the Transport (Scotland) Act 2001 s.41, s.81. In force: April 23, 2002; £2.00.

These Regulations establish the Bus User Complaints Tribunal and provide for the determination of written complaints under the Transport (Scotland) Act 2001 s.41 in connection with the operation of local services.

6130. Disabled persons—Mobility and Access Committee—establishment

MOBILITY AND ACCESS COMMITTEE FOR SCOTLAND REGULATIONS 2002, SSI 2002 69; made under the Transport (Scotland) Act 2001 s.72, s.81. In force: March 22, 2002; £1.75.

These Regulations establish the Mobility and Access Committee for Scotland which will consider such matters relating to the needs of disabled persons in connection with transport and also give advice to the Scottish Ministers in relation to such matters as the committee thinks appropriate. They provide details of the appointment and tenure of office for members of the committee, for administrative arrangements, for the constitution and procedure for the committee and that the committee is to prepare a report to Scottish Ministers which provides Scottish Ministers with advice on matters relating to the needs of disabled persons in connection with transport as the committee thinks appropriate.

6131. Disabled persons—motor vehicles—badges

DISABLED PERSONS (BADGES FOR MOTOR VEHICLES) (SCOTLAND) AMENDMENT REGULATIONS 2002, SSI 2002 451; made under the Chronically Sick and Disabled Persons Act 1970 s.21. In force: November 8, 2002; £1.50.

These Regulations amend the Disabled Persons (Badges for Motor Vehicles) (Scotland) Regulations 2000 (SSI 2000 59) to enable disabled person's badges issued in Northern Ireland or any Member State to be displayed as if they were badges issued by a local authority in Scotland.

6132. Disabled persons—taxis—carriage of guide dogs

TAXI DRIVERS' LICENCES (CARRYING OF GUIDE DOGS AND HEARING DOGS) (SCOTLAND) AMENDMENT REGULATIONS 2002, SSI 2002 521; made under the Civic Government (Scotland) Act 1982 s.20. In force: December 2, 2002; £1.75.

These Regulations amend the Taxi Drivers' Licences (Carrying of Guide Dogs and Hearing Dogs) (Scotland) Regulations 2002 (SSI 2002 500) to correct a technical inconsistency.

6133. Disabled persons—taxis—carriage of guide dogs

TAXI DRIVERS' LICENCES (CARRYING OF GUIDE DOGS AND HEARING DOGS) (SCOTLAND) REGULATIONS 2002, SSI 2002 500; made under the Civic Government (Scotland) Act 1982 s.20. In force: December 2, 2002; £2.00.

These Regulations, which place a duty on taxi drivers, through the imposition of a condition in a taxi driver's licence, to carry a disabled passenger's guide dog, hearing dog or assistance dog, provide that the taxi driver must allow the dog to remain with the disabled person and not make any additional charge for carrying the dog. The Regulations also prescribe certain dogs helping people with epilepsy and people with certain general physical disabilities as dogs to which this obligation applies and provide that a taxi driver may be exempted from the obligation to carry a disabled passenger's guide dog, hearing dog or assistance dog on medical grounds. They prescribe the form of the exemption notice which must, in those circumstances, be displayed and the manner of its display in the taxi. They also provide for the giving of reasons for, and appeals against, decisions of licensing authorities on applications for exemption.

6134. Dissolution–Scottish Transport Group

SCOTTISH TRANSPORT GROUP (DISSOLUTION) ORDER 2002, SSI 2002 263; made under the Transport (Scotland) Act 1989 s.14. In force: June 7, 2002; £2.00.

This Order, which amends the Industrial Development Act 1966, the Transport Act 1968, the House of Commons Disqualifications Act 1975, the Transport Act 1981, the Transport Act 1982, the Miscellaneous Financial Provisions Act 1983 and the National Audit Act 1983, provides for the dissolution of the Scottish Transport Group.

6135. International carriage by road–subcontractors–liability

[Convention for the International Carriage of Goods by Road 1956 Art.34.]

P sought damages from C in respect of the loss of goods belonging to P which were the subject of a contract of carriage entered into between P and another company, PWR, for delivery of those goods from Tokyo to Scotland. P claimed that PWR subcontracted part of the work to C through an intermediary, T, a fact he was not made aware of at the time. He also claimed that, of a total of 129 boxes in the consignment, one box went missing which contained a computer and associated equipment. P also claimed that the contract was one for the international carriage of goods to which the Convention for the International Carriage of Goods by Road 1956 applied. C argued that the contract was one for the removal of furniture to which the Convention did not apply and that even if it did, as T did not supply C with a consignment note in accordance with the terms of the Convention, C would have no liability under the terms of the Convention. They argued that the purpose of a consignment note was to make succeeding carriers aware that the contract was subject to the terms of the Convention and that formal acceptance of the note was required. Even if they were wrong, C argued, P had failed to demonstrate that C had any knowledge that the contract fell within the terms of the Convention. In those circumstances, C maintained that they were no liable as succeeding carriers under Art.34 of the Convention. P argued that, in order to determine whether a contract was one for the removal of furniture, it was appropriate to look at the tasks being undertaken, which did not, in this case, involve any element of packing or unpacking or movement of furniture and that the mere existence of items which could be regarded as furnishings within the consignment did not render the contract one for removal. P also argued that the elements for constituting a successive carrier as a party to the original contract were the acceptance of goods by the carrier and knowledge that the carriage of those goods was international, and absence of, or defects in, a consignment note were irrelevant.

Held, dismissing the action, that (1) the carriage of goods internationally was different from the removal of furniture by virtue of the nature of the tasks undertaken by the carriers and as the contract did not involve any degree of packing or unpacking of the goods or movement or arrangement of the goods within the delivery building, it could not be deemed to be a contract for removals, but rather a contract for carriage to which the Convention did apply; (2) the consignment note was irrelevant to the establishment of the contract between P and PWR, but was crucial to the constitution of the obligations the continuing carrier in making him party to the original contract of carriage, and (3) P's inability to aver that C had accepted the consignment note was fatal to his claim that C was liable in terms of Art.34. PARR v. CLARK & ROSE LTD 2002 S.C.L.R. 222, James Tierney, Sh Ct.

6136. Motor vehicles–competitions and trials–fees

MOTOR VEHICLES (COMPETITIONS AND TRIALS) (SCOTLAND) AMENDMENT REGULATIONS 2002, SSI 2002 14; made under the Road Traffic Act 1988 s.13. In force: March 1, 2002; £1.50.

These Regulations, which revoke the Motor Vehicles (Competition and Trials) (Scotland) Amendment Regulations 1992 (SI 1992 747), amend the Motor Vehicles (Competitions and Trials) (Scotland) Regulations 1976 (SI 1976 2019) so as to increase the fees to be submitted to the Royal Scottish Automobile Club with applications for the authorisation of events.

6137. Parking–parking adjudicators–appeals

ROAD TRAFFIC (PARKING ADJUDICATORS) (PERTH AND KINROSS COUNCIL) REGULATIONS 2002, SSI 2002 400; made under the Road Traffic Act 1991 s.73. In force: October 1, 2002; £2.50.

These Regulations prescribe the procedure to be followed in relation to appeals before parking adjudicators against decisions of the parking authority under a decriminalised parking regime in Perth and Kinross Council area.

6138. Parking–special parking areas–designation–Edinburgh

ROAD TRAFFIC (PERMITTED PARKING AREA AND SPECIAL PARKING AREA) (CITY OF EDINBURGH) DESIGNATION AMENDMENT ORDER 2002, SSI 2002 188; made under the Road Traffic Act 1991 Sch.3 para.1, para.2, para.3. In force: May 17, 2002; £1.50.

This Order amends the Road Traffic (Permitted Parking Area and Special Parking Area) (City of Edinburgh) Designation Order 1998 (1998 1539) by making a further modification to the provisions of the Road Traffic Act 1991. The effect of the modification is to make further provision with regard to when a penalty charge is payable.

6139. Parking–special parking areas–designation–Glasgow

ROAD TRAFFIC (PERMITTED PARKING AREA AND SPECIAL PARKING AREA) (CITY OF GLASGOW) DESIGNATION AMENDMENT ORDER 2002, SSI 2002 187; made under the Road Traffic Act 1991 Sch.3 para.1, para.2, para.3. In force: May 17, 2002; £1.50.

This Order amends the Road Traffic (Permitted Parking Area and Special Parking Area) (City of Glasgow) Designation Order 1999 (SSI 1999 59) by making a further modification to the provisions of the Road Traffic Act 1991. The effect of the modification is to make further provision with regard to when a penalty charge is payable.

6140. Parking–special parking areas–designation–Perth and Kinross

ROAD TRAFFIC (PERMITTED PARKING AREA AND SPECIAL PARKING AREA) (PERTH AND KINROSS COUNCIL) DESIGNATION ORDER 2002, SSI 2002 398; made under the Road Traffic Act 1991 Sch.3 para.1, para.2, para.3. In force: October 1, 2002; £2.50.

This Order, which amends the Road Traffic Regulation Act 1984 and the Road Traffic Act 1991, extends to Perth and Kinross new arrangements for enforcing parking controls already available in London and certain other areas in England and in Edinburgh and Glasgow. It designates Perth and Kinross, with certain specified exceptions, as a permitted parking area and as a special parking area.

6141. Passenger vehicles–local services–registration–fees

PUBLIC SERVICE VEHICLES (REGISTRATION OF LOCAL SERVICES) (SCOTLAND) AMENDMENT REGULATIONS 2002, SSI 2002 548; made under the Public Passenger Vehicles Act 1981 s.60. In force: January 15, 2003; £1.50.

These Regulations amend the Public Service Vehicles (Registration of Local Services) (Scotland) Regulations 2001 (SSI 2001 219) Reg.13 by increasing the fee for an application to register or vary particulars of a bus service (other than a community bus service) from £38 to £40.

6142. Road safety–school crossing patrol sign

SCHOOL CROSSING PATROL SIGN (SCOTLAND) REGULATIONS 2002, SSI 2002 549; made under the Road Traffic Regulation Act 1984 s.28. In force: January 15, 2003; £1.75.

These Regulations which amend the Traffic Signs Regulations and General Directions 1994 (SI 1994 1519), prescribe the size, colour and type of the sign which, in accordance with the Road Traffic Regulations Act 1984 s.28, a school crossing patrol may exhibit so as to require traffic to stop when approaching a place where a person is crossing or seeking to cross a road. These Regulations were notified in draft to the European Commission in accordance with Directive 98/34 ([1998] OJ L204/37) as amended by Directive 98/48 ([1998] OJ L217/18).

6143. Road safety–traffic authorities–home zones–designation

HOME ZONES (SCOTLAND) REGULATIONS 2002, SSI 2002 177; made under the Transport (Scotland) Act 2001 s.74, s.81. In force: May 20, 2002; £2.50.

These Regulations make provisions as to the procedures that local traffic authorities have to follow prior to designating as a home zone any road for which they are the traffic authority.

6144. Road safety–traffic authorities–home zones–designation

HOME ZONES (SCOTLAND) (NO.2) REGULATIONS 2002, SSI 2002 292; made under the Transport (Scotland) Act 2001 s.74, s.81. In force: July 1, 2002; £2.50.

These Regulations, which revoke the Home Zones (Scotland) Regulations 2002 (SSI 2002 177), make provisions as to the procedures that local traffic authorities have to follow prior to designating as a home zone any road for which it is the traffic authority. They specify classes of road that may be designated; detail the consultation procedures to be followed prior to designation; specify where the proposals are to be published following a consultation, the content of the proposals and where they will be available for public inspection; specify the procedures for dealing with objections and hearing of objections; and provide where an objection has been made and a hearing held no designation can be made unless the designation is first confirmed by the Scottish Ministers.

6145. Road safety–traffic calming–road humps

ROAD HUMPS AND TRAFFIC CALMING (SCOTLAND) AMENDMENT REGULATIONS 2002, SSI 2002 419; made under the Roads (Scotland) Act 1984 s.38, s.39B, s.143. In force: October 1, 2002; £1.75.

These Regulations amend the Roads (Traffic Calming) (Scotland) Regulations 1994 (SI 1994 2488), which prescribe the traffic calming works which a roads authority may construct in a road maintained by them; and the Road Humps (Scotland) Regulations 1998 (SI 1998 1448) which make provision as to the construction and maintenance of road humps. The Regulations make amendments so that the signing provisions relating to the warning of the presence of traffic calming works do not apply to traffic calming works on a road designated as a home zone; and so that signing and lighting provisions and certain provisions relating to the placing of road humps do not apply to a road hump on a road designated as a home zone.

6146. Road traffic–speed limits–A9

A9 TRUNK ROAD (BALLINLUIG) (TEMPORARY 50MPH SPEED LIMIT) (CONTINUATION) ORDER 2002, SSI 2002 371; made under the Road Traffic Regulation Act 1984 s.88. In force: September 2, 2002; £1.50.

This Order continues in force the provisions of the A9 Trunk Road (Ballinluig) (Temporary 50mph Speed Limit) Order 2001 (SSI 2001 296) which would otherwise cease to have effect at midnight on September 1, 2002. It imposes a temporary 50 mph speed limit on two lengths of the A9 Trunk Road at Ballinluig.

6147. Road transport-establishment-Forth Estuary Transport Authority

FORTH ESTUARY TRANSPORT AUTHORITY ORDER 2002, SSI 2002 178; made under the Transport (Scotland) Act 2001 s.69, s.81. In force: April 1, 2002; £2.50.

This Order, which amends the Forth Road Bridge Order Confirmation Act 1947, the Forth Road Bridge Order Confirmation Act 1958, the Forth Road Bridge Order 1960 and the Forth Road Bridge (Toll Period) Extension Order 1997, revokes the Forth Road Bridge Order Confirmation Act 1950, the Forth Road Bridge Order Confirmation Act 1954 and the Forth Road Bridge Order Confirmation Act 1961. It dissolves the Forth Road Bridge Joint Board and replaces it with a new body to be known as the Forth Estuary Transport Authority which will be able to fund road and public transport measures that will improve travel across the Forth.

6148. Traffic wardens-uniforms

PARKING ATTENDANTS (WEARING OF UNIFORMS) (PERTH AND KINROSS COUNCIL PARKING AREA) REGULATIONS 2002, SSI 2002 399; made under the Road Traffic Regulation Act 1984 s.63A. In force: October 1, 2002; £1.75.

These Regulations prescribe functions during the exercise of which, a parking attendant must wear such uniform as the Scottish Ministers may determine.

6149. Transport (Scotland) Act 2001 (asp 2)-Commencement No.3 and Transitional Provisions Order

TRANSPORT (SCOTLAND) ACT 2001 (COMMENCEMENT NO.3 AND TRANSITIONAL PROVISIONS) ORDER 2002, SSI 2002 291; made under the Transport (Scotland) Act 2001 s.81, s.84. Commencement details: bringing into force various provisions of the 2001 Act on July 1, 2002; £1.75.

This Order, which brings into force certain provisions of the Transport (Scotland) Act 2001, contains transitional provisions which preserve the power of the traffic commissioners to impose penalties under the Transport Act 1985 s.111 where breaches of the relevant legislation have occurred before July 1, 2002. The Order also limits the power of the traffic commissioners to impose penalties to the amount which could have been imposed if the penalty relates to breaches occurring partly before and partly on or after July 1, 2002.

TRUSTS

6150. Liferent and fee-neglecting property-proper remedy

Executors of a deceased, as fiars of a house, sought decree of specific implement against the liferenter that he carry out certain repairs to a house, or alternatively damages. The defender sought dismissal of the action as incompetent. The sheriff upheld the defender's plea on the basis that he was bound by the statement in Erskine, Institute, II ix 59, inter alia, that "where waste is already committed, no action is competent to him who stands presently in the fee for recovering damages", and the only remedy open to a proper liferenter was to seek cautio usufructuaria. The pursuers appealed to the Court of Session and argued that (1) Erskine had been misinterpreted and did not mean that the present action was incompetent where there had been partial damage to the heritage caused by the wrongful act or omission of the liferenter; (2) if Erskine, properly construed, did so state, it was incorrect since it neither reflected Roman law nor the domestic law on liferent and fee, and (3) even if Erskine was good law, changes in the law and society meant it was no longer binding on the court: the cautio usufructuaria had in effect fallen into desuetude and it was inequitable to deny the appellants the remedies sought.

Held, refusing the appeal, that (1) Erskine had been read too broadly and meant that a presumptive heir, in whom the fee had not yet vested, could not competently seek damages from the liferenter for breach of his duty to use the estate salva rei substantia so long as the liferent subsisted, since a decree might be misdirected if the heir died before the liferenter; but (2) Scots law had not adopted all the remedies available under Roman law to a fiar who, as in the present case, had an indefeasibly vested right, and a fiar was entitled to remedies such as declarator, interdict, damages and specific implement only in respect of those parts of the estate in which he had a present beneficial interest, and (3) the appellants had not specified any particular societal changes which might have rendered the approach in Erskine out of date and while the cautio usufructuaria was very rarely used, changes in society or equitable considerations had not resulted in its falling into desuetude.

STRONACH'S EXECUTORS v. ROBERTSON 2002 S.L.T.1044, Lady Paton, Lord Cullen L.P., Lord Dawson, 1 Div.

6151. Books

Chalmers, James–Trusts. Paperback: £39.00. ISBN 0-414-01337-9. W.Green & Son.

UNJUSTIFIED ENRICHMENT

6152. Recompence–occupancy of heritable property–standard security unenforceable by virtue of mistake

G acted for T and her husband, H, in the purchase of a house occupied by T. G made a mistake in the preparation of the standard security which meant it was enforceable by the building society lender on H's default. G averred that as the disposition and standard security were supposed to have been in the joint names of T and H, T's continued occupation of the premises without paying rent meant that she had been unjustifiably enriched. G had made a settlement with the building society which assigned its rights under the standard security.

Held, granting decree of absolvitor, that (1) if the principle of actio de in rem verso had ever formed part of Scottish law, it was not now; (2) G had failed to demonstrate that T had no legal justification for retaining her share in the property it having been legally given to her by her husband; (3) even if T had been unjustifiably enriched, it would not have been equitable for her to pay rent in respect of her occupation of the property when the fault lay with G; (4) G failed in relation to each branch of the test laid down by the House of Lords in *Dollar Land (Cumbernauld) Ltd v. CIN Properties Ltd* 1998 S.C. (H.L.) 90, [1998] C.L.Y. 6034 and the case should be viewed simply as a loss to the building society as a result of lending to a bad debtor, the remedy for which was an action for recovery of debt from the husband, and (5) in relation to prescription, the cause of the action arose when G failed to obtain a valid standard security in favour of the building society and the loss occurred when the cheque was issued, or at latest cashed in January 1992, making the action time-barred.

GW TAIT & SONS v. TAYLOR 2002 S.L.T.1285, Lord Dawson, OH.

6153. Repetition–overpayment under contract–claim assigned–prior settlement of claim

S were employed by A to manage certain construction work. S subcontracted R as a consulting engineer who completed the required work and submitted invoices which were paid by A. A dispute arose between A and S with regard to how much was due and S made repayments to A. A then assigned their right to recover any "overcharge" from R, to S and S sought payment from R. R argued that S had no title to sue, A could not have assigned any right to S since their right had been extinguished upon repayment in full by S. R also argued that S's pleadings were irrelevant, they had not set out that the overpayment was as the result of error, nor how the error arose. A proof before answer was allowed and R appealed to the sheriff principal seeking dismissal.

Held, allowing the appeal, that S's payment to A would provide a complete defence to R, should A instigate proceedings against R. Accordingly, the assignation by A to S was, in effect, an empty vessel which could not give S a meaningful claim against R.

SMITHS GORE v. REILLY (T/A BOOTH AND REILLY CONSULTING ENGINEERS) 2003 S.L.T. (Sh Ct) 15, CGB Nicholson Q.C., Sheriff Principal, Sh Ct.

UTILITIES

6154. **Dissolution—utilities—New Water and Sewerage Authorities**

NEW WATER AND SEWERAGE AUTHORITIES DISSOLUTION (SCOTLAND) ORDER 2002, SSI 2002 277; made under the Water Industry (Scotland) Act 2002 s.24. In force: June 29, 2002; £1.50.

This Order dissolves the new water and sewerage authorities established under the Local Government etc. (Scotland) Act 1994.

6155. **Electricity generation—non fossil fuel sources**

ELECTRICITY FROM NON-FOSSIL FUEL SOURCES (SCOTLAND) SAVING ARRANGEMENTS (MODIFICATION) ORDER 2002, SSI 2002 93; made under the Utilities Act 2000 s.67. In force: March 31, 2002; £1.75.

This Order amends the Electricity from Non-Fossil Fuel Sources (Scotland) Saving Arrangements Order 2001 (SI 2001 3269) to make it a requirement that the supply successor company puts arrangements in place to sell on the open market benefits attaching to any electricity received by him under the SRO Orders. The arrangements are to be approved by the Authority and the Scottish Ministers. The requirements will allow for the electricity benefits to be auctioned by a third party and the proceeds of sale used to reduce the Fossil Fuel Levy paid by electricity consumers.

6156. **Electricity supply industry—fossil fuel levy**

FOSSIL FUEL LEVY (SCOTLAND) AMENDMENT REGULATIONS 2002, SSI 2002 94; made under the Electricity Act 1989 s.33, s.60. In force: March 31, 2002; £1.50.

These Regulations, which amend the Fossil Fuel Levy (Scotland) Regulations 1996 (SI 1996 293), require any benefits attaching to renewable sources of electricity to be taken into account when calculating the Fossil Fuel Levy to be paid. The amendment to the formula will result in less levy being paid by consumers.

6157. **Electricity supply industry—renewable energy—renewables obligation**

RENEWABLES OBLIGATION (SCOTLAND) ORDER 2002, SSI 2002 163; made under the Electricity Act 1989 s.32, s.32A, s.32B, s.32C. In force: April 1, 2002; £3.00.

This Order imposes an obligation on all electricity suppliers, which are licensed under the Electricity Act 1989, to supply to customers in Great Britain specified amounts of electricity generated by using renewable sources. As alternatives, in respect of all or part of an electricity supplier's renewables obligation, an electricity supplier is permitted to provide evidence that other licensed electricity suppliers have supplied electricity generated using renewable sources instead of it or to make a payment to the Gas and Electricity Markets Authority. Renewable sources include sources of energy such as wind, water, solar and biomass.

6158. Water industry–transfer of functions–Scottish Water

WATER INDUSTRY (SCOTLAND) ACT 2002 (CONSEQUENTIAL AND SAVINGS PROVISIONS) ORDER 2002, SSI 2002 166; made under the Water Industry (Scotland) Act 2002 s.24, s.68, s.69. In force: April 1, 2002; £1.75.

This Order, which amends the Council Tax (Administration and Enforcement) (Scotland) Regulations 1992 (SI 1992 1332), the Water Services Charges (Billing and Collection) (Scotland) Order 2002 (SSI 2002 33) and the Domestic Water and Sewerage Charges (Reduction) (Scotland) Regulations 2002 (SSI 2002 47), sets out additional provisions relating to the transfer of functions, property and liabilities from the new water and sewerage authorities to Scottish Water. It makes provision to save the current charges schemes and codes of practice made under the provisions of Local Government etc. (Scotland) Act 1994 until a replacement scheme and code can be made under the provisions of the Water Industry (Scotland) Act 2002 and makes consequential provisions relating to the billing and collection of water and sewerage charges by local authorities. It also makes consequential provisions arising from the provisions of a domestic water and sewerage charges reduction scheme.

6159. Water industry–transfer of functions–Scottish Water–rate of return

SCOTTISH WATER (RATE OF RETURN) (SCOTLAND) ORDER 2002, SSI 2002 165; made under the Water Industry (Scotland) Act 2002 s.41. In force: April 1, 2002; £1.75.

Responsibility for the provision of water and sewerage services in Scotland will transfer from the new water and sewerage authorities to Scottish Water established under the Water Industry (Scotland) Act 2002. This Order makes provision as to the rate of return on the value of its average net assets which Scottish Water requires to achieve for the financial year beginning with April 1, 2002.

6160. Water industry–transfer of functions–Scottish Water–tax provisions

SCOTTISH WATER (TRANSFER OF FUNCTIONS, ETC.) (TAX PROVISIONS) ORDER 2002, SI 2002 653; made under the Scotland Act 1998 s.104, s.112, s.126. In force: April 1, 2002; £1.75.

This Order makes provision consequential on the Water Industry (Scotland) Act 2002 to ensure that the transfer of functions, property and liabilities from the three Scottish water authorities to Scottish Water does not give rise to any adverse or beneficial tax consequences. It treats Scottish Water, for all purposes of corporation tax, as being the same person as each of the three Scottish water authorities, and vice versa. The Order provides the three Scottish water authorities shall be treated as together having carried on a single trade before April 1, 2002, that Scottish Water shall be treated as having acquired the assets transferred to it from the three Scottish water authorities at the time when they were acquired by those authorities, and that expenditure incurred by any of those authorities on any of those assets shall be treated, in computing the chargeable gain or allowable loss on a subsequent disposal by Scottish Water of that asset, as if it had been incurred by Scottish Water. In addition, the Order provides that no transfer from the three Scottish water authorities to Scottish Water effected by virtue of the 2002 Act shall give rise to any liability to stamp duty.

6161. Water Industry (Scotland) Act 2002 (asp 3)

This Act of the Scottish Parliament makes further provision in relation to the Water Industry Commissioner for Scotland and provides for the establishment of Water Customer Consultation Panels; makes further provision in relation to the regulation of the quality of drinking water; makes provision for the establishment of Scottish Water, transfers to Scottish Water the functions of the water and sewerage authorities established by the Local Government etc. (Scotland) Act 1994 s.62(1) and the dissolution of those authorities and in relation to the functions of

Scottish Water and makes further amendments of the law relating to water and sewerage.

This Act received Royal Assent on March 1, 2002.

6162. Water Industry (Scotland) Act 2002 (asp 3)–Commencement Order

WATER INDUSTRY (SCOTLAND) ACT 2002 (COMMENCEMENT AND SAVINGS) ORDER 2002, SSI 2002 118; made under the Water Industry (Scotland) Act 2002 s.68, s.72. Commencement details: bringing into force various provisions of the 2002 Act on March 8, 2002 and April 1, 2002; £1.75.

This Order brings into force specified provisions of the Water Industry (Scotland) Act 2002 which brings Scottish Water into being, establishes Water Customer Consultation Panels and allows the appointment of the Drinking Water Quality Regulator.

6163. Water supply–sewerage–charges–exemption

WATER AND SEWERAGE CHARGES (EXEMPTION) (SCOTLAND) REGULATIONS 2002, SSI 2002 167; made under the Water Industry (Scotland) Act 2002 s.40. In force: April 1, 2002; £1.75.

These Regulations provide that persons, which includes individuals, companies, incorporated bodies and partnerships, shall be exempt from charges for water and sewerage services if specified conditions are fulfilled. The exemption applies from the financial year in which the statement and information provided for are given to Scottish Water until March 31, 2006. The exemption is lost if the statement or information is inaccurate or misleading.

6164. Scottish Water–civil emergency–directions–Secretary of State and Scottish Ministers

See CONSTITUTIONAL LAW. §5395

VAT

6165. Exemptions–cash dispensers–issue of banknotes to other banks' customers through ATM–reciprocity fee

[Value Added Tax Act 1994 (c.23) Sch.8 Part II Group 11 Item 1, Sch.9 Part II Group 5 Item 1.]

B, a bank, appealed against a decision of the VAT and duties tribunal that for VAT purposes the supplies made by B to other banks through use by customers of other banks of its cash dispensing machines (ATMs) in Scotland were exempt and not zero rated. B had entered into two agreements with counterparty banks regulating the use of participants' ATMs, commission charges (referred to as reciprocity fees) being payable by the banks to each other. While B's ATMs in England dispensed Bank of England notes (being notes already in circulation), their Scottish ATMs dispensed B's banknotes (being an issue of the notes). The tribunal held that no material distinction could be made between dispensing cash from a Scottish ATM and from an English ATM, and that what was supplied in consideration of the reciprocity fee was the service of providing customers of counterparty banks with the facility to obtain money, which was an exempt supply under the Value Added Tax Act 1994 Sch.9 Group 5 item 1. The reciprocity fee was not a consideration payable for the issue of banknotes by B. B argued that the reciprocity fee was payable for the service of dispensing cash to the counterparty bank's customers through an ATM, and that an issue of their own banknotes was a zero rated supply in terms of Sch.8 Group 11 item 1 to the Act.

Held, dismissing the appeal, that the tribunal had correctly identified the nature of the supply as the provision of a service to the counterparty bank, even though that involved the provision of a service to a third party customer which was an "issue" of banknotes, as under the contractual arrangements the obligation to provide that service was owed directly to the counterparty bank, and the reciprocity fee was payable to B in consideration of its providing to the counterparty bank a supply consisting of a service to that bank's customers in the form of a facility.

ROYAL BANK OF SCOTLAND GROUP PLC v. CUSTOMS AND EXCISE COMMISSIONERS (RECIPROCITY FEES) [2002] S.T.C. 575, Lord Gill L.J.C., Lord Coulsfield, Lord Sutherland, 2 Div.

6166. Supply of services–possession of land–date of supply–major interest in land–when "made available"

[Value Added Tax Act 1994 (c.23) s.6(2)(b), s.96(1)(a).]

C, a development corporation, appealed against the decision of a VAT and duties tribunal that an assessment to VAT made by the CEC had been served timeously. C and D, a golf club, had concluded a minute of agreement dated January 28 and February 17, 1994 whereby they agreed to exchange adjacent tracts of land. C had given D occupation of the relevant land on May 1, 1996 and delivered the feu disposition on March 6, 1997 at which time D delivered the disposition of the other piece of land to C. The parties reached an agreement that the consideration for the piece of land which C had given to D, as the relevant taxable supply, should be valued at £1,505,000 and the CEC gave notice of assessment on that basis by letter dated July 12, 1999. On appeal, the VAT and duties tribunal held that the date of supply of the land to D was the date on which the feu disposition was delivered, therefore the assessment had been made timeously. C argued that the tribunal had failed to give effect to the Value Added Tax Act 1994 s.6(2)(b) as the land had been "made available" to D on May 1, 1996.

Held, dismissing the appeal, that having regard to the definition in s.96(1)(a), "major interest in land" referred to ownership in land, and although the relevant land had been made available on May 1, 1996 insofar as the club was given occupation, the interest of the proprietor of the dominium utile was not made available until March 6, 1997 which, for the purpose of the legislation, was the relevant date of supply.

CUMBERNAULD DEVELOPMENT CORP v. CUSTOMS AND EXCISE COMMISSIONERS [2002] S.T.C. 226, Lord Gill L.J.C., Lord Coulsfield, Lord MacLean, 2 Div.

WATER LAW

6167. Water industry–establishment–Water Customer Consultation Panels

WATER CUSTOMER CONSULTATION PANELS (SCOTLAND) ORDER 2002, SSI 2002 473; made under the Water Industry (Scotland) Act 2002 s.2, s.68. In force: November 20, 2002; £1.75.

This Order establishes Water Customer Consultation Panels.

6168. Water supply–sewerage–charges–reduction

DOMESTIC WATER AND SEWERAGE CHARGES (REDUCTION) (SCOTLAND) REGULATIONS 2002, SSI 2002 47; made under the Local Government etc. (Scotland) Act 1994 s.81. In force: April 1, 2002; £1.75.

These Regulations provide for reductions in water and sewerage charges in Scotland from April 1, 2002 until March 31, 2003 and make provision for a reduction in the water and sewerage charges due to a local authority for those in receipt of council tax benefit. The reduction applies to charges in a range from a threshold of £198 to the charges payable for properties in council tax Band E. There is no provision for reductions in charges due in the relevant year which fall either below £198 or above the Band E level. Within that range the Regulations provide that the proportion of the water and sewerage charge liability above the threshold attracts relief proportionate to council tax benefit received by virtue of the Social Security Contributions and Benefits Act 1992.

6169. Water supply–water services charges–billing and collection

WATER SERVICES CHARGES (BILLING AND COLLECTION) (SCOTLAND) ORDER 2002, SSI 2002 33; made under the Local Government etc. (Scotland) Act 1994 s.79. In force: April 1, 2002; £2.00.

Responsibility for water and sewerage services in Scotland rests with the three water authorities established under the Local Government etc. (Scotland) Act 1994. This Order provides, as regards financial years 2002-2003 to 2004-2005, for each local authority in Scotland to be responsible for demanding and recovering charges payable in respect of services provided by the water authorities to dwellings in the area of the local authority.

A that the proportion of the water and sewerage charges liability above the threshold attracts relief proportionate to council tax benefit received by virtue of the Social Security Contributions and Benefits Act 1992.

8193. Water supply—water services charges—billing and collection

WATER SERVICES CHARGES (BILLING AND COLLECTION) (SCOTLAND) ORDER 2002, SSI 2002/33, made under the Local Government etc. (Scotland) Act 1994 s.79. In force: April 1, 2002; £2.00.

Responsibility for water and sewerage services in Scotland rests with the three water authorities established under the Local Government etc. (Scotland) Act 1994. This Order provides, as regards financial years 2002-2003 to 2004-2005 (a) each local authority in Scotland is to be responsible for maintaining and recovering charges payable in respect of services provided by the water authorities to dwellings in the area of the local authority.

WORDS AND PHRASES

The table below is a cumulative guide to words and phrases judicially considered in 2002:

(N) refers to a case in the Northern Ireland section.

(S) refers to a case in the Scottish section.

adoption order, 1613
aims of a civic nature, 4757
all subcontractors, 2744
apply compulsorily, 4093
arrangements involving an intermediary, 4227, 4228
as shall survive me, 4331
bargain at arm's length, 4365
bodily injury, 5305(S)
body administered on an essentially voluntary basis, 4758
connection, 4729
debtor's estate, 5889(S)
demise together with me, 4339
destruction, 766
disability, 5569(S)
discard, 1519
dishonest concealment of material facts, 789
display, 3710
embryo, 3864
family proceedings, 2660
farmer practising farming as his main occupation, 111
fault, 4541
fixed base, 4389
good reason, 480
habitually resident, 4208
impairment, 1322
incentive, 2907
insecticidal activity, 2794
interception, 746, 3774
in the course of any of the operations of embarking, 243
land, 1445, 3842
lawful, 3644
miscarriage, 1824

necessary disbursement, 2718, 4382
non contractual overtime, 3396
non profit making organisations, 4756
obligation in question, 622
other proceedings, 2647, 4636
premises in a particular locality, 4727
property obtained, 809
proposes to dismiss, 1402
protected building, 4816
public authorities of all descriptions, 767
qualifying bodies, 1395
reasonable sufficiency, 863
recognised as refugee, 2632
reconstruction, 4358
recorded sounds, 3137
refugee, 5877(S)
relevant date, 4076
reorganisation, 4361
sale, 5971(S)
same damage, 325
scandalous conduct, 1361
severely disabled person, 4214
sufficient time to arrange a defence, 638
supervised study, 4215
supply, 698, 4661
temporarily, 2838
the other universities in Scotland, 5928(S)
to rent, 3072
trade organisation, 1324
trading regulations, 4107
training, 3791
transactions in securities, 4369
waste, 1519, 1520, 1521, 4466
week's pay, 1374
with a view to, 2908

Law books

published during 2002

Abbell, Michael–International Prisoner Transfer. Looseleaf/ring bound: £120.99. ISBN 1-57105-217-8. Transnational Publishers, Inc.

Abbell, Michael–Obtaining Evidence Abroad in Criminal Cases. Looseleaf/ring bound: £133.50. ISBN 1-57105-215-1. Transnational Publishers, Inc.

Abbey, Robert; Richards, Mark–Blackstone's Guide to the Land Registration Act 2002. Blackstone's Guide Series. Paperback: £29.95. ISBN 0-19-925796-5. Oxford University Press.

Abbott, Keith; Pendlebury, Norman; Wardman, Kevin–Business Law. 7th Ed. Paperback: £18.99. ISBN 0-8264-5860-2. Continuum International Publishing Group.

Abbott; Pendlebury; Wardman–Business Law. 7th Ed. Hardback: £60.00. ISBN 0-8264-5916-1. Continuum International Publishing Group.

Abeyratne, Ruwantissa I.R.–Frontiers of Aerospace Law. Hardback: £65.00. ISBN 0-7546-1949-4. Ashgate Publishing Limited.

Abrahamson, Debbie–Bar Manual: Professional Conduct 2002/2003. Blackstone Bar Manual. Paperback: £21.99. ISBN 0-19-925505-9. Oxford University Press.

Acer, Yucel–Aegean Maritime Disputes and International Law. Hardback: £55.00. ISBN 0-7546-2273-8. Dartmouth.

Adedayo, Morakinyo–Disused Offshore Installations and Pipelines. International Energy and Resources Law and Policy, 17. Hardback: £55.00. ISBN 90-411-1739-3. Kluwer Law International.

Adediran, Peter–Practical Guide to Business, Law and the Internet. Hardback: £25.00. ISBN 0-7494-3734-0. Kogan Page.

Agnew, Crispin; Baillie, Heather M.–Licensing (Scotland) Act 1976: Combined Set Of: Licensing (Scotland) Act and Scottish Civic Government Law. 5th Ed. Greens Annotated Acts. Paperback: £85.00. ISBN 0-414-01509-6. W.Green & Son.

Agnew, Crispin; Baillie, Heather M.–Licensing (Scotland) Act 1976. 5th Ed. Greens Annotated Acts. Paperback: £48.00. ISBN 0-414-01488-X. W.Green & Son.

Agreement for the Creation of an Assured Shorthold Tenancy. Paperback: £9.50. RICS Books.

Aikin, Olga–Managing Business Transfers: Takeovers, Mergers and Outsourcing. Paperback: £37.00. ISBN 0-7545-1661-X. Tolley Publishing.

Al-Azzawi, Ayad H.A.–Crime of International Maritime Fraud. Hardback: £50.00. ISBN 0-7546-2101-4. Ashgate Publishing Limited.

Alberstein, Michal–Pragmatism and Law-From Philosophy to Dispute Resolution. Law, Justice and Power. Hardback: £55.00. ISBN 0-7546-2208-8. Dartmouth.

Albors-Llorens, Albertina–EC Competition Law and Policy. Hardback: £40.00. ISBN 1-903240-75-1. Paperback: £17.99. ISBN 1-903240-74-3. Willan Publishing.

Alder, John–General Principles of Constitutional and Administrative Law. 4th Ed. Palgrave Law Masters. Paperback: £16.99. ISBN 0-333-97164-7. Palgrave Macmillan.

Aldridge, Trevor M.–Commonhold Law. Looseleaf/ring bound: £185.00. ISBN 0-421-75880-5. Sweet & Maxwell.

Aleinikoff, T. Alexander–Semblances of Sovereignty-The Constitution, the State and American Citizenship. Hardback: £30.95. ISBN 0-674-00745-X. Harvard University Press.

Alexander, Larry; Sherwin, Emily–Rule of Rules-Morality, Rules, and the Dilemmas of Law. Hardback: £34.95. ISBN 0-8223-2736-8. Duke University Press.

Alexy, Robert–Theory of Constitutional Rights. Hardback: £70.00. ISBN 0-19-825821-6. Oxford University Press.

Ali, Paul–Law of Secured Finance. Hardback: £110.00. ISBN 0-19-829902-8. Oxford University Press.

Allan, James Plunkett–Sympathy and Antipathy. Hardback: £50.00. ISBN 0-7546-2289-4. Dartmouth.

Allen, Christopher; Inns of Court School of Law–Bar Manual: Evidence 2002/2003. Blackstone Bar Manual. Paperback: £21.99. ISBN 0-19-925502-4. Oxford University Press.

Allen, Michael; Thompson, Brian–Cases and Materials on Constitutional and Administrative Law. Cases and Materials. Paperback: £24.99. ISBN 0-19-925525-3. Oxford University Press.

Allen, Simon; Bowley, Ivan; Davies, Hugh–APIL Guide to Damages. Paperback: £35.00. ISBN 0-85308-765-2. Jordans.

Allinson, J.R. Julian–Understanding Patent Law. Hardback: £40.00. ISBN 1-85521-811-9. Paperback: £16.50. ISBN 1-85521-706-6. Dartmouth.

Alschuler, Albert W.–Law Without Values-The Life, Work, and Legacy of Justice Holmes. Paperback: £11.50. ISBN 0-226-01521-1. University of Chicago Press.

Alter, Karen–Establishing the Supremacy of European Law. Oxford Studies in European Law. Paperback: £19.99. ISBN 0-19-926099-0. Oxford University Press.

Ambrose, Clare; Maxwell, Karen–London Maritime Arbitration. Hardback: £175.00. ISBN 1-84311-146-2. LLP Professional Publishing.

Amerasinghe, Chittharanjan F.–Jurisdiction of International Tribunals. Hardback: £135.00. ISBN 90-411-1838-1. Kluwer Law International.

Andenas, Mads; Roth, Wulf-Henning–Services and Free Movement in EU Law. Hardback: £60.00. ISBN 0-19-829938-9. Oxford University Press.

Andersen–Tolley's Guide to the UK/US Double Tax Treaty. Paperback: £75.00. ISBN 0-7545-1723-3. Tolley Publishing.

Anderson, David; Demetriou, Marie–References to the European Court. 2nd Ed. Litigation Library. Hardback: £160.00. ISBN 0-421-75350-1. Sweet & Maxwell.

Anderson, Ellen Mary–Judging Bertha Wilson-Law As Large As Life. Osgoode Society for Canadian Legal History. Hardback: £32.00. ISBN 0-8020-3648-1. University of Toronto Press Inc.

Anderson, Richard N.M.–Personal Services Companies: a Practical Guide. 2nd Ed. Paperback: £39.95. ISBN 0-7545-1516-8. Tolley Publishing.

Ando, Nisuke; McWhinney, Edward; Wolfrum, Rudiger; Roben, Betsy Baker–Liber Amicorum Judge Shigeru Oda. Hardback: £252.00. ISBN 90-411-1790-3. Kluwer Law International.

Anglade, Lelia–International Arbitration: Documents and Cases. Paperback. ISBN 1-85800-202-8. Round Hall Ltd.

Annuaire: 2000, Vol 4. Paperback: £50.00. ISBN 90-411-1761-X. Kluwer Law International.

Anson, William Reynell; Beatson, Jack–Anson's Law of Contract. 28th Ed. Paperback: £27.99. ISBN 0-19-876576-2. Oxford University Press Inc, USA.

Antczak, Gina–Tolley's Tax Essentials: Employment and Benefits. Tolley's Tax Essentials. Paperback: £35.00. ISBN 0-7545-1329-7. Tolley Publishing.

Antell, John—Employment Status. Paperback: £59.95. ISBN 0-7545-1812-4. Butterworths Law.

Anthony, Gordon—UK Public Law and European Law-The Dynamics of Legal Integration. Hardback: £35.00. ISBN 1-84113-148-2. Hart Publishing.

Antoine, Rose-Marie—Confidentiality in Offshore Financial Law. Hardback: £95.00. ISBN 0-19-925012-X. Oxford University Press.

Apap, Joanna—Rights of Immigrant Workers in the European Union. Hardback: £64.00. ISBN 90-411-1922-1. Kluwer Law International.

Appelbaum, Richard; Felstiner, William; Gessner, Volkmar—Rules and Networks-The Legal Culture of Global Business Transactions. Hardback: £45.00. ISBN 1-84113-295-0. Paperback: £20.00. ISBN 1-84113-296-9. Hart Publishing.

Appelbe, Gordon E.; Wingfield, Joy; Taylor, Lyndsay M.—Practical Exercises in Pharmacy Law and Ethics. 2nd Ed. Paperback: £19.95. ISBN 0-85369-522-9. Pharmaceutical Press.

Applebey, George—Contract Law. Textbook Series. Paperback: £24.95. ISBN 0-421-57120-9. Sweet & Maxwell.

Arden, Andrew; Hunter, Caroline; Dymond, Andrew; Carter, David—Housing Law Reports: 2001. Hardback: £310.00. ISBN 0-421-77110-0. Sweet & Maxwell.

Arden, A.; Hunter, C.—Homelessness and Allocations. Paperback: £39.00. ISBN 1-903307-04-X. The Legal Action Group.

Arlidge, Anthony; Parry, Jacques; Gatt, Ian—Arlidge and Parry on Fraud: 2nd Supplement to the 2nd Edition. Paperback: £55.00. ISBN 0-421-79680-4. Sweet & Maxwell.

Armstrong, Elizabeth—Before Copyright. Cambridge Studies in Publishing and Printing History. Paperback: £21.95. ISBN 0-521-89315-1. Cambridge University Press.

Arnold-Baker, Charles; Clayden, Paul—Arnold-Baker: Local Council Administration. Paperback: £45.00. ISBN 0-406-95298-1. Butterworths Law.

Arnold, Richard—Entertainment and Media Law Reports: 2001. Hardback: £430.00. ISBN 0-421-75670-5. Sweet & Maxwell.

Arnull, Anthony; Wincott, Daniel—Accountability and Legitimacy in the European Union. Oxford Studies in European Law. Hardback: £65.00. ISBN 0-19-925560-1. Paperback: £30.00. ISBN 0-19-925710-8. Oxford University Press.

Arsalidou, Demetra—Impact of Modern Influences on the Traditional Duties of Care, Skill and Diligence of Company Directors. Studies in Comparative Corporate and Financial Law, 13. Hardback: £59.00. ISBN 90-411-9851-2. Kluwer Law International.

Ashley-Norman, Jonathan—Ashley-Norman on Fraud. Hardback: £125.00. ISBN 0-406-94908-5. Butterworths Law.

Ashton, District Judge Gordon R.—Ashton: Elderly People and the Law. Paperback: £40.00. ISBN 0-406-94152-1. Butterworths Law.

Ashworth, Andrew—Serious Crime, Human Rights and Criminal Procedure. Hardback: £34.95. ISBN 0-421-78290-0. Paperback: £17.95. ISBN 0-421-78300-1. Sweet & Maxwell.

Asif H. Qureshi—Perspectives in International Economic Law. Hardback: £79.00. ISBN 90-411-9866-0. Kluwer Law International.

Atherton, Rosalind F.—Papers of the International Academy of Estate and Trust Law-2000. The International Academy of Estate and Trust Law Yearbook, Vol 2. Hardback: £69.00. ISBN 90-411-9855-5. Kluwer Law International.

Atherton, Rosalind F.—Papers of the International Academy of Estate and Trust Law: 2001. The International Academy of Estate and Trust Law Yearbook, Vol 3. Hardback: £72.00. ISBN 90-411-9880-6. Kluwer Law International.

Atria, Fernando—On Law and Legal Reasoning. Hardback: £35.00. ISBN 1-84113-275-6. Hart Publishing.

Austin, John; Campbell, Robert—Lectures on Jurisprudence: 2 Volumes (1879 Ed.). Hardback: £175.00. ISBN 1-85506-962-8. Thoemmes Press.

Baatz, Nicholas; Clay, Robert; Walker, Steven J.—Technology and Construction Law Reports. Hardback: £245.00. ISBN 0-421-77120-8. Sweet & Maxwell.

Babington, Anthony—For the Sake of Example. Rev Ed. Classic Military History. Paperback (C format): £6.99. ISBN 0-14-139100-6. Penguin Books.

Bace, Rebecca Gurley; Smith, Fred Chris—Guide to Forensic Testimony. Paperback: £37.99. ISBN 0-201-75279-4. Addison Wesley.

Bahaa Ali El-Dean—Privatisation and the Creation of a Market Based Legal System. Social, Economic and Political Studies of the Middle East and Asia, 82. Hardback. ISBN 90-04-12580-9. Brill.

Bailey, Edward—Voluntary Arrangements. Paperback: £30.00. ISBN 0-406-94600-0. Butterworths Law.

Bailey, Stephen; Gunn, Michael—Smith, Bailey and Gunn on the Modern English Legal System. 4th Ed. Paperback: £30.00. ISBN 0-421-74130-9. Sweet & Maxwell.

Bailey, Stephen; Gunn, Michael—Smith, Bailey and Gunn on the Modern English Legal System. Paperback: £14.95. ISBN 0-421-75080-4. Sweet & Maxwell International Student Editions.

Bainbridge, David I.—Intellectual Property. Paperback: £34.99. ISBN 0-582-47314-4. Longman.

Bainbridge, David I.—Patent Law. Hardback: £125.00. ISBN 1-85811-140-4. EMIS Professional Publishing.

Baker, Philip—Transfer Pricing and Taxation. Hardback. ISBN 0-421-49910-9. Sweet & Maxwell.

Banakar, Reza; Travers, Max—Introduction to Law and Social Theory. Hardback: £40.00. ISBN 1-84113-208-X. Paperback: £20.00. ISBN 1-84113-209-8. Hart Publishing.

Bankowski, Zenon—Living Lawfully: Love in Law and Law in Love. Law and Philosophy Library, 53. Hardback: £55.00. ISBN 0-7923-7180-1. Kluwer Academic Publishers.

Banks, Robert—Banks on Sentencing. Paperback: £38.00. ISBN 0-406-95130-6. Paperback: £38.00. ISBN 0-406-95130-6. Butterworths Law.

Bantekas, Ileas—Principles of Direct and Superior Responsibility in International Humanitarian Law. Melland Schill Studies in International Law. Hardback: £45.00. ISBN 0-7190-6080-X. Manchester University Press.

Bantekas, Ilias—Public International Law. Statutes Series. Paperback: £16.95. ISBN 0-421-79410-0. Sweet & Maxwell.

Barber, John—Building and Civil Engineering Claims. 4th Ed. Hardback: £120.00. ISBN 0-421-72510-9. Sweet & Maxwell.

Barber, Susan—Company Law. 1999-2000 Suggested Solutions. Paperback: £6.95. ISBN 1-85836-442-6. Old Bailey Press.

Barcroft, Charles; Jenney, Hugo—BDO Stoy Hayward's Orange Tax Guide 2002-03. Paperback: £47.95. ISBN 0-406-95033-4. Butterworths Tolley.

Barendt, Eric M.—Privacy. International Library of Essays in Law and Legal Theory (Second Series). Hardback: £100.00. ISBN 0-7546-2071-9. Dartmouth.

Barendt, Eric; Firth, Alison—Yearbook of Copyright and Media Law: Vol 6. 2001-02. Hardback: £95.00. ISBN 0-19-924584-3. Oxford University Press.

Barker, D.L.—Law. 11th Ed. Made Simple Series. Paperback: £14.99. ISBN 0-7506-5405-8. Butterworth-Heinemann.

Barlow, Anne—Barlow: Cohabitants and the Law. 3rd Ed. Paperback: £47.00. ISBN 0-406-94151-3. Butterworths Law.

Barnard, Catherine; Scott, Joanne—Law of the Single European Market-Unpacking the Premises. Hardback: £45.00. ISBN 1-84113-271-3. Paperback: £22.50. ISBN 1-84113-344-2. Hart Publishing.

Barnes, David; Stone, Tim—Practitioner's Guide to Legacies. Paperback: £45.00. ISBN 0-7545-1454-4. Tolley Publishing.

Barnes, Michael—Hill and Redmans Guide to Rent Review. Paperback: £60.00. ISBN 0-406-93756-7. Butterworths Law.

Barnett, Daniel; Scrope, Henry—Employment Law Handbook. Paperback: £44.95. ISBN 1-85328-716-4. Law Society Publications.

Barnett, Daniel—Managing Dismissal. Paperback: £35.00. ISBN 0-7545-1255-X. Tolley Publishing.

Barraclough, Fraser R.—Practical Guide to Rent Review of Agricultural Holdings in Scotland. Paperback: £20.00. ISBN 0-414-01506-1. W.Green & Son.

Barrett, Scott—Environment and Statecraft. Hardback: £27.50. ISBN 0-19-925733-7. Oxford University Press.

Barrow, Charles—Industrial Relations Law. 2nd Ed. Paperback: £31.95. ISBN 1-85941-563-6. Cavendish Publishing Ltd.

Basedow, Jurgen—European Private Law/Droit Prive Europeen/Europaisches Privatrecht/Diritto Privato Europeo-Sources/quellen/fonti, III. Hardback: £164.00. ISBN 90-411-1329-0. Kluwer Law International.

Bass, Gary Jonathan—Stay the Hand of Vengeance. Princeton Studies in International History and Politics. Paperback: £13.95. ISBN 0-691-09278-8. Princeton University Press.

Bassiouni, M. Cherif—International Terrorism-A Compilation of U.N. Documents and Regional Conventions, 1970-2000. International and Comparative Law. Hardback: £237.99. ISBN 1-57105-227-5. Transnational Publishers, Inc.

Bassiouni, M. Cherif—International Terrorism. International and Comparative Law. Hardback: £116.99. ISBN 1-57105-149-X. Transnational Publishers, Inc.

Bates, Phil—Butterworths Core Text: Family Law. Butterworths Core Text. Paperback: £12.95. ISBN 0-406-92954-8. Butterworths Law.

Bauman, Richard W.—Ideology and Community in the First Wave of Critical Legal Studies. Paperback: £18.00. ISBN 0-8020-8341-2. University of Toronto Press Inc.

Bazley, Stuart; Blunden, Tony; Haynes, Andrew—Butterworths Compliance Series: Compliance. Butterworths Compliance Series. Paperback: £45.00. ISBN 0-406-93250-6. Butterworths Law.

Beale, Hugh—Contract Law. Casebooks for the Common Law of Europe. Paperback: £32.50. ISBN 1-84113-237-3. Hart Publishing.

Beatson, Jack—Anson's Law of Contract. Hardback: £55.00. ISBN 0-19-925603-9. Oxford University Press.

Beaumont, C.H.—Planning Appeal Decisions: 2001. Hardback: £405.00. ISBN 0-421-75660-8. Sweet & Maxwell.

Beaumont, Paul; Lyons, Carole; Walker, Neil—Convergence and Divergence in European Public Law. Hardback: £35.00. ISBN 1-84113-211-X. Hart Publishing.

Beck, Robert A; Ambrosio, Thomas—International Law and the Rise of Nations. Paperback: £28.95. ISBN 1-889119-30-X. Chatham House Publishers of Seven Bridges Press, LLC.

Bederman, David J.—Spirit of International Law. The Spirit of the Laws. Hardback: £33.95. ISBN 0-8203-2404-3. University of Georgia Press.

Beigbeder, Yves—Judging Criminal Leaders. Nijoff Law Specials, 55. Hardback: £50.00. ISBN 90-411-1815-2. Martinus Nijhoff Publishers.

Belitz, Hina; Crossley-Holland, Dominic—Penguin Guide to Employment Rights. Paperback (B format): £8.99. ISBN 0-14-100045-7. Penguin Books.

Bell, Andrew—Forum Shopping and Venue in Transnational Litigation. Oxford Private International Law Series. Hardback: £75.00. ISBN 0-19-924818-4. Oxford University Press.

Bell, Cedric D.—Land: the Law of Real Property. Revision Workbook. Paperback: £9.95. ISBN 1-85836-376-4. Old Bailey Press.

Bell, Cedric D.–Land. 150 Leading Cases. Paperback: £11.95. ISBN 1-85836-457-4. Old Bailey Press.

Bell, Cedric D.–Real Property: Cases and Statutes. Cracknell's Companion Cases and Statutes. Paperback: £11.95. ISBN 1-85836-301-2. Old Bailey Press.

Bell, Mark–Anti-discrimination Law and the European Union. Oxford Studies in European Law. Hardback: £40.00. ISBN 0-19-924450-2. Oxford University Press Inc, USA.

Beloff, Michael–International Sports Law Review: 2000. Hardback. ISBN 0-421-78700-7. Sweet & Maxwell.

Belson, Jeffrey–Certification Marks. Special Reports. Hardback: £150.00. ISBN 0-421-75820-1. Sweet & Maxwell.

Benedek, Wolfgang; Kisaakye, Esther Mayambala; Oberleitner, Gerd–Human Rights of Women-International Instruments and African Experiences. Paperback: £16.95. ISBN 1-84277-045-4. Zed Books.

Benedek, Wolfgang–Human Rights of Women-International Instruments and African Experiences. Hardback: £50.00. ISBN 1-84277-044-6. Zed Books.

Benitah, Marc–Law of Subsidies Under the GATT/WTO System. Hardback: £69.00. ISBN 90-411-9827-X. Kluwer Law International.

Benjamin, Joanna; Yates, Madeleine–Legal Risk Management in Global Securities Investment and Collateral. Hardback: £170.00. ISBN 0-406-94721-X. Butterworths Law.

Bennion, Francis A.R.–Bennion: Statutory Interpretation. 4th Ed. Hardback: £275.00. ISBN 0-406-94305-2. Butterworths Law.

Berg, Alan–Common Law in Practice: Understanding Common Problems. ISBN 1-84311-001-6. LLP Professional Publishing.

Berk-Seligson, Susan–Bilingual Courtroom. Paperback: £14.50. ISBN 0-226-04378-9. University of Chicago Press.

Berman, Bruce–From Ideas to Assets: Investing Wisely in Intellectual Property. Hardback: £44.50. ISBN 0-471-40068-8. John Wiley & Sons Inc.

Bermingham, Vera–Nutcases-tort. 3rd Ed. Nutcases. Paperback: £5.95. ISBN 0-421-76740-5. Sweet & Maxwell.

Berns, Sandra–Women Going Backwards: Law and Change in Family Unfriendly Society. Applied Legal Philosophy. Hardback: £50.00. ISBN 0-7546-2303-3. Dartmouth.

Berry, Christopher; Bailey, Edward; Schaw-Miller, Stephen–Berry, Bailey and Schaw-Miller: Personal Insolvency-law and Practice. 3rd Ed. Paperback: £145.00. ISBN 0-406-08153-0. Butterworths Law.

Berson, Ilene R.; Berson, Michael J.; Cruz, Barbara C.–Cross Cultural Perspectives in Child Advocacy. Research in Global Child Advocacy, 1. Paperback: £25.50. ISBN 1-930608-04-7. Information Age Publishing.

Beyleveld, David; Brownsword, Roger–Human Dignity in Bioethics and Biolaw. Hardback: £45.00. ISBN 0-19-826826-2. Oxford University Press.

Billington, Michael J.; Powell-Smith, Vincent–Means of Escape from Fire-An Illustrated Guide to the Law. Hardback: £39.50. ISBN 0-632-03203-0. Blackwell Science (UK).

Binder, Sarah–Stalemate-Causes and Consequences of Legislative Gridlock. Hardback: £29.25. ISBN 0-8157-0910-2. Paperback: £12.50. ISBN 0-8157-0911-0. The Brookings Institution.

Bindman, Geoffrey; Bamforth, Nicholas; Malik, Maleiha–Discrimination. Socio Legal Series. Paperback: £15.95. ISBN 0-421-55440-1. Sweet & Maxwell.

Bird, Roger; Salter, David–Family Law Precedents Service. Looseleaf/ring bound: CD-ROM: £150.00. ISBN 0-85308-727-X. Family Law.

Bird, Roger–Ancillary Relief Handbook. 3rd Ed. Paperback: £45.00. ISBN 0-85308-739-3. Family Law.

Bird, Roger–Child Support-The New Law. Paperback: £32.50. ISBN 0-85308-761-X. Family Law.

Birks, Peter—English Private Law-Main Volumes and First Cumulative Supplement (Updated Ed). Oxford English Law. Hardback: £175.00. ISBN 0-19-925576-8. Oxford University Press.

Birks, Peter—English Private Law: First Cumulative Supplement. English Private Law Series. Paperback: £30.00. ISBN 0-19-924754-4. Oxford University Press.

Birnie, Patricia; Boyle, Alan—International Law and the Environment. Reissued 2nd Ed. Paperback: £29.99. ISBN 0-19-876553-3. Oxford University Press.

Black, Helen; Waller, Phillip; White, Ken—Black, Waller and White: Family Proceedings-a Guide for Urgent Business and Emergencies. Hardback: Floppy disk: £75.00. ISBN 0-406-99294-0. Butterworths Law.

Black, Trevor—IP in the Digital Era. Special Reports. Hardback: £150.00. ISBN 0-421-82410-7. Sweet & Maxwell.

Blackburn, Robert; Kennon, Andrew—Griffith & Ryle on Parliament. Hardback: £65.00. ISBN 0-421-60910-9. Sweet & Maxwell.

Blackburn, Robert; Polakiewicz, Jorg—Fundamental Rights in Europe. Hardback: £100.00. ISBN 0-19-924348-4. Oxford University Press.

Blackett-Ord, Mark—Blackett-Ord: Partnership-the Modern Law of Partnership and Limited Liability Partnership. Hardback: £195.00. ISBN 0-406-94644-2. Butterworths Law.

Blackie, John W.G.; Patrick, Hilary—Mental Health-the Law in Scotland. Paperback (C format): £45.00. ISBN 0-406-07756-8. Butterworths Law (Scotland).

Blackstone's Police Manual: Road Traffic 2003. Blackstone's Police Manual. Paperback: £10.99. ISBN 0-19-925490-7. Blackstone Press.

Blackstone, William—Commentaries on the Laws of England-A Facsimile of the First Edition of 1765-1769. Hardback: £123.00. ISBN 0-226-05547-7. University of Chicago Press.

Blair, William; Allison, Austin; Morton, Guy; Palmer, Keith; Richards-Carpenter, Peter—Blair: Banking and Financial Services Regulation. 3rd Ed. Hardback: £195.00. ISBN 0-406-94987-5. Butterworths Law.

Blake, Susan—Bar Manual: Remedies 2002/2003. Blackstone Bar Manual. Paperback: £21.99. ISBN 0-19-925506-7. Oxford University Press.

Blakemore, Timothy; Greene, Brendan—Law for Legal Executives: Part One Year One. 6th Ed. Paperback: £21.99. ISBN 0-19-925526-1. Oxford University Press.

Blanpain, Roger—Involvement of Employees in the European Union. Bulletin of Comparative Labour Relations, 42. Paperback: £69.00. ISBN 90-411-1760-1. Kluwer Law International.

Blue Book 2002: the Directory of the Law Society of Scotland. Paperback: £36.00. ISBN 0-406-94755-4. Butterworths Law (Scotland).

Bobb-Semple, Colin; Inns of Court School of Law—Bar Manual: Criminal Litigation and Sentencing 2002/2003. Blackstone Bar Manual. Paperback: £21.99. ISBN 0-19-925499-0. Oxford University Press.

Bogdanovic, Slavko—International Law of Water Resources. International and National Water Law and Policy Series, 4. Hardback: £100.00. ISBN 90-411-1623-0. Kluwer Law International.

Bohan, Brian—Bohan: Capital Acquisitions Tax. Reissued 2nd Ed. Hardback: £70.18. ISBN 1-85475-762-8. Butterworths Law (Ireland).

Bond, Robert—Bond: E-licences and Software Contracts: Law, Practice and Precedents. Paperback/CD-ROM: £99.00. ISBN 0-406-95652-9. Butterworths Law.

Bonner, David; Hooker Ian—Social Security Legislation 2002: Non-means Tested Benefits, Vol 1. Paperback: £63.00. ISBN 0-421-79120-9. Sweet & Maxwell.

Born, Gary B.—International Commercial Arbitration: Student Edition. Hardback: £68.99. ISBN 1-57105-175-9. Transnational Publishers, Inc.

Borrows, Jane–Current Issues in Securitisation. Special Reports. Hardback: £150.00. ISBN 0-7520-0585-5. Sweet & Maxwell.

Bottomley, Anne–Feminist Perspectives on the Foundational Subjects of Law. Feminist Perspectives. Paperback: £32.95. ISBN 1-85941-590-3. Cavendish Publishing Ltd.

Bottomley, Stephen; Kinley, David–Commercial Law and Human Rights. Hardback: £50.00. ISBN 0-7546-2136-7. Dartmouth.

Bouchet-Saulnier, Francois–Practical Guide to Humanitarian Law-First English Language Edition. Hardback: £65.00. ISBN 0-7425-1062-X. Rowman & Littlefield Publishers.

Bowers, John; Brown, Damian; Mansfield, Gavin–Employment Tribunal Practice and Procedure. Paperback: £130.00. ISBN 0-421-78780-5. Sweet & Maxwell.

Bowers, John; Brown, Damian; Mead, Geoffrey–Employment Tribunal Practice and Procedure: 2001 Supplement to Volume 2 of the 3rd Edition. Common Law Library. Paperback: £85.00. ISBN 0-421-76770-7. Sweet & Maxwell.

Bowers–On Employment Law. Paperback: £37.95. ISBN 0-19-925451-6. Oxford University Press.

Boyle, Alan; Bowman, Michael–Environmental Damage in International and Comparative Law-Problems of Definition and Valuation. Hardback: £65.00. ISBN 0-19-925573-3. Oxford University Press.

Boyle, A.J.–Minority Shareholders' Remedies. Cambridge Studies in Corporate Law. Hardback: £40.00. ISBN 0-521-79106-5. Cambridge University Press.

Bradley, A.; Ewing, K.–Constitutional and Administrative Law. Paperback: £32.99. ISBN 0-582-43807-1. Longman.

Bradshaw, Joseph; Goodie, Howard–House Buying, Selling & Conveyancing and Buying Bargains At Property Auctions. Hardback: £24.99. ISBN 1-902646-87-8. Law Pack Publishing.

Braithwaite, John–Restorative Justice and Responsive Regulation. Studies in Crime and Public Policy. Book (details unknown): £37.95. ISBN 0-19-513639-X. Oxford University Press Inc, USA.

Brammer, Alison–Social Work Law. Paperback: £19.99. ISBN 0-582-43831-4. Longman.

Bramwell, Richard; James, Alun; Hardwick, Mike; Lindsay, John–Taxation of Companies and Company Reconstructions. 8th Ed. Looseleaf/ring bound: £295.00. ISBN 0-421-82720-3. Sweet & Maxwell.

Bray, Judith; Martin, Jacqueline; Turner, Chris–Key Facts: Land Law. Key Facts for Law. Paperback: £4.99. ISBN 0-340-84585-6. Hodder & Stoughton Educational.

Breen, P.J.–Round Hall's Consolidated Superior Court Rules. Hardback. ISBN 1-85800-303-2. Round Hall Ltd.

Brennan, Gabriel–Landlord and Tenant Law. Paperback: £34.99. ISBN 0-19-925555-5. Oxford University Press.

Breslin, Mary Lou; Yee, Silvia; Mayerson, Arlene–Disability Rights Law and Policy. Hardback: £76.99. ISBN 1-57105-239-9. Transnational Publishers, Inc.

Brett, Hugh; Sullivan, Rory–European Intellectual Property Review: 2001. Hardback: £555.00. ISBN 0-421-75590-3. Sweet & Maxwell.

Bridge, Caroline; Swindells, Heather–Adoption. Paperback: £29.50. ISBN 0-85308-762-8. Family Law.

Bridge, Michael–Personal Property Law. 3rd Ed. Clarendon Law Series. Paperback: £15.99. ISBN 0-19-925476-1. Oxford University Press.

Bridges, Mark; Way, David–Tolley's Guide to International Succession Laws. Looseleaf/ring bound: £115.00. ISBN 0-7545-1246-0. Looseleaf/ring bound: £145.00. ISBN 0-7545-1447-1. Tolley Publishing.

Brieger, N.–Test Your Professional English Law. PENG. Paperback: £6.00. ISBN 0-582-46898-1. Longman.

Briggs, Adrian–Conflict of Laws. Clarendon Law Series. Paperback: £17.99. ISBN 0-19-876333-6. Oxford University Press.

Brockman, Joan–Gender in the Legal Profession-Fitting or Breaking the Mould. Paperback: £25.50. ISBN 0-7748-0835-7. University of British Columbia Press.

Brooks, Richard O.; Jones, Ross; Virginia, Ross A.–Law and Ecology and the Rise of the Ecosystem Regime. Ecology and Law in Modern Society. Paperback: £25.00. ISBN 0-7546-2316-5. Dartmouth.

Broomhall, Bruce–International Justice and the International Criminal Court. Oxford Monographs in International Law. Hardback: £60.00. ISBN 0-19-925600-4. Oxford University Press.

Brown, Alastair N.–Brown: Criminal Evidence and Procedure: An Introduction. Paperback: £40.00. ISBN 0-406-95230-2. Butterworths Law (Scotland).

Brown, Alastair N.–Regulation of Investigatory Powers in Scotland. Green's Essential Legislation. Paperback: £39.00. ISBN 0-414-01490-1. W.Green & Son.

Brown, Anne–Human Rights and the Borders of Suffering. New Approaches to Conflict Analysis. Hardback: £45.00. ISBN 0-7190-6105-9. Manchester University Press.

Brown, Ian; Cracknell, D. G.; Cracknell, D.G., Brown, Ian–Conflict of Laws. Cracknell's Statutes. Paperback: £11.95. ISBN 1-85836-473-6. Old Bailey Press.

Brown, Ian; Cracknell, D. G.; Cracknell, D.G.; Brown, Ian–Public International Law. Cracknell's Statutes. Paperback: £11.95. ISBN 1-85836-476-0. Old Bailey Press.

Brown, Ian–Conflict of Laws. Revision Workbook. Paperback: £9.95. ISBN 1-85836-425-6. Old Bailey Press.

Brown, Ian–Conflict of Law. 150 Leading Cases. Paperback: £11.95. ISBN 1-85836-420-5. Old Bailey Press.

Brown, Michael–Butterworths Insurance Law Handbook. 7th Ed. Paperback: £82.00. ISBN 0-406-94577-2. Butterworths Law.

Brown, Vincent; Aitchison, Karen–Brown and Aitchison: Environmental Law and Commercial Property Transactions in Scotland. Paperback: £65.00. ISBN 0-406-92758-8. Butterworths Law.

Brownlie Ian; Goodwin-Gill, Guy S.–Basic Documents on Human Rights. 4th Ed. Paperback: £25.99. ISBN 0-19-924944-X. Oxford University Press.

Brownlie, Ian–Basic Documents in International Law. 5th Ed. Paperback: £19.99. ISBN 0-19-924942-3. Oxford University Press.

Bryer, Lanning G; Seminsky, Melvin–Intellectual Property Assets in Mergers and Acquisitions. Hardback: £55.95. ISBN 0-471-41437-9. John Wiley & Sons Inc.

Bryer, Lanning G; Seminsky, Melvin–Intellectual Property. Hardback: £55.95. ISBN 0-471-41437-9. John Wiley and Sons Inc.

Buckley, Richard A.–Illegality and Public Policy. Hardback: £125.00. ISBN 0-421-64790-6. Sweet & Maxwell.

Budget Tax Tables 2002. Paperback: £9.95. ISBN 0-406-95032-6. Butterworths Tolley.

Building Law Reports: 2001. Hardback: £230.00. ISBN 1-84311-136-5. LLP Professional Publishing.

Bunn-Livingstone, Sandra L.; Jennings, Robert C.–Juricultural Pluralism Vis-a-vis Treaty Law. Developments in International Law, 42. Hardback: £63.00. ISBN 90-411-1779-2. Martinus Nijhoff Publishers.

Bunter, Michael A.G.–Promotion and Licensing of Petroleum Prospective Acreage. International Energy and Resources Law and Policy, 16. Hardback: £83.00. ISBN 90-411-1712-1. Kluwer Law International.

Burn, Suzanne; Terrett, Andrew–Client Participation in Civil Litigation (Reissue). Paperback: £45.00. ISBN 0-406-98582-0. Butterworths Law.

Burrows, Andrew—Burrows: the Law of Restitution. 2nd Ed. Paperback: £28.95. ISBN 0-406-93244-1. Butterworths Law.

Burrows, D.—Funding Family Proceedings. Paperback: £25.00. ISBN 0-85308-790-3. Paperback: £25.00. ISBN 0-85308-790-3. Family Law.

Burton, Frances—Principles of Family Law. Principles of Law. Paperback: £22.95. ISBN 1-85941-471-0. Cavendish Publishing Ltd.

Burton, Frank; Nelson-Jones, Rodney—Nelson-Jones and Burton: Clinical Negligence Case Law 3rd Ed. Hardback: £120.00. ISBN 0-406-91959-3. Butterworths Law.

Burton, Michael—Civil Appeals. Looseleaf release (unbound): £250.00. ISBN 1-858-11284-2. Spiral/comb bound: £275.00. ISBN 1-858-11284-2. EMIS Professional Publishing.

Burton, Nicholas—Highway Law: a Practical Guide. Paperback: £28.00. ISBN 1-85811-267-2. EMIS Professional Publishing.

Butler, Desmond—Employer Liability for Workplace Trauma. Hardback: £50.00. ISBN 0-7546-2287-8. Dartmouth.

Butler, Frances—Human Rights Protection-Methods and Effectiveness. The British Institute of Human Rights Library. Hardback: £60.00. ISBN 90-411-1702-4. Kluwer Law International.

Butler, Julie M.—Tax Planning for Agriculture and Land Diversification. Paperback: £49.95. ISBN 0-7545-1769-1. Tolley Publishing.

Butterworths Student Statutes: EC Law. Butterworths Student Statutes. Paperback: £12.95. ISBN 0-406-91636-5. Butterworths Law.

Bygrave, Lee A.—Data Protection Law. Information Law Series, Vol 10. Hardback: £75.00. ISBN 90-411-9870-9. Kluwer Law International.

Byrne, John; Glover, Leigh; Martinez, Celia—Environmental Justice: International Discourses in Political Economy, Energy and Environmental Policy, Volume 2. Energy and Environmental Policy Series, Vol 8. Paperback: £22.95. ISBN 0-7658-0751-3. Transaction Publishers.

Cahill, Eamonn, SC—Discovery and Disclosure. 2nd Ed. Hardback: £59.00. ISBN 1-85800-233-8. Round Hall Ltd.

Cain, Brian—Law of Gene Technology. Hardback: £150.00. ISBN 0-406-94593-4. Butterworths Law.

Cain, George H.—Law Partnership Revisited. Hardback: £46.95. ISBN 1-59031-032-2. American Bar Association.

Cain, Paul—Claims Against Uninsured and Untraced Drivers. Hardback: £70.00. ISBN 0-421-79500-X. Sweet & Maxwell.

Cairns, Walter—Introduction to European Union Law. Paperback: £16.95. ISBN 1-85941-679-9. Cavendish Publishing Ltd.

Caller, Russell—ADR and Commercial Disputes. Dispute Resolution Series. Hardback: £85.00. ISBN 0-421-76300-0. Sweet & Maxwell.

Cameron, Gordon—Delict LawBasics. Greens Law Basics. Paperback: £9.95. ISBN 0-414-01233-X. W.Green & Son.

Camp, Peter—Solicitors and Financial Services-A Compliance Handbook. 3rd Ed. Paperback: £69.95. ISBN 1-85328-805-5. Law Society Publications.

Campbell, Andrea—Making Crime Pay-An Author's Guide to Criminal Law, Evidence, and Procedure. Paperback: £14.95. ISBN 1-58115-216-7. Allworth Press.

Campbell, Andrew; Cartwright, Peter—Banks in Crisis-The Legal Response. Hardback: £45.00. ISBN 1-84014-442-4. Dartmouth.

Campbell, Emily—Campbell: Varying International Domestic Trusts. Paperback: £60.00. ISBN 0-406-94023-1. Butterworths Law.

Campbell, Tom D.; Stone, Adrienne—Law and Democracy. International Library Essays in Law and Legal Theory. Hardback: £100.00. ISBN 0-7546-2214-2. Dartmouth.

Campbell, Tom; Ewing, Keith; Tomkins, Adam—Sceptical Essays on Human Rights. Paperback: £16.99. ISBN 0-19-924668-8. Oxford University Press.

Campbell, T.C.; McKay, Reg–The Wilderness Years. Paperback (C format): £9.99. ISBN 1-84195-331-8. Canongate Books Ltd.

Cane, Peter–Administrative Law. International Library of Essays in Law and Legal Theory: Second Series. Hardback: £110.00. ISBN 0-7546-2181-2. Dartmouth.

Cane, Peter–Responsibility in Law and Morality. Hardback: £25.00. ISBN 1-841-13321-3. Hart Publishing.

Cann, Simon; Churchill, Philip; Fallon, Liz; Head, Simon–Tolly's Basic Guide to Pensions. Paperback: £26.99. ISBN 0-7545-0745-9. Tolley Publishing.

Cannon, Patrick–Practical Guide to Stamp Duty and E-conveyancing. Paperback: £19.95. ISBN 0-7545-1485-4. Tolley Publishing.

Cannon, Patrick–Tolley's Stamp Duties and Stamp Duty Reserve Tax 2001-02. Paperback: £59.95. ISBN 0-7545-1205-3. Tolley Publishing.

Cannon, Patrick–Tolley's Stamp Duties and Stamp Duty Reserve Tax 2002-03. Paperback: £74.95. ISBN 0-7545-1677-6. Tolley Publishing.

Cannon, Patrick–Tolley's Tax Essentials: Stamp Duties. Tolley's Tax Essentials. Spiral/comb bound: £35.00. ISBN 0-7545-1295-9. Tolley Publishing.

Canny, James–Construction and Building Law. Hardback: £75.00. ISBN 1-85800-225-7. Round Hall Ltd.

Card, Richard; James, Jennifer–Card and James: Law for Accountancy Students. 7th Ed. Paperback: £19.95. ISBN 0-406-94681-7. Butterworths Law.

Carey, Peter; Ustaran, Eduardo; Paisner, Berwin Leighton–E-privacy and Online Data Protection. Book (details unknown): CD-ROM: £95.00. ISBN 0-406-94588-8. Butterworths Law.

Carman, Dominic–No Ordinary Man. Paperback: £7.99. ISBN 0-340-82099-3. Coronet.

Carroll, Alex–Constitutional and Administrative Law. 2nd Ed. Foundation Studies in Law. Paperback: £26.99. ISBN 0-582-43808-X. Longman.

Cartledge, Paul; Millett, Paul; Todd, Stephen–Nomos-Essays in Athenian Law, Politics and Society. Paperback: £18.95. ISBN 0-521-52209-9. Cambridge University Press.

Cartwright, John–Misrepresentation. Contract Law Library. Hardback: £135.00. ISBN 0-421-62670-4. Sweet & Maxwell.

Cassell, Elizabeth–Equity and Trusts. 150 Leading Cases. Paperback: £11.95. ISBN 1-85836-452-3. Old Bailey Press.

Castellino, Joshua; Allen, Steve–Title to Territory in International Law. Law, Social Change and Development. Hardback: £60.00. ISBN 0-7546-2224-X. Dartmouth.

Cato, D. Mark–Arbitration Practice and Procedure. Hardback: £220.00. ISBN 1-84311-139-X. LLP Professional Publishing.

Catt, Hilton; Scudamore, Pat–Know Your Employment Rights in a Week. In a Week Series. Paperback: £6.99. ISBN 0-340-84914-2. Hodder & Stoughton Educational.

Chalmers, James–Trusts. Paperback: £39.00. ISBN 0-414-01337-9. W.Green & Son.

Chapman, Michael D.–Waterlow's Solicitors' & Barristers' Directory: 2002. Hardback: £61.95. ISBN 1-85783-982-X. Waterlow Professional Publishing.

Chappell, David–Parris's Standard Form of Building Contract JCT 98. Hardback: £49.50. ISBN 0-632-02195-0. Blackwell Science (UK).

Charitable Arbitrator-How to Mediate and Arbitrate in Louis XIV's France. Hardback: £40.00. ISBN 0-9537730-2-7. Holo Books.

Charman, Mary–Contract Law. Paperback: £14.99. ISBN 1-903240-85-9. Willan Publishing.

Cheeseman, Henry–Legal and Regulatory Environment of Business: Study Guide. Paperback: £12.99. ISBN 0-13-060703-7. Prentice Hall.

Chen-Wishart, Mindy–Law of Contract. Butterworth's Core Text. Paperback: £12.95. ISBN 0-406-03311-0. Butterworths Law.

Chesterman, Simon–Just War or Just Peace? Oxford Monographs in International Law. Paperback: £19.99. ISBN 0-19-925799-X. Oxford University Press.

Cheyne, Ann–Legal Secretary's Guide. Paperback: £25.99. ISBN 0-19-925422-2. Oxford University Press.

Chigwada-Bailey, Ruth–Race, Gender & Criminal Justice. Paperback: £19.50. ISBN 1-872870-52-X. Waterside Press.

Childs, Penny–Nutcases-criminal Law. Nutcases. Paperback: £5.95. ISBN 0-421-76760-X. Sweet & Maxwell.

Chill, R.–Executry Practice. Paperback. ISBN 0-414-01386-7. W. Green & Son.

Chissick, Michael–Electronic Commerce-Law and Practice. 3rd Ed. Hardback: £155.00. ISBN 0-421-76430-9. Sweet & Maxwell.

Christie, Michael G.A.; Gordon, Gerald H.–Criminal Law of Scotland: Vol 2. Scottish Universities Law Institute. Hardback: £150.00. ISBN 0-414-01399-9. W. Green & Son.

Christou, Richard–Boilerplate: Practical Clauses. Practitioner Series. Hardback: £75.00. ISBN 0-421-78280-3. Sweet & Maxwell.

Church, Clive H.; Phinnemore, David–Penguin Guide to the European Treaties. Paperback: £30.00. ISBN 0-14-028973-9. Penguin Books.

CIMA Paper 3b-stage 1: Business Law (FBLW): MCQ Cards (2002). Educational cards: £5.95. ISBN 0-7517-3753-4. BPP Business Education Ltd.

CIMA Paper 3B Stage 1: Business Law (FBLW): Study Text (2002). CIMA Study Text: Foundation Paper. Paperback: £20.95. ISBN 0-7517-3752-6. BPP Business Education Ltd.

Clarke-Williams, Jeremy–Clarke-Williams: Defamation Law. Paperback: £60.00. ISBN 0-406-08132-8. Butterworths Law.

Clarke, Barry–Challenging Racism-A Handbook on the Human Rights Act. Paperback: £22.50. ISBN 0-85315-931-9. Lawrence & Wishart.

Clarke, David; Wells, Andrew–Leasehold Enfranchisement. 2nd Ed. Paperback: £32.50. ISBN 0-85308-426-2. Jordans.

Clarke, David–Commonhold-The New Law. Paperback: £35.00. ISBN 0-85308-774-1. Jordans.

Clarke, Giles–Clarke: Offshore Tax Planning. Paperback: £89.95. ISBN 0-406-95039-3. Butterworths Tolley.

Clarke, Ian–Land Registration Act 2002-a Practical Guide. Paperback: £35.00. ISBN 0-421-78690-6. Sweet & Maxwell.

Clarke–Contracts of Carriage by Air. Transport Law Series. Hardback: £180.00. ISBN 1-84311-148-9. LLP Professional Publishing.

Clay, Andrew; Donovan, Colleen–Tolley's IP Handbook. Paperback: £49.95. ISBN 0-7545-1591-5. Tolley Publishing.

Clayden, Paul–Law of Allotments. 5th Ed. Paperback: £18.95. ISBN 0-7219-0143-3. Shaw & Sons.

Clayton, Nigel–Administration of Trusts. Paperback: £30.00. ISBN 0-85297-605-4. Paperback: £30.00. ISBN 0-85297-605-4. Financial World Publishing.

Clayton, Richard and Tomlinson, Hugh–Civil Actions Against the Police. Hardback: £135.00. ISBN 0-421-63090-6. Sweet & Maxwell.

Clayton, Richard; Tomlinson, Hugh–Law of Human Rights. Law of Human Rights Series. Book: £195.00. ISBN 0-19-925822-8. Paperback: £49.50. ISBN 0-19-925431-1. Oxford University Press.

Cleland, Alison; Hall-Dick, Anne–Child Centred Practice in Family Law. Paperback: £19.99. ISBN 0-414-01388-3. W. Green & Son.

Cleland, Alison; Mcdiarmid, Claire; Sutherland, Elaine; et al; Scoular, Jane–Family Dynamics: Contemporary Issues in Family Law. Paperback: £35.00. ISBN 0-406-93239-5. Butterworths Law.

Cochrane, F. Michael–Tolley's Accounting Principles for Tax Purposes. Paperback: £53.95. ISBN 0-7545-0260-0. Tolley Publishing.

Cochrane, Mike–Tolley's Taper Relief. 2nd Ed. Paperback: £64.95. ISBN 0-7545-1299-1. Tolley Publishing.

Cockburn, David–Commercial Leases. Paperback: £40.00. ISBN 0-406-94712-0. Butterworths Law (Scotland).

Cohen, Jean L.–Regulating Intimacy-A New Legal Paradigm. Hardback: £24.95. ISBN 0-691-05740-0. Princeton University Press.

Cohen, Steve–No One Is Illegal. Hardback: £17.99. ISBN 1-85856-291-0. Trentham Books.

Cohn, Marjorie; Dow, David–Cameras in the Courtroom. Paperback: £14.95. ISBN 0-7425-2023-4. Rowman & Littlefield Publishers.

Cole, Daniel H.–Pollution and Property-Comparing Ownership Institutions for Environmental Protection. Hardback: £45.00. ISBN 0-521-80637-2. Paperback: £16.95. ISBN 0-521-00109-9. Cambridge University Press.

Cole, Robin–Cole on Property Finance. Paperback: £125.00. ISBN 0-406-90519-3. Butterworths Law.

Coleman, Jules L.–Markets, Morals, and the Law. Paperback: £25.00. ISBN 0-19-925360-9. Oxford University Press.

Coleman, Jules L.–Risks and Wrongs. Paperback: £25.00. ISBN 0-19-925361-7. Oxford University Press.

Coleman, Martin; Grenfell, Michael–Competition Act 1998: Law and Practice-Second Cumulative Supplement. Paperback: £65.00. ISBN 0-19-829956-7. Oxford University Press.

Coles, Joanne–European Union Law-1999-2000 LLB Examination Questions and Suggested Solutions: University of London External Examinations. 1999-2000 Suggested Solutions. Paperback: £6.95. ISBN 1-85836-443-4. Old Bailey Press.

Coles, Richard; Ready, Nigel–Ship Registration: Law and Practice. Lloyd's Shipping Law Library. Hardback: £185.00. ISBN 1-84311-119-5. Lloyd's List.

Collar, Neil–Planning and Human Rights. Paperback: £39.00. ISBN 0-414-01432-4. W.Green & Son.

Collateral Warranties. 2nd Ed. Hardback: £55.00. ISBN 0-632-03896-9. Blackwell Science (UK).

Collin, P.H.–Pocket German Law Dictionary-English-German/German-English. Paperback: £6.95. ISBN 1-903856-26-4. Peter Collin Publishing.

Collin, P.H.–Pocket Spanish Law Dictionary. Paperback: £6.95. ISBN 1-903856-25-6. Peter Collin Publishing.

Collins, Hugh–Regulating Contracts. Paperback: £19.99. ISBN 0-19-925801-5. Oxford University Press.

Commercial Law. 3rd Ed. LawCards Series. Paperback: £6.95. ISBN 1-85941-519-9. Cavendish Publishing Ltd.

Commercial Property. Looseleaf/ring bound. ISBN 0-414-01421-9. W.Green & Son.

Company Law. LawCards Series. Paperback: £6.95. ISBN 1-85941-709-4. Cavendish Publishing Ltd.

Conaghan, Joanne; Fischl, Richard Michael; Klare, Karl–Labour Law in an Era of Globalization-Transformative Practices and Possibilities. Hardback: £60.00. ISBN 0-19-924247-X. Oxford University Press.

Congressional Quarterly's Congressional Staff Directory: March 2002/Spring. 63rd Ed. Paperback: £167.00. ISBN 0-87289-194-1. CQ Press.

Congressional Quarterly's Judicial Staff Directory: December 2001/Winter. 19th Ed. Paperback: £167.00. ISBN 0-87289-193-3. CQ Press.

Conneely, Sinead–Family Mediation in Ireland. Hardback: £50.00. ISBN 0-7546-2219-3. Ashgate Publishing Limited.

Connelly, Claire–Criminal. Greens Law Basics. Paperback: £9.95. ISBN 0-414-01231-3. W.Green & Son.

Constitutional Law. 3rd Ed. LawCards Series. Paperback: £6.00. ISBN 1-85941-716-7. Cavendish Publishing Ltd.

Constitutional Law. Paperback: £37.99. ISBN 0-19-571726-0. Oxford University Press Southern Africa.

Contracts of Employment. 2nd Ed. Legal Essentials. Paperback: £32.99. ISBN 0-85292-951-X. Chartered Institute of Personnel and Development (CIPD).

Conveyancing Statutes 2002. Paperback: £29.95. ISBN 0-414-01493-6. W.Green & Son.

Cook, Philip J.; Ludwig, Jens–Gun Violence. Studies in Crime and Public Policy. Paperback: £14.99. ISBN 0-19-515384-7. Oxford University Press Inc, USA.

Cook, Trevor–Cook: a User's Guide to Patents. Users' Guide, 3. Paperback: £65.00. ISBN 0-406-90003-5. Butterworths Law.

Cook, Trevor–Cook: Pharmaceuticals, Biotechnology and the Law. Hardback: £125.00. ISBN 0-406-91441-9. Butterworths Law.

Cooper, Jeremy–Care Homes Legal Handbook. Paperback: £13.95. ISBN 1-84310-064-9. Jessica Kingsley Publishers.

Cooter, Robert; Ulen, Thomas–Law and Economics. Hardback: £31.99. ISBN 0-201-77025-3. Addison Wesley.

Cornish, Graham–Copyright in a Week. In a Week Series. Paperback: £6.99. ISBN 0-340-84944-4. Hodder & Stoughton Educational.

Corporate Fraud: Prevention and Detection. Paperback: £39.95. ISBN 0-7545-1298-3. Tolley Publishing.

Cossman, Brenda; Fudge, Judy–Privatization, Law, and the Challenge of Feminism. Hardback: £48.00. ISBN 0-8020-3699-6. Paperback: £22.50. ISBN 0-8020-8509-1. University of Toronto Press Inc.

Cotterill, Janet–Language in the Legal Process. Hardback: £50.00. ISBN 0-333-96902-2. Macmillan.

Cotterrell, Roger–Politics of Jurisprudence. 2nd Ed. Paperback: £22.95. ISBN 0-406-93055-4. Butterworths Law.

Cousins, Mel–Irish Social Welfare System. Paperback. ISBN C. Round Hall Ltd.

Cowan, Jane K.; Dembour, Marie Benedicte; Wilson, Richard–Culture and Rights-Anthropological Perspectives. Hardback: £45.00. ISBN 0-521-79339-4. Paperback: £15.95. ISBN 0-521-79735-7. Cambridge University Press.

Cox, Sue; Janes, Bill; Walker, Deborah; Wenham, David–Tolley's Office Health and Safety Handbook. Paperback: £50.00. ISBN 0-7545-1267-3. Tolley Publishing.

Cracknell, D. G.; Hollick, P. N.; Cracknell, D.G.–Criminal Law. Cracknell's Statutes. Paperback: £11.95. ISBN 1-85836-474-4. Old Bailey Press.

Cracknell, D. G.–Employment Law. Cracknell's Statutes. Paperback: £11.95. ISBN 1-85836-475-2. Old Bailey Press.

Cracknell, D.G.–Commercial Law. Cracknell's Statutes. Paperback: £11.95. ISBN 1-85836-472-8. Old Bailey Press.

Cracknell, D.G.–Obligations. 150 Leading Cases. Paperback: £11.95. ISBN 1-85836-458-2. Old Bailey Press.

Cracknell, D.G.–Obligations. 150 Leading Cases. Paperback: £11.95. ISBN 1-85836-459-0. Old Bailey Press.

Craig, Paul; de Burca, Grainne–EU Law. Paperback: £32.99. ISBN 0-19-924943-1. Oxford University Press.

Craig, William–Taxation of E-commerce. Paperback: £71.95. ISBN 0-7545-1213-4. Tolley Publishing.

Cranston, Ross–Principles of Banking Law. Paperback: £32.99. ISBN 0-19-925331-5. Oxford University Press.

Crawford, James; Lowe, Vaughan–British Yearbook of International Law: Vol 72. 2001. British Yearbook of International Law. Hardback: £125.00. ISBN 0-19-925401-X. Oxford University Press.

Cretney, Stephen M.; Masson, Judith; Bailey-Harris, Rebecca–Principles of Family Law. Paperback: £30.00. ISBN 0-421-71760-2. Sweet & Maxwell.

Criminal Law Statutes: 2002. A Parliament House Book. Paperback: £33.00. ISBN 0-414-01492-8. W.Green & Son.

Criminal Law. 3rd Ed. LawCards Series. Paperback: £6.00. ISBN 1-85941-515-6. Cavendish Publishing Ltd.

Cripps, Yvonne and Newiss, Hilary–Biotechnology-The Intellectual Property Law. Hardback: £145.00. ISBN 0-421-57500-X. Sweet & Maxwell.

Crofts, Thomas–Criminal Responsibility of Children and Young Persons. Hardback: £60.00. ISBN 0-7546-2265-7. Ashgate Publishing Limited.

Crone, Tom; Alberstat, Philip; Cassels, Tom–Law and the Media. 4th Ed. Paperback: £19.99. ISBN 0-240-51629-X. Focal Press.

Cross, Claire; Loades, David; Scarisbrick, J.J.–Law and Government in Tudor England-Essays Presented to Sir Geoffrey Elton. Paperback: £18.95. ISBN 0-521-89363-1. Cambridge University Press.

Cruz, Julio Baquero–Between Competition and Free Movement. Hardback: £35.00. ISBN 1-84113-336-1. Hart Publishing.

Crystal, Michael; Phillips, Mark; Davis, Glen–Butterworths Insolvency Law Handbook. 6th Ed. Paperback: £67.00. ISBN 0-406-94409-1. Butterworths Law.

Curnutt, Jordan–Animals and the Law-A Dictionary. Contemporary Legal Issues. Hardback: £35.95. ISBN 1-57607-147-2. ABC CLIO (Reference Books).

Current Law Statutes: 2001. Vol 2. Hardback: £130.00. ISBN 0-421-78870-4. Sweet & Maxwell.

Current Law Statutes: Vol 1. 2001. Hardback: £130.00. ISBN 0-421-78860-7. Sweet & Maxwell.

Curtis, Richard; Donnelly, Tracy–Tax Office Directory 2002: Six Monthly. Spiral/comb bound: £19.95. ISBN 0-7545-1433-1. Tolley Publishing.

Cusine, Douglas J., NP; Forte, A.D.M.–Scottish Cases and Materials in Commercial Law. Paperback: £35.00. ISBN 0-406-04658-1. Butterworths Law (Scotland).

C.I.P.A. Guide to the Patents Acts: 2nd Supplement to the 5th Edition. Intellectual Property Library. Paperback: £50.00. ISBN 0-421-79490-9. Sweet & Maxwell.

Dailly, Mike–Housing Law in Practice. Paperback: £40.00. ISBN 0-414-01500-2. W.Green & Son.

Daintith, Terence; Page, Alan–Executive in the Constitution. Paperback: £16.99. ISBN 0-19-925578-4. Oxford University Press.

Dan-Cohen, Meir–Harmful Thoughts-Essays on Law, Self, and Morality. Hardback: £45.00. ISBN 0-691-09006-8. Paperback: £13.95. ISBN 0-691-09007-6. Princeton University Press.

Darbyshire, Penny–Eddey and Darbyshire on the English Legal System. 7th Ed. Paperback: £14.95. ISBN 0-421-75070-7. Sweet & Maxwell.

Dashwood, Alan; Ward, Angela; Spencer, John; Hillion, Christopher–Cambridge Yearbook of European Legal Studies: Vol 3. 2001. Hardback: £65.00. ISBN 1-84113-240-3. Hart Publishing.

David, Martyn R.–Natural Gas Agreements. Hardback: £200.00. ISBN 0-421-76800-2. Sweet & Maxwell.

Davies, Iwan R.–Journal of International Commercial Law: Vol 1, No 1. Hardback: £140.00. ISBN 0-7546-2298-3. Ashgate Publishing Limited.

Davies, Iwan–Security Interests in Mobile Equipment. Hardback: £55.00. ISBN 1-84014-792-X. Dartmouth.

Davies, Rt Hon Denzil–Booth: Residence, Domicile and UK Taxation. Paperback: £89.95. ISBN 0-7545-1685-7. Tolley Publishing.

Davis, Anthony C.R.–Tolley's Taxation in Corporate Insolvency. 5th Ed. Spiral/comb bound: £61.95. ISBN 0-7545-1211-8. Tolley Publishing.

Davis, Colin; Sutherland, Mike; Eastaway, Nigel–BDO Stoy Hayward's Yellow Tax Guide 2002-03. Paperback: £67.95. ISBN 0-406-95036-9. Butterworths Tolley.

Davis, Glen; Phillips, Mark–Butterworths Insolvency Law Manual. Paperback: £95.00. ISBN 0-406-94643-4. Butterworths Law.

Dawn, Renata–International Policing in Peace Operations. SIPRI Research Report, 18. Paperback: £12.99. ISBN 0-19-925241-6. Oxford University Press.

DCG: Law: 2002/2003. Paperback: £5.50. ISBN 1-86017-937-1. Hobsons plc.

de Burca, Grainne–Constitutional Limits of EU Action. Collected Courses of the Academy of European Law, V. 9, No. 3. Hardback: £45.00. ISBN 0-19-829957-5. Oxford University Press.

de Cruz, Peter–Family Law, Sex and Society. Paperback: £32.95. ISBN 1-85941-638-1. Cavendish Publishing Ltd.

De Cruz, Peter–Nutshells-medical Law. Nutshells. Paperback: £5.95. ISBN 0-421-78670-1. Sweet & Maxwell.

De Lacy, John–Reform of UK Company Law. Hardback: £65.00. ISBN 1-85941-693-4. Cavendish Publishing Ltd.

de Sadeleer, Nicolas–Environmental Principles. Hardback: £60.00. ISBN 0-19-925474-5. Oxford University Press.

De Than, Claire; Shorts, Edwin–International Criminal Law and Human Rights. Paperback: £24.95. ISBN 0-421-72250-9. Sweet & Maxwell.

De Than, Claire; Shorts, Edwin–Public Law and Human Rights. Statutes Series. Paperback: £14.95. ISBN 0-421-78680-9. Paperback: £14.95. ISBN 0-421-78680-9. Sweet & Maxwell.

De Wilde, Robin–Facts and Figures: 2002. Paperback: £35.00. ISBN 0-421-78230-7. Sweet & Maxwell.

Delany, Hilary; Mcgrath, Declan–Civil Procedure in the Superior Courts. Hardback: £125.00. ISBN 1-85800-241-9. Round Hall Ltd.

Dellapenna, Joseph W.–Suing Foreign Governments and Their Corporations. Hardback: £100.99. ISBN 1-57105-131-7. Transnational Publishers, Inc.

Delmas-Marty, Mireille; Spencer, J. R.–European Criminal Procedures. Cambridge Studies in International and Comparative Law. Hardback: £100.00. ISBN 0-521-59110-4. Cambridge University Press.

Dennis, Ian–Criminal Law. Statutes Series. Paperback: £10.95. ISBN 0-421-78080-0. Sweet & Maxwell.

Dennis, Ian–Law of Evidence. 2nd Ed. Paperback: £27.95. ISBN 0-421-74200-3. Sweet & Maxwell.

Denyer, Roderick–Denyer: Children and Personal Injury Litigation. 2nd Ed. Paperback: £29.00. ISBN 0-406-93917-9. Butterworths Law.

Denza, Eileen–Intergovernmental Pillars of the European Union. Hardback: £60.00. ISBN 0-19-829935-4. Oxford University Press.

Derham, Rory–Law of Set-off. Hardback: £165.00. ISBN 0-19-829800-5. Oxford University Press.

Dershowitz, Alan–Letters to a Young Lawyer. The Art of Mentoring Series. Hardback: £15.99. ISBN 0-465-01631-6. Basic Books.

Desta, Melaku Geboye–Law of International Trade in Agricultural Products. Hardback: £99.00. ISBN 90-411-9865-2. Kluwer Law International.

Dicey, A.V.; Morris, J.H.C.; Collins, Lawrence–Dicey and Morris on the Conflict of Laws: Second Supplement to the 13th Edition. Paperback: £45.00. ISBN 0-421-78990-5. Sweet & Maxwell.

Dillon, Sara–International Trade and Economic Law and the European Union. Paperback: £25.00. ISBN 1-84113-113-X. Hart Publishing.

Dine, Janet–Company Law. Textbook Series. Paperback: £24.95. ISBN 0-421-65280-2. Sweet & Maxwell.

Directory of Local Authorities: 2002 (CD-ROM). CD-ROM: £80.00. ISBN 0-421-77230-1. Sweet & Maxwell.

Directory of Local Authorities: 2002 (special Bundle Offer). Paperback: CD-ROM: £99.00. ISBN 0-421-77240-9. Sweet & Maxwell.

Directory of Local Authorities: 2002. Paperback: £38.50. ISBN 0-421-77220-4. Sweet & Maxwell.

Dispute Settlement Reports 1999. World Trade Organization Dispute Settlement Reports. Paperback: £30.00. ISBN 0-521-00565-5. Cambridge University Press.

Dispute Settlement Reports 1999: Volume I. World Trade Organization Dispute Settlement Reports. Hardback: £75.00. ISBN 0-521-80320-9. Paperback: £30.00. ISBN 0-521-00562-0. Cambridge University Press.

Dispute Settlement Reports 1999: Volume II. World Trade Organization Dispute Settlement Reports. Hardback: £75.00. ISBN 0-521-80321-7. Paperback: £30.00. ISBN 0-521-00564-7. Cambridge University Press.

Dispute Settlement Reports 1999: Volume III. World Trade Organization Dispute Settlement Reports. Hardback: £75.00. ISBN 0-521-80322-5. Cambridge University Press.

Dixon, John C.–Tolley's Trading in the European Union: a Guide to Business and Taxation. 4th Ed. Paperback: £65.00. ISBN 0-7545-1157-X. Tolley Publishing.

Dixon, Martin–Principles of Land Law. 4th Ed. Principles of Law Series. Paperback: £19.95. ISBN 1-85941-472-9. Cavendish Publishing Ltd.

Dixon, Martin–Q&A Land Law. 4th Ed. Questions and Answers. Paperback: £10.95. ISBN 1-85941-627-6. Cavendish Publishing Ltd.

Dnes, Antony; Rowthorn, Robert–Law and Economics of Marriage and Divorce. Hardback: £45.00. ISBN 0-521-80933-9. Paperback: £15.95. ISBN 0-521-00632-5. Cambridge University Press.

Dobson, Paul–Nutshells: Criminal Law. 6th Ed. Nutshells. Paperback: £5.95. ISBN 0-421-76510-0. Sweet & Maxwell.

Dodds, Malcolm–Family Law. 1999-2000 Suggested Solutions. Paperback: £6.95. ISBN 1-85836-445-0. Old Bailey Press.

Dodds, Malcolm–Family Law. Revision Workbook. Paperback: £9.95. ISBN 1-85836-464-7. Old Bailey Press.

Doherty, Michael–Criminology. 2nd Ed. Sourcebook. Paperback: £11.95. ISBN 1-85836-450-7. Old Bailey Press.

Doherty, Michael–Equity and Trusts. Revision Workbook. Paperback: £9.95. ISBN 1-85836-462-0. Old Bailey Press.

Doherty, Michael–Jurisprudence, 2nd Edition. Sourcebook. Paperback: £11.95. ISBN 1-85836-456-6. Old Bailey Press.

Doherty, Michael–Jurisprudence. Revision Workbook. Paperback: £9.95. ISBN 1-85836-427-2. Old Bailey Press.

Dolton, Alan; Saunders, Glyn–Tolley's Tax Cases 2002. Paperback: £69.00. ISBN 0-7545-1783-7. Tolley Publishing.

Dolton, Alan; Wareham, Robert–Tolley's VAT Cases 2002. Paperback: £89.95. ISBN 0-7545-1688-1. Tolley Publishing.

Donnelly, Aileen; Walsh, Majella–Enforcement of Revenue. Paperback: £57.97. ISBN 1-85475-687-7. Butterworths Law.

Dorsen, Norman–Unpredictable Constitution. Hardback: £40.00. ISBN 0-8147-1948-1. New York University Press.

Douglas-Scott, Sionaidh–Constitutional Law of the European Union. Law in Focus. Paperback: £29.99. ISBN 0-582-31717-7. Longman.

Douglas, Andrew–National Lottery: Its Regulation Process, Problems and Personalities. Hardback: £40.00. ISBN 0-485-11572-7. Continuum International Publishing Group-Athlone Press.

Dowding, Nicholas–Landlord and Tenant Reports 2001. Hardback: £265.00. ISBN 0-421-75630-6. Sweet & Maxwell.

Doyle, Christopher–The Company Secretary. Hardback. ISBN 1-85800-290-7. Round Hall Ltd.

Drabble, Richard; Maurici, James–Local Authorities and Human Rights. Blackstone's Human Rights Act Series. Paperback: £25.00. ISBN 1-84174-135-3. Blackstone Press.

Drahos, Peter; Mayne, Ruth–Global Intellectual Property Rights. Hardback: £47.50. ISBN 0-333-99027-7. Paperback: £15.99. ISBN 0-333-99028-5. Palgrave Macmillan.

Driscoll, James; Williams, Del; Boston, Charles–Handbook of Residential Tenancies. Looseleaf/ring bound: £195.00. ISBN 0-421-70310-5. Sweet & Maxwell.

Dugdale, Anthony–Clerk and Lindsell on Torts: 1st Supplement to the 18th Ed. Common Law Library. Paperback: £38.00. ISBN 0-421-76250-0. Sweet & Maxwell.

Dugdale, Anthony–Clerk & Lindsell on Torts: 2nd Supplement to the 18th Edition. Common Law Library. Paperback: £40.00. ISBN 0-421-79580-8. Sweet & Maxwell.

Duggan, Michael–Wrongful Dismissal-Law Practice and Precedents. Paperback: £42.00. ISBN 1-85811-232-X. EMIS Professional Publishing.

Duncan, Nigel–Bar Manual: Case Preparation 2002/2003. Blackstone Bar Manual. Paperback: £21.99. ISBN 0-19-925497-4. Oxford University Press.

Dunkley, Mark–Practitioner's Guide to Drafting Trusts. Paperback: £45.00. ISBN 0-7545-1245-2. Tolley Publishing.

Dutfield, Graham–Intellectual Property Rights, Trade and Biodiversity. Paperback: £24.95. ISBN 1-85383-903-5. Earthscan.

Duxbury, Neil–Random Justice: on Lotteries and Legal Decision Making. Paperback: £19.99. ISBN 0-19-925353-6. Oxford University Press.

Duxbury, Robert; Morton, Sandra–Blackstone's Statutes on Environmental Law (Rev Ed). Blackstone's Statutes Series. Paperback: £14.99. ISBN 0-19-925528-8. Oxford University Press.

Duxbury, R.M.C.–Telling and Duxbury: Planning Law and Procedure. 12th Ed. Paperback: £23.95. ISBN 0-406-94796-1. Butterworths Law.

Dworkin, Ronald–Sovereign Virtue. Paperback: £13.95. ISBN 0-674-00810-3. Harvard University Press.

Dyson, Kenneth–European States and the Euro. Paperback: £18.99. ISBN 0-19-925025-1. Oxford University Press.

Eady, David; Smith, A.T.H.–Arlidge, Eady and Smith on Contempt: 2nd Supplement to the Second Edition. Common Law Library. Paperback: £48.00. ISBN 0-421-76910-6. Sweet & Maxwell.

Earle, Murray–Data Protection in the NHS. Book (details unknown): £165.00. ISBN 1-84311-117-9. Informa Healthcare.

Eastaway, Nigel; Richards, Ian–Tax Adviser's Guide to Trusts. Paperback: £75.00. ISBN 0-7545-1223-1. Tolley Publishing.

Echaore-McDavid, Susan–Career Opportunities in Law and the Legal Industry. Career Opportunities Series. Hardback: £38.50. ISBN 0-8160-4552-6. Paperback: £14.95. ISBN 0-8160-4553-4. Facts on File Inc.

Ede, Roger–Criminal Defence. Paperback: £44.95. ISBN 1-85328-830-6. Law Society Publications.

Edelman, James–Gain-based Damages-Contract, Tort, Equity and Intellectual Property. Hardback: £30.00. ISBN 1-841-13334-5. Hart Publishing.

Edgeworth, Brendan–Law, Modernity, Postmodernity: Legal Change in Advanced Societies. Hardback: £45.00. ISBN 1-84014-009-7. Dartmouth.

Edwards, Richard; Stockwell, Nigel–Trusts and Equity. 5th Ed. Foundation Studies in Law. Paperback: £26.99. ISBN 0-582-43810-1. Longman.

Edwards, R.–Introduction to Paralegal Studies and the Law. Paperback: £38.00. ISBN 0-7668-3589-8. Delmar.

Eeckhout, Piet; Tridimas, Takis–Yearbook of European Law: Vol 20. 2001. Yearbook of European Law. Hardback: £115.00. ISBN 0-19-924340-9. Oxford University Press.

Efthymiou, Sarah—Revenue Law, 3rd Edition. Revision Workbook. Paperback: £9.95. ISBN 1-85836-468-X. Old Bailey Press.

Egan, Suzanne—Immigration and Refugee Law in Ireland. Paperback: £70.00. ISBN 1-85475-270-7. Butterworths Law (Ireland).

Ehlers, Peter N.; Hos, Cristina Mann-Borgese, Elisabeth; Wolfrum, Rudiger—Marine Issues: From a Scientific, Political and Legal Perspective. Hardback: £64.00. ISBN 90-411-1740-7. Kluwer Law International.

Eicke, Tim; Grief, Nicholas—European Human Rights Reports: Consolidated Index. Hardback: £90.00. ISBN 0-421-76960-2. Sweet & Maxwell.

Eicke, Tim; Grief, Nicholas—European Human Rights Reports: Vol 30. Hardback: £520.00. ISBN 0-421-79350-3. Sweet & Maxwell.

Elkin-Koren, Niva; Netanel, Neil Weinstock—Commodification of Information. Information Law Series, 11. Hardback: £85.00. ISBN 90-411-9876-8. Kluwer Law International.

Ellinger, E.P.; Hooley, Richard—Modern Banking Law. 3rd Ed. Paperback: £32.99. ISBN 0-19-924831-1. Oxford University Press Inc, USA.

Elliott, Catherine; Quinn, Frances—AS Law. Paperback: £19.99. ISBN 0-582-47319-5. Longman.

Elliott, Catherine; Quinn, Frances—Criminal Law. 4th Ed. Paperback: £15.99. ISBN 0-582-47312-8. Longman.

Elliott, Catherine; Quinn, Francis—English Legal System. 4th Ed. Paperback: £19.99. ISBN 0-582-47313-6. Longman.

Ellis, Peter; Welham, Mike; Welham, Jacqui; Bateman, Mike—Tolley's Risk Assessment Workbook Series-the Retail Trade. Tolley's Risk Assessment Workbook Series. Paperback: £60.00. ISBN 0-7545-1890-6. Tolley Publishing.

Ellison, Louise—Adversarial Process and the Vulnerable Witness. Oxford Monographs on Criminal Law and Justice. Hardback: £45.00. ISBN 0-19-829909-5. Oxford University Press.

Elvin, David; Karas, Jonathan—Unlawful Interference with Land-Nuisance, Trespass, Covenants and Statutes. 2nd Ed. Hardback: £145.00. ISBN 0-421-72730-6. Sweet & Maxwell.

Emmet, David—Bar Manual: Drafting 2002/2003. Blackstone Bar Manual. Paperback: £21.99. ISBN 0-19-925501-6. Oxford University Press.

Emmins, Christopher J.; Sprack, John—Emmins on Criminal Procedure. Paperback: £23.95. ISBN 0-19-925350-1. Oxford University Press.

Employee Health Handbook 2002. Paperback: £50.00. ISBN 0-7545-1249-5. Tolley Publishing.

Employment 2003. Plastic-reinforced paperback: CD-ROM (e-book): £57.00. ISBN 0-9540581-2-7. FL Memo.

Employment Law. 3rd Ed. LawCards Series. Paperback: £6.95. ISBN 1-85941-714-0. Cavendish Publishing Ltd.

English Legal System. 3rd Ed. LawCards Series. Paperback: £6.00. ISBN 1-85941-711-6. Cavendish Publishing Ltd.

Epstein—Wiley IAS 2002: Interpretation and Application of International Accounting Standards 2002. Paperback: £52.95. ISBN 0-471-44121-X. John Wiley & Sons Inc.

Eskridge Jr., William N.—Equality Practice-Civil Unions and the Future of Gay Rights. Hardback: £50.00. ISBN 0-415-93072-3. Paperback: £11.99. ISBN 0-415-93073-1. Routledge, an imprint of Taylor & Francis Books Ltd.

Esmaeili, Hossein—Legal Regime of Offshore Oil Rigs in International Law. Hardback: £60.00. ISBN 0-7546-2193-6. Dartmouth.

Estella, Antonio—EU Principle of Subsidiarity and Its Critique. Oxford Studies in European Law. Hardback: £40.00. ISBN 0-19-924242-9. Oxford University Press.

Estreicher, Samuel; Katz, Harry C.; Kaufman, Bruce E.—Internal Governance and Organizational Effectiveness of Labor Unions. Hardback: £115.00. ISBN 90-411-8868-1. Kluwer Law International.

European Community Law. 3rd Ed. LawCards Series. Paperback: £6.00. ISBN 1-85941-517-2. Cavendish Publishing Ltd.

Evitts, Adrian–Drugs and the Criminal Law. Paperback: £48.40. ISBN 1-85941-645-4. Cavendish Publishing Ltd.

Exall, Gordon–APIL Guide to Fatal Injury Claims. Paperback: £30.00. ISBN 0-85308-757-1. Jordans.

Exall, Gordon–Practice Notes on Personal Injury. 3rd Ed. Practice Notes. Paperback: £19.95. ISBN 1-85941-577-6. Cavendish Publishing Ltd.

Facilities Management Handbook. Looseleaf in binder: £50.00. ISBN 0-7545-0230-9. Tolley Publishing.

Fairpo, Anne–Taxation of Intellectual Property. Paperback: £65.00. ISBN 0-7545-1980-5. Butterworths Law.

Faludi, Andreas; Waterhout, Bas–Making of the European Spatial Development Perspective. The RTPI Library. Hardback: £65.00. ISBN 0-415-27263-7. Paperback: £24.99. ISBN 0-415-27264-5. Routledge, an imprint of Taylor & Francis Books Ltd.

Family Law Statutes 2002. A Parliament House Book. Paperback: £14.00. ISBN 0-414-01428-6. W. Green & Son.

Farber, Daniel A.; Sherry, Suzanna–Desperately Seeking Certainty-The Misguided Quest for Constitutional Foundations. Hardback: £16.00. ISBN 0-226-23808-3. University of Chicago Press.

Farr, Sebastian; Oakley, Vanessa–EU Communications Law. Paperback: £52.00. ISBN 1-902558-50-2. Palladian Law Publishing Ltd.

Feldman, David–Civil Liberties and Human Rights in England and Wales. 2nd Ed. Paperback: £29.99. ISBN 0-19-876503-7. Oxford University Press.

Feldman, David–Civil Liberties and Human Rights in England and Wales. Reissued 2nd Ed. Hardback: £75.00. ISBN 0-19-876559-2. Oxford University Press.

Felson, Richard B.–Violence and Gender Reexamined. Law and Public Policy: Psychology and the Social Sciences. Hardback: £33.95. ISBN 1-55798-895-1. American Psychological Association.

Fenwick and Phillipson: Media Freedom and the Human Rights Act. Paperback. ISBN 0-406-94289-7. Butterworths Law.

Fenwick, Helen; Phillipson, Gavin–Sourcebook on Public Law. Sourcebook Series. Paperback: £32.95. ISBN 1-85941-655-1. Cavendish Publishing Ltd.

Fenwick, Helen–Civil Liberties and Human Rights. 3rd Ed. Paperback: £31.95. ISBN 1-85941-493-1. Cavendish Publishing Ltd.

Fenwick, Helen–Q&A Constitutional and Administrative Law. Questions and Answers. Paperback: £10.95. ISBN 1-85941-622-5. Cavendish Publishing Ltd.

Ferguson, Peter W.–Statutory Controlled Substance Offences. Green's Essential Legislation. Paperback: £32.00. ISBN 0-414-01491-X. W. Green & Son.

Ferran, Eilis; Goodhart, Charles A.E.–Regulating Financial Services and Markets in the 21st Century. Hardback: £50.00. ISBN 1-84113-279-9. Hart Publishing.

Ficsor, Mihaly–Law of Copyright and the Internet. Hardback: £125.00. ISBN 0-19-829901-X. Oxford University Press.

Finch, Vanessa–Corporate Insolvency Law. Hardback: £95.00. ISBN 0-521-62256-5. Paperback: £34.95. ISBN 0-521-62685-4. Cambridge University Press.

Fionda, Julia–Legal Concepts of Childhood. Hardback: £25.00. ISBN 1-84113-150-4. Hart Publishing.

Firth, Judith; Nickson, Susan–Privacy and Communications. Legal Essentials. Paperback: £29.99. ISBN 0-85292-942-0. Chartered Institute of Personnel and Development (CIPD).

Fleming, Macklin–Lawyers, Money, and Success-The Consequences of Dollar Obsession. Paperback: £20.95. ISBN 1-56720-595-X. Quorum Books.

Fletcher, Ian F.–Law of Insolvency. 3rd Ed. Sweet & Maxwell's Insolvency Library. Hardback: £175.00. ISBN 0-421-68410-0. Sweet & Maxwell.

Fletcher, Ian; Higham, John; Tower, William–Fletcher, Higham & Trower: Corporate Administrations and Rescue Procedures. 2nd Ed. Hardback: £120.00. ISBN 0-406-93757-5. Butterworths Law.

Fletcher, Roland–Commercial Law. Revision Workbook. Paperback: £11.95. ISBN 1-85836-419-1. Paperback: £9.95. ISBN 1-85836-424-8. Old Bailey Press.

Flushman–Demystifying Land Boundaries Adjacent to Tidal or Navigable Water: Practical Rules for Establishing the Location of Property Boundaries of Lands Adjacent to Tidal or Navigable Water Bodies. Hardback: £74.50. ISBN 0-471-40391-1. John Wiley & Sons Inc.

Foot, Rosemary; Gaddis, John Lewis; Hurrell, Andrew–Order and Justice in International Relations. Hardback: £50.00. ISBN 0-19-925120-7. Paperback: £16.99. ISBN 0-19-925119-3. Oxford University Press.

Ford, Michael–Redgrave's Health and Safety. 4th Ed. Paperback: £150.00. ISBN 0-406-95813-0. Butterworths Law.

Foreign Exchange Tax Team–Tolley's Taxation of Foreign Exchange Gains and Losses. Paperback: £79.95. ISBN 0-7545-1221-5. Tolley Publishing.

Forlin, Gerard–Butterworths Corporate Manslaughter Service. Looseleaf/ring bound: £375.00. ISBN 0-406-93176-3. Looseleaf/ring bound: £395.00. ISBN 0-406-93176-3. Butterworths Law.

Forster, Malcolm; Hattan, Elizabeth–Contaminated Land. Paperback: £58.00. ISBN 1-902558-40-5. Palladian Law Publishing Ltd.

Fortson, Rudi–Misuse of Drugs and Drug Trafficking Offences. 4th Ed. Criminal Practice. Paperback: £70.00. ISBN 0-421-76330-2. Sweet & Maxwell.

Foskett, David–Law and Practice of Compromise. 5th Ed. Litigation Library. Hardback: £145.00. ISBN 0-421-76600-X. Sweet & Maxwell.

Foster, Charles–Tripping and Slipping Cases-a Practitioner's Guide. 3rd Ed. Personal Injury Library. Paperback: £55.00. ISBN 0-421-77850-4. Sweet & Maxwell.

Foster, Nigel; Sule, Satish–German Legal System and Laws. 3rd Ed. Paperback: £29.99. ISBN 0-19-925483-4. Oxford University Press.

Foster, Nigel–EC Legislation. Blackstone's Statutes Series. Paperback: £12.99. ISBN 0-19-925486-9. Oxford University Press.

Fox Jr, Willian F.–International Electronic Commerce: Resolving the Legal Issues. Hardback: £100.99. ISBN 1-57105-193-7. Transnational Publishers, Inc.

Fox, Bill–Tolley's Managing Violence in the Workplace. Hardback: £65.00. ISBN 0-7545-1967-8. Tolley Publishing.

Fox, Hazel–Law of State Immunity. Hardback: £80.00. ISBN 0-19-829836-6. Oxford University Press.

Franck, Thomas M.–Recourse to Force-State Action Against Threats and Armed Attacks. Hersch Lauterpacht Memorial Lectures. Hardback: £40.00. ISBN 0-521-82013-8. Cambridge University Press.

Frase, Dick; Parry, Helen–Exchanges and Alternative Trading Systems-Law and Regulation. Hardback: £150.00. ISBN 0-421-73930-4. Sweet & Maxwell.

Fraser, Marge–Michigan Real Estate. Paperback: £26.99. ISBN 0-324-14374-5. South Western College Publishing.

Freckelton, Ian; Mendelson, Danuta–Causation in Law and Medicine. Hardback: £65.00. ISBN 0-7546-2204-5. Dartmouth.

Fredman, Sandra–Discrimination Law. Clarendon Law Series. Paperback: £16.99. ISBN 0-19-876566-5. Oxford University Press.

Freedman, David; Walden, Ian–Walden and Freedman: Information Law. Looseleaf/ring bound: £175.00. ISBN 0-406-91623-3. Butterworths Law.

Freeman, Michael–Current Legal Problems: Vol 54. 2001. Current Legal Problems. Hardback: £65.00. ISBN 0-19-924780-3. Oxford University Press.

Freeman, Michael–Lloyd's Introduction to Jurisprudence. 7th Ed. Paperback: £17.95. ISBN 0-421-75330-7. Sweet & Maxwell International Student Editions. Paperback: £36.00. ISBN 0-421-69020-8. Sweet & Maxwell.

French, Derek–Statutes on Company Law. Blackstone's Statutes Series. Paperback: £14.99. ISBN 0-19-925529-6. Oxford University Press.

Friedmann, Dan; Barak-Erez, Daphne–Human Rights in Private Law. Hardback: £45.00. ISBN 1-84113-213-6. Hart Publishing.

Furber John; Karas, Jonathan; Evans Jonathan; Scott, Tiffany–Furber: Commonhold and Leasehold Reform Act 2002. Butterworth's New Law Guides. Paperback: £35.00. ISBN 0-406-94557-8. Butterworths Law.

Furber, John; Karas, Jonathan; Evans, Jonathan; Scott, Tiffany–Commonhold Leasehold Reform Act (2001). Butterworth's New Law Guides. Paperback: £35.00. ISBN 0-406-94557-8. Butterworths Law.

Furse, Mark–Competition Law of the UK and EC. Paperback: £21.99. ISBN 0-19-925487-7. Oxford University Press.

Furze, Mark; Nash, Susan–Essential Human Rights Cases. Paperback: £45.00. ISBN 0-85308-800-4. Paperback: £45.00. ISBN 0-85308-800-4. Jordans.

Fysh, Michael; Wilson-Thomas, R.–Intellectual Property Citator: 1st Supplement. Paperback: £85.00. ISBN 0-421-76450-3. Sweet & Maxwell.

Garner, Bryan A.–Elements of Legal Style. 2nd Ed. Hardback: £21.99. ISBN 0-19-514162-8. Oxford University Press Inc, USA.

Garner–Practical Approach to Landlord and Tenant Law. Paperback: £24.95. ISBN 0-19-925452-4. Oxford University Press.

Garnett, George; Hudson, John–Law and Government in Medieval England and Normandy. Paperback: £25.95. ISBN 0-521-52009-6. Cambridge University Press.

Garnett, Kevin; Davies, Gillian; Rayner James, Jonathan–Copinger and Skone James on Copyright. 14th Ed. Hardback: £415.00. ISBN 0-421-75810-4. Sweet & Maxwell.

Garnett, Kevin; James, Jonathan Rayner; Davies, Gillian–Copinger and Skone James on Copyright: 1st Supplement. 14th Ed. Paperback: £120.00. ISBN 0-421-75800-7. Sweet & Maxwell.

Garnett, Kevin; Davies, Gillian–Moral Rights. Hardback: £150.00. ISBN 0-421-72940-6. Sweet & Maxwell.

Gaunt, Jonathan; Morgan, Paul–Gale on the Law of Easements. Property and Conveyancing Library. Hardback: £195.00. ISBN 0-421-77960-8. Sweet & Maxwell.

Geary, Roger–Understanding Criminal Law. Paperback: £8.95. ISBN 1-85941-749-3. Cavendish Publishing Ltd.

Ghandhi, Sandy–International Human Rights Documents. Blackstone's Statutes Series. Paperback: £15.99. ISBN 0-19-925530-X. Oxford University Press.

Gharavi, Hamid G.–International Effectiveness of the Annulment of an Arbitral Award. International Arbitration Law Library, 7. Hardback: £54.00. ISBN 90-411-1717-2. Kluwer Law International.

Gibbons, John–Forensic Linguistics. Language in Society. Hardback: £55.00. ISBN 0-631-21246-9. Paperback: £16.99. ISBN 0-631-21247-7. Blackwell Publishers.

Giblin, B.H.–Irish Tax Reports 2001 Cases, Cumulative Tables, Index, and Determinations of the Appeal Commissioners. Paperback: £45.76. ISBN 1-85475-217-0. Butterworths Law.

Gibraltar-international Finance Centre. Paperback: £55.00. ISBN 0-7545-1340-8. Tolley Publishing.

Gilboa, Eytan–Media and Conflict-Framing Issues, Making Policy, Shaping Opinions. Hardback: £28.50. ISBN 1-57105-270-4. Paperback: £28.50. ISBN 1-57105-276-3. Transnational Publishers, Inc.

Gillespie, J.–Immigration Appeals Practice: 2001. Hardback: £100.00. ISBN 0-85308-447-5. Jordans.

Gillies, David; Roger, Marshall–Telecommunications Law. Hardback: £210.00. ISBN 0-406-95129-2. Butterworths Law.

Gilliom, John–Overseers of the Poor-Surveillance, Resistance, and the Limits of Privacy. Hardback: £25.00. ISBN 0-226-29360-2. University of Chicago Press.

Gilliom, John–Overseers of the Poor. Paperback: £10.50. ISBN 0-226-29361-0. University of Chicago Press.

Gillroy, John Martin–Justice and Nature-Kantian Philosophy, Environmental Policy, and the Law. American Governance and Public Policy. Paperback: £26.00. ISBN 0-87840-796-0. Georgetown University Press.

Ginzburg, Carlo–Judge and the Historian: Marginal Notes on a Late-twentieth Century Miscarriage of Justice. Paperback: £11.00. ISBN 1-85984-371-9. Verso Books.

Glachant, Matthieu–Implementing European Environmental Policy-The Impacts of Directives in the Member States. New Horizons in Environmental Economics. Hardback: £49.95. ISBN 1-84064-659-4. Edward Elgar.

Gladstone, Alan; Bar-Niv, Zvi H.; Aaron, Benjamin; Sigeman, Tore; Verdier, Jean-Maurice; Lord Wedderburn of Charlton; Weiss, Manfred–International Labour Law Reports: Vol 20. International Labour Law Reports, 20. Hardback: £126.00. ISBN 90-411-1732-6. Martinus Nijhoff Publishers.

Glaser, Maric–Tolley's VAT Business by Business Guide 2001-02. Paperback: £79.95. ISBN 0-7545-1290-8. Tolley Publishing.

Glazebrook, Peter–Blackstone's Statutes on Criminal Law. 12th Ed. Blackstone's Statute Book Series. Paperback: £10.99. ISBN 0-19-925531-8. Oxford University Press.

Glover-Thomas, Nicola–Glover-Thomas: Reconstructing Mental Health Law and Policy. Law in Context Series. Paperback: £24.95. ISBN 0-406-94677-9. Butterworths Law.

Goldspink, Bob; Cole, Jeremy–International Commercial Fraud. Hardback: £295.00. ISBN 0-7520-0617-7. Sweet & Maxwell.

Goldstein, Norm; Goldstein, Norma–Associated Press Stylebook and Briefing on Media Law. New Ed. Paperback: £12.99. ISBN 0-7382-0740-3. Perseus Books.

Goldsworthy, Jeffrey; Campbell, Tom–Legal Interpretation in Democratic States. Applied Legal Philosophy. Hardback: £55.00. ISBN 0-7546-2215-0. Dartmouth.

Goo, S.H.–Land Law. 3rd Ed. Sourcebook Series. Paperback: £32.95. ISBN 1-85941-188-6. Cavendish Publishing Ltd.

Goodman, Richard A.; Rothstein, Mark A.; Hoffman, Richard E.; Lopez, Wilfredo; Matthews, Gene W.–Law in Public Health Practice. Hardback: £47.50. ISBN 0-19-514871-1. Oxford University Press Inc, USA.

Gordon, Richard; Venne, Roger; Le Sueur, Andrew–Administrative Court Digest 2001. Hardback. ISBN 0-421-77910-1. Sweet & Maxwell.

Goriely, Tamara–Civil Legal Aid. Socio-legal Studies. Hardback: £40.00. ISBN 1-85521-476-8. Dartmouth.

Gower, Jackie–European Union Handbook. 2nd Ed. Regional Handbooks of Economic Development. Hardback: £35.00. ISBN 1-57958-223-0. Fitzroy Dearborn.

Graham, Toby; Elliott, Nicholas; Bell, Evan–Butterworths Compliance Series: Money Laundering and Financial Services. Butterworth's Compliance Series. Paperback: £45.00. ISBN 0-406-93248-4. Butterworths Law.

Grana, Sheryl J.; Ollenburger Jane C.; Nicholas, Mark–Social Context of Law. 2nd Ed. Paperback: £24.99. ISBN 0-13-041374-7. Prentice Hall.

Grant, Beryl–Employment Law-A Guide for Human Resource Management. Paperback: £24.99. ISBN 1-86152-756-X. Thomson Learning.

Gravells, Nigel P.–Property Law. Statutes Series. Paperback: £12.95. ISBN 0-421-78090-8. Sweet & Maxwell.

Gravestock, Peter; Hear, William–Tolley's Guide to Self-assessment 2001-02. Paperback: £45.95. ISBN 0-7545-1204-5. Tolley Publishing.

Gray, Barry; Jackson, Robin–Advocacy and Learning Difficulties. Paperback: £24.95. ISBN 1-85302-942-4. Jessica Kingsley Publishers.

Green's Guide to the Sheriff Court Districts. Paperback. ISBN 0-414-01494-4. W. Green & Son.

Greenaway, A. Roger–How to Obtain Air Quality Permits. Environmental Permitting. Hardback: CD-ROM: £82.45. ISBN 0-07-137975-4. McGraw-Hill Education.

Greenberg, Daniel; Milbrook, Alexandra–Stroud's Judicial Dictionary of Words and Phrases: 2nd Supplement to the 6th Edition. Paperback: £55.00. ISBN 0-421-82880-3. Sweet & Maxwell.

Greene, Abner S.–Understanding the 2000 Election: A Guide to the Legal Battles That Decided the Presidency. Hardback: £20.00. ISBN 0-8147-3148-1. New York University Press.

Greene, J.H.; Fletcher, I.M.–Greene & Fletcher: the Law and Practice of Receivership in Scotland. 3rd Ed. Paperback: £110.00. ISBN 0-406-94451-2. Butterworths Law (Scotland).

Greenhill, John–Work of a Magistrate. 6th Ed. Paperback: £13.95. ISBN 0-7219-0563-3. Shaw & Sons.

Greens Annotated Rules of the Court of Session 2002. Paperback: £59.00. ISBN 0-414-01463-4. W. Green & Son.

Greenstreet, Bob; Chappell, David; Dunn, Michael–Legal and Contractual Procedures for Architects. Paperback: £24.99. ISBN 0-7506-5408-2. Paperback: £24.99. ISBN 0-7506-5408-2. Architectural Press.

Grier, Nicholas–Company Law. Greens Concise Scots Law. Paperback: £32.00. ISBN 0-414-01496-0. Paperback: £32.00. ISBN 0-414-01496-0. W. Green & Son.

Griffiths-Baker, Janine–Serving Two Masters. Onati International Series in Law and Society. Hardback: £30.00. ISBN 1-84113-229-2. Hart Publishing.

Griffiths, Margaret–Law for Purchasing and Supply. 3rd Ed. Paperback: £29.99. ISBN 0-273-64679-6. FT Prentice Hall.

Griggs, Lyndon; Clark, Eugene; Iredale, Ian–Managers and the Law. Lawbook Company. Paperback: £44. ISBN 0-455-21845-5. Sweet & Maxwell.

Grove, Trevor–Magistrate's Tale. Hardback: £14.99. ISBN 0-7475-6055-2. Bloomsbury.

Grubb, Andrew–Law of Tort. 2nd Ed. Butterworths Common Law. Hardback: £195.00. ISBN 0-406-89672-0. Butterworths Law.

Guest, A.G.–Benjamin's Sale of Goods. Common Law Library. Hardback: £310.00. ISBN 0-421-72950-3. Sweet & Maxwell.

Guidelines for the Assessment of General Damages. Paperback: £19.95. ISBN 0-19-925795-7. Oxford University Press.

Guild, Elspeth; Harlow, Carol–Implementing Amsterdam. Hardback: £45.00. ISBN 1-84113-116-4. Hart Publishing.

Guthrie, Tom–Statutory Sexual Offences. Green's Essential Legislation. Paperback: £28.00. ISBN 0-414-01473-1. W. Green & Son.

Guttenplan, D.D.–Holocaust on Trial: History, Justice and the David Irving Libel Case. Paperback (B format): £9.99. ISBN 1-86207-486-0. Granta Books.

Hadjucki, A.; Stuart, S.–Scottish Civic Government Licensing Law. Paperback: £48.00. ISBN 0-414-01497-9. W. Green & Son.

Halberstam, Simon; Brook, Joanne; Turner, Jonathan D.C.–Domain Names: a Practical Guide. Paperback: £39.95. ISBN 0-7545-1491-9. Tolley Publishing.

Hale; Pearl, David; Cooke, Elizabeth; Bates, Philip–Hoggett, Pearl, Cooke and Bates: Family, Law and Society-Cases and Materials. 5th Ed. Paperback: £29.95. ISBN 0-406-98587-1. Butterworths Law.

Haley, Michael–Which? Way to Buy, Own and Sell a Flat. Which? Consumer Guides. Paperback: £10.99. ISBN 0-85202-900-4. Which? Books.

Hall-Dick, Anne; Ballantine, Tom–Science of Family Law. Paperback: £35.00. ISBN 0-414-01370-0. W.Green & Son.

Halpin, Andrew–Reasoning with Law. Hardback: £25.00. ISBN 1-84113-070-2. Paperback: £20.00. ISBN 1-84113-244-6. Hart Publishing.

Halsbury's Statutes Citator 2002. Paperback: £103.00. ISBN 0-406-94620-5. Butterworths Law.

Hamburger, Philip–Separation of Church and State. Hardback: £34.50. ISBN 0-674-00734-4. Harvard University Press.

Hamilton, Carolyn; Perry, Alison–Hamilton: Family Law in Europe. 2nd Ed. Hardback: £120.00. ISBN 0-406-94150-5. Butterworths Law.

Hamilton, Penny–Environmental Taxes Handbook. Paperback: £65.00. ISBN 0-7545-1787-X. Tolley Publishing.

Hamilton, Penny–Hamilton on VAT and Duty Appeals. Paperback: £74.95. ISBN 0-7545-1484-6. Tolley Publishing.

Hamilton, W.; Kennedy, P.; Kilpatrick, A.; Mclaughlin, R.–Scottish Building Regulations. Paperback: £27.50. ISBN 0-632-04945-6. Blackwell Science (UK).

Hammer, Leonard M.–International Human Right to Freedom of Conscience-Some Suggestions for Its Development and Application. Hardback: £55.00. ISBN 0-7546-2132-4. Dartmouth.

Hannabuss, Stuart–Information Liability and Negligence: Legal and Ethical Issues for Library and Information Professionals. Paperback: £29.95. ISBN 1-85604-423-8. Library Association Publishing.

Hannibal, Martin; Mountford, Lisa–Law of Criminal and Civil Evidence. Paperback: £27.99. ISBN 0-582-43720-2. Longman.

Harcourt, Amanda; Parker, Nigel–Music Business. Paperback: £52.00. ISBN 1-902558-42-1. Palladian Law Publishing Ltd.

Harpum, Charles; Bignell, Janet–Registered Land-the New Law-A Guide to the Land Registration Act 2002. Paperback: £35.00. ISBN 0-85308-759-8. Jordans.

Harpwood, Vivienne–Complaints in Healthcare. Paperback: £38.95. ISBN 1-85941-669-1. Cavendish Publishing Ltd.

Harris, Donald Renshaw; Campbell, I. David; Halson, Roger–Harris, Campbell and Halson: Remedies in Contract and Tort. 2nd Ed. Law in Context. Paperback: £23.95. ISBN 0-406-90410-3. Butterworths Law.

Harris, Douglas C.–Fish, Law, and Colonialism-The Legal Capture of Salmon in British Columbia. Hardback: £45.00. ISBN 0-8020-3598-1. University of Toronto Press Inc.

Harris, Douglas C.–Fish, Law, and Colonialism. Paperback: £18.00. ISBN 0-8020-8453-2. University of Toronto Press Inc.

Harris, Jonathan–Hague Trusts Convention-The Private International Law of Trusts. Hardback: £65.00. ISBN 1-841-13110-5. Hart Publishing.

Harris, J.W.–Property and Justice. Paperback: £18.99. ISBN 0-19-925140-1. Oxford University Press.

Harris, Phil–Harris: An Introduction to Law. 6th Ed. Law in Context. Paperback: £15.95. ISBN 0-406-94672-8. Butterworths Law.

Hartogh, Govert A. den–Mutual Expectations-A Conventionalist Theory of Law. Law and Philosophy Library. Hardback: £61.00. ISBN 90-411-1796-2. Kluwer Law International.

Harvey, Mark–APIL Guide to Conditional Fee Agreements. Paperback: £30.00. ISBN 0-85308-754-7. Jordans.

Haslanger, Sally; Witt, Charlotte–View from Home. Feminist Theory and Politics. Hardback: £46.99. ISBN 0-8133-6616-X. Westview Press.

Hawke, Neil; Parpworth, Neil; Thompson, Katharine–Environmental Health Law Reports 2001. Hardback: £180.00. ISBN 0-421-75550-4. Sweet & Maxwell.

Hawke, Neil–Environmental Policy: Implementation and Enforcement. Paperback: £25.00. ISBN 0-7546-2311-4. Avebury Technical.

Hawke, Neil–Environmental Policy. Hardback: £60.00. ISBN 0-7546-2067-0. Dartmouth.

Hawkins, Alan J.; Wardle, Lynn D.; Coolidge, David Orgon–Revitalizing the Institution of Marriage for the Twenty-first Century-An Agenda for Strengthening Marriage. Hardback: £53.95. ISBN 0-275-97272-0. Paperback: £20.95. ISBN 0-275-97273-9. Praeger Publishers.

Hayden, Patrick–John Rawls-Towards a Just World Order. Political Philosophy Now. Hardback: £30.00. ISBN 0-7083-1729-4. Paperback: £14.99. ISBN 0-7083-1728-6. University of Wales Press.

Hayes, Mary; Williams, Catherine–Family Law. Paperback: £25.95. ISBN 0-406-94680-9. Butterworths Law.

Haynes, Andrew–Butterworths Financial Services Law Guide. 2nd Ed. Paperback: £95.00. ISBN 0-406-93913-6. Butterworths Law.

Hayton, David J.–Extending the Boundaries of Trust and Similar Ring-fenced Funds. Hardback: £100.00. ISBN 90-411-9879-2. Kluwer Law International.

Hayton, David–European Succession Laws. Hardback: £99.00. ISBN 0-85308-816-0. Jordans.

Hayward, John; Ure, Alec–Tolley's SSAS-SIPPS-FURBS: Directors' Retirement Benefits. 5th Ed. Paperback: £54.95. ISBN 0-7545-1225-8. Tolley Publishing.

Hazell, Robert; French, Alan–State of the Nations 2001-The Second Year of Devolution in the United Kingdom. Paperback: £14.95. ISBN 0-907845-19-3. Imprint Academic.

Health and Safety. Legal Essentials. Paperback: £33.99. ISBN 0-85292-966-8. Chartered Institute of Personnel and Development (CIPD).

Heath, Christopher; Sanders, Anselm Kamperman–Intellectual Property in the Digital Age. Hardback: £53.00. ISBN 90-411-9847-4. Kluwer Law International.

Hedges, Lawrence–Facing the Challenge of Liability in Psychotherapy-Practicing Defensively. Hardback: CD-ROM: £94.95. ISBN 0-7657-0290-8. Jason Aronson.

Hedley, Steve–Butterworths Core Text: Tort. 3rd Ed. Butterworths Core Text. Paperback: £12.95. ISBN 0-406-95002-4. Butterworths Law.

Hedley, Steve–Law of Restitution. Butterworths Common Law Series. Hardback: £195.00. ISBN 0-406-98261-9. Butterworths Law.

Hedley, Steven; Aplin, Tanya–Blackstone's Statutes on IT and E-commerce. Paperback: £15.99. ISBN 0-19-925823-6. Oxford University Press.

Helgeson, Edward–International Convention on the Settlement of Investment Disputes Reports: Volume 5: Hardback: £170.00. ISBN 0-521-81383-2. Cambridge University Press.

Hellawell, Trevor–Environmental Law Handbook. Paperback: £34.95. ISBN 1-85328-891-8. Law Society Publications.

Henderson, Schuyler K.–Henderson on Derivatives. Hardback: £140.00. ISBN 0-406-94988-3. Butterworths Law.

Hennessy, Charles–Practical Advocacy in the Sheriff Court. Paperback: £25.00. ISBN 0-414-01503-7. W. Green & Son.

Henriques, Jack; Winter, Richard–Henriques and Winter on Local Authority Prosecutions. Paperback: £45.00. ISBN 1-85941-697-7. Cavendish Publishing Ltd.

Herbert, Rebecca–Personal Injury Claims Manual. Looseleaf/ring bound: £225.00. ISBN 0-421-79990-0. Sweet & Maxwell.

Herring, Jonathan; Cremona, Marise–Criminal Law. 3rd Ed. Palgrave Law Masters. Paperback: £15.99. ISBN 0-333-98770-5. Palgrave Macmillan.

Hewitson, Russell–Conveyancer's Yearbook 2002. Paperback: £21.00. ISBN 0-7219-1564-7. Shaw & Sons.

Hewitt, Ian–Joint Ventures. 2nd Ed. Hardback: Floppy disk: £130.00. ISBN 0-421-73980-0. Sweet & Maxwell.

Higgins, Mark–Scottish Repossessions. Paperback: £55.00. ISBN 0-414-01465-0. W.Green & Son.

Hill, Mark–Religious Liberty and Human Rights. Hardback: £35.00. ISBN 0-7083-1758-8. University of Wales Press.

Hill, Robert; Wood, Helen; Fine, Suzanne–Practical Guide to Civil Litigation. Hardback: £45.00. ISBN 0-85308-818-7. Jordans.

Hinterseer, Kris–Criminal Finance-The Political Economy of Money Laundering in a Comparative Legal Context. Studies in Comparative Corporate and Financial Law. Hardback: £100.00. ISBN 90-411-9864-4. Kluwer Law International.

Hiram, Hilary–Scots Law of Succession. Paperback: £34.00. ISBN 0-406-90040-X. Butterworths Law (Scotland).

Hirsch, Andrew von; Roberts, Julian; Bottoms, Anthony E.–Restorative Justice & Criminal Justice. Hardback: £35.00. ISBN 1-84113-273-X. Hart Publishing.

Hobsons Guide to Careers in Law: 2003. Hobsons Casebooks. Paperback: £9.99. ISBN 1-86017-946-0. Hobsons plc.

Hodge, Sue–Tort Law. 2nd Ed. Paperback: £14.99. ISBN 1-903240-87-5. Willan Publishing.

Hoecke, Mark Van–Law As Communication. European Academy of Legal Theory Series. Hardback: £35.00. ISBN 1-84113-341-8. Hart Publishing.

Hogan, Greer–Nutshells: Constitutional and Administrative Law. 6th Ed. Nutshells. Paperback: £5.95. ISBN 0-421-76500-3. Sweet & Maxwell.

Hoggett, Brenda–Parents and Children. Reissued 5th Ed. Paperback: £40.00. ISBN 0-421-69070-4. Sweet & Maxwell.

Homer, Arnold; Burrows, Rita; Deeks, Sarah–Tolley's Partnership Taxation. 5th Ed. Paperback: £56.95. ISBN 0-7545-1199-5. Tolley Publishing.

Homer, Arnold; Burrows, Rita; Gravestock, Peter–Tolley's Taxwise II 2002-03. Paperback: £39.95. ISBN 0-7545-1681-4. Tolley Publishing.

Homer, Arnold; Burrows, Rita–Tolley's Tax Guide 2002-03. Hardback: £44.95. ISBN 0-7545-1686-5. Tolley Publishing.

Honeyball, Simon; Bowers, John–Textbook on Labour Law. 7th Ed. Textbook Series. Paperback: £21.99. ISBN 0-19-925547-4. Oxford University Press.

Honore, Tony–Ulpian: Pioneer of Human Rights. 2nd Ed. Hardback: £55.00. ISBN 0-19-924424-3. Oxford University Press.

Hood, Roger–Death Penalty. Hardback: £45.00. ISBN 0-19-925129-0. Oxford University Press.

Hopkins, John–Devolution in Context-Regional, Federal and Devolved Government in the EU. Paperback: £48.40. ISBN 1-85941-637-3. Cavendish Publishing Ltd.

Hovey, Craig–Patent Process. Paperback: £18.50. ISBN 0-471-44217-8. John Wiley & Sons Inc.

Howard, Michael; Hochberg, Daniel; Mirfield, Peter; Grevling, Katharine; Hollander, Charles; Pattenden, Rosemary–Phipson on Evidence: 1st Supplement to the 15th Edition. Common Law Library. Paperback: £40.00. ISBN 0-421-76270-5. Sweet & Maxwell.

Howard, Michael; Hochberg, Daniel; Mirfield, Peter; Grevling, Katharine; Hollander, Charles; Pattenden, Rosemary–Phipson on

Evidence: 2nd Supplement to the 15th Edition. Common Law Library. Paperback: £45.00. ISBN 0-421-82800-5. Sweet & Maxwell.

Howarth, William; McGillivray, Donald−Water Pollution and Water Quality Law. Hardback: £85.00. ISBN 0-7219-1102-1. Shaw & Sons.

Howarth, William−Flood Defence Law. Paperback: £45.00. ISBN 0-7219-1610-4. Shaw & Sons.

Howarth, William−Legal Aspects of Flooding and Land Drainage. Paperback: £29.95. ISBN 0-7219-1610-4. Shaw & Sons.

Hughes, David; Parpworth, Neil; Jewell, Tim; Prez, Paula de; Lowther, Jason−Hughes: Environmental Law. 4th Ed. Paperback: £27.95. ISBN 0-406-94291-9. Butterworths Law.

Hughesdon, John; Russell, Neville−Butterworths Solicitors Accounts and Financial Management. Looseleaf/ring bound: £90.00. ISBN 0-406-05370-7. Butterworths Tolley.

Hull, John−Commercial Secrecy-Law and Practice. 2nd Ed. Hardback: £130.00. ISBN 0-421-74770-6. Sweet & Maxwell.

Human Rights Law. LawCards Series. Paperback: £6.95. ISBN 1-85941-728-0. Cavendish Publishing Ltd.

Hunter, Ian; Saunders, David; Hunter, Ian; Saunders, David−Natural Law and Civil Sovereignty-Moral Right and State Authority in Early Modern Political Thought. Hardback: £45.00. ISBN 0-333-96459-4. Palgrave Macmillan.

Hunter, Robert L.−Law of Arbitration in Scotland. 2nd Ed. Paperback: £60.00. ISBN 0-406-94887-9. Butterworths Law (Scotland).

Huntley, John a K−Contract-Cases and Materials. 2nd Ed. Cases & Materials. Paperback: £45.00. ISBN 0-414-01281-X. W. Green & Son.

Huntley, John a K−Contract. Cases & Materials. Paperback: £45.00. ISBN 0-414-01281-X. W. Green & Son.

Hurst, Peter−Civil Costs: Second Supplement to the 2nd Edition. Litigation Library. Paperback: £65.00. ISBN 0-421-79030-X. Sweet & Maxwell.

Huscroft, Grant; Rishworth, Paul−Litigating Rights-Perspectives from Domestic and International Law. Hardback: £30.00. ISBN 1-84113-194-6. Hart Publishing.

Huse, Joseph−Understanding and Negotiating Turnkey and EPC Contracts. Hardback: £150.00. ISBN 0-421-67410-5. Sweet & Maxwell.

Hutchinson, Dennis J.; Strauss, David A.; Stone, Geoffrey R.−Supreme Court Review: 2001. Hardback: £34.50. ISBN 0-226-36250-7. University of Chicago Press.

Hutton, Matthew−Tolley's Tax Essentials: Trusts and Estates 2001. Tolley's Tax Essentials. Paperback: £39.00. ISBN 0-7545-1393-9. Tolley Publishing.

Hutton, Matthew−Tolley's Tax Essentials: Trusts and Estates 2002-03. Spiral / comb bound: £39.00. ISBN 0-7545-1707-1. Tolley Publishing.

Hutton, Matthew−Tolley's UK Taxation of Trusts. Paperback: £89.95. ISBN 0-7545-1675-X. Tolley Publishing.

Hyatt−Law of Tax-exempt Healthcare Organizations: 2002 Supplement. Nonprofit Law, Finance, and Management Series. Paperback: £66.95. ISBN 0-471-41942-7. John Wiley & Sons Inc.

Ibusuki, Makoto−Transnational Cyberspace Law. Hardback: £65.00. ISBN 1-84113-163-6. Hart Publishing.

Iller, Martin−Civil Evidence. Paperback: £55.00. ISBN 1-902558-46-4. Palladian Law Publishing Ltd.

Ingman, Terence−English Legal Progress. 9th Ed. Paperback: £19.99. ISBN 0-19-925495-8. Oxford University Press.

Institute of Trade Mark Attorneys; Chartered Institute of Patent Agents−Community Trade Mark Handbook. Looseleaf/ring bound: £295.00. ISBN 0-421-75150-9. Sweet & Maxwell.

Intellectual Property Law. 3rd Ed. LawCards Series. Paperback: £6.95. ISBN 1-85941-708-6. Cavendish Publishing Ltd.

International Construction Law Review: 2001. Hardback: £95.00. ISBN 1-84311-118-7. LLP Professional Publishing.

International Directory of Construction Law: 2001. Book (details unknown): £60.00. ISBN 1-84311-067-9. LLP Professional Publishing.

International Handbook of Corporate and Personal Finance. 6th Ed. Paperback: £79.95. ISBN 0-7545-1150-2. Tolley Publishing.

International Initiatives Affecting Financial Havens. Paperback: £175.00. ISBN 0-406-94264-1. Butterworths Tolley.

International IP Directory: 2002. Paperback: £120.00. ISBN 1-84311-068-7. Informa Business Publishing.

International Leasing. 2nd Ed. Paperback: £85.00. ISBN 0-7545-1296-7. Tolley Publishing.

Irvin, Carol; Irvin, James–Ohio Real Estate Law. 7th Ed. Paperback: £37.99. ISBN 0-324-14383-4. South Western College Publishing.

Is It in Force? 2002. Paperback: £45.00. ISBN 0-406-94710-4. Butterworths Law.

Jackson, David; Warr, George–Immigration Law and Practice. Looseleaf/ring bound: £185.00. ISBN 0-421-74750-1. Sweet & Maxwell.

Jackson, Paul; Leopold, Patricia–O. Hood Phillips & Jackson's Constitutional and Administrative Law. Paperback: £14.95. ISBN 0-421-57650-2. Sweet & Maxwell International Student Editions.

Jackson, Vicki C.; Tushnet, Mark–Defining the Field of Comparative Constitutional Law. Hardback: £54.50. ISBN 0-275-97069-8. Praeger Publishers.

Jaconelli, Joseph–Open Justice: Critique of the Public Trial. Hardback: £50.00. ISBN 0-19-825258-7. Oxford University Press.

Jaeger, Paul T.; Bowman, Cynthia Ann–Disability Matters. Hardback: £51.95. ISBN 0-89789-909-1. Praeger Publishers.

James, Susan; Palmer, Stephanie–Visible Women-Essays on Feminist Legal Theory and Political Philosophy. Hardback: £25.00. ISBN 1-84113-195-4. Hart Publishing.

Jensen–Construction Law. Hardback. ISBN 0-13-083806-3. US Imports & PHIPEs.

Jervis, Nick; Dawson, Judy–Jervis & Dawson: a Practical Guide to Motor Accident Claims. Paperback: £65.00. ISBN 0-406-91780-9. Butterworths Law.

Joerges, Christian; Dehousse, Renaud–Good Governance in Europe's Integrated Market. Collected Courses of the Academy of European Law, V. 11, No. 1. Hardback: £45.00. ISBN 0-19-924608-4. Oxford University Press.

Johnson, Sterling–Peace Without Justice. Hardback: £45.00. ISBN 0-7546-2075-1. Dartmouth.

Johnston, David; Hutton, Glenn–Blackstone's Police Manual: Evidence and Procedure 2003. Blackstone's Police Manual. Paperback: £10.99. ISBN 0-19-925488-5. Oxford University Press.

Johnston, David; Zimmermann, Reinhard–Comparative Law of Unjust Enrichment. Hardback: £80.00. ISBN 0-521-80820-0. Cambridge University Press.

Jones, Christopher; Van Der Woude, Marc–EC Competition Law Handbook 2002/2003. Paperback: £155.00. ISBN 0-421-82940-0. Sweet & Maxwell.

Jones, Gareth–Law of Restitution. Common Law Library. Hardback: £225.00. ISBN 0-421-82820-X. Sweet & Maxwell.

Jones, Hugh; Benson, Chris–Publishing Law. 2nd Ed. Hardback: £65.00. ISBN 0-415-26153-8. Paperback: £24.99. ISBN 0-415-26154-6. Routledge, an imprint of Taylor & Francis Books Ltd.

Jones, Michael–Law of Damages. Common Law Series. Paperback: £195.00. ISBN 0-406-98170-1. Butterworths Tolley.

Jones, Michael–Textbook on Torts. 8th Ed. Textbook. Paperback: £19.99. ISBN 0-19-925533-4. Oxford University Press.

Jongsma, Arthur E; McInnis, William P; Myers, Michell et al–Juvenile Justice and Residential Care Treatment Planner. Paperback: £37.50. ISBN 0-471-43320-9. John Wiley & Sons Inc.

Jordan, David–Understanding VAT on Property. Paperback: £39.95. ISBN 1-85328-860-8. Law Society Publications.

Jourdan, Stephen–Adverse Possession. Hardback: £55.00. ISBN 0-406-98251-1. Butterworths Law.

Jurisprudence. 3rd Ed. LawCards Series. Paperback: £6.95. ISBN 1-85941-518-0. Cavendish Publishing Ltd.

Kaczorowska, Alina–Public International Law: Textbook. 2nd Ed. Old Bailey Press Textbooks. Paperback: £14.95. ISBN 1-85836-416-7. Old Bailey Press.

Kaczorowska, Alina–Public International Law. 150 Leading Ases. Paperback: £11.95. ISBN 1-85836-422-1. Old Bailey Press.

Kamel, Hossain; Besselink, Leonard F.M.; Haile Gebre Selassie; Volker, Edmond–Human Rights Commissions and Ombudsman Offices. Hardback: £126.00. ISBN 90-411-1586-2. Kluwer Law International.

Kamina, Pascal–Film Copyright in the European Union. Cambridge Studies in International Property Rights. Hardback: £55.00. ISBN 0-521-77053-X. Cambridge University Press.

Kamstra, Gerry; Scott-Ram, Nick; Sheard, Andrew; Doring, Marc; Wixon, Henry–Patents on Biotechnological Inventions. Special Reports. Hardback: £150.00. ISBN 0-75200-706-8. Sweet & Maxwell.

Kaplow, Louis; Shavell, Steven–Fairness Versus Welfare. Hardback: £30.95. ISBN 0-674-00622-4. Harvard University Press.

Kapp, Marshall B.–Lessons in Law and Aging. Hardback: £38.95. ISBN 0-8261-1411-3. Springer Publishing Company.

Kay, D.–Bar Manual: Solicitors Accounts/practice Guide 2002/2003. 6th Ed. Blackstone Bar Manual. Paperback: £22.99. ISBN 0-19-925508-3. Oxford University Press.

Kayser, Valerie–Launching Space Objects: Issues of Liability and Future Prospects. Space Regulations Library Series, 1. Hardback: £91.00. ISBN 1-4020-0061-8. Kluwer Academic Publishers.

Keating, Albert–Construction of Wills. Hardback: £78.00. ISBN 1-85800-231-1. Round Hall Ltd.

Keating, Albert–Probate Law and Practice. Brehon Library. Hardback. ISBN 1-85800-300-8. Round Hall Ltd.

Keenan, Denis; Bisacre, Josephine–Smith and Keenan's Company Law for Students: with Scottish Supplement. 12th Ed. Paperback: £30.99. ISBN 0-582-47316-0. Longman.

Keenan, Denis–English Law Update: Bulletin No 1:September 2001. Paperback. ISBN 0-582-47306-3. Longman.

Keenan, Denis–Smith and Keenan's Company Law. 12th Ed. Paperback: £29.99. ISBN 0-582-47315-2. Longman.

Kellett, Peter; Farthing, Julia; Marshall, Bridget–Pollution Prevention and Control-the New Regime. Hardback: £45.00. ISBN 0-406-95811-4. Tolley Publishing.

Kelly, Jacky–Asset Securitisation. Hardback: £125.00. ISBN 0-85308-636-2. Jordans.

Kelsey, Jane–International Economic Regulation. The Library of Essays in International Law. Hardback: £110.00. ISBN 0-7546-2225-8. Dartmouth.

Kennedy, Ian; Grubb, Andrew–Principles of Medical Law. Kennedy and Grubb: Principles of Medical Law Series. Hardback: £150.00. ISBN 0-19-924583-5. Oxford University Press.

Kennedy, T.P.–European Law. Paperback: £34.99. ISBN 0-19-925484-2. Paperback: £34.99. ISBN 0-19-925484-2. Oxford University Press.

Kenner, Jeff–EU Employment Law. Paperback: £45.00. ISBN 1-901362-69-8. Hart Publishing.

Keogh, Andrew–CLSA Duty Solicitor's Handbook. Paperback: £44.95. ISBN 1-85328-856-X. Law Society Publications.

Kerr, Anthony–Employment Rights Legislation (2001 Ed.). Paperback: £28.00. ISBN 1-85800-211-7. Round Hall Ltd.

Kerr, Michael–As Far As I Remember. Hardback: £22.50. ISBN 1-901362-87-6. Hart Publishing.

Kerridge, R.–Parry and Clark: the Law of Succession. Paperback: £29.95. ISBN 0-421-74110-4. Sweet & Maxwell.

Kerrigan, Kevin–Guide to Criminal Cases: Review Commission. Paperback. ISBN 1-872870-94-5. Waterside Press.

Kerson, Toba Schwaber–Boundary Spanning-An Ecological Reinterpretation of Social Work Practice in Health and Mental Health Systems. Hardback: £39.50. ISBN 0-231-11036-7. Columbia University Press.

Kessler, James–Drafting Trusts and Will Trusts. Hardback: CD-ROM: £99.00. ISBN 0-421-79310-4. Sweet & Maxwell.

Kevan, Tim; Adamson, Dominic–Sports Personal Injury. Paperback: £70.00. ISBN 0-421-77840-7. Sweet & Maxwell.

Kevan, Tim–Kevan on Claims for Credit Hire. 2nd Ed. Paperback: £48.00. ISBN 1-85811-275-3. EMIS Professional Publishing.

Key Issues in Planning and Environmental Law. Hardback: £61.02. ISBN 1-85475-254-5. Butterworths Law.

Khan, Malcolm; Robson, Michelle–Clinical Negligence. 2nd Ed. Paperback: £52.95. ISBN 1-85941-492-3. Cavendish Publishing Ltd.

Khor, Martin–Intellectual Property, Biodiversity and Sustainable Development. Hardback: £35.95. ISBN 1-84277-234-1. Paperback: £12.95. ISBN 1-84277-235-X. Zed Books.

Kidner, Richard–Statutes on Employment Law. (Rev Ed). Blackstone's Statutes Series. Paperback: £14.99. ISBN 0-19-925534-2. Oxford University Press.

Kiikeri, Markku–Comparative Legal Reasoning and European Law. Law and Philosophy Library, 50. Hardback: £79.00. ISBN 0-7923-6884-3. Kluwer Academic Publishers.

Kinzie, Mark; Hart, Christine–Product Liability for the Professional. Paperback: £29.99. ISBN 0-7668-2035-1. Delmar.

Kirk, David N.; Woodcock, Anthony J.J.–Kirk and Woodcock: Serious Fraud, Investigation and Trial. Hardback: £170.00. ISBN 0-406-94595-0. Butterworths Law.

Kirk, Jonathan; Gumpert, Benjamin; Bojarski, Andrzej–Proceeds of Crime Act 2002. Paperback: £35.00. ISBN 0-85308-806-3. Paperback: £35.00. ISBN 0-85308-806-3. Jordans.

Kirkbride, James; Olowofoyeku, Abimbola A.; Butler, Debbie–Revenue Law. Hardback: £60.00. ISBN 1-903499-05-4. Paperback: £24.95. ISBN 1-903499-09-7. Liverpool Academic Press.

Kirkbride; Olowofoyeku; Butler–The Law and Theory of Income Tax. Paperback: £24.95. ISBN 1-90349-900-3. Liverpool Academic Press.

Klip, Andre; Sluiter, Goran–Annotated Leading Cases of the International Criminal Tribunals: Vol 111. The International Criminal Tribunal for the Former Yugoslavia 1997-1999. Paperback: £70.00. ISBN 90-5095-141-4. Intersentia Publishers.

Knop, Karen–Diversity and Self-determination in International Law. Cambridge Studies in International and Comparative Law. Hardback: £55.00. ISBN 0-521-78178-7. Cambridge University Press.

Koch, Hugh–Interface Between Medical Expert and Lawyer. Spiral/comb bound: £165.00. ISBN 1-84311-028-8. LLP Professional Publishing.

Kodilinye, Gilbert–Commonwealth Caribbean Law of Trusts. 2nd Ed. Paperback: £48.40. ISBN 1-85941-540-7. Cavendish Publishing Ltd.

Koivurova, Timo–Environmental Impact Assessment (EIA) in the Arctic. Hardback: £55.00. ISBN 0-7546-2283-5. Dartmouth.

Kolah, Ardi—Essential Law for Marketers. Paperback: £25.00. ISBN 0-7506-5500-3. Butterworth-Heinemann.

Kollmer, Louise; Lark, Susan—EU Origin of Goods. Hardback: £58.00. ISBN 1-902558-35-9. Palladian Law Publishing Ltd.

Kolm, Serge-Christophe—Modern Theories of Justice. Paperback: £26.50. ISBN 0-262-61180-5. The MIT Press.

Komesar, Neil—Law's Limits: The Role of Courts, the Rule of Law, and the Supply and Demand of Rights. Hardback: £45.00. ISBN 0-521-80629-1. Cambridge University Press.

Kono, Toshiyuki; Paulus, Christoph G.; Rajak, Harry—Selected Legal Issues of E-commerce. Law and Electronic Commerce, Vol 16. Hardback: £41.00. ISBN 90-411-1898-5. Kluwer Law International.

Koo, John—English Legal System. 2nd Ed. 150 Leading Cases. Paperback: £11.95. ISBN 1-85836-451-5. Old Bailey Press.

Koppen, Peter J. Van; Penrod, Steven D.—Adversarial Versus Inquisitorial Justice. Perspectives in Law & Psychology, 17. Hardback: £50.00. ISBN 0-306-47362-3. Kluwer Academic / Plenum Publishers.

Korah, Valentine; O'Sullivan, Denis—Distribution Agreements Under the EC Competition Rules. Hardback: £75.00. ISBN 1-84113-239-X. Hart Publishing.

Koskenniemi, Martti—Gentle Civilizer of Nations-The Rise and Fall of Modern International Law, 1870-1960. Cambridge Studies in International and Comparative Law, 14. Hardback: £65.00. ISBN 0-521-62311-1. Cambridge University Press.

Kraeuter, David W.—Radio Patent Lists and Index, 1830-1980. Hardback: £89.95. ISBN 0-7734-7520-6. Edwin Mellen Press.

Kramer, Ludwig—Casebook on EU Environmental Law. 2nd Ed. Paperback: £35.00. ISBN 1-84113-172-5. Hart Publishing.

Kreijen, Gerard—State, Sovereignty, and International Governance. Hardback: £70.00. ISBN 0-19-924538-X. Oxford University Press.

Kreppel, Amie—European Parliament and Supranational Party System-A Study in Institutional Development. Cambridge Studies in Comparative Politics. Hardback: £40.00. ISBN 0-521-80625-9. Paperback: £14.95. ISBN 0-521-00079-3. Cambridge University Press.

Krishnan, Vickneswaren—English Legal System. 2nd Ed. Revision Workbook. Paperback: £9.95. ISBN 1-85836-426-4. Old Bailey Press.

Krishnan, Vickneswaren—Obligations. Revision Workbook. Paperback: £9.95. ISBN 1-85836-354-3. Old Bailey Press.

Krishnan, Vickneswaren—Obligations. Revision Workbook. Paperback: £9.95. ISBN 1-85836-467-1. Old Bailey Press.

Kritzer, Herbert M.—Legal Systems of the World-A Political, Social, and Cultural Encyclopedia. Hardback: £265.50. ISBN 1-57607-231-2. ABC CLIO (Reference Books).

Kurer, Martin; Codoni, Stefano; Gunther, Klaus; Neves, Jorge Santiago; Teh, Lawrence—Warranties and Disclaimers: Limitations of Liability in Consumer-related Transactions. International Bar Association Series. Hardback: £143.00. ISBN 90-411-9856-3. Kluwer Law International.

Ladeur, Karl-Heinz—Europeanisation of Administrative Law-Transforming National Decision-making Procedure. Hardback: £45.00. ISBN 0-7546-2223-1. Dartmouth.

Lai, Jerry—Tolley's Company Secretary's Handbook 2001-02. 11th Ed. Paperback: £49.95. ISBN 0-7545-1265-7. Tolley Publishing.

Lai, Jerry—Tolley's Company Secretary's Handbook. Paperback: £49.95. ISBN 0-7545-1789-6. Tolley Publishing.

Laken, Elaine; et al—Family Bench Handbook. Looseleaf/ring bound: £65.00. ISBN 1-904380-00-X. Waterside Press.

Land Lawcards. 3rd Ed. LawCards Series. Paperback: £6.00. ISBN 1-85941-715-9. Cavendish Publishing Ltd.

Langlois, Anthony J.–Politics of Justice and Human Rights-Southeast Asia and Universalist Theory. Cambridge Asia-Pacific Studies. Hardback: £45.00. ISBN 0-521-80785-9. Cambridge University Press.

Lasok, Paul; Paines, Nicholas–Common Market Law Reports 2001: Vol 1. Hardback: £250.00. ISBN 0-421-79320-1. Sweet & Maxwell.

Lasok, Paul; Paines, Nicholas–Common Market Law Reports 2001: Vol 2. Hardback: £250.00. ISBN 0-421-79340-6. Sweet & Maxwell.

Lasok, Paul; Paines, Nicholas–Common Market Law Reports 2001: Vol 3. Hardback: £250.00. ISBN 0-421-79360-0. Sweet & Maxwell.

Lasok, Paul; Paines, Nicholas–Common Market Law Reports: Antitrust Supplement 2001, Vol 1. Hardback: £207.50. ISBN 0-421-79540-9. Sweet & Maxwell.

Latham, Charles–Practitioner's Guide to the Competition Act 1998. Competition on Law in Practice. Hardback: £85.00. ISBN 0-421-62090-0. Hardback: £95.00. ISBN 0-421-62090-0. Sweet & Maxwell.

Latzer, Barry–Death Penalty Cases. Paperback: £20.99. ISBN 0-7506-7594-2. Butterworth-Heinemann.

Lauterbach, T.–EU Law Basics. Greens Law Basics. Paperback: £9.95. ISBN 0-414-01403-0. W. Green & Son.

Lauterpacht, E.; Greenwood, C. J.–International Law Reports: Volume 119: International Law Reports. Hardback: £110.00. ISBN 0-521-66122-6. Cambridge University Press.

Lauterpacht, Elihu; Greenwood, Christopher J.–International Law Reports: Volume 120. International Law Reports. Hardback: £110.00. ISBN 0-521-66123-4. Cambridge University Press.

Lauterpacht, Elihu; Greenwood, Christopher J.–International Law Reports: Volume 121. International Law Reports. Hardback: £110.00. ISBN 0-521-80774-3. Cambridge University Press.

Lauterpacht, Elihu; Greenwood, Christopher J.–International Law Reports: Volume 122: International Law Reports. Hardback: £110.00. ISBN 0-521-80775-1. Cambridge University Press.

Law and Cyberspace. Paperback: £8.99. ISBN 0-85092-658-0. Commonwealth Secretariat.

Law Society's Directory of Solicitors and Barristers 2002-2003. 11th Ed. Hardback: £94.95. ISBN 1-85328-811-X. Law Society Publications.

Law Update 2002. Paperback: £9.95. ISBN 1-85836-435-3. Old Bailey Press.

Lawson, F.H.; Rudden, Bernard–Law of Property. Revised Ed. Clarendon Law Series. Paperback: £18.99. ISBN 0-19-829993-1. Oxford University Press.

Lawson, R.G.; Bertram, A.D.W.–Business Tax and Law Handbook. Zurich. Hardback: £29.99. ISBN 0-273-66216-3. Financial Times Prentice Hall.

Lawson, Virginia–Contracts for the Real Estate Professional. Paperback: £9.99. ISBN 0-324-15373-2. South Western College Publishing.

Layton, Alexander–O'Malley and Layton: European Civil Practice. Hardback: £295.00. ISBN 0-421-60860-9. Sweet & Maxwell.

Le Prestre, Philippe G.–Governing Global Biodiversity. Global Environmental Governance. Hardback: £39.95. ISBN 0-7546-1744-0. Ashgate Publishing Limited.

Le Prestre, Philippe G.–Governing Global Biodiversity. Global Environmental Governance. Hardback: £45.00. ISBN 0-7546-1744-0. Ashgate Publishing Limited.

Le Sueur, Andrew; Marshall, G.; Yeats, I.; Armstrong, K.–Public Law: 2001. Hardback: £150.00. ISBN 0-421-77360-X. Sweet & Maxwell.

Leech, Mark; Cheney, Deborah–Prisons Handbook: 2002. 6th Ed. Paperback: £62.50. ISBN 1-872870-16-3. Waterside Press.

Leighton, Patricia; Proctor, Giles–Recruiting Within the Law. 2nd Ed. Legal Essentials. Paperback: £32.99. ISBN 0-85292-957-9. Chartered Institute of Personnel and Development (CIPD).

Lerner–Essentials of Intellectual Property. Paperback: £25.95. ISBN 0-471-20942-2. John Wiley & Sons Inc.

Letterman, G. Gregory–Basics of International Sales of Goods. The Basics of International Law. Paperback: £76.99. ISBN 1-57105-255-0. Transnational Publishers, Inc.

Levi, Michael; Pithouse, Andrew–White Collar Crime and Its Victims. Clarendon Studies in Criminology. Hardback: £45.00. ISBN 0-19-826254-X. Clarendon Press.

Lewis, David; Sargeant, Malcolm–Essentials of Employment Law. 7th Ed. People and Organizations. Paperback: £25.99. ISBN 0-85292-939-0. Chartered Institute of Personnel and Development (CIPD).

Lewis, Robyn–Geiriadur Newydd Y Gyfraith/The New Legal Dictionary. Hardback: £75.00. ISBN 1-84323-101-8. Gomer Press.

Leyland, Peter; Woods, Terry–Textbook on Administrative Law. 4th Ed. Paperback: £21.99. ISBN 0-19-925536-9. Oxford University Press.

Linarelli, John–Linarelli: International Economic Law. Paperback: £29.95. ISBN 0-406-98584-7. Butterworths Law.

Lindley, Nathaniel; Banks, R.C.–Lindley and Banks on Partnership. 18th Ed. Hardback: £210.00. ISBN 0-421-67390-7. Sweet & Maxwell.

Lindrup, Garth–Competition Law Handbook. Paperback: £75.00. ISBN 0-406-95762-2. Butterworths Law.

Livingstone, Stephen–European Convention on Human Rights. Paperback: £26.99. ISBN 0-19-876337-9. Oxford University Press Inc, USA.

Llewelyn, Margaret–Intellectual Property Quarterly: 2001. Hardback: 235.00. ISBN 0-421-75560-1. Sweet & Maxwell.

Lloyd's Law Reports: Medical: 2001. Hardback: £107.00. ISBN 1-84311-134-9. LLP Professional Publishing.

Lloyd's Law Reports: Professional Negligence: 2001. Hardback: £107.00. ISBN 1-84311-137-3. LLP Professional Publishing.

Lloyd's Law Reports: Vol 2. 2001. Hardback: £120.00. ISBN 1-84311-132-2. LLP Professional Publishing.

Lloyd's Maritime & Commercial Law Quarterly: 2001. Hardback: £96.00. ISBN 1-84311-138-1. LLP Professional Publishing.

Lloyd, Stephen; Bleasdale, Marie-Claire–Practitioner's Guide to Powers and Duties of Trustees. Paperback: £49.00. ISBN 0-7545-1489-7. Paperback: £49.00. ISBN 0-7545-1489-7. Tolley Publishing.

Lodder, Arno R.; Kaspersen, Henrik W.K.–E-Directives: Guide to European Union Law on E-commerce. Law and Electronic Commerce, 14. Hardback: £44.00. ISBN 90-411-1752-0. Kluwer Law International.

Longdin, Ian–Legal Aspects of Purchasing and Supply. Hardback: £16.99. ISBN 1-903499-08-9. Hardback: £16.99. ISBN 1-90349-908-9. Liverpool Academic Press.

Longrigg, William; Higgins, Sarah–Longrigg & Higgins: Family Breakdown and Trusts. Hardback: £50.00. ISBN 0-406-94829-1. Butterworths Law.

Lord Reed; Murdoch, James L.–Guide to Human Rights Law in Scotland. Paperback: £40.00. ISBN 0-406-92320-5. Butterworths Law.

Loux, Andrea; Boyle, Alan; Himsworth, Chris; MacQueen, Hector–Human Rights and Scots Law–Comparative Perspectives on the Incorporation of the ECHR. Hardback: £40.00. ISBN 1-84113-044-3. Hart Publishing.

Love, Gavin; Head, Nicholas–European Union Law. Statutes Series. Paperback: £14.95. ISBN 0-421-79210-8. Sweet & Maxwell.

Luba, Jan; Davies, Liz–Homelessness Act 2002. Paperback: £30.00. ISBN 0-85308-825-X. Family Law.

Luba, Jan–Housing and the Human Rights Act. Paperback: £25.00. ISBN 0-85308-769-5. Jordans.

Luba, J.; Madge, N.; McConnell, D.–Defending Possession Proceedings. 5th Ed. Paperback: £42.00. ISBN 1-903307-06-6. The Legal Action Group.

Lugard, Paul–Vertical Restraints Under EC Competition Law. Hardback: £35.00. ISBN 1-84113-151-2. Hart Publishing.

Lush, Master Denzil–Heywood and Massey: Court of Protection Practice. 13th Ed. Looseleaf/ring bound: £195.00. ISBN 0-421-82680-0. Sweet & Maxwell.

Lutzker, Arnold P.–Content Rights for Creative Professionals. Paperback: CD-ROM: £27.50. ISBN 0-240-80484-8. Paperback: CD-ROM: £27.50. ISBN 0-240-80484-8. Focal Press.

Lynn, Michael–Media Law in Ireland. Hardback. ISBN 1-85475-209-X. Butterworths Law (Ireland).

Lyon, Christina; Cobley, Cathy; Petrie, Stephanie; Reid, Carline–Child Abuse. 3rd Ed. Paperback: £30.00. ISBN 0-85308-576-5. Family Law.

Lyons, Peter–Tolley's Businesswise: Financial Planning for the Small and Medium-sized Enterprise 2002. Paperback: £42.00. ISBN 0-7545-1785-3. Tolley Publishing.

Lyons, Timothy–EC Customs Law. Oxford European Community Law Library. Hardback: £95.00. ISBN 0-19-876492-8. Oxford University Press.

Maas, Robert W.–Tolley's Property Taxes 2001-02. Paperback: £65.95. ISBN 0-7545-1201-0. Tolley Publishing.

Maas, Robert–Tolley's Taxation of Employments. 8th Ed. Paperback: £65.95. ISBN 0-7545-1220-7. Tolley Publishing.

Macdonald, Lynda–Managing Fixed-term and Part-time Workers: a Practical Guide to Temporary, Seasonal and Contract Employees. Paperback: £35.00. ISBN 0-7545-1662-8. Tolley Publishing.

Macdonald, Roderick A.–Lessons of Everyday Law. Hardback: £49.90. ISBN 0-88911-913-9. Paperback: £18.90. ISBN 0-88911-915-5. McGill-Queen's University Press.

MacDowell, Laurel Sefton–Renegade Lawyer. Osgoode Society for Canadian Legal History. Hardback: £42.00. ISBN 0-8020-3513-2. University of Toronto Press Inc.

Mackay, Malcolm R.; Simon, Shona–Employment Law. 2nd Ed. Greens Concise Scots Law. Hardback: £95.00. ISBN 0-414-01402-2. W.Green & Son.

Mackenzie, G. Calvin; Hafken, Michael–Scandal Proof-Do Ethics Laws Make Government Ethical? Hardback: £29.25. ISBN 0-8157-5402-7. Paperback: £12.50. ISBN 0-8157-5403-5. The Brookings Institution.

MacKenzie, Judith-Anne; Phillips, Mary–Textbook on Land Law. Textbook. Paperback: £19.99. ISBN 0-19-925537-7. Oxford University Press.

MacKey, Thomas C.–Pornography on Trial. On Trial. Hardback: £39.95. ISBN 1-57607-275-4. ABC CLIO.

Macleod, John–Consumer Sales Law. Paperback: £28.95. ISBN 1-85941-700-0. Cavendish Publishing Ltd.

MacMillan, Fiona–WTO and the Environment. International Trade Law Series. Hardback: £130.00. ISBN 0-421-82420-4. Sweet & Maxwell.

Maitland-Walker, Julian; Evans, Jonathan; Harding, Geoffrey; Hanker, Michael; Poole, Jill; Wareham, Philip–European Competition Law Review: 2001. Hardback: £435.00. ISBN 0-421-77310-3. Sweet & Maxwell.

Manning, J.; Kilpatrick, A.–Judicial Review Proceedings. 2nd Ed. Paperback: £32.00. ISBN 0-905099-96-6. The Legal Action Group.

Marciano, Alain; Josselin, Jean-Michel–Economics of Harmonizing European Law. New Horizons in Law and Economics. Hardback: £59.95. ISBN 1-84064-608-X. Edward Elgar.

Marett, Paul–Information Law in Practice. 2nd Ed. Hardback: £50.00. ISBN 0-566-08390-6. Ashgate Publishing Limited.

Mars, Gerald–Occupational Crime-Reissue. International Library of Criminology, Criminal Justice and Penology. Hardback: £95.00. ISBN 1-85521-382-6. Dartmouth.

Marsh, James L.–Unjust Legality. New Critical Theory. Hardback. ISBN 0-7425-1260-6. Rowman & Littlefield Publishers.

Martin, Elizabeth A.–Dictionary of Law. 5th Ed. Oxford Paperback Reference. Paperback: £9.99. ISBN 0-19-860399-1. Oxford University Press.

Martin, Jacqueline; Gibbins, Mary–Complete A-Z Law Handbook. 2nd Ed. Complete A-Z. Paperback: £9.99. ISBN 0-340-84716-6. Hodder & Stoughton Educational.

Martin, Jacqueline; Turner, Chris–Key Facts: European Law. Key Facts for Law. Paperback: £4.99. ISBN 0-340-84584-8. Hodder & Stoughton Educational.

Martin, Jacqueline–AQA Law for AS. Paperback: £14.99. ISBN 0-340-84741-7. Hodder & Stoughton Educational.

Martino, Tony; Miskin, Claire–Entertainment Law Review 2001. Hardback: £435.00. ISBN 0-421-77320-0. Sweet & Maxwell.

Mason, J.K.; Smith, R.A. Mccall; Laurie, G.T.–Mason & Mccall Smith: Law and Medical Ethics. 6th Ed. Paperback: £19.95. ISBN 0-406-94995-6. Butterworths Law.

Matthews, Jan; Eastaway, Nigel–Corporation Tax Self-assessment. 3rd Ed. Paperback: £65.95. ISBN 0-7545-1288-6. Tolley Publishing.

Matthews, Jan; Eastaway, Nigel–Tolley's Self-assessment 2001-02. Paperback: £69.95. ISBN 0-7545-1203-7. Tolley Publishing.

Matthews, Paul; Malek, Hodge M.–Disclosure: 1st Supplement to the Second Edition. Litigation Library. Paperback: £45.00. ISBN 0-421-79000-8. Sweet & Maxwell.

Maugham, Jolyon; Peacock, Jonathan–Taxation for Personal Injury Specialists. Paperback: £49.95. ISBN 0-406-94802-X. Butterworths Tolley.

Mayson, Stephen; French, Derek; Ryan, Christopher–Mayson, French and Ryan on Company Law. 19th Ed. Paperback: £29.99. ISBN 0-19-925538-5. Oxford University Press.

McAlhone, Christina; Stockdale, Michael–Nutshells: Evidence. 3rd Ed. Nutshells. Paperback: £5.95. ISBN 0-421-76520-8. Sweet & Maxwell.

Mcallister, Angus–Scottish Law of Leases. Paperback: £36.00. ISBN 0-406-93238-7. Butterworths Law.

McAuslan, Patrick–Bringing the Law Back in. Hardback: £50.00. ISBN 0-7546-2060-3. Dartmouth.

McConnell, Michael W.; Cochran Jr, Robert F.; Carmella, Angela C.–Christian Perspectives on Legal Thought. Hardback: £35.00. ISBN 0-300-08749-7. Paperback: £18.95. ISBN 0-300-08750-0. Yale University Press.

McConville, Mike; Wilson, Geoffrey–Handbook of the Criminal Justice Process. Hardback: £69.99. ISBN 0-19-925460-5. Paperback: £26.99. ISBN 0-19-925395-1. Oxford University Press.

McDonald, Laughlin–Voting Rights Odyssey. Hardback: £37.50. ISBN 0-521-81232-1. Paperback: £13.95. ISBN 0-521-01179-5. Cambridge University Press.

McEldowney, J.F.–Public Law. Paperback: £27.95. ISBN 0-421-78070-3. Sweet & Maxwell.

McGee, Andrew–McGee: Limitation Periods. 4th Ed. Litigation Library. Hardback: £185.00. ISBN 0-421-77940-3. Sweet & Maxwell.

McGhee, John–Snell's Equity: 2nd Supplement to the 30th Edition. 30th Ed. Paperback: £45.00. ISBN 0-421-76420-1. Sweet & Maxwell.

Mcghee, Robin–Offshore Practice and Administration. 3rd Ed. Paperback: £30.00. ISBN 0-85297-674-7. Financial World Publishing.

McGregor, Harvey–McGregor on Damages: 4th Supplement to the 16th Edition. Common Law Library. Paperback: £45.00. ISBN 0-421-79020-2. Sweet & Maxwell.

McGregor, Lindsay–Tolley's Director's Handbook: 1999-2000. Paperback: £59.95. ISBN 0-7545-0239-2. Tolley Publishing.

McKendrick, Ewan—Contract, Tort, Restitution Law. Statutes Series. Paperback: £12.95. ISBN 0-421-78100-9. Sweet & Maxwell.

McLeod, Ian—Legal Method. 4th Ed. Palgrave Law Masters. Paperback: £14.99. ISBN 0-333-97025-X. Palgrave Macmillan.

McLoughlin, Patrick—Commercial Leases and Insolvency. 3rd Ed. Paperback: £40.00. ISBN 0-406-91347-1. Butterworths Law.

McMahon, Bryan M.E.; Binchy, William—McMahon and Binchy: Casebook on Irish Law of Torts. 3rd Ed. Paperback: £39.66. ISBN 1-85475-203-0. Butterworths Law.

McMullen, John; Smith, Ian—McMullen & Smith: Breach of the Employment Contract and Wrongful Dismissal. Hardback: £65.00. ISBN 0-406-11841-8. Butterworths Law.

McPeake, Robert—Bar Manual: Advocacy 2002/2003. Blackstone Bar Manual. Paperback: £21.99. ISBN 0-19-925496-6. Oxford University Press.

McQuater, John—APIL Model Letters for Personal Injury Lawyers. Paperback/ Floppy disk: £47.00. ISBN 0-85308-766-0. Paperback: Floppy disk: £40.00. ISBN 0-85308-766-0. Jordans.

Medical Records for Lawyers. Paperback: £42.00. ISBN 1-85811-259-1. EMIS Professional Publishing.

Meek, Alison; Wood, John; Meadway, Susannagh; Evans, Nicola—Practitioner's Guide to Contentious Trusts and Estates. Paperback: £49.00. ISBN 0-7545-1658-X. Tolley Publishing.

Meeks, Alastair—Tolley's Pensions Cases. Paperback: £64.95. ISBN 0-7545-1273-8. Tolley Publishing.

Megantz—Technology Management: Developing and Implementing Effective Licensing Programs. Hardback: £48.50. ISBN 0-471-20018-2. John Wiley & Sons Inc.

Menell, Peter—Environmental Law. International Library of Essays in Law and Legal Theory: Second Series -. Hardback: £100.00. ISBN 0-7546-2134-0. Ashgate Publishing Limited.

Menuge, Noel James—Medieval English Wardship in Romance and Law. Hardback: £40.00. ISBN 0-85991-632-4. D.S. Brewer.

Merkin, Robert—Colinvaux's Law of Insurance: 2nd Supplement to the 7th Edition. Insurance Practitioners Library Series. Paperback: £80.00. ISBN 0-421-67420-2. Sweet & Maxwell.

Merritt, Jonathan—Introduction to Business Law. Paperback: £24.95. ISBN 1-9034-9904-6. Liverpool Academic Press.

Merritt, Jonathan—Modern Business Law. Paperback: £19.50. ISBN 1-90349-907-0. Liverpool Academic Press.

Meston, Michael—Succession (Scotland) Act 1964. 5th Ed. Greens Annotated Acts. Paperback: £40.00. ISBN 0-414-01453-7. W.Green & Son.

Michaels, Amanda—Practical Guide to Trade Mark Law. 3rd Ed. Hardback: £95.00. ISBN 0-421-74760-9. Sweet & Maxwell.

Michalos, Christina—Law of Photography and Digital Images. Hardback: £125.00. ISBN 0-421-76470-8. Sweet & Maxwell.

Middleton, Kirsty—Blackstone's UK and EC Competition Documents. 2nd Ed. Blackstone's Statutes. Paperback: £16.99. ISBN 0-19-925539-3. Oxford University Press.

Miller, Phillip—Media Law for Producers. 4th Ed. Paperback: £27.50. ISBN 0-240-80478-3. Focal Press.

Milmo, Marina—European Commercial Cases 2001. Hardback: £530. ISBN 0-421-78390-7. Sweet & Maxwell.

Milmo, Marina—International Litigation Procedure: 2001. Hardback: £415.00. ISBN 0-421-78650-7. Sweet & Maxwell.

Milmo, Patrick; Rogers, W.V.H.—Gatley on Libel and Slander: 1st Supplement to the 9th Edition. Common Law Library. Paperback: £40.00. ISBN 0-421-75930-5. Sweet & Maxwell.

Milovanovic, Dragan–Critical Criminology At the Edge. Praeger Series in Criminology and Crime Control Policy. Hardback: £53.95. ISBN 0-275-96828-6. Praeger Publishers.

Mitchell, Andrew R; Talbot, Kennedy; Taylor, Susan M.–Mitchell, Taylor and Talbot on Confiscation and the Proceeds of Crime. 3rd Ed. Criminal Law Library. Looseleaf/ring bound: £175.00. ISBN 0-421-78200-5. Sweet & Maxwell.

Mitchell, Barry; Farrar, Salim–Statutes on Criminal Justice and Sentencing. Blackstone's Statute Series. Paperback: £14.99. ISBN 0-19-925485-0. Oxford University Press.

Moir, Lindsay–Law of Internal Armed Conflict. Cambridge Studies in International and Comparative Law. Hardback: £45.00. ISBN 0-521-77216-8. Cambridge University Press.

Molan, Michael T.–Administrative Law. Old Bailey Press Revision Workbook. Paperback: £9.95. ISBN 1-85836-338-1. Old Bailey Press.

Molan, Michael T.–Constitutional and Administrative Law. 150 Leading Cases. Paperback: £11.95. ISBN 1-85836-448-5. Old Bailey Press.

Molan, Michael T.–Constitutional Law. Revision Workbook. Paperback: £9.95. ISBN 1-85836-460-4. Old Bailey Press.

Molan, Michael T.–Criminal Law. Revision Workbook. Paperback: £11.95. ISBN 1-85836-449-3. Paperback: £9.95. ISBN 1-85836-461-2. Old Bailey Press.

Moloney, Niamh–EC Securities Regulation. Oxford European Community Law Library. Hardback: £110.00. ISBN 0-19-826891-2. Oxford University Press.

Montagu–Legal Practice Companion 2002-2003. Paperback: £29.99. ISBN 0-19-925540-7. Oxford University Press.

Montgomery, Jonathan–Health Care Law. Paperback: £23.99. ISBN 0-19-876574-6. Oxford University Press.

Moore, Randy–Evolution in the Courtroom. Hardback: £55.95. ISBN 1-57607-420-X. ABC CLIO (Reference Books).

Moore, Terence–Anthony and Berryman's Magistrates Court Guide. Paperback: £35.00. ISBN 0-406-96239-1. Butterworths Law.

Moore, Victor–Practical Approach to Planning Law. 8th Ed. A Practical Approach. Paperback: £28.95. ISBN 0-19-925595-4. Oxford University Press.

Morgan, Adrienne; Granville, Andrew; Copley, James–Disciplinary and Regulatory Tribunals. Hardback: £125.00. ISBN 0-406-90260-7. Butterworths Law.

Morgan, Owen–International Protection of Performers Rights. Hardback: £35.00. ISBN 1-84113-285-3. Hart Publishing.

Morgan, Richard; Burden, Kit–Legal Protection of Software. Hardback: £48.00. ISBN 1-85811-294-X. EMIS Professional Publishing.

Moriarty, Jane–Role of Mental Illness in Criminal Trials: 1. Hardback: £85.00. ISBN 0-8153-4062-1. Routledge, an imprint of Taylor & Francis Books Ltd.

Moriarty, Jane–Role of Mental Illness in Criminal Trials: 2. Hardback: £85.00. ISBN 0-8153-4063-X. Routledge, an imprint of Taylor & Francis Books Ltd.

Moriarty, Jane–Role of Mental Illness in Criminal Trials: 3. Hardback: £85.00. ISBN 0-8153-4064-8. Routledge, an imprint of Taylor & Francis Books Ltd.

Moriarty, Jane–Role of Mental Illness in Criminal Trials. Hardback: £250.00. ISBN 0-8153-3573-3. Garland Publishing, Inc.

Morison, John; Livingstone, Steven; Morrow, Karen–Introduction to Constitutional and Administrative Law. Hardback: £30.00. ISBN 1-901362-57-4. Paperback: £12.99. ISBN 1-901362-58-2. Hart Publishing.

Morris, Glynis–Finance Director's Handbook. Paperback: £55.00. ISBN 0-7545-1259-2. Tolley Publishing.

Morris, Gordon–Shaw's Directory of Courts in the United Kingdom: 2002/03. Paperback: £39.50. ISBN 0-7219-1409-8. Shaw & Sons.

Morrish, Peter; McLean, Ian; Selwood, David–Crown Court Index: 2002. Hardback: £75.00. ISBN 0-421-76820-7. Sweet & Maxwell.

Morse, Geoffrey–Palmer's Limited Liability Partnership Law. Hardback: £125.00. ISBN 0-421-74000-0. Sweet & Maxwell.

Moss, Gabriel; Isaacs, Stuart; Fletcher, Ian–EC Regulation on Insolvency Proceedings. Hardback: £125.00. ISBN 0-19-925109-6. Hardback: £125.00. ISBN 0-19-925109-6. Oxford University Press.

Mostyn, Nicholas–Butterworths Child's Pay: the Complete Guide to Child Support Law and Practice. Hardback/Compact disk: £95.00. ISBN 0-406-95111-X. Butterworths Law.

Muir, Ian; Brandi-Dohrn, Matthias; Gruber, Stephan–European Patent Law. Hardback: £55.00. ISBN 0-19-925427-3. Oxford University Press.

Mumford, Ann–Taxing Culture: Towards a Theory of Tax Collection Law. Socio-legal Studies. Hardback: £55.00. ISBN 1-84014-710-5. Dartmouth.

Mundy, Martha–Law and Anthropology. International Library of Essays in Law and Legal Theory: Second Series. Hardback: £115.00. ISBN 0-7546-2082-4. Dartmouth.

Murdoch, Joyce; Price, Deb–Courting Justice. Paperback: £14.99. ISBN 0-465-01514-X. Basic Books.

Murphy, Liam; Nagel, Thomas–Myth of Ownership-Taxes and Justice. Hardback: £17.99. ISBN 0-19-515016-3. Oxford University Press Inc, USA.

Murphy–Counting Nine Analyzing the Supreme Court. Paperback: £33.99. ISBN 0-205-29008-6. Allyn & Bacon.

Murray, Jeff–Children's Rights and the Children's Act 1989. Hardback: £30.00. ISBN 1-84113-145-8. Hart Publishing.

Murray, Len–Pleader-An Autobiography. Hardback: £15.99. ISBN 1-84018-642-9. Mainstream Publishing.

Musker, David–Community Design Law-Principles and Practice. Hardback: £125.00. ISBN 0-421-79060-1. Sweet & Maxwell.

Mynors, Charles–Law of Trees, Forests and Hedgerows. Hardback: £75.00. ISBN 0-421-59040-8. Sweet & Maxwell.

Naffine, Ngaire; Owens, Rosemary J.; Williams, John–Intention in Law and Philosophy. Applied Legal Philosophy. Hardback: £50.00. ISBN 0-7546-2171-5. Dartmouth.

Naffine, Ngaire–Gender and Justice. International Library of Essays in Law and Legal Theory: Second Series. Hardback: £110.00. ISBN 0-7546-2087-5. Dartmouth.

Nafziger, James A.R.; Symeonides, Symeon–Law and Justice in a Multi-state World. Hardback: £149.50. ISBN 1-57105-118-X. Transnational Publishers, Inc.

Nakajima, Chizu; Sheffield, Elizabeth; Alexander Richard–Butterworths Compliance Series: Conflicts of Interest and Chinese Walls. Butterworths Compliance Series. Paperback: £50.00. ISBN 0-406-93751-6. Butterworths Law.

Navarro, Edurne; Font, Andres; Folguera, Jaime; Briones, Juan–Merger Control in the EU. Hardback: £95.00. ISBN 0-19-924470-7. Oxford University Press.

Nelken, David; Feest, Johannes–Adapting Legal Cultures. Onati International Series in Law and Society. Hardback: £45.00. ISBN 1-84113-291-8. Paperback: £20.00. ISBN 1-84113-292-6. Hart Publishing.

Neumann, Michael–Rule of Law-Politicizing Ethics. Ashgate New Critical Thinking in Philosophy. Hardback: £40.00. ISBN 0-7546-0525-6. Ashgate Publishing Limited.

Newman, Peter–New Palgrave Dictionary of Economics and the Law. Paperback: £150.00. ISBN 0-333-99756-5. Palgrave Macmillan.

Newton, Justin–Uniform Interpretation of the Brussels and Lugano Conventions. Hardback: £75.00. ISBN 1-84113-323-X. Hart Publishing.

Newton–Bankruptcy and Insolvency Taxation: 2002 Cumulative Supplement. 2nd Ed. Paperback: £70.50. ISBN 0-471-41928-1. John Wiley & Sons Inc.

Nicholls, Doug–Employment Practice and Policies in Youth and Community Work. 2nd Ed. Paperback: £16.95. ISBN 1-898924-63-5. Russell House Publishing Ltd.

Nicol, Danny–EC Membership and the Judicialization of British Politics. Oxford Studies in European Law. Hardback: £35.00. ISBN 0-19-924779-X. Oxford University Press.

Nielsen, Ruth; Szyszczak, Erika–EU Labour Law. Hardback: £34.00. ISBN 87-630-0057-1. Copenhagen Business School Press.

Nolff, Markus–TRIPS, PCT and Global Patent Procurement. Hardback: £59.00. ISBN 90-411-9740-0. Kluwer Law International.

Norman, Helen E.–Law of Patents in the United Kingdom and the European Community. European Community Law. Hardback: £65.00. ISBN 0-485-70015-8. Continuum International Publishing Group-Athlone Press.

O'Brien, John–Public International Law. 1999-2000 Suggested Solutions. Paperback: £6.95. ISBN 1-85836-446-9. Old Bailey Press.

O'Floinn, Benedict; Gannon, The Hon Mr Justice Sean–Practice and Procedure in the Superior Courts. Hardback: £91.54. ISBN 1-85475-263-4. Butterworths Law (Ireland).

O'Leary, Siofra–Employment Law in the European Court of Justice. Hardback: £30.00. ISBN 1-84113-233-0. Hart Publishing.

Oakley, A.J.–Megarry's Manual of the Law of Real Property. 8th Ed. Paperback: £27.95. ISBN 0-421-71790-4. Sweet & Maxwell.

Ogle, Robbin S.; Jacobs, Susan–Self-defense and Battered Women Who Kill. Hardback: £53.95. ISBN 0-275-96711-5. M.E. Sharpe.

Ogloff, James R.P.–Taking Psychology and Law Into the Twenty-first Century. Perspectives in Law & Psychology. Hardback: £55.00. ISBN 0-306-46760-7. Kluwer Academic / Plenum Publishers.

Oldham, Mika–Blackstone's Statutes on Family Law. 11th Ed. Blackstone's Statutes Series. Paperback: £14.99. ISBN 0-19-925541-5. Oxford University Press.

Omar, Paul J.–Procedures to Enforce Foreign Judgments. Association of European Lawyers. Hardback: £40.00. ISBN 0-7546-2010-7. Dartmouth.

Orange Tax Handbook 2002-03. Paperback: £51.95. ISBN 0-406-95034-2. Butterworths Tolley.

Orentlicher, David–Matters of Life and Death. Hardback: £29.95. ISBN 0-691-08946-9. Paperback: £13.95. ISBN 0-691-08947-7. Princeton University Press.

Ormerod, David; Rodgers, Jon; Gunn, Michael–Criminal Litigation and Sentencing. Paperback: £27.95. ISBN 1-85941-335-8. Cavendish Publishing Ltd.

Osborne–Civil Litigation 2002/2003. Legal Practice Course Guides. Paperback: £22.99. ISBN 0-19-925511-3. Oxford University Press.

Osin, Paul–Point of Law: PACE Explained. The Point of Law. Paperback: £25.00. ISBN 0-11-702836-3. The Stationery Office Books.

Ovey, Clare; White, Robin, C.A.–Jacobs and White, The European Convention on Human Rights-Third Edition by Clare Ovey and Robin White. (Revised Ed.). Paperback: £25.99. ISBN 0-19-876580-0. Oxford University Press.

Owen, Nicholas–Human Rights, Human Wrongs. Oxford Amnesty Lectures. Paperback: £9.99. ISBN 0-19-280219-4. Oxford Paperbacks.

Padfield, Nicky–Butterworths Core Text: Criminal Law. 3rd Ed. Butterworths Core Text Series. Paperback: £12.95. ISBN 0-406-94999-9. Butterworths Law.

Padfield, Nicola; Biggs, Stuart; Farrell, Simon–Padfield, Biggs and Farrell: the Proceeds of Crime Act 2002. Butterworths New Law Guides. Paperback: £35.00. ISBN 0-406-95653-7. Butterworths Law.

Paget's Law of Banking 12th Ed. Hardback: £325.00. ISBN 0-406-91343-9. Butterworths Law.

Painter, Richard; Holmes, Anne–Cases and Materials: Employment Law. Paperback: £28.99. ISBN 0-19-925481-8. Oxford University Press.

Palfreyman, David; Warner, David—Higher Education Law. 2nd Ed. Hardback: £49.50. ISBN 0-85308-730-X. Jordans.

Pallis, Athanasios A.—Common EU Maritime Transport Policy: Policy Europeanisation in the 1990s. Transport and Mobility. Hardback: £45.00. ISBN 0-7546-1913-3. Ashgate Publishing Limited.

Palmer, Martin; Dewhurst, John—UK International Holding Companies. Hardback: £100.00. ISBN 0-85308-792-X. Jordans.

Palmer, Robert C.—Selling the Church. Studies in Legal History. Hardback: £42.95. ISBN 0-8078-2743-6. The University of North Carolina Press.

Park, Patricia D.—Energy Law and the Environment. Hardback: £75.00. ISBN 0-415-27188-6. Paperback: £29.99. ISBN 0-415-27189-4. Taylor & Francis.

Parker, Nigel—Music Business. Paperback: £52.00. ISBN 1-902558-42-1. Palladian Law Publishing Ltd.

Parpworth, Neil—Butterworths Core Text: Constitutional and Administrative Law. Butterworths Core Text Series. Paperback: £12.95. ISBN 0-406-95001-6. Butterworths Law.

Parrington, Sheila—Whillans Tax Tables 2001-02. Paperback: £13.95. ISBN 0-406-94457-1. Butterworths Tolley.

Parrington, Sheila; Antczak, Gina—Whillan's Tax Tables 2002-03. Paperback: £15.95. ISBN 0-406-95028-8. Butterworths Tolley.

Parrington, Sheila; Antczak, Gina—Whillans's Tax Tables 2002-03. 63rd Ed. Paperback: £15.95. ISBN 0-406-95027-X. Butterworths Tolley.

Parry, Chris; McNeil, Iain—Corporate Banking Law and Practice. Paperback: £19.95. ISBN 0-85297-672-0. Paperback: £19.95. ISBN 0-85297-672-0. Financial World Publishing.

Parry, Chris; McNeil, Iain—Corporate Lending and Securities. Paperback: £19.95. ISBN 0-85297-673-9. Paperback: £19.95. ISBN 0-85297-673-9. Financial World Publishing.

Parry, Rebecca—Transaction Avoidance in Insolvencies. Hardback: £125.00. ISBN 0-19-829890-0. Oxford University Press.

Party Wall Legislation and Procedure. Paperback: £23.00. ISBN 1-84219-073-3. RICS Books.

Pawlowski, Mark; Brown, James—Undue Influence and the Family Home. Hardback: £65.00. ISBN 1-85941-720-5. Cavendish Publishing Ltd.

Payne, Jennifer—Takeovers in English and German Law. Hardback: £45.00. ISBN 1-84113-340-X. Hart Publishing.

Peach, Lucinda—Legislating Morality. Hardback: £32.50. ISBN 0-19-514371-X. Oxford University Press Inc, USA.

Pearce, Robert A.; Stevens, John—Pearce and Stevens: Trusts and Equitable Obligations. 3rd Ed. Hardback: £26.95. ISBN 0-406-94683-3. Butterworths Law.

Pegg, Samantha—Good Web Guide to Legal Advice Online. Paperback: £9.99. ISBN 1-903282-41-1. Paperback: £9.99. ISBN 1-903282-41-1. The Good Web Guide.

Peglow, Michael—Law of Financial Futures. Hardback: £95.00. ISBN 0-19-826075-X. Oxford University Press.

Penn, Christopher N.—Noise Control. Paperback: £34.95. ISBN 0-7219-0832-2. Shaw & Sons.

Penn, Graham A.—Banking Supervision. Reissued 2nd Ed. Hardback: £130.00. ISBN 0-406-05212-3. Butterworths Law.

Perry, James and Hill, Jeremy—Financial Services and Markets Act-A Practical Legal Guide. Hardback: £70.00. ISBN 0-421-67990-5. Sweet & Maxwell.

Perry, Michael J.—We the People: The Fourteenth Amendment and the Supreme Court. Paperback: £15.99. ISBN 0-19-515125-9. Oxford University Press Inc, USA.

Personalised Client Publications-tax Facts Cards. Printed stationery. ISBN 0-7545-1649-0. Butterworths Law.

Pertegas Sender, Marta–Cross-border Enforcement of Patent Rights. Oxford Private International Law Series. Hardback: £85.00. ISBN 0-19-924969-5. Oxford University Press.

Petersen, Shannon C.–Acting for Endangered Species-The Statutory Ark. Hardback: £25.50. ISBN 0-7006-1172-X. University Press of Kansas.

Philips Fred–Commonwealth Caribbean Constitutional Law. Paperback: £49.50. ISBN 1-85941-691-8. Cavendish Publishing Ltd.

Phillips, Alfred–Lawyer's Language-The Distinctiveness of Legal Language. Hardback: £50.00. ISBN 0-7007-1688-2. RoutledgeCurzon.

Phillips, Jeremy–European Trade Mark Reports: 2001. Hardback: £470.00. ISBN 0-421-77100-3. Sweet & Maxwell.

Phillips, Jeremy–Phillips: Licensing Law Guide. 3rd Ed. Paperback: £45.00. ISBN 0-406-95226-4. Butterworths Law.

Pianca, Andrew; Dawes, Greyham–Charity Accounts-A Practical Guide to the Charities SORP. 2nd Ed. Paperback: £50.00. ISBN 0-85308-737-7. Jordans.

Pitt, M and Bowman, E–Valuation: Law and Practice. Greens Law Basics. Paperback: £25.00. ISBN 0-414-01298-4. W.Green & Son.

Plant, Charles Smith; Rose, William; Sime, Stuart; French, Derek–Blackstone's Civil Practice 2002. Hardback: £145.00. ISBN 0-19-925677-2. Oxford University Press.

Platts-Mills, John–Muck, Silk and Socialism. Hardback: £28.00. ISBN 0-9539949-0-2. Paper Publishing, London.

Pleming, Nigel; Stern, Kristina; Richards, Jenni; Foster, Alison; Grey, Eleanor; Morris, Fenella–Public Law and Health Care. Hardback: £30.00. ISBN 1-84113-155-5. Hart Publishing.

Plowden, Philip; Kerrigan, Kevin–Advocacy and the Human Rights Act. Paperback: £40.00. ISBN 1-85941-690-X. Cavendish Publishing Ltd.

Plunkett, Christopher; Ecob, Jo–APIL Guide to Evidence. Paperback: £35.00. ISBN 0-85308-756-3. Jordans.

Pointing, John; Malcolm, Rosalind–Statutory Nuisance: Law and Practice. Hardback: £45.00. ISBN 0-19-924246-1. Oxford University Press.

Poos, Lawrence R.–Lower Ecclesiastical Jurisdiction in Late-medieval England-The Courts of the Dean and Chapter of Lincoln, 1336-1349, and the Deanery of Wisbech, 1458-1484. Records of Social and Economic History, 32. Hardback: £50.00. ISBN 0-19-726245-7. Oxford University Press.

Porter, Tony–Technology, Governance and Political Conflict in International Industries. Routledge Advances in International Political Economy. Hardback: £50.00. ISBN 0-415-27009-X. Routledge, an imprint of Taylor & Francis Books Ltd.

Poskanzer, Steven G.–Higher Education Law. Hardback: £30.00. ISBN 0-8018-6748-7. Paperback: £13.50. ISBN 0-8018-6749-5. The Johns Hopkins University Press.

Posner, Eric A.–Law and Social Norms. Paperback: £12.95. ISBN 0-674-00814-6. Harvard University Press.

Posner, Martin–Effective Credit Control and Debt Recovery Handbook. Paperback: £65.00. ISBN 0-7545-1737-3. Tolley Publishing.

Posner, Richard A.; Parisi, Francesco–Economic Foundations of Private Law. An Elgar Critical Writings Reader. Paperback: £35.00. ISBN 1-84376-071-1. Edward Elgar.

Posner, Richard–Problematics of Moral and Legal Theory. Paperback: £13.95. ISBN 0-674-00799-9. Harvard University Press.

Post, Robert; Appiah, Anthony; Butler, Judith; et al–Prejudicial Appearances-The Logic of American Antidiscrimination Law. Hardback: £41.95. ISBN 0-8223-2702-3. Duke University Press.

Postema, Gerald J.–Philosophy and the Law of Torts. Cambridge Studies in Philosophy and Law. Hardback: £40.00. ISBN 0-521-62282-4. Cambridge University Press.

Postgraduate Guide: Business, Economics and Law: Vol 1. 2003. Paperback: £6.50. ISBN 1-86017-955-X. Hobsons plc.

Potok, Richard–Cross Border Collateral: Legal Risk and the Conflict of Laws. Hardback: £135.00. ISBN 0-406-92941-6. Butterworths Law.

Pound, R.W.–History of Stikeman Elliott. Hardback: £37.90. ISBN 0-7735-2411-8. McGill-Queen's University Press.

Powell, John; Stewart, Roger; Jackson, The Honourable Mr Justice–Jackson and Powell on Professional Negligence. 5th Ed. Common Law Library. Hardback: £225.00. ISBN 0-421-82600-2. Sweet & Maxwell.

Powers, Stephen P.; Rothman, Stanley–The Least Dangerous Branch? Hardback: £58.50. ISBN 0-275-97536-3. Praeger Publishers.

Pre-contract Practice and Contract Administration for the Building Team. Paperback: £19.99. ISBN 0-632-05485-9. Paperback: £19.99. ISBN 0-632-05485-9. Blackwell Science (UK).

Priban, Jiri–Dissidents of Law-On the 1989 Revolutions, Legitimations, Fictions of Legality and Contemporary Version of the Social Contract. Law, Justice and Power. Paperback: £50.00. ISBN 0-7546-2284-3. Dartmouth.

Price, John–Tolley's Taxation 2001: VAT. Spiral/comb bound: £35.00. ISBN 0-7545-1294-0. Tolley Publishing.

Proceedings of the 43rd Colloquium on the Law of Outer Space. AIAA Conference Proceedings. Hardback: £67.50. ISBN 1-56347-488-3. AIAA American Institute of Aeronautics and Astronautics.

Proctor, Giles; Miles, Lilian–Corporate Governance. Paperback: £48.40. ISBN 1-85941-651-9. Cavendish Publishing Ltd.

Property Disputes in Practice. 5th Ed. Paperback: £22.95. ISBN 1-84174-318-6. Blackstone Press.

Provost, Rene–International Human Rights and Humanitarian Law. Cambridge Studies in International and Comparative Law. Hardback: £55.00. ISBN 0-521-80697-6. Cambridge University Press.

Pugh-Smith, John; Sinclair, Graham; Upton, William–Neighbours and the Law. 3rd Ed. Hardback: £55.00. ISBN 0-421-69320-7. Sweet & Maxwell.

Puttick, Keith–Child Support Law-Parents, the CSA and the Courts. Paperback/Internet resource: £24.00. ISBN 1-85811-293-1. EMIS Professional Publishing.

Puttick, Keith–Welfare Benefits: 2000-2001. Welfare Benefits. Paperback: £14.99. EMIS Professional Publishing.

Quantum: Supplement 4. Paperback: £34.00. ISBN 0-406-94693-0. Butterworths Law.

Quarrell, John; Beaumont, Sue–Tolleys Pension Scheme Investment: a Practical Guide to the Law. Hardback: £55.00. ISBN 0-7545-1268-1. Tolley Publishing.

Quinn, Gerard; Flynn, Leo–EU Charter on Fundamental Rights. Paperback: £15.00. ISBN 0-19-924667-X. Oxford University Press.

Racheter, Donald P.; Wagner, Richard E.–Politics, Taxation, and the Rule of Law. Hardback: £78.00. ISBN 1-4020-7154-X. Kluwer Academic Publishers.

Raic, David–Statehood and the Law of Self-determination. Developments in International Law, 43. Hardback: £79.00. ISBN 90-411-1890-X. Kluwer Law International.

Rajak, Harry; Davis, Richard–Insolvency-a Business by Business Guide. Paperback: £70.00. ISBN 0-406-02231-3. Butterworths Law.

Ramage, Roderick W.–Kelly's Draftsman. Hardback: CD-ROM: £194.02. ISBN 0-406-94834-8. Butterworths Law.

Ramage, Roderick W.–Underhill and Hayton: Law Relating to Trustees. Hardback: CD-ROM: £295.00. ISBN 0-406-93884-9. Butterworths Law.

Ramsey, Lynn; Macaulay, Mark–Construction and Procurement Law. Greens Practice Library. Paperback: £85.00. ISBN 0-414-01348-4. W. Green & Son.

Randall, Helen–Local Government Contracts and Procurement. Hardback: £115.00. ISBN 0-406-94897-6. Hardback: £115.00. ISBN 0-406-94897-6. Butterworths Law.

Randolph, Fergus; Davey, Jonathan–Guide to Commercial Agents' Regulations. Paperback: £40.00. ISBN 1-84113-156-3. Paperback: £40.00. ISBN 1-84113-156-3. Hart Publishing.

Ravitch–Employment Discrimination Law. Hardback: £32.99. ISBN 0-13-974866-0. US Imports & PHIPEs.

Ray, Ralph; Hitchmough, Andrew; Wilson, Elizabeth–Ray's Practical Inheritance Tax Planning. 6th Ed. Paperback: £69.95. ISBN 0-406-94284-6. Butterworths Tolley.

Ray, Ralph–Wills and Post-death Tax Planning. 3rd Ed. Paperback: £38.00. ISBN 1-858-11286-9. EMIS Professional Publishing.

Rayney, Peter; Cave, Rebecca–Tolley's Tax Planning for Family and Owner-managed Companies. 5th Ed. Paperback: £54.95. ISBN 0-7545-1215-0. Tolley Publishing.

Rayney, Peter–Tolley's Tax Planning for Family and Owner-managed Companies. Paperback: £59.95. ISBN 0-7545-1683-0. Tolley Publishing.

Raynor, Peter; Vanstone, Maurice–Understanding Community Penalties. Crime and Justice. Hardback: £50.00. ISBN 0-335-20626-3. Paperback: £16.99. ISBN 0-335-20625-5. Open University Press.

Reay, Rosamund–Evidence. 1999-2000 Suggested Solutions. Paperback: £6.95. ISBN 1-85836-444-2. Old Bailey Press.

Reay, Rosamund–Evidence. Revision Workbook. Paperback: £9.95. ISBN 1-85836-463-9. Old Bailey Press.

Reeb, Matthieu–Digest of CAS Awards II, 1998-2000. Digest of CAS Awards Series, 2. Hardback: £82.00. ISBN 90-411-1730-X. Kluwer Law International.

Reed, Chris–Reed: Internet Law: Text and Materials. 2nd Ed. Butterworths Law in Context. Paperback: £26.95. ISBN 0-406-95391-0. Butterworths Law.

Reed, Penelope–Trust and Estates Handbook. Paperback: £49.95. ISBN 0-7545-1946-5. Butterworths Law.

Rees, Edward; Hall, Andrew–Blackstone's Guide to the Proceeds of Crime Act 2002. Paperback: £30.00. ISBN 0-19-925454-0. Oxford University Press Inc, USA.

Reeve, Rosalind–CITES and Compliance. Hardback: £50.00. ISBN 1-85383-875-6. Paperback: £19.95. ISBN 1-85383-880-2. Earthscan.

Rehman, Javaid–International Human Rights Law. Paperback: £27.99. ISBN 0-582-43773-3. Longman.

Reid, Brian C.; Jones, Jessica–European Patent Office Reports 2001. Hardback: £460.00. ISBN 0-421-75480-X. Sweet & Maxwell.

Reid, Colin T.–Nature Conservation Law. 2nd Ed. Paperback: £39.00. ISBN 0-414-01355-7. W. Green & Son.

Reid, Kenneth G.C.; Gretton, George L.–Conveyancing 2001. Paperback: £22.00. ISBN 0-406-95703-7. Butterworths Law (Scotland).

Reid, Kenneth–Execution of Deeds. Greens Practice Library. Hardback. ISBN 0-414-01138-4. W. Green & Son.

Rennie, Michele T.; et al–Computer and Telecommunications Law Review 2002. Hardback. ISBN 0-421-83300-9. Sweet & Maxwell.

Rescher, Nicholas–Fairness: Theory and Practice of Distributive Justice. Hardback: £29.50. ISBN 0-7658-0110-8. Transaction Publishers.

Reynolds, Kirk; Clark, Wayne–Renewal of Business Tenancies. 2nd Ed. Hardback: £175.00. ISBN 0-421-74030-2. Sweet & Maxwell.

Richardson, James; Thomas, David–Archbold: Criminal Pleading, Evidence and Practice 2003: CD and Print Pack. Paperback: CD-ROM: £320.00. ISBN 0-421-79080-6. Sweet & Maxwell.

Richardson, James; Thomas, David–Archbold: Criminal Pleading, Evidence and Practice 2003: Print Bundle. Looseleaf/ring bound: £250.00. ISBN 0-421-79090-3. Sweet & Maxwell.

Riches, J.; Dancaster, C.–Construction Adjudication. 2nd Ed. Book (details unknown): £88.00. ISBN 1-84311-000-8. LLP Professional Publishing.

Riddall, John G.–Riddall: Law of Trusts. Paperback: £23.95. ISBN 0-406-94286-2. Butterworths Law.

Rider, Barry; Alexander, Kern; Linklater, Lisa–Rider, Alexander and Linklater: Market Abuse and Insider Dealing. Butterworth's Compliance Series. Paperback: £45.00. ISBN 0-406-93249-2. Butterworths Law.

Ridgway, Philip–Principles of Revenue Law. 2nd Ed. Principles of Law. Paperback: £27.95. ISBN 1-85941-385-4. Cavendish Publishing Ltd.

Ridout, P.–Care Standards. Paperback: £45.00. ISBN 0-85308-823-3. Jordans.

Riesenfeld, Stefan A.; Pakter, Walter J.–Casebook on Comparative Law. Hardback: £68.99. ISBN 1-57105-220-8. Transnational Publishers, Inc.

Roberts, J. Timmons–Chronicles from the Environmental Justice Frontline. Hardback: £40.00. ISBN 0-521-66062-9. Paperback: £14.95. ISBN 0-521-66900-6. Cambridge University Press.

Robertson, Geoffrey; Nicol, Andrew–Media Law. 4th Ed. Paperback (C format): £30.00. ISBN 0-14-024769-6. Penguin Books.

Robertson, Geoffrey–Crimes Against Humanity-The Struggle for Global Justice (New Ed.). Paperback (B format): £10.99. ISBN 0-14-101014-2. Penguin Books.

Robinson, Alan–Tolley's Social Security and Family Benefit Law: a Practical Guide. Paperback: £39.95. ISBN 0-7545-1895-7. Tolley Publishing.

Robinson, Duncan; Butterfield, Roger; Chambers, David–Entertainments Licensing Law and Practice. 2nd Ed. Paperback: £9.95. ISBN 1-85836-436-1. Old Bailey Press.

Robison, Wade L.–Legal Essays of Michael Bayles. Law and Philosophy Library. Hardback: £60.00. ISBN 90-411-1835-7. Kluwer Law International.

Rodway, Susan; Levene, Simon–Clinical Litigation-Managing Medical Disputes. Hardback: £65.00. ISBN 1-902558-48-0. Palladian Law Publishing Ltd.

Roesch, Ronald; Corrado, Raymond; Dempster, Rebecca–Psychology in the Courts: International Advances in Knowledge. Hardback: £38.00. ISBN 90-5823-123-2. Harwood Academic (Medical, Reference and Social Sciences).

Rogers, Christopher P.–Rodgers: Housing Law, Residential Security and Enfranchisement. Paperback: £60.00. ISBN 0-406-91103-7. Butterworths Law.

Rogers, James Steven–Early History of the Law of Bills and Notes. Cambridge Studies in English Legal History. Paperback: £18.95. ISBN 0-521-52204-8. Cambridge University Press.

Rogers, W.V.H.–Winfield and Jolowicz on Tort. 16th Ed. Paperback: £30.00. ISBN 0-421-76850-9. Sweet & Maxwell.

Rohatgi, Roy–Basic International Taxation. Hardback: £138.60. ISBN 90-411-9852-0. Kluwer Law International.

Rollins, Joe–Ironic Jurisprudence. Hardback: £22.99. ISBN 0-312-24006-6. Palgrave Macmillan.

Rose, Francis–Blackstone's Statutes on Contract, Tort and Restitution. 13th Ed. Blackstone's Statutes Series. Paperback: £12.99. ISBN 0-19-925543-1. Oxford University Press.

Rose, Francis–Kennedy and Rose on Law of Salvage. British Shipping Laws. Hardback: £215.00. ISBN 0-421-60230-9. Sweet & Maxwell.

Rose, Francis–Statutes on Commercial and Consumer Law. 11th Ed. Blackstone's Statutes Series. Paperback: £16.99. ISBN 0-19-925544-X. Oxford University Press.

Rose, William–Pleading Without Tears-A Guide to Legal Drafting Under the Civil Procedure Rules. 6th Ed. Paperback: £19.95. ISBN 0-19-925438-9. Oxford University Press.

Rosenheim, Margaret K.; Zimring, Franklin E.; Tanenhaus, David S.; Dohrn, Bernardine–Century of Juvenile Justice. Hardback: £26.50. ISBN 0-226-72783-1. University of Chicago Press.

Rosenthal, Dennis–Rosenthal: A Guide to Consumer Credit Law and Practice. Reissued 2nd Ed. Paperback: £50.00. ISBN 0-406-90321-2. Butterworths Law.

Ross, Kenneth–Contaminated Land for Conveyancers. Paperback: £38.00. ISBN 0-414-01289-5. W.Green & Son.

Rotherham, Craig–Proprietary Remedies in Context. Hardback: £35.00. ISBN 1-84113-165-2. Hart Publishing.

Rovati, Veena Kanda–Succession. Revision Workbook. Paperback: £9.95. ISBN 1-85836-469-8. Old Bailey Press.

Rowan-Robinson, Jeremy–Planning Law and Procedure. Scottish Universities Law Institute. Hardback: £165.00. ISBN 0-414-01430-8. W.Green & Son.

Rowland, Mark; White, Robin–Social Security Legislation: Administration, Adjudication and the European Dimension, Vol 3. Paperback: £63.00. ISBN 0-421-79140-3. Sweet & Maxwell.

Rowley, Graham; Stevenson, Janet; Greene, Brendan; Blakemore, Timothy–Law for Legal Executives: Part One Year Two. 6th Ed. Paperback: £21.99. ISBN 0-19-925527-X. Oxford University Press.

Ruff, Anne–Nutcases-contract Law. Nutcases. Paperback: £5.95. ISBN 0-421-76750-2. Sweet & Maxwell.

Ruff, Anne–Ruff: Education Law-text, Cases and Materials. Paperback: £26.95. ISBN 0-406-92407-4. Butterworths Law.

Ruiter, Dick W.P.–Legal Institutions. Law and Philosophy Library, 55. Hardback: £56.00. ISBN 1-4020-0186-X. Kluwer Academic Publishers.

Rush, Jonathan–Understand and Negotiate Contracts. Paperback: £9.99. ISBN 1-85703-798-7. HowTo Books.

Russomanno, Joseph–Speaking Our Minds-Conversations with the People Behind Landmark First Amendment Cases. Hardback: £51.50. ISBN 0-8058-3767-1. Paperback: £25.50. ISBN 0-8058-3768-X. Lawrence Erlbaum Associates, Inc.

Rutherford, Andrew–Growing out of Crime. 2nd Ed. Paperback: £17.50. ISBN 1-872870-49-X. Waterside Press.

Sabalot, Deborah A.–Butterworths Financial Services Law Handbook. 4th Ed. Paperback: £85.00. ISBN 0-406-93140-2. Butterworths Law.

Sabalot, Deborah–Guide to the Financial Services and Markets Act 2000. Paperback: £35.00. ISBN 0-406-93141-0. Butterworths Law.

Sacker, Tony–Practical Partnership Agreements. 2nd Ed. Hardback: CD-ROM: £60.00. ISBN 0-85308-640-0. Jordans.

Sadat, Leila–International Criminal Court and the Transformation of International Law-Justice for the New Millenium. International and Comparative Law. Hardback: £100.99. ISBN 1-57105-133-3. Transnational Publishers, Inc.

Sage, Gill–TUPE-A Practical Guide. Paperback: £34.95. ISBN 1-85328-815-2. Law Society Publications.

Saintier, Severine–Commercial Agency Law-A Comparative Analysis. Hardback: £55.00. ISBN 0-7546-2191-X. Dartmouth.

Sale of Goods and Consumer Credit in Practice. 5th Ed. Paperback: £22.95. ISBN 1-84174-316-X. Blackstone Press.

Salter, David; Snape, John–Easson: Cases and Materials on Revenue Law. Paperback: £40.00. ISBN 1-85941-726-4. Cavendish Publishing Ltd.

Salter, David–Humphreys' Family Proceedings. Practitioner Series. Hardback: £85.00. ISBN 0-421-74820-6. Sweet & Maxwell.

Salter, David–Pensions and Insurance on Family Breakdown. 3rd Ed. Hardback: Floppy disk: £45.00. ISBN 0-85308-698-2. Family Law.

Sampson, Fraser–Blackstone's Police Manual: Crime 2003. Blackstone's Police Manuals. Paperback: £10.99. ISBN 0-19-925489-3. Blackstone Press.

Sampson, Fraser–Blackstone's Police Manual: General Police Duties 2003- (Human Rights Ed). Blackstone's Police Manual. Paperback: £10.99. ISBN 0-19-925491-5. Blackstone Press.

Sampson, Fraser–Preparing for Police Duty. Paperback: £8.99. ISBN 0-19-925556-3. Oxford University Press.

Sanders, Catherine–Declarations of Trust. 2nd Ed. Paperback: £49.00. ISBN 0-7520-0605-3. Sweet & Maxwell.

Santos, Boaventura De Sousa–Toward a New Common Sense. 2nd Ed. Paperback: £34.95. ISBN 0-406-94997-2. Butterworths Law.

Sara, Colin–Boundaries and Easements. 3rd Ed. Hardback: £155.00. ISBN 0-421-75840-6. Sweet & Maxwell.

Sarat, A.; Ewick, P.–Studies in Law, Politics and Society: Vol 26. Studies in Law, Politics and Society, Vol 26. Hardback. ISBN 0-7623-0894-X. JAI Press.

Saunders, Glyn; Antczak, Gina–Tolley's Corporation Tax 2002-03: Main Annual. Paperback: £59.95. ISBN 0-7545-1711-X. Tolley Publishing.

Saunders, Glyn; Smailes, David; Antczak, Gina–Tolley's Income Tax 2002-03: Main Annual. Paperback: £59.95. ISBN 0-7545-1710-1. Tolley Publishing.

Saunders, Glyn; Smailes, David; Walton, Kevin–Tolley's Capital Gains Tax Workbook 2001-02. Paperback: £24.95. ISBN 0-7545-1285-1. Tolley Publishing.

Saunders, Glyn; Smailes, David; Walton, Kevin–Tolley's Income Tax Workbook 2001-02. Paperback: £24.95. ISBN 0-7545-1286-X. Tolley Publishing.

Saunders, Glyn–Tolley's Taxation in the Republic of Ireland 2002. Paperback: £59.95. ISBN 0-7545-1672-5. Tolley Publishing.

Savage, David–Construction Law Yearbook 2000/2001. Paperback: £45.00. ISBN 0-7545-1545-1. Tolley Publishing.

Scamell, E.H.–Butterworths Property Law Handbook. 5th Ed. Paperback: £49.00. ISBN 0-406-94327-3. Butterworths Law.

Schabas, William A.–Abolition of the Death Penalty in International Law. Hardback: £80.00. ISBN 0-521-81491-X. Paperback: £29.95. ISBN 0-521-89344-5. Cambridge University Press.

Scheiber, Harry N.–State and Freedom of Contract. The Making of Modern Freedom. Paperback: £17.95. ISBN 0-8047-4191-3. Stanford University Press.

Schmalleger–Criminal Law Today. 2nd Ed. Paperback: £12.99. ISBN 0-13-093681-2. Prentice Hall.

Schmitz, Andrew; Furtan, Hartley; Baylis, Katherine–Agricultural Policy, Agribusiness, and Rent-seeking Behaviour. Hardback: £60.00. ISBN 0-8020-4846-3. University of Toronto Press Inc.

Schneider, Elizabeth M.–Battered Women and Feminist Lawmaking. Paperback: £12.95. ISBN 0-300-09411-6. Yale University Press.

Schofield, Gareth; Middleton, Jonathan; Bethel, Fiona; Stone, Nick; Salter, David; Bull, Alison; Way, Philip–Debt and Insolvency on Family Breakdown. Paperback: £45.00. ISBN 0-85308-645-1. Family Law.

Schuit, Steven R.–Corporate Law and Practice of the Netherlands. Allen & Overy Legal Practice, 12. Paperback: £35.50. ISBN 90-411-1906-X. Kluwer Law International.

Schulze, Reiner–Casebook on European Consumer Law. Paperback: £25.00. ISBN 1-84113-227-6. Hart Publishing.

Schwarz, Jonathan–Law of UK Tax Treaties. Hardback: £120.00. ISBN 0-421-72490-0. Sweet & Maxwell.

Scott, I.R.–Civil Justice Quarterly: 2001. Hardback: £160.00. ISBN 0-421-75650-0. Sweet & Maxwell.

Scott, M.–Conveyancing Factfinder. Paperback: £11.95. ISBN 0-85308-797-0. Paperback: £11.95. ISBN 0-85308-797-0. Jordans.

Scottish Landlord & Tenant Fact Book. Looseleaf/ring bound. ISBN 0-414-01380-8. W.Green & Son.

Scottish Law Directory: the White Book 2002. 111th Ed. Hardback: £36.00. ISBN 0-406-94888-7. Butterworths Law (Scotland).

Sealy, Len; Milman, David—Annotated Guide to the Insolvency Legislation. Company Law Books. Paperback: £70.00. ISBN 0-421-82790-4. Sweet & Maxwell.

Sedgewick, Peter; Jones, Christopher—The Future of Criminal Justice. Paperback: £16.99. ISBN 0-281-05483-5. SPCK (Society for Promoting Christian Knowledge).

Self, Roger—Tolley's Pension Fund Trustee Handbook. 7th Ed. Paperback: £29.95. ISBN 0-7545-1648-2. Tolley Publishing.

Sellman, Pamela; Evans, Judith—Law of International Trade. Old Bailey Press Leading Cases. Paperback: £11.95. ISBN 1-85836-364-0. Old Bailey Press.

Sellman, Pamela—Law of International Trade. Revision Workbook. Paperback: £9.95. ISBN 1-85836-465-5. Old Bailey Press.

Selwyn, Norman—Selwyn's Law of Employment. Paperback: £24.95. ISBN 0-406-94996-4. Butterworths Law.

Seneviratne, Mary—Seneviratne: Ombudsmen: Public Services and Administrative Justice. Butterworths Law in Context Series. Paperback: £23.95. ISBN 0-406-94676-0. Butterworths Law.

Seward, Karen; Baldwinson, Lucy; Carr, Jonathan; et al—Maternity and Parental Rights: a Practical Guide to Parental, Maternity and Dependant Care Leave. Paperback: £49.95. ISBN 0-7545-1427-7. Butterworths Law.

Sex and Race Discrimination. Legal Essentials. Paperback: £33.99. ISBN 0-85292-964-1. Chartered Institute of Personnel and Development (CIPD).

Shannon, Geoffrey—Health and Safety Law. Paperback: £57.00. ISBN 1-85800-277-X. Round Hall Ltd.

Sheikh, Saleem—Employment Law and Practice. Paperback: £14.95. ISBN 1-874241-79-1. Cavendish Publishing Ltd.

Sheldon, David—Evidence: Cases and Materials. 2nd Ed. Paperback: £41.50. ISBN 0-414-01387-5. W.Green & Son.

Shepherd, Chris—Company Law. 150 Leading Cases. Paperback: £11.95. ISBN 1-85836-447-7. Old Bailey Press.

Sheriff Court Rules 2002. A Parliament House Book. Paperback: £28.00. ISBN 0-414-01495-2. W.Green & Son.

Sherrin, C.H.; Barlow, R.F.D.; Wallington, R.A.; Meadway, Susannah L.; Waterworth, Michael—Williams on Wills. 8th Ed. Hardback: £295.00. ISBN 0-406-93391-X. Butterworths Law.

Sherwin, Richard K.—When Law Goes Pop. Paperback: £12.00. ISBN 0-226-75292-5. University of Chicago Press.

Shilling—Essentials of Trademarks and Unfair Competition. Paperback: £22.50. ISBN 0-471-20941-4. John Wiley & Sons Inc.

Shiva, Vandana—Protect or Plunder?-Understanding Intellectual Property Rights. Global Issues Series. Hardback: £32.95. ISBN 1-84277-108-6. Paperback: £9.99. ISBN 1-84277-109-4. Zed Books.

Short, Martin—Secrets of the Jury Room. Paperback. ISBN 0-00-638776-4. HarperCollins.

Shrubsall, Vivien—Transfer of Undertakings. Hardback: £60.00. ISBN 1-902558-20-0. Palladian Law Publishing Ltd.

Shute, Stephen; Simester, Andrew—Criminal Law Theory-Doctrines of the General Part. Oxford Monographs on Criminal Law and Justice. Hardback: £45.00. ISBN 0-19-924349-2. Oxford University Press.

Shuy, Roger—Linguistic Battles in Trademark Disputes. Hardback: £42.50. ISBN 0-333-99758-1. Palgrave Macmillan.

Shytov, Alexander Nikolaevich—Conscience and Love in Making Judicial Decisions. Law and Philosophy Library, 54. Hardback: £56.00. ISBN 1-4020-0168-1. Kluwer Academic Publishers.

Siedel, George J.–Using the Law for Competitive Advantage. University of Michigan Business School Management Series. Hardback: £18.95. ISBN 0-7879-5623-6. Jossey Bass Wiley.

Sime, Stuart–Bar Manual: Civil Litigation 2002/2003. Blackstone Bar Manual. Paperback: £21.99. ISBN 0-19-925498-2. Oxford University Press.

Sime, Stuart–Practical Approach to Civil Procedure. 5th Ed. Paperback: £26.00. ISBN 0-19-925351-X. Oxford University Press Inc, USA.

Sime, Stuart–Practical Approach to Civil Procedure. A Practical Approach. Paperback: £28.95. ISBN 0-19-925437-0. Oxford University Press.

Simensky, Melvin; Bryer, Lanning; Wilkof, Neil–Intellectual Property in the Global Marketplace: 2001 Cumulative Supplement. 2nd Ed. Wiley Intellectual Property Series. Paperback: £44.50. ISBN 0-471-39031-3. John Wiley and Sons.

Simma, Bruno–Charter of the United Nations: a Commentary. Hardback: £250.00. ISBN 0-19-925377-3. Oxford University Press.

Simon, David R.–Elite Deviance. 7th Ed. Paperback: £26.99. ISBN 0-205-32176-3. Allyn & Bacon.

Simons, Alan; Harmer, Caroline–Practical Guide to the Small Claims Court. Paperback: £22.95. ISBN 0-754-51760-8. Butterworths Law.

Simpson, Gerry–Nature of International Law. The Library of Essays in International Law. Hardback: £120.00. ISBN 0-7546-2065-4. Dartmouth.

Simpson, John; Rover, Jan-Hendrik; Fairgrieve, Duncan–Comparative Law of Security and the EBRD Model. Hardback: £75.00. ISBN 0-19-826013-X. Oxford University Press.

Sinclair, John H.–Sinclair: Handbook of Conveyancing Practice in Scotland. 4th Ed. Paperback: £42.00. ISBN 0-406-95705-3. Butterworths Law (Scotland).

Sinclair, William–Drafting. Hardback: £19.95. ISBN 0-414-01284-4. W.Green & Son.

Singer, Mr Justice; Parker, Judith, Wildblood, Stephen; Eaton, Deborah: Cobb, Stephen Amos, Tim; Anderson, Nicholas Cusworth, David Davidson, Deborah Dinan-Hayward, Michael Horowitz, Charles Hyde, Daniel Leafe, Marcus Scot–Essential Family Practice 2002: Text and CD Set. Looseleaf/ring bound: CD-ROM: £142.00. ISBN 0-406-95692-8. Butterworths Law.

Singer, Mr Justice; Parker, Judith–Essential Family Practice 2002. Hardback: £98.00. ISBN 0-406-95689-8. Butterworths Law.

Singleton, Susan; Lawson, Richard–Tolley's Sale & Purchase Agreements. Paperback: CD-ROM: £59.95. ISBN 0-7545-1948-1. Tolley Publishing.

Singleton, Susan–ECommerce: a Practical Guide to the Law. Hardback: £45.00. ISBN 0-566-08276-4. Gower Publishing Limited.

Singleton, Susan–Tolley's Data Protection Handbook. Paperback: £49.95. ISBN 0-7545-1242-8. Tolley Publishing.

Slovenko, Ralph–Law in Psychiatry. Hardback. ISBN 0-415-93364-1. Brunner-Routledge.

Slovenko, Ralph–Psychiatry in Law / Law in Psychiatry. 2 Volume Set. Hardback: £99.95. ISBN 0-415-93365-X. Brunner-Routledge.

Smailes, David K.; Walton, Kevin–Tolley's Capital Gains Tax Workbook 2001-02. Paperback: £24.95. ISBN 0-7545-1284-3. Tolley Publishing.

Smailes, David; Walton, Kevin–Tolley's Tax Losses. Paperback: £59.95. ISBN 0-7545-1745-4. Tolley Publishing.

Smale, David A.–Davies' Law of Burial, Cremation and Exhumation. Paperback: £39.95. ISBN 0-7219-0065-8. Shaw & Sons.

SME Handbook. Paperback: £45.00. ISBN 0-7545-1275-4. Tolley Publishing.

Smith, A.T.H.–Learning the Law. 12th Ed. Paperback: £9.95. ISBN 0-421-74420-0. Sweet & Maxwell.

Smith, Gordon V; Parr, Russell L.–Valuation of Intellectual Property and Intangible Assets: 2002: Cumulative Supplement. 3rd Ed. Intellectual Property. Paperback: £48.50. ISBN 0-471-41943-5. John Wiley & Sons Inc.

Smith, Graham J.H.–Internet Law and Regulation. 3rd Ed. Hardback: £145.00. ISBN 0-421-70590-6. Sweet & Maxwell.

Smith, J.C.–Law of Contract. 4th Ed. Fundamental Principles of Law. Paperback: £15.95. ISBN 0-421-78170-X. Sweet & Maxwell.

Smith, P.F.–Evans and Smith: the Law of Landlord and Tenant. 6th Ed. Paperback: £23.95. ISBN 0-406-94679-5. Butterworths Law.

Smith, Rodger; Newton Clive R.–Jackson's Matrimonial Finance and Taxation. 7th Ed. Paperback: £139.00. ISBN 0-406-94149-1. Butterworths Law.

Smith, Rosemary S.–Bar Manual: Conference Skills 2002/2003. Blackstone Bar Manual. Paperback: £21.99. ISBN 0-19-925500-8. Oxford University Press.

Smith, Simon–Image, Persona and the Law. Special Reports. Hardback: £150.00. ISBN 0-421-74800-1. Sweet & Maxwell.

Smith, Stephen A.–Introduction to Contract Theory. Clarendon Law Series. Paperback: £13.99. ISBN 0-19-876561-4. Oxford University Press.

Snell, Jukka–Goods and Services in EC Law-A Study of the Relationship Between the Freedoms. Hardback: £65.00. ISBN 0-19-925009-X. Oxford University Press.

Snyder, Francis–Regional and Global Regulation of International Trade. Hardback: £35.00. ISBN 1-84113-218-7. Hart Publishing.

Soares, Patrick–VAT Planning for Property Transactions. 8th Ed. Hardback: £120.00. ISBN 0-421-77460-6. Sweet & Maxwell.

Social Housing Law-A Practical Guide. Hardback: £65.00. ISBN 0-406-90314-X. Butterworths Law.

Solicitors' Professional Handbook 2002. A Parliament House Book. Paperback: £24.00. ISBN 0-414-01499-5. W.Green & Son.

Somerville, Ian; Lewis, Susan–VAT for Retailers and E-tailers. Paperback: £49.95. ISBN 0-7545-0991-5. Butterworths Law.

Somerville, Margaret–Death Talk-The Case Against Euthanasia and Physician Assisted Suicide. Hardback: £57.00. ISBN 0-7735-2201-8. Paperback: £18.90. ISBN 0-7735-2245-X. McGill-Queen's University Press.

Somsen, Han–Yearbook of European Environmental Law. Hardback: £100.00. ISBN 0-19-924778-1. Oxford University Press Inc, USA.

Sosa, Ernest–Philosophical Issues: Vol 11. Philosophy of Law and Social Philosophy. Philosophical Issues, 11, 2002. Paperback: £19.99. ISBN 0-631-23029-7. Blackwell Publishers.

Southern, David–Taxation of Corporate Debt and Financial Instruments. Paperback: £65.95. ISBN 0-7545-1219-3. Tolley Publishing.

Spence, Michael–European National Patent Reports 2001. Hardback: £325.00. ISBN 0-421-75680-2. Sweet & Maxwell.

Stainforth, Paul; Seymour, Mavis; Murgatroyd, Bob; Walton, Kevin–Enterprise Investment Schemes, Venture Capital Scheme and the Corporate Venturing Scheme. Paperback: £65.00. ISBN 0-7545-1459-5. Tolley Publishing.

Stauder, Dieter–Singer and Stauder: the European Patent Convention: Vol 1. Substantive Patent Law. Hardback: £120.00. ISBN 0-421-83150-2. Sweet & Maxwell.

Stebbings, Chantal–Private Trustee in Victorian England. Cambridge Studies in English Legal History. Hardback: £45.00. ISBN 0-521-78185-X. Cambridge University Press.

Stefan, Susan, JD–Hollow Promises-Employment Discrimination Against People with Mental Disabilities. Eating Disorders. Hardback: £41.95. ISBN 1-55798-792-0. American Psychological Association.

Steiner, Eva–French Legal Method. Paperback: £24.99. ISBN 1-84174-185-X. Oxford University Press.

Stephens–Criminal Justice. 2nd Ed. Paperback: £19.99. ISBN 0-205-32153-4. Allyn & Bacon.

Stetson, Dorothy McBride–Abortion Politics, Women's Movements, and the Democratic State-A Comparative Study of State Feminism. Gender and Politics. Hardback: £45.00. ISBN 0-19-924265-8. Oxford University Press.

Stevens, Robert–English Judges-Their Role in the Changing Constitution. Hardback: £22.50. ISBN 1-84113-226-8. Hart Publishing.

Stevens, Robert–Restitution in Private International Law. Oxford Monographs in Private International Law. Hardback: £65.00. ISBN 0-19-829843-9. Oxford University Press.

Steverson, Janet W.–Children and the Law: 3 Volume Set. Controversies in Constitutional Law. Hardback: £240.00. ISBN 0-415-93803-1. Routledge, Inc.

Steverson, Janet W.–Children and the Law: Child Versus State: Vol 3. Hardback: £90.00. ISBN 0-415-93806-6. Routledge, Inc.

Steverson, Janet W.–Children and the Law: Parent, State and Child-parenting of Children: Vol 1. Hardback: £90.00. ISBN 0-415-93804-X. Routledge, Inc.

Steverson, Janet W.–Children and the Law: Parent, State and Child-the Schooling of Children: Vol 2. Hardback: £90.00. ISBN 0-415-93805-8. Routledge, Inc.

Stewart, Andrew F.–Cautionary Obligations. Greens Practice Library. Hardback: £80.00. ISBN 0-414-01311-5. W. Green & Son.

Stokes, Simon; Lyons, Tarlo–Stokes: Digital Copyright-law and Practice. Paperback: £69.00. ISBN 0-406-94702-3. Butterworths Law.

Stone, Richard–Modern Law of Contract. 5th Ed. Paperback: £20.95. ISBN 1-85941-667-5. Cavendish Publishing Ltd.

Stone, Richard–Textbook on Civil Liberties and Human Rights. Textbook. Paperback: £22.99. ISBN 0-19-925514-8. Oxford University Press.

Storey, Nicholas; Bloom, Margaret–Health Service-law and Practice. Looseleaf/ring bound: £140.00. ISBN 0-406-94024-X. Butterworths Law.

Strasser, Mark–On Same-sex Marriages, Civil Unions, and the Rule of Law. Issues on Sexual Diversity and the Law. Hardback: £37.95. ISBN 0-275-97761-7. Praeger Publishers.

Strawson, John–Law After Ground Zero-1st Ed. Glasshouse Series. Paperback: £19.95. ISBN 1-904385-02-8. The Glasshouse Press.

Styles, Scott–Butterworths Glossary of Scottish and European Legal Terms. Paperback: £20.00. ISBN 0-406-94947-6. Butterworths Law (Scotland).

Sullivan, Amanda–International Employee Payroll. Paperback: £74.95. ISBN 0-7545-1416-1. Tolley Publishing.

Sunnucks, James H.G.–Williams, Mortimer & Sunnucks-executors, Administrators and Probate: 1st Supplement to the 18th Edition. Property and Conveyancing Library. Paperback: £40.00. ISBN 0-421-77000-7. Sweet & Maxwell.

Supperstone, Michael; Knapman, Lynn–Administrative Court Practice: Judicial Review. Hardback: £65.00. ISBN 0-406-94353-2. Butterworths Law.

Supperstone, Michael; Pitt-Payne, Timothy–Guide to the Freedom of Information Act 2000. Paperback: £35.00. ISBN 0-406-93145-3. Butterworths Law.

Suzuki, Kenji–Competition Law Reform in Britain and Japan-Comparative Analysis of Policy Network. European Institute of Japanese Studies East Asian Economics and Business, 3. Hardback: £55.00. ISBN 0-415-25587-2. Routledge, an imprint of Taylor & Francis Books Ltd.

Sweet, Robert–Commercial Leases: Tenants' Amendments. 4th Ed. Paperback: £65.00. ISBN 0-421-77210-7. Sweet & Maxwell.

Sydenham, Angela; Monnington, Bruce–Essential Law for Landowners and Farmers. 4th Ed. Paperback: £32.50. ISBN 0-632-05796-3. Blackwell Science (UK).

Sykes, John; Scarisbrick, John–Valuation of Intellectual Property Assets. Hardback: £95.00. ISBN 1-858-11281-8. Hardback: £95.00. ISBN 1-858-11281-8. EMIS Professional Publishing.

Sylvan, Donald A.; Keren, Michael–Dilemmas of International Intervention-Sovereignty Versus Responsibility. Paperback: £17.50. ISBN 0-7146-8194-6. Paperback: £17.50. ISBN 0-7146-8194-6. Frank Cass Publishers.

Symes, Mark; Jorro, Peter–Symes & Jorro: the Law Relating to Asylum in the UK. Paperback: £65.00. ISBN 0-406-98378-X. Butterworths Law.

Sze Ping-fat–Carrier's Liability Under the Hague, Hague-Visby and Hamburg Rules. Hardback: £60.00. ISBN 90-411-1676-1. Kluwer Law International.

Taggart, Michael–Abuse of Property Rights and Industrialisation. Oxford Studies in Modern Legal History. Hardback: £45.00. ISBN 0-19-925687-X. Oxford University Press.

Tate, C. Neal–Comparative Judicial Systems. Hardback: £117.00. ISBN 1-56802-684-6. CQ Press.

Tax Annuals Set 2001-02. Paperback: £180.00. ISBN 0-406-94116-5. Butterworths Tolley.

Tax Annuals Set 2002-03. Paperback: £199.00. ISBN 0-406-95046-6. Butterworths Tolley.

Taylor, Jonathan; Lewis, Adam–Taylor and Lewis: Sport: Law and Practice. Hardback: £120.00. ISBN 0-406-94592-6. Hardback: £120.00. ISBN 0-406-94592-6. Butterworths Law.

Taylor, Margot–Bar Manual: Negotiation 2002/2003. Blackstone Bar Manual. Paperback: £21.99. ISBN 0-19-925503-2. Oxford University Press.

Taylor, Rodney–Tolley's Double Taxation Relief. 4th Ed. Paperback: £85.00. ISBN 0-7545-0261-9. Tolley Publishing.

Teece, David J.–Managing Intellectual Capital-Organizational, Strategic, and Policy Dimensions (Reissue). Clarendon Lectures in Management Studies. Paperback: £14.99. ISBN 0-19-829542-1. Oxford University Press.

Teitel, Ruti G.–Transitional Justice. Paperback: £15.99. ISBN 0-19-515126-7. Oxford University Press Inc, USA.

Terrell, Martin–Practitioner's Guide to the Court of Protection. Paperback: £45.00. ISBN 0-7545-1623-7. Tolley Publishing.

Tettenborn, Andrew; Jackson, Justice; Asif, Jalil; Plunkett, Christopher; Goodman, Andrew–Professional Negligence and Liability Reports 2001. Hardback: £195.00. ISBN 0-421-82750-5. Sweet & Maxwell.

The Green Book-form of Contract, Reimbursable Contracts. Paperback: £45.00. ISBN 0-85295-444-1. Institution of Chemical Engineers.

The Lawyer's Remembrancer 2003. Paperback: £36.00. ISBN 0-406-95927-7. Butterworths Law.

The Tolley Editorial Team–Tolley's Tax Computations 2001-02. Paperback: £59.95. ISBN 0-7545-1206-1. Tolley Publishing.

Thomas, David–Sentencing Referencer: 2002. Paperback: £20.00. ISBN 0-421-78610-8. Sweet & Maxwell.

Thomas, D. Rhidian–Modern Law of Marine Insurance: Vol 2. Hardback: £140.00. ISBN 1-84311-120-9. LLP Professional Publishing.

Thomas, Meryl–Statutes on Property Law. Blackstone's Statutes Series. Paperback: £12.99. ISBN 0-19-925546-6. Oxford University Press.

Thompson, P.K.; Mambro, Louise di–Civil Court Practice 2002. Hardback: £260.00. ISBN 0-406-95222-1. Butterworths Law.

Thomson, Joseph M.–Family Law in Scotland. Paperback: £39.00. ISBN 0-406-95567-0. Butterworths Law.

Thornberry, Patrick–Cultural Rights of Indigenous People. Melland Schill Studies in International Law. Hardback: £80.00. ISBN 0-7190-3793-X. Paperback: £29.95. ISBN 0-7190-3794-8. Manchester University Press.

Thorne, Clive; Hull, John–Guide to Intellectual Property in the Financial Services Market. Hardback: £100.00. ISBN 0-406-93143-7. Butterworths Law.

Thorne, James; Prentice, Dan–Butterworths Company Law Guide. 4th Ed. Paperback: £70.00. ISBN 0-406-93758-3. Butterworths Law.

Thurston, John–Practitioner's Guide to Executorship and Administration. Paperback: £42.00. ISBN 0-7545-1697-0. Tolley Publishing.

Thurston, John–Practitioner's Guide to Inheritance Claims. Paperback: £37.00. ISBN 0-7545-1247-9. Tolley Publishing.

Tian, Kelly; Keep, Bill–Customer Fraud and Business Responses-Let the Marketer Beware. Hardback: £53.95. ISBN 1-56720-387-6. Quorum Books.

Tiernan, Ralph–Nutshells-tort. 6th Ed. Nutshells. Paperback: £5.95. ISBN 0-421-76530-5. Sweet & Maxwell.

Tillman, Robert–Global Pirates-Fraud in the Offshore Insurance Industry. Hardback: £39.95. ISBN 1-55553-506-2. Paperback: £16.95. ISBN 1-55553-505-4. Northeastern University Press.

Tingley, K.R.–Tolley's Roll-over, Hold-over and Retirement Reliefs. 11th Ed. Paperback: £68.95. ISBN 0-7545-1202-9. Tolley Publishing.

Tingley, K.R.–Tolley's Roll-over, Hold Over and Retirement Reliefs. Paperback: £69.95. ISBN 0-7545-1676-8. Tolley Publishing.

Todd, Paul–Cases and Materials on International Trade Law. Paperback: £40.00. ISBN 0-421-82710-6. Sweet & Maxwell.

Tolley's Capital Gains Tax 2001-02. Tolley's Tax Annuals. Paperback: £54.95. ISBN 0-7545-1390-4. Tolley Publishing.

Tolley's Charities Administration Handbook. Paperback: £46.95. ISBN 0-7545-1192-8. Tolley Publishing.

Tolley's Dictionary of Tax and Accountancy. Paperback: £14.95. ISBN 0-7545-1009-4. Tolley Publishing.

Tolley's Directors' Handbook: 1999-2000. Paperback: £59.95. ISBN 0-7545-0239-2. Tolley Publishing.

Tolley's Employment Cases. Paperback: £59.95. ISBN 0-7545-1761-6. Tolley Publishing.

Tolley's Employment Handbook 2001-02: Plus Supplement. 15th Ed. Paperback: £65.00. ISBN 0-7545-1266-5. Tolley Publishing.

Tolley's Guide to Managing Employee Health 2002. Paperback: £50.00. ISBN 0-7545-1249-5. Tolley Publishing.

Tolley's Inheritance Tax 2001-02. Tolley's Tax Annuals. Paperback: £53.95. ISBN 0-7545-1188-X. Tolley Publishing.

Tolley's Insurance Handbook. 3rd Ed. Paperback: £49.95. ISBN 0-7545-1258-4. Tolley Publishing.

Tolley's International Handbook of Corporate and Personal Taxes. 6th Ed. Paperback: £79.95. ISBN 0-406-94627-2. Butterworths Tolley.

Tolley's International Tax Planning. 5th Ed. Paperback: £195.00. ISBN 0-7545-1510-9. Tolley Publishing.

Tolley's Leasing in the UK 2001. Paperback: £59.95. ISBN 0-7545-1198-7. Tolley Publishing.

Tolley's National Insurance Contributions: 2001-02. Tolley's Tax Annuals. Paperback: CD-ROM: £69.95. ISBN 0-7545-1187-1. Tolley Publishing.

Tolley's Payroll Management Handbook 2002. Paperback: £58.95. ISBN 0-7545-1261-4. Tolley Publishing.

Tolley's Pensions Law Handbook. 4th Ed. Paperback: £49.95. ISBN 0-7545-1257-6. Tolley Publishing.

Tolley's Professional Partnership Handbook. 4th Ed. Paperback: £59.95. ISBN 0-7545-1200-2. Tolley Publishing.

Tolley's Stakeholder Pensions. Paperback: £45.00. ISBN 0-7545-1618-0. Paperback: £45.00. ISBN 0-7545-1618-0. Tolley Publishing.

Tolley's Tax Essentials: Family Taxation 2001. Tolley's Tax Essentials. Spiral/comb bound: £35.00. ISBN 0-7545-1297-5. Tolley Publishing.

Tolley's Tax Investigations. Paperback: £56.95. ISBN 0-7545-1212-6. Tolley Publishing.

Tolley's Tax Planning 2001-02. Paperback: £139.00. ISBN 0-7545-1214-2. Tolley Publishing.

Tolley's Tax Planning 2002-03. Paperback: £145.00. ISBN 0-7545-1732-2. Tolley Publishing.

Tolley's Taxation in the Channel Islands and the Isle of Man 2001-02. Paperback: £55.00. ISBN 0-7545-1281-9. Tolley Publishing.

Tolley's Taxation of Lloyd's Underwriters. Hardback: £89.95. ISBN 0-7545-1678-4. Tolley Publishing.

Tomkins, Nigel; Edwards, Claire–CFAs and Risk Assessment in Practice. Hardback: £75.00. ISBN 0-421-78620-5. Sweet & Maxwell.

Tonge, Kate; Hirst, Lyn–Housing and Housing Benefit Law: a Practical Guide. Paperback: £35.00. ISBN 0-7545-1405-6. Butterworths Law.

Tonge, Kate–Social Security and State Benefits: a Practical Guide. 2nd Ed. Paperback: £40.00. ISBN 0-7545-1657-1. Tolley Publishing.

Tonge, Kate–Tolley's Practical Guide to State Benefits and Personal Injury Awards. Paperback: £45.00. ISBN 0-7545-1625-3. Tolley Publishing.

Tonry, Michael–Crime and Justice: 29. Hardback: £38.00. ISBN 0-226-80861-0. Newberry Library.

Tookey, Michael–Revenue Law: Textbook. 3rd Ed. Old Bailey Press Textbooks. Paperback: £14.95. ISBN 1-85836-417-5. Old Bailey Press.

Tort Law. 3rd Ed. LawCards Series. Paperback: £6.00. ISBN 1-85941-718-3. Cavendish Publishing Ltd.

Towse, Ruth; Holzhauer, Rudi–Economics of Intellectual Property. The International Library of Critical Writings in Economics (ILCWE), 145. Hardback: £530.00. ISBN 1-84064-351-X. Edward Elgar.

Towse, Ruth–Copyright in the Cultural Industries. Hardback: £59.95. ISBN 1-84064-661-6. Edward Elgar.

Treitel, Guenter–Some Landmarks of Twentieth Century Contract Law. Clarendon Law Lectures. Hardback: £25.00. ISBN 0-19-925575-X. Oxford University Press.

Tremml, B.; Buecker, B.–Key Aspects of German Business Law-A Practical Manual. 2nd Ed. Hardback: £42.00. ISBN 3-540-43411-9. Springer-Verlag Berlin and Heidelberg GmbH & Co. KG.

Tristram and Cootes: Probate Practice. Hardback: £285.00. ISBN 0-406-94720-1. Butterworths Law.

Tritton, Guy–Intellectual Property in Europe. 2nd Ed. Hardback: £145.00. ISBN 0-421-64150-9. Hardback: £170.00. ISBN 0-421-64150-9. Sweet & Maxwell.

Trouwborst, Arie–Evolution and Status of the Precautionary Principle in International Law. International Environmental Law and Policy, 62. Hardback: £70.00. ISBN 90-411-1785-7. Kluwer Law International.

Trusts Law. 3rd Ed. LawCards Series. Paperback: £6.00. ISBN 1-85941-710-8. Cavendish Publishing Ltd.

Tugendhat, Michael; Christie, Iain–Law of Privacy and the Media. Hardback: £145.00. ISBN 0-19-925430-3. Oxford University Press.

Tunkel, Daniel; Auger, David–Butterworths Compliance Series: Managed Funds. Butterworths Compliance Series. Paperback: £45.00. ISBN 0-406-93749-4. Butterworths Law.

Tuori, Kaarlo–Critical Legal Positivism. Applied Legal Philosophy. Hardback: £60.00. ISBN 0-7546-2272-X. Dartmouth.

Tur, Richard–Different Concept of Law. Paperback: £22.00. ISBN 1-85941-641-1. Cavendish Publishing Ltd.

Turczynowicz, Antoni; O'Reilly, Toby; Sherratt, Antonia–VAT in Central and Eastern Europe. Paperback: £49.95. ISBN 0-7545-0838-2. Tolley Publishing.

Turlington, Shannon–Cyberscams. Behind the Headlines. Paperback: £3.50. ISBN 1-902932-10-2. South Street Press.

Turner, Chris–Key Facts: Employment. Key Facts for Law. Paperback: £4.99. ISBN 0-340-84583-X. Hodder & Stoughton Educational.

Turner, Jonathan D.C.; Whaite, Robin; Toutoungi, Adrian–EU Rules on the Exploitation of Intellectual Property. Hardback: £85.00. ISBN 0-406-90026-4. Butterworths Law.

Turner; Goldrein–Ship Sale and Purchase. 4th Ed. Hardback: £170.00. ISBN 1-84311-145-4. LLP Professional Publishing.

Turpin, Colin–Turpin: British Government and the Constitution. 5th Ed. Law in Context. Paperback: £25.95. ISBN 0-406-94671-X. Butterworths Law.

Twining, William L.–Great Juristic Bazaar-Juristic Texts and Lawyers' Stories. Collected Essays in Law. Hardback: £60.00. ISBN 0-7546-2211-8. Dartmouth.

Twining, William; Hampsher-Monk, Iain–Evidence and Inference in History and Law-Interdisciplinary Dialogues. Hardback: £75.50. ISBN 0-8101-1893-9. Paperback: £24.95. ISBN 0-8101-1756-8. Northwestern University Press.

Uglow, Stephen; Cheney, Deborah; Dickson, Lisa–Criminal Justice. Paperback: £24.95. ISBN 0-421-73840-5. Sweet & Maxwell.

Underwood, Kerry–No Win, No Fee, No Worries! (New Ed.). Paperback: £38.00. ISBN 1-858-11216-8. EMIS Professional Publishing.

Upex, Robert–Law of Termination of Employment. 6th Ed. Hardback: CD-ROM: £80.00. ISBN 0-85308-731-8. Jordans.

Urbina, Sebastian–Legal Method and the Rule of Law. Law and Philosophy Library, 59. Hardback: £56.00. ISBN 90-411-1870-5. Kluwer Law International.

Ure, Alex; Firth, John; Templeton, Andrew; Sleziak, Douglas–Taxation of Retirement Benefits: 1999. Paperback: £85.00. ISBN 0-7545-0134-5. Tolley Publishing.

Usher, John A.–EC Agricultural Law. 2nd Ed. Oxford European Community Law Library. Hardback: £60.00. ISBN 0-19-826882-3. Oxford University Press.

Valdes, Francisco; Culp, Jerome McCristal; Harris, Angela P.–Crossroads, Directions, and a New Critical Race Theory. Hardback: £66.95. ISBN 1-56639-929-7. Paperback: £24.95. ISBN 1-56639-930-0. Temple University Press.

Van Caenegem, R.C.–Unity and Diversity: European Law in the Past and the Future. Paperback: £14.95. ISBN 0-521-80938-X. Paperback: £14.95. ISBN 0-521-00648-1. Cambridge University Press.

Van der Mei, A. Pieter–Free Movement of Persons Within the European Community. Hardback: £45.00. ISBN 1-84113-288-8. Hart Publishing.

Van Houtte, Hans–Law of International Trade. 2nd Ed. Hardback: £140.00. ISBN 0-421-76480-5. Sweet & Maxwell. Paperback: £40.00. ISBN 0-421-76490-2. Sweet & Maxwell International Student Editions.

van Pelt, Robert–Case for Auschwitz-Evidence from the Irving Trial. Hardback: £34.50. ISBN 0-253-34016-0. Indiana University Press.

Veale Wasbrough; J Bradford–Property Development and Investment. Paperback: £95.00. ISBN 0-406-94517-9. Butterworths Law.

Verheij, B.; Lodder, A.R.; Loui, R.P.; Muntjewerff, A.–Legal Knowledge and Information Systems. Frontiers in Artificial Intelligence and Applications, Vol 70. Hardback: £48.00. ISBN 1-58603-201-1. IOS Press.

Vickers, Lucy–Freedom of Speech and Employment. Oxford Monographs on Labour Law. Hardback: £45.00. ISBN 0-19-826830-0. Oxford University Press.

Viscusi, W. Kip–Regulation Through Litigation. Hardback: £41.00. ISBN 0-8157-0610-3. Paperback: £18.50. ISBN 0-8157-0609-X. The Brookings Institution.

Vitoria, Mary—Fleet Street Reports-cases on Intellectual Property Law: 2001. Hardback: £550.00. ISBN 0-421-77080-5. Sweet & Maxwell.

Voller, Mike—Tolley's Taxation of Lloyds Underwriters. 10th Ed. Hardback: £89.95. ISBN 0-7545-1282-7. Tolley Publishing.

Waite, John-Paul; Isted, Barry; Traylen, Claire—Tolley's Employment Tribunals Handbook: Successful Strategies for Managing Disputes. Paperback: £49.95. ISBN 0-7545-1488-9. Tolley Publishing.

Walgrave, Lode—Restorative Justice and the Law. Hardback: £45.00. ISBN 1-903240-97-2. Paperback: £25.00. ISBN 1-903240-96-4. Willan Publishing.

Walker, Andrew—Administration of Estates. Paperback: £30.00. ISBN 0-85297-604-6. Financial World Publishing.

Walker, Andrew—Conveyancing Lso Leading Cases. Old Bailey Press Leading Cases. Paperback: £11.95. ISBN 1-85836-421-3. Old Bailey Press.

Walker, George Alexander—International Banking Regulation. International Banking, Finance and Economic Law, 19. Hardback: £123.00. ISBN 90-411-9794-X. Kluwer Law International.

Wall, Wilson—Genetics and DNA Technology: Legal Aspects. Paperback: £49.50. ISBN 1-85941-682-9. Cavendish Publishing Ltd.

Wallace, Rebecca M.M.—International Law. Paperback: £22.95. ISBN 0-421-76880-0. Sweet & Maxwell.

Wallington, Peter; Lee, Robert G.—Statutes on Public Law and Human Rights. Blackstone's Statutes Series. Paperback: £13.99. ISBN 0-19-925535-0. Oxford University Press.

Wallington, Peter—Butterworths Employment Law Handbook. 10th Ed. Paperback: £49.00. ISBN 0-406-94878-X. Butterworths Law.

Wallis, Peter; McCormac, Kevin; Niekirk, Paul—Wilkinson's Road Traffic Offences: 1st Supplement to the 20th Edition. Paperback: £40.00. ISBN 0-421-78210-2. Sweet & Maxwell.

Wallis, Peter; McCormac, Kevin; Niekirk, Paul—Road Traffic Offences: 2nd Supplement to the 20th Edition. Paperback: £57.00. ISBN 0-421-79720-7. Sweet & Maxwell.

Walton, Christopher; Cooper, Roger; Wood, Simon E.; Percy, R.A.—Charlesworth & Percy on Negligence: 1st Supplement to the 10th Edition. The Common Law Library, No.6. Paperback: £35.00. ISBN 0-421-79400-3. Sweet & Maxwell.

Walton, Douglas N.—Legal Argumentation and Evidence. Hardback: £51.95. ISBN 0-271-02177-2. Penn State University Press.

Walton, Kevin; Smailes, David—Tolley's Capital Allowances 2001-02. Paperback: £54.95. ISBN 0-7545-1193-6. Tolley Publishing.

Walzer, Lee—Gay Rights on Trial. Hardback: £29.95. ISBN 1-57607-254-1. ABC CLIO (Reference Books).

Ward, John—Judge Irish Income Tax 2002. Butterworth's Irish Tax Library. Paperback: £79.33. ISBN 1-85475-648-6. Butterworths Law (Ireland).

Wareham, Robert; Dolton, Alan—Tolley's Value Added Tax 2002. 2nd Ed. Paperback: £69.00. ISBN 0-7545-1706-3. Tolley Publishing.

Wareham, Robert; Smailes, David; Antczak, Gina—Tolley's Tax Data 2002-03 (six-monthly) Budget/Finance Act Editions-Budget 2002 Ed. Spiral/comb bound: £29.95. ISBN 0-7545-1699-7. Tolley Publishing.

Wareham, Robert—Tolley's Company Law Handbook 2002-2003. 9th Ed. Paperback: £55.00. ISBN 0-7545-1490-0. Tolley Publishing.

Wareham, Robert—Tolley's VAT Planning 2001-02. Paperback: £74.95. ISBN 0-7545-1291-6. Tolley Publishing.

Wareham, Robert—Tolley's VAT Planning 2002-03. Paperback: £84.95. ISBN 0-7545-1689-X. Tolley Publishing.

Warnock-Smith, S.; Legge, Henry; Tidmarsh Christopher—Practitioner's Guide to Variations of Trusts. Paperback: £48.00. ISBN 0-7545-1244-4. Tolley Publishing.

Wasbrough, Veale–Property Development. Paperback: £95.00. ISBN 0-406-94517-9. Butterworths Law.

Watkins, Michael; Gordon, Winston–Sentence of the Court. Revised 3rd Ed. Paperback: £17.00. ISBN 1-904380-01-8. Waterside Press.

Watson, Brian–Litigation Liabilities. Hardback: £105.00. ISBN 1-902558-52-9. Palladian Law Publishing Ltd.

Webb, Julian–LPC Lawyer Skills 2002/2003. 9th Ed. Blackstone Bar Manual. Paperback: £22.99. ISBN 0-19-925509-1. Oxford University Press.

Webber, Gary; Dovar, Daniel–Residential Possession Proceedings. 6th Ed. Practitioner Series. Paperback: £85.00. ISBN 0-421-76410-4. Sweet & Maxwell.

Weiler, Paul–Leveling the Playing Field. Paperback: £12.50. ISBN 0-674-00687-9. Harvard University Press.

Weinrib, Ernest Joseph–Tort Law. International Library of Essays in Law and Legal Theory (second Series). Hardback: £100.00. ISBN 0-7546-2142-1. Hardback: £110.00. ISBN 0-7546-2142-1. Dartmouth.

Weisgard, Geoffrey M.–Company Voluntary Arrangements. Hardback: £60.00. ISBN 0-85308-733-4. Hardback: £60.00. ISBN 0-85308-733-4. Jordans.

Weitekamp, Elmar; Kerner, Hans-Jurgen–Restorative Justice in Context. Hardback: £45.00. ISBN 1-903240-73-5. Willan Publishing.

Welch, Jeanie M.–Tokyo Trial. Hardback: £62.95. ISBN 0-313-31598-1. Greenwood Press.

Welch, Michael–Detained. Hardback: £49.95. ISBN 1-56639-977-7. Paperback: £15.95. ISBN 1-56639-978-5. Temple University Press.

Welham, Michael–Corporate Killing: the New Law. Paperback: £50.00. ISBN 0-7545-1066-2. Tolley Publishing.

Wellens, Karel–Remedies Against International Organisations. Cambridge Studies in International and Comparative Law, 21. Hardback: £45.00. ISBN 0-521-81249-6. Cambridge University Press.

Whalan, Mark–Limitation in Personal Injury Actions. Paperback: £42.00. ISBN 1-85811-273-7. EMIS Professional Publishing.

Wheeler, John–English Legal System. Frameworks Series. Paperback: £21.99. ISBN 0-582-42405-4. Longman.

Wheeler, Sally–Corporations and the Third Way. Paperback: £20.00. ISBN 1-901362-63-9. Hart Publishing.

Whitbourn, Simon–Special Education Needs and Disability in Education-a Legal Guide. Hardback: £55.00. ISBN 0-406-94635-3. Butterworths Law.

White Book Service 2002: Network CD-ROM. CD-ROM: £250.00. ISBN 0-421-78500-4. Sweet & Maxwell.

White, G. Edward–Constitution and the New Deal. Paperback: £13.95. ISBN 0-674-00831-6. Harvard University Press.

White, Jeremy–Customs Duties Handbook 2002. Paperback: £99.00. ISBN 0-406-95114-4. ButterworthsTolley.

White, Richard; Carr, A.P.; Lowe, Nigel–White, Carr and Lowe: Children Act in Practice. Paperback: £30.00. ISBN 0-406-94003-7. Butterworths Law.

White, Richard; Lowe, Nigel–Adoption and Children Act 2002. Butterworths New Law Guides. Paperback: £30.00. ISBN 0-406-95654-5. Paperback: £30.00. ISBN 0-406-95654-5. Butterworths Law.

White, Robin C.A.; Arnull, Anthony–European Law Review: 2001. Hardback: £370.00. ISBN 0-421-75720-5. Sweet & Maxwell.

Whitehouse, Chris; Hassall, Nicholas–Whitehouse and Hassall: Principles of Trust and Will Drafting. Paperback: £50.00. ISBN 0-406-91444-3. Butterworths Law.

Whitehouse, Chris; Watson, Loraine; Narain, Lakshmi; Lee, Natalie; Farley, Andrew–Whitehouse: Revenue Law-Principles and Practice. 20th Ed. Paperback: £55.00. ISBN 0-406-95026-1. ButterworthsTolley.

Whiteman, Peter; Gammie, Malcolm; Herbert, Mark–Whiteman on Capital Gains Tax: 12th Supplement to the 4th Edition. British Tax Library. Paperback: £95.00. ISBN 0-421-76780-4. Sweet & Maxwell.

Whiteman, Peter; Gammie, Malcolm; Herbert, Mark–Whiteman on Capital Gains Tax: 13th Supplement to the 4th Edition. British Tax Library. Paperback: £115.00. ISBN 0-421-79050-4. Sweet & Maxwell.

Whiteman, Peter; Goy, David; Sandison, Francis; Sherry, Michael–Whiteman on Income Tax: 12th Supplement to the 3rd Edition. British Tax Library. Paperback: £110.00. ISBN 0-421-76790-1. Sweet & Maxwell.

Wicken, William C.–Mi'kmaq Treaties on Trial-History, Land, and Donald Marshall Jr. Hardback: £35.00. ISBN 0-8020-0718-X. Paperback: £18.00. ISBN 0-8020-7665-3. University of Toronto Press Inc.

Wickham, Gary; Pavlich, George–Rethinking Law Society and Governance-Foucault's Bequest. Onati International Series in Law and Society. Hardback: £45.00. ISBN 1-84113-293-4. Paperback: £20.00. ISBN 1-84113-294-2. Hart Publishing.

Wikeley, N.J.–Wikely, Ogus & Barendt: the Law of Social Security. Paperback: £35.95. ISBN 0-406-98585-5. Butterworths Law.

Wilde, Mark–Civil Liability for Environmental Damage. Comparative Environmental Law & Policy Series, 4. Hardback: £70.00. ISBN 90-411-1891-8. Kluwer Law International.

Wilde, Peter; Butt, Paul–Which? Guide to Renting and Letting. Revised Ed. Which? Consumer Guides. Paperback (C format): £11.99. ISBN 0-85202-894-6. Which? Books.

Wilken, Sean–Law of Waiver, Variation and Estoppel. Hardback: £95.00. ISBN 0-19-925321-8. Oxford University Press.

Wilkinson, David–Environment and Law. Routledge Introductions to the Environment. Hardback: £55.00. ISBN 0-415-21567-6. Paperback: £17.99. ISBN 0-415-21568-4. Routledge, an imprint of Taylor & Francis Books Ltd.

Wilkinson, Jacqueline; Barber, Susan–Company Law. Revision Workbook. Paperback: £9.95. ISBN 1-85836-369-1. Old Bailey Press.

Williams, Lucy A.–Welfare Law. International Library of Essays in Law and Legal Theory (second Series). Hardback: £100.00. ISBN 0-7546-2096-4. Dartmouth.

Williams, Melanie–Empty Justice: One Hundred Years of Law, Literature and Philosophy. Feminist Perspectives. Paperback: £40.00. ISBN 1-85941-614-4. Cavendish Publishing Ltd.

Wilson, Caroline–Nutshells: Intellectual Property Law. Nutshells. Paperback: £5.95. ISBN 0-421-78000-2. Sweet & Maxwell.

Wilson, Martin–Tolley's Capital Allowances: Transactions and Planning 2001-0.2. 4th Ed. Paperback: £71.95. ISBN 0-7545-1194-4. Tolley Publishing.

Winston, Kenneth–Fuller's Principles of Social Order. Paperback: £25.00. ISBN 1-84113-234-9. Hart Publishing.

Winter, Steven L.–Clearing in the Forest-Law, Life, and Mind. Hardback: £24.00. ISBN 0-226-90221-8. University of Chicago Press.

Wintgens, Luc–Legisprudence. Hardback: £50.00. ISBN 1-84113-342-6. Hardback: £50.00. ISBN 1-84113-342-6. Hart Publishing.

Wittman, Donald–An Economic Analysis of the Law. Hardback: £60.00. ISBN 0-631-23157-9. Paperback: £21.99. ISBN 0-631-23158-7. Blackwell Publishers.

Wolfgarten, Alison–Bar Manual: Opinion Writing 2002/2003. Blackstone Bar Manual. Paperback: £21.99. ISBN 0-19-925504-0. Oxford University Press.

Wong, Glenn M.–Essentials of Sports Law. Hardback: £54.50. ISBN 0-275-97121-X. Praeger Publishers.

Wood, Penny; Wikeley, Nick; Paynter, Richard; Bonner, David–Social Security Legislation 2002: Income Support, Jobseeker's Allowance, Tax Credits and the Social Fund, Vol 2. Paperback: £64.00. ISBN 0-421-79130-6. Sweet & Maxwell.

Woolf, Lord–Zamir and Woolf: The Declaratory Judgement. 3rd Ed. Litigation Library. Hardback: £130.00. ISBN 0-421-71710-6. Sweet & Maxwell.

World Trade Organization–WTO Agreements on CD-ROM Issue 1-The Legal Texts (English, French and Spanish) and Schedules: Services (English Only). World Trade Organization Schedules. CD-ROM: £406.35. ISBN 0-521-79645-8. Cambridge University Press.

Yalof, David Alistair–Pursuit of Justices-Presidential Politics and the Selection of Supreme Court Nominees. Paperback: £11.50. ISBN 0-226-94546-4. University of Chicago Press.

Yearbook: 2000, Vol 4. Paperback: £50.00. ISBN 90-411-1762-8. Kluwer Law International.

Yellow Tax Handbook 2002-03. Paperback: £57.95. ISBN 0-406-95035-0. Butterworths Tolley.

Yokoi-Arai, Mamiko–Financial Stability Issues. International Banking, Finance and Economic Law, 24. Hardback: £94.00. ISBN 90-411-9878-4. Kluwer Law International.

Young, Kirsten A.–Law and Process of the U.N. Human Rights Committee. Proceedural Aspects of International Law Monograph Series, 26. Hardback: £100.99. ISBN 1-57105-063-9. Transnational Publishers, Inc.

Young, Simon–Limited Liability Partnerships Handbook. Paperback: £55.00. ISBN 0-7545-1181-2. Tolley Publishing.

Youngs, Raymond–Sourcebook on German Law. 2nd Ed. SOURCEBOOK SERIES. Paperback: £35.95. ISBN 1-85941-678-0. Cavendish Publishing Ltd.

Yudof, Mark G.; Kirp, David; Levin, Betsy–Educational Policy and the Law. 4th Ed. Hardback: £28.99. ISBN 0-534-57375-4. Wadsworth.

Zanettin, Bruno–Cooperation Between Antitrust Agencies At the International Level. Hardback: £50.00. ISBN 1-84113-351-5. Hart Publishing.

Zegveld, Liesbeth–Accountability of Armed Opposition Groups in International Law. Cambridge Studies in International and Comparative Law. Hardback: £45.00. ISBN 0-521-81130-9. Cambridge University Press.

Zerbe Jr, Richard O.–Economic Efficiency in Law and Economics. New Horizons in Law and Economics. Paperback: £25.00. ISBN 1-84064-611-X. Edward Elgar.

Zimmermann, Reinhard–Comparative Foundations of a European Law of Set-off and Prescription. Hardback: £37.50. ISBN 0-521-81461-8. Cambridge University Press.

Zindani, Jeffrey–Health and Safety Law: a Modern Guide. Paperback: £65.00. ISBN 1-85811-217-6. EMIS Professional Publishing.

INDEX 2002

abatement notices
noise
lack of sufficient judicial reasoning, 02/3321
nuisance from dogs
enforcement notice regarding unauthorised
change of use, 02/1524
abortion
certificates of opinion
form, 02/1605
Wales, 02/1606
abuse of process
claim for nervous shock, 02/280
contempt proceedings
trial on same facts
abuse of process, 02/842
delay
relevant considerations, 02/843
extradition
magistrates court
jurisdiction to determine lawfulness of
detention, 02/1593
injunction staying proceedings in Turkey, 02/640
legal proceedings
issues already subject of judgment of other
court, 02/282
negotiations between parties, 02/281
Part 20 claims amounting to attempt to relitigate,
02/281
relitigation of issues determined by Commission
failure to seek annulment of Commission
decisions, 02/279
access to justice
issuing of public safety certificate
disproportionate breach of ECHR, 02/4822NI
access to the countryside
local access forums
establishment, 02/3854
sites of special scientific interest
appeals
Wales, 02/1466
accommodation
homelessness
priority need, 02/2335
accountancy
accountants
negligent misrepresentation
economic loss not established, 02/3276
books, 02/1
accounts
directors remuneration
reports, 02/523
summary financial statements
directors remuneration, 02/524
acquisitions
imported goods, 02/4731

Acts of Adjournal
rules
adults with incapacity
applications and appeals, 02/5992S
extradition
forms of notice, 02/5482S
life imprisonment, 02/5484S
terrorist cash
High Court applications, 02/5512S
Acts of Sederunt
Court of Session
personal injuries
procedure, 02/5214S
rules
applications for power of arrest, 02/5215S
solicitors, shorthand writers and witnesses
fees, 02/5216S
Lands Valuation Appeal Court
judicial appointments, 02/5219S
sheriff courts
fees
sheriff officers, 02/5229S
rules
applications for detention of cash, 02/
5362S
power of arrest applications, 02/5361S
warrants for appeals, 02/5363S
small claims, 02/5231S
summary causes, 02/5232S, 5233S
fees, 02/5234S
summary proceedings
recovery of cash, 02/5501S
summary warrants, 02/5235S
adjudication
adjudicators
appointment of adjudicator from approved list,
02/653
awards
discretion to refuse enforcement, 02/655
enforcement of adjudicator's decision
error of law, 02/5397S
failure to inform parties of analytical method
adopted
requirement to observe rules of natural justice,
02/662
jurisdiction
consideration of more than one dispute in
single adjudication, 02/5398S
contract allowing for staged payments, 02/
658
contract concluded after provisions of
Housing Grants
validity of adjudicator's award, 02/656
errors of law
enforceability, 02/660
legal nature of adjudicator's decision, 02/661

agriculture -*cont.*
agricultural land -*cont.*
development -*cont.*
fairness of appeal, 02/3703
agricultural policy
agricultural support
Tir Mynydd Scheme, 02/71
direct support schemes
appeals, 02/72
subsidies
hill farming, 02/75
wine, 02/5252S
agricultural processing and marketing
grants, 02/4839NI
agricultural property
agricultural occupancies
forms, 02/3012
animal products
beef
premiums, 02/4841NI
bone in beef
despatch to domestic market, 02/2967, 5038NI, 5905S
diseases and disorders
BSE, 02/5256S
TSE, 02/87, 88, 89, 4842NI, 5257S
import and export controls, 02/93, 2970, 5039NI, 5906S, 5907S
Wales, 02/94, 2971
TSE
Wales, 02/90
artificial insemination of cattle
foot and mouth disease
Wales, 02/114
beef
slaughter of calves originating in UK
extent of powers conferred on national authorities, 02/108
bone in beef
despatch to domestic market
Wales, 02/2968, 2969
books, 02/188, 5293S
cattle
foot and mouth disease
artificial insemination, 02/115, 5261S
identification and registration, 02/106
movement control, 02/5260S
Wales, 02/107
premiums
extensification payment, 02/5276S
cereals
intervention agencies
Commission Regulation 336/2003, 02/76
common agricultural policy
information measures
Commission Regulation 2208/2002, 02/110
community aid
milk
Commission Regulation 2238/2002, 02/147
compensation
slaughter of calves originating in UK
extent of powers conferred on national authorities, 02/116

agriculture -*cont.*
farmers
inclusion on Farmers' Register, 02/111
farming
animal welfare
laying hens, 02/192, 4868NI, 5294S
feedingstuffs, 02/4847NI
additives
Commission Regulation 2188/2002, 02/1770
maximum levels, 02/5262S
Wales, 02/96
zootechnical products, 02/97, 4848NI
felling of trees
licences
electronic communication, 02/1799
Horticultural Development Council
horticultural produce
levies, 02/113
infectious disease control
animal movements
interim measures, 02/5264S
disposal by burning
compensation to farmers, 02/70
movement of animals
interim measures, 02/5274S, 5275S
livestock
extensification payment, 02/5276S
machinery
tractors
emissions, 02/1475
marketing standards
eggs
Commission Regulation 2003/326, 02/146
medicated feedingstuffs
zootechnical products
fees, 02/98, 4849NI
Milk Marketing Board
dissolution, 02/148
milk quotas
expiry of non marketing undertaking
claim for compensation time barred, 02/151
prohibition on milk production, 02/150
requirements for damages claim, 02/149
nitrate sensitive areas
aid
rates of payment, 02/73
pesticides
maximum residue levels
Commission Directive 2002/100, 02/152
pig industry
capital grants, 02/5279S
non-capital grants, 02/5280S
poultry
breeding flocks and hatcheries
fees, 02/176, 5290S
public health
relationship between establishment of MRL and marketing authorisation, 02/203
reorganisation
Milk Marketing Board, 02/4865NI
rural development
Less Favoured Area Support Scheme, 02/5291S
sheep

banking and finance -cont.
  individual savings accounts
    chargeable event gains
      insurance policies, 02/256
    transfer or withdrawal instructions
      time limits, 02/258
  overdrafts
    interest rates
      disparity with loan account interest rate, 02/262

bankruptcy
  abuse of process
    multiple petitions
      grant of leave, 02/2652
  annulment
    jurisdiction to review decision of General Commissioners, 02/2653
  bankruptcy orders
    adjournment
      adjournment of bankruptcy petition, 02/2671
    jurisdiction to go behind judgment, 02/2673
  bankruptcy petitions
    setting aside
      costs payable, 02/2665
  bankruptcy proceedings
    impartiality and equality of arms, 02/2408
  bankrupts
    breach of trust
      liability for breaches made after discharge of bankruptcy, 02/2675
  causes of action
    settlement monies paid to bankrupt, 02/2654
  consent orders
    jurisdiction to set aside, 02/2655
  death
    hearing of petition after death of bankrupt
      appointment of personal representative, 02/311
  debts
    financial provision
      husband in arrears of maintenance order made in Hong Kong, 02/2674
  dissipation of assets
    failing to account for loss of property, 02/2664
  fraud
    fraudulent transfer of assets to avoid creditors
      contingent liabilities, 02/2657
  gambling resulting in bankruptcy
    strict liability, 02/2662
  gifts
    requirement of valid gift, 02/2658
  gratuitous alienations
    disposition for "love, favour and affection", 02/5886S
  interim orders
    application for review of order, 02/2659
  limitations
    limitation period for contractual claim involving fraud, 02/2661
  offences
    defence of lack of intention
      burden of proof, 02/2663
  sequestration

bankruptcy -cont.
  sequestration -cont.
    disposition prior to sequestration
      rights of holder, 02/5890S
    recall
      payment of trustee's fees, 02/5889S
      timeous observance of procedural rules, 02/5887S
  statutory demands
    setting aside
      counterclaims, 02/2666
      evidence of genuine dispute, 02/2667
  trustees in bankruptcy
    application to reject proof of debt
      correct procedure, 02/2670
    setting aside
      transactions at an undervalue, 02/2668

banks. See also **banking and finance**

Barbados
  constitutional rights
    denial of legal representation at criminal trial, 02/646

Barclays Group Reorganisation Act 2002 (c.iv), 02/248

barristers
  appointment of Queens Counsel
    fees, 02/3101
  expenses
    claim for expenses incurred travelling to scene of crime, 02/3083
  fees
    travelling expenses
      case reference with client on remand, 02/3082

Belize
  death penalty
    mandatory sentence for murder by shooting
      compatibility with constitutional rights, 02/3917

benefits. See also **attendance allowance; child benefit; incapacity benefit; social security**
  approved work
    computation of earnings, 02/5104NI
  carers allowance, 02/5106NI, 5119NI
  child care charges
    computation of earnings, 02/4140
  child support maintenance
    deductions, 02/4141
  children and young persons
    personal allowances, 02/5105NI
      increase, 02/4142
  entitlement
    capital disregards, 02/5113NI
  hospital in-patients, 02/4150, 5115NI
  housing benefit
    Council Tax Benefit, 02/4152
  income related benefits
    funeral payments
      entitlement, 02/4235, 5151NI
  income support
    job seekers allowance, 02/4152
  invalid care allowance, 02/4169, 5119NI
    carer premium
      entitlement, 02/5120NI
  loss of benefits, 02/4156

Budget Act (Northern Ireland) 2002 (c.3), 02/5181NI

Budget (No.2) Act (Northern Ireland) Act 2002 (c.7), 02/5182NI

Budget (Scotland) Act 2002 (asp7), 02/6123S

building and engineering contracts. *See also* **arbitration**
claim for liquidated damages
stay of proceedings, 02/492
construction contracts
interim certificates
prescription
when obligation enforceable, 02/6055S
payments
interim certificate issued by architect
sums due under contract, 02/5407S

building regulations
building inspectors
sound insulation testing, 02/664
local authorities
requirements, 02/665
local authorities powers and duties, 02/665
rooms for residential purposes, 02/666
sound insulation testing
rooms for residential purposes, 02/666

burials and cremation
cemeteries
petition for authority to disinter
right of lairholder, 02/5969S
fees
parochial fees, 02/974

bus services
London service permits
appeals procedure, 02/4573
service subsidy agreements
exceptions to tendering requirement, 02/4650
Wales, 02/4651
written complaints
tribunals
establishment, 02/6129S

buses
community bus permit
fees, 02/4562
permits
fees, 02/4563

business tenancies. *See also* **leases**
access
renewal of tenancy
property treated as landlocked for purposes of fixing rent, 02/3018
assignment of lease
reasonableness of authorised guarantee agreements, 02/3019
contract terms
no commencement date in lease, 02/3020
grant
demolition and reconstruction works
landlord's opposition to new lease, 02/3022
licensed premises
surrender of equitable tenancy, 02/3024
local authorities
refusal to consent to change of use of premises, 02/3025
rent reviews

business tenancies -*cont.*
rent reviews -*cont.*
appointment of independent surveyor, 02/3023
repair covenants
interpretation of clause, 02/3028
right of access
estoppel or positive right over landlord's property, 02/3017
tenancies at will
implied intentions of parties, 02/3029
termination
effect of tenant vacating before term date, 02/3030
notice returned to sender after despatch by recorded delivery
validity of notice, 02/3031
underleases
obligation to keep premises open during trading hours, 02/5927S
validity of notice
delayed payment of rent
post dated cheques, 02/3026

Canada
charitable trusts
unincorporated associations
sale of assets to satisfy damages claim, 02/4672
creation of trust
agreements lacking certainty of subject and object, 02/4680
double taxation
US resident providing training services to Canadian resident company
meaning of "fixed base", 02/4389
letters of credit
expert evidence relied on in foreign court, 02/275
patents
infringement
purposive interpretation of claim, 02/2841, 2842
professional negligence
solicitors
duty of care owed to beneficiaries, 02/3297
tax planning
company in liquidation transferring losses
sale of share in partnership, 02/4497
swap agreements
composite transaction creating capital gain, 02/4500

capital allowances
energy conservation
machinery, 02/4353

capital finance
local government finance
private finance transactions
disposal of property, 02/3206

capital gains tax
assessment
company reconstruction
effect of reissue of shares, 02/4358
double taxation
reliefs

capital gains tax -*cont.*
  double taxation -*cont.*
    reliefs -*cont.*
      Lithuania, 02/4385
      South Africa, 02/4386
      Taiwan, 02/4387
      United States, 02/4388
  exempt amount
    2002-2003, 02/4359
  gilt edged securities
    exemptions, 02/4360
  reduction of capital
    cancellation of class of share capital
      meaning of "reorganisation", 02/4361
  sale of assets
    calculation of expenditure on new asset
      roll over relief, 02/4362
  share option schemes
    date of exercising option under capital gains
      tax, 02/4365
caravan sites. *See* **planning permission**
care
  care orders
    allegation of child abuse against proposed
    carer
      admissibility of hearsay evidence of social
      worker, 02/1639
    mother suffering from psychological problems
      risk of harm to children, 02/1642
    responsibility between courts and local
    authorities
      compatibility with ECHR, 02/1615
  care proceedings
    allegation of bias against judge, 02/1618
    allegations of sexual abuse abandoned during
    proceedings
      guidance as to future practice, 02/1621
    children of diplomatic staff
      jurisdiction to grant interim care orders, 02/
      1624
    retrials
      reopening of preliminary issue following
      confession, 02/1626
    unmarried father seeking disclosure of all
    documents, 02/1622
    witnesses
      social worker's application to give evidence
      anonymously, 02/1628
  children
    local authority assistance
      Wales, 02/4259
  health care
    registration
      Wales, 02/4261
  regulation of care
    applications and provision of advice, 02/
    6100S
    appointments and procedure, 02/6101S
    care service requirements, 02/6102S
    excepted services, 02/6103S
    fees, 02/6104S
    registration and registers, 02/6105S
    staff transfer scheme, 02/6106S
  social and health care
    registration

care -*cont.*
  social and health care -*cont.*
    registration -*cont.*
      fees, 02/4260
      Wales, 02/4261
  social care
    registration
      Wales, 02/4261
  standards
    establishments and agencies
      miscellaneous amendments, 02/4262
care plans
  reasonableness
    exclusion of parents from decision making
    process, 02/1617
care proceedings
  disclosure of documents
    criminal investigation into cause of child's
    injuries, 02/1619
  documents used in proceedings
    order for limited discovery of document, 02/
    1623
care standards
  social care worker
    extension of meaning
      Wales, 02/4264
Care Standards Act 2000 (c.14)
  Commencement and Transitional Provisions
  Order
    England, 02/4265, 4266
  Commencement No.8 and Transitional, Savings
  and Consequential Provisions Order
    Wales, 02/4267
  Commencement No.9
    Wales, 02/4268
  Commencement No.11 Order, 02/4269
  Commencement No.12 Order
    England, 02/4270
  Commencement No.13 Order
    England, 02/4271
  Commencement No.14
    England, 02/4272
  Commencement No.15 and Transitional
  Provisions Order
    England, 02/4273
  Commencement No.16 Order
    England, 02/4274
careless driving *See* **sentencing**
Carers and Direct Payments Act (Northern Ireland) 2002 (c.6), 02/5169NI
carriage by air. *See also* **air transport; transport**
  carriers liabilities
    psychiatric illness, 02/5305S
  domestic flight
    post traumatic stress disorder
      meaning of "bodily injury", 02/5305S
  passengers
    personal injury
      meaning of "in the course of any of the
      operations of embarking", 02/243
carriage by rail
  dangerous goods
    radioactive substances, 02/2228

child support -*cont.*
  decisions and appeals -*cont.*
    miscellaneous amendments, 02/5129NI
  enforcement
    liability order
      compatibility with ECHR, 02/1646
  maintenance orders
    jurisdiction of courts
      appeals, 02/4174, 4955NI
    reciprocal arrangements, 02/5130NI, 5131NI
  temporary compensation scheme
    modification of dates, 02/5132NI
    recovery of arrears, 02/4175
Child Support, Pensions and Social Security Act 2000 (c.19)
  Commencement No.11 Order, 02/4275
  Commencement No.8 Order, 02/5133NI
  Commencement No.7 Order, 02/5170NI
childcare
  tax credits
    new category, 02/4366
children. *See also* **child abduction; child support; childrens welfare**
  aliment
    variation of minute of agreement, 02/5611S
  anti social behaviour orders
    child subject to order interviewed by BBC
      appropriateness, 02/1648
  care
    health assessments
      Wales, 02/1649
    standards
      Wales, 02/4258
  care orders
    allegation of child abuse against carer
      admissibility of hearsay evidence of social worker, 02/1639
    appropriateness
      judge making final order in favour of local authority, 02/1640
    baby sustaining acute subdural haematomas
      threshold conditions, 02/1643
    mother suffering from psychological problems
      threshold criteria, 02/1642
  care proceedings
    absence of legal representation
      compatibility with ECHR, 02/2525
    appropriateness
      direction for residence at mother and baby unit, 02/1625
    disclosure of child sex abuse
      housing association's need to protect tenants, 02/1620
    father seeking permission to be joined as party
      compatibility with ECHR, 02/1627
    non accidental injury
      burden of proving parent inflicted harm rested on local authority, 02/1636
    unmarried father seeking disclosure of all documents, 02/1622
  change of name
    divorced Muslim mother and Sikh father
      knowledge of Sikh heritage vital, 02/1651

children -*cont.*
  change of name -*cont.*
    legality of multiple registrations with different names, 02/1629
    unmarried mother changing child's surname without father's consent, 02/1652
  child abduction
    place of habitual residence of dependent children, 02/1635
    stay on order to return child pending decision on contact, 02/1631
    surrogacy
      Californian arrangement, 02/1634
  child abuse
    expert witnesses
      burden of proving non accidental injury, 02/1637
  child protection
    care standards
      tribunal procedure, 02/1653
    domestic violence
      approval of care plan for adoption, 02/1645
    tribunal procedure, 02/1653
  child protection orders
    unborn children
      caveat to receive intimation of application, 02/5607S, 5608S
  childminders
    local authority's decision to cancel registration
      right to hearing de novo, 02/1647
    registration
      Wales, 02/1644
  childminding and day care
    certificates of registration
      Wales, 02/1654
  childrens hearings. *See also* children
    fair hearing
      unavailability of legal aid, 02/5619S
    supervision orders
      suspension of condition by hearing, 02/5622S
  childrens welfare. *See also* children
    acquisition of accommodation
      power of local authority to provide financial assistance, 02/4278
    childrens homes
      Wales, 02/1667
    contact orders
      threat of harm from father, 02/1659
    family proceedings, 02/1668
    local authorities
      failure to address long term care needs, 02/1669
  contact
    child subject to local authority supervision requirement
      intimation of appeal, 02/5612S
  contact orders
    fear of violence and emotional harm, 02/1656
    foreign judgments
      application to vary order made in Spanish court, 02/1655
    litigants in person
      appropriateness of order, 02/1658

children -*cont.*
  contact orders -*cont.*
    parental alienation syndrome
      views of children, 02/1657
  fostering
    local authorities
      payments to short term carers, 02/1700
  interim care orders
    alleged abuse by father
      threshold criteria, 02/1641
  learning difficulties
    confidential information
      disclosure sought by mother, 02/3229
  leaving care
    local authority assistance
      Wales, 02/4259
  names
    change of name
      requirement of paternal consent, 02/5614S
  parental contact
    reports
      status of report, 02/5613S
  parental responsibility orders
    order conferring status as relevant person, 02/5615S
    whether in child's best interests, 02/5616S
  secure accommodation
    absconding
      relevant considerations, 02/4956NI
  sexual abuse
    action to be taken by children and family reporter, 02/1665
    indirect contact order
      expert evidence, 02/1666
  witnesses
    failure to challenge reliability, 02/5526S
Children (Leaving Care) Act (Northern Ireland) 2002 (c.11), 02/4957NI
Children (Scotland) Act 1995 (c.36)
  Commencement No.5 Order, 02/5618S
childrens hearings
  legal representation, 02/5620S, 5621S
  relevant person
    immediate effect of parental responsibility and rights orders, 02/5615S
childrens tax credit
  qualifying person
    entitlement, 02/4367
childrens welfare
  care
    accommodation, 02/4276
      Wales, 02/1649, 4277
    standards
      Wales, 02/4258
  multiple occupation
    licensing, 02/5806S
Chiropractors Act 1994 (c.17)
  Commencement No.6 Order, 02/1821
choice of forum. *See also* **choice of law; conflict of laws; jurisdiction**
  contract of employment
    breach of duty as director, 02/620
    cook employed on mining vessels within different jurisdictions, 02/621
  contract terms

choice of forum -*cont.*
  contract terms -*cont.*
    interpretation of exclusive jurisdiction clauses, 02/5381S
    place of performance, 02/622
  contracts
    claimant issuing proceedings in English courts
      appropriate forum, 02/623
    rigs supplied by US corporation to Iranian customers, 02/625
    Scottish office of company with main office in England
      applicable law, 02/626
  contractual disputes
    Protection and Indemnity Clubs
      undertakings, 02/627
  derivative claim
    service out of jurisdiction
      procedural requirements, 02/619
  foreign jurisdictions
    incorporation of jurisdiction clause into contract of reinsurance, 02/2756
  jurisdiction
    road traffic accident claim
      proceedings in English court for further damages, 02/629
  jurisdiction clauses
    motion for reconsideration, 02/4103
  sist
    proceedings in other jurisdiction
      motion after record closed, 02/5366S
  stay of proceedings
    relevant considerations by Canadian court, 02/632
  trusts fund
    administration of trust funds set up in India
      governing law Bermuda, 02/633
choice of law. *See also* **choice of forum; conflict of laws; jurisdiction**
  contracts
    place of business, 02/5384S
Church of Scotland
  female associate minister
    dismissal for misconduct, 02/5576S
churches
  lighting
    installation of floodlighting
      effect on bats, 02/970
  noise levels created by church bell
    claim in private nuisance not actionable against bishop of diocese, 02/971
cinemas
  safety on premises, 02/3218
City of London (Ward Elections) Act 2002 (c.vi), 02/1207
Civil Defence (Grant) Act 2002 (c.5), 02/3151
civil engineers
  duty of care
    duty to third party purchaser of dwellinghouse, 02/6002S
civil evidence
  admissibility
    appeals
      insurance claim for fire damage, 02/271

confiscation orders -*cont.*
  postponement of hearing -*cont.*
    validity of extension beyond six months after
      conviction, 02/3892
  procedure
    independent power to consider confiscation
      validity of notice, 02/862
  smuggling
    tax evasion
      existence of derivation of benefit, 02/3898
conflict of laws. *See also* **choice of forum;**
choice of law; jurisdiction
  action involving English companies
    determination of jurisdiction issues, 02/624
  books, 02/644
  choice of law
    proceedings instituted in America
      determination of appropriate forum, 02/
        2736
  divorce
    separation agreements
      estoppel as to jurisdiction, 02/628
  fatal accident at sea
    compensation
      applicable law, 02/634
  foreign judgments
    enforcement contrary to public policy, 02/636
    registration of French judgment in Bahamas
      reciprocal enforcement, 02/637
      service, 02/638
  residence
    acquisition of domicile of choice, 02/5385S,
      5386S
consent orders
  restraint of trade
    variation of unenforceable terms, 02/323
conservation. *See also* **environmental**
protection
  biocidal products, 02/4945NI
  birds
    wild bird hunting
      failure to fulfil obligations under Council
        Directive 79/409, 02/1464
  military vessels
    designation
      protected places, 02/4106
  seals, 02/5296S
  sites of special scientific interest
    appeals
      Wales, 02/1466
Consolidated Fund Act 2002 (c.10), 02/1804
Consolidated Fund (No.2) Act 2002 (c.43),
02/1805
constitutional law. *See also* **Parliament**
  books, 02/652
  constitutional rights
    denial of legal representation at criminal trial,
      02/646
    infringement
      procedure for redress, 02/647
  corporal punishment
    sentence of flogging
      validity under Bahamas constitution, 02/
        645
  devolution

constitutional law -*cont.*
  devolution -*cont.*
    Scottish Administration
      offices, 02/5731S
    local authorities
      conduct of referendums, 02/3174
    Northern Ireland Assembly
      suspension of devolved government, 02/
        4885NI
      members salaries, 02/4884NI
    Pitcairn Islands
      Court of Appeal
        form of judicial affirmation, 02/649
      courts and judicial authorities, 02/650
    Scottish devolution
      cross border public authorities, 02/5391S
    Scottish Ministers
      agency arrangements, 02/5734S, 5735S
      directions
        national security, 02/5395S
      transfer of functions, 02/5393S
    Scottish Parliament
      legislative competence, 02/5392S
    Secretary of State
      directions
        national security, 02/5395S
    territorial waters
      boundaries, 02/4886NI
    Turks and Caicos Islands
      capital punishment, 02/651
    water boundaries
      British fishery limits, 02/4886NI
construction contracts. *See also* **building and**
engineering contracts
  arbitration
    further reference after award
      jurisdiction of arbiter, 02/5401S
  breach
    defective performance by subcontractor
      entitlement to compensation, 02/5402S
  causation
    requirement to establish global claim for loss
      and expense, 02/5404S
  defective premises
    failure to issue final certificate
      estoppel, 02/667
  design and build contracts
    contract disputes
      terms of settlement, 02/672
  interim certificates
    late issue by architect
      nature of certification duties, 02/668
  JCT standard form
    arbitration
      negotiations to form contract, 02/676
    asbestos
      payemts for removal, 02/677
    jurisdiction of arbitrator, 02/675
    subcontractors
      conclusion of management contract with
        developer, 02/673
  letters of intent
    contract terms
      obligation to pay sub contractor for
        defective work, 02/674

customs duty. *See also* **Customs and Excise;**
excise duty
origin of goods
petroleum products, 02/2980
damages. *See also* **compensation; measure of**
damages
award exceeding tender when interest added,
02/5532S
bereavement
variation of sum, 02/926, 4897NI
books, 02/950
fatal accidents
death of child's mother in road accident
value of substitute support from child's
father, 02/939
dependency claims
inclusion of damages relating to value of
services, 02/938
liquidated damages
constitution of penalty clause, 02/5403S
loss of earnings
financial support
amount of deceased's earnings to be
allocated to widow, 02/5534S
inability to provide gratuitous care
entitlement to recovery, 02/3411
loss of society
children
death of eldest son in Muslim family, 02/
5533S
mental distress
burials and cremation
entitlement to mental distress damages,
02/941
mitigation
misrepresentation
liability of third party for hire charges, 02/
932
motor insurance
recovery of hire charges
mitigation of loss, 02/933
motor vehicles
recovery of hire charges
charges extending beyond basic hire, 02/
5411S
mitigation of loss, 02/935
negligent misrepresentation
fall in value of shares, 02/5421S
psychiatric harm
secondary victims
pathological grief reaction of mother to
death of child, 02/948
rate of return
personal injuries, 02/5536S
dangerous driving. *See also* **road traffic**
offences
causing death, 02/5458S
unduly lenient sentence, 02/4055
consecutive sentences
multiple deaths caused by drunken driver
offences arising out of single incident, 02/
3908
inflicting grievous bodily harm on victims in
revenge attack, 02/3913
sentence length

dangerous driving -*cont.*
sentence length -*cont.*
causing death of 12 year old cyclist
poor driving record, 02/3909
data protection
Information Commissioner
appeals, 02/23
Information Tribunal
appeals, 02/23
prohibition on processing of sensitive personal
data
exemptions, 02/2640
death
fees, 02/5240S
registration
fees, 02/59, 4838NI, 5248S
Debt   Arrangement   and   Attachment
(Scotland) Act 2002 (asp 17), 02/5306S
debts
assignation
whether   liability   under   counterclaim
transferred, 02/5412S
delay
interest
commercial transactions, 02/5368S
interest rates
excepted contracts, 02/512
qualifying creditors, 02/511, 5369S
deception. *See also* **theft**
declarators
competency
prevention of enforcement of foreign decree,
02/5387S
decrees
joint and several
competency
whether same grounds of action, 02/
5328S
defamation
books, 02/963
libel
alleged publication of affidavit
correct approach to issues of conduct and
motivation, 02/952
ambiguity of defamatory words
qualified privilege, 02/953
damages awarded by jury
interference with excessive awards, 02/
956
defamatory publication
defence of qualified privilege, 02/960
defences
meaning of words complained of, 02/954
newspapers
successful claimant guilty of dishonest
conduct, 02/958
qualified privilege
preliminary issues, 02/961
qualified privilege
malice
relevancy, 02/5328S
slander
liability of original tortfeasor, 02/962

Employee Share Schemes Act 2002 (c.34), 02/4391
employees rights
consultation
redundancy
codes of practice, 02/4915NI
disciplinary and grievance procedures
codes of practice, 02/4913NI
industrial action ballots
codes of practice, 02/4914NI
employers liability. See also **health and safety at work; vicarious liability**
duty of care
accident at work
common law and statutory breach, 02/6001S
manual handling operations
risk of injury
relevancy of averments of risk, 02/5770S
employment. See also **employees rights; employers liability; redundancy; transfer of undertakings; unfair dismissal**
"trust and confidence" agreements
employees liabilities, 02/1317
annual leave
casual workers entitlement to paid leave, 02/1373
arbitration
Labour Relations Agency Arbitration Scheme, 02/4911NI
books, 02/1444, 5579S
codes of practice
disciplinary and grievance procedures, 02/4913NI
industrial action ballots, 02/4914NI
redundancy consultation and procedures, 02/4915NI
collective bargaining
appropriateness of structure proposed by union, 02/1423
conditions of employment
annual leave, 02/4916NI
police officers, 02/3756, 3757
promotion, 02/3758
special constables, 02/3760
teachers, 02/1183, 1184
Construction Industry Training Board
levy on employers, 02/669, 4887NI
constructive dismissal
failure to allow sufficient time for consultative process, 02/1312
continuity of employment
permanent employment of seconded employees
transfer of undertaking over a period, 02/1430
contract of employment
employment duties
breach of implied trust and confidence, 02/1318
registrars
power to dismiss, 02/1315
sportspersons
effect of "entire agreement" clause on contract, 02/1316

employment -cont.
contractual duty of fidelity
breach of duty
knowledge of damage, 02/5564S
criminal record
applications for certificates
fees, 02/5566S
certificates
protection of vulnerable adults, 02/1319, 5567S
registration
fees, 02/1320, 5568S
disability discrimination
medical evidence
physical or mental impairment, 02/1326
psychiatric illness
absence of medical evidence to support claim, 02/1328
disciplinary procedures
medical profession
criteria governing categorisation of conduct, 02/1872
dismissal
European Commission employees
publishing book without prior censorship, 02/1372
employees
bullying at work
damages for psychiatric harm, 02/1334
employees rights
holiday pay
payment by way of extra pay every week, 02/1376
increase of limits to certain payments, 02/1336, 4918NI
statutory adoption leave, 02/1337, 4919NI
statutory adoption leave and pay, 02/4928NI
statutory adoption pay, 02/4186, 4920NI
employers liabilities, 02/1338, 4921NI
entitlement, 02/4162, 4912NI
Health and Personal Social Services employees, 02/4922NI
NHS employees, 02/1339
persons abroad, 02/1340, 4923NI
weekly rates, 02/1341, 4924NI
statutory maternity leave, 02/4928NI
statutory paternity leave, 02/1337, 4919NI
statutory paternity leave and pay, 02/4928NI
statutory paternity pay, 02/4186, 4920NI
employers liabilities, 02/1338, 4921NI
entitlement, 02/4162, 4912NI
Health and Personal Social Services employees, 02/4922NI
NHS employees, 02/1339
persons abroad, 02/1340, 4923NI
weekly rates, 02/1341, 4924NI
employers
failure to offer enhanced redundancy entitlement to employee, 02/1407
stress at work
liability for employmees psychiatric illness, 02/3264
employers duties
asbestos, 02/2224
consent orders

employment -*cont.*
  unfair dismissal -*cont.*
    compensation
      impact of statutory minimum wage, 02/
        1438
      premature dismissal, 02/1439
    employee accessing pornography from office
      computer
      range of reasonable responses, 02/1441
    limited grounds of appeal, 02/1350
    withdrawal of claim
      intention of applicant, 02/1309
    variation of contract of employment
      burden of proof, 02/1409
Employment Act 2002 (c.22), 02/1343
  Commencement No.1 Order, 02/1344
  Commencement No.2 Order, 02/1345
  Commencement No.3 and Transitional and
    Saving Provisions Order, 02/1346
Employment Appeal Tribunal
  bias
    independence of lay members, 02/1347
employment protection
**Employment Relations (Northern Ireland)
  Order 1999 (SI 1999 2790 (NI.9))**
  Commencement No.5 and Transitional
    Provisions, 02/4925NI
  Commencement No.6 and Transitional
    Provisions, 02/4926NI
employment tribunals
  adjournment
    tribunal's duties, 02/1352
  estoppel
    complaint dismissed following withdrawal by
      applicant, 02/1354
  hearings
    deliberate delay of hearing
      appropriateness, 02/1356
  jurisdiction
    duality of proceedings
      financial limitations on common law claim,
        02/1357
    electoral matters
      refusal of job share application, 02/5571S
    executors
      right to pursue claims on behalf of
        deceased, 02/5572S
  legal representation
    power to interfere with representation, 02/
      1358
  procedural impropriety
    authorities referred to in judgment
      failure to invite parties to make submission,
        02/1359
  procedure
    costs warning given to claimant
      proportionality of tribunal's action, 02/1353
    notification of hearing
      relevant statutory provisions, 02/1355
  service of documents
    guidance on postal service, 02/1360
  sex discrimination proceedings
    criteria for award of aggravated damages, 02/
      1412
  time limits

employment tribunals -*cont.*
  time limits -*cont.*
    tribunal's approach to extension of time limit,
      02/1351
**Employment (Northern Ireland) Order 2002
  (SI 2002 2386 (NI.2))**
  Commencement, Transitional and Savings
    Provisions Order, 02/4927NI
energy. *See also* **electricity industry; gas
  industry; oil and gas industry**
  books, 02/1457
  electricity lines
    wayleaves
      meaning of "land", 02/1445
  electricity supply industry
    licences
      exemption, 02/1447
  energy conservation
    grants, 02/1470, 4938NI
  hydrocarbon oil
    registered dealers, 02/919
  nuclear power
    special constables
      powers and privileges, 02/1451
energy conservation
  building standards, 02/5400S
  buildings
    Council Directive 2002/91, 02/1448
enforcement notices
  appeals
    liability for expenses incurred, 02/6036S
    locus standi of applicants, 02/3669
  breach
    extent of authority of prosecuting solicitor
      agreement to withdraw, 02/3670
  change of use
    proof of date of change, 02/6034S
    validity of enforcement notice, 02/3671
  estoppel
    impact of estoppel upon obligation to enforce
      planning regulation, 02/3672
  interpretation
    consideration of documents directly referred
      to in notice, 02/3675
  land registration
    ownership of land following transfer, 02/3673
  listed buildings
    misapplication of annexation test, 02/3693
    outbuildings not within curtilage of listed
      building, 02/3694
  mobile homes
    ambit of defence for non-compliance
      defendant's inaction, 02/3674
  planning control
    appeals, 02/3734
      determination by inspectors, 02/3735
      hearings procedure, 02/3736
      inquiries procedure, 02/3737
      written representations, 02/3738
  time limits
    lack of development within time limit, 02/
      3676
    meaning of "substantially completed", 02/
      3677
  variation

environmental impact assessments -cont.
planning permission -cont.
applications -cont.
procedural requirements, 02/5584S
uncultivated land and semi-natural areas, 02/5585S
requirements for consent
Wales, 02/1472
environmental protection. See also conservation; pollution control
Antarctica
restricted areas, 02/1473
biocidal products, 02/4945NI
combustion plants
emissions, 02/1474, 5586S
emissions
agricultural or forestry tractors, 02/1476
non road mobile machinery, 02/1477
financial assistance, 02/1495, 5589S
Aggregates Levy Sustainability Fund, 02/1478
fixed penalties
dog fouling, 02/1479
litter, 02/1480
hunting
restriction on use of lead shot, 02/1481
Wales, 02/1482
lead shot
prohibition, 02/1481
national parks
Peak District
agricultural operations, 02/1483
odours
rendering of animals
lawfulness of "odour boundary condition", 02/1484
offshore chemicals
control system, 02/1485
ozone depletion
controlled substances, 02/1486
pollution control
landfill sites, 02/1506
pollution control regime, 02/1490, 1491
Council Directive, 02/4943NI
emissions, 02/1487, 5587S
permit applications, 02/1488, 1489
waste
packaging, 02/1492, 4946NI, 5588S
Wales, 02/1493
waste recycling payments, 02/1494
water pollution
nitrate vulnerable zones, 02/5595S, 5596S
designation, 02/1522
equal opportunities
public authorities, 02/4929NI
equal pay. See also sex discrimination
comparators
comparators employed more than six years prior to claim, 02/1362
Scottish education service
use of comparator from different authority, 02/5574S
maternity pay
entitlement to benefit of pay rise

equal pay -cont.
maternity pay -cont.
entitlement to benefit of pay rise -cont.
reference to European Court of Justice, 02/1364
equal treatment
fixed term contracts
failure to inform employer of pregnancy at recruitment, 02/1368
fixed term employees
prevention of less favourable treatment, 02/1365, 4930NI
part time employees
prevention of less favourable treatment, 02/1366, 4931NI
pension schemes
lawfulness of disparity in treatment, 02/1367
pregnancy
non renewal of fixed term contracts
direct effect of Council Directive 92/85, 02/1369
equipment
pressure equipment, 02/2232
equitable interests in land. See real property
equity. See also equitable interests in land; trusts
books, 02/1533
fraudulent misrepresentation
setting aside
legal charge procured by husband's equitable fraud, 02/3840
estoppel
misrepresentation
estoppel precluding limitation defence, 02/1529
ethics. See professional conduct
European Communities (Amendment) Act 2002 (c.3), 02/1550
European Court of Justice
appeals
Court of First Instance
breach of procedure, 02/1538
order for disclosure by Court of First Instance, 02/1551
preliminary rulings
Austria's trading rules restricting intra community trade, 02/1570
deduction of tax paid on inputs
compatibility with EC law, 02/4737
European Economic Area
free movement of persons
Switzerland, 02/2617
european ombudsman
appointment
Commission Decision 2003/104, 02/47
European Parliamentary Elections Act 2002 (c.24), 02/1219
European Patents. See patents
European Union. See also EC law
books, 02/1592
Commission documents
refusal to grant access
validity under EC law, 02/1544
Community institutions
European Common Aviation Area

European Union -cont.
  Community institutions -cont.
    European Common Aviation Area -cont.
      compatibility of proposed agreement with EC law, 02/1537
    Court of First Instance
      jurisdiction
        judicial review of Commission decision, 02/1540
        suspension of order pending full hearing, 02/1539
    European Court of Justice
      preliminary rulings
        interpretation of 1994 TRIPS Agreement, 02/2906
    European Economic Area agreement
      non compliance by Ireland
        UK's locus standi to intervene, 02/1554
    European Parliament
      fraud investigations
        powers conferred on European Anti Fraud Office, 02/1556
      legality
        formation of political group by Members without political affinity, 02/1557
    freedom to provide services
      cross border vehicle leasing
        testing requirements, 02/1583
    ministers
      power to make regulations, 02/1811, 1812, 1813, 1814
    treaties
      agreement on trade, development and cooperation
        South Africa, 02/2959
      Macedonia, 02/2958
      South Africa, 02/2959
evidence. See also corroboration; criminal evidence; witnesses
  asylum
    treatment of uncertain evidence, 02/5874S
  books, 02/278, 5312S
  burden of proof
    access to croft
      access of necessity, 02/5918S
  letters of request
    disclosure of without prejudice negotiations
      access to confidential statement, 02/276
excise duty. See also Customs and Excise; customs duty; vehicle excise duty
  beer
    reduced rates
      small breweries, 02/4392
  beer and tobacco products, 02/4393
  excise duty points
    movement of excise goods
      accompanying documents, 02/4394
  forfeiture
    consignment of goods belonging to different owners
      right to challenge Customs, 02/923
  fuel
    rates, 02/4395
  gaming duty rates, 02/4396
  hydrocarbon oil

excise duty -cont.
  hydrocarbon oil -cont.
    industrial relief, 02/4397
    registered dealers, 02/919
    relief, 02/4398
  personal reliefs
    revocation, 02/4399, 4400
  relief
    alcohol
      France, 02/4401
    tobacco products
      France, 02/4401
executive agencies
  domiciliary care agencies
    quality of services, 02/4279
  National Care Standards Commission
    residential family centres
      registration and inspection, 02/4284
expenses
  abandonment of action
    decree of absolvitor
      expenses not paid, 02/5325S
  caution
    failure to find in Land Court action
      appropriate order, 02/5922S
  caution for expenses
    appeal
      whether statable case, 02/5328S
  civil legal aid
    assessment of liability
      modification, 02/5934S
  divorce
    financial provision
      considerations relevant to award, 02/5623S
  Land Court
    legal aid
      modification of award, 02/5932S
  legal aid
    civil legal aid
      assessment of liability, 02/5933S
  time
    tender
      time for acceptance, 02/5330S
explosives
  fireworks
    licences, 02/4892NI
Export Control Act 2002 (c.28), 02/2984
exports
  export controls
    dual use goods, 02/2985
      Americium, 02/2986
    weapons
      Yugoslavia, 02/2988, 2989
  sanctions
    Yugoslavia, 02/2999
    Zimbabwe, 02/3000
extradition
  applicant on charge of murder
    magistrate's power to admit confessions, 02/1595
  bail
    court's power to order forfeiture of recognisance, 02/1594
  British overseas territories, 02/2935

food safety -*cont.*
scallops -*cont.*
emergency prohibitions -*cont.*
amnesic shellfish poisoning, 02/4983NI,
5713S, 5714S, 5715S
diarrhetic shellfish poisoning, 02/4984NI
football
spectators
world cup
control period, 02/4302
**Football (Disorder) (Amendment) Act 2002
(c.12),** 02/791
Commencement Order, 02/792
foreign exchange
tax treatment
gains and losses
bringing into account, 02/4409
loan relationships, 02/4408
foreign judgments
enforcement
declarator that foreign decree fraudulently
obtained, 02/5387S
garnishee orders
jurisdiction to enforce judgment debt, 02/
635
forestry
environmental impact assessments
summary offences, 02/4944NI
forests
reproductive material
marketing, 02/4993NI
fostering
placement of children, 02/1660
fraud
burden of proof
concealment of debts of company
anticipation of winding up, 02/795
Counter Fraud and Security Management
Service
establishment and constitution, 02/770
fraudulent trading
directors
company winding up with financial losses,
02/3954
request for information
specified organisations, 02/4187, 5137NI
free movement of capital
privatisation
government controls on share ownership in
privatised undertakings, 02/1561
reservation of state controls over privatised
energy company
proportionality, 02/1562
retention of controlling powers over privatised
petroleum company, 02/1563
free movement of goods
imports
French ban on British beef
validity under EC law, 02/1566
labelling
perfumes and aromatic goods
compatibility with Council Directive 76/
768, 02/1567
oil and gas industry
compulsory storage of petroleum products

free movement of goods -*cont.*
oil and gas industry -*cont.*
compulsory storage of petroleum products -
cont.
lawfulness, 02/1569
quality labels granted to German forestry goods
effect on intra Community trade, 02/1568
tax rates
reduced VAT rate levied on books in Icelandic
compatibility with EFTA agreement, 02/
4794
free movement of persons
migrant workers
eligibility for occupational disability pension,
02/4199
freedom of association
membership of freemasons
validity of disciplinary measures taken against
judge, 02/2372
political parties
dissolution of party advocating Sharia law,
02/2374
freedom of establishment
air transport
lawfulness of air services agreement between
UK and US, 02/1572
architects, 02/1573
application for registration
mutual recognition of qualifications within
EU, 02/1573
association agreements
direct effect
right of Member State to restrict entry, 02/
1574, 1575
corporation tax
non resident EU companies
exemption from wealth tax, 02/4374
EFTA
residence requirement
breach of equal treatment principle, 02/
1577
European Economic Interest Groupings
fees
microfiche based information, 02/515, 558
supply of services
prostitution pursued in self employed capacity,
02/1578
freedom of expression
conviction for defacing American flag
compatibility with ECHR, 02/825
convictions for spreading propaganda
politics, 02/2377
journalists
conviction for criminal libel, 02/2380
conviction of conveying propaganda
compatibility with ECHR, 02/2381
newspapers
solicitor's alleged conflict of interest
interim interdict, 02/5334S
publications
refusal to register titles
compatibility with ECHR, 02/2383
television broadcasting
refusal of licence to operate TV transmitter
compatibility with ECHR, 02/2376

government administration -cont.
ministers -cont.
refusal to nominate Sinn Fein ministers -cont.
unlawful exercise of discretionary powers, 02/4997NI
Ministry of Agriculture, Fisheries and Food
dissolution, 02/1815
public expenditure
accountability, 02/5307S
access to documents and information, 02/5308S
designation of bodies, 02/1818
efficiency and effectiveness of examinations, 02/5309S
Royal Mint Trading Fund
gifts and collectible items, 02/1803
trading funds
Queen Elizabeth II Conference Centre, 02/1808
government aid
African Development Fund
additional subscriptions, 02/2992
special development fund
Caribbean Development Bank, 02/250
government securities
Irish registers
closure and transfer, 02/254
grants
aided places scheme
St Mary's Music School, 02/5548S
Assembly Learning Grant Scheme
Wales, 02/1048, 1049
assisted places
incidental expenses, 02/1050
Wales, 02/1051
qualifying income limits, 02/1052
remission of fees
qualifying income levels, 02/5542S
Wales, 02/1053
dentistry, 02/5754S
disabled persons
postgraduate students, 02/986, 4898NI
education
mandatory awards, 02/1057, 1058, 1070
schools for performing arts, 02/1060
voluntary aided schools, 02/1069
education maintenance allowances, 02/1054
education standards, 02/1055
educational purposes
Wales, 02/1076
energy conservation, 02/1470, 4938NI
fishing industry, 02/4974NI
Wales, 02/1742
further or higher education
post-compulsory education awards
Wales, 02/1078
healthcare students
eligibility, 02/1056
housing relocation grants
forms, 02/2329
forms of application
Wales, 02/2330
housing renewal grants
forms, 02/2331
Wales, 02/2332

grants -cont.
housing renewal grants -cont.
means test, 02/2333
Wales, 02/2334
housing support grant
aggregate amount and apportionment, 02/5814S
local government, 02/5056NI
local government finance
central funds, 02/5052NI, 5053NI
mandatory awards
health authorities, 02/1059
marketing
agricultural processing and marketing, 02/4839NI
agricultural produce, 02/4840NI
national lottery
Awards For All joint scheme
local community groups, 02/267
parliamentary elections
political parties, 02/1277
police grant, 02/6045S
students, 02/4902NI, 4903NI
change of course
transfer of eligibility, 02/1061
eligibility, 02/1062, 1063, 1064, 1179, 4899NI, 4900NI
higher education, 02/1066
performing arts, 02/1067
teacher training, 02/1196, 1197, 1198, 1199
Greece
films
cinematic co-production agreements, 02/231
Greenham and Crookham Commons Act 2002 (c.i), 02/3824
Grenada
criminal evidence
sexual offences
need for corroboration warning, 02/750
grievous bodily harm
affray
striking victim's head repeatedly with metal bar, 02/3955
joint enterprise
other assailant remaining unapprehended
unduly lenient sentence, 02/3958
juvenile offenders
failure to impose extended licence on release
unduly lenient sentence, 02/4000
knives
violent criminal record
unduly lenient sentence, 02/3960
sentence length
provocation
loss of sight, 02/3961
unprovoked attack
victim kicked while lying on ground, 02/3957
sportspersons
injuries inflicted during rugby match, 02/3962
ground rent
leaseholds
redemption money
multiplier, 02/5041NI

health and safety at work -*cont.*
  hazardous substances -*cont.*
    colouring agents in paraffin -*cont.*
      safety, 02/2229
    controls, 02/2234, 2235
    dangerous goods, 02/2227
    explosive atmospheres, 02/2236
    handling
      specified quantities, 02/2237
    marketing and use, 02/1467, 1468
    packaging and labelling, 02/1469, 4888NI
  Health and Safety Executive
    fees, 02/2238
  industrial injuries
    noise induced hearing loss, 02/462
  lead
    employers duties, 02/2239
  manual handling
    breach of statutory duty
      slip on wet magazine, 02/5771S
    foreseeability
      risk of injury, 02/5771S
    reduction of risk, 02/5768S
    risk assessment
      evidence on causation, 02/2222
  manual handling operations
    breach of duty, 02/5769S
    risk of injury
      relevancy of averments of risk, 02/5770S
  occupational health
    exposure to known health hazard
      duty of care owed to employees, 02/2226
  offshore installations, 02/2242
    safety zones, 02/1453, 1454
  personal protective equipment, 02/2231
  workplace
    duty owed to customer shop premises
      relevancy, 02/5775S
Health and Social Care Act 2001 (c.15)
  Commencement No.2 Order
    Wales, 02/1854
  Commencement No.3 Order
    Wales, 02/1855
  Commencement No.8 Amendment Order, 02/1856
  Commencement No.8 Order, 02/1857
  Commencement No.9 Order, 02/1858
    Scotland, 02/5742S
  Commencement No.10 Order
    England, 02/1859
health authorities. *See also* **National Health Service**
  education
    grants
      mandatory awards, 02/1059
  establishment and abolition, 02/1860
  Falmouth & Truro Port Health Authority
    expenses contributions, 02/1861
  functions
    provision of services and appraisal, 02/1862
  functions and administration arrangements, 02/1863
  renaming
    consequential amendments, 02/1928
  Retained Organs Commission, 02/1865

health care
  appointments
    members, 02/1866
health services
  dentistry
    dental services
      fees, 02/5005NI
  employees rights
    statutory paternity and adoption pay, 02/4922NI
  general medical services
    doctors
      Hepatitis B, 02/5006NI
    prescription of drugs, 02/5007NI
heavy goods vehicles
  carriage by road
    community authorisations, 02/4570
  licensing
    fees, 02/4571
  testing
    fees, 02/5192NI
heritable property
  constitution of servitude
    sufficiency of averments, 02/5791S
  creditors
    positive prescription
      subjects left vacant by heritable creditor, 02/6057S
  disposition
    breach of warrandice
      rectification of register, 02/5777S
    sequestration prior to registration of title, 02/5890S
  guarantees
    enforcement
      undue influence by debtor against co-debtor, 02/5794S
  heritable creditors
    sale of land
      duty to obtain best price, 02/5785S
  land obligations
    real burdens
      remedy for breach, 02/5333S
    variation and discharge
      compensation, 02/5779S
      footpath over garden, 02/5782S
      prevention of development, 02/5780S, 5781S
  land registration
    rectification of register, 02/5783S
  missives
    non-supersession clause
      effect where no settlement, 02/5787S
      failure to state commencement date, 02/5788S
  standard securities
    calling up notice
      relevancy, 02/5792S
    failure to oppose calling up, 02/5793S
Heritable property (Scotland)
  books, 02/5796S
High court
  family proceedings
    fees, 02/4963NI

human rights -*cont.*
intervention -*cont.*
power of Human Rights Commission to
intervene in legal proceedings, 02/4826NI
prisoners rights
mail interception
compatibility with ECHR, 02/2387
prison media ban policy
compatibility with ECHR, 02/3351
privacy
strip searches
application of retrospective legislation, 02/4554
property rights
extension to entertainment licence
refusal closing business, 02/5965S
remedies
failure to exhaust domestic remedies, 02/2389
repatriation
risk of torture
compatibility with ECHR, 02/2544
risk of torture on return to Turkey, 02/2545
retrospective legislation
homicide conviction of former senior GDR
politicians
compatibility with ECHR, 02/2390
strip searches
drug trafficking
requirement to show reasonable and
probable grounds, 02/912
surveillance
authorisations
cancellation, 02/5869S
torture
asylum seekers
no evidence of threat from authorities if
returned to Sri Lanka, 02/2540
decision to return Kurdish asylum seeker to
Syria
no evidence of threat from State
authorities, 02/2539
injuries sustained on arrest
failure to prosecute officials involved, 02/2542
Turkish authorities
failure to investigate and identify officers
responsible, 02/2543
torture in detention
Turkish teacher disciplined for giving
statement to press, 02/2379
trade union membership
financial incentives offered in return for
renouncing of union representation
compatibility with ECHR, 02/2375
Turkey
compensation proceedings
statutory interest for delay, 02/2371
hunting
controlling use of property
consideration of foxhunting as activity of
private life, 02/5866S
illegal entrants. *See also* **entry clearances**
carriers liabilities
penalties, 02/2620

illegal entrants -*cont.*
directions for removal
immigration officers, 02/2626
facilitating illegal entry of immigrants into UK,
02/3971
immigration. *See also* **asylum; entry
clearances; illegal entrants; refugees**
adjudicators
reversal of oral decision in written
determination
status of written determination, 02/2555
appeals
family visitor, 02/2609
review of fairness of proceedings
powers of adjudicator, 02/5881S
asylum
one stop notices
time limits, 02/2554
asylum seekers
accommodation, 02/2606
short term holding facilities
contracting out, 02/2579
support
applications, 02/2598
vouchers, 02/2601
travel assistance, 02/2606
books, 02/2635, 5029NI
carriers liabilities
clandestine entrants
penalties, 02/2621
deportation
marriage as compassionate factor, 02/5882S
overstayer married to EC national
compatibility with EC law, 02/2607
setting aside
IAT's failure to determine all grounds of
appeal, 02/2550
validity of removal arrangement, 02/2593
entry clearances
Commonwealth citizen
reentry requirements, 02/2610
family visitor, 02/2609
legality of ban imposed on alien, 02/2612
marriage termination
legitimate expectation of grant of indefinite
leave to remain, 02/2611
reasonableness
officer's approach to circumstances of
applicant's family life, 02/5883S
travel bans
exemptions, 02/2614, 2615, 2616
European Economic Area
free movement of persons
Switzerland, 02/2617
foreign nationals
travel documents
exemption of fees, 02/2618
housing
accommodation
eligibility, 02/2351
illegal entrants
carriers liabilities
penalties, 02/2620, 2621
judicial review
delay in seeking relief, 02/2622

local authorities. *See also* **housing; local government**

abuse of power
　exercise of statutory power for improper purpose, 02/3185
access to meetings and documents
　period of notice, 02/3162
alternative arrangements
　proposals
　　Wales, 02/3183
best value
　analyses and improvement plans
　　Wales, 02/3144
　performance indicators
　　Wales, 02/3145
　performance indicators and standards, 02/3146
　performance plans and reviews, 02/3148
building regulations
　requirements, 02/665
cemeteries
　maintenance of graves
　　necessity for obtaining faculty for safety works, 02/967
change of district name
　Lisburn Borough, 02/5054NI
childrens welfare
　failure to address long term care needs, 02/1669
companies
　credit cover
　　Wales, 02/3171
　Greater London Authority, 02/3172
conduct
　model codes of practice, 02/3173
conduct of referendums, 02/3174
contracting out
　income related benefits, 02/3143
council meetings
　access and disclosure, 02/3175
　modification of enactments, 02/3176
　　Wales, 02/3177
data protection
　unlawful use of data held on computer
　　liability of local authority, 02/3188
duties
　specified medical treatments, 02/5988S
　　neurosurgery, 02/5989S
　supervision of welfare guardians, 02/5990S
duty of care
　duty to community service worker, 02/6004S
executive arrangements
　access to information, 02/3175
　discharge of functions
　　Wales, 02/3178, 3179
　functions and responsibilities
　　Wales, 02/3180
　modification of enactments, 02/3181
　powers and duties
　　Wales, 02/3182
　proposals
　　Wales, 02/3183
failure to issue exemption notice
　duties of Local Government Ombudsman, 02/3208

local authorities *-cont.*
fly posting
　entitlement to claim cost of removal from election agent, 02/63
grants, 02/5056NI
gypsies
　order to vacate plot
　　compatibility with ECHR, 02/3682
housing support grant
　aggregate amount and apportionment, 02/5814S
local authorities powers and duties
　prohibition of public procession
　　reasonableness, 02/5978S, 5979S
　system of inspection of housing department land
　　tenants duty to report disrepair, 02/3278
local government officers
　allowances and expenses, 02/5981S
local government pension scheme, 02/3369
members
　allowances
　　Wales, 02/3163
motor salvage operators
　registration
　　specified offences, 02/804
motor vehicles
　salvage operators
　　registration, 02/803
powers and duties
principal councils
　inspection of documents
　　public notice, 02/3162
　meetings
　　public notice, 02/3162
renovation grant
　refusal to grant, 02/2327
roads
　pedestrian crossings
　　duty to notify affected residents, 02/2260
sale of land
　obligation to obtain highest price
　　commercial value of consideration, 02/3195
structured settlements
　liability to provide residential care after conclusion of settlement, 02/949
supply of goods and services
　designation of public bodies, 02/3213, 3214
　　Wales, 02/3215
traffic orders, 02/5800S
　exemptions, 02/5798S, 5799S
waste disposal
　mistaken removal of property by refuse collectors
　　no breach of duty, 02/3196
local authority housing
disposals
　deregulation, 02/2352
eviction
　anti social behaviour
　　tenant's spouse convicted of drugs offence, 02/5820S
living accommodation
　assistance, 02/2354

local authority housing -*cont.*
  right to buy
    failure to disclose defects prior to purchase
      measure of damages, 02/2355
local education authorities
  budget statements, 02/1074
    Wales, 02/1075
  duty of care
    supervision of pupils leaving school, 02/6005S
  expenditure
    outturn statements, 02/1077
  finance
    individual schools budget
      sixth form, 02/1130, 1131
    local schools budget
      individual schools budget, 02/1129, 1132
      Wales, 02/1134
    maintained schools
      expenditure on community facilities, 02/1133
  post compulsory education awards
    further or higher education
      Wales, 02/1078
  school admissions
    role of appeals panels
      perversity of admission decision in light of policy, 02/1099
  school exclusions
    pupil referral units
      appeals, 02/1107, 1108
  schools
    information and prospectuses, 02/1124
  transfer of assets
    London Residuary Body, 02/1079, 1080
local elections. *See also* **elections**
  election of councillors
    Scotland, 02/5561S
  Local Government Commission
    winding up, 02/1246
local government. *See also* **local authorities**
  best value
    performance plans and reviews, 02/3148
  books, 02/3216
  boundaries
    Blaenau Gwent and Caerphilly
      Wales, 02/3164
    Cardiff
      Wales, 02/3165
    Carmarthenshire
      Wales, 02/3166
    Ceredigion
      Wales, 02/3167
    Neath Port Talbot and Swansea
      Wales, 02/3168
    Newport
      Wales, 02/3169
    Pembrokeshire
      Wales, 02/3166, 3167
    Rhondda Cynon Taff
      Wales, 02/3170
    Vale of Glamorgan
      Wales, 02/3165, 3170
  councillors
    wilful misconduct

local government -*cont.*
  councillors -*cont.*
    wilful misconduct -*cont.*
      nature of remedy available to local authority, 02/3161
  elected mayor and mayor's assistant, 02/1212
  local authorities
    supply of goods and services
      designation of public bodies, 02/3184
  Local Government Commission
    electoral process
      winding up, 02/1246
  local government officers
    allowances and expenses, 02/5981S
    redundancy
      continuity of employment, 02/1406
  local government pension scheme, 02/3369, , 02/3370, 5060NI, 6017S
    fund management, 02/3371
    investment principles
      written statements, 02/3371
  maladministration
    disabled tenants
      failure of local authority to provide suitably adapted accommodation, 02/3192
  street trading
    tenancies
      power to grant tenancy over highway, 02/3212
  termination of employment
    discretionary payments, 02/1380
Local Government Act 2000 (c.22)
  Commencement No.3 Order
    Wales, 02/3198
  Commencement No.8 Order, 02/3199
local government finance. *See also* **community charge; council tax; rates**
  billing authorities
    calculations, 02/3201
  budget requirements
    amendment to calculations
      Wales, 02/3202
  calculation of housing revenue account, 02/5819S
  capital finance
    investments, 02/3203
      Wales, 02/3204
    investments and contracts
      Wales, 02/3205
    private finance transactions
      disposal of property, 02/3206
    rate of discount, 02/3149
      Wales, 02/3150
  grants
    central funds, 02/5052NI, 5053NI
    council tax calculations
      Greater London Authority, 02/3200
  public expenditure
    limits, 02/3207
  revenue support grant
    determination for 2002/03, 02/5983S, 5984S

Local Government in Scotland Act 2003 (asp 1), 02/5980S
Local Government (Best Value) Act (Northern Ireland) 2002 (c.4), 02/5055NI
local plans
  proposed structure plans
    examination in public
      reasonableness of refusal, 02/6041S
London
  service permits
    appeals procedure, 02/4573
lotteries. *See also* **gambling**
  fees
    Gaming Board, 02/3140
  national lottery
    licence fees
      prescribed sum, 02/3141
Macedonia
  treaties
    European Union, 02/2958
magistrates. *See also* **magistrates courts**
  committal orders
    council tax
      justices' powers to remit fine, 02/855
magistrates courts
  anti social behaviour orders, 02/887
  bias
    evidence of witness intimidation in prior application, 02/888
  commission areas
    West Mercia, 02/30
  committals
    legitimate expectation of summary sentence, 02/859
  detention and forfeiture of cash
    applications procedure, 02/889
  extradition proceedings
    notice of consent form, 02/31
  family proceedings
    declarations of parentage, 02/4962NI
    fees, 02/4832NI
  Greater London Magistrates' Courts Authority
    occupational pensions, 02/3357
  proof of parentage
    blood tests, 02/4967NI
  rules
    special measures directions
      video evidence, 02/32
    terrorist assets
      detention and forfeiture, 02/4895NI
  sex offender orders
    procedure, 02/890
  size and chairmanship of bench, 02/33
  summary procedure
    rejection of submission of no case to answer, 02/891
maintenance. *See also* **financial provision**
manslaughter
  diminished responsibility
    Court of Appeal
      power to substitute conviction of alternative offence, 02/807
  drug addiction
    administration of heroin injection to drug addict, 02/4023

manslaughter -*cont.*
  drugs
    aiding and abetting victim who self injected, 02/801
  illegal entrants
    immigration manslaughter case
      defence of joint illegality, 02/802
  intoxication
    lump of wood used as weapon
      public interest issues regarding violent offences, 02/4024
  perverting the course of justice
    sentence length
      uninsured driver with defective vision, 02/4026
  rape
    administration of drug for purposes of sexual assault
      life sentence, 02/4029
  robbery
    sentence length
      street attacks on elderly persons, 02/4032
  street violence
    single unprovoked punch to victim's head
      unduly lenient sentence, 02/4021
  violence
    consumption of drugs and alcohol prior to stabbing
      unduly lenient sentence, 02/4033
    sentence length
      infliction of two blows to victim's head, 02/4034
marine insurance. *See also* **insurance**
  declaration of risk
    implied terms
      obligatory nature of risk, 02/2747
  evidence
    destination of ship at time of sailing
      liability for loss of cargo, 02/4122
  exclusion clauses
    interpretation of phrase "customs regulations", 02/2749
  implied terms
    declaration of risk
      charterers liability, 02/2748
  salvage
    limits on evidential challenge as to causation, 02/4123
marketing
  potatoes
    British Potato Council
      registration and levies, 02/175
  standards
    eggs
      Commission Regulation 2003/326, 02/146
  veterinary medicines
    authorisations, 02/202
marriage. *See also* **civil marriage; divorce**
  civil marriages
    approval of places
      application procedures, 02/5970S
  fees, 02/5240S
    parochial fees, 02/974
  irregular marriage
    cohabitation with habit and repute, 02/5634S

marriage -*cont.*
nullity
arranged marriage
lack of consent to marry, 02/5635S
pre marital agreements
parties privy to agreement, 02/1713
registration
fees, 02/59, 4838NI, 5248S
Marriage (Scotland) Act 2002 (asp 8), 02/5636S
Commencement Order, 02/5637S
matrimonial home. *See also* financial provision; matrimonial property
joint tenancies
transfer of joint tenancy, 02/5639S
occupancy rights
time limits, 02/5638S
wife primary carer of child
statutory entitlement to be rehoused, 02/1706
matrimonial property. *See also* financial provision; matrimonial home
property adjustment orders
protection against order for sale, 02/1707
Mauritius
newspapers
alleged publication of false news report
requirement to establish likelihood of breach of public order, 02/826
measure of damages. *See also* personal injuries
clinical negligence
knee operation
loss of earnings, 02/3416
death from asbestosis
calculated at date of death or date of trial, 02/3418
discounts
correct rate for quantification of future losses, 02/3417
risk of osteoarthritis shortening career as miner, 02/5997S
solatium
loss of earnings
injury preventing active involvement in restaurant business, 02/5535S
wrongful birth
cerebral palsy
future cost of care and loss of earnings, 02/3432
media. *See also* broadcasting; films; newspapers
books, 02/3227
newspapers
report on celebrity's drug addiction
public interest, 02/951
Press Complaints Commission
judicial review
threshold for interference, 02/3223
publications
anonymity
effect of investigative journalism on presumption of innocence, 02/3224
medical equipment
in vitro medical devices
mutual recognition, 02/2110

medical profession. *See also* clinical negligence dentistry; medical treatment; National Health Service; opticians
chiropractors
General Chiropractic Council
elections, 02/1870
registration, 02/1871
doctors
out of hours medical services, 02/1911
European qualifications
approval
Specialist Training Authority, 02/1873
Family Practitioner Committees
dentists
allegations of breach of terms of service, 02/1828
determination of preliminary jurisdictional issue, 02/1834
procedure for conduct of enquiries into complaint, 02/1829
General Dental Council
constitution, 02/1847, 1848
General Medical Council
committees
fitness to practise, 02/1849
constitution, 02/1850, 1874
general medical services
protection of health care workers and patients
Hepatitis B, 02/5006NI
Health Professions Council
consequential amendments, 02/1875
nurses, midwives and health visitors
amendments, 02/1876
professional conduct, 02/1877, 1878, 5008NI, 5009NI, 5743S, 5744S
Nursing and Midwifery Council
consequential amendments, 02/1879
optical appliances
vouchers, 02/2098, 2099
Wales, 02/2100, 2101, 2102
opticians
opthalmic list
Wales, 02/2105
optical appliances, 02/5014NI
vouchers, 02/2097, 5015NI, 5016NI, 5760S, 5761S, 5762S
provision of ophthalmic services, 02/2104
osteopaths
General Osteopathic Council
elections, 02/1880
registers
Health Professions Council
transitional provisions, 02/1881
Nursing and Midwifery Council
transitional provisions, 02/1882
regulatory bodies, 02/2218
Council for Professions Supplementary to Medicine
transfer of staff, 02/2217
nurses and midwives, 02/2219
appointments and procedure, 02/5013NI
transfer of staff
Nursing and Midwifery Council, 02/2220
services

medical profession -cont.
  services -cont.
    pharmaceutical services and general medical
     services, 02/5010NI
medical treatment. *See also* medical
  negligence
  failure to pay Health Service charge
    civil penalty charges, 02/5001NI
  persistent vegetative state
    artificial feeding and hydration, 02/1888
  travelling expenses
    remission of charges, 02/5019NI
medicines. *See also* medical negligence;
  medical profession; medical treatment;
  National Health Service; pharmacy
  medicinal products
    codification amendments, 02/1892
mens rea. *See also* diminished responsibility;
  insanity; provocation
mental health. *See also* community care;
  mental patients; nervous shock
  adults with incapacity
    rules
      applications and appeals, 02/5992S
    welfare guardians
      non compliance of decisions, 02/5996S
  books, 02/3244
  hospital authority
    abolition
      Ashworth, 02/1894
  hospital orders
    Crown Courts
      power to make order, 02/3228
  mental hospitals
    decision of hospital managers regarding
     nature of care
      susceptibility to judicial review, 02/3232
  mental patients
    discharge
      reconsideration by tribunal of deferred
       decision, 02/3239
    ethics committee
      membership and qualifications, 02/5993S
    guardianship and intervention orders
      reports, 02/5994S
    infectious disease control
      no "real and immediate threat to life", 02/
       3236
    late term abortion
      procedure not in patient's best interest, 02/
       3233
    local authorities
      entitlement to charge for after care
       services, 02/3237
      specified medical treatments, 02/5988S,
       5989S
      supervision of welfare guardians, 02/
       5990S
    medical treatment certificates, 02/5991S
    powers of guardians
      recall, 02/5995S
    procedure for challenging continued
     detention, 02/2485
    public guardians
      fees, 02/5733S

mental health -cont.
  mental patients -cont.
    validity
      decision to administer medical treatment to
       non consenting patient, 02/3234
    mental patients rights
      criteria for renewal of detention, 02/3238
      cross dressing
       detention, 02/3241
      justification
       referral of case of restricted patient, 02/
        3235
      seclusion of patient in non secure hospital
       compatibility with ECHR, 02/3240
      transfer from care home
       right to respect for private and family life,
        02/3242
    psychological overlay
      meaning of physical or mental impairment,
       02/1322
    restricted patients
      deferred conditional discharge
       compatibility with ECHR, 02/3243
    tribunals
      mental health review tribunals
       reasonableness of decision to discharge
        patient, 02/3230
mergers
  merger report
    Bass PLC
      revocation, 02/603
    Interbrew SA
      revocation, 02/603
messengers at arms
  fees, 02/5221S, 5222S
middle schools
  classification
    primary or secondary schools, 02/1138
migrant workers. *See* free movement of
  persons; immigration
Milford Haven Port Authority Act 2002 (c.v),
  02/4126
military occupation
  Cyprus
    Turkish invasion of Cyprus
      alleged human rights violations, 02/2386
milk quotas. *See; agriculture*
mining
  duty of care
    breach of statutory duty
      slippery walkway, 02/5997S
ministerial functions
  transfer and modification, 02/4996NI
misrepresentation. *See also* fraud
  negligent misrepresentation
    special relationship, 02/5421S
Mobile Telephones (Re-progamming) Act
  2002 (c.31)
  Commencement Order, 02/4533
Mobile Telephones (Re-programming) Act
  2002 (c.31), 02/4534
mode of trial. *See* jury trial; magistrates
  courts
mortgages
  facility letters

national parks -*cont.*
Loch Lomond and the Trossachs -*cont.*
designation, 02/5591S
elections, 02/5592S
Peak District
agricultural operations
restriction, 02/1483
Nationality, Immigration and Asylum Act 2002 (c.41), 02/2629
Commencement No.1 Order, 02/2630
natural justice
licensing
renewal of public house licence
objection by local authority, 02/5964S
planning permission
interest of member of planning committee, 02/6039S
navigation
river Bann, 02/4947NI
river Wye, 02/1503
negligence. *See also* **clinical negligence; duty of care; professional negligence**
accidents
primary schools
injury caused by sharpened pencil, 02/3272
banks
loan provided for refurbishment of property
role of bank as insurance broker, 02/247
books, 02/3319
causation
damage to water main during construction work
duty of water company to provide accurate mapping, 02/3257
fatal mesothelioma
full liability consent order prior to death, 02/3245
cause of action for negligent misstatement, 02/3277
clinical negligence
indemnity scheme
Mental Welfare Commission, 02/5748S
contributory negligence
giving ambiguous instructions, 02/5773S
road traffic accidents
failure to place child in restraint seat, 02/3258
damage to property
subsidence caused by street trees
liability of local authority, 02/3318
duty of care
motorcycle event organisers
causative effect of mixed ability groupings, 02/3246
economic loss
claim against local authority
justification for trial, 02/3316
foreseeability
personal injury
sustained at holiday camp, 02/3265
schools
pupil injured on bannister, 02/3274
independent contractors
occupier's duty to enquire into insurance

position of independent contractor, 02/4549
negligence -*cont.*
intervening events
children removing petrol from garage
foreseeability of accident, 02/3273
local authorities
statutory powers
no duty over road markings, 02/3315
medical treatment
exemplary damages
criteria for award, 02/931
prison officers
injury caused by inmate, 02/6022S
psychiatric harm
foreseeability
recoverability of damages, 02/3275
road traffic accidents
agricultural vehicles
duty to take exceptional steps, 02/3269
standard of care
road traffic accidents
defendant approaching ice cream van at low speed, 02/3312
statutory duty
duties of local authority in relation to inquiries, 02/3317
teachers
school skiing trips
extent and nature of duty of care, 02/3270
water companies
failure to repair drainage system
liability for damage to property, 02/942
New Roads and Street Works Act 1991 (c.22)
Commencement No.7 Order
England, 02/2259
New Zealand
constructive trusts
assets
transfer out of jurisdiction awarding judgment debt, 02/4677
legitimate expectation
equal distribution of superannuation funds, 02/4674
criminal appeals
legal aid applications
procedure for judicial determination, 02/848
income tax
tax planning
tax avoidance scheme, 02/4499
life assurance companies
interest on late premiums
deductibility, 02/4426
negligence
medical treatment
exemplary damages, 02/931
supply of services
tax rates
rest home subsidy schemes, 02/4502
surgical procedures
fairness of composition of report, 02/39
newspapers
freedom of expression
solicitor's alleged conflict if interest

newspapers -cont.
  freedom of expression -cont.
    solicitor's alleged conflict if interest -cont.
      interim interdict, 02/5334S
NHS trusts
  change of name
    Basildon and Thurrock General Hospitals, 02/1939
    Bournewood Community and Mental Health, 02/1940
    Brent, Kensington, Chelsea and Westminster Mental Health, 02/1969
    Cornwall Healthcare, 02/1970
    Eastbourne and County, 02/1971, 1972
    Leeds Community and Mental Health Services Teaching, 02/1941
    Leicestershire and Rutland Healthcare, 02/1973
    Lincolnshire Healthcare, 02/1942
    North and East Devon Partnership, 02/1974
    Rushmoor and Hart Primary Care Trust, 02/1943
    Sheffield Children's Hospital, 02/1975
    South Essex Mental Health and Community Care, 02/1976
    South Yorkshire Metropolitan Ambulance and Paramedic Service, 02/1944
    Southampton East Healthcare, 02/1977
    Southern Derbyshire Mental Health, 02/1978
    Worcestershire Community and Mental Health, 02/1979
  dissolution, 02/1945, 1946
    Barnsley Community and Priority Services, 02/1947
    Blackburn, Hyndburn and Ribble Valley Health Care, 02/1961
    Blackpool Victoria Hospital, 02/1957
    Blackpool, Wyre and Fylde Community Health Services, 02/1957
    Bradford Community Health, 02/1980
    Burnley Health Care, 02/1961
    Bury Health Care, Rochdale Healthcare, Oldham, and the North Manchester Healthcare, 02/1987
    Cheshire Community Healthcare, 02/1948
    Chester and Halton Community, 02/1949
    City Hospital, 02/1988
    CommuniCare, 02/1950
    Community Health Care Service (North Derbyshire), 02/1978
    Community Healthcare Bolton, 02/1951
    Dewsbury Health Care, 02/1986
    Invicta Community Care, 02/1991
    Lifespan Health Care Cambridge, 02/1983
    Lifespan Health Care Cambridge and the North West Anglia Health Care, 02/1984
    Mid Sussex, 02/1981
    North Durham Health Care, 02/1985
    North Mersey Community, 02/1952
    North West Anglia Health Care, 02/1983
    Northallerton Health Services, 02/1953
    Pinderfields and Pontefract Hospitals, 02/1986
    Preston Acute Hospitals, 02/1962
    Priority Healthcare Wearside, 02/1989

NHS trusts -cont.
  dissolution -cont.
    Rotherham Priority Health Services, 02/1954
    Sandwell Healthcare, 02/1988
    South Buckinghamshire, 02/1982
    South Durham Health Care, 02/1985
    St. Helens and Knowsley Community Health, 02/1955
    Stoke Mandeville Hospital, 02/1982
    Sussex Weald and Downs, 02/1992
    Thames Gateway, 02/1991
    Wakefield and Pontefract Community, 02/1990
    Wiltshire and Swindon Health Care, 02/1956
    Wirral and West Cheshire Community, 02/1959
    Worthing Priority, 02/1992
  establishment
    Blackpool, Fylde and Wyre Hospitals, 02/1957
    Bradford District Care Trust, 02/1980
    Brent, Kensington, Chelsea and Westminster Mental Health, 02/1969
    Brighton and Sussex University Hospitals, 02/1981
    Buckinghamshire Hospitals, 02/1982
    Cambridgeshire and Peterborough Mental Health Partnership, 02/1983, 1984
    Camden and Islington Mental Health, 02/1958
    Cheshire and Wirral Partnership, 02/1959
    Chorley and South Ribble, 02/1962
    Cornwall Healthcare, 02/1970
    County Durham and Darlington Acute Hospitals, 02/1985
    Doncaster Healthcare, 02/1960
    East Lancashire Hospitals, 02/1961
    Eastbourne and County, 02/1971, 1972
    Leicestershire and Rutland Healthcare, 02/1973
    Manchester Mental Health and Social Care Trust, 02/1963
    Mid Yorkshire Hospitals, 02/1986
    North and East Devon Partnership, 02/1974
    Pennine Acute Hospitals, 02/1987
    Sandwell and West Birmingham Hospitals, 02/1988
    Sheffield Children's Hospital, 02/1975
    South Buckinghamshire, 02/1964
    South Essex Mental Health and Community Care, 02/1976
    South of Tyne and Wearside Mental Health, 02/1989
    South Tees Acute Hospitals, 02/1965
    South West Yorkshire Mental Health, 02/1990
    Southampton East Healthcare, 02/1977
    Southern Derbyshire Mental Health, 02/1978
    Velindre
      Wales, 02/1966, 1967
    West Kent NHS and Social Care Trust, 02/1991
    West Sussex Health and Social Care, 02/1992
    Witham, Braintree and Halstead, 02/1968
    Worcestershire Community and Mental Health, 02/1979
  originating capital, 02/1993

NHS trusts -*cont.*
  transfer of assets -*cont.*
    West Yorkshire Health Authority, 02/2093
    Wiltshire and Swindon Health Care, 02/2094
    Worcestershire Health Authority, 02/2095
nobile officium
  abandoned appeal
    reinstatement
      alternative remedy, 02/5485S
  competency
    extension of time limit for leave to appeal, 02/5486S
noise. *See also* **abatement notices**
  noise pollution
    codes of practice for construction works
      Wales, 02/1508
    construction works
      codes of practice, 02/1507, 4948NI, 5593S
non domestic rates. *See also* **rates**
  calculation of contributions
    amendment of rules, 02/3789
      Wales, 02/3790
  rateable value
    electricity lands and generators
      variation, 02/6063S
  valuation list
    2003, 02/5091NI
non molestation orders
  breach
    appropriate sentence length, 02/1708
Northern Ireland
  modification, 02/4998NI
Northern Ireland Arms Decommissioning (Amendment) Act 2002 (c.6), 02/4883NI
Northern Ireland Criminal Injuries Compensation Scheme 2002
  Commencement No.1 Order, 02/5079NI
nuclear power
  prescribed substances
    Americium, 02/1450
nuisance. *See also* **abatement notices; noise**
  abatement
    tree felling
      duty to abate nuisance to neighbouring property, 02/3320
  books, 02/3325
  culpa
    persistent ingress of water allegedly affecting custom
    claim for economic loss, 02/6013S
  public nuisance
    obstruction of highway
      magistrate's discretion to make order, 02/3322
  statutory nuisance
    defective premises
      condensation dampness, 02/6014S
  trees
    objective test for statutory nuisance, 02/3324
nursery education. *See also* **education**
  early years
    development plan, 02/1083
  prescribed children, 02/5545S

nurses
  nursing agencies
    statement of purpose, 02/2096
occupational pensions. *See also* **pensions**
  addition of employment
    Invest Northern Ireland, 02/5073NI
  armed forces
    disablement or death in service, 02/3356
  bankruptcy, 02/3381, 5064NI
  benefits
    revaluation percentages
  contracting-out, 02/3359
  disclosure of information, 02/3361, 5058NI
  equal treatment
    widower's pension entitlement, 02/3363
  fund trustees
    allegations of maladministration
      validity of Ombudsman's directions, 02/3360
  guaranteed minimum pensions
    increase, 02/3364, 5059NI
  ill health
    rule governing retirement, 02/3365
  incapacity benefit
    entitlement
      medical evidence of extent of incapacity, 02/3366
  income tax
    payments to unpaid non executive director, 02/4430
  judiciary
    office holders, 02/3368
  local government pension scheme, 02/3369, 3370, 5060NI, 5061NI, 6017S
    discretionary payments, 02/1380
    fund management, 02/3371
    maternity leave, 02/5062NI
  Metropolitan Police Authority
    civil staff, 02/3372
  minimum funding requirement, 02/3373, 5063NI
  National Health Service
    additional voluntary contributions, 02/3374
    compensation
      premature retirement, 02/3375
    transfer of undertakings, 02/3376
  Parliament
    Members of Parliament, 02/3378, 3379
  pensionable age
    normal retirement date
      request for directions by scheme trustee, 02/3380
  police
    pension sharing on divorce, 02/3382
    unpaid leave
      maternity and sick leave, 02/5065NI, 5066NI
  revaluation of benefits, 02/5067NI
  sex discrimination
    compatibility with EC law, 02/3362
  surplus
    distribution
      entitlement of former members to participate, 02/3384
  teachers, 02/3385
  transfer of assets

occupational pensions -cont.
transfer of assets -cont.
trustee company's personal liability, 02/3386
trustees
compromise of statutory debt due from employer, 02/3388
duty to advise on alternative options, 02/3389
power to deal with disposable surplus, 02/3390
trustees and directors
appointments
alternative arrangements, 02/3387, 5068NI
warrant enforcement staff, 02/3391
winding up notices and reports, 02/3392, 5069NI
withdrawal of guaranteed annuity rates
interpretation of "increase in insurance", 02/3367
occupiers liability
duty of care
adequacy of warning signs in bowling alley, 02/4550
duty to fence reservoir, 02/6009S
slipping accident in supermarket, 02/4551
slipping accident on slippery stairway
sufficiency of averments, 02/6001S
tripping hazards
supermarkets, 02/4552
foreseeability
injuries sustained by falling against glass panel, 02/4548
landlord not in occupation
landlord's duty to tenant, 02/6010S
OFCOM
membership, 02/4535
off licences. See **licensing**
offences
Official Secrets Act
defence of disclosure in public interest, 02/814
sale of goods
offensive weapons, 02/810, 5454S
offences against the person. See also **assault; actual bodily harm; grievous bodily harm**
offensive weapons. See also **firearms**
sale or supply
criminal offence, 02/810, 5454S
Office of Communications Act 2002 (c.11), 02/1816
Commencement No.1 Order, 02/4536
Commencement No.2 Order, 02/4537
offshore installations
emergency pollution control, 02/1452
safety zones, 02/1453, 1454
oil
excise duty
hydrocarbon oil
registered dealers, 02/919
marine voyages relief, 02/4397
marking requirements
rebates and relief, 02/4398
marked oil
storage and labelling, 02/4398

oil and gas industry. See also **oil, oil pollution**
offshore installations, 02/2242
safety zones, 02/1453
oil pollution
compensation
acceptance of offer, 02/5417S
ombudsmen
Assembly Ombudsman
salaries, 02/4837NI
Commissioner for Complaints
salaries, 02/4837NI
investigation of complaints
Wales, 02/1817
investigations
removal from list
traffic commissioner, 02/5737S
public services
payment of expenses, 02/5736S
Open-Ended Investment Companies Act (Northern Ireland) 2002 (c.13), 02/4882NI
opticians
general opthalmic services
opthalmic list
Wales, 02/2105
General Optical Council
registration and enrolment
fees, 02/2103
optical appliances
vouchers, 02/2097, 2098, 2099, 5014NI, 5015NI, 5016NI, 5760S, 5761S, 5762S
Wales, 02/2100, 2101, 2102
origin marking
animal products
third country imports, 02/2973, 2974, 2975, 5259S, 5908S
Brazil, 02/1755
China, 02/2976
veterinary checks, 02/5040NI
Wales, 02/2977, 2978, 2979
origin of goods
petroleum products
revocation, 02/2980
Osteopaths Act 1993 (c.21)
Commencement No.7 Order, 02/2106
ownership
possession
presumption, 02/5998S
ozone depletion
controlled substances
unlawful imports, 02/1486
PACE codes of practice. See also **criminal evidence; police**
package holidays. See also **holidays**
absence of heated swimming pool
offer of unsuitable alternatives, 02/2321
misleading nature of brochure
loss of enjoyment, 02/2323
parental contact. See also **parental rights**
reports
application to test in court report findings, 02/1709
status of report, 02/5613S
parental leave
cut off date for entitlement

parental leave -*cont.*
cut off date for entitlement -*cont.*
implementation of Council Directive 96/34, 02/
1388
period leave, 02/4932NI
period of leave, 02/1381, 4933NI, 4934NI
parental responsibility
parental dispute as to child's schooling
scope of court's function to resolve dispute,
02/1710
parental rights
artificial insemination
application by donor father, 02/5640S
parking. *See also* **highway control**
parking adjudicators
appeals, 02/6137S
special parking areas
Basingstoke and Deane, 02/4589
Brentwood, 02/4590, 4591
Bury, 02/4592
Chelmsford, 02/4593
Colchester, 02/4594
designation
Edinburgh, 02/6138S
Glasgow, 02/6139S
Perth and Kinross, 02/6140S
East Dorset, 02/4595
Eden, 02/4596
Epping Forest, 02/4597
Harrogate, 02/4598
Hart, 02/4599
Liverpool, 02/4600
Milton Keynes, 02/4601
North Dorset, 02/4602
Norwich, 02/4603
Nottingham, 02/4604
Poole, 02/4605
Purbeck, 02/4606
Rushmoor, 02/4607
South Lakeland, 02/4608
Southampton, 02/4609
Sunderland, 02/4610
West Dorset, 02/4611
Weymouth and Portland, 02/4612
Worcester, 02/4613
traffic wardens
uniforms
Scotland, 02/6148S
Parliament
occupational pensions
Members of Parliament, 02/3378, 3379
Part 20 proceedings
entitlement to contribution
liability of parties for same damage, 02/469
Part 36 offers
claimant beating offer
offer made prior to issue of proceedings, 02/
351
conflicting evidence
withdrawal of pre-action offer after
acceptance, 02/470
indemnity costs
claimant's offer included term as to costs, 02/
352

partnerships
books, 02/3333
insolvency proceedings
entitlement to petition, 02/2702
voluntary arrangement procedures, 02/2703
limited liability partnerships
confidentiality orders, 02/3326, 3327
fees, 02/3328, 3329
forms, 02/3330
maximum size restrictions
removal, 02/3331
unrestricted size
exemptions
investment companies, 02/3332
passenger vehicles. *See also* **bus services;
railways; taxis**
accessibility requirements
disabled persons, 02/4614, 4615
conduct of drivers and conductors, 02/
4616
buses
guided busway
Chester, 02/4617
licensing
fees, 02/5202NI
local services
compulsory registration, 02/4619
fees, 02/4620
registration
fees, 02/6141S
public hire vehicles
conditions of fitness, 02/5204NI
roadworthiness
fees, 02/4621
tachographs
fees, 02/4618, 5203NI
taxis
licensing
fees, 02/5202NI
passing off. *See also* **trade marks; service
marks**
business names
music group called "Liberty"
sufficiency of reputation, 02/2780
significantly different activities
descriptive nature of name, 02/2781
domain names
expressed intention to continue use
order to transfer name appropriate, 02/
2782
good will
false product endorsement, 02/2783
personal bar
failure to assert rights in the past, 02/5901S
pressure groups
use of group name in local election
goodwill capable of protection, 02/2784
trade names
business selling similar goods
own name defence, 02/2785
passports
fees, 02/2631
patents. *See also* **European Patent**
amendments
delay

pensions -cont.
stakeholder pensions -cont.
annual declaration, 02/3403, 3404, 5071NI
trustees powers and duties, 02/5072NI
state pension credit
income, 02/4231
miscellaneous provisions, 02/4232
state retirement pension
legality
exclusion of non resident UK pensioner in
annual uprating, 02/3405
low earnings threshold, 02/4245, 5162NI
miscellaneous amendments, 02/3406
superannuation
additional voluntary contributions
Health and Personal Social Services, 02/
5074NI
consideration of superannuation fund as trust
scheme, 02/6019S
Health and Personal Social Services, 02/
5075NI
teachers
compensation for redundancy and retirement,
02/4936NI
war pensions
payments to civilians, 02/3408
Pensions Appeal Tribunals
judicial offices
Deputy President, 02/3397
performance bonds. *See also* **guarantees;
surety**
personal injuries. *See also* **damages; industrial
injuries; measure of damages**
books, 02/3634
contributory negligence
claimant's awareness of hazard, 02/3256
contribution to extent of injuries, 02/943
Court of Session
rules, 02/5214S
damages
rate of return, 02/5536S
disabled persons
residential care
recovery of costs by local authority, 02/
930
horse racing
jockeys
duty of care, 02/3281
immunisation
compensation for vaccine damage, 02/1867
leg
late tackle in football match
liability, 02/3280
limitations
date when pursuer aware injury was
"sufficiently serious", 02/5345S
identification of members of unincorporated
association, 02/5346S
subjective or objective factors determining
injuries, 02/5347S
measure of damages
provisional damages
risk of osteoarthritis shortening career as
miner, 02/5997S
mitigation

personal injuries -cont.
mitigation -cont.
decision to refuse medical treatment
burden of proving reasonableness, 02/944
negligent medical advice
causation, 02/3279
occupiers liability
standard of care required to prevent risk of
injury, 02/4553
tripping injury
flagstone, 02/3278
pensions
payments to civilians injured during war, 02/
3408
prescription
commencement date of prescriptive period,
02/6053S
statutory duty
extent of duty to maintain highway, 02/3314
tripping injury
local authority's negligent inspection, 02/
3256
personal property
books, 02/3635
**Personal Social Services (Preserved Rights)
Act (Northern Ireland) 2002 (c.5),** 02/5174NI
Commencement Order, 02/5175NI
pesticides
crops
maximum residue levels
EC limits, 02/154, 155, 4851NI, 4852NI,
4853NI, 5277S, 5278S
feeding stuffs
maximum residue levels
EC limits, 02/4851NI
food
maximum residue levels
EC limits, 02/154, 155, 4851NI, 4853NI,
5277S
maximum residue levels
azoxystrobin
Commission Directive 2002/100, 02/152
parallel imports
control arrangements by Pesticides
Directorate, 02/153
pharmaceutical industry
registration of premises
fees
increase, 02/2109
pharmacy
drugs and appliances
fees, 02/1904, 1905, 1906, 5011NI, 5750S
medical devices
registration
fees, 02/1889
medicines
drugs, 02/1908
general sale list
marketing authorisation, 02/1890
glucosamine sulphate products
Wales, 02/1913
nurse prescribers
drugs and appliances, 02/5012NI
restricted availability appliances, 02/5758S
prescription of drugs, 02/5007NI, 5753S

race discrimination -*cont.*
councillors
selection of candidates by labour party, 02/1395
mental patients
temporary contract workers
assessment of mental state, 02/1396
police officers
vicarious liability of chief constable, 02/1397
procedural impropriety
grounds for overturning tribunal decision, 02/1398
public authorities
statutory duties
code of practice, 02/2388
Race Equality Scheme, 02/5845S
refusal to provide reference for former employee
jurisdiction of employment tribunal, 02/1401
sex discrimination
lack of specific allegations, 02/1399
statutory duties
code of practice, 02/5846S
time limits
exhaustion of internal grievance procedure, 02/1400
race relations
statutory duties
code of practice, 02/5846S
radioactive substances
natural gas
exemptions, 02/1455
planning control
use classes
Wales, 02/3702
Railway Safety Act (Northern Ireland) Act 2002 (c.8), 02/5205NI
railways
accessibility
disabled persons, 02/4625, 4626
exemptions, 02/4627, 4628, 4629, 4630, 4631, 4632, 4633, 4634, 4635
Bitton
maintenance and operation, 02/4637
Channel Tunnel Rail Link
Thames Tunnel Approach, 02/4638
Heathrow Express
exemptions, 02/4639
interoperability
high speed, 02/4641
light railways
East Lancashire
Heywood extension, 02/4643
Greater Manchester
Trafford depot, 02/4644
Merseyrail Electrics
passenger services, 02/4624
Strand Road, Preston
transfer of ownership, 02/4646
Wear Valley
safety provisions, 02/4647
rape
actus reus
use of force, 02/5455S
aiding and abetting
victim five month old baby

rape -*cont.*
aiding and abetting -*cont.*
victim five month old baby -*cont.*
unduly lenient sentence, 02/4049
consent
use of force, 02/5455S
intoxicated persons
previous convictions for indecent assault
unduly lenient sentence, 02/4051
juvenile offenders
child victim, 02/4007
life imprisonment
exceptional circumstances, 02/4052
sentence length
rape of child by step father, 02/4050
repeated rape of estranged wife at knifepoint, 02/4053
sustained and sadistic attack on victim, 02/4054
two sisters aged 16 raped at knifepoint, 02/6083S
rates. *See also* **community charge; council tax**
determination of rateable value, 02/5090NI
non domestic rates
alteration of lists, 02/3787
Wales, 02/3788
annual value
office qualifying as hereditament, 02/3798
appeals, 02/3787
Wales, 02/3788
billing authorities, 02/3789
Wales, 02/3790
calculation of contributions, 02/3789
Wales, 02/3790
demand notices, 02/3786
electricity lands and generators
variation, 02/6063S
exemptions
detoxification and counselling clinic, 02/3791
flats
alteration of non domestic rating lists, 02/3792
local authorities
application for single liability order, 02/3796
rate for 2002/03, 02/6061S, 6062S
rateable value
water undertakings, 02/6064S
rural rate relief
Wales, 02/3210
sports facilities
local authority leisure centres, 02/3799
surrender of lease
validity of magistrates reasoning, 02/3795
valuation
exemptions, 02/6065S
valuation date
Wales, 02/3800
rateable value
golf course site under construction, 02/3793
receivers
liability for non domestic rates of company premises, 02/3797
valuation

rates -*cont.*
  valuation -*cont.*
    holiday cottages
      evidence of value, 02/3794
    shops
      allowance for cost of repair, 02/5089NI
  valuation list
    2003, 02/5091NI
  valuation officers
    retrospective alteration
      duty to maintain accurate list, 02/3801
real property. *See also* **landlord and tenant; easements; land registration; sale of land**
  adverse possession
    effect of loss of possession on human rights, 02/3803
    establishing squatter's intention to possess, 02/3805
    meaning of possession, 02/3805
    squatting
      acknowledgement of title, 02/3804
  books, 02/3859
  conveyancing
    completion
      validity of notice requiring completion, 02/3812
  easements
    dedication of land as public highway
      evidence of unrestricted public use, 02/3822
    prescription
      right to park, 02/3819
    use of land as communal garden
      scope of rights created by easement, 02/3817
    use of right of way to access parking space, 02/3820
  equitable interests
    payment of mortgage instalments
      extent of beneficial interest, 02/3823
  freeholds
    industrial units
      rent charge payable, 02/3846
  interest
    request for vendor to deduce title, 02/3813
  land charges
    failure to register
      proprietary interest of mortgagee in proceeds of sale, 02/3837
  leases
    assignment
      standard conditions of sale, 02/3045
  local land charges
    non registration
      assessment of compensation, 02/3833
  negative equity
    home improvements
      claim for refund of monies spent, 02/3845
  overriding interests
    proprietary estoppel
      rights accruing to managing director of company in occupation, 02/3843
  restrictive covenants
    planning permission
      houses, 02/3847

real property -*cont.*
  restrictive covenants -*cont.*
    residential developments
      discharge and modification of restrictive covenants, 02/3849
      use restricted to "single private dwelling", 02/3848
  rights of way
    access to petrol station
      commercial efficacy, 02/3821
    acquiescence
      lost modern grant, 02/3852
    bridleways
      burden of rebutting statutory presumption, 02/3850
  sale of land
    conditions of sale
      validity of notice to complete, 02/3811
    Land Charges Register
      effect of retrospective rectification, 02/3844
    tenant's option to purchase property
      valuation criteria, 02/4322
  searches
    error in certificate of official search of index map
      liability of Land Registrar, 02/3814
  tenancies in common
    availability of estoppel
      requirement for reliance, 02/3857
  treasure
    designation, 02/3858
recreational services
  sports grounds
    designation for criminal law purposes, 02/6119S
recruitment
  police officers, 02/4935NI
redundancy
  consultation
    duty to consult employee representative in good time, 02/1402
  continuity of employment
    pre arranged childcare break, 02/1404
  part time employment
    teachers
      consultation procedure, 02/1405
  redundancy payments
    continuity of employment in local government, 02/1406
refugees. *See* **asylum**
registration
  births, deaths and marriages
    armed forces
      corrections to register, 02/58
    service departments
      procedure for corrections, 02/58
Regulation of Care (Scotland) Act 2001 (asp 8)
  Commencement No.2 and Transitional Provisions Order, 02/6114S
Regulation of Investigatory Powers
  public authorities, 02/5026NI

reinsurance. *See* **insurance**

remuneration. *See also* **equal pay**
teachers, 02/1192
wages
minimum wage
increase, 02/1385

rent. *See also* **service charges**
registered rents
increase, 02/5043NI
rent review
time limits
meaning of rent review clause, 02/3063
rent reviews
student accommodation
construction of clause, 02/5928S
time limits
meaning of rent review clause, 02/3064
underleases
interpretation of terms, 02/3065
scope of principle of retention
relevant defence, 02/5929S

reparation (Scotland)
books, 02/6068S

repossession
rent arrears
part payment of arrears, 02/5824S

residence orders
appropriateness
shared residence with "care and control", 02/1663
children
intimation to child previously dispensed with
effect of lapse of time, 02/5617S
expert evidence
father's emotional instability
validity of judge's rejection of uncontested evidence, 02/1662
varying contact arrangements
welfare of child, 02/1664

residential accommodation
family centres
care standards, 02/4284
remission of charges
capital limits, 02/5002NI

residential care
care homes and nursing homes
Wales, 02/4291
transfer of assets
independence of review panel, 02/4294

residential tenancies
forms, 02/3068

residential tenancies. *See* **assured tenancies**

restitution
books, 02/3860

restraint orders
receivers
remuneration from assets, 02/907
without notice applications
relevant criteria, 02/906

restrictive trade practices. *See also* **restraint of trade**
broadcasting
agreement between French TV companies, 02/607

right to buy
application forms, 02/5835S
approved lending institutions
Wales, 02/2359
green belt
discretion to consider broad planning considerations, 02/3074
houses liable to demolition
information requirements, 02/5808S
qualifying occupation
effect of interruption, 02/5839S
rate of discount, 02/2360
rural areas
Ribble Valley, 02/2361

right to effective remedy
sexual abuse claim
lack of redress in domestic court, 02/2391
torture
failure to conduct proper investigation
denial of effective remedy, 02/2392

right to fair trial
access to justice
confiscation of personal property and passport, 02/2393
court fees
excessive level of impeding access to court, 02/2394
intervention in criminal appeal by Supreme Court judge, 02/2395
limitations
statutory provision requiring written notice, 02/2397
sex discrimination claim against US Embassy
state immunity, 02/2398
treaty restricting jurisdiction of German Courts
compatibility with ECHR, 02/2396
acquiescence
hearing by independent and impartial tribunal, 02/5493S
ambassador accused of irregularities
delay
absence of public hearing, 02/2418
annulment
Vatican court
decision annulling marriage confirmed by secular court, 02/2436
appeals
appeal against conviction
right to independent tribunal, 02/2399
refusal of legal aid
compatibility with ECHR, 02/2406
removal of appeal from list
compatibility with ECHR, 02/2403
requirement to make payment into court, 02/2407
application for leave
sheriffs
independence and impartiality, 02/5237S
bankruptcy proceedings
impartiality and equality of arms, 02/2408
bias
independence of court martial, 02/2411
investigating judge sitting as judge at first instance
compatibility with ECHR, 02/2410

robbery -cont.

pleas

discounts granted to defendants pleading guilty, 02/4068

sentence length

theft of mobile phone

possession of imitation firearm and issue of threats to kill, 02/4057

wounding with intent

victims attacked in own homes, 02/4084

threatening to kill

use of loose blade

unduly lenient sentence, 02/4069

Romania

films

cinematic co-production agreements, 02/232

rural areas

countryside access

appeals procedures

Wales, 02/3853

local access forums, 02/3854

maps, 02/3855

Wales, 02/1509

less favoured areas

compensatory allowances, 02/4866NI

safety at sea

diving safety

duty of care, 02/4129

miscellaneous amendments, 02/4130

seamen

medical fitness certificates, 02/4131

sale of goods

books, 02/3862

defective goods

fitness for purpose

recovery of cost for recalling product, 02/513

hire purchase and conditional sale agreements

VAT

margin scheme, 02/4778

mail order

consideration

contribution to postal charge for delivery by third party, 02/4785

unfair terms

guarantees, 02/696

sale of land

completion

conditions of sale

validity of notice to complete, 02/3811

rectification

transfer failing to reserve rights in flats to vendor, 02/3856

sanctions

British overseas territories

Zimbabwe

restrictive measures, 02/2987

scallops

several fishery rights

Little Loch Broom, 02/5652S

Loch Ewe, Isle of Ewe, Wester Ross, 02/5653S

School Education (Amendment) (Scotland) Act 2002

Commencement Order

School Education (Amendment) (Scotland) Act 2002 -cont.

Commencement Order -cont.

Scotland, 02/5547S

schools. *See also* **education; middle schools; special educational needs; students; teachers**

aided places scheme

St Mary's Music School, 02/5548S

appeals

pupils

school exclusions, 02/1135

assessment

special educational needs

Wales, 02/1157

assisted places

incidental expenses

Wales, 02/1051

assisted places scheme

grants

incidental expenses, 02/1050

qualifying income limits, 02/1052

remission of fees, 02/5542S

boarding schools

annual fees

Wales, 02/980

closure

lawfulness of challenge by child rather than parent, 02/1119

disability discrimination

special educational needs

tribunal procedures, 02/985

disabled persons

accessibility plans, 02/987

duty of care

bullying outside school

scope of duty, 02/1120

Education Act 2002

modification of provisions, 02/1121, 1122

Wales, 02/1155

education action zones

extension and variation

Dudley Partnership for Achievement, 02/1020

East Manchester, 02/1021

Greenwich, 02/1022

Hackney, 02/1023

Hastings and St Leonards, 02/1024

Heart of Slough, 02/1025

New Horizons Kent-Somerset Virtual, 02/1026

North East Derbyshire Coalfields, 02/1027

Oxfordshire, 02/1028

Southend, 02/1029

Telford and Wrekin, 02/1030

Wednesbury, 02/1031

Widening Horizons-North Islington, 02/1032

Wythenshawe, 02/1033

education standards

improvement plans, 02/1086

educational achievements

information

Wales, 02/1087

governors reports

social security -*cont.*
  benefits -*cont.*
    miscellaneous amendments, 02/4159, 4160, 4161, 5123NI, 5124NI
    New Deal Scheme
      employment option, 02/4148, 5112NI
    paternity and adoption
      entitlement, 02/4162, 4912NI
    paternity leave
      computation of earnings, 02/4163, 5104NI
    re rating, 02/4221
    statutory maternity pay, 02/4164, 5125NI, 5126NI
    statutory sick pay, 02/4164, 5125NI, 5126NI
    up rating, 02/4165, 5127NI
      child dependency, 02/4166
    work focused interviews, 02/4167
      lone parents, 02/4168, 5128NI
  books, 02/4256
  carers
    invalid care allowance
      meaning of "severely disabled person", 02/4214
  carers allowance, 02/4169
    disabled people, 02/4170
  child benefit
    discrimination
      sharing of benefit between separated parents, 02/4173
    electronic communications, 02/4172
  contributions
    Class 1 contributions
      business travel, 02/4176
    earnings period, 02/4177
    employers, 02/4178
    intermediaries, 02/4179
      Northern Ireland, 02/5134NI
    payments to be disregarded
      non cash vouchers, 02/4180
    statutory maternity pay, 02/4181
    statutory sick pay, 02/4181
    teachers
      student loans, 02/4180
  council tax benefit
    water and sewerage charges
      reduction, 02/6168S
  decisions and appeals
    miscellaneous amendments, 02/5129NI
  disability living allowance
    mental disability
      conditions of entitlement, 02/4183, 5136NI
  disabled persons tax credit
    claims and payments, 02/4487, 5187NI
    miscellaneous amendments, 02/4250
  earnings factors
    calculation of additional pension, 02/4184, 5149NI
  employment programmes
    New Deal Scheme
      employment option, 02/4148, 5112NI
  energy conservation
    grants, 02/1470, 4938NI
  fraud
    request for information
      specified organisations, 02/4187, 5137NI

social security -*cont.*
  funeral payments
    entitlement, 02/4235, 5151NI
  guardians allowance
    custodial sentences, 02/4188, 5138NI
  housing benefit
    local authorities powers and duties
      criteria relevant to restriction of benefit, 02/4194
    tenancies
      referrals, 02/4196
    tenancy
      size of dwelling, 02/5139NI
  incapacity
    entitlement, 02/4200
  incapacity benefit
    allowances, 02/4198, 5140NI, 5141NI
    discriminatory effect of age differential, 02/4202
    entitlement
      statutorily prescribed procedure, 02/4201
  income
    capital
      assessment, 02/4203
    residential accommodation
      assessment of resources, 02/4205
  income and capital
    assessment
      Wales, 02/4204
  income related benefits
    students, 02/4247, 4248, 5163NI, 5164NI
    subsidy to authorities, 02/4206, 4207
  income related benefits benefits
    contracting out
      local authorities, 02/3143
  income support
    loans
      interest rate, 02/4210, 5144NI, 5145NI
    meaning of "habitual residence", 02/4208
  industrial diseases
    entitlement to benefits, 02/4153, 5117NI
    workers compensation, 02/5023NI
  industrial injuries
    dependants
      permitted earnings limits, 02/4213, 5147NI
    incapacity allowance
      compensation, 02/4212, 5146NI
  invalid care allowance, 02/4169
    carer premium
      entitlement, 02/5120NI
  migrant workers
    eligibility for occupational disability pension, 02/4199
  national insurance
    compulsory insurance schemes
      definition of concept of undertaking, 02/4220
    contributions
      re rating, 02/4221
  national insurance contributions
    agency workers
      meaning of "arrangements involving an intermediary", 02/4227
    earning limits and threshold, 02/4222
    school fees

social security -cont.
  national insurance contributions -cont.
    school fees -cont.
      payment by company for director's children, 02/4229
    self employment in different Member States
      effect on social security, 02/4225
  old age insurance
    calculation, 02/4244
  pensions
    low earnings threshold, 02/4245, 5162NI
    state pension credit
      income, 02/4231
      miscellaneous provisions, 02/4232
  reciprocal arrangements, 02/5130NI, 5131NI
  reduction in income support entitlement, 02/5154NI
  social fund
    cold weather payments
      weather stations, 02/5150NI
      weather stations and postcode districts, 02/4234
    crisis loans
      applications, 02/4235, 5151NI
  Social Security Commissioners
    tax credits
      appeals, 02/4237
  stateless persons
    right to benefits while resident in Member State, 02/4171
  statutory adoption pay
    electronic communications, 02/4185
  statutory maternity pay
    compensation of employers
      reduction, 02/4246
    electronic communications, 02/4185
  statutory paternity pay
    electronic communications, 02/4185
  tax credits
    appeals, 02/4481
    disabled persons tax credit, 02/4249, 4484, 4485, 4486, 5185NI, 5186NI
      decisions and appeals, 02/5184NI
    employers
      payments, 02/4493
    Inland Revenue Board
      payments, 02/4491
    up rating, 02/4489
    working families tax credit, 02/4249, 4484, 4485, 4486, 5185NI, 5186NI
      decisions and appeals, 02/5184NI
  widows benefits
    settlement between widower and UK government, 02/4254
  working families tax credit
    claims and payments, 02/4487, 5187NI
    miscellaneous amendments, 02/4250
Social Security Act (Northern Ireland) 2002 (c.10), 02/5159NI
  Commencement No.1 Order, 02/5152NI
  Commencement No.2 and Transitional and Saving Provisions Order, 02/5153NI
Social Security Fraud Act 2001 (c.11)
  Commencement No.3 Order, 02/4238
  Commencement No.4 Order, 02/4239

Social Security Fraud Act 2001 (c.11) -cont.
  Commencement No.5 Order, 02/4240
Social Security Fraud Act (Northern Ireland) 2001 (c.17)
  Commencement No.2 Order, 02/5155NI
  Commencement No.3 Order, 02/5156NI
  Commencement No.4 Order, 02/5157NI
  Commencement No.5 Order, 02/5158NI
Social Security Tribunals
  judicial review
    material error of fact
      inevitability of result, 02/5244S
social services
  community care
    accommodation, 02/6117S
  health and welfare
    VAT, 02/4781
  personal social services
    preserved rights, 02/5176NI
  Social Care Council
    appointments and procedure, 02/5177NI
  Social Services Council
    appointments, procedure and access to the register, 02/6118S
social welfare
  books, 02/4298, 5178NI
  care
    child protection
      Wales, 02/4258
  care plans
    child with mixed religious and cultural heritage
      suitability of placement with Jewish adopters, 02/1607
    local authorities
      proposal to send child to residential school 350 miles from mother, 02/4263
  care standards
    establishments and agencies
      miscellaneous amendments, 02/4262
    social welfare
      Wales, 02/4264
  children
    care
      accommodation, 02/4276
  children in care
    accommodation
      Wales, 02/1649, 4277
  community care
    additional payments, 02/6107S
    assessment of needs
      relevant person, 02/6108S
    deferred payment of accommodation costs, 02/6109S
    disregard of resources, 02/6110S
    personal care and nursing care, 02/6111S
  Community Care and Health (Scotland) Act 2002
    consequential amendment, 02/5763S
  day care
    registration fees
      Wales, 02/4260
  disciplinary procedures
    social workers
      alleged breach of duty of care, 02/4297
  domiciliary care agencies

social welfare -cont.
  domiciliary care agencies -cont.
    quality of services, 02/4279
  food
    milk, 02/4285, 5171NI
  health care
    private health care
      Wales, 02/4286
    voluntary health care
      Wales, 02/4286
  invalid care allowance
    entitlement when in full time education, 02/4215
  local authorities
    transfer of staff
      consultation, 02/6113S
  mental patients
    local authority's failure to provide suitable accommodation, 02/4257
  National Care Standards Commission
    children's rights director, 02/1692
    director of private and voluntary health care, 02/1846
    fees and frequency of inspections
      registration, 02/4280
    inspection of schools and colleges, 02/4281
    registration fees, 02/4282, 4283
    residential family centres
      registration and inspection, 02/4284
  personal social services
    preserved rights, 02/5176NI
  regulation of care
    applications and provision of advice, 02/6100S
    care service requirements, 02/6102S
    excepted services, 02/6103S
    fees, 02/6104S
    local authorities and health boards, 02/6113S
    registration and registers, 02/6105S
  residential accommodation
    community financial assistance
      need caused by destitution, 02/4287
    remission of charges
      capital limits, 02/5002NI
    sums for personal requirements, 02/4233, 6115S
    Wales, 02/4290
  residential care
    care homes and nursing homes
      Wales, 02/4291
    closure of home for elderly persons
      relevant considerations, 02/4293
    provision of accommodation by voluntary sector
      performance of public function, 02/4292
    public funding
      assessment of needs, 02/6116S
  social and health care
    registration
      Wales, 02/4261
  social services
    community care
      accommodation, 02/6117S
  social work
    education and training

social welfare -cont.
  social work -cont.
    education and training -cont.
      abolition of Central Council, 02/4295
  social workers
    investigation procedure regarding sexual abuse allegations
      appropriate forum for appeal, 02/4296
solicitors. See also professional negligence
  breach of trust
    dishonesty by failing to act, 02/249
    personal liability
      misapplication of loan monies, 02/249
  confidential information
    privilege
      solicitor previously acting for defendants' group of companies, 02/3111
  conflict of interest
    previous role in proceedings
      disclosure of confidential material, 02/3108
  contempt of court
    duty to arrange counsel in criminal trial, 02/5210S
  costs
    assessment of bills submitted by solicitor, 02/3109
  disciplinary procedures
    delay, 02/5953S
  disciplinary proceedings
    criminal conviction
      review of trial, 02/5955S
    statutory demands
      alleged negligence on part of investigating accountant, 02/3107
  discipline tribunal
    privilege, 02/5328S
  duty to client
    duty to inform of court order, 02/5915S
  fees
    adequacy of information provided to client in bill, 02/3110
    Court of Session, 02/5216S
    sheriff courts, 02/5225S, 5226S, 5227S
    Law Society's intervention powers
      recovery of outstanding fees, 02/3104
  mortgage fraud
    claim for indemnity against Solicitors Indemnity Fund, 02/3113
  practising certificates
    fees, 02/3106
  professional misconduct
    penalties
      applicable test for court on appeal, 02/5954S
  professional negligence
    failure to raise action, 02/6012S
  retainers
    solicitor continuing to act for company after death of sole director, 02/3112
  Solicitors Disciplinary Tribunal
    appropriate respondent to appeal against Tribunal's finding, 02/3115
  undertakings
    change of circumstances
      enforcement of undertaking, 02/3114

torts -*cont.*
  conversion -*cont.*
    Iraq
      wrongful interference with aircraft, 02/4540
  deceit
    fraudulent misrepresentation
      contributory negligence not available as defence to action in deceit, 02/4541
  false imprisonment
    erroneous warrant
      liability of prison governors and Registrar, 02/4543
  joint tortfeasors
    directors liabilities
      procuring copyright infringements pursuant to common design, 02/4544
  misfeasance in public office
    abuse of position as public officer
      exploration of facts, 02/4547
    personal injury claim
      locus standi of victims, 02/4546
  negligent misstatement
    occupational pensions
      damages for negligent misstatement on benefits, 02/1432
  product contamination
    damage during manufacturing process
      limit of liability, 02/695
  Rylands v Fletcher liability
    proprietary interest required, 02/3323
  tortious liability
    personal liability for negligent misstatement, 02/4542
trade marks. *See also* **passing off; service marks; trade names**
  appeals
    correct approach
      test for admission of new evidence, 02/2859
    opposition to registration
      admission of fresh evidence, 02/2860
  classification
    request to transfer application to different class
      extent to which amendment permitted, 02/2862
  community trade mark
    registration
      jurisdiction to consider validity of opponent's mark, 02/2863
  Community trade marks
    applications
      amendment to correct typographical error, 02/2864
      language requirement discriminatory, 02/2865
    distinctiveness
      colour combination trade marks, 02/2875
      internet advertising services, 02/2876
      registration of three dimensional mark, 02/2888
      registration of word mark "IDEAL" for rubber stamps, 02/2882
      rugby jersey with rose design, 02/2886

trade marks -*cont.*
  Community trade marks -*cont.*
    distinctiveness -*cont.*
      three dimensional dishwasher tablet, 02/2887
      three dimensional shape in respect of torches, 02/2879
    evidence of prior use
      declaration of invalidity, 02/2892
    marks for data transmission services
      likelihood of confusion, 02/2894
    medicines
      effect of marketing authorisation on repackaging, 02/2890
    minor departure from word "GLASS"
      likelihood of confusion, 02/2869
    passing off
      application to strike out claim, 02/2891
    procedural impropriety
      declaration of invalidity, 02/2889
    registration
      distinctiveness of mark for clothing, 02/2877
      distinctiveness of three dimensional mark, 02/2878
      evidence and burden of proof in invalidity proceedings, 02/2893
    registration of "DLC" as trade mark for razors
      likelihood of confusion, 02/2881
    registration of mark "TED BAKER"
      likelihood of confusion, 02/2866
    registration of three dimensional mark
      likelihood of confusion, 02/2883
    registration of toy dolls
      assessment of distinctiveness, 02/2880
    registration of word "LIFESOURCE"
      likelihood of confusion, 02/2870
    registration of word "PRIVATE" likelihood of confusion, 02/2884
    registration of word "SAVOY"
      likelihood of confusion, 02/2871
    registration of word mark "BUY.COM"
      likelihood of confusion, 02/2873
    registration of word mark "FOX"
      likelihood of confusion, 02/2868
    registration of word mark "Hollywood"
      likelihood of confusion, 02/2872
    registration of words "Canaletto Cassa Girelli"
      likelihood of confusion, 02/2867
    registration of words "TINY PENIS"
      morality as mark for clothing, 02/2920
    revocation for lack of distinctiveness, 02/2885
    word mark "Pebble Beach"
      likelihood of confusion, 02/5903S
  comparative advertising
    use of distinguishing marks in catalogue by competitor supplier, 02/2895
  Comptroller of Patents Designs and Trade Marks
    Jurisdiction to grant summary judgment, 02/2787
    power to decide on revocation, 02/2850
  distinctiveness
    detergent in tablet form
      likelihood of confusion, 02/2900

transport -cont.
  bus services -cont.
    bus service operators
        grants, 02/4558, 6127S
      fares
        travel concessions, 02/4560, 6128S
      travel concessions
        Wales, 02/4561
    buses
      community bus permit
        fees, 02/4562
      permits
        fees, 02/4563
    carriage by road
      dangerous goods
        radioactive material, 02/4565
    disabled persons
      Mobility and Access Committee
        establishment, 02/6130S
    driving licences
      designation
        Guernsey, 02/4567
      exchangeable licences
        Kenya, 02/4568, 5190NI
        Korea, 02/4569
        Monaco, 02/4569
    international carriage by air
      aviation safety
        Montreal Convention 1999, 02/245
    motor vehicles
      authorised weight vehicles, 02/5194NI
    passenger vehicles
      buses
        guided busway, 02/4617
    railway passenger services
      Merseyrail Electrics, 02/4624
    railways
      Heathrow Express Railway
        extension, 02/4640
      light railways
        Docklands Light Railway, 02/4642
      London Underground
        Piccadilly Line, 02/4645
    road user charging
      charges
        enforcement, 02/2267
    Scottish Transport Group
      dissolution, 02/6134S
    transport policy
      quality partnership schemes
        Wales, 02/4657
Transport Act 2000 (c.38)
  Commencement No.2 Order
    Wales, 02/4653
  Commencement No.8 and Transitional Provisions
    Order
      amendment, 02/4654
  Commencement No.8 Order, 02/4655
  Commencement No.9 and Transitional Provisions
    Order
      England, 02/4656
transport tribunal
  registrar of approved driving instructors
    appeals, 02/42

Transport (Scotland) Act 2001 (asp 2)
  Commencement No.3 and Transitional Provisions
    Order, 02/6149S
Travel Concessions (Eligibility) Act 2002 (c.4),
  02/4658
  Commencement Order
    England, 02/4659
    Wales, 02/4660
travellers. See gypsies
treasure
  designation, 02/3858
treaties
  European Union
    Macedonia, 02/2958
    South Africa, 02/2959
trees. See also forests
  infectious disease control
    treatment of spruce bark, 02/1801
trespass. See also adverse possession;
  possession of land
trials. See also criminal procedure; hearings;
  juries; jury trials; mode of trial; witnesses
  attendance
    meaning of "good reason" for failure to attend
      trial, 02/480
  delay
    compatibility with ECHR, 02/5514S, 5517S
    criminal appeals
      remedies, 02/5515S
    devolution issues
      lack of police resources, 02/5494S
    period between charge and trials
      compatibility with ECHR, 02/5516S
    summary complaint changed to petition
      18 months not unreasonable, 02/5495S
    trial not brought within reasonable time
      proper remedy, 02/5488S
  desertion
    evidence allegedly tainted, 02/5518S
  excessive interruptions by judge
    fairness of trial, 02/2415
  fairness
    comment for co-accused on accused's silence
      at judicial examination and trial, 02/5513S
  interviews
    justification
      placing before jury co accused taped
        interview, 02/5519S
  judges
    judicial examination
      comments on failure to state defence, 02/
        5523S
    misdirection
      evidence relating to charges withdrawn,
        02/5520S
      hearsay evidence wrongly admitted, 02/
        5522S
      reference to evidence led, 02/5521S
      unnecessary elaboration of verdicts, 02/
        5524S
  jury trial
    awards
      compatibility with ECHR, 02/5343S
  legal representation
    right of audience

trusts -cont.

resulting trusts

joint mortgagees

no contribution to purchase price of property, 02/4691

property transferred by father to children

rebuttal presumption of advancement, 02/4690

settlements

validity of settlement created under Jersey law, 02/4692

trust funds

appointment of receiver to protect trust property, 02/4698

bankrupts

beneficial interest in retirement plan, 02/4696

trustee seeking directions from court

relevant considerations, 02/4709

trustees

bank acting as trustee and banker

extent of fiduciary duty, 02/4712

beneficiaries' informed consent to variation of trust

equitable jurisdiction to set aside, 02/4713

breach of trust

delay in prosecution of action, 02/4699

payments made by trustees out of deceased estates, 02/4667

conflict of interest

appointing spouse as beneficiary and trustee, 02/4707

indemnity

fraudulent transfer of assets, 02/4700

indemnity costs orders

indemnification from trust funds, 02/4702, 4703

insolvency of beneficiaries

indemnity, 02/4701

occupational pensions

power to distribute demutualisation windfall to members, 02/4711

requirements for valid trust of personalty, 02/4705

trustees powers and duties

exercise of discretionary powers, 02/4708

trusts of land

rights of reverter, 02/4333

variation

tax planning purposes

Jersey, 02/4694

variation of trusts

proposed variation to avoid capital gains tax on settlors, 02/4663

Turkey

compensation proceedings

statutory interest for delay, 02/2371

Turks and Caicos Islands

constitution, 02/651

underwriting. See insurance

undue influence

guarantees

creditor's duties, 02/5794S

unemployment benefit. See jobseekers allowance

unfair dismissal

compensation

calculation of loss of earnings

impact of statutory minimum wage, 02/1438

offer of reemployment

mitigation of loss, 02/1442

disability discrimination

inferences drawn from findings of fact, 02/1332

disclosure

public interest

disclosure made prior to commencement of statutory protection, 02/5578S

dismissal by receivers

economic and organisational reason for dismissal, 02/1437

gross misconduct

application of range of reasonable responses test, 02/1440

employee accessing pornography from office computer

range of reasonable responses, 02/1441

redundancy

calculation of compensatory award, 02/1403

trust and confidence

breach of implied terms of trust, 02/1313

whistleblowers

protected disclosures

jurisdiction of tribunal, 02/1443

unincorporated associations. See also clubs; building societies; credit unions; friendly societies; industrial and provident societies

duty of care

liability for historic acts, 02/5360S

United Nations

immunities and privileges

International Court of Justice, 02/2960

International Labour Organization, 02/2961

sanctions

Somalia, 02/2962

Channel Islands, 02/2963

Isle of Man, 02/2964

overseas territories, 02/2965

United States

choice of forum

jurisdiction clauses

motion for reconsideration, 02/4102, 4103

University of St. Andrews (Postgraduate Medical Degrees) Act 2002 (asp 15), 02/5558S

unjustified enrichment

actio de in rem verso, 02/6152S

occupancy of land

mistake in standard security, 02/6152S

pleadings

relevancy, 02/6152S

recompence

occupancy of heritable property

standard security unenforceable by virtue of mistake, 02/6152S

repetition

assignation of claim

unjustified enrichment -*cont.*
  repetition -*cont.*
    assignation of claim -*cont.*
      prior settlement, 02/6153S
utilities. *See also* **electricity industry; gas industry; water industry; water supply**
  electricity and gas supply industries
    determination of turnover for penalties, 02/4716
  electricity supply industry
    connection charges, 02/1446, 4715
    fossil fuel levy, 02/6156S
    renewables obligation, 02/4718, 6157S
    standards of performance, 02/4720, 4721
  gas supply industry
    recovery of expenses
      time extension, 02/4722
    standards of performance, 02/4723, 4724
  New Water and Sewerage Authorities
    dissolution, 02/6154S
  sewers and drains
    water supply
      conversion and change of use of connected premises, 02/4729
VAT. *See also* **VAT and duties tribunals**
  acquisitions
    imported goods, 02/4731
  air transport
    zero rating, 02/4810
  amendment, 02/4796
  assessment
    best judgment challenge
      requirement for material inaccuracy, 02/4732
    cheque exchanged for gambling chips
      duty payable, 02/4759
    recovery of undeclared tax, 02/4761
    restricted access to court
      compatibility with South Africa's constitution, 02/4735
    retail schemes
      zero rated stock sold below expected price, 02/4734
  assets
    allocation of business assets for private use
      liability under Sixth Council Directive 77/388, 02/4736
  bad debt relief
    input tax, 02/4797
  books, 02/4817
  car sales
    hire purchase and conditional sale agreements, 02/4779
  carriage by ship
    zero rating, 02/4810
  consideration
    motor dealers
      discount scheme by motor dealer on part exchanges, 02/4733
  exempt supply
    assignment of lease
      consideration paid to assignee, 02/4749
  exemptions
    affinity credit cards

VAT -*cont.*
  exemptions -*cont.*
    affinity credit cards -*cont.*
      agreement between professional institute and card issuer, 02/4743
    banks
      issue of banknotes to other banks' customers through ATM, 02/6165S
    credit card schemes
      commissions payable by bank to subsidiary regarding use of credit card, 02/4744
    educational institutions
      profit making body supplying higher education services, 02/4740
    general practitioners
      supply of pharmaceutical services to patients unable to access pharmacist, 02/4745
    holding companies
      supply of auditing, legal and tax services, 02/4746
    information provided on behalf of financial institution
      applicability of Council Directive, 02/4755
    insurance companies
      pension misselling review conducted by insurance agent, 02/4748
    meaning of "non profit making organisations" within Council Directive 77/388, 02/4756
    non provision for international coach travel
      equal treatment, 02/4742
    opticians
      supply of services, 02/4750
    partners
      transaction between partner and partnership, 02/4752
    provision and maintenance of cemeteries by local authority, 02/4739
    residential care
      homes operated on profit making basis, 02/4753
    residential tenancies
      national law imposing VAT on all leaseholds with exemption for residential property, 02/4754
    Students' Union as integral part of university, 02/4741
    supply of services
      meaning of "aims of a civic nature", 02/4757
    used car imported from Cyprus
      liability to import tax, 02/4747
    voluntary organisations
      meaning of "body administered on an essentially voluntary basis", 02/4758
  fuel
    private use
      rates, 02/4800
  grants
    improvements to private sector housing
      refund of tax, 02/4774
  heating systems
    reduced rate, 02/4801
  input tax
    acquisition of high value cars for business use

Welfare Reform and Pensions Act 1999 (c.30)
  Commencement No.13 Order, 02/4251
  Commencement No.14 Order, 02/4252
  Commencement No.15 Order, 02/4253
Welfare Reform and Pensions (Northern Ireland) Order 1 (SI 1 3147 NI.11))
  Commencement No.11 Order, 02/5166NI
  Commencement No.10 Order, 02/5167NI
  Commencement No.12 Order, 02/5168NI
Welsh language
  forms
    attestation of constables, 02/3778
wills. *See also* **gifts; inheritance tax; succession; trusts**
  beneficiaries
    intention
      grandson as beneficiary under grandfather's will, 02/4335
    representation orders
      approval of compromise settlement between beneficiaries, 02/4336
  capacity
    elderly testatrix
      lack of requisite knowledge and approval, 02/4328
    relationship between elderly employer and housekeeper
      presumption of undue influence, 02/4330
  entail
    codicils
      date of execution, 02/6121S
  intention
    executors
      burden of dispelling suspicion, 02/4338
  mistake
    husband executing wife's will
      rectification, 02/4341
  mutual wills
    ability of survivor to deal with capital of estate, 02/4321
    subsequent change to disposition by survivor
      burden of proof, 02/4320
  probate
    proceedings for revocation of grant, 02/4340
    validity of revocation clause, 02/4326
  wife predeceasing testator
    meaning of "demise together with me", 02/4339
winding up. *See also* **corporate insolvency; insolvency**
  administration orders
    company voluntary arrangements
      opposition of creditors, 02/2716
  appointment of liquidators
    dispute as to extent of debt, 02/5894S
  creditors
    proof of debt
      right of creditor to challenge, 02/2717
  disputed debts
    petitioner having different legal personality than party to agreement, 02/2724

winding up *-cont.*
  expenses
    corporation tax
      post liquidation profits, 02/2718
  liquidators
    examination of officers of company
      court's discretion to order examination, 02/2693
  petitions
    application to restrain petition on basis of cross claim, 02/2720, 2721
  cross claims
    dismissal of petition, 02/2723
    reasonableness, 02/2722
  property transfer
    chargee's application for validation, 02/2726
  public interest
    improper conduct of business
      grounds for winding up, 02/2725
  unfair preferences
    form of remedy, 02/5891S
witnesses. *See also* **criminal evidence; evidence**
  children
    child abuse
      expert evidence of reliability of child abuse complainers, 02/5426S
  cohabitation
    compellability of unmarried partner, 02/914
  devolution issues
    right to prepare for trial
      confidentiality of witness reports, 02/5442S
  disclosure
    death inquests, 02/4823NI
  expert witnesses
    appointment of single joint expert
      relevant considerations, 02/430
working families tax credit
  period of awards, 02/5165NI
writs. *See* **service of process**
young offender institutions
  disciplinary offences
    punishment, 02/3354
  supervision levels, 02/6016S
Youth Justice and Criminal Evidence Act 1999 (c.23)
  Commencement No.7 Order
    England and Wales, 02/43
Yugoslavia
  weapons
    export controls, 02/2988, 2989
Zimbabwe
  criminal law
    offences
zoos
  wild animals
    animal welfare, 02/194